COBUILD

COLLINS Birmingham University International Language Database

STUDENT'S DICTIONARY
and
GRAMMAR

**THE UNIVERSITY
OF BIRMINGHAM**

**COLLINS
COBUILD**

HarperCollinsPublishers

HarperCollins Publishers
77-85 Fulham Palace Road
Hammersmith
London W6 8JB

COBUILD is a trademark of William Collins Sons & Co Ltd

ISBN 0 00 375042 6

Computer typeset by C.R. Barber & Partners, Wrotham and Promenade Graphics,
Cheltenham
Printed and bound in Great Britain by Clays Ltd, St Ives PLC

NOTE Entered words that we have reason to believe constitute trademarks have been
designated as such. However, neither the presence nor absence of such designation
should be regarded as affecting the legal status of any trademark.

Acknowledgements
The author and publishers are grateful to the late Roald Dahl and Jonathan Cape Ltd
and Penguin Ltd for the extract from *The Hitch-Hiker* from *The Marvellous Story of
Henry Sugar and Six Others*.

Corpus Acknowledgements
We would like to thank those authors and publishers who kindly gave permission for
copyright material to be used in the Bank of English. We would also like to thank
Times Newspapers Ltd.

Every effort has been made to contact owners of copyright material. If there are any
omissions, the publishers will be glad to rectify these, when the title is reprinted.

Contents

The Appendix of verb forms and the Index can be found
at the back of the book.

Editorial Team

Editor-in-Chief	John Sinclair
Editorial Director	Gwyneth Fox

Dictionary
Senior Editor	Rosamund Moon
Editors	Elizabeth Manning John Todd Deborah Yuill
Assistant Editors	Ann Hewings Jenny Watson

Grammar
Senior Editor	Ramesh Krishnamurthy
Editor	Jenny Watson
Assistant Editors	Christina Rammell Keith Stuart

Computational Assistance
Tim Lane, Zoe James, Stephen Bullon

Secretarial Staff
Sue Smith, Sue Crawley, Kirsty Haynes

HarperCollins Publishers
Annette Capel, Lorna Heaslip, Marina Maher, Douglas Williamson

Illustrators
John Batten, Gillian Martin, David Parkins, Clyde Pearson,
Peter Schrank

We would like to thank Ela Bullon, Janet Hilsden, Alyson McGee, Elaine Pollard, and Sue Sutton for their valuable contribution to the Dictionary; Sylvia Chalker, Sue Inkster, and Dave Willis for their detailed comments and suggestions on the Grammar text; Richard Fay and Paschalena Groutka for their part in the original drafting of the Grammar Units; Sue Inkster, Anthony Harvey, John Curtin, John Dyson, Tom Stableford, Bob Walker, David Evans, and Angus Oliver for their comments on the initial list of Units.

We would also like to thank all the people who contributed to previous COBUILD dictionaries and to the COBUILD *English Grammar*, whose original work provided the impetus for this book.

Introduction

The *Student's Dictionary and Grammar* presents a great deal of information about the English Language. The information comes from the Birmingham Collection of English Text, which contains about twenty million words of spoken and written English from a variety of sources including conversations, literature, and journalism. (The Birmingham Collection now forms part of the Bank of English.)

From this unique evidence we have chosen the most useful words for inclusion in the Dictionary, and noted their grammatical patterns and the words that often occur with them. Where appropriate, we have also included other information, for instance about the formality of a particular word.

Similarly, in the Grammar, we have picked out the most important patterns and shown the grammatical structures that people actually use.

In both sections we have used real examples taken from our collection of texts.

Based on the successful *Student's Dictionary* and *Student's Grammar*, both of these recently-revised learning tools are now available in one volume. Both are suitable for students from intermediate level upward, and form a useful reference book for teachers.

I would be glad to receive any comments on this or on any other COBUILD publications.

John Sinclair
Professor of Modern English Language
University of Birmingham
Editor-in-Chief
COBUILD

How to use the Dictionary

1 Finding words

1.1 Main entries

The order of entries is alphabetical, with no notice being taken of capital letters, hyphens, or spaces between words. So the order of words in a small section of 'G' is:

golden
goldfish
gold medal
goldmine
gold-plated
golf

1.2 Phrasal verbs

Phrasal verbs are put towards the end of the entry for the simple verb. For example, you will find **clean out** and **clean up** in the entry for **clean**, at the end of it. The dictionary entries at this point are:

clean
  clean out
  clean up
cleaner

1.3 Phrases

Phrases are combinations of words which have their own special meanings, so that you cannot normally guess the meaning from the individual words.

Phrases are printed in bold type in the entry for the most important word in the phrase. When the phrase is close in meaning to another meaning of the word, the phrase will be found in the same part of the entry as that meaning, but will be introduced by a ●. For example, in the entry for **bee**:

> COUNT N A **bee** is an insect that makes a buzzing noise as it flies and usually has a yellow and black striped body. Bees make honey, and live in large groups.
> ● If you **have a bee in your bonnet**, you are so enthusiastic or worried about something that you keep mentioning it or thinking about it.

In other cases, phrases are given as separate meanings. If there are several phrases in the same entry, they are put together in a separate paragraph at the end of the entry.

> PHRASES ● Something that makes your <u>hair stand on end</u> shocks or horrifies you. *She did it with an ease that made his hair stand on end.* ● If you <u>let your hair down</u>, you relax completely and enjoy yourself. ● If you say that someone is <u>splitting hairs</u>, you mean that they are making unnecessary distinctions or paying too much attention to unimportant details. *Am I splitting hairs here? I think not, because this is an important distinction.*

1.4 Cross-references

If you cannot find the explanation of a phrase or compound at the word you have looked up, you will often find a note telling you which entry has the explanation. You may look up a phrase like **I beg your pardon** at **beg**, but the dictionary explains it at **pardon**. In such cases, you will often find a cross-reference. For example, at the entry for **beg**, **beg 3**, reads:

> **3 I beg your pardon**: see **pardon**.

Cross-references are also used to help you find compounds. For example, at the end of the entry for **glass** you will find:

> **3** See also **dark glasses, magnifying glass**.

At the end of **get away 2** you will find:

> ● See also **getaway**.

1.5 Words which are defined together

Sometimes the meaning of a word does not change although the form of the word may change when an ending is added. For example, **eager** ADJ and **eagerly** ADV and **eagerness** UNCOUNT N have the same meaning, although they have different grammatical functions. In these cases, the meaning is only given for the main word, and the other words are introduced by ♦.

> **eager** /íːgə/. ADJ If you are **eager** to do or have something, you very much want to do it or have it. *The majority were eager for change.* ♦ **eagerly** ADV ...*eagerly waiting for news of a victory.* ♦ **eagerness** UNCOUNT N ...*my eagerness to learn.*

The different endings that can be added to form the new words are all explained in alphabetical order in the text of the dictionary. So there are entries for **-ly**, **-ness**, **-ation**, and so on.

If there is a difference in meaning, the words are treated separately and will be found in their correct alphabetical place. So there are different entries for words such as **hopeful** and **hopefully**, and **sure** and **surely**.

Sometimes a word is used with the same meaning in two word classes, but there is no special ending. The new word class is introduced by the word 'Also'. For example, the entry for **crackle**:

> **crackle** /krǽkəl/. **crackles, crackling, crackled.** VB If something **crackles**, it makes a series of short, harsh noises. *The loudspeaker crackled.* Also SING N ...*the crackle of the fire.*

2 Forms and spelling

The spelling for each form of a word is given in bold letters at the beginning of an entry. For example:

> **earthquake** /ɜːθkweɪk/, **earthquakes.**
> **echo** /ɛkəʊ/, **echoes, echoing, echoed.**
> **easy** /íːziʲ/, **easier, easiest.**
> **dry** /draɪ/, **drier** or **dryer, driest; dries, drying, dried.**

The forms of a verb are listed in the order: base form, third person form of the present tense (*-s* form), present participle (*-ing* form), past tense (*-ed* form), and past participle (*-ed* or *-en* form), if this is different from the past tense form. The forms for an adjective are listed in the order: comparative form (*-er* form), superlative form (*-est* form). If a word is both a count noun and a verb, and has the same form for both the plural of the noun and the third person form of the present tense, then we only give this form once.

If there is anything unusual about the use of the forms, this is explained in a note. For example:

> **hit** /hɪt/, **hits, hitting.** The form **hit** is used in the present tense and is the past tense and past participle.

If the word is spelled differently in British and American English, this is also explained in a note. For example:

> **label** /léɪbəl/, **label, labelling, labelled**; spelled **labeling** and **labeled** in American English.

3 Pronunciation

The pronunciation is normally given after the first form of the word. For example:

> **key** /kiː/, **keys.**

But if the word is pronounced in different ways, this is explained after all the forms. For example:

> **bow, bows, bowing, bowed**; pronounced /baʊ/ for meanings 1 to 4 and for the phrasal verbs, and /bəʊ/ for meanings 5, 6, and 7.

When the pronunciation of one of the forms is very different from the first form given, then its pronunciation is also given immediately after it. For example:

> **give** /gɪv/, **gives, giving, gave** /geɪv/, **given.**

For further information about pronunciation and a key to the symbols used, see page x.

4 Grammar

In this dictionary, grammatical information is given just before the explanation of each word or meaning. Words that are introduced by ♦ in the text (see section 1.5 above) have no explanations. The grammatical information comes just after the word form. We do not give grammatical information for individual phrases in the paragraphs of phrases, and phrasal verbs are simply labelled PHR VB. The grammatical labels that we use are explained on pages vii to ix.

5 Explanations

Words are explained in simple English. If you read the explanations carefully, you should be able to use the word yourself in good, natural English. The explanation of each word or meaning shows you how the word is typically used. For example, the explanation of the adjective **bleary** reads:

> If your eyes are **bleary**, they are red and watery, usually because you are tired.

This tells you that you use **bleary** to describe eyes, rather than anything else.

The explanations of words show you what other words are typically used in association with them, and what kinds of structures they are used in. The explanations of verbs give you information about the kinds of thing that are mentioned as their subjects and objects. The entry for **crawl** reads as follows:

crawl /krɔːl/, **crawls, crawling, crawled. 1** VB When you **crawl**, you move forwards on your hands and knees. *Her baby is crawling about now.* **2** VB When an insect or vehicle **crawls**, it moves slowly. *A spider was crawling up my leg.* **3** VB If you say that a place **is crawling** with people or things, you mean that it is full of them. *The forecourt was crawling with security men.* **4** VB If you **crawl** to someone, you try to please them in order to gain some advantage; an informal use. *Let's see who comes crawling to whom.* **5** SING N The **crawl** is a swimming stroke where you lie on your front, swinging first one arm over your head, and then the other arm.

From these explanations, you can see that there is typically a human subject with the first meaning, but that with the second meaning, the subject is more likely to refer to something such as an insect or vehicle. The third explanation shows you that for this meaning, the subject typically refers to a place, and that it is followed by a prepositional phrase beginning with the word 'with'. In addition, the expression 'you say' in the explanation indicates that this use of the word normally expresses an opinion, rather than a simple statement of fact. The fourth explanation shows you that in this use, the subject is typically human, and that it is followed by a prepositional phrase beginning with 'to'. Finally, the fifth explanation shows you that you typically use the determiner 'the' in front of this noun.

6 Examples

The dictionary contains a large number of examples, showing how the words have been used by English writers and speakers. The examples have been chosen to show the most typical patterns of grammar and vocabulary in which the words are used, and also to show the situations in which you are most likely to find each word being used. Examples are

printed in italic type after the explanation of meaning. For example, in the entry for **leave**:

1 VB WITH OR WITHOUT OBJ When you **leave** a place, you go away from it. *They left the house to go for a walk after tea... My train leaves at 11.30.*

7 Style and Usage

This dictionary also has information about how and when you should use a word or meaning of a word. For example, some words are mainly used in informal situations, or by American speakers and writers, or in technical writing, while others are used to indicate someone's attitude or opinion. Information of this kind is usually placed after the explanation, if it only applies to that use or if there is only one use of the word:

abode /əbəʊd/, **abodes**, COUNT N Your **abode** is the place where you live; a formal use.
care for 2 If you say that you do not **care for** something, you mean that you do not like it; an old-fashioned use.
copper 2 COUNT N A **copper** is a policeman or policewoman; an informal use.
sponge off or **sponge on**. PHR VB Someone who **sponges off** other people or **sponges on** other people reguarly gets money from them without giving anything in return; an informal use showing disapproval. *He sponged on his friends.*

Some words have several meanings which are all used in the same sort of situation: for example, some words are only used in formal situations. In such cases, information about this is given at the beginning of the entry, after the forms:

extinguish /ɪkstɪŋgwɪʃ/, **extinguishes, extinguishing, extinguished**; a formal word. **1** VB WITH OBJ If you **extinguish** a fire or a light, you stop it burning or shining. **2** VB WITH OBJ To **extinguish** an idea or feeling means to destroy it. *We have to extinguish the memory of the defeat.*

The explanations for many words tell you the situations in which you would be likely to use the word or hear it used. So, if a word is used mainly by someone who is angry or worried or frightened, then the explanation says so. For example, in the entry for **help**, you find:

9 CONVENTION You shout 'Help!' when you are in danger, in order to attract someone's attention.

Grammatical Information in the Dictionary

The labels that we use in this dictionary are explained in the following list. Some words or meanings have to be used in particular structures or patterns, and we show this in the grammatical information. For example, **belong 1** has the label VB WITH PREP 'to', and this means that **belong** is an intransitive verb and is followed by the preposition 'to'. *The land belongs to a big family.* Similarly, **enable** has the label VB WITH OBJ AND TO-INF, which means that **enable** is a transitive verb and is followed by an infinitive with 'to': *I made arrangements which enabled me to continue working.* And **fit 10** has the label COUNT N WITH 'of', which means that **fit** is a count noun here and is followed by the preposition 'of': *In a fit of rage, he had flung Paul's violin out of the window.*

Many words or meanings typically follow the same grammatical pattern, and so they only have one label, for example COUNT N, ADJ, or VB WITH OBJ. Sometimes, however, words or meanings can follow more than one pattern, and in this case we show more than one pattern. The alternative patterns are separated with 'or'. For example, **pudding 1** has the grammar label COUNT N OR UNCOUNT N, which means that it is used either as a count noun or an uncount noun; **claim 4** has the label VB WITH OBJ OR ADJUNCT, which means that it is used either with an object or an adjunct; **quite 1** has the label SUBMOD OR ADV, which means that it is used either as a submodifier or as an adverb; and **after 1** has the label PREP, ADV, OR CONJ, which means that **after** can be used as a preposition or an adverb or a conjunction.

ADJ means adjective. Adjectives are words such as **beautiful, blue, small,** and **old** which tell you more about a thing, such as its appearance, colour, size, or other qualities. Adjectives can come in front of nouns: *There was a faint smell of gas.* They can also come after link verbs: *She was fair and blue-eyed.* Some adjectives can only come in one of these positions, and in this case they are labelled as ATTRIB ADJ or as PRED ADJ: see the separate explanations. A few adjectives always follow nouns, for example **galore**: *...restaurants and night clubs galore.* They are labelled ADJ AFTER N.

ADJUNCT. An adjunct is a word or group of words such as an adverb or a prepositional phrase that is added to a clause in order to give more information about time, place, or manner. Grammar labels such as VB

WITH ADJUNCT mean that the verb must be used with an adjunct. See separate entries for **VB WITH ADJUNCT, VB WITH OBJ AND ADJUNCT,** and **VB WITH OR WITHOUT OBJ, WITH ADJUNCT.**

ADV means adverb. Adverbs are words such as **now, quickly, up, here, sadly,** and **officially** which give you more information about time, place, or manner. See also the separate entries for **SUBMOD** and **SENTENCE ADV.**

ATTRIB ADJ means attributive adjective. Attributive adjectives can only come in front of nouns, and not after verbs. **Classical 2, classical 3** and **coastal** are examples of adjectives with this label: *...plays set in classical times. ...coastal waters.*

AUX means auxiliary verb. The auxiliary verbs are **be, do,** and **have,** and they are used with main verbs to form tenses, negatives, questions, and so on. See also the entry for **MODAL.**

COLL N means collective noun. Collective nouns are words such as **audience** and **committee** which refer to groups of people or things. In the singular, a collective noun takes a determiner, but you can use either the singular or plural forms of verbs and pronouns with it. For example, you can say *The audience was very enthusiastic* or *The audience were very enthusiastic.*

COMPLEMENT. A complement is a group consisting of at least a noun or an adjective. It comes after a verb and gives you more information about the subject or object of the verb. Grammar labels such as VB WITH ADJUNCT OR COMPLEMENT mean that the verb must be followed by an adjunct or a complement. See separate entries for **VB WITH COMPLEMENT,** and **VB WITH OBJ AND COMPLEMENT.**

CONJ means conjunction. Conjunctions are words such as **and, but, if,** and **when** which relate clauses to each other. You use subordinating conjunctions to relate subordinate clauses to main clauses: for example, **because** in *I couldn't see Helen's expression, because her head was turned.* You use co-ordinating conjunctions to relate two clauses which are of the same grammatical type: for example, **and** in *I came here in 1972 and have lived here ever since.* Co-ordinating conjunctions are also commonly used to relate groups or words: for example **and** in *...my father and mother.*

CONVENTION. Conventions are words or ready-made phrases that you use in conversation, for example when you are meeting someone, greeting them, or thanking them. Examples of conventions include **Hello** and **Thank you.**

COUNT N means count noun. Count nouns are nouns such as **box, car, tree,** or **woman** which have both a singular and a plural form. You usually form the plural by adding **-s** to the singular. In this dictionary the plural form is shown at the beginning of the entry. When you use a count noun in the singular, you must put a determiner in front of it, and if it is in subject position, you use the singular form of the verb. For example, *Donald's car was in the garage... I stood under a tree.*

DET means determiner. Determiners are words such as **a, the, my,** and **every** which are used at the beginning of a noun group in order to say which particular thing or person you are referring to.

ERG VB means ergative verb. An ergative verb occurs in both transitive and intransitive clauses. The object of the transitive clause can be found as the subject of the intransitive clause. **Break** is an example of an ergative verb. You can say that someone breaks something, or you can say that something breaks. For example, *He has broken a window... The string broke.* The two uses of ergative verbs are similar to the active and passive uses of transitive verbs. For example, *Father broke a plate... The bell was broken.*

INDEF PRON means indefinite pronoun. Indefinite pronouns are pronouns such as **anyone, nobody,** and **something** which you use to refer to people or things in a general way. You cannot put a determiner in front of an indefinite pronoun, and you use it with the singular form of a verb.

INF means infinitive. Verbs in English have two infinitive forms. One is the simple or base form of the verb, such as 'see': in this dictionary, it is referred to as INF. The other is the simple form of the verb with 'to' in front of it, and in this dictionary, it is referred to as TO-INF: see separate entry for **TO-INF**. Labels such as VB WITH INF mean that the verb must be followed by the base form of another verb, without 'to'. For example, **make 2** has the label VB WITH OBJ AND INF: *A sudden noise made Brody jump.*

-ING is used in labels such as VB WITH -ING or PRED ADJ WITH -ING, to say that a word is followed by the '-ing' form of a verb. See the separate entry for **VB WITH -ING.**

LINK VB means link verb. Link verbs are verbs such as **be, become,** and **seem** which you use to link the subject of a verb with a complement or prepositional phrase which describes or identifies the subject: see the explanation of **COMPLEMENT.** The following sentences contain link verbs: *There is a single cottage at the roadside... She was slightly disappointed... The smell became stronger and stronger.*

MASS N means mass noun. In this dictionary, mass nouns are nouns such as **acid, beer,** and **cheese** which are usually used as uncount nouns. However, they can also be used as count nouns when they refer to quantities or types of something. For example, you can either say that someone ordered two cups of coffee or that they ordered two coffees. See the explanations for **COUNT N** and **UNCOUNT N.**

MOD means noun modifier. In this dictionary, modifiers are nouns which are frequently used in front of other nouns. For example, **beauty 5** has the grammar label MOD, because when **beauty** is used to describe things that are concerned with making women look attractive, it is usually used in front of another noun, as in *beauty products.*

MODAL means modal verb. The modals are the verbs **can, could, may, might, must, ought, shall, should, will,** and **would** which you use to express attitudes and ideas such as possibility, obligation, prediction, or deduction. You usually use a modal verb with a main verb. The main verb is in its base form. For example, *Neither of them can swim... He will come.* However, the modal **ought** is always followed by a 'to'-infinitive. Modal verbs do not inflect – that is, the form of a modal verb never changes.

N means noun. Nouns are words which refer to people, things, and abstract ideas such as feelings and qualities. The abbreviation N is used in this dictionary in grammar labels such as COUNT N, UNCOUNT N, and N WITH NUMBER.

NUMBER. Numbers are words such as 'one', 'eleven', and 'forty-two', which say precisely how many things there are. NUMBER is used in the grammar labels N WITH NUMBER and VB WITH NUMBER.

PASSIVE VB means passive verb. Passive verbs are verbs which are always or nearly always used in the passive, and they consist of the

auxiliary **be** together with the past participle of the verb. **Base 4, born 1,** and **daze 2** are examples of verbs which are labelled PASSIVE VB in this dictionary: *I was based in London... Mary was born in Glasgow... She was dazed by the news.*

PAST PARTICIPLE. The past participle of a verb is a form which usually ends in '-ed' or '-en'. It is used to form perfect tenses and passives.

PHR VB means phrasal verb. A phrasal verb is a combination of a verb with an adverb or preposition that has a single meaning. **Give up, go on,** and **put off** are examples of phrasal verbs. *She never completely gave up hope... I went on writing... Nothing would put her off once she had made up her mind.* In this dictionary, phrasal verbs are put towards the end of the entry for the simple verb.

PHRASE. A phrase is a group of words that you use together. Phrases have meanings which may be difficult to guess, even if you know the meanings of individual words. For example, **out of the blue** and **to have butterflies in your stomach** are phrases: see **blue 2** and **butterfly 2.** Many words are used in several phrases, and the phrases are all grouped together in a separate paragraph towards the end of the entry, with the heading PHRASES.

PLURAL N means plural noun. Plural nouns are nouns such as **armed forces, clothes, means 11, police,** and **trousers.** They are only used in the plural. You can use them with a determiner in front of them.

POSS means possessive. Labels such as COUNT N WITH POSS or SING N WITH POSS mean that the noun must be used with a possessive. The possessive comes in front of the noun if it is in the form of a determiner such as 'my' or 'her', or the possessive form of a name or noun such as 'John's' or 'the writer's'. The possessive can also follow the noun if it is in the form of a prepositional phrase beginning with 'of'. The labels for **birthplace** and **colouring 2** include POSS: *...Tom Hood's birthplace. ...the birthplace of President Eisenhower... Her son had inherited her colouring.*

PRED ADJ means predicative adjective. Predicative adjectives can only come after link verbs, and not in front of nouns. **Afraid** and **alone** are examples of this: *Don't be afraid to ask questions... I wanted to be alone.*

PREDET means predeterminer. The predeterminers are **all, both, double, half, such, twice,** and **what** which you put in front of a determiner in a noun group, as in *...all the girls* and *...both her parents.*

PREFIX. A prefix is a group of letters such as **anti-, ex-,** or **un-** which is added to the beginning of a word in order to change its meaning. For example, you can add **un-** to the beginning of some adjectives in order to form other adjectives with the opposite meaning.

PREP means preposition. Prepositions are words such as **by, from,** and **with** which are always followed by a noun group or by a clause built around the '-ing' form of a verb.

PRON means pronoun. Pronouns are words which you use instead of a noun group to refer to someone or something. You use personal pronouns such as **me, she, it,** and **you** to refer to people or things. Other words which are labelled PRON in this dictionary include **none, some,** and **this.** In many cases, they can also be used as determiners, in front of a noun group. See separate entries for **INDEF PRON** and **REFL PRON.**

PROPER N means proper noun. A proper noun refers to a particular person, place, or institution. It is usually spelled with a capital letter, and it does not usually have a plural form. Some proper nouns have to be used after the determiner *the.* For example, you have to say **the Bible** and **the Far East.** The explanation and examples show you if you need to use *the* with a proper noun.

QUANTIF means quantifier. Quantifiers are words such as **half, few,** and **many** which express ideas of quantity or amount. You use them in noun groups, before 'of' and a noun group. For example, *...a few of the teams. ...half of the patients.* You can also use quantifiers on their own, without 'of' and the noun group, providing that the context makes it clear what you are referring to. For example, you can say *A few were smoking* instead of *A few of the people were smoking.*

RECIP VB means reciprocal verb. Reciprocal verbs describe actions that involve two people or two groups of people. Verbs that are labelled RECIP VB in this dictionary can be used in several possible patterns. In each case, the explanations and examples will show you which patterns are possible. The commonest pattern is the one used in **agree 1, argue 1,** and **collide.** The verb is intransitive. You can mention both people or groups as the subject of the verb: *They were arguing about who should sit in front.* You can also mention one of them as the subject and the other in a prepositional phrase after 'with': *Don't argue with me,*

George, just do as you're told. In a few cases, a different preposition is used; for example, you use 'from' with **differ 1**. The next commonest pattern is used in **marry 1** and **meet**. You can mention both people or groups as the subject of an intransitive verb: *They are in love with each other and wish to marry.* You can also mention one of them as the subject of a transitive verb and the other as the object: *I want to marry you.* The third pattern is used in **compare 1** and **mix 1**. The verb is transitive. You can mention both people or groups as the object of the verb: *It's interesting to compare the two prospectuses.* You can also mention one of them as the object and the other in a prepositional phrase, usually after 'with': *...studies comparing Russian children with those in Britain.*

REFL PRON means reflexive pronoun. The reflexive pronouns are **myself**, **yourself**, **himself**, **herself**, **itself**, **oneself**, **ourselves**, **yourselves**, and **themselves** which you use as the object of a verb or preposition when you are referring to someone who has already been mentioned as the subject of the clause.

REFL VB means reflexive verb. Reflexive verbs describe actions in which the subject and the object of the verb are the same, and they take reflexive pronouns as their objects. **Behave 2**, **commit 3**, and **occupy 5** are examples of reflexive verbs: *He's old enough to behave himself... I really wouldn't like to commit myself.*

REPORT VB means reporting verb. Reporting verbs are verbs such as **announce**, **believe**, **say**, and **see** which describe acts of saying, of thinking, or of perception. They are followed by a clause which tells you what someone is saying, thinking, or perceiving. The clause typically begins with the conjunction 'that', although 'that' is often omitted: *I said that I would rather work in the forest... She said she would like to go with him... I thought I would have to stop... Etta could see that he wasn't listening.* They are also often followed by a clause beginning with a wh- word such as 'who' or 'what': *We asked what had happened... She knew who I was. ...when you have decided what you want to do.* Many of these verbs can also be used with an object rather than a clause. The object refers to the type of thing that was said or perceived, or the topic: *Dillon asked a question... Shirley said something insulting... He explained his problem.* Many reporting verbs can be used with a clause which consists of a quotation or the actual words that someone spoke: *'There is Tim,' said Kate... 'Where are we going?' I asked.* Not all the verbs that are labelled REPORT VB in this dictionary can be used in all these ways, but you can see from the explanations and examples which structures are frequently used. With some reporting verbs such as **ask 1** and **tell 1**, you mention the person who is being addressed as the object of the verb, and in this case the grammar label will also say WITH OBJ: *I asked him what he wanted... He told her all about it... 'Wait here,' she told Ash.*

SEMI-MODAL. The semi-modals are the verbs **dare**, **need** and **used to**. They can be used like modals, in which case they do not inflect and are followed by the base form of a verb. **Dare** and **need** can also be used as ordinary verbs, in which case they inflect in the normal way and can be used with auxiliaries and modals.

SENTENCE ADV means sentence adverb. Sentence adverbs are adverbs such as **actually**, **however**, and **generally** which you use to link clauses or to make a comment on the whole clause, not just on part of it.

SING N means singular noun. Singular nouns are only used in the singular, and they must have determiners in front of them. **Background 3** and **business 5** are labelled SING N: *In the background is a tall cypress tree... That's his business and no one else's.*

SUBMOD means submodifier. Submodifiers are adverbs such as **awfully**, **quite**, and **very** which express ideas of degree. You use them in front of an adjective or another adverb in order to strengthen or weaken its meaning. For example, *He was awfully cold... The reason is quite simple... I left for London very early the next morning.*

SUFFIX. A suffix is a group of letters such as **-able**, **-er**, or **-ly** which is added to the end of a word in order to change its grammar or its meaning. For example, you add **-ly** or **-ness** to adjectives in order to form adverbs or nouns with related meanings. You can add **-ish** to adjectives to form other adjectives which say that something has a particular quality to only a slight extent.

SUPP means supporting word or words, and it occurs in labels such as COUNT N WITH SUPP or SING N WITH SUPP. This means that the noun is not usually used on its own in this meaning. It either needs an adjective in front of it, or a relative clause or prepositional phrase after it. **Accomplishment 2** and **case 1** are examples of words where the label includes SUPP: *The accomplishment of this task filled him with satisfaction. ...a classic case of people living in harmony with their environment.*

TITLE. Titles are special words or expressions that you use when you are addressing or referring to someone with a particular role or position.

For example, **excellency** and **highness** are labelled TITLE in this dictionary because they are only used in titles such as 'Your Excellency' and 'Her Royal Highness'.

TO-INF means infinitive. Verbs in English have two infinitive forms. One is the simple or base form of the verb with 'to' in front of it, for example 'to see': in this dictionary it is referred to as TO-INF. The other is the simple or base form of the verb without 'to', and in this dictionary it is referred to as INF: see separate entry for INF. Labels such as VB WITH TO-INF or PRED ADJ WITH TO-INF mean that the word must be followed by the base form of a verb, with 'to' in front of it. For example, the labels for **able 1** and **mean 6** include TO-INF: *I wasn't able to do these quizzes... I meant to ring you but I'm afraid I forgot.*

UNCOUNT N means uncount noun. Uncount nouns are nouns such as **furniture**, **information**, **rice**, and **sadness** which only have one form and which refer to a general kind of thing, rather than an individual item. You cannot use numbers with these nouns, and they do not have a plural form. You use them with the singular form of a verb. *...stew with rice... It filled me with sadness... Sea water tastes nasty... Electricity is potentially dangerous.* You do not use a determiner such as **the** in front of them unless you are giving extra information or being specific. For example, *All this information is useful... Where is the money you stole?*

VB means verb. Verbs are words which you use with a subject in order to say what someone or something does, or what happens to them. In this dictionary, VB is often followed by another label, to show that you must use the verb in a particular structure, and the commonest of these labels are explained below. If there is no other label, it means that the verb is intransitive, and so it is not followed by an object. **Act**, **go**, and **talk** are examples of intransitive verbs: *They had acted so strangely... Let us go away from here... We all stopped talking.*

VB WITH ADJUNCT means that the verb must be used with an adverb or prepositional phrase. For example, **climb 2**, **do 12**, and **get 3** have the label VB WITH ADJUNCT: *She climbed into her car... I didn't do very well in my exams... He got into trouble with the police.*

VB WITH COMPLEMENT means that the verb must be used with a complement which refers back to the subject of the verb: see the explanation of **COMPLEMENT** above. For example, **equal 6** and **look 6** have the label VB WITH COMPLEMENT: *79 minus 14 equals 65... You look very pale.*

VB WITH -ING means that the verb is followed by the -ing form of another verb. For example, **avoid 2**, **get 14**, and **go 2** have the label VB WITH -ING: *Thomas turned his head, trying to avoid breathing in the smoke... We can't seem to get moving... Let's go fishing.*

VB WITH OBJ means that the verb is transitive: that is, it takes an object. The object consists of a noun group. Most transitive verbs can be used in the passive. **Admire**, **carry**, **hit**, and **make** are examples of verbs which are labelled as VB WITH OBJ: *I admire courage... He picked up his suitcase and carried it into the bedroom... The truck had hit a wall... I made the wrong decision.*

VB WITH OBJ AND ADJUNCT means that the verb must be used with both an object and an adjunct. **Bring 5**, **dab**, and **put** are examples of verbs with this label: *He brought the car to a stop... She dabbed some powder on her nose... Marsha put her cup down.*

VB WITH OBJ AND COMPLEMENT means that the verb must be used with both an object and a complement. The complement refers to the same person or thing as the object of the verb. **Call 1**, **find 3**, and **make 3** are examples of verbs with this label: *All my friends call him Jo... I found him a disappointment... I'd like to make the world a better place.*

VB WITH OBJ AND OBJ means that the verb is used with two objects, an indirect object and a direct object. In many cases, the verb can also be used with just one object and a prepositional phrase beginning with 'to' or 'for' instead of an indirect object. **Cause 3**, **forgive 1**, **give**, and **owe** are examples of verbs with this label: *What's causing you so much concern?... I forgave him everything... Give me your key... I still owe you seven pounds.*

VB WITH OR WITHOUT OBJ means that the verb can be either transitive or intransitive: that is, it can take an object, but does not have to. **Answer**, **dance 1**, **drive 1**, and **eat** are examples of verbs with this label: *It is her turn to drive the car... I have never learned to drive... He began to eat his sandwich... He said he would eat at his hotel.*

VB WITH OR WITHOUT OBJ, WITH ADJUNCT means that the verb must be used with an adjunct. It can take an object, but does not have to. **Last 9** and **lean 2** are examples of verbs with this label: *He leaned against a tree... He leaned the bike against a railing.*

VOCATIVE. A vocative is a word that you use when you are speaking to someone, just as if it were their name. **Dad**, **mum**, and **darling** are examples of vocatives.

Pronunciation

In this dictionary a guide is given to the pronunciation of English words using the International Phonetic Alphabet. The accent represented is Received Pronunciation, or RP for short, which is an accent used by many speakers of Southern British English. There are several other accents of English, but RP is perhaps the most widely used as a norm for teaching purposes.

Two kinds of information are needed if a word is to be appropriately pronounced. We need to know about each of the sounds that make up the word, and we need to know about stress. In each of the pronunciations shown in this dictionary, at least one vowel symbol is in heavier type and underlined. Sometimes more than one vowel is in heavier type and underlined:

result /rɪzʌlt/
disappointing /dɪsəpɔɪntɪŋ/

Heavy type and underlining give important information both about stress and the sounds that make up a word.

When a word is spoken in isolation, stress falls on all the syllables that contain vowels that are in heavier type and underlined. When two syllables are marked in this way, the second syllable has primary stress while the first has secondary stress; if only one is marked, it has primary stress. A word spoken in isolation is called the citation form.

When a word is used in context, either or both of the stresses found in the citation form may be absent. The one-stress or two-stress patterns of English speech are associated not with individual words but with the information units that a speaker constructs:

The result was disappointing
/ðə rɪzʌlt wəz dɪsəpɔɪntɪŋ/

A disappointing result
/ə dɪsəpɔɪntɪŋ rɪzʌlt/

Very disappointing indeed
/vɛri dɪsəpɔɪntɪŋ ɪndiːd/

Because stress patterns are associated with linguistic units larger than the word, a dictionary cannot state in advance which of the stresses present in a citation form will be absent when a word is used in context.

Vowels that are in heavier type and underlined are called protected vowels. This means that, irrespective of whether a vowel is stressed or unstressed in a particular context, there is very little variation in the way a speaker pronounces it. Unprotected vowels, conversely, which are always unstressed, may show considerable variation in the way they are pronounced.

In this dictionary, the range of possible variation is shown by the tiny superscript numbers printed just above and to the right of the vowel symbol. In the word /sɪti¹/ (city), for example, the protected vowel is always pronounced /ɪ/, irrespective of whether it is stressed or not. Conversely, the key at the bottom of the page shows that the pronunciation of the protected vowel may be made in the range between /iː/ and /ɪ/. In the word /juːslɪs/ (useless) the protected vowel is always pronounced /uː/, irrespective of whether it is stressed or not, while the pronunciation of the unprotected vowel may be made in the range between /ɪ/ and /ɛ/.

Some unprotected vowels are pronounced in only one way. For example, the second vowel in /hɔːlmɑːk/ (hallmark) is stressed neither in its citation form nor when the word is used in context, but there is still very little variation in the way it is pronounced.

Some sounds, both vowels and consonants, are heard only in rather slow and careful speech. /juːʒuəl/ (usual) and /kɒləmnɪst/ (columnist) are often heard as /juːʒəl/ and /kɒləmnɪst/. In such cases, the superscript ° indicates that the sound in question is often omitted:

usual /juːʒ°əl/
columnist /kɒləmn°ɪst/

All superscripts and the variations they stand for are given in the key below.

Pronunciation Key

Vowels

ɑː	heart, start, calm.
æ	act, mass, lap.
aɪ	dive, cry, mind.
aɪə	fire, tyre, buyer.
aʊ	out, down, loud.
aʊə	flour, tower, sour.
ɛ	met, lend, pen.
eɪ	say, main, weight.
ɛə	fair, care, wear.
ɪ	fit, win, list.
iː	feed, me, beat.
ɪə	near, beard, clear.
ɒ	lot, lost, spot.
əʊ	note, phone, coat.
ɔː	more, cord, claw.
ɔɪ	boy, coin, joint.
ʊ	could, stood, hood.
uː	you, use, choose.
ʊə	sure, pure, cure.
ɜː	turn, third, world.
ʌ	but, fund, must.
ə	*the weak vowel in* butter, about, forgotten.

Consonants

b	bed
d	done
f	fit
g	good
h	hat
j	yellow
k	king
l	lip
m	mat
n	nine
p	pay
r	run
s	soon
t	talk
v	van
w	win
x	loch
z	zoo
ʃ	ship
ʒ	measure
ŋ	sing
tʃ	cheap
θ	thin
ð	then
dʒ	joy

Superscripts

ə⁶	(ə ⇔ 0)
ə⁵	(ə ⇔ ɪ)
ə⁴	(ə ⇔ ɛ)
ə³	(ə ⇔ æ)
ə²	(ə ⇔ ʊ)
ə⁶	(ə ⇔ ɜː)
ə⁶	(ə ⇔ əʊ)
ə⁷	(ə ⇔ ɒ)
ə⁶	(ə ⇔ ɔː)
ə³	(ə ⇔ ʌ)
ɪ⁶	(ɪ ⇔ 0)
ɪ¹	(ɪ ⇔ ɪ)
ɪ²	(ɪ ⇔ ɛ)
ɪ³	(ɪ ⇔ æ)
ɪ⁵	(ɪ ⇔ aɪ)
iⁱ	(ɪ ⇔ iː)
ɛ¹	(ɛ ⇔ ɪ)
mⁱ	(m ⇔ n)
ŋ¹	(ŋ ⇔ n)

° after a consonant symbol indicates probable omission: k°, t°, h°, etc

x

How to use the Grammar

This section is designed so that you can find the answers to particular problems of English grammar. You are not expected to start at Unit 1 and study the Units one by one, or study a whole Unit at a time. Different people have different problems, so they need to look at different points in different Units.

Finding what you want

Contents

There is a complete list of Grammar Units on pages xvi and xvii. This gives the numbers and titles of all the Units. The Units are grouped under various headings to help you, for example 'Nouns', 'Prepositions', and 'Modals'.

Index

There is an Index at the back of the book which is an alphabetical list of the points covered in this section. For each point, the Index gives the unit number and paragraph number where the point is explained. Grammar terms such as 'adjectives', 'nouns', and 'verbs' are in **bold** letters. The ideas that you can express, such as 'ability' and 'certainty', are also in **bold** letters. The actual words and forms explained in the grammar, such as 'able' and 'this', are in *italic* letters.

Glossary

There is a Glossary on pages xii to xv. The Glossary explains the meaning of the grammar terms used in the grammar section, with examples. The terms are listed in alphabetical order.

Using the grammar units

Main points

Each page has two columns. At the top of the first column you will find a section headed 'Main points'. This is a summary of the important information given in the Unit. Each main point is introduced by a large bold dot. You will find more detailed information about the point in the numbered paragraphs on the same page.

Numbered paragraphs

The rest of the page is divided into numbered paragraphs. These give more detailed information about the topic covered in the Unit.

Example sentences

Each point is illustrated with example sentences printed in italic letters. When particular words in the example sentences show the point that is being explained, the words are underlined.

Lists

With many rules and patterns, a number of words are used in the same way. When this is the case, a list of words is given. For some points, a complete list of the words would be very long, so only the commonest words are included.

Warnings

Some points of English grammar frequently cause learners to make mistakes. Sometimes they are exceptions to a rule. Sometimes the rules are different in other languages. We have used the label 'WARNING' before such points.

Cross-references

Sometimes, more information about a rule or pattern is contained in another Unit. When this is the case, we tell you which Unit to refer to.

Glossary of terms used in the Grammar

Note: entries in **bold** are terms used in this grammar.

abstract noun a noun used to refer to a quality, idea, feeling, or experience, rather than a physical object; EG *size, reason, joy.*

active voice verb groups such as 'gives', 'took', 'has made', which are used when the subject of the verb is the person or thing doing the action or responsible for it. Compare with **passive voice.**

adjective a word used to tell you more about a person or thing, such as their appearance, colour, size, or other qualities; EG *...a **pretty blue** dress.*

adjunct another name for **adverbial.**

adverb a word that gives more information about when, how, where, or in what circumstances something happens; EG *quickly, now.*

adverbial an adverb, or an adverb phrase, prepositional phrase, or noun group which does the same job as an adverb, giving more information about when, how, where, or in what circumstances something happens; EG *then, very quickly, in the street, the next day.*

adverbial of degree an adverbial which indicates the amount or extent of a feeling or quality; EG *She felt **extremely** tired.*

adverbial of duration an adverbial which indicates how long something continues or lasts; EG *He lived in London **for six years.***

adverbial of frequency an adverbial which indicates how often something happens; EG *She **sometimes** goes to the cinema.*

adverbial of manner an adverbial which indicates the way in which something happens or is done; EG *She watched **carefully.***

adverbial of place an adverbial which gives more information about position or direction; EG *They are **upstairs**... Move **closer.***

adverbial of probability an adverbial which gives more information about how sure you are about something; EG *I've **probably** lost it.*

adverbial of time an adverbial which gives more information about when something happens; EG *I saw her **yesterday.***

adverb phrase two adverbs used together; EG *She spoke **very quietly**... He did not play **well enough** to win.*

affirmative A clause or sentence in the affirmative has the subject followed by the verb.

apostrophe s an ending ('s) added to a noun to indicate possession; EG *...Harriet**'s** daughter... the professor**'s** husband... the Managing Director**'s** secretary.*

article see **definite article, indefinite article.**

auxiliary another name for **auxiliary verb.**

auxiliary verb one of the verbs 'be', 'have', and 'do' when they are used with a main verb to form tenses, negatives, and questions. Some grammars include modals in the group of auxiliary verbs.

base form the form of a verb without any endings added to it, which is used in the 'to'-infinitive and for the imperative; EG *walk, go, have, be.* The base form is the form you look up in a dictionary.

cardinal number a number used in counting; EG *one, seven, nineteen.*

clause a group of words containing a verb. See also **main clause** and **subordinate clause.**

collective noun a noun that refers to a group of people or things, which can be used with a singular or plural verb; EG *committee, team, family.*

comparative an adjective or adverb with '-er' on the end or 'more' in front of it; EG *slower, more important, more carefully.*

complement a noun group or adjective which comes after a link verb such as 'be' and gives more information about the subject of the clause; EG *She is **a teacher**... She is **tired**.*

complex sentence a sentence consisting of a main clause and a subordinate clause; EG *She wasn't thinking very quickly because she was tired.*

compound sentence a sentence consisting of two or more main clauses linked by 'and', 'or', or 'but'; EG *They picked her up and took her into the house.*

contrast clause a subordinate clause, usually introduced by 'although' or 'in spite of the fact that', which contrasts with a main clause; EG ***Although I like her**, I find her hard to talk to.*

conditional clause a subordinate clause, usually starting with 'if' or 'unless', which is used to talk about possible situations and their results; EG *They would be rich **if they had taken my advice**... We'll go to the park, **unless it rains**.*

conjunction a word such as 'and', 'because', or 'nor', that links two clauses, groups, or words.

continuous tense a tense which contains a form of the verb 'be' and a present participle; EG *She **was laughing**... They **had been playing** badminton.*

coordinating conjunction a conjunction such as 'and', 'but', or 'or', which links two main clauses.

count noun a noun which has both singular and plural forms; EG *dog/dogs, lemon/lemons, foot/ feet.*

countable noun another name for **count noun.**

declarative another name for **affirmative.**

defining relative clause a relative clause which identifies the person or thing that is being talked about; EG *...the lady **who lives next door**... I wrote down everything **that she said**.*

definite article the determiner 'the'.

delexical verb a common verb such as 'give', 'have', 'make', or 'take', which has very little meaning in itself and is used with a noun as object that describes the action; EG *She **gave** a small cry... I've just **had** a bath.*

demonstrative one of the words 'this', 'that', 'these', and 'those'; EG *...**this** woman... ...**that** tree... **That** looks interesting... **This** is fun.*

descriptive adjective an adjective which describes a person or thing, for example indicating their size, age, shape, or colour, rather than expressing your opinion of that person or thing. Compare with **opinion adjective.**

determiner one of a group of words including 'the', 'a', 'some', and 'my', which are used at the beginning of a noun group.

direct object a noun group referring to the person or thing affected by an action, in a clause with a verb in the active voice; EG *She wrote **her name**... I shut **the windows***.

direct speech the actual words spoken by someone.

ditransitive verb another name for a verb with two objects, such as 'give', 'take', or 'sell'; EG *She **gave** me a kiss*.

double-transitive verb another name for a verb with two objects.

'-ed' adjective an adjective which has the same form as the '-ed' form of a regular verb, or the past participle of an irregular verb; EG ...***boiled** potatoes... ...a **broken** wing*.

'-ed' form the form of a regular verb used for the past simple and for the past participle.

ellipsis the leaving out of words when they are obvious from the context.

emphasizing adverb an adverb such as 'absolutely' or 'utterly', which modifies adjectives that express extreme qualities, such as 'astonishing' and 'wonderful'; EG *You were **absolutely** wonderful*.

ergative verb a verb which is both transitive and intransitive in the same meaning. The object of the transitive use is the subject of the intransitive use; EG *He **boiled** a kettle... The kettle **boiled***.

first person see **person**.

gerund another name for the '-ing' form when it is used as a noun.

'if'-clause see **conditional clause**.

imperative the form of a verb used when giving orders and commands, which is the same as its base form; EG ***Come** here... **Take** two tablets every four hours... **Enjoy** yourself*.

impersonal 'it' 'it' used as an impersonal subject to introduce new information; EG ***It's** raining... **It's** ten o'clock*.

indefinite article the determiners 'a' and 'an'.

indefinite adverb a small group of adverbs including 'anywhere' and 'somewhere' which are used to indicate place in a general way.

indefinite pronoun a small group of pronouns including 'someone' and 'anything' which are used to refer to people or things without saying exactly who or what they are.

indirect object an object used with verbs that take two objects. For example, in 'I gave him the pen' and 'I gave the pen to him', 'him' is the indirect object and 'pen' is the direct object. Compare **direct object**.

indirect question a question used to ask for information or help; EG *Do you know **where Jane is?**... I wonder **which hotel it was***.

indirect speech the words you use to report what someone has said, rather than using their actual words. Also called reported speech.

infinitive the base form of a verb; EG *I wanted to **go**... She helped me **dig** the garden*.

'-ing' adjective an adjective which has the same form as the present participle of a verb; EG... *a **smiling** face... ...a **winning** streak*.

'-ing' form a verb form ending in '-ing' which is used to form verb tenses, and as an adjective or a noun. Also called the present participle.

interrogative pronoun one of the pronouns 'who', 'whose', 'whom', 'what', and 'which', when they are used to ask questions.

interrogative sentence a sentence in the form of a question.

intransitive verb a verb which does not take an object; EG *She **arrived**... I was **yawning***.

irregular a word or form which does not follow the normal rules.

irregular verb a verb that has three forms or five forms, or whose forms do not follow the normal rules.

link verb a verb which takes a complement rather than an object; EG *be, become, seem, appear*.

main clause a clause which does not depend on another clause, and is not part of another clause.

main verb all verbs which are not auxiliaries or modals.

manner clause a subordinate clause which describes the way in which something is done, usually introduced with 'as' or 'like'; EG *She talks **like her mother used to***.

modal a verb such as 'can', 'might', or 'will', which is always the first word in a verb group and is followed by the base form of a verb. Modals are used to express requests, offers, suggestions, wishes, intentions, politeness, possibility, probability, certainty, obligation, and so on.

mood The mood of a clause is the way in which the verb forms are used to show whether the clause is a statement, command, or question.

negative a negative clause, question, sentence, or statement is one which has a negative word such as 'not', and indicates the absence or opposite of something, or is used to say that something is not the case; EG *I don't know you... I'll never forget*. Compare with **positive**.

negative word a word such as 'never', 'no', 'not', 'nothing', or 'nowhere', which makes a clause, question, sentence, or statement negative.

non-defining relative clause a relative clause which gives more information about someone or something, but which is not needed to identify them because we already know who or what they are; EG *That's Mary, **who was at university with me***. Compare with **defining relative clause**.

non-finite clause a 'to'-infinitive clause, '-ed' clause, or '-ing' clause.

noun a word which refers to people, things, ideas, feelings, or qualities; EG *woman, Harry, guilt*.

noun group a group of words which acts as the subject, complement, or object of a verb, or as the object of a preposition.

object a noun group which refers to a person or thing that is affected by the action described by a verb. Compare with **subject**. Prepositions also have noun groups as objects.

object pronoun one of a set of pronouns including 'me', 'him' and 'them', which are used as the object of a verb or preposition. Object pronouns are also used as complements after 'be'; EG *I hit **him**... It's **me***.

opinion adjective an adjective which you use to express your opinion of a person or thing, rather then just describing them. Compare with **descriptive adjective**.

ordinal number a number used to indicate where something comes in an order or sequence; EG *first, fifth, tenth, hundredth*.

participle a verb form used for making different tenses. Verbs have two participles, a present participle and a past participle.

particle an adverb or preposition which combines with verbs to form phrasal verbs.

passive voice verb groups such as 'was given', 'were taken', 'had been made', which are used when the subject of the verb is the person or thing that is affected by the action. Compare with **active voice**.

past form the form of a verb, often ending in '-ed', which is used for the past simple tense.

past participle a verb form which is used to form perfect tenses and passives. Some past participles are also used as adjectives; EG *watched, broken, swum*.

past tense see **tense**.

perfect tense see **tense**.

person one of the three classes of people who can be involved in something that is said. The person who is speaking or writing is called the first person. The people who are listening or reading are called the second person. The people or things that are being talked about are called the third person.

personal pronoun one of the group of words including 'I', 'you', and 'me', which are used to refer back to yourself, the people you are talking to, or the people or things you are talking about. See also **object pronoun** and **subject pronoun**.

phrasal verb a combination of a verb and a particle, which together have a different meaning to the verb on its own; EG *back down, hand over, look forward to*.

plural the form of a count noun or verb, which is used to refer to or talk about more than one person or thing; EG *Dogs have ears... The women were outside*.

plural noun a noun which is normally used only in the plural form; EG *trousers, scissors*.

positive a postive clause, question, sentence, or statement is one which does not contain a negative word such as 'not'.

possessive one of the determiners 'my', 'your', 'his', 'her', 'its', 'our', or 'their', which is used to show that one person or thing belongs to another; EG *your car*.

possessive adjective another name for **possessive**.

possessive pronoun one of the pronouns 'mine', 'yours', 'hers', 'his', 'ours', or 'theirs'.

preposition a word such as 'by', 'with' or 'from', which is always followed by a noun group.

prepositional phrase a structure consisting of a preposition followed by a noun group as its object; EG *on the table, by the sea*.

present participle see **'-ing' form**.

present tense see **tense**.

pronoun a word which you use instead of a noun, when you do not need or want to name someone or something directly; EG *it, you, none*.

progressive tense another name for **continuous tense**.

proper noun a noun which is the name of a particular person, place, organization, or building. Proper nouns are always written with a capital letter; EG *Nigel, Edinburgh, the United Nations, Christmas*.

purpose clause a subordinate clause which is used to talk about the intention that someone has when they do something; EG *I came here in order to ask you out to dinner*.

qualifier a word or group or words, such as an adjective, prepositional phrase, or relative clause, which comes after a noun and gives more information about it; EG *...the person involved... ...a book with a blue cover... ...the shop that I went into*.

question a sentence which normally has the verb in front of the subject, and which is used to ask someone about something; EG *Have you any money?*

question tag an auxiliary or modal with a pronoun, which is used to turn a statement into a question; EG *He's very friendly, isn't he?... I can come, can't I?*

reason clause a subordinate clause, usually introduced by 'because', 'since', or 'as', which is used to explain why something happens or is done; EG *Since you're here, we'll start*.

reciprocal verb a verb which describes an action which involves two people doing the same thing to each other; EG *I met you at the dance... We've met one another before... They met in the street*.

reflexive pronoun a pronoun ending in '-self' or '-selves', such as 'myself' or 'themselves', which you use as the object of a verb when you want to say that the object is the same person or thing as the subject of the verb in the same clause; EG *He hurt himself*.

reflexive verb a verb which is normally used with a reflexive pronoun as object; EG *He contented himself with the thought that he had the only set of keys*.

regular verb a verb that has four forms, and follows the normal rules.

relative clause a subordinate clause which gives more information about someone or something mentioned in the main clause. See also **defining relative clause** and **non-defining relative clause**.

relative pronoun 'that' or a 'wh'-word such as 'who' or 'which', when it is used to introduce a relative clause; EG *...the girl who was carrying the bag*.

reported clause the clause in a report structure which indicates what someone has said; EG *She said that I couldn't see her*.

reported question a question which is reported using a report structure rather than the exact words used by the speaker. See also **indirect question**.

reported speech the words you use to report what someone has said, rather than using their actual words. Also called indirect speech.

reporting clause the clause in a report structure which contains the reporting verb.

reporting verb a verb which describes what people say or think; EG; *suggest, say, wonder*.

report structure a structure which is used to report what someone says or thinks, rather than repeating their exact words; EG *She told me she'd be late*.

result clause a subordinate clause introduced by 'so', 'so...that', or 'such...(that)', which indicates the result of an action or situation; EG *I don't think there's any more news, **so I'll finish**.*

second person see **person**.

semi-modal a term used by some grammars to refer to the verbs 'dare', 'need', and 'used to', which behave like modals in some structures.

sentence a group of words which express a statement, question, or command. A sentence usually has a verb and a subject, and may be a simple sentence with one clause, or a compound or complex sentence with two or more clauses. In writing, a sentence has a capital letter at the beginning and a full-stop, question mark, or exclamation mark at the end.

short form a form in which one or more letters are omitted and two words are joined together, for example an auxiliary or modal and 'not', or a subject pronoun and an auxiliary or modal; EG *aren't, couldn't, he'd, I'm, it's, she's.*

simple tense a present or past tense formed without using an auxiliary verb; EG *I **wait**... she **sang**.*

singular the form of a count noun or verb which is used to refer to or talk about one person or thing; EG *A **dog was** in the **back** of the **car**... That **woman is** my **mother**.*

singular noun a noun which is normally used only in the singular form; EG *the sun, a bath.*

strong verb another name for **irregular verb.**

subject the noun group in a clause that refers to the person or thing who does the action expressed by the verb; EG *We were going shopping.*

subject pronoun one of the set of pronouns including 'I', 'she', and 'they', which are used as the subject of a verb.

subordinate clause a clause which must be used with a main clause and is not usually used alone, for example a time clause, conditional clause, relative clause, or result clause, and which begins with a subordinating conjunction such as 'because' or 'while'.

subordinating conjunction a conjunction such as 'although', 'as if', 'because' or 'while', which you use to begin a subordinate clause.

superlative an adjective or adverb with '-est' on the end or 'most' in front of it; EG *thinnest, quickest, most beautiful.*

tag question a statement to which a question tag has been added; EG *She's quiet, isn't she?*

tense the form of a verb which shows whether you are referring to the past, present, or future.

future 'will' or 'shall' with the base form of the verb, used to refer to future events; EG *She **will come** tomorrow.*

future continuous 'will' or 'shall' with 'be' and a present participle, used to refer to future events; EG *She **will be going** soon.*

future perfect 'will' or 'shall' with 'have' and a past participle, used to refer to future events; EG *I **shall have finished** by tomorrow.*

future perfect continuous 'will' or 'shall' with 'have been' and a present participle, used to refer to future events; EG *I **will have been walking** for three hours by then.*

past simple the past form of a verb, used to refer to past

events; EG *They **waited**.*

past continuous 'was' or 'were' with a present participle, usually used to refer to past events; EG *They **were worrying** about it yesterday.*

past perfect 'had' with a past participle, used to refer to past events; EG *She **had finished**.*

past perfect continuous 'had been' with a present participle, used to refer to past events; EG *He **had been waiting** for hours.*

present simple the base form and the third person singular form of a verb, usually used to refer to present events; EG *I **like** bananas... My sister **hates** them.*

present continuous the present simple of 'be' with a present participle, usually used to refer to present events; EG *Things **are improving**.*

present perfect 'have' or 'has' with a past participle, used to refer to past events which exist in the present; EG *She **has loved** him for ten years.*

present perfect continuous 'have been' or 'has been' with a present participle, used to refer to past events which continue in the present; EG *We **have been sitting** here for hours.*

'that'-clause a clause starting with 'that', used mainly when reporting what someone has said; EG *She said **that she'd wash up for me**.*

third person see **person**.

time clause a subordinate clause which indicates the time of an event; EG *I'll phone you **when I get back**.*

time expression a noun group used as an adverbial of time; EG *last night, the day after tomorrow, the next time.*

'to'-infinitive the base form of a verb preceded by 'to'; EG *to go, to have, to jump.*

transitive verb a verb which takes an object; EG *She's **wasting** her money.*

uncount noun a noun which has only one form, takes a singlar verb, and is not used with 'a' or numbers. Uncount nouns often refer to substances, qualities, feelings, activities, and abstract ideas; EG *coal, courage, anger, help, fun.*

verb a word which is used with a subject to say what someone or something does, or what happens to them; EG *sing, spill, die.*

verb group a main verb, or a main verb with one or more auxiliaries, a modal, or a modal and an auxiliary, which is used with a subject to say what someone does, or what happens to them; EG *I'**ll show** them... She'**s been** sick.*

'wh'-question a question which expects the answer to give more information than just 'yes' or 'no'; EG *What happened?... Where did he go?* Compare with **'yes/no'-question.**

'wh'-word one of a group of words starting with 'wh-', such as 'what', 'when' or 'who', which are used in 'wh'-questions. 'How' is also called a 'wh'-word because it behaves like the other 'wh'-words.

'yes/no'-question a question which can be answered by just 'yes' or 'no', without giving any more information; EG *Would you like some more tea?* Compare with **'wh'-question.**

List of Grammar Units

Aa

a /eɪ/ or /ə/, **an** /æn/ or /ən/. 1 DET You use **a** or **an** when you are referring to someone or something for the first time, or when you do not want to be specific. *Tom could see a hallway... She wanted to be an actress.* 2 DET You can use **a** or **an** instead of the number 'one'. *...in an hour's time.* 3 DET When you express rates, prices, and measurements, you can use **a** or **an** to say how many units apply to each of the items being measured. *He charges 100 dollars an hour.* 4 DET You can use **a** or **an** in front of uncount nouns when they are preceded by adjectives or followed by words that describe the uncount noun more fully. *...a happiness that he couldn't quite hide.*

aback /əbæk/. See **take aback.**

abacus /æbəkəs/, **abacuses.** COUNT N An **abacus** is a frame used for counting. It has rods with sliding beads on them.

abandon /əbændən/, **abandons, abandoning, abandoned.** 1 VB WITH OBJ If you **abandon** a place, thing, or person, you leave them permanently or for a long time. *You're not supposed to abandon your car on the motorway.* ♦ **abandonment** /əbændənmə2nt/ UNCOUNT N *...the abandonment of farms.* 2 VB WITH OBJ To **abandon** an activity or idea means to stop doing it or thinking about it before it is finished. *I abandoned the search.* ♦ **abandonment** UNCOUNT N *She disagreed with the abandonment of the project.* 3 REFL VB WITH PREP 'to' If you **abandon** yourself to an emotion, you feel it strongly and do not try to control it. *She abandoned herself to grief.* 4 UNCOUNT N If you do something with **abandon,** you do it in a carefree way.

abate /əbeɪt/, **abates, abating, abated.** VB When something **abates,** it becomes much less strong or widespread; a formal use. *My terror abated a little.*

abattoir /æbətwɑː/, **abattoirs.** COUNT N An **abattoir** is a place where animals are killed for meat.

abbey /æbi1/, **abbeys.** COUNT N An **abbey** is a church with buildings attached to it in which monks or nuns live.

abbot /æbət/, **abbots.** COUNT N An **abbot** is a monk in charge of the other monks in a monastery or abbey.

abbreviate /ə3briːvieɪt/, **abbreviates, abbreviating, abbreviated.** 1 VB WITH OBJ If you **abbreviate** a piece of writing or speech, you make it shorter. *Don't be afraid to abbreviate, to cut a paragraph here and there.* 2 VB WITH OBJ A word or phrase that **is abbreviated** is made shorter by leaving out some of the letters or by using only the first letters of each word.

abbreviation /ə3briːvieɪʃə0n/, **abbreviations.** COUNT N An **abbreviation** is a short form of a word or phrase, made by leaving out some of the letters or by using only the first letters of each word.

abdicate /æbdɪkeɪt/, **abdicates, abdicating, abdicated.** 1 VB If a king or queen **abdicates,** he or she resigns. *...the day Edward VIII abdicated* ♦ **abdication** /æbdɪkeɪʃə0n/ UNCOUNT N *...the abdication crisis of 1936.* 2 VB WITH OBJ If you **abdicate** responsibility for something, you refuse to accept the responsibility for it any longer. *We would be abdicating our responsibility to the local community.* ♦ **abdication** UNCOUNT N *...an abdication of political responsibility.*

abdomen /æbdə6mən/, **abdomens.** COUNT N Your **abdomen** is the part of your body below your chest where your stomach and intestines are. ♦ **abdominal** /ə3bdɒmɪ1nə0l/ ADJ *...a patient suffering from abdominal pains.*

abduct /ə3bdʌkt/, **abducts, abducting, abducted.** VB WITH OBJ If someone **abducts** another person, they take the person away illegally. *He was afraid of being abducted by a rival gang.*

aberration /æbəreɪʃə0n/, **aberrations.** COUNT N An **aberration** is an action or way of behaving that is not normal.

abet /əbet/, **abets, abetting, abetted.** VB WITH OBJ If you **abet** someone, you help or encourage them to do something wrong. *...aiding and abetting the enemy.*

abhor /ə3bhɔː/, **abhors, abhorring, abhorred.** VB WITH OBJ If you **abhor** something, you hate it very much; a formal use.

abhorrent /ə3bhɒrənt/. ADJ If something is **abhorrent** to you, you hate it and find it unacceptable; a formal use. *...a ruthless and utterly abhorrent system.*

abide /əbaɪd/, **abides, abiding, abided.** 1 PHRASE If you **can't abide** something, you dislike it very much. *He likes you but he can't abide Dennis.* 2 VB If something **abides,** it continues to happen or exist for a long time.

abide by. PHR VB If you **abide by** a law, agreement, or decision, you do what it says. *Both parties must agree to abide by the court's decision.*

ability /əbɪlə1ti1/, **abilities.** COUNT N OR UNCOUNT N Your **ability** to do something is the quality or skill that makes it possible for you to do it. *...the ability to see... ...his ability as a journalist.*

-ability. SUFFIX **-ability** is added in place of '-able' at the end of adjectives to form nouns referring to a quality or state. Nouns of this kind are often not defined but are treated with the related adjectives. *...the suitability of particular courses... ...their vulnerability to criticism.*

abject /æbdʒekt/. 1 ATTRIB ADJ You use **abject** to say that a situation or quality is shameful or depressing. *...abject poverty.* 2 ADJ Someone who is **abject** shows no self-respect or courage.

ablaze /əbleɪz/. 1 PRED ADJ Something that is **ablaze** is burning fiercely. 2 PRED ADJ WITH 'with' If a place is **ablaze** with lights or colours, it is very bright.

able /eɪbə0l/, **abler, ablest.** 1 PRED ADJ WITH TO-INF If someone or something is **able** to do something, they have the skill, knowledge, means, or opportunity to do it. *The frog is able to jump three metres... I wasn't able to do these quizzes.* 2 ADJ An **able** person is clever or good at doing something. *He was an unusually able detective.*

-able. SUFFIX **-able** is added to some verbs to form adjectives which describe someone or something as able to have something done to them. For example, something that is identifiable can be identified. *They are both immediately recognizable.*

ably /eɪbli1/. ADV **Ably** means skilfully and successfully. *They were ably supported by the Party members.*

abnormal /æbnɔːmə0l/. ADJ Someone or something that is **abnormal** is unusual or exceptional, especially in a worrying way. *Maybe my child is abnormal... ...an abnormal interest in food.* ♦ **abnormally** ADV *...people who are behaving abnormally.*

aboard /əbɔːd/. PREP OR ADV If you are **aboard** a ship or plane, you are on or in it. *The plane crashed, killing all 271 aboard.*

abode /əbəʊd/, **abodes.** COUNT N Your **abode** is the place where you live; a formal use.

abolish /əbɒlɪʃ/, **abolishes, abolishing, abolished.** VB WITH OBJ If you **abolish** a system or practice, you put an end to it. *They believed the death penalty should be abolished.* ♦ **abolition** /æbəlɪʃə0n/ UNCOUNT N WITH SUPP *...the abolition of slavery.*

abominable /əbɒmɪnəbə0l/. ADJ Something that is **abominable** is very unpleasant or very bad.

aboriginal /æbərɪdʒɪ1nə0l/, **aboriginals.** COUNT N An **aboriginal** is a member of one of the tribes which were living in Australia when Europeans arrived.

abort /əbɔːt/, **aborts, aborting, aborted.** 1 VB WITH OR WITHOUT OBJ If a woman's pregnancy **is aborted** or if she **aborts,** her pregnancy is ended deliberately and the baby dies. 2 ERG VB If you **abort** a process, plan, or activity, you stop it before it is finished.

abortion /əbɔːʃə0n/, **abortions.** COUNT N OR UNCOUNT N If a woman has an **abortion,** the pregnancy is ended deliberately and the baby dies.

abortive /əbɔːtɪv/. ATTRIB ADJ An **abortive** attempt or action is unsuccessful.

abound /əbaʊnd/, **abounds, abounding, abounded.** VB If a place **abounds** with things, there are very large numbers of them; a formal use.

about /əbaʊt/. 1 PREP The thing that you talk, write, or think **about** is the subject of what you are saying, writing, or thinking. *I'll have to think about that... This is a book about India.* 2 PREP If you do something **about** a problem, you take action to solve it. *They knew they had to do something about their mother's unhappiness.* 3 PREP When you say that there is a particular quality **about** someone or something, you mean that they have this quality. *There's something peculiar about him.* 4 ADV **About** in front of a number means approximately. *We went about forty miles.* 5 ADV If someone or something moves **about,** they keep moving in different directions. *We saw them walking about.* 6 PRED ADJ If someone or something is **about,** they are present or available. *There was no money about.* 7 PHRASE If you **are about to** do something, you are going to do it soon. *Her father is about to retire.*

above /əbʌv/. 1 PREP OR ADV If one thing is **above** another one, it is directly over it or higher than it. *...the branches above their heads... A noise was coming from the bedroom above.* 2 ADJ OR SING N You use **above** in writing to refer to something that has already been mentioned. *All the above items can be obtained from Selfridges... The above is a fair description of teaching machines.* 3 PREP OR ADV If an amount or measurement is **above** a particular level, it is greater than that level. *...children above the age of 5.* 4 PREP If someone is **above** you, they are in a position of authority over you. *He will have an executive above him to whom he reports.* 5 PREP If someone thinks that they are **above** a particular activity, they do not approve of it and refuse to become involved in it. *They consider themselves above such mercenary transactions.* 6 PREP If someone is **above** criticism or suspicion, they cannot be criticized or suspected because of their good qualities or their position. *...those whose loyalty and morals were above reproach.*

abrasion /əbreɪʒə0n/, **abrasions.** COUNT N An **abrasion** is an area of scraped or damaged skin; a formal use. *...abrasions to the side of the neck.*

abrasive /əbreɪsɪv/. 1 ADJ An **abrasive** person is unkind and rude. *He could be abrasive and insensitive.* 2 ADJ An **abrasive** substance is rough and can be used to clean hard surfaces.

abreast /əbrest/. 1 ADV If people or things walk or move **abreast,** they are side by side. *...carts pulled by donkeys three abreast.* 2 PREP If you keep **abreast of** a subject, you know all the most recent facts about it. *The press kept abreast of each development.*

abridged /əbrɪdʒd/. ADJ A book or play that has been **abridged** has been made shorter by removing some parts of it. *...an abridged version of the novel.*

abroad /əbrɔːd/. ADV If you go **abroad,** you go to a foreign country. *...a holiday abroad... I just got back from abroad.*

abrupt /əbrʌpt/. 1 ADJ An **abrupt** action is very sudden and often unpleasant. *It came to an abrupt end.* ♦ **abruptly** ADV *I had to apply the brakes abruptly.* 2 ADJ Someone who is **abrupt** is rather rude and unfriendly. *...David's abrupt and bullying manner.* ♦ **abruptly** ADV *I wouldn't have spoken so abruptly if I'd realized you were ill.*

abscess /æbsɪ2s/, **abscesses.** COUNT N An **abscess** is a painful, pus-filled swelling.

absence /æbsəns/, **absences.** 1 UNCOUNT N OR COUNT N Someone's **absence** from a place is the fact of their not being there. *...frequent absences from school.* 2 SING N The **absence** of something is the fact that it is not there. *The absence of electricity made matters worse.*

absent /æbsə2nt/. 1 ADJ If someone or something is **absent** from a place or situation, they are not there. *You have been absent twenty minutes.* 2 ADJ If someone appears **absent,** they are not paying attention. *...an absent stare.* ♦ **absently** ADV *'Did you?' Boylan said absently.*

absentee /æbsə2ntiː/, **absentees.** COUNT N An **absentee** is a person who should be in a particular place but who is not there. *...absentees from school.*

absent-minded. ADJ An **absent-minded** person is very forgetful. *She is so absent-minded and careless.* ♦ **absent-mindedly** ADV *...if you absent-mindedly drop a ring down the sink.*

absolute /æbsə6luːt/, **absolutes.** 1 ATTRIB ADJ **Absolute** means total and complete. *...the necessity for absolute secrecy.* 2 ATTRIB ADJ You use **absolute** to emphasize what you are saying. *The script is an absolute mess.* 3 ADJ An **absolute** ruler has complete power and authority over his or her country. 4 ATTRIB ADJ **Absolute** rules and principles are believed to be true or right for all situations. *...absolute doctrines.* Also COUNT N *...rigid absolutes, such as 'divorce is always wrong'.*

absolutely /æbsə6luːtli1/. 1 ADV OR SUBMOD **Absolutely** means totally and completely. *That's an absolutely fascinating piece of work.* 2 CONVENTION You say **absolutely** as an emphatic way of agreeing with someone. *'She's excellent, though.'—'Absolutely.'*

absolve /ə3bzɒlv/, **absolves, absolving, absolved.** VB WITH OBJ If someone **is absolved** from blame or responsibility, a formal statement is made that they are not guilty or are not to blame.

absorb /ə3bsɔːb, -zɔːb/, **absorbs, absorbing, absorbed.** 1 VB WITH OBJ To **absorb** a substance means to soak it up or take it in. *Frogs absorb water through their skins.* 2 VB WITH OBJ If a group **is absorbed** into a larger group, it becomes part of the larger group. *Small businesses are absorbed by larger ones.* 3 VB WITH OBJ If a system or society **absorbs** changes or effects, it is able to cope with them. 4 VB WITH OBJ If you **absorb** information, you learn and understand it. 5 VB WITH OBJ If something **absorbs** you, it interests you and gets all your attention. ♦ **absorbed** ADJ *I was utterly absorbed in what I was doing.* ♦ **absorbing** ADJ *The work is absorbing.*

absorbent /ə3bsɔːbənt, -zɔː-/. ADJ **Absorbent** material soaks up liquid easily. *Dry it inside with an absorbent cloth.*

absorption /ə3bsɔːpʃə0n, -zɔːp-/. 1 SING N WITH SUPP If you have an **absorption** in something, you are very interested in it. 2 UNCOUNT N WITH SUPP **Absorption** is the action of absorbing something. *...the absorption of foreign minorities.*

abstain /ə^{3}bsteɪn/, **abstains, abstaining, abstained.** 1 VB If you **abstain** from doing something, you deliberately do not do it. 2 VB If you **abstain** during a vote, you do not vote.

abstention /ə^{3}bstenʃə^{0}n/, **abstentions.** COUNT N OR UNCOUNT N An **abstention** is a formal act of not voting. *There were 4 abstentions... We have the right of abstention.*

abstinence /æbstɪ^{1}nəns/. UNCOUNT N **Abstinence** is the practice of not having something you enjoy, such as alcoholic drinks.

abstract, abstracts, abstracting, abstracted; pronounced /æbstrækt/ when it is an adjective or noun, and /ə^{3}bstrækt/ when it is a verb. 1 ADJ An **abstract** idea or argument is based on general ideas rather than on particular things and events. *...our capacity for abstract reasoning.* 2 ATTRIB ADJ **Abstract** is a style of art using shapes and colours rather than representing people or things. *...abstract sculptures.* 3 ATTRIB ADJ An **abstract** noun describes a quality or idea rather than a physical object. 4 COUNT N An **abstract** of an article or speech is a short piece of writing that summarizes the main points of it. 5 VB WITH OBJ If you **abstract** information from an article or other piece of writing, you make a summary of the main points in it.

abstracted /ə^{3}bstræktɪ^{2}d/. ADJ Someone whose behaviour is **abstracted** does not notice what is happening around them. *...a dreamy, abstracted stare.*

abstraction /ə^{3}bstrækʃə^{0}n/, **abstractions.** COUNT N An **abstraction** is a general idea rather than one relating to a specific thing. *...abstractions of philosophy and religion.*

absurd /ə^{3}bsɜːd/. ADJ Something that is **absurd** is ridiculous. *It seemed absurd to try to carry a twenty-five-pound camera about.* ♦ **absurdity** /ə^{3}bsɜːdɪ^{1}ti^{1}/ COUNT N OR UNCOUNT N *...the oddities and absurdities of the language... ...a feeling of absurdity.* ♦ **absurdly** ADV OR SUBMOD *...an absurdly low rent.*

abundance /əbʌndəns/. 1 SING N An **abundance** of something is a large quantity of it. *...an abundance of evidence.* 2 PHRASE If something is **in abundance,** there is a lot of it. *There was grass in abundance.*

abundant /əbʌndə^{2}nt/. ADJ Something that is **abundant** is present in large quantities. *...an abundant supply of food.*

abundantly /əbʌndə^{2}ntli^{1}/. SUBMOD If something is **abundantly** obvious, it is extremely obvious. *It has become abundantly clear that there is no time to lose.*

abuse, abuses, abusing, abused; pronounced /ə^{3}bjuːs/ when it is a noun and /ə^{3}bjuːz/ when it is a verb. 1 UNCOUNT N **Abuse** is rude and unkind things that people say when they are angry. *The girls shrieked abuse at the lawyers.* 2 VB WITH OBJ If someone **abuses** you, they say rude or unkind things to you or treat you cruelly and violently. *He did not like to hear Elaine abused or criticized... The patients were often physically abused.* 3 UNCOUNT N WITH SUPP **Abuse** of someone is cruel and violent treatment of them. *...found guilty of gross neglect and abuse.* 4 VB WITH OBJ If you **abuse** something, you use it in a wrong way or for a bad purpose. 5 UNCOUNT N **Abuse** of something is the use of it in a wrong way or for a bad purpose. *...drug abuse.*

abusive /ə^{3}bjuːsɪv/. ADJ Someone who is **abusive** says rude or unkind things. *...abusive language.*

abysmal /əbɪzmə^{0}l/. ADJ **Abysmal** means very bad or poor in quality. *...abysmal wages... ...an abysmal failure.* ♦ **abysmally** ADV *He failed abysmally.*

abyss /ə^{3}bɪs/, **abysses.** 1 COUNT N An **abyss** is a very deep hole in the ground. *We looked down into the abyss.* 2 COUNT N WITH SUPP A very frightening or threatening situation can be referred to as an **abyss;** a literary use. *The world was teetering on the edge of the abyss of World War III.*

AC /eɪ siː/. **AC** is used to refer to an electric current that continually changes direction as it flows. **AC** is an abbreviation for 'alternating current'.

academic /ækədemɪk/, **academics.** 1 ATTRIB ADJ **Academic** work is work done in schools, colleges, and universities. *...the academic system.* ♦ **academically** ADV *...people who are well qualified academically.* 2 ADJ Someone who is **academic** is good at studying. 3 COUNT N An **academic** is a member of a university or college who teaches or does research. 4 ADJ You also use **academic** to say that you think a particular point has no real effect on or relevance to what is happening. *It was all academic, because there were never any profits to share out.*

academy /ə^{3}kædə^{2}mi^{1}/, **academies.** COUNT N A school or college specializing in a particular subject is sometimes called an **academy.** *...the Royal Academy of Dramatic Art.*

accede /ə^{3}ksiːd/, **accedes, acceding, acceded.** VB If you **accede** to someone's request or opinion, you allow it or agree with it; a formal use.

accelerate /ə^{3}kseləreɪt/, **accelerates, accelerating, accelerated.** VB When the rate or speed of something **accelerates,** it increases. *Inflation rates began to accelerate.* ♦ **acceleration** /ə^{3}kseləreɪʃə^{0}n/ UNCOUNT N *...the acceleration of economic growth.*

accelerator /ə^{3}kseləreɪtə/, **accelerators.** COUNT N The **accelerator** in a vehicle is the pedal which is pressed to make the vehicle go faster.

accent, accents, accenting, accented; pronounced /æksə^{2}nt/ when it is a noun and /æksent/ when it is a verb. 1 COUNT N Someone who speaks with a particular **accent** pronounces the words of a language in a way that indicates their country, region, or social class. *She has a strong Irish accent.* 2 COUNT N An **accent** is also a mark written above or below certain letters in some languages to show how they are pronounced. 3 SING N If the **accent** is on a particular feature of something, that feature is its most important part. *The accent is on presentation in this contest.* 4 VB WITH OBJ If you **accent** a word or a musical note, you emphasize it.

accentuate /ə^{3}ksentʃueɪt/, **accentuates, accentuating, accentuated.** VB WITH OBJ To **accentuate** something means to emphasize it. *These laws accentuate inequality and exploitation.*

accept /ə^{3}ksept/, **accepts, accepting, accepted.** 1 VB WITH OR WITHOUT OBJ If you **accept** something that you have been offered, agree to take it. *He accepted our invitation... I thanked him and accepted.* ♦ **acceptance** /ə^{3}kseptəns/ UNCOUNT N *...the acceptance of foreign aid.* 2 VB WITH OBJ If you **accept** someone's advice or suggestion, you agree to do what they say. *I knew that they would accept my proposal.* 3 REPORT VB If you **accept** a story or statement, you believe it. *The panel accepted her version of the story... The majority do not accept that there has been any discrimination.* 4 VB WITH OBJ To **accept** a difficult or unpleasant situation means to recognize that it cannot be changed. *...unwillingness to accept bad working conditions.* ♦ **acceptance** UNCOUNT N *...their acceptance of their plight.* 5 VB WITH OBJ If you **accept** the blame or responsibility for something, you admit that you are responsible for it. 6 VB WITH OBJ When an institution or organization **accepts** someone, they give them a job or allow them to join. *I was accepted by the Open University.* ♦ **acceptance** UNCOUNT N *...a letter of acceptance.* 7 VB WITH OBJ If a group **accepts** you, they begin to think of you as part of the group. *The children gradually begin to accept her.* ♦ **acceptance** UNCOUNT N *...her speedy acceptance into the San Diego community.* 8 See also **accepted.**

acceptable /ə^{3}kseptəbə^{0}l/. 1 ADJ If a situation or action is **acceptable,** people generally approve of it or allow it to happen. *In war killing is acceptable.* ♦ **acceptability** /əkseptə^{1}bɪlɪ^{1}ti^{1}/ UNCOUNT N *The proof of the doctrine is its acceptability to the man in the street.* ♦ **acceptably** ADV *...an acceptably low heat loss.* 2 ADJ If you think that something such as an action, a plan or a piece of work is **acceptable,** you consider it to be good enough. *To my relief he found the article acceptable... ...a strategy acceptable to all classes and interests.*

accepted /ə^{3}kseptɪ^{2}d/. ATTRIB ADJ **Accepted** ideas are generally agreed to be correct. *...the accepted wisdom about old age.*

access /ækses/, **accesses, accessing, accessed.** 1 UNCOUNT N If you gain **access** to a building or other place, you succeed in getting into it; a formal use. *They attempted to gain access through a side entrance... The entrance door gives access to a living room.* 2 UNCOUNT N **Access** is also the opportunity or right to use or see something or someone. *I demanded access to a telephone... Has Donald got access to the child?* 3 VB WITH OBJ If you **access** information from a computer, you get it.

accessible /ə^{3}ksesə^{1}bə^{0}l/. 1 ADJ If a place is **accessible,** you are able to reach it. *The hidden room was accessible only through a secret back entrance.* ♦ **accessibility** /əksesə^{1}bɪlɪ^{1}ti^{1}/ UNCOUNT N 2 PRED ADJ WITH PREP 'to' If something is **accessible** to people, they are able to use it or understand it. *...computers cheap enough to be accessible to virtually everyone.*

accessory /ə^{3}ksesəri^{1}/, **accessories.** 1 COUNT N **Accessories** are extra parts added to a machine or tool to make it more efficient or useful. *...an attractive range of accessories such as built-in tape decks and radios.* 2 COUNT N **Accessories** are also articles such as belts or handbags which you wear or carry but which are not part of your main clothing. 3 COUNT N An **accessory** to a crime is a person who knows who committed the crime but does not tell the police; a legal use. *They are all accessories to murder.*

accident /æksɪdə^{2}nt/, **accidents.** 1 COUNT N An **accident** is an event which happens completely by chance. *The fact that there is a university here is due to a historic accident.* 2 COUNT N An **accident** is also something unpleasant and unfortunate that happens and that often leads to injury or death. *She was killed in a motor accident.* 3 PHRASE If something happens **by accident,** it happens completely by chance. *I only came to Liverpool by accident.*

accidental /æksɪdentə^{0}l/. ADJ Something that is **accidental** happens by chance. *The evidence doesn't suggest accidental death.* ♦ **accidentally** ADV *We accidentally found an ideal solution.*

acclaim /əkleɪm/, **acclaims, acclaiming, acclaimed.** VB WITH OBJ If someone or something **is acclaimed,** they are praised enthusiastically; a formal use. *He has been widely acclaimed for his paintings.* Also UNCOUNT N *His book was published in 1919 and met with unusual acclaim.*

acclimatize /əklaɪmətaɪz/, **acclimatizes, acclimatizing, acclimatized;** also spelled **acclimatise.** VB OR REFL VB When you **acclimatize** to something or **acclimatize** yourself to it, you become used to it. *Once you've acclimatized to the heat you won't feel so tired.*

accolade /ækə^{6}leɪd/, **accolades.** COUNT N WITH SUPP An **accolade** is praise or an award given publicly to someone who is greatly admired; a formal use. *This was the highest accolade he could receive.*

accommodate /əkɒmədeɪt/, **accommodates, accommodating, accommodated.** 1 VB WITH OBJ If you **accommodate** someone, you provide them with a place where they can stay, live, or work. *She can't accommodate guests at the moment.* 2 VB WITH OBJ To **accommodate** someone also means to help them. *The bank is accommodating its customers more than it used to.* ♦ **accommodating** ADJ *The warder was always accommodating in allowing visitors in.* 3 VB WITH OBJ If a building can **accommodate** a number of people or things, it has enough room for them.

accommodation /əkɒmədeɪʃə^{0}n/. UNCOUNT N **Accommodation** is a room or building to stay in, work in, or live in. *There is a shortage of accommodation.*

accompaniment /əkʌmpə^{0}nɪmə^{2}nt/, **accompaniments.** 1 UNCOUNT N The **accompaniment** to a song or tune is the music that is played at the same time to form a background. *...a guitar accompaniment.* 2 COUNT N An **accompaniment** to something is another thing that happens or exists at the same time. *This sauce is often served as an accompaniment to fish.*

accompanist /əkʌmpə^{0}nɪst/, **accompanists.** COUNT N An **accompanist** is a musician who plays one part of a piece of music while someone else sings or plays the main tune.

accompany /əkʌmpəni^{1}/, **accompanies, accompanying, accompanied.** 1 VB WITH OBJ If you **accompany** someone, you go somewhere with them. *She asked me to accompany her to the church.* 2 VB WITH OBJ If one thing **accompanies** another, the two things happen or exist at the same time. *A high fever often accompanies a mild infection.* 3 VB WITH OBJ OR REFL VB When you **accompany** a singer or a musician, you play one part of a piece of music while they sing or play the main tune.

accomplice /əkɒmplɪs, əkʌm-/, **accomplices.** COUNT N An **accomplice** is a person who helps to commit a crime.

accomplish /əkɒmplɪʃ, əkʌm-/, **accomplishes, accomplishing, accomplished.** VB WITH OBJ If you **accomplish** something, you succeed in doing it. *I never seem to accomplish anything.*

accomplished /əkɒmplɪʃt, əkʌm-/. ADJ If someone is **accomplished,** they are very good at something. *...an accomplished cook.*

accomplishment /əkɒmplɪʃmə^{2}nt, əkʌm-/, **accomplishments.** 1 COUNT N Your **accomplishments** are the things you do well. *One of her few accomplishments was the ability to do cartwheels.* 2 UNCOUNT N WITH SUPP The **accomplishment** of a task or plan is the fact of finishing it; a formal use. *The accomplishment of this task filled him with satisfaction.* 3 COUNT N WITH SUPP An **accomplishment** is something remarkable that has been done or achieved.

accord /ə^{3}kɔːd/, **accords, according, accorded.** 1 PHRASE When you do something **of your own accord,** you do it freely and because you want to. *She knew they would leave of their own accord.* 2 UNCOUNT N If people are in **accord,** they agree about something. *There are few issues on which the two are in perfect accord.* 3 VB WITH OBJ AND OBJ OR PREP 'to' To **accord** someone a particular kind of treatment means to treat them in that way. *Newsmen accorded her the kind of coverage normally reserved for film stars... They are given more importance than we would accord to them if left to ourselves.*

accordance /ə^{3}kɔːdəns/. PHRASE If something is done **in accordance with** a rule or system, it is done in the way that the rule or system says it should be done. *...in accordance with Islamic law.*

accordingly /ə^{3}kɔːdɪŋli^{1}/. ADV You use **accordingly** to say that one thing happens as the result of another thing. *He wanted to be treated like any other star entertainer, and paid accordingly.*

according to. 1 PREP If something is true **according to** a particular person or book, that person or book claims that it is true. *According to Dr Santos, the cause of death was drowning.* 2 PREP If something is done **according to** a particular principle or plan, this principle or plan is used as the basis for the way it is done. *Each person was given tasks according to their skills... There are six classes organized according to age.*

accordion /ə[3]kɔːdɪən/, **accordions.** COUNT N An **accordion** is a box-shaped musical instrument which is played by pressing buttons and moving the two sides together and apart.

accost /əkɒst/, **accosts, accosting, accosted.** VB WITH OBJ If you **accost** someone, you stop them and speak to them. *In the hall he was accosted by two men.*

account /əkaʊnt/, **accounts, accounting, accounted.** 1 COUNT N An **account** is a written or spoken report of something that has happened. *There were accounts of the incident in the paper.* 2 COUNT N **Accounts** are detailed records of all the money that a person or business receives and spends. *He had to submit accounts of his expenditure.* 3 COUNT N If you have an **account** with a bank, you leave money with it and withdraw it when you need it. 4 COUNT N If you have an **account** with a shop or company, you can get goods or services from there and pay at a later time.

PHRASES • If you **take** something **into account** you consider it when you are thinking about a situation. • If you do something **on account of** something or someone, you do it because of that thing or person. *'Auntie told me not to run,' he explained, 'on account of my asthma.'* • If you say that something should **on no account** be done, you mean that it should not be done under any circumstances. *On no account must strangers be let in.* • If something is **of no account,** it does not matter at all.

account for. PHR VB 1 If you **account for** something, you explain how it happened. *How do you account for the dent in the car?* 2 If something **accounts for** a particular part or proportion of a whole thing, it is what that part or proportion consists of. *Computer software accounts for some 70 per cent of our range of products.*

accountable /əkaʊntəbə[0]l/. PRED ADJ If you are **accountable** for something that you do, you are responsible for it. *They cannot be held accountable for what they did.* ♦ **accountability** UNCOUNT N *...the need for greater accountability of the police.*

accountancy /əkaʊntənsi[1]/. UNCOUNT N **Accountancy** is the work of keeping financial accounts.

accountant /əkaʊntənt/, **accountants.** COUNT N An **accountant** is a person whose job is to keep financial accounts.

accredit /ə[3]krɛdɪt/, **accredits, accrediting, accredited.** VB WITH OBJ If someone **is accredited** in a particular position or job, their position or job is officially recognized. *...an accredited shop steward.*

accumulate /ə[3]kjuːmjə[4]leɪt/, **accumulates, accumulating, accumulated.** ERG VB When you **accumulate** things, they collect or gather over a period of time. *...the things I had accumulated over the last four years.* ♦ **accumulation** /ə[3]kjuːmjə[4]leɪʃə[0]n/, COUNT N *...an accumulation of facts.*

accuracy /ækjə[4]rəsi[1]/. 1 UNCOUNT N **Accuracy** is the ability to perform a task without making a mistake. *...the speed and accuracy with which she typed.* 2 UNCOUNT N **Accuracy** is also the quality of being true or correct. *...the reputation of The Times for accuracy.*

accurate /ækjə[4]rə[1]t/. 1 ADJ An **accurate** account or description gives a true idea of what someone or something is like. *...an accurate picture of social history.* ♦ **accurately** ADV *The story is accurately told.* 2 ADJ A person, device, or machine that is **accurate** is able to perform a task without making a mistake. *Missiles are becoming more accurate... She is accurate in punctuation and spelling.* ♦ **accurately** ADV *I have not drawn it accurately enough.*

accusation /ækjə[4]zeɪʃə[0]n/, **accusations.** 1 COUNT N An **accusation** is a statement that someone has done something wrong. *...accusations of cheating.* 2 UNCOUNT N **Accusation** is the quality of showing by your behaviour that you think someone has done something wrong. *Her eyes were full of accusation.*

accuse /ə[3]kjuːz/, **accuses, accusing, accused.** 1 VB WITH OBJ If you **accuse** someone of something, you say they have done something wrong. *He was accused of incompetence.* 2 VB WITH OBJ If someone **is accused** of a crime, they have been charged with the crime and are on trial for it. *He is accused of killing ten young women.*

accused /ə[3]kjuːzd/. **Accused** is the singular and plural. COUNT N The **accused** refers to the person or people being tried in a court for a crime. *Will the accused please stand?*

accusing /ə[3]kjuːzɪŋ/. ADJ If your expression or tone of voice is **accusing,** it indicates that you think someone has done something wrong. *She gave him an accusing look.* ♦ **accusingly** ADV *'You liked him,' he said accusingly.*

accustom /ə[3]kʌstəm/, **accustoms, accustoming, accustomed.** REFL VB OR VB WITH OBJ If you **accustom** yourself to something different, you make yourself get used to it. *He sat very still, trying to accustom himself to the darkness... I think it is preferable to accustom babies to sleeping on the stomach.* ♦ **accustomed** PRED ADJ WITH PREP 'to' *I am not accustomed to being interrupted.*

ace /eɪs/, **aces.** COUNT N An **ace** is a playing card with a single symbol on it.

ache /eɪk/, **aches, aching, ached.** 1 VB If you **ache** or if a part of your body **aches,** you feel a dull steady pain. *I was tired, aching, and miserable... His leg ached.* 2 VB If you **ache** for something or **ache** to do something, you want it very much. *She was aching for a cigarette... I was aching to tell you all my news.* 3 COUNT N An **ache** is a dull steady pain in a part of your body. *...my usual aches and pains.*

achieve /ə[3]tʃiːv/, **achieves, achieving, achieved.** VB WITH OBJ If you **achieve** a particular aim or effect, you succeed in obtaining it. *The riots achieved nothing.*

achievement /ə[3]tʃiːvmə[2]nt/, **achievements.** 1 COUNT N WITH SUPP An **achievement** is something which someone has succeeded in doing, especially after a lot of effort. *It was an astonishing achievement.* 2 UNCOUNT N **Achievement** is the process of achieving something. *This fact did not lessen her sense of achievement.*

acid /æsɪd/, **acids.** 1 MASS N An **acid** is a liquid or substance with a pH value of less than 7. Strong acids can damage your skin and clothes. *Dab it with a solution of weak acid.* Also ADJ *...an acid soil.* 2 ADJ An **acid** fruit or drink has a sour or sharp taste. 3 ADJ An **acid** remark is unkind or critical. *...her acid wit.*

acidic /ə[3]sɪdɪk/. ADJ Something that is **acidic** contains acid or has a pH value of less than 7.

acidity /ə[3]sɪdɪ[1]ti[1]/. 1 UNCOUNT N **Acidity** is the quality of having a pH value lower than 7. *...the acidity of the wine.* 2 UNCOUNT N **Acidity** is also the making of unkind or critical remarks. *I noticed a certain acidity in his comments.*

acknowledge /ə[3]knɒlɪdʒ/, **acknowledges, acknowledging, acknowledged.** 1 VB WITH OBJ If a fact or a situation **is acknowledged,** it is accepted as true or correct. *He was acknowledged as America's finest writer... Most people will now acknowledge that there is a crisis.* 2 VB WITH OBJ If you **acknowledge** someone, you show that you have seen and recognized them. 3 VB WITH OBJ If you **acknowledge** a message, letter, or parcel, you tell the person who sent it that you have received it. *You have to sign here and acknowledge receipt.*

acknowledgement /ə[3]knɒlɪdʒmə[2]nt/, **acknowledgements;** also spelled **acknowledgment.** 1 UNCOUNT N OR COUNT N **Acknowledgement** of something is admitting or accepting that it is true. *...his acknowledgement of his guilt... There was some acknowledgement that his parents had to be involved.* 2 UNCOUNT N **Acknowledgement** is the expression of gratitude for something that someone has done or said. *...her acknowledgement of their offerings.* 3 UNCOUNT N **Acknowledgement** of someone is showing that you have seen and recognized them. *One of the men raised an arm in acknowledgement.* 4 UNCOUNT N OR COUNT N **Acknowledgement** of a message, letter, or parcel is telling the sender that it has arrived. *...in acknowledgement of telephone orders.* 5 PLURAL N The **acknowledgements** in a book are the parts in which the author thanks the people who have helped.

acne /ækni[1]/. UNCOUNT N Someone who has **acne** has a lot of spots on their face and neck.

acorn /eɪkɔːn/, **acorns.** COUNT N An **acorn** is a pale oval nut that is the fruit of an oak tree.

acoustic /əkuːstɪk/, **acoustics.** 1 ATTRIB ADJ **Acoustic** means relating to sound or hearing. *Acoustic contact had been made.* 2 PLURAL N The **acoustics** of a room are the structural features which determine how well you can hear music or speeches in it. *The theatre was large, with good acoustics.*

acquaint /əkweɪnt/, **acquaints, acquainting, acquainted.** VB WITH OBJ AND 'with' If you **acquaint** someone with something, you tell them about it; a formal use. *I will acquaint you with the facts.*

acquaintance /əkweɪntəns/, **acquaintances.** 1 COUNT N An **acquaintance** is someone who you have met but do not know well. *My cousin is an acquaintance of Lord Northcliffe.* 2 SING N WITH SUPP Your **acquaintance** with a subject is your knowledge or experience of it. *...her acquaintance with modern art.*

PHRASES • When you **make** someone's **acquaintance,** you meet them for the first time. • If you have a **nodding** or **passing acquaintance** with someone, you know them slightly but not very well.

acquainted /əkweɪntɪ[2]d/. PRED ADJ If you are **acquainted** with someone, you know them slightly but they are not a close friend. *Mrs Oliver is acquainted with my mother... The families were acquainted.*

acquiesce /ækwiɛs/, **acquiesces, acquiescing, acquiesced.** VB If you **acquiesce** to something, you agree to do it; a formal use. *He acquiesced to the demand.*

acquiescence /ækwi[1]ɛsə[0]ns/. UNCOUNT N **Acquiescence** is agreement to do what someone wants or acceptance of what they do.

acquire /ə[3]kwaɪə/, **acquires, acquiring, acquired.** 1 VB WITH OBJ If you **acquire** something, you obtain it. *I tried to acquire the information I needed.* 2 VB WITH OBJ If you **acquire** a skill or habit, you learn it or develop it. *It is a habit well worth acquiring.* ♦ **acquired** ADJ *...hereditary and acquired characteristics.*

acquisition /ækwi[1]zɪʃə[0]n/, **acquisitions.** 1 COUNT N An **acquisition** is something that you have obtained. *He invited me to inspect his latest acquisition.* 2 UNCOUNT N WITH SUPP The **acquisition** of something is the process of getting it or being given it. *...the acquisition of land.* 3 UNCOUNT N WITH SUPP The **acquisition** of a skill or habit is the process of learning it or developing it. *...the acquisition of knowledge.*

acquit /əkwɪt/, **acquits, acquitting, acquitted.** 1 VB WITH OBJ If someone **is acquitted** of a crime, it is formally declared in court that they did not commit it. *The jury acquitted her of theft... Campbell was acquitted on all charges.* 2 REFL VB If you **acquit** yourself in a particular way, other people feel that you behave in that way; a formal use. *She acquitted herself well.*

acquittal /əkwɪtə[0]l/, **acquittals.** UNCOUNT N OR COUNT N **Acquittal** is a formal declaration that someone who has been accused of a crime is innocent.

acre /eɪkə/, **acres.** COUNT N An **acre** is a unit of area equal to 4840 square yards or approximately 4047 square metres.

acrid /ækrɪd/. ADJ An **acrid** smell or taste is strong, sharp, and unpleasant. *...acrid smoke.*

acrimonious /ækrɪ[1]məʊnɪəs/. ADJ **Acrimonious** words or quarrels are bitter and angry; a formal use. *An acrimonious dispute broke out.*

acrimony /ækrɪ[1]məni[1]/. UNCOUNT N **Acrimony** is bitterness and anger about something; a formal use. *...acrimony over the involvement of the police.*

acrobat /ækrə[6]bæt/, **acrobats.** COUNT N An **acrobat** is an entertainer who performs difficult jumps, somersaults, and balancing acts.

acrobatic /ækrə[6]bætɪk/, **acrobatics.** 1 ADJ An **acrobatic** movement or display involves difficult jumps, somersaults, and balancing acts. 2 PLURAL N **Acrobatics** are acrobatic movements.

acronym /ækrə[6]nɪm/, **acronyms.** COUNT N An **acronym** is a word made of the initial letters of the words in a phrase, especially when this is the name of something. An example of an acronym is NATO.

across /əkrɒs/. 1 PREP OR ADV If you go or look **across** somewhere, you go or look from one side of it to the other. *We ran across the bridge... He turned his head and looked across at me.* 2 PREP Something that is situated or stretched **across** something else is situated or stretches from one side to the other. *...a banner stretched across the street... A straight line was ruled across the map.* 3 PREP Something that is situated **across** a street or river is on the other side of it. *He stared at the houses across the street.* 4 ADV **Across** is used to indicate the width of something. *The bomb blasted a hole 200 kilometres across.*

acrylic /əkrɪlɪk/. ATTRIB ADJ **Acrylic** material is man-made, manufactured by a chemical process.

act /ækt/, **acts, acting, acted.** 1 VB When you **act,** you do something for a particular purpose. *We have to act quickly... He acted alone in the shooting.* 2 VB WITH ADJUNCT If someone **acts** in a particular way, they behave in that way. *We acted as if we had never seen each other before.* 3 VB WITH 'as' OR 'like' If one thing **acts** as another, it functions as that other thing. *The shark can twist its fins to act as brakes.* 4 VB WITH OR WITHOUT OBJ If you **act** in a play or film, you have a part in it. 5 COUNT N WITH SUPP An **act** is a single action or thing that someone does. *Sometimes the act of writing down the problems straightens out your thinking.* • If you are **in the act of** doing something, you are doing it. *He saw Jones in the act of snatching a gun.* 6 SING N If you say that someone's behaviour is an **act,** you mean that it does not express their real feelings. *She appeared calm and confident but it was just an act.* 7 COUNT N An **Act** is a law passed by the government. *...the 1944 Education Act.* 8 COUNT N An **act** in a play, opera, or ballet is one of the main parts into which it is divided. 9 COUNT N An **act** in a show is one of the short performances in the show. *...comedy acts.*

act up. PHR VB If someone or something **is acting up,** they are not working or behaving properly. *Her car has started acting up again.*

acting /æktɪŋ/. 1 UNCOUNT N **Acting** is the activity or profession of performing in plays or films. *...the brilliant acting of Hawtrey.* 2 ATTRIB ADJ You use **acting** before the title of a job to indicate that someone is only doing that job temporarily. *...Yassin, acting Director of Education.*

action /ækʃə^{0}n/, **actions.** 1 UNCOUNT N **Action** is doing something for a particular purpose. *The government was already taking action.* 2 COUNT N An **action** is something that you do on a particular occasion. *Surely resigning was rather a rash action?* 3 SING N The **action** refers to all the important and exciting things that are happening in a situation. *They want to be where the action is... The whole action of the book takes place in one day.* 4 UNCOUNT N **Action** is also fighting in a war. *...reports of military action... Henry had been killed in action.*

PHRASES ● If you **put** an idea or policy **into action,** you begin to use it. ● If a machine is **out of action,** it does not work.

activate /æktɪ^{1}veɪt/, **activates, activating, activated.** VB WITH OBJ If a device or process **is activated,** something causes it to start working. *The gates will open automatically when the detection equipment is activated.*

active /æktɪv/. 1 ADJ An **active** person is energetic and always busy or moving about. *...active and noisy children.* 2 ADJ If someone is **active** in an organization or cause, they are involved in it and work hard for it. *He was active in drawing public attention to our problems.* ♦ **actively** ADV *He had not actively participated in politics.* 3 ATTRIB ADJ You use **active** to say that something is done with energy or enthusiasm. *The proposal is under active discussion.* ♦ **actively** ADV *Such qualities were actively discouraged.* 4 ADJ An **active** volcano has erupted recently.

activist /æktɪvɪst/, **activists.** COUNT N An **activist** is a person who works to bring about political or social changes.

activity /æktɪvɪ^{1}ti^1/, **activities.** 1 UNCOUNT N **Activity** is a situation in which a lot of things are happening. *There was a flurry of activity in the hall.* 2 COUNT N An **activity** is something that you spend time doing. *I find tennis a very enjoyable activity.* 3 PLURAL N WITH SUPP The **activities** of a group are the things they do to achieve their aims. *...the activities of trade unions.*

actor /æktə/, **actors.** COUNT N An **actor** is someone whose job is acting in plays or films.

actress /æktrɪ^{2}s/, **actresses.** COUNT N An **actress** is a woman whose job is acting in plays or films.

actual /æktʃ^{0}uəl/. 1 ATTRIB ADJ **Actual** is used to emphasize that a place, object, or person is real and not imaginary. *The predicted results and the actual results are very different.* 2 ATTRIB ADJ You can also use **actual** to indicate that you are referring only to the specific thing mentioned and not to other things associated with it. *The actual wedding procession starts at 10 a.m.*

actually /æktʃ^{0}uəli^1/. 1 ADV You use **actually** to indicate that a situation exists in real life or that it is true or correct. *No one actually saw this shark... He actually died in exile, didn't he?* 2 SENTENCE ADV You also use **actually** as a way of being more polite, especially when you are correcting or contradicting someone, advising them, or when you are introducing a new topic of conversation. *Actually, it was more complicated than that... Actually it might be a good idea to stop recording now... Actually, Dan, before I forget, she asked me to give you this.*

acumen /ækjʊmen/. UNCOUNT N **Acumen** is the ability to make good judgements and quick decisions. *...a man with big ideas and keen business acumen.*

acute /ə^{3}kju:t/. 1 ADJ If something such as a situation, feeling, or illness is **acute,** it is very severe or intense. *...acute staff shortages... These problems have become more acute.* 2 ADJ If your sight, hearing, or sense of smell is **acute,** it is sensitive and powerful. 3 ADJ In geometry, an **acute** angle is less than 90°.

acutely /ə^{3}kju:tli^1/. 1 ADV If you feel something **acutely,** you feel it very strongly. *They were acutely aware of the difficulties.* 2 ADV If a feeling or quality is **acutely** unpleasant, it is very unpleasant. *It was acutely embarrassing.*

ad /æd/, **ads.** COUNT N An **ad** is an advertisement; an informal use.

AD /eɪ di:/. You use **AD** in dates to indicate a number of years or centuries since the year in which Jesus Christ is believed to have been born. *...2000 AD.*

adamant /ædəmənt/. ADJ If you are **adamant** about something, you are determined not to change your mind. *He is adamant that we must put less emphasis on nationalism.* ♦ **adamantly** ADV *He adamantly refused to be moved to a hospital.*

Adam's apple /ædəmz æpə^{0}l/, **Adam's apples.** COUNT N Your **Adam's apple** is the lump that sticks out of the front of your neck.

adapt /ə^{3}dæpt/, **adapts, adapting, adapted.** 1 VB OR REFL VB If you **adapt** to a new situation or **adapt** yourself to it, you change in order to deal with it. *He cannot adapt himself to being free.* 2 VB WITH OBJ If you **adapt** something, you change it to make it suitable for a new purpose or situation. *Reformers attempted to adapt traditional religion.* 3 VB WITH OBJ If you **adapt** a book or play, you change it so that it can be made into a film or a television programme. *Mortimer is adapting the novel for television.*

adaptable /ə^{3}dæptəbə^{0}l/. ADJ Someone who is **adaptable** is able to change their ideas or behaviour in order to deal with new situations. *The rural areas are losing their brightest, most educated and adaptable members to the cities.* ♦ **adaptability** /ə^{3}dæptəbɪlɪ^{1}ti^1/ UNCOUNT N *...adaptability to his environment.*

adaptation /ædə^{3}pteɪʃə^{0}n/, **adaptations.** UNCOUNT N A **adaptation** of a story or novel is a play or film based on it. *...a new television adaptation of 'A Tale of Two Cities'.*

adapted /ə^{3}dæptɪ^{2}d/. PRED ADJ If something is **adapted** for a particular purpose, it is made so that it is especially suitable for it. *The cleaner is well adapted for use in the home and car... ...a Regency period residence, skilfully adapted to the needs of a modern hotel.*

add /æd/, **adds, adding, added.** 1 VB WITH OBJ If you **add** one thing to another, you put it with the other thing. *She added a tree to the picture.* 2 VB WITH OR WITHOUT OBJ If you **add** numbers or amounts, you calculate their total. 3 VB WITH OR WITHOUT OBJ, WITH PREP 'to' If one thing **adds** to another, it makes the other thing greater in degree or amount. *He is given answers that only add to his confusion... This process adds an extra £3 to the cost.* ♦ **added** ATTRIB ADJ *There are added complications.* 4 REPORT VB If you **add** something when you are speaking, you say something more. *He added that the fee would be £100.*

add up. PHR VB 1 If you **add up** several numbers, you calculate their total. 2 If facts or events **add up,** they make you understand the true nature of the situation. *It all added up. I became aware that Halliday was the thief.*

add up to. PHR VB If amounts **add up to** a particular total, they result in that total when they are put together. *This adds up to 75,000 miles of new streets.*

addict /ædɪkt/, **addicts.** 1 COUNT N An **addict** is someone who cannot stop taking harmful drugs. *...a Swiss drug addict.* 2 COUNT N WITH SUPP An **addict** is also someone who is very keen about something. *...a radio addict.*

addicted /ə^{3}dɪktɪ^{2}d/. 1 PRED ADJ Someone who is **addicted** to a harmful drug cannot stop taking it. *He became addicted to drink.* 2 PRED ADJ If you are **addicted** to something, you like it a lot. *He was probably addicted to peppermints.*

addiction /ə^{3}dɪkʃə^{0}n/. 1 UNCOUNT N **Addiction** is the condition of taking harmful drugs and being unable to stop. *...heroin addiction.* 2 SING N An **addiction** to something is a very strong desire for it. *...an addiction to sweets.*

addictive /ə^{3}dɪktɪv/. ADJ If a drug is **addictive,** people who start taking it find that they cannot stop.

addition /ə^{3}dɪʃə^{0}n/, **additions.** 1 PHRASE You use **in addition** to add to what you have already said. *In addition, there were meetings with trade unionists.* 2 COUNT N WITH SUPP An **addition** to something is a thing or amount which is added to it. *They can also award a weekly addition for extra heating.* 3 UNCOUNT N WITH SUPP The **addition** of something is also the fact or process of adding it as an extra. *These houses have been improved by the addition of bathrooms.* 4 UNCOUNT N **Addition** is the process of calculating the total of two or more numbers.

additional /ə^{3}dɪʃə^{0}nəl, -ʃənə^{0}l/. ADJ **Additional** things are extra things that are added to the ones that are already present. *...additional troops.*

additionally /ə^{3}dɪʃə^{0}nəli^1, -ʃənə^{0}li^1/. 1 SENTENCE ADV You use **additionally** to introduce an extra fact. *Additionally, there was a substantial bill.* 2 ADV If something happens **additionally,** it happens to a greater extent than before. *There was no point in additionally burdening her with this news.*

additive /ædɪtɪv/, **additives.** COUNT N An **additive** is a substance which is added to food by the manufacturer for a particular purpose, such as colouring it.

address /ədres/, **addresses, addressing, addressed.** 1 COUNT N Your **address** is the number of the house, the name of the street, and the town where you live. *The address is 70 Brompton Road, London SW1.* 2 VB WITH OBJ If a letter **is addressed** to you, your name and address are written on it. 3 COUNT N An **address** is also a formal speech. *He gave an address to the Psychological Association.* 4 VB WITH OBJ If you **address** a group of people, you give a speech to them. *He addressed a meeting in Bristol.* 5 VB WITH OBJ To **address** a problem means to deal with it. *He has not addressed the issue of the strike.*

adept /ə^{3}dept/. ADJ Someone who is **adept** at something does it well. *...adept at filling in forms.*

adequacy /ædɪ^{1}kwəsi^1/. 1 UNCOUNT N **Adequacy** is the state of being great enough in amount. *...the adequacy of resources.* 2 UNCOUNT N **Adequacy** is also the quality of being acceptable or usable. *...proof of the adequacy of the principles.*

adequate /ædɪ^{1}kwə^{1}t/. 1 ADJ If an amount is **adequate,** there is just enough of it. *The pay was adequate... ...a country with adequate rainfall.* ♦ **adequately** ADV *The children are not adequately fed.* 2 ADJ If something is **adequate,** it is good enough to be used or accepted. *She could not think of an adequate answer.* ♦ **adequately** ADV *This has never been adequately explained.*

adhere /ə^{3}dhɪə/, **adheres, adhering, adhered.** 1 VB WITH PREP 'to' If a substance **adheres** to a surface or object, it sticks to it. *This helps the plaster to adhere to the wall.* 2 VB WITH PREP 'to' If you **adhere** to a rule or agreement, you act in the way that it says you should. *The fire regulations have been adhered to.* 3 VB WITH PREP 'to' If you **adhere** to an opinion or belief, you support it. *She has adhered to the view that it is my responsibility.*

adherence /ə^{3}dhɪərə^{2}ns/. 1 UNCOUNT N WITH PREP 'to' **Adherence** is the fact of adhering to a particular rule or agreement. *Do they question our adherence to the treaty?* 2 UNCOUNT N **Adherence** is also the fact of supporting a particular belief or opinion. *...their adherence to democratic or totalitarian systems.*

adhesive /ə^{3}dhi:sɪv/, **adhesives.** 1 MASS N An **adhesive** is a substance which is used to make things stick together. *Make sure you stick them on with the correct adhesive.* 2 ADJ Something that is **adhesive** sticks firmly to something else. *...adhesive plasters.*

ad hoc /æd hɒk/. ATTRIB ADJ An **ad hoc** arrangement takes place only because a situation has made it necessary and was not planned in advance. *Rescue work continued on an ad hoc basis... The men agreed to set up an ad hoc committee.*

adjacent /ə^{3}dʒeɪsə^{0}nt/. ADJ If two things are **adjacent,** they are next to each other. *The bench was adjacent to the court... ...the adjacent room.*

adjective /ædʒəktɪv/, **adjectives.** COUNT N An **adjective** is a word such as 'old', 'red', or 'ugly' which gives more information about a thing, such as its colour, size, or other qualities.

adjoin /ə^{3}dʒɔɪn/, **adjoins, adjoining, adjoined.** VB WITH OBJ If one room, place, or object **adjoins** another, they are next to each other; a formal use. *Her bedroom adjoined Guy's room.* ♦ **adjoining** ATTRIB ADJ *The adjoining room is Professor Marvin's office.*

adjourn /ə^{3}dʒɜ:n/, **adjourns, adjourning, adjourned.** ERG VB If a meeting or trial **adjourns,** it is stopped for a short time. *The trial would be adjourned until the next morning.* ♦ **adjournment** /ə^{3}dʒɜ:nmə^{2}nt/ COUNT N *An adjournment was called.*

adjudicate /ə^{3}dʒu:dɪkeɪt/, **adjudicates, adjudicating, adjudicated.** VB WITH OR WITHOUT OBJ If you **adjudicate** on a dispute or problem, you make an official decision about it; a formal use. *The boards adjudicate on the punishment of prisoners... It should adjudicate individual grievances and complaints against all the broadcasting systems.*

adjunct /ædʒʌŋkt/, **adjuncts.** 1 COUNT N WITH PREP 'to' OR 'of' An **adjunct** is something that is connected with a larger or more important thing. *Duncan's survey was an adjunct to the current population survey.* 2 COUNT N In grammar, an **adjunct** is one of the main elements of a clause which gives information about time, place, or manner.

adjust /ə^{3}dʒʌst/, **adjusts, adjusting, adjusted.** 1 VB When you **adjust** to a new situation, you get used to it by changing your behaviour or your ideas. *Couples do not give themselves time to adjust to marriage before a baby arrives.* ♦ **adjustment** /ə^{3}dʒʌstmə^{2}nt/ COUNT N OR UNCOUNT N *Foreign students have problems of adjustment to living in Britain... Thousands of young marines have made the adjustment from combat.* 2 VB WITH OBJ If you **adjust** something, you correct or alter its position or setting. *He spent several minutes adjusting his tie... I went to adjust the television set.* ♦ **adjustment** COUNT N OR UNCOUNT N *He spent weeks making repairs and adjustments... Tappet adjustment has to be made with the engine cold.*

adjustable /ə3dʒʌstəbə0l/. ADJ If something is **adjustable,** it can be changed to different positions. *...an adjustable spanner.*

adjusted /ə3dʒʌstɪ2d/. ADJ A well **adjusted** person can control their behaviour and deal with the problems of life. A badly **adjusted** person cannot.

ad-lib /ædlɪb/, **ad-libs, ad-libbing, ad-libbed.** VB WITH OR WITHOUT OBJ If you **ad-lib** in a play or a speech, you say something which has not been prepared beforehand. *They ad-libbed so much and broke down in chuckles so often... I tried to ad-lib a joke I'd heard but my timing was completely wrong.* Also ADV *We discussed the result ad lib.*

administer /ə3dmɪnɪstə/, **administers, administering, administered.** 1 VB WITH OBJ To **administer** a country, company, or institution means to be responsible for managing it. *She had a huge department to administer.* 2 VB WITH OBJ To **administer** something also means to ensure that it is done or carried out correctly. *Experts administer the tests and publish the results... The prison officers helped to administer a sedative to him.*

administration /ə3dmɪnɪstreɪʃə0n/. 1 SING N WITH SUPP The **administration** of a company, institution, or country is the group of people who organize and supervise it. *...the University administration... ...the Reagan Administration.* 2 UNCOUNT N **Administration** is the range of activities connected with the organization or supervision of a company, institution, or country. *They need to spend less on administration.*

administrative /ə3dmɪnɪstrətɪv/. ADJ **Administrative** work involves organizing and supervising a country, company, or institution.

administrator /ə3dmɪnɪstreɪtə/, **administrators.** COUNT N An **administrator** is a person who manages and organizes a country, company, or institution.

admirable /ædmərəbə0l/. ADJ An **admirable** quality or action deserves to be praised and admired. *The trains ran with admirable precision.* ♦ **admirably** ADV *It fulfills its purpose admirably.*

admiral /ædmərəl/, **admirals.** COUNT N OR TITLE An **admiral** is a naval officer of the highest rank.

admiration /ædmə1reɪʃə0n/. UNCOUNT N **Admiration** is a feeling of great liking and respect. *Benson had enormous admiration for them all.*

admire /ə3dmaɪə/, **admires, admiring, admired.** 1 VB WITH OBJ If you **admire** someone or something, you like and respect them. *I admire courage... They had been admired for their discipline.* ♦ **admiring** ADJ *She gave me one of her rare admiring looks.* ♦ **admiringly** ADV *Ralph glanced at them admiringly.* 2 VB WITH OBJ You can also say you **admire** something when you look with pleasure at it. *He went along the lane admiring the crocuses.*

admirer /ə3dmaɪə0rə/, **admirers.** 1 COUNT N WITH POSS A woman's **admirers** are the men who are attracted to her. 2 COUNT N WITH POSS If you are an **admirer** of someone, you like and respect them or their work. *I am not myself an admirer of Hogarth.*

admission /ə3dmɪʃə0n/, **admissions.** 1 UNCOUNT N OR COUNT N **Admission** is permission given to a person or group of people to enter a place or join an organization. *No admission allowed after 10 pm... His Act tightened up the admission of immigrants into Britain.* 2 UNCOUNT N The **admission** fee is the amount of money you pay to enter a place. 3 COUNT N An **admission** is a statement that something bad, unpleasant, or embarrassing is true. *He submitted his resignation, together with an admission of his guilt.*

admit /ə3dmɪt/, **admits, admitting, admitted.** 1 REPORT VB OR VB WITH -ING OR PREP 'to' If you **admit** something bad, unpleasant, or embarrassing, you agree that it is true. *'I don't know,' he admitted... The President admitted taking bribes.* 2 VB WITH OBJ If someone **is admitted** to a place or organization, they are allowed to enter it or join it. *Junior members of staff are not admitted.* 3 VB WITH OBJ If someone **is admitted** to hospital, they are kept there until they are well enough to go home.

admittance /ə3dmɪtə0ns/. UNCOUNT N **Admittance** is the act of entering a place or the right to enter it. *How was he to gain admittance?*

admittedly /ə3dmɪtɪ1dli1/. SENTENCE ADV You use **admittedly** when you say something which weakens your previous statement. *Admittedly, economists often disagree among each other.*

admonish /ə3dmɒnɪʃ/, **admonishes, admonishing, admonished.** VB WITH OBJ If you **admonish** someone, you tell them sternly that they have done something wrong; a formal use. *They are frequently admonished for their failure to act quickly.*

ado /ədu:/. PHRASE If you do something **without further ado,** you do it at once; an old-fashioned use.

adolescence /ædə7lesəns/. UNCOUNT N **Adolescence** is the period of your life in which you develop from being a child into an adult.

adolescent /ædə7lesə2nt/, **adolescents.** COUNT N An **adolescent** is a young person who is no longer a child but who is not yet an adult. Also ATTRIB ADJ *...a father with an adolescent son.*

adopt /ədɒpt/, **adopts, adopting, adopted.** 1 VB WITH OBJ If you **adopt** someone else's child, you take it into your own family and make it legally your own. ♦ **adopted** ADJ *...parents of adopted children.* ♦ **adoption** /ədɒpʃə0n/ UNCOUNT N OR COUNT N *...the shortage of children available for adoption... ...the commitment involved in the adoption of a child.* 2 VB WITH OBJ If you **adopt** an attitude, position, or way of behaving, you begin to have it. *I had to adopt other methods of persuasion.* ♦ **adoption** UNCOUNT N WITH 'of' *This would complicate the adoption of a rule.*

adorable /ədɔ:rəbə0l/. ADJ If you say that a child or animal is **adorable,** you feel great affection for them. *...an adorable kitten.*

adoration /ædə8reɪʃə0n/. UNCOUNT N **Adoration** is a feeling of great admiration and love. *He did not tell anyone of his adoration for her.*

adore /ədɔ:/, **adores, adoring, adored.** 1 VB WITH OBJ If you **adore** someone, you love and admire them. *She adored her sister.* 2 VB WITH OBJ If you **adore** something, you like it very much. *People will adore this film.*

adorn /ədɔ:n/, **adorns, adorning, adorned.** 1 VB WITH OBJ If you **adorn** something, you make it more beautiful by adding things to it; a literary use. *The container is adorned with semi-precious stones.* 2 VB WITH OBJ If things **adorn** a place, they make it more attractive. *Oil paintings adorned the walls.* ♦ **adornment** /ədɔ:nmə2nt/ COUNT N OR UNCOUNT N *...adornments such as make-up and jewellery... Styles of adornment have changed over the centuries.*

adrenalin /ə3drenəlɪn/; also spelled **adrenaline.** UNCOUNT N **Adrenalin** is a substance produced by your body which makes your heart beat faster and gives you more energy.

adrift /ədrɪft/. PRED ADJ If a boat is **adrift,** it is floating on the water without being controlled.

adroit /ə3drɔɪt/. ADJ Someone who is **adroit** is quick and skilful in their thoughts or actions; a formal use. *Jamie was adroit at flattering others.* ♦ **adroitly** ADV *The young men picked up the papers adroitly.*

adulation /ædjə4leɪʃə0n/. UNCOUNT N **Adulation** is very great and uncritical admiration and praise. *He was greeted with adulation.*

adult /ædʌlt, ə3dʌlt/, **adults.** 1 COUNT N An **adult** is a mature, fully developed person or animal. *A happy home is one in which children and adults have equal rights.* Also ATTRIB ADJ *...adult insects.* 2 ADJ Something that is **adult** is suitable for adult people. *Children can assist in adult work at an early age.*

adulterate /ə3dʌltəreɪt/, **adulterates, adulterating, adulterated.** VB WITH OBJ If you **adulterate** drink or food, you make its quality worse by adding water to it. *The champagne had been adulterated.*

adultery /ə3dʌltə0ri1/. UNCOUNT N If a married person commits **adultery,** they have sex with someone that they are not married to.

adulthood /ædʌlthʊd/. UNCOUNT N **Adulthood** is the state of being an adult. *There is no reason why she shouldn't survive into healthy adulthood.*

advance /ə3dvɑ:ns/, **advances, advancing, advanced.** 1 VB To **advance** means to move forward. *She advanced on him, shouting and waving her ticket.* ♦ **advancing** ADJ *...rows of advancing enemy tanks.* 2 VB If you **advance** in something you are doing, you make progress in it. *This student has advanced in reading and writing.* Also COUNT N OR UNCOUNT N *...radical advances in computer design.* 3 VB WITH OBJ AND OBJ If you **advance** someone a sum of money, you give it to them earlier than arranged. *Axel advanced him the money for a suit.* 4 COUNT N An **advance** is money which is lent or given to someone before they are due to receive it. *...a twenty pound advance.* 5 ATTRIB ADJ **Advance** booking or warning is done or given before an event happens. *There was no advance warning of the President's departure.* 6 PHRASE If you do something **in advance,** you do it before a particular date or event. *You should book well in advance, preferably six weeks before.*

advanced /ə3dvɑ:nst/. 1 ADJ An **advanced** student has learned the basic facts of a subject and is doing more difficult work. 2 ADJ A country that is **advanced** has reached a high level of industrial or technological development.

advancement /ə3dvɑ:nsmə2nt/. 1 UNCOUNT N **Advancement** is promotion in your job, or to a higher social class. *...opportunity for personal advancement.* 2 UNCOUNT N WITH SUPP The **advancement** of something is the process of helping it to progress. *...the advancement of knowledge.*

advantage /ə3dvɑ:ntɪdʒ/, **advantages.** 1 COUNT N An **advantage** is something that puts you in a better position than other people. *As a scientist I have a slight advantage over him.* 2 COUNT N An **advantage** is also a benefit that is likely to result from something. *The advantages of electricity are the lack of fumes and the ease of distribution.*

PHRASES ● If something is **to your advantage,** it will be useful for you or will benefit you. ● If you **take advantage of** someone, you treat them unfairly for your own benefit. ● If you **take advantage of** something, you make good use of it while you can.

advantageous /ædvə3nteɪdʒəs/. ADJ Something that is **advantageous** to you is likely to benefit you. *Economic growth is inevitable and advantageous.*

advent /ædvə2nt/. SING N WITH POSS The **advent** of something is the fact of it starting or coming into existence; a formal use. *...the advent of computers.*

adventure /ə3dventʃə/, **adventures.** COUNT N OR UNCOUNT N An **adventure** is a series of events that you become involved in and that are unusual, exciting, and perhaps dangerous. *...my Arctic adventures... They were bored, and looking for adventure.*

adventurer /ə3dventʃərə/, **adventurers.** COUNT N An **adventurer** is a person who enjoys adventure.

adventurous /ə3dventʃərəs/. ADJ An **adventurous** person is willing to take risks and eager to have new experiences.

adverb /ædvɜ:b/, **adverbs.** COUNT N In grammar, an **adverb** is a word which gives more information about time, place, or manner.

adversary /ædvəsə2ri1/, **adversaries.** COUNT N Your **adversary** is someone you are competing with, or arguing or fighting against. *She had two potential political adversaries.*

adverse /ædvɜ:s/. ATTRIB ADJ **Adverse** decisions, conditions, or effects are unfavourable to you. *Falling prices had an adverse effect on business... ...adverse weather conditions.* ♦ **adversely** ADV *The majority of children are adversely affected.*

adversity /ə3dvɜ:sɪ1ti1/. UNCOUNT N **Adversity** is a very difficult or unfavourable situation. *They continue to fight in the face of adversity.*

advert /ædvɜ:t/, **adverts.** COUNT N An **advert** is the same as an advertisement; an informal use.

advertise /ædvətaɪz/, **advertises, advertising, advertised.** 1 VB WITH OBJ If you **advertise** a product, event, or job, you tell people about it publicly, for example in newspapers or on television, in order to encourage them to buy that product, go to that event, or apply for that job. *...deodorants she had seen advertised on television... ...a leaflet advertising a fishing competition.* 2 VB If you **advertise** for something that you want or if you **advertise** for a person to do a job, you announce in a newspaper, on television, or on a notice board that you want that thing or want someone to do that job. *The Council advertised for accountants.*

advertisement /ə3dvɜ:tɪsmə2nt/, **advertisements.** COUNT N An **advertisement** is a public announcement, for example in a newspaper or on television, that tells people about a product, event, or job vacancy. *...an advertisement for Adler shoes.*

advertiser /ædvətaɪzə/, **advertisers.** COUNT N An **advertiser** is a person or company that pays for something to be advertised on television, in a newspaper, or on posters.

advertising /ædvətaɪzɪŋ/. UNCOUNT N **Advertising** is the activity of telling people about products, events, or job vacancies, and making them want to buy the products, go to the events, or apply for the jobs.

advice /ə3dvaɪs/. UNCOUNT N If you give someone **advice,** you tell them what you think they should do. *She promised to follow his advice... They want advice on how to do it.*

advisable /ə3dvaɪzəbə0l/. ADJ If a course of action is **advisable,** it is sensible or is likely to achieve the result you want. *It's advisable to ring up first to make an appointment.*

advise /ə3dvaɪz/, **advises, advising, advised.** 1 VB WITH OBJ If you **advise** someone to do something, you tell them what you think they should do. *He advised me not to buy it... Their job involves advising people how to avoid this disease... I would strongly advise you against it.* 2 VB WITH OR WITHOUT OBJ If you **advise** people on a particular subject, you give them help and information on it. *A panel of bishops has been appointed to advise on matters of religious policy.*

adviser /ə3dvaɪzə/, **advisers;** also spelled **advisor.** COUNT N An **adviser** is someone who gives people help and information, especially on a particular subject. *...an independent legal adviser... ...the President's advisers.*

advisory /ə3dvaɪzə0ri1/. ADJ Someone who has an **advisory** role gives people help and information, especially on a particular subject. *Most of the advisory work is carried out over the phone... ...the National Women's Advisory Committee.*

advocate, advocates, advocating, advocated; pronounced /ædvə6keɪt/ when it is a verb and /ædvə6kət/ when it is a noun. 1 REPORT VB If you **advocate** a particular action or plan, you support it publicly. *He advocated that Britain should join the alliance.* 2 COUNT N WITH 'of' An **advocate** of a particular action or plan is someone who supports it publicly. *...the advocates of women's rights... ...a strong advocate of nuclear power.* 3 COUNT N An **advocate** is a lawyer who speaks in favour of someone or defends them in a court of law; a legal use.

aerial /ɛərɪəl/, **aerials.** 1 ATTRIB ADJ You use **aerial** to describe things that are above the level of the ground or that happen in the air. *An aerial railway had been erected... ...aerial warfare.* 2 ATTRIB ADJ **Aerial** photographs are taken from aeroplanes of things on the ground. 3 COUNT N An **aerial** is a piece of wire that receives television or radio signals; a British use.

aerodynamic /ɛərə6daɪnæmɪk/. ATTRIB ADJ **Aerodynamic** effects and principles are concerned with the way in which objects move through the air. *...aerodynamic improvements in design.*

aeroplane /ɛərə6pleɪn/, **aeroplanes.** COUNT N An **aeroplane** is a vehicle with wings and engines that enable it to fly through the air; a British use.

aerosol /ɛərə6sɒl/, **aerosols.** COUNT N An **aerosol** is a pressurized container holding a liquid such as paint or deodorant. When you press a button, the liquid is forced out as a fine spray.

aesthetic /i1sθɛtɪk/; spelled **esthetic** in American English. ADJ **Aesthetic** means involving beauty or art, and people's appreciation of beautiful things. *...a purely aesthetic appeal.* ♦ **aesthetically** ADV *...aesthetically appealing products.*

afar /əfɑː/. PHRASE **From afar** means from a long way away; a literary use. *...visitors from afar.*

affable /æfəbə0l/. ADJ Someone who is **affable** is pleasant and friendly; a literary use.

affair /əfɛə/, **affairs.** 1 COUNT N WITH SUPP You refer to an event as an **affair** when you are talking about it generally. *The wedding was a quiet affair.* 2 PLURAL N WITH SUPP You can use **affairs** to refer to the important facts or activities connected with a particular subject; a formal use. *...a specialist in Eastern European affairs... ...affairs of state.* ● See also **current affairs, state of affairs.** 3 PLURAL N WITH POSS Your **affairs** are your private and personal concerns. *What had induced her to meddle in his affairs?* 4 PHRASE If you say to someone that something is **their own affair,** you mean that you do not want to want to know about or become involved in their activities. *What went on behind that door was your own affair.* 5 COUNT N If two people who are not married to each other are having an **affair,** they have a sexual relationship.

affect /ə3fɛkt/, **affects, affecting, affected.** 1 VB WITH OBJ When one thing **affects** another, it influences it or causes it to change. *...the ways in which computers can affect our lives.* 2 VB WITH OBJ If a disease **affects** you, it causes you to become ill. *The disease primarily affected Jane's lungs.* 3 VB WITH OBJ OR TO-INF If you **affect** a particular characteristic, you pretend that it is natural for you; a formal use. *She affected a lisp... He affected to despise every Briton he met.*

affectation /æfekteɪʃə0n/, **affectations.** COUNT N OR UNCOUNT N An **affectation** is an attitude or type of behaviour that is not genuine, but which is intended to impress other people. *His film star affectations had disappeared... ...elegance without affectation.*

affected /ə3fɛktɪ2d/. ADJ Someone who is **affected** behaves in an unnatural way that is intended to impress other people. *He was affected and conceited.*

affection /ə3fɛkʃə0n/. UNCOUNT N **Affection** is a feeling of fondness and caring that you have for another person. *She gazed with deep affection at him.*

affectionate /ə3fɛkʃənə1t/. ADJ If you are **affectionate,** you show your fondness for another person in your behaviour. *They were an affectionate couple.* ♦ **affectionately** ADV *He stroked her affectionately.*

affinity /əfɪnɪ1ti1/, **affinities.** 1 COUNT N OR UNCOUNT N If you have an **affinity** with someone or something, you feel that you belong with them and understand them. *I had this tremendous sense of affinity with the place.* 2 COUNT N If people or things have an **affinity** with each other, they are similar in some ways. *In anatomical structure, Prehistoric Man has close affinities with modern humans.*

affirm /ə3fɜːm/, **affirms, affirming, affirmed;** a formal word. 1 REPORT VB If you **affirm** a fact, you state that it is definitely true. *I affirmed my innocence.* 2 VB WITH OBJ If you **affirm** an idea or belief, you indicate clearly that you have this idea or belief. *They affirm a policy of religious toleration.*

affirmative /ə3fɜːmətɪv/. ATTRIB ADJ An **affirmative** word or gesture indicates that you agree with someone; a formal use.

afflict /ə3flɪkt/, **afflicts, afflicting, afflicted.** VB WITH OBJ If pain, illness, or sorrow **afflicts** someone, it makes them suffer. *Cameron had been afflicted with blindness.*

affliction /ə3flɪkʃə0n/, **afflictions.** COUNT N OR UNCOUNT N An **affliction** is something which causes suffering. *...the horrors and afflictions of his time in prison.*

affluent /æfluənt/. ADJ If you are **affluent,** you have a lot of money. *...affluent young professionals.* ♦ **affluence** /æfluəns/ UNCOUNT N *...the general affluence of a consumer society.*

afford /əfɔːd/, **affords, affording, afforded.** 1 VB WITH OBJ OR TO-INF If you can **afford** something, you are able to pay for it. *...families who can afford cars... I can't afford to rent this flat.* 2 VB WITH OBJ OR TO-INF If you cannot **afford** to allow something to happen, it would be harmful or embarrassing to you if it happened. *We can't afford another scandal... He could not afford to be associated with them.*

affront /əfrʌnt/, **affronts, affronting, affronted.** 1 VB WITH OBJ If you **are affronted** by something, you feel insulted and hurt by it. *They were deeply affronted by their abrupt dismissal.* 2 COUNT N If something is an **affront** to you, it is an obvious insult to you.

afield /əfiːld/. PHRASE If someone comes from **far afield,** they come from a long way away. *Groups from as far afield as Scotland have sent deputations.*

afloat /əfləʊt/. 1 PRED ADJ When someone or something is **afloat,** they remain partly above the surface of water and do not sink. *By kicking constantly he could stay afloat.* 2 PRED ADJ If you stay **afloat** or if you keep a business **afloat,** you have just enough money to run your business. *They have kept Vickers afloat during the recession.*

afoot /əfʊt/. PRED ADJ If a plan or scheme is **afoot,** it is already happening or being planned, often secretly. *There was a plan afoot to have her sent to a camp.*

aforementioned /əfɔːmenʃənd/. ATTRIB ADJ When you refer to the **aforementioned** person or subject, you mean the person or subject that has already been mentioned; a formal use. *...the works of all the aforementioned writers.*

afraid /əfreɪd/. 1 PRED ADJ If you are **afraid** of someone or **afraid** to do something, you are frightened because you think that something horrible is going to happen. *They were afraid of you... He was afraid even to turn his head.* 2 PRED ADJ If you are **afraid** that something unpleasant will happen, you are worried that it may happen. *She was afraid that I might be embarrassed... He was terribly afraid of offending anyone... Don't be afraid to ask questions.* 3 CONVENTION When you want to apologize to someone or to disagree with them in a polite way, you can begin by saying **I'm afraid.** *I'm afraid I can't agree.*

afresh /əfrɛʃ/. ADV If you do something **afresh,** you do it again in a different way. *I'm too old to start afresh.*

African /æfrɪkən/, **Africans.** 1 ADJ **African** means belonging or relating to Africa. *...the African population of Johannesburg.* 2 COUNT N An **African** is a person who comes from Africa.

after /ɑːftə/. 1 PREP, ADV, OR CONJ If something happens **after** a particular date or event, it happens later than that date or event. *She arrived just after breakfast... Soon after, Faraday began his research into electricity... He was ill after eating the meal.* 2 PREP If you go **after** someone, or if you are **after** them, you follow or chase them. *She ran after him into the courtyard... The Germans were after him.* 3 PREP If you are **after** something, you are trying to get it for yourself. *Those youngsters are after my job.* 4 PREP To be named **after** someone means to be given the same name as them. *...a street named after my grandfather.* 5 PREP Americans use **after** to tell the time. For example, if they say it is ten **after** six, the time is ten minutes past six. 6 PHRASE If something happens **day after day** or **year after year,** it happens every day or every year. *Some jokes go round school year after year.*

after-effect, after-effects. COUNT N The **after-effects** of an activity or event are the conditions which result from it. *100,000 died from the after-effects of radiation over the next few decades.*

aftermath /ɑːftəmɑːθ, -mæθ/. SING N WITH POSS The **aftermath** of an important event is the situation that results from it. *In the immediate aftermath of the accident, no one knew who had been hurt.*

afternoon /ɑːftənuːn/, **afternoons.** COUNT N OR UNCOUNT N The **afternoon** is the part of each day which begins at lunchtime and ends at about six o'clock.

afterthought /ɑːftəθɔːt/, **afterthoughts.** COUNT N An **afterthought** is a remark or action which you do or say as an addition to something else, but perhaps without careful thought. *After a while she said as an afterthought, 'I could do that.'*

afterwards /ɑːftəwədz/. **Afterward** is also used, especially in American English. SENTENCE ADV If something is done or happens **afterwards,** it is done or happens later than a particular event or time that has already been described. *Afterwards we all helped with the washing up... She died soon afterwards.*

again /əgɛn, əgeɪn/. 1 ADV If you do something **again,** you do it once more. *Try again in half an hour... Let's do it, I may never have the chance again.* 2 ADV When something is in a particular state or place **again,** it has returned to the state or place that it was before. *At last the assembly was silent again.* 3 SENTENCE ADV When you are asking someone to repeat something that they have already told you, you can add **again** to the end of your question. *What's his name again?* 4 SENTENCE ADV You can use **again** to emphasize a similarity between the subject you are talking about now and a previous subject. *My last question is again a personal one.*

against /əgɛnst, əgeɪnst/. 1 PREP If something is leaning or pressing **against** something else, it is touching it. *Ralph leaned against a tree... She was pressing her nose against the window.* 2 PREP If you compete **against** someone in a game, you try to beat them. *He played in the first Test Match against Australia.* 3 PREP If you do something **against** someone or something, you do something that might harm them. *They were not allowed to use arms against their enemies.* 4 PREP OR ADV If you are **against** an idea, policy, or system, you are opposed to it. *He was fanatically against American intervention in the war.* 5 PREP Something that is **against** the law is forbidden by law. 6 PREP If you take action **against** a possible future event, you try to prevent it. *He has taken certain precautions against burglary.* 7 PREP If you are moving **against** a current, tide, or wind, you are moving in the opposite direction to it. 8 PREP OR ADV The chances or odds **against** something happening are the chances or odds that it will not happen. *The odds against another attack were astronomical.*

age /eɪdʒ/, **ages, ageing** or **aging, aged.** 1 UNCOUNT N WITH SUPP Your **age** is the number of years that you have lived. *He is eighty years of age... He died at the age of forty.* 2 UNCOUNT N **Age** is the state of being old. *Her age and frailty are giving him cause for concern... ...medals stained with age.* 3 ERG VB When someone **ages,** they become or seem much older. *She was dismayed to see how much he had aged... The strain of looking after her had aged him.* ♦ **ageing** ADJ *...an ageing film star.* 4 COUNT N An **age** is a period in history. *...the great age of Greek sport... ...a detailed study of woman's role throughout the ages.* 5 SING N OR PLURAL N You can say **an age** or **ages** to mean a very long time; an informal use. *She took an age to dress... I've known him for ages.*

PHRASES ● Someone who is **under age** is not legally old enough to do something, for example to buy an alcoholic drink. ● When someone **comes of age,** they become legally an adult. In Britain, young people come of age when they are 18.

aged; pronounced /eɪdʒd/ for meaning 1 and /eɪdʒɪ2d/ for meanings 2 and 3. 1 PRED ADJ You use **aged** followed by a number to say how old someone is. *...men aged 60 and over.* ● See also **middle-aged.** 2 ADJ Someone or something that is **aged** is very old. *...his aged aunt.* 3 PLURAL N You can refer to all people who are very old as **the aged.**

agency /eɪdʒənsi1/, **agencies.** 1 COUNT N An **agency** is a business which provides services for another business. *...an advertising agency.* 2 COUNT N In the United States, an **agency** is an administrative organization run by a government. *...the Central Intelligence Agency.*

agenda /ədʒɛndə/, **agendas.** COUNT N An **agenda** is a list of items to be discussed at a meeting. *What is on the agenda today?*

agent /eɪdʒə2nt/, **agents.** 1 COUNT N An **agent** is someone who arranges work or business for someone else, especially actors or musicians. *I phoned my agent in London about the job.* 2 COUNT N An **agent** is also someone who works for a country's secret service. *...an enemy agent.* 3 COUNT N WITH SUPP You can refer to the cause of a particular effect as its **agent.** *...the agent of change.*

age-old. ATTRIB ADJ An **age-old** story, tradition, or connection has existed for a very long time.

aggravate /ægrəveɪt/, **aggravates, aggravating, aggravated.** 1 VB WITH OBJ If you **aggravate** a situation, you make it worse. *National poverty was aggravated by rapid population growth.* 2 VB WITH OBJ To **aggravate** someone means to make them annoyed; an informal use. *Thomas had a great deal to aggravate him at present.*

aggregate /ægrɪ2gət/, **aggregates.** COUNT N An **aggregate** is an amount made up of several smaller amounts. *He had spent an aggregate of fifteen years in various jails.*

aggression /ə[3]grɛʃə[0]n/. UNCOUNT N If you behave with **aggression,** you behave angrily or violently towards someone. *Barbara defended herself with a sudden new aggression... ...an act of aggression.*

aggressive /ə[3]grɛsɪv/. 1 ADJ Someone who is **aggressive** shows aggression. *She was in a highly aggressive mood.* ♦ **aggressively** ADV *She strode aggressively into the office.* 2 ADJ If you are **aggressive** in your work or other activities, you behave in a forceful way because you are eager to succeed. *...aggressive businessmen.*

aggressor /ə[3]grɛsə/, **aggressors.** COUNT N The **aggressor** is the person or country that starts a fight.

aggrieved /ə[3]griːvd/. ADJ If you feel **aggrieved,** you feel upset and angry because of the way you have been treated.

aghast /əgɑːst/. PRED ADJ If you are **aghast,** you are filled with horror and surprise.

agile /ædʒaɪl/. 1 ADJ Someone who is **agile** can move with surprising ease and speed. *He was as agile as a monkey.* ♦ **agility** /ədʒɪlɪ[1]ti[1]/ UNCOUNT N *He leaped out of the car with surprising agility.* 2 ADJ If you have an **agile** mind, you think quickly and intelligently. ♦ **agility** UNCOUNT N *...tests of mental agility.*

agitate /ædʒɪteɪt/, **agitates, agitating, agitated.** 1 VB If you **agitate** for something, you talk and campaign enthusiastically in order to get it. *...a group agitating against the use of chemical fertilizers.* ♦ **agitation** /ædʒɪteɪʃə[0]n/ UNCOUNT N *...anti-imperialist agitation.* 2 VB WITH OBJ If something **agitates** you, it worries you and makes you unable to think clearly. *I don't want to agitate him unduly.* ♦ **agitated** /ædʒɪteɪtɪ[2]d/ ADJ *He looked dishevelled and agitated.* ♦ **agitation** UNCOUNT N *I saw Peter glancing at his watch in some agitation.*

agitator /ædʒɪteɪtə/, **agitators.** COUNT N An **agitator** is someone who tries to bring about political or social change by making speeches and campaigning in public. *...political agitators.*

agnostic /ægnɒstɪk/, **agnostics.** COUNT N An **agnostic** believes that it is not possible to know whether God exists or not. Also ADJ *She remained agnostic.*

ago /əgəʊ/. ADV You use **ago** to refer to past time. For example, if something happened one year **ago,** it is one year since it happened. *Five years ago, I went to the tropics... How long ago was that?*

agonize /ægə[7]naɪz/, **agonizes, agonizing, agonized;** also spelled **agonise.** VB If you **agonize** over something, you feel anxious and spend a long time thinking about it.

agonized /ægə[7]naɪzd/; also spelled **agonised.** ADJ **Agonized** describes something that you say or do when you are in great physical or mental pain. *...agonised moans.*

agonizing /ægə[7]naɪzɪŋ/; also spelled **agonising.** 1 ADJ Something that is **agonizing** causes you to feel great physical or mental pain. *...agonizing feelings of shame and guilt.* ♦ **agonizingly** ADV *The sound was agonisingly painful.* 2 ADJ **Agonizing** decisions and choices are very difficult to make.

agony /ægəni[1]/, **agonies.** UNCOUNT N OR PLURAL N **Agony** is great physical or mental pain. *The blow made him scream in agony.*

agree /əgriː/, **agrees, agreeing, agreed.** 1 RECIP VB If you **agree** with someone, you have the same opinion about something. *Do you agree with him about this?... People agree that the law is behind the times.* 2 VB If you **agree** to do something, you say that you will do it. *She agreed to let us use her flat while she was away.* 3 PRED ADJ If people are **agreed** about something, they have reached a decision about it. *Are we agreed, gentlemen?* 4 VB WITH 'with' If you **agree** with an action or a suggestion, you approve of it. *I agree with what they are doing.* 5 RECIP VB If two stories, accounts, or totals **agree,** they are the same as each other. *This bill doesn't agree with my calculations.*

agreeable /əgriːəbə[0]l/. 1 ADJ If something is **agreeable,** it is pleasant. *...an agreeable sensation.* 2 ADJ If someone is **agreeable,** they are pleasant and try to please people. *She always made a point of being agreeable to them.* 3 PRED ADJ If you are **agreeable** to something or if it is **agreeable** to you, you are willing to do it or to allow it.

agreement /əgriːmə[2]nt/, **agreements.** 1 COUNT N An **agreement** is a decision that two or more people have reached together. *Half of the land was given away under the same agreement.* 2 UNCOUNT N **Agreement** is the act of reaching a decision, or of indicating that you will accept something. *There was no general agreement on the timing.* ● If you are **in agreement** with someone, you have the same opinion as they have.

agriculture /ægrɪkʌltʃə/. UNCOUNT N **Agriculture** is farming and the methods used to look after crops and animals. ♦ **agricultural** /ægrɪkʌltʃə[0]rəl/ ADJ *...modern agricultural methods.*

ahead /əhɛd/. 1 ADV If something is **ahead,** it is in front of you. *The road ahead is foggy... She stared ahead.* 2 ADV If you are **ahead** of someone in your work or achievements, you have made more progress than they have. 3 PRED ADJ If a person or a team is **ahead** in a competition, they are winning. 4 ADV WITH 'of' If someone arrives at a place **ahead** of you, they arrive there before you. ● If someone goes **on ahead** or is sent **on ahead,** they leave for a place before other people. *Our parents had gone on ahead in father's car.* 5 ADV **Ahead** also means in the future. *I haven't had time to think far ahead.* 6 See also **go ahead.**

aid /eɪd/, **aids, aiding, aided.** 1 UNCOUNT N WITH SUPP **Aid** is money, equipment, or services that are provided for people in need. *...food and medical aid.* 2 COUNT N An **aid** is something that makes things easier to do. *...a valuable aid to digestion.* 3 VB WITH OBJ If you **aid** a person or an organization, you help them. *He crossed the border aided by a priest.*

PHRASES ● If an activity or event is **in aid of** a particular cause, it raises money for that cause. *...a cricket match in aid of cancer relief.* ● If you do something **with the aid of** a particular person or thing, they help you to do it. *The programmes had been prepared with the aid of various broadcasters.* ● If you go **to the aid of** someone, you try to help them. *They had rushed to her aid.*

aide /eɪd/, **aides.** COUNT N An **aide** is an assistant to a person with an important job, especially in government or in the armed forces.

AIDS /eɪdz/. UNCOUNT N **AIDS** is an illness which destroys the natural system of protection that the body has against disease.

ailing /eɪlɪŋ/. 1 ADJ If someone is **ailing,** they are ill and not getting better. 2 ADJ If an organization is **ailing,** it is in difficulty and is becoming weaker.

ailment /eɪlmə[2]nt/, **ailments.** COUNT N An **ailment** is an illness, especially one that is not very serious.

aim /eɪm/, **aims, aiming, aimed.** 1 VB WITH OR WITHOUT OBJ If you **aim** a weapon or object at something, you point it in the direction of the thing. *Roger picked up a stone, aimed it, and threw it at Henry... He aimed at the far wall and squeezed the trigger.* Also UNCOUNT N WITH SUPP *He leaned against a tree to steady his aim.* 2 PHRASE If you **take aim** at someone or something, you point a weapon or object at them, ready to shoot or throw. 3 VB If you **aim** at something or **aim** to do it, you plan or hope to achieve it. *We are aiming at a higher production level... A good solid job is the thing to aim for.* 4 PASSIVE VB WITH 'at' If an action or plan **is aimed** at achieving something, it is intended to achieve it. *...policies aimed at securing mass support.* 5 COUNT N WITH SUPP An **aim** is the thing that an action or plan is intended to achieve. *It is our aim to set up a workshop.* 6 VB WITH OBJ AND 'at' If your action **is aimed** at a particular person, you intend it to affect and influence them. *This anti-smoking campaign is mainly aimed at young teenagers.*

aimless /eɪmlɪ[1]s/. ADJ A person or activity that is **aimless** has no clear purpose or plan. *...drawing aimless doodles in the sand.* ♦ **aimlessly** ADV *She wandered aimlessly along the beach.*

ain't /eɪnt/. **Ain't** is used in some dialects of English instead of 'am not', 'aren't', or 'isn't'.

air /ɛə/, **airs, airing, aired.** 1 UNCOUNT N **Air** is the mixture of gases which forms the earth's atmosphere and which we breathe. *She took a gulp of air.* 2 SING N The **air** is the space around things that is above the ground. *My dog was lying on the floor with its feet in the air... The smell of cooking filled the air.* 3 UNCOUNT N **Air** is used to refer to travel in aircraft. *The fare by air from London to Luxembourg is £145 return... ...air travel.* 4 SING N WITH SUPP If someone or something has a particular **air,** they give this general impression. *He has a faintly old-fashioned air.* 5 VB WITH OBJ If you **air** your opinions, you make them known to people. *He spoke on the radio, airing his views to the nation.* 6 VB WITH OBJ If you **air** a room, you let fresh air into it. 7 ERG VB When you **air** clothing or when it **airs,** you put it somewhere warm so it becomes completely dry. 8 See also **airing.**

PHRASES ● To disappear **into thin air** means to disappear completely. ● To appear **out of thin air** means to appear suddenly and mysteriously. ● If someone is **on the air,** they are broadcasting on radio or television.

airborne /ɛəbɔːn/. ADJ **Airborne** means flying in the air or coming from the air. *...airborne attacks.*

air-conditioned. ADJ If a room is **air-conditioned,** the air in it is kept cool and dry by means of a special machine called an 'air-conditioner'.

aircraft /ɛəkrɑːft/. **Aircraft** is the singular and plural. COUNT N An **aircraft** is a vehicle which can fly, for example an aeroplane or a helicopter.

airfield /ɛəfiːld/, **airfields.** COUNT N An **airfield** is a small area of ground where aircraft take off and land.

air force, air forces. COUNT N An **air force** is the part of a country's military organization that is concerned with fighting in the air.

airing /ɛərɪŋ/. 1 SING N If you give a room an **airing,** you let fresh air into it. 2 SING N If you give clothing an **airing,** you put it somewhere warm so that it becomes completely dry. 3 SING N If you give your opinions an **airing,** you make them known to people.

airline /ɛəlaɪn/, **airlines.** COUNT N An **airline** is a company which provides regular services carrying people or goods in aeroplanes.

airliner /ɛəlaɪnə/, **airliners.** COUNT N An **airliner** is a large aeroplane used for carrying passengers.

airmail /ɛəmeɪl/. UNCOUNT N **Airmail** is the system of sending letters, parcels, and goods by air. *She gave him a letter to post by airmail.*

airplane /ɛəpleɪn/, **airplanes.** COUNT N An **airplane** is the same as an aeroplane; an American use.

airport /ɛəpɔːt/, **airports.** COUNT N An **airport** is a place where aircraft land and take off, usually with a lot of buildings and facilities.

air raid, air raids. COUNT N An **air raid** is an attack by enemy aircraft in which bombs are dropped.

airspace /ɛəspeɪs/. UNCOUNT N A country's **airspace** is the part of the sky that is over that country and is considered to belong to the country. *The plane crashed just after entering British airspace.*

air terminal, air terminals. COUNT N An **air terminal** is a building at an airport where you check in and wait for your flight, or arrive after your flight.

airtight /ɛətaɪt/. ADJ If a container is **airtight,** its lid fits so tightly that no air can get in or out.

airwaves /ɛəweɪvz/. PLURAL N **Airwaves** are the radio waves used in radio and television broadcasting.

airy /ɛəri[1]/. 1 ADJ If a building is **airy,** it is large and has plenty of fresh air inside. *The church was airy and light inside.* 2 ADJ You can use **airy** to describe someone who is light-hearted and casual about things which should be taken seriously. *He applied in an airy way for the job of assistant manager.* ♦ **airily** ADV *...talking airily of this and that.*

aisle /aɪl/, **aisles.** COUNT N An **aisle** is a long narrow gap that people can walk along between rows of seats or between rows of shelves in a supermarket.

ajar /ədʒɑː/. PRED ADJ If a door is **ajar,** it is slightly open. *She left the door ajar.*

akin /əkɪn/. PRED ADJ WITH PREP 'to' If one thing is **akin** to another, it is similar to it in some way; a formal use. *She had answered with something akin to anger.*

-al. SUFFIX **-al** is added to nouns to form adjectives indicating what something relates to or what kind of thing something is. Adjectives of this kind are often not defined but are treated with the related nouns. *...agricultural workers... ...departmental running costs.*

alacrity /əlækrɪ[1]ti[1]/. UNCOUNT N If you do something with **alacrity,** you do it quickly and eagerly; a formal use.

alarm /əlɑːm/, **alarms, alarming, alarmed.** 1 UNCOUNT N **Alarm** is a sudden feeling of fear or anxiety. *She looked round in alarm.* 2 COUNT N An **alarm** is an automatic device that warns you of danger. *The alarm went off... ...a burglar alarm.* ● If you **sound** or **raise the alarm,** you warn people of danger. 3 VB WITH OBJ If something **alarms** you, it makes you suddenly afraid or anxious. *The sight of the school alarmed her.* ♦ **alarmed** ADJ *She looked alarmed.*

alarm clock, alarm clocks. COUNT N An **alarm clock** is a clock that you can set so that it wakes you up at a particular time.

alarming /əlɑːmɪŋ/. ADJ Something that is **alarming** makes you worried or concerned. *The world's forests are shrinking at an alarming rate.* ♦ **alarmingly** ADV *Her sight had begun to deteriorate alarmingly.*

alarmist /əlɑːmɪst/. ADJ **Alarmist** means causing unnecessary alarm. *Don't be too alarmist.*

alas /ə[3]læs/. SENTENCE ADV You use **alas** to say that you think that the facts you are talking about are sad, unfortunate, or regrettable; a formal use. *There was, alas, no shortage of assassinations.*

albatross /ælbətrɒs/, **albatrosses.** COUNT N An **albatross** is a very large white sea bird.

albeit /ɔːlbiːɪt/. CONJ You can use **albeit** to introduce a fact or comment which contrasts in some way with what you have just said; a formal use. *It continues to publish, albeit irregularly, two journals.*

albino /ælbiːnəʊ/, **albinos.** COUNT N An **albino** is a person or animal with very white skin, white hair, and pink eyes.

album /ælbəm/, **albums.** 1 COUNT N An **album** is a record with about 25 minutes of music or speech on each side. 2 COUNT N WITH SUPP An **album** is also a book in which you put photographs, stamps, or other things that you have collected.

alcohol /ælkə[6]hɒl/. 1 UNCOUNT N **Alcohol** is drink such as beer, wine, and whisky that can make people drunk. 2 UNCOUNT N **Alcohol** is also a colourless liquid which is found in drinks such as beer, wine, and whisky and which can be used as a solvent.

alcoholic /ælkə[6]hɒlɪk/, **alcoholics.** 1 ADJ An **alcoholic** drink contains alcohol. 2 COUNT N Someone who is an **alcoholic** is addicted to alcohol.

alcoholism /ælkə[6]hɒlɪzə[0]m/. UNCOUNT N **Alcoholism** is a kind of poisoning caused by drinking too much alcohol over a long period of time.

alcove /ælkəʊv/, **alcoves.** COUNT N An **alcove** is a small area of a room which is formed when one part of a wall is built farther back than the rest of it.

ale /eɪl/. MASS N Ale is a kind of beer.

alert /əlɜːt/, **alerts, alerting, alerted.** 1 ADJ If you are **alert,** you are paying full attention to what is happening. *We have to be alert all the time and look for our opportunity.* ♦ **alertness** UNCOUNT N *The job requires constant alertness and vigilance.* 2 PRED ADJ If you are **alert** to something, you are fully aware of it. *They were both alert to the dangers.* 3 COUNT N An **alert** is a situation in which people prepare themselves for danger. *The city centre was on a nuclear alert.* ● If you are **on the alert,** you are ready to deal with anything that might happen. 4 VB WITH OBJ If you **alert** someone, you warn them of danger or trouble. *He pressed the horn of the vehicle to alert the squadron.*

A level, A levels. COUNT N An **A level** is a British educational qualification which schoolchildren take when they are seventeen or eighteen years old.

algebra /ældʒɪ[2]brə/. UNCOUNT N **Algebra** is a type of mathematics in which letters are used to represent possible quantities.

alias /eɪlɪəs/, **aliases.** 1 COUNT N An **alias** is a false name, especially one used by a criminal. 2 PREP You use **alias** when you mention someone's false name. *...Dr Christopher Pallis, alias Martin Grainger.*

alibi /ælɪbaɪ/, **alibis.** COUNT N If you have an **alibi,** you can prove that you were somewhere else when a crime was committed.

alien /eɪljən, eɪlɪən/, **aliens.** 1 ATTRIB ADJ Something that is **alien** belongs to a different country, race, or group. *...adjusting to an alien society.* 2 ADJ If you describe something as **alien,** you mean that it seems strange and perhaps frightening, because it is not part of your normal experience. *...a totally alien and threatening environment.* 3 ADJ If something is **alien** to your normal feelings or behaviour, it is not the way you would normally feel or behave. *There were things about this new life that were not only alien to him, but horrifying.* 4 COUNT N An **alien** is someone who is not a legal citizen of the country in which they live. 5 COUNT N An **alien** is also a creature from outer space.

alienate /eɪljəneɪt, eɪlɪə-/, **alienates, alienating, alienated.** 1 VB WITH OBJ If you **alienate** someone, you make them become unfriendly or unsympathetic towards you. *I managed to alienate Dennis, who earlier on had been so friendly.* ♦ **alienation** /eɪljəneɪʃə[0]n, eɪlɪə-/ UNCOUNT N *...alienation on the part of many workers.* 2 VB WITH OBJ If someone **is alienated** from something, they are emotionally or intellectually separated from it. *People have been alienated from their roots.* ♦ **alienation** UNCOUNT N *...a growing feeling of despair and alienation.*

alight /əlaɪt/, **alights, alighting, alighted.** 1 PRED ADJ If something is **alight,** it is burning. *The boats were set alight.* 2 PRED ADJ If you describe someone's face or expression as **alight,** you mean that they look excited. *She was looking at him, her eyes alight.* 3 VB If a bird or insect **alights** somewhere, it lands there. *It flew across to the tree and alighted on a branch.* 4 VB When you **alight** from a train or bus, you get out of it after a journey; a formal use.

align /əlaɪn/, **aligns, aligning, aligned.** 1 PASSIVE VB OR REFL VB If you **are aligned** with a particular group, you support them in the same political aim. *They have avoided aligning themselves with any one political party.* ♦ **alignment** /əlaɪnmə[2]nt/ COUNT N *...political alignments with foreign powers.* 2 VB WITH OBJ If you **align** two objects, you place them in a particular position in relation to each other, usually parallel. *He aligned his papers in geometrical patterns on his desk.* ♦ **alignment** UNCOUNT N *Something had slipped out of alignment.*

alike /əlaɪk/. 1 PRED ADJ If two or more things are **alike,** they are similar. *They all look alike to me.* 2 ADV **Alike** also means in a similar way. *The children are all treated alike.* 3 ADV You use **alike** after mentioning a group in order to emphasize that you are referring to the whole of it. *The strike is damaging to managers and workers alike.*

alimony /ælɪmən[1]/. UNCOUNT N **Alimony** is money that someone has to pay regularly to their former wife or husband after they have been divorced.

alive /əlaɪv/. 1 PRED ADJ If people or animals are **alive,** they have life. *I think his father is still alive.* 2 PRED ADJ If you describe someone as **alive,** you mean that they are lively and enjoy everything that they do. 3 PRED ADJ If you describe an activity or situation as **alive,** you mean that it exists or is functioning well. *Theatre outside London is very much alive.* 4 PRED ADJ WITH 'with' If a place is **alive** with something, a lot of people or things are there and it seems busy or exciting. *The ditches beside the fields were alive with frogs.* 5 PRED ADJ WITH PREP 'to' If you are **alive** to a problem or situation, you are aware of it and realize its importance. *As you can see, I am fully alive to the problems facing the industry.*

PHRASES ● If a story or description **comes alive,** it becomes interesting, lively, or realistic. ● If people or places **come alive,** they start to be active or lively again.

alkali /ælkəlaɪ/, **alkalis.** MASS N An **alkali** is a substance with a pH value of more than 7.

all /ɔːl/. 1 PREDET, DET, OR PRON You use **all** to indicate that you are referring to the whole of a group or thing. *All the girls think it's great... They carried all the stuff into the hall... All of the defendants were proved guilty... They all live together... All was quiet in the gaol.* 2 ADV You also use **all** to emphasize the extent to which something happens or is true. *He spilled coffee all over himself... I'm all alone.* 3 ADV You also use **all** when you are talking about an equal score in a game. For example, if the score is three **all,** both players or teams have three points.

PHRASES ● You say **above all** to emphasize that a particular thing is more important than others. *Relax, and above all don't panic.* ● You say **after all** to draw attention to something that other people might have forgotten or that you had not previously realized. *Could it be true, after all, that money did not bring happiness?* ● You use **all in all** to introduce a summary or generalization. *All in all, I'm not in favour.* ● If you say that something is not **all that** good or not **all that** important, you mean that it is not very good or not very important; used mainly in speech. *I don't know him all that well.* ● **All the** more or **all the** better mean even more or even better than before. *You must work all the more quickly now.* ● You use **at all** to emphasize a negative or a question. *We didn't go there at all... Haven't you got any at all?* ● You use **for all** to say that a particular fact does not affect or contradict what you are saying, although you know that it may seem to do so. *For all her sensitivity, she's extremely tough.* ● **In all** means in total. *There were nine in all.* ● You say **in all** seriousness or **in all** honesty to emphasize that you are being completely serious or honest. *I say this in all seriousness.* ● You use **of all** to emphasize the words 'first' or 'last', or a superlative adjective or adverb. *I asked them first of all if they were Welsh... This view is the best of all.*

Allah /ælə/. PROPER N **Allah** is the name of God in Islam.

allay /ə[3]leɪ/, **allays, allaying, allayed.** VB WITH OBJ If you **allay** someone's fears or doubts, they stop feeling afraid or doubtful; a formal use.

allegation /ælɪ[2]geɪʃə[0]n/, **allegations.** COUNT N An **allegation** is a statement suggesting that someone has done something wrong. *...allegations of improper business dealings.*

allege /ə[3]lɛdʒ/, **alleges, alleging, alleged.** REPORT VB If you **allege** that something is true, you say it but do not prove it. *The reports alleged that the motive was financial.*

alleged /ə[3]lɛdʒd/. ATTRIB ADJ An **alleged** fact has been stated but not proved to be true. *...alleged police brutality.* ♦ **allegedly** ADV *...the crimes he had allegedly committed.*

allegiance /ə[3]liːdʒəns/, **allegiances.** UNCOUNT N OR COUNT N Your **allegiance** to a group, person, or belief is your support for and loyalty to them. *...their traditional allegiances.*

allegorical /ælɪ[2]gɒrɪkə[0]l/. ADJ An **allegorical** story, poem, or painting uses allegory.

allegory /ælɪ[2]gə[0]ri[1]/, **allegories.** COUNT N OR UNCOUNT N An **allegory** is a story, poem, or painting in which the characters and events are symbols of something else.

allergy /ælədʒi[1]/, **allergies.** COUNT N OR UNCOUNT N An **allergy** is an illness that you have when you eat, smell, or touch a substance which does not normally make people ill. *He had an allergy to milk.* ♦ **allergic** /ə[3]lɜːdʒɪk/ ADJ *Are you allergic to dogs?*

alleviate /ə[3]liːvieɪt/, **alleviates, alleviating, alleviated.** VB WITH OBJ If something **alleviates** pain or suffering, it makes it less severe. ♦ **alleviation** /ə[3]liːvieɪʃə[0]n/ UNCOUNT N *...the alleviation of pain.*

alley /æli[1]/, **alleys.** COUNT N An **alley** or **alleyway** is a narrow path or street.

alliance /əlaɪəns/, **alliances.** COUNT N An **alliance** is a relationship in which two or more people or groups work together for some purpose.

allied /ælaɪd/. 1 ATTRIB ADJ **Allied** countries, political parties, or other groups are united by a political or military agreement. 2 ATTRIB ADJ **Allied** describes things that are related to other things because they have particular qualities or characteristics in common. *The aircraft and allied industries were nationalized.* 3 See also **ally.**

alligator /ælɪgeɪtə/, **alligators.** COUNT N An **alligator** is a large animal, similar to a crocodile.

allocate /ælə[6]keɪt/, **allocates, allocating, allocated.** VB WITH OBJ If something **is allocated** to a person or for a purpose, it is given to that person or used for that purpose. *You've been allocated room 426.* ♦ **allocation** /ælə[6]keɪʃə[0]n/ UNCOUNT N *...the allocation of responsibilities.*

allot /ə[3]lɒt/, **allots, allotting, allotted.** VB WITH OBJ If something **is allotted** to someone, it is given to them as their share. *All seats in the Public Gallery are allotted in advance by ticket.* ♦ **allotted** ATTRIB ADJ *...our allotted sum of money.*

allotment /ə[3]lɒtmə[2]nt/, **allotments.** 1 COUNT N An **allotment** is a small area of land which a person rents to grow vegetables on; a British use. 2 SING N WITH 'of' An **allotment** of something is a share of it.

all-out. ATTRIB ADJ An **all-out** attack is aggressive and determined.

allow /əlaʊ/, **allows, allowing, allowed.** 1 VB WITH OBJ If you **are allowed** to do something, it is all right for you to do it. *He agreed to allow me to take the course.* 2 VB WITH OBJ AND OBJ If you **are allowed** something, you are given permission to have it or are given it. *Sometimes, we were allowed a special treat.* 3 VB WITH OBJ AND TO-INF If you **allow** something to happen, you do not prevent it. *The further this process is allowed to go, the more difficult it will be to reverse it.* 4 VB WITH OBJ AND TO-INF If something **allows** a particular thing to happen, it makes it possible. *The creatures had warm blood, which allowed them to be active at night.* 5 REPORT VB If you **allow** that something is true, you admit that it is true; a formal use. *He allowed that even world leaders could make mistakes.*

allow for. PHR VB If you **allow for** certain problems or expenses, you include extra time or money in your planning in order to deal with them if they occur.

allowable /əlaʊəbə[0]l/. ADJ If something is **allowable,** it is all right for you to do it. *...allowable departures from the norms of behaviour.*

allowance /əlaʊəns/, **allowances.** 1 COUNT N WITH SUPP An **allowance** is money that is given regularly to someone, to help them pay for things they need. 2 PHRASE If you **make allowances** for something, you take it into account in your plans or actions.

all-powerful. ADJ Someone or something that is **all-powerful** has a very great deal of power or influence.

all right; also spelled **alright.** 1 PRED ADJ OR ADV If you say that something is **all right,** you mean that it is satisfactory or acceptable. *'Do you like this champagne?'—'It's all right.'... He's getting on all right.* 2 PRED ADJ If someone is **all right,** they are well or safe. *Someone should see if she's all right.* 3 CONVENTION You say **'all right'** when you are agreeing to something. *'Can you help?'—'All right. What do you want me to do?'* 4 PHRASE You also say **'all right?'** to someone when you are checking that they have understood what you have just said. *If you feel dizzy again put your head in your hands, all right?*

all-rounder, all-rounders. COUNT N An **all-rounder** is someone who has a lot of different skills or is good at many sports; a British use.

allude /ə[3]lj[0]uːd/, **alludes, alluding, alluded.** VB WITH PREP 'to' If you **allude** to something, you mention it in an indirect way; a formal use. *I have already alluded to the energy problem.*

allure /ə[3]lj[0]ʊə/. SING N The **allure** of something is a pleasing or exciting quality that it has. *...the allure of foreign travel.*

alluring /ə[3]lj[0]ʊərɪŋ/. ADJ Someone or something that is **alluring** is very attractive.

allusion /ə[3]lj[0]uːʒə[0]n/, **allusions.** COUNT N OR UNCOUNT N An **allusion** to something is an indirect or vague reference to it. *...allusions to Latin and Greek authors.*

ally, allies, allying, allied; pronounced /ælaɪ/ when it is a noun and /ə[3]laɪ/ when it is a verb. 1 COUNT N An **ally** is a country, organization, or person that helps and supports another. *...our European allies.* 2 REFL VB WITH 'with' If you **ally** yourself with someone, you support them. 3 See also **allied.**

almighty /ɔːlmaɪti/. 1 PROPER N The **Almighty** is another name for God. *...the mercy of the Almighty.* Also ATTRIB ADJ *...Almighty God.* 2 ATTRIB ADJ An **almighty** row, problem, or mistake is a very great or serious one; an informal use. *She made the most almighty fuss.*

almond /ɑ:mənd/, **almonds.** COUNT N An **almond** is a kind of pale oval nut.

almost /ɔ:lməust/. ADV **Almost** means very nearly, but not completely. *I spent almost a month in China... He is almost blind... I had almost forgotten about the trip... In Oxford Street, you can buy almost anything.*

aloft /əlɒft/. ADV Something that is **aloft** is in the air or off the ground; a literary use.

alone /ələun/. 1 PRED ADJ When you are **alone,** you are not with any other people. *I wanted to be alone... Barbara spent most of her time alone in the flat.* 2 PRED ADJ A person who is **alone** is also someone who has no family or friends. *I had never felt so alone and without hope in my life.* 3 PRED ADJ If one person is **alone** with another, they are together, with nobody else present. *I was alone with the attendant... We'd never spent such a long time alone together.* 4 ADV If you do something **alone,** you do it without help from other people. *I was left to bring up my two children alone.* 5 ADJ AFTER N If you **alone** do something, you are the only person who does it. *Simon alone knew the truth.* 6 ADJ AFTER N If something consists of one idea or feature **alone,** nothing else is involved. *Pride alone prevented her from giving up.*

along /əlɒŋ/. 1 PREP If you move or look **along** something, you move or look towards one end of it. *He was driving along a lane... She glanced along the corridor.* 2 PREP OR ADV If something is situated **along** a road, river, or corridor, it is situated in it or beside it. *...an old house along the Lanark Road... Room 64 was half way along on the right.* 3 ADV When someone or something moves **along,** they keep moving steadily. *I put my arm around him as we walked along.* 4 ADV If something is going **along** in a particular way, it is progressing in that way. *It was going along nicely.* 5 ADV If you take someone **along** when you go somewhere, you take them with you. *Why don't you come along too?*
PHRASES • You use **all along** to say that something has existed or been the case throughout a period of time. *Perhaps they had been mistaken all along.* • If you do something **along with** someone else, you both do it. If you take one thing **along with** another, you take both things. *Along with thousands of others, he fled the country... The eggs were delivered along with the milk.*

alongside /əlɒŋsaɪd/. 1 PREP OR ADV If something is **alongside** something else, it is next to it. *There was a butcher's shop alongside the theatre... A car drew up alongside.* 2 PREP If you work **alongside** other people, you are working in the same place and are co-operating with them. *The idea is to get them working on simple things alongside other people.* 3 PREP If one thing exists **alongside** another, the two things are both present in a situation. *I cannot imagine two political systems less likely to live at peace alongside each other.*

aloof /əlu:f/. 1 ADJ Someone who is **aloof** likes to be alone and does not talk much. 2 PRED ADJ If you stay **aloof** from something, you do not become involved with it.

aloud /əlaud/. ADV When you speak or read **aloud,** you speak so that other people can hear you. *She read aloud to us from the newspaper.*

alphabet /ælfəbet/, **alphabets.** COUNT N The **alphabet** is the set of letters in a fixed order which is used for writing the words of a language.

alphabetical /ælfəbetɪkəºl/. ATTRIB ADJ **Alphabetical** means arranged according to the normal order of the letters in the alphabet. *...an alphabetical list.*

alpine /ælpaɪn/. ATTRIB ADJ **Alpine** means existing in or relating to mountains. *...alpine meadows.*

already /ɔ:lredi¹/. 1 ADV If something has **already** happened, it has happened before the present time. *I've had tea already, thank you.* 2 ADV You also use **already** to indicate that something happened earlier than expected. *By the time he got home, Julie was already in bed.*

alright /ɔ:lraɪt/. See **all right.**

also /ɔ:lsəu/. 1 ADV You use **also** when you are giving more information about a person or thing. *Tony Nuttall is Vice-Chancellor and also a Professor of English at Sussex... ...also available in blue and green.* 2 ADV You can use **also** to say that the same fact applies to someone or something else. *His first wife was also called Margaret.*

altar /ɒltə/, **altars.** COUNT N An **altar** is a holy table in a church or temple.

alter /ɒltə/, **alters, altering, altered.** ERG VB If something **alters** or if you **alter** it, it changes. *The weather could alter violently... America must radically alter its economic policy.* ♦ **alteration** /ɒltəreɪʃəºn/ COUNT N *It is not possible to make major alterations to existing arrangements.*

alternate, alternates, alternating, alternated; pronounced /ɒltəneɪt/ when it is a verb and /ɒltɜ:nət/ when it is an adjective. 1 VB WITH 'between' When you **alternate** between two things, you regularly do or use one thing and then the other. *They alternated between patronising us and ignoring us.* 2 VB WITH 'with' When one thing **alternates** with another, the two things regularly occur in turn. *The Third World suffers from an annual cycle of drought alternating with flood.* ♦ **alternation** /ɒltəneɪʃəºn/ UNCOUNT N *...an alternation of right-wing and left-wing governments.* 3 ATTRIB ADJ **Alternate** actions, events, or processes regularly occur after each other. *...the alternate contraction and relaxation of muscles.* ♦ **alternately** ADV *Each piece of material is washed alternately in soft water and coconut oil.* 4 ATTRIB ADJ If something happens on **alternate** days, it happens on one day, then does not happen on the next day, then happens again on the day after it, and so on. In the same way, something can happen in **alternate** weeks or years. *We saw each other on alternate Sunday nights.*

alternative /ɒltɜ:nətɪv/, **alternatives.** 1 COUNT N An **alternative** is something that can exist or you can do instead of something else. *Are there alternatives to prison?* Also ATTRIB ADJ *But still people try to find alternative explanations.* 2 ATTRIB ADJ **Alternative** is also used to describe something that is different from the usual things of its kind, especially when it is simpler or more natural, or not part of the establishment. *...sources of alternative energy.*

alternatively /ɒltɜ:nətɪvli¹/. SENTENCE ADV You use **alternatively** to suggest or mention something different from what has just been mentioned. *Alternatively, you can use household bleach.*

although /ɔ:lðəu/. 1 CONJ You use **although** to introduce a subordinate clause which contains a statement that makes the main clause seem surprising. *Although he was late he stopped to buy a sandwich... Gretchen kept her coat on, although it was warm in the room.* 2 CONJ **Although** also introduces a subordinate clause, often containing 'not', that modifies the main clause and corrects a wrong impression that someone might get from it. *I have a lot of my grandfather's features, although I'm not so tall as he was.*

altitude /æltɪtju:d/, **altitudes.** UNCOUNT N OR COUNT N If something is at a particular **altitude,** it is at that height above sea level. *...flying at high altitude.*

alto /æltəu/, **altos.** 1 COUNT N An **alto** is a woman with a low singing voice. 2 ATTRIB ADJ An **alto** musical instrument has a range of musical notes of medium pitch.

altogether /ɔ:ltəgeðə/. 1 ADV If something stops **altogether,** it stops completely. *He abandoned his work altogether.* 2 ADV If one thing is **altogether** different from another, the two things are completely different. *...an altogether different kind of support.* 3 SENTENCE ADV You can use **altogether** to summarize something you have been talking about. *Yes, it's quite a pleasant place altogether.* 4 ADV You also use **altogether** to indicate that the amount you are mentioning is a total. *Altogether, he played in 44 matches.*

altruism /æltru:ɪzəºm/. UNCOUNT N **Altruism** is unselfish concern for other people's happiness and welfare.

altruistic /æltru:ɪstɪk/. ADJ **Altruistic** means unselfish and concerned for other people's happiness and welfare. *My invitation was not completely altruistic.*

aluminium /æljə⁴mɪnɪəm/; spelled **aluminum** /əlu:mɪnəm/ in American English. UNCOUNT N **Aluminium** is a lightweight metal used for making things such as cooking equipment and aircraft parts.

always /ɔ:lwɪ³z/. 1 ADV If you **always** do a particular thing, you do it all the time. *I shall always love you.* 2 ADV If something is **always** the case, it is the case all the time. *I had always been poor.* 3 ADV If you say that someone can **always** take a particular course of action, you mean that they can try it if all other methods are unsuccessful. *Oh well, I can always come back later.*

am /æm/. **Am** is the first person singular of the present tense of **be.**

a.m. /eɪ em/. **a.m.** after a number indicates that the number refers to a particular time between midnight and noon.

amalgamate /ə³mælgəmeɪt/, **amalgamates, amalgamating, amalgamated.** RECIP VB When two or more organizations **amalgamate** or **are amalgamated,** they become one large organization. *...the Variety Artists Federation, which has since amalgamated with Equity.* ♦ **amalgamation** /ə³mælgəmeɪʃəºn/ UNCOUNT N *...the amalgamation of several large businesses.*

amass /əmæs/, **amasses, amassing, amassed.** VB WITH OBJ If you **amass** something such as money, you gradually get a lot of it.

amateur /æmətjºuºə, -tʃə/, **amateurs.** 1 COUNT N An **amateur** is someone who does something as a hobby, not as a job. *...a good amateur viola player.* 2 ADJ **Amateur** can also mean the same as amateurish.

amateurish /æmətjºuºərɪʃ/. ADJ If you describe something as **amateurish,** you mean it is not skilfully made or done.

amaze /əmeɪz/, **amazes, amazing, amazed.** VB WITH OBJ If something **amazes** you, it surprises you very much. *She was amazed that I was only twenty.* ♦ **amazed** ADJ *I saw her amazed look.*

amazement /əmeɪzmə³nt/. UNCOUNT N **Amazement** is what you feel if you are very surprised by something. *Her eyes were wide with amazement.*

amazing /əmeɪzɪŋ/. ADJ If something is **amazing,** it is very surprising and makes you feel pleasure or admiration. *New York is an amazing city.* ♦ **amazingly** SUBMOD *Our holiday was amazingly cheap.*

ambassador /æmbæsədə/, **ambassadors.** COUNT N An **ambassador** is an important official living in a foreign country who represents his or her government.

amber /æmbə/. 1 UNCOUNT N **Amber** is a hard yellowish-brown substance used for making jewellery. 2 ADJ Something that is **amber** in colour is orange or yellowish-brown.

ambience /æmbi¹əns/; also spelled **ambiance.** SING N The **ambience** of a place is its character and atmosphere; a literary use.

ambiguity /æmbɪgju:ɪ¹ti¹/, **ambiguities.** UNCOUNT N OR COUNT N You say that there is **ambiguity** when something can be understood in more than one way. *...a speech which was a masterpiece of ambiguity.*

ambiguous /æmbɪgju⁴əs/. ADJ Something that is **ambiguous** can be understood in more than one way. *There was nothing ambiguous in the message.* ♦ **ambiguously** ADV *The announcement was ambiguously worded.*

ambition /æmbɪʃəºn/, **ambitions.** 1 COUNT N If you have an **ambition** to achieve something, you want very much to achieve it. *Her ambition was to be a teacher.* 2 UNCOUNT N OR PLURAL N If someone has **ambition** or **ambitions,** they want to be successful, rich, or powerful. *...men of energy and ambition.*

ambitious /æmbɪʃəs/. 1 ADJ Someone who is **ambitious** wants to be successful, rich, or powerful. 2 ADJ An **ambitious** idea or plan is on a large scale and needs a lot of work to be successful.

ambivalent /æmbɪvələnt/. ADJ If you are **ambivalent** about something, you have opposing feelings about it. *...an ambivalent attitude towards women.*

amble /æmbəºl/, **ambles, ambling, ambled.** VB When you **amble,** you walk slowly and in a relaxed manner. *I ambled home through the village.*

ambulance /æmbjə⁴ləns/, **ambulances.** COUNT N An **ambulance** is a vehicle for taking people to and from hospital.

ambush /æmbuʃ/, **ambushes, ambushing, ambushed.** VB WITH OBJ If people **ambush** their enemies, they attack them after hiding and waiting for them. *Weyler's troops successfully ambushed a rebel force.* Also COUNT N *A whole battalion got caught in an ambush.*

amen /eɪmen, ɑ:men/. CONVENTION **Amen** is said or sung by Christians at the end of a prayer.

amenable /ə³mi:nəbəºl/. ADJ If you are **amenable** to something, you are willing to do or accept it.

amend /ə³mend/, **amends, amending, amended.** 1 VB WITH OBJ If you **amend** something that has been written or said, you change it. *Last year the regulations were amended to allow other awards to be made.* 2 PHRASE If you **make amends** when you have harmed someone, you show you are sorry by doing something to please them.

amendment /ə³mendmə³nt/, **amendments.** 1 COUNT N An **amendment** is a section that is added to a law or rule in order to change it. *...amendments to the Industrial Relations Bill.* 2 COUNT N An **amendment** is also a correction to a piece of writing. *She made a few amendments to the letter.*

amenity /əmi:nɪ¹ti¹/, **amenities.** COUNT N An **amenity** is something such as a shopping centre or sports facility that is provided for people's convenience or enjoyment.

American /əmerɪkən/, **Americans.** 1 ADJ **American** means belonging or relating to the United States of America. 2 COUNT N An **American** is a person who comes from the United States of America. 3 ADJ **American** also means belonging or relating to North, Central or South America. *...the white man's treatment of the American Indian... ...the livelihoods of several Central American and South American states.*

amiable /eɪmɪəbə^{0}l/. ADJ Someone who is **amiable** is friendly and pleasant. *...her amiable manner.* ♦ **amiably** ADV *He chatted amiably with Dorothy.*

amicable /æmɪkəbə^{0}l/. ADJ When people have an **amicable** relationship, they are pleasant to each other and solve their problems without quarrelling. *We hope to settle the dispute in an amicable way.* ♦ **amicably** ADV *They parted amicably.*

amid /əmɪd/. 1 PREP If something happens **amid** other things, it happens while the other things are happening. *Suddenly, amid the cries, I heard some words.* 2 PREP If something is **amid** other things, it is surrounded by them; a literary use. *Tombstones stood amid the swaying grass.*

amidst /ə^{3}mɪdst/. **Amidst** means the same as amid.

amiss /əmɪs/. PRED ADJ If you say that something is **amiss,** you mean there is something wrong. *I immediately sensed something amiss.*
PHRASES ● If someone **takes** a remark **amiss,** they are offended and upset by it. *You mustn't take anything I say amiss.* ● If you say that something would **not come amiss,** you mean it would be welcome and useful. *A little calm wouldn't come amiss.*

ammonia /əməʊnɪə, -njə/. UNCOUNT N **Ammonia** is a colourless liquid or gas with a strong, sharp smell. It is used in making household cleaning substances.

ammunition /æmjə^{4}nɪʃə^{0}n/. 1 UNCOUNT N **Ammunition** is bullets and rockets that are made to be fired from guns. 2 UNCOUNT N **Ammunition** can also refer to information that may be used against someone. *The letters might be used as ammunition by reactionary groups.*

amnesia /æmniːzɪə/. UNCOUNT N If someone is suffering from **amnesia,** they have lost their memory.

amnesty /æmnɪ^{2}sti^1/, **amnesties.** 1 COUNT N An **amnesty** is an official pardon granted to a prisoner by the state. 2 COUNT N An **amnesty** is also a period of time during which people can confess to a crime or give up weapons without being punished.

among /əmʌŋ/. 1 PREP A person or thing that is **among** a group of people or things is surrounded by them. *We stood there among piles of wooden boxes.* 2 PREP If you are **among** a group of people, you are in their company. *I was among friends.* 3 PREP If you say that one person **among** others did something, you are saying that other people also did it, and not just that one person. *Bluestone, among other union leaders, argued against a strike.* 4 PREP If an opinion, or state exists **among** a group of people, they have it or experience it. *He has always been popular among MPs.* 5 PREP If something is divided **among** three or more people, they all get a part of it.

amongst /əmʌŋst/. PREP **Amongst** means the same as among. *They sat amongst monstrous cans of tomato soup.*

amoral /æmɒrəl, eɪ-/. ADJ Someone who is **amoral** does not care whether what they do is right or wrong; used showing disapproval.

amorous /æmə^{8}rəs/. ADJ **Amorous** feelings and behaviour involve sexual desire.

amorphous /əmɔːfəs/. ADJ Something that is **amorphous** has no clear shape or structure.

amount /əmaʊnt/, **amounts, amounting, amounted.** 1 COUNT N An **amount** of something is how much of it you have, need, or get. *...the amount of potatoes that people buy... I was horrified by the amount of work I had to do.* 2 VB WITH PREP 'to' If something **amounts** to a particular total, all the parts of it add up to that total. *...very high fees which amount to £2,000.*

amphibian /æmfɪbɪən/, **amphibians.** COUNT N An **amphibian** is an animal such as a frog that can live both on land and in water.

amphibious /æmfɪbɪəs/. ADJ An **amphibious** animal can live both on land and in water.

ample /æmpə^{0}l/. 1 ADJ If there is an **ample** amount of something, there is enough of it and some extra. *This leaves her ample time to prepare.* ♦ **amply** ADV *This has been amply demonstrated over the past few years.* 2 ATTRIB ADJ **Ample** also means large. *There was provision for an ample lawn.*

amplifier /æmplɪfaɪə/, **amplifiers.** COUNT N An **amplifier** is an electronic device in a radio or stereo system, which causes sounds or signals to become louder.

amplify /æmplɪfaɪ/, **amplifies, amplifying, amplified.** 1 VB WITH OBJ If you **amplify** a sound, you make it louder. *These signals are then amplified.* 2 VB WITH OBJ If you **amplify** an idea, statement, or piece of writing, you explain it more fully. ♦ **amplification** /æmplɪfɪkeɪʃə^{0}n/ UNCOUNT N *His story needed confirmation and amplification.*

amputate /æmpjə^{4}teɪt/, **amputates, amputating, amputated.** VB WITH OBJ To **amputate** someone's arm or leg means to cut it off. *They had to amputate his leg.* ♦ **amputation** /æmpjə^{4}teɪʃə^{0}n/ UNCOUNT N *Punishment for a thief was amputation of a hand.*

amuse /ə^{3}mjuːz/, **amuses, amusing, amused.** 1 VB WITH OBJ If something **amuses** you, it makes you want to laugh or smile. *He laughed as if the idea amused him.* ♦ **amused** ADJ *I was highly amused by a comment Shaw made.* 2 REFL VB OR VB WITH OBJ If you **amuse** yourself, or if someone **amuses** you, you do something in order to pass the time and not become bored. *Sam amused himself by throwing branches into the fire.*

amusement /ə^{3}mjuːzmə^{2}nt/, **amusements.** 1 UNCOUNT N **Amusement** is the feeling that you have when you think that something is funny. *She smiled in amusement.* 2 UNCOUNT N **Amusement** is the pleasure that you get from being entertained or from doing something interesting. *Every kind of facility was laid on for their amusement.* 3 COUNT N **Amusements** are ways of passing the time pleasantly. *What amusements have you found to keep a young boy out of mischief?* 4 PLURAL N **Amusements** are the games, rides, and other things that you can enjoy at a fairground or holiday resort.

amusing /ə^{3}mjuːzɪŋ/. ADJ Someone or something that is **amusing** makes you laugh or smile. *There was an amusing story in the paper.* ♦ **amusingly** ADV *He talked lightly and amusingly.*

an /æn/ or /ən/. DET **An** is used instead of 'a', the indefinite article, in front of words that begin with vowel sounds: see **a.**

anachronism /ə^{3}nækrə^{7}nɪzə^{0}m/, **anachronisms.** COUNT N You say that something is an **anachronism** when you think that it is old-fashioned. *The English public schools are an anachronism.* ♦ **anachronistic** /ə^{3}nækrə^{7}nɪstɪk/ ADJ *...a peculiarly anachronistic view of communism.*

anaemia /ə^{3}niːmɪə/; also spelled **anemia.** UNCOUNT N If you have **anaemia,** you have too few red cells in your blood, so that you feel tired and look pale.

anaemic /ə^{3}niːmɪk/; also spelled **anemic.** ADJ Someone who is **anaemic** suffers from anaemia.

anaesthetic /ænəsθetɪk/, **anaesthetics;** also spelled **anesthetic.** COUNT N An **anaesthetic** is a drug that stops you feeling pain, particularly during an operation.

anaesthetist /ə^{3}niːsθətɪst/, **anaesthetists;** also spelled **anesthetist.** COUNT N An **anaesthetist** is a doctor who specializes in giving anaesthetics.

anaesthetize /ə^{3}niːsθətaɪz/, **anaesthetizes, anaesthetizing, anaesthetized;** also spelled **anaesthetise** or **anesthetize.** VB WITH OBJ To **anaesthetize** someone means to make them unconscious by giving them an anaesthetic.

anal /eɪnə^{0}l/. ATTRIB ADJ **Anal** means relating to the anus.

analogous /ənælə^{7}gəs/. ADJ If one thing is **analogous** to another, the two things are similar in some way.

analogy /ənælə^{7}dʒi^1/, **analogies.** 1 COUNT N If you make or draw an **analogy** between two things, you show that they are similar. *He made an analogy between parental and judicial discipline.* 2 PHRASE If you explain something **by analogy,** you explain it by describing something else that is similar. *The models are meant to show, by analogy, how matter is built up.*

analyse /ænəlaɪz/, **analyses, analysing, analysed;** also spelled **analyze.** VB WITH OBJ If you **analyse** something, you consider it or examine it in order to understand it or to find out what it consists of.

analysis /ənælɪ^{1}sɪs/, **analyses** /ənælɪ^{1}siːz/. 1 UNCOUNT N OR COUNT N **Analysis** is the process of considering something in order to understand it or to find out what it consists of. *...linguistic analysis.* 2 COUNT N An **analysis** is an explanation that is the result of considering something. *He offers a calm analysis of the situation.* 3 PHRASE You say **in the final analysis** or **in the last analysis** to indicate that the statement you are making is about the basic facts of a situation. *In the final analysis power rested in the hands of one man.*

analyst /ænəlɪst/, **analysts.** 1 COUNT N An **analyst** is a person whose job is to analyse a subject and give opinions about it. 2 COUNT N An **analyst** is also someone who examines and treats people who are emotionally disturbed.

analytic /ænəlɪtɪk/. ADJ **Analytic** means using logical reasoning. *...an analytic process.*

analytical /ænəlɪtɪkə^{0}l/. ADJ **Analytical** means the same as analytic.

analyze /ænəlaɪz/. See **analyse.**

anarchism /ænəkɪzə^{0}m/. UNCOUNT N **Anarchism** is the belief that the laws and power of governments should be replaced by people working together freely. ♦ **anarchist** /ænəkɪst/ COUNT N *Anarchists oppose the organised violence of war.*

anarchy /ænəki^1/. UNCOUNT N **Anarchy** is a situation where nobody obeys rules or laws; *...his will to reverse the drift into anarchy and economic chaos.*
♦ **anarchic** ADJ *The system is economically inefficient and politically anarchic.*

anatomical /ænətɒmɪkə^{0}l/. ATTRIB ADJ **Anatomical** means relating to the structure of the bodies of people and animals.

anatomy /ə^{3}nætə^{7}mi^1/, **anatomies.** 1 UNCOUNT N **Anatomy** is the study of the structure of the bodies of people or animals. 2 COUNT N An animal's **anatomy** is the structure of its body.

-ance. SUFFIX **-ance** and **-ancy** are added to adjectives, usually in place of '-ant', to form nouns. These nouns usually refer to states, qualities, or behaviour. Nouns of this kind are often not defined but are treated with the related adjectives. *...his academic brilliance... ...the buoyancy of the economy.*

ancestor /ænsɛstə/, **ancestors.** 1 COUNT N Your **ancestors** are the people from whom you are descended. 2 COUNT N An **ancestor** of something modern is an earlier thing from which it developed. *These creatures are the ancestors of modern man.*

ancestral /ænsɛstrəl/. ATTRIB ADJ **Ancestral** means relating to your family in former times.

ancestry /ænsɛstri^1/, **ancestries.** COUNT N Your **ancestry** is the people from whom you are descended. *...American citizens of Japanese ancestry.*

anchor /æŋkə/, **anchors, anchoring, anchored.** 1 COUNT N An **anchor** is a heavy hooked object that is dropped from a boat into the water at the end of a chain to make the boat stay in one place. 2 ERG VB When a boat **anchors** or when you **anchor** it, its anchor is dropped into the water to make it stay in one place. 3 VB WITH OBJ If you **anchor** an object, you prevent it from moving by, for example, tying it down. *We anchored his wheelchair to a huge stone.*

ancient /eɪnʃənt/. 1 ADJ You use **ancient** to describe things that belong to the distant past. *...ancient Greece and Rome.* 2 ADJ You also use **ancient** to describe things that are very old or that have a long history. *He came from an ancient Catholic family.*

ancillary /ænsɪləri^1/. ATTRIB ADJ The **ancillary** workers in an institution are the people such as the cleaners, whose work supports the main work of the institution.

-ancy. See **-ance.**

and /ə^{3}nd/. 1 CONJ You use **and** to link two or more words, groups, or clauses. *...my mother and father... I came here in 1972 and have lived here ever since.* 2 CONJ You also use **and** to link two identical words or phrases to emphasize their degree or to suggest that something continues or increases over a period of time. *He became more and more annoyed.* 3 CONJ **And** indicates that two numbers are to be added together. *Two and two is four.* 4 CONJ **And** links two statements about events which follow each other. *He opened the car door and got out.* 5 CONJ You also use **and** to interrupt yourself in order to make a comment on what you are saying. *Finally—and I really ought to stop in a minute—I wish to tell a little story.* 6 CONJ You use **and** in some numbers. *...three hundred and fifty people.*

anecdotal /ænɪ^{2}kdəʊtə^{0}l/. ADJ **Anecdotal** speech or writing is full of anecdotes or is based on anecdotes. *...anecdotal evidence.*

anecdote /ænɪ^{2}kdəʊt/, **anecdotes.** COUNT N An **anecdote** is a short, entertaining account of something that has happened. *She told him anecdotes about the hospital and the patients.*

anemia /əniːmɪə/. See **anaemia.**

anemic /əniːmɪk/. See **anaemic.**

anesthetic /ænəsθetɪk/. See **anaesthetic.**

anesthetist /ə^{3}niːsθətɪst/. See **anaesthetist.**

anesthetize /ə^{3}niːsθətaɪz/. See **anaesthetize.**

anew /ə^{3}njuː/. ADV If you do something **anew,** you do it again, often in a different way; a literary use. *...starting life anew in a fresh place.*

angel /eɪndʒə^{0}l/, **angels.** COUNT N **Angels** are spiritual beings that some people believe are God's messengers and servants in heaven.

angelic /ændʒelɪk/. ADJ You can describe someone as **angelic** when they are very good, kind, and gentle.

anger /æŋgə/, **angers, angering, angered.** 1 UNCOUNT N **Anger** is the strong emotion that you feel when you think someone has behaved in such an unfair, cruel, or insulting way that you want to express your feelings towards them in a forceful way. *'You're a fool.'—'Am I?' he said, red with anger.* 2 VB WITH OBJ If someone or something **angers** you, they make you angry. *His hostile attitude angered her.*

angle /æŋgə^{0}l/, **angles, angling, angled.** 1 COUNT N An **angle** is the difference in direction between two lines or surfaces. Angles are measured in degrees. ● See also **right angle.** 2 COUNT N An **angle** is the shape that is created where two lines or surfaces join together. 3 COUNT N An **angle** is the direction from which you look at something. *He held the vase close to his face, peering at it from all angles.* 4 COUNT N WITH

SUPP You can refer to a way of presenting something, for example in a newspaper, as a particular **angle.** *The play's pacifist angle had a great appeal.* **5** VB WITH 'for' If you **angle** for something, you try to make someone offer it to you without asking for it directly. *He got the invitation to Washington he had been angling for.*

angler /æŋglə/, **anglers.** COUNT N An **angler** is someone who fishes with a fishing rod as a hobby.

angling /æŋglɪŋ/. UNCOUNT N **Angling** is the activity of fishing with a fishing rod.

Anglo-. PREFIX **Anglo-** is added to adjectives indicating nationality to form adjectives describing something which involves relations between Britain and another country. *...the 1921 Anglo-Irish treaty.*

angry /æŋgri1/, **angrier, angriest.** ADJ When you are **angry,** you feel strong emotion about something that you consider unfair, cruel, or insulting. *He was angry at Sally for accusing him.* ♦ **angrily** ADV *The story was angrily denied by the dead man's family.*

anguish /æŋgwɪʃ/. UNCOUNT N **Anguish** is great mental or physical suffering. *...a quarrel which caused her intense unhappiness and anguish.*

anguished /æŋgwɪʃt/. ADJ **Anguished** means feeling or showing great mental or physical suffering. *The anguished cries continued.*

angular /æŋgjə4lə/. ATTRIB ADJ **Angular** things have shapes that seem to contain a lot of straight lines and sharp points. *...his angular face.*

animal /ænɪmə0l/, **animals. 1** COUNT N An **animal** is a living creature such as a dog, or horse, rather than a bird, fish, insect, or human. *They used to hunt wild animals.* **2** COUNT N An **animal** is also any living thing that is not a plant, including people. *Man is a very weak animal... ...the animal kingdom.* **3** ATTRIB ADJ **Animal** qualities or feelings relate to your physical nature and instincts rather than your mind. *Animal instinct warned me to tread carefully.*

animate /ænɪmət/. ADJ Something that is **animate** has life, in contrast to things like stones and machines which do not.

animated /ænɪmeɪtɪ2d/. **1** ADJ Someone or something that is **animated** is lively and interesting. *The conversation was animated.* **2** ADJ An **animated** film has been filmed by means of animation. *...an animated cartoon.*

animation /ænɪmeɪʃə0n/. **1** UNCOUNT N **Animation** is the process of making films in which drawings or puppets appear to move. **2** UNCOUNT N Someone with **animation** behaves in a lively way.

animosity /ænɪmɒsɪ1ti1/. UNCOUNT N **Animosity** is a feeling of strong dislike and anger.

ankle /æŋkə0l/, **ankles.** COUNT N Your **ankle** is the joint where your foot joins your leg.

annex /ænɛks/, **annexes, annexing, annexed;** also spelled **annexe. 1** COUNT N An **annex** is a building which is joined to or is next to a larger main building. **2** VB WITH OBJ If a country **annexes** another country or an area of land, it seizes it and takes control of it. ♦ **annexation** /ænɛkseɪʃə0n/ UNCOUNT N *...the annexation of Hawaii.*

annihilate /ənaɪəleɪt/, **annihilates, annihilating, annihilated.** VB WITH OBJ If something **is annihilated,** it is destroyed completely. *What would happen if the human race should be annihilated?* ♦ **annihilation** /ənaɪəleɪʃə0n/ UNCOUNT N *...threatening the total annihilation of the planet.*

anniversary /ænə1vɜːsə0ri1/, **anniversaries.** COUNT N An **anniversary** is a date which is remembered or celebrated because a special event happened on that date in a previous year. *...his wedding anniversary.*

announce /ə3naʊns/, **announces, announcing, announced. 1** REPORT VB If you **announce** something, you tell people about it publicly or officially. *Mr Heath announced his decision.* **2** REPORT VB If you **announce** something, you say it in a deliberate and rather aggressive way. *'I am Mrs Jones,' she announced.*

announcement /ə3naʊnsmə3nt/, **announcements. 1** COUNT N An **announcement** is a public statement which gives information about something that has or will happen. *The Government announcement gave details of small increases in taxes.* **2** SING N The **announcement** of something is the act of telling people about it. *...the events which follow the announcement of your resignation.*

announcer /ə3naʊnsə/, **announcers.** COUNT N An **announcer** is someone who introduces programmes on radio or television.

annoy /ə3nɔɪ/, **annoys, annoying, annoyed.** VB WITH OBJ If someone **annoys** you, they make you fairly angry and impatient. *You're just saying that to annoy me.*

annoyance /ə3nɔɪəns/. UNCOUNT N **Annoyance** is the feeling that you get when someone annoys you.

annoyed /ə3nɔɪd/. PRED ADJ If you are **annoyed,** you are fairly angry about something. *She shook her head, annoyed with herself for forgetting.*

annoying /ə3nɔɪɪŋ/. ADJ An **annoying** person or action makes you feel fairly angry and impatient. *It was annoying to be corrected by him all the time.*

annual /ænjʊ0əl/, **annuals. 1** ATTRIB ADJ **Annual** means happening or done once every year. *...her annual holiday.* ♦ **annually** ADV *Independence day is celebrated annually.* **2** ATTRIB ADJ **Annual** means calculated over a period of one year. *...an annual income of twelve thousand dollars.* ♦ **annually** ADV *They import 500 million tonnes of crude oil annually.* **3** COUNT N An **annual** is a book or magazine that is published once a year.

annul /ənʌl/, **annuls, annulling, annulled.** VB WITH OBJ If a contract or marriage **is annulled,** it is declared invalid, so that legally it is considered never to have existed.

annum /ænəm/. See **per annum.**

anomalous /ənɒmələs/. ADJ Something that is **anomalous** is different from what is normal; a formal use. *These calculations have given anomalous results.*

anomaly /ənɒməli1/, **anomalies.** COUNT N If something is an **anomaly,** it is different from what is normal or usual; a formal use.

anon. **Anon.** means anonymous; often written after poems or other writing whose author is not known.

anonymity /ænə7nɪmɪ1ti1/. **1** UNCOUNT N **Anonymity** is the state of not having your name or identity known. *...a benefactor who insisted on anonymity.* **2** UNCOUNT N WITH SUPP The **anonymity** of something is the fact that it hides your identity. *...the anonymity of life in big cities.* **3** UNCOUNT N WITH SUPP The **anonymity** of a place is its lack of interesting features. *...the anonymity of a hotel room.*

anonymous /ə3nɒnɪməs/. **1** ADJ If you remain **anonymous** when you do something, you do not let people know that you were the person who did it. *...anonymous letters.* ♦ **anonymously** ADV *Anyone who wanted to make a complaint could do so anonymously.* **2** ADJ Something that is **anonymous** does not reveal who you are. *A taxi is anonymous. Nobody knows who's inside.* **3** ADJ Something that is **anonymous** has no interesting features. *...an anonymous little town.*

anorak /ænə8ræk/, **anoraks.** COUNT N An **anorak** is a warm waterproof jacket, usually with a hood.

another /ənʌðə/. **1** DET OR PRON **Another** means additional. *We walked another hundred metres.* **2** DET OR PRON **Another** can also be used to mean a different thing or person from the one just mentioned. *Parents say one thing and do another.* **3** PHRASE You use **one another** to indicate that each member of a group does something to or for the other members. *Members usually meet in one another's homes.*

answer /ɑːnsə/, **answers, answering, answered. 1** VB WITH OR WITHOUT OBJ, OR REPORT VB When you **answer** someone who has asked you something, you say something back to them. *'Did he win?'—'No,' I answered... He answered that the price would be three pounds.* **2** VB WITH OR WITHOUT OBJ If you **answer** a letter or advertisement, you write to the person who wrote it. **3** COUNT N An **answer** is something that you say or write when you answer someone. *The answer to your question is no!* **4** VB WITH OR WITHOUT OBJ When you **answer** the telephone, you pick it up when it rings. When you **answer** the door, you open it when you hear a knock or the bell. Also COUNT N *I rang the doorbell, but there was no answer.* **5** COUNT N An **answer** to a problem is a possible solution to it. **6** COUNT N The **answer** to a question in a test is something that a student writes or says in an attempt to give the facts. **7** VB WITH OBJ When you **answer** a question in a test, you give the answer to it. *You have to answer four questions.*

answer back. PHR VB If someone, especially a child, **answers** you **back** or **answers back,** they speak rudely to you when you speak to them.

answerable /ɑːnsə0rəbə0l/. **1** PRED ADJ WITH PREP 'to' If you are **answerable** to someone, you have to report and explain your actions to them. **2** PRED ADJ WITH 'for' If you are **answerable** for your actions or for someone else's actions, you are considered to be responsible for them.

ant /ænt/, **ants.** COUNT N **Ants** are small crawling insects that live in large groups.

antagonism /æntægənɪzə0m/. UNCOUNT N **Antagonism** is hatred or hostility.

antagonist /æntægənɪst/, **antagonists.** COUNT N Your **antagonist** is your opponent or enemy.

antagonistic /æntægənɪstɪk/. ADJ Someone who is **antagonistic** shows hostility towards you. *Many of them are antagonistic towards the President.*

antagonize /æntægənaɪz/, **antagonizes, antagonizing, antagonized;** also spelled **antagonise.** VB WITH OBJ If you **antagonize** someone, you make them feel angry or hostile towards you.

antecedent /æntɪsiːdənt/, **antecedents. 1** COUNT N An **antecedent** of something is a similar thing that happened or existed before it. *...the prehistoric antecedents of the horse.* **2** PLURAL N Your **antecedents** are your ancestors.

antelope /æntɪləʊp/, **antelopes. Antelope** can also be the plural. COUNT N An **antelope** is an animal like a deer with long legs and horns.

antenna /æntɛnə/, **antennae** /æntɛnaɪ/ or **antennas.** For meaning 2 the plural is usually **antennas. 1** COUNT N The **antennae** of an insect are the two long, thin parts attached to its head that it uses to feel things with. **2** COUNT N An **antenna** is also an aerial; an American use.

anthem /ænθəm/, **anthems.** COUNT N An **anthem** is a song or hymn written for a special occasion. ● See also **national anthem.**

anthology /ænθɒlədʒi1/, **anthologies.** COUNT N An **anthology** is a collection of writings by different writers published together in one book.

anthropology /ænθrəpɒlədʒi1/. UNCOUNT N **Anthropology** is the study of people, society, and culture. ♦ **anthropologist** COUNT N *...an English anthropologist, Colin Turnbull.*

anti-. 1 PREFIX **Anti-** is used to form adjectives that describe people as opposing something such as a group of people or a practice. *...the anti-apartheid movement.* **2** PREFIX **Anti-** is also used to form words that mean intended to prevent something from happening or to destroy something harmful. *...anti-aircraft guns... ...anti-freeze.*

antibiotic /ænti1baɪɒtɪk/, **antibiotics.** COUNT N **Antibiotics** are drugs that are used in medicine to kill bacteria and to cure infections.

anticipate /æntɪsɪpeɪt/, **anticipates, anticipating, anticipated. 1** VB WITH OBJ If you **anticipate** an event, you realize in advance that it may happen and you are prepared for it. *The Secretary had anticipated the question.* ♦ **anticipation** /æntɪsɪpeɪʃə0n/ UNCOUNT N *Petrol coupons were issued in anticipation of rationing.* **2** VB WITH OBJ If you **anticipate** something pleasant or exciting that is going to happen, you look forward to it with pleasure. *She had often pleasurably anticipated the moment when she would hand in her resignation.* ♦ **anticipation** UNCOUNT N *'Please!' the children cried, jumping up and down in anticipation.*

anticlimax /ænti1klaɪmæks/, **anticlimaxes.** COUNT N OR UNCOUNT N If something is an **anticlimax,** it disappoints you because it is not as exciting as you expected, or because it happens after something that was very exciting. *Polling day was a bit of an anticlimax... ...a sense of anticlimax.*

anti-clockwise /ænti1klɒkwaɪz/. ADV OR ATTRIB ADJ When something moves **anti-clockwise,** it moves in a circle in the opposite direction to the hands of a clock; a British use.

antics /æntɪks/. PLURAL N **Antics** are funny, silly or unusual ways of behaving.

antidote /ænti1dəʊt/, **antidotes. 1** COUNT N An **antidote** is a chemical substance that controls the effect of a poison. **2** COUNT N An **antidote** to a difficult situation is something that helps you to deal with the situation. *Work is a wonderful antidote to misery.*

antipathy /æntɪpəθi1/. UNCOUNT N **Antipathy** is a strong feeling of dislike or hostility.

antiquated /æntɪkweɪtɪ2d/. ADJ **Antiquated** things seem very old or old-fashioned.

antique /æntiːk/, **antiques.** COUNT N An **antique** is an old object which is valuable because of its beauty or rarity. *...antique furniture.*

antiquity /æntɪkwɪ1ti1/, **antiquities. 1** UNCOUNT N **Antiquity** is the distant past, especially the time of the ancient Egyptians, Greeks, and Romans. *...the great lost paintings of antiquity.* **2** COUNT N **Antiquities** are interesting old things, such as buildings and statues, that you can go and see.

anti-Semitism /ænti1sɛmɪ1tɪzə0m/. UNCOUNT N **Anti-Semitism** is prejudice against Jewish people.

antiseptic /ænti1sɛptɪk/. MASS N **Antiseptic** is a substance that kills harmful bacteria.

anti-social. 1 ADJ Someone who is **anti-social** is unwilling to meet and be friendly with other people. **2** ADJ **Anti-social** behaviour is annoying or upsetting to other people.

antithesis /æntɪθə1sɪs/, **antitheses** /æntɪθə1siːz/. COUNT N The **antithesis** of something is its exact opposite; a formal use.

antler /æntlə/, **antlers.** COUNT N A male deer's **antlers** are the branched horns on its head.

anus /eɪnəs/, **anuses.** COUNT N A person's **anus** is the hole between their buttocks, from which faeces leave their body; a medical use.

anvil /ænvɪl/, **anvils.** COUNT N An **anvil** is a heavy iron block on which hot metals are beaten into shape.

anxiety /æŋzaɪ^{1}ti^1/, **anxieties. 1** UNCOUNT N **Anxiety** is a feeling of nervousness or worry. *'What do you think?' asked the Belgian with a touch of anxiety.* **2** COUNT N An **anxiety** is something which causes you to feel nervous or worried. *...major financial anxieties.*

anxious /æŋkəʃəs/. **1** ADJ If you are **anxious,** you are nervous or worried about something. *She was anxious about her job.* ♦ **anxiously** ADV *'I'm not boring you?' she asked anxiously.* **2** ATTRIB ADJ An **anxious** time or situation is one during which you feel nervous and worried. *You must have had an anxious day.* **3** PRED ADJ If you are **anxious** to do something or **anxious** that something should happen, you very much want to do it or want it to happen. *She's anxious to go abroad.*

any /ɛni^1/. **1** DET OR PRON You use **any** in negative statements, for example with 'not' or 'never', to mean none of a particular thing. *I don't like any of this.* **2** DET OR PRON You use **any** in questions and conditional clauses to ask if there is some of a particular thing or to suggest that there might be. *Were you in any danger?... They will retaliate if any of their ships are attacked.* **3** DET OR PRON You use **any** in positive statements when you are referring to something or someone without saying exactly what, who, or which kind you mean. *Any big tin container will do... ...things that any man might do under pressure.* **4** ADV You can also use **any** to emphasize a comparative adjective or adverb in a negative statement. *I couldn't stand it any longer.*

anybody /ɛnibə^{7}di^1/. See **anyone.**

anyhow /ɛnihaʊ/. **1** ADV **Anyhow** means the same as anyway. **2** ADV If you do something **anyhow,** you do it in a careless or untidy way. *They were all shoved in anyhow.*

anymore /ɛnimɔː/. **Anymore** means the same as 'any more': see **more.**

anyone /ɛniwə^{9}n/ or **anybody** /ɛnibə^{7}di^1/. **1** INDEF PRON You use **anyone** or **anybody** in negative statements, for example with 'not' or 'never', to say that nobody is present or involved in an action. *There wasn't anyone there.* **2** INDEF PRON You use **anyone** or **anybody** in questions and conditional clauses to ask or talk about whether someone is present or doing something. *Was there anyone behind you?... If anyone asks where you are I'll say you've just gone out.* **3** INDEF PRON You also use **anyone** and **anybody** to refer to a person or to people in general, when you do not want to say which particular person or people you are referring to. *He took longer than anybody else.*

anything /ɛniθɪŋ/. **1** INDEF PRON You use **anything** in negative statements, for example with 'not' or 'never', to say that nothing is present or an action or event does not happen. *I did not say anything.* **2** INDEF PRON You use **anything** in questions and conditional clauses to ask or talk about whether something is present or happening. *I've told her to come to you if she wants anything.* **3** INDEF PRON You can use **anything** to refer to a thing, an event, or an idea without saying exactly which one you mean. *Lemon gives a fresh flavour to almost anything.* **4** ADV You can use **anything** for emphasis, when you are saying that something is not at all like something else. *It didn't taste anything like soup... The total wasn't anything near what we'd expected.*

anyway /ɛniweɪ/ or **anyhow** /ɛnihaʊ/. **1** SENTENCE ADV You use **anyway** or **anyhow** to indicate that a statement explains or supports a previous point. *We ought to spend less on the defence missiles, which I reckon are pretty useless anyway.* **2** SENTENCE ADV You use **anyway** or **anyhow** to suggest that a statement is true or relevant in spite of other things that have been said. *'I can give you a lift.'—'No, I'll walk. Thanks, anyway.'* **3** SENTENCE ADV You use **anyway** or **anyhow** to correct or modify a statement, for example to limit it to what you definitely know to be true. *'All of them?' I asked. 'Some, anyway.'* **4** SENTENCE ADV You use **anyway** or **anyhow** to change the topic or return to a previous topic. *What are you phoning for, anyway?... Anyway, I'll see you later.*

anywhere /ɛniwεə/. **1** ADV You can use **anywhere** in negative statements, questions, and conditional clauses to refer to a place without saying exactly where you mean. *Is there an ashtray anywhere?* **2** ADV You can use **anywhere** in positive statements to emphasize an expression that refers to a place or area. *They are the oldest rock paintings anywhere in North America.*

apart /əpɑːt/. **1** ADV WITH 'from' When something is **apart** from something else, there is a space between them. *I was sitting apart from the rest.* **2** PRED ADJ If two things are a particular distance **apart,** they are that distance from each other. *Their faces were a couple of inches apart.* **3** ADV If two things move **apart** or are pulled **apart,** they move away from each other. **4** PRED ADJ If two people are **apart,** they are not living together or spending time together. **5** ADV If you take something **apart,** you separate it into the pieces that it is made of. If it comes or falls **apart,** its parts separate from each other. **6** ADV If something such as an organization or relationship falls **apart,** it can no longer continue because it has serious difficulties. *Their marriage began to fall apart.*

PHRASES ● If you **can't tell** two people or things **apart,** they look exactly the same to you. *He couldn't tell the boys apart.* ● You use **apart from** when you are giving an exception to a general statement. *Apart from Ann, the car was empty.* ● You use **apart from** to say that you want to ignore one aspect of a situation so that you can talk about another aspect. *Quite apart from the expense, I don't think I would want to fly anyway.*

apartheid /əpɑːthəaɪt, -həeɪt/. UNCOUNT N **Apartheid** is a political system in South Africa in which people of different races are kept apart by law.

apartment /əpɑːtmə^{2}nt/, **apartments. 1** COUNT N An **apartment** is a flat, especially in America. **2** COUNT N An **apartment** is one of a set of large rooms used by an important person such as a king, queen, or president. *...splendid apartments of state.*

apathetic /æpəθɛtɪk/. ADJ Someone who is **apathetic** is not interested in anything.

apathy /æpəθi^1/. UNCOUNT N **Apathy** is a state of mind in which you are not interested in or enthusiastic about anything.

ape /eɪp/, **apes, aping, aped. 1** COUNT N **Apes** are animals such as chimpanzees or gorillas. **2** VB WITH OBJ If you **ape** someone's speech or behaviour, you imitate it.

aperture /æpətʃə/, **apertures.** COUNT N An **aperture** is a narrow hole or gap, for example the opening in a camera through which light passes into it.

apex /eɪpɛks/, **apexes.** COUNT N The **apex** of something is its pointed top or end.

apiece /əpiːs/. ADV If people have a particular number of things **apiece,** they have that number each; an old-fashioned use. *He gave his daughters £200 apiece.*

aplomb /əplɒm/. UNCOUNT N If you do something with **aplomb,** you do it with great confidence.

apolitical /eɪpəlɪtɪkəl/. ADJ Someone who is **apolitical** is not interested in politics.

apologetic /əpɒlədʒɛtɪk/. ADJ If you are **apologetic,** you show or say that you are sorry that you have hurt someone or caused trouble for them. *He had been apologetic about his behaviour at dinner.* ♦ **apologetically** ADV *He smiled apologetically.*

apologize /əpɒlədʒaɪz/, **apologizes, apologizing, apologized;** also spelled **apologise.** VB When you **apologize** to someone, you say that you are sorry that you have hurt them or caused trouble for them. *I apologise for my late arrival.*

apology /əpɒlədʒi^1/, **apologies.** COUNT N OR UNCOUNT N An **apology** is something that you say or write in order to tell someone that you are sorry that you have hurt them or caused trouble for them.

apostrophe /əpɒstrəfi^1/, **apostrophes.** COUNT N An **apostrophe** is a mark written to indicate that one or more other letters have been omitted from a word, as in 'can't' and 'he'll'. An apostrophe is also written before or after an 's' at the end of a word to indicate that what follows belongs or relates to the word, as in 'the cat's whiskers' and 'the players' entrance'.

appal /əpɔːl/, **appals, appalling, appalled;** spelled **appall** and **appalls** in American English. VB WITH OBJ If something **appals** you, it shocks and disgusts you because it is so bad. *The levels of ignorance appalled me.* ♦ **appalled** ADJ *I was absolutely appalled at the quality of the reporting.*

appalling /əpɔːlɪŋ/. ADJ Something that is **appalling** is so bad that it shocks you. *These people live in appalling conditions.* ♦ **appallingly** ADV *The situation has deteriorated appallingly since 1951.*

apparatus /æpəreɪtəs/. **1** UNCOUNT N **Apparatus** is the equipment which is used to do a particular job or activity. **2** UNCOUNT N WITH SUPP The **apparatus** of an organization is its structure and method of operation. *...the whole apparatus of the welfare state.*

apparent /əpærənt/. **1** ATTRIB ADJ An **apparent** situation, quality, or feeling seems to exist, although you cannot be certain that it exists. *...the apparent success of their marriage.* **2** PRED ADJ If something is **apparent** to you, it is clear and obvious to you. *It was becoming increasingly apparent to me that he disliked me.*

apparently /əpærəntli^1/. SENTENCE ADV OR ADV You use **apparently** to refer to something that seems to be the case although it may not be. *She was standing by the window, apparently quite calm and relaxed.*

apparition /æpərɪʃən/, **apparitions.** COUNT N An **apparition** is something that you think you see but that is not really there.

appeal /əpiːl/, **appeals, appealing, appealed. 1** VB WITH 'for' OR REPORT VB If you **appeal** for something that you need, you make a serious and urgent request for it. *He was appealing for funds to build a new school.* **2** COUNT N An **appeal** is a serious and urgent request. *A radio appeal asking for money for cancer research, raised £75,000.* **3** VB WITH PREP 'to' If you **appeal** to someone's reason or feelings, you suggest that they should do what you ask if they want to seem reasonable or compassionate. *They are confident they can appeal to her sense of duty.* Also COUNT N *...an appeal to her maternal feelings.* **4** VB If you **appeal** to someone in authority against a decision, you formally ask them to change it. **5** COUNT N An **appeal** is a formal request for a decision to be changed. *The Supreme Court turned down our appeal.* **6** VB WITH PREP 'to' If something **appeals** to you, you find it attractive or interesting. *The idea appealed to him.* ♦ **appealing** ADJ *She had an appealing sense of humour.* **7** UNCOUNT N WITH SUPP The **appeal** of something is a quality that it has which people find attractive or interesting.

appear /əpɪə/, **appears, appearing, appeared. 1** VB When something **appears,** it moves into a position where you can see it. *A glow of light appeared over the sea.* **2** VB When something new **appears,** it begins to exist or becomes available. *His second novel appeared under the title 'Getting By'.* **3** VB WITH 'in' When someone **appears** in a play or show, they take part in it. **4** VB When someone **appears** before a court of law, they go there to answer charges or to give information. **5** VB WITH TO-INF OR COMPLEMENT, OR REPORT VB If you say that something **appears** to be the way that you describe it, you mean that you believe it to be that way. *Their offer appears to be the most attractive.*

appearance /əpɪərəns/, **appearances. 1** SING N WITH SUPP The **appearance** of someone in a place is their arrival there, especially when it is unexpected. *The fight was soon stopped, thanks to the prompt appearance of the police.* **2** UNCOUNT N Someone or something's **appearance** is the way that they look to people. *I had ceased to worry about my appearance.* **3** SING N WITH SUPP The **appearance** of something new is its coming into existence or into use. *With the appearance of credit cards more people got into debt.* **4** COUNT N When someone makes an **appearance** in a play or show, they take part in it. *She has made several television appearances recently.*

PHRASES ● If you **put in an appearance** at an event, you go to it for a short time but do not stay. ● If something is true **to all appearances** or **by all appearances,** it seems from what you know about it that it is true. *To all appearances he doesn't work hard.*

appease /əpiːz/, **appeases, appeasing, appeased.** VB WITH OBJ If you try to **appease** someone, you try to stop them being angry by giving them what they want; a formal use. *He had to do something to appease the Republicans.* ♦ **appeasement** UNCOUNT N *...a policy of appeasement.*

appendicitis /əpɛndɪ^{1}saɪtɪ^{1}s/. UNCOUNT N **Appendicitis** is an illness in which your appendix is infected and painful.

appendix /ə^{3}pɛndɪks/, **appendices** /ə^{3}pɛndɪsiːz/ or **appendixes. 1** COUNT N Your **appendix** is a small closed tube inside your body at the end of your digestive system. **2** COUNT N An **appendix** to a book is extra information that is placed at the end of it.

appetite /æpə^{1}taɪt/, **appetites. 1** COUNT N OR UNCOUNT N Your **appetite** is your desire to eat. *All that work has given me an appetite... ...his loss of appetite.* **2** COUNT N If you have an **appetite** for something, you have a strong desire for it. *...the appetite for power.*

appetizing /æpə^{1}taɪzɪŋ/; also spelled **appetising.** ADJ Food that is **appetizing** looks and smells nice, so that you want to eat it.

applaud /əplɔːd/, **applauds, applauding, applauded. 1** VB WITH OR WITHOUT OBJ When a group of people **applaud,** they clap their hands in order to show approval, for example when they have enjoyed a play. **2** VB WITH OBJ When an action or attitude **is applauded,** people praise it.

applause /əplɔːz/. UNCOUNT N **Applause** is an expression of praise or appreciation by a group of people, in which they clap their hands.

apple /æpə^{0}l/, **apples.** COUNT N OR UNCOUNT N An **apple** is a round fruit with a smooth skin and firm white flesh.

appliance /əplaɪəns/, **appliances.** COUNT N An **appliance** is a device or machine that does a particular job in your home, for example a vacuum cleaner or a washing machine.

applicable /æplɪkəbə^{0}l, əplɪkə-/. ADJ Something that is **applicable** to a particular situation is relevant to it. *The following special regulations are applicable to overseas students.*

applicant /æplɪkənt/, **applicants.** COUNT N An **applicant** for a job is someone who formally asks to be given it.

application /æplɪkeɪʃə0n/, **applications. 1** COUNT N OR UNCOUNT N An **application** for a job or a place at a college is a formal written request to be given it. **2** UNCOUNT N OR COUNT N The **application** of a rule or piece of knowledge is the use of it in a particular situation. *Do the results have any practical application?* **3** UNCOUNT N **Application** is hard work and concentration on what you are doing.

applied /ə3plaɪd/. ATTRIB ADJ An **applied** subject of study is practical rather than theoretical. *...applied psychology.*

apply /əplaɪ/, **applies, applying, applied. 1** VB If you **apply** to have something or to do something, you write asking formally to be allowed to have it or do it. *I've applied for another job.* **2** REFL VB OR VB WITH OBJ If you **apply** yourself to something, you concentrate hard on it. *He tried to apply his mind to Rose's problems.* **3** VB If something **applies** to a person or a situation, it is relevant to the person or situation. **4** VB WITH OBJ If you **apply** a rule, system, or skill, you use it in a situation or activity. *...the capacity to develop and apply technology.* **5** VB WITH OBJ If you **apply** a name to someone or something, you refer to them by that name. **6** VB WITH OBJ If you **apply** something to a surface, you put it onto the surface or rub it into it; a formal use. *Apply a little liquid wax polish.*

appoint /əpɔɪnt/, **appoints, appointing, appointed. 1** VB WITH OBJ If you **appoint** someone to a job or post, you formally choose them for it. **2** VB WITH OBJ If you **appoint** a time or place for something to happen, you decide when or where it will happen; a formal use. *I arrived at the appointed time.*

appointment /əpɔɪntmə2nt/, **appointments. 1** UNCOUNT N The **appointment** of a person to do a particular job is the choice of that person to do it. **2** COUNT N An **appointment** is a job or position of responsibility. **3** COUNT N If you have an **appointment** with someone, you have arranged to see them at a particular time. *The doctor's appointment was for 11 am.*

appraisal /əpreɪzə0l/, **appraisals.** COUNT N OR UNCOUNT N If you make an **appraisal** of something, you consider it carefully and form an opinion about it.

appraise /əpreɪz/, **appraises, appraising, appraised.** VB WITH OBJ If you **appraise** something, you consider it carefully and form an opinion about it.

appreciable /əpriːʃɪ0əbə0l, -sɪ-/. ATTRIB ADJ An **appreciable** amount or effect is large enough to be important or clearly noticed. *There had been appreciable progress recently.* ♦ **appreciably** SUBMOD *The following week it was appreciably colder.*

appreciate /əpriːʃɪeɪt, -sɪ-/, **appreciates, appreciating, appreciated. 1** VB WITH OBJ If you **appreciate** something, you like it because you recognize its good qualities. **2** REPORT VB If you **appreciate** a situation or problem, you understand it and know what it involves. *I appreciate that this is not a fair comparison.* **3** VB WITH OBJ If you say that you **appreciate** what someone has done for you, you mean that you are grateful to them for it. **4** VB If something **appreciates** over a period of time, its value increases. *These diamonds should appreciate in value.*

appreciation /əpriːʃɪeɪʃə0n, -sɪ-/, **appreciations. 1** UNCOUNT N **Appreciation** of something is recognition and enjoyment of its good qualities. *He had little appreciation of great plays.* **2** UNCOUNT N If you show your **appreciation** for something that someone has done for you, you express your gratitude for it. **3** COUNT N An **appreciation** of someone such as an artist is a discussion and evaluation of their achievements.

appreciative /əpriːʃɪ0ətɪv/. ADJ An **appreciative** reaction or expression shows pleasure or gratitude. *...appreciative laughter... 'Thank you,' I said, flashing him an appreciative smile.* ♦ **appreciatively** ADV *'Want a lift?' she asked. I nodded appreciatively.*

apprehension /æprɪhenʃə0n/, **apprehensions.** UNCOUNT N OR COUNT N **Apprehension** is a feeling of fear that something terrible may happen; a formal use. *His mother trembled with apprehension.*

apprehensive /æprɪhensɪv/. ADJ Someone who is **apprehensive** is afraid that something terrible may happen. *I felt a bit apprehensive at first.* ♦ **apprehensively** ADV *She looked up apprehensively.*

apprentice /ə3prentɪs/, **apprentices.** COUNT N An **apprentice** is a young person who works with someone in order to learn their skill.

apprenticeship /ə3prentɪs0ʃɪp/, **apprenticeships.** COUNT N OR UNCOUNT N A young person's **apprenticeship** is a fixed period of time during which they work with someone in order to learn their skill.

approach /əprəʊtʃ/, **approaches, approaching, approached. 1** VB WITH OR WITHOUT OBJ When someone **approaches** you, they come nearer to you. *He opened the car door for her as she approached.* Also COUNT N WITH SUPP *The dogs began to bark as if aware of our approach.* **2** COUNT N An **approach** to a place is a road or path that leads to it. **3** VB WITH OBJ If you **approach** someone about something, you speak to them about it for the first time. *They had approached us about working with their party.* **4** VB WITH OBJ AND ADJUNCT When you **approach** a situation or problem in a particular way, you think about it or deal with it in that way. *Governments must approach the subject of disarmament in a new spirit.* **5** COUNT N An **approach** to a situation or problem is a way of thinking about it or of dealing with it. *We need a new approach to this problem.* **6** ERG VB When a future event or date **approaches** or when you **approach** it, it gradually becomes nearer. *We are approaching the day of the race.* Also SING N WITH SUPP *...the approach of winter.* **7** VB WITH OBJ If something **approaches** a particular level or state, it almost reaches that level or state. *These rocket planes approached speeds of 4000 mph.*

appropriate, appropriates, appropriating, appropriated; pronounced /ə3prəʊprɪət/ when it is an adjective and /ə3prəʊprɪeɪt/ when it is a verb. **1** ADJ Something that is **appropriate** is suitable or acceptable for a particular situation. *It seemed appropriate to end with a joke.* ♦ **appropriately** ADV *He reminded himself to thank Louis appropriately.* **2** VB WITH OBJ If you **appropriate** something which does not belong to you, you take it for yourself; a formal use. *The materials are exported and other countries appropriate the profits.*

approval /ə3pruːvə0l/. **1** UNCOUNT N If a plan or request gets **approval,** someone agrees to allow it. *I was given McPherson's approval for the plan.* **2** UNCOUNT N **Approval** also means admiration. *Oliver looked at Simon with approval.*

approve /ə3pruːv/, **approves, approving, approved. 1** VB If you **approve** of an action, event, or suggestion, you are pleased about it. *My grandfather did not approve of my father's marriage.* **2** VB If you **approve** of someone or something, you like and admire them. *He doesn't approve of me.* **3** VB WITH OBJ If someone in authority **approves** a plan or idea, they formally agree to it.

approved /ə3pruːvd/. **1** ADJ An **approved** method or course of action is generally or officially accepted as appropriate. **2** ADJ Someone who is **approved** in a particular position has been formally accepted by people in authority. *...lists of approved candidates.*

approving /ə3pruːvɪŋ/. ADJ An **approving** reaction or expression shows support for something, or satisfaction with it. *There were a few approving nods and smiles.* ♦ **approvingly** ADV *His wife watched approvingly.*

approximate, approximates, approximating, approximated; pronounced /ə3prɒksə1mə1t/ when it is an adjective and /ə3prɒksə1meɪt/ when it is a verb. **1** ADJ An **approximate** number, time, or position is close to the correct number, time, or position, but is not exact. *She gave me some approximate figures.* ♦ **approximately** ADV *We have approximately 40 pupils.* **2** VB WITH OBJ OR PREP 'to' If something **approximates** to something else, it is similar to it but not exactly the same. *...social conditions approximate those of the early thirties... ...stories which vaguely approximated to the truth.*

approximation /ə3prɒksɪ1meɪʃə0n/, **approximations. 1** COUNT N An **approximation** is a fact, object, or description which is similar to something else but not exactly the same. *...an approximation to the truth.* **2** COUNT N An **approximation** is also a number, calculation, or position that is not exact.

apricot /eɪprɪkɒt/, **apricots.** COUNT N An **apricot** is a small, soft, round fruit with yellowish-orange flesh and a stone inside.

April /eɪprə1l/. UNCOUNT N **April** is the fourth month of the year in the Western calendar.

apron /eɪprən/, **aprons.** COUNT N An **apron** is a piece of clothing that you put on over the front of your normal clothes to prevent them from getting dirty.

apt /æpt/. **1** ADJ **Apt** means suitable. *...a very apt description.* ♦ **aptly** ADV *...the aptly named village of Cold Weston.* **2** PRED ADJ WITH TO-INF If someone is **apt** to behave in a particular way, they often behave in that way. *I was apt to fidget during a long performance.*

aptitude /æptɪtjuːd/, **aptitudes.** COUNT N If you have an **aptitude** for something, you are able to learn it quickly and do it well.

aquarium /əkweərɪəm/, **aquariums. 1** COUNT N An **aquarium** is a glass tank filled with water, in which people keep fish. **2** COUNT N An **aquarium** is also a building, often in a zoo, where fish and underwater animals are kept.

aquatic /əkwætɪk/. **Aquatic** means existing or happening in water. *...aquatic plants... ...aquatic sports.*

Arab /ærəb/, **Arabs.** COUNT N An **Arab** is a member of a people who live in the Middle East and North Africa. *...his early life among the Arabs.* Also ADJ *The Ambassadors of several Arab countries were invited.*

Arabian /əreɪbɪən/. ATTRIB ADJ **Arabian** means belonging or relating to Arabia, especially to Saudi Arabia.

Arabic /ærəbɪk/. **1** UNCOUNT N **Arabic** is a language spoken in the Middle East and in parts of North Africa. **2** ADJ Something that is **Arabic** belongs or relates to the language, writing, or culture of the Arabs. **3** ATTRIB ADJ An **Arabic** numeral is one of the written figures, such as 1, 2, 3, or 4.

arable /ærəbə0l/. ADJ **Arable** is used to describe things relating to growing crops. *...arable farming.*

arbiter /ɑːbɪtə/, **arbiters.** COUNT N An **arbiter** is a person or institution that judges and settles a quarrel between people or groups; a formal use.

arbitrary /ɑːbɪtrəri1, ɑːbɪtri1/. ADJ An **arbitrary** decision or action is not taken for any particular reason. *...the brutal and arbitrary expulsion of immigrants.* ♦ **arbitrarily** ADV *The victim has almost always been arbitrarily arrested.*

arbitrate /ɑːbɪtreɪt/, **arbitrates, arbitrating, arbitrated.** VB When someone **arbitrates** between two people who are in dispute, they consider all the facts and decide who is right. ♦ **arbitration** /ɑːbɪtreɪʃə0n/ UNCOUNT N *...arbitration between employers and unions.*

arc /ɑːk/, **arcs. 1** COUNT N An **arc** is a smoothly curving shape or line of movement. **2** COUNT N In mathematics, an **arc** is a section of the circumference of a circle.

arcade /ɑːkeɪd/, **arcades.** COUNT N An **arcade** is a covered passageway where there are shops.

arch /ɑːtʃ/, **arches, arching, arched. 1** COUNT N An **arch** is a structure that has a curved roof or top supported on either side by a pillar or wall. *...a house beneath the railway arches.* **2** ERG VB When something **arches,** it forms a curved shape or line. *Trees arched over the sidewalks... He arched his back.* **3** ATTRIB ADJ An **arch** look is mysterious and mischievous; a literary use. **4** See also **arched.**

archaeology /ɑːki1ɒlədʒi1/; also spelled **archeology.** UNCOUNT N **Archaeology** is the study of the past by examining the remains of things such as buildings and tools. ♦ **archaeological** /ɑːki1əlɒdʒɪkəl/ ADJ *...the most dramatic archaeological discovery of this century.* ♦ **archaeologist** /ɑːki1ɒlədʒɪst/ COUNT N *Archaeologists date the fragment between 4650 and 4500.*

archaic /ɑːkeɪɪk/. ADJ Things that are **archaic** are very old or very old-fashioned.

archbishop /ɑːtʃbɪʃəp/, **archbishops.** COUNT N An **archbishop** is a bishop of the highest rank, who is in charge of all the bishops and priests in a region.

arched /ɑːtʃt/. ADJ An **arched** roof, window, or doorway has a curved top.

archeology. /ɑːki1ɒlədʒi1/. See **archaeology.**

archer /ɑːtʃə/, **archers.** COUNT N An **archer** is someone who shoots with a bow and arrow.

archery /ɑːtʃə0ri1/. UNCOUNT N **Archery** is a sport in which people shoot at a target with a bow and arrow.

archetype /ɑːki1taɪp/, **archetypes.** COUNT N The **archetype** of a kind of person or thing is a perfect example of it. *He is said to be the archetype of the modern journalist.* ♦ **archetypal** ATTRIB ADJ *...the archetypal romantic heroes: Beethoven and Byron.*

archipelago /ɑːkɪpeləgəʊ/, **archipelagos.** COUNT N An **archipelago** is a group of small islands.

architect /ɑːkɪtekt/, **architects. 1** COUNT N An **architect** is a person who designs buildings. **2** COUNT N The **architect** of an idea or event is the person who invented it or made it happen. *He was the real architect of the country's independence.*

architecture /ɑːkɪtektʃə/. **1** UNCOUNT N **Architecture** is the art of designing and constructing buildings. ♦ **architectural** /ɑːki1tektʃərə0l/ ATTRIB ADJ *...architectural drawings.* **2** UNCOUNT N WITH SUPP The **architecture** of a building is the style in which it is constructed.

archive /ɑːkaɪv/, **archives.** COUNT N OR PLURAL N **Archives** are collections of documents and records that contain information about the history of an organization or group of people.

ardent /ɑːdə0nt/. ADJ Someone who is **ardent** about something is very enthusiastic or passionate about it. *...an ardent socialist.* ♦ **ardently** ADV *No woman desired more ardently to educate her sons.*

ardour /ɑːdə/; spelled **ardor** in American English. UNCOUNT N **Ardour** is an intense and passionate feeling of love or enthusiasm.

arduous /ɑːdjuːəs/. ADJ Something that is **arduous** is tiring and involves a lot of effort. *...a long and arduous journey.*

are /ɑː/. **Are** is the plural and the second person singular of the present tense of **be.**

area /ɛəriə/, **areas.** 1 COUNT N An **area** is a particular part of a city, a country, or the world. *...a dry area that gets only a few months of rain a year... ...the Brighton area.* 2 COUNT N WITH SUPP A particular **area** of a room or other place is a part that is used for a particular activity. *...an outdoor play area.* 3 COUNT N The **area** of a shape or piece of land is the amount that it covers, expressed in a measurement such as square metres or hectares. 4 COUNT N WITH SUPP An **area** of knowledge or activity is a particular subject or kind of activity. *His special interest lies in the area of literature.*

arena /əriːnə/, **arenas.** COUNT N An **arena** is a place where sports and other public events take place. It has seats around it where people sit and watch.

aren't /ɑːnt/. 1 **Aren't** is the usual spoken form of 'are not'. *We aren't ready... They are coming, aren't they?* 2 **Aren't** is used instead of 'am not' in negative questions. *I'm right, aren't I?*

arguable /ɑːgjuəbə0l/. 1 ADJ An idea, point, or comment that is **arguable** is not obviously true or correct and should be questioned. *Whether he was right or not is arguable.* 2 ADJ If you say that it is **arguable** that something is true, you mean that there are good reasons for thinking that it is true. *It is arguable that western civilisation was saved by his actions.* ♦ **arguably** SENTENCE ADV *Deforestation is arguably the most serious environmental issue of our time.*

argue /ɑːgjuː/, **argues, arguing, argued.** 1 RECIP VB If you **argue** with someone, you say things which show that you disagree with them, sometimes speaking angrily. *Don't argue with me, George, just do as you're told... They were arguing about who should sit in front.* 2 REPORT VB If you **argue** that something is the case, you say that you think it is the case and give reasons why. *There are those who argue that the existence of nuclear weapons has helped to maintain peace.* 3 VB WITH ADJUNCT If you **argue** for or **argue** against something, you give reasons why it should or should not happen. *Some politicians argued against giving women the vote.*

argument /ɑːgjə4mə2nt/, **arguments.** 1 COUNT N OR UNCOUNT N An **argument** is a disagreement between two or more people, sometimes resulting in them shouting at each other. *He and David had been drawn into a ferocious argument... Wrangling, argument, and law suits followed.* 2 COUNT N An **argument** is also a set of statements that you use to try to convince people that your opinion is correct. *There are strong arguments against these measures.*

argumentative /ɑːgjə4mentə1tɪv/. ADJ Someone who is **argumentative** is always ready to disagree.

arid /ærɪd/. ADJ Land that is **arid** is so dry that very few plants can grow on it.

arise /əraɪz/, **arises, arising, arose** /ərəʊz/, **arisen** /ərɪzə0n/. VB When something such as an opportunity, problem, or new state of affairs **arises,** it begins to exist. *A serious problem has arisen.*

aristocracy /ærɪstɒkrəsi1/, **aristocracies.** COLL N The **aristocracy** is a class of people in some countries who have a high social rank and special titles.

aristocrat /ærɪstə6kræt/, **aristocrats.** COUNT N An **aristocrat** is someone whose family has a high social rank, especially someone with a title.

aristocratic /ærɪstə6krætɪk/. ADJ **Aristocratic** means belonging to the aristocracy, or typical of them. *...young aristocratic girls.*

arithmetic /ə3rɪθmə2tɪk/. UNCOUNT N **Arithmetic** is the part of mathematics that deals with the addition, subtraction, multiplication, and division of numbers.

arm /ɑːm/, **arms.** 1 COUNT N Your **arms** are the two long parts of your body that are attached to your shoulders and that have your hands at the end. 2 COUNT N The **arms** of a chair are the parts on which you rest your arms. 3 COUNT N WITH SUPP An **arm** of an organization is a section of it. *...the political arm of a trade union movement.* 4 PLURAL N **Arms** are weapons that are used in a war.

PHRASES • If you are walking **arm in arm** with someone, your arm is linked through their arm. • If you welcome an event or change **with open arms,** you are very pleased about it. • If you hold something **at arm's length,** you hold it as far as possible from your body. • If you **keep** someone **at arm's length,** you avoid becoming too friendly or involved with them. • If someone is **up in arms** about something, they are protesting strongly about it.

armaments /ɑːməmə2nts/. PLURAL N **Armaments** are weapons and military equipment belonging to an army or country.

armchair /ɑːmtʃɛə/, **armchairs.** COUNT N An **armchair** is a comfortable chair with a support on each side for your arms.

armed /ɑːmd/. 1 ADJ Someone who is **armed** is carrying a weapon. *He was seized by armed men.* 2 ATTRIB ADJ An **armed** attack or conflict involves people fighting with guns. 3 PRED ADJ WITH 'with' If you are **armed** with something useful such as information or a skill, you have it. *Armed with secretarial skills, she will easily find a job.*

armed forces. PLURAL N The **armed forces** of a country are its army, navy, and air force.

armful /ɑːmfʊl/, **armfuls.** COUNT N An **armful** of something is the amount that you can carry in one or both of your arms.

armistice /ɑːmɪ1stɪs/, **armistices.** COUNT N OR UNCOUNT N An **armistice** is an agreement between countries who are at war to stop fighting and to discuss ways of making a peaceful settlement.

armour /ɑːmə/; spelled **armor** in American English. 1 UNCOUNT N **Armour** is the metal clothing that soldiers used to wear for protection. 2 SING N WITH SUPP **Armour** is also a hard covering that protects some animals from attack. *...an armour of horny scales.*

armoured /ɑːməd/; spelled **armored** in American English. ADJ An **armoured** vehicle has a metal covering that protects it from gunfire and other missiles.

armpit /ɑːmpɪt/, **armpits.** COUNT N Your **armpit** is the area under your arm where your arm joins your shoulder.

army /ɑːmi1/, **armies.** 1 COLL N An **army** is a large organized group of people who are armed and trained to fight. 2 COUNT N An **army** of people, animals, or things is a large number of them together. *...an army of ants.*

aroma /ərəʊmə/, **aromas.** COUNT N WITH SUPP An **aroma** is a strong, pleasant smell.

aromatic /ærə6mætɪk/. ADJ A plant or food that is **aromatic** has a strong, pleasant smell.

arose /ərəʊz/. **Arose** is the past tense of **arise.**

around /əraʊnd/. 1 ADV OR PREP **Around** can be an adverb or preposition, and is often used instead of **round** as the second part of a phrasal verb. Examples of these uses of **around** are explained at **round.** 2 PHRASE If someone or something **is around,** they are present or available. *It's a gadget which has been around for years.* 3 ADV **Around** also means approximately. *He owns around 200 acres.*

arousal /əraʊzə0l/. UNCOUNT N WITH SUPP If something causes the **arousal** of a feeling, it causes people to have this feeling. *...the arousal of interest.*

arouse /əraʊz/, **arouses, arousing, aroused.** 1 VB WITH OBJ If something **arouses** a feeling in you, it causes you to have this feeling. *It may arouse his interest in the subject.* 2 VB WITH OBJ If something **arouses** people, it makes them angry. 3 VB WITH OBJ If something **arouses** you from sleep, it wakes you up; a literary use.

arrange /ə3reɪndʒ/, **arranges, arranging, arranged.** 1 VB WITH OBJ If you **arrange** an event or meeting, you make plans for it to happen. *They arrange holidays in Eastern Europe.* 2 VB WITH 'with' OR TO-INF If you **arrange** with someone to do something, you make plans together to do it. *I've arranged with somebody else to go there... We had arranged to meet in the street outside.* 3 VB WITH OBJ If you **arrange** something for someone, you make it possible for them to have it or to do it. *We can arrange loans.* 4 VB WITH OBJ AND ADJUNCT If you **arrange** a number of objects, you put them in a particular position or order. *...four chairs arranged around the table.*

arranged /ə3reɪnʒd/. ADJ In an **arranged** marriage, the parents choose the person who their son or daughter will marry.

arrangement /ə3reɪnʒmə2nt/, **arrangements.** 1 PLURAL N **Arrangements** are plans and preparations which you make so that something will happen or be possible. *I've made all the arrangements for the conference.* 2 COUNT N WITH SUPP An **arrangement** of things, for example flowers or furniture, is a group of them displayed in a particular way. *There was an arrangement of books in the window.*

array /əreɪ/. COUNT N An **array** of different things is a large number of them. *Sutherland studied the array of sandwiches on the tray.*

arrears /ərɪəz/. PLURAL N **Arrears** are amounts of money that someone owes.

PHRASES • If someone is **in arrears,** they have not paid the regular amounts of money that they should have paid. • If you are paid **in arrears,** your wages are paid to you at the end of the period of time in which you earned them.

arrest /ərest/, **arrests, arresting, arrested.** 1 VB WITH OBJ When the police **arrest** someone, they catch them and take them somewhere in order to decide whether they should be charged with an offence. 2 UNCOUNT N OR COUNT N When the police make an **arrest,** they arrest someone. *A number of arrests were made.* • If someone is **under arrest,** they have been caught by the police and are not allowed to go free. 3 VB WITH OBJ To **arrest** something means to stop it happening; a formal use. *He tried to arrest the course of destruction.*

arrival /əraɪvə0l/, **arrivals.** 1 UNCOUNT N Your **arrival** at a place is the act of arriving there. *I apologise for my late arrival.* 2 SING N If you talk about the **arrival** of something new, you are referring to the fact that it has begun to exist or happen. *Industry has been revolutionized by the arrival of the computer.* 3 SING N The **arrival** of a baby is its birth. 4 COUNT N An **arrival** is someone who has just arrived at a place. *One of the new arrivals at the college was an old friend.*

arrive /əraɪv/, **arrives, arriving, arrived.** 1 VB When you **arrive** at a place, you reach it at the end of a journey, or you come to it for the first time in order to stay or live there. *He arrived back at his hotel... Since arriving in England in 1979, she has established herself as a major writer.* 2 VB When a letter or piece of news **arrives,** it reaches you. 3 VB WITH 'at' When you **arrive** at an idea, decision, or conclusion, you reach it or decide on it. 4 VB When a baby **arrives,** it is born. 5 VB When a time or event that you have been waiting for **arrives,** it happens.

arrogant /ærəgənt/. ADJ Someone who is **arrogant** behaves in a proud, unpleasant way because they believe they are more important than other people. *They are arrogant and aggressive people.* ♦ **arrogantly** ADV *They regarded me arrogantly.* ♦ **arrogance** /ærəgəns/ UNCOUNT N *...a reputation for arrogance.*

arrow /ærəʊ/, **arrows.** 1 COUNT N An **arrow** is a long, thin weapon with a sharp point at one end which is shot from a bow. 2 COUNT N An **arrow** is also a written sign which points in a particular direction to indicate where something is.

arsenic /ɑːsə0nɪk/. UNCOUNT N **Arsenic** is a very strong poison which can kill people.

arson /ɑːsə0n/. UNCOUNT N **Arson** is the crime of deliberately setting fire to a building.

art /ɑːt/, **arts.** 1 UNCOUNT N **Art** is the making of paintings, drawings, and sculpture which are beautiful or which express an artist's ideas. *...the development of post-war American art.* 2 UNCOUNT N **Art** is also used to refer to the paintings, drawings, and sculpture produced by artists. *...a great art collection.* 3 PLURAL N The **arts** refers to the creation or performance of drama, music, poetry, or painting, especially in a particular country or region. *How much will they spend on sport, how much on the arts?* 4 PLURAL N **Arts** is used to refer to subjects such as history or languages in contrast to scientific subjects. *...an arts degree.* 5 SING N You describe an activity as an **art** when it requires a lot of skill. *...the art of camouflage.*

artefact /ɑːtɪ1fækt/, **artefacts;** also spelled **artifact.** COUNT N An **artefact** is an ornament, tool, or other object made by a human being.

artery /ɑːtəri1/, **arteries.** COUNT N Your **arteries** are the tubes that carry blood from your heart to the rest of your body.

artful /ɑːtfʊl/. ADJ Someone who is **artful** is clever and skilful, often in a cunning way. *They became the most artful of all the hunters.* ♦ **artfully** ADV *The lighting was artfully arranged to flatter people's faces.*

arthritic /ɑːθrɪtɪk/. ADJ A person who is **arthritic** has arthritis.

arthritis /ɑːθraɪtɪ1s/. UNCOUNT N **Arthritis** is a condition in which the joints in someone's body are swollen and painful.

artichoke /ɑːtɪtʃəʊk/, **artichokes.** 1 COUNT N An **artichoke** or a **globe artichoke** is a round, green vegetable with fleshy leaves, of which you eat the bottom part. 2 COUNT N An **artichoke** or a **Jerusalem artichoke** is a small, yellowish-white vegetable that grows underground and looks like a potato.

article /ɑːtɪkə0l/, **articles.** 1 COUNT N An **article** is a piece of writing in a newspaper or magazine. 2 COUNT N You can use **article** to refer generally to an object. *He was ordered to pay for the articles he had stolen.* 3 COUNT N An **article** of a formal document is a section dealing with a particular point. *The invasion contravened article 51 of the UN charter.* 4 See also **definite article** and **indefinite article.**

articulate, articulates, articulating, articulated; pronounced /ɑːtɪkjə4lə1t/ when it is an adjective and /ɑːtɪkjə4leɪt/ when it is a verb. 1 ADJ If you are **articulate,** you are able to express yourself well. *He was the most articulate among them.* 2 VB WITH OBJ When you **articulate** your ideas or feelings, you say in words what you think or feel; a formal use.

articulated /ɑːtɪkjə4leɪtɪ1d/. ATTRIB ADJ An **articulated** vehicle is made in two sections which are joined so that the vehicle can turn corners more easily.

articulation /ɑːtɪkjə4leɪʃə0n/. 1 UNCOUNT N The **articulation** of an idea or feeling is its expression in words; a formal use. *...the articulation of an alternative housing policy.* 2 UNCOUNT N The **articulation** of a sound or word is the way it is spoken.

artifact. See artefact.

artificial /ɑ:tɪfɪʃəl/. 1 ADJ An **artificial** state or situation is not natural and exists because people have created it. *These results appear only in very artificial conditions.* ♦ **artificially** ADV *The government keeps prices artificially high.* ♦ **artificiality** /ɑ:tɪfɪʃi^{1}ælɪti^{1}/ UNCOUNT N *There was a strong element of artificiality in this movement.* 2 ADJ **Artificial** objects or materials do not occur naturally and are created by people. *...artificial flowers.* 3 ATTRIB ADJ An **artificial** arm or leg is made of metal or plastic and is fitted to someone's body when their own arm or leg has been removed. 4 ADJ If someone's behaviour is **artificial,** they are pretending to have attitudes and feelings which they do not really have. *They jumped at the suggestion with artificial enthusiasm.*

artillery /ɑ:tɪləri^{1}/. UNCOUNT N **Artillery** consists of large, powerful guns which are transported on wheels and used by an army.

artist /ɑ:tɪst/, **artists.** 1 COUNT N An **artist** is someone who draws, paints, or produces other works of art. 2 COUNT N You can refer to a musician, actor, dancer, or other performer as an **artist.** *She has acted with great artists like Edith Evans.*

artiste /ɑ:ti:st/, **artistes.** COUNT N An **artiste** is a professional entertainer, for example a singer or dancer.

artistic /ɑ:tɪstɪk/. 1 ADJ You say that someone is **artistic** when they can produce good paintings or other works of art, although they may not be a professional artist. *Artistic people are in a tiny minority in this country.* ♦ **artistically** ADV *She was artistically gifted.* 2 ADJ **Artistic** also means relating to art or artists. *...artistic freedom.* 3 ADJ A design or arrangement that is **artistic** is attractive.

artistry /ɑ:tɪstri^{1}/. UNCOUNT N **Artistry** is the great skill with which something is done. *He acted the final scenes with superb artistry.*

as /ə^{3}z/. 1 CONJ If something happens **as** something else happens, it happens at the same time. *She wept bitterly as she told her story.* 2 PREP You use the structure **as...as** when you are comparing things. *I'm as good a cook as she is.* 3 PREP You use **as** to introduce a prepositional phrase referring to something's appearance or function. *You regard the whole thing as a joke... Hydrogen gas can be used as a fuel... Over the summer she worked as a waitress.* 4 CONJ You use **as** when you are saying how something is done. *I like the freedom to organize my day as I want to.* 5 CONJ You can also use **as** to mean 'because'. *She bought herself an iron, as she felt she couldn't keep borrowing Anne's.*

PHRASES ● You use **as if** and **as though** when you are comparing one situation to another. *The furniture looked as though it had come out of somebody's attic... He looked at me as if I were mad.* ● You use **as for** to introduce a slightly different subject. *That's the answer. As for the cause, how do I know?* ● You use **as to** to indicate what something refers to; a British use. *John had been given no directions as to what to write.* ● You say **as it were** in order to make what you are saying sound less definite. *That was as it were part of the job.*

asbestos /æsbestɒs/. UNCOUNT N **Asbestos** is a grey material which does not burn.

ascend /əsend/, **ascends, ascending, ascended.** 1 VB If something **ascends,** it goes upwards; a literary use. 2 VB WITH OBJ If you **ascend** a hill or a staircase, you go up it; a literary use.

ascendant /əsendənt/. PHRASE If someone or something is **in the ascendant,** they are increasing in power, influence, or popularity. *His party was now in the ascendant.*

ascending /əsendɪŋ/. ATTRIB ADJ If a group of things is arranged in **ascending** order, each thing is higher in position or greater in amount or importance than the thing before it.

ascent /əsent/, **ascents.** COUNT N An **ascent** is a steep upward slope, or a journey up a steep slope. *The final ascent took an hour.*

ascertain /æsəteɪn/, **ascertains, ascertaining, ascertained.** REPORT VB If you **ascertain** that something is the case, you find out that it is the case; a formal use. *I ascertained that Lo was still sound asleep.*

ascetic /əsetɪk/, **ascetics.** ADJ People who are **ascetic** have a way of life that is simple and strict, usually because of their religious beliefs. Also COUNT N *...a Christian ascetic.*

ascribe /ə^{3}skraɪb/, **ascribes, ascribing, ascribed.** 1 VB WITH OBJ AND PREP 'to' If you **ascribe** an event or state of affairs to a particular factor, you consider that it is caused by that factor. *...headaches which may be ascribed to stress.* 2 VB WITH OBJ AND PREP 'to' If you **ascribe** a quality to someone, you consider that they have it. *Husbands are often mistaken in the virtues they ascribe to their wives.*

ash /æʃ/, **ashes.** 1 UNCOUNT N OR PLURAL N **Ash** is the grey powder-like substance that is left after something is burnt. *...cigarette ash... Ashes blew into Ralph's face from the dead fire.* 2 COUNT N An **ash** is a kind of tree.

ashamed /əʃeɪmd/. 1 PRED ADJ If you are **ashamed** of something you have done, you feel embarrassed or guilty because of it. *She was ashamed of her tears.* 2 PRED ADJ WITH TO-INF If you are **ashamed** to do something, you do not want to do it because you feel embarrassed about it. *I bet that's what happened, and you're ashamed to admit it.* 3 PRED ADJ WITH 'of' If you are **ashamed** of someone you are connected with, you feel embarrassed because of their behaviour. *He was ashamed of her for writing such lies.*

ashore /əʃɔ:/. ADV Something that comes **ashore** comes from the sea onto the shore. *He managed to swim ashore.*

ashtray /æʃtreɪ/, **ashtrays.** COUNT N An **ashtray** is a small dish in which people put the ash from their cigarettes and cigars.

Asian /eɪʃən, eɪʒən/, **Asians.** 1 ADJ **Asian** means belonging or relating to Asia. 2 COUNT N An **Asian** is a person who comes from India, Pakistan, or some other part of Asia.

aside /əsaɪd/. 1 ADV If you move something **aside,** you move it to one side of you. *He threw the manuscript aside.* 2 ADV If you take someone **aside,** you take them away from a group of people in order to talk to them in private. 3 ADV If you move **aside,** you get out of someone's way.

ask /ɑ:sk/, **asks, asking, asked.** 1 VB WITH OBJ OR REPORT VB If you **ask** someone something, you say something in the form of a question because you want some information. *I asked him what he wanted... 'Why?' he asked... He started asking questions.* 2 VB WITH OBJ If you **ask** someone to do something, you say to them that you want them to do it. *He asked her to marry him.* 3 VB WITH OR WITHOUT OBJ If you **ask** someone's permission or forgiveness, you try to obtain it. *I asked permission to leave.* 4 VB WITH OBJ AND ADJUNCT If you **ask** someone somewhere, you invite them there. *She asked me in.*

PHRASES ● If something is yours **for the asking,** you can have it simply by saying that you would like it. ● You can say **'if you ask me'** to emphasize that you are stating your personal opinion. *The whole thing's stupid if you ask me.*

ask after. PHR VB If you **ask after** someone, you ask how they are.

ask for. PHR VB 1 If you **ask for** someone, you say that you would like to speak to them. *He rang the office and asked for Cynthia.* 2 If you **ask for** something, you say that you would like it.

askew /əskju:/. PRED ADJ Something that is **askew** is not straight or level.

asleep /əsli:p/. PRED ADJ Someone who is **asleep** is sleeping.

PHRASES ● When you **fall asleep,** you start sleeping. ● Someone who is **fast asleep** or **sound asleep** is sleeping deeply.

asparagus /əspærəgəs/. UNCOUNT N **Asparagus** is a vegetable with green shoots that you cook and eat.

aspect /æspekt/, **aspects.** 1 COUNT N WITH SUPP An **aspect** of something is one of the parts of its character or nature. *The most terrifying aspect of nuclear bombing is radiation.* 2 COUNT N WITH SUPP A room or a window with a particular **aspect** faces in that direction; a formal use. *...an office with a south-west aspect.*

asphalt /æsfælt, -fɔ:lt/. UNCOUNT N **Asphalt** is a black substance used to make surfaces on things such as roads and playgrounds.

asphyxiate /æsfɪksieɪt/, **asphyxiates, asphyxiating, asphyxiated.** VB WITH OBJ If someone **is asphyxiated** by smoke or a poisonous gas, they breathe it in and die.

aspiration /æspə^{1}reɪʃə^{0}n/, **aspirations.** COUNT N OR UNCOUNT N Someone's **aspirations** are their ambitions to achieve something.

aspire /əspaɪə/, **aspires, aspiring, aspired.** VB WITH PREP 'to' OR TO-INF If you **aspire** to something such as an important job, you have a strong desire to have it. *Edward has always aspired to leadership.* ♦ **aspiring** ATTRIB ADJ *...an aspiring concert pianist.*

aspirin /æspɪ^{0}rɪn/, **aspirins.** UNCOUNT N OR COUNT N **Aspirin** is a mild drug which reduces pain and fever. It is sold in the form of tablets called **aspirins.**

ass /æs/, **asses.** COUNT N An **ass** is an animal similar to a horse but smaller and with long ears.

assail /əseɪl/, **assails, assailing, assailed.** VB WITH OBJ If you **are assailed** by unpleasant thoughts or problems, you are greatly troubled by a lot of them; a literary use. *They are assailed by doubts.*

assailant /əseɪlənt/, **assailants.** COUNT N Someone's **assailant** is a person who physically attacks them; a formal use.

assassin /əsæsɪn/, **assassins.** COUNT N An **assassin** is a person who assassinates someone.

assassinate /əsæsɪneɪt/, **assassinates, assassinating, assassinated.** VB WITH OBJ When someone important **is assassinated,** they are murdered as a political act. *The president was assassinated as he left the building.* ♦ **assassination** /əsæsɪneɪʃə^{0}n/ UNCOUNT N OR COUNT N *...the assassination of Martin Luther King.*

assault /əsɔ:lt/, **assaults, assaulting, assaulted.** 1 COUNT N An **assault** by an army is a strong attack made against an enemy. 2 COUNT N OR UNCOUNT N An **assault** on a person is a physical attack. *There have been several assaults recently... They arrested him for assault.* 3 VB WITH OBJ To **assault** someone means to attack them physically. *She was found guilty of assaulting a police officer.* 4 COUNT N An **assault** on someone's beliefs is a strong criticism of them. *...an all-out assault on racism.*

assemble /ə^{3}sembə^{0}l/, **assembles, assembling, assembled.** 1 VB When people **assemble,** they gather together in a group, usually for a particular purpose. *The witnesses would assemble in the Detective Sergeant's room.* ♦ **assembled** ADJ *She announced to the assembled relatives that she intended to move abroad.* 2 VB WITH OBJ If you **assemble** something, you fit its parts together. *Tractors are being assembled.* 3 VB WITH OBJ If you **assemble** a number of objects or facts, you bring them together. *She began to assemble her belongings... His job was to assemble the facts.*

assembly /ə^{3}sembli^{1}/, **assemblies.** 1 COUNT N An **assembly** is a large number of people gathered together, especially a group of people who meet regularly to make laws. *The assembly was shocked into silence.* 2 UNCOUNT N **Assembly** is the gathering together of people for a particular purpose. *They are demanding rights of assembly.* 3 UNCOUNT N The **assembly** of a machine or device is the process of fitting its parts together.

assembly line, assembly lines. COUNT N An **assembly line** is an arrangement of workers and machines in a factory where the product passes from one worker to another until it is finished.

assent /ə^{3}sent/, **assents, assenting, assented.** 1 UNCOUNT N If someone gives their **assent** to something that has been suggested, they agree to it. 2 VB WITH PREP 'to' To **assent** to something means to agree to it; a formal use. *They all assented to the proposition.*

assert /ə^{3}sɜ:t/, **asserts, asserting, asserted.** 1 REPORT VB If you **assert** a fact or belief, you state it firmly. *The protesters asserted their right to be heard.* ♦ **assertion** /ə^{3}sɜ:ʃə^{0}n/ COUNT N OR UNCOUNT N *I challenge that assertion.* 2 VB WITH OBJ If you **assert** your authority, you make it clear that you have it. *He wished to assert his authority in his own house.* ♦ **assertion** UNCOUNT N *...an assertion of power.* 3 REFL VB If you **assert** yourself, you speak and act in a forceful way so that people take notice of you.

assertive /ə^{3}sɜ:tɪv/. ADJ Someone who is **assertive** speaks and acts in a forceful way so that people take notice of them.

assess /ə^{3}ses/, **assesses, assessing, assessed.** 1 VB WITH OBJ When you **assess** a person, feeling, or situation, you consider them and make a judgement about them. *They meet monthly to assess the current political situation.* ♦ **assessment** /ə^{3}sesmə^{2}nt/ COUNT N WITH SUPP *...the assessment of his academic progress.* 2 VB WITH OBJ When you **assess** the amount of money that something is worth or that should be paid, you calculate or estimate it. *She looked the house over and assessed its rough market value.* ♦ **assessment** COUNT N *...assessments made by the tax man.*

asset /æset/, **assets.** 1 COUNT N If something that you have is an **asset,** it is useful to you. *He was a great asset to the committee.* 2 PLURAL N The **assets** of a company or a person are all the things that they own.

assiduous /əsɪdju:əs/. ADJ Someone who is **assiduous** works hard. *...an assiduous student.* ♦ **assiduously** ADV *He kept on painting assiduously.*

assign /əsaɪn/, **assigns, assigning, assigned.** 1 VB WITH OBJ If you **assign** a task or function to someone, you give it to them. *She kept calling him up to assign some new task to him... Mother and father play out the roles assigned to them.* 2 VB WITH OBJ If you **are assigned** to a place or group, you are sent to work in the place or with the group. *She was assigned to the men's wards.*

assignation /æsɪgneɪʃə^{0}n/, **assignations.** COUNT N An **assignation** is a secret meeting with someone, especially a lover; a literary use.

assignment /əsaɪnmə^{2}nt/, **assignments.** 1 COUNT N An **assignment** is a piece of work that you are given to do, as part of your job or studies. 2 UNCOUNT N WITH POSS You can refer to someone being given a task or job as their **assignment** to the task or job.

assimilate /əsɪmɪleɪt/, **assimilates, assimilating, assimilated.** 1 VB WITH OBJ If you **assimilate** ideas, customs, or methods, you learn them and make use of them. *He was quick to assimilate new ideas.* ♦ **assimilation** /ə3sɪmɪleɪʃə0n/ UNCOUNT N *...the rapid assimilation of new techniques in industry.* 2 ERG VB When immigrants **are assimilated** into a community, they become an accepted part of it. ♦ **assimilation** UNCOUNT N *...the assimilation of the new arrivals.*

assist /əsɪst/, **assists, assisting, assisted.** 1 VB WITH OR WITHOUT OBJ If you **assist** someone, you help them. *We may be able to assist with the tuition fees... He was asked to assist in keeping the hotel under surveillance.* 2 VB WITH OR WITHOUT OBJ If something **assists** you with a task, it makes it easier for you.

assistance /əsɪstəns/. UNCOUNT N If you give someone **assistance,** you help them. *He thanked me for my assistance.* ● Someone or something that is **of assistance** to you is helpful or useful to you.

assistant /əsɪstənt/, **assistants.** 1 COUNT N WITH POSS Someone's **assistant** is a person who helps them in their work. 2 ATTRIB ADJ **Assistant** is used in front of titles or jobs to indicate a slightly lower rank. For example, an **assistant** director is one rank lower than a director. 3 COUNT N An **assistant** or a **shop assistant** is a person who sells things in a shop.

associate, associates, associating, associated; pronounced /ə3səʊsi1eɪt/ when it is a verb and /əsəʊsi1ət/ when it is a noun. 1 VB WITH OBJ AND 'with' If you **associate** one thing with another, the two things are connected in your mind. *Dignity is the quality which I associate mostly with her... Zuse worked on problems associated with aircraft design.* 2 VB WITH OBJ AND 'with' If you **are associated** with an organization, cause, or point of view, or if you **associate** yourself with it, you support it publicly. 3 VB WITH 'with' If you **associate** with a group of people, you spend a lot of time with them. 4 COUNT N Your **associates** are your business colleagues.

association /ə3səʊsi1eɪʃə0n, -ʃi1-/, **associations.** 1 COUNT N An **association** is an official group of people with a common occupation, aim, or interest. *...the British Medical Association.* 2 UNCOUNT N WITH SUPP Your **association** with a person, group, or organization is the connection that you have with them. ● If someone does something **in association with** someone else, they do it together. 3 COUNT N WITH SUPP If something has a particular **association** for you, it is connected in your mind with a particular memory or feeling.

assorted /ə3sɔːtɪ2d/. ATTRIB ADJ A group of **assorted** things of a particular kind have different sizes, colours, or qualities. *...a bunch of assorted wild flowers.*

assortment /əsɔːtmə2nt/, **assortments.** COUNT N An **assortment** is a group of similar things that have different sizes, colours, or qualities. *...an assortment of plastic bags.*

assume /ə3sjuːm/, **assumes, assuming, assumed.** 1 REPORT VB OR VB WITH OBJ AND TO-INF If you **assume** that something is true, you suppose that it is true, sometimes wrongly. *I assume you don't drive... I was mistakenly assumed to be a Welshman.* 2 VB WITH OBJ If someone **assumes** power or responsibility, they begin to have power or responsibility. 3 VB WITH OBJ If you **assume** a particular expression, quality, or way of behaving, you start to look or behave in this way.

assuming /ə3sjuːmɪŋ/. CONJ You use **assuming** or **assuming that** when you are supposing that something is true, so that you can think about what the consequences would be. *Keep your goods (assuming that you have any) separate from his.*

assumption /ə3sʌmp0ʃə0n/, **assumptions.** 1 COUNT N If you make an **assumption,** you suppose that something is true, sometimes wrongly. *His suggestions are based on an assumption that the system is out of date.* 2 UNCOUNT N WITH 'of' Someone's **assumption** of power or responsibility is their taking of it.

assurance /ə3ʃʊərəns/, **assurances.** 1 COUNT N OR UNCOUNT N If you give someone an **assurance** about something, you say that it is definitely true or will definitely happen, in order to make them less worried. *One must be content with assurances that progress is being made... ...the assurance of full employment.* 2 UNCOUNT N If you do something with **assurance,** you do it with confidence and certainty. *'She'll like that,' said Lally with assurance.* 3 UNCOUNT N **Assurance** is also insurance that provides for events which are certain to happen, such as death.

assure /ə3ʃʊə/, **assures, assuring, assured.** 1 VB WITH OBJ If you **assure** someone that something is true or will happen, you tell them that it is definitely true or will definitely happen, to make them less worried. *Kurt assured me that he was an excellent climber.* 2 VB WITH OBJ AND OBJ OR 'of' If you **are assured** of something, you will definitely get it. *This film had assured him a place in movie history.*

assured /ə3ʃʊəd/. ADJ Someone who is **assured** is very confident and feels at ease.

assuredly /ə3ʃʊərə1dli1/. ADV OR SENTENCE ADV If something is **assuredly** true, it is definitely true.

asterisk /æstə0rɪsk/, **asterisks.** COUNT N An **asterisk** is the sign *.

asthma /æsmə/. UNCOUNT N **Asthma** is an illness which affects the chest and makes breathing difficult.

asthmatic /æsmætɪk/. ADJ Someone who is **asthmatic** suffers from asthma.

astonish /ə3stɒnɪʃ/, **astonishes, astonishing, astonished.** VB WITH OBJ If something **astonishes** you, it surprises you very much. *He used to astonish me with the clarity of his recollections.*

astonished /ə3stɒnɪʃt/. ADJ If you are **astonished,** you are very surprised about something. *They were astonished at the extraordinary beauty of the pictures.*

astonishing /ə3stɒnɪʃɪŋ/. ADJ Something that is **astonishing** is very surprising. *The shape of their bodies changes with astonishing speed.* ♦ **astonishingly** SUBMOD OR SENTENCE ADV *Birth rates there are astonishingly high.*

astonishment /ə3stɒnɪʃmə2nt/. UNCOUNT N **Astonishment** is a feeling of great surprise. *John stared at him in astonishment.*

astound /ə3staʊnd/, **astounds, astounding, astounded.** VB WITH OBJ If something **astounds** you, you are amazed by it. *The sheer volume of work astounds us.* ♦ **astounding** ADJ *It seemed an astounding decision.*

astray /əstreɪ/.
PHRASES ● If you **lead** someone **astray,** you make them behave in a bad or foolish way. ● If something **goes astray,** it gets lost.

astride /əstraɪd/. PREP If you sit or stand **astride** something, you sit or stand with one leg on each side of it. *Karen sat astride a large white horse.*

astringent /əstrɪndʒə2nt/, **astringents.** 1 COUNT N An **astringent** is a substance that makes your skin less greasy or stops it bleeding. Also ADJ *...an astringent lotion.* 2 ADJ **Astringent** comments are forceful and critical.

astrologer /ə3strɒlədʒə/, **astrologers.** COUNT N An **astrologer** is a person who uses astrology to tell you things about your character and future.

astrology /ə3strɒlədʒi1/. UNCOUNT N **Astrology** is the study of the movements of the planets, sun, moon, and stars in the belief that they can influence people's lives.

astronaut /æstrə7nɔːt/, **astronauts.** COUNT N An **astronaut** is a person who travels in a spacecraft.

astronomer /ə3strɒnəmə/, **astronomers.** COUNT N An **astronomer** is a scientist who studies the stars, planets, and other natural objects in space.

astronomical /æstrə7nɒmɪkə0l/. 1 ADJ If you describe a value, price, or amount as **astronomical,** you mean that it is very large indeed. 2 ADJ **Astronomical** also means relating to astronomy.

astronomy /ə3strɒnəmi1/. UNCOUNT N **Astronomy** is the scientific study of the stars, planets, and other natural objects in space.

astute /ə3stjuːt/. ADJ Someone who is **astute** is clever and skilful at understanding behaviour and situations.

asylum /ə3saɪləm/, **asylums.** 1 COUNT N An **asylum** is a mental hospital. 2 UNCOUNT N **Asylum** is protection given to foreigners who have left their own country for political reasons.

asymmetrical /eɪsɪmetrɪkə0l/. ADJ Something that is **asymmetrical** has two sides or halves that are different.

at /ə3t/. 1 PREP You use **at** to say where something happens or is situated. *The play takes place at a beach club... There was a knock at his door.* 2 PREP If you look **at** something or someone, you look towards them. If you direct something **at** someone, you direct it towards them. *They were staring at a garage roof... Supporters threw petals at his car.* 3 PREP You use **at** to say when something happens. *She leaves her house every day at 11 a.m.* 4 PREP You use **at** to say how quickly or regularly something happens. *He hurtles through the air at 600 miles per hour... The high technology companies have grown at an astonishing rate.* 5 PREP If you buy or sell something **at** a particular price, you buy it or sell it for that price. *The book is published at $7.95.* 6 PREP If you are **at** lunch, dinner, or any other meal, you are eating it. 7 PREP If you are working **at** something, you are dealing with it. If you are aiming **at** something, you are trying to achieve it. *It means working harder at your thesis.* 8 PREP If something is done **at** someone's command or invitation, it is done as a result of it. 9 PREP You use **at** to say that someone or something is in a particular state or condition. *He remains at liberty... The two nations are at war.* 10 PREP You use **at** to say how something is done. *Guardsmen herded them back at gun point.* 11 PREP You use **at** after a verb to indicate that something is being done in a tentative way. *Rudolph sipped at his drink.* 12 PREP If you are good **at** something, you do it well. If you are bad **at** something, you do it badly. *They seemed to be very good at reading.* 13 PREP If you are delighted, pleased, or appalled **at** something, that is the effect it has on you.

ate /eɪt, et/. **Ate** is the past tense of **eat.**

atheism /eɪθi1ɪzə0m/. UNCOUNT N **Atheism** is the belief that there is no God. ♦ **atheist** /eɪθi1ɪst/ COUNT N *He is a convinced atheist.*

athlete /æθliːt/, **athletes.** COUNT N An **athlete** is a person who takes part in athletics competitions.

athletic /æθletɪk/, **athletics.** 1 UNCOUNT N **Athletics** consists of sports such as running, the high jump, and the javelin. 2 ATTRIB ADJ **Athletic** means relating to athletes and athletics. 3 ADJ An **athletic** person is fit, healthy, and active.

-ation, -ations. SUFFIX **-ation, -tion,** and **-ion** are added to verbs to form nouns referring to an action or the result of an action. Nouns of this kind are often not defined but are treated with the related verbs. *...upon completion of their studies... We will make such alterations as we consider necessary.*

atlas /ætləs/, **atlases.** COUNT N An **atlas** is a book of maps.

atmosphere /ætməsfɪə/, **atmospheres.** 1 COUNT N A planet's **atmosphere** is the layer of air or other gas around it. ♦ **atmospheric** /ætməsferɪk/ ATTRIB ADJ *...atmospheric pollution.* 2 SING N The **atmosphere** of a place is the air that you breathe there. *...the polluted atmosphere of towns and cities.* 3 SING N WITH SUPP You can also refer to the general impression that you get of a place as its **atmosphere.** *It's got such a friendly atmosphere.*

atom /ætə0m/, **atoms.** COUNT N An **atom** is the smallest amount of a substance that can take part in a chemical reaction.

atom bomb, atom bombs. COUNT N An **atom bomb** or an **atomic bomb** causes an explosion by the sudden release of energy that results from splitting atoms.

atomic /ə3tɒmɪk/. 1 ATTRIB ADJ **Atomic** means relating to the power produced by splitting atoms. 2 ATTRIB ADJ **Atomic** also means relating to the atoms that substances consist of.

atone /ətəʊn/, **atones, atoning, atoned.** VB WITH 'for' If you **atone** for something that you have done, you do something to show that you are sorry you did it; a formal use.

atrocious /ətrəʊʃəs/. ADJ Something that is **atrocious** is extremely bad. *...speaking French with an atrocious accent.* ♦ **atrociously** ADV *The farm animals are treated atrociously.*

atrocity /ətrɒsɪ1ti1/, **atrocities.** COUNT N An **atrocity** is a very cruel, shocking action.

attach /ətætʃ/, **attaches, attaching, attached.** 1 VB WITH OBJ If you **attach** something to an object, you join it or fasten it to the object. 2 VB WITH OBJ If someone **is attached** to an organization, they are working for it, usually for a short time. *Hospital officers would be temporarily attached to NHS hospitals.* 3 VB WITH OBJ AND PREP 'to' If you **attach** a quality to something or someone, you consider that they have that quality. *Don't attach too much importance to what he said.*

attaché /ətæʃeɪ/, **attachés.** COUNT N An **attaché** is a member of the staff in an embassy.

attached /ətætʃt/. PRED ADJ WITH PREP 'to' If you are **attached** to someone or something, you are very fond of them.

attachment /ətætʃmə2nt/, **attachments.** 1 COUNT N An **attachment** to someone or something is a fondness for them. *...a romantic attachment.* 2 COUNT N An **attachment** is a device that can be fixed onto a machine in order to enable it to do different jobs. *...a special attachment for cleaning upholstery.*

attack /ətæk/, **attacks, attacking, attacked.** 1 VB WITH OR WITHOUT OBJ If you **attack** someone, you try to hurt them using physical violence. *The court decided that he was insane when he attacked the women.* Also COUNT N *...a worrying increase in attacks on old people.* 2 VB WITH OBJ If you **attack** a person, belief, or idea, you criticize them strongly. *The senator attacked the press for misleading the public.* Also COUNT N OR UNCOUNT N *...attacks on various aspects of apartheid... Burt's work came under violent attack.* 3 VB WITH OBJ If you **attack** a job or a problem, you start to deal with it in an energetic way. 4 VB When players **attack** in a game such as football, they try to score a goal. 5 COUNT N An **attack** of an illness is a short period in which you suffer badly from it. *...an attack of smallpox.*

attacker /ətækə/, **attackers.** COUNT N Someone's **attacker** is the person who attacks them. *He described his attacker to the police.*

attain /ətéɪn/, attains, attaining, attained. VB WITH OBJ If you **attain** something, you achieve it, often after a lot of effort. ...the qualities which enabled him to attain his ambitions.

attainment /ətéɪnmənt/, attainments. 1 UNCOUNT N WITH SUPP The **attainment** of something is the achieving of it; a formal use. ...the attainment of independence. 2 COUNT N An **attainment** is a skill you have learned, or something you have achieved; a formal use.

attempt /ətémpt/, attempts, attempting, attempted. VB WITH OBJ OR TO-INF If you **attempt** something or **attempt** to do something, you try to do it. A long time had elapsed since I had attempted any serious study... Some of the crowd attempted to break through police cordons. Also COUNT N The young birds manage to fly several kilometres at their first attempt.

attempted /ətémptɪd/. ATTRIB ADJ An **attempted** crime is an unsuccessful effort to commit a crime. He was charged with attempted murder.

attend /əténd/, attends, attending, attended. 1 VB WITH OBJ If you **attend** a meeting or other event, you are present at it. I stopped off in London to attend a conference. 2 VB WITH OBJ If you **attend** an institution such as a school or church, you go to it regularly. 3 VB WITH PREP 'to' If you **attend** to something, you deal with it.

attendance /əténdəns/, attendances. 1 COUNT N OR UNCOUNT N The **attendance** at a meeting is the number of people who are present there. 2 UNCOUNT N If you talk about someone's **attendance** at an institution, you are referring to the fact that they go there regularly. She was allowed to resume her attendance at the High School.

attendant /əténdənt/, attendants. COUNT N An **attendant** is someone whose job is to serve people in a place such as a petrol station or a museum.

attention /əténʃə⁰n/. 1 UNCOUNT N If you give something your **attention**, you look at it, listen to it, or think about it carefully. When he felt he had their attention, he began. 2 UNCOUNT N If something is getting **attention**, it is being dealt with. They needed medical attention.
PHRASES ● If someone **brings** something **to** your **attention** or **draws** your **attention to** it, they point it out to you. ● If something **attracts** your **attention** or **catches** your **attention**, you suddenly notice it. ● If you **pay attention** to something, you watch it, listen to it, or take notice of it. There's far too much attention being paid to these hooligans. ● When soldiers **stand to attention**, they stand up straight with their feet together and their arms at their sides.

attentive /əténtɪv/. 1 ADJ If you are **attentive**, you are paying close attention to what is being said or done. ...an attentive audience. ♦ **attentively** ADV He was listening attentively. 2 ADJ To be **attentive** also means to be helpful and polite. He was unfailingly attentive.

attest /ətést/, attests, attesting, attested. VB WITH OBJ OR PREP 'to' To **attest** something or to **attest** to it means to show that it is true; a formal use. The perfection of their design is attested by the fact that they survived for thousands of years... Historic documents attest to the truth of this.

attic /ætɪk/, attics. COUNT N An **attic** is a room at the top of a house just below the roof.

attire /ətáɪə/. UNCOUNT N Your **attire** is the clothes you are wearing; a literary use.

attitude /ætɪtjuːd/, attitudes. 1 COUNT N WITH SUPP Your **attitude** to something is the way you think and feel about it. 2 COUNT N WITH POSS Your **attitude** to someone is the way you behave when you are dealing with them. I resented his attitude. 3 COUNT N WITH SUPP An **attitude** is also a position in which you hold your body. ...with her arms flung out in an attitude of surrender.

attorney /ətɜ́ːnɪ/, attorneys. COUNT N In the United States, an **attorney** is a lawyer.

attract /ətrǽkt/, attracts, attracting, attracted. 1 VB WITH OBJ If something **attracts** people or animals, it has features that cause them to come to it. The show attracted large crowds this year... Moths are attracted to lights. 2 VB WITH OBJ If someone or something **attracts** you, they have qualities which cause you to like or admire them. You can also say that their qualities **attract** you to them. She didn't attract me physically... What attracted me to Valeria was her sense of humour. ♦ **attracted** PRED ADJ WITH PREP 'to' I was becoming attracted to a girl from the next office. 3 VB WITH OBJ If something **attracts** support or publicity, it gets it. 4 VB WITH OBJ If something **attracts** your attention, you notice it. 5 VB WITH OBJ If something magnetic **attracts** an object, it causes the object to move towards it.

attraction /ətrǽkʃə⁰n/, attractions. 1 UNCOUNT N **Attraction** is a feeling of liking someone, and often of being sexually interested in them. ...the attraction between the sexes. 2 SING N WITH SUPP **Attraction** is also the quality of being interesting or desirable. The attraction of the house lay in its simplicity. 3 COUNT N An **attraction** is a feature that makes something interesting or desirable. One of the main attractions of the city was its superb transport system. 4 COUNT N An **attraction** is also something that people can go to for interest or enjoyment, for example a famous building. ...tourist attractions.

attractive /ətrǽktɪv/. 1 ADJ A person who is **attractive** is pretty or handsome. ...a remarkably attractive girl. ♦ **attractiveness** UNCOUNT N ...youthful attractiveness. 2 ADJ Something that is **attractive** has a pleasant appearance or sound. ...attractive illustrations. 3 ADJ You also say that something is **attractive** when it seems desirable. The company offers more time off and attractive pay.

attribute, attributes, attributing, attributed; pronounced /ətrɪbjuːt/ when it is a verb and /ætrɪbjuːt/ when it is a noun. 1 VB WITH OBJ AND PREP 'to' If you **attribute** something to an event or situation, you think that it was caused by that event or situation. Economists attributed the lack of progress to poor cooperation. 2 VB WITH OBJ AND PREP 'to' If you **attribute** a remark, a piece of writing, or a work of art to someone, you say that they said it, wrote it, or produced it. 3 VB WITH OBJ AND PREP 'to' If you **attribute** a particular quality or feature to someone or something, you think they have it. Here we are attributing human feelings to animals. ♦ **attribution** /ætrɪbjúːʃə⁰n/ UNCOUNT N ...the attribution of mysterious powers to these men. 4 COUNT N An **attribute** is a quality or feature. ...her physical attributes.

attuned /ətjúːnd/. 1 PRED ADJ WITH PREP 'to' If you are **attuned** to something, you can understand and appreciate it. The public is not quite attuned to this kind of art. 2 PRED ADJ WITH PREP 'to' If your ears are **attuned** to a sound, you can hear it and recognize it quickly.

aubergine /óʊbədʒiːn/, aubergines. COUNT N An **aubergine** is a vegetable with a smooth purple skin.

auburn /óːbə⁰n/. ADJ **Auburn** hair is reddish brown.

auction /óːkʃə⁰n/, auctions, auctioning, auctioned. 1 COUNT N OR UNCOUNT N An **auction** is a public sale where goods are sold to the person who offers the highest price. The big house was sold by auction. 2 VB WITH OBJ If you **auction** something, you sell it in an auction. They are going to auction the pictures at the end of the month.
auction off. PHR VB If you **auction off** a number of things, you get rid of them all by selling them at an auction.

auctioneer /ɔːkʃənɪə/, auctioneers. COUNT N An **auctioneer** is a person in charge of an auction.

audacious /ɔːdéɪʃəs/. ADJ **Audacious** behaviour is bold or cheeky. ...a series of audacious adventures. ♦ **audacity** /ɔːdǽsɪtɪ/ UNCOUNT N He had the audacity to blame Baldwin for their failure.

audible /óːdɪbə⁰l/. ADJ An **audible** sound can be heard. ♦ **audibly** ADV The clock ticked audibly.

audience /óːdɪəns/, audiences. 1 COLL N The **audience** is all the people who are watching or listening to something such as a play, concert, film, or television programme. 2 COLL N You can also use **audience** to refer to the people who read someone's books or hear about their ideas. ...the need for intellectuals to communicate their ideas to a wider audience. 3 COUNT N If you have an **audience** with someone important, you have a formal meeting with them.

audio /óːdɪəʊ/. ATTRIB ADJ **Audio** equipment is used for recording and reproducing sound.

audio-visual. ATTRIB ADJ **Audio-visual** teaching aids involve both recorded sound and pictures.

audit /óːdɪt/, audits, auditing, audited. VB WITH OBJ When an accountant **audits** an organization's accounts, he or she examines them officially to make sure that they are correct. Also COUNT N We're going to conduct a full audit.

audition /ɔːdɪ́ʃə⁰n/, auditions, auditioning, auditioned. 1 COUNT N An **audition** is a short performance that someone gives so that a director can decide if they are good enough to be in a play, film, or orchestra. 2 ERG VB If you **audition** or if someone **auditions** you, you perform an audition.

auditor /óːdɪtə/, auditors. COUNT N An **auditor** is an accountant who officially examines the accounts of organizations.

auditorium /ɔːdɪtóːrɪəm/, auditoriums or auditoria /ɔːdɪtóːrɪə/. COUNT N In a theatre or concert hall, the **auditorium** is the part of the building where the audience sits.

augment /ɔːgmént/, augments, augmenting, augmented. VB WITH OBJ To **augment** something means to make it larger by adding something to it; a formal use. They hit upon another idea to augment their income.

August /óːgəst/. UNCOUNT N **August** is the eighth month of the year in the Western calendar.

aunt /ɑːnt/, aunts. COUNT N Your **aunt** is the sister of your mother or father, or the wife of your uncle. ...Aunt Alice.

au pair /əʊpéə/, au pairs. COUNT N An **au pair** is a young foreign woman who lives for a time with a family in order to learn the language and to help with the children and housework.

aura /óːrə/, auras. COUNT N An **aura** is a quality or feeling that seems to surround a person or place. ...an aura of glamour and prestige.

auspices /óːspɪsɪz/. PHRASE If something is done **under the auspices of** a particular person or organization, it is done with their support and approval; a formal use.

austere /ɒstɪ́ə/. 1 ADJ Something that is **austere** is plain and not decorated. The interior of the church is sober and austere. ♦ **austerity** /ɒstérɪtɪ/ UNCOUNT N ...the austerity of these surroundings. 2 ADJ An **austere** person is strict and serious. 3 ADJ An **austere** way of life is simple and has no luxuries.

Australian /ɒstréɪlɪən/, Australians. 1 ADJ **Australian** means belonging or relating to Australia. 2 COUNT N An **Australian** is a person who comes from Australia.

authentic /ɔːθéntɪk/. 1 ADJ If a letter or painting is **authentic**, it is genuine rather than a forgery or an imitation. ♦ **authenticity** /ɔːθentɪ́sɪtɪ/ UNCOUNT N He challenged the authenticity of the letter. 2 ADJ If information or an account is **authentic**, it is reliable and accurate. ...an authentic account of the war. ♦ **authenticity** UNCOUNT N No historian has ever doubted the authenticity of Haldane's account.

authenticate /ɔːθéntɪkeɪt/, authenticates, authenticating, authenticated. VB WITH OBJ If you **authenticate** something, you establish that it is genuine after examining it. These stories seem to be well authenticated.

author /óːθə/, authors. 1 COUNT N The **author** of a piece of writing is the person who wrote it. 2 COUNT N An **author** is a person whose occupation is writing books.

authorise /óːθə⁰raɪz/. See authorize.

authoritarian /ɔːθɒrɪtéərɪən/, authoritarians. ADJ Someone who is **authoritarian** wants to control other people rather than letting them decide things themselves; used showing disapproval. Also COUNT N The old rulers were authoritarians.

authoritative /ɔːθɒrɪtətɪv/. 1 ADJ If someone behaves in an **authoritative** way, they give an impression of power and importance. ...an authoritative display of discipline. ♦ **authoritatively** ADV 'Don't do that,' he said authoritatively. 2 ADJ An **authoritative** piece of writing is based on a lot of knowledge or facts. ...his authoritative study of the Commonwealth.

authority /ɔːθɒ́rɪtɪ/, authorities. 1 COUNT N An **authority** is an official organization or government department that has the power to make decisions. She sold the house to the local authority... The authorities have got to clamp down on people like this. 2 UNCOUNT N If you have **authority** over someone, you have the power to control them. He made efforts to reassert his authority over them... He would be reported to those in authority. 3 UNCOUNT N **Authority** is official permission to do something. Have you been ordering taxis without signed authority? 4 COUNT N Someone who is an **authority** on a subject knows a lot about it. He is an authority on India.

authorize /óːθəraɪz/, authorizes, authorizing, authorized; also spelled **authorise**. VB WITH OBJ If someone in authority **authorizes** something, they give their official permission for it to happen. The president authorized the bombings. ♦ **authorization** /ɔːθəraɪzéɪʃə⁰n/ UNCOUNT N They will have to phone your branch for authorization.

auto /óːtəʊ/, autos. COUNT N In North America, cars are sometimes called **autos**.

autobiographical /ɔːtəbaɪəgrǽfɪkə⁰l/. ADJ A piece of writing that is **autobiographical** relates to events in the life of the person who has written it.

autobiography /ɔːtəbaɪɒ́grəfɪ/, autobiographies. COUNT N OR UNCOUNT N Your **autobiography** is an account of your life, which you write yourself.

autocratic /ɔːtəkrǽtɪk/. ADJ Someone who is **autocratic** has complete power and makes decisions without asking anyone else's advice.

autograph /óːtəgrɑːf/, autographs, autographing, autographed. 1 COUNT N If you ask someone famous for their **autograph**, you ask them to write their signature for you. 2 VB WITH OBJ When a famous person **autographs** something, they put their signature on it. ♦ **autographed** ADJ He gave me an autographed copy of his book.

automate /ɔ:tə6meɪt/, **automates, automating, automated.** VB WITH OBJ To **automate** a factory, office, or industrial process means to install machines which can do the work instead of people. ♦ **automation** /ɔ:tə6meɪʃə0n/ UNCOUNT N *This is an age of high technology and automation.*

automatic /ɔ:tə6mætɪk/, **automatics. 1** ADJ An **automatic** machine does not need anyone to operate it. *...automatic washing machines.* ♦ **automatically** ADV *The lights come on automatically.* **2** COUNT N An automatic gun, car, or washing machine can be called an **automatic. 3** ADJ An **automatic** action is one that you do without thinking about it. *Most of our decisions are automatic.* ♦ **automatically** ADV *Billy found himself automatically walking up to the house.* **4** ADJ If something such as an action or a punishment is **automatic,** it happens as the normal result of something else. *These offences carry automatic fines.* ♦ **automatically** ADV *Once people retire they automatically cease to be union members.*

automobile /ɔ:təmə6bi:l/, **automobiles.** COUNT N In North America, cars are sometimes called **automobiles.**

autonomous /ɔ:tɒnəməs/. ADJ An **autonomous** country, organization, or group governs or controls itself rather than being controlled by anyone else.

autonomy /ɔ:tɒnəmi1/. UNCOUNT N **Autonomy** is the control of a country, organization, or group by itself, rather than by others. *They wanted more autonomy.*

autopsy /ɔ:tɒpsi1, ɔ:tə7p-/, **autopsies.** COUNT N An **autopsy** is an examination of a dead body by a doctor who cuts it open in order to try to discover the cause of death.

autumn /ɔ:təm/, **autumns.** UNCOUNT N OR COUNT N **Autumn** is the season between summer and winter. In the autumn the weather becomes cooler. *The rain began in the late autumn... ...autumn leaves.*

autumnal /ɔ:tʌmnə0l/. ADJ Something that is **autumnal** has features that are characteristic of autumn.

auxiliary /ɔ:gzɪljəri1, -lə0ri1/, **auxiliaries. 1** COUNT N An **auxiliary** is a person who is employed to help other people. Auxiliaries are often medical workers or members of the armed forces. *...nursing auxiliaries.* Also ATTRIB ADJ *...six auxiliary squadrons.* **2** ATTRIB ADJ **Auxiliary** equipment is extra equipment that is used when necessary. *...auxiliary scaffolding.* **3** COUNT N In grammar, the **auxiliary verbs** are 'be', 'have', and 'do'. They are used with a main verb to form tenses, negatives, questions, and so on.

avail /əveɪl/. PHRASE If an action is **of no avail** or is done **to no avail,** it does not achieve what you want. *Speeches and protests were of no avail... They were fighting to no avail.*

available /əveɪləbə0l/. **1** ADJ If something is **available,** you can use it or obtain it. *...the amount of money available for spending.* ♦ **availability** /əveɪləbɪlɪ1ti1/ UNCOUNT N *...the availability of oil.* **2** ADJ Someone who is **available** is not busy and is therefore free to talk to you or spend time with you.

avalanche /ævəlɑ:ntʃ/, **avalanches. 1** COUNT N An **avalanche** is a large mass of snow or rock that falls down the side of a mountain. **2** COUNT N WITH SUPP You can refer to a large quantity of things that arrive or happen at the same time as an **avalanche** of them. *...an avalanche of tourists.*

avant-garde /ævɒŋgɑ:d/. ADJ **Avant-garde** art, theatre, and writing is modern and experimental.

avarice /ævərɪs/. UNCOUNT N **Avarice** is extreme greed for money.

avaricious /ævərɪʃəs/. ADJ Someone who is **avaricious** is very greedy for money.

avenge /ə3vendʒ/, **avenges, avenging, avenged.** VB WITH OBJ If you **avenge** a wrong or harmful act, you hurt or punish the person who did it. *He was determined to avenge his father's death.*

avenue /ævɪ1nju:/, **avenues. 1** COUNT N An **avenue** is a wide road with trees on either side. **2** COUNT N An **avenue** is also a way of getting something done. *We are exploring a number of avenues.*

average /ævə0rɪdʒ/, **averages, averaging, averaged. 1** COUNT N An **average** is the result you get when you add several amounts together and divide the total by the number of amounts. *These pupils were examined in 39 subjects, an average of 6.5 subjects for each pupil.* Also ATTRIB ADJ *The average age of the group was thirty-nine years.* **2** VB WITH COMPLEMENT To **average** a particular amount means to be that amount as an average over a period of time. *Price increases during these years averaged around 20%.* **3** ATTRIB ADJ **Average** is sometimes used to mean normal in size or quality. *...a sheet of paper of average thickness... Their language development is below average.* **4** PHRASE You say **on average** to indicate that a number is the average of several numbers. *We can discover how many words, on average, a person reads in a minute.*

average out. PHR VB When you **average out** a set of numbers, you work out the average.

averse /ə3vɜ:s/. PRED ADJ WITH PREP 'to' If you say that you are not **averse** to something, you mean that you quite like it or quite want to do it; a formal use.

aversion /ə3vɜ:ʃə0n/, **aversions. 1** COUNT N If you have an **aversion** to someone or something, you dislike them very much. *She had a great aversion to children.* **2** COUNT N Your **aversion** is something that you strongly dislike. *His current aversion is pop music.*

avert /ə3vɜ:t/, **averts, averting, averted. 1** VB WITH OBJ To **avert** something unpleasant means to prevent it from happening. *There must be immediate action if total chaos is to be averted.* **2** VB WITH OBJ If you **avert** your eyes from something, you look away from it.

aviary /eɪvjəri1/, **aviaries.** COUNT N An **aviary** is a large cage or covered area in which birds are kept.

aviation /eɪvieɪʃə0n/. UNCOUNT N **Aviation** is the operation and production of aircraft.

avid /ævɪd/. **1** ATTRIB ADJ You use **avid** to describe someone who is very keen and enthusiastic about something. *...an avid reader of movie magazines.* ♦ **avidly** ADV *They listened avidly.* **2** PRED ADJ WITH 'for' Someone who is **avid** for something is eager to get it.

avocado /ævə6kɑ:dəʊ/, **avocados.** COUNT N OR UNCOUNT N An **avocado** or **avocado pear** is a tropical fruit in the shape of a pear with a dark green skin and a large stone inside it.

avoid /əvɔɪd/, **avoids, avoiding, avoided. 1** VB WITH OBJ If you **avoid** something that might happen, you take action in order to prevent it from happening. *...a book on how to avoid a heart attack.* **2** VB WITH -ING If you **avoid** doing something, you make a deliberate effort not to do it. *Thomas turned his head, trying to avoid breathing in the smoke.* **3** VB WITH OBJ If you **avoid** someone or something, you keep away from them.

avoidance /əvɔɪdəns/. UNCOUNT N **Avoidance** of someone or something is the act of avoiding them. *...the avoidance of responsibilities.*

avowal /əvaʊə0l/, **avowals.** COUNT N An **avowal** of something is an admission or declaration of it; a formal use. *He made a shy avowal of love.*

avowed /əvaʊd/. **1** ATTRIB ADJ If you are an **avowed** supporter or opponent of something, you have declared that you support it or oppose it; a formal use. *...avowed enemies.* **2** ATTRIB ADJ An **avowed** belief or aim is one that you hold very strongly.

await /əweɪt/, **awaits, awaiting, awaited. 1** VB WITH OBJ If you **await** someone or something, you wait for them. *I returned to the States to find the FBI awaiting me.* **2** VB WITH OBJ Something that **awaits** you is going to happen to you in the future. *...the adventures that awaited him.*

awake /əweɪk/, **awakes, awaking, awoke** /əwəʊk/, **awoken** /əwəʊkə0n/. **1** PRED ADJ Someone who is **awake** is not sleeping. *He lay awake all night.* **2** ERG VB When you **awake** or when something **awakes** you, you wake up; a literary use. *I awoke from a deep sleep.*

awaken /əweɪkə0n/, **awakens, awakening, awakened;** a literary word. **1** VB WITH OBJ To **awaken** a feeling in a person means to cause them to have this feeling. *My first visit to a theatre awakened an interest which never left me.* **2** ERG VB WITH PREP 'to' When you **awaken** to a fact or when someone **awakens** you to it, you become aware of it. *Gradually people are awakening to their responsibilities.* **3** ERG VB When you **awaken** or when something **awakens** you, you wake up.

awakening /əweɪkə0nɪŋ/. **1** SING N The **awakening** of a feeling or realization in someone is the start of it. **2** PHRASE If you have a **rude awakening,** you are suddenly made aware of an unpleasant fact.

award /əwɔ:d/, **awards, awarding, awarded. 1** COUNT N An **award** is a prize or certificate that a person is given for doing something well. **2** COUNT N An **award** is also a sum of money that a court of law decides should be given to someone as compensation. **3** VB WITH OBJ To **award** something to someone means to give it to them as a prize, reward, or compensation.

aware /əweə/. **1** PRED ADJ If you are **aware** of a fact or situation, you know about it. *He was aware that he had drunk too much whisky... I was quite aware of this before we married.* ♦ **awareness** UNCOUNT N *...the public awareness of the need for conservation.* **2** PRED ADJ If you are **aware** of something that is present or happening, you know that it is present or happening because you can hear it, see it, smell it, or feel it. *Ralph was aware of the heat for the first time.* **3** ADJ If you say that someone is **aware,** you mean that they notice what is happening around them. *Some people are more politically aware.*

away /əweɪ/. **1** ADV If you move **away** from a place, you move so that you are no longer there. *He rose and walked away.* **2** ADV If you look or turn **away** from something, you move your head so that you are no longer looking at it. **3** ADV **Away** from a person or place means at a distance from that person or place. *...a pleasant picnic spot away from the city.* **4** ADV If you put something **away,** you put it in a safe place. *Tom put the book away... The report is not yet ready to be filed away.* **5** ADV If someone is **away,** they are not in the place where people expect them to be. *Is he at home or has he gone away?* **6** ADV You also use **away** to talk about future events. For example, if an event is a week **away,** it will happen in a week. **7** ADV If you give something **away** or if someone takes it **away** from you, you no longer have it. **8** ATTRIB ADJ When a sports team plays an **away** game, it plays on its opponents' ground. **9** ADV You can use **away** to say that something slowly disappears, or changes so that it is no longer the same. *The snow had all melted away.* **10** ADV **Away** is also used to emphasize that an action is continuous or repeated. *Howard was still working away in the university library... She was coughing away.*

awe /ɔ:/, **awes, awed. 1** UNCOUNT N **Awe** is the respect and amazement that you feel when you are faced with something wonderful and rather frightening. *The child stared at him in silent awe.* **2** PHRASE If you are **in awe of** someone, you have a lot of respect for them and are slightly afraid of them. **3** VB WITH OBJ If you **are awed** by someone or something, you are impressed by them and rather frightened of them. ♦ **awed** ADJ *...talking in an awed whisper.*

awe-inspiring. ADJ Something that is **awe-inspiring** is amazing and rather frightening.

awesome /ɔ:səm/. ADJ Something that is **awesome** is very impressive and frightening. *...an awesome weapon.*

awful /ɔ:fə4l/. **1** ADJ If you say that something is **awful,** you mean that it is very unpleasant or bad. *Isn't the weather awful?... ...that awful war.* **2** PRED ADJ If you look or feel **awful,** you look or feel ill. **3** ATTRIB ADJ You can use **awful** to emphasize how large an amount is; an informal use. *It must have taken an awful lot of courage.*

awfully /ɔ:fə4li1/. SUBMOD You use **awfully** to emphasize how much of a quality someone or something has; an informal use. *She was awfully nice... I'm awfully sorry.*

awhile /əwaɪl/. ADV **Awhile** means for a short time; a literary use. *Can't you just wait awhile?*

awkward /ɔ:kwəd/. **1** ADJ An **awkward** movement or position is uncomfortable or clumsy. *...an awkward gesture.* ♦ **awkwardly** ADV *He fell and lay awkwardly, covered in mud.* **2** ADJ Someone who is **awkward** behaves in a shy or embarrassed way. *I hated the big formal dances and felt very awkward.* ♦ **awkwardly** ADV *I said, 'How do you do?' awkwardly.* ♦ **awkwardness** UNCOUNT N *There was no awkwardness between them.* **3** ADJ You also say that someone is **awkward** when they are unreasonable and difficult to live with or deal with. **4** ADJ An **awkward** job is difficult to do. *Getting the wheel off can be awkward.* **5** ADJ An **awkward** situation is embarrassing and difficult to deal with. *McPherson started making things awkward for him... He asked a lot of awkward questions.*

awning /ɔ:nɪŋ/, **awnings.** COUNT N An **awning** is a piece of material attached to a caravan or building which provides shelter from the rain or sun.

awoke /əwəʊk/. **Awoke** is the past tense of **awake.**

awoken /əwəʊkə0n/. **Awoken** is the past participle of **awake.**

awry /əraɪ/. **1** PRED ADJ If something is **awry,** it is not in its normal or proper position. *His tie was awry.* **2** PRED ADJ If something goes **awry,** it does not happen in the way it was planned and it goes wrong.

axe /æks/, **axes, axing, axed. 1** COUNT N An **axe** is a tool used for cutting wood. It consists of a blade attached to the end of a long handle. **2** VB WITH OBJ If the government or a company **axes** a project or plan, it suddenly ends it.

axiom /æksɪəm/, **axioms.** COUNT N An **axiom** is a statement or idea which people accept as being true; a formal use.

axis /æksɪs/, **axes** /æksi:z/. **1** COUNT N An **axis** is an imaginary line through the middle of something. *The earth's axis is tilted at an angle of about 23°.* **2** COUNT N An **axis** of a graph is one of the two lines on which the scales of measurement are marked.

axle /æksə0l/, **axles.** COUNT N An **axle** is a rod connecting a pair of wheels on a car or other vehicle.

aye /aɪ/. CONVENTION In some British dialects, **aye** means yes.

azure /æʒʊ0ə, eɪ-/. ADJ **Azure** means bright blue.

Bb

B.A. /biː eɪ/, **B.A.s.** A **B.A.** is an arts degree or a social sciences degree. **B.A.** is an abbreviation for 'Bachelor of Arts'.
babble /bæbəˈl/, **babbles, babbling, babbled.** VB If you **babble**, you talk in a confused or excited way. *He babbled on about old enemies.* Also SING N *...the babble of women's voices.*
babe /beɪb/, **babes.** 1 COUNT N A **babe** is the same as a baby; an old-fashioned use. 2 VOCATIVE Some people use **babe** as an affectionate way of addressing someone; an informal, American use.
baboon /bəbuːn/, **baboons.** COUNT N A **baboon** is a type of monkey.
baby /beɪbiˈ/, **babies.** 1 COUNT N A **baby** is a very young child that cannot yet walk or talk. 2 VOCATIVE Some people use **baby** as an affectionate way of addressing someone; an informal American use. *Don't worry, baby, I'll think of something.*
babyish /beɪbiˈɪʃ/. ADJ **Babyish** things are suitable for a baby, or typical of a baby.
baby-sit, baby-sits, baby-sitting, baby-sat. VB If you **baby-sit**, you look after someone's children while they are out. ♦ **baby-sitter** COUNT N *Can't you find a baby-sitter?*
bachelor /bætʃəˈlə/, **bachelors.** COUNT N A **bachelor** is a man who has never married.
Bachelor of Arts, Bachelors of Arts. COUNT N A **Bachelor of Arts** is a person with a first degree in an arts or social science subject.
Bachelor of Science, Bachelors of Science. COUNT N A **Bachelor of Science** is a person with a first degree in a science subject.
back /bæk/, **backs, backing, backed.** 1 ADV If someone moves **back**, they move in the opposite direction to the one in which they are facing. *The child stepped back nervously... She pushed back her chair.* 2 ADV You use **back** to say that someone or something returns to a particular place or state. *I went back to the kitchen... She put it back on the shelf... He went back to sleep.* 3 ADV If you get something **back**, you get it again after not having it for a while. *You'll get the money back.* 4 ADV If you do something **back**, you do to someone what they have done to you. *He looked at her, and the girl stared back... I shall make some enquiries and call you back.* 5 ADV If someone or something is kept or situated **back** from a place, they are at a distance from it. *Police struggled to keep the crowd back... The house is set back from the road.* 6 ADV You use **back** to indicate that you are talking or thinking about something that happened in the past. *I invested in the company way back in 1971... Think back to what we've said.* 7 COUNT N Your **back** is the part of your body from your neck to your waist that is on the opposite side to your chest, stomach, and face. 8 COUNT N WITH SUPP The **back** of something is the part of it that is towards the rear or farthest from the front. *Sign on the back of the prescription form... He went to the small counter at the back of the store.* Also ATTRIB ADJ *The back wheels were spinning in the mud.* 9 COUNT N WITH SUPP The **back** of a chair is the part that you lean against. 10 ATTRIB ADJ A **back** road is small with very little traffic. 11 ERG VB When a car **backs** or when you **back** it, it moves backwards. *She backed out of the driveway.* 12 VB WITH OBJ If you **back** someone, you give them support or money. *The organization is backed by the U.N.* 13 VB WITH OBJ If you **back** a particular person, team, or horse in a competition, you bet money that they will win. 14 See also **backing.**
PHRASES • If someone moves **back and forth,** they repeatedly move in one direction and then in the opposite one. *Someone was pacing back and forth behind the curtains.* • If you are wearing something **back to front,** you are wearing it with the back of it on the front of your body. • If you do something **behind** someone's **back,** you do it without them knowing about it. • If you **turn** your **back on** someone or something, you ignore them or refuse to help them. *We have turned our backs on the very principles we were elected to uphold.*
back away. PHR VB If you **back away,** you move away because you are nervous or frightened.
back down. PHR VB If you **back down,** you withdraw a claim or demand that you made earlier.
back off. PHR VB If you **back off,** you move away in order to avoid problems or a fight.
back out. PHR VB If you **back out,** you decide not to do something that you previously agreed to do.
back up. PHR VB 1 If you **back up** a statement, you supply evidence to show it is true. 2 If you **back** someone **up,** you help and support them. 3 See also **back-up.**
backache /bækeɪk/. UNCOUNT N **Backache** is a pain in your back.
backbencher /bækbentʃə/, **backbenchers.** COUNT N In Britain, a **backbencher** is an MP who does not hold an official position in the government or its opposition.
backbiting /bækbaɪtɪŋ/. UNCOUNT N **Backbiting** is the saying of unpleasant things about someone who is not there.
backbone /bækbəʊn/, **backbones.** COUNT N Your **backbone** is the column of small linked bones along the middle of your back.
back-breaking. ADJ **Back-breaking** work is very hard physical work.
backer /bækə/, **backers.** COUNT N WITH SUPP A **backer** is someone who gives support or financial help to a person or project.
backfire /bækfaɪə/, **backfires, backfiring, backfired.** 1 VB If a plan **backfires,** it has the opposite result to the one that was intended. 2 VB When a motor vehicle or its engine **backfires,** there is an explosion in the exhaust pipe.
background /bækgraʊnd/, **backgrounds.** 1 COUNT N WITH SUPP Your **background** is the kind of family you come from and the kind of education you have had. *...people from working-class backgrounds.* 2 SING N WITH SUPP The **background** to an event or situation consists of the facts that explain what caused it. *...background information.* 3 SING N The **background** also refers to things, shapes, colours, or sounds that are less noticeable or less important and are often partly hidden by other things. *In the background is a tall cypress tree... ...blue flowers on a grey background... ...background music.*
backhand /bækhænd/, **backhands.** COUNT N A **backhand** is a shot in tennis or squash which you make with your arm across your body.
backing /bækɪŋ/, **backings.** 1 COUNT N OR UNCOUNT N **Backing** is a layer of strong material that is put onto the back of something in order to protect it. 2 SING N The **backing** of a popular song is the music which is sung or played to accompany the main tune. 3 UNCOUNT N WITH SUPP **Backing** is also money, resources, or support given to a person or organization. *Mr Yasser Arafat had received the full backing of the U.S..*
backlash /bæklæʃ/. SING N A **backlash** is a sudden, strong reaction against a tendency or development in society or politics. *...a backlash against the Thatcher government.*
backlog /bæklɒg/, **backlogs.** COUNT N A **backlog** is a number of things which have not yet been done, but which need to be done.
backpack /bækpæk/, **backpacks.** COUNT N A **backpack** is the same as a rucksack.
back pay. UNCOUNT N **Back pay** is money which an employer owes an employee for work that was done in the past.
backside /bæksaɪd/, **backsides.** COUNT N Your **backside** is the part of your body that you sit on; an informal use.
backstage /bæksteɪdʒ/. ADV In a theatre, **backstage** refers to the areas behind the stage. *He went backstage... ...a nasty incident backstage.*
backstreet /bækstriːt/. ATTRIB ADJ **Backstreet** activities are unofficial, secret, and often illegal. *...backstreet abortions.*
backstroke /bækstrəʊk/. SING N **Backstroke** is a swimming stroke which you do lying on your back.
back-up. 1 UNCOUNT N **Back-up** is extra help from people or machines which you need in order to be able to achieve something. *...the computer back-up which each mission required.* 2 UNCOUNT N If you have something such as a second set of plans as **back-up,** you have arranged for them to be available for use in case the first one does not work.
backward /bækwəd/, **backwards.** In normal British English, **backwards** is an adverb and **backward** is an adjective. In formal British English and in American English, **backward** is both an adjective and an adverb. 1 ADV If you move or look **backwards,** you move or look in the direction that your back is facing. *She stepped backwards onto a coffee cup.* Also ATTRIB ADJ *...a backward jerk of her head.* 2 ADV If you do something **backwards,** you do it in the opposite way to the usual way. *Listen to the tape backwards.* 3 PHRASE If you **know** something **backwards,** you know it very well. 4 ADJ A **backward** country or society does not have modern industries and machines. *...a backward, agrarian society.* 5 ADJ A **backward** child has difficulty in learning.
backwater /bækwɔːtə/, **backwaters.** COUNT N A **backwater** is a place or an institution that is isolated from modern ideas or influences; often used showing disapproval. *...a cultural backwater.*
backwoods /bækwʊdz/. PLURAL N Someone who lives in the **backwoods** lives a long way from large towns, and is isolated from modern life and modern ideas. *...peasants in the backwoods.* Also ATTRIB ADJ *...this tiny backwoods community.*
bacon /beɪkən/. UNCOUNT N **Bacon** is salted or smoked meat taken from the back or sides of a pig.
bacteria /bæktɪərɪə/. PLURAL N **Bacteria** are very small organisms which can cause disease.
bad /bæd/, **worse** /wɜːs/, **worst** /wɜːst/. • See also separate entries at **worse** and **worst.** 1 ADJ You describe something as **bad** if it is undesirable, unpleasant, or of poor quality. *I have some very bad news... Candy is bad for your teeth... Is the pain bad?* 2 ADJ Someone who is **bad** at doing something is not very skilful at it. *I was bad at sports... ...a bad actor.* 3 PRED ADJ Food that has gone **bad** has started to decay. 4 ADJ If you have a **bad** leg, heart, or eye, there is something wrong with it. 5 ATTRIB ADJ If you call a child **bad,** you mean that he or she is naughty and disobedient. 6 ADJ If you are in a **bad** mood, you are cross and behave unpleasantly to people.
PHRASES • If you say that something is **not bad,** you mean that it is quite good or acceptable. *It was an awful job, but the money wasn't bad.* • If you **feel bad** about something, you feel rather sorry and sad about it. • If you say **'too bad',** you are indicating in a rather harsh way that nothing can be done to change the situation. *'I want to speak to the director.'—'Too bad,' Castle said. 'You can't.'* • **bad blood:** see **blood.** • **bad luck:** see **luck.**
bade /bæd, beɪd/. **Bade** is the past tense of some senses of **bid.**
badge /bædʒ/, **badges.** 1 COUNT N A **badge** is a small piece of metal or cloth which you attach to your clothes for decoration. 2 COUNT N Any feature which is regarded as a sign of a particular quality can be referred to as a **badge** of that quality. *Wisdom is the badge of maturity.*
badger /bædʒə/, **badgers, badgering, badgered.** 1 COUNT N A **badger** is a wild animal with a white head with two wide black stripes on it. Badgers live underground. 2 VB WITH OBJ If you **badger** someone, you repeatedly tell them to do something or repeatedly ask them questions.
badly /bædliˈ/, **worse** /wɜːs/, **worst** /wɜːst/. 1 ADV If something is done **badly,** it is done with very little success or effect. *The party did badly in the election.* 2 ADV If someone or something is **badly** hurt or **badly** affected, they are severely hurt or affected. *The house was badly damaged.* 3 ADV If you need or want something **badly,** you need or want it very much. *We need the money badly.* 4 ADV You can use **badly** to say that something harms the reputation of someone or something, or affects them in a harmful way. *The story reflected badly on Amity... He got badly confused.* 5 See also **worse, worst.**
badly off, worse off, worst off. PRED ADJ If you are **badly off,** you do not have much money. *In the cities, the poor are as badly off as they were in the villages.*
badminton /bædmɪntən/. UNCOUNT N **Badminton** is a game played using rackets to hit a small, feathered object called a shuttlecock over a net.
bad-tempered /bædtempəd/. ADJ **Bad-tempered** people become angry very easily.
baffle /bæfəˈl/, **baffles, baffling, baffled.** VB WITH OBJ If you **are baffled** by something, you cannot understand it or explain it. *I was baffled by his refusal.* ♦ **baffling** ADJ *...the baffling array of new problems.*
bag /bæg/, **bags.** 1 COUNT N A **bag** is a container made of paper, plastic, or leather which is used to carry things. *...a paper bag... He packed his bags and drove to the airport.* 2 COUNT N You can use **bag** to refer to a bag and its contents, or to the contents only. *He ate a whole bag of sweets.* 3 PLURAL N **Bags** under your eyes are folds of skin, usually caused by not having enough sleep. 4 PHRASE If you say that something is **in the bag,** you mean that you are certain to get it or achieve it; an informal use.
baggage /bægɪdʒ/. UNCOUNT N Your **baggage** consists of the suitcases and bags that you take with you when you travel.
baggy /bægiˈ/. ADJ If a piece of clothing is **baggy,** it hangs loosely on your body.
bagpipes /bægpaɪps/. PLURAL N **Bagpipes** are a musical instrument consisting of a leather bag and several pipes.
bail /beɪl/, **bails, bailing, bailed;** also spelled **bale, bales, baling, baled** for meaning 2 and for **bail out 2.** 1 UNCOUNT N **Bail** is permission for an arrested person to be released after a sum of money has been paid to a law court. You can also refer to the sum of money

as **bail.** *She was released on $2,500 bail... The judge refused to grant bail.* **2** VB WITH OR WITHOUT OBJ If you **bail** water from a boat, you remove it using a container.

bail out. PHR VB **1** If you **bail** someone **out,** you pay bail on their behalf. **2** You can also say that you **bail** someone **out** when you help them in a difficult situation.

bailiff /beɪlɪf/, **bailiffs.** COUNT N A **bailiff** is a law officer who makes sure that the decisions of a court are obeyed; a British use.

bait /beɪt/, **baits, baiting, baited. 1** UNCOUNT N **Bait** is food which you put on a hook or in a trap in order to catch fish or animals. *I took a slice of white bread to use as bait.* **2** VB WITH OBJ When you **bait** a hook or trap, you put bait on it. **3** SING N A person or thing that is used as **bait** is used to tempt or encourage someone to do something. *He's using my papers as a bait.* **4** VB WITH OBJ If you **bait** someone, you deliberately try to make them angry by teasing them.

baize /beɪz/. UNCOUNT N **Baize** is a thick, green, woollen material used for covering snooker tables and card tables.

bake /beɪk/, **bakes, baking, baked. 1** VB OR ERG VB When you **bake** food or when it **bakes,** you cook it in an oven without using extra liquid or fat. *She said she would bake a cake... I cleaned the kitchen while the bread was baking.* ♦ **baked** ADJ *...baked potatoes.* **2** ERG VB When earth or clay **bakes,** it becomes hard and dry because of the heat of the sun. *The ground was baked hard.* **3** See also **baking.**

baked beans. PLURAL N **Baked beans** are beans cooked in tomato sauce.

baker /beɪkə/, **bakers. 1** COUNT N A **baker** is a person whose job is to bake and sell bread and cakes. **2** COUNT N A **baker** or a **baker's** is a shop where bread and cakes are sold.

bakery /beɪkə^{r}ri^{1}/, **bakeries.** COUNT N A **bakery** is a building where bread and cakes are baked.

baking /beɪkɪŋ/. ADJ If you say that a place is **baking,** you mean that it is very hot indeed; an informal use.

balance /bæləns/, **balances, balancing, balanced. 1** ERG VB If a person or thing **balances** or **is balanced,** they are steady and do not fall over. *An ashtray was balanced on the arm of her chair... Balancing on one leg is an excellent exercise.* **2** UNCOUNT N **Balance** is the stability that someone or something has when they are balanced on something. *She lost her balance.* **3** SING N WITH SUPP **Balance** is a situation in which all the different things involved are equal or correct in size, strength, or importance. *...the ecological balance of the lake.* **4** RECIP VB If you **balance** one thing with another or if several things **balance** each other, each of the things has the same weight, strength, or importance. *Any escapism in the magazine is balanced by more practical items.* **5** SING N In a game or contest, if the **balance** swings in your favour, you start winning. **6** ERG VB To **balance** a budget or **balance** the books means to make sure that the amount of money that is spent is not greater than the amount that is received. **7** COUNT N The **balance** in a bank account is the amount of money in it.

PHRASES ● If you are **off balance,** you are in an unsteady position and about to fall. *I pulled her off balance and she slipped down.* ● If something is **in the balance,** it is uncertain whether it will happen or continue. *The destiny of our race lies in the balance.* ● You can say **on balance** to indicate that you are stating an opinion only after considering all the relevant facts or arguments.

balanced /bælənst/. **1** ADJ A **balanced** account or report is a fair and reasonable one. *...a balanced summary of the debate.* **2** ADJ Something that is **balanced** is effective because its parts have been used or arranged skilfully and in the correct proportions. *...a beautifully balanced play... ...a balanced diet.*

balcony /bælkəni^{1}/, **balconies. 1** COUNT N A **balcony** is a platform on the outside of a building with a wall or railing around it. **2** COUNT N The **balcony** in a theatre or cinema is an area of seats upstairs.

bald /bɔːld/, **balder, baldest. 1** ADJ Someone who is **bald** has little or no hair on the top of their head. *You're going bald... He has a large bald patch.* ♦ **baldness** UNCOUNT N *I think you'll suffer from early baldness.* ♦ **balding** ADJ *...a trim, balding man in his early 60's.* **2** ADJ A **bald** tyre has become very smooth and is no longer safe to use. **3** ATTRIB ADJ A **bald** statement, question, or account has no unnecessary words in it. *Those bald figures mask the size of the operation.* ♦ **baldly** ADV *Stated baldly like this, these comments seem rather obvious.*

bale /beɪl/, **bales, baling, baled. 1** COUNT N A **bale** is a large quantity of something such as cloth, paper, or hay, tied into a tight bundle. **2** See also **bail.**

baleful /beɪlful/. ADJ Something that is **baleful** is likely to have harmful effects, or expresses someone's harmful intentions; a literary use. *We saw his baleful eye fixed on us.*

balk /bɔː^{l}k/, **balks, balking, balked;** also spelled **baulk.** VB If you **balk** at something, you are very reluctant to do it. *They would have balked at the idea of a socialist society.*

ball /bɔːl/, **balls. 1** COUNT N A **ball** is a round object used in games such as tennis, cricket, and football. **2** COUNT N A **ball** is also something that has a round shape. *He rolled the socks into a ball.* **3** COUNT N The **ball** of your foot is the rounded part where your toes join your foot. **4** COUNT N A **ball** is also a large, formal, social event at which people dance.

PHRASES ● If someone is **on the ball,** they are very alert and aware of what is happening. ● If you **start the ball rolling,** or **set the ball rolling,** you start something happening. *The banks set the ball rolling when they reduced their lending rates.*

ballad /bæləd/, **ballads.** COUNT N A **ballad** is a long song or poem which tells a story.

ballast /bæləst/. UNCOUNT N **Ballast** is used in ships or hot-air balloons to make them more stable.

ball bearing, ball bearings. COUNT N **Ball bearings** are small metal balls used to make the moving parts of a machine run smoothly.

ballerina /bæləriːnə/, **ballerinas.** COUNT N A **ballerina** is a woman ballet dancer.

ballet /bæleɪ, bæleɪ/, **ballets. 1** UNCOUNT N **Ballet** is a type of skilled and artistic dancing with carefully planned movements. *...a ballet dancer.* **2** COUNT N A **ballet** is an artistic work performed by ballet dancers.

ball game, ball games. 1 COUNT N A **ball game** is a baseball match; an American use. **2** PHRASE If a situation is **a whole new ball game,** it is completely different from the previous one; an informal use.

ballistics /bə^{3}lɪstɪks/. UNCOUNT N **Ballistics** is the study of the movement of objects that are shot or thrown through the air.

balloon /bəluːn/, **balloons, ballooning, ballooned. 1** COUNT N A **balloon** is a small, thin, rubber bag that you blow air into so that it becomes larger. Balloons are used as toys or decorations. **2** COUNT N A **balloon** is also a large, strong bag filled with gas or hot air, which can carry passengers in a basket or compartment underneath it. **3** VB When something **balloons,** it quickly becomes bigger and rounder in shape. *She crossed the park, her skirt ballooning in the wind.*

ballot /bælət/, **ballots, balloting, balloted. 1** COUNT N A **ballot** is a secret vote in which people select a candidate in an election, or express their opinion about something. **2** VB WITH OBJ If you **ballot** a group of people, you find out what they think about something by organizing a secret vote.

ballot box, ballot boxes. COUNT N A **ballot box** is the box into which ballot papers are put after people have voted.

ballpoint /bɔːlpɔɪnt/, **ballpoints.** COUNT N A **ballpoint** is a pen with a small metal ball at the end which transfers the ink onto the paper.

ballroom /bɔːlru^{4}m/, **ballrooms.** COUNT N A **ballroom** is a very large room used for dancing or formal balls.

balustrade /bæləstreɪd/, **balustrades.** COUNT N A **balustrade** is a railing or wall on a balcony or staircase.

bamboo /bæmbuː/, **bamboos.** UNCOUNT N OR COUNT N **Bamboo** is a tall tropical plant with hard, hollow stems. The young shoots of the plant are eaten, and the stems are used to make furniture and fences.

ban /bæn/, **bans, banning, banned. 1** VB WITH OBJ If something is **banned,** it is not allowed to be done, shown, or used. *His play was banned by the BBC.* **2** COUNT N A **ban** is an official statement showing that something is forbidden. *There was no ban on smoking.* **3** VB WITH OBJ If you **are banned** from doing something, you are officially prevented from doing it.

banal /bə^{3}nɑːl/. ADJ Something that is **banal** is so ordinary that it is not at all effective or interesting. *...banal songs.* ♦ **banality** /bə^{3}nælɪ^{1}ti^{1}/ UNCOUNT N *Throughout the film, there are moments of banality.*

banana /bənɑːnə/, **bananas.** COUNT N OR UNCOUNT N A **banana** is a long curved fruit with a yellow skin and cream-coloured flesh.

band /bænd/, **bands, banding, banded. 1** COUNT N A **band** is a group of musicians who play jazz, rock, or pop music, or a group who play brass instruments together. **2** COUNT N A **band** of people is a group of people who have joined together because they share an interest or belief. *...a small band of revolutionaries.* **3** COUNT N A **band** is also a flat, narrow strip of cloth which you wear round your head or wrists, or round a piece of clothing. *...a panama hat with a red band.* **4** COUNT N WITH SUPP A range of numbers or values within a system of measurement can also be referred to as a **band.** *...a very wide band of radio frequencies.*

band together. PHR VB If people **band together,** they meet and act as a group in order to try and achieve something. *Everywhere women banded together to talk about liberation.*

bandage /bændɪdʒ/, **bandages, bandaging, bandaged. 1** COUNT N A **bandage** is a long strip of cloth which is wrapped around a wounded part of someone's body to protect it. *She was wearing a bandage round her head.* **2** VB WITH OBJ If you **bandage** a wound or part of someone's body, you tie a bandage around it. ♦ **bandaged** ADJ *...a man with a bandaged arm.*

bandit /bændɪt/, **bandits.** COUNT N A **bandit** is an armed robber; an old-fashioned use.

bandstand /bændstænd/, **bandstands.** COUNT N A **bandstand** is a platform with a roof where a military band or a brass band can play in the open air.

bandwagon /bændwægən/. PHRASE If you say that someone has **jumped on the bandwagon,** you mean that they have become involved in an activity only because it has become fashionable.

bandy /bændi^{1}/, **bandies, bandying, bandied.** VB WITH OBJ AND ADJUNCT If ideas or words **are bandied** about or around, they are mentioned or used by a lot of people. *Various suggestions were bandied around.*

bandy-legged. ADJ Someone who is **bandy-legged** has legs which curve outwards at the knees.

bang /bæŋ/, **bangs, banging, banged. 1** COUNT N A **bang** is a loud noise such as the noise of an explosion. *She slammed the drawer shut with a bang.* **2** ERG VB If you **bang** a door or if it **bangs,** it closes violently with a loud noise. **3** VB WITH OR WITHOUT OBJ, WITH ADJUNCT If you **bang** on something or if you **bang** it, you hit it so that it makes a loud noise. **4** ERG VB If you **bang** part of your body against something, you accidentally knock into it and hurt yourself. *I bang my head against it every time.* Also COUNT N *Did you suffer any bangs or bumps?*

PHRASES ● If something goes **with a bang,** it is very successful. ● If you say that something is **bang** in a particular position, you mean that it is in exactly that position. *Emory University is bang in the middle of Atlanta.*

banger /bæŋə/, **bangers;** an informal word used in British English. **1** COUNT N A **banger** is a sausage. **2** COUNT N Old cars are sometimes called **bangers.**

bangle /bæŋgə^{0}l/, **bangles.** COUNT N A **bangle** is a bracelet or band that you wear round your wrist or ankle.

banish /bænɪʃ/, **banishes, banishing, banished.** VB WITH OBJ If someone or something **is banished,** they are sent away from a place or got rid of altogether. *They were banished to the penal colony... Tobacco had been banished from polite society.* ♦ **banishment** /bænɪʃmə^{2}nt/ UNCOUNT N *They ordered the banishment of political and tribal leaders.*

banister /bænɪstə/, **banisters;** also spelled **bannister.** COUNT N A **banister** is a rail supported by posts and fixed along the side of a staircase.

banjo /bændʒəʊ/, **banjos** or **banjoes.** COUNT N A **banjo** is a musical instrument with a circular body and four or more strings.

bank /bæŋk/, **banks, banking, banked. 1** COUNT N A **bank** is a place where you can keep your money in an account. **2** COUNT N WITH SUPP You use **bank** to refer to a store of something. For example, a blood **bank** or a data **bank** is a store of blood or a store of data that is kept ready for use. **3** COUNT N A **bank** is also the raised ground along the edge of a river or lake. *...the river bank.* **4** COUNT N WITH SUPP A **bank** of something is a long, high row or mass of it. *...a bank of fog.*

bank on. PHR VB If you **bank on** something happening, you rely on it happening. *He may come, but I'm not banking on it.*

bank account, bank accounts. COUNT N A **bank account** is an arrangement with a bank which allows you to keep your money in the bank and to withdraw it when you need it.

banker /bæŋkə/, **bankers.** COUNT N A **banker** is someone involved in banking at a senior level.

bank holiday, bank holidays. COUNT N A **bank holiday** is a public holiday; a British use.

banking /bæŋkɪŋ/. UNCOUNT N **Banking** is the business activity of banks and similar institutions.

banknote /bæŋknəʊt/, **banknotes.** COUNT N A **banknote** is a piece of paper money.

bankrupt /bæŋkrə^{9}pt/, **bankrupts, bankrupting, bankrupted. 1** ADJ People or organizations that are **bankrupt** do not have enough money to pay their debts. *The company has gone bankrupt.* **2** VB WITH OBJ To **bankrupt** a person or company means to make them go bankrupt. **3** COUNT N A **bankrupt** is a person who has been legally declared bankrupt. **4** ADJ Something that is **bankrupt** is completely lacking in a particular quality. *...the mindless, intellectually bankrupt leadership.*

bankruptcy /bæŋkrəptsi/. UNCOUNT N **Bankruptcy** is the state of being bankrupt. *A really big strike will throw the firm into bankruptcy.*

bank statement, bank statements. See **statement.**

banner /bænə/, **banners.** COUNT N A **banner** is a long strip of cloth with a message or slogan on it. *Crowds filled the streets carrying banners.*

bannister /bænɪstə/. See **banister.**

banquet /bæŋkwɪt/, **banquets.** COUNT N A **banquet** is a grand formal dinner.

banter /bæntə/. UNCOUNT N **Banter** is teasing or joking talk that is amusing and friendly.

baptism /bæptɪzəm/, **baptisms.** COUNT N OR UNCOUNT N A **baptism** is a Christian ceremony in which a person is baptized.

baptize /bæptaɪz/, **baptizes, baptizing, baptized;** also spelled **baptise.** VB WITH OBJ When someone **is baptized,** water is sprinkled on them or they are immersed in water as a sign that they have become a member of a Christian Church.

bar /bɑː/, **bars, barring, barred. 1** COUNT N A **bar** is a place where alcoholic drinks are bought and drunk. *Norris was drinking at a bar in San Francisco... He called for the menu and ordered in the bar while they were finishing their drinks.* **2** COUNT N A **bar** is also the counter on which alcoholic drinks are served. *Sally serves behind the bar.* **3** COUNT N A **bar** is also a long, straight, rigid piece of metal. *...an iron bar... We beat on the bars of our cells.* **4** COUNT N WITH SUPP A **bar** of something is a roughly rectangular piece of it. *...a bar of soap.* **5** VB WITH OBJ If you **bar** someone from going somewhere or doing something, you prevent them from going there or doing it. *I turned to go. Stryker barred my way... ...restrictions barring the use of US-supplied weapons.* **6** PREP You can use **bar** to mean 'except'. For example, all the work **bar** the washing means all the work except the washing; a formal use. **7** COUNT N In music, a **bar** is one of the several short parts of the same length into which a piece of music is divided. **8** See also **barring.**

barb /bɑːb/, **barbs. 1** COUNT N A **barb** is a sharp curved point on the end of an arrow or fish-hook. **2** COUNT N A **barb** is also an unkind remark.

barbarian /bɑːbeərɪən/, **barbarians.** COUNT N **Barbarians** were members of wild and violent tribes in former times.

barbaric /bɑːbærɪk/. ADJ **Barbaric** behaviour is extremely cruel. *...the barbaric sport of hunting.*

barbarism /bɑːbərɪzəm/. UNCOUNT N **Barbarism** is cruel or uncivilized behaviour. *War is barbarism.*

barbarous /bɑːbərəs/. ADJ Something that is **barbarous** is rough and uncivilized, or very cruel. *...the most barbarous atrocities.*

barbecue /bɑːbɪkjuː/, **barbecues. 1** COUNT N A **barbecue** is a grill used to cook food outdoors. **2** COUNT N A **barbecue** is also an outdoor party at which people eat food cooked on a barbecue.

barbed /bɑːbd/. ADJ A **barbed** remark or joke seems humorous or polite, but contains a cleverly hidden criticism. *...a barbed compliment.*

barbed wire. UNCOUNT N **Barbed wire** is strong wire with sharp points sticking out of it, which is used to make fences.

barber /bɑːbə/, **barbers. 1** COUNT N A **barber** is a man who cuts men's hair. **2** SING N The shop where a barber works is called the **barber's.**

bare /beə/, **barer, barest; bares, baring, bared. 1** ADJ If a part of your body is **bare,** it is not covered by any clothing. *...her bare feet.* ● If someone does something **with their bare hands,** they do it without using weapons or tools. *He killed those two men with his bare hands.* **2** ADJ If an object is **bare,** it is not covered or decorated with anything. *The doctor stood uneasily on the bare floor... The trees were almost bare.* **3** ADJ If a room, cupboard, or shelf is **bare,** it is empty. **4** ATTRIB ADJ The **bare** minimum or the **bare** essentials are the very least things that are necessary. *She packed the barest minimum of clothing.* **5** VB WITH OBJ If you **bare** something, you uncover it. *She bared her teeth.*

bareback /beəbæk/. ADV If you ride **bareback,** you ride a horse without a saddle.

barefoot /beəfʊt/. ADJ Someone who is **barefoot** or **barefooted** is not wearing anything on their feet. Also ADV *She ran barefoot through the field.*

barely /beəli/. ADV If something is **barely** true or possible, it is only just true or possible. *He was so drunk that he could barely stand.*

bargain /bɑːgɪn/, **bargains, bargaining, bargained. 1** COUNT N A **bargain** is a business agreement in which two people or groups agree what each of them will do, pay, or receive. *We shook hands on the bargain.* **2** VB When people **bargain** with each other, they discuss what each of them will do, pay, or receive. *Trade unions bargain with employers for better conditions.* ♦ **bargaining** UNCOUNT N *...the kind of bargaining that goes on in industry.* **3** COUNT N A **bargain** is also something which is sold at a lower price than it would be normally. *He couldn't resist a bargain.*

bargain for. PHR VB If you say that someone **had** not **bargained for** something, you mean that they did not expect it to happen. *They had not bargained for such opposition.*

barge /bɑːdʒ/, **barges, barging, barged. 1** VB WITH OR WITHOUT OBJ, WITH ADJUNCT If you **barge** into a place or person, you rush into it or push past them in a rude or rough way; an informal use. *Arthur barged into the garden... ...barging his way through the crowd.* **2** COUNT N A **barge** is a boat with a flat bottom, used for carrying heavy loads.

barge in. PHR VB If you **barge in,** you rudely interrupt what someone else is doing or saying; an informal use. *I'm sorry to barge in on you.*

baritone /bærɪtəʊn/, **baritones.** COUNT N A **baritone** is a man with a fairly deep singing voice.

bark /bɑːk/, **barks, barking, barked. 1** VB When a dog **barks,** it makes a short, loud noise, once or several times. *The dogs began to bark.* Also COUNT N *His spaniel gave a sudden bark.* **2** VB WITH OR WITHOUT OBJ If you **bark** at someone, you shout at them in a loud, rough voice. *He barked an order at us.* **3** UNCOUNT N **Bark** is the tough material that covers the outside of a tree.

barley /bɑːli/. UNCOUNT N **Barley** is a tall, grass-like plant or the grain produced by it that is grown for food and for the production of beer and whisky.

barmaid /bɑːmeɪd/, **barmaids.** COUNT N A **barmaid** is a woman who serves drinks in a bar or pub.

barman /bɑːmən/, **barmen.** COUNT N A **barman** is a man who serves drinks in a bar or pub.

barn /bɑːn/, **barns.** COUNT N A **barn** is a large building on a farm in which crops or animal food can be kept.

barometer /bərɒmɪtə/, **barometers.** COUNT N A **barometer** is an instrument that measures air pressure and shows when the weather is changing.

baron /bærən/, **barons. 1** COUNT N OR TITLE A **baron** is a man who is a member of the nobility. **2** COUNT N WITH SUPP You use **baron** to refer to someone who controls a large amount of an industry and who is therefore extremely powerful. *...oil and wheat barons.*

baroness /bærənɪs/, **baronesses.** COUNT N OR TITLE A **baroness** is a woman who has the same rank as a baron, or who is the wife of a baron.

baronet /bærənɪt/, **baronets.** COUNT N A **baronet** is a man who is given the honorary British title 'baronet' by the King or Queen, and can pass the title on to his son.

baroque /bərɒk, bərəʊk/. **1** ATTRIB ADJ **Baroque** art is an elaborate style of art that was used in Europe from the late 16th to the early 18th century. **2** ATTRIB ADJ **Baroque** music is a style of European music that was written in the 18th century.

barrack /bærək/, **barracks, barracking, barracked. Barracks** is the singular and plural of the noun. **1** VB WITH OR WITHOUT OBJ If you **barrack** someone, you shout loudly in order to interrupt them when they are making a speech. *The Prime Minister was barracked as she offered her sympathy to the relatives.* ♦ **barracking** UNCOUNT N *The barracking was led by a bearded man in jeans.* **2** COUNT N A **barracks** is a building or group of buildings where members of the armed forces live and work.

barrage /bærɑːʒ/, **barrages.** COUNT N WITH SUPP If you get a lot of questions or complaints about something, you can say that you are getting a **barrage** of them. *...a barrage of criticism.*

barred /bɑːd/. ADJ A **barred** window or door has bars on it to prevent people from getting in or out.

barrel /bærəl/, **barrels. 1** COUNT N A **barrel** is a round container for liquids. Barrels are wider in the middle than at the top and bottom and are usually made of wood. *...a wine barrel.* **2** COUNT N You can use **barrel** to refer to a barrel and its contents, or to the contents only. *...a barrel of beer.* **3** COUNT N The **barrel** of a gun is the long, cylindrical part through which the bullet moves when the gun is fired.

barren /bærən/. **1** ADJ **Barren** land has soil of such poor quality that plants cannot grow on it. **2** ADJ A **barren** woman is unable to have babies; an old-fashioned use.

barricade /bærɪkeɪd/, **barricades, barricading, barricaded. 1** COUNT N A **barricade** is a line of vehicles or other objects placed across a road or passage to stop people getting past. **2** VB WITH OBJ If you **barricade** a road or passage, you put something across it to stop people reaching it. **3** VB WITH OBJ AND ADJUNCT If you **barricade** yourself inside a room or building, you put something heavy against the door so that other people cannot get in. *We rushed into the bedroom and barricaded ourselves in... They were barricaded behind concrete slabs.*

barrier /bærɪə/, **barriers. 1** COUNT N A **barrier** is a fence or wall that prevents people or things from moving from one area to another. **2** COUNT N A **barrier** to the happening or achievement of something is something that makes it difficult or impossible for it to happen or to be achieved. *Pollution is not a barrier to future economic growth.*

barring /bɑːrɪŋ/. PREP You use **barring** to indicate that the person, thing, or event that you are mentioning is an exception to the point that you are making. *It is hard to imagine anyone, barring a lunatic, starting a war.*

barrister /bærɪstə/, **barristers.** COUNT N A **barrister** is a lawyer who speaks in the higher courts of law on behalf of either the defence or the prosecution; a British use.

barrow /bærəʊ/, **barrows. 1** COUNT N A **barrow** is a wheelbarrow. **2** COUNT N A **barrow** is also a cart from which fruit or other goods are sold in the street.

bartender /bɑːtendə/, **bartenders.** COUNT N A **bartender** is a person who serves drinks in a bar; an American use.

barter /bɑːtə/, **barters, bartering, bartered.** VB WITH OR WITHOUT OBJ If you **barter** goods, you exchange them for other goods, rather than selling them for money. *They bring meat, grain, and vegetables to sell or barter.* Also UNCOUNT N *Metal discs and chains were used for barter.*

base /beɪs/, **bases** /beɪsɪz/, **basing, based. 1** COUNT N The **base** of something is its lowest edge or part, or the part at which it is attached to something else. *...at the base of a cliff... ...the scar at the base of his thumb.* **2** COUNT N A position or thing that is a **base** for something is one from which that thing can be developed or achieved. *This innovation was regarded as a sensible base for teaching and research... The League had no real power base on which it could build.* **3** VB WITH OBJ AND 'on' OR 'upon' If one thing **is based** on another, the first thing is developed from the second one. *The new agreement is based on the original United Nations proposal... ...movies based on British life.* **4** PASSIVE VB If you **are based** in a particular place, that is the place where you live or do most of your work. *I was based in London.* **5** COUNT N OR UNCOUNT N A military **base** is a place which part of an army, navy, or air force works from. *...the new air base at Buzaruto... The submarines abandoned the chase and returned to base.* **6** COUNT N Your **base** is the main place where you work, stay, or live. *The company made Luxembourg city their base.*

baseball /beɪsbɔːl/. UNCOUNT N **Baseball** is a game played by two teams of nine players. Each player hits a ball with a bat and then tries to run round all four bases before the other team can get the ball back.

basement /beɪsmənt/, **basements.** COUNT N The **basement** of a building is a floor built partly or wholly below ground level.

bases. Bases is the plural of **base** or **basis.**

bash /bæʃ/, **bashes, bashing, bashed. 1** VB WITH OBJ If you **bash** someone or something, you deliberately hit them hard; an informal use. *She was bashing him over the head with a saucepan.* **2** VB WITH ADJUNCT If you **bash** into something or against something, you hit it or bump into it accidentally with a lot of force; an informal use. *He bashed into a tree.* Also COUNT N *...a bash on the nose.* **3** PHRASE If you **have a bash** at something or if you **give it a bash,** you try to do it; an informal use. *She was going to have a bash at swimming the Channel.*

bashful /bæʃfʊl/. ADJ A **bashful** person is shy and easily embarrassed. *Most parents are bashful about asking questions.* ♦ **bashfully** ADV *He smiled bashfully.*

basic /beɪsɪk/, **basics. 1** ATTRIB ADJ You use **basic** to describe the thing which is the most important or the simplest part of something. *The basic theme of these stories never varies... ...people with only a basic education.* **2** PRED ADJ An activity, situation, or plan that is **basic** to the achievement or success of something else is necessary for it. *There are certain things that are absolutely basic to a good relationship.* **3** ADJ You describe something as **basic** when it has only the most important features and no luxuries. *The facilities are terribly basic.* **4** PLURAL N The **basics** of a subject or activity are the simplest and most important aspects of it. *For a year I learnt the basics of journalism.*

basically /beɪsɪkəli/. SENTENCE ADV You use **basically** to indicate what the most important feature of something is or to give a general description of something complicated. *There are basically three types of vacuum cleaner... Basically, I think Britain shouldn't have gone into the Common Market.*

basin /beɪsən/, **basins. 1** COUNT N A **basin** is a deep bowl used for mixing or storing food. **2** COUNT N A **basin** is also a washbasin. **3** COUNT N The **basin** of a large river is the area of land around it from which water and streams run down into it. *...the Amazon basin.*

basis /beɪsɪs/, **bases** /beɪsi:z/. 1 COUNT N The **basis** of something is the central and most important part of it, from which it can be further developed. *This was the basis of the final design.* 2 COUNT N The **basis** for something is the thing that provides a reason for it. *...arguments which had no logical basis.* 3 PHRASE If something happens or is done **on a** particular **basis,** it happens or is done in that way or using that method. *We run the service on a voluntary basis... The Chairman is paid on a part-time basis.*

bask /bɑ:sk/, **basks, basking, basked.** VB If you **bask** in the sunshine, you lie in it and enjoy its warmth.

basket /bɑ:skɪt/, **baskets.** COUNT N A **basket** is a container made of thin strips of cane woven together. *...a shopping basket.*

basketball /bɑ:skɪtbɔ:l/. UNCOUNT N **Basketball** is a game in which two teams of five players each try to score goals by throwing a large ball through a circular net fixed to a metal ring at each end of the court.

bass /beɪs/, **basses.** 1 COUNT N A **bass** is a man with a deep singing voice. 2 ATTRIB ADJ A **bass** musical instrument has a range of notes of low pitch.

bassoon /bəsu:n/, **bassoons.** COUNT N A **bassoon** is a woodwind musical instrument which can produce a very deep sound.

bastard /bɑ:stəd, bæs-/, **bastards.** 1 COUNT N A **bastard** is someone whose parents were not married to each other when he or she was born; an old-fashioned use. 2 COUNT N OR VOCATIVE If you call someone a **bastard,** you are insulting them; an offensive use.

bastion /bæstɪən/, **bastions.** COUNT N WITH SUPP A **bastion** is a system or organization that is regarded as being important and effective in defending a particular way of life; a literary use. *They regard the wealth-producing system as a bastion of capitalistic privilege.*

bat /bæt/, **bats, batting, batted.** 1 COUNT N A **bat** is a specially shaped piece of wood that is used for hitting the ball in cricket, baseball, or table tennis. *...a cricket bat.* 2 VB When you **bat,** you have a turn at hitting the ball with a bat in cricket or baseball. 3 COUNT N A **bat** is also a small flying animal that looks like a mouse with leathery wings. Bats fly at night.

batch /bætʃ/, **batches.** COUNT N A **batch** of things or people is a group of them, especially one that is dealt with at the same time. *Another batch of letters came in... ...the next batch of trainees.*

bath /bɑ:θ/, **baths, bathing, bathed.** 1 COUNT N A **bath** is a long, rectangular container which you fill with water and sit in while you wash your body. 2 COUNT N When you have a **bath** or take a **bath,** you wash your body while sitting in a bath filled with water. 3 VB WITH OBJ If you **bath** a child or other person, you wash them in a bath. *She will show you how to bath the baby.*

bathe /beɪð/, **bathes, bathing, bathed.** 1 VB When you **bathe** in a sea, river, or lake, you swim or play there. *It is dangerous to bathe in the sea here.* Also SING N *Let's go for a bathe.* 2 VB When you **bathe,** you have a bath; an American use. 3 VB WITH OBJ When you **bathe** a wound, you wash it gently. 4 VB WITH OBJ AND ADJUNCT If a place is **bathed** in light, it is very bright. *The room was bathed in sunlight.*

bathing suit /beɪðɪŋ sju:t/, **bathing suits.** COUNT N A **bathing suit** is a tight-fitting garment worn by a woman when she goes swimming; an American use.

bathing trunks /beɪðɪŋ trʌŋks/. PLURAL N **Bathing trunks** are shorts worn by a man when he goes swimming; a British use.

bathrobe /bɑ:θrəʊb/, **bathrobes.** COUNT N A **bathrobe** is a loose piece of clothing which you wear before or after you have a bath or a swim.

bathroom /bɑ:θrum/, **bathrooms.** 1 COUNT N A **bathroom** is a room in a house that contains a bath or shower, a washbasin, and sometimes a toilet. 2 SING N People sometimes refer to a toilet as the **bathroom.**

bathtub /bɑ:θtʌb/, **bathtubs.** COUNT N A **bathtub** is the same as a bath; an old-fashioned use.

baton /bætɒn/, **batons.** 1 COUNT N A **baton** is a light, thin stick. 2 COUNT N A **baton** is also a short heavy stick used as a weapon by a policeman.

batsman /bætsmən/, **batsmen.** COUNT N In a game of cricket, the **batsman** is the person who is batting.

battalion /bətælɪən/, **battalions.** COUNT N A **battalion** is a large group of soldiers consisting of three or more companies.

batter /bætə/, **batters, battering, battered.** 1 VB WITH OBJ To **batter** someone or something means to hit them many times. *Such parents have been known to batter their children... The ship was being battered by the waves.* 2 UNCOUNT N **Batter** is a mixture of flour, eggs, and milk used to make pancakes.

battered /bætəd/. ADJ Something that is **battered** is old, worn, and damaged. *...a battered old hat.*

battering /bætərɪŋ/, **batterings.** COUNT N A **battering** is an experience in which someone suffers badly through being attacked. *The Eighth Army had taken the worst battering.*

battery /bætəri/, **batteries.** 1 COUNT N A **battery** is a device that produces the electricity in something such as a torch or radio. 2 COUNT N A **battery** of things, people, or events is a large number of them. *Batteries of cameras were set to record the event.* 3 ATTRIB ADJ **Battery** hens are kept in small cages and made to produce large numbers of eggs.

battle /bætəl/, **battles, battling, battled.** 1 COUNT N OR UNCOUNT N In a war, a **battle** is a fight between armies or between groups of ships or planes. *...the Battle of Balaclava... The general was killed in battle.* 2 COUNT N A **battle** is also a process in which two people or two groups compete for power or try to achieve opposite things. *...the battle between the sexes... ...his battle for control of the administration.* 3 VB WITH ADJUNCT To **battle** means to fight very hard. *Dad was soon battling for his life.*

battlefield /bætəlfi:ld/, **battlefields.** COUNT N A **battlefield** is a place where a battle is fought.

battleground /bætəlgraund/, **battlegrounds.** 1 COUNT N A **battleground** is a battlefield. 2 COUNT N You can also refer to a subject over which people disagree or compete as a **battleground.** *The theory of evolution is no longer a battleground.*

battlements /bætəlmənts/. PLURAL N The **battlements** of a castle or fortress consist of a wall built round the top, with gaps through which guns or arrows can be fired.

battleship /bætəlʃɪp/, **battleships.** COUNT N A **battleship** is a very large, heavily armoured warship.

baulk /bɔ:lk/. See **balk.**

bawdy /bɔ:di/. ADJ A **bawdy** story or joke contains humorous references to sex; an old-fashioned use. *...bawdy songs.*

bawl /bɔ:l/, **bawls, bawling, bawled.** 1 VB If you **bawl,** you shout or sing something loudly and harshly. *They bawl down the telephone at me.* 2 VB If a child **bawls,** it cries loudly. *Josephine started bawling.*

bawl out. PHR VB If someone **bawls** you **out,** they scold you angrily for doing something wrong; an informal use. *I was regularly bawled out at school for not doing homework.*

bay /beɪ/, **bays, baying, bayed.** 1 COUNT N A **bay** is a part of a coastline where the land curves inwards. *Hearst sailed from San Francisco across the bay to Oakland.* 2 COUNT N A **bay** is also a space or area used for a particular purpose. *...the corridor beyond the loading bay.* 3 PHRASE If you **keep** something frightening or upsetting **at bay,** you prevent it from reaching you. *...lighting a fire to keep dangerous animals at bay.* 4 VB When a dog or wolf **bays,** it howls.

bayonet /beɪənɪt/, **bayonets.** COUNT N A **bayonet** is a long, sharp blade that can be fixed to the end of a rifle and used as a weapon.

bay window, bay windows. COUNT N A **bay window** is a window that sticks out from the outside wall of a house.

bazaar /bəzɑ:/, **bazaars.** 1 COUNT N A **bazaar** is an area with many small shops and stalls, especially in the Middle East and India. 2 COUNT N A **bazaar** is also a sale to raise money for charity. *Our local church is having a Christmas bazaar.*

BC /bi: si:/. You use **BC** in dates to indicate a number of years or centuries before the year in which Jesus Christ is believed to have been born. *...1600 BC... ...the fifth century BC.*

be /bi:/, **am, are, is; was, were; being, been.** For explanations of the use of the inflected forms, see the individual entries. 1 AUX **Be** is used in front of a present participle to form the continuous tense of a verb. *The Government is considering the introduction of student loans.* 2 VB WITH TO-INF **Be** is also used in front of an infinitive to talk about future events. *Mr Sandy Saunders is to be chairman... She is to appeal against the decision.* 3 AUX You use **be** to form the passive voice. *Some milk products have been found to contain aluminium... Mr Harris was elected by the Council last month.* 4 LINK VB **Be** is used in front of an adjective, a noun, or a prepositional phrase in order to give more information about the subject of a sentence. For example, you may want to name a person or place, or to give information about their qualities, features, age, and so on. *She was slightly disappointed with her Grade C pass... I'm from Dortmund originally... The iron was in her left hand... The head of the Corporation is Mr Paul Simpson.* 5 LINK VB You use **be** with 'it' as the subject in order to describe something, or mention one of its qualities. You can do this in as a single sentence as in 'It's so cold today' or as a way of commenting on a sentence, as in 'It's a pity we can't go later.' *It was terribly hot and airless... It's a shame she didn't enjoy the film.* 6 LINK VB **Be** is also used with 'it' or 'what' as the subject in order to delay the final part of the sentence. For example, you can change the statement 'John bought the car' into 'It was John who bought the car' when you want to emphasise the person or thing that performs the action of the verb. *What I'm talking about is the satellite that fell out of its orbit... It was Ted who broke the news to me.* 7 LINK VB **Be** is used with 'there' as the subject to say that something exists or happens. *There was a rustling of papers... There is no such thing as a happy marriage.* 8 AUX OR LINK VB **Be** is used on its own in co-ordinating structures where the subject of the second clause is different from the subject of the first. *She wasn't enjoying it, but the children were... He's exactly the same age as I am.* 9 AUX OR LINK VB **Be** can also be used on its own in a response to a question. *'Rose, are you interested in underdeveloped countries at all?'—'Yes, I am.'* 10 AUX OR LINK VB **Be** is also used in expressions such as 'isn't it?' and 'aren't you?' which are added to the end of a statement and change it into a question. *She's Welsh, isn't she?... I hear things are much better in Liverpool, aren't they?*

beach /bi:tʃ/, **beaches.** COUNT N A **beach** is an area of sand or pebbles by the sea.

beacon /bi:kən/, **beacons.** COUNT N A **beacon** is a light or a fire on a hill or tower, which acts as a signal or a warning.

bead /bi:d/, **beads.** 1 COUNT N **Beads** are small pieces of coloured glass, wood, or plastic with a hole through the middle which are used for jewellery or decoration. *...strings of beads.* 2 COUNT N A **bead** of liquid or moisture is a small drop of it. *Beads of perspiration began to form on his brow.*

beady /bi:di/. ADJ **Beady** eyes are small, round, and bright.

beak /bi:k/, **beaks.** COUNT N A bird's **beak** is the hard curved or pointed part of its mouth.

beaker /bi:kə/, **beakers.** COUNT N A **beaker** is a plastic cup used for drinking.

beam /bi:m/, **beams, beaming, beamed.** 1 VB If you **beam,** you smile because you are happy. *He beamed at Ralph.* Also COUNT N *...a beam of satisfaction.* 2 COUNT N WITH SUPP A **beam** of light is a line of light that shines from an object such as a torch or the sun. *I could see the beam of his flashlight.* 3 VB WITH OBJ AND ADJUNCT If you **beam** a signal or information to a place, you send it by means of radio waves. *We were able to beam pictures of the riots out to Denmark.* 4 COUNT N A **beam** is also a long thick bar of wood, metal, or concrete, especially one which is used to support the roof of a building. *...the low oak beams.*

bean /bi:n/, **beans.** 1 COUNT N **Beans** are the pods of a climbing plant, or the seeds that the pods contain, which are eaten as a vegetable. 2 COUNT N **Beans** are also the seeds of various plants which are used for different purposes, for example to make drinks such as coffee or cocoa, or to produce oil. 3 PHRASE If someone is **full of beans,** they are very lively and full of energy and enthusiasm; an informal use.

bear /beə/, **bears, bearing, bore** /bɔ:/, **borne** /bɔ:n/. 1 COUNT N A **bear** is a large, strong wild animal with thick fur and sharp claws. ● See also **polar bear.** ● **Teddy bear:** see **teddy.** 2 VB WITH OBJ If you **bear** something, you carry it; a formal use. *Camels and donkeys bear those goods inland... She arrived bearing a large bunch of grapes.* 3 VB WITH OBJ If something **bears** the weight of something else, it supports the weight of that thing. *His ankle now felt strong enough to bear his weight.* 4 VB WITH OBJ If something **bears** a particular mark or characteristic, it has that mark or characteristic. *The scene bore all the marks of a country wedding.* 5 VB WITH OBJ If you **bear** something difficult, you accept it and are able to deal with it. *Their policies are putting a greater strain on the economic system than it can bear.* ● **Grin and bear it:** see **grin.** 6 VB WITH OBJ When a plant or tree **bears** flowers, fruit, or leaves, it produces them. 7 VB WITH OBJ AND OBJ If you **bear** someone a feeling such as love or hate, you feel that emotion towards them; a formal use. *He bore his children no malice.* 8 PHRASE If you **bring** pressure or influence **to bear** on someone, you use it to try and persuade them to do something. *The group's aim is to bring pressure to bear on Parliament to get the law changed.* 9 VB WITH ADJUNCT If you **bear** left or **bear** right when you are driving or walking along, you turn slightly in that direction.

bear out. PHR VB If something **bears** someone **out** or **bears out** what they are saying, it supports what they are saying. *The claims are not borne out by the evidence.*

bear with. PHR VB If you ask someone to **bear with** you, you are asking them to be patient. *I hope you'll bear with me as I explain.*

bearable /bɛərəbəl/. ADJ If something is **bearable,** you can accept it, although it is rather unpleasant. *The heat was just bearable.*

beard /bɪəd/, **beards.** COUNT N A man's **beard** is the hair that grows on his chin and cheeks. *He had a long grey beard.* ♦ **bearded** /bɪədɪd/ ADJ *...a bearded man.*

bearer /bɛərə/, **bearers.** 1 COUNT N A **bearer** is a person who carries a stretcher or coffin. *The four bearers lifted the coffin slowly.* 2 COUNT N The **bearer** of something such as a letter, a document, or a piece of news is the person who has in their possession, and who brings it to you. *...the bearer of the invitation... The document contains the bearer's fingerprints.* 3 COUNT N The **bearer** of a name or title is the person who has it.

bearing /bɛərɪŋ/, **bearings.** 1 PHRASE If something **has a bearing on** a situation or event, it is relevant to it. *That is all in the past. It has no bearing on what is happening today.* 2 SING N Someone's **bearing** is the way in which they move or stand; a formal use. 3 PHRASE If you **get** or **find** your **bearings,** you find out where you are or what you should do next. If you **lose** your **bearings** , you do not know where you are or what you should do next. *They stopped to get their bearings.*

beast /biːst/, **beasts.** COUNT N A **beast** is an animal, especially a large one.

beastly /biːstli/. ADJ **Beastly** means very unpleasant, unkind, or spiteful; an old-fashioned use. *It's so beastly there.*

beat /biːt/, **beats, beating, beaten. Beat** is used in the present tense and is the past tense of the verb. 1 VB WITH OR WITHOUT OBJ If you **beat** someone or something, you hit them very hard. *His stepfather used to beat him... The rain beat against the window.* 2 ERG VB When a bird or insect **beats** its wings or when its wings **beat,** its wings move up and down. *Some birds beat their wings as fast as 80 times a second.* Also COUNT N *Flies can move their wings at 1000 beats per second.* 3 VB When your heart or pulse **beats,** it is continually making movements with a regular rhythm. 4 COUNT N The **beat** of your heart or pulse is a single movement of it. *He could feel the beat of her heart.* 5 SING N The **beat** of a piece of music is the main rhythm that it has. 6 VB WITH OBJ If you **beat** eggs, cream, or butter, you mix them thoroughly using a fork or whisk. 7 VB WITH OBJ To **beat** someone in a competition means to defeat them or to do better than them.

PHRASES ● You use **beat** in expressions such as 'It beats me' to indicate that you cannot understand or explain something; an informal use. *What beats me is where they get the money from.* ● A police officer **on the beat** is on duty, walking around the area for which he or she is responsible. ● **to beat about the bush:** see **bush.**

beat down. PHR VB 1 When the sun **beats down,** it is very hot and bright. 2 When the rain **beats down,** it rains very hard. 3 When you **beat down** a person who is selling you something, you force them to accept a lower price for it.

beat up. PHR VB If someone **beats** a person **up,** they hit or kick the person many times. *He told us that he had been beaten up by the police.*

beating /biːtɪŋ/, **beatings.** 1 COUNT N If you are given a **beating,** you are hit hard many times. 2 SING N If a team takes a **beating,** it is defeated by a large amount in a competition.

beating up, beatings up. COUNT N A **beating up** is an attack on someone in which they are hit and kicked so that they are very badly hurt. *They gave him an awful beating up.*

beautiful /bjuːtɪful/. 1 ADJ You say that someone or something is **beautiful** when you find them very attractive or pleasant. *The table looked beautiful... ...a very beautiful girl.* ♦ **beautifully** ADV *...beautifully dressed young men.* 2 ADJ You can describe something that someone does as **beautiful** when they do it very skilfully. *It was a beautiful shot.* ♦ **beautifully** ADV *Doesn't he play the piano beautifully?*

beautify /bjuːtɪfaɪ/, **beautifies, beautifying, beautified.** VB WITH OBJ If you **beautify** something, you make it look more beautiful; a formal use.

beauty /bjuːti/, **beauties.** 1 UNCOUNT N **Beauty** is the state or quality of being beautiful. *Her beauty grew in her old age... She learned to appreciate beauty.* 2 COUNT N A **beauty** is a beautiful woman. *Vita had turned into a beauty.* 3 COUNT N WITH SUPP The **beauties** of something are its attractive qualities or features. *...the beauties of nature.* 4 SING N If you say that a particular feature is the **beauty** of something, you mean that this feature is what makes the thing so good. *That's the beauty of the plan—it's so simple.* 5 MOD **Beauty** is used to describe people, products, and activities that are concerned with making women look attractive. *...beauty products... ...the magazine's beauty editor.*

beauty spot, beauty spots. COUNT N A **beauty spot** is a place that is popular because of its beautiful countryside.

beaver /biːvə/, **beavers, beavering, beavered.** COUNT N A **beaver** is a furry animal like a large rat with a big flat tail.

beaver away. PHR VB If you **are beavering away** at something, you are working very hard at it.

became /bɪˈkeɪm/. **Became** is the past tense of **become.**

because /bɪˈkɔz/. 1 CONJ You use **because** to introduce a subordinate clause which gives a reason. *I couldn't see Helen's expression, because her head was turned.* 2 PREP You also use **because of** at the beginning of a prepositional phrase which gives a reason. *He retired last month because of illness.*

beck /bɛk/. PHRASE If someone wants you to be **at** their **beck and call,** they want you to be constantly available and ready to do what they ask.

beckon /bɛkən/, **beckons, beckoning, beckoned.** 1 VB WITH OR WITHOUT OBJ If you **beckon** to someone, you signal to them to come to you. *Claus beckoned to him excitedly... He beckoned me to follow him.* 2 VB WITH OR WITHOUT OBJ If something **beckons** you, it is so attractive that you feel you must become involved in it. *No restaurants beckoned late diners into the area.*

become /bɪˈkʌm/, **becomes, becoming, became** /bɪˈkeɪm/. **Become** is used in the present tense and is the past participle. 1 LINK VB If something **becomes** a particular thing, it starts being that thing. *The smell became stronger and stronger... It became clear that the Conservatives were not going to win... We became good friends at once.* 2 PHRASE If you wonder **what has become of** someone, you wonder where they are and what has happened to them.

becoming /bɪˈkʌmɪŋ/. ADJ A piece of clothing, a colour, or a hairstyle that is **becoming** makes the person who is wearing it look attractive; an old-fashioned use.

bed /bɛd/, **beds.** 1 COUNT N OR UNCOUNT N A **bed** is a piece of furniture that you lie on when you sleep. *He sat down on the bed... He went to bed at ten.* 2 PHRASE If you **go to bed with** someone, you have sex with them. 3 COUNT N WITH SUPP A flower **bed** is an area of earth in which you grow plants. 4 COUNT N WITH SUPP The sea **bed** or a river **bed** is the ground at the bottom of the sea or of a river.

bed and breakfast. UNCOUNT N **Bed and breakfast** is a system of accommodation in a hotel or guest house in which you pay for a room for the night and for breakfast the following morning. *...£15.50 a night for bed and breakfast.*

bedclothes /bɛdkləʊðz/. PLURAL N **Bedclothes** are the sheets and covers which you put over you when you get into bed.

bedding /bɛdɪŋ/. UNCOUNT N **Bedding** is sheets, blankets, and other covers used on beds. *She changed the bedding.*

bedfellow /bɛdfɛləʊ/, **bedfellows.** COUNT N You refer to two people or things as **bedfellows** when they have become associated or related in some way. *The oddest of enemies might become bedfellows.*

bedlam /bɛdləm/. UNCOUNT N If you say that a place or situation is **bedlam,** you mean that it is very noisy and disorderly.

bedraggled /bɪˈdrægəld/. ADJ Someone or something that is **bedraggled** is untidy and disorderly, because they have got wet or dirty.

bedridden /bɛdrɪdən/. ADJ Someone who is **bedridden** is so ill or disabled that they cannot get out of bed.

bedrock /bɛdrɒk/. UNCOUNT N The **bedrock** of something refers to all the principles, ideas, or facts on which it is based. *The Act reaffirmed family values as the moral bedrock of the nation.*

bedroom /bɛdrum/, **bedrooms.** COUNT N A **bedroom** is a room which is used for sleeping in.

bedside /bɛdsaɪd/. SING N Your **bedside** is the area beside your bed. *An excellent breakfast had been left on the tray by his bedside... ...a bedside light.*

bedsitter /bɛdsɪtə/, **bedsitters.** COUNT N A **bedsitter** or **bedsit** is a single furnished room in a house, which you pay rent for and in which you live and sleep; a British use.

bedspread /bɛdsprɛd/, **bedspreads.** COUNT N A **bedspread** is a decorative cover which is put over a bed, on top of the sheets and blankets.

bedtime /bɛdtaɪm/. UNCOUNT N Your **bedtime** is the time when you usually go to bed.

bee /biː/, **bees.** COUNT N A **bee** is an insect that makes a buzzing noise as it flies and usually has a yellow-and-black striped body. Bees make honey, and live in large groups. ● If you **have a bee in** your **bonnet,** you are so enthusiastic or worried about something that you keep mentioning it or thinking about it.

beech /biːtʃ/, **beeches.** COUNT N OR UNCOUNT N A **beech** is a tree with a smooth grey trunk.

beef /biːf/. UNCOUNT N **Beef** is the meat of a cow, bull, or ox.

beefy /biːfi/. ADJ Someone, especially a man, who is **beefy** is strong and muscular; an informal use.

beehive /biːhaɪv/, **beehives.** COUNT N A **beehive** is a place where bees are kept so that someone can collect the honey that they produce.

been /biːn, bɪn/. 1 **Been** is the past participle of **be.** 2 PAST PARTICIPLE You use **been** after the auxiliaries 'has', 'have', and 'had' to say that someone has gone to a place or has visited it. *I haven't been to Birmingham... Has the milkman been yet?*

beer /bɪə/, **beers.** 1 MASS N **Beer** is a bitter alcoholic drink made from grain. *We drank a few pints of beer.* 2 COUNT N A **beer** is a glass, bottle, or can containing beer. *He'd had two beers.*

beet /biːt/. UNCOUNT N **Beet** is a root vegetable that is used as food for animals.

beetle /biːtəl/, **beetles.** COUNT N A **beetle** is an insect with a hard covering to its body.

beetroot /biːtruːt/, **beetroots.** UNCOUNT N OR COUNT N **Beetroot** is a dark red root vegetable which can be cooked or pickled, and eaten in salads.

befall /bɪˈfɔːl/, **befalls, befalling, befell** /bɪˈfɛl/, **befallen.** VB WITH OBJ If something bad or unlucky **befalls** you, it happens to you; a literary use. *She knew no harm would ever befall her.*

before /bɪˈfɔː/. 1 PREP OR CONJ If something happens **before** a time or event, it happens earlier than that time or event. *We arrived just before two o'clock... Can I see you before you go, Helen?... A dozen ideas were considered before he decided on this plan.* 2 ADJ AFTER N If something happens the day **before,** it happened during the previous day. *It had rained the night before.* 3 ADV If someone has done something **before,** they have done it on a previous occasion. *Have you been to Greece before?* 4 PREP If someone is **before** something, they are in front of it; a formal use. *He stood before the door to the cellar... He will appear before the magistrate.* 5 PREP When you have a task or difficult situation **before** you, you have to deal with it. *Let's get started. I have a difficult job before me.*

beforehand /bɪˈfɔːhænd/. ADV If you do something **beforehand,** you do it earlier than a particular event. *Kathleen got married without telling anyone beforehand.*

befriend /bɪˈfrɛnd/, **befriends, befriending, befriended.** VB WITH OBJ If you **befriend** someone, you make friends with them. *I befriended a lonely little boy in the village.*

befuddle /bɪˈfʌdəl/, **befuddles, befuddling, befuddled.** VB WITH OBJ If something **befuddles** you, it confuses you. *His words were sufficient to befuddle the girls.*

beg /bɛg/, **begs, begging, begged.** 1 VB WITH OR WITHOUT OBJ If you **beg** someone to do something, you ask them anxiously or eagerly to do it. *I begged him to stay, but he wouldn't... He begged for help... 'Tell me all the news,' I begged.* 2 VB WITH OR WITHOUT OBJ When someone **begs,** they ask people to give them food or money because they are poor. *...children in the streets begging for money... Kids were begging milk from the governor.* 3 **I beg your pardon:** see **pardon.**

began /bɪˈgæn/. **Began** is the past tense of **begin.**

beggar /bɛgə/, **beggars.** COUNT N A **beggar** is someone who lives by asking people for money or food.

begin /bɪˈgɪn/, **begins, beginning, began** /bɪˈgæn/, **begun** /bɪˈgʌn/. 1 VB WITH TO-INF OR -ING If you **begin to** do something, you start doing it. *The actors began to rehearse a scene... I began eating the grapes.* 2 VB OR ERG VB When something **begins** or when you **begin** it, it takes place from a particular time onwards. *The concerts begin at 8 pm... Malcolm began his speech... They began by looking at the problems.* 3 VB WITH ADJUNCT You say that a place or region **begins** somewhere when you are indicating where its edges are. *The ocean begins here.* 4 PHRASE You use **to begin with** to talk about the first event or stage in a process, or to introduce the first thing you want to say. *To begin with, they just take your name and address.*

beginner /bɪˈgɪnə/, **beginners.** COUNT N A **beginner** is someone who has just started learning to do something and cannot do it well yet. *This is the sort of thing that beginners write.*

beginning /bɪˈgɪnɪŋ/, **beginnings.** 1 COUNT N The **beginning** or the **beginnings** of something is the first part of it. *I say this at the beginning of my book... ...the beginnings of a new relationship.* 2 SING N The **beginning** of a period of time is when it starts. *I came back at the beginning of the term... The number had increased by the beginning of the following year.*

begrudge /bɪ1grʌdʒ/, **begrudges, begrudging, begrudged.** VB WITH OBJ AND OBJ If you say that you do not **begrudge** someone something, you mean that you do not feel angry, upset, or jealous that they have got it. *I do not begrudge her that happiness.*

beguiling /bɪ1gaɪlɪŋ/. ADJ Something that is **beguiling** seems attractive, but may be dangerous or harmful. *...this beguiling idea.*

begun /bɪ1gʌn/. **Begun** is the past participle of **begin.**

behalf /bɪ1hɑ:f/. PHRASE If someone does something **on** your **behalf,** they do it as your representative. *Wilkins spoke on behalf of the Labour Party.*

behave /bɪ1heɪv/, **behaves, behaving, behaved.** 1 VB WITH ADJUNCT If you **behave** in a particular way, you do things in that way. *In New York, he had behaved in a very strange way... You are behaving like a silly child.* 2 VB OR REFL VB If you **behave** yourself, you act in the way that people think is correct and proper. *Their startled boyfriends got warnings to behave... He's old enough to behave himself.*

behaviour /bɪ1heɪvjə/; spelled **behavior** in American English. 1 UNCOUNT N A person's **behaviour** is the way they behave. *I had been puzzled by his behaviour... ...the obstinate behaviour of a small child.* 2 UNCOUNT N The **behaviour** of something is the way in which it acts, functions, or changes. *...the behaviour of the metal as we heat it.*

behead /bɪ1hɛd/, **beheads, beheading, beheaded.** VB WITH OBJ If someone **is beheaded,** their head is cut off.

beheld /bɪ1hɛld/. **Beheld** is the past tense and past participle of **behold.**

behind /bɪ1haɪnd/, **behinds.** 1 PREP OR ADV If you are **behind** a thing or person, you are facing the back of that thing or person. *There were two boys sitting behind me... Joe was limping along behind his wife... He followed a few paces behind.* 2 ADV If you stay **behind,** you remain in a place after other people have gone. 3 ADV If you leave something **behind,** you do not take it with you when you go. 4 ADV OR PREP When someone or something is **behind,** they are delayed or are making less progress than other people think they should. *I got more and more behind... The bus was badly behind schedule.* 5 PREP OR ADV If an experience is **behind** you, it is finished. *...now that the war is behind us... We must leave adolescence behind and grow up.* 6 PREP The reason or person **behind** something caused that thing or is responsible for it. *These were the reasons behind Macleod's statement... ...the man behind the modernizing of the station.* 7 PREP If you are **behind** someone, you support them. *The country was behind the President.* 8 COUNT N Your **behind** is the part of your body that you sit on.

behold /bɪ1həʊld/, **beholds, beholding, beheld** /bɪ1hɛld/. VB WITH OBJ If you **behold** someone or something, you look at them; a literary use. *She was a terrible sight to behold.*

beholder /bɪhəʊldə/, **beholders.** COUNT N The **beholder** of something is the person looking at it; an old-fashioned use. *The picture was very pleasing to beholders.*

beige /beɪʒ/. ADJ Something that is **beige** is pale brown.

being /bi:ɪŋ/, **beings.** 1 **Being** is the present participle of **be.** 2 PHRASE Something that is **in being** exists. *...laws already in being... The Polytechnic came into being in 1971.* 3 COUNT N You can refer to any real or imaginary creature as a **being;** a literary use. *...beings from outer space.* ● See also **human being.**

belated /bɪ1leɪtɪ2d/. ATTRIB ADJ A **belated** action happens later than it should have done; a formal use. *Please accept my belated thanks for your kind gift.* ♦ **belatedly** ADV *Bill belatedly agreed to call in the police.*

belch /bɛltʃ/, **belches, belching, belched.** VB If someone **belches,** they make a sudden noise in their throat because air has risen up from their stomach. *The baby drank his milk and belched.* Also COUNT N *'Amazing,' said Brody, stifling a belch.*

beleaguered /bɪ1li:gəd/. ATTRIB ADJ A **beleaguered** person is experiencing a lot of difficulties, problems, or criticism; a formal use. *The beleaguered prime minister explained this to an angry crowd.*

belfry /bɛlfri1/, **belfries.** COUNT N The **belfry** of a church is the top part of the tower, where the bells are.

belie /bɪ1laɪ/, **belies, belying, belied.** 1 VB WITH OBJ If one thing **belies** another, it makes the other thing seem very surprising. *The young face belied the grey hair above it.* 2 VB WITH OBJ You can also say that something **belies** another when it proves that the other thing is not genuine or true. *Their social attitudes belie their words.*

belief /bɪ1li:f/, **beliefs.** COUNT N OR UNCOUNT N **Belief** is a feeling of certainty that something exists, is true, or is good. *...belief in God... It is my belief that more people could have been helped... ...religious beliefs.*

believable /bɪ1li:vəbə0l/. ADJ Something that is **believable** makes you think that it could be true or real. *...the only believable explanation for the disappearance of the plane.*

believe /bɪ1li:v/, **believes, believing, believed.** 1 REPORT VB OR VB WITH OBJ If you **believe** that something is true, you think that it is true. *It is believed that two prisoners have escaped... I couldn't believe what I had heard... We believed him dead... I believed him to be right.* 2 VB WITH OBJ If you **believe** someone, you accept that they are telling the truth. *I didn't believe him... Don't believe a word he says.* 3 VB WITH 'in' If you **believe** in things such as God, fairies, or miracles, you are sure that they exist or happen. *I don't believe in ghosts.* 4 VB WITH 'in' If you **believe** in something, you are in favour of it because you think it is good or right. *...all those who believe in democracy... He did not believe in educating women.*

believer /bɪ1li:və/, **believers.** 1 COUNT N WITH 'in' If you are a **believer** in something, you think that it is good or right. *...the true believer in democracy... Bob is a great believer in jogging.* 2 COUNT N A **believer** is someone who is sure that their religion is true. *Of course you, as a believer, try to convert others?*

belittle /bɪ1lɪtə0l/, **belittles, belittling, belittled.** VB WITH OBJ If you **belittle** someone or something, you make them seem unimportant or not very good. *The press gave the election no publicity and belittled its significance... Don't think I'm trying to belittle Turner. He was a genius.*

bell /bɛl/, **bells.** 1 COUNT N A **bell** is a device that makes a ringing sound which is used to attract people's attention. *He approached the front door and rang the bell.* 2 COUNT N A **bell** is also a hollow metal object shaped like a cup which has a piece hanging inside it that hits the sides and makes a sound. *In the distance a church bell was ringing.* 3 PHRASE If you say that something **rings a bell,** you mean that it reminds you of something else, but you cannot remember exactly what; an informal use. *The name rings a bell.*

belligerent /bɪ2lɪdʒə0rənt/. ADJ **Belligerent** people are eager to defend themselves and their opinions in a fairly aggressive way. *Not even the belligerent Leggett was willing to face that mob.* ♦ **belligerently** ADV *Mr Kidley looked at him belligerently.*

bellow /bɛləʊ/, **bellows, bellowing, bellowed.** 1 VB WITH OR WITHOUT OBJ If someone **bellows,** they shout in a loud, deep voice. *The president bellowed with laughter... 'Thirty-two!' bellowed Mrs Pringle.* Also COUNT N *He raised his voice to a bellow.* 2 VB When an animal **bellows,** it makes a loud, deep sound. *The cow charged across the farmyard with the bull bellowing after it.* 3 COUNT N A **bellows** is a device used for blowing air into a fire in order to make it burn more fiercely. The plural is also 'bellows'.

belly /bɛli1/, **bellies.** 1 COUNT N Your **belly** is your stomach; a British use. 2 COUNT N The **belly** of an animal is the lower part of its body. *...lions creeping on their bellies.*

belong /bɪ1lɒŋ/, **belongs, belonging, belonged.** 1 VB WITH PREP 'to' If something **belongs** to you, you own it or it is yours. *The land belongs to a big family... ...a myth belonging to some tribe in Western Australia.* 2 VB WITH PREP 'to' If someone or something **belongs** to a particular group, they are a member of that group. *She belongs to the Labour Party.* 3 VB If a person or thing **belongs** in a particular place, that is where they should be. *The plates don't belong in that cupboard.*

belongings /bɪ1lɒŋɪŋz/. PLURAL N Your **belongings** are the things that you own and that you have with you or have in your house. *She was tidying up her belongings.*

beloved /bɪ1lʌvɪ2d/; also pronounced /bɪ1lʌvd/ when used after a noun or after the verb 'be'. ADJ A **beloved** person, thing, or place is one that you feel great affection for. *He withdrew to his beloved Kent... ...Marilyn Monroe, beloved of men in their millions.*

below /bɪ1ləʊ/. 1 PREP OR ADV If something is **below** something else, it is in a lower position. *The sun had just sunk below the horizon... Their office is on the floor below... The fish attacked from below.* 2 PREP If something is **below** a particular amount, rate, or level, it is less than that amount, rate, or level. *The temperature was below freezing... Their reading ability is below average.* 3 ADV You use **below** in a piece of writing to refer to something that is mentioned later. *Get legal advice on how to do this (see below).*

belt /bɛlt/, **belts, belting, belted.** 1 COUNT N A **belt** is a strip of leather or cloth that you fasten round your waist. ● See also **safety belt, seat-belt.** 2 COUNT N A **belt** is also a circular strip of rubber used in machines to drive moving parts or to move objects along. *A belt snapped in the vacuum cleaner.* ● See also **conveyor belt.** 3 COUNT N WITH SUPP A **belt** of land or sea is a long, narrow area of it that has some special feature. *...the cotton belt of the USA.* 4 VB WITH OBJ If someone **belts** you, they hit you very hard; an informal use. 5 VB WITH ADJUNCT If you **belt** somewhere, you move or travel there very fast; an informal use. *I came belting out of the woods.*

bemoan /bɪ1məʊn/, **bemoans, bemoaning, bemoaned.** VB WITH OBJ If you **bemoan** something, you express sorrow or dissatisfaction about it; a formal use. *The farmer bemoaned his loss.*

bemused /bɪ1mju:zd/. ADJ If you are **bemused,** you are slightly puzzled or confused.

bench /bɛntʃ/, **benches.** 1 COUNT N A **bench** is a long seat of wood or metal. 2 COUNT N A **bench** is also a long, narrow table in a factory, laboratory, or workshop.

bend /bɛnd/, **bends, bending, bent** /bɛnt/. 1 VB When someone **bends** or **bends** down, they move the top part of their body towards the ground. *...bending over the basin... He bent down and undid his shoelaces.* ♦ **bent** PRED ADJ *Dan is bent over the fireplace.* 2 ERG VB When you **bend** a part of your body such as your arm or leg, you change its position so that it is no longer straight. *Bend the arm at the elbow.* ♦ **bent** ADJ *Keep your knees bent.* 3 ERG VB When you **bend** something that is flat or straight, you use force to make it curved or angular. *...pliers for bending wire.* ♦ **bent** ADJ *...two bent pipes.* 4 COUNT N A **bend** in a road, river, or pipe is a curved part of it. *I was out of sight around the next bend.* 5 See also **bent.**

PHRASES ● If you say that someone or something is driving you **round the bend,** you mean that they are annoying you or upsetting you very much; an informal use. ● If you **bend the rules,** you interpret them in a way that allows you to do something that they really forbid. ● **to bend double:** see **double.**

beneath /bɪ1ni:θ/. 1 PREP Something that is **beneath** another thing is under the other thing. *She concealed the bottle beneath her mattress.* 2 PREP If you talk about what is **beneath** the surface of something, you are talking about the aspects of it which are hidden or not obvious. *Beneath the veneer of civilization, he was a very vulgar man.*

benefactor /bɛnɪ2fæktə/, **benefactors.** COUNT N Your **benefactor** is a person who helps you by giving you money.

beneficial /bɛnɪ1fɪʃə0l/. ADJ Something that is **beneficial** helps people or improves their lives. *Such a system will be beneficial to society.*

beneficiary /bɛnɪ1fɪʃə0ri1/, **beneficiaries.** COUNT N A **beneficiary** of something is a person who receives it or is helped by it. *Who are the main beneficiaries of the changes?*

benefit /bɛnɪ1fɪt/, **benefits, benefiting, benefited.** 1 ERG VB If something **benefits** you or if you **benefit** from it, it helps you or improves your life. *...a medical service which will benefit rich and poor... The firm benefited from his ingenuity.* 2 COUNT N The **benefits** of something are the advantages that it brings to people. *...the benefits of modern technology.* 3 UNCOUNT N **Benefit** is money given by the government to people who are poor, ill, or unemployed. *You are entitled to child benefit.*

PHRASES ● If something is **to your benefit** or is **of benefit** to you, it helps you or improves your life. *This will be of benefit to the country as a whole.* ● If you **have the benefit of** something, it gives you an advantage. *I had the benefit of a good education.* ● If you do something **for the benefit of** someone, you do it specially for them. *He smiled for the benefit of the reporters.* ● If you **give** someone **the benefit of the doubt,** you accept what they say as true, because you cannot prove that it is not true.

benevolent /bɪ1nɛvələnt/. ADJ A **benevolent** person is kind, helpful, and tolerant. *My aunt and uncle were looking benevolent and prepared to forgive me.* ♦ **benevolently** ADV *He smiled benevolently.* ♦ **benevolence** /bɪ1nɛvələns/ UNCOUNT N *...the benevolence of the Vicar's smile.*

benign /bɪ1naɪn/. 1 ADJ Someone who is **benign** is kind, gentle, and harmless. *They are among the most benign people on earth... His face was calm and benign.* ♦ **benignly** ADV *He smiled benignly at his guest.* 2 ADJ A **benign** disease or substance will not cause death or serious harm; a technical use. *...women with benign breast disease.*

bent /bɛnt/. 1 **Bent** is the past tense and past participle of **bend.** 2 ADJ If a person or thing is **bent,** they are curved and no longer have their normal shape. *...bent saucepans... He was bent with arthritis.* 3 PRED ADJ WITH 'on' OR 'upon' If you are **bent** on doing something, you are determined to do it. *They are bent on improving existing weapon systems.* 4 SING N WITH SUPP If you have a **bent** for something, you have a natural interest in it or a natural ability to do it. *...a boy with a mechanical bent.*

bequeath /biˈkwiːð/, **bequeaths, bequeathing, bequeathed.** VB WITH OBJ AND OBJ OR PREP 'to' If you **bequeath** money or property to someone, you legally state that they should have it when you die; a formal use. *...the forty million dollars he bequeathed Phoebe... He bequeathed his collection to the nation.*

bequest /biˈkwest/, **bequests.** COUNT N A **bequest** is money or property which you legally leave to someone when you die; a formal use. *Except for a few small bequests to relatives, he left all his property to charity.*

bereaved /biˈriːvd/. ADJ A **bereaved** person is one who had a relative or close friend who has recently died; a formal use. ♦ **bereavement** /biˈriːvməᵊnt/ UNCOUNT N OR COUNT N *...bereavement in old age.*

bereft /bɪreft/. PRED ADJ WITH 'of' If a person or thing is **bereft** of something, they no longer have it; a literary use. *Her cheeks were bereft of colour... ...crumbling slums bereft of basic amenities.*

beret /bereɪ/, **berets.** COUNT N A **beret** is a circular, flat hat that is made of soft material and has no brim.

berry /beriˈ/, **berries.** COUNT N A **berry** is a small, round fruit that grows on a bush or a tree.

berserk /bəzɜːk, -sɜːk/. PRED ADJ If someone goes **berserk,** they lose control of themselves and become very violent. *One night she went berserk and wrecked her room.*

berth /bɜːθ/, **berths.** 1 PHRASE If you **give** someone or something **a wide berth,** you avoid them because they are unpleasant or dangerous. 2 COUNT N A **berth** is a space in a harbour where a ship stays for a period of time. 3 COUNT N A **berth** is also a bed in a boat, train, or caravan.

beseech /biˈsiːtʃ/, **beseeches, beseeching, beseeched** or **besought** /biˈsɔːt/. VB WITH OBJ If you **beseech** someone to do something, you ask them very insistently and desperately; a literary use. *I beseech you to tell me.* ♦ **beseeching** ADJ *She was staring at me with great beseeching eyes.* ♦ **beseechingly** ADV *Larsen looked beseechingly at Rudolph.*

beset /biˈset/, **besets, besetting. Beset** is used in the present tense and is the past tense and past participle. VB WITH OBJ If someone or something **is beset** by problems or fears, they have many of them; a formal use. *She had been beset by doubts... The policy is beset with problems.*

beside /biˈsaɪd/. 1 PREP Something that is **beside** something else is at the side of it or next to it. *I sat down beside my wife.* 2 See also **besides.**

PHRASES • If you are **beside yourself** with anger or excitement, you are extremely angry or excited. • **beside the point:** see **point.**

besides /biˈsaɪdz/. The form **beside** can be used for meaning 1. 1 PREP OR ADV **Besides** or **beside** something means in addition to it. *What languages do you know besides English?... He needed so much else besides... Thomas was the only blond in the family, beside the mother.* 2 SENTENCE ADV You use **besides** to make an additional point or give an additional reason. *Would these figures prove anything? And besides, who keeps such statistics?*

besiege /biˈsiːdʒ/, **besieges, besieging, besieged.** 1 VB WITH OBJ If you **are besieged** by people, many people want something from you and continually bother you. *I am besieged with visitors from abroad.* 2 VB WITH OBJ If soldiers **besiege** a place, they surround it and wait for the people in it to surrender.

besought /biˈsɔːt/. **Besought** is a past tense and past participle of **beseech.**

best /best/. 1 ADJ **Best** is the superlative of **good.** *That was one of the best films I've seen... ...my best friend... It's best to be as clear as possible... I want her to have the very best.* 2 ADV **Best** is also the superlative of **well.** *I think mine would suit her best.* 3 SING N Your **best** is the greatest effort or the highest achievement that you are capable of. *They are trying their best to discourage them.* 4 ADV OR ADJ If you like something **best** or like it the **best,** you prefer it. *Which did you like best—the Vivaldi or the Schumann?* 5 You use **best** to form the superlative of compound adjectives beginning with 'good' and 'well'. *...the best-looking women... ...the best-known author of books for children.* 6 See also **second-best.**

PHRASES • You use **at best** to indicate that even if you describe something as favourably as possible, it is still not very good. • If you **make the best of** an unsatisfactory situation, you accept it and try to be cheerful about it. *There is nowhere else to go, so make the best of it.* • **to know best:** see **know.** • **the best part of** something: see **part.** • **the best of both worlds:** see **world.**

bestial /bestɪəl/. ADJ **Bestial** behaviour is very unpleasant or disgusting; a literary use.

bestow /biˈstəʊ/, **bestows, bestowing, bestowed.** VB WITH OBJ If you **bestow** something on someone, you give it to them; a formal use. *The Duke bestowed this property on him... ...the attention bestowed upon her son.*

best-seller, best-sellers. COUNT N A **best-seller** is a book of which a very large number of copies have been sold.

bet /bet/, **bets, betting. Bet** is used in the present tense of the verb, and is the past tense and past participle. 1 VB WITH OR WITHOUT OBJ If you **bet** on a future event, you make an agreement with someone which means that you receive money if you are right about what happens, and lose money if you are wrong. *He bet me a hundred pounds that I wouldn't get through.* Also COUNT N *I didn't put a bet on.* ♦ **betting** UNCOUNT N *They spend their money on betting.* 2 PHRASE You say **'You bet'** as an emphatic way of saying 'yes' or of emphasizing a statement; an informal use. *'Are you coming?'—'You bet!'... You bet I'm getting out.*

betray /biˈtreɪ/, **betrays, betraying, betrayed.** 1 VB WITH OBJ If you **betray** someone who thinks you support or love them, you do something which harms them, often by helping their enemies or opponents. *His best friend betrayed him.* 2 VB WITH OBJ If you **betray** a secret, you tell it to people who you should not tell it to. 3 VB WITH OBJ If you **betray** your feelings or thoughts, you show them without intending to. *People learned never to betray their anger.*

betrayal /biˈtreɪəᵊl/. COUNT N OR UNCOUNT N A **betrayal** is an action that betrays someone or something. *...the betrayal of socialist principles.*

betrothed /biˈtrəʊðd/. ADJ If you are **betrothed** to someone, you are engaged to be married to them; an old-fashioned use.

better /betə/. 1 ADJ **Better** is the comparative of **good.** *The results were better than expected... Milk is much better for you than lemonade.* 2 ADV **Better** is also the comparative of **well.** *Some people can ski better than others.* 3 ADV If you like one thing **better** than another, you like it more. *I love this place better than anywhere else.* 4 PRED ADJ If you are **better** after an illness or injury, you are less ill. *Her cold was better.* 5 You use **better** to form the comparative of compound adjectives beginning with 'good' or 'well.' *My husband was better-looking than that... She's much better known in Europe.*

PHRASES • If you say that someone **had better** do something, you mean that they ought to do it. *I'd better go.* • If someone **is better off,** they are in a pleasanter situation than before. *They are much better off than they were two years ago... She will be better off in hospital.* • If something changes **for the better,** it improves. *The weather had changed for the better.* • If something **gets the better of** you, you are unable to resist it. *My curiosity got the better of me.* • **to know better:** see **know.** • **the better part of:** see **part.** • **to think better of it:** see **think.**

between /biˈtwiːn/. 1 PREP OR ADV If something is **between** two things or is **in between** them, it has one of the things on one side of it and the other thing on the other side. *She put the cigarette between her lips and lit it... ...Penn Close, Court Road, and all the little side streets in between.* 2 PREP If people or things are moving **between** two places, they are moving regularly from one place to the other and back again. *I have spent a lifetime commuting between Britain and the United States.* 3 PREP A relationship, discussion, or difference **between** two people, groups, or things is one that involves them both or relates to them both. *...a clash between the two gangs... I asked whether there was much difference between British and European law.* 4 PREP If people have a particular amount of something **between** them, this is the total amount that they have. *They have both been married before and have five children between them.* 5 PREP When something is divided or shared **between** people, they each have a share of it. *The land was divided equally between them.* 6 PREP If something is **between** or **in between** two amounts or ages, it is greater or older than the first one and smaller or younger than the second one. *...at temperatures between 36 and 39°C.* 7 PREP If something stands **between** you and what you want, it prevents you from having it. *These men stand between you and the top jobs.* 8 PREP If something happens **between** or **in between** two times or events, it happens after the first time or event and before the second one. *The house was built between 1840 and 1852... Between sessions I spent my time with my husband.* 9 PREP If you must choose **between** two things, you must choose one thing or the other one. *The choice is between defeat or survival.*

beverage /bevəᵊrɪdʒ/, **beverages.** COUNT N A **beverage** is a drink; a formal use.

bevy /beviˈ/. SING N A **bevy** of people or things is a group of them. *...a bevy of village girls.*

beware /biˈweə/. If you tell someone to **beware** of a person or thing, you are warning them that the person or thing may harm them. *Beware of the dog!... I would beware of companies which depend on one product only.*

bewildered /biˈwɪldəd/. ADJ If you are **bewildered,** you are very confused and cannot understand something or decide what to do. *His wife watched him, bewildered... I was bewildered by the volume of noise.*

bewildering /biˈwɪldəᵊrɪŋ/. ADJ Something that is **bewildering** is confusing and difficult to understand or make a decision about. *There is a bewildering variety of activities... ...a bewildering and upsetting experience.* ♦ **bewilderment** /biˈwɪldəməᵊnt/ UNCOUNT N *To my complete bewilderment, she rang and offered to buy the place.*

bewitch /biˈwɪtʃ/, **bewitches, bewitching, bewitched.** VB WITH OBJ If someone or something **bewitches** you, you find them so attractive that you cannot think about anything else. *...bewitching the audience with her singing.* ♦ **bewitching** ADJ *...a bewitching smile.*

beyond /biˈjɒnd/. 1 PREP OR ADV If something is **beyond** a place, it is on the other side of it. *...a farm beyond Barnham... He indicated the street beyond.* 2 PREP To extend, continue, or progress **beyond** a particular thing or point means to extend or continue further than that thing or point. *Few children remain in the school beyond the age of 16.* 3 PREP If someone or something is **beyond** understanding, control, or help, they have become impossible to understand, control, or help. *The situation has changed beyond recognition.* 4 PREP If you say that something is **beyond** you, you mean that you cannot understand it. *How he managed to find us is beyond me.*

bias /baɪəs/, **biases.** UNCOUNT N OR COUNT N Someone who shows **bias** is unfair in their judgements or decisions, because they allow themselves to be influenced by their own opinions, rather than considering the facts. *You're accusing me of bias in my marking... There's an intense bias against women.*

biased /baɪəst/. 1 PRED ADJ Someone or something that is **biased** towards one thing is more concerned with it than with other things. *The university is biased towards the sciences.* 2 ADJ If someone is **biased,** they show favouritism towards a particular person or group, and so do not judge things fairly. *I am biased in favour of Eisenhower.*

bib /bɪb/, **bibs.** COUNT N A **bib** is a piece of cloth or plastic worn by very young children while they are eating, to protect their clothes.

bible /baɪbəᵊl/, **bibles.** 1 PROPER N The **Bible** is the sacred book of the Christian religion. *...a new translation of the Bible.* ♦ **biblical** /bɪblɪkəᵊl/ ATTRIB ADJ *...the biblical account of creation.* 2 COUNT N A **bible** is a copy of the Bible.

bibliography /bɪbliˈɒgrəfiˈ/, **bibliographies.** 1 COUNT N A **bibliography** is a list of books on a particular subject. 2 COUNT N A **bibliography** is also a list of the books and articles referred to in a particular book.

biceps /baɪseps/. **Biceps** is the singular and plural. COUNT N Your **biceps** are the large muscles at the front of the upper part of your arms.

bicker /bɪkə/, **bickers, bickering, bickered.** VB When people **bicker,** they argue or quarrel about unimportant things. ♦ **bickering** UNCOUNT N *...after months of bickering and confusion.*

bicycle /baɪsɪkəᵊl/, **bicycles.** COUNT N A **bicycle** is a vehicle with two wheels which you ride by sitting on it and pushing two pedals with your feet.

bid /bɪd/, **bids, bidding, bade** /bæd, beɪd/, **bidden. Bid** is used in the present tense of all meanings of the verb, and is the past tense and past participle in meaning 3. 1 COUNT N A **bid** is an attempt to obtain or do something. *He made a bid for power... Brandt failed in a bid to see Reagan.* 2 COUNT N A **bid** is also an offer to pay a particular amount of money to buy something. *...bids for other oil companies.* 3 VB WITH OR WITHOUT OBJ If you **bid** for something that is being sold, you offer to pay a particular amount of money for it. *He bid a quarter of a million pounds for the portrait.* 4 VB WITH OBJ AND OBJ OR PREP 'to' If you **bid** someone good morning, you say hello to them; a formal use. *I bid you good night, young man.* 5 VB WITH OBJ AND INF If you **bid** someone do something, you ask or invite them to do it; a literary use.

bidder /bɪdə/. PHRASE If you sell something to the **highest bidder,** you sell it to the person who offers most money for it.

bide /baɪd/, **bides, biding, bided.** PHRASE If you **bide** your **time,** you wait for a good opportunity before doing something. *He never showed this anger but bided his time.*

bidet /biːdeɪ/, **bidets.** COUNT N A **bidet** is a low basin in a bathroom which you wash your bottom in.

big /bɪg/, **bigger, biggest.** 1 ADJ Something that is **big** is large in size or great in degree, extent, or importance. *He was holding a big black umbrella... The* *biggest problem at the moment is unemployment... You're making a big mistake.* used in questions and statements about size. *'It's a shark.'—'How big?'* **2** ATTRIB ADJ You can refer to your older brother or sister as your **big** brother or sister; an informal use.

bigot /bɪgət/, **bigots.** COUNT N A **bigot** is someone who is bigoted.

bigoted /bɪgətɪ[2]d/. ADJ Someone who is **bigoted** has strong and often unreasonable opinions and will not change them, even when they are proved to be wrong. *He was a bigoted, narrow-minded fanatic.*

bigotry /bɪgətri[1]/. UNCOUNT N **Bigotry** is the possession or expression of strong and often unreasonable opinions. *...campaigns against bigotry and racism.*

bike /baɪk/, **bikes.** COUNT N A **bike** is a bicycle or a motorcycle; an informal use.

bikini /bɪkiːni[1]/, **bikinis.** COUNT N A **bikini** is a two-piece swimming costume worn by women.

bile /baɪl/. UNCOUNT N **Bile** is a liquid produced by your liver which helps you to digest fat.

bilingual /baɪlɪŋgwəl/. **1** ADJ **Bilingual** means involving or using two languages. *...bilingual dictionaries... ...bilingual street signs.* **2** ADJ Someone who is **bilingual** can speak two languages fluently.

bilious /bɪlɪəs/. **1** ADJ **Bilious** means unpleasant and rather disgusting. **2** ADJ If you feel **bilious,** you feel sick and have a headache. *...bilious attacks.*

bill /bɪl/, **bills, billing, billed. 1** COUNT N A **bill** is a written statement of money that you owe for goods or services. *...an enormous electricity bill.* **2** COUNT N A **bill** is also a piece of paper money; an American use. *...a dollar bill.* **3** COUNT N In parliament, a **bill** is a formal statement of a proposed new law that is discussed and then voted on. *The Bill was defeated by 238 votes to 145.* **4** SING N The **bill** of a show or concert is the people who are going to appear in it, or the items of entertainment that a show or concert consists of. *There were some famous names on the bill... The Chamber Opera is offering a double bill of Mozart and Haydn.* **5** VB WITH OBJ If a performer or show **is billed** as a particular thing, they are advertised as that thing. *...what was being billed as the greatest show on earth.* **6** COUNT N A bird's **bill** is its beak.

billboard /bɪlbɔːd/, **billboards.** COUNT N A **billboard** is a very large board on which posters are displayed.

billiards /bɪliədz/. The form **billiard** is used in front of another noun. UNCOUNT N **Billiards** is a game played on a large table, in which you use a long stick called a cue to hit balls against each other or into pockets around the sides of the table. *...a game of billiards... ...a billiard table.*

billion /bɪljən/, **billions. 1** A **billion** is a thousand million. **2** COUNT N You can also use **billions** and **billion** to mean an extremely large amount. *...billions of tons of ice... They printed the papers off by the billion.*

billow /bɪləʊ/, **billows, billowing, billowed. 1** VB When something made of cloth **billows,** it swells out and flaps slowly in the wind. **2** VB When smoke or cloud **billows,** it moves slowly upwards or across the sky. *Clouds of white dust billowed out.*

bin /bɪn/, **bins.** COUNT N A **bin** is a container that you use to put rubbish in, or to store things in. *She threw both letters in the bin.*

binary /baɪnə[0]ri[1]/. ATTRIB ADJ The **binary** system expresses numbers using only the two digits 0 and 1. It is used especially in computing.

bind /baɪnd/, **binds, binding, bound** /baʊnd/. **1** VB WITH OBJ If you **bind** something, you tie string or rope tightly round it so that it is held firmly. *His hands were bound behind the post.* **2** VB WITH OBJ If a duty or legal order **binds** you to a course of action, it forces you to do it. *This oath binds you to secrecy.* **3** VB WITH OBJ When a book **is bound,** the pages are joined together and the cover is put on. **4** SING N If something is a **bind,** it is unpleasant and boring to do; an informal use. *It's a terrible bind to have to cook your own meals.* **5** See also **binding, bound.**

binder /baɪndə/, **binders.** COUNT N A **binder** is a hard cover with metal rings inside, which is used to hold loose pieces of paper.

binding /baɪndɪŋ/, **bindings. 1** ADJ If a promise or agreement is **binding,** it must be obeyed or carried out. *...a Spanish law that is still binding in California.* **2** COUNT N OR UNCOUNT N The **binding** of a book is its cover. *...books in ugly economy bindings... ...durable leather binding.*

binge /bɪndʒ/, **binges.** COUNT N If you go on a **binge,** you go somewhere and drink a lot of alcohol; an informal use.

bingo /bɪŋgəʊ/. UNCOUNT N **Bingo** is a game in which each player has a card with numbers on. Someone calls out numbers and if you are the first person to have all your numbers called out, you win the game.

binoculars /bɪ[5]nɒkjə[4]ləz/. PLURAL N **Binoculars** consist of two small telescopes joined together side by side, which you look through in order to see things that are a long way away.

biochemistry /baɪə[6]kɛmɪstri[1]/. UNCOUNT N **Biochemistry** is the study of the chemistry of living things.

biographer /baɪɒgrəfə/, **biographers.** COUNT N Someone's **biographer** is a person who writes an account of their life.

biographical /baɪə[6]græfɪkə[0]l/. ADJ You use **biographical** to describe something which gives information about a person's life. *...a brief biographical sketch.*

biography /baɪɒgrəfi[1]/, **biographies.** COUNT N A **biography** of a person is an account of their life, written by someone else. *...a biography of Dylan Thomas.*

biological /baɪəlɒdʒɪkə[0]l/. **1** ADJ A **biological** process, system, or product is connected with or produced by natural processes in plants, animals, and other living things. *...the effect of heat on biological activity.* ♦ **biologically** ADV *These beings were biologically different from man.* **2** ATTRIB ADJ **Biological** studies and discoveries are connected with research in biology. *...recent biological breakthroughs.* **3** ATTRIB ADJ **Biological** weapons and **biological** warfare involve the use of organisms which damage living things. *...the stockpiling of biological weapons.*

biology /baɪɒlədʒɪ/. UNCOUNT N **Biology** is the science which is concerned with the study of living things. ♦ **biologist** /baɪɒlədʒɪst/ COUNT N *This has puzzled biologists for a long time.*

birch /bɜːtʃ/, **birches. 1** COUNT N OR UNCOUNT N A **birch** or a **birch tree** is a tall tree with thin branches. **2** SING N The **birch** is a punishment in which someone is hit with a wooden cane.

bird /bɜːd/, **birds.** COUNT N A **bird** is a creature with feathers and wings. Most birds can fly.

PHRASES • If you say that **a bird in the hand is worth two in the bush,** you mean that it is better to keep what you already have than to risk losing it by trying to achieve something else. • If you say that something will **kill two birds with one stone,** you mean that two things are achieved rather than just one.

Biro /baɪrəʊ/, **Biros.** COUNT N A **Biro** is a ballpoint; a trademark.

birth /bɜːθ/, **births. 1** UNCOUNT N OR COUNT N When a baby is born, you refer to this event as its **birth.** *...a girl deaf from birth... ...the birth of her first child.* **2** SING N WITH SUPP You can refer to the beginning or origin of something as its **birth.** *...the birth of television.*

PHRASES • When a woman **gives birth,** she produces a baby from her body. *Betta gave birth to our third child.* • You use **by birth** after your nationality in order to indicate where you or your parents were born. *Dr Cort's father is a Russian by birth.* • See also **date of birth.**

birth control. UNCOUNT N **Birth control** is the same as contraception.

birthday /bɜːθdeɪ/, **birthdays.** COUNT N Your **birthday** is the anniversary of the date on which you were born. *Happy birthday!*

birthplace /bɜːθpleɪs/, **birthplaces. 1** COUNT N WITH POSS Your **birthplace** is the place where you were born. **2** SING N WITH POSS The **birthplace** of something is the place where it began or originated. *...the birthplace of the Renaissance.*

birth rate, birth rates. COUNT N The **birth rate** in a place is the number of babies born there for every 1000 people during a particular period of time.

biscuit /bɪskɪt/, **biscuits.** COUNT N A **biscuit** is a small, flat cake that is crisp and usually sweet; a British use.

bisect /baɪsɛkt/, **bisects, bisecting, bisected.** VB WITH OBJ If something **bisects** an area or line, it divides the area or line in half. *The main north-south road bisects the town.*

bishop /bɪʃəp/, **bishops. 1** COUNT N A **bishop** is a clergyman of high rank, especially in the Roman Catholic, Anglican, and Orthodox churches. **2** COUNT N In chess, a **bishop** is a piece which is moved diagonally across the board.

bistro /biːstrəʊ/, **bistros.** COUNT N A **bistro** is a small restaurant or bar.

bit /bɪt/, **bits. 1** COUNT N A **bit** of something is a small amount or piece of it; an informal use. *...a little bit of cheese... I really enjoyed your letter, especially the bits about Dr O'Shea.* **2** COUNT N You also use **bit** to refer to an item or thing of a particular kind; an informal use. *...a bit of furniture.* **3** COUNT N In computing, a **bit** is the smallest unit of information that is held in a computer's memory. **4 Bit** is also the past tense of **bite.**

PHRASES • **A bit** means to a small extent or degree; an informal use. *He was a bit deaf.* • You can use **a bit of** to make a statement less extreme. For example, the statement 'It's a bit of a nuisance' is less extreme than 'It's a nuisance'. • You can say that someone's behaviour is **a bit much** when you are annoyed about it; an informal use. *It's asking a bit much to expect a lift.* • You say that something is **every bit as** good, interesting, or worthwhile as something else to emphasize that they are just as good or interesting as each other. *She wanted to prove to them that she was every bit as clever as they were.* • If you do something **for a bit,** you do it for a short period of time; an informal use. *Why can't we stay here for a bit?* • You use **not a bit** when you want to make a strong negative statement; an informal use. *It was all very clean and tidy, not a bit like his back garden.* • **Quite a bit** of something is quite a lot of it; an informal use. *...a rich Irishman who's made quite a bit of money.*

bitch /bɪtʃ/, **bitches, bitching, bitched. 1** COUNT N If you call a woman a **bitch,** you mean that she behaves in a very unpleasant way; a rude and offensive use. **2** VB If someone **bitches,** they complain about something in a nasty way; an informal use. *You haven't done a thing except bitch ever since we got here.* **3** COUNT N A **bitch** is also a female dog.

bite /baɪt/, **bites, biting, bit** /bɪt/, **bitten** /bɪtə[0]n/. **1** VB WITH OBJ OR ADJUNCT When a person or animal **bites** something, they use their teeth to cut into it or through it. *My dog bit me... She bit into her rock cake.* Also COUNT N *Madeleine took a bite. 'It's delicious.'* **2** VB WITH OBJ When an insect or a snake **bites** you, it pierces your skin and causes an area of your skin to itch or be painful. Also COUNT N *My hands are covered with mosquito bites.* **3** VB When an action or policy begins to **bite,** it begins to have a significant or harmful effect. *The sanctions are beginning to bite.* **4** SING N If you have a **bite** to eat, you have a small meal; an informal use.

biting /baɪtɪŋ/. **1** ADJ A **biting** wind is extremely cold. **2** ADJ **Biting** speech or writing is sharp and clever in a way that makes people feel uncomfortable. *...a writer with a biting wit.*

bitten /bɪtə[0]n/. **Bitten** is the past participle of **bite.**

bitter /bɪtə/, **bitterest; bitters. 1** ADJ If someone is **bitter,** they feel angry and resentful. *He was a jealous, slightly bitter man.* ♦ **bitterly** ADV *'I'm glad somebody's happy,' he said bitterly.* ♦ **bitterness** UNCOUNT N *He remembers with bitterness how his father was cheated.* **2** ATTRIB ADJ If you have a **bitter** disappointment or experience, you feel angry or unhappy about it. *I have had long and bitter experience of dealing with people like that.* **3** ADJ In a **bitter** argument, war, or struggle, people argue or fight fiercely and angrily. **4** ADJ A **bitter** wind or **bitter** weather is extremely cold. ♦ **bitterly** SUBMOD *...a bitterly cold New Year's Day.* **5** ADJ Something that tastes **bitter** has a sharp, unpleasant taste. **6** MASS N **Bitter** is a kind of British beer. *...two pints of bitter.*

bitterly /bɪtəli[1]/. ADV **Bitterly** means strongly and intensely. You use it to describe strong emotions such as anger, hatred, or shame. *No man could have hated the old order more bitterly.* • See also **bitter.**

bizarre /bɪ'zɑː/. ADJ Something that is **bizarre** is very odd and strange. *...bizarre gadgets.*

black /blæk/, **blacker, blackest; blacks, blacking, blacked. 1** ADJ Something that is **black** is of the darkest colour that there is, the colour of the sky at night when there is no light at all. *...a black leather coat.* • Someone who is **black and blue** is badly bruised. **2** ADJ Someone who is **black** belongs to a race of people with dark skins, especially a race from Africa. *...black musicians.* Also COUNT N *He was the first black to be elected to the Congress.* **3** ADJ **Black** coffee or tea has no milk or cream added to it. **4** ADJ If you describe a situation as **black,** you mean that it is bad and not likely to improve. *I don't think the future is as black as that.* **5** ATTRIB ADJ **Black** magic involves communicating with evil spirits. **6** ATTRIB ADJ **Black** humour involves jokes about things that are sad or unpleasant. *...a black comedy.* **7** VB WITH OBJ When a group **blacks** particular goods or people, it refuses to handle the goods or to have dealings with the people. *Their members had blacked these goods at the London Docks.*

black out. PHR VB If you **black out,** you lose consciousness for a short time. • See also **blackout.**

black and white. ADJ In a **black and white** photograph or film, everything is shown in black, white, and grey. *I saw it in black and white.* • You say that something is **in black and white** when it has been written or printed, and not just spoken. *I want to see that agreement written down in black and white.*

blackberry /blækbəri[1]/, **blackberries.** COUNT N A **blackberry** is a small black or dark purple fruit.

blackbird /blækbɜːd/, **blackbirds.** COUNT N A **blackbird** is a common European bird with black or brown feathers.

blackboard /blækbɔːd/, **blackboards.** COUNT N A **blackboard** is a dark-coloured board which teachers write on with chalk.

blackcurrant /blækkʌrənt/, **blackcurrants.** COUNT N **Blackcurrants** are very small dark purple fruits that grow in bunches.

blacken /blækən/, **blackens, blackening, blackened.** VB WITH OBJ To **blacken** something means to make it black or very dark in colour. *His face was blackened with charcoal.*

black eye, black eyes. COUNT N A **black eye** is a dark-coloured bruise around the eye.

blackmail /blækmeɪl/, **blackmails, blackmailing, blackmailed.** 1 UNCOUNT N **Blackmail** is the action of threatening to do something unpleasant to someone, for example to reveal a secret about them, unless they give you money or behave in the way you want them to. *The statements amounted to blackmail.* ♦ **blackmailer** /blækmeɪlə/ COUNT N *...the blackmailer's cruelty to his victim.* 2 VB WITH OBJ If someone **blackmails** you, they try to make you give them money by threatening to reveal something about you or by doing something unpleasant to you.

black market, black markets. COUNT N If something is bought or sold on the **black market,** it is bought or sold illegally. *He whispered that he could change money on the black market.*

blackout /blækaʊt/, **blackouts.** 1 COUNT N A **blackout** is a period of time during a war in which a place is made dark for safety reasons. *We couldn't get home before the blackout.* 2 COUNT N If you have a **blackout,** you temporarily lose consciousness.

black sheep. SING N If you refer to someone as the **black sheep** of a group, you mean that everyone else in the group is good, but that person is bad.

blacksmith /blæksmɪθ/, **blacksmiths.** COUNT N A **blacksmith** is someone whose job is making things out of metal, for example horseshoes or farm tools.

bladder /blædə/, **bladders.** COUNT N Your **bladder** is the part of your body where urine is held until it leaves your body. ● See also **gall bladder.**

blade /bleɪd/, **blades.** 1 COUNT N The **blade** of a knife, axe, or saw is the sharp part. 2 COUNT N The **blades** of a propeller are the parts that turn round. 3 COUNT N The **blade** of an oar is the thin, flat part that you put into the water. 4 See also **razor blade, shoulder blade.**

blame /bleɪm/, **blames, blaming, blamed.** 1 VB WITH OBJ If you **blame** a person or thing for something bad, you think or say that they are responsible for it. *I was blamed for the theft.* Also UNCOUNT N *You haven't said a word of blame.* 2 UNCOUNT N The **blame** for something bad that has happened is the responsibility for causing it or letting it happen. *He had to take the blame for everything.* 3 VB WITH OBJ If you say that you do not **blame** someone for doing something, you mean that it was a reasonable thing to do in the circumstances. *I can't really blame him for wanting to make me suffer.*

blameless /bleɪmlɪ[2]s/. ADJ Someone who is **blameless** has not done anything wrong.

blanch /blɑːntʃ/, **blanches, blanching, blanched.** VB If you **blanch,** you suddenly become very pale.

bland /blænd/, **blander, blandest.** 1 ADJ Someone who is **bland** is calm and polite, and does not react in an excited way. *...bland, middle-of-the-road, evasive men.* ♦ **blandly** ADV *Mr Jones blandly dismissed their arguments.* 2 ADJ **Bland** things are dull and uninteresting. *...bland cheeses.*

blandishments /blændɪʃmə[2]nts/. PLURAL N **Blandishments** are pleasant things that you say to someone in order to persuade them to do something; a formal use. *He remained impervious to all Nell's blandishments.*

blank /blæŋk/, **blanker, blankest.** 1 ADJ Something that is **blank** has nothing on it. *...a blank sheet of paper... ...a blank wall.* 2 ADJ If you look **blank,** your face shows no feeling, understanding, or interest. *Her face went blank.* ♦ **blankly** ADV *I sat quietly, staring blankly ahead.* 3 SING N If your mind or memory is a **blank,** you cannot think of anything or remember anything. 4 See also **point-blank.**

blanket /blæŋkɪ[2]t/, **blankets, blanketing, blanketed.** 1 COUNT N A **blanket** is a large piece of thick cloth, especially one which you put on a bed to keep you warm. 2 VB WITH OBJ If something such as snow **blankets** an area, it covers it. Also SING N *...a blanket of cloud.* 3 ATTRIB ADJ You use **blanket** to describe something which affects or refers to every person or thing in a group. *...our blanket acceptance of everything they say.*

blare /bleə/, **blares, blaring, blared.** VB When something such as a siren or radio **blares,** it makes a loud, unpleasant noise. *The TV set was blaring in the background.* Also SING N *...the blare of conversation.*

blasé /blɑːzeɪ/. ADJ If you are **blasé** about something which other people find exciting, you show no excitement in it, because you have experienced it before. *You sound very blasé about it.*

blaspheme /blæsfiːm/, **blasphemes, blaspheming, blasphemed.** VB If someone **blasphemes,** they say rude or disrespectful things about God.

blasphemous /blæsfə[1]məs/. ADJ Words or actions that are **blasphemous** show disrespect for God. *...a blasphemous poem.*

blasphemy /blæsfə[1]mi[1]/, **blasphemies.** UNCOUNT N OR COUNT N If someone says or does something that shows disrespect for God, you can say that what they are saying or doing is **blasphemy.** *Any attempt to violate that image is blasphemy... It would be regarded as a blasphemy.*

blast /blɑːst/, **blasts, blasting, blasted.** 1 COUNT N A **blast** is a big explosion. *Nobody had been hurt in the blast.* 2 VB WITH OBJ If people or things **blast** something, they destroy or damage it with a bomb or an explosion. *Tunnels have been blasted through bedrock beneath the city.* 3 COUNT N A **blast** is also a sudden strong rush of air or wind, or a short, loud sound carried by the wind. *...icy blasts... Ralph blew a series of short blasts.* 4 PHRASE If a machine is on **at full blast,** it is producing as much sound or heat as it is able to. *She insists on having the radio on at full blast.* 5 **Blast** is a mild swear word that people use when they are irritated or annoyed about something.

blast off. PHR VB When a space rocket **blasts off,** it leaves the ground at the start of its journey.

blast-off. UNCOUNT N **Blast-off** is the moment when a rocket or space shuttle leaves the ground and rises into the air.

blatant /bleɪtə[0]nt/. ADJ **Blatant** is used to describe something bad which is obvious and not concealed in any way. *...blatant discrimination.* ♦ **blatantly** ADV *They blatantly ignored the truce agreement.*

blaze /bleɪz/, **blazes, blazing, blazed.** 1 VB When a fire **blazes,** it burns strongly and brightly. 2 COUNT N A **blaze** is a large fire in which things are damaged. *You never saw such a blaze.* 3 VB Something that **blazes** with light or colour is extremely bright. *The flower beds blazed with colour.* 4 COUNT N WITH SUPP A **blaze** of light or colour is a large amount of it. *...a blaze of sunlight.* 5 SING N WITH 'of' A **blaze** of publicity or attention is a great amount of it. *She eventually retired in a blaze of glory.*

blazer /bleɪzə/, **blazers.** COUNT N A **blazer** is a kind of jacket, especially one worn by schoolchildren or members of a sports team.

blazing /bleɪzɪŋ/. 1 ATTRIB ADJ You use **blazing** to describe the weather or a place when it is very hot and sunny. *...the blazing beach... ...the blazing heat of the plain.* 2 ATTRIB ADJ When people have a **blazing** row, they quarrel in a noisy and excited way.

bleach /bliːtʃ/, **bleaches, bleaching, bleached.** 1 ERG VB To **bleach** material or hair means to make it white or pale, either with a chemical or by leaving it in the sun. *He bleaches his hair... I left the cloth in the sun to bleach.* 2 UNCOUNT N **Bleach** is a chemical that is used to make cloth white, or to clean things thoroughly. *...a strong household bleach.*

bleak /bliːk/, **bleaker, bleakest.** 1 ADJ If a situation is **bleak,** it is bad, and seems unlikely to improve. *The future looked bleak.* ♦ **bleakness** UNCOUNT N *...the bleakness of the post war years.* 2 ADJ If something is **bleak,** it looks cold and bare. *...the bleak coastline... ...the bleak winters.* 3 ADJ If someone looks or sounds **bleak,** they seem depressed, hopeless, or unfriendly. *...his bleak features.* ♦ **bleakly** ADV *He stared bleakly ahead.*

bleary /blɪəri[1]/. ADJ If your eyes are **bleary,** they are red and watery, usually because you are tired.

bleat /bliːt/, **bleats, bleating, bleated.** 1 VB When a sheep or goat **bleats,** it makes the sound that sheep and goats usually make. Also COUNT N *...the bleat of a goat.* 2 VB When people **bleat,** they speak in a weak, high, complaining voice. *They bleat about how miserable they are.*

bleed /bliːd/, **bleeds, bleeding, bled.** VB When you **bleed,** you lose blood from your body as a result of injury or illness. *His feet had begun to bleed... He was bleeding heavily.* ♦ **bleeding** UNCOUNT N *Has the bleeding stopped?*

blemish /blemɪʃ/, **blemishes, blemishing, blemished.** 1 COUNT N A **blemish** is a mark that spoils the appearance of something. 2 VB WITH OBJ If something **blemishes** your reputation, it spoils it.

blend /blend/, **blends, blending, blended.** 1 RECIP VB When you **blend** substances together, you mix them together so that they become one substance. *Blend the cornflour with a little cold water... Next, blend the tomatoes, garlic, and cream to form a paste.* Also COUNT N *...a blend of different oils.* 2 RECIP VB When colours or sounds **blend,** they come together or are combined in a pleasing way. *...their voices blending marvellously as they sing in harmony.*

blend into or **blend in.** PHR VB If something **blends into** the background or **blends in,** it is so similar to the background in appearance or sound that it is difficult to see or hear it separately. *Tree snakes blend well into foliage.*

blender /blendə/, **blenders.** COUNT N A **blender** is a machine used in the kitchen for mixing liquids and soft foods together at high speed.

bless /bles/, **blesses, blessing, blessed** or **blest** /blest/. 1 VB WITH OBJ When a priest **blesses** people or things, he asks for God's favour and protection for them. 2 PASSIVE VB WITH 'with' If someone **is blessed** with a particular good quality or skill, they have it. *She is blessed with immense talent and boundless energy.*

PHRASES ● When people say **God bless** or **bless you** to someone, they are expressing their affection, thanks, or good wishes. *Bless you, it's terribly good of you to come.* ● You can say **bless you** to someone who has just sneezed.

blessed /blesɪ[2]d, blest/. ATTRIB ADJ You use **blessed** to describe something that you think is wonderful, and that you are thankful for or relieved about. *...blessed freedom.* ♦ **blessedly** SUBMOD *...the blessedly cool oasis of the airport.*

blessing /blesɪŋ/, **blessings.** 1 COUNT N A **blessing** is something good that you are thankful for. *Health is a blessing that money cannot buy.* 2 COUNT N WITH POSS If something is done with someone's **blessing,** they approve of it. *She did it with the full blessing of her parents.* 3 PHRASE If you say that a situation is a **mixed blessing,** you mean that it has disadvantages as well as advantages.

blew. /bluː/. **Blew** is the past tense of **blow.**

blight /blaɪt/, **blights, blighting, blighted.** 1 COUNT N You can refer to something as a **blight** when it causes great difficulties, and damages or spoils other things. *We think of pollution as a modern blight, but it is not.* 2 VB WITH OBJ If something **blights** your life or your expectations, it damages and spoils them. *Her career has been blighted by clashes with the authorities.*

blind /blaɪnd/, **blinds, blinding, blinded.** 1 ADJ Someone who is **blind** cannot see because their eyes are damaged. *The accident had left him almost totally blind.* ♦ **blindness** UNCOUNT N *Eye damage can result in temporary or permanent blindness.* 2 PLURAL N You can refer to people who are blind as the **blind.** 3 VB WITH OBJ If something **blinds** you, you become unable to see, either for a short time or permanently. *My eyes were momentarily blinded by flash bulbs.* 4 PRED ADJ WITH PREP 'to' If you are **blind** to a fact or situation, you take no notice of it or are unaware of it. *He was blind to everything except his immediate needs.* 5 VB WITH OBJ AND PREP 'to' If something **blinds** you to the real situation, it prevents you from noticing or being aware of its reality. *We have to beware that missionary zeal doesn't blind us to the realities here.* 6 ATTRIB ADJ You describe someone's beliefs or actions as **blind** when they take no notice of the facts or behave in an unreasonable way. *...her blind faith in the wisdom of her Church... She had driven him into a blind rage.* 7 ADJ A **blind** corner is one that you cannot see round. 8 COUNT N A **blind** is a roll of cloth or paper which you pull down over a window to keep out the light. 9 See also **colour blind, Venetian blind.**

blindfold /blaɪndfəʊld/, **blindfolds, blindfolding, blindfolded.** 1 COUNT N A **blindfold** is a strip of cloth that is tied over someone's eyes so that they cannot see. 2 VB WITH OBJ If you **blindfold** someone, you tie a blindfold over their eyes. *I was blindfolded and taken away in an unmarked car.*

blinding /blaɪndɪŋ/. 1 ADJ A **blinding** light is extremely bright. *There came a blinding flash.* 2 ATTRIB ADJ You use **blinding** to emphasize that something is very obvious. *...the blinding obviousness of the advantage.* ♦ **blindingly** SUBMOD *Isn't it blindingly obvious?*

blindly /blaɪndli[1]/. 1 ADV If you do something **blindly,** you do it when you cannot see properly. *He ran blindly across the clearing.* 2 ADV You can also use **blindly** to say that you do something without enough information, or without thinking much about it. *With the information we have now, we can only speculate blindly.*

blind spot, blind spots. COUNT N If you have a **blind spot** about something, you cannot understand it.

blink /blɪŋk/, **blinks, blinking, blinked.** 1 VB OR ERG VB When you **blink** or when you **blink** your eyes, you shut your eyes and very quickly open them again. *They looked at him without blinking... The girl blinked her eyes several times.* Also COUNT N *It was his guilty blink that gave him away.* 2 VB When a light **blinks,** it flashes on and off. *Dots and dashes blinked out from a signal light.*

blinkered /blɪŋkəd/. ADJ A **blinkered** view, attitude, or approach considers only a narrow point of view and does not take into account other people's opinions; a British use. ...*blinkered self-interest.*

blinkers /blɪŋkəz/. PLURAL N **Blinkers** are two pieces of leather which are placed at the side of a horse's eyes so that it can only see straight ahead; a British use.

bliss /blɪs/. UNCOUNT N **Bliss** is a state of complete happiness, or a time or situation in which you are very happy. *For a couple of months, weekends were bliss.*

blissful /blɪsfʊl/. ADJ A **blissful** time or state is a very happy one. *They sat there together in blissful silence.* ♦ **blissfully** ADV *His eyes shut blissfully and he smiled.*

blister /blɪstə/, **blisters, blistering, blistered.** 1 COUNT N A **blister** is a painful swelling containing clear liquid on the surface of your skin. 2 ERG VB When your skin **blisters**, blisters appear on it as a result of burning or rubbing. *Blistering can be prevented by using foot powder... My face was blistered with a crimson rash.* 3 ERG VB When paint or rubber **blisters**, small bumps appear on its surface.

blistering /blɪstəʳrɪŋ/. 1 ADJ When the weather or the sun is **blistering**, it is extremely hot. ...*the blistering days of midsummer.* 2 ADJ A **blistering** remark expresses great anger or sarcasm. ...*had recently been exposed to a blistering attack.*

blithe /blaɪð/. ADJ You use **blithe** to indicate that something is done casually, without serious or careful thought. *I made a blithe comment about the fine weather.* ♦ **blithely** ADV ...*the blessing of good health which we blithely take for granted.*

blizzard /blɪzəd/, **blizzards.** COUNT N A **blizzard** is a storm in which snow falls heavily and there are strong winds.

bloated /bləʊtɪᵈd/. ADJ Something that is **bloated** is much larger than normal because it has a lot of liquid or gas inside it. ...*bloated corpses.*

blob /blɒb/, **blobs.** 1 COUNT N A **blob** of thick or sticky liquid is a small amount of it. ...*a blob of melted wax.* 2 COUNT N You describe something that you cannot see very clearly, for example because it is far away, as a **blob.** ...*a blob of grey in the distance.*

bloc /blɒk/, **blocs.** COUNT N WITH SUPP A **bloc** is a group of countries with similar political aims and interests acting together. ...*an Eastern bloc country.* ● See also **en bloc.**

block /blɒk/, **blocks, blocking, blocked.** 1 COUNT N A **block** of flats or offices is a large building containing them. ...*a large office block.* 2 COUNT N A **block** in a town is an area of land with streets on all its sides. *The store was three blocks away.* 3 COUNT N A **block** of a substance is a large rectangular piece of it. ...*a block of ice.* 4 VB WITH OBJ To **block** a road, channel, or pipe means to put something across or in it so that nothing can get past. *The Turks had blocked the land routes.* ♦ **blocked** ADJ *The road was completely blocked.* 5 VB WITH OBJ If something **blocks** your view, it prevents you from seeing something by being between you and that thing. *The driver blocked his view.* 6 VB WITH OBJ If you **block** something that is being arranged, you prevent it from being done. *The Council blocked his plans.*

block out. PHR VB If you **block out** a thought, you try not to think about it. *They attempt to withdraw from the world, to block it out.*

block up. PHR VB If you **block** something **up** or if it **blocks up**, it becomes completely blocked so that nothing can get through it. *Never block up ventilators... The sink keeps blocking up.*

blockade /blɒkeɪd/, **blockades, blockading, blockaded.** COUNT N A **blockade** is an action that is taken to prevent goods from reaching a place. ...*the blockade of Berlin.* Also VB WITH OBJ *The Atlantic Squadron promptly blockaded Santiago.*

blockage /blɒkɪdʒ/, **blockages.** COUNT N OR UNCOUNT N A **blockage** in a pipe, tube, or tunnel is something that is blocking it. *Perhaps there was a blockage in the fuel line.*

block capitals. PLURAL N **Block capitals** or **block letters** are simple capital letters that are not decorated in any way.

bloke /bləʊk/, **blokes.** COUNT N A **bloke** is a man; an informal British use.

blonde /blɒnd/, **blondes;** also spelled **blond.** 1 ADJ A **blonde** person has pale yellow-coloured hair. ...*a tall, blond Englishman... ...her long blonde hair.* 2 COUNT N A **blonde** is a person, especially a woman, who has blonde hair.

blood /blʌd/. 1 UNCOUNT N **Blood** is the red liquid that flows inside your body. 2 UNCOUNT N WITH SUPP You can use **blood** to refer to the race or social class of someone's parents or ancestors. *There was eastern blood on her mother's side.*

PHRASES ● **Bad blood** refers to feelings of hate and anger between groups of people. *The rebels hoped to create bad blood between Spain and the United States.* ● If something violent and cruel is done **in cold blood,** it is done deliberately and in an unemotional way. ● If a quality or talent is **in** your **blood,** it is part of your nature, and other members of your family have it too. *Music is in her blood.* ● If something **makes** your **blood boil,** it makes you very angry. ● If something **makes** your **blood run cold,** it makes you feel very frightened. ● New people who are introduced into an organization and whose fresh ideas are likely to improve it are referred to as **new blood, fresh blood,** or **young blood.**

bloodless /blʌdlɪˢs/. 1 ADJ If you describe someone's face or skin as **bloodless,** you mean that it is very pale. 2 ADJ A **bloodless** coup or victory is one in which nobody is killed.

blood pressure. UNCOUNT N Your **blood pressure** is a measure of the amount of force with which your blood flows around your body. *I have high blood pressure and heart trouble.*

bloodshed /blʌdʃɛd/. UNCOUNT N **Bloodshed** is violence in which people are killed or wounded. *There was no evidence of bloodshed or attack.*

bloodshot /blʌdʃɒt/. ADJ If your eyes are **bloodshot,** the parts that are usually white are red or pink.

blood sport, blood sports. COUNT N **Blood sports** are sports such as hunting in which animals are killed.

bloodstained /blʌdsteɪnd/. ADJ Something that is **bloodstained** is covered with blood.

bloodstream /blʌdstriːm/, **bloodstreams.** COUNT N Your **bloodstream** is your blood as it flows around your body. ...*a drug that dissolves in the bloodstream.*

bloodthirsty /blʌdθɜːsti¹/. ADJ A **bloodthirsty** person is eager to use violence or to see other people use violence.

blood vessel, blood vessels. COUNT N **Blood vessels** are the narrow tubes through which your blood flows.

bloody /blʌdi¹/, **bloodier, bloodiest.** 1 **Bloody** is a swear word, used to emphasize how annoyed or angry you are; a British use. 2 ADJ A situation or event that is **bloody** is one in which there is a lot of violence and people are killed. *The effects will be violent, disruptive, and probably bloody.* 3 ADJ Something that is **bloody** has a lot of blood on it. *Orest raises his bloody hands to heaven.*

bloom /bluːm/, **blooms, blooming, bloomed.** 1 COUNT N A **bloom** is the flower on a plant. ...*great scarlet hibiscus blooms.* ● A plant or tree that is **in bloom** has flowers on it. 2 VB When a plant or tree **blooms,** it produces flowers. When a flower **blooms,** the flower bud opens. *This variety of rose blooms late into the autumn.*

blossom /blɒsəᵒm/, **blossoms, blossoming, blossomed.** 1 UNCOUNT N OR COUNT N **Blossom** is the flowers that appear on a tree before the fruit. *The trees were heavy with yellow blossom... ...the tender white blossoms on the blackthorn.* ● A tree that is **in blossom** has blossom on it. 2 VB When a tree **blossoms,** it produces blossom. 3 VB You say that a person **blossoms** when they develop attractive qualities or abilities. *She had blossomed into a real beauty.*

blot /blɒt/, **blots, blotting, blotted.** 1 COUNT N A **blot** is a drop of liquid, especially ink, that has been spilled on a surface and has dried. 2 VB WITH OBJ If you **blot** a surface, you remove liquid from it by pressing a piece of soft paper or cloth onto it.

blot out. PHR VB If one thing **blots out** another thing, it is in front of the other thing and prevents it from being seen. *The resulting dust cloud blotted out the sun.*

blotch /blɒtʃ/, **blotches.** COUNT N A **blotch** is a small area of colour, for example on someone's skin. *There were purple blotches around her eyes.*

blotchy /blɒtʃi¹/. ADJ Something that is **blotchy** has blotches on it.

blotting paper. UNCOUNT N **Blotting paper** is thick, soft paper that you use for soaking up and drying ink on a piece of paper.

blouse /blaʊz/, **blouses.** COUNT N A **blouse** is a kind of shirt worn by a girl or woman.

blow /bləʊ/, **blows, blowing, blew** /bluː/, **blown** /bləʊn/. 1 VB When a wind or breeze **blows,** the air moves. *The winds had been blowing form the west.* 2 ERG VB If something **blows** somewhere or if the wind **blows** it there, it is moved there by the wind. *The dust blew all over the decks... The wind blew his papers away.* 3 VB If you **blow,** you send out a stream of air from your mouth. *Eric put his lips close to the hole and blew softly.* 4 VB WITH OBJ If you **blow** bubbles, you make them by blowing air out of your mouth through liquid. 5 VB WITH OBJ When you **blow** a whistle or a horn, you make a sound by blowing into it. 6 VB WITH OBJ When you **blow** your nose, you force air out of it through your nostrils in order to clear it. 7 COUNT N If you give someone a **blow,** you hit them. *He knocked Thomas unconscious with one blow of his fist.* 8 COUNT N A **blow** is also something that happens which makes you very disappointed or unhappy. *It must have been a fearful blow to him.* 9 COUNT N A **blow** for a particular cause or principle is an action that makes it more likely to succeed. A **blow** against it makes it less likely to succeed. *He struck a blow for liberty.* 10 VB WITH OBJ AND ADJUNCT **Blow** is used as a verb to describe the violent effects of an explosion. *He would have blown his hand off if he'd fired the gun... It blew a hole in the roof.* 11 VB WITH OBJ If you **blow** a large amount of money, you spend it quickly on things that you do not really need; an informal use.

blow out. PHR VB If you **blow out** a flame or a candle, you blow at it so that it stops burning.

blow over. PHR VB If something such as trouble or an argument **blows over,** it comes to an end.

blow up. PHR VB 1 If you **blow** something **up** or if it **blows up,** it is destroyed by an explosion. 2 If you **blow up** something such as a balloon or a tyre, you fill it with air.

blow-by-blow. ATTRIB ADJ A **blow-by-blow** account of an event describes every stage of it in detail.

blown /bləʊn/. **Blown** is the past participle of **blow.**

bludgeon /blʌdʒəᵒn/, **bludgeons, bludgeoning, bludgeoned.** VB WITH OBJ AND 'into' If someone **bludgeons** you into doing something, they make you do it by bullying or threatening you.

blue /bluː/, **bluer, bluest; blues.** 1 ADJ Something that is **blue** is the colour of the sky on a sunny day. 2 PHRASE Something that happens **out of the blue** happens suddenly and unexpectedly. 3 UNCOUNT N The **blues** is a type of music which is similar to jazz, but is always slow and sad. 4 ADJ **Blue** films, stories, or jokes are mainly about sex.

blue-black. ADJ Something that is **blue-black** is very dark blue.

bluebottle /bluːbɒtəᵒl/, **bluebottles.** COUNT N A **bluebottle** is a large fly with a shiny dark-blue body.

blue-collar. ADJ **Blue-collar** workers work in industry, doing physical work, rather than in offices.

blueprint /bluːprɪnt/, **blueprints.** COUNT N A **blueprint** for something is an original plan or description of how it is expected to work.

bluff /blʌf/, **bluffs, bluffing, bluffed.** 1 COUNT N OR UNCOUNT N A **bluff** is an attempt to make someone believe that you will do something when you do not really intend to do it. *The boy was thinking up a clever bluff... His threats are merely bluff.* ● If you **call** someone's **bluff,** you tell them to do what they have been threatening to do, because you are sure that they will not really do it. 2 VB WITH OR WITHOUT OBJ If you **bluff** someone, you make them believe that you will do something although you do not really intend to do it. *She wasn't bluffing him... You're just bluffing.*

bluish /bluːɪʃ/. ADJ Something that is **bluish** is slightly blue.

blunder /blʌndə/, **blunders, blundering, blundered.** 1 VB If you **blunder,** you make a stupid or careless mistake. Also COUNT N *I might have committed some dreadful blunder.* 2 VB WITH ADJUNCT If you **blunder** somewhere, you move there in a clumsy and careless way. *She blundered into a tree.*

blunt /blʌnt/, **blunter, bluntest; blunts, blunting, blunted.** 1 ADJ If you are **blunt,** you say exactly what you think without trying to be polite. *Let me ask a blunt question.* ♦ **bluntly** ADV *He told them bluntly what was acceptable.* ♦ **bluntness** UNCOUNT N *Trueman is famous for his bluntness.* 2 ADJ A **blunt** object has a rounded or flat end rather than a sharp one. ...*a wooden spoon or similar blunt instrument.* 3 ADJ A **blunt** knife is no longer sharp and does not cut well. 4 VB WITH OBJ If something **blunts** an emotion or feeling, it weakens it. *This side of his personality has been blunted by toil.*

blur /blɜː/, **blurs, blurring, blurred.** 1 COUNT N A **blur** is a shape or area which you cannot see clearly because it has no distinct outline or because it is moving very fast. 2 ERG VB When a thing **blurs** or **is blurred,** you cannot see it clearly because its edges are no longer distinct. ♦ **blurred** ADJ ...*a blurred snapshot.* 3 VB WITH OBJ If something **blurs** an idea or a concept, the idea or concept no longer seems clear. *It blurred our essential message of racial reconciliation.* ♦ **blurred** ADJ *The distinction between reform and revolution had become blurred in his mind.*

blurt /blɜːt/, **blurts, blurting, blurted.**

blurt out PHR VB If you **blurt** something **out,** you say it suddenly, after trying hard to keep quiet or to keep it secret.

blush /blʌʃ/, **blushes, blushing, blushed.** VB When you **blush,** your face becomes redder than usual because you are ashamed or embarrassed. *Philip blushed and laughed uneasily.* Also COUNT N *'I made it myself,' Mr Solomon informed them with a modest blush.*

bluster /blʌstə/, **blusters, blustering, blustered.** VB When someone **blusters,** they speak angrily and aggressively because they are angry or offended. *They blustered and swore the pictures were fakes.* Also UNCOUNT N *She simply ignored his bluster.*

blustery /blʌstə^{0}ri^1/. ADJ **Blustery** weather is rough and windy.

boa /bəʊə/, **boas.** COUNT N A **boa** is a large snake that kills animals by squeezing them.

boa constrictor /bəʊə kənstrɪktə/, **boa constrictors.** COUNT N A **boa constrictor** is the same as a boa.

boar /bɔː/, **boars.** 1 COUNT N A **boar** is a male pig. 2 COUNT N A **boar** or a **wild boar** is a wild pig. The plural can be 'boar' or 'boars'.

board /bɔːd/, **boards, boarding, boarded.** 1 COUNT N A **board** is a flat piece of wood which is used for a particular purpose. *...a chopping board... ...a drawing board.* 2 SING N You can refer to a blackboard, chessboard, or notice board as the **board.** *I'll write the sum up on the board.* 3 COUNT N The **board** of a company or organization is the group of people who control it. *...members of the board.* 4 VB WITH OBJ If you **board** a train, ship, or aircraft, you get on it in order to travel somewhere; a formal use. *That same afternoon I boarded the plane at Kastrup.* ● When you are **on board** a train, ship, or aircraft, you are on it or in it. *He looked around at the other people on board.* 5 UNCOUNT N **Board** is the food which is provided when you stay somewhere, for example in a hotel. ● See also **full board, half board.**

PHRASES ● An arrangement or deal that is **above board** is legal and is being carried out honestly and openly. ● If a policy or a situation applies **across the board,** it affects everything or everyone in a particular group. *We're aiming for a 20% reduction across the board.* ● If an arrangement or plan **goes by the board,** it is not used or does not happen.

board up. PHR VB If you **board up** a door or window, you fix pieces of wood over it so that it is covered up.

boarding house, boarding houses. COUNT N A **boarding house** is a house where people pay to stay for a short time.

boarding school, boarding schools. COUNT N A **boarding school** is a school where the pupils live during the term.

boardroom /bɔːdruːm, -rʊm/, **boardrooms.** COUNT N The **boardroom** is a room where the board of a company meets.

boast /bəʊst/, **boasts, boasting, boasted.** VB If you **boast** about something that you have done or that you own, you talk about it in a way that shows that you are proud of it. *Williams boasted of his influence on the Prime Minister.* Also COUNT N *It is his boast that he has read the entire works of Trollope.*

boastful /bəʊstfʊl/. ADJ If someone is **boastful,** they talk too proudly about something that they have done or own. *They are rather boastful about their equipment.*

boat /bəʊt/, **boats.** 1 COUNT N A **boat** is a small vehicle for travelling across water. 2 COUNT N You can refer to a passenger ship as a **boat;** an informal use. *She was intending to take the boat to Stockholm.*

PHRASES ● If you say that someone is **rocking the boat,** you mean that they are upsetting a calm situation and causing trouble; an informal use. ● If two or more people are **in the same boat,** they are in the same unpleasant situation.

boating /bəʊtɪŋ/. UNCOUNT N If you go **boating,** you go on a lake or river in a small boat for pleasure.

bob /bɒb/, **bobs, bobbing, bobbed.** 1 VB If something **bobs,** it moves up and down, like something does when it is floating on water. 2 COUNT N In informal speech, people used to refer to a shilling as a **bob.** The plural form was also 'bob'. 3 COUNT N A **bob** is also a hair style in which a woman's hair is cut level with her chin.

bobbed /bɒbd/. ADJ If a woman's hair is **bobbed,** it is cut in a bob.

bode /bəʊd/, **bodes, boding, boded.** PHRASE If something **bodes ill, bodes no good,** or **does not bode well,** it makes you think that something bad will happen; a literary use.

bodice /bɒdɪs/, **bodices.** COUNT N The **bodice** of a dress is the part above the waist.

bodily /bɒdɪli^1/. 1 ATTRIB ADJ Your **bodily** needs and functions are the needs and functions of your body. *They have no interests beyond their bodily needs.* 2 ADV You use **bodily** to refer to actions that involve the whole of someone's body. *He hurled himself bodily at the Prince.*

body /bɒdi^1/, **bodies.** 1 COUNT N Your **body** is all your physical parts, including your head, arms, and legs. *His whole body felt as if it were on fire.* 2 COUNT N You can also refer to the main part of your body, excluding your head, arms, and legs, as your **body.** *They respond with slow movements of their arms, legs, and bodies.* 3 COUNT N A **body** is a dead person's body. 4 COUNT N A **body** is also an organized group of people who deal with something officially. *They are members of a larger body called the Senate Committee.* 5 COUNT N The **body** of a car or aeroplane is the main part of it, excluding its engine, wheels, and wings.

bodyguard /bɒdi^{1}gɑːd/, **bodyguards.** COUNT N Someone's **bodyguard** is the person or group of people employed to protect them. *He came striding into the room followed by his two bodyguards... ...one of the Rajah's personal bodyguard.*

bodywork /bɒdi^{1}wɜːk/. UNCOUNT N The **bodywork** of a motor vehicle is the outside part of it.

bog /bɒg/, **bogs.** COUNT N A **bog** is an area of land which is very wet and muddy.

bogged down /bɒgd daʊn/. PRED ADJ If you are **bogged down** in something, it prevents you from making progress or getting something done; an informal use. *Don't get bogged down in details.*

boggle /bɒgə^{0}l/, **boggles, boggling, boggled.** ERG VB If you find something difficult to imagine or understand, you can say that it **boggles** your mind or that your mind **boggles;** an informal use. *The questions raised by the new biology simply boggle the mind.*

boggy /bɒgi^1/. ADJ **Boggy** land is very wet and muddy.

bogus /bəʊgəs/. ADJ You say that something is **bogus** when you know that it is not genuine. *...bogus names.*

bohemian /bəʊhiːmɪən/, **bohemians.** COUNT N Artistic people who live in an unconventional way are sometimes referred to as **bohemians.** *Brian saw Tim as a romantic bohemian.* Also ADJ *My parents disapproved of the bohemian life I led.*

boil /bɔɪl/, **boils, boiling, boiled.** 1 ERG VB When a hot liquid **boils** or when you **boil** it, bubbles appear in it and it starts to change into steam or vapour. *When the water has boiled, let it cool... Boil the solution in the pan for five minutes.* 2 SING N When you bring a liquid to the **boil,** you heat it until it boils. 3 ERG VB When you **boil** a kettle, you heat it until the water inside it boils. When a kettle **is boiling,** the water inside it is boiling. 4 VB WITH OBJ When you **boil** food, you cook it in boiling water. *She didn't know how to boil an egg.* 5 ADJ If something is very hot, you can say that it is **boiling** or **boiling hot.** *I immersed my boiling body in a cool pool.* 6 VB If you **are boiling** with anger, you are very angry. 7 COUNT N A **boil** is a red, painful swelling on your skin.

boil away. PHR VB When a liquid **boils away,** all of it changes into steam or vapour.

boil down to. PHR VB If you say that a situation or problem **boils down to** a particular thing, you mean that this is the most important aspect of it. *What it all seemed to boil down to was money.*

boil over. PHR VB When a liquid that is being heated **boils over,** it rises and flows over the edge of the container.

boiler /bɔɪlə/, **boilers.** COUNT N A **boiler** is a device which burns gas, oil, electricity, or coal to provide hot water, especially for central heating.

boisterous /bɔɪstə^{1}rəs/. ADJ Someone who is **boisterous** is noisy, lively, and full of energy.

bold /bəʊld/, **bolder, boldest.** 1 ADJ Someone who is **bold** is not afraid to do things which involve risk or danger. *...a bold action.* ♦ **boldly** ADV *...boldly going where no man had gone before.* ♦ **boldness** UNCOUNT N *For any success, boldness is required.* 2 ADJ You also say that someone is **bold** when they are not shy or embarrassed in the company of other people. *Mary was surprisingly bold for a girl who seemed so young.* ♦ **boldly** ADV *He returned her gaze boldly.* 3 ADJ **Bold** lines or designs are painted or drawn in a clear, strong way. *...bold handwriting.*

bollard /bɒlɑːd, bɒləd/, **bollards.** COUNT N **Bollards** are short, thick posts that are used to prevent cars from going on to someone's land or on to part of a road.

bolster /bəʊlstə/, **bolsters, bolstering, bolstered.** VB WITH OBJ If you **bolster** someone's confidence or courage, you make them more confident or more courageous.

bolster up. PHR VB If you **bolster** something **up,** you help or support it in order to make it stronger. *To bolster up their case, they quoted a speech by Ray Gunter.*

bolt /bəʊlt/, **bolts, bolting, bolted.** 1 COUNT N A **bolt** is a long metal object which screws into a nut and is used to fasten things together. 2 VB WITH OBJ When you **bolt** one thing to another, you fasten the two things together firmly using a bolt. *...an iron cot bolted to the floor.* 3 COUNT N A **bolt** on a door or window is a metal bar that you slide across in order to fasten the door or window. 4 VB WITH OBJ When you **bolt** a door or window, you slide the bolt across to fasten it. 5 VB If a person or animal **bolts,** they suddenly start to run very fast, often because something has frightened them. 6 VB WITH OBJ If you **bolt** your food or **bolt** it down, you eat it very quickly. 7 PHRASE If someone is sitting or standing **bolt upright,** they are sitting or standing very straight.

bomb /bɒm/, **bombs, bombing, bombed.** 1 COUNT N A **bomb** is a device which explodes and damages or destroys a large area. 2 SING N Nuclear weapons are sometimes referred to as the **bomb.** *Ban the bomb!* 3 VB WITH OBJ When people **bomb** a place, they attack it with bombs. *They bombed the airports in three cities.* ♦ **bombing** UNCOUNT N OR COUNT N *It replaced the building destroyed by bombing in 1940... ...the current wave of bombings.*

bomb out. PHR VB If a building **is bombed out,** it is destroyed by a bomb. If people **are bombed out,** their houses are destroyed by bombs.

bombard /bɒmbɑːd/, **bombards, bombarding, bombarded.** 1 VB WITH OBJ If you **bombard** someone with questions or criticism, you keep asking questions or criticizing them. 2 VB WITH OBJ When soldiers **bombard** a place, they attack it with continuous heavy gunfire or bombs. ♦ **bombardment** /bɒmbɑːdmə^{2}nt/ UNCOUNT N *...increasingly heavy artillery bombardment.*

bomber /bɒmə/, **bombers.** 1 COUNT N A **bomber** is an aircraft which drops bombs. 2 COUNT N A **bomber** is also a person who causes a bomb to explode in a public place.

bona fide /bəʊnəfaɪdi^1/. ATTRIB ADJ **Bona fide** means genuine; a formal use. *...bona fide applications.*

bonanza /bənænzə/, **bonanzas.** COUNT N You can refer to a time or situation when people suddenly become much richer as a **bonanza.** *...an oil bonanza.*

bond /bɒnd/, **bonds, bonding, bonded.** 1 COUNT N A **bond** between people is a strong feeling of friendship, love, or shared beliefs that unites them. *...the bond between mother and child.* 2 PASSIVE VB When people or animals **are bonded,** they unite to help and protect each other; a formal use. *Societies have always been bonded together by a threat from outside.* 3 PLURAL N WITH SUPP **Bonds** are feelings, duties, or customs that force you to behave in a particular way. *...the bonds of party discipline.* 4 VB WITH OBJ When you **bond** two things, you stick them together using glue. 5 COUNT N A **bond** is also a certificate issued by a government or company which shows that you have lent them money and that they will pay you interest.

bondage /bɒndɪdʒ/. UNCOUNT N **Bondage** is the condition of belonging to someone as their slave; a literary use.

bone /bəʊn/, **bones, boning, boned.** 1 COUNT N OR UNCOUNT N Your **bones** are the hard parts inside your body which together form your skeleton. *...hip bones... Its eye sockets are encircled by bone.* 2 VB WITH OBJ If you **bone** a piece of meat or fish, you remove the bones from it before cooking it. 3 ADJ A **bone** tool or ornament is made of bone.

PHRASES ● If you **feel** or **know** something **in** your **bones,** you are certain about it, although you cannot explain why; an informal use. *He felt in his bones he could do it.* ● If you **make no bones** about doing something unpleasant or difficult, you do it without hesitation; an informal use.

bonfire /bɒnfaɪə/, **bonfires.** COUNT N A **bonfire** is a fire that is made outdoors, usually to burn rubbish.

bonnet /bɒnɪt/, **bonnets.** 1 COUNT N The **bonnet** of a car is the metal cover over the engine at the front; a British use. 2 COUNT N A baby's or woman's **bonnet** is a hat tied under their chin. ● to **have a bee in** your bonnet: see **bee.**

bonny /bɒni^1/; also spelled **bonnie.** ADJ **Bonny** means nice to look at; a Scottish use.

bonus /bəʊnəs/, **bonuses.** 1 COUNT N A **bonus** is an amount of money that is added to someone's usual pay, usually because they have worked very hard. 2 COUNT N A **bonus** is also something good that you get in addition to something else. *Any sort of party after work was a bonus.*

bony /bəʊni^1/. ADJ A **bony** person is very thin. *He was tall, thin, and bony... ...his long bony fingers.*

boo /buː/, **boos, booing, booed.** VB WITH OR WITHOUT OBJ If you **boo** a speaker or performer, you shout 'boo' to show that you do not like them, their opinions, or their performance. Also COUNT N *There were loud boos.*

booby prize /buːbi^1 praɪz/, **booby prizes.** COUNT N The **booby prize** is a prize given to the person who comes last in a competition.

booby-trap, /buːbi^1 træp/, **booby-traps, booby-trapping, booby-trapped.** 1 COUNT N A **booby-trap** is something such as a bomb which is hidden or disguised and which causes death or injury when it is touched. 2 VB WITH OBJ If something is **booby-trapped,** a booby-trap is placed in it or on it.

book /bʊk/, **books, booking, booked.** 1 COUNT N A **book** consists of a number of pieces of paper, usually with words printed on them, which are fastened

together and fixed inside a cover of stronger paper or cardboard. 2 COUNT N A **book** of something such as stamps, matches, or tickets is a small number of them fastened together between thin cardboard or plastic covers. 3 PLURAL N A company's or organization's **books** are written records of money that has been spent and earned, or of the names of people who belong to it. *He's going to help me go over my books and check the totals... His name is no longer on our books.* 4 VB WITH OBJ When you **book** something such as a hotel room or a ticket, you arrange to have it or use it at a particular time; a British use. *I'd like to book a table for four for tomorrow night.* ● See also **booking.**
PHRASES ● If a hotel, restaurant, or theatre is **booked up** or **fully booked,** it has no rooms, tables, or tickets left for a particular time or date. ● If you are **in** someone's **bad books,** they are annoyed with you. If you are **in** their **good books,** they are pleased with you.

book into or **book in.** PHR VB When you **book into** a hotel or **book in,** you officially state that you have arrived to stay there, usually by signing your name in a register; a British use.

bookcase /bʊkkeɪs/, **bookcases.** COUNT N A **bookcase** is a piece of furniture with shelves for books.

booking /bʊkɪŋ/, **bookings.** COUNT N A **booking** is the arrangement that you make when you book something such as a theatre seat or a hotel room.

bookish /bʊkɪʃ/. ADJ Someone who is **bookish** spends a lot of time reading serious books.

bookkeeping /bʊkki:pɪŋ/. UNCOUNT N **Bookkeeping** is the job of keeping an accurate record of the money spent and received by an organization.

booklet /bʊkle^{1}t/, **booklets.** COUNT N A **booklet** is a small book with a paper cover that gives you information.

bookmaker /bʊkmeɪkə/, **bookmakers.** COUNT N A **bookmaker** is a person whose job is to take your money when you bet and to pay you money if you win.

bookmark /bʊkmɑ:k/, **bookmarks.** COUNT N A **bookmark** is a narrow piece of card or leather that you put between the pages of a book so that you can find a particular page easily.

bookshelf /bʊkʃelf/, **bookshelves.** COUNT N A **bookshelf** is a bookcase, or a shelf on which you keep books.

bookstall /bʊkstɔ:l/, **bookstalls.** COUNT N A **bookstall** is a small shop with an open front where books and magazines are sold.

boom /bu:m/, **booms, booming, boomed.** 1 COUNT N WITH SUPP If there is a **boom** in something, there is a fast increase or development in it. *...the population boom.* Also VB *The gardening industry is booming.* 2 VB When something such as a big drum, a cannon, or someone's voice **booms,** it makes a loud, deep, echoing sound. *The cannon boomed again.* Also COUNT N *The boom of the drum echoed along the street.*

boomerang /bu:məræŋ/, **boomerangs.** COUNT N A **boomerang** is a curved piece of wood which comes back to you if you throw it the correct way. Boomerangs were used by Australian natives as weapons.

boon /bu:n/, **boons.** COUNT N You say that something is a **boon** when it makes life better or easier for someone. *The bus service is a great boon to old people.*

boor /bʊə/, **boors.** COUNT N A **boor** is a boorish person; an old-fashioned use.

boorish /bʊərɪʃ/. ADJ Someone who is **boorish** behaves in a rough, impolite, clumsy way.

boost /bu:st/, **boosts, boosting, boosted.** 1 VB WITH OBJ If one thing **boosts** another, it causes it to increase. *This new technology will boost food production.* Also COUNT N *This will be a great boost to the economy.* 2 VB WITH OBJ If something **boosts** your confidence or morale, it improves it. Also COUNT N *...a boost to self-confidence.*

boot /bu:t/, **boots, booting, booted.** 1 COUNT N **Boots** are shoes that cover your whole foot and the lower part of your leg. 2 COUNT N **Boots** are also strong, heavy shoes which cover your ankle and which have thick soles. 3 COUNT N The **boot** of a car is a covered space at the back, in which you carry things such as luggage and shopping; a British use.
PHRASES ● To **put the boot in** means to repeatedly kick someone who is lying on the ground. It also means to say something cruel to someone who is already upset; an informal use. ● If someone says that you **are getting too big for** your **boots,** they mean that you are becoming too proud and pleased with yourself; an informal use. ● If you **get the boot** or **are given the boot,** you are dismissed from your job; an informal use.

boot out. PHR VB If you **are booted out** of a job, organization, or place, you are forced to leave it; an informal use.

booth /bu:ð/, **booths.** 1 COUNT N A **booth** is a small area separated from a larger public area by screens or thin walls where, for example, you can make a telephone call. 2 COUNT N A **booth** is also a small tent or stall, usually at a fair, in which you can buy goods or watch some entertainment.

booty /bu:ti^{1}/. UNCOUNT N **Booty** consists of valuable things taken from a place, especially by soldiers after a battle; a literary use.

booze /bu:z/, **boozes, boozing, boozed.** 1 UNCOUNT N **Booze** is alcoholic drink; an informal use. 2 VB When people **booze,** they drink alcohol; an informal use.

border /bɔ:də/, **borders, bordering, bordered.** 1 COUNT N The **border** between two countries is the dividing line between them. *They crossed the border into Mexico.* 2 COUNT N A **border** is also a strip or band around the edge of something. *It's painted in white with a gold border.* 3 COUNT N In a garden, a **border** is a strip of ground planted with flowers along the edge of a lawn. 4 VB WITH OBJ If something **borders** something else, it forms a line along the edge of it. *Huge elm trees bordered the road.* 5 VB WITH 'on' When you say that something **borders** on a particular state, you mean that it has almost reached that state. *I was in a state of excitement bordering on insanity.*

borderline /bɔ:dəlaɪn/. 1 ADJ You use **borderline** to say that something is only just acceptable as a member of a class or group. *He is a borderline candidate for a special school.* 2 SING N The **borderline** between two conditions or qualities is the division between them. *...the narrow borderline between laughter and tears.*

bore /bɔ:/, **bores, boring, bored.** 1 VB WITH OBJ If something **bores** you, you find it dull and uninteresting. *Most of the book had bored him... I won't bore you with the details.* ♦ **bored** ADJ *Tom was bored with the film.* ♦ **boring** ADJ *...a boring journey.* ● If something **bores** you **to tears, bores** you **to death,** or **bores** you **stiff,** it bores you very much indeed; an informal use. 2 COUNT N You describe someone as a **bore** when you think that they talk in a very uninteresting way. 3 SING N You can describe a situation as a **bore** when you find it annoying or a nuisance. 4 VB WITH OBJ If you **bore** a hole in something, you make a deep round hole in it using a special tool. 5 **Bore** is also the past tense of **bear.**

boredom /bɔ:də^{4}m/. UNCOUNT N **Boredom** is the state of being bored. *Many of the audience walked out through sheer boredom.*

born /bɔ:n/. 1 PASSIVE VB When a baby **is born,** it comes out of its mother's body. *Mary was born in Glasgow.* 2 ATTRIB ADJ You use **born** to talk about something that someone can do well and easily. For example, a **born** cook has a natural ability to cook well.

-born. SUFFIX **-born** is added to the name of a place or nationality to indicate where a person was born. *...Lennox Lewis of Canada, the British-born Olympic boxing champion.*

borne /bɔ:n/. **Borne** is the past participle of **bear.**

borough /bʌrə/, **boroughs.** COUNT N A **borough** is a town, or a district within a large town, which has its own council. *...the London Borough of Lewisham.*

borrow /bɒrəʊ/, **borrows, borrowing, borrowed.** VB WITH OBJ If you **borrow** something that belongs to someone else, you take it intending to return it, usually with their permission. *Could I borrow your car?... I need to borrow five thousand pounds.* ♦ **borrowing** UNCOUNT N *Lowering interest rates will make borrowing cheaper.*

borrower /bɒrəʊə/, **borrowers.** COUNT N A **borrower** is a person or organization that borrows money.

borstal /bɔ:stə^{0}l/, **borstals.** COUNT N OR UNCOUNT N In Britain, prisons for young criminals used to be known as **borstals.**

bosom /bʊzə^{0}m/, **bosoms.** 1 COUNT N A woman's **bosom** is her breasts; an old-fashioned use. *...hugging the cat to her bosom.* 2 SING N WITH SUPP If you are in the **bosom** of your family or of a community, you are among people who love and protect you; a literary use. 3 COUNT N WITH POSS Strong feelings are sometimes described as being in your **bosom;** a literary use. *...some dark, sinful passion you're nursing in your bosom.* 4 MOD A **bosom** friend is a very close friend; an old-fashioned use.

boss /bɒs/, **bosses, bossing, bossed.** 1 COUNT N Your **boss** is the person in charge of the organization where you work. 2 PHRASE If you **are** your **own boss,** you work for yourself or do not have to ask other people for permission to do something. 3 VB WITH OBJ If someone **bosses** you, they keep telling you what to do. *They've bossed us around enough.*

bossy /bɒsi^{1}/. ADJ A **bossy** person enjoys telling other people what to do; used showing disapproval. *...one of those large, bossy women.* ♦ **bossiness** UNCOUNT N *His bossiness didn't worry her unduly.*

botanic /bə^{7}tænɪk/. **Botanic** gardens are large gardens where plants are grown and studied.

botanical /bə^{7}tænɪkə^{0}l/. ATTRIB ADJ **Botanical** books, research, and activities relate to the scientific study of plants. *...botanical gardens.*

botany /bɒtəni^{1}/. UNCOUNT N **Botany** is the scientific study of plants. ♦ **botanist** /bɒtənɪst/ COUNT N

botch /bɒtʃ/, **botches, botching, botched.** VB WITH OBJ If you **botch** a piece of work or **botch** it up, you do it badly or clumsily; an informal use.

both /bəʊθ/. 1 PREDET, DET, OR QUANTIF You use **both** when you are referring to two people or things and saying something about each of them. *Both her parents were dead... Both policies made good sense.* Also PRON *He got angry with both of them... Most of them speak either English or German or both... We were both young.* 2 You use the structure **both...and** when you are giving two facts or alternatives and emphasizing that each of them is true or possible. *These are dangers that threaten both men and women... The prospects both excited and worried me.*

bother /bɒðə/, **bothers, bothering, bothered.** 1 VB If you do not **bother** to do something, you do not do it, because you think it is unnecessary or would involve too much effort. *I never bother to iron my shirts... Don't bother with the washing-up.* 2 PHRASE If you say that you **can't be bothered** to do something, you mean that you are not going to do it because you think it is unnecessary or would involve too much effort. 3 UNCOUNT N **Bother** is trouble, fuss, or difficulty. *We found the address without any bother.* 4 SING N If a task or a person is a **bother,** they are boring or irritating; an informal use. *Sorry to be a bother, but could you sign this for me?* 5 VB WITH OBJ OR 'about' If something **bothers** you or if you **bother** about it, you are worried, concerned, or upset about it. *Is something bothering you?... I didn't bother about what I looked like.* ♦ **bothered** PRED ADJ *She was bothered about Olive.* 6 VB WITH OBJ If you **bother** someone, you talk to them or interrupt them when they are busy. *Don't bother me with little things like that.*

bottle /bɒtə^{0}l/, **bottles, bottling, bottled.** 1 COUNT N A **bottle** is a glass or plastic container for keeping liquids in. *...a scent bottle.* 2 COUNT N You can use **bottle** to refer to a bottle and its contents, or to the contents only. *She drank half a bottle of whisky a day.* 3 VB WITH OBJ To **bottle** wine or beer means to put it into bottles. 4 COUNT N A **bottle** is also a drinking container used by babies. It has a special rubber part through which the baby sucks.

bottle up. PHR VB If you **bottle up** strong feelings, you do not express them or show them. *...all the rage that had been bottled up in him for so long.*

bottled /bɒtə^{0}ld/. ADJ **Bottled** drinks are sold in bottles. *...bottled beer.*

bottom /bɒtə^{0}m/, **bottoms, bottoming, bottomed.** 1 COUNT N The **bottom** of something is the lowest part of it. *I stood there at the bottom of the steps... It sank to the bottom of the lake.* 2 ATTRIB ADJ The **bottom** thing in a series of things is the lowest one. *...the bottom button of my waistcoat.* 3 COUNT N The **bottom** of a place such as a street or garden is the end farthest from the entrance. *...down at the bottom of the meadow.* 4 PRED ADJ If you are **bottom** of the class or come **bottom** in a test, you are the worst student in the class or get the lowest marks in the test. 5 PHRASE If you **get to the bottom of** something, you discover the real truth about it or the real cause of it. 6 COUNT N Your **bottom** is the part of your body that you sit on.

bottom out. PHR VB When something that has been getting worse **bottoms out,** it stops getting worse, and remains at a particular level. *Even if the recession has bottomed out, it will not help the unemployed.*

bough /baʊ/, **boughs.** COUNT N A **bough** is a large branch of a tree; a literary use.

bought /bɔ:t/. **Bought** is the past tense and past participle of **buy.**

boulder /bəʊldə/, **boulders.** COUNT N A **boulder** is a large rounded rock.

boulevard /bu:lə^{0}vɑ:d^{0}/, **boulevards.** COUNT N A **boulevard** is a wide street in a city, usually with trees along each side.

bounce /baʊns/, **bounces, bouncing, bounced.** 1 VB When something such as a ball **bounces,** it moves upwards or away immediately after hitting a surface. *Enormous hailstones bounced off the pavements.* 2 VB WITH OBJ When you **bounce** a ball, you throw it hard against a surface so that it immediately moves away. 3 VB If sound or light **bounces** off a surface, it reaches the surface and is reflected back. *Its flickering light bounced off the walls.* 4 VB You can say that something **bounces** when it swings or moves up and down. *The rucksack bounced and jingled on my shoulders.* 5 VB WITH ADJUNCT If you **bounce** on something, you jump up and down on it repeatedly. *...bouncing on a trampoline.* 6 VB WITH ADJUNCT If someone **bounces**

somewhere, they move in an energetic way, because they are feeling happy. *He came bouncing in, grinning.* 7 VB If a cheque **bounces,** the bank refuses to accept it and pay out the money, because there is not enough money in the account.

bouncer /baʊnsə/, **bouncers.** COUNT N A **bouncer** is a man who is employed to prevent unwanted people from coming into a club and to throw people out if they cause trouble.

bouncy /baʊnsi^1/. ADJ Someone who is **bouncy** is very lively and enthusiastic. *...a bouncy little man.*

bound /baʊnd/, **bounds, bounding, bounded.** 1 PRED ADJ WITH TO-INF If something is **bound** to happen, it is certain to happen. *We are bound to win.* 2 PRED ADJ If you are **bound** by an agreement or law, you have a duty to obey it. *We are bound by the government's pay policy.* 3 PLURAL N **Bounds** are limits which restrict what can be done. *It is not outside the bounds of possibility.* 4 VB WITH OBJ If an area of land **is bounded** by something, that thing is situated around its edge. *The plantation was bounded by marsh.* 5 PRED ADJ WITH 'for' If a vehicle is **bound** for a particular place, it is travelling towards it. *He put her aboard the steamer bound for New York.* 6 VB When animals or people **bound,** they move quickly with large leaps. *He bounded up the stairs.* 7 **Bound** is also the past tense and past participle of **bind.**

PHRASES • You can say **'I am bound to say'** or **'I am bound to admit'** when mentioning a fact which you regret. *Sometimes, I'm bound to say, they are a hopeless muddle.* • If one thing is **bound up with** another, it is closely connected with it. *All this was bound up with what was happening in Egypt.* • If a place is **out of bounds,** people are forbidden to go there.

boundary /baʊndə^{0}ri^1/, **boundaries.** COUNT N The **boundary** of an area of land is an imaginary line that separates it from other areas. *You have to stay within your county boundary.*

boundless /baʊndlı^{2}s/. ADJ If you describe something as **boundless,** you mean that there seems to be no end or limit to it. *...her boundless energies.*

bounty /baʊnti^1/; a literary word. 1 SING N WITH POSS Someone's **bounty** is their generosity in giving something. *They must accept the colonel's bounty.* 2 UNCOUNT N **Bounty** is also something provided in large amounts.

bouquet /bəʊkeɪ, bu:-/, **bouquets.** COUNT N A **bouquet** is a bunch of flowers arranged in an attractive way, especially one given as a present. *...a bouquet of roses.*

bourbon /bɜ:bə^{0}n/, **bourbons.** MASS N **Bourbon** is a type of whisky that is made mainly in America.

bourgeois /bʊəʒwa:/. 1 ADJ If you describe something, for example an attitude, as **bourgeois,** you mean it is typical of fairly rich middle-class people; used showing disapproval. 2 ADJ Communists use **bourgeois** when referring to the capitalist system and to the social class who own most of the wealth in that system. *She condemns modern bourgeois society.*

bourgeoisie /bʊəʒwa:zi:/. COLL N In Marxist theory, the **bourgeoisie** are the middle-class people who own most of the wealth in a capitalist system.

bout /baʊt/, **bouts.** 1 COUNT N If you have a **bout** of something such as an illness, you have it for a short period. *...a bout of flu.* 2 COUNT N A **bout** of activity is a short time during which you put a lot of effort into doing something. *...frenzied bouts of writing.*

boutique /bu:ti:k/, **boutiques.** COUNT N A **boutique** is a small shop that sells fashionable clothes, shoes, or jewellery.

bow, bows, bowing, bowed; pronounced /baʊ/ for meanings 1 to 4 and for the phrasal verbs, and /bəʊ/ for meanings 5, 6, and 7. 1 VB When you **bow** to someone, you briefly bend your body towards them as a formal way of greeting them or showing respect. Also COUNT N *He opened the door with a bow.* 2 VB WITH OBJ If you **bow** your head, you bend it downwards so that you are looking towards the ground. 3 VB WITH PREP 'to' If you **bow** to someone's wishes or **bow** to pressure, you agree to do what someone wants you to do; a formal use. 4 COUNT N OR PLURAL N The front part of a ship is called the **bow** or the **bows.** 5 COUNT N A **bow** is a knot with two loops and two loose ends that is used in tying shoelaces and ribbons. 6 COUNT N A **bow** is also a weapon for shooting arrows, consisting of a long piece of wood bent into a curve by a string attached to both its ends. 7 COUNT N The **bow** of a violin or other stringed instrument is a long, thin piece of wood with hair from a horse's tail stretched along it, which you move across the strings of the instrument in order to play it.

bow down. PHR VB If you **bow down,** you bow very low to show great respect.

bow out. PHR VB If you **bow out** of something, you stop taking part in it. *We may do one more performance before we bow out.*

bowed; pronounced /bəʊd/ for meaning 1 and /baʊd/ for meaning 2. 1 ADJ Something that is **bowed** is curved. *He had slightly bowed legs.* 2 ADJ If someone is **bowed,** their body is bent forward, usually because they are very old. *I remember seeing an old man bent and bowed walking slowly along Queen Anne Street.*

bowel /baʊə^{0}l/, **bowels.** 1 PLURAL N OR SING N Your **bowels** or your **bowel** are the tubes in your body through which digested food passes from your stomach to your anus. 2 PLURAL N WITH SUPP You can refer to the parts deep inside something as its **bowels.** *...deep in the bowels of the earth.*

bowl /bəʊl/, **bowls, bowling, bowled.** 1 COUNT N A **bowl** is a circular container with a wide, uncovered top. Bowls are used, for example, for serving food. *...a china bowl.* 2 COUNT N You can use **bowl** to refer to a bowl and its contents, or to the contents only. *I ate a big bowl of porridge.* 3 COUNT N The **bowl** of a lavatory or a tobacco pipe is the hollow, rounded part of it. 4 VB When someone **bowls** in cricket, they throw the ball down the pitch towards the batsman. *He had bowled badly.* 5 UNCOUNT N **Bowls** is a game in which the players try to roll large wooden balls as near as possible to a small ball. 6 See also **bowling.**

bowl over. PHR VB 1 If you **bowl** someone **over,** you knock them down by accidentally hitting them when you are moving very quickly. 2 If you **are bowled over** by something, you are very impressed or surprised by it. *I was bowled over by the beauty of Malawi.*

bow-legged /bəʊ legı^{1}d/. ADJ Someone who is **bow-legged** has legs that curve apart.

bowler /bəʊlə/, **bowlers.** 1 COUNT N In a game of cricket, the **bowler** is the person who is bowling. 2 COUNT N A **bowler** or a **bowler hat** is a round, stiff hat with a narrow curved brim.

bowling /bəʊlıŋ/. UNCOUNT N **Bowling** is a game in which you roll a heavy ball down a long, narrow track towards a group of wooden objects and try to knock them down.

bow tie /bəʊ taɪ/, **bow ties.** COUNT N A **bow tie** is a man's tie in the form of a bow, worn especially for formal occasions.

box /bɒks/, **boxes, boxing, boxed.** 1 COUNT N A **box** is a container which has stiff sides and which sometimes has a lid. *...a cardboard box.* 2 COUNT N You can use **box** to refer to a box and its contents, or to the contents only. *...a box of chocolates.* 3 COUNT N A **box** on a form that you fill in is a square or rectangular space in which you have to write something. 4 COUNT N A **box** in a theatre is a separate area like a little room where a small number of people can sit to watch the performance. 5 VB To **box** means to fight someone according to the rules of the sport of boxing.

box in. PHR VB If you **are boxed in,** you are unable to move from a particular place because you are surrounded by other people or cars.

boxer /bɒksə/, **boxers.** COUNT N A **boxer** is a sportsman whose sport is boxing.

boxing /bɒksıŋ/. UNCOUNT N **Boxing** is a sport in which two men wearing large padded gloves fight according to special rules, by punching each other.

Boxing Day. UNCOUNT N In Britain, **Boxing Day** is December 26th, the day after Christmas Day.

box office, box offices. 1 COUNT N The **box office** in a theatre, cinema, or concert hall is the place where the tickets are sold. 2 SING N OR MOD **Box office** is also used to refer to the degree of success of a film, play, or actor in terms of the number of tickets sold. *She was a very hot box office attraction indeed.*

boy /bɔɪ/, **boys.** 1 COUNT N A **boy** is a male child. 2 CONVENTION Some Americans express excitement or admiration by saying **'Boy'** or **'Oh boy'.** *Boy, was that some party!*

boycott /bɔɪkɒt/, **boycotts, boycotting, boycotted.** VB WITH OBJ When people **boycott** a country, organization, or event, they refuse to be involved with it, because they strongly disapprove of it. *He urged all citizens to boycott the polls.* Also COUNT N *...an Olympic boycott.*

boyfriend /bɔɪfrend/, **boyfriends.** COUNT N Someone's **boyfriend** is the man with whom they are having a romantic or sexual relationship.

boyish /bɔɪɪʃ/. ADJ If you say that someone is **boyish,** you mean that they are like a boy in their appearance or behaviour. *He still seemed boyish... ...her boyish clothes.* ♦ **boyishly** ADV *He grinned boyishly.*

bra /brɑ:/, **bras.** COUNT N A **bra** is a piece of underwear that a woman wears to support her breasts.

brace /breɪs/, **braces, bracing, braced.** 1 REFL VB If you **brace** yourself for something unpleasant or difficult, you prepare yourself for it. *She had braced herself to read the letter.* 2 VB WITH OBJ AND 'against' If you **brace** a part of your body against something, you press the part of your body against it, to steady yourself or to avoid falling. *He braced a hand against a doorpost.* 3 VB WITH OBJ If you **brace** your shoulders or legs, you keep them stiffly in a particular position. *He stood to attention, his shoulders braced.* 4 COUNT N A **brace** is a metal device fastened to a child's teeth to help them grow straight. 5 COUNT N A **brace** is also a device attached to a person's leg to strengthen or support it. 6 PLURAL N **Braces** are a pair of straps that you wear over your shoulders to prevent your trousers from falling down; a British use. 7 COUNT N You can refer to two things of the same kind as a **brace,** especially two wild birds that have been killed for sport or food. The plural is also 'brace'. *...a brace of pheasants.*

bracelet /breɪslı^{2}t/, **bracelets.** COUNT N A **bracelet** is a chain or band that you wear round your wrist.

bracing /breɪsıŋ/. ADJ If you describe a place, climate, or activity as **bracing,** you mean that it makes you feel fit and full of energy.

bracken /brækə^{0}n/. UNCOUNT N **Bracken** is a plant like a large fern that grows on hills and in woods.

bracket /brækı^{2}t/, **brackets, bracketing, bracketed.** 1 COUNT N **Brackets** are a pair of written marks such as ( ) that you place round a word, expression, or sentence in order to indicate that you are giving extra information. 2 VB WITH OBJ To **bracket** a word, expression, or sentence means to put brackets round it. *...a bracketed question mark.* 3 COUNT N WITH SUPP If you say that something is in a particular **bracket,** you mean that it is within a particular range, for example a range of prices or ages. *...the 14-16 age bracket.* 4 VB WITH OBJ AND 'together' OR 'with' When you **bracket** two or more things or people together, you consider them as being similar or related in some way. 5 COUNT N A **bracket** is also a piece of metal, wood, or plastic that is fastened to a wall to support something such as a shelf.

brag /bræg/, **brags, bragging, bragged.** VB If you **brag,** you say in a very proud way that you have something or have done something. *He bragged to two nurses that he had killed a man.*

braid /breɪd/, **braids, braiding, braided.** 1 UNCOUNT N **Braid** is a narrow piece of decorated cloth or twisted threads, which is used to decorate clothes or curtains. *...a cap with gold braid on it.* 2 VB WITH OBJ If you **braid** hair, you plait it; an American use. 3 COUNT N A **braid** is a length of hair which has been plaited and tied; an American use. *Carole was plump, with long braids.*

Braille /breɪl/. UNCOUNT N **Braille** is a system of printing for blind people. The letters are printed as groups of raised dots that you feel with your fingers.

brain /breɪn/, **brains.** 1 COUNT N Your **brain** is the organ inside your head that enables you to think and to feel things such as heat and pain. 2 COUNT N You also use **brain** to refer to your mind and the way you think. *He had one clear wish in his confused brain.* 3 COUNT N If you say that someone has **brains** or a good **brain,** you mean that they have the ability to learn and understand things quickly, to solve problems, and to make good decisions. *He'd got brains but wouldn't use them... She has a very capable business brain.* 4 COUNT N Very clever people are sometimes referred to as **brains;** an informal use. *Not even the great brains of Cambridge can solve his problem.* 5 SING N The person who plans the activities of an organization can be referred to as its **brains;** an informal use. *She was the brains of the company.*

PHRASES • If you **pick** someone's **brains,** you ask them to help you with a problem because they know a lot about the subject; an informal use. to • **rack** your brains: see **rack.**

brainchild /breɪntʃaɪld/. SING N WITH POSS Someone's **brainchild** is an idea or invention that they have thought up or created.

brainless /breɪnlı^{2}s/. ADJ If you say that someone is **brainless,** you mean that they are very silly.

brainwash /breɪnwɒʃ/, **brainwashes, brainwashing, brainwashed.** VB WITH OBJ If you **brainwash** someone, you force them to believe something by continually telling them that it is true, and preventing them from thinking about it properly.

brainwave /breɪnweɪv/, **brainwaves.** COUNT N If you have a **brainwave,** you suddenly think of a clever idea.

brainy /breɪni^1/, **brainier, brainiest.** ADJ Someone who is **brainy** is clever and good at learning; an informal use.

brake /breɪk/, **brakes, braking, braked.** 1 COUNT N A vehicle's **brakes** are devices that make it go slower or stop. 2 VB When the driver of a vehicle **brakes,** or when the vehicle **brakes,** the driver makes the vehicle slow down or stop by using the brakes. *Try to avoid sudden braking.*

bramble /bræmbə^{0}l/, **brambles.** COUNT N **Brambles** are wild, thorny bushes that produce blackberries.

bran /bræn/. UNCOUNT N **Bran** is the small brown flakes that are left when wheat grains have been used to make white flour.

branch /brɑːntʃ/, **branches, branching, branched.** 1 COUNT N The **branches** of a tree are the parts that grow out from its trunk and that have leaves, flowers, or fruit growing on them. 2 COUNT N A **branch** of a business or other organization is one of the offices, shops, or local groups which belong to it. 3 COUNT N WITH SUPP A **branch** of a subject is a part or type of it. *...specialists in particular branches of medicine.*

branch off. PHR VB A road or path that **branches off** from another one starts from it and goes in a slightly different direction.

branch out. PHR VB If you **branch out,** you do something different from your normal activities or work. *She decided to branch out alone and launch a campaign.*

brand /brænd/, **brands, branding, branded.** 1 COUNT N A **brand** of a product is the version made by one particular manufacturer. *...a preference for one brand of soft drink rather than another.* 2 COUNT N WITH 'of' You can refer to a kind of thought, behaviour, or writing as a particular **brand** of it. *...their brand of politics.* 3 VB WITH OBJ AND COMPLEMENT OR 'as' If you **are branded** as something bad, people decide and say that you are that thing. *His political supporters had been branded traitors... Hamburgers have been branded as junk food.* 4 VB WITH OBJ When an animal **is branded,** a permanent mark is burned on its skin, in order to indicate who it belongs to.

brandish /brændɪʃ/, **brandishes, brandishing, brandished.** VB WITH OBJ If you **brandish** something, especially a weapon, you wave it vigorously. *They sprang high into the air brandishing their spears.*

brand name, brand names. COUNT N The **brand name** of a product made by a particular manufacturer is the name that appears on it.

brand-new. ADJ Something that is **brand-new** is completely new.

brandy /brændi^{1}/, **brandies.** MASS N **Brandy** is a strong alcoholic drink, usually made from wine.

brash /bræʃ/, **brasher, brashest.** ADJ If someone's behaviour is **brash,** they are being too confident and aggressive. *...these brash children.*

brass /brɑːs/. 1 UNCOUNT N **Brass** is a yellow metal made from copper and zinc. It is used especially for making ornaments and musical instruments. 2 PLURAL N The section of an orchestra which consists of brass wind instruments such as trumpets and horns is called the **brass.** 3 PHRASE If you **get down to brass tacks,** you discuss the basic facts of a situation.

brassiere /bræsɪə, bræz-/, **brassieres.** COUNT N A **brassiere** is a bra; an old-fashioned use.

brat /bræt/, **brats.** COUNT N If you call a child a **brat,** you mean that he or she behaves badly or annoys you; an informal use.

bravado /brəvɑːdəʊ/. UNCOUNT N **Bravado** is an appearance of courage that someone shows in order to impress other people. *...a display of bravado.*

brave /breɪv/, **braver, bravest; braves, braving, braved.** 1 ADJ Someone who is **brave** is willing to do things which are dangerous, and does not show fear in difficult or dangerous situations. *...the brave young men who have fallen in the struggle... I think you were very brave to defy convention.* ♦ **bravely** ADV *He fought bravely at the Battle of Waterloo.* 2 PHRASE If you say that someone is **putting a brave face on** a difficult situation, you mean that they are pretending that they are happy. 3 VB WITH OBJ If you **brave** a difficult or dangerous situation, you deliberately experience it, in order to achieve something. *Farmers braved wintry conditions to rescue the sheep.*

bravery /breɪvə^{ə}ri^{1}/. UNCOUNT N **Bravery** is brave behaviour or the quality of being brave.

bravo /brɑːvəʊ/. CONVENTION You say **'Bravo'** to express appreciation when someone has done something well.

brawl /brɔːl/, **brawls, brawling, brawled.** 1 COUNT N A **brawl** is a rough fight or struggle. *A wild brawl followed.* 2 VB When people **brawl,** they take part in a brawl. *They were brawling in the street.*

brawny /brɔːni^{1}/. ADJ Someone who is **brawny** is strong and muscular. *...a brawny worker.*

bray /breɪ/, **brays, braying, brayed.** VB When a donkey **brays,** it makes the loud, harsh sound that donkeys make. Also COUNT N *...the bray of a donkey.*

brazen /breɪzə^{ə}n/, **brazens, brazening, brazened.** ADJ If you describe someone as **brazen,** you mean that they are very bold and do not care if other people think that they are behaving wrongly. *...his brazen breaking of the law.* ♦ **brazenly** ADV *No industry is more brazenly orientated towards quick, easy profits.*

brazen out. PHR VB If you have done something wrong and you **brazen** it **out,** you behave confidently in order not to appear ashamed.

brazier /breɪzɪə/, **braziers.** COUNT N A **brazier** is a large metal container in which people make a fire when they are outside in cold weather.

breach /briːtʃ/, **breaches, breaching, breached;** a formal word. 1 COUNT N OR UNCOUNT N A **breach** of a law or agreement is an act of breaking it. *It was a breach of regulations... They were alleging breach of contract.* 2 COUNT N A **breach** in a relationship is a serious disagreement which often results in the relationship ending. *This was the most profound breach in our marriage.* 3 VB WITH OBJ If you **breach** a barrier, you make a gap in it in order to get through it. *He breached the enemy barbed wire.* 4 COUNT N A **breach** in a barrier is a gap or crack in it. *They rush to defend any breach in the walls.*

bread /brɛd/. UNCOUNT N **Bread** is a very common food made from flour, water, and often yeast. The mixture is made into a soft dough and baked in an oven. *...some bread and cheese... ...a loaf of bread.*

breadcrumbs /brɛdkrʌmz/. PLURAL N **Breadcrumbs** are tiny pieces of bread.

breadth /brɛdθ/. 1 UNCOUNT N The **breadth** of something is the distance between its two sides. *...six yards in breadth and fifty yards long.* 2 UNCOUNT N WITH SUPP **Breadth** is also the quality of consisting of or involving many different things. *The very breadth of the subject gives it an added interest... ...his breadth of vision.* 3 See also **hair's breadth.**

breadwinner /brɛdwɪnə/, **breadwinners.** COUNT N In a family, the **breadwinner** is the person who earns the money that the family needs.

break /breɪk/, **breaks, breaking, broke** /brəʊk/, **broken** /brəʊkə^{ə}n/. 1 ERG VB When an object **breaks** or when you **break** it, it suddenly separates into two or more pieces, often because it has been hit or dropped. *The string broke... He has broken a window.* 2 ERG VB When a tool or piece of machinery **breaks** or when you **break** it, it is damaged and no longer works. 3 VB WITH OBJ If you **break** a rule, promise, or agreement, you do something that disobeys it. *We're not breaking the law.* 4 VB WITH OBJ To **break** a connection or situation that has existed for some time means to end it suddenly. *They cannot break the habit.* 5 VB WITH ADJUNCT If you **break** with a group of people, you stop being involved with them. If you **break** with a way of doing things, you stop doing things that way. *He broke with precedent by making his maiden speech on a controversial subject.* Also COUNT N *...their break with the Labour Party in 1968.* 6 VB WITH OBJ To **break** something also means to reduce its impact. *Fortunately, the tree broke her fall.* 7 VB WITH OBJ To **break** someone means to destroy their success or career. 8 ERG VB If you **break** a piece of news to someone, you tell it to them. *It was Ted who broke the news to me.* 9 VB WITH 'for' If you **break** for a meal, you stop what you are doing in order to have the meal. *We broke for tea.* 10 COUNT N A **break** is also a short period of time when you have a rest or a change from what you are doing. *We all met in the pub during the lunch break... The doctors had worked without a break.* 11 COUNT N A **break** is also a lucky opportunity; an informal use. *His big break came last spring in Australia.* 12 VB WITH OBJ If you **break** a record, you do better than the previous record for a particular achievement. *Oliver Barrett was out to break his New York-Boston speed record.* 13 VB When day **breaks,** it starts to grow light after the night has ended. 14 VB When a wave **breaks,** the highest part of it falls down. 15 VB WITH OBJ If you **break** a secret code, you work out how to read it. 16 VB When a boy's voice **breaks,** it becomes permanently deeper. 17 VB WITH OBJ In tennis, if you **break** your opponent's serve, you win a game in which your opponent is serving. 18 See also **broke, broken.**

PHRASES ● If you **break free** or **break** someone's **hold,** you free yourself by force from someone who is holding you. *He was trying to break free... He had my hands behind my back in a hold that was impossible to break.* ● When a company **breaks even,** it makes neither a profit nor a loss.

break down. PHR VB 1 When a machine or a vehicle **breaks down,** it stops working. *The car broke down three miles outside Winchester.* 2 When a system, plan, or discussion **breaks down,** it fails because of a problem or disagreement. *The talks broke down over differences on doctrine.* 3 When a substance **breaks down** or when something **breaks** it **down,** it changes into a different form because of a chemical process. *Enzymes break down proteins by chemical action.* 4 If someone **breaks down,** they start crying. 5 If you **break down** a door or barrier, you hit it so hard that it falls down. 6 See also **breakdown.**

break in. PHR VB 1 If someone **breaks in,** they get into a building by force. 2 If you **break in** on someone's conversation or activity, you interrupt them. 3 See also **break-in.**

break into. PHR VB 1 If someone **breaks into** a building, they get into it by force. 2 You can also use **break into** to indicate that someone suddenly starts doing something. *Rudolph broke into a run... The boys broke into applause.* 3 If you **break into** a new area of activity, you become involved in it. *...women wanting to break into the labour market.*

break off. PHR VB 1 When part of something **breaks off** or when you **break it off,** it is snapped off or torn away. *Garroway broke off another piece of bread.* 2 If you **break off** when you are doing or saying something, you suddenly stop doing it or saying it. 3 If you **break off** a relationship, you end it. *She broke off her engagement.*

break out. PHR VB 1 If something such as a fight or disease **breaks out,** it begins suddenly. 2 If you **break out** in a rash or a sweat or if it **breaks out,** it appears on your skin. *She felt the sweat break out on her forehead.*

break through. PHR VB 1 If you **break through** a barrier, you succeed in forcing your way through. *I broke through the bushes.* 2 See also **breakthrough.**

break up. PHR VB 1 When something **breaks up** or when you **break it up,** it separates or is divided into several smaller parts. *The wood broke up into a shower of fragments... ...bacteria that break up decaying vegetation.* 2 If you **break up** with your wife, husband, girlfriend, or boyfriend, you end your relationship with them; an informal use. 3 If an activity **breaks up** or if you **break it up,** it is brought to an end. *The party had just broken up... The policemen broke the fight up.* 4 When schools or their pupils **break up,** the term ends and the pupils start their holidays. 5 See also **break-up.**

breakable /breɪkəbə^{ə}l/. ADJ **Breakable** objects are easy to break by accident.

breakage /breɪkɪdʒ/, **breakages.** UNCOUNT N OR COUNT N **Breakage** is the act or result of breaking something; a formal use. *Accidental breakage of your household glass will be covered by the policy... ...the cost of breakages.*

breakaway /breɪkəweɪ/. ATTRIB ADJ A **breakaway** group is a group of people who have separated from a larger group. *...a breakaway party.*

breakdown /breɪkdaʊn/, **breakdowns.** 1 COUNT N OR UNCOUNT N WITH SUPP The **breakdown** of a system, plan, or discussion is its failure or ending. *There was a serious breakdown of communications... ...industrial and social breakdown.* 2 COUNT N If you suffer a **breakdown,** you become so depressed that you cannot cope with life. 3 COUNT N If you have a **breakdown** when travelling by car, your car stops working. 4 COUNT N A **breakdown** of something is a list of its separate parts. *Mr Willis gave the following breakdown.*

breaker /breɪkə/, **breakers.** COUNT N **Breakers** are large sea waves.

breakfast /brɛkfəst/, **breakfasts, breakfasting, breakfasted.** 1 UNCOUNT N OR COUNT N **Breakfast** is the first meal of the day, which is usually eaten early in the morning. 2 VB When you **breakfast,** you have breakfast; a formal use.

break-in, break-ins. COUNT N When there is a **break-in,** someone gets into a building by force.

breakneck /breɪknɛk/. ATTRIB ADJ Something that happens or travels at **breakneck** speed happens or travels very fast.

breakthrough /breɪkθruː/, **breakthroughs.** COUNT N A **breakthrough** is an important development or achievement. *Scientists are on the brink of a major breakthrough.*

break-up, break-ups. UNCOUNT N OR COUNT N The **break-up** of a group, relationship, or system is its end. *This caused the break-up of the coalition.*

breakwater /breɪkwɔːtə/, **breakwaters.** COUNT N A **breakwater** is a wooden or stone wall that extends from the shore into the sea. It is built to protect a harbour or beach from the force of the waves.

breast /brɛst/, **breasts.** 1 COUNT N A woman's **breasts** are the two soft, round pieces of flesh on her chest that can produce milk to feed a baby. 2 COUNT N A person's chest can be referred to as his or her **breast;** an old-fashioned or literary use. *The bullet pierced Joel's breast.* 3 COUNT N WITH SUPP When someone experiences an emotion, you can say that they feel it in their **breast;** an old-fashioned or literary use. *...the creation of national pride in the breasts of Frenchmen.* 4 COUNT N A bird's **breast** is the front part of its body. 5 PHRASE If you **make a clean breast** of something, you tell someone the truth about yourself or about something wrong that you have done.

breastbone /brɛstbəʊn/, **breastbones.** COUNT N Your **breastbone** is the long vertical bone in the centre of your chest.

breast-feed, breast-feeds, breast-feeding, breast-fed. VB WITH OBJ When a woman **breast-feeds** her baby, she feeds it with milk from her breasts, rather than from a bottle. *...babies who cannot be breast-fed.* ♦ **breast-feeding** UNCOUNT N *A big advantage of breast-feeding is that the milk is always pure.*

breaststroke /brestrəuk/. UNCOUNT N **Breaststroke** is a swimming stroke which you do lying on your front, moving your arms and legs horizontally.

breath /breθ/, **breaths.** 1 COUNT N OR UNCOUNT N Your **breath** is the air which you take into and let out of your lungs when you breathe. *You could smell the whisky on his breath.* 2 COUNT N When you take a **breath,** you breathe in.
PHRASES ● If you are **out of breath,** you are breathing quickly and with difficulty because you have been doing something energetic. ● When you **get** your **breath** back after doing something energetic, you start breathing normally again. ● If you **hold** your **breath,** you stop breathing for a short while. ● If you say something **under** your **breath,** you say it in a very quiet voice. *I was cursing him under my breath.* ● If you get **a breath of fresh air,** you go outside because it is stuffy indoors. ● If you say that something **takes** your **breath away,** you mean that it is extremely beautiful or amazing.

breathalyze /breθəlaɪz/, **breathalyzes, breathalyzing, breathalyzed;** also spelled **breathalyse.** VB WITH OBJ When the police **breathalyze** a driver, they ask the driver to breathe into a special bag to see if he or she has drunk too much alcohol.

breathe /briːð/, **breathes, breathing, breathed.** 1 VB WITH OR WITHOUT OBJ When people or animals **breathe,** they take air into their lungs and let it out again. *I breathed deeply... When we breathed the air, it smelt sweet.* ♦ **breathing** UNCOUNT N *He could hear her deep, regular breathing.* 2 VB WITH OBJ AND ADJUNCT If you **breathe** smoke or fumes over someone, you send smoke or fumes out of your mouth towards them. 3 PHRASE If you say that someone **is breathing down** your **neck,** you mean that they are paying such careful attention to everything you do that you feel uncomfortable and unable to act freely. 4 REPORT VB If someone says something very quietly, you can say that they **breathe** it; a literary use. *'Frank,' she breathed. 'Help me, please.'* 5 VB WITH OBJ Someone who **breathes** life, confidence, or excitement into something gives this quality to it; a literary use.
breathe in. PHR VB When you **breathe in,** you take some air into your lungs.
breathe out. PHR VB When you **breathe out,** you send air out of your lungs through your nose or mouth.

breather /briːðə/, **breathers.** COUNT N If you take or have a **breather,** you stop what you are doing for a short time and have a rest; an informal use.

breathing space. SING N A **breathing space** is a short period of time in which you can recover from one activity and prepare for a second one.

breathless /breθlɪ^{2}s/. ADJ If you are **breathless,** you have difficulty in breathing properly, for example because you have been running. *She opened the door, a little breathless from climbing the stairs.* ♦ **breathlessly** ADV *'Miss Crabbe's on the telephone,' I said breathlessly.* ♦ **breathlessness** UNCOUNT N *Obesity causes breathlessness.*

breathtaking /breθteɪkɪŋ/. ADJ If you say that something is **breathtaking,** you mean that it is extremely beautiful or amazing. *...breathtaking scenery.* ♦ **breathtakingly** SUBMOD *...breathtakingly beautiful gowns.*

bred /bred/. **Bred** is the past tense and past participle of **breed.**

breeches /brɪtʃɪz/. PLURAL N **Breeches** are trousers which reach as far as your knees.

breed /briːd/, **breeds, breeding, bred** /bred/. 1 COUNT N A **breed** of animal is a particular type of it. For example, terriers are a breed of dog. *Different breeds of sheep give wool of varying lengths.* 2 VB WITH OBJ If you **breed** animals or plants, you keep them for the purpose of producing more animals or plants with particular qualities, in a controlled way. *Strains of the plant have been bred that resist more diseases.* ♦ **breeding** UNCOUNT N *We retain a small proportion of bulls for breeding purposes.* 3 VB When animals **breed,** they mate and produce offspring. ♦ **breeding** UNCOUNT N *The breeding season is a very long one.* 4 VB WITH OBJ If something **breeds** a situation or feeling, it causes it to develop; a literary use. *The rumours bred hope.* 5 PHRASE Someone who was **born and bred** in a particular place was born there and spent their childhood there. 6 COUNT N WITH SUPP A particular **breed** of person is a type of person, with special qualities or skills. *This required a whole new breed of actors.*

breeding /briːdɪŋ/. UNCOUNT N Someone who has **breeding** has been taught how to behave correctly with good manners, and is often upper-class. *She certainly lacked breeding.*

breeze /briːz/, **breezes, breezing, breezed.** 1 COUNT N A **breeze** is a gentle wind. 2 VB WITH ADJUNCT If you **breeze** into a place, you enter it suddenly, in a very casual manner. *I just breezed into her room, flinging the door wide.*

breezy /briːzi^1/. 1 ADJ Someone who is **breezy** behaves in a brisk, casual, cheerful, and confident manner. 2 ADJ When the weather is **breezy,** there is a fairly strong but pleasant wind blowing.

brethren /breðrɪ^{2}n/. **Brethren** is an old-fashioned plural of **brother.**

brevity /brevɪ^{1}ti^1/. UNCOUNT N The **brevity** of something is the fact that it lasts for only a short time; a formal use. *...the brevity and frailty of human existence.*

brew /bruː/, **brews, brewing, brewed.** 1 ERG VB When you **brew** tea or coffee or when it **brews,** it is made by letting hot water take the flavour of tea leaves or ground coffee. 2 COUNT N A **brew** is a drink made by mixing something such as tea with hot water. *...herbal brews.* 3 VB WITH OBJ When people **brew** beer, they make it. 4 VB If an unpleasant situation **is brewing,** it is starting to develop. *A crisis was brewing.*

brewer /bruːə/, **brewers.** COUNT N A **brewer** is a person who makes beer or who owns a brewery.

brewery /brʊəri^1/, **breweries.** COUNT N A **brewery** is a company which makes beer, or a place where beer is made.

bribe /braɪb/, **bribes, bribing, bribed.** 1 COUNT N A **bribe** is a sum of money or something valuable given to an official in order to persuade the official to do something. *The Vice President admitted taking bribes.* 2 VB WITH OBJ If someone **bribes** an official, they give the official a bribe. *The attempt to bribe the clerk had failed.*

bribery /braɪbə^{0}ri^1/. UNCOUNT N **Bribery** is the action of giving an official a bribe. *The court found Williams guilty of bribery.*

bric-a-brac /brɪkəbræk/. UNCOUNT N **Bric-a-brac** consists of small ornamental objects of no great value.

brick /brɪk/, **bricks, bricking, bricked.** COUNT N OR UNCOUNT N **Bricks** are rectangular blocks of baked clay used for building walls. *...a massive old building of crumbling red brick.*
brick up. PHR VB If you **brick up** a door or window, you close it with a wall of bricks.

bricklayer /brɪkleɪə/, **bricklayers.** COUNT N A **bricklayer** is a person whose job is to build walls using bricks.

brickwork /brɪkwɜːk/. UNCOUNT N You can refer to the bricks in the walls of a building as the **brickwork.**

bridal /braɪdə^{0}l/. ATTRIB ADJ **Bridal** means relating to a bride or a wedding. *...her bridal costume.*

bride /braɪd/, **brides.** COUNT N A **bride** is a woman who is getting married or who has just got married.

bridegroom /braɪdgru^{4}m/, **bridegrooms.** COUNT N A **bridegroom** is a man who is getting married.

bridesmaid /braɪdzmeɪd/, **bridesmaids.** COUNT N A **bridesmaid** is a woman or a girl who helps and accompanies a bride on her wedding day.

bridge /brɪdʒ/, **bridges.** 1 COUNT N A **bridge** is a structure built over a river, road, or railway so that people or vehicles can cross from one side to the other. *...the little bridge over the stream.* 2 COUNT N Something that is a **bridge** between two groups or things makes it easier for the differences between them to be overcome. *We need to build a bridge between East and West.* 3 COUNT N The **bridge** of a ship is the high part from which the ship is steered. 4 UNCOUNT N **Bridge** is a card game for four players.

bridle /braɪdə^{0}l/, **bridles, bridling, bridled.** 1 COUNT N A **bridle** is a set of straps that is put around a horse's head and mouth so that the person riding or driving the horse can control it. 2 VB WITH OBJ When you **bridle** a horse, you put a bridle on it.

brief /briːf/, **briefer, briefest; briefs, briefing, briefed.** 1 ADJ Something that is **brief** lasts for only a short time. *There was a brief scuffle.* 2 PRED ADJ If you are **brief,** you say what you want to say in as few words as possible. 3 ADJ A **brief** skirt or pair of shorts is very short. 4 PLURAL N **Briefs** are pants or knickers. 5 VB WITH OBJ When you **brief** someone, you give them information that they need before they do something.

briefcase /briːfkeɪs/, **briefcases.** COUNT N A **briefcase** is a case for carrying documents.

briefing /briːfɪŋ/, **briefings.** COUNT N A **briefing** is a meeting at which information or instructions are given to people, usually just before they do something.

briefly /briːfli^1/. 1 ADV Something that happens **briefly** happens for a very short period of time. *He smiled briefly.* 2 ADV If you say something **briefly,** you use very few words or give very few details. *She told them briefly what had happened.* 3 SENTENCE ADV You can say **briefly** to indicate that you are about to say something in as few words as possible. *The facts, briefly, are these.*

brigade /brɪgeɪd/, **brigades.** COLL N A **brigade** is one of the groups which an army is divided into. ● See also **fire brigade.**

brigadier /brɪgədɪə/, **brigadiers.** COUNT N OR TITLE A **brigadier** is an army officer of high rank.

bright /braɪt/, **brighter, brightest.** 1 ADJ A **bright** colour is strong and noticeable, and not dark. *Her eyes were bright blue.* ♦ **brightly** ADV *...brightly coloured silk blouses.* 2 ADJ A **bright** light is shining strongly. *The sun was bright and hot.* ♦ **brightly** ADV *The sun shone brightly.* ♦ **brightness** UNCOUNT N *Already the stars were losing their brightness.* 3 ADJ **Bright** people are quick at learning things. *...the brightest girls in the school.* 4 ATTRIB ADJ A **bright** idea is clever and original. 5 PRED ADJ If someone looks or sounds **bright,** they look or sound cheerful. ♦ **brightly** ADV *'Fine!' I said brightly.* 6 ADJ If the future is **bright,** it is likely to be pleasant and successful. *The economic outlook is bright.* 7 PHRASE **Bright and early** means very early in the morning. *I was up bright and early, eager to be off.*

brighten /braɪtə^{0}n/, **brightens, brightening, brightened.** 1 VB If you **brighten** or if your face **brightens,** you suddenly look happier. *Her face brightened. 'Oh, hi! It's you.'* 2 VB WITH OBJ To **brighten** a situation means to make it more pleasant and enjoyable. *You girls brighten our Sundays.* 3 ERG VB When a light **brightens** a place, the place becomes brighter or lighter. *Stars brighten the night sky... The grey sky brightened with the flash of their guns.*
brighten up. PHR VB 1 If you **brighten up,** you look happier. 2 To **brighten up** a place means to make it more colourful and attractive. *These flowers will brighten up your garden.*

brilliant /brɪljənt/. 1 ADJ If you describe people or ideas as **brilliant,** you mean that they are extremely clever. *...a brilliant young engineer.* ♦ **brilliantly** ADV *He acted brilliantly in a wide range of parts.* ♦ **brilliance** /brɪljəns/ UNCOUNT N *...a writer of tremendous brilliance.* 2 ADJ People also say that something is **brilliant** when they are very pleased with it or think it is very good; an informal British use. 3 ATTRIB ADJ A **brilliant** career is very successful. *He predicted a brilliant future for the child.* 4 ATTRIB ADJ A **brilliant** light or colour is extremely bright. *...a brilliant yellow flame.* ♦ **brilliantly** ADV *Many of them are brilliantly coloured.*

brim /brɪm/, **brims, brimming, brimmed.** 1 COUNT N The **brim** of a hat is the wide part that sticks outwards at the bottom. 2 PHRASE If a container is filled **to the brim** with something, it is filled right up to the top. *The pool was full to the brim with brown water.* 3 VB If something **is brimming** with things of a particular kind, it is full of them. *...a group of youngsters, all brimming with ideas... Her eyes brimmed with tears.*
brim over. PHR VB 1 When a container or the liquid in it **brims over,** the liquid spills out. *He poured wine into Daniel's glass until it brimmed over.* 2 If you **are brimming over** with a pleasant feeling, you behave in a way that shows how pleased you are. *She rushed to her mother, brimming over with joy and pride.*

brine /braɪn/. UNCOUNT N **Brine** is salty water that is used for preserving food.

bring /brɪŋ/, **brings, bringing, brought** /brɔːt/. 1 VB WITH OBJ If you **bring** someone or something with you when you come to a place, they come with you or you have them with you. *He would have to bring Judy with him... Please bring your calculator to every lesson.* 2 VB WITH OBJ AND ADJUNCT If you **bring** something to a different place or position, you move it there. *He opened the case and brought out a pair of glasses... Sheldon brought his right hand to his head.* 3 VB WITH OBJ AND OBJ If you **bring** something to someone, you fetch it for them or carry it to them. *Bring me a glass of wine.* 4 VB WITH OBJ AND ADJUNCT When something causes people to come to a place, you can say that it **brings** them there. *The festival brings a great many people to Glastonbury.* 5 VB WITH OBJ AND ADJUNCT To **bring** someone or something into a particular state or condition means to cause them to be in that state or condition. *These ideas had brought him into conflict with Stalin... The wind had brought several trees down... He brought the car to a stop.* 6 VB WITH OBJ If something **brings** a particular feeling, situation, or quality, it causes it. *Could it be true that money did not bring happiness?... The biting wind brought tears to her eyes.* 7 REFL VB WITH TO-INF If you cannot **bring** yourself to do something, you cannot make yourself do it. *I could not bring myself to touch him.* 8 VB WITH OBJ If you **bring** a legal action against someone, you officially accuse them of doing something unlawful.
bring about. PHR VB To **bring** something **about** means to cause it to happen. *The Administration helped bring about a peaceful settlement.*
bring along. PHR VB If you **bring** someone or some-

thing **along,** you bring them with you when you come to a place. *Bring your friends along.*

bring back. PHR VB **1** If something **brings back** a memory, it makes you start thinking about it. *Losing a husband can bring back memories of childhood loss.* **2** When people **bring back** a fashion or practice that existed at an earlier time, they introduce it again. *Many of the students appear to be trying to bring back the crew cut.*

bring down. PHR VB To **bring down** a government or ruler means to cause them to lose power. *A national strike would bring the government down.*

bring forward. PHR VB **1** To **bring forward** a meeting or lecture means to arrange for it to take place at an earlier time than had been planned. *The meeting has been brought forward to Tuesday.* **2** If you **bring forward** an argument or proposal, you state it so that people can consider it.

bring in. PHR VB **1** When a government or organization **brings in** a new law or system, they introduce it. *The government intends to bring in legislation to control their activities.* **2** To **bring in** money means to earn it; an informal use. *Tourism is a big industry, bringing in £7 billion a year.*

bring off. PHR VB If you **bring off** something difficult, you succeed in doing it; an informal use.

bring out. PHR VB **1** When a person or company **brings out** a new product, they produce it and sell it. *I've just brought out a book on Dostoevski.* **2** Something that **brings out** a particular kind of behaviour in you causes you to behave in that way. *These dreadful circumstances bring out the worst in everybody.*

bring round or **bring to.** PHR VB If you **bring round** someone who is unconscious or **bring** them **to,** you make them become conscious again.

bring up. PHR VB **1** To **bring up** a child means to look after it until it is grown up. *Tony was brought up strictly.* **2** If you **bring up** a particular subject, you introduce it into a discussion or conversation. **3** If you **bring up** food, you vomit; an informal use.

brink /brɪŋk/. SING N If you are on the **brink** of something important, terrible, or exciting, you are just about to do it or experience it. *The country was on the brink of civil war... I was on the brink of losing my temper.*

brisk /brɪsk/, **brisker, briskest. 1** ADJ Someone who is **brisk** behaves in a busy, confident way which shows that they want to get things done quickly. *Lynn's tone was brisk.* ♦ **briskly** ADV *'We've been into that,' said Posy briskly.* **2** ADJ A **brisk** action is done quickly and in an energetic way. *I went for a brisk swim.* ♦ **briskly** ADV *He walked briskly down the street.* **3** ADJ If trade or business is **brisk,** things are being sold very quickly and a lot of money is being made. *They are doing a brisk trade in cars.* **4** ADJ If the weather is **brisk,** it is cold and refreshing. *...brisk winds.*

bristle /brɪsə^{0}l/, **bristles, bristling, bristled. 1** COUNT N OR UNCOUNT N **Bristles** are thick, strong animal hairs that are sometimes used to make brushes. *...hog's bristles... ...a bristle toothbrush.* **2** PLURAL N The **bristles** of a brush are the thick hairs or hair-like pieces of plastic attached to the handle. **3** PLURAL N The **bristles** on the chin of a man who has shaved recently are the short hairs growing there. **4** VB If the hair on your body **bristles,** it rises away from your skin because you are cold, frightened, or angry. *I felt the hairs bristle along the back of my neck.* **5** VB If you **bristle** at something, you react to it angrily. *Eddie bristled at being called a 'girl'.*

bristle with. PHR VB If a place **bristles with** objects or people, there are a lot of them there. *The hotel was bristling with policemen.*

bristly /brɪsli^1/. **1** ADJ **Bristly** hair is rough, coarse, and thick. **2** ADJ If a man's chin is **bristly,** it is covered with bristles because he has not shaved recently.

British /brɪtɪʃ/. **1** ADJ **British** means belonging or relating to Great Britain. *...British textile companies.* **2** PLURAL N The **British** are the people who come from Great Britain. *The British are very good at sympathy.*

Briton /brɪtə^{0}n/, **Britons.** COUNT N A **Briton** is a person who comes from Great Britain.

brittle /brɪtə^{0}l/. **1** ADJ A **brittle** object or substance is hard but easily broken. *...dry sticks as brittle as candy.* **2** ADJ A **brittle** sound is short, loud, and sharp. *There was a sharp, brittle tinkling.*

broach /brəʊtʃ/, **broaches, broaching, broached.** VB WITH OBJ When you **broach** a subject, you mention it in order to start a discussion on it.

broad /brɔːd/, **broader, broadest. 1** ADJ Something that is **broad** is wide. *The streets of this town are broad... He was tall, with broad shoulders.* **2** ADJ You also use **broad** to describe something that involves many different things or people. *She had a broader range of interests than Jane... This syllabus is a broad one... ...a broad feeling that the West lacks direction.* **3** ATTRIB ADJ A **broad** description is general rather than detailed. *The book gives a broad introduction to linguistics.* **4** ATTRIB ADJ You use **broad** to describe a hint or sarcastic remark and indicate that its meaning is very obvious. *Broad hints were aired that the paper should be closed down.* **5** ADJ A **broad** accent is strong and noticeable. *He has a broad Wiltshire accent.* **6** PHRASE A crime that is committed **in broad daylight** is committed during the day, rather than at night.

broad bean, broad beans. COUNT N **Broad beans** are flat, light green beans.

broadcast /brɔːdkɑːst/, **broadcasts, broadcasting, broadcasted.** The past tense and past participle can be **broadcasted** or **broadcast. 1** COUNT N A **broadcast** is something that you hear on the radio or see on television. *He was criticized for making these broadcasts.* **2** VB WITH OR WITHOUT OBJ To **broadcast** a programme means to send it out by radio waves, so that it can be heard on the radio or seen on television. *Episode One was broadcast last night.* ♦ **broadcasting** UNCOUNT N *...the purpose of educational broadcasting.*

broadcaster /brɔːdkɑːstə/, **broadcasters.** COUNT N A **broadcaster** is someone who gives talks or takes part in discussions on radio or television.

broaden /brɔːdə^{0}n/, **broadens, broadening, broadened. 1** VB When something **broadens,** it becomes wider. *Her smile broadened a little.* **2** ERG VB If you **broaden** something, you make it involve or affect more things or people. *He made another attempt to broaden his appeal... ...a time of broadening horizons.* • If an experience **broadens** your **mind,** it makes you more willing to accept other people's beliefs and customs.

broadly /brɔːdli^1/. **1** SENTENCE ADV You can use **broadly** or **broadly speaking** to indicate that although there may be a few exceptions to what you are saying, it is true in almost all cases. *You can see that, broadly speaking, it is really quite straightforward.* **2** ADV You can also use **broadly** to say that something is true to a large extent. *I was broadly in favour of it.* **3** ADV If someone smiles **broadly,** their mouth is stretched very wide because they are very pleased or amused.

broadminded /brɔːdmaɪndɪ^{2}d/. ADJ Someone who is **broadminded** does not disapprove of actions or attitudes that many other people disapprove of. *She assured me that her parents were broadminded.*

brocade /brə^{6}keɪd/. UNCOUNT N **Brocade** is a thick, expensive material, often made of silk, with a raised pattern on it.

broccoli /brɒkəli^1/. UNCOUNT N **Broccoli** is a vegetable with green stalks and green or purple flower buds.

brochure /brəʊʃ^{0}ʊ^{0}ə/, **brochures.** COUNT N A **brochure** is a magazine or booklet with pictures that gives you information about a product or service. *...travel brochures.*

broke /brəʊk/. **1 Broke** is the past tense of **break. 2** PRED ADJ If you are **broke,** you have no money; an informal use. **3** PHRASE If a company **goes broke,** it loses money and is unable to continue in business.

broken /brəʊkə^{0}n/. **1 Broken** is the past participle of **break. 2** ADJ An object that is **broken** has split into pieces or has cracked, for example because it has been hit or dropped. *He sweeps away the broken glass under the window... He was rushed to hospital with a broken back.* **3** ADJ A **broken** tool or piece of machinery is damaged and no longer works. *The telephone is broken.* **4** ADJ A **broken** line, sound, or process is interrupted rather than continuous. *...a broken curve.* **5** ADJ A **broken** promise or contract has not been kept or obeyed. **6** ATTRIB ADJ A **broken** marriage has ended in divorce. **7** ATTRIB ADJ If someone talks, for example, in **broken** French, they speak slowly and make a lot of mistakes because they do not know the language very well.

broken-down. ADJ A **broken-down** vehicle or machine no longer works because it has something wrong with it. *...two men pushing a broken-down car.*

broken-hearted. ADJ Someone who is **broken-hearted** is very sad and upset because they have had a serious disappointment.

broken home, broken homes. COUNT N If you say that someone comes from a **broken home,** you mean that their family did not live together, because their parents were separated or divorced.

broker /brəʊkə/, **brokers.** COUNT N A **broker** is a person whose job is to buy and sell shares, foreign money, or goods for other people. *...an insurance broker.*

brolly /brɒli^1/, **brollies.** COUNT N A **brolly** is an umbrella; a British use.

bronchial tubes. PLURAL N Your **bronchial tubes** are the two tubes which connect your windpipe to your lungs.

bronchitis /brɒŋkaɪtɪ^{1}s/. UNCOUNT N **Bronchitis** is an illness in which your bronchial tubes become sore and infected.

bronze /brɒnz/, **bronzes. 1** UNCOUNT N **Bronze** is a yellowish-brown metal made from copper and tin. **2** ADJ Something that is **bronze** is yellowish-brown. *...bronze hair.*

bronzed /brɒnzd/. ADJ Someone who is **bronzed** is sun-tanned in an attractive way.

bronze medal, bronze medals. COUNT N A **bronze medal** is a medal made of bronze which is awarded as third prize in a contest or competition.

brooch /brəʊtʃ/, **brooches.** COUNT N A **brooch** is a small piece of jewellery which a woman attaches to her clothing.

brood /bruːd/, **broods, brooding, brooded. 1** COLL N A **brood** is a group of baby birds belonging to the same mother. *...a brood of ducklings.* **2** VB If someone **broods** about something, they think about it a lot, seriously and often unhappily. *He brooded on his failure.*

brooding /bruːdɪŋ/. ADJ Something that is **brooding** is disturbing and threatening; a literary use. *Once or twice the grey, brooding sky rumbled and flashed.*

broody /bruːdi^1/. **1** ADJ You say that someone is **broody** when they are thinking a lot about something in an unhappy way. *Frustrated workers become broody and resentful.* **2** ADJ A **broody** hen is ready to lay or sit on eggs.

brook /brʊk/, **brooks.** COUNT N A **brook** is a small stream.

broom /bru^{4}m/, **brooms.** COUNT N A **broom** is a long-handled brush which is used to sweep the floor.

broomstick /bru^{4}mstɪk/, **broomsticks.** COUNT N A **broomstick** is a broom with a bundle of twigs at the end. Witches are said to fly on broomsticks.

broth /brɒθ/. UNCOUNT N **Broth** is soup, often with meat or vegetables floating in it.

brothel /brɒθə^{0}l/, **brothels.** COUNT N A **brothel** is a building where men pay to have sex with prostitutes.

brother /brʌðə/, **brothers.** The old-fashioned form **brethren** /brɛðrɪ^{1}n/ is also used as the plural for meanings 2 and 3. **1** COUNT N Your **brother** is a boy or a man who has the same parents as you. *I have two brothers and one sister.* • See also **half-brother. 2** COUNT N Some people describe a man as their **brother** when he belongs to the same religion or trade union that they belong to. **3** TITLE **Brother** is a title given to a man who belongs to a religious institution such as a monastery. *...Brother Michael.*

brotherhood /brʌðəhʊd/, **brotherhoods. 1** UNCOUNT N **Brotherhood** is the affection and loyalty that you feel for people who you have something in common with. *...a deepening sense of brotherhood.* **2** COUNT N A **brotherhood** is an organization whose members all have the same political aims and beliefs or the same job or profession.

brother-in-law, brothers-in-law. COUNT N Your **brother-in-law** is the brother of your husband or wife, or the man who is married to your sister or to your wife's or husband's sister.

brotherly /brʌðəli^1/. ATTRIB ADJ **Brotherly** feelings are the feelings of love and loyalty which you expect a brother to show.

brought /brɔːt/. **Brought** is the past tense and past participle of **bring.**

brow /braʊ/, **brows. 1** COUNT N Your **brow** is your forehead. *He mopped his sweating brow.* **2** COUNT N Your **brows** are your eyebrows. • **to knit** your brows: see **knit. 3** COUNT N The **brow** of a hill is the top of it.

browbeat /braʊbiːt/, **browbeats, browbeating, browbeaten. Browbeat** is used in the present tense and is the past tense. VB WITH OBJ If you **browbeat** someone, you bully them and try to force them to do what you want. *She browbeat her parents into letting her go.*

brown /braʊn/, **browner, brownest; browns, browning, browned. 1** ADJ Something that is **brown** is the colour of earth or wood. *...long brown hair.* **2** ADJ You can say that someone is **brown** when their skin is darker than usual because they have been in the sun. **3** ERG VB When something **browns** or **is browned,** it becomes browner in colour. *Her hands had been browned by the sun.*

brownish /braʊnɪʃ/. ADJ Something that is **brownish** is slightly brown. *...a patch of brownish lawn.*

browse /braʊz/, **browses, browsing, browsed. 1** VB If you **browse** through a book or magazine, you look through it in a casual way. **2** VB If you **browse** in a shop, you look at things in a casual way, without intending to buy anything. *She browses a while, then picks up a glossy magazine.* Also COUNT N WITH SUPP *I had a browse in the children's picture book section.* **3** VB When animals **browse,** they feed on plants.

bruise /bruːz/, **bruises, bruising, bruised. 1** COUNT N A **bruise** is an injury produced when a part of your body is hit and a purple mark appears. **2 ERG VB** When a part of your body **is bruised,** it is hit so that a purple mark appears. *They were jostled, bruised, and scratched... I bruise easily.*

brunette /bru:nɛt/, **brunettes. COUNT N** A **brunette** is a white-skinned woman or girl with dark brown hair.

brunt /brʌnt/. **PHRASE** If someone **bears the brunt** or **takes the brunt** of something unpleasant, they suffer the main part or force of it. *It will be the poorest families who bear the brunt of the attack.*

brush /brʌʃ/, **brushes, brushing, brushed. 1 COUNT N** A **brush** is an object with a large number of bristles fixed to it. You use some brushes for sweeping, and others for tidying your hair or painting. *...a paint brush.* **2 VB WITH OBJ** When you **brush** something, you clean it or tidy it using a brush. *I'm going to brush my teeth.* Also **SING N** *Give the carpet a hard brush.* **3 VB WITH OBJ AND ADJUNCT** If you **brush** something away, you remove it by pushing it lightly with your hand. *She brushed back the hair from her eyes.* **4 VB WITH OBJ OR ADJUNCT** To **brush** something or **brush** against it means to touch it lightly while passing it. *The girl's hair brushed his cheek... An arm brushed against hers.*

brush aside. PHR VB If you **brush aside** an idea, remark, or feeling, you refuse to consider it because you think it is not important. *She brushed his protests aside.*

brush up. PHR VB If you **brush up** a subject or **brush up on** it, you revise or improve your knowledge of it. *They need to brush up their French.*

brushwood /brʌʃwʊd/. **UNCOUNT N Brushwood** consists of small branches and twigs that have broken off trees and bushes.

brusque /bru:sk, -ʊsk/. **ADJ** Someone who is **brusque** wastes no time when dealing with things and does not show much consideration for other people. *She had a brusque manner.* ♦ **brusquely ADV** *'Sorry—no time to waste,' she said brusquely.*

brussels sprouts /brʌsᵊlz sprauts/; also spelled **brussel sprouts. PLURAL N Brussels sprouts** are vegetables which look like very small cabbages.

brutal /bru:tᵊl/. **ADJ** Someone who is **brutal** is cruel and violent. *...the government's brutal treatment of political prisoners.* ♦ **brutally ADV** *Richard II was brutally murdered.* ♦ **brutality** /bru:tælɪtiⁱ/ **UNCOUNT N OR COUNT N** *There is so much brutality shown on the television screen... I abhor the brutalities of the regime.*

brutalize /bru:tᵊlaɪz/, **brutalizes, brutalizing, brutalized;** also spelled **brutalise. VB WITH OBJ** If an unpleasant experience **brutalizes** someone, it makes them cruel or violent.

brute /bru:t/, **brutes. 1 COUNT N** If you call a man a **brute,** you mean that he is rough and insensitive. **2 COUNT N** You can also call a large animal a **brute.** *...the poor half-starved brutes.* **3 ATTRIB ADJ** When you refer to **brute** strength or force, you are contrasting it with gentler methods or qualities. *We will never yield to brute force.*

brutish /bru:tɪʃ/. **ADJ** If you describe human conditions or actions as **brutish,** you mean that they seem like an animal's; used showing disapproval. *Man's life is nasty, brutish and short.*

B.Sc. /bi: ɛs si:/, **B.Sc.s.** A **B.Sc.** is a science degree. **B.Sc.** is an abbreviation for 'Bachelor of Science'.

bubble /bʌbᵊl/, **bubbles, bubbling, bubbled. 1 COUNT N** A **bubble** is a ball of air in a liquid. *Tiny bubbles were rising from the dissolving tablets.* **2 COUNT N** A **bubble** is also a hollow, delicate ball of soapy liquid floating in the air or standing on a surface. **3 VB** When a liquid **bubbles,** bubbles form in it, because it is boiling, fizzy, or moving quickly. *The champagne bubbled in her glass.* **4 VB** If you are **bubbling** with a feeling, you are full of it. *I was bubbling with excitement.*

bubble gum. UNCOUNT N Bubble gum is chewing gum that you can blow into the shape of a bubble.

bubbly /bʌbliⁱ/, **bubblier, bubbliest. 1 ADJ** A **bubbly** liquid is full of bubbles. **2 UNCOUNT N Bubbly** is champagne; an informal use. **3 ADJ** Someone who is **bubbly** is very lively and cheerful. *...a bubbly little girl.*

buck /bʌk/, **bucks, bucking, bucked. 1 COUNT N** A **buck** is a US or Australian dollar; an informal use. *It cost me four bucks.* **2 COUNT N** A **buck** is also the male of various animals, including the deer and rabbit. **3 VB** If a horse **bucks,** it jumps into the air wildly with all four feet off the ground.

PHRASES • When someone **makes a fast buck,** they make a lot of money quickly, especially by doing something dishonest; an informal use. • If you **pass the buck,** you refuse to accept responsibility for something, and say that someone else is responsible; an informal use.

buck up. PHR VB 1 If you **buck up** or if something **bucks** you **up,** you become more cheerful. *I need something to buck my spirits up today.* **2** If you tell someone to **buck up,** you are telling them to hurry up; an informal use.

bucket /bʌkɪt/, **buckets. 1 COUNT N** A **bucket** is a round metal or plastic container with a handle. Buckets are often used for holding and carrying water. *The hotel cleaner entered carrying a bucket and mop.* **2 COUNT N** You can use **bucket** to refer to a bucket and its contents, or to the contents only. *...a bucket of warm water.*

bucketful /bʌkɪᵗfʊl/, **bucketfuls. COUNT N** A **bucketful** of something is the amount contained in a bucket. *...a bucketful of cold water.*

buckle /bʌkᵊl/, **buckles, buckling, buckled. 1 COUNT N** A **buckle** is a piece of metal or plastic attached to one end of a belt or strap and used to fasten it. *...shoes fastened with big metal buckles.* **2 VB WITH OBJ** If you **buckle** a belt or strap, you fasten it. *The cuffs of the raincoat are tightly buckled.* **3 ERG VB** If an object **buckles** or if something **buckles** it, it becomes bent as a result of severe heat or force. *There was an explosion. The door buckled and swung inwards... The forces within the earth have buckled the strata.* **4 VB** If your legs or knees **buckle,** they bend because they have become very weak or tired. *His knees almost buckled under him.*

buckle down. PHR VB If you **buckle down** to something, you start working seriously at it.

bud /bʌd/, **buds, budding, budded. 1 COUNT N** A **bud** is a small pointed lump that appears on a tree or plant and develops into a leaf or flower. **2 VB** When a tree or plant **buds,** buds appear on it. **3 PHRASE** To **nip** something **in the bud** means to put an end to it at an early stage; an informal use. *This incident very nearly nipped his political career in the bud.* **4** See also **budding.**

Buddhism /bʊdɪzᵊm/. **UNCOUNT N Buddhism** is a religion which teaches that the way to end suffering is by overcoming your desires.

Buddhist /bʊdɪst/, **Buddhists. 1 COUNT N** A **Buddhist** is a person whose religion is Buddhism. **2 ADJ Buddhist** means relating to Buddhism. *...Buddhist philosophy.*

budding /bʌdɪŋ/. **ATTRIB ADJ** A **budding** poet, artist, or musician is one who is just beginning to develop and be successful. *...a budding writer.*

buddy /bʌdiⁱ/, **buddies. 1 COUNT N** A man's **buddy** is his close friend; an informal use. **2 VOCATIVE** In America, men sometimes address other men as **buddy.** *Keep going, buddy.*

budge /bʌdʒ/, **budges, budging, budged. 1 VB** If someone will not **budge** on a matter, they refuse to change their mind or to compromise. *He refuses to budge on his design principles.* **2 ERG VB** If you cannot move something, you can say that it will not **budge** or that you cannot **budge** it. *The screw just will not budge... She could not budge the wheel.*

budgerigar /bʌdʒᵊrɪgɑ:/, **budgerigars. COUNT N Budgerigars** are small, brightly-coloured birds that people keep in their houses as pets.

budget /bʌdʒɪᵗt/, **budgets, budgeting, budgeted. 1 COUNT N** A **budget** is a plan showing how much money a person or organization has available and how it should be spent. *Work out a weekly budget... Education budgets have been cut.* **2 VB** If you **budget,** you plan carefully how much you are going to spend on each thing you want. ♦ **budgeting UNCOUNT N** *Through careful budgeting they had equipped the entire school.* **3 ATTRIB ADJ Budget** is used in advertising to suggest that something is being sold cheaply. *...budget prices.*

budget for. PHR VB If you **budget** for something, you take account of it in your budget. *These expenses can all be budgeted for.*

budgie /bʌdʒiⁱ/, **budgies. COUNT N** A **budgie** is the same as a budgerigar; an informal use.

buff /bʌf/, **buffs. 1 ADJ** Something that is **buff** is pale brown. **2 COUNT N WITH SUPP** You can use **buff** to talk about people who know a lot about a particular subject. For example, someone who is a film **buff** knows a lot about films; an informal use.

buffalo /bʌfələʊ/, **buffaloes. Buffalo** can also be the plural. **COUNT N** A **buffalo** is a wild animal like a large cow with long curved horns.

buffer /bʌfə/, **buffers. 1 COUNT N** A **buffer** is something that prevents something else from being harmed. *The world lacks the buffer of large international grain reserves.* **2 COUNT N** The **buffers** on a train or at the end of a railway line are two metal discs on springs that reduce the shock when they are hit.

buffet, buffets, buffeting, buffeted; pronounced /bʊfeɪ/ for meanings 1 and 2, and /bʌfət/ for meaning 3. **1 COUNT N** A **buffet** is a café in a station. **2 COUNT N** A **buffet** is also a meal of cold food at a party or public occasion. Guests usually help themselves to the food. *We found a huge buffet laid out.* **3 VB WITH OBJ** If the wind or the sea **buffets** something, it pushes against it suddenly and violently. *The vessel was buffeted by huge waves.*

buffet car /bʊfeɪ kɑ:/, **buffet cars. COUNT N** A **buffet car** is a carriage on a train where you can buy drinks and snacks.

bug /bʌg/, **bugs, bugging, bugged. 1 COUNT N** A **bug** is a tiny insect, especially one that causes damage. **2 COUNT N** A **bug** is also a minor illness such as a cold that people catch from each other; an informal use. *There must be a bug going around.* **3 VB WITH OBJ** If a place **is bugged,** tiny microphones are hidden there to secretly record what people are saying. **4 VB WITH OBJ** If something **bugs** you, it worries or annoys you; an informal use. **5 PHRASE** You can say that someone **is bitten by** a **bug** when they suddenly become very enthusiastic about something; an informal use. *She's been bitten by the skiing bug.*

bugle /bju:gᵊl/, **bugles. COUNT N** A **bugle** is a simple brass instrument that looks like a small trumpet.

build /bɪld/, **builds, building, built** /bɪlt/. **1 VB WITH OBJ** If you **build** a structure, you make it by joining things together. *John had built a house facing the river... They were building a bridge.* **2 VB WITH OBJ** If people **build** an organization or a society, they gradually form it. *They struggled to build a more democratic society.* **3 UNCOUNT N WITH SUPP** Your **build** is the shape that your bones and muscles give to your body. *She was in her early thirties, with a lean, athletic build.* • See also **built.**

build into. PHR VB 1 If you **build** something **into** a wall or object, you make it in such a way that it is in the wall or object, or is part of it. *There was a cupboard built into the whitewashed wall.* **2** If you **build** something **into** a policy, system, or product, you make it a part of it. *...the inequalities built into our system of financing.*

build on or **build upon. PHR VB 1** If you **build** an organization, system, or product **on** something, you base it on it. *...the principles on which these organizations are built... ...an economy built upon manufacturing industry.* **2** If you **build on** or **build upon** the success of something, you take advantage of this success in order to make further progress. *We must try to build on the success of these growth industries.*

build up. PHR VB 1 If an amount of something **builds up** or if you **build it up,** it gradually gets bigger as a result of more being added to it. *Mud builds up in the lake... We're trying to build up a collection of herbs and spices.* **2** If you **build up** someone's trust or confidence, you gradually make them more trusting or confident. **3** To **build** someone **up** means to cause them to be their normal weight again after they have been ill. **4** See also **build-up, built-up.**

build upon. PHR VB See **build on.**

builder /bɪldə/, **builders. COUNT N** A **builder** is a person whose job is to build houses and other buildings.

building /bɪldɪŋ/, **buildings. COUNT N** A **building** is a structure with a roof and walls, for example a house or a factory.

building society, building societies. COUNT N In Britain, a **building society** is a business which will lend you money to buy a house. You can also invest money in a building society.

build-up, build-ups. COUNT N A **build-up** is a gradual increase in something. *...a massive build-up of nuclear weapons.*

built /bɪlt/. **1 Built** is the past tense and past participle of **build. 2 ADJ** If you say that someone is **built** in a particular way, you are describing the kind of body they have. *He didn't look as if he was built for this kind of work.* • See also **well-built.**

built-in. ATTRIB ADJ Built-in devices or features are included in something as an essential part of it. *...a dishwasher with a built-in waste disposal unit.*

built-up. ADJ A **built-up** area is an area where there are many buildings.

bulb /bʌlb/, **bulbs. 1 COUNT N** A **bulb** or **light bulb** is the glass part of an electric lamp. **2 COUNT N** A **bulb** is also an onion-shaped root that grows into a plant.

bulbous /bʌlbəs/. **ADJ** Something that is **bulbous** is round and fat in a rather ugly way. *...people with great bulbous noses.*

bulge /bʌldʒ/, **bulges, bulging, bulged. 1 VB** If something **bulges,** it sticks out from a surface. *Guns bulged on their hips.* **2 VB** If something **is bulging** with things, it is very full of them. *The shelves were bulging with knick-knacks.* ♦ **bulging ATTRIB ADJ** *He arrived in the office with a bulging briefcase.* **3 COUNT N** A **bulge** is a lump on a surface that is otherwise flat.

bulk /bʌlk/, **bulks. 1 COUNT N** A **bulk** is a large mass of something. *...the dark bulk of the building.* **2 SING N** If you refer to the **bulk** of something, you mean most of it. *...the bulk of the population.* **3 PHRASE** If you buy or sell something **in bulk,** you buy or sell it in large quantities.

bulky /bʌlki[1]/, **bulkier, bulkiest.** ADJ Something that is **bulky** is large and heavy. *...bulky equipment.*

bull /bʊl/, **bulls.** 1 COUNT N A **bull** is a male animal of the cow family. 2 COUNT N Male elephants and whales are also called **bulls.**

bulldog /bʊldɒg/, **bulldogs.** COUNT N A **bulldog** is a type of dog with a large square head and short hair.

bulldoze /bʊldəʊz/, **bulldozes, bulldozing, bulldozed.** VB WITH OBJ To **bulldoze** something such as a small building means to knock it down with a bulldozer.

bulldozer /bʊldəʊzə/, **bulldozers.** COUNT N A **bulldozer** is a large, powerful tractor with a broad metal blade at the front, used for moving large amounts of earth or rubble..

bullet /bʊlɪ[1]t/, **bullets.** COUNT N A **bullet** is a small piece of metal which is fired from a gun.

bulletin /bʊlɪ[1]tɪn/, **bulletins.** 1 COUNT N A **bulletin** is a short news report on radio or television. 2 COUNT N A **bulletin** is also a regular newspaper or leaflet produced by an organization such as a school or church.

bullet-proof. ADJ If something is **bullet-proof,** bullets cannot pass through it. *...bullet-proof glass.*

bullfight /bʊlfaɪt/, **bullfights.** COUNT N In Spain and some other countries, a **bullfight** is a public entertainment in which a bull is made angry and then killed with a sword.

bullion /bʊlɪ[0]jən/. UNCOUNT N **Bullion** is gold or silver in the form of lumps or bars.

bullock /bʊlək/, **bullocks.** COUNT N A **bullock** is a young bull that has been castrated.

bull's-eye, bull's-eyes. 1 SING N The **bull's-eye** is the small circular area at the centre of a target. 2 COUNT N A **bull's-eye** is a shot or throw that hits the bull's-eye.

bully /bʊli[1]/, **bullies, bullying, bullied.** 1 COUNT N A **bully** is someone who uses their strength or power to hurt or frighten people. 2 VB WITH OBJ If someone **bullies** you, they use their strength or power to hurt or frighten you. *For the first month at my new school I was bullied constantly.* ♦ **bullying** UNCOUNT N *All cases of bullying will be severely dealt with.* 3 VB WITH OBJ If someone **bullies** you into doing something, they make you do it by using force or threats. *He had been bullied into driving her home.*

bulwark /bʊlwək/, **bulwarks.** COUNT N A **bulwark** is something strong that protects you against unpleasant or dangerous situations. *The fund is a bulwark against your benefits being cut.*

bum /bʌm/, **bums;** an informal word. 1 COUNT N In America, a **bum** is a tramp. 2 COUNT N Americans also say that someone is a **bum** when they are worthless or irresponsible. 3 COUNT N Your **bum** is the part of your body which you sit on; an informal British use.

bumble /bʌmbə[0]l/, **bumbles, bumbling, bumbled.** VB To **bumble** means to behave in a confused way and make a lot of mistakes. ♦ **bumbling** ATTRIB ADJ *Michael Hordern plays the bumbling Englishman yet again.*

bump /bʌmp/, **bumps, bumping, bumped.** 1 VB WITH ADJUNCT If you **bump** into something, you accidentally hit it while you are moving. *The canoe bumped against the bank.* 2 VB WITH ADJUNCT If a vehicle **bumps** over a surface, it travels in a rough, bouncing way because the surface is very uneven. 3 COUNT N A **bump** is a minor car accident in which you hit something. 4 COUNT N A **bump** on a road is a raised, uneven part.

bump into. PHR VB If you **bump into** someone you know, you meet them by chance; an informal use.

bump off. PHR VB To **bump** someone **off** means to kill them; an informal use.

bumper /bʌmpə/, **bumpers.** 1 COUNT N In British English, **bumpers** are bars at the front and back of a vehicle which protect it if it bumps into something. 2 ATTRIB ADJ A **bumper** crop or harvest is larger than usual.

bumpy /bʌmpi[1]/, **bumpier, bumpiest.** 1 ADJ A **bumpy** road or path has a lot of bumps on it. 2 ADJ If a journey in a vehicle is **bumpy,** it is uncomfortable, because you are travelling over an uneven surface.

bun /bʌn/, **buns.** 1 COUNT N A **bun** is a small cake or bread roll, often containing currants or spices. 2 COUNT N If a woman has her hair in a **bun,** it is fastened into a round shape at the back of her head.

bunch /bʌntʃ/, **bunches, bunching, bunched.** 1 COUNT N A **bunch** of people or similar things is a group of them. *They're a bunch of tired old men... ...a big bunch of keys.* 2 COUNT N A **bunch** of flowers is a number of them held or tied together. 3 COUNT N A **bunch** of bananas, grapes, or other fruit is a group of them growing on the same stem. 4 VB If people **bunch** together or **bunch** up, they stay close together in a group.

bundle /bʌndə[0]l/, **bundles, bundling, bundled.** 1 COUNT N A **bundle** is a number of things tied together or wrapped in a cloth so that they can be carried or stored. *He tied the wood into a bundle.* 2 VB WITH OBJ AND ADJUNCT If you **bundle** someone somewhere, you push them there in a rough and hurried way. *They bundled him into the ambulance.*

bundle off. PHR VB If you **bundle** someone **off** somewhere, you send them there in a hurry. *Jack was bundled off to Ely to stay with friends.*

bung /bʌŋ/, **bungs, bunging, bunged.** 1 COUNT N A **bung** is a round piece of wood, cork, or rubber used to close the hole in a barrel or flask. 2 VB WITH OBJ AND ADJUNCT If you **bung** something somewhere, you put it there in a quick and careless way; an informal use. *I bunged the books on the shelf.*

bungalow /bʌŋgələʊ/, **bungalows.** COUNT N A **bungalow** is a house with only one storey.

bunged up. PRED ADJ If a hole is **bunged up,** it is blocked; an informal use.

bungle /bʌŋgə[0]l/, **bungles, bungling, bungled.** VB WITH OR WITHOUT OBJ If you **bungle** something, you fail to do it properly, because you make mistakes or are clumsy. *They bungled the whole operation.* ♦ **bungled** ADJ *...the bungled murder of Bernard Lustig.* ♦ **bungling** ADJ *...this bungling administration.*

bunk /bʌŋk/, **bunks.** 1 COUNT N A **bunk** is a bed fixed to a wall, especially in a ship or caravan. 2 PHRASE If you **do a bunk,** you suddenly leave a place without telling anyone; an informal British use.

bunker /bʌŋkə/, **bunkers.** 1 COUNT N A **bunker** is a place, usually underground, built with strong walls to protect it against heavy gunfire and bombing. 2 COUNT N A **bunker** is also a container for coal or other fuel.

bunny /bʌni[1]/, **bunnies.** COUNT N Small children call a rabbit a **bunny** or a **bunny rabbit.**

bunting /bʌntɪŋ/. UNCOUNT N **Bunting** consists of rows of small coloured flags that are used to decorate streets and buildings on special occasions.

buoy /bɔɪ/, **buoys, buoying, buoyed.** COUNT N A **buoy** is a floating object that shows ships and boats where they can go and warns them of danger.

buoy up. PHR VB If you **buoy** someone **up,** you keep them cheerful in a situation in which they might feel depressed.

buoyant /bɔɪənt/. 1 ADJ If you are **buoyant,** you feel cheerful and behave in a lively way. *He suddenly smiled, feeling buoyant and at ease.* ♦ **buoyancy** /bɔɪənsi[1]/ UNCOUNT N *Without Alfred's buoyancy and originality we would never have succeeded.* 2 ADJ Something that is **buoyant** floats on a liquid or in the air. *...a row of buoyant cylinders.* ♦ **buoyancy** UNCOUNT N *New chambers were added to provide buoyancy.*

burden /bɜːdə[0]n/, **burdens.** 1 COUNT N Something that is a **burden** causes you a lot of worry or hard work. *...the burden of state secrets he carried with him.* 2 COUNT N A **burden** is also a heavy load that is difficult to carry; a formal use.

burdened /bɜːdə[0]nd/. PRED ADJ If you are **burdened** with something, it causes you a lot of worry or hard work. *He was burdened with endless paperwork.*

bureau /bjʊərəʊ/, **bureaux** or **bureaus.** 1 COUNT N In Britain, a **bureau** is a desk with drawers and a lid that opens to form a writing surface. 2 COUNT N In America, a **bureau** is an office, organization, or government department that collects and distributes information.

bureaucracy /bjʊərɒkrəsi[1]/, **bureaucracies.** 1 COUNT N A **bureaucracy** is an administrative system operated by a large number of officials following rules and procedures. 2 UNCOUNT N **Bureaucracy** is all the rules and procedures followed by government departments and similar organizations; often used showing disapproval. *One of the problems is the bureaucracy the claimant has to face.*

bureaucrat /bjʊərə[6]kræt/, **bureaucrats.** COUNT N A **bureaucrat** is an official who works in a bureaucracy, especially one who seems to follow rules and procedures too strictly. *...endless paperwork dished out by bureaucrats.*

bureaucratic /bjʊərə[6]krætɪk/. ADJ **Bureaucratic** rules and procedures are complicated and can cause long delays.

bureaux /bjʊərəʊz/. **Bureaux** is a plural of **bureau.**

burglar /bɜːglə/, **burglars.** COUNT N A **burglar** is a thief who breaks into a house and steals things.

burglar alarm, burglar alarms. COUNT N A **burglar alarm** is a device that makes a bell ring loudly if someone tries to break into a building.

burglary /bɜːgləri[1]/, **burglaries.** COUNT N OR UNCOUNT N If someone carries out a **burglary** or commits **burglary,** they break into a building and steal things. *Contact the police as soon as possible after a burglary... He was found guilty of burglary.*

burgle /bɜːgə[0]l/, **burgles, burgling, burgled.** VB WITH OBJ If a house **is burgled,** someone breaks in and steals things.

burial /bɛri[1]əl/, **burials.** COUNT N OR UNCOUNT N A **burial** is the ceremony that takes place when a dead body is put into a grave. *...the burial of an important person... The bodies are brought home for burial.*

burly /bɜːli[1]/. ADJ A **burly** man has a broad body and strong muscles.

burn /bɜːn/, **burns, burning, burned** or **burnt** /bɜːnt/. 1 VB If something **is burning,** it is on fire. *The stubble was burning in the fields.* ♦ **burning** UNCOUNT N *There was a smell of burning.* ♦ **burnt** ADJ *...a charred bit of burnt wood.* 2 VB WITH OBJ If you **burn** something, you destroy it with fire. *We couldn't burn the rubbish because it was raining.* 3 VB WITH OBJ If you **burn** yourself, you are injured by fire or by something very hot. *'What's the matter with your hand?'—'I burned it on my cigar.'* Also COUNT N *Many had serious burns over much of their bodies.* 4 VB WITH 'with' If you **are burning** with an emotion such as anger, you feel it very strongly. *...letters burning with indignation.* 5 ERG VB If the sun **burns** your skin, it makes it red or brown.

burn down. PHR VB If a building **burns down** or **is burned down,** it is completely destroyed by fire.

burner /bɜːnə/, **burners.** COUNT N A **burner** is a device which produces heat or a flame, especially as part of a cooker or heater.

burning /bɜːnɪŋ/. ATTRIB ADJ If something is extremely hot, you can say that it is **burning** or **burning hot.** ● See also **burn.**

burnished /bɜːnɪʃt/. ADJ **Burnished** means bright or smooth; a literary use. *...her burnished skin.*

burnt /bɜːnt/. **Burnt** is a past tense and past participle of **burn.**

burp /bɜːp/, **burps, burping, burped.** VB When someone **burps,** they make a noise because air from their stomach has been forced up through their throat. Also COUNT N *A slight burp interrupted her flowing speech.*

burrow /bʌrəʊ[0]/, **burrows, burrowing, burrowed.** 1 COUNT N A **burrow** is a tunnel or hole in the ground dug by an animal such as a rabbit. 2 VB When an animal **burrows,** it digs a tunnel or hole in the ground.

bursary /bɜːsə[0]ri[1]/, **bursaries.** COUNT N A **bursary** is a sum of money given to someone to allow them to study in a college or university.

burst /bɜːst/, **bursts, bursting. Burst** is used in the present tense of the verb, and is the past tense and past participle. 1 ERG VB When something **bursts** or when you **burst** it, it suddenly splits open, and air or some other substance comes out. *As he braked, a tyre burst... She burst the balloon... ...a burst water pipe.* 2 VB WITH 'open' When a door or lid **bursts** open, it opens very suddenly because of the pressure behind it. 3 VB WITH ADJUNCT If you **burst** into or through something, you suddenly go into it or through it with a lot of energy. *O'Shea burst in through the opposite door.* 4 COUNT N WITH 'of' A **burst** of something is a sudden short period of it. *...a burst of automatic rifle fire.*

burst in on. PHR VB If you **burst in on** someone, you suddenly enter the room that they are in.

burst into. PHR VB If you **burst into** tears or laughter, you suddenly begin to cry or laugh. ● **to burst into flames:** see **flame.**

burst out. PHR VB If you **burst out** laughing or crying, you suddenly begin laughing or crying loudly.

bursting /bɜːstɪŋ/; an informal word. 1 PRED ADJ WITH 'with' If a place is **bursting** with people or things, it is full of them. *...parks bursting with flowers.* 2 PRED ADJ WITH 'with' If you are **bursting** with a feeling, you are full of it. *Claud was bursting with pride and excitement.* 3 PRED ADJ WITH TO-INF If you are **bursting** to do something, you are very eager to do it. *I was bursting to tell someone.*

bury /bɛri[1]/, **buries, burying, buried.** 1 VB WITH OBJ When a dead person **is buried,** their body is put into a grave and covered with earth. 2 VB WITH OBJ To **bury** something means to put it into a hole in the ground and cover it up, often in order to hide it. *Reptiles bury their eggs in holes.* 3 VB WITH OBJ If you **are buried** under something that falls on top of you, you are completely covered and may not be able to get out. *People were buried beneath mountains of rubble.* 4 VB WITH OBJ AND ADJUNCT If you **bury** your face in something, you try to hide your face by pressing it against that thing. *She buried her face in her hands.* 5 REFL VB WITH 'in' If you **bury** yourself in your work or an activity, you concentrate hard on it.

bury away. PHR VB If something **is buried away** somewhere, you cannot easily find it or see it.

bus /bʌs/, **buses.** COUNT N A **bus** is a large motor vehicle which carries passengers from one place to another.

bus conductor, bus conductors. COUNT N A **bus conductor** is an official on a bus who sells tickets.

bush /bʊʃ/, **bushes.** 1 COUNT N A **bush** is a plant which is like a very small tree. 2 SING N The wild parts of some hot countries are referred to as the **bush.** *I went for a walk in the bush.* 3 PHRASE If you say **'Don't beat about the bush',** you mean that you want someone to tell you something immediately and directly rather than trying to avoid doing so.

bushy /bʊʃi^1/, **bushier, bushiest.** ADJ **Bushy** hair or fur grows very thickly. *...bushy eyebrows.*

busily /bɪzili^1/. ADV If you do something **busily,** you do it in a very active way. *I went on writing busily.*

business /bɪznɪs/, **businesses. 1** UNCOUNT N **Business** is work relating to the production, buying, and selling of goods or services. *There are good profits to be made in the hotel business... Are you in San Francisco for business or pleasure?* **2** COUNT N A **business** is an organization which produces and sells goods or provides a service. *He set up a small travel business.* **3** PHRASE If a shop or company goes **out of business,** it has to stop trading because it is not making enough money. **4** UNCOUNT N You can use **business** to refer to any activity, situation, or series of events. *She got on with the business of clearing up... The whole business affected him profoundly.* **5** SING N WITH POSS If you say that something is your **business,** you mean that it concerns you personally and that other people should not get involved in it. *That's his business and no one else's.*

PHRASES ● If you say that someone **has no business** to do something, you mean that they have no right to do it. *She had no business to publish his letters.* ● If you say to someone **'Mind your own business'** or **'It's none of your business',** you are telling them not to ask about something that does not concern them; an informal use. ● If someone **means business,** they are serious and determined about what they are doing; an informal use.

businesslike /bɪznɪslaɪk/. ADJ Someone who is **businesslike** deals with things in an efficient way without wasting time.

businessman /bɪznɪsmə^{3}n/, **businessmen. 1** COUNT N A **businessman** is a man who works in business, for example by running a firm. **2** COUNT N WITH SUPP If you describe a man as a good **businessman,** you mean that he knows how to deal with money and how to make good deals.

businesswoman /bɪznɪswʊmən/, **businesswomen.** COUNT N A **businesswoman** is a woman who works in business, for example by running a firm.

busker /bʌskə/, **buskers.** COUNT N In Britain, a **busker** is a person who plays music or sings for money in city streets or stations.

bus stop, bus stops. COUNT N A **bus stop** is a place on a road where buses stop to let people get on and off.

bust /bʌst/, **busts, busting, busted.** The past tense and past participle can be **busted** or **bust. 1** VB WITH OBJ When you **bust** something, you damage it so badly that it cannot be used; an informal use. **2** PRED ADJ If something is **bust,** it is broken or very badly damaged; an informal use. *The television's bust.* **3** PHRASE If a company **goes bust,** it loses so much money that it is forced to close down; an informal use. **4** COUNT N A **bust** is a statue of someone's head and shoulders. **5** COUNT N A woman's **bust** is her breasts.

bustle /bʌsə^{0}l/, **bustles, bustling, bustled. 1** VB WITH ADJUNCT If someone **bustles** somewhere, they move there in a hurried and determined way. *I watched housewives bustle in and out of a supermarket.* ♦ **bustling** ATTRIB ADJ *...the bustling curator of the museum.* **2** VB A place that **is bustling** is full of people and is very busy and lively. *The station was bustling with activity.* ♦ **bustling** ATTRIB ADJ *Fraserburgh is a bustling fishing town.* **3** UNCOUNT N **Bustle** is busy, noisy activity. *...the bustle of the airport.*

busy /bɪzi^1/, **busier, busiest; busies, busying, busied. 1** ADJ If you are **busy,** you are working hard or concentrating on a task, so that you are not free to do anything else. *She's going to be busy till Friday.* **2** PRED ADJ WITH -ING If you are **busy** doing something, it is taking all your attention. **3** REFL VB If you **busy** yourself with something, you occupy yourself by dealing with it. *I decided to busy myself with our untidy lawn.* **4** ADJ A **busy** time is a time when you have a lot of things to do. *I've had a busy day.* **5** ADJ A **busy** place is full of people who are doing things or moving about. *...a busy office.*

busybody /bɪzi^{1}bɒdi^1/, **busybodies.** COUNT N If you call someone a **busybody,** you mean that they interfere in other people's affairs.

but /bʌt, bət/. **1** CONJ You use **but** to introduce something which contrasts with what you have just said. *It was a long walk but it was worth it... We'll have a meeting. But not today... ...a cheap but incredibly effective carpet cleaner.* **2** CONJ You also use **but** when you are adding something or changing the subject. *Later I'll be discussing this with Dr Peter Unsworth. But first let me remind you of some of the issues.* **3** CONJ You also use **but** to link an excuse or apology with what you are about to say. *I'm sorry, but she's not in at the moment... Forgive my ignorance, but just what is Arista?* **4** PREP **But** also means 'except'. *It hurt nobody but himself... It could do everything but stop.* **5** ADV In formal English, **but** can mean 'only'. *Low cost and high speed are but two of the advantages of electronic data handling.*

PHRASES ● You use **but then** before a remark which slightly contradicts what you have just said. *Iron would do the job better. But then you can't bend iron so easily.* ● You also use **but then** before indicating that what you have just said is not surprising. *They're very close. But then, they've known each other for years and years.* ● You use **but for** to introduce the only factor that causes a particular thing not to happen or not to be completely true. *But for his ice-blue eyes, he looked like a bearded, wiry Moor.*

butcher /bʊtʃə/, **butchers, butchering, butchered. 1** COUNT N A **butcher** is a shopkeeper who sells meat. **2** COUNT N A **butcher** or a **butcher's** is a shop where meat is sold. *There's a family butcher at the end of our road.* **3** VB WITH OBJ To **butcher** a lot of people means to kill them in a cruel way.

butchery /bʊtʃəri^1/. UNCOUNT N You can refer to the cruel killing of a lot of people as **butchery.**

butler /bʌtlə/, **butlers.** COUNT N A **butler** is the most important male servant in a house.

butt /bʌt/, **butts, butting, butted. 1** COUNT N The **butt** of a weapon is the thick end of its handle. *...the padded butt of the rifle.* **2** COUNT N The **butt** of a cigarette or cigar is the small part that is left when you have finished smoking it. **3** COUNT N A **butt** is a large barrel used for collecting or storing liquid. *...a water butt.* **4** SING N If you are the **butt** of teasing or criticism, people keep teasing you or criticizing you. *They made him the butt of endless practical jokes.* **5** VB WITH OBJ If you **butt** something, you hit it with your head. *He butted Stuart in the chest.*

butt in. PHR VB If you **butt in,** you rudely join in a private conversation or activity without being asked to.

butter /bʌtə/, **butters, buttering, buttered. 1** UNCOUNT N **Butter** is a yellowish substance made from cream which you spread on bread or use in cooking. **2** VB WITH OBJ When you **butter** bread or toast, you spread butter on it. **3** PHRASE If you say that **butter wouldn't melt in** someone's **mouth,** you mean that they look very innocent but you know that they have done something wrong or are intending to.

butter up. PHR VB If you **butter** someone **up,** you praise them or try to please them, because you want to ask them a favour; an informal use.

buttercup /bʌtəkʌp/, **buttercups.** COUNT N A **buttercup** is a small plant with bright yellow flowers.

butterfly /bʌtəflaɪ/, **butterflies. 1** COUNT N A **butterfly** is an insect with large colourful wings and a thin body. **2** PHRASE If you have **butterflies in** your **stomach,** you are very nervous about something; an informal use. **3** UNCOUNT N **Butterfly** is a swimming stroke which you do lying on your front, bringing your arms together over your head.

buttock /bʌtə^{0}k/, **buttocks.** COUNT N Your **buttocks** are the part of your body that you sit on.

button /bʌtə^{0}n/, **buttons, buttoning, buttoned. 1** COUNT N **Buttons** are small, hard objects sewn on to shirts, coats, or other pieces of clothing. You fasten the clothing by pushing the buttons through holes called buttonholes. **2** VB WITH OBJ If you **button** a shirt, coat, or other piece of clothing, you fasten it by pushing its buttons through the buttonholes. **3** COUNT N A **button** is also a small object on a machine that you press in order to operate the machine. *I couldn't remember which button turns it off.*

button up. PHR VB If you **button up** a shirt, coat, or other piece of clothing, you fasten it completely by pushing all its buttons through the buttonholes.

buttonhole /bʌtə^{0}nhəʊl/, **buttonholes, buttonholing, buttonholed. 1** COUNT N A **buttonhole** is the hole that you push a button through. **2** COUNT N In Britain, a **buttonhole** is also a flower worn on the collar or lapel of your jacket. **3** VB WITH OBJ If you **buttonhole** someone, you stop them and make them listen to you. *I was just on my way out and he buttonholed me.*

buttress /bʌtrɪs/, **buttresses, buttressing, buttressed. 1** COUNT N **Buttresses** are supports, usually made of stone or brick, that support a wall. **2** VB WITH OBJ To **buttress** an argument or system means to give it support and strength. *The present system serves to buttress the social structure in Britain.*

buxom /bʌksə^{0}m/. ADJ A **buxom** woman is large, healthy, and attractive.

buy /baɪ/, **buys, buying, bought** /bɔːt/. **1** VB WITH OBJ, OR VB WITH OBJ AND OBJ OR 'for' If you **buy** something, you obtain it by paying money for it. *She could not afford to buy it... Let me buy you a drink... Many people have their cars bought for them by their firm.* **2** COUNT N WITH SUPP If you say that something is a good **buy,** you mean that it is of good quality and can be bought cheaply. *Other good buys include cameras and toys.*

buy out. PHR VB If you **buy** someone **out,** you buy their share of something that you previously owned together. *He sold off the shops to buy out his partner.*

buy up. PHR VB If you **buy up** land or property, you buy large quantities of it, or all of it that is available.

buyer /baɪə/, **buyers. 1** COUNT N A **buyer** is a person who is buying something or who intends to buy it. *I have a buyer for the house.* **2** COUNT N A **buyer** is also someone employed by a large store to decide what goods will be bought from manufacturers to be sold in the store.

buzz /bʌz/, **buzzes, buzzing, buzzed. 1** SING N A **buzz** is a continuous sound, like the sound of a bee when it is flying. **2** VB When a bee **buzzes,** it makes the continuous sound that bees make when they are flying. **3** VB WITH ADJUNCT If thoughts **are buzzing** round your head, you are thinking about a lot of things. *Anne's head buzzed with angry, crazy thoughts.* **4** VB If a place **is buzzing,** a lot of people are talking there. *The room buzzed with excited questions.* Also SING N *...the buzz of conversation around her.*

buzz off. PHR VB If you say **'buzz off'** to someone, you are telling them rudely to go away.

buzzard /bʌzəd/, **buzzards.** COUNT N A **buzzard** is a large bird of prey.

buzzer /bʌzə/, **buzzers.** COUNT N A **buzzer** is a device that makes a buzzing sound, for example in an alarm clock or an office telephone.

by /baɪ/. **1** PREP If something is done **by** a person or thing, that person or thing does it. *He was brought up by an aunt... I was startled by his anger... ...the use of pocket calculators by schoolchildren.* **2** PREP WITH -ING If you achieve one thing **by** doing another thing, your action enables you to achieve the first thing. *By bribing a nurse I was able to see some files... They were making a living by selling souvenirs to the tourists.* **3** PREP **By** is used to say how something is done. *The money will be paid by cheque... We heard from them by phone... I always go by bus.* **4** PREP If you say that a book, a piece of music, or a painting is **by** someone, you mean that they wrote it or created it. *...three books by a great Australian writer.* **5** PREP Something that is **by** something else is beside it and close to it. *I sat by her bed.* **6** PREP OR ADV If something passes **by** you, it moves past without stopping. *People rushed by us... They watched the cars whizzing by.* **7** PREP If something happens **by** a particular time, it happens at or before that time. *He can be out by seven... By 1940 the number had grown to 185 millions.* **8** PREP If you are **by** yourself, you are alone. If you do something **by** yourself, you do it without anyone helping you. *He was standing by himself in a corner of the room... She did not think she could manage by herself.* **9** PREP Things that are made or sold **by** the million or **by** the dozen are made or sold in those quantities. *Books can be mailed by the dozen.* **10** PREP You use **by** in expressions such as 'day by day' to say that something happens gradually. *The university gets bigger year by year... The children had one by one fallen asleep.* **11** PREP If something increases or decreases **by** a particular amount, that amount is gained or lost. *Its grant is to be cut by more than 40 per cent.* **12** PREP If you hold someone or something **by** a particular part of them, you hold that part. *My mother took me firmly by the hand.*

bye /baɪ/. CONVENTION **'Bye'** and **'bye-bye'** are informal ways of saying goodbye.

bye-law /baɪlɔː/. See **by-law.**

by-election, by-elections. COUNT N A **by-election** is an election that is held to choose a new member of parliament when a member has resigned or died.

bygone /baɪgɒn/. ATTRIB ADJ **Bygone** means happening or existing a very long time ago; a literary use. *...empires established in bygone centuries.*

by-law, by-laws; also spelled **bye-law.** COUNT N A **by-law** is a law made by a local authority which applies only in that authority's area.

bypass, /baɪpɑːs/, **bypasses, bypassing, bypassed. 1** VB WITH OBJ If you **bypass** someone in authority, you avoid asking their permission to do something. *This is what happens when the worker bypasses his foreman.* **2** VB WITH OBJ If you **bypass** a difficulty, you avoid dealing with it. **3** COUNT N A **bypass** is a main road which takes traffic round the edge of a town rather than through its centre. *...the Oxford bypass.* **4** VB WITH OBJ If you **bypass** a place, you go round it rather than through it.

by-product, by-products. COUNT N A **by-product** is something which is made during the manufacture or processing of another product. *Oxygen is released as a by-product of the photosynthesis.*

bystander /baɪstændə/, **bystanders.** COUNT N A **bystander** is a person who is present when something happens and who sees it but does not take part in it. *...curious bystanders watching from a distance.*

byte /baɪt/, **bytes.** COUNT N A **byte** is a unit of storage in a computer.

byword /baɪwɜːd/, **bywords.** COUNT N WITH 'for' Something that is a **byword** for a particular quality is well known for having that quality. *The department had become a byword for obstinacy and brutality.*

Cc

C, c. 1 **C** is an abbreviation for 'century' or 'centuries'. You put 'C' before or after a number which refers to a particular century. *...living in the C14... ...the 14th C.* 2 **c.** is written in front of a date or number to indicate that it is approximate. *He was born c. 834 A.D.* 3 **C** is also an abbreviation for 'centigrade'.

cab /kæb/, **cabs.** 1 COUNT N A **cab** is a taxi. 2 COUNT N The **cab** of a lorry is the part in which the driver sits.

cabaret /kæbəreɪ/, **cabarets.** COUNT N OR UNCOUNT N A **cabaret** is a show of dancing, singing, or comedy acts. *The cabaret was just finishing... ...a cabaret artiste.*

cabbage /kæbɪdʒ/, **cabbages.** COUNT N OR UNCOUNT N A **cabbage** is a large green leafy vegetable.

cabin /kæbɪn/, **cabins.** 1 COUNT N A **cabin** is a small room in a boat or plane. *...the First Class cabin.* 2 COUNT N A **cabin** is also a small wooden house.

cabinet /kæbɪ^{1}nɪ^{2}t/, **cabinets.** 1 COUNT N A **cabinet** is a cupboard used for storing things such as medicines or alcoholic drinks. ● See also **filing cabinet.** 2 COLL N The **Cabinet** is a group of the most senior ministers in a government. *...the first man to be appointed to the Kennedy cabinet.*

cable /keɪbə^{0}l/, **cables.** 1 COUNT N A **cable** is a strong, thick rope. 2 COUNT N OR UNCOUNT N A **cable** is also a bundle of electrical wires inside a rubber or plastic covering. *...ten metres of electrical cable.*

cable car, cable cars. COUNT N A **cable car** is a vehicle for taking people up mountains. It is pulled by a moving cable.

cable television. UNCOUNT N **Cable television** is a television system in which signals are sent along wires, rather than by radio waves.

cache /kæʃ/, **caches.** COUNT N A **cache** is a quantity of things that have been hidden. *...an arms cache.*

cackle /kækə^{0}l/, **cackles, cackling, cackled.** VB If you **cackle**, you laugh in a loud unpleasant way. *She cackled with delight.* Also SING N *He gave a malicious cackle.*

cacophony /kəkɒfəni^1/. SING N You can describe a loud, unpleasant mixture of sounds as a **cacophony;** a formal use. *...a cacophony of squeaks and rattles.*

cactus /kæktəs/, **cactuses** or **cacti** /kæktaɪ/. COUNT N A **cactus** is a thick, fleshy desert plant, often with spikes.

cadence /keɪdə^{0}ns/, **cadences.** COUNT N The **cadence** of your voice is the way it goes up and down as you speak; a formal use.

cadet /kədet/, **cadets.** COUNT N A **cadet** is a young person who is being trained in the armed forces or police.

cadge /kædʒ/, **cadges, cadging, cadged.** VB WITH OR WITHOUT OBJ If you **cadge** something from someone, or **cadge** off them, you ask them for food, money, or help, and succeed in getting it; an informal British use that shows disapproval. *He only came to cadge free drinks... ...living by cadging off relatives.*

café /kæfeɪ/, **cafés.** COUNT N A **café** is a place where you can buy and have light meals and drinks.

cafeteria /kæfɪ^{1}tɪərɪə/, **cafeterias.** COUNT N A **cafeteria** is a self-service restaurant in a large shop or workplace.

caffeine /kæfiːn/; also spelled **caffein.** UNCOUNT N **Caffeine** is a substance found in coffee and tea which makes you more active.

cage /keɪdʒ/, **cages.** COUNT N A **cage** is a structure of wire or metal bars in which birds or animals are kept.

caged /keɪdʒd/. ADJ A **caged** bird or animal is inside a cage. *He felt like a caged lion.*

cagey /keɪdʒi^1/. ADJ If people are being **cagey,** they are careful not to reveal too much information. *They were so cagey about Lucy and her new job.*

cajole /kədʒəʊl/, **cajoles, cajoling, cajoled.** VB WITH OBJ If you **cajole** someone into doing something, you persuade them to do it by flattering them; a formal use.

cake /keɪk/, **cakes.** 1 COUNT N OR UNCOUNT N A **cake** is a sweet food made by baking a mixture of flour, eggs, sugar, and fat. *She cut the cake and gave me a piece... ...a slice of cake.* 2 COUNT N A **cake** of soap is a small block of it.

PHRASES ● If something is **a piece of cake,** it is very easy; an informal use. ● If things are **selling like hot cakes,** people are buying a lot of them; an informal use. ● **the icing on the cake:** see **icing.**

caked /keɪkt/. 1 ADJ If a substance is **caked,** it has changed into a dry layer or lump. *... dried blood caked in his hair.* 2 PRED ADJ If a surface is **caked** with a substance, it is covered with a solid layer of it. *...heavy farm shoes caked with mud.*

calamitous /kəlæmɪ^{1}təs/. ADJ A **calamitous** event is very unfortunate or serious; a formal use.

calamity /kəlæmɪ^{1}ti^1/, **calamities.** COUNT N A **calamity** is an event that causes a great deal of damage or distress; a formal use.

calcium /kælsɪəm/. UNCOUNT N **Calcium** is a soft white element found in bones, teeth, and limestone.

calculate /kælkjə^{4}leɪt/, **calculates, calculating, calculated.** 1 VB WITH OR WITHOUT OBJ If you **calculate** a number or amount, you work it out by doing some arithmetic. *The number of votes cast will then be calculated.* 2 REPORT VB If you **calculate** the effects of something, you consider what they will be. *...actions whose consequences can in no way be calculated... She calculated that the risks were worth taking.* 3 PASSIVE VB WITH TO-INF If something **is calculated** to have a particular effect, it is done in order to have that effect. *... a cool dignified attitude that was calculated to discourage familiarity.* ♦ **calculated** ADJ *...the deliberate, calculated use of violence.*

calculating /kælkjə^{4}leɪtɪŋ/. ADJ A **calculating** person arranges situations and controls people in order to get what he or she wants. *...calculating and selfish men.*

calculation /kælkjə^{4}leɪʃə^{0}n/, **calculations.** 1 COUNT N OR UNCOUNT N A **calculation** is something that you think about and work out mathematically. *I did a rapid calculation... ...a technique for quick calculation.* 2 UNCOUNT N **Calculation** is behaviour in which someone thinks only of themselves and not of other people. *His behaviour seems free of all calculation.*

calculator /kælkjə^{4}leɪtə/, **calculators.** COUNT N A **calculator** is a small electronic device used for doing mathematical calculations.

caldron /kɔːldrən/, **caldrons.** See **cauldron.**

calendar /kælɪ^{1}ndə/, **calendars.** 1 COUNT N A **calendar** is a chart showing the dates on which the days, weeks, and months of a year fall. 2 ATTRIB ADJ A **calendar** month is one of the twelve periods of time that a year is divided into. *It costs one hundred dollars per calendar month.* 3 COUNT N A **calendar** is also a list of dates within a year that are important for a particular organization or activity. *...a major event in the theatrical calendar.*

calf /kɑːf/, **calves** /kɑːvz/. 1 COUNT N A **calf** is a young cow. 2 COUNT N Some other young animals, such as young elephants, giraffes, and whales, are also called **calves.** 3 COUNT N Your **calves** are the backs of your legs between your ankles and knees.

calibre /kælɪbə/, **calibres;** spelled **caliber** in American English. 1 UNCOUNT N WITH SUPP The **calibre** of a person is the quality or standard of their ability or intelligence, especially when this is high. *...directors of the right calibre.* 2 COUNT N WITH SUPP The **calibre** of a gun is the width of the inside of its barrel.

call /kɔːl/, **calls, calling, called.** 1 VB WITH OBJ AND COMPLEMENT If someone or something **is called** a particular name, that is their name or title. *...a novel called 'Memoirs of a Survivor'... All his friends call him Jo.* 2 VB WITH OBJ AND COMPLEMENT If you **call** a person or situation something, that is how you describe them. *President Nixon called his opponents traitors.* 3 VB WITH OR WITHOUT OBJ If you **call** someone's name, you say it loudly to get their attention. *Children are as likely to call for their father as for their mother... 'Edward!' she called.* 4 VB WITH OR WITHOUT OBJ If you **call** someone, you telephone them. *He promised to call me soon... 'I want to speak to Mr Landy, please.'—'Who is calling?'* 5 VB WITH OBJ To **call** someone also means to ask them to come to you by shouting to them or telephoning them. *When Margaret collapsed, I called the doctor.* 6 COUNT N When you make a phone **call,** you phone someone. 7 VB WITH OBJ If you **call** a meeting, you arrange for it to take place. 8 VB WITH ADJUNCT If you **call** somewhere, you make a short visit there. *We called at the Vicarage.* 9 COUNT N If you pay a **call** on someone, you visit them briefly. *Doctors have no time these days to make regular calls.* 10 COUNT N OR UNCOUNT N A **call** for something is a demand or desire for it to be done or provided. *Labour MPs renewed their call for the abolition of the House of Lords... There is little call for his services.* 11 COUNT N A bird's **call** is the sound that it makes. 12 **to call it a day:** see **day.**

call for. PHR VB 1 If you **call for** someone or something, you go to collect them. *I'll call for you about eight... I called at the station for my luggage.* 2 If you **call for** an action, you demand that it should happen. *The declaration called for an immediate ceasefire.* 3 If something **calls for** a particular action or quality, it needs it to be successful. *Controlling a class calls for all your skill as a teacher.*

call in. PHR VB If you **call** someone **in,** you ask them to come and do something for you. *We called in the police.*

call off. PHR VB If you **call** something **off,** you cancel it. *We had to decide whether classes should be called off.*

call on or **call upon.** PHR VB 1 If you **call on** someone to do something or **call upon** them to do it, you appeal to them to do it; a formal use. *The Opposition called on the Prime Minister to stop the arms deal.* 2 To **call on** someone also means to pay them a short visit.

call out. PHR VB 1 If you **call** something **out,** you shout it. *'Where shall I put them?' I called out... ...calling out to the porter that she'd arrived.* 2 If you **call** someone **out,** you order them to come to help, especially in an emergency. *The National Guard has been called out.*

call up. PHR VB 1 If you **call** someone **up,** you telephone them. 2 If someone **is called up,** they are ordered to join the armed forces.

call upon. PHR VB See **call on.**

call box, call boxes. COUNT N A **call box** is a telephone box.

caller /kɔːlə/, **callers.** COUNT N A **caller** is a person who comes to see you for a short visit.

calling /kɔːlɪŋ/, **callings.** COUNT N A **calling** is a profession or career, especially one which involves helping other people. *Teaching is said to be a worthwhile calling.*

callous /kæləs/. ADJ A **callous** person or action is cruel and shows no concern for other people.

calm /kɑːm/, **calmer, calmest; calms, calming, calmed.** 1 ADJ A **calm** person does not show any worry or excitement. *Gary was a calm and reasonable man... Sit down and keep calm.* ♦ **calmly** ADV *She calmly wiped the blood away.* 2 UNCOUNT N **Calm** is a state of being quiet and peaceful. *...the calm of the vicarage.* 3 ADJ If the weather or sea is **calm,** there is no wind and so the trees are not moving or the water is not moving. *...a calm, sunny evening.* 4 VB WITH OBJ If you **calm** someone or **calm** their fears, you do something to make them less upset, worried, or excited. *Mitchell tried to calm her, but she didn't hear him.*

calm down. PHR VB If you **calm down** or if someone **calms** you **down,** you become less upset, excited, or lively. *'Calm down. Let me explain.'*

calorie /kæləri^1/, **calories.** COUNT N A **calorie** is a unit of measurement for the energy value of food. *...a diet of only 1,700 calories a day.*

calves. **Calves** is the plural of **calf.**

camaraderie /kæmərɑːdəri^1/. UNCOUNT N **Camaraderie** is a feeling of trust and friendship among a group of people; a formal use.

came /keɪm/. **Came** is the past tense of **come.**

camel /kæmə^{0}l/, **camels.** COUNT N A **camel** is a large animal which lives in the desert. It has a long neck and one or two humps on its back.

cameo /kæmɪəʊ/, **cameos.** 1 COUNT N A **cameo** is a short descriptive piece of acting or writing. *He gave cameos of debates with exquisite touches of irony.* 2 COUNT N A **cameo** is also a brooch with a raised stone design on a flat stone of another colour.

camera /kæmə^{0}rə/, **cameras.** COUNT N A **camera** is a piece of equipment for taking photographs or for making a film.

cameraman /kæmə^{0}rəmə^{3}n/, **cameramen.** COUNT N A **cameraman** is a person who operates a television or film camera.

camouflage /kæməflɑːʒ/. 1 UNCOUNT N **Camouflage** consists of things such as leaves, branches, or paint, used to make military forces difficult to see. ♦ **camouflaged** /kæməflɑːʒd/ ADJ *The gun crews were in camouflaged bunkers.* 2 UNCOUNT N **Camouflage** is also the way in which some animals are coloured and shaped to blend in with their natural surroundings.

camp /kæmp/, **camps, camping, camped.** 1 COUNT N OR UNCOUNT N A **camp** is a place where people live or stay in tents. *We set up camp near the bay.* 2 VB If you **camp** somewhere, you stay there in a tent or caravan. *I camped in the hills.* ♦ **camping** UNCOUNT N *I don't like camping.* 3 COUNT N A **camp** is also a collection of buildings for people such as soldiers, refugees, or prisoners. 4 COUNT N WITH SUPP You can use **camp** to refer to a group of people with a particular idea or belief. *...two clear-cut camps, reformists and reactionaries.*

campaign /kæmpeɪn/, **campaigns, campaigning, campaigned.** 1 COUNT N A **campaign** is a set of activities planned to achieve something such as social or political change. *...the campaign against world hunger.* ♦ **campaigner** COUNT N *...anti-apartheid campaigners.* 2 VB WITH ADJUNCT To **campaign** means to carry out activities planned to achieve something such as social or political change. *He campaigned for political reform.* 3 COUNT N In a war, a **campaign** is a series of planned movements by armed forces.

camp bed, camp beds. COUNT N A **camp bed** is a small folding bed.

camper /kæmpə/, **campers.** 1 COUNT N A **camper** is a person who goes camping. 2 COUNT N A **camper** is also a van equipped with beds and cooking equipment.

campsite /kæmpsaɪt/, **campsites.** COUNT N A **campsite** is a place where people can stay in tents or caravans.

campus /kæmpəs/, **campuses.** COUNT N OR UNCOUNT N A university or college **campus** is the area of land containing its main buildings. *...the university campus... How many students live on campus?*

can, cans, canning, canned. For meanings 1 to 5, **can** is pronounced /kæn/ or /kən/ ; for meanings 6 to 8, it is always pronounced /kæn/. **Canned** is used as the past tense and past participle of the verb in meaning 7. **Could** is sometimes considered to be the past tense of the modal **can,** but in this dictionary the two words are dealt with separately. 1 MODAL If you **can** do something, it is possible for you to do it or you are allowed to do it. *Many people cannot afford telephones... 'Will you stay for lunch?'—'I can't.'... You can borrow that pen if you want to.* 2 MODAL If you **can** do something, you have the skill or ability to do it. *Some people can ski better than others... My wife can't sew.* 3 MODAL You use **can** in questions as a polite way of asking someone to do something. *Can you tell me the time?* 4 MODAL If you say that something **cannot** be true or **cannot** happen, you mean that you feel sure that it is not true or will not happen. *This cannot be the whole story... He can hardly have read the report with much care... He can't have said that.* 5 MODAL You use **can't** and **can...not** in questions in order to ask people to do something. *Can't we talk about it?... Can't you keep your voice down?* 6 COUNT N A **can** is a sealed metal container for food, drink, or paint. *...beer cans.* 7 COUNT N You can use **can** to refer to a can and its contents, or to the contents only. *...cans of beans.* 8 VB WITH OBJ When food or drink **is canned,** it is put into a metal container and sealed. ♦ **canned** ADJ *...canned beer.* 9 See also **canned.**

canal /kənæl/, **canals.** COUNT N A **canal** is a long, narrow, man-made stretch of water.

canary /kənɛəri^1/, **canaries.** COUNT N **Canaries** are small yellow birds that sing and are often kept as pets.

cancel /kænsəl/, **cancels, cancelling, cancelled;** spelled **canceling, canceled** in American English. 1 VB WITH OBJ If you **cancel** something that has been arranged, you stop it from happening. *The performances were cancelled because the leading man was ill.* ♦ **cancellation** /kænsə^{1}leɪʃə^{0}n/ UNCOUNT N OR COUNT N *...the cancellation of the tour.* 2 VB WITH OBJ If you **cancel** something such as a hotel room or theatre seat, you tell the management that you no longer want it. ♦ **cancellation** COUNT N *I've had two cancellations already this morning... ...a cancellation charge.* 3 VB WITH OBJ If you **cancel** a cheque or a business arrangement, you cause it to be no longer valid.

cancel out. PHR VB If two things **cancel** each other **out,** they have opposite effects which combine to produce no real effect. *These political factions cancelled each other out.*

cancer /kænsə/, **cancers.** UNCOUNT N OR COUNT N **Cancer** is a serious illness in which abnormal body cells increase, producing growths. *He had cancer of the throat... ...lung cancer... Most cancers are preventable.*

cancerous /kænsərəs/. ADJ **Cancerous** growths are the result of cancer. *...cancerous cells.*

candid /kændɪd/. ADJ When you are **candid** with someone, you speak honestly to them. *...candid comments.* ♦ **candidly** ADV *Charlie got him to talk candidly about his life.*

candidacy /kændɪdəsi^1/. UNCOUNT N Someone's **candidacy** is their position of being a candidate in an election. *He announced his candidacy.*

candidate /kændɪdeɪt, -də^{1}t/, **candidates.** 1 COUNT N A **candidate** is someone who is being considered for a position, for example in an election or for a job. *...a parliamentary candidate.* 2 COUNT N A **candidate** is also someone taking an examination. 3 COUNT N A **candidate** can also be a person or thing regarded as suitable for a particular purpose. *Small companies are likely candidates for take-over.*

candle /kændə^{0}l/, **candles.** COUNT N A **candle** is a stick of hard wax with a wick through the middle. The lighted wick gives a flame that provides light.

candlelight /kændə^{0}llaɪt/. UNCOUNT N **Candlelight** is the light from a candle. *...writing by candlelight.*

candlestick /kændə^{0}lstɪk/, **candlesticks.** COUNT N A **candlestick** is a holder for a candle.

candour /kændə/; spelled **candor** in American English. UNCOUNT N **Candour** is the quality of speaking honestly and openly about things.

candy /kændi^1/, **candies.** COUNT N OR UNCOUNT N A **candy** is a sweet; an American use. *There was a bowl of candies on his desk... You eat too much candy.*

cane /keɪn/, **canes, caning, caned.** 1 UNCOUNT N **Cane** is the long, hollow stems of a plant such as bamboo. *...sugar cane.* 2 UNCOUNT N **Cane** is also strips of cane used for weaving. 3 COUNT N A **cane** is a long narrow stick. 4 SING N When schoolchildren used to be given the **cane,** they were hit with a cane as a punishment. *I got the cane for smoking.* 5 VB WITH OBJ If a child **was caned** at school, he or she was hit with a cane as a punishment.

canine /keɪnaɪn, kæn-/. ATTRIB ADJ **Canine** means relating to or resembling a dog.

canister /kænɪstə/, **canisters.** COUNT N A **canister** is a metal container.

cannabis /kænəbɪs/. UNCOUNT N **Cannabis** is a drug which some people smoke. It is illegal in many countries.

canned /kænd/. ADJ **Canned** music, laughter, or applause on the television or radio has been recorded beforehand. ● See also **can.**

cannibal /kænɪbə^{0}l/, **cannibals.** COUNT N A **cannibal** is a person who eats human flesh.

cannibalism /kænɪ^{1}bəlɪzə^{0}m/. UNCOUNT N People who practise **cannibalism** eat human flesh.

cannon /kænən/, **cannons. Cannon** can also be the plural. 1 COUNT N A **cannon** is a large gun on wheels, formerly used in battles. 2 COUNT N A **cannon** is also a heavy automatic gun, especially one fired from an aircraft.

cannon ball, cannon balls. COUNT N A **cannon ball** is a heavy metal ball that was fired from a cannon.

cannot /kænɒt, kænɒt/. **Cannot** means 'can not'. ● See **can.**

canoe /kənuː/, **canoes.** COUNT N A **canoe** is a small, narrow boat that you row using a paddle.

canoeing /kənuːɪŋ/. UNCOUNT N **Canoeing** is the sport of racing and performing tests of skill in canoes.

canon /kænən/, **canons.** 1 COUNT N A **canon** is one of the clergy on the staff of a cathedral. 2 COUNT N WITH SUPP A **canon** is also a basic rule or principle; a formal use.

canopy /kænəpi^1/, **canopies.** 1 COUNT N A **canopy** is a decorated cover above something such as a bed or throne. 2 COUNT N WITH SUPP A **canopy** is also a layer of something that covers an area, for example branches and leaves at the top of a forest. *The leaves created a dense canopy that cut out much of the light.*

can't /kɑːnt/. **Can't** is the usual spoken form of 'cannot'.

canteen /kæntiːn/, **canteens.** COUNT N A **canteen** is a place in a factory, office or shop where the workers can have lunch or other meals.

canter /kæntə/, **canters, cantering, cantered.** VB When a horse **canters,** it moves at a speed between a gallop and a trot. Also SING N *It broke into an easy canter.*

canvas /kænvəs/, **canvases.** 1 UNCOUNT N **Canvas** is strong, heavy cloth used for making tents, sails, and bags. 2 PHRASE If you are living and sleeping **under canvas,** you are living and sleeping in a tent. 3 COUNT N OR UNCOUNT N A **canvas** is also a piece of canvas on which an oil painting is done, or the painting itself. *...oil paintings on canvas... ...the canvases of Hieronymus Bosch.*

canvass /kænvəs/, **canvasses, canvassing, canvassed.** 1 VB If you **canvass** for a particular person or political party, you try to persuade people to vote for them. *He had canvassed for Mr Foot in the leadership election.* ♦ **canvassing** UNCOUNT N *...house-to-house canvassing.* 2 VB WITH OBJ If you **canvass** opinion, you find out how people feel about something.

canyon /kænjən/, **canyons.** COUNT N A **canyon** is a long, narrow valley with very steep sides.

cap /kæp/, **caps, capping, capped.** 1 COUNT N A **cap** is a soft, flat hat usually worn by men or boys. 2 COUNT N The **cap** of a bottle is its lid. 3 COUNT N A **cap** is also a contraceptive device placed inside a woman's vagina. 4 COUNT N **Caps** are very small explosives used in toy guns. 5 VB WITH OBJ If you **cap** an action, you do something that is better. *He capped his performance by telling the funniest joke I have ever heard.*

capability /keɪpəbɪlə^{1}ti^1/, **capabilities.** 1 UNCOUNT N OR COUNT N If you have the **capability** to do something, you are able to do it. *The work may be beyond his capability... She may worry about her capabilities as a parent.* 2 UNCOUNT N A country's military **capability** is its ability to fight in a war.

capable /keɪpəbə^{0}l/. 1 PRED ADJ WITH 'of' If you are **capable** of doing something, you are able to do it. *...a man capable of killing... ...a mind capable of original ideas.* 2 ADJ Someone who is **capable** has the ability to do something well. *Basil proved a capable cricketer.* ♦ **capably** ADV *...a capably performed dance.*

capacious /kəpeɪʃəs/. ADJ Something that is **capacious** has a lot of room. *...capacious pockets.*

capacity /kəpæsə^{1}ti^1/, **capacities.** 1 UNCOUNT N WITH SUPP The **capacity** of something is the amount that it can hold or produce. *The pipeline has a capacity of 1.2m barrels a day.* ● If something is filled **to capacity,** it is as full as possible. 2 MOD A **capacity** crowd completely fills a theatre or stadium. 3 COUNT N WITH SUPP Your **capacity** to do something is your ability to do it. *...the capacity to read and write... People have different capacities for learning.* 4 UNCOUNT N WITH SUPP Someone's **capacity** for food or drink is the amount that they can eat or drink. 5 PHRASE If someone does something **in a** particular **capacity,** they do it as part of their duties. *I was involved in an advisory capacity.* 6 UNCOUNT N In industry, **capacity** is the quantity that can be produced. *We need to raise productivity and expand capacity.*

cape /keɪp/, **capes.** 1 COUNT N A **cape** is a large piece of land that sticks out into the sea. 2 COUNT N A **cape** is also a short cloak.

capillary /kəpɪləri^1/, **capillaries.** COUNT N **Capillaries** are tiny blood vessels.

capital /kæpɪtə^{0}l/, **capitals.** 1 UNCOUNT N **Capital** is a large sum of money used in a business or invested to make more money. 2 MOD In industry, **capital** investment or expenditure is money spent on equipment and buildings. 3 PHRASE If you **make capital out of** a situation, you use it for personal gain; a formal use. 4 COUNT N The **capital** of a country is the city where its government meets. 5 COUNT N A **capital** or a **capital** letter is the large form of a letter used at the beginning of sentences and names. *...written in capitals.* 6 ATTRIB ADJ A **capital** offence is one that is punished by death.

capitalise /kæpɪtəlaɪz/. See **capitalize.**

capitalism /kæpɪtəlɪzm/. UNCOUNT N **Capitalism** is an economic and political system in which property, business, and industry are owned by private individuals and not by the state.

capitalist /kæpɪtəlɪst/, **capitalists.** 1 ADJ A **capitalist** country or system supports or is based on the principles of capitalism. *...a modern capitalist economy.* 2 COUNT N A **capitalist** is someone who believes in and supports the principles of capitalism.

capitalize /kæpɪtəlaɪz/, **capitalizes, capitalizing, capitalized;** also spelled **capitalise.** VB If you **capitalize** on a situation, you use it to gain some advantage. *Mr Healey has been capitalising on the anxiety expressed throughout the House.*

capital punishment. UNCOUNT N **Capital punishment** is punishment which involves the legal killing of a person who has committed a serious crime.

capitulate /kəpɪtjə^{4}leɪt/, **capitulates, capitulating, capitulated.** VB If you **capitulate,** you stop resisting and do what someone else wants you to do. *Economic pressures finally forced the Government to capitulate to our demands.* ♦ **capitulation** /kəpɪtjə^{4}leɪʃə^{0}n/ UNCOUNT N *...the capitulation of the city without a struggle.*

capricious /kə^{3}prɪʃəs/. ADJ A **capricious** person often changes their mind unexpectedly. *Authoritarian rulers are typically capricious.*

capsize /kæpsaɪz/, **capsizes, capsizing, capsized.** ERG VB If you **capsize** a boat or if it **capsizes,** it turns upside down in the water. *Ships capsize when struck by these waves... ...a capsized boat.*

capsule /kæpsjuːl/, **capsules.** 1 COUNT N A **capsule** is a small container with powdered medicine inside which you swallow. 2 COUNT N The **capsule** of a spacecraft is the part in which the astronauts travel.

captain /kæptɪn/, **captains, captaining, captained.** 1 COUNT N The **captain** of an aeroplane or ship is the officer in charge of it. 2 COUNT N OR TITLE In the army, a **captain** is an officer of fairly low rank. 3 COUNT N The **captain** of a sports team is its leader. 4 VB WITH OBJ If you **captain** a sports team, you are its leader. *Willis is probably the best player to have captained England.*

caption /kæpʃə^{0}n/, **captions.** COUNT N The **caption** of a picture or cartoon is the words printed underneath.

captivate /kæptə^{1}veɪt/, **captivates, captivating, captivated.** VB WITH OBJ If you **are captivated** by someone or something, you find them fascinating and attractive. *At eighteen he had been captivated by a charming brunette.*

captive /kæptɪv/, **captives.** 1 COUNT N A **captive** is a prisoner; a literary use. *The troops took the women and children as captives.* 2 PHRASE If you **take** someone **captive,** you take them as a prisoner.

captivity /kæptɪvɪ^{1}ti^1/. UNCOUNT N **Captivity** is the state of being kept as a captive. *...wild birds raised in captivity.*

capture /kæptʃə/, **captures, capturing, captured.** 1 VB WITH OBJ If you **capture** someone, you take them prisoner. *They had been captured and thrown in chains.* Also UNCOUNT N *...the night before his capture.* **2** VB WITH OBJ When military forces **capture** an area, they take control of it by force. *The city took 24 days to capture.* Also UNCOUNT N *...the capture of the city.* **3** VB WITH OBJ To **capture** something also means to gain control of it. *Overseas firms captured almost 41 per cent of the market.* **4** VB WITH OBJ If someone **captures** the atmosphere or quality of something, they represent it successfully in pictures, music, or words.

car /kɑː/, **cars. 1** COUNT N A **car** is a motor vehicle with room for a small number of passengers. *He parked the car about a hundred yards from the gates... They usually go by car.* **2** COUNT N In American English, railway carriages are called **cars. 3** COUNT N WITH SUPP In British English, railway carriages are called **cars** when they are used for a particular purpose. *...the dining car.* **4** See also **cable car.**

carafe /kəræf, -rɑːf/, **carafes.** COUNT N A **carafe** is a glass container for water or wine.

caramel /kærəmə⁰l, -mɛl/, **caramels. 1** COUNT N A **caramel** is a kind of toffee. **2** UNCOUNT N **Caramel** is burnt sugar used for colouring and flavouring food.

carat /kærət/, **carats. 1** COUNT N A **carat** is a unit equal to 0.2 grams used for measuring the weight of diamonds and other precious stones. **2** COUNT N A **carat** is also a unit for measuring the purity of gold. The purest gold is 24-carat gold.

caravan /kærəvæn/, **caravans. 1** COUNT N A **caravan** is a vehicle in which people live or spend their holidays. It is usually pulled by a car. *He lived in a caravan on the outskirts of the town.* **2** COUNT N A **caravan** is also a group of people and animals that travel together in deserts and other similar places. *...a caravan of twelve thousand camels.*

carbohydrate /kɑːbəʊhaɪdreɪt/, **carbohydrates.** UNCOUNT N OR COUNT N **Carbohydrate** is a substance found in foods such as sugar and bread that gives you energy. *Most fish are free from carbohydrate.*

carbon /kɑːbə⁰n/. UNCOUNT N **Carbon** is a chemical element that diamonds and coal are made of.

carbon copy, carbon copies. COUNT N A **carbon copy** is a copy of a piece of writing that is made using carbon paper.

carbon dioxide /kɑːbən daɪɒksaɪd/. UNCOUNT N **Carbon dioxide** is a gas that animals and people breathe out.

carbon monoxide /kɑːbən mə⁷nɒksaɪd/. UNCOUNT N **Carbon monoxide** is a poisonous gas produced for example by cars.

carbon paper. UNCOUNT N **Carbon paper** is thin paper coated with a dark substance. You use it to make copies of letters and other papers.

carcass /kɑːkəs/, **carcasses;** also spelled **carcase.** COUNT N A **carcass** is the body of a dead animal.

card /kɑːd/, **cards. 1** COUNT N OR UNCOUNT N A **card** is a piece of stiff paper or plastic containing specific information. *Put all the details on the card... Make a second copy on card or paper.* **2** COUNT N A **card** is also a piece of stiff paper with a picture and a message which you send to someone on a special occasion. *...a Christmas card.* **3** COUNT N **Cards** are thin pieces of cardboard decorated with numbers or pictures used to play various games. *The General liked her because she played cards well.* **4** COUNT N WITH SUPP You can also use **card** to refer to something that gives you an advantage in a particular situation. *Her chief card was her perfect memory.*

cardboard /kɑːdbɔːd/. UNCOUNT N **Cardboard** is thick, stiff paper used to make boxes and other containers.

cardiac /kɑːdiæk/. ATTRIB ADJ **Cardiac** means relating to the heart; a medical use. *...death caused by cardiac failure.*

cardigan /kɑːdɪgən/, **cardigans.** COUNT N A **cardigan** is a knitted woollen garment that fastens at the front.

cardinal /kɑːdɪnə⁰l/, **cardinals. 1** COUNT N A **cardinal** is a priest of high rank in the Catholic church. **2** ATTRIB ADJ **Cardinal** means extremely important; a formal use. *...a cardinal part of the scheme... ...a fact of cardinal importance.*

care /kɛə/, **cares, caring, cared. 1** VB If you **care** about something, you are concerned about it or interested in it. *...people who care about the environment... She couldn't care less what they thought... You can go with Roger for all I care.* **2** UNCOUNT N **Care** is the act of providing what a person needs to keep them healthy, or to make them well after they have been ill. *...the care of mental patients... ...the children in her care.* **3** VB WITH TO-INF To **care** to do something means to want or choose to do it; a formal use. *It's wrong whichever way you care to look at it... It's not a problem I'd care to face myself.* **4** UNCOUNT N If you do something with **care,** you do it with great attention to avoid mistakes or damage. *He chose every word with care.* **5** COUNT N **Cares** are worries. *...without a care in the world.* **6** See also **caring.**

PHRASES ● Children who are **in care** are being looked after by the state. ● If you **take care of** something or someone, you look after them. *He takes good care of my goats.* ● You can say **'Take care'** when saying goodbye to someone; an informal use.

care for. PHR VB **1** If you **care for** someone or something, you look after them. *You must learn how to care for children.* **2** If you say that you do not **care for** something, you mean that you do not like it; an old-fashioned use. *I didn't much care for the way he looked at me.*

career /kərɪə/, **careers.** COUNT N A **career** is a job or profession. *...a career in accountancy... ...a political career.*

carefree /kɛəfriː/. ADJ If someone is **carefree,** they have no problems or responsibilities. *...his normally carefree attitude.*

careful /kɛəfʊl/. **1** CONVENTION If you say **'Be careful'** to someone, you are warning them of a danger or a problem. *Be careful or you'll fall!... Please be careful with the washing machine.* **2** ADJ If you are **careful,** you do something with a lot of attention to make sure that you do it well or correctly. *This law will encourage more careful driving... He made a careful copy of the notes... ...careful preparation.* ♦ **carefully** ADV *He walked carefully around the broken glass.*

careless /kɛəlɪ²s/. **1** ADJ If you are **careless,** you do not pay enough attention to what you are doing, and so you make mistakes. *We are rather careless about the way we cook... I had been careless and let him wander off on his own.* ♦ **carelessly** ADV *...a gate left carelessly ajar.* ♦ **carelessness** UNCOUNT N *There seems to have been some carelessness recently at the office.* **2** ADJ You do something in a **careless** way when you are relaxed or confident. *...a careless laugh... ...her simplicity and careless grace.* ♦ **carelessly** ADV *'I'll give him a ring later,' Rudolph said, carelessly.* ♦ **carelessness** UNCOUNT N *She handled it with the carelessness of an expert.*

caress /kərɛs/, **caresses, caressing, caressed.** RECIP VB OR VB WITH OBJ If you **caress** someone, you stroke them gently and affectionately. *I caressed her hair and we kissed... They caressed and looked into each other's eyes.* Also COUNT N *...a loving caress.*

caretaker /kɛəteɪkə/, **caretakers.** COUNT N A **caretaker** is a person who looks after a large building such as a school or a block of flats.

cargo /kɑːgəʊ/, **cargoes.** COUNT N OR UNCOUNT N The **cargo** of a ship or plane is the goods that it is carrying. *...a cargo of wool... The port is still handling cargo.*

caricature /kærɪkətjʊə/, **caricatures, caricaturing, caricatured. 1** COUNT N OR UNCOUNT N A **caricature** is a drawing or description of someone that exaggerates their appearance or behaviour. *...a caricature of Max Beerbohm... ...a master of caricature.* **2** VB WITH OBJ If you **caricature** someone, you portray them in a way that exaggerates their features or their personality in order to make people laugh. *Lawson caricatured his boss in his cartoons.* **3** COUNT N A **caricature** of an event or situation is a very exaggerated account of it. *...an outrageous caricature of the truth.*

caring /kɛərɪŋ/. **1** ADJ A **caring** person is affectionate, helpful, and sympathetic. *...a caring parent... We need a more caring society.* **2** UNCOUNT N **Caring** is affection, help, and sympathy. *...love and caring between a man and a woman.*

carnage /kɑːnɪdʒ/. UNCOUNT N When there is **carnage,** a lot of people are killed; a literary use. *Refugees crossed the border to escape the carnage.*

carnal /kɑːnə⁰l/. ATTRIB ADJ **Carnal** means involving sexual feelings or activity; a literary use which shows disapproval. *...carnal desires.*

carnation /kɑːneɪʃə⁰n/, **carnations.** COUNT N A **carnation** is a plant with white, pink, red, or yellow flowers that often smell sweet.

carnival /kɑːnɪvə⁰l/, **carnivals.** COUNT N A **carnival** is a public festival with music, processions, and dancing.

carnivore /kɑːnɪvɔː/, **carnivores.** COUNT N A **carnivore** is an animal that eats meat rather than plants; a formal use. *...carnivores like the lion and the cheetah.*

carnivorous /kɑːnɪvə⁰rəs/. ADJ **Carnivorous** animals eat meat. *Snakes are carnivorous.*

carol /kærəl/, **carols.** COUNT N **Carols** are Christian religious songs that are sung at Christmas.

carp /kɑːp/. **Carp is the singular and plural.** COUNT N A **carp** is a large fish that lives in lakes and rivers.

car park, car parks. COUNT N A **car park** is an area or building where people can leave their cars; a British use. *...the multi-storey car park.*

carpenter /kɑːpɪntə/, **carpenters.** COUNT N A **carpenter** is a person whose job is making and repairing wooden things.

carpentry /kɑːpɪntri¹/. UNCOUNT N **Carpentry** is the skill or the work of a carpenter.

carpet /kɑːpɪt/, **carpets. 1** COUNT N A **carpet** is a thick covering for a floor, made of wool or a similar material. *He asked what the marks were on the stair carpet.* ♦ **carpeted** /kɑːpɪtɪ²d/ ADJ *The corridor was carpeted.* **2** COUNT N WITH SUPP A **carpet** of something is a layer of it covering the ground. *There was a carpet of snow everywhere.* ♦ **carpeted** ADJ *The ground was carpeted with flowers.*

carriage /kærɪdʒ/, **carriages. 1** COUNT N A **carriage** is one of the separate sections of a train that carries passengers; a British use. **2** COUNT N A **carriage** is also an old-fashioned vehicle which is pulled by horses. *...a procession of eight carriages led by the Queen.*

carried away /kæri¹d əweɪ/. PRED ADJ If you are **carried away,** you are so enthusiastic about something that you behave in a foolish way. *She can get so carried away that she forgets the time.*

carrier /kærɪə/, **carriers. 1** COUNT N A **carrier** is a vehicle or device used for carrying things. *...a new luggage carrier for bicycles... ...an aircraft carrier.* **2** COUNT N A **carrier** is also someone who is infected with a disease and so can make other people ill. *...mothers identified from blood tests as carriers.* **3** COUNT N A **carrier** or a **carrier bag** is a paper or plastic bag with handles; a British use.

carrion /kærɪən/. UNCOUNT N **Carrion** is the decaying flesh of dead animals.

carrot /kærət/, **carrots. 1** COUNT N OR UNCOUNT N A **carrot** is a long, thin, orange-coloured vegetable that grows under the ground. **2** COUNT N You can use **carrot** to refer to something that is offered to people in order to persuade them to do something. *The free cottage is the carrot which makes him accept his low wage.*

carry /kæri¹/, **carries, carrying, carried. 1** VB WITH OBJ If you **carry** something, you take it with you, holding it so that it does not touch the ground. *He picked up his suitcase and carried it into the bedroom.* **2** VB WITH OBJ To **carry** something also means to have it with you wherever you go. *I always carry a gun.* **3** VB WITH OBJ If something **carries** a person or thing somewhere, it takes them there. *A gentle current carried him slowly to the shore... ...trucks that carried casualties.* **4** VB WITH OBJ If someone or something **carries** a disease, they are infected with it and can pass it on to people or animals. *Rats carry very nasty diseases.* **5** VB WITH OBJ If an action **carries** a particular quality or consequence, it involves it. *Any job carries with it periods of boredom... Adultery carried the death penalty.* **6** VB WITH OBJ AND ADJUNCT If you **carry** an idea or a method to a particular extent, you use or develop it to that extent. *George carried this idea one step further.* **7** VB WITH OBJ If a newspaper or poster **carries** a picture or an article, it contains it. *A poster carried a portrait of Churchill.* **8** VB WITH OBJ If a proposal or motion **is carried** in a debate, a majority of people vote in favour of it. *The motion was carried by 259 votes to 162.* **9** VB If a sound **carries,** it can be heard a long way away. *...a faint voice which carried no farther than the front row.* **10** VB WITH OBJ If a woman is pregnant, you can say that she **is carrying** a child.

carry on. PHR VB **1** If you **carry on** doing something, you continue to do it. *I carried on without their support.* **2** If you **carry on** an activity, you take part in it. *Our work is carried on in an informal atmosphere.*

carry out. PHR VB If you **carry out** a task or order, you do it. *They also have to carry out many administrative duties... He was simply carrying out the instructions he had received.*

carry over. PHR VB If you **carry** something **over** from one situation to another, you make it continue to exist in the new situation. *The habit of obedience is carried over from the war.*

carry through. PHR VB If you **carry** a plan **through,** you put it into practice. *...the task of carrying through the necessary reforms.*

carrycot /kæri¹kɒt/, **carrycots.** COUNT N A **carrycot** is a cot for small babies with handles for carrying it; a British use.

cart /kɑːt/, **carts, carting, carted. 1** COUNT N A **cart** is an old-fashioned wooden vehicle, usually pulled by an animal. *...a cart loaded with hay.* **2** VB WITH OBJ AND ADJUNCT If you **cart** things or people somewhere, you carry or transport them there, often with difficulty; an informal use. *It took several trips to cart it all back up the stairs... He was carted off to hospital.*

cartilage /kɑːtɪ⁰lɪdʒ/. UNCOUNT N **Cartilage** is a strong, flexible substance which surrounds the joints in your body.

carton /kɑːtə⁰n/, **cartons. 1** COUNT N A **carton** is a plastic or cardboard container in which food or drink is sold. **2** COUNT N A **carton** is also a large, strong cardboard box; an American use.

cartoon /kɑːtuːn/, **cartoons.** 1 COUNT N A **cartoon** is a humorous drawing in a newspaper or magazine. 2 COUNT N A **cartoon** is also a film in which all the characters and scenes have been drawn rather than being real people or objects.

cartoonist /kɑːtuːnɪst/, **cartoonists.** COUNT N A **cartoonist** is a person whose job is to draw cartoons for newspapers and magazines.

cartridge /kɑːtrɪdʒ/, **cartridges.** COUNT N A **cartridge** is a tube containing a bullet and an explosive substance.

cartwheel /kɑːtwiːl/, **cartwheels.** COUNT N If you turn a **cartwheel,** you do a fast, circular movement by falling sideways, supporting your body with one hand after the other until you are standing again.

carve /kɑːv/, **carves, carving, carved.** 1 VB WITH OBJ If you **carve** an object, you cut it out of stone or wood. *The statue was carved by John Gibson.* ♦ **carved** ATTRIB ADJ *Pat loved the carved Buddhas.* 2 VB WITH OR WITHOUT OBJ If you **carve** a design on an object, you cut it into the surface. *He begins to carve his initials on the tree... ...an intricately carved door.* 3 VB WITH OR WITHOUT OBJ If you **carve** meat, you cut slices from it.

carve out. PHR VB If you **carve out** something for yourself, you create or obtain it, often with difficulty. *The company is carving out a huge slice of the electronics market.*

carve up. PHR VB If you **carve** something **up,** you divide it into smaller areas or pieces. *When the old man died the estate was carved up and sold.*

carving /kɑːvɪŋ/, **carvings.** COUNT N A **carving** is an object that has been cut out of stone or wood.

carving knife, carving knives. COUNT N A **carving knife** is a large knife used for cutting cooked meat.

cascade /kæskeɪd/, **cascades, cascading, cascaded.** 1 COUNT N A **cascade** is a waterfall; a literary use. 2 VB WITH ADJUNCT When water **cascades,** it pours downwards very fast and in large quantities. *The water is cascading through the air.*

case /keɪs/, **cases.** 1 COUNT N WITH SUPP A **case** is a particular situation or instance. *In Catherine's case, it led to divorce... These tribes are a classic case of people living in harmony with their environment... All cases of bullying will be severely dealt with.* 2 COUNT N Doctors sometimes refer to a patient as a **case.** *...road accident cases.* 3 COUNT N A crime, or a trial that takes place after a crime, can be called a **case.** *...one of Sherlock Holmes' cases... He had lost the case.* 4 COUNT N In an argument, the **case** for or against something consists of the facts and reasons used to support or oppose it. *...a book arguing the case for better adult education... He stated his case.* 5 COUNT N A **case** is also a container that is specially designed to hold or protect something. *...scissors in a leather case.* 6 COUNT N A suitcase can be referred to as a **case.** *They unload their trunks and cases.*

PHRASES ● You say **in that case** or **in which case** to indicate that you are assuming that a previous statement is correct or true. *'The bar is closed,' the waiter said. 'In that case,' McFee said, 'I'll go to another hotel.'* ● When you say that a job or task **is a case of** doing a particular thing, you mean that the job or task consists of doing that thing. *There's very little work involved. It's just a case of drafting the summons.* ● If you say that something **is a case in point,** you mean that it is a good example of a general statement you have just made. ● You say **in any case** when you are adding another reason for something you have said or done. *I couldn't ask him all the time, and in any case he wasn't always there.* ● You say **in case** to indicate that you have something or are doing something because a particular thing might happen or might have happened. *I've got the key in case we want to go inside... I have a phone number in case of emergency.*

case history, case histories. COUNT N A person's **case history** is the record of past events or problems that have affected them; a formal use. *They had no case history of illness... She was making out a case-history for each child.*

cash /kæʃ/, **cashes, cashing, cashed.** 1 UNCOUNT N **Cash** is money in the form of notes and coins rather than cheques. *...four hundred dollars in cash.* 2 VB WITH OBJ If you **cash** a cheque, you exchange it at a bank for the amount of money that it is worth. *Cheques up to 50 pounds may be cashed at any of our branches.*

cash in. PHR VB If you **cash in** on a situation, you use it to gain an advantage for yourself; an informal use. *They cashed in on the public's growing suspicion.*

cashier /kə^{3}ʃɪə/, **cashiers.** COUNT N A **cashier** is the person that customers pay money to or get money from in a shop, bank, or garage.

casing /keɪsɪŋ/, **casings.** COUNT N A **casing** is a substance or object that covers something and protects it. *...the outer casing of a vacuum flask.*

casino /kəsiːnəʊ/, **casinos.** COUNT N A **casino** is a place where people play gambling games.

cask /kɑːsk/, **casks.** COUNT N A **cask** is a wooden barrel used for storing alcoholic drink.

casket /kɑːskɪ^{2}t/, **caskets.** 1 COUNT N A **casket** is a small box in which you keep valuable things. 2 COUNT N A **casket** is also a coffin; an American use.

casserole /kæsərəʊl/, **casseroles.** 1 COUNT N OR UNCOUNT N A **casserole** is a dish made by cooking food in liquid in an oven. *Use this stock in soups or casseroles... There's lamb casserole for dinner.* 2 COUNT N A **casserole** is also a large, heavy container with a lid which is used to cook food.

cassette /kə^{3}sɛt/, **cassettes.** COUNT N A **cassette** is a small, flat rectangular plastic container with magnetic tape inside which is used for recording and playing back sounds. *...a storage rack for cassettes.*

cassette recorder, cassette recorders. COUNT N A **cassette recorder** is a machine used for recording and listening to cassettes.

cast /kɑːst/, **casts, casting. Cast** is used in the present tense of the verb, and is the past tense and past participle. 1 COLL N The **cast** of a play or film is all the people who act in it. *The whole cast worked wonderfully together.* 2 VB WITH OBJ To **cast** an actor means to choose them to act a particular role. *I was cast as the husband, a man of about fifty.* 3 VB WITH OBJ AND ADJUNCT If you **cast** your eyes somewhere, you look there. *He cast a quick glance at his friend.* 4 VB WITH OBJ If you **cast** doubt or suspicion on something, you make other people unsure about it. *He had cast doubt on our traditional beliefs.* 5 PHRASE If you **cast** your **mind back,** you think about things in the past or try to remember them. *He cast his mind back over the day.* 6 VB WITH OBJ When you **cast** your vote in an election, you vote. *Will had cast his vote for the President.* 7 VB WITH OBJ To **cast** an object means to make it by pouring hot, liquid metal into a container and leaving it there until it becomes hard. 8 See also **casting.**

cast about or **cast around.** PHR VB If you **cast about** or **cast around** for something, you try to find it; a literary use. *I cast around for some place to hide.*

cast aside. PHR VB If you **cast** someone or something **aside,** you get rid of them; a formal use which shows disapproval. *His country cast him aside and disgraced him.*

cast off. PHR VB 1 If you **cast** something **off,** you get rid of it or no longer use it; a formal use. *Organizations must cast off old-fashioned practices in order to survive.* ● See also **cast-off.** 2 If you are on a boat and you **cast off,** you untie the rope that fastens it to the shore; a technical use. *We cast off as quietly as we could.*

caste /kɑːst/, **castes.** COUNT N OR UNCOUNT N A **caste** is one of the social classes into which people in a Hindu society are divided. *Sushma came from a lower caste... Duties were determined by caste.*

caster /kɑːstə/. See **castor.**

castigate /kæstɪgeɪt/, **castigates, castigating, castigated.** VB WITH OBJ If you **castigate** someone or something, you scold or criticize them severely; a formal use. *They castigated the report as inadequate.*

casting /kɑːstɪŋ/. UNCOUNT N **Casting** is the activity of choosing actors to play particular roles. *...people doing the casting for films.*

cast-iron. 1 ATTRIB ADJ **Cast-iron** objects are made of a special type of iron containing carbon. *...a cast-iron stove.* 2 ATTRIB ADJ A **cast-iron** excuse, guarantee, or solution is absolutely certain to be effective.

castle /kɑːsə^{0}l/, **castles.** 1 COUNT N A **castle** is a large building with thick, high walls, built by important people in former times, for protection during wars and battles. 2 COUNT N In chess, a **castle** is a piece which can move forwards, backwards, or sideways. A **castle** is also called a **rook.**

castor /kɑːstə/, **castors;** also spelled **caster.** COUNT N **Castors** are small wheels fitted to a piece of furniture.

castrate /kæstreɪt/, **castrates, castrating, castrated.** VB WITH OBJ To **castrate** a male animal means to remove its testicles; a formal use. *The two bulls had to be castrated.* ♦ **castration** /kæstreɪʃə^{0}n/ UNCOUNT N *They used castration of men as a form of punishment.*

casual /kæʒjuᵒəl/. 1 ADJ If you are **casual,** you are relaxed and do things without great attention. *He tried to appear casual as he asked her to dance... ...a casual glance.* ♦ **casually** ADV *...saying goodbye as casually as I could.* ♦ **casualness** UNCOUNT N *...working with apparent casualness.* 2 ADJ Something that is **casual** happens by chance or without planning. *...a casual friendship... It is not open to casual visitors.* ♦ **casually** ADV *...any casually assembled group of men.* 3 ATTRIB ADJ **Casual** clothes are ones that you normally wear at home or on holiday, and not for formal occasions. *She wears casual clothes in bright colours.* ♦ **casually** ADV *The students dress casually, in jeans and sweat shirts.* 4 ATTRIB ADJ **Casual** work is done for short periods and not permanently. *...a casual labourer.*

casualty /kæʒjuᵒəltiⁱ/, **casualties.** 1 COUNT N A **casualty** is a person who is injured or killed in a war or an accident. *No casualties were reported... There were heavy casualties on both sides.* 2 COUNT N A **casualty** of an event or situation is a person or a thing that has suffered badly as a result of it. *She was one of the casualties of the system.* 3 ATTRIB ADJ The **casualty** ward of a hospital is the place where very sudden illnesses and injuries are treated.

cat /kæt/, **cats.** 1 COUNT N A **cat** is a small, furry animal with a tail, whiskers, and sharp claws. Cats are often kept as pets. 2 COUNT N A **cat** is also any larger animal that is a type of cat, such as a lion or tiger.

cataclysm /kætəklɪsə^{0}m/, **cataclysms.** COUNT N A **cataclysm** is a disaster or violent change; a literary use. *Europe is approaching a terrible cataclysm.* ♦ **cataclysmic** /kætəklɪsmɪk/ ADJ *...a cataclysmic effect on British politics.*

catalogue /kætəlɒg/, **catalogues, cataloguing, catalogued;** spelled **catalog** in American English. 1 COUNT N A **catalogue** is a book containing a list of goods that are available from a company, or a list of objects that are in a museum. *...expensive illustrated catalogues... ...catalogues from publishers.* 2 VB WITH OBJ To **catalogue** things means to make a list of them. *Books are catalogued on white cards filed alphabetically.* 3 COUNT N WITH 'of' A **catalogue** of things is a number of them considered one after another. *Mrs Zapp recited a catalogue of her husband's sins.* 4 VB WITH OBJ If you **catalogue** a series of similar events or qualities, you list them. *They had been cataloguing the many discomforts of life in India.*

catalyst /kætəlɪst/, **catalysts.** 1 COUNT N A **catalyst** is something that causes a change or event to happen; a formal use. *Nuclear power served as a catalyst for the emergence of the Greens as a political force.* 2 COUNT N In chemistry, a **catalyst** is a substance that causes a reaction to take place; a technical use.

cataract /kætərækt/, **cataracts.** COUNT N A **cataract** is a layer that has grown over a person's eye that prevents them from seeing properly.

catastrophe /kətæstrəfiⁱ/, **catastrophes.** COUNT N OR UNCOUNT N A **catastrophe** is an unexpected event that causes great suffering or damage. *Unemployment is a personal catastrophe... ...an overwhelming sense of catastrophe.*

catastrophic /kætəstrɒfɪk/. ADJ **Catastrophic** means extremely bad or serious, often causing great suffering or damage. *The impact on Belgium has already been catastrophic... ...catastrophic mistakes.*

catch /kætʃ/, **catches, catching, caught** /kɔːt/. 1 VB WITH OBJ If you **catch** an animal or person, you capture them. *I went fishing and caught a nice little trout... ...a wild otter caught in a trap... We can get six months in prison if they catch us.* 2 VB WITH OBJ To **catch** an object which is moving through the air means to take hold of it or collect it while it is moving. *'Catch,' said Howard. He threw the book over to her... The wind caught her hat.* 3 VB WITH OBJ If you **catch** someone doing something wrong or, you discover them doing it. *A gardener was sacked if he was caught smoking... Don't let him catch you at it.* 4 VB WITH OBJ If one object **catches** another one, it hits the other object with a lot of force. *The wave caught the trawler on her bow.* 5 ERG VB If something **catches** on an object, it becomes trapped by it. *There was a bit of rabbit's fur caught on the fence... He caught his fingers in the spokes of the wheel.* 6 VB WITH OBJ If you **catch** a bus, train, or plane, you get on it to travel somewhere. *She caught a train to Boston.* 7 VB WITH OBJ If you cannot **catch** something that someone has said, you do not manage to hear it. *She whispered something he could not catch.* 8 VB WITH OBJ If something **catches** your interest, imagination, or attention, you notice it or become interested in it. *A poster caught her attention.* 9 PASSIVE VB WITH 'in' If you **are caught** in a storm or other unpleasant situation, it happens when you cannot avoid its effects. *They were caught in an earthquake.* 10 VB WITH OBJ If you **catch** a cold or a disease, you become ill with it. 11 VB WITH OBJ If something **catches** the light or if the light **catches** it, it reflects the light and looks bright or shiny. *The grass is sparkling where the sunlight catches small drops from the rain.* 12 COUNT N A **catch** on a window or door is a device that fastens it. *He put his hand through the hole in the glass and released the catch.* 13 SING N A **catch** is also a hidden problem or difficulty in a plan or course of action. *'There's a catch in this.'—'There's no catch, Gordon. I swear it.'* 14 to **catch** someone's eye: see **eye.** ● to **catch fire:** see **fire.**

catch at. PHR VB If you **catch at** something, you quickly take hold of it. *The children caught at my skirts and tugged me back.*

catch on. PHR VB 1 If you **catch on** to something, you understand it, or realize that it is happening. *You were expected to catch on quick... They finally caught on to our game.* **2** If something **catches on,** it becomes popular. *Ballroom dancing caught on.*

catch out. PHR VB If you **catch** someone **out,** you make them make a mistake, often by an unfair trick. *Are you trying to catch me out?*

catch up. PHR VB **1** If you **catch up** with someone, you reach them by walking faster than them. *Tim had just reached the corner when Judy caught up with him... She stood still, allowing him to catch her up.* **2** To **catch up** with someone also means to reach the same standard or level that they have reached. *Most leaders were obsessed with catching up with the West.* **3** If you **catch up** on an activity that you have not had much time to do, you spend time doing it. *They went to the office to catch up on correspondence... I was catching up on my sleep.* **4** If you **are caught up** in something, you are involved in it, usually unwillingly. *He was determined not to get caught up in any publicity nonsense.*

catch up with. PHR VB **1** When people **catch up with** someone who has done something wrong, they succeed in finding them. *When Birmingham authorities finally caught up with her, she had spent all the money.* **2** If something **catches up with** you, you find yourself in an unpleasant situation which you have been able to avoid but which you are now forced to deal with. *I am sure that the truth will catch up with him.*

categorical /kætə1gɒrɪkə0l/. ADJ If you are **categorical** about something, you state your views with certainty and firmness. *On this point we can be clear and categorical.* ♦ **categorically** ADV *The proposals had been categorically rejected.*

categorize /kætə1gəraɪz/, **categorizes, categorizing, categorized;** also spelled **categorise.** VB WITH OBJ If you **categorize** people or things, you divide them into sets. *Animals can be categorised according to the food they eat.* ♦ **categorization** /kætɪgə0raɪzeɪʃə0n/ UNCOUNT N OR COUNT N *We don't think it's necessary to have such rigid categorization.*

category /kætə1gəri0/, **categories.** COUNT N If people or things are divided into **categories,** they are divided into groups according to their qualities and characteristics. *They divided the nation into six social categories... There are three categories of machine.*

cater /keɪtə/, **caters, catering, catered.** VB WITH 'for' OR PREP 'to' To **cater** for people means to provide them with the things they need. *We can cater for all age groups... ...theatres catering to a white middle-class audience.*

caterer /keɪtərə/, **caterers.** COUNT N A **caterer** is a person or a company that provides food and drink in a particular place or on a special occasion. *...a hotel caterer.*

catering /keɪtə0rɪŋ/. UNCOUNT N **Catering** is the activity or business of providing food and drink for people. *'Who did the catering?'—'A firm in Arundel.'*

caterpillar /kætəpɪlə/, **caterpillars.** COUNT N A **caterpillar** is a small, worm-like animal that eventually develops into a butterfly or moth.

cathedral /kəθiːdrə0l/, **cathedrals.** COUNT N A **cathedral** is a large important church which has a bishop in charge of it.

Catholic /kæθə0lɪk/, **Catholics.** COUNT N A **Catholic** is someone who belongs to the branch of the Christian church which accepts the Pope as its leader. *...four million Ukrainian Catholics... ...the Catholic Church.*

Catholicism /kəθɒlɪsɪzə0m/. UNCOUNT N **Catholicism** is the set of Christian beliefs held by Catholics.

cattle /kætə0l/. PLURAL N **Cattle** are cows and bulls.

caucus /kɔːkəs/, **caucuses.** COUNT N A **caucus** is an influential group of people within an organization sharing similar aims and interests; a formal use. *...the California caucus at the National Convention.*

caught /kɔːt/. **Caught** is the past tense and past participle of **catch.**

cauldron /kɔːldrən/, **cauldrons;** spelled **caldron** in American English. COUNT N A **cauldron** is a very large round metal pot used for cooking over a fire.

cauliflower /kɒlɪflaʊə/, **cauliflowers.** COUNT N OR UNCOUNT N A **cauliflower** is a large round white vegetable surrounded by green leaves.

causal /kɔːzə0l/. ATTRIB ADJ **Causal** means connected by a relationship of cause and effect. *There may be no causal link... It is hard to see how such a causal relationship could be proved.*

causation /kɔːzeɪʃə0n/. UNCOUNT N **Causation** is the relationship of cause and effect; a formal word. *From what is our knowledge of causation received?*

cause /kɔːz/, **causes, causing, caused. 1** COUNT N The **cause** of an event is the thing that makes it happen. *Nobody knew the cause of the explosion... The men died of natural causes.* **2** UNCOUNT N WITH 'for' OR TO-INF If you have **cause** for a particular feeling or action, you have good reasons for it. *Years of training gave him every cause for confidence... I have no cause to go back.* **3** VB WITH OBJ, OR VB WITH OBJ AND OBJ To **cause** something means to make it happen. *...difficulties caused by price increases... What's causing you so much concern?... The sound caused her to step aside.* **4** COUNT N A **cause** is also an aim which a group of people supports or is fighting for. *...the cause of world peace.*

caustic /kɔːstɪk/. **1** ADJ **Caustic** chemical substances can dissolve other substances. *Do not use a caustic cleaner on enamel.* **2** ADJ A **caustic** remark is extremely critical or bitter. *...her caustic sense of humour.*

caution /kɔːʃə0n/, **cautions, cautioning, cautioned. 1** UNCOUNT N **Caution** is great care taken in order to avoid danger. *You must proceed with extreme caution.* **2** VB WITH OBJ OR REPORT VB If someone **cautions** you, they warn you. *I cautioned him not to reveal too much to anyone... The doctor cautioned that any such state of tension could be highly dangerous.* Also UNCOUNT N *...a word of caution.* **3** VB WITH OBJ When the police **caution** someone, they warn them that anything that they say may be used as evidence in a trial.

cautionary /kɔːʃənə0ri1/. ATTRIB ADJ A **cautionary** story or tale is intended to give a warning.

cautious /kɔːʃəs/. ADJ A **cautious** person acts very carefully in order to avoid danger. *Her husband is reserved and cautious.* ♦ **cautiously** ADV *We moved cautiously forward.*

cavalier /kævəlɪə/. ADJ Someone who behaves in a **cavalier** way does not consider other people's feelings or the seriousness of a situation.

cavalry /kævəlri1/. SING N In an army, the **cavalry** used to be the group of soldiers who rode horses. Nowadays, it is usually the part of the army that uses armoured vehicles.

cave /keɪv/, **caves, caving, caved.** COUNT N A **cave** is a large hole in the side of a cliff or hill, or under the ground.

cave in. PHR VB **1** When a roof or wall **caves in,** it collapses inwards. **2** If you **cave in,** you suddenly stop arguing or resisting.

cavern /kævə0n/, **caverns.** COUNT N A **cavern** is a large deep cave.

cavernous /kævənəs/. ADJ A **cavernous** building is very large inside.

caviar /kæviɑː, kæviɑː/; also spelled **caviare.** UNCOUNT N **Caviar** is the salted eggs of a fish called the sturgeon.

cavity /kævə1ti1/, **cavities.** COUNT N A **cavity** is a small space or hole in something solid. *...the filling of tooth cavities.*

cavort /kə3vɔːt/, **cavorts, cavorting, cavorted.** VB When people **cavort,** they leap about in a noisy and excited way.

cc. cc. is an abbreviation for 'cubic centimetres', used when referring to the volume or capacity of something.

CD /siː diː/, **CDs.** COUNT N A **CD** is a compact disc. *...a CD player.*

cease /siːs/, **ceases, ceasing, ceased;** a formal word. **1** VB If something **ceases,** it stops happening. *Hostilities must cease at once.* **2** VB WITH TO-INF OR -ING If you **cease** to do something, you stop doing it. *Once people retire they cease to be union members... The vicar sighed as he ceased speaking.* **3** VB WITH OBJ To **cease** something that is being produced or provided means to stop producing or providing it. *They threatened to cease financial support to the university.*

ceasefire /siːsfaɪə/, **ceasefires.** COUNT N A **ceasefire** is an arrangement in which countries at war agree to stop fighting for a time.

ceaseless /siːslɪ2s/. ATTRIB ADJ **Ceaseless** means continuing for ever or for a long time; a formal use. *...the ceaseless traffic.* ♦ **ceaselessly** ADV *Clarissa was talking ceaselessly.*

cedar /siːdə/, **cedars.** COUNT N A **cedar** is a kind of large evergreen tree.

cede /siːd/, **cedes, ceding, ceded.** VB WITH OBJ If you **cede** something to someone, you let them have it; a formal use. *The colony was ceded to Spain in 1762.*

ceiling /siːlɪŋ/, **ceilings. 1** COUNT N A **ceiling** is the top inside surface of a room. *...a large room with a high ceiling.* **2** COUNT N WITH SUPP A **ceiling** is also an official upper limit on prices or wages. *...a ceiling on business rate increases.*

celebrate /seɪə1breɪt/, **celebrates, celebrating, celebrated. 1** VB WITH OR WITHOUT OBJ If you **celebrate** an event or anniversary, you do something special and enjoyable because of it. *His victory was celebrated with music and dancing... The company was celebrating its fiftieth birthday... We ought to celebrate; let's have a bottle of champagne.* ♦ **celebration** /selə1breɪʃə0n/ UNCOUNT N OR COUNT N *...a time of celebration... ...its tenth anniversary celebrations.* **2** VB WITH OBJ When priests **celebrate** Holy Communion or Mass, they officially perform the actions and ceremonies that are involved.

celebrated /selə1breɪtɪ2d/. ADJ Someone or something that is **celebrated** is famous. *...a celebrated actress.*

celebrity /sə1lebrɪ1ti1/, **celebrities.** COUNT N A **celebrity** is someone who is famous.

celery /seləri1/. UNCOUNT N **Celery** is a vegetable with long pale green stalks.

celestial /sɪ2lestɪəl/. ATTRIB ADJ **Celestial** is used to describe things connected with heaven; a formal use.

celibacy /selə1bəsi1/. UNCOUNT N **Celibacy** is the state of being celibate; a formal use. *...vows of poverty and celibacy and obedience.*

celibate /selɪbə1t/. ADJ Someone who is **celibate** does not marry or have sex; a formal use. *The celibate life was beginning to appeal to him.*

cell /sel/, **cells. 1** COUNT N A **cell** is the smallest part of an animal or plant. Animals and plants are made up of millions of cells. **2** COUNT N A **cell** is also a small room in which a prisoner is locked, or one in which a monk or nun lives.

cellar /selə/, **cellars.** COUNT N A **cellar** is a room underneath a building, often used for storing things in.

cello /tʃeləʊ/, **cellos.** COUNT N A **cello** is a musical instrument that looks like a large violin. You hold it upright and play it sitting down.

cellophane /selə6feɪn/. UNCOUNT N **Cellophane** is a thin transparent material, used to wrap things.

cellular /seljə4lə/. **1** ATTRIB ADJ **Cellular** means relating to the cells of animals or plants. *...cellular structure.* **2** ATTRIB ADJ **Cellular** fabrics are loosely woven and keep you warm.

celluloid /seljə4lɔɪd/. **1** UNCOUNT N **Celluloid** is a type of plastic. **2** UNCOUNT N You can use **celluloid** to refer to films and the cinema; a literary use. *...the celluloid world of Hollywood.*

Celsius /selsɪəs/. UNCOUNT N **Celsius** is a scale for measuring temperature, in which water freezes at 0° and boils at 100°.

cement /sɪment/, **cements, cementing, cemented. 1** UNCOUNT N **Cement** is a grey powder which is mixed with sand and water in order to make concrete. *...a sack of cement.* **2** VB WITH OBJ If you **cement** an area, you cover it with cement. **3** VB WITH OBJ If things **are cemented** together, they are stuck or fastened together. *The lumps were cemented to the reef with coral.* **4** VB WITH OBJ Something that **cements** a relationship or agreement makes it stronger.

cemetery /semə1tri1/, **cemeteries.** COUNT N A **cemetery** is a place where dead people are buried.

censor /sensə/, **censors, censoring, censored. 1** VB WITH OBJ If someone **censors** a letter, report, book, play, or film, they officially examine it and cut out any parts that they consider unacceptable. *He was censoring his platoon's mail.* **2** COUNT N A **censor** is a person who has been officially appointed to censor books, plays, and films.

censorship /sensəʃɪp/. UNCOUNT N When there is **censorship,** books, plays, films, letters, or reports are censored. *...the censorship of bad news in wartime.*

censure /senʃə/, **censures, censuring, censured.** VB WITH OBJ If you **censure** someone, you tell them that you strongly disapprove of what they have done; a formal use. *He had been censured for showing cowardice in the battle.* Also UNCOUNT N *The result exposed him to official censure.*

census /sensəs/, **censuses.** COUNT N A **census** is an official survey of the population of a country.

cent /sent/, **cents.** COUNT N A **cent** is a small unit of money in many countries, worth one hundredth of the main unit. ● See also **per cent.**

centenary /sentiːnə0ri1/, **centenaries.** COUNT N A **centenary** is a year when people celebrate something important that happened one hundred years earlier. *1928 was the centenary of Ibsen's birth.*

center /sentə/. See **centre.**

Centigrade /sentɪgreɪd/. UNCOUNT N **Centigrade** is a scale for measuring temperature, in which water freezes at 0° and boils at 100°.

centimetre /sentɪmiːtə/, **centimetres;** spelled **centimeter** in American English. COUNT N A **centimetre** is a unit of length equal to ten millimetres or one-hundredth of a metre.

centipede /sentɪpiːd/, **centipedes.** COUNT N A **centipede** is a long, thin insect with a lot of legs.

central /sentrəl/. **1** ADJ Something that is **central** is in the middle of a place or area. *The houses are arranged around a central courtyard... ...a film about central Poland.* ♦ **centrally** ADV *The pin is centrally positioned on the circle.* **2** ADJ A place that is **central** is easy to reach because it is in the centre of a city. *The cafe was near Oxford Street, very central for her.* ♦ **centrally** ADV *...a centrally located flat.* **3** ATTRIB ADJ A **central** group or organization makes all the important decisions for a larger organization or country. *Their activities are strictly controlled by a central committee... ...local and central government.* ♦ **centrally** ADV *France has a centrally organized system.* 4 ADJ The **central** person or thing in a particular situation is the most important one. *These statistics were central to the debate.*

central heating. UNCOUNT N **Central heating** is a heating system in which water or air is heated and passed round a building through pipes and radiators.

centralization /sɛntrəlaɪzeɪʃə^{0}n/; also spelled **centralisation.** UNCOUNT N **Centralization** is the process of changing a system or organization so that it is controlled by one central group. *Large-scale technology brings centralization.*

centralized /sɛntrəlaɪzd/; also spelled **centralised.** ADJ If a country or system is **centralized,** it is controlled by one central group. *We believe in a strong centralized state.*

centrally heated. ADJ A building that is **centrally heated** has central heating.

centre /sɛntə/, **centres, centring, centred;** spelled **center, centers, centering, centered** in American English. 1 COUNT N The **centre** of something is the middle of it. *He moved the table over to the centre of the room.* Also ATTRIB ADJ *...a black wig with a centre parting... The centre section was coloured pink.* 2 COUNT N A **centre** is a place where people have meetings, get help of some kind, or take part in a particular activity. *...a new arts centre... ...the university's health centre.* 3 COUNT N WITH SUPP If an area or town is a **centre** for an industry or activity, that industry or activity is very important there. *The region began as a centre for sheep-farming.* 4 COUNT N WITH SUPP The **centre** of a situation is the most important thing involved. *Smith was right in the centre of the action.* 5 COUNT N WITH SUPP If something is the **centre** of attention or interest, people are giving it a lot of attention. *She was the centre of public admiration.* 6 SING N In politics, the **centre** refers to political groups and beliefs that are neither left-wing nor right-wing. Also ATTRIB ADJ *...a relatively small centre party called the Free Democrats.* 7 PASSIVE VB Someone or something that **is centred** in a particular place is based there. *They were now centred in the new Royal Observatory at Greenwich.*

centre around or **centre on.** PHR VB If something **centres around** a person or thing or **centres on** them, that person or thing is the main feature or subject of attention. *The workers' demands centred around pay and conditions... Attention was for the moment centred on Michael Simpson.*

century /sɛntʃəri^1/, **centuries.** 1 COUNT N A **century** is the period of a hundred years that is used when stating a date. For example, the 19th century was the period from 1801 to 1900. 2 COUNT N A **century** is also any period of a hundred years.

ceramic /sɪ^{1}ræmɪk/, **ceramics.** 1 ATTRIB ADJ **Ceramic** objects are made of clay that has been heated to a very high temperature. *...ceramic tiles.* 2 COUNT N **Ceramics** are ceramic objects. *...Chinese ceramics.*

cereal /sɪərɪəl/, **cereals.** 1 COUNT N OR UNCOUNT N A **cereal** is a plant such as wheat, maize, or rice that produces grain. *...chemicals used to control mildew and mould in cereals, fruit and vegetables... ...cereal crops.* 2 COUNT N OR UNCOUNT N A **cereal** is also a food made from grain, usually mixed with milk and eaten for breakfast.

cerebral /sɛrə^{1}brəl/. 1 ADJ **Cerebral** means relating to thought or reasoning rather than to emotions; a formal use. *...the cerebral challenge of police work.* 2 ATTRIB ADJ **Cerebral** also means relating to the brain; a technical use. *...a cerebral hemorrhage.*

ceremonial /sɛrə^{1}məʊnɪəl/, **ceremonials.** 1 ADJ Something that is **ceremonial** is used in a ceremony or relates to a ceremony. *...a ceremonial robe from Africa... ...ceremonial dances.* 2 UNCOUNT N OR COUNT N **Ceremonial** consists of all the impressive things that are done, said, or worn on very formal occasions. *...the splendid ceremonial of Whitehall on great occasions... He loved parades and ceremonials.*

ceremony /sɛrə^{1}məni^1/, **ceremonies.** 1 COUNT N A **ceremony** is a formal event such as a wedding or a coronation. *...a graduation ceremony.* 2 UNCOUNT N **Ceremony** consists of the special things that are said and done on very formal occasions. 3 UNCOUNT N **Ceremony** is also very formal and polite behaviour. *At the BBC she was received with respectful ceremony.*

certain /sɜ:tə^{0}n/. 1 ADJ To be **certain** means to be definite and without doubt. *He felt certain that she would disapprove... I'm absolutely certain of that... She's certain to be late... Such a vote would mean the certain defeat of the government.* 2 ATTRIB ADJ You use **certain** to indicate that you are referring to one particular thing, person, or group, although you are not saying exactly which it is. *She arranged to meet him at three o'clock on a certain afternoon... Certain areas in Sussex are better than others for keeping bees.* Also PRON WITH 'of' *Certain of our judges have claimed that this is the case.*

PHRASES ● If you know something **for certain,** you have no doubt at all about it. *It is not known for certain where they are now.* ● When you **make certain** that something happens, you take action to ensure that it happens. ● If something is done or achieved **to a certain extent,** it is only partly done or achieved. *That takes care of my anxieties to a certain extent.*

certainly /sɜ:tə^{0}nli^1/. 1 ADV You use **certainly** to emphasize what you are saying when you are making a statement. *If nothing is done there will certainly be an economic crisis... It certainly looks wonderful, doesn't it?* 2 CONVENTION You also use **certainly** when you are agreeing with what someone has said or suggested. *'Would you agree that it is still a difficult world for women to live in?'—'Oh certainly.'* 3 CONVENTION You say **certainly not** when you want to say 'no' in a strong way. *'Had you forgotten?'—'Certainly not.'*

certainty /sɜ:tə^{0}nti^1/, **certainties.** 1 UNCOUNT N **Certainty** is the state of being definite or of having no doubts at all. *Answers to such questions would never be known with certainty... ...the certainty of death in battle.* 2 COUNT N A **certainty** is something that nobody has any doubts about. *It's by no means a certainty that we'll win... ...probabilities rather than certainties.*

certificate /sətɪfɪ^{1}kə^{1}t/, **certificates.** COUNT N A **certificate** is an official document which states that particular facts are true, or which you receive when you have successfully completed a course of study or training. *...a medical certificate... ...your birth certificate.*

certify /sɜ:tɪfaɪ/, **certifies, certifying, certified.** 1 VB WITH OBJ To **certify** something means to declare formally that it is true. *...a piece of paper certifying the payment of his taxes.* 2 VB WITH OBJ To **certify** someone means to give them a certificate stating that they have successfully completed a course of training. 3 VB WITH OBJ AND COMPLEMENT OR 'as' To **certify** someone insane means to officially declare that they are insane.

cessation /sɛseɪʃə^{0}n/. UNCOUNT N WITH SUPP The **cessation** of something is the stopping of it; a formal use. *...a cessation of hostilities.*

chafe /tʃeɪf/, **chafes, chafing, chafed.** 1 VB OR ERG VB When your skin **is chafed** by something, it becomes sore as a result of being rubbed by it. *Baby powder helps to avoid chafing.* 2 VB If you **chafe** at a restriction or delay, you feel annoyed and impatient about it; a formal use.

chaff /tʃæf/. UNCOUNT N **Chaff** consists of the outer parts of grain such as wheat that are removed.

chagrin /ʃægrɪn/. UNCOUNT N **Chagrin** is a feeling of annoyance or disappointment; a formal use. *Thomas discovered to his great chagrin that he was too late.*

chain /tʃeɪn/, **chains, chaining, chained.** 1 COUNT N OR UNCOUNT N A **chain** consists of metal rings connected together in a line. *She wore a silver chain... ...a length of chain.* 2 VB WITH OBJ When you **chain** a person or thing to something, you fasten them to it with a chain. *I chained my bike to some railings... They chained themselves to the fence.* 3 COUNT N WITH SUPP A **chain** of things is a group of them arranged in a line. *...the island chains of the Pacific.* 4 COUNT N WITH SUPP A **chain** of shops or hotels is a number of them owned by the same company. 5 COUNT N WITH SUPP A **chain** of events is a series of them happening one after another. *...the brief chain of events that led up to her death.*

chain-smoke, chain-smokes, chain-smoking, chain-smoked. VB Someone who **chain-smokes** smokes cigarettes continuously.

chain store, chain stores. COUNT N A **chain store** is one of many similar shops owned by the same company.

chair /tʃɛə/, **chairs, chairing, chaired.** 1 COUNT N A **chair** is a piece of furniture for one person to sit on. **Chairs** have backs and four legs. *I sat in a low chair by the fire, reading.* 2 COUNT N At a university, a **chair** is the post of professor. 3 VB WITH OBJ If you **chair** a meeting, you are the chairperson. 4 COUNT N The **chair** of a meeting is the chairperson.

chairman /tʃɛəmə^{3}n/, **chairmen.** COUNT N The **chairman** of a meeting, committee, or organization is the person in charge of it.

chairperson /tʃɛəpɜ:sə^{0}n/, **chairpersons.** COUNT N The **chairperson** of a meeting, committee, or organization is the person in charge of it.

chairwoman /tʃɛəwʊmən/, **chairwomen.** COUNT N The **chairwoman** of a meeting, committee, or organization is the woman in charge of it.

chalet /ʃæleɪ/, **chalets.** COUNT N A **chalet** is a small wooden house, especially in a mountain area or holiday camp.

chalk /tʃɔ:k/, **chalks, chalking, chalked.** 1 UNCOUNT N **Chalk** is soft white rock. You can use small pieces of it for writing or drawing with. *He took a piece of chalk from his pocket... ...the chalk uplands of Wiltshire.* 2 COUNT N **Chalks** are small pieces of chalk used for writing or drawing with. 3 VB WITH OBJ OR ADJUNCT If you **chalk** something, you draw or write it using a piece of chalk. *A line was chalked round the body... ...a young man chalking on the blackboard.*

chalk up. PHR VB If you **chalk up** a success, you achieve it. *They chalked up several victories.*

chalky /tʃɔ:ki^1/. ADJ Something that is **chalky** contains chalk or is covered with chalk. *...the white, chalky road.*

challenge /tʃælɪ^{2}ndʒ/, **challenges, challenging, challenged.** 1 COUNT N OR UNCOUNT N A **challenge** is something new and difficult which will require great effort and determination. *Mount Everest presented a challenge to Hillary... ...the challenge of the unknown.* 2 COUNT N OR UNCOUNT N A **challenge** to something is a questioning of its truth, value, or authority. *There will inevitably be challenges to the existing order... These ideas are open to challenge.* 3 VB WITH OBJ If you **challenge** someone, you invite them to fight or compete with you. *They had challenged and beaten the best teams in the world.* 4 VB WITH OBJ To **challenge** ideas or people means to question their truth, value, or authority. *The idea has never been challenged... He challenged the minister to produce evidence.*

challenger /tʃælɪ^{2}ndʒə/, **challengers.** COUNT N A **challenger** is someone who competes for a position or title, for example a sports championship. *...a challenger to Mitterrand's leadership.*

challenging /tʃælɪ^{2}ndʒɪŋ/. 1 ADJ A **challenging** job or activity requires great effort and determination. *Life as a housewife does not seem very challenging to the highly educated girl.* 2 ADJ **Challenging** behaviour seems to be inviting people to argue or compete. *...a suspicious challenging look.*

chamber /tʃeɪmbə/, **chambers.** 1 COUNT N A **chamber** is a large room that is used for formal meetings, or that is designed and equipped for a particular purpose. *...the Council Chamber... He led the way to the torture chamber.* 2 COUNT N WITH 'of' A **Chamber** of Commerce or **Chamber** of Trade is a group of business people who work together to improve business in their town. 3 PLURAL N **Chambers** are offices used by judges and barristers.

chambermaid /tʃeɪmbəmeɪd/, **chambermaids.** COUNT N A **chambermaid** is a woman who cleans and tidies the bedrooms in a hotel.

chamber music. UNCOUNT N **Chamber music** is classical music written for a small number of instruments.

chameleon /kəmi:lɪən/, **chameleons.** COUNT N A **chameleon** is a lizard whose skin changes colour to match its surroundings.

champagne /ʃæmpeɪn/. UNCOUNT N **Champagne** is a good quality white wine from France, with lots of bubbles in it.

champion /tʃæmpɪən/, **champions, championing, championed.** 1 COUNT N A **champion** is someone who has won the first prize in a competition. *...the school tennis champion.* 2 COUNT N WITH SUPP If you are a **champion** of a cause or principle, you support or defend it. *...a champion of liberty.* 3 VB WITH OBJ If you **champion** a cause or principle, you support or defend it.

championship /tʃæmpɪənʃɪp/, **championships.** COUNT N A **championship** is a competition to find the best player or team in a particular sport. A **championship** is also the title or status of the winner. *...the first round of the U.S open golf championship... ...the heavyweight championship of the world.*

chance /tʃɑ:ns/, **chances, chancing, chanced.** 1 COUNT N OR UNCOUNT N If there is a **chance** of something happening, it is possible that it will happen. *We've got a good chance of winning... What are her chances of getting the job?... There's little chance that the situation will improve.* 2 COUNT N When you take a **chance,** you try to do something although there is a risk of danger or failure. 3 UNCOUNT N Something that happens by **chance** was not planned. *Almost by chance I found myself talking to him.* Also ADJ *...a chance meeting.* 4 VB WITH TO-INF If you **chance** to do something, you do it although you had not planned to; a formal use. *I chanced to overhear them.*

chancellor /tʃɑ:nsələ/, **chancellors.** 1 COUNT N OR TITLE In several European countries, the **Chancellor** is the head of government. *...Chancellor Kohl.* 2 COUNT N The official head of a British university is also called the **Chancellor.**

chandelier /ʃændəˈlɪə/, **chandeliers.** COUNT N A **chandelier** is an ornamental frame hanging from a ceiling, which holds light bulbs or candles.

change /tʃeɪndʒ/, **changes, changing, changed.** 1 COUNT N OR UNCOUNT N If there is a **change** in something, it becomes different. *...a radical change in attitudes... ...the changes that had taken place since he had left China... There had been little change.* 2 ERG VB When something **changes** or when you **change** it, it becomes different. *Her disdain changed to surprised respect... They can be used to change uranium into plutonium... A bird changes direction by dipping one wing and lifting the other.* ♦ **changed** ADJ *He returned to parliament a changed man.* ♦ **changing** ADJ *...a report on changing fashions in food.* 3 VB WITH OBJ To **change** something also means to replace it with something new or different. *His doctor advised that he change his job.* 4 COUNT N WITH SUPP If there is a **change** of something, it is replaced. *...a change of government... That motorcycle needs a change of oil.* 5 VB WITH OR WITHOUT OBJ When you **change** your clothes, you take them off and put on different ones. *She changed into her street clothes... I want to change my socks.* 6 COUNT N WITH 'of' A **change** of clothes is an extra set of clothes that you take with you when you go away. 7 VB WITH OBJ When you **change** a baby or **change** its nappy, you take off its dirty nappy and put on a clean one. 8 VB WITH OR WITHOUT OBJ When you **change** buses or trains, you get off one and get on to another to continue your journey. *Don't forget to change at Crewe... They were waiting to change trains.* 9 UNCOUNT N Your **change** is the money that you receive when you pay for something with more money than it costs. *Morris handed Hooper his change.* 10 UNCOUNT N **Change** is coins, rather than notes. *We only had 80p in change.* 11 UNCOUNT N WITH 'for' If you have **change** for a note or a large coin, you have the same amount of money in smaller notes or coins. *Have you got change for a fiver?* 12 VB WITH OBJ When you **change** money, you exchange it for the same amount of money in different coins or notes. *Can anyone change a ten pound note?... Do you change foreign currency?*

PHRASES ● If you say that something is happening **for a change,** you mean that it is different from what usually happens. *They were glad to leave their cars and walk for a change.* ● If you say that an experience **makes a change,** you mean that it is enjoyable and different from what you are used to. *Being out in the country made a refreshing change.* ● **to change hands:** see **hand.** ● **to change your mind:** see **mind.**

change over. PHR VB If you **change over** from one thing to another, you stop doing one thing and start doing the other. *They had been Liberal till several years ago, then they changed over to Conservative.*

changeable /tʃeɪndʒəbəl/. ADJ **Changeable** means likely to change. *...as changeable as the weather.*

channel /tʃænəl/, **channels, channelling, channelled;** spelled **channeling** and **channeled** in American English. 1 COUNT N A **channel** is a wavelength on which television programmes are broadcast. *He switched to the other channel.* 2 COUNT N WITH SUPP If something has been done through particular **channels,** that particular group of people have arranged for it to be done. *I notified the authorities through the normal channels.* 3 VB WITH OBJ If you **channel** money into something, you arrange for it to be used for that purpose. *...the need to channel North Sea oil revenues into industry.* 4 COUNT N A **channel** is also a passage along which water flows, or a route used by boats. *...irrigation channels... The main channels had been closed by enemy submarines.* 5 PROPER N The **Channel** or the **English Channel** is the narrow area of water between England and France.

chant /tʃɑːnt/, **chants, chanting, chanted.** 1 COUNT N A **chant** is a word or group of words that is repeated over and over again. *The assembly broke into a chant: 'What's your name? What's your name?'* 2 COUNT N A **chant** is also a religious song or prayer that is sung on only a few notes. 3 VB WITH OR WITHOUT OBJ When you **chant,** you repeat the same words over and over again, or you sing a religious song or prayer. *They marched to their coach chanting slogans.*

chaos /keɪɒs/. UNCOUNT N **Chaos** is a state of complete disorder and confusion. *...economic chaos.*

chaotic /keɪɒtɪk/. ADJ If a situation is **chaotic,** it is disordered and confused. *...a chaotic jumble of motor vehicles.*

chap /tʃæp/, **chaps.** COUNT N You can use **chap** to refer to a man or boy; an informal use.

chapel /tʃæpəl/, **chapels.** 1 COUNT N A **chapel** is a part of a church which has its own altar and which is used for private prayer 2 COUNT N A **chapel** is also a small church in a school, hospital, or prison. 3 COUNT N A **chapel** is also a building used for worship by members of some Protestant churches. *...a Methodist chapel.*

chaperone /ʃæpərəʊn/, **chaperones.** also spelled **chaperon.** COUNT N In former times, **chaperones** were women who used to accompany young unmarried women on social occasions.

chaplain /tʃæplɪn/, **chaplains.** COUNT N A **chaplain** is a member of the Christian clergy who does religious work in a hospital, school, or prison.

chapped /tʃæpt/. ADJ If your skin is **chapped,** it is dry, cracked, and sore.

chapter /tʃæptə/, **chapters.** 1 COUNT N OR N WITH NUMBER A **chapter** is one of the parts that a book is divided into. *...the subjects of the next two chapters... I'd nearly finished chapter 8.* 2 COUNT N WITH SUPP You can refer to a part of your life or a period in history as a **chapter;** a literary use. *A new chapter of my career as a journalist was about to commence.*

character /kærəktə/, **characters.** 1 COUNT N WITH SUPP The **character** of a person or place consists of all the qualities they have that make them distinct. *There was another side to his character... ...the character of New York.* 2 PHRASE If someone behaves **in character,** they behave in the way you expect them to. If they behave **out of character,** they do not behave as you expect. *It's quite in character for Carey to use a word like that.* 3 UNCOUNT N WITH SUPP You use **character** when you are mentioning a particular quality that something has. *...the radical character of our demands... ...purely negative in character.* 4 COUNT N The **characters** in a film, book, or play are the people in it. 5 COUNT N You can refer to a person as a **character,** especially when describing their qualities; an informal use. *He's a strange character, Evans.* 6 COUNT N A **character** is also a letter, number, or symbol that is written or printed; a technical use.

characteristic /kærəktərɪstɪk/, **characteristics.** 1 COUNT N A **characteristic** is a quality or feature that is typical of someone or something. *Ambition is a characteristic of all successful businessmen.* 2 ADJ If something is **characteristic** of a person, thing, or place, it is typical of them. *...those large brick tiles so characteristic of East Anglia.* ♦ **characteristically** ADV *He proposed a characteristically brilliant solution.*

characterize /kærəktəraɪz/, **characterizes, characterizing, characterized;** also spelled **characterise.** VB WITH OBJ To **characterize** someone or something means to be typical of them. *...the incessant demand for change that characterizes our time... The relationship between them was characterized by tension and rivalry from the first.*

charade /ʃərɑːd/, **charades.** COUNT N A **charade** is a pretence which is so obvious that nobody is deceived.

charcoal /tʃɑːkəʊl/. UNCOUNT N **Charcoal** is a black substance obtained by burning wood without much air. **Charcoal** is used as a fuel and also for drawing.

charge /tʃɑːdʒ/, **charges, charging, charged.** 1 VB WITH OBJ AND OBJ, OR VB WITH OBJ If you **charge** someone an amount of money, you ask them to pay that amount for something that you have provided or sold to them. *'How much do you charge?'—'£6 a night.'... You can be sure he's going to charge you something for the service.* 2 VB WITH OBJ AND PREP 'to' If you **charge** goods or services to a person or organization, you arrange for the bill to be sent to them. *Please charge the bill to my account.* 3 COUNT N The **charge** for something is the price that you have to pay for it. *...increases in postal and telephone charges... No charge is made for repairs.* 4 COUNT N A **charge** is a formal accusation that someone has committed a crime. *...a charge of conspiracy to murder... ...a murder charge.* 5 VB WITH OBJ When the police **charge** someone, they formally accuse them of having committed a crime. *He was arrested and charged with a variety of offences.* 6 UNCOUNT N If you have **charge** of something or someone, you have responsibility for them. *She intended to take charge of the boy herself.* ● If you are **in charge** of something or someone, you have responsibility for them. *You had left me in charge.* 7 VB If you **charge** towards someone or something, you move quickly and aggressively towards them. 8 VB WITH OBJ When you **charge** a battery, you pass an electrical current through it to make it more powerful.

charged /tʃɑːdʒd/. ADJ **Charged** means filled with emotion and therefore very tense or excited. *...a highly charged silence... His voice was charged with suppressed merriment.*

chariot /tʃærɪət/, **chariots.** COUNT N In ancient times, **chariots** were fast-moving vehicles with two wheels that were pulled by horses.

charisma /kərɪzmə/. UNCOUNT N If someone has **charisma,** they can attract, influence, and inspire people by their personal qualities. ♦ **charismatic** /kærɪzmætɪk/ ADJ *...a charismatic politician.*

charitable /tʃærɪtəbəl/. 1 ADJ Someone who is **charitable** is kind and tolerant. *She was being unusually charitable to me... ...a charitable remark.* 2 ATTRIB ADJ A **charitable** organization or activity helps and supports people who are ill, handicapped, or poor.

charity /tʃærɪti/, **charities.** 1 COUNT N A **charity** is an organization which raises money to help people who are ill, handicapped, or poor. *The proceeds will go to charities.* 2 UNCOUNT N **Charity** is also money or gifts given to poor people; a formal use. *He's too proud to accept charity.* 3 UNCOUNT N **Charity** is a kind and generous attitude towards other people; a formal use. *She found the charity in her heart to forgive them.*

charm /tʃɑːm/, **charms, charming, charmed.** 1 UNCOUNT N OR COUNT N **Charm** is the quality of being attractive and pleasant. *He bowed with infinite grace and charm... ...the charms of the exotic.* 2 VB WITH OBJ If you **charm** someone, you please them. *I was charmed by his courtesy.* 3 COUNT N A **charm** is a small ornament that is fixed to a bracelet or necklace. 4 COUNT N A **charm** is also an action, saying, or object that is believed to be lucky or to have magic powers.

charming /tʃɑːmɪŋ/. ADJ If someone or something is **charming,** they are very pleasant and attractive. *Celia is a charming girl.* ♦ **charmingly** ADV *...a charmingly medieval atmosphere.*

charred /tʃɑːd/. ADJ Something that is **charred** is partly burnt and made black by fire.

chart /tʃɑːt/, **charts, charting, charted.** 1 COUNT N A **chart** is a diagram or graph which makes information easy to understand. *...large charts illustrating world poverty.* 2 COUNT N A **chart** is also a map of the sea or stars. 3 PLURAL N The **charts** are the official lists that show which pop records have sold the most copies each week. 4 VB WITH OBJ If you **chart** something, you observe and record it carefully. *We charted their movements.*

charter /tʃɑːtə/, **charters, chartering, chartered.** 1 COUNT N A **charter** is a document describing the rights or principles of an organization. *...the Working Women's Charter... It contravened article 51 of the UN charter.* 2 ATTRIB ADJ A **charter** plane or boat is hired for use by a particular person or group. *He is travelling on a charter flight.* 3 VB WITH OBJ If you **charter** a vehicle, you hire it for your private use. *We plan to charter a special train for London.*

chartered /tʃɑːtəd/. ATTRIB ADJ **Chartered** is used to describe someone who has formally qualified in their profession. *...a chartered accountant.*

chase /tʃeɪs/, **chases, chasing, chased.** 1 VB WITH OR WITHOUT OBJ If you **chase** someone, you run after them or follow them in order to catch them or drive them away. *Youngsters chase one another up trees... A dozen soldiers chased after the car... They were chased from the village.* Also COUNT N *They abandoned the chase and returned home.* 2 VB WITH OBJ OR 'after' If you **chase** something such as work or money, you try hard to get it. *We are getting more and more applicants chasing fewer and fewer jobs.*

chasm /kæzəm/, **chasms.** 1 COUNT N A **chasm** is a very deep crack in rock or ice. 2 COUNT N If there is a **chasm** between two things or between two groups, there is a very large difference between them. *...the chasm between rich and poor.*

chaste /tʃeɪst/. ADJ A **chaste** person does not have sex with anyone, or only has sex with their husband or wife; an old-fashioned use which shows approval. *She was a holy woman, innocent and chaste.* ♦ **chastity** /tʃæstɪti/ UNCOUNT N *A monk makes vows of poverty, chastity and obedience.*

chasten /tʃeɪsən/, **chastens, chastening, chastened.** VB WITH OBJ If you **are chastened** by something, it makes you regret your behaviour; a formal use. *I left the cafe secretly chastened.*

chastise /tʃæstaɪz/, **chastises, chastising, chastised.** VB WITH OBJ If you **chastise** someone, you scold or punish them; a formal or old-fashioned use. *He chastised members at the Conference for not taking things seriously enough.*

chat /tʃæt/, **chats, chatting, chatted.** 1 VB When people **chat,** they talk in an informal and friendly way. *We sat by the fire and chatted all evening.* 2 COUNT N OR UNCOUNT N A **chat** is an informal, friendly talk. *We had a nice long chat about our schooldays... ...entertaining them with light chat.*

chat up. PHR VB If you **chat** someone **up,** you talk to them in a friendly way because you are attracted to them; an informal British use. *She was being chatted up by this bloke.*

château /ʃætəʊ/, **châteaux.** COUNT N A **château** is a large country house in France.

chatter /tʃætə/, **chatters, chattering, chattered.** 1 VB If you **chatter,** you talk quickly and continuously about unimportant things. *Off we set, with Bill chattering away all the time.* Also UNCOUNT N *At teatime there was much excited chatter.* 2 VB When birds and small animals **chatter,** they make a series of short, high-pitched noises. 3 VB If your teeth **chatter,** they rattle together because you are cold.

chatty /tʃæti¹/. ADJ Someone who is **chatty** talks a lot in a friendly way.

chauffeur /ʃəʊfə, ʃəʊfɜː/, **chauffeurs, chauffeuring, chauffeured.** 1 COUNT N A **chauffeur** is a person whose job is to drive and look after another person's car. 2 VB WITH OBJ If you **chauffeur** someone somewhere, you drive them there in a car, usually as part of your job.

chauvinism /ʃəʊvɪnɪzə⁰m/. UNCOUNT N **Chauvinism** is a strong and unreasonable belief that your own country is the best and most important. *...racism and national chauvinism.* ♦ **chauvinist** /ʃəʊvɪnɪst/ COUNT N OR MOD *...chauvinist pride.* ● See also **male chauvinism.**

cheap /tʃiːp/, **cheaper, cheapest.** 1 ADJ **Cheap** goods or services do not cost very much money. *...cheap plastic buckets... A solid fuel cooker is cheap to run.* ♦ **cheaply** ADV *He decorated my home cheaply and efficiently.* 2 ADJ **Cheap** behaviour and remarks are unkind and unnecessary. *He could not resist making cheap jokes at their expense.*

cheat /tʃiːt/, **cheats, cheating, cheated.** 1 VB When someone **cheats,** they lie or behave dishonestly in order to get or achieve something. *We all used to cheat in exams.* ♦ **cheating** UNCOUNT N *...accusations of cheating.* 2 VB WITH OBJ If someone **cheats** you out of something, they get it from you by behaving dishonestly. *She cheated her sister out of some money.* 3 COUNT N If you call someone a **cheat,** you mean that they behave dishonestly in order to get what they want.

check /tʃɛk/, **checks, checking, checked.** 1 VB WITH OR WITHOUT OBJ If you **check** something, you make sure that it is satisfactory, safe, or correct. *Did you check the engine?... Tony came in from time to time, to check on my progress... He needed a chance to check with Hooper to see if his theory was plausible... He checked that both rear doors were safely shut.* 2 COUNT N A **check** is an examination or inspection to make sure that everything is correct or safe. *Checks on cars and televisions are thorough... ...security checks.* 3 VB WITH OBJ To **check** something also means to stop it from continuing or spreading. *The destruction of the bridge checked the enemy's advance.* 4 REFL VB OR VB WITH OBJ If you **check** yourself or if something **checks** you, you suddenly stop what you are doing or saying. *He began to saunter off, then checked himself and turned back... Sudhir held up his hand to check him.* 5 PHRASE If you keep something **in check,** you keep it under control. *He had not conquered inflation but he had held it in check.* 6 COUNT N In a restaurant in America, your **check** is your bill. 7 UNCOUNT N OR COUNT N **Check** is a pattern consisting of squares. *...the simplest of stripes and checks.* Also ADJ *...a tall man in a check suit.* 8 See also **cheque.**

check in or **check into.** PHR VB 1 When you **check into** a hotel or **check in,** you fill in the necessary forms before staying there. *He checked into a small boarding house... I checked in at the Gordon Hotel.* 2 When you **check in** at an airport, you arrive and show your ticket before going on a flight. *He had already checked in for his return flight.* ● See also **check-in.**

check out. PHR VB 1 When you **check out** of the hotel where you have been staying, you pay the bill and leave. *Mr Leonard checked out this afternoon, Miss.* 2 If you **check** something **out,** you find out about it. *It might be difficult to transfer your money, so check it out with the manager.* 3 See also **checkout.**

check up. PHR VB If you **check up** on someone or something, you obtain information about them. ● See also **check-up.**

checkered /tʃɛkəd/. See **chequered.**

check-in, check-ins. COUNT N At an airport, a **check-in** is a place where you check in.

checkmate /tʃɛkmeɪt/. UNCOUNT N In chess, **checkmate** is a situation in which you cannot stop your king being captured and so you lose the game.

checkout /tʃɛkaʊt/, **checkouts.** COUNT N In a supermarket, a **checkout** is a counter where you pay for the things you have bought.

checkpoint /tʃɛkpɔɪnt/, **checkpoints.** COUNT N A **checkpoint** is a place where traffic has to stop and be checked.

check-up, check-ups. COUNT N A **check-up** is a routine examination by a doctor or dentist.

cheek /tʃiːk/, **cheeks.** 1 COUNT N Your **cheeks** are the sides of your face below your eyes. 2 UNCOUNT N You say that someone has **cheek** when you are annoyed about something unreasonable that they have done; an informal use. *You've got a cheek, coming in here.*

cheekbone /tʃiːkbəʊn/, **cheekbones.** COUNT N Your **cheekbones** are the two bones in your face just below your eyes.

cheeky /tʃiːki¹/. ADJ Someone who is **cheeky** is rude or disrespectful. *They're such cheeky boys.*

cheer /tʃɪə/, **cheers, cheering, cheered.** 1 VB WITH OR WITHOUT OBJ When you **cheer,** you make a loud noise with your voice to show approval or encouragement. *The home crowd cheered their team enthusiastically.* Also COUNT N *I heard a great cheer go up.* 2 VB WITH OBJ If you **are cheered** by something, it makes you happier or less worried. *We were cheered by her warmth and affection.* ♦ **cheering** ADJ *It was very cheering to have her here.* 3 CONVENTION People say **'Cheers'** just before they drink an alcoholic drink.

cheer on. PHR VB If you **cheer** someone **on,** you cheer loudly in order to encourage them.

cheer up. PHR VB When you **cheer up,** you stop feeling depressed and become more cheerful. *She cheered up a little... Her friends tried to cheer her up.*

cheerful /tʃɪəfʊl/. 1 ADJ Someone who is **cheerful** is happy and joyful. *She remained cheerful throughout the trip.* ♦ **cheerfully** ADV *He smiled cheerfully at everybody.* ♦ **cheerfulness** UNCOUNT N *They worked with great energy and cheerfulness.* 2 ADJ **Cheerful** things are pleasant and make you feel happy. *...literature of a more cheerful nature.*

cheerio /tʃɪəri¹əʊ/. CONVENTION **Cheerio** is an informal way of saying 'goodbye'.

cheerless /tʃɪəlɪ²s/. ADJ Something that is **cheerless** is gloomy and depressing. *It was a cold, cheerless morning.*

cheery /tʃɪəri¹/. ADJ **Cheery** means cheerful and happy; an old-fashioned use. *I wrote cheery letters home.* ♦ **cheerily** ADV *'Hello!' I shouted cheerily.*

cheese /tʃiːz/, **cheeses.** MASS N **Cheese** is a solid food made from milk.

cheetah /tʃiːtə/, **cheetahs.** COUNT N A **cheetah** is a wild animal like a large cat with black spots. Cheetahs can run very fast.

chef /ʃɛf/, **chefs.** COUNT N A **chef** is a cook in a restaurant or hotel.

chemical /kɛmɪkə⁰l/, **chemicals.** 1 ATTRIB ADJ **Chemical** means concerned with chemistry or made by a process in chemistry. *...the chemical composition of the atmosphere... ...chemical fertilizers.* ♦ **chemically** ADV *Chemically, this substance is similar to cellulose.* 2 COUNT N A **chemical** is a substance that is used in or made by a chemical process.

chemist /kɛmɪst/, **chemists.** 1 COUNT N In Britain, a **chemist** or a **chemist's** is a shop where you can buy medicine, cosmetics, and some household goods. 2 COUNT N In Britain, a **chemist** is also a person who is qualified to sell medicines prescribed by a doctor. 3 COUNT N A **chemist** is also a scientist who does research in chemistry.

chemistry /kɛmɪstri¹/. UNCOUNT N **Chemistry** is the scientific study of the characteristics and composition of substances.

cheque /tʃɛk/, **cheques;** spelled **check** in American English. COUNT N A **cheque** is a printed form on which you write an amount of money and say who it is to be paid to. Your bank then pays the money to that person from your account.

chequebook /tʃɛkbʊk/, **chequebooks;** spelled **checkbook** in American English. COUNT N A **chequebook** is a book of cheques.

chequered /tʃɛkəd/; spelled **checkered** in American English. ATTRIB ADJ If a person or organization has had a **chequered** career or history, they have had a varied past with both good and bad parts. *The Journal was a paper with a chequered history.*

cherish /tʃɛrɪʃ/, **cherishes, cherishing, cherished.** 1 VB WITH OBJ If you **cherish** a hope or a memory, you keep it in your mind so that it gives you happy feelings. *I cherish a hope that one day we will be reunited.* ♦ **cherished** ADJ *...cherished memories.* 2 VB WITH OBJ If you **cherish** someone, you care for them in a loving way. *Comfort and cherish those you love.* 3 VB WITH OBJ If you **cherish** a right or a privilege, you regard it as important and try hard to keep it. *Can he preserve the values he cherishes?* ♦ **cherished** ADJ *One of our cherished privileges is the right of free speech.*

cherry /tʃɛri¹/, **cherries.** 1 COUNT N **Cherries** are small, round fruit with red or black skins. 2 COUNT N A **cherry** or a **cherry tree** is a tree that cherries grow on.

chess /tʃɛs/. UNCOUNT N **Chess** is a game for two people, played on a chessboard. Each player has 16 pieces, including a king. You try to move your pieces so that your opponent cannot prevent his or her king from being taken.

chessboard /tʃɛsbɔːd/, **chessboards.** COUNT N A **chessboard** is a square board on which you play chess.

chest /tʃɛst/, **chests.** 1 COUNT N Your **chest** is the top part of the front of your body. *He folded his arms on his chest... She has severe pains in her chest.* 2 ● If you **get** something **off** your **chest,** you say what you have been worrying about; an informal use. 3 COUNT N A **chest** is a large, heavy box. 4 COUNT N A **chest** is also a chest of drawers.

chestnut /tʃɛsnʌt/, **chestnuts.** 1 COUNT N **Chestnuts** are reddish-brown nuts. The tree they grow on is also called a **chestnut.** 2 ADJ Something that is **chestnut** or **chestnut-brown** is reddish-brown.

chest of drawers, chests of drawers. COUNT N A **chest of drawers** is a piece of furniture with drawers.

chew /tʃuː/, **chews, chewing, chewed.** VB WITH OR WITHOUT OBJ When you **chew** food, you break it up with your teeth and make it easier to swallow. ● If you say that someone **has bitten off more than** they **can chew,** you mean that they are trying to do something which is too difficult for them.

chew over. PHR VB If you **chew over** a problem, you think carefully about it; an informal use.

chewing gum. UNCOUNT N **Chewing gum** is a kind of sweet which you chew for a long time but do not swallow.

chic /ʃiːk, ʃɪk/. ADJ **Chic** people and things are fashionable and sophisticated.

chick /tʃɪk/, **chicks.** COUNT N A **chick** is a baby bird.

chicken /tʃɪkɪn/, **chickens, chickening, chickened.** 1 COUNT N A **chicken** is a type of bird which is kept for its eggs and its meat. 2 UNCOUNT N **Chicken** is the meat of a chicken.

chicken out. PHR VB If you **chicken out** of something, you decide not to do it because you are afraid; an informal use.

chickenpox /tʃɪkɪnpɒks/. UNCOUNT N **Chickenpox** is a disease which gives you a high temperature and red spots.

chicory /tʃɪkəri¹/. UNCOUNT N **Chicory** is a vegetable with crunchy, sharp-tasting leaves.

chide /tʃaɪd/, **chides, chiding, chided.** VB WITH OBJ If you **chide** someone, you scold them; an old-fashioned use. *Maurice chided him for his carelessness.*

chief /tʃiːf/, **chiefs.** 1 COUNT N The **chief** of an organization is the person in charge of it. *...the current CIA chief... ...the chief of the Presidential Security Corps.* 2 COUNT N The **chief** of a tribe is its leader. *He was the last of the Apache chiefs.* 3 ATTRIB ADJ **Chief** is used to describe the most important worker of a particular kind in an organization. *...the chief cashier.* 4 ATTRIB ADJ The **chief** cause, part, or member of something is the main or most important one. *The 1902 Education Act was the chief cause of the Progressives' downfall... I was his chief opponent.*

chiefly /tʃiːfli¹/. 1 ADV OR SENTENCE ADV You use **chiefly** to indicate the most important cause or feature of something. *The experiment was not a success, chiefly because the machine tools were of poor quality... They were chiefly interested in making money.* 2 ADV If something is done **chiefly** in a particular way or place, it is done mainly in that way or place. *They lived chiefly by hunting.*

chieftain /tʃiːftə¹n/, **chieftains.** COUNT N A **chieftain** is the leader of a tribe.

chiffon /ʃɪfɒn, ʃɪfɒn/. UNCOUNT N **Chiffon** is a kind of very thin silk or nylon cloth that you can see through.

child /tʃaɪld/, **children** /tʃɪldrən/. 1 COUNT N A **child** is a human being who is not yet an adult. 2 PLURAL N Someone's **children** are their sons and daughters of any age. *Their children are all married.*

childbirth /tʃaɪldbɜːθ/. UNCOUNT N **Childbirth** is the act of giving birth to a child. *His mother died in childbirth.*

childhood /tʃaɪldhʊd/. UNCOUNT N A person's **childhood** is the time when they are a child.

childish /tʃaɪldɪʃ/. ADJ You describe someone as **childish** when they behave in a silly and immature way. *I thought her nice but rather childish.* ♦ **childishly** ADV *'It's too hot here,' he complained childishly.*

childless /tʃaɪldlɪ²s/. ADJ Someone who is **childless** has no children. *...childless couples.*

childlike /tʃaɪldlaɪk/. ADJ You describe someone as **childlike** when they seem like a child in their appearance or behaviour.

childminder /tʃaɪldmaɪndə/, **childminders.** COUNT N A **childminder** is someone who is paid to use their own home to look after other people's children.

children /tʃɪldrən/. **Children** is the plural of **child.**

chili /tʃɪli¹/. See **chilli.**

chill /tʃɪl/, **chills, chilling, chilled.** 1 VB WITH OBJ When you **chill** something, you lower its temperature without freezing it. *White wine should be slightly chilled.* 2 VB WITH OBJ When something **chills** you, it makes you feel very cold or frightened. *She was chilled by his callousness.* ♦ **chilling** ADJ *A chilling wind swept round them... The thought was chilling.* 3 COUNT N A **chill** is a mild illness which can give you a slight fever.

chilli /tʃɪli^1/, **chillies;** also spelled **chili.** COUNT N OR UNCOUNT N **Chillies** are small red or green seed pods with a hot, spicy taste.

chilly /tʃɪli^1/. 1 ADJ **Chilly** means rather cold and unpleasant. *A draught of chilly air entered the room.* 2 PRED ADJ If you feel **chilly,** you feel cold.

chime /tʃaɪm/, **chimes, chiming, chimed.** VB When church bells or clocks **chime,** they make ringing sounds to show the time. Also COUNT N *...the silvery chime of the old stable clock.*

chime in. PHR VB When someone **chimes in,** they say something just after someone else has spoken. *Bill chimed in with 'This is an emergency situation.'*

chimney /tʃɪmni^1/, **chimneys.** COUNT N A **chimney** is a pipe above a fireplace or furnace through which smoke can go up into the air.

chimney pot, chimney pots. COUNT N A **chimney pot** is a short pipe on top of a chimney stack.

chimney stack, chimney stacks. COUNT N A **chimney stack** is the brick or stone part of a chimney on the roof of a building; a British use.

chimney sweep, chimney sweeps. COUNT N A **chimney sweep** is a person whose job is to clean the soot out of chimneys.

chimpanzee /tʃɪmpə^{3}nziː/, **chimpanzees.** COUNT N A **chimpanzee** is a kind of small African ape.

chin /tʃɪn/, **chins.** COUNT N Your **chin** is the part of your face below your mouth and above your neck.

china /tʃaɪnə/. 1 UNCOUNT N **China** or **china clay** is a very thin clay from which cups, plates, and ornaments are made. 2 UNCOUNT N Cups, plates, and ornaments made of china are referred to as **china.** *She laid out a small tray with the best china.*

Chinese /tʃaɪniːz/. **Chinese** is the singular and plural. 1 ADJ **Chinese** means belonging or relating to China. 2 COUNT N A **Chinese** is a person who comes from China. 3 UNCOUNT N **Chinese** is one of the languages spoken by people who live in China.

chink /tʃɪŋk/, **chinks, chinking, chinked.** 1 COUNT N A **chink** is a very narrow opening. *Through a chink she could see a bit of blue sky.* 2 VB When objects **chink,** they touch each other, making a short, light, ringing sound. *Empty bottles chinked as the milkman put them into his crate.* Also SING N WITH 'of' *...the chink of money.*

chintz /tʃɪnts/. UNCOUNT N **Chintz** is a cotton fabric with bright patterns on it. *...chintz curtains.*

chip /tʃɪp/, **chips, chipping, chipped.** 1 COUNT N In Britain, **chips** are long, thin pieces of fried potato. 2 COUNT N In America, **chips** or **potato chips** are very thin slices of potato that have been fried until they are hard and crunchy. 3 COUNT N A **chip** or **silicon chip** is a very small piece of silicon with electric circuits on it which is part of a computer. 4 VB WITH OBJ When you **chip** something, you accidentally damage it by breaking a small piece off it. ♦ **chipped** ADJ *...a chipped mug.* 5 COUNT N **Chips** are also small pieces which have been broken off something. *...granite chips.* 6 PHRASE If someone has a **chip on** their **shoulder,** they behave rudely and aggressively because they feel they have been treated unfairly; an informal use.

chip in. PHR VB 1 When a number of people **chip in,** each person gives some money so that they can pay for something together; an informal use. *They all chipped in to pay the doctor's bill.* 2 When someone **chips in** during a conversation, they interrupt it; an informal use.

chiropodist /kɪrɒpədɪst/, **chiropodists.** COUNT N A **chiropodist** is a person whose job is to treat people's feet.

chirp /tʃɜːp/, **chirps, chirping, chirped.** VB When a bird or insect **chirps,** it makes short high-pitched sounds.

chisel /tʃɪzə^{0}l/, **chisels, chiselling, chiselled;** spelled **chiseling, chiseled** in American English. 1 COUNT N A **chisel** is a tool that has a long metal blade with a sharp edge at the end. It is used for cutting and shaping wood and stone. 2 VB WITH OBJ If you **chisel** wood or stone, you cut and shape it using a chisel. *The men chisel the blocks out of solid rock.*

chivalrous /ʃɪvəlrəs/. ADJ **Chivalrous** men are polite, kind, and unselfish, especially towards women. *They were treated with chivalrous consideration.*

chivalry /ʃɪvəlri^1/. UNCOUNT N **Chivalry** is chivalrous behaviour. *...small acts of chivalry.*

chlorine /klɔːriːn/. UNCOUNT N **Chlorine** is a strong-smelling gas that is used to disinfect water and to make cleaning products.

chlorophyll /klɒrəfɪl/. UNCOUNT N **Chlorophyll** is a green substance in plants which enables them to use the energy from sunlight in order to grow.

chocolate /tʃɒkə^{0}lə^{1}t/, **chocolates.** 1 UNCOUNT N **Chocolate** is a sweet hard brown food made from cocoa beans. *...a bar of chocolate... ...chocolate cake.* 2 COUNT N A **chocolate** is a sweet or nut covered with a layer of chocolate. *...a box of chocolates.* 3 MASS N **Chocolate** is also a hot drink made from a powder containing chocolate.

choice /tʃɔɪs/, **choices; choicer, choicest.** 1 COUNT N If there is a **choice,** there are several things from which you can choose. *There's a choice of eleven sports... ...the choice between peace and war.* 2 COUNT N Your **choice** is the thing or things that you choose. *He congratulated the chef on his choice of dishes.* 3 ATTRIB ADJ You use **choice** to describe things that are of high quality. *...choice cuts of meat.*

PHRASES ● The thing or person **of** your **choice** is the one that you choose. *She was prevented from marrying the man of her choice.* ● If you **have no choice** but to do something, you cannot avoid doing it. *The President had no choice but to agree.*

choir /kwaɪə/, **choirs.** COUNT N A **choir** is a group of people who sing together.

choirboy /kwaɪəbɔɪ/, **choirboys.** COUNT N A **choirboy** is a boy who sings in a church choir.

choke /tʃəʊk/, **chokes, choking, choked.** 1 ERG VB When you **choke,** you cannot breathe properly because something is blocking your windpipe. *Philip choked on his drink... The pungent smell of sulphur choked him.* ♦ **choking** ADJ *They were enveloped in a cloud of choking dust.* 2 VB WITH OBJ To **choke** someone means to squeeze their neck until they are dead. *An old woman was found choked to death.* 3 PASSIVE VB If a place **is choked** with things or people, it is full of them and nothing can move. *The centre of the city was choked with cars.* 4 COUNT N The **choke** in a car or other vehicle is a device that reduces the amount of air going into the engine and makes it easier to start.

choke back. PHR VB If you **choke back** an emotion, you force yourself not to show it.

cholera /kɒlərə/. UNCOUNT N **Cholera** is a serious disease that affects your digestive organs.

choose /tʃuːz/, **chooses, choosing, chose** /tʃəʊz/, **chosen** /tʃəʊzə^{0}n/. 1 VB WITH OBJ If you **choose** something from all the things that are available, you decide to have that thing. *I chose a yellow dress... I had been chosen to be trained as editor.* ♦ **chosen** ATTRIB ADJ *They undergo training in their chosen professions.* 2 VB If you **choose** to do something, you do it because you want to or because you feel that it is right. *They could fire employees whenever they chose.* 3 PHRASE If there is **little to choose** between things or **not much to choose** between them, it is difficult to decide which is better. *There's nothing to choose between the two countries.*

choosy /tʃuːzi^1/. ADJ A **choosy** person will only accept something if it is exactly right or of very high quality; an informal use. *I'm very choosy about my whisky.*

chop /tʃɒp/, **chops, chopping, chopped.** 1 VB WITH OBJ If you **chop** something, you cut it into pieces with an axe or a knife. *I don't like chopping wood... Peel, slice, and chop the apple.* 2 COUNT N A **chop** is a small piece of meat cut from the ribs of a sheep or pig. *...lamb chops.* 3 PHRASE When people **chop and change,** they keep changing their minds about what to do; an informal use.

chop down. PHR VB If you **chop down** a tree, you cut through its trunk with an axe so that it falls to the ground.

chop up. PHR VB If you **chop** something **up,** you chop it into small pieces. *Chop up some tomatoes and add them to the onion.*

chopper /tʃɒpə/, **choppers;** an informal word. 1 COUNT N A **chopper** is a helicopter. 2 COUNT N A **chopper** is also an axe.

choppy /tʃɒpi^1/. ADJ When water is **choppy,** there are a lot of small waves on it. *The sea suddenly turned from smooth to choppy.*

chopstick /tʃɒpstɪk/, **chopsticks.** COUNT N **Chopsticks** are a pair of thin sticks used by people in the Far East for eating food.

choral /kɔːrəl/. ATTRIB ADJ **Choral** music is sung by a choir.

chord /kɔːd/, **chords.** COUNT N A **chord** is a number of musical notes played or sung together with a pleasing effect.

chore /tʃɔː/, **chores.** COUNT N A **chore** is an unpleasant task. *Does your husband do his fair share of the household chores?*

choreographer /kɒrɪɒgrəfə/, **choreographers.** COUNT N A **choreographer** is someone who invents the movements for a ballet and tells the dancers how to perform them.

choreography /kɒrɪɒgrəfi^1/. UNCOUNT N **Choreography** is the inventing of movements for ballets.

chorus /kɔːrəs/, **choruses, chorusing, chorused.** 1 COUNT N A **chorus** is a large group of people who sing together. 2 COUNT N The **chorus** of a song is the part which is repeated after each verse. 3 SING N WITH SUPP When there is a **chorus** of disapproval or satisfaction, these attitudes are expressed by many people. *In recent weeks the chorus of complaint has been growing.* 4 REPORT VB When people **chorus** something, they say or sing it together. *'Shall I tell you a story?'—'Please!' the children would chorus.*

chose /tʃəʊz/. **Chose** is the past tense of **choose.**

chosen /tʃəʊzə^{0}n/. **Chosen** is the past participle of **choose.**

christen /krɪsə^{0}n/, **christens, christening, christened.** 1 VB WITH OBJ, WITH OR WITHOUT COMPLEMENT When a baby **is christened,** he or she is given Christian names during a christening. *She was christened Victoria Mary... Charles II was christened in this church.* 2 VB WITH OBJ AND COMPLEMENT To **christen** a place or an object means to choose a name for it and to start calling it by that name; an informal use. *The crew christened the hot geysers the 'black smokers'.*

christening /krɪsə^{0}nɪŋ/, **christenings.** COUNT N A **christening** is a ceremony in which a baby is made a member of the Christian church and is officially given his or her Christian names.

Christian /krɪstʃən/, **Christians.** COUNT N A **Christian** is a person who believes in Jesus Christ and follows his teachings. Also ADJ *...Christian virtues.*

Christianity /krɪstɪænɪ^{1}ti^1/. UNCOUNT N **Christianity** is a religion based on the teachings of Jesus Christ and on the belief that he was the son of God.

Christian name, Christian names. COUNT N A person's **Christian names** are the names given to them when they are born or when they are christened. *Do all your students call you by your Christian name?*

Christmas /krɪsməs/, **Christmases.** UNCOUNT N OR COUNT N **Christmas** is the Christian festival when the birth of Jesus Christ is celebrated on the 25th of December. *Merry Christmas and a Happy New Year!... ...Christmases in her childhood.*

Christmas Day. UNCOUNT N **Christmas Day** is December 25th, when Christmas is celebrated.

Christmas Eve. UNCOUNT N **Christmas Eve** is December 24th, the day before Christmas Day.

Christmas tree, Christmas trees. COUNT N A **Christmas tree** is a fir tree, or an artificial tree that looks like a fir tree, which people put in their houses at Christmas and decorate with lights and balls.

chrome /krəʊm/. UNCOUNT N **Chrome** is a hard silver-coloured metal.

chromium /krəʊmɪəm/. UNCOUNT N **Chromium** is the same as chrome.

chromosome /krəʊməsəʊm/, **chromosomes.** COUNT N A **chromosome** is a part of a cell in an animal or plant. It contains genes which determine what characteristics the animal or plant will have.

chronic /krɒnɪk/. 1 ADJ A **chronic** illness lasts for a very long time. *Her father was dying of chronic asthma.* ♦ **chronically** SUBMOD *...pensions for the chronically sick.* 2 ATTRIB ADJ You describe someone's bad habits or behaviour as **chronic** when they have behaved like that for a long time and do not seem able to stop themselves. *...chronic drunkenness.* 3 ADJ A **chronic** situation is very severe and unpleasant. *...chronic food shortages.* ♦ **chronically** SUBMOD *...an education service that is chronically short of finance.*

chronicle /krɒnɪkə^{0}l/, **chronicles, chronicling, chronicled;** a formal word. 1 VB WITH OBJ If you **chronicle** a series of events, you write about them in the order in which they happened. *Xenophon chronicled the Persian Wars.* 2 COUNT N A **chronicle** is a formal account or record of a series of events.

chronological /krɒnəlɒdʒɪkə^{0}l/. ADJ If you describe a series of events in **chronological** order, you describe them in the order in which they happened. ♦ **chronologically** ADV *They proceeded to examine developments chronologically.*

chrysalis /krɪsəlɪs/, **chrysalises.** COUNT N A **chrysalis** is a butterfly or moth in the stage between being a larva and an adult.

chrysanthemum /krɪsænθəməm/, **chrysanthemums.** COUNT N A **chrysanthemum** is a large garden flower with many long, thin petals.

chubby /tʃʌbi^1/. ADJ A **chubby** child is rather fat.

chuck /tʃʌk/, **chucks, chucking, chucked;** an informal word. VB WITH OBJ AND ADJUNCT When you **chuck** something somewhere, you throw it there in a casual or careless way. *Chuck my tights across, please.*

chuck away or **chuck out.** PHR VB If you **chuck** something **away** or **chuck it out,** you throw it away.

chuckle /tʃʌkə^{0}l/, **chuckles, chuckling, chuckled.** VB When people **chuckle,** they laugh quietly. *They were chuckling over the photographs.* Also COUNT N *He shook his head with a soft chuckle.*

chug /tʃʌg/, **chugs, chugging, chugged.** VB When a vehicle **chugs** somewhere, its engine makes short thudding sounds. *A small fishing boat comes chugging towards them.*

chum /tʃʌm/, **chums;** an old-fashioned informal use. 1 COUNT N Your **chum** is your friend. *In Dublin he met an old school chum.* 2 VOCATIVE Men sometimes address each other as **chum,** usually in a slightly aggressive or unfriendly way.

chunk /tʃʌŋk/, **chunks. 1** COUNT N A **chunk** of something is a piece of it. *...a great chunk of meat.* **2** COUNT N A **chunk** is also a large amount or part of something; an informal use. *Research and development now take up a sizeable chunk of the military budget.*

chunky /tʃʌŋki[1]/. ADJ A **chunky** person or thing is large and heavy. *A chunky waitress came waddling towards him... ...great chunky cardigans.*

church /tʃɜ:tʃ/, **churches. 1** COUNT N OR UNCOUNT N A **church** is a building in which Christians worship. *There were no services that day, and the church was empty... His parents go to church now and then.* **2** COUNT N A **Church** is one of the groups of people within the Christian religion, for example Catholics. *Jane had been received into the Church a month previously.*

churchman /tʃɜ:tʃmə[3]n/, **churchmen.** COUNT N A **churchman** is the same as a clergyman; a formal use.

churchyard /tʃɜ:tʃjɑ:d/, **churchyards.** COUNT N A **churchyard** is an area of land around a church where dead people are buried.

churlish /tʃɜ:lɪʃ/. ADJ **Churlish** behaviour is unfriendly, bad-tempered, or impolite.

churn /tʃɜ:n/, **churns, churning, churned. 1** COUNT N A **churn** is a container used for making butter. **2** VB WITH OBJ To **churn** milk or cream means to stir it vigorously in order to make butter. **3** VB WITH OBJ If something **churns** mud or water or **churns** it up, it moves it about violently. *The bulldozers were churning the mud... The wind churned up the water into a swirling foam.*

churn out. PHR VB To **churn** things **out** means to produce large numbers of them very quickly; an informal use. *His organization began churning out tracts and posters.*

chute /ʃu:t/, **chutes.** COUNT N A **chute** is a steep, narrow slope down which people or things can slide.

chutney /tʃʌtni[1]/. UNCOUNT N **Chutney** is a strong-tasting mixture of fruit, vinegar, sugar, and spices.

cider /saɪdə/. UNCOUNT N **Cider** is an alcoholic drink made from apples.

cigar /sɪgɑ:/, **cigars.** COUNT N **Cigars** are rolls of dried tobacco leaves which people smoke.

cigarette /sɪgə[0]rɛt/, **cigarettes.** COUNT N **Cigarettes** are small tubes of paper containing tobacco which people smoke.

cinder /sɪndə/, **cinders.** COUNT N **Cinders** are the pieces of material that are left after wood or coal has burned. ● If something has been burned **to a cinder,** it has been burned until it is black.

cinema /sɪnə[1]mə/, **cinemas. 1** COUNT N A **cinema** is a place where people go to watch films. **2** UNCOUNT N **Cinema** is the business and art of making films that are shown in cinemas. *...one of the classic works of Hollywood cinema.*

cinnamon /sɪnəmən/. UNCOUNT N **Cinnamon** is a spice used for flavouring sweet food and in curries.

cipher /saɪfə/, **ciphers;** also spelled **cypher.** COUNT N OR UNCOUNT N A **cipher** is a secret system of writing. *The necessary codes and ciphers will be included in your orders... They had been corresponding with one another in cipher.*

circa /sɜ:kə/. PREP If you write **circa** in front of a year, you mean that the date is approximate. *...an old British newspaper, circa 1785.*

circle /sɜ:kə[0]l/, **circles, circling, circled. 1** COUNT N A **circle** is a round shape. Every part of its edge is the same distance from the centre. *The students sit in a circle on the floor... Stand the paint tin on a circle of aluminium foil.* **2** VB If a bird or aircraft **circles,** it moves round in a circle. *Hawks circled overhead looking for prey.* **3** COUNT N WITH SUPP You can refer to a group of people as a **circle.** *I have widened my circle of acquaintances... This proposal caused an uproar in parliamentary circles.* **4** SING N The **circle** in a theatre or cinema is an area of seats on the upper floor.

circuit /sɜ:kɪt/, **circuits. 1** COUNT N An electrical **circuit** is a complete route which an electric current can flow around. **2** COUNT N WITH SUPP A **circuit** is also a series of places that are visited regularly by a person or group. *...the American college lecture circuit.* **3** COUNT N A racing **circuit** is a track on which cars or motorbikes race.

circuitous /sə[5]kju:ɪtəs/. ADJ A **circuitous** route is long and complicated; a formal use. *...a long and circuitous journey by train and boat.*

circular /sɜ:kjə[4]lə/, **circulars. 1** ADJ Something that is **circular** is shaped like a circle. *...a circular pond.* **2** ADJ If you make a **circular** journey, you go somewhere and then return by a different route. **3** ADJ A **circular** argument or theory is not valid because it uses a statement to prove the conclusion and the conclusion to prove the statement. **4** COUNT N A **circular** is a letter or advertisement which is sent to a large number of people at the same time.

circulate /sɜ:kjə[4]leɪt/, **circulates, circulating, circulated. 1** ERG VB When a piece of writing **circulates** or **is circulated,** copies of it are passed round among a group of people. *The report was circulated to all the members... A union newspaper was circulating at the congress.* ♦ **circulation** /sɜ:kjə[4]leɪʃə[0]n/ UNCOUNT N *...the circulation of illegal books.* **2** ERG VB When a joke or a rumour **circulates,** people tell it to each other. *Stories about him circulated at his club... A wicked rumour had been circulated that she was a secret drinker.* **3** VB When a substance **circulates,** it moves easily and freely within a closed place or system. *We are governed by the hormones that circulate around our bodies.* ♦ **circulation** UNCOUNT N *...the circulation of air.* **4** VB If you **circulate** at a party, you move among the guests and talk to different people.

circulation /sɜ:kjə[4]leɪʃə[0]n/, **circulations. 1** COUNT N WITH SUPP The **circulation** of a newspaper or magazine is the number of copies sold each time it is produced. *The local paper had a circulation of only six thousand.* **2** SING N Your **circulation** is the movement of blood around your body. *He stamped his feet from time to time to keep the circulation going.* **3** UNCOUNT N Money that is in **circulation** is being used by the public.

circumcise /sɜ:kəmsaɪz/, **circumcises, circumcising, circumcised.** VB WITH OBJ If a man or boy **has been circumcised,** the loose skin has been cut off the end of his penis for religious or medical reasons. ♦ **circumcision** /sɜ:kəmsɪʒə[0]n/ UNCOUNT N

circumference /səkʌmfə[0]rəns/, **circumferences.** COUNT N WITH SUPP The **circumference** of a circle, place, or round object is the distance around its edge. *The area has a circumference of 54 miles.*

circumscribe /sɜ:kəmskraɪb/, **circumscribes, circumscribing, circumscribed.** VB WITH OBJ If someone's power or freedom **is circumscribed,** it is limited; a formal use.

circumspect /sɜ:kəmspɛkt/. ADJ If you are **circumspect,** you avoid taking risks; a formal use. *Physicians are now more circumspect about making recommendations for surgery.*

circumstance /sɜ:kəmstə[3]ns/, **circumstances. 1** PLURAL N WITH SUPP **Circumstances** are the conditions which affect what happens in a particular situation. *In normal circumstances I would have resigned immediately... She died without ever learning the circumstances of her grandfather's death.* ● You can emphasize that something will not happen by saying that it will not happen **under any circumstances.** *Under no circumstances whatsoever will I support Mr Baldwin.* **2** PLURAL N WITH POSS Your **circumstances** are the conditions of your life, especially the amount of money that you have. *...the change in George's circumstances.*

circumstantial /sɜ:kəmstænʃə[0]l/. ADJ **Circumstantial** evidence makes it seem likely that something happened, but does not prove it. *The circumstantial evidence is overwhelming.*

circus /sɜ:kəs/, **circuses.** COUNT N A **circus** is a travelling show performed in a large tent, with clowns, acrobats, and trained animals.

cistern /sɪstən/, **cisterns.** COUNT N A **cistern** is a container which holds water, for example to flush a toilet or to store the water supply of a building.

citadel /sɪtədə[2]l/, **citadels.** COUNT N A **citadel** is a strongly fortified building in a city.

citation /saɪteɪʃə[0]n/, **citations;** a formal word. **1** COUNT N A **citation** is an official document or speech which praises a person for something brave or special that they have done. *The policemen subsequently received citations for their action.* **2** COUNT N A **citation** from a book or piece of writing is a quotation from it.

cite /saɪt/, **cites, citing, cited;** a formal word. **1** VB WITH OBJ If you **cite** something, you quote it or mention it, especially as an example or proof of what you are saying. *Low wages were cited as the main cause for dissatisfaction... The most commonly cited example of a primitive device is the abacus.* **2** VB WITH OBJ To **cite** someone or something in a legal action means to officially name them.

citizen /sɪtɪzən/, **citizens. 1** COUNT N WITH SUPP If someone is a **citizen** of a country, they are legally accepted as belonging to that country. *...a Swedish citizen.* **2** COUNT N WITH SUPP The **citizens** of a town are the people who live there. *...the citizens of Bristol.* **3** See also **senior citizen.**

citizenship /sɪtɪzənʃɪp/. UNCOUNT N WITH SUPP If you have **citizenship** of a country, you are legally accepted as belonging to it.

citrus fruit /sɪtrəs fru:t/, **citrus fruits.** COUNT N OR UNCOUNT N A **citrus fruit** is a juicy, sharp-tasting fruit such as an orange, lemon, or grapefruit.

city /sɪti[1]/, **cities. 1** COUNT N A **city** is a large town. *...the city of Birmingham... ...a modern city centre.* **2** PROPER N The **City** is the part of London where many financial institutions have their main offices.

civic /sɪvɪk/. ATTRIB ADJ **Civic** means having an official status in a town, or relating to the town you live in. *...the civic centre... ...civic pride.*

civil /sɪvə[0]l/. **1** ATTRIB ADJ You use **civil** to describe things that relate to the people of a country, and their rights and activities, often in contrast with the armed forces. *...wars or civil disturbances... ...a supersonic civil airliner... ...the defence of civil liberties and human rights.* **2** ADJ A **civil** person is polite. *He'd been careful to be civil to everyone.* ♦ **civilly** ADV *He was somewhat upset but he answered civilly enough.*

civilian /sɪvɪljən/, **civilians.** COUNT N A **civilian** is anyone who is not a member of the armed forces. *They tried to avoid bombing civilians.*

civilise /sɪvɪ[1]laɪz/. See **civilize.**

civility /sɪvɪlɪ[1]ti[1]/. UNCOUNT N **Civility** is behaviour which is polite but not very friendly. *She was treated with civility and consideration.*

civilization /sɪvɪ[1]laɪzeɪʃə[0]n/, **civilizations;** also spelled **civilisation. 1** COUNT N OR UNCOUNT N A **civilization** is a human society with its own social organization and culture which makes it distinct from other societies. *...the earliest great civilizations: Egypt, Sumer, Assyria... ...the entire history of Western civilisation.* **2** UNCOUNT N **Civilization** is the state of having an advanced level of social organization and a comfortable way of life. *The Romans brought civilization to much of Europe.*

civilize /sɪvɪ[1]laɪz/, **civilizes, civilizing, civilized;** also spelled **civilise.** VB WITH OBJ To **civilize** a person or society means to educate them and improve their way of life. *...their mission of civilizing and modernizing that society.*

civilized /sɪvɪ[1]laɪzd/; also spelled **civilised. 1** ADJ A **civilized** society has an advanced level of social organization. *They aim to create an orderly, just and civilised society.* **2** ADJ A **civilized** person or behaviour is polite and reasonable. *...a civilized discussion.*

civil servant, civil servants. COUNT N A **civil servant** is a person who works in the Civil Service.

Civil Service. COLL N The **Civil Service** of a country consists of the government departments and the people who work in them.

civil war, civil wars. COUNT N OR UNCOUNT N A **civil war** is a war which is fought between different groups of people living in the same country. *...the Spanish Civil War... There might be civil war again.*

clad /klæd/. ADJ If you are **clad** in particular clothes, you are wearing them; a literary use. *...beggars clad in dirty white rags.*

claim /kleɪm/, **claims, claiming, claimed. 1** REPORT VB OR VB WITH TO-INF You use **claim** to report what someone says when you are not sure whether what they are saying is true. *He claimed that he found the money in the forest... They claimed to have shot down twenty-two planes.* **2** COUNT N A **claim** is something which a person says but which cannot be proved and which may be false. *Forecasts do not support the government's claim that the economy is picking up.* **3** VB WITH OBJ If someone **claims** responsibility or credit for something, they say that they are responsible for it. *The rebels claimed responsibility for the bombing.* **4** VB WITH OBJ OR ADJUNCT If you **claim** something such as money or property, you ask for it because you have a right to it. *Voluntary workers can claim travelling expenses... Don't forget to claim for a first-class rail ticket to London.* **5** COUNT N A **claim** is also a demand for something that you think you have a right to. *...a pay claim... ...a claim for compensation.* **6** VB WITH OBJ If a fight or disaster **claims** someone's life, they are killed in it; a formal use. *The wave of bombings and street clashes is claiming new lives every day.* **7** COUNT N WITH 'on' OR 'upon' If you have a **claim** on someone, you have a right to demand things from them. *She realized that she had no claims on the man.* **8** PHRASE If you **lay claim to** something, you say that it is yours; a formal use. ● **to stake a claim:** see **stake.**

claimant /kleɪmənt/, **claimants.** COUNT N A **claimant** is someone who asks to be given something which they think they are entitled to.

clam /klæm/, **clams.** COUNT N A **clam** is a kind of shellfish.

clamber /klæmbə/, **clambers, clambering, clambered.** VB WITH ADJUNCT If you **clamber** somewhere, you climb there with difficulty. *We clambered up the hill.*

clammy /klæmi[1]/. ADJ Something that is **clammy** is unpleasantly damp and sticky. *His handshake is cold and clammy.*

clamour /klæmə/, **clamours, clamouring, clamoured;** spelled **clamor** in American English. **1** VB WITH 'for' If people **clamour** for something, they demand it noisily or angrily; a formal use. *...changes in the law for which people are clamouring.* Also UNCOUNT N WITH SUPP *The public clamour could not be silenced.*

2 UNCOUNT N WITH SUPP If people are talking or shouting together loudly, you can refer to the noise as a **clamour;** a literary use. *...the clamour of voices.*

clamp /klæmp/, **clamps, clamping, clamped.** 1 COUNT N A **clamp** is a device that holds two things firmly together. 2 VB WITH OBJ When you **clamp** one thing to another, you fasten them together with a clamp. *...trays that were clamped to the arm of a chair.* 3 VB WITH OBJ AND ADJUNCT To **clamp** something in a particular place means to put it there firmly and tightly. *He picked up his bowler hat and clamped it upon his head.*

clamp down. PHR VB To **clamp down** on something means to stop it or control it. *The authorities have got to clamp down on these trouble-makers.*

clan /klæn/, **clans.** COLL N A **clan** is a group of families related to each other. *...the Issas, a Somali clan.*

clandestine /klændɛstɪ^{5}n/. ADJ Something that is **clandestine** is hidden or secret, and often illegal; a formal use. *...a clandestine radio station.*

clang /klæŋ/, **clangs, clanging, clanged.** ERG VB When large metal objects **clang,** they make a loud, deep noise. *...the sound of the bells clanging... She clanged the gates behind her.* Also SING N *The door opened with a heavy clang.*

clank /klæŋk/, **clanks, clanking, clanked.** VB When metal objects **clank,** they make a loud noise because they are banging together or against something hard. *All about him he heard chains clanking.*

clap /klæp/, **claps, clapping, clapped.** 1 VB WITH OR WITHOUT OBJ When you **clap,** you hit your hands together to express appreciation or attract attention. *The audience clapped enthusiastically and called for more... The vicar clapped his hands for silence.* Also SING N *He called them to order with a clap of his hands.* 2 VB WITH OBJ AND ADJUNCT If you **clap** an object or your hand onto something, you put it there quickly and firmly. *He claps his hands to his head... ...clapping his cap firmly on his head.* 3 VB WITH OBJ AND ADJUNCT If you **clap** someone on the back or shoulder, you hit them with your hand in a friendly way. *He clapped her on the back and laughed.* 4 COUNT N WITH 'of' A **clap** of thunder is a sudden loud noise of thunder.

claret /klærət/, **clarets.** MASS N **Claret** is a type of red French wine.

clarify /klærɪfaɪ/, **clarifies, clarifying, clarified.** VB WITH OBJ To **clarify** something means to make it easier to understand. *Ask the speaker to clarify the point.* ♦ **clarification** /klærɪfɪkeɪʃə^{6}n/ UNCOUNT N *We must wait for clarification of the situation.*

clarinet /klærɪnɛt/, **clarinets.** COUNT N A **clarinet** is a woodwind instrument with a single reed in its mouthpiece.

clarity /klærɪ^{1}ti^1/. 1 UNCOUNT N WITH SUPP **Clarity** is the quality of being well explained and easy to understand. *...the clarity of her explanation.* 2 UNCOUNT N **Clarity** is also the ability to think clearly. *She was forcing me to think with more clarity about what I had seen.*

clash /klæʃ/, **clashes, clashing, clashed.** 1 RECIP VB When people **clash,** they fight, argue, or disagree with each other. *Youths clashed with police in the streets around the ground... The delegates clashed from the first day of the congress.* Also COUNT N *...the first public clash between the two party leaders.* 2 RECIP VB Beliefs, ideas, or qualities that **clash** are very different from each other and are therefore opposed. *This belief clashes with all that we know about human psychology.* Also COUNT N *...a personality clash.* 3 RECIP VB If two events **clash,** they happen at the same time so you cannot go to both of them. *A religious convention had clashed with a flower show.* 4 RECIP VB When colours or styles **clash,** they look ugly together. *...a pink jacket which clashed violently with the colour of her hair.* 5 VB When metal objects **clash,** they make a lot of noise by being hit together. Also SING N *...a clash of cymbals.*

clasp /klɑːsp/, **clasps, clasping, clasped.** 1 VB WITH OBJ If you **clasp** someone or something, you hold them tightly. *The woman was clasping the sleeping baby in her arms.* 2 COUNT N A **clasp** is a small metal fastening.

class /klɑːs/, **classes, classing, classed.** 1 COUNT N A **class** is a group of pupils or students who are taught together. *If classes were smaller, children would learn more.* 2 COUNT N A **class** is also a short period of teaching in a particular subject. *Peggy took evening classes in French.* 3 COUNT N OR UNCOUNT N **Class** is used to refer to the division of people in a society according to their social status. *...the ruling class... ...other children of the same age and class... ...the British class system.* 4 COUNT N WITH SUPP A **class** of things is a group of them with similar characteristics. *We can identify several classes of fern.* 5 UNCOUNT N If someone has **class,** they are elegant and sophisticated; an informal use. 6 VB WITH OBJ If you **class** someone or something as a particular thing, you consider them as belonging to that group of things. *At nineteen you're still classed as a teenager.*

PHRASES ● If you do something **in class,** you do it during a lesson in school. ● If you say that someone is **in a class of their own,** you mean that they have more of a particular skill or quality than anyone else. ● See also **middle class, upper class, working class.**

-class. SUFFIX **-class** is added to words like 'first' and 'executive' to indicate that something is of a particular standard. *...a second-class stamp... I prefer to travel first class.*

classic /klæsɪk/, **classics.** 1 ATTRIB ADJ A **classic** example of something has all the features which you expect that kind of thing to have. *London is the classic example of the scattered city.* 2 ATTRIB ADJ A **classic** film or piece of writing is of high quality and has become a standard against which similar things are judged. *...one of the classic works of the Hollywood cinema.* 3 COUNT N A **classic** is a book which is well-known and of a high literary standard. *...a great classic of Brazilian literature.* 4 UNCOUNT N **Classics** is the study of ancient Greek and Roman civilizations, especially their languages, literature, and philosophy.

classical /klæsɪkə^{0}l/. 1 ADJ You use **classical** to describe something that is traditional in form, style, or content. *...classical ballet... ...the classical Hindu scheme of values.* 2 ATTRIB ADJ **Classical** music is considered to be serious and of lasting value. 3 ATTRIB ADJ **Classical** also means relating to ancient Greek or Roman civilization. *...plays set in classical times.*

classified /klæsɪfaɪd/. ADJ **Classified** information is officially secret.

classify /klæsɪfaɪ/, **classifies, classifying, classified.** VB WITH OBJ When things such as animals or plants **are classified,** they are divided into groups so that ones with similar characteristics are in the same group. *Twenty-two of these plants are now classified as rare... The books have been classified according to subject.* ♦ **classification** UNCOUNT N OR COUNT N *The cataloguing and classification of the plants on the island took several months... The broad outlines of most classifications are quite similar.*

classless /klɑːslɪ^{2}s/. ADJ In a **classless** society, everyone has the same social and economic status.

classmate /klɑːsmeɪt/, **classmates.** COUNT N Your **classmates** are students in the same class as you at school or college.

classroom /klɑːsru^{4}m/, **classrooms.** COUNT N A **classroom** is a room in a school where lessons take place.

classy /klɑːsi^1/. ADJ If someone or something is **classy,** they are stylish and sophisticated; an informal use. *...eating out in classy places.*

clatter /klætə/, **clatters, clattering, clattered.** 1 SING N A **clatter** is a series of loud sounds made by things knocking each other. *...the clatter of dishes being washed.* 2 VB When something **clatters,** it makes a series of loud sounds. *The door clattered open.*

clause /klɔːz/, **clauses.** 1 COUNT N A **clause** is a section of a legal document. 2 COUNT N In grammar, a **clause** is a group of words containing a verb.

claustrophobia /klɒstrə^{6}fəʊbɪə, klɔːs-/. UNCOUNT N **Claustrophobia** is a fear of small or enclosed places.

claustrophobic /klɒstrə^{6}fəʊbɪk, klɔː-/. 1 ADJ If you feel **claustrophobic,** you feel uncomfortable or nervous when you are in a small or enclosed place. 2 ADJ You describe a place or situation as **claustrophobic** when it makes you feel restricted, and nervous or unhappy. *...a small claustrophobic restaurant.*

claw /klɔː/, **claws, clawing, clawed.** 1 COUNT N The **claws** of a bird or animal are the thin, curved nails on its feet. *...a cat sharpening its claws.* 2 COUNT N The **claws** of a lobster, crab, or scorpion are two pointed parts at the end of one of its legs, used for grasping things. 3 VB WITH OBJ If an animal **claws** something, it scratches or damages it with its claws. *He had been clawed by the cat.* 4 VB If you **claw** at something, you try to damage it or get hold of it with your nails or fingers. *I fought and clawed and bit and kicked... ...scrabbling and clawing at the rock as I fell.*

clay /kleɪ/. UNCOUNT N **Clay** is a type of earth that is soft when it is wet and hard when it is baked dry. Clay is used to make things such as pots. *...modelling in clay... ...clay pots.*

clean /kliːn/, **cleaner, cleanest; cleans, cleaning, cleaned.** 1 ADJ Something that is **clean** is free from dirt and unwanted marks. *...clean white shirts... Knives should be wiped clean after use.* 2 ADJ People or animals that are **clean** keep themselves or their surroundings clean. *He looked clean and healthy.* 3 VB WITH OBJ If you **clean** something, you make it free from dirt and unwanted marks, for example by washing or wiping it. *Clean the bathroom and lavatory thoroughly... ...the industrial fluid used to clean grease from the hands.* ♦ **cleaning** UNCOUNT N *We have a landlady who does our cooking and our cleaning.* 4 ATTRIB ADJ **Clean** humour is decent and not offensive. *...clean jokes.* 5 ADJ If someone's reputation or record is **clean,** they have never done anything wrong. *Applicants must have a clean driving licence.* 6 PHRASE If you **come clean** about something that you have been keeping secret, you admit it; an informal use. 7 ADV **Clean** also means directly, completely or thoroughly; an informal use. *The ninth shot went clean through the forehead... The thief got clean away... I'd clean forgotten.*

clean out. PHR VB 1 If you **clean out** a cupboard or room, you clean and tidy it thoroughly. *I was cleaning out my desk.* 2 If you **clean** someone **out,** you take all their money; an informal use. *I've got no more money—they cleaned me out.*

clean up. PHR VB If you **clean up** something, you clean it thoroughly. *Clean up food spills at once.*

cleaner /kliːnə/, **cleaners.** 1 COUNT N A **cleaner** is someone who is employed to clean the rooms in a building, or to clean a particular type of thing. *...our window cleaner.* 2 COUNT N OR UNCOUNT N A **cleaner** is also a substance or device for cleaning things. *...a spray oven cleaner.* ● See also **vacuum cleaner.** 3 SING N The **cleaner's** is a shop where clothes and curtains are dry-cleaned.

cleanliness /klɛnlɪnə^{2}s/. UNCOUNT N **Cleanliness** is the habit of keeping yourself clean.

cleanly /kliːnli^1/. ADV **Cleanly** means smoothly and completely. *The porcelain top of the ornament broke cleanly off.*

cleanse /klɛnz/, **cleanses, cleansing, cleansed.** VB WITH OBJ To **cleanse** something means to make it completely free from dirt or unpleasant or unwanted things; a formal use. *...to cleanse the kidneys... ...his vow to cleanse Washington of subversives.*

cleanser /klɛnzə/, **cleansers.** MASS N A **cleanser** is a liquid that you use for cleaning.

clean-shaven. ADJ A **clean-shaven** man does not have a beard or a moustache.

clear /klɪə/, **clearer, clearest; clears, clearing, cleared.** 1 ADJ Something that is **clear** is easy to see, hear, or understand. *The line of its footprints is still clear... I gave a clear, frank account of the incident... It was clear from his letter that he was not interested.* ♦ **clearly** ADV *Make sure that all your luggage is clearly labelled... I couldn't see him clearly... Clearly, it is very important for a solution to be found quickly.* 2 PRED ADJ If you are **clear** about something, you understand it completely. *I'm not clear from what you said whether you support the idea or not.* 3 ADJ If you have a **clear** mind or way of thinking, you are sensible and logical. *You need clear thought and action.* ♦ **clearly** ADV *Wait until you can think more clearly.* 4 ADJ If a substance is **clear,** you can see through it. *...a clear glue... ...a small creek with cold, clear water.* 5 ADJ If a surface or place is **clear,** it is free from obstructions or unwanted objects. *The road was clear... ...a patch of floor that has been swept clear.* 6 ADJ If it is a **clear** day, there is no mist, rain, or cloud. 7 ADJ If your conscience is **clear,** you do not feel guilty about anything. 8 PRED ADJ If one thing is **clear** of another, the two things are not touching. *Raise the jack until the wheel is clear of the ground.* 9 VB WITH OBJ When you **clear** a place, you remove unwanted things from it. *The children were helping me clear weeds from the pond... Will you clear the table when you've finished eating?* 10 VB WITH OBJ If an animal or person **clears** a fence, wall, or hedge, they jump over it without touching it. 11 VB When fog or mist **clears,** it gradually disappears. 12 VB WITH OBJ If a course of action **is cleared,** people in authority give permission for it to happen. *The proposals haven't been cleared by the local authority yet.* 13 VB WITH OBJ If someone **is cleared** of a crime or mistake, they are proved to be not guilty of it. *I have every confidence that I will be cleared of the crime.* 14 See also **clearing.**

PHRASES ● If you **stay clear** or **steer clear** of a person or place, you do not go near them. ● If someone is **in the clear,** they are free from blame, suspicion, or danger; an informal use. ● When you **clear** your **throat,** you cough slightly in order to make it easier to speak. ● **the coast is clear:** see **coast.**

clear away. PHR VB When you **clear away,** you put away things that you have been using. *Brody began to clear away the soup bowls.*

clear off. PHR VB If you tell someone to **clear off,** you are telling them in a rude way to go away; an informal use.

clear out. PHR VB 1 If you **clear out** of a place, you leave; an informal use. *Just clear out and leave me in peace!* 2 If you **clear out** a cupboard or room, you tidy it and throw away unwanted things.

clear up. PHR VB 1 When you **clear up,** you tidy a place and put things away. *Go and clear up your room.* 2 When a problem or misunderstanding **is cleared**

up, it is settled or explained. *I trembled until the misunderstanding was cleared up.* **3** When bad weather **clears up,** it stops raining or being cloudy.

clearance /klɪərəns/. **1** UNCOUNT N **Clearance** is the removal of old or unwanted buildings, trees, or other things from an area. *He was responsible for slum clearance and rehousing programmes.* **2** UNCOUNT N If you get **clearance** for something, you get official permission for it. *They were still awaiting clearance to start the engines.*

clear-cut. ADJ Something that is **clear-cut** is easy to understand and definite or distinct. *It was a clear-cut decision.*

clearing /klɪərɪŋ/, **clearings.** COUNT N A **clearing** is a small area of grass or bare ground in a wood.

cleavage /kliːvɪdʒ/, **cleavages. 1** COUNT N A woman's **cleavage** is the space between her breasts. **2** COUNT N A **cleavage** between people is a division or disagreement between them; a formal use. *...a political cleavage between the classes.*

clef /klɛf/, **clefs.** COUNT N A **clef** is the symbol at the beginning of a line of music that indicates its pitch.

cleft /klɛft/, **clefts.** COUNT N A **cleft** in a rock or ground is a narrow opening in it. *He could see the valley through a cleft in the rocks.*

clemency /klɛmənsi^{1}/. UNCOUNT N If someone is shown **clemency** , they receive kind and merciful treatment from someone who has authority to punish them; a formal use. *...appeals for clemency.*

clench /klɛntʃ/, **clenches, clenching, clenched. 1** VB WITH OBJ When you **clench** your fist, you curl your fingers up tightly. *Ralph clenched his fist and went very red.* **2** VB WITH OBJ When you **clench** your teeth, you squeeze them together firmly. *She hissed through clenched teeth, 'Get out of here.'* **3** VB WITH OBJ If you **clench** something in your hand or teeth, you hold it tightly. *There he sat, pipe clenched in his mouth, typing away.*

clergy /klɜːdʒi^{1}/. PLURAL N The **clergy** are the religious leaders of a Christian church.

clergyman /klɜːdʒɪmə^{3}n/, **clergymen.** COUNT N A **clergyman** is a male member of the clergy.

clerical /klɛrɪkə^{0}l/. **1** ADJ **Clerical** jobs and workers are concerned with work in offices. *...routine clerical work.* **2** ADJ **Clerical** also means relating to the clergy; a formal use. *...a priest in a clerical grey suit.*

clerk /klɑːk/, **clerks.** COUNT N A **clerk** works in an office, bank, or law court and looks after the records or accounts.

clever /klɛvə/, **cleverer, cleverest. 1** ADJ A **clever** person is intelligent and able to understand things easily or to plan things well. *My sister was very clever and passed all her exams at school... How clever of you to know that.* ♦ **cleverly** ADV *They had gone about the scheme cleverly.* ♦ **cleverness** UNCOUNT N *I admire cleverness—and courage too.* **2** ADJ An idea, book, or invention that is **clever** is extremely effective and skilful. *This is a very clever way of running a college... ...a clever gadget.*

cliché /kliːʃeɪ/, **clichés;** also spelled **cliche.** COUNT N A **cliché** is an idea or phrase which has been used so much that it no longer has any real effect.

click /klɪk/, **clicks, clicking, clicked. 1** ERG VB When something **clicks,** it makes a short, sharp sound. *His camera was clicking away... He clicked the switch on the radio.* Also COUNT N *The lock opened with a click.* **2** VB When you suddenly understand something, you can say that it **has clicked;** an informal use.

client /klaɪənt/, **clients.** COUNT N A **client** is someone for whom a professional person or organization is providing a service or doing some work. *...a solicitor and his client.*

clientele /kliːɒntɛl/. COLL N The **clientele** of a place or business are its customers or clients. *...a restaurant with a predominantly upper-class clientele.*

cliff /klɪf/, **cliffs.** COUNT N A **cliff** is a high area of land with a very steep side, especially one next to the sea.

climate /klaɪmə^{1}t/, **climates. 1** COUNT N OR UNCOUNT N The **climate** of a place is the typical weather conditions that occur there. *...the English climate... ...changes in climate... ...very cold climates.* **2** COUNT N WITH SUPP You can use **climate** when referring to people's attitudes or opinions. *...this changing climate of public opinion.*

climax /klaɪmæks/, **climaxes.** COUNT N The **climax** of something is the most exciting or important moment in it, usually near the end. *This proved to be the climax of his political career.*

climb /klaɪm/, **climbs, climbing, climbed. 1** VB WITH OR WITHOUT OBJ If you **climb** something such as a tree, mountain, or ladder, you move towards the top of it. *We started to climb the hill... We climbed to the top of the mountain.* Also COUNT N *We were still out of breath from the climb.* **2** VB WITH ADJUNCT If you **climb** somewhere, you move there carefully and often awkwardly, often because there is not much room to move. *She climbed into her car... Four men climbed down through the hatch.* **3** VB To **climb** also means to move upwards or to increase in level or value. *The plane climbed steeply and banked... The cost has climbed to a staggering £35 billion.*

climber /klaɪmə/, **climbers. 1** COUNT N A **climber** is someone who climbs rocks or mountains as a sport. **2** COUNT N A **climber** is also a plant that grows upwards by attaching itself to other plants or objects.

climbing /klaɪmɪŋ/. UNCOUNT N **Climbing** is the sport of climbing rocks or mountains.

clinch /klɪntʃ/, **clinches, clinching, clinched.** VB WITH OBJ To **clinch** an agreement or argument means to settle it; an informal use.

cling /klɪŋ/, **clings, clinging, clung** /klʌŋ/. **1** VB WITH ADJUNCT If you **cling** to someone or something, you hold onto them tightly. *I clung to the door to support myself.* **2** VB WITH ADJUNCT Clothes that **cling** stay pressed against your body when you move. *The dress clung tight to Etta's waist.* **3** VB WITH PREP 'to' If you **cling** to someone, you do not allow them enough freedom or independence. *A working woman is not so likely to cling to her children when they leave home.* ♦ **clinging** ADJ *There was something weak and clinging in his nature.* **4** VB WITH PREP 'to' If you **cling** to an idea or way of behaving, you continue to believe in its value or importance, even though it may no longer be valid or useful. *They cling to all the old, inefficient methods of doing things.*

clinic /klɪnɪk/, **clinics.** COUNT N A **clinic** is a building where people receive medical advice or treatment.

clinical /klɪnɪkə^{0}l/. **1** ATTRIB ADJ **Clinical** refers to the direct medical treatment of patients, as opposed to theoretical research; a medical use. *Doctors are hoping to start clinical tests next month.* ♦ **clinically** ADV *On examination she looked well and was not clinically anaemic.* **2** ADJ **Clinical** thought or behaviour is very logical, detached, and unemotional; used showing disapproval. *She adopted an icy, impersonal, clinical attitude.* **3** ADJ A **clinical** room or building is very plain, or is too neat and clean, so that people do not enjoy being in it. *...tiny offices painted clinical white.*

clink /klɪŋk/, **clinks, clinking, clinked.** ERG VB When glass or metal objects **clink,** they touch each other and make a short, light sound. *The milk bottles clinked... She clinked her glass against Rudolph's.* Also SING N *...the clink of glasses.*

clip /klɪp/, **clips, clipping, clipped. 1** COUNT N A **clip** is a small metal or plastic device that is used for holding things together. *He wore three pencils held by metal clips in his top pocket... ...hair clips.* **2** VB WITH OBJ AND ADJUNCT If you **clip** one thing to another, you fasten it there with a clip. *Keep the list clipped to that notebook.* **3** VB WITH OBJ If you **clip** something, you cut small pieces from it. *Mr Willet had come to clip the hedges.* **4** COUNT N A **clip** of a film or television programme is a short section of it shown by itself. *They were shown film clips depicting murders.*

clipboard /klɪpbɔːd/, **clipboards.** COUNT N A **clipboard** is a board with a clip at the top, used to hold together pieces of paper and provide a firm base on which to write.

clipped /klɪpt/. **1** ADJ If a man's hair or moustache is **clipped,** it is neatly trimmed. **2** ADJ If you have a **clipped** way of speaking, you speak with quick, short sounds. *He talked with a clipped, upper-class accent.*

clippers /klɪpəz/. PLURAL N **Clippers** are a tool used for cutting small amounts from something. *...a pair of nail clippers.*

clipping /klɪpɪŋ/, **clippings.** COUNT N A **clipping** is an article, picture, or advertisement that has been cut from a newspaper or magazine. *Dawlish read the newspaper clipping I gave him.*

clique /kliːk, klɪk/, **cliques.** COLL N A **clique** is a small group of people who spend a lot of time together and are unfriendly towards other people.

cloak /kləʊk/, **cloaks, cloaking, cloaked. 1** COUNT N A **cloak** is a wide, loose coat that fastens at the neck and does not have sleeves. **2** COUNT N WITH SUPP You can use **cloak** to refer to something which is intended to hide the truth. *He could be using the story as a cloak for more sinister activities.* **3** VB WITH OBJ To **cloak** something means to cover it or hide it. *The hills were cloaked by thick mists.*

cloakroom /kləʊkru^{4}m/, **cloakrooms.** COUNT N A **cloakroom** is a small room where you can leave your coat and hat in a public building. It is also a room containing toilets and washbasins.

clobber /klɒbə/, **clobbers, clobbering, clobbered;** an informal word. **1** UNCOUNT N You can refer to someone's belongings as their **clobber.** *...bits of old army clobber.* **2** VB WITH OBJ If you **clobber** someone, you hit them. *If that dog bites me I'll clobber it.*

clock /klɒk/, **clocks, clocking, clocked. 1** COUNT N A **clock** is an instrument, for example in a room or on a wall, that shows you what the time is. *...the ticking of the clock... The church clock struck eleven.* ● If you work **round the clock,** you work all day and all night without stopping. **2** COUNT N A **clock** or time **clock** on a piece of equipment is a device that causes things to happen automatically at particular times. *Set the time clock on your central heating system to give heat only when it is needed.* **3** COUNT N The **clock** in a car is an instrument that shows the distance that the car has travelled. *...a Mini with 5,000 miles on the clock.* **4** VB WITH 'in' OR 'out' When workers **clock** in at a factory or office, they record the time that they arrive by putting a special card into a device. When they **clock** out, they record the time that they leave.

clock up. PHR VB To **clock up** a large number or total means to reach that total; an informal use. *He has clocked up more than 171,750 miles.*

clockwise /klɒkwaɪz/. ATTRIB ADJ OR ADV When something moves in a **clockwise** direction, it moves in a circle, in the same direction as the hands on a clock. *He pushed the bolt back in and twisted it clockwise.*

clockwork /klɒkwɜːk/. **1** UNCOUNT N **Clockwork** is machinery in some toys or models that makes them move or operate when they are wound up with a key. **2** PHRASE If something happens **like clockwork,** it happens without problems or delays.

clod /klɒd/, **clods.** COUNT N A **clod** is a large lump of earth.

clog /klɒg/, **clogs, clogging, clogged. 1** VB WITH OBJ When something **clogs** a hole, it blocks it so that nothing can pass through. *His rifle was clogged with sand.* **2** COUNT N **Clogs** are heavy leather or wooden shoes with thick wooden soles.

clog up. PHR VB When something **is clogged up,** it is blocked and no longer works properly. *If the cooling unit gets clogged up with ice it can't do its job efficiently... Their lungs may progressively clog up.*

cloister /klɔɪstə/, **cloisters.** COUNT N A **cloister** is a paved, covered area round a square in a monastery or a cathedral.

cloistered /klɔɪstəd/. ADJ If you lead a **cloistered** way of life, you live quietly and have little contact with other people.

clone /kləʊn/, **clones, cloning, cloned. 1** COUNT N A **clone** is an animal or plant that has been produced artificially from the cells of another animal or plant, and is identical to the original one. **2** VB WITH OBJ To **clone** an animal or plant means to produce it as a clone.

close, closes, closing, closed; closer, closest; pronounced /kləʊz/ when it is a verb and also in meaning 4, and /kləʊs/ when it is an adjective or adverb. **1** ERG VB When you **close** a door, window, or lid, you move it to cover an opening or gap, so that it is no longer open. *He opened the door and closed it behind him... It took a bit of pressure to make the lid close.* ♦ **closed** ADJ *I fell asleep with my window closed tight... He was sitting with closed eyes.* **2** ERG VB When a place **closes,** people cannot use it, or all work stops there. *Many libraries close on Saturdays at 1 p.m... Shotton Steelworks was closed with the loss of nearly 8,000 jobs.* ♦ **closed** ADJ *It was Sunday and the garage was closed.* **3** VB WITH OBJ To **close** an event or matter means to bring it to an end. *He spoke as though he wanted to close the conversation.* **4** SING N The **close** of a period of time or an activity is the end of it; a formal use. *...towards the close of the day... The war in Europe drew to a close.* **5** VB If you **close** on someone who you are following, you get nearer to them. *The boat was about 200 yards away from us but closing fast.* **6** PRED ADJ Something that is **close** to something else is near to it. *Their two heads were close together... I got close enough to see what the trouble was... He moved a bit closer.* ♦ **closely** ADV *The crowd moved in more closely around him.* **7** ADJ People who are **close** know each other well and like each other a lot. *They felt very close to each other... ...my closest friends.* ♦ **closeness** UNCOUNT N *They felt a new closeness in relationships with their friends.* **8** ATTRIB ADJ Your **close** relatives are the members of your family most directly related to you, for example your parents, brothers, or sisters. **9** ATTRIB ADJ **Close** contact or co-operation involves seeing or communicating with someone often. *My sons have maintained extremely close ties with a college friend.* ♦ **closely** ADV *Every doctor works closely with the Child Health Service.* **10** ADJ If there is a **close** link or resemblance between two things, they are strongly connected or similar. *...the close link between love and fear... She regarded Lomax with something that was close to fear.* ♦ **closely** ADV *Status was closely linked with wealth... ...a creature that closely resembles a newt.* **11** ATTRIB ADJ **Close** inspection or observation of something is careful and thorough. *These events deserve closer examination.* ♦ **closely** ADV *He studied the photographs very closely.* **12** ADJ When a competition or election is **close,** it is only won or lost by a small amount. *The vote was close.* **13** PRED ADJ If an event is **close** or if you are **close** to it, it is likely to happen soon. *An agreement seems close... The Government several times came close to defeat... She was close to tears.* **14** ADJ If the atmosphere in a place is **close,** it is uncomfortably warm with not enough air; a British use. **15** See also **closing.**

PHRASES • Something that is **close by** or **close at hand** is near to you. *There was a small lamp on the table close by.* • If you look at something **close up** or **close to,** you look at it when you are very near to it. *It was my first glimpse of him close to.* • If something is **close to** or **close on** a particular amount or distance, it is slightly less than that amount or distance. *...a bill of close to £8,000... The pile of wood was close on ten feet in height.* • If you describe an event as **a close shave, a close thing,** or **a close call,** you mean that an accident or a disaster nearly happened. *It was a very close shave. The car only just missed me.*

close down. PHR VB If a factory or a business **closes down,** all work or activity stops there, usually for ever. *The magazine was forced to close down... The mines had been closed down.*

close in. PHR VB If people **close in** on a person or place, they come nearer and gradually surround them. *As the enemy closed in, the resistance of the villagers shrank to nothing.*

closed-circuit television. UNCOUNT N **Closed-circuit television** is a television system that is used inside a building, for example to film customers in a shop so that thieves can be identified.

closed shop, closed shops. COUNT N A **closed shop** is a factory, shop, or other business in which employees must be members of a particular trade union.

closet /klɒzɪt/, **closets, closeted. 1** COUNT N A **closet** is a cupboard; an American use. **2** VB WITH OBJ If you **are closeted** with someone, you are talking privately to them. **3** ATTRIB ADJ You use **closet** to describe beliefs, habits, or feelings that people keep private and secret, often because they are embarrassed about them. *...closet fears... ...closet alcoholics.*

close-up /kləʊs ʌp/, **close-ups.** COUNT N A **close-up** is a photograph or film that shows a lot of detail because it was taken very near to the subject. *The team anxiously awaited close-ups of the moon.*

closing /kləʊzɪŋ/. ATTRIB ADJ The **closing** part of an activity or period of time is its final part. *...the closing stages of the election campaign.*

closure /kləʊʒə/, **closures. 1** UNCOUNT N OR COUNT N The **closure** of a business or factory is the permanent shutting of it. *...newspapers that are threatened with closure... ...the closures of less profitable factories.* **2** UNCOUNT N WITH SUPP The **closure** of a road or border is the blocking of it to prevent people from using it.

clot /klɒt/, **clots, clotting, clotted. 1** COUNT N A **clot** is a sticky lump that forms when a liquid, especially blood, dries and becomes hard. *...a blood clot.* **2** VB When blood **clots,** it becomes thick and forms a lump. ♦ **clotted** ADJ *...clotted blood.*

cloth /klɒθ/, **cloths. 1** MASS N **Cloth** is fabric which is made by weaving, knitting, or some other similar process. *...strips of cotton cloth.* **2** COUNT N A **cloth** is a piece of cloth used for a particular purpose, such as cleaning. *Clean with a soft cloth dipped in warm soapy water.*

clothe /kləʊð/, **clothes, clothing, clothed. 1** PLURAL N **Clothes** are the things that people wear, such as shirts, coats, trousers, dresses, and underwear. *I took off all my clothes... They hadn't got any clothes on.* **2** ADJ If you are **clothed** in something, you are dressed in it. *Mrs Travers was clothed in green.* **3** VB WITH OBJ To **clothe** someone means to provide them with clothes. *Are we not better fed, better clothed, and better housed than ever before?*

clothes line, clothes lines. COUNT N A **clothes line** is a rope on which you hang washing to dry.

clothes peg, clothes pegs. COUNT N A **clothes peg** is a small wooden or plastic device, used to fasten clothes to a clothes line.

clothing /kləʊðɪŋ/. **1** UNCOUNT N **Clothing** is the clothes people wear. *...loans to pay for food and clothing... ...waterproof clothing.* **2** ATTRIB ADJ You use **clothing** to refer to the business of designing, manufacturing, or selling clothes. *...a clothing factory.*

cloud /klaʊd/, **clouds, clouding, clouded. 1** COUNT N OR UNCOUNT N A **cloud** is a mass of water vapour that is seen as a white or grey mass in the sky. *There were little white clouds high in the blue sky... There will be heavy cloud over many areas.* **2** COUNT N A **cloud** of smoke or dust is a mass of it floating in the air. **3** ERG VB If something **clouds,** it becomes less easy to see through. *He lit a cigar and soon clouded the room in smoke... My glasses kept clouding up.* **4** VB WITH OBJ If one thing **clouds** another, it makes it more difficult to understand. *His explanations clouded the issue.* **5** VB WITH OBJ If something **clouds** an event or situation, it makes it more unpleasant. *Insanity clouded the last years of his life.*

cloud over. PHR VB **1** If your face or eyes **cloud over,** you suddenly look sad or angry. *His face clouded over with anguish.* **2** If it **clouds over,** the sky becomes covered with clouds.

cloudless /klaʊdlɪ²s/. ADJ If the sky is **cloudless,** there are no clouds in it.

cloudy /klaʊdi¹/. **1** ADJ If it is **cloudy,** there are a lot of clouds in the sky. *It was a cloudy day.* **2** ADJ If a liquid is **cloudy,** it is less clear than it should be. *...cloudy water.* **3** ADJ Ideas or opinions that are **cloudy** are confused or uncertain. *Their policies seem fairly cloudy.*

clout /klaʊt/, **clouts, clouting, clouted;** an informal word. **1** VB WITH OBJ If you **clout** someone, you hit them *Then he clouted me across the face.* Also COUNT N *...a clout on the head.* **2** UNCOUNT N **Clout** is also influence and power. *The commission lacks the clout to force him to resign... ...political clout.*

clove /kləʊv/, **cloves. 1** COUNT N **Cloves** are small dried flower buds used as a spice. **2** COUNT N A **clove** of garlic is one of the small sections of a garlic bulb.

clover /kləʊvə/. UNCOUNT N **Clover** is a small plant with pink or white ball-shaped flowers.

clown /klaʊn/, **clowns, clowning, clowned. 1** COUNT N A **clown** is a performer who wears funny clothes and bright make-up, and does silly things to make people laugh. **2** VB If you **clown,** you do silly things to make people laugh. *He clowned and joked with the children.*

cloying /klɔɪɪŋ/. ADJ Something that is **cloying** is unpleasant because it is too sweet and sickly, or too sentimental. *...the cloying scent of flowers... ...cloying sentimentality.*

club /klʌb/, **clubs, clubbing, clubbed. 1** COUNT N A **club** is an organization of people who are all interested in a particular activity. *Have you joined the Swimming Club?* **2** COUNT N A **club** is also a place where the members of a particular club or organization meet. *I'll see you at the club.* **3** COUNT N A **club** is also a thick heavy stick that can be used as a weapon. **4** VB WITH OBJ If you **club** someone, you hit them with something blunt and heavy. *They were going to club him to death.* **5** COUNT N A golf **club** is a long thin stick which is used to hit a golf ball. **6** UNCOUNT N **Clubs** is one of the four suits in a pack of playing cards.

club together. PHR VB If people **club together,** they all give money in order to share the cost of something. *We all clubbed together to buy her a present.*

cluck /klʌk/, **clucks, clucking, clucked. 1** VB When a hen **clucks,** it makes the noise that hens typically make. **2** VB WITH ADJUNCT If you **cluck** over someone or something, you say things in a disapproving or fussy way. *The women clucked disapprovingly over her hair.*

clue /klu:/, **clues. 1** COUNT N A **clue** to a problem, mystery, or puzzle is something that helps you find the answer. *The clue to solving our energy problem lies in conservation... The police searched all the houses but found no clues... ...a crossword clue.* **2** PHRASE If you **haven't a clue** about something, you know nothing about it. *I hadn't got a clue how to spell it.*

clump /klʌmp/, **clumps, clumping, clumped. 1** COUNT N WITH SUPP A **clump** of plants or buildings is a small group of them close together. *...a clump of thistles... ...clumps of young fir trees.* **2** VB WITH ADJUNCT If someone **clumps** about, they walk with heavy clumsy footsteps. *My sister came clumping back in her wellingtons.*

clumsy /klʌmzi¹/, **clumsier, clumsiest. 1** ADJ A **clumsy** person moves or handles things in an awkward way, often so that they knock things over or break them. *I wanted to dance, but I felt stupid and clumsy... I held the tweezers, but my fingers were too clumsy to handle them properly.* ♦ **clumsily** ADV *She stumbled clumsily, as though drunk, and sat down.* ♦ **clumsiness** UNCOUNT N *The older boys would laugh loudly at his clumsiness.* **2** ADJ A **clumsy** remark is tactless and likely to upset people. *Haldane's efforts at reconciliation were clumsy and naive.* ♦ **clumsily** ADV *...a clumsily phrased apology.* **3** ADJ An **clumsy** object is ugly and awkward to use. *Mechanical switches are often clumsy and unreliable... ...a clumsy weapon.* ♦ **clumsily** ADV *The furniture was clumsily designed.*

clung /klʌŋ/. **Clung** is the past tense and past participle of **cling.**

cluster /klʌstə/, **clusters, clustering, clustered. 1** COUNT N A **cluster** of people or things is a small group of them close together. *There was a little cluster of admirers round the guest speaker... ...clusters of white flowers.* **2** VB If people or things **cluster** together, they gather together or are found together in small groups. *The guests immediately clustered around the table.*

clutch /klʌtʃ/, **clutches, clutching, clutched. 1** VB WITH OBJ OR ADJUNCT If you **clutch** something, you hold it very tightly. *Myra came in, clutching her handbag... Her pony stumbled, and she clutched at the reins.* **2** PLURAL N If you are in the **clutches** of another person, that person has power or control over you; an informal use. *He escaped the clutches of the law.* **3** COUNT N In a car, the **clutch** is the pedal that you press before you change gear, and the mechanism that it operates.

clutter /klʌtə/, **clutters, cluttering, cluttered. 1** UNCOUNT N **Clutter** is a lot of unnecessary or useless things in an untidy state. *The rooms were full of clutter.* **2** VB WITH OBJ If things **clutter** a place, they fill it in an untidy way. *Cluttering the table were papers, books, and ashtrays.* ♦ **cluttered** ADJ *He glanced around the small, cluttered room.*

cm. cm. is an abbreviation for 'centimetre'. *...two rolls of sterile bandage 5 cm. wide.*

c/o. You write **c/o** before an address on an envelope when you are sending it to someone who is staying or working at that address, often for only a short time. **c/o** is an abbreviation for 'care of'. *Mr A D Bright, c/o Sherman Ltd, 62 Burton Road, Bristol 8.*

co- /kəʊ/. PREFIX **Co-** is used to form words that refer to people sharing things or doing things together. *...the co-author of a cookery book... The two countries coexist peacefully.*

Co. /kəʊ/. **Co.** is used as an abbreviation for 'company' in the names of companies. *...Morris, Marshall, Faulkner & Co.*

coach /kəʊtʃ/, **coaches, coaching, coached. 1** COUNT N A **coach** is a bus that carries passengers on long journeys; a British use. *The coach leaves Cardiff at twenty to eight... We usually go there by coach.* **2** COUNT N A **coach** on a train is one of the separate sections for passengers. **3** COUNT N A **coach** is also an enclosed four-wheeled vehicle pulled by horses. **4** VB WITH OBJ If you **coach** someone, you help them to become better at a particular sport or subject. *She had been coached by a former Wimbledon champion.* **5** COUNT N A **coach** is also someone who coaches a person or sports team.

coagulate /kəʊægjə⁴leɪt/, **coagulates, coagulating, coagulated.** VB When paint or blood **coagulates,** it becomes very thick.

coal /kəʊl/, **coals.** UNCOUNT N **Coal** is a hard black substance taken from underground and burned as fuel. *...a lump of coal... ...the coal mining industry.*

coalesce /kəʊəlɛs/, **coalesces, coalescing, coalesced.** RECIP VB If things **coalesce,** they join to form a larger group or system; a formal use. *There is a tendency for industrial systems to coalesce into large units.*

coalition /kəʊəlɪʃəⁿn/, **coalitions. 1** COUNT N A **coalition** is a government consisting of people from two or more political parties. *...the fall of Asquith's Coalition Government.* **2** COUNT N A **coalition** is also a group consisting of people from different political or social groups who are co-operating to achieve a particular aim. *...a broad coalition of community groups in the area.*

coalminer /kəʊlmaɪnə/, **coalminers.** COUNT N A **coalminer** is a person whose job is mining coal.

coarse /kɔ:s/, **coarser, coarsest. 1** ADJ Something that is **coarse** has a rough texture. *...coarse white cloth... ...coarse black hair.* **2** ADJ A **coarse** person talks and behaves in a rude, offensive way. *He objected to her coarse remarks.* ♦ **coarsely** ADV *She speaks rather coarsely.* ♦ **coarseness** UNCOUNT N *With deliberate coarseness, he wiped his mouth with his hand.*

coarsen /kɔ:səⁿn/, **coarsens, coarsening, coarsened.** VB If someone **coarsens,** they become less polite. *My whole nature had coarsened in a way that horrified me.*

coast /kəʊst/, **coasts. 1** COUNT N The **coast** is an area of land next to the sea. *...a trawler fishing off the coast of Portugal... We had made up our minds to stay on the East Coast.* **2** PHRASE If you say that **the coast is clear,** you mean that there is nobody around to see you or catch you.

coastal /kəʊstəⁿl/. ATTRIB ADJ **Coastal** means in the sea or on the land near a coast. *...coastal waters.*

coastguard /kəʊstgɑ:d/, **coastguards.** COUNT N A **coastguard** is an official who watches the sea near a coast, in order to get help when it is needed.

coastline /kəʊstlaɪn/, **coastlines.** COUNT N A country's **coastline** is the edge of its coast. *...a rocky and treacherous coastline.*

coat /kəʊt/, **coats, coating, coated. 1** COUNT N A **coat** is a piece of clothing with long sleeves worn over your other clothes when you go outside. **2** COUNT N An animal's **coat** is its fur or hair. *It has a long shaggy* *coat.* **3** VB WITH OBJ If you **coat** something with a substance, you cover it with a thin layer of the substance. *The sweets are then coated with chocolate.* **4** COUNT N A **coat** of paint or varnish is a thin layer of it.

coat hanger, coat hangers. COUNT N A **coat hanger** is a curved piece of wood, metal, or plastic for hanging clothes on.

coating /kəʊtɪŋ/, **coatings.** COUNT N WITH SUPP A **coating** of a substance is a thin layer of it. *...a coating of dust.*

coat of arms, coats of arms. COUNT N A **coat of arms** is a design in the form of a shield used as an emblem by a family, a town, or an organization.

coax /kəʊks/, **coaxes, coaxing, coaxed.** VB WITH OBJ If you **coax** someone to do something, you gently try to persuade them to do it. *She might be coaxed into giving their marriage another chance.*

cobbler /kɒblə/, **cobblers.** COUNT N A **cobbler** is a person whose job is to make or mend shoes; an old-fashioned use.

cobblestone /kɒbə^{0}lstəʊn/, **cobblestones.** COUNT N **Cobblestones** are stones with a rounded upper surface which were once used for making streets.

cobra /kəʊbrə/, **cobras.** COUNT N A **cobra** is a kind of poisonous snake.

cobweb /kɒbwɛb/, **cobwebs.** COUNT N A **cobweb** is the fine net that a spider makes in order to catch insects.

cocaine /kə^{6}keɪn/. UNCOUNT N **Cocaine** is an addictive drug which people take for pleasure. In most countries it is illegal to take cocaine.

cock /kɒk/, **cocks, cocking, cocked.** **1** COUNT N A **cock** is an adult male chicken; a British use. **2** VB WITH OBJ If you **cock** your head or your leg, you lift it sideways. *He stepped back, his head cocked to one side, to admire his work... A stray dog cocked his leg against a lamp-post.*

cockatoo /kɒkətuː, kɒkətuː/, **cockatoos.** COUNT N A **cockatoo** is a kind of parrot with a crest on its head.

cockerel /kɒkə^{0}rəl/, **cockerels.** COUNT N A **cockerel** is a young cock.

cockle /kɒkə^{0}l/, **cockles.** COUNT N **Cockles** are a kind of small shellfish.

cockney /kɒkni^1/, **cockneys.** **1** COUNT N A **cockney** is a person who was born in the East End of London. **2** UNCOUNT N **Cockney** is the dialect and accent of the East End of London.

cockpit /kɒkpɪt/, **cockpits.** COUNT N The **cockpit** in a small plane or racing car is the part where the pilot or driver sits.

cockroach /kɒkrəʊtʃ/, **cockroaches.** COUNT N A **cockroach** is a large brown insect found in dirty rooms.

cocktail /kɒkteɪl/, **cocktails.** **1** COUNT N A **cocktail** is an alcoholic drink containing several ingredients. *...a champagne cocktail.* **2** COUNT N WITH SUPP Something which is made by combining a number of different things can be called a **cocktail.** *...a shrimp cocktail.*

cocky /kɒki^1/. ADJ A **cocky** person is very self-confident and pleased with themselves; an informal use. *Don't be too cocky, you were only third.*

cocoa /kəʊkəʊ/. **1** UNCOUNT N **Cocoa** is a brown powder made from the seeds of a tropical tree, which is used in making chocolate. **2** UNCOUNT N **Cocoa** is also a hot drink made with cocoa powder and milk.

coconut /kəʊkənʌt/, **coconuts.** COUNT N A **coconut** is a very large nut with a hairy shell, white flesh and milky juice inside.

cocoon /kəkuːn/, **cocoons.** **1** COUNT N A **cocoon** is a covering of silky threads made by the larvae of moths and other insects before they grow into adults. **2** COUNT N WITH SUPP You can use **cocoon** to describe a safe and protective environment. *I lived in a cocoon of love and warmth.*

cocooned /kəkuːnd/. **1** ADJ If someone is **cocooned** in blankets or clothes, they are completely wrapped in them. **2** ADJ If you say that someone is **cocooned,** you mean that they are isolated and protected from everyday life and problems.

cod /kɒd/. **Cod** is the singular and plural. UNCOUNT N **Cod** is a kind of fish. *Their diet centres upon cod and fried chicken.*

code /kəʊd/, **codes, coding, coded.** **1** COUNT N A **code** is a set of rules about how people should behave. *...accepted codes of behaviour... ...the IBA's code of advertising standards and practice.* **2** COUNT N OR UNCOUNT N A **code** is also a system of sending secret messages by replacing letters and words with other letters or words. *It is a code that even I can crack... The messages were typed in code.* **3** VB WITH OBJ If you **code** a message, you change it by replacing the letters or symbols with different letters or symbols so that people who do not know the code cannot understand it. *...abstracting information and coding it.* ♦ **coded** ADJ *For several hours now coded messages had been going out by telephone.* **4** COUNT N A group of numbers or letters used to identify something is also called a **code.** *My university course code is E5L21.* **5** VB WITH OBJ To **code** something means to identify it by a short group of numbers or letters. *The data on fathers' occupation are not coded in the same way.*

code name, code names. COUNT N A **code name** is a name used for someone or something in order to keep their identity secret. *He is listed in the files by his code-name, the Jackal.*

codify /kəʊdɪfaɪ, kɒ-/, **codifies, codifying, codified.** VB WITH OBJ If you **codify** a set of rules, you present them in a clear and ordered way. *When were the rules of snooker codified?*

co-ed /kəʊɛd/. ATTRIB ADJ A **co-ed** school is the same as a co-educational school.

co-educational /kəʊɛdjə^{4}keɪʃə^{0}nəl, -ʃənə^{0}l/. ADJ A **co-educational** school is attended by both boys and girls.

coerce /kəʊɜːs/, **coerces, coercing, coerced.** VB WITH OBJ If you **coerce** someone into doing something, you force them to do it; a formal use. *They tried to coerce me into changing my appearance.* ♦ **coercion** /kəʊɜːʃə^{0}n/ UNCOUNT N *No one was using coercion.*

coexist /kəʊɪ^{2}gzɪst/, **coexists, coexisting, coexisted.** RECIP VB If two or more things **coexist,** they exist at the same time or in the same place. *Large numbers of species coexist here... The forest peoples can coexist with the forest.* ♦ **coexistence** /kəʊɪ^{2}gzɪstəns/ UNCOUNT N *...the need for peaceful coexistence.*

coffee /kɒfi^1/, **coffees.** **1** MASS N **Coffee** is a hot brown drink made with boiling water and the roasted and ground seeds of a tropical tree. *...a cup of coffee... ...three coffees please.* **2** UNCOUNT N **Coffee** is also the roasted seeds or powder from which the drink is made.

coffee bar, coffee bars. COUNT N A **coffee bar** is a small café where drinks and snacks are sold.

coffee pot, coffee pots. COUNT N A **coffee pot** is a tall narrow jug in which coffee is made or served.

coffee table, coffee tables. COUNT N A **coffee table** is a small, low table in a living-room.

coffers /kɒfəz/. PLURAL N When people refer to the **coffers** of an organization, they are talking about its money. *...the flow of taxes into the government's coffers.*

coffin /kɒfɪn/, **coffins.** **1** COUNT N A **coffin** is a box in which a dead body is buried or cremated. **2** PHRASE If you say that one thing is a **nail in** another thing's **coffin,** you mean that it will help bring about its end or failure. *Credit cards are the first nails in the coffin of traditional financial methods.*

cog /kɒg/, **cogs.** COUNT N A **cog** is a wheel with teeth around the edge, used in a machine to turn another wheel or part.

cogent /kəʊdʒənt/. ADJ A **cogent** reason, argument, or example is strong and convincing; a formal use. *He put forward a cogent objection to our analysis.* ♦ **cogently** ADV *His opinions were always cogently expressed.*

cognac /kɒnjæk/, **cognacs.** MASS N **Cognac** is a kind of brandy.

cognitive /kɒgnɪtɪv/. ATTRIB ADJ **Cognitive** means relating to the mental process of learning; a technical use. *...a study of the cognitive functions in learning to read.*

cohabit /kəʊhæbɪt/, **cohabits, cohabiting, cohabited.** RECIP VB If two people **are cohabiting,** they are living together and have a sexual relationship, but are not married; a formal use. ♦ **cohabitation** UNCOUNT N *We were thinking of marriage, or at least cohabitation.*

coherent /kəʊhɪərənt/. **1** ADJ If something is **coherent,** it is clear and easy to understand. *They can offer no coherent answer... ...a coherent theory.* ♦ **coherence** /kəʊhɪərəns/ UNCOUNT N *The theory possesses a certain intellectual coherence.* **2** ADJ If someone is **coherent,** they are talking in a clear and calm way. *At last his sister was coherent enough to explain.* ♦ **coherently** ADV *Is she able to talk coherently now?*

cohesion /kəʊhiːʒə^{0}n/. UNCOUNT N **Cohesion** is a state in which all the parts of something fit together well and form a united whole. *We lack a sense of national purpose and social cohesion.*

cohesive /kəʊhiːsɪv/. ADJ Something that is **cohesive** consists of parts that fit together well and form a united whole. *The poor do not see themselves as a cohesive group.*

coil /kɔɪl/, **coils, coiling, coiled.** **1** COUNT N A **coil** of rope or wire is a length of it wound into a series of loops. **2** COUNT N A **coil** is a single loop that is one of a series into which something has been wound. *Pythons kill by tightening their coils so that their victim cannot breathe.* **3** ERG VB If something **coils,** or if you **coil** it up, it curves into a series of loops or into the shape of a ring. *Thick smoke coiled up over the fields... He coiled up the hose.* ♦ **coiled** ADJ *The base is made of coiled springs.*

coin /kɔɪn/, **coins, coining, coined.** **1** COUNT N A **coin** is a small piece of metal used as money. *...a 10p coin... ...notes and coins.* **2** VB WITH OBJ If you **coin** a word or a phrase, you invent it. *Schumacher coined the slogan 'Small is beautiful'.* **3** PHRASE If you say that two things are **two sides of the same coin,** you mean that they are two different aspects of the same situation.

coinage /kɔɪnɪdʒ/. UNCOUNT N **Coinage** consists of the coins used in a country. *...decimal coinage.*

coincide /kəʊɪnsaɪd/, **coincides, coinciding, coincided.** **1** RECIP VB If events **coincide,** they happen at the same time. *Macmillan's departure coincided with Benn's return... I'm afraid our holidays don't coincide this year.* **2** RECIP VB If the opinions or ideas of two or more people **coincide,** they are the same. *On the whole their views coincided... This coincided with my own private opinion.* **3** RECIP VB If two or more lines or points **coincide,** they are in exactly the same place. *The boundary of the L.E.A. coincides with a county boundary.*

coincidence /kəʊɪnsɪ^{3}dəns/, **coincidences.** COUNT N OR UNCOUNT N A **coincidence** happens when two or more things occur at the same time by chance. *It was quite a coincidence that my sister was on the same train... Is it coincidence that so many of these complaints are made by teachers?*

coincidental /kəʊɪnsɪdɛntə^{0}l/. ADJ Something that is **coincidental** is the result of a coincidence and has not been deliberately arranged. *Any similarity to real people is purely coincidental.* ♦ **coincidentally** /kəʊɪnsɪdɛntə^{0}li^1/ SENTENCE ADV *These players, coincidentally, are all left-handed.*

coke /kəʊk/, **cokes.** UNCOUNT N **Coke** is a solid black substance produced from coal and burned as fuel.

cold /kəʊld/, **colder, coldest; colds.** **1** ADJ Something that is **cold** has a low temperature. *Wash delicate fabrics in cold water... ...a cold winter's day... The building was cold and draughty.* **2** SING N The **cold** is cold weather or a low temperature. *My fingers are so stiff from the cold.* **3** PRED ADJ If you are **cold,** you feel that your body is at an unpleasantly low temperature. *Can I light the fire? I'm cold.* **4** ADJ A **cold** person does not show much emotion or affection. *She seemed cold and uncaring.* ♦ **coldly** ADV *'It's yours,' I said, politely, but coldly.* ♦ **coldness** UNCOUNT N *Kay was stunned by the coldness in his voice.* **5** COUNT N A **cold** is a mild, very common illness which makes you sneeze a lot and gives you a sore throat or a cough.

PHRASES ● If you **catch cold,** you become ill with a cold. ● If something **leaves** you **cold,** it fails to interest you. *Her performance left me cold.* ● If you **have** or **get cold feet** about something that you were intending to do, you are now frightened of doing it. ● **in cold blood:** see **blood.** ● **to make** your **blood run cold:** see **blood.**

cold-blooded. ADJ Someone who is **cold-blooded** shows no pity or emotion. *...a cold-blooded murderer.*

cold war. SING N The **cold war** is a state in which two countries are politically unfriendly towards each other, although they are not actually fighting.

colic /kɒlɪk/. UNCOUNT N If a baby has **colic,** it has pain in its stomach and bowels.

collaborate /kəlæbəreɪt/, **collaborates, collaborating, collaborated.** **1** VB When people **collaborate,** they work together on a particular project. *Antony and I are collaborating on a paper... The university hopes to collaborate with industry.* ♦ **collaboration** /kəlæbəreɪʃə^{0}n/ UNCOUNT N *...photographs published by Collins in collaboration with the War Museum.* ♦ **collaborator** /kəlæbəreɪtə/ COUNT N *My collaborator Roy Lewis and I did a series of articles for Radio 4.* **2** RECIP VB If someone **collaborates** with enemies, he or she helps them; used showing disapproval. *I believe he collaborated with the Nazis.* ♦ **collaborator** COUNT N *...violence against alleged collaborators.*

collaborative /kəlæbə^{0}rətɪv/. ATTRIB ADJ A **collaborative** piece of work is done by two or more people working together; a formal use. *The project is a collaborative one.*

collage /kə^{7}lɑːʒ, kɒlɑːʒ/, **collages.** COUNT N A **collage** is a picture made by sticking pieces of paper and cloth onto paper.

collapse /kəlæps/, **collapses, collapsing, collapsed.** **1** VB If something **collapses,** it suddenly falls down or falls inwards. If a person **collapses,** they suddenly fall down because they are ill or tired. *These flimsy houses are liable to collapse in a heavy storm... As we walked into the hotel, Jane collapsed.* Also UNCOUNT N *The collapse of buildings trapped thousands of people... Upon her collapse she was rushed to hospital.* **2** VB If a system or institution **collapses,** it fails completely and suddenly. *Their marriage had collapsed.* Also UNCOUNT N *...a company on the verge of collapse.*

collar /kɒlə/, **collars.** 1 COUNT N The **collar** of a shirt or coat is the part which fits round the neck and is usually folded over. 2 COUNT N A **collar** is also a leather band which is put round the neck of a dog or cat.

collarbone /kɒləbəun/, **collarbones.** COUNT N Your **collarbone** is one of the two long bones which run from the base of your neck to your shoulder.

collate /kə^{7}leɪt/, **collates, collating, collated.** VB WITH OBJ When you **collate** pieces of information, you gather them all together and examine them. *All the new evidence had been collated.*

collateral /kə^{6}lætərəl/. UNCOUNT N **Collateral** is money or property which is used as a guarantee that someone will repay a loan; a formal use. *They have nothing to offer as collateral.*

colleague /kɒli:g/, **colleagues.** COUNT N Your **colleagues** are the people you work with, especially in a professional job.

collect /kəlɛkt/, **collects, collecting, collected.** 1 VB WITH OBJ If you **collect** a number of things, or **collect** them up, you bring them together from several places. *They're collecting wood for the fire... They collected up their gear.* 2 VB WITH OBJ If you **collect** things as a hobby, you get a large number of them because you are interested in them. *Do you collect antiques?* ♦ **collecting** UNCOUNT N *...stamp collecting.* 3 VB WITH OBJ When you **collect** someone, you go and fetch them from somewhere. *I have to collect the children from school.* 4 VB WITH ADJUNCT When things **collect** somewhere, they gather there over a period of time. *Damp leaves collect in gutters.* 5 VB WITH ADJUNCT If you **collect** for a charity or for a present, you ask people to give you money for it. *How much have you collected so far?* 6 REFL VB OR VB WITH OBJ If you **collect** yourself or **collect** your thoughts, you make an effort to calm or prepare yourself. *I had five minutes in which to collect my thoughts before the interview.*

collected /kəlɛktɪ^{2}d/. ADJ Someone's **collected** works are all their works published together. *...the collected works of Proust.*

collection /kəlɛkʃə^{0}n/, **collections.** 1 COUNT N A **collection** of things is a group of similar or related things. *Davis had a large collection of pop records... ...a collection of Scott Fitzgerald's short stories.* 2 UNCOUNT N **Collection** is the act of collecting something from a place or from people. *...the collection of national taxes... Your curtains are ready for collection.* 3 COUNT N A **collection** is also the organized collecting of money from people for charity, or the amount of money that is collected. *They organized dances and collections which raised £450.*

collective /kəlɛktɪv/. ATTRIB ADJ **Collective** means shared by or involving every member of a group of people. *It was a collective decision.* ♦ **collectively** ADV *They were collectively responsible.*

collector /kəlɛktə/, **collectors.** 1 COUNT N WITH SUPP A **collector** is a person who collects things as a hobby. *...an art collector.* 2 COUNT N WITH SUPP A **collector** is also someone whose job is to take something such as money or tickets from people. For example, a rent **collector** collects rent from tenants.

college /kɒlɪdʒ/, **colleges.** 1 COUNT N OR UNCOUNT N A **college** is an institution where students study after they have left school. *...the local technical college... What do you plan to do after college?* 2 COUNT N A **college** in a university is one of the institutions which some British universities are divided into. *...Jesus College, Cambridge.*

collide /kəlaɪd/, **collides, colliding, collided.** RECIP VB If people or vehicles **collide,** they bump into each other. *The two vehicles collided... He almost collided with me when I stopped.*

collie /kɒli^{1}/, **collies.** COUNT N A **collie** is a kind of dog, often used for controlling sheep.

colliery /kɒljəri^{1}/, **collieries.** COUNT N A **colliery** is a coal mine; a British use.

collision /kəlɪʒə^{0}n/, **collisions.** 1 COUNT N OR UNCOUNT N A **collision** occurs when a moving object hits something. *...a mid-air collision... Henry and a window came into chance collision.* 2 COUNT N OR UNCOUNT N A **collision** of cultures or ideas occurs when two very different cultures or people meet and conflict. *...a collision of egos... ...the collision of private and public interests.*

colloquial /kələukwɪəl/. ADJ **Colloquial** words and phrases are informal and are used in conversation. *...a course in colloquial Greek.* ♦ **colloquially** ADV *This game is colloquially known as 'Buzz off, Buster'.*

collude /kə^{7}lu:d/, **colludes, colluding, colluded.** RECIP VB To **collude** with someone means to co-operate with them secretly; used showing disapproval. *Some groups have colluded with the unions in avoiding a ballot.* ♦ **collusion** /kə^{7}lu:ʒə^{0}n/ UNCOUNT N *She was in collusion with him for financial reasons.*

cologne /kələun/. UNCOUNT N **Cologne** is a kind of weak perfume.

colon /kəulə^{7}n/, **colons.** 1 COUNT N A **colon** is the punctuation mark (:). 2 COUNT N Your **colon** is the part of your intestine above your rectum.

colonel /kɜ:nə^{0}l/, **colonels.** COUNT N OR TITLE A **colonel** is an army officer of fairly high rank.

colonial /kələunɪəl/. ATTRIB ADJ **Colonial** means relating to countries that are colonies, or to colonialism. *...the liberation of oppressed peoples from colonial rule.*

colonialism /kələunɪəlɪzə^{0}m/. UNCOUNT N **Colonialism** is the practice by which a powerful country directly controls less powerful countries. *The politics of the Third World had their origins in colonialism.*

colonist /kɒlə^{7}nɪst/, **colonists.** COUNT N A **colonist** is someone who starts a colony. *...the Australian colonists.*

colonize /kɒlə^{7}naɪz/, **colonizes, colonizing, colonized;** also spelled **colonise.** VB WITH OBJ When large numbers of people or animals **colonize** a place, they go to live there and make it their home. *...the Europeans who colonized North America... The plains were colonised by ant-eaters and other species.*

colony /kɒlə^{7}ni^{1}/, **colonies.** 1 COUNT N A **colony** is a country which is controlled by a more powerful country. *...the formation of the Gold Coast as a colony.* 2 COUNT N A **colony** is also a group of people or animals of a particular sort living together. *...a leper colony.*

color /kʌlə/. See **colour.**

colossal /kəlɒsə^{0}l/. ADJ Something that is **colossal** is very large. *...colossal sums of money.*

colour /kʌlə/, **colours, colouring, coloured;** spelled **color** in American English. 1 COUNT N OR UNCOUNT N The **colour** of something is the appearance that it has as a result of reflecting light. Red, blue, and green are colours. *All the rooms were painted different colours... His face was greyish in colour.* ♦ **coloured** ADJ *The sky was mauve-coloured.* 2 UNCOUNT N Someone's **colour** is the normal colour of their skin. *It was illegal to discriminate on the grounds of colour.* 3 ATTRIB ADJ A **colour** television, film, or photograph is one that shows things in all their colours, and not just in black and white. *...marvellous colour illustrations.* ♦ **coloured** ADJ *...in coloured chalks.* 4 UNCOUNT N **Colour** is also a quality that makes something interesting or exciting. *The audiences liked the romance and colour of 'The Lady's Not for Burning'.* 5 VB WITH OBJ If something **colours** your opinion, it affects your opinion. *Anger had coloured her judgement.* 6 PHRASE If you achieve something **with flying colours,** you achieve it in an extremely successful way.

colour blind. ADJ Someone who is **colour blind** cannot distinguish clearly between some colours.

coloured /kʌləd/; spelled **colored** in American English. ADJ A person who is **coloured** belongs to a race of people who do not have white or pale skins.

colourful /kʌləful/; spelled **colorful** in American English. 1 ADJ Something that is **colourful** has bright colours. *...colourful posters of Paris and Venice.* 2 ADJ **Colourful** also means interesting and exciting. *Many colourful stories were told about him.*

colouring /kʌlərɪŋ/, **colourings;** spelled **coloring** in American English. 1 UNCOUNT N The **colouring** of something is the colours that it has. *...its rounded fins and distinctive green colouring.* 2 SING N WITH POSS Someone's **colouring** is the colour of their hair, skin, and eyes. 3 MASS N **Colouring** is a substance that is used to give colour to food.

colourless /kʌləlɪ^{2}s/; spelled **colorless** in American English. 1 ADJ Something that is **colourless** is dull and uninteresting. *He spoke in the same colourless, plodding voice.* 2 ADJ **Colourless** things have no colour at all. *...a colourless and tasteless liquid.*

colt /kɒlt/, **colts.** COUNT N A **colt** is a young male horse.

column /kɒləm/, **columns.** 1 COUNT N A **column** is a tall solid cylinder, especially one supporting part of a building. 2 COUNT N A **column** is also something that has a tall narrow shape. *...columns of smoke.* 3 COUNT N A **column** of people or animals is a group of them moving in a line. *Behind the brass band came a column of workers.* 4 COUNT N In a newspaper or magazine, a **column** is a vertical section of writing, or a regular section written by the same person. *Bill used to write a column for the Bristol Evening News.*

columnist /kɒləmn^{0}ɪst/, **columnists.** COUNT N A **columnist** is a journalist who writes a regular article in a newspaper or magazine. *...gossip columnists.*

coma /kəumə/, **comas.** COUNT N If someone is in a **coma,** they are deeply unconscious.

comb /kəum/, **combs, combing, combed.** 1 COUNT N A **comb** is a flat piece of plastic or metal with long thin pointed parts, which you use to tidy your hair. 2 VB WITH OBJ When you **comb** your hair, you tidy it using a comb. *They could see Mr Baker busily combing his hair.* 3 VB WITH OBJ If you **comb** a place for something, you search thoroughly for it. *It might amuse her to comb the town for antiques.*

combat, combats, combating, combated; pronounced /kɒmbæt/ when it is a noun, and /kə^{7}mbæt/ when it is a verb. 1 UNCOUNT N OR COUNT N **Combat** is fighting that takes place in a war; a formal use. *He was awarded the Military Cross for gallantry in combat... ...the mighty combats between the West and the East.* 2 VB WITH OBJ If people in authority **combat** something, they try to stop it happening. *The basic problem is that of combating poverty.*

combatant /kɒmbətə^{0}nt, kʌm-/, **combatants.** COUNT N A **combatant** is someone who takes part in a fight or a war.

combination /kɒmbɪneɪʃə^{0}n/, **combinations.** 1 COUNT N A **combination** is a mixture of things. *All actors use a combination of these techniques.* 2 COUNT N The **combination** of a lock is the series of letters or numbers used to open it. *I can't remember the combination... ...a combination lock.*

combine, combines, combining, combined; pronounced /kə^{7}mbaɪn/ when it is a verb, and /kɒmbaɪn/ when it is a noun. 1 RECIP VB If you **combine** two or more things or if they **combine,** they exist or join together. *We would all prefer to combine liberty with order... Later the two teams were combined.* ♦ **combined** ATTRIB ADJ *The combined efforts of police and military were at last successful.* 2 COUNT N A **combine** is a group of people or organizations that are working together. *...a newspaper combine.* 3 RECIP VB If someone or something **combines** two qualities or features, they have both of them. *Carbon fibre combines flexibility with immense strength... Morality and national pride combine in his public statements.* ♦ **combined** ADJ *...a perfect example of professional expertise combined with personal charm... His eyes were wide with amazement and adoration combined.* 4 RECIP VB If someone **combines** two activities, they do them both at the same time. *It's difficult to combine family life with a career... One person combines the work of both District Nurse and Health Visitor.*

combustion /kəmbʌstʃə^{0}n/. UNCOUNT N **Combustion** is the act of burning something or the process of burning; a formal use. *...the combustion of fossil fuels.*

come /kʌm/, **comes, coming, came** /keɪm/. **Come** is used in the present tense and is the past participle. 1 VB You use **come** to say that someone or something arrives somewhere, or moves towards you. *She looked up when they came into the room... She eventually came to the town of Pickering.* 2 VB WITH ADJUNCT If something **comes** to a particular point, it reaches it. *Her hair came right down to her waist... Mum doesn't even come up to my shoulder.* 3 VB WITH ADJUNCT You use **come** in expressions which state what happens to someone or something. *It just came apart in my hands... They had come to power ten years earlier... Ordinary sticky tape comes unstuck.* 4 VB WITH TO-INF If someone **comes** to do something, they gradually start to do it. *I have come to like him quite a lot.* 5 VB When a particular time or event **comes,** it arrives or happens. *The time has come for a full campaign against the government's spending cuts.* 6 PHRASE You say **'Come to think of it'** to indicate that you have suddenly realized something. *Come to think of it, why should I apologize?* 7 VB WITH 'from' OR 'out of' If someone or something **comes** from a particular place or thing, that is their source or starting point. *'Where do you come from?'—'India.'... Information coming out of the country was unreliable... Did you know the word 'idea' comes from Greek?* 8 VB WITH 'from' OR 'of' Something that **comes** from something else is the result of it. *...the warm glow that comes from working co-operatively... I'll let you know what comes of the meeting.* 9 VB WITH COMPLEMENT If someone or something **comes** first, next, or last, they are first, next, or last in a series, list, or competition. *What comes next then?... I was never in any race in which I didn't come last.* 10 VB WITH ADJUNCT If a product **comes** in a particular range of colours, styles, or sizes, it is available in any of those colours, styles, or sizes. *The van came in two colours, medium brown or medium grey.* 11 See also **coming.**

come about. PHR VB The way that something **comes about** is how it happens. *The discovery of adrenalin came about through a mistake.*

come across. PHR VB 1 If you **come across** or **come upon** someone or something, you meet or find them by chance. *I came across a letter from Brunel the other day... They rounded a turn and came upon a family of lions.* 2 The way that someone **comes across** is the impression they make on other people. *He wasn't coming across as the idiot I had expected him to be.* 3 When an idea or meaning **comes across,** you understand exactly what is meant by it. *Do you think this idea comes across in the play?*

come along. PHR VB When something **comes along,** it arrives or happens, perhaps by chance. *A new generation of planners came along who were much more scientifically based.* ● See also **come on 1, 3.**

come at. PHR VB If a person or animal **comes at** you or **comes for** you, they move towards you in a threatening way. *The bear came at me... Jake was coming for me with a knife.*

come back. PHR VB 1 If you **come back** to a topic or point, you return to it. *We'll come back to that question a little later.* 2 If something that you had forgotten **comes back** to you, you remember it. 3 When something **comes back,** it becomes fashionable again. *She was pleased to see that mini skirts were coming back.* 4 See also **comeback.**

come by. PHR VB To **come by** something means to find or obtain it. *He had not come by these things through his own labour... Jobs were hard to come by.*

come down. PHR VB 1 If the cost, level, or amount of something **comes down,** it becomes less than it was before. *Inflation is starting to come down.* 2 If a structure such as a building or a tree **comes down,** it falls to the ground. *In the storm a tree came down.*

come down on. PHR VB To **come down on** someone means to criticize them. *Social workers like me come down harder on parents than on their children.*

come down to. PHR VB If a problem or decision **comes down to** a particular thing, that thing is the most important factor involved. *Your final choice of kitchen may well come down to cost.*

come down with. PHR VB If you **come down with** an illness, you get it. *She came down with pneumonia.*

come for. PHR VB See **come at.**

come forward. PHR VB If someone **comes forward,** they offer to do something. *More coloured men are now coming forward to join the police.*

come in. PHR VB 1 If information or a report **comes in,** you receive it. *Reports are coming in from Mexico of a major earthquake.* 2 If you have money **coming in,** you receive it regularly as your income. 3 If someone **comes in** on a discussion or an arrangement, they join in. *He should come in on the deal.* 4 If someone or something **comes in** or **comes into** a situation, it is involved in it. *Where does your husband come in?... Prestige comes into it as much as other factors.*

come in for. PHR VB If someone or something **comes in for** criticism or blame, they receive it.

come into. PHR VB 1 If someone **comes into** money or property, they inherit it. *She was going to come into some more money on her mother's death.* 2 See also **come in 4.**

come off. PHR VB If something **comes off,** it is successful or effective. *Sotheby's publicity stunt came off brilliantly.*

come on. PHR VB 1 You say **'Come on'** or **'Come along'** to someone to encourage them to do something or to make them hurry up. *Come on, Wendy, you say something... Come along, now, drink this.* 2 If you have got a cold or a headache **coming on,** it is just starting. *I felt a cold coming on.* 3 If something **is coming on** or **coming along,** it is developing or making progress. *My new book is coming on quite well.* 4 When a machine or appliance **comes on,** it starts working. *The lights came on.*

come on to. PHR VB When you **come on to** a particular topic, you start discussing it. *I want to come on to the question of disease in a minute.*

come out. PHR VB 1 If information **comes out,** it is revealed or made public. *All the facts came out after Seery's death.* 2 When something such as a book **comes out,** it is published or becomes available to the public. *She asked me to send her any new stamps which might come out.* 3 To **come out** in a particular way means to be in the position or state described at the end of a process or event. *Who do you think will come out on top?... The press was coming out of the affair very badly.* 4 If you **come out** for something, you declare that you support it. *He came out in support of the claim.* 5 If a photograph **comes out,** it is developed successfully. 6 When the sun, moon, or stars **come out,** they appear in the sky.

come out in. PHR VB If you **come out in** spots, you become covered with them.

come over. PHR VB 1 If a feeling **comes over** you, it affects you. *She wondered what could have come over him all of a sudden.* 2 When someone **comes over,** they call at your house for a short time. *You can come over tomorrow at four.*

come round. PHR VB 1 If you **come round** to an idea, you eventually change your mind and accept it. *He knew I would have to come round to his way of thinking in the end.* 2 When something **comes round,** it happens as a regular or predictable event. *Don't wait for April to come round before planning your vegetable garden.* 3 When someone who is unconscious **comes round** or **comes to,** they become conscious again. *That's about all I remember, until I came to in a life-raft.*

come through. PHR VB 1 If you **come through** a dangerous or difficult situation, you survive it. *Most of the troops came through the fighting unharmed.* 2 If something **comes through,** you receive it. *Has my visa come through yet?* 3 If a quality or impression **comes through,** you perceive it. *I think the teacher's own personality has got to come through.*

come to. PHR VB 1 If a thought or idea **comes to** you, you suddenly realize it. *The answer came to him just before noon... It came to me suddenly that what was wrong was that I was tired.* 2 If something such as a sum **comes to** a particular number or amount, it adds up to it. *My income now comes to £65 a week.* 3 See **come round 3.**

come under. PHR VB 1 If something **comes under** a particular authority, it is managed by that authority. *Day Nurseries come under the Department of Health and Social Security.* 2 If you **come under** criticism or attack, you are criticized or attacked. *British produce came under pressure from foreign competition.* 3 If something **comes under** a particular heading, it is in the category mentioned. *Records and tapes come under published material.*

come up. PHR VB 1 If a topic **comes up** in a conversation or meeting, or if you **come up with** it, it is mentioned or discussed. *His name came up at a buffet lunch... I hope to come up with some of the answers.* 2 If an event **is coming up,** it is about to happen or take place. *There's a royal wedding coming up.* 3 If something **comes up,** it happens unexpectedly. *I can't see you tonight. Something's come up.* 4 When someone **comes up** for election, it is time for them to take part in an election again. *A third of my colleagues will come up for election next May.* 5 When a matter or policy **comes up** for review, it is time to discuss it again. *The pension scheme has come up for review.* 6 When the sun or moon **comes up,** it rises. *The sun comes up in the East.*

come up against. PHR VB If you **come up against** a problem or difficulty, you have to deal with it. *Everyone comes up against discrimination sooner or later.*

come upon. PHR VB See **come across 1.**

come up to. PHR VB To **be coming up to** a time or state means to be getting near to it. *Some of them are coming up to retirement... It was just coming up to ten o'clock.*

comeback /kʌmbæk/, **comebacks.** COUNT N If something or someone makes a **comeback,** they become popular or successful again. *Wigs and elaborate hairstyles made a comeback.*

comedian /kəmiːdɪən/, **comedians.** COUNT N A **comedian** is an entertainer whose job is to make people laugh by telling jokes.

comedy /kɒmə^{0}di^1/, **comedies.** 1 COUNT N A **comedy** is an amusing play or film. *...a revival of Maugham's comedy Caroline.* 2 UNCOUNT N You can refer to amusing things in a play or film as **comedy.** *The play had plenty of excitement as well as comedy... ...her rare gift for comedy on the stage.*

comet /kɒmɪ^{2}t/, **comets.** COUNT N A **comet** is an object that travels around the sun leaving a bright trail behind it.

comfort /kʌmfət/, **comforts, comforting, comforted.** 1 UNCOUNT N **Comfort** is the state of being physically or mentally relaxed. *She longed to stretch out in comfort... ...a hard narrow chair not made for comfort... I found comfort in his words.* 2 UNCOUNT N You can refer to a pleasant style of life in which you have everything you need as **comfort.** *She wanted a life of reasonable comfort.* 3 COUNT N **Comforts** are things that make your life more pleasant or help you stop worrying. *It will be a comfort to know that you are standing by... I longed for the comforts of home.* 4 VB WITH OBJ To **comfort** someone means to make them feel less worried or unhappy. *Jeannie came to comfort him.* ♦ **comforting** ADJ *It's a comforting thought that we have a few days before it starts.*

comfortable /kʌmfə^{0}təbə^{0}l/. 1 ADJ Something that is **comfortable** makes you feel physically relaxed. *That chair is quite comfortable.* 2 ADJ If you are **comfortable,** you are physically relaxed and at ease, and not worried, afraid, or embarrassed. *He did not feel comfortable with strangers.* ♦ **comfortably** ADV *They were too cold to sleep comfortably.* 3 PRED ADJ When an ill or injured person is said to be **comfortable,** they are in a stable physical condition and are not getting worse. 4 ADJ A **comfortable** job or task is one which you can do without difficulty. *It's a comfortable two hours' walk from here.* ♦ **comfortably** ADV *I can manage the work comfortably.*

comic /kɒmɪk/, **comics.** 1 ADJ Something that is **comic** or **comical** makes you want to laugh. *...a story rich in comic and dramatic detail... There is something slightly comical about him.* 2 COUNT N A **comic** is a person who tells jokes to make people laugh. *When the comic comes on they'll all laugh.* 3 COUNT N A **comic** is also a magazine that contains stories told in pictures; a British use.

coming /kʌmɪŋ/. ATTRIB ADJ A **coming** event or time will happen soon. *The real struggle will take place in the coming weeks.*

comma /kɒmə/, **commas.** COUNT N A **comma** is the punctuation mark (,).

command /kəmɑːnd/, **commands, commanding, commanded.** 1 VB WITH OBJ If you **command** someone to do something, you order them to do it. *'Stay here!' he commanded... She commanded me to lie down and relax.* Also COUNT N *They waited for their master's command.* 2 VB WITH OBJ If you **command** something, you order it. *The king had commanded his presence at court.* 3 VB WITH OBJ If you **command** something such as obedience or attention, you obtain it as a result of being popular or important. *She was no longer in a position to command obedience or admiration.* 4 VB WITH OBJ An officer who **commands** part of an army, navy, or air force is in charge of it. *He commanded a regiment of cavalry in Algiers.* Also UNCOUNT N *He had been in command of HMS Churchill for a year.* 5 UNCOUNT N **Command** is control over a particular situation. *Lady Sackville took command... He was looking more relaxed and in command than ever before.* 6 UNCOUNT N Your **command** of something is your knowledge of it and ability to use it. *...a good command of spoken English.*

commandant /kɒməndænt/, **commandants.** COUNT N A **commandant** is an army officer in charge of a particular place or group of people.

commandeer /kɒməndɪə/, **commandeers, commandeering, commandeered.** VB WITH OBJ If the army **commandeer** a building or vehicle, they take it officially in order to use it.

commander /kəmɑːndə/, **commanders.** COUNT N A **commander** is an officer in charge of a military operation.

commanding /kəmɑːndɪŋ/. 1 ATTRIB ADJ If you are in a **commanding** position, you are able to control people and events. *Britain had lost her commanding position in the world.* 2 ADJ If you have a **commanding** voice or manner, you seem powerful and confident. 3 ATTRIB ADJ A building that has a **commanding** position is high up with good views of the surrounding area. *The University stands in a commanding position overlooking the bay.*

commandment /kəmɑːndmə^{2}nt/, **commandments.** COUNT N The Ten **Commandments** are the rules of behaviour which, according to the Old Testament of the Bible, people should obey.

commando /kəmɑːndəʊ/, **commandos.** COUNT N **Commandos** are specially trained soldiers.

commemorate /kəmeməreɪt/, **commemorates, commemorating, commemorated.** 1 VB WITH OBJ An object that **commemorates** a person or an event is intended to remind people of that person or event. *...a monument commemorating a great soldier.* 2 VB WITH OBJ If you **commemorate** an event, you do something special to show that you remember it. *...a Jewish holiday commemorating the destruction of the Temple.*

commence /kəmens/, **commences, commencing, commenced.** VB WITH OR WITHOUT OBJ To **commence** means to begin; a formal use. *He had been in prison for nine months when his trial commenced... Laurie commenced running in his late twenties... I commenced a round of visits... The officer commenced duty earlier than usual.* ♦ **commencement** /kəmensmə^{2}nt/ UNCOUNT N *...the commencement of the present century.*

commend /kəmend/; **commends, commending, commended;** a formal word. 1 VB WITH OBJ If you **commend** someone or something, you praise them formally to other people. *I was commended for my reports... Rothermere commended Baldwin to his readers as a great man.* ♦ **commendation** /kɒmendeɪʃə^{0}n/ UNCOUNT N OR COUNT N *His action earned the personal commendation of the prime minister... ...a degree of duty and devotion which deserves commendation.* 2 REFL VB WITH PREP 'to' If something **commends** itself to you, you approve of it. *The defence would scarcely commend itself even to other lawyers.*

commendable /kəmendəbə^{0}l/. ADJ **Commendable** behaviour is admired and praised. *The committee acted with commendable fairness.*

commensurate /kəmensərə^{1}t, -ʃə-/. PRED ADJ WITH 'with' If one amount is **commensurate** with another, it is in proportion to the second amount; a formal use. *...action commensurate with the gravity of what has happened.*

comment /kɒmɛnt/, **comments, commenting, commented. 1** VB OR REPORT VB If you **comment** on something, you give your opinion of it. *Both girls commented on Chris's size... 'It needs washing,' she commented... Someone commented that Brian changes his mind every day.* **2** COUNT N OR UNCOUNT N A **comment** is a statement which expresses your opinion of something. *People in the town started making rude comments... He was not available for comment yesterday.* CONVENTION People say **'no comment'** as a way of refusing to answer a question during an interview. *'Do you intend to keep them in prison?'—'No comment.'*

commentary /kɒməntə^{0}ri^1/, **commentaries. 1** COUNT N A **commentary** is a description of an event that is broadcast on radio or television while the event is taking place. *We were gathered round a radio to hear the commentary.* **2** COUNT N OR UNCOUNT N A **commentary** is also a book or article which explains or discusses something. *...political commentaries... The programme linked commentary from the BBC correspondent with first-hand accounts.*

commentator /kɒmənteɪtə/, **commentators. 1** COUNT N A **commentator** is a broadcaster who gives a commentary on an event. **2** COUNT N A **commentator** is also someone who often writes or broadcasts about a particular subject. *...Peter Jenkins, an experienced commentator on political affairs.*

commerce /kɒmɜ:s/. UNCOUNT N **Commerce** is the activity of buying and selling things on a large scale.

commercial /kəmɜ:ʃə^{0}l/, **commercials. 1** ATTRIB ADJ **Commercial** means relating to commerce and business. *...commercial and industrial organisations.* **2** ATTRIB ADJ A **commercial** activity involves producing goods to make a profit. *...commercial agriculture... ...a big commercial bakery.* ♦ **commercially** ADV *Slate was quarried commercially here.* **3** ATTRIB ADJ **Commercial** television and radio are paid for by the broadcasting of advertisements between programmes. **4** COUNT N A **commercial** is an advertisement broadcast on television or radio.

commercialized /kəmɜ:ʃəlaɪzd/; also spelled **commercialised.** ADJ If something such as an activity is **commercialized,** people use it as an opportunity for making money rather than for any other purpose. *The ceremonies have degenerated into vulgar, commercialized spectacles.*

commiserate /kəmɪzəreɪt/, **commiserates, commiserating, commiserated.** VB If you **commiserate** with someone, you show pity or sympathy for them; a formal use. *I commiserated with him over the recent news.* ♦ **commiseration** /kəmɪzəreɪʃə^{0}n/ UNCOUNT N *...a look of commiseration.*

commission /kəmɪʃə^{0}n/, **commissions, commissioning, commissioned. 1** VB WITH OBJ If you **commission** a piece of work, you formally arrange to pay for someone to do it for you. *The Times commissioned a Public Opinion Poll... I was immediately commissioned to write another book.* Also COUNT N *Red House was Webb's first commission as an architect.* **2** UNCOUNT N OR COUNT N **Commission** is a sum of money paid to a person selling goods for every sale that he or she makes. *They get commission on top of their basic salary.* **3** COLL N A **commission** is also a group of people appointed to find out about something or to control something. *A commission was appointed to investigate the assassination of the President.*

commissionaire /kəmɪʃənɛə/, **commissionaires.** COUNT N A **commissionaire** is a person employed by a hotel, theatre, or cinema to open doors and help customers.

commissioner /kəmɪʃə^{0}nə/, **commissioners.** COUNT N A **commissioner** is an important official in an organization. *...the Church Commissioners.*

commit /kəmɪt/, **commits, committing, committed. 1** VB WITH OBJ If someone **commits** a crime or a sin, they do it. *He has committed a criminal offence... Margaret had no intention of committing suicide.* **2** VB WITH OBJ To **commit** money or resources to something means to use them for a particular purpose. *Rolls Royce must commit its entire resources to the project.* **3** REFL VB If you **commit** yourself to a course of action, you definitely decide that you will do it. *I really wouldn't like to commit myself.* **4** VB WITH OBJ If someone **is committed** to a hospital or prison, they are officially sent there. *She was committed to a mental hospital.* **5** PHRASE If you **commit** something **to memory,** you memorize it.

commitment /kəmɪtmə^{2}nt/, **commitments. 1** UNCOUNT N **Commitment** is a strong belief in an idea or system. *There is no doubting his enthusiasm or his commitment.* **2** COUNT N A **commitment** is a regular task which takes up some of your time. *She's got family commitments.* **3** COUNT N If you give a **commitment** to something, you promise faithfully that you will do it; a formal use. *He gave a clear commitment to reopen disarmament talks.*

committal /kəmɪtə^{0}l/. UNCOUNT N **Committal** is the process of officially sending someone to prison or to hospital. *Mr Chung sought to delay the committal on two grounds.*

committee /kəmɪti^1/, **committees.** COLL N A **committee** is a group of people who represent a larger group or organization and make decisions for them.

commodity /kəmɒdɪti^1/, **commodities.** COUNT N A **commodity** is something that is sold for money; a formal use. *He dealt in all domestic commodities—clothes, hardware, and furniture.*

common /kɒmən/, **commoner, commonest; commons. 1** ADJ If something is **common,** it is found in large numbers or it happens often. *Durand is a common name there... It was quite common for dogs to be poisoned this way.* ♦ **commonly** ADV *The most commonly used argument is that clients do not like long delays.* **2** ADJ If something is **common** to several people, it is possessed, done, or used by them all. *We shared a common language... It suppressed the desire for freedom common to all people.* **3** ATTRIB ADJ **Common** is also used to indicate that something is ordinary and not special. *Sodium chloride is better known as common salt.* **4** ADJ A **common** person behaves in a way that shows lack of taste, education, and good manners. **5** COUNT N A **common** is a public area of grassy land near a village.

PHRASES ● Something that is done **for the common good** is done for the benefit of everyone. ● **Common ground** is something which several people agree about. *There is no common ground upon which dialogue can be based.* ● If two or more things have something **in common,** they have the same characteristics or features. *In common with many other companies, we advertise in the local press.*

commoner /kɒmənə/, **commoners.** COUNT N A **commoner** is a person who is not a member of the nobility.

common-law. ATTRIB ADJ A **common-law** relationship is regarded as a marriage because it has lasted a long time, although no official marriage contract has been signed. *...common-law marriage... ...his common-law wife.*

commonplace /kɒmənpleɪs/. ADJ Something that is **commonplace** happens often. *Air travel has now become commonplace.*

common room, common rooms. COUNT N A **common room** is a room in a university or school where people can sit, talk, and relax.

common sense. UNCOUNT N **Common sense** is the natural ability to make good judgements and behave sensibly. *Use your common sense.* Also ATTRIB ADJ *...a few common-sense steps to help the situation.*

Commonwealth /kɒmənwɛlθ/. PROPER N The **Commonwealth** is an association of countries that used to belong to the British Empire.

commotion /kəməʊʃə^{0}n/. SING N OR UNCOUNT N A **commotion** is a lot of noise and confusion. *Suddenly there was a commotion at the other end of the bar... We reached home, where there was much commotion.*

communal /kɒmjə^{4}nə^{0}l/. ADJ Something that is **communal** is shared by a group of people. *...a communal dining-room... ...a communal style of life.* ♦ **communally** ADV *The mills are owned communally.*

commune /kɒmju:n/, **communes.** COLL N A **commune** is a group of people who live together and share everything.

communicate /kəmju:nɪkeɪt/, **communicates, communicating, communicated. 1** RECIP VB OR REPORT VB If you **communicate** with someone, you give them information, for example, by speaking, writing, or sending radio signals. *He communicates with Miami by radio... Anthony and I hadn't communicated for years... Through signs she communicated that she wanted a drink.* **2** VB WITH OBJ If you **communicate** an idea or a feeling to someone, you make them aware of it. *...the failure of intellectuals to communicate their ideas to a wider audience.* **3** RECIP VB If people can **communicate,** they understand each other's feelings or attitudes. *Cliff talked to me a few times but we couldn't really communicate... ...his tough background and ability to communicate.*

communication /kəmju:nɪkeɪʃə^{0}n/, **communications. 1** UNCOUNT N **Communication** is the activity or process of giving information to other people or living things. *Insects such as ants have a highly effective system of communication.* **2** PLURAL N **Communications** are the systems and processes that are used to communicate or broadcast information. *...large numbers of communications satellites.* **3** COUNT N A **communication** is a letter or telephone call; a formal use. *...a secret communication from the Foreign Minister.*

communicative /kəmju:nɪkətɪv/. ADJ Someone who is **communicative** is able to talk to people easily. *He was as friendly and communicative as taxi-drivers commonly are.*

communion /kəmju:njən/. UNCOUNT N **Communion** is also the Christian ceremony in which people eat bread and drink wine as a symbol of Christ's death and resurrection.

communiqué /kəmju:nɪkeɪ/, **communiqués.** COUNT N A **communiqué** is an official statement. *On his desk were a dozen communiqués from various government departments.*

communism /kɒmjə^{4}nɪzə^{0}m/. UNCOUNT N **Communism** is the political belief that the state should control the means of producing everything, and that there should be no private property. ♦ **communist** /kɒmjə^{4}nɪst/ COUNT N OR MOD *...a young communist from Cleveland, Ohio... ...national communist factions.*

community /kəmju:nɪ^{1}ti^1/, **communities.** COLL N A **community** is a group of people who live in a particular area or are alike in some way. *Members are drawn from all sections of the local community.*

commute /kəmju:t/, **commutes, commuting, commuted.** VB If you **commute,** you travel a long distance every day between your home and your place of work. ♦ **commuter** /kəmju:tə/ COUNT N *...a crowd of commuters on the London Underground.*

compact, compacts, compacting, compacted; pronounced /kɒmpækt/ or /kə^{7}mpækt/ when it is an adjective, and /kə^{7}mpækt/ when it is a verb. **1** ADJ Something that is **compact** takes up very little space. *The kitchen was small, compact, and immaculately clean... ...smaller, more compact computers.* **2** VB WITH OBJ To **compact** something means to press it so that it becomes more dense; a formal use. *The tractor wheels compact the soil to a damaging extent.*

compact disc /kɒmpækt dɪsk/, **compact discs.** COUNT N **Compact discs** are played on special machines which use lasers to read their signals and convert the signals into sound of a very high quality. 'Compact disc' is often abbreviated to 'CD'.

companion /kə^{7}mpænjən/, **companions.** COUNT N A **companion** is someone who you spend time with or travel with.

companionable /kəmpænjənəbə^{0}l/. ADJ A person who is **companionable** is friendly and pleasant.

companionship /kəmpænjənʃɪp/. UNCOUNT N **Companionship** is the state of being with someone you know and like, rather than being on your own. *She missed her mother's companionship and love.*

company /kʌmpəni^1/, **companies. 1** COLL N A **company** is a business organization that makes money by selling goods or services. **2** COLL N A theatre or dance **company** is a group of performers who work together. *...the Royal Shakespeare Company.* **3** UNCOUNT N **Company** is the state of having someone with you, rather than being on your own. *Are you expecting company?... She preferred his company to that of most people.* **4** PHRASE If you **keep** someone **company,** you spend time with them and stop them feeling lonely or bored.

comparable /kɒmpərəbə^{0}l/. ADJ If two or more things are **comparable,** they are as good as each other, or similar in size, or quality. *The sums of money involved were not, of course, comparable... They have much lower fuel consumption than comparable petrol-engined cars.* ♦ **comparability** /kɒmpərəbɪlɪti^1/ UNCOUNT N *There are problems over the comparability of data.*

comparative /kə^{7}mpærə^{1}tɪv/, **comparatives. 1** ATTRIB ADJ You add **comparative** to indicate that something is true only when compared to what is normal. *He hoped they could spend the night in comparative safety.* ♦ **comparatively** SUBMOD *There was comparatively little pressure for change.* **2** ATTRIB ADJ A **comparative** study involves the comparison of similar things. *...a comparative study of Indian and Western food.* **3** ADJ OR COUNT N In grammar, the **comparative** form of an adjective or adverb is the form, usually ending in '-er', which indicates that something is greater in quality, size, or amount than the average or than previously.

compare /kə^{7}mpɛə/, **compares, comparing, compared. 1** RECIP VB When you **compare** things, you consider them and discover their differences or similarities. *It's interesting to compare the two prospectuses... ...studies comparing Russian children with those in Britain... The fee is low, compared with that at many other independent schools.* **2** VB WITH OBJ AND PREP 'to' If you **compare** one person or thing to another, you say that they are similar. *As an essayist he is compared frequently to Paine and Hazlitt.*

comparison /kə^{7}mpærɪsən/, **comparisons.** COUNT N OR UNCOUNT N When you make a **comparison,** you consider two or more things and discover their differences and similarities. *We have to find out more* *before we can make a proper comparison... Here, for comparison, is the French version.*

compartment /kə^{7}mpɑ:tmə^{2}nt/, **compartments.** 1 COUNT N A **compartment** is one of the separate sections of a railway carriage. 2 COUNT N A **compartment** is also one of the separate parts of an object used for keeping things in. *He tucked the ticket into the inner compartment of his wallet.*

compass /kʌmpəs/, **compasses.** 1 COUNT N A **compass** is an instrument with a magnetic needle which always points north. It is used for finding directions. 2 PLURAL N **Compasses** are a hinged V-shaped instrument used for drawing circles.

compassion /kə^{7}mpæʃə^{0}n/. UNCOUNT N **Compassion** is a feeling of pity and sympathy. *The suffering of the Cubans aroused their compassion.*

compassionate /kə^{7}mpæʃənə^{1}t/. ADJ A **compassionate** person feels pity and sympathy. *She was among the most compassionate of women.* ♦ **compassionately** ADV *Liz looked at her compassionately.*

compatible /kə^{7}mpætəbə^{0}l/. ADJ If people or things are **compatible,** they can live or exist together happily or safely. *These programs no longer seem compatible with European society... We assumed that all these objectives were compatible.* ♦ **compatibility** /kə^{7}mpætəbɪlɪti^1/ UNCOUNT N *They failed to achieve any compatibility of planning aims.*

compatriot /kə^{7}mpætrɪət/, **compatriots.** COUNT N Your **compatriots** are people from your own country.

compel /kə^{7}mpel/, **compels, compelling, compelled.** VB WITH OBJ AND TO-INF If something **compels** you to act or behave in a particular way, it forces you to do it. *...illnesses which compel people to change their diet.*

compelling /kə^{7}mpelɪŋ/. ADJ A **compelling** argument or reason for something convinces you that it is true or right. *I had ended a man's life for no compelling reason.*

compensate /kɒmpə^{2}nseɪt/, **compensates, compensating, compensated.** 1 VB WITH OBJ To **compensate** someone for something means to give them money to replace it. *The allowance should be paid to compensate people for loss of earnings.* 2 VB To **compensate** for the bad effect of something means to do something that cancels out this effect. *Fish compensate for the current by moving their fins.*

compensation /kɒmpə^{2}nseɪʃə^{0}n/, **compensations.** 1 UNCOUNT N **Compensation** is money that you claim from a person or organization to compensate you for something unpleasant that has happened to you. *If you were killed, your dependants could get compensation.* 2 COUNT N OR UNCOUNT N A **compensation** is something that cancels out another thing that has had a bad effect. *Look for some of the compensations your body has to make... Letters that began to arrive from Nell were some compensation.*

compensatory /kɒmpə^{2}nseɪtə^{0}ri^1/. ATTRIB ADJ Something that is **compensatory** involves helping people by giving them money or resources to compensate for something bad that has happened. *There must be compensatory payments to the farmers.*

compete /kə^{7}mpi:t/, **competes, competing, competed.** 1 VB When people or organizations **compete** with each other, they try to get something for themselves. *This would enable British shipbuilders to compete with foreign yards... Senior members of staff competed eagerly for the honour of representing the company.* 2 VB WITH ADJUNCT If you **compete** in a contest or a game, you take part in it. *Dave Moorcroft has now competed in two Olympics.* 3 RECIP VB If two statements or ideas **compete,** they cannot both be right or acceptable. ♦ **competing** ATTRIB ADJ *Various competing theories are compared and discussed.*

competent /kɒmpə^{1}tənt/. ADJ Someone who is **competent** is efficient and effective. *He was a competent amateur pilot... It was a highly competent piece of work.* ♦ **competently** ADV *He carved the bird roughly, but competently.* ♦ **competence** /kɒmpə^{1}təns/ UNCOUNT N *He will be expected to show competence in the relevant methods of research.*

competition /kɒmpə^{1}tɪʃə^{0}n/, **competitions.** 1 UNCOUNT N **Competition** is a situation in which two or more people or groups are trying to get something which not everyone can have. *Competition for admission to the college is keen... Part of the reason for the drop in sales is competition from overseas suppliers.* 2 COUNT N A **competition** is an event in which people take part in order to find out who is best at a particular activity.

competitive /kə^{7}mpetɪtɪv/. 1 ADJ Something that is **competitive** involves people or firms competing with each other. *...a highly competitive society.* 2 ADJ A **competitive** person is eager to be more successful than other people. *I realize how awfully competitive I am.* ♦ **competitiveness** UNCOUNT N *Why should we put such an emphasis on individualism and competitiveness?* 3 ADJ Goods that are **competitive** are cheaper than similar goods. *...a competitive car for the 1980s.* ♦ **competitively** ADV *...competitively priced newspapers.*

competitor /kə^{7}mpetɪtə/, **competitors.** 1 COUNT N Companies that are **competitors** sell similar kinds of goods. *...Austin-Rover's challenge to its foreign competitors.* 2 COUNT N A **competitor** is a person who takes part in a competition.

compilation /kɒmpɪleɪʃə^{0}n/, **compilations.** COUNT N A **compilation** is a book, record, or programme containing many different things. *...a compilation of Victorian poetry.*

compile /kəmpaɪl/, **compiles, compiling, compiled.** VB WITH OBJ When you **compile** a book, report, or film, you produce it by putting together pieces of information. *The programme was compiled and presented by Dr Brian Smith.* ♦ **compilation** /kɒmpɪleɪʃə^{0}n/ UNCOUNT N *One of the first steps was the compilation of a report.*

complacent /kə^{7}mpleɪsənt/. ADJ If you are **complacent** about a situation, you do not feel that you need to worry or do anything. *We cannot afford to be complacent about the energy problem.* ♦ **complacently** ADV *Her mother smiled complacently.* ♦ **complacency** /kə^{7}mpleɪsənsi^1/ UNCOUNT N *No one has any cause for complacency.*

complain /kə^{7}mpleɪn/, **complains, complaining, complained.** 1 VB OR REPORT VB If you **complain** about something, you express the fact that you are not satisfied with it. *People had complained to Uncle Harold about his fights... 'He never told me, sir,' Watson complained... She complained that the office was not 'businesslike'.* 2 VB WITH 'of' OR REPORT VB If you **complain** of pain or illness, you say you have it. *He complained of pain in the chest.*

complaint /kə^{7}mpleɪnt/, **complaints.** 1 COUNT N OR UNCOUNT N A **complaint** is a statement of dissatisfaction or a reason for it. *There were the usual complaints of violence... She wrote a letter of complaint to the manufacturer.* 2 COUNT N A **complaint** is also an illness. *...a minor complaint.*

complement /kɒmplə^{1}mə^{2}nt/, **complements, complementing, complemented.** 1 VB WITH OBJ If people or things **complement** each another, they go well together. *Crisp pastry complements the juicy fruit of an apple pie.* Also COUNT N *The exercises are an ideal complement to my usual rehearsal methods.* 2 COUNT N In grammar, a **complement** is one of the elements of clause structure which gives information about the subject or the object of the verb.

complementary /kɒmplə^{1}mentə^{0}ri^1/. ADJ If two different things are **complementary,** they form a complete unit when they are brought together, or fit well together. *These two approaches are complementary.*

complete /kə^{7}mpli:t/, **completes, completing, completed.** 1 ADJ If something is **complete,** it contains all the parts that it should contain. *This is not a complete list... ...an almost complete skeleton of a dinosaur.* 2 ADJ You use **complete** to indicate that something is as great in degree or amount as it possibly can be. *...a complete change of diet... They were in complete agreement.* ♦ **completely** ADV *He was completely bald.* 3 VB WITH OBJ If you **complete** something, you finish doing, making, or producing it. *The cathedral was begun in 1240 and completed forty years later.* ♦ **completion** /kə^{7}mpli:ʃə^{0}n/. UNCOUNT N *The house was due for completion in 1983.* 4 PRED ADJ If a task is **complete,** it is finished. *The harvesting was complete.* 5 VB WITH OBJ If something **completes** a set, it is the last item needed to make it whole or finished. *A black silk tie completed the outfit.* 6 VB WITH OBJ To **complete** a form means to write the necessary information on it. 7 PHRASE Something that is **complete with** a particular thing includes that thing as an extra part. *...a lovely mansion, complete with swimming pool.*

complex /kɒmpleks/, **complexes.** 1 ADJ **Complex** things have many different parts and are hard to understand. *...complex lace patterns... It is a complex problem.* 2 COUNT N WITH SUPP A **complex** is a group of many things which are connected with each other in a complicated way. *...a complex of little roads... Conflicts usually develop out of a complex of causes.* 3 COUNT N A **complex** is also a group of buildings used for a particular purpose. *...a splendid new sports and leisure complex.* 4 COUNT N If you have a **complex,** you have a mental or emotional problem caused by an unpleasant experience in the past. *I am developing a guilt complex about it.*

complexion /kə^{7}mplekʃə^{0}n/, **complexions.** COUNT N Your **complexion** is the natural quality of the skin on your face. *She said I had a good complexion.*

complexity /kə^{7}mpleksɪ^{1}ti^1/, **complexities.** 1 UNCOUNT N **Complexity** is the state of having many different parts related to each other in a complicated way. *...problems of varying complexity.* 2 PLURAL N The **complexities** of something are its connected parts, which make it difficult to understand. *...the complexities of tax law.*

compliance /kə^{7}mplaɪəns/. UNCOUNT N **Compliance** is doing what you have been asked to do; a formal use. *...Melanie's compliance with these terms.*

complicate /kɒmplɪkeɪt/, **complicates, complicating, complicated.** VB WITH OBJ To **complicate** something means to make it more difficult to understand or deal with. *Just to complicate matters, I have to be back by the end of the month.*

complicated /kɒmplɪkeɪtɪ^{2}d/. ADJ Something that is **complicated** has many parts and is difficult to understand. *I find the British legal system extremely complicated... The situation is much more complicated than that.*

complication /kɒmplɪkeɪʃə^{0}n/, **complications.** COUNT N A **complication** is a problem or difficulty. *Finally, there is the complication that wages help to determine the level of inflation.*

complicity /kə^{7}mplɪsɪ^{1}ti^1/. UNCOUNT N **Complicity** is involvement in an illegal activity; a formal use. *She suspected him of complicity in Ashok's escape.*

compliment /kɒmplə^{1}mə^{2}nt/, **compliments, complimenting, complimented.** 1 COUNT N If you pay someone a **compliment,** you say something nice about them. *He had just been paid a great compliment.* 2 VB WITH OBJ If you **compliment** someone, you praise them or tell them how much you like something that they own or that they have done. *He complimented Morris on his new car.* 3 PLURAL N **Compliments** is used in expressing good wishes or respect; a formal use. *The Secretary of State presents his compliments.*

complimentary /kɒmplə^{1}mentə^{0}ri^1/. 1 ADJ If you are **complimentary** about something, you express admiration for it. *In Russia a rhythmic slow handclap can be highly complimentary.* 2 ATTRIB ADJ A **complimentary** seat, ticket, or book is free.

comply /kə^{7}mplaɪ/, **complies, complying, complied.** VB If you **comply** with an order or rule, you do what you are required to do; a formal use. *New vehicles must comply with certain standards.*

component /kə^{7}mpəʊnənt/, **components.** COUNT N The **components** of something are its parts. *The factory makes components for cars.*

compose /kə^{7}mpəʊz/, **composes, composing, composed.** 1 PASSIVE VB The things that something **is composed** of are its parts or members. *The book is composed of essays written over the last twenty years... The National Committee was composed of 22 manual workers and 6 white-collar workers.* 2 VB WITH OR WITHOUT OBJ When someone **composes** music, a speech, or letter, they write it. *Mr Morris sat down to compose his letter of resignation... He conducts and composes.* 3 REFL VB If you **compose** yourself, you become calm after being angry or excited. *She lay on her bed and cried and then she composed herself and went downstairs.* ♦ **composed** ADJ *I felt calmer and more composed than I had in a long time.*

composer /kə^{7}mpəʊzə/, **composers.** COUNT N A **composer** is a person who writes music.

composite /kɒmpəzɪt/. ATTRIB ADJ A **composite** object or item is made up of several different things or parts; a formal use. *...the composite annual fee.*

composition /kɒmpəzɪʃə^{0}n/, **compositions.** 1 UNCOUNT N The **composition** of something is the things that it consists of and the way that they are arranged. *...the chemical composition of the atmosphere.* 2 COUNT N A **composition** is a piece of work you write at school on a particular subject. 3 COUNT N A composer's **compositions** are the pieces of music he or she has written. 4 UNCOUNT N **Composition** is also the act of composing something such as a piece of music or a poem. *...a poem of his own composition.*

compost /kɒmpɒst/. UNCOUNT N **Compost** is a mixture of decaying plants and manure which is used to improve soil. *...a compost heap.*

composure /kə^{7}mpəʊʒə/. UNCOUNT N **Composure** is the ability to stay calm; a formal use. *He had recovered his composure.*

compound, compounds, compounding, compounded; pronounced /kɒmpaʊnd/ when it is a noun, and /kə^{7}mpaʊnd/ when it is a verb. 1 COUNT N A **compound** is an enclosed area of land used for a particular purpose. *He led the men into the prison compound.* 2 COUNT N In chemistry, a **compound** is a substance consisting of two or more elements. 3 COUNT N If something is a **compound** of different things, it consists of those things. *The new threat was a compound of nationalism and social revolution.* 4 VB WITH OBJ To **compound** a problem means to make it worse by increasing it in some way; a formal use. *Her uncertainty was now compounded by fear.*

comprehend /kɒmprɪhɛnd/, **comprehends, comprehending, comprehended.** VB OR REPORT VB If you cannot **comprehend** something, you cannot fully understand or appreciate it; a formal use. *...a failure to comprehend the huge power of computers... They did not comprehend how hard he had struggled.*

comprehensible /kɒmprɪhɛnsə1bə0l/. ADJ If something is **comprehensible,** it is easily understood. *The object is to make our research comprehensible.*

comprehension /kɒmprɪhɛnʃə0n/, **comprehensions. 1** UNCOUNT N **Comprehension** is the ability to understand or appreciate something fully. *The problems of solar navigation seem beyond comprehension.* **2** COUNT N A **comprehension** is an exercise to find out how well you understand a piece of text.

comprehensive /kɒmprɪhɛnsɪv/, **comprehensives. 1** ADJ Something that is **comprehensive** includes everything necessary or relevant. *...a comprehensive list of all the items in stock.* **2** COUNT N A **comprehensive school** is one where children of all abilities are taught together; a British use.

compress /kə7mprɛs/, **compresses, compressing, compressed.** ERG VB When you **compress** something, you squeeze it or make it smaller or shorter. *I could feel my lips compress into a white line... I soon finished a paper, which I compressed to minimum length.* ♦ **compression** /kə7mprɛʃə0n/ UNCOUNT N *...the compression of air by the piston.*

comprise /kə7mpraɪz/, **comprises, comprising, comprised.** VB WITH COMPLEMENT OR PASSIVE VB WITH 'of' If something **comprises** a number of things or people, it has them as its parts or members; a formal use. *The Privy Council comprised 283 members... The fountain was comprised of three stone basins.*

compromise /kɒmprəmaɪz/, **compromises, compromising, compromised. 1** COUNT N OR UNCOUNT N A **compromise** is an agreement in which people agree to accept less than they originally wanted. *It was necessary for members to make compromises to ensure party unity... Delegates predict that some compromise will be reached.* **2** VB If you **compromise,** you reach an agreement with another person or group in which you both give up something that you originally wanted. *The best thing to do is to compromise.* **3** REFL VB OR VB WITH OBJ If you **compromise** yourself or your beliefs, you do something which makes people doubt your sincerity or honesty. *They claim he has already compromised himself... The Government had compromised its principles.*

compulsion /kə7mpʌlʃə0n/, **compulsions. 1** COUNT N A **compulsion** is a strong desire to do something. *She feels a compulsion to tidy up all the time.* **2** UNCOUNT N If someone uses **compulsion** to get you to do something, they force you to do it. *We are not entitled to use compulsion.*

compulsive /kə7mpʌlsɪv/. **1** ADJ You use **compulsive** to describe people who cannot stop doing something. *...a compulsive gambler.* ♦ **compulsively** ADV *He steals compulsively.* **2** ADJ If a book or television programme is **compulsive,** it is so interesting that you do not want to stop reading or watching it.

compulsory /kə7mpʌlsə0ri1/. ADJ If something is **compulsory,** you must do it. *In most schools, sports are compulsory... ...compulsory retirement.*

compute /kə7mpjuːt/, **computes, computing, computed.** VB WITH OBJ To **compute** a quantity or number means to calculate it. *It is difficult to compute the loss in revenue.* ♦ **computation** /kɒmpjə4teɪʃə0n/ UNCOUNT N OR COUNT N *There had been a sudden advance in the field of automatic computation... He sat over his adding machine making rapid computations.*

computer /kə7mpjuːtə/, **computers.** COUNT N A **computer** is an electronic machine which makes quick calculations and deals with large amounts of information. *Portable computers can be plugged into TV sets... The entire process is done by computer... ...computer games.*

computerize /kə7mpjuːtəraɪz/, **computerizes, computerizing, computerized;** also spelled **computerise.** VB WITH OBJ To **computerize** a system or type of work means to arrange for it to be done by computers. *We are currently computerizing the Inland Revenue.* ♦ **computerized** ADJ *He had just introduced a computerized filing system into the office.* ♦ **computerization** /kə7mpjuːtəraɪzeɪʃə0n/ UNCOUNT N *...the economic benefits of computerization.*

computing /kə7mpjuːtɪŋ/. UNCOUNT N **Computing** is the activity of using a computer and writing programs for it.

comrade /kɒmrɪ3d, -æd/, **comrades. 1** VOCATIVE Socialists or communists sometimes call each other **comrade,** especially in meetings. *This is what I propose, Comrades.* **2** COUNT N Someone's **comrades** are their friends or companions; an old-fashioned use.

con /kɒn/, **cons, conning, conned.** VB WITH OBJ If someone **cons** you, they trick you into doing or believing something by saying things that are not true; an informal use. *A lot of people are conned into thinking that they can't fight back.* Also COUNT N *The whole thing was a big con.* ● **Pros and cons:** see **pro.**

concave /kɒŋ1keɪv, kɒŋ1keɪv/. ADJ A surface that is **concave** curves inwards in the middle.

conceal /kə7nsiːl/, **conceals, concealing, concealed.** VB WITH OBJ If you **conceal** something, you hide it or keep it secret. *She concealed the bottle beneath her mattress... He might be concealing a secret from me.* ♦ **concealment** UNCOUNT N *The trees offered concealment and protection... ...the concealment of truth.*

concede /kə7nsiːd/, **concedes, conceding, conceded.** REPORT VB OR VB If you **concede** something, you admit it or accept that it is true. *The company conceded that an error had been made... The government was forced to concede defeat... Another strike will force the government to concede.*

conceit /kə7nsiːt/. UNCOUNT N **Conceit** is very great pride in your abilities or achievements; used showing disapproval. *His recent movies have shown signs of arrogance and conceit.* ♦ **conceited** ADJ *...a conceited old fool.*

conceivable /kə7nsiːvəbə0l/. ADJ If something is **conceivable,** you can imagine it or believe that it is possible. *Jenny learned every conceivable recipe for pasta... It is conceivable that he drowned.* ♦ **conceivably** SENTENCE ADV *It might conceivably be useful.*

conceive /kə7nsiːv/, **conceives, conceiving, conceived. 1** VB WITH 'of' OR OBJ If you can **conceive** of something, you can imagine it or believe it. *He could never conceive of such a thing happening... A politician conceives the world as a variety of conflicts.* **2** VB WITH OBJ If you **conceive** a plan or idea, you think of it and work out how it can be done. *A Prices and Incomes policy was boldly conceived.* **3** VB WITH OR WITHOUT OBJ When a woman **conceives,** she becomes pregnant.

concentrate /kɒnsə2ntreɪt/, **concentrates, concentrating, concentrated. 1** VB If you **concentrate** on something, you give all your attention to it. *Concentrate on your driving.* ♦ **concentration** /kɒnsə2ntreɪʃə0n/ UNCOUNT N *It requires considerable concentration.* **2** VB WITH OBJ When something **is concentrated** in one place, it is all there rather than being spread around. *Modern industry has been concentrated in a few large urban centres.* ♦ **concentration** COUNT N OR UNCOUNT N *...the concentration of power in the hands of a single group... ...the densest concentrations of people in the Third World.*

concentrated /kɒnsə2ntreɪtɪ2d/. **1** ADJ A **concentrated** liquid has been increased in strength by having water removed from it. **2** ADJ A **concentrated** activity is directed with great intensity in one place. *...a heavily concentrated attack.*

concentric /kə7nsɛntrɪk/. ATTRIB ADJ **Concentric** circles have the same centre. *...concentric circles of stones.*

concept /kɒnsɛpt/, **concepts.** COUNT N A **concept** is an idea or abstract principle. *...the concept of trade unionism... Of course, it's a difficult concept.*

conception /kə7nsɛpʃə0n/, **conceptions. 1** COUNT N OR UNCOUNT N A **conception** is an idea or the forming of an idea in your mind. *He had a definite conception of how he wanted things arranged... The plan was very imaginative in conception.* **2** UNCOUNT N **Conception** is also the process in which a woman becomes pregnant. *...the nine months between conception and birth.*

conceptual /kə7nsɛptʃuə0l/. ATTRIB ADJ **Conceptual** means related to ideas and concepts formed in the mind; a formal use. *Most people have little conceptual understanding of computers.*

concern /kə7nsɜːn/, **concerns, concerning, concerned. 1** UNCOUNT N OR COUNT N **Concern** is a feeling of worry. *...the growing public concern over Britain's poor economic performance... My concern is that many of these cases are going unnoticed.* **2** VB WITH OBJ If something **concerns** you, it worries you. *One of the things that concerns me is the rise in vandalism.* ♦ **concerned** ADJ *He was concerned about the level of unemployment.* **3** REFL VB OR VB WITH OBJ If you **concern** yourself with something, you give attention to it because you think that it is important. *I don't want you to concern yourself with it... We are more concerned with efficiency than expansion.* **4** UNCOUNT N WITH SUPP Your **concern** for someone is a feeling that you want them to be happy, safe, and well. *She shows a true concern for others.* **5** VB WITH OBJ If a situation, event, or activity **concerns** you, it affects or involves you. *These are matters which some of my colleagues would think do not concern them.* ♦ **concerned** ADJ AFTER N *It was a perfect arrangement for all concerned.* **6** SING N WITH POSS If a situation or problem is your **concern,** it is your duty or responsibility. *That's your concern, I'm afraid.* **7** VB WITH OBJ OR PASSIVE VB WITH 'with' If a book, speech, or piece of information **concerns** a particular subject or **is concerned** with it, it is about that subject. *This chapter is concerned with changes that are likely to take place.* **8** COUNT N A **concern** is also a company or business. *...the giant West German chemical concern, Hoechst.*

PHRASES ● You say **as far as** something **is concerned** to indicate the subject that you are talking about. *We have rather a poor record as far as regional studies are concerned.* ● You say **'as far as I'm concerned'** to indicate that you are giving your own opinion. *This is all rubbish as far as I'm concerned.*

concerning /kə7nsɜːnɪŋ/. PREP You use **concerning** to indicate what something is about. *He refused to answer questions concerning his private life.*

concert /kɒnsət/, **concerts.** COUNT N A **concert** is a performance of music. *...pop concerts.*

concerted /kə7nsɜːtɪ2d/. ATTRIB ADJ A **concerted** action is done by several people together. *Everyone makes a concerted effort to help.*

concerto /kə7ntʃɛətəʊ/, **concertos.** COUNT N A **concerto** is a piece of music for a solo instrument and an orchestra.

concession /kə7nsɛʃə0n/, **concessions.** COUNT N A **concession** is something that you agree to let someone do or have, especially after a disagreement or as a special privilege. *The Prime Minister had been urged to make a concession by the government.*

conciliation /kə7nsɪlieɪʃə0n/. UNCOUNT N **Conciliation** is trying to end a disagreement. *Did you make any efforts at conciliation?*

conciliatory /kə7nsɪljətri1/. ADJ When you are **conciliatory,** you are willing to end a disagreement with someone. *She spoke in a conciliatory tone.*

concise /kə7nsaɪs/. ADJ Something that is **concise** gives all the necessary information in a very brief form. *...a concise survey of English literature.* ♦ **concisely** ADV *Write clearly and concisely.*

conclude /kə7ŋ1kluːd/, **concludes, concluding, concluded. 1** REPORT VB OR VB WITH 'from' If you **conclude** that something is true, you decide that it is true because of other things that you know. *Darwin concluded that men were descended from apes... What do you conclude from all that?* **2** ERG VB When you **conclude** something or when it **concludes,** it finishes; a formal use. *I will conclude this chapter with a quotation... 'That,' he concluded, 'is why we're so poor.'* ♦ **concluding** ATTRIB ADJ *...his concluding remark.* **3** VB WITH OBJ If you **conclude** a treaty or business deal, you arrange or settle it finally; a formal use.

conclusion /kə7ŋ1kluːʒə0n/, **conclusions. 1** COUNT N A **conclusion** is something that you decide is true after careful thought. *I came to the conclusion that I didn't really like civil engineering.* **2** SING N The **conclusion** of something is its ending. *We tried an experiment which had an interesting conclusion.* **3** ● You can describe something that seems certain to happen as a **foregone conclusion.**

conclusive /kə7ŋ1kluːsɪv/. ADJ **Conclusive** evidence or facts show that something is certainly true. *The evidence is not conclusive.* ♦ **conclusively** ADV *This has been difficult to prove conclusively.*

concoct /kə7ŋ1kɒkt/, **concocts, concocting, concocted. 1** VB WITH OBJ If you **concoct** an excuse, you invent one. **2** VB WITH OBJ If you **concoct** something, you make it by mixing several things together. *Nancy had concocted a red wine sauce.* ♦ **concoction** COUNT N *Chutney is a concoction of almost any fruit or vegetable you like.*

concomitant /kə7ŋ1kɒmɪtənt/. ADJ Something that is **concomitant** with another thing happens at the same time and is connected with it; a formal use. *...the growth of bureaucracy, with its concomitant dangers of corruption.*

concord /kɒŋ1kɔːd/. UNCOUNT N **Concord** is the state of being in agreement with others; a formal use. *...this religion of peace and concord.*

concrete /kɒŋ1kriːt/. **1** UNCOUNT N **Concrete** is a substance used for building made from cement, sand, small stones, and water. **2** ADJ Something that is **concrete** is definite or real. *There were no specific, concrete proposals placed before the people.*

concur /kə7ŋ1kɜː/, **concurs, concurring, concurred.** VB When you **concur,** you agree with an opinion or statement; a formal use. *The judge concurred with earlier findings.*

concurrent /kə7ŋ1kʌrənt/. ADJ If two things are **concurrent,** they happen at the same time. *The two events were concurrent.* ♦ **concurrently** ADV *Two subjects will be studied concurrently.*

concussed /kə7ŋ1kʌst/. ADJ If you are **concussed** by a blow to your head, you lose consciousness or feel sick or confused.

concussion /kə7ŋ1kʌʃə0n/. UNCOUNT N If you suffer **concussion** after a blow to your head, you lose consciousness or feel sick or confused. *She was in Newcastle Infirmary with concussion.*

condemn /kəˈndem/, **condemns, condemning, condemned.** 1 VB WITH OBJ If you **condemn** something, you say that it is bad and unacceptable. *He condemned the report as partial and inadequate.* ♦ **condemnation** /kɒndemneɪʃən/ UNCOUNT N OR COUNT N *...their strong condemnation of her conduct.* 2 VB WITH OBJ AND PREP 'to' OR TO-INF If someone **is condemned** to a punishment, they are given it. *Susan was condemned to death.* 3 VB WITH OBJ AND PREP 'to' OR TO-INF If you **are condemned** to something unpleasant, you have to suffer it. *Most of the applicants are condemned to spend all morning waiting to be seen.* 4 VB WITH OBJ If a building **has been condemned,** the authorities have decided that it is not safe and must be pulled down.

condemned /kəˈndemd/. ATTRIB ADJ A **condemned** prisoner is going to be executed.

condensation /kɒndenseɪʃən/. UNCOUNT N **Condensation** is a coating of tiny drops of water which form on a cold surface.

condense /kəˈndens/, **condenses, condensing, condensed.** 1 VB WITH OBJ If you **condense** a piece of writing or speech, you make it shorter, by removing the less important parts. *I tried to condense every report into as few words as possible.* 2 ERG VB When a gas or vapour **condenses** or when you **condense** it, it changes into a liquid.

condescend /kɒndɪsend/, **condescends, condescending, condescended.** 1 VB If you **condescend** to people, you behave in a way which shows them that you think you are superior to them; a formal use. *He never condescended, never spoke down to me.* ♦ **condescending** ADJ *She addressed him with the same condescending tone.* ♦ **condescension** UNCOUNT N *He spoke to the labourers with no condescension.* 2 VB WITH TO-INF If you **condescend** to do something, you agree to do it, but in a way which shows that you think you are doing people a favour. *She did not condescend to have dinner with him.*

condition /kəˈndɪʃən/, **conditions, conditioning, conditioned.** 1 SING N WITH SUPP The **condition** of someone or something is the state they are in. *You can't go home in that condition... Keep your car exterior in good condition.* 2 PLURAL N WITH SUPP The **conditions** in which people live or do things are the qualities or factors that affect their comfort, safety, or success. *...adverse weather conditions... ...appalling living conditions.* 3 COUNT N A **condition** is something which must happen in order for something else to be possible. *You have to live there as a condition of your job.* 4 PHRASE When you agree to do something **on condition that** something else happens, you mean that you will only do it if this other thing happens or is agreed to first. *He has agreed to come on condition that there won't be any publicity.* 5 COUNT N WITH SUPP You can refer to an illness or other medical problem as a particular **condition.** *He has a heart condition.* 6 VB WITH OBJ If someone **is conditioned** to think or do something in a particular way, they do it as a result of their upbringing or training. *Men had been conditioned to regard women as their inferiors.* ♦ **conditioning** UNCOUNT N *It is very difficult to overcome your early conditioning.* 7 PHRASE If someone is **out of condition,** they are unhealthy and unfit.

conditional /kəˈndɪʃənəl, -ʃənəl/. ADJ If a situation or agreement is **conditional** on something, it will only happen if this thing happens. *Their support is conditional upon further reduction in public expenditure.*

condolence /kəˈndəʊləns/, **condolences.** UNCOUNT N OR PLURAL N **Condolence** is sympathy that you express for someone whose friend or relative has died. *...letters of condolence... She wished to offer her condolences.*

condom /kɒndəˈm/, **condoms.** COUNT N A **condom** is a rubber covering which a man wears on his penis as a contraceptive during sexual intercourse.

condone /kəˈndəʊn/, **condones, condoning, condoned.** VB WITH OBJ If someone **condones** behaviour that is morally wrong, they accept it and allow it to happen. *We cannot condone the daily massacre of innocent people.*

conducive /kəˈndjuːsɪv/. PRED ADJ If one thing is **conducive** to another, it makes the other thing likely to happen. *Competition is not conducive to human happiness.*

conduct, conducts, conducting, conducted; pronounced /kəˈndʌkt/ when it is a verb and /kɒndʌkt/ when it is a noun. 1 VB WITH OBJ When you **conduct** an activity or task, you organize it and do it. *We have been conducting a survey of the region.* Also UNCOUNT N *Secrets are essential to the conduct of a war.* 2 REFL VB WITH ADJUNCT The way you **conduct** yourself is the way you behave; a formal use. *He instructed them in how to conduct themselves inside the mosque.* Also UNCOUNT N *The minister had several good reasons for his conduct.* 3 VB WITH OR WITHOUT OBJ When someone **conducts** an orchestra or choir, they stand in front of it and direct its performance. *I remember when I first conducted in London.* 4 VB WITH OBJ If something **conducts** heat or electricity, it allows heat or electricity to pass through it.

conductor /kəˈndʌktə/, **conductors.** COUNT N The **conductor** of an orchestra or choir and is the person who conducts it. ● See also **bus conductor.**

cone /kəʊn/, **cones.** 1 COUNT N A **cone** is a three-dimensional shape similar to a pyramid but with a circular base. *...build a big cone of wood over it.* 2 COUNT N The **cones** of a pine or fir tree are its fruit. They consist of a cluster of woody scales containing seeds.

confectionery /kəˈnfekʃənəri/. UNCOUNT N You can refer to sweets and chocolates as **confectionery.**

confederate /kəˈnfedərət/, **confederates.** COUNT N Someone's **confederates** are the people they are working with in a secret activity.

confederation /kəˈnfedəreɪʃən/, **confederations.** COUNT N A **confederation** is an organization of groups for political or business purposes. *We are in favour of a loose confederation of states.*

confer /kəˈnfɜː/, **confers, conferring, conferred.** 1 RECIP VB When you **confer** with someone, you discuss something with them in order to make a decision. *He went home to confer with his wife... The jury conferred for only twelve minutes.* 2 VB WITH OBJ If something **confers** an advantage, it gives that advantage; a formal use. *The system had conferred great benefits.*

conference /kɒnfərəns/, **conferences.** 1 COUNT N A **conference** is a meeting at which formal discussions take place. *The Managing Director has daily conferences with the other staff members.* ● If someone is **in conference,** they are having a formal meeting. *...the time he must spend in conference listening to reports.* 2 COUNT N A **conference** is also a meeting where people discuss a particular subject, often lasting a few days.

confess /kəˈnfes/, **confesses, confessing, confessed.** 1 REPORT VB OR VB WITH PREP 'to' If you **confess** something that you are ashamed of, you admit it. *Perhaps I shouldn't confess this, but I did on one occasion forge Tony's signature... I confess to a certain weakness for puddings... He once confessed to Vita that he really hated parties* 2 VB WITH OR WITHOUT OBJ If you **confess** to a crime, you admit that you have committed it. *Bianchi had confessed to five of the murders.*

confession /kəˈnfeʃən/, **confessions.** 1 COUNT N If you make a **confession,** you admit that you have committed a crime or done something wrong. *I have a confession to make.* 2 UNCOUNT N **Confession** is also a religious act in which you tell a priest about your sins and ask for forgiveness. *He had gone to confession.*

confetti /kəˈnfeti/. UNCOUNT N **Confetti** is small pieces of coloured paper thrown over the bride and bridegroom at a wedding.

confidant /kɒnfɪdænt/, **confidants;** spelled **confidante** when referring to a woman. COUNT N Someone's **confidant** or **confidante** is a person who they discuss their private problems with; an old-fashioned use.

confide /kəˈnfaɪd/, **confides, confiding, confided.** VB If you **confide** in someone or **confide** something to them, you tell them a secret. *May I confide in you?... I never confided my fear to anyone... He had confided to me that he wasn't an Irishman at all.* ♦ **confiding** ADJ *At first she was suspicious, then she became confiding.*

confidence /kɒnfɪdəns/, **confidences.** 1 UNCOUNT N If you have **confidence** in someone, you feel you can trust them. *I have a lot of confidence in him.* 2 UNCOUNT N If you have **confidence,** you feel sure about your abilities, qualities, or ideas. *I was full of confidence.* 3 UNCOUNT N **Confidence** is also a situation in which you tell someone a secret that they should not tell to anyone else. *I'm telling you this in the strictest confidence.* ● If you **take** someone **into** your **confidence,** you tell them a secret. 4 COUNT N A **confidence** is a secret that you tell someone.

confident /kɒnfɪdənt/. 1 ADJ If you are **confident** about something, you are certain that it will happen in the way you want it to. *He said he was confident that the scheme would be successful.* ♦ **confidently** ADV *One could confidently rely on him.* 2 ADJ People who are **confident** feel sure of their own abilities, qualities, or ideas. *...a witty, young and confident lawyer.* ♦ **confidently** ADV *I strode confidently up the hall.*

confidential /kɒnfɪdenʃəl/. 1 ADJ Information that is **confidential** is meant to be kept secret. *This arrangement is to be kept strictly confidential.* ♦ **confidentially** ADV *I wrote to you confidentially about this on 30th September 1987.* ♦ **confidentiality** /kɒnfɪdenʃiˈæləˈti/ UNCOUNT N *Please respect the confidentiality of this information.* 2 ADJ If you talk to someone in a **confidential** way, you talk to them quietly because what you are saying is secret. *He became very confidential.* ♦ **confidentially** ADV *She leaned forward and whispered to him confidentially.*

configuration /kəˈnfɪgjəˈreɪʃən/, **configurations.** COUNT N A **configuration** is an arrangement of a group of things; a formal use.

confine, confines, confining, confined; pronounced /kəˈnfaɪn/ when it is a verb and /kɒnfaɪnz/ when it is a noun. 1 VB WITH OBJ If something **is confined** to only one place, situation, or person, it only exists there or only affects that person. *The problem appears to be confined to the tropics.* 2 REFL VB OR VB WITH OBJ AND PREP 'to' If you **confine** yourself to something, you do only that thing. *They confine themselves to discussing the weather... Confine your messages to official business.* 3 VB WITH OBJ To **confine** someone means to keep them in a place which they cannot leave. *William was confined to an institution for some years.* ♦ **confinement** UNCOUNT N *...his many years in confinement.* 4 PLURAL N The **confines** of an area are its boundaries; a formal use. *...within the confines of the Gallery.*

confined /kəˈnfaɪnd/. ADJ A **confined** space is small and enclosed by walls.

confirm /kəˈnfɜːm/, **confirms, confirming, confirmed.** 1 REPORT VB If something **confirms** what you believe, it shows that it is definitely true. *My suspicions were confirmed... He glanced round to confirm that he was alone.* ♦ **confirmation** /kɒnfəmeɪʃən/ UNCOUNT N *This discovery was a confirmation of Darwin's proposition.* 2 REPORT VB If you **confirm** something, you say that it is true. *She asked me if it was my car and I confirmed that it was.* ♦ **confirmation** UNCOUNT N *She turned to Jimmie for confirmation and he nodded.* 3 REPORT VB If you **confirm** an arrangement or appointment, you say that it is definite. *...a letter confirming that they expect you on the twelfth.* ♦ **confirmation** UNCOUNT N *All times are approximate and subject to confirmation.* 4 VB WITH OBJ When someone **is confirmed,** they are formally accepted as a member of a Christian church. ♦ **confirmation** UNCOUNT N *I went to my sister's confirmation last week.*

confirmed /kəˈnfɜːmd/. ATTRIB ADJ You use **confirmed** to describe someone who has a particular habit or belief that they are unlikely to change. *I am a confirmed non-smoker.*

confiscate /kɒnfɪskeɪt/, **confiscates, confiscating, confiscated.** VB WITH OBJ If you **confiscate** something from someone, you take it away from them, often as a punishment. *We had instructions to confiscate all their cameras.* ♦ **confiscation** /kɒnfɪskeɪʃən/ UNCOUNT N *I faced two years' jail plus the confiscation of the tapes.*

conflict, conflicts, conflicting, conflicted; pronounced /kɒnflɪkt/ when it is a noun and /kəˈnflɪkt/ when it is a verb. 1 UNCOUNT N OR COUNT N **Conflict** is disagreement and argument. *...the familiar conflict between government and opposition... ...a number of conflicts in the engineering industry.* 2 COUNT N OR UNCOUNT N A **conflict** is a war or battle. *A conventional conflict might escalate to a nuclear confrontation... Europe was encircled by conflict.* 3 RECIP VB If ideas, interests, or accounts **conflict,** they are very different from each other and it seems impossible for them to exist together or to both be true. *There is some research that conflicts with this view... These criteria might undoubtedly conflict.* ♦ **conflicting** ADJ *The evidence seems to be conflicting.*

conform /kəˈnfɔːm/, **conforms, conforming, conformed.** 1 VB If you **conform,** you behave in the way that you are expected to behave. *You must be prepared to conform.* 2 VB WITH PREP 'to' OR 'with' If something **conforms** to a law or someone's wishes, it is what is required or wanted. *Such a change would not conform to the wishes of the people.*

conformist /kəˈnfɔːmɪst/, **conformists.** COUNT N A **conformist** is someone who behaves like everyone else rather than doing original things. Also ADJ *The school had grown more conformist and cautious.*

conformity /kəˈnfɔːmɪˈti/. UNCOUNT N **Conformity** is behaviour, thought, or appearance that is the same as that of most other people. *All that seems to be required of us is conformity.*

confound /kəˈnfaʊnd/, **confounds, confounding, confounded.** VB WITH OBJ If something **confounds** you, it makes you confused or surprised. *...speaking French to confound their friends.*

confront /kəˈnfrʌnt/, **confronts, confronting, confronted.** 1 VB WITH OBJ If you **are confronted** with a problem or task, you have to deal with it. *...typical problems that confront Germans learning English.* 2 VB WITH OBJ If you **confront** an enemy, you meet them face to face. *They were confronted by a line of* *guardsmen.* 3 VB WITH OBJ AND 'with' If you **confront** someone with facts or evidence, you present it to them in order to accuse them of something. *I decided to confront her with the charges of racism.*

confrontation /kɒnfrənteɪʃə⁰n/, **confrontations.** COUNT N OR UNCOUNT N A **confrontation** is a dispute, fight, or battle. *...a confrontation between the pickets and police... ...a time of confrontation.*

confuse /kə⁷nfjuːz/, **confuses, confusing, confused.** 1 VB WITH OBJ If you **confuse** two things, you get them mixed up, so that you think one is the other. *You must be confusing me with someone else.* 2 VB WITH OBJ To **confuse** someone means to make it difficult for them to know what to do. *You're trying to confuse me.* 3 VB WITH OBJ To **confuse** a situation means to make it more complicated or difficult to understand. *To confuse matters further, her sister is married to her husband's uncle.* ♦ **confusing** ADJ *The plot is fairly confusing.*

confused /kə⁷nfjuːzd/. 1 ADJ Something that is **confused** does not have any order or pattern and is difficult to understand. *My thoughts were confused.* 2 ADJ If you are **confused,** you do not understand what is happening or you do not know what to do. *She was bewildered and confused.*

confusion /kə⁷nfjuːʒə⁰n/, **confusions.** 1 UNCOUNT N **Confusion** is making a mistake about a person or thing and thinking that they are another person or thing. *There is danger of confusion between them.* 2 UNCOUNT N **Confusion** is also a situation where it is not clear what is happening. *In all the confusion, both men managed to grab me.* 3 UNCOUNT N If your mind is in a state of **confusion,** you do not know what to believe or what you should do. *Her answers to his questions have only added to his confusion.*

congeal /kə⁷ndʒiːl/, **congeals, congealing, congealed.** VB When a liquid **congeals,** it becomes very thick and sticky and almost solid.

congenial /kə⁷ndʒiːnjəl, -nɪəl/. ADJ Someone or something that is **congenial** is pleasant; a formal use. *...congenial company.*

congenital /kə⁷ndʒɛnɪtə⁰l/. ADJ A **congenital** illness is one that a person has had from birth, but is not inherited; a medical use. *The brain damage was congenital.*

congested /kə⁷ndʒɛstɪ²d/. ADJ A road or area that is **congested** is very crowded.

congestion /kə⁷ndʒɛstʃə⁰n/. UNCOUNT N If there is **congestion** in a place, the place is very crowded.

conglomerate /kə⁷nglɒmərə¹t/, **conglomerates.** COUNT N A **conglomerate** is a large business consisting of several different companies.

conglomeration /kə⁷nglɒməreɪʃə⁰n/, **conglomerations.** COUNT N WITH SUPP A **conglomeration** is a group of many different things. *...a conglomeration of white buildings.*

congratulate /kəngrætjə⁴leɪt/, **congratulates, congratulating, congratulated.** VB WITH OBJ If you **congratulate** someone, you express pleasure for something good that has happened to them, or praise them for something they have achieved. *Friends came to congratulate the parents and to see the baby... I must congratulate you on a successful interview.* ♦ **congratulation** /kə⁷ngrætjə⁴leɪʃə⁰n/ UNCOUNT N *...a letter of congratulation.*

congratulations /kə⁷ngrætjə⁴leɪʃə⁰nz/. CONVENTION You say **'congratulations'** to someone in order to congratulate them. *'Congratulations,' the doctor said. 'You have a son.'... I offered him my heartiest congratulations.*

congregate /kɒŋgrɪ²geɪt/, **congregates, congregating, congregated.** VB When people **congregate,** they gather together. *The crowds congregated around the pavilion.*

congregation /kɒŋgrɪ²geɪʃə⁰n/, **congregations.** COLL N The people who attend a church service are the **congregation.** *There were only ten in the congregation.*

congress /kɒŋgrɛs/, **congresses.** COUNT N A **congress** is a large meeting held to discuss ideas and policies. *...the second Congress of Writers and Artists.*

conical /kɒnɪkə⁰l/. ADJ A **conical** object is shaped like a cone. *...a small conical shell.*

conifer /kəʊnɪfə, kɒn-/, **conifers.** COUNT N A **conifer** is a tree that has needle-like leaves and produces cones.

conjecture /kə⁷ndʒɛktʃə/. UNCOUNT N **Conjecture** is the formation of opinions from incomplete or doubtful information; a formal use. *The exact figure is a matter for conjecture.*

conjugal /kɒndʒə⁴gə⁰l/. ATTRIB ADJ **Conjugal** means relating to marriage and the relationship between a husband and wife; a formal use. *...conjugal happiness.*

conjunction /kə⁷ndʒʌŋk⁰ʃə⁰n/, **conjunctions.** 1 COUNT N A **conjunction** of things is a combination of them; a formal use. *The cause of suicide is a nasty conjunction of personal and social factors.* ● If two or more things are done **in conjunction,** they are done together rather than separately. *This course can only be taken in conjunction with course 234.* 2 COUNT N In grammar, a **conjunction** is a word that joins together words, groups, or clauses. For example, 'and' and 'or' are conjunctions.

conjure /kʌndʒə/, **conjures, conjuring, conjured.** VB WITH OBJ If you **conjure** something into existence, you make it appear as if by magic. *He appeared with a small bucket he'd apparently conjured from nowhere.*

conjure up. PHR VB If you **conjure up** a memory, picture, or idea, you create it in your mind. *To many people, the name Kalahari conjures up images of a desert of unrelenting aridity.*

conjurer /kʌndʒə⁰rə/, **conjurers;** also spelled **conjuror.** COUNT N A **conjurer** is an entertainer who does magic tricks.

conjuring trick, conjuring tricks. COUNT N A **conjuring trick** is a trick in which something is made to appear or disappear as if by magic.

con-man, con-men. COUNT N A **con-man** is a man who persuades people to give him money or property by lying to them.

connect /kə⁷nɛkt/, **connects, connecting, connected.** 1 VB WITH OBJ To **connect** one thing to another means to join them together. *Connect the fishing line to the hook.* ♦ **connecting** ATTRIB ADJ *The rooms had connecting doors between them.* 2 VB WITH OBJ If a piece of equipment **is connected,** it is joined by a wire to an electricity supply or to another piece of equipment. *...a telephone line connected to their terminal.* 3 VB WITH OBJ If a telephone operator **connects** you, he or she enables you to speak to another person by telephone. *I'm trying to connect you, sir.* 4 VB If a train, plane, or bus **connects** with another form of transport, it arrives at a time which allows passengers to change to the other form of transport to continue their journey. 5 VB WITH OBJ If you **connect** a person or thing with something, you realize that there is a link between them. *There is no evidence to connect Griffiths with the murder.*

connected /kə⁷nɛktɪ²d/. ADJ If one thing is **connected** with another, there is a relationship or link between them. *There are serious questions connected with radioactive waste disposal.*

connection /kə⁷nɛkʃə⁰n/, **connections;** also spelled **connexion.** 1 COUNT N A **connection** is a relationship between two things. *I do not think there is any logical connection between the two halves of the question.* 2 PHRASE If you talk to someone **in connection with** something, you talk to them about that thing. *The police wanted to interview him in connection with the murder.* 3 COUNT N A **connection** is also the joint where two wires or pipes are joined together. 4 COUNT N If you get a **connection** at a station or airport, you continue your journey by catching another train, bus, or plane. *I missed my connection.*

connive /kənaɪv/, **connives, conniving, connived.** VB WITH 'at' If you **connive** at something, you allow it to happen even though you know that it is wrong. *He was assisted by his mother who connived at his laziness.* ♦ **connivance** /kə⁷naɪvəns/ UNCOUNT N *He kept out of jail with the connivance of corrupt police.*

connoisseur /kɒnə¹sɜː/, **connoisseurs.** COUNT N A **connoisseur** is someone who knows a lot about the arts, food, or drink. *...a connoisseur of Italian music.*

connotation /kɒnə⁶teɪʃə⁰n/, **connotations.** COUNT N WITH SUPP The **connotations** of a word are the ideas or qualities that it makes you think of. *...strong religious connotations.*

conquer /kɒŋkə/, **conquers, conquering, conquered.** 1 VB WITH OR WITHOUT OBJ If one country or group of people **conquers** another, they take complete control of their land. *...the white people who had conquered their land... Britain was conquered by the Romans.* ♦ **conqueror** /kɒŋkərə/ COUNT N *...the European conquerors of Mexico.* 2 VB WITH OBJ If you **conquer** something difficult or dangerous, you succeed in destroying it or getting control of it. *...a tremendous international effort to conquer cancer.*

conquest /kɒŋ¹kwɛst/, **conquests.** 1 UNCOUNT N **Conquest** is the act of conquering a country or group of people. *Negotiations are preferable to conquest.* 2 COUNT N A **conquest** is land that has been conquered in war. 3 SING N The **conquest** of something difficult or dangerous is success in getting control of it. *...the conquest of space.*

conscience /kɒnʃəns/, **consciences.** 1 COUNT N Your **conscience** is the part of your mind that tells you if what you are doing is wrong. *My conscience told me to vote against the others.* ● If you have a guilty **conscience,** you feel guilty because you have done something wrong. 2 UNCOUNT N **Conscience** is doing what you believe is right even though it might be unpopular, difficult, or dangerous. *In all conscience, I couldn't make things difficult for him... The exercise of conscience is an individual act.*

conscientious /kɒnʃɪɛnʃəs/. ADJ Someone who is **conscientious** always does their work properly. *He was a very conscientious minister.* ♦ **conscientiously** ADV *He'd been doing his job conscientiously.*

conscious /kɒnʃəs/. 1 PRED ADJ If you are **conscious** of something, you notice it or are aware of it. *She became conscious of Rudolph looking at her... I was conscious that he had changed his tactics.* 2 ADJ **Conscious** is used in expressions such as 'socially conscious' and 'politically conscious' to describe someone who believes that a particular aspect of life is important. *Hundreds of women had become politically conscious.* 3 ATTRIB ADJ A **conscious** action or effort is done deliberately. *He made a conscious effort to look pleased.* ♦ **consciously** ADV *She couldn't believe that Mr Foster would ever consciously torment her.* 4 PRED ADJ Someone who is **conscious** is awake rather than asleep or unconscious. *The patient was fully conscious during the operation.*

consciousness /kɒnʃəsnɪ²s/. 1 SING N Your **consciousness** is your mind and thoughts, beliefs and attitudes. *Doubts were starting to enter into my consciousness... ...the awakening political consciousness of Africans.* 2 UNCOUNT N If you lose **consciousness,** you are unconscious rather than awake. If you have regained **consciousness,** you are awake again rather than unconscious.

conscript, conscripts, conscripting, conscripted; pronounced /kə⁷nskrɪpt/ when it is a verb and /kɒnskrɪpt/ when it is a noun. 1 VB WITH OBJ If someone **is conscripted,** they are officially made to join the armed forces. *Nine countries decided to let women be conscripted.* ♦ **conscription** /kə⁷nskrɪpʃə⁰n/ UNCOUNT N *The president has ended conscription.* 2 COUNT N A **conscript** is a person who has been made to join the armed forces of a country.

consecrate /kɒnsɪ²kreɪt/, **consecrates, consecrating, consecrated.** VB WITH OBJ When a building, place, or object **is consecrated,** it is officially declared to be holy. *King Edward consecrated the original church here in 1065.* ♦ **consecrated** ADJ *He was refused burial in consecrated ground.* ♦ **consecration** /kɒnsɪ²kreɪʃə⁰n/ UNCOUNT N *...the consecration of the church.*

consecutive /kə⁷nsɛkjə⁴tɪv/. ADJ **Consecutive** periods of time or events happen one after the other without interruption. *...three consecutive victories.*

consensus /kə⁷nsɛnsəs/. UNCOUNT N **Consensus** is general agreement amongst a group of people. *There was some consensus of opinion.*

consent /kə⁷nsɛnt/, **consents, consenting, consented.** 1 UNCOUNT N **Consent** is permission given to someone to do something. *She had threatened to marry without her parents' consent.* 2 UNCOUNT N **Consent** is also agreement about something between people. *By common consent they stopped.* 3 VB If you **consent** to something, you agree to do it or to allow it to be done.

consequence /kɒnsɪkwəns/, **consequences.** 1 COUNT N A **consequence** of something is a result or effect of it. *...the economic consequences of the computer revolution.* 2 UNCOUNT N Someone or something that is of **consequence** is important or valuable. Someone or something that is of little **consequence** is not important.

consequent /kɒnsɪkwənt/. ATTRIB ADJ **Consequent** means happening as a direct result of something; a formal use. *...the non-publication of the report and the consequent absence of public discussion.* ♦ **consequently** SENTENCE ADV *Absolute secrecy is essential. Consequently, the fewer who are aware of the plan the better.*

conservation /kɒnsəveɪʃə⁰n/. UNCOUNT N **Conservation** is the preservation and protection of the environment. *...the present public awareness of the need for conservation.* ♦ **conservationist** COUNT N *Mike Holland, soil conservationist, was also with VSO.*

conservatism /kə⁷nsɜːvətɪzə⁰m/. UNCOUNT N **Conservatism** is unwillingness to accept changes and new ideas. *...the conservatism of President Reagan.*

conservative /kə⁷nsɜːvətɪv/, **conservatives.** 1 ADJ Someone who is **conservative** is unwilling to accept changes and new ideas. *Publishers in Britain are more conservative than their continental counterparts.* ♦ **conservatively** ADV *He dresses conservatively.* 2 COUNT N A **conservative** is someone with right-wing political views. *...leading conservatives in the Senate.* Also ADJ *...conservative voters.* 3 ADJ A **conservative** estimate or guess is very cautious. *How long will it last? Three hundred years at a fairly conservative estimate.*

conservatory /kə⁷nsɜːvətrɪ¹/, **conservatories.** COUNT N A **conservatory** is a glass room, attached to a house, in which plants are kept.

conserve /kə7nsɜːv/, **conserves, conserving, conserved. 1** VB WITH OBJ If you **conserve** a supply of something, you use it carefully so that it lasts longer. *They made themselves wait quietly, conserving their strength.* **2** VB WITH OBJ To **conserve** something means to keep it in its original form and protect it from harm, loss, or change. *Such laws exist only to conserve the privilege of this selfish minority.*

consider /kə7nsɪdə/, **considers, considering, considered. 1** VB WITH OBJ OR REPORT VB If you **consider** a person or thing to be something, this is your opinion of them. *They consider themselves to be very lucky... Some British generals considered the attack a mistake... I consider that one is enough.* **2** VB WITH OBJ If you **consider** something, you think about it carefully. *He had no time to consider the matter.* **3** VB WITH OBJ If you **consider** a person's needs, wishes, or feelings, you pay attention to them. ● See also **consideration, considered, considering.**

considerable /kə7nsɪdə0rəbə0l/. ADJ Something that is **considerable** is great in amount or degree. *The building suffered considerable damage.* ♦ **considerably** ADV *His work had improved considerably.*

considerate /kə7nsɪdə0rə1t/. ADJ A **considerate** person pays attention to the needs, wishes, or feelings of other people.

consideration /kə7nsɪdəreɪʃə0n/, **considerations. 1** UNCOUNT N **Consideration** is careful thought about something. *After careful consideration, her parents gave her permission.* **2** UNCOUNT N Someone who shows **consideration** pays attention to the needs, wishes, or feelings of other people. *He showed no consideration for his daughters.* **3** COUNT N A **consideration** is something that should be thought about, when you are planning or deciding something. *An important consideration is the amount of time it will take.*

PHRASES ● If you **take** something **into consideration,** you think about it because it is relevant to what you are doing. *The first thing one has to take into consideration is the cost.* ● Something that is **under consideration** is being discussed. *The case was still under consideration.*

considered /kə7nsɪdəd/. ATTRIB ADJ A **considered** opinion or act is the result of careful thought. *...a considered change of mind.*

considering /kə7nsɪdə0rɪŋ/. CONJ OR PREP You use **considering** to indicate that you are taking a particular fact into account when giving an opinion. *Considering that he received no help, his results are very good... Considering her dislike of Martin, it was surprising that she invited him.*

consign /kə7nsaɪn/, **consigns, consigning, consigned.** VB WITH OBJ AND PREP 'to' If you **consign** something to a particular place, you put it there to get rid of it; a formal use. *I discovered some wheels that had been consigned to the loft.*

consignment /kə7nsaɪnmə2nt/, **consignments.** COUNT N A **consignment** of goods is a load that is being delivered to a place or person.

consist /kə7nsɪst/, **consists, consisting, consisted.** VB WITH 'of' Something that **consists** of particular things is formed from them. *The committee consists of scientists and engineers.*

consistency /kə7nsɪstənsi1/. **1** UNCOUNT N **Consistency** is the condition of being consistent. *...consistency and continuity in government policy.* **2** UNCOUNT N The **consistency** of a substance is the extent to which it is thick or smooth. *Small children dislike food with a sticky consistency.*

consistent /kə7nsɪstənt/. **1** ADJ A **consistent** person always behaves or responds in the same way. *Brook was Baldwin's most dangerous and consistent adversary.* ♦ **consistently** ADV *Hearst consistently opposed Roosevelt's policies.* **2** ADJ An idea or argument that is **consistent** is organized so that each part of it agrees with all the other parts.

console, consoles, consoling, consoled; pronounced /kə7nsəʊl/ when it is a verb and /kɒnsəʊl/ when it is a noun. **1** VB WITH OBJ If you **console** someone who is unhappy, you try to make them more cheerful. *She tried to console me by saying that I'd probably be happier in a new job.* ♦ **consoling** ADJ *Dad laid a consoling hand on his shoulder.* ♦ **consolation** /kɒnsəleɪʃə0n/ UNCOUNT N *...a few words of consolation.* **2** COUNT N A **console** is a panel with switches or knobs used to operate a machine.

consolidate /kə7nsɒlɪdeɪt/, **consolidates, consolidating, consolidated. 1** VB WITH OBJ If you **consolidate** power or a plan, you strengthen it so that it becomes more effective or secure. *The new middle class consolidated its wealth and power.* ♦ **consolidation** /kə7nsɒlɪdeɪʃə0n/ UNCOUNT N *...the long-term consolidation of party power.* **2** VB WITH OBJ To **consolidate** a number of small groups or firms means to make them into one large organization. *They consolidated the states of the north into a unified Northern region.* ♦ **consolidation** UNCOUNT N *...a dangerous trend toward consolidation that could destroy small businesses.*

consonant /kɒnsənənt/, **consonants.** COUNT N A **consonant** is a sound such as 'p' or 'f' which you pronounce by stopping the air flowing freely through your mouth.

consort, consorts, consorting, consorted; pronounced /kə7nsɔːt/ when it is a verb and /kɒnsɔːt/ when it is a noun. **1** VB WITH 'with' If someone **consorts** with a particular person or group, they spend a lot of time with them; a formal use which is often used showing disapproval. *Daddy would never approve of her consorting with drug addicts.* **2** COUNT N A **consort** is the wife or husband of the ruling monarch.

consortium /kə7nsɔːtɪəm/, **consortia** /kə7nsɔːtɪə/ or **consortiums.** COLL N A **consortium** is a group of people or firms who have agreed to work together. *...a consortium of Birmingham businessmen.*

conspicuous /kə7nspɪkjʊəs/. ADJ If something is **conspicuous,** people can see or notice it very easily. *Her freckles were more conspicuous than usual.* ♦ **conspicuously** ADV *He had been conspicuously successful.*

conspiracy /kə7nspɪrəsi1/, **conspiracies.** UNCOUNT N OR COUNT N **Conspiracy** is the secret planning by a group of people to do something illegal, usually for political reasons. *The police arrested her on a charge of conspiracy to murder... Very few people knew the details of the conspiracy.*

conspirator /kə7nspɪrətə/, **conspirators.** COUNT N A **conspirator** is a person who joins a conspiracy.

conspiratorial /kə7nspɪrətɔːrɪəl/. **1** ADJ If you are **conspiratorial,** you behave as if you are sharing a secret with someone. *...a conspiratorial nod.* **2** ADJ Something that is **conspiratorial** is secret and illegal, often with a political purpose.

conspire /kə7nspaɪə/, **conspires, conspiring, conspired. 1** RECIP VB If you **conspire,** you secretly agree with other people to do something illegal or harmful. *I disliked the feeling of conspiring with her father... My enemies are conspiring against me.* **2** VB If events **conspire** towards a particular result, they seem to cause this result; a literary use. *Everything had conspired to make him happy.*

constable /kʌnstəbə0l/, **constables.** COUNT N A **constable** is a police officer of the lowest rank in Britain.

constabulary /kənstæbjə4ləri1/, **constabularies.** COUNT N In Britain, a **constabulary** is the police force of a particular area. *...the Wiltshire Constabulary.*

constant /kɒnstənt/. **1** ADJ Something that is **constant** happens all the time or is always there. *He was in constant pain.* ♦ **constantly** ADV *The world around us is constantly changing.* **2** ADJ An amount or level that is **constant** stays the same over a particular period of time. *...a constant voltage.* ♦ **constancy** /kɒnstənsi1/ UNCOUNT N *...the constancy of the temperature.*

constellation /kɒnstr2leɪʃə0n/, **constellations.** COUNT N A **constellation** is a named group of stars.

consternation /kɒnstəneɪʃə0n/. UNCOUNT N **Consternation** is a feeling of anxiety or fear. *We looked at each other in consternation.*

constipated /kɒnstɪpeɪtɪ2d/. ADJ Someone who is **constipated** has difficulty in defecating.

constipation /kɒnstɪpeɪʃə0n/. UNCOUNT N **Constipation** is a medical condition which causes people to have difficulty defecating.

constituency /kə7nstɪtjʊənsi1/, **constituencies.** COUNT N A **constituency** is an area which is officially allowed to elect someone to represent them in parliament. *There were 14,000 voters in the constituency.*

constituent /kə7nstɪtjʊənt/, **constituents. 1** COUNT N A **constituent** is someone who lives in a particular constituency, especially someone who is eligible to vote in an election. **2** COUNT N A **constituent** of something is one of the things that it is made from. *Nitrogen is one of the essential constituents of living matter.*

constitute /kɒnstɪtjuːt/, **constitutes, constituting, constituted. 1** VB WITH COMPLEMENT If something **constitutes** a particular thing, it can be regarded as being that thing. *Conifers constitute about a third of the world's forests.* **2** VB WITH OBJ To **constitute** something also means to form it from a number of parts or elements; a formal use. *...the way in which the modern artist constitutes his images.*

constitution /kɒnstɪtjuːʃə0n/, **constitutions. 1** COUNT N The **constitution** of a country or organization is the system of laws which formally states people's rights and duties. *...the US constitution.* ♦ **constitutional** /kɒnstɪtjuːʃə0nəl, -ʃənə0l/ ADJ *...a major constitutional change.* **2** COUNT N Your **constitution** is your health. *He has a strong constitution.* **3** SING N The **constitution** of something is also what it is made of, and how its parts are arranged. *Questions were asked concerning the constitution and scope of the proposed commission.*

constrain /kə7nstreɪn/, **constrains, constraining, constrained;** VB WITH OBJ To **constrain** someone or something means to limit their development or force them to behave in a particular way; a formal use. *Papa had told her that he would not constrain her in any way.* ♦ **constrained** PRED ADJ *He felt constrained to apologize.*

constraint /kə7nstreɪnt/, **constraints;** a formal word. **1** COUNT N A **constraint** is something that limits or controls the way you behave. *The constraint on most doctors is lack of time.* **2** UNCOUNT N **Constraint** is control over the way you behave which prevents you from doing what you want to do. *The list of instructions and guidelines brings with it a flavour of constraint.*

constrict /kə7nstrɪkt/, **constricts, constricting, constricted. 1** VB WITH OBJ To **constrict** something means to squeeze it tightly. *He rubbed his ankles where the bindings had constricted him.* ♦ **constriction** /kə7nstrɪkʃə0n/ UNCOUNT N *Some snakes kill, not by constriction, but by poison.* **2** VB WITH OBJ If something **constricts** you, it limits your actions so that you cannot do what you want to do. *...the constricting structure of schools.* ♦ **constriction** COUNT N *...the constrictions of family life.*

construct, constructs, constructing, constructed; pronounced /kə7nstrʌkt/ when it is a verb and /kɒnstrʌkt/ when it is a noun. **1** VB WITH OBJ If you **construct** something, you build, make or create it. *We constructed a raft... ...a building constructed of brick.* **2** COUNT N A **construct** is a complex idea; a formal use. *...theoretical constructs.*

construction /kə7nstrʌkʃə0n/, **constructions. 1** UNCOUNT N **Construction** is the building or creating of something. *...the construction of the Panama Canal.* **2** COUNT N A **construction** is an object that has been made or built. *These wigs are complicated constructions of real and false hair.* **3** UNCOUNT N You use the word **construction** to talk about how things have been built. For example, if something is of simple **construction,** it is simply built. *The main walls of the building are of solid brick construction.*

constructive /kə7nstrʌktɪv/. ADJ **Constructive** advice or criticism is useful and helpful. *I did not have anything constructive to say.* ♦ **constructively** ADV *You must channel your anger constructively.*

consul /kɒnsə0l/, **consuls.** COUNT N A **consul** is a government official who lives in a foreign city and looks after all the people there who are from his or her own country. ♦ **consular** /kɒnsjə4lə/ ATTRIB ADJ *...the British Consular authorities in Barcelona.*

consulate /kɒnsjə4lə1t/, **consulates.** COUNT N A **consulate** is the place where a consul works.

consult /kə7nsʌlt/, **consults, consulting, consulted. 1** VB WITH OBJ OR 'with' If you **consult** someone, you ask them for their opinion and advice. *If your baby is losing weight, you should consult your doctor promptly... They would have to consult with their allies.* **2** VB WITH OBJ If you **consult** a book or a map, you refer to it for information.

consultancy /kə7nsʌltənsi1/, **consultancies.** COUNT N A **consultancy** is a group of people who give professional advice on a particular subject.

consultant /kə7nsʌltə2nt/, **consultants. 1** COUNT N A **consultant** is an experienced doctor specializing in one area of medicine. *I was the first woman consultant on the staff of Charing Cross Hospital.* **2** COUNT N A **consultant** is also a person who gives expert advice to people who need professional help. *...a firm of public relations consultants.*

consultation /kɒnsə0lteɪʃə0n/, **consultations. 1** COUNT N A **consultation** is a meeting held to discuss something. **2** UNCOUNT N **Consultation** is discussion between people, especially when advice is given. *This is a matter for the Prime Minister to decide in consultation with the Ministry of Defence.*

consulting room, consulting rooms. COUNT N A **consulting room** is a room in which a doctor sees patients.

consume /kə7nsj0uːm/, **consumes, consuming, consumed. 1** VB WITH OBJ If you **consume** something, you eat or drink it; a formal use. *They spend their evenings consuming vodka.* **2** VB WITH OBJ To **consume** an amount of fuel, energy, or time means to use it up. *The ship consumed a great deal of fuel.* **3** VB WITH OBJ If a feeling or desire **consumes** you, it affects you very strongly; a literary use.

consumer /kə7nsj0uːmə/, **consumers.** COUNT N A **consumer** is a person who buys things or uses services. *The consumer is entitled to products that give value for money... ...gas consumers.*

consuming /kə7nsj0uːmɪŋ/. ATTRIB ADJ A **consuming** passion or interest is more important to you than anything else. *Politics is the consuming passion of half the town.*

consummate, consummates, consummating, consummated; a formal word, pronounced /kɒnsj^{0}ə^{4}meɪt/ when it is a verb and /kɒnsj^{0}ə^{4}mət/ when it is an adjective. **1** VB WITH OBJ If two people **consummate** a marriage or relationship, they make it complete by having sex. ♦ **consummation** UNCOUNT N *...the consummation of their marriage.* **2** VB WITH OBJ To **consummate** something means to do something which makes it complete. *We need to consummate what we have so far achieved.* ♦ **consummation** UNCOUNT N *This expedition was the consummation of what he regarded as his life's work.* **3** ATTRIB ADJ You use **consummate** to describe someone who is extremely skilful. *He was a fighter of consummate skill.*

consumption /kə^{7}nsʌmpʃə^{0}n/. **1** UNCOUNT N WITH SUPP The **consumption** of fuel or energy is the amount of it that is used or the act of using it. *Oil used to make up 10 per cent of our total energy consumption... ...our consumption of energy.* **2** UNCOUNT N **Consumption** is the act of eating or drinking something; a formal use. *The water was unfit for consumption.* **3** UNCOUNT N **Consumption** is also the act of buying and using things. *...new patterns of consumption.*

contact /kɒntækt/, **contacts, contacting, contacted. 1** UNCOUNT N OR COUNT N **Contact** involves meeting or communicating with someone, especially regularly. *There is little contact between governors and parents... My first contact with him was about twenty-five years ago.* **2** VB WITH OBJ If you **contact** someone, you telephone them or write to them. *As soon as we find out, we'll contact you.* **3** COUNT N A **contact** is someone you know, for example a person in an organization or profession, who helps you or gives you information. *He had contacts in America... ...business contacts.* **4** UNCOUNT N **Contact** also refers to the fact of things touching each other. *Close physical contact is important for a baby.*

PHRASES ● If you are **in contact** with someone, you regularly meet them or communicate with them. *I'm in contact with a number of schools.* ● When things are **in contact,** they are touching each other. *One foot must always be in contact with the ground.* ● If you **come into contact with** someone, you happen to meet them in the course of your work or other activities. *Everyone who came into contact with her liked her.* ● If one thing **comes into contact with** another, the first thing touches the second. *My hand came into contact with a small lump.* ● If you **make contact** with someone, you find out where they are and talk or write to them. ● If you **lose contact** with someone, you stop meeting them or writing to them.

contact lens, contact lenses. COUNT N **Contact lenses** are small lenses that you put on your eyes to help you to see better, instead of wearing glasses.

contagious /kə^{7}nteɪdʒəs/. **1** ADJ A **contagious** disease can be caught by touching people or things that are infected with it. **2** ADJ A **contagious** feeling or attitude spreads quickly among a group of people. *Quint's confidence was contagious.*

contain /kə^{7}nteɪn/, **contains, containing, contained. 1** VB WITH OBJ If something such as a box or a room **contains** things, those things are inside it. *...a basket containing groceries... The urban areas contain several million people.* **2** VB WITH OBJ If something **contains** a particular substance, that substance is part of it. *...chemical compounds containing mercury.* **3** VB WITH OBJ To **contain** something such as a feeling, problem, or activity means to control it and prevent it from increasing; a formal use. *He could hardly contain his eagerness to leave... ...measures to contain population growth.*

container /kə^{7}nteɪnə/, **containers. 1** COUNT N A **container** is something such as a box or bottle that is used to hold or store things. *...a soap container.* **2** MOD **Container** ships and lorries transport goods in very large sealed metal boxes called containers.

contaminate /kə^{7}ntæmɪneɪt/, **contaminates, contaminating, contaminated.** VB WITH OBJ When something **is contaminated** by dirt, chemicals, or radiation, it becomes impure or harmful. *Many wells have been contaminated by chemicals... ...foods that are easily contaminated with poisonous bacteria.* ♦ **contaminated** ADJ *...contaminated water.* ♦ **contamination** /kə^{7}ntæmɪneɪʃə^{0}n/ UNCOUNT N *...infections caused by the contamination of milk.*

contemplate /kɒntə^{2}mpleɪt/, **contemplates, contemplating, contemplated. 1** VB WITH OBJ OR -ING If you **contemplate** doing something, you wonder whether to do it or not. *Lawrence contemplated publishing the book.* **2** VB WITH OBJ If you **contemplate** an idea or subject, you think about it carefully and for a long time. *We have to pause and contemplate what we are talking about.* ♦ **contemplation** /kɒntə^{2}mpleɪʃə^{0}n/ UNCOUNT N *...religious contemplation.* **3** VB WITH OBJ To **contemplate** something or someone means to look at them for a long time. *They contemplated each other in silence.*

contemplative /kə^{7}ntemplətɪv/. ADJ **Contemplative** people think deeply in a serious and calm way.

contemporary /kə^{7}ntemprəri^1/, **contemporaries. 1** ATTRIB ADJ **Contemporary** means happening or existing now or at the time you are talking about. *...contemporary writers... ...a contemporary account of the trial.* **2** COUNT N A person's **contemporaries** are people who are approximately the same age as them, or who lived at approximately the same time as them. *...Darwin's contemporary, Sir James Simpson.*

contempt /kə^{7}ntempt/. UNCOUNT N If you have **contempt** for someone or something, you have no respect for them. *The women would often look at us with contempt... ...his contempt for the truth.* ● If you **hold** someone or something **in contempt,** you feel contempt for them.

contemptible /kə^{7}ntemptəbə^{0}l/. ADJ If you feel that someone or something is **contemptible,** you feel strong dislike and disrespect for them. *You are showing a contemptible lack of courage.*

contemptuous /kə^{7}ntemptjuəs/. ADJ If you are **contemptuous** of someone or something, you do not like or respect them at all; a formal use. *Hamilton gave me a contemptuous look.* ♦ **contemptuously** ADV *He tossed the paper contemptuously on to the table.*

contend /kə^{7}ntend/, **contends, contending, contended. 1** VB WITH 'with' To **contend** with a problem or difficulty means to deal with it or overcome it. *The girls had problems of their own at home to contend with.* **2** RECIP VB If you **contend** with someone for something such as power or a championship, you compete with them in order to get it. *...new worlds contending with old for mastery... Three parties are contending for power.* ♦ **contending** ATTRIB ADJ *Those decisions were fought out between contending groups.* ♦ **contender** /kə^{7}ntendə/ COUNT N *...a contender in the Presidential election.* **3** REPORT VB If you **contend** that something is true, you state or argue that it is true; a formal use. *She contended that the report was deficient.*

content, contents, contenting, contented; pronounced /kɒntent/ for meanings 1 to 4, and /kə^{7}ntent/ for meanings 5 to 8. **1** PLURAL N The **contents** of something such as a box or room are the things inside it. *He drank the contents of his glass in one gulp... ...the contents of the bag.* **2** PLURAL N The **contents** of something such as a document or a tape are the things written or recorded on it. *He knew by heart the contents of the note.* **3** UNCOUNT N The **content** of a piece of writing, speech, or television programme is its subject and the ideas expressed in it. *I was disturbed by the content of some of the speeches.* **4** SING N WITH SUPP The amount or proportion of something that a substance contains is referred to as its **content** of that thing. *No other food has such a high iron content.* **5** PRED ADJ If you are **content,** you are happy and satisfied. *However hard up they were, they stayed content.* ♦ **contentment** /kə^{7}ntentmə^{3}nt/ UNCOUNT N *I sighed with contentment.* **6** PRED ADJ If you are **content** with something, you are satisfied with it. If you are **content** to do something, you do it willingly. *Children are not content with glib explanations... A few teachers were content to pay the fines.* **7** REFL VB WITH 'with' If you **content** yourself with something, you accept it and do not try to do or have other things. *She didn't take part in the discussion, but contented herself with smoking cigarettes.* **8 to** your **heart's content:** see **heart.**

contented /kə^{7}ntentɪ^{2}d/. ADJ If you are **contented,** you are happy and satisfied. *...firms with a loyal and contented labour force.* ♦ **contentedly** ADV *She plays contentedly by herself.*

contention /kə^{7}ntenʃə^{0}n/, **contentions;** a formal word. **1** COUNT N Someone's **contention** is the idea or opinion that they are expressing. *My contention is that we must offer all our children the same opportunities.* **2** UNCOUNT N **Contention** is disagreement or argument about something. *This is an issue of great contention at the moment.* **3** PHRASE If you are **in contention** in a contest, you have a chance of winning it.

contentious /kə^{7}ntenʃəs/. ADJ A **contentious** subject or opinion causes disagreement and arguments. *...his contentious view that mental illness is a myth.*

contest, contests, contesting, contested; pronounced /kɒntest/ when it is a noun and /kə^{7}ntest/ when it is a verb. **1** COUNT N A **contest** is a competition or game. *...a fishing contest.* **2** COUNT N A **contest** is also a struggle to win power or control. *He won the contest for the deputy leadership.* **3** VB WITH OBJ To **contest** an election or competition means to take part in it in order to win. *There was an election contested by six candidates.* **4** VB WITH OBJ If you **contest** a statement or decision, you disagree with it formally. *We hotly contest the idea that any of them were ours.*

contestant /kə^{7}ntestənt/, **contestants.** COUNT N The **contestants** in a competition or quiz are the people taking part in it. *...the contestants in the world championship.*

context /kɒntekst/, **contexts. 1** COUNT N OR UNCOUNT N The **context** of an idea or event is the general situation in which it occurs. *We need to place present events in some kind of historical context.* **2** COUNT N OR UNCOUNT N The **context** of a word or sentence consists of the words or sentences before it and after it.

continent /kɒntɪnənt/, **continents. 1** COUNT N A **continent** is a very large area of land, such as Africa or Asia. *...the North American continent.* ♦ **continental** /kɒntɪnentə^{0}l/ ADJ *Defence should be organized on a continental scale.* **2** PROPER N In Britain, the mainland of Europe is sometimes referred to as the **Continent.** *British artists are very well known on the Continent.* ♦ **Continental** ATTRIB ADJ *...a Continental holiday.*

contingency /kə^{7}ntɪndʒənsi^1/, **contingencies.** COUNT N A **contingency** is something that might happen in the future. *He had anticipated all contingencies... ...contingency plans for nuclear attack.*

contingent /kə^{7}ntɪndʒənt/, **contingents. 1** COUNT N A **contingent** is a group of people representing a country or organization. *...a contingent of European scientists.* **2** COUNT N A **contingent** of police or soldiers is a group of them. *Police contingents were ordered into the area.* **3** PRED ADJ WITH 'on' If an event is **contingent** on something, it can only happen if that thing happens or exists; a formal use. *The raid was contingent on the weather.*

continual /kə^{7}ntɪnju^{0}əl/. ATTRIB ADJ **Continual** means happening without stopping, or happening again and again. *...a continual movement of air... He ignored the continual warnings of his nurse.* ♦ **continually** ADV *Tom was continually asking me questions.*

continuance /kə^{7}ntɪnjuəns/. UNCOUNT N The **continuance** of something is its continuation; a formal use. *...the continuance of the war.*

continuation /kə^{7}ntɪnju:eɪʃə^{0}n/. **1** UNCOUNT N The **continuation** of something is the fact that it continues to happen or exist. *People take for granted the continuation of economic growth.* **2** SING N If one thing is a **continuation** of another, it is next to it or happens after it and forms an extra part of it. *The carpet seemed a continuation of the lawn.*

continue /kə^{7}ntɪnju:/, **continues, continuing, continued. 1** VB WITH TO-INF OR -ING If you **continue** to do something, you keep doing it. *The orchestra continued to play... He continued talking.* **2** VB OR ERG VB If something **continues,** it does not stop. *The battle continued for an hour... They want to continue their education.* **3** VB OR ERG VB You also say that something **continues** when it starts again after stopping for a period of time. *The next day the performance continued... He arrived in Norway, where he continued his campaign.* **4** VB WITH 'with' If you **continue** with something, you keep doing it or using it. *The girls should continue with their mathematics.* **5** VB OR REPORT VB To **continue** also means to begin speaking again after a pause or interruption. *'I mean Phil,' she continued, 'It's for him.'* **6** VB WITH ADJUNCT To **continue** in a particular direction means to keep going in that direction. *I continued up the path.*

continuity /kɒntɪnju:ɪ^{1}ti^1/. UNCOUNT N The **continuity** of something is the fact that it happens, exists, or develops without stopping or changing suddenly. *...the importance of continuity in government policy.*

continuous /kə^{7}ntɪnju:əs/. **1** ADJ Something that is **continuous** happens or exists without stopping. *...the continuous increase in their military capacity.* ♦ **continuously** ADV *The volcano had been erupting continuously since March.* **2** ATTRIB ADJ A **continuous** line or surface has no gaps in it. **3** ADJ In English grammar, the **continuous** form of verbs is formed by the auxiliary 'be' and the '-ing' form of a verb.

continuum /kə^{7}ntɪnjuəm/. SING N A **continuum** is a series of events considered as a single process; a formal use. *...the continuum of the seasons.*

contort /kə^{7}ntɔ:t/, **contorts, contorting, contorted.** ERG VB When something **contorts,** it changes into an unnatural and unattractive shape. *...contorting his features into an expression of agony.* ♦ **contorted** ADJ *...his mad contorted smile.* ♦ **contortion** /kə^{7}ntɔ:ʃə^{0}n/ COUNT N OR UNCOUNT N *...the child's ceaseless contortions.*

contour /kɒntʊə/, **contours. 1** COUNT N The **contours** of something are its shape or outline. *Pain altered the contours of his face.* **2** COUNT N On a map, a **contour** is a line joining points of equal height.

contraband /kɒntrəbænd/. UNCOUNT N Goods brought into a country illegally are called **contraband.** *He might be carrying contraband.*

contraception /kɒntrəsɛpʃə0n/. UNCOUNT N Methods of preventing pregnancy are called **contraception.**

contraceptive /kɒntrəsɛptɪv/, **contraceptives.** COUNT N A **contraceptive** is a device or pill that prevents a woman from becoming pregnant.

contract, contracts, contracting, contracted; pronounced /kɒntrækt/ when it is a noun, and /kə7ntrækt/ when it is a verb. 1 COUNT N A **contract** is a written legal agreement, especially one connected with the sale of something or with the carrying out of a job of work. *We won a contract to build fifty-eight planes.* ♦ **contractual** /kə7ntræktju0əl/ ATTRIB ADJ *The union had a contractual agreement with the company.* 2 VB WITH TO-INF If you **contract** with someone to do something, you legally agree to do it; a formal use. *They contracted to supply us with horses.* 3 ERG VB When something **contracts,** it becomes smaller or shorter. *Metals expand with heat and contract with cold.* ♦ **contraction** /kə7ntrækʃə0n/ COUNT N OR UNCOUNT N *...the contraction of the muscles.* 4 VB WITH OBJ If you **contract** an illness, you become ill; a formal use.

contractor /kɒntræktə, kəntræk-/, **contractors.** COUNT N A **contractor** is a person or company that does work for other people or companies. *...houses built by private contractors.*

contradict /kɒntrədɪkt/, **contradicts, contradicting, contradicted.** 1 VB WITH OBJ If you **contradict** someone, you say that what they have just said is untrue. *I took care not to contradict her... 'No,' contradicted her sister, 'it's because he doesn't care.'* 2 VB WITH OBJ If one statement **contradicts** another, the statements cannot both be true. *Perfectly reputable books may contradict each other.*

contradiction /kɒntrədɪkʃə0n/, **contradictions.** COUNT N OR UNCOUNT N A **contradiction** is a difference between two things or two parts of something which reduce their effect or make them difficult to understand. *There is a contradiction between the two laws... There is no contradiction in this approach... I hate to admit all these contradictions in myself.* ● If you say that something is a **contradiction in terms,** you mean that it is described as having a quality that it cannot have. *A rational religion is almost a contradiction in terms.*

contradictory /kɒntrədɪktə0ri1/. ADJ If two ideas or statements are **contradictory,** they are opposite. *The government had made two contradictory promises.*

contralto /kə7ntræltəʊ/, **contraltos.** COUNT N A **contralto** is a woman with a low singing voice.

contraption /kə7ntræpʃə0n/, **contraptions.** COUNT N A **contraption** is a strange-looking device or machine. *Over his door was a contraption with a sliding shutter.*

contrary /kɒntrəri1/. 1 ADJ **Contrary** ideas or opinions are opposed to each other and cannot be held by the same person. *They happily tolerated the existence of opinions contrary to their own.* 2 PREP If you say that something is true **contrary to** what someone else believes or says, you are saying that it is true and that they are wrong. *Contrary to what is generally assumed, the adjustment is easily made.*
PHRASES ● You say **on the contrary** when you are contradicting what has just been said. *'You'll get tired of it.'—'On the contrary. I shall enjoy it.'* ● Evidence or statements **to the contrary** contradict what you are saying or what someone else has said. *This method, despite statements to the contrary, has no damaging effects.*

contrast, contrasts, contrasting, contrasted; pronounced /kɒntrɑːst/ when it is a noun, and /kə7ntrɑːst/ when it is a verb. 1 COUNT N A **contrast** is a great difference between two or more things. *...the contrast between his public image and his private life.* 2 COUNT N If one thing is a **contrast** to another, it is very different from it. *The atmosphere of the Second War was a complete contrast to that of the First.* 3 VB WITH 'with' If one thing **contrasts** with another, it is very different from it. *...a willingness to promote change, which contrasts strongly with the previous government's conservatism.* ♦ **contrasting** ATTRIB ADJ *...their contrasting attitudes... ...contrasting colours.* 4 PHRASE You say **by contrast** or **in contrast** when you are mentioning something that contrasts with what you have just said. *By contrast, our use of oil has increased enormously... This second movement, in contrast, reached a membership of 100,000 in two years.* 5 VB WITH OBJ If you **contrast** things, you show the differences between them. *The book contrasts the methods used in America and Russia.*

contravene /kɒntrəviːn/, **contravenes, contravening, contravened.** VB WITH OBJ To **contravene** a law or rule means to do something that is forbidden by it; a formal use. *They contravened the drug laws.* ♦ **contravention** /kɒntrəvɛnʃə0n/ UNCOUNT N OR COUNT N *The advert was in contravention of the Race Relations Act... ...contraventions of the ban.*

contribute /kə7ntrɪbjuːt/, **contributes, contributing, contributed.** 1 VB WITH OR WITHOUT OBJ If you **contribute** to something, you help to make it successful. *The elderly have much to contribute to the community.* ♦ **contribution** /kɒntrɪbjuːʃə0n/ COUNT N *...the BBC's contribution to the adult literacy campaign.* 2 VB WITH OR WITHOUT OBJ If you **contribute** money, you help to pay for something. *She persuaded friends to contribute $5,000 to the fund... George was already contributing to Democratic Party funds.* ♦ **contributor** /kə7ntrɪbjə4tə/ COUNT N *...contributors to a fund to save the house.* ♦ **contribution** COUNT N *The United Kingdom had to make a contribution of £1,000 million to the EEC budget.* 3 VB If something **contributes** to a situation, it is one of its causes. *Soaring land prices contribute to the high cost of housing.* 4 VB WITH OR WITHOUT OBJ If you **contribute** to a magazine or book, you write things that are published in it. *Distinguished writers had contributed to its pages... She contributed anonymous items to the Chronicle.* ♦ **contributor** COUNT N *...a contributor of short stories to a national weekly.*

contributory /kəntrɪbjə4tə0ri1/. ADJ A **contributory** factor is one of the causes of something; a formal use. *The inefficient use of oil was a major contributory factor.*

contrite /kə7ntraɪt, kɒntraɪt/. ADJ If you are **contrite,** you are ashamed and apologetic because you have done something wrong; a formal use. *I tried to look contrite.* ♦ **contrition** /kə7ntrɪʃə0n/ UNCOUNT N *They tell lies and show no sign of contrition.*

contrivance /kə7ntraɪvəns/, **contrivances.** COUNT N A **contrivance** is a strange-looking device. *...a contrivance of wood and wire.*

contrive /kə7ntraɪv/, **contrives, contriving, contrived;** a formal word. 1 VB WITH TO-INF If you **contrive** to do something difficult, you succeed in doing it. *I shall contrive to see you again... Mike contrived to grin without taking his cigar out of his mouth.* 2 VB WITH OBJ If you **contrive** an event or situation, you succeed in making it happen. *Confidential talks with professors were contrived by reporters posing as students.*

contrived /kə7ntraɪvd/. ADJ **Contrived** behaviour is false and unnatural. *...a contrived smile.*

control /kə7ntrəʊl/, **controls, controlling, controlled.** 1 VB WITH OBJ Someone who **controls** a country or organization has the power to take all the important decisions about the way it is run. *The Australians controlled the island.* ♦ **controlling** ATTRIB ADJ *The family had a controlling interest in the firm.* 2 UNCOUNT N **Control** is power or authority. *The rebels took control of a television station... ...political control over colonies.* 3 VB WITH OBJ To **control** a machine, process, or system means to make it work in the way that is required. *Computer systems control the lighting and heating.* 4 UNCOUNT N **Control** of a machine, process, or system is the fact of making it work in the way required. *You should have control of your vehicle at all times.* 5 REFL VB OR VB WITH OBJ If you **control** yourself or your feelings, you make yourself behave calmly when you are feeling angry, excited, or upset. 6 UNCOUNT N **Control** over yourself is the ability to make yourself behave calmly. *He told himself that he mustn't lose control.* 7 VB WITH OBJ To **control** something dangerous means to prevent it from becoming worse or spreading. *...a way of controlling cancer.* 8 COUNT N A **control** is a device used to operate a machine. *Just turn the volume control.* 9 PLURAL N **Controls** are the methods a government uses to restrict increases, for example in prices or wages.
PHRASES ● If you are **in control** of something that is happening, you are able to decide how it develops. *Those who begin the revolution rarely stay in control to complete the process.* ● If something is **beyond** your **control** or **outside** your **control,** you do not have any power to affect or change it. *The service is being withdrawn for reasons outside anyone's control.* ● If something is **out of control,** nobody has any power over it. *Inflation got out of control.* ● If something harmful is **under control,** it is being dealt with successfully and is unlikely to cause any more harm. *The fever was brought under control.* ● If something is **under** your **control,** you have the power to decide what will happen to it.

controller /kə7ntrəʊlə/, **controllers.** COUNT N A **controller** is a person with responsibility for a particular task. *...an air traffic controller... ...the financial controller.*

controversial /kɒntrəvɜːʃə0l/. ADJ Someone or something that is **controversial** causes a lot of discussion and disagreement. *Many of the new taxes are controversial... He is a controversial politician.*

controversy /kɒntrəvɜːsi1, kə7ntrɒvəsi1/, **controversies.** UNCOUNT N OR COUNT N **Controversy** is a lot of discussion and disagreement about something. *The government tried to avoid controversy... ...a violent controversy over a commercial treaty.*

conurbation /kɒnə5beɪʃə0n/, **conurbations.** COUNT N A **conurbation** is a large urban area formed by several towns that have spread towards each other.

convalesce /kɒnvəlɛs/, **convalesces, convalescing, convalesced.** VB If you **are convalescing,** you are resting and regaining your health after an illness or operation. *The fever is gone and the child is convalescing.*

convalescent /kɒnvəlɛsənt/. ATTRIB ADJ **Convalescent** means relating to regaining health. *...a convalescent home.* ♦ **convalescence** /kɒnvəlɛsəns/ UNCOUNT N *Clem wasn't allowed to visit me during my convalescence.*

convene /kə7nviːn/, **convenes, convening, convened;** a formal word. 1 VB WITH OBJ If you **convene** a meeting, you arrange for it to take place. 2 VB If a group of people **convene,** they come together for a meeting. *The grand jury did not convene until February.*

convenience /kə7nviːnɪəns/, **conveniences.** 1 UNCOUNT N WITH POSS If something is done for your **convenience,** it is done in a way that is useful or suitable for you. *The entire event had been arranged for their convenience.* 2 COUNT N A **convenience** is something useful. *...a house with every modern convenience.* ● See also **public convenience.**

convenient /kə7nviːnɪənt/. ADJ Something that is **convenient** is useful or suitable for a particular purpose. *It will be more convenient to stick to a three-hour timetable... ...a convenient place to live.* ♦ **conveniently** ADV *The amount of fuel is displayed conveniently on a gauge.* ♦ **convenience** /kə7nviːnɪəns/ UNCOUNT N *We use frozen food for convenience.*

convent /kɒnvə7nt/, **convents.** COUNT N A **convent** is a building where nuns live, or a school run by nuns.

convention /kə7nvɛnʃə0n/, **conventions.** 1 COUNT N OR UNCOUNT N A **convention** is an accepted way of behaving or of doing something. *...the everyday conventions... ...his arrogance and rejection of convention.* 2 COUNT N A **convention** is also an official agreement between countries or organizations. *They signed the convention in 1905.* 3 COUNT N A **convention** is also a large meeting of an organization or political group. *He left New York before the convention ended.*

conventional /kə7nvɛnʃə0nəl, -ʃənə0l/. 1 ADJ **Conventional** people behave in an ordinary and normal way. *...the conventional housewife.* ♦ **conventionally** ADV *...a more conventionally acceptable life.* 2 ATTRIB ADJ A **conventional** method or product is the one that is usually used. *...the abolition of conventional examinations... ...conventional fuels.* ♦ **conventionally** ADV *...conventionally educated students.* 3 ATTRIB ADJ **Conventional** wars and weapons do not involve nuclear explosives.

converge /kə7nvɜːdʒ/, **converges, converging, converged.** 1 VB When roads or lines **converge,** they meet or join. *The paths converge under the trees.* 2 VB When people or vehicles **converge** on a place, they move towards it from different directions. *The guards converged on her and flung her to the ground.* 3 VB When ideas or societies **converge,** they gradually become similar to each other. *Two radically different types of society were converging.* ♦ **convergence** /kə7nvɜːdʒəns/ UNCOUNT N *There was some convergence of views.*

conversant /kə7nvɜːsə0nt/. PRED ADJ If you are **conversant** with something, you are familiar with it; a formal use. *The designer must be conversant with all the aspects of the problem.*

conversation /kɒnvəseɪʃə0n/, **conversations.** 1 COUNT N OR UNCOUNT N If you have a **conversation** with someone, you talk to each other. *Roger and I had a conversation about the risks... He spent some hours in conversation with me.* 2 PHRASE When you **make conversation,** you talk to someone in order to be polite rather than because you want to. *He didn't like having to make conversation.*

conversational /kɒnvəseɪʃə0nəl, -ʃənə0l/. ATTRIB ADJ **Conversational** means relating to conversation or informal talk. *...their brilliant conversational powers.* ♦ **conversationally** ADV *'Tell me,' she said conversationally, 'does he bite?'*

converse, converses, conversing, conversed; pronounced /kə7nvɜːs/ when it is a verb, and /kɒnvɜːs/ when it is a noun or adjective. 1 RECIP VB If you **converse** with someone, you talk to each other; a formal use. *I consider it a privilege to have conversed with you... After the meeting, members conversed in small groups.* 2 SING N **The converse** of a statement or fact is the opposite of it, or a reversed form of it. For example, the converse of 'Investment stimulates growth' is 'Growth stimulates investment'. Also ATTRIB ADJ *Political power is used to win economic power. But the converse process is just as common.* ♦ **conversely** /kəˀnvɜːsli¹/ SENTENCE ADV *You can use beer yeast for bread-making. Conversely, you can use bread yeast in beer-making.*

convert, converts, converting, converted; pronounced /kəˀnvɜːt/ when it is a verb, and /kɒnvɜːt/ when it is a noun. 1 VB WITH OBJ To **convert** one thing into another means to change the first into the second. *A solar cell takes radiation from the sun and converts it into electricity... The house has been converted into two apartments... ...the formula for converting kilometres to miles.* ♦ **converted** ATTRIB ADJ *The theatre is a converted squash court.* ♦ **conversion** /kəˀnvɜːʃəⁿn/ COUNT N OR UNCOUNT N *...the conversion of coal into oil and gas.* 2 VB WITH OBJ If someone **converts** you, they persuade you to change your religious or political beliefs. *...since he was converted to Roman Catholicism.* ♦ **conversion** COUNT N OR UNCOUNT N *...his recent conversion to Christianity.* 3 COUNT N A **convert** is someone who has changed their religious or political beliefs. *...a Catholic convert.*

convertible /kəˀnvɜːtəbəⁿl/, **convertibles.** 1 COUNT N A **convertible** is a car with a soft roof that can be folded down or removed. 2 ADJ **Convertible** money can be easily exchanged for other forms of money. *The loan is freely convertible into dollars.*

convex /kɒnvɛks, kɒnvɛks/. ADJ A **convex** object curves outwards at its centre. *...a convex lens.*

convey /kəˀnveɪ/, **conveys, conveying, conveyed.** 1 REPORT VB To **convey** information or feelings means to cause them to be known or understood. *Newspapers convey the impression that the war is over... ...trying to convey that it did not really matter.* 2 VB WITH OBJ To **convey** someone or something to a place means to transport them there; a formal use. *...the truck conveying Daniel and the work crew.*

conveyor belt /kəˀnveɪə bɛlt/, **conveyor belts.** COUNT N A **conveyor belt** is a continuously moving strip which is used in factories for moving objects along.

convict, convicts, convicting, convicted; pronounced /kəˀnvɪkt/ when it is a verb and /kɒnvɪkt/ when it is a noun. 1 VB WITH OBJ To **convict** someone of a crime means to find them guilty of it in a court of law. *He was convicted of spying.* ♦ **convicted** ADJ *...convicted criminals.* 2 COUNT N A **convict** is someone who is in prison; an old-fashioned use. *...an escaped convict.*

conviction /kəˀnvɪkʃəⁿn/, **convictions.** 1 COUNT N OR UNCOUNT N A **conviction** is a strong belief or opinion. *...his conviction that he could run a newspaper... 'Yes,' I said without much conviction.* 2 COUNT N OR UNCOUNT N A **conviction** is also the act of finding someone guilty in a court of law. *...his record of previous convictions... ...the trial and conviction of Ward.*

convince /kəˀnvɪns/, **convinces, convincing, convinced.** VB WITH OBJ To **convince** someone of something means to make them believe that it is true or that it exists. *It took them a few days to convince me that it was possible... This had convinced her of the problems.* ♦ **convinced** PRED ADJ *He was convinced that her mother was innocent... I am convinced of your loyalty.*

convincing /kəˀnvɪnsɪŋ/. ADJ If someone or something is **convincing**, you believe them. *...a more convincing explanation.* ♦ **convincingly** ADV *She must speak more convincingly.*

convivial /kəˀnvɪvɪəl/. ADJ **Convivial** people and events are pleasant and friendly; a formal use. *The meal was a convivial one... ...a happy and convivial group.* ♦ **conviviality** UNCOUNT N *...the atmosphere of conviviality.*

convoluted /kɒnvəluːtɪ²d/. ADJ **Convoluted** sentences are complicated and difficult to understand.

convoy /kɒnvɔɪ/, **convoys.** COUNT N A **convoy** is a group of ships or other vehicles travelling together. *...a convoy of police cars.* ● If a group of vehicles are travelling **in convoy**, they are travelling together.

convulse /kəˀnvʌls/, **convulses, convulsing, convulsed.** ERG VB If someone **convulses**, their body moves suddenly in an uncontrolled way. *He convulsed in pain... A quiver convulsed his body.*

convulsion /kəˀnvʌlʃəⁿn/, **convulsions.** COUNT N If someone has a **convulsion** or **convulsions**, they suffer uncontrollable movements of their muscles.

convulsive /kəˀnvʌlsɪv/. ADJ A **convulsive** movement or action is sudden and uncontrollable. *I gave his hand a convulsive squeeze.* ♦ **convulsively** ADV *He shivered convulsively.*

coo /kuː/, **coos, cooing, cooed.** VB When a dove or pigeon **coos**, it makes soft sounds.

cook /kʊk/, **cooks, cooking, cooked.** 1 ERG VB OR VB When you **cook** food, you prepare it and then heat it, for example in an oven or in a saucepan. *I could smell vegetables cooking in the kitchen... Mildred cooks remarkably well.* 2 COUNT N A **cook** is a person who prepares and cooks food. *Are you a good cook?* 3 See also **cooking.**

cook up. PHR VB If someone **cooks up** a dishonest scheme, they plan it; an informal use. *They cook up all sorts of little deals.*

cooker /kʊkə/, **cookers.** COUNT N A **cooker** is a large box-shaped object used for cooking food either inside it or on top of it. *The milk was warming in a saucepan on the cooker.*

cookery /kʊkəⁿri¹/. UNCOUNT N **Cookery** is the activity of preparing and cooking

cookie /kʊki¹/, **cookies.** COUNT N A **cookie** is a biscuit; an American use.

cooking /kʊkɪŋ/. 1 UNCOUNT N **Cooking** is the activity of preparing and cooking food. *My mother was fond of cooking.* 2 UNCOUNT N WITH SUPP You can also use **cooking** to refer to cooked food of a particular type. *She loves your cooking... I like Portuguese cooking.*

cool /kuːl/, **cooler, coolest; cools, cooling, cooled.** 1 ADJ Something that is **cool** has a low temperature but is not cold. *The air was cool and fresh... ...a cool drink.* ♦ **coolness** UNCOUNT N *...the coolness of the room.* 2 ADJ **Cool** clothing is made of thin material. *I'll just change into a cooler frock.* 3 ERG VB When something **cools**, it becomes lower in temperature. *The water began to cool... Cool your feet in the stream.* 4 ADJ If you stay **cool** in a difficult situation, you remain calm. ♦ **coolly** ADV *He drove coolly and carefully.* ♦ **coolness** UNCOUNT N *...the coolness with which he dealt with a crisis.* 5 ADJ If someone is **cool** towards you, they are unfriendly. If they are **cool** towards an idea or suggestion, they are not enthusiastic about it. ♦ **coolly** ADV *'I'm not asking you,' she informed him coolly.* ♦ **coolness** UNCOUNT N *Hagen was hurt by my coolness.*

cool down. PHR VB 1 If something **cools down,** it becomes cooler until it reaches the temperature you want. *The engine will take half an hour to cool down.* 2 If someone **cools down,** they become less angry.

cool off. PHR VB If you **cool off,** you make yourself cooler after being too hot. *We cooled off with a refreshing swim.*

co-op /kəʊɒp/, **co-ops.** COUNT N A **co-op** is a co-operative; an informal use. *I'm in the food co-op.*

cooped up /kuːpt ʌp/. PRED ADJ If someone is **cooped up,** they are kept in a place which is too small or which does not allow them much freedom. *I hate being cooped up in the flat every day.*

co-operate /kəʊɒpəreɪt/, **co-operates, co-operating, co-operated.** 1 RECIP VB When people **co-operate,** they work or act together. *The workers cooperated with the management and the police.* ♦ **co-operation** /kəʊɒpəreɪʃəⁿn/ UNCOUNT N *...co-operation between staff and parents.* 2 VB To **co-operate** also means to do what someone asks you to do. *You're not co-operating!* ♦ **co-operation** UNCOUNT N *Thank you for your co-operation.*

co-operative /kəʊɒpəⁿrətɪv/, **co-operatives.** 1 COUNT N A **co-operative** is a business or organization run by the people who work for it, who share its benefits and profits. *...a food co-operative.* 2 ADJ A **co-operative** activity is done by people working together. *...co-operative forms of ownership.* ♦ **co-operatively** ADV *The work is carried on co-operatively.* 3 ADJ Someone who is **co-operative** does what you ask them to. *Her children are considerate and co-operative.* ♦ **co-operatively** ADV *'Okay,' she said co-operatively.*

co-opt /kəʊɒpt/, **co-opts, co-opting, co-opted.** VB WITH OBJ If the people on a committee **co-opt** you, they make you a member of it. *Committees can always co-opt members.*

co-ordinate /kəʊɔːdɪneɪt/, **co-ordinates, co-ordinating, co-ordinated;** 1 VB WITH OBJ If you **co-ordinate** an activity, you organize it. *They were asked to coordinate the election campaign... ...a co-ordinated attack.* ♦ **co-ordination** /kəʊɔːdɪneɪʃəⁿn/ UNCOUNT N *...the co-ordination of public transport.* ♦ **co-ordinator** /kəʊɔːdɪneɪtə/ COUNT N *...the co-ordinator of a project in Cornwall.* 2 VB WITH OBJ If you **co-ordinate** the parts of your body, you make them work together efficiently. *The children could not co-ordinate their movements.* ♦ **co-ordination** UNCOUNT N

cop /kɒp/, **cops;** an informal word. COUNT N A **cop** is a policeman or policewoman.

cope /kəʊp/, **copes, coping, coped.** VB If you **cope** with a problem, task, or difficult situation, you deal with it successfully. *John and Sally coped with all their problems cheerfully... ...a computer capable of coping with domestic requirements.*

co-pilot, co-pilots. COUNT N The **co-pilot** of an aeroplane is a pilot who assists the chief pilot.

copious /kəʊpɪəs/. ADJ A **copious** amount is a large amount; a formal use. *Plants need copious sunshine... She made copious notes.* ♦ **copiously** ADV *He cried copiously.*

copper /kɒpə/, **coppers.** 1 UNCOUNT N **Copper** is a soft reddish-brown metal. *...a copper mine... ...copper wire.* 2 COUNT N A **copper** is a policeman or policewoman; an informal use. 3 COUNT N A **copper** is also a brown metal coin of low value. *It only cost a few coppers.*

copse /kɒps/, **copses.** COUNT N A **copse** is a small group of trees.

copulate /kɒpjə⁴leɪt/, **copulates, copulating, copulated.** RECIP VB When animals **copulate,** they have sex; a formal use. ♦ **copulation** /kɒpjə⁴leɪʃəⁿn/ UNCOUNT N

copy /kɒpi¹/, **copies, copying, copied.** 1 COUNT N A **copy** is something that has been made to look the same as something else. *I will send you a copy of the letter.* 2 VB WITH OBJ If you **copy** something that has been written, you write it down. *...a comment she had copied from his notes.* 3 VB WITH OBJ If you **copy** a person or their ideas, you behave like them. *Our scheme has been copied by other universities.* 4 COUNT N A **copy** of a book, newspaper, or record is one of many identical ones. *Sixty thousand copies of the record were sold.*

copy down. PHR VB If you **copy down** what someone says or writes, you write it down yourself. *I shouldn't bother to copy these figures down.*

copy out. PHR VB If you **copy out** a long piece of writing, you write it all down. *I remember copying out the whole play.*

copyright /kɒpi¹raɪt/, **copyrights.** COUNT N OR UNCOUNT N If someone has the **copyright** on a piece of writing or music, it cannot be reproduced or performed without their permission. *Who holds the copyright of the song?*

coral /kɒrəⁿl/, **corals.** UNCOUNT N **Coral** is a hard substance formed from the skeletons of very small sea animals. **Coral** is used to make jewellery.

cord /kɔːd/, **cords.** 1 UNCOUNT N OR COUNT N **Cord** is strong, thick string. *...a piece of cord... She tied a cord around her box.* 2 COUNT N A **cord** is also a long piece of electrical wire covered in rubber or plastic. *...a small electric heater on a long cord.* 3 PLURAL N **Cords** are trousers made of corduroy.

cordial /kɔːdɪəl/, **cordials;** a formal word. 1 ADJ **Cordial** behaviour is warm and friendly. *Relations between the two men were far from cordial.* ♦ **cordially** ADV *She shook hands cordially with Charley.* 2 MASS N **Cordial** is a sweet drink made from fruit juice. *...lime juice cordial.*

cordon /kɔːdəⁿn/, **cordons, cordoning, cordoned.** COUNT N A **cordon** is a line of police, soldiers, or vehicles preventing people from entering or leaving an area. *The crowd attempted to break through the police cordons.*

cordon off. PHR VB If police or soldiers **cordon off** an area, they prevent people from entering or leaving it. *The area surrounding the office had been cordoned off.*

corduroy /kɔːdəⁿrɔɪ, kɔːdəⁿrɔɪ/. UNCOUNT N **Corduroy** is thick cotton cloth with parallel raised lines on the outside. *...a corduroy jacket.*

core /kɔː/, **cores.** 1 COUNT N The **core** of a fruit is the hard central part containing seeds or pips. *...the core of an apple.* 2 COUNT N The **core** of something is the central or most important part. *The planet probably has a molten core... ...the core of industry's problems.*

cork /kɔːk/, **corks.** 1 UNCOUNT N **Cork** is the soft, light, spongy bark of a Mediterranean tree. *...cork table mats... ...a floor covering such as cork.* 2 COUNT N A **cork** is a piece of cork or plastic that is pushed into the end of a bottle to close it. *He removed the cork from the wine bottle.*

corkscrew /kɔːkskruː/, **corkscrews.** COUNT N A **corkscrew** is a device for pulling corks out of bottles.

corn /kɔːn/, **corns.** 1 UNCOUNT N In British English, **corn** refers to crops such as wheat and barley, or their seeds. *...a field of corn... ...sacks of corn.* 2 UNCOUNT N **Corn** is also maize. *...corn bread.* 3 COUNT N A **corn** is a small, painful area of hard skin which can form on your foot.

corner /kɔːnə/, **corners, cornering, cornered.** 1 COUNT N A **corner** is a place where two sides or edges of something meet. *...a television set in the corner of the room.* 2 COUNT N A **corner** is also a place where a road bends sharply or meets another road. *There's a telephone box on the corner.* 3 VB WITH OBJ If you **corner** a person or animal, you get them into a place or situation that they cannot escape from. *The police and cornered the wrong car.* ♦ **cornered** ADJ *She had me cornered between the front porch and her car.* 4 VB WITH OBJ If you **corner** a market or other area of activity, you gain control of it so that nobody else can succeed in it.

PHRASES ● If you are **in a corner,** you are in a difficult situation; an informal use. ● If you **cut corners,** you do something quickly by doing it less thoroughly than you should.

cornerstone /kɔ:nəstəʊn/, **cornerstones.** COUNT N The **cornerstone** of something is the basis of its existence or success; a formal use.

cornet /kɔ:nɪ^{2}t/, **cornets. 1** COUNT N A **cornet** is a musical instrument that looks like a small trumpet. **2** COUNT N A **cornet** is also a cone-shaped wafer with ice cream in it.

cornflour /kɔ:nflaʊə/. UNCOUNT N **Cornflour** is a very fine white maize flour.

corny /kɔ:ni^1/. ADJ Something that is **corny** is very obvious or sentimental. *...corny old jokes.*

corollary /kərɒləri^1/, **corollaries.** COUNT N A **corollary** of something is an idea or fact that results directly from it; a formal use.

coronary /kɒrənə^{0}ri^1/, **coronaries.** COUNT N If someone has a **coronary**, blood cannot reach their heart because of a blood clot. *He died of a massive coronary.*

coronation /kɒrəneɪʃə^{0}n/, **coronations.** COUNT N A **coronation** is the ceremony at which a king or queen is crowned.

coroner /kɒrənə/, **coroners.** COUNT N A **coroner** is an official responsible for investigating sudden or unusual deaths.

coronet /kɒrənɪ^{1}t/, **coronets.** COUNT N A **coronet** is a small crown.

corporal /kɔ:pə^{0}rəl/, **corporals.** COUNT N OR TITLE A **corporal** is a non-commissioned officer of low rank in the army or air force.

corporal punishment. UNCOUNT N **Corporal punishment** is the punishment of people by beating them.

corporate /kɔ:pə^{0}rə^{1}t/. ATTRIB ADJ **Corporate** means owned or shared by all the members of a group or organization. *...a corporate identity.*

corporation /kɔ:pəreɪʃə^{0}n/, **corporations. 1** COUNT N A **corporation** is a large business or company. **2** COUNT N The **corporation** of a town or city is the authority responsible for running it; a British use.

corps /kɔ:/. **Corps** is the singular and plural. **1** COUNT N A **corps** is a part of the army which has special duties. *...the Royal Army Ordnance Corps.* **2** COUNT N WITH SUPP A **corps** is also a small group of people who do a special job. *...the diplomatic corps.*

corpse /kɔ:ps/, **corpses.** COUNT N A **corpse** is a dead body.

corpuscle /kɔ:pʌsə^{0}l/, **corpuscles.** COUNT N A **corpuscle** is a red or white blood cell.

correct /kərekt/, **corrects, correcting, corrected. 1** ADJ Something that is **correct** is accurate and has no mistakes. *That's the correct answer.* ♦ **correctly** ADV *I hope I pronounced his name correctly.* ♦ **correctness** UNCOUNT N *This confirmed the correctness of my decision.* **2** PRED ADJ If you are **correct**, what you have said or thought is true. *Jenkins is correct. We've got to change our strategy.* **3** ATTRIB ADJ The **correct** thing is the right or most suitable one. *Make sure you ask for the correct fuse.* ♦ **correctly** ADV *Rice, correctly cooked and prepared, is delicious.* **4** VB WITH OBJ If you **correct** a mistake, problem, or fault, you put it right. *I wish to correct a false impression which may have been created.* **5** VB WITH OBJ OR REFL VB If you **correct** someone, you say something which is more accurate or appropriate than what they have just said. *'I'm a fighter like your dad is—or was,' Mr Cupples corrected himself.* **6** VB WITH OBJ When someone **corrects** a piece of writing, they mark the mistakes in it. **7** ADJ **Correct** behaviour is considered socially acceptable. *Charter's dealings with him have been wholly correct.* ♦ **correctly** ADV *We tried to behave correctly.* ♦ **correctness** UNCOUNT N *Such a person should be treated with polite correctness.*

correction /kərekʃə^{0}n/, **corrections. 1** COUNT N OR UNCOUNT N A **correction** is something which puts right something that is wrong. *A couple of mistakes need correction.* **2** UNCOUNT N OR COUNT N **Correction** is the changing of something so that it is no longer faulty or unsatisfactory. *Deaf children need speech correction.*

corrective /kərektɪv/, **correctives.** ADJ **Corrective** measures are intended to put right something that is wrong. *...corrective surgery.* Also COUNT N *This analysis provides an important corrective to the traditional view.*

correlate /kɒrə^{1}leɪt/, **correlates, correlating, correlated.** RECIP VB If two things **correlate** or if they are **correlated**, they are closely connected or influence each other. *In Britain, class and region are strongly correlated.* ♦ **correlation** /kɒrə^{1}leɪʃə^{0}n/ COUNT N *There was a definite correlation between rates of unemployment and wage stability.*

correspond /kɒrɪspɒnd/, **corresponds, corresponding, corresponded. 1** RECIP VB If one thing **corresponds** with another or if the two things **correspond**, they have a similar purpose, position or status. *This view corresponds less and less with reality... His job in Moscow corresponds to her position here.* **2** RECIP VB If two numbers or amounts **correspond**, they are the same. *Check the telephone numbers in case they don't correspond... The date of her birth corresponded with her father's visit.* **3** RECIP VB If two people **correspond**, they write letters to each other. *I've been corresponding with Tim.*

correspondence /kɒrɪspɒndəns/, **correspondences. 1** UNCOUNT N **Correspondence** is the act of writing letters to someone. *The judges' decision is final and no correspondence will be entered into.* **2** UNCOUNT N **Correspondence** also refers to the letters that someone receives. *The letter had been among his correspondence that morning.* **3** COUNT N If there is a **correspondence** between two things, there is a close relationship or similarity between them. *In African languages there is a close correspondence between sounds and letters.*

correspondent /kɒrɪspɒndənt/, **correspondents.** COUNT N A **correspondent** is a television or newspaper reporter.

corresponding /kɒrɪspɒndɪŋ/. ATTRIB ADJ You use **corresponding** to indicate that one thing is similar or related to another; a formal use. *In France they study to the same standard and take the corresponding examinations... Any increase in complexity brings with it a corresponding probability of error.* ♦ **correspondingly** SENTENCE ADV *The new edition is bigger and correspondingly more expensive.*

corridor /kɒrɪdɔ^8/, **corridors.** COUNT N A **corridor** is a long passage in a building or train.

corroborate /kərɒbəreɪt/, **corroborates, corroborating, corroborated.** VB WITH OBJ If someone or something **corroborates** an idea, account, or argument, they provide evidence to support it; a formal use. *Abrams and Rose corroborated this view in their influential study of the subject.* ♦ **corroboration** /kərɒbəreɪʃə^{0}n/ UNCOUNT N *Evangelina's story was later published without corroboration.*

corrode /kərəʊd/, **corrodes, corroding, corroded.** ERG VB When metal **corrodes**, it is gradually destroyed by rust or a chemical. *Vinegar will corrode metal.* ♦ **corroded** ADJ *The generator was badly corroded.*

corrosion /kərəʊʒə^{0}n/. UNCOUNT N **Corrosion** is the damage that is caused when something is corroded. *Check that the terminals of the battery are free from dirt and corrosion.*

corrosive /kərəʊsɪv/. ADJ A **corrosive** substance can destroy solid materials as a result of a chemical reaction. *...a corrosive poison.*

corrugated /kɒrə^{4}geɪtɪ^{2}d/. ATTRIB ADJ **Corrugated** metal or cardboard has parallel folds in it to make it stronger. *...a corrugated iron roof.*

corrupt /kərʌpt/, **corrupts, corrupting, corrupted. 1** ADJ A **corrupt** person behaves dishonestly or illegally in return for money or power. *...corrupt politicians... ...corrupt practices.* **2** VB WITH OR WITHOUT OBJ To **corrupt** someone means to make them dishonest or immoral. *Young people in prison are corrupted by hardened criminals... It is claimed that television corrupts.*

corruption /kərʌpʃə^{0}n/. **1** UNCOUNT N **Corruption** is dishonesty and illegal behaviour by people in positions of authority or power. *...police corruption.* **2** UNCOUNT N The **corruption** of someone is the process of making them behave in a way that is morally wrong. *His whole life seemed dedicated to the corruption of the young.*

corset /kɔ:sɪ^{2}t/, **corsets.** COUNT N A **corset** is a stiff piece of underwear, worn by some women around their hips and waist to make them look slimmer.

cosmetic /kɒzmetɪk/, **cosmetics. 1** COUNT N **Cosmetics** are substances such as lipstick or face powder. **2** ADJ **Cosmetic** measures or changes improve the appearance of something without changing its basic character or without solving a basic problem.

cosmic /kɒzmɪk/. ATTRIB ADJ **Cosmic** means belonging or relating to the universe.

cosmonaut /kɒzmə^{6}nɔ:t/, **cosmonauts.** COUNT N A **cosmonaut** is an astronaut from the former USSR.

cosmopolitan /kɒzmə^{6}pɒlɪtə^{0}n/. ADJ **Cosmopolitan** means influenced by many different countries and cultures. *...a cosmopolitan street.*

cosmos /kɒzmɒs/. SING N The **cosmos** is the universe; a technical use.

cosset /kɒsɪt/, **cossets, cosseting, cosseted.** VB WITH OBJ If you **cosset** someone, you do everything for them and protect them too much.

cost /kɒst/, **costs, costing. Cost** is used in the present tense of the verb, and is the past tense and past participle. **1** COUNT N The **cost** of something is the amount of money needed to buy, do, or make it. *The total cost of the holiday was £300... The building was restored at a cost of £500,000... ...the huge increases in fuel costs.* **2** VB WITH OBJ OR VB WITH OBJ AND OBJ You use **cost** to talk about the amount of money that you have to pay for things. *Those books cost £2.95 each... A two-day stay there cost me $125... A freezer doesn't cost much to run.* **3** SING N The **cost** of achieving something is the loss, damage or injury involved in achieving it. *The cost in human life had been enormous.* **4** VB WITH OBJ AND OBJ, OR VB WITH OBJ If an event or mistake **costs** you something, you lose that thing because of it. *A single error here could cost you your life.* **5** PHRASE You say that something must be done **at all costs** to emphasize the importance of doing it.

co-star, co-stars. COUNT N WITH SUPP An actor or actress who is a **co-star** of a film has one of the most important parts in it.

cost-effective. ADJ Something that is **cost-effective** saves or makes a lot of money in comparison with the costs involved. *...more cost-effective methods of production.*

costly /kɒstli^1/, **costlier, costliest. 1** ADJ Something that is **costly** is very expensive. *...a costly mistake.* **2** ADJ **Costly** also describes things that take a lot of time or effort. *That route will be too costly in time.*

cost of living. SING N The **cost of living** is the average amount of money that people need to spend on food, housing, and clothing.

costume /kɒstju:m/, **costumes. 1** COUNT N A **costume** is a set of clothes worn by an actor. *...theatrical costumes.* **2** UNCOUNT N **Costume** is the clothing worn in a particular place or during a particular period. *...17th-century costume.*

cosy /kəʊzi^1/, **cosier, cosiest; cosies;** spelled **cozy** in American English. **1** ADJ **Cosy** means comfortable and warm. *A hot water bottle will make you feel cosier.* ♦ **cosily** ADV *We were all sitting cosily in the recreation room.* **2** ADJ You use **cosy** to describe activities that are pleasant and friendly. *I had a cosy chat with him.* ♦ **cosily** ADV *We spent the afternoon cosily gossiping.* **3** COUNT N WITH SUPP A tea **cosy** is a soft cover used to keep a teapot warm.

cot /kɒt/, **cots. 1** COUNT N In British English, a **cot** is a baby's bed with bars or panels round it. **2** COUNT N In American English, a **cot** is a small, narrow bed.

cottage /kɒtɪdʒ/, **cottages.** COUNT N A **cottage** is a small house in the country.

cotton /kɒtə^{0}n/, **cottons, cottoning, cottoned. 1** MASS N **Cotton** is cloth made from the soft fibres of a plant. *...a cotton dress.* **2** UNCOUNT N The plant grown for these fibres is also called **cotton.** *...cotton fields.* **3** MASS N In British English, **cotton** is also sewing thread. *...reels of cotton.*

cotton on. PHR VB If you **cotton on** to something, you understand it or realize it; an informal use. *At long last he has cottoned on to the fact that I don't want him!*

cotton wool. UNCOUNT N **Cotton wool** is soft, fluffy cotton, often used for applying liquids or creams to your skin.

couch /kaʊtʃ/, **couches, couching, couched. 1** COUNT N A **couch** is a long, soft piece of furniture for sitting or lying on. **2** VB WITH OBJ If a statement **is couched** in a particular style of language, it is expressed in that language; a formal use. *...a resolution couched in forthright terms.*

cough /kɒf/, **coughs, coughing, coughed. 1** VB When you **cough**, air is forced out of your throat with a sudden, harsh noise. *Mr Willet coughed nervously.* Also COUNT N *There was a muffled cough outside the study door.* ♦ **coughing** UNCOUNT N *They suffered abdominal pains and intense coughing.* **2** VB WITH OBJ If you **cough** blood or phlegm, you force it out of your throat with a sudden, harsh noise. **3** COUNT N A **cough** is also an illness in which you cough often and your chest or throat hurts.

cough up. PHR VB If you **cough up** money, you give someone money; an informal use. *How can he persuade the authorities to cough up for the private education of his children?*

could /kʊd, kəd/. **Could** is sometimes considered to be the past tense of **can**, but in this dictionary the two words are dealt with separately. **1** MODAL If you **could** do something, you were able to do it. *They complained that they couldn't sleep... When I was young you could buy a packet for two shillings.* **2** MODAL **Could** is used in indirect speech to indicate that someone has said that something is allowed or possible. *She said I could go... I asked if we could somehow get a car.* **3** MODAL If something **could** happen, it is possible that it will happen or it is possible to do it. If something **could** have happened, it was possible, but it did not actually happen. *The river could easily overflow, couldn't it?... We could do a great deal more in this country to educate people... If one could measure this sort of thing, one might understand it better... You were lucky. It could have been awful.* **4** MODAL If something **could** be the case, it is possibly the case. If something **could** have been the case, it was possibly the case in the past. *It could be a* *symbol, couldn't it?... It couldn't possibly be poison... He couldn't have rowed away.* 5 MODAL You use **could** when you are making suggestions. *You could phone her... Couldn't you just build more factories?... I could ask her, I suppose.* 6 MODAL You also use **could** when you are making polite requests. *Could you just switch the projector on?... Could we put this fire on?... Could I speak to Sue, please?*

couldn't /kʊdəⁿnt/. **Couldn't** is the usual spoken form of 'could not'.

could've /kʊdəᵒv/. **Could've** is the usual spoken form of 'could have', especially when 'have' is an auxiliary verb.

council /kaʊnsəˡl/, **councils.** 1 COLL N A **council** is a group of people elected to run a town or other area; a British use. *...Wiltshire County Council... ...council meetings.* 2 COLL N Some other advisory or administrative groups are also called **councils;** a British use. *...the Arts Council.* 3 MOD A **council** house or flat is owned by the local council. You pay rent to live in it. *...council estates... ...a council tenant.* 4 COUNT N A **council** is also a specially organized meeting. *A council of ministers and generals was held at No. 10.*

councillor /kaʊnsəᵒlə/, **councillors.** COUNT N A **councillor** is a member of a local council.

counsel /kaʊnsəl/, **counsels, counselling, counselled;** spelled **counseling** and **counseled** in American English. 1 UNCOUNT N **Counsel** is careful advice; a formal use. *...giving counsel in times of stress.* 2 VB WITH OBJ If you **counsel** someone to do something, you advise them to do it; a formal use. *'Ignore them,' Mrs Jones counselled... Some wanted to fight. Others counselled caution.* 3 VB WITH OBJ If you **counsel** people, you give them advice about their problems. *Part of her work is to counsel families when problems arise.* ♦ **counselling** UNCOUNT N *...psychiatric counselling.* 4 COUNT N OR TITLE A **counsel** is a lawyer who gives advice on a legal case and fights the case in court.

counsellor /kaʊnsəᵒlə/, **counsellors;** spelled **counselor** in American English. COUNT N A **counsellor** is a person whose job is to give advice to people who need it. *The hospital has trained counsellors who are used to dealing with depressed patients.*

count /kaʊnt/, **counts, counting, counted.** 1 VB WITH OR WITHOUT OBJ When you **count,** you say all the numbers in order up to a particular number. *I'm going to count up to three... After counting sixty the rest set off in pursuit.* 2 VB WITH OBJ If you **count** all the things in a group, you add them up to see how many there are. *He withdrew to his office to count the money.* 3 COUNT N A **count** is a number that you get by counting a particular set of things. *The official government count has now risen to eight million.* 4 VB The thing that **counts** in a particular situation is the most important thing. *What counts is how you feel about yourself.* 5 VB WITH 'for' If a particular thing **counts** for something, it is valuable or important. *I felt that all my years there counted for nothing.* 6 ERG VB If something **counts** as a particular thing, it is regarded as being that thing. *These benefits do not count as income for tax purposes... They can hardly be counted as friends.* 7 COUNT N OR TITLE A **count** is also a European nobleman with the same rank as a British earl.

PHRASES ● If you **keep count** of a number of things, you keep a record of how many have occurred. If you **lose count** of a number of things, you cannot remember how many have occurred. ● If something is wrong **on** a number of **counts,** it is wrong for that number of reasons. *The use of these tests is criticized on two counts... They are right on the first count but wrong on the second.*

count against. PHR VB If something **counts against** you, it may cause you to be punished or rejected.

count on or **count upon.** PHR VB To **count on** or **count upon** someone or something means to rely on them. *Doctors could now count on a regular salary.*

count out. PHR VB If you **count out** a sum of money, you count it as you put the notes or coins in a pile.

count up. PHR VB If you **count up** all the things in a group, you count them. *I counted up my years of teaching experience.*

count upon. PHR VB See **count on.**

countable noun /kaʊntəˡbəˡl naʊn/, **countable nouns.** COUNT N A **countable noun** is the same as a count noun.

countdown /kaʊntdaʊn/, **countdowns.** COUNT N A **countdown** is the counting aloud of numbers in reverse order before something happens.

countenance /kaʊntɪ²nəns/, **countenances.** COUNT N Someone's **countenance** is their face; a literary use.

counter /kaʊntə/, **counters, countering, countered.** 1 COUNT N A **counter** in a shop is a long, flat surface where goods are displayed or sold. 2 VB WITH OBJ If you **counter** something that is being done, you take action to make it less effective. *To counter this the police will equip themselves with riot shields and tear gas.* 3 VB If you **counter** something that has just been said, you say something in reaction to it or in opposition to it; a formal use. *I countered by enquiring whether she actually knew this man.* 4 COUNT N A **counter** is also a small, flat, round object used in board games.

counteract /kaʊntərækt/, **counteracts, counteracting, counteracted.** VB WITH OBJ To **counteract** something means to reduce its effect by doing something that has the opposite effect.

counter-attack, counter-attacks. COUNT N OR UNCOUNT N A **counter-attack** is an attack on a person or group that has already attacked you. *...counter-attacks against enemy civilians.*

counterbalance /kaʊntəbæleⁿns/, **counterbalances, counterbalancing, counterbalanced.** VB WITH OBJ To **counterbalance** something means to balance or correct it with something that has an equal but opposite effect. *...sufficient salt in the diet to counterbalance the amount of salt lost in sweat.*

counterclockwise /kaʊntəklɒkwaɪz/. ADV OR ATTRIB ADJ **Counterclockwise** means the same as anticlockwise; an American use.

counterfeit /kaʊntəfiˡt/, **counterfeits, counterfeiting, counterfeited.** 1 ADJ Something that is **counterfeit** is not genuine, but has been made to look genuine to deceive people. 2 VB WITH OBJ To **counterfeit** something means to make a counterfeit version of it.

counterfoil /kaʊntəfɔɪl/, **counterfoils.** COUNT N A **counterfoil** is the part of a cheque or receipt that you keep.

counterpart /kaʊntəpɑːt/, **counterparts.** COUNT N WITH POSS The **counterpart** of something is another thing with a similar function in a different place. *...the English merchant bank and its American counterpart, the Wall Street investment bank.*

counter-productive. ADJ Something that is **counter-productive** has the opposite effect from what you intend.

countess /kaʊntɪ²s/, **countesses.** COUNT N OR TITLE A **countess** is a woman with the same rank as a count or earl, or who is the wife of a count or earl.

countless /kaʊntlɪ²s/. ATTRIB ADJ **Countless** means very many.

count noun, count nouns. COUNT N A **count noun** is a noun that has a singular and a plural form and is always used after a determiner when singular.

country /kʌntriˡ/, **countries.** 1 COUNT N A **country** is one of the political areas which the world is divided into. *The level of unemployment in this country is too high... Forests cover about one third of the country.* 2 SING N You can also refer to the people who live in a particular country as the **country.** *The country was stunned.* 3 SING N The **country** is land away from towns and cities. *We live in the country.* Also ATTRIB ADJ *...country roads.* 4 UNCOUNT N WITH SUPP **Country** is used to refer to an area with particular characteristics or connections. *...mountain country.* 5 ATTRIB ADJ **Country** music is a style of popular music from the USA.

country house, country houses. COUNT N A **country house** is a large house in the country owned by a rich or noble family.

countryman /kʌntrɪməᵌn/, **countrymen.** COUNT N Your **countrymen** are people from your own country.

countryside /kʌntrɪsaɪd/. SING N OR UNCOUNT N The **countryside** is land away from towns and cities. *...the English countryside... It's very nice countryside around there.*

county /kaʊntiˡ/, **counties.** COUNT N A **county** is a region of Britain, Ireland, or the USA with its own local government.

coup /kuː/, **coups.** 1 COUNT N A **coup** is the same as a coup d'état. 2 COUNT N A **coup** is also an achievement thought to be especially brilliant because of its difficulty. *Brooke went on to bigger things, his next notable coup being the case of Robert Scott.*

coup d'état /kuː deɪtɑː/, **coups d'état.** The plural is pronounced the same as the singular. COUNT N When there is a **coup d'état,** a group of people seize power in a country.

couple /kʌpəᵒl/, **couples, coupling, coupled.** 1 COLL N A **couple** is two people who are married, living together, or having a sexual or romantic relationship. 2 COLL N You can also use **couple** to describe two people who you see together on a particular occasion. *...a couple on the dance floor.* 3 COUNT N A **couple** of people or things means two people or things. *He met her a couple of years ago.* 4 VB WITH OBJ AND 'with' If one thing **is coupled** with another, the two things are done or dealt with together. *Strong protests were made, coupled with demands for an international inquiry.*

coupon /kuːpɒn/, **coupons.** 1 COUNT N A **coupon** is a piece of printed paper which allows you to pay less than usual for something. 2 COUNT N A **coupon** is also a small form which you fill in and send off to ask for information or to enter a competition.

courage /kʌrɪdʒ/. UNCOUNT N **Courage** is the quality shown by someone who does something difficult or dangerous, even though they may be afraid; used showing approval. *She would never have had the courage to defy him.*

courageous /kəreɪdʒəs/. ADJ Someone who is **courageous** shows courage. *...his courageous attempt to get the facts published.* ♦ **courageously** ADV *She fought courageously for her principles.*

courgette /kʊəʒɛt/, **courgettes.** COUNT N **Courgettes** are small marrows, eaten as a vegetable.

courier /kʊərɪə/, **couriers.** 1 COUNT N A **courier** is someone employed by a travel company to look after holidaymakers. 2 COUNT N A **courier** is also someone paid to take a special letter from one place to another.

course /kɔːs/, **courses, coursing, coursed.** 1 COUNT N A **course** is a series of lessons or lectures. 2 COUNT N WITH 'of' A series of medical treatments is also called a **course.** *Another course of injections was prescribed.* 3 COUNT N A **course** is also one part of a meal. *...a three-course dinner.* 4 COUNT N The **course** of a ship or aircraft is its route. 5 SING N You can refer to the way that events develop as the **course** of history, nature, or events. 6 VB If a liquid **courses** somewhere, it flows quickly; a literary use. *Tears coursed down my face.* 7 See also **golf course, racecourse.**

PHRASES ● You say **of course** when you are saying something that you expect other people to realize or understand. *There is of course an element of truth in this argument.* ● You also use **of course** when you are talking about an event or situation that does not surprise you. *He never writes to me, of course.* ● **Of course** is also a polite way of giving permission or agreeing with someone. *'Could I make a telephone call?' he said. 'Of course,' Boylan said.* ● You use **of course** to emphasize what you are saying. *'Do you love him, Dolly?'—'Of course I do. He's wonderful.'... 'Do you think he was killed?'—'No, no, of course not.'* ● A **course of action** is one of the things you can do in a situation. ● If you do something **as a matter of course,** you do it as part of your normal work or way of life. ● If something happens **in the course of** a period of time, it happens during that time. ● If a ship or aircraft is **on course,** it is travelling along the correct route. If it is **off course,** it is no longer travelling along the correct route. ● If something **runs its course** or **takes its course,** it develops naturally and comes to a natural end. *The illness was allowed to run its course.* ● **in due course:** see **due.**

court /kɔːt/, **courts.** 1 COUNT N A **court** is a place where legal matters are decided by a judge and jury or by a magistrate. 2 COUNT N You can also refer to the judge and jury or magistrates as the **court.** *The court dismissed the charges.* 3 COUNT N A **court** is also an area in which you play a game such as tennis, badminton, or squash. 4 COUNT N The **court** of a king or queen is the place where he or she lives and carries out ceremonial or administrative duties.

PHRASES ● If someone is **in court,** they are in a court while a trial is taking place. ● If you **go to court** or **take** someone **to court,** you take legal action against them. ● When someone is **at court,** they are present at the king's or queen's residence.

courteous /kɜːtɪəs/. ADJ Someone who is **courteous** is polite, respectful, and considerate. *He was the kindest, most courteous gentleman to work for.* ♦ **courteously** ADV *The jailer received me courteously.*

courtesy /kɜːtɪsiˡ/, **courtesies.** 1 UNCOUNT N **Courtesy** is polite, respectful, and considerate behaviour. *He replied with promptness and courtesy.* 2 PLURAL N **Courtesies** are polite and respectful things that you say or do; a formal use. *...a brief exchange of courtesies.* 3 PHRASE If something is done **by courtesy of** someone, it is done with their permission. If something happens **by courtesy of** a situation, that situation makes it possible.

courthouse /kɔːthaʊs/, **courthouses.** COUNT N A **courthouse** is a building in which a law court meets; an American use.

courtier /kɔːtɪə/, **courtiers.** COUNT N **Courtiers** were noblemen and women at the court of a king or queen.

court-martial, court-martials, court-martialling, court-martialled. VB WITH OBJ To **court-martial** a member of the armed forces means to try them in a military court. *The colonel threatened to court-martial him.* Also COUNT N *They arrested General Lee for disobedience, and ordered a court-martial.*

court of appeal, courts of appeal. COUNT N A **court of appeal** is a court which deals with appeals against legal judgements.

courtroom /kɔːtru⁴m/, **courtrooms.** COUNT N A **courtroom** is a room in which a law court meets.

courtship /kɔːtʃɪp/. UNCOUNT N **Courtship** is an activity in which a man and a woman spend a lot of time together, because they are intending to get married; a formal use.

courtyard /kɔːtjɑːd/, **courtyards.** COUNT N A **courtyard** is a flat open area of ground surrounded by buildings or walls.

cousin /kʌzə^{0}n/, **cousins.** COUNT N Your **cousin** is the child of your uncle or aunt.

cove /kəʊv/, **coves.** COUNT N A **cove** is a small bay on the coast.

covenant /kʌvə^{0}nənt/, **covenants.** COUNT N A **covenant** is a formal written promise to pay a sum of money each year for a fixed period.

cover /kʌvə/, **covers, covering, covered.** **1** VB WITH OBJ If you **cover** something, you place something else over it to protect it or hide it. *She covered her face with her hands.* **2** VB WITH OBJ If something **covers** something else, it forms a layer over it. *Her hand was covered with blood.* **3** VB WITH OBJ If you **cover** a particular distance, you travel that distance. *I covered approximately twenty miles a day.* **4** VB WITH OBJ An insurance policy that **covers** a person or thing guarantees that money will be paid in relation to that person or thing. Also UNCOUNT N *This policy gives unlimited cover for hospital charges.* **5** VB WITH OBJ If a law **covers** a particular set of people, things, or situations, it applies to them. **6** VB WITH OBJ If you **cover** a particular topic, you discuss it in a lecture, course, or book. *We've covered a wide range of subjects today.* **7** VB WITH OBJ If reporters, newspapers, or television companies **cover** an event, they report on it. **8** VB WITH OBJ If a sum of money **covers** something, it is enough to pay for it. *I'll give you a cheque to cover the cost of your journey.* **9** COUNT N A **cover** is something which is put over an object, usually in order to protect it. **10** COUNT N If respectable or normal behaviour is a **cover** for secret or illegal activities, it is intended to hide them. *...a cover for murder.* **11** PLURAL N Bed **covers** are the sheet, blankets, and bedspread that you have on top of you. **12** COUNT N The **cover** of a book or a magazine is its outside. **13** UNCOUNT N **Cover** is trees, rocks, or other places where you shelter from the weather or hide from someone. *They crossed to the other side of the stream in search of cover.*

PHRASES • If you **take cover,** you shelter from the weather or from gunfire. • If you do something **under cover of** a particular condition, this enables you to do it without being noticed. *The attack usually takes place under cover of darkness.*

cover up. PHR VB **1** If you **cover** something **up,** you put something else over it to protect it or hide it. **2** If you **cover up** something that you do not want people to know about, you hide it from them. *She tried to cover up for Willie.* • See also **cover-up.**

coverage /kʌvə^{0}rɪdʒ/. UNCOUNT N The **coverage** of something in the news is the reporting of it. *They put an immediate ban on all television coverage of their operations.*

covering /kʌvə^{0}rɪŋ/, **coverings.** COUNT N OR UNCOUNT N A **covering** is a layer of something over something else. *Kitchen floor covering should be non-slip.*

covering letter, **covering letters.** COUNT N A **covering letter** is a letter that you send with a parcel or with another document to give extra information.

covert /kʌvət/. ADJ Something that is **covert** is secret or hidden; a formal use. *...a covert involvement in activist politics.* ♦ **covertly** ADV *She watched Marina covertly.*

cover-up, **cover-ups.** COUNT N A **cover-up** is an attempt to hide a crime or mistake.

covet /kʌvə^{1}t/, **covets, coveting, coveted.** VB WITH OBJ If you **covet** something, you badly want it for yourself; a formal use. *It was an honour he had long coveted.*

covetous /kʌvə^{1}təs/. ATTRIB ADJ **Covetous** feelings and actions involve a strong desire to possess something; a formal use.

cow /kaʊ/, **cows, cowing, cowed.** **1** COUNT N A **cow** is a large female animal kept on farms for its milk. **2** COUNT N A **cow** is also any animal of this species, either male or female. *...a herd of cows.* **3** VB WITH OBJ If someone **is cowed,** they are frightened into behaving in a particular way; a formal use. *People shouldn't allow themselves to be cowed into this.* ♦ **cowed** ADJ *...his tragically cowed and battered wife.*

coward /kaʊəd/, **cowards.** COUNT N A **coward** is someone who is easily frightened and avoids dangerous or difficult situations.

cowardice /kaʊədɪs/. UNCOUNT N **Cowardice** is cowardly behaviour. *He despised them for their cowardice and ignorance.*

cowardly /kaʊədli^{1}/. ADJ Someone who is **cowardly** is easily frightened and so avoids doing dangerous or difficult things. *...a cowardly refusal to face reality.*

cowboy /kaʊbɔɪ/, **cowboys.** **1** COUNT N A **cowboy** is a man employed to look after cattle in America. **2** COUNT N A **cowboy** is also a male character in a western.

cower /kaʊə/, **cowers, cowering, cowered.** VB If you **cower,** you bend downwards or move back because you are afraid. *Bernadette cowered in her seat.*

coy /kɔɪ/. **1** ADJ If someone is **coy,** they pretend to be shy and modest. *...a coy little smile.* ♦ **coyly** ADV *They were looking at us coyly through their elegant lashes.* ♦ **coyness** UNCOUNT N *There is no false modesty or coyness about her.* **2** ADJ **Coy** can also mean unwilling to say something, in a way that people find slightly irritating. *Let us not be coy about the identity of this great man.*

cozy /kəʊzi^{1}/. See **cosy.**

crab /kræb/, **crabs.** COUNT N A **crab** is a sea creature with a flat round body covered by a shell, and five pairs of legs with claws on the front pair.

crack /kræk/, **cracks, cracking, cracked.** **1** ERG VB If something **cracks** or if you **crack** it, it becomes slightly damaged, with lines appearing on its surface. *If you hold a glass under the hot tap, it may crack.* **2** VB If someone **cracks,** they finally give in or have a nervous breakdown; an informal use. *I thought I might crack if I didn't get away soon.* **3** VB WITH OBJ If you **crack** a problem or a code, you solve it, especially after a lot of thought. *They were eager to crack the codes.* **4** VB WITH OBJ If you **crack** a joke, you tell it. **5** COUNT N A **crack** is a very narrow gap between two things. *...the cracks between the boards of the ceiling.* **6** COUNT N A **crack** is also a line appearing on the surface of something when it is slightly damaged or partly broken. *She found a crack in one of the teacups.* **7** COUNT N A **crack** is also a sharp sound like the sound of something suddenly breaking. *...the crack of a whip.* **8** COUNT N A **crack** is also a slightly rude or cruel joke. **9** ATTRIB ADJ A **crack** soldier or sportsman is highly trained and very skilful. **10** See also **cracked.**

PHRASES • If you do something **at the crack of dawn,** you do it very early in the morning. • If you **have a crack at** something, you make an attempt to do it; an informal use.

crack down. PHR VB If people in authority **crack down** on a group of people, they become stricter in making them obey rules or laws. • See also **crackdown.**

crack up. PHR VB If someone **cracks up,** they are under such a lot of emotional strain that they become mentally ill; an informal use.

crackdown /krækdaʊn/, **crackdowns.** COUNT N A **crackdown** is strong official action taken to punish people who break laws. *...a crackdown on criminals.*

cracked /krækt/. ADJ A **cracked** object has lines on its surface because it has been damaged or partly broken.

cracker /krækə/, **crackers.** **1** COUNT N A **cracker** is a thin, crisp biscuit often eaten with cheese. **2** COUNT N A **cracker** is also a small paper-covered tube that is pulled apart with a bang to reveal a small toy and a paper hat.

crackle /krækə^{0}l/, **crackles, crackling, crackled.** VB If something **crackles,** it makes a series of short, harsh noises. *The loudspeaker crackled.* Also SING N *...the crackle of the fire.*

crackpot /krækpɒt/, **crackpots.** COUNT N A **crackpot** is someone who has strange and crazy ideas; an informal use.

cradle /kreɪdə^{0}l/, **cradles, cradling, cradled.** **1** COUNT N A **cradle** is a small box-shaped bed for a baby. **2** SING N WITH SUPP The **cradle** of something is the place where it began; a literary use. *New England saw itself as the cradle of American technology.* **3** VB WITH OBJ If you **cradle** something in your arms, you hold it carefully. *She cradled a child in her arms.*

craft /krɑːft/, **crafts. Craft** is used as the plural in meaning 3. **1** COUNT N A **craft** is an activity such as weaving, carving, or pottery that involves making things skilfully with your hands. *...traditional crafts such as thatching and weaving... ...a craft festival.* **2** COUNT N You can use **craft** to refer to any activity or job that involves doing something skilfully. *He was still learning his journalistic craft.* **3** COUNT N You can refer to a boat, a spacecraft, or an aircraft as a **craft.** *There were eight destroyers and fifty smaller craft.*

craftsman /krɑːftsmən/, **craftsmen.** COUNT N A **craftsman** is someone who makes things skilfully with their hands.

craftsmanship /krɑːftsmənʃɪp/. **1** UNCOUNT N **Craftsmanship** is the skill of making beautiful things with their hands. **2** UNCOUNT N **Craftsmanship** is also the quality that something has when it is beautiful and has been carefully made. *I bent down to examine the exquisite craftsmanship.*

crafty /krɑːfti^{1}/. ADJ **Crafty** means achieving things by deceiving people in a clever way. *...the crafty tactics of journalists.* ♦ **craftily** ADV *Several ploys are being craftily developed.*

crag /kræg/, **crags.** COUNT N A **crag** is a steep, rocky cliff or part of a mountain.

craggy /krægi^{1}/. ADJ A **craggy** mountain is steep and rocky.

cram /kræm/, **crams, cramming, crammed.** VB WITH OBJ AND ADJUNCT If you **cram** people or things into a place, you push as many of them in it as possible. *Thirty of us were crammed into a small dark room... He crammed the bank notes into his pockets.*

crammed /kræmd/. PRED ADJ If a place is **crammed** with things or people, it is very full of them. *...a concrete bunker crammed full of radio equipment.*

cramp /kræmp/, **cramps, cramping, cramped.** **1** UNCOUNT N OR PLURAL N If you have **cramp** or **cramps,** you feel a strong pain caused by a muscle suddenly contracting. *I had the most excruciating cramp in my leg... She had severe stomach cramps.* **2** PHRASE If you **cramp** someone's **style,** your presence restricts their behaviour in some way; an informal use.

cramped /kræmpt/. ADJ A **cramped** room or building is not big enough for the people or things in it. *...bringing up children in cramped high-rise flats.*

crane /kreɪn/, **cranes, craning, craned.** **1** COUNT N A **crane** is a large machine that moves heavy things by lifting them in the air. **2** COUNT N A **crane** is also a kind of large bird with a long neck and long legs. **3** VB WITH OBJ If you **crane** your neck, you stretch it to see or hear something better. *He craned his neck out of the window.*

crank /kræŋk/, **cranks, cranking, cranked.** **1** COUNT N A **crank** is someone with peculiar ideas who behaves in a strange way; an informal use. **2** VB WITH OBJ If you **crank** a device or machine, you make it move by turning a handle. *She cranked down the window.*

cranny /kræni^{1}/. **every nook and cranny:** see **nook.**

crash /kræʃ/, **crashes, crashing, crashed.** **1** COUNT N A **crash** is an accident in which a moving vehicle hits something and is damaged or destroyed. *Her mother was killed in a car crash.* **2** VB OR ERG VB If a moving vehicle **crashes,** it hits something and is damaged or destroyed. *The plane crashed within seconds of taking off... He crashed his car into the bar.* **3** VB To **crash** also means to move or fall violently, making a loud noise. *The door crashed open... A glass crashed to the floor.* **4** SING N A **crash** is also a sudden, loud noise. *...a terrific crash of thunder.* **5** COUNT N The **crash** of a business is its serious failure. *...one of the most spectacular financial crashes of the decade.*

crash helmet, **crash helmets.** COUNT N A **crash helmet** is a helmet worn by motor cyclists to protect their heads.

crass /kræs/. ADJ **Crass** behaviour is stupid and insensitive.

crate /kreɪt/, **crates.** COUNT N A **crate** is a large box used for transporting or storing things. *...a crate of oranges.*

crater /kreɪtə/, **craters.** COUNT N A **crater** is a large hole in the ground, caused by an explosion or by something large that hits it. *...bomb craters.*

cravat /krəvæt/, **cravats.** COUNT N A **cravat** is a piece of cloth like a scarf which a man wears around his neck and tucked inside the collar of his shirt.

crave /kreɪv/, **craves, craving, craved.** VB WITH OBJ OR 'for' If you **crave** something or **crave** for it, you want to have it very much. *She craved luxury... Baker was craving for a smoke.* ♦ **craving** COUNT N *Both the sisters had a craving for sweets... ...their powerful craving to succeed.*

crawl /krɔːl/, **crawls, crawling, crawled.** **1** VB When you **crawl,** you move forward on your hands and knees. *Her baby is crawling about now.* **2** VB When an insect or vehicle **crawls,** it moves slowly. *A spider was crawling up my leg.* **3** VB If you say that a place **is crawling** with people or things, you mean that it is full of them. *The forecourt was crawling with security men.* **4** VB If you **crawl** to someone, you try to please them in order to gain some advantage; an informal use. *Let's see who comes crawling to whom.* **5** SING N The **crawl** is a swimming stroke where you lie on your front, swinging first one arm over your head, and then the other arm.

crayon /kreɪə^{7}n/, **crayons.** COUNT N A **crayon** is a pencil containing coloured wax or clay. *...a box of crayons.* Also UNCOUNT N *...drawing in crayon.*

craze /kreɪz/, **crazes.** COUNT N A **craze** is something that is very popular for a very short time. *...the latest dance craze from America.*

crazed /kreɪzd/. ATTRIB ADJ **Crazed** behaviour is wild and uncontrolled. *She fought with crazed ferocity.*

crazy /kreɪzi^{1}/, **crazier, craziest;** an informal word. **1** ADJ A **crazy** person or idea seems very strange or foolish. *My fellow students thought I was crazy... It's crazy to have a picnic in October.* ♦ **crazily** ADV *A man rushed past him shouting crazily.* **2** PRED ADJ OR ADJ AFTER N If you are **crazy** about something, you are very enthusiastic about it. *They are crazy about football... Everyone was jazz crazy.* 3 PRED ADJ If something makes or drives you **crazy,** it makes you extremely annoyed or upset.

creak /kri:k/, **creaks, creaking, creaked.** VB If something **creaks,** it makes a harsh sound when it moves. *The door creaked.* Also COUNT N WITH SUPP *The creak of the mattress did not wake her.*

cream /kri:m/, **creams, creaming, creamed.** 1 UNCOUNT N **Cream** is a thick liquid that is produced from milk. You can use it in cooking or put it on fruit or puddings. *...strawberries and cream.* 2 UNCOUNT N **Cream** is also an artificial food that looks and tastes like cream. *...chocolates with cream fillings.* 3 MASS N **Cream** is also a thick substance that you rub into your skin. *She wiped the cream off her face.* 4 ADJ Something that is **cream** in colour is yellowish-white. 5 SING N WITH SUPP You can refer to the best people or things in a group as the **cream** of it. *They were the cream of their generation.*

cream off. PHR VB If you **cream off** part of a group of people, you separate them and treat them differently, because you think they are better than the rest. *The best pupils would be creamed off and given a superior training.*

creamy /kri:mi^1/. 1 ADJ Something that is **creamy** is yellowish-white. 2 ADJ Food or drink that is **creamy** contains a lot of cream.

crease /kri:s/, **creases, creasing, creased.** 1 COUNT N **Creases** are lines or folds that appear in cloth or paper when it is crushed. *She smoothed down the creases in her dress.* 2 ERG VB When cloth or paper **creases** or **is creased,** lines or folds appear in it because it has been crushed. ♦ **creased** ADJ *His suit had become creased.* 3 ERG VB If your face **creases** or **is creased,** lines appear on it because you are frowning or smiling. *A wrinkle of doubt creased her forehead.*

create /kri:eɪt/, **creates, creating, created.** VB WITH OBJ To **create** something means to cause it to happen or exist. *His work created enormous interest in England... They opened windows and doors to create a draught.*

creation /kri:eɪʃə^{0}n/, **creations.** 1 UNCOUNT N The **creation** of something is the act of bringing it into existence. *They proposed the creation of Welsh and Scottish parliaments... ...a job creation scheme.* 2 PROPER N In the Bible, the **Creation** is the making of the universe, earth, and creatures by God. 3 UNCOUNT N People sometimes refer to the entire universe as **creation.** *They look upon everything in creation as material for exploitation.* 4 COUNT N A **creation** is something that has been made or produced; a literary use. *...his ceramic creations.*

creative /kri:eɪtɪv/. 1 ADJ A **creative** person has the ability to invent and develop original ideas, especially in art. **Creative** activities involve inventing and developing original ideas. *He has more time to be creative... ...creative writing.* ♦ **creativity** /kri:eɪtɪvɪ^{1}ti^1/ UNCOUNT N *...adults who want to express their own creativity.* 2 ADJ If you use something in a **creative** way, you use it in a new way that produces interesting and unusual results. *...the creative use of language.*

creator /kri:eɪtə/, **creators.** 1 COUNT N The **creator** of something is the person who made it or invented it. 2 PROPER N God is sometimes referred to as the **Creator.**

creature /kri:tʃə/, **creatures.** 1 COUNT N A **creature** is a living thing such as an animal, bird, or insect. *Worms are very simple creatures.* 2 COUNT N WITH SUPP You can also use **creature** to talk about people. For example, you call someone a stupid **creature** to emphasize that they are stupid. *She was a weak and helpless creature.*

crèche /krɛʃ/, **crèches.** COUNT N A **crèche** is a place where small children are left and looked after while their parents are working.

credence /kri:də^{0}ns/. UNCOUNT N If something lends **credence** to a theory or story, it makes it easier to believe. *These latest discoveries give credence to Burke's ideas.*

credentials /krɪ^{2}dɛnʃə^{0}lz/; a formal word. 1 PLURAL N Your **credentials** are your previous achievements, training, and general background, which indicate that you are qualified to do something. *His credentials as a journalist were beyond dispute.* 2 PLURAL N **Credentials** are also a letter or certificate that proves your identity or qualifications. *Didn't you ask for his credentials?*

credibility /krɛdɪ^{1}bɪlɪ^{1}ti^1/. UNCOUNT N If someone or something has **credibility,** people believe in them and trust them. *He felt that he had lost credibility.*

credible /krɛdɪ^{1}bə^{0}l/. ADJ If someone or something is **credible,** you can believe or trust them. *No politicians seem credible these days.*

credit /krɛdɪt/, **credits, crediting, credited.** 1 UNCOUNT N **Credit** is a system where you pay for goods or services several weeks or months after you have received them. *...the availability of cheap long-term credit... They sold grain on credit during times of famine.* 2 UNCOUNT N If you get the **credit** for something, people praise you for it. *Some of the credit should go to Nick.* 3 VB WITH OBJ If you **are credited** with an achievement or if it **is credited** to you, people believe that you were responsible for it. *...the woman who is often credited with originating the movement.* 4 VB WITH OBJ If you cannot **credit** something, you cannot believe it; a formal use. *There must be many of you who find this case hard to credit.* 5 PLURAL N The list of people who helped to make a film, a record, or a television programme is called the **credits.**

PHRASES ● If someone or their bank account is **in credit,** their bank account has money in it. ● If something **does** you **credit,** you should be respected or admired for it. ● If something is **to your credit,** you deserve praise for it. *Price, to his credit, denounced in private the brutalities of the regime.* ● If you have one or more achievements **to your credit,** you have achieved them.

creditable /krɛdɪtəbə^{0}l/. 1 ADJ Something that is **creditable** is of a reasonably high standard. *He polled a creditable 44.8 per cent.* 2 ADJ If someone's behaviour is **creditable,** it should be respected or admired. *...some of the less creditable features of his past.*

credit card, credit cards. COUNT N A **credit card** is a plastic card that you use to buy goods on credit or to borrow money.

creditor /krɛdɪtə/, **creditors.** COUNT N Your **creditors** are the people who you owe money to.

credulity /krɪ^{2}dju:lɪ^{1}ti^1/. UNCOUNT N **Credulity** is willingness to believe that something is real or true; a formal use. *Don't stretch my credulity too far.*

credulous /krɛdjə^{4}ləs/. ADJ If you are **credulous,** you are always ready to believe what people tell you, and are easily deceived.

creed /kri:d/, **creeds.** 1 COUNT N A **creed** is a set of beliefs or principles that influence the way people live or work. *They never embraced any particular creed.* 2 COUNT N A **creed** is also a religion; a formal use. *...the Christian creed.*

creek /kri:k/, **creeks.** 1 COUNT N A **creek** is a narrow inlet where the sea comes a long way into the land. *...the muddy creeks of my home coast.* 2 COUNT N A **creek** is also a small stream or river; an American use. *By early summer the creek was almost dry.*

creep /kri:p/, **creeps, creeping, crept** /krɛpt/. 1 VB WITH ADJUNCT When people **creep** somewhere, they move quietly and slowly. *I heard my landlady creeping stealthily up to my door.* 2 VB WITH ADJUNCT If something **creeps** somewhere, it moves slowly so that you hardly notice it; a literary use. *Here and there, little breezes crept over the water.* 3 COUNT N You call someone a **creep** to show you dislike them, especially because they flatter people; an informal use.

creep in. PHR VB If a new idea or custom **creeps in,** it gradually becomes used.

creep up on. PHR VB 1 If you **creep up on** someone, you move slowly closer to them without being seen. 2 If a feeling or situation **creeps up on** you, you hardly notice that it is happening to you or affecting you. *Fame has crept up on her almost by accident.*

creeper /kri:pə/, **creepers.** COUNT N A **creeper** is a plant with long stems that wind themselves around things.

creepy /kri:pi^1/. ADJ Something that is **creepy** gives you a strange, unpleasant feeling of fear; an informal use. *It was very creepy in the woods.*

cremate /krɪ^{1}meɪt/, **cremates, cremating, cremated.** VB WITH OBJ When someone **is cremated,** their dead body is burned.

cremation /krɪ^{1}meɪʃə^{0}n/, **cremations.** 1 COUNT N A **cremation** is a funeral service during which a dead body is cremated. 2 UNCOUNT N **Cremation** is the process of burning a dead body at a funeral.

crematorium /krɛmətɔ:rɪəm/, **crematoria** /krɛmətɔ:rɪə/ or **crematoriums.** COUNT N A **crematorium** is a building in which bodies are cremated.

crepe /kreɪp/. UNCOUNT N **Crepe** is a thin fabric made of cotton, silk, or wool with an uneven, wrinkled surface.

crept /krɛpt/. **Crept** is the past tense and past participle of **creep.**

crescendo /krɪ^{2}ʃɛndəʊ/. SING N A **crescendo** is the fact of a noise getting louder or being very loud. *The noise reached a crescendo.*

crescent /krɛsə^{0}nt, -zə^{0}nt/, **crescents.** COUNT N A **crescent** is a curved shape that is wider in the middle than at its ends, like the moon in its first and last quarters.

crest /krɛst/, **crests.** 1 COUNT N The **crest** of a hill or a wave is the highest part of it. *We had reached the crest of the hill.* 2 COUNT N A **crest** is also a design that is the sign of a noble family, a town, or an organization.

crestfallen /krɛstfɔ:lən/. PRED ADJ Someone who looks **crestfallen** looks sad and disappointed.

crevice /krɛvɪs/, **crevices.** COUNT N A **crevice** is a narrow crack in a rock. *The insects are hidden in rock crevices.*

crew /kru:/, **crews.** 1 COLL N The people who work on and operate a ship, aeroplane, or spacecraft are called the **crew.** *The 'Maine' carried a crew of three hundred and fifty.* 2 COLL N You also use **crew** to refer to people with special technical skills who work together on a task or project. *...TV crews.*

crew cut, crew cuts. COUNT N A **crew cut** is a hairstyle where the hair is cut very short.

crib /krɪb/, **cribs.** COUNT N A **crib** is a baby's cot; an American use. *She used to throw her toys out of her crib.*

crick /krɪk/. SING N If you have a **crick** in your neck, you have a pain caused by stiff muscles.

cricket /krɪkɪt/, **crickets.** 1 UNCOUNT N **Cricket** is an outdoor game played two teams who try to score points, called runs, by hitting a ball with a wooden bat. 2 COUNT N A **cricket** is a small jumping insect that produces sharp sounds by rubbing its wings together.

cricketer /krɪkɪtə/, **cricketers.** COUNT N A **cricketer** is a person who plays cricket.

crime /kraɪm/, **crimes.** 1 COUNT N OR UNCOUNT N A **crime** is an illegal action for which a person can be punished by law. *A crime has been committed... ...the crime of murder... ...a life of crime.* 2 COUNT N You can also refer to an action which seems morally wrong as a **crime.** *To waste good food is a crime against nature.*

criminal /krɪmɪnə^{0}l/, **criminals.** 1 COUNT N A **criminal** is a person who has committed a crime. *...one of the country's ten most wanted criminals.* 2 ADJ Something that is **criminal** is connected with crime. *He had done nothing criminal... ...a criminal offence.* ♦ **criminally** SUBMOD *...criminally responsible for the loss of lives.* 3 ADJ **Criminal** also means morally wrong. *To refuse medical aid would be criminal.*

crimson /krɪmzə^{0}n/. ADJ Something that is **crimson** is dark purplish-red.

cringe /krɪndʒ/, **cringes, cringing, cringed.** 1 VB If you **cringe** from someone or something, you back away because of fear. *She cringed against the wall.* 2 VB You say that people **cringe** when they are very embarrassed. *Cringing under the stares of passers-by, I tried to read my newspaper.*

crinkle /krɪŋkə^{0}l/, **crinkles, crinkling, crinkled.** 1 ERG VB When something **crinkles** or **is crinkled,** it becomes slightly creased or folded. *His face crinkled into a smile... Carl crinkled his brow... ...brown crinkled leaves.* 2 COUNT N **Crinkles** are small creases or folds. *There were crinkles at the outer corners of his eyes.*

cripple /krɪpə^{0}l/, **cripples, crippling, crippled.** 1 COUNT N A **cripple** is someone who cannot move properly because of illness or injury. 2 VB WITH OBJ If something **cripples** you, you are seriously injured so that you cannot move properly. *...several painful falls that crippled him.* ♦ **crippled** ADJ *...his crippled mother.* 3 VB WITH OBJ If something **cripples** an organization, it prevents it from working properly. *The government had done much to cripple national enterprise.*

crippling /krɪplɪŋ/. 1 ATTRIB ADJ A **crippling** illness or disability severely damages your health or body. *...the dread of crippling disablement.* 2 ADJ **Crippling** prices or taxes have a serious effect on the people who have to pay them.

crisis /kraɪsɪs/, **crises** /kraɪsi:z/. 1 COUNT N OR UNCOUNT N A **crisis** is a serious or dangerous situation which could cause death or great hardship. *...an economic crisis... ...times of crisis.* 2 COUNT N OR UNCOUNT N A **crisis** in someone's life is a time when they have serious personal problems. *He had an emotional crisis... Who can you turn to in time of crisis?*

crisp /krɪsp/, **crisper, crispest; crisps.** 1 ADJ Something that is **crisp** is pleasantly stiff and fresh. *...crisp bacon... ...crisp new bank notes.* 2 COUNT N **Crisps** are very thin slices of potato that have been fried until they are hard and crunchy; a British use. *...a packet of crisps.* 3 ADJ **Crisp** air or weather is pleasantly fresh, cold, and dry. *...a crisp October morning.* 4 ADJ A **crisp** remark or response is brief and perhaps unfriendly. *He sent off two crisp telegrams.* ♦ **crisply** ADV *'What did she want?' Etta said crisply. 'Money?'*

criss-cross /krɪskrɒs/, **criss-crosses, criss-crossing, criss-crossed.** 1 VB WITH OR WITHOUT OBJ If things **criss-cross,** they create a pattern of crossed lines. *...the freeways that criss-cross the whole of Los Angeles.* 2 ATTRIB ADJ A **criss-cross** pattern or design has lines crossing each other. *...a criss-cross pattern of tree trunks.*

criterion /kraɪtɪərɪən/, **criteria** /kraɪtɪərɪə/. COUNT N A **criterion** is a standard by which you judge or decide something. *My own criterion of success is the ability to work joyfully... ...the criteria for defining mental illness.*

critic /krɪtɪk/, **critics.** **1** COUNT N A **critic** is a person who writes reviews and expresses opinions about books, films, music, and art. *...television critics.* **2** COUNT N WITH SUPP A **critic** of a person or system disapproves of them and criticizes them publicly. *...critics of the Trade Union Movement.*

critical /krɪtɪkə^{0}l/. **1** ADJ If you are **critical** of someone or something, you criticize them. *He had long been critical of Conservative policy.* ♦ **critically** ADV *She had mentioned the book critically to friends.* **2** ATTRIB ADJ A **critical** approach to something involves careful examination and judgement of it. *...each player regarding the other with critical interest.* ♦ **critically** ADV *The problem should be analysed more critically.* **3** ADJ A **critical** time or situation is extremely important. *This was a critical moment in his career... The twelve weeks of summer were critical to most of the restaurants and pubs.* ♦ **critically** ADV *The distribution of resources is critically important.* **4** ADJ **Critical** also means very serious and dangerous. *...the critical state of the economy.* ♦ **critically** ADV *He became critically ill.*

criticism /krɪtɪsɪzə^{0}m/, **criticisms.** **1** UNCOUNT N **Criticism** is the expression of disapproval of someone or something. *Some fierce public criticism of the plan had been voiced.* **2** UNCOUNT N **Criticism** of a book, play, or other work of art is a serious examination and judgement of it. *...literary criticism.* **3** COUNT N A **criticism** is a comment in which you say that something has a particular fault. *One of the main criticisms against him is that he is lazy.*

criticize /krɪtɪsaɪz/, **criticizes, criticizing, criticized;** also spelled **criticise.** VB WITH OBJ If you **criticize** someone or something, you express your disapproval of them by saying what you think is wrong with them. *Please don't get angry if I criticize you... He was criticized for pursuing a policy of conciliation.*

critique /krɪtiːk/, **critiques.** COUNT N A **critique** of something is a written examination and judgement of it; a formal use.

croak /krəʊk/, **croaks, croaking, croaked.** **1** VB When animals or birds **croak,** they utter harsh, low sounds. *A bullfrog was croaking in the distance.* Also SING N *...the croak of a raven.* **2** REPORT VB When someone **croaks** something, they say it in a hoarse, rough voice. *'Brandy,' he croaked.* Also SING N *His voice was a weak croak.*

crochet /krəʊʃɪ^{3}/. UNCOUNT N **Crochet** is a way of making clothes and other things out of thread by using a needle with a small hook at the end.

crockery /krɒkə^{0}ri^{1}/. UNCOUNT N **Crockery** is plates, cups, and saucers. *...a sink overflowing with dirty crockery.*

crocodile /krɒkədaɪl/, **crocodiles.** COUNT N A **crocodile** is a large reptile with a long body. Crocodiles live in rivers and eat meat.

crocus /krəʊkəs/, **crocuses.** COUNT N **Crocuses** are small white, yellow, or purple flowers that are grown in gardens in the early spring.

crony /krəʊni^{1}/, **cronies.** COUNT N Your **cronies** are the friends who you spend a lot of time with; an informal use.

crook /krʊk/, **crooks, crooking, crooked.** **1** COUNT N A **crook** is a criminal or dishonest person; an informal use. *The accountants turned out to have been crooks.* **2** COUNT N The **crook** of your arm or leg is the soft inside part where you bend your elbow or knee. *She buried her face in the crook of her arm.* **3** VB WITH OBJ If you **crook** your arm or finger, you bend it.

crooked /krʊkɪ^{2}d/. **1** ADJ Something that is **crooked** is bent or twisted. *My back is so crooked and painful that I cannot stand upright.* **2** ADJ Someone who is **crooked** is dishonest or a criminal. *...a crooked cop.*

croon /kruːn/, **croons, crooning, crooned.** VB If you **croon** something, you sing or say it quietly and gently. *He sat there, crooning to himself... 'You little charmer,' he crooned.*

crop /krɒp/, **crops, cropping, cropped.** **1** COUNT N **Crops** are plants such as wheat and potatoes that are grown in large quantities for food. *...vast fields of crops.* **2** COUNT N The plants that are collected at harvest time are referred to as a **crop.** *They get two crops of rice a year.* **3** COUNT N WITH SUPP You can also refer to a group of people or things that appear together as a **crop;** an informal use. *What do you think of the current crop of school-leavers?* **4** VB WITH OBJ If your hair **is cropped,** it is cut very short. *...a boy with closely cropped hair.* **5** VB WITH OBJ When an animal **crops** grass or leaves, it eats them.

crop up. PHR VB If something **crops up,** it happens or appears unexpectedly; an informal use.

croquet /krəʊkɪ^{3}/. UNCOUNT N **Croquet** is a game in which the players use long-handled wooden mallets to hit balls through metal arches stuck in a lawn.

cross /krɒs/, **crosses, crossing, crossed; crosser, crossest.** **1** VB WITH OBJ If you **cross** a room, road, or area of land, you move or travel to the other side of it. *He crossed the room slowly.* **2** VB If you **cross** to a place, you go across an area of land or water to reach it. *He stood up at once and crossed to the door... Where and how did you cross into Swaziland?* **3** RECIP VB Lines or roads that **cross** meet and go across each other. *...a place where four canyons crossed... Brook Street runs west, crossing Bond Street.* **4** VB WITH OBJ If you **cross** your arms, legs, or fingers, you put one of them on top of the other. *She sat back and crossed her legs.* **5** VB WITH OBJ If an expression **crosses** someone's face, it appears briefly on their face; a literary use. *A flicker of unconcealed distaste crossed his features.* **6** PHRASE When a thought **crosses** your **mind,** you think of something or remember something. *It had not crossed my mind to tell them I was leaving.* **7** COUNT N A **cross** is a shape that consists of a vertical line with a shorter horizontal line across it. It is the most important Christian symbol. **8** COUNT N A **cross** is also a written mark in the shape of an X. *The reader has to indicate the answer with a cross or a tick.* **9** ADJ Someone who is **cross** is angry. *We all get cross with our children.* ♦ **crossly** ADV *'Don't ask me,' the post office lady replied, crossly.* **10** COUNT N Something that is a **cross** between two things is neither one thing nor the other, but a mixture of both. *A Barbary duck is a cross between a wild duck and an ordinary duck.*

cross off. PHR VB If you **cross off** items on a list, you draw a line through them. *...crossing off those who were no longer interested.*

cross out. PHR VB If you **cross out** words, you draw a line through them. *She saw her name and crossed it out.*

crossbar /krɒsbɑː/, **crossbars.** **1** COUNT N A **crossbar** is a horizontal piece of wood attached to two upright pieces, for example the top part of the goal in the game of football. **2** COUNT N The **crossbar** on a man's bicycle is the horizontal metal bar between the handlebars and the saddle.

cross-country. **1** ATTRIB ADJ OR ADV If you go somewhere **cross-country,** you use paths or less important routes, rather than main roads. *...a cross-country bicycle trip... He walked cross-country to the hospital.* **2** UNCOUNT N **Cross-country** is the sport of running across open countryside.

cross-examine, cross-examines, cross-examining, cross-examined. VB WITH OBJ If you **are cross-examined** during a trial in a court of law, you are questioned about evidence that you have already given. ♦ **cross-examination** UNCOUNT N OR COUNT N *Mr Fairbairn, in cross-examination, took the matter further.*

cross-eyed. ADJ A person who is **cross-eyed** has eyes that seem to look towards each other.

crossing /krɒsɪŋ/, **crossings.** **1** COUNT N A **crossing** is a journey by boat to the other side of a sea. *...the night ferry crossing to Esbjerg.* **2** COUNT N A **crossing** is also the same as a pedestrian crossing.

cross-legged /krɒslegɪ^{1}d, krɒslegd/. ADJ If someone is sitting **cross-legged,** they are sitting with their legs bent close to their body, their knees pointing outwards, and their feet pointing inwards.

cross-purposes. PHRASE When people are **at cross-purposes,** they do not understand each other because they are talking about different things without realizing it. *They are bound to be at cross-purposes.*

cross-reference, cross-references. COUNT N A **cross-reference** is a note in a book which tells you that there is relevant or more detailed information in another part of the book.

crossroads /krɒsrəʊdz/. **Crossroads is the singular and plural.** COUNT N A **crossroads** is a place where two roads meet and cross each other.

cross-section, cross-sections. **1** COUNT N A **cross-section** of something such as a group of people is a typical or representative sample. *It attracts a remarkable cross-section of the public.* **2** COUNT N WITH SUPP A **cross-section** of an object is what you would see if you cut straight through the middle of it. *...a cross-section of a human brain.*

crossword /krɒswɜːd/, **crosswords.** COUNT N A **crossword** or **crossword puzzle** is a word game in which you work out answers to clues, and write the answers in the white squares of a pattern of black and white squares. *I do the crossword first.*

crotch /krɒtʃ/, **crotches.** **1** COUNT N Your **crotch** is the part of your body between the tops of your legs. **2** COUNT N The **crotch** of a pair of trousers or pants is the part that covers the area between the tops of your legs.

crouch /kraʊtʃ/, **crouches, crouching, crouched.** **1** VB If you **are crouching,** your legs are bent under you so that you are close to the ground and leaning forward slightly. *He crouched down among the tangled foliage.* **2** VB If you **crouch** over something, you bend over it so that you are very near to it. *Her stout form crouched over a typewriter.*

crow /krəʊ/, **crows, crowing, crowed.** **1** COUNT N A **crow** is a kind of large black bird which makes a loud, harsh noise. **2** VB When a cock **crows,** it utters a loud sound early in the morning. *The cocks crowed again.* **3** VB If someone **crows** about or over something, they keep telling people proudly about it; an informal use, that often shows disapproval. *Now perhaps that is something to crow about.*

crowbar /krəʊbɑː/, **crowbars.** COUNT N A **crowbar** is a heavy iron bar which is used as a lever.

crowd /kraʊd/, **crowds, crowding, crowded.** **1** COUNT N A **crowd** is a large group of people who have gathered together. *The crowd was silent... ...crowds of tourists.* **2** COUNT N A **crowd** is also a group of friends, or people with the same interests or occupation; an informal use. *They were mostly women, the usual crowd.* **3** VB When people **crowd** round someone or something, they gather closely together around them. *We crowded round eagerly.* **4** VB WITH OBJ OR ADJUNCT If a group of people **crowd** a place or **crowd** into it, they fill it completely. *Mobs of movie stars were crowding the bar... The TV men crowded in, examining our equipment.*

crowded /kraʊdɪ^{2}d/. ADJ A **crowded** place is full of people or things. *The bar was very crowded... The centre of Birmingham was crowded with shoppers.*

crown /kraʊn/, **crowns, crowning, crowned.** **1** COUNT N A **crown** is a circular ornament for the head, usually made of gold and jewels, which kings and queens wear at official ceremonies. **2** PROPER N The monarchy of a particular country is referred to as the **Crown** when it is regarded as an institution. *...a senior Minister of the Crown.* **3** VB WITH OBJ, WITH OR WITHOUT COMPLEMENT When someone **is crowned,** a crown is placed on their head as part of a ceremony in which they are officially made king or queen. **4** VB WITH OBJ If something **crowns** something else, it is on the top of it; a literary use. *...the shattered rocks that crowned the hill.* **5** COUNT N Your **crown** is the top part of your head, at the back. **6** VB WITH OBJ An achievement, event, or quality that **crowns** something is the best part of it. *The evening was crowned by a dazzling performance from Maria Ewing.* ♦ **crowning** ATTRIB ADJ *...the crowning achievement of 16 years of research.*

crucial /kruːʃə^{0}l/. ADJ Something that is **crucial** is extremely important. *Success or failure here would be crucial to his future prospects.* ♦ **crucially** ADV *The answer will depend crucially on the kind of data collected.*

crucifix /kruːsɪfɪks/, **crucifixes.** COUNT N A **crucifix** is a cross with a figure of Christ on it.

crucifixion /kruːsɪfɪkʃə^{0}n/, **crucifixions.** UNCOUNT N OR COUNT N In the Roman Empire, **crucifixion** was a way of executing people by crucifying them. The **Crucifixion** was the death of Christ by this method.

crucify /kruːsɪfaɪ/, **crucifies, crucifying, crucified.** VB WITH OBJ To **crucify** someone means to kill them by tying or nailing them to a cross and leaving them to die.

crude /kruːd/, **cruder, crudest.** **1** ADJ Something that is **crude** is simple, rough, and unsophisticated. *...crude methods of administration.* ♦ **crudely** ADV *...crudely sewn shirts.* **2** ADJ **Crude** language is rude and offensive. *Do you have to be so crude?*

crude oil. UNCOUNT N **Crude oil** is oil in its natural state before it has been processed.

cruel /kruːəl/, **crueller, cruellest.** ADJ Someone who is **cruel** deliberately causes pain or distress. *She had cruel parents.* ♦ **cruelly** ADV *They treated him cruelly.*

cruelty /kruːəlti^{1}/. UNCOUNT N **Cruelty** is behaviour that deliberately causes pain or distress to people or animals. *...cruelty to animals.*

cruise /kruːz/, **cruises, cruising, cruised.** **1** COUNT N A **cruise** is a holiday spent on a large ship which visits a number of places. **2** VB If a car or a ship **cruises,** it moves at a constant moderate speed. *The taxi cruised off down the Cromwell Road.*

cruise missile, cruise missiles. COUNT N A **cruise missile** is a missile which carries a nuclear warhead and which is guided by a computer.

cruiser /kruːzə/, **cruisers.** **1** COUNT N A **cruiser** is a motor boat with a cabin for people to sleep in. **2** COUNT N A **cruiser** is also a large, fast warship.

crumb /krʌm/, **crumbs.** COUNT N **Crumbs** are very small pieces of bread or cake.

crumble /krʌmbəl/, **crumbles, crumbling, crumbled.** 1 ERG VB When something soft, brittle, or old **crumbles,** it breaks into a lot of little pieces. *The bread crumbled in my fingers... The flakes can be easily crumbled into small pieces... The villages are crumbling into ruin.* 2 VB When a society, organization, or relationship **crumbles,** it fails and comes to an end. *His first Labour Government crumbled.*

crumbly /krʌmbli[1]/. ADJ Something that is **crumbly** is easily broken into a lot of little pieces.

crumple /krʌmpəl/, **crumples, crumpling, crumpled.** 1 VB WITH OBJ If you **crumple** paper or cloth, you squash it and it becomes full of creases and folds. *He took the letter and crumpled it in his hand.* ♦ **crumpled** ADJ *He was dressed in crumpled clothes.* 2 VB If someone or something **crumples,** they collapse suddenly in an untidy and helpless way. *He crumpled into a heap.*

crunch /krʌntʃ/, **crunches, crunching, crunched.** VB WITH OBJ If you **crunch** something with your teeth or feet, you crush it noisily. *He put seven or eight pieces into his mouth and began crunching them... I crunched a wine glass underfoot.* Also COUNT N WITH SUPP *...the crunch of footsteps on the gravel.*

crunchy /krʌntʃi[1]/. ADJ **Crunchy** food is hard or crisp, and makes a noise when you eat it.

crusade /kru:seɪd/, **crusades.** COUNT N WITH SUPP A **crusade** is a long and determined attempt to achieve something. *...the great crusade to fight and conquer cancer.* ♦ **crusader** /kru:seɪdə/ COUNT N WITH SUPP *...a moral crusader.*

crush /krʌʃ/, **crushes, crushing, crushed.** 1 VB WITH OBJ If you **crush** an object, you press it very hard so that you break it or destroy its shape. 2 VB WITH OBJ If you **crush** a substance, you make it into a powder by pressing and grinding it. *To get the oil out you will have to crush the seeds.* 3 VB WITH OBJ To **crush** an army or a political organization means to defeat it completely. *The government still think they can crush the unions.* ♦ **crushing** ATTRIB ADJ *...a crushing defeat.* 4 COUNT N A **crush** is a dense crowd of people. *A reporter made his way through the crush.* 5 COUNT N If you have a **crush** on someone, you are strongly attracted to them for a short time; an informal use. *I had a crush on the violin master.*

crust /krʌst/, **crusts.** 1 COUNT N OR UNCOUNT N The **crust** on a loaf of bread is the hard, crisp outside part of it. 2 COUNT N A **crust** is also the hard upper layer of something. *The snow had a fine crust on it.* 3 COUNT N WITH SUPP The earth's **crust** is its outer layer.

crusty /krʌsti[1]/. ADJ Something that is **crusty** has a hard, crisp outer layer. *...crusty bread.*

crutch /krʌtʃ/, **crutches.** 1 COUNT N A **crutch** is a support like a stick, which you lean on to help you to walk when you have injured your foot or leg. 2 COUNT N Someone's **crutch** is their crotch.

crux /krʌks/. SING N The **crux** of a problem or argument is the most important or difficult part, which affects everything else. *Here we come to the crux of the matter.*

cry /kraɪ/, **cries, crying, cried.** 1 VB When you **cry,** you produce tears because you are unhappy or hurt. *Helen began to cry... He kept on crying.* Also SING N *I think she had had a good cry.* 2 REPORT VB To **cry** something means to shout it or say it loudly. *'Come on!' he cried.* Also COUNT N *I heard a cry for help... Claud let out a cry of horror.* 3 COUNT N You can describe a loud sound made by a bird as a **cry.** *A sea bird flapped upwards with a hoarse cry.* 4 PHRASE Something that is **a far cry** from something else is very different from it. *The tropical grasslands are a far cry from the lush green pastures of Ireland.*

cry off. PHR VB If you **cry off,** you decide not to do something that you had arranged to do; an informal use. *I'm afraid I cried off at the last moment.*

cry out. PHR VB If you **cry out,** you call out or say something loudly, for example because you are anxious or frightened. *I heard Mary cry out in fright... 'Father! You must stop that!' he suddenly cried out.*

cry out for. PHR VB If you say that one thing **is crying out for** another, you mean that it needs that thing very much. *There is a vast surplus of workers crying out for employment.*

crypt /krɪpt/, **crypts.** COUNT N A **crypt** is an underground room beneath a church or cathedral.

cryptic /krɪptɪk/. ADJ A **cryptic** remark or message contains a hidden meaning. *I didn't ask what this cryptic remark was intended to convey.* ♦ **cryptically** ADV *'I have taken precautions,' she said cryptically.*

crystal /krɪstəl/, **crystals.** 1 COUNT N A **crystal** is a mineral that has formed naturally into a regular symmetrical shape. *Pure copper is made up of layers of crystals.* 2 UNCOUNT N **Crystal** is a transparent rock used in jewellery and ornaments. 3 UNCOUNT N **Crystal** is also very high quality glass, usually with its surface cut into patterns. *...a shimmering crystal chandelier.*

crystal clear. ADJ An explanation that is **crystal clear** is very easy to understand. *He challenged every point which he did not find crystal clear.*

crystallize /krɪstəlaɪz/, **crystallizes, crystallizing, crystallized;** also spelled **crystallise.** 1 ERG VB When an opinion or idea **crystallizes,** it becomes fixed and definite in your mind. *My thoughts began to crystallize... This experience crystallized his attitude to democracy.* 2 VB When a substance **crystallizes,** it turns into crystals.

cub /kʌb/, **cubs.** COUNT N A **cub** is a young wild animal such as a lion, wolf, or bear. *...a leopard cub.*

cubby-hole /kʌbi[1] həʊl/, **cubby-holes.** COUNT N A **cubby-hole** is a very small room or space for storing things.

cube /kju:b/, **cubes.** 1 COUNT N A **cube** is a three-dimensional shape with six square surfaces which are all the same size. 2 COUNT N The **cube** of a number is another number that is produced by multiplying the first number by itself twice. For example, the cube of 2 is 8.

cubic /kju:bɪk/. ATTRIB ADJ **Cubic** is used in front of units of length to form units of volume such as 'cubic metre' and 'cubic foot'.

cubicle /kju:bɪkəl/, **cubicles.** COUNT N A **cubicle** is a small enclosed area in a public building which is used for a particular purpose, for example changing your clothes or talking to someone privately.

cuckoo /kʊku:/, **cuckoos.** COUNT N A **cuckoo** is a grey bird with a call of two quick notes. Cuckoos lay their eggs in other birds' nests.

cucumber /kju:kʌmbə/, **cucumbers.** COUNT N A **cucumber** is a long vegetable with a dark green skin and white flesh.

cud /kʌd/. PHRASE When cows **chew the cud,** they chew their partly digested food over and over again.

cuddle /kʌdəl/, **cuddles, cuddling, cuddled.** RECIP VB If you **cuddle** someone, you put your arms round them and hold them close. *A baby must be cuddled a lot.* Also COUNT N *Give them a few cuddles and talk nicely to them.*

cuddly /kʌdli[1]/. ADJ You say that people, animals, or toys are **cuddly** when you like them and want to cuddle them.

cue /kju:/, **cues.** 1 COUNT N A **cue** is something said or done by a performer that is a signal for another performer to begin speaking or doing something. *The violinist was late for her cue.* 2 COUNT N A **cue** is also a long stick used in snooker, billiards, and pool.

PHRASES ● If you **take your cue** from someone, you use their behaviour as an indication of what you should do. *Michael took his cue from the Duke's tone.* ● If you say that something happened **on cue,** you mean that it happened just when it was expected to happen. *Then, right on cue, the coach broke down.*

cuff /kʌf/, **cuffs, cuffing, cuffed.** 1 COUNT N The **cuffs** of a piece of clothing are the end parts of the sleeves. 2 ● If you are making a statement **off the cuff,** you have not prepared what you are saying. *I can't answer that question off the cuff.* 3 VB WITH OBJ If you **cuff** someone, you hit them lightly with your hand.

cufflink /kʌflɪŋk/, **cufflinks.** COUNT N **Cufflinks** are small decorative objects used for holding together a shirt cuff.

cuisine /kwɪzi:n/. UNCOUNT N WITH SUPP The **cuisine** of a region is its characteristic style of cooking. *...the delights of the Paris cuisine.*

cul-de-sac /kʌldəsæk, kʊl-/, **cul-de-sacs.** COUNT N A **cul-de-sac** is a road which is closed at one end.

culinary /kʌlɪnəri[1]/. ATTRIB ADJ **Culinary** means concerned with cooking. *...culinary skills.*

cull /kʌl/, **culls, culling, culled.** 1 VB WITH OBJ If you **cull** ideas or information, you gather them so that you can use them. *...materials that I'd culled from all sorts of places.* 2 VB WITH OBJ To **cull** a group of animals means to kill some of them in order to reduce their numbers. *They start to cull the herds in dry years.* Also COUNT N *...a big elephant cull in Zimbabwe.*

culminate /kʌlmɪneɪt/, **culminates, culminating, culminated.** VB WITH 'in' If a situation **culminates** in an event, this event is the end result of the situation. *The struggle between King and Parliament had culminated in the Civil War.* ♦ **culmination** /kʌlmɪneɪʃən/ UNCOUNT N *Marriage is seen as the culmination of a successful relationship.*

culpable /kʌlpəbəl/. PRED ADJ You say that someone is **culpable** when they are responsible for something wrong or unpleasant that has happened; a formal use.

culprit /kʌlprɪt/, **culprits.** COUNT N When some harm has been done, the **culprit** is the person who did it. *The main culprits were caught and heavily sentenced.*

cult /kʌlt/, **cults.** 1 COUNT N A **cult** is a religious group with special rituals which worships a particular person. *The 'Moonies' cult gained adherents at an alarming rate.* 2 COUNT N When a person, object, or activity becomes a **cult,** they become very popular or fashionable. *The Beatles became the heroes of a world-wide cult... ...a cult figure.*

cultivate /kʌltɪveɪt/, **cultivates, cultivating, cultivated.** 1 VB WITH OBJ To **cultivate** land means to prepare it and grow crops on it. *He retired to his estate near Bordeaux to cultivate his vineyard.* ♦ **cultivated** ADJ *Only 1 per cent of the cultivated area was under irrigation.* ♦ **cultivation** /kʌltɪveɪʃən/ UNCOUNT N *Some extra land is being brought under cultivation in Asia.* 2 VB WITH OBJ If you **cultivate** a feeling, idea, or attitude, you develop it and make it stronger. *He was anxious to cultivate the trust of moderate Tories.* ♦ **cultivation** UNCOUNT N WITH 'of' *...the cultivation of good taste.* 3 VB WITH OBJ If you **cultivate** someone, you try to develop a friendship with them. *Their cooperation is vital, so cultivate them assiduously.*

cultivated /kʌltɪveɪtɪ[2]d/. 1 ADJ Someone who is **cultivated** has had a good education, and shows this in their behaviour. 2 ATTRIB ADJ **Cultivated** plants have been developed for growing on farms or in gardens. *...cultivated wheat... ...cultivated mushrooms.*

cultural /kʌltʃərəl/. ATTRIB ADJ **Cultural** means relating to the arts generally, or to the arts and customs of a particular society. *...cultural activities such as plays, concerts, and poetry readings.* ♦ **culturally** ADV *They had little in common culturally with us.*

culture /kʌltʃə/, **cultures.** 1 UNCOUNT N OR COUNT N **Culture** consists of the ideas, customs, and art produced by a particular society. *He was specially interested in culture and history... ...African culture.* 2 COUNT N WITH SUPP A **culture** is a particular society or civilization. *We must respect the practices of cultures different from our own.* 3 COUNT N In science, a **culture** is a group of bacteria or cells grown in a laboratory as part of an experiment.

cultured /kʌltʃəd/. ADJ Someone who is **cultured** has good manners, is well educated, and knows a lot about the arts. *...a highly cultured man.*

culture shock. UNCOUNT N **Culture shock** is a feeling of anxiety, loneliness, and confusion that people sometimes experience when they first arrive in another country.

-cum-. You put **-cum-** between two words to form a compound noun referring to something or someone that is partly one thing and partly another. *...a dining-cum-living room.*

cumbersome /kʌmbəsəm/. 1 ADJ Something that is **cumbersome** is large and heavy and therefore difficult to carry, wear, or handle. *...a cumbersome piece of machinery.* 2 ADJ A **cumbersome** system or process is complicated and inefficient.

cumulative /kju:mjə[4]lətɪv/. ADJ Something that is **cumulative** keeps increasing in quantity or degree. *It was an accelerating, cumulative process.*

cunning /kʌnɪŋ/. 1 ADJ A **cunning** person is clever and deceitful. *He knew nothing of the cunning means employed to get him out of his job.* 2 UNCOUNT N **Cunning** is the ability to plan things cleverly, often by deceiving people. *They achieved their aim by stealth and cunning.*

cup /kʌp/, **cups, cupping, cupped.** 1 COUNT N A **cup** is a small, round container with a handle, which you drink from. *...a china cup.* 2 COUNT N You can use **cup** to refer to a cup and its contents, or to the contents only. *I've just made some tea. Would you like a cup?... I had a cup of hot flavourless coffee.* 3 COUNT N A **cup** is also something which is small, round, and hollow, like a cup. *....an egg cup... She tipped a pile of raisins into the cup of his hand.* 4 COUNT N A **cup** is also a large metal cup given as a prize to the winner of a game or competition. 5 VB WITH OBJ If you **cup** something in your hands, you hold it with your hands touching all round it. *....his hands were cupped around his lighter.*

cupboard /kʌbəd/, **cupboards.** COUNT N A **cupboard** is a piece of furniture with doors at the front and usually shelves inside. *...a kitchen cupboard.*

cupful /kʌpfʊl/, **cupfuls.** COUNT N A **cupful** of something is the amount which one cup can hold. *...a cupful of rice.*

curable /kjʊərəbəl/. ADJ A **curable** disease or illness can be cured.

curate /kjʊərə[1]t/, **curates.** COUNT N A **curate** is a clergyman who helps a vicar or priest.

curator /kjʊəreɪtə/, **curators.** COUNT N The **curator** of a museum or art gallery is the person in charge of the exhibits or works of art.

curb /kɜ:b/, **curbs, curbing, curbed.** 1 VB WITH OBJ If you **curb** something, you control it and keep it within fixed limits. *...proposals to curb the powers of the Home Secretary.* Also COUNT N *This requires a curb on public spending.* 2 See also **kerb.**

curdle /kɜ:dəl/, **curdles, curdling, curdled.** ERG VB When milk **curdles** or when something **curdles** it, it becomes sour.

curds /kɜ:dz/. PLURAL N **Curds** are the thick white substance formed when milk turns sour.

cure /kjʊə/, **cures, curing, cured.** 1 VB WITH OBJ To **cure** an illness means to make it end. *...the girl whose headache he cured... There are few diseases that these modern drugs cannot cure.* 2 VB WITH OBJ To **cure** a sick or injured person means to make them well again. *Her patients appear to be cured.* 3 VB WITH OBJ To **cure** a problem means to deal with it successfully. *The bishop had done nothing to cure the widespread lack of faith.* 4 VB WITH OBJ AND 'of' To **cure** someone of a habit or attitude means to make them give it up. *The shock of losing my purse cured me of my former carelessness.* 5 VB WITH OBJ When food, tobacco, or animal skin **is cured,** it is treated by being dried, smoked, or salted so that it will last for a long time. ♦ **cured** ADJ *...cured ham.* 6 COUNT N A **cure** is a medicine or other treatment that cures an illness. *There's no known cure for a cold.* 7 COUNT N A **cure** for a problem is a way of dealing with it successfully. *The only cure for her unhappiness was to leave home.*

curfew /kɜ:fju:/, **curfews.** COUNT N A **curfew** is a law stating that people must stay inside their houses after a particular time at night. *An emergency curfew was enforced.*

curiosity /kjʊərɪɒsɪ^{1}ti^1/, **curiosities.** 1 UNCOUNT N **Curiosity** is a desire to know about things. *She looked at me, eyes wide open and full of curiosity... I have very little curiosity about anything.* 2 COUNT N **Curiosities** are things which are interesting and fairly rare. *...old but natural curiosities like fossils.*

curious /kjʊərɪəs/. 1 ADJ If you are **curious** about something, you are interested in it and want to learn more about it. *He seemed awfully curious about Robertson's day-to-day routine... She was curious to see what would happen.* ♦ **curiously** ADV *They stopped and looked at her curiously.* 2 ADJ Something that is **curious** is unusual and interesting or surprising. *Not long after our arrival, a curious thing happened... It is curious how two such different problems can be solved so similarly.* ♦ **curiously** ADV OR SENTENCE ADV *She had a curiously husky voice... Curiously, Hearst worked energetically during his mental breakdown.*

curl /kɜ:l/, **curls, curling, curled.** 1 COUNT N **Curls** are lengths of hair shaped in curves and circles. *...a little girl with golden curls.* 2 VB If something **curls,** it has tight curves or becomes tightly curved. *Her hair curled about her head like a child's... The bark was curling and falling away from the trunk.* 3 VB WITH ADJUNCT If something **curls** somewhere, it moves in circles or spirals. *Smoke was curling out of kitchen chimneys.* Also COUNT N *...curls of smoke.*

curl up. PHR VB 1 When someone who is lying down **curls up,** they bring their arms, legs, and head in towards their stomach. *He was lying curled up with his back to us.* 2 When something such as a leaf or a piece of paper **curls up,** its edges bend up or towards its centre.

curler /kɜ:lə/, **curlers.** COUNT N **Curlers** are small plastic or metal tubes that women roll their hair round in order to make it curly.

curly /kɜ:li^1/, **curlier, curliest.** 1 ADJ **Curly** hair is full of curls. 2 ADJ **Curly** objects are curved or spiral-shaped; an informal use. *What are these curly bits of paper for?*

currant /kʌrənt/, **currants.** COUNT N **Currants** are small dried grapes which are often put into cakes.

currency /kʌrənsi^1/, **currencies.** 1 COUNT N OR UNCOUNT N The money used in a country is referred to as its **currency.** *Sterling has once again become one of the stronger currencies... Do you change foreign currency?* 2 UNCOUNT N If ideas, expressions, or customs have **currency** at a particular time, they are generally used and accepted by people at that time; a formal use. *They have seen many of their basic ideas gain wide currency.*

current /kʌrənt/, **currents.** 1 COUNT N A **current** is a steady, continuous, flowing movement of water or air. *The child had been swept out to sea by the current.* 2 COUNT N An electric **current** is electricity flowing through a wire or circuit. 3 ADJ Something that is **current** is happening, being done, or being used at the present time. *Our current methods of production are too expensive... The words 'light pollution' are in current use among astronomers.* ♦ **currently** ADV *...experiments currently in progress.*

current account, current accounts. COUNT N A **current account** is a bank account which you can take money out of at any time using your cheque book or cheque card; a British use.

current affairs. PLURAL N **Current affairs** are political and social events which are happening at the present time. *...the BBC's current affairs programmes.*

curriculum /kərɪkjə^{4}ləm/, **curriculums** or **curricula** /kərɪkjə^{4}lə/. 1 COUNT N In a school, college, or university, the **curriculum** consists of all the different courses of study that are taught there. *Social studies have now been added to the curriculum.* 2 COUNT N A particular course of study can also be referred to as a **curriculum.** *...our English curriculum.*

curriculum vitae /kərɪkjə^{4}ləm vi:taɪ/. SING N Your **curriculum vitae** is a brief written account of your personal details, your education, and the jobs you have had.

curried /kʌrɪd/. ATTRIB ADJ **Curried** food has been flavoured with hot spices. *...curried eggs.*

curry /kʌri^1/, **curries.** MASS N **Curry** is an Indian or Asian dish made with hot spices. *...a vegetable curry.*

curse /kɜ:s/, **curses, cursing, cursed.** 1 VB If you **curse,** you swear or say rude words because you are angry about something. *He missed the ball and cursed violently.* Also COUNT N *With a curse he disentangled his head from the netting.* 2 VB WITH OBJ If you **curse** someone, you say insulting things to them because you are angry with them. *I was cursing him under my breath for his carelessness.* 3 VB WITH OBJ If you **curse** something, you complain angrily about it, especially using rude language. *Cursing my plight, I tried to find shelter for the night.* 4 COUNT N If you say that there is a **curse** on someone, you mean that a supernatural power is causing unpleasant things to happen to them. *There is a curse on this family.* 5 COUNT N WITH SUPP You can also refer to something that causes a lot of trouble or unhappiness as a **curse.** *Loneliness in old age is the curse of modern society.*

cursory /kɜ:sə^{0}ri^1/. ADJ A **cursory** glance or examination is a brief one in which you do not pay much attention to detail.

curt /kɜ:t/. ADJ If someone is **curt,** they speak in a brief and rather rude way. *He had been curt with Gertrude.* ♦ **curtly** ADV *Marsha said curtly, 'You're supposed to be on watch.'*

curtail /kə^{5}teɪl/, **curtails, curtailing, curtailed.** VB WITH OBJ If you **curtail** something, you reduce or restrict it. *Countries are under pressure to curtail public expenditure... ...further legislation to curtail basic union rights.* ♦ **curtailment** /kə^{5}teɪlmə^{2}nt/ UNCOUNT N *...the curtailment of military aid.*

curtain /kɜ:tə^{0}n/, **curtains.** 1 COUNT N **Curtains** are hanging pieces of material which you can pull across a window to keep light out or prevent people from looking in. *He drew the curtains.* 2 SING N In a theatre, the **curtain** is a large piece of material that hangs in front of the stage until a performance begins. *There was a burst of applause as the curtain went up.*

curtsy /kɜ:tsi^1/, **curtsies, curtsying, curtsied;** also spelled **curtsey.** VB When a woman **curtsies,** she lowers her body briefly, bending her knees and holding her skirt with both hands, as a way of showing respect. *The ladies curtsied to him.* Also COUNT N *I bobbed him a curtsy.*

curve /kɜ:v/, **curves, curving, curved.** 1 COUNT N A **curve** is a smooth, gradually bending line, for example part of the edge of a circle. *The beach stretched away before them in a gentle curve.* 2 VB WITH ADJUNCT If something **curves,** it is shaped like a curve, or moves in a curve. *The lane curved round to the right... The missile curved gracefully towards its target.* ♦ **curved** ADJ *...the curved tusks of a walrus.*

cushion /kʊʃə^{0}n/, **cushions, cushioning, cushioned.** 1 COUNT N A **cushion** is a fabric case filled with soft material, which you put on a seat to make it more comfortable. 2 VB WITH OBJ To **cushion** an impact means to reduce its effect. *The pile of branches cushioned his fall.*

custard /kʌstəd/. UNCOUNT N **Custard** is a sweet yellow sauce made from milk and eggs or from milk and a powder. You eat custard with puddings.

custodial /kʌstəʊdɪəl/. ADJ **Custodial** means relating to the custody of people in prison; a formal use. *...offences which called for custodial sentences.*

custodian /kʌstəʊdɪən/, **custodians.** COUNT N The **custodian** of a collection, art gallery, or museum is the person in charge of it.

custody /kʌstədi^1/. 1 UNCOUNT N **Custody** is the legal right to look after a child, especially the right given to the child's father or mother when they become divorced. *Divorce courts usually award custody to mothers.* 2 PHRASE Someone who is **in custody** has been arrested and is being kept in prison until they can be tried. *...people who have been quite wrongly held in custody.*

custom /kʌstə^{0}m/, **customs.** 1 COUNT N A **custom** is a traditional activity or festivity. *My wife likes all the old English customs.* 2 SING N If something is the **custom,** it is usually done in particular circumstances. *It is the custom to take chocolates or fruit when visiting a patient in hospital... It is Howard's custom to take his class for coffee afterwards.* 3 UNCOUNT N OR MOD **Customs** is the place where people arriving from a foreign country have to declare goods that they bring with them. *At Kennedy airport I went through the customs... ...a customs officer.* 4 UNCOUNT N If a shop has your **custom,** you regularly buy things there; a formal use. *Many local services depend on the University's custom.*

customary /kʌstəmə^{0}ri^1/. ADJ **Customary** means usual. *...her customary calm... It was customary for our children to curtsy to the gentlemen.* ♦ **customarily** ADV *...the civil exchange of letters which customarily marks the departure of a minister.*

customer /kʌstəmə/, **customers.** COUNT N A **customer** is someone who buys something. *She's one of our regular customers.*

custom-made. ADJ Something that is **custom-made** is made according to people's special requirements. *...custom-made cars.*

cut /kʌt/, **cuts, cutting. Cut** is used in the present tense of the verb, and is the past tense and past participle. 1 VB WITH OBJ If you **cut** something, you push a knife or similar tool into it in order to remove a piece of it or to mark or damage it. *She cut the cake and gave me a piece... His wife killed herself by cutting her wrists.* Also ADJ *...thinly cut rye bread.* 2 REFL VB OR VB WITH OBJ If you **cut** yourself, you accidentally injure yourself on a sharp object and you bleed. *Robert cut his knee quite badly.* 3 VB WITH ADJUNCT To **cut** across or through an area means to move through it easily. *I cut across country for the next hundred miles... The big canoe was cutting through the water.* 4 VB WITH OBJ To **cut** an amount means to reduce it. *She cut her costs by half.* 5 VB WITH OBJ When a part of a piece of writing **is cut,** it is not printed or broadcast. *Her publishers insisted on cutting several stories out of her memoirs.* Also COUNT N *He agreed to make a few minor changes and cuts in the play.* 6 VB WITH OBJ If you **cut** someone's hair, you shorten it using scissors. *Tell him to get his hair cut.* 7 ADJ Well **cut** clothes have been well designed and well made. *He wears beautifully cut suits.* 8 COUNT N If you make a **cut** in something, you push a knife or similar tool into it in order to mark or damage it. *He made a deep cut in the wood.* 9 COUNT N A **cut** is also the injury caused when a sharp object makes you bleed. *I had some cuts and bruises but I'm OK.* 10 COUNT N A **cut** of meat is a large piece of it. 11 COUNT N A **cut** in an amount is a reduction in it. *...large cuts in government spending.* 12 PHRASE If something is **a cut above** other things of the same kind, it is better than them. *The meals they serve are a cut above most pub food.* 13 See also **cutting.**

cut back. PHR VB If you **cut back** some money that you are spending or **cut back on** it, you reduce it. *Congress cut back the funds.* ● See also **cutback.**

cut down. PHR VB 1 If you **cut down** on an activity, you do it less often. *She had cut down on smoking.* 2 If you **cut** a tree **down,** you cut through its trunk so that it falls to the ground.

cut in. PHR VB If you **cut in** on someone, you interrupt them when they are speaking. *Mrs Travers began a reply, but Mrs Patel cut in again.*

cut off. PHR VB 1 If you **cut** something **off,** you remove it by cutting it. *Lexington cut off a small piece of meat... ...egg sandwiches with the crusts cut off.* 2 To **cut off** a place or a person means to separate them from things they are normally connected with. *The town was cut off... We have cut ourselves off from the old ways of thinking.* Also PRED ADJ *She is completely cut off from friends.* 3 If a supply of something **is cut off,** it stops being provided. *Gas supplies had now been cut off... They are threatening to cut off funds.* 4 If you **cut** someone **off** when they are having a telephone conversation, you disconnect them. 5 See also **cut-off.**

cut out. PHR VB 1 If you **cut out** part of something, you remove it using a tool with a sharp edge. *Badly decayed timber should be cut out and replaced.* 2 If you **cut out** something that you are doing or saying, you stop doing or saying it. *Cut out waste... He's cut out the drinking altogether.* 3 If an object **cuts out** the light, it prevents light from reaching a place. 4 When an engine **cuts out,** it suddenly stops working. *It keeps cutting out when I stop.* ● See also **cut-out.**

cut up. PHR VB If you **cut** something **up,** you cut it into several pieces. ● See also the separate entry **cut up.**

cut-and-dried. ADJ A **cut-and-dried** answer or solution is clear and obvious. *There is no cut-and-dried formula which can answer these questions.*

cutback /kʌtbæk/, **cutbacks.** COUNT N A **cutback** is a reduction in something. *...the cutback in public services.*

cute /kju:t/, **cuter, cutest.** ADJ **Cute** means pretty or attractive; an American use. *...a cute little girl.*

cut glass UNCOUNT N OR MOD **Cut glass** is glass with patterns cut into its surface. *...a cut-glass bowl.*

cutlery /kʌtləri^1/. UNCOUNT N The knives, forks, and spoons that you eat with are referred to as **cutlery.**

cutlet /kʌtlə[2]t/, **cutlets.** COUNT N A **cutlet** is a small piece of meat, or a mixture of vegetables and nuts pressed into a rounded shape. Cutlets are usually fried or grilled. *...veal cutlets... ...a nut cutlet.*

cut-off, cut-offs. COUNT N The **cut-off** or **cut-off point** is the level or limit at which something should stop happening.

cut-out, cut-outs. 1 COUNT N A **cut-out** is an automatic device that turns off a motor. *...a cut-out to prevent the battery from overcharging.* **2** COUNT N A cardboard **cut-out** is a shape cut from card. **3** PRED ADJ WITH 'for' If you are **cut out** for a particular type of work, you have the qualities needed to do it. *I'm not really cut out for this job.*

cut-price. ADJ A **cut-price** item is for sale at a reduced price. *We enjoy going shopping and taking advantage of cut-price offers.*

cutter /kʌtə/, **cutters.** COUNT N OR PLURAL N A **cutter** or a pair of **cutters** is a tool that you use for cutting something. *...a glass cutter... ...a pair of wire cutters.*

cut-throat. ADJ In a **cut-throat** situation, people all want the same thing and do not care if they harm each other in getting it. *...cut-throat competition.*

cutting /kʌtɪŋ/, **cuttings. 1** COUNT N A **cutting** is a piece of writing cut from a newspaper or magazine. *...press cuttings.* **2** COUNT N A **cutting** is also a piece of stalk that you cut from a plant and use to grow a new plant. *They are easy roses to grow from cuttings.* **3** ADJ A **cutting** remark is unkind and likely to hurt someone's feelings.

cut up. PRED ADJ If you are **cut up** about something, you are very unhappy because of it; an informal use. *She's still terribly cut up about his death.* ● See also **cut.**

CV /siː viː/, **CV's. CV** is an abbreviation for 'curriculum vitae'.

cwt, cwts. cwt can also be the plural. **cwt** is an abbreviation for 'hundredweight'. *...75 cwt of wheat.*

cyanide /saɪənaɪd/. UNCOUNT N **Cyanide** is a substance which is highly poisonous.

cycle /saɪkə[0]l/, **cycles, cycling, cycled. 1** VB If you **cycle,** you ride a bicycle. *I decided to cycle into town.* ♦ **cycling** UNCOUNT N *We recommend cycling as a good form of exercise.* **2** COUNT N A **cycle** is a bicycle or a motorcycle. **3** COUNT N WITH SUPP A **cycle** is also a series of events that is repeated again and again, always in the same order. *...the endless cycle of the seasons.* **4** COUNT N In an electrical, electronic, or mechanical process, a **cycle** is a single complete series of movements. *...50 cycles per second.* **5** COUNT N WITH SUPP A **cycle** of songs or poems is a series of them, intended to be performed or read one after the other.

cyclic /saɪklɪk, sɪklɪk/ or **cyclical** /sɪklɪkə[0]l/. ADJ A **cyclic** or **cyclical** process happens again and again in cycles. *...a cyclic process... ...cyclical fluctuations.*

cyclist /saɪklɪst/, **cyclists.** COUNT N A **cyclist** is someone who rides a bicycle.

cyclone /saɪkləʊn/, **cyclones.** COUNT N A **cyclone** is a violent storm in which air circulates rapidly in a clockwise direction.

cylinder /sɪlɪndə/, **cylinders. 1** COUNT N A **cylinder** is a shape or container with flat circular ends and long straight sides. *...the hot water cylinder.* **2** COUNT N In an engine, a **cylinder** is a piece of machinery shaped like a cylinder, in which a piston moves backwards and forwards. *...a five cylinder engine.*

cylindrical /sɪlɪndrɪkə[0]l/. ADJ Something that is **cylindrical** has flat circular ends and long straight sides. *...two cylindrical tanks.*

cymbal /sɪmbə[0]l/, **cymbals.** COUNT N A **cymbal** is a flat circular brass object used as a musical instrument. You hit it with a stick or hit two cymbals together.

cynic /sɪnɪk/, **cynics.** COUNT N A **cynic** is someone who always thinks the worst of people or things.

cynical /sɪnɪkə[0]l/. ADJ Someone who is **cynical** or who has a **cynical** attitude always thinks the worst of people or things. *You are taking a rather cynical view of marriage.* ♦ **cynically** ADV *Grant smiled cynically.*

cynicism /sɪnɪsɪzə[0]m/. UNCOUNT N **Cynicism** is an attitude in which you always think the worst of people or things. *The mood of political cynicism and despair deepened.*

cypher /saɪfə/. See **cipher.**

cypress /saɪprəs/, **cypresses.** COUNT N A **cypress** is a type of evergreen tree.

cyst /sɪst/, **cysts.** COUNT N A **cyst** is a growth containing liquid that appears inside your body or under your skin.

Dd

-'d. SUFFIX **-'d** is a short form of 'would' or 'had' used in spoken English and informal written English, especially when 'had' is an auxiliary verb. *I knew there'd be trouble... I'd heard it many times.*

dab /dæb/, **dabs, dabbing, dabbed. 1** VB WITH OBJ AND ADJUNCT If you **dab** a substance onto a surface, you put it there with quick, light, strokes. If you **dab** a surface with something, you touch it quickly and lightly with that thing. *She dabbed some powder on her nose... He dabbed the cuts with disinfectant.* **2** COUNT N A **dab** of something is a small amount of it that is put onto a surface. *She returned wearing a dab of rouge on each cheekbone.* **3** PHRASE If you are a **dab hand** at something, you are good at doing it; an informal British use.

dabble /dæbə[0]l/, **dabbles, dabbling, dabbled.** VB WITH 'in' If you **dabble** in an activity, you take part in it but are not seriously involved. *They dabble in politics.*

dad /dæd/, **dads.** VOCATIVE OR COUNT N Your **dad** is your father. *Hey, Dad, what's for dinner?*

daddy /dædi[1]/, **daddies.** VOCATIVE OR COUNT N **Daddy** means father; an informal word used especially by children. *Daddy, why do we grow old?*

daffodil /dæfədɪl/, **daffodils.** COUNT N A **daffodil** is a yellow flower that blooms in the spring.

daft /dɑːft/, **dafter, daftest.** ADJ **Daft** means stupid and not sensible; an informal use. *Don't be daft.*

dagger /dægə/, **daggers.** COUNT N A **dagger** is a weapon like a knife with two sharp edges.

daily /deɪli[1]/, **dailies. 1** ADV OR ATTRIB ADJ If something happens **daily,** it happens every day. *He wrote to her almost daily... ...Margaret's daily visits.* **2** ATTRIB ADJ **Daily** also means relating to a single day or to one day at a time. *Daily wage rates were around two dollars.* **3** ATTRIB ADJ OR COUNT N A **daily** newspaper or a **daily** is a newspaper that is published every day except Sunday.

dainty /deɪnti[1]/. ADJ A **dainty** movement, person, or object is small, neat, or pretty. *...walking with neat, dainty steps... ...a dainty little girl.* ♦ **daintily** ADV *She raised a plump arm, fingers daintily extended.*

dairy /deəri[1]/, **dairies. 1** COUNT N A **dairy** is a shop or company that sells milk, butter, and cheese. **2** COUNT N A **dairy** on a farm is a building where milk is kept or cream, butter, and cheese are made. **3** MOD **Dairy** products are foods made from milk, for example butter and cheese. **4** MOD **Dairy** also refers to the use of cattle to produce milk rather than meat. *...a dairy herd of 105 cattle.*

dais /deɪɪs/. SING N A **dais** is a raised platform in a hall.

daisy /deɪzi[1]/, **daisies.** COUNT N A **daisy** is a small wild flower with a yellow centre and white petals.

dam /dæm/, **dams, damming, dammed. 1** COUNT N A **dam** is a wall built across a river to stop the flow of the water and make a lake. **2** VB WITH OBJ To **dam** a river means to build a dam across it.

dam up. PHR VB To **dam up** a river means to dam it or block it completely

damage /dæmɪdʒ/, **damages, damaging, damaged. 1** VB WITH OBJ To **damage** something means to injure or harm it. *A fire had severely damaged part of the school... Unofficial strikes were damaging the British economy.* ♦ **damaging** ADJ *The incident was damaging to his career and reputation.* **2** UNCOUNT N **Damage** is injury or harm that is caused to something. *It can cause lethal damage to the liver... He could not repair the damage done to the party's credibility.* **3** PLURAL N When a court of law awards **damages** to someone, it orders money to be paid to them by a person who has harmed their reputation or property, or who has injured them. *He finally got £4,000 in damages.*

damask /dæməsk/. UNCOUNT N **Damask** is a type of heavy cloth with a pattern woven into it.

dame /deɪm/, **dames. 1** COUNT N A **dame** is a woman; an informal American use. *Remember, some of these dames are very powerful in movies.* **2** TITLE In Britain, **Dame** is a title given to a woman as a special honour because of important service or work that she has done. *...Dame Flora Robson.*

damn /dæm/. **Damn** is a swear word.

damnation /dæmneɪʃə[0]n/. UNCOUNT N According to some religions, if someone suffers **damnation,** they are condemned to stay in hell for ever after death because of their sins. *...eternal damnation.*

damned /dæmd/. PLURAL N According to some religions, the **damned** are people condemned to stay in hell for ever after they have died.

damning /dæmɪŋ/. ADJ Something that is **damning** suggests strongly that someone is guilty of a crime or error. *...damning evidence.*

damp /dæmp/, **damper, dampest; damps, damping, damped. 1** ADJ **Damp** means slightly wet. *The building was cold and damp... She wiped the table with a damp cloth.* ♦ **dampness** UNCOUNT N *...the cold and dampness of winter.* **2** UNCOUNT N **Damp** is slight moisture in the air or on the walls of a house.

damp down. PHR VB To **damp down** a difficult situation means to make it calmer or less intense. *Neighbouring countries had been of no help in damping down the crisis.*

dampen /dæmpə[0]n/, **dampens, dampening, dampened. 1** VB WITH OBJ To **dampen** something means to make it less lively or intense. *The prospect of an election in no way dampened his spirits... The flaps can be opened or closed so as to increase or dampen the sound.* **2** VB WITH OBJ If you **dampen** something, you make it slightly wet.

dance /dɑːns/, **dances, dancing, danced. 1** VB WITH OR WITHOUT OBJ When you **dance,** you move around in time to music. *John danced with Julie... ...girls dancing the can-can.* ♦ **dancing** UNCOUNT N *The music and dancing lasted for hours.* **2** COUNT N A **dance** is a series of steps and rhythmic movements which you do to music. It is also a piece of music which people can dance to. *Before we knew it, we were doing this dance.* **3** COUNT N A **dance** is also a social event where people dance with each other. **4** UNCOUNT N **Dance** is the activity of performing dances as a public entertainment. *They are supreme artists of dance and theatre.* **5** VB To **dance** also means to move about lightly and quickly. *Ralph danced out into the street.*

dancer /dɑːnsə/, **dancers.** COUNT N A **dancer** is a person who earns money by dancing, or a person who is dancing. *He always wanted to be a dancer.*

dandelion /dændɪ[1]laɪən/, **dandelions.** COUNT N A **dandelion** is a wild plant which has yellow flowers first, then fluffy balls of seeds.

dandruff /dændrə[9]f/. UNCOUNT N **Dandruff** refers to small white pieces of dead skin in someone's hair.

danger /deɪndʒə/, **dangers. 1** UNCOUNT N **Danger** is the possibility that someone may be harmed or killed. *The child is too young to understand danger... I was in no danger.* **2** COUNT N A **danger** is something or someone that can hurt or harm you. *Cigarette smoking is a danger to health... ...the dangers of making assumptions.* **3** SING N WITH SUPP If there is a **danger** that something unpleasant will happen, it is possible that it will happen. *There is no danger of fire... There was a danger that she might marry the wrong man.*

dangerous /deɪndʒə[0]rəs/. ADJ If something is **dangerous,** it may hurt or harm you. *...a dangerous animal... It is dangerous to drive with a dirty windscreen.* ♦ **dangerously** ADV *She was dangerously close to the fire.*

dangle /dæŋgə[0]l/, **dangles, dangling, dangled.** ERG VB If something **dangles** or **is dangled,** it hangs or swings loosely. *Huge wooden earrings dangled from her ears... Charlie was leaning across my desk dangling the long roll of paper.*

dank /dæŋk/. ADJ A **dank** place is damp, cold, and unpleasant. *I slept in the dank basement room.*

dapper /dæpə/. ADJ A **dapper** man is slim and neat.

dappled /dæpə[0]ld/. ADJ Something that is **dappled** has light and dark patches, or patches of light and shade; a literary use. *...dappled leafy sunlight.*

dare /deə/, **dares, daring, dared. 1** VB WITH TO-INF OR SEMI-MODAL **Dare** is used both as a main verb and as a semi-modal. If you **dare** to do something, you have enough courage to do it. *She did not dare to look at him... He dared not show that he was pleased... I can't do that—I simply wouldn't dare.* **2** VB WITH OBJ If you **dare** someone to do something, you suggest that they do it in order to prove how brave they are. *He looked round fiercely, daring them to contradict.* **3** COUNT N A **dare** is a challenge to do something dangerous or frightening. *It was many years since James had accepted a dare.*

PHRASES ● You say **'Don't you dare'** when you are angrily telling someone not to do something. *Don't you dare throw it away.* ● You say **I dare say** or **I daresay** to show that you think something is probably true. *I daresay you've spent all your money by now.*

daren't /deənt/. **Daren't** is the usual spoken form of 'dare not'.

daresay /deəseɪ/. See the phrases at **dare.**

daring /deərɪŋ/. **1** ADJ A **daring** person does things which might be dangerous or shocking. *He was the most daring of contemporary writers of fiction... ...a daring raid.* **2** UNCOUNT N **Daring** is the courage to do things which might be dangerous or shocking. *...the efficiency and daring shown by our armed forces.*

dark /dɑːk/, **darker, darkest. 1** ADJ When it is **dark,** there is not enough light to see properly. *Luckily it* *was too dark for anyone to see me blushing... The room was dark and empty.* ♦ **darkness** UNCOUNT N *The lights went out and the hall was plunged into darkness.* 2 SING N The **dark** is the lack of light in a place. *He was sitting in the dark at the back of the theatre.* 3 ADJ Something that is **dark** has one of the colours that things seem to have when they are in shadow. *...long dark hair... ...dark red curtains.* 4 ADJ Someone who is **dark** has brown or black hair, and often brown skin. *He was a tall, dark, and undeniably handsome man.* 5 ATTRIB ADJ A **dark** period of time is unpleasant or frightening. *...the dark days of high unemployment.* 6 ATTRIB ADJ **Dark** looks or remarks suggest that something horrible is going to happen. ♦ **darkly** ADV *Another of the men hinted darkly that there would be violence.*

PHRASES ● If you do something **before dark,** you do it before the sun sets. If you do something **after dark,** you do it when night has begun. ● If you are **in the dark** about something, you do not know anything about it.

darken /dɑ:kə°n/, **darkens, darkening, darkened.** 1 ERG VB If something **darkens,** it becomes darker in colour. *The sky darkened... His hair was darkened by the rain.* 2 VB WITH OBJ If someone's face **darkens,** they suddenly look angry.

dark glasses. PLURAL N **Dark glasses** are glasses with dark lenses to protect your eyes in the sunshine.

darkroom /dɑ:kru⁴m/, **darkrooms.** COUNT N A **darkroom** is a room which is lit only by red light, so that photographs can be developed there.

darling /dɑ:lɪŋ/, **darlings.** 1 VOCATIVE You call someone **darling** if you love them or like them very much. *You're looking marvellous, darling.* 2 ATTRIB ADJ You can use **darling** to describe someone that you love or like very much. *...her darling baby brother.* 3 COUNT N WITH POSS The **darling** of a group of people is someone who is especially liked by that group. *She quickly became the darling of the crowds.*

darn /dɑ:n/, **darns, darning, darned.** 1 VB WITH OR WITHOUT OBJ When you **darn** something made of cloth, you mend a hole in it by sewing stitches across the hole and then weaving stitches in and out of them. *I offered to darn Sean's socks... She started darning.* 2 COUNT N A **darn** is the part of a piece of clothing that has been darned. *Her jumper had a darn at the bottom.*

dart /dɑ:t/, **darts, darting, darted.** 1 VB If a person or animal **darts** somewhere, they move there suddenly and quickly. *...butterflies darting from one flower to another.* 2 VB WITH OBJ AND ADJUNCT If you **dart** a glance at something, you look at it very quickly. *She darted a glance at her teacher.* 3 COUNT N A **dart** is a small, narrow object with a sharp point which you can throw or shoot. *They killed the elephants with tiny poisoned darts.* 4 UNCOUNT N **Darts** is a game in which you throw darts at a round board with numbers on it.

dash /dæʃ/, **dashes, dashing, dashed.** 1 VB WITH ADJUNCT If you **dash** somewhere, you go there quickly and suddenly. *People dashed out into the street to see what was happening.* Also SING N *He made a dash for the door.* 2 SING N A **dash** of a liquid is a small quantity of it added to food or a drink. *Some soups are delicious served cold with a dash of cream.* 3 VB WITH OBJ AND ADJUNCT If you **dash** something somewhere, you throw it or push it violently. *She picked up his photograph and dashed it to the ground.* 4 VB WITH OBJ If your hopes **are dashed,** something makes it impossible for you to get what you hope for. 5 COUNT N A **dash** is also a short horizontal line (—) used in writing.

dash off. PHR VB If you **dash off** a letter, you write it quickly without thinking much about it.

dashboard /dæʃbɔ:d/, **dashboards.** COUNT N The **dashboard** in a car is the panel facing the driver's seat where most of the instruments and switches are.

dashing /dæʃɪŋ/. ADJ Someone who looks **dashing** is stylish and attractive. *She felt very dashing in her yellow suit.*

data /deɪtə, dɑ:tə/. UNCOUNT N OR PLURAL N **Data** is information, usually in the form of facts or statistics that you can analyse. *The data was being processed at the Census Office... It isn't present in the data when they are received.*

database /deɪtəbeɪs/, **databases.** COUNT N A **database** is a collection of data stored in a computer in such a way that it is easy to obtain.

date /deɪt/, **dates, dating, dated.** 1 COUNT N A **date** is a particular day, for example 7th June 1990, or year, for example 1066. *No date was announced for the talks.* ● **To date** means up until the present time. *Their effects to date have been limited.* 2 VB WITH OBJ When you **date** something, you give the date when it began or was made. *How can we date these fossils?* 3 VB WITH OBJ When you **date** a letter or a cheque, you write the day's date on it. *The letter was dated September 18 1952.* 4 SING N At a particular **date** means at a particular time or stage. *The matter may be worth pursuing at a later date.* 5 VB If something **dates,** it goes out of fashion. 6 COUNT N A **date** is also an appointment to meet someone or go out with them, especially someone of the opposite sex. *Sorry I can't come—I have a date with Jill.* 7 COUNT N Your **date** is someone of the opposite sex that you have a date with; an American use. *Her date says that he doesn't know either.* 8 VB WITH OBJ If you **are dating** someone of the opposite sex, you go out regularly with them; an American use. 9 COUNT N A **date** is also a small, sticky, dark brown fruit. Dates grow on palm trees. 10 See also **out of date, up-to-date.**

date back or **date from.** PHR VB If something **dates back** to a particular time or **dates from** that time, it started or was made then. *The present city hall dates back to the 1880s... ...a manuscript dating from the eleventh century.*

dated /deɪtɪ²d/. ADJ **Dated** things seem old-fashioned, although they were once fashionable. *...dated clothes.*

date of birth, dates of birth. COUNT N Your **date of birth** is the exact date on which you were born, including the year. *Give your name, age, and date of birth.*

daub /dɔ:b/, **daubs, daubing, daubed.** VB WITH OBJ AND ADJUNCT When you **daub** a substance on something, you carelessly spread it on that thing. *...daubing walls with paint.*

daughter /dɔ:tə/, **daughters.** COUNT N Your **daughter** is your female child. *She is the daughter of a retired Army officer.*

daughter-in-law, daughters-in-law. COUNT N Your **daughter-in-law** is the wife of your son.

daunt /dɔ:nt/, **daunts, daunting, daunted.** VB WITH OBJ If something **daunts** you, it makes you feel afraid or worried about dealing with it. *They may be daunted by the size of the task.* ♦ **daunting** ADJ *...a daunting prospect.*

dawdle /dɔ:də°l/, **dawdles, dawdling, dawdled.** VB If you **dawdle,** you spend more time than is necessary doing something or going somewhere. *Billy dawdled behind her, balancing on the cracks in the pavement.*

dawn /dɔ:n/, **dawns, dawning, dawned.** 1 UNCOUNT N OR COUNT N **Dawn** is the time of day when light first appears in the sky, before the sun rises. *Tom woke me at dawn.* 2 VB When a day **dawns,** they sky grows light after the night. 3 SING N WITH SUPP The **dawn** of a period of time or a situation is the beginning of it; a literary use. *This marked the dawn of a new era in human history.* 4 VB If something **is dawning,** it is beginning to develop or appear; a literary use. *The age of the answering machine is just dawning... ...the dawning hopes of reconciliation in Western Europe.*

dawn on or **dawn upon.** PHR VB If a fact or idea **dawns on** you or **dawns upon** you, you realize it. *Then it dawned on me that they were speaking Spanish.*

day /deɪ/, **days.** 1 COUNT N A **day** is one of the seven twenty-four hour periods of time in a week. *The attack occurred six days ago... Can you go any day of the week? What about Monday?* 2 COUNT N OR UNCOUNT N **Day** is the part of a day when it is light. *They had waited three days and nights for this opportunity... They hunt by day.* 3 COUNT N WITH SUPP You can refer to a period in history as a particular **day.** *This is the main problem of the present day... Are students interested in religion these days?*

PHRASES ● If you **call it a day,** you stop what you are doing and leave it to be finished later. ● If something happens **day and night** or **night and day,** it happens all the time without stopping. ● If something **makes** your **day,** it makes you feel very happy; an informal use. ● **One day, some day,** or **one of these days** means at some future time. *We're all going to be old one day.* ● If it is a year **to the day** since something happened, it happened exactly a year ago.

daybreak /deɪbreɪk/. UNCOUNT N **Daybreak** is the time in the morning when light first appears. *They had to leave at daybreak.*

daydream /deɪdri:m/, **daydreams, daydreaming, daydreamed.** 1 COUNT N A **daydream** is a series of pleasant thoughts, especially about things that you would like to happen. *He drifted off into another daydream.* 2 VB When you **daydream,** you think about pleasant things that you would like to happen. *Boys and girls daydream about what they want to be.*

daylight /deɪlaɪt/. UNCOUNT N **Daylight** is the light during the day, or the time of day when it is light. *We've got at least two more hours of daylight... The ship sailed into harbour before daylight on 1 May.* ● **in broad daylight:** see **broad.**

daytime /deɪtaɪm/. UNCOUNT N OR SING N **Daytime** is the part of a day when it is light. *The forests were dark even in the daytime.*

day-to-day. ATTRIB ADJ **Day-to-day** means happening every day as part of ordinary life. *...the day-to-day life of the village.*

daze /deɪz/, **dazed.** 1 PHRASE If you are **in a daze,** you feel confused or upset. 2 PASSIVE VB If you **are dazed** by a sudden injury or unexpected event, you are unable to think clearly. *She was dazed by the news.* ♦ **dazed** ADJ *He seemed dazed and bewildered.*

dazzle /dæzə°l/, **dazzles, dazzling, dazzled.** 1 VB WITH OBJ If something **dazzles** you, you are extremely impressed by its quality or beauty. *She had clearly been dazzled by the evening's performance.* ♦ **dazzling** ADJ *She gave him a dazzling smile... ...his dazzling political career.* 2 UNCOUNT N The **dazzle** of a light is its sudden brightness, so you cannot see properly. *They both blinked in the sudden dazzle.* 3 VB WITH OBJ If a bright light **dazzles** you, you cannot see properly. ♦ **dazzling** ADJ *...the dazzling sun.*

DC /di: si:/. **DC** is used to refer to an electric current that always flows in the same direction. **DC** is an abbreviation for 'direct current'.

DDT /di: di: ti:/. UNCOUNT N **DDT** is a poisonous substance used for killing insects.

dead /ded/. 1 ADJ A **dead** person, animal, or plant is no longer living. *He was shot dead in a gunfight... Mary threw away the dead flowers.* 2 PLURAL N The **dead** are people who are dead or have been killed. *Among the dead was Captain Burroughs.* 3 PRED ADJ If your arm or leg goes **dead,** you lose the sense of feeling in it for a short time. 4 PRED ADJ If a telephone or other device is **dead,** it is not functioning. *The phone went dead.* 5 ATTRIB ADJ **Dead** can mean complete or absolute, especially with the words 'silence', 'centre', and 'stop'. *There was dead silence... The table was placed in the dead centre of the room.* Also ADV OR SUBMOD *I was staring dead ahead.* 6 SUBMOD **Dead** also means very or very much; an informal use. *It's dead easy... They were dead against the idea.*

PHRASES ● The **dead of night** is the middle part of it, when it is dark and quiet. *They came at dead of night.* ● If something **stops dead,** it stops suddenly.

deaden /dedə°n/, **deadens, deadening, deadened.** VB WITH OBJ If something **deadens** a feeling or sound, it makes it less strong or loud. *Drugs deaden the pangs of hunger.*

dead end, dead ends. 1 COUNT N If a street is a **dead end,** there is no way out at one end of it. 2 COUNT N A job or course of action that is a **dead end** does not lead to further developments. *The investigation has reached a dead end... ...a dead-end job.*

dead heat, dead heats. COUNT N If a race ends in a **dead heat,** two or more competitors reach the finishing line first at exactly the same time.

deadline /dedlaɪn/, **deadlines.** COUNT N A **deadline** is a time or date before which a particular task must be finished. *We must meet the deadline.*

deadlock /dedlɒk/. UNCOUNT N **Deadlock** is a state of affairs in an argument or dispute in which neither side is willing to give in, and so no agreement can be reached. *The meeting between management and unions ended in deadlock.*

deadly /dedli¹/, **deadlier, deadliest.** 1 ADJ If something is **deadly,** it is likely or able to kill. *This is one of nature's deadliest poisons... ...deadly spiders.* 2 SUBMOD You use **deadly** to emphasize an unpleasant or serious quality. *The air was deadly cold... He was deadly serious.* 3 ADJ You can also use **deadly** to say that something is great in degree and effective, especially in the context of hurting someone. *...the deadliest insult he could think of... ...deadly accuracy.*

deadpan /dedpæn/. ADV If you do something **deadpan,** you appear to be serious and are hiding the fact that you are joking or teasing. *She looked at me deadpan.* Also ADJ *He speaks in a deadpan way.*

dead weight, dead weights. COUNT N A **dead weight** is a load which is heavy and difficult to lift.

deaf /def/, **deafer, deafest.** 1 ADJ Someone who is **deaf** is unable to hear anything or unable to hear very well. *...a school for deaf children... He was very deaf.* ♦ **deafness** UNCOUNT N *They finally diagnosed her deafness when she was thirteen.* 2 PLURAL N The **deaf** are people who are deaf. 3 PRED ADJ WITH PREP 'to' If you are **deaf** to something, you refuse to pay attention to it. *He was deaf to the public's complaints.* 4 PHRASE If you **turn a deaf ear** to something that someone says, you refuse to pay attention to it.

deafen /defə°n/, **deafens, deafening, deafened.** VB WITH OBJ If you **are deafened** by a noise, it is so loud that you cannot hear anything else. *She was momentarily deafened by the din.* ♦ **deafening** ADJ *The noise was deafening.*

deal /di:l/, **deals, dealing, dealt** /delt/. 1 QUANTIF A **good deal** or a **great deal** of something is a lot of it. *There was a great deal of concern about energy shortages... They talked a great deal... The teaching of the older children is a good deal better.* 2 COUNT N A **deal** is an agreement or arrangement, especially in business. *He certainly hadn't done badly on the deal.* 3 COUNT N AFTER ADJ If someone has had a bad **deal,**

they have been unfortunate or have been treated unfairly. *He has had a lousy deal out of life.* 4 VB WITH OBJ AND OBJ OR PREP 'to' If you **deal** someone a blow, you hit them or harm them in some way. *This woman dealt him an alarming series of blows... The growth of modern industry had dealt a heavy blow to their way of life.* 5 VB WITH OR WITHOUT OBJ When you **deal** cards, you give them out to the players in a game of cards. *Deal seven cards to each player... Whose turn is it to deal?*

deal in. PHR VB To **deal in** a type of goods means to sell that type of goods. *The shop deals only in trousers.*

deal out. PHR VB When you **deal out** cards, you give them out to the players in a game of cards.

deal with. PHR VB 1 When you **deal with** a situation or problem, you do what is necessary to achieve the result you want. *They learned to deal with any sort of emergency.* 2 If a book, speech, or film **deals with** a subject, it is concerned with it. *The film deals with a strange encounter between two soldiers.*

dealer /diːlə/, **dealers.** COUNT N A **dealer** is a person whose business involves buying and selling things. *...a dealer in antique furniture.*

dealing /diːlɪŋ/, **dealings.** 1 PLURAL N Your **dealings** with a person or organization are the relations that you have with them or your business with them. *Ford insists that Carter's dealings with him have been totally correct... He was questioned about his past business dealings.* 2 UNCOUNT N **Dealing** refers to the buying and selling of things as a business. For example, antique **dealing** involves buying and selling antiques.

dean /diːn/, **deans.** 1 COUNT N A **dean** in a university or college is an important administrator there. 2 COUNT N A **dean** in a large church is a priest who is its main administrator.

dear /dɪə/, **dearer, dearest; dears.** 1 VOCATIVE You can call someone **dear** as a sign of affection. *How are you, dear?... Now, my dears, come with me.* 2 ATTRIB ADJ **Dear** is written at the beginning of a letter, followed by the name or title of the person you are writing to. *Dear Mum, I was glad to get your letter... Dear Sir, I regret to inform you that I cannot accept your kind invitation.* 3 ATTRIB ADJ You use **dear** to describe someone or something that feel affection for. *...dear old Aunt Elizabeth... ...a dear friend.* 4 PRED ADJ WITH PREP 'to' If something is **dear** to you, you care deeply about it. *Sussex was very dear to him... ...a cause that is very dear to her heart.* 5 PHRASE You say **'Oh dear'** when you are sad or upset about something. *Oh dear, I'm late.* 6 PRED ADJ Something that is **dear** costs a lot of money. *Firewood is getting dearer.*

dearest /dɪərɪ^{2}st/. 1 VOCATIVE You can call someone **dearest** when you are very fond of them; an old-fashioned use. *It's too late now, my dearest.* 2 ADJ You can use **dearest** to describe something that is very important to you. *His dearest wish was to become a civil servant... ...my cherished dreams and dearest hopes.*

dearly /dɪəli^1/; a formal word. 1 ADV If you love someone **dearly**, you love them very much. 2 ADV If you would **dearly** like to do or have something, you would very much like to do it or have it. *I dearly wish I had more money.* 3 PHRASE If you **pay dearly** for doing something, you suffer a lot as a result. *He paid dearly for his mistake.*

dearth /dɜːθ/. SING N If there is a **dearth** of something, there is not enough of it; a formal use. *There is a dearth of good children's plays.*

death /deθ/, **deaths.** UNCOUNT N OR COUNT N **Death** is the end of the life of a person or animal. *...after the death of her parents... He bled to death... The two deaths could have been prevented.*

PHRASES ● If something **frightens** or **worries** you **to death,** it frightens or worries you very much; an informal use. *He was frightened to death of her.* ● If you are **sick to death** of a situation, you feel very angry about it and want it to stop; an informal use. ● If someone **is put to death,** they are executed; a literary use.

deathbed /deθbed/. SING N If someone is on their **deathbed,** they are in bed and are about to die. *On his deathbed he asked her forgiveness.*

deathly /deθli^1/. ATTRIB ADJ **Deathly** is used to indicate that something that is as cold, pale, or quiet as a dead person. *A deathly hush lay in the streets.* Also SUBMOD *Her feet were deathly cold.*

death penalty. SING N The **death penalty** is the punishment of death, used in some countries for people who have committed very serious crimes.

debacle /deɪbɑːkə^{0}l, dɪ-/, **debacles;** also spelled **débâcle.** COUNT N A **debacle** is an event or attempt that is a complete failure. *...the debacle of the TV series.*

debase /di^{1}beɪs/, **debases, debasing, debased.** VB WITH OBJ If something **is debased,** its value or quality is reduced; a formal use. *The quality of life can only be debased by such a system.*

debatable /di^{1}beɪtəbə^{0}l/. ADJ Something that is **debatable** is not definitely true or not certain. *'They won't notice it's gone.'—'Well. That's debatable.'*

debate /di^{1}beɪt/, **debates, debating, debated.** 1 COUNT N OR UNCOUNT N A **debate** is a discussion in which people express different opinions about a subject. *...a debate on education... There was a great deal of debate about the national health service.* 2 VB WITH OBJ When people **debate** something, they discuss it fairly formally, putting forward different views. *These issues have been widely debated... They debated the motion that capital punishment should be re-introduced.* 3 VB If you **debate** what to do, you think about possible courses of action before deciding what to do. *He turned round, debating whether to go back.* 4 PHRASE If something is **open to debate,** it has not been proved to be true.

debauchery /di^{1}bɔːtʃəri^1/. UNCOUNT N **Debauchery** is excessive drunkenness or sexual activity; a formal use.

debilitating /dɪ^{1}bɪlɪteɪtɪŋ/. ADJ A **debilitating** illness, situation, or action makes you weak; a formal use. *...the debilitating effects of the fast... ...economically debilitating subsidies.*

debility /dɪ^{1}bɪlɪti^1/. UNCOUNT N **Debility** is physical or mental weakness, especially weakness caused by illness; a formal use. *...the debility produced by old age.*

debit /debɪt/, **debits, debiting, debited.** 1 VB WITH OBJ When your bank **debits** your account, money is taken from it and paid to someone else. 2 COUNT N A **debit** is a record of the money taken from your bank account, for example when you write a cheque. *...a statement showing all the credits and debits.*

debris /deɪbri^1, debri^1/. UNCOUNT N **Debris** consists of pieces of things that have been destroyed, or rubbish that is lying around. *She began clearing up the debris.*

debt /det/, **debts.** 1 COUNT N A **debt** is a sum of money that you owe someone. *You must spend less until your debts are paid off.* 2 UNCOUNT N **Debt** is the state of owing money. *He began getting deeper and deeper into debt.* 3 PHRASE If you are **in** someone's **debt,** you are grateful to them for something, and you feel that you ought to do something for them in return; a formal use.

debtor /detə/, **debtors.** COUNT N A **debtor** is a person who owes money.

debunk /diːbʌŋk/, **debunks, debunking, debunked.** VB WITH OBJ If you **debunk** an idea or belief, you show that it is false or not important.

debut /deɪbjuː, debjuː/, **debuts.** COUNT N The **debut** of a singer, musician, footballer, or other performer is his or her first public performance or recording. *She made her debut in this theatre.*

decade /dekeɪd, dɪ^{2}keɪd/, **decades.** COUNT N A **decade** is a period of ten years, especially one that begins with a year ending in 0, for example 1980 to 1989. *By the end of the decade he had acquired international fame.*

decadent /dekədə^{2}nt/. ADJ If someone or something is **decadent**, they show low standards, especially low moral standards. *...decadent values.* ♦ **decadence** /dekədə^{2}ns/ UNCOUNT N *...moral decadence.*

decaffeinated /di^{1}kæfə^{1}neɪtɪ^{2}d/. ADJ **Decaffeinated** coffee has had most of the caffeine removed.

decant /dɪ^{2}kænt/, **decants, decanting, decanted.** VB WITH OBJ If you **decant** wine, you pour it slowly from its bottle into another container before serving it.

decanter /dɪ^{2}kæntə/, **decanters.** COUNT N A **decanter** is a glass container that you use for serving wine, sherry, and so on.

decapitate /di^{1}kæpɪteɪt/, **decapitates, decapitating, decapitated.** VB WITH OBJ If someone **is decapitated,** their head is cut off; a formal use.

decay /dɪ^{2}keɪ/, **decays, decaying, decayed.** 1 VB When something **decays,** it rots and starts to fall apart. *The body had already started to decay... ...a smell of decaying meat.* ♦ **decayed** ADJ *...a decayed tooth.* 2 UNCOUNT N **Decay** is the process of something rotting. *...dental decay.* 3 VB If buildings **decay,** their condition becomes worse because they have not been looked after and repaired. *The old palace decayed badly during Cromwell's time... ...decaying urban centres.* Also UNCOUNT N *...saving houses from falling into decay.* 4 VB If a society or culture **decays,** it gradually becomes weaker or more corrupt. Also UNCOUNT N *...a religion in the final stages of decay.*

deceased /di^{1}siːst/; a formal word. 1 SING N A person who has recently died can be referred to as the **deceased.** *...the property of the deceased.* 2 ADJ A **deceased** person is one who has recently died. *...the relatives of the deceased couple.*

deceit /dɪsiːt/, **deceits.** UNCOUNT N **Deceit** is lying, or behaviour that is intended to make people believe something which is not true. *...marriages in which deceit was commonplace.*

deceitful /dɪsiːtfʊl/. ADJ Someone who is **deceitful** tries to make people believe things that are not true.

deceive /dɪsiːv/, **deceives, deceiving, deceived.** 1 VB WITH OBJ To **deceive** someone means to cause them to believe something that is not true. *He tried to deceive me... His unkempt appearance deceived the staff into believing that he was a student.* 2 REFL VB If you **deceive** yourself, you do not admit to yourself something that you know is true. *They try to deceive themselves that everything is all right.*

December /di^{1}sembə/. UNCOUNT N **December** is the twelfth and last month of the year in the Western calendar.

decency /diːsə^{0}nsi^1/. 1 UNCOUNT N **Decency** is behaviour which follows accepted moral standards. *They tried to restore some sense and decency to the Administration.* 2 UNCOUNT N **Decency** is also kind and considerate behaviour. *Why hadn't they had the decency to ask him if he'd like to join in?*

decent /diːsə^{0}nt/. 1 ADJ **Decent** means acceptable in standard or quality. *...decent wages... ...a decent night's rest.* ♦ **decently** ADV *The farm animals are decently treated.* 2 ATTRIB ADJ **Decent** also means morally correct or acceptable. *He would marry her as soon as a decent amount of time had elapsed.* ♦ **decently** ADV *They only want the chance to live their lives decently.* 3 ATTRIB ADJ **Decent** people are honest and respectable and behave morally. *...decent, hard-working citizens.*

decentralize /di^{1}sentrəlaɪz/, **decentralizes, decentralizing, decentralized;** also spelled **decentralise.** VB WITH OBJ To **decentralize** a large organization means to move some of its departments away from the main administrative area, or to give more power to local departments. *He accused the Minister of seeking to decentralise the Commission.* ♦ **decentralized** ADJ *...a decentralized health service.* ♦ **decentralization** /di^{1}sentrəlaɪzeɪʃə^{0}n/ UNCOUNT N *...the decentralization of government.*

deception /di^{1}sepʃə^{0}n/, **deceptions.** 1 COUNT N A **deception** is something that you say or do in order to deceive someone. *He would quickly have seen through Mary's deceptions.* 2 UNCOUNT N **Deception** is the act of deceiving someone. *...his part in the deception of the British public.*

deceptive /di^{1}septɪv/. ADJ If something is **deceptive,** it might cause you to believe something which is not true. *Its fragile appearance was deceptive.* ♦ **deceptively** SUBMOD OR ADV *It all looks deceptively simple... It was deceptively presented as a scientific study.*

decibel /desɪbel/, **decibels.** COUNT N A **decibel** is a unit of measurement of how loud something is. *He lowered his voice a few decibels.*

decide /di^{1}saɪd/, **decides, deciding, decided.** 1 VB WITH TO-INF OR ADJUNCT, OR REPORT VB If you **decide** to do something, you choose to do it. *What made you decide to get married?... I'm glad you decided against a career as a waiter... She decided that she would leave... He has a month to decide whether he's going to stay.* 2 VB WITH OBJ When something **is decided,** people choose what should be done. *The case is to be decided by the International Court.* 3 VB WITH OBJ If an event or fact **decides** something, it makes a particular result definite or unavoidable. *It was this that decided the fate of the company.* ♦ **deciding** ATTRIB ADJ *I suppose cost shouldn't be a deciding factor.* 4 REPORT VB If you **decide** that something is the case, you form that opinion after considering the facts. *He decided that the doorbell was broken... I couldn't decide whether she was joking or not.*

decide on or **decide upon.** PHR VB If you **decide on** something or **decide upon** it, you choose it from two or more possibilities. *He decided on a career in the army.*

decided /di^{1}saɪdɪ^{2}d/. ATTRIB ADJ **Decided** means clear and definite. *This gave them a decided advantage over their opponents.*

decidedly /di^{1}saɪdɪ^{2}dli^1/. 1 SUBMOD **Decidedly** means to a great extent and in a way that is obvious. *The men looked decidedly uncomfortable.* 2 ADV If you say something **decidedly,** you say it in a way that suggests you are unlikely to change your mind. *'It's time things were altered,' said Mrs Moffat decidedly.*

deciduous /di^{1}sɪdjuːəs/. ADJ A **deciduous** tree loses its leaves in autumn every year.

decimal /desɪmə^{0}l/, **decimals.** 1 ATTRIB ADJ A **decimal** system involves counting in units of ten. 2 COUNT N A **decimal** is a fraction written in the form of a dot followed by one or more numbers representing tenths, hundredths, and so on: for example .5, .51, .517.

decimal point, decimal points. COUNT N A **decimal point** is the dot in front of a decimal fraction.

decimate /desɪmeɪt/, **decimates, decimating, decimated.** VB WITH OBJ To **decimate** a group of people or animals means to destroy a very large number of them. *The soldiers would be decimated long before they reached the beaches.*

decipher /di1saɪfə/, **deciphers, deciphering, deciphered.** VB WITH OBJ If you **decipher** a piece of writing, you work out what it says, even though it is difficult to read or understand.

decision /di1sɪʒə0n/, **decisions. 1** COUNT N When you make a **decision,** you choose what should be done or which is the best of various alternatives. *I think that I made the wrong decision... A decision on the issue might not be necessary... ...difficult decisions.* **2** UNCOUNT N **Decision** is the act of deciding something. *Philip laced up his shoes slowly, delaying the moment of decision.* **3** UNCOUNT N **Decision** is also the ability to decide quickly and definitely what to do. *...a man of decision and action.*

decisive /di1saɪsɪv/. **1** ADJ If a fact, action, or event is **decisive,** it makes it certain that there will be a particular result. *...a decisive battle... This promise was not a decisive factor in the election.* ♦ **decisively** ADV *Thornton was decisively defeated.* **2** ADJ If someone is **decisive,** they have the ability to make quick decisions. *...a decisive leader.* ♦ **decisively** ADV *'Can I see him?' Edgar shook his head decisively.*

deck /dek/, **decks, decking, decked. 1** COUNT N A **deck** on a bus or ship is a downstairs or upstairs area. *They got on the bus and sat on the top deck.* **2** SING N The **deck** of a ship is also a floor in the open air which you can walk on. *I'm going back up on deck.* **3** COUNT N A record **deck** is a piece of equipment on which you play records. **4** COUNT N A **deck** of cards is a pack of playing cards. **5** VB WITH OBJ AND 'with' If something **is decked** with attractive things, it is decorated with them; a literary use. *The graves are decked with flowers.*

deck out. PHR VB If you **deck** someone or something **out,** you decorate them or make them look attractive; a literary use. *I decked myself out in a suit and tie.*

deckchair /dektʃeə/, **deckchairs.** COUNT N A **deckchair** is a simple folding chair which is used out of doors.

declaration /dekləreɪʃə0n/, **declarations. 1** COUNT N A **declaration** is a firm, emphatic statement. *He seemed embarrassed by her declaration of love... ...his earlier declarations that things were improving.* **2** COUNT N A **declaration** is also an official announcement or statement. *...the day after the declaration was signed... ...formal declarations of war.*

declare /di1kleə/, **declares, declaring, declared. 1** REPORT VB If you **declare** that something is the case, you say it in a firm, deliberate way. *'I like it,' she declared... They were heard to declare that they would never steal again.* **2** VB WITH OBJ If you **declare** an attitude or intention, or if you **declare** yourself as having this attitude or intention, you make it known that you have it. *He declared his intention to fight... Mr Bell has declared his support... He declared himself strongly in favour of the project.* ♦ **declared** ATTRIB ADJ *...his declared intention to resign.* **3** VB WITH OBJ If you **declare** something, you state it officially and formally. *The French declared war on England... At his trial he was declared innocent.* **4** VB WITH OBJ When you **declare** goods that you have bought abroad or money that you have earned, you tell customs or tax officials about it so that you can pay tax on it.

decline /di1klaɪn/, **declines, declining, declined. 1** VB If something **declines,** it becomes smaller, weaker, or worse. *The number of congress members declined from 371 to 361... Since 1971 the party's influence has declined.* ♦ **declining** ATTRIB ADJ *...a steadily declining income... ...declining industries.* **2** COUNT N OR UNCOUNT N If there is a **decline** in something, it becomes smaller, weaker, or worse. *...a decline in standards... ...the decline of the motor industry.* **3** PHRASE If something is **in decline** or **on the decline,** it is growing smaller, weaker or worse. *The city's population is in decline... Organized religion seems to be on the decline.* **4** VB WITH OR WITHOUT OBJ OR VB WITH TO-INF If you **decline** something or **decline** to do something, you politely refuse to accept it or do it; a formal use. *He has declined the invitation... Mr Santos declined to comment on the news.*

decode /di:kəʊd/, **decodes, decoding, decoded.** VB WITH OBJ If you **decode** a message that has been written or spoken in code, you change it into ordinary language.

decompose /di:kə7mpəʊz/, **decomposes, decomposing, decomposed.** VB When something that has died **decomposes,** it changes chemically and begins to rot. *Shellfish decompose very quickly after death.* ♦ **decomposition** /di:kɒmpəzɪʃə0n/ UNCOUNT N *...the decomposition of organic matter.*

decor /deɪkɔ:/. UNCOUNT N The **decor** of a house or room is the style in which it is furnished and decorated. *...the pine decor of the kitchen.*

decorate /dekə7reɪt/, **decorates, decorating, decorated. 1** VB WITH OBJ If you **decorate** something, you make it look more attractive by adding things to it. *The walls were all decorated with posters.* **2** VB WITH OR WITHOUT OBJ If you **decorate** a building or room, you paint it or wallpaper it. *...a newly decorated room.* ♦ **decorating** UNCOUNT N *We said we would do the decorating.*

decoration /dekə7reɪʃə0n/, **decorations. 1** COUNT N OR UNCOUNT N **Decorations** are features added to something to make it look more attractive. *...Christmas decorations... ...dresses that are free of all decoration.* **2** UNCOUNT N The **decoration** of a room or building is the furniture, wallpaper, and ornaments there. *...the style of decoration typical of the 1920s.* **3** COUNT N A **decoration** is a medal given to someone as an official honour.

decorative /dekə0rətɪv/. ADJ Something that is **decorative** is intended to look pretty or attractive.

decorator /dekəreɪtə/, **decorators.** COUNT N A **decorator** is a person whose job is to paint houses or put wallpaper on the walls.

decorous /dekə7rəs/. ADJ Behaviour that is **decorous** is polite and correct and does not offend people; a formal use. *He gave his wife a decorous kiss.* ♦ **decorously** ADV *...teenage lovers strolling decorously.*

decorum /dɪ2kɔ:rəm/. UNCOUNT N **Decorum** is behaviour that people consider to be correct and polite; a formal use.

decoy /di:kɔɪ/, **decoys, decoying, decoyed. 1** COUNT N A **decoy** is a person or object that you use to lead someone away from where they intended to go, especially so that you can catch them. **2** VB WITH OBJ AND ADJUNCT If you **decoy** someone, you lead them away from where they intended to go, often by means of a trick. *Eight of the missiles were decoyed away from targets.*

decrease /di1kri:s/, **decreases, decreasing, decreased. 1** ERG VB When something **decreases,** it becomes smaller. *The number of marriages has decreased by forty per cent... To save money, decrease the temperature.* ♦ **decreasing** ATTRIB ADJ *...a life of increasing labour and decreasing leisure.* **2** COUNT N A **decrease** is a reduction in the quantity or size of something.

decree /di1kri:/, **decrees, decreeing, decreed. 1** REPORT VB If someone in authority **decrees** that something must happen, they order this officially. **2** COUNT N A **decree** is an official order, especially one made by the ruler of a country.

decrepit /di1krepɪt/. ADJ Something that is **decrepit** is very old and in bad condition.

decry /di1kraɪ/, **decries, decrying, decried.** VB WITH OBJ If you **decry** something, you say that it is bad; a formal use.

dedicate /dedɪkeɪt/, **dedicates, dedicating, dedicated. 1** REFL VB WITH PREP 'to' If you **dedicate** yourself to something, you give a lot of time and effort to it because you think it is important. *...a man who had dedicated himself to his work.* **2** VB WITH OBJ AND PREP 'to' If you **dedicate** something such as a book or a piece of music to someone, you say that the work is written for them, as a sign of affection or respect. *She dedicated her first book to her husband.*

dedicated /dedɪkeɪtɪ2d/. ADJ If you are **dedicated** to something, you give a lot of time and effort to it because you think it is important. *...people dedicated to social or political change... ...a dedicated surgeon.*

dedication /dedɪkeɪʃə0n/, **dedications. 1** UNCOUNT N If you show **dedication** to something, you give a lot of time and effort to it because you think it is important. *I admired her dedication to her family.* **2** COUNT N A **dedication** is a message written at the beginning of a book as a sign of affection or respect for someone.

deduce /dɪdju:s/, **deduces, deducing, deduced.** REPORT VB If you **deduce** that something is true, you reach that conclusion because of what you know to be true. *What do you deduce from all this?*

deduct /di1dʌkt/, **deducts, deducting, deducted.** VB WITH OBJ When you **deduct** an amount from a total, you reduce the total by that amount. *Tax will be deducted automatically from your wages.*

deduction /di1dʌkʃə0n/, **deductions. 1** COUNT N OR UNCOUNT N A **deduction** is a conclusion that you reach because of what you know to be true. **2** COUNT N OR UNCOUNT N A **deduction** is also an amount subtracted from a total. *...national insurance deductions.*

deed /di:d/, **deeds. 1** COUNT N A **deed** is something that is done, especially something very good or very bad; a literary use. **2** COUNT N WITH SUPP A **deed** is also a legal document containing an agreement or contract.

deem /di:m/, **deems, deeming, deemed.** VB WITH OBJ If you **deem** something to be the case, you consider that it is the case; a formal use. *This was deemed to detract from the dignity of the republic... Force was deemed necessary.*

deep /di:p/, **deeper, deepest. 1** ADJ OR ADV If something is **deep,** it extends a long way down from the surface. *The sea is not very deep there... They dug deep down into the earth.* ♦ **deeply** ADV *His face was deeply lined.* **2** ADJ AFTER N You use **deep** to talk about measurements. For example, if something is two feet **deep,** it measures two feet from top to bottom, or from front to back. **3** ADJ OR ADV **Deep** in an area means a long way inside it. *...deep in the forest... Guerrilla forces were advancing deep into enemy territory.* **4** ATTRIB ADJ You use **deep** for emphasis. *This was a matter of deep concern.* ♦ **deeply** SUBMOD *...deeply religious people.* **5** ATTRIB ADJ If you are in a **deep** sleep, you are sleeping and it is difficult to wake you. **6** ATTRIB ADJ A **deep** breath or sigh uses the whole of your lungs. *She took a deep breath and put her head under the water.* ♦ **deeply** ADV *She sighed deeply.* **7** ADJ A **deep** colour is strong. *The sky was a deep purple.* **8** ADJ A **deep** sound is a low one. *He sang in a deep voice.* **9** ADJ **Deep** thoughts are serious thoughts.

PHRASES ● If you are **deep in thought,** you are thinking very hard about something. ● If you say that something **goes** or **runs deep,** you mean that it is very serious and hard to change. *The crisis in the prisons goes deep.*

deepen /di:pə0n/, **deepens, deepening, deepened. 1** VB WITH OBJ To **deepen** something means to make it deeper. *The authority wants to widen and deepen the River Soar.* **2** VB Where a river or a sea **deepens,** the water gets deeper. **3** ERG VB If a situation or emotion **deepens,** it becomes more intense. *The crisis deepened.* **4** ERG VB If you **deepen** your knowledge of a subject, you learn more about it. *Their object was to deepen man's understanding of the universe.* **5** ERG VB When a sound **deepens,** it becomes lower in tone. *The engine sound deepened from a steady whine to a thunderous roar.*

deep freeze, deep freezes. COUNT N A **deep freeze** is a very cold refrigerator in which frozen food is stored.

deep-rooted. ADJ An idea or feeling that is **deep-rooted** or **deeply rooted** is so firmly fixed in a person or a society that it is difficult to change or remove. *...a deep-rooted prejudice.*

deep-sea. ATTRIB ADJ **Deep-sea** activities take place in areas of the sea that are a long way from the coast. *...deep-sea diving.*

deep-seated. ADJ A **deep-seated** feeling or problem is very strong or basic, and difficult to change.

deer /dɪə/. **Deer** is the singular and plural. COUNT N A **deer** is a large wild animal. Male deer usually have large, branching horns.

deface /di1feɪs/, **defaces, defacing, defaced.** VB WITH OBJ If someone **defaces** something such as a wall or a notice, they spoil it by writing or drawing on it. *...books with pages torn out or defaced with graffiti.*

defamation /defəmeɪʃə0n/. UNCOUNT N **Defamation** is the damaging of someone's reputation by saying something bad and untrue about them; a legal use.

default /di1fɔ:lt/, **defaults, defaulting, defaulted. 1** VB If you **default,** you fail to do something that you are legally supposed to do, such as make a payment that you owe. *He said he had been right to default on that loan.* Also UNCOUNT N *...default of payment.* **2** PHRASE If something happens **by default,** it happens only because something else has not happened.

defeat /di1fi:t/, **defeats, defeating, defeated. 1** VB WITH OBJ If you **defeat** someone, you win a victory over them in a battle, game, or contest. *Arsenal were defeated on Saturday.* **2** VB WITH OBJ If a proposal or a motion in a debate **is defeated,** more people vote against it than vote for it. *The motion was defeated by 221 votes to 152.* **3** VB WITH OBJ If a task or a problem **defeats** you, it is so difficult that you cannot do it or solve it. *...a complex sum which defeats many adults as well as children.* **4** VB WITH OBJ To **defeat** an action or plan means to cause it to fail. *He would like to see the strike defeated.* **5** UNCOUNT N OR COUNT N **Defeat** is the state of being beaten in a battle, game, or contest, or of failing to achieve what you wanted to. *The bad weather contributed to the defeat of the navy... These defeats came as a setback for Thorne... Her friend finally gave up in defeat.*

defeatism /di1fi:tɪzə0m/. UNCOUNT N **Defeatism** is a way of thinking or talking which suggests that you expect to be unsuccessful. *We were accused of defeatism.* ♦ **defeatist** /di1fi:tɪst/ COUNT N OR MOD *I was in a defeatist mood... Was she a defeatist?*

defecate /defə1keɪt/, **defecates, defecating, defecated.** VB To **defecate** means to get rid of waste matter from the body through the anus; a formal use.

defect, defects, defecting, defected; pronounced /di:fekt/ when it is a noun and /di1fekt/ when it is a verb. **1** COUNT N A **defect** is a fault or imperfection in a person or thing. 2 VB If you **defect,** you leave your own country, political party, or other group, and join an opposing one. *Several of the Labour MPs defected to the new party.* ♦ **defection** /diˈfɛkʃən/ COUNT N OR UNCOUNT N *The number of defections has increased in recent years.* ♦ **defector** COUNT N *...defectors from the Liberal Party.*

defective /diˈfɛktɪv/. ADJ If a piece of machinery is **defective,** there is something wrong with it.

defence /diˈfɛns/, **defences;** spelled **defense** in American English. 1 UNCOUNT N **Defence** is action taken to protect someone or something from attack. *...the defence of civil liberties.* ● If you say something **in defence,** you say it in order to support ideas or actions that have been criticized. 2 COUNT N A **defence** is something that people or animals can use or do to protect themselves. *The jellyfish has had to develop this deadly poison as a defence... He had found coldness his only defence against despair.* 3 COUNT N A **defence** is also something that you say in support of ideas or actions that have been criticized. *His economists have drawn up a defence of his policy.* 4 UNCOUNT N **Defence** is also used to refer to a country's armies and weapons, and their activities. *...the Ministry of Defence... ...defence spending.* 5 PLURAL N The **defences** of a country or region are its armed forces and weapons. 6 COUNT N In a court of law, a person's **defence** is their denial of a charge against them. *He decided to conduct his own defence.* 7 SING N The **defence** is the case presented by a lawyer in a trial for the person who has been accused of a crime, or the lawyers for this person. 8 COLL N In a sports team, the **defence** is the group of players who try to stop the opposing team scoring a goal or a point.

defenceless /diˈfɛnsləs/; spelled **defenseless** in American English. ADJ If someone is **defenceless,** they are weak and cannot defend themselves.

defend /diˈfɛnd/, **defends, defending, defended.** 1 VB WITH OBJ OR REFL VB If you **defend** someone or something, you take action to protect them. *The village had to defend itself against raiders.* 2 VB WITH OBJ OR REFL VB If you **defend** someone or something when they have been criticized, you argue in support of them. *The bank has defended its actions in these cases.* ♦ **defender** COUNT N *...a defender of right-wing views.* 3 VB WITH OBJ A lawyer who **defends** a person in court tries to show that the charges against the person are not true or that there was an excuse for the crime. 4 VB WITH OR WITHOUT OBJ If a sports champion **defends** his or her title, he or she plays a match or a game against someone who will become the new champion if they win.

defendant /diˈfɛndənt/, **defendants.** COUNT N The **defendant** in a trial is the person accused of a crime.

defense /diˈfɛns/. See **defence.**

defensible /diˈfɛnsəbəl/. ADJ An opinion, system, or action that is **defensible** is one that people can argue is right or good. *He gave a very defensible definition of socialism.*

defensive /diˈfɛnsɪv/. 1 ATTRIB ADJ You use **defensive** to describe things that are intended to protect someone or something. *...defensive measures.* 2 PHRASE If you are **on the defensive,** you are trying to protect yourself or your interests because you feel unsure or threatened. 3 ADJ Someone who is **defensive** is behaving in a way that shows that they feel unsure or threatened. *He had the defensive humour of a lonely man.* ♦ **defensively** ADV *'I'm in no hurry,' said Rudolph defensively.*

defer /diˈfɜː/, **defers, deferring, deferred;** a formal word. 1 VB WITH OBJ OR -ING If you **defer** an event or action, you arrange that it will take place at a later date than was planned. *They offered to defer his appointment for a year.* 2 VB WITH PREP 'to' If you **defer** to someone, you accept their opinion or do what they want because you respect them. *'He's a medical man and we'd be fools not to defer to him in medical matters.'*

deference /dɛfərəns/. UNCOUNT N **Deference** is a polite and respectful attitude to someone. *She is treated with deference.*

deferential /dɛfərɛnʃəl/. ADJ A **deferential** person is polite and respectful. *I made every effort to be pleasant and deferential to Mr Thoms.*

defiance /diˈfaɪəns/. 1 UNCOUNT N **Defiance** is behaviour which shows that you are not willing to obey someone or are not worried about their disapproval. *In a gesture of defiance, I wore a black mini-skirt.* 2 PHRASE If you do something **in defiance of** a rule, you do it even though it is forbidden. *The houses were erected in defiance of all building regulations.*

defiant /diˈfaɪənt/. ADJ If you are **defiant,** you refuse to obey someone or you ignore their disapproval of you. *The girl sat down with a defiant look at Judy.* ♦ **defiantly** ADV *She announced defiantly that she intended to stay.*

deficient /diˈfɪʃənt/. 1 ADJ If someone or something is **deficient** in a particular thing, they do not have as much of it as they need. *...old people deficient in vitamin C.* ♦ **deficiency** /diˈfɪʃənsi/ COUNT N OR UNCOUNT N *...vitamin deficiency.* 2 ADJ Something that is **deficient** is not good enough; a formal use. *...increasingly deficient public services.* ♦ **deficiency** COUNT N OR UNCOUNT N *The deficiency of the answers was obvious to everybody.*

deficit /dɛfɪsɪt/, **deficits.** COUNT N A **deficit** is the amount by which the money received by a country or organization is less than the money it has spent. *The Post Office's deficit totalled 150m pounds.*

defile /diˈfaɪl/, **defiles, defiling, defiled.** VB WITH OBJ If you **defile** something precious or holy, you spoil it or damage it. *...secret thoughts which defiled her purity.*

define /diˈfaɪn/, **defines, defining, defined.** VB WITH OBJ If you **define** something, you say exactly what it is or means. *Each object had clearly defined functions... My dictionary defines 'crisis' as a 'turning point'.*

definite /dɛfɪnɪt/. 1 ADJ If something is **definite,** it is firm and clear, and unlikely to be changed. *There's a definite date for the wedding.* 2 ADJ **Definite** also means true rather than being someone's opinion or guess. *There was no definite evidence.*

definite article, definite articles. COUNT N In grammar, the word 'the' is sometimes called the **definite article.** In this dictionary, 'the' is called a determiner.

definitely /dɛfɪnɪtli/. 1 SENTENCE ADV You use **definitely** to emphasize that something is certainly the case. *They were definitely not for sale.* 2 ADV If something has **definitely** been decided, the decision will not be changed. *I haven't definitely decided on going to law school.*

definition /dɛfɪnɪʃən/, **definitions.** 1 COUNT N A **definition** of a word or term is a statement giving its meaning, especially in a dictionary. 2 PHRASE If you say that something has a particular quality **by definition,** you mean that it has this quality simply because of what it is. 3 UNCOUNT N **Definition** is the quality of being clear and distinct. *They lack definition and identity as a class.*

definitive /dəˈfɪnɪtɪv/. 1 ADJ Something that is **definitive** provides a firm, unquestionable conclusion. *...a definitive verdict.* ♦ **definitively** ADV *'Hearts of Darkness' will definitively establish McCullin as a writer.* 2 ADJ A book or performance that is **definitive** is thought to be the best of its kind that has ever been done or that will ever be done.

deflate /diˈfleɪt/, **deflates, deflating, deflated.** 1 VB WITH OBJ If you **deflate** someone, you take away their confidence or make them seem less important. ♦ **deflated** ADJ *If that left us feeling deflated, worse was to come.* 2 ERG VB When a tyre or balloon **deflates,** or when you **deflate** it, all the air comes out of it.

deflation /diˈfleɪʃən/. UNCOUNT N **Deflation** is a reduction in economic activity in a country that leads to lower industrial production and lower prices.

deflect /diˈflɛkt/, **deflects, deflecting, deflected.** 1 VB WITH OBJ If you **deflect** something such as someone's attention or criticism, you cause them to turn their attention to something else or to do something different. *Their main purpose was to deflect attention from the Government's proposals.* 2 VB WITH OBJ If you **deflect** something that is moving, you make it go in a slightly different direction, for example by hitting or pushing it. *Our goalie deflected their shot... The two streams of water are deflected.*

deform /diˈfɔːm/, **deforms, deforming, deformed.** VB WITH OBJ If something **deforms** a person's body or an object, it causes it to have an unnatural shape or appearance. *Badly fitting shoes can deform the feet.* ♦ **deformed** ADJ *The drug may have caused deformed babies.*

deformity /diˈfɔːmɪti/, **deformities.** 1 COUNT N A **deformity** is a part of someone's body which is the wrong shape. 2 UNCOUNT N **Deformity** is the condition of having a deformity. *Many cases of deformity and death occurred in the villagers who ate the fish.*

defrost /diːfrɒst, diˈfrɒst/, **defrosts, defrosting, defrosted.** 1 ERG VB When you **defrost** a fridge or freezer or when it **defrosts,** you switch it off so that the ice inside it can melt. 2 ERG VB When you **defrost** frozen food or when it **defrosts,** you allow it to melt so that you can eat it.

deft /dɛft/. ADJ A **deft** action is skilful and often quick. *The deft fingers massaged his scalp.* ♦ **deftly** ADV *He deftly slit open the envelope.*

defunct /dɪfʌŋkt/. ADJ If something is **defunct,** it no longer exists or it is no longer functioning. *...long defunct local authorities.*

defuse /diˈfjuːz/, **defuses, defusing, defused.** 1 VB WITH OBJ If you **defuse** a dangerous or tense situation, you make it less dangerous or tense. *Lester's casual attitude defused the situation.* 2 VB WITH OBJ If someone **defuses** a bomb, they remove the fuse from it so that it cannot explode.

defy /diˈfaɪ/, **defies, defying, defied.** 1 VB WITH OBJ If you **defy** people or laws, you refuse to obey them. 2 VB WITH OBJ AND TO-INF If you **defy** someone to do something which you think is impossible, you challenge them to do it. *I defy anyone to disprove it.* 3 VB WITH OBJ If something **defies** description or understanding, it is so strange or surprising that it is almost impossible to describe or understand. *...forces within the human character which defy rational analysis.*

degenerate, degenerates, degenerating, degenerated; pronounced /diˈdʒɛnəreɪt/ when it is a verb and /diˈdʒɛnərət/ when it is an adjective or noun. 1 VB To **degenerate** means to become worse. *The discussion degenerated into a row.* ♦ **degeneration** /dɪdʒɛnəreɪʃən/ UNCOUNT N *This disease causes physical and mental degeneration.* 2 ADJ If someone is **degenerate,** they show very low standards of morality. 3 COUNT N A **degenerate** is someone who shows very low standards of morality. *The world is full of degenerates.*

degradation /dɛgrədeɪʃən/. UNCOUNT N **Degradation** is a state of poverty and dirt. *They forgot the squalor and degradation around them.*

degrade /diˈgreɪd/, **degrades, degrading, degraded.** VB WITH OBJ To **degrade** someone means to make them seem less respectable or important; used showing disapproval. *...films that degrade women.* ♦ **degrading** ADJ *...the vicious and degrading cult of violence.*

degree /diˈgriː/, **degrees.** 1 COUNT N WITH SUPP You use **degree** to indicate the extent to which something happens or is felt. *This has been tried with varying degrees of success... The number of police carrying guns has increased to an alarming degree.* ● If something happens **by degrees,** it happens gradually. 2 COUNT N A **degree** is a unit of measurement for temperatures, angles, and longitude and latitude; often written as '°', for example 23°. 3 COUNT N A **degree** at a university or polytechnic is a qualification gained after completing a course of study there. *He had taken a degree in music at Cambridge.*

dehydrate /diːhaɪdreɪt/, **dehydrates, dehydrating, dehydrated.** 1 VB WITH OBJ When something **is dehydrated,** water is removed from it. *...packets of dehydrated soup.* 2 VB WITH OBJ If you **are dehydrated,** you feel ill because you have lost too much water from your body.

deign /deɪn/, **deigns, deigning, deigned.** VB WITH TO-INF If you **deign** to do something, you do it even though you think you are too important to do it; a formal use.

deity /diːɪtɪ, deɪ-/, **deities.** COUNT N A **deity** is a god or goddess; a formal use.

dejected /diˈdʒɛktɪd/. ADJ If you are **dejected,** you feel unhappy or disappointed; a formal use. *He had a dejected, saddened look.* ♦ **dejectedly** ADV *'I can't do it,' said the girl dejectedly.*

dejection /diˈdʒɛkʃən/. UNCOUNT N **Dejection** is unhappiness and disappointment; a formal use.

delay /diˈleɪ/, **delays, delaying, delayed.** 1 VB WITH OR WITHOUT OBJ If you **delay** doing something, you do not do it until a later time. *Try and persuade them to delay some of the changes.* 2 VB WITH OBJ To **delay** someone or something means to make them late or slow them down. *I'm afraid I was slightly delayed... The shock of the operation delayed his recovery.* 3 COUNT N OR UNCOUNT N If there is a **delay,** something does not happen until later than planned or expected. *We shall inform you without delay.*

delectable /diˈlɛktəbəl/. ADJ Something that is **delectable** is very pleasant; a formal use.

delegate, delegates, delegating, delegated; pronounced /dɛləgət/ when it is a noun and /dɛləgeɪt/ when it is a verb. 1 COUNT N A **delegate** is a person chosen to make decisions on behalf of a group of people, especially at a meeting. *...delegates to the annual party conference.* 2 VB WITH OBJ If you **delegate** someone to do something, you formally ask them to do it on your behalf. *The Bishop delegated me to approach the local press.* 3 VB WITH OR WITHOUT OBJ If you **delegate** duties or responsibilities, you tell someone to do them on your behalf.

delegation /dɛlɪˈgeɪʃən/, **delegations.** COUNT N A **delegation** is a group of people chosen to represent a larger group of people.

delete /diˈliːt/, **deletes, deleting, deleted.** VB WITH OBJ If you **delete** something that has been written down, you cross it out or remove it.

deliberate, deliberates, deliberating, deliberated; pronounced /diˈlɪbərət/ when it is an adjective and /diˈlɪbəreɪt/ when it is a verb. 1 ADJ If something that you do is **deliberate,** you intended to do it. *He told his mother a deliberate lie.* ♦ **deliberately** ADV *The terms* *of the agreement were left deliberately vague.* 2 ADJ A **deliberate** action or movement is slow and careful. *His manner was quiet, his speech deliberate.* ♦ **deliberately** ADV *He climbed the stairs slowly and deliberately.* 3 VB If you **deliberate,** you think about something carefully before making a decision. *We had been waiting for two days while the jury deliberated.*

deliberation /dɪ1lɪbəreɪʃə0n/, **deliberations.** 1 UNCOUNT N **Deliberation** is careful consideration of a subject. *After considerable deliberation, I decided to accept the job.* 2 PHRASE If you do something **with deliberation,** you do it slowly and carefully. 3 PLURAL N **Deliberations** are formal discussions. *I left the committee to its deliberations.*

delicacy /delɪkəsi1/, **delicacies.** 1 UNCOUNT N If something has **delicacy,** it is graceful and attractive. *...delicacy of their features.* 2 UNCOUNT N If you do or say something with **delicacy,** you do or say it carefully and tactfully because you do not want to offend anyone. 3 COUNT N A **delicacy** is a rare or expensive food, considered especially nice to eat.

delicate /delɪkə1t/. 1 ADJ Something that is **delicate** is narrow and graceful or attractive. *She had long delicate fingers.* ♦ **delicately** ADV *...delicately veined pale skin.* 2 ADJ A **delicate** colour, taste, or smell is pleasant and not intense. *...a delicate pale cream colour.* 3 ADJ A **delicate** object is fragile and needs to be handled carefully. *...delicate china.* 4 ADJ A **delicate** movement is gentle, controlled, and not at all clumsy. *...delicate ballet steps.* ♦ **delicately** ADV *The princess took the pot delicately from him.* 5 ADJ Someone who is **delicate** is often ill; an old-fashioned use. *She was a very delicate child.* 6 ADJ A **delicate** situation or problem needs very careful and tactful treatment. *...the delicate sphere of race relations.* ♦ **delicately** ADV *...highly sensitive and delicately balanced economic systems.* 7 ADJ A **delicate** sense or scientific instrument is capable of noticing very small changes or differences. *Bees have a delicate sense of smell.*

delicatessen /delɪkətesə0n/, **delicatessens.** COUNT N A **delicatessen** is a shop that sells unusual or foreign foods.

delicious /dɪ2lɪʃəs/. 1 ADJ Food that is **delicious** has an extremely pleasant taste. *...a delicious cake.* 2 ADJ A **delicious** sensation is also extremely pleasant; an informal use. *...a delicious feeling.* ♦ **deliciously** SUBMOD *The sun felt deliciously warm.*

delight /dɪ1laɪt/, **delights, delighting, delighted.** 1 UNCOUNT N **Delight** is a feeling of very great pleasure. *Frank discovered to his delight that the gun was real.* 2 PHRASE If someone **takes a delight** or **takes delight** in doing something, they get a lot of pleasure from doing it. 3 COUNT N You can refer to someone or something that gives you great joy or pleasure as a **delight.** *Mrs Travers was a delight to interview.* 4 VB WITH OBJ If something **delights** you, it gives you a lot of pleasure. *The thought of divorce neither distressed nor delighted her.* 5 VB WITH 'in' OR 'at' If you **delight** in something, you get a lot of pleasure from it. *Morris delighted in hard manual work.*

delighted /dɪ1laɪtɪ2d/. ADJ If you are **delighted,** you are extremely pleased and excited about something. *He was grinning, delighted with his achievement.* ♦ **delightedly** ADV *She laughed delightedly.*

delightful /dɪlaɪtfʊl/. ADJ Someone or something that is **delightful** is very pleasant. *...a delightful room.* ♦ **delightfully** SUBMOD *...a delightfully smooth soup.*

delinquency /dɪ2lɪŋkwənsi1/. UNCOUNT N **Delinquency** is criminal behaviour, especially that of young people. *...children taken into care because of their delinquency.*

delinquent /dɪ2lɪŋkwənt/, **delinquents.** ADJ You use **delinquent** to describe young people who repeatedly commit minor crimes; a formal use. *...delinquent behaviour.* Also COUNT N *A few months of this may deter some potential delinquents.* ● See also **juvenile delinquent.**

delirious /dɪlɪrɪəs/. 1 ADJ Someone who is **delirious** is unable to think or speak in a rational way, usually because they have a fever. 2 ADJ **Delirious** also means extremely excited and happy.

delirium /dɪlɪrɪəm/. UNCOUNT N If someone is suffering from **delirium,** they cannot think or speak in a rational way, usually because they have a fever.

deliver /dɪ2lɪvə/, **delivers, delivering, delivered.** 1 VB WITH OBJ If you **deliver** something, you take it to someone's house or office. *He delivered newspapers as a boy.* 2 VB WITH OBJ AND ADJUNCT To **deliver** something also means to give it to someone; a formal use. *Chance delivered his enemy into his hands.* 3 VB WITH OBJ If you **deliver** a lecture or speech, you give it. *He delivered an emotional speech on the horrors of war.* 4 VB WITH OBJ When someone **delivers** a baby, they help the woman who is giving birth.

delivery /dɪ2lɪvə0ri1/, **deliveries.** 1 UNCOUNT N **Delivery** is the bringing of letters, parcels, or goods to someone's house or office. *All goods must be paid for before delivery.* 2 COUNT N A **delivery** of something is an amount of it that is delivered. *...an extra delivery of coal.* 3 UNCOUNT N Someone's **delivery** of a speech is the way in which they give it. *His delivery was slow and ponderous.* 4 COUNT N OR UNCOUNT N **Delivery** is also the process of giving birth to a baby. *It was a simple, routine delivery.*

delta /deltə/, **deltas.** COUNT N A **delta** is an area of flat land where a river spreads out into several smaller rivers before entering the sea.

delude /dɪ1lj0u:d/, **deludes, deluding, deluded.** VB WITH OBJ OR REFL VB If you **delude** someone, you make them believe something that is not true. *It was no good deluding myself that he loved me.*

deluge /delju:dʒ/, **deluges, deluging, deluged.** 1 COUNT N A **deluge** is a sudden, very heavy fall of rain. 2 SING N A **deluge** of things is a very large number of them which arrive at the same time. *...a deluge of petitions.* 3 VB WITH OBJ If you **are deluged** with things, a very large number of them arrive at the same time. *They were deluged with requests to play the song.*

delusion /dɪ1lu:ʒən/, **delusions.** COUNT N OR UNCOUNT N A **delusion** is a false belief. *Had it really happened? Was it a delusion?... I've suffered from delusion enough these past months.*

de luxe /dɪ1 lʌks/. ADJ You use **de luxe** to describe things that are better and more expensive than other things of the same kind. *...a de luxe coach tour.*

delve /delv/, **delves, delving, delved.** 1 VB WITH ADJUNCT If you **delve** into a question or problem, you try to discover more information about it. *She couldn't delve too deeply into the past.* 2 VB WITH ADJUNCT If you **delve** inside something such as a cupboard or bag, you search inside it.

demand /dɪ1mɑ:nd/, **demands, demanding, demanded.** 1 REPORT VB OR VB WITH TO-INF If you **demand** something, you ask for it very forcefully. *I demand to see a doctor... She had been demanding that he visit her.* 2 REPORT VB To **demand** also means to ask a question in a forceful way. *'What have I done?' he demanded.* 3 VB WITH OBJ If a job or situation **demands** something, that thing is necessary for it. *He has most of the qualities demanded of a leader.* 4 COUNT N A **demand** is a firm request. *...his demand for stronger armed forces.* 5 UNCOUNT N If there is **demand** for something, a lot of people want to buy it or have it. *The demand for health care is unlimited.* 6 COUNT N The **demands** of an activity, process, or situation are the things that have to be done or provided for it. *...the demands of family life... The body's fuel demands are very low.*

PHRASES ● If someone or something **makes demands** on you, they require you to do things which need a lot of time, energy, or money. *The system has always made heavy demands on those working in it.* ● If something is **in demand,** a lot of people want to buy it or have it. ● If something is available **on demand,** you can have it whenever you ask for it.

demanding /dɪ1mɑ:ndɪŋ/. 1 ADJ A **demanding** job or task requires a lot of time, energy, or attention. 2 ADJ Someone who is **demanding** always wants something and is not easily satisfied.

demarcation /di:mɑ:keɪʃə0n/. MOD OR UNCOUNT N **Demarcation** refers to a boundary or limit which separates two areas, groups, or activities. *...the demarcation lines between ethnic groups... There is no identifiable area of demarcation.*

demean /dɪ1mi:n/, **demeans, demeaning, demeaned.** REFL VB OR VB WITH OBJ If you **demean** yourself or **demean** something, you behave in a way which makes people have less respect for you or for that thing; a formal use. ♦ **demeaning** ADJ *They regard these jobs as demeaning and degrading.*

demeanour /dɪ1mi:nə/; spelled **demeanor** in American English. UNCOUNT N Your **demeanour** is the way you behave, which gives people an impression of your character and feelings; a formal use. *...his usual calm demeanour.*

demented /dɪ1mentɪ2d/. ADJ Someone who is **demented** behaves in a wild or violent way, often because they are mad.

demise /dɪ1maɪz/. SING N WITH SUPP The **demise** of something or someone is their end or death; a formal use.

democracy /dɪ2mɒkrəsi1/, **democracies.** 1 UNCOUNT N **Democracy** is a system of government or organization in which the citizens or members choose leaders or make other important decisions by voting. 2 COUNT N A **democracy** is a country in which the people choose their government by voting for it.

democrat /deməˆ6krӕt/, **democrats.** COUNT N A **democrat** is a person who believes in democracy.

democratic /demə6krӕtɪk/. ADJ A **democratic** country, organization, or system is one in which leaders are chosen or decisions are made by voting. *...democratic government.* ♦ **democratically** ADV *...a democratically elected government.*

demolish /dɪ1mɒlɪʃ/, **demolishes, demolishing, demolished.** 1 VB WITH OBJ When a building **is demolished,** it is knocked down, often because it is old or dangerous. *The old prison was demolished in 1890.* ♦ **demolition** /deməlɪʃə0n, di:-/ UNCOUNT N *...the demolition of the old YMCA building.* 2 VB WITH OBJ If you **demolish** someone's idea, argument, or belief, you prove that it is completely wrong. *He soon demolished Mr Stewart's suggestions.* ♦ **demolition** UNCOUNT N *...the demolition of a beloved theory.*

demon /di:mə0n/, **demons.** COUNT N A **demon** is an evil spirit. *Frederica seemed sometimes possessed by a demon.* ♦ **demonic** /dɪ1mɒnɪk/ ADJ *...demonic forces.*

demonstrable /dɪ2mɒnstrəbə0l/. ADJ Something that is **demonstrable** can be shown to exist or to be true. *The economic advantages are clearly demonstrable.* ♦ **demonstrably** ADV *Their vehicles are demonstrably more reliable than ours.*

demonstrate /demənstreɪt/, **demonstrates, demonstrating, demonstrated.** 1 VB WITH OBJ To **demonstrate** a fact or theory means to make it clear to people. *Her latest book demonstrates how important freedom is.* 2 VB WITH OBJ If you **demonstrate** something to someone, you show them how to do it or how it works. *She has been demonstrating how you make bread.* 3 VB WITH OBJ If you **demonstrate** a skill, quality, or feeling, you show that you have it. *She has not demonstrated much generosity.* 4 VB When people **demonstrate,** they take part in a march or a meeting to show that they oppose or support something. *Why don't you go and demonstrate outside the embassy?* ♦ **demonstrator** COUNT N *...crowds of demonstrators.*

demonstration /demənstreɪʃə0n/, **demonstrations.** 1 COUNT N A **demonstration** is a public meeting or march held by people to show that they oppose or support something. 2 COUNT N A **demonstration** of something is a talk in which someone shows you how to do it or how it works. 3 COUNT N OR UNCOUNT N A **demonstration** is also a proof that something exists or is true. *It was an unforgettable demonstration of the power of reason.* 4 COUNT N OR UNCOUNT N **Demonstration** of a quality or feeling is an expression of it. *...spontaneous demonstrations of affection.*

demonstrative /dɪ2mɒnstrətɪv/. ADJ A **demonstrative** person shows affection freely and openly.

demoralize /dɪ1mɒrəlaɪz/, **demoralizes, demoralizing, demoralized;** also spelled **demoralise.** VB WITH OBJ If something **demoralizes** you, it makes you lose confidence and feel depressed. ♦ **demoralized** ADJ *...the stream of desperate and demoralized people seeking work.* ♦ **demoralization** /dɪ1mɒrəlaɪzeɪʃə0n/ UNCOUNT N *...the growing mood of doubt and demoralisation.*

demote /dɪ1məʊt/, **demotes, demoting, demoted.** VB WITH OBJ If someone in authority **demotes** you, they reduce your rank, often as a punishment.

demur /dɪmɜ:/, **demurs, demurring, demurred.** VB If you **demur,** you say that you do not agree with something, or do not want to do it; a formal use. *Morris invited her out for a meal. She demurred.*

demure /dɪ1mjʊə/. ADJ A woman who is **demure** is quiet and rather shy, and behaves very correctly.

den /den/, **dens.** COUNT N The **den** of a fox or wolf is its home.

denial /dɪ2naɪəl/, **denials.** 1 COUNT N OR UNCOUNT N A **denial** of something such as an accusation is a statement that it is not true. *He made a personal denial of all the charges against him... ...the government's policy of denial.* 2 UNCOUNT N If there is **denial** of something that people think they have a right to, they are not allowed to have it. *They protested against the continued denial of civil liberties.*

denigrate /denɪ2greɪt/, **denigrates, denigrating, denigrated.** VB WITH OBJ If you **denigrate** someone or something, you criticize them in order to damage their reputation; a formal use.

denim /denɪm/, **denims.** 1 UNCOUNT N OR MOD **Denim** is a thick cotton cloth used to make clothes. *...denim jeans.* 2 PLURAL N **Denims** are denim trousers.

denomination /dɪ1nɒmɪneɪʃə0n/, **denominations.** COUNT N A **denomination** is a religious group within a particular religion.

denote /dɪ1nəʊt/, **denotes, denoting, denoted** a formal word. 1 VB WITH OBJ If one thing **denotes** another, it is a sign or indication of it. 2 VB WITH OBJ What a word or name **denotes** is what it means or refers to. *'Basic', as its name denotes, is a very straightforward set of computer instructions.*

denounce /dɪ1naʊns/, **denounces, denouncing, denounced.** VB WITH OBJ If you **denounce** someone or something, you criticize them severely and publicly.

dense /dens/, **denser, densest.** 1 ADJ Something that is **dense** contains a lot of things or people in a small area. *...dense forest.* ♦ **densely** ADV *...the most densely populated region in the country.* **2** ADJ **Dense** fog or smoke is thick and difficult to see through. **3** PRED ADJ If you say that someone is **dense,** you mean they are stupid and take a long time to understand things; an informal use.

density /dɛnsi1ti1/, **densities. 1** UNCOUNT N OR COUNT N The **density** of something is the extent to which it fills a place. *Traffic density was increasing.* **2** UNCOUNT N OR COUNT N The **density** of a substance or object is the relation of its mass to its volume; a technical use. *...the density of water.*

dent /dɛnt/, **dents, denting, dented. 1** VB WITH OBJ If you **dent** something, you damage its surface by hitting it and making a hollow in it. *I drove into a post and dented the bumper slightly.* **2** COUNT N A **dent** is a hollow in the surface of something which has been caused by hitting it.

dental /dɛntə0l/. ATTRIB ADJ **Dental** is used to describe things relating to teeth. *...free dental treatment.*

dentist /dɛntɪst/, **dentists.** COUNT N A **dentist** is a person qualified to treat people's teeth.

dentures /dɛntʃəz/. PLURAL N **Dentures** are false teeth.

denunciation /di1nʌnsiɛɪʃən/, **denunciations.** UNCOUNT N OR COUNT N **Denunciation** of someone or something is severe public criticism of them. *...repeating their denunciations of violence... There has been enough denunciation of Government proposals.*

deny /dɪ2naɪ/, **denies, denying, denied. 1** REPORT VB OR VB WITH -ING If you **deny** something such as an accusation, you say that it is not true. *He denied that he was involved... Green denied doing anything illegal.* **2** VB WITH OBJ If you **deny** someone something that they want or have a right to, you do not let them have it. *Freedom is denied to the young.*

deodorant /di:əʊdə0rənt/, **deodorants.** MASS N **Deodorant** is a substance that you put on your body to reduce the smell of perspiration.

depart /di1pɑ:t/, **departs, departing, departed. 1** VB To **depart** from a place means to leave it. *She prepared to depart for Italy.* **2** VB WITH 'from' If you **depart** from the normal way of doing something, you do something slightly different.

departed /di1pɑ:tɪ2d/. ADJ If you talk about **departed** friends or relatives, you mean the ones who have died; a formal use.

department /di1pɑ:tmə2nt/, **departments.** COUNT N WITH SUPP A **department** is one of the sections of a large shop or organization such as a university. *...the cosmetics department of Harrods... ...a Professor in the English department... ...the Department of Health.* ♦ **departmental** /di:pɑ:tmɛntə0l/ ATTRIB ADJ *...a departmental meeting.*

department store, department stores. COUNT N A **department store** is a large shop which sells many different kinds of goods.

departure /di1pɑ:tʃə/, **departures. 1** COUNT N OR UNCOUNT N **Departure** is the act of leaving a place. *...the week before their departure.* **2** COUNT N If an action is a **departure** from what was previously planned or what is usually done, it is different from it. *Does the budget represent a departure from stated Government policy?*

depend /di1pɛnd/, **depends, depending, depended. 1** VB WITH 'on' OR 'upon' If you **depend** on someone or something, you need them to survive. *These factories depend upon natural resources.* **2** VB WITH 'on' OR 'upon' If you can **depend** on someone or something, you know that they will help you when you need them. *I knew I could depend on you.* **3** VB If you say that something **depends** on something else, you mean that it will only happen if the circumstances are right. *The success of the meeting depends largely on whether the chairman is efficient.*

PHRASES ● You use an expression such as **'It depends'** to indicate that you are not sure what will happen or what is the best answer to give. *'What will you do?'—'I don't know. It depends.'* ● You use **depending on** to say that what happens varies according to the circumstances. *This training takes a variable time, depending on the chosen speciality.*

dependable /di1pɛndəbə0l/. ADJ If someone or something is **dependable,** you know that they will always do what you need or expect them to do. *...a dependable sort of car.*

dependant /di1pɛndənt/, **dependants;** also spelled **dependent.** COUNT N Your **dependants** are the people who you support financially, such as your children.

dependence /di1pɛndəns/. UNCOUNT N WITH 'on' OR 'upon' **Dependence** is a constant need for something in order to be able to live or work properly. *...the increasing dependence of police forces on computers.*

dependent /di1pɛndənt/. ADJ If you are **dependent** on someone or something, you need them to survive. *West Europe was still heavily dependent on Middle Eastern oil.*

depict /di1pɪkt/, **depicts, depicting, depicted. 1** VB WITH OBJ If you **depict** someone or something, you draw them in a painting or cartoon. *...an art calendar depicting some ancient legend.* **2** VB WITH OBJ To **depict** someone or something also means to describe them in words. *Women are constantly depicted as inferior to men.*

depiction /di1pɪkʃə0n/, **depictions.** COUNT N OR UNCOUNT N A **depiction** of something is a picture of it or a written description of it. *...depictions of the burial of Christ... ...the media depiction of the Havana summit.*

deplete /di1pli:t/, **depletes, depleting, depleted.** VB WITH OBJ If you **deplete** something, you reduce the amount of it that is available to be used. *We must be careful as we deplete our stocks of resources.* ♦ **depletion** /di1pli:ʃə0n/ UNCOUNT N *...the depletion of raw material reserves.*

deplorable /di1plɔ:rəbə0l/. ADJ If you say that something is **deplorable,** you mean that it is extremely bad or unpleasant; a formal use.

deplore /di1plɔ:/, **deplores, deploring, deplored.** VB WITH OBJ If you **deplore** something, you think that it is wrong or immoral; a formal use.

deploy /di1plɔɪ/, **deploys, deploying, deployed.** VB WITH OBJ To **deploy** troops or resources means to organize or position them so that they can be used effectively. *Oman could deploy regular forces of some 15,000.* ♦ **deployment** /di1plɔɪmə2nt/ UNCOUNT N *...the deployment of nuclear weapons.*

deport /di1pɔ:t/, **deports, deporting, deported.** VB WITH OBJ When a government **deports** foreigners, it sends them out of the country because they have committed a crime or because they are there without official permission. *He was deported to France.* ♦ **deportation** /di:pɔ:teɪʃə0n/ UNCOUNT N OR COUNT N *They were prepared to risk deportation.*

deportment /di1pɔ:tmə2nt/. UNCOUNT N Your **deportment** is the way you behave, especially the way you walk and move; a formal use.

depose /di1pəʊz/, **deposes, deposing, deposed.** VB WITH OBJ If a ruler or leader **is deposed,** they are removed from their position by force.

deposit /di1pɒzɪt/, **deposits, depositing, deposited. 1** VB WITH OBJ If you **deposit** something somewhere, you put it there, often so that it will be safe until it is needed again. *He deposited the case in the left luggage office.* **2** COUNT N A **deposit** is a sum of money which you put in a bank account or other savings account. **3** COUNT N A **deposit** is also money given in part payment for goods or services. *We've saved enough for the deposit on a house.* **4** COUNT N A **deposit** is also a sum of money which you give a person you rent or hire something from. The money is returned to you if you do not damage the goods. **5** VB WITH OBJ If a substance **is deposited** somewhere, it is left there as a result of a chemical or geological process. *Layers of sand were deposited on top of the peat.* **6** COUNT N A **deposit** is an amount of a substance that has been left somewhere as a result of a chemical or geological process. *...rich mineral deposits.*

depot /dɛpəʊ/, **depots. 1** COUNT N A **depot** is a place where goods and vehicles are kept when they are not being used. **2** COUNT N A **depot** is also a bus station or a railway station; an American use.

depraved /di1preɪvd/. ADJ Someone who is **depraved** is morally bad. *Few mothers are depraved enough to kill their children.* ♦ **depravity** /di1prævɪ1ti1/ UNCOUNT N *...a world of depravity and torture.*

deprecating /dɛprəkeɪtɪŋ/. ADJ A **deprecating** gesture or remark shows that you think something is not very good; a formal use. *Tom waved a deprecating hand.*

depreciate /di1pri:ʃieɪt/, **depreciates, depreciating, depreciated.** VB When something **depreciates,** it loses some of its value. *...an investment that was certain to depreciate.* ♦ **depreciation** /di1pri:si1eɪʃə0n/ UNCOUNT N WITH SUPP *...the depreciation of currency.*

depress /di1prɛs/, **depresses, depressing, depressed. 1** VB WITH OBJ If something **depresses** you, it makes you feel sad and disappointed. **2** VB WITH OBJ If something **depresses** prices or wages, it causes them to drop in value.

depressed /di1prɛst/. **1** ADJ If you are **depressed,** you feel sad and disappointed. **2** ADJ A place that is **depressed** does not have as much business or employment as it used to. *...depressed city areas.*

depressing /di1prɛsɪŋ/. ADJ Something that is **depressing** makes you feel sad and disappointed. *This was depressing news.* ♦ **depressingly** SUBMOD *It was all depressingly clear.*

depression /di1prɛʃə0n/, **depressions. 1** UNCOUNT N OR COUNT N **Depression** is a mental state in which someone feels unhappy and has no energy or enthusiasm. **2** COUNT N A **depression** is a time when there is very little economic activity, which results in a lot of unemployment. *...the depression of the 1930's.* **3** COUNT N On a surface, a **depression** is an area which is lower than the rest of the surface.

deprive /di1praɪv/, **deprives, depriving, deprived.** VB WITH OBJ AND 'of' If you **deprive** someone of something, you take it away from them or prevent them from having it. *...to deprive a peasant of his land.* ♦ **deprivation** /dɛprɪ2veɪʃə0n/ UNCOUNT N OR COUNT N *...suffering years of deprivation and poverty.*

deprived /di1praɪvd/. ADJ If you describe someone as **deprived,** you mean they do not have the things that are essential in life.

dept. Dept is a written abbreviation for 'department'.

depth /dɛpθ/, **depths. 1** UNCOUNT N OR COUNT N The **depth** of something such as a river is the distance between its top and bottom surfaces. *None of the lakes was more than a few yards in depth.* **2** UNCOUNT N OR COUNT N The **depth** of a solid structure is the distance between its front and back. *...things buried in the depths of your store cupboard.* **3** UNCOUNT N WITH SUPP The **depth** of an emotion is its great intensity. *The depth of his concern was evident enough.* **4** PLURAL N The **depths** of the ocean are the parts which are a long way below the surface. **5** PLURAL N WITH SUPP If you are in the **depths** of despair, you are extremely unhappy. **6** PLURAL N WITH SUPP In the **depths** of winter means in the middle of winter, when it is coldest.

PHRASES ● If you deal with a subject **in depth,** you deal with it very thoroughly and consider all the aspects of it. ● If you are **out of** your **depth,** you are trying to deal with something that is too difficult for you.

deputation /dɛpjə4teɪʃə0n/, **deputations.** COUNT N A **deputation** is a small group of people sent to speak or act on behalf of others.

deputize /dɛpjə4taɪz/, **deputizes, deputizing, deputized;** also spelled **deputise.** VB If you **deputize** for someone, you do something on their behalf, for example attend a meeting. *The budget was delivered by Mr Lynch, deputizing for Mr Haughey.*

deputy /dɛpjə4ti1/, **deputies.** COUNT N OR MOD A **deputy** is the second most important person in an organization or department. Someone's **deputy** often acts on their behalf when they are not there. *He and his deputy co-operated well... ...the Deputy Chairman of the Commission.*

deranged /di1reɪndʒd/. ADJ Someone who is **deranged** behaves in a wild or strange way, often as a result of mental illness.

derelict /dɛrə1lɪkt/. ADJ A **derelict** building or area of land has not been used for some time and is in a bad condition. *...a derelict tower block.*

deride /di1raɪd/, **derides, deriding, derided.** VB WITH OBJ If you **deride** someone or something, you laugh at them in an unkind way; a formal use. *His sense of superiority makes him deride her opinions.*

derision /di1rɪʒə0n/. UNCOUNT N If you speak of someone or something with **derision,** you show contempt for them. *They speak with derision of amateurs.*

derisive /di1raɪsɪv/. ADJ A **derisive** noise, expression, or remark shows the contempt that you have for someone or something. *Maureen rocked with derisive laughter.* ♦ **derisively** ADV *Desiree snorted derisively.*

derisory /di1raɪzəri/. ADJ Something that is **derisory** is so small or inadequate that it seems silly or not worth considering. *Fines for cruelty to animals are derisory.*

derivation /dɛrə1veɪʃə0n/, **derivations.** COUNT N The **derivation** of a word is the original word or expression that it comes from.

derivative /dɪrɪvətɪv/, **derivatives. 1** COUNT N A **derivative** is something which has developed from something else. *...the modern derivative of the fairy story.* **2** ADJ A work or idea that is **derivative** is not new or original, but copies ideas that have been used before; used showing disapproval.

derive /di1raɪv/, **derives, deriving, derived. 1** VB WITH OBJ If you **derive** a particular feeling from someone or something, you get it from them; a formal use. **2** ERG VB WITH 'from' If something **derives** or is **derived** from another thing, it comes from that thing. *The word 'detergent' is derived from the Latin word for 'cleaner'.*

derogatory /dɪrɒgətə0ri1/. ADJ A **derogatory** remark expresses your low opinion of someone or something.

descend /di1sɛnd/, **descends, descending, descended. 1** VB WITH OR WITHOUT OBJ If you **descend** or if you **descend** something, you move downwards; a formal use. *The valley becomes more exquisite as we* *descend... They descended the stairs.* 2 VB If silence or unhappiness **descends** on people or places, it occurs or starts to affect them; a literary use. *Gloom began to descend on all of them.* 3 VB If people **descend** on a place, they arrive suddenly. *The whole family descended on us without any warning.* 4 VB WITH PREP 'to' If you **descend** to something, you behave in a way that is considered unworthy of you. *All too soon they will descend to spreading scandal and gossip.*

descendant /di[1]sɛndə[2]nt/, **descendants.** COUNT N Someone's **descendants** are the people in later generations who are related to them.

descended /di[1]sɛndɪ[2]d/. PRED ADJ WITH 'from' A person who is **descended** from someone who lived a long time ago is related to them.

descending /di[1]sɛndɪŋ/. ATTRIB ADJ When a group of things is arranged in **descending** order, each thing is smaller or less important than the thing before it.

descent /di[1]sɛnt/, **descents.** 1 COUNT N A **descent** is a movement from a higher to a lower level. *He saw an aircraft making a very steep descent.* 2 UNCOUNT N WITH SUPP Your **descent** is your family's origins. *...Americans of Irish descent.*

describe /dɪ[2]skraɪb/, **describes, describing, described.** REPORT VB When you **describe** a person, thing, or event, you say what they are like or what happened. *His ideas could hardly be described as original... He described how he was kidnapped.*

description /dɪ[2]skrɪpʃə[0]n/, **descriptions.** 1 COUNT N A **description** is an account of what someone or something is like. *...a detailed description of the house.* 2 UNCOUNT N **Description** is the act of saying what someone or something is like. *The relationships in his family are so complex that description is almost impossible.* 3 SING N Something of a particular **description** is something of that kind. *Her dress was too tight to have concealed a weapon of any description.*

descriptive /dɪ[2]skrɪptɪv/. ADJ **Descriptive** writing describes what something is like. *...a descriptive article about Venice.*

desecrate /dɛsɪkreɪt/, **desecrates, desecrating, desecrated.** VB WITH OBJ If someone **desecrates** something considered sacred or special, they deliberately damage it. *The men in Rodez had desecrated the church.* ♦ **desecration** /dɛsəkreɪʃə[0]n/ UNCOUNT N *...the desecration of religious sites.*

desert, deserts, deserting, deserted; pronounced /dɛzət/ when it is a noun and /di[1]zɜːt/ when it is a verb. 1 COUNT N A **desert** is a large area of land where there is very little water or rain and very few plants. *...the Sahara Desert.* 2 VB WITH OBJ If people **desert** a place, they leave it and it becomes empty. ♦ **deserted** ADJ *...a deserted village.* 3 VB WITH OBJ If someone **deserts** you, they leave you and no longer help or support you. *She deserted her family.* ♦ **desertion** UNCOUNT N *She could get a divorce on the grounds of desertion.* 4 VB If someone **deserts** from the armed forces, they leave without permission. ♦ **desertion** /di[1]zɜːʃə[0]n/ UNCOUNT N *...the desertion of young conscripts.* ♦ **deserter** /di[1]zɜːtə/ COUNT N *...a deserter from the British army.*

deserve /di[1]zɜːv/, **deserves, deserving, deserved.** VB WITH OBJ OR TO-INF If you say that someone **deserves** a reward or punishment, you mean that they should be given this reward or punishment because of their qualities or actions. *These people deserve recognition for their talents... He deserves to get the sack.* ♦ **deserved** ADJ *It was a richly deserved honour.*

deservedly /di[1]zɜːvɪ[1]dli[1]/. ADV You use **deservedly** to indicate that something that happened was deserved. *The first prize was won, most deservedly, by Mrs Jones.*

deserving /di[1]zɜːvɪŋ/. ADJ If someone or something is **deserving**, they should be helped; a formal use. *There are hordes of deserving people in this world.*

design /di[1]zaɪn/, **designs, designing, designed.** 1 VB WITH OBJ When you **design** something new, you plan what it should be like. *The house was designed by local builders... Tests have been designed to assess mathematical ability.* 2 UNCOUNT N **Design** is the process of planning the form of a new object. *...graphic and industrial design.* 3 UNCOUNT N The **design** of a manufactured object is its form or the way it has been made. *The awkward design of the handles made it difficult to use.* 4 COUNT N A **design** is a drawing of the proposed form of a new object. *He is submitting a design for the new building.* 5 COUNT N A **design** is also a decorative pattern of lines, flowers, or shapes. 6 PASSIVE VB If something **is designed** for a purpose, it is intended for that purpose. *The laws were designed to protect women.*

designate, designates, designating, designated; pronounced /dɛzɪ[2]gneɪt/ when it is a verb and /dɛzɪ[2]gnət/ when it is an adjective. 1 VB WITH OBJ When you **designate** someone or something, you formally give them a description or name. *The area was designated a national monument.* 2 VB WITH OBJ When you **designate** someone to do a particular job, you formally choose them for that job. *I had been designated to read the lesson.* 3 ADJ AFTER N **Designate** is used to describe someone who has been formally chosen to do a job, but has not yet started doing it. *Mr Bell had been Attorney General designate.*

designation /dɛzɪgneɪʃə[0]n/, **designations.** COUNT N A **designation** is a description or name given to a person or thing; a formal use.

designer /di[1]zaɪnə/, **designers.** COUNT N A **designer** is a person whose job involves planning the form of a new object. *...a dress designer.*

desirable /di[1]zaɪərəbə[0]l/. 1 ADJ Something that is **desirable** is worth having or doing. *After an injury an X-ray is often desirable.* ♦ **desirability** /di[1]zaɪrəbɪlɪ[1]ti[1]/ UNCOUNT N *...the desirability of an official policy.* 2 ADJ Someone who is **desirable** is sexually attractive.

desire /di[1]zaɪə/, **desires, desiring, desired.** 1 VB WITH OBJ OR TO-INF If you **desire** something, you want it. *He passionately desired to continue his career in politics... They desire peace.* ♦ **desired** ADJ *This did not produce the desired effect.* 2 COUNT N A **desire** is a wish to do or have something. *He had not the slightest desire to go on holiday... ...his desire for justice.* 3 VB WITH OBJ If you **desire** someone, you want to have sex with them. 4 UNCOUNT N OR COUNT N **Desire** for someone is a feeling of wanting to have sex with them.

desist /dɪzɪst, -sɪst/, **desists, desisting, desisted.** VB If you **desist** from doing something, you stop doing it; a formal use. *Only then may you desist from your enquiries.*

desk /dɛsk/, **desks.** COUNT N A **desk** is a table, often with drawers, which you sit at in order to write or work.

desolate /dɛsə[7]lət/. 1 ADJ A **desolate** place is empty of people and looks depressing. *...dark and desolate caves.* 2 ADJ If someone is **desolate**, they feel very lonely and depressed.

desolation /dɛsə[7]leɪʃə[0]n/. 1 UNCOUNT N The **desolation** of a place is its depressing emptiness. *...the horror and desolation of the camp.* 2 UNCOUNT N **Desolation** is also a feeling of great unhappiness.

despair /dɪ[2]spɛə/, **despairs, despairing, despaired.** 1 UNCOUNT N **Despair** is a feeling of hopelessness. *I was in despair.* 2 VB If you **despair**, you lose hope. *She despaired at the thought of it.* 3 VB WITH 'of' If you **despair** of something, you feel that there is no hope that it will happen or improve. *She had despaired of completing her thesis.*

despatch /dɪspætʃ/. See **dispatch.**

desperate /dɛspə[0]rə[1]t/. 1 ADJ If you are **desperate**, you are in such a bad or frightening situation that you will try anything to change it. *She killed him in a desperate attempt to free herself.* ♦ **desperation** /dɛspəreɪʃə[0]n/ UNCOUNT N *Sam's desperation grew worse as the day approached.* ♦ **desperately** ADV *He will fight even more desperately if trapped.* 2 PRED ADJ If you are **desperate** for something, you want to have it or do it very much indeed. *I was desperate for the money... She was desperate to find a job.* ♦ **desperately** ADV *I desperately wanted to be on my own.* 3 ADJ A **desperate** situation is very difficult or dangerous.

despicable /dɛspɪkəbə[0]l, dɪspɪk-/. ADJ A **despicable** person or action is extremely nasty.

despise /dɪ[2]spaɪz/, **despises, despising, despised.** VB WITH OBJ If you **despise** someone or something, you have a very low opinion of them. *They despise them for their ignorance.*

despite /dɪ[2]spaɪt/. 1 PREP You use **despite** to introduce a fact which makes the other part of the sentence surprising. *Despite the difference in their ages they were close friends.* 2 PREP If you do something **despite** yourself, you do it although you did not really intend to. *Rose, despite herself, had to admit that she was impressed.*

despondent /dɪ[2]spɒndə[2]nt/. ADJ If you are **despondent**, you are unhappy because you have difficulties that seem hard to overcome. *She felt too despondent to go downstairs.* ♦ **despondently** ADV *Fanny sighed despondently.* ♦ **despondency** /dɪ[2]spɒndə[2]nsi[1]/ UNCOUNT N *He was unable to hide his despondency.*

despot /dɛspɒt/, **despots.** COUNT N A **despot** is a ruler or other person who has a lot of power and uses it unfairly or cruelly; a formal use.

despotic /də[2]spɒtɪk/. ADJ **Despotic** rulers or governments use their power in an unfair or cruel way; a formal use.

dessert /dɪzɜːt/, **desserts.** UNCOUNT N OR COUNT N **Dessert** is something sweet, such as fruit or a pudding, that you eat at the end of a meal.

destination /dɛstɪneɪʃə[0]n/, **destinations.** COUNT N Your **destination** is the place you are going to.

destined /dɛstɪnd/. ADJ If someone or something is **destined** for a particular experience, and it cannot be prevented. *The station was destined for demolition... She felt she was destined to be unhappy for the rest of her life.*

destiny /dɛstɪ[1]ni[1]/, **destinies.** 1 COUNT N WITH SUPP Someone's **destiny** is everything that will happen to them, especially when it is considered to be controlled by someone or something else. 2 UNCOUNT N **Destiny** is the force which some people believe controls the things that happen to you.

destitute /dɛstɪtjuːt/. ADJ Someone who is **destitute** has no money or possessions; a formal use. *...destitute immigrants.* ♦ **destitution** /dɛstɪtjuːʃə[0]n/ UNCOUNT N *The peasantry hovered on the brink of destitution.*

destroy /dɪ[2]strɔɪ/, **destroys, destroying, destroyed.** VB WITH OBJ To **destroy** something means to damage it so much that it is completely ruined or ceases to exist. *Several buildings were destroyed by the bomb... They want to destroy the State.*

destroyer /dɪ[2]strɔɪə/, **destroyers.** COUNT N A **destroyer** is a small warship with a lot of guns.

destruction /dɪ[2]strʌkʃə[0]n/. UNCOUNT N **Destruction** is the act of destroying something. *It will cause pollution and the destruction of our seas and rivers.*

destructive /dɪ[2]strʌktɪv/. ADJ Something that is **destructive** causes great damage or distress. *Jealousy is destructive and undesirable.* ♦ **destructiveness** UNCOUNT N *...the destructiveness of the problem child.*

desultory /dɛsəltə[0]rɪ/. ADJ A **desultory** action is done without enthusiasm and in a disorganized way; a formal use. *There were some desultory attempts to defend him.*

detach /di[1]tætʃ/, **detaches, detaching, detached.** VB WITH OBJ If you **detach** something from the thing that it is fixed to, you remove it. *The handle of the saucepan can be detached.*

detachable /di[1]tætʃəbə[0]l/. ADJ Something that is **detachable** is made so that it can be removed from a larger object. *...detachable collars.*

detached /di[1]tætʃt/. 1 ADJ A **detached** house is not joined to any other house. 2 ADJ If you are **detached** about something, you are not personally involved in it. *...the detached view that writers must take.*

detachment /di[1]tætʃmə[2]nt/. UNCOUNT N **Detachment** is the feeling of not being personally involved in something.

detail /diːteɪl/, **details, detailing, detailed.** 1 COUNT N A **detail** is an individual feature or element of something. *I can still remember every single detail of that night... He described it down to the smallest detail.* 2 UNCOUNT N **Detail** consists of small features which are often not noticed. *Attention to detail is vital in this job.* 3 PLURAL N **Details** about someone or something are items of information about them. *You can get details of nursery schools from the local authority.* 4 VB WITH OBJ If you **detail** things, you list them or give full information about them; a formal use.

detailed /diːteɪld/. ADJ Something that is **detailed** contains a lot of details. *They gave a detailed account of what they had seen.*

detain /di[1]teɪn/, **detains, detaining, detained.** 1 VB WITH OBJ When people such as the police **detain** someone, they keep them in a place under their control. *We shall be obliged to detain you here while we continue the investigation.* 2 VB WITH OBJ To **detain** someone also means to delay them, for example by talking to them.

detect /di[1]tɛkt/, **detects, detecting, detected.** VB WITH OBJ If you **detect** something, you notice it or find it. *These animals seem able to detect a shower of rain falling five miles away... The submarines had to be detected and destroyed.* ♦ **detection** /di[1]tɛkʃə[0]n/ UNCOUNT N *The main detection device is sonar.*

detective /di[1]tɛktɪv/, **detectives.** COUNT N A **detective** is someone, usually a police officer, whose job is to discover the facts about a crime or other situation.

detector /di[1]tɛktə/, **detectors.** COUNT N A **detector** is an instrument which is used to find or measure something. *...a metal detector.*

detente /deɪtɒnt/; also spelled **détente.** UNCOUNT N **Detente** is a state of friendly relations between two countries when previously there had been problems between them; a formal use.

detention /di[1]tɛnʃə[0]n/. UNCOUNT N **Detention** is the arrest or imprisonment of someone.

deter /di[1]tɜː/, **deters, deterring, deterred.** VB WITH OBJ To **deter** someone from doing something means to make them unwilling to do it. *Such discrimination may deter more women from seeking work.*

detergent /di[1]tɜːdʒə[2]nt/, **detergents.** MASS N **Detergent** is a chemical used for washing things such as clothes or dishes.

deteriorate /di[1]tɪərɪəreɪt/, **deteriorates, deteriorating, deteriorated.** VB If something **deteriorates**, it becomes worse. *His sight had begun to deteriorate...*

The weather had deteriorated. ♦ **deterioration** /di^{1}tɪərɪəreɪʃə^{0}n/ UNCOUNT N *She had suffered progressive deterioration of health.*

determination /di^{1}tɜːmɪneɪʃə^{0}n/. UNCOUNT N **Determination** is great firmness about doing what you have decided to do. *Seeing my determination to leave, she demanded her money.*

determine /di^{1}tɜːmɪn/, **determines, determining, determined;** a formal word. **1** VB WITH OBJ If something **determines** what will happen, it controls it. *Economic factors determine the progress which a society can make.* **2** REPORT VB To **determine** the truth about something means to discover it. *It was in the public interest to determine exactly what happened.* **3** REPORT VB If you **determine** something, you decide it or settle it. *The date of the match is yet to be determined... ...to determine how their money should be spent.*

determined /di^{1}tɜːmɪnd/. ADJ If you are **determined** to do something, you have made a firm decision to do it and will not let anything stop you. *He is determined to win in the end.* ♦ **determinedly** ADV *She determinedly kept the conversation going.*

determiner /di^{1}tɜːmɪnə/, **determiners.** COUNT N In grammar, a **determiner** is a word that is used before a noun to indicate which particular thing or person you are referring to. 'The', 'my', and 'every' are determiners.

deterrence /di^{1}tɛrəns/. UNCOUNT N **Deterrence** is the prevention of war by having weapons that are so powerful that people will not dare to attack you. *They believe that NATO's policy of deterrence is justified.*

deterrent /di^{1}tɛrənt/, **deterrents. 1** COUNT N A **deterrent** is something that makes people afraid to do something. *Severe punishment is the only true deterrent.* Also ATTRIB ADJ *...the deterrent effect of nuclear weapons.* **2** COUNT N A **deterrent** is also a weapon that is intended to make enemies afraid to attack. *...the nuclear deterrent.*

detest /di^{1}tɛst/, **detests, detesting, detested.** VB WITH OBJ If you **detest** someone or something, you dislike them very much.

detestable /di^{1}tɛstəbə^{0}l/. ADJ If you say that someone or something is **detestable,** you mean that you dislike them very strongly.

detonate /dɛtə^{7}neɪt/, **detonates, detonating, detonated.** ERG VB If you **detonate** a bomb, it explodes. ♦ **detonation** /dɛtə^{7}neɪʃə^{0}n/ UNCOUNT N *...the possible detonation of a nuclear weapon.*

detour /diːtʊə/, **detours.** COUNT N If you make a **detour** on a journey, you do not go straight to your destination, but visit another place on the way.

detract /di^{1}trækt/, **detracts, detracting, detracted.** VB WITH 'from' If something **detracts** from something else, it makes the other thing seem less good or impressive. *This fact did not detract from her sense of achievement.*

detriment /dɛtrə^{1}mə^{2}nt/. PHRASE If something happens **to** your **detriment,** it harms you; a formal use. *This discovery has been exploited to the detriment of the poor peasants.*

detrimental /dɛtrɪmɛntə^{0}l/. ADJ Something that is **detrimental** has harmful or damaging effects; a formal use. *...actions which may be detrimental to the company.*

devalue /diːvæljuː/, **devalues, devaluing, devalued. 1** VB WITH OBJ If you **devalue** something, you cause it to be thought less important and worthy of respect. *Scientific expertise has been devalued.* **2** VB WITH OBJ To **devalue** the currency of a country means to reduce its value in relation to other currencies. *The President has devalued the dollar.* ♦ **devaluation** /diːvæljuːeɪʃə^{0}n/ UNCOUNT N *...the devaluation of sterling in November 1967.*

devastate /dɛvəsteɪt/, **devastates, devastating, devastated.** VB WITH OBJ If something **devastates** a place, it damages it very badly. *A hurricane had devastated the plantation.* ♦ **devastation** /dɛvəsteɪʃə^{0}n/ UNCOUNT N *...the threat of nuclear devastation.*

devastated /dɛvəsteɪtɪ^{2}d/. PRED ADJ If you are **devastated** by something, you are very shocked and upset.

devastating /dɛvəsteɪtɪŋ/. **1** ADJ Something that is **devastating** severely damages something. *...devastating bombing raids.* **2** ADJ If you find something **devastating,** it makes you feel very shocked and upset. *It was a devastating announcement.*

develop /dɪvɛləp/, **develops, developing, developed. 1** ERG VB When something **develops,** it grows or changes over a period of time into a better, more advanced, or more complete form. *The bud develops into a flower... Her friendship with Harold developed slowly... We had hopes of developing tourism on a big scale.* ♦ **developing** ATTRIB ADJ *...supplying developing countries with new technology.* **2** VB WITH OBJ To **develop** an area of land means to build houses or factories on it. **3** VB WITH OBJ If someone **develops** a new machine, they produce it by improving the original design. **4** VB WITH OBJ To **develop** a characteristic, illness, or fault means to begin to have it. *She developed an enormous appetite.* **5** VB WITH OBJ When a photographic film **is developed,** prints or negatives are made from it.

developer /dɪvɛlə^{7}pə/, **developers. 1** COUNT N A **developer** is a person or a company that buys land in order to build new houses or factories on it. **2** COUNT N WITH SUPP If a child is an early **developer** or a late **developer,** he or she develops physically or mentally earlier or later than others of the same age.

development /dɪvɛlə^{7}pmə^{2}nt/, **developments. 1** UNCOUNT N WITH SUPP **Development** is the gradual growth or formation of something. *...a child's psychological development... ...rapid economic development.* **2** UNCOUNT N OR COUNT N **Development** is also the process or result of improving a basic design. *...research and development... ...developments in aircraft engines.* **3** UNCOUNT N WITH SUPP **Development** is also the process of making an area of land or water more useful or profitable. *...Japanese ventures for the development of Siberia.* **4** COUNT N A **development** is an event which is likely to have an effect on a situation. *Recent developments in Latin America suggest that the situation may be improving.* **5** COUNT N A **development** is also an estate of houses or other buildings which have been built by property developers.

deviant /diːvɪənt/, **deviants.** COUNT N A **deviant** is someone whose behaviour or beliefs are not considered acceptable by most people. *...social deviants.* Also ADJ *To light a cigarette in company is becoming a deviant act.*

deviate /diːvɪeɪt/, **deviates, deviating, deviated.** VB To **deviate** from a way of thinking or behaving means to think or behave differently. *He has not deviated from his view that war can never be justified.* ♦ **deviation** /diːvɪeɪʃə^{0}n/ UNCOUNT N OR COUNT N *There was to be no deviation from the ruling ideology.*

device /di^{1}vaɪs/, **devices. 1** COUNT N A **device** is an object that has been made or built for a particular purpose, for example for recording or measuring something. *...a device for processing information.* **2** COUNT N A **device** is also a method of achieving something. *They used television advertising as a device for stimulating demand.* **3** PHRASE If you **leave** someone **to their own devices,** you leave them alone to do as they wish.

devil /dɛvə^{0}l/, **devils. 1** PROPER N In Christianity, the **Devil** is the most powerful evil spirit. **2** COUNT N A **devil** is any evil spirit. **3** COUNT N WITH SUPP You can also use **devil** when showing your opinion of someone. For example, you can call someone a silly **devil** or a lucky **devil;** an informal use.

devilish /dɛvə^{0}lɪʃ/. ADJ A **devilish** idea or action is cruel or wicked.

devious /diːvɪəs/. **1** ADJ A **devious** person is dishonest and does things in a secretive, often complicated way. *...consultants who are prepared to use devious means to justify their actions.* **2** ADJ A **devious** route or path to a place involves many changes in direction.

devise /di^{1}vaɪz/, **devises, devising, devised.** VB WITH OBJ If you **devise** a plan, system, or machine, you work it out or design it. *It has been necessary to devise a system of universal schooling.*

devoid /di^{1}vɔɪd/. PRED ADJ If someone or something is **devoid** of a quality, they have none of it at all; a formal use. *...people who are completely devoid of humour.*

devolution /diːvə^{7}luːʃə^{0}n/. UNCOUNT N **Devolution** is the transfer of authority or power from a central organization or government to smaller organizations or local governments.

devolve /di^{1}vɒlv/, **devolves, devolving, devolved.** ERG VB If a responsibility **devolves** or **is devolved** upon a person or group, it is transferred to them from people with greater authority; a formal use. *The necessity for making decisions devolves upon him.*

devote /di^{1}vəʊt/, **devotes, devoting, devoted.** REFL VB OR VB WITH OBJ If you **devote** yourself, your time, or your energy to something, you spend a lot of your time or energy on it. *He devoted himself to his studies... They have devoted all their time to helping the sick.*

devoted /di^{1}vəʊtɪ^{2}d/. ADJ If you are **devoted** to someone or something, you love them very much. *He's devoted to his mother.*

devotee /dɛvə^{6}tiː/, **devotees.** COUNT N A **devotee** of a subject or activity is someone who is very enthusiastic about it. *The building has an enormous appeal for devotees of history.*

devotion /di^{1}vəʊʃə^{0}n/. UNCOUNT N **Devotion** is great love for a person or thing. *...their devotion to their children... ...total devotion to the cause.*

devour /di^{1}vaʊə/, **devours, devouring, devoured.** VB WITH OBJ To **devour** something means to eat it; a literary use. *We came upon a black snake devouring a large frog.*

devout /di^{1}vaʊt/. ADJ Someone who is **devout** has deep religious beliefs. *...a devout Catholic.*

dew /djuː/. UNCOUNT N **Dew** is small drops of water that form on the ground during the night.

dexterous /dɛkstrəs/; also spelled **dextrous.** ADJ Someone who is **dexterous** is very skilful with their hands; a formal use. *He was a born cook. He was dexterous and quick.* ♦ **dexterity** /dɛkstɛrɪ^{1}ti^1/ UNCOUNT N *...weaving in and out with great dexterity.*

diabetes /daɪəbiːtɪs, -tiːz/. UNCOUNT N **Diabetes** is a condition in which someone's body is unable to control the level of sugar in their blood.

diabetic /daɪəbɛtɪk/, **diabetics.** COUNT N A **diabetic** is a person who suffers from diabetes. Also ATTRIB ADJ *...in a diabetic coma.*

diabolical /daɪəbɒlɪkə^{0}l/. ADJ **Diabolical** means very bad; an informal use. *It gave men the pretext for all sorts of diabolical behaviour.*

diagnose /daɪəgnəʊz/, **diagnoses, diagnosing, diagnosed.** VB WITH OBJ When a doctor **diagnoses** an illness that someone has, he or she identifies what is wrong. *The doctor has diagnosed it as rheumatism.*

diagnosis /daɪəgnəʊsɪs/, **diagnoses** /daɪəgnəʊsiːz/. UNCOUNT N OR COUNT N **Diagnosis** is identifying what is wrong with someone who is ill. *...instant diagnosis... Joan's fever led to a diagnosis of pneumonia.*

diagnostic /daɪəgnɒstɪk/. ADJ **Diagnostic** devices or methods are used for discovering what is wrong with people who are ill.

diagonal /daɪægənə^{0}l/. ADJ A **diagonal** line goes between opposite corners. ♦ **diagonally** ADV *We drove diagonally across the airfield.*

diagram /daɪəgræm/, **diagrams.** COUNT N A **diagram** is a drawing which is used to explain something. *...a simple diagram showing compass directions.*

dial /daɪl/, **dials, dialling, dialled;** spelled **dialing** and **dialed** in American English. **1** COUNT N The **dial** of a clock or meter is the part where the time or a measurement is indicated. *The figures on the dial can be seen.* **2** COUNT N On a radio, the **dial** is the controlling part which you move in order to change the frequency. **3** COUNT N The **dial** on some telephones is a circle with holes in it which you turn several times in order to phone someone. **4** VB WITH OR WITHOUT OBJ If you **dial** a number, you move the circle or press the buttons on a telephone in order to phone someone. *He dialled five times with no response.*

dialect /daɪəlɛkt/, **dialects.** COUNT N OR UNCOUNT N A **dialect** is a form of a language spoken in a particular area. *...old ballads written in northern dialect.*

dialogue /daɪəlɒg/, **dialogues;** spelled **dialog** in American English. **1** UNCOUNT N OR COUNT N **Dialogue** is communication or discussion between groups. *The union continued to seek dialogue with the authorities... ...the dialogue between rich nations and poor.* **2** COUNT N OR UNCOUNT N A **dialogue** is a conversation. *...500 words of movie dialogue... Their dialogue was interrupted by Philip's voice.*

diameter /daɪæmə^{1}tə/, **diameters.** COUNT N The **diameter** of a circle or sphere is the length of a straight line through the middle of it. *...a giant planet over 30,000 miles in diameter.*

diametrically /daɪəmɛtrɪkli^1/. PHRASE If two things are **diametrically opposed** or **diametrically opposite,** they are completely different from each other. *The two systems are diametrically opposed.*

diamond /daɪəmənd/, **diamonds. 1** COUNT N A **diamond** is a hard, bright precious stone. *...diamond brooches.* **2** COUNT N A **diamond** is also a shape with four straight sides of equal length which are not at right angles to each other. **3** UNCOUNT N **Diamonds** is one of the four suits in a pack of playing cards.

diaper /daɪəpə/, **diapers.** COUNT N A **diaper** is a nappy; an American use.

diaphragm /daɪəfræm/, **diaphragms. 1** COUNT N Your **diaphragm** is a muscle between your lungs and your stomach. **2** COUNT N A **diaphragm** is a small, round contraceptive device that a woman places inside her vagina.

diarrhoea /daɪərɪə/; also spelled **diarrhea.** UNCOUNT N When someone has **diarrhoea,** a lot of liquid faeces comes out of their body because of an illness.

diary /daɪəri^1/, **diaries.** COUNT N A **diary** is a book which has a separate space for each day of the year. You use a diary to write down things you plan to do, or to record what happens in your life.

dice /daɪs/, **dices, dicing, diced. Dice** is the singular and plural of the noun. **1** COUNT N A **dice** is a small cube with one to six spots on each face. You throw dice in games to decide, for example, how many moves you can make. *They roll dice to see who will go first.* **2** VB

WITH OBJ When you **dice** food, you cut it into small cubes. *Peel and finely dice the onion.* ♦ **diced** ADJ *...diced potatoes.*

dichotomy /daɪkɒtə^{7}mi^{1}/, **dichotomies.** COUNT N If there is a very great difference between two things, you can say that there is a **dichotomy** between them; a formal use. *The clearest dichotomy is between the winners and the losers.*

dictate, dictates, dictating, dictated; pronounced /dɪkteɪt/ when it is a verb and /dɪkteɪt/ when it is a noun. 1 VB WITH OR WITHOUT OBJ If you **dictate** something, you say it aloud for someone else to write down. *It took him a long time to dictate this letter... Walk about as you dictate.* 2 VB WITH PREP 'to', OR REPORT VB If you **dictate** to someone, you tell them what they must do. *The unions are hardly in a position to dictate to the Labour party... Landlords can dictate their own conditions... The law dictated that his right hand be cut off.* 3 COUNT N A **dictate** is an order which you have to obey; a formal use. *They obeyed the union's dictates and went on strike.*

dictation /dɪkteɪʃə^{0}n/, **dictations.** 1 UNCOUNT N **Dictation** is the speaking aloud of words for someone else to write down. *Jill took down a story from Frank's dictation.* 2 COUNT N OR UNCOUNT N A **dictation** is a test of your knowledge of a foreign language, in which you write down a text that is read aloud to you.

dictator /dɪkteɪtə/, **dictators.** COUNT N A **dictator** is a ruler who has complete power in a country; used showing disapproval.

dictatorial /dɪktətɔːrɪəl/. ADJ **Dictatorial** people use their power too forcefully. *...dictatorial regimes... ...their dictatorial attitude.*

dictatorship /dɪkteɪtə^{8}ʃɪp/, **dictatorships.** 1 UNCOUNT N **Dictatorship** is government by a dictator. *Democracy soon gave way to dictatorship.* 2 COUNT N A **dictatorship** is a country ruled by a dictator.

diction /dɪkʃə^{0}n/. UNCOUNT N Someone's **diction** is how clearly they speak or sing.

dictionary /dɪkʃənə^{0}rɪ/, **dictionaries.** COUNT N A **dictionary** is a book which lists the words of a language in alphabetical order and gives their meanings or corresponding words of another language. *...an English-French dictionary.*

did /dɪd/. **Did** is the past tense of **do.**

didactic /dɪ^{5}dæktɪk/. ADJ Something that is **didactic** is intended to teach people a moral lesson; a formal use.

didn't /dɪdə^{0}nt/. **Didn't** is the usual spoken form of 'did not'.

die /daɪ/, **dies, dying, died.** 1 VB When people, animals, and plants **die,** they stop living. *He died of a heart attack.* ● If someone **dies** a violent or unnatural **death,** they die in a violent or unnatural way. *I don't believe Davis died a natural death.* 2 VB When something **dies, dies** away, or **dies** down, it becomes less intense and disappears; a literary use. *True love never dies... Now that the cheers had died away, it seemed oddly quiet... The wind has died down.* 3 See also **dying.**
PHRASES ● If you are **dying for** something or **dying to** do something, you want very much to have it or to do it; an informal use. *I'm dying for a drink... They were all dying to go to Paris.* ● If an idea or custom **dies hard,** it changes or disappears very slowly. *Colonial traditions die hard.*

die out. PHR VB If something **dies out,** it becomes less and less common and eventually disappears. *Many species died out.*

diesel /diːzə^{0}l/, **diesels.** 1 COUNT N A **diesel** is a vehicle which has an engine in which a mixture of air and heavy oil is made to burn by pressure rather than by an electric spark. 2 UNCOUNT N **Diesel** or **diesel oil** is the heavy oil used in a diesel engine.

diet /daɪət/, **diets, dieting, dieted.** 1 COUNT N OR UNCOUNT N Someone's **diet** is the kind of food they eat. *Her diet consisted of bread and lentils.* 2 COUNT N If you are on a **diet,** you are eating special kinds of food because you want to lose weight. *...people who aren't able to stick to a diet.* Also ATTRIB ADJ *...diet drinks.* 3 VB If you **are dieting,** you are on a diet.

dietary /daɪətə^{0}rɪ/. ATTRIB ADJ **Dietary** means relating to the kind of food people eat. *We are working on changing dietary habits.*

differ /dɪfə/, **differs, differing, differed.** 1 RECIP VB If one thing **differs** from another or if they **differ,** they are unlike each other in some way. *Modern cars differ from the early ones in many ways.* 2 VB If people **differ** about something, they disagree with each other about it. *We differ about moral standards.*

difference /dɪfə^{0}rəns/, **differences.** 1 COUNT N OR UNCOUNT N The **difference** between things is the way in which they are different from each other. *There is an essential difference between computers and humans... Look at their difference in size.* 2 SING N The **difference** between two amounts is the amount by which one is less than the other. 3 COUNT N If people have their **differences,** they disagree about things. 4 PHRASE If you say that something **makes a difference,** you mean that it changes a situation. *It makes no difference whether he is a citizen or not.*

different /dɪfə^{0}rənt/. 1 ADJ If one thing is **different** from another, it is unlike the other thing in some way. *The meeting was different from any that had gone before... His message is very different to theirs.* ♦ **differently** ADV *...people who feel very differently about things.* 2 ATTRIB ADJ When you refer to two or more **different** things of a particular kind, you mean two or more separate things of that kind. *I visited 21 different schools.*

differentiate /dɪfərɛnʃɪeɪt/, **differentiates, differentiating, differentiated.** 1 VB WITH 'between' If you **differentiate** between things, you recognize or show the difference between them. *How can you differentiate between moral and religious questions?* 2 VB WITH OBJ If a feature **differentiates** one thing from another, it makes the two things different. *What differentiates a sculpture from an object?* ♦ **differentiation** /dɪfərɛnʃɪeɪʃə^{0}n/ UNCOUNT N *...the differentiation of classes.*

difficult /dɪfɪkə^{0}lt/. 1 ADJ Something that is **difficult** is not easy to do, understand, or solve. *That's a very difficult question... Why is it so difficult for the rich to help the poor?* 2 ADJ Someone who is **difficult** behaves in an unreasonable and unhelpful way.

difficulty /dɪfɪkə^{0}ltɪ^{1}/, **difficulties.** 1 COUNT N A **difficulty** is a problem. *There are lots of difficulties that have to be overcome.* 2 UNCOUNT N If you have **difficulty** doing something, you are not able to do it easily. *I was having difficulty breathing... She spoke with difficulty.* 3 PHRASE If you are **in difficulty** or **in difficulties,** you are having a lot of problems. *He went to the aid of a swimmer in difficulty.*

diffident /dɪfɪdə^{2}nt/. ADJ Someone who is **diffident** is nervous and lacks confidence. *...a rather diffident, uncommunicative man.* ♦ **diffidently** ADV *He approached the desk diffidently.* ♦ **diffidence** /dɪfɪdə^{2}ns/ UNCOUNT N *She walked up with some diffidence.*

diffuse, diffuses, diffusing, diffused; a formal word, pronounced /dɪfjuːz/ when it is a verb and /dɪfjuːs/ when it is an adjective. 1 ERG VB If light or knowledge **diffuses** or **is diffused,** it spreads. *The light was diffused by leaves... The sun diffuses through the trees.* ♦ **diffusion** /dɪ^{1}fjuːʒə^{0}n/ UNCOUNT N *...the diffusion of scientific knowledge.* 2 ADJ Something that is **diffuse** is spread over a large area rather than concentrated in one place. *...a broad, diffuse organization... ...a faint and diffuse glow of light.*

dig /dɪg/, **digs, digging, dug** /dʌg/. 1 VB WITH OR WITHOUT OBJ If you **dig,** you push a spade into the ground, to break up the earth or to make a hole. *I was digging my garden... He dug a little hole in the ground.* 2 ERG VB WITH ADJUNCT If you **dig** one thing into another, you press the first thing hard into the second. *She dug her needle into her sewing.* 3 COUNT N A **dig** is a remark which is intended to hurt or embarrass someone. *Whenever she can, she takes a dig at me.*

dig out. PHR VB If you **dig** something **out,** you find it after it has been hidden or stored for a long time. *We dug out our tour books and maps for the holiday.*

dig up. PHR VB If you **dig up** information that is not widely known, you discover it. *Journalists have dug up some hair-raising facts about the company.*

digest /dɪ^{5}dʒɛst/, **digests, digesting, digested.** VB WITH OBJ When you **digest** food, your stomach removes the substances that your body needs and gets rid of the rest. ♦ **digestion** /dɪ^{5}dʒɛstʃə^{0}n/ UNCOUNT N *A good walk aids digestion.*

digestive /dɪ^{5}dʒɛstɪv/. ATTRIB ADJ **Digestive** refers to the digestion of food. *...the digestive system.*

digit /dɪdʒɪt/, **digits.** COUNT N A **digit** is a written symbol for any of the ten numbers from 0 to 9. *...a two digit number.*

digital /dɪdʒə^{1}tə^{0}l/. ATTRIB ADJ **Digital** watches or clocks show the time by displaying numbers rather than by using hands on a traditional clock face.

dignified /dɪgnɪfaɪd/. ADJ **Dignified** means calm, impressive, and worthy of respect. *She was tall, handsome, very dignified... ...a dignified letter.*

dignitary /dɪgnɪtə^{0}rɪ^{1}/, **dignitaries.** COUNT N A **dignitary** is someone who has a high rank in government or in the Church.

dignity /dɪgnɪtɪ^{1}/. 1 UNCOUNT N If someone has **dignity,** their behaviour or appearance is serious, calm, and controlled. 2 UNCOUNT N **Dignity** is also the quality of being worthy of respect. *Don't discount the importance of human dignity.*

digress /daɪgrɛs/, **digresses, digressing, digressed.** VB If you **digress,** you stop talking about your main subject and talk about something different for a while; a formal use. *I will digress slightly at this stage.* ♦ **digression** /daɪgrɛʃə^{0}n/ COUNT N *This long digression has led me away from my main story.*

dike /daɪk/. See **dyke.**

dilapidated /dɪ^{1}læpɪdeɪtɪ^{2}d/. ADJ A building that is **dilapidated** is old and in bad condition.

dilate /dɪ^{5}leɪt/, **dilates, dilating, dilated.** ERG VB When the pupils of your eyes **dilate,** they become bigger.

dilemma /dɪ^{5}lɛmə/, **dilemmas.** COUNT N A **dilemma** is a difficult situation in which you have to choose between two or more alternatives. *It put me in a difficult moral dilemma.*

diligent /dɪlɪ^{2}dʒə^{2}nt/. ADJ Someone who is **diligent** works hard and carefully. *...diligent research.* ♦ **diligently** ADV *He read the Bible diligently.* ♦ **diligence** /dɪlɪ^{2}dʒə^{2}ns/ UNCOUNT N *I had been hoping to impress my new boss with my diligence.*

dilute /daɪlj^{0}uːt/, **dilutes, diluting, diluted.** VB WITH OBJ When you **dilute** a liquid, you add water or another liquid to it in order to make it weaker.

dim /dɪm/, **dimmer, dimmest; dims, dimming, dimmed.** 1 ADJ A **dim** place is rather dark because there is not much light in it. *...a dim hallway.* ♦ **dimly** ADV *...the dimly lit department store.* 2 ADJ Something that is **dim** is not very easy to see. *Bernard peered at the dim figure by the bus-stop.* 3 ADJ If your memory of something is **dim,** you can hardly remember it at all. *I only have a dim recollection of the production.* 4 ADJ Someone who is **dim** is stupid; an informal use. 5 ERG VB If a light **dims** or if you **dim** it, it becomes less bright. *Then the lights dimmed and the movie began.*

dimension /dɪ^{5}mɛnʃə^{0}n/, **dimensions.** 1 COUNT N A **dimension** of a situation is a fact or event that affects it. *Most of us were Catholic, and this added an extra dimension to the tension.* 2 PLURAL N You can refer to the measurements of something as its **dimensions.** *...the dimensions of a standard brick.*

diminish /dɪmɪnɪʃ/, **diminishes, diminishing, diminished.** ERG VB When something **diminishes** or is **diminished,** its size, importance, or intensity in reduced; a formal use. *As she turned the knob, the sound diminished... ...the diminishing importance of universities.*

diminutive /dɪmɪnjuːtɪv/. ADJ **Diminutive** means very small indeed; a formal use. *...Mrs Bradley, a diminutive figure in black.*

dimple /dɪmpə^{0}l/, **dimples.** COUNT N A **dimple** is a small hollow in someone's cheek or chin, often one that you can see when they smile.

dimpled /dɪmpə^{0}ld/. ADJ Something that is **dimpled** has small hollows in it. *...the child's dimpled cheeks.*

din /dɪn/. SING N A **din** is a very loud and unpleasant noise. *They were unable to sleep because of the din coming from the bar.*

dine /daɪn/, **dines, dining, dined.** VB When you **dine,** you have dinner; a formal use. *They dined at a Hungarian restaurant.*

diner /daɪnə/, **diners.** 1 COUNT N A **diner** in a restaurant is someone who is having a meal there. 2 COUNT N A **diner** is also a small, cheap restaurant; an American use.

dinghy /dɪŋɪ^{1}/, **dinghies.** COUNT N A **dinghy** is a small boat that you sail or row.

dingy /dɪndʒɪ^{1}/. ADJ A **dingy** place or thing is dirty or rather dark. *...a dingy suburb of north-east Paris.*

dining room, dining rooms. COUNT N The **dining room** is the room in a house or hotel where people have their meals.

dinner /dɪnə/, **dinners.** 1 UNCOUNT N OR COUNT N **Dinner** is the main meal of the day. 2 COUNT N A **dinner** is a formal social event in the evening at which a meal is served. *Mrs Thatcher attended a dinner at the Mansion House last night.*

dinner jacket, dinner jackets. COUNT N A **dinner jacket** is a black jacket that a man wears with a bow tie at formal social events.

dinner party, dinner parties. COUNT N A **dinner party** is a social event where a small group of people are invited to have dinner and spend the evening at someone's house.

dinosaur /daɪnəsɔː/, **dinosaurs.** COUNT N **Dinosaurs** were large reptiles which lived in prehistoric times.

diocese /daɪə^{7}sɪs/, **dioceses.** COUNT N A **diocese** is the area over which a bishop has control.

dip /dɪp/, **dips, dipping, dipped.** 1 VB WITH OBJ If you **dip** something into a liquid, you put it in and then quickly take it out again. *He dipped his pen in the ink.* 2 VB If something **dips,** it makes a downward movement. *The plane's nose dipped.* 3 COUNT N A **dip** in a surface is a place that is lower than the rest of the surface. *...a small dip in the ground.* 4 COUNT N OR UNCOUNT N A **dip** is a thick creamy mixture which you eat by scooping it up with raw vegetables or biscuits. *...tasty cheese dips.*

diploma /dɪpləʊmə/, **diplomas.** COUNT N A **diploma** is a qualification lower than a degree which is awarded by a university or college. *...a diploma in theology.*

diplomacy /dɪpləʊməsi[1]/. 1 UNCOUNT N **Diplomacy** is the management of relations between countries. *...high-level diplomacy.* 2 UNCOUNT N **Diplomacy** is also the skill of saying or doing things without offending people.

diplomat /dɪplə[6]mæt/, **diplomats.** COUNT N A **diplomat** is a government official, usually in an embassy, who negotiates with another country on behalf of his or her own country.

diplomatic /dɪplə[6]mætɪk/. 1 ATTRIB ADJ **Diplomatic** means relating to diplomacy and diplomats. *...its diplomatic links with Britain.* 2 ADJ Someone who is **diplomatic** is able to be tactful and say or do things without offending people.

dire /daɪə/. ADJ Something that is **dire** is very bad. *...the dire consequences of his actions.*

direct /dɪ[5]rɛkt/, **directs, directing, directed.** 1 ADJ OR ADV **Direct** means going or aimed straight towards a place or object. *Are there any direct flights to Athens?... Why hadn't he gone direct to the lounge?* 2 ATTRIB ADJ OR ADV **Direct** actions are done openly or without involving anyone else. *...the direct intervention of the managing director... This move is a direct challenge to the government.* ♦ **directness** UNCOUNT N *Such directness embarrassed Ian.* 3 VB WITH OBJ AND ADJUNCT Something that **is directed** at a particular person or thing is aimed at them or is intended to affect them. *...a question that John had evidently directed at me... This is a fundamental question to which we should all be directing our attention.* 4 VB WITH OBJ If you **direct** someone somewhere, you tell them how to get there; a formal use. *Can you direct me to the cemetery?* 5 VB WITH OBJ If someone **directs** a project or a group of people, they organize it and are in charge of it. *No one seemed to be directing the operation.* 6 VB WITH OR WITHOUT OBJ If someone **directs** a film, play, or television programme, they decide how it should be made and performed.

direction /dɪ[5]rɛkʃə[0]n/, **directions.** 1 COUNT N A **direction** is the general line that someone or something is moving or pointing in. *We ended up going in the opposite direction from them.* 2 PLURAL N **Directions** are instructions that tell you what to do or how to get to a place. *Follow the directions that your doctor gives you... I asked a policeman for directions to the hospital.* 3 PHRASE If you do something **under** someone else's **direction,** they tell you what to do.

directive /dɪ[5]rɛktɪv/, **directives.** COUNT N A **directive** is an official instruction; a formal use. *The government is obliged to take action because of EEC directives.*

directly /dɪ[5]rɛktli[1]/. 1 ADV **Directly** means straight towards something. *She turned her head and looked directly at them.* 2 ADV If you do something **directly,** you do it openly or without involving anyone else. *She never directly asked for money.* 3 ADV If something is **directly** above, below, or in front of something, it is in exactly that position. *The sun was almost directly overhead.* 4 ADV OR CONJ **Directly** means very soon or immediately. *I'll move back into my old room directly... Directly he heard the door close he picked up the telephone.*

director /dɪ[5]rɛktə/, **directors.** 1 COUNT N A **director** is someone who decides how a film, play, or television programme is made or performed. 2 COUNT N A **director** is also someone who is on the board of a company or is in charge of group, institution, or project. *...the Director of the Scottish Prison Service.*

directory /dɪ[5]rɛktə[0]ri[1]/, **directories.** COUNT N A **directory** is a book which gives lists of information such as people's names, addresses, and telephone numbers, usually arranged in alphabetical order. *...a telephone directory.*

dirt /dɜ:t/. 1 UNCOUNT N If there is **dirt** on something, there is dust, mud, or a stain on it. *...sweeping up the dirt.* 2 UNCOUNT N **Dirt** is also the earth on the ground. *...rough dirt roads.*

dirty /dɜ:ti[1]/, **dirtier, dirtiest; dirties, dirtying, dirtied.** 1 ADJ Something that is **dirty** has dust, mud, or stains on it. *...dirty marks on the walls.* 2 VB WITH OBJ To **dirty** something means to make it dirty. 3 ATTRIB ADJ A **dirty** action is unfair or dishonest. *They will use any dirty trick.* 4 ADJ **Dirty** jokes, books, or language refer to sex in a way that many people find offensive.

dis-. PREFIX **Dis-** is added to words to form other words which refer to an opposite process, quality, or state. *The ball disappeared into the river... ...crowds of discontented people... There was disagreement on the ideal course.*

disability /dɪsəbɪlə[1]ti[1]/, **disabilities.** COUNT N OR UNCOUNT N A **disability** is a physical or mental condition that severely affects your life; a formal use. *...the disabilities suffered by the elderly.*

disabled /dɪseɪbə[0]ld/. PLURAL N The **disabled** are people who have a physical or mental condition that severely affects their lives. *...the variety of help available to the disabled.* Also ADJ *She has to look after a disabled relative.*

disadvantage /dɪsə[3]dvɑ:ntɪdʒ/, **disadvantages.** 1 COUNT N A **disadvantage** is a part of a situation which causes problems. *...the disadvantages of living in cities.* 2 PHRASE If you are **at a disadvantage,** you have a problem that other people do not have. *These restrictions put banks at a disadvantage.*

disadvantaged /dɪsə[3]dvɑ:ntɪdʒd/. ADJ People who are **disadvantaged** live in bad conditions and cannot easily improve their situation.

disadvantageous /dɪsædvɑ:nteɪdʒəs/. ADJ Something that is **disadvantageous** to you puts you in a worse position than other people. *This made the 1988 agreement disadvantageous to the British.*

disaffected /dɪsəfɛktɪ[2]d/. ADJ People who are **disaffected** are dissatisfied with an organization or idea and no longer support it. *Our party gained four disaffected UP members.*

disaffection /dɪsəfɛkʃə[0]n/. UNCOUNT N **Disaffection** is a feeling of dissatisfaction that people have with an organization or idea, so that they no longer support it; a formal use. *They were worried about the possibility of disaffection in the army.*

disagree /dɪsəgri:/, **disagrees, disagreeing, disagreed.** 1 RECIP VB If you **disagree** with someone, you have a different opinion about something. *She and I disagree about it... I disagree completely with John Taylor.* 2 VB WITH 'with' If you **disagree** with an action or decision, you disapprove of it. *Benn disagreed with the abandonment of the project.* 3 VB WITH 'with' If food or drink **disagrees** with you, you feel ill after you have eaten or drunk it; an informal use.

disagreeable /dɪsəgri:əbə[0]l/. 1 ADJ Something that is **disagreeable** is unpleasant or annoying. *...a very disagreeable smell.* 2 ADJ A **disagreeable** person is unfriendly or unpleasant.

disagreement /dɪsəgri:mə[2]nt/, **disagreements.** 1 UNCOUNT N **Disagreement** is a situation in which people have different opinions about something. *The experts find themselves in total disagreement.* 2 COUNT N A **disagreement** is an argument. *We had a serious disagreement about business.*

disappear /dɪsəpɪə/, **disappears, disappearing, disappeared.** 1 VB If someone or something **disappears,** they go where they cannot be seen or found. *I saw him disappear round the corner.* ♦ **disappearance** /dɪsəpɪərəns/ UNCOUNT N OR COUNT N *...the mysterious disappearance of Halliday... ...a series of disappearances in the Carribean.* 2 VB To **disappear** also means to stop existing or happening. ♦ **disappearance** UNCOUNT N *...the disappearance of the dinosaurs.*

disappoint /dɪsəpɔɪnt/, **disappoints, disappointing, disappointed.** VB WITH OBJ If things or people **disappoint** you, they are not as good as you had hoped, or do not do what you want. *The results disappointed him... We must not disappoint the hopes of the people.* ♦ **disappointing** ADJ *...a disappointing book.*

disappointed /dɪsəpɔɪntɪ[2]d/. ADJ If you are **disappointed,** you are sad because something has not happened or because something is not as good as you hoped it would be. *She was disappointed that Ted had not come... My father was bitterly disappointed in me.*

disappointment /dɪsəpɔɪntmə[2]nt/, **disappointments.** 1 UNCOUNT N **Disappointment** is the state of feeling disappointed. *To my disappointment, she came with her mother.* 2 COUNT N A **disappointment** is something which makes you feel disappointed. *That defeat was a surprise and a disappointment.*

disapproval /dɪsəpru:və[0]l/. UNCOUNT N If you express **disapproval** of something, you indicate that you do not like it or that you think it is wrong. *...his disapproval of the President's policy.*

disapprove /dɪsəpru:v/, **disapproves, disapproving, disapproved.** VB If you **disapprove** of something, you do not like it or you think it is wrong. *The other teachers disapproved of his methods.* ♦ **disapproving** ADJ *...a disapproving glance.*

disarm /dɪsɑ:m/, **disarms, disarming, disarmed.** 1 VB WITH OBJ To **disarm** people means to take away their weapons. *The officer captured and disarmed the two men.* 2 VB If a country **disarms,** it gets rid of some of its weapons. 3 VB WITH OBJ To **disarm** someone also means to cause them to feel less angry or hostile. *They were so kind that it surprised and disarmed her.* ♦ **disarming** ADJ *...a disarming smile.*

disarmament /dɪsɑ:məmə[2]nt/. UNCOUNT N **Disarmament** is the process in which countries agree to reduce the number of weapons that they have.

disarray /dɪsəreɪ/. PHRASE If people or things are **in disarray** they have become confused and disorganized; a formal use. *The Democratic Party was in disarray.*

disassociate /dɪsəsəʊʃieɪt/, **disassociates, disassociating, disassociated.** REFL VB WITH 'from' If you **disassociate** yourself from a person or situation, you show that you are not involved with them; a formal use. *Democratic politicians wanted to disassociate themselves from the President.*

disaster /dɪzɑ:stə/, **disasters.** 1 COUNT N A **disaster** is an unexpected event which causes a lot of damage or suffering. 2 COUNT N If something is **a disaster,** it is very unsuccessful or unpleasant. *The last day at the hotel was a disaster.* 3 UNCOUNT N **Disaster** is a situation which affects you very badly. *They had led the country into economic disaster.*

disastrous /dɪzɑ:strəs/. 1 ADJ A **disastrous** event causes a lot of damage or suffering. *...disastrous floods.* ♦ **disastrously** ADV *These diseases have increased disastrously.* 2 ADJ **Disastrous** also means very unsuccessful or unpleasant. *...a disastrous holiday.* ♦ **disastrously** ADV *The team performed disastrously.*

disband /dɪsbænd/, **disbands, disbanding, disbanded.** ERG VB When an organization **is disbanded,** it officially ceases to exist. *The regiment had been disbanded... They began to disband.*

disbelief /dɪsbə[1]li:f/. UNCOUNT N **Disbelief** is not believing that something is true or real. *He shook his head in disbelief... I looked at it with disbelief.*

disbelieve /dɪsbə[1]li:v/, **disbelieves, disbelieving, disbelieved.** VB WITH OBJ If you **disbelieve** someone, you think that they are telling lies; a formal use.

disc /dɪsk/, **discs;** spelled **disk** in American English. 1 COUNT N A **disc** is a flat, circular shape or object. *...a metal disc with a number stamped on it.* 2 COUNT N A **disc** is also a piece of cartilage between the bones in your spine. 3 COUNT N A **disc** is also a gramophone record. 4 See also **disk.**

discard /dɪskɑ:d/, **discards, discarding, discarded.** VB WITH OBJ If you **discard** something, you get rid of it because it is not wanted. *Pull off and discard the outer leaves.* ♦ **discarded** ADJ *...discarded newspapers.*

discern /dɪsɜ:n/, **discerns, discerning, discerned;** a formal word. 1 VB WITH OBJ If you can **discern** something, you can see it by looking carefully. *I could dimly discern his figure.* 2 REPORT VB To **discern** something also means to notice or understand it by careful thought or study. *Posy had not discerned the real reason... He is unable to discern what is actually happening.*

discernible /dɪsɜ:nəbə[0]l/. 1 ADJ If something is **discernible,** you can see it by looking carefully. *Each pebble was clearly discernible.* 2 ADJ If a quality, characteristic, or effect is **discernible,** you can notice it or understand it by careful thought or study. *An element of envy is discernible in his attitude... Privatizing the electricity will not result in discernible improvements.*

discerning /dɪsɜ:nɪŋ/. ADJ A **discerning** person is good at judging the quality of something. *...discerning readers.*

discharge, discharges, discharging, discharged; pronounced /dɪstʃɑ:dʒ/ when it is a verb and /dɪstʃɑ:dʒ/ when it is a noun. 1 VB WITH OBJ When someone **is discharged** from hospital, prison, or the armed forces, they are allowed to leave. Also UNCOUNT N *...from the time of his discharge until his re-arrest.* 2 VB WITH OBJ If someone **discharges** their duties or responsibilities, they carry them out; a formal use. *He is unable to discharge the duties of his office.* 3 VB WITH OBJ To **discharge** an object or substance means to send it out from a place; a formal use. *The city's sewage is discharged into huge lakes.* Also COUNT N *...the discharge of mercury from industrial premises.* 4 COUNT N A **discharge** is also the quantity of a substance that comes out from a place; a technical use. *...a discharge from the nose.*

disciple /dɪsaɪpə[0]l/, **disciples.** COUNT N A **disciple** is someone who believes, supports, and uses the ideas of their leader or superior.

disciplinary /dɪsɪplɪnəri[1]/. ATTRIB ADJ **Disciplinary** matters are concerned with rules, making sure that people obey them, and punishing people who do not. *...forcing them to take disciplinary action against their own members.*

discipline /dɪsɪplɪn/, **disciplines, disciplining, disciplined.** 1 UNCOUNT N **Discipline** is the practice of making people obey rules and punishing them when they do not. *She was a harsh mother and imposed severe discipline.* 2 VB WITH OBJ To **discipline** someone means to punish them for behaving badly or breaking rules. *They could be disciplined by the union if they refused to strike.* 3 UNCOUNT N **Discipline** is also the quality of always behaving or working in a controlled way. *They admired our patience and discipline.* ♦ **disciplined** ADJ *Baker lives a disciplined life.*

4 UNCOUNT N OR COUNT N A **discipline** is a particular activity or subject; a formal use. *...graduates of all disciplines.*

disclaim /dɪskleɪm/, **disclaims, disclaiming, disclaimed.** VB WITH OBJ If you **disclaim** knowledge of something or **disclaim** responsibility for it, you say that you did not know about it or are not responsible for it. *Tess disclaimed any knowledge of it.*

disclose /dɪskləʊz/, **discloses, disclosing, disclosed.** REPORT VB If you **disclose** new or secret information, you tell it to someone. *I had no intention of disclosing their names... The English newspaper disclosed that the treaty had been signed.*

disclosure /dɪskləʊʒə/, **disclosures.** UNCOUNT N OR COUNT N **Disclosure** is the act of revealing new or secret information. *He feared it might lead to the disclosure of his visit to Rome... There were more disclosures about Casey in the press.*

disco /dɪskəʊ/, **discos.** COUNT N A **disco** is a place where people dance to pop records.

discolour /dɪskʌlə/, **discolours, discolouring, discoloured;** spelled **discolor** in American English. ERG VB If something **discolours**, its original colour changes and it looks unattractive. *The pans may discolour inside.* ♦ **discoloured** ADJ *...discoloured teeth.*

discomfort /dɪskʌmfə^{8}t/, **discomforts.** 1 UNCOUNT N **Discomfort** is an unpleasant or painful feeling in a part of your body. *He was conscious only of physical discomfort.* 2 UNCOUNT N **Discomfort** is also a feeling of worry or embarrassment. *I no longer experienced discomfort in their presence.* 3 PLURAL N WITH SUPP **Discomforts** are conditions which make you feel pain or unease. *...the physical discomforts of filming.*

disconcert /dɪskə^{7}nsɜːt/, **disconcerts, disconcerting, disconcerted.** VB WITH OBJ If something **disconcerts** you, it makes you feel worried or embarrassed. *Her cold stare disconcerted me.* ♦ **disconcerting** ADJ *...his disconcerting habit of pausing before he spoke.*

disconnect /dɪskə^{7}nekt/, **disconnects, disconnecting, disconnected.** 1 VB WITH OBJ If you **disconnect** things that are joined, you pull them apart. *Can you disconnect all these tubes?* 2 VB WITH OBJ If you **disconnect** a piece of equipment, you detach it from its source of power. *I bent down to disconnect the plug.* 3 VB WITH OBJ If a gas, electricity, water, or telephone company **disconnects** you, it turns off the connection to your house.

disconnected /dɪskə^{2}nektɪ^{2}d/. ADJ **Disconnected** things are not linked in any way. *...a series of disconnected events.*

disconsolate /dɪskɒnsələ^{1}t/. ADJ Someone who is **disconsolate** is very unhappy or disappointed; a formal use. ♦ **disconsolately** ADV *He walked disconsolately down the path.*

discontent /dɪskə^{7}ntent/. UNCOUNT N **Discontent** is the feeling of not being satisfied with your situation. *...their discontent with pay and conditions.*

discontented /dɪskə^{7}ntentɪ^{2}d/. ADJ If you are **discontented**, you are not satisfied with your situation. *Most of the people he saw looked discontented.*

discontinue /dɪskə^{7}ntɪnjuː/, **discontinues, discontinuing, discontinued.** VB WITH OBJ If you **discontinue** an activity, you stop doing it; a formal use.

discord /dɪskɔːd/, **discords.** UNCOUNT N **Discord** is disagreement; a literary use. *He's been a source of discord and worry.*

discordant /dɪskɔːdə^{0}nt/; a formal word. 1 ADJ Things that are **discordant** are different from each other in an unpleasant way. *...the discordant state of industrial relations.* 2 ADJ A **discordant** sound is unpleasant to listen to.

discotheque /dɪskə^{6}tek/, **discotheques.** COUNT N A **discotheque** is a disco; a formal use.

discount, discounts, discounting, discounted; pronounced /dɪskaʊnt/ when it is a noun and /dɪskaʊnt/ when it is a verb. 1 COUNT N A **discount** is a reduction in the price of something. *Our clients receive a 50 per cent discount.* 2 VB WITH OBJ If you **discount** something, you reject or ignore it. *I decided to discount the risks.*

discourage /dɪskʌrɪdʒ/, **discourages, discouraging, discouraged.** 1 VB WITH OBJ If someone or something **discourages** you, they cause you to lose your enthusiasm or become unwilling to do something. *Don't let friends discourage you.* ♦ **discouraging** ADJ *...a difficult and discouraging task.* ♦ **discouraged** ADJ *Whenever I feel discouraged, I read that letter.* 2 VB WITH OBJ To **discourage** an action or to **discourage** someone from doing it means to try and persuade them not to do it. *She wanted to discourage him from marrying the girl.*

discouragement /dɪskʌrɪdʒmə^{2}nt/. 1 UNCOUNT N **Discouragement** is the act of trying to persuade someone not to do something. *When I first started, I encountered opposition and discouragement.* 2 SING N A **discouragement** is something that makes you unwilling to do something because you are afraid of the consequences. *The submarines were a constant discouragement to naval movements.*

discourse, /dɪskɔːs/, **discourses;** a formal word. 1 COUNT N A **discourse** is a talk or written communication that teaches or explains something. *They listened to his discourse on human relations.* 2 UNCOUNT N **Discourse** is spoken or written communication between people. *Let us switch the area of discourse to politics.*

discover /dɪskʌvə/, **discovers, discovering, discovered.** 1 VB WITH OBJ OR REPORT VB When you **discover** something, you find it or find out about it, especially for the first time. *Herschel discovered a new planet... I discovered that Zapp is Melanie's father... He was dead before anyone discovered him.* ♦ **discoverer** /dɪskʌvərə/ COUNT N *...the discoverer of penicillin, Sir Alexander Fleming.* 2 VB WITH OBJ If an artist or athlete **is discovered,** someone realizes how talented they are and helps them to become famous.

discovery /dɪskʌvə^{0}ri^1/, **discoveries.** 1 COUNT N OR UNCOUNT N A **discovery** is the finding of an object or fact that nobody knew about. *New scientific discoveries are being made every day... Further discovery can be made about his condition.* 2 COUNT N A **discovery** is also something that you find or learn about. *...the discovery that he wanted to hurt her.*

discredit /dɪskredɪt/, **discredits, discrediting, discredited;** a formal word. 1 VB WITH OBJ To **discredit** someone means to cause other people to stop trusting or respecting them. *...efforts to discredit the government.* ♦ **discredited** ADJ *...the discredited ambassador.* 2 VB WITH OBJ To **discredit** an idea or belief means to make it appear false or doubtful. *Scientific discoveries have discredited religious belief.* ♦ **discredited** ADJ *...discredited theories.* 3 UNCOUNT N **Discredit** is shame and disapproval. *It may bring discredit to our city.*

discreet /dɪskriːt/. 1 ADJ If you are **discreet,** you avoid causing embarrassment when dealing with secret or private matters. *Make discreet enquiries at his place of employment... I'll certainly be most discreet in my conversation.* ♦ **discreetly** ADV *The king came discreetly up the back stairs.* 2 ADJ Something that is **discreet** is intended to avoid attracting attention. ♦ **discreetly** ADV *...the discreetly shaded light.*

discrepancy /dɪskrepənsi^1/, **discrepancies.** COUNT N A **discrepancy** is a difference between things that ought to be the same. *...discrepancies between school records and examination results.*

discrete /dɪskriːt/. ATTRIB ADJ **Discrete** things are separate from each other; a formal use. *...the two discrete hemispheres of the brain.*

discretion /dɪskreʃə^{0}n/. 1 UNCOUNT N **Discretion** is the quality of not causing embarrassment or difficulties when dealing with secret or private matters. *The plan was carried out with maximum speed and discretion.* 2 UNCOUNT N **Discretion** is also the ability to judge a situation and to take suitable decisions or actions. *Use your discretion!* 3 PHRASE If a decision is **at the discretion of** someone in authority, it depends on them and not on a fixed rule. *The issue of these cards is at the discretion of your bank manager.*

discretionary /dɪskreʃənə^{0}rɪ/. ADJ **Discretionary** matters are not fixed by rules but are decided by the people in authority. *The University has funds for discretionary awards in special cases.*

discriminate /dɪskrɪmɪneɪt/, **discriminates, discriminating, discriminated.** 1 VB If you can **discriminate** between two things, you can recognize the difference between them. *...to discriminate between right and wrong.* ♦ **discrimination** /dɪskrɪmɪneɪʃə^{0}n/ UNCOUNT N *...discrimination between the important and the trivial problems.* 2 VB To **discriminate** against someone or in favour of them means to unfairly treat them worse or better than other people. *The law discriminated against women.* ♦ **discrimination** UNCOUNT N *...discrimination against the poor.*

discriminating /dɪskrɪmɪneɪtɪŋ/. ADJ If you are **discriminating**, you recognize and like things that are of good quality. *We offer choices to discriminating readers.*

discrimination /dɪskrɪmɪneɪʃə^{0}n/. UNCOUNT N **Discrimination** is the ability to recognize and like things that are of good quality.

discursive /dɪskɜːsɪv/. ADJ If speech or writing is **discursive,** the ideas in it are not carefully arranged and include unnecessary details; a formal use.

discus /dɪskəs/, **discuses.** COUNT N A **discus** is a heavy, circular object that is thrown as a sport.

discuss /dɪskʌs/, **discusses, discussing, discussed.** VB WITH OBJ If you **discuss** something, you talk about it seriously with other people.

discussion /dɪskʌʃə^{0}n/, **discussions.** 1 UNCOUNT N **Discussion** is the act of talking seriously about something with other people. *Ten hours were spent in discussion of Boon's papers.* 2 COUNT N A **discussion** is a serious conversation. *I had been involved in discussions about this with Ken and Frank.* 3 PHRASE If something is **under discussion,** it is being talked about and no decision about it has been reached yet.

disdain /dɪsdeɪn/, **disdains, disdaining, disdained;** a formal word. 1 UNCOUNT N If you feel **disdain** for someone or something, you think that they have little value or importance. *He spoke of the rebels with disdain.* 2 VB WITH OBJ OR TO-INF If you **disdain** something or **disdain** to do something, you reject it or refuse to do it because you think that it is not important or is not good enough for you. *...disdaining the help of his son... Claire disdained to reply.*

disdainful /dɪsdeɪnfʊl/. ADJ If you are **disdainful** of someone or something, you think they have little value or importance. *They tend to be disdainful of their colleagues.* ♦ **disdainfully** ADV *She looked away disdainfully.*

disease /dɪziːz/, **diseases.** COUNT N OR UNCOUNT N A **disease** is an illness in living things caused by infection or by a fault inside them. *I have a rare eye disease... ...conditions that cause disease and starvation.*

diseased /dɪziːzd/. ADJ Someone or something that is **diseased** is affected by a disease. *...an old diseased tree.*

disembark /dɪsɪ^{2}mbɑːk/, **disembarks, disembarking, disembarked.** VB When you **disembark** from a ship or aeroplane, you get off it at the end of your journey; a formal use.

disenchanted /dɪsɪntʃɑːntɪ^{2}d/. ADJ If you are **disenchanted** with something, you no longer think that it is good or worthwhile. *Some young people are disenchanted with school.*

disenchantment /dɪsɪntʃɑːntmə^{2}nt/. UNCOUNT N **Disenchantment** is the feeling of being disappointed with something and no longer thinking that it is good or worthwhile. *...public disenchantment with the war.*

disengage /dɪsɪ^{2}ngeɪdʒ/, **disengages, disengaging, disengaged.** VB WITH OBJ If you **disengage** things that are linked or connected, you separate them; a formal use. *Melanie attempted to disengage her arms from his grip... He disengaged himself and jumped up.*

disentangle /dɪsɪ^{2}ntæŋgə^{0}l/, **disentangles, disentangling, disentangled.** VB WITH OBJ If you **disentangle** something, you separate it from other things that it has become attached to. *She disentangled her jacket from the coat-hanger... Tom disentangled himself from his wife's arms.*

disfavour /dɪsfeɪvə/; spelled **disfavor** in American English. UNCOUNT N **Disfavour** is dislike or disapproval of someone or something. *...looking with disfavour at the glass in his hand.*

disfigure /dɪsfɪgə/, **disfigures, disfiguring, disfigured.** VB WITH OBJ To **disfigure** someone or something means to spoil their appearance; a formal use. *His nose was disfigured in an accident.*

disgrace /dɪsgreɪs/, **disgraces, disgracing, disgraced.** 1 UNCOUNT N **Disgrace** is a state in which people disapprove of someone or no longer respect them. *My uncle brought disgrace on the family.* ● If you are **in disgrace,** you have done something which makes people disapprove of you or stop respecting you. *He was sent back to his village in disgrace.* 2 SING N Something that is a **disgrace** is totally unacceptable. *The state of Britain's roads is a disgrace!* 3 SING N You say that someone is a **disgrace** to someone else when their behaviour harms the other person's reputation. *You're a disgrace to the Italians.* 4 VB WITH OBJ OR REFL VB If you **disgrace** someone, you behave in a way that causes them to be disapproved of. *Fanny disgraced herself in London.*

disgraceful /dɪsgreɪsfʊl/. ADJ If you say that something is **disgraceful,** you think it is totally unacceptable. *...the disgraceful state of the prisons.* ♦ **disgracefully** ADV *She behaved disgracefully.*

disgruntled /dɪsgrʌntə^{0}ld/. ADJ If you are **disgruntled,** you are cross and dissatisfied about something.

disguise /dɪsgaɪz/, **disguises, disguising, disguised.** 1 COUNT N A **disguise** is a change in your appearance that is intended to prevent people from recognizing you. *...the disguise he wore when he escaped.* ● If you are **in disguise,** you have changed your appearance to prevent people recognizing you. *The Emperor came aboard the ship in disguise.* 2 REFL VB If you **disguise** yourself, you dress like someone else and behave like them in order to deceive people. *I disguised myself as a French priest.* 3 VB WITH OBJ If you **disguise** something, you change it so that people do not recognize it or know about it. *He tried to disguise his voice... It proved difficult to disguise her anxiety.*

disgust /dɪsgʌst/, **disgusts, disgusting, disgusted.** VB WITH OBJ Something that **disgusts** you causes you to have a strong feeling of dislike or disapproval. *The* *attitudes of the tourists disgusted him even more.* Also UNCOUNT N *Many expressed disgust at the use of such weapons... He returned downstairs in disgust.*

disgusted /dɪsgʌstɪ[2]d/. ADJ If you are **disgusted,** you have a strong feeling of dislike or disapproval. *She was disgusted with herself.*

disgusting /dɪsgʌstɪŋ/. ADJ **Disgusting** means extremely unpleasant. *The food was disgusting.* ♦ **disgustingly** SUBMOD *She was disgustingly fat.*

dish /dɪʃ/, **dishes, dishing, dished. 1** COUNT N A **dish** is a shallow container used for cooking or serving food. **2** COUNT N A **dish** is also food prepared in a particular style. *...the traditional British dish of eggs and bacon.* **dish up.** PHR VB If you **dish up** food, you serve it.

dishcloth /dɪʃklɒθ/, **dishcloths.** COUNT N A **dishcloth** is a cloth used for washing dishes and cutlery.

disheartened /dɪshɑːtə[0]nd/. ADJ If you are **disheartened,** you feel disappointed and have less hope or confidence.

disheartening /dɪshɑːtə[0]nɪŋ/. ADJ If something is **disheartening,** it makes you feel disappointed and have less hope or confidence. *Such a defeat is inevitably disheartening.*

dishevelled /dɪʃɛvə[0]ld/; spelled **disheveled** in American English. ADJ If someone is **dishevelled,** their appearance is very untidy. *...dirty and dishevelled travellers.*

dishonest /dɪsɒnɪ[2]st/. ADJ Someone who is **dishonest** lies, cheats, or does illegal things, and cannot be trusted. *The smugglers could be regarded as pretty dishonest men.* ♦ **dishonestly** ADV *In my opinion, they have acted dishonestly.*

dishonesty /dɪsɒnə[1]sti[1]/. UNCOUNT N **Dishonesty** is dishonest behaviour.

dishonour /dɪsɒnə/, **dishonours, dishonouring, dishonoured;** spelled **dishonor** in American English. **1** VB WITH OBJ If you **dishonour** someone, you behave in a way that damages their good reputation; a formal use. *He taught her never to dishonour her family.* **2** UNCOUNT N **Dishonour** is a state in which people disapprove of you and have no respect for you. *There are people who prefer death to dishonour.*

dishwasher /dɪʃwɒʃə/, **dishwashers.** COUNT N A **dishwasher** is a machine that washes dishes.

disillusion /dɪsə[1]luːʒə[0]n/, **disillusions, disillusioning, disillusioned. 1** VB WITH OBJ If something **disillusions** you, it makes you realize that something is not as good as you thought. *They were bitterly disillusioned by the performance.* ♦ **disillusioned** ADJ *My father was thoroughly disillusioned with me.* ♦ **disillusioning** ADJ **2** UNCOUNT N **Disillusion** is the same as disillusionment. *...her growing disillusion with her husband.*

disillusionment /dɪsə[1]luːʒə[0]nmə[2]nt/. UNCOUNT N **Disillusionment** is a feeling of disappointment when you discover that someone or something is not as good as you thought. *...public disillusionment with politics.*

disinclination /dɪsɪŋklɪneɪʃə[0]n/. UNCOUNT N **Disinclination** is a feeling that you do not want to do something. *...a disinclination to go out on winter evenings.*

disinclined /dɪsɪŋklaɪnd/. PRED ADJ If you are **disinclined** to do something, you do not want to do it. *She was disinclined to talk about that.*

disinfect /dɪsɪnfɛkt/, **disinfects, disinfecting, disinfected.** VB WITH OBJ If you **disinfect** something, you clean it using a liquid that kills germs.

disinfectant /dɪsɪnfɛktənt/. MASS N **Disinfectant** is a liquid which contains chemicals that kill germs.

disinherit /dɪsɪnhɛrɪt/, **disinherits, disinheriting, disinherited.** VB WITH OBJ If you **disinherit** your children, you legally arrange that, when you die, they do not receive any of your money or property.

disintegrate /dɪsɪntɪ[2]greɪt/, **disintegrates, disintegrating, disintegrated. 1** VB If an object **disintegrates,** it breaks into many small pieces. *There was an explosion and the boat disintegrated.* **2** VB If a relationship or organization **disintegrates,** it becomes very weak and unsuccessful. *They had seen marriages disintegrate under such pressure.* ♦ **disintegration** /dɪsɪntɪ[2]greɪʃə[0]n/ UNCOUNT N *...the disintegration of the army.*

disinterest /dɪsɪntə[0]rɪ[2]st/. UNCOUNT N **Disinterest** is a lack of interest or enthusiasm. *...the Government's disinterest in conservation.*

disinterested /dɪsɪntə[0]rɪ[2]stɪ[2]d/. ADJ Someone who is **disinterested** is not involved in a situation and can make fair decisions or judgements about it. *I'm a disinterested observer.*

disjointed /dɪsdʒɔɪntɪ[2]d/. ADJ **Disjointed** words or ideas are not connected in a sensible way and are difficult to understand. *...a number of disjointed statements.*

disk /dɪsk/. **1** COUNT N A **disk** is part of a large computer which stores information. **2** COUNT N A **disk** is also a small, circular, flexible piece of plastic with a magnetic surface which is used with small computers to store information.

dislike /dɪslaɪk/, **dislikes, disliking, disliked. 1** VB WITH OBJ If you **dislike** someone or something, you think they are unpleasant and do not like them. **2** UNCOUNT N **Dislike** is the feeling of not liking someone or something. *...their dislike of authority.* **3** PHRASE If you **take a dislike to** someone or something, you begin to dislike them. **4** PLURAL N Your **dislikes** are the things that you do not like. *She has her likes and dislikes, as we all have.*

dislocate /dɪslə[7]keɪt/, **dislocates, dislocating, dislocated.** VB WITH OBJ If you **dislocate** a part of your body, it is forced out of its normal position and causes you pain. *I had a nasty fall and dislocated my arm.*

dislodge /dɪslɒdʒ/, **dislodges, dislodging, dislodged.** VB WITH OBJ **To dislodge** someone or something means to cause them to move from a place. *Burr put his feet on the table, dislodging papers and books.*

disloyal /dɪslɔɪə[0]l/. ADJ If you are **disloyal** to your friends, family, or country, you do not support them and or do things that could harm them. *You wanted me to be disloyal to Gareth.*

disloyalty /dɪslɔɪə[0]lti[1]/. UNCOUNT N **Disloyalty** is disloyal behaviour. *...Haldane's disloyalty to the nation.*

dismal /dɪzmə[0]l/. **1** ADJ Something that is **dismal** is unattractive and depressing. *...one dark, dismal day.* **2** ADJ You can also use **dismal** to describe something that is unsuccessful. *Their record over the last decade has been dismal.*

dismantle /dɪsmæntə[0]l/, **dismantles, dismantling, dismantled.** VB WITH OBJ If you **dismantle** a machine or structure, you separate it into its parts.

dismay /dɪsmeɪ/, **dismays, dismaying, dismayed. 1** VB WITH OBJ If something **dismays** you, it makes you feel afraid, worried, or disappointed. *He dismayed his friends by his vicious attacks on the English way of life.* ♦ **dismayed** ADJ *Barbara seemed dismayed at my views.* **2** UNCOUNT N **Dismay** is a strong feeling of fear, worry, or disappointment. *I realised with dismay that he had gone.*

dismember /dɪsmɛmbə/, **dismembers, dismembering, dismembered.** VB WITH OBJ To **dismember** a person or animal means to tear their body to pieces; a formal use. *...a wild animal dismembering its prey.*

dismiss /dɪsmɪs/, **dismisses, dismissing, dismissed. 1** VB WITH OBJ If you **dismiss** something, you decide or say that it is not important enough or not good enough for you to think about. *This plan was dismissed as foolish.* **2** VB WITH OBJ If you **are dismissed** from your job, your employers get rid of you. *They were dismissed for refusing to join a union.* **3** VB WITH OBJ If someone in authority **dismisses** you, they give you permission to go away; a formal use. *Dismissing the other children, she told me to wait.*

dismissal /dɪsmɪsə[0]l/, **dismissals. 1** UNCOUNT N OR COUNT N **Dismissal** is the act of getting rid of an employee. *They discussed the dismissal of a teacher... ...a tribunal dealing with unfair dismissals.* **2** UNCOUNT N **Dismissal** is also the act of deciding or stating that something is not important or not good enough. *...this dismissal of the computer's potential.*

dismissive /dɪsmɪsɪv/. ADJ If you are **dismissive** of something, your attitude indicates that you think they are not important or not good enough; a formal use. *She is dismissive of the school.*

dismount /dɪsmaʊnt/, **dismounts, dismounting, dismounted.** VB If you **dismount** from a horse or a vehicle, you get down from it; a formal use. *The police officer dismounted from his bicycle.*

disobedience /dɪsə[6]biːdɪəns/. UNCOUNT N **Disobedience** is deliberately not doing what you are told to do by a person in authority. *She would tolerate no argument or disobedience.*

disobedient /dɪsə[6]biːdɪənt/. ADJ If you are **disobedient,** you deliberately do not do what you are told to do. *...a disobedient child.*

disobey /dɪsə[6]beɪ/, **disobeys, disobeying, disobeyed.** VB WITH OR WITHOUT OBJ If you **disobey** a person in authority or an order, you deliberately do not do what you are told to do. *It never occurred to them that they could disobey their parents.*

disorder /dɪsɔːdə/, **disorders. 1** UNCOUNT N Something that is in **disorder** is very untidy, badly prepared, or badly organized. *The room was in dreadful disorder.* **2** UNCOUNT N **Disorder** is a situation in which people behave violently. *...a serious risk of public disorder.* **3** COUNT N A **disorder** is a problem or illness which affects a person's mind or body. *...painful stomach disorders.*

disordered /dɪsɔːdəd/. **1** ADJ Something that is **disordered** is untidy and not neatly arranged. *...the small disordered room.* **2** ADJ Someone who is mentally **disordered** has an illness which affects their mind. *...the care of mentally disordered patients.*

disorderly /dɪsɔːdəli[1]/. **1** ADJ Something that is **disorderly** is very untidy. *...their disorderly bedroom.* **2** ADJ People who are **disorderly** behave in an uncontrolled or violent way.

disorganized /dɪsɔːgənaɪzd/; also spelled **disorganised. 1** ADJ Something that is **disorganized** is in a confused and badly prepared state. *Everything was disorganised because he had got back late.* **2** ADJ If you are **disorganized,** you do not plan or arrange things well.

disorientated /dɪsɔːrɪə[2]nteɪtɪ[2]d/. ADJ **Disorientated** means the same as disoriented.

disorientation /dɪsɔːrɪə[2]nteɪʃə[0]n/. UNCOUNT N **Disorientation** is a feeling of extreme confusion.

disoriented /dɪsɔːrɪə[2]ntɪ[2]d/. ADJ If you are **disoriented,** you are confused or lost and are not sure where you are. *I woke up that afternoon, totally disoriented.*

disown /dɪsəʊn/, **disowns, disowning, disowned.** VB WITH OBJ If you **disown** someone or something, you formally end your connection with them. *If it happened again her family would disown her.*

disparage /dɪspærɪdʒ/, **disparages, disparaging, disparaged.** VB WITH OBJ If you **disparage** someone or something, you talk about them with disapproval or lack of respect; a formal use. ♦ **disparagement** /dɪspærɪdʒmə[2]nt/ UNCOUNT N *...Bernstein's disparagement of the myth.*

disparaging /dɪspærɪdʒɪŋ/. ADJ A **disparaging** remark or comment is critical and scornful. *The newspaper had made disparaging remarks about his wife.*

disparate /dɪspərə[1]t/. ADJ **Disparate** is used to describe things that are very different from each other; a formal use. *...disparate social groups.*

disparity /dɪspærə[1]ti[1]/, **disparities.** COUNT N OR UNCOUNT N A **disparity** between things is a difference between them; a formal use. *...the disparity between rich and poor.*

dispassionate /dɪspæʃə[0]nə[1]t/. ADJ Someone who is **dispassionate** is calm, reasonable, and not influenced by their emotions. *...a dispassionate observer.* ♦ **dispassionately** ADV *I shall judge your problems dispassionately.*

dispatch /dɪspætʃ/, **dispatches, dispatching, dispatched;** a formal word, also spelled **despatch** in British English. **1** VB WITH OBJ If you **dispatch** someone or something to a place, you send them there. *Troops were dispatched to the north coast.* **2** COUNT N A **dispatch** is an official report sent to a person or organization by their representative in another place. *...a dispatch from their office in Rome.*

dispel /dɪspɛl/, **dispels, dispelling, dispelled.** VB WITH OBJ To **dispel** an idea or feeling that someone has means to stop them believing in it or feeling it. *All such doubts were now dispelled.*

dispensable /dɪspɛnsəbə[0]l/. ADJ Someone or something that is **dispensable** is not really needed. *These were dispensable luxuries.*

dispensation /dɪspɛnseɪʃə[0]n/, **dispensations.** COUNT N OR UNCOUNT N A **dispensation** is special permission to do something that is normally not allowed; a formal use. *For centuries royal dispensation was required to hunt here.*

dispense /dɪspɛns/, **dispenses, dispensing, dispensed. 1** VB WITH OBJ To **dispense** something means to give it to people; a formal use. *...a clinic at which advice was dispensed.* **2** VB WITH OBJ Someone who **dispenses** medicine prepares it and gives it to people. **dispense with.** PHR VB If you **dispense with** something, you stop using it or get rid of it because it is not needed. *We decided to dispense with the services of Mrs Baggot.*

dispenser /dɪspɛnsə/, **dispensers.** COUNT N WITH SUPP A **dispenser** is a machine or container from which you can get things. *...cash dispensers.*

disperse /dɪspɜːs/, **disperses, dispersing, dispersed. 1** ERG VB When a group of people **disperse,** they go away in different directions. *The crowd was dispersing... Police used tear gas to disperse the mob.* **2** ERG VB When something **disperses** it spreads over a wide area. *Most of the pieces had dispersed... ...an effective means of dispersing oil at sea.*

dispirited /dɪspɪrɪtɪ[2]d/. ADJ If you are **dispirited,** you have lost your confidence or enthusiasm.

displace /dɪspleɪs/, **displaces, displacing, displaced. 1** VB WITH OBJ If one thing **displaces** another, it forces the other thing out and occupies its position. *London displaced Antwerp as the commercial capital of Europe.* **2** VB WITH OBJ If someone **is displaced,** they are forced to move away from the area where they live. *...Greek Cypriots displaced from the North.* ♦ **displacement** /dɪspleɪsmə[2]nt/ UNCOUNT N *...the displacement of large masses of people.*

display /dɪspleɪ/, **displays, displaying, displayed.** 1 VB WITH OBJ If you **display** something, you put it in a place where people can see it. *...a small museum where they could display the collection.* Also UNCOUNT N *He has all his tools on display.* 2 VB WITH OBJ If you **display** a quality or emotion, you behave in a way which shows that you have it. Also COUNT N *...a spontaneous display of affection.* 3 COUNT N A **display** is something which is intended to attract people's attention, such as an event, or attractive arrangement of different things. *...displays of sausages and cheese... ...a firework display.*

displease /dɪspliːz/, **displeases, displeasing, displeased.** VB WITH OBJ If someone or something **displeases** you, they make you dissatisfied, annoyed, or upset. *What he saw did not displease him.* ♦ **displeased** PRED ADJ *Why are you displeased with me?*

displeasure /dɪspleʒə/. UNCOUNT N **Displeasure** is a feeling of dissatisfaction or annoyance. *Professor Aitken looked at me with displeasure.*

disposable /dɪspəʊzəb^{0}l/. ADJ **Disposable** things are designed to be thrown away after use. *...disposable nappies.*

disposal /dɪspəʊzə^{0}l/. 1 PHRASE If you have something **at your disposal**, you can use it at any time. *...a cottage put at her disposal by a friend.* 2 UNCOUNT N **Disposal** is the act of getting rid of something. *...the safe disposal of radioactive waste.*

dispose /dɪspəʊz/, **disposes, disposing, disposed.**
dispose of. PHR VB If you **dispose of** something that you no longer want or need, you get rid of it. *He could dispose of the house and car.*

disposed /dɪspəʊzd/; a formal word. 1 PRED ADJ WITH TO-INF If you are **disposed** to do something, you are willing to do it. 2 PHRASE If you are **well disposed** to someone, you feel friendly towards them.

disposition /dɪspəzɪʃə^{0}n/, **dispositions.** 1 COUNT N Your **disposition** is your character or mood. *Waddell was of a cheerful disposition.* 2 UNCOUNT N WITH TO-INF A **disposition** to do something is a willingness to do it; a formal use. *Adam showed no disposition to move.*

dispossess /dɪspə^{6}zes/, **dispossesses, dispossessing, dispossessed.** VB WITH OBJ If you **are dispossessed** of land or property, it is taken from you. *Landowners could not be legally dispossessed.*

disproportionate /dɪsprəpɔːʃə^{0}nə^{1}t/. ADJ Something that is **disproportionate** is surprising or unreasonable in amount or size. *A disproportionate number of people die shortly after retiring.* ♦ **disproportionately** ADV *There were disproportionately high costs.*

disprove /dɪspruːv/, **disproves, disproving, disproved.** REPORT VB If you **disprove** an idea or belief, you show that it is not true. *They can neither prove nor disprove that it is genuine.*

dispute, disputes, disputing, disputed; pronounced /dɪspjuːt/ when it is a noun and /dɪspjuːt/ when it is a verb. 1 COUNT N OR UNCOUNT N A **dispute** is a disagreement or quarrel between people or groups. *...disputes between unions and employers... There is some dispute about this.* 2 PHRASE If people are **in dispute,** they disagree with each other. 3 PHRASE If something is **in dispute,** people disagree about it. 4 REPORT VB If you **dispute** an opinion, you say that you think it is incorrect. *I don't dispute that children need love.* ♦ **disputed** ADJ *...a disputed decision.* 5 VB WITH OBJ When people **dispute** something, they fight for control of it. *They continued to dispute the ownership of the territory.* ♦ **disputed** ADJ *...the disputed provinces.*

disqualify /dɪskwɒlɪfaɪ/, **disqualifies, disqualifying, disqualified.** VB WITH OBJ If someone **is disqualified,** they are officially stopped from doing something because they have broken a law or rule. *They were disqualified from driving.* ♦ **disqualification** /dɪskwɒlɪfɪkeɪʃə^{0}n/ UNCOUNT N OR COUNT N *He is liable to disqualification from all official events.*

disquiet /dɪskwaɪət/. UNCOUNT N **Disquiet** is a feeling of worry or anxiety; a formal use.

disregard /dɪsrɪ^{2}gɑːd/, **disregards, disregarding, disregarded.** VB WITH OBJ To **disregard** something means to ignore it or not take it seriously. *Men who disregarded the warning were beaten severely.* Also UNCOUNT N *The centre was built with an obvious disregard for cost.*

disreputable /dɪsrepjə^{4}təbə^{0}l/. ADJ If someone is **disreputable,** they are not respectable or trustworthy. *...Ash and his disreputable friends.*

disrepute /dɪsrɪ^{2}pjuːt/. PHRASE If something is **brought** or **falls into disrepute,** it loses its good reputation; a formal use. *He brought his profession into disrepute.*

disrespect /dɪsrɪ^{2}spekt/. UNCOUNT N If someone shows **disrespect** for a person, law, or custom, they do not behave towards them in a respectful way. *I don't think he intended any disrespect.*

disrespectful /dɪsrɪ^{1}spekt^{0}fə^{4}l/. ADJ Someone who is **disrespectful** shows disrespect. *They are arrogant and disrespectful to me.*

disrupt /dɪsrʌpt/, **disrupts, disrupting, disrupted.** VB WITH OBJ To **disrupt** an activity or system means to prevent it from continuing normally. *...attempts to disrupt meetings.*

disruption /dɪsrʌpʃə^{0}n/, **disruptions.** COUNT N OR UNCOUNT N When there is **disruption** of an event, system, or process, it is prevented from proceeding or operating easily or peacefully. *...the disruption of rail communications... ...disruptions in routine.*

disruptive /dɪsrʌptɪv/. ADJ Someone who is **disruptive** prevents an activity or system from continuing normally. *...children who are disruptive in school.*

dissatisfaction /dɪssætɪsfækʃə^{0}n/. UNCOUNT N If you feel **dissatisfaction** with something, you are not satisfied with it. *There is widespread dissatisfaction with the existing political parties.*

dissatisfied /dɪssætɪsfaɪd/. ADJ If you are **dissatisfied,** you are not contented, or are not satisfied with something. *All of them had been dissatisfied with their lives.*

dissect /dɪ^{5}sekt/, **dissects, dissecting, dissected.** VB WITH OBJ To **dissect** a dead body means to cut it up in order to examine it. ♦ **dissection** /dɪ^{5}sekʃə^{0}n/ UNCOUNT N *...the dissection of the earthworm.*

disseminate /dɪsemɪneɪt/, **disseminates, disseminating, disseminated.** VB WITH OBJ To **disseminate** information means to distribute it to many people; a formal use. *...disseminating information among the villages.* ♦ **dissemination** /dɪsemɪneɪʃə^{0}n/ UNCOUNT N *...the printing and dissemination of news.*

dissension /dɪsenʃə^{0}n/. UNCOUNT N **Dissension** is disagreement and argument; a formal use.

dissent /dɪsent/, **dissents, dissenting, dissented.** 1 VB If someone **dissents,** they express strong disagreement with established ideas; a formal use. *...anyone dissenting from the prevailing view.* ♦ **dissenting** ATTRIB ADJ *There have been dissenting voices.* 2 UNCOUNT N **Dissent** is strong disagreement or dissatisfaction with a proposal or with established ideas or values. *Healthy societies can tolerate dissent.*

dissenter /dɪsentə/, **dissenters.** COUNT N A **dissenter** is someone who expresses disagreement with established ideas; a formal use. *...political and religious dissenters.*

dissertation /dɪsəteɪʃə^{0}n/, **dissertations.** COUNT N A **dissertation** is a long, formal piece of writing, especially for a university degree. *She wrote a dissertation on industrial development.*

disservice /dɪssɜːvɪs/. COUNT N If you do someone a **disservice,** you do something that harms them; a formal use. *They are guilty of a disservice to their community.*

dissident /dɪsɪdə^{2}nt/, **dissidents.** COUNT N A **dissident** is someone who criticizes their government or organization; a formal use. *...political dissidents.*

dissimilar /dɪsɪmɪlə/. ADJ If two things are **dissimilar,** they are different from each other; a formal use. *...a proposal not dissimilar to that now adopted by the Government.*

dissipate /dɪsɪpeɪt/, **dissipates, dissipating, dissipated;** a formal word. 1 ERG VB If something **dissipates** or **is dissipated** by something else, it gradually becomes less or disappears. *The heat was dissipated by cooling systems.* 2 VB WITH OBJ If someone **dissipates** money, time, or effort, they waste it in a foolish way.

dissociate /dɪsəʊʃɪeɪt, -sɪ-/, **dissociates, dissociating, dissociated.** 1 REFL VB WITH 'from' If you **dissociate** yourself from someone or something, you say that you are not connected with them. *He did all he could to dissociate himself from the Government.* 2 VB WITH OBJ AND 'from' If you **dissociate** one thing from another, you consider them separately. *It is often difficult to dissociate cause from effect.*

dissolution /dɪsəluːʃə^{0}n/. UNCOUNT N The **dissolution** of an organization or legal relationship is the act of officially ending it; a formal use.

dissolve /dɪzɒlv/, **dissolves, dissolving, dissolved.** 1 ERG VB If you **dissolve** a solid substance, you mix it with a liquid until it disappears. *Dissolve the sugar in the water... Stir over a low heat until the sugar has dissolved.* 2 VB WITH OBJ To **dissolve** an organization or legal relationship means to officially end it; a formal use. *They wish to dissolve their union with the United States.*
dissolve in or **dissolve into.** PHR VB If you **dissolve into** tears or laughter, you begin to cry or laugh, because you cannot control yourself; a literary use. *Kiri dissolved in tears.*

dissuade /dɪsweɪd/, **dissuades, dissuading, dissuaded.** VB WITH OBJ If you **dissuade** someone from doing something, you persuade them not to do it; a formal use. *I tried to dissuade David from going.*

distance /dɪstəns/, **distances.** 1 COUNT N OR UNCOUNT N The **distance** between two places is the amount of space between them. *The town is some distance from the sea... Farmers were travelling long distances to get supplies.* 2 PHRASE If you are **at a distance** from something, or if you see it or remember it **from a distance,** you are a long way away from it in space or time. *From a distance, he heard Jack's whisper... Remembering this disaster at a distance, I think that it was not her fault.*

distant /dɪstənt/. 1 ADJ Something that is **distant** is far away. *...a distant country.* 2 ADJ An event or time that is **distant** is far away in the past or future. *He may return in the not too distant future.* 3 ADJ A **distant** relative is one that you are not closely related to. ♦ **distantly** ADV *...an Italian family to whom he was distantly related.* 4 ADJ Someone who is **distant** is unfriendly. *Boylan was polite but distant.* 5 ADJ You also use **distant** to say that someone is not paying attention because they are thinking about something else. *His eyes took on a distant look.* ♦ **distantly** ADV *Jennifer looked at herself, smiling distantly.*

distaste /dɪsteɪst/. SING N WITH SUPP **Distaste** is a feeling of dislike or disapproval. *She looked at him with distaste... ...his distaste for money.*

distasteful /dɪsteɪstfʊl/. ADJ If something is **distasteful** to you, you dislike or disapprove of it. *...work that is distasteful to him.*

distended /dɪstendɪ^{2}d/. ADJ If a part of someone's body is **distended,** it is swollen and unnaturally large; a formal use. *He had a grossly distended stomach.*

distil /dɪstɪl/, **distils, distilling, distilled;** spelled **distill** in American English. VB WITH OBJ When a liquid **is distilled,** it is purified or concentrated by being heated until it becomes steam and then being cooled until it becomes liquid again. ♦ **distilled** ADJ *Top up the car battery with distilled water.* ♦ **distillation** /dɪstɪleɪʃə^{0}n/ UNCOUNT N *Separate the alcohol from the water by distillation.*

distinct /dɪstɪŋkt/. 1 ADJ If one thing is **distinct** from another, there is an important difference between them. *Our interests were quite distinct from those of the workers.* 2 PHRASE You use **as distinct from** to indicate exactly which thing you mean by contrasting it with something else. *...parliamentary (as distinct from presidential) systems.* 3 ADJ If something is **distinct,** you hear or see it clearly. ♦ **distinctly** ADV *Jones was distinctly seen at the back door.* 4 ATTRIB ADJ You can use **distinct** to emphasize that something is great enough to be noticeable or important. *...a distinct possibility of war.* ♦ **distinctly** SUBMOD *...a Frenchwoman with a distinctly un-Latin temperament.*

distinction /dɪstɪŋkʃə^{0}n/, **distinctions.** 1 COUNT N A **distinction** is a difference between similar things. *Remember the distinction between those words.* 2 PHRASE If you **draw** or **make a distinction** between two things, you say that they are different. *I must make a distinction here between travellers and tourists.* 3 UNCOUNT N **Distinction** is the quality of being excellent. *He is a man of distinction.*

distinctive /dɪstɪŋktɪv/. ADJ Something that is **distinctive** has special qualities that make it easily recognizable. *Irene had a very distinctive voice.* ♦ **distinctively** ADV *...a distinctively African culture.*

distinguish /dɪstɪŋgwɪʃ/, **distinguishes, distinguishing, distinguished.** 1 VB WITH OBJ OR 'between' If you can **distinguish** one thing from another, you can see or understand the difference between them. *...animals that cannot distinguish colours... He had never been capable of distinguishing between his friends and his enemies.* 2 VB WITH OBJ AND 'from' If a feature or quality **distinguishes** one thing from another, it causes the things to be recognized as different. *What distinguishes totalitarian governments from authoritarian ones?* ♦ **distinguishing** ATTRIB ADJ *He had no scars or distinguishing marks.* 3 VB WITH OBJ If you can **distinguish** something, you are just able to see it, hear it, or taste it. *The photograph was poor and few details could be distinguished.* 4 REFL VB If you **distinguish** yourself, you do something that makes you famous, important, or admired. *...prisoners who had distinguished themselves in battle.*

distinguished /dɪstɪŋgwɪʃt/. ADJ A **distinguished** person is very successful, famous or important. *...rushing to meet the distinguished visitors.*

distort /dɪstɔːt/, **distorts, distorting, distorted.** 1 VB WITH OBJ To **distort** a fact or idea means to represent it wrongly. *You're distorting his argument.* ♦ **distorted** ADJ *They get a distorted picture of what's going on.* ♦ **distortion** /dɪstɔːʃə^{0}n/ UNCOUNT N OR COUNT N *...this distortion of history... The report contained a number of distortions.* 2 VB WITH OBJ If something **is distorted,** it becomes twisted into a different shape. *The objects were scorched and distorted.* ♦ **distorted** ADJ *...her* *distorted limbs.* ♦ **distortion** UNCOUNT N OR COUNT N *...the distortion of his face.*

distract /dɪstrækt/, **distracts, distracting, distracted.** VB WITH OBJ If something **distracts** you or **distracts** your attention, it stops you concentrating. *It distracted them from their work.* ♦ **distracting** ADJ *...distracting details.*

distracted /dɪstrækt^{2}d/. ADJ If you are **distracted,** you are very worried or not concentrating. *During classes he was distracted and strangely troubled.* ♦ **distractedly** ADV *She began looking distractedly about her.*

distraction /dɪstrækʃə^{0}n/, **distractions.** 1 COUNT N OR UNCOUNT N A **distraction** is something that takes your attention away from what you are doing. *It would be a distraction from his political labours... She needed to work without interruption or distraction.* 2 COUNT N OR UNCOUNT N A **distraction** is also an object or activity that is intended to entertain people. *...the various distractions provided for them.*

distraught /dɪstrɔːt/. ADJ If someone is **distraught,** they are extremely upset or worried. *'What can we do?' she asked, turning a distraught face to me.*

distress /dɪstrɛs/, **distresses, distressing, distressed.** 1 UNCOUNT N **Distress** is extreme anxiety, sorrow, or pain. *Delays may cause distress to your family... He was breathing fast and in obvious distress.* 2 UNCOUNT N **Distress** is also the state of being in extreme danger and needing urgent help. *...an aircraft in distress.* 3 VB WITH OBJ If someone or something **distresses** you, they cause you to be upset or worried. *I hate to distress you like this, but it is important.* ♦ **distressed** ADJ *She was distressed about having to leave home.* ♦ **distressing** ADJ *It was a distressing experience for me.*

distribute /dɪstrɪbjuːt, dɪstrɪbjuːt/, **distributes, distributing, distributed.** 1 VB WITH OBJ If you **distribute** things such as leaflets, you hand them to people. 2 VB WITH OBJ When goods **are distributed,** they are supplied to the shops or businesses that use or sell them. *They needed trucks to distribute their produce over New York City.* ♦ **distribution** /dɪstrɪbjuːʃə^{0}n/ UNCOUNT N *...the manufacture and distribution of products.* 3 VB WITH OBJ To **distribute** something also means to share it among the members of a group. ♦ **distribution** UNCOUNT N *...a fairer distribution of wealth.*

distributor /dɪstrɪbjə^{4}tə/, **distributors.** COUNT N A **distributor** is a person or company that supplies goods to shops and businesses.

district /dɪstrɪkt/, **districts.** 1 COUNT N WITH SUPP A **district** is an area of a town or country. *...doctors in country districts... ...a working class district of Paris.* 2 COUNT N A **district** is also an administrative area of a town or country. *...district councils.*

distrust /dɪstrʌst/, **distrusts, distrusting, distrusted.** VB WITH OBJ If you **distrust** someone or something, you think that they are not honest, reliable, or safe. *He keeps his savings under his mattress because he distrusts the banks.* Also UNCOUNT N *...their distrust of politicians.*

distrustful /dɪstrʌstfʊl/. ADJ If you are **distrustful** of someone or something, you think that they are not honest, reliable, or safe. *Both parties were distrustful of his policies.*

disturb /dɪstɜːb/, **disturbs, disturbing, disturbed.** 1 VB WITH OBJ If you **disturb** someone, you interrupt what they are doing and cause them inconvenience. *If she's asleep, don't disturb her.* 2 VB WITH OBJ If something **disturbs** you, it makes you feel upset or worried. *I was disturbed by some of the speeches.* 3 VB WITH OBJ To **disturb** something means to change its position or appearance. *The sand had not been disturbed.*

disturbance /dɪstɜːbəns/, **disturbances.** 1 COUNT N A **disturbance** is an event in which people behave violently in public. *...violent disturbances in Liverpool.* 2 UNCOUNT N OR COUNT N **Disturbance** is the act of making a situation less peaceful, organized, or stable. *This would cause disturbance to the public... ...a disturbance of the social order.* 3 COUNT N You can use **disturbance** to refer to extreme unhappiness or mental illness. *...serious emotional disturbance.*

disturbed /dɪstɜːbd/. ADJ Someone who is **disturbed** is extremely worried, unhappy, or mentally ill. *...emotionally disturbed youngsters... ...his disturbed childhood.*

disturbing /dɪstɜːbɪŋ/. ADJ Something that is **disturbing** makes you feel worried or upset. *She has written two disturbing books.* ♦ **disturbingly** SUBMOD *The radiation levels are disturbingly high.*

disuse /dɪsjuːs/. UNCOUNT N **Disuse** is the state of being no longer used. *These methods have fallen into disuse.*

disused /dɪsjuːzd/. ADJ A **disused** place or building is no longer used. *...a disused airfield near Lincoln.*

ditch /dɪtʃ/, **ditches, ditching, ditched.** 1 COUNT N A **ditch** is a long, narrow channel cut into the ground at the side of a road or field. *...a muddy ditch.* 2 VB WITH OBJ If you **ditch** something, you get rid of it; an informal use. *He had decided to ditch the car.*

dither /dɪðə/, **dithers, dithering, dithered.** VB If you **are dithering,** you are hesitating because you are unable to make a quick decision. *After dithering about helplessly for a bit, he picked up the phone.*

ditto /dɪtəʊ/. You use **ditto** to represent a word or phrase that you have just used to avoid repeating it. In written lists, **ditto** can be represented by a symbol (ɘ) underneath the word or phrase that you want to repeat.

divan /dɪvæn/, **divans.** COUNT N A **divan** or **divan bed** is a bed with a thick base under the mattress.

dive /daɪv/, **dives, diving, dived.** In American English **dove** /dəʊv/ is sometimes used as the past tense. 1 VB If you **dive,** you jump head-first into water with your arms straight above your head. Also COUNT N *Ralph did a dive into the pool.* 2 VB To **dive** also means to go under the surface of the sea or a lake, using special breathing equipment. ♦ **diver** /daɪvə/ COUNT N ♦ **diving** UNCOUNT N *...deep-sea diving.* 3 VB When birds and animals **dive,** they go quickly downwards, head-first, through the air or water. 4 VB WITH ADJUNCT If you **dive** in a particular direction, you jump or rush in that direction. *He dived after the ball.* Also SING N *He made a dive for the bag.* 5 VB WITH ADJUNCT If you **dive** into a bag or cupboard, you put your hands into it quickly in order to get something out. *He suddenly dived into the chest and produced a shirt.*

diverge /daɪvɜːdʒ/, **diverges, diverging, diverged.** 1 VB When things **diverge,** they are different, or become different. *Their interests diverge from those of pensioners.* 2 VB When roads or paths **diverge,** they begin leading in different directions.

divergent /daɪvɜːdʒənt/. ADJ Things that are **divergent** are different from each other. *...widely divergent religious groups.* ♦ **divergence** /daɪvɜːdʒəns/ UNCOUNT N OR COUNT N *...a sharp divergence of opinion.*

diverse /daɪvɜːs, daɪvɜːs/. ADJ People or things that are **diverse** are very different from each other. *...a man of diverse talents.*

diversify /daɪvɜːsə^{1}faɪ/, **diversifies, diversifying, diversified.** VB WITH OR WITHOUT OBJ When an organization **diversifies,** it increases the variety of the things that it makes or does. *Many car manufacturers are diversifying as rapidly as they can.* ♦ **diversification** /daɪvɜːsə^{1}fɪkeɪʃə^{0}n/ UNCOUNT N *...a diversification of interests.*

diversion /daɪvɜːʃə^{0}n/, **diversions.** 1 COUNT N A **diversion** is something that distracts your attention and makes you think about something else. 2 COUNT N A **diversion** is also a special route arranged for traffic when the normal route cannot be used. 3 UNCOUNT N OR COUNT N The **diversion** of something involves changing its course or destination, or changing the thing that it is used for. *Inflation and diversion of investment were having a bad effect... Possible diversions of the troop convoys were considered.*

diversity /daɪvɜːsə^{1}ti^{1}/. UNCOUNT N **Diversity** is a range of different conditions, qualities, or types. *...the rich diversity of cultures and societies in the world.*

divert /daɪvɜːt/, **diverts, diverting, diverted.** 1 VB WITH OBJ To **divert** people or vehicles means to change their course or destination. *The police were diverting the traffic.* 2 VB WITH OBJ AND ADJUNCT To **divert** something such as money means to cause it to be used for a different purpose. *We feel it desirable to divert funds from armaments to health and education.* 3 VB WITH OBJ If you **divert** someone's attention, you stop them thinking about something by making them think about something else.

divest /daɪvɛst/, **divests, divesting, divested;** a formal word. 1 REFL VB WITH 'of' If you **divest** yourself of something, you get rid of it. *She divested herself of her bag.* 2 VB WITH OBJ AND 'of' If you **divest** something of a quality or function, you cause it to lose it. *...divesting public housing of its welfare role.*

divide /di^{1}vaɪd/, **divides, dividing, divided.** 1 ERG VB To **divide** something means to separate it into two or more parts. *...an attempt to divide the country into two social classes... The children are divided into three age groups... The cells begin to divide rapidly.* ♦ **divided** PRED ADJ *The houses in Florence St are all divided into flats.* 2 VB WITH OBJ If you **divide** something among a number of people, you give each of them part of it. *The land was divided between the two brothers.* 3 VB WITH OBJ If something **divides** two areas or **divides** an area into two, it forms a barrier or boundary between the two areas. *A line of rocks seemed to divide the cave into two.* 4 ERG VB If people **divide** over something, they disagree about it. *This question is dividing the people of Wales.* ♦ **divided** ADJ *The conference was divided on many issues.* 5 VB WITH OBJ If you **divide** a larger number by a smaller number, you calculate how many times the smaller number can go exactly into the larger number. 6 COUNT N A **divide** is a significant difference between two groups. *The divide between rich and poor was great.*

divide up. PHR VB If you **divide** something **up,** you share it out among a number of people. *The proceeds had to be divided up among about four hundred people.*

dividend /dɪvɪdə^{2}nd/, **dividends.** COUNT N A **dividend** is part of a company's profits which is paid to people who have shares in the company. ● If something **pays dividends,** it brings advantages at a later date. *The time she had spent learning German now paid dividends.*

divine /di^{1}vaɪn/. ADJ Something that is **divine** belongs or relates to a god or goddess. *These men had been operating under divine inspiration.* ♦ **divinely** ADV *...a divinely appointed prophet.*

diving board, diving boards. COUNT N A **diving board** is a board high above a swimming pool from which people can dive into the water.

divinity /dɪvɪnɪ^{1}ti^{1}/, **divinities.** 1 UNCOUNT N **Divinity** is the study of the Christian religion. 2 UNCOUNT N **Divinity** is also the quality of being divine. *The divinity of the Pharoah was not doubted.* 3 COUNT N A **divinity** is a god or goddess.

divisible /dɪvɪzə^{1}bə^{0}l/. PRED ADJ A number that is **divisible** by another number can be divided by that number.

division /dɪvɪʒə^{0}n/, **divisions.** 1 UNCOUNT N The **division** of something is the act of separating it into two or more different parts. *...the division of physical science into chemistry and physics.* 2 UNCOUNT N The **division** of something is also the sharing of it among a number of people. *...the division of responsibility.* 3 UNCOUNT N **Division** is the mathematical process of dividing one number by another. 4 COUNT N A **division** is a difference or conflict between two groups of people. *...class divisions... ...a division of opinion.* 5 COUNT N A **division** is also a department in a large organization. *...the BBC's engineering division.*

division sign, division signs. COUNT N A **division sign** is the sign (÷) which is put between two numbers to show that the first number is being divided by the second.

divisive /di^{1}vaɪsɪv/. ADJ Something that is **divisive** causes hostility between people; a formal use. *...the Government's divisive policy of confrontation.*

divorce /dɪvɔːs/, **divorces, divorcing, divorced.** 1 RECIP VB When someone **divorces** their husband or wife, their marriage is legally ended. ♦ **divorced** ADJ *...a divorced lady... ...when my parents got divorced.* 2 COUNT N OR UNCOUNT N A **divorce** is the legal ending of a marriage. *I want a divorce... Divorce is on the increase.* 3 VB WITH OBJ If you **divorce** one thing from another, you treat the two things as separate from each other; a formal use. *I don't think it is possible to divorce sport from politics.*

divorcee /di^{1}vɔːsiː/, **divorcees.** COUNT N A **divorcee** is a person, especially a woman, who is divorced.

divulge /daɪvʌldʒ/, **divulges, divulging, divulged.** REPORT VB If you **divulge** a piece of information, you tell someone about it; a formal use. *I shall divulge the details to no one... He divulged that he had heard reports about Sharp's misbehaviour.*

D.I.Y. /diː aɪ waɪ/. UNCOUNT N **D.I.Y.** is the activity of making or repairing things yourself, especially in your home. **D.I.Y.** is an abbreviation for 'do-it-yourself'. *...D.I.Y. experts.*

dizzy /dɪzi^{1}/. ADJ If you feel **dizzy,** you feel that you are losing your balance and are about to fall. *I can't climb trees—I get dizzy.* ♦ **dizziness** UNCOUNT N *She was overcome by nausea and dizziness.*

do /duː/, **does** /dʌz/, **doing, did** /dɪd/, **done** /dʌn/. 1 AUX **Do** is used to form the negative of main verbs, by putting 'not' or '-n't' after the auxiliary and before the main verb in its infinitive form. *You don't have to go.* 2 AUX **Do** is used to form questions, by putting the subject after the auxiliary and before the main verb in its infinitive form. *What did he say?... Do you think that's possible?* 3 AUX **Do** is used to stand for, and refer back to, a previous verbal group. *She meets lots more people than I do... I like cooking and so does John.* 4 AUX **Do** is used in question tags. *She made a lot of mistakes, didn't she?* 5 AUX **Do** is used to give emphasis to the main verb when there is no other auxiliary. *I did buy a map but I must have lost it... Do sit down.* 6 AUX **Do** is used with '-n't' or 'not' to tell someone not to behave in a certain way. *Don't speak to me like that.* 7 VB WITH OBJ When you **do** something, you perform an action, activity, or task. *What are you doing?... I do the cooking and Brian does the cleaning.* 8 VB WITH OBJ You use **do** with a noun referring to a thing when you are talking about something regularly done to that thing. For example, if you **do** your teeth, you brush your teeth. *She had done her hair for the party... We have a man to do the garden.* **9** VB WITH OBJ To **do** something about a problem means to try to solve it. *They promised that they were going to do something about immigration.* **10** VB WITH OBJ You use **do** to say that something has a particular result or effect. *Their policies have done more harm for the working class than ours... They are afraid of what it might do to the children.* **11** VB WITH OBJ If you ask someone what they **do**, you are asking what their job is. *What do you want to do when you leave school?* **12** VB WITH ADJUNCT If someone **does** well or badly, they are successful or unsuccessful. *I didn't do very well in my exams... It all depends how the Labour Party do at this next election.* **13** VB WITH OBJ If you **do** a subject, you study it at school or college. *I'm doing biology.* **14** VB WITH NUMBER You use **do** when referring to the speed that something achieves or can achieve. *The car's already doing 70 miles per hour.* **15** VB WITH OR WITHOUT OBJ If you say that something will **do**, you mean that it is satisfactory. *No other school will do... Two thousand will do me very well.* **16** See also **doings, done.**

PHRASES ● If you ask someone **what they did with** something, you are asking where they put it. *What did you do with the keys?* ● If you ask **what** someone **is doing** in a particular place, you are expressing surprise that they are there. *What are you doing here? I thought you were still in London.* ● If you say that someone **would do well** to do something, you mean that they ought to do it. *She would do well to steer clear of men.* ● What something **has to do with** or **is to do with** is what it is connected or concerned with. *The basic argument has nothing to do with agriculture... It's got something to do with an economic crisis.* ● If you say that you **could do with** something, you mean that you need it. *I think we could all do with a good night's sleep.* ● **'How do you do?'** is a formal way of greeting someone.

do away with. PHR VB To **do away with** something means to get rid of it. *Modern medicines have not done away with disease.*

do out of. PHR VB If you **do** someone **out of** something, you unfairly cause them not to have it; an informal use. *He did me out of £500.*

do up. PHR VB **1** If you **do** something **up**, you fasten it. *He did his shoelaces up.* **2** To **do up** an old building means to repair and decorate it; an informal use.

do without. PHR VB If you **do without** something, you manage or survive in spite of not having it. *Many Victorian households did without a bathroom altogether... If you don't have cigarettes, you must simply do without.*

docile /dəʊsaɪl/. ADJ A **docile** person or animal is quiet and easily controlled.

dock /dɒk/, **docks, docking, docked. 1** COUNT N A **dock** is an enclosed area of water where ships are loaded, unloaded, or repaired. **2** VB When a ship **docks,** it comes into a dock. *They docked at Southampton.* **3** SING N In a law court, the **dock** is the place where the person accused of a crime stands or sits. **4** VB WITH OBJ If you **dock** someone's wages, you do not give them some of the money. *He docked her pocket money until the debt was paid off.*

docker /dɒkə/, **dockers.** COUNT N A **docker** is a person who works in docks.

doctor /dɒktə/, **doctors, doctoring, doctored. 1** COUNT N A **doctor** is someone qualified in medicine who treats sick or injured people. **2** COUNT N **Doctor** is also the title given to someone who has been awarded the highest academic degree by a university. **3** VB WITH OBJ To **doctor** something means to deliberately change it, usually in order to deceive people. *The despatch from Davis had been doctored.*

doctorate /dɒktə0rə1t/, **doctorates.** COUNT N A **doctorate** is the highest degree awarded by a university.

doctrinaire /dɒktrɪnɛə/. ADJ Someone who is **doctrinaire** accepts particular theories or principles without considering arguments against them; a formal use. *Their attitudes were condemned as doctrinaire.*

doctrine /dɒktrɪn/, **doctrines.** COUNT N OR UNCOUNT N A **doctrine** is a principle or belief, or a set of principles or beliefs. *...the doctrine of permanent revolution... ...Christian doctrine.* ♦ **doctrinal** /dɒktraɪnə0l/ ATTRIB ADJ *...doctrinal arguments between rival factions.*

document /dɒkjəmə2nt/, **documents, documenting, documented. 1** COUNT N A **document** is an official piece of paper with writing on it. *...travel documents.* **2** VB WITH OBJ If you **document** something, you make a detailed record of it on film, tape, or paper.

documentary /dɒkjə4mɛntə0ri1/, **documentaries. 1** COUNT N A **documentary** is a radio or television programme or a film, which gives information about a particular subject. *...a television documentary on the lives of the Royal Family.* **2** ATTRIB ADJ **Documentary** evidence consists of documents.

documentation /dɒkjə4mɛnteɪʃə0n/. UNCOUNT N **Documentation** consists of documents that provide proof or evidence of something.

dodge /dɒdʒ/, **dodges, dodging, dodged. 1** VB If you **dodge** somewhere, you move there suddenly to avoid being hit, caught, or seen. *He dodged into the post office.* **2** VB WITH OBJ If you **dodge** a moving object, you avoid it by quickly moving aside. *The Minister had to dodge flying tomatoes.* **3** VB WITH OBJ If you **dodge** a problem, you avoid thinking about it or dealing with it. *This issue should not be dodged.*

doe /dəʊ/, **does.** COUNT N A **doe** is an adult female deer, rabbit, or hare.

does /dʌz/ **Does** is the third person singular of the present tense of **do.**

doesn't /dʌzə0nt/. **Doesn't** is the usual spoken form of 'does not'.

dog /dɒg/, **dogs, dogging, dogged. 1** COUNT N A **dog** is an animal that is often kept as a pet or used to guard or hunt things. **2** COUNT N When you are mentioning the sex of a dog or fox, you refer to the male animal as a **dog. 3** VB WITH OBJ If problems or injuries **dog** you, they keep affecting you. *The project has been dogged by a number of technical problems... Bad luck has dogged me all year.*

dog-collar, dog-collars. COUNT N A **dog-collar** is a white collar worn by Christian priests and ministers; an informal use.

dog-eared. ADJ A **dog-eared** book or piece of paper has been used so much that the corners of the pages are turned down or crumpled.

dogged /dɒgɪd/. ATTRIB ADJ **Dogged** means showing determination to continue with something, even if it is very difficult. *...his dogged refusal to admit defeat.* ♦ **doggedly** ADV *Karen doggedly continued to search.*

dogma /dɒgmə/, **dogmas.** COUNT N OR UNCOUNT N A **dogma** is a belief or system of beliefs held by a religious or political group. *He had no time for political or other dogmas... ...Christianity in the early days when there was less dogma.*

dogmatic /dɒgmætɪk/. ADJ Someone who is **dogmatic** about something is convinced that they are right and does not consider other points of view. *She was not impressed by his dogmatic assertions.* ♦ **dogmatically** ADV *'This stone,' he said dogmatically, 'is far older than the rest.'*

dogsbody /dɒgzbɒdi1/, **dogsbodies.** COUNT N A **dogsbody** is someone who does the boring jobs that nobody else wants to do; an informal British use. *I was employed as a general dogsbody on the project.*

doings /duːɪŋz/. PLURAL N Someone's **doings** are their activities. *...a magazine about the doings of royalty.*

do-it-yourself. UNCOUNT N **Do-it-yourself** is the activity of making or repairing things in your home yourself, rather than employing other people.

doldrums /dɒldrəmz/. PHRASE If an area of activity is **in the doldrums,** nothing new or exciting is happening. *The American market is in the doldrums.*

dole /dəʊl/, **doles, doling, doled. 1** SING N The **dole** is money given regularly by the government to people who are unemployed; a British use. *...lengthening dole queues.* **2** PHRASE Someone who is **on the dole** is unemployed and receives money regularly from the government.

dole out. PHR VB If you **dole** something **out,** you give a certain amount of it to each person in a group.

doleful /dəʊlfʊl/. ADJ A **doleful** expression or manner is depressed and miserable. *...a doleful sigh.*

doll /dɒl/, **dolls.** COUNT N A **doll** is a child's toy which looks like a small person or baby.

dollar /dɒlə/, **dollars.** COUNT N A **dollar** is a unit of money in the USA, Canada, and some other countries. *They spent half a million dollars on the campaign.*

dolled up /dɒld ʌp/. PRED ADJ When a woman gets **dolled up,** she puts on smart clothes in order to look attractive; an informal use. *She was all dolled up in the latest fashion.*

dollop /dɒləp/, **dollops.** COUNT N A **dollop** of soft or sticky food is an amount of it served in a lump; an informal use. *...a dollop of ice-cream.*

dolphin /dɒlfɪn/, **dolphins.** COUNT N A **dolphin** is a mammal which lives in the sea and looks like a large fish.

domain /də7meɪn/, **domains;** a formal word. **1** COUNT N WITH SUPP A **domain** is a particular area of activity or interest. *This question comes into the domain of philosophy.* **2** COUNT N WITH POSS Someone's **domain** is the area where they have control or influence. *His domain extended to New York.*

dome /dəʊm/, **domes.** COUNT N A **dome** is a round roof. *...the dome of St Peter's.*

domestic /də6mɛstɪk/. **1** ATTRIB ADJ **Domestic** means concerning matters within a country, rather than its relations with other countries. *...foreign and domestic policy.* **2** ATTRIB ADJ **Domestic** also means concerning your home and family. *...domestic responsibilities.* **3** ATTRIB ADJ **Domestic** items and services are used in people's homes rather than in factories or offices. *...domestic appliances.* **4** ADJ **Domestic** animals are not wild, and are kept as pets or on farms.

domesticated /də6mɛstɪkeɪtɪ2d/. **1** ADJ **Domesticated** animals are kept on farms and used for work or food. *There were no domesticated animals for ploughing.* **2** ADJ If someone is **domesticated,** they willingly do household tasks such as cleaning.

domesticity /dəʊmɛstɪsɪ1ti1, dɒm-/. UNCOUNT N **Domesticity** is the habit of spending a lot of time at home with your family; a formal use.

dominance /dɒmɪnəns/. **1** UNCOUNT N If someone has **dominance** over a person, place, or group, they have power or control over them. *The treaty gave them dominance of the sea routes.* **2** UNCOUNT N If something has **dominance,** it is regarded as more important than other similar things. *...the dominance of economics in social sciences.*

dominant /dɒmɪnənt/. ADJ Someone or something that is **dominant** is more powerful, important, or noticeable than similar people or things. *The dominant personality in our firm was John Brown.*

dominate /dɒmɪneɪt/, **dominates, dominating, dominated. 1** VB WITH OBJ To **dominate** a situation means to be the most powerful or important person or thing in it. *These issues dominated the election.* ♦ **domination** /dɒmɪneɪʃə0n/ UNCOUNT N *...the company's increasing domination of the UK market.* **2** VB WITH OBJ If one country **dominates** another, it has power over it. ♦ **domination** UNCOUNT N *...the domination of Europe over the rest of the world.*

dominating /dɒmɪneɪtɪŋ/. ADJ Someone who is **dominating** has a strong personality and influences other people a great deal.

domineering /dɒmɪnɪərɪŋ/. ADJ Someone who is **domineering** tries to control other people; used showing disapproval.

dominion /də6mɪnjən/. UNCOUNT N **Dominion** is control or authority; a formal use. *They now had dominion over a large part of southern India.*

domino /dɒmɪnəʊ/, **dominoes.** UNCOUNT N OR COUNT N **Dominoes** is a game played using small rectangular blocks marked with two groups of spots on one side. These blocks are called **dominoes.**

don /dɒn/, **dons, donning, donned. 1** COUNT N A **don** is a lecturer at Oxford or Cambridge University. **2** VB WITH OBJ If you **don** a piece of clothing, you put it on; a literary use. *The two men donned white cotton gloves.*

donate /dəʊneɪt/, **donates, donating, donated.** VB WITH OBJ If you **donate** something to a charity or other organization, you give it to them. *The van was donated to us by a local firm.*

donation /dəʊneɪʃə0n/, **donations.** COUNT N A **donation** is an amount of money given to a charity or other organization. *They received a large donation from one of the unions.*

done /dʌn/. **1 Done** is the past participle of **do. 2** PRED ADJ A task that is **done** has been completed. *When her errand was done she ran home.* ● If you say that a situation or task is **over and done with,** you mean that it is finished and you can forget about it.

donkey /dɒŋki1/, **donkeys.** COUNT N A **donkey** is an animal like a small horse with long ears.

donor /dəʊnə/, **donors. 1** COUNT N A **donor** is someone who lets blood or an organ be taken from their body so that it can be given to a patient who needs it. *...kidney donors.* **2** COUNT N A **donor** is also someone who gives something such as money to a charity or other organization. *About half this amount comes from individual donors.*

don't /dəʊnt/. **Don't** is the usual spoken form of 'do not'.

doodle /duːdə0l/, **doodles, doodling, doodled.** COUNT N A **doodle** is a pattern or picture that you draw when you are bored or thinking about something else. Also VB *I used to doodle on my papers.*

doom /duːm/. UNCOUNT N **Doom** is a terrible state or event in the future which you cannot prevent. *I felt as if I were going to my doom.*

doomed /duːmd/. **1** PRED ADJ If someone is **doomed** to an unpleasant or undesirable experience, they are certain to suffer it. *They are doomed to failure... He was doomed to be killed in a car crash.* **2** ADJ Something that is **doomed** is certain to fail or be destroyed. *They informed the Prime Minister that his government was doomed.*

door /dɔː/, **doors. 1** COUNT N A **door** is a swinging or sliding piece of wood, glass, or metal, which is used to open and close the entrance to a building, room, cupboard, or vehicle. **2** COUNT N A **door** is also a doorway. *As they passed through the door, they saw Tom at the end of the room.*

PHRASES • **Next door** refers to the house next to yours. *She put a notice in the shop next door... ...our next-door neighbour, Joan.* • When you are **out of doors,** you are in the open air, rather than inside a building.

doorbell /dɔːbel/, **doorbells.** COUNT N A **doorbell** is a bell which you ring when you want the people inside a house to open the door.

doorknob /dɔːnɒb/, **doorknobs.** COUNT N A **doorknob** is a round handle on a door.

doormat /dɔːmæt/, **doormats.** COUNT N A **doormat** is a mat by a door which people can wipe their shoes on before coming into the house.

doorstep /dɔːstep/, **doorsteps.** COUNT N A **doorstep** is a step on the outside of a building, in front of a door. • If a place is **on your doorstep,** it is very near to where you live.

door-to-door. ATTRIB ADJ **Door-to-door** activities involve going from one house to another along a street, often in order to try and sell something.

doorway /dɔːweɪ/, **doorways.** COUNT N A **doorway** is the space in a wall when a door is open. *A child stood in the doorway.*

dope /dəʊp/, **dopes, doping, doped. 1** UNCOUNT N **Dope** is an illegal drug such as cannabis; an informal use. **2** VB WITH OBJ If someone **dopes** you, they put a drug into your food or drink to make you unconscious.

dormant /dɔːmənt/. ADJ Something that is **dormant** has not been active or used for a long time. *The idea had lain dormant in Britain during the fifties.*

dormitory /dɔːmə[1]tə[0]ri[1]/, **dormitories.** COUNT N A **dormitory** is a large bedroom where several people sleep, for example in a boarding school.

dormouse /dɔːmaʊs/, **dormice** /dɔːmaɪs/. COUNT N A **dormouse** is a small furry animal like a mouse.

dosage /dəʊsɪdʒ/, **dosages.** COUNT N The **dosage** of a medicine or drug is the amount that should be taken. *...a daily dosage of 150 mg.*

dose /dəʊs/, **doses, dosing, dosed. 1** COUNT N A **dose** of a medicine or drug is a measured amount of it. *This is lethal to rats in small doses.* **2** VB WITH OBJ OR REFL VB If you **dose** someone, you give them a medicine or drug. *He dosed himself with pills.*

dossier /dɒsieɪ, -sɪə/, **dossiers.** COUNT N A **dossier** is a collection of papers containing information on a particular subject.

dot /dɒt/, **dots. 1** COUNT N A **dot** is a very small round mark. **2** PHRASE If something happens **on the dot,** it happens at exactly the right time.

dote /dəʊt/, **dotes, doting, doted.** VB WITH 'on' OR 'upon' If you **dote** on someone, you love them very much and cannot see their faults. ♦ **doting** ATTRIB ADJ *...doting relatives who keep spoiling them with presents.*

dotted /dɒtɪ[2]d/. ATTRIB ADJ **Dotted** lines are made of a row of dots. *The boundaries are shown on the map by dotted lines.*

dotty /dɒti[1]/. ADJ Someone who is **dotty** is slightly mad; an informal use.

double /dʌbə[0]l/, **doubles, doubling, doubled. 1** PREDET OR QUANTIF If something is **double** the amount or size of another thing, it is twice as large. *We paid her double what she was getting before.* **2** ATTRIB ADJ You use **double** to describe a quantity of food or drink that is twice the normal size. *...a double gin.* **3** ATTRIB ADJ **Double** before a number or letter indicates that it occurs twice. *My phone number is nine, double three, two, four.* **4** ATTRIB ADJ **Double** is also used to describe a pair of similar things. *The double doors were open.* **5** ATTRIB ADJ A **double** room or bed is intended to be used by two people. **6** ERG VB If something **doubles,** it becomes twice as large. *The world population is doubling every thirty-five years... If every performance sold out, he would double his investment.* **7** VB WITH 'as' If something **doubles** as something else, it is used for it in addition to its main use. *This bedroom doubles as a study.* **8** UNCOUNT N **Doubles** is a game of tennis or badminton in which two people play against two other people. **9** PHRASE If you **bend double,** you bend right over. If you **are bent double,** you are bending right over. **10 double figures:** see **double.**

double up. PHR VB If you **double up** with laughter or pain, you bend your body right over. ♦ **doubled up** PRED ADJ *I was doubled up in pain.*

double bass, double basses. COUNT N A **double bass** is a large stringed instrument shaped like a violin, which you play standing up.

double-breasted /dʌbə[0]lbrestɪ[1]d/. ADJ A **double-breasted** jacket or coat has two wide sections at the front which overlap when you button them up.

double-check, double-checks, double-checking, double-checked. VB WITH OR WITHOUT OBJ If you **double-check** something, you check it a second time to make sure that it is completely correct or safe.

double chin, double chins. COUNT N Someone who has a **double chin** has a fold of fat under their chin.

double-cross, double-crosses, double-crossing, double-crossed. VB WITH OBJ If someone **double-crosses** you, they betray you, instead of doing what you had planned together; an informal use.

double-dealing. UNCOUNT N **Double-dealing** is deceitful behaviour.

double-decker /dʌbə[0]ldekə/, **double-deckers.** COUNT N A **double-decker** is a bus with two floors.

double-glazing. UNCOUNT N **Double-glazing** is an extra layer of glass fitted to a window to keep a room warmer or quieter.

doubly /dʌbli[1]/. **1** SUBMOD You use **doubly** to say that something has two aspects or features. *He is doubly disadvantaged, both by his age and by his nationality.* **2** SUBMOD You also use **doubly** to say that something happens or is true to a greater degree than usual. *It was doubly difficult for Dora at her age.*

doubt /daʊt/, **doubts, doubting, doubted. 1** COUNT N OR UNCOUNT N If you have **doubts** about something, you have feelings of uncertainty about it. *Frank had no doubts about the outcome of the trial... I had moments of doubt.* **2** REPORT VB If you **doubt** whether something is true or possible, you think it is probably not true or possible. *I doubt if they will ever want vanilla pudding again... Maybe he changed his mind, but I doubt it.* **3** VB WITH OBJ If you **doubt** something, you think it might not be true or might not exist. *...men who never doubt their own superiority.* **4** VB WITH OBJ If you **doubt** someone or **doubt** their word, you think they might not be telling the truth.

PHRASES • If you say there is **no doubt** about something, you are emphasizing that it is true. *Rose was mad, there was no doubt about it.* • You also use **no doubt** to say that you are assuming that something is true. *As Jennifer has no doubt told you, we are leaving tomorrow.* • You use **without doubt** or **without a doubt** to emphasize that something is true. *Hugh Scanlon became without doubt one of the most powerful men in Britain.* • If something is shown to be true **beyond a doubt,** it is shown to be definitely true. *We have established the ownership beyond all doubt.* • If something is **in doubt** or is **open to doubt,** it is uncertain. *Devaluation had put Concorde's future in doubt.* • If you are **in doubt** about something, you feel unsure about it. *If in doubt, call the doctor.* • **to give** someone **the benefit of the doubt:** see **benefit.**

doubtful /daʊtfʊl/. **1** ADJ Something that is **doubtful** seems unlikely or uncertain. *It is doubtful whether the Chairman would approve... The organisation has a doubtful future.* **2** ADJ If you are **doubtful** about something, you are unsure about it. *I was a little doubtful about accepting the job.* ♦ **doubtfully** ADV *Ralph looked at him doubtfully.*

doubtless /daʊtlɪ[2]s/. SENTENCE ADV **Doubtless** means probably or almost certainly. *Over 2,500 species are known and doubtless more are still to be discovered.*

dough /dəʊ/. UNCOUNT N **Dough** is a mixture of flour and water, and sometimes also sugar and fat, which can be cooked to make bread, pastry, or biscuits.

doughnut /dəʊnʌt/, **doughnuts.** COUNT N A **doughnut** is a lump or ring of sweet dough cooked in hot fat.

dour /dʊə/. ADJ Someone who is **dour** has a severe and unfriendly manner. *She faced me with her usual dour expression.*

douse /daʊs/, **douses, dousing, doused;** also spelled **dowse. 1** VB WITH OBJ If you **douse** a fire or light, you stop it burning or shining. **2** VB WITH OBJ If you **douse** something with liquid, you throw the liquid over it. *She had doused herself with perfume.*

dove, doves; pronounced /dʌv/ for meaning 1 and /dəʊv/ for meaning 2. **1** COUNT N A **dove** is a type of pigeon. Doves are often used as a symbol of peace. **2** In American English, **dove** is a past tense of **dive.**

dowdy /daʊdi[1]/. ADJ Someone who is **dowdy** is wearing dull and unfashionable clothes.

down /daʊn/. **1** PREP OR ADV **Down** means towards the ground or a lower level, or in a lower place. *They walked down the steps... Shall I lift your suitcase down?... The rain came down in sheets... ...the house down below.* **2** ADV You use **down** with verbs such as 'fall' or 'pull' to say that something is destroyed or falls to the ground. *The house fell down a week later... He burnt down his school.* **3** ADV If you put something **down,** you put it somewhere, so that you are no longer holding it. *Put that book down.* **4** PREP OR ADV If you go **down** a road, you go along it. *He walked down the road reading a newspaper... The library is halfway down the street... Farther down she stopped at the chemist's.* **5** PREP If you go **down** a river, you go along it in the direction that it flows. *...floating down the river.* **6** ADV **Down** is often used to mean in the south or towards the south. *There's a man down in Baltimore who does that.* **7** ADV If the amount or level of something goes **down,** it decreases. *Sheila was trying to get her weight down.* **8** PRED ADJ If something is **down** on paper, it has been written on the paper. *That date wasn't down on our news sheet.* **9** PRED ADJ If you are feeling **down,** you are feeling unhappy or depressed; an informal use. **10** UNCOUNT N **Down** is the small, soft feathers on young birds. Down is used to make pillows or quilts.

PHRASES • **Down to** a particular detail means including everything, even that detail. *Successful suicides seem to have been planned down to the last detail.* • If you **go down with** an illness or **are down with** it, you have that illness; an informal use. *She's down with the flu.* • **up and down, ups and downs:** see **up.**

downcast /daʊnkɑːst/. **1** ADJ If you are **downcast,** you are feeling sad and pessimistic. **2** ADJ If your eyes are **downcast,** you are looking towards the ground. *The girl could only nod, her eyes downcast.*

downfall /daʊnfɔːl/. **1** UNCOUNT N The **downfall** of a person or institution is their failure or loss of power. *...the downfall of a dictator.* **2** UNCOUNT N If something was someone's **downfall,** it caused their failure or loss of power. *Bad publicity was our downfall.*

downgrade /daʊngreɪd/, **downgrades, downgrading, downgraded.** VB WITH OBJ If you **downgrade** something, you give it less importance. *They were reluctant to downgrade the nuclear element of their defence.*

downhill /daʊnhɪl/. **1** ADV OR ATTRIB ADJ If something is moving **downhill,** it is moving down a slope. *The children were racing downhill on their sledges.* **2** ADV You also say that something is going **downhill** when it is deteriorating.

downpour /daʊnpɔː/, **downpours.** COUNT N A **downpour** is a heavy fall of rain.

downright /daʊnraɪt/. SUBMOD OR ATTRIB ADJ You use **downright** to emphasize that something is bad or unpleasant. *Some of the jobs were downright disgusting... That's a downright lie.*

downstairs /daʊnsteəz/. **1** ADV If you go **downstairs** in a building, you go down a staircase towards the ground floor. **2** ADV If something is **downstairs,** it is on the ground floor. *...the photograph on the piano downstairs.* **3** ATTRIB ADJ A **downstairs** room or object is on the ground floor. *...the downstairs phone.*

downstream /daʊnstriːm/. ADV Something that is moving **downstream** is moving along a river towards its mouth. *The soil is washed downstream.*

down-to-earth. ADJ **Down-to-earth** people are concerned with practical things, rather than with theories. *...his warm, down-to-earth manner.*

downtown /daʊntaʊn/. ADV OR ATTRIB ADJ **Downtown** means in or towards the centre of a city. *We went downtown... ...downtown Belfast.*

downtrodden /daʊntrɒdə[0]n/. ADJ **Downtrodden** people are treated very badly by the people with power.

downturn /daʊntɜːn/, **downturns.** COUNT N If there is a **downturn** in something such as a country's economy, it becomes worse or less successful. *...a downturn in manufacturing and industry.*

downward /daʊnwəd/, **downwards.** In normal British English, **downwards** is an adverb and **downward** is an adjective. In formal British English and in American English, **downward** is both an adjective and an adverb. **1** ADV If you move or look **downwards,** you move or look towards the ground or a lower level. *It glides gently downwards... My dad was lying face downward.* Also ATTRIB ADJ *...a downward glance.* **2** ADV If an amount or rate moves **downwards,** it decreases. *Benefit levels in the national assistance scheme were revised downwards.* Also ATTRIB ADJ *Prices started a downward plunge.*

downwind /daʊnwɪnd/. ADJ If you are **downwind** of something, the wind is blowing through it or past it towards you.

downy /daʊni[1]/. ADJ Something that is **downy** is filled or covered with small, soft feathers, or covered with very fine hairs. *...thick downy feather beds... ...the downy head of the sleeping baby.*

dowry /daʊəri[1]/, **dowries.** COUNT N A woman's **dowry** is money or goods which her family give to the man that she marries.

dowse /daʊs/. See **douse.**

doze /dəʊz/, **dozes, dozing, dozed.** VB When you **doze,** you sleep lightly or for a short period. *Thomas dozed in the armchair.* Also COUNT N *I had a short doze at ten o'clock.*

doze off. PHR VB If you **doze off,** you fall into a light sleep. *He dozed off in front of the fire.*

dozen /dʌzə[0]n/, **dozens. 1** NUMBER A **dozen** means twelve. *...a dozen eggs.* **2** QUANTIF You can use **dozens** to refer vaguely to a large number. *There had been dozens of attempts at reform.*

Dr, Drs. Dr is a written abbreviation for 'Doctor'. *...Dr Franz.*

drab /dræb/, **drabber, drabbest.** ADJ Something that is **drab** is dull and not attractive or exciting. *...the drab old building... ...a drab brown dress.*

draconian /drə^{3}kəʊnɪən/. ATTRIB ADJ **Draconian** laws or measures are extremely harsh; a formal use.

draft /drɑːft/, **drafts, drafting, drafted. 1** COUNT N A **draft** of a letter, book, or speech is an early version of it. **2** VB WITH OBJ When you **draft** a letter, book, or speech, you write the first version of it. *They drafted a letter to the local newspaper.* **3** VB WITH OBJ If you **are drafted,** you are ordered to serve in one of your country's armed forces; an American use. *I was drafted into the navy.* **4** VB WITH OBJ When people **are drafted** somewhere, they are moved there to do a particular job. *Extra staff were drafted from Paris to Rome.* **5** See also **draught.**

draftsman /drɑːftsmən/. See **draughtsman.**

drafty /drɑːfti^1/. See **draughty.**

drag /dræg/, **drags, dragging, dragged. 1** VB WITH OBJ If you **drag** something or someone somewhere, you pull them there with difficulty. *He listened as the body was dragged up the stairs... She grabbed her husband by the wrist and dragged him away.* **2** VB WITH OBJ AND ADJUNCT To **drag** someone somewhere also means to make them go there; an informal use. *I'm sorry to drag you to the telephone, but something awful has happened.* **3** REFL VB WITH ADJUNCT If you **drag** yourself somewhere, you move there slowly because you feel ill or weak or because you do not want to go. *I was able to drag myself shakily to my feet.* **4** VB If an event **drags,** it is very boring and seems to last a long time. *The part of the play which drags is the last half-hour.* **5** PHRASE If a man is **in drag,** he is wearing women's clothes; an informal use.

drag out. PHR VB If you **drag** something **out,** you make it last for longer than necessary. *How could we prevent them from dragging out the talks?*

dragon /drægən/, **dragons.** COUNT N In stories and legends, a **dragon** is an animal like a big lizard. It has wings and claws, and breathes out fire.

dragonfly /drægənflaɪ/, **dragonflies.** COUNT N A **dragonfly** is a colourful insect which is often found near water.

drain /dreɪn/, **drains, draining, drained. 1** ERG VB When something **drains,** liquid gradually flows out of it or off it. *...the problem of draining the marshes.* **2** VB WITH ADJUNCT When liquid **drains** somewhere, it flows there gradually. *The sewage drains off into the river.* **3** COUNT N A **drain** is a pipe that carries water or sewage away from a place. **4** COUNT N A **drain** is also a metal grid in a road, through which rainwater can flow away. **5** VB WITH OBJ If you **drain** a glass, you drink the whole of its contents. **6** VB WITH OBJ If something **drains** your strength or resources, it uses them up. *The project is draining the charity's funds.* ♦ **drained** ADJ *She looked tired and drained.* **7** SING N If something is a **drain** on your resources, it uses them up. *The banks are facing a large drain on their funds.*

drainage /dreɪnɪdʒ/. UNCOUNT N **Drainage** is the system or process by which water or other liquids are drained from a place. *...drainage ditches.*

draining board, draining boards. COUNT N A **draining board** is a sloping area next to a sink where you put cups, plates, and cutlery to drain.

drainpipe /dreɪnpaɪp/, **drainpipes.** COUNT N A **drainpipe** is a pipe attached to the side of a building, through which water flows from the roof into a drain.

drake /dreɪk/, **drakes.** COUNT N A **drake** is a male duck.

drama /drɑːmə/, **dramas. 1** COUNT N A **drama** is a serious play for the theatre, television, or radio. **2** UNCOUNT N You refer to plays in general as **drama.** *...an expert on modern drama.* **3** UNCOUNT N OR COUNT N You can refer to exciting aspects of a real situation as its **drama.** *...the drama of politics... ...the dramas of this village life.*

dramatic /drəmætɪk/, **dramatics. 1** ADJ A **dramatic** change is sudden and noticeable. *I expect to see dramatic improvements.* ♦ **dramatically** ADV *The way in which information is transmitted has changed dramatically.* **2** ADJ You describe something as **dramatic** when it is very exciting. *Landing on the moon was one of the most dramatic scientific adventures of this century.* **3** ADJ If you say or do something **dramatic,** you are trying to surprise and impress people. *...a dramatic gesture.* ♦ **dramatically** ADV *He paused dramatically.* **4** ATTRIB ADJ **Dramatic** art or writing is connected with plays and the theatre. *...Browning's dramatic works.* **5** UNCOUNT N **Dramatics** is the performing of plays. *...amateur dramatics.*

dramatist /dræmətɪst/, **dramatists.** COUNT N A **dramatist** is someone who writes plays.

dramatize /dræmətaɪz/, **dramatizes, dramatizing, dramatized;** also spelled **dramatise. 1** VB WITH OBJ If you **dramatize** a book or story, you rewrite it as a play. ♦ **dramatization** /dræmətaɪ-zeɪʃə^{0}n/ COUNT N *...a dramatization of the story of Ali Baba.* **2** VB WITH OBJ If you **dramatize** an event or situation, you try to make it seem more serious or exciting than it really is.

drank /dræŋk/. **Drank** is the past tense of **drink.**

drape /dreɪp/, **drapes, draping, draped. 1** VB WITH OBJ AND ADJUNCT If you **drape** a piece of cloth somewhere, you place it there so that it hangs down. *He began to drape the shawl over Gertrude's shoulders.* **2** VB WITH OBJ If something **is draped** with a piece of cloth, it is covered by it. *...coffins draped with American flags.* **3** PLURAL N **Drapes** are curtains; an American use.

drastic /dræstɪk/. **1** ADJ A **drastic** course of action is extreme and is usually taken urgently. *This may force the Government to take drastic measures.* **2** ADJ A **drastic** change is very significant and noticeable. *...the drastic decline in flat-building.* ♦ **drastically** ADV *Because of the snow, visibility was drastically reduced.*

draught /drɑːft/, **draughts;** spelled **draft** in American English. **1** COUNT N A **draught** is a current of air coming into a room or vehicle. *The draught from the window stirred the papers on her desk.* **2** COUNT N A **draught** of liquid is a large amount that you swallow. *He gulped the brandy down in one draught.* **3** ATTRIB ADJ **Draught** beer is served from barrels. **4** UNCOUNT N **Draughts** is a game for two people, played with round pieces on a board; a British use.

draughtsman /drɑːftsmən/, **draughtsmen;** spelled **draftsman** in American English. COUNT N A **draughtsman** is someone whose job is to prepare technical drawings.

draughty /drɑːfti^1/, **draughtier, draughtiest;** spelled **drafty** in American English. ADJ If a room or building is **draughty,** it has currents of cold air blowing into it.

draw /drɔː/, **draws, drawing, drew** /druː/, **drawn** /drɔːn/. **1** VB WITH OR WITHOUT OBJ If you **draw** a picture, pattern, or diagram, you make it using a pencil, pen, or crayon. *She used to draw funny pictures.* **2** VB WITH ADJUNCT When vehicles or people **draw** away or **draw** near, they move away or move near. *The cab drew away from the kerb... Jack and Roger drew near.* **3** VB WITH OBJ AND ADJUNCT If you **draw** someone or something in a particular direction, you pull them there. *He draws the document from its folder.* **4** VB WITH OBJ When an animal **draws** a cart or other vehicle, it moves along pulling the vehicle. **5** VB WITH OBJ If you **draw** a curtain or blind, you pull it across a window to cover it or uncover it. **6** PHRASE When an event or period of time **draws to an end** or **draws to a close,** it finishes. **7** VB WITH OR WITHOUT OBJ If someone **draws** a gun, sword, or knife, they pull it out of its holder so that it is ready to use. **8** VB WITH OBJ If you **draw** a deep breath, you breathe in deeply. **9** VB WITH OBJ AND ADJUNCT If you **draw** money out of a bank or building society, you take it out so that you can use it. **10** VB WITH OBJ If something **is drawn** from a thing or place, it is obtained from that thing or place. *The committee members are drawn from all sections of the local community.* **11** VB WITH OBJ If you **draw** a conclusion, distinction, or comparison, you decide that it exists or is true. *Unfortunately, they drew the wrong conclusions.* **12** VB WITH OBJ If something that you do **draws** a particular reaction, that is the way that people react to it. *The mayor drew criticism for these excesses.* **13** PHRASE If you **draw** people's **attention** to something, you make them aware of it. *He drew attention to the rising unemployment rates.* **14** RECIP VB In a game or competition, if one person or team **draws** with another one, they get the same number of points and nobody wins. Also COUNT N *The fifth game ended in a draw.* **15** See also **drawing, drawn.**

draw into. PHR VB If you **draw** someone **into** something, you cause them to become involved in it. *She refused to be drawn into the conversation.*

draw on. PHR VB **1** If you **draw on** or **upon** something, you use it. *...the kind of information an expert draws on.* **2** When someone **draws on** a cigarette, they breathe in through it and inhale the smoke.

draw up. PHR VB **1** When you **draw up** a document, list, or plan, you prepare it and write it out. *I was busy drawing up plans for the new course.* **2** When a vehicle **draws up,** it comes to a place and stops.

draw upon. PHR VB See **draw on 1.**

drawback /drɔːbæk/, **drawbacks.** COUNT N A **drawback** is an aspect of something that makes it less acceptable. *The major drawback of the system is that the funds are administered centrally.*

drawer /drɔːə^0/, **drawers.** COUNT N A **drawer** is a part of a desk or other piece of furniture that is shaped like a rectangular box. You pull it towards you to open it.

drawing /drɔːɪŋ/, **drawings. 1** COUNT N A **drawing** is a picture made with a pencil, pen, or crayon. **2** UNCOUNT N **Drawing** is the skill or work of drawing pictures. *She had a passion for drawing and painting.*

drawing pin, drawing pins. COUNT N A **drawing pin** is a short nail with a broad, flat top used for attaching papers to a vertical surface; a British use.

drawing room, drawing rooms. COUNT N A **drawing room** is a room in a large house where people sit and relax, or entertain guests; an old-fashioned use.

drawl /drɔːl/, **drawls, drawling, drawled.** VB If someone **drawls,** they speak slowly, with long vowel sounds. Also SING N *McCord spoke in a soft drawl.*

drawn /drɔːn/. **1 Drawn** is the past participle of **draw. 2** ADJ A **drawn** curtain or blind has been pulled over a window to cover it. **3** ADJ If someone looks **drawn,** they look very tired or ill. *There was a drawn and haggard look about his eyes.*

drawn-out. ADJ You describe something as **drawn-out** when it lasts longer than you think it should. *He was tired of the long drawn-out arguments.*

dread /dred/, **dreads, dreading, dreaded.** VB WITH OBJ OR -ING If you **dread** something unpleasant which may happen, you feel anxious about it. *She had begun to dread these excursions... Fanny dreaded seeing Thomas again.* Also UNCOUNT N *Her dread of returning to school gets stronger.*

dreaded /dredɪ^{2}d/. ATTRIB ADJ **Dreaded** means terrible and greatly feared. *Consumption was the most dreaded disease of the time.*

dreadful /dredfʊl/. **1** ADJ If you say that something is **dreadful,** you mean that it is very unpleasant or very poor in quality. *The weather was dreadful.* ♦ **dreadfully** ADV *Things could have gone dreadfully wrong.* **2** ATTRIB ADJ You can use **dreadful** to emphasize the degree or extent of something bad. *I was a dreadful coward... It'll be a dreadful waste.* ♦ **dreadfully** SUBMOD *The girls were dreadfully dull companions.*

dream /driːm/, **dreams, dreaming, dreamed** or **dreamt** /dremt/. **1** COUNT N A **dream** is an imaginary series of events that you experience in your mind while you are asleep. *In his dream he was sitting in a theatre watching a play.* **2** VB If you **dream** when you are asleep, you experience imaginary events in your mind. *I dreamt that I was beaten up by Ernest Hemingway.* **3** COUNT N A **dream** is also something which you often think about because you would like it to happen. *His dream of being champion had come true... ...a dream world.* **4** VB If you **dream,** you think about a situation or event that you would very much like to happen. *She dreamed of having a car.* Also ATTRIB ADJ *...a dream house.* **5** PHRASE If you say you **would not dream of** doing something, you are emphasizing that you would not do it. *A lot of the boys would never dream of going away for residential courses.*

dream up. PHR VB If someone **dreams up** a plan, they invent it. *He would never dream up a desperate scheme like that on his own.*

dreamer /driːmə/, **dreamers.** COUNT N Someone who is a **dreamer** looks forward to pleasant things that may never happen, rather than being realistic and practical.

dreamily /driːmili^1/. ADV If you do something **dreamily,** you do it without concentrating, because you are thinking about something else.

dreamy /driːmi^1/, **dreamier, dreamiest.** ADJ Someone with a **dreamy** expression looks as if they are thinking about something very pleasant. *A dreamy look came into her eyes.*

dreary /drɪəri^1/, **drearier, dreariest.** ADJ If something is **dreary,** it is so dull that it makes you feel bored or depressed. *They don't realise how dull and dreary their world is... They do only the dreariest jobs.*

dredge /dredʒ/, **dredges, dredging, dredged.** VB WITH OBJ To **dredge** a harbour or river means to clear a channel by removing mud from the bottom.

dregs /dregz/. **1** PLURAL N The **dregs** of a liquid are the last drops left at the bottom of a container, together with any solid bits that have sunk to the bottom. **2** PLURAL N WITH SUPP The **dregs** of a society or community are the people who you consider to be the worst or the most useless people in it.

drenched /drentʃt/. ADJ If you are **drenched,** you have become very wet. *Joseph was drenched with sweat.*

dress /dres/, **dresses, dressing, dressed. 1** COUNT N A **dress** is a piece of clothing worn by a woman or girl which covers her body and extends down over her legs. *She was wearing a short black dress.* **2** UNCOUNT N You can refer to a set of clothes worn by a man or a woman as a particular kind of **dress.** *He was in evening dress.* **3** VB OR REFL VB When you **dress** or **dress** yourself, you put on your clothes. *When he had shaved and dressed, he went down to the kitchen.* **4** PRED ADJ If you are **dressed,** you are wearing clothes rather than being naked. *Both men were fully dressed... Get dressed.* **5** PRED ADJ If you are **dressed** in a particular way, you are wearing clothes of a particular kind or colour. *He was dressed in a black suit.*

dress up. PHR VB If you **dress up,** you put on different clothes, in order to look smarter or to disguise yourself.

dresser /dresə/, **dressers.** 1 COUNT N In British English, a **dresser** is a piece of furniture with cupboards or drawers in the lower part and shelves in the top part. 2 COUNT N In American English, a **dresser** is a chest of drawers, usually with a mirror on the top; 3 COUNT N WITH SUPP You also use **dresser** to refer to the kind of clothes that a person wears. For example, if you say that someone is a neat dresser, you mean that they dress neatly.

dressing /dresɪŋ/, **dressings.** 1 COUNT N A **dressing** is a protective covering that is put on a wound. 2 MASS N A salad **dressing** is a mixture of oil, vinegar, and herbs, which you pour over a salad.

dressing gown, dressing gowns. COUNT N A **dressing gown** is a loose-fitting coat worn over pyjamas or a nightdress when you are not in bed.

dressing room, dressing rooms. COUNT N A **dressing room** is a room in a theatre where actors prepare for a performance.

dressing table, dressing tables. COUNT N A **dressing table** is a small table in a bedroom with drawers and a mirror.

dressmaker /dresmeɪkə/, **dressmakers.** COUNT N A **dressmaker** is a person who is paid to make women's or children's clothes.

drew /druː/. **Drew** is the past tense of **draw.**

dribble /drɪbə⁰l/, **dribbles, dribbling, dribbled.** 1 ERG VB When a liquid **dribbles** down a surface, it moves down it in a thin stream. *Condensation dribbled down the glass.* 2 VB When a person or animal **dribbles,** saliva trickles from their mouth.

dried /draɪd/. 1 **Dried** is the past tense and past participle of **dry.** 2 ATTRIB ADJ **Dried** food has been preserved by the removal of liquid from it. *...dried milk.*

drier /draɪə/. See **dryer.**

drift /drɪft/, **drifts, drifting, drifted.** 1 VB WITH ADJUNCT When something **drifts** somewhere, it is carried there by the wind or by water. *The clouds drifted away... A fishing boat was drifting slowly along.* 2 VB WITH ADJUNCT When people **drift** somewhere, they move there slowly. *The crowd started to drift away.* 3 VB WITH ADJUNCT To **drift** towards a bad situation means to slowly reach that situation. *We are drifting towards disaster.* Also SING N WITH SUPP *...the drift to violence.* 4 VB When someone **drifts** or **drifts** around, they travel from place to place without a settled way of life. ♦ **drifter** /drɪftə/ COUNT N *She was a drifter with no family and no close friends.* 5 COUNT N A **drift** is the same as a snowdrift. *There were two-foot drifts in some places.*

drift off. PHR VB If you **drift off** to sleep, you gradually fall asleep.

driftwood /drɪftwʊd/. UNCOUNT N **Driftwood** is wood which is floating on the sea or a river, or which has been carried by the water onto the shore.

drill /drɪl/, **drills, drilling, drilled.** 1 COUNT N A **drill** is a tool for making holes. *...an electric drill.* 2 VB WITH OR WITHOUT OBJ When you **drill** into something or **drill** a hole in something, you make a hole using a drill. 3 VB When people **drill** for oil or water, they search for it by drilling deep holes in the ground or in the seabed. 4 COUNT N A **drill** is also a way of learning something by repeating a routine exercise. *...spelling drills... ...a fire drill.* Also VB WITH OBJ *The band were as tightly drilled as you might expect.*

drily /draɪli¹/. See **dry.**

drink /drɪŋk/, **drinks, drinking, drank** /dræŋk/, **drunk** /drʌŋk/. 1 VB WITH OR WITHOUT OBJ When you **drink** a liquid, you take it into your mouth and swallow it. *We sat drinking coffee... He drank eagerly.* 2 COUNT N A **drink** is an amount of a liquid which you drink. *I asked for a drink of water.* 3 VB To **drink** also means to drink alcohol. *You shouldn't drink and drive.* ♦ **drinking** UNCOUNT N *There had been some heavy drinking at the party.* 4 UNCOUNT N **Drink** is alcohol, for example beer, wine, or whisky. *He eventually died of drink.* 5 COUNT N A **drink** is also an alcoholic drink. *He poured himself a drink.* 6 See also **drunk.**

drink to. PHR VB If you **drink to** someone or something, you raise your glass before drinking, and say that you hope they will be happy or successful. *They agreed on their plan and drank to it.*

drinker /drɪŋkə/, **drinkers.** 1 COUNT N A **drinker** is someone who drinks a lot of alcohol. *She had become a secret drinker.* 2 COUNT N WITH SUPP You can use **drinker** to say what kind of drink someone regularly drinks. For example, a beer drinker is someone who regularly drinks beer.

drip /drɪp/, **drips, dripping, dripped.** 1 VB When liquid **drips,** it falls in small drops. *The rain was dripping down our necks.* 2 VB When something **drips,** drops of liquid fall from it. *...the dripping of the tap.* 3 COUNT N **Drips** are drops of liquid falling from a place. *She placed a cup under the leak to catch the drips.*

drive /draɪv/, **drives, driving, drove** /drəʊv/, **driven** /drɪvə⁰n/. 1 VB WITH OR WITHOUT OBJ To **drive** a vehicle means to control it so that it goes where you want it to go. *It is her turn to drive the car... I have never learned to drive.* 2 VB WITH OBJ AND ADJUNCT If you **drive** someone somewhere, you take them there in a car. *Can I drive you to the airport?* 3 COUNT N A **drive** is a journey in a vehicle such as a car. *It'll be a thirty mile drive.* 4 COUNT N A **drive** is also a private road leading from a public road to a house. *There were several cars parked in the drive.* 5 VB WITH OBJ If something **drives** a machine, it supplies the power that makes it work. *Steam can be used to drive generators.* 6 VB WITH OBJ AND ADJUNCT If you **drive** a post or a nail into something, you force it in by hitting it with a hammer. 7 VB WITH OBJ AND ADJUNCT If people or animals **are driven** somewhere, or **driven** to do something, they are forced to go there or do it. *Half a million people had been driven out... The farming venture drove the company into debt.* 8 VB WITH OBJ If someone **is driven** by a feeling or need, this is what makes them behave as they do. *...a man driven by greed or envy.* 9 UNCOUNT N **Drive** is energy and determination. *Northcliffe had great ability and drive.* 10 SING N WITH SUPP A **drive** is also a special effort by a group of people to achieve something. *The Poles launched a tremendous investment drive.* 11 PHRASE If you understand **what** someone **is driving at,** you understand what they are trying to say. *She knew at once what I was driving at.* 12 See also **driving, drove.**

driver /draɪvə/, **drivers.** COUNT N A **driver** is someone who drives a motor vehicle.

driveway /draɪvweɪ/, **driveways.** COUNT N A **driveway** is a private road that leads from a public road to a house or garage.

driving /draɪvɪŋ/. 1 UNCOUNT N **Driving** is the activity of driving a car, or the way that you drive it. *She was found guilty of dangerous driving.* 2 ATTRIB ADJ The **driving** force behind something is the person or group mainly responsible for it. *The union is the driving force behind the revolution.*

driving licence, driving licences. COUNT N A **driving licence** is a card showing that you are qualified to drive; a British use.

drizzle /drɪzə⁰l/, **drizzles, drizzling, drizzled.** UNCOUNT N **Drizzle** is light rain falling in very small drops. Also VB *It was drizzling as I walked home.*

drone /drəʊn/, **drones, droning, droned.** VB If something **drones,** it makes a low, continuous humming noise. *The engine droned on and on.* Also SING N *...the drone of a bee.*

drool /druːl/, **drools, drooling, drooled.** 1 VB If someone **drools,** they let saliva fall from their mouth. 2 VB If you **drool** over someone or something, you look at them with uncontrolled pleasure; used showing disapproval. *Gaskell's drooling over you all the time.*

droop /druːp/, **droops, drooping, drooped.** VB If something **droops,** it hangs or leans downwards with no strength or firmness. *His shoulders drooped.* ♦ **drooping** ADJ *...drooping purple flowers.*

drop /drɒp/, **drops, dropping, dropped.** 1 ERG VB If you **drop** something, or if it **drops,** it falls straight down. *Planes dropped huge quantities of incendiary bombs... He dropped his cigar... Ash dropped from his cigarette.* 2 VB If a level or amount **drops,** it quickly becomes less. *The temperature of their bodies dropped ten degrees.* Also COUNT N *...a drop in income.* 3 ERG VB If your voice **drops** or if you **drop** your voice, you speak more quietly. 4 VB WITH OBJ AND ADJUNCT If the driver of a vehicle **drops** you somewhere, or **drops** you off, he or she stops the vehicle and you get out. 5 VB WITH OBJ If you **drop** what you are doing or dealing with, you stop doing it or dealing with it. *The charges against him were dropped... I was certain he would drop everything to help.* 6 VB WITH OBJ If you **drop** a hint, you give someone a hint in a casual way. 7 PHRASE If you **drop** someone **a line,** you write them a short letter; an informal use. 8 COUNT N A **drop** of a liquid is a very small amount of it shaped like a little ball. *A drop of blood slid down his leg.* 9 COUNT N WITH SUPP You use **drop** to talk about vertical distances. For example, a thirty-foot **drop** is a distance of thirty feet between the top of a cliff or wall and the bottom of it.

drop by or **drop in.** PHR VB If you **drop by** or **drop in,** you visit someone informally. *If there's anything you want to see, just drop by... I thought I'd just drop in and see how you were.*

drop off. PHR VB If you **drop off** to sleep, you go to sleep.

drop out. PHR VB If you **drop out** of college or university, you leave without finishing your course.

drop-out, drop-outs; an informal word. 1 COUNT N **Drop-outs** are people who reject the accepted ways of a society, for example by not having a regular job. 2 COUNT N **Drop-outs** are also young people who have left school or college before finishing their studies. *...a high-school dropout.*

droppings /drɒpɪŋz/. PLURAL N **Droppings** are the faeces of birds and small animals. *...mouse droppings.*

drought /draʊt/, **droughts.** UNCOUNT N OR COUNT N A **drought** is a long period of time during which no rain falls. *...the effects of famine and drought... Local problems include diseases and periodic droughts.*

drove /drəʊv/, **droves.** 1 **Drove** is the past tense of **drive.** 2 PLURAL N **Droves** of people are very large numbers of them.

drown /draʊn/, **drowns, drowning, drowned.** 1 ERG VB When someone **drowns** or **is drowned,** they die because they have gone under water and cannot breathe. *A man fell from a bridge and drowned... I couldn't make myself drown the poor creature.* 2 VB WITH OBJ If something **drowns** a sound, it is louder than the sound and makes it impossible to hear it. *...the heckling which drowned his speech.*

drowse /draʊz/, **drowses, drowsing, drowsed.** VB If you **are drowsing,** you are almost asleep or just asleep.

drowsy /draʊzi¹/, **drowsier, drowsiest.** ADJ If you are **drowsy,** you feel sleepy and cannot think clearly. *I became pleasantly drowsy.* ♦ **drowsily** ADV *I shook my head drowsily.* ♦ **drowsiness** UNCOUNT N *The sound of the waves lulled me into drowsiness.*

drudge /drʌdʒ/, **drudges.** COUNT N A **drudge** is someone who has to do a lot of uninteresting work.

drudgery /drʌdʒəri¹/. UNCOUNT N **Drudgery** is uninteresting work that must be done.

drug /drʌg/, **drugs, drugging, drugged.** 1 COUNT N A **drug** is a chemical substance given to people to treat or prevent illness or disease. 2 COUNT N **Drugs** are also substances that some people smoke or inject into their blood because of their stimulating effects. In most countries, these uses of drugs are illegal. *He was on drugs... She takes drugs.* 3 VB WITH OBJ If you **drug** a person or animal, you give them a chemical substance in order to make them sleepy or unconscious. ♦ **drugged** ADJ *She spoke as if she was half asleep or drugged.* 4 VB WITH OBJ If food or drink **is drugged,** a chemical substance is added to it in order to make someone unconscious when they eat or drink it.

drugstore /drʌgstɔː/, **drugstores.** COUNT N In America, a **drugstore** is a shop where you can buy medicines and other goods and also get drinks and snacks.

drum /drʌm/, **drums, drumming, drummed.** 1 COUNT N A **drum** is a musical instrument consisting of a skin stretched tightly over a round frame. It is played by beating it rhythmically with sticks or with your hands. 2 COUNT N A **drum** is also a large cylindrical container in which fuel is kept. *...oil drums.* 3 VB If something **is drumming** on a surface, it is hitting it regularly, making a continuous beating sound. *We sat listening to the rain drumming on the roof.*

drum into. PHR VB If you **drum** something **into** someone, you keep saying it to make them understand or remember it. *These facts had been drummed into him.*

drum up. PHR VB To **drum up** support means to do things that attract and win people's support.

drummer /drʌmə/, **drummers.** COUNT N A **drummer** is a person who plays a drum or drums in a band or group.

drunk /drʌŋk/, **drunks.** 1 **Drunk** is the past participle of **drink.** 2 ADJ If someone is **drunk,** they have drunk so much alcohol that they cannot speak clearly or behave sensibly. *He was so drunk he couldn't write a word.* 3 COUNT N A **drunk** is someone who is drunk or who often gets drunk.

drunkard /drʌŋkəd/, **drunkards.** COUNT N A **drunkard** is someone who often gets drunk.

drunken /drʌŋkə⁰n/. ATTRIB ADJ **Drunken** behaviour is clumsy, noisy, or foolish behaviour by someone who is drunk. *A long drunken party had just broken up.* ♦ **drunkenly** ADV *Their parents fought drunkenly with each other.* ♦ **drunkenness** /drʌŋkənnə²s/ UNCOUNT N *They acquired a reputation for drunkenness.*

dry /draɪ/, **drier** or **dryer, driest; dries, drying, dried.** 1 ADJ Something that is **dry** has no water or other liquid on it or in it. ♦ **dryness** UNCOUNT N *...the dryness of the air.* 2 ERG VB When you **dry** something or when it **dries,** it becomes dry. *He dried his feet with the towel... The washing hung drying in the sun.* 3 ADJ When the weather is **dry,** there is no rain. *The night was dry and clear.* 4 PHRASE If you are on **dry land,** you are on the shore, rather than in a ship or boat. 5 ADJ **Dry** humour is subtle and sarcastic. *I enjoyed her dry accounts of her work experiences.* ♦ **drily** or **dryly** ADV *'Thank you,' I said drily. 'It must be nice to be so culturally enlightened.'* 6 ADJ **Dry** sherry or wine does not taste sweet. *I'll have a dry* *sherry, please.* 7 See also **dried, dryer.**

dry out. PHR VB If something **dries out,** it becomes completely dry.

dry up. PHR VB 1 If something **dries up,** it loses all its water or moisture. *The pool dried up in the summer... My mouth always dries up when I'm nervous.* ♦ **dried-up** ADJ *...a dried-up piece of cake.* 2 When you **dry up** after a meal or **dry** the dishes **up,** you wipe the water off the cutlery and dishes when they have been washed. *Would you like me to dry up?* 3 If a supply or series of things **dries up,** it stops.

dry-clean, dry-cleans, dry-cleaning, dry-cleaned. VB WITH OBJ When clothes **are dry-cleaned,** they are cleaned with a liquid chemical rather than with water. ♦ **dry-cleaning** MOD *I'm taking a load of things to the dry-cleaning shop.*

dryer /draɪə/, **dryers;** also spelled **drier.** 1 COUNT N A **dryer** is a machine for drying clothes. 2 **Dryer** and **drier** are also the comparative forms of **dry.**

dual /dju:əl/. ATTRIB ADJ **Dual** means having two parts, functions, or aspects. *The committee has a dual function... ...dual nationality.*

dual carriageway /dju:əl kærɪdʒweɪ/, **dual carriageways.** COUNT N OR UNCOUNT N A **dual carriageway** is a road with a strip of grass or concrete down the middle to separate traffic going in opposite directions; a British use.

dub /dʌb/, **dubs, dubbing, dubbed.** 1 VB WITH OBJ AND COMPLEMENT If something **is dubbed** a particular name, it is given that name. *London was dubbed 'the insurance capital of the world'.* 2 VB WITH OBJ If a film **is dubbed,** the voices on the soundtrack are not those of the actors, but the voices of other actors speaking in a different language.

dubious /dju:bɪəs/. 1 ADJ You describe something as **dubious** when you think it is not completely honest, safe, or reliable. *...goods of dubious origin.* 2 PRED ADJ If you are **dubious** about something, you are unsure about it. *She was dubious about Baker's choice of pilot.* ♦ **dubiously** ADV *They looked at him dubiously, not knowing how much to believe.*

duchess /dʌtʃɪ^{2}s/, **duchesses.** COUNT N OR TITLE A **duchess** is a woman who has the same rank as a duke, or is a duke's wife or widow. *...the Duchess of Marlborough.*

duck /dʌk/, **ducks, ducking, ducked.** 1 COUNT N A **duck** is a common water bird with short legs, webbed feet, and a large flat beak. The plural form of 'duck' is either 'ducks' or 'duck'. 2 UNCOUNT N **Duck** refers to the meat of a duck when it is cooked and eaten. 3 VB WITH OR WITHOUT OBJ If you **duck,** you move your head quickly downwards to avoid being seen or hit. *A gull flew so close that she ducked.* 4 VB WITH ADJUNCT If you **duck** into a place, you move there quickly, especially to escape danger. *I ducked into the shrubbery.* 5 VB WITH OBJ If you **duck** a duty or responsibility, you avoid it.

duck out. PHR VB If you **duck out** of something that you are supposed to do, you avoid doing it.

duckling /dʌklɪŋ/, **ducklings.** COUNT N A **duckling** is a young duck.

duct /dʌkt/, **ducts.** 1 COUNT N A **duct** is a pipe, tube, or channel through which a liquid or gas is sent. 2 COUNT N A **duct** is also a tube in your body that a liquid such as tears or bile can pass through.

dud /dʌd/, **duds.** ADJ OR COUNT N You say that something is **dud** or a **dud** when it does not work properly; an informal use. *...dud light bulbs... The new system is a dud.*

due /dju:/, **dues.** 1 PREP If an event or situation is **due to** something else, it happens or exists as a result of it. *Over 40 per cent of deaths were due to this disease.* 2 PRED ADJ If something is **due** at a particular time, it is expected to happen or to arrive at that time. *What time is the bus due?... The committee was due to meet on 22 August.* 3 PHRASE If you say that something will happen **in due course,** you mean that it will happen eventually, when the time is right; a formal use. *All will be attended to in due course.* 4 PLURAL N **Dues** are sums of money that you pay regularly to an organization that you belong to. 5 PRED ADJ If some money is **due** to you, you have a right to it. *You may get slightly less than the full amount due to you.* 6 ATTRIB ADJ If you give something **due** consideration, you give it the consideration it deserves. *After due consideration of the evidence, the meeting decided that no one had been to blame.* 7 ADV You use **due** to talk about exact compass directions. For example, **due** north means exactly to the north of where you are.

duel /dju:əl/, **duels.** 1 COUNT N A **duel** is a fight between two people in which they use guns or swords in order to settle a quarrel. 2 COUNT N You can refer to any conflict between two people as a **duel.**

duet /dju:ɛt/, **duets.** COUNT N A **duet** is a piece of music sung or played by two people.

duffel coat /dʌfəl kəʊt/, **duffel coats;** also spelled **duffle coat.** COUNT N A **duffel coat** is a heavy coat with buttons shaped like rods and a hood.

dug /dʌg/. **Dug** is the past tense and past participle of **dig.**

duke /dju:k/, **dukes.** COUNT N OR TITLE A **duke** is a man with a rank just below that of a prince. *...the Duke of York.*

dull /dʌl/, **duller, dullest; dulls, dulling, dulled.** 1 ADJ Something or someone that is **dull** is not interesting. *I thought the book dull and unoriginal.* ♦ **dullness** UNCOUNT N *...the dullness of his life.* 2 ADJ You say that someone is **dull** when they show no interest in anything. *She became dull and silent.* ♦ **dully** ADV *They stared dully at the ground.* 3 ATTRIB ADJ A **dull** colour or light is not bright. *The sea had been a dull grey.* ♦ **dully** ADV *The lights of the houses gleamed dully.* 4 ADJ You say that the weather is **dull** when it is rather cloudy. *It was a dull morning.* 5 ADJ A **dull** sound is not clear or loud. *...a dull thud.* 6 ATTRIB ADJ **Dull** feelings are weak and not intense. *The dull ache in her side began again.* ♦ **dully** ADV *His ankle throbbed dully.* 7 VB WITH OBJ If something **dulls** a pain or feeling, it causes it to seem less intense.

duly /dju:li^1/. ADV If something is **duly** done, it is done in the correct way; a formal use. *She was declared duly elected to Parliament.*

dumb /dʌm/, **dumber, dumbest.** 1 ADJ Someone who is **dumb** is completely unable to speak. 2 PRED ADJ If someone is **dumb** on a particular occasion, they cannot speak because they are angry, shocked, or surprised. *We were struck dumb with horror.* 3 ADJ **Dumb** also means stupid; an informal use.

dumbfounded /dʌmfaʊndɪ^{2}d/. ADJ If you are **dumbfounded,** you are so surprised that you cannot speak. *He was watching, dumbfounded.*

dummy /dʌmi^1/, **dummies.** 1 COUNT N A baby's **dummy** is a rubber or plastic object that you give to it to suck so that it feels comforted; a British use. 2 COUNT N A tailor's **dummy** is a model of a person that is used to display clothes. 3 ATTRIB ADJ You use **dummy** to describe things that are not real. For example, a **dummy** car is not a real car, but has been made to look or behave like a real car.

dump /dʌmp/, **dumps, dumping, dumped.** 1 VB WITH OBJ When unwanted waste matter **is dumped,** it is put somewhere and is intended to remain there for ever. ♦ **dumping** UNCOUNT N *...the dumping of acid wastes in the North Sea.* 2 VB WITH OBJ If you **dump** something somewhere, you put it there quickly and carelessly. *She dumped her bag on Judy's table.* 3 COUNT N A **dump** or a **rubbish dump** is a place where rubbish is left, for example on open ground outside a town. 4 COUNT N If you refer to a place as a **dump,** you mean it is unattractive and unpleasant to live in; an informal use.

dumpling /dʌmplɪŋ/, **dumplings.** COUNT N A **dumpling** is a lump of dough cooked with meat and vegetables.

dumpy /dʌmpi^1/. ADJ A **dumpy** person is short and fat.

dun /dʌn/. ADJ Something that is **dun** is a dull grey-brown colour.

dune /dju:n/, **dunes.** COUNT N A **dune** or a sand **dune** is a hill of sand near the sea or in a desert.

dung /dʌŋ/. UNCOUNT N **Dung** is faeces from large animals.

dungarees /dʌŋgəri:z/. PLURAL N **Dungarees** are trousers attached to a piece of cloth which covers your chest and has straps going over your shoulders.

dungeon /dʌndʒən/, **dungeons.** COUNT N A **dungeon** is a dark underground prison in a castle.

dunk /dʌŋk/, **dunks, dunking, dunked.** VB WITH OBJ If you **dunk** something in a liquid, you put it there for a short time before swallowing it; an informal use. *I dunked my bread in the cocoa.*

dupe /dju:p/, **dupes, duping, duped.** 1 VB WITH OBJ If someone **dupes** you, they trick you. *I was duped into expressing my thoughts.* 2 COUNT N A **dupe** is someone who has been tricked.

duplicate, duplicates, duplicating, duplicated; pronounced /dju:plɪkeɪt/ when it is a verb and /dju:plɪkə^{1}t/ when it is a noun or adjective. 1 VB WITH OBJ If you **duplicate** a piece of writing or a drawing, you make exact copies of it using a machine. 2 COUNT N A **duplicate** is something that is identical to something else. Also ATTRIB ADJ *...a duplicate key.* 3 PHRASE If you have something **in duplicate,** you have two identical copies of it. 4 VB WITH OBJ When an activity is **duplicated,** two people or two groups do the same thing. ♦ **duplication** /dju:plɪkeɪʃən/ UNCOUNT N *We try to avoid duplication of work.*

durable /djʊərəbəl/. ADJ Something that is **durable** is strong and lasts a long time. *...durable products.* ♦ **durability** /djʊərəbɪlɪ^{1}ti^1/ UNCOUNT N *...the durability of their love.*

duration /djʊreɪʃən/. SING N The **duration** of something is the length of time that it lasts for. *He was prepared to do this for the duration of the campaign.*

duress /djʊərɛs/. PHRASE If you do something **under duress,** you are forced to do it.

during /djʊərɪŋ/. 1 PREP Something that happens **during** a period of time happens continuously or repeatedly in that period. *She heated the place during the winter with a huge wood furnace... Fred had worked with her at Oxford during the war.* 2 PREP You also use **during** to say that something happens at some point in a period of time. *He had died during the night.*

dusk /dʌsk/. UNCOUNT N **Dusk** is the time just before night when it is not completely dark.

dusky /dʌski^1/. ADJ Something that is **dusky** is rather dark. *...her dusky cheeks.*

dust /dʌst/, **dusts, dusting, dusted.** 1 UNCOUNT N **Dust** is dry, fine powder such as particles of earth, dirt, or pollen. *Each car threw up a cloud of white dust... ...the dust on the coffee table.* 2 VB WITH OR WITHOUT OBJ When you **dust** furniture or other objects, you remove dust from them using a duster. *She lifted the jugs as she dusted the shelf... He washed, tidied, and dusted.* 3 VB WITH OBJ If you **dust** a surface with a powder, you cover it lightly with the powder.

dustbin /dʌstbɪn/, **dustbins.** COUNT N A **dustbin** is a large container that you put rubbish in; a British use.

duster /dʌstə/, **dusters.** COUNT N A **duster** is a cloth used for removing dust from furniture and other objects.

dustman /dʌstmə^{3}n/, **dustmen.** COUNT N A **dustman** is a person whose job is to empty dustbins; a British use.

dusty /dʌsti^1/, **dustier, dustiest.** ADJ Something that is **dusty** is covered with dust. *...a dusty mountain track... ...a room full of dusty, broken furniture.*

Dutch /dʌtʃ/. 1 ADJ **Dutch** means belonging or relating to the Netherlands. 2 UNCOUNT N **Dutch** is the language spoken by people who live in the Netherlands. 3 PLURAL N The **Dutch** are the people who come from the Netherlands.

dutiful /dju:tɪfʊl/. ADJ If you are **dutiful,** you do everything that you are expected to do. *He was a dutiful son.* ♦ **dutifully** ADV *The audience dutifully applauded.*

duty /dju:ti^1/, **duties.** 1 UNCOUNT N **Duty** is the work that you have to do as your job. *He reported for duty at the manager's office.* 2 PHRASE When policemen, doctors, or nurses are **on duty,** they are working. When they are **off duty,** they are not working. *A police constable on duty became suspicious... You can go off duty now.* 3 PLURAL N Your **duties** are the tasks you do as part of your job. *A young woman was going to give instruction in her duties.* 4 SING N WITH POSS If you say that something is your **duty,** you mean that you ought to do it because it is your responsibility. *As a doctor, it was my duty to preserve life.* 5 COUNT N **Duties** are taxes which you pay to the government on goods that you buy. *The government increased the duty on petrol.*

duty-free. ADJ **Duty-free** goods are bought at airports or on planes or ships at a cheaper price than usual because they are not taxed.

duvet /du:veɪ/, **duvets.** COUNT N A **duvet** is a large bag filled with feathers or similar material, which you use to cover yourself in bed; a British use.

dwarf /dwɔ:f/, **dwarfs, dwarfing, dwarfed.** 1 VB WITH OBJ If one thing **dwarfs** another thing, it makes the other thing look small. *David was dwarfed by a huge desk.* 2 ATTRIB ADJ **Dwarf** plants or animals are much smaller than other plants or animals of the same kind. 3 COUNT N A **dwarf** is a person who is much smaller than most people.

dwell /dwɛl/, **dwells, dwelling, dwelled** or **dwelt** /dwɛlt/. VB WITH ADJUNCT If you **dwell** somewhere, you live there; an old-fashioned use.

dwell on. PHR VB If you **dwell on** something or **dwell upon** it, you think, speak, or write about it a great deal. *She began to dwell on memories of her mother... So far we have dwelt upon the negative elements in the situation.*

dweller /dwɛlə/, **dwellers.** COUNT N WITH SUPP You use **dweller** to say where someone lives. For example, a city **dweller** is someone who lives in a city.

dwelling /dwɛlɪŋ/, **dwellings.** COUNT N A **dwelling** is a house or other place where someone lives; a formal use. *They were five miles from the nearest dwelling.*

dwindle /dwɪndəl/, **dwindles, dwindling, dwindled.** VB If something **dwindles,** it becomes smaller or less strong. *Their small hoard of money dwindled.* ♦ **dwindling** ADJ *...an area of rapidly dwindling forest.*

dye /daɪ/, **dyes, dyeing, dyed.** 1 VB WITH OBJ If you **dye** hair or cloth, you change its colour by soaking it in a coloured liquid. ♦ **dyed** ADJ *...a woman with dyed red* *hair.* **2** MASS N A **dye** is a substance which is mixed into a liquid and used to change the colour of cloth or hair.

dying /daɪɪŋ/. **1** **Dying** is the present participle of **die. 2** PLURAL N The **dying** are people who are so ill or so badly injured that they are likely to die soon. *She cared for the poor, the diseased and the dying.* **3** ATTRIB ADJ A **dying** tradition or industry is becoming less important and is likely to end altogether.

dyke /daɪk/, **dykes;** also spelled **dike.** COUNT N A **dyke** is a thick wall that prevents water flooding onto land from a river or from the sea.

dynamic /daɪnæmɪk/, **dynamics. 1** ADJ A **dynamic** person is full of energy. *The new President is a dynamic and able man.* ♦ **dynamically** ADV *We would like to see them participate more dynamically.* **2** PLURAL N The **dynamics** of a society or a situation are the forces that cause it to change. *...the dynamics of industrial development.*

dynamism /daɪnəmɪzə^{0}m/. UNCOUNT N Someone's **dynamism** is their energy or ability to produce new ideas.

dynamite /daɪnəmaɪt/. UNCOUNT N **Dynamite** is an explosive. *...rebels wielding sticks of dynamite.*

dynamo /daɪnəməʊ/, **dynamos.** COUNT N A **dynamo** is a device that uses the movement of a machine to produce electricity.

dynasty /dɪnəsti^1/, **dynasties.** COUNT N A **dynasty** is a series of rulers of a country who all belong to the same family.

dysentery /dɪsə^{0}ntri^1/. UNCOUNT N **Dysentery** is an infection that causes severe diarrhoea.

dyslexia /dɪslɛksɪə/. UNCOUNT N **Dyslexia** is difficulty with reading, caused by a slight disorder of the brain. ♦ **dyslexic** /dɪslɛksɪk/ ADJ *...dyslexic pupils.*

Ee

E. E is a written abbreviation for 'east'.

each /iːtʃ/. **1** DET OR PRON If you refer to **each** thing or person in a group, you are referring to every member and considering them as individuals. *Each county is subdivided into several districts... There were peaches and pears. I opened two tins of each.* **2** PRON You use **each** to emphasize that you are referring to every individual thing or person in a group. *They cost eight pounds each.* **3** PRON You use **each other** when you are saying that each member of a group does something to the others. *She and John looked at each other.*

eager /iːgə/. ADJ If you are **eager** to do or have something, you very much want to do it or have it. *The majority were eager for change.* ♦ **eagerly** ADV *...eagerly waiting for news of a victory.* ♦ **eagerness** UNCOUNT N *...my eagerness to learn.*

eagle /iːgə^{0}l/, **eagles.** COUNT N An **eagle** is a large bird that lives by eating small animals.

ear /ɪə/, **ears. 1** COUNT N Your **ears** are the two parts of your body, one on each side of your head, with which you hear. **2** SING N WITH SUPP You can use **ear** to refer to a person's willingness to listen to someone. *He tried to give a sympathetic ear at all times.* **3** COUNT N The **ears** of a cereal plant such as wheat are the top parts containing the seeds.

PHRASES ● If you **keep** or **have** your **ear to the ground,** you make sure that you are well informed about what is happening. ● If you can **play** a piece of music **by ear,** you can play it after listening to it, rather than by reading printed music. ● If you **turn a deaf ear** to something that is being said, you ignore it. ● When someone forgets what you tell them, you can say that it **goes in one ear and out the other.**

eardrum /ɪədrʌm/, **eardrums.** COUNT N Your **eardrums** are thin pieces of skin inside your ears, which vibrate so that you can hear sounds.

earl /ɜːl/, **earls.** COUNT N OR TITLE An **earl** is a British nobleman.

earlier /ɜːli^{1}ə/. ADV OR ADJ **Earlier** is the comparative of **early.** It is also used to refer to a time before the present or before the one you are talking about. *Her parents had died of cholera four years earlier... ...in earlier times, when this fashion was popular.*

early /ɜːli^1/, **earlier, earliest. 1** ADV OR ATTRIB ADJ **Early** means near the beginning of a period of time, a process, or a piece of work. *I got up early... ...early last week... ...in the early 1980s.* **2** ADV OR ADJ If someone or something arrives or happens **early,** they arrive or happen before the expected or normal time. *The day's practice ended early because of bad light... ...her husband's early death.*

PHRASES ● **As early as** means at a particular time that is surprisingly early. *As early as 1978 the United States had taken steps to counteract this.* ● **At the earliest** means not before the date or time mentioned. *No developments were expected before August at the earliest.* ● **bright and early:** see **bright.** ● **early night:** see **night.**

earmark /ɪəmɑːk/, **earmarks, earmarking, earmarked.** VB WITH OBJ If something **is earmarked** for a particular purpose, it has been reserved for that purpose.

earn /ɜːn/, **earns, earning, earned. 1** VB WITH OBJ If you **earn** money, you receive it in return for work that you do. *...the average worker, earning $15,058... They have to earn a living somehow.* ♦ **earner** /ɜːnə/, COUNT N WITH SUPP *Most wage earners can afford it.* **2** VB WITH OBJ If something **earns** money, it produces money as profit. **3** VB WITH OBJ If you **earn** something such as praise, you get it because you deserve it. *He has earned his place in history.*

earnest /ɜːnɪ^{2}st/. **1** ADJ **Earnest** people are very serious. *...an earnest young man from the University... It is my earnest wish that you use this money to further your research.* ♦ **earnestly** ADV *He was in a corner of the room talking earnestly to Julie.* **2** PHRASE If you are **in earnest,** you are sincere. *Is the President in earnest about the desire to negotiate?* **3** PHRASE If something happens **in earnest,** it happens to a greater extent than before. *Work on the tunnel began in earnest soon after.*

earnings /ɜːnɪŋz/. PLURAL N Your **earnings** are the money that you earn by working.

earphone /ɪəfəʊn/, **earphones.** COUNT N **Earphones** are a piece of equipment which you wear over or inside your ears, so that you can listen to a radio or a cassette recorder in private.

earring /ɪərɪŋ/, **earrings.** COUNT N **Earrings** are pieces of jewellery which hang from your ears.

earshot /ɪəʃɒt/. PHRASE If you are **within earshot** of something, you are close enough to be able to hear it. If you are **out of earshot,** you are too far away to hear it. *There was no one within earshot... Keep him out of earshot if possible.*

earth /ɜːθ/, **earths. 1** PROPER N The **earth** is the planet on which we live. **2** SING N The **earth** is also the land surface on which we live and move about. *For twenty minutes the earth shook.* **3** UNCOUNT N **Earth** is the substance in which plants grow. **4** COUNT N An **earth** is an electrical wire which passes from an appliance into the ground to make the appliance safe.

PHRASES ● You use **on earth** with words such as 'how', 'why', 'what', or 'where', or with negatives, to emphasize that there is no obvious answer to a question or problem. *How on earth do we raise half a million dollars?... He was wondering what on earth he should do.* ● If something costs **the earth,** it costs a very large amount of money; an informal use. *If you go to a commercial photographer he'll charge the earth for it.* ● See also **down-to-earth.**

earthen /ɜːθə^{0}n/. **1** ATTRIB ADJ **Earthen** pots are made of baked clay. **2** ATTRIB ADJ An **earthen** floor is made of hard earth.

earthenware /ɜːθə^{0}nweə/. ATTRIB ADJ **Earthenware** pots are made of baked clay. *...a big earthenware jar.* Also UNCOUNT N *...bowls of glazed earthenware.*

earthly /ɜːθli^1/. **1** ATTRIB ADJ **Earthly** means happening in the material world and not in any spiritual life or life after death. *She believed that our earthly life is all that matters.* **2** ATTRIB ADJ If you say that there is no **earthly** reason for something, you are emphasizing that there is no reason for it.

earthquake /ɜːθkweɪk/, **earthquakes.** COUNT N An **earthquake** is a shaking of the ground caused by movement of the earth's crust.

earthworm /ɜːθwɜːm/, **earthworms.** COUNT N An **earthworm** is a worm that lives under the ground.

earthy /ɜːθi^1/. **1** ADJ Someone who is **earthy** does not mind talking openly about things such as sex that other people find embarrassing. **2** ADJ Something that is **earthy** looks, smells, or feels like earth. *...the subtle, earthy fragrance of wild thyme.*

ease /iːz/, **eases, easing, eased. 1** UNCOUNT N **Ease** is lack of difficulty. *She performed this trick with ease.* **2** PHRASE If you are **at ease,** you feel confident and comfortable. If you are **ill at ease,** you are anxious or worried. *He was at ease with strangers... Brody felt ill at ease and patronized.* **3** VB WITH OBJ If something **eases** an unpleasant situation, it makes it less unpleasant. *The bungalows were built to ease the housing shortage... ...a powder which eased the pain.* **4** ERG VB If something **eases** or **eases** off, it reduces in degree, quantity, or intensity. *Crude oil prices have eased slightly... The rain had eased off.* **5** VB WITH OBJ AND ADJUNCT If you **ease** something somewhere, you move it there slowly and carefully. *I eased the back door open.*

easel /iːzə^{0}l/, **easels.** COUNT N An **easel** is a wooden frame that supports a picture which an artist is painting.

easily /iːzɪli^1/. **1** ADV If something can be done **easily,** it can be done without difficulty. *A baby buggy can be easily carried on a bus or in a car.* **2** ADV You use **easily** to emphasize that something is very likely to happen, or is certainly true. *She might easily decide to cancel the whole thing... This car is easily the most popular model.* **3** ADV You also use **easily** to say that something happens more quickly than normal. *He tired very easily.*

east /iːst/. **1** SING N The **east** is the direction in which you look to see the sun rise. *Ben noticed the first faint streaks of dawn in the east.* **2** SING N The **east** of a place is the part which is towards the east. *...old people in the east of Glasgow.* Also ATTRIB ADJ *...East Africa.* **3** ADV **East** means towards the east, or to the east of a place or thing. *They were heading almost due east.* **4** ATTRIB ADJ An **east** wind blows from the east. **5** SING N The **East** is used to refer either to the countries in the southern and eastern part of Asia, including India, China, and Japan, or to the former USSR and other countries in eastern Europe. *He was deeply interested in meditation, the East, and yoga... ...a breakthrough in East-West relations.* **6** See also **Far East, Middle East.**

Easter /iːstə/. UNCOUNT N **Easter** is a religious festival when Christians celebrate the resurrection of Christ after his death.

Easter egg, Easter eggs. COUNT N An **Easter egg** is a chocolate egg given as a present at Easter.

easterly /iːstəli^1/. **1** ADJ **Easterly** means towards the east. **2** ADJ An **easterly** wind blows from the east.

eastern /iːstə^{5}n/. **1** ATTRIB ADJ **Eastern** means in or from the east of a region or country. *...a small town in Eastern Portugal.* **2** ATTRIB ADJ **Eastern** also means coming either from the people or countries of the East, such as India, China, and Japan, or from the countries in the East of Europe and the former USSR. *...Eastern philosophy... ...the Eastern bloc.*

eastward /iːstwəd/ or **eastwards. 1** ADV **Eastward** or **eastwards** means towards the east. *They travelled eastwards.* **2** ATTRIB ADJ **Eastward** is used to describe things which are moving towards the east or which face towards the east. *...a grassy eastward slope.*

easy /iːzi^1/, **easier, easiest. 1** ADJ Something that is **easy** can be done without difficulty. *The house is easy to keep clean... This new dancing looked easy.* **2** ADJ **Easy** also means relaxed. *They have a natural, easy confidence.* **3** ADJ An **easy** life or time is comfortable and without any problems. *I wanted to make life easier for you.*

PHRASES ● If you **take it easy** or **take things easy,** you relax and do very little; an informal use. ● If you **go easy on** something, you avoid using too much of it; an informal use. ● You can say **easier said than done** to indicate that it is difficult to do what someone has just suggested.

easy chair, easy chairs. COUNT N An **easy chair** is a large, comfortable chair.

easy-going. ADJ An **easy-going** person is not easily annoyed or upset.

eat /iːt/, **eats, eating, ate,** /eɪt, ɛt/, **eaten.** VB WITH OR WITHOUT OBJ When you **eat** something, you put it into your mouth, chew it, and swallow it. *He began to eat his sandwich... He said he would eat at his hotel.*

eat into. PHR VB If a substance such as acid or rust **eats into** something, it destroys the surface of the thing.

eat out. PHR VB When you **eat out,** you have a meal at a restaurant.

eat up. PHR VB If you **eat up** your food, you eat it all.

eater /iːtə/, **eaters.** COUNT N WITH SUPP You use **eater** to refer to someone who eats in a particular way or eats a particular thing. *...a slow eater... ...a meat eater.*

eaves /iːvz/. PLURAL N **The eaves** of a house are the lower edges of its roof.

eavesdrop /iːvzdrɒp/, **eavesdrops, eavesdropping, eavesdropped.** VB If you **eavesdrop** on someone, you listen secretly to what they are saying.

ebb /ɛb/, **ebbs, ebbing, ebbed. 1** VB If a feeling or a person's strength **ebbs,** it weakens; a literary use. *Only then did the strength ebb from his fingers.* **2** PHRASE If something is **at a low ebb,** it is not being very successful or profitable. *George's fortunes at this time were at a low ebb.* **3** VB When the tide or the sea **ebbs,** its level falls. Also SING N *...the stormy ebb and flow of the sea.*

ebony /ɛbəni^1/. **1** UNCOUNT N **Ebony** is a very hard, dark-coloured wood. **2** ADJ Something that is **ebony** in colour is very deep black.

ebullient /i^{1}bʌli^{1}ənt/. ADJ An **ebullient** person is lively and full of enthusiasm; a formal use.

EC /iː siː/. PROPER N The **EC** is the former name of the European Union, the organization of European countries that have joint policies on matters such as trade, agriculture, and human rights. 'EC' is an abbreviation for 'European Community'.

eccentric /ɪ2ksɛntrɪk/, **eccentrics.** 1 ADJ An **eccentric** person has habits or opinions that other people think strange. *...a slightly eccentric Frenchman.* ♦ **eccentricity** /ɛksɛntrɪsɪ1ti1/ UNCOUNT N OR COUNT N *...the eccentricity of Rose's behaviour... ...her husband's eccentricities.* 2 COUNT N An **eccentric** is a person with strange habits or opinions. *...a bunch of harmless eccentrics.*

ecclesiastical /ɪ2kliːziæstɪkə0l/. ADJ **Ecclesiastical** means belonging to or connected with the Christian Church.

echelon /ɛʃə0lɒn/, **echelons.** COUNT N WITH SUPP An **echelon** is a level of power or responsibility in an organization; a formal use. *...the higher echelons of the party.*

echo /ɛkəʊ/, **echoes, echoing, echoed.** 1 COUNT N An **echo** is a sound caused by a noise being reflected off a surface such as a wall. *Judy listened to the echo of her shoes clicking on the marble floors.* 2 VB If a sound **echoes,** a reflected sound can be heard after it. *Our footsteps echoed through the large hollow lobby.* 3 VB In a place that **echoes,** a sound is repeated after the original sound has stopped. *The bamboo grove echoed with the screams of monkeys.* ♦ **echoing** ADJ *...echoing halls.* 4 COUNT N An **echo** is also an expression of an attitude, opinion, or statement which has already been expressed. *The echo of public sentiment in Congress was inevitable.* 5 VB WITH OBJ If you **echo** someone's words, you repeat them or express the same thing. *Todd's disappointment was echoed by Ian Stark.* 6 COUNT N WITH SUPP A detail or feature which reminds you of something else can also be referred to as an **echo.** *...echoes of the past.*

eclectic /ɪ2klɛktɪk/. ADJ **Eclectic** means using what seems to be best from different ideas or beliefs; a formal use. *...an eclectic mixture of Western and Asian thought.*

eclipse /ɪ1klɪps/, **eclipses, eclipsing, eclipsed.** 1 COUNT N When there is an **eclipse,** one planet, sun, or moon passes in front of another and hides it partially or completely from view. *...an eclipse of the sun.* 2 SING N If someone or something suffers an **eclipse,** they lose some or all of their importance or influence. *...the eclipse of the radical press.* 3 VB WITH OBJ If one thing **eclipses** another, the first thing becomes more important so that the second thing is no longer noticed. *Less talented artists were totally eclipsed.*

ecology /ɪ1kɒləd3i1/. 1 UNCOUNT N When you talk about the **ecology** of a place, you are referring to the relationships between living things and their environment. *...the delicate ecology of the rainforest.* ♦ **ecological** /iːkəlɒdʒɪkə0l/, ATTRIB ADJ *Use of nitrogen fertilizers has damaged the ecological balance in the lake.* ♦ **ecologically** SUBMOD *...an ecologically sound system of farm management.* 2 UNCOUNT N **Ecology** is the study of the relationship between living things and their environment. *...the most recent research in ecology.* ♦ **ecologist** /ɪ1kɒlə7dʒɪst/ COUNT N *Ecologists estimate that half of the ancient woodlands in Britain are in danger of extinction.*

economic /iːkənɒmɪk, ɛk-/, **economics.** 1 ATTRIB ADJ **Economic** means concerned with the organization of the money, industry, and trade of a country, region, or social group. *...a period of economic and industrial crisis.* ♦ **economically** ADV *...an economically stable society.* 2 ADJ A business that is **economic** produces a profit. 3 UNCOUNT N **Economics** is the study of the way in which money, industry, and trade are organized in a society. 4 UNCOUNT N WITH SUPP The **economics** of a society or industry is the system of organizing money and trade in it. *...the economics of the timber trade.*

economical /iːkənɒmɪkə0l, ɛk-/. 1 ADJ Something that is **economical** does not require a lot of money to operate. *This system was extremely economical because it ran on half-price electricity.* ♦ **economically** ADV *This service could be most economically operated.* 2 ADJ If someone is **economical,** they spend money carefully and sensibly. ♦ **economically** ADV *We live very economically.* 3 ADJ **Economical** also means using the minimum amount of something that is necessary. *She spoke in short, economical sentences.*

economist /ɪ1kɒnəmɪst/, **economists.** COUNT N An **economist** is a person who studies, teaches, or writes about economics.

economize /ɪ1kɒnəmaɪz/, **economizes, economizing, economized;** also spelled **economise.** VB If you **economize,** you save money by spending it very carefully. *The loss of business was so great that they had to economize on staff.*

economy /ɪ1kɒnəmi1/, **economies.** 1 COUNT N The **economy** of a country or region is the system by which money, industry, and trade are organized. *New England's economy is still largely based on manufacturing.* 2 COUNT N The wealth obtained by a country or region from business and industry is also referred to as its **economy.** *Unofficial strikes were damaging the British economy.* 3 UNCOUNT N **Economy** is careful spending or the careful use of things to save money. *His house was small, for reasons of economy.*

ecstasy /ɛkstəsi1/, **ecstasies.** UNCOUNT N **Ecstasy** is a feeling of very great happiness.

ecstatic /ɪ2kstætɪk/. ADJ If you are **ecstatic,** you feel very enthusiastic and happy. *Eddie was ecstatic over his new rifle... ...a wild ecstatic happiness.* ♦ **ecstatically** ADV *...children jumping ecstatically up and down.*

ecumenical /iːkjuːmɛnɪkə0l, ɛk-/. ADJ **Ecumenical** is used to describe ideas and movements which try to unite different Christian Churches; a formal use.

-ed. 1 SUFFIX **-ed** is used to form the past tense of most verbs. *He blinked in the bright light... Tim dodged round the car.* 2 SUFFIX **-ed** is also used to form the past participle of most verbs. The past participles of transitive verbs are often used as adjectives indicating that something has been affected in some way. The past participles of a few intransitive verbs are used as adjectives indicating that a person or thing has done something. Adjectives of this kind are often not defined but are treated with the related verbs. *They had arrived two hours earlier... ...fried eggs... ...an escaped prisoner.* 3 SUFFIX **-ed** is also added to nouns to form adjectives which describe someone or something as having a particular feature. For example, a bearded man is a man with a beard. Adjectives of this kind are sometimes not defined but are treated with the related nouns. *...gabled houses.*

eddy /ɛdi1/, **eddies, eddying, eddied.** VB If water or wind **eddies,** it moves round and round in no particular direction. *The wind whipped and eddied around the buildings.* Also COUNT N *...every eddy of the tide.*

edge /ɛdʒ/, **edges, edging, edged.** 1 COUNT N The **edge** of something is the place or line where it stops and another thing begins. *Little children played at the water's edge.* 2 COUNT N The **edge** of a flat, thin object is its long side. *...the edge of a ruler.* 3 VB WITH OBJ If something **is edged** with a particular thing, it has that thing along its edge. *...a beautiful garden edged with flowering trees.* 4 VB WITH OR WITHOUT OBJ, WITH ADJUNCT If you **edge** somewhere, or **edge your way** there, you move there very slowly. *He edged away from the thug... I edged my way to the window.* 5 SING N If people are on the **edge** of an event, it is likely to happen soon. *The world had been brought to the edge of war.* 6 PHRASE If you are **on edge,** you are nervous and unable to relax. *The prospect was setting his nerves on edge.* 7 SING N If you have an **edge** over someone, you have an advantage over them. *Europe's edge over the rest of the world became marked.*

edging /ɛdʒɪŋ/, **edgings.** COUNT N An **edging** is something that is put along the sides of something else to make it look attractive. *...a blouse trimmed with bows and lace edgings.*

edgy /ɛdʒi1/. ADJ When you are **edgy,** you are nervous and anxious.

edible /ɛdɪ1bə0l/. ADJ Something that is **edible** is safe to eat and not poisonous. *...edible mushrooms.*

edict /iːdɪkt/, **edicts.** COUNT N An **edict** is a command given by someone in authority; a formal use. *I told the factory inspector we would defy his edict.*

edifice /ɛdɪfɪs/, **edifices;** a formal word. 1 COUNT N An **edifice** is a large and impressive building; 2 COUNT N An **edifice** is also a system of beliefs or a traditional institution. *The whole edifice of modern civilization is beginning to sway.*

edify /ɛdɪfaɪ/, **edifies, edifying, edified.** VB WITH OBJ If something **edifies** you, it teaches you something useful or interesting; a formal use. *...a series of popular talks intended to edify and entertain.* ♦ **edifying** ADJ *He may come out with all sorts of edifying sentiments.* ♦ **edification** /ɛdɪfɪkeɪʃə0n/ UNCOUNT N *...books bought for instruction or edification.*

edit /ɛdɪt/, **edits, editing, edited.** 1 VB WITH OR WITHOUT OBJ If you **edit** a text, you correct it so that it is suitable for publication. 2 VB WITH OBJ If you **edit** a book, you collect pieces of writing by different authors and prepare them for publication. *...'The Save and Prosper Book of Money,' edited by Margaret Allen.* 3 VB WITH OBJ If you **edit** a film or a television or radio programme, you choose material for it and arrange it in a particular order. 4 VB WITH OBJ Someone who **edits** a newspaper or magazine is in charge of it and makes decisions concerning the contents.

edition /ɪ2dɪʃə0n/, **editions.** 1 COUNT N WITH SUPP An **edition** is a particular version of a book, magazine, or newspaper that is printed at one time. *...the city edition of the New York Times.* 2 COUNT N WITH SUPP An **edition** is also a television or radio programme that is one of a series. *...tonight's edition of Kaleidoscope.*

editor /ɛdɪtə/, **editors.** 1 COUNT N An **editor** is a person in charge of a newspaper or magazine, or a section of a newspaper or magazine, who makes decisions concerning the contents. *....the editor of a local newspaper... ...the foreign editor.* 2 COUNT N An **editor** is also a person who checks and corrects texts before they are published. 3 COUNT N A person who selects recorded material for a film or for radio or television programmes is also called an **editor.**

editorial /ɛdɪtɔːrɪəl/, **editorials.** 1 ATTRIB ADJ **Editorial** means involved in preparing a newspaper, magazine, or book for publication. *Hearst expanded his editorial staff.* 2 ATTRIB ADJ **Editorial** also means involving the attitudes, opinions, and contents of a newspaper, magazine, or television programme. *...the paper's editorial policy.* 3 COUNT N An **editorial** is an article in a newspaper which gives the opinion of the editor or publisher on a particular topic.

educate /ɛdjə4keɪt/, **educates, educating, educated.** 1 VB WITH OBJ When someone **is educated,** he or she is taught at a school or college. 2 ADJ **Educated** people have reached a high standard of learning. 3 VB WITH OBJ To **educate** people also means to teach them better ways of doing something or a better way of living. *Not enough is being done to educate smokers about the benefits of stopping the habit.*

education /ɛdjə4keɪʃə0n/. UNCOUNT N **Education** consists of teaching people various subjects at a school or college.

educational /ɛdjə4keɪʃə0nəl, -ʃənə0l/. ADJ **Educational** means concerned with and related to education. *...an educational institution.* ♦ **educationally** ADV *...a school for the educationally subnormal.*

educationalist /ɛdjə4keɪʃə0nəlɪst/, **educationalists.** COUNT N An **educationalist** is a specialist in the theories and methods of education.

EEC /iː iː siː/. PROPER N The **EEC** is a former name of the European Union; see **EC.**

eel /iːl/, **eels.** COUNT N An **eel** is a long, thin, snake-like fish.

eerie /ɪəri1/. ADJ Something that is **eerie** is strange and frightening. *...the eerie feeling that someone was watching me.* ♦ **eerily** ADV *The lights gleamed eerily.*

efface /ɪ1feɪs/, **effaces, effacing, effaced.** VB WITH OBJ To **efface** something means to remove it completely; a formal use. *In the sand, all the footprints had effaced one another... He hoped to efface the memory of an embarrassing speech.*

effect /ɪ1fɛkt/, **effects, effecting, effected.** 1 COUNT N OR UNCOUNT N An **effect** is a change, reaction, or impression that is caused by something or is the result of something. *This has the effect of separating students from teachers... ...the effect of noise on people in the factories... Don't move, or you'll destroy the whole effect.* 2 VB WITH OBJ If you **effect** something, you succeed in causing it to happen; a formal use. *Production was halted until repairs could be effected.* PHRASES ● If you do something **for effect,** you do it in order to impress people. *...a pause for effect.* ● You add **in effect** to a statement to indicate that it is not precisely accurate but it is a reasonable summary of a situation. *In effect he has no choice.* ● You use **to this effect, to that effect,** or **to the effect that** when you are summarizing what someone has said, rather than repeating their actual words. *...a rumour to the effect that he had been drunk... He said, 'No, you fool, the other way!' or words to that effect.* ● When something **takes effect** or **is put into effect,** it starts to happen. *The tax cuts take effect on July 1st... Signing the agreement was one thing, putting it into effect was another.* ● See also **sound effect.**

effective /ɪ1fɛktɪv/. 1 ADJ Something that is **effective** produces the intended results. *...the most effective ways of reducing pollution.* ♦ **effectively** ADV *...an attempt to make the system work more effectively.* ♦ **effectiveness** UNCOUNT N *Methods vary in effectiveness.* 2 ATTRIB ADJ **Effective** also means having a particular role or result in practice, though not officially. *He assumed effective command of the armed forces.* 3 PRED ADJ When a law or an agreement becomes **effective,** it begins officially to apply.

effectively /ɪ1fɛktɪvli1/. ADV You use **effectively** to indicate that what you are saying is a reasonable summary of a situation, although it is not precisely accurate. *The television was on, effectively ruling out conversation.*

effeminate /ɪ1fɛmɪnə1t/. ADJ When people describe a man as **effeminate,** they mean that he behaves, looks, or sounds like a woman.

efficient /ɪ1fɪʃə0nt/. ADJ Something or someone that is **efficient** does a job successfully, without wasting time or energy. *Engines and cars can be made more efficient... You need a very efficient production manager.* ♦ **efficiently** ADV *You must work more efficiently.* ♦ **efficiency** /ɪ1fɪʃə0nsi1/ UNCOUNT N *...an increase in business efficiency.*

effigy /ɛfɪ1dʒi1/, **effigies.** 1 COUNT N An **effigy** is a roughly made figure that represents someone you strongly dislike. *The students burned effigies of the president.* 2 COUNT N An **effigy** is also a statue or carving of a famous person; a formal use. *...unusually good fifteenth-century alabaster effigies.*

effluent /ɛfluənt/, **effluents.** UNCOUNT N OR COUNT N **Effluent** is liquid waste material that comes out of factories or sewage works; a formal use.

effort /ɛfət/, **efforts. 1** UNCOUNT N OR COUNT N If you make an **effort** to do something, you try hard to do it. *...the efforts of governments to restrain inflation... It's a waste of effort.* **2** UNCOUNT N If you do something with **effort,** it is difficult for you to do. *Robert spoke with effort.* **3** COUNT N AFTER ADJ If you describe an object or an action as a poor or feeble **effort,** you mean it has not been well made or well done. *It was a rather amateurish effort.* **4** SING N If you say that an action is an **effort,** you mean that an unusual amount of physical or mental energy is needed to do it. *Getting up was an effort.*

effortless /ɛfətlɪ²s/. ADJ You describe an action as **effortless** when it is achieved very easily. *His rise in politics appears to have been effortless.* ♦ **effortlessly** ADV *He slipped back effortlessly into his old ways.*

effrontery /i¹frʌntə⁰ri¹/. UNCOUNT N **Effrontery** is bold, rude, or cheeky behaviour; a formal use. *He has the effrontery to use my office without asking.*

effusive /i¹fjuːsɪv/. ADJ An **effusive** person expresses pleasure, gratitude, or approval enthusiastically. *Mrs Schiff was effusive in her congratulations... ...an effusive welcome.* ♦ **effusively** ADV *The doctor thanked him effusively.*

EFL /iː ɛf ɛl/. **EFL** is used to describe things that are connected with the teaching of English to people whose first language is not English. **EFL** is an abbreviation for 'English as a Foreign Language'. *...EFL dictionaries.*

e.g. /iː dʒiː/. **e.g.** is an abbreviation that means 'for example'. It is used before a noun, or to introduce another sentence. *...woollens and other delicate fabrics (e.g. lace)... He specialised in trivial knowledge, e.g. that three MPs had glass eyes.*

egalitarian /i¹gælɪtɛərɪən/. ADJ In an **egalitarian** system or society, all people are equal and have the same rights. *...a more egalitarian educational system.*

egg /ɛg/, **eggs, egging, egged. 1** COUNT N An **egg** is the rounded object produced by a female bird from which a baby bird later emerges. Some other creatures, such as reptiles and fish, also produce eggs. **2** COUNT N OR UNCOUNT N An **egg** is also a hen's egg considered as food. *...bacon and egg.* **3** COUNT N An **egg** is also a cell in a female person or animal which can develop into a baby.

egg on. PHR VB If you **egg** someone **on,** you encourage them to do something daring or foolish.

eggshell /ɛgʃɛl/, **eggshells.** COUNT N OR UNCOUNT N **Eggshell** or an **eggshell** is the hard covering round a bird's egg.

ego /iːgəʊ, ɛgəʊ/, **egos.** COUNT N Your **ego** is your opinion of your own worth. *It was a blow to my ego.*

egoism /iːgəʊɪzə⁰m, ɛg-/. UNCOUNT N **Egoism** is the same as egotism.

egoist /iːgəʊɪst, ɛg-/, **egoists.** COUNT N An **egoist** is the same as an egotist.

egoistic /iːgəʊɪstɪk, ɛg-/. ADJ **Egoistic** means the same as egotistic.

egotism /iːgətɪzə⁰m, ɛg-/. UNCOUNT N **Egotism** is selfish behaviour which shows that you believe you are more important than other people. *It was a piece of blatant egotism.*

egotist /iːgətɪst, ɛg-/, **egotists.** COUNT N An **egotist** is a person who acts selfishly and believes that he or she is more important than other people. ♦ **egotistic** /iːgətɪstɪk, ɛg-/. ADJ *Success makes a man egotistic.*

eiderdown /aɪdədaʊn/, **eiderdowns.** COUNT N An **eiderdown** is a bed covering filled with feathers or warm material.

eight /eɪt/, **eights. Eight** is the number 8.

eighteen /eɪtiːn/. **Eighteen** is the number 18.

eighteenth /eɪtiːnθ/. ADJ The **eighteenth** item in a series is the one that you count as number eighteen.

eighth /eɪtθ/, **eighths. 1** ADJ The **eighth** item in a series is the one that you count as number eight. *...his room on the eighth floor.* **2** COUNT N An **eighth** is one of eight equal parts of something. *It was about an eighth of an inch thick.*

eightieth /eɪti¹ɪθ/. ADJ The **eightieth** item in a series is the one that you count as number eighty.

eighty /eɪti¹/, **eighties. Eighty** is the number 80.

either /aɪðə, iːðə/. **1** CONJ You use **either** in front of the first of two or more alternatives, when you are stating the only possibilities or choices that there are. The other alternatives are introduced by 'or'. *I was expecting you either today or tomorrow... You either love him or you hate him.* **2** CONJ You can use **either** in a negative statement in front of the first of two alternatives, when you are emphasizing that the negative statement refers to both the alternatives. *Dr Kirk, you're not being either frank or fair... I wouldn't dream of asking either Mary or my mother to take on the responsibility.* **3** PRON OR DET **Either** refers to one of two possible things, when you want to say that it does not matter which one is chosen. *Either is acceptable... Either way, I can't lose.* **4** PRON OR DET You can also use **either** in a negative statement to refer to each of two things when you are emphasizing that the negative statement includes both of them. *'Which one do you want?'—'I don't want either.'... She could not see either man.* **5** ADV **Either** is used by itself at the end of a negative statement to indicate that there is a similarity or connection between a person or thing that you have just mentioned and one that was mentioned earlier. *'I haven't got that address.'—'No, I haven't got it either.'... Not only was he ugly, he was not very interesting either.* **6** DET You can use **either** before a noun that refers to each of two things when you are talking about both of them. *The two ladies sat in large armchairs on either side of the stage... In either case the answer is the same.*

eject /i¹dʒɛkt/, **ejects, ejecting, ejected. 1** VB WITH OBJ To **eject** something means to push or send it out forcefully. *The machine ejected a handful of cigarettes.* **2** VB WITH OBJ If you **eject** someone from a place, you force them to leave.

eke /iːk/, **ekes, eking, eked.**

eke out. PHR VB **1** If you **eke** something **out,** you make your supply of it last as long as possible. *Migrants send home cash that helps eke out low village incomes.* **2** If you **eke out** a living, you manage to survive with very little money.

elaborate, elaborates, elaborating, elaborated; pronounced /i¹læbərə¹t/ when it is an adjective and /i¹læbəreɪt/ when it is a verb. **1** ADJ Something that is **elaborate** is very complex because it has a lot of different parts. *...the elaborate network of canals.* ♦ **elaborately** ADV *Every inch of its surface was elaborately decorated.* **2** VB WITH 'on' OR OBJ If you **elaborate** on an idea, or if you **elaborate** it, you give more details about it. *It isn't a statement I want to elaborate on... Some of these points will have to be further elaborated as we go along.* ♦ **elaboration** /i¹læbəreɪʃə⁰n/ COUNT N OR UNCOUNT N *An elaboration of this idea will follow in Chapter 12.* **3** VB WITH OBJ To **elaborate** something also means to make it more complex. *This type of plan could be elaborated.*

elapse /i¹læps/, **elapses, elapsing, elapsed.** VB When a period of time **elapses,** it passes; a formal use. *Too much time had elapsed since I had attempted any serious study.*

elastic /i¹læstɪk/. **1** UNCOUNT N **Elastic** is a rubber material that stretches when you pull it and returns to its original size when you let it go. *It snapped back like a piece of elastic.* **2** ADJ Something that is **elastic** stretches easily. *...a softer, more elastic and lighter material.* ♦ **elasticity** /iːlæstɪsɪ¹ti¹, ɪlæstɪsɪ¹ti¹/ UNCOUNT N *The skin eventually loses its elasticity.* **3** ADJ **Elastic** ideas and policies can change in order to suit new circumstances. *Liberal policy was sufficiently elastic to accommodate both views.*

elastic band, elastic bands. COUNT N An **elastic band** is the same as a rubber band.

elated /i¹leɪtɪ²d/. ADJ If you are **elated,** you are extremely happy and excited. *The members left the meeting elated.*

elation /i¹leɪʃə⁰n/. UNCOUNT N **Elation** is a feeling of great happiness and excitement. *This little incident filled me with elation.*

elbow /ɛlbəʊ/, **elbows, elbowing, elbowed. 1** COUNT N Your **elbow** is the part in the middle of your arm where it bends. *She sat with her elbows on the table.* **2** VB WITH OBJ AND ADJUNCT If you **elbow** someone away, you push them aside with your elbow.

elder /ɛldə/, **elders. 1** ADJ The **elder** of two people is the one who was born first. *...his elder brother.* **2** COUNT N The **elders** of a society or religious organization are the older members who have influence and authority, or who hold positions of responsibility; a formal use.

elderly /ɛldəli¹/. **1** ADJ **Elderly** people are old. *The coach was full of elderly ladies.* **2** PLURAL N You can refer to old people in general as the **elderly.** *...unless the elderly are adequately cared for.*

eldest /ɛldɪ²st/. ADJ The **eldest** person in a group is the one who was born before all the others. *Her eldest son was killed in the First War.*

elect /i¹lɛkt/, **elects, electing, elected. 1** VB WITH OBJ OR VB WITH OBJ AND COMPLEMENT When people **elect** someone, they choose that person to represent them, by voting. *They met to elect a president... Why should we elect him Mayor?* ♦ **elected** ATTRIB ADJ *...a democratically elected government.* **2** VB WITH TO-INF If you **elect** to do something, you choose to do it; a formal use.

election /i¹lɛkʃə⁰n/, **elections. 1** COUNT N OR UNCOUNT N An **election** is a process in which people vote to choose a person or group of people to hold an official position. *Labour did badly in the election... I may vote for her at the next election.* ● See also **by-election, general election. 2** SING N The **election** of a person or a political party is their success in winning an election. *...the election of Mr Heath's government in 1970.*

elector /i¹lɛktə/, **electors.** COUNT N The **electors** are the people who have the right to vote in an election.

electoral /i¹lɛktə⁰rəl/. ATTRIB ADJ **Electoral** is used to refer to things that are connected with an election. *...a contribution to their electoral funds... ...electoral success.*

electorate /i¹lɛktə⁰rə¹t/, **electorates.** COUNT N The **electorate** of a country is the people there who have the right to vote in an election.

electric /i¹lɛktrɪk/. **1** ADJ An **electric** device or machine works by means of electricity. *...an electric fan.* **2** ATTRIB ADJ **Electric** is used to describe other things that relate to electricity. *...electric current.* **3** ADJ If a situation is **electric,** people are very excited. *When Drew arrived, the atmosphere was already electric.*

electrical /i¹lɛktrɪkə⁰l/. **1** ADJ **Electrical** devices or machines work by means of electricity. *...electrical equipment.* ♦ **electrically** ADV *...electrically operated windows.* **2** ATTRIB ADJ **Electrical** engineers and industries are involved in the production or maintenance of electricity or electrical goods.

electrician /ɪlɛktrɪʃə⁰n, iːlɛk-/, **electricians.** COUNT N An **electrician** is a person whose job is to install and repair electrical equipment.

electricity /ɪlɛktrɪsɪ¹ti¹, iːlɛk-/. UNCOUNT N **Electricity** is a form of energy used for heating and lighting, and to provide power for machines. *They generate the electricity in power stations.*

electric shock, electric shocks. COUNT N If you get an **electric shock,** you feel a sudden sharp pain when you touch something connected to a supply of electricity.

electrify /i¹lɛktrɪfaɪ/, **electrifies, electrifying, electrified. 1** VB WITH OBJ If something **electrifies** you, it excites you a lot. *...the news that had electrified the world.* ♦ **electrifying** ADJ *...an electrifying speech.* **2** VB WITH OBJ When something **is electrified,** it is connected to a supply of electricity. *I toyed with the idea of electrifying the railings.* ♦ **electrified** ATTRIB ADJ *...electrified wire netting.*

electrocute /i¹lɛktrə⁶kjuːt/, **electrocutes, electrocuting, electrocuted.** VB WITH OBJ OR REFL VB If you **are electrocuted** or if you **electrocute** yourself, you are killed or badly injured by touching something connected to a source of electricity.

electrode /i¹lɛktrəʊd/, **electrodes.** COUNT N An **electrode** is a small piece of metal that takes an electric current to or from a source of power or a piece of equipment.

electromagnetic /i¹lɛktrəʊmægnɛtɪk/. ADJ **Electromagnetic** is used to describe magnetic forces and effects produced by an electric current. *...electromagnetic waves.*

electron /i¹lɛktrɒn/, **electrons.** COUNT N An **electron** is a tiny particle of matter smaller than an atom.

electronic /ɪlɛktrɒnɪk, iːlɛk-/, **electronics. 1** ADJ An **electronic** device has transistors, silicon chips, or valves which control and change the electric current passing through it. *...electronic equipment.* **2** ATTRIB ADJ An **electronic** process involves the use of electronic devices. *...electronic surveillance.* ♦ **electronically** ADV *Each vehicle might be electronically tracked.* **3** UNCOUNT N **Electronics** is the technology of using transistors, silicon chips, or valves to make radios, televisions, and computers. *...the British electronics industry.* **4** PLURAL N **Electronics** also refers to the equipment that consists of electronic devices. *The boat carries a mass of sophisticated electronics.*

elegant /ɛlɪgənt/. **1** ADJ **Elegant** means pleasing and graceful in appearance. *...a tall, elegant woman... ...the little church with its elegant square tower.* ♦ **elegantly** ADV *...an elegantly dressed woman.* ♦ **elegance** /ɛlɪgəns/ UNCOUNT N *The street had retained some of its old elegance.* **2** ADJ An **elegant** idea or plan is simple, clear, and clever. *His proposal has an elegant simplicity.*

element /ɛlə¹mə⁰nt/, **elements. 1** COUNT N WITH SUPP An **element** of something is one of the single parts which combines with others to make up a whole. *...the different elements in the play.* **2** PLURAL N WITH SUPP The **elements** of a subject are the basic and most important points. *...the elements of reading.* **3** COUNT N WITH SUPP When you talk about **elements** within a society, you are referring to groups of people with similar aims or habits. *...sympathetic elements outside the party.* **4** COUNT N If something has an **element** of a particular quality, it has a certain amount of it. *It contains an element of truth.* **5** COUNT N The **element** in an electrical appliance is the metal part which changes the electric current into heat. 6 PLURAL N You can refer to stormy weather as the **elements.** *Her raincoat was buttoned tight against the elements.* 7 PHRASE If someone is **in** their **element,** they are doing something that they enjoy and do well.

elemental /ɛlə1mɛntə0l/. ADJ **Elemental** feelings and behaviour are simple and forceful; a literary use. *...outbursts of elemental rage.*

elementary /ɛlə1mɛntə0ri1/. ADJ Something that is **elementary** is very simple, straightforward, and basic. *Most towns had taken some elementary precautions... ...elementary maths.*

elephant /ɛlı1fənt/, **elephants.** COUNT N An **elephant** is a very large animal with a long trunk.

elevate /ɛlıveıt/, **elevates, elevating, elevated.** 1 VB WITH OBJ When people or things **are elevated,** they are given greater status or importance. *The series elevated Johnson from obscurity to stardom.* ♦ **elevated** ADJ *...some elevated person like the Home Secretary.* 2 VB WITH OBJ To **elevate** something means to raise it to a higher level. *Earth movements elevated great areas of the seabed.* ♦ **elevated** ADJ *...the elevated dual carriageway at Brentford.*

elevation /ɛlı1veıʃə0n/, **elevations;** a formal word. 1 UNCOUNT N WITH POSS The **elevation** of someone or something is the act of raising them to a position of greater importance. *...the elevation of the standards of the average man... ...his elevation to the peerage.* 2 COUNT N The **elevation** of a place is its height above sea level. *...a fairly flat plateau at an elevation of about a hundred feet.*

elevator /ɛlə1veıtə/, **elevators.** COUNT N An **elevator** is the same as a lift. *I went down in the elevator.*

eleven /ılɛvə0n/. **Eleven** is the number 11.

eleventh /ı1lɛvə0nθ/. ADJ The **eleventh** item in a series is the one that you count as number eleven.

eleventh hour. SING N The **eleventh hour** is the last possible moment before something happens. *I was asked, at the eleventh hour, to direct the play.*

elicit /ı1lısıt/, **elicits, eliciting, elicited;** a formal word. 1 VB WITH OBJ If you **elicit** a response or a reaction, you do something which makes other people respond or react. *Threats to reinstate the tax elicited jeers from the opposition.* 2 VB WITH OBJ If you **elicit** a piece of information, you get it by asking careful questions. *In five minutes she had elicited all the Herriard family history.*

eligible /ɛlıdʒə1bə0l/. 1 ADJ Someone who is **eligible** for something is qualified or suitable for it. *You may be eligible for a grant... She is only just eligible to vote.* ♦ **eligibility** /ɛlıdʒəbılıti1/ UNCOUNT N *...the eligibility of applicants.* 2 ADJ An **eligible** man or woman is not yet married but is considered to be a suitable partner. *...an eligible bachelor.*

eliminate /ı1lımı1neıt/, **eliminates, eliminating, eliminated.** 1 VB WITH OBJ To **eliminate** something means to remove it completely. *Poverty must be eliminated.* ♦ **elimination** /ı1lımıneıʃə0n/ UNCOUNT N *...the elimination of spelling errors.* 2 VB WITH OBJ When a person or team **is eliminated** from a competition, they are defeated and so take no further part in it. *Four minor candidates were eliminated in the first round.*

elite /ı3li:t/, **elites.** 1 COLL N An **elite** is a group of the most powerful, rich, or talented people in a society. 2 ATTRIB ADJ **Elite** people or organizations are considered to be the best of their kind. *...elite training establishments.*

elitism /ı3li:tızə0m/. UNCOUNT N **Elitism** is the belief that a society should be ruled by a small group of people who are considered by some to be superior to everyone else. *This kind of elitism is even more marked in public schools.* ♦ **elitist** /ı3li:tıst/ COUNT N OR ADJ *Conservationists are often branded as elitists... It had been a very elitist society.*

ellipse /ı1lıps/, **ellipses.** COUNT N An **ellipse** is an oval shape like a flattened circle.

elm /ɛlm/, **elms.** COUNT N OR UNCOUNT N An **elm** is a kind of tree with broad leaves which it loses in winter.

elocution /ɛləkju:ʃə0n/. UNCOUNT N **Elocution** is the art of speaking clearly in public with a standard accent. *He taught elocution at a junior college.*

elongated /i:lɒŋgeıtı2d/. ADJ Something that is **elongated** is very long and thin.

elope /ı1ləʊp/, **elopes, eloping, eloped.** RECIP VB When two people **elope,** they go away secretly together to get married. *Is it true you eloped with her to Florida?*

eloquent /ɛləkwə2nt/. ADJ **Eloquent** people express themselves well in speech or writing. *He was tall, eloquent, and had fine manners... ...eloquent descriptions.* ♦ **eloquently** ADV *They spoke eloquently of their concern.* ♦ **eloquence** /ɛləkwəns/ UNCOUNT N *He may have inherited his eloquence from his father.*

else /ɛls/. 1 ADV You use **else** after words such as 'anywhere', 'someone', and 'what' to refer vaguely to another place, person, or thing. *Let's go somewhere else... I had nothing else to do... ...someone else's house... Who else was there?* 2 CONJ You use **or else** when you are indicating the unpleasant results that will occur if someone does not do something. *You've got to be very careful or else you'll miss the turn-off into our drive.* 3 CONJ You also use **or else** to introduce the second of two possibilities, when you do not know which one is true. *I think I was at school, or else I was staying with a friend.*

elsewhere /ɛlswɛə/. ADV **Elsewhere** means in other places or to another place. *...in Europe and elsewhere... He can go elsewhere.*

ELT /i: ɛl ti:/. **ELT** is used to describe things that are connected with the teaching of English. **ELT** an abbreviation for 'English Language Teaching'.

elucidate /ı1lj0u:sıdeıt/, **elucidates, elucidating, elucidated.** VB WITH OBJ If you **elucidate** something, you make it clear and understandable; a formal use. *...a lesson elucidating the points that have been made in the previous lecture.*

elude /ı1lu:d/, **eludes, eluding, eluded;** a formal word. 1 VB WITH OBJ If a fact or idea **eludes** you, you cannot understand or remember it. 2 VB WITH OBJ If you **elude** someone or something, you manage to escape from them. *...the problems of eluding the police.*

elusive /ı1lu:sıv/. ADJ Something or someone that is **elusive** is difficult to find, achieve, describe, or remember; a formal use. *Happiness is an elusive quality.*

emaciated /ı1meısıeıtı2d/. ADJ An **emaciated** person is extremely thin because of illness or lack of food.

emanate /ɛməneıt/, **emanates, emanating, emanated.** VB WITH 'from' If a quality, idea, or feeling **emanates** from you, it comes from you; a formal use. *These ideas are said to emanate from Henry Kissinger.*

emancipate /ı1mænsıpeıt/, **emancipates, emancipating, emancipated.** VB WITH OBJ To **emancipate** someone means to free them from unpleasant social, political, or legal restrictions; a formal use. *...a government determined to emancipate the poor.* ♦ **emancipation** /ı1mænsıpeıʃə0n/ UNCOUNT N *Marx spoke of the emancipation of mankind.*

embalm /ı2mbɑ:m/, **embalms, embalming, embalmed.** VB WITH OBJ When a dead person **is embalmed,** their body is preserved using special substances.

embankment /ɛmbæŋkmə2nt/, **embankments.** COUNT N An **embankment** is a thick wall built of earth, often supporting a railway line.

embargo /ɛmbɑ:gəʊ/, **embargoes.** COUNT N An **embargo** is an order made by a government to stop trade with another country. *The states imposed an embargo on oil shipments... ...a trade embargo.*

embark /ı2mbɑ:k/, **embarks, embarking, embarked.** 1 VB WITH 'on' OR 'upon' If you **embark** on something new, you start doing it. *Peru embarked on a massive programme of reform.* 2 VB When you **embark** on a ship, you go on board before the start of a voyage. *She had embarked on the S.S. Gordon Castle at Tilbury.*

embarrass /ı2mbærəs/, **embarrasses, embarrassing, embarrassed.** 1 VB WITH OBJ If something **embarrasses** you, it makes you feel shy or ashamed. *It embarrasses me even to think about it.* ♦ **embarrassed** ADJ *I felt really embarrassed about it... She had been too embarrassed to ask her friends.* 2 VB WITH OBJ If something **embarrasses** a politician, it causes political problems for them. *The march could embarrass the government.*

embarrassing /ı2mbærəsıŋ/. ADJ Something that is **embarrassing** makes you feel shy or ashamed. *He said something that would be embarrassing for me to repeat.* ♦ **embarrassingly** SUBMOD *Their possessions were embarrassingly few.*

embarrassment /ı2mbærəsmə2nt/, **embarrassments.** 1 UNCOUNT N **Embarrassment** is a shy feeling or a feeling of shame. *His cheeks were hot with embarrassment.* 2 COUNT N Someone or something that embarrasses people can be referred to as an **embarrassment.** *It was a political embarrassment.*

embassy /ɛmbəsi1/, **embassies.** 1 COUNT N An **embassy** is a group of officials, headed by an ambassador, who represent their government in a foreign country. *She was attached to the Canadian embassy.* 2 COUNT N The building in which an ambassador and his or her officials work is also called an **embassy.**

embattled /ı2mbætə0ld/. ADJ An **embattled** person or group is having a lot of problems. *...supporting an embattled Labour Government.*

embedded /ı2mbɛdıd/. 1 PRED ADJ WITH 'in' If an object is **embedded** in something, it is fixed there firmly and deeply. *The boat lay with its rudder embedded in mud.* 2 ADJ If an attitude or feeling is **embedded** in a society or in someone's personality, it has become a permanent feature of it. *...a deeply embedded feeling of guilt.*

embellish /ı2mbɛlıʃ/, **embellishes, embellishing, embellished;** a formal word. 1 VB WITH OBJ If something **is embellished** with other things, they are added to make it more attractive. *...a dress embellished with tiny circular mirrors.* ♦ **embellishment** /ı2mbɛlıʃmə2nt/ COUNT N OR UNCOUNT N *...the embellishment of the church at Chambery.* 2 VB WITH OBJ If you **embellish** a story, you make it more interesting by adding details which may be untrue. *...embellished accounts of the day's events.* ♦ **embellishment** COUNT N *...copying articles from other papers and repeating them with embellishments.*

ember /ɛmbə/, **embers.** COUNT N **Embers** are glowing pieces of wood or coal from a dying fire.

embezzle /ı2mbɛzə0l/, **embezzles, embezzling, embezzled.** VB WITH OBJ If someone **embezzles** money, they steal it from an organization that they work for. ♦ **embezzlement** UNCOUNT N *He was prosecuted for embezzlement.*

embitter /ı2mbıtə/, **embitters, embittering, embittered.** VB WITH OBJ If someone **is embittered** by what happens to them, they feel angry and resentful because of it. ♦ **embittered** ADJ *...an embittered man.*

emblem /ɛmblə2m/, **emblems.** 1 COUNT N An **emblem** is a design representing a country or organization. 2 COUNT N WITH SUPP An **emblem** is also something representing a quality or idea. *...a ruler's staff, an emblem of kingship.*

embodiment /ı2mbɒdi1mə2nt/. SING N If you describe someone or something as the **embodiment** of a quality or idea, you mean that it is their most noticeable characteristic or the basis of all they do; a formal use. *She was the embodiment of loyalty.*

embody /ı2mbɒdi1/, **embodies, embodying, embodied.** 1 VB WITH OBJ To **embody** a quality or idea means to have it as your most noticeable characteristic or as the basis of all you do. *...the institutions which embody traditional values.* 2 VB WITH OBJ If something **embodies** a particular thing, it contains or consists of that thing. *These proposals were embodied in the Industrial Relations Act.*

emboldened /ı2mbəʊldə0nd/. PRED ADJ If you are **emboldened** by something that happens, it makes you feel confident enough to behave in a particular way.

embossed /ɛmbɒst/. ADJ An **embossed** design or word sticks up slightly from the surface it has been added to. *...embossed writing paper.*

embrace /ı2mbreıs/, **embraces, embracing, embraced.** 1 RECIP VB When you **embrace** someone, you put your arms around them in order to show your affection for them. *Before she could embrace him he stepped away... We embraced each other.* Also COUNT N *They greeted us with warm embraces.* 2 VB WITH OBJ If something **embraces** a group of people, things, or ideas, it includes them; a formal use. *The course embraces elements of chemistry, physics, and engineering.* 3 VB WITH OBJ If you **embrace** a religion, political system, or idea, you start believing wholeheartedly in it; a formal use.

embroider /ı2mbrɔıdə/, **embroiders, embroidering, embroidered.** VB WITH OR WITHOUT OBJ If you **embroider** fabric, you sew a decorative design onto it. ♦ **embroidered** ADJ *...an embroidered shirt.*

embroidery /ı2mbrɔıdə0ri1/. 1 UNCOUNT N **Embroidery** consists of designs sewn onto fabric. 2 UNCOUNT N **Embroidery** is also the activity of sewing designs onto fabric.

embroil /ı2mbrɔıl/, **embroils, embroiling, embroiled.** VB WITH OBJ When someone **is embroiled** in an argument or fight, they become deeply involved in it; a formal use.

embryo /ɛmbrıəʊ/, **embryos.** COUNT N An **embryo** is an animal or human in the very early stages of development in the womb.

embryonic /ɛmbrıɒnık/. ATTRIB ADJ **Embryonic** means in a very early stage of development; a formal use. *Embryonic peasant movements began to emerge.*

emerald /ɛmə0rəld/, **emeralds.** 1 COUNT N An **emerald** is a bright green precious stone. 2 ADJ Something that is **emerald** in colour is bright green.

emerge /ı1mɜ:dʒ/, **emerges, emerging, emerged.** 1 VB When you **emerge,** you come out from a place where you could not be seen. *I saw the woman emerge from a shop.* 2 VB WITH 'from' If you **emerge** from a difficult or bad experience, you come to the end of it. *Few emerge from the experience unscathed.* 3 VB WITH 'from' OR REPORT VB If a fact **emerges** from a discussion or investigation, it becomes known as a result of it. *One really interesting thing emerged from this research... It emerged that she had been drinking.* 4 VB When something such as an industry or a political movement **emerges**, it comes into existence. *Large-scale industry emerged only gradually.*

emergence /ɪ'mɜːdʒəns/. SING N The **emergence** of something is the process or event of its coming into existence. *...the emergence of new ideas.*

emergency /ɪ'mɜːdʒənsɪ/, **emergencies**. COUNT N OR UNCOUNT N An **emergency** is an unexpected and dangerous situation, which must be dealt with quickly. *The bells were only used in emergencies... ...what to do in case of emergency.* Also MOD *The plane made an emergency landing.*

emergent /ɪ'mɜːdʒənt/. ATTRIB ADJ An **emergent** country, political group, or way of life is becoming powerful or is coming into existence; a formal use.

emigrate /'emɪgreɪt/, **emigrates**, **emigrating**, **emigrated**. VB If you **emigrate**, you leave your native country to live in another country. *He received permission to emigrate to Canada.* ♦ **emigration** /emɪ'greɪʃəⁿn/ UNCOUNT N *...the encouragement given to peasant emigration.*

eminent /'emɪnənt/. ADJ **Eminent** people are important and respected. *...one of the most eminent scientists in Britain.* ♦ **eminence** /'emɪnəns/ UNCOUNT N *...a statesman of great eminence.*

eminently /'emɪnəntlɪ/. SUBMOD **Eminently** means very, or to a great degree; a formal use. *Children are eminently practical.*

emissary /'emɪsəⁿrɪ/, **emissaries**. COUNT N An **emissary** is a messenger or representative sent by a government or leader; a formal use.

emission /ɪ'mɪʃəⁿn/, **emissions**. COUNT N OR UNCOUNT N When there is an **emission** of gas or radiation, it is released into the atmosphere; a formal use.

emit /ɪ'mɪt/, **emits**, **emitting**, **emitted**. VB WITH OBJ To **emit** a sound, smell, substance, heat, or light means to produce it or send it out; a formal use. *...the rays of heat that are emitted by the warm earth.*

emotion /ɪ'məʊʃəⁿn/, **emotions**. COUNT N OR UNCOUNT N An **emotion** is a feeling such as fear or love. *It wasn't proper for a man to show his emotions... She looked around her without emotion.*

emotional /ɪ'məʊʃəⁿnəl, -ʃənⁿl/. 1 ADJ **Emotional** means relating to your feelings. *...the emotional needs of children.* ♦ **emotionally** ADV *He felt physically and emotionally exhausted.* 2 ADJ When someone is **emotional**, they experience a strong emotion and show it openly, especially by crying.

emotive /ɪ'məʊtɪv/. ADJ Something that is **emotive** is likely to make people feel strong emotions. *...emotive language.*

empathy /'empəθɪ/. UNCOUNT N **Empathy** is the ability to share another person's feelings as if they were your own; a formal use.

emperor /'empəⁿrə/, **emperors**. COUNT N An **emperor** is a man who rules an empire.

emphasis /'emfəsɪs/. UNCOUNT N OR SING N **Emphasis** is special importance or extra stress given to something. *Too much emphasis is being placed on basic research... 'They had four cars,' he repeated with emphasis.*

emphasize /'emfəsaɪz/, **emphasizes**, **emphasizing**, **emphasized**; also spelled **emphasise**. REPORT VB To **emphasize** something means to indicate that it is particularly important or true, or to draw special attention to it. *Mr Thompson was at pains to emphasize that he was threatening nobody.*

emphatic /ɪm'fætɪk/. 1 ADJ An **emphatic** statement is made forcefully. *...an emphatic refutation.* 2 PRED ADJ If you are **emphatic**, you use forceful language, to show that what you are saying is important.

emphatically /ɪm'fætɪkəⁿlɪ/. 1 ADV If you say something **emphatically**, you say it in a way that shows that you feel strongly about it. *'I hope it does,' she said emphatically.* 2 SENTENCE ADV You also use **emphatically** to indicate that something is definitely true. *She is emphatically not a recluse.*

empire /'empaɪə/, **empires**. 1 COUNT N An **empire** is a group of countries controlled by one country. 2 COUNT N You can also refer to a large group of companies controlled by one person as an **empire**. *His publishing empire was flourishing.*

empirical /ɪm'pɪrɪkəⁿl/. ADJ **Empirical** knowledge or study is based on practical experience rather than theories; a formal use. ♦ **empirically** ADV *The theory could be tested empirically.*

employ /ɪm'plɔɪ/, **employs**, **employing**, **employed**. 1 VB WITH OBJ If you **employ** someone, you pay them to work for you. *He was employed as a research assistant.* 2 VB WITH OBJ To **employ** something means to use it; a formal use. *You will need to employ a great deal of tact.*

employee /emplɔɪ'iː, ɪm'plɔɪiː/, **employees**. COUNT N An **employee** is a person who is paid to work for an organization or for another person.

employer /ɪm'plɔɪə/, **employers**. COUNT N Your **employer** is the organization or person that you work for.

employment /ɪm'plɔɪmə²nt/. UNCOUNT N **Employment** is the position of having a paid job. *He had retired from regular employment.*

empower /ɪm'paʊə/, **empowers**, **empowering**, **empowered**. VB WITH OBJ AND TO-INF When someone is **empowered** to do something, they have the authority or power to do it; a formal use. *The police are empowered to stop anyone to search for illegal drugs.*

empress /'emprɪs/, **empresses**. COUNT N An empress is a woman who rules an empire, or the wife of an emperor.

emptiness /'empⁿtɪnɪ²s/. 1 UNCOUNT N A feeling of **emptiness** is an unhappy or frightening feeling that nothing is worthwhile. *...the inner sense of emptiness she felt.* 2 UNCOUNT N The **emptiness** of a place is the fact that it has nothing in it. *...the largely unexplored emptiness of the Indian Ocean.*

empty /'empⁿtɪ/, **emptier**, **emptiest**; **empties**, **emptying**, **emptied**. 1 ADJ An **empty** place, vehicle, or container has no people or things in it. *The room was empty.* 2 ADJ A gesture, threat, or relationship that is **empty** has no real value or meaning. *They ignored his threats as empty rhetoric.* 3 ADJ If you describe a person's life or a period of time as **empty**, you mean that nothing interesting or valuable happens in it. *How shall I exist during the empty days ahead?* 4 VB WITH OBJ If you **empty** a container, you remove its contents. *She picked up an ashtray and emptied it into a wastepaper basket.* 5 VB WITH OBJ AND ADJUNCT If you **empty** a substance or object out of a container, you pour or tip it out of the container. *Empty the water out of those boots.* 6 VB If a room **empties**, everyone in it goes out. *The play was over and the auditorium began to empty.* 7 VB If a container **empties**, everything in it flows out or disappears from it.

empty-handed. PRED ADJ If you come back from somewhere **empty-handed**, you have failed to get what you intended to get.

emulate /'emjəleɪt/, **emulates**, **emulating**, **emulated**. VB WITH OBJ If you **emulate** someone or something, you imitate them because you admire them; a formal use.

-en. SUFFIX **-en** is used instead of '-ed' to form the past participle of some verbs, such as 'take' and 'give'. See **-ed**.

enable /ɪ'neɪbⁿl/, **enables**, **enabling**, **enabled**. VB WITH OBJ AND TO-INF If someone or something **enables** you to do something, they make it possible for you to do it; a formal use. *...the feathers that enable a bird to fly.*

enact /ɪ'nækt/, **enacts**, **enacting**, **enacted**. 1 VB WITH OBJ When a government **enacts** a proposal, they make it into a law; a technical use. 2 VB WITH OBJ If people **enact** a story or play, they act it; a formal use.

enamel /ɪ'næmⁿl/. 1 UNCOUNT N **Enamel** is a substance like glass which can be heated and used to decorate or protect metal, glass, or pottery. ♦ **enamelled** /ɪ'næmⁿld/ ADJ *...scissors with enamelled handles.* 2 UNCOUNT N **Enamel** is also the hard white substance that forms the outer part of a tooth.

en bloc /ɒn 'blɒk/. ADV **En bloc** means as a group; a formal use. *...a system which teaches the young, en bloc, a number of beliefs.*

encapsulate /ɪn'kæpsjə'leɪt/, **encapsulates**, **encapsulating**, **encapsulated**. VB WITH OBJ If something **encapsulates** facts or ideas, it contains or represents them in a very small space or in a single object or event; a formal use. *A play was written, encapsulating the main arguments.*

encase /ɪn'keɪs/, **encases**, **encasing**, **encased**. VB WITH OBJ If something is **encased** in a container or material, it is completely enclosed within it or covered by it. *Her feet were encased in a pair of old baseball boots.*

-ence. SUFFIX **-ence** and **-ency** are added to adjectives, usually in place of '-ent', to form nouns. These nouns usually refer to states, qualities, or behaviour. Nouns of this kind are often not defined but are treated with the related adjectives. *...signs of affluence... ...the prevention of delinquency.*

enchanted /ɪn'tʃɑːntɪd/. 1 ADJ If you are **enchanted** by something, you think it is very pleasing. 2 ADJ If you describe a place or event as **enchanted**, you mean that it seems as lovely or strange as something in a fairy story. *...an enchanted island.*

enchanting /ɪn'tʃɑːntɪŋ/. ADJ **Enchanting** means lovely or very pleasing. *...the most enchanting smile.*

encircle /ɪn'sɜːkⁿl/, **encircles**, **encircling**, **encircled**. VB WITH OBJ To **encircle** someone or something means to surround them completely. *'Not now,' she said, encircling me with her arms.*

enclave /'enkleɪv/, **enclaves**. COUNT N An **enclave** is a place that is different in some way from the areas

surrounding it, for example because the people there are from a different culture; a formal use.

enclose /ɪn'kləʊz/, **encloses**, **enclosing**, **enclosed**. 1 VB WITH OBJ If an object is **enclosed** by something solid, it is completely surrounded by it. *The statue is enclosed in a heavy glass cabinet.* ♦ **enclosed** ADJ *The reaction takes place within an enclosed space.* 2 VB WITH OBJ If you **enclose** something with a letter, you put it in the same envelope. *I enclose a small cheque.* ♦ **enclosed** ADJ *...the enclosed list.*

enclosure /ɪn'kləʊʒə/, **enclosures**. COUNT N An **enclosure** is an area of land surrounded by a wall or fence and used for a special purpose. *...the public enclosure of a racecourse.*

encode /ɪn'kəʊd/, **encodes**, **encoding**, **encoded**. VB WITH OBJ If you **encode** a message or some information, you put it into code.

encompass /ɪn'kʌmpəs/, **encompasses**, **encompassing**, **encompass**. VB WITH OBJ If something **encompasses** certain things, it includes all of them; a formal use. *...a policy which encompasses all aspects of conservation.*

encore /'ɒnkɔː/, **encores**. CONVENTION An audience shouts **'Encore!'** at the end of a concert when they want the performer to perform an extra item. Also COUNT N *...and lastly, for the encore, a Brahms waltz.*

encounter /ɪn'kaʊntə/, **encounters**, **encountering**, **encountered**; a formal word. 1 VB WITH OBJ If you **encounter** someone, you meet them. *On their journey they encountered an English couple.* Also COUNT N *That was my first encounter with the great man.* 2 VB WITH OBJ If you **encounter** something, you experience it. *They've never encountered any discrimination.* Also COUNT N *In their earliest encounters with stories, children want action.*

encourage /ɪn'kʌrɪdʒ/, **encourages**, **encouraging**, **encouraged**. 1 VB WITH OBJ If you **encourage** someone to do something, you tell them that you think that they should do it, or that they should continue doing it. *Her husband encouraged her to get a car.* ♦ **encouragement** /ɪn'kʌrɪdʒmə²nt/ UNCOUNT N *Many people sent messages of encouragement.* 2 VB WITH OBJ If you **encourage** a particular activity, you support it actively. *Group meetings in the factory were always encouraged.* 3 VB WITH OBJ If something **encourages** an attitude or a kind of behaviour, it makes it more likely to happen. *This encouraged the growth of Marxism.*

encouraging /ɪn'kʌrɪdʒɪŋ/. ADJ Something that is **encouraging** gives you hope or confidence. *...a piece of encouraging news.* ♦ **encouragingly** ADV *Rachel smiled encouragingly.*

encroach /ɪn'krəʊtʃ/, **encroaches**, **encroaching**, **encroached**. VB To **encroach** on a place or on your time or rights means to gradually take up or take away more and more of these things. *The new law doesn't encroach on the rights of the citizen.* ♦ **encroachment** /ɪn'krəʊtʃmə²nt/ COUNT N OR UNCOUNT N *...an encroachment on their property.*

encrusted /ɪn'krʌstɪ²d/. ADJ If a surface is **encrusted** with something, it is covered with it. *The statues are encrusted with jewels.*

encumber /ɪn'kʌmbə/, **encumbers**, **encumbering**, **encumbered**. VB WITH OBJ If you are **encumbered** with something, you find it difficult to move or to do something; a formal use. *...passengers who were encumbered with suitcases.*

encumbrance /ɪn'kʌmbrəns/, **encumbrances**. COUNT N An **encumbrance** is something or someone that encumbers you; a formal use.

-ency. See **-ence**.

encyclopedia /ɪn'saɪklə�ⁿ'piːdɪə/, **encyclopedias**; also spelled **encyclopaedia**. COUNT N An **encyclopedia** is a book or set of books in which many facts are arranged for reference, usually in alphabetical order.

end /end/, **ends**, **ending**, **ended**. 1 SING N The **end** of a period of time, event, or piece of writing is the last part of it. *...at the end of August... He urged an immediate end to all armed attacks... She read the first draft from beginning to end.* 2 COUNT N WITH SUPP The **end** of something is the point of it that is farthest from the centre. *Sharpen a stick at both ends... ...at the other end of the social scale.* 3 COUNT N WITH SUPP You can refer to a place that you are telephoning or travelling to as the other **end**. *The phone at the other end rang.* 4 COUNT N An **end** is the purpose for which something is done. *...their use of industrial power for political ends.* 5 COUNT N Someone's **end** is their death; a literary use. *He did not deserve such a cruel end.* 6 ERG VB If something **ends** or if you **end** it, it stops. *He refused to end his nine-week-old hunger strike... The play ends with all the children playing and reciting... The trail ends one mile from Bakewell.* 7 VB WITH 'with' OR 'in' An object that **ends** with or in something has that thing on its tip or as its last part. *Each finger ends with a sharp claw.* 8 See also **ending**.

PHRASES ● If something is **at an end**, it is finished. ● If something **comes to an end,** it stops. ● **In the end** means finally, after a considerable time. *She went back to England in the end.* ● If something is **an end in itself,** it is desirable, even though you may achieve nothing by it. ● You say **at the end of the day** when you are talking about what appears to be the case after you have considered the relevant facts. *The question at the end of the day is whether the house is actually worth that amount.* ● If you manage to **make ends meet,** you have just enough money to live on. ● **No end** means a lot; an informal use. *She had no end of trouble at school.* ● When something happens for days or weeks **on end,** it happens continuously during that time. ● **to get the wrong end of the stick:** see **stick.** ● **at a loose end:** see **loose.** ● See also **dead end, odds and ends.**

end up. PHR VB If you **end up** in a particular place or situation, you are in that place or situation after a series of events, even though you did not intend to be. *Many of their friends have ended up in prison... We ended up taking a taxi there.*

endanger /ɪ^{2}ndeɪndʒə/, **endangers, endangering, endangered.** VB WITH OBJ If you **endanger** someone or something, you cause them to be in a dangerous situation in which they might be harmed. *The herbicides did not endanger human life.* ♦ **endangered** ADJ *...endangered species of animals.*

endear /ɪ^{2}ndɪə/, **endears, endearing, endeared.** VB WITH OBJ AND PREP 'to' OR REFL VB WITH PREP 'to' If someone's behaviour **endears** them to you, it makes you fond of them; a formal use. *This sort of talk did not endear him to Mr Lincoln.* ♦ **endearing** ADJ *...an endearing smile.* ♦ **endearingly** ADV *...endearingly childish behaviour.*

endearment /ɪ^{2}ndɪəmə^{2}nt/, **endearments.** COUNT N OR UNCOUNT N **Endearments** are words or phrases that you use to show affection; a formal use. *...murmuring endearments... ...terms of endearment.*

endeavour /ɪ^{2}ndevə/, **endeavours, endeavouring, endeavoured;** spelled **endeavor** in American English. 1 VB WITH TO-INF If you **endeavour** to do something, you try to do it; a formal use. *He endeavoured to adopt a positive but realistic attitude.* 2 COUNT N OR UNCOUNT N An **endeavour** is an attempt to do something, especially if it is new and original. *We must wish him good fortune in his endeavours... ...this exciting new field of endeavour.*

endemic /ɛndemɪk/. ADJ A condition or illness that is **endemic** in a particular place is found naturally or commonly among the people there; a formal use. *Until the 1940's, malaria was endemic in Ceylon.*

ending /ɛndɪŋ/, **endings.** COUNT N The **ending** of something such as a story or a play is the last part of it. *...a happy ending.*

endless /ɛndlı^{2}s/. 1 ADJ If you describe something as **endless,** you mean that it lasts so long that it seems as if it will never end. *...an endless search for food.* ♦ **endlessly** ADV *She used to nag me endlessly.* 2 ADJ **Endless** also means very large or long, with no variation. *...an endless sandy waste.*

endorse /ɪ^{2}ndɔːs/, **endorses, endorsing, endorsed.** VB WITH OBJ If you **endorse** someone or something, you say publicly that you support or approve of them. *The Germans and Italians endorsed the plan.* ♦ **endorsement** /ɪ^{2}ndɔːsmə^{2}nt/ COUNT N OR UNCOUNT N *...their public endorsement of Liberal candidates.*

endow /ɪ^{2}ndaʊ/, **endows, endowing, endowed.** 1 VB WITH OBJ If someone or something **is endowed** with a quality, they have it or are given it; a formal use. *O'Neill had been endowed with film star looks.* 2 VB WITH OBJ If someone **endows** an institution, they give it a large amount of money.

endowment /ɪ^{2}ndaʊmə^{2}nt/, **endowments.** 1 COUNT N An **endowment** is a gift of money that is made to an institution such as a school or hospital. *Every penny of our endowment is spent on equipment.* 2 COUNT N Someone's **endowments** are their natural qualities and abilities; a formal use. *His natural endowments made him specially suited to the work.*

end product. SING N The **end product** of an activity or process is the thing that it produces.

end result. SING N You can describe the result of a lengthy process or activity as its **end result.**

endurance /ɪ^{2}ndj^{0}ʊərəns/. UNCOUNT N **Endurance** is the ability to bear an unpleasant or painful situation calmly and patiently. *They admired the troops for their courage and endurance.*

endure /ɪ^{2}ndj^{0}ʊə/, **endures, enduring, endured.** 1 VB WITH OBJ If you **endure** a painful or difficult situation, you bear it calmly and patiently. *It was more than I could endure.* 2 VB If something **endures,** it continues to exist. *...a city which will endure for ever.* ♦ **enduring** ADJ *...hopes for an enduring peace.*

enemy /ɛnəmi^1/, **enemies.** 1 COUNT N You can describe someone who intends to harm you as your **enemy.** *...an enemy of society.* 2 COLL N In a war, the **enemy** is the army or country that you are fighting. *...the enemy had been forced back... ...enemy aircraft.*

energetic /ɛnədʒɛtɪk/. 1 ADJ Someone who is **energetic** shows a lot of enthusiasm and determination. *He is an energetic campaigner in the cause of road safety.* ♦ **energetically** ADV *This right is energetically denied.* 2 ADJ An **energetic** person or activity does or involves a lot of physical movement. *...energetic young children... Do something energetic, play golf, swim, or ski.* ♦ **energetically** ADV *...acrobats energetically tumbling across the stage.*

energy /ɛnədʒi^1/, **energies.** 1 UNCOUNT N **Energy** is the ability and willingness to be active, because you do not feel tired. *He has neither the time nor the energy to play with the children.* 2 COUNT N WITH POSS Your **energies** are your effort and attention, which you direct towards a particular aim. *Men like Muhammed Abdu poured their energies into religious reform.* 3 UNCOUNT N **Energy** is also power obtained from sources such as electricity, coal, or water, that makes machines work or provides heat. *...nuclear energy.*

enfold /ɪ^{2}nfəʊld/, **enfolds, enfolding, enfolded.** 1 VB WITH OBJ If you **enfold** something in your hand or in your arms, you put your hand or arms around it; a formal use. *Their arms reached out to enfold him.* 2 VB WITH OBJ If something **enfolds** you, it surrounds you; a literary use. *...this darkness that enfolds me.*

enforce /ɪ^{2}nfɔːs/, **enforces, enforcing, enforced.** 1 VB WITH OBJ If people in a position of authority **enforce** a law or rule, they make sure that it is obeyed. *...officials who refused to enforce the immigration laws.* ♦ **enforcement** /ɪ^{2}nfɔːsmə^{2}nt/ UNCOUNT N *...the enforcement of public laws and regulations.* 2 VB WITH OBJ If you **enforce** a particular condition, you force it to be done or to happen. *He enforced high standards.* ♦ **enforced** ATTRIB ADJ *...a life of enforced inactivity.* ♦ **enforcement** /ɪ^{2}nfɔːsmə^{2}nt/ UNCOUNT N *...the enforcement of discipline.*

engage /ɪ^{2}ŋ^{1}geɪdʒ/, **engages, engaging, engaged;** a formal word. 1 VB OR PASSIVE VB WITH 'in' OR 'on' If you **engage** in an activity, you do it. If you **are engaged** in it, you are doing it. *It was considered inappropriate for a former President to engage in commerce... The work we're engaged on is a study of heat transfer.* 2 VB WITH OBJ If something **engages** you or **engages** your attention or interest, it keeps you interested in it and thinking about it. *Boredom has a chance to develop if the child's interest is not engaged.* 3 PHRASE If you **engage** someone **in conversation,** you have a conversation with them. 4 VB WITH OBJ If you **engage** someone to do a particular job, you appoint them to do it.

engaged /ɪ^{2}ŋ^{1}geɪdʒd/. 1 ADJ If two people are **engaged,** they have agreed to marry each other. 2 ADJ If someone's telephone is **engaged,** they are already using it and so you cannot speak to them. 3 PRED ADJ If a public toilet is **engaged,** it is already being used.

engagement /ɪ^{2}ŋ^{1}geɪdʒmə^{2}nt/, **engagements.** 1 COUNT N An **engagement** is an appointment that you have with someone; a formal use. 2 COUNT N An **engagement** is also an agreement that two people have made to get married, or the period during which they are engaged. *Their engagement was officially announced on 5th August.*

engaging /ɪ^{2}ŋ^{1}geɪdʒɪŋ/. ADJ An **engaging** person is pleasant and charming.

engender /ɪ^{2}ndʒɛndə/, **engenders, engendering, engendered.** VB WITH OBJ If someone or something **engenders** a particular feeling, atmosphere, or situation, they cause it to occur; a formal use. *This engenders a sense of responsibility.*

engine /ɛndʒɪn/, **engines.** 1 COUNT N The **engine** of a vehicle is the part that produces the power to make it move. 2 COUNT N An **engine** is also the large vehicle that pulls a railway train.

engineer /ɛndʒɪ^{1}nɪə/, **engineers, engineering, engineered.** 1 COUNT N An **engineer** is a skilled person who uses scientific knowledge to design and construct machinery, electrical devices, or roads and bridges. 2 COUNT N An **engineer** is also a person who repairs mechanical or electrical devices. *...a telephone engineer.* 3 VB WITH OBJ If you **engineer** an event or situation, you cause it to happen in a clever or indirect way. *It was Dr Martin who had engineered Miss Jackson's dismissal.*

engineering /ɛndʒɪ^{1}nɪ^{1}ərɪŋ/. UNCOUNT N **Engineering** is the work involved in designing and constructing machinery, electrical devices, or roads and bridges.

English /ɪŋglɪʃ/. 1 ADJ **English** means belonging or relating to England. *...the English countryside.* 2 UNCOUNT N **English** is the language spoken by people who live in Great Britain and Ireland, the United States, Canada, Australia, and many other countries. *Half the letter was in Swedish and the rest in English.* 3 PLURAL N The **English** are the people who come from England.

Englishman /ɪŋglɪʃmə^{3}n/, **Englishmen.** COUNT N An **Englishman** is a man who comes from England.

Englishwoman /ɪŋglɪʃwʊmən/, **Englishwomen.** COUNT N An **Englishwoman** is a woman who comes from England.

engrave /ɪ^{2}ŋ^{1}greɪv/, **engraves, engraving, engraved.** 1 VB WITH OBJ If you **engrave** something with a design or inscription or if you **engrave** a design on it, you cut the design into its surface. ♦ **engraved** ADJ *...engraved copper trays.* 2 VB WITH OBJ AND 'on' If you say that something **is engraved** on your mind, memory, or heart, you mean that you will never forget it; a literary use.

engraving /ɪ^{2}ŋ^{1}greɪvɪŋ/, **engravings.** COUNT N An **engraving** is a picture or design that has been either cut into a surface or printed from an engraved plate.

engrossed /ɪ^{2}ŋ^{1}grəʊst/. PRED ADJ If you are **engrossed** in something, it holds your attention completely. *She was engrossed in her book.*

engulf /ɪ^{2}ŋ^{1}gʌlf/, **engulfs, engulfing, engulfed;** a literary word. 1 VB WITH OBJ To **engulf** something means to completely cover and hide it. *The town was quickly engulfed in volcanic ash.* 2 VB WITH OBJ If something such as a feeling **engulfs** you, you are strongly affected by it. *...a world engulfed in hatred and intolerance.*

enhance /ɪ^{2}nhɑːns/, **enhances, enhancing, enhanced.** VB WITH OBJ To **enhance** something means to improve it. *It would enhance his standing in the community.*

enigma /ɪ^{2}nɪgmə/, **enigmas.** COUNT N Someone or something that is an **enigma** is mysterious and difficult to understand. *Mrs Yule remains an enigma, revealing nothing of herself.*

enigmatic /ɛnɪgmætɪk/. ADJ **Enigmatic** means mysterious and difficult to understand. *Donne is the most enigmatic of all our poets... ...an enigmatic smile.* ♦ **enigmatically** ADV *'You can try,' he said enigmatically.*

enjoy /ɪ^{2}ndʒɔɪ/, **enjoys, enjoying, enjoyed.** 1 VB WITH OBJ OR -ING If you **enjoy** something, it gives you pleasure and satisfaction. *Painting is something that I really enjoy doing.* 2 VB WITH OBJ To **enjoy** something also means to be lucky enough to have it. *They enjoyed exceptional living standards.* 3 REFL VB If you **enjoy** yourself, you do something you like doing. *He is thoroughly enjoying himself.*

enjoyable /ɪ^{2}ndʒɔɪəbə^{0}l/. ADJ Something that is **enjoyable** gives you pleasure. *We had an enjoyable day.*

enjoyment /ɪ^{2}ndʒɔɪmə^{2}nt/, **enjoyments.** UNCOUNT N **Enjoyment** is the feeling of pleasure you get from something you enjoy. *...the enjoyment that reading brings.*

enlarge /ɪ^{2}nlɑːdʒ/, **enlarges, enlarging, enlarged.** ERG VB If you **enlarge** something or if it **enlarges,** it becomes bigger. *The original windows were enlarged by Christopher Wren.* ♦ **enlarged** ADJ *...abnormally enlarged tonsils.*

enlarge on or **enlarge upon.** PHR VB If you **enlarge on** or **enlarge upon** a subject, you give more details about it; a formal use. *He enlarged on the glorious future he had in mind.*

enlargement /ɪ^{2}nlɑːdʒmə^{2}nt/, **enlargements.** 1 UNCOUNT N **Enlargement** is the process or result of making something larger. *The X-ray showed moderate enlargement of the heart.* 2 COUNT N An **enlargement** is a photograph that has been made bigger.

enlighten /ɪ^{2}nlaɪtə^{0}n/, **enlightens, enlightening, enlightened.** VB WITH OBJ To **enlighten** someone means to give them more knowledge about something; a formal use. *The object is to amuse and enlighten the reader.* ♦ **enlightening** ADJ *...a most enlightening book.* ♦ **enlightenment** /ɪ^{2}nlaɪtə^{0}nmə^{2}nt/ UNCOUNT N *The talks were intended to bring culture and enlightenment to the hearers.*

enlightened /ɪ^{2}nlaɪtə^{0}nd/. ADJ If you describe someone as **enlightened,** you mean that they have sensible, modern attitudes and ways of dealing with things. *Our enlightened social policies are much admired.*

enlist /ɪ^{2}nlɪst/, **enlists, enlisting, enlisted.** 1 ERG VB If someone **enlists,** they join the armed forces. *He had enlisted in the Marines... They were enlisted into the 21st Regiment.* 2 VB WITH OBJ If you **enlist** someone or **enlist** their help, you persuade them to help you.

enliven /ɪ^{2}nlaɪvə^{0}n/, **enlivens, enlivening, enlivened.** VB WITH OBJ If something **enlivens** an event or situation, it makes it more lively or cheerful. *The journey was enlivened by noisy goings-on in the next carriage.*

en masse /ɒn mæs/. ADV If a group of people do something **en masse,** they all do it together. *They threatened to resign en masse.*

enmeshed /ɪ^{2}nmɛʃt/. PRED ADJ If you are **enmeshed** in a situation, you are involved in it and find it difficult to escape; a formal use. *He was being enmeshed in the family business against his will.*

enmity /ɛnmɪ[1]ti[1]/. UNCOUNT N **Enmity** is a long-lasting feeling of hatred towards someone; a formal use. *It had earned him the enduring enmity of the farmers.*

ennoble /ɪ[2]nəʊbə[0]l/, **ennobles, ennobling, ennobled.** VB WITH OBJ To **ennoble** someone or something means to make them more noble and dignified; a formal use. *Suffering does not ennoble people.*

enormity /i[1]nɔːmɪ[1]ti[1]/. SING N The **enormity** of a problem or difficulty is its great size and seriousness. *Smith did not grasp the enormity of the danger involved.*

enormous /i[1]nɔːməs/. ADJ **Enormous** means extremely large in size, amount, or degree. *...an enormous cat... To his enormous delight he was elected.* ♦ **enormously** ADV *I admired her enormously.*

enough /i[1]nʌf/. **1** DET OR PRON **Enough** means as much as you need. *I haven't enough room... I hope it's enough... I had not seen enough of his work.* Also ADJ AFTER N *The fact that he did so much is proof enough.* **2** PRON OR DET If you say that something is **enough,** you mean that you do not want it to continue or get any worse. *I've had enough of the both of you... Don't tell me. I've got enough problems.* Also ADV *This thing is complicated enough already.* **3** ADV You use **enough** to say that someone or something has the necessary amount of a quality, or that something is happening to the necessary extent. *He was old enough to understand... The student isn't trying hard enough.*
PHRASES ● You use expressions such as **strangely enough** and **interestingly enough** to indicate that you think a fact is strange or interesting. *Oddly enough, I do believe you.* ● **sure enough:** see **sure.**

enquire /ɪ[2]n[1]kwaɪə/. See **inquire.**

enquiry /ɪ[2]n[1]kwaɪəri[1]/. See **inquiry.**

enrage /ɪ[2]nreɪdʒ/, **enrages, enraging, enraged.** VB WITH OBJ If something **enrages** you, it makes you very angry. *She was enraged by these remarks.* ♦ **enraged** ADJ *Letters flooded in to MPs from enraged constituents.*

enrich /ɪ[2]nrɪtʃ/, **enriches, enriching, enriched. 1** VB WITH OBJ To **enrich** something means to improve its quality by adding something to it. *He enriched drab lives.* ♦ **enriched** ADJ *...enriched breakfast cereals.* ♦ **enrichment** /ɪ[2]nrɪtʃmə[2]nt/ UNCOUNT N *...the enrichment of human experience.* **2** VB WITH OBJ To **enrich** someone means to make them richer; a formal use. *The purpose of the colonies was to enrich the colonists.*

enrol /ɪ[2]nrəʊl/, **enrols, enrolling, enrolled;** spelled **enroll** in American English. ERG VB If you **enrol** on a course, you officially join it and pay a fee. *I enrolled at the University of Vienna.* ♦ **enrolment** /ɪ[2]nrəʊlmə[2]nt/ UNCOUNT N *...the enrolment of pupils.*

en route /ɒn ruːt/. ADV If you are **en route** to a place, you are travelling there. *You'll see plenty to interest you en route.*

enshrined /ɪ[2]nʃraɪnd/. ADJ If something such as an idea or a right is **enshrined** in a society or a law, it is permanent and protected; a formal use. *The universities' autonomy is enshrined in their charters.*

enslave /ɪ[2]nsleɪv/, **enslaves, enslaving, enslaved. 1** VB WITH OBJ To **enslave** someone means to make them into a slave. *He was enslaved and ill-treated.* ♦ **enslaved** ADJ *...enslaved peoples.* ♦ **enslavement** /ɪ[2]nsleɪvmə[2]nt/ UNCOUNT N *...the enslavement of the whole population.* **2** VB WITH OBJ To **enslave** people also means to keep them in a difficult situation from which they cannot escape. *Men were enslaved by developing industrialism.*

ensue /ɪ[2]nsj[0]uː/, **ensues, ensuing, ensued.** VB If something **ensues,** it happens immediately after something else; a formal use. *A shouting match ensued between us and the bus driver.* ♦ **ensuing** ATTRIB ADJ *...the ensuing months.*

ensure /ɪ[2]nʃʊə, -ʃɔː/, **ensures, ensuring, ensured;** spelled **insure** /ɪnʃʊə, -ʃɔː/ in American English. REPORT VB To **ensure** that something happens means to make certain that it happens. *I shall try to insure that your stay is a pleasant one... The door did not lock, but at least it ensured a reasonable amount of privacy.*

entail /ɪ[2]nteɪl/, **entails, entailing, entailed.** VB WITH OBJ If one thing **entails** another, it necessarily involves it or causes it. *The move entailed radical changes in lifestyle.*

entangled /ɪ[2]ntæŋgə[0]ld/. **1** PRED ADJ If an object becomes **entangled** in something such as a rope or a net, it is caught and held by it. *The oar got entangled in the weeds.* **2** PRED ADJ If you are **entangled** in a difficult situation, you find it difficult to escape from it. *The country became entangled in a grave economic crisis.* **3** PRED ADJ If you are **entangled** with someone, you are involved in a relationship with them that causes you problems. *She got entangled with a crook.*

entanglement /ɪ[2]ntæŋgə[0]lmə[2]nt/, **entanglements.** COUNT N OR UNCOUNT N An **entanglement** is a relationship with someone, often a sexual one, which you wish to escape from.

enter /ɛntə/, **enters, entering, entered. 1** VB WITH OR WITHOUT OBJ When you **enter** a place, you come or go into it. *They stopped talking as soon as they saw Brody enter... Tom timidly entered the bedroom.* **2** VB WITH OBJ When you **enter** an organization, institution, or profession, you become a member of it or become involved in it. *He decided to enter college... She entered politics.* **3** VB WITH OBJ If a new quality or feature **enters** something, it appears in it. *A note of resolution entered the bishop's voice.* **4** VB WITH OBJ When something **enters** a new period in its development or history, it begins this period. *The industry entered a period of lower growth.* **5** VB WITH OBJ OR 'for' If you **enter** a competition or race or if you **enter** for it, you take part in it. **6** VB WITH OBJ When you **enter** something in a book or computer, you write or type it in. *Enter it in the cash book.*
enter into. PHR VB **1** When you **enter into** something important or complicated, you start doing it or become involved in it. *The Labour Government refused to enter into negotiations.* **2** Something that **enters into** something else is a factor in it. *Obviously personal relationships enter into it.*

enterprise /ɛntəpraɪz/, **enterprises. 1** COUNT N An **enterprise** is a company or business. *...large industrial enterprises.* **2** COUNT N An **enterprise** is also something new, difficult, or important that you do or try to do. *He had doubts about the whole enterprise.* **3** UNCOUNT N **Enterprise** is a system of business, especially one in a particular country. *...private enterprise.* **4** UNCOUNT N **Enterprise** is also willingness to try out new ways of doing and achieving things. *...men of enterprise, energy, and ambition.* ♦ **enterprising** /ɛntəpraɪzɪŋ/ ADJ *You are no longer the enterprising cook that once you were.*

entertain /ɛntəteɪn/, **entertains, entertaining, entertained. 1** VB WITH OR WITHOUT OBJ If you **entertain** people, you do something that amuses or interests them. *We entertained the guests with a detailed description of the party.* **2** VB WITH OR WITHOUT OBJ To **entertain** people also means to give them food and hospitality, for example at your house. *He entertained all the eminent people... She never entertained.* **3** VB WITH OBJ If you **entertain** an idea or suggestion, you consider it; a formal use. *I wondered what could have led me to entertain so ludicrous a suspicion.*

entertainer /ɛntəteɪnə/, **entertainers.** COUNT N An **entertainer** is a person whose job is to entertain audiences, for example by telling jokes, singing, or dancing.

entertaining /ɛntəteɪnɪŋ/. **1** ADJ People or things that are **entertaining** are amusing or interesting and give you pleasure. *Films should be entertaining.* **2** UNCOUNT N **Entertaining** involves giving guests food and talking to them. *...business entertaining.*

entertainment /ɛntəteɪnmə[2]nt/, **entertainments. 1** UNCOUNT N **Entertainment** consists of performances or activities that give an audience pleasure. *...the entertainment business.* **2** COUNT N An **entertainment** is a performance which people watch. *...extravagant musical entertainments.*

enthral /ɪ[2]nθrɔːl/, **enthrals, enthralling, enthralled;** spelled **enthraling** and **enthraled** in American English. VB WITH OBJ To **enthral** someone means to hold their attention and interest completely. ♦ **enthralled** ADJ *400 people listened enthralled to an account of their journey.* ♦ **enthralling** ADJ *...an enthralling story.*

enthuse /ɪ[2]nθj[0]uːz/, **enthuses, enthusing, enthused.** VB If you **enthuse** over something, you say excitedly how wonderful or pleasing it is. *...enthusing over a weekend spent in the Lake District... 'Brilliant,' he enthused.*

enthusiasm /ɪ[2]nθj[0]uːzɪæzə[0]m/. UNCOUNT N **Enthusiasm** is great eagerness to do something or to be involved in something. *He had embarked with great enthusiasm on an ambitious project... ...her enthusiasm for the theatre.*

enthusiast /ɪ[2]nθj[0]uːzɪæst/, **enthusiasts.** COUNT N An **enthusiast** is a person who is very interested in a particular activity or subject. *...a soccer enthusiast.*

enthusiastic /ɪ[2]nθj[0]uːzi[1]æstɪk/. ADJ If you are **enthusiastic** about something, you want to do it very much or like it very much, and show this in an excited way. *Sarah is very enthusiastic about learning to read.* ♦ **enthusiastically** ADV *I responded very enthusiastically.*

entice /ɪ[2]ntaɪs/, **entices, enticing, enticed.** VB WITH OBJ To **entice** someone means to try to persuade them to go somewhere or to do something. *He wants to create a Church that can entice reasonable people back into it.*

enticing /ɪ[2]ntaɪsɪŋ/. ADJ Something that is **enticing** is extremely attractive; a literary use. *Tanya's invitation seemed too enticing to refuse.*

entire /ɪ[2]ntaɪə/. ATTRIB ADJ **Entire** is used to refer to the whole of something. *He had spent his entire career on Wall Street.*

entirely /ɪ[2]ntaɪəli[1]/. ADV **Entirely** means completely. *It was entirely my own fault... I agree entirely... He had told them something entirely different.*

entirety /ɪ[2]ntaɪərɪ[1]ti[1]/. PHRASE If you refer to something **in its entirety,** you mean all of it; a formal use. *If published, it must be published in its entirety.*

entitle /ɪ[2]ntaɪtə[0]l/, **entitles, entitling, entitled. 1** VB WITH OBJ AND PREP 'to' OR TO-INF If something **entitles** you to have or do something, it gives you the right to have it or do it. *Their qualifications entitle them to a higher salary.* **2** PRED ADJ You use **entitled** when you are mentioning the title of a book, film, or painting. *...a report entitled 'Attitudes Towards Geriatrics'.*

entitlement /ɪ[2]ntaɪtə[0]lmə[2]nt/, **entitlements.** COUNT N OR UNCOUNT N An **entitlement** to something is the right to have or do it; a formal use. *...entitlements to welfare and tax benefits... Manual workers were limited to a shorter period of entitlement.*

entity /ɛntɪ[1]ti[1]/, **entities.** COUNT N An **entity** is something that exists separately from other things and has a clear identity; a formal use. *Increasingly, inner cities and suburbs are separate entities.*

entourage /ɒntʊrɑːʒ/, **entourages.** COUNT N The **entourage** of someone famous or important is the group of assistants or other people who travel with them. *Among his entourage was a retired general.*

entrails /ɛntreɪlz/. PLURAL N The **entrails** of people or animals are their intestines; a literary use.

entrance, entrances, entrancing, entranced; pronounced /ɛntrəns/ when it is a noun, and /ɪ[2]ntrɑːns/ when it is a verb. **1** COUNT N An **entrance** is a way into a place, for example a door or gate. *...the entrance to the National Gallery.* **2** COUNT N Someone's **entrance** is their arrival in a room. *Her father would make a sudden entrance.* **3** UNCOUNT N If you gain **entrance** to a place, profession or institution, you are able to go into it or are accepted as a member of it. *I denied him entrance... Entrance to the professions is open to many more people.* **4** VB WITH OBJ If something **entrances** you, it makes you feel delight and wonder. *He was entirely entranced by her.* ♦ **entranced** ADJ *Everyone sat entranced.*

entrant /ɛntrənt/, **entrants.** COUNT N An **entrant** is a person who officially enters a competition or institution. *Each entrant plays the music of their choice.*

entrenched /ɪ[2]ntrɛntʃt/. ADJ If something such as power, a custom, or an idea is **entrenched,** it is firmly established and difficult to change; a formal use. *...strongly entrenched ideas.*

entrepreneur /ɒntrəprənɜː/, **entrepreneurs.** COUNT N An **entrepreneur** is a person who sets up businesses.

entrust /ɪ[2]ntrʌst/, **entrusts, entrusting, entrusted.** VB WITH OBJ AND PREP 'to' OR 'with' If you **entrust** something important to someone or if you **entrust** them with it, you make them responsible for it. *Children are too young to be entrusted with family money... It was a task the Foreign Secretary had entrusted to him.*

entry /ɛntri[1]/, **entries. 1** COUNT N An **entry** is something that you do in order to take part in a competition, for example a piece of work or the answers to a set of questions. *...the five winning entries.* **2** COUNT N Something written under a particular heading in a diary, account book, dictionary, or encyclopedia is also called an **entry.** *Let me look up the entries for mid-June.* **3** COUNT N An **entry** is also a way into a place, for example a door or gate. *...the pretty screen at the entry to Hyde Park.* **4** COUNT N WITH POSS A person's **entry** is their arrival in a room. *At Derek's entry a few heads turned.* **5** UNCOUNT N If you are allowed **entry** into a country or place, you are allowed to go in it. *Many of his associates were refused entry to Britain.* **6** UNCOUNT N Someone's **entry** into a society or group is the act of joining it. *...her entry into national politics.* **7** UNCOUNT N **Entry** in a competition is the act of taking part in it. *Entry is free to all readers.*

entwine /ɪ[2]ntwaɪn/, **entwines, entwining, entwined.** ERG VB If you **entwine** something with something else, you twist it in and around it. *One second later her fingers were entwined in my own.*

enumerate /i[1]njuːməreɪt/, **enumerates, enumerating, enumerated.** VB WITH OBJ When you **enumerate** a list of things, you name each one in turn; a formal use.

enunciate /i[1]nʌnsieɪt/, **enunciates, enunciating, enunciated;** a formal word. **1** VB WITH OR WITHOUT OBJ

When you **enunciate** a word or part of a word, you pronounce it clearly. **2** VB WITH OBJ When you **enunciate** a thought, idea, or plan, you express it clearly and formally. *I enunciated a general principle.*

envelop /ɪ2nvɛləp/, **envelops, enveloping, enveloped.** VB WITH OBJ If something soft **envelops** an object, it covers or surrounds it completely. *Mist was rising, enveloping the grey tree trunks.*

envelope /ɛnvələʊp, ɒn-/, **envelopes.** COUNT N An **envelope** is the rectangular paper cover in which you send a letter through the post.

enviable /ɛnvɪəbə0l/. ADJ You describe something such as a quality as **enviable** when someone else has it and you wish that you had it yourself. *She learned to speak foreign languages with enviable fluency.*

envious /ɛnvɪəs/. ADJ Someone who is **envious** of someone else envies them. ♦ **enviously** ADV *They were watched enviously by the rest of the crowd.*

environment /ɪ2nvaɪrən0mə2nt/, **environments.** **1** COUNT N OR UNCOUNT N Your **environment** is everything around you that affects your daily life, for example where you live and the people and things that affect you. *Could the college provide a stimulating environment?... Are we more influenced by environment or heredity?* **2** SING N The **environment** is the natural world of land, sea, air, plants, and animals. *We are fighting pollution to protect the environment.*

environmental /ɪ2nvaɪrən0mɛntə0l/. **1** ATTRIB ADJ **Environmental** means concerned with or relating to the natural world. *...environmental pollution.* **2** ATTRIB ADJ **Environmental** also means relating to the surroundings in which a person or animal lives. *Corals are very demanding in their environmental requirements.*

environmentalist /ɪ2nvaɪrən0mɛntəlɪst/, **environmentalists.** COUNT N An **environmentalist** is a person who wants to protect and preserve the natural environment.

envisage /ɪ2nvɪzɪdʒ/, **envisages, envisaging, envisaged.** REPORT VB If you **envisage** a situation or event, you imagine it, or think that it is likely to happen. *The last forecast envisaged inflation falling to about 10 per cent... The party envisages that socialism can come without civil war.*

envoy /ɛnvɔɪ/, **envoys.** COUNT N An **envoy** is a diplomat sent to a foreign country.

envy /ɛnvi1/, **envies, envying, envied.** **1** VB WITH OBJ OR VB WITH OBJ AND OBJ If you **envy** someone, you wish that you had the same things or qualities that they have. *It would be unfair to envy him his good fortune.* **2** UNCOUNT N **Envy** is the feeling you have when you wish you had the same thing or quality that someone else has. *Her undisputed good looks caused envy and admiration.* **3** PHRASE If you have something that other people wish they had, you can say that it is **the envy of** these people. *It has a robust economy that is the envy of its neighbours.*

ephemeral /i1fɛmə0rəl/. ADJ Something that is **ephemeral** lasts only for a short time; a literary use.

epic /ɛpɪk/, **epics.** **1** COUNT N An **epic** is a long book, poem, or film which usually tells a story of heroic deeds. **2** ADJ Something that is described as **epic** is considered very impressive or ambitious. *...his triumphant return after his epic voyage.*

epidemic /ɛpɪdɛmɪk/, **epidemics.** COUNT N An **epidemic** is an occurrence of a disease which spreads quickly and affects a large number of people.

epilepsy /ɛpɪlɛpsi1/. UNCOUNT N **Epilepsy** is a brain condition which causes a person to lose consciousness and have fits.

epileptic /ɛpɪlɛptɪk/, **epileptics.** **1** ADJ Someone who is **epileptic** suffers from epilepsy. Also COUNT N *He is an epileptic.* **2** ATTRIB ADJ **Epileptic** also means caused by epilepsy. *...an epileptic fit.*

epilogue /ɛpɪlɒg/, **epilogues.** COUNT N An **epilogue** is a passage added to the end of a book or play as a conclusion.

episcopal /i1pɪskəpə0l/. ATTRIB ADJ **Episcopal** means belonging or relating to a bishop; a formal use.

episode /ɛpɪsəʊd/, **episodes.** **1** COUNT N An **episode** is an important or memorable event or series of events. *A wartime episode had demonstrated his judgement of men.* **2** COUNT N An **episode** is also one of the programmes in a serial on television or radio.

epitaph /ɛpɪtɑːf, -tæf/, **epitaphs.** COUNT N An **epitaph** is something written on a person's gravestone, or a sentence or short poem that summarizes a dead person's character.

epithet /ɛpɪθɛt/, **epithets.** COUNT N An **epithet** is an adjective or a short descriptive phrase; a formal use.

epitome /i1pɪtəmi1/. SING N If you say that someone or something is the **epitome** of a particular thing, you mean that they are a perfect example of it; a formal use. *He was considered the epitome of a gentleman.*

epitomize /i1pɪtəmaɪz/, **epitomizes, epitomizing, epitomized;** also spelled **epitomise.** VB WITH OBJ If you say that someone or something **epitomizes** a particular thing, you mean that they are a perfect example of it. *His failure epitomizes that of the whole movement.*

epoch /iːpɒk/, **epochs.** COUNT N An **epoch** is a long period of time in history; a formal use. *We are at the end of a historical epoch.*

equable /ɛkwəbə0l/. ADJ An **equable** person is calm and reasonable, and does not get angry quickly. ♦ **equably** ADV *'It suits me,' I said equably.*

equal /iːkwəl/, **equals, equalling, equalled;** spelled **equaling** and **equaled** in American English. **1** ADJ If two things are **equal** or if one thing is **equal** to another, they are the same in size, amount, or degree. *The cake was divided into twelve equal parts... They paid fines of 250 rupees each (equal to about three months' wages).* **2** ATTRIB ADJ If people have **equal** rights, they have the same rights as each other. *...equal opportunities for men and women.* **3** PRED ADJ If you say that people are **equal,** you mean that everyone has or should have the same rights and opportunities. **4** COUNT N WITH POSS Someone who is your **equal** has the same ability, status, or rights that you have. *We treat our enemies as equals.* **5** PHRASE If two people do something **on equal terms,** neither person has any advantage over the other. *This law enables British shipbuilders to compete on equal terms with foreign yards.* **6** VB WITH COMPLEMENT If something **equals** a particular amount, it is equal to it. *79 minus 14 equals 65.* **7** VB WITH OBJ To **equal** something or someone means to be as good or as great as them. *There are few film artists who can equal this man for sheer daring.* **8** PRED ADJ WITH PREP 'to' If someone is **equal** to a job or situation, they have the necessary abilities, strength, or courage to deal successfully with it; a formal use.

equality /i1kwɒlɪ1ti1/. UNCOUNT N **Equality** is a situation or state where all the members of a society or group have the same status, rights, and opportunities. *...equality between men and women.*

equally /iːkwəli1/. **1** ADV **Equally** means in sections, amounts, or spaces that are the same size as each other. *On his death the land was divided equally between them.* **2** SUBMOD OR ADV **Equally** also means to the same degree or extent. *He was a superb pianist. Irene was equally brilliant... Are parents meant to love all their children equally?* **3** SENTENCE ADV **Equally** is used to introduce a comment which balances or contrasts with another comment that has just been made. *Each country must find its own solution to unemployment. Equally, each must find its own way of coping with inflation.*

equals sign, equals signs. COUNT N An **equals sign** is the sign (=).

equanimity /ɛkwənɪmɪ1ti1/. UNCOUNT N **Equanimity** is a calm state of mind; a formal use. *They were content to accept their defeat with equanimity.*

equate /i1kweɪt/, **equates, equating, equated.** VB WITH OBJ AND 'with' OR PREP 'to' If you **equate** one thing with another, you say or believe that it is the same thing; a formal use. *War should on no account be equated with glory.*

equation /i1kweɪʒə0n/, **equations.** COUNT N An **equation** is a mathematical statement saying that two amounts or values are the same, for example 6×4=12×2.

equator /i1kweɪtə/. PROPER N The **equator** is an imaginary line round the middle of the earth, halfway between the North and South poles.

equatorial /ɛkwətɔːrɪəl/. ATTRIB ADJ **Equatorial** is used to describe places and conditions near or at the equator.

equestrian /ɪ2kwɛstrɪən/. ATTRIB ADJ **Equestrian** means connected with the activity of riding horses; a formal use.

equidistant /iːkwɪdɪstənt/. PRED ADJ A place that is **equidistant** from two other places is the same distance from each of them.

equilibrium /iːkwɪlɪbrɪəm/. UNCOUNT N **Equilibrium** is a balance between several different forces, groups, or aspects of a situation; a formal use. *I believe this state of equilibrium will be maintained.*

equip /ɪ2kwɪp/, **equips, equipping, equipped.** **1** REFL VB OR VB WITH OBJ If you **equip** yourself with something, or if someone **equips** you with it, you obtain it for a particular purpose. *They equip themselves with a great variety of gadgets... The enemy troops were equipped with tanks, aircraft and missiles.* ♦ **equipped** ADJ *By contrast, their competitors were superbly equipped.* **2** VB WITH OBJ If something **is equipped** with a particular feature, it has it. *The card will be equipped with a built-in computer chip.* **3** VB WITH OBJ If something **equips** you for a task or experience, it prepares you mentally for it. *Little in their history has equipped them for coping with this problem.* ♦ **equipped** ADJ *They were ill equipped to deal with the situation.*

equipment /i1kwɪpmə2nt/. UNCOUNT N **Equipment** consists of the things which are needed for a particular activity. *...kitchen equipment.*

equitable /ɛkwɪtəbə0l/. ADJ In an **equitable** system, everyone is treated equally; a formal use.

equivalence /i1kwɪvələns/. UNCOUNT N If there is **equivalence** between two things, they have the same use, function, size, or value.

equivalent /i1kwɪvələ2nt/, **equivalents.** ADJ If things are **equivalent,** they have the same use, function, size, or value. *Women were paid less than men doing equivalent work... His job was roughly equivalent to that of the State Department's chief.* Also COUNT N *A good quilt is the equivalent of at least three blankets.*

equivocal /i1kwɪvəkə0l/. ADJ If something that you say or do is **equivocal,** it is deliberately ambiguous or hard to understand; a formal use. *He limited himself to an equivocal grunt.*

-er, -ers. **1** SUFFIX You add **-er** to adjectives with one or two syllables to form comparative adjectives. You also add it to some adverbs that do not end in '-ly' to form comparative adverbs. *They are faced with a much harder problem... Alf kept putting bigger and bigger locks on the door... He apologized for not returning sooner.* **2** SUFFIX **-er** is added to verbs to form nouns referring to people or things that perform a particular action. For example, a reader is someone who reads. Nouns of this kind are often not defined but are treated with the related verbs. *...successive waves of invaders.* **3** SUFFIX **-er** is also used to form nouns that refer to a person with a particular job or of a particular kind. *My grandfather was a miner... ...elderly pensioners.*

era /ɪərə/, **eras.** COUNT N An **era** is a period of time that is considered as a single unit because it has a particular feature. *...the post-war era... Her candidacy marked the beginning of a new era for the party.*

eradicate /ɪrædɪkeɪt/, **eradicates, eradicating, eradicated.** VB WITH OBJ To **eradicate** something means to destroy or remove it completely; a formal use. *...the failure of the welfare state to eradicate poverty.* ♦ **eradication** /ɪ2rædɪkeɪʃə0n/ UNCOUNT N *...the eradication of apartheid.*

erase /ɪreɪz/, **erases, erasing, erased.** **1** VB WITH OBJ If you **erase** a thought or feeling, you get rid of it. *He cannot erase the memories of childhood.* **2** VB WITH OBJ If you **erase** writing, you remove it by rubbing it. **3** VB WITH OBJ To **erase** something also means to remove it so that it no longer exists; a formal use. *...a campaign to erase hunger from the world.*

eraser /ɪreɪzə/, **erasers.** COUNT N An **eraser** is a piece of rubber used for rubbing out writing.

erect /ɪrɛkt/, **erects, erecting, erected.** **1** VB WITH OBJ If you **erect** something, you build it or set it up so that it can be used; a formal use. *It would be splendid to erect a memorial to the regiment... This kind of tent is easily erected.* ♦ **erection** /ɪrɛkʃə0n/ UNCOUNT N *The building was badly damaged shortly after its erection.* **2** ADJ People or things that are **erect** are straight and upright. *In the door, small but erect, stood an old man... She held herself erect.*

erode /i1rəʊd/, **erodes, eroding, eroded.** **1** ERG VB If something **is eroded,** it is gradually destroyed or removed. *Confidence in the dollar has eroded... Our freedom is being eroded.* **2** ERG VB If rock or soil **erodes** or **is eroded** by water or the weather, it is gradually destroyed or removed. *The river has eroded the rocks.*

erosion /i1rəʊʒə0n/. UNCOUNT N **Erosion** is the gradual removal or destruction of something. *...the erosion of individual freedom... ...the loss of farmland by erosion.*

erotic /i1rɒtɪk/. **1** ADJ **Erotic** feelings and activities involve sexual pleasure or desire. *...erotic dreams... ...an erotic experience.* **2** ADJ **Erotic** paintings, books, and films are intended to produce feelings of sexual pleasure. *...an anthology of erotic verse.*

err /ɜː/, **errs, erring, erred.** **1** VB If you **err,** you make a mistake; a formal use. *Undoubtedly we have erred in giving such low status to our nurses.* **2** PHRASE If you **err on the side of** a particular way of behaving, you tend to behave in that way. *Often one finds that advisers err on the side of caution.*

errand /ɛrənd/, **errands.** COUNT N If you go on an **errand** for someone, you go a short distance in order to do something for them, for example to buy something from a shop.

erratic /ɪ2rætɪk/. ADJ Something that is **erratic** does not follow a regular pattern, but happens at unexpected times or moves in an irregular way. *...the country's erratic attempts to move into the future... I made my erratic way through the dining room.* ♦ **erratically** ADV *Bullets whiz past erratically.*

erroneous /ɪ2rəʊnɪəs/. ADJ **Erroneous** beliefs or opinions are incorrect; a formal use. ♦ **erroneously**

ADV *They erroneously imagined that they had become wiser.*

error /ɛrə/, **errors.** 1 COUNT N OR UNCOUNT N An **error** is a mistake. *The doctor committed an appalling error of judgement... A degree of error is inevitable.* 2 PHRASE If something happens **in error,** it happens by mistake. *Another village had been wiped out in error.* **3 trial and error:** see **trial.**

erudite /ɛrju:daɪt/. ADJ **Erudite** people show great academic knowledge.

erupt /ɪ'rʌpt/, **erupts, erupting, erupted.** 1 VB When something **erupts,** it happens suddenly and unexpectedly. *The Cuban Missile Crisis had erupted... ...the urban riots that erupted this summer in Britain.* ♦ **eruption** /ɪ'rʌpʃən/ UNCOUNT N OR COUNT N *This may have stopped the eruption of a major war between the superpowers.* 2 VB WITH ADJUNCT When people in a place suddenly become angry or violent, you can say that they **erupt** or that the place **erupts.** *The inhabitants had erupted in massive protests... The room erupted.* 3 VB When a volcano **erupts,** it throws out lava, ash, and steam. ♦ **eruption** UNCOUNT N OR COUNT N *...the most violent eruption of Mount Etna.*

escalate /ɛskəleɪt/, **escalates, escalating, escalated.** ERG VB If an unpleasant situation **escalates,** it becomes worse. *There is a danger that the conflict might escalate to a nuclear confrontation.* ♦ **escalation** /ɛskəleɪʃən/ UNCOUNT N *...a steady escalation of violence.*

escalator /ɛskəleɪtə/, **escalators.** COUNT N An **escalator** is a moving staircase.

escape /ɪ'skeɪp/, **escapes, escaping, escaped.** 1 VB WITH OR WITHOUT OBJ If you **escape** from something or someone, you succeed in avoiding them. *Ralph was thankful to have escaped responsibility... The two other burglars were tipped off by a lookout and escaped.* 2 VB If you **escape** from a place, you succeed in getting away from it. *On 7 October Eva escaped from prison... He escaped to Britain.* ♦ **escaped** ATTRIB ADJ *He had shot and killed two escaped convicts.* 3 UNCOUNT N OR COUNT N An **escape** is the act of escaping from a particular place or situation. *They were now able to make their escape.* 4 VB WITH COMPLEMENT OR ADJUNCT You can say that you **escape** when you survive something such as an accident. *Fortunately we all escaped unhurt... The minister escaped without a scratch.* 5 VB WITH OBJ If something **escapes** you or **escapes** your attention, you do not know about it or do not remember it. *I doubt that such tactics escaped their notice... Their names escaped him.* 6 COUNT N An **escape** is a way of avoiding difficulties or responsibilities. *Reading is an escape from reality.* 7 VB When a gas or liquid **escapes,** it leaks from a pipe or container. *...air escaping from a tyre.* 8 See also **fire escape.**

escapism /ɪ'skeɪpɪzəm/. UNCOUNT N **Escapism** consists of thoughts or activities involving pleasant ideas instead of the boring aspects of your life. *Thinking about the future is a form of escapism.* ♦ **escapist** /ɪ'skeɪpɪst/ ADJ *...an escapist fantasy.*

escort, escorts, escorting, escorted; pronounced /ɛskɔ:t/ when it is a noun, and /ɪ'skɔ:t/ when it is a verb. 1 COUNT N An **escort** is a person who goes somewhere with you to protect you. *...a police escort.* ● If someone is taken somewhere **under escort,** they are accompanied by guards, either because they have been arrested or because they are very important. 2 VB WITH OBJ AND ADJUNCT If you **escort** someone somewhere, you go there with them to make sure that they leave a place or get to their destination. *He escorted me to the door.*

ESL /i: ɛs ɛl/. UNCOUNT N **ESL** is used to describe things that are connected with the teaching of English to people whose first language is not English and who need to speak and write English because it is an important or official language in their country. **ESL** is an abbreviation for 'English as a second language'.

esoteric /ɛsəʊtɛrɪk/. ADJ Something that is **esoteric** is understood by only a small number of people with special knowledge; a formal use. *...an esoteric script that few people can read.*

ESP /i: ɛs pi:/. UNCOUNT N **ESP** is used to describe things that are connected with the teaching of English to people who need it for a particular purpose. **ESP** is an abbreviation for 'English for specific purposes' or 'English for special purposes'.

especial /ɪ'spɛʃəl/. ATTRIB ADJ If something is **especial,** it is exceptional or special in some way; a formal use. *He took especial care to vary his routine.*

especially /ɪ'spɛʃəli/. 1 SENTENCE ADV You use **especially** to indicate that what you are saying applies more to one thing than to any other. *He was kind to his staff, especially those who were sick or in trouble... Double ovens are a good idea, especially if you are cooking several meals at once.* 2 SUBMOD You use **especially** with an adjective to emphasize a quality. *He found his host especially irritating... They didn't find it especially hard.*

espionage /ɛspɪənɑ:ʒ/. UNCOUNT N **Espionage** is the activity of finding out the political, military, or industrial secrets of your enemies or rivals. *The Swiss threatened to throw them in jail for espionage.*

espouse /ɪ'spaʊz/, **espouses, espousing, espoused.** VB WITH OBJ If you **espouse** a policy or plan, you support it; a formal use.

Esq. Esq. is sometimes written after a man's name if he has no other title. It is an abbreviation for 'esquire'. *...James Dickson, Esq.*

essay /ɛseɪ/, **essays.** COUNT N An **essay** is a piece of writing on a particular subject. *I had to produce an essay on Herrick for my tutor... ...a volume of essays.*

essence /ɛsəns/. 1 SING N The **essence** of something is its basic and most important characteristic which gives it an individual identity. *Competition is the essence of all games.* 2 SENTENCE ADV You use **in essence** to indicate that you are talking about the most important aspect of something; a formal use. *But this is not in essence a book about religion.*

essential /ɪ'sɛnʃəl/, **essentials.** 1 ADJ Something that is **essential** is absolutely necessary. *Land is essential for food and for work... ...an essential qualification for a journalist... It is essential to set your targets realistically.* 2 COUNT N **Essentials** are things that are absolutely necessary. *...other essentials such as fuel and clothing... I had only the bare essentials.* 3 ATTRIB ADJ The **essential** aspects of something are its most basic or important aspects. *...the essential feature of the situation.* 4 PLURAL N **Essentials** are also the most important parts or facts of a particular subject. *Their laws deal with essentials, not appearances.*

essentially /ɪ'sɛnʃəli/. 1 ADV OR SENTENCE ADV You use **essentially** to emphasize a quality that something or someone has, and to say that this quality is their most important one. *Phyllis was essentially a soft, caring person.* 2 ADV You also use **essentially** to indicate that what you are saying is generally true, and that other factors are not necessary for you to make your point. *Such theories are essentially correct.*

-est. SUFFIX You add **-est** to adjectives that have one or two syllables to form superlatives. You also add it to some adverbs that do not end in -ly. *...the prettiest girl she had ever seen... It's the winning blow that strikes hardest.*

establish /ɪ'stæblɪʃ/, **establishes, establishing, established.** 1 VB WITH OBJ If you **establish** an organization or a system, you create it. *He had set out to establish his own business.* ♦ **established** ATTRIB ADJ *...the established institutions of society.* ♦ **establishment** /ɪ'stæblɪʃmənt/ SING N *...the establishment of free trade unions.* 2 VB WITH OBJ If you **establish** contact with a group of people, you start to have discussions with them. 3 REPORT VB If you **establish** that something is true, you prove that it is definitely true. *A court of enquiry established that there were faults on both sides... So far they have been unable to establish the cause of death.*

establishment /ɪ'stæblɪʃmənt/, **establishments.** 1 COUNT N WITH SUPP An **establishment** is a shop or business; a formal use. 2 SING N You refer to a group of people as the **establishment** when they have special power and influence in the running of a country or organization. *...the British Establishment... ...the university establishment.*

estate /ɪ'steɪt/, **estates.** 1 COUNT N An **estate** is a large area of land in the country owned by one person or organization. 2 COUNT N WITH SUPP A housing **estate** or factory **estate** is a large area of land with houses or factories on it. ● See also **real estate.** 3 COUNT N Someone's **estate** is the money and property they leave when they die. *She left her estate to her grandchildren.*

estate agent, estate agents. COUNT N An **estate agent** is someone who works for a company selling houses and land; a British use.

estate car, estate cars. COUNT N An **estate car** is a car with a long body, a door at the rear, and space behind the back seats; a British use.

esteem /ɪ'sti:m/. UNCOUNT N **Esteem** is admiration and respect; a formal use. *I know the high esteem you feel for our colleague here... Zapp had no great esteem for his fellow lecturers.*

esthetic /ɛsθɛtɪk/. See **aesthetic.**

estimate, estimates, estimating, estimated; pronounced /ɛstɪmeɪt/ when it is a verb, and /ɛstɪmət/ when it is a noun. 1 VB WITH OBJ OR REPORT VB If you **estimate** an amount or a quantity, you calculate it approximately or say what it is likely to be. *They were not able to estimate the cost... He estimated he would do the hundred miles by noon.* ♦ **estimated** ADJ *In 1975 there were an estimated 6,000 children in community homes.* 2 COUNT N An **estimate** is an approximate calculation. *According to some estimates the number of farms has increased by 50 per cent.* 3 COUNT N An **estimate** is also a judgement made about a person or a situation. *Thomas wasn't living up to my estimate of him.*

estimation /ɛstɪmeɪʃən/, **estimations.** 1 SING N Your **estimation** of a person or situation is your opinion of them. *His comments were, in my estimation, correct and most useful.* 2 COUNT N An **estimation** is an approximate calculation, or the result obtained by it. *...an estimation of the speed of the air leaving the lungs.*

estranged /ɪ'streɪndʒd/. 1 ADJ If you are **estranged** from your husband or wife, you no longer live with them. *...her estranged husband.* 2 PRED ADJ If you are **estranged** from your family or friends, you have quarrelled with them and no longer speak to them. *He knows I am estranged from my father.*

estuary /ɛstjuəri/, **estuaries.** COUNT N An **estuary** is the wide part of a river where it joins the sea.

etc /ɪt'sɛtərə/. **etc** is used at the end of a list to indicate that there are other items which you could mention if you had enough time or space. *...window frames, floorboards, beams, etc... She had to cook, do the cleaning, make beds etc, etc.*

etch /ɛtʃ/, **etchs, etching, etched.** 1 VB WITH OR WITHOUT OBJ If you **etch** a design or pattern on a surface, you cut it into the surface using a sharp tool. *The artists must have spent many hours etching the images on the walls.* 2 VB WITH OBJ If something is **etched** on your memory, it has made a very deep impression on you. *His face will remain permanently etched on my memory.*

etching /ɛtʃɪŋ/, **etchings.** COUNT N An **etching** is a picture printed from a metal plate that has had a design cut into it.

eternal /ɪ'tɜ:nəl/. 1 ADJ If something is **eternal,** it lasts for ever. *...the promise of eternal bliss.* ♦ **eternally** ADV *Something remained eternally unspoiled in him.* 2 ADJ **Eternal** truths and values never change and are thought to be true in all situations. *...a society which lives by eternal principles.*

eternity /ɪ'tɜ:nɪti/, **eternities.** 1 UNCOUNT N **Eternity** is time without an end, or a state of existence that is outside time, especially the state which some people believe they will pass into after they have died. *The preacher promised us eternity.* 2 COUNT N You can refer to a period of time as an **eternity** when it seems very long; an informal use. *I lay there for an eternity, coughing and gasping.*

ethic /ɛθɪk/, **ethics.** 1 SING N WITH SUPP A particular **ethic** is a moral belief that influences people's behaviour, attitudes, and ideas. *...the American ethic of expansion and opportunity.* 2 PLURAL N **Ethics** are moral beliefs and rules about right and wrong.

ethical /ɛθɪkəl/. ATTRIB ADJ **Ethical** means influenced by a system of moral beliefs about right and wrong. *She had no ethical objection to drinking.*

ethnic /ɛθnɪk/. ATTRIB ADJ **Ethnic** means connected with different racial or cultural groups of people. *...the ethnic composition of the voters of New York... ...ethnic minorities.*

ethos /i:θɒs/. SING N The **ethos** of a group of people is the set of ideas and attitudes associated with it.

etiquette /ɛtɪket/. UNCOUNT N **Etiquette** is a set of customs and rules for polite behaviour. *...a book on etiquette.*

eulogy /ju:lədʒi/, **eulogies.** COUNT N A **eulogy** is a speech or piece of writing praising someone or something; a formal use. *Countless eulogies have been written about her.*

euphemism /ju:fɪmɪzəm/, **euphemisms.** COUNT N OR UNCOUNT N A **euphemism** is a polite word or expression that people use to talk about something they find unpleasant or embarrassing, such as death or sex.

euphemistic /ju:fɪ'mɪstɪk/. ADJ **Euphemistic** language consists of polite words or expressions for things that people find unpleasant or embarrassing. ♦ **euphemistically** ADV *Then came what the French euphemistically call 'the events of May'—the student revolution.*

euphoria /ju:fɔ:rɪə/. UNCOUNT N **Euphoria** is a feeling of great happiness. *She shared Dan's euphoria over the play.*

euphoric /ju:fɒrɪk/. ADJ If you are **euphoric,** you feel extremely happy. *...a euphoric moment.*

European /jʊərəpi:ən/, **Europeans.** 1 ADJ **European** means coming from or relating to Europe. 2 COUNT N A **European** is a person who comes from Europe.

euthanasia /ju:θəneɪzɪə/. UNCOUNT N **Euthanasia** is the practice of painlessly killing a sick or injured person to relieve their suffering when they cannot be cured.

evacuate /i^{1}vækju^{4}eɪt/, **evacuates, evacuating, evacuated.** VB WITH OBJ If people **are evacuated** from a place, they move out of it because it has become dangerous. *The entire complex was being evacuated... I was evacuated to Swindon in 1941.* ♦ **evacuation** /i^{1}vækju^{4}eɪʃə^{0}n/. UNCOUNT N *Orders went out to prepare for the evacuation of the city.*

evade /i^{1}veɪd/, **evades, evading, evaded. 1** VB WITH OBJ If you **evade** something that you do not want to be involved with, you avoid it. *I evaded the issue... He had found a way of evading responsibility.* **2** VB WITH OBJ If you **evade** someone or something that is moving towards you, you succeed in not being touched by them. *Tim tried to catch her arm but she evaded him.* **3** VB WITH OBJ If something such as success or love **evades** you, you never manage to achieve it. *Military glory had evaded him throughout his long career.*

evaluate /i^{1}vælju^{4}eɪt/, **evaluates, evaluating, evaluated.** VB WITH OBJ If you **evaluate** something, you decide how valuable it is after considering all its features. *He was asked to evaluate the situation.* ♦ **evaluation** /i^{1}vælju^{4}eɪʃə^{0}n/ COUNT N OR UNCOUNT N *...a realistic evaluation of the working of Britain's economy... They can help develop our powers of critical evaluation.*

evaporate /i^{1}væpəreɪt/, **evaporates, evaporating, evaporated. 1** VB When a liquid **evaporates,** it changes into a gas, usually because it has been heated. *All the water has evaporated.* ♦ **evaporation** /i^{1}væpəreɪʃə^{0}n/ UNCOUNT N *Be careful not to lose too much liquid by evaporation.* **2** VB If a feeling or attitude **evaporates,** it gradually becomes less and eventually disappears. *My nervousness evaporated.*

evasion /i^{1}veɪʒə^{0}n/, **evasions.** UNCOUNT N OR COUNT N **Evasion** consists of deliberately not doing something that you ought to do. *He is guilty of gross tax evasion... ...an evasion of our responsibilities... He continued with his evasions and lies.*

evasive /i^{1}veɪsɪv/. ADJ If you are being **evasive,** you are deliberately not talking about something. *...an evasive answer.* ♦ **evasively** ADV *The Count had answered evasively.*

eve /iːv/, **eves.** COUNT N The **eve** of an event is the day before it. *...a devastating attack on the eve of the election.* ● See also **Christmas Eve, New Year's Eve.**

even /iːvə^{0}n/, **evens, evening, evened. 1** SENTENCE ADV You use **even** to emphasize that what precedes it or follows it in the sentence is surprising. *Even Anthony enjoyed it... She liked him even when she was quarrelling with him... I often lend her money even now.* **2** PHRASE You use **even so** to introduce a surprising fact that relates to what you have just said. *Their feathers are regularly shed and renewed. Even so they need constant care.* **3** ADV You use **even** with comparative adjectives for emphasis. *Barber had something even worse to tell me... ...an even brighter light... I must be even more tired than I thought.* **4** CONJ You use **even if** or **even though** to indicate that a particular fact does not make the rest of your statement untrue. *Even if you disagree with her, she's worth listening to... I was always rather afraid of men, even though I had lots of boyfriends.* **5** ADJ If a measurement or rate is **even,** it stays at about the same level. *...an even body temperature.* ♦ **evenly** ADV *Mary was breathing quietly and evenly.* **6** ADJ **Even** surfaces are smooth and flat. **7** ADJ If there is an **even** distribution or division of something, each person, group, or area involved has an equal amount. *The distribution of land was much more even than in Latin America.* ♦ **evenly** ADV *Opinion seems to be fairly evenly divided.* **8** ADJ If a contest or competition is **even,** the people taking part are all equally skilful. *It was a pretty even game.* ♦ **evenly** ADV *Government and rebel soldiers are evenly matched.* **9** PHRASE If you say you will **get even** with someone, you mean you intend to harm them because they have harmed you; an informal use. *I always knew that one day I would get even with her.* **10** ADJ If there is an **even** chance of something happening, it is equally likely to happen or not to happen. *She would have had only an even chance of being saved.* **11** ADJ An **even** number can be divided exactly by the number two.

even out. PHR VB When an amount of something **evens out** or when you **even it out,** it becomes more evenly distributed or steadier. *Irrigation systems help to even out the supply of water over the growing season.*

evening /iːvnɪŋ/, **evenings.** COUNT N OR UNCOUNT N The **evening** is the part of each day between the end of the afternoon and the time you go to bed. *He arrived about six in the evening... Each evening he runs 5 miles... He was silently finishing his evening meal.*

evening class, evening classes. COUNT N An **evening class** is a course for adults that is taught in the evening.

event /i^{1}vent/, **events. 1** COUNT N An **event** is something that happens, especially something unusual or important. *Next day the newspapers reported the event... ...the most important event in family life.* **2** PLURAL N You can refer to all the things that are happening in a particular situation as **events.** *Events now moved swiftly... The authorities were quite unable to control events.* **3** COUNT N In sport, an **event** is one of the activities that are part of an organized occasion. *Lord Exeter presented the medals for this event.*

eventful /i^{1}ventfʊl/. ADJ An **eventful** period of time is full of exciting or important events. *...the most exhausting and eventful day of his life.*

eventual /i^{1}ventʃ^{0}ʊ^{0}əl/. ATTRIB ADJ The **eventual** result of something is what happens at the end of it. *...the company's eventual collapse in 1971.*

eventuality /i^{1}ventʃʊælɪ^{1}ti^1/, **eventualities.** COUNT N An **eventuality** is a possible future event; a formal use. *We are insured against all eventualities.*

eventually /i^{1}ventʃʊ^{0}əli^1/. **1** ADV OR SENTENCE ADV If something happens **eventually,** it happens after a lot of delays or problems. *Rodin eventually agreed that Casson was right... Eventually they got through to the hospital.* **2** ADV **Eventually** also means happening as the final result of a process or series of events. *The three firms eventually became Imperial Airways.*

ever /evə/. **1** ADV **Ever** means at any time in the past. *I don't think I'll ever be homesick here... I am happier than I have ever been.* **2** ADV **Ever** is used in expressions like 'ever-increasing' and 'ever-present' to indicate that something exists or continues all the time. *...an ever-increasing prison population... ...an ever-present sense of danger.* **3** ADV You also use **ever** in questions beginning with words such as 'why', 'when', and 'which' when you want to emphasize your surprise or shock. *'I'm sorry. I'd rather not say.'—'Why ever not?.'... Who ever would have thought that?*

PHRASES ● You use **ever since** to emphasize that something has been true all the time since the time mentioned, and is still true now. *'How long have you lived here?'—'Ever since I was married.'* ● You use **ever so** and **ever such** to emphasize the degree of something; an informal use. *They are ever so kind... I had ever such a nice letter from her.*

evergreen /evəgriːn/, **evergreens.** COUNT N An **evergreen** is a tree or bush which never sheds its leaves.

everlasting /evəlɑːstɪŋ/. ADJ Something that is **everlasting** never ends or never seems to change; a literary use. *...the everlasting snows of the mighty Himalayas.* ♦ **everlastingly** ADV *He was everlastingly optimistic.*

every /evri^1/. **1** DET You use **every** to indicate that you are referring to all the members of a group or all the parts of something. *She spoke to every person at the party... I loved every minute of it.* **2** DET You also use **every** to indicate that something happens at regular intervals. *They met every day... I visit her once every six months... Every so often, she spends a weekend in London.* **3** PHRASE You use **every** to say how often something happens. For example, if something happens **every second** day or **every other** day, it happens on one day in each period of two days. *We only take a vacation every other year.* **4** DET You use **every** before a number to say what proportion of people or things something applies to. *One woman in every two hundred is a sufferer... Since 1976, nine women have lost jobs for every five men.* **5** DET If something shows **every** sign of happening, or if there is **every** chance that it will happen, it is very likely to happen. *They show every sign of continuing to succeed.* **6** DET If someone has **every** reason to do something, they would be justified in doing it. *She had every reason to be pleased.*

everybody /evrɪbɒdi^1/. See **everyone.**

everyday /evrɪdeɪ/. **1** ATTRIB ADJ You use **everyday** to describe something which is part of normal life, and is not especially interesting. *People could resume a normal everyday life... ...their role in everyday affairs.* **2** ATTRIB ADJ You also use **everyday** to refer to something that happens or is used each day. *Exercise is part of my everyday routine.*

everyone /evrɪwə^{0}n/. **1** INDEF PRON **Everyone** or **everybody** means all the people in a group. *Everybody in the office laughed... She was genuinely interested in everyone she met.* **2** INDEF PRON You can use **everyone** or **everybody** to refer to all the people in the world. *Everyone has their own ideas about it.*

everything /evrɪθɪŋ/. **1** INDEF PRON You use **everything** to refer to all the objects, activities, or facts in a situation. *I don't agree with everything he says... I will arrange everything.* **2** INDEF PRON You can also use **everything** to refer to all possible or likely actions, activities, or situations. *That's your answer to everything... You think of everything.* **3** INDEF PRON **Everything** also means life in general. *Is everything all right?... Everything went on just as before.*

everywhere /evrɪweə/. **1** ADV You use **everywhere** to refer to a whole area or to all the places in a particular area. *Everywhere in Asia it is the same... People everywhere are becoming aware of the problem.* **2** ADV You also use **everywhere** to refer to all the places that someone goes to. *Everywhere I went, people were angry or suspicious... She always carried a gun with her everywhere.*

evict /i^{1}vɪkt/, **evicts, evicting, evicted.** VB WITH OBJ When people **are evicted,** they are officially forced to leave the house where they are living. *If evicted, they would have nowhere else to go.* ♦ **eviction** /i^{1}vɪkʃə^{0}n/ UNCOUNT N OR COUNT N *The family faces eviction for non-payment of rent... She described the evictions as 'an outrage'.*

evidence /evɪdəns/. **1** UNCOUNT N **Evidence** is the things you see, experience, or are told which make you believe that something is true. *We saw evidence everywhere that a real effort was being made to promote tourism... There was no evidence of quarrels between them.* **2** PHRASE If you **give evidence** in a court of law, you say what you know about something. **3** PHRASE If someone or something is **in evidence,** they are present and can be clearly seen. *Violence was particularly in evidence in the towns.*

evident /evɪdənt/. ADJ If it is **evident** that something exists or is true, people can easily see that it exists or is true. *It was evident that his faith in the Government was severely shaken.*

evidently /evɪdəntli^1/. SENTENCE ADV You use **evidently** to say that something is true. *They said it would come, but evidently they failed to send it... I found her in bed, evidently in great pain.*

evil /iːvə^{0}l/, **evils. 1** UNCOUNT N **Evil** is all the wicked and bad things that happen in the world. **2** COUNT N The **evils** of a situation are all the bad or harmful things in it. *...the evils of drink.* **3** ADJ An **evil** person is wicked and cruel. **4** ADJ Something that is **evil** is harmful. *Slavery was the most evil system of labour ever devised.*

evocation /iːvəkeɪʃə^{0}n/, **evocations.** COUNT N OR UNCOUNT N An **evocation** of a place or a past event is an experience in which you are reminded of it. *...evocations of rural America... It was disturbing, this evocation of her youth.*

evocative /i^{1}vɒkətɪv/. ADJ Something that is **evocative** makes you think about a place or a past event. *...an evocative description.*

evoke /i^{1}vəʊk/, **evokes, evoking, evoked.** VB WITH OBJ If something **evokes** an emotion, memory, or response, it causes it; a formal use. *The quarrel seemed to evoke the bitterest passions.*

evolution /iːvəluːʃə^{0}n/. **1** UNCOUNT N **Evolution** is a process of gradual change during which animals and plants change some of their characteristics and sometimes develop into new species. *The processes of evolution are still going on... ...the thousands of years of man's evolution.* **2** UNCOUNT N WITH SUPP You can use **evolution** to refer to any gradual process of change and development. *...the evolution of parliamentary democracy.*

evolutionary /iːvəluːʃənə^{0}ri^1/. ATTRIB ADJ **Evolutionary** means related to the evolution of animals and plants. *...evolutionary theory.*

evolve /i^{1}vɒlv/, **evolves, evolving, evolved. 1** VB When animals and plants **evolve,** they gradually change and develop into different forms or species. *The earliest fish have evolved into some 30,000 different species.* **2** ERG VB When something **evolves,** it gradually develops from something simpler. *It was fascinating to see how the film evolved... How did Giotto evolve his very personal and original style?*

ewe /juː/, **ewes.** COUNT N A **ewe** is an adult female sheep.

ex-. PREFIX **Ex-** is added to nouns to indicate that someone or something is no longer the thing referred to by the noun. For example, an ex-farmer is someone who is no longer a farmer.

exacerbate /ɪ^{2}gzæsəbeɪt, ɪ^{2}ksæs-/, **exacerbates, exacerbating, exacerbated.** VB WITH OBJ If something **exacerbates** a bad situation, it makes it worse; a formal use.

exact /ɪ^{2}gzækt/, **exacts, exacting, exacted. 1** ADJ Something that is **exact** is correct, accurate, and complete in every way. *He noted the exact time... ...an exact replica of Hamburg airport.* ♦ **exactness** UNCOUNT N *He expressed himself with great exactness.* **2** PHRASE You say **to be exact** when you want give more detailed information. *I thought that this would be possible, or to be more exact, I could see no reason why it should not be so.* **3** VB WITH OBJ If someone **exacts** something from you, they demand and obtain it, because they are more powerful than you are; a formal use. *They exacted absolute obedience from their followers.*

exacting /ɪ[2]gzæktɪŋ/. ADJ An **exacting** person or task requires you to work very hard. *...an exacting job... The state of repair failed to measure up to their exacting standards.*

exactly /ɪ[2]gzæktli[1]/. 1 ADV **Exactly** means precisely, and not just approximately. *You've exactly one hour to do this... That's exactly what they told me.* 2 ADV If you do something **exactly,** you do it very accurately. *Sam answered the owl's cry, imitating it exactly.* 3 ADV You can use **exactly** to emphasize how similar two things are. *He's exactly like a little baby.* 4 CONVENTION You can say **'Exactly'** to agree with what has just been said. *'Do you mean that we are stuck here?'—'Exactly, my dear.'* 5 ADV OR CONVENTION You can use **not exactly** to indicate that something is not quite true. *He didn't exactly block me, but he didn't move either... 'She's taken the day off.'—'Is she sick?'—'Not exactly.'*

exaggerate /ɪ[2]gzædʒəreɪt/, **exaggerates, exaggerating, exaggerated.** 1 VB WITH OR WITHOUT OBJ If you **exaggerate,** you make the thing that you are talking about seem bigger or more important than it actually is. *I am exaggerating a little... It is impossible to exaggerate the horrors of the system.* ♦ **exaggeration** /ɪ[2]gzædʒəreɪʃə[0]n/ COUNT N OR UNCOUNT N *Isn't that a bit of an exaggeration?... One can speak, without exaggeration, of a peaceful revolution.* 2 VB WITH OBJ To **exaggerate** something such as a gesture means to make it very obvious. *Ballet exaggerates ordinary body movements.* ♦ **exaggerated** ADJ *Brody heaved an exaggerated sigh.*

exalted /ɪ[2]gzɔːltɪ[2]d/. ADJ An **exalted** person is very important; a literary use. *...someone in his exalted position.*

exam /ɪ[2]gzæm/, **exams.** COUNT N An **exam** is the same as an examination; an informal use.

examination /ɪ[2]gzæmɪneɪʃə[0]n/, **examinations.** COUNT N An **examination** is a formal test taken to show your knowledge of a subject. *...a three-hour written examination.*

examine /ɪ[2]gzæmɪn/, **examines, examining, examined.** 1 VB WITH OBJ If you **examine** something, you look at it or consider it carefully. *I examined the lighter, then handed it back... Government experts were still examining the wreckage of the plane.* ♦ **examination** /ɪ[2]gzæmɪneɪʃə[0]n/ UNCOUNT N OR COUNT N *Mrs Oliver devoted herself to an examination of the address book... ...an important case which deserves closer examination.* 2 VB WITH OBJ If a doctor **examines** you, he or she looks at your body to check your health. *Each child is medically examined.* ♦ **examination** /ɪ[2]gzæmɪneɪʃə[0]n/ UNCOUNT N OR COUNT N *...a full examination of the chest.* 3 VB WITH OBJ If a teacher **examines** you, he or she finds out how much you know by asking you questions or by making you take an examination.

examiner /ɪ[2]gzæmɪnə/, **examiners.** COUNT N An **examiner** is a person who sets or marks an examination.

example /ɪ[2]gzɑːmpə[0]l/, **examples.** 1 COUNT N An **example** is something which represents or is typical of a particular group of things. *It's a very fine example of traditional architecture... Could you give me an example?* 2 COUNT N If someone is an **example** to other people or sets an **example,** they behave in a way that other people should copy. *They are a shining example to progressive people everywhere... She set such a good example to us all.*

PHRASES ● You use **for example** to show that you are giving an example of a particular kind of thing. *Japan, for example, has two languages.* ● If you **follow** someone's **example,** you copy their behaviour.

exasperate /ɪ[2]gzɑːspəreɪt/, **exasperates, exasperating, exasperated.** VB WITH OBJ If someone or something **exasperates** you, they annoy you and make you feel frustrated. *She frequently exasperates her friends.* ♦ **exasperated** ADJ *He had an exasperated look on his face.* ♦ **exasperating** ADJ *I have seldom had a more exasperating day.* ♦ **exasperation** /ɪ[2]gzɑːspəreɪʃə[0]n/ UNCOUNT N *He looked at the little boy in exasperation.*

excavate /ɛkskəveɪt/, **excavates, excavating, excavated.** VB WITH OR WITHOUT OBJ To **excavate** a piece of land means to remove earth carefully from it and look for the remains of pots or buildings, in order to find out about the past. ♦ **excavation** /ɛkskəveɪʃə[0]n/ COUNT N OR UNCOUNT N *...the excavation of a Neolithic village.*

exceed /ɪ[2]ksiːd/, **exceeds, exceeding, exceeded.** 1 VB WITH OBJ If something **exceeds** a particular amount, it is greater than that amount. *Average annual temperatures exceed 20° centigrade.* 2 VB WITH OBJ If you **exceed** a limit, you go beyond it. *A motorist was caught exceeding the speed limit... The company is not allowed to exceed its budget.*

exceedingly /ɪ[2]ksiːdɪŋli[1]/. SUBMOD **Exceedingly** means very much indeed; an old-fashioned use. *The Colonel was exceedingly wealthy.*

excel /ɪ[2]ksɛl/, **excels, excelling, excelled.** VB If someone **excels** at or in something, they are very good at it. *He excels at sports.*

excellence /ɛksələns/. UNCOUNT N **Excellence** is the quality of being extremely good at something. *Sport is an area in which excellence is still treasured.*

Excellency /ɛksələnsi[1]/, **Excellencies.** TITLE People use **Your Excellency, His Excellency,** or **Excellency** to refer to or address important officials. *His Excellency desires to see you... I shall do my best, Your Excellency.*

excellent /ɛksələnt/. ADJ Something that is **excellent** is very good indeed. *I think the teaching here is excellent... That's an excellent idea.* ♦ **excellently** ADV *The system works excellently.*

except /ɪ[2]ksɛpt/. PREP OR CONJ You use **except** or **except for** to introduce the only thing or person that a statement does not apply to. *All the boys except Piggy started to giggle... There was little I could do except wait.*

excepted /ɪ[2]ksɛptɪd/. ADJ AFTER N You use **excepted** after you have mentioned a person or thing to show that you do not include them in a group mentioned in your statement. *...a gentleman for whom other people—Rhoda excepted—put on their biggest smiles.*

excepting /ɪ[2]ksɛptɪŋ/. PREP You use **excepting** to introduce the only thing that prevents a statement from being completely true. *He was the only human male for miles around (excepting an old handyman).*

exception /ɪ[2]ksɛpʃə[0]n/, **exceptions.** COUNT N An **exception** is a thing, person, or situation that is not included in a general statement. *Women, with a few exceptions, are not involved in politics.*

PHRASES ● You use **without exception** to indicate that your statement is true in all cases. *Almost without exception, the fastest-growing cities are in Africa.* ● If you **take exception to** something, you feel offended or annoyed by it. *There are three things you've just said that I take exception to.*

exceptional, /ɪ[2]ksɛpʃə[0]nəl, -ʃənə[0]l/. 1 ADJ An **exceptional** person is unusually talented or clever. *My brother isn't exceptional; there are plenty of youngsters like him.* ♦ **exceptionally** SUBMOD *Ian is an exceptionally gifted musician.* 2 ADJ **Exceptional** situations or events are unusual or rare. *Permission will be granted only in very exceptional circumstances.* ♦ **exceptionally** SENTENCE ADV *Exceptionally, a degree will be awarded to a candidate who did not take all the exams.*

excerpt /ɛksɜːpt/, **excerpts.** COUNT N An **excerpt** is a short piece of writing or music taken from a larger piece. *Here are a few excerpts from her diary... You'll hear the oboe in this final excerpt.*

excess, excesses; pronounced /ɛksɛs/ when it is an adjective, and /ɪ[2]ksɛs/ or /ɛksɛs/ when it is a noun. 1 SING N An **excess** of something is a larger amount than is necessary or normal. *Inflation results from an excess of demand over supply... This report should discourage us all from eating an excess of fat.* Also ATTRIB ADJ *The body gets rid of excess water through the urine.* 2 PHRASE If you do something **to excess,** you do it too much. *He spent all his time cleaning and tidying to excess.* 3 PLURAL N **Excesses** are acts which are extreme, cruel, or immoral. *...the worst excesses of the French Revolution.*

excessive /ɪ[2]ksɛsɪv/. ADJ If something is **excessive,** it is too great in amount or degree. *Their profits were excessive.* ♦ **excessively** ADV *He walked excessively fast.*

exchange /ɪ[2]kstʃeɪnd[0]ʒ/, **exchanges, exchanging, exchanged.** 1 VB WITH OBJ If people **exchange** things, they give them to each other at the same time. *The three of us exchanged addresses... Gertie and Dolly exchanged glances.* Also COUNT N *...an exchange of information.* 2 VB WITH OBJ If you **exchange** one thing for another, you replace the first thing with the second. *The sales girl refused to exchange the sweater... She exchanged the jewels for money.* 3 PHRASE If you give someone one thing **in exchange for** another thing, you give it to them because they are giving the other thing to you. *They sold textiles in exchange for agricultural products.* 4 COUNT N An **exchange** is a brief conversation; a formal use. *Throughout these exchanges I had a curious feeling of detachment.* 5 See also **stock exchange, telephone exchange.**

exchange rate, exchange rates. COUNT N The **exchange rate** is the rate at which a sum of money of your country's currency is exchanged for an equivalent sum of money of another country's currency.

excise /ɛksaɪz/. UNCOUNT N **Excise** is a tax that the government of a country puts on goods produced for sale in that country; a technical use.

excitable /ɪ[2]ksaɪtəbə[0]l/. ADJ An **excitable** person becomes excited very easily.

excite /ɪ[2]ksaɪt/, **excites, exciting, excited.** 1 VB WITH OBJ If something **excites** you, it makes you interested and enthusiastic. *The idea of journalism excited me.* 2 VB WITH OBJ If something **excites** a feeling or reaction, it causes it; a formal use. *These rumours excited suspicion.*

excited /ɪ[2]ksaɪtɪ[2]d/. ADJ If you are **excited,** you are looking forward to something very eagerly. *He was so excited he could hardly sleep.* ♦ **excitedly** ADV *They were excitedly discussing plans.*

excitement /ɪ[2]ksaɪtmə[2]nt/, **excitements.** 1 UNCOUNT N **Excitement** is the state of being excited. *Struggling to conceal his excitement, he accepted her invitation.* 2 COUNT N **Excitements** are things that cause you to feel excited; a literary use. *...all the excitements of London.*

exciting /ɪ[2]ksaɪtɪŋ/. ADJ Something that is **exciting** makes you feel excited. *Growing up in the heart of London was exciting.*

exclaim /ɪ[2]kskleɪm/, **exclaims, exclaiming, exclaimed.** REPORT VB OR VB When you **exclaim,** you say something suddenly because you are excited, shocked, or angry. *'Oh, you poor child!' exclaimed Mrs Socket... All of the women exclaimed at how well formed the baby was.*

exclamation /ɛkskləmeɪʃə[0]n/, **exclamations.** COUNT N An **exclamation** is a sound, word, or sentence that is spoken suddenly and emphatically in order to express excitement, admiration, shock, or anger. *He drew back with a sharp exclamation... They embraced him with exclamations of joy.*

exclamation mark, exclamation marks. COUNT N An **exclamation mark** is the punctuation mark (!).

exclude /ɪ[2]ksklu:d/, **excludes, excluding, excluded.** 1 VB WITH OBJ If you **exclude** something from an activity or discussion, you deliberately do not include that thing in it. *The retail prices index, excluding housing costs, rose by 646.6 per cent.* 2 VB WITH OBJ If you **exclude** a possibility, you reject it. *A fake call from some local phone box was not excluded.* 3 VB WITH OBJ If you **exclude** someone from a place or activity, you prevent them from entering the place or taking part in the activity. *...jobs from which the majority of workers are excluded.*

excluding /ɪ[2]ksklu:dɪŋ/. PREP You use **excluding** before mentioning a person or thing to show that you are not including them in your statement. *We are open seven days a week, excluding Christmas Day.*

exclusion /ɪ[2]ksklu:ʒə[0]n/. 1 UNCOUNT N The **exclusion** of something from a speech, piece of writing, or activity is the act of deliberately not including it. *...the exclusion of any mention of her good qualities.* 2 UNCOUNT N When someone is prevented from entering a place or from taking part in an activity, you can refer to this as their **exclusion** from the place or activity. *...the laws relating to the admission and exclusion of aliens.*

exclusive /ɪ[2]ksklu:sɪv/. 1 ADJ Something that is **exclusive** is available only to people who are rich or who belong to a high social class. *...an exclusive residential district.* 2 ATTRIB ADJ **Exclusive** means used or owned by only one person or group. *They have exclusive use of the machine.* 3 ADJ If two things are mutually **exclusive,** they cannot exist together. *There is no reason why these two functions should be mutually exclusive.*

exclusively /ɪ[2]ksklu:sɪvli[1]/. ADV You use **exclusively** to refer to situations that involve only the things mentioned, and nothing else. *...young people who devote their lives exclusively to sport.*

excrement /ɛkskrɪ[1]mə[2]nt/. UNCOUNT N **Excrement** is the solid waste matter that is passed out of your body through your bowels; a formal use.

excrete /ɪ[2]kskri:t/, **excretes, excreting, excreted.** VB WITH OR WITHOUT OBJ When you **excrete** waste matter from your body, you get rid of it, usually through your bowels; a formal use.

excruciating /ɪ[2]kskru:ʃieɪtɪŋ/. 1 ADJ **Excruciating** pain is very painful indeed. 2 ADJ An **excruciating** situation or experience is extremely difficult to bear. *...excruciating unhappiness.*

excursion /ɪ[2]ksk3:ʃə[0]n/, **excursions.** 1 COUNT N An **excursion** is a short journey. *...a shopping excursion.* 2 COUNT N An **excursion** into a new activity is an attempt to develop it or understand it. *...a rare excursion into contemporary music.*

excuse, excuses, excusing, excused; pronounced /ɪ[2]kskju:s/ when it is a noun and /ɪ[2]kskju:z/ when it is a verb. 1 COUNT N An **excuse** is a reason which you give to explain why something has been done, has not been done, or will not be done. *There is no excuse for this happening in a new building.* 2 REFL VB OR VB WITH OBJ If you **excuse** yourself or **excuse** something wrong that you have done, you say why you did it, in an attempt to defend yourself. *The Vice-President admitted taking bribes, excusing it as a momentary weakness.* **3** VB WITH OBJ OR VB WITH OBJ AND OBJ If you **excuse** someone for something wrong that they have done, you forgive them for it. *Such delays cannot be excused... I excused him much of his prejudice.* **4** VB WITH OBJ If you **excuse** someone from a duty or responsibility, you free them from it. *...a certificate excusing him from games at school.* **5** VB WITH OBJ If you ask someone to **excuse** you, you are asking them to allow you to leave.

PHRASES ● You say **excuse me** to attract someone's attention when you want to ask them a question. *Excuse me, but is there a fairly cheap restaurant near here?* ● You also say **excuse me** before correcting someone. *Excuse me, but I think you have misunderstood.* ● You also say **excuse me** to apologize for disturbing or interrupting someone, or for doing something slightly impolite such as burping.

execute /ɛksɪkju:t/, **executes, executing, executed.** **1** VB WITH OBJ To **execute** someone means to kill them as a punishment. *...the last woman to be executed in Britain.* ♦ **execution** /ɛksɪkju:ʃə^{0}n/ COUNT N OR UNCOUNT N *...the execution of Charles 1.* **2** VB WITH OBJ If you **execute** a plan, you carry it out; a formal use. *...a carefully executed crime.* ♦ **execution** UNCOUNT N *...obstructing an officer in the execution of his duty.* **3** VB WITH OBJ If you **execute** a difficult action or movement, you perform it. *The pilot began to execute a series of aerobatics.*

executioner /ɛksɪkju:ʃə^{0}nə/, **executioners.** COUNT N An **executioner** is a person who has the job of executing criminals.

executive /ɪ^{2}gzɛkjə^{4}tɪv/, **executives.** **1** COUNT N An **executive** is someone employed by a company at a senior level. **2** ATTRIB ADJ The **executive** sections and tasks of an organization are concerned with making important decisions. **3** COLL N The **executive** of an organization is a committee which has the authority to make important decisions. *...the executive of the National Union of Teachers.*

exemplary /ɪ^{2}gzɛmpləri^1/. ADJ **Exemplary** means excellent; a formal use. *...an exemplary father.*

exemplify /ɪ^{2}gzɛmplɪfaɪ/, **exemplifies, exemplifying, exemplified.** **1** VB WITH OBJ If you say that someone or something **exemplifies** a situation or quality, you mean that they are a typical example of it. *He exemplified the new liberalism.* **2** VB WITH OBJ If you **exemplify** something, you give an example of it. *I'm going to exemplify one or two of these points.*

exempt /ɪ^{2}gzɛmp^{0}t/, **exempts, exempting, exempted.** **1** PRED ADJ If you are **exempt** from a rule or duty, you do not have to obey it or perform it. *Harold was exempt from military service.* **2** VB WITH OBJ To **exempt** a person from a rule or duty means to state officially that they do not have to obey it or perform it. *Farmers were exempted from rates.* ♦ **exemption** /ɪ^{2}gzɛmp^{0}ʃə^{0}n/ UNCOUNT N OR COUNT N *...exemption from jury service.*

exercise /ɛksəsaɪz/, **exercises, exercising, exercised.** **1** COUNT N OR UNCOUNT N **Exercises** are energetic movements which you do to make yourself fit and healthy. *...gymnastic exercises... I have had all the exercise I need for one day.* **2** COUNT N **Exercises** are also repeated actions in which you practise something, for example playing a musical instrument. **3** COUNT N An **exercise** is a short piece of work which is designed to help you learn something. *...grammatical exercises.* **4** COUNT N **Exercises** are also operations or manoeuvres performed by the armed forces. **5** COUNT N WITH SUPP An **exercise** in something is an activity intended to achieve a particular purpose. *The rally was organized by the state as an exercise in patriotism.* **6** VB When you **exercise**, you move your body energetically in order to become fit and healthy. **7** VB WITH OBJ To **exercise** authority, rights, or responsibilities means to use them; a formal use. *They exercise considerable influence in all western countries.* Also SING N *...the exercise of personal responsibility.* **8** VB WITH OBJ If something **exercises** your mind, you think about it a great deal; a formal use.

exercise book, exercise books. COUNT N An **exercise book** is a small book with blank pages used for doing school work.

exert /ɪ^{2}gzɜ:t/, **exerts, exerting, exerted.** **1** VB WITH OBJ If you **exert** influence or pressure, you use it to achieve something. *These departments exert pressure on the schools to get them to agree.* **2** REFL VB If you **exert** yourself, you make a physical or mental effort to do something. *He had to exert himself to make conversation with the visitor.*

exertion /ɪ^{2}gzɜʃə^{0}n/, **exertions.** UNCOUNT N OR COUNT N **Exertion** is physical effort or exercise. *He was panting with exertion.*

exhale /ɪ^{2}gzh^{0}eɪl/, **exhales, exhaling, exhaled.** VB WITH OR WITHOUT OBJ When you **exhale**, you breathe out; a formal use. *He exhaled slowly and smiled.*

exhaust /ɪ^{2}gzɔ:st/, **exhausts, exhausting, exhausted.** **1** VB WITH OBJ If something **exhausts** you, it makes you very tired. *His efforts exhausted him.* ♦ **exhausted** ADJ *All three men were hot, dirty, and exhausted.* ♦ **exhausting** ADJ *...a difficult and exhausting job.* **2** VB WITH OBJ If you **exhaust** money or food, you finish it all. *They soon exhausted the food resources.* **3** VB WITH OBJ If you **exhaust** a subject, you talk about it so much that there is nothing else to say. **4** COUNT N An **exhaust** or an **exhaust pipe** is a pipe which carries the gas out of the engine of a motor vehicle. **5** UNCOUNT N **Exhaust** is the gas produced by the engine of a motor vehicle.

exhaustion /ɪ^{2}gzɔ:stʃə^{0}n/. UNCOUNT N **Exhaustion** is the state of being so tired that you have no energy left. *She was almost fainting with exhaustion.*

exhaustive /ɪ^{2}gzɔ:stɪv/. ADJ An **exhaustive** study or search is very thorough. *You might have to make many more exhaustive surveys.* ♦ **exhaustively** ADV *...exhaustively researched evidence.*

exhibit /ɪ^{2}gzɪbɪt/, **exhibits, exhibiting, exhibited.** **1** VB WITH OBJ If you **exhibit** an ability or feeling, it can be seen clearly by other people; a formal use. *He still exhibited signs of stress.* **2** VB WITH OBJ When something **is exhibited**, it is put in a public place for people to look at. *The paintings are exhibited in chronological sequence.* **3** COUNT N An **exhibit** is something shown in a museum or art gallery. *Our local museum has over a thousand exhibits.* **4** COUNT N An **exhibit** is also something shown in a court as evidence. *Exhibit number two is a diary belonging to the accused.*

exhibition /ɛgzɪbɪʃə^{0}n/, **exhibitions.** **1** COUNT N An **exhibition** is a collection of pictures or other objects shown in a public place. *Did you see the Shakespeare exhibition?* **2** UNCOUNT N **Exhibition** is the showing of pictures or other objects in a public place. *The film was refused a licence for public exhibition.*

exhibitionism /ɛgzɪbɪʃə^{0}nɪzə^{0}m/. UNCOUNT N **Exhibitionism** is a type of behaviour in which someone tries to get people's attention all the time; a formal use. ♦ **exhibitionist** COUNT N *As a child I was inclined to be an exhibitionist.*

exhibitor /ɪ^{2}gzɪbɪtə/, **exhibitors.** COUNT N An **exhibitor** is a person whose work is being exhibited.

exhilarate /ɪ^{2}gzɪləreɪt/, **exhilarates, exhilarating, exhilarated.** VB WITH OBJ If you **are exhilarated** by something, you feel great happiness and excitement. *The refugees were exhilarated by the news.* ♦ **exhilarating** ADJ *...an exhilarating experience.* ♦ **exhilaration** /ɪ^{2}gzɪləreɪʃə^{0}n/ UNCOUNT N *There was a sense of exhilaration about being alone on the beach.*

exhort /ɪ^{2}gzɔ:t/, **exhorts, exhorting, exhorted.** VB WITH OBJ If you **exhort** someone to do something, you try hard to persuade them to do it; a formal use. *I exhorted the men not to drink too much.* ♦ **exhortation** /ɛgzɔ:teɪʃə^{0}n/ COUNT N OR UNCOUNT N *...fervent exhortations to revolutionary action.*

exhume /ɛksh^{0}ju:m/, **exhumes, exhuming, exhumed.** VB WITH OBJ When a body **is exhumed**, it is taken out of the ground where it is buried; a formal use.

exile /ɛgzaɪl, ɛksaɪl/, **exiles, exiling, exiled.** **1** UNCOUNT N If someone lives in **exile**, they live in a foreign country because they cannot live in their own country, usually for political reasons. *...eight whole months of exile.* **2** VB WITH OBJ If someone **is exiled**, they are sent away from their own country and are not allowed to return. *I was exiled from Ceylon for a year.* ♦ **exiled** ADJ *...the exiled King.* **3** COUNT N An **exile** is someone who lives in exile. *...political exiles.*

exist /ɪ^{2}gzɪst/, **exists, existing, existed.** **1** VB If something **exists**, it is present in the world as a real or living thing. *Communities who live by hunting still exist.* **2** See also **existing.**

existence /ɪ^{2}gzɪstəns/, **existences.** **1** UNCOUNT N **Existence** is the state of existing. *Do you believe in the existence of God?* **2** COUNT N WITH SUPP You can use **existence** to refer to someone's way of life. *The family lived a more or less vagabond existence.*

existential /ɛgzɪstɛnʃə^{0}l/. ADJ **Existential** means relating to human existence and experience; a formal use.

existing /ɪ^{2}gzɪstɪŋ/. ATTRIB ADJ You use **existing** to describe something which is now in use or in operation. *We have to find ways of making the existing system work better.*

exit /ɛgzɪt, ɛksɪt/, **exits.** **1** COUNT N An **exit** is a door through which you can leave a public building. *He hurried towards the exit.* **2** COUNT N An **exit** is also a place where traffic can leave a motorway. **3** PHRASE If you **make an exit** from a room, you leave it; a formal use. *He made a hasty exit from the Men's Room.*

exodus /ɛksədəs/. SING N When there is an **exodus**, a lot of people leave a place together. *...the massive exodus of refugees from the North.*

exonerate /ɪ^{2}gzɒnəreɪt/, **exonerates, exonerating, exonerated.** VB WITH OBJ To **exonerate** someone means to show that they are not responsible for something wrong that has happened; a formal use. *His evidence might exonerate me from the crimes they had charged me with.*

exorbitant /ɪ^{2}gzɔ:bɪtənt/. ADJ If you describe something as **exorbitant**, you mean that it is much more expensive than it should be. *...an exorbitant rent.*

exorcism /ɛksɔ:sɪzə^{0}m/. UNCOUNT N OR COUNT N **Exorcism** is the removing of evil spirits from a place or person by using prayer.

exorcize /ɛksɔ:saɪz/, **exorcizes, exorcizing, exorcized;** also spelled **exorcise.** VB WITH OBJ To **exorcize** an evil spirit or to **exorcize** a place or person means to force the spirit to leave the place or person by means of prayers and religious ceremonies.

exotic /ɪ^{2}gzɒtɪk/. ADJ Something that is **exotic** is unusual and interesting because it comes from a distant country. *...rich exotic foods.*

expand /ɪ^{2}kspænd/, **expands, expanding, expanded.** ERG VB When something **expands**, it becomes larger. *The city's population expanded by 12 per cent... Natural materials expand with heat... ...major measures to expand the Royal Air Force.*

expand on or **expand upon.** PHR VB If you **expand on** or **expand upon** something, you give more information or details about it. *Perhaps you could expand on this a little bit.*

expanse /ɪ^{2}kspæns/, **expanses.** COUNT N WITH 'of' An **expanse** of sea, sky, or land is a very large area of it; a literary use. *...the wide expanse of snowy fields.*

expansion /ɪ^{2}kspænʃə^{0}n/. UNCOUNT N **Expansion** is the process of becoming greater in size or amount. *...the rapid expansion of British agriculture.*

expansive /ɪ^{2}kspænsɪv/. ADJ If you are **expansive**, you talk a lot, because you are happy and relaxed.

expatriate /ɛkspætri^{1}ət/, **expatriates.** COUNT N An **expatriate** is someone who lives in a country which is not their own.

expect /ɪ^{2}kspɛkt/, **expects, expecting, expected.** **1** VB OR REPORT VB If you **expect** something to happen, you believe that it will happen. *Nobody expected the strike to succeed... He didn't expect to be so busy... When do you expect that this material will be available?* **2** VB WITH OBJ If you **are expecting** something, you believe that it is going to happen or arrive. *We are expecting rain... Dr Willoughby was expecting him.* ♦ **expected** ADJ *We would resist this expected attack.* **3** VB WITH OBJ OR TO-INF If you **expect** something, you believe that it is your right to get it or have it. *We expect sincerity from our politicians... I expect to be treated with respect.* **4** VB WITH OBJ AND TO-INF If you **expect** someone to do something, you require them to do it as a duty or obligation. *He is expected to put his work before his family.* **5** VB WITH OR WITHOUT OBJ If a woman **is expecting**, she is pregnant; an informal use. *She's expecting her third baby.*

expectancy /ɪ^{2}kspɛktənsi^1/. UNCOUNT N **Expectancy** is a feeling that something exciting is about to happen. ● See also **life expectancy.**

expectant /ɪ^{2}kspɛktənt/. **1** ADJ If you are **expectant**, you think something is going to happen. ♦ **expectantly** ADV *She looked at him expectantly.* **2** ATTRIB ADJ An **expectant** mother or father is someone whose baby is going to be born soon.

expectation /ɛkspɛkteɪʃə^{0}n/, **expectations.** COUNT N OR UNCOUNT N **Expectations** are hopes or beliefs that something will happen. *The plan has succeeded beyond our expectations... I was watched in the expectation that I would go too far.*

expediency /ɪ^{2}kspi:dɪənsi^1/. UNCOUNT N **Expediency** is behaviour in which you do what is convenient, rather than what is morally right; a formal use. *...torn between principle and expediency.*

expedient /ɪ^{2}kspi:dɪənt/, **expedients;** a formal word. **1** COUNT N An **expedient** is an action that achieves a particular purpose, but may not be morally acceptable. *Incomes controls were used only as a short-term expedient.* **2** ADJ If it is **expedient** to do something, it is useful or convenient to do it. *The President did not find it expedient to attend the meeting.*

expedition /ɛkspɪ^{1}dɪʃə^{0}n/, **expeditions.** COUNT N An **expedition** is a journey made for a particular purpose. *...the British expedition to Mount Everest... ...a shopping expedition.*

expel /ɪ^{2}kspɛl/, **expels, expelling, expelled.** **1** VB WITH OBJ If someone **is expelled** from a school or organization, they are officially told to leave because they have behaved badly. *He had been expelled from his previous school for stealing.* **2** VB WITH OBJ When people **are expelled** from a place, they are made to leave it, usually by force. *Peasants were expelled from their villages.* **3** VB WITH OBJ If a gas or liquid **is expelled** from a place, it is forced out of it; a formal use. *Water is sucked in at one end and expelled at the other.*

expend /ɪ[2]kspɛnd/, **expends, expending, expended.** VB WITH OBJ To **expend** energy, time, or money means to spend or use it; a formal use.

expendable /ɪ[2]kspɛndəbə[0]l/. ADJ Something that is **expendable** is no longer needed and can be got rid of; a formal use.

expenditure /ɪ[2]kspɛndɪtʃə/. **1** UNCOUNT N OR COUNT N Your **expenditure** on something is the total amount of money you spend on it. *We restricted our expenditure on food... ...public expenditure.* **2** UNCOUNT N WITH SUPP **Expenditure** of energy or time is energy or time used for a particular purpose. *This was done with a minimum expenditure of energy.*

expense /ɪ[2]kspɛns/, **expenses. 1** UNCOUNT N OR COUNT N **Expense** is the money that something costs. *...the roads they're building at vast expense... ...household expenses.* **2** PLURAL N Your **expenses** are the money you spend while doing something connected with your work, which is paid back to you afterwards. *...travelling expenses.*
PHRASES ● If you do something **at** someone's **expense,** they provide the money for it. *He circulated the document at his own expense.* ● If you make a joke **at** someone's **expense,** you do it to make them seem foolish. ● If you achieve something **at** someone's **expense,** you do it in a way that harms them. *They increase their own income at the expense of the rural masses.*

expensive /ɪ[2]kspɛnsɪv/. ADJ **Expensive** things cost a lot of money. *...expensive clothes.* ♦ **expensively** ADV *We can do that fairly easily and not too expensively.*

experience /ɪ[2]kspɪərɪəns/, **experiences, experiencing, experienced. 1** UNCOUNT N If you have had **experience** of something, you have seen it, done it, or felt it. *The new countries have no experience of democracy... I had no military experience.* **2** UNCOUNT N You can refer to all the things that have happened to you as **experience.** *Everyone learns best from his own experience... ...speaking from personal experience.* **3** COUNT N WITH SUPP An **experience** is something that happens to you or something you do. *Moving house can be a traumatic experience.* **4** VB WITH OBJ If you **experience** a situation or feeling, it happens to you or you are affected by it. *Similar problems have been experienced by other students.*

experienced /ɪ[2]kspɪərɪənst/. ADJ **Experienced** is used to describe someone who has done a particular job for a long time. *...an experienced lecturer.*

experiment /ɪ[2]kspɛrə[1]mə[2]nt/, **experiments, experimenting, experimented. 1** COUNT N OR UNCOUNT N An **experiment** is a scientific test done to prove or discover something. **2** VB If you **experiment** with something or **experiment** on it, you do a scientific test on it. *He experimented with young white rats.* ♦ **experimentation** /ɪ[2]kspɛrə[1]menteɪʃə[0]n/ UNCOUNT N *...medical experimentation.* **3** COUNT N OR UNCOUNT N If you do something new to see what effects it has, you can describe your action as an **experiment.** *...the failure of this great experiment in industrial democracy.* Also VB *...small businesses anxious to experiment with computers.*

experimental /ɪ[2]kspɛrə[1]mɛntə[0]l/. **1** ADJ **Experimental** means involving the use of new ideas or methods. *...experimental forms of teaching.* ♦ **experimentally** ADV *...the first parking meters, introduced experimentally in 1958.* **2** ADJ **Experimental** also means relating to scientific experiments. ♦ **experimentally** ADV *They are measured experimentally and the results compared.*

expert /ɛkspɜːt/, **experts. 1** COUNT N An **expert** is a person who is very skilled at doing something or who knows a lot about a particular subject. *Experts were called in to dismantle the bomb... ...an expert on Eastern philosophy.* **2** ADJ Someone who is **expert** at doing something is very skilled at it. *...expert acrobats.* ♦ **expertly** ADV *Burke drove expertly.*

expertise /ɛkspɜːtiːz/. UNCOUNT N **Expertise** is special skill or knowledge. *...managerial expertise.*

expire /ɪ[2]kspaɪə/, **expires, expiring, expired. 1** VB When something **expires,** it reaches the end of the period of time for which it is valid; a formal use. *My passport is due to expire in three months.* **2** VB When someone **expires,** they die; a literary use.

expiry /ɪ[2]kspaɪəri[1]/. UNCOUNT N The **expiry** of something such as a licence or passport is the fact of it ceasing to be valid; a formal use. *The French licences have no expiry date.*

explain /ɪ[2]kspleɪn/, **explains, explaining, explained. 1** REPORT VB If you **explain** something, you give details about it so that it can be understood. *John went on to explain the legal situation... I explained that I was trying to write a book.* **2** VB WITH OR WITHOUT OBJ If you **explain** something that has happened, you give reasons for it. *He never wrote to me to explain his decision.*

explanation /ɛkspləneɪʃə[0]n/, **explanations.** COUNT N OR UNCOUNT N If you give an **explanation,** you say why something happened, or describe something in detail. *...a scientific explanation of the universe... ...a note of explanation.*

explanatory /ɪ[2]ksplænətə[0]ri[1]/. ADJ Something that is **explanatory** explains something by giving details about it. *They produce free explanatory leaflets on heating.*

explicable /ɛksplɪkəbə[0]l, ɪ[2]ksplɪk-/. ADJ Something that is **explicable** can be explained and understood; a formal use. *For no explicable reason your mind goes blank.*

explicit /ɪ[2]ksplɪsɪt/. **1** ADJ Something that is **explicit** is shown or expressed clearly and openly, without hiding anything. *...the explicit support of the Prime Minister.* ♦ **explicitly** ADV *...explicitly violent scenes.* **2** ADJ If you are **explicit** about something, you express yourself clearly and openly. *She was not explicit about what she really felt.* ♦ **explicitly** ADV *This was explicitly admitted by the Minister.*

explode /ɪ[2]kspləʊd/, **explodes, exploding, exploded. 1** ERG VB When a bomb **explodes,** it bursts with great force. *A bomb had exploded in the next street... They exploded a nuclear device.* **2** VB WITH ADJUNCT You can say that a person **explodes** when they express strong feelings suddenly and violently. *She exploded with rage.* **3** VB WITH OBJ If you **explode** a theory, you prove that it is wrong or impossible.

exploit, exploits, exploiting, exploited; pronounced /ɪksplɔɪt/ when it is a verb and /ɛksplɔɪt/ when it is a noun. **1** VB WITH OBJ If someone **exploits** you, they unfairly use your work or ideas and give you little in return. ♦ **exploitation** /ɛksplɔɪteɪʃə[0]n/ UNCOUNT N *...to protect the public from commercial exploitation.* **2** VB WITH OBJ To **exploit** something such as a raw material or an idea means to develop it in order to make money out of it. ♦ **exploitation** UNCOUNT N *...the exploitation of the Earth's resources.* **3** COUNT N Someone's **exploits** are the brave or interesting things they have done. *...his exploits in the War.*

exploitative /ɪ[2]ksplɔɪtətɪv/. ADJ An **exploitative** person or organization treats people unfairly by using their work or ideas and giving them very little in return. *...exploitative employment agencies.*

exploratory /ɪ[2]ksplɒrətə[0]ri[1]/. ADJ **Exploratory** actions are done to discover something or to learn something; a formal use. *...an exploratory expedition.*

explore /ɪ[2]ksplɔː/, **explores, exploring, explored. 1** VB WITH OBJ If you **explore** a place, you travel in it to find out what it is like. *He explored three continents by canoe.* ♦ **exploration** /ɛkspləreɪʃə[0]n/ UNCOUNT N *...voyages of exploration.* ♦ **explorer** /ɪ[2]ksplɔːrə/ COUNT N *...an Arctic explorer.* **2** VB WITH OBJ If you **explore** something with your hands, you touch it so that you can feel what it is like. *With widespread hands he explored the wet grass.* **3** VB WITH OBJ If you **explore** an idea, you think about it carefully to decide whether it is a good one. *The conference explored the possibility of closer trade links.*

explosion /ɪ[2]kspləʊʒə[0]n/, **explosions. 1** COUNT N An **explosion** is a sudden, violent burst of energy, for example one caused by a bomb. *Twenty men were killed in the explosion.* **2** COUNT N WITH SUPP An **explosion** of something is a large and rapid increase of it. *...the population explosion.* **3** COUNT N An **explosion** of anger is a sudden, violent expression of it.

explosive /ɪ[2]kspləʊsɪv/, **explosives. 1** COUNT N OR UNCOUNT N An **explosive** is a substance or device that can cause an explosion. **2** ADJ Something that is **explosive** is capable of causing an explosion. *...a powerful explosive device.* **3** ADJ A sudden loud noise can be described as **explosive.** *The final applause was explosive.* **4** ADJ An **explosive** situation is likely to have serious or dangerous effects. *Unemployment has become the most explosive political issue.*

exponent /ɪ[2]kspəʊnənt/, **exponents. 1** COUNT N WITH SUPP An **exponent** of an idea, theory, or plan is someone who speaks or writes in support of it. *...the leading exponents of apartheid.* **2** COUNT N WITH SUPP An **exponent** of a particular kind of writing or music is someone who writes in that way or performs music of that kind; a formal use. *...the supreme exponent of the English humorous essay.*

exponential /ɛkspə[6]nɛnʃə[0]l/. ADJ **Exponential** means growing or increasing very rapidly; a formal use. *...a period of exponential growth.*

export, exports, exporting, exported; pronounced /ɛkspɔt/ when it is a noun and /ɪ[2]kspɔt/ when it is a verb. **1** VB WITH OBJ To **export** goods means to sell them to another country and send them there. *Raw materials are exported at low prices.* Also UNCOUNT N *They grow coffee and bananas for export.* **2** COUNT N **Exports** are goods which are sold to another country and sent there. **3** VB WITH OBJ To **export** ideas or values means to introduce them into other countries.

exporter /ɛkspɔːtə/, **exporters.** COUNT N An **exporter** is a country, firm, or person that sells and sends goods to another country.

expose /ɛkspəʊz/, **exposes, exposing, exposed. 1** VB WITH OBJ To **expose** something means to uncover it and make it visible. *The rocks are exposed at low tide.* **2** VB WITH OBJ AND PREP 'to' If you **are exposed** to something dangerous, you are put in a situation in which it might harm you. *They had been exposed to radiation.* **3** VB WITH OBJ To **expose** someone means to reveal the truth about them, especially when it involves dishonest or shocking behaviour. **4** ADJ An **exposed** place has no natural protection against bad weather or enemies. *...a very exposed position.*

exposé /ɛkspəʊzeɪ/, **exposés.** COUNT N An **exposé** is a piece of writing which reveals the truth about something, especially something involving dishonest or shocking behaviour.

exposition /ɛkspə[6]zɪʃə[0]n/, **expositions.** COUNT N An **exposition** of an idea or theory is a detailed explanation of it; a formal use.

expostulate /ɪ[2]kspɒstjə[4]leɪt/, **expostulates, expostulating, expostulated.** VB If you **expostulate,** you express strong disagreement with someone; a formal use. *He was expostulating with the porter.*

exposure /ɪ[2]kspəʊʒə/, **exposures. 1** UNCOUNT N **Exposure** to something dangerous means being in a situation where are you affected by it. *He was suffering from exposure to nuclear radiation.* **2** UNCOUNT N **Exposure** is also the harmful effect on your body caused by very cold weather. *The group's leader died of exposure.* **3** UNCOUNT N **Exposure** is also publicity. *...giving the widest possible exposure to scenes of casualties and damage.* **4** UNCOUNT N The **exposure** of a well-known person is the revealing of the truth about them, especially when it involves dishonest or shocking behaviour. **5** COUNT N In photography, an **exposure** is a single photograph. *...a camera capable of taking a hundred exposures before the film needs changing.*

expound /ɪ[2]kspaʊnd/, **expounds, expounding, expounded.** VB WITH OBJ If you **expound** an idea or opinion, you give a clear and detailed explanation of it; a formal use.

express /ɪ[2]kspres/, **expresses, expressing, expressed. 1** VB WITH OBJ OR REFL VB When you **express** an idea or feeling, you show what you think or feel by saying or doing something. *I expressed myself better in French.* **2** REFL VB If an idea or feeling **expresses** itself in some way, it can be clearly seen in someone's actions; a formal use. *That increased confidence expressed itself in other ways.* **3** VB WITH OBJ If you **express** a quantity in a particular form, you write it down in that form. *Here it is expressed as a percentage.* **4** ATTRIB ADJ An **express** command or order is stated clearly; a formal use. ♦ **expressly** ADV *Jefferson had expressly asked her to invite Freeman.* **5** ATTRIB ADJ An **express** intention or purpose is deliberate or specific. *She came with the express purpose of causing trouble.* ♦ **expressly** ADV *They bought the house expressly for her.* **6** ATTRIB ADJ An **express** service is one in which things are done faster than usual. *...an express letter.* **7** COUNT N An **express** is a fast train or coach which stops at very few places.

expression /ɪ[2]kspreʃə[0]n/, **expressions. 1** COUNT N An **expression** is a word or phrase. *...slang expressions.* **2** UNCOUNT N OR COUNT N The **expression** of ideas or feelings is the showing of them through words, actions, or art. *We parted with many expressions of goodwill.* **3** COUNT N OR UNCOUNT N Your **expression** is the way that your face shows what you are thinking or feeling.

expressionless /ɪ[2]kspreʃə[0]nlɪ[2]s/. ADJ If someone's face or voice is **expressionless,** it does not show their feelings.

expressive /ɪ[2]kspresɪv/. **1** ADJ Something that is **expressive** indicates clearly a person's feelings or intentions. *She had given Lynn an expressive glance.* ♦ **expressively** ADV *He drew a finger expressively across his throat.* **2** ADJ Someone's **expressive** ability is their ability to speak or write clearly and interestingly. *...evaluating the child's expressive powers.*

expressway /ɪ[2]kspreswei/, **expressways.** COUNT N An **expressway** is a wide road designed so that a lot of traffic can move along it very quickly.

expropriate /ɛkspr əʊprieɪt/, **expropriates, expropriating, expropriated.** VB WITH OBJ If someone **expropriates** something, they take it away from its owner; a formal use. *The surplus will be expropriated by the government.*

expulsion /ɪ[2]kspʌlʃə[0]n/, **expulsions;** a formal word. **1** UNCOUNT N OR COUNT N **Expulsion** is the expelling of someone from a school or organization. *...his expulsion from the university.* **2** UNCOUNT N OR COUNT N **Expulsion** is also the act of forcing people to leave a place. *...the expulsion of military advisers.*

exquisite /ɪ2kskwɪzɪt, ɛkskwɪzɪt/. 1 ADJ **Exquisite** means extremely beautiful. *She has the most exquisite face... ...exquisite jewellery.* ♦ **exquisitely** ADV *Their children were exquisitely dressed.* 2 ADJ **Exquisite** pleasure or pain is very great. *...sipping the water slowly with exquisite relief.*

extant /ɛkstænt, ɛkstənt/. ADJ Something that is **extant** still exists although it is very old; a formal use. *...one Spanish law that is still extant in California.*

extend /ɪ2kstɛnd/, **extends, extending, extended.** 1 VB WITH ADJUNCT If something **extends** for a particular distance, it continues for that distance. *The road now extends two kilometres beyond the River.* 2 VB WITH ADJUNCT If an object **extends** from a surface, it sticks out from it. *...metal slabs extending from the wall.* 3 VB WITH ADJUNCT If an event or activity **extends** for a period of time, it continues for that time. *His working day often extends well into the evening.* 4 VB WITH ADJUNCT If a situation **extends** to particular people or things, it includes or affects them. *The consequences of unemployment extend well beyond the labour market.* 5 VB WITH OBJ If you **extend** something, you make it bigger, or make it last longer or include more. *Have you ever thought of extending your house?... The authorities extended her visa... Congress wants the law extended to cover all states.* 6 VB WITH OBJ If you **extend** a part of your body, you straighten it or stretch it out. *He extended his hand, and Brody shook it.* 7 VB WITH OBJ To **extend** an offer or invitation to someone means to make it; a formal use.

extension /ɪ2kstɛnʃə0n/, **extensions.** 1 COUNT N An **extension** is a new room or building which is added to an existing building. *...a new extension to the library.* 2 COUNT N OR UNCOUNT N An **extension** is also an extra period of time for which something continues to exist or be valid. *He asked for extension of his residence permit.* 3 COUNT N OR UNCOUNT N The **extension** of something is its development to include or affect more things. *Nationalist leaders demanded the extension of democratic rights.* 4 COUNT N A telephone **extension** is one of several telephones connected to the switchboard of an organization, each with its own number.

extensive /ɪ2kstɛnsɪv/. 1 ADJ If something is **extensive** in area, it covers a large area. *...an extensive Roman settlement in north-west England.* 2 ADJ **Extensive** means very great in effect. *Many buildings suffered extensive damage in the blast.* ♦ **extensively** ADV *The aircraft were extensively modified.* 3 ADJ **Extensive** also means covering many details, ideas, or items. *We had fairly extensive discussions.* ♦ **extensively** ADV *I have quoted extensively from it in the following pages.*

extent /ɪ2kstɛnt/. 1 SING N WITH POSS The **extent** of something is its length, area, or size. *...to expand the empire to its largest extent.* 2 SING N WITH POSS The **extent** of a situation or difficulty is its size or scale. *The full extent of the problem is not yet known.*
PHRASES ● You use phrases such as **to a large extent, to some extent,** or **to a certain extent** to indicate that something is partly but not entirely true. *Well I think to a certain extent it's true.* ● You use phrases such as **to what extent, to that extent,** or **to the extent that** when discussing how true a statement is. *To what extent are diseases linked with genes?... A computer is intelligent only to the extent that it can store information.* ● You use phrases such as **to the extent of** or **to such an extent that** to indicate that a situation has reached a particular stage. *Sanitary conditions had deteriorated to such an extent that there was widespread danger of disease.*

exterior /ɪ2kstɪərɪə/, **exteriors.** 1 COUNT N The **exterior** of something is its outside surface. *Keep your car exterior in good condition.* 2 COUNT N WITH SUPP Your **exterior** is your usual outward appearance and behaviour. *Beneath his professional doctor's exterior, he was wildly fun-loving and reckless.* 3 ATTRIB ADJ **Exterior** means situated or happening outside a person or thing. *Exterior drains must be kept clear.*

exterminate /ɪ2kstɜːmɪneɪt/, **exterminates, exterminating, exterminated.** VB WITH OBJ When a group of animals or people **is exterminated,** they are all killed. *Fishing must stop before the species is completely exterminated.* ♦ **extermination** /ɪ2kstɜːmɪneɪʃə0n/ UNCOUNT N *...a way to prevent the extermination of these animals.*

external /ɪ2kstɜːnə0l/, **externals.** 1 ADJ **External** means happening, coming from, or existing outside a place, person, or area of activity. *...the external walls of the chimneys... They did it in response to external pressures.* ♦ **externally** ADV *It should be applied externally.* 2 ATTRIB ADJ **External** is used to describe people who come into an organization from outside to do a job there. *Their accounts are audited by a firm of external auditors.* 3 PLURAL N The **externals** of a situation are features in it which are obvious but not important; a formal use. *The popular historian is concerned only with externals.*

extinct /ɪ2kstɪŋkt/. 1 ADJ If a species of animals is **extinct,** it no longer has any living members. *The dodo became extinct about 300 years ago.* 2 ADJ An **extinct** volcano does not erupt or is unlikely to erupt.

extinction /ɪ2kstɪŋk0ʃə0n/. UNCOUNT N The **extinction** of a species of animal is the death of all its remaining members. *Apes are in danger of extinction.*

extinguish /ɪ2kstɪŋgwɪʃ/, **extinguishes, extinguishing, extinguished;** a formal word. 1 VB WITH OBJ If you **extinguish** a fire or a light, you stop it burning or shining. 2 VB WITH OBJ To **extinguish** an idea or feeling means to destroy it.

extinguisher /ɪ2kstɪŋgwɪʃə/. See also **fire extinguisher.**

extol /ɪ2kstəʊl/, **extols, extolling, extolled.** VB WITH OBJ If you **extol** something, you praise it enthusiastically; a formal use. *He was extolling the virtues of female independence.*

extort /ɪ2kstɔːt/, **extorts, extorting, extorted.** VB WITH OBJ If someone **extorts** money from you, they get it by using force or threats. ♦ **extortion** /ɪ2kstɔːʃə0n/ UNCOUNT N *He faces trial on extortion charges.*

extortionate /ɪ2kstɔːʃə0nət/. ADJ **Extortionate** demands or prices are greater than you consider to be fair.

extra /ɛkstrə/, **extras.** 1 QUANTIF OR ADV An **extra** thing, person, or amount is another one that is added to others of the same kind. *Take an extra pair of shoes... You have to pay extra for breakfast.* 2 COUNT N **Extras** are things that are not necessary but make something more comfortable, useful, or enjoyable. *With the extras, the car cost £4,000.* 3 PLURAL N **Extras** are also additional amounts of money added to the basic price of something. *There are no hidden extras.* 4 COUNT N An **extra** is a person who plays an unimportant part in a film. 5 SUBMOD If you are **extra** polite or **extra** careful, you are more polite or careful than usual. *He was extra polite to his superiors.*

extract, extracts, extracting, extracted; pronounced /ɪ2kstrækt/ when it is a verb and /ɛkstrækt/ when it is a noun. 1 VB WITH OBJ If you **extract** something from a place, you take or pull it out; a formal use. *Mrs Oliver extracted a small notebook from her bag.* 2 VB WITH OBJ To **extract** a raw material means to get it from the ground or to separate it from another substance. *The Japanese extract ten million tons of coal each year.* 3 VB WITH OBJ If you **extract** information from someone, you get it from them with difficulty. *Sir James had extracted from Francis a fairly detailed account.* 4 VB WITH OBJ AND 'from' If someone **extracts** advantage from a situation, they use the situation in order to gain advantage; a formal use. *They will extract the maximum propaganda value from this affair.* 5 COUNT N An **extract** from a piece of writing or music is a small part of it that is printed or played separately.

extraction /ɪ2kstrækʃə0n/. 1 UNCOUNT N Your **extraction** is the country or people that your family originally comes from; a formal use. *Alistair was of Scottish extraction.* 2 UNCOUNT N The **extraction** of something is the act or process of removing it. *...mineral extraction.*

extractor /ɪ2kstræktə/, **extractors.** COUNT N An **extractor** or **extractor fan** is a device in a window or wall which draws steam or hot air out of a room or building.

extra-curricular /ɛkstrə kərɪkjə4lə/. ADJ **Extra-curricular** activities are activities for students that are not part of their course; a formal use.

extradite /ɛkstrədaɪt/, **extradites, extraditing, extradited.** VB WITH OBJ If someone **is extradited,** they are officially sent back to their own country to be tried for a crime that they have been accused of; a formal use. ♦ **extradition** /ɛkstrədɪʃə0n/ UNCOUNT N OR COUNT N *France requested their extradition from the United States.*

extramarital /ɛkstrəmærɪtə0l/. ADJ You use **extramarital** to describe a sexual relationship between a married person and someone who is not their husband or wife; a formal use.

extra-mural. ATTRIB ADJ You use **extra-mural** to refer to courses in a college or university which are involved mainly with part-time students. *...the Department of Extra-mural Studies.*

extraneous /ɪ2kstreɪnɪəs/. ADJ Something that is **extraneous** happens or concerns things outside the situation or subject that you are talking about; a formal use. *We must avoid all extraneous issues.*

extraordinary /ɪ2kstrɔːdə0nə0ri1/. 1 ADJ If you describe someone or something as **extraordinary,** you mean that they have some special or extreme qualities. *My grandfather was a most extraordinary man.* ♦ **extraordinarily** SUBMOD *...an extraordinarily beautiful girl.* 2 ADJ You can also say that something is **extraordinary** when it is unusual or surprising. *What an extraordinary thing to say.* ♦ **extraordinarily** SUBMOD *...extraordinarily high levels of radiation.* 3 ATTRIB ADJ An **extraordinary** meeting is arranged specially to deal with a particular problem.

extravagance /ɪ2kstrævə1gəns/, **extravagances.** 1 UNCOUNT N **Extravagance** is the spending of more money than is reasonable or than you can afford. *It is easy to criticize governments for extravagance and waste.* 2 COUNT N An **extravagance** is something that you spend money on but cannot really afford. *It was a little extravagance of my father to buy new plants every year.*

extravagant /ɪ2kstrævə1gənt/. 1 ADJ An **extravagant** person spends more money than they can afford or uses more of something than is reasonable. *He was extravagant and liked to live well... She considered him extravagant with electricity.* ♦ **extravagantly** ADV *I lived extravagantly, taking cabs everywhere.* 2 ADJ Something that is **extravagant** costs more money than you can afford or uses more of something than is reasonable. *...extravagant gifts... ...machines that are extravagant in their requirements of energy.* ♦ **extravagantly** SUBMOD *...merchandise known to be extravagantly priced.* 3 ADJ **Extravagant** behaviour is exaggerated and is done to create a particular effect; a formal use. *He raised his eyebrows in extravagant surprise.* ♦ **extravagantly** SUBMOD *Harold was extravagantly affectionate with his daughters.* 4 ADJ **Extravagant** ideas or dreams are unrealistic and impractical; a formal use. 5 ADJ **Extravagant** entertainments or designs are elaborate and impressive.

extreme /ɪ2kstriːm/, **extremes.** 1 ATTRIB ADJ **Extreme** means very great in degree or intensity. *He died in extreme poverty... You must proceed with extreme caution.* ♦ **extremely** SUBMOD *...an extremely difficult task... Ralph and I always got on extremely well.* 2 ADJ **Extreme** also means very severe, unusual, or unreasonable. *People are capable of surviving in extreme conditions... Their methods may seem extreme... ...the extreme Right Wing of the Party.* 3 ATTRIB ADJ The **extreme** point or edge of something is its farthest point or edge. *...the extreme south of the country.*
PHRASES ● If someone **is going to extremes,** or **is taking** something **to extremes,** their behaviour is exaggerated and unacceptable. ● You use **in the extreme** to emphasize how bad or undesirable something is. *I thought the suggestion dangerous in the extreme.*

extremism /ɪ2kstriːmɪzə0m/. UNCOUNT N **Extremism** is the behaviour or beliefs of extremists. *...political extremism.*

extremist /ɪ2kstriːmɪst/, **extremists.** COUNT N An **extremist** is a person who wishes to bring about political or social change by using severe or unreasonable methods. *...a bomb planted by Nationalist extremists.* Also ADJ *...extremist views.*

extremity /ɪ2kstrɛmɪ1ti1/, **extremities.** 1 COUNT N The **extremities** of something are its farthest points or edges; a formal use. *...the northern extremity of the cathedral.* 2 PLURAL N Your **extremities** are the farthest parts of your body, especially your hands and feet. *The warmth spread outwards till it reached his extremities.* 3 COUNT N An **extremity** is a very serious situation; a formal use. *She tried to remember how things had ever reached such an extremity.* 4 UNCOUNT N If someone talks or behaves in an extreme way, you can talk about the **extremity** of their views or behaviour; a formal use.

extricate /ɛkstrɪkeɪt/, **extricates, extricating, extricated,** a formal word. 1 VB WITH OBJ OR REFL VB If you **extricate** someone from a difficult situation, you free them from it. *She found it impossible to extricate herself from the relationship.* 2 VB WITH OBJ OR REFL VB If you **extricate** someone from a place where they are trapped, you get them out. *It was exceedingly difficult to extricate her from the hole.*

extrovert /ɛkstrəvɜːt/, **extroverts.** COUNT N An **extrovert** is a person who is active, lively, and sociable. Also ADJ *...a rather extrovert student.*

extrude /ɪ2kstruːd/, **extrudes, extruding, extruded.** ERG VB When something **extrudes** or **is extruded,** it is forced or squeezed out through a small opening; a formal use.

exuberant /ɪ2gzjuːbə0rənt/. ADJ Someone who is **exuberant** is full of energy, excitement, and cheerfulness. *...the exuberant director of the Theatre Royal.* ♦ **exuberance** /ɪ2gzjuːbə0rəns/, UNCOUNT N *She always greeted him with the same exuberance.*

exude /ɪ2gzjuːd/, **exudes, exuding, exuded;** a formal word. 1 VB WITH OBJ If someone **exudes** a quality or feeling, they show that they have it to a great extent. *She exuded vitality, enthusiasm, and generosity.* 2 ERG VB If something **exudes** a liquid or smell, the liquid or smell comes out of it.

exult /ɪ^{2}gzʌlt/, **exults, exulting, exulted.** VB If you **exult,** you feel and show great pleasure because of a success that you have had. *I exulted at my fortune... 'I've never played golf like I did last week,' he exulted.*

exultant /ɪ^{2}gzʌltənt/. ADJ If you are **exultant,** you feel very happy and triumphant; a formal use. *Her voice was loud and exultant.*

eye /aɪ/, **eyes, eyeing** or **eying, eyed. 1** COUNT N Your **eyes** are the two things in your face that you see with. *She opened her eyes.* **2** SING N WITH 'for' If you have an **eye** for something, you can recognize it and make good judgements about it. *...a marvellous eye for detail.* **3** VB WITH OBJ If you **eye** something, you look at it carefully or suspiciously. *Posy was eyeing the man thoughtfully.*

PHRASES ● If you **cast** or **run** your **eye over** something, you look quickly at every part of it. *He ran his eye over the article.* ● If something **catches** your **eye,** you suddenly notice it. *The flowers in your window caught my eye.* ● If you try to **catch** someone's **eye,** you try to attract their attention. ● If someone **has** their **eye on** you, they are watching you and making judgements about you. ● If something is true **in** your **eyes,** this is your opinion. *Her children could do no wrong in her eyes.* ● If you **keep an eye on** someone or something, you watch them and make sure they are safe. *Can you keep an eye on the baby while I go shopping?* ● If there is **more to** a situation **than meets the eye,** it is more complicated than it seemed at first. ● If an event **opens** your **eyes,** it makes you aware that something is different from the way you thought it was. ● If you don't **see eye to eye** with someone, you disagree with them. ● If you are **up to** your **eyes in** something, you are very busy with it. *Sal is still up to her eyes in kids and housework.*

eyeball /aɪbɔːl/, **eyeballs.** COUNT N Your **eyeballs** are the parts of your eyes that are like white balls.

eyebrow /aɪbraʊ/, **eyebrows.** COUNT N Your **eyebrows** are the lines of hair which grow above your eyes. ● If something causes you to **raise an eyebrow** or to **raise** your **eyebrows,** it causes you to feel surprised or disapproving. *Eyebrows were raised at their behaviour.*

eyelash /aɪlæʃ/, **eyelashes.** COUNT N Your **eyelashes** are the hairs which grow on the edges of your eyelids.

eyelid /aɪlɪd/, **eyelids.** COUNT N Your **eyelids** are the two flaps of skin which cover your eyes when they are closed.

eye-shadow. UNCOUNT N **Eye-shadow** is a substance which women put on their eyelids to colour them.

eyesight /aɪsaɪt/. UNCOUNT N Your **eyesight** is your ability to see. *His eyesight was excellent.*

eye-witness /aɪwɪtnɪ^{1}s/, **eye-witnesses.** COUNT N An **eye-witness** is a person who has seen an event and can therefore describe it, for example in a law court. *...an eye-witness account.*

Ff

F. F is an abbreviation for 'Fahrenheit'.

fable /feɪbə^{0}l/, **fables.** COUNT N A **fable** is a traditional story which teaches a moral lesson.

fabric /fæbrɪk/, **fabrics. 1** MASS N A **fabric** is a type of cloth. *...silks and other soft fabrics... ...a bit of fabric.* **2** SING N **The fabric** of a society is its structure and customs; a formal use. **3** SING N **The fabric** of a building is its walls, roof, and other parts; a formal use.

fabricate /fæbrɪkeɪt/, **fabricates, fabricating, fabricated.** VB WITH OBJ If you **fabricate** information, you invent it in order to deceive people; a formal use. *They fabricated evidence and threatened witnesses.* ♦ **fabrication** /fæbrɪkeɪʃə^{0}n/ COUNT N OR UNCOUNT N *The story was a fabrication... ...a tissue of lies and fabrication.*

fabulous /fæbjə^{4}ləs/. ADJ You use **fabulous** to say how wonderful or impressive something is; an informal use. *What a fabulous place this is!* ♦ **fabulously** SUBMOD *...a fabulously rich family.*

facade /fə^{3}sɑːd/, **facades;** also spelled **façade. 1** COUNT N The **facade** of a large building is the outside of its front wall. *...the ornate facade of the Palace.* **2** SING N You say that something is a **facade** when it gives a wrong impression of the true nature of a situation. *...the grim facts behind the facade of gaiety.*

face /feɪs/, **faces, facing, faced. 1** COUNT N Your **face** is the front of your head from your chin to your forehead. *Her face was sad... ...the expression on her face.* **2** COUNT N A **face** of a mountain is a steep side of it. *...the north face of the Eiger.* **3** COUNT N The **face** of a clock or watch is the surface which shows the time. **4** SING N The **face** of a place or organization is its appearance or nature; a literary use. *The face of a city can change completely in a year.* **5** VB WITH OBJ OR ADJUNCT If someone or something **faces** in a particular direction, their front is towards that direction. *The boys faced each other... The seats face forward.* **6** VB WITH OBJ If you **face** something difficult or unpleasant, or if you **face** the truth, you accept it and try to deal with it. *It is the biggest problem he has ever faced... They face a sentence of ten years in prison... We simply must face facts.* **7** VB WITH OBJ OR -ING If you cannot **face** something, you do not feel able to deal with it because it seems so difficult or unpleasant. *I just couldn't face the idea of going back there... She could not face speaking to them.*

PHRASES ● If something is **face down,** its front points downwards. If it is **face up,** its front points upwards. ● If two people are **face to face,** they are looking directly at each other. *I suddenly came face to face with Karen.* ● If you are brought **face to face** with an unpleasant fact, you cannot avoid it and have to deal with it. *It brings patients face to face with their problems.* ● If you **make** or **pull a face,** you put on an ugly expression to show your dislike of something. ● If you **lose face,** people lose respect for you. If you do something to **save face,** you do it in order to avoid losing people's respect. ● If you do something **in the face of** a particular problem or difficulty, you do it even though this problem or difficulty exists. *They carry on smiling in the face of adversity.* ● You say **on the face of it** to indicate that you are describing what something seems to be like but that its real nature may be different. *On the face of it, it sounds like a good idea.* ● **at face value:** see **value.**

face up to. PHR VB If you **face up to** a difficult situation, you accept it and deal with it. *They had to face up to many setbacks.*

faceless /feɪslɪ^{2}s/. ATTRIB ADJ **Faceless** people are dull and boring, and have no individuality. *...faceless bureaucrats in the Civil Service.*

facet /fæsɪ^{2}t/, **facets. 1** COUNT N A **facet** of something is a part or aspect of it. *...an interesting facet of his character.* **2** COUNT N The **facets** of a stone are the flat surfaces on its outside.

facetious /fəsiːʃəs/. ADJ If someone is being **facetious,** they are making humorous remarks in a serious situation. *Mrs Pringle ignored this facetious interruption.*

facial /feɪʃə^{0}l/. ATTRIB ADJ **Facial** is used to describe things that relate to your face. *...facial muscles.*

facile /fæsaɪl/. ADJ A **facile** remark or argument is simple and obvious, and has not been carefully thought about. *It would be facile to call it a conspiracy.*

facilitate /fəsɪlɪteɪt/, **facilitates, facilitating, facilitated.** VB WITH OBJ To **facilitate** a process means to make it easier; a formal use. *...legislation to facilitate the sale of homes.*

facility /fəsɪlɪ^{1}ti^1/, **facilities. 1** COUNT N **Facilities** are buildings or equipment provided for a particular purpose. *...play facilities for young children.* **2** COUNT N WITH SUPP A **facility** is a useful feature in something. *...a computer with a message-swapping facility.*

facsimile /fæksɪmɪli^1/, **facsimiles.** COUNT N A **facsimile** of something is an exact model or copy of it.

fact /fækt/, **facts. 1** COUNT N A **fact** is a statement or piece of information that is true. *The report is full of facts and figures... He told me a few facts about her.* **2** COUNT N You also use **fact** when referring to a situation that exists or something that happened. *...the fact of belonging to a certain race... ...to investigate the facts of the killing.* **3** UNCOUNT N If you say that a story or statement is **fact,** you mean that it is true. *How much of the novel is fiction and how much is fact?* **4** PHRASE You say **in fact, in point of fact, in actual fact,** or **as a matter of fact** to emphasize that something really happened or is true, or to introduce some information, especially more precise information. *This is, in fact, what happened... In actual fact, we don't have all that much more leisure time than we used to... It was terribly cold weather—a blizzard in fact... As a matter of fact, I just got it this afternoon.*

faction /fækʃə^{0}n/, **factions.** COLL N A **faction** is an organized group of people within a larger group, who oppose some of the ideas of the larger group. *...arguments between rival factions.*

factor /fæktə/, **factors.** COUNT N WITH SUPP A **factor** is one of the things that affects an event, decision, or situation. *Confidence is the key factor in any successful career... ...social and economic factors.*

factory /fæktə^{0}ri^1/, **factories.** COUNT N A **factory** is a large building or group of buildings where machines are used to make goods in large quantities.

factual /fæktʃu^{0}əl/. ADJ Something that is **factual** contains or refers to facts rather than theories or opinions. *...a factual account.*

faculty /fækə^{0}lti^1/, **faculties. 1** COUNT N Your **faculties** are your physical and mental abilities. *...the faculty of imagination.* **2** COUNT N A **faculty** in a university or college is a group of related departments. *...the Arts Faculty.*

fad /fæd/, **fads.** COUNT N A **fad** is something which is very popular for a short time. *...taking up the latest fad about 'whole foods' or 'biological farming'.*

fade /feɪd/, **fades, fading, faded. 1** VB If something **fades,** it slowly becomes less bright, less loud, or less intense. *The afternoon light was fading... The applause faded... Interest in the story will fade.* **2** ERG VB When a coloured object **fades,** it gradually becomes paler in colour. *The wallpaper may have faded... How can I stop the sun from fading the carpet?* ♦ **faded** ADJ *...an old man in a faded blue shirt.*

fade away or **fade out.** PHR VB When something **fades away** or **fades out,** it slowly becomes less intense or strong until it ends completely. *Your enthusiasm for running will soon fade away... This sort of protest tends to fade out quickly.*

faeces /fiːsiːz/; spelled **feces** in American English. UNCOUNT N **Faeces** is the solid waste that people get rid of from their body when they go to the toilet; a formal use.

fag /fæg/, **fags.** COUNT N A **fag** is a cigarette; an informal British use. *...a packet of fags.*

Fahrenheit /færənh^{0}aɪt/. UNCOUNT N **Fahrenheit** is a scale for measuring temperature, in which water freezes at 32° and boils at 212°. *...a temperature of 50° Fahrenheit.*

fail /feɪl/, **fails, failing, failed. 1** VB If someone **fails** to do something that they were trying to do, they do not succeed in doing it. *Their party failed to win a single seat.* ♦ **failed** ATTRIB ADJ *He was a failed novelist and poet.* **2** VB WITH TO-INF If someone **fails** to do something that they should have done, they do not do it. *He was fined for failing to complete the census form.* **3** VB WITH OR WITHOUT OBJ If someone **fails** a test or examination, they do not reach the standard that is required. *I passed the written part but failed the oral section.* **4** VB If something **fails,** it stops working properly. *Her lighter failed... ...people whose sight is failing.* ♦ **failing** ATTRIB ADJ *He had given up his job because of failing health.* **5** VB WITH OBJ If someone **fails** you, they do not do what you expected or trusted them to do. *Our leaders have failed us.*

failing /feɪlɪŋ/, **failings. 1** COUNT N A **failing** is a fault or unsatisfactory feature. *The present system has many failings.* **2** PHRASE You say **failing that** to introduce an alternative, in case what you previously said is not possible. *Wear your national dress or, failing that, a suit.*

failure /feɪljə/, **failures. 1** UNCOUNT N **Failure** is a lack of success in doing or achieving something. *...a desperate initiative which ended in failure.* **2** COUNT N Someone who is a **failure** at something has not succeeded with it or at anything, or at what they were trying to do. *I felt such a failure.* **3** COUNT N If something is a **failure,** it is unsuccessful. *The meeting was a failure.* **4** UNCOUNT N WITH TO-INF Your **failure** to do something is the fact that you do not do it although you were expected to. *They remarked on his failure to appear at the party.* **5** UNCOUNT N OR COUNT N WITH SUPP When there is a **failure** of something, it stops working or functioning properly. *...engine failure.*

faint /feɪnt/, **fainter, faintest; faints, fainting, fainted. 1** ADJ Something that is **faint** is not strong or intense. *There was a faint smell of gas... Her cries grew fainter... ...a faint hope... ...a faint smile.* ♦ **faintly** ADV *It was faintly possible... She turned and smiled faintly.* **2** VB If you **faint,** you lose consciousness for a short time. *He nearly fainted from the pain.* **3** ADJ Someone who feels **faint** feels dizzy and unsteady.

fair /feə/, **fairer, fairest; fairs. 1** ADJ Something or someone that is **fair** is reasonable, right, and just. *It wouldn't be fair to disturb the children... She won't get a fair trial.* ♦ **fairness** UNCOUNT N *Even a child sees the fairness of reasonable penalties.* **2** ATTRIB ADJ You use **fair** to say that something is quite good, quite large, or quite likely. *We've got a fair number of postgraduate students... ...a fair-sized bedroom... I've think I've got a fair chance of evading them altogether.* **3** ADJ Someone who is **fair** or who has **fair** hair has light, gold-coloured hair. *She was fair and blue-eyed.* **4** ADJ **Fair** skin is pale in colour. *Unprotected fair skin gets sunburned quickly.* **5** ADJ When the weather is **fair,** it is not cloudy or rainy; a formal use. *It will be fair and warm.* **6** COUNT N A **fair** is an event held in a park or field at which people pay to ride on various machines for amusement or try to win prizes in games; a British use. *...the doll I won at the fair.* **7** COUNT N A **fair** is also an event at which people display or sell goods; a British use. *...the Leipzig Trade Fair.*

fairground /fɛəgraʊnd/, **fairgrounds.** COUNT N A **fairground** is an area of land where a fair is being held.

fairly /fɛəli¹/. 1 SUBMOD **Fairly** means to quite a large degree. *The information was fairly accurate... I wrote the first part fairly quickly.* 2 ADV If something is said or done **fairly,** it seems reasonable and just. *The car could fairly be described as sluggish and noisy.*

fairy /fɛəri¹/, **fairies.** COUNT N **Fairies** are small, imaginary creatures with magical powers.

fairy tale, fairy tales. COUNT N A **fairy tale** or a **fairy story** is a story for children involving magical events and imaginary creatures.

fait accompli /feɪt ə³kɒmpli:/. SING N If something is a **fait accompli,** it has already been done and cannot be changed; a formal use. *You've presented us with a fait accompli.*

faith /feɪθ/, **faiths.** 1 UNCOUNT N If you have **faith** in someone or something, you feel confident about their ability or goodness. *I had faith in Alan—I knew he could take care of me.* 2 COUNT N A **faith** is a particular religion, such as Christianity or Buddhism. *...its tolerant attitude to other faiths.* 3 UNCOUNT N **Faith** is strong religious belief. *...her deep religious faith.*

PHRASES ● If you **break faith** with someone, you fail to behave in the way that you promised or were expected to. If you **keep faith** with them, you continue to behave as you promised or were expected to. ● If you do something **in good faith,** you sincerely believe that it is the right thing to do in the circumstances.

faithful /feɪθfʊl/. 1 ADJ If you are **faithful** to a person, organization, or idea, you remain firm in your support for them. *Bond remained faithful to his old teacher.* ♦ **faithfully** ADV *The party rallied round him faithfully.* 2 ADJ Someone who is **faithful** to their husband, wife, or lover does not have a sexual relationship with anyone else. *She has been a faithful wife to him.* 3 ADJ A **faithful** account, translation, or adaptation of a book represents the facts or the original book accurately. *Do you think the film was faithful to the book?* ♦ **faithfully** ADV *Their activities were faithfully described in the newspapers.*

faithfully /feɪθfə⁴li¹/. CONVENTION You write **Yours faithfully** before your signature at the end of a letter which you have started with 'Dear Sir' or 'Dear Madam'.

fake /feɪk/, **fakes, faking, faked.** 1 COUNT N A **fake** is something that is made to look like something valuable or real in order to deceive people. *They swore that the pictures were fakes.* Also ADJ *...a fake passport.* 2 VB WITH OBJ If someone **fakes** something, they make it look like something valuable or real in order to deceive people. *...faking the fine furniture of the century before.* 3 VB WITH OBJ If you **fake** a feeling or reaction, you pretend that you are experiencing it. *Thomas faked a yawn.*

falcon /fɔ:l⁰kən/, **falcons.** COUNT N A **falcon** is a bird of prey that can be trained to hunt other birds and animals.

fall /fɔ:l/, **falls, falling, fell** /fel/, **fallen** /fɔ:lən/. 1 VB If someone or something **falls** or **falls** down, they move quickly downwards onto or towards the ground. *The cup fell from her hand and shattered on the floor... Tears fell from Mother's eyes... Part of the ceiling fell down... The snow was still falling.* Also SING N *He was rushed to hospital after a 40-foot fall.* 2 VB If someone or something that is standing **falls,** or if they **fall** down or **fall** over, they accidentally move or are pushed, and they end up lying on the ground. *She lost her balance and fell... He tripped and fell down... ...a falling tree.* ♦ **fallen** ATTRIB ADJ *...to rescue people trapped inside fallen buildings.* 3 VB If people in a position of power **fall,** they suddenly lose that position. If a place **falls** in a war or election, an enemy army or a different political party takes control of it. *The regime had fallen... Greater London will fall to Labour.* Also SING N WITH POSS *This led to the Government's fall... ...the fall of France.* 4 VB If someone **falls** in battle, they are killed; a literary use. 5 VB If something **falls** in amount, value, or strength, it decreases. *The value of the dollar has fallen... Their voices could be heard rising and falling.* Also SING N *...a fall in moral standards.* ♦ **falling** ADJ *Some nations were uneasy about their falling birth rates.* 6 VB When night or darkness **falls,** night begins and it becomes dark. 7 VB WITH ADJUNCT When light or shadow **falls** on something, it covers it. *A shadow fell over her book and she looked up.* 8 VB WITH ADJUNCT If your eyes **fall** on something, you suddenly see or notice it. *His gaze fell on a small white bundle.* 9 VB If silence or a feeling of sadness or tiredness **falls** on a group of people, they become silent, sad, or tired; a literary use. *An expectant hush fell on the gathering.* 10 VB WITH COMPLEMENT OR ADJUNCT You can use **fall** to show that someone or something passes into another state. For example, if someone **falls** ill, they become ill. *After a while I fell asleep... The crowd fell silent... He fell in love with her.* 11 VB WITH ADJUNCT To **fall** into a particular group or category means to belong in that group or category. *Human beings fall into two types.* 12 PLURAL N You can refer to a waterfall as the **falls.** *...Niagara Falls.* 13 UNCOUNT N OR COUNT N The **fall** is autumn; an American use. 14 to **fall flat**: see **flat.**

fall apart. PHR VB 1 If something **falls apart,** it breaks into pieces because it is old or badly made. *...cheap beds that fell apart.* 2 If an organization or system **falls apart,** it becomes disorganized and unable to work effectively. *The nation is falling apart.*

fall back. PHR VB If you **fall back,** you move quickly away from someone or something. *I saw my husband fall back in horror.*

fall back on. PHR VB If you **fall back on** something, you do it or use it after other things have failed. *Often you give up and fall back on easier solutions.*

fall behind. PHR VB If you **fall behind,** you do not make progress or move forward as fast as other people. *...children who fall behind with their reading.*

fall down. PHR VB See **fall 1, 2.**

fall for. PHR VB 1 If you **fall for** someone, you are strongly attracted to them and start loving them. *Richard fell for her the moment he set eyes on her.* 2 If you **fall for** a lie or trick, you believe it even though it is not true; an informal use. *The working class were not going to fall for this one.*

fall in. PHR VB If a roof or ceiling **falls in,** it collapses and falls to the ground.

fall in with. PHR VB If you **fall in with** an idea, plan, or system, you accept it and do not try to change it. *Instead of challenging the lie, she falls in with it.*

fall off. PHR VB If the degree, amount, or rate of something **falls off,** it decreases. *We knew that the numbers of overseas students would fall off drastically.*

fall out. PHR VB 1 If a person's hair or a tooth **falls out,** it becomes loose and separates from their body. *After about two weeks, the victim's hair starts to fall out.* 2 If you **fall out** with someone, you have an argument with them and stop being friendly. *I've fallen out with certain members of the band.* 3 See also **fallout.**

fall over. PHR VB See **fall 2.**

fall through. PHR VB If an arrangement **falls through,** it fails to happen. *We wanted to book a villa but it fell through.*

fall to. PHR VB If a responsibility or duty **falls to** someone, it becomes their responsibility or duty; a formal use. *It fell to Philip to act the part of host.*

fallacy /fæləsi¹/, **fallacies.** COUNT N A **fallacy** is an idea or argument which is incorrect or illogical; a formal use. *It is a fallacy that women are more pure-minded than men.*

fallen /fɔ:lən/. **Fallen** is the past participle of **fall.**

fallible /fælı¹bə⁰l/. 1 ADJ If you say that someone is **fallible,** you mean that they may make mistakes; a formal use. 2 ADJ If something is **fallible,** it may be wrong or unreliable; a formal use. *Mary was conscious how fallible this method was.*

fallout /fɔ:laʊt/. UNCOUNT N **Fallout** is the radiation that affects an area after a nuclear explosion.

fallow /fæləʊ/. ADJ If land is lying **fallow,** no crops have been planted in it, so that the soil has a chance to rest and improve. *...plots of fallow land.*

false /fɒls, fɔ:ls/. 1 ADJ If something is **false,** it is untrue or based on a mistake or wrong information. *What you're saying is false... I had a false impression of him... ...to save her from false imprisonment.* ♦ **falsely** ADV *...falsely accusing him of a crime.* ● **under false pretences:** see **pretence.** 2 ADJ **False** things are made so that they appear real although they are not. *...false teeth.* 3 ADJ Behaviour that is **false** is not sincere *...a false smile... ...false modesty.* ♦ **falsely** ADV *She laughed, falsely, to cheer him up.*

false alarm, false alarms. COUNT N When you are warned of something dangerous and it does not happen, you say that the warning was a **false alarm.**

falsehood /fɒlshʊd, fɔ:l-/, **falsehoods.** 1 UNCOUNT N The **falsehood** of something is the fact that it is untrue; a formal use. *We must establish the truth or falsehood of the various rumours.* 2 COUNT N A **falsehood** is a lie; a formal use.

falsify /fɒlsıfaı, fɔ:l-/, **falsifies, falsifying, falsified.** VB WITH OBJ If someone **falsifies** information, they change it so that it is no longer true, in order to deceive people. *The facts concerning my birth have been falsified.* ♦ **falsification** /fɒlsıfıkeıʃə⁰n, fɔ:l-/ UNCOUNT N OR COUNT N *...falsification of accounts.*

falter /fɒltə, fɔ:ltə/, **falters, faltering, faltered.** 1 VB If something **falters,** it becomes weaker or slower, and may stop completely. *The engines faltered and the plane lost height.* 2 VB If you **falter,** you hesitate and become unsure or unsteady. *From that moment onwards he never faltered in his resolve... Looking to his left, he saw Percy faltering.*

fame /feɪm/. UNCOUNT N If you achieve **fame,** you become well known and admired by many people. *She was jealous of Ellen's fame... He rose rapidly to fame.*

famed /feɪmd/. ADJ If you are **famed** for something, you are well known and admired because of it; a literary use. *The women there were famed for the pots they made.*

familiar /fəmıljə/. 1 ADJ If someone or something is **familiar** to you, you recognize them or know them well. *His name was familiar to me... ...my pleasure at seeing all the familiar faces again.* ♦ **familiarity** /fəmılıærı¹ti¹/ UNCOUNT N *...the familiarity of the surroundings.* 2 PRED ADJ WITH 'with' If you are **familiar** with something, you know it well. *I am of course familiar with your work.* ♦ **familiarity** UNCOUNT N *...his familiarity with the system gave him a considerable advantage.* 3 ADJ If you behave in a **familiar** way towards someone, you treat them very informally, so that you may offend them if you are not close friends. *...disliking intensely the burly man's familiar tone.* ♦ **familiarly** ADV *He spoke of them casually and familiarly by their first names.* ♦ **familiarity** UNCOUNT N *They greeted him with familiarity.*

familiarize /fəmıljəraız/, **familiarizes, familiarizing, familiarized;** also spelled **familiarise.** VB WITH OBJ AND 'with' OR REFL VB If someone **familiarizes** you with something, you learn all about it and get to know it. *He had to familiarize himself with the ship... ...to familiarize their colleagues with the principles.*

family /fæmı⁰li¹/, **families.** 1 COLL N OR UNCOUNT N A **family** is a group of people who are related to each other, especially parents and their children. *...an English family on holiday... ...help offered by family and friends.* 2 COLL N OR UNCOUNT N When parents talk about their **family,** they mean their children. *...mothers with large families.* 3 MOD You use **family** to describe things which can be used or enjoyed by both parents and children. *...a family car... ...family entertainment.* 4 COLL N Your **family** is also one line of your ancestors. *Her mother's family had lived there for generations... Ben worked in the family business.*

family planning. UNCOUNT N **Family planning** is the practice of using contraception to control the number of children in a family.

family tree, family trees. COUNT N A **family tree** is a chart that shows all the people in your family over many generations and their relationships between them.

famine /fæmın/, **famines.** UNCOUNT N OR COUNT N A **famine** is a serious shortage of food in a country, which may cause many deaths. *...the effects of famine and drought.*

famished /fæmıʃt/. ADJ If you say that you are **famished,** you mean that you are very hungry; an informal use.

famous /feɪməs/. ADJ Someone or something that is **famous** is very well known. *...a famous writer... California is famous for raisins.*

fan /fæn/, **fans, fanning, fanned.** 1 COUNT N If you are a **fan** of someone or something, you admire them and support them. *...football fans.* 2 COUNT N A **fan** is a flat object that you hold in your hand and wave in order to move the air and make yourself cooler. 3 COUNT N A **fan** is also a piece of electrical equipment with revolving blades which keeps a room or machine cool or gets rid of unpleasant smells. 4 REFL VB If you **fan** yourself, you wave a fan or other flat object in order to move the air and make yourself cooler. *She took up some sheets of paper and fanned herself with them.* 5 VB WITH OBJ To **fan** a fire means to create a current of air so that the fire burns more strongly. *...fires that were fanned by the outward moving winds.*

fan out. PHR VB When people or things **fan out,** they move forwards together from the same point, while moving farther apart from each other. *The five of us fanned out at intervals of not more than fifteen feet.*

fanatic /fənætık/, **fanatics.** 1 COUNT N A **fanatic** is a person with strong religious or political beliefs who behaves in an extreme or violent way. 2 COUNT N A **fanatic** is also a person who is very enthusiastic about a subject or activity. *...a sports fanatic.*

fanatical /fənætıkə⁰l/. ADJ Someone who is **fanatical** feels very strongly about something and behaves in an extreme way because of this. *...fanatical rebels.*

fanaticism /fənætısızə⁰m/. UNCOUNT N **Fanaticism** is fanatical behaviour. *He took to abstract painting with an obsessive fanaticism.*

fanciful /fænsıfʊl/. 1 ADJ **Fanciful** ideas or stories are based on someone's imagination and not on reality. *He had heard fanciful tales about their work.* 2 ADJ Something that is **fanciful** is unusual and elaborate rather than plain; used showing disapproval. *He considered this name far too fanciful.*

fancy /fænsi¹/, **fancies, fancying, fancied; fancier, fanciest.** 1 VB WITH OBJ OR -ING If you **fancy** something, you want to have it or do it; an informal use. *She* *fancied a flat of her own... I don't fancy going back alone.* 2 VB WITH OBJ If you **fancy** someone, you feel attracted to them in a sexual way; an informal use. 3 REFL VB If you **fancy** yourself, you think that you are especially clever, attractive, or good at something; an informal use, showing disapproval. *I've heard that this man Bond fancies himself with a pistol... We all fancied ourselves as leaders.* 4 CONVENTION You say **'fancy'** when you want to express surprise; an informal use. *Fancy seeing you here!* 5 REPORT VB If you **fancy** that something is the case, you think or suppose that it is true; a formal use. *I fancied I could hear a baby screaming.* 6 COUNT N OR UNCOUNT N A **fancy** is an idea that is unlikely or untrue; a formal use. *His mind was filled with weird fancies... It is difficult to separate fact from fancy.* 7 ADJ Something that is **fancy** is unusual and elaborate; an informal use. *...good plain food: nothing fancy.*

PHRASES ● If you **take a fancy to** someone or something, you start liking them, usually for no understandable reason; an informal use. ● If something **takes** your **fancy** when you see or hear it, you like it quite a lot; an informal use.

fancy dress. UNCOUNT N **Fancy dress** is clothing that you wear for a party where people dress to look like particular characters, for example from history or stories, and so on. *...ladies in fancy dress.*

fanfare /fænfɛə/, **fanfares.** COUNT N A **fanfare** is a short, loud tune played on trumpets to announce a special event.

fang /fæŋ/, **fangs.** COUNT N An animal's **fangs** are its long, sharp teeth.

fantasize /fæntəsaɪz/, **fantasizes, fantasizing, fantasized;** also spelled **fantasise.** VB If you **fantasize,** you think imaginatively about something that you would like to happen but that is unlikely. *I have often fantasized about these occasions.*

fantastic /fæntæstɪk/. 1 ADJ People say that something is **fantastic** when they like or admire it very much; an informal use. *He chewed it and said, 'Fantastic!'... He scored the most fantastic goal I have ever seen.* 2 ATTRIB ADJ You use **fantastic** to emphasize the size, amount, or degree of something. *...a fantastic amount of time... ...her fantastic power.* ♦ **fantastically** SUBMOD *They were fantastically strict.* 3 ADJ You describe something as **fantastic** when it seems strange and wonderful or unlikely. *...fantastic images of gods... He was in love with her—fantastic though that may seem.* ♦ **fantastically** SUBMOD *...fantastically shaped islands.*

fantasy /fæntəsi^1/, **fantasies.** 1 COUNT N A **fantasy** is a situation or event that you think about or imagine, although it is unlikely to happen or be true. *That's supposed to be every schoolgirl's fantasy.* 2 UNCOUNT N OR COUNT N **Fantasy** refers to the activity of imagining things, or the things that you imagine. *To a child, fantasy and reality are very close to each other... His novels were fantasies.*

far /fɑː/, **farther** /fɑːðə/ or **further** /fɜːðə/, **farthest** /fɑːðɪ^{2}st/ or **furthest** /fɜːðɪ^{2}st/. **Farther** and **farthest** are used mainly when talking about distance. ● See separate entries for **further** and **furthest.** 1 ADV If one place, thing, or person is **far** away from another, there is a great distance between them. *He sat far away from the others... ...a villa not far from Hotel Miranda... ...a little farther south.* used in questions and statements about distance. *How far is Amity from here?... Vita went as far as Bologna.* 2 ATTRIB ADJ You use **far** to refer to the part of an area that is the greatest distance from the centre in a particular direction. *...in the far north of the country... ...on the far right of the page.* 3 ATTRIB ADJ When there are two similar things somewhere, you use **far** to refer to the one that is a greater distance from you. *...the far end of the room.* 4 ADV WITH ADJUNCT A time or event that is **far** in the future or the past is a long time from the present. *The Fourth of July isn't far off... ...as far back as the twelfth century.* 5 ADV You use **far** to indicate the extent or degree to which something happens. *Prices will not come down very far... None of us would trust them very far... ...using her methods as far as possible.* used in questions and statements about extent or degree. *How far have you got in developing this?* 6 ADV You can use **far** in comparisons to emphasize that one thing is much greater or better than another. *...a far greater problem... It was far more than I expected... The firm had far outstripped its rivals.*

PHRASES ● If something happens **far and wide,** it happens in a lot of places or over a large area. *People would come from far and wide to hear him.* ● You can use **by far** or **far and away** in comparisons to emphasize that something is better or greater than anything else. *She was by far the camp's best swimmer... This is far and away the most important point.* ● If an answer or idea is **not far wrong, not far out,** or **not far off,** it is almost correct. ● You can use **far from** to emphasize that something is the opposite of what it could have been or of what you expected. *His hands were far from clean... Far from speeding up, the tank slithered to a halt.* ● **So far** means up until the present point in time or in a situation. *What do you think of the town so far?* ● If you say that someone is going **too far,** you mean that they are behaving in an unacceptable or extreme way; an informal use. ● **as far as** something is concerned: see **concern.** ● **few and far between:** see **few.** ● **in so far as:** see **insofar.**

faraway /fɑːr^{0}əweɪ/. 1 ATTRIB ADJ **Faraway** means a long distance away from you. *...news from far-away villages... ...the faraway sound of a waterfall.* 2 ATTRIB ADJ If someone has a **faraway** look, they seem to be thinking deeply and are not paying attention to what is happening.

farce /fɑːs/, **farces.** 1 COUNT N A **farce** is a humorous play in which the characters become involved in unlikely and complicated situations. 2 COUNT N If you say that something is a **farce,** you mean that it is very disorganized or unsatisfactory. *His education had been a farce.*

farcical /fɑːsɪkə^{0}l/. ADJ If you describe a situation or event as **farcical,** you mean that it is completely ridiculous. *The next ten minutes were farcical.*

fare /fɛə/, **fares, faring, fared.** 1 COUNT N The **fare** is the money that you pay for a journey by bus, taxi, train, boat, or aeroplane. *Coach fares are cheaper than rail fares.* 2 UNCOUNT N The **fare** served at a restaurant is the food that is served there; an old-fashioned use. *Army kitchens serve better fare than some hotels.* 3 VB WITH ADJUNCT If you **fare** badly in a particular situation, you are unsuccessful or are treated badly. If you **fare** well, you are successful or are treated well; an old-fashioned use. *They fared badly in the 1978 elections.*

Far East. PROPER N The **Far East** consists of all the countries of Eastern Asia, including China and Japan.

farewell /fɛəwɛl/, **farewells.** CONVENTION **Farewell** means goodbye; an old-fashioned use. *Farewell, my dear child... He bade farewell to his family.* Also COUNT N *...tearful farewells.*

far-fetched. ADJ A **far-fetched** story, idea, or plan is exaggerated or unlikely. *The theory is too far-fetched to be considered.*

far-flung. 1 ATTRIB ADJ **Far-flung** places are a long distance away. *...some far-flung corner of the world.* 2 ATTRIB ADJ Something that is **far-flung** covers a very wide area or extends to distant places. *...the produce of a far-flung empire.*

farm /fɑːm/, **farms, farming, farmed.** 1 COUNT N A **farm** is an area of land consisting of fields and buildings, where crops are grown or animals are raised. *My father worked on a farm.* 2 VB WITH OR WITHOUT OBJ If you **farm** an area of land, you grow crops or raise animals on it. *The hill land is farmed by Mike Keeble.* ♦ **farming** UNCOUNT N *...an economy based on farming and tourism... ...sheep farming.*

farmer /fɑːmə/, **farmers.** COUNT N A **farmer** is a person who owns or manages a farm.

farmhouse /fɑːmhaʊs/, **farmhouses.** COUNT N A **farmhouse** is a house on a farm, especially one where a farmer lives.

farmland /fɑːmlænd/. UNCOUNT N **Farmland** is land which is farmed or is suitable for farming.

farmyard /fɑːmjɑːd/, **farmyards.** COUNT N A **farmyard** is an area on a farm surrounded by buildings or walls.

far-off. 1 ADJ A **far-off** place is a long distance away. *...a far-off country.* 2 ADJ A **far-off** time is a long time away in the future or past. *...looking back at that far-off day.*

far-reaching. ADJ **Far-reaching** means affecting something greatly, in many ways. *It could have far-reaching implications for the economy.*

far-sighted. ADJ If someone is **far-sighted,** they are good at guessing what will happen in the future and making suitable plans.

farther /fɑːðə/. **Farther** is a comparative of **far.**

farthest /fɑːðɪ^{2}st/. **Farthest** is a superlative of **far.**

fascinate /fæsɪneɪt/, **fascinates, fascinating, fascinated.** VB WITH OBJ If something or someone **fascinates** you, you find them very interesting. *I love history, it fascinates me.* ♦ **fascinated** ADJ *He became fascinated with their whole way of life.* ♦ **fascinating** ADJ *It's a fascinating book.*

fascination /fæsɪneɪʃə^{0}n/. UNCOUNT N **Fascination** is the state of being greatly interested in and delighted by something. *...a fascination with Hokkaido's wild country.*

fascism /fæʃɪzə^{0}m/. UNCOUNT N **Fascism** is a right-wing political philosophy that believes in the importance of having strong rules, state control, and the prevention of political opposition.

fascist /fæʃɪst/, **fascists.** 1 COUNT N A **fascist** is someone who supports or believes in fascism. 2 COUNT N If you call someone a **fascist,** you mean that their opinions are very right-wing.

fashion /fæʃə^{0}n/, **fashions, fashioning, fashioned.** 1 SING N WITH SUPP If you do something in a particular **fashion,** you do it in that way. *He greeted us in his usual friendly fashion.* 2 UNCOUNT N **Fashion** is the area of activity that involves styles of clothing and appearance. *...the fashion industry.* 3 COUNT N A **fashion** is a style of clothing or a way of behaving that is popular at a particular time. *...the latest Parisian fashions.* ● If something is **in fashion,** it is popular and approved of at a particular time. If it is **out of fashion,** it is not popular or approved of. 4 VB WITH OBJ If you **fashion** something, you make it; an old-fashioned use. *The crew fashioned a raft from the wreckage.* 5 See also **old-fashioned.**

fashionable /fæʃə^{0}nəbə^{0}l/. ADJ Something that is **fashionable** is popular or approved of at a particular time. *...the striped shirts that were fashionable in 1963.* ♦ **fashionably** ADV *...fashionably dressed ladies.*

fast /fɑːst/, **faster, fastest; fasts, fasting, fasted.** 1 ADJ OR ADV **Fast** means moving, acting, or happening with great speed. *...a fast car... ...producing goods at a faster rate... I ran as fast as I could... News travels pretty fast.* used in questions and statements about speed. *...looking out of the windows to see how fast we were going.* 2 ADV **Fast** also means happening without any delay. *She needed medical help fast... Treat stains as fast as possible.* 3 PRED ADJ If a watch or clock is **fast,** it is showing a time that is later than the real time. 4 ADV If something is held or fixed **fast,** it is held or fixed very firmly. *He saw a small man, his leg held fast in the lion trap, making desperate efforts to free himself.* 5 VB If you **fast,** you eat no food for a period of time, usually for religious reasons. *He fasts for a whole day every week.* Also COUNT N *During my fast I lost fifteen pounds.*

PHRASES ● Someone who is **fast asleep** is completely asleep. ● If you **hold fast** to an idea or course of action, you firmly continue believing it or doing it. *He was determined to hold fast to his beliefs.* ● to **make a fast buck:** see **buck.** ● **thick and fast:** see **thick.** ● See also **hard and fast.**

fasten /fɑːsə^{0}n/, **fastens, fastening, fastened.** 1 ERG VB If you **fasten** something, you fix it in a closed position with a button, strap, or other device. *He fastened his seat-belt... The case fastened at the top.* 2 VB WITH OBJ AND ADJUNCT If you **fasten** one thing to another, you attach the first thing to the second. *The bench had been fastened to the pavement.* 3 ERG VB OR VB, WITH ADJUNCT If you **fasten** your hands round something, or if you **fasten** onto it, you grasp it firmly. *He fastened his hands round the spear... Her hands fastened on the climbing rope.*

fasten on. PHR VB If you **fasten on** to someone or something, you concentrate your attention or efforts on them. *Once she had fastened on to a scheme she did not let go.*

fastening /fɑːsə^{0}nɪŋ/, **fastenings.** COUNT N A **fastening** is a device that keeps something fixed or closed. *...the fastenings of her gown.*

fast food. UNCOUNT N **Fast food** is hot food that is prepared and served quickly after you order it.

fastidious /fæstɪdɪəs/. ADJ Someone who is **fastidious** is fussy and likes things to be clean, tidy, and properly done. *...with noses wrinkled in fastidious distaste.* ♦ **fastidiously** ADV *The process was fastidiously checked.*

fat /fæt/, **fatter, fattest; fats.** 1 ADJ A **fat** person has a lot of flesh on their body and weighs too much. *...a small fat man.* ♦ **fatness** UNCOUNT N *He was embarrassed to hear her discussing his fatness.* 2 UNCOUNT N **Fat** in the bodies of animals and people is the layer of flesh which is used to store energy and to keep them warm. 3 MASS N **Fat** is a substance contained in many foods and used by your body to produce energy. *...a diet containing protein, fats, carbohydrates, and vitamins.* 4 MASS N **Fat** is also a substance used in cooking which is obtained from vegetables or the flesh of animals. *...a smell of fried fat.* 5 ADJ A **fat** book, case, or other object is very thick or wide. *...a fat briefcase.* 6 ATTRIB ADJ A **fat** profit is a large one.

fatal /feɪtə^{0}l/. 1 ADJ A **fatal** action has undesirable results. *I made the fatal mistake of letting her talk.* ♦ **fatally** ADV *...men in whom he had fatally trusted.* 2 ADJ A **fatal** accident or illness causes someone's death. *...Pollock's fatal car crash.* ♦ **fatally** ADV *Four men were fatally stabbed.*

fatalism /feɪtəlɪzə^{0}m/. UNCOUNT N **Fatalism** is the belief that people cannot prevent or control events. *...the fatalism of the masses.*

fatalistic /feɪtəlɪstɪk/. ADJ Someone who is **fatalistic** believes that human beings cannot influence or control events. *She had a far more fatalistic approach.*

fatality /fətælɪ1ti1/, **fatalities. 1** COUNT N A **fatality** is a person's death, caused by an accident or violence. **2** UNCOUNT N **Fatality** is the feeling or belief that people cannot prevent or control events; a formal use. *The modern world is dominated by a sense of fatality.*

fate /feɪt/, **fates. 1** UNCOUNT N **Fate** is a power believed by some people to control everything that happens. *Fate was against me.* **2** COUNT N WITH SUPP Someone's **fate** is what happens to them. *Several other companies suffered a similar fate.*

fated /feɪtɪ2d/. ADJ If you say that someone is **fated** to do something, or that an event is **fated,** you mean that nothing can be done to prevent what will happen. *We were fated to dislike one another.*

fateful /feɪtfʊl/. ATTRIB ADJ If you describe an action or event as **fateful,** you mean that it had important, and often bad, effects on later events. *The President made his fateful announcement.*

father /fɑːðə/, **fathers, fathering, fathered. 1** COUNT N OR VOCATIVE Your **father** is your male parent. **2** VB WITH OBJ When a man **fathers** a child, he makes a woman pregnant and their child is born; a literary use. **3** SING N The **father** of something is the man who invented or started it. *Chaucer is often said to be the father of English poetry.* **4** TITLE In some Christian churches, priests are addressed or referred to as **Father. 5** PROPER N OR VOCATIVE Christians often refer to God as our **Father** or address him as **Father.** *Heavenly Father, hear our prayers.*

Father Christmas. PROPER N **Father Christmas** is an imaginary old man with a long white beard and a red coat. Young children believe that he brings their Christmas presents.

fatherhood /fɑːðəhʊd/. UNCOUNT N **Fatherhood** is the state of being a father. *Attitudes to fatherhood are changing.*

father-in-law, fathers-in-law. COUNT N Your **father-in-law** is the father of your husband or wife.

fatherless /fɑːðəlɪ2s/. ADJ You describe children as **fatherless** when their father has died or does not live with them.

fatherly /fɑːðəli1/. ATTRIB ADJ You say that someone behaves in a **fatherly** way when they behave like a kind father. *Let me give you some fatherly advice.*

fathom /fæðə0m/, **fathoms, fathoming, fathomed. 1** COUNT N A **fathom** is a unit of length used for describing the depth of the sea. One fathom is equal to 6 feet or approximately 1.8 metres. **2** VB WITH OBJ If you **fathom** something or **fathom** it out, you understand it as a result of thinking about it carefully. *I couldn't fathom the meaning of her remarks... She couldn't fathom why McCurry was causing such a scene.*

fatigue /fətiːg/, **fatigues, fatiguing, fatigued. 1** UNCOUNT N **Fatigue** is a feeling of extreme physical or mental tiredness. *He was dizzy with hunger and fatigue.* **2** VB WITH OBJ If something **fatigues** you, it makes you extremely tired; a formal use. ♦ **fatigued** ADJ *She was utterly fatigued.* **3** UNCOUNT N Metal **fatigue** is a weakness caused by repeated stress. It can cause the metal to break.

fatten /fætə0n/, **fattens, fattening, fattened.** ERG VB If you **fatten** an animal or if it **fattens,** it becomes fatter as a result of eating more. *Soya is excellent for fattening pigs.*

fatten up. PHR VB If you **fatten up** an animal, you feed it more so that it reaches the desired weight. *Their cattle take twice as long to fatten up as European cattle.*

fattening /fætə0nɪŋ/. ADJ **Fattening** food tends to make people fat.

fatty /fæti1/. ADJ **Fatty** food contains a lot of fat.

fatuous /fætjʊəs/. ADJ If you say that a remark, action, or plan is **fatuous,** you mean that it is extremely foolish.

faucet /fɔːsɪt/, **faucets.** COUNT N A **faucet** is a tap, for example on a sink or bath; an American use.

fault /fɔːlt/, **faults, faulting, faulted. 1** SING N WITH POSS If a bad situation is your **fault,** you caused it or are responsible for it. *It was entirely my own fault.* **2** COUNT N A **fault** in something is a weakness or imperfection in it. *Computer faults are commonplace.* **3** VB WITH OBJ If you say that you cannot **fault** someone, you mean that they are doing something so well that you cannot criticize them for it. *I couldn't fault him on that one.* **4** COUNT N A **fault** is also a large crack in the earth's surface; a technical use.

PHRASES ● If you are **at fault,** you are incorrect or have done something wrong. *It was 1976, I believe, if my memory is not at fault.* ● If you **find fault** with something, you complain about it.

faultless /fɔːltlɪ2s/. ADJ Something that is **faultless** contains no mistakes. *...faultless German.*

faulty /fɔːlti1/. ADJ A **faulty** machine or piece of equipment is not working properly. *...a faulty transformer.*

fauna /fɔːnə/. PLURAL N The **fauna** in a place are all the animals, birds, fish, and insects there; a formal use. *...the flora and fauna of Africa.*

favour /feɪvə/, **favours, favouring, favoured;** spelled **favor** in American English. **1** UNCOUNT N If you regard something or someone with **favour,** you like or support them. *I think the company will look with favour on your plan... Is this just an attempt to win his favour?* **2** COUNT N If you do someone a **favour,** you do something for them even though you do not have to. *I've come to ask a favour.* **3** VB WITH OBJ If you **favour** something, you prefer it to the other choices available. *...those who favour disarmament.* **4** VB WITH OBJ Something that **favours** a person or event make it easier for that person to be successful or for that event to happen. *The weather favoured the attacking army.* **5** VB WITH OBJ If you **favour** someone, you treat them better than you treat other people. *Parents may favour the youngest child in the family.* **6** VB WITH OBJ AND 'with' If you **favour** someone with your attention or presence, you give it to them; a formal use. *The minister favoured us with an interview.*

PHRASES ● If you are **in favour** of something, you think that it is a good thing. *They are in favour of reforming the tax laws.* ● If someone makes a judgement **in** your **favour,** they say that you are right. *The umpire ruled in her favour.* ● Something that is **in** your **favour** gives you an advantage. *The system is biased in favour of young people.* ● If one thing is rejected **in favour of** another, the second thing is done or chosen instead of the first one. *The plans for a new airport have been scrapped in favour of an extension to the old one.* ● If something is **in favour,** people like or support it. If something is **out of favour,** people no longer like or support it. *Their views are very much out of favour now.*

favourable /feɪvə0rəbə0l/; spelled **favorable** in American English. **1** ADJ If you are **favourable** to something, you agree with it or approve of it. *Her request met with a favourable response.* ♦ **favourably** ADV *Many reacted favourably to the plan.* **2** ADJ If something makes a **favourable** impression on you, you like it or approve of it. ♦ **favourably** ADV *Her application had impressed him very favourably.* **3** ADJ If you present something in a **favourable** light, you try to make people like it or approve of it. **4** ADJ **Favourable** conditions make something more likely to succeed. *This creates an atmosphere favourable to expansion.* **5** ADJ If you make a **favourable** comparison between two things, you say that the first is at least as good as the second. ♦ **favourably** ADV *...a service which compares favourably with that of other countries.*

favourite /feɪvə0rɪt/, **favourites;** spelled **favorite** in American English. **1** ADJ Your **favourite** thing of a particular type is the one that you like most. *What is your favourite television programme?* **2** COUNT N The **favourite** in a race or contest is the person or animal expected to win.

favouritism /feɪvə0rɪtɪzm/; spelled **favoritism** in American English. UNCOUNT N **Favouritism** is the practice of unfairly helping or supporting one person or group more than another. *There must be no favouritism in the allocation of contracts.*

fawn /fɔːn/, **fawns, fawning, fawned. 1** ADJ Something that is **fawn** is pale yellowish-brown. **2** COUNT N A **fawn** is a very young deer. **3** VB If people **fawn** on powerful or rich people, they flatter them to get something for themselves.

fear /fɪə/, **fears, fearing, feared. 1** UNCOUNT N **Fear** is the unpleasant feeling of worry that you get when you think that you are in danger or that something horrible is going to happen. *They huddled together, quaking with fear... She was brought up with no fear of animals.* **2** COUNT N A **fear** is a thought that something unpleasant might happen or might have happened. *My worst fears were quickly realized.* **3** PHRASE If you do not do something **for fear** of something happening, you do not do it because you do not wish that thing to happen. *They did not mention it for fear of offending him.* **4** VB WITH OBJ If you **fear** someone or something, they make you feel nervous or worried; a formal use. *He fears nothing.* **5** REPORT VB If you **fear** something unpleasant, you are worried that it might happen, or might have happened; a formal use. *An epidemic of plague was feared... They fear that their new-found independence might be lost.* **6** VB WITH 'for' If you **fear** for something, you worry that it might be in danger; a formal use. *Morris began to fear for the life of Mrs Reilly.* **7** VB If you say that you **fear** that something is the case, you mean that you are sorry or sad about it; a formal use. *It is usually, I fear, the parents who are responsible.*

fearful /fɪəfʊl/; a formal word. **1** ADJ A **fearful** person is afraid. *They are fearful of letting their feelings take over.* ♦ **fearfully** ADV *The boys looked at each other fearfully.* **2** ADJ Something that is **fearful** is very unpleasant or bad. *...the fearful risks of the operation.*

fearless /fɪəlɪ2s/. ADJ A **fearless** person or animal is not afraid. *...fearless reporters.*

fearsome /fɪəsəm/. ADJ A **fearsome** thing is terrible or frightening; an old-fashioned use. *The dog had a fearsome set of teeth.*

feasible /fiːzəbə0l/. ADJ Something that is **feasible** can be done, made, or achieved. *The electric car is technically feasible.* ♦ **feasibility** /fiːzəbɪlɪti1/ UNCOUNT N *...the technical feasibility of a supersonic aircraft.*

feast /fiːst/, **feasts, feasting, feasted;** a literary word. **1** COUNT N A **feast** is a large and special meal. *...a wedding feast.* **2** VB If you **feast,** you take part in a feast. *He sprawled there, feasting off cold roast duck.* ♦ **feasting** UNCOUNT N *The feasting went on for hours.* **3** PHRASE If you **feast** your **eyes** on something, you look at it for a long time because you like it very much. *I feasted my eyes upon her lovely face.*

feat /fiːt/, **feats.** COUNT N WITH SUPP A **feat** is an impressive and difficult act or achievement. *...a brilliant feat of engineering.*

feather /feðə/, **feathers.** COUNT N A bird's **feathers** are the light, soft things covering its body. *...ostrich feathers.* ♦ **feathered** /feðəd/ ATTRIB ADJ *...feathered head-dresses.*

feathery /feðə0ri1/. ADJ If something is **feathery,** it reminds you of feathers, for example because of its softness or shape. *...feathery palm trees.*

feature /fiːtʃə/, **features, featuring, featured. 1** COUNT N WITH SUPP A **feature** of something is an interesting or important part or characteristic of it. *Every car will have built-in safety features... ...the natural features of the landscape.* **2** PLURAL N Your **features** are your eyes, nose, mouth, and other parts of your face. **3** VB WITH OBJ When a film or exhibition **features** someone or something, they are an important part of it. *This film features two of my favourite actors.* **4** VB WITH 'in' If you **feature** in something, you are an important and noticeable part of it. *This is not the first time he has featured in allegations of violence.* **5** COUNT N A **feature** is also a special article in a newspaper or magazine, or a special programme on radio or television. *The local newspaper ran a feature on drug abuse.* **6** COUNT N A full-length film in a cinema is also called a **feature** or a **feature** film.

February /febrʊəri1/. UNCOUNT N **February** is the second month of the year in the western calendar.

feces /fiːsiːz/. See **faeces.**

feckless /feklɪ2s/. ADJ A **feckless** person lacks strength of character, and cannot run their life properly; a formal use. *...children with drunken or feckless parents.*

fed /fed/. **Fed** is the past tense and past participle of **feed.** ● See also **fed up.**

federal /fedə0rəl/. ATTRIB ADJ In a **federal** country or system, a group of states is controlled by a central government. *...the Federal Republic of Germany.*

federation /fedəreɪʃə0n/, **federations.** COUNT N A **federation** is a group of organizations or states that have joined together for a common purpose. *...the National Federation of Women's Institutes.*

fed up. PRED ADJ Someone who is **fed up** is bored or annoyed; an informal use. *You sound a bit fed up.*

fee /fiː/, **fees. 1** COUNT N A **fee** is a sum of money that you pay to be allowed to do something. *...an entrance fee.* **2** COUNT N A **fee** is also the money paid for a particular job or service. *Agencies charge a fee to find an au pair.*

feeble /fiːbə0l/, **feebler, feeblest.** ADJ **Feeble** means having very little power, energy or effectiveness. *The creature is physically feeble, with poor vision and dull senses... ...a feeble joke.* ♦ **feebly** ADV *'They seemed all right to me,' I explained feebly.*

feed /fiːd/, **feeds, feeding, fed** /fed/. **1** VB WITH OBJ OR VB WITH OBJ AND OBJ If you **feed** a baby or an animal, you give it food. *She fed the baby some milk.* Also COUNT N *What time is his next feed?* **2** VB When an animal or baby **feeds,** it eats something. *Not all bats feed on insects.* **3** MASS N **Feed** is food that is given to an animal. **4** VB WITH OBJ OR REFL VB If you **feed** your family or a community, you supply or prepare food for them. *The farmers grew too little to feed even their own families... Are you feeding yourself properly?* **5** VB WITH 'on' OR OBJ If something **feeds** on something else or **is fed** by it, it grows stronger as a result of it. *Anger feeds on disappointment... The fires were being fed by escaping gas.* **6** VB WITH OBJ If you **feed** something into a container, store, or other object, you gradually put it in. *This data is fed into the computer.*

feedback /fiːdbæk/. UNCOUNT N When you get **feedback,** you get comments about something that you have done or made.

feel /fiːl/, **feels, feeling, felt** /fɛlt/. **1** VB WITH OBJ OR LINK VB If you **feel** an emotion or a sensation, you experience it. *Mrs Oliver felt a sudden desire to burst out crying... I was feeling hungry... She felt a fool... I felt like a murderer.* **2** REPORT VB, VB WITH COMPLEMENT, OR VB WITH OBJ AND COMPLEMENT If you **feel** that something is the case, it is your opinion that it is the case. *He felt I was making a terrible mistake... I felt obliged to invite him in... He felt it necessary to explain why he had come.* **3** VB WITH ADJUNCT If you **feel** a particular way about something, you have that attitude or reaction to it. *She knew how I felt about totalitarianism.* **4** VB WITH COMPLEMENT OR 'like' If you talk about how an experience **feels**, you are talking about the emotions and sensations connected with it. *It felt good to be back... What does it feel like to watch yourself on TV?* **5** VB WITH COMPLEMENT OR 'like' The way something **feels** is the way it seems to you when you touch or hold it. *It feels like a normal fabric.* Also SING N WITH SUPP *...the cool feel of armchair leather.* **6** VB WITH OBJ OR REFL VB If you **feel** something, you are aware that it is touching or happening to your body. *They felt the wind on their damp faces... He could feel himself blushing.* **7** VB WITH OBJ To **feel** something also means to be aware of it, even though you cannot see or hear it. *He had felt Binta's presence in the hut.* **8** VB WITH OBJ If you **feel** a physical object, you touch it deliberately, in order to find out what it is like. *Eric felt his face. 'I'm all rough. Am I bleeding?'* **9** VB WITH 'for' If you **feel** for an object, you try to find it using your hands rather than your eyes. *She felt in her bag for her key.* **10** VB WITH OBJ If you **feel** the effect or result of something, you experience it. *We shan't feel the effect of the change for some years.* **11** SING N WITH SUPP The **feel** of something, for example a place, is the general impression that it gives. *The Brazilian Amazon has the feel of a tropical wild west.* **12** See also **feeling, felt.**

PHRASES ● If you **feel like** doing or having something, you want to do or have it. *I feel like a stroll.* ● If you **do not feel yourself,** you feel slightly ill.

feeling /fiːlɪŋ/, **feelings. 1** COUNT N OR UNCOUNT N A **feeling** is an emotion or attitude. *A feeling of panic was rising in him... She tried to hide her feelings... ...a voice rich in real feeling.* **2** COUNT N WITH SUPP A **feeling** is also is a physical sensation. *...an itchy feeling... ...feelings of nausea.* **3** UNCOUNT N If you have no **feeling** in a part of your body, you do not know when that part is being touched. **4** COUNT N If you have a **feeling** that something is the case, you think that it is probably the case. *My feeling is that it would work very well... I have a nasty feeling you're right.* **5** UNCOUNT N **Feeling** for someone or something is affection for them. *He may be moved by feeling for his fellow-citizens.*

PHRASES ● **Bad feeling** is resentment or hostility between people. ● If you **hurt** someone's **feelings,** you upset them. ● If you have no **hard feelings** towards someone who has upset you, you do not feel angry with them.

feet /fiːt/. **Feet** is the plural of **foot.**

feign /feɪn/, **feigns, feigning, feigned.** VB WITH OBJ If you **feign** a feeling, you pretend to experience it; a literary use. *Her efforts to feign cheerfulness weren't convincing.* ♦ **feigned** ADJ *...with feigned surprise.*

feline /fiːlaɪn/. **1** ADJ **Feline** means belonging or relating to the cat family. **2** ADJ A **feline** person looks or moves like a cat. *...her feline charm.*

fell /fɛl/, **fells, felling, felled. 1 Fell** is the past tense of **fall. 2** VB WITH OBJ If you **fell** a tree, you cut it down.

fellow /fɛləʊ/, **fellows. 1** COUNT N A **fellow** is a man; an informal use. *Doug is an exceedingly amiable fellow.* **2** ATTRIB ADJ You use **fellow** to describe people who have something in common with you. *...a fellow passenger.* Also PLURAL N WITH POSS *He sought the approval of his fellows.* **3** COUNT N A **fellow** of a society or academic institution is a senior member of it.

fellowship /fɛlə⁶ʃɪp/, **fellowships. 1** UNCOUNT N **Fellowship** is a feeling of friendship that people have when they are doing something together. *...the atmosphere of cheerful good fellowship.* **2** COUNT N WITH SUPP A **fellowship** is a group of people that join together for a common purpose. *...the Socialist Fellowship.*

felony /fɛləni¹/, **felonies.** COUNT N A **felony** is a very serious crime such as armed robbery; a legal use.

felt /fɛlt/. **1 Felt** is the past tense and past participle of **feel. 2** UNCOUNT N **Felt** is a type of thick cloth made by pressing short threads together.

female /fiːmeɪl/, **females. 1** COUNT N You can refer to any creature that can produce babies from its body or lay eggs as a **female.** Also ADJ *...a female toad.* **2** COUNT N Women and girls are sometimes referred to as **females**; some people find this use offensive. *...a lone female staying at a hotel.* **3** ATTRIB ADJ **Female** means concerning or relating to women, or being a woman.. *...traditionally female areas of work... There are only nineteen female members of parliament.*

feminine /fɛmɪnɪn/. ADJ **Feminine** means relating to women or considered typical of or suitable for them. *...feminine clothes.* ♦ **femininity** /fɛmɪnɪni¹ti¹/ UNCOUNT N *The fashion industry responded to the new mood of femininity.*

feminism /fɛmɪnɪzə⁰m/. UNCOUNT N **Feminism** is the belief that women should have the same rights, power, and opportunities as men.

feminist /fɛmɪnɪst/, **feminists.** COUNT N A **feminist** is a person who believes in and supports feminism. *Claudia thought of herself as a feminist.* Also MOD *...the feminist response to the new law.*

fence /fɛns/, **fences, fencing, fenced. 1** COUNT N A **fence** is a barrier made of wood or wire supported by posts. **2** VB WITH OBJ If you **fence** an area of land, you surround it with a fence. ♦ **fenced** ADJ *...a fenced enclosure.* **3** PHRASE If you **sit on the fence,** you avoid supporting any side in a discussion or argument.

fence in. PHR VB If you **fence** something **in,** you surround it with a fence.

fence off. PHR VB If you **fence off** an area of land, you build a fence round it.

fencing /fɛnsɪŋ/. **1** UNCOUNT N **Fencing** is a sport in which two competitors fight using very thin swords. **2** UNCOUNT N **Fencing** is also materials used to make fences. *...cedar wood fencing.*

fend /fɛnd/, **fends, fending, fended.** PHRASE If you **fend for yourself,** you look after yourself without relying on help from anyone else. *Grown up children should leave home and fend for themselves.*

fend off. PHR VB **1** If you **fend off** someone who is attacking you, you use your arms or a stick to defend yourself. **2** If you **fend off** questions or requests, you avoid answering them. *She fended off all these claims.*

ferment, ferments, fermenting, fermented; pronounced /fɜːmɛnt/ when it is a noun and /fə⁵mɛnt/ when it is a verb. **1** UNCOUNT N **Ferment** is excitement and unrest caused by change or uncertainty. *Portugal was in ferment.* **2** ERG VB When wine, beer, or fruit **ferments** or **is fermented,** a chemical change takes place in it. ♦ **fermented** ADJ *...the whiff of fermented apples.* ♦ **fermentation** /fɜːmɛnteɪʃə⁰n/ UNCOUNT N *...the fermentation of wines.*

fern /fɜːn/, **ferns.** COUNT N A **fern** is a plant with long stems, feathery leaves, and no flowers.

ferocious /fərəʊʃəs/. ADJ A **ferocious** animal, person, or action is fierce and violent. *...two years of ferocious fighting.* ♦ **ferociously** ADV *The buck shook his antlers ferociously.*

ferocity /fərɒsi¹ti¹/. UNCOUNT N When something is done with **ferocity,** it is done in a fierce and violent way. *The attack was resumed with a new ferocity.*

ferret /fɛrɪt/, **ferrets, ferreting, ferreted.** COUNT N A **ferret** is a small, fierce animal used for hunting rabbits and rats.

ferret out. PHR VB If you **ferret out** information, you discover it by searching thoroughly; an informal use.

ferry /fɛri¹/, **ferries, ferrying, ferried. 1** COUNT N A **ferry** is a boat that carries passengers or vehicles across a river or a narrow bit of sea. *We got back to London by train and ferry.* **2** VB WITH OBJ To **ferry** people or goods somewhere means to transport them there. *They were ferried from one building to another.*

fertile /fɜːtaɪl/. **1** ADJ Land is **fertile** if plants grow easily in it. *...light, fertile soil.* ♦ **fertility** /fɜːtɪlɪti¹/ UNCOUNT N *...soil fertility.* **2** ATTRIB ADJ If someone has a **fertile** mind or imagination, they produce a lot of good or original ideas. **3** ADJ You describe a place or situation as **fertile** ground when you think that something is likely to succeed or develop there. *Britain is not fertile ground for news magazines.* **4** ADJ A woman who is **fertile** can have babies. ♦ **fertility** UNCOUNT N *Fertility rates have declined.*

fertilize /fɜːtɪlaɪz/, **fertilizes, fertilizing, fertilized**; also spelled **fertilise. 1** VB WITH OBJ When an egg or plant **is fertilized,** the process of reproduction begins by sperm joining with the egg, or by pollen coming into contact with the reproductive part of a plant. ♦ **fertilized** ADJ *The fertilised egg remains where it is for one more week.* ♦ **fertilization** /fɜːtɪlaɪzeɪʃə⁰n/ UNCOUNT N *...the small amount of pollen necessary for fertilization.* **2** VB WITH OBJ To **fertilize** land means to spread manure or chemicals on it to make plants grow well.

fertilizer /fɜːtɪlaɪzə/, **fertilizers**; also spelled **fertiliser.** MASS N **Fertilizer** is a substance that you spread on the ground to make plants grow more successfully.

fervent /fɜːvənt/. ADJ Someone who is **fervent** about something has strong and enthusiastic feelings about it. *...a fervent belief in God.* ♦ **fervently** ADV *'Oh, I am glad!' Scylla said fervently.*

fervour /fɜːvə/; spelled **fervor** in American English. UNCOUNT N **Fervour** is a very strong feeling in favour of something; a formal use. *'She's marvellous,' said Mrs Moffatt with fervour.*

fester /fɛstə/, **festers, festering, festered. 1** VB When a wound **festers,** it becomes infected and produces pus. *...a festering sore.* **2** VB If an unpleasant situation, feeling, or thought **festers,** it grows worse. *...the bitter row still festering between them.*

festival /fɛstɪvə⁰l/, **festivals. 1** COUNT N A **festival** is an organized series of events and performances. *...the London Film Festival.* **2** COUNT N A **festival** is also a day or period when people have a holiday and celebrate some special event, often a religious one.

festive /fɛstɪv/. ADJ Something that is **festive** is full of colour and happiness, especially because of a holiday or celebration. *...a festive occasion.*

festivity /fɛstɪvɪ¹ti¹/, **festivities. 1** UNCOUNT N **Festivity** is the celebrating of something in a happy way. *...four days of festivity.* **2** PLURAL N **Festivities** are things that people do to celebrate something. *The week is crammed with festivities.*

festooned /fɛstuːnd/. PASSIVE VB WITH 'with' If something **is festooned** with objects, the objects are hanging across it in large numbers. *The counters were festooned with rainbow-coloured scarves.*

fetch /fɛtʃ/, **fetches, fetching, fetched. 1** VB WITH OBJ OR VB WITH OBJ AND OBJ If you **fetch** something or someone, you go and get them from where they are. *He fetched a bucket of water from the pond... Scylla ran to fetch her guardian a long cool drink.* **2** VB WITH OBJ If something **fetches** a particular amount of money, it is sold for that amount. *His pictures fetch very high prices.* **3** See also **far-fetched.**

fetch up. PHR VB If you **fetch up** somewhere, you arrive there, usually without intending to; an American use.

fetching /fɛtʃɪŋ/. ADJ If a woman looks **fetching,** she looks attractive. *Melanie looked remarkably fetching in a white dress.*

fête /feɪt/, **fêtes, fêting, fêted**; also spelled **fete. 1** COUNT N A **fête** is an event held out of doors that includes competitions, entertainments, and the selling of home-made goods. *...the church fête.* **2** VB WITH OBJ If someone important **is fêted,** a public welcome is provided for them. *In New York, Karen Blixen was being fêted by everyone who knew her work.*

fetid /fɛtɪd, fiː-/. ADJ **Fetid** water or air has a strong, unpleasant smell; a formal use.

fetter /fɛtə/, **fetters, fettering, fettered**; a literary word. **1** VB WITH OBJ If something **fetters** you, it prevents you from behaving in a free and natural way. *...the forces that fetter our souls.* **2** COUNT N **Fetters** are things that prevent you from behaving in a free and natural way. *...freed from the fetters of control.*

fetus /fiːtəs/. See **foetus.**

feud /fjuːd/, **feuds, feuding, feuded. 1** COUNT N A **feud** is a long-lasting and bitter dispute. *His feud with the Premier proceeded remorselessly.* **2** RECIP VB If two people or groups **feud,** there is a feud between them. *They are constantly feuding amongst themselves.*

feudal /fjuːdə⁰l/. ATTRIB ADJ **Feudal** means relating to feudalism. *...a feudal society.*

feudalism /fjuːdə⁰lɪzə⁰m/. UNCOUNT N **Feudalism** was a system in which people were given land or protection by people of higher rank, and worked and fought for them in return.

fever /fiːvə/, **fevers. 1** COUNT N OR UNCOUNT N If you have a **fever,** your temperature is higher than usual because you are ill. ● See also **hay fever, scarlet fever, yellow fever. 2** COUNT N A **fever** is also extreme excitement or agitation. *He stayed calm through the fever of the campaign.*

feverish /fiːvə⁰rɪʃ/. **1** ADJ **Feverish** emotion or activity shows great excitement or agitation. *...the feverish excitement in his voice... ...a feverish race against time.* ♦ **feverishly** ADV *They worked feverishly.* **2** ADJ If you are **feverish,** you are suffering from a fever.

few /fjuː/, **fewer, fewest. 1** QUANTIF OR PRON **Few** is used to indicate a small number of things or people. *The window opened a few inches... A few were smoking.* **2** QUANTIF OR PRON **Few** is also used to indicate that a number of things or people is smaller than is desirable or than was expected. *Very few people survived... There are fewer trains at night... Few of them ever reach their potential.*

PHRASES ● Things that are **few and far between** are very rare or uncommon. ● You use **no fewer than** to suggest that a number is surprisingly large. *No fewer than five cameramen lost their lives.* ● You use **quite a few** and **a good few** when you are referring to quite a lot of things or people. *We had quite a few friendly arguments... I spent a good few years of my life there.*

fiancé /fi¹ɒnseɪ/, **fiancés**; spelled **fiancée** when referring to a woman. COUNT N Your **fiancé** or **fiancée** is the person you are engaged to.

fiasco /fi¹æskəʊ/, **fiascos.** COUNT N When something fails completely, you can describe it as a **fiasco,**

especially if it seems ridiculous or disorganized. *The meeting was a fiasco.*

fib /fɪb/, **fibs, fibbing, fibbed;** an informal word. **1** COUNT N A **fib** is a small lie which is not very important. **2** VB If you **are fibbing,** you are telling lies. *It isn't true! You're fibbing!*

fibre /faɪbə/, **fibres;** spelled **fiber** in American English. **1** COUNT N A **fibre** is a thin thread of a natural or artificial substance, especially one used to make cloth or rope. **2** UNCOUNT N **Fibre** consists of the parts of plants that your body cannot digest and absorb. *Scientists are recommending people to eat more fibre.* **3** COUNT N A **fibre** is also a thin piece of flesh like a thread which connects nerve cells in your body or which muscles are made of. *...nerve fibres.*

fibreglass /faɪbəglɑːs/; spelled **fiberglass** in American English. UNCOUNT N **Fibreglass** is plastic strengthened with short threads of glass.

fibrous /faɪbrəs/. ADJ Something that is **fibrous** contains a lot of fibres. *They eat a great deal of fibrous twigs and woody material.*

fickle /fɪkəˀl/. ADJ A **fickle** person keeps changing their mind about what they like or want.

fiction /fɪkʃəˀn/, **fictions. 1** UNCOUNT N **Fiction** is stories about imaginary people and events. *I enjoy reading fiction.* **2** UNCOUNT N OR COUNT N A **fiction** is something you pretend is true, although you know it is not. *We had to keep up the fiction of being a normal couple.*

fictional /fɪkʃəˀnəl, -ʃənəˀl/. **1** ADJ **Fictional** people and events are not real, but occur in stories, plays, and films. *...a fictional composer called Moony Shapiro.* **2** ATTRIB ADJ **Fictional** means relating to novels and stories. *...the fictional treatment of adultery.*

fictitious /fɪktɪʃəs/. ADJ Something that is **fictitious** is false or does not exist. *They bought the materials under fictitious names.*

fiddle /fɪdəˀl/, **fiddles, fiddling, fiddled. 1** VB If you **fiddle** with something, you keep moving it or touching it with your fingers. *He sat nervously fiddling with his spectacles.* **2** VB WITH OBJ When people **fiddle** something such as an account, they alter it dishonestly to get money for themselves; an informal use. *He had fiddled the figures in the transaction.* ♦ **fiddling** UNCOUNT N *A lot of fiddling goes on in these companies.* **3** COUNT N A **fiddle** is a dishonest action or scheme to get money. *Laing had worked some fiddle.* **4** COUNT N A **fiddle** is also a violin. **5** PHRASE If you **play second fiddle** to someone, your position is less important than theirs in something that you are doing together.

fiddly /fɪdliˡ/. ADJ Something that is **fiddly** is difficult to do or use, because it involves small or complicated objects; an informal use. *...a very fiddly job.*

fidelity /fɪdelɪˡtiˡ/; a formal word. **1** UNCOUNT N **Fidelity** is the quality of remaining firm in your beliefs and loyalties. *There's nothing like a dog's fidelity.* **2** UNCOUNT N The **fidelity** of a report, translation, or adaptation is its degree of accuracy. *...fidelity to the author's intentions.*

fidget /fɪdʒɪt/, **fidgets, fidgeting, fidgeted.** VB If you **fidget,** you keep moving your hands or feet or changing position slightly, because you are nervous or bored. *The children are starting to fidget.*

field /fiːld/, **fields, fielding, fielded. 1** COUNT N A **field** is an enclosed area of land where crops are grown or animals are kept. *...fields of wheat.* **2** COUNT N A sports **field** is a grassy area where sports are played. *...a football field.* **3** COUNT N WITH SUPP A magnetic or gravitational **field** is an area in which magnetism or gravity has an effect. **4** COUNT N WITH SUPP Your **field** of vision is the area that you can see without turning your head. *A brown figure dressed in red crept into her field of vision.* **5** COUNT N WITH SUPP A particular **field** is a subject or area of interest. *...the political field.* **6** ATTRIB ADJ A **field** trip or a **field** study involves research that is done in a real, natural environment rather than in a theoretical way. **7** VB The team that is **fielding** in a game of cricket or baseball is the team trying to catch the ball.

field-glasses. PLURAL N **Field-glasses** are binoculars.

field marshal, field marshals. COUNT N OR TITLE A **field marshal** is an army officer of the highest rank. *...Field Marshal Montgomery.*

fiend /fiːnd/, **fiends. 1** COUNT N If you call someone a **fiend,** you mean that they are very wicked or cruel; a literary use. *I have no idea who this murderous fiend may be.* **2** COUNT N AFTER N You can use **fiend** to describe someone who is very interested in a particular thing or who likes it very much; an informal use. *...that health fiend.*

fiendish /fiːndɪʃ/. **1** ADJ A **fiendish** person is very cruel. *...a fiendish despot.* **2** ADJ A **fiendish** problem or task is very difficult; an informal use. *...a task of fiendish complexity.*

fierce /fɪəs/, **fiercer, fiercest. 1** ADJ **Fierce** means very aggressive or angry. *...fierce dogs.* ♦ **fiercely** ADV *'Don't assume anything!' said Martha fiercely.* **2** ADJ **Fierce** also means extremely strong or intense. *...the fierce loyalty of these people... ...a fierce storm.* ♦ **fiercely** ADV *...a fiercely dedicated group of people.*

fiery /faɪəriˡ/. **1** ADJ Something that is **fiery** is burning strongly or contains fire. *...clouds of fiery gas.* **2** ADJ **Fiery** also means bright red. *The tonsils become fiery red and swollen.* **3** ADJ A **fiery** person behaves or speaks in an angry way. *...this fiery young man... ...a fiery speech.*

fifteen /fɪftiːn/. **Fifteen** is the number 15.

fifteenth /fɪftiːnθ/. ADJ The **fifteenth** item in a series is the one that you count as number fifteen.

fifth /fɪfθ/, **fifths. 1** ADJ The **fifth** item in a series is the one that you count as number five. **2** COUNT N A **fifth** is one of five equal parts of something. *Only one fifth of the surface area of Africa is farmland.*

fiftieth /fɪftiˡəθ/. ADJ The **fiftieth** item in a series is the one that you count as number fifty.

fifty /fɪftiˡ/, **fifties. Fifty** is the number 50.

fifty-fifty. 1 ADV OR ADJ When something is divided **fifty-fifty** between two people, each person gets half. *Profits were to be split fifty-fifty between us.* **2** ADJ If the chances of something happening are **fifty-fifty,** it is equally likely to happen as not to happen. *...a fifty-fifty chance of survival.*

fig /fɪg/, **figs.** COUNT N A **fig** is a soft, sweet fruit full of tiny seeds. Figs grow on trees in hot countries.

fig., figs. Fig. is used to refer to a particular diagram. It is an abbreviation for 'figure'. *The piston moves into a horizontal position (see fig. 3).*

fight /faɪt/, **fights, fighting, fought** /fɔːt/. **1** VB WITH OR WITHOUT OBJ If you **fight** something, you try in a determined way to stop it. *You can't fight against progress.* Also COUNT N *...the fight against illegal drugs.* **2** VB If you **fight** for something, you try in a determined way to get it or achieve it. *They will fight for their rights.* Also COUNT N *...the fight for equality.* **3** VB WITH OR WITHOUT OBJ When people **fight,** they try to hurt each other physically. *I learned how to fight other boys... He had fought in the First World War.* ♦ **fighting** UNCOUNT N *We were only metres away from the fighting.* **4** COUNT N A **fight** is a situation in which people hit or try to hurt each other physically. *There would be fights sometimes between the workers.* **5** VB WITH OR WITHOUT OBJ When people **fight** about something, they quarrel. *They fought about money... It's nice not having to fight you about housework.* **6** VB WITH OBJ When politicians **fight** an election, they try to win it. **7** VB WITH OBJ When you **fight** an emotion or desire, you try very hard not to feel it, show it, or act on it. *He fought the urge to cry.*

PHRASES • If you **fight** your **way** somewhere, you get there with difficulty, usually because there are a lot of people in your way. • If you **put up a fight,** you fight strongly against someone who is stronger than you are.

fight back. PHR VB **1** If you **fight back** against someone who has attacked you or made difficulties for you, you try to protect yourself and stop them or beat them. *The importing countries could fight back with laws of their own.* **2** When you **fight back** an emotion, you try very hard not to feel it, show it, or act on it. *She fought back the tears.*

fight off. PHR VB **1** If you **fight off** something such as an illness or unpleasant feeling, you succeed in getting rid of it. *We can fight off most minor ailments.* **2** If you **fight off** someone who has attacked you, you succeed in driving them away by fighting them.

fight out. PHR VB When two people or groups **fight** something **out,** they fight or argue until one of them wins. *...while the European nations were fighting it out on the battlefield.*

fighter /faɪtə/, **fighters. 1** COUNT N A **fighter** or a **fighter plane** is a fast military aircraft used for destroying other aircraft. **2** COUNT N A **fighter** is also someone who fights.

figment /fɪgməˀnt/, **figments.** COUNT N If you say that something is a **figment** of someone's imagination, you mean that it does not really exist and they are imagining it.

figuratively /fɪgəˀrətɪvliˡ/. ADV When someone is speaking **figuratively,** they are using a word or expression with a more abstract or imaginative meaning than its usual one. *'She said I killed him.'—'She was speaking figuratively.'*

figure /fɪgə/, **figures, figuring, figured. 1** COUNT N A **figure** is a particular amount expressed as a number, especially a statistic. *...unemployment figures.* **2** COUNT N A **figure** is also any of the ten written symbols from 0 to 9 that are used to represent a number. *...a three-figure number.* **3** COUNT N A **figure** is the shape of a person you cannot see clearly. *I could see a small female figure advancing towards us.* **4** COUNT N WITH SUPP Someone who is referred to as a particular type of **figure** is well-known and important in some way. *He was a key figure in the independence struggle.* **5** COUNT N WITH SUPP If you say that someone is, for example, a mother **figure** or a hero **figure,** you mean that they have the qualities typical of mothers or heroes. *...authority figures.* **6** COUNT N Your **figure** is the shape of your body. *She's got a fabulous figure.* **7** COUNT N A **figure** is also a drawing or diagram in a book. *The original design was modified (see Figure 4.)* **8** REPORT VB If you **figure** that something is the case, you think or guess that it is the case; an informal use. *They figured it was better to stay where they were.* **9** VB A thing or person that **figures** in something appears in it or is included in it. *Loneliness figures quite a lot in his conversation.*

PHRASES • A number in **double figures** is between ten and ninety-nine. A number in **single figures** is between nought and nine. • When you **put a figure on** an amount, you say exactly how much it is. *They said defence spending should be raised but put no figure on the increase they wanted.*

figure out. PHR VB If you **figure out** a solution to a problem or the reason for something, you work it out; an informal use. *She had not yet figured out what she was going to do.*

figurehead /fɪgəhed/, **figureheads.** COUNT N If you refer to the leader of a movement or organization as a **figurehead,** you mean that he or she has little real power.

figure of speech, figures of speech. COUNT N A **figure of speech** is an expression or word that is used with a more abstract or imaginative meaning than its original one.

filament /fɪləməˀnt/, **filaments.** COUNT N A **filament** is a very thin piece or thread of something.

filch /fɪltʃ/, **filches, filching, filched.** VB WITH OBJ If someone **filches** something, they steal it; an informal use.

file /faɪl/, **files, filing, filed. 1** COUNT N A **file** is a box or folder in which documents are kept. *He closed the file and looked up at Rodin.* **2** VB WITH OBJ When you **file** a document, you put it in the correct file. *Bills are not filed under B; but under U for unpleasant.* **3** COUNT N In computing, a **file** is a set of related data with its own name. **4** VB WITH OBJ OR 'for' When you **file** a complaint or request, you make it officially. *...a lawsuit they have filed... I'm filing for divorce.* **5** VB WITH ADJUNCT When a group of people **files** somewhere, they walk one behind the other in a line. *They filed out in silence.* **6** COUNT N A **file** is also a tool with rough surfaces, used for smoothing and shaping hard materials. **7** VB WITH OBJ If you **file** an object, you smooth or shape it with a file. *...filing her fingernails.*

PHRASES • Something that is **on file** or **on the files** is recorded in a collection of information. *The police had both men on their files.* • A group of people who are moving along **in single file** are in a line, one behind the other.

filial /fɪljəl/. ADJ **Filial** means relating to the status or duties of a son or daughter; a formal use. *...a sense of filial obligation.*

filing cabinet, filing cabinets. COUNT N A **filing cabinet** is a piece of office furniture with deep drawers in which files are kept.

fill /fɪl/, **fills, filling, filled. 1** VB WITH OBJ If you **fill** a container or area, you put a large amount of something into it, so that it is full. *Fill the teapot with boiling water.* **2** VB WITH OBJ If something **fills** a space, it is so large that there is very little room left. *Enthusiastic crowds filled the streets.* ♦ **filled** PRED ADJ *...a large hall filled with rows of desks.* **3** VB To **fill** means to become full of things, people, or a substance. *Madeleine's eyes filled with tears.* **4** VB WITH OBJ If something **fills** you with an emotion or if an emotion **fills** you, you experience this emotion strongly. *His son's lies filled him with anger.* **5** VB WITH OBJ If something **fills** a need or gap, its activity or existence satisfies or stops it. *The Alliance filled the political vacuum.* **6** VB WITH OBJ Something that **fills** a role or position performs a particular function or has a particular place within a system. *It has filled this role in a most satisfactory way for many years.* **7** PHRASE If you **have had your fill** of something, you do not want to experience it or do it any more. **8** See also **filling.**

fill in. PHR VB **1** When you **fill in** a form, you write information in the spaces on it. *Fill in your name and address.* **2** If you **fill** someone **in,** you give them detailed information about something. *I'll fill you in on the details now.* **3** If you **fill in** for someone else, you do their job for them in their absence.

fill out. PHR VB **1** When you **fill out** a form, you write information in the spaces on it. *I've filled out the death certificate.* **2** If a thin person **fills out,** he or she becomes fatter.

fill up. PHR VB **1** If you **fill up** a container, you put a large amount of something into it, so that it is full. *Fill up his seed bowl twice a day.* 2 If a place **fills up,** it becomes full of things or people. *His office began to fill up with people.*

fillet /fɪlɪt/, **fillets.** COUNT N OR UNCOUNT N A **fillet** of fish or meat is a piece that has no bones in it.

filling /fɪlɪŋ/, **fillings.** 1 COUNT N A **filling** is a small amount of metal or plastic that a dentist puts in a hole in a tooth. 2 MASS N The **filling** in a pie, chocolate, sandwich or cake is the mixture inside it. *...delicious chocolates with cream fillings.* 3 ADJ Food that is **filling** makes you feel full when you have eaten it.

filling station, filling stations. COUNT N A **filling station** is a place where you can buy petrol and oil for your car.

film /fɪlm/, **films, filming, filmed.** 1 COUNT N OR UNCOUNT N A **film** consists of moving pictures that have been recorded so that they can be shown in a cinema or on television. *Shall we go and see a film?... The broadcast began with close-up film of babies crying.* 2 VB WITH OR WITHOUT OBJ If you **film** someone or something, you use a camera to take moving pictures which can be shown in a cinema or on television. *The TV crews couldn't film at night.* 3 COUNT N OR UNCOUNT N A **film** is also the roll of thin plastic that you use in a camera to take photographs. *...a roll of film.* 4 COUNT N A **film** of powder, liquid, or grease is a very thin layer of it.

filming /fɪlmɪŋ/. UNCOUNT N **Filming** is the activity of making a film, including acting, directing, and operating of the cameras. *I found filming exhausting.*

filter /fɪltə/, **filters, filtering, filtered.** 1 VB WITH OBJ To **filter** a substance means to pass it through a device which is designed to remove particles from it. *Water would have to be filtered many times to remove any radioactive matter.* 2 COUNT N A **filter** is a device through which something is filtered. 3 VB WITH ADJUNCT When light or sound **filters** into a place, it comes in faintly. *...with the morning light already filtering through the curtains.* 4 VB WITH ADJUNCT When news or information **filters** through to people, it gradually reaches them. *Disturbing rumours filtered back from the East.*

filter out. PHR VB To **filter out** something from a substance means to remove it by passing the substance through a filter. *First we would have to filter out some of the tar particles.*

filth /fɪlθ/. 1 UNCOUNT N **Filth** is a large amount of dirt that disgusts you. *...the filth and decay of the villages.* 2 UNCOUNT N People refer to words or pictures as **filth** when they think that they describe or represent something such as sex or nudity in a disgusting way.

filthy /fɪlθiˡ/, **filthier, filthiest.** 1 ADJ Something that is **filthy** is very dirty indeed. *...a really filthy oven.* 2 ADJ People describe words or pictures as **filthy** when they think that they describe or represent sex or nudity in a disgusting way. *...a filthy book.*

fin /fɪn/, **fins.** COUNT N A fish's **fins** are the flat objects which stick out of its body and help it to swim.

final /faɪnəl/, **finals.** 1 ATTRIB ADJ In a series of events, things, or people, the **final** one is the last one, or the one that happens at the end. *...on the final morning of the festival... We made our final attempt to beat the record... The final applause was explosive.* 2 ATTRIB ADJ **Final** also means the greatest or most severe that is possible. *He paid the final penalty for his crime.* 3 ADJ If a decision is **final,** it cannot be changed or questioned. *The judges' decision is final.* 4 COUNT N WITH SUPP A **final** is the last game or contest in a series which decides the overall winner. *I'm trying to get tickets for the Cup Final.* 5 PLURAL N **Finals** are the last and most important examinations in a university or college course.

finale /fɪnɑːliˡ/, **finales.** COUNT N The **finale** is the last section of a show or a piece of music. *...the Finale of Beethoven's Violin Concerto.*

finalist /faɪnəlɪst/, **finalists.** COUNT N A **finalist** is someone who takes part in the final of a competition. *...an Olympic finalist.*

finality /faɪnælɪˡtiˡ/. UNCOUNT N If you say something with **finality,** it is clear that you will not say anything else relating to that matter. *Margaret said quietly but with finality: 'Well, we'll just have to disagree over this.'*

finalize /faɪnəlaɪz/, **finalizes, finalizing, finalized;** also spelled **finalise.** VB WITH OBJ If you **finalize** something that you are arranging, you complete the arrangements for it. *I'm hoping to finalize things with the builders next week.*

finally /faɪnəliˡ/. 1 ADV If you say that something **finally** happened, you mean that it happened after a long delay. *They finally realized that the whole thing was a joke.* 2 ADV You use **finally** to indicate that something is the last in a series. *Trotsky lived in Turkey, France, Norway and finally Mexico.* 3 SENTENCE ADV You also use **finally** to introduce a final point, question, or topic. *Finally, Carol, are you encouraged by the direction education is taking?... Let's come finally to the question of pensions.*

finance /fɪnæns, faɪnæns/, **finances, financing, financed.** 1 VB WITH OBJ To **finance** a project or purchase means to provide money for it. *A private company will finance and build the pipeline.* 2 UNCOUNT N **Finance** for a project or purchase is the money needed to pay for it. *The Group raises finance for oil drilling.* 3 UNCOUNT N **Finance** is also the management of money, especially on a national level. *...public-sector finance... ...a successful job in high finance.* 4 PLURAL N Your **finances** are the amount of money that you have. *Whether it can be done depends, of course, on your finances.*

financial /fɪˢnænʃəˡl/. ADJ **Financial** means relating to or involving money. *The company was in deep financial difficulties.* ♦ **financially** SUBMOD *The venture was not financially successful.*

financier /fɪˢnænsɪə/, **financiers.** COUNT N A **financier** is a person who provides money for projects or enterprises.

finch /fɪntʃ/, **finches.** COUNT N A **finch** is a small bird with a short strong beak.

find /faɪnd/, **finds, finding, found** /faʊnd/. 1 VB WITH OBJ If you **find** something that you are looking for, you discover it, see it, or learn where it is. *She found a crack in one of the tea-cups... She looked up to find Tony standing there.* 2 VB WITH OBJ If you **find** something that you need or want, you succeed in getting it. *He cannot find work... I had not yet found the answer.* 3 REPORT VB OR VB WITH OBJ AND COMPLEMENT If you **find** that something is the case, you become aware of it or realize it. *When I got back, I found that the reading lamp would not work... I don't find that funny at all... I found him a disappointment... Others may find them of value.* 4 REFL VB WITH -ING If you **find** yourself doing something, you do it without intending to. *He found himself giggling uncontrollably.* 5 PASSIVE VB If you say that something **is found** in a particular place, you mean that it is in that place. *Four different species of lungfish are found in Africa.* 6 PHRASE If you **find** your **way** somewhere, you get there by choosing the right way to go. 7 VB WITH OBJ If you **find** the time to do something, you manage to do it even though you are busy. *How do you find time to write these books?* 8 VB WITH OBJ AND COMPLEMENT When a court or jury **finds** a person guilty or not guilty, they decide if that person is guilty or innocent. *He was found guilty of murder.* 9 COUNT N If you describe something that has been discovered as a **find,** you mean that it is interesting, good, or useful. *Among the finds so far are pottery and jewellery... Liz Pym, who plays the heroine, is a real find.* 10 to **find fault:** see **fault.** 11 See also **found.**

find out. PHR VB 1 If you **find** something **out,** you learn it, often by making a deliberate effort. *I found out the train times.* 2 If you **find** someone **out,** you discover they have been doing something dishonest.

finding /faɪndɪŋ/, **findings.** COUNT N Someone's **findings** are the information they get as the result of an investigation or some research. *...the findings of the committee.*

fine /faɪn/, **finer, finest; fines, fining, fined.** 1 ADJ You use **fine** to describe something that is very good. *From the top there is a fine view.* 2 PRED ADJ If something is **fine,** it is satisfactory or acceptable. *'Do you want it stronger than that?'—'No, that's fine.'* Also ADV *We get on fine.* 3 CONVENTION If you say that you are **fine,** you mean that you are feeling well and quite happy. *'How are you?'—'Fine, thanks.'* 4 ADJ Something that is **fine** consists of very small or narrow parts. *...fine hair... ...handfuls of fine sand.* ♦ **finely** ADV *...finely chopped meat.* 5 ADJ A **fine** adjustment or distinction is very delicate or exact. *Their eyes are trained to see the fine detail.* ♦ **finely** ADV *...finely balanced systems.* 6 ADJ When the weather is **fine,** it is sunny and not raining. *...a fine summer's day.* 7 VB WITH OBJ If you **are fined,** you are punished by being ordered to pay a sum of money. *The demonstrators were fined £5 each for breach of the peace.* 8 COUNT N A **fine** is a sum of money which someone has to pay as a punishment. *He paid a £10,000 fine for income tax evasion.*

fine art, fine arts. UNCOUNT N OR PLURAL N **Fine art** is painting, sculpture, and objects which are made to be admired rather than to be useful. *...a fine art course... He was no expert in the fine arts.*

finery /faɪnəˡriˡ/. UNCOUNT N **Finery** is beautiful and impressive clothing and jewellery. *The ladies were dressed up in all their finery.*

finesse /fɪnɛs/. UNCOUNT N If you do something with **finesse,** you do it with great skill and elegance.

finger /fɪŋgə/, **fingers, fingering, fingered.** 1 COUNT N Your **fingers** are the four long parts at the end of each of your hands. *She ran her fingers through the cool grass... He held it between his finger and thumb.* 2 VB WITH OBJ If you **finger** something, you touch or feel it with your finger. *Eric fingered his split lip.*

PHRASES ● If you **put** your **finger on** a reason or problem, you identify it. *He immediately put his finger on what was wrong.* ● To **point the finger** at someone means to blame them or accuse them of something. ● to have **green fingers:** see **green.**

fingernail /fɪŋgəneɪl/, **fingernails.** COUNT N Your **fingernails** are the hard areas on the ends of your fingers.

fingerprint /fɪŋgəprɪnt/, **fingerprints.** COUNT N A **fingerprint** is a mark made by the tip of your finger showing the lines on the skin. *He was careful, leaving no fingerprints.* ● When the police **take** your **fingerprints,** they make you press your fingers onto an inky pad and then onto paper, so that they can see what your fingerprints look like.

fingertip /fɪŋgətɪp/, **fingertips.** COUNT N Your **fingertips** are the ends of your fingers.

finish /fɪnɪʃ/, **finishes, finishing, finished.** 1 VB WITH OBJ When you **finish** something, you reach the end of it and complete it. *I've finished reading your book... Brody finished his sandwich.* ● The **finishing touches** are the last, detailed thing you have to do in order to complete something. *She had been putting the finishing touches to her make-up.* 2 VB When something **finishes,** it ends. *The course starts in October and finishes in June.* 3 SING N The **finish** of something is the the last part of it. *In a thrilling finish, she won by two shots.* 4 VB WITH OBJ If you **finish** work at a particular time, you stop working or studying at that time. *I finish work at 3.* 5 VB WITH ADJUNCT OR COMPLEMENT In a race or competition, the position that someone **finishes** in is the position they are in at the end. *He finished fifth.* 6 UNCOUNT N OR COUNT N An object's **finish** is the appearance or texture of its surface. *Metallic finish is standard on this car... ...a fabric which has a special finish.* 7 See also **finished.**

finish off. PHR VB 1 When you **finish** something **off,** you do the last part of it. *He finished off his thesis.* 2 When you **finish off** something that you have been eating or drinking, you eat or drink the last part of it. *He finished off the wine with a couple of swallows.*

finish up. PHR VB If you **finish up** in a particular place or situation, you are in that place or situation after doing something. *She'll be starting in Southampton and finishing up in London... They finished up serving in a shop.*

finish with. PHR VB When you **finish with** someone or something, you stop being involved with them. *I haven't finished with you yet.*

finished /fɪnɪʃt/. 1 PRED ADJ If you are **finished** with something, you are no longer dealing with it, or are no longer interested in it. *He won't be finished for at least half an hour... He was finished with marriage.* 2 PRED ADJ If someone or something is **finished,** they no longer exist or are no longer important. *All that is finished now... If that happens, Richard is finished.*

finishing school, finishing schools. COUNT N OR UNCOUNT N A **finishing school** is a private school where upper-class young women are taught manners and other social skills.

finite /faɪnaɪt/. ADJ Something that is **finite** has a limited size which cannot be increased; a formal use. *We have a finite number of places.*

fir /fɜː/, **firs.** COUNT N A **fir** is a tall, pointed, evergreen tree.

fire /faɪə/, **fires, firing, fired.** 1 UNCOUNT N **Fire** is the hot, bright flames produced by things that are burning. 2 COUNT N OR UNCOUNT N A **fire** is an occurrence of uncontrolled burning. *A fire had severely damaged the school... His neighbour's house is not insured against fire.* 3 COUNT N A **fire** is also a burning pile of fuel that you have set light to. *He lit a fire and cooked a meal.* 4 COUNT N A device that uses electricity or gas to give out heat is also called a **fire.** 5 VB WITH OR WITHOUT OBJ If someone **fires** a gun or **fires** a bullet, they cause a bullet to be sent from a gun. *I fired three or four times in quick succession.* ♦ **firing** SING N *The firing stopped.* 6 UNCOUNT N Shots fired from a gun or guns are referred to as **fire.** *We climbed up the hill under fire.* 7 VB WITH OBJ If you **fire** questions at someone, you say a lot of them quickly. 8 VB WITH OBJ If your employer **fires** you, he or she dismisses you from your job; an informal use. *Graffman fired him for incompetence.*

PHRASES ● Something that is **on fire** is burning and is being destroyed. *Two vehicles were on fire.* ● If something **catches fire,** it starts burning. ● If you **set fire** to something, you start it burning. *He set fire to the church.*

firearm /faɪərɑːm/, **firearms.** COUNT N **Firearms** are guns.

fire brigade, fire brigades. COUNT N The **fire brigade** is an organization which puts out fires.

fire engine, fire engines. COUNT N A **fire engine** is a large vehicle used to carries firemen and their equipment.

fire escape, fire escapes. COUNT N A **fire escape** is a metal staircase on the outside of a building which people can use to escape from a fire in the building.

fire extinguisher, fire extinguishers. COUNT N A **fire extinguisher** is a metal cylinder containing water or chemicals which can put out fires.

firelight /faɪəlaɪt/. UNCOUNT N **Firelight** is the light that comes from a fire.

fireman /faɪəmə^{3}n/, **firemen.** COUNT N A **fireman** is a person whose job is to put out fires. *Firemen turned their hoses on the flames.*

fireplace /faɪəpleɪs/, **fireplaces.** COUNT N A **fireplace** is an opening in the wall of a room where you can light a fire. *There was a portrait of his wife over the fireplace.*

firepower /faɪəpaʊə/. UNCOUNT N The **firepower** of an army, ship, tank, or aircraft is the amount of ammunition it can fire.

fireproof /faɪəpru:f/. ADJ **Fireproof** things cannot be damaged by fire. *...fireproof clothing.*

fireside /faɪəsaɪd/, **firesides.** COUNT N If you sit by the **fireside** in a room, you sit near the fire. *...sitting comfortably by his fireside... ...a fireside chat.*

fire station, fire stations. COUNT N A **fire station** is a building where fire engines are kept.

firewood /faɪəwʊd/. UNCOUNT N **Firewood** is wood that has been prepared for burning on a fire.

firework /faɪəwɜ:k/, **fireworks.** COUNT N **Fireworks** are small objects with chemicals inside them that burn with coloured sparks or smoke when you light them. *A few fireworks went off... ...a firework display.*

firing squad, firing squads. COUNT N A **firing squad** is a group of soldiers ordered to shoot dead a person who has been sentenced to death.

firm /fɜ:m/, **firms; firmer, firmest.** 1 COUNT N A **firm** is a business selling or producing something. *He was a partner in a firm of solicitors.* 2 ADJ Something that is **firm** does move easily when pressed, pushed, or shaken. *...a firm mattress... ...a firm ladder.* ♦ **firmly** ADV *Each block rested firmly on the block below it.* 3 ADJ A **firm** grasp or push is one which is strong and controlled. *I took a firm hold on the rope... ...firm pressure.* ♦ **firmly** ADV *She grasped the cork firmly.* 4 ADJ A **firm** decision, opinion, or piece of information is definite and unlikely to change. *...a person with firm views... No firm evidence had come to light.* ♦ **firmly** ADV *His sister was firmly of the belief that he was crazy.* 5 ADJ A **firm** person behaves with authority and shows that they will not change their mind. *...firm leadership... 'No,' said Mother in a firm voice.* ♦ **firmly** ADV *I shall tell her quite firmly that it is not any business of hers.* ♦ **firmness** UNCOUNT N *She treated the children with kindliness and firmness.*

first /fɜ:st/. 1 ADJ The **first** thing, person, event, or period of time is the one that is earlier than all the others of the same kind. *...the first man in space... ...the first two years of life.* 2 ADV If you do something **first,** you do it before anyone else does it, or before you do anything else. *Ralph spoke first... First I went to see the editor of the Dispatch.* 3 ADJ OR ADV When something happens or is done for the **first** time, it has never happened or been done before. *For the first time in our lives something really exciting has happened... Vita and Harold first met in the summer of 1910.* 4 SING N An event that is described as a **first** has never happened before. *It's a first for me too.* 5 ADJ The **first** thing, person, or place in a line is the one that is nearest to the front or nearest to you. *They took their seats in the first three rows.* 6 PRON The **first** you hear of or know about something is the time when you first become aware of it. *The first Mr Walker knew about it was when he saw it in the local paper.* 7 PHRASE You use **at first** when you are talking about what happens in the early part of an event or experience, in contrast to what happens later. *At first I was reluctant.* 8 SENTENCE ADV You say **first** when you are about to mention the first in a series of items. *There were several reasons for this. First, four submarines had been sighted.* 9 ADJ **First** refers to the best or most important thing or person of a particular kind. *She won first prize... The first duty of the state is to ensure that law and order prevail.* 10 ADV If you put someone or something **first,** you treat them as more important than anything else. *Put your career first... Your family must always come first.*

first aid. UNCOUNT N **First aid** is medical treatment given as soon as possible to a sick or injured person. *The wounded were given first aid... ...my first-aid kit.*

first-class. 1 ADJ Something or someone that is **first-class,** is of the highest quality. *...a first-class administrator... ...a first class honours degree in applied chemistry.* 2 ADJ **First-class** accommodation on public transport is the best and most expensive type of accommodation. *...a first-class rail ticket.* Also ADV *...flying first class.* 3 ADJ OR ADV **First-class** postage is the quicker and more expensive type of postage.

first floor. 1 SING N In British English, the **first floor** of a building is the floor immediately above the ground floor. 2 SING N In American English, the **first floor** of a building is the ground floor.

first-hand. ATTRIB ADJ **First-hand** information or experience is gained directly, rather than from other people or from books. *They have first-hand experience of charitable organizations.* Also ADV *This sort of experience can only be gained first-hand.*

firstly /fɜ:stli^1/. SENTENCE ADV You use **firstly** when you are about to mention the first in a series of items. *There are two reasons. Firstly I have no evidence that the original document has been destroyed.*

first name, first names. COUNT N Your **first name** is the first of the names that you were given when you were born, as opposed to your surname. *Nobody called Daintry by his first name because nobody knew it.*

first-rate. ADJ If someone or something is **first-rate,** they are excellent and of the highest quality. *...a first-rate golfer... ...first-rate performances.*

first school, first schools. COUNT N In Britain, a **first school** is a school for children aged between five and nine.

fiscal /fɪskə^{0}l/. ATTRIB ADJ **Fiscal** is used to describe something relating to government taxes; a technical use. *...fiscal controls.*

fish /fɪʃ/, **fishes, fishing, fished.** The plural of the noun is usually **fish,** but **fishes** is also used. 1 COUNT N A **fish** is a creature with a tail and fins that lives in water. 2 UNCOUNT N **Fish** is the flesh of a fish eaten as food. *...fish and chips.* 3 VB If you **fish,** you try to catch fish. *They went fishing and caught half a dozen trout.* 4 VB WITH OBJ If you **fish** a particular area of water, you try to catch fish there. *It was the first trawler ever to fish those waters.* 5 VB If you **fish** for information or praise, you try to get it indirectly. *I think he was just fishing for compliments.* 6 VB WITH OBJ AND ADJUNCT If you **fish** something out of a liquid or a container, you remove it; an informal use. *He fished a gold watch from his pocket.*

fisherman /fɪʃəmə^{3}n/, **fishermen.** COUNT N A **fisherman** is a man who catches fish as a job or for sport.

fishery /fɪʃə^{0}ri^1/, **fisheries.** COUNT N **Fisheries** are areas of the sea where many fish are caught.

fishing /fɪʃɪŋ/. UNCOUNT N **Fishing** is the sport, hobby, or business of catching fish. *Fishing has been a profitable industry lately... ...a small fishing boat.*

fishing rod, fishing rods. COUNT N A **fishing rod** is a pole with a line and hook attached to it which is used for fishing.

fishmonger /fɪʃmʌŋgə/, **fishmongers.** COUNT N A **fishmonger** is a shopkeeper who sells fish; a British use.

fishy /fɪʃi^1/. 1 ADJ Something that smells or tastes **fishy** smells or tastes like fish. *It had a fishy flavour.* 2 ADJ If something seems **fishy** to you, it seems dishonest or suspicious; an informal use. *The film world is full of barmy and fishy people.*

fission /fɪʃə^{0}n/. UNCOUNT N Nuclear **fission** is the splitting of the nucleus of an atom to produce a large amount of energy.

fissure /fɪʃə/, **fissures.** COUNT N A **fissure** is a deep crack in rock or in the ground; a formal use.

fist /fɪst/, **fists.** COUNT N You refer to someone's hand as their **fist** when they have bent their fingers towards their palm. *I shook my fist... The Marine held it tightly in his fist.*

fistful /fɪstfʊl/, **fistfuls.** COUNT N A **fistful** of things is the number of them that you can hold in your fist. *He handed me a fistful of letters.*

fit /fɪt/, **fits, fitting, fitted; fitter, fittest.** In American English **fit** can also be used for the past tense and past participle of the verb. 1 VB WITH OR WITHOUT OBJ Something that **fits** is the right size and shape for a particular person or object, or is suitable for them in some way. *The boots fitted Rudolph perfectly... The metal cover fits over the tap... The description fits women better than it fits men.* 2 SING N If something is a good **fit,** it fits well. 3 VB WITH ADJUNCT If something **fits** into something else, it is small enough to be able to go in it. *All my clothes fit into one suitcase.* 4 VB WITH OBJ AND ADJUNCT If you **fit** something into the right space or place, you put it there. *Philip fitted his key into the lock.* 5 VB WITH OBJ If you **fit** something somewhere, you put it there carefully and securely. *Castors can be fitted to a bed to make it easier to pull... The kitchen has been fitted with a stainless steel sink.* 6 PRED ADJ If someone or something is **fit** for a particular purpose, they are suitable or appropriate for it. *The houses are now fit for human habitation... She regarded herself as fit to be a governess.* 7 ADJ Someone who is **fit** is healthy and physically strong. *She works hard at keeping fit.* ♦ **fitness** UNCOUNT N *They were trained to a peak of physical fitness.* 8 COUNT N If someone has a **fit,** they suddenly lose consciousness and their body makes uncontrollable movements. *...an epileptic fit.* 9 COUNT N WITH SUPP If you have a **fit** of coughing or laughter, you suddenly start coughing or laughing in an uncontrollable way. *She had a coughing fit.* 10 COUNT N WITH 'of' If you do something in a **fit** of anger or panic, you are very angry or afraid when you do it. *In a fit of rage, he had flung Paul's violin out of the window.* 11 See also **fitted, fitter, fitting.**

PHRASES ● If someone **sees fit** to do something, they decide that it is the right thing to do; a formal use. *The present government has seen fit to cut back on spending.* ● Something that happens **in fits and starts** keeps happening and then stopping again. ● **not in a fit state:** see **state.**

fit in or **fit into.** PHR VB 1 If you **fit** something **in** or **fit** something **into** your schedule, you find time to do it. *You seem to fit in an enormous amount every day.* 2 If you **fit in** or if you **fit into** a group, you are similar to the other people in the group. *These children are unable to fit into ordinary society when they leave school.*

fitful /fɪtfʊl/. ADJ Something that is **fitful** happens for irregular periods of time. *He dozed off into a fitful sleep.*

fitted /fɪtɪ^{2}d/. 1 PRED ADJ If you are **fitted** to something or **fitted** to do something, you have the right qualities for it; a formal use. *Those best fitted to their surroundings will survive.* 2 ATTRIB ADJ **Fitted** clothes or furnishings are designed to be exactly the right size for their purpose. *Dolly wore a grey dress with a fitted bodice... ...a fitted carpet.* 3 ATTRIB ADJ **Fitted** furniture is designed to fill a particular space and is fixed in place. *...fitted wardrobes.*

fitter /fɪtə/, **fitters.** COUNT N A **fitter** is a person whose job is to put together or install machinery or equipment. *He got a job as an electrical fitter.*

fitting /fɪtɪŋ/, **fittings.** 1 ADJ If something is **fitting,** it is right or suitable. *As I was the eldest, it was fitting that I should go first.* 2 COUNT N A **fitting** is a small part on the outside of a piece of equipment or furniture, such as a handle or a tap. 3 PLURAL N **Fittings** are things such as cookers or electric fires that are fixed inside a building but can be removed to another building. *Make sure you know what fixtures and fittings will be left at your new home.*

five /faɪv/, **fives. Five** is the number 5.

fiver /faɪvə/, **fivers.** COUNT N A **fiver** is five pounds, or a note worth five pounds; an informal use. *You owe me a fiver.*

fix /fɪks/, **fixes, fixing, fixed.** 1 VB WITH OBJ AND ADJUNCT If you **fix** something somewhere, you attach it or put it there firmly and securely. *He had the sign fixed to the gate... She fixed a jewelled brooch on her dress.* 2 VB WITH OBJ AND 'on' If you **fix** your eyes or attention on something, you look at it or think about it with complete attention. *She fixed her brown eyes on him.* 3 VB WITH OBJ If you **fix** the date or amount of something, you decide and arrange exactly what it will be. *All that remained was to fix the date of the wedding.* 4 VB WITH OBJ To **fix** something means to repair it. *I learned how to fix radios in the Army.* 5 VB WITH OBJ If a race or a competition **was fixed,** it was won unfairly or dishonestly; an informal use. 6 VB WITH OBJ To **fix** someone a drink or some food means to prepare it for them; an informal use. *Would you like me to fix you a drink?* 7 COUNT N A **fix** is an injection of an addictive drug such as heroin; an informal use. 8 See also **fixed.**

fix up. PHR VB 1 If you **fix** someone **up** with something they need, you provide it. *They told me that they could fix me up with tickets.* 2 If you **fix** something **up,** you arrange it. *The holiday is all fixed up.*

fixation /fɪkseɪʃə^{0}n/, **fixations.** COUNT N A **fixation** is an extreme or obsessive interest in something. *...the sport fixation of the British.*

fixed /fɪkst/. 1 ADJ A **fixed** amount, pattern, method, or opinion always stays the same. *The signal goes on sounding at fixed intervals... ...a fixed pattern of behaviour... Children can be raised without fixed ideas and prejudices.* 2 PRED ADJ If something is **fixed** in your mind, you remember it well. *The scene was firmly fixed in all our minds.*

fixedly /fɪksə^{1}dli^1/. ADV If you stare **fixedly** at someone or something, you look at them steadily and continuously.

fixture /fɪkstʃə/, **fixtures.** 1 COUNT N A **fixture** is a piece of furniture or equipment which is fixed inside a building and which remains there when you move. *...the light fixture on the ceiling.* 2 COUNT N If something or someone is a **fixture** in a particular place, they are always there. *Pool seems likely to become a fixture in working-class pubs.* 3 COUNT N In sport, a **fixture** is a competition arranged for a particular date; a British use. *We had to cancel a lot of fixtures... Most athletic clubs produce their own fixture lists.*

fizz /fɪz/, **fizzes, fizzing, fizzed.** VB If a liquid, especially a drink, **fizzes,** it produces lots of little bubbles of gas.

fizzle /fɪzə°l/, **fizzles, fizzling, fizzled.**

fizzle out PHR VB If something **fizzles out,** it ends in a weak or disappointing way; an informal use. *The strike fizzled out after three days.*

fizzy /fɪzi¹/. ADJ A **fizzy** drink is full of little bubbles of gas. *...fizzy lemonade.*

flabbergasted /flæbəgɑ:stɪ²d/. ADJ If you are **flabbergasted,** you are extremely surprised; an informal use. *I stared at him, flabbergasted.*

flabby /flæbi¹/. ADJ **Flabby** people are fat and have loose flesh on their bodies. *...her flabby arms.*

flag /flæg/, **flags, flagging, flagged. 1** COUNT N A **flag** is a piece of coloured cloth used as a sign or a signal, or a symbol of something such as a country. *...a ship flying a foreign flag... The guard blew his whistle and waved his flag.* **2** VB If you **flag,** you begin to lose enthusiasm or energy. *They showed signs of flagging.* ♦ **flagging** ADJ *She tried to revive their flagging energies.*

flag down. PHR VB If you **flag down** a vehicle, you signal to the driver to stop.

flagon /flægə°n/, **flagons.** COUNT N A **flagon** is a large wide bottle or jug for cider or wine.

flagpole /flægpəʊl/, **flagpoles.** COUNT N A **flagpole** is a tall pole used to display a flag.

flagrant /fleɪgrənt/. ATTRIB ADJ **Flagrant** actions or situations are openly shocking and bad. *...a flagrant violation of human rights... ...flagrant injustices.*

flagship /flægʃɪp/, **flagships.** COUNT N A **flagship** is the most important ship in a fleet.

flagstone /flægstəʊn/, **flagstones.** COUNT N **Flagstones** are big, flat, square pieces of stone used for paving.

flail /fleɪl/, **flails, flailing, flailed.** ERG VB If your arms or legs **flail** about, they wave about wildly. *The baby flailed her little arms... ...his flailing arms.*

flair /fleə/. **1** SING N OR UNCOUNT N A **flair** for doing something is a natural ability to do it. *He had a flair for this branch of law... Wilson was impressed by his political flair.* **2** UNCOUNT N **Flair** is also the ability to do things in an original, interesting, and stylish way. *She showed her usual flair and cunning.*

flak /flæk/. **1** UNCOUNT N **Flak** is a large number of explosive shells being fired at planes from the ground. *I saw one of the Dakotas hit by flak.* **2** UNCOUNT N You can also refer to severe criticism as **flak;** an informal use.

flake /fleɪk/, **flakes, flaking, flaked. 1** COUNT N A **flake** is a small thin piece of something that has broken off a larger piece. *...flakes of burnt paper from a bonfire.* **2** COUNT N A **flake** is also a snowflake. **3** VB If paint **flakes,** small pieces of it come off. *The paint was flaking off the walls.*

flake out. PHR VB If you **flake out,** you collapse or go to sleep because you are very tired; an informal use.

flamboyant /flæmbɔɪənt/. **1** ADJ **Flamboyant** people behave in a very noticeable, confident, and exaggerated way. *He has been accused of being too flamboyant on stage.* **2** ADJ Something that is **flamboyant** is very brightly coloured and noticeable. *...a flamboyant quilted bathrobe.*

flame /fleɪm/, **flames.** COUNT N OR UNCOUNT N A **flame** is a long, pointed stream of burning gas that comes from something that is burning. *The flames and smoke rose hundreds of feet into the air... The aircraft disappeared in a ball of flame.*

PHRASES ● If something is **in flames,** it is on fire. *My parents' home was in flames.* ● If something **bursts into flames,** it suddenly starts burning. *The satellite burst into flames and disintegrated.*

flaming /fleɪmɪŋ/. **1** ATTRIB ADJ **Flaming** things are burning and producing flames. *...planes diving down with flaming wings.* **2** ADJ Something that is **flaming** red or **flaming** orange is very bright in colour. *She had flaming red hair.*

flamingo /flə³mɪŋgəʊ/, **flamingos** or **flamingoes.** COUNT N A **flamingo** is a bird with pink feathers, long thin legs, and a curved beak.

flammable /flæməbə°l/. ADJ Something that is **flammable** catches fire easily.

flan /flæn/, **flans.** COUNT N OR UNCOUNT N A **flan** is a kind of tart made of pastry and filled with fruit or something savoury. *...onion flan.*

flank /flæŋk/, **flanks, flanking, flanked. 1** VB WITH OBJ If something **is flanked** by things, it has them on both sides of it. *Billy was seated at the table, flanked by the two women.* **2** COUNT N An animal's **flanks** are its sides. *Their legs gripped the flanks of the ponies.* **3** COUNT N The **flank** of an army or fleet is the part at one side of it when it is ready for battle. *Their fire on the enemy's flank could not stop his southward advance.*

flannel /flænə°l/, **flannels. 1** UNCOUNT N **Flannel** is a lightweight cloth used for making clothes. *...a grey flannel suit.* **2** COUNT N A **flannel** is a small cloth used for washing yourself; a British use.

flap /flæp/, **flaps, flapping, flapped. 1** ERG VB OR VB WITH ADJUNCT If something attached at one end **flaps,** the other end moves quickly up and down or from side to side. *She flapped her arms... Its wings flapped weakly... His long robes flapped in the breeze.* **2** COUNT N A **flap** is a flat piece of something that moves freely because it is attached by only one edge. *...looking out through a tent flap.* **3** PHRASE Someone who is **in a flap** is very excited or frightened; an informal use.

flare /fleə/, **flares, flaring, flared. 1** COUNT N A **flare** is a small device that produces a bright flame. *He stood ready to fire a warning flare.* **2** VB If a fire **flares,** the flames suddenly become larger. *The candle flared to a bright light.* **3** VB If something such as violence, conflict, or anger **flares,** it becomes worse. *From time to time violence flared... The fighting flared up when a blockade was imposed.* **4** VB If clothes **flare,** they spread outwards at one end to form a wide shape. *She pirouetted, making the skirt flare out.* ♦ **flared** ATTRIB ADJ *...flared trousers.*

flash /flæʃ/, **flashes, flashing, flashed. 1** COUNT N A **flash** of light is a sudden, short burst of light. *Suddenly there was a flash of lightning.* **2** ERG VB If a light **flashes** it shines brightly and suddenly. *I'll flash my headlights to make sure he sees us.* **3** VB WITH ADJUNCT If something **flashes** past you, it moves very fast. *Something white flashed past the van.* **4** VB WITH 'through' If something **flashes** through your mind, you think of it suddenly and briefly. *It flashed through his mind that he might never get back.* **5** COUNT N WITH SUPP If you have a **flash** of intuition or insight, you suddenly realize something. **6** VB WITH OBJ AND 'at' If you **flash** a look or a smile at someone, you look or smile at them quickly and briefly; a literary use. *He flashed a conspiratorial grin at them.*

flashback /flæʃbæk/, **flashbacks.** COUNT N A **flashback** is a scene in a film, play, or book where the story suddenly goes back to events in the past.

flashlight /flæʃlaɪt/, **flashlights.** COUNT N A **flashlight** is a large torch.

flashy /flæʃi¹/, **flashier, flashiest.** ADJ **Flashy** things look smart, bright, and expensive in a rather vulgar way; an informal use. *...a flashy sports car.*

flask /flɑːsk/, **flasks. 1** COUNT N A **flask** is a bottle used for carrying alcoholic or hot drinks around with you. **2** COUNT N You can use **flask** to refer to a flask and its contents, or to the contents only. *...a flask of coffee.*

flat /flæt/, **flats; flatter, flattest. 1** COUNT N In Britain, a **flat** is a set of rooms for living in, usually on one floor of a large building. *...a block of flats.* **2** ADJ Something that is **flat** is not sloping, curved, or pointed. *Every flat surface in our house is covered with junk... He took the handkerchief and smoothed it flat.* **3** ADV WITH ADJUNCT If something is **flat** against a surface, all of it is touching the surface. *She let the blade of her oar rest flat upon the water.* **4** ADJ A **flat** tyre does not have enough air inside it. **5** ATTRIB ADJ A **flat** refusal, denial, or rejection is definite and firm. *Their earnest request met with a flat refusal.* ♦ **flatly** ADV *She has flatly refused to go.* **6** ADJ A **flat** voice is cold and unemotional. ♦ **flatly** ADV *'She is dead,' said Ash flatly.* **7** ADV If something is done in a particular amount of time **flat,** it is done in exactly that amount of time. *They will be able to hit the targets in four minutes flat.* **8** PHRASE If an event or attempt to do something **falls flat,** it fails. **9** COUNT N OR ADJ AFTER N In music, a **flat** is the note a semitone lower than the note described by the same letter. It is usually represented by the symbol 'b' after the letter. *...B flat.* **10** ADV OR ADJ If a musical note is played or sung **flat,** it is slightly lower in pitch than it should be. **11** ATTRIB ADJ A **flat** charge or fee is the same for everyone whatever the circumstances are. **12** ADJ A **flat** battery has lost some or all of its electrical power.

flatmate /flætmeɪt/, **flatmates.** COUNT N Someone's **flatmate** is the person who shares a flat with them.

flatten /flætə°n/, **flattens, flattening, flattened. 1** ERG VB If you **flatten** something, or **flatten** it out, it becomes flat or flatter. *The steel rod had been slightly flattened... The lump had flattened out, almost.* ♦ **flattened** ADJ *...flattened paper cups.* **2** REFL VB WITH ADJUNCT If you **flatten** yourself against something, you press yourself flat against it. *She flattened herself against the door to avoid detection.* **3** VB WITH OBJ To **flatten** buildings or crops means to destroy them by knocking them down. *Huge areas of Queen Victoria Street were flattened by bombs.*

flatter /flætə/, **flatters, flattering, flattered. 1** VB WITH OBJ If you **flatter** someone, you praise them in an exaggerated way, either to please them or to persuade them to do something. *Ginny knew that he was saying all this just to flatter her.* **2** PASSIVE VB If you **are flattered** by something, you are pleased because it makes you feel important. *I was flattered that he remembered my name.* **3** REFL VB If you **flatter** yourself that something is the case, you believe, perhaps wrongly, something good about yourself. *I flatter myself on being a good judge of character.*

flattering /flætərɪŋ/. **1** ADJ If someone's behaviour towards you is **flattering,** it is pleasing because it shows that they have a high opinion of you. *They listened to him with a flattering interest.* **2** ADJ If a picture or piece of clothing is **flattering,** it makes you appear more attractive than you usually do. *It is not a flattering picture.*

flattery /flætə°ri¹/. UNCOUNT N **Flattery** is flattering words or behaviour. *He was immune to the flattery of political leaders.*

flaunt /flɔːnt/, **flaunts, flaunting, flaunted.** VB WITH OBJ If you **flaunt** something that you possess, you display it in a very obvious way. *They flaunt their engagement rings... The leader of the group wanted to flaunt his authority.*

flavour /fleɪvə/, **flavours, flavouring, flavoured;** spelled **flavor** in American English. **1** COUNT N OR UNCOUNT N The **flavour** of a food or drink is its taste. *Raw fish has a very delicate flavour... You can try adding salt to give it some flavour.* **2** VB WITH OBJ If you **flavour** food or drink, you add something to give it a particular taste. *Milk can be flavoured with vanilla.* **3** UNCOUNT N You can refer to a special quality that something has as its **flavour.** *Pimlico has its own peculiar flavour and atmosphere.*

flavouring /fleɪvə°rɪŋ/, **flavourings;** spelled **flavoring** in American English. MASS N **Flavouring** is a substance used in food or drink to give it a particular taste.

flaw /flɔː/, **flaws. 1** COUNT N A **flaw** in something is a fault or mistake in it that spoils it or makes it unsatisfactory. *There is a flaw in this policy... The law contained a flaw which made it unworkable.* ♦ **flawed** ADJ *...flawed arguments... Certainly, these are flawed paintings.* **2** COUNT N A **flaw** in someone's character is an undesirable quality which they have.

flawless /flɔːlɪ²s/. ADJ Something that is **flawless** is perfect. *...a flawless performance... ...her flawless complexion.*

flax /flæks/. UNCOUNT N **Flax** is a plant used for making rope and cloth.

flay /fleɪ/, **flays, flaying, flayed.** VB WITH OBJ If someone **flays** a dead animal, they cut off its skin.

flea /fliː/, **fleas.** COUNT N A **flea** is a small jumping insect that sucks human or animal blood.

fleck /flek/, **flecks.** COUNT N **Flecks** are small marks on a surface, or objects that look like small marks. *...the grey flecks in his eyes... Little flecks of white powder floated on top.* ♦ **flecked** PRED ADJ *Her eyes were flecked with dots of milky white.*

fled /fled/. **Fled** is the past tense and past participle of **flee.**

fledgling /fledʒlɪŋ/, **fledglings. 1** COUNT N A **fledgling** is a young bird. **2** ATTRIB ADJ You use **fledgling** to describe an inexperienced person or a new organization; a literary use. *...fledgling industries.*

flee /fliː/, **flees, fleeing, fled** /fled/. **1** VB If you **flee,** you run away from someone or something. *He had to flee to Tanzania.* **2** VB WITH OBJ If you **flee** a place, you run away from it. *He fled the country.*

fleece /fliːs/, **fleeces, fleecing, fleeced. 1** COUNT N A sheep's **fleece** is its wool. **2** COUNT N A **fleece** is a sheep's wool when it is cut off in one piece. **3** VB WITH OBJ If you **are fleeced,** someone gets a lot of money from you dishonestly; an informal use. *The pensioners feel they are being fleeced.*

fleet /fliːt/, **fleets. 1** COUNT N A **fleet** is an organized group of ships. *Britain had to increase her battle fleet... ...a trawling fleet.* **2** COUNT N You can also refer to a group of vehicles as a **fleet.** *...fleets of buses.*

fleeting /fliːtɪŋ/. ATTRIB ADJ **Fleeting** is used to describe things which last for only a very short time. *I got only fleeting glimpses of them.* ♦ **fleetingly** ADV *...a way to assert power, however fleetingly.*

flesh /fleʃ/, **fleshes, fleshing, fleshed. 1** UNCOUNT N Your **flesh** is the soft part of your body between your bones and your skin. *The fangs are driven into the victim's flesh.* **2** UNCOUNT N You can also refer to a person's skin as their **flesh.** *...the whiteness of her flesh.* **3** PHRASE Someone who is your **own flesh and blood** is a member of your own family. ● See also **flesh-and-blood. 4** UNCOUNT N The **flesh** of a fruit or vegetable is the soft inner part.

flesh out. PHR VB If you **flesh** something **out,** you add more details to it. *We're now seeing the proposal fleshed out for the first time.*

flesh-and-blood. ATTRIB ADJ **Flesh-and-blood** means real and alive, rather than imaginary or artificial. *...a game between a computer and a flesh-and-blood chess master.*

fleshy /flɛʃi/. 1 ADJ **Fleshy** people have a lot of flesh on their bodies. 2 ADJ **Fleshy** leaves or stalks are thick.

flew /flu:/. **Flew** is the past tense of **fly.**

flex /flɛks/, **flexes, flexing, flexed.** 1 COUNT N OR UNCOUNT N A **flex** is a long plastic tube with two or three wires inside which is used for carrying electricity. *...a length of flex.* 2 VB WITH OBJ If you **flex** part of your body, you bend, move, or stretch it to exercise it.

flexible /flɛksɪbəl/. 1 ADJ A **flexible** object or material can be bent easily without breaking. *The tube is flexible but tough.* 2 ADJ A **flexible** arrangement can be adapted to different conditions. *...flexible working hours.* ♦ **flexibility** /flɛksəbɪlɪti/ UNCOUNT N *This called for some flexibility of approach.*

flick /flɪk/, **flicks, flicking, flicked.** 1 ERG VB WITH ADJUNCT If something **flicks** in a particular direction, it moves with a short, sudden movement. *Its tongue flicks in and out of its tiny mouth... ...flicking its tail backwards and forwards.* Also COUNT N *...a quick upward flick of the arm.* 2 VB WITH OBJ AND ADJUNCT If you **flick** something away, you remove it with a quick movement of your finger or hand. *He flicked the dust from his suit... She sat there, flicking ash into the ashtray.* 3 VB WITH OBJ If you **flick** something such as a whip or a towel, you hold one end and move your hand quickly up and then forward, so that the other end moves. *He flicked their bare arms with a tea towel.* Also COUNT N *He gave a flick of the whip.* 4 VB WITH OBJ You also **flick** something when you hit it sharply with your fingernail by pressing the fingernail against your thumb and suddenly releasing it. *I flicked the hollow door with my finger.* 5 VB WITH OBJ If you **flick** a switch or catch, you press it sharply so that it moves. *She flicked on the lamp.* 6 VB WITH OBJ OR ADJUNCT If you **flick** through a book or magazine, you turn the pages quickly. *He flicked through the passport, not understanding a word.* Also COUNT N WITH SUPP *...a quick flick through the pages.*

flicker /flɪkə/, **flickers, flickering, flickered.** 1 VB If a light or flame **flickers,** it shines unsteadily. *The candle flickered by the bed.* Also COUNT N *...a faint flicker of lightning.* 2 COUNT N A **flicker** of feeling is a brief experience of it. *There was a flicker of fear in the man's eyes.* 3 VB WITH ADJUNCT If an expression **flickers** across your face, it appears briefly. *A rather sad smile flickered across her face.* 4 VB You can also say that something **flickers** when it moves lightly and quickly, especially up and down or backwards and forwards. *Her eyelids flickered and closed again.*

flight /flaɪt/, **flights.** 1 COUNT N A **flight** is a journey made by flying, especially in an aeroplane. *It had been his first flight.* 2 COUNT N A **flight** is also an aeroplane carrying passengers on a particular journey. *Can you tell me what time Flight No. 172 arrives?* 3 UNCOUNT N **Flight** is the action of flying. *...a bird in flight... Supersonic flight is very expensive.* 4 COUNT N A **flight** of birds is a group of them flying together. *...a flight of duck.* 5 UNCOUNT N **Flight** is also the act of running away from a dangerous or unpleasant situation. *He was born at sea during his parents' flight from the revolution.* 6 COUNT N A **flight** of steps is a row of them leading from one level to another. *She led the way down a short flight of steps.*

flimsy /flɪmzi/, **flimsier, flimsiest.** 1 ADJ Something that is **flimsy** is easily damaged because it is badly made or made of a weak material. *Poor people can afford only flimsy houses of mud and straw.* 2 ADJ **Flimsy** cloth or clothing is thin and does not give much protection. 3 ADJ A **flimsy** excuse or **flimsy** evidence is not very good or convincing.

flinch /flɪntʃ/, **flinches, flinching, flinched.** 1 VB If you **flinch** when you are startled or hurt, you make a small, sudden movement without meaning to. 2 VB If you **flinch** from something unpleasant, you are unwilling to do it or think about it. *They flinched from the prospect of starting again.*

fling /flɪŋ/, **flings, flinging, flung** /flʌŋ/. 1 VB WITH OBJ AND ADJUNCT If you **fling** something somewhere, you throw it there. *She was flinging a few things into her handbag.* 2 REFL VB WITH ADJUNCT If you **fling** yourself somewhere, you move or jump there with a lot of force. *He flung himself down at Jack's feet.* 3 COUNT N If you have a **fling,** you enjoy yourself a lot for a short time, for example by doing something very energetic or having a brief sexual relationship; an informal use. *She had a brief fling while her husband was away.*

flint /flɪnt/, **flints.** UNCOUNT N OR COUNT N **Flint** is a very hard, greyish-black stone which produces sparks when struck. *...the grey flint parish church.*

flip /flɪp/, **flips, flipping, flipped.** 1 VB WITH 'through' If you **flip** through a book or file, you turn the pages quickly. 2 VB WITH OBJ AND ADJUNCT If you **flip** something into a different position, you quickly push it into that position. *He flipped open his notebook.*

flippant /flɪpənt/. ADJ If you are being **flippant,** you are making remarks which show that you are not taking something seriously. *John was offended by the doctor's flippant attitude.* ♦ **flippancy** /flɪpənsi/ UNCOUNT N *'This is no time for flippancy,' he said angrily.*

flipper /flɪpə/, **flippers.** 1 COUNT N The **flippers** of an animal such as a seal are the two or four flat limbs that it uses for swimming. 2 COUNT N **Flippers** are also flat pieces of rubber that you can wear on your feet to help you swim more quickly.

flirt /flɜ:t/, **flirts, flirting, flirted.** 1 RECIP VB If you **flirt** with someone, you behave as if you are sexually attracted to them, in a not very serious way. *She never even flirted with other men.* ♦ **flirtation** /flɜ:teɪʃən/ COUNT N OR UNCOUNT N *He had a mild flirtation with two Danish blondes.* 2 COUNT N A **flirt** is someone who flirts a lot. 3 VB WITH 'with' If you **flirt** with the idea of doing or having something, you consider doing or having it, without making any definite plans. *Burlington has flirted for years with the idea of a wood-burning electrical generator.*

flirtatious /flɜ:teɪʃəs/. ADJ If someone is flirting, you can say they are being **flirtatious.** *She kept giving him flirtatious looks.*

flit /flɪt/, **flits, flitting, flitted.** 1 VB WITH ADJUNCT To **flit** about means to fly or move quickly from one place to another. *Bats flitted about.* 2 VB WITH ADJUNCT If an expression **flits** across your face or if an idea **flits** through your mind, it is there for only a short time.

float /fləʊt/, **floats, floating, floated.** 1 VB If something **is floating** in a liquid, it is lying or moving slowly on the surface. *There was seaweed floating on the surface of the water.* 2 VB Something that **floats** through the air moves slowly through it, because it is very light. *Six dollar bills floated down on to the table.* 3 COUNT N A **float** is a light object that is used to help someone or something float in water.

floating voter, floating voters. COUNT N A **floating voter** is a person who is not a firm supporter of any political party.

flock /flɒk/, **flocks, flocking, flocked.** 1 COUNT N A **flock** of birds, sheep, or goats is a group of them. *...a flock of seagulls.* 2 COLL N WITH POSS Someone's **flock,** especially a clergyman's, is the group of people that they are responsible for; an old-fashioned use. 3 VB WITH ADJUNCT OR TO-INF If people **flock** to a place or event, a lot of them go there, because it is pleasant or interesting. *Crowds flocked to see the treasures.*

flog /flɒg/, **flogs, flogging, flogged.** 1 VB WITH OBJ If you **flog** something, you sell it; an informal use. 2 VB WITH OBJ To **flog** someone means to hit them hard with a whip or stick as a punishment. ♦ **flogging** UNCOUNT N OR COUNT N *He was sentenced to receive a public flogging.*

flood /flʌd/, **floods, flooding, flooded.** 1 COUNT N If there is a **flood,** a large amount of water covers an area which is usually dry, for example when a river overflows. *In 1975, floods in north-eastern India made 233,000 people homeless.* 2 ERG VB If a place **floods,** it becomes covered with water. *When we took the plug out the kitchen flooded... The rice fields were flooded.* ♦ **flooding** UNCOUNT N *There has been heavy rain in many areas, resulting in widespread flooding.* 3 VB If a river **floods,** it overflows, usually after very heavy rain. 4 COUNT N A **flood** of things is a large number of them. *She received a flood of grateful letters.* 5 VB WITH ADJUNCT If people or things **flood** into a place, large numbers of them come there. *This brought more and more migrants flooding into the cities.*

floodlight /flʌdlaɪt/, **floodlights.** COUNT N **Floodlights** are powerful lamps which are used to light sports grounds and the outsides of public buildings when it is dark.

floodlit /flʌdlɪt/. ADJ If a building or place is **floodlit,** it is lit by floodlights. *The cathedral is floodlit at night.*

floor /flɔ:/, **floors, flooring, floored.** 1 COUNT N The **floor** of a room is the flat part that you walk on. *The book fell to the floor.* 2 COUNT N A **floor** of a building is all the rooms on a particular level. *My office is on the second floor.* 3 VB WITH OBJ If a remark or question **floors** you, you are so surprised or confused by it that you cannot answer it. ● See also **shop floor.**

floorboard /flɔ:bɔ:d/, **floorboards.** COUNT N **Floorboards** are the long pieces of wood that a floor is made of.

flop /flɒp/, **flops, flopping, flopped.** 1 VB WITH ADJUNCT If you **flop** onto something, you sit or lie down suddenly and heavily because you are tired. *She flopped into an armchair.* 2 COUNT N Something that is a **flop** is a total failure; an informal use. *His first play was a disastrous flop.* 3 VB If something **flops,** it is a total failure; an informal use. *One of their space projects flopped.*

floppy /flɒpi/. ADJ Something that is **floppy** is loose rather than stiff, and tends to hang downwards. *...ladies in floppy hats.*

flora /flɔ:rə/. PLURAL N The **flora** in a place are all the plants there; a formal use. *...the flora and fauna of our countryside.*

floral /flɔ:rəl/. 1 ATTRIB ADJ **Floral** cloth, paper, or china has a pattern of flowers on it. *...floral dresses.* 2 ATTRIB ADJ You also use **floral** to describe something that is made of flowers. *...floral decorations.*

florid /flɒrɪd/. 1 ADJ Something that is **florid** is complicated and extravagant rather than plain and simple; a literary use. *...florid verse.* 2 ADJ Someone who is **florid** has a red face. *...a large man with a florid complexion.*

florist /flɒrɪst/, **florists.** 1 COUNT N A **florist** is a shopkeeper who sells flowers and indoor plants. 2 COUNT N A **florist** or a **florist's** is a shop where flowers and indoor plants are sold.

flounce /flaʊns/, **flounces, flouncing, flounced.** VB WITH ADJUNCT When people **flounce** somewhere, they walk there quickly in an angry way, trying to draw attention to themselves. *She flounced into the bedroom, slamming the door behind her.*

flounder /flaʊndə/, **flounders, floundering, floundered.** 1 VB If you **flounder** in water or mud, you move in an uncontrolled way, trying not to sink. 2 VB You can also say that someone **is floundering** when they cannot think what to say or do. *Suddenly she asked me: 'What do you think?' I floundered for a moment.*

flour /flaʊə/. UNCOUNT N **Flour** is a white or brown powder that is made by grinding grain. It is used to make bread, cakes, and pastry.

flourish /flʌrɪʃ/, **flourishes, flourishing, flourished.** 1 VB If something **flourishes,** it grows well or is successful because the conditions are right for it. *In these waters, bacteria flourish... Democracy cannot possibly flourish in such circumstances.* ♦ **flourishing** ADJ *...flourishing industries.* 2 VB WITH OBJ If you **flourish** an object, you wave it about so that people notice it. *She rushed in flourishing a document.* 3 COUNT N If you do something with a **flourish,** you do it with a bold sweeping movement. *Jack drew his knife with a flourish.*

flout /flaʊt/, **flouts, flouting, flouted.** VB WITH OBJ If you **flout** a law, order, or rule of behaviour, you deliberately disobey it.

flow /fləʊ/, **flows, flowing, flowed.** 1 VB WITH ADJUNCT If a liquid, gas, or electrical current **flows** somewhere, it moves steadily and continuously. *The tears flowed down his cheeks.* Also COUNT N WITH SUPP *The blood flow is cut off.* 2 VB WITH ADJUNCT You can also say that people or things **flow** somewhere when they move freely or steadily from one place to another. *The river flows south-west to the Atlantic Ocean.* Also COUNT N WITH SUPP *There's a good flow of information.* 3 VB WITH ADJUNCT If someone's hair or clothing **flows** about them, it hangs freely and loosely. ♦ **flowing** ADJ *...women in long flowing robes.* 4 VB WITH 'from' If a quality or situation **flows** from something, it results naturally from it; a literary use. *The love for one another flows from that unity.*

flower /flaʊə/, **flowers, flowering, flowered.** 1 COUNT N The **flowers** on a plant are the coloured parts that grow on its stems, as opposed to its leaves. 2 COUNT N **Flowers** are also small plants that are grown for their flowers, as opposed to trees, shrubs, and vegetables. *He planted flowers on the banks.* 3 VB When a plant or tree **flowers,** its flowers appear and open. 4 VB When an idea, artistic style, or political movement **flowers,** it develops fully and is successful; a literary use. ♦ **flowering** UNCOUNT N *...the flowering of socialist thought.*

flowerbed /flaʊəbɛd/, **flowerbeds.** COUNT N A **flowerbed** is an area of earth in which you grow plants.

flowered /flaʊəd/. ADJ **Flowered** cloth, paper, or china has a pattern of flowers on it.

flowering /flaʊərɪŋ/. ATTRIB ADJ **Flowering** shrubs, trees, or plants produce flowers.

flowerpot /flaʊəpɒt/, **flowerpots.** COUNT N A **flowerpot** is a small container which a plant is grown in.

flowery /flaʊəri/. 1 ADJ Something that is **flowery** has a pattern of flowers on it or smells of flowers. *...a flowery apron.* 2 ADJ **Flowery** speech or writing contains long, complicated words and literary expressions.

flown /fləʊn/. **Flown** is the past participle of **fly.**

flu /flu:/. UNCOUNT N **Flu** is an illness which is like a bad cold. When you have flu, you feel weak and your muscles ache.

fluctuate /flʌktjʊeɪt/, **fluctuates, fluctuating, fluctuated.** VB If something **fluctuates,** its amount, level, or nature keeps changing. *Prices fluctuated between 1970 and 1972.* ♦ **fluctuation** /flʌktjʊeɪʃən/ COUNT N OR UNCOUNT N *...fluctuations in temperature.*

flue /flu:/, **flues.** COUNT N A **flue** is a chimney or a pipe that acts as a chimney.

fluent /flu:ənt/. 1 ADJ Someone who is **fluent** in a foreign language can speak or write it easily and correctly. *She was fluent in Spanish.* ♦ **fluently** ADV *He spoke both languages fluently.* ♦ **fluency** /flu:ənsi[1]/ UNCOUNT N *She could speak German with great fluency.* 2 ADJ Someone whose speech, reading, or writing is **fluent** speaks, reads, or writes easily and clearly. ♦ **fluently** ADV *By the time she was six she could read fluently.*

fluff /flʌf/, **fluffs, fluffing, fluffed.** 1 UNCOUNT N **Fluff** is the small masses of soft, light thread that you find on clothes or in dusty corners of a room. *He brushed some fluff from his jacket.* 2 VB WITH OBJ If you **fluff** something or **fluff** it out, you shake it or brush it in order to make it seem larger and lighter. *She fluffed her hair out in big waves.*

fluffy /flʌfi[1]/. ADJ Something that is **fluffy** is very soft and furry. *...a fluffy kitten.*

fluid /flu:ɪd/, **fluids.** 1 COUNT N OR UNCOUNT N A **fluid** is a substance that can flow, especially a liquid. *...petrol and cleaning fluids.* Also PRED ADJ *After a month it was still completely fluid at the centre.* 2 ADJ A situation, idea, or arrangement that is **fluid** is likely to change, or can be changed. *Opinion in the trade unions is very fluid as regards this question.* ♦ **fluidity** /flu:ɪdɪ[1]ti[1]/ UNCOUNT N *...the fluidity of the situation.*

fluid ounce, fluid ounces. COUNT N A **fluid ounce** is a unit of volume for liquids. There are twenty fluid ounces in an imperial pint, and sixteen in an American pint.

fluke /flu:k/, **flukes.** COUNT N If something good that happens is a **fluke**, it happens accidentally rather than because of someone's skill or plan; an informal use.

flung /flʌŋ/. **Flung** is the past tense and past participle of **fling.**

fluorescent /flʊərɛsə[0]nt/. ATTRIB ADJ A **fluorescent** light shines with a very hard, bright light.

fluoride /flʊəraɪd/. UNCOUNT N **Fluoride** is a mixture of chemicals that is sometimes added to a water supply or to toothpaste because it is good for people's teeth.

flurry /flʌri[1]/, **flurries.** 1 COUNT N A **flurry** of activity or speech is a short, energetic amount of it. *The decision raised a flurry of objections.* 2 COUNT N A **flurry** of snow or wind is a small amount of it that moves suddenly and quickly along. *...snow flurries.*

flush /flʌʃ/, **flushes, flushing, flushed.** 1 VB If you **flush**, your face goes red because you are embarrassed or hot. 2 SING N If there is a **flush** in your face, it is slightly red. *There was a flush in his cheeks.* ♦ **flushed** ADJ *Her face was flushed.* 3 ERG VB When you **flush** a toilet or when it **flushes**, the handle is pressed or pulled and water flows into the toilet bowl. 4 VB WITH OBJ AND ADJUNCT If you **flush** people or animals out of a place, you force them to come out. *They went into the area to flush out guerrillas who were sheltering there.* 5 PRED ADJ If something is **flush** with a surface, it is level with it and does not stick up.

flushed /flʌʃt/. PRED ADJ Someone who is **flushed** with success or pride is very pleased and excited as a result of achieving something.

fluster /flʌstə/, **flusters, flustering, flustered.** VB WITH OBJ If something **flusters** you, it makes you feel nervous and confused. ♦ **flustered** ADJ *He was so flustered he forgot to close the door.*

flute /flu:t/, **flutes.** COUNT N A **flute** is a musical instrument in the shape of a long tube with holes in it. You play it by blowing over a hole near one end.

fluted /flu:tɪ[2]d/. ADJ Something that is **fluted** has long grooves cut or shaped into it. *...fluted columns.*

flutter /flʌtə/, **flutters, fluttering, fluttered.** 1 ERG VB If something **flutters** it waves up and down or from side to side. *His long robe fluttered in the wind.* 2 VB If something light **flutters** somewhere, it moves through the air with small quick movements. *The pieces of paper flutter down like butterflies.*

flux /flʌks/. UNCOUNT N If something is in a state of **flux**, it is changing constantly. *...years of political flux.*

fly /flaɪ/, **flies, flying, flew** /flu:/, **flown** /fləʊn/. 1 COUNT N A **fly** is a small insect with two wings. 2 VB When a bird, insect, or aircraft **flies**, it moves through the air. *My canary flew away.* 3 VB If you **fly** somewhere, you travel there in an aircraft. *You can fly from Cardiff to Ostend.* 4 VB WITH OR WITHOUT OBJ When someone **flies** an aircraft, they control its movement in the air. *Once I was flying my plane and ran into a storm over San Francisco.* ♦ **flying** UNCOUNT N *Why don't you take up flying?* 5 VB WITH OBJ AND ADJUNCT If you **fly** something somewhere, you send it there by plane. *Exotic fruits were specially flown in for the occasion.* 6 VB If something **flies** about, it moves about freely and loosely. *He jumped onto the platform with his cloak flying.* 7 ERG VB When a flag **is flying** or when people **fly** a flag, it is displayed at the top of a pole. 8 VB WITH ADJUNCT If something **flies** in a particular direction, it moves there with a lot of speed or force. *His glasses flew off and smashed on the rocks.* 9 VB WITH 'at' If you **fly** at someone or let **fly** at them, you attack them, either by hitting them or by insulting them. *One day the man flew at me in a temper.* 10 COUNT N The front opening on a pair of trousers is referred to as the **fly** or the **flies.**
PHRASES ● If you say that **time flies,** you mean that it seems to pass very quickly. ● If you take a **flying leap,** you run forward and jump. *She took a flying leap at the fence.* ● A **flying visit** is a visit that lasts for a very short time. ● If you **get off to a flying start,** you start something very well, for example a race or a new job. ● **with flying colours:** see **colour.** ● **to fly off the handle:** see **handle.**

fly into. PHR VB If you **fly into** a rage or a panic, you suddenly become very angry or anxious. *She flies into a temper if I make a mistake.*

flying saucer, flying saucers. COUNT N **Flying saucers** are round flat spacecraft from other planets, which some people say they have seen.

flyover /flaɪəʊvə/, **flyovers.** COUNT N A **flyover** is a structure which carries one road above another one.

foal /fəʊl/, **foals.** COUNT N A **foal** is a very young horse.

foam /fəʊm/, **foams, foaming, foamed.** 1 UNCOUNT N **Foam** consists of a mass of small bubbles. It is formed when air and a liquid are mixed together violently. *...the line of white foam where the waves broke.* 2 UNCOUNT N **Foam** or **foam rubber** is soft rubber full of small holes which is used, for example, to make mattresses and cushions. 3 VB If a liquid **is foaming**, it has lots of small bubbles in it or on its surface.

fob /fɒb/, **fobs, fobbing, fobbed.**

fob off PHR VB If you ask for something and **are fobbed off** with something else, the thing that you are given is not very good or is not really what you want; an informal use. *He may try to fob you off with a prescription for pills.*

focal point /fəʊkə[0]l pɔɪnt/. SING N The **focal point** of people's interest or activity is the thing they concentrate on or the place they are most active. *Dinner was the focal point of my day... The focal point of these celebrations was the local church.*

focus /fəʊkəs/, **focuses, focusing, focused.** The spellings **focusses, focussing,** and **focussed** are also used. 1 VB WITH OBJ When you **focus** a camera you adjust it so that it will take clear photographs. ● If a photograph or telescope is **in focus,** the photograph or the thing you are looking at is clear and sharp. If it is **out of focus,** the photograph or the thing you are looking at is blurred. *The only part of the picture which was in clear focus was a small child.* 2 ERG VB When you **focus** your eyes, you adjust them so that you can see clearly. *His eyes would not focus.* 3 VB WITH OBJ If you **focus** a ray of light, you direct it towards a particular point. *I focused the beam of the spotlight on them.* 4 ERG VB If you **focus** your attention on something, you concentrate on it. *Attention focused on the election.* 5 UNCOUNT N If special attention is being paid to something, you can say that it is the **focus** of interest or attention. *Changes in the urban environment are the focus of public interest and discussion.*

fodder /fɒdə/. UNCOUNT N **Fodder** is food that is given to animals such as cows or horses.

foe /fəʊ/, **foes.** COUNT N Your **foe** is your enemy; an old-fashioned use.

foetus /fi:təs/, **foetuses;** also spelled **fetus.** COUNT N A **foetus** is an unborn animal or human being in its later stages of development.

fog /fɒg/, **fogs.** UNCOUNT N OR COUNT N When there is **fog,** there are tiny drops of water in the air which form a thick cloud and make it difficult to see things. *Around midday, the fog lifted.*

foggy /fɒgi[1]/, **foggier, foggiest.** ADJ When it is **foggy,** there is fog. *...a foggy day.*

foible /fɔɪbə[0]l/, **foibles.** COUNT N A **foible** is a rather strange or foolish habit which is not serious. *She knows his moods and foibles.*

foil /fɔɪl/, **foils, foiling, foiled.** 1 UNCOUNT N **Foil** is metal in the form of a thin sheet. *...the foil wrapper of a bar of chocolate.* 2 VB WITH OBJ If you **foil** someone's plan or attempt at something, you prevent it from being successful. 3 SING N Something that is a good **foil** for something else contrasts with it and makes its good qualities more noticeable. *She had bronzed skin, for which her yellow swimsuit was a perfect foil.*

foist /fɔɪst/, **foists, foisting, foisted.**

foist on PHR VB If you **foist** something **on** someone, you force them to have it or experience it. *They were out to foist their views on the people.*

fold /fəʊld/, **folds, folding, folded.** 1 VB WITH OBJ If you **fold** a piece of paper or cloth, you bend it so that one part covers another part. 2 VB WITH OBJ If you **fold** something or fold it up, you make it into a smaller shape by folding it several times. *They folded the tent neatly.* 3 COUNT N A **fold** is one of the curved shapes that are formed in a piece of cloth when it is not lying flat. *Snow had collected in the folds of my clothes.* 4 ERG VB If you **fold** a piece of furniture or equipment, you change its shape by bending or closing parts of it. *The rear seat folds down.* 5 VB WITH OBJ If you **fold** your arms or hands, you bring them together and cross them or link them. *He sat with his arms folded across his chest.* 6 VB If a business or organization **folds,** it is unsuccessful and has to close. *The project folded.* ● See also **folding.**

-fold. 1 SUFFIX **-fold** is added to a number to say that something has a particular number of kinds or parts. *The problems were two-fold: it was difficult to get finance, and there weren't enough trained people available.* 2 SUFFIX **-fold** is also used to indicate that something is multiplied a particular number of times. *Even if we multiplied it ten-fold, that would still only be thirty per cent.*

folder /fəʊldə/, **folders.** COUNT N A **folder** is a thin piece of cardboard folded into the shape of a container or cover, in which you can keep documents. *He took a sealed envelope from the folder on his desk.*

folding /fəʊldɪŋ/. ATTRIB ADJ A **folding** table, bicycle, or other object can be folded into a smaller shape to make it easier to carry or store. *...folding chairs.*

foliage /fəʊli[1]ɪdʒ/. UNCOUNT N The leaves of plants and trees can be referred to as **foliage.**

folk /fəʊk/, **folks.** 1 PLURAL N You can refer to people as **folk.** *...old folk.* 2 PLURAL N Your **folks** are your close relatives, especially your parents; an informal American use. *I don't even have time to write letters to my folks.* 3 ATTRIB ADJ **Folk** music, art, and customs are traditional or typical of a particular community or nation. *...Russian folk songs.*

folklore /fəʊklɔ:/. UNCOUNT N The traditional stories and customs of a community or nation are referred to as its **folklore.**

follow /fɒləʊ/, **follows, following, followed.** 1 VB WITH OR WITHOUT OBJ If you **follow** someone who is moving, you move along behind them. *He followed Sally into the yard... Marsha followed.* 2 VB WITH OR WITHOUT OBJ If you **follow** someone who has gone to a place, you go there yourself. *He followed them to Venice.* 3 VB WITH OR WITHOUT OBJ Something that **follows** a particular event happens after it. *In the days that followed, Keith could talk of nothing else... ...outings to the cinema followed by tea at Lyons Corner House.* 4 VB If you say that something **follows,** you mean that it is true because something else is true. *Just because they are old, it doesn't follow that they have to be patronized.* 5 PHRASE You use **as follows** to introduce a list of things or a description of the way something is done. *The contents are as follows: one black desk, one grey wastepaper bin, two red chairs.* 6 VB WITH OBJ If you **follow** a path or river, you go along it. 7 VB WITH OBJ If you **follow** someone's instructions, advice, or example, you do what they say or do what they have done. *She promised to follow his advice.* 8 VB WITH OBJ If you **follow** a particular course of action, you do something in a planned way. *This forced them to follow a tight money policy.* 9 VB WITH OR WITHOUT OBJ If you can **follow** an explanation or the plot of a story, you can understand it. *They were having some difficulty in following the plot.* 10 VB WITH OBJ If you **follow** a series of events or a television serial, you take an interest in it and keep informed about what happens. ● **to follow suit:** see **suit.**

follow up. PHR VB If you **follow** something **up,** you try to find out more about it. *It's an idea which has been followed up by a group of researchers at Birmingham.* ● See also **follow-up.**

follower /fɒləʊə/, **followers.** COUNT N The **followers** of a person or belief are the people who support the person or accept the belief. *...the followers of Chinese communism.*

following /fɒləʊɪŋ/. 1 ATTRIB ADJ The **following** day, week, or year is the day, week, or year after the one you have just mentioned. *He died the following day... She intended to come on the following Friday.* 2 PREP **Following** a particular event means after that event. *...the election of Harold Wilson to the leadership following Gaitskell's death.* 3 ATTRIB ADJ You can refer to the things that you are about to mention as the **following** things. *This could be achieved in the following way.* 4 SING N A person or organization that has a **following** has a group of people who support their beliefs or actions.

follow-up, follow-ups. ATTRIB ADJ **Follow-up** work or action is done as a continuation of something. *...follow-up treatment... ...a follow-up survey.* Also COUNT N *This conference is a follow-up to an earlier one.*

folly /fɒli[1]/, **follies.** UNCOUNT N OR COUNT N If you say that an action or way of behaving is **folly** or a **folly,**

you mean that it is foolish. *It would be folly to continue.*

fond /fɒnd/, **fonder, fondest. 1** PRED ADJ WITH 'of' If you are **fond** of someone, you feel affection for them. *I'm very fond of you.* **2** PRED ADJ WITH 'of' If you are **fond** of something, you like it. *I am not fond of salad... Etta was fond of shopping.* ♦ **fondness** UNCOUNT N *...my fondness for red wine.* **3** ATTRIB ADJ You use **fond** to describe people or their behaviour when they show affection. *His fond parents looked on... ...looking at me with fond eyes.* ♦ **fondly** ADV *He used to gaze at the old car fondly.* **4** ATTRIB ADJ **Fond** hopes, wishes, or expectations are a little bit foolish and unlikely to be fulfilled. *One fond dream has been to harness the sun's rays.* ♦ **fondly** ADV *He had fondly imagined that it would be a simple matter.*

fondle /fɒndəᵒl/, **fondles, fondling, fondled.** VB WITH OBJ If you **fondle** someone, you touch them or stroke them gently, usually to show your affection.

font /fɒnt/, **fonts.** COUNT N The **font** in a church is a bowl which holds the water used for baptisms.

food /fuːd/, **foods.** MASS N **Food** is what people and animals eat.

foodstuff /fuːdstʌf/, **foodstuffs.** COUNT N **Foodstuffs** are substances which people eat. *They produce sugar and other basic foodstuffs.*

fool /fuːl/, **fools, fooling, fooled. 1** COUNT N OR VOCATIVE If you call someone a **fool,** you mean that they are silly or have done something silly. *You stupid fool!* **2** VB WITH OBJ If you **fool** someone, you deceive or trick them. *He fooled them with false promises.*

PHRASES ● If you **make a fool of** someone, you make them appear silly by telling people about something silly that they have done, or by tricking them. ● If you **make a fool of yourself,** you behave in a way that makes you appear silly. *He had never learned to dance and was not prepared to make a fool of himself.* ● If you **play the fool,** you behave in a playful and silly way; a British use.

fool about or **fool around.** PHR VB If you **fool about** or **fool around,** you behave in a playful and silly way. *He was always fooling about.*

foolhardy /fuːlhɑːdi¹/; an old-fashioned word. ADJ **Foolhardy** behaviour is foolish because it involves taking risks.

foolish /fuːlɪʃ/. **1** ADJ If you say that someone's behaviour is **foolish,** you mean that it is not sensible. *It would be foolish to tell such things to a total stranger.* ♦ **foolishly** ADV OR SENTENCE ADV *They have acted a little foolishly... Foolishly, we said we would do the decorating.* ♦ **foolishness** UNCOUNT N *Have I killed him by my foolishness?* **2** ADJ You can also say that people are **foolish** when they are so silly that they make you want to laugh. *They looked foolish.* ♦ **foolishly** ADV *Would the whole thing appear foolishly melodramatic?*

foolproof /fuːlpruːf/. ADJ A plan, system, or machine that is **foolproof** is so good or easy to use that it cannot go wrong or be used wrongly. *...foolproof safety devices.*

foot /fʊt/, **feet; foots, footing, footed. Feet** is the plural of the noun. **Foots** is the third person singular, present tense, of the verb in the final phrase. **1** COUNT N Your **feet** are the parts of your body that are at the ends of your legs and that you stand on. **2** SING N The **foot** of something is the bottom or lower end of it. *...at the foot of the stairs... He sat at the foot of her bed.* **3** COUNT N A **foot** is a unit of length, equal to 12 inches or approximately 30.48 centimetres. The plural can be either 'foot' or 'feet'. *We were a few feet away from the edge... ...a 40-foot fall.* ● to **have** or **get cold feet:** see **cold.**

PHRASES ● If you go somewhere **on foot,** you walk, rather than use any form of transport. *The city should be explored on foot.* ● When you are **on your feet,** you are standing up. ● When someone is **on** their **feet** again after an illness or a difficult period of time, they have recovered. *...an economic programme to put the country back on its feet.* ● If you get **to your feet,** you stand up. *He rose hurriedly to his feet.* ● To **set foot** in a place means to go there. *It was a long time before I set foot in a theatre again.* ● If someone in authority **puts** their **foot down,** they say that something must not happen or continue. ● If you **put** your **foot in it,** you cause embarrassment by doing or saying something tactless; an informal use. ● If someone has to **stand on** their **own two feet,** they have to manage without help from other people. ● If you **foot the bill** for something, you pay for it. *They may no longer be willing to foot the bills.*

football /fʊtbɔːl/, **footballs. 1** UNCOUNT N **Football** is a game played between two teams of eleven players who kick a ball around a field in an attempt to score goals. *The children are playing football.* **2** COUNT N A **football** is the large ball which is used in the game of football.

footballer /fʊtbɔːlə/, **footballers.** COUNT N A **footballer** is a person who plays football.

foothills /fʊthɪlz/. PLURAL N **Foothills** are hills at the base of a mountain. *...the foothills of the Himalayas.*

foothold /fʊthəʊld/, **footholds. 1** COUNT N **Footholds** are ledges or hollows where you can put your feet when you are climbing. *He cut footholds in the side of the ravine.* **2** SING N If you get a **foothold** when you are trying to achieve something, you establish yourself in a strong position from which you can make progress. *I tried to gain a foothold in the organization.*

footing /fʊtɪŋ/. **1** UNCOUNT N If you lose your **footing,** your feet slip, and you fall. *He lost his footing, and stumbled to the floor.* **2** SING N WITH SUPP You use **footing** to describe the basis on which something is done. *We've had to get this on a more official footing.* **3** SING N Your **footing** with someone is your relationship with them. *The school's constitution puts parents on an equal footing with staff.*

footnote /fʊtnəʊt/, **footnotes.** COUNT N A **footnote** is a note at the bottom of a page which gives more information about something on the page.

footpath /fʊtpɑːθ/, **footpaths.** COUNT N A **footpath** is a path for people to walk on, especially in the country.

footprint /fʊtprɪnt/, **footprints.** COUNT N **Footprints** are the marks that your feet leave in soft ground or when they are wet. *...footprints in the snow.*

footstep /fʊtstɛp/, **footsteps.** COUNT N Your **footsteps** are the sounds that your feet make when you walk. *They heard footsteps and turned.* ● If you **follow in** someone's **footsteps,** you do the same things as they did earlier. *I followed in my father's footsteps and became a gamekeeper.*

footwear /fʊtwɛə/. UNCOUNT N **Footwear** refers to shoes, boots, and sandals.

for /fɔː/. **1** PREP If something is **for** someone, they are intended to have it or benefit from it. *He left a note for her on the table... I am doing everything I can for you.* **2** PREP You use **for** when you are describing the purpose of something, the reason for something, or the cause of something. *...a knife for cutting lino-leum... This area is famous for its spring flowers.* **3** PREP If you work **for** someone, you are employed by them. *He works for British Rail.* **4** PREP If you speak or act **for** someone, you do it on their behalf. *We are speaking for the majority of the British people.* **5** PREP You use **for** when you are saying how something affects someone. *I knew it was difficult for him to talk like this... It was a frightening experience for a boy.* **6** PREP You also use **for** when you are mentioning a person or thing that you have feelings about. *I felt sorry for my wife... ...Kurt's contempt for people.* **7** PREP You use **for** when you are mentioning two things that are equivalent or can be substituted in some way. *'Carte' is the French word for card... ...a substitute for natural rubber.* **8** PREP You also use **for** when you are saying that there is enough of something. *There was room for a table... He didn't have the concentration required for doing the job.* **9** PREP You use **for** to say how long something lasts or continues. *I have known you for a long time.* **10** PREP You also use **for** to say how far something extends. *Black cliffs rose sheer out of the water for a hundred feet or more.* **11** PREP If something is planned **for** a particular time, it is planned to happen then. *The meeting has been scheduled for August 30.* **12** PREP If you leave **for** a place or if you take a train, plane, or boat **for** a place, you are going there. *...one morning, before he left for the fields.* **13** PREP You use **for** when you are talking about the cost of something. *You can buy the paperback for about two pounds.* **14** PREP You also use **for** when you state the second part of a ratio. *About nine women have lost their jobs for every five men.* **15** PREP If you are **for** something, you are in favour of it. *There was a majority of 294 for war, with only 6 voting against.* **16** CONJ **For** is sometimes used to mean 'because'; an old-fashioned use. *This was where he spent his free time, for he had nowhere else to go.*

PHRASES ● You use an expression such as **for the first time** when you are saying on which occasion something has happened. *The guide returned for the third time.* ● If you are **all for** something, you are very much in favour of it. ● **as for:** see **as.** ● **but for:** see **but.** ● **for all:** see **all.**

forage /fɒrɪdʒ/, **forages, foraging, foraged. 1** VB When animals **forage,** they search for food. **2** VB WITH ADJUNCT If you **forage** for something, you search busily for it.

foray /fɒreɪ/, **forays.** COUNT N If a group of soldiers make a **foray** into an area, they make a quick attack there, usually in order to steal supplies.

forbade /fəbæd, -beɪd/. **Forbade** is the past tense of **forbid.**

forbid /fəᵊbɪd/, **forbids, forbidding, forbade** /fəbæd, -beɪd/, **forbidden. 1** VB WITH OBJ If you **forbid** someone to do something, you order them not to do it. *I forbid you to tell her.* **2** VB WITH OBJ If something **forbids** an event or course of action, it makes it impossible for it to happen; a formal use. *Mexico City's altitude forbids such exertions.*

forbidden /fəᵊbɪdəᵒn/. **1** PRED ADJ If something is **forbidden,** you are not allowed to do it or have it. *It is forbidden to bathe in the sea here... Indoor football is forbidden.* **2** ADJ A **forbidden** place is one that you are not allowed to visit or enter. *...forbidden ground.* **3** ADJ A **forbidden** subject is one that you must not mention.

forbidding /fəᵊbɪdɪŋ/. ADJ Someone or something that is **forbidding** has a severe and unfriendly appearance. *...a bleak, forbidding stretch of grey water.*

force /fɔːs/, **forces, forcing, forced. 1** VB WITH OBJ If you **force** someone to do something, you cause them to do it, although they are unwilling. *They forced him to resign... She forced herself to kiss her mother's cheek... ...the campaign to force the closure of the factory... Weekend gales forced him to change his plans.* **2** VB WITH OBJ AND ADJUNCT If you **force** something into a particular position, you use a lot of strength to make it move there. *I forced his head back.* **3** VB WITH OBJ If you **force** a lock, door, or safe, you break the lock in order to open it. **4** UNCOUNT N **Force** is power or strength. *We have renounced the use of force to settle our disputes... I hit him with all the force I could muster.* **5** COUNT N Someone or something that is a **force** in a situation has a great effect or influence on it. *Britain is re-establishing itself as a powerful force in world affairs.* **6** COUNT N OR UNCOUNT N A **force** in physics is the pulling or pushing effect that one thing has on another. *...magnetic forces.* **7** COUNT N A **force** is also an organized group of soldiers or other armed people. *...the United States armed forces... ...a guerrilla force.*

PHRASES ● If you **force** your **way** into a place, you push or break things that are in your way in order to get there. ● If you do something from **force of habit,** you do it because you have always done it in the past. ● A law or system that is **in force** exists or is being used. *...when the system comes into force.* ● If you **join forces** with someone, you work together to achieve a common aim or purpose.

forced /fɔːst/. **1** ATTRIB ADJ A **forced** action is one that you only do because you have no choice. *They promised to abolish forced labour.* **2** ADJ Something that is **forced** does not happen naturally and easily. *...a forced smile.*

forceful /fɔːsfʊl/. **1** ADJ Someone who is **forceful** expresses their opinions in a strong and confident way. *...a forceful and assertive man.* ♦ **forcefully** ADV *Her views were forcefully expressed.* **2** ADJ Something that is **forceful** causes you to think or feel something very strongly. *...a forceful reminder of the risks involved.*

forceps /fɔːsɪ²ps/. PLURAL N A pair of **forceps** is an instrument consisting of two long narrow arms which is used by a doctor for holding things.

forcible /fɔːsəbəᵒl/. **1** ATTRIB ADJ **Forcible** actions involve physical force or violence. *...the forcible imposition of military control.* ♦ **forcibly** ADV *Children were taken forcibly from their mothers.* **2** ATTRIB ADJ A **forcible** reminder, example, or statement is very powerful or emphatic. *The survey made certain very forcible recommendations.* ♦ **forcibly** ADV *This point has been forcibly expressed by Tories.*

ford /fɔːd/, **fords.** COUNT N A **ford** is a shallow place in a river or stream where you can cross safely on foot or in a vehicle.

fore /fɔː/. When something or someone comes **to the fore,** they suddenly become important or popular.

forearm /fɔːrɑːm/, **forearms.** COUNT N Your **forearms** are the parts of your arms between your elbows and your wrists.

forebears /fɔːbɛəz/. COUNT N Your **forebears** are your ancestors; a formal use. *...the lands from which their forebears had been driven.*

foreboding /fɔːbəʊdɪŋ/, **forebodings.** UNCOUNT N OR COUNT N **Foreboding** is a strong feeling that something terrible is going to happen. *Tim's absence filled her with foreboding... ...dismal forebodings.*

forecast /fɔːkɑːst/, **forecasts, forecasting, forecasted.** The past tense and past participle of the verb can be **forecasted** or **forecast. 1** COUNT N A **forecast** is a prediction of what is expected to happen in the future. *...forecasts of military involvement in British politics... ...the weather forecast.* **2** VB WITH OBJ If you **forecast** future events, you say what you think is going to happen. *Some warm weather had been forecast.*

forecourt /fɔːkɔːt/, **forecourts.** COUNT N The **forecourt** of a large building is an open area at the front.

forefather /fɔːfɑːðə/, **forefathers.** COUNT N Your **forefathers** are your ancestors, especially your male ancestors; a formal use.

forefinger /fɔ:fɪŋgə/, **forefingers.** COUNT N Your **forefinger** is the finger next to your thumb.

forefront /fɔ:frʌnt/. SING N Someone or something that is in the **forefront** of an activity is important in its development. *This was to place the company in the forefront of computer manufacture.*

forego /fɔ:gəʊ/, **foregoes, foregoing** /fɔ:gəʊɪŋ/, **forewent** /fɔ:wɛnt/, **foregone** /fɔ:gɒn/; also spelled **forgo.** VB WITH OBJ If you **forego** something, you give it up or do not insist on having it; a formal use. *Lilian agreed to forego her holiday.*

foregoing /fɔ:gəʊɪŋ/. SING N You can refer to something that has just been said as the **foregoing;** a formal use. *In the foregoing we have seen how people differ in their approach to problems.* Also ATTRIB ADJ *...the foregoing analysis.*

foregone /fɔ:gɒn/. PHRASE If the result of something is **a foregone conclusion,** it is certain what the result will be. *The outcome was assumed to be a foregone conclusion.*

foreground /fɔ:graʊnd/. SING N The **foreground** of a picture is the part that seems nearest to you.

forehand /fɔ:hænd/, **forehands.** COUNT N A **forehand** is a shot in tennis or squash in which the palm of your hand faces the direction in which you are hitting the ball.

forehead /fɒrɪd, fɔ:hɛd/, **foreheads.** COUNT N Your **forehead** is the flat area at the front of your head above your eyebrows and below where your hair grows. *He wiped his forehead with his hand.*

foreign /fɒrɪ^{1}n/. **1** ADJ Something that is **foreign** belongs or relates to a country that is not your own. *...a policy of restricting foreign imports... ...children from foreign countries.* **2** ATTRIB ADJ A **foreign** minister is a government minister who deals with matters involving other countries besides his or her own. **3** ATTRIB ADJ A **foreign** object has got into something, usually by accident, and should not be there; a formal use. *...food containing foreign matter.* **4** ADJ You can say that something is **foreign** to a person or thing when it is not typical of them; a formal use. *...that strange gloomy mood that was so foreign to him.*

foreigner /fɒrɪ^{1}nə/, **foreigners.** COUNT N You refer to someone as a **foreigner** when they belong to a country that is not your own. *More than a million foreigners visit the USA every year.*

foreman /fɔ:mə^{3}n/, **foremen.** COUNT N A **foreman** is a person who is in charge of a group of workers.

foremost /fɔ:məʊst/. **1** ADJ The **foremost** of a group of things is the most important or best. *...India's foremost centre for hand-made shoes.* **2** PHRASE **First and foremost** means more than anything else. *Rugby is first and foremost a team game.*

forename /fɔ:neɪm/, **forenames.** COUNT N Your **forenames** are your first names, as opposed to your surname; a formal use.

forensic /fərɛnsɪk/. ATTRIB ADJ When a **forensic** analysis is done, objects are examined scientifically in order to discover information about a crime. *...forensic tests for detecting the presence of blood.*

forerunner /fɔ:rʌnə/, **forerunners.** COUNT N The **forerunner** of something is a similar thing that existed before it. *...the forerunners of the International Socialists.*

foresee /fɔ:si:/, **foresees, foreseeing, foresaw** /fɔ:sɔ:/, **foreseen** /fɔ:si:n/. REPORT VB If you **foresee** something, you believe that it is going to happen. *Do you foresee any problems with the new system?... It was possible to foresee that the coming winter would be a hard one.*

foreseeable /fɔ:si:əbə^{0}l/. PHRASE When you talk about **the foreseeable future,** you are referring to the period of time in the future during which it is possible to say what will happen. *Nobody is likely to find a cure in the foreseeable future.*

foreshadow /fɔ:ʃædəʊ/, **foreshadows, foreshadowing, foreshadowed.** VB WITH OBJ If one thing **foreshadows** another, it suggests that the other thing will happen. *These later movements had been foreshadowed in much of the work of the late 1950s.*

foresight /fɔ:saɪt/. UNCOUNT N **Foresight** is the ability to see what is likely to happen, which is shown in the action that someone takes. *He showed remarkable foresight... ...a lack of foresight.*

forest /fɒrɪ^{2}st/, **forests.** COUNT N OR UNCOUNT N A **forest** is a large area where trees grow close together. *...a clearing in the forest.*

forestall /fɔ:stɔ:l/, **forestalls, forestalling, forestalled.** VB WITH OBJ If you **forestall** someone, you realize what they were intending to do and prevent them from doing it.

forestry /fɒrɪstri^1/. UNCOUNT N **Forestry** is the science or skill of growing trees in forests.

foretaste /fɔ:teɪst/. SING N WITH 'of' You say that an event is a **foretaste** of a future situation when it suggests to you what that future situation will be like. *The episode was a foretaste of the bitter struggle that was to come.*

foretell /fɔ:tɛl/, **foretells, foretelling, foretold** /fɔ:təʊld/. REPORT VB If you **foretell** something, you say correctly that it will happen in the future; a literary use. *Who could ever foretell that Paul would turn traitor?*

forethought /fɔ:θɔ:t/. UNCOUNT N **Forethought** is the practice of thinking carefully about what will be needed, or about what the consequences of something will be. *With a bit of forethought, life can be made a lot easier.*

forever /fə^{8}rɛvə/. The form **for ever** is also used, except for meaning 3. **1** ADV Something that will happen or continue **forever** will always happen or continue. *They thought that their empire would last forever.* **2** ADV Something that has gone **forever** has gone and will never reappear. *This innocence is lost forever.* **3** ADV WITH -ING If you say that someone is **forever** doing something, you mean that they do it very often; an informal use which often shows disapproval. *Babbage was forever spotting errors in their calculations.*

forewarn /fɔ:wɔ:n/, **forewarns, forewarning, forewarned.** VB WITH OBJ If you **forewarn** someone, you warn them that something is going to happen. *We were forewarned that the food would be unusual.*

foreword /fɔ:wɜ:d/, **forewords.** COUNT N The **foreword** to a book is an introduction by the author or by someone else.

forfeit /fɔ:fɪt/, **forfeits, forfeiting, forfeited.** VB WITH OBJ If you **forfeit** a right, privilege, or possession, you have to give it up because you have done something wrong. *He has forfeited the right to be the leader of this nation.*

forgave /fəgeɪv/. **Forgave** is the past tense of **forgive.**

forge /fɔ:dʒ/, **forges, forging, forged. 1** VB WITH OBJ If someone **forges** banknotes, documents, or paintings, they copy them or make false ones in order to deceive people. *I learnt how to forge someone else's signature.* ♦ **forger** /fɔ:dʒə/ COUNT N *We're dealing with the work of a forger.* **2** VB WITH OBJ If you **forge** an alliance or relationship, you succeed in creating it. *They forged links with the French Communist Party.* **3** COUNT N A **forge** is a place where metal things such as horseshoes are made.

forge ahead. PHR VB If you **forge ahead** with something, you make a lot of progress.

forgery /fɔ:dʒə^{0}ri^1/, **forgeries. 1** UNCOUNT N **Forgery** is the crime of forging things such as banknotes, documents, or paintings. **2** COUNT N You can refer to a forged banknote, document, or painting as a **forgery.**

forget /fəgɛt/, **forgets, forgetting, forgot** /fəgɒt/, **forgotten** /fəgɒtə^{0}n/. **1** VB WITH OBJ OR REPORT VB If you **forget** something or **forget** how to do something, you cannot think of it, although you knew it in the past. *I never forget a face... She had forgotten how to ride a bicycle.* ♦ **forgotten** ADJ *...a forgotten event in her past.* **2** VB WITH OR WITHOUT OBJ If you **forget** to do something, you do not remember to do it. *I meant to see her on Friday, but I forgot all about it... I forgot to mention that John is a musician.* **3** VB WITH OBJ If you **forget** something that you had intended to bring with you, you do not remember to bring it. *Sorry to disturb you—I forgot my key.* **4** VB WITH OBJ You also say that someone **forgets** something when they deliberately do not think about it any more. *If you want my advice I think you ought to forget her.* **5** REFL VB If you **forget** yourself, you behave in an uncontrolled or unacceptable way; a formal use.

forgetful /fəgɛtfʊl/. ADJ Someone who is **forgetful** often forgets things. *I had been hopelessly vague, forgetful and sloppy.* ♦ **forgetfulness** UNCOUNT N *...his growing forgetfulness.*

forgive /fəgɪv/, **forgives, forgiving, forgave** /fəgeɪv/, **forgiven. 1** VB WITH OBJ OR VB WITH OBJ AND OBJ If you **forgive** someone who has done something wrong, you stop being angry with them. *I'll never forgive you for what you did... I forgave him everything.* **2** PASSIVE VB If you say that someone could **be forgiven** for doing a particular thing, you mean that you can understand the reasons for such behaviour. *We could be forgiven for thinking that we were still in London.*

forgiveness /fəgɪvnɪ^{2}s/. UNCOUNT N If you ask someone for their **forgiveness,** you are asking them to forgive you for something wrong that you have done.

forgiving /fəgɪvɪŋ/. ADJ Someone who is **forgiving** is willing to forgive people. *...a forgiving father.*

forgo /fɔ:gəʊ/. See **forego.**

forgot /fəgɒt/. **Forgot** is the past tense of **forget.**

forgotten /fəgɒtə^{0}n/. **Forgotten** is the past participle of **forget.**

fork /fɔ:k/, **forks, forking, forked. 1** COUNT N A **fork** is a tool that you eat food with. It consists of three or four prongs on the end of a handle. **2** COUNT N A **fork** is also a tool that you dig your garden with. It consists of three or four long prongs attached to a long handle. **3** COUNT N A **fork** in a road, path, or river is the point at which it divides into two parts in the shape of a 'Y'. **4** VB If something such as a path or river **forks,** it divides into two parts in the shape of a 'Y'. *...where the road forks.* ♦ **forked** ADJ *...an adder's forked tongue.*

fork out. PHR VB If you **fork out** for something, you pay for it; an informal use. *...the fortune I had already had to fork out on her education.*

forlorn /fəlɔ:n/. **1** ADJ If you are **forlorn,** you are lonely and unhappy. *The child looked very forlorn... ...a forlorn cry.* ♦ **forlornly** ADV *He was standing forlornly by the ticket office.* **2** ATTRIB ADJ A **forlorn** attempt or hope has no chance of success. *...the forlorn hope of achieving full employment.*

form /fɔ:m/, **forms, forming, formed. 1** COUNT N WITH SUPP A **form** of something is a type or kind of it. *He begged for any form of transport that would take him to the ferry... ...money in the form of notes or cheques... The broadcast took the form of an interview.* **2** ERG VB When people or things **form** a particular shape, they move or are arranged so that this shape is made. *They formed a ring... Long queues had formed.* **3** COUNT N The **form** of something is its shape. *The middle finger was touching the end of the thumb in the form of a letter O.* **4** COUNT N You can refer to someone or something that you see as a **form;** a literary use. *She gazed with deep affection at his slumbering form.* **5** VB WITH COMPLEMENT If something **forms** a thing with a particular structure or function, it has this structure or function. *The chair folds back to form a couch... ...red rocks forming a kind of cave.* **6** VB WITH COMPLEMENT The things or people that **form** a particular thing are what it consists of. *The contents of the house will form the basis of a major exhibition.* **7** VB WITH OBJ If you **form** an organization, group, or company, you start it. *The League was formed in 1959.* **8** ERG VB When something **forms** or **is formed,** it begins to exist. *The islands are volcanic and were formed comparatively recently... He formed the habit of taking long solitary walks.* **9** COUNT N A **form** is a piece of paper with questions on it. You write the answers on the same piece of paper. *Fill in this form... ...application forms.* **10** COUNT N In a school, a **form** is a class, or all the classes containing children of a similar age. *...the fifth form.*

PHRASES ● Someone who is **on form** is performing their usual activity very well. Someone who is **off form** is not performing as well as they usually do. ● If someone's behaviour is **true to form,** it is typical of them. *Watson, true to form, made an instant decision.*

formal /fɔ:mə^{0}l/. **1** ADJ **Formal** speech or behaviour is correct, rather than relaxed and friendly, and is used especially in official situations. *The letter was stiff and formal.* ♦ **formally** ADV *Everyone was formally lined up to meet the king.* ♦ **formality** /fə^{8}mælɪ^{1}ti^1/ UNCOUNT N *The elders conversed with strict formality.* **2** ATTRIB ADJ A **formal** statement or action is one that is done officially. *No formal declaration of war had been made.* ♦ **formally** ADV *He had already formally announced his candidacy.* **3** ADJ **Formal** occasions are ones at which people wear smart clothes and behave correctly rather than casually. **Formal** clothes are clothes suitable for formal occasions. *...a formal dinner.* ♦ **formally** ADV *He dressed rather formally.* **4** ADJ A **formal** garden or room is arranged in a neat and regular way. *...formal flowerbeds.* **5** ATTRIB ADJ **Formal** education or training is given officially, usually in a school or college. *...formal qualifications.*

formality /fə^{8}mælɪti^1/, **formalities. 1** COUNT N **Formalities** are formal actions that are carried out on particular occasions. *The pre-funeral formalities had to be attended to.* **2** See also **formal.**

formalize /fɔ:məlaɪz/, **formalizes, formalizing, formalized;** also spelled **formalise.** VB WITH OBJ If you **formalize** a plan or arrangement, you make it official. *Their marriage vows will be formalized.*

format /fɔ:mæt/, **formats.** COUNT N The **format** of something is the way it is arranged and presented. *They're producing material in different formats.*

formation /fə^{8}meɪʃə^{0}n/, **formations. 1** UNCOUNT N WITH SUPP The **formation** of something is its start or creation. *...the formation of the United Nations... ...the physical process of rock formation... ...the formation of new ideas.* **2** UNCOUNT N If things are in a particular **formation,** they are arranged in a particular pattern. *...aircraft flying in formation.* **3** COUNT N A rock **formation** or a cloud **formation** is rock or clouds of a particular shape.

formative /fɔ:mətɪv/. ATTRIB ADJ A **formative** period in your life has an important influence on your character and attitudes. *...my formative years.*

former /fɔːmə/. 1 ATTRIB ADJ **Former** is used to indicate what someone or something used to be, but no longer is. *...former President Richard Nixon... ...their former home.* 2 ATTRIB ADJ If something happened or existed in **former** days or **former** years, it happened or existed in the past. *...a selection of items published in former years.* 3 SING N OR PLURAL N When two people or things have just been mentioned, you can refer to the first of them as the **former.** *The former believe in a strong centralized government.* Also ADJ *Lack of space forbids the former alternative.*

formerly /fɔːməli[1]/. ADV If something happened **formerly,** it happened in the past. *Some of my salesmen formerly worked for this company.*

formidable /fɔːmɪdəbə[0]l, fə[8]mɪdəbə[0]l/. 1 ADJ Something that is **formidable** is difficult to deal with or overcome. *He had earned the reputation of being a formidable opponent.* 2 ADJ **Formidable** also means impressive because it is so good or great. *...the formidable army of brains that are at the Prime Minister's disposal.*

formless /fɔːmlɪ[2]s/. ADJ Something that is **formless** does not have a clear shape or structure; a formal use. *...formless chaos.*

formula /fɔːmjə[4]lə/, **formulae** /fɔːmjə[4]liː/ or **formulas.** 1 COUNT N A **formula** is a group of letters, numbers, or other symbols which represents a scientific or mathematical rule. *He knew the formula for converting kilometres into miles.* 2 COUNT N The **formula** for a substance tells you what amounts of other substances are needed in order to make that substance. 3 COUNT N A **formula** is a plan that is made as a way of dealing with a problem. *...a peace formula.*

formulate /fɔːmjə[4]leɪt/, **formulates, formulating, formulated.** 1 VB WITH OBJ If you **formulate** a plan or proposal, you develop it, thinking about the details carefully. *We had formulated our own strategy.* ♦ **formulation** /fɔːmjə[4]leɪʃə[0]n/ UNCOUNT N OR COUNT N *...the formulation of policy.* 2 VB WITH OBJ If you **formulate** a thought or opinion, you express it in words.

forsake /fə[8]seɪk/, **forsakes, forsaking, forsook** /fə[8]sʊk/, **forsaken;** a literary word. 1 VB WITH OBJ If you **forsake** someone, you stop helping them or stop looking after them. *Their leaders have forsaken them.* 2 VB WITH OBJ If you **forsake** something, you stop doing or having it. *...if you forsake religion.*

forsaken /fə[8]seɪkə[0]n/. ADJ A **forsaken** place is no longer lived in or no longer looked after; a literary use. *...a dusty, forsaken prairie village.*

fort /fɔːt/, **forts.** COUNT N A **fort** is a strong building that is used as a military base.

forte /fɔːteɪ/, **fortes.** COUNT N WITH SUPP You can say that an activity is your **forte** if you are very good at it. *Cooking is hardly my forte.*

forth /fɔːθ/; a literary word. 1 ADV To go **forth** from a place means to leave it. *The goats came bounding forth from their pens.* 2 ADV When something is brought **forth,** it is brought out into a place where you can see it. *He reached into his briefcase and brought forth a file.* 3 **and so forth:** see **so.** ● **back and forth:** see **back.**

forthcoming /fɔːθkʌmɪŋ/; a formal word. 1 ATTRIB ADJ A **forthcoming** event is going to happen soon. *...the forthcoming election.* 2 PRED ADJ When something such as help or information is **forthcoming,** it is provided or made available. *No evidence was forthcoming.* 3 PRED ADJ If someone is **forthcoming,** they willingly give you information when you ask. *He was not forthcoming on the way in which he had risen to power.*

forthright /fɔːθraɪt/. ADJ Someone who is **forthright** says clearly and strongly what they think. *...his forthright opposition to the war.*

forthwith /fɔːθwɪθ, -wɪð/. ADV **Forthwith** means immediately; a literary use. *He would take up his new duties forthwith.*

fortieth /fɔːtɪ[2]θ/. ADJ The **fortieth** item in a series is the one that you count as number forty.

fortification /fɔːtɪfɪkeɪʃə[0]n/, **fortifications.** 1 COUNT N **Fortifications** are buildings, walls, or ditches that are built to protect a place against attack. 2 UNCOUNT N The **fortification** of a place is the act of fortifying it; a formal use. *...the fortification of Florence.*

fortify /fɔːtɪfaɪ/, **fortifies, fortifying, fortified.** 1 VB WITH OBJ If people **fortify** a place, they make it better and less easy to attack, often by building a wall or ditch round it. *...the tiny fortified town.* 2 VB WITH OBJ Things such as food or drinks that **fortify** you make you feel stronger and more full of energy.

fortitude /fɔːtɪtjuːd/. UNCOUNT N If someone who is in pain or danger shows **fortitude,** they do not complain and remain brave and calm; a formal use.

fortnight /fɔːtnaɪt/, **fortnights.** COUNT N A **fortnight** is a period of two weeks. *I went to Rothesay for a fortnight.*

fortnightly /fɔːtnaɪtli[1]/. ATTRIB ADJ OR ADV A **fortnightly** event or magazine happens or appears once a fortnight. *...a fortnightly newspaper... The group meets fortnightly.*

fortress /fɔːtrɪ[2]s/, **fortresses.** COUNT N A **fortress** is a castle or other large strong building which is difficult for enemies to enter.

fortuitous /fə[8]tjuːɪtəs/. ADJ You describe an event as **fortuitous** when it happens by chance and helps someone; a formal use. *...a fortuitous discovery.*

fortunate /fɔːtʃə[4]nə[1]t/. 1 ADJ Someone who is **fortunate** is lucky. *...those who are fortunate enough to get jobs.* 2 ADJ You say that an event is **fortunate** when it is lucky for someone. *It was fortunate for Mr Fox that he decided to wait.* ♦ **fortunately** /fɔːtʃə[4]nətli[1]/ SENTENCE ADV *Fortunately she didn't mind.*

fortune /fɔːtʃə[4]n/, **fortunes.** 1 UNCOUNT N **Fortune** or good **fortune** is good luck. Ill **fortune** is bad luck. *He has since had the good fortune to be promoted.* 2 PLURAL N WITH POSS If you talk about someone's **fortunes,** you are referring to the extent to which they are doing well or being successful. *In the following years, Victor's fortunes improved considerably.* 3 PHRASE When someone **tells** your **fortune,** they tell you what will happen to you in the future. 4 COUNT N A **fortune** is a very large amount of money. *His father left him an immense fortune.*

forty /fɔːti[1]/, **forties. Forty** is the number 40.

forum /fɔːrəm/, **forums.** COUNT N A **forum** is a place or event in which people exchange ideas and discuss things. *...Parliament's role as a forum for debate.*

forward /fɔːwəd/, **forwards, forwarding, forwarded. Forward** can be used as an adverb, an adjective, or a verb. **Forwards** is only used as an adverb. 1 ADV OR ATTRIB ADJ **Forward** or **forwards** is the direction in front of you. *Suddenly she leaned forward... ...his forward movement.* 2 ADV OR ADJ AFTER N **Forward** or **forwards** is also used to indicate that something progresses or becomes more modern. *Obviously it's a great step forward for you... ...moving society forward into a better world.* 3 ADV OR ATTRIB ADJ If you look **forward** in time, you look into the future. *When I was your age I could only look forward... ...forward planning.* ● See also **look forward to.** 4 VB WITH OBJ If you **forward** a letter that has been sent to someone who has moved, you send it to them at the place where they are now living.

fossil /fɒsə[0]l/, **fossils.** COUNT N A **fossil** is the hardened remains of a prehistoric animal or plant, or a print that it leaves in rock.

fossil fuel, fossil fuels. MASS N **Fossil fuels** are fuels such as coal, oil, and peat that are formed from the decayed remains of plants and animals.

fossilized /fɒsɪlaɪzd/; also spelled **fossilised.** ADJ A **fossilized** animal or plant is one whose remains have become hard and formed a fossil in prehistoric times. *...fossilized bones.*

foster /fɒstə/, **fosters, fostering, fostered.** 1 ATTRIB ADJ **Foster** parents are people who officially take a child into their family for a period of time, without becoming the child's legal parents. The child is referred to as their **foster** child. 2 VB WITH OR WITHOUT OBJ If you **foster** children, you take them into your family for a period of time, without becoming their legal parents. *When they are fostered, boys have more behaviour problems than girls.* 3 VB WITH OBJ If you **foster** a feeling, activity, or idea, you help it to develop. *The local council has a policy of fostering music, drama, and crafts.*

fought /fɔːt/. **Fought** is the past tense and past participle of **fight.**

foul /faʊl/, **fouler, foulest; fouls, fouling, fouled.** 1 ADJ Something that is **foul** is dirty or smells unpleasant. *The water in the pools became tepid and foul.* 2 ADJ **Foul** language contains swear words or rude words. 3 ADJ If someone has a **foul** temper, they become angry or violent suddenly and easily. 4 PHRASE If you **fall foul of** someone or something, you accidentally do something which gets you into trouble with them. 5 VB WITH OBJ If you **foul** something, you make it dirty; a formal use. *The deck would soon be fouled with blood.* 6 COUNT N In a game or sport, a **foul** is an action that is against the rules. *The team's record of fouls was among the worst.*

foul up. PHR VB If you **foul up** something such as a plan, you spoil it by doing something wrong or stupid; an informal use.

foul play. UNCOUNT N **Foul play** is criminal violence or activity that results in someone's death. *There was no evidence of foul play.*

found /faʊnd/, **founds, founding, founded.** 1 **Found** is the past tense and past participle of **find.** 2 VB WITH OBJ If someone **founds** a town or an organization, they cause it to be built or to exist. *The Constituency Labour Party was founded in 1918 by Walter Ayles and others... The theatre was founded in 1720.* 3 VB WITH OBJ AND 'on' OR 'upon' If something **is founded** on a particular thing, it is based on it. *...a political system founded on force.* ● See also **well-founded.**

foundation /faʊndeɪʃə[0]n/, **foundations.** 1 COUNT N WITH SUPP The **foundation** of something such as a belief or way of life is the idea, attitude, or experience on which it is based. *Respect for the law is the foundation of civilised living.* 2 PLURAL N The **foundations** of a building or other structure are the layers of bricks or concrete below the ground that it is built on. 3 SING N When a new institution or organization is created, you can refer to this event as its **foundation.** *...since the foundation of the university.* 4 COUNT N A **foundation** is an organization which provides money for a special purpose. *...the National Foundation for Educational Research.* 5 UNCOUNT N If a story, idea, or argument has no **foundation,** there are no facts to prove that it is true. *The suggestion is absurd and without foundation.*

founder /faʊndə/, **founders, foundering, foundered.** 1 COUNT N The **founder** of a town or organization is the person who caused it to be built or exist. *...Thomas Kemp, the founder of Kemp Town.* 2 VB If something **founders,** it fails. *Without their assistance the arrangement would have foundered.* 3 VB If a ship **founders,** it fills with water and sinks.

foundry /faʊndri[1]/, **foundries.** COUNT N A **foundry** is a place where metal or glass is melted and formed into particular shapes.

fountain /faʊntɪn/, **fountains.** COUNT N A **fountain** is an ornamental feature in a pool which consists of a jet of water that is forced up into the air by a pump.

fountain pen, fountain pens. COUNT N A **fountain pen** is a pen with a container inside which you fill with ink.

four /fɔː/, **fours.** 1 **Four** is the number 4. 2 PHRASE If you are **on all fours,** you are crawling or leaning on your hands and knees. *Claud slipped through the hedge on all fours.*

foursome /fɔːsəm/, **foursomes.** COUNT N A **foursome** is a group of four people. *We functioned well as a foursome.*

fourteen /fɔːtiːn/. **Fourteen** is the number 14.

fourteenth /fɔːtiːnθ/. ADJ The **fourteenth** item in a series is the one that you count as number fourteen.

fourth /fɔːθ/, **fourths.** 1 ADJ The **fourth** item in a series is the one that you count as number four. 2 COUNT N A **fourth** is one of four equal parts of something; an old-fashioned use. *They conceded him three-fourths or more of the spending cuts he sought.*

fowl /faʊl/, **fowls. Fowl** can also be the plural. COUNT N A **fowl** is a bird, especially one that can be eaten as food.

fox /fɒks/, **foxes, foxing, foxed.** 1 COUNT N A **fox** is a wild animal which looks like a dog and has reddish-brown fur. 2 VB WITH OBJ If something **foxes** you, you cannot understand it or solve it; an informal use. *We were foxed by the calculations.*

foyer /fɔɪeɪ, fɔɪə/, **foyers.** COUNT N The **foyer** of a theatre, cinema, or hotel is the large area just inside the main doors where people meet or wait.

fracas /frækɑː/. SING N A **fracas** is a rough, noisy quarrel or fight; a formal use. *They got involved in another fracas.*

fraction /frækʃə[0]n/, **fractions.** 1 COUNT N You can refer to a small amount or proportion of something as a **fraction** of it. *For a fraction of a second, I hesitated... The door opened a fraction.* 2 COUNT N In arithmetic, a **fraction** is an exact division of a number. For example, ½ and ⅓ are fractions of 1.

fractionally /frækʃə[0]nəlɪ[1], -ʃənə[0]lɪ[1]/. ADV **Fractionally** means very slightly. *They're only fractionally different.*

fracture /fræktʃə/, **fractures, fracturing, fractured.** 1 COUNT N A **fracture** is a crack or break in something, especially a bone. *...a fracture of the left shoulder blade.* 2 ERG VB If something such as a bone **fractures** or **is fractured,** it breaks. *...a fractured ankle.*

fragile /frædʒaɪl/. ADJ **Fragile** things are easily broken or harmed. *...constructions built of fragile materials... ...extremely fragile economies.* ♦ **fragility** /frə[3]dʒɪlɪ[1]ti[1]/ UNCOUNT N *...the softness and fragility of baby animals.*

fragment, fragments, fragmenting, fragmented; pronounced /frægmə[0]nt/ when it is a noun and /frægment/ when it is a verb. 1 COUNT N A **fragment** of something is a small piece or part of it. *...a small fragment of bone... This was only a fragment out of a long conversation with John.* 2 ERG VB If something **fragments** or **is fragmented,** it breaks or separates into small pieces. *Farms are constantly being fragmented into smaller holdings.* ♦ **fragmentation**

/frægmenteɪʃə[0]n/ UNCOUNT N *This led to its fragmentation into eight independent parties.*

fragmentary /frægmə[2]ntə[0]ri[1]/. ADJ Something that is **fragmentary** is made up of small or unconnected pieces. *...the fragmentary evidence for this story.*

fragmented /frægmentɪd/. ADJ Something that is **fragmented** consists of a lot of different parts which seem unconnected with each other. *It's a book that is very fragmented in its structure.*

fragrance /freɪgrəns/, **fragrances.** COUNT N OR UNCOUNT N You can refer to a sweet or pleasant smell as a **fragrance.**

fragrant /freɪgrənt/. ADJ Something that is **fragrant** has a sweet or pleasant smell. *...fragrant flowers.*

frail /freɪl/, **frailer, frailest.** 1 ADJ A **frail** person is not strong or healthy. *...a frail old man.* 2 ADJ Something that is **frail** is easily broken or damaged. *...a frail structure.*

frailty /freɪlti[1]/, **frailties.** 1 PLURAL N OR UNCOUNT N If you talk about someone's **frailties** or **frailty,** you are referring to their weaknesses. *...our vanities and frailties.* 2 UNCOUNT N **Frailty** is also the condition of being weak in health. *...the advanced age and frailty of some of the inhabitants.*

frame /freɪm/, **frames, framing, framed.** 1 COUNT N A **frame** is a structure inside which you can fit something such as a window, door, or picture. *...gold-painted picture frames.* 2 COUNT N A **frame** is also an arrangement of bars that give an object its shape and strength. *...a bunk made of canvas laced to a steel frame.* 3 PLURAL N The **frames** of a pair of glasses are the wire or plastic part which holds the lenses in place. 4 COUNT N If someone has a big or small **frame,** they have a big or small body. *His big frame was gaunt and weak.* 5 VB WITH OBJ If you **frame** a picture or photograph, you put it in a frame. *...a framed photograph of her mother.* 6 VB WITH OBJ AND ADJUNCT If you **frame** something in a particular kind of language, you express it in that way. *Laws are invariably framed in tortuous jargon.* 7 VB WITH OBJ If you **are framed** by someone, they make it seem that you have committed a crime, although you have not; an informal use. *I was framed by the authorities.*

frame of mind. SING N Your **frame of mind** is the mood that you are in at a particular time. *I'm not in the right frame of mind for riddles.*

framework /freɪmwɜːk/, **frameworks.** 1 COUNT N A **framework** is a structure that forms a support or frame for something. *There are nine large panels set in a richly carved framework.* 2 COUNT N WITH SUPP A **framework** is also a set of rules, ideas, or beliefs which you use in order to decide how to behave. *They were able to absorb these changes within the framework of traditional institutions and ideas.*

franchise /fræntʃaɪz/, **franchises.** 1 SING N The **franchise** is the right to vote in an election, especially one to elect a parliament. *...a policy of universal franchise.* 2 COUNT N A **franchise** is an authority that is given by a company to someone, allowing them to sell its goods or services.

frank /fræŋk/, **franker, frankest.** ADJ If someone is **frank,** they state things in an open and honest way. *...a frank discussion.* ♦ **frankness** UNCOUNT N *He seemed to be speaking with complete frankness.*

frankly /fræŋkli[1]/. 1 SENTENCE ADV You use **frankly** when boldly stating a feeling or opinion. *Frankly, this has all come as a bit of a shock.* 2 ADV If you say or do something **frankly,** you say or do it in an open and honest way. *He asked me to tell him frankly what I wished to do.*

frantic /fræntɪk/. 1 ADJ If you are **frantic,** you behave in a wild and desperate way because you are frightened or worried. *We were frantic with worry.* ♦ **frantically** ADV *...frantically searching for David.* 2 ADJ When there is **frantic** activity, things are done hurriedly and in a disorganized way. *...a frantic week of high-level discussions.* ♦ **frantically** ADV *They worked frantically throughout the day.*

fraternal /frə[3]tɜːnə[0]l/. ADJ **Fraternal** means having strong links of friendship with another group of people; a formal use. *Fraternal greetings were received from the Communist Party of the Soviet Union.*

fraternity /frə[3]tɜːnɪti[1]/, **fraternities;** a formal word. 1 UNCOUNT N **Fraternity** refers to feelings of friendship between groups of people. 2 COUNT N WITH SUPP You can refer to a group of people with the same profession or interests as a **fraternity.** *...the banking fraternity.*

fraud /frɔːd/, **frauds.** 1 UNCOUNT N **Fraud** is the crime of gaining money by deceit or trickery. *His closest adviser is under indictment for fraud.* 2 COUNT N A **fraud** is something that deceives people in an illegal or immoral way. 3 COUNT N Someone who is a **fraud** is not the person they pretend to be or does not have the abilities or status they pretend to have.

fraudulent /frɔːdjə[4]lənt/. ADJ Something that is **fraudulent** is deliberately deceitful, dishonest, or untrue. *The promise Mrs Haze had made was a fraudulent one.*

fraught /frɔːt/. 1 PRED ADJ WITH 'with' If something is **fraught** with problems or difficulties, it is full of them. *Any further moves would be fraught with danger.* 2 ADJ Someone who is **fraught** is very worried or anxious. *Everyone's rather tense and fraught tonight.*

fray /freɪ/, **frays, fraying, frayed.** 1 ERG VB If something such as cloth or rope **frays,** its threads or strands become worn and it is likely to tear or break. *His shirts were frayed.* 2 SING N You can refer to an exciting activity or argument that you are involved in as the **fray.** *I returned to the fray with renewed vigour.*

freak /friːk/, **freaks.** 1 COUNT N People call someone a **freak** when their behaviour or attitudes are unusual or when they are physically abnormal in some way. *A woman is considered a freak if she puts her career first... ...hair-raising freaks, including a two-headed Indian.* 2 MOD A **freak** event or action is unusual and unlikely to happen. *My mother died in a freak accident, struck by lightning at a picnic.*

freckled /frekə[0]ld/. ADJ Someone who is **freckled** has freckles. *...her freckled face.*

freckles /frekə[0]lz/. PLURAL N **Freckles** are small, light brown spots on someone's skin, especially their face. *She had red hair and freckles.*

free /friː/, **freer** /friːə/, **freest** /friː[2]st/; **frees, freeing, freed.** 1 ADJ Someone or something that is **free** is not controlled or limited. *Within the EEC there is free movement of labour... ...a free press.* 2 ADJ OR ADV Someone who is **free** is no longer a prisoner or a slave. *I wish to return to London, this time as a free man... One prisoner in seven had been set free.* 3 VB WITH OBJ If you **free** a prisoner or a slave, you release them. *She was arrested but freed after three weeks.* 4 VB WITH OBJ If you **free** someone of something unpleasant or restricting, you get rid of it for them. *...the attempt to free France of the Dictator.* 5 PRED ADJ A person or thing that is **free** of something unpleasant does not have it or is not affected by it. *The area will be free of pollution by the year 2000... ...free from all financial worry.* 6 VB WITH OBJ If you **free** something such as money or resources, you make it available for a task or purpose. *We could cut defence expenditure, freeing vital resources for more useful purposes.* 7 ADJ If you have a **free** period of time or are **free** at a particular time, you are not busy then. *They don't have much free time... Are you free for lunch?* 8 ADJ A place, seat, or machine that is **free** is not occupied or not being used. 9 ADJ If something is **free,** you can have it or use it without paying. *...free school meals.* 10 ADV If something is cut or pulled **free,** it is moved so that it is no longer attached to something or trapped. *I shook my jacket free and hurried off.* 11 VB WITH OBJ If you **free** something that is fixed or trapped, you remove or loosen it from the place where it was. *He freed his arms.* 12 to give someone **a free hand:** see **hand.**

-free. **-free** is added to nouns to form adjectives that indicate that something does not have the thing mentioned. *Each submarine reported a trouble-free launch... ...error-free computer programs.*

freedom /friːdəm/, **freedoms.** 1 UNCOUNT N OR COUNT N **Freedom** is the state of being allowed to do or say what you want. *Political freedom is still rare... ...freedom of speech... ...the erosion of basic freedoms.* 2 UNCOUNT N When slaves or prisoners escape or are released, you can say that they gain their **freedom.** *Many slaves buy their freedom with what they save from farming.* 3 UNCOUNT N When someone or something has **freedom** of movement, they can move about without restriction. 4 UNCOUNT N WITH 'from' When there is **freedom** from something unpleasant, people are not affected by it. *...freedom from hunger and starvation.*

freedom fighter, freedom fighters. COUNT N **Freedom fighters** are people who try to overthrow the government of their country, using violent methods; used showing approval.

free enterprise. UNCOUNT N **Free enterprise** is an economic system in which businesses compete for profit without much government control.

free kick, free kicks. COUNT N When there is a **free kick** in a game of football or rugby, the ball is given to a member of one side to kick without opposition because a member of the other side has broken a rule.

freelance /friːlɑːns/. ADJ OR ADV A **freelance** journalist or photographer is not employed by one organization, but is paid for each piece of work that they do by the organization that they do it for. *...freelance writing... I work freelance.*

freely /friːli[1]/. 1 ADV You say that something is done **freely** when it is done often or in large quantities. *He spends fairly freely... ...perspiring freely.* 2 ADV Someone or something that can move or act **freely** is not controlled or limited by anything. *British goods were allowed to move freely from one state to another.* 3 ADV If you can talk **freely,** you do not need to be careful about what you say. *We are all comrades here and I may talk freely.* 4 SUBMOD Something that is **freely** available can be obtained easily. *These drugs are freely available in most cities.* 5 ADV Something that is given or done **freely** is given or done willingly. *...freely given affection.*

freer /friːə/. **Freer** is the comparative of **free.**

free-range. ADJ **Free-range** eggs are produced by hens that can move and feed freely on an area of open ground.

freest /friː[2]st/. **Freest** is the superlative of **free.**

freestyle /friːstaɪl/. SING N **Freestyle** refers to sports competitions, especially swimming and wrestling, in which competitors can use any style or method they like. *She won the 100 metres freestyle.*

freeway /friːweɪ/, **freeways.** COUNT N A **freeway** is a road with several lanes and controlled places where vehicles join it, so that people can travel quickly; an American use. *He turned off the freeway.*

free will. 1 UNCOUNT N If you believe in **free will,** you believe that people are able to choose what they do and that their actions are not decided in advance by God or Fate. 2 PHRASE If you do something **of** your **own free will,** you do it by choice and not because you are forced. *He has come back of his own free will.*

freeze /friːz/, **freezes, freezing, froze** /frəʊz/, **frozen** /frəʊzə[0]n/. 1 ERG VB When a liquid **freezes** or when something **freezes** it, it becomes solid because it is so cold. *The water froze in the wells.* 2 VB WITH OBJ If you **freeze** food, you preserve it by storing it at a temperature below freezing point. 3 VB When it **freezes** outside, the temperature falls below freezing point. 4 VB If you **freeze,** you become very cold; an informal use. *You'll freeze to death out there.* 5 VB You can also say that someone **freezes** when they suddenly stop moving and become completely still and quiet. *Then she sensed something moving about. She froze.* 6 VB WITH OBJ To **freeze** something such as wages or prices means to state officially that they will not be allowed to increase during a particular period of time. *Various attempts to control or freeze wages have failed.* Also COUNT N *...a freeze in the nuclear arms race.* 7 See also **deep freeze, freezing, frozen.**

freezer /friːzə/, **freezers.** COUNT N A **freezer** is a large container in which you can store food for long periods of time, because the temperature inside is kept below freezing point.

freezing /friːzɪŋ/. 1 ADJ If something is **freezing,** it is very cold indeed. *It's freezing outside... The water was freezing.* 2 PRED ADJ If you are **freezing,** you feel unpleasantly cold. 3 UNCOUNT N **Freezing** is the same as freezing point. *The air temperature was now well below freezing.*

freezing point. 1 UNCOUNT N **Freezing point** is 0° Celsius, the temperature at which water freezes. *The temperature was well above freezing point.* 2 COUNT N The **freezing point** of a particular substance is the temperature at which it freezes.

freight /freɪt/. 1 UNCOUNT N **Freight** refers to the movement of goods by lorries, trains, ships, or aeroplanes. *It is going by air freight.* 2 UNCOUNT N **Freight** is the goods that are transported by lorries, trains, ships, or aeroplanes. *...eight thousand tons of freight.*

freighter /freɪtə/, **freighters.** COUNT N A **freighter** is a ship or aeroplane designed to carry goods.

French /frent[0]ʃ/. 1 ADJ **French** means belonging or relating to France. 2 UNCOUNT N **French** is the language spoken by people who live in France and in parts of Belgium, Canada, and Switzerland. 3 PLURAL N **The French** are the people who come from France.

French fries. PLURAL N **French fries** are thin sticks of potato fried in oil.

French horn, French horns. See **horn.**

French window, French windows. COUNT N **French windows** are glass doors which lead onto a garden or balcony.

frenetic /frɪ[2]netɪk/. ADJ **Frenetic** activity or behaviour is fast, energetic, and uncontrolled.

frenzied /frenzɪd/. ADJ **Frenzied** actions are wild, excited, and uncontrolled. *...frenzied cheers... ...a frenzied mob of students.*

frenzy /frenzi[1]/, **frenzies.** COUNT N OR UNCOUNT N Someone who is in a **frenzy** is very excited and violent or uncontrolled. *It would drive Thomas into a frenzy... There was an element of frenzy and desperation in the singing.*

frequency /friːkwənsi[1]/, **frequencies.** 1 UNCOUNT N The **frequency** of an event is the number of times it happens. *Disasters appear to be increasing in fre-*

quency... ...the frequency of their appearance. **2** COUNT N OR UNCOUNT N The **frequency** of a sound or radio wave is the rate at which it vibrates; a technical use.

frequent, frequents, frequenting, frequented; pronounced /fri:kwənt/ when it is an adjective, and /fri'kwεnt/ when it is a verb. **1** ADJ You say that something is **frequent** when it happens often. George's absences were frequent... They move at frequent intervals. ♦ **frequently** ADV This question is frequently asked. **2** VB WITH OBJ If you **frequent** a place, you go there often. Jo liked to frequent the bars.

fresco /frεskəʊ/, **frescoes.** COUNT N A **fresco** is a picture painted onto a wet plastered wall; a technical use.

fresh /frεʃ/, **fresher, freshest. 1** ATTRIB ADJ A **fresh** thing or amount replaces or is added to a previous one. He poured himself a fresh drink... Rose had given him fresh instructions. **2** ADJ Something that is **fresh** has been done or experienced recently. ...fresh footprints in the snow... Memories of the war are fresh in both countries. **3** ADJ **Fresh** food has been produced or picked recently, and has not been preserved. ...fresh vegetables. **4** ADJ If you describe something as **fresh**, you mean you like it because it is new and exciting. He has a fresh approach. ♦ **freshness** UNCOUNT N This gives the novel freshness and charm. **5** ADJ If something smells, tastes, or feels **fresh**, it is pleasant and refreshing. If something looks **fresh**, it is pleasantly clean in appearance. The air is cool and fresh... ...the fresh dawn light. **6** ADJ **Fresh** water is water that is not salty, for example the water in streams and lakes. **7** ADJ If the weather is **fresh**, it is fairly cold and windy. **8** PRED ADJ If you are **fresh** from a place, you have been there very recently. ...coming fresh from the junior school.

freshen /frεʃ⁰n/, **freshens, freshening, freshened. 1** VB WITH OBJ If you **freshen** something, you make it cleaner and fresher. The air freshened his lungs... Keith freshened himself with a wash. **2** VB If the wind **freshens**, it becomes stronger.

freshen up. PHR VB If you **freshen up**, you have a quick wash and tidy yourself up. Sarah and Barry returned to their hotel to freshen up.

freshly /frεʃli¹/. ADV Something that is **freshly** done has been done recently. ...freshly cooked food.

freshwater /frεʃwɔːtə/. **1** ATTRIB ADJ A **freshwater** lake or pool contains water that is not salty. **2** ATTRIB ADJ A **freshwater** fish lives in a river, lake, or pool that is not salty.

fret /frεt/, **frets, fretting, fretted.** VB If you **fret** about something, you worry about it. Daniel was fretting about money... Don't fret. He'll be all right.

fretful /frεtfʊl/. ADJ If someone is **fretful**, they behave in a way that shows that they are worried or uncomfortable. ...fretful babies.

friar /fraɪə/, **friars.** COUNT N A **friar** is a member of a Catholic religious order.

friction /frɪkʃ⁰n/, **frictions. 1** UNCOUNT N **Friction** is the force that prevents things from moving freely when they are touching each other. **2** UNCOUNT N **Friction** is also the rubbing of one thing against another. **3** UNCOUNT N OR PLURAL N **Friction** between people is disagreement and quarrels. ...friction between Healy and his colleagues... ...family frictions.

Friday /fraɪdi¹/, **Fridays.** UNCOUNT N OR COUNT N **Friday** is the day after Thursday and before Saturday.

fridge /frɪdʒ/, **fridges.** COUNT N A **fridge** is a large metal container for storing food at low temperatures to keep it fresh; a British use.

friend /frεnd/, **friends. 1** COUNT N Your **friends** are the people you know well and like spending time with. He was my best friend at Oxford... ...an old friend of the family. **2** PLURAL N If you are **friends** with someone, you like each other and enjoy spending time together. You used to be friends with him, didn't you? **3** PHRASE If you **make friends** with someone, you begin a friendship with them. **4** PLURAL N The people who help and support a cause or a country are often referred to as its **friends**. All friends of Ireland should support us.

friendless /frεndli¹s/. ADJ A **friendless** person has no friends. She remained friendless and miserable.

friendly /frεndli¹/, **friendlier, friendliest; friendlies. 1** ADJ A **friendly** person is kind and pleasant. The women had been friendly to Lyn... ...a friendly smile. ♦ **friendliness** UNCOUNT N The friendliness was gone from his voice. **2** ADJ If you are **friendly** with someone, you like each other and enjoy spending time together. I became friendly with a young engineer. **3** ADJ A **friendly** place or object makes you feel comfortable. ...a small room lit by friendly lamps. **4** ADJ A **friendly** fight or argument is not serious. **5** COUNT N A **friendly** is a sports match that is played for practice and not as part of a competition.

friendship /frεndʃɪp/, **friendships. 1** COUNT N OR UNCOUNT N A **friendship** is a relationship or state of friendliness between two people who like each other. My friendship with her had taught me a great deal... Friendship is based on shared interests. **2** UNCOUNT N **Friendship** between countries is a relationship in which they help and support each other. ...his efforts to promote Anglo-German friendship.

frieze /fri:z/, **friezes.** COUNT N A **frieze** is a long, narrow decorative feature along the top of a wall.

frigate /frɪgə¹t/, **frigates.** COUNT N A **frigate** is a small, fast ship used by the navy to protect other ships.

fright /fraɪt/, **frights. 1** UNCOUNT N **Fright** is a sudden feeling of fear. I heard Amy cry out in fright... He was paralysed with fright. **2** PHRASE If someone **takes fright**, they experience a sudden feeling of fear. The animals took fright and ran away. **3** COUNT N A **fright** is an experience which gives you a sudden feeling of fear. She gave me a nasty fright with those rabbits.

frighten /fraɪt⁰n/, **frightens, frightening, frightened.** VB WITH OBJ If something **frightens** you, it makes you feel afraid, nervous, or worried. Rats and mice don't frighten me. ♦ **frightened** ADJ The men led their frightened families to safety... I was frightened of making a fool of myself. ♦ **frightening** ADJ ...the most frightening sight he had ever seen... It is frightening to think what a complete search would reveal.

frighten away. PHR VB If you **frighten** someone **away**, you scare them so that they go away and do not harm you. He waved his torch to frighten away some animal.

frighten into. PHR VB If you **frighten** someone **into** doing something, you force them to do it by making them afraid. They tried to frighten me into talking.

frighten off. PHR VB To **frighten** a person **off** means to make them unwilling to become involved in something. Cliff was less encouraging, seeking to frighten him off.

frightful /fraɪtfʊl/. ADJ Something that is **frightful** is very bad or unpleasant; an informal use. The smell was frightful. ♦ **frightfully** ADV She had behaved frightfully.

frigid /frɪdʒɪd/. ADJ If a woman is **frigid**, she does not easily become sexually aroused.

frill /frɪl/, **frills. 1** COUNT N A **frill** is a long, narrow, folded strip of cloth which is attached to something as a decoration. ...a white pillow with a blue frill round it. ♦ **frilled** /frɪld/ ADJ ...a white frilled blouse. **2** PLURAL N If something has no **frills**, it is simple and has no unnecessary or additional features. ...a house with no frills... ...the necessities of life but none of the frills.

frilly /frɪli¹/. ADJ **Frilly** clothes or objects are decorated with many frills. ...a frilly nightdress.

fringe /frɪndʒ/, **fringes. 1** COUNT N A **fringe** is hair which is cut so that it hangs over your forehead. **2** COUNT N A **fringe** is also a decoration attached to clothes and other objects, consisting of a row of hanging threads. ...silk shawls with fringes. **3** COUNT N The **fringes** of a place are the parts farthest from the centre. ...on the western fringe of London. **4** COUNT N If you refer to the **fringes** of an activity or organization, you mean the least typical parts of it. ...the radical fringe of the Labour Party... ...fringe theatre.

fringed /frɪndʒ⁰d/. ADJ **1** **Fringed** clothes are decorated with a fringe. ...a fringed leather jacket. **2** PRED ADJ WITH ADJUNCT If a place or object is **fringed** with things, they are situated along its edges. Her eyes were large, fringed with long eyelashes... ...a bay of blue water fringed by palm trees.

frisk /frɪsk/, **frisks, frisking, frisked. 1** VB WITH OBJ If someone **frisks** you, they search you quickly with their hands to see if you are hiding a weapon; an informal use. Two policemen grabbed his arms while another one frisked him. **2** VB When animals **frisk**, they run around in a happy, energetic way. ...his nine dogs frisking round him.

fritter /frɪtə/, **fritters, frittering, frittered.** COUNT N **Fritters** consist of fruit or vegetables dipped in batter and fried.

fritter away. PHR VB If you **fritter away** time or money, you waste it on unimportant things. She would not fritter away her vacation on reading.

frivolity /frɪvɒlɪ¹ti¹/. UNCOUNT N **Frivolity** is silly, light-hearted behaviour. Harry tolerated the younger man's frivolity.

frivolous /frɪvələs/. **1** ADJ A **frivolous** person is being silly when they should be serious or sensible. Forgive me. I didn't mean to sound frivolous. **2** ADJ **Frivolous** objects and activities are amusing or silly, rather than useful. I spend a lot of my salary on frivolous things.

frizzy /frɪzi¹/. ADJ **Frizzy** hair has stiff, wiry curls. ...a youth with a mop of frizzy hair.

fro /frəʊ/. **to and fro:** see to.

frock /frɒk/, **frocks.** COUNT N A **frock** is a woman's or girl's dress; an old-fashioned use.

frog /frɒg/, **frogs. 1** COUNT N A **frog** is a small creature with smooth skin, big eyes, and long back legs which it uses for jumping. **2** PHRASE If you **have a frog in** your **throat**, you cannot speak properly because your throat is partly blocked by mucus; an informal use.

frogman /frɒgmə³n/, **frogmen.** COUNT N A **frogman** is a person whose job involves working underwater.

frog-march, frog-marches, frog-marching, frog-marched. VB WITH OBJ If you **are frog-marched** somewhere, you are forced to walk there by two people, each holding one of your arms. I was frog-marched down to the police station.

frolic /frɒlɪk/, **frolics, frolicking, frolicked. 1** VB When animals or children **frolic**, they run around and play in a lively way. The children frolicked on the sand. **2** COUNT N A **frolic** is lively, happy, and carefree behaviour. What started as a frolic might turn into something different.

from /frɒm/. **1** PREP You use **from** to say what the source, origin, or starting point of something is. ...wisps of smoke from a small fire... She came from Ilford... Get the leaflet from a post office... ...a song from his latest film... The shafts were cut from heavy planks of wood. **2** PREP If someone or something moves or is taken **from** a place, they leave it or are removed, so that they are no longer there. They drove down from Leeds... We scrambled from our trucks and ran after them... We went around clearing rubbish from the fields. **3** PREP If you take something **from** an amount, you reduce the amount by that much. This will be deducted from your pension. **4** PREP If you are away **from** a place, you are not there. They were away from home. **5** PREP If you return **from** doing something, you return after doing it. The men had not yet come back from fishing. **6** PREP If you see or hear something **from** a particular position, you are in that position when you see it or hear it. From the top of the bus you could look down on people below. **7** PREP Something that sticks out or hangs **from** an object is attached to it or touches it. ...buckets hanging from a bamboo pole. **8** PREP You can use **from** when giving distances. For example, if one place is fifty miles **from** another, the distance between them is fifty miles. **9** PREP If a road goes **from** one place to another, you can travel along it between the two places. ...on the main road from Paris to Marseilles. **10** PREP If something happens **from** a particular time, it begins to happen then. She was deaf from birth... We had no rain from March to October. **11** PREP If something changes **from** one thing to another, it stops being the first thing and becomes the second thing. They enlarged the committee from 17 members to 30... ...translating from one language to another. **12** PREP If one thing happens **from** another, it happens as a result of it. From nervousness she said a few more stupid things... My eyes hurt from the wind. **13** PREP You use **from** to give the reason for an opinion. I could see from her face that she felt disappointed... I am speaking from personal experience. **14** PREP You say **from** one thing to another when you are stating the range of things that are possible. The process takes from two to five weeks... The flowers may be anything from pink to crimson.

frond /frɒnd/, **fronds.** COUNT N **Fronds** are long spiky leaves. ...palm fronds.

front /frʌnt/, **fronts. 1** COUNT N The **front** of something is the part of it that faces you or faces forward. ...jackets with six buttons down the front... The policeman searched the front of the car. Also ATTRIB ADJ ...the front gate... One of his front teeth was gone. **2** PREP If you do something **in front of** someone, you do it in their presence. I couldn't tell you in front of Sam. **3** COUNT N In a war, the **front** is the place where two armies are fighting. ...fourteen miles from the front. **4** COUNT N If something happens on a particular **front**, it happens with regard to a particular situation or activity. On the intellectual front, little advance has been made. **5** SING N If someone puts on a **front**, they pretend to have feelings which they do not have. ...presenting a united front to the world. **6** COUNT N A **front** is also the line where a mass of cold air meets a mass of warm air; a technical use.

PHRASES ● If someone or something is **in front**, they are ahead of other people or things who are in the same group or who are doing the same activity. Jay walked in front and Simon and Val behind him... ...a lady in the row in front. ● If you are **in front** in a competition or contest, you are winning. After two missed penalty strokes, England were in front. ● If someone or something is **in front of** a particular thing, they are facing it or close to the front part of it. A car was drawing up in front of the house... There was a man standing in front of me.

frontage /frʌntɪdʒ/, **frontages.** COUNT N The **frontage** of a building is the side facing the street. ...the Victorian frontage of the Treasury.

frontal /frʌntə^{0}l/. 1 ATTRIB ADJ A **frontal** attack is direct and obvious. *...a frontal attack on the unions.* 2 ATTRIB ADJ **Frontal** also means concerning the front of something. *...a frontal view.*

frontier /frʌntɪə/, **frontiers.** 1 COUNT N A **frontier** is a border between two countries. 2 COUNT N WITH SUPP The **frontiers** of a subject are the limits to which it can be known or done. *They are doing work on the frontiers of discovery... ...crossing social frontiers.*

front line. SING N The **front line** is the place where two armies are fighting each other. *We came to within a mile of the front line... ...front-line troops.*

frost /frɒst/, **frosts.** 1 COUNT N OR UNCOUNT N When there is a **frost,** the outside temperature drops below freezing and the ground is covered with ice crystals. *There was a touch of frost this morning... Even into April the frosts continued.* 2 UNCOUNT N **Frost** is the thin layer of ice crystals which forms on the ground when it is very cold. *The lawn was sparkling with frost.*

frostbite /frɒstbaɪt/. UNCOUNT N **Frostbite** is a condition caused by extreme cold which can damage your fingers, toes, and ears. *He was crippled with frostbite.*

frosted /frɒstɪ^{2}d/. ATTRIB ADJ **Frosted** glass has a rough surface that you cannot see through. *...the frosted glass pane in the door.*

frosty /frɒsti^1/. 1 ADJ If the weather is **frosty,** the temperature is below freezing. *...a still and frosty night.* 2 ADJ A **frosty** person is unfriendly. *...a frosty glance.*

froth /frɒθ/, **froths, frothing, frothed.** 1 VB If a liquid **froths,** small bubbles appear on the surface. *...the water frothing at his feet.* 2 UNCOUNT N **Froth** is a mass of small bubbles on the surface of a liquid. *...a ring of white froth appeared on the surface.*

frothy /frɒθi^1/. ADJ A **frothy** liquid has lots of bubbles on its surface. *...frothy beer.*

frown /fraʊn/, **frowns, frowning, frowned.** VB If you **frown,** you move your eyebrows close together because you are annoyed, worried, or thinking hard. *He frowned as though deep in thought.* Also COUNT N *...a frown of disappointment.*

frown on or **frown upon.** PHR VB If something **is frowned on** or **is frowned upon,** people disapprove of it. *Non-membership of a union is frowned upon.*

froze /frəʊz/. **Froze** is the past tense of **freeze.**

frozen /frəʊzə^{0}n/. 1 **Frozen** is the past participle of **freeze.** 2 ADJ If water is **frozen** or **frozen** over, its surface has turned into ice because it is very cold. *...the frozen canal... The Missouri was frozen over.* 3 ADJ **Frozen** food has been preserved by freezing. *...a packet of frozen peas.* 4 ADJ If you are **frozen,** you are very cold. *'Poor Oliver,' she said. 'You're frozen.'*

frugal /fruːgə^{0}l/. 1 ADJ Someone who is **frugal** spends very little money. *She lived a careful, frugal life.* ♦ **frugality** /fruːgælɪ^{1}ti^1/ UNCOUNT N *...the tendency towards frugality and simplicity.* 2 ADJ A **frugal** meal is small and cheap. *...his frugal breakfast.*

fruit /fruːt/, **fruits.** The plural is usually **fruit,** but **fruits is also used.** 1 COUNT N OR UNCOUNT N A **fruit** is something which grows on a tree or a bush and which contains seeds or a stone covered by a substance that you can eat. Apples, oranges, and bananas are all fruit. 2 UNCOUNT N OR PLURAL N The **fruit** or **fruits** of an action are its results, especially good ones. *...the fruit of his visits to China... The fruits of our labours were tremendous.* ● If an action **bears fruit,** it produces good results; a formal use. *The good work of this year will continue to bear fruit.*

fruitcake /fruːtkeɪk/, **fruitcakes.** COUNT N OR UNCOUNT N A **fruitcake** is a cake containing dried fruit.

fruitful /fruːtfʊl/. ADJ Something that is **fruitful** produces good and useful results. *...hours of fruitful discussion... ...the fruitful use of funds.*

fruition /fruːɪʃə^{0}n/. PHRASE When something **comes to fruition,** it starts to produce the intended results; a formal use. *At last his efforts were coming to fruition.*

fruitless /fruːtlɪ^{2}s/. ADJ Something that is **fruitless** does not produce any results or achieve anything worthwhile. *...making fruitless inquiries... ...their fruitless search for the plane.*

fruit machine, fruit machines. COUNT N A **fruit machine** is a machine used for gambling which pays out money when you get a particular pattern of symbols on a screen; a British use.

fruity /fruːti^1/, **fruitier, fruitiest.** 1 ADJ Something that is **fruity** smells or tastes of fruit. *...cheap, fruity wines.* 2 ADJ A **fruity** laugh or voice is rich and deep.

frustrate /frʌstreɪt/, **frustrates, frustrating, frustrated.** 1 VB WITH OBJ If a situation **frustrates** you, it stops you doing what you want to do, and it angers or upsets you. *The lack of money depressed and frustrated him.* ♦ **frustrated** ADJ *...the sobbing wife and the angry, frustrated husband.* ♦ **frustrating** ADJ *It was frustrating to live at the sea's edge and be unable to swim.* 2 VB WITH OBJ To **frustrate** something such as a plan means to prevent it. *The government have frustrated further advance towards European union.* ♦ **frustrated** ADJ *Many frustrated poets end up as teachers.*

frustration /frʌstreɪʃə^{0}n/, **frustrations.** 1 UNCOUNT N OR COUNT N **Frustration** is a feeling of anger or distress because you cannot do what you want to do. *...screaming with frustration... ...the frustrations of poverty.* 2 UNCOUNT N WITH SUPP **Frustration** is also the prevention of a plan or hope that should have taken place. *...the frustration of hopes.*

fry /fraɪ/, **fries, frying, fried.** 1 ERG VB When you **fry** food, you cook it in a pan containing hot fat. *Ellen was frying an egg... ...the smell of frying onions.* ♦ **fried** ADJ *...fried potatoes.* 2 See also **small fry.**

frying pan, frying pans. COUNT N A **frying pan** is a flat, metal pan with a long handle, used for frying food.

ft. **ft** is a written abbreviation for 'foot' or 'feet' in measurements. *...cages less than 4 ft high.*

fudge /fʌdʒ/, **fudges, fudging, fudged.** 1 UNCOUNT N **Fudge** is a soft, brown sweet made from butter, milk, and sugar. 2 VB WITH OBJ If you **fudge** something, you avoid making clear or definite decisions about it. *...an attempt to fudge this issue by concealing the facts.*

fuel /fjʊəl/, **fuels, fuelling, fuelled;** spelled **fueling, fueled** in American English. 1 MASS N **Fuel** is a substance such as wood or petrol that is burned to supply heat or power. *The cost of fuel is a worry for old people... ...the increase in world fuel consumption.* ● See also **fossil fuel.** 2 VB WITH OBJ A machine or vehicle that **is fuelled** by a particular substance works by burning that substance. *...boilers fuelled by coal.* 3 VB WITH OBJ If something **fuels** a bad situation or feeling, it makes it worse. *Hugh's anger was fuelled by resentment.*

fugitive /fjuːdʒɪtɪv/, **fugitives.** COUNT N OR MOD A **fugitive** is someone who is avoiding their enemies or an unpleasant situation. *...political fugitives from Algeria... ...a fugitive American.*

-ful, -fuls. SUFFIX **-ful** is used to form nouns referring to the amount of a substance that an object contains. *...two cupfuls of sugar... ...every mouthful of food.*

fulcrum /fʌlkrəm, fʊlkrəm/. SING N A **fulcrum** is the point at which something is balancing or pivoting; a technical use.

fulfil /fʊlfɪl/, **fulfils, fulfilling, fulfilled;** spelled **fulfill, fulfills** in American English. 1 VB WITH OBJ If you **fulfil** a promise or hope, you carry it out or achieve it. *They failed to fulfil their promises to revive the economy... I had fulfilled many of my ambitions.* 2 VB WITH OBJ OR REFL VB If what you are doing **fulfils** you or if you **fulfil** yourself, you feel happy and satisfied. *This way of life no longer fulfils the individuals concerned.* ♦ **fulfilling** ADJ *...creative and fulfilling jobs.* ♦ **fulfilled** ADJ *The children gain if both parents are living fulfilled lives.* 3 VB WITH OBJ To **fulfil** a role or function means to do what is required by it. *He could no longer fulfil his function as breadwinner for the family... Helicopters fulfilled a variety of roles.*

fulfilment /fʊlfɪlmə^{2}nt/; spelled **fulfillment** in American English. 1 UNCOUNT N **Fulfilment** is a feeling of satisfaction that you get from doing or achieving something. *People find fulfilment in working for a common goal.* 2 UNCOUNT N The **fulfilment** of a promise or hope is the fact of it happening. *...the fulfilment of their dreams.*

full /fʊl/, **fuller, fullest.** 1 ADJ Something that is **full** contains as much of a substance or as many objects as it can. *The bucket's almost full... All the car parks are absolutely full.* 2 PRED ADJ WITH 'of' If a place is **full** of things or people, it contains a large number of them. *...a garden full of pear and apple trees.* 3 PRED ADJ WITH 'of' If someone or something is **full** of a feeling or quality, they have a lot of it. *I was full of confidence.* 4 ATTRIB ADJ You can use **full** to indicate the greatest possible amount of something. *...a return to full employment... Make full use of your brains.* 5 ATTRIB ADJ You can use **full** to emphasize that you are referring to the whole of something, or to emphasize the amount of a quality that it has. *I haven't got his full name... ...my last full day in Warsaw... ...the full squalor of the buildings.* 6 ADV When machinery or equipment is **full** on, it is working at its greatest power. *The gas fire was full on.* 7 ADJ If someone has a **full** life, they are always busy. 8 ADJ When there is a **full** moon, the moon appears as a bright circle.

PHRASES ● Something that has been done **in full** has been done or finished completely. *The bill has been paid in full.* ● to be **full of beans:** see **bean.**

full-blooded. ATTRIB ADJ **Full-blooded** is used to describe things that are intense or complete. *...without the full-blooded support of the Opposition parties.*

full-blown. ATTRIB ADJ **Full-blown** things are complete and fully developed. *...a full-blown military operation.*

full board. UNCOUNT N If a hotel provides **full board,** you can get all your meals there.

full-length. 1 ATTRIB ADJ Something that is **full-length** is the normal length, rather than being shorter than normal. *There was a full-length mirror in the bedroom... ...a full-length television documentary.* 2 ADV Someone who is lying **full-length** is lying down flat and stretched out.

full marks. PLURAL N If you get **full marks** in a test or exam, you answer every question correctly.

fullness /fʊlnɪ^{2}s/. 1 UNCOUNT N If you talk about the **fullness** of something, you mean that it is very intense, or full of many things; a literary use. *...the fullness of her love... ...life in all its fullness.* 2 PHRASE If something will happen **in the fullness of time,** it will eventually happen after a long time.

full-scale. ATTRIB ADJ **Full-scale** things have all the features that are possible and are done to the greatest possible extent. *...a full-scale war.*

full-size. 1 ADJ **Full-size** or **full-sized** things have finished growing and will not become any larger. *...full-size trees.* 2 ATTRIB ADJ You can also use **full-size** to describe things that are the same size as the thing they represent. *...a full-size model of a vehicle.*

full stop, full stops. COUNT N A **full stop** is the punctuation mark (.); a British use.

full-time. 1 ADJ OR ADV **Full-time** work or study takes up the whole of each normal working week. *...a full-time job... Bob and I worked full time.* 2 UNCOUNT N In games such as football **full time** is the end of a match.

full up. PRED ADJ If something is **full up,** it contains as much of something as it can. *The town's full up.*

fully /fʊli^1/. 1 ADV **Fully** means to the greatest degree or extent possible. *The secrets of its success are still not fully understood.* 2 ADV You use **fully** to indicate that a process is completely finished, and that no details have been omitted or forgotten. *It was weeks before he fully recovered... She answered his questions fully.*

fully-fledged /fʊli^{1}fledʒd/. ATTRIB ADJ **Fully-fledged** means having completely developed into the type of thing or person mentioned. *...fully-fledged members of the association.*

fumble /fʌmbə^{0}l/, **fumbles, fumbling, fumbled.** VB If you **fumble** with an object or **fumble** in a container, you handle the object or search in it clumsily. *His awkwardness made him fumble with the key... He fumbled in his pocket for his whistle.*

fume /fjuːm/, **fumes, fuming, fumed.** 1 PLURAL N **Fumes** are unpleasantly strong or harmful gases or smells. *...the exhaust fumes of a car... ...tobacco fumes.* 2 VB If you **fume,** you show impatience and anger. *I was fuming with rage.*

fun /fʌn/. 1 UNCOUNT N **Fun** is pleasant, enjoyable, and light-hearted activity or amusement. *It's fun working for him... Tests are no fun.* 2 UNCOUNT N If you have **fun,** you enjoy yourself. *She wanted a bit more fun out of life.* 3 UNCOUNT N If someone is **fun,** they are good company because they are interesting or amusing. *She was great fun... He was fun to be with.*

PHRASES ● If you do something **for fun** or **for the fun of it,** you do it for amusement. *...things that you do for fun in your spare time... You don't come to work just for the fun of it.* ● If you **make fun of** someone or something, you tease them or make jokes about them. *Don't make fun of my father.*

function /fʌŋk^{0}ʃə^{0}n/, **functions, functioning, functioned.** 1 COUNT N The **function** of something or someone is its purpose or role. *The essential function of trade unions is to bargain with employers... The brain performs three functions: recording, recalling, and analysing.* 2 VB If a machine or system **functions,** it works. *The phone didn't function at all... ...an idea of how the civil service functions.* 3 VB WITH 'as' If someone or something **functions** as a particular thing, they do the work or fulfil the purpose of that thing. *The room had previously functioned as a playroom... I found myself functioning as an ambassador.* 4 COUNT N If one thing is a **function** of another, its amount or nature depends on the other thing; a formal use. *The supply of money was a function of the amount of gold discovered.* 5 COUNT N A **function** is also a large formal dinner or party. *He had been invited to a function at the college.*

functional /fʌŋk^{0}ʃə^{0}nəl, -ʃənə^{0}l/. 1 ADJ **Functional** things are useful rather than attractive. *...functional modern furniture.* 2 ADJ If a machine is **functional,** it is working properly. *How long has the machine been functional?* 3 ADJ **Functional** also means relating to the way something works. *...a functional description of the motorcycle... ...functional efficiency.*

fund /fʌnd/, **funds, funding, funded.** 1 PLURAL N **Funds** are amounts of money that are available for spending. *...how to raise funds for a commercial project.* 2 COUNT N A **fund** is an amount of money that is collected for a particular purpose. *He made a generous donation to our campaign fund.* 3 COUNT N If you have a **fund** of something, you have a lot of it. *...a large fund of scientific knowledge.* 4 VB WITH OBJ To **fund** something means to provide money for it. *The work is being funded both by governments and private industry.* ♦ **funding** UNCOUNT N *They provide funding in the form of loans.*

fundamental /fʌndəmentə^{0}l/, **fundamentals.** 1 ADJ If something is **fundamental**, it is very important or basic. *...the fundamental principles on which it is based... The differences are in some respects fundamental.* 2 PLURAL N The **fundamentals** of a subject or activity are its most important and basic parts. *...the fundamentals of police work... Their test really gets down to fundamentals.*

fundamentalism /fʌndəmentəlɪzə^{0}m/. UNCOUNT N **Fundamentalism** is belief in the original form of a religion, without accepting any later ideas. ♦ **fundamentalist** /fʌndəmentəlɪst/ COUNT N OR MOD *...a fundamentalist Christian.*

fundamentally /fʌndəmentəli^1/. ADV OR SENTENCE ADV You use **fundamentally** to indicate that you are talking about the real or basic nature of something. *Our criminal code is based fundamentally on fear... I disagreed fundamentally with the Party... Fundamentally, we are not a part of the community.*

fund-raising. UNCOUNT N **Fund-raising** is the activity of collecting money for a particular purpose.

funeral /fjuːnə^{0}rəl/, **funerals.** COUNT N A **funeral** is a ceremony for the burial or cremation of someone who has died. *Both actresses attended the funeral... ...a funeral service.*

fungus /fʌŋgəs/, **fungi** /fʌngaɪ/. COUNT N OR UNCOUNT N **Fungi** are plants such as mushrooms and mould which have no leaves.

funnel /fʌnə^{0}l/, **funnels, funnelling, funnelled;** spelled **funneling, funneled** in American English. 1 COUNT N A **funnel** is an object with a wide top and a tube at the bottom, which is used to pour substances into a container. *Fill a bottle through a funnel.* 2 COUNT N A **funnel** is also a chimney on a ship or railway engine. *...a ship with a yellow funnel.* 3 ERG VB If something **is funnelled** somewhere, it is directed through a narrow space. *...gales funnelling between the islands.* 4 VB WITH OBJ AND ADJUNCT If you **funnel** money or resources somewhere, you send them there from several sources. *...funneling aid to the resistance groups.*

funnily /fʌnɪli^1/. PHRASE You say **funnily enough** to indicate that something is surprising, but true. *Funnily enough, old people seem to love bingo.*

funny /fʌni^1/, **funnier, funniest.** 1 ADJ You say that something is **funny** when it is strange, surprising, or puzzling. *...a funny little white hat... It's a funny thing to write... The funny thing is, we went to Arthur's house just yesterday.* 2 ADJ **Funny** things are amusing and make you smile or laugh. *...funny stories... It did look funny upside down... She laughed. 'What's funny?' he asked.* 3 PRED ADJ If you feel **funny**, you feel slightly ill; an informal use.

fur /fɜː/, **furs.** 1 UNCOUNT N **Fur** is the thick hair that grows on the bodies of many animals. *Moles have short silky fur.* 2 MASS N You use **fur** to refer to the fur-covered skin of an animal used to make clothes or rugs. *...a fur coat.* 3 UNCOUNT N **Fur** is also a soft, artificial material that resembles fur. 4 COUNT N A **fur** is a coat made from real or artificial fur.

furious /fjʊərɪəs/. 1 ADJ If someone is **furious**, they are extremely angry. *I was furious and told them to get out of my house... She was furious with him.* ♦ **furiously** ADV *'Who is this man?' the Prince exclaimed furiously.* 2 ATTRIB ADJ You can use **furious** to indicate that something involves great energy, speed, or violence. *...a furious battle... ...the furious efforts they were making.* ♦ **furiously** ADV *She ran furiously up the hill.*

furnace /fɜːnɪ^{1}s/, **furnaces.** COUNT N A **furnace** is a container for a very hot fire used to melt metal or burn rubbish. *Gradually, coal furnaces were replaced by gas and electric ones.*

furnish /fɜːnɪʃ/, **furnishes, furnishing, furnished.** 1 VB WITH OBJ When you **furnish** a room, you put furniture in it. *Do you enjoy decorating and furnishing a house?* ♦ **furnished** ADJ *...a large room furnished with low tables and cushions... They were living in a furnished flat near Finchley Station.* 2 VB WITH OBJ To **furnish** something means to provide it or supply it; a formal use. *They were not prepared to furnish the necessary troops... Luckily, they have furnished us with a translation.*

furnishings /fɜːnɪʃɪŋz/. PLURAL N The **furnishings** of a room are the furniture in it. *The tables and stools were the sole furnishings of the room.*

furniture /fɜːnɪtʃə/. UNCOUNT N **Furniture** consists of the large movable objects in a room such as tables or chairs. *She arranged the furniture... The only piece of furniture was an old wardrobe.*

furrow /fʌrəʊ/, **furrows, furrowing, furrowed.** 1 COUNT N A **furrow** is a long line in the earth made for planting seeds. *...a field with parallel furrows running down it.* 2 COUNT N The **furrows** in someone's skin are deep folds or lines. *...the deep furrows in his cheeks.* 3 ERG VB When you **furrow** your brow, you frown. *The pain caused him to furrow his brow... His brow furrowed in anguish.*

furry /fɜːri^1/, **furrier, furriest.** 1 ADJ A **furry** animal is covered with thick, soft hair. *It had a long furry tail.* 2 ADJ Something that is **furry** resembles fur. *...a furry coat.*

further /fɜːðə/, **furthers, furthering, furthered.** **Further** is a comparative of **far,** and it is also a verb. 1 ADV **Further** means to a greater degree or extent. *The situation was further complicated by uncertainty about the future... He sank further into debt.* 2 ADV If someone or something goes **further** or takes something **further,** they progress to a more advanced or detailed stage. *They never got any further... He hoped the new offer would develop matters a stage further.* 3 ADJ OR ADJ AFTER N A **further** thing or amount is an additional one. *We need a further five hundred pounds... Do you have nothing further to say?* 4 PHRASE **Further to** is used in business letters to indicate that you are referring to a previous letter or conversation; a formal use. *Further to your enquiry of the 16th, I am happy to enclose the new contract.* 5 ADV **Further** means a greater distance than before or than something else. *I walked further than I intended.* 6 VB WITH OBJ If you **further** something, you help it to progress or to be successful. *...a plot by Morris to further his career.*

further education. UNCOUNT N **Further education** is education received at a college after leaving school, but not at a university or polytechnic; a British use. *The state is pouring money into further education... ...further education courses.*

furthermore /fɜːðəmɔː/. SENTENCE ADV **Furthermore** is used to introduce a statement adding to or supporting the previous one. *He carried out orders without questioning them. Furthermore, he was not bothered by hard work... It is nearly dark, and furthermore it's going to rain.*

furthest /fɜːðɪ^{1}st/. **Furthest** is a superlative of **far.** 1 ADV OR ADJ **Furthest** means to a greater extent or degree than ever before. *...countries where commercialized farming has advanced furthest... ...the furthest limits of democracy.* 2 ADJ OR ADV The **furthest** one of a number of things is the one that is the greatest distance away. *...the fields which lay furthest from his farm.*

furtive /fɜːtɪv/. ADJ **Furtive** behaviour is secretive and sly. *They suddenly looked furtive... ...a furtive glance.* ♦ **furtively** ADV *He looked round, furtively.*

fury /fjʊəri^1/. UNCOUNT N **Fury** is very strong anger. *He clenched his fists in fury... There was fury in Miss Lenaut's dark eyes.*

fuse /fjuːz/, **fuses, fusing, fused.** 1 COUNT N In an electrical appliance, a **fuse** is a wire safety device which melts and stops the electric current if there is a fault. *Have you checked the fuse?* 2 ERG VB When an electric device **fuses,** it stops working because of a fault. *Several of the street lamps had fused... If the cables had met, they would have fused the lights.* 3 COUNT N A **fuse** is also part of a bomb or firework which delays the explosion and gives people time to move away. 4 ERG VB When objects **fuse** they join together because of heat or a biological process. *During fertilization the sperm and egg fuse... Some pieces of gold coin had fused together in the blaze.* 5 ERG VB To **fuse** ideas, methods, or systems means to combine them. *...the attempt to fuse new and old... His dances are not so much set to music as fused to it.*

fuselage /fjuːzɪlɑːʒ/, **fuselages.** COUNT N The **fuselage** of an aeroplane or rocket is its main part.

fusion /fjuːʒə^{0}n/, **fusions.** 1 UNCOUNT N OR COUNT N When two ideas, methods, or systems are combined, you can say that there is a **fusion** of them. *...the fusion of radical and socialist ideals... The painting is a rich fusion of several elements.* 2 UNCOUNT N The process in which atomic particles combine to produce nuclear energy is called nuclear **fusion;** a technical use.

fuss /fʌs/, **fusses, fussing, fussed.** 1 SING N OR UNCOUNT N **Fuss** is unnecessarily anxious or excited behaviour. *They're making a fuss about the wedding... He accepted the statement without fuss.* 2 VB When people **fuss,** they behave in an unnecessarily anxious or excited way. *Stop fussing, mother... Ted fussed with his camera.* 3 PHRASE If you **make a fuss of** someone, you pay a lot of attention to them. *They like to be flattered and made a fuss of.*

fuss over. PHR VB If you **fuss over** someone or something, you pay them too much attention or worry about them too much. *She was inclined to fuss over her health.*

fussy /fʌsi^1/, **fussier, fussiest.** 1 ADJ Someone who is **fussy** is much too nervous, concerned with details, or careful in choosing things. *I am very fussy about my food... ...a fat and fussy lady.* 2 ADJ **Fussy** clothes or furniture are too elaborate or detailed. *...fussy lace curtains.*

futile /fjuːtaɪl/. ADJ A **futile** action is one which is not successful, and is unlikely ever to be successful. *...a series of costly and futile wars... Lucy knew how futile it was to argue with her father.* ♦ **futility** /fjuːtɪlɪ^{1}ti^1/ UNCOUNT N *...the futility of their attempts.*

future /fjuːtʃə/, **futures.** 1 SING N The **future** is the period of time after the present. *It might be possible in the future... What plans do you have for the future?* Also ATTRIB ADJ *Let's meet again at some future date... ...future generations.* 2 PHRASE You use **in future** when you are telling someone what you want or expect to happen from now on. *Be more careful in future.* 3 COUNT N Your **future** is your life or career after the present time. *I decided that my future lay in medicine.* 4 SING N Something that has a **future** is likely to be successful. *Does the engine have a future?*

future tense. SING N In grammar, the **future tense** is used to refer to things that will come after the present.

fuzz /fʌz/. UNCOUNT N **Fuzz** is a mass of short curly hairs or threads. *...the light, blond fuzz on his cheeks.*

fuzzy /fʌzi^1/, **fuzzier, fuzziest.** 1 ADJ **Fuzzy** hair sticks up in a soft, curly mass. 2 ADJ A **fuzzy** picture or image is blurred and unclear. *These photographs were less fuzzy.* 3 ADJ If you or your thoughts are **fuzzy,** you are confused and cannot think clearly. *My mind was tired and a bit fuzzy.*

Gg

g. g is used after a number as an abbreviation for 'gram'. *...257g.*

gabble /gæbə^{0}l/, **gabbles, gabbling, gabbled.** VB If you **gabble,** you talk so quickly that it is difficult for people to understand you. *'Look here,' he gabbled, 'It's about the Harvest Festival.'* Also SING N *There was a gabble of conversation in the pub.*

gable /geɪbə^{0}l/, **gables.** COUNT N A **gable** is the triangular part at the top of the end wall of a building, between the two sloping sides of the roof. ♦ **gabled** /geɪbə^{0}ld/ ADJ *...small gabled houses.*

gadget /gædʒɪ^{2}t/, **gadgets.** COUNT N A **gadget** is a small machine or device. *...household gadgets.*

gaffe /gæf/, **gaffes.** COUNT N A **gaffe** is something that you say or do which is considered socially incorrect. *I had no idea of the gaffe which I was committing.*

gag /gæg/, **gags, gagging, gagged.** 1 COUNT N A **gag** is a piece of cloth that is tied round or put inside someone's mouth to stop them from speaking. 2 VB WITH OBJ If someone **gags** you, they tie a piece of cloth round your mouth. 3 COUNT N A **gag** is also a joke told by a comedian; an informal use.

gaiety /geɪə^{2}ti^1/. UNCOUNT N **Gaiety** is a feeling or attitude of being lively and fun. *...fresh youthful gaiety.*

gaily /geɪli^1/. 1 ADV If you do something **gaily,** you do it in a lively, happy way. *Off we set, with Pam chattering gaily all the way.* 2 ADV Something that is **gaily** decorated is decorated in a bright, pretty way.

gain /geɪn/, **gains, gaining, gained.** 1 VB WITH OBJ OR 'in' If you **gain** a quality, you get it gradually. *The speaker began to gain confidence... The opposition party is gaining in popularity.* 2 VB WITH OR WITHOUT OBJ If you **gain** from something, you get some advantage from it. *It is not only banks who will gain from the coming of electronic money... What has Britain gained by being a member of the EEC?* 3 COUNT N A **gain** is an improvement or increase. *The company has made notable gains in productivity.* 4 UNCOUNT N If you do something for **gain,** you do it in order to get some profit for yourself; a formal use. *He did it for financial gain.* 5 VB WITH OR WITHOUT OBJ If a clock or watch **is gaining,** the hands are moving round slightly faster than they should.

gain on. PHR VB If you **are gaining on** someone or something, you are gradually catching them up.

gait /geɪt/, **gaits.** COUNT N Someone's **gait** is their way of walking; a formal use.

gala /gɑːlə/, **galas.** COUNT N A **gala** is a special public celebration, entertainment, or performance. *...the special guest on a gala occasion.*

galactic /gəlæktɪk/. ATTRIB ADJ **Galactic** means relating to galaxies.

galaxy /gæləksi1/, **galaxies.** COUNT N A **galaxy** is a huge group of stars and planets extending over millions of miles.

gale /geɪl/, **gales.** COUNT N A **gale** is a very strong wind.

gall /gɔːl/, **galls, galling, galled.** 1 SING N If someone has the **gall** to do something dangerous or dishonest, they have the daring to do it; used showing disapproval. *They haven't the gall to steal.* 2 VB WITH OBJ If something **galls** you, it makes you angry or annoyed; an old-fashioned use. *It galled him to have to ask permission.*

gallant /gælənt/. 1 ADJ A **gallant** person is very brave and honourable when in danger or difficulty. *They have put up a gallant fight over the years.* ♦ **gallantly** ADV *Gallantly they battled on.* 2 ADJ A **gallant** man is polite and considerate towards women. ♦ **gallantly** ADV *He gallantly offered to carry her cases to the car.*

gallantry /gæləntri1/. 1 UNCOUNT N **Gallantry** is bravery shown by someone who is in danger, especially in a war. *He was awarded the Military Cross for gallantry in combat.* 2 UNCOUNT N **Gallantry** is also polite and considerate behaviour by men towards women. *...expectations of old-fashioned gallantry.*

gall bladder, gall bladders. COUNT N Your **gall bladder** is the organ in your body which stores bile. It is next to your liver.

gallery /gælə0ri1/, **galleries.** 1 COUNT N A **gallery** is a building or room where works of art are exhibited, and sometimes sold. *...the National Gallery.* 2 COUNT N In a theatre or large hall, the **gallery** is a raised area at the back or sides where the audience can sit. *...the public gallery at Parliament.*

galley /gæli1/, **galleys.** COUNT N A **galley** is a kitchen in a ship or an aircraft.

gallon /gælən/, **gallons.** 1 COUNT N In Britain, a **gallon** is a unit of volume for liquids equal to eight imperial pints or approximately 4.55 litres. *...three gallons of water.* 2 COUNT N In America, a **gallon** is a unit of volume for liquids equal to eight American pints or approximately 3.79 litres.

gallop /gæləp/, **gallops, galloping, galloped.** 1 VB When a horse **gallops,** it runs very fast so that all four legs are off the ground at the same time. *The horse galloped down the road.* Also SING N *All the animals broke into a gallop.* 2 VB WITH OR WITHOUT OBJ If you **gallop,** you ride a horse that is galloping. *He swung onto his horse, saluted, and galloped off.* 3 COUNT N A **gallop** is also a ride on a galloping horse. *...a brisk morning's gallop.*

galloping /gæləpɪŋ/. ATTRIB ADJ **Galloping** is used to describe something that is increasing or developing very fast and is difficult to control. *The oil crisis brought galloping inflation on an international scale.*

gallows /gæləʊz/. **Gallows** is the singular and plural. COUNT N A **gallows** is a wooden frame on which criminals used to be hanged.

galore /gəlɔː/. ADJ AFTER N **Galore** means existing in very large numbers. *...restaurants and night clubs galore.*

galoshes /gəlɒʃɪz/. PLURAL N **Galoshes** are waterproof shoes worn over ordinary shoes.

galvanize /gælvənaɪz/, **galvanizes, galvanizing, galvanized;** also spelled **galvanise.** VB WITH OBJ To **galvanize** someone means to cause them to do something suddenly by making them feel excited, afraid, or angry. *The lecture galvanized several others into action.*

galvanized /gælvənaɪzd/; also spelled **galvanised.** ATTRIB ADJ **Galvanized** metal has been covered with zinc to protect it from rust. *...galvanized iron.*

gambit /gæmbɪt/, **gambits.** COUNT N A **gambit** is something that you do or say for a particular purpose. *...a good gambit for attracting attention.*

gamble /gæmbə0l/, **gambles, gambling, gambled.** 1 SING N A **gamble** is a risky action or decision taken in the hope of gaining money or success. *We took a gamble, and lost... ...a gamble that paid off for us.* Also VB WITH OR WITHOUT OBJ *I was gambling on the assumption that the file had been lost.* 2 VB WITH OR WITHOUT OBJ If you **gamble,** you bet money in a game or on the result of a race or competition. *He gambled heavily on the horses.* ♦ **gambling** UNCOUNT N *He used the firm's money to pay off gambling debts.* ♦ **gambler** COUNT N *...a compulsive gambler.*

game /geɪm/, **games.** 1 COUNT N A **game** is an enjoyable activity with a set of rules which is played by individuals or teams against each other. *You need two people to play this game... ...word games.* 2 COUNT N A **game** is also a particular occasion on which a game is played. *Did you go to the baseball game?* 3 COUNT N Part of a match, consisting of a fixed number of points, is also called a **game.** *Becker leads by four games to one.* 4 PLURAL N **Games** are sports played at school or in a competition. *I was hopeless at games at school... ...the Olympic Games.* 5 COUNT N A **game** is also the equipment needed to play a particular indoor game. *...a box of toys and games.* 6 COUNT N You can describe a way of behaving as a **game** when it is used to try to gain advantage. *...these games that politicians play.* 7 UNCOUNT N **Game** is wild animals or birds that are hunted for sport or food. 8 ADJ Someone who is **game** is willing to do something new, unusual, or risky. *I'm game for anything!*
PHRASES ● If you beat someone **at their own game,** you use their own methods to gain an advantage over them. ● If someone or something **gives the game away,** they reveal a secret.

gamekeeper /geɪmkiːpə/, **gamekeepers.** COUNT N A **gamekeeper** is a person employed to look after game animals and birds on someone's land.

gammon /gæmən/. UNCOUNT N **Gammon** is smoked or salted meat from a pig, similar to bacon.

gamut /gæmə4t/. SING N WITH 'of' You use **gamut** to refer to the whole range of things in a varied situation or activity; a literary use. *...the entire gamut of London politics.*

gang /gæŋ/, **gangs, ganging, ganged.** COLL N A **gang** is a group of people who join together for some purpose, often criminal. *...a gang of terrorists.*
gang up. PHR VB If people **gang up** on you, they unite against you; an informal use. *National groups are ganging up to claim their rights.*

gangling /gæŋglɪŋ/. ADJ A **gangling** young person is tall, thin, and clumsy; used in written English.

gangrene /gæŋgriːn/. UNCOUNT N **Gangrene** is decay in part of a person's body, caused by insufficient blood flowing to it.

gangster /gæŋstə/, **gangsters.** COUNT N A **gangster** is a member of a group of violent criminals.

gangway /gæŋweɪ/, **gangways.** 1 COUNT N A **gangway** is a passage left between rows of seats for people to walk along; a British use. 2 COUNT N A **gangway** is also a short bridge or platform leading onto a ship.

gaol /dʒeɪl/. See **jail.**

gaoler /dʒeɪlə/. See **jailer.**

gap /gæp/, **gaps.** 1 COUNT N A **gap** is a space between two things or a hole in something solid. *She had gaps in her teeth... ...a gap in the hedge.* 2 COUNT N A **gap** is also a period of time when you are not doing what you normally do. *After a gap of two years, she went back to college.* 3 COUNT N If there is something missing from a situation which prevents it from being satisfactory or complete, you can also say that there is a **gap.** *This book fills a major gap.* 4 COUNT N A **gap** is also a great difference between two things, people, or ideas. *The gap between rich and poor regions widened.* ● See also **generation gap.**

gape /geɪp/, **gapes, gaping, gaped.** 1 VB If you **gape,** you look at someone or something in surprise, with your mouth open. *Jackson gaped in astonishment at the result.* ♦ **gaping** ADJ *...gaping tourists.* 2 VB If something **gapes,** it opens wide or comes apart. *The shirt gaped to reveal his chest.* ♦ **gaping** ATTRIB ADJ *The dressing gown had a gaping hole in it.*

garage /gærɑːʒ, -rɪdʒ/, **garages.** 1 COUNT N A **garage** is a building in which you keep a car. 2 COUNT N A **garage** is also a place where you can get your car repaired, buy a car, or buy petrol.

garb /gɑːb/. SING N WITH SUPP Someone's **garb** is the clothes they are wearing; a literary use.

garbage /gɑːbɪdʒ/. 1 UNCOUNT N **Garbage** is rubbish, especially kitchen waste; an American use. *...the garbage in the streets.* 2 UNCOUNT N You can refer to ideas that are stupid or worthless as **garbage;** an informal use. *He talked a lot of garbage on the subject.*

garbled /gɑːbə0ld/. ADJ If a message or explanation is **garbled,** the details are confused or wrong. *I got a garbled telephone message.*

garden /gɑːdə0n/, **gardens, gardening.** 1 COUNT N A **garden** is an area of land next to a house, with plants, trees and grass. *...sitting in the back garden... ...the vegetable garden.* 2 VB If you **are gardening,** you are doing work in your garden such as weeding or planting. ♦ **gardening** UNCOUNT N *It is too hot to do any gardening.* 3 COUNT N **Gardens** are a park with plants, trees, and grass. *...the botanical gardens.*

gardener /gɑːdə0nə/, **gardeners.** COUNT N A **gardener** is someone who looks after a garden, either as a job or a hobby. *...a keen gardener.*

garden party, garden parties. COUNT N A **garden party** is a formal party held in a large private garden, usually in the afternoon.

gargantuan /gɑːgæntju4ən/. ADJ Something that is **gargantuan** is very large; a literary use.

gargle /gɑːgə0l/, **gargles, gargling, gargled.** VB When you **gargle,** you wash your mouth by filling it with liquid, tilting your head back, and breathing out through your mouth, making a bubbling noise.

garish /geərɪʃ/. ADJ Something that is **garish** is very bright and harsh to look at. *...a garish yellow tie.*

garland /gɑːlənd/, **garlands.** COUNT N A **garland** is a circle of flowers and leaves, worn round the neck or head. *He hung a garland of flowers round my neck.*

garlic /gɑːlɪk/. UNCOUNT N **Garlic** is the small round white bulb of an onion-like plant with a very strong smell and taste. *Add a crushed clove of garlic.*

garment /gɑːmə2nt/, **garments.** COUNT N A **garment** is a piece of clothing; a formal use.

garner /gɑːnə/, **garners, garnering, garnered.** VB WITH OBJ If you **garner** information, you collect it, often with some difficulty; a formal use.

garnish /gɑːnɪʃ/, **garnishes, garnishing, garnished.** 1 COUNT N OR UNCOUNT N A **garnish** is a small amount of food used to decorate food. *...a garnish of parsley.* 2 VB WITH OBJ To **garnish** food means to decorate it with small amounts of a different food. *Garnish the fish with cucumber slices.*

garret /gæri2t/, **garrets.** COUNT N A **garret** is a very small room at the top of a house.

garrison /gærɪsə0n/, **garrisons.** COUNT N A **garrison** is a group of soldiers whose job is to guard a town or building.

garrulous /gærə4ləs/. ADJ A **garrulous** person talks a lot. *...a foolish, garrulous woman.*

garter /gɑːtə/, **garters.** COUNT N A **garter** is a piece of elastic worn round the top of a stocking or sock to prevent it slipping down.

gas /gæs/, **gases; gasses, gassing, gassed. Gases** is the plural of the noun. **Gasses** is the 3rd person singular, present tense of the verb. 1 UNCOUNT N **Gas** is a substance like air that is neither liquid nor solid and burns easily. It is used as a fuel for heating and cooking. *He remembered to turn the gas off before leaving home.* 2 COUNT N OR UNCOUNT N A **gas** is any air-like substance that is neither liquid nor solid, such as oxygen or hydrogen. *Helium is a gas at room temperature.* ● See also **tear gas.** 3 MOD **Gas** fires and **gas** cookers use gas as a fuel. 4 UNCOUNT N **Gas** is also the same as petrol; an American use. 5 VB WITH OBJ OR REFL VB To **gas** a person or animal means to kill them with poisonous gas. *She tried to gas herself.*

gaseous /gæsɪəs, geɪʃəs/. ATTRIB ADJ **Gaseous** describes substances which are neither solid nor liquid; a formal use. *...liquid or gaseous fuels.*

gash /gæʃ/, **gashes, gashing, gashed.** 1 COUNT N A **gash** is a long, deep cut. *Zeleika had a large gash in her head.* 2 VB WITH OBJ If you **gash** something, you make a long, deep cut in it. *He gashed his arm on a window last night.*

gasoline /gæsəli1n/. UNCOUNT N **Gasoline** is the same as petrol; an American use.

gasp /gɑːsp/, **gasps, gasping, gasped.** 1 COUNT N A **gasp** is a short quick intake of breath through your mouth, especially when you are surprised or in pain. *I listened to him breathing in short gasps... ...a gasp of horrified surprise.* 2 VB If you **gasp,** you take a short, quick breath through your mouth, especially when you are surprised or in pain. *He was gasping for air... 'Call the doctor!' she gasped.*

gas station, gas stations. COUNT N A **gas station** is a place where petrol is sold; an American use.

gastric /gæstrɪk/. ATTRIB ADJ **Gastric** describes processes, pains, or illnesses occurring in the stomach. *...a gastric ulcer.*

gastronomic /gæstrə6nɒmɪk/. ATTRIB ADJ **Gastronomic** means concerned with good food; a formal use. *...the gastronomic reputation of France.*

gate /geɪt/, **gates.** 1 COUNT N A **gate** is a door-like structure used at the entrance to a field, a garden, or the grounds of a building. *The prison gates closed behind him.* 2 COUNT N In an airport, a **gate** is an exit through which passengers reach their aeroplane.

gatecrash /geɪtkræʃ/, **gatecrashes, gatecrashing, gatecrashed.** VB WITH OR WITHOUT OBJ If you **gatecrash** a party, you go to it when you have not been invited; an informal use.

gateway /geɪtweɪ/, **gateways.** 1 COUNT N A **gateway** is an entrance where there is a gate. *They passed through an arched gateway.* 2 COUNT N WITH PREP 'to' Something that is considered the entrance to a larger or more important thing can be described as the **gateway** to the larger thing. *...examinations are the gateways to some professions.*

gather /gæðə/, **gathers, gathering, gathered.** 1 ERG VB When people **gather** somewhere, they come together in a group. *The villagers gathered around him... He whistled to gather the whole squad in a group.* 2 VB WITH OBJ If you **gather** things, you collect them or bring them together in one place. *I gathered my maps together and tucked them into the folder... The team worked for about a year and a half to gather data.* 3 PHRASE Something that **is gathering**

dust is not being used regularly. *My briefcase was already beginning to gather dust.* 4 VB WITH OBJ If something **gathers** speed, momentum, or force, it gradually becomes faster or stronger. *The train gathered speed as it left the town.* 5 REPORT VB If you **gather** that something is true, you learn from what someone says that it is true. *I gathered that they were not expected to eat with us... His wife had been ill, I gather, for some time.* 6 VB WITH OBJ If you **gather** a piece of cloth, you sew a thread through it and then pull the thread tight so that the cloth forms very small folds or pleats.

gather up. PHR VB If you **gather up** a number of things, you bring them together into a group. *She watched Willie gather up the papers.*

gathering /gæðə^{0}rɪŋ/, **gatherings.** COUNT N A **gathering** is a group of people meeting for a particular purpose. *...political and social gatherings.*

gauche /gəʊʃ/. ADJ Someone who is **gauche** is awkward and uncomfortable in the company of other people. *She seemed rather gauche and fat and to have grown much shyer.*

gaudy /gɔːdi^1/. ADJ Something that is **gaudy** is very brightly coloured; used showing disapproval. *...young men in gaudy shirts.*

gauge /geɪdʒ/, **gauges, gauging, gauged.** 1 VB WITH OBJ If you **gauge** something, you measure or judge it. *With a modern machine, you can gauge the number of stitches... I couldn't gauge how it would affect me.* 2 COUNT N A **gauge** is a device that shows the amount of something. *The fuel gauge dropped swiftly towards zero.* 3 COUNT N WITH SUPP A **gauge** is also a fact that can be used to judge a situation. *The increase in attendance was used as a gauge of the course's success.*

gaunt /gɔːnt/. 1 ADJ A **gaunt** person looks very thin and unhealthy. *She looked very weak, her face gaunt and drawn.* 2 ADJ Something that is **gaunt** looks bare and unattractive. *...the gaunt outlines of the houses.*

gauntlet /gɔːntlɪ^{2}t/, **gauntlets.** COUNT N **Gauntlets** are long, thick, protective gloves.

PHRASES • If you **throw down the gauntlet,** you challenge someone to argue or compete with you. If you **pick up the gauntlet,** you accept someone's challenge. • If you **run the gauntlet,** you go through an unpleasant experience in which a lot of people criticize or attack you.

gauze /gɔːz/. UNCOUNT N **Gauze** is a light, soft cloth with tiny holes in it.

gave /geɪv/. **Gave** is the past tense of **give.**

gawky /gɔːki^1/. ADJ A **gawky** person stands and moves awkwardly and clumsily. *...a gawky young woman.*

gawp /gɔːp/, **gawps, gawping, gawped.** VB If you are **gawping** at someone or something, you are staring at them in a rude or stupid way.

gay /geɪ/, **gays; gayer, gayest.** 1 ADJ A **gay** person is homosexual. Also COUNT N *...a holiday spot for gays.* 2 ATTRIB ADJ **Gay** organizations and magazines are for homosexual people. *...an active Gay Group.* 3 ADJ **Gay** also means lively and bright; an old-fashioned use. *What gay and exciting place are you taking me to?*

gaze /geɪz/, **gazes, gazing, gazed.** 1 VB WITH ADJUNCT If you **gaze,** you look steadily at someone or something for a long time. *She turned to gaze admiringly at her husband... He gazed down into the water.* 2 COUNT N Someone's **gaze** is the long and steady way they are looking at someone or something. *He sat without shifting his gaze from the television.*

gazelle /gə^{3}zel/, **gazelles.** COUNT N A **gazelle** is a kind of small antelope.

GCE /dʒiː siː iː/. **GCE** is an abbreviation for 'General Certificate of Education', an examination taken by British school students at Advanced level when leaving school and before going to university. Until 1988, British students also took GCE examinations at Ordinary level, but now they take GCSEs instead. In some other countries, both the Ordinary level and Advanced level GCE examinations are still taken. • See also **A level, O level.**

GCSE /dʒiː siː es iː/, **GCSEs.** 1 **GCSE** is an abbreviation for 'General Certificate of Secondary Education', an examination introduced in Britain in 1988 to replace the GCE O level examination. 2 COUNT N A **GCSE** is a GCSE examination in a particular subject, or a pass in it.

gear /gɪə/, **gears, gearing, geared.** 1 COUNT N A **gear** is a piece of machinery, for example in a car or on a bicycle, which controls the rate at which energy is converted into motion. *John checked the gear on the bicycle.* 2 COUNT N OR UNCOUNT N A **gear** is also one of the different ranges of speed or power which a machine or vehicle has. *We slow down to first gear and ten miles an hour.* 3 UNCOUNT N The **gear** for a particular activity is the equipment and special clothes that you use. *...camping gear.* 4 VB WITH OBJ AND ADJUNCT If someone or something **is geared** to a particular purpose, they are organized or designed to be suitable for it. *They were not geared to armed combat... ...a policy geared towards rehabilitation.*

gear up. PHR VB If someone **is geared up** to do something, they are prepared and able to do it. *Hotels like this are not geared up to cater for parties.*

gearbox /gɪəbɒks/, **gearboxes.** COUNT N A **gearbox** is the system of gears in an engine or vehicle.

geese /giːs/. **Geese** is the plural of **goose.**

gel /dʒel/, **gels, gelling, gelled;** also spelled **jell.** 1 VB If a liquid **gels,** it changes into a thicker, firmer, jelly-like substance. 2 VB If an unclear shape, thought, or idea **gels,** it becomes clearer or easier to understand. *After talking to you things really began to gel.* 3 MASS N **Gel** is a smooth, soft, jelly-like substance, especially one used to keep your hair tidy.

gelatine /dʒeləti^{1}n/. MASS N **Gelatine** is a clear, tasteless powder used to make liquids firm.

gelignite /dʒelɪgnaɪt/. UNCOUNT N **Gelignite** is an explosive similar to dynamite.

gem /dʒem/, **gems.** 1 COUNT N A **gem** is a jewel. *...a bracelet of solid gold, studded with gems.* 2 COUNT N You can refer to someone or something as a **gem** if they are especially good or pleasing. *...this gem of wisdom... This house is a gem.*

gender /dʒendə/, **genders.** UNCOUNT N OR COUNT N The **gender** of a person or animal is their characteristic of being male or female. *...differences of race or gender.*

gene /dʒiːn/, **genes.** COUNT N **Genes** are parts of cells which control the physical characteristics, growth, and development of living things. They are passed on from one generation to another.

genealogy /dʒiːni^{1}ælədʒi^1/, **genealogies;** a formal word. 1 UNCOUNT N **Genealogy** is the study of the history of families. ♦ **genealogist** COUNT N *...an amateur genealogist attempting to trace the family of his wife.* 2 COUNT N A **genealogy** is the history of a particular family, describing who each person married and who their children were.

genera /dʒenərə/. **Genera** is the plural of **genus.**

general /dʒenə^{0}rəl/, **generals.** 1 ATTRIB ADJ You use **general** when describing something that relates to the whole of something, or to most of it, rather than to its details or parts. *The general standard of education there is very high... ...general business expenses... Principles have to be stated in very general terms.* ♦ **generally** ADV OR SENTENCE ADV *His account was generally accurate... It's wonderful for information on things generally... Generally speaking, your pronunciation of English is very good.* 2 ADJ You also use **general** to describe something that involves or affects most people in a group. *There was a general movement to leave the table... ...a topic of general interest.* ♦ **generally** ADV *When will this material become generally available?* 3 ATTRIB ADJ **General** also describes a statement or opinion that is true or suitable in most situations. *As a general rule, consult the doctor if the baby has a temperature.* 4 ATTRIB ADJ You also use **general** to describe an organization or business that offers a variety of services or goods. *...a general grocery store.* 5 ATTRIB ADJ **General** is also used to describe someone's job, to indicate that they have complete responsibility for the administration of an organization. *...the general manager of the hotel.* 6 ATTRIB ADJ **General** is also used to describe a person who does a variety of unskilled jobs. *...unskilled general labourers.* 7 COUNT N OR TITLE A **general** is an army officer of very high rank.

PHRASES • You say **in general** when you are talking about the whole of a situation without going into details, or when you are referring to most people or things in a group. *They want shorter shifts, and shorter working hours in general... ...his contemptuous attitude to society in general.* • **In general** is also used to indicate that a statement is true in most cases. *The industrial processes, in general, are based on man-made processes.*

general election, general elections. COUNT N A **general election** is an election for a new government, in which all the citizens of a country may vote. *A general election was called.*

generality /dʒenəræli^{1}ti^1/, **generalities.** COUNT N OR UNCOUNT N A **generality** is a statement that is not very detailed; a formal use. *She spoke in short simple generalities.*

generalize /dʒenə^{0}rəlaɪz/, **generalizes, generalizing, generalized;** also spelled **generalise.** VB If you **generalize,** you say something that is true in most cases. *I don't think you can generalize about that.* ♦ **generalization** COUNT N OR UNCOUNT N *It is easy to make sweeping generalizations about someone else's problems... We all know women who diverge from this generalisation.*

generalized /dʒenə^{0}rəlaɪzd/; also spelled **generalised.** ADJ **Generalized** means relating to a large number or variety of people, things, or situations. *The problem is one of generalized human needs... ...generalised remarks about the futility of love.*

general knowledge. UNCOUNT N **General knowledge** is knowledge about many different things, rather than about one particular subject. *Her general knowledge is amazing.*

general practice, general practices. 1 UNCOUNT N **General practice** is the work of a doctor who treats people at a surgery or in their homes, and who does not specialize; a British use. 2 COUNT N A **general practice** is a place where such a doctor works.

general practitioner. See **GP.**

general public. COLL N The **general public** is all the people in a society. *The lecture will interest both musicians and members of the general public.*

generate /dʒenəreɪt/, **generates, generating, generated.** 1 VB WITH OBJ To **generate** something means to cause it to begin and develop; a formal use. *This book will continue to generate excitement for a long time.* 2 VB WITH OBJ To **generate** electricity or other forms of energy means to produce it.

generation /dʒenəreɪʃə^{0}n/, **generations.** 1 COUNT N A **generation** is all the people in a group or country who are of a similar age. *...an older generation of intellectuals... Few actresses of her generation could play the part well.* 2 COUNT N A **generation** is also the period of time, usually considered to be about thirty years, that it takes for children to grow up and become adults and have children of their own. *We have had a generation of peace in Europe.* 3 COUNT N WITH SUPP A stage of development in the design and manufacture of machines or equipment is also called a **generation.** *...the new generation of missiles.* 4 UNCOUNT N The **generation** of energy is its production. *Electric power generation had ceased.*

generation gap. SING N A **generation gap** is a difference in attitude and behaviour between older people and younger people.

generator /dʒenəreɪtə/, **generators.** COUNT N A **generator** is a machine which produces electricity.

generic /dʒɪ^{2}nerɪk/. ATTRIB ADJ **Generic** means applying to a whole group of similar things; a formal use. *Software is a generic term for the sets of programs which control a computer.*

generosity /dʒenərɒsɪ^{1}ti^1/. UNCOUNT N Someone's **generosity** is their characteristic of doing or giving more than is usual or expected. *You shouldn't take advantage of his generosity.*

generous /dʒenə^{0}rəs/. 1 ADJ A **generous** person gives more of something, especially money, than is usual or expected. *That's very generous of you... They aren't very generous with pensions.* ♦ **generously** ADV *She was paid generously.* 2 ADJ **Generous** also means friendly, helpful, and willing to see the good qualities in people or things. *She was a kind and generous soul... The most generous interpretation is that he didn't know.* ♦ **generously** ADV *Mrs Hutchins has generously agreed to be with us today.* 3 ADJ Something that is **generous** is much larger than is usual or necessary. *...a generous measure of cognac.* ♦ **generously** ADV *...a generously illustrated book.*

genetic /dʒɪ^{2}netɪk/, **genetics.** 1 UNCOUNT N **Genetics** is the study of how characteristics are passed from one generation to another by means of genes. 2 ADJ **Genetic** means concerned with genetic or genes. *...genetic defects.* ♦ **genetically** ADV *...genetically programmed behaviour.*

genial /dʒiːnɪəl/. ADJ A **genial** person is kind and friendly. *...a genial smile.* ♦ **genially** ADV *He waved genially to people as they passed.* ♦ **geniality** /dʒiːniæli^{1}ti^1/. UNCOUNT N *...his general air of geniality.*

genital /dʒenɪtə^{0}l/, **genitals.** 1 PLURAL N Someone's **genitals** are their external sexual organs. 2 ATTRIB ADJ **Genital** means relating to a person's external sexual organs.

genius /dʒiːnɪəs/, **geniuses.** 1 UNCOUNT N **Genius** is very great ability or skill in something. *...his genius for improvisation.* 2 UNCOUNT N **Genius** is also an excellent quality which makes something distinct from everything else. *That is the genius of the system.* 3 COUNT N A **genius** is a highly intelligent, creative, or talented person. *Beethoven was a genius.*

genocide /dʒenə^{6}saɪd/. UNCOUNT N **Genocide** is the murder of a whole community or race; a formal use.

genre /ʒɑːnrə/, **genres.** COUNT N A **genre** is a particular style of literature, art, or music; a formal use. *...a whole new genre of sentimental fiction.*

gent /dʒent/, **gents.** COUNT N A **gent** is a gentleman; an informal use. *They are very tough gents.*

genteel /dʒentiːl/. ADJ A **genteel** person is polite, respectable, and refined.

gentle /dʒentə^{0}l/, **gentler, gentlest.** 1 ADJ A **gentle** person is kind, mild, and pleasantly calm. *...a gentle, sweet man... ...gentle blue eyes.* ♦ **gently** ADV *'You have nothing to worry about,' he said gently.* ♦ **gentleness** UNCOUNT N *...the virtues of gentleness and* *compassion.* **2** ADJ **Gentle** movements are even and calm. *...the gentle rocking of his mother's chair... There was a gentle breeze.* ♦ **gently** ADV *I shook her gently and she opened her eyes.* **3** ADJ **Gentle** scenery has soft shapes and colours that people find pleasant and relaxing. *The beach stretched away in a gentle curve.* ♦ **gently** ADV *...gently sloping hills.* **4** ATTRIB ADJ **Gentle** jokes or hints are kind and not intended to hurt people. *...a very gentle parody of American life.*

gentleman /dʒɛntə^{0}lmə^{3}n/, **gentlemen. 1** COUNT N A **gentleman** is a man from a family of high social standing. *...a country gentleman.* **2** COUNT N A **gentleman** is also a man who is polite and well-educated. *He was a terribly nice man—a real gentleman.* **3** COUNT N You can refer politely to men as **gentlemen.** *Good afternoon, ladies and gentlemen.*

gentlemanly /dʒɛntə^{0}lmə^{3}nli^1/. ADJ A man who is **gentlemanly** behaves very politely and kindly. *...a courteous, gentlemanly gesture.*

gentry /dʒɛntri^1/. PLURAL N The **gentry** are people of high social status; a formal use.

genuine /dʒɛnjʊɪn/. **1** ADJ Something that is **genuine** is real and exactly what it appears to be. *...genuine Ugandan food... She looked at me in genuine astonishment.* ♦ **genuinely** ADV *...genuinely democratic countries.* **2** ADJ Someone who is **genuine** is honest and sincere. *They seemed nice, genuine fellows.*

genus /dʒi:nəs/, **genera** /dʒɛnərə/. COUNT N A **genus** is a class or group of similar animals or plants; a technical use.

geographic /dʒi:ə^{6}græfɪk/ or **geographical** /dʒi:ə^{6}græfɪkə^{0}l/. ADJ Something that is **geographic** or **geographical** involves geography. *...geographic and political boundaries... ...the characteristics of any geographical region.* ♦ **geographically** ADV *...geographically separated species.*

geography /dʒɪɒgrəfi^1/. **1** UNCOUNT N **Geography** is the study of the countries of the world and of such things as land formations, seas, climate, towns, and populations. ♦ **geographer** COUNT N *...professional geographers.* **2** UNCOUNT N The **geography** of a place is the way that its physical features are arranged within it. *...the geography of the United States.*

geology /dʒɪɒlədʒi^1/. **1** UNCOUNT N **Geology** is the study of the earth's structure, surface, and origins. ♦ **geological** /dʒi:ə^{6}lɒdʒɪkə^{0}l/ ADJ *...an interesting geological site.* ♦ **geologist** COUNT N *For many years these questions puzzled geologists.* **2** UNCOUNT N The **geology** of an area is the structure of its land.

geometric /dʒi:ə^{6}mɛtrɪk/ or **geometrical** /dʒi:ə^{6}mɛtrɪkə^{0}l/. **1** ATTRIB ADJ **Geometric** or **geometrical** is used to refer to something which relates to geometry. *...a geometrical problem.* **2** ADJ **Geometric** or **geometrical** designs and shapes consist of regular shapes and lines, and sharp angles. *...abstract geometrical designs.*

geometry /dʒɪɒmɪ^{2}tri^1/. UNCOUNT N **Geometry** is a mathematical science concerned with the measurement of lines, angles, curves, and shapes.

geranium /dʒɪ^{2}reɪnɪəm/, **geraniums.** COUNT N A **geranium** is a plant with small red, pink, or white flowers, often grown in houses.

geriatric /dʒɛri^{1}ætrɪk/. ADJ **Geriatric** is used to describe very old people, their illnesses, and their treatment; a technical use. *...a geriatric ward.*

germ /dʒɜ:m/, **germs. 1** COUNT N A **germ** is a very small organism that causes disease. *...a flu germ.* **2** COUNT N WITH SUPP The **germ** of an idea or plan is the beginning of it.

German /dʒɜ:mən/, **Germans. 1** ADJ **German** means belonging or relating to Germany. **2** COUNT N A **German** is a person who comes from Germany. **3** UNCOUNT N **German** is the language spoken by people who live in Germany, Austria, and parts of Switzerland.

German measles. UNCOUNT N **German measles** is a disease which gives you red spots and a sore throat.

germinate /dʒɜ:mɪneɪt/, **germinates, germinating, germinated. 1** ERG VB If a seed **germinates** or **is germinated,** it starts to grow. *You need cool, moist weather for the seed to germinate.* ♦ **germination** /dʒɜ:mɪneɪʃə^{0}n/ UNCOUNT N *Temperature is most important for seed germination.* **2** ERG VB If an idea, plan, or feeling **germinates,** or if it **is germinated,** it comes into existence and begins to develop; a formal use. *New concepts germinate before your eyes.*

gestation /dʒɛsteɪʃə^{0}n/. **1** UNCOUNT N **Gestation** is the process in which babies grow inside their mother's body before they are born; a technical use. *...the gestation period.* **2** UNCOUNT N **Gestation** is also the process in which an idea or plan develops; a literary use. *The road had been sixty years in gestation.*

gesticulate /dʒɛstɪkjə^{4}leɪt/, **gesticulates, gesticulating, gesticulated.** VB If you **gesticulate,** you move your hands and arms around while you are talking; a formal use. *Stuart gesticulated angrily.* ♦ **gesticulation** /dʒɛstɪkjə^{4}leɪʃə^{0}n/ UNCOUNT N OR COUNT N *...the gesticulations that accompany conversation.*

gesture /dʒɛstʃə/, **gestures, gesturing, gestured. 1** COUNT N A **gesture** is a movement that you make with your hands or your head to express emotion or to give information. *She made an angry gesture with her fist.* **2** REPORT VB OR VB WITH ADJUNCT If you **gesture,** you use your hands or your head to express emotion or to give information. *She gestured that I ought to wait... He gestured to me to lie down... She gestured towards the bookshelves.* **3** COUNT N A **gesture** is also something that you say or do in order to express your attitude or intentions. *The demonstration is a gesture of defiance.*

get /gɛt/, **gets, getting, got** /gɒt/. The form **gotten** /gɒtə^{0}n/ is often used in American English for the past participle. 'Get' is a fairly informal word. **1** VB WITH COMPLEMENT **Get** often has the same meaning as 'become'. For example, if something **gets** cold, it becomes cold. *She began to get suspicious... If things get worse, you'll have to come home... It's getting late.* **2** AUX WITH PAST PARTICIPLE **Get** can be used instead of 'be' to form passives. *Suppose someone gets killed... He failed to get re-elected.* **3** VB WITH ADJUNCT If you **get** into a particular state or situation, you start being in that state or situation. *He got into trouble with the police... I began to get in a panic.* **4** VB WITH ADJUNCT To **get** also means to move or arrive somewhere. *When the train stopped, he got off... Nobody can get past... When we got to Firle Beacon we had a rest... What time do they get back?* **5** VB WITH OBJ AND ADJUNCT OR COMPLEMENT If you **get** someone or something into a particular position, state, or situation, you cause them to be in that position, state, or situation. *I got Allen into his bunk... The girl finally got the door open... He got her pregnant.* **6** VB WITH OBJ AND TO-INF If you **get** someone to do something, you ask or tell them to do it, and they do it. *She gets Stuart to help her.* **7** VB WITH OBJ AND PAST PARTICIPLE If you **get** something done, you cause it to be done. *I got safety belts fitted.* **8** VB WITH OBJ If you **get** something, you obtain it or receive it. *He's trying to get a flat... I got the anorak for Christmas... He was with us when we got the news... Get advice from your local health department.* **9** VB WITH OBJ AND OBJ, OR VB WITH OBJ AND 'for' If you **get** something for someone, you bring it to them or obtain it for them. *Get me a glass of water... He got her a job with the telephone company.* **10** VB WITH OBJ If you **get** the time or opportunity to do something, you have the time or opportunity to do it. *We get little time for sewing.* **11** VB WITH OBJ If you **get** a particular idea or feeling, you have it or experience it. *I got the impression he'd had a sleepless night... She got a lot of fun out of sweeping the front porch.* **12** VB WITH OBJ If you **get** an illness or disease, you become ill with it. *She got chicken pox.* **13** VB WITH TO-INF If you **get** to do something, you eventually do it. *The Prime Minister got to hear of the rumours... I got to like the whole idea... We never got to see the play.* **14** VB WITH -ING If you **get** moving or **get** going, you begin to move or to do something. *We can't seem to get moving.* **15** VB WITH ADJUNCT If you **get** to a particular stage in an activity, you reach that stage. *You have got to an important stage in your career... I got as far as dismantling the plug.* **16** VB WITH OBJ When you **get** a train or bus, you make a journey by train or bus. *We got the train to Colchester.* **17** VB WITH OBJ If you **get** a person or an animal, you catch, trap, or shoot them; used mainly in speech. *The police got him in the end.* **18** VB WITH OBJ If something **gets** you, it annoys you; used mainly in speech. *What gets me is the way Janet implies that I'm lazy.* **19** VB WITH OBJ If you **get** a joke or **get** the point of something, you understand it. *I don't really get the point of the story.* **20** See also **got.**

PHRASES ● People often say **'you get'** instead of 'there is' or 'there are' when they are saying that something exists, happens, or can be experienced. *You get some rather curious effects.* ● to **get** your **way:** see **way.** ● to **get used to** something: see **used.**

get about. PHR VB See **get around.**

get across. PHR VB If you **get** an idea or argument **across,** you succeed in making people understand it.

get along. PHR VB If you **get along** with someone, you have a friendly relationship with them. *The two men get along well.*

get around. PHR VB **1** If you **get around,** you go to a lot of different places as part of your way of life. **2** If news **gets around, gets about,** or **gets round,** it is told to lots of people and becomes well known. *The news got around... Startling rumours began to get about.* **3** If you **get around** or **get round** a difficulty or restriction, you manage to avoid it or you deal with it. *To help get around this problem, some tanks are now equipped with radar.*

get around to. PHR VB See **get round to.**

get at. PHR VB **1** If you **get at** something, you manage to reach it or obtain it. *The goats bent down to get at the short grass.* **2** If you ask someone what they **are getting at,** you ask them to explain what they mean; an informal use. *I don't know what you are getting at.* **3** If someone **is getting at** you, they are criticizing or teasing you in an unkind way; an informal use.

get away. PHR VB **1** If you **get away** from somewhere, you succeed in leaving it. *You've got to get away from home.* **2** If you **get** someone **away** or if they **get away,** they escape. *They got away through Mrs Barnett's garden.* ● See also **getaway.**

get away with. PHR VB If you **get away with** something that you should not have done, you are not punished for doing it. *He bribed her—and got away with it.*

get back. PHR VB **1** If you **get back** something that you used to have, you have it once again. *He hoped he would get back his old job.* **2** If you tell someone to **get back,** you are telling them to move away.

get back to. PHR VB **1** If you **get back** to what you were doing before, you start doing it again. *Eddie wanted to get back to sleep... He got back to work again.* **2** To **get back to** a previous state or level means to return to it. *Things would soon get back to normal.*

get by. PHR VB If you **get by** in a situation, you succeed in surviving or in dealing with it. *He had managed to get by without much reading or writing.*

get down to. PHR VB When you **get down to** something, you start doing it. *I got down to work.*

get in. PHR VB **1** When a train, bus, or plane **gets in,** it arrives. *What time does the coach get in?* **2** When a political party or a politician **gets in,** they are elected. **3** In a conversation, if you **get** a remark **in,** you eventually manage to say something. *'What I wanted to say,' I finally got in, 'is that I've a set of instructions at home.'*

get in on. PHR VB If you **get in on** an activity, you start taking part in it, perhaps without being invited; an informal use. *'He even gets in on the photography shows,' she said indignantly.*

get into. PHR VB **1** If you **get into** an activity, you start doing it or being involved in it. *I always get into arguments with people... He was determined to get into politics.* **2** If you **get into** a school, college, or university, you are accepted there as a pupil or student. **3** You ask what has **got into** someone when they are behaving in an unexpected way; an informal use.

get off. PHR VB **1** If you **get** something **off,** you remove it. *Get your shirt off... I got most of the mud off your clothes.* **2** If someone is given a very small punishment for breaking a law or rule, you can say that they **got off** with this punishment. *He expressed relief that he had got off so lightly.* **3** PHRASE You say **'Get off'** or **'Get your hands off'** to someone when you are telling them not to touch something.

get off with. PHR VB If you **get off with** someone, you begin a romantic or sexual relationship with them; an informal use. *Mike thinks I'm trying to get off with his girlfriend.*

get on. PHR VB **1** If you **get** a piece of clothing **on,** you put it on. *Get your coat on.* **2** If you **get on** with someone, you have a friendly relationship with them. *Mother and I get on very well.* **3** If you **get on** with an activity, you continue doing it or start doing it. *Perhaps we can get on with the meeting now.* **4** If someone **is getting on** well or badly, they are making good or bad progress. *I always get on far better if I can draw a diagram.* **5** To **get on** also means to be successful in your career. *She's got to study to get on.* **6** If you say that someone **is getting on,** you mean that they are old; an informal use. **7** PHRASE If something is **getting on for** a particular amount, it is nearly that amount; an informal use. *They have getting on for a hundred stores.*

get on to. PHR VB **1** If you **get on to** a particular topic, you start talking about it. *Somehow we got on to grandparents.* **2** If you **get on to** someone, you contact them. *I'll get on to her right away.*

get out. PHR VB **1** If you **get out** of a place or organization, you leave it. *I'm going to get out of New York... The Alliance? The sooner we get out the better.* **2** If you **get** something **out,** you take it from the place where it is kept. *He got out a book and read.* **3** If you **get out** of doing something, you avoid doing it. *She always got out of washing up.* **4** If news or information **gets out,** it becomes known. *The word got out that he would go ahead with the merger.* **5** If you **get** a stain **out,** you remove it.

get over. PHR VB **1** If you **get over** an unpleasant experience or an illness, you recover from it. *Have you got over the shock?* **2** If you **get over** a problem, you manage to deal with it. *One mother got over this problem by leaving her baby with someone else.*

get over with. PHR VB If you decide to **get** something unpleasant **over with,** you decide to do it or endure it. *Can we just get this questioning over with?*

get round. PHR VB See **get around.**
get round to. PHR VB If you **get round** or **get around to.** doing something, you do it after a delay, because you were previously too busy or were reluctant to do it.
get through. PHR VB 1 If you **get through** a task, you succeed in completing it. *It is extremely difficult to get through this amount of work in such a short time.* **2** If you **get through** an unpleasant experience or time, you manage to live through it. *They helped me to get through that time.* **3** If you **get through** a large amount of something, you completely use it up. *I got through about six pounds worth of drink.* **4** If you **get through** to someone, you succeed in making them understand what you are trying to say; an informal use. *Howard, how do I get through to you?* **5** When you are telephoning someone, if you **get through,** you succeed in contacting them. *I finally got through at twenty past ten.*
get together. PHR VB 1 When people **get together,** they meet in order to discuss something or to spend time together. ● See also **get-together. 2** If you get something **together,** you make it or organize it. *He's spent a whole afternoon trying to get the thing together.*
get up. PHR VB **1** If you are sitting or lying and then **get up,** you rise to a standing position. *The woman got up from her chair with the baby in her arms.* **2** When you **get up** in the morning, you get out of bed and dress. *You've got to get up at eight o'clock.* **3** See also **get-up.**
get up to. PHR VB What someone **gets up to** is what they do, especially when it is something that you do not approve of; an informal use. *When I found out what they used to get up to I was horrified.*
getaway /gɛtəweɪ/, **getaways.** COUNT N When someone makes a **getaway,** they leave a place in a hurry, often after committing a crime; an informal use. *Duffield was already making his getaway down the stairs.*
get-together, get-togethers. COUNT N A **get-together** is an informal meeting or party; an informal use. *We must have a get-together some evening.*
get-up, get-ups. COUNT N A **get-up** is a strange or unusual set of clothes; an informal use. *She was wearing her arty get-up.*
geyser /giːzə/, **geysers.** COUNT N A **geyser** is a hole in the Earth's surface from which hot water and steam are forced out.
ghastly /gɑːstli^1/. **1** ADJ You describe things, situations, or people as **ghastly** when they are very unpleasant or when you dislike them a lot. *...the ghastly news of the murder... ...ghastly office blocks.* **2** PRED ADJ You can say that someone looks **ghastly** when they look very ill; an informal use.
ghetto /gɛtəʊ/, **ghettos** or **ghettoes.** COUNT N A **ghetto** is a part of a city which is inhabited by many people of a particular nationality, colour, religion, or class. *...a black kid growing up in the ghetto.*
ghost /gəʊst/, **ghosts.** COUNT N When people think that they see a **ghost,** they think that they can see the spirit of a dead person. *...the ghost of Mrs Dowell.*
ghostly /gəʊstli^1/. ADJ Something that is **ghostly** is frightening because it does not seem real or natural. *...ghostly rumbling noises.*
GI /dʒiː aɪ/, **GIs.** COUNT N A **GI** is a soldier in the United States army.
giant /dʒaɪənt/, **giants. 1** COUNT N In myths and children's stories, a **giant** is a huge, very strong person. *...stories of cruel giants.* **2** COUNT N You can use **giant** to refer to something much larger than usual. *...a giant of a man... ...the electronics giant, Hitachi.* Also ATTRIB ADJ *...giant Christmas trees.*
gibberish /dʒɪbə^{0}rɪʃ/. UNCOUNT N **Gibberish** is talk which does not make any sense. *He was talking gibberish.*
gibbon /gɪbən/, **gibbons.** COUNT N A **gibbon** is an ape with very long arms.
gibe /dʒaɪb/. See **jibe.**
giblets /dʒɪblɪ^{2}ts/. PLURAL N The **giblets** of a chicken or other bird are the parts such as its heart and liver that you remove before you cook it.
giddy /gɪdi^1/. **1** ADJ If you feel **giddy,** you feel that you are about to fall over, usually because you are not well. *He had a headache and felt giddy.* ♦ **giddiness** UNCOUNT N *...a sensation of extreme giddiness.* **2** ADJ If something makes you **giddy,** you find it confusing.
gift /gɪft/, **gifts. 1** COUNT N A **gift** is something that you give someone as a present. *...a gift from the Russian ambassador to Charles II... ...the gift of a handful of primroses.* **2** COUNT N If someone has a **gift** for a particular activity, they have a natural ability for doing it. *John has a real gift for conversation... ...his gifts as a story-teller.*
gifted /gɪftɪ^{2}d/. **1** ADJ A **gifted** person has a natural ability for a particular activity. *...a gifted actress.* **2** ADJ A **gifted** child is very intelligent or talented.
gig /gɪg/, **gigs.** COUNT N A **gig** is a performance by pop musicians; an informal use. *They started out doing free gigs in bars.*
gigantic /dʒaɪgæntɪk/. ADJ Something that is **gigantic** is extremely large. *...a gigantic rubbish heap... ...a gigantic effort.*
giggle /gɪgə^{0}l/, **giggles, giggling, giggled.** VB If you **giggle,** you make quiet laughing noises, because you are amused or because you are nervous or embarrassed. *The absurd sound made her giggle... 'Oh dear,' she giggled, 'I forgot.'* Also COUNT N *...a nervous giggle.*
gilded /gɪldɪd/. ADJ If something is **gilded,** it has been covered with a thin layer of gold or gold paint. *...the ornate gilded mirror.*
gill /gɪl/, **gills.** COUNT N **Gills** are the organs on the sides of a fish through which it breathes.
gilt /gɪlt/. **1** ADJ Something that is **gilt** is covered with a thin layer of gold or gold paint. *...paintings in dark gilt frames.* **2** UNCOUNT N **Gilt** is a thin layer of gold or gold paint that you use to decorate something. *The gilt had been chipped.*
gimmick /gɪmɪk/, **gimmicks.** COUNT N A **gimmick** is an unusual action, object, or device which is intended to attract attention or publicity. *The manufacturer needed a new sales gimmick.*
gin /dʒɪn/, **gins.** MASS N **Gin** is a colourless alcoholic drink.
ginger /dʒɪndʒə/. **1** UNCOUNT N **Ginger** is the root of a plant which has a spicy hot flavour and is used in cooking. **2** ADJ Something that is **ginger** in colour is bright orange-brown. *...a man with ginger hair... ...a ginger cat.*
ginger ale, ginger ales. MASS N **Ginger ale** is a fizzy non-alcoholic drink flavoured with ginger, which is often mixed with an alcoholic drink.
ginger beer, ginger beers. MASS N **Ginger beer** is a fizzy drink flavoured with ginger and sometimes slightly alcoholic.
gingerly /dʒɪndʒəli^1/. ADV If you do something **gingerly,** you do it carefully and perhaps nervously. *They walked gingerly over the rotten floorboards.*
gipsy /dʒɪpsi^1/, **gipsies.** See **gypsy.**
giraffe /dʒə^{1}rɑːf, -ræf/, **giraffes.** COUNT N A **giraffe** is an African animal with a very long neck, long legs, and dark patches on its body.
girder /gɜːdə/, **girders.** COUNT N A **girder** is a long, thick piece of steel or iron that is used in the frameworks of buildings and bridges.
girdle /gɜːdə^{0}l/, **girdles.** COUNT N A **girdle** is a piece of woman's underwear that fits tightly around her stomach and hips.
girl /gɜːl/, **girls. 1** COUNT N A **girl** is a female child. *...when you were a little girl... She has two girls and a boy... ...a girls' school.* **2** COUNT N You can also refer to a young woman as a **girl.** *There were a lot of pretty girls there.*
girlfriend /gɜːlfrɛnd/, **girlfriends. 1** COUNT N A man's or boy's **girlfriend** is the woman or girl with whom he is having a romantic or sexual relationship. **2** COUNT N A woman's **girlfriend** is a female friend. *She went to the movies with some girlfriends.*
girlish /gɜːlɪʃ/. ADJ If you say that a woman is **girlish,** you mean that she is like a young girl in appearance or behaviour. *...a girlish laugh.*
giro /dʒaɪrəʊ/. UNCOUNT N **Giro** is a system by which a bank or post office can transfer money from one account to another; a British use.
girth /gɜːθ/, **girths.** COUNT N **The girth** of something is the measurement around it; a formal use. *...a 52-inch girth.*
gist /dʒɪst/. SING N **The gist** of a speech, conversation, or piece of writing is its general meaning. *We began to get the gist of her remarks.*
give /gɪv/, **gives, giving, gave** /geɪv/, **given. 1** VB WITH OBJ, OR VB WITH OBJ AND OBJ **Give** is often used with nouns that describe actions, especially physical actions. The whole expression refers to the performing of the action. For example, 'She gave a smile' means almost the same as 'She smiled'. *Jill gave an immense sigh... She gave Etta a quick, shrewd glance... She gave the door a push... Any aircraft carrying the Prime Minister is given a thorough check.* **2** VB WITH OBJ AND OBJ, OR VB WITH OBJ AND PREP 'to' You use **give** to say that a person does a particular thing for someone else. For example, if you **give** someone help, you help them. *He gave her a lift back to London... ...a tutor who came to give lessons to my son.* **3** VB WITH OBJ, VB WITH OBJ AND OBJ, OR VB WITH OBJ AND PREP 'to' You also use **give** with nouns that refer to information, opinions, or greetings. For example, if you **give** someone some news, you tell it to them. *That's the best advice I can give... Castle gave the porter the message... Give my regards to your daughter.* **4** VB WITH OBJ If you **give** a speech or a performance, you speak or perform in public. *He was due to give a lecture that evening.* **5** VB WITH OBJ AND PREP 'to', OR VB WITH OBJ AND OBJ If you **give** attention or thought to something, you concentrate on it, deal with it, or think about it. *She hadn't bothered to give it particular thought.* **6** VB WITH OBJ AND OBJ, VB WITH OBJ AND PREP 'to', OR VB WITH OBJ If you **give** someone something, you offer it to them as a present and they take it. *They gave me a handsome little wooden box... He gave it to me, it's mine... It was the only thing she had to give.* **7** VB WITH OBJ AND OBJ, OR VB WITH OBJ AND PREP 'to' To **give** someone something also means to hand it over to them or to provide them with it. *Give me your key... ...without having been given the opportunity to defend himself... He gave a card to Beynon.* **8** VB WITH OBJ AND OBJ If something **gives** you a particular feeling, quality, idea, or right, it causes you to have it or experience it. *Working on the car has given me an appetite... What gave you that idea?... His leadership gives him the right to command.* **9** VB WITH OBJ If you **give** a party, you organize it. *Every year he gives a lunch for his family and friends.* **10** VB WITH OBJ AND OBJ You also use **give** to say that you estimate something to be a particular amount, level, or value. *The polls had given the President a 10 to 15 point lead.* **11** VB If something **gives,** it collapses or breaks under pressure. *His legs gave beneath him.* **12** See also **given.**
PHRASES ● If you would **give anything** or would **give your right arm** to do or have something, you are very keen to do or have it. *She said she would give anything to stay in China.* ● If someone **gives as good as** they get in a fight or argument, they fight or argue as hard as their opponent. ● If one thing **gives way** to another, it is replaced by it. *Her look of joy gave way to one of misery.* ● If a structure **gives way,** it collapses. *The floor gave way.* ● If you **give way** to someone, you agree to allow them to do something, although you do not really want to. *In the long run it proved easier to give way to his demands.* ● If you **give way** when you are driving a car, you slow down or stop in order to allow other traffic to go in front of you. ● **Give or take** is used to indicate that an amount is approximate. For example, if something is fifty years old **give or take** a few years, it is approximately fifty years old.
give away. PHR VB **1** If you **give** something **away,** you give it to someone, often because you no longer want it. *She has given away jewellery worth millions of pounds.* **2** If you **give away** information that should be kept secret, you reveal it to other people.
give back. PHR VB If you **give** something **back,** you return it to the person who gave it to you. *If I didn't need the money, I would give it back again.*
give in. PHR VB When you **give in,** you agree to do something you do not want to, or accept that you will not be able to do it. *We mustn't give in to threats... I resolved not to give in.*
give off. PHR VB If something **gives off** heat, smoke, or a smell, it produces it and sends it out into the air. *...the tremendous heat given off by the fire.*
give out. PHR VB If you **give out** a number of things, you distribute them among a group of people. *Howard gave out drinks to his guests.*
give over. PHR VB If something **is given over** to a particular use, it is used only for that purpose. *...land given over to agriculture.*
give up. PHR VB **1** If you **give up** something, you stop doing it or having it. *He gave up smoking to save money... She never completely gave up hope.* **2** If you **give up,** you admit that you cannot do a particular thing and stop trying to do it. *I don't know. I give up.* **3** If you **give up** your job, you resign from it.
give-and-take. UNCOUNT N **Give-and-take** is willingness to listen to other people's opinions and to make compromises.
give-away. SING N A **give-away** is something that reveals a truth that someone is trying to hide. *...a give-away remark.*
given /gɪvə^{0}n/. **1 Given** is the past participle of **give. 2** ATTRIB ADJ A **given** date or time is one that has been fixed or decided on previously. *At a given moment we all cheered.* **3** PHRASE If you talk about **any given** society or **any given** moment, you mean any society or time that can be mentioned. *One cannot look at the problems of any given society in isolation from the rest of the world... Often people don't know what's happening at any given moment.* **4** PREP OR CONJ If something is the case **given** a particular thing, it is the case if you take that thing into account. *It seemed churlish to send him away, given that he only wanted to take photographs.* **5** PRED ADJ WITH PREP 'to' If you say that someone is **given** to doing something, you mean that they often do it; a formal use. *He was given to claiming that he was related to the Queen.*
glacial /gleɪsjə^{0}l/. ATTRIB ADJ **Glacial** means relating to glaciers or ice. *...a glacial landscape.*
glacier /glæsjə/, **glaciers.** COUNT N A **glacier** is a huge mass of ice which moves very slowly, often down a mountain valley.

glad /glæd/. 1 PRED ADJ If you are **glad** about something, you are happy and pleased about it. *I'm so glad that your niece was able to use the tickets... Ralph was glad of a chance to change the subject.* ♦ **gladly** ADV *He gladly accepted their invitation.* 2 PRED ADJ WITH TO-INF If you say that you are **glad** to do something, you mean that you are willing to do it. *Many people would be glad to work half time.* ♦ **gladly** ADV *We will gladly do it if it is within our power.*

glade /gleɪd/, **glades.** COUNT N A **glade** is a grassy space without trees in a wood or forest; a literary use.

glamorous /glæmərəs/. ADJ People, places, or jobs that are **glamorous** are attractive and exciting. *...the most glamorous star in motion pictures.*

glamour /glæmə/; spelled **glamor** in American English. UNCOUNT N People, places, or jobs that have **glamour** are attractive and exciting. *...the superficial glamour of television.*

glance /glɑːns/, **glances, glancing, glanced.** 1 VB WITH ADJUNCT If you **glance** at something, you look at it very quickly and then look away. *Jacqueline glanced at her watch... Rudolph glanced around to make sure nobody was watching.* Also COUNT N *He cast a quick glance at his friend.* 2 VB WITH 'through' OR 'at' If you **glance** through or at a newspaper or book, you spend a short time looking at it without reading it carefully. *During breakfast he glances through the morning paper.* 3 PHRASE If you can see or recognize something **at a glance,** you can see or recognize it immediately. *She can tell at a glance whether they are married.*

glancing /glɑːnsɪŋ/. ATTRIB ADJ A **glancing** blow hits something at an angle rather than from directly in front. *It hit him a glancing blow on the forehead.*

gland /glænd/, **glands.** COUNT N **Glands** are organs in your body that make substances for your body to use or that allow substances to pass out of your body. *...the thyroid gland.*

glandular /glændjə^{4}lə/. ATTRIB ADJ **Glandular** means relating to your glands. *...glandular changes.*

glare /gleə/, **glares, glaring, glared.** 1 VB If you **glare** at someone, you look at them angrily. *The two brothers glared at each other.* Also SING N *He shot a suspicious glare at me.* 2 VB If a light **glares,** it shines very brightly and makes it difficult to see. *A harsh light glared through the windows... ...the glaring lights of the fairground.* Also SING N *The windows were tinted to reduce the glare.* 3 SING N If you are in the **glare** of publicity or public attention, you are constantly being watched and talked about by people. *At home he can relax once he's away from the glare of publicity.*

glaring /gleərɪŋ/. ADJ If you refer to something bad as **glaring,** you mean that it is very obvious. *...glaring inequalities of wealth.* ♦ **glaringly** ADV *It was glaringly obvious that he had no idea what he was doing.*

glass /glɑːs/, **glasses.** 1 UNCOUNT N **Glass** is the hard transparent substance that windows and bottles are made from. *He sweeps away the broken glass... They crept up to the glass doors and peeped inside.* 2 COUNT N A **glass** is a container made of glass which you can drink from. Most glasses do not have handles. *I put down my glass and stood up.* 3 COUNT N You can use **glass** to refer to a glass and its contents, or to the contents only. *He poured Ellen a glass of wine.* 4 UNCOUNT N Glass objects that you have in your house can be referred to as **glass.** *...a house crammed with beautiful furniture, glass and china.* 5 PLURAL N **Glasses** are two lenses in a frame that some people wear in front of their eyes in order to see better. *...a girl with glasses... ...a pair of glasses.* 6 See also **dark glasses, magnifying glass.**

glasshouse /glɑːshaus/, **glasshouses.** COUNT N A **glasshouse** is a large greenhouse.

glassy /glɑːsi^1/. 1 ADJ Something that is **glassy** is smooth and shiny, like glass; a literary use. *...the glassy sea.* 2 ADJ If someone's eyes are **glassy,** they show no feeling or understanding in their expression. *He gazed at the street with dull, glassy eyes.*

glaze /gleɪz/, **glazes, glazing, glazed.** COUNT N A **glaze** is a thin layer of a hard shiny substance on a piece of pottery.

glaze over. PHR VB If someone's eyes **glaze over,** they become dull and lose all expression, usually because of boredom.

glazed /gleɪzd/. 1 ADJ If someone's eyes are **glazed,** their expression is dull or dreamy, because they are tired or are having difficulty concentrating. *His eyes took on a slightly glazed, distant look.* 2 ADJ If pottery is **glazed,** it is covered with a thin layer of a hard shiny substance. *...glazed clay pots.* 3 ADJ A **glazed** window or door has glass in it.

gleam /gliːm/, **gleams, gleaming, gleamed.** 1 VB If an object or a surface **gleams,** it shines because it is reflecting light. *He polished the gold until it gleamed.* Also SING N *...a gleam of water.* 2 VB When a small light shines brightly, you can say that it **gleams.** *The lighthouses of the islands gleam and wink above the surf.* 3 VB If your face or eyes **gleam** with a particular feeling, they show it. *His eyes gleamed with pleasure.* Also SING N *A gleam of triumph crossed the woman's face.*

glean /gliːn/, **gleans, gleaning, gleaned.** VB WITH OBJ If you **glean** information about something, you obtain it slowly and with difficulty. *Much of the information he gleaned was of no practical use.*

glee /gliː/. UNCOUNT N **Glee** is a feeling of joy and excitement. *...the glee with which the media report scientific calamities.*

gleeful /gliːful/. ADJ Someone who is **gleeful** is happy or excited, often because of someone else's foolishness or failure. *...clicking her teeth in gleeful disapproval.* ♦ **gleefully** ADV *He gleefully rubbed his hands.*

glen /glen/, **glens.** COUNT N A **glen** is a deep, narrow valley, especially in Scotland or Ireland.

glib /glɪb/. ADJ You describe someone's behaviour as **glib** when they talk too quickly and confidently, making difficult things sound easy, so that you feel that you cannot trust them. *MacIver was always ready with glib promises.* ♦ **glibly** ADV *They still talk glibly of a return to full employment.*

glide /glaɪd/, **glides, gliding, glided.** 1 VB If you **glide** somewhere, you move there smoothly and silently. *Tim glided to the door and down the stairs... The canoes glided by.* 2 VB When birds or aeroplanes **glide,** they float on air currents. *...an owl gliding silently over the fields.*

glider /glaɪdə/, **gliders.** COUNT N A **glider** is an aircraft without an engine which flies by floating on air currents.

glimmer /glɪmə/, **glimmers, glimmering, glimmered.** 1 VB If something **glimmers,** it produces a faint, often unsteady light. *The pearl glimmered faintly as she moved.* Also SING N *The sky was pink with the first, far-off glimmer of the dawn.* 2 COUNT N WITH SUPP A **glimmer** or a **glimmering** of something is a faint sign of it. *He showed no glimmer of interest in them... ...the first glimmerings of hope.*

glimpse /glɪmp^{0}s/, **glimpses, glimpsing, glimpsed.** 1 VB WITH OBJ If you **glimpse** something, you see it very briefly and not very well. *...a village they had glimpsed through the trees.* Also COUNT N *...the first glimpse I caught of Fanny.* 2 VB WITH OBJ You can also say that you **glimpse** something when you experience or think about it briefly, and begin to understand it better. *She glimpses something of what life ought to be about.* Also COUNT N *...glimpses of his kindness.*

glint /glɪnt/, **glints, glinting, glinted.** 1 VB If something **glints,** it produces or reflects a quick flash of light. *His spectacles glinted in the sunlight... The sun glinted on the walls.* Also SING N *...a glint of metal.* 2 VB If someone's eyes **glint,** they shine and express a particular emotion. *Her green eyes glinted with mockery.* Also SING N *There was an ironic glint in his eyes.*

glisten /glɪsə^{0}n/, **glistens, glistening, glistened.** VB If something **glistens,** it shines, because it is smooth, wet, or oily. *His face glistened with sweat.* ♦ **glistening** ADJ *...glistening lips.*

glitter /glɪtə/, **glitters, glittering, glittered.** 1 VB If something **glitters,** it shines and sparkles. *Her jewellery glittered under the spotlight... Stars glittered in a clear sky.* Also SING N *...the glitter of the sea.* 2 VB If someone's eyes **glitter,** they are very bright and shiny because they are feeling a particular emotion. *Tony gazed with glittering eyes around him.*

glittering /glɪtə^{0}rɪŋ/. ATTRIB ADJ You can describe something as **glittering** when it is very impressive. *...a glittering career.*

gloat /gləut/, **gloats, gloating, gloated.** VB When someone **gloats,** they show great pleasure at their own success or at other people's failure. *They were gloating over my bankruptcy.*

global /gləubə^{0}l/. ADJ **Global** means concerning or including the whole world. *...protests on a global scale.*

globe /gləub/, **globes.** 1 SING N You can refer to the Earth as the **globe.** *...countries on the far side of the globe.* 2 COUNT N A **globe** is a spherical object with a map of the world on it. 3 COUNT N Any object shaped like a ball can be referred to as a **globe.** *...the orange globe of the sun.*

globule /glɒbjuːl/, **globules.** COUNT N A **globule** of a liquid is a tiny round drop of it; a formal use. *...a globule of blood.*

gloom /gluːm/. 1 SING N **Gloom** is partial darkness in which there is still a little light. *He peered through the gloom at the dim figure... ...the gloom of their cell.* 2 UNCOUNT N **Gloom** is also a feeling of unhappiness or despair. *He viewed the future with gloom.*

gloomy /gluːmi^1/, **gloomier, gloomiest.** 1 ADJ Something that is **gloomy** is dark and rather depressing. *...the gloomy prison... ...a gloomy day.* 2 ADJ If someone is **gloomy,** they are unhappy and have no hope. *He looked gloomy... There was a gloomy silence.* ♦ **gloomily** ADV *'Trouble,' Rudolph said gloomily.* 3 ADJ If a situation is **gloomy,** it does not give you much hope of success or happiness.

glorified /glɔːrɪfaɪd/. ATTRIB ADJ You use **glorified** to say that something is not really any more important or impressive than its name suggests. For example, if you describe a lake as a glorified pond, you mean that it is really no bigger than a pond. *I can't stay here, though. I'm just a sort of glorified lodger.*

glorify /glɔːrɪfaɪ/, **glorifies, glorifying, glorified.** VB WITH OBJ If you **glorify** someone or something, you praise them or make them seem important. *His newspapers glorified his charitable donations.*

glorious /glɔːrɪəs/. 1 ADJ Something that is **glorious** is very beautiful and impressive. *...the most glorious flowers I have ever seen.* ♦ **gloriously** SUBMOD *...gloriously embroidered pictures.* 2 ADJ Things that are **glorious** are very pleasant and make you happy. *...a glorious carefree feeling of joy... We had glorious sunshine.* ♦ **gloriously** SUBMOD *We got gloriously drunk... The first few days were gloriously hot.* 3 ADJ **Glorious** events or periods involve great fame or success. *...the glorious future opening before them.*

glory /glɔːri^1/, **glories, glorying, gloried.** 1 UNCOUNT N **Glory** is fame and admiration that you get for an achievement. *The warriors valued glory and honour above life itself... I did it for the theatre, not for my own personal glory.* 2 UNCOUNT N WITH SUPP The **glory** of something is the fact of its being very beautiful or impressive. *...the glory of the classical theatre.* 3 PLURAL N WITH SUPP The **glories** of a person or group are the occasions on which they have done something famous or admirable. *...a shrine to the glories of the French Army.* 4 PLURAL N WITH SUPP The **glories** of a culture or place are the things that people find most attractive about it. *...the glories of Venice.*

glory in. PHR VB If you **glory in** a situation or activity, you enjoy it very much. *The women were glorying in this new-found freedom.*

gloss /glɒs/, **glosses, glossing, glossed.** SING N A **gloss** is a bright shine on a surface. *The wood has a high gloss.*

gloss over. PHR VB If you **gloss over** a problem or mistake, you try to make it seem unimportant by ignoring it or by dealing with it very quickly. *...callously glossing over the facts of misery and malnutrition.*

glossary /glɒsə^{0}ri^1/, **glossaries.** COUNT N The **glossary** of a book or a subject is an alphabetical list of the special or technical words used in it, with explanations of their meanings.

glossy /glɒsi^1/. 1 ADJ Something that is **glossy** is smooth and shiny. *She had glossy brown hair.* 2 ATTRIB ADJ **Glossy** magazines and photographs are produced on expensive, shiny paper.

glove /glʌv/, **gloves.** COUNT N A **glove** is a piece of clothing which covers your hand and wrist and has individual sections for each finger. *He pulled his gloves on.*

glow /gləu/, **glows, glowing, glowed.** 1 COUNT N A **glow** is a dull, steady light. *...the blue glow of a police station light.* 2 SING N A **glow** on someone's face is the pink colour that it has when they are excited or when they have done some exercise. *The conversation brought a glow to her cheeks.* 3 SING N A **glow** is also a strong feeling of pleasure or satisfaction. *I felt a glow of pleasure.* 4 VB If something **glows,** it produces a dull, steady light or looks bright by reflecting light. *A cluster of stars glowed above us... They blew into the charcoal until it glowed red... ...children's faces glowing in the light of the fire.* 5 VB If someone **glows** or if their face **glows,** their face is pink as a result of excitement or physical exercise. *Aunt Agnes glowed with joy... Her face glowed with a healthy red sheen.*

glower /glauə/, **glowers, glowering, glowered.** VB If you **glower** at someone, you look at them angrily. *He glowered resentfully at Ash.*

glowing /gləuɪŋ/. ADJ A **glowing** description of someone or something praises them very highly. *...the book, of which I had read such glowing reports.*

glucose /gluːkəuz, -əus/. UNCOUNT N **Glucose** is a type of sugar that gives you energy.

glue /gluː/, **glues, glueing** or **gluing, glued.** 1 MASS N **Glue** is a sticky substance used for joining things together. *The hat seems to be stuck on with glue.* 2 VB WITH OBJ AND ADJUNCT If you **glue** one object to another, you stick them together using glue. *A new piece was glued into place.*

glued /gluːd/; an informal word. 1 PRED ADJ You can use **glued** to say that one thing is firmly fixed to another. *...a chop glued to the plate by a thick sauce.* 2 PRED ADJ If someone is **glued** to the television or radio, they are giving it all their attention. 3 PRED ADJ If someone's eyes are **glued** to a particular thing, they are watching it with all their attention. *Their eyes were glued to the scene below.*

glum /glʌm/. ADJ Someone who is **glum** is sad and quiet, because they are depressed. *Don't look so glum... ...his glum face.* ♦ **glumly** ADV *'It's no use,' Eddie said glumly.*

glut /glʌt/, **gluts.** COUNT N If there is a **glut** of something such as goods or raw materials, there is so much of it that it cannot all be sold or used. *The oil glut has forced price cuts.*

glutton /glʌtəºn/, **gluttons. 1** COUNT N Someone who is a **glutton** is greedy and eats too much. **2** COUNT N WITH 'for' If someone keeps having or doing something which you consider undesirable, you can say that they are a **glutton** for it. *He was a glutton for work.*

gluttony /glʌtəºni¹/. UNCOUNT N **Gluttony** is the habit or act of eating too much.

glycerine /glɪsəºri¹n/; spelled **glycerin** in American English. UNCOUNT N **Glycerine** is a thick, colourless liquid that is used in making medicine and explosives.

gnarled /nɑːld/. ADJ If something is **gnarled,** it is old, rough, and twisted. *...gnarled and twisted trees... ...gnarled peasant's hands.*

gnash /næʃ/, **gnashes, gnashing, gnashed.** VB WITH OBJ If you **gnash** your teeth, you grind them together hard because you are angry or in pain. *I lay gnashing my teeth in despair.*

gnat /næt/, **gnats.** COUNT N A **gnat** is a small flying insect that bites.

gnaw /nɔː/, **gnaws, gnawing, gnawed. 1** VB WITH OBJ OR ADJUNCT If animals or people **gnaw** something or **gnaw** at it, they bite it repeatedly. *...watching her puppy gnaw a bone... The ant tried to gnaw through the thread.* **2** VB WITH ADJUNCT If a feeling **gnaws** at you or **gnaws** away at you, it causes you to keep worrying; a literary use. *These desires gnaw away at us constantly.* ♦ **gnawing** ATTRIB ADJ *...gnawing doubts about the future of civilisation.*

gnome /nəʊm/, **gnomes.** COUNT N In children's stories, a **gnome** is a tiny old man with a beard and pointed hat.

go /gəʊ/, **goes, going, went** /wɛnt/, **gone** /gɒn/. In most cases the past participle of **go** is 'gone', but in meanings 1, 2, 3, and 4 'been' is sometimes used: see **been. 1** VB When you **go** somewhere, you leave a place and move or travel somewhere else. *I went to Stockholm... 'I must go,' she said... She went into the sitting-room... He went to get some fresh milk... Our train went at 2.25.* **2** VB WITH -ING OR 'for' You use **go** to say that you take part in an activity. *Let's go fishing... They went for a walk.* **3** VB WITH 'and' AND INF If you **go** and do a particular thing, you move from one place to another in order to do it. *I'll go and see him in the morning.* **4** VB WITH PREP 'to' If you **go** to school, church, or work, you attend regularly. *She went to London University for three years.* **5** VB WITH ADJUNCT If a road **goes** somewhere, it leads to that place. *There's a little road that goes off to the right.* **6** VB WITH COMPLEMENT OR ADJUNCT You can also use **go** to say that something changes or becomes something else. For example, if your hair **is going** grey, it is becoming grey. *The village thought we had gone crazy... The average age of farmers has gone down.* **7** VB WITH COMPLEMENT You can use **go** to say that someone chooses to be in a particular state. For example, if someone is not wearing any clothes, you can say they are **going** naked. **Go** is often used with negative words in this sense. *Halliday's absence had gone unnoticed... Her decision went unchallenged.* **8** VB WITH ADJUNCT **Go** is also used to say how a particular event, activity, or period of time passes. *How did school go?... Everything went pretty smoothly... The days went by slowly.* **9** VB You say that a machine or device **is going** when it is in operation. *The tape recorder was still going.* **10** VB When a bell or alarm **goes,** it makes a noise. **11** VB You can say that something **is going** or **has gone** when it no longer works. *Her eyesight is going... I think the batteries must have gone.* **12** VB WITH ADJUNCT If money or resources **go** into or on something such as a plan or project, they support or finance it. *Most of the aid has gone into urban projects... 40% of his income goes on rent.* **13** VB WITH PREP 'to' If something **goes** to someone, it is given to them. *The job is to go to a private contractor.* **14** RECIP VB If two things **go** together, they match or are appropriate to each other. *I got the shoes to go with my coat... The colours go so very well together.* **15** VB WITH ADJUNCT If something **goes** in a particular place, it fits in that place or belongs there. *The silencer went on easily... Where do the pans go?* **16** VB You can use **go** before a word representing a noise or before quoting something. *As the song goes: I fell in love with eyes of blue... ...American sirens which instead of going 'Ow-wow' go 'Whoop-whoop'.* **17** COUNT N A **go** is an attempt to do something. *He passed the test first go... I'll have a go at mending it.* **18** See also **going, gone.**

PHRASES ● If there is a particular thing **to go,** it remains to be done. If there is a particular period of time **to go,** it has not yet passed. *There are still two years to go.* ● You say **there goes** a particular thing to express disappointment that you cannot have it; an informal use. *There goes my chance of a job.* ● If you say that something **goes to show** or **goes to prove** something interesting, you mean that it shows or proves it. *All of which goes to show that people haven't changed.* ● To **have a go** at someone means to criticize them; an informal use. ● If something happens **from the word go,** it happens throughout a situation. *She complained from the word go.* ● If someone **makes a go** of a business or relationship, they try very hard to make it successful; an informal use. ● If someone is always **on the go,** they are busy and active; an informal use. ● If you have a particular project or activity **on the go,** you are dealing with it or are involved in it. *She's always got several schemes on the go.* ● to **go easy on** something: see **easy.** ● to **go without saying:** see **say.** ● **there you go:** see **there.**

go about. PHR VB **1** If you **go about** a task or your usual activities, you deal with them. *She told me how to go about it.* **2** See also **go around.**

go after. PHR VB If you **go after** something, you try to get it. *My husband had gone after a job.*

go against. PHR VB **1** If something **goes against** an idea, it conflicts with it. *When things go against my wishes, I threaten to resign.* **2** If you **go against** someone's advice, you do something different from what they want you to do. *She went against the advice of her Cabinet and called a general election.* **3** If a decision **goes against** someone, for example in a court of law, they lose.

go ahead. PHR VB **1** If someone **goes ahead** with a plan or idea, they begin to do it. *They are going ahead with the missile... 'Would you like to hear it?'—'Go ahead.'* **2** If an organized event **goes ahead,** it takes place. *The May Day marches could go ahead.* **3** See also **go-ahead.**

go along with. PHR VB If you **go along with** a decision or idea, you accept it and obey it. *How could you go along with such a plan?*

go around. PHR VB **1** If you **go around, go round,** or **go about** doing something that other people disapprove of, you have the habit of doing it. *I don't go around deliberately hurting people's feelings.* **2** If you **go around, go round,** or **go about** with a person or group of people, you regularly meet them as friends. *He had no intention of letting her go around with those scruffy students.* **3** If a piece of news or a joke **is going around, is going round,** or **is going about,** it is being told by many people.

go back on. PHR VB If you **go back on** a promise, you do not do what you promised to do.

go back to. PHR VB **1** If you **go back to** a task or a particular topic, you start doing it again or talking about it again. *She had gone back to staring out of the window... Going back to your point about standards, I agree that they have fallen.* **2** If something **goes back** to a particular time in the past, it was made or built then. *The shop goes back to 1707.*

go before. PHR VB Something that **has gone before** has happened or been discussed at an earlier time. *The meeting was unlike any that had gone before.*

go by. PHR VB **1** If a period of time **has gone by,** it has passed. *Eight years went by and the children grew up.* **2** If you **go by** something, you use it as a basis for a judgement or action. *I try to go by reason as far as possible.*

go down. PHR VB **1** If an amount or level **goes down,** it becomes lower. *The average age of farmers has gone down.* **2** If a speech or performance **goes down** well, people like it. **3** When the sun **goes down,** it sets.

go down with. PHR VB If you **go down with** an illness, you catch it.

go for. PHR VB **1** If you **go for** a particular type of product or method, you choose it. *...a tendency to go for grand projects.* **2** If you **go for** someone, you attack them. *He went for me with the bread-knife.* **3** If a statement about one person or thing **goes for** another, it is also true of the second person or thing. *The same goes for Bardolph.*

go in for. PHR VB If you **go in for** something, you decide to do it or have it on a regular basis. *I thought of going in for teaching... They go in for vintage port.*

go into. PHR VB **1** If you **go into** something, you describe it or examine it in detail. *I won't go into what I've suffered.* **2** If you **go into** a particular occupation, you decide to do it as your career. *Have you ever thought of going into journalism?* **3** The amount of time, effort, or money that **goes into** something is the amount that produces it. *Three years of research went into the making of those films.* **4** If a vehicle **goes into** a particular movement, it starts moving in that way. *The plane went into a nose dive.*

go off. PHR VB **1** If you **go off** someone or something, you stop liking them. *He's suddenly gone off the idea.* **2** If something **goes off,** it explodes or makes a sudden loud noise. *I could hear the bombs going off... The alarm went off.* **3** If a device or machine **goes off,** it stops operating. *The light only goes off at night.*

go off with. PHR VB If someone **goes off with** something belonging to another person, they take it away with them. *She had let him go off with her papers.*

go on. PHR VB **1** If you **go on** doing something, you continue to do it. *I went on writing... They can't go on with their examinations.* **2** If you **go on** to do something, you do it after you have done something else. *He went on to get his degree.* **3** If you **go on** to a place, you go to it from the place that you have reached. *We had gone on to Clare's house.* **4** If you **go on,** you continue talking. *'You know,' he went on, 'it's extraordinary.'... 'Sounds serious,' I said. 'Go on.'* **5** If you **go on** about something or **go on** at someone, you keep talking in a boring way; an informal use. *Don't go on about it... I went on at my father to have safety belts fitted.* **6** If a particular activity **is going on,** it is taking place. *There's a big argument going on... A lot of cheating goes on.* ● See also **goings-on. 7** You say **'Go on'** to someone to encourage them to do something. *Go on, have a biscuit.* **8** If you **go on** a piece of information, you base your opinion on it. *It's not much to go on.* **9** If a device or machine **goes on,** it starts operating. *The light goes on automatically.*

go out. PHR VB **1** If you **go out** with someone, you spend time with them socially and often have a romantic or sexual relationship with them. *I went out with him a long time ago.* **2** If something that produces light or heat **goes out,** it stops producing light or heat. *The lights went out in the big tent... The fire went out... My cigar's gone out.* **3** If something **goes out,** it stops being popular. *Steam went out and diesel was introduced.*

go over. PHR VB If you **go over** something, you examine or consider it very carefully. *He went over this in his mind.*

go over to. PHR VB **1** If someone **goes over to** a different method, they change to it. *We went over to the American system.* **2** If you **go over to** an organization, you join them after previously belonging to one with very different ideas. *Anyone joining the police is going over to the other side.*

go round. PHR VB **1** If there is enough of something to **go round,** there is enough of it for everyone. **2** See also **go around.**

go through. PHR VB **1** If you **go through** an unpleasant event, you experience it. *I'm too old to go through that again.* **2** If you **go through** a number of things, you look at them or describe each of them in turn. *Go through the files again... You'd better go through the names.* **3** If a law or official decision **goes through,** it is officially approved. *The adoption went through.*

go through with. PHR VB If you **go through with** something difficult or unpleasant, you do it. *Would he go through with the assassination?*

go towards. PHR VB If an amount of money **goes towards** something, it is used as part of the cost of that thing. *It will go towards a deposit on the flat.*

go under. PHR VB If a business **goes under,** it fails.

go up. PHR VB **1** If an amount or level **goes up,** it increases. *The price of food will go up.* **2** When a building or other structure **goes up,** it is built. **3** If something **goes up,** it explodes or starts to burn fiercely. *In seconds it had gone up in flames.*

go with. PHR VB If one thing **goes with** another, you always get the first thing if you get the second one. *The house went with the job.*

go without. PHR VB If you **go without** something, you do not get it or have it. *If they couldn't get coal, they had to go without... The family went without food all day.*

goad /gəʊd/, **goads, goading, goaded.** VB WITH OBJ If you **goad** someone, you make them feel angry, often causing them to react by doing something. *She was being goaded into denouncing her own friend.*

goad on. PHR VB If you **goad** someone **on,** you encourage them. *...the spontaneous uprising of masses goaded on by student activists.*

go-ahead. 1 SING N If you give someone the **go-ahead,** you give them permission to do something. **2** ADJ A **go-ahead** person or organization tries hard to succeed, often by using new methods.

goal /gəʊl/, **goals. 1** COUNT N A **goal** in games such as football or hockey is the space into which the players try to get the ball in order to score a point for their team. *Robson completely missed his kick in front of the goal.* **2** COUNT N You also use **goal** to refer to an instance in which a player succeeds in getting the ball into the goal, and the point they score by doing this. *It was his guile that gave Chelsea the decisive goal.* **3** COUNT N WITH SUPP Your **goal** is something that you hope to achieve. ...*their goal of landing a man on the moon.*

goalkeeper /gəʊlki:pə/, **goalkeepers.** COUNT N A **goalkeeper** is the player in a sports team whose job is to guard the goal.

goalpost /gəʊlpəʊst/, **goalposts.** COUNT N A **goalpost** is one of the two upright posts connected by a crossbar which form the goal in games like football and hockey.

goat /gəʊt/, **goats.** COUNT N A **goat** is an animal which is a bit bigger than a sheep and has horns.

gobble /gɒbəl/, **gobbles, gobbling, gobbled.** VB WITH OBJ If you **gobble** food or **gobble** it down, you eat it quickly and greedily. *Still hungry, I gobbled a second sandwich... He gobbled down the eggs.*

go-between, go-betweens. COUNT N A **go-between** is a person who takes messages between people who are not able or willing to meet each other.

goblet /gɒblɪt/, **goblets.** COUNT N A **goblet** is a type of cup without handles and a long stem.

god /gɒd/, **gods. 1** PROPER N The name **God** is given to the spirit or being who is worshipped as the creator and ruler of the world, especially by Christians, Jews, and Muslims. **2** CONVENTION People sometimes use **God** in exclamations for emphasis, or to express surprise, fear, or excitement. Some people find this offensive. **3** COUNT N A **god** is one of the spirits or beings believed in many religions to have power over an aspect of the world. ...*the Saxon god of war.*

PHRASES ● If you say **God knows,** you are emphasizing that you don't know something or that you find a fact very surprising. *He was interested in shooting and God knows what else... God knows how they knew I was coming.* ● **for God's sake:** see **sake.** ● **thank God:** see **thank.**

godchild /gɒdtʃaɪld/, **godchildren** /gɒdtʃɪldrən/. COUNT N If someone is your **godchild,** you are their godparent, which means that you have agreed to take responsibility for their religious upbringing.

goddaughter /gɒddɔ:tə/, **goddaughters.** COUNT N A **goddaughter** is a female godchild.

goddess /gɒdɪs/, **goddesses.** COUNT N A **goddess** is a female god.

godfather /gɒdfɑ:ðə/, **godfathers.** COUNT N A **godfather** is a male godparent.

godless /gɒdlɪs/. ADJ A **godless** person does not believe in God and has no moral principles; used showing disapproval. *These men were dirty, drunken, and both godless and lawless.*

godmother /gɒdmʌðə/, **godmothers.** COUNT N A **godmother** is a female godparent.

godparent /gɒdpeərənt/, **godparents.** COUNT N Someone's **godparent** is a man or woman who agrees to take responsibility for their religious upbringing.

godsend /gɒdsend/. SING N If you describe something as a **godsend,** you mean that it helps you very much. *The extra twenty dollars a week was a godsend.*

godson /gɒdsʌn/, **godsons.** COUNT N A **godson** is a male godchild.

-goer /gəʊə/, **-goers.** SUFFIX **-goer** is added to words such as 'church' and 'film' to form nouns that refer to people who regularly go to a particular place or event. *They were both enthusiastic playgoers.*

goggle /gɒgəl/, **goggles, goggling, goggled. 1** VB If you **goggle** at something, you stare at it with your eyes wide open; an informal use. *She goggled at the dreadful suit.* **2** PLURAL N **Goggles** are large glasses that fit closely to your face around your eyes to protect them. *She was wearing big green-tinted snow goggles.*

going /gəʊɪŋ/. **1** VB WITH TO-INF You use **be going to** to express future time. For example, if you say that something **is going to** happen, you mean that it will happen or that you intend it to happen. *She told him she was going to leave her job... I'm not going to be made a scapegoat.* **2** UNCOUNT N The **going** is the conditions that affect your ability to do something. ...*when the going gets tough... It was hard going at first.* **3** ATTRIB ADJ The **going** rate for something is the usual and expected rate for it. *The going rate is about £1,000 a head.* **4** See also **go.**

PHRASES ● If you **get going,** you start doing something after a delay. ● If you **keep going,** you continue doing something difficult or tiring. ● If you **have** something **going for** you, you have an advantage or useful quality. *She had so much going for her in the way of wealth and success.*

goings-on. PLURAL N **Goings-on** are strange, amusing, or improper activities.

gold /gəʊld/, **golds. 1** UNCOUNT N **Gold** is a valuable yellow-coloured metal used for making jewellery. It is also used as an international currency. ...*a fixed exchange rate for the dollar against gold... ...gold bracelets.* **2** UNCOUNT N **Gold** is also jewellery and other things that are made of gold. *They stole an estimated 12 million pounds worth of gold and jewels.* **3** ADJ Something that is **gold** in colour is bright yellow. ...*a cap with gold braid all over it.*

PHRASES ● If someone has **a heart of gold,** they are very good, kind, and considerate. ● If a child or an animal is **as good as gold,** it behaves very well.

golden /gəʊldən/. **1** ADJ Something that is **golden** in colour is bright yellow. ...*a girl with bright golden hair.* **2** ADJ **Golden** things are made of gold. *She wore a golden cross.* **3** ADJ You use **golden** to describe something that is excellent or ideal. *It's a golden opportunity.*

goldfish /gəʊldfɪʃ/. **Goldfish** is the singular and plural. COUNT N A **goldfish** is a small orange-coloured fish which people keep in ponds or bowls.

gold medal, gold medals. COUNT N A **gold medal** is a medal made of gold which is awarded as first prize in a contest or competition. *David Wilkie won the gold medal for the 200 metres breaststroke.*

goldmine /gəʊldmaɪn/, **goldmines.** COUNT N If you call a business a **goldmine,** you mean that it produces large profits.

gold-plated. ADJ Something that is **gold-plated** is covered with a very thin layer of gold.

golf /gɒlf/. UNCOUNT N **Golf** is a game in which you use long sticks called clubs to hit a ball into holes that are spread out over a large area of grass.

golf club, golf clubs. 1 COUNT N A **golf club** is a stick which you use to hit the ball in golf. **2** COUNT N A **golf club** is also an organization whose members play golf, or the place where they play golf.

golf course, golf courses. COUNT N A **golf course** is a large area of grass where people play golf.

golfer /gɒlfə/, **golfers.** COUNT N A **golfer** is a person who plays golf for pleasure or as a profession.

gone /gɒn/. **1 Gone** is the past participle of **go. 2** PRED ADJ Someone or something that is **gone** is no longer present or no longer exists. *He turned the corner and was gone... The days are gone when women worked for half pay.* **3** PREP If it is **gone** a particular time, it is later than that time. *It's gone tea-time.*

gong /gɒŋ/, **gongs.** COUNT N A **gong** is a flat, circular piece of metal that you hit with a hammer to make a loud sound.

gonna /gɒnə/. **Gonna** is used in written English to represent the words 'going to' when they are pronounced informally. *What are we gonna do?*

good /gʊd/, **better** /betə/, **best** /best/; **goods.** ● See also separate entries at **better** and **best. 1** ADJ Something that is **good** is pleasant, acceptable, or satisfactory. *They had a good time... Hello! It's good to see you... ...a very good school... She speaks good English... Both policies make good sense... It's good that there are places like this.* **2** ATTRIB ADJ Someone who is in a **good** mood is cheerful and pleasant to be with. **3** ADJ If you are **good** at something, you are skilful and successful at it. *Alex is a good swimmer... Marcus was good with his hands... You were never any good at Latin.* **4** ADJ A **good** person is kind and thoughtful. *He's always been good to me... It's good of you to come.* **5** ADJ You also use **good** to describe someone who is morally correct in their attitudes and behaviour. *There was no trace of evil in her—she was good.* **6** ADJ A child or animal that is **good** is well-behaved. *Were the kids good?* **7** UNCOUNT N **Good** is moral and religious correctness. ...*the conflict between good and evil.* **8** SING N WITH POSS If something is done for the **good** of a person or organization, it is done in order to benefit them. *Casey should quit for the good of the agency... It was for her own good.* **9** UNCOUNT N You use **good** with a negative to say that something will not succeed or be of any use. *It's no good worrying any more tonight... Even if I came, what good would it do?* **10** ATTRIB ADJ You use **good** to emphasize the extent or degree of something. *He took a good long look at it... ...a good while ago.* **11** PLURAL N **Goods** are things that are made to be sold. ...*a wide range of electrical goods.*

PHRASES ● If you say **it's a good thing** or **it's a good job** that something is the case, you mean it is fortunate. *It's a good thing I wasn't there.* ● People say **'Good for you'** to express approval. ● If something happens **for good,** the situation it produces will never change. *They had gone for good.* ● You use **as good as** before an adjective or a verb to indicate that something is almost true. *Without her glasses she was as good as blind... He had as good as abdicated.* ● If you **make good** some damage or a loss, you repair the damage or replace what has been lost. ● If you **deliver the goods** or **come up with the goods,** you do what is expected of you. *Such an unwieldy system is unable to deliver the goods.* ● **in good time:** see **time.**

good afternoon. CONVENTION You say **'Good afternoon'** in the afternoon when you are greeting someone; a formal use. *Good afternoon. Could I speak to Mr Duff, please.*

goodbye /gʊdbaɪ/. CONVENTION You say **'Goodbye'** to someone when leaving, or at the end of a telephone conversation. *We said good-bye to Charlie and walked back.*

good evening. CONVENTION You say **'Good evening'** in the evening when you are greeting someone; a formal use. *Good evening, Mr Castle. I'm sorry I'm late.*

good-humoured. ADJ Someone who is **good-humoured** is pleasant and cheerful.

goodie /gʊdi/. See **goody.**

good-looking. ADJ A **good-looking** person has an attractive face.

good morning. CONVENTION You say **'Good morning'** in the morning when you are greeting someone. *Good morning, darling. Another beautiful day.*

good-natured. ADJ A person or animal that is **good-natured** is friendly, pleasant, and has an even temper.

goodness /gʊdnɪs/. **1** CONVENTION People say **'My goodness'** or **'Goodness'** to express surprise. *My goodness, this is a difficult one.* ● **thank goodness:** see **thank. 2** UNCOUNT N **Goodness** is the quality of being kind and considerate. ...*a belief in the goodness of human nature.*

goodnight /gʊdnaɪt/. CONVENTION You say **'Goodnight'** to someone late in the evening, before going home or going to sleep. *We all said good night and went to our rooms.*

goods train, goods trains. COUNT N A **goods train** is a train that transports goods and not people.

good-tempered. ADJ A **good-tempered** person is cheerful and does not easily get angry.

goodwill /gʊdwɪl/. UNCOUNT N **Goodwill** is kindness and helpfulness. ...*the goodwill and cooperation of all who are involved.*

goody /gʊdi/, **goodies;** an informal word, also spelled **goodie. 1** CONVENTION Children, say **'goody'** to express pleasure. *Oh goody, there's some cake!* **2** COUNT N A **goody** is a person in a film or book who supports the people or ideas that you approve of. **3** PLURAL N **Goodies** are pleasant, exciting, or attractive things. *She opened the bag of goodies.*

goose /gu:s/, **geese** /gi:s/. COUNT N A **goose** is a large bird with a long neck and webbed feet.

gooseberry /gʊzbəri/, **gooseberries. 1** COUNT N A **gooseberry** is a small, round, green fruit that grows on a bush. **2** PHRASE If someone is **playing gooseberry,** they are with two other people who are in love and who want to be alone together.

gore /gɔ:/, **gores, goring, gored. 1** VB WITH OBJ If an animal **gores** someone, it wounds them badly with its horns or tusks. ...*if a bull gores someone to death.* **2** UNCOUNT N **Gore** is unpleasant-looking blood from a wound. ...*a horror film full of gore.*

gorge /gɔ:dʒ/, **gorges, gorging, gorged. 1** COUNT N A **gorge** is a narrow steep-sided valley. *The road winds through rocky gorges and hills.* **2** VB OR REFL VB If you **gorge** or **gorge** yourself, you eat a lot of food very greedily. *They gorged themselves on rich food.*

gorgeous /gɔ:dʒəs/. ADJ Someone or something that is **gorgeous** is extremely pleasant or attractive; an informal use. *'Look what David gave me.'—'Oh it's absolutely gorgeous.'... Isn't it a gorgeous day?*

gorilla /gərɪlə/, **gorillas.** COUNT N A **gorilla** is an animal which resembles a very large ape.

gorse /gɔ:s/. UNCOUNT N **Gorse** is a dark green bush which has sharp prickles and yellow flowers.

gory /gɔ:ri/. ADJ **Gory** situations involve people being injured or dying in a horrible way. *The film contains no gory violence.*

gosh /gɒʃ/. CONVENTION You say **'Gosh'** to indicate surprise or shock; an informal use.

gosling /gɒzlɪŋ/, **goslings.** COUNT N A **gosling** is a baby goose.

go-slow, go-slows. COUNT N A **go-slow** is a protest by workers in which they deliberately work slowly.

gospel /gɒspəl/, **gospels. 1** COUNT N **The Gospels** are the four books of the Bible describing the life and teachings of Jesus Christ. ...*the Gospel according to St Mark.* **2** COUNT N WITH SUPP A **gospel** is also a set of ideas that someone believes in very strongly. *They continue to preach their gospel of self-reliance.* **3** ADJ If you regard something as **gospel** or as **gospel** truth, you believe strongly that it is true. *You can take it as gospel truth that he is busy.*

gossamer /gɒsəmə/. **1** UNCOUNT N **Gossamer** is the very light, fine thread that spiders use to make cobwebs. **2** UNCOUNT N **Gossamer** is very thin and delicate cloth; a literary use.

gossip /gɒsɪp/, **gossips, gossiping, gossiped. 1** UNCOUNT N OR COUNT N **Gossip** is informal conversation, often about other people's private affairs. ...*spreading scandal and gossip about their colleagues... ...friendly gossips over our garden gates.* **2** VB If you **gossip** with someone, you talk informally with them about local people and events. *I mustn't* *stay gossiping with you any longer.* 3 COUNT N A **gossip** is a person who enjoys talking about other people's private affairs.

gossip column, gossip columns. COUNT N A **gossip column** is the part of a newspaper or magazine where the activities of famous people are discussed.

got /gɒt/. 1 **Got** is the past tense and past participle of **get.** 2 VB WITH OBJ You can use **have got** instead of the more formal 'have' when talking about possessing things: see **have.** *We haven't got a car... Have you got any brochures on Holland?... I've got nothing to hide... That door's got a lock on it.* 3 VB WITH TO-INF You can use **have got to** instead of the more formal 'have to' or 'must' when talking about something that must be done. *We've got to get up early tomorrow... There's got to be some motive.*

gotta /gɒtə/. **Gotta** is used in written English to represent the words 'got to' when they are pronounced informally, as a way of saying 'have to' or 'must'. *I've gotta get back.*

gotten /gɒtə^{r}n/. **Gotten** is often used for the past participle of **get** in American English.

gouge /gaʊdʒ/, **gouges, gouging, gouged.** VB WITH OBJ If you **gouge** something, you make a hole in it with a pointed object. *...gouging a trough in the lawn.*

gouge out. PHR VB If you **gouge** something **out,** you force it out of a hole using your fingers or a sharp tool. *...gouging out the dirt with a knife.*

gourd /gʊəd/, **gourds.** COUNT N A **gourd** is a large fruit that is similar to a marrow, or a container made from a gourd.

gourmet /gʊəmeɪ/, **gourmets.** COUNT N A **gourmet** is a person who enjoys good food and who knows a lot about cooking and wine.

gout /gaʊt/. UNCOUNT N **Gout** is an illness which causes swollen joints.

govern /gʌvə^{r}n/, **governs, governing, governed.** 1 VB WITH OR WITHOUT OBJ Someone who **governs** a country rules it, for example by making and revising the laws, managing the economy, and controlling public services. *Many civil servants are sure that they can govern better than the politicians.* 2 VB WITH OBJ Something that **governs** an event or situation has control and influence over it. *Poverty governed our lives... ...rules governing the conduct of students.*

governess /gʌvənɪ^{2}s/, **governesses.** COUNT N A **governess** is a woman employed by a family to live with them and educate their children.

government /gʌvən^{r}mə^{2}nt/, **governments.** 1 COLL N A **government** is the group of people who are responsible for governing a country or state. *The Wilson Government came to power in 1964... The government has had to cut back on public expenditure.* 2 UNCOUNT N **Government** is the organization and methods involved in governing a country or state. *Most of his ministers had no previous experience of government... ...a cut in government spending.* ♦ **governmental** /gʌvən^{r}mentə^{r}l/ ADJ *...the governmental system.*

governor /gʌvə^{r}nə/, **governors.** COUNT N A **governor** is a person who is responsible for the political administration of a region, or for the administration of an institution. *...Governor John Connally of Texas.*

gown /gaʊn/, **gowns.** 1 COUNT N A **gown** is a long dress which women wear on formal occasions. *...a wedding gown.* 2 COUNT N A **gown** is also a loose black cloak which is worn on formal occasions by people such as judges and lawyers.

GP, GPs. COUNT N A **GP** is a doctor who treats all types of illness, instead of specializing in one area of medicine. **GP** is an abbreviation for 'general practitioner'. *...the GP's surgery.*

grab /græb/, **grabs, grabbing, grabbed.** 1 VB WITH OBJ OR 'at' If you **grab** something, or **grab** at it, you take it or pick it up roughly. *She grabbed my arm... She fell on her knees to grab at the money.* Also COUNT N *He made a grab for the knife.* 2 VB WITH OBJ If you **grab** some food or sleep, you manage to get some quickly. *I'll grab a sandwich before I go.* 3 VB WITH OBJ OR 'at' If you **grab** an opportunity, you take advantage of it eagerly. *Why didn't you grab the chance to go to New York?*

grace /greɪs/, **graces.** 1 UNCOUNT N Someone's **grace** is the smooth, elegant and attractive way they move. *She moved with an extraordinary grace.* 2 TITLE You use expressions such as **Your Grace** and **Her Grace** to address or referring to a duke, duchess, or archbishop. 3 PHRASE If you do something unpleasant **with good grace,** you do it without complaining.

graceful /greɪsful/. 1 ADJ Someone or something that is **graceful** moves in a smooth and elegant way or has an attractive, pleasing shape. *They're very graceful animals... ...graceful curves... ...graceful writing.* ♦ **gracefully** ADV *Learn how to move gracefully on a stage.* 2 ADJ **Graceful** behaviour is polite, kind, and pleasant. *She turned with graceful solicitude to Anthea.* ♦ **gracefully** ADV *He accepted gracefully and gratefully.*

graceless /greɪslɪ^{2}s/. 1 ADJ Something that is **graceless** is unattractive and dull, rather than elegant. *...a large, graceless industrial city.* 2 ADJ If someone is **graceless,** they behave in an impolite way; a formal use. *He was so graceless, so eager to shock.*

gracious /greɪʃəs/. 1 ADJ If someone is **gracious,** they are polite and pleasant, especially towards people who have a lower social position than them. ♦ **graciously** ADV *The lady assured him graciously that it had all been a mistake.* 2 ATTRIB ADJ You use **gracious** to describe the comfortable way of life of wealthy people, especially in former times. *...places of recreation and gracious living.* 3 CONVENTION You can use **'Good gracious!'** and **'Goodness gracious!'** to express surprise or annoyance; an informal, old-fashioned use.

gradation /grədeɪʃə^{r}n/, **gradations.** COUNT N WITH SUPP A **gradation** is a small change, or one of the stages in the process of change. *...the subtle colour gradations.*

grade /greɪd/, **grades, grading, graded.** 1 VB WITH OBJ If you **grade** things, you judge or measure their quality. *The reports are graded 1 to 6.* 2 COUNT N The **grade** of a product is its quality. *...ordinary grade petrol.* 3 COUNT N Your **grade** in an examination is the mark that you get. *She passed the exams with good grades.* 4 COUNT N WITH SUPP Your **grade** in a company or organization is your level of importance or your rank. *...separate dining rooms for different grades of staff.* 5 COUNT N A **grade** in an American school is a group of classes in which all the children are of a similar age. *She had entered the sixth grade at eleven.* 6 PHRASE If you **make the grade,** you succeed in something by reaching the required standard; an informal use.

graded /greɪdɪ^{2}d/. ATTRIB ADJ **Graded** is used to describe something that is gradually sloping or changing. *...a nicely graded curve.*

gradient /greɪdɪənt/, **gradients.** COUNT N A **gradient** is a slope or the angle of a slope. *The floor has a minimum gradient of one in five... ...roads with sharp bends and varying gradients.*

gradual /grædjʊ^{r}əl/. ADJ Something that is **gradual** happens over a long period of time rather than suddenly. *It's a process of gradual development.* ♦ **gradually** ADV *Things change gradually in engineering.*

graduate, graduates, graduating, graduated; pronounced /grædjʊət/ when it is a noun or modifier and /grædjueɪt/ when it is a verb. 1 COUNT N A **graduate** is a student who has successfully completed a first degree at a university or college. *...a psychology graduate of Stanford University.* 2 COUNT N WITH SUPP In the United States, a **graduate** is a student who has successfully completed high school. 3 MOD **Graduate** means the same as postgraduate. *...graduate students in the philosophy department.* 4 VB When a student **graduates,** he or she has successfully completed a degree course at a university or college and receives a certificate that shows this. *She recently graduated from law school.* 5 VB In the United States, when someone **graduates,** they have successfully completed high school and receive a certificate or diploma that shows this. 6 VB If you **graduate** from one thing to another, you go from a less important job or position to a more important one. *Start on a local paper, and then graduate to a provincial paper.*

graduated /grædueɪtɪ^{2}d/. ADJ **Graduated** is used to describe something that increases by regular amounts or grades. *...graduated pensions.*

graduation /grædjueɪʃə^{r}n/. 1 UNCOUNT N **Graduation** is the successful completion of a course of study at a university or college. *He should get a good job after graduation.* 2 COUNT N The ceremony at which students from university or college receive their degrees or diplomas is also called a **graduation.** *He had just attended his daughter's graduation.*

graffiti /grə^{3}fi:ti^1/. UNCOUNT N OR PLURAL N **Graffiti** is words or pictures that are written or drawn on walls, signs, and posters in public places. Graffiti is usually rude, funny, or contains a political message.

graft /grɑ:ft/, **grafts, grafting, grafted.** 1 VB WITH OBJ If you **graft** a part of one plant onto another, you join them so that they will grow together and become one plant. 2 VB WITH OBJ If you **graft** one idea or system onto another, you try to join one to the other. *...modern federal structures grafted on to ancient cultural divisions.* 3 VB WITH OBJ If doctors **graft** a piece of healthy tissue to a damaged part of your body, they attach it by a medical operation in order to replace the damaged part. *...new veins grafted to his heart.* Also COUNT N *Laverne had skin grafts on her thighs.*

grain /greɪn/, **grains.** 1 COUNT N A **grain** of wheat, rice, or other cereal crop is a seed from it. *...no bigger than grains of rice.* 2 MASS N **Grain** is a cereal crop, especially wheat or corn, that has been harvested for food. 3 COUNT N A **grain** of sand or salt is a tiny hard piece of it. 4 SING N A **grain** of a quality is a very small amount of it; a literary use. *He did not have a grain of humour... ...a grain of truth.* 5 COUNT N The **grain** in wood is the natural pattern and direction of lines on its surface. 6 PHRASE If an idea or action **goes against the grain,** it is very difficult to accept it or do it, because it conflicts with your beliefs.

grainy /greɪni^1/. ATTRIB ADJ Something that is **grainy** has a rough surface or texture. *...the grainy wood of the table.*

gram /græm/, **grams;** also spelled **gramme.** COUNT N A **gram** is a unit of weight equal to one thousandth of a kilogram. *...500 grams of flour.*

grammar /græmə/, **grammars.** 1 UNCOUNT N **Grammar** is the rules of a language which describe how sentences are formed. 2 UNCOUNT N You can also refer to someone's **grammar** when you are describing the way in which they either obey or do not obey the rules of grammar when they write or speak. *I'm constantly having to correct their grammar.* 3 COUNT N A **grammar** is a book that describes the rules of a language. *...an old French grammar.*

grammar school, grammar schools. COUNT N A **grammar school** is a school in Britain for children aged between eleven and eighteen with a high academic ability.

grammatical /grəmætɪkə^{r}l/. 1 ATTRIB ADJ **Grammatical** is used to describe something that relates to grammar. *This sentence is very complex in its grammatical structure.* ♦ **grammatically** ADV *His English was usually grammatically correct.* 2 ADJ If someone's language is **grammatical,** it is correct because it obeys the rules of grammar. *He speaks perfectly grammatical English.*

gramme /græm/. See **gram.**

gramophone /græməfəʊn/, **gramophones.** COUNT N A **gramophone** is an old-fashioned type of record player.

gran /græn/, **grans.** COUNT N OR VOCATIVE Your **gran** is your grandmother; an informal use.

granary /grænəri^1/, **granaries.** COUNT N A **granary** is a building in which grain is stored.

grand /grænd/, **grander, grandest.** 1 ADJ **Grand** buildings are splendid or impressive. *...a grand palace... ...grand architecture.* ♦ **grandly** ADV *Its interior is grandly elegant.* 2 ATTRIB ADJ Plans and actions that are **grand** are intended to achieve important results. *...the grand plot that you two are hatching.* 3 ADJ People, jobs, or appearances that are **grand** seem important or socially superior. *...all sorts of grand people... The job isn't as grand as it sounds.* ♦ **grandly** ADV *He announced grandly that he 'had no time for women.'* 4 ATTRIB ADJ **Grand** moments or activities are exciting and important. *Finally, the grand moment comes when you make your first solo flight.* 5 ATTRIB ADJ A **grand** total is the final amount of something. *In 1886 Levers, the soap firm, spent a grand total of 50 pounds on advertising.*

grandad /grændæd/, **grandads;** also spelled **granddad.** COUNT N OR VOCATIVE Your **grandad** is your grandfather; an informal use.

grandchild /grænd^{r}tʃaɪld/, **grandchildren** /grænd^{r}tʃɪldrən/. COUNT N Your **grandchild** is the child of your son or daughter.

granddaughter /grændɔ:tə/, **granddaughters.** COUNT N Your **granddaughter** is the daughter of your son or daughter.

grandeur /grændʒə/. 1 UNCOUNT N **Grandeur** is the quality in something which makes it seem impressive and elegant. *...the grandeur of Lansdowne House.* 2 UNCOUNT N A person's **grandeur** is the great importance and social status that they have. *His wealth gave him grandeur.*

grandfather /grænd^{r}fɑ:ðə/, **grandfathers.** COUNT N Your **grandfather** is the father of your father or mother.

grandfather clock, grandfather clocks. COUNT N A **grandfather clock** is a clock in a tall wooden case which stands on the floor.

grandiose /grændɪəʊs/. ADJ **Grandiose** is used to describe something which is bigger or more elaborate than necessary and therefore seems ridiculous. *...grandiose architecture... ...grandiose schemes to recycle everything.*

grandma /grænd^{r}mɑ:/, **grandmas.** COUNT N OR VOCATIVE Your **grandma** is your grandmother; an informal use.

grandmother /grænd^{r}mʌðə/, **grandmothers.** COUNT N Your **grandmother** is the mother of your father or mother.

grandpa /grænd^{r}pɑ:, græmpɑ:/, **grandpas.** COUNT N OR VOCATIVE Your **grandpa** is your grandfather; an informal use.

grandparent /grænd^{0}peərənt/, **grandparents.** COUNT N Your **grandparents** are the parents of your father or mother.

grand piano, grand pianos. COUNT N A **grand piano** is a large piano.

grandson /grænd^{0}sʌn/, **grandsons.** COUNT N Your **grandson** is the son of your son or daughter.

grandstand /grænd^{0}stænd/, **grandstands.** COUNT N A **grandstand** is a covered stand for spectators at sporting events.

granite /grænɪt/. UNCOUNT N **Granite** is a very hard rock used in building.

granny /græni^1/, **grannies;** also spelled **grannie.** COUNT N OR VOCATIVE Your **granny** is your grandmother; an informal use.

grant /grɑːnt/, **grants, granting, granted.** 1 COUNT N A **grant** is an amount of money that the government gives to a person or an organization for a particular purpose such as education or home improvements. *You may be eligible for a grant to help you study.* 2 VB WITH OBJ AND OBJ, OR VB WITH OBJ AND PREP 'to' If someone in authority **grants** you something, they give it to you. *Proposals have been made to grant each displaced family £25,000... He was finally granted a visa.* 3 REPORT VB OR VB WITH OBJ If you **grant** that something is true, you admit that it is true. *That joy ride, I grant you, was a silly stunt.*
PHRASES • If you **take it for granted** that something is true, you believe that it is true without thinking about it. *It is taken for granted that every child should learn mathematics.* • If you **take** someone **for granted,** you benefit from them without showing that you are grateful. *He just takes me absolutely for granted.*

granulated /grænjə^{4}leɪtɪ^{2}d/. ATTRIB ADJ **Granulated** sugar is in the form of coarse grains.

granule /grænjə^{4}l/, **granules.** COUNT N A **granule** is a small round piece of something. *...sea salt sold in the form of granules.*

grape /greɪp/, **grapes.** COUNT N **Grapes** are small green or purple fruit that can be eaten raw or used for making wine. *...a bunch of grapes.*

grapefruit /greɪpfruːt/, **grapefruits. Grapefruit** can also be the plural. COUNT N OR UNCOUNT N A **grapefruit** is a large, round, yellow fruit, similar to an orange, that has a sharp, sour taste.

grapevine /greɪpvaɪn/, **grapevines.** 1 COUNT N A **grapevine** is a climbing plant on which grapes grow. 2 PHRASE If people hear news **on the grapevine,** the news is passed from one person to another in casual conversation.

graph /grɑːf, græf/, **graphs.** COUNT N A **graph** is a mathematical diagram, usually a line or curve, which shows the relationship between two or more sets of numbers or measurements. *...a temperature graph.*

graphic /græfɪk/, **graphics.** 1 ADJ **Graphic** descriptions or accounts are very clear and detailed. *...his graphic stories of persecution.* ♦ **graphically** ADV *The cruelty of this is graphically described by the old farmer.* 2 ATTRIB ADJ Something that is **graphic** is concerned with drawing, especially the use of strong lines and colours. *...graphic and industrial design.* 3 PLURAL N **Graphics** are drawings and pictures that are made using simple lines and sometimes strong colours. *...computer generated graphics.*

graphite /græfaɪt/. UNCOUNT N **Graphite** is a hard black substance that is a form of carbon. It is used to make the centre part of pencils.

grapple /græpə^{0}l/, **grapples, grappling, grappled.** 1 VB If you **grapple** with someone, you struggle or fight with them. *We grappled with him and took the guns from him.* 2 VB WITH 'with' If you **grapple** with a problem, you try hard to solve it. *I grappled with this moral dilemma.*

grasp /grɑːsp/, **grasps, grasping, grasped.** 1 VB WITH OBJ If you **grasp** something, you hold it firmly. *Edward grasped Castle's arm.* 2 SING N WITH SUPP A **grasp** is a firm hold or grip. *The animal had a powerful grasp.* 3 REPORT VB If you **grasp** something complicated, you understand it. *The concepts were difficult to grasp... I grasped quite soon what was going on.* 4 SING N WITH SUPP If you have a **grasp** of something, you have an understanding of it. *He had a sound grasp of tactics.*
PHRASES • If something is **within** your **grasp,** it is likely that you will achieve it. *A peaceful solution was within his grasp.* • If something is **in** your **grasp,** you hold it or control it. If something escapes or slips **from** your **grasp,** you no longer hold it or control it.

grasping /grɑːspɪŋ/. ADJ A **grasping** person wants to get as much money as possible; used showing disapproval. *...a grasping woman who would stoop to any device to lay her hands on Sir John's money.*

grass /grɑːs/, **grasses.** 1 UNCOUNT N **Grass** is a very common green plant with narrow leaves that forms a layer covering an area of ground. *They lay on the grass.* 2 MASS N **Grasses** are different types of grass, especially ones that grow wild. *...prairie grasses.*

grasshopper /grɑːsh^{0}ɒpə/, **grasshoppers.** COUNT N A **grasshopper** is an insect with long back legs that jumps high into the air and makes a high, vibrating sound.

grassland /grɑːslə^{3}nd/, **grasslands.** UNCOUNT N OR COUNT N **Grassland** is land covered with wild grass.

grass roots. PLURAL N The **grass roots** of an organization are the ordinary people in it, rather than its leaders. *...to strengthen democracy at the grass roots.*

grassy /grɑːsi^1/. ADJ A **grassy** area of land is covered in grass. *...a steep grassy slope.*

grate /greɪt/, **grates, grating, grated.** 1 COUNT N A **grate** is a framework of metal bars in a fireplace. *A fire was burning in the grate.* 2 VB WITH OBJ When you **grate** food, you shred it into very small pieces using a grater. *...grated lemon peel.* 3 ERG VB When something **grates** or you **grate** it, it rubs against something else, making a harsh, unpleasant sound. *He could hear her shoes grating on the steps... He grated his teeth.* 4 VB If a noise **grates** on you, it irritates you. *That shrill laugh grated on her mother.* 5 See also **grating.**

grateful /greɪtful/. ADJ If you are **grateful** for something that someone has given you or done for you, you are pleased and wish to thank them. *I am ever so grateful to you for talking to me... I'd be so grateful if you could do it.* ♦ **gratefully** ADV *He accepted the money gratefully.*

grater /greɪtə/, **graters.** COUNT N A **grater** is a small metal tool with a rough surface which is used for grating food.

gratify /grætɪfaɪ/, **gratifies, gratifying, gratified;** a formal word. 1 VB WITH OBJ If you **are gratified** by something, it gives you pleasure or satisfaction. *He was gratified that his guess had been proved right.* ♦ **gratifying** ADJ *It was gratifying to see so many people present... It makes a gratifying change.* ♦ **gratification** /grætɪfɪkeɪʃə^{0}n/ UNCOUNT N *To my immense gratification, he fell into the trap.* 2 VB WITH OBJ If you **gratify** a desire, you satisfy it. *His smallest wish must be gratified.* ♦ **gratification** UNCOUNT N *...action directed towards the gratification of desire.*

grating /greɪtɪŋ/, **gratings.** 1 COUNT N A **grating** is a metal frame with rows of bars across it fastened over a hole in a wall or in the ground. 2 ADJ A **grating** sound is harsh and unpleasant. *...a grating voice.*

gratitude /grætɪtjuːd/. UNCOUNT N **Gratitude** is the state of feeling grateful. *I must express my gratitude to the BBC.*

gratuitous /grətjuːɪtəs/. ADJ An action that is **gratuitous** is unnecessary; a formal use. *...gratuitous acts of vandalism.* ♦ **gratuitously** ADV *She had no wish to wound his feelings gratuitously.*

grave /greɪv/, **graves; graver, gravest.** 1 COUNT N A **grave** is a place where a dead person is buried. *Flowers had been put on the grave.* 2 ADJ A situation that is **grave** is very serious. *I had the gravest suspicions about the whole enterprise.* ♦ **gravely** ADV *His father was gravely ill.*

gravel /grævə^{0}l/. UNCOUNT N **Gravel** consists of very small stones. It is often used to make paths. *...the sound of his feet on the gravel.*

gravelled /grævə^{0}ld/; spelled **graveled** in American English. ADJ A **gravelled** path has a surface made of gravel.

gravelly /grævə^{0}li^1/. ADJ An area of land that is **gravelly** is covered in small stones.

gravestone /greɪvstəʊn/, **gravestones.** COUNT N A **gravestone** is a large stone with words carved into it, which is placed on a grave.

graveyard /greɪvjɑːd/, **graveyards.** COUNT N A **graveyard** is an area of land where dead people are buried.

gravitate /grævɪteɪt/, **gravitates, gravitating, gravitated.** VB WITH PREP 'to' OR 'towards' If you **gravitate** towards a place or activity, you are attracted by it. *The best reporters gravitate towards the centres of power.*

gravitation /grævɪteɪʃə^{0}n/. UNCOUNT N **Gravitation** is the force which causes objects to be attracted towards each other; a technical use. ♦ **gravitational** /grævɪteɪʃə^{0}nəl -ʃənə^{0}l/ ATTRIB ADJ *...the earth's gravitational force.*

gravity /grævɪ^{1}ti^1/. 1 UNCOUNT N **Gravity** is the force which makes things fall when you drop them. 2 UNCOUNT N WITH SUPP The **gravity** of a situation is its importance and seriousness. *...the gravity of the threat to shipping.*

gravy /greɪvi^1/. UNCOUNT N **Gravy** is a thin savoury sauce that is served with meat.

gray /greɪ/. See **grey.**

graze /greɪz/, **grazes, grazing, grazed.** 1 ERG VB OR VB WITH OBJ When an animal **grazes,** it eats grass. *The horses graze peacefully... The people of the town fought for the right to graze cattle on the Common... ...land grazed by sheep and cattle.* 2 VB WITH OBJ If you **graze** a part of your body, you injure the skin by scraping against something. *I grazed my legs as he pulled me up.* Also COUNT N *...cuts and grazes.*

grease /griːs/, **greases, greasing, greased.** 1 UNCOUNT N **Grease** is a thick substance used to oil the moving parts of machines. 2 UNCOUNT N **Grease** is an oily substance produced by your skin. 3 UNCOUNT N **Grease** is also animal fat produced by cooking meat. 4 VB WITH OBJ If you **grease** something, you put grease or fat on it. *Clean and grease the valve thoroughly.*

greaseproof paper /griːspruːf peɪpə/. UNCOUNT N **Greaseproof paper** does not allow grease to pass through it. It is used especially when cooking.

greasy /griːsi^1, -zi^1/. ADJ Something that is **greasy** is covered with grease or contains a lot of grease. *...greasy tools... ...greasy hamburgers.*

great /greɪt/, **greater, greatest.** 1 ADJ You use **great** to describe something that is very large. *...a great black cloud of smoke... There is a great amount of conflict... He had great difficulty in selling his house.* 2 ADJ Something or someone important, famous, or exciting can be described as **great.** *...the great cities of the Rhineland... ...the great issues of the day... ...a great actor.* ♦ **greatness** UNCOUNT N *...the greatness of Germany... ...Boltzmann's greatness as a physicist.* 3 ADJ If something is **great,** it is very good; an informal use. *It's a great idea.* Also CONVENTION *Great! Thanks very much.* 4 ADV WITH ADJ OR ATTRIB ADJ You also use **great** for emphasis. *...a great big gaping hole... He was a great friend of Huxley.*

great-. PREFIX **Great-** is used before nouns referring to relatives, such as 'aunt' or 'grandson', to indicate that a relative is one generation farther away than the one that the noun refers to. For example, someone's great-grandson is the grandson of their son or daughter.

greatly /greɪtli^1/. ADV You use **greatly** to emphasize the degree of something. *I was greatly influenced by Sullivan... He was not greatly surprised.*

greed /griːd/. UNCOUNT N **Greed** is a desire for more of something than is necessary or fair.

greedy /griːdi^1/, **greedier, greediest.** ADJ Someone who is **greedy** wants more of something than is necessary or fair. *People got richer and also greedier.* ♦ **greedily** ADV *They were eating greedily.*

Greek /griːk/, **Greeks.** 1 ADJ **Greek** means belonging or relating to Greece. 2 COUNT N A **Greek** is a person who comes from Greece. 3 UNCOUNT N **Greek** is the language spoken by people living in Greece now; also the language spoken in Greece in ancient times.

green /griːn/, **greener, greenest; greens.** 1 ADJ Something that is **green** is the colour of grass or leaves. *She had blonde hair and green eyes.* 2 ADJ A place that is **green** is covered with grass and trees. 3 ADJ **Green** is used to describe political movements that are particularly concerned about protecting the environment. 4 COUNT N **Greens** are members of green political movements. *...the success of the Greens in Germany.* 5 COUNT N A **green** is an area of grass in a town or village. *...the village green.* 6 COUNT N A **green** is also a smooth, flat area of grass around a hole on a golf course. 7 PLURAL N You can refer to cooked cabbage as **greens.** 8 PRED ADJ WITH 'with' If someone is **green** with envy, they are very envious indeed. 9 ADJ If someone is **green,** they are inexperienced. *...green recruits, new to the traditions.* 10 PHRASE If someone has **green fingers** or, in American English, **a green thumb,** they are very good at gardening.

greenery /griːnə^{0}ri^1/. UNCOUNT N Plants that make a place look attractive are referred to as **greenery.** *...the lush greenery of the region.*

greengrocer /griːngrəʊsə/, **greengrocers.** COUNT N A **greengrocer** or **greengrocer's** is a shop where you can buy fruit and vegetables; a British use.

greenhouse /griːnhaʊs/, **greenhouses.** COUNT N A **greenhouse** is a glass building in which you grow plants that need to be protected from bad weather.

greenish /griːnɪʃ/. ADJ **Greenish** means slightly green. *...a greenish blue.*

greet /griːt/, **greets, greeting, greeted.** 1 VB WITH OBJ When you meet someone, you **greet** them by saying something friendly such as 'Hello'. 2 VB WITH OBJ If you **greet** something in a particular way, you react to it in that way. *The news will be greeted with shock and surprise.* 3 VB WITH OBJ If something **greets** you, it is the first thing you notice in a place; used in written English. *The smell of coffee greeted us as we entered.*

greeting /griːtɪŋ/, **greetings.** COUNT N OR UNCOUNT N A **greeting** is something friendly that you say or do on meeting someone. *...a friendly greeting... She smiled in greeting.*

gregarious /grɪ^{2}geərɪəs/. ADJ Someone who is **gregarious** enjoys being with other people.

grenade /grɪ^{2}neɪd/, **grenades.** COUNT N A **grenade** is a small bomb that can be thrown by hand.

grew /gruː/. **Grew** is the past tense of **grow.**

grey /greɪ/, **greyer, greyest; greys, greying;** spelled **gray** in American English. **1** ADJ Something that is **grey** is the colour of ashes or of clouds on a rainy day. *...a grey suit... ...the grey-haired driver.* **2** ADJ If someone is going **grey**, their hair is becoming grey. *She went grey in about a year.* Also VB *Her hair was greying... ...a small, greying man.* **3** ADJ If someone looks **grey**, they look pale and ill. *He had gone grey and his hands trembled slightly.* ♦ **greyness** UNCOUNT N *There was an awful greyness about his face.*

grey area, grey areas. COUNT N A **grey area** is an aspect of something that people are not sure how to deal with because it is not clearly defined.

greyhound /greɪhaʊnd/, **greyhounds.** COUNT N A **greyhound** is a thin dog that can run very fast.

greyish /greɪɪʃ/; spelled **grayish** in American English. ADJ **Greyish** means slightly grey.

grid /grɪd/, **grids.** COUNT N A **grid** is a pattern of straight lines that cross over each other to form squares. *...a grid of small streets.*

grief /gri:f/; a formal word. **1** UNCOUNT N **Grief** is extreme sadness. *That helped to ease his grief.* **2** PHRASE If someone or something **comes to grief,** they fail or are harmed. *I ran away once but came to grief.*

grievance /gri:vəns/, **grievances.** COUNT N OR UNCOUNT N A **grievance** is a reason for complaining. *They may well have a genuine grievance... ...my family's grievance against Mr Geard.*

grieve /gri:v/, **grieves, grieving, grieved;** a formal word. **1** VB If you **grieve,** you feel very sad about something that has happened. *She was grieving for the dead baby.* **2** VB WITH OBJ If something **grieves** you, it makes you feel sad. *I was grieved to hear that he had been captured.*

grievous /gri:vəs/. ADJ Something that is **grievous** is extremely serious or worrying in its effects. *...a grievous mistake.* ♦ **grievously** ADV *He had been grievously wounded.*

grill /grɪl/, **grills, grilling, grilled.** **1** ERG VB When you **grill** food, you cook it using strong heat directly above or below it. *I usually grill or fry beef.* ♦ **grilled** ADJ *...a grilled chop.* **2** COUNT N A **grill** is a part of a cooker where food is cooked by strong heat from above. **3** COUNT N A **grill** is also a flat frame of metal bars on which you cook food over a fire. **4** COUNT N OR UNCOUNT N A **grill** is also a dish which consists of food that has been grilled. **5** VB WITH OBJ If you **grill** someone, you ask them many questions in an intense way; an informal use. *At the police station, she was grilled for twenty-four hours.*

grille /grɪl/, **grilles.** COUNT N A **grille** is a framework of metal bars or wire placed in front of a window or a piece of machinery, for protection.

grim /grɪm/, **grimmer, grimmest.** **1** ADJ A situation or news that is **grim** is unpleasant. *...the grim facts... ...the grim aftermath of World War I.* **2** ADJ A **grim** place is unattractive and depressing. **3** ADJ If someone is **grim,** they are very serious or stern. *...his grim determination not to cry... ...grim-faced guards.* ♦ **grimly** ADV *'Smoke,' Eddie announced grimly.*

grimace /grɪmeɪs, grɪmə^1s/, **grimaces, grimacing, grimaced.** COUNT N A **grimace** is a twisted, ugly expression on your face that shows you are displeased, disgusted, or in pain. *Thomas made a little grimace. Perhaps he thought the wine was sour.* Also VB *She made a bad gear-change and grimaced.*

grime /graɪm/. UNCOUNT N **Grime** is dirt on the surface of something. *The windows were thick with grime.*

grimy /graɪmi^1/. ADJ Something **grimy** is very dirty. *...a grimy office.*

grin /grɪn/, **grins, grinning, grinned.** **1** VB If you **grin,** you smile broadly. *He grinned at her.* Also COUNT N *The pilot was unhurt and climbed out with a cheerful grin.* **2** PHRASE If you **grin and bear it,** you accept a difficult or unpleasant situation without complaining; an informal use. *I'd just have to grin and bear it for the next two hours.*

grind /graɪnd/, **grinds, grinding, ground** /graʊnd/. **1** VB WITH OBJ When something such as corn or coffee **is ground,** it is crushed until it becomes a fine powder. *...freshly ground black pepper.* **2** VB WITH OBJ AND ADJUNCT If you **grind** something into a surface, you press it hard into the surface. *He ground his cigarette in the ashtray.* **3** VB If a machine **grinds,** it makes a harsh scraping noise. *The lift grinds in the shaft.* **4** PHRASE If something large **grinds to a halt** or **comes to a grinding halt,** it stops. *The huge coal cart would grind to a halt at our front door... Why doesn't the whole economy grind to a halt?* **5** SING N You can refer to tiring, boring and routine work as the **grind.** *...the long and tiresome grind of preparing themselves for college entrance.* **6** See also **grinding, ground.**

grind down. PHR VB If you **grind** someone **down,** you treat them very harshly, so that they do not have the will to resist you.

grinder /graɪndə/, **grinders.** COUNT N A **grinder** is a machine or device which crushes something into small pieces. *...a coffee grinder.*

grinding /graɪndɪŋ/. ATTRIB ADJ **Grinding** describes a situation that never seems to change, and makes you feel unhappy, tired, or bored. *...grinding poverty.*

grip /grɪp/, **grips, gripping, gripped.** **1** VB WITH OBJ If you **grip** something, you hold it firmly. *Lomax gripped the boy's arm.* Also COUNT N *I tightened my grip on the handrail.* **2** SING N WITH SUPP A **grip** on someone or something is control over them. *He now took a firm grip on the management side of the newspaper... She felt herself in the grip of a sadness she could not understand.* **3** VB WITH OBJ If something **grips** you, it suddenly affects you strongly. *He seemed to be gripped by a powerful desire to laugh.* **4** VB WITH OBJ If you are **gripped** by something, your attention is concentrated on it. *I was really gripped by the first few pages.* ♦ **gripping** ADJ *...a gripping film.*

PHRASES ● If you **get** or **come to grips with** a problem, you start taking action to deal with it. *It's taken us eighteen years to get to grips with our inadequacies.* ● If you **are losing** your **grip,** you are becoming less able to deal with things.

gripe /graɪp/, **gripes, griping, griped.** VB If you **gripe** about something, you keep complaining about it; an informal use.

grisly /grɪzli^1/. ADJ Something that is **grisly** is extremely nasty and horrible. *...a grisly experiment.*

gristle /grɪsə^0l/. UNCOUNT N **Gristle** is a tough, rubbery substance found in meat.

grit /grɪt/, **grits, gritting, gritted.** **1** UNCOUNT N **Grit** consists of tiny pieces of stone. **2** VB WITH OBJ If people **grit** a road, they put grit on it to make it less slippery in icy or snowy weather. **3** UNCOUNT N If you say that someone has **grit** they have determination and courage. *He has grit.*

PHRASES ● If you **grit** your **teeth,** you press your upper and lower teeth together. *She nodded at me sternly. I gritted my teeth, but she didn't notice my anger.* ● If you **grit** your **teeth** in a difficult situation, you decide to carry on.

gritty /grɪti^1/. ADJ Something that is **gritty** is covered with grit or has a texture like grit. *...the gritty carpet.*

groan /grəʊn/, **groans, groaning, groaned.** **1** VB If you **groan,** you make a long, low sound of pain, unhappiness or disapproval. *'I'm sick,' he groaned.* Also COUNT N *A chorus of groans greeted his joke.* **2** VB If wood **groans,** it makes a loud creaking sound. *The wind roared, the trees groaned.*

grocer /grəʊsə/, **grocers.** COUNT N A **grocer** or **grocer's** is a shop where you can buy foods such as flour, sugar, and tinned foods.

grocery /grəʊsə^0ri^1/, **groceries.** **1** COUNT N In America, a grocer's shop is called a **grocery.** **2** PLURAL N **Groceries** are foods such as flour, sugar, and tinned foods. *...a shopping-basket containing groceries.*

groggy /grɒgi^1/. ADJ If you feel **groggy,** you feel weak and ill; an informal use. *I expect you're feeling a bit groggy with the injections.*

groin /grɔɪn/, **groins.** COUNT N Your **groin** is the part of your body where your legs meet.

groom /gru^4m/, **grooms, grooming, groomed.** **1** COUNT N A **groom** is a person who looks after horses in a stable. **2** COUNT N A **groom** is also the same as a bridegroom. *The wedding feast went on until midnight but the bride and groom left before that.* **3** VB WITH OBJ If you **groom** an animal, you brush its fur. **4** VB WITH OBJ If you **groom** a person for a special job, you prepare them by teaching them the skills they will need. *I had been chosen to be groomed as editor.*

groomed /gru:md/. ADJ Someone who is well **groomed** is clean and smart.

groove /gru:v/, **grooves.** COUNT N A **groove** is a line cut into a surface. *...a steel plate with grooves cut in it.* ♦ **grooved** /gru:vd/ ADJ *...the grooved rock.*

grope /grəʊp/, **gropes, groping, groped.** **1** VB If you **grope** for something that you cannot see, you search for it with your hands. *I groped for the timetable I had in my pocket.* **2** VB WITH OR WITHOUT OBJ, WITH ADJUNCT If you **grope** your way to a place, you move there using your hands to feel the way because you cannot see anything. *I groped my way out of bed and downstairs.* **3** VB If you **grope** for something such as the solution to a problem, you try to think of it, when you have no real idea what it could be. *We are groping for ways to get the communities together.*

gross /grəʊs/, **grosser, grossest. Gross** is the singular and plural of the noun. **1** ATTRIB ADJ You use **gross** to describe something unacceptable or unpleasant that is very great in amount or degree. *...children whose parents are guilty of gross neglect.* ♦ **grossly** ADV *They were both grossly overweight.* **2** ADJ Speech or behaviour that is **gross** shows lack of taste, or is very rude. *He felt he had said something gross, indecent.* **3** ADJ Something that is **gross** is very large and ugly. *...the gross architecture of the Piccadilly frontages.* **4** ATTRIB ADJ OR ADV **Gross** is used to describe a total amount of something, after all relevant amounts have been added but before any deductions have been made. *His gross income will very likely exceed $900,000 this year... ...the gross national product.* **5** ATTRIB ADJ OR ADV **Gross** describes the total weight of something, including its container. *...8,000 merchant ships with a gross tonnage of 20 million.* **6** COUNT N A **gross** is a group of 144 things. *He bought them by the gross.*

grotesque /grəʊtɛsk/. **1** ADJ Something that is **grotesque** is exaggerated and ridiculous or frightening. *...grotesque comedy.* ♦ **grotesquely** ADV *I knew I had been perfectly ridiculous, over-acting grotesquely.* **2** ADJ If something is **grotesque,** it is very ugly. *...grotesque figures carved into the stonework.*

grotto /grɒtəʊ/, **grottoes** or **grottos.** COUNT N A **grotto** is a small attractive cave.

grotty /grɒti^1/. ADJ Something **grotty** is unpleasant or of poor quality; an informal use. *...a grotty little building.*

grouchy /graʊtʃi^1/. ADJ Someone **grouchy** is bad-tempered and complains a lot; an informal use.

ground /graʊnd/, **grounds, grounding, grounded.** **1** SING N The **ground** is the surface of the earth. *He set down his bundle carefully on the ground.* **2** UNCOUNT N **Ground** is land. *...a rocky piece of ground.* **3** COUNT N WITH SUPP A **ground** is an area which is used for a particular purpose. *...a burial ground... ...fishing grounds... ...football grounds.* **4** PLURAL N The **grounds** of a building are the land which surrounds it and belongs with it. *...the school grounds.* **5** UNCOUNT N WITH SUPP You can also use **ground** to refer to a subject or range of things when you are considering it as an area to be covered or dealt with. *This course covers the same ground as the undergraduate degree in Social Administration.* **6** PLURAL N WITH SUPP Something that is **grounds** for something else is a reason or justification for it. *You have no real grounds for complaint.* **7** UNCOUNT N If you gain **ground,** you make progress or get an advantage. *Godley's views are gaining political ground... He tried to regain lost ground.* **8** VB WITH OBJ If aircraft or pilots **are grounded,** they are not allowed to fly. **9** VB WITH OBJ If an argument or opinion **is grounded** in or on something, it is based on that thing. *...a delusion grounded in fear.* **10 Ground** is also the past tense and past participle of **grind.**

PHRASES ● **On grounds of, on the grounds of,** and **on the grounds that** introduce the reason for a particular action. *He was always declining their invitations on grounds of ill health.* ● If you **go to ground,** you hide somewhere for a period of time. *All the people involved have gone to ground in cheap hotels.* ● If you **run** something **to ground,** you find it after a long, difficult search. *It was run to ground in the nearby woods.* ● If you **break fresh ground** or **break new ground,** you make a discovery or start a new activity. ● If you **get** something **off the ground,** you get it started. *There was a hurry to get the new film off the ground.* ● If you **stand** or **hold** your **ground,** you do not retreat or give in when people are opposing you. ● **to have your ear to the ground:** see **ear.** ● **thin on the ground:** see **thin.** ● See also **home ground.**

ground floor. SING N In Britain the **ground floor** of a building is the floor that is level with the ground outside.

grounding /graʊndɪŋ/. SING N A **grounding** in a subject is instruction in the basic facts or principles of it. *Schools must provide a firm grounding in the basics, reading, writing, arithmetic.*

groundless /graʊndlɪ^2s/. ADJ A fear or suspicion that is **groundless** is not based on reason or evidence; a formal use. *Your fears are groundless... His allegations, when investigated, proved groundless.*

ground level. UNCOUNT N **Ground level** is used to refer to the ground or to the floor of a building which is at the same level as the ground.

ground rules. PLURAL N **Ground rules** are the basic principles on which future action will be based. *They sat down to work out the ground rules for the project.*

groundsheet /graʊndʃi:t/, **groundsheets.** COUNT N A **groundsheet** is a piece of waterproof material put on the ground to sleep on when camping.

groundsman /graʊndzmən/, **groundsmen.** COUNT N A **groundsman** is a person whose job is to look after a park or sports ground.

groundwork /graʊndwɜ:k/. SING N If you do the **groundwork** on something, you do the early work which forms the basis for further work. *They had already provided the groundwork for economic progress.*

group /gru:p/, **groups, grouping, grouped.** **1** COLL N A **group** is a number of people or things which are together in one place at one time. *...a group of buildings... ...standing in a group in the centre of the room.* 2 COLL N WITH SUPP A **group** is a set of people or things which have something in common. *...children of his age group... ...a parents' action group.* ● See also **pressure group.** 3 COLL N A **group** is also a number of musicians who perform pop music together. 4 ERG VB When you **group** a number of things or people, they all come together in some way. *They encouraged workers and consumers to group together... Occupations are grouped into separate categories.*

grouping /gruːpɪŋ/, **groupings.** COUNT N WITH SUPP A **grouping** of people or things is a set of them with something in common. *Lawyers and government officials were the largest groupings.*

grouse /graʊs/, **grouses, grousing, groused.** **Grouse** is the singular and plural of the noun. 1 COUNT N A **grouse** is a small fat bird. Grouse are often shot for sport and can be eaten. 2 VB If you **grouse,** you complain. *It was a sad end to her career but she never grumbled or groused.*

grove /grəʊv/, **groves.** COUNT N A **grove** is a group of trees that are close together. *...an olive grove.*

grovel /grɒvəl/, **grovels, grovelling, grovelled;** spelled **groveling** and **groveled** in American English. 1 VB If you **grovel,** you behave very humbly towards someone because you think they are important. *They are going to make you grovel.* ♦ **grovelling** ADJ *He sent a letter of grovelling apology to the publisher.* 2 VB WITH ADJUNCT To **grovel** also means to crawl on the floor, for example in order to find something. *He was grovelling under his desk for a dropped pencil.*

grow /grəʊ/, **grows, growing, grew** /gruː/, **grown** /grəʊn/. 1 VB If something **grows,** it increases in size, amount or degree. *Babies who are small at birth grow faster... Jobs in industry will grow by 11 per cent... ...the fast-growing New York investment bank.* 2 VB If a plant or tree **grows** in a particular place, it is alive there. *An oak tree grew at the edge of the lane.* 3 VB WITH OBJ When you **grow** plants, you put them in the ground and look after them as they develop. *The district grew peas on a large scale.* ♦ **grower** COUNT N WITH SUPP *My father was a great rose grower.* 4 VB WITH OBJ If a man **grows** a beard or a moustache, he lets it develop by not shaving. 5 VB WITH COMPLEMENT, TO-INF, OR ADJUNCT If something **grows** into a particular state, it changes gradually until it is in that state. *The sun grew so hot that they were forced to stop working... I grew to dislike working for the cinema.* 6 VB If one idea **grows** out of another, it develops from it. *My own idea grew out of seeing this film.* 7 See also **grown.**

grow into. PHR VB When children **grow into** a piece of clothing that is too big for them, they get bigger so that it fits them properly.

grow on. PHR VB If something **grows on** you, you start to like it more and more; an informal use. *She was someone whose charm grew very slowly on you.*

grow out of. PHR VB 1 If you **grow out of** a type of behaviour, you stop behaving in that way. 2 When children **grow out of** a piece of clothing, they become so big that it no longer fits them.

grow up. PHR VB 1 When someone **grows up,** they gradually change from being a child into being an adult. *They grew up in the early days of television.* 2 If something **grows up,** it becomes stronger. *The idea has grown up that science cannot be wrong.* 3 See also **grown-up.**

growl /graʊl/, **growls, growling, growled.** 1 VB When an animal **growls,** it makes a low rumbling noise, usually because it is angry. *The dog growled at me.* Also COUNT N *He did not hear the growl of the leopard.* 2 VB If someone **growls,** they use a low, rough, rather angry voice. *'There's a visitor here,' he growled.* Also COUNT N *'Yeah,' said John in a low growl.*

grown /grəʊn/. 1 **Grown** is the past participle of **grow.** 2 ATTRIB ADJ A **grown** man or woman is an adult.

grown-up, grown-ups. 1 COUNT N **Grown-up** is a children's word for an adult. *Until the grown-ups come to fetch us we'll have fun.* 2 ADJ Someone who is **grown-up** is adult or behaves in an adult way even though he or she is still a child. *...older couples with grown-up children... Your brother's awfully grown-up for his age.*

growth /grəʊθ/, **growths.** 1 UNCOUNT N WITH SUPP The **growth** of something is its increase or development in size, wealth, or importance. *Its economic growth rate is second only to Japan's... ...the growth of political opposition... ...India's population growth.* 2 UNCOUNT N **Growth** in a person, animal, or plant is the process of increasing in size and development. *He noticed that this drug seemed to inhibit bacterial growth.* 3 COUNT N A **growth** is an abnormal lump that grows inside or on a person, animal, or plant.

grub /grʌb/, **grubs, grubbing, grubbed.** 1 COUNT N A **grub** is a worm-like young insect which has just come out of an egg. 2 UNCOUNT N **Grub** is food; an informal use. 3 VB WITH ADJUNCT If you **grub** about for something, you search for it by moving things or digging. *The fish grubs around on the river bed.*

grubby /grʌbi/, **grubbier, grubbiest.** ADJ Something that is **grubby** is rather dirty; an informal use. *...their grubby hands.*

grudge /grʌdʒ/, **grudges, grudging, grudged.** 1 COUNT N OR UNCOUNT N If you have a **grudge** against someone, you have unfriendly feelings towards them because they have harmed you in the past. *They had to do it, and I bear them no grudge... It isn't in her nature to hold grudges.* 2 VB WITH OBJ AND OBJ, OR VB WITH OBJ AND PREP 'to' If you **grudge** someone something, you give it to them unwillingly or are not pleased that they have it. *We need not grudge them their mindless pleasures... Not that I grudge the use of my kitchen to you.*

grudging /grʌdʒɪŋ/. ADJ A **grudging** action is one that you do very unwillingly. *Others stood watching with grudging respect.* ♦ **grudgingly** ADV *'Okay,' he said grudgingly, 'I suppose I was to blame.'*

gruelling /grʊəlɪŋ/; spelled **grueling** in American English. ADJ Something that is **gruelling** is extremely difficult and tiring. *I was exhausted after a gruelling week.*

gruesome /gruːsəm/. ADJ Something that is **gruesome** involves death or injury and is very shocking. *...gruesome tales of child murder.*

gruff /grʌf/. ADJ A **gruff** voice is low, rough, and unfriendly. *He hid his feelings behind a kind of gruff abruptness.* ♦ **gruffly** ADV *She said gruffly, 'Put on your clothes.'*

grumble /grʌmbəl/, **grumbles, grumbling, grumbled.** VB If you **grumble,** you complain about something, usually in a low voice and not forcefully. *They will grumble about having to do the work.* Also COUNT N *There were angry grumbles from the British ranks.*

grumpy /grʌmpi/. ADJ A **grumpy** person is bad-tempered and miserable; an informal use. *Don't be so grumpy and cynical about it.*

grunt /grʌnt/, **grunts, grunting, grunted.** VB If a person or a pig **grunts,** they make a low, rough noise. *His father looked up and grunted, then went back to his work.* Also COUNT N *He gave a sceptical grunt... It sounded like a pig's grunt.*

guarantee /gærəntiː/, **guarantees, guaranteeing, guaranteed.** 1 VB WITH OBJ If one thing **guarantees** another, the first is certain to cause the second thing to happen. *This method guarantees success.* 2 VB WITH OBJ OR VB WITH OBJ AND OBJ If you **guarantee** something, you promise that it will definitely happen, or that you will do or provide it. *I'm not guaranteeing that this will work... They guarantee to hold interest rates down until next year... Advertisers were guaranteed a weekly circulation of 250,000.* 3 REPORT VB If you say that you **guarantee** that something will happen, or that it **is guaranteed** to happen, you mean that you are certain that it will happen. *You should have one evening off a week, but you can't guarantee it... This state of affairs is guaranteed to continue indefinitely.* 4 COUNT N Something that is a **guarantee** of a particular thing makes it certain that it will happen or that it is true. *There is no guarantee that they are telling the truth... The jury system is one of the guarantees of democracy.* 5 COUNT N A **guarantee** is also a promise that something will happen. *We want some guarantee that an enquiry will be held... ...guarantees of full employment.* 6 VB WITH OBJ If a company **guarantees** work, they give a written promise that if it has any faults within a particular time it will be repaired or replaced free of charge. 7 COUNT N A **guarantee** is also a written promise by a company that if their work has any faults within a particular time, it will be repaired or replaced free of charge. *How long does the guarantee last?*

guard /gɑːd/, **guards, guarding, guarded.** 1 VB WITH OBJ If you **guard** a place, person, or object, you watch them carefully, either to protect them or to stop them from escaping. *Scotland Yard sent an officer to guard his house... She had been locked in her room and was guarded night and day.* 2 COUNT N OR COLL N A **guard** is a person or group of people that protect or watch someone or something. *They will give him an armed guard.* 3 COUNT N A **guard** is also a railway official on a train. 4 VB WITH OBJ If you **guard** something important or secret, you protect or hide it. *The professions, as you might expect, guard their secrets closely.* ♦ **guarded** ADJ *The contents of the lists were a closely guarded secret.* 5 COUNT N A **guard** is also a cover for something dangerous. *When the guard is taken off the motor the machine can't start.*

PHRASES ● If you **stand guard** over someone or something, you guard them. *You will be expected to stand guard over the village.* ● Someone who is **on guard** is responsible for guarding a particular place or person. ● If you are **on** your **guard,** you are being careful because a situation might become difficult or dangerous. *Busy parents have to be on their guard against being bad-tempered with their children.* ● If you **catch** someone **off guard,** you surprise them by doing something when they are not expecting it.

guard against. PHR VB If you **guard against** something, you are careful to avoid it happening or avoid being affected by it. *...ideas which the trained mind of a judge knows to guard against.*

guarded /gɑːdɪd/. ADJ Someone who is **guarded** is careful not to show their feelings or give away information. *His statements were guarded.*

guardian /gɑːdɪən/, **guardians.** 1 COUNT N A **guardian** is someone who has been legally appointed to look after a child. *He became the legal guardian of his brother's daughter.* 2 COUNT N A **guardian** is also someone who is considered a protector or defender of things. *...guardians of morality.*

guerrilla /gərɪlə/, **guerrillas;** also spelled **guerilla.** COUNT N A **guerrilla** is a person who fights as part of an unofficial army.

guess /gɛs/, **guesses, guessing, guessed.** 1 REPORT VB OR VB If you **guess** something, you give an answer or an opinion about something when you do not know whether it is correct. *She guessed that she was fifty yards from shore... We can only guess at the number of deaths it has caused... My salary is, I would guess, about half of yours.* 2 VB WITH OR WITHOUT OBJ If you **guess** something, you give the correct answer to a problem or question when you did not know the answer for certain. *How did you guess?... I had guessed the identity of her lover.* 3 COUNT N A **guess** is an attempt to give the right answer to something when you do not know what the answer is. *I don't know the name but I'll take a guess at it.* 4 PHRASE You say **I guess** to indicate that you think that something is true or likely; an informal American use. *'What's that?'—'Some sort of blackbird, I guess.'... 'Sure?'—'I guess so.'*

guesswork /gɛswɜːk/. UNCOUNT N **Guesswork** is the process or result of trying to guess something. *This is pure guesswork at this stage.*

guest /gɛst/, **guests.** 1 COUNT N A **guest** is someone who is staying in your home or is attending an event because they have been invited. *...wedding guests... We're here as guests of the National Theatre.* 2 COUNT N A **guest** is also someone who is staying in a hotel.

guest house, guest houses. COUNT N A **guest house** is a small hotel.

guffaw /gəfɔː/, **guffaws, guffawing, guffawed.** COUNT N A **guffaw** is a very loud laugh. *Martin let out a delighted guffaw.* Also VB *He guffawed and thumped his friend on the shoulder.*

guidance /gaɪdəns/. UNCOUNT N **Guidance** is help and advice. *...guidance from an expert.*

guide /gaɪd/, **guides, guiding, guided.** 1 COUNT N A **guide** is someone who shows tourists round places such as museums or cities. 2 VB WITH OBJ If you **guide** someone round a city or building, you show it to them and explain points of interest. ♦ **guided** ATTRIB ADJ *We went on a guided tour of Paris.* 3 COUNT N A **guide** is also someone who leads the way through difficult country. 4 VB WITH OBJ To **guide** someone or something means to cause them to move in the right direction. *Men crossing the ocean would use the stars to guide them.* 5 COUNT N A **guide** is the same as a guidebook. *...a guide to New York City.* 6 COUNT N A **guide** is also a book which gives you information or instructions to help you do or understand something. *This book is meant to be a practical guide to healthy living.* 7 COUNT N A **guide** or a **girl guide** is a member of the Girl Guides Association which encourages girls to become disciplined and to learn practical skills; a British use. 8 VB WITH OBJ If you **guide** someone, you influence their actions or decisions. *Politicians will in the end always be guided by changes in public opinion.*

guidebook /gaɪdbʊk/, **guidebooks.** COUNT N A **guidebook** is a book which gives information for tourists about a town, area, or country.

guideline /gaɪdlaɪn/, **guidelines.** COUNT N A **guideline** is a piece of advice about how to do something. *...government pay guidelines.*

guild /gɪld/, **guilds.** COUNT N A **guild** is an organization of people who do the same job or who share an interest; a formal use.

guile /gaɪl/. UNCOUNT N **Guile** is cunning and deceit. *He was a man without guile.*

guillotine /gɪlətiːn/, **guillotines.** 1 COUNT N A **guillotine** is a device which was used to execute people by cutting off their heads, especially in France in the past. 2 COUNT N A **guillotine** is also a device used for cutting and trimming paper.

guilt /gɪlt/. 1 UNCOUNT N **Guilt** is an unhappy feeling that you have because you have done something wrong. *I had agonizing feelings of shame and guilt.* 2 UNCOUNT N **Guilt** is the fact that you have done something wrong or illegal. *He at last made a public admission of his guilt.*

guilty /gɪlti[1]/. 1 ADJ If you feel **guilty,** you feel unhappy because you have done something wrong. *They feel guilty about seeing her so little.* ♦ **guiltily** ADV *I blushed and looked away guiltily.* 2 ATTRIB ADJ You use **guilty** to describe an action or fact that you feel guilty about. *...a guilty secret.* 3 ADJ If someone is **guilty,** they have committed a crime or done something wrong. *He was found guilty of passing on secret papers to a foreign power.*

guinea /gɪni[1]/, **guineas.** COUNT N A **guinea** is an old British unit of money worth £1.05.

guinea pig, guinea pigs. 1 COUNT N A **guinea pig** is a small furry animal without a tail which is often kept as a pet. 2 COUNT N A **guinea pig** is also a person that is used in an experiment. *...experimentation on human guinea pigs.*

guise /gaɪz/, **guises.** COUNT N WITH SUPP **Guise** refers to the outward appearance or form of something. *A lot of nonsense was talked, under the guise of philosophy.*

guitar /gɪtɑː/, **guitars.** COUNT N A **guitar** is a wooden musical instrument with six strings which are plucked or strummed.

guitarist /gɪtɑːr[0]ɪst/, **guitarists.** COUNT N A **guitarist** is someone who plays the guitar.

gulf /gʌlf/, **gulfs.** 1 COUNT N A **gulf** is an important difference between two people, things, or groups. *The gulf between the cultures was too great to be easily bridged.* 2 COUNT N A **gulf** is also a very large bay. *...the Gulf of Mexico.*

gull /gʌl/, **gulls.** COUNT N A **gull** is a common sea bird.

gullet /gʌlɪ[2]t/, **gullets.** COUNT N Your **gullet** is the tube from your mouth to your stomach.

gullible /gʌləbə[0]l/. ADJ A **gullible** person is easily tricked.

gully /gʌli[1]/, **gullies.** COUNT N A **gully** is a long narrow valley with steep sides.

gulp /gʌlp/, **gulps, gulping, gulped.** 1 VB WITH OBJ If you **gulp** something, or **gulp** it down, you swallow large quantities of it at the same time. *She gulped her coffee... After gulping down his breakfast, he hurried to the station.* Also COUNT N *She took a gulp of whisky.* 2 VB If you **gulp,** you swallow air, usually because you are nervous. *He gulped and stammered for me to call back.* Also COUNT N *I gave a little gulp.*

gum /gʌm/, **gums, gumming, gummed.** 1 UNCOUNT N **Gum** is a kind of sweet which you chew but do not swallow. ● See also **bubble gum, chewing gum.** 2 UNCOUNT N **Gum** is also a type of glue that you use to stick paper together. 3 VB WITH OBJ AND ADJUNCT If you **gum** one thing to another, you stick them together. 4 COUNT N Your **gums** are the areas of firm, pink flesh inside your mouth, which your teeth grow out of.

gumboot /gʌmbuːt/, **gumboots.** COUNT N **Gumboots** are long, waterproof, rubber boots.

gun /gʌn/, **guns, gunning, gunned.** COUNT N A **gun** is a weapon from which bullets are fired.

PHRASES ● If you **jump the gun,** you do something before the proper time; an informal use. *Newspapers began to jump the gun and talk about resignations.* ● If you **stick to** your **guns,** you continue to have your own opinion about something even though other people disagree; an informal use.

gun down. PHR VB If you **gun** someone **down,** you shoot at them and kill or injure them.

gunfire /gʌnfaɪə/. UNCOUNT N **Gunfire** is the repeated shooting of guns. *...listening for the bursts of gunfire.*

gunman /gʌnmə[3]n/, **gunmen.** COUNT N A **gunman** is someone who uses a gun to commit a crime.

gunner /gʌnə/, **gunners.** COUNT N A **gunner** is a member of the armed forces who is trained to use guns.

gunpoint /gʌnpɔɪnt/. PHRASE If someone does something to you **at gunpoint,** they threaten to shoot you if you do not obey them. *He held the three men at gunpoint.*

gunpowder /gʌnpaʊdə/. UNCOUNT N **Gunpowder** is an explosive substance.

gunshot /gʌnʃɒt/, **gunshots.** COUNT N A **gunshot** is the firing of a gun. *...the sound of gunshots.*

gurgle /gɜːgə[0]l/, **gurgles, gurgling, gurgled.** 1 VB When water **gurgles,** it makes a bubbling sound. 2 VB When a baby **gurgles,** it makes bubbling sounds in its throat. *Kicking and gurgling, his little brother looked up at him.* Also COUNT N *...gurgles of pleasure.*

guru /gu[4]ruː/, **gurus.** 1 COUNT N A **guru** is a spiritual leader and teacher, especially in Hinduism. 2 COUNT N A **guru** is also a respected adviser.

gush /gʌʃ/, **gushes, gushing, gushed.** 1 VB WITH ADJUNCT When liquid **gushes** out of something, it flows out very quickly and in large quantities. *Tears were gushing from her closed eyes.* Also SING N *...a gush of blood.* 2 VB If someone **gushes,** they express their admiration or pleasure in an exaggerated way. *'Amy!' he gushed. 'How good to see you again.'* ♦ **gushing** ADJ *...a large gushing female.*

gust /gʌst/, **gusts.** 1 COUNT N A **gust** is a short, strong rush of wind. *...a sudden gust of wind.* 2 SING N WITH 'of' If you feel a **gust** of emotion, you feel the emotion suddenly and intensely. *A gust of pure happiness swept through her.*

gusto /gʌstəʊ/. PHRASE If you do something **with gusto,** you do it with energy and enthusiasm.

gut /gʌt/, **guts, gutting, gutted.** 1 PLURAL N Your **guts** are your internal organs, especially your intestines. 2 SING N The **gut** is the tube inside your body through which food passes while it is being digested. 3 VB WITH OBJ If you **gut** a fish, you remove the organs from inside it. 4 UNCOUNT N **Guts** is courage; an informal use. *Sam hasn't got the guts to leave.* 5 MOD A **gut** feeling is based on instinct or emotion rather than on reason. *My immediate gut reaction was to refuse.* 6 VB WITH OBJ If a building **is gutted,** the inside is destroyed. *The whole house was gutted by fire.*

gutter /gʌtə/, **gutters.** 1 COUNT N The **gutter** is the edge of a road next to the pavement, where rain collects and flows away. *The motorbike lay on its side in the gutter.* 2 COUNT N A **gutter** is also a plastic or metal channel fixed to the edge of a roof, which rain water drains into.

guy /gaɪ/, **guys;** an informal word. 1 COUNT N A **guy** is a man. *...the guy who drove the bus.* 2 VOCATIVE Americans sometimes address a group of people as **guys** or **you guys.**

guzzle /gʌzə[0]l/, **guzzles, guzzling, guzzled.** VB WITH OR WITHOUT OBJ If you **guzzle** something, you drink or eat it quickly and greedily; an informal use.

gym /dʒɪm/, **gyms.** 1 COUNT N A **gym** is a gymnasium. *He was always at the gym.* 2 UNCOUNT N **Gym** means gymnastics. *We did an hour of gym.*

gymkhana /dʒɪmkɑːnə/, **gymkhanas.** COUNT N A **gymkhana** is an event in which people ride horses in competitions.

gymnasium /dʒɪmneɪzɪəm/, **gymnasiums.** COUNT N A **gymnasium** is a room with equipment for physical exercise.

gymnast /dʒɪmnæst/, **gymnasts.** COUNT N A **gymnast** is someone who is trained in gymnastics.

gymnastic /dʒɪmnæstɪk/, **gymnastics.** 1 PLURAL N **Gymnastics** are physical exercises, which develop your agility and strength. 2 ATTRIB ADJ **Gymnastic** is used to describe things relating to gymnastics. *...gymnastic ability.*

gynaecology /gaɪnəkɒlədʒi[1]/; also spelled **gynecology.** UNCOUNT N **Gynaecology** is the branch of medical science which deals with women's diseases and medical conditions; a technical use.

gypsy /dʒɪpsi[1]/, **gypsies;** also spelled **gipsy.** COUNT N A **gypsy** is a member of a race of people who travel from place to place in caravans rather than living in one place.

Hh

habit /hæbɪt/, **habits.** 1 COUNT N OR UNCOUNT N A **habit** is something that you do often or regularly. *It became a habit for the fans to use the office... More out of habit than anything else, I stopped and went in.* ● If you are **in the habit of** doing something, or if you **make a habit** of doing it, you do it regularly and often. *Once a month Castle was in the habit of taking Sarah for an excursion... They made a habit of lunching together twice a week.* 2 COUNT N A **habit** is also an action which is considered bad that someone does repeatedly and finds difficult to stop doing. *He had a nervous habit of biting his nails.* 3 COUNT N WITH SUPP A drug **habit** is an addiction to a drug. *Groups exist to help those who want to kick the marijuana habit.*

habitable /hæbɪtəbə[0]l/. ADJ If a place is **habitable,** it is suitable for people to live in.

habitat /hæbɪtæt/, **habitats.** COUNT N WITH SUPP The **habitat** of an animal or plant is its natural environment. *...the open woodland that is their natural habitat.*

habitation /hæbɪteɪʃə[0]n/, **habitations.** 1 UNCOUNT N **Habitation** is the human activity of living somewhere. *...to see whether the houses are fit for human habitation.* 2 COUNT N A **habitation** is a place where people live; a formal use. *...squalid human habitations.*

habitual /hə[3]bɪtjʊ[0]əl/. ADJ A **habitual** action is one that someone usually does or often does. *'Sorry I'm late,' David said with his habitual guilty grin.* ♦ **habitually** ADV *Anybody who habitually keeps his office door shut is suspect.*

hack /hæk/, **hacks, hacking, hacked.** 1 VB WITH OBJ OR ADJUNCT If you **hack** something, you cut it with a sharp tool, using strong, rough strokes. *They were ambushed and hacked to death... ...hacking away at the branches.* 2 COUNT N A **hack** is a professional writer who produces work fast, without worrying about its quality; an informal use. *...a hack writer.* 3 VB When someone **hacks** into a computer system, they try to break into it in order to get secret information. ♦ **hacker** /hækə/ COUNT N *He was well known as a hacker.* ♦ **hacking** UNCOUNT N *The act of hacking is not an offence.*

hackneyed /hæknɪd/. ADJ A **hackneyed** expression is meaningless because it has been used too often. *'Of course I love you. With all my heart.' The hackneyed phrase came unintended to his lips.*

had /hæd/. **Had** is the past tense and past participle of **have.**

haddock /hædək/. **Haddock** is the singular and plural. COUNT N OR UNCOUNT N A **haddock** is a sea fish.

hadn't /hædə[0]nt/. **Hadn't** is the usual spoken form of 'had not'.

haemoglobin /hiːmə[6]gləʊbɪn, hem-/; also spelled **hemoglobin.** UNCOUNT N **Haemoglobin** is a substance that carries oxygen in red blood cells; a technical use.

haemophilia /hiːmə[6]fɪlɪə, hem-/; also spelled **hemophilia.** UNCOUNT N **Haemophilia** is a disease in which a person's blood does not clot properly, so that they bleed for a long time if they are injured.

haemorrhage /hemə[0]rɪdʒ/, **haemorrhages;** also spelled **hemorrhage.** COUNT N OR UNCOUNT N A **haemorrhage** is serious bleeding inside a person's body. *He had died of a brain haemorrhage... ...repeated haemorrhages from no apparent cause.*

hag /hæg/, **hags.** COUNT N A **hag** is an ugly and unpleasant woman; an offensive use.

haggard /hægəd/. ADJ A **haggard** person looks very tired and worried. *There was a haggard look about his eyes.*

haggle /hægə[0]l/, **haggles, haggling, haggled.** RECIP VB If you **haggle,** you argue about the cost of something that you are buying. *They haggled with shopkeepers in the bazaar.*

ha ha /hɑː hɑː/. CONVENTION **Ha ha** is used in writing to represent laughter.

hail /heɪl/, **hails, hailing, hailed.** 1 SING N **Hail** consists of tiny balls of ice that fall from the sky. *The hail battered on the windows.* 2 VB When it **hails,** hail falls from the sky. *It hailed all afternoon.* 3 SING N A **hail** of small objects is a large number of them that fall down on you at the same time with great force. *He was dead, killed in a hail of bullets.* 4 VB WITH OBJ If you **hail** someone, you call to them; a literary use. *A voice hailed him from the steps.* 5 VB WITH OBJ If you **hail** a taxi, you signal to the driver to stop. 6 VB WITH OBJ WITH 'as' If you **hail** a person, event, or achievement as important or successful, you praise them publicly. *They were hailed as heroes... The discovery was hailed as the scientific sensation of the century.*

hailstone /heɪlstəʊn/, **hailstones.** COUNT N **Hailstones** are tiny balls of ice that fall from the sky when it hails.

hair /heə/, **hairs.** 1 UNCOUNT N Your **hair** is the large number of hairs that grow in a mass on your head. *...a young woman with long blonde hair.* 2 COUNT N **Hairs** are the long, fine strands that grow in large numbers on your head and on other parts of your body. *...black hairs on the back of his hands.* 3 COUNT N **Hairs** are also very fine thread-like strands that grow on some insects and plants. *The adult beetle has silken hairs on its body.*

PHRASES ● Something that **makes your hair stand on end** shocks or horrifies you. *She did it with an ease that made his hair stand on end.* ● If you **let your hair down,** you relax completely and enjoy yourself. ● If you say that someone **is splitting hairs,** you mean that they are making unnecessary distinctions or paying too much attention to unimportant details. *Am I splitting hairs here? I think not, because this is an important distinction.*

hairbrush /heəbrʌʃ/, **hairbrushes.** COUNT N A **hairbrush** is a brush that you use to brush your hair.

haircut /heəkʌt/, **haircuts.** 1 COUNT N If you have a **haircut,** someone cuts your hair for you. *He needed a haircut.* 2 COUNT N A **haircut** is also the style in which your hair has been cut. *The girls had short, neat haircuts.*

hairdresser /heədresə/, **hairdressers.** 1 COUNT N A **hairdresser** is a person who cuts, washes, and styles people's hair. 2 COUNT N A **hairdresser's** is a place where you can have your hair cut, washed, or styled.

hairdryer /heədraɪə/, **hairdryers;** also spelled **hairdrier.** COUNT N A **hairdryer** is a machine that you use to dry your hair.

hairless /heəlɪ[2]s/. ADJ A part of your body that is **hairless** has no hair on it. *...his hairless chest.*

hairline /hɛəlaɪn/, **hairlines. 1** COUNT N Your **hairline** is the edge of the area where your hair grows on the front part of your head. *His hairline was receding.* **2** ATTRIB ADJ A **hairline** crack or gap is very narrow or fine. *...a tiny hairline fracture.*

hairpin /hɛəpɪn/, **hairpins. 1** COUNT N A **hairpin** is a thin piece of bent metal used to hold hair in position. **2** COUNT N A **hairpin** bend is a very sharp bend in a road. *We laboured slowly up the hairpin bends.*

hair-raising. ADJ Something that is **hair-raising** is very frightening or disturbing. *The ride was bumpy and at times hair-raising.*

hair's breadth. PHRASE If something happens **by a hair's breadth,** it nearly did not happen at all. *A national strike has been averted by no more than a hair's breadth.*

hairstyle /hɛəstaɪl/, **hairstyles.** COUNT N Your **hairstyle** is the style in which your hair has been cut or arranged. *...a new hairstyle.*

hairy /hɛəri[1]/, **hairier, hairiest. 1** ADJ Someone or something that is **hairy** is covered with hair. *...a big, hairy man.* **2** ADJ If you describe a situation as **hairy,** you mean that it is exciting but rather frightening; an informal use. *Gordon's birth had been a hairy affair.*

halcyon /hælsiən/. ATTRIB ADJ A **halcyon** time is a peaceful or happy one; a formal use.

half /hɑːf/, **halves** /hɑːvz/. **1** QUANTIF, PREDET, PRON, OR COUNT NOUN **Half** of an amount or object is one of the two equal parts that together make up the whole amount or object. *I went to Poland four and a half years ago... Half of the patients are not receiving the drug... Half his front teeth are missing... Roughly half are French... The changes will have repercussions for both halves of Germany.* **2** ATTRIB ADJ You also use **half** to refer to a half of something. *...a half chicken... The film wouldn't end for another half hour.* **3** ADV You also use **half** to say that something is only partly the case or happens to only a limited extent. *He half expected to see Davis there... His eyes were half-closed... ...his half empty glass.* **4** SUBMOD You can use **half** to say that someone has parents of different nationalities. For example, if you are **half** German, one of your parents is German. **5** ADV You use **half** with 'past' to refer to a time that is thirty minutes after a particular hour. For example, if it is **half** past two, thirty minutes have passed since two o'clock.

PHRASES ● If you increase something **by half,** half of the original amount is added to it. If you decrease it **by half,** half of the original amount is taken away from it. *She reckoned she cut her costs by half.* ● If something is divided **in half,** it is divided into two equal parts. *He tore it in half.* ● If two people **go halves,** they divide the cost of something equally between them. *Janet is going halves with Cheryl.*

half-baked. ADJ **Half-baked** ideas or plans have not been properly thought out, and so are usually stupid or impractical. *...your half-baked political opinions.*

half board. UNCOUNT N If you have **half board** at a hotel, you have your breakfast and evening meal there, but not your lunch.

half-brother, half-brothers. COUNT N Your **half-brother** is a boy or man with either the same mother or the same father as you.

half-caste. ADJ Someone who is **half-caste** has parents of different races; an old-fashioned word which some people now find offensive.

half-hearted. ADJ Someone or something that is **half-hearted** shows no real effort or enthusiasm. *She made a half-hearted attempt to break away.* ♦ **half-heartedly** ADV *I stayed home, studying half-heartedly.*

half-life, half-lives. COUNT N The **half-life** of a radioactive substance is the time that it takes to lose half its radioactivity; a technical use.

half-mast. PHRASE If a flag is flying **at half-mast,** it is flying from the middle of the pole as a sign of mourning.

half-sister, half-sisters. COUNT N Your **half-sister** is a girl or woman with either the same mother or the same father as you.

half-term. UNCOUNT N **Half-term** is a short holiday in the middle of a school term.

half-timbered /hɑːftɪmbəd/. ADJ Buildings that are **half-timbered** have a framework of wooden beams which you can see from the outside.

half-time. UNCOUNT N **Half-time** is the short break between the two parts of a sports match, when the players have a rest.

halfway /hɑːfweɪ/. **1** ADV **Halfway** means at the middle of a place or in between two points. *She was half-way up the stairs.* **2** ADV **Halfway** also means at the middle of a period of time or an event. *Dr O'Shea usually fell asleep halfway through the programme.* **3** PHRASE If you **meet** someone **halfway,** you accept some of the points they are making so that you can come to an agreement.

hall /hɔːl/, **halls. 1** COUNT N A **hall** is the area just inside the front door of a house. **2** COUNT N A **hall** is also a large room or building used for public events such as concerts, exhibitions, and meetings. *We organized a concert in the village hall... ...the town hall.* **3** PHRASE Students who live **in hall** live in university or college accommodation.

hallelujah /hælɪ[2]luːjə/; also spelled **halleluiah** and **alleluia.** CONVENTION Some Christians say **hallelujah** in church as an exclamation of praise and thanks to God.

hallmark /hɔːlmɑːk/, **hallmarks. 1** COUNT N WITH SUPP A **hallmark** is the most typical quality or feature of something or someone. *...the kind of subtlety that was the hallmark of Elgar.* **2** COUNT N A **hallmark** is also an official mark put on objects made of precious metals which indicates their value, origin, and quality.

hallo /hə[3]ləʊ/. See **hello.**

hall of residence, halls of residence. COUNT N **Halls of residence** are blocks of rooms or flats belonging to universities or colleges which are used by students.

hallowed /hæləʊd/. ADJ If something is **hallowed,** it is respected, usually because it is old or important; a literary use. *...those hallowed offices on State Street.*

Halloween /hæləuiːn/; also spelled **Hallowe'en.** UNCOUNT N **Halloween** is October 31st. It is traditionally said to be the night on which ghosts and witches can be seen.

hallucinate /hə[3]luːsɪneɪt/, **hallucinates, hallucinating, hallucinated.** VB If you **hallucinate,** you see things that are not really there, either because you are ill or because you have taken a drug. *She barked at me and I knew she must be hallucinating.*

hallucination /hə[3]luːsɪneɪʃə[0]n/. COUNT N OR UNCOUNT N A **hallucination** is the experience of seeing something that is not really there because you are ill or have taken a drug. *...a bizarre hallucination... He was filled with excitement and hallucination.*

hallway /hɔːlweɪ/, **hallways.** COUNT N A **hallway** is the entrance hall of a house or other building.

halo /heɪləʊ/, **haloes** or **halos.** COUNT N A **halo** is a circle of light that is drawn in pictures round the head of a holy figure such as a saint or angel.

halt /hɒlt, hɔːlt/, **halts, halting, halted. 1** ERG VB When you **halt** or when something **halts** you, you stop moving. *He took a step and halted... He tried to push past, but the girl halted him.* **2** ERG VB When growth, development, or activity **halts** or when you **halt** it, it stops completely. *...if population growth were to halt overnight... The firm halted its imports of nylon.*

halting /hɒltɪŋ, hɔːl-/. ADJ If you speak in a **halting** way, you speak uncertainly with a lot of pauses. *...his halting admission of guilt.*

halve /hɑːv/, **halves, halving, halved. 1** ERG VB When you **halve** something or when it **halves,** it is reduced to half its previous size or amount. *This could halve rail fares... If that happened, sales would halve overnight.* **2** VB WITH OBJ If you **halve** something, you divide it into two equal parts. *Halve the avocado pears and remove the stones.* **3 Halves** is the plural of **half.**

ham /hæm/. UNCOUNT N **Ham** is salted meat from a pig's leg. *...legs of ham hanging behind the counter.*

hamburger /hæmbɜːgə/, **hamburgers.** COUNT N A **hamburger** is a flat round mass of minced beef, fried and eaten in a bread roll.

hamlet /hæmlɪ[2]t/, **hamlets.** COUNT N A **hamlet** is a small village.

hammer /hæmə/, **hammers, hammering, hammered. 1** COUNT N A **hammer** is a tool used for hitting things, consisting of a heavy piece of metal at the end of a handle. **2** VB WITH OBJ If you **hammer** something, you hit it with a hammer. *I hammered a peg into the crack.* **3** VB WITH OBJ OR ADJUNCT If you **hammer** a surface or **hammer** on it, you hit it several times. *He hammered the table and told us he wanted results... Men used to hammer on our door late at night.* **4** COUNT N A **hammer** is also a heavy weight attached to a piece of wire, that is thrown as a sport. **5** VB WITH OBJ AND ADJUNCT If you **hammer** an idea into people, you keep repeating it in order to influence them. *...ideas hammered into their heads by a stream of movies.*

hammer out. PHR VB If you **hammer out** something such as an agreement or plan, you reach an agreement about it after a long or difficult discussion. *...procedures hammered out over recent years.*

hammock /hæmək/, **hammocks.** COUNT N A **hammock** is a piece of strong cloth which is hung between two supports and used as a bed.

hamper /hæmpə/, **hampers, hampering, hampered. 1** VB WITH OBJ If you **hamper** a person or their actions, you make it difficult for them to move or make progress. *They were hampered by a constant stream of visitors.* **2** COUNT N A **hamper** is a large basket with a lid, used for carrying food.

hamstring /hæmstrɪŋ/, **hamstrings, hamstringing, hamstrung. 1** COUNT N A **hamstring** is a tendon behind your knee joining the muscles of your thigh to the bones of your lower leg. *...a hamstring injury.* **2** VB WITH OBJ If you **hamstring** someone, you make it very difficult for them to take any action; a literary use. *The economic growth of the West is hamstrung by the lack of purchasing power.*

hand /hænd/, **hands, handing, handed. 1** COUNT N Your **hands** are the parts of your body at the end of your arms. Each hand has four fingers and a thumb. *He took her hand and squeezed it.* **2** COUNT N The **hands** of a clock or watch are the thin pieces of metal or plastic that indicate what time it is. **3** SING N If you ask someone for a **hand** with something, you are asking them to help you. *Give me a hand with this desk, will you?* **4** COUNT N A **hand** is someone who is employed to do hard physical work. **5** VB WITH OBJ AND OBJ If you **hand** something to someone, you give it to them. *Could you hand me that piece of wood?... He scribbled four lines and handed the note to the Field Marshal.*

PHRASES ● You use **on the one hand** when mentioning one aspect of a situation. Then you use **on the other hand** when mentioning another, contrasting aspect. *John had great difficulties playing cricket. But on the other hand, he was an awfully good rugby player.* ● If you have a responsibility or problem **on your hands,** you have to deal with it. *They've still got an economic crisis on their hands.* ● The job or problem **in hand** is the one that you are currently dealing with. *Let's get on with the job in hand.* ● If you have some time **in hand,** you have some time free. *He arrived with half an hour in hand and went for a walk.* ● If someone is **on hand,** they are near and ready to help. ● If you have something **to hand,** you have it ready to use when needed. *...using the material most readily to hand.* ● Something that is **at hand** or **close at hand** is very near in time or place. *I picked up a book that happened to lie at hand.* ● If you do something **by hand,** you do it using your hands rather than a machine. ● Two people who are **hand in hand** are holding each other's hand. ● Two things that **go hand in hand** are closely connected. *Military superiority went hand in hand with organizational superiority.* ● If you **know** a place **like the back of** your **hand,** you know it extremely well. ● If you **try** your **hand** at a new activity, you attempt to do it. *I had tried my hand at milking years ago.* ● If you **have a hand** in a situation, you are actively involved in it. *I had a hand in drafting the appeal.* ● If you **take** someone **in hand,** you take control of them. ● If someone gives you a **free hand,** they allow you to do a particular task exactly as you want. ● If you reject an idea **out of hand,** you reject it immediately and completely. ● If a person or a situation **gets out of hand,** you are no longer able to control them or it. ● If a possession **changes hands,** it is sold or given away. ● If you **wash** your **hands** of someone or something, you refuse to take any more responsibility for them.

hand down or **hand on.** PHR VB If you **hand** something **down,** or **hand** it **on,** you pass it on to people of a younger generation. *Such knowledge was handed down from father to son... Property is something handed on from generation to generation.*

hand in. PHR VB If you **hand in** a written paper, you give it to someone in authority. *I haven't yet marked the work you handed in... I was tempted to hand in my resignation at once.*

hand on. PHR VB See **hand down.**

hand out. PHR VB **1** If you **hand** something **out,** you give it to people. *Hand out the books... Family doctors handed out information on treatment.* **2** See also **handout.**

hand over. PHR VB **1** If you **hand** something **over** to someone, you give it to them. *Samuel was clearly about to hand over large sums of money to this man.* **2** If you **hand over** to someone, you make them responsible for something which you were previously responsible for. *Sir John handed over to his deputy and left.*

handbag /hændbæg/, **handbags.** COUNT N A **handbag** is a small bag used mainly by women.

handbook /hændbʊk/, **handbooks.** COUNT N A **handbook** is a book giving advice or instructions.

handbrake /hændbreɪk/, **handbrakes.** COUNT N A **handbrake** is a brake in a car which is operated by hand. *Mr Boggis released the handbrake.*

handcuff /hændkʌf/, **handcuffs, handcuffing, handcuffed. 1** PLURAL N **Handcuffs** are two metal rings linked by a short chain which are locked round a prisoner's wrists. **2** VB WITH OBJ If you **handcuff** someone, you put handcuffs around their wrists. *They were searched and handcuffed.*

handful /hændfʊl/, **handfuls. 1** COUNT N A **handful** of something is a small quantity of it that you can hold in one hand. *Roger gathered a handful of stones.* **2** SING N If there is only a **handful** of people or things, there are not very many of them. *The firm employs only a* *handful of workers.* 3 COUNT N If you describe a child as a **handful,** you mean that he or she is difficult to control; an informal use.

handicap /hændɪkæp/, **handicaps, handicapping, handicapped.** 1 COUNT N A **handicap** is a physical or mental disability. *These changes have made the campus an easier place for people with handicaps.* 2 COUNT N A **handicap** is also a situation that makes it harder for you to do something. *His chief handicap is that he comes from a broken home.* 3 VB WITH OBJ If an event or a situation **handicaps** someone, it makes it difficult for them to act or to do something. *We were handicapped by the darkness.* 4 COUNT N A **handicap** is also a disadvantage given to someone who is good at a particular sport, in order to make the competition between them and the other competitors more equal.

handicapped /hændɪkæpt/. 1 ADJ Someone who is **handicapped** has a physical or mental disability. *A friend of his had a handicapped daughter.* 2 PLURAL N You can refer to people who are handicapped as **the handicapped.** *...establishments for the mentally or physically handicapped.*

handiwork /hændiwɜːk/. UNCOUNT N WITH POSS If you refer to something as your **handiwork,** you mean that you made it yourself. *He stood back and surveyed his handiwork.*

handkerchief /hæŋkətʃiˡf/, **handkerchiefs.** COUNT N A **handkerchief** is a small square of fabric used when you blow your nose.

handle /hændəˡl/, **handles, handling, handled.** 1 COUNT N A **handle** is the part of an object that you hold in order to carry it or operate it. *He tugged at the metal handle... ...a broom handle.* 2 PHRASE If you **fly off the handle,** you completely lose your temper; an informal use. 3 VB WITH OBJ When you **handle** something, you hold it and move it about in your hands. *The child handled the ornaments carefully and seldom broke anything.* 4 ERG VB WITH ADJUNCT When you **handle** something such as a weapon, car, or horse, you use or control it effectively. *She had handled a machine gun herself.* 5 VB WITH OBJ If you **handle** a problem or a particular area of work, you deal with it or are responsible for it. *You don't have to come. Hendricks and I can handle it... He handles all the major accounts.* ♦ **handling** UNCOUNT N *His handling of these important issues was condemned by the opposition.* 6 VB WITH OBJ If you can **handle** people, you are good at getting them to respect you and do what you want them to. *The principal was a genius in the way he handled us.*

handlebar /hændəˡlbɑː/, **handlebars.** COUNT N The **handlebars** of a bicycle consist of the curved metal bar with handles at each end which are used for steering.

handler /hændlə/, **handlers.** COUNT N WITH SUPP A **handler** is someone whose job is to be in charge of a particular type of thing. *...baggage handlers.*

handmade /hændmeɪd/. ADJ If something is **handmade,** it is made without using machines. *...beautiful handmade clothes.*

handout /hændaʊt/, **handouts.** 1 COUNT N A **handout** is money, clothing, or food which is given free to poor people. *We said that we wouldn't be relying on handouts from anyone for our future.* 2 COUNT N A **handout** is also a document which gives information about an organization or event. *...a pile of unread public relations handouts and shiny magazines.*

hand-picked. ADJ If someone is **hand-picked,** they have been carefully chosen for a particular purpose or job. *Each of the officers had been hand-picked by the general.*

handrail /hændreɪl/, **handrails.** COUNT N A **handrail** is a long piece of metal or wood fixed near stairs or high places.

handshake /hændʃeɪk/, **handshakes.** COUNT N If you give someone a **handshake,** you grasp their right hand with your right hand and move it up and down as a sign of greeting or to show that you have agreed about something.

handsome /hænsəm/. 1 ADJ A **handsome** man has an attractive face with regular features. *He was a tall, dark, and undeniably handsome man.* 2 ADJ A woman who is **handsome** has an attractive, smart appearance with large, regular features rather than small, delicate ones. *...a strikingly handsome woman.* 3 ATTRIB ADJ A **handsome** sum of money is a large or generous amount; a formal use. *The rate of return on these farmers' outlay was a handsome 57 per cent.*

handstand /hændstænd/, **handstands.** COUNT N If you do a **handstand,** you balance upside down on your hands with your body and legs straight up in the air.

hand-to-hand. ATTRIB ADJ A **hand-to-hand** fight is one in which people are fighting very close together, with their hands or knives.

hand-to-mouth. ATTRIB ADJ A **hand-to-mouth** existence is a way of life in which you have hardly enough food or money to live on. *Humboldt's tired of living like a hand-to-mouth Bohemian.*

handwriting /hændraɪtɪŋ/. UNCOUNT N Your **handwriting** is your style of writing with a pen or pencil. *He looked at his son's laborious handwriting.*

handwritten /hændrɪtəˡn/. ADJ A piece of writing that is **handwritten** is one that has been written using a pen or pencil rather than a typewriter or other machine.

handy /hændiˡ/, **handier, handiest.** 1 ADJ Something that is **handy** is useful and easy to use. *An electric kettle is very handy.* 2 ADJ Someone who is **handy** with a particular tool is skilful at using it; an informal use. *...village boys who had a handy way with horses.* 3 ADJ A thing or place that is **handy** is nearby and convenient; an informal use. *I looked to see whether there was a glass handy.*

handyman /hændiˡmæn/, **handymen.** COUNT N A **handyman** is a man who is good at making or repairing things.

hang /hæŋ/, **hangs, hanging, hung** /hʌŋ/ or **hanged. Hanged** is used as the past tense and past participle in meaning 3. 1 VB WITH OBJ AND ADJUNCT If you **hang** something somewhere, you attach it to a high point so that it is above the ground. *He was hanging his coat in the hall.* 2 VB WITH ADJUNCT If something **is hanging** somewhere, the top of it is attached to something and the rest of it is free and not supported. *...some washing hanging on a line.* 3 VB WITH OBJ OR REFL VB To **hang** someone means to kill them by tying a rope around their neck and taking away the support from under their feet so that they hang in the air. *Rebecca Smith was hanged in 1849... He tried to hang himself.* 4 VB WITH 'over' If a future event or a possibility **hangs** over you, it worries you. *...the threat of universal extinction hanging over all the world today.* 5 PHRASE If you **get the hang of** something, you begin to understand how to do it; an informal use. *Once you have got the hang of it, you'll be alright.* 6 See also **hanging.**

hang about, hang around, or **hang round.** PHR VB If you **hang about, hang around,** or **hang round** somewhere, you stay or wait there; an informal use. *We would have to hang around for a while... I enjoyed hanging around Parliament listening to debates.*

hang on. PHR VB 1 If you ask someone to **hang on,** you mean you want them to wait for a moment; an informal use. *Hang on a minute.* 2 If you **hang on,** you manage to survive until a situation improves. *I can't keep hanging on here much longer.* 3 If one thing **hangs on** another, it depends on it. *Everything hangs on money at the moment.*

hang onto. PHR VB 1 If you **hang onto** something, you hold it very tightly. *Claude hung on to Tom's shoulder.* 2 If you **hang onto** a position that you have, you try to keep it. *Fear is a powerful motive for hanging onto power.*

hang out. PHR VB When you **hang out** washing, you hang it on a clothes line to dry.

hang round. PHR VB See **hang around.**

hang up. PHR VB 1 If you **hang** something **up,** you place it so that its highest part is supported and the rest of it is not. *Howard hangs up his scarf on the hook behind the door.* 2 Something that **is hanging up** somewhere has been put there so that it does not touch the ground. *There are some old tools hanging up in the shed.* 3 If you **hang up** when you are on the phone, you end the phone call.

hang up on. PHR VB If you **hang up on** someone, you end a phone call to them suddenly and unexpectedly by putting the receiver back on the rest.

hangar /hæŋə/, **hangars.** COUNT N A **hangar** is a large building where aircraft are kept.

hanger /hæŋə/, **hangers.** COUNT N A **hanger** is curved piece of metal or wood used for hanging clothes on.

hanger-on, hangers-on. COUNT N A **hanger-on** is a person who tries to be friendly with a richer or more important person or group, especially for his or her own advantage. *...a small group of writers, artists and assorted hangers-on.*

hanging /hæŋɪŋ/, **hangings.** 1 UNCOUNT N **Hanging** is the practice of executing people by hanging them. *Every one of them was in favour of hanging.* 2 COUNT N OR UNCOUNT N A **hanging** is the act of killing a person by hanging them. *The crowds at Tyburn used to find a hanging entertaining.* 3 COUNT N A **hanging** is also a piece of cloth used as a decoration on a wall. *...silk and damask hangings.*

hangman /hæŋməˡn/, **hangmen.** COUNT N A **hangman** is a man whose job is to execute people by hanging them.

hangover /hæŋəʊvə/, **hangovers.** 1 COUNT N A **hangover** is a headache and feeling of sickness that you have after drinking too much alcohol. 2 COUNT N WITH SUPP A **hangover** from the past results from ideas which people had but which are no longer generally held. *...a hangover from earlier, more primitive times.*

hang-up, hang-ups. COUNT N If you have a **hang-up** about something, you have a feeling of embarrassment or anxiety about it; an informal use. *He's got a hang-up about flying.*

hank /hæŋk/, **hanks.** COUNT N A **hank** is a length of loosely-wound wool, rope, or string; a technical use.

hanker /hæŋkə/, **hankers, hankering, hankered.** VB WITH 'after' OR 'for' If you **hanker** after something or **hanker** for it, you want it very much. *We always hankered after a bungalow of our own.*

hankering /hæŋkəˡrɪŋ/, **hankerings.** COUNT N WITH 'for' A **hankering** for something is a great desire for it. *If you give way to this hankering for food you will become fat.*

haphazard /hæphæzəd/. ADJ Something that is **haphazard** is not organized according to a plan. *It was done on a haphazard basis.* ♦ **haphazardly** ADV *...all the papers haphazardly strewn on desks.*

hapless /hæplɪˡs/. ATTRIB ADJ A **hapless** person is unlucky; a literary use. *...the hapless victim of a misplaced murder attempt.*

happen /hæpəˡn/, **happens, happening, happened.** 1 VB When something **happens,** it occurs or is done without being planned. *The explosion had happened at one in the morning... ...a court of inquiry into what happened.* 2 VB WITH PREP 'to' When something **happens** to you, it takes place and affects you. *...all the ghastly things that had happened to him.* 3 VB WITH TO-INF If you **happen** to do something, you do it by chance. *He happened to be at their base when the alert began.* 4 PHRASE You say **as it happens** before a statement in order to introduce a new fact. *As it happens, I brought the note with me.*

happening /hæpəˡnɪŋ/, **happenings.** COUNT N A **happening** is something that happens, often in an unexpected way. *...some very bizarre happenings in Europe.*

happy /hæpiˡ/, **happier, happiest.** 1 ADJ Someone who is **happy** feels pleasure, often because something nice has happened. *The old man's not very happy... I was happy to hear that you passed your exam.* ♦ **happily** ADV *We laughed and chatted happily together.* ♦ **happiness** UNCOUNT N *Money did not bring happiness.* 2 ADJ A time or place that is **happy** is full of pleasant and enjoyable feelings, or has an atmosphere in which people feel happy. *...a happy childhood... ...the happiest time of their lives.* 3 PRED ADJ If you are **happy** about a situation or arrangement, you are satisfied with it. *We are not too happy about this turn of events... Are you happy with that, Diana?* 4 PRED ADJ WITH TO-INF If you are **happy** to do something, you are willing to do it. *I was happy to work with George.* 5 ATTRIB ADJ You use **happy** in greetings to say that you hope someone will enjoy a special occasion. *Happy birthday!... Happy New Year!* ● **many happy returns:** see **return.** 6 ATTRIB ADJ You use **happy** to describe something that is appropriate or lucky; a formal use. *I appreciate that this is not a happy comparison... By a happy coincidence, we were all on the same train.* ♦ **happily** SENTENCE ADV *That trend reversed itself, happily.*

harangue /həˡræŋ/, **harangues, haranguing, harangued.** 1 COUNT N A **harangue** is a long, forceful, persuasive speech. *...blazing harangues about the wickedness of the Government.* 2 VB WITH OBJ If someone **harangues** you, they try to persuade you to accept their opinions or ideas in a forceful way. *Smith harangued his fellow students and persuaded them to walk out.*

harass /hærəs/, **harasses, harassing, harassed.** VB WITH OBJ If you **harass** someone, you continually trouble them or annoy them. *Some governments have chosen to harass and persecute the rural poor.* ♦ **harassment** /hærəsməˡnt/ UNCOUNT N *...alleged police brutality and harassment.*

harassed /hærəst/. ADJ Someone who is **harassed** feels worried because they have too much to do. *As the pressure gets worse, people get more harassed.*

harassing /hærəsɪŋ/. ADJ Something that is **harassing** makes you feel worried because you have too much to do. *I have had a particularly busy and harassing day.*

harbour /hɑːbə/, **harbours, harbouring, harboured;** spelled **harbor** in American English. 1 COUNT N A **harbour** is an area of deep water which is protected from the sea by land or walls, so that boats can be left there safely. 2 VB WITH OBJ If you **harbour** an emotion, you have it for a long period of time; a literary use. *I was unable to dismiss the fears I harboured for my safety.* 3 VB WITH OBJ If you **harbour** someone who is wanted by the police, you hide them secretly in your house. *You could get into trouble for harbouring her.*

hard /hɑːd/, **harder, hardest.** 1 ADJ If something feels **hard** when you touch it, it is very firm and is not easily bent, cut, or broken. *The green fruits were as hard as rocks... The ground was baked hard.* ♦ **hardness** UNCOUNT N *We gave them cushions to ease the hardness of the benches.* 2 ADJ If something is **hard** to do or to understand, it is difficult to do or understand. *He found it hard to make friends... That is a very hard question to answer.* 3 ADV If you try **hard** or work **hard,** you make a great effort to achieve something. *I cannot stand upright, no matter how hard I try... He had worked hard all his life... Think hard about what I'm offering.* 4 ADJ **Hard** work involves a lot of effort. *This has been a long hard day... It was very hard work in the shop.* 5 ADV **Hard** also means with a lot of force. *She slammed the door hard... The government's first reaction to the riots was to clamp down hard.* 6 ADJ Someone who is **hard** shows no kindness or pity. *His hard grey eyes began to soften a little.* 7 PRED ADJ WITH 'on' To be **hard** on someone or something means to cause them suffering or damage. *Don't be hard on her... It seemed rather hard on the women... This work's hard on the feet.* 8 ADJ If your life is **hard,** it is difficult and unpleasant. 9 ADJ A **hard** winter or **hard** frost is very cold or severe. 10 ATTRIB ADJ **Hard** facts are definitely true. *We have no hard evidence to indicate that he is the culprit.* 11 ATTRIB ADJ **Hard** drugs are strong illegal drugs such as heroin or cocaine. 12 ATTRIB ADJ You can refer to very extreme members of political parties as the **hard** left or the **hard** right.

PHRASES ● If you feel **hard done by,** you feel you have been treated unfairly. ● to **follow hard on the heels** of someone: see **heel.**

hard and fast. ATTRIB ADJ **Hard and fast** rules cannot be changed. *There isn't any hard and fast rule about this.*

hardback /hɑːdbæk/, **hardbacks.** COUNT N OR UNCOUNT N A **hardback** is a book which has a stiff cover. *...a hardback edition... It was published in hardback.*

hardboard /hɑːdbɔːd/. UNCOUNT N **Hardboard** is a thin, flexible sheet of wood made by pressing wood fibres very closely together.

hard cash. UNCOUNT N **Hard cash** is money in the form of notes and coins rather than a cheque or a credit card.

hard core. SING N You can refer to the members of a group who are most involved with it as the **hard core.** *...hard-core members.*

harden /hɑːdəᵊn/, **hardens, hardening, hardened.** 1 ERG VB When something **hardens,** it becomes stiff or firm. *The glue dries very fast and hardens in an hour.* 2 ERG VB When your ideas or attitudes **harden,** they become fixed and you become determined not to change them. *The organization has hardened its attitude to the crisis.* ♦ **hardening** UNCOUNT N *It would almost certainly result in a hardening of Allied opposition and determination.* 3 ERG VB When events **harden** people or when people **harden,** they become less sympathetic and gentle than they were before. *Life in the camp had hardened her considerably.*

hard-headed. ADJ A **hard-headed** person is practical and determined. *...this hard-headed brother of mine.*

hard-hearted /hɑːd hɑːtɪd/. ADJ A **hard-hearted** person is unsympathetic and does not care.

hard labour; spelled **hard labor** in American English. UNCOUNT N **Hard labour** is hard physical work which people have to do as punishment for a crime. *He was condemned to six months hard labour.*

hard line. SING N If someone takes a **hard line** on something, they have a firm policy which they refuse to change. *He applauded the president's hard line on the issue.*

hard luck. CONVENTION You can say **'Hard luck'** to someone to say that you are sorry they have not got what they wanted; an informal use.

hardly /hɑːdli[1]/. 1 ADV You use **hardly** to say that something is only just true. *I was beginning to like Sam, though I hardly knew him... The boy was hardly more than seventeen... She had hardly any money... Her bedroom was so small that she could hardly move in it.* 2 ADV If you say **hardly** had one thing happened when something else happened, you mean that the first event was followed immediately by the second. *Hardly had he uttered the words when he began laughing.* 3 ADV You can use **hardly** in an ironic way to emphasize that something is certainly not true. *In the circumstances, it is hardly surprising that he resigned.*

hard of hearing. ADJ If someone is **hard of hearing,** they are deaf.

hardship /hɑːdʃɪp/, **hardships.** UNCOUNT N OR COUNT N **Hardship** is a situation in which someone suffers from difficulties and problems, often because they do not have enough money. *...a period of considerable hardship and unhappiness... You know the hardships we have suffered.*

hard shoulder. SING N The **hard shoulder** is the area at the side of a motorway where you are allowed to stop if your car has broken down.

hard-up. ADJ If you are **hard-up,** you have very little money; an informal use.

hardware /hɑːdweə/. 1 UNCOUNT N **Hardware** is tools and equipment for use in the home and garden. 2 UNCOUNT N Computer **hardware** is the machinery of a computer as opposed to the programs that are written for it. *In addition to the basic hardware and software, several other components will be needed.*

hard-wearing. ADJ Something that is **hard-wearing** is strong and lasts for a long time. *These blankets are hard-wearing, but not so warm as wool.*

hardy /hɑːdi[1]/, **hardier, hardiest.** ADJ People, animals, and plants that are **hardy** are strong and able to endure difficult conditions. *Their children are remarkably hardy... Strawberries are hardy and easy to grow in all soils.*

hare /heə/, **hares.** COUNT N A **hare** is an animal like a large rabbit with long ears, long legs, and a small tail.

harebrained /heəbreɪnd/. ADJ **Harebrained** plans or ideas are foolish and unlikely to succeed. *...harebrained schemes.*

harem /heərəm, hɑːriːm/, **harems.** COUNT N A **harem** is a group of wives or mistresses belonging to one man, especially in Muslim societies.

hark /hɑːk/, **harks, harking, harked.**

hark back. PHR VB If someone or something **harks back** to an event or situation in the past, they remember it or remind you of it. *Increasingly she harked back to our 'dear little cottage'.*

harm /hɑːm/, **harms, harming, harmed.** 1 VB WITH OBJ To **harm** someone or something means to injure or damage them. *I stood very still, hoping they wouldn't harm my sister and me... Washing cannot harm the fabric.* 2 UNCOUNT N **Harm** is physical injury or damage which is caused to someone or something. *He went in danger of physical harm... Do prisons do more harm than good?*

PHRASES ● If you say that someone or something will **come to no harm** or that **no harm will come** to them, you mean that they will not be hurt or damaged. ● If someone or something is **out of harm's way,** they are in a safe place. ● If you say that **there is no harm in** doing something, you mean that you want to do it and you do not think that it is wrong. *There's no harm in asking.*

harmful /hɑːmfʊl/. ADJ Something that is **harmful** has a bad effect on someone or something else. *Too much salt can be harmful to a young baby.*

harmless /hɑːmlɪ[2]s/. 1 ADJ Something that is **harmless** is safe to use, touch, or be near. *...harmless butterflies.* ♦ **harmlessly** ADV *The rocket thudded harmlessly to the ground.* 2 ADJ A **harmless** action is unlikely to annoy or worry other people. *Singing in the bath gives him a little harmless pleasure.* ♦ **harmlessly** ADV *His column deals harmlessly with the antics of film stars.*

harmonica /hɑːmɒnɪkə/, **harmonicas.** COUNT N A **harmonica** is a small musical instrument which you play by moving it across your lips and blowing and sucking air through it.

harmonious /hɑːməʊnɪəs/. 1 ADJ A relationship, agreement, or discussion that is **harmonious** is friendly and peaceful. *...a generally harmonious debate.* ♦ **harmoniously** ADV *Harold and I worked harmoniously together.* 2 ADJ Something that is **harmonious** has parts which go well together. *The different parts of the garden fit together in a harmonious way.*

harmonize /hɑːmənaɪz/, **harmonizes, harmonizing, harmonized;** also spelled **harmonise.** VB If two or more things **harmonize** with each other, they fit in well with each other. *Such events harmonized with one's view of society.*

harmony /hɑːməni[1]/, **harmonies.** 1 UNCOUNT N If people are living in **harmony** with each other, they are in a state of peaceful agreement and co-operation. *Industry and the universities have worked together in harmony.* 2 UNCOUNT N OR COUNT N **Harmony** is the pleasant combination of different notes of music played at the same time. *They sing in harmony... ...the harmonies of Ravel and Debussy.* 3 SING N WITH SUPP The **harmony** of something is the way in which its parts are combined into a pleasant arrangement. *...the harmony of nature.*

harness /hɑːnɪ[2]s/, **harnesses, harnessing, harnessed.** 1 VB WITH OBJ If you **harness** something such as a source of energy, you bring it under your control and use it. *Techniques harnessing the energy of the sun are being developed.* 2 COUNT N A **harness** is a set of straps which fit under a person's arms and round their body to hold equipment or to prevent them from moving too much. *...your safety harness.* 3 COUNT N A **harness** is also a set of leather straps and metal links fastened round a horse's head or body so that it can pull a carriage, cart, or plough. 4 VB WITH OBJ If you **harness** a horse, you put a harness on it.

harp /hɑːp/, **harps, harping, harped.** COUNT N A **harp** is a large musical instrument consisting of a triangular frame with vertical strings which you pluck with your fingers.

harp on. PHR VB If you **harp on** about something, you keep talking about it; used showing disapproval. *She continued to harp on the theme of her wasted life.*

harpoon /hɑːpuːn/, **harpoons.** COUNT N A **harpoon** is a spear with a long rope attached to it. It is fired from a gun by people hunting whales.

harrowing /hærəʊɪŋ/. ADJ A **harrowing** situation or experience is very upsetting or disturbing. *The film is deeply harrowing.*

harsh /hɑːʃ/, **harsher, harshest.** 1 ADJ A **harsh** condition or way of life is severe and difficult. *His family wouldn't survive the harsh winter.* ♦ **harshness** UNCOUNT N *...the harshness of their nomadic life.* 2 ADJ **Harsh** behaviour and actions are cruel and unkind. *...her harsh, cold, contemptuous attitude.* ♦ **harshly** ADV *You've marked his essay rather harshly.* ♦ **harshness** UNCOUNT N *Disobedience is treated with special harshness.* 3 ADJ A **harsh** light or sound is unpleasantly bright or loud. *Harsh daylight fell into the room... She spoke in a harsh whisper.* ♦ **harshly** ADV *'What is it?' he said harshly.*

harvest /hɑːvɪ[2]st/, **harvests, harvesting, harvested.** 1 SING N The **harvest** is the cutting and gathering of a crop. *Their stock of rice wouldn't last until the harvest.* Also VB WITH OBJ *We harvested what we could before the rains came.* 2 COUNT N A crop is called a **harvest** when it is gathered. *Their sons always came home to help bring in the harvest.*

has /hæz/. **Has** is the third person singular of the present tense of **have.**

has-been, has-beens. COUNT N A **has-been** is a person who used to be important or successful, but is not now; an informal use. *...a political has-been.*

hash /hæʃ/. PHRASE If you **make a hash of** a job, you do it very badly; an informal use.

hasn't /hæzəᵊnt/. **Hasn't** is the usual spoken form of 'has not'.

hassle /hæsəᵊl/, **hassles, hassling, hassled;** an informal word. 1 COUNT N OR UNCOUNT N If you say that something is a **hassle,** you mean that it is difficult or causes trouble. *I didn't want any hassle from the other women.* 2 VB WITH OBJ If someone **hassles** you, they keep annoying you, for example by telling you to do things that you do not want to.

haste /heɪst/. 1 UNCOUNT N **Haste** is the act of doing things quickly. *I immediately regretted my haste... It was written quickly and published in haste.* 2 PHRASE To **make haste** means to hurry; an old-fashioned use.

hasten /heɪsəᵊn/, **hastens, hastening, hastened;** a formal word. 1 VB WITH OBJ If you **hasten** something, you make it happen faster or sooner. *Two factors hastened the formation of the new party.* 2 VB WITH TO-INF If you **hasten** to do something, you are quick to do it. *He hastened to remark that he was not against television.* 3 VB WITH ADJUNCT If you **hasten** somewhere, you hurry there. *He hastened back into the forest.*

hasty /heɪsti[1]/. 1 ADJ If you are **hasty,** you do things suddenly and quickly, often without thinking properly about them. *He made a hasty, unsuitable marriage.* ♦ **hastily** ADV *Philip hastily changed the subject.* 2 ADJ A **hasty** action is done quickly because you do not have much time. *...a hasty meal.* ♦ **hastily** ADV *He dressed himself hastily.*

hat /hæt/, **hats.** COUNT N A **hat** is a covering that you wear on your head.

hatch /hætʃ/, **hatches, hatching, hatched.** 1 ERG VB When an egg **hatches,** or when a bird, insect, or other animal **hatches** or **is hatched,** the egg breaks open and the baby animal comes out. *The larva hatches out and lives in the soil... ...newly hatched chicks... After ten days, the eggs hatch.* 2 VB WITH OBJ To **hatch** a plot or scheme means to plan it. *I've heard about the grand plot that you two gentlemen are hatching.* 3 COUNT N A **hatch** is a small covered opening in a floor, wall, or ceiling.

hatchet /hætʃɪ[2]t/, **hatchets.** COUNT N A **hatchet** is a small axe.

hate /heɪt/, **hates, hating, hated.** 1 VB WITH OBJ, -ING, OR TO-INF If you **hate** someone or something, you have an extremely strong feeling of dislike for them. *She was aware of what she was doing and she hated herself for it... I used to hate going to lectures... I hate milk... I would hate to move to another house.* ♦ **hated** ADJ *...the most hated man in America.* 2 UNCOUNT N **Hate** is an extremely strong feeling of dislike for someone or something. *He was a violent bully, destructive and full of hate.* 3 PHRASE You say **'I hate to say it'** to introduce something that you regret having to say because it is unpleasant. *There is unfortunately—I hate to say it—a substantial amount of racism in our cities.*

hateful /heɪtfʊl/. ADJ **Hateful** means extremely unpleasant; an old-fashioned use. *It was going to be a hateful week.*

hatred /heɪtrɪ²d/. UNCOUNT N **Hatred** is an extremely strong feeling of dislike. *...their hatred of technology... She felt hatred towards his sister.*

haughty /hɔːti¹/. ADJ **Haughty** people think that they are better than others; used showing disapproval. *He had an air of haughty aloofness.* ♦ **haughtily** ADV *'Very well,' he replied haughtily.*

haul /hɔːl/, **hauls, hauling, hauled. 1** VB WITH OBJ OR REFL VB, WITH ADJUNCT If you **haul** something heavy somewhere, you pull it there with a great effort. *They hauled the pilot clear of the wreckage... Ralph hauled himself onto the platform.* **2** PHRASE If something is a **long haul,** it takes a long time and a lot of effort. *We began the long haul up the cobbled street... ...as women begin the long haul to equality.*

haul up. PHR VB If someone **is hauled up** before a court of law, they are made to appear before the court; an informal use. *He got hauled up in court for assaulting a student.*

haunch /hɔːntʃ/, **haunches.** COUNT N Your **haunches** are your buttocks and the tops of your legs. *He squatted down on his haunches.*

haunt /hɔːnt/, **haunts, haunting, haunted. 1** VB WITH OBJ If a place **is haunted,** people believe that a ghost appears there regularly. ♦ **haunted** ADJ *...a haunted house.* **2** VB WITH OBJ If something unpleasant **haunts** you, you keep thinking or worrying about it over a long period of time. *...a mystery that had haunted me for most of my life.* ♦ **haunted** ADJ *Her face took on a haunted quality.* **3** COUNT N WITH SUPP Someone's **haunts** are places which they often visit. *Their old haunts have been ruined by becoming too popular.*

haunting /hɔːntɪŋ/. ADJ Something that is **haunting** remains in your thoughts because it is very beautiful or sad. *He repeated the haunting melody.*

have /hæv/, **has, having, had** /hæd/. **Have** is often contracted to **'ve, has** to **'s,** and **had** to **'d. 1** AUX WITH PAST PARTICIPLE You use **have** as an auxiliary in order to form the present perfect tense of a verb. *We have already done that... I've never heard of it... It hasn't rained for a month.* **2** AUX WITH PAST PARTICIPLE You use **had** as an auxiliary in order to form the past perfect tense of a verb. *Officials said that the two men had at last signed an agreement... I had just finished when you arrived.* **3** AUX WITH PAST PARTICIPLE The form **having** is used to introduce a clause that mentions an action which had already happened before another related action began. *Quite a few of the shop fronts were still boarded up, having closed down in 1930 or 1931... We were back in Edinburgh at ten past twelve having driven straight across the bridge again.* **4** VB WITH TO-INF You can use **have** followed by an infinitive with 'to' to say that something must be done or must happen. 'Have got' is also used in this way: see **got.** *Then he had to sit down because he felt dizzy... I have to speak to your father... There are plenty of jobs; she doesn't have to go to Canada.* **5** VB WITH OBJ You can use **have** with nouns which describe actions in order to emphasize that an action has a definite beginning or an end, or in order to give more information about the action. *You go and have a look... I had a little stroll round the garden this morning... We're having a meeting. Come and join in... I had a lot of comments on my work.* **6** VB WITH OBJ In normal speech or writing, you often use **have** where in more formal language you would use a specific verb. For example, you normally say 'I have a sandwich every lunchtime' rather than 'I eat a sandwich every lunchtime'. *I had a boring afternoon... They all had an injection when they left Britain... Boylan had his back to the window.* **7** VB WITH OBJ **Have** is often used in structures where the meaning would be the same if you used the verb 'be', because you are talking about attributes, qualities, or characteristics of someone or something. *He had beautiful manners... It's nice to have an excuse... ...machines which have dangerous moving parts.* **8** VB WITH OBJ You can use **have** to say that you own something, or to talk about things and people that are associated with you. 'Have got' is also used in this way: see **got.** *What's the point in having a mink coat?... He had a small hotel... They don't have any money... I have lots of friends.* **9** VB WITH OBJ AND PAST PARTICIPLE **Have** is used in front of a past participle to say that you arrange for something to happen, or to say that something happens to you without your doing anything about it. *You should have your car cleaned... Isn't it time you had your hair cut?... She had her purse stolen... Children love to have stories read to them.* **10** VB WITH OBJ AND TO-INF You use **have** with an object and an infinitive with 'to' to say that you are responsible for something. *She had a huge department to administer... I've never had so much work to finish.*

PHRASES ● If you **have it in for** someone, you are determined to make life difficult for them because you dislike them or are angry with them. *He had it in for me.* ● If you **have been had,** you have been deliberately tricked by someone, who has, for example, sold you something at too high a price. ● If you say that someone **has had it,** you mean that they will be in trouble because of something they have done. ● If you say that you **have had it,** you mean that you are too exhausted to continue with what you were doing. *They both look as if they've about had it.* ● If you **are had up** for something, you appear in court for a crime that you have committed. *He was had up for indecent exposure.* ● If you **are having someone on,** you are teasing them; an informal use.

haven /heɪvə⁰n/, **havens.** COUNT N A **haven** is a place where people feel safe and secure. *They have made the park a haven for weary Londoners.*

haven't /hævə⁰nt/. **Haven't** is the usual spoken form of 'have not'.

haversack /hævəsæk/, **haversacks.** COUNT N A **haversack** is a canvas bag worn on your back and used for carrying things when you are out walking.

havoc /hævək/. **1** UNCOUNT N **Havoc** is a state of great disorder. *After the havoc of the war, England had to be rebuilt.* **2** PHRASE To **play havoc with** something means to cause great disorder and confusion.

hawk /hɔːk/, **hawks, hawking, hawked. 1** COUNT N A **hawk** is a large bird with a hooked bill, sharp claws, and very good eyesight. *A hawk hovered, motionless, in the blue sky.* **2** VB WITH OBJ If you **hawk** something around, you try to sell it by taking it from place to place; often used showing disapproval. *His writings were being hawked round German publishers.*

hay /heɪ/. UNCOUNT N **Hay** is grass which has been cut and dried so that it can be used to feed animals. *...40 bales of hay.*

hay fever. UNCOUNT N **Hay fever** is an allergy to pollen and grass which makes people sneeze a lot.

haystack /heɪstæk/, **haystacks. 1** COUNT N A **haystack** is a large neat pile of hay, usually in a field. **2** PHRASE If you say that trying to find something is like looking for **a needle in a haystack,** you mean that it is extremely difficult or impossible to find.

hazard /hæzəd/, **hazards, hazarding, hazarded. 1** COUNT N A **hazard** is something which could be dangerous to you. *...a natural hazard, like an earth tremor... Drinking alcohol is a real health hazard if carried to excess.* **2** REPORT VB If you **hazard** a guess, you make a suggestion which is only a guess. *As to the author of the letter, I will hazard a guess that it is Howard... 'How much do you think he makes a year?'—'Fifteen thousand,' Rudolph hazarded.*

hazardous /hæzədəs/. ADJ Something that is **hazardous** is dangerous to people's health or safety. *...hazardous chemicals... Breathing smoky air may be hazardous to health.*

haze /heɪz/. COUNT N WITH SUPP A **haze** is a kind of mist caused by heat or dust in the air. *The room became cloudy with a blue haze of smoke.*

hazel /heɪzə⁰l/, **hazels. 1** COUNT N OR UNCOUNT N A **hazel** is a small tree which produces nuts. **2** ADJ **Hazel** eyes are greenish-brown.

hazy /heɪzi¹/, **hazier, haziest. 1** ADJ When the sky or a view is **hazy,** you cannot see it clearly because there is a haze. *...a hazy blue view beyond railings on a mountain pass.* **2** PRED ADJ If you are **hazy** about things or if your thoughts are **hazy,** you are unclear or confused. *She was hazy about her mother's origins... The details are getting a bit hazy in my mind now.*

he /hiː/. **He** is used as the subject of a verb. **1** PRON You use **he** to refer to a man, boy, or male animal that has already been mentioned, or whose identity is known. *Bill had flown back from New York and he and his wife took me out to dinner.* **2** PRON **He** can also be used to refer to a person whose sex is not known or stated; an old-fashioned use. *A teacher should do whatever he thinks best.*

head /hɛd/, **heads, heading, headed. 1** COUNT N Your **head** is the part of your body which has your eyes, mouth, and brain in it. *She shook her head.* **2** SING N WITH SUPP The **head** of something is the top, start, or most important end. *Howard stood at the head of the stairs... ...standing at the head of the queue.* **3** COUNT N The **head** of an organization, school, or department is the person in charge of it. *...the head of the English department.* Also ATTRIB ADJ *...the head gardener.* **4** ADV When you toss a coin and it comes down **heads,** you can see the side of the coin with a person's head on it. **5** VB WITH OBJ If something **heads** a list, it is at the top of it. *...with Tower Hamlets heading the list.* **6** VB WITH OBJ If you **head** an organization, you are in charge of it. *The firm is headed by John Murray.* **7** VB WITH OBJ AND COMPLEMENT You can mention the title of a piece of writing by saying how it **is headed.** *...an article headed 'An Open Letter to the Prime Minister.'* **8** VB WITH ADJUNCT If you **head** in a particular direction, you go in that direction. *Julie headed for the cupboard.* **9** VB WITH 'for' If you **are heading** for an unpleasant situation, you are behaving in a way that makes the situation more likely. *You may be heading for disaster.* **10** VB WITH OBJ When you **head** a ball, you hit it with your head. **11** See also **heading.**

PHRASES ● The cost or amount **a head** or **per head** is the cost or amount for each person. ● If you are speaking **off the top of** your **head,** the information you are giving may not be accurate, because you have not had time to check it or think about it. ● If you are laughing, crying, or shouting your **head off,** you are doing it very noisily; an informal use. ● If you **bite** or **snap** someone's **head off,** you speak to them very angrily; an informal use. ● If something **comes** or **is brought to a head,** it reaches a state where you have to do something urgently about it. ● If alcohol **goes to** your **head,** it makes you drunk. ● If praise or success **goes to your head,** it makes you conceited. ● If you **keep** your **head,** you stay calm. If you **lose** your **head,** you panic. ● If you cannot **make head nor tail of** something, you cannot understand it at all; an informal use.

headache /hɛdeɪk/, **headaches. 1** COUNT N If you have a **headache,** you have a pain in your head. **2** COUNT N If you say that something is a **headache,** you mean that it causes you difficulty or worry. *Rivalry between the two industries presents a big headache for government.*

headdress /hɛddrɛs/, **headdresses.** COUNT N A **headdress** is something worn on a person's head for decoration. *The dancers wore face masks and tall head-dresses.*

head-first. ADV If you fall somewhere **head-first,** your head is the part of your body that is furthest forward as you fall. *He had fallen head-first into the ditch.*

headgear /hɛdgɪə/. UNCOUNT N You can refer to hats or other things worn on people's heads as **headgear.**

heading /hɛdɪŋ/, **headings.** COUNT N A **heading** is the title of a piece of writing, written or printed at the top of it. *The figures were put forward under the heading 'World Fuel Requirements in the 1990s'.*

headlamp /hɛdlæmp/, **headlamps.** COUNT N A **headlamp** is a headlight.

headland /hɛdlə³nd/, **headlands.** COUNT N A **headland** is a narrow piece of land which sticks out into the sea.

headlight /hɛdlaɪt/, **headlights.** COUNT N A car's **headlights** are the large bright lights at the front.

headline /hɛdlaɪn/, **headlines. 1** COUNT N A **headline** is the title of a newspaper story, printed in large letters. *The headlines that day were full of news of the kidnapping.* **2** PLURAL N The **headlines** are also the main points of the news which are read on radio or television. *And now for the main headlines again.*

headlong /hɛdlɒŋ/. **1** ADV If you move **headlong** in a particular direction, you move there very quickly. *The frightened elephants ran headlong through the forest.* **2** ADV OR ADJ If you rush **headlong** into something, you do it quickly without thinking carefully about it. *They dropped headlong into trouble... ...a headlong rush to sell.*

headmaster /hɛdmɑːstə/, **headmasters.** COUNT N A **headmaster** is a man who is the head teacher of a school.

headmistress /hɛdmɪstrɪ²s/, **headmistresses.** COUNT N A **headmistress** is a woman who is the head teacher of a school.

head of state, heads of state. COUNT N A **head of state** is the leader of a country, for example a president, king, or queen.

head-on. 1 ADV OR ATTRIB ADJ If two vehicles hit each other **head-on,** they hit each other with their front parts pointing towards each other. *The motor cycle ran head-on into the lorry... ...a head-on collision.* **2** ATTRIB ADJ OR ADV A **head-on** disagreement is firm and direct and has no compromises. *...a head-on confrontation with the unions... It had to meet the threat head-on.*

headphones /hɛdfəʊnz/. PLURAL N **Headphones** are small speakers which you wear over your ears in order to listen to music or other sounds without other people hearing.

headquarters /hɛdkwɔːtəz/. PLURAL N The **headquarters** of an organization are its main offices. *Captain Meadows was ordered to report to headquarters the following day.*

headroom /hɛdru⁴m/. UNCOUNT N **Headroom** is the amount of space below a roof or bridge.

head start, head starts. COUNT N If you have a **head start** on other people, you have an advantage over them in a competition or race. *A university degree would give you a head start in getting a job.*

headstone /hedstəʊn/, **headstones.** COUNT N A **headstone** is a large stone at one end of a grave, showing the name of the dead person.

headstrong /hedstrɒŋ/. ADJ A **headstrong** person is determined to do what they want and will not let anyone stop them. *Luce was stubborn and headstrong.*

headway /hedweɪ/. PHRASE If you **make headway,** you make progress towards achieving something. *The emergency services began to make some headway in restoring order to the devastated area.*

headwind /hedwɪnd/, **headwinds.** COUNT N A **headwind** is a wind blowing in the opposite direction to the way you are moving.

heady /hedi[1]/. ADJ A **heady** drink, atmosphere, or experience strongly affects your senses, for example by making you feel drunk or excited. *...heady perfumes... ...the heady days of the sixties.*

heal /hi:l/, **heals, healing, healed.** 1 ERG VB When something **heals** or **is healed,** it becomes healthy and normal again. *...damage to the ecology that would take a hundred years to heal... This ointment should heal the cut in no time.* 2 VB WITH OBJ If someone **heals** you when you are ill, they make you well again. *He had been miraculously healed of his illness.* ♦ **healer** COUNT N *...traditional healers.*

heal up. PHR VB When an injury **heals up,** it becomes completely healthy again.

health /helθ/. 1 UNCOUNT N Your **health** is the condition of your body. *Cigarette smoking is dangerous to your health... My mother was in poor health.* 2 UNCOUNT N **Health** is a state in which you are fit and well. *They were glowing with health... ...a soldier who was nursed back to health.* 3 PHRASE When you **drink to** someone's **health** or **drink** their **health,** you drink as a sign of wishing them health and happiness. 4 UNCOUNT N WITH SUPP The **health** of an organization or system is the success that it has and the fact that it is working well. *...the health of the British film industry.*

health food, health foods. COUNT N OR MOD **Health foods** are natural foods without artificial ingredients which people buy because they consider them to be good for them.

healthy /helθi[1]/, **healthier, healthiest.** 1 ADJ A **healthy** person is well and not suffering from any illness. *As a result of the diet, he feels fitter and healthier.* ♦ **healthily** ADV *It is perfectly possible to live healthily on a meat-free diet.* 2 ADJ If a feature or quality that you have is **healthy,** it shows that you are well. *The children have healthy appetites... ...healthy skin.* ♦ **healthily** SUBMOD *...the dreamless slumber of the healthily tired man.* 3 ADJ Something that is **healthy** is good for you and likely to make you fit and strong. *...healthy seaside air.* 4 ADJ A **healthy** organization or system is successful. *...a healthy economy.* 5 ADJ A **healthy** amount of something is a large amount that shows success. *...healthy profits.*

heap /hi:p/, **heaps, heaping, heaped.** 1 COUNT N A **heap** of things is an untidy pile of them. ● If someone collapses **in a heap,** they fall heavily and do not move. 2 VB WITH OBJ AND ADJUNCT If you **heap** things in a pile, you arrange them in a large pile. *...food heaped on platters.* 3 VB WITH OBJ AND 'on' OR 'upon' If you **heap** praise or criticism on someone or something, you give them a lot of praise or criticism. 4 QUANTIF **Heaps** or a **heap** of something is a large quantity of it; an informal use. *We've got heaps of time.*

heap up. PHR VB If you **heap** things **up,** you make them into a pile.

heaped /hi:pt/. 1 ADJ A **heaped** spoonful has the contents of the spoon piled up above the edge. *Add one heaped tablespoon of salt.* 2 ADJ If a surface is **heaped** with things, it has a lot of them on it in a pile. *The desk was heaped with magazines.*

hear /hɪə/, **hears, hearing, heard** /hɜ:d/. 1 VB WITH OR WITHOUT OBJ When you **hear** sounds, you are aware of them because they reach your ears. *He heard a distant voice shouting... She could hear clearly.* 2 VB WITH OBJ When a judge or a court **hears** a case or **hears** evidence, they listen to it officially in order to make a decision about it. 3 VB WITH 'from' If you **hear** from someone, you receive a letter or a telephone call from them. *They'll be delighted to hear from you again.* 4 REPORT VB OR VB If you **hear** some news or information, you learn it because someone tells it to you or it is mentioned on the radio or television. *My first meeting with the woman confirmed everything I had heard about her... I was glad to hear that things are quietening down... He came to hear of their difficulties.*

PHRASES ● If you **won't hear of** someone doing something, you refuse to let them do it. ● If you **have** never **heard of** someone or something, you do not know anything about them. *Nobody had ever heard of him.*

hearer /hɪərə/, **hearers.** COUNT N Your **hearers** are the people who are listening to you speak; a formal use.

hearing /hɪərɪŋ/, **hearings.** 1 UNCOUNT N **Hearing** is the sense which makes it possible for you to be aware of sounds. *Her limbs were weak, her hearing almost gone.* 2 COUNT N A **hearing** is an official meeting held to collect facts about an incident or problem.

PHRASES ● If you are **in** or **within** someone's **hearing,** you are so close to them that they can hear what you are saying. *She began to grumble about it within his hearing.* ● If someone gives you **a hearing** or **a fair hearing,** they listen to you when you give your opinion about something. ● See also **hard of hearing.**

hearing aid, hearing aids. COUNT N A **hearing aid** is a device that helps deaf people to hear better.

hearsay /hɪəseɪ/. UNCOUNT N **Hearsay** is information which you have been told indirectly, but which you do not personally know to be true.

hearse /hɜ:s/, **hearses.** COUNT N A **hearse** is a large car that carries the coffin at a funeral.

heart /hɑ:t/, **hearts.** 1 COUNT N Your **heart** is the organ in your chest that pumps the blood around your body. *She could hear her heart beating.* 2 COUNT N You can also talk about someone's **heart** to refer to their emotions or character. *...the troubled heart of the younger man... He's got a very soft heart.* 3 UNCOUNT N **Heart** is used in various expressions referring to courage and determination. *It was a bad time and people were losing heart... No one had the heart to tell her.* 4 SING N WITH 'of' The **heart** of something is the most central or important part of it. *...the heart of the problem... Thousands of protesters marched into the heart of San Francisco.* 5 COUNT N A **heart** is also a shape like a real heart, used especially as a symbol of love. 6 UNCOUNT N **Hearts** is one of the four suits in a pack of playing cards.

PHRASES ● If someone is a particular kind of person **at heart,** this is what they are really like. *He was at heart a kindly man.* ● If you know something such as a poem **by heart,** you can remember it perfectly. ● If you have a **change of heart,** your feelings about something change. ● If you say something **from the heart** or **from the bottom of** your **heart,** you are being sincere. ● If your **heart isn't in** what you are doing, you have very little enthusiasm for it. ● If someone can do something **to their heart's content,** they can do it as much as they want. ● If someone or something **breaks** your **heart,** they make you very unhappy. ● If something is **close to** or **dear to** your **heart,** you care deeply about it. ● If your **heart leaps,** you suddenly feel very excited and happy. If your **heart sinks,** you suddenly feel very disappointed or unhappy. ● If you have **set** your **heart on** something, you want it very much. *She had set her heart on going.* ● If you **take** an experience **to heart,** you are deeply affected and upset by it.

heart attack, heart attacks. COUNT N If someone has a **heart attack,** their heart begins to beat irregularly or stops completely.

heartbeat /hɑ:tbi:t/, **heartbeats.** 1 SING N Your **heartbeat** is the regular movement of your heart as it pumps blood around your body. *He could hear the pounding rhythm of her heartbeat.* 2 COUNT N A **heartbeat** is one of the movements of your heart.

heartbreak /hɑ:tbreɪk/. UNCOUNT N **Heartbreak** is very great sadness or unhappiness. *...tragedy and heartbreak.*

heartbreaking /hɑ:tbreɪkɪŋ/. ADJ Something that is **heartbreaking** makes you feel extremely sad and upset. *...a heartbreaking letter from an American friend whose wife had died.*

heartbroken /hɑ:tbrəʊkə[0]n/. ADJ Someone who is **heartbroken** is extremely sad and upset. *Sylvia would be heartbroken if one of her cats died.*

hearten /hɑ:tə[0]n/, **heartens, heartening, heartened.** VB WITH OBJ If you are **heartened** by something, it encourages you and makes you cheerful. *I am very heartened by her success.* ♦ **heartening** ADJ *...some heartening news.*

heartfelt /hɑ:tfelt/. ATTRIB ADJ You use **heartfelt** to indicate that someone feels or believes something deeply and sincerely. *...a heartfelt wish that it will never happen.*

hearth /hɑ:θ/, **hearths.** COUNT N A **hearth** is the floor of a fireplace. *A bright fire was burning in the hearth.*

heartland /hɑ:tlænd/, **heartlands.** COUNT N OR PLURAL N WITH SUPP The **heartland** or **heartlands** of a country, region, or continent are the most central parts of it. *...the industrial heartlands of western Europe.*

heartless /hɑ:tlɪ[2]s/. ADJ If someone is **heartless,** they are cruel and unkind. *...a heartless cynic.* ♦ **heartlessly** ADV *...defenceless creatures being heartlessly destroyed.*

heartrending /hɑ:trendɪŋ/. ADJ If something is **heartrending,** it makes you feel great sadness and pity. *Isabel's sigh was heartrending.*

hearty /hɑ:ti[1]/, **heartier, heartiest.** 1 ADJ **Hearty** people or actions are loud, cheerful, and energetic. *...hearty soccer fans... He had a big hearty laugh.* ♦ **heartily** ADV *Etta laughed heartily.* 2 ATTRIB ADJ **Hearty** feelings or opinions are strongly felt or strongly held. *I have a hearty hatred of all examinations.* ♦ **heartily** ADV *Why should one pretend to like people one actually heartily dislikes?*

heat /hi:t/, **heats, heating, heated.** 1 VB WITH OBJ When you **heat** something, you raise its temperature. *Don't heat more water than you need... ...accommodation that is difficult to heat.* 2 UNCOUNT N **Heat** is warmth or the quality of being hot. *Water retains heat much longer than air... ...loss of body heat... You shouldn't go out in this heat.* 3 UNCOUNT N WITH SUPP **Heat** is also the temperature of something that is warm. *It should be equivalent to blood heat.* 4 SING N **Heat** is also a source of heat, for example a cooking ring. *Don't put pans straight on to a high heat.* 5 UNCOUNT N WITH SUPP You also use **heat** to refer to a state of strong emotional feeling, especially anger or excitement. *'You're a fool,' Boylan said, without heat.* 6 COUNT N A **heat** is a race or competition whose winners take part in another one, against winners of similar races or competitions. ● See also **dead heat.** 7 See also **heated, heating.**

heat up. PHR VB 1 When something **heats up,** it gradually becomes hotter. 2 When you **heat up** food that has already been cooked, you make it hot again.

heated /hi:tɪ[2]d/. ADJ If someone is **heated** about something, they are angry and excited about it. *...a heated argument.* ♦ **heatedly** ADV *Naturalists argued heatedly about the issue for nearly a century.*

heater /hi:tə/, **heaters.** COUNT N A **heater** is a piece of equipment which is used to warm a room or to heat water. *Mel had left the car heater on.* ● See also **immersion heater.**

heath /hi:θ/, **heaths.** COUNT N A **heath** is an area of open land covered with rough grass or heather.

heathen /hi:ðə[0]n/, **heathens.** COUNT N Christians used to refer to people from other countries who were not Christians as **heathens;** an old-fashioned use. Also ADJ *...the ancient heathen inhabitants of this place.*

heather /heðə/. UNCOUNT N **Heather** is a plant with small flowers that grows wild on hills and moorland.

heating /hi:tɪŋ/. UNCOUNT N **Heating** is the process or equipment involved in keeping a building warm. *The rent was £7 a week including heating.* ● See also **central heating.**

heatwave /hi:tweɪv/, **heatwaves.** COUNT N A **heatwave** is a period when the weather is much hotter than usual.

heave /hi:v/, **heaves, heaving, heaved.** 1 VB WITH OR WITHOUT OBJ To **heave** something means to push, pull, or lift it using a lot of effort. *Lee heaved himself with a groan from his chair.* Also COUNT N *With one single determined heave I pulled everything down.* 2 VB If something **heaves,** it moves up and down or in and out with large regular movements. *His shoulders heaved silently.* 3 VB To **heave** also means to vomit or feel sick.

heaven /hevə[0]n/, **heavens.** 1 PROPER N **Heaven** is where God is believed to live, and where good people are believed to go when they die. 2 PLURAL N The **heavens** are the sky; a literary use. *The moon was high in the heavens.*

PHRASES ● You say **'heaven knows'** to emphasize that you do not know something or that you find something very surprising. *Heaven knows what I would do without it... He ended up, heaven knows why, in the Geological Museum.* ● You say **'good heavens'** or **'heavens'** to express surprise or to emphasize that you agree or disagree. *Heavens, is that the time?... 'Oh, good heavens, no,' said Etta.* ● **thank heavens:** see **thank.** ● **for heaven's sake:** see **sake.**

heavenly /hevə[0]nli[1]/. 1 ATTRIB ADJ **Heavenly** describes things relating to heaven. *The heavenly spirits were displeased with the people.* 2 ADJ If you describe something as **heavenly,** you mean that it is very pleasant and enjoyable; an informal use. *...a big steaming pot of the most heavenly stew.*

heaven-sent. ADJ Something that is **heaven-sent** is unexpected but very welcome because it happens at just the right time. *...a heaven-sent opportunity.*

heavily /hevɪli[1]/. ADV If someone says something **heavily,** they say it in a slow way, showing sadness, tiredness, or annoyance. *'I don't understand you,' he said heavily.*

heavy /hevi[1]/, **heavier, heaviest.** 1 ADJ Something that is **heavy** weighs a lot. *He dumped the heavy suitcases by the door.* 2 ADJ **Heavy** also means great in amount, degree, or intensity. *There would be heavy casualties... ...a heavy responsibility.* ♦ **heavily** ADV *It* *began to rain more heavily.* **3** ADJ You also use **heavy** to describe something that has a solid, thick appearance or texture. *...spectacles with heavy black frames... ...heavy clay soil.* ♦ **heavily** ADV *I've never seen anyone so heavily built move quite so fast.* **4** PRED ADJ WITH 'with' Something that is **heavy** with things is full of them or loaded with them; a literary use. *The trees were heavy with fruit and blossoms.* **5** ADJ **Heavy** breathing is very loud and deep. *She lay sleeping, her breathing heavy.* ♦ **heavily** ADV *She sighed heavily.* **6** ATTRIB ADJ A **heavy** movement or action is done with a lot of force or pressure. *A heavy blow with a club knocked him senseless.* ♦ **heavily** ADV *He sat down heavily.* **7** ADJ If you have a **heavy** schedule, you have a lot of work. *I've had a heavy week.* **8** ADJ **Heavy** work requires a lot of physical strength. *I cannot do heavy work in the fields.* **9** ADJ **Heavy** air or weather is unpleasantly still, hot, and damp. **10** ADJ If your heart is **heavy**, you are sad about something. **11** to **make heavy weather** of something: see **weather.**

heavy-duty. ATTRIB ADJ A **heavy-duty** machine is strong and can be used a lot.

heavy-handed. ADJ Someone who is **heavy-handed** acts or speaks forcefully and thoughtlessly. *We are incensed at the government's heavy-handed economic policies.*

heavy industry, heavy industries. UNCOUNT N OR COUNT N **Heavy industry** is industry in which large machines are used to produce raw materials or to make large objects.

heavy metal. UNCOUNT N **Heavy metal** is a type of loud, fast rock music with a strong beat.

heavyweight /hevi^{1}weɪt/, **heavyweights.** COUNT N A **heavyweight** is a boxer or wrestler in the heaviest class.

Hebrew /hi:bru:/. UNCOUNT N **Hebrew** is a language spoken by Jews in former times. A modern form of Hebrew is spoken now in Israel.

heckle /hekə^{0}l/, **heckles, heckling, heckled.** VB WITH OR WITHOUT OBJ If people **heckle** public speakers, they interrupt them by making rude remarks. *He went to heckle at their meetings.* ♦ **heckling** UNCOUNT N *Despite the heckling, the meeting was a success.* ♦ **heckler** COUNT N *...a crowd of hecklers.*

hectare /hektɛə/, **hectares.** COUNT N A **hectare** is a unit of area equal to 10,000 square metres.

hectic /hektɪk/. ADJ A **hectic** situation involves a lot of rushed activity. *Monday morning is a hectic time.*

he'd /hi:d/. **He'd** is the usual spoken form of 'he had', especially when 'had' is an auxiliary verb. **He'd** is also a spoken form of 'he would'. *He said he'd told them... He said that he'd give me a lift.*

hedge /hedʒ/, **hedges, hedging, hedged. 1** COUNT N A **hedge** is a row of bushes along the edge of a garden, field, or road. **2** VB If you **hedge,** you avoid answering a question or committing yourself to something. *Politicians are known for hedging on promises.* **3** PHRASE If you **hedge** your **bets,** you avoid the risk of losing a lot by supporting more than one person or thing; an informal use.

hedgehog /hedʒhɒg/, **hedgehogs.** COUNT N A **hedgehog** is a small brown animal with sharp spikes covering its back.

hedgerow /hedʒrəʊ/, **hedgerows.** COUNT N A **hedgerow** is a row of bushes, trees, and plants, usually growing along a country lane or between fields.

hedonism /hi:də^{0}nɪzə^{0}m, hed-/. COUNT N **Hedonism** is the belief that gaining pleasure is the most important thing in life; a formal use. ♦ **hedonistic** /hi:də^{0}nɪstɪk hed-/ ADJ *...lives of unending hedonistic delight.*

heed /hi:d/, **heeds, heeding, heeded. 1** VB WITH OBJ If you **heed** someone's advice, you pay attention to it; a formal use. *David wished that he had heeded his father's warnings.* **2** PHRASE If you **take heed of** what someone says or if you **pay heed to** them, you consider carefully what they say.

heedless /hi:dlɪ^{2}s/. ADJ If you are **heedless** of someone or something, you do not take any notice of them; a formal use. *She stood glued to the radio, heedless of the bustle about her... ...heedless passers-by hurrying through the market place.*

heel /hi:l/, **heels. 1** COUNT N Your **heel** is the back part of your foot, just below your ankle. **2** COUNT N The **heel** of a sock or shoe is the part covering or below the heel. *All I could hear was the click of my own heels.* PHRASES ● If you **dig** your **heels in,** you refuse to be persuaded to do something. ● If one event or situation **follows hard on the heels of** another, it happens very quickly after it. ● If you **take to** your **heels,** you run away; a literary use.

hefty /hefti^1/, **heftier, heftiest.** ADJ **Hefty** means very large in size, weight, or amount; an informal use. *...a broad, hefty Irish nurse... We sell them at a hefty profit.*

heifer /hefə/, **heifers.** COUNT N A **heifer** is a young cow.

height /haɪt/, **heights. 1** UNCOUNT N OR COUNT N WITH SUPP The **height** of a person or thing is their measurement from bottom to top. *The redwood grows to 100 metres in height... He was of medium height... This enables them to grow to considerable heights.* **2** UNCOUNT N **Height** is the quality of being tall. *You'll recognize her because of her height.* **3** UNCOUNT N OR COUNT N WITH SUPP A particular **height** is the distance that something is above the ground. *The aircraft reaches its maximum height of 80,000 feet in about ten minutes... The bag had been dropped from about shoulder height.* **4** PLURAL N You use **heights** to refer to the top of a hill or cliff. *...fierce fighting on the heights above the bay.* **5** SING N WITH SUPP Something that is at its **height** is at its most successful, powerful, or intense. *The group had at its height 500 members... It is the height of the tourist season.* **6** SING N WITH 'of' You can use **height** to emphasize how extreme a quality is. For example, if you say that something is the **height** of absurdity, you mean that it is extremely absurd; a formal use. *It seemed to me the height of luxury.*

heighten /haɪtə^{0}n/, **heightens, heightening, heightened.** ERG VB When something **heightens** a feeling or state or when it **heightens,** it increases in degree or intensity; a formal use. *As their hardship heightened, so did their desperation and anger.* ♦ **heightened** ATTRIB ADJ *She is in a state of heightened emotion.*

heinous /heɪnəs, hi:-/. ADJ **Heinous** means extremely evil; a formal use. *...heinous crimes.*

heir /ɛə/, **heirs.** COUNT N Someone's **heir** is the person who will inherit their money, property, or title when they die. *...Thompson's son and heir... The Prince of Wales is heir to the throne.*

heiress /ɛərɪ^{2}s/, **heiresses.** COUNT N An **heiress** is a woman who will inherit property, money, or a title.

heirloom /ɛəlu:m/, **heirlooms.** COUNT N An **heirloom** is an object that has belonged to a family for a very long time. *...jewels and other family heirlooms.*

held /held/. **Held** is the past tense and past participle of **hold.**

helicopter /helɪkɒptə/, **helicopters.** COUNT N A **helicopter** is an aircraft with no wings, but with large blades which rotate above it.

hell /hel/. **1** PROPER N **Hell** is the place where wicked people are believed to go when they die. **2** UNCOUNT N If you say that a situation is **hell,** you mean that it is extremely unpleasant; an informal use. *It's been hell.* **3** CONVENTION **Hell** is also used as a swear word. PHRASES The following phrases are all informal. ● If you say that **all hell broke loose,** you mean that there was suddenly a lot of arguing or fighting. ● If someone **gives** you **hell,** they are very severe and cruel to you. ● To **play hell** with something means to have a bad effect on it. *The new extension will play hell with the plumbing.* ● If someone does something **for the hell of it,** they do it for fun or for no particular reason. ● People use **a hell of** or **one hell of** to emphasize the amount or size of something. *There was a hell of a lot of traffic.* ● Some people use **like hell** to emphasize how strong an action or quality is. *It hurt like hell.*

he'll /hi:l/. **He'll** is the usual spoken form of 'he will'.

hellish /helɪʃ/. ADJ If something is **hellish,** it is extremely unpleasant; an informal use. *It's hellish being a student without a grant.*

hello /hə^{2}ləʊ/, **hellos;** also spelled **hallo** and **hullo.** CONVENTION You say **'Hello'** when you are greeting someone or starting a telephone conversation. *'Hello,' said the girl.* Also COUNT N *Do come over and say hello to the group.*

helmet /helmɪt/, **helmets.** COUNT N A **helmet** is a hard hat which you wear to protect your head.

help /help/, **helps, helping, helped. 1** VB WITH OR WITHOUT OBJ If you **help** someone, you make something easier for them, for example by doing part of their work or by giving them advice or money. *Something went wrong with his machine so I helped him fix it... The courier helped everyone out of the coach.* **2** VB WITH OR WITHOUT OBJ If something **helps,** it makes it easier for you to get something, do something, or bear something. *I've got 40 pence, will that help?... Good weather helped the clean-up operations on the East Coast.* **3** VB WITH TO-INF OR INF If something **helps** to achieve a particular result, it is one of the things that together achieve it. *One of the things that can help to keep prices down is high productivity... Having a job helps keep them off the streets.* **4** REFL VB If you **help** yourself, you serve yourself some food or drink. *Mr Stokes helped himself to some more rum.* **5** VB WITH OBJ OR -ING If you can't **help** the way you feel or the way you behave, you cannot change it or stop it happening. *You can't help who you fall in love with... I can't help feeling that it was a mistake to let him go.* **6** UNCOUNT N If you give **help** to someone, you help them. *The organization gives help to single women.* **7** SING N If someone or something is a **help,** they help you to do something. *He was a great help with some of the problems.* **8** PHRASE If something **is of help,** it makes things easier or better. *Having a sober mind around might prove to be of some help.* **9** CONVENTION You shout **'Help!'** when you are in danger, in order to attract someone's attention.

help out. PHR VB If you **help out** or **help** someone **out,** you help them by doing some work for them or lending them money.

helper /helpə/, **helpers.** COUNT N A **helper** is a person who helps another person or group, usually with an organised activity. *All the helpers for this organization are voluntary.*

helpful /helpfʊl/. **1** ADJ If someone is **helpful,** they help you by doing work for you or by giving you advice or information. *They were all very pleasant and extremely kind and helpful.* ♦ **helpfully** ADV *Doctor Percival said helpfully, 'I'd advise you not to go'.* ♦ **helpfulness** UNCOUNT N *I was greatly impressed by the efficiency and helpfulness of the stage crew.* **2** ADJ Something that is **helpful** makes a situation more pleasant or easier to tolerate. *It is often helpful during an illness to talk to other sufferers.*

helping /helpɪŋ/, **helpings.** COUNT N A **helping** of food is the amount that you get in a single serving. *I gave him a second helping of pudding.*

helpless /helplɪ^{2}s/. ADJ If you are **helpless,** you are unable to do anything useful or to protect yourself, for example because you are very weak. *...a helpless baby... Sam raised his arms in a helpless gesture.* ♦ **helplessly** ADV *She stood there helplessly crying.* ♦ **helplessness** UNCOUNT N *She took advantage of my utter helplessness.*

hem /hem/, **hems, hemming, hemmed. 1** COUNT N The **hem** of a garment or piece of cloth is an edge which is folded over and sewn. **2** VB WITH OBJ If you **hem** a piece of cloth, you fold the edge over and sew it to make it neat. *She had hemmed a set of handkerchiefs.*

hem in. PHR VB If you **are hemmed in** by something, you are completely surrounded by it so that you cannot move.

hemisphere /hemɪsfɪə/, **hemispheres.** COUNT N A **hemisphere** is one half of the earth; a formal use. *...the greatest empires in the western hemisphere.*

hemoglobin /hi:mə^{6}gləʊbɪn, hem-/. See **haemoglobin.**

hemophilia /hi:mə^{6}fɪlɪə, hem-/. See **haemophilia.**

hemorrhage /hemə^{5}rɪdʒ/. See **haemorrhage.**

hen /hen/, **hens. 1** COUNT N **Hens** are female chickens, often kept for their eggs. **2** COUNT N OR MOD A **hen** is also any female bird. *...a hen pheasant.*

hence /hens/; a formal word. **1** SENTENCE ADV **Hence** means for the reason just mentioned. *The computer has become smaller and cheaper and hence more available to a greater number of people.* **2** ADV If something will happen a particular length of time **hence,** it will happen that length of time from now. *The tunnel will open in 1993, seven years hence.*

henceforth /hensfɔ:θ/. SENTENCE ADV **Henceforth** means from this time on; a formal use. *Henceforth his life would never be the same again.*

henchman /hentʃmə^{0}n/, **henchmen.** COUNT N WITH POSS The **henchmen** of a powerful person are people employed by that person to do violent or dishonest work; used showing disapproval. *He signed the papers and left it to his henchmen to do the work.*

hepatitis /hepətaɪtɪs/. UNCOUNT N **Hepatitis** is a serious disease which affects the liver.

her /hɜ:/. **1** PRON **Her** is used as the object of a verb or preposition. You use **her** to refer to a woman, girl, or female animal that has already been mentioned, or whose identity is known. *I knew your mother. I was at school with her... They gave her the job.* **2** DET You also use **her** to indicate that something belongs or relates to a woman, girl, or female animal that has already been mentioned, or whose identity is known. *She opened her bag... Her name is Cynthia.* **3** DET You also use **her** in some titles. *...Her Majesty the Queen.*

herald /herəld/, **heralds, heralding, heralded. 1** VB WITH OBJ Something that **heralds** a future event or situation is a sign that it is going to happen or appear. *His rise to power heralded the end of the liberal era.* **2** COUNT N WITH 'of' The **herald** of a future event or situation is a sign of it. *The festival was the herald of a new age.*

herb /hɜ:b/, **herbs.** COUNT N A **herb** is a plant which is used to flavour food, or as a medicine. *...dried herbs and spices.* ♦ **herbal** /hɜ:bə^{0}l/ ATTRIB ADJ *...herbal medicine.*

herd /hɜ:d/, **herds, herding, herded. 1** COUNT N A **herd** is a large group of animals of one kind that live together. *...a herd of goats.* **2** VB WITH OBJ If you **herd** people or animals, you make them move together to form a group. *...men herding cattle... The chained people were herded back into the dark cellar.*

here /hɪə/. 1 ADV **Here** refers to the place where you are or to a place which has been mentioned. *She left here at eight o'clock... Elizabeth, come over here... You've been here for a number of years.* 2 ADV You use **here** when you are referring to a place, person or thing that is near you. *You have to sign here and acknowledge the receipt... I have here a very important message that has just arrived.* 3 ADV You can also use **here** to refer to a particular time, situation, or subject. *The autumn's really here at last... I think that what we're talking about here is role-playing.* 4 ADV You can use **here** at the beginning of a sentence in order to draw attention to something or to introduce something. *Now here is the News... Here she is... Here's how it's done.* 5 CONVENTION You can say **'here'** when you are offering or giving something to someone. *He pushed a piece of paper across the table. 'Here you are. My address.'... Here, hold this while I go and get a newspaper.*

PHRASES ● You say **'Here's to us'** or **'Here's to your new job'**, for example, as a toast in order to wish someone success or happiness. ● Something that is happening **here and there** is happening in several different places at the same time. *Panic here and there was only to be expected.*

hereby /hɪəbaɪ/. ADV **Hereby** is used in formal statements and documents to emphasize that they are official; a formal use. *I hereby resign.*

hereditary /hɪ^{2}rɛdɪtə^{0}ri^{1}/. 1 ADJ A **hereditary** characteristic or illness is passed on to a child from its parents before it is born. *...a progressive, hereditary disease of certain glands.* 2 ADJ A **hereditary** title or position in society is passed on as a right from parent to child. *...the hereditary right to belong to the House of Lords.*

heredity /hɪ^{2}rɛdɪ^{1}ti^{1}/. UNCOUNT N **Heredity** is the process by which characteristics are passed on from parents to their children before the children are born. *Do you think we are influenced more by environment or heredity?*

heresy /hɛrə^{1}si^{1}/, **heresies.** UNCOUNT N OR COUNT N **Heresy** is a belief or way of behaving that disagrees with generally accepted beliefs, especially religious ones. *...bitter complaints about the heresies of the group.*

heretic /hɛrə^{1}tɪk/, **heretics.** COUNT N A **heretic** is a person whose beliefs, especially religious ones, are thought to be wrong. *They were denounced as heretics.* ♦ **heretical** /hɪ^{2}rɛtɪkə^{0}l/ ADJ *The bishops jailed him for heretical and blasphemous words.*

heritage /hɛrɪtɪdʒ/. SING N WITH POSS A country's **heritage** consists of all the qualities and traditions that have continued over many years, especially when they are considered to be of historical importance. *...Britain's national heritage.*

hermit /hɜːmɪt/, **hermits.** COUNT N A **hermit** is a person who deliberately lives alone, away from people and society.

hero /hɪərəʊ/, **heroes.** 1 COUNT N The **hero** of a book, play, or film is its main male character, who is admired for his good qualities. 2 COUNT N A **hero** is also someone who has done something brave or good and is admired by a lot of people. *...one of the heroes of the Battle of Britain.* 3 COUNT N WITH POSS If you describe someone as your **hero,** you mean that you admire them greatly. *Bill Hook was my first rugby hero.*

heroic /hɪ^{2}rəʊɪk/. ADJ **Heroic** actions or people are brave, courageous, and determined. *...truly heroic work by army engineers... They are heroic figures in the fight against cancer.* ♦ **heroically** ADV *They fought heroically.*

heroin /hɛrəʊɪn/. UNCOUNT N **Heroin** is a powerful drug which some people take for pleasure, but which they can become addicted to.

heroine /hɛrəʊɪn/, **heroines.** 1 COUNT N A **heroine** of a book, play, or film is its main female character, who is admired for her good qualities. 2 COUNT N A **heroine** is also a woman who has done something brave or good and is admired by a lot of people. *...the heroine of their great 1967 election triumph.*

heroism /hɛrəʊɪzə^{0}m/. UNCOUNT N **Heroism** is great courage and bravery. *...an act of heroism.*

heron /hɛrən/, **herons.** COUNT N A **heron** is a large bird which eats fish.

herring /hɛrɪŋ/, **herrings. Herring** can also be the plural. 1 COUNT N OR UNCOUNT N A **herring** is a long silver-coloured fish that lives in the sea. 2 See also **red herring.**

hers /hɜːz/. PRON You use **hers** to indicate that something belongs or relates to a woman, girl, or female animal that has already been mentioned, or whose identity is known. **Hers** is also sometimes used to indicate that something belongs or relates to a nation, ship, or car. *He laid his hand on hers... You were an old friend of hers.*

herself /hə^{5}sɛlf/. 1 REFL PRON You use **herself** as the object of a verb or preposition to refer to the same woman, girl, or female animal that is mentioned as the subject of the clause, or as a previous object in the clause. *She groaned and stretched herself out flat on the sofa... Barbara stared at herself in the mirror... On the way home Rose bought herself a piece of cheese for lunch.* 2 REFL PRON You also use **herself** to emphasize the female subject or object of a clause, and to make it clear who you are referring to. *Sally herself came back... How strange that he should collide with Melanie Byrd herself... Their audience was of middle-aged women like herself.* 3 REFL PRON If a girl or woman does something **herself,** she does it without any help or interference from anyone else. *She had printed the little card herself.*

he's /hiːz/. 1 **He's** is the usual spoken form of 'he is'. *He's a reporter... He's going away soon.* 2 **He's** is also the usual spoken form of 'he has', especially when 'has' is an auxiliary verb. *I hope he's got some money left... He's gone.*

hesitancy /hɛzɪtənsi^{1}/. UNCOUNT N **Hesitancy** is unwillingness to do something. *There was no hesitancy in his words.*

hesitant /hɛzɪtə^{0}nt/. ADJ If you are **hesitant** about doing something, you do not do it quickly or immediately, for example because you are uncertain, embarrassed, or worried. *He was hesitant about accepting the invitation... He seemed hesitant to confirm the bad news... ...a hesitant, almost boyish smile.* ♦ **hesitantly** ADV *'Maybe you could teach me,' said Marsha hesitantly.*

hesitate /hɛzɪteɪt/, **hesitates, hesitating, hesitated.** 1 VB If you **hesitate,** you pause slightly while you are doing something or just before you do it, usually because you are uncertain, embarrassed, or worried. *She put her hand on the phone, hesitated for a moment, then picked up the receiver.* 2 VB WITH TO-INF If you **hesitate** to do something, you are unwilling to do it because you are not certain whether it is correct or right. *Don't hesitate to go to a doctor if you have any unusual symptoms.*

hesitation /hɛzɪteɪʃə^{0}n/, **hesitations.** 1 UNCOUNT N OR COUNT N **Hesitation** is a pause or slight delay in something that you are doing, usually because you are uncertain, embarrassed, or worried. *'Well, no,' Karen said, with some hesitation... ...a slight hesitation.* 2 UNCOUNT N OR COUNT N **Hesitation** is also an unwillingness to do something because you are uncertain, embarrassed, or worried. *After some hesitation he agreed to allow me to write the article... Bamuthi's hesitations were overcome.*

heterogeneous /hɛtə^{0}rə^{6}dʒiːnɪəs/. ADJ Something that is **heterogeneous** consists of many different types of things; a formal use. *Arts and sciences are contained in one heterogeneous collection.*

heterosexual /hɛtə^{0}rə^{6}sɛksjʊ^{0}əl/. 1 ADJ A **heterosexual** relationship is a sexual one between a man and a woman. 2 ADJ Someone who is **heterosexual** is sexually attracted to people of the opposite sex.

het up /hɛt ʌp/. PRED ADJ If you get **het up,** you get very excited or anxious about something; an informal use. *...when he gets all het up about some business problem.*

hey /heɪ/. CONVENTION You say or shout **'hey'** to attract someone's attention or show surprise, interest, or annoyance; an informal use. *'Hey, Ben!' he called. There was no reply.*

heyday /heɪdeɪ/. SING N WITH POSS The **heyday** of a person, nation, or organization is the time when they are most powerful, successful, or popular. *...the heyday of Christianity.*

hi /haɪ/. CONVENTION You say **'hi'** when you are greeting someone; an informal use. *'Hi, Uncle Harold,' Thomas said.*

hiatus /haɪeɪtəs/. SING N A **hiatus** is a pause in which nothing happens; a formal use. *There came a pause, a hiatus. He stared out of the window.*

hibernate /haɪbəneɪt/, **hibernates, hibernating, hibernated.** VB Animals that **hibernate** spend the winter in a state like a deep sleep. *Squirrels don't hibernate.* ♦ **hibernation** /haɪbəneɪʃə^{0}n/ UNCOUNT N *...a brown bear emerging from hibernation.*

hiccup /hɪkʌp/, **hiccups, hiccupping, hiccupped;** also spelled **hiccough.** 1 COUNT N If you have **hiccups,** a spasm causes repeated sharp sounds in your throat, often because you have been eating or drinking too quickly. 2 VB When you **hiccup,** you make one of the repeated sharp sounds in your throat that are sometimes caused by eating or drinking too quickly. *She turned over on her side, hiccupped once or twice and went to sleep.*

hidden /hɪdə^{0}n/. 1 ADJ Something that is **hidden** is not easily noticed. *...the hidden disadvantages of a cheque book.* 2 ADJ A place that is **hidden** is difficult to find. *...hidden valleys.*

hide /haɪd/, **hides, hiding, hid** /hɪd/, **hidden** /hɪdə^{0}n/. 1 VB WITH OBJ To **hide** something means to cover it or put it somewhere so that it cannot be seen. *The women managed to steal and hide a few knives... Much of his face was hidden by a beard.* 2 VB OR REFL VB If you **hide,** you go somewhere where you cannot easily be seen or found. *There was nowhere to hide... He went off and hid himself from them.* 3 VB WITH OBJ If you **hide** what you feel or know, you keep it a secret, so that nobody else knows about it. *I couldn't hide this fact from you.* 4 COUNT N OR UNCOUNT N A **hide** is the skin of a large animal, used for making leather.

hideous /hɪdi^{1}əs/. ADJ Something that is **hideous** is extremely unpleasant or ugly. *...the hideous conditions of trench warfare... They're ugly, hideous brutes.* ♦ **hideously** SUBMOD *...hideously mutilated bodies... ...a hideously difficult task.*

hiding /haɪdɪŋ/, **hidings.** 1 UNCOUNT N If someone is in **hiding,** they have secretly gone somewhere where they cannot be found. *He has not been heard from since going into hiding in June.* 2 COUNT N If you give someone a **hiding,** you beat them as a punishment; an informal use. *He told us to stop, or else we'd get a good hiding.*

hierarchy /haɪərɑːki^{1}/, **hierarchies.** 1 COUNT N A **hierarchy** is a system in which people have different ranks or positions depending on how important they are; a formal use. *...the hierarchy of the Episcopal Church.* ♦ **hierarchical** /haɪərɑːkɪkə^{0}l/ ADJ *...ancient hierarchical societies.* 2 COUNT N The **hierarchy** of an organization is the group of people who manage and control it; a formal use. *The university hierarchy decided that it was best to ignore the situation.*

hi-fi /haɪfaɪ/, **hi-fis.** COUNT N A **hi-fi** is a set of stereo equipment which you use to play records, tapes, and compact discs. *...listening to music on the hi-fi.*

high /haɪ/, **higher, highest; highs.** 1 ADJ A **high** structure or mountain measures a great amount from the bottom to the top. *...the high walls of the prison.* Also ADJ OR ADJ AFTER N used in questions and statements about height. *How high are the walls?... ...a 200 foot high crag.* 2 ADJ If something is **high,** it is a long way above the ground, above sea level, or above a person. *The bookshelf was too high for him to reach... I threw the shell high up into the air.* 3 ADJ **High** also means great in amount, degree, or intensity. *Her works fetch high prices... ...areas of high unemployment... ...high-quality colour photographs.* 4 ADJ **High** is also used with numbers. For example, if a number or level is in the **high** eighties, it is more than eighty-five, but not as much as ninety. 5 ATTRIB ADJ **High** also means advanced or complex. *...a successful job in high finance... The questions he'd asked were at a higher level than other people's.* 6 ADJ A **high** position in a profession or society is an important one. *She is high enough up in the company to be able to help you... ...high social status.* 7 ADJ If people have a **high** opinion of you, they respect you very much. 8 ADJ If someone has **high** principles or standards, they are morally good. 9 ADJ A **high** sound is close to the top of a range of notes. *...a high squeaky voice.* 10 ADJ If your spirits are **high,** you are happy and confident about the future. *They were not at all depressed, but in high spirits.* 11 ADJ If you are **high** on drugs, you are under the influence of them; an informal use. 12 COUNT N WITH SUPP A **high** is the greatest level or amount that something reaches. *Prices on the stock exchange reached another record high last week.* 13 PHRASE If you say that **it is high time** something was done, you mean that it should be done now, and that it should have been done before now.

highbrow /haɪbraʊ/. ADJ If you describe something as **highbrow,** you mean that it is intellectual, academic, and difficult to understand. *...highbrow radio programmes.*

high-class. ADJ Something that is **high-class** is of very good quality and high social status. *...big hotels and high-class restaurants.*

higher /haɪə/. 1 **Higher** is the comparative form of **high.** 2 ATTRIB ADJ A **higher** exam or qualification is of an advanced standard or level. *They have their first degrees and are studying for higher degrees.*

higher education. UNCOUNT N **Higher education** is education at universities, colleges, and polytechnics.

high-heeled /haɪ hiːld/. ADJ **High-heeled** shoes have a narrow high heel at the back. They are usually worn by women.

high jump. SING N The **high jump** is an athletics event which involves jumping over a high bar.

highlands /haɪləndz/. PLURAL N **Highlands** are mountainous areas. *...the highlands of New Guinea.*

highlight /haɪlaɪt/, **highlights, highlighting, highlighted.** 1 VB WITH OBJ If you **highlight** a point or problem, you draw attention to it. *The survey highlighted the needs of working women.* 2 COUNT N WITH SUPP A **highlight** is the most interesting or exciting part of something. *This visit provided the real highlight of the morning.* 3 PLURAL N **Highlights** are light-coloured streaks in someone's hair.

highly /haɪli[1]/. 1 SUBMOD You use **highly** to emphasize that a particular quality exists to a great degree. *The report is highly critical of these policies... It is highly improbable that they will accept... ...highly-educated people.* 2 SUBMOD **Highly** is also used to indicate that something is very important. *...a highly placed negotiator... ...a very highly classified document.* 3 ADV If you praise someone **highly** or speak **highly** of them, you praise them a lot. *They spoke highly of Harold... Ross Thompson obviously thought very highly of him.*

highly-strung. ADJ Someone who is **highly-strung** is very nervous and easily upset.

high-minded. ADJ Someone who is **high-minded** has strong moral principles. *...high-minded idealists from overseas.*

Highness /haɪnɪ[2]s/, **Highnesses.** TITLE You use expressions such as **Your Highness** and **His Highness** to address or refer to a prince or princess. *...Her Royal Highness, Princess Alexandra.*

high-pitched. ADJ A sound that is **high-pitched** is high and shrill. *...a high-pitched whine.*

high point, high points. COUNT N WITH SUPP The **high point** of an event or period of time is the most exciting or enjoyable part of it. *His speech was the high point of the evening.*

high-powered. 1 ADJ A **high-powered** machine or piece of equipment is powerful and efficient. *...high-powered microscopes.* 2 ADJ A **high-powered** activity is very advanced and successful. *...high-powered advertising... The course is high-powered.*

high-rise. ATTRIB ADJ **High-rise** buildings are very tall modern buildings. *...high-rise flats.*

high school, high schools. 1 COUNT N OR UNCOUNT N In Britain, a **high school** is a school for people aged between eleven and eighteen. 2 COUNT N OR UNCOUNT N In the United States, a **high school** is a school for people aged between fifteen and eighteen.

high-spirited. ADJ Someone who is **high-spirited** is very lively.

high street, high streets. COUNT N The **high street** of a town is the main street where most of the shops and banks are. *They had a little flat off Kensington High Street.*

high tea. UNCOUNT N **High tea** is a large meal that some people eat in the late afternoon, often with tea to drink; a British use.

high technology. UNCOUNT N **High technology** is the development and use of advanced electronics and computers. *...a new leap forward into an age of high technology... ...high-technology equipment.*

high tide. UNCOUNT N At the coast, **high tide** is the time when the sea is at its highest level. *...a pool which the sea only reached at high tide.*

highway /haɪweɪ/, **highways.** 1 COUNT N A **highway** is a large road that connects towns or cities; an American use. *...inter-state highways.* 2 COUNT N A **highway** is also a main road; a formal use. *She was charged with obstructing the highway.*

hijack /haɪdʒæk/, **hijacks, hijacking, hijacked.** VB WITH OBJ If someone **hijacks** a plane, they illegally take control of it by force while it is flying from one place to another.

hike /haɪk/, **hikes, hiking, hiked.** 1 COUNT N A **hike** is a long walk in the country. *We're going on a four mile hike tomorrow.* 2 VB If you **hike,** you go on long country walks for pleasure. *She was in Switzerland, hiking.* ♦ **hiker** COUNT N *I watched the hikers scrambling up the gully.* ♦ **hiking** UNCOUNT N *We have maps of the area where we hope to do some hiking.*

hilarious /hɪlɛ̲ərɪəs/. ADJ Something that is **hilarious** is extremely funny and makes you laugh a lot. *...the hilarious tale of how Harold got stuck in a lift.*

hilarity /hɪlærɪ[1]ti[1]/. UNCOUNT N **Hilarity** is great amusement and laughter. *The noise of hilarity in the restaurant below kept him awake.*

hill /hɪl/, **hills.** COUNT N A **hill** is an area of land that is higher than the land that surrounds it, but not as high as a mountain. *I started to walk up the hill... ...the Malvern Hills of Worcestershire.*

hillside /hɪlsaɪd/, **hillsides.** COUNT N A **hillside** is the side of a hill. *...the steep hillsides of North Wales... ...a hillside town.*

hilltop /hɪltɒp/, **hilltops.** COUNT N A **hilltop** is the top of a hill. *...the hilltop village of Combe.*

hilly /hɪli[1]/. ADJ **Hilly** land has many hills. *They drove around the hilly area behind the town.*

hilt /hɪlt/, **hilts.** 1 COUNT N The **hilt** of a sword or knife is its handle. 2 PHRASE If you support or defend someone **to the hilt,** you give them all the support that you can; an informal use. *She had backed me to the hilt in all my projects.*

him /hɪm/. **Him** is used as the object of a verb or preposition. 1 PRON You use **him** to refer to a man, boy, or male animal that has already been mentioned or whose identity is known. *He asked if you'd ring him back when you got in... There's no need for him to worry.* 2 PRON **Him** can also be used to refer to someone whose sex is not known or stated; an old-fashioned use.

himself /hɪmse̲lf/. 1 REFL PRON You use **himself** as the object of a verb or preposition to refer to the same man, boy, or male animal that is mentioned as the subject of the clause, or as a previous object in the clause. *Mr Boggis introduced himself... ...his lack of confidence in himself.* 2 REFL PRON You also use **himself** to emphasize the male subject or object of a clause, and to make it clear who you are referring to. *Forman himself became Minister of International Affairs... It was easy for a clever young man like himself to make a good living.* 3 REFL PRON If a man or boy does something **himself,** he does it without any help or interference from anyone else.

hind /haɪnd/. ATTRIB ADJ The **hind** legs of an animal are at the back.

hinder /hɪndə/, **hinders, hindering, hindered.** VB WITH OBJ If something **hinders** you, it makes it more difficult for you to carry out a task or plan. *Her career was not hindered by the fact that she had three children.*

hindrance /hɪndrəns/, **hindrances.** 1 COUNT N A **hindrance** is a person or thing that makes it more difficult for you to do something. *New ideas may be more of a hindrance than an asset.* 2 UNCOUNT N **Hindrance** is the act of hindering someone or something. *Now they can construct tunnel systems without hindrance.*

hindsight /ha̲ɪndsaɪt/. UNCOUNT N **Hindsight** is the ability to understand something after it has happened. *With hindsight, what could we learn from their mistakes?*

Hindu /hɪnduː, hɪndu̲ː/, **Hindus.** COUNT N A **Hindu** is a person who believes in Hinduism. Also ADJ *...Hindu civilization.*

Hinduism /hɪnduːɪzə[0]m/. UNCOUNT N **Hinduism** is an Indian religion, which has many gods and teaches that people have another life after they die.

hinge /hɪndʒ/, **hinges, hinging, hinged.** COUNT N A **hinge** is a moveable joint made of metal, wood, or plastic that joins two things so that one of them can swing freely. *The door was ripped from its hinges.*

hinge on or **hinge upon.** PHR VB If something **hinges on** or **hinges upon** a fact or event, it depends on it. *Everything hinged on what happened to the United States economy.*

hinged /hɪnd[0]ʒd/. ADJ An object that is **hinged** is joined to another object with a hinge. *...the hinged flap of the counter.*

hint /hɪnt/, **hints, hinting, hinted.** 1 COUNT N A **hint** is a suggestion about something that is made in an indirect way. *As yet no hint had appeared as to who was going to be the next Foreign Secretary.* ● If you **drop a hint,** you suggest something in an indirect way. *He had dropped several hints that he knew where Mary was.* ● If you **take a hint,** you understand something that is suggested indirectly. *She may take the hint and become more organized.* 2 VB WITH 'at' OR REPORT VB If you **hint** at something, you suggest something in an indirect way. *Harold hinted at what she had already guessed... I tried to hint that I deserved an increase in salary.* 3 COUNT N A **hint** is also a helpful piece of advice. *The magazine had the usual hints on fashion and cookery.* 4 SING N A **hint** of something is a very small amount of it. *There was a hint of disapproval in her face.*

hip /hɪp/, **hips.** COUNT N Your **hips** are the two areas at the sides of your body between the tops of your legs and your waist.

hippie /hɪpi[1]/, **hippies;** also spelled **hippy.** COUNT N A **hippie** is someone who has rejected conventional ideas and wants to live a life based on peace and love.

hippo /hɪpəʊ/, **hippos.** COUNT N A **hippo** is a hippopotamus.

hippopotamus /hɪpəpɒ̲təməs/, **hippopotamuses** or **hippopotami.** COUNT N A **hippopotamus** is a large African animal with short legs and thick, wrinkled skin which lives near water.

hippy /hɪpi[1]/. See **hippie.**

hire /haɪə̲/, **hires, hiring, hired.** 1 VB WITH OBJ If you **hire** something, you pay money to use it for a period of time. *We hired a car and drove across the island.* Also UNCOUNT N WITH SUPP *Hire of a van costs about £30 a day.* 2 PHRASE If something is **for hire,** you can hire it. *...boats for hire.* 3 VB WITH OBJ If you **hire** someone, you pay them to do a job for you. *You've got to hire a private detective to make enquiries.*

hire out. PHR VB If you **hire out** something, you allow it to be used in return for payment. *Holborn library hires out pictures.*

his /hɪz/. 1 DET You use **his** to indicate that something belongs or relates to a man, boy, or male animal that has already been mentioned, or to refer to someone whose sex is not known or stated. *He had his hands in his pockets... To each according to his need.* Also PRON *Willie had a job on a magazine that a friend of his had just started.* 2 DET You also use **his** in titles when you are referring to a man. *...his Lordship.*

hiss /hɪs/, **hisses, hissing, hissed.** 1 VB To **hiss** means to make a sound like a long 's'. *If you shove a hot frying pan into water it will hiss and buckle.* Also SING N *...the soft hiss of roasting meat.* 2 VB If you **hiss,** you say something in a strong, angry whisper. *He pointed a shaking finger at my friend and hissed through clenched teeth: 'You, you get out!'* 3 VB WITH OR WITHOUT OBJ When an audience **hisses,** they express their dislike of a performance by making long loud 's' sounds. *His public appearances were hissed.*

historian /hɪstɔ̲ːrɪən/, **historians.** COUNT N A **historian** is a person who studies history.

historic /hɪstɒ̲rɪk/. ADJ Something that is **historic** is important in history. *...a historic change.*

historical /hɪstɒ̲rɪkə[0]l/. 1 ATTRIB ADJ **Historical** people or situations existed in the past and are considered to be a part of history. *...actual historical events... ...autographs and manuscripts of historical interest.* ♦ **historically** ADV *Historically, Labour was strongly opposed to the powers of the Lords.* 2 ATTRIB ADJ **Historical** books and pictures describe or represent real people or things that existed in the past. *...historical novels.*

history /hɪstə[0]ri[1]/, **histories.** 1 UNCOUNT N You can refer to the events of the past as **history.** *...one of the most dramatic moments in Polish history... Each city has its own history and character.* 2 UNCOUNT N **History** is also the study of the past. *I adored history and hated geography... ...a history book, not a novel.* 3 COUNT N WITH SUPP A **history** is a description of the important events that have happened in a particular subject. *...a television history of the United States.* 4 COUNT N WITH SUPP Someone's **history** is a set of facts or a particular fact that is known about their past. *I'd like to look at his medical history... There is a family history of coronary heart disease.* 5 See also **natural history.**

histrionic /hɪstri[1]ɒ̲nɪk/. ATTRIB ADJ **Histrionic** behaviour is very dramatic and exaggerated, but is not sincere; a formal use.

hit /hɪ̲t/, **hits, hitting. Hit** is used in the present tense of the verb, and is the past tense and past participle. 1 VB WITH OBJ To **hit** someone or something means to strike or touch them forcefully. *He hit the burglar on the head with a candlestick... He never hit the ball very far... The truck had hit a wall... Enormous hailstones hit the roof of the car.* 2 VB WITH OBJ If a bomb or other missile **hits** its target, it reaches it. *Three ships were hit.* 3 COUNT N A **hit** is the action or fact of a bomb or other missile hitting its target. *The tanks were designed to withstand anything except a direct hit.* 4 VB WITH OBJ If something **hits** a person, place, or thing, it affects them badly. *Spectator sport has been badly hit by the increase in ticket prices.* 5 VB WITH OBJ When a feeling or an idea **hits** you, it suddenly comes into your mind. *The shock of her death kept hitting me afresh... Suddenly it hit me: my diary had probably been read by everyone in the office.* 6 COUNT N A **hit** is a record, play, or film that is very popular and successful. *The play became a tremendous hit.*

hit on or **hit upon.** PHR VB If you **hit on** an idea or **hit upon** it, you think of it. *He hit on the idea of cutting a hole in the door to let the cat in.*

hit and miss. ADJ Something that is **hit and miss** happens in a disorganized way.

hit-and-run. ATTRIB ADJ A **hit-and-run** car accident is one in which the driver does not stop.

hitch /hɪ̲tʃ/, **hitches, hitching, hitched.** 1 COUNT N A **hitch** is a slight problem or difficulty. *There had also been one or two technical hitches.* 2 VB WITH OR WITHOUT OBJ If you **hitch** a lift, you hitch-hike. *He hitched south towards Italy.* 3 VB WITH OBJ AND ADJUNCT If you **hitch** something onto an object, you fasten it there. *...ponies hitched to rails.*

hitch up. PHR VB If you **hitch up** a piece of clothing, you pull it up into a higher position.

hitch-hike, hitch-hikes, hitch-hiking, hitch-hiked. VB If you **hitch-hike,** you travel by getting lifts from passing vehicles. *She went off with a friend intending to hitch-hike to Turkey.* ♦ **hitch-hiker** COUNT N *...foreign hitch-hikers in Sardinia.*

hi tech /haɪ te̲k/. ADJ Something that is **hi tech** uses very modern methods and equipment.

hitherto /hɪ̲ðətu̲ː/. ADV If something has been happening **hitherto,** it has been happening until now; a formal use. *She had hitherto been nice to me.*

hit list, hit lists. COUNT N A **hit list** is a list that terrorists have of the people they intend to kill.

hit or miss. ADJ Something that is **hit or miss** happens in a disorganized way.

hive /haɪv/, **hives. 1** COUNT N A **hive** is a beehive. **2** COUNT N WITH 'of' You describe a place as a **hive** of a particular kind of activity when there is a lot of that activity there. *Calcutta is a hive of industry and trade.*

hoard /hɔːd/, **hoards, hoarding, hoarded. 1** VB WITH OBJ If you **hoard** things, you save or store them. *Is it better to spend your money today or hoard every penny in the bank for tomorrow?* **2** SING N A **hoard** is a store of things you have saved. *...a small hoard of coins.*

hoarding /hɔːdɪŋ/, **hoardings.** COUNT N A **hoarding** is a large board used for advertising which stands at the side of a road. *I scanned the hoardings for election posters.*

hoarse /hɔːs/, **hoarser, hoarsest.** ADJ If your voice is **hoarse,** it sounds rough and unclear. *When he spoke his voice was hoarse with rage.* ♦ **hoarsely** ADV *'Go in there,' he whispered hoarsely.* ♦ **hoarseness** UNCOUNT N *I noticed a peculiar hoarseness in Johnny's voice.*

hoary /hɔːri¹/. ADJ Something that is **hoary** is old; a literary use.

hoax /həʊks/, **hoaxes.** COUNT N A **hoax** is a trick in which someone tells people something that is not true. *It wasn't a hoax, there really was a fire.*

hob /hɒb/, **hobs.** COUNT N A **hob** is a surface on top of a cooker which can be heated.

hobble /hɒbə⁰l/, **hobbles, hobbling, hobbled. 1** VB If you **hobble,** you walk in an awkward way because you are in pain. *He hobbled along as best he could.* **2** VB WITH OBJ If you **hobble** an animal, you tie its legs together so that it cannot run away.

hobby /hɒbi¹/, **hobbies.** COUNT N A **hobby** is something that you enjoy doing in your spare time. *Music is his chief hobby.*

hockey /hɒki¹/. UNCOUNT N **Hockey** is an outdoor game played between two teams using long curved sticks to hit a small ball. ● See also **ice hockey.**

hoe /həʊ/, **hoes, hoeing, hoed. 1** COUNT N A **hoe** is a long-handled gardening tool which is used to remove small weeds. **2** VB WITH OR WITHOUT OBJ If you **hoe** a field, you use a hoe to remove the weeds there.

hog /hɒg/, **hogs, hogging, hogged. 1** COUNT N A **hog** is a castrated male pig. **2** VB WITH OBJ If you **hog** something, you take all of it in a selfish or impolite way; an informal use. *...a huge lorry hogging the centre of the road.*

hoist /hɔɪst/, **hoists, hoisting, hoisted. 1** VB WITH OBJ AND ADJUNCT If you **hoist** something somewhere, you lift it or pull it up there. *She hoisted the child onto her shoulder.* **2** VB WITH OBJ If you **hoist** a flag or a sail, you pull it up to its correct position using ropes. *The American flag was hoisted.* **3** COUNT N A **hoist** is a machine for lifting heavy things. *...an electric hoist.*

hold /həʊld/, **holds, holding, held** /hɛld/. **1** VB WITH OBJ When you **hold** something, you carry or support it, usually using your fingers or your arms. *He was holding a bottle of milk... I held the picture up to the light... He held her in his arms.* **2** UNCOUNT N If you take **hold** of something, you put your hand tightly round it. *She took hold of my wrist... He still had hold of my jacket.* Also SING N *She resumed her hold on the rope.* **3** VB WITH OBJ OR REFL VB If you **hold** your body or part of your body in a particular position, you keep it in that position. *Etta held her head back... Mrs Patel held herself erect.* **4** VB WITH OR WITHOUT OBJ If one thing **holds** another thing, it keeps it in position. *There was just a rail holding it... The glue held.* **5** VB WITH OBJ If something **holds** a particular amount of something, it can contain that amount. *The theatre itself can hold only a limited number of people.* **6** VB WITH OBJ OR VB WITH OBJ AND OBJ If you **hold** someone, you keep them as a prisoner. *I was held overnight in a cell... The young private had been held a prisoner by the guerrillas.* **7** VB WITH OBJ If you **hold** power or office, you have it. *The reins of power are held by a restricted group of Shi'ite clergy... ...one of the greatest Prime Ministers who ever held office.* **8** SING N If you have a **hold** over someone, you have power or control over them. *The party tightened its hold on the union... The farmer had a hold over me. He had discovered my illegal whiskey still.* **9** VB WITH OBJ If you **hold** a qualification, licence or other official document, you have it. *You need to hold a work permit... She held a BA degree in psychology.* **10** VB WITH OBJ If you **hold** an event, you organize it and it takes place. *He had promised he would hold elections in June.* **11** VB WITH OBJ If you **hold** a conversation with someone, you talk with them. **12** VB WITH OBJ You can use **hold** to say that something has a particular quality or characteristic. *These legends hold a romantic fascination for many Japanese... We will have to see what the future holds.* **13** REPORT VB If you **hold** a particular opinion, that is your opinion. *People who hold this view are sometimes dismissed as cranks... Marxists hold that people are all naturally creative.* **14** VB WITH OR WITHOUT OBJ If someone asks you to **hold** the line when you have made a telephone call, they are asking you to wait until they can connect you. *The line's engaged; will you hold?* **15** VB WITH OBJ If you **hold** someone's interest or attention, you keep them interested. **16** VB If an offer or invitation still **holds,** it is still available. *Will you tell her the offer still holds?* **17** VB If your luck **holds** or if the weather **holds,** it remains good. *If my luck continues to hold, I think I've got a fair chance.* **18** COUNT N The **hold** of a ship or aeroplane is the place where cargo is stored.

PHRASES ● If you **hold tight,** you hold something very firmly. ● When something **takes hold,** it starts to have a great effect. *Then the fire took hold.* ● If you **get hold of** something or someone, you manage to get them or find them. *Can you get hold of a car this weekend?* ● If you say **'Hold it'** or **'Hold everything',** you are telling someone to stop what they are doing. ● If you **hold** your **own,** you are not defeated by someone. *She was still able to hold her own with the Prime Minister.*

hold against. PHR VB If someone has done something wrong and you **hold** it **against** them, you treat them more severely because they did it. *His refusal to cooperate will be held against him.*

hold back. PHR VB **1** If you **hold back,** you hesitate before doing something. *Police have held back from going into such a holy place.* **2** If you **hold** someone or something **back,** you prevent them from advancing or increasing. *If she is ambitious, don't try to hold her back... The rise in living standards has been held back for so long.* **3** If you **hold** something **back,** you do not tell someone the full details about it. *I want the truth now, with nothing held back.*

hold down. PHR VB If you **hold down** a job, you manage to keep it. *He was surprised to find her holding down a successful job in high finance.*

hold off. PHR VB If you **hold** something **off,** you prevent it from reaching you. *The French and British wanted to hold off Portuguese textile competition.*

hold on. PHR VB **1** If you **hold on,** you keep your hand firmly round something. *He tried to pull free but she held on tight.* **2** If you ask someone to **hold on,** you are asking them to wait for a short time. *Hold on a moment, please.*

hold onto. PHR VB **1** If you **hold onto** something, you keep your hand firmly round it. *He has to hold onto something to steady himself.* **2** To **hold onto** something also means to keep it and not lose it. *Politicians want to hold on to power at all costs.*

hold out. PHR VB **1** If you **hold out** your hand or something that is in your hand, you move it towards someone. *'John?' Esther held out the phone.* **2** If you **hold out,** you stand firm and manage to resist opposition. *Women all over the country are holding out for more freedom... I can't hold out forever.*

hold up. PHR VB If someone or something **holds** you **up,** they delay you. *The whole thing was held up about half an hour.* ● See also **hold-up.**

hold with. PHR VB If you do not **hold with** something, you do not approve of it. *...a man who did not hold with these notions.*

holder /həʊldə/, **holders. 1** COUNT N A **holder** is a container in which you put an object. *The cup was held in a brown plastic holder.* **2** COUNT N A **holder** is also someone who owns, controls, or has something. *...ticket-holders... ...holders of anti-government opinions... ...Luton town, the Littlewoods cup holders.*

holding /həʊldɪŋ/, **holdings. 1** COUNT N WITH SUPP If you have a **holding** in a company, you own shares in it. *We should sell the government holding in British Gas.* **2** COUNT N A **holding** is also an area of farm land rented or owned by the person who cultivates it. *78 per cent of holdings are below 5 hectares.* **3** ATTRIB ADJ You use **holding** to describe a temporary action which is intended to prevent a situation from becoming worse. *The rest of the campaign was a holding operation.*

hold-up, hold-ups. 1 COUNT N A **hold-up** is a situation in which someone is threatened with a weapon in order to make them hand over money. *...the victim of a masked hold-up.* **2** COUNT N A **hold-up** is also something which causes a delay. *...traffic hold-ups.*

hole /həʊl/, **holes, holing, holed. 1** COUNT N A **hole** is an opening or hollow space in something solid. *What do you recommend for filling holes and cracks?... ...a deep hole in the ground... He was wearing grey socks with holes in them.* **2** PHRASE If you **pick holes in** an argument or theory, you find weak points in it; an informal use. **3** COUNT N You can describe an unpleasant place as a **hole;** an informal use. *Why don't you leave this awful hole and come to live with me?* **4** VB WITH OBJ If a building or a ship **is holed,** holes are made in it. *The buildings were holed by shrapnel.*

holiday /hɒlɪdi³/, **holidays. 1** COUNT N OR UNCOUNT N A **holiday** is a period of time spent away from home for relaxation. *I went to Marrakesh for a holiday... Remember to turn off the gas when you go on holiday.* **2** COUNT N OR UNCOUNT N A **holiday** is also a period of time during which you are not working. *New Year's Day is a national holiday... The company offers three weeks paid holiday.* ● See also **bank holiday.**

holidaymaker /hɒlɪdi³meɪkə/, **holidaymakers.** COUNT N A **holidaymaker** is a person who is away from home on holiday.

holiness /həʊlɪnɪ²s/. **1** UNCOUNT N **Holiness** is the state or quality of being holy. *She could feel the holiness of the place.* **2** TITLE You use expressions such as **Your Holiness** and **His Holiness** to address or refer to the Pope or to leaders of some other religions.

holler /hɒlə/, **hollers, hollering, hollered.** VB If you **holler,** you shout or weep loudly; an informal American use. *You should have heard him holler!*

hollow /hɒləʊ/, **hollows, hollowing, hollowed. 1** ADJ Something that is **hollow** has a hole or space inside it. *...a hollow tube... ...a large hollow container.* **2** ADJ A surface that is **hollow** curves inwards or downwards. *...a lean, hollow-cheeked man.* **3** COUNT N A **hollow** is an area that is lower than the surrounding surface. *Davis hid in a hollow surrounded by bracken.* **4** ADJ A **hollow** situation or opinion has no real value, worth, or effectiveness; a formal use. *Their independence is hollow... His outward optimism rang hollow.* **5** ATTRIB ADJ If someone gives a **hollow** laugh, they laugh in a way that shows that they do not really find something funny. ♦ **hollowly** ADV *He laughed hollowly. 'And what a mess we made of that!'* **6** ADJ A **hollow** sound is dull and echoing. *The door closed with a hollow clang behind him.* ♦ **hollowly** ADV *His footsteps sounded hollowly on the uncarpeted stairs.*

hollow out. PHR VB If you **hollow** something **out,** you remove the inside part of it. *The kids had hollowed out tunnels through the maize.*

holly /hɒli¹/. UNCOUNT N **Holly** is a small evergreen tree with prickly leaves and red berries.

holocaust /hɒləkɔːst/, **holocausts.** COUNT N OR UNCOUNT N A **holocaust** is very great destruction and loss of life, especially in war or by fire. *...a nuclear holocaust... ...a danger of war and holocaust.*

holster /həʊlstə/, **holsters.** COUNT N A **holster** is a holder for a gun worn on a belt.

holy /həʊli¹/, **holier, holiest. 1** ADJ Something that is **holy** relates to God or to a particular religion. *...holy pictures and statues.* **2** ADJ Someone who is **holy** is religious and leads a pure and good life.

homage /hɒmɪdʒ/. UNCOUNT N **Homage** is a way of behaving towards someone that shows respect. *The soldiers gathered to pay homage to the heroes.*

home /həʊm/, **homes, homing, homed. 1** UNCOUNT N, COUNT N, OR MOD Your **home** is the place or country where you live or feel that you belong. *The old man wants to die in his own home... ...a normal home life... He stayed at home to care for the children... My own home town is thousands of miles away.* **2** ADV **Home** means to or at the place where you live. *I want to go home... Here we are, home at last.* **3** PHRASE If you are **at home** in a particular situation, you feel comfortable and relaxed in it. *I felt at home at once, because I recognized familiar faces.* **4** MOD OR UNCOUNT N **Home** also means relating to your own country rather than to foreign countries. *The government had promised to maintain an expanding home market... Newspapers both at home and abroad ignored the incident.* **5** COUNT N A **home** is also a building where people who cannot care for themselves are looked after. *...a children's home... ...a home for the elderly.* **6** SING N WITH SUPP The **home** of something is the place where it began or where it is found. *...that home of free enterprise, the United States.* **7** PHRASE If you **bring** or **drive** something **home to** someone, you make them understand how important it is. *He raised his voice to drive home the point.* **8** ATTRIB ADJ A **home** game is played on your team's own ground. *They watched every single game, home or away.* **9** See also **homing.**

home in. PHR VB If a missile **homes in** on something, it finds it. *It can thus home in on the target with pinpoint accuracy.*

homecoming /həʊmkʌmɪŋ/, **homecomings.** COUNT N Your **homecoming** is your return to your home or country after you have been away for a long time. *There were 120,000 people at his homecoming.*

home economics. UNCOUNT N **Home economics** is a school subject dealing with how to run a house well and efficiently.

home ground. PHRASE If you are **on home ground** in a particular situation, you know exactly what to do.

home help, home helps. COUNT N A **home help** is a person employed by a local government authority to help sick or old people with their housework.

homeland /həʊmlə3nd/, **homelands.** COUNT N Your **homeland** is your native country.

homeless /həʊmlı2s/. 1 ADJ If people are **homeless,** they have nowhere to live. *Floods in north-eastern India made 233,000 people homeless.* ♦ **homelessness** UNCOUNT N *For a growing number of young people, homelessness is becoming a way of life.* 2 PLURAL N You can refer to people who are homeless as **the homeless.** *We were running homes for the homeless.*

homely /həʊmli1/. ADJ If something is **homely,** it is simple and ordinary. *We stayed in the Hotel Claravallis, a homely and comfortable establishment.*

home-made. ADJ Something that is **home-made** has been made in someone's home, rather than in a shop or factory. *...homemade bread.*

homeopathy /həʊmi1ɒpəθi1/; also spelled **homoeopathy.** UNCOUNT N **Homeopathy** is a way of treating illness in which the patient is given very small amounts of drugs which are prepared from natural substances. ♦ **homeopathic** /həʊmi1ə6pæθık/ ADJ *...homeopathic remedies.*

homesick /həʊmsık/. ADJ If you are **homesick,** you are unhappy because you are away from home. *The smell of the grass made her homesick for her parents' farm.* ♦ **homesickness** UNCOUNT N *...a sudden spasm of homesickness.*

home truth, home truths. COUNT N **Home truths** are unpleasant facts that you learn about yourself, usually from someone else.

homeward /həʊmwəd/, **homewards.** In normal British English, **homewards** is an adverb and **homeward** is an adjective. In formal British English and in American English, **homeward** is both an adjective and an adverb. ADV **Homewards** or **homeward** means towards home. *The time had come to drive the goats homewards.* Also ATTRIB ADJ *The tank blew up on its homeward journey.*

homework /həʊmwɜ:k/. 1 UNCOUNT N **Homework** is work that teachers give pupils to do at home. *He never did any homework and he got terrible results in school.* 2 UNCOUNT N **Homework** is also research that is done in preparation for a written article or speech. *Aiken did his homework and worked out a convincing commercial case.*

homicidal /hɒmısaıdə0l/. ADJ Someone who is **homicidal** is likely to commit murder. *...homicidal maniacs.*

homicide /hɒmısaıd/, **homicides.** UNCOUNT N OR COUNT N **Homicide** is the crime of murder; an American use. *...the persons who have committed these homicides.*

homing /həʊmıŋ/. 1 ATTRIB ADJ A weapon that has a **homing** system is able to guide itself to a target. *Even small missiles have built-in homing devices.* 2 ATTRIB ADJ An animal that has a **homing** instinct is able to remember a place and return there.

homogeneity /hɒmə6dʒıni:ı1ti1, həʊ-/. UNCOUNT N **Homogeneity** is the quality of being homogeneous. *...emphasis on the unity of the nation and the homogeneity of society.*

homogeneous /hɒmə6dʒi:niəs, həʊ-/. ADJ A thing or group that is **homogeneous** has parts or members which are all the same. *The working class is not very homogeneous.*

homogenous /həmɒdʒənəs/. ADJ **Homogenous** means the same as homogeneous.

homosexual /həʊmə6sɛksju0əl, hɒm-/, **homosexuals.** ADJ Someone who is **homosexual** is sexually attracted to people of the same sex. Also COUNT N *...clubs and bars for homosexuals.* ♦ **homosexuality** /həʊmə6sɛksju:ælıti1 hɒm-/ UNCOUNT N *...the reform of the laws on homosexuality.*

honest /ɒnıst/. 1 ADJ Someone who is **honest** about something is completely truthful about it. *At least you're honest about why you want the money... To be perfectly honest, up until three weeks ago I had never set foot in a nightclub... Not all scientists are as honest as Pasteur was.* ♦ **honestly** ADV *Philip had answered them honestly.* 2 ADJ Someone who is **honest** does not cheat or break the law and can be trusted with valuable things. *He's very honest in money matters.* ♦ **honestly** ADV *If he couldn't get rare shrubs honestly, he would steal them.* 3 SENTENCE ADV You say **'honest'** to emphasize that you are telling the truth; an informal use. *It's true as I'm sitting here, Mabel, honest it is.*

honestly /ɒnı2stli1/. 1 ADV OR SENTENCE ADV You use **honestly** to emphasize that you are telling the truth. *He didn't honestly think he would miss them... I'll go if you like. I don't mind, honestly.* 2 CONVENTION You also use **honestly** to indicate annoyance or impatience. *Honestly, Flora, this is getting ridiculous.*

honesty /ɒnı2sti1/. UNCOUNT N **Honesty** is the quality of being honest. *...the need for complete honesty.*

honey /hʌni1/. UNCOUNT N **Honey** is a sweet sticky substance made by bees. You eat honey and use it as a sweetener. *...tea sweetened with honey.*

honeycomb /hʌni1kəʊm/, **honeycombs.** COUNT N OR UNCOUNT N A **honeycomb** is a wax structure consisting of rows of six-sided holes where bees store honey.

honeymoon /hʌnımu:n/, **honeymoons.** 1 COUNT N A **honeymoon** is a holiday taken by a newly-married couple. *They spent their honeymoon at Petersburg, Florida.* 2 COUNT N A **honeymoon** is also a period of time after the start of a new job or government when everyone is pleased with the people concerned. *The honeymoon period is over.*

honeysuckle /hʌnısʌkə0l/. UNCOUNT N **Honeysuckle** is a climbing plant with sweet-smelling flowers.

honk /hɒŋk/, **honks, honking, honked.** ERG VB If you **honk** the horn of a vehicle, it produces a short loud sound.

honor /ɒnə/. See **honour.**

honorable /ɒnə0rəbə0l/. See **honourable.**

honorary /ɒnə0rəri1/. 1 ATTRIB ADJ An **honorary** title is given to someone as a mark of respect and does not require the usual qualifications. *...an honorary degree.* 2 ATTRIB ADJ An **honorary** job is an official job that is done without payment. *...the honorary Treasurer.*

honour /ɒnə/, **honours, honouring, honoured;** spelled **honor** in American English. 1 UNCOUNT N **Honour** is behaviour in which you behave in accordance with your ideas or beliefs, so that other people respect you. *A debt is a thing of family honour... He was able to withdraw from the battle with honour.* 2 COUNT N An **honour** is a special award or job that is given to someone for something they have done. *It was a richly deserved honour.* 3 SING N If you describe something that has happened to you as an **honour,** you mean that you are pleased and proud about it; a formal use. *He is one of the most interesting people I have had the honour of meeting... She did me the honour of attending my exhibition.* 4 UNCOUNT N **Honours** is a type of university degree which is of a higher standard than an ordinary degree; a British use. *...a first class honours degree in French.* 5 VB WITH OBJ If you **honour** someone, you give them public praise or a medal for something they have done. *The people came to honour their leader... In 1949, he was honoured with the Grand Cross.* 6 VB WITH OBJ To **honour** someone also means to treat them with special attention and respect. *When President Gorbachev lunches with the Queen today, he will become the first Soviet leader to be so honoured.* ♦ **honoured** ATTRIB ADJ *Rose was the honoured guest.* 7 VB WITH OBJ If you **honour** an arrangement or promise, you keep to it; a formal use. *The government has solemn commitments and must honour them.*
PHRASES ● If something is arranged **in honour of** an event, it is arranged to celebrate that event. *The ceremony was held in honour of the Queen's birthday.* ● You address a judge in court as **your honour;** an American use.

honourable /ɒnə0rəbə0l/; spelled **honorable** in American English. ADJ Someone who is **honourable** is honest and worthy of respect. *...an honourable man... Major Vane had always tried to do the honourable thing.* ♦ **honourably** ADV *He served his master honourably until his death.*

hood /hʊd/, **hoods.** 1 COUNT N A **hood** is a part of a coat which covers your head. *He held both sides of the hood closed against the snow.* 2 COUNT N A **hood** is also a covering on a vehicle or a piece of equipment, which is usually curved and can be moved. *...a pram which had its hood folded down.* 3 COUNT N In American English, the **hood** is the bonnet of a car.

hooded /hʊdı2d/. 1 ATTRIB ADJ A **hooded** piece of clothing has a hood. *...a hooded duffel coat.* 2 ATTRIB ADJ Someone with **hooded** eyes has large eyelids that are partly closed.

hoodwink /hʊdwıŋk/, **hoodwinks, hoodwinking, hoodwinked.** VB WITH OBJ If you **hoodwink** someone, you trick or deceive them. *He is too often hoodwinked by flashy external appearances.*

hoof /hu:f/, **hoofs** or **hooves** /hu:vz/. COUNT N The **hooves** of an animal such as a horse are the hard parts of its feet.

hook /hʊk/, **hooks, hooking, hooked.** 1 COUNT N A **hook** is a bent piece of metal or plastic used for holding things. *Howard hangs up his coat on the hook behind the door... ...curtain hooks.* 2 VB WITH OBJ AND ADJUNCT If you **hook** one thing onto another, you attach it there using a hook. *One after the other they were hooked to the moving cable.*
PHRASES ● If you take the phone **off the hook,** you take the receiver off the part that it normally rests on, so that the phone will not ring. ● If someone **gets off the hook,** they manage to get out of a difficult or dangerous situation; an informal use. *He felt he had got off the hook perhaps too easily.*

hook up. PHR VB If you **hook up** a computer or other electronic machine, you connect it to other similar machines or to a central power supply.

hooked /hʊkt/. 1 ADJ Something that is **hooked** is shaped like a hook. *...huge hooked claws... ...a long, rather hooked nose.* 2 PRED ADJ If you are **hooked** on something, you enjoy it so much that it takes up a lot of your interest and attention; an informal use. *They're the sweetest kids ever. I'm really hooked on those kids.* 3 PRED ADJ If you are **hooked** on a drug, you are addicted to it.

hooker /hʊkə/, **hookers.** COUNT N In American English, a **hooker** is a prostitute; an informal use.

hook-up, hook-ups. COUNT N A **hook-up** is an electronic or radio connection between computers, satellites, or radios.

hooligan /hu:lıgən/, **hooligans.** COUNT N A **hooligan** is a young person who behaves in a noisy and violent way in public places.

hooliganism /hu:lıgənızə0m/. UNCOUNT N **Hooliganism** is the behaviour and action of hooligans. *...an increase in football hooliganism.*

hoop /hu:p/, **hoops.** COUNT N A **hoop** is a large ring made of wood, metal, or plastic. *...boys holding hoops, kites, and marbles.*

hooray /hə4reı/; also spelled **hurray.** CONVENTION People sometimes shout **'Hooray!'** when they are very happy and excited.

hoot /hu:t/, **hoots, hooting, hooted.** 1 VB WITH OR WITHOUT OBJ If you **hoot** the horn on a vehicle, it makes a loud noise. *Tug boats hooted at it... He hoots the horn.* Also COUNT N *I heard a hoot and saw Martin driving by.* 2 VB If you **hoot,** you make a loud high-pitched noise when you are laughing. *They pointed and hooted with enjoyment.* Also COUNT N *At this Etta gave a hoot of laughter.* 3 VB When an owl **hoots,** it makes a sound like a long 'oo'. *Outside, an owl hooted among the pines.* Also SING N *He heard the hoot of an owl.*

hoover /hu:və/, **hoovers, hoovering, hoovered.** 1 COUNT N A **Hoover** is a vacuum cleaner; a trademark. *There was no Hoover for the carpets.* 2 VB WITH OR WITHOUT OBJ If you **hoover** a carpet, you clean it using a vacuum cleaner.

hooves /hu:vz/. **Hooves** is a plural of **hoof.**

hop /hɒp/, **hops, hopping, hopped.** 1 VB If you **hop,** you move along by jumping on one foot. *...hopping clumsily up and down in their chains.* Also COUNT N *They began jumping up and down together in short hops.* 2 VB When birds and some small animals **hop,** they move in small jumps using both feet together. *A hare hopped straight into the doorway.* Also COUNT N *...a bird so heavy that it could make only short, low hops through the brush.* 3 VB WITH ADJUNCT If you **hop** somewhere, you move there quickly or suddenly; an informal use. *He hopped out of bed... Let's hop in my car and drive out there.* 4 COUNT N **Hops** are flowers that are dried and used for making beer. *...the hop gardens of Sussex.*

hope /həʊp/, **hopes, hoping, hoped.** 1 REPORT VB OR VB WITH TO-INF OR 'for' If you **hope** that something is true or will happen, you want it to be true or to happen. *She hoped she wasn't going to cry... I sat down, hoping to remain unnoticed... He paused, hoping for evidence of interest... 'You haven't lost the ticket, have you?'—'I hope not.'* 2 UNCOUNT N OR COUNT N **Hope** is a feeling of confidence that what you want to happen might happen. *She never completely gave up hope... ...his hopes of a reconciliation.* 3 SING N WITH SUPP If there is a **hope** of something desirable happening, it is likely to happen. *Co-operation is the only hope for progress.*
PHRASES ● If you do something **in the hope** of achieving a particular thing, you do it because you want to achieve that thing. *Tourists were waiting outside the palace in the hope of getting a look at the king.* ● If something **raises** your **hopes,** it makes you feel that what you want to happen will happen. *The new agreement raised hopes for conditions of prosperity.*

hopeful /həʊpfʊl/, **hopefuls.** 1 ADJ If you are **hopeful,** you are fairly confident that something that you want to happen will happen. *He sounded hopeful that she would come.* 2 ADJ An outcome, method, or event that is **hopeful** makes you feel that what you want to happen will happen. *...the most astonishing and hopeful results... This seems to be a hopeful way of tacking the problem.* 3 COUNT N If you refer to someone as a **hopeful,** you mean that they have an ambition and it is possible that they will achieve it. *Almost a hundred hopefuls stood in a queue outside the theatre.*

hopefully /həʊpfəli1/. 1 ADV If you do something **hopefully,** you do it in a way which shows that you are fairly confident that what you want to happen will happen. *He smiled hopefully.* 2 SENTENCE ADV **Hopefully** is often used when mentioning something that you hope and are fairly confident will happen. Some careful speakers of English think that this use of

hopefully is incorrect. *The new legislation, hopefully, will lead to some improvements.*

hopeless /həʊplɪ^{2}s/. 1 ADJ If you feel **hopeless,** you feel desperate because there seems to be no possibility of comfort or success. *I walked away in an agony of hopeless grief and pity.* ♦ **hopelessly** ADV *She shook her head hopelessly.* ♦ **hopelessness** UNCOUNT N *...the hopelessness of the poor.* 2 ADJ Someone or something that is **hopeless** is certain to be unsuccessful. *I knew my love was as hopeless as ever... The situation was hopeless... He was hopeless at games.* 3 ATTRIB ADJ You use **hopeless** to emphasize how bad an event or situation is. *Her room is in a hopeless muddle.* ♦ **hopelessly** SUBMOD *She was hopelessly impulsive.*

horde /hɔːd/, **hordes.** COUNT N A **horde** is a large crowd of people. *...hordes of screaming children... ...rioting hordes.*

horizon /həraɪzə^{0}n/, **horizons.** 1 COUNT N The **horizon** is the distant line where the sky seems to touch the land or the sea. *...the smoke on the horizon.* 2 PHRASE If something is **on the horizon,** it is going to happen or appear soon. *A new type of drug is on the horizon.* 3 COUNT N Your **horizons** are the limits of what you want to do or of what you are involved in. *...the spontaneous expansion of human horizons.*

horizontal /hɒrɪzɒntə^{0}l/. ADJ Something that is **horizontal** is flat and level with the ground, rather than at an angle to it. *...horizontal stripes.* ♦ **horizontally** ADV *The lower branches spread out almost horizontally.*

hormone /hɔːməʊn/, **hormones.** COUNT N A **hormone** is a chemical produced by your body. *...the male hormone testosterone.* ♦ **hormonal** /hɔːməʊnə^{0}l/ ADJ *...hormonal changes.*

horn /hɔːn/, **horns.** 1 COUNT N The **horn** on a vehicle is the thing that makes a loud noise as a signal or warning. *A car passed him at top speed, sounding its horn.* 2 COUNT N **Horns** are the hard pointed things that stick out of the heads of cows, deer, and some other animals. *...the horns of a bull.* 3 UNCOUNT N **Horn** is the hard substance that the horns of animals are made of. 4 COUNT N A **horn** or a **French horn** is a musical instrument consisting of a long brass tube wound round in a circle with a funnel at the end.

horoscope /hɒrəskəʊp/, **horoscopes.** COUNT N Your **horoscope** is a forecast of future events, based on the position of the stars when you were born.

horrendous /hə^{7}rendəs/. ADJ Something that is **horrendous** is extremely unpleasant and shocking. *...the horrendous murder of a prostitute.*

horrible /hɒrə^{1}bə^{0}l/. 1 ADJ Something that is **horrible** is very unpleasant and causes you to feel shock, fear, or disgust. *The hotel was horrible... I've never had such a horrible meal.* ♦ **horribly** ADV *The man had begun to scream horribly.* 2 ATTRIB ADJ You use **horrible** to emphasize how bad something is. *Everything's in a horrible muddle... I've got a horrible suspicion this thing won't work.* ♦ **horribly** SUBMOD *Everything has gone horribly wrong.*

horrid /hɒrɪd/. ADJ Something or someone that is **horrid** is very unpleasant; an informal use. *...a horrid little flat... I don't mean to be horrid to you.*

horrific /hə^{7}rɪfɪk/. ADJ Something that is **horrific** is so unpleasant that people are horrified and shocked by it. *It was one of the most horrific experiences of my life.*

horrify /hɒrɪfaɪ/, **horrifies, horrifying, horrified.** VB WITH OBJ If you **are horrified** by something, it makes you feel alarmed and upset. *He was horrified by their poverty... Both Mr Faulds and his daughter were horrified at the proposal.* ♦ **horrifying** ADJ *...horrifying stories.*

horror /hɒrə/, **horrors.** 1 UNCOUNT N **Horror** is a strong feeling of alarm caused by something extremely unpleasant. *The boys shrank away in horror.* 2 SING N If you have a **horror** of something, you are afraid of it or dislike it strongly. *Despite a horror of violence, John allowed himself to be drafted into the army.* 3 COUNT N You can refer to extremely unpleasant experiences as **horrors.** *His mind would dwell on the horrors he had been through.* 4 MOD A **horror** film or story is intended to be very frightening.

hors d'oeuvre /ɔːdɜːv/, **hors d'oeuvres.** PLURAL N **Hors d'oeuvres** are dishes of cold food eaten before the main course of a meal.

horse /hɔːs/, **horses.** COUNT N A **horse** is a large animal which you can ride. Some horses are used for pulling ploughs and carts.

horseback /hɔːsbæk/. PHRASE If you are **on horseback,** you are riding a horse. *The crowds were dispersed by policemen on horseback.*

horseshoe /hɔːsʃuː/, **horseshoes.** COUNT N A **horseshoe** is a piece of metal shaped like a U which is fixed to a horse's hoof.

horticulture /hɔːtɪkʌltʃə/. UNCOUNT N **Horticulture** is the study and practice of growing plants. ♦ **horticultural** /hɔːti^{1}kʌltʃərəl/ ADJ *...the Royal Horticultural Society.*

hose /həʊz/, **hoses, hosing, hosed.** 1 COUNT N A **hose** is a long, flexible pipe through which water is carried. 2 VB WITH OBJ If you **hose** something, you wash it or spread water on it using a hose. *Hose the soil well immediately after planting rose bushes.*

hospice /hɒspɪs/, **hospices.** COUNT N A **hospice** is a hospital where dying people receive special care.

hospitable /hɒspɪtəbə^{0}l, hɒspɪt-/. ADJ If you are **hospitable,** you are friendly and welcoming to guests or strangers. *Mr Steinberg was a good-natured and hospitable man... She behaved in a generous and hospitable fashion.*

hospital /hɒspɪtə^{0}l/, **hospitals.** COUNT N OR UNCOUNT N A **hospital** is a place where sick people are looked after by doctors and nurses. *...a psychiatric hospital... I used to visit him in hospital.*

hospitality /hɒspɪtælɪ^{1}ti^{1}/. UNCOUNT N **Hospitality** is friendly, welcoming behaviour towards guests or strangers. *I thanked him for his hospitality.*

hospitalize /hɒspɪtəlaɪz/, **hospitalizes, hospitalizing, hospitalized.** VB WITH OBJ If someone **is hospitalized,** they are sent to hospital; an American use. *She contracted pneumonia and had to be hospitalized.* ♦ **hospitalization** /hɒspɪtəlaɪzeɪʃə^{0}n/ UNCOUNT N *Psychiatrists play safe and opt for hospitalization.*

host /həʊst/, **hosts.** 1 COUNT N The **host** at a party is the person who has invited the guests. *Drinks were being prepared by the host.* 2 MOD A **host** country or organization provides the facilities for an event, or gives people from another country a place to live. *...the attitude of the host community to the refugees.* 3 COUNT N The **host** of a radio or television show is the person who introduces it and talks to the people taking part. 4 SING N A **host** of things is a lot of them; a formal use. *...a host of questions for our experts.*

hostage /hɒstɪdʒ/, **hostages.** COUNT N A **hostage** is someone who has been captured by a person or organization and who may be killed or injured if people do not do what the person or organization wants. *An agreement was reached that freed the 52 hostages* ● If someone **is taken hostage** or **is held hostage,** they are captured and kept as a hostage. *He had been taken hostage by terrorists... They are being held hostage until our demands are met.*

hostel /hɒstə^{0}l/, **hostels.** COUNT N A **hostel** is a house owned by local government authorities or charities where people can stay cheaply for a short time.

hostess /həʊstɪ^{2}s/, **hostesses.** COUNT N The **hostess** at a party is the woman who has invited the guests.

hostile /hɒstaɪl/. 1 ADJ A **hostile** person is unfriendly and aggressive. *Frank was a reserved, almost hostile person... I was in a depressed and hostile mood.* 2 ADJ If you are **hostile** to someone or something, you disagree with them or disapprove of them. *...a new government that is hostile to us.* 3 ADJ **Hostile** situations and conditions make it difficult for you to achieve something. *...hostile weather... ...the problem of running machinery in hostile environments.*

hostility /hɒstɪlɪ^{1}ti^{1}/, **hostilities.** 1 UNCOUNT N **Hostility** is unfriendly and aggressive behaviour. *Their friendship is regarded with suspicion and hostility.* 2 UNCOUNT N **Hostility** is also opposition to something you do not approve of. *American spokesmen made clear their hostility to the new proposals.* 3 PLURAL N You can refer to fighting between two countries or groups as **hostilities;** a formal use. *Both sides wanted a cessation of hostilities.*

hot /hɒt/, **hotter, hottest; hots, hotting, hotted.** 1 ADJ If something is **hot,** it has a high temperature. *The metal is so hot I can't touch it..... ...a fine, hot August day.* 2 PRED ADJ If you are **hot,** your body is at an unpleasantly high temperature. *Hot and perspiring, John toiled up the hill.* 3 ADJ Food that is **hot** has a strong, burning taste caused by spices. *...hot curries.* 4 PRED ADJ If someone is **hot** on something, they know a lot about it; an informal use. *I'm not so hot on linguistic theory.* 5 ADJ Someone with a **hot** temper gets angry very easily.

hot dog, hot dogs. COUNT N A **hot dog** is a long bread roll with a sausage in it.

hotel /h^{0}əʊtel/, **hotels.** COUNT N A **hotel** is a building where people stay, for example when they are on holiday, and pay for their rooms and meals.

hotelier /h^{0}əʊtelɪə/, **hoteliers.** COUNT N A **hotelier** is a person who owns or manages a hotel.

hot line, hot lines. COUNT N A **hot line** is a direct telephone line between heads of government for use in an emergency.

hotly /hɒtli^{1}/. 1 ADV If you say something **hotly,** you say it angrily. *'I don't mind going,' said Jack hotly... ...a claim which the USA has hotly denied.* 2 ADV If something is **hotly** discussed, people discuss it in a lively way, because they feel strongly about it. *...the hotly debated question of abortion.*

hot-water bottle, hot-water bottles. COUNT N A **hot-water bottle** is a rubber container which you fill with hot water and use to warm a bed.

hound /haʊnd/, **hounds, hounding, hounded.** 1 COUNT N A **hound** is a type of dog used for hunting or racing. *...large packs of hounds.* 2 VB WITH OBJ If someone **hounds** you, they constantly disturb you or criticize you. *He was hounded by the press.*

hour /aʊə/, **hours.** 1 COUNT N An **hour** is a period of sixty minutes. *They slept for two hours... We talked for hours.* 2 PLURAL N You can refer to the period of time that something happens each day as the **hours** that it happens. *...our demands for shorter working hours.*

PHRASES ● Something that happens **on the hour** happens at one o'clock, at two o'clock, and so on at regular intervals of one hour. *Buses for London leave on the hour.* ● If something happens in **the small hours,** it happens in the early morning after midnight. *The noise kept him awake until the small hours.* ● See also **eleventh hour, rush hour.**

hourly /aʊəli^{1}/. 1 ATTRIB ADJ An **hourly** event happens once every hour. *There is an hourly bus service.* 2 ATTRIB ADJ Your **hourly** earnings are the amount of money that you earn each hour. *Their average hourly earnings were £5.00.*

house, houses, housing, housed; pronounced /haʊs/ when it is a singular noun and /haʊz/ when it is a verb. The plural of the noun is pronounced /haʊzɪ^{2}z/. 1 COUNT N A **house** is a building in which people live. *He has a house in Pimlico.* ● See also **boarding house, public house.** 2 COUNT N WITH SUPP A **house** is also a company, especially one which publishes books, lends money, or designs clothes. *...a University Publishing House.* 3 COUNT N The people who make a country's laws are often referred to as a **House;** a formal use. *...the House of Assembly... ...twenty-two members drawn from both Houses.* 4 COUNT N In a theatre or cinema, the **house** is the part where the audience sits. *We stood at the back of the packed house.* 5 VB WITH OBJ When someone **is housed,** they are provided with a house or flat. *They are better housed than ever before.* 6 VB WITH OBJ If a building **houses** something, that thing is kept in the building; a formal use. *This is the building which houses the library.*

housebound /haʊsbaʊnd/. ADJ Someone who is **housebound** is unable to leave their house because they are ill or old.

household /haʊshəʊld/, **households.** 1 COUNT N A **household** consists of all the people in a family or group who live together in a house. *He loved being part of a huge household... Only 8 per cent of households owned a fridge.* 2 SING N The **household** is your home and everything connected with looking after it. *My daughter managed the entire household... ...household chores.*

householder /haʊshəʊldə/, **householders.** COUNT N A **householder** is the legal owner or tenant of a house.

housekeeper /haʊskiːpə/, **housekeepers.** COUNT N A **housekeeper** is a person employed to cook and clean a house for its owner.

housekeeping /haʊskiːpɪŋ/. 1 UNCOUNT N **Housekeeping** is the work and organization involved in running a home. 2 SING N The **housekeeping** is the money that you use each week to buy food, cleaning materials, and other things for your home. *She spent all the housekeeping on a new coat.*

house-to-house. ATTRIB ADJ If the police carry out a **house-to-house** search, they search all the houses in an area. *We've not got the manpower to do a house-to-house check.*

housewife /haʊswaɪf/, **housewives.** COUNT N A **housewife** is a married woman who does not have a job outside her home.

housework /haʊswɜːk/. UNCOUNT N **Housework** is the work such as cleaning and cooking that you do in your home. *The men shared all the housework.*

housing /haʊzɪŋ/. 1 COUNT N **Housing** is the buildings that people live in. *...bad housing and poverty... There is a severe housing shortage.* 2 COUNT N OR MOD **Housing** is also the job of providing houses for people to live in. *...the housing department.*

housing estate, housing estates. COUNT N A **housing estate** is a large number of houses or flats built close together at the same time.

hovel /hʌvə^{0}l, hɒv-/, **hovels.** COUNT N A **hovel** is a small, dirty hut or house that people live in and that is in bad condition. *They lived in overcrowded hovels.*

hover /hɒvə/, **hovers, hovering, hovered.** 1 VB When a bird or insect **hovers,** it stays in the same position in the air. 2 VB If someone **is hovering,** they are hesitating about doing something because they cannot make a decision. *A figure hovered uncertainly in the doorway... We hovered between the two possibilities.*

hovercraft /hɒvəkrɑːft/. **Hovercraft** is the singular and plural. COUNT N A **hovercraft** is a vehicle that travels across water by floating on a cushion of air.

how /haʊ/. 1 ADV OR CONJ You use **how** to ask about or refer to the way in which something is done. *How did you know about this?... Tell me how to get there... A lot depends on how the Americans handle the situation.* 2 ADV You use **how** in questions when you are asking someone whether something was successful or enjoyable. *'How did school go?'... How was Paris?* 3 ADV You also use **how** to ask about or refer to someone's health. *'How are you?'—'Fine, thanks.'... I'm going to see how Davis is.* 4 ADV You can use **how** in exclamations to emphasize an adjective, adverb, or statement. *How pretty you look!... How I dislike that man!* 5 ADV You use **how** to ask about or refer to a measurement, amount, or quantity. *How old are you?... How far is Amity from here?... How much does this lot cost?... That shows how much energy is available.* 6 CONVENTION You can say **'How about you?'** when you are asking someone their opinion. *How about you, Dorothy, what do you want?*

however /haʊɛvə/. 1 SENTENCE ADV You use **however** when you are adding a comment which contrasts with what has just been said. *Losing at games doesn't matter to some women. Most men, however, can't stand it.* 2 ADV You can use **however** to emphasize that the degree or extent of something cannot change a situation. *She could not remember, however hard she tried.* 3 PHRASE You use **however many** or **however much** after 'or' at the beginning of a clause to indicate that you do not know the exact quantity or size of something, and that it is not important; an informal use. *...the twelve or eleven people on the jury or however many there are.*

howl /haʊl/, **howls, howling, howled.** 1 VB If a wolf or a dog **howls,** it utters a long, loud crying sound. *Jackals howled among the ruins.* 2 VB If a person **howls,** they weep loudly. *I put back my head and howled.* Also COUNT N *...a howl of pain.* 3 VB When the wind **howls,** it blows hard and makes a loud noise.

howl down. PHR VB If people **howl** you **down,** they shout loudly to stop you speaking. *He was howled down by monarchists.*

HQ, HQs. COUNT N **HQ** is an abbreviation for 'headquarters'.

hr, hrs. hr is a written abbreviation for 'hour'. *He won the Cardiff run in 2hrs 26mins 4secs.*

HRH. TITLE **HRH** is a written abbreviation for 'His Royal Highness' or 'Her Royal Highness'. It is used as part of the title of a prince or princess. *...HRH Prince Charles.*

hub /hʌb/, **hubs.** 1 COUNT N The **hub** of a wheel is the part at the centre. *Attach your lamp to the hub and spin the wheel.* 2 COUNT N WITH 'of' If you describe a place as the **hub** of a district, you mean that it is the most important part. *Amity would one day be the hub of commerce on Long Island.*

huddle /hʌdəl/, **huddles, huddling, huddled.** 1 VB WITH ADJUNCT If you **huddle** somewhere, you sit, stand, or lie there holding your arms and legs close to your body, because you are cold or frightened. *She huddled among the untidy bedclothes.* ♦ **huddled** ADJ *In the evening he would sit huddled near the stove.* 2 COUNT N A **huddle** of people or things is a small group standing or sitting close together. *They flopped down in a huddle... ...a huddle of huts.*

hue /hjuː/, **hues.** COUNT N A **hue** is a colour; a literary use. *Mrs Partridge's face took on a deeper hue.*

huff /hʌf/. PHRASE If someone is **in a huff,** they are behaving in a bad-tempered way because they are annoyed or offended. *The people all left in a huff.*

hug /hʌg/, **hugs, hugging, hugged.** 1 RECIP VB When you **hug** someone, you put your arms around them and hold them tightly because you like them or are pleased to see them. *During our infancy, our parents cuddle and hug us... In an instant we were hugging and kissing.* Also COUNT N *He greeted his mother with a hug.* 2 VB WITH OBJ If you **hug** something, you hold it close to your body with your arms tightly round it. *...a basket which she hugged tight on her lap.*

huge /hjuːdʒ/. ADJ Something that is **huge** is extremely large in size, amount, or degree. *A huge industry has been built up... Huge numbers of children are leaving school.* ♦ **hugely** ADV *...a hugely expensive machine... Gardener was enjoying himself hugely.*

hulk /hʌlk/, **hulks.** COUNT N You can refer to something or someone that is large, clumsy, and heavy as a **hulk.** *The Abbey is a great cross-shaped, blackish hulk.*

hull /hʌl/, **hulls.** COUNT N The **hull** of a boat or ship is the main part of its body.

hullo /həˈləʊ/. See **hello.**

hum /hʌm/, **hums, humming, hummed.** 1 VB If something **hums,** it makes a low continuous noise. *The air-conditioning hummed.* Also SING N *The only sound she heard was the hum of a machine in the basement.* 2 VB WITH OR WITHOUT OBJ When you **hum,** you sing a tune with your lips closed. *I began to hum... She continued to hum the song.*

human /hjuːmən/, **humans.** 1 ADJ **Human** means relating to or concerning people. *He had no regard for human life... ...the human body... ...one of the most exciting periods in human history.* 2 COUNT N You can refer to people as **humans** when you are comparing them with animals or machines. *Could a computer ever beat a human at chess?*

human being, human beings. COUNT N A **human being** is a man, woman, or child.

humane /hjuːmeɪn/. ADJ Someone who is **humane** is kind, thoughtful, and sympathetic. *He's one of the most humane people I have ever worked with... ...the humane treatment of psychiatric patients.* ♦ **humanely** ADV *Animals must be killed humanely.*

humanism /hjuːmənɪzəm/. UNCOUNT N **Humanism** is the belief that people can achieve happiness and fulfilment without having a religion. ♦ **humanist** COUNT N *...the humanist's belief in man.*

humanitarian /hjuːmænɪtɛərɪən/, **humanitarians.** COUNT N A **humanitarian** is someone who works to improve the welfare of mankind. Also ADJ *...liberal and humanitarian opinions.*

humanity /hjuːmænɪti/, **humanities.** 1 UNCOUNT N **Humanity** is the same as **mankind.** *...a crime against humanity.* 2 UNCOUNT N A person's **humanity** is their state of being a human being, rather than an animal or an object; a formal use. *They denied him his humanity.* 3 UNCOUNT N **Humanity** is also the quality of being kind, thoughtful, and sympathetic. *...a man of remarkable humanity.* 4 PLURAL N The **humanities** are subjects such as literature, philosophy, and history which are concerned with human ideas and behaviour. *She has a background in humanities and modern languages.*

humanly /hjuːmənli/. PHRASE If something is **humanly possible,** it is possible or reasonable for people to do it. *You were asked to reply within twenty-four hours whenever this was humanly possible.*

human nature. UNCOUNT N **Human nature** is the natural qualities and behaviour that most people have. *You can't change human nature.*

human race. SING N You can refer to the whole of mankind as the **human race.** *The future of the human race might now be at stake.*

human rights. PLURAL N **Human rights** are the basic rights which all people should have. *...a violation of human rights.*

humble /hʌmbəl/, **humbler, humblest.** 1 ADJ A **humble** person is not proud and does not believe that they are better than other people. *We were taught to be humble, truthful, and generous... Jim bore this with humble patience.* ♦ **humbly** ADV *'You know much more about it, Sir, than I do,' said John humbly.* 2 ADJ People with low social status are sometimes described as **humble;** an old-fashioned use. *...men and women from very humble backgrounds.*

humbug /hʌmbʌg/, **humbugs.** 1 COUNT N A **humbug** is a hard striped sweet that tastes of peppermint. 2 UNCOUNT N **Humbug** is speech or writing that is dishonest and intended to deceive people; an old-fashioned use. *...parliamentary humbug.*

humdrum /hʌmdrʌm/. ADJ Something that is **humdrum** is ordinary and dull. *...their humdrum lives.*

humid /hjuːmɪd/. ADJ In **humid** places, the weather is hot and damp. *...humid jungles.*

humidity /hjuːmɪdɪti/. UNCOUNT N **Humidity** is dampness in the air. *...diseases and weeds, encouraged by heat and humidity.*

humiliate /hjuːmɪlieɪt/, **humiliates, humiliating, humiliated.** VB WITH OBJ If you **humiliate** someone, you say or do something that makes them feel ashamed or foolish. *She had humiliated him in front of his friends.* ♦ **humiliated** ADJ *I could die. I feel so humiliated.*

humiliation /hjuːmɪlieɪʃən/, **humiliations.** UNCOUNT N **Humiliation** is the experience of feeling helpless or stupid. *The prisoners suffered constant public humiliation.*

humility /hjuːmɪlɪti/. UNCOUNT N Someone who has **humility** is not proud and does not believe that they are better than other people. *He has sufficient humility to acknowledge his own imperfections.*

humor /hjuːmə/. See **humour.**

humorous /hjuːmərəs/. ADJ If someone or something is **humorous,** they are amusing and witty. *...humorous books... The pupils were imaginative, quick, and humorous.* ♦ **humorously** ADV *They often humorously referred to themselves as caretakers.*

humour /hjuːmə/, **humours, humouring, humoured;** spelled **humor** in American English. 1 UNCOUNT N **Humour** is the ability to see when something is funny and to say amusing things. *He appealed to them with his direct style and wry humour... ...a great sense of humour.* 2 UNCOUNT N If something has **humour,** it is funny and makes you want to laugh. *She could appreciate the humour of the remark.* 3 UNCOUNT N WITH SUPP If you are in a good **humour,** you feel happy and cheerful. *The work was proceeding with efficiency and good humour.* 4 VB WITH OBJ If you **humour** someone who is behaving strangely, you try to please them, so that they will not become upset. *He had bought it to humour Julie.*

humourless /hjuːməlɪs/; spelled **humorless** in American English. ADJ Someone who is **humourless** is very serious and does not find things amusing.

hump /hʌmp/, **humps, humping, humped.** 1 COUNT N A **hump** is a small hill or raised piece of ground. *...the humps and hollows of the old golf course.* 2 COUNT N A camel's **hump** is the large lump on its back. 3 VB WITH OBJ If you **hump** something heavy somewhere, you carry it there with difficulty; an informal use. *You will probably have to hump your own luggage.*

hunch /hʌntʃ/, **hunches, hunching, hunched.** 1 COUNT N If you have a **hunch** that something is true, you think that it is likely to be true; an informal use. *Morris had a hunch that she was a good cook... Watson frequently acted on a hunch.* 2 VB If you **hunch** somewhere, you draw your shoulders towards each other and lower your chin towards your chest. *I was cold as I hunched over my meagre fire.*

hundred /hʌndrəd/, **hundreds.** 1 A **hundred** or one **hundred** is the number 100. *There are more than two hundred languages spoken in Nigeria.* 2 PLURAL N You can use **hundreds** to mean an extremely large number. *He handed me hundreds of forms.* 3 PHRASE If you say that something is **a hundred per cent** true, you mean that it is completely true; an informal use. *Your assessment of Otto is a hundred per cent wrong... I agree one hundred per cent with Carol.*

hundredth /hʌndrədθ/, **hundredths.** 1 ADJ The **hundredth** item in a series is the one that you count as number one hundred. *...the hundredth anniversary of tennis championships at Wimbledon.* 2 COUNT N A **hundredth** is one of a hundred equal parts of something. *...one hundredth of a second.*

hundredweight /hʌndrədweɪt/, **hundredweights. Hundredweight** can also be the plural. COUNT N A **hundredweight** is a unit of weight equal to 112 pounds in Britain and 100 pounds in the United States. *The tenor bell in St Paul's Cathedral weighs sixty-two hundredweight.*

hung /hʌŋ/. **Hung** is the past tense and past participle of most senses of **hang.**

hunger /hʌŋgə/, **hungers, hungering, hungered.** 1 UNCOUNT N **Hunger** is the feeling of weakness or discomfort that you get when you need something to eat. *Babies show their hunger by waking up to be fed.* 2 UNCOUNT N **Hunger** is also a serious lack of food which causes suffering or death. *There were families dying of hunger and disease.* 3 VB If you **hunger** for or **hunger** after something, you want it very much; a formal use. *...Spaniards who hunger for Flamenco music.* Also UNCOUNT N *What gives people the hunger for power?*

hungry /hʌŋgri/, **hungrier, hungriest.** 1 ADJ When you are **hungry,** you want food. *I'm tired and hungry and I want some supper... ...a hungry baby.* ♦ **hungrily** ADV *I ate hungrily.* 2 ADJ If you are **hungry** for something, you want it very much. *They were hungry for news.*

hung up. ADJ If you are **hung up** on something or **hung up** about it, you are anxious about it; an informal use. *You're hung up about your father.*

hunk /hʌŋk/, **hunks.** COUNT N A **hunk** of something is a large piece of it. *...a hunk of brown bread.*

hunt /hʌnt/, **hunts, hunting, hunted.** 1 VB WITH OR WITHOUT OBJ When people or animals **hunt,** they chase wild animals and kill them. *The men had gone to the forest to hunt wild game... Hyenas usually hunt at night.* Also COUNT N *They sighted a zebra and the hunt began.* 2 VB WITH OR WITHOUT OBJ If you **hunt** for someone or something, you search for them. *Two helicopters were hunting a submarine... The kids hunted for treasure.* Also COUNT N *...the hunt for the missing child.*

hunt down. PHR VB If you **hunt** someone or something **down,** you succeed in finding them after searching for them. *They had hunted down their victims.*

hunter /hʌntə/, **hunters.** 1 COUNT N A **hunter** is a person who hunts wild animals for food or as a sport. 2 COUNT N WITH SUPP People who search for things of a particular kind are often referred to as **hunters.** *...bargain hunters... ...fossil hunters.*

hurdle /hɜːdəl/, **hurdles.** 1 COUNT N A **hurdle** is a difficulty that you must overcome in order to achieve something. *The Government had got over their first important hurdle.* 2 COUNT N **Hurdles** are fences that runners jump over in some races.

hurl /hɜːl/, **hurls, hurling, hurled. 1** VB WITH OBJ If you **hurl** something, you throw it with a lot of force. *I took all his books and hurled them out of the window.* **2** VB WITH OBJ If you **hurl** abuse or insults at someone, you shout abuse or insults at them. *Abuse was hurled at the police.*

hurray /həreɪ/. See **hooray.**

hurricane /hʌrɪkə^{0}n, -keɪn/, **hurricanes.** COUNT N A **hurricane** is a very violent wind or storm. *The island is in the path of the hurricane.*

hurried /hʌrɪd/. ADJ Something that is **hurried** is done very quickly or suddenly. *...a hurried lunch... ...a hurried glance.* ♦ **hurriedly** ADV *He had dressed hurriedly.*

hurry /hʌri^1/, **hurries, hurrying, hurried. 1** VB If you **hurry** somewhere, you go there quickly. *He hurried off down the street... The people hurried home.* **2** VB If you **hurry** to do something, you start doing it as soon as you can. *They hurried to help him.* **3** VB WITH OBJ If you **hurry** someone or something, you try to make them do something more quickly. *Efforts to hurry them only make them angry.* **4** SING N If you are in a **hurry**, you need to do something quickly. If you do something in a **hurry**, you do it quickly. *She was always in a hurry... Otto had to leave in a great hurry... In the middle of all this hurry, he dropped the bag.*

hurry up. PHR VB **1** If you tell someone to **hurry up**, you are telling them to do something more quickly. *Hurry up, it's getting late.* **2** If you **hurry** something **up**, you make it happen faster or sooner than it would have done. *You can hurry the process up by leaving the door open.*

hurt /hɜːt/, **hurts, hurting. Hurt** is used in the present tense of the verb, and is the past tense and past participle. **1** REFL VB OR VB WITH OBJ If you **hurt** yourself or **hurt** a part of your body, you injure yourself. *How did you hurt your finger?* **2** VB If a part of your body **hurts**, you feel pain there. *My leg was beginning to hurt.* **3** VB WITH OBJ If you **hurt** someone else, you cause them pain or upset them. *Did I hurt you?... She was easily hurt by an unkindness... He didn't want to hurt her feelings.* **4** ADJ If you are **hurt**, you have been injured. *The soldier was obviously badly hurt.* **5** ADJ You can also say you are **hurt** when you are upset because of something that someone has said or done. *His mother was deeply hurt... ...a tone of hurt surprise.* **6** UNCOUNT N A feeling of **hurt** is a feeling that you have when you have been treated badly. *...feelings of anger and hurt.* **7** VB WITH OBJ You can say that something **hurts** someone or something when it has a bad effect on them. *These policies could destroy small businesses and hurt consumers.*

hurtful /hɜːtfʊl/. ADJ **Hurtful** remarks or actions upset people. *Some of the things they say are hurtful.*

hurtle /hɜːtə^{0}l/, **hurtles, hurtling, hurtled.** VB If something **hurtles** somewhere, it moves very quickly, often in a dangerous way. *He watched the plane as it hurtled down the runway.*

husband /hʌzbənd/, **husbands.** COUNT N A woman's **husband** is the man she is married to.

hush /hʌʃ/, **hushes, hushing, hushed. 1** CONVENTION If you say **'Hush!'** to someone, you are telling them to be quiet. **2** SING N You say that there is a **hush** when it is quiet and peaceful. *An expectant hush fell on the gathering.*

hush up. PHR VB If people in authority **hush** something **up**, they prevent the public from knowing about it. *The police had hushed the matter up.*

hushed /hʌʃt/; a literary word. **1** ADJ A **hushed** place is quiet and peaceful. *We walked in silence through the hushed valley.* **2** ADJ If you say something in a **hushed** voice, you say it very quietly; *In the hotel lobby, people were talking in hushed tones.*

husk /hʌsk/, **husks.** COUNT N **Husks** are the outer coverings of grains or seeds.

husky /hʌski^1/, **huskier, huskiest.** ADJ If someone's voice is **husky**, it sounds rough or hoarse.

hustle /hʌsə^{0}l/, **hustles, hustling, hustled.** VB WITH OBJ If you **hustle** someone, you make them move quickly, usually by pulling or pushing them. *He hustled Fanny through the door.*

hut /hʌt/, **huts.** COUNT N A **hut** is a small, simple building, often made of wood, mud, or grass.

hybrid /haɪbrɪd/, **hybrids. 1** COUNT N A **hybrid** is an animal or plant bred from two different types of animal or plant; a technical use. Also ADJ *...hybrid roses.* **2** COUNT N Anything that is a mixture of two different things can be called a **hybrid.** *...a hybrid of business and art.* Also ADJ *...hybrid systems of heat storage.*

hydrant /haɪdrənt/, **hydrants.** COUNT N A fire **hydrant** is a pipe in the street which supplies water for putting out fires.

hydro-electric /haɪdrəʊ ɪ^{1}lɛktrɪk/. ATTRIB ADJ **Hydro-electric** power is electrical power obtained from the energy of running water.

hydrogen /haɪdrədʒə^{0}n/. UNCOUNT N **Hydrogen** is the lightest gas and the simplest chemical element in nature.

hygiene /haɪdʒiːn/. UNCOUNT N **Hygiene** is the practice of keeping yourself and your surroundings clean, especially to avoid illness or the spread of diseases. *...personal hygiene.* ♦ **hygienic** /haɪdʒiːnɪk/ ADJ *It's more hygienic to use disposable paper tissues.*

hymn /hɪm/, **hymns.** COUNT N A **hymn** is a song sung by Christians to praise God.

hyper-. PREFIX **Hyper-** is used to form adjectives that describe someone as having too much of a particular quality. For example, someone who is hyper-cautious is too cautious. *Emily is fastidious and hypersensitive.*

hypermarket /haɪpəmɑːkɪt/, **hypermarkets.** COUNT N A **hypermarket** is a very large supermarket.

hyphen /haɪfə^{0}n/, **hyphens.** COUNT N A **hyphen** is a punctuation mark used to join words together. For example, the word 'left-handed' has a hyphen in the middle of it.

hypnosis /hɪpnəʊsɪs/. UNCOUNT N **Hypnosis** is the practice or skill of hypnotizing people. ● If you are **under hypnosis,** you have been hypnotized. *Is it true that a person could be made to commit a crime under hypnosis?*

hypnotic /hɪpnɒtɪk/. ADJ Something that is **hypnotic** makes you feel as if you have been hypnotized. *The rhythmic clapping was having a hypnotic effect on Ginny.*

hypnotism /hɪpnətɪzə^{0}m/. COUNT N **Hypnotism** is the same as **hypnosis.**

hypnotize /hɪpnətaɪz/, **hypnotizes, hypnotizing, hypnotized;** also spelled **hypnotise. 1** VB WITH OBJ If someone **hypnotizes** you, they put you into a state in which you seem to be asleep but in which you can still respond to things that are said to you. *I was able to hypnotize him into doing things against his own will.* **2** VB WITH OBJ If you **are hypnotized** by something, you are so fascinated by it that you cannot think of anything else. *The child was hypnotized by the machine.*

hypochondriac /haɪpəkɒndriæk/, **hypochondriacs.** COUNT N A **hypochondriac** is someone who worries about their health, often when there is nothing wrong with them. *He was a bit of a hypochondriac.*

hypocrisy /hɪpɒkrəsi^1/. UNCOUNT N **Hypocrisy** is behaviour in which someone pretends to have beliefs, principles, or feelings that they do not really have; used showing disapproval. *Many people have dismissed his criticism as hypocrisy.*

hypocrite /hɪpəkrɪt/, **hypocrites.** COUNT N A **hypocrite** is someone who pretends to have beliefs, principles, or feelings that they do not really have; used showing disapproval.

hypocritical /hɪpəkrɪtɪkə^{0}l/. ADJ If someone is being **hypocritical,** they are pretending to have beliefs, principles, or feelings that they do not really have; used showing disapproval. *They send you their love. It would be hypocritical of me to do the same.*

hypodermic /haɪpədɜːmɪk/. ADJ A **hypodermic** needle or syringe is a medical instrument with a hollow needle, which is used to give injections.

hypothesis /haɪpɒθ^{1}sɪs/, **hypotheses** /haɪpɒθ^{1}siːz/. COUNT N A **hypothesis** is an explanation or theory which has not yet been proved to be correct; a formal use. *People have proposed all kinds of hypotheses about what these things are.*

hypothetical /haɪpəθɛtɪkə^{0}l/. ADJ Something that is **hypothetical** is based on possible situations rather than actual ones; a formal use. *Let me put a hypothetical question to you.*

hysteria /hɪstɪərɪə/. **1** UNCOUNT N **Hysteria** among a group of people is a state of uncontrolled excitement, anger, or panic. *...a growing climate of hysteria and racialism... ...this current hysteria about shortage of petrol.* **2** UNCOUNT N A person who is suffering from **hysteria** is in a state of violent and disturbed emotion as a result of shock; a medical use.

hysterical /hɪstɛrɪkə^{0}l/. **1** ADJ Someone who is **hysterical** is in a state of uncontrolled excitement, or of violent and disturbed emotion, for example as a result of shock. *...a mob of hysterical vigilantes... ...Farlow's hysterical letter... ...stress leading to irrational and hysterical behaviour.* ♦ **hysterically** ADV *A man was screaming hysterically.* **2** ADJ **Hysterical** laughter is loud and uncontrolled. ♦ **hysterically** ADV *We laughed hysterically at their startled expressions.* **3** ADJ If you describe something as **hysterical,** you mean that you think it is extremely funny. ♦ **hysterically** SUBMOD *...jokes which people find hysterically funny.*

hysterics /hɪstɛrɪks/. **1** PLURAL N If someone is in **hysterics** or is having **hysterics,** they are in a state of uncontrolled excitement, anger, or panic. *If she didn't get home early, there would probably be hysterics from her mother.* **2** PLURAL N You can also say that someone is in **hysterics** or is having **hysterics** when they are laughing uncontrollably; an informal use. *The audience was in hysterics.*

Ii

I /aɪ/. PRON **I** is used as the subject of a verb. A speaker or writer uses **I** to refer to himself or herself. *I like your dress... He and I were at school together.*

-ibility, -ibilities. SUFFIX **-ibility** is added in place of '-ible' at the end of adjectives to form nouns. Nouns of this kind are often not defined but are treated with the related adjectives. *...the need to provide flexibility... ...the impossibility of any change.*

-ic. SUFFIX **-ic** is added to nouns to form adjectives indicating that someone or something has a particular quality or relates to a particular thing. Adjectives of this kind are often not defined but are treated with the related nouns. *...parasitic insects... ...an opportunistic foreign policy.*

ice /aɪs/, **ices, icing, iced. 1** UNCOUNT N **Ice** is frozen water. **2** UNCOUNT N **Ice** is also pieces of ice used to keep food or drink cool. *...two tall glasses of pineapple juice, soda and ice.* ♦ **iced** ATTRIB ADJ *...an iced beer.* **3** VB WITH OBJ To **ice** cakes means to cover them with icing. **4** COUNT N An **ice** is an ice cream. **5** PHRASE If you **break the ice,** you make people feel relaxed, for example at the beginning of a party. **6** See also **icing.**

ice over or **ice up.** PHR VB If something **ices over** or **ices up,** it becomes covered with ice. *The road becomes treacherous when it is iced over.*

iceberg /aɪsbɜːg/, **icebergs.** COUNT N An **iceberg** is a large, tall mass of ice floating in the sea. ● **tip of the iceberg:** see **tip.**

ice-box, ice-boxes. COUNT N An **ice-box** is a refrigerator; an American use.

ice-cold. ADJ **Ice-cold** means very cold indeed. *...ice-cold beer.*

ice cream, ice creams. 1 UNCOUNT N **Ice cream** is a very cold sweet food made from milk. **2** COUNT N An **ice cream** is a portion of ice cream, usually wrapped in paper or in a container.

ice cube, ice cubes. COUNT N An **ice cube** is a small block of ice that you put into a drink to make it cold.

ice hockey. UNCOUNT N **Ice hockey** is a game like hockey played on ice.

ice lolly, ice lollies. COUNT N An **ice lolly** is a piece of flavoured ice or ice cream on a stick.

ice-skate, ice-skates. COUNT N **Ice-skates** are shoes with metal bars attached to them that you wear when you skate on ice.

ice-skating. UNCOUNT N **Ice-skating** is the activity of skating on ice.

icicle /aɪsɪkə^{0}l/, **icicles.** COUNT N An **icicle** is a long pointed piece of ice hanging from a surface.

icing /aɪsɪŋ/. UNCOUNT N **Icing** is a sweet substance made from powdered sugar that is used to cover cakes. ● If you describe something as **the icing on the cake,** you mean that it is an attractive but unnecessary addition to something.

icon /aɪkɒn/, **icons;** also spelled **ikon.** COUNT N An **icon** is a picture of Christ or a saint painted on a wooden panel. Icons are regarded as holy by some Christians.

icy /aɪsi^1/. **1** ADJ **Icy** air or water is extremely cold. *As I opened the door a gust of icy air struck me.* **2** ADJ An **icy** road has ice on it. **3** ADJ You say that someone's behaviour is **icy** when they show their dislike or anger in a quiet, controlled way. *Bowman spoke with an icy calm.* ♦ **icily** ADV *'That is quite out of the question,' said Thomas icily.*

I'd /aɪd/. **I'd** is the usual spoken form of 'I had', especially when 'had' is an auxiliary verb. **I'd** is also a spoken form of 'I would'. *I'd just had a letter from her... I'd like to make my views clear.*

idea /aɪdɪə/, **ideas. 1** COUNT N An **idea** is a plan or possible course of action. *It's a good idea to get some instruction... I don't like the idea of going to ask for money.* **2** COUNT N Your **idea** of something is your belief about what it is like or what it should be like. *People had some odd ideas about village children... What's your idea of a good party?... They had many ideas on how films should be made.* **3** SING N WITH SUPP If you have an **idea** of something, you know about it to some extent. *He has a good idea of how the Civil Service functions... Have you any idea how much it would cost?* **4** SING N WITH SUPP If you have an **idea** that something is the case, you suspect that it is the case.

My friends had an idea that something was wrong. **5** SING N The **idea** of an action or activity is its aim or purpose. *The idea is to try and avoid further expense.*

ideal /aɪdɪəl/, **ideals. 1** COUNT N An **ideal** is a principle, idea, or standard that seems very good so that you try to achieve it. *He believed in parliamentary democracy as an ideal.* **2** SING N Your **ideal** of something is the person or thing that seems to you to be the best possible example of it. *He idolizes her as his feminine ideal.* **3** ADJ The **ideal** person or thing for a particular purpose is the best one for it. *He is the ideal person for the job.* **4** ATTRIB ADJ An **ideal** society or world is the best possible one that you can imagine.

idealise /aɪdɪəlaɪz/. See **idealize.**

idealism /aɪdɪəlɪzə^{0}m/. UNCOUNT N **Idealism** is the behaviour and beliefs of someone who has ideals and tries to follow them. ♦ **idealist** /aɪdɪəlɪst/. COUNT N *He was an idealist, too good for the world of action.*

idealistic /aɪdɪəlɪstɪk/. ADJ **Idealistic** people base their behaviour on ideals.

idealize /aɪdɪəlaɪz/, **idealizes, idealizing, idealized;** also spelled **idealise.** VB WITH OR WITHOUT OBJ If you **idealize** someone or something, you think of them as perfect or much better than they really are. *Romantic love and motherhood are sentimentally idealized.*

ideally /aɪdɪəli^1/. **1** SENTENCE ADV If you say that **ideally** something should happen, you mean that you would like it to happen, although it may not be possible. *The government should ideally be run by the people.* **2** ADV If someone is **ideally** suited for something, they are as suitable for it as possible. *He considered himself ideally suited for the job.*

identical /aɪdentɪkə^{0}l/. ADJ Things that are **identical** are exactly the same, or are so similar that they seem the same. *...two women in identical pinafores.* ♦ **identically** ADV *All of them were identically dressed for the occasion.*

identical twin, identical twins. COUNT N **Identical twins** are twins of the same sex who look exactly the same.

identifiable /aɪdentɪfaɪəbə^{0}l/. ADJ Something that is **identifiable** can be recognized. *...a much more easily identifiable hand signal.*

identification /aɪdentɪfɪkeɪʃə^{0}n/. **1** UNCOUNT N The **identification** of people or things is the process of recognizing or choosing them. *...the identification of requirements and resources.* **2** UNCOUNT N When someone asks for your **identification,** they are asking to see something such as a driving licence which proves who you are. **3** UNCOUNT N WITH 'with' **Identification** with someone or something is a feeling of sympathy and support for them. *...identification with the People's Republic of China.*

identify /aɪdentɪfaɪ/, **identifies, identifying, identified. 1** VB WITH OBJ If you can **identify** someone or something, you can recognize them and say who or what they are. *The guard had been identified as Victor Kowalski.* **2** VB WITH OBJ If something **identifies** you, it makes it possible for people to recognize you. *Wear on your third finger an iron ring, which will identify you.* **3** VB WITH OBJ If you **identify** with someone or something, you feel that you understand them. *He couldn't identify with other people's troubles.* **4** VB WITH OBJ AND 'with' If you **identify** one thing with another, you consider them to be the same thing; a formal use.

identity /aɪdentɪ^{1}ti^1/, **identities. 1** COUNT N WITH POSS Your **identity** is who you are. *Glenn whipped off the mask to reveal his identity.* **2** COUNT N OR UNCOUNT N The **identity** of a place is the characteristics that it has that distinguish it from other places. *...a region with its own cultural identity.*

identity card, identity cards. COUNT N An **identity card** is a card with a person's name, age, and other information on it, which people in some countries have to carry in order to prove who they are.

ideology /aɪdi^{1}ɒlədʒi^1/, **ideologies.** COUNT N WITH SUPP OR UNCOUNT N An **ideology** is a set of beliefs, especially the political beliefs on which people, parties, or countries base their actions. *...the capitalist ideology of the West.* ♦ **ideological** /aɪdɪəlɒdʒɪkə^{0}l/. ADJ *...the ideological aspects of the dispute.*

idiocy /ɪdɪəsi^1/. UNCOUNT N The **idiocy** of something is the fact that it is very stupid; a formal use. *...the idiocy of the plan.*

idiom /ɪdɪəm/, **idioms.** COUNT N An **idiom** is a group of words which have a different meaning when used together from the one they would have if you took the meaning of each word individually. For example, 'Don't beat about the bush' is an idiom.

idiomatic /ɪdi^{1}ə^{6}mætɪk/. ADJ In **idiomatic** speech or writing, words are used in a way that sounds natural to native speakers of the language. *Her English was fluent and idiomatic.*

idiosyncrasy /ɪdi^{1}ə^{6}sɪnkrəsi^1/, **idiosyncrasies.** COUNT N Someone's **idiosyncrasies** are their own rather unusual habits or likes and dislikes. *She adjusted to her husband's many idiosyncrasies.*

idiosyncratic /ɪdi^{1}ə^{6}sɪnkrætɪk/. ADJ If someone's behaviour or likes and dislikes are **idiosyncratic,** they are personal to them, and are often rather unusual. *...Michelangelo's highly idiosyncratic style of painting.*

idiot /ɪdɪət/, **idiots.** COUNT N If you call someone an **idiot,** you mean that they are very stupid. *That idiot Antonio has gone and locked our door.*

idiotic /ɪdi^{1}ɒtɪk/. ADJ **Idiotic** means very stupid. *It was an idiotic question to ask.*

idle /aɪdə^{0}l/, **idles, idling, idled. 1** ADJ Someone who is **idle** is not doing anything, especially when they should be doing something. *...long, idle conversations.* ♦ **idly** ADV *...those who sit idly by while you slave over a hot stove.* ♦ **idleness** UNCOUNT N *No one can afford to pay troops to sit about in idleness.* **2** PRED ADJ Machines or factories that are **idle** are not being used. *The machinery could not be converted, and so stood idle.* **3** ADJ If you say that it would be **idle** to do something, you mean that nothing useful would be achieved by it; a formal use. *It would be idle to look for a solution at this stage.* **4** ATTRIB ADJ You use **idle** to describe something that you do for no particular reason, often because you have nothing better to do. *Sudhir and Judy carried on long, idle conversations.* ♦ **idly** ADV *She glanced idly down the list of contents.*

idle away. PHR VB If you **idle away** a period of time, you spend it doing very little.

idol /aɪdə^{0}l/, **idols. 1** COUNT N An **idol** is someone such as a film star or pop star, who is greatly admired or loved by the public. *...young pop idols.* **2** COUNT N An **idol** is also a statue that is worshipped by people who believe that it is a god.

idolatry /aɪdɒlətri^1/. UNCOUNT N Someone who practises **idolatry** worships idols; a formal use.

idolize /aɪdəlaɪz/, **idolizes, idolizing, idolized;** also spelled **idolise.** VB WITH OBJ If you **idolize** someone such as a film star or a pop star, you admire them very much. *They idolize Bob Dylan.*

idyll /ɪdɪl/, **idylls.** COUNT N An **idyll** is an idyllic situation. *...the myth of an unchanging idyll of rural England.*

idyllic /ɪ^{5}dɪlɪk/. ADJ Something that is **idyllic** is extremely pleasant and peaceful without any difficulties. *...an idyllic place to raise a young child.*

i.e. /aɪ iː/. **i.e.** is used to introduce a word or sentence expressing what you have just said in a different and clearer way. *To keep a dog costs twice as much, i.e. £110 a year.*

if /ɪf/. **1** CONJ You use **if** in conditional sentences to mention an event or situation that might happen, might be happening, or might have happened. *If all goes well, Voyager 2 will head on to Uranus... If any questions occur to you, then don't hesitate to write... If I could afford it I would buy a boat.* **2** CONJ You also use **if** in indirect questions. *I asked her if I could help her... I wonder if you'd give the children a bath?*
PHRASES ● You use **if not** to suggest, for example, that an amount might be bigger or that a time might be sooner than one you have just mentioned. *They have hundreds of thousands if not millions of pounds of investment... I'd like to see you tonight, if not sooner.* ● You can say **'if I were you'** when you are giving someone advice. *If I were you I'd take the money.* ● You use **'if anything'** when you are saying something which confirms a negative statement that you have just made. *It certainly wasn't an improvement. We were, if anything, worse off than before.* ● You use **if only** when you are mentioning a reason for doing something. *I'll have a glass myself, if only to stop you from drinking it all.* ● You also use **if only** to express a wish or desire, especially one that cannot be fulfilled. *If only she could have lived a little longer.* ● You use **as if** when you are describing the way something is done by comparing it with something else. *She folded her arms as if she were cold.*

igloo /ɪgluː/, **igloos.** COUNT N An **igloo** is a round house made from blocks of snow.

ignite /ɪgnaɪt/, **ignites, igniting, ignited.** ERG VB When you **ignite** something, it starts burning. *The device was supposed to ignite the fireworks.*

ignition /ɪgnɪʃə^{0}n/. SING N The **ignition** is the part of a car's engine which ignites the fuel and starts the car. It is also the keyhole where you put a key in order to start the engine. *Have you switched the ignition on?*

ignoble /ɪgnəʊbə^{0}l/. ADJ An **ignoble** person behaves in a cowardly or morally unacceptable way which makes people lose respect for them; a formal use.

ignominious /ɪgnə^{6}mɪnɪəs/. ADJ **Ignominious** means shameful; a formal use. *The marriage was considered especially ignominious since she was of royal descent.* ♦ **ignominiously** ADV *They were ignominiously defeated in the general election.*

ignorant /ɪgnərənt/. **1** ADJ You say that people are **ignorant** when they behave in a rude way. *She is an ignorant woman.* ♦ **ignorance** /ɪgnərəns/ UNCOUNT N *...the elimination of hunger, sickness, and ignorance.* **2** ADJ If you are **ignorant** of something, you do not know about it. *The masses were largely ignorant of the options open to them.* ♦ **ignorance** UNCOUNT N *Individuals suffer through ignorance of their rights.*

ignore /ɪgnɔː/, **ignores, ignoring, ignored.** VB WITH OBJ If you **ignore** someone or something, you deliberately take no notice of them. *I ignored him and looked at Judith... Ralph ignored Jack's question.*

ikon /aɪkɒn/. See **icon.**

ill /ɪl/, **ills. Worse** is sometimes used as the comparative for meaning 1. **1** ADJ Someone who is **ill** is suffering from a disease or health problem. *I feel ill... She is ill with cancer.* **2** PLURAL N Difficulties or problems can be referred to as **ills;** a literary use. *...the ills of old age.* **3** ADV **Ill** means badly; a literary use. *The programme was ill researched.* **4** ATTRIB ADJ **Ill** also means harmful; a formal or literary use. *Did you get any ill effects when you had your blood transfusion?... ...protection against ill fortune.*
PHRASES ● If you **fall ill** or **are taken ill,** you become ill suddenly. ● If you **speak ill of** someone, you criticize them. ● **ill at ease:** see **ease.**

I'll /aɪl/. **I'll** is the usual spoken form of 'I will' or 'I shall'. *I'll ring you tomorrow morning.*

ill-. Ill- is added to words, especially adjectives and past participles, to add the meaning 'badly' or 'inadequately'. For example, 'ill-written' means badly written.

ill-advised. ADJ An **ill-advised** action is not sensible or wise.

illegal /ɪliːgə^{0}l/. **1** ADJ If an activity, possession, or organization is **illegal,** the law says that it is not allowed. *It is illegal in many countries for women to work on night shifts... Marijuana is illegal in the United States.* ♦ **illegally** ADV *...illegally parked cars.* **2** ATTRIB ADJ An **illegal** immigrant is a person who has entered a country without official permission.

illegible /ɪledʒɪbə^{0}l/. ADJ **Illegible** writing is so unclear that you cannot read it.

illegitimacy /ɪlɪdʒɪtɪməsi^1/. UNCOUNT N **Illegitimacy** is the fact of being born illegitimate. *Victoria was not told of her illegitimacy until she was ten.*

illegitimate /ɪlɪdʒɪtɪmə^{1}t/. **1** ADJ A person who is **illegitimate** was born of parents who were not legally married to each other. *...an illegitimate child.* **2** ADJ Something that is **illegitimate** is not allowed by law. *All parties regarded the treaty as illegitimate.*

ill-equipped. ADJ Someone who is **ill-equipped** to do something does not have the ability, qualities, or equipment necessary to do it. *The police were plainly ill-equipped to deal with the riot.*

ill-fated. ADJ If you describe something as **ill-fated,** you mean that it ended in an unfortunate or tragic way; a literary use. *Alice recounted the story of her ill-fated boating expedition.*

ill-health. UNCOUNT N Someone who suffers from **ill-health** is often ill.

illicit /ɪlɪsɪt/. ATTRIB ADJ An **illicit** activity or substance is not allowed by law, or is not acceptable according to the social customs of a country. *They were prosecuted for illicit liquor selling.*

illiteracy /ɪlɪtə^{0}rəsi^1/. UNCOUNT N **Illiteracy** is the inability of people to read or write. *...the elimination of illiteracy.*

illiterate /ɪlɪtərə^{1}t/. ADJ Someone who is **illiterate** cannot read or write. *40 per cent of the country is reckoned to be illiterate.*

illness /ɪlnɪ^{2}s/, **illnesses. 1** UNCOUNT N **Illness** is the fact or experience of being ill. *I haven't been able to work because of illness.* **2** COUNT N An **illness** is a particular disease such as a cold, measles, or pneumonia. *She died of a mysterious illness.*

illogical /ɪlɒdʒɪkə^{0}l/. ADJ An **illogical** feeling or action is not reasonable or sensible. *It is clearly illogical to maintain such a proposition.*

ill-treat, ill-treats, ill-treating, ill-treated. VB WITH OBJ If someone **ill-treats** you, they treat you cruelly.

illuminate /ɪluːmɪneɪt/, **illuminates, illuminating, illuminated. 1** VB WITH OBJ To **illuminate** something means to shine light on it. *Lamps were arranged to illuminate his work.* ♦ **illuminated** ADJ *...Vienna's most spectacularly illuminated church.* **2** VB WITH OBJ If you **illuminate** something that is difficult to understand, you make it clearer by explaining it or giving examples. *Their doctrine illuminates much that might seem obscure in the Muslim teaching.* ♦ **illuminating** ADJ *...his illuminating book on the subject.*

illumination /ɪluːmɪneɪʃə^{0}n/, **illuminations. 1** UNCOUNT N **Illumination** is the lighting that a place has. *The dusty bulb gave barely adequate illumination.* **2** PLURAL N **Illuminations** are coloured lights which are put up in towns, especially at Christmas, as a decoration.

illusion /ɪlu:ʒən/, **illusions.** 1 COUNT N OR UNCOUNT N An **illusion** is a false idea or belief. *We have an illusion of freedom.* 2 COUNT N An optical **illusion** is something that looks like one thing but is really something else or is not there at all.

illusory /ɪlu:zəri/; a formal word. 1 ADJ Something that is **illusory** seems to exist, but does not really exist. *The difference is largely illusory.* 2 ADJ An **illusory** hope or belief makes you believe in something that does not exist or is not possible. *...illusory hopes that he would soon find a new job.*

illustrate /ɪləstreɪt/, **illustrates, illustrating, illustrated.** 1 VB WITH OBJ If you **illustrate** a point, you make it clear by using examples or stories. *The Muslims tell a story to illustrate the fact that power changes people.* 2 VB WITH OBJ To **illustrate** a book means to put pictures or diagrams into it. ♦ **illustrated** ADJ *...illustrated books of fairy tales.*

illustration /ɪləstreɪʃən/, **illustrations.** 1 COUNT N An **illustration** is an example or story used to make a point clear. *I've included a few specific examples as illustrations of the difficulty of our work.* 2 COUNT N An **illustration** in a book is a picture or diagram. *...a cookery book with marvellous colour illustrations.*

illustrator /ɪləstreɪtə/, **illustrators.** COUNT N An **illustrator** is an artist who draws pictures and diagrams for books and magazines. *...an illustrator of children's books.*

illustrious /ɪlʌstrɪəs/. ATTRIB ADJ An **illustrious** person is famous and distinguished; a formal use.

ill-will. UNCOUNT N **Ill-will** is a feeling of hostility. *He assured me he felt no ill-will toward me.*

I'm /aɪm/. **I'm** is the usual spoken form of 'I am'. *I'm not blaming you... I'm afraid I can't come.*

image /ɪmɪdʒ/, **images.** 1 COUNT N If you have an **image** of someone or something, you have a picture or idea of them in your mind. *To most people, the term 'industrial revolution' conjures up images of smoky steel mills or clanking machines.* 2 COUNT N The **image** of a person or organization is the way that they appear to other people. *His attempts to improve the Post Office's image were criticised as 'gimmicks'.* 3 COUNT N An **image** is also a picture or reflection of someone or something. *He began to dress, never taking his eyes off his image in the mirror.*

imagery /ɪmɪdʒri/. UNCOUNT N **Imagery** is the mental pictures or ideas created by poetic language, art, or music.

imaginable /ɪmædʒɪnəbəl/. ATTRIB ADJ OR ADJ AFTER N You use **imaginable** when referring to the most extreme example of a particular thing that you can think of. *...the narrowest imaginable range of interests... ...the most horrible punishments imaginable.*

imaginary /ɪmædʒɪnəri/. ADJ Something that is **imaginary** exists only in your mind. *Many children develop fears of imaginary dangers.*

imagination /ɪmædʒɪneɪʃən/, **imaginations.** COUNT N OR UNCOUNT N Your **imagination** is your ability to form new ideas or to think about things which do not exist in real life. *He has a marvellous imagination... ...a failure of imagination.*

imaginative /ɪmædʒɪnətɪv/. ADJ Someone who is **imaginative** is able to form ideas of new or exciting things. *...an imaginative writer... ...imaginative and original theories.* ♦ **imaginatively** ADV *...an imaginatively designed bathroom.*

imagine /ɪmædʒɪn/, **imagines, imagining, imagined.** 1 REPORT VB OR VB WITH -ING If you **imagine** a situation, you think about it. *It's hard to imagine a greater biological threat,... Try to imagine you're sitting on a cloud... Can you imagine standing up there and giving a speech?* 2 REPORT VB If you say that someone **imagined** something, you mean that they thought they saw or heard it, although it did not really happen or exist. *'I saw a thing on the mountain.'—'You only imagined it.'* 3 REPORT VB If you say that you **imagine** something is true, you mean that you think it is true. *I should imagine he wants you to hold his hand.*

imbalance /ɪmbæləns/, **imbalances.** COUNT N OR UNCOUNT N If there is an **imbalance** in a situation, things are not evenly or fairly arranged. *...the imbalance between the rich and poor countries.*

imbecile /ɪmbɪsi:l, -saɪl/, **imbeciles.** COUNT N An **imbecile** is a stupid person. *For two years that imbecile spent his money like water.*

imbue /ɪmbju:/, **imbues, imbuing, imbued.** VB WITH OBJ If you **imbue** something with a quality, you fill it with the quality; a formal use. *...Mondrian's desire to imbue his art with mystical properties.*

imitate /ɪmɪteɪt/, **imitates, imitating, imitated.** VB WITH OBJ If you **imitate** someone or something, you copy what they say or do. *He tried to imitate the girl's voice.* ♦ **imitator** /ɪmɪteɪtə/ COUNT N *...successful designers and their imitators.*

imitation /ɪmɪteɪʃən/, **imitations.** 1 COUNT N An **imitation** is a copy of something else. *Computers so far are just bad imitations of our brains.* 2 COUNT N OR UNCOUNT N If you give an **imitation** of someone, you copy the way they speak or behave. *'Come here, my dear,' she said, giving a reasonable imitation of Isabel Travers... Boys can be seen to pat one another on the head in imitation of what their fathers do.* 3 ATTRIB ADJ **Imitation** things are not genuine but are made to look genuine. *...a pocket diary bound in black imitation leather.*

immaculate /ɪmækjələt/. 1 ADJ **Immaculate** means perfectly clean or tidy. *Her apartment was immaculate.* ♦ **immaculately** ADV *Sir Oswald was immaculately dressed.* 2 ADJ **Immaculate** also means without any mistakes. *Your timing and technique will have to be immaculate.*

immaterial /ɪmətɪərɪəl/. ADJ Something that is **immaterial** is not important or not relevant; a formal use. *The price was immaterial.*

immature /ɪmətjʊə, -tʃʊə/. 1 ADJ Something that is **immature** is not yet fully developed. *...the baby's immature digestive system.* 2 ADJ If you describe someone as **immature,** you mean that they do not behave in a sensible and adult way. *...an immature desire to shock.* ♦ **immaturity** /ɪmətjʊərɪti/ UNCOUNT N *...complaints about my immaturity and lack of judgement.*

immeasurable /ɪmeʒərəbəl/. ADJ An amount or distance that is **immeasurable** is too large to be measured or counted. *The gap between them now seems immeasurable.*

immeasurably /ɪmeʒərəbli/. SUBMOD You use **immeasurably** to emphasize that something has a particular quality to a very great extent. *Paul Getty had always been immeasurably wealthy.*

immediacy /ɪmi:dɪəsi/. UNCOUNT N When you talk about the **immediacy** of something, you mean that it seems to be happening now or that it makes you feel directly involved with it; a formal use. *It is the immediacy of events which makes television so popular.*

immediate /ɪmi:dɪət/. 1 ADJ **Immediate** means happening without any delay. *They called for an immediate meeting of the Security Council.* 2 ATTRIB ADJ **Immediate** needs and concerns must be dealt with quickly. *He was occupied with more immediate matters.* 3 ATTRIB ADJ **Immediate** also means next in time or position. *Charlie was more honest than his immediate predecessor... To the immediate south we can see the mountains.* 4 ATTRIB ADJ Your **immediate** family are your close relatives such as your parents, brothers, and sisters.

immediately /ɪmi:dɪətli/. 1 ADV If something happens **immediately,** it happens without any delay. *I have to go to Brighton immediately. It's very urgent.* 2 CONJ You also use **immediately** when you are saying that something happens as soon as something else has happened. *Immediately I finish the show I get changed and go home.* 3 ADV **Immediately** also means next in time or position. *The church is immediately on your right... The sequence of events immediately preceding the tragedy is uncertain.*

immemorial /ɪmɪmɔ:rɪəl/. ATTRIB ADJ You use **immemorial** to describe things which are so old that nobody can remember a time when they did not exist. *...the immemorial custom of all Western societies.* ● If something has been happening **from time immemorial,** it has been happening for longer than anyone can remember.

immense /ɪmens/. ADJ **Immense** means extremely large. *Squids grow to an immense size... This development has been of immense importance.* ♦ **immensity** /ɪmensɪti/. UNCOUNT N WITH SUPP *...the immensity of the building.*

immensely /ɪmensli/. ADV **Immensely** means to a very great extent or degree. *The issue is immensely complex... I enjoyed the course immensely.*

immerse /ɪmɜ:s/, **immerses, immersing, immersed.** 1 REFL VB WITH 'in' If you **immerse** yourself in something, you become completely involved in it. *That year I immersed myself totally in my work.* 2 VB WITH OBJ If you **immerse** something in a liquid, you put it into the liquid so that it is completely covered. ♦ **immersion** /ɪmɜ:ʃən/ UNCOUNT N *You must be baptized by total immersion in our pool.*

immersion heater, immersion heaters. COUNT N An **immersion heater** is an electric heater which provides hot water.

immigrant /ɪmɪgrənt/, **immigrants.** COUNT N An **immigrant** is a person who has come to live in a country from another country. *...a Russian immigrant.*

immigration /ɪmɪgreɪʃən/. 1 UNCOUNT N **Immigration** is the coming of people into a country in order to live and work there. *...government controls on immigration.* 2 UNCOUNT N **Immigration** is also the place at a port, airport, or border where officials check the passports of people coming into a country.

imminent /ɪmɪnənt/. ADJ Something that is **imminent** will happen very soon. *I believed that war was imminent... ...his imminent departure.*

immobile /ɪməʊbaɪl/. ADJ **Immobile** means not moving, or unable to move. *Boylan sat immobile, staring straight ahead... Sea-snakes have fangs that are short and immobile.* ♦ **immobility** /ɪməʊbɪlɪti/ UNCOUNT N *She had drugged herself into immobility.*

immobilize /ɪməʊbɪlaɪz/, **immobilizes, immobilizing, immobilized;** also spelled **immobilise.** VB WITH OBJ If someone or something **is immobilized,** they are unable to move. *When you ring the alarm it immobilizes the lift.*

immodest /ɪmɒdɪst/. 1 ADJ **Immodest** behaviour is embarrassing because people think it is rude. *Breast feeding in public may seem immodest to some people.* 2 ADJ **Immodest** also means boastful. *He said it might be immodest for him to quote the next two lines of the review.*

immoral /ɪmɒrəl/. ADJ If you describe someone or their behaviour as **immoral,** you mean that they are morally wrong. *...the cruel and immoral use of animals in medical research.* ♦ **immorality** /ɪmərælɪti/ UNCOUNT N *...a denunciation of other people's immorality.*

immortal /ɪmɔ:təl/. 1 ADJ When people say that something is **immortal,** they mean that it is famous and will be remembered for a long time. *The play contained one immortal line.* ♦ **immortality** /ɪmɔ:tælɪti/ UNCOUNT N *You're not going to achieve immortality by writing a book like that.* 2 ADJ In stories, someone who is **immortal** lives for ever. *...old legends of immortal creatures.*

immortalize /ɪmɔ:təlaɪz/, **immortalizes, immortalizing, immortalized;** also spelled **immortalise.** VB WITH OBJ To **immortalize** someone or something means to cause them to be remembered for a very long time. *We talked about her gangster parts immortalised on film.*

immovable /ɪmu:vəbəl/. 1 ADJ An **immovable** object is fixed and cannot be moved. *...an immovable pillar.* 2 ADJ **Immovable** attitudes or opinions are firm and will not change. *...immovable conservatism.*

immune /ɪmju:n/. 1 PRED ADJ If you are **immune** to a disease, you cannot be made ill by it. *She thought that women might be immune to lung cancer.* ♦ **immunity** /ɪmju:nɪti/ UNCOUNT N *Babies receive immunity to a variety of infections.* 2 PRED ADJ If you are **immune** to something harmful, it cannot affect you or happen to you. *He was immune to the flattery of political leaders... ...targets that the West had considered immune from air attack.* ♦ **immunity** UNCOUNT N *He had been granted immunity from prosecution.*

immunize /ɪmjənaɪz/, **immunizes, immunizing, immunized;** also spelled **immunise.** VB WITH OBJ If you **are immunized** against a disease, you are made immune to it, usually by being given an injection. *They should have their children immunised against diphtheria.* ♦ **immunization** /ɪmjənaɪzeɪʃən/. UNCOUNT N *Measles can be prevented by immunization.*

immutable /ɪmju:təbəl/. ADJ Something that is **immutable** will never change; a formal use. *...behaving according to a set of immutable rules.*

impact /ɪmpækt/, **impacts.** 1 COUNT N WITH SUPP If something makes an **impact** on a situation or person, it has a strong effect on them. *...the impact of computing on routine office work... British authors make relatively little impact abroad.* 2 UNCOUNT N The **impact** of one object on another is the force with which it hits it. *Many modern bullets produce an explosive effect upon impact.*

impair /ɪmpeə/, **impairs, impairing, impaired.** VB WITH OBJ If you **impair** something, you damage it so that it stops working properly; a formal use. *His digestion had been impaired by his recent illness.* ♦ **impaired** ADJ *...children with impaired hearing.*

impale /ɪmpeɪl/, **impales, impaling, impaled.** VB WITH OBJ OR REFL VB If you **impale** something, you stick a sharp pointed object through it; a formal use. *He cut off a piece of the meat and impaled it on his fork.*

impart /ɪmpɑ:t/, **imparts, imparting, imparted;** a formal word. 1 VB WITH OBJ If you **impart** information to someone, you tell it to them. *He had a terrible piece of news to impart.* 2 VB WITH OBJ If something **imparts** a particular quality, it gives that quality to something else. *Carrots impart a delicious flavour to stews.*

impartial /ɪmpɑ:ʃəl/. ADJ Someone who is **impartial** is able to act fairly because they are not personally involved in a situation. *He gave an impartial view of the state of affairs in Northern Ireland.* ♦ **impartially** ADV *These men will judge the people impartial-*

ly. ♦ **impartiality** /ɪmpɑːʃiælɪ¹ti¹/ UNCOUNT N *The BBC was dedicated to impartiality.*

impassable /ɪmpɑːsəbə⁰l/. ADJ If a road or path is **impassable,** you cannot use it because it is blocked or in bad condition.

impasse /ɒmpæs/. SING N An **impasse** is a difficult situation in which it is impossible to make any progress; a formal use. *The government had reached an impasse.*

impassioned /ɪmpæʃənd/. ADJ When you speak in an **impassioned** way, you express powerful emotion; a formal use. *After three hours of impassioned debate the motion was defeated.*

impassive /ɪmpæsɪv/. ADJ If your face is **impassive,** it does not show any emotion.

impatient /ɪmpeɪʃənt/. 1 ADJ If you are **impatient,** you are annoyed because you have had to wait too long for something. *The Englishman became impatient.* ♦ **impatiently** ADV *Oliver stood waiting impatiently.* ♦ **impatience** /ɪmpeɪʃəns/ UNCOUNT N *Chris watched me with some impatience.* 2 ADJ If you are **impatient** to do something, you are eager to do it. If you are **impatient** for something to happen, you want it to happen immediately. *Philip was impatient to inspect his place of work.* ♦ **impatiently** ADV *He looked forward impatiently to Kumar's next visit.* ♦ **impatience** UNCOUNT N *He was awaiting the outcome with impatience.*

impeccable /ɪmpekəbə⁰l/. ADJ Something that is **impeccable** is perfect. *He had impeccable manners.* ♦ **impeccably** ADV *As usual, he was impeccably dressed.*

impede /ɪmpiːd/, **impedes, impeding, impeded.** VB WITH OBJ To **impede** someone or something means to make their movement or development difficult; a formal use. *...procedures that would impede an effective investigation.*

impediment /ɪmpedɪmə²nt/, **impediments.** 1 COUNT N If something is an **impediment** to a person or thing, it makes their movement or development difficult; a formal use. *The new taxes were a major impediment to economic growth.* 2 COUNT N A speech **impediment** is a disability such as a stammer which makes speaking difficult.

impel /ɪmpel/, **impels, impelling, impelled.** VB WITH OBJ When an emotion **impels** you to do something, you feel forced to do it; a formal use. *I feel impelled to express grave doubts about the project.*

impending /ɪmpendɪŋ/. ATTRIB ADJ You use **impending** to describe something that will happen very soon; a formal use. *...impending disaster.*

impenetrable /ɪmpenɪtrəbə⁰l/. 1 ADJ An **impenetrable** wall or barrier is impossible to get through. 2 ADJ **Impenetrable** also means impossible to understand. *The law seems mysterious and impenetrable.*

imperative /ɪmperətɪv/, **imperatives.** 1 ADJ If you say that it is **imperative** that something is done, you are emphasizing that it must be done. *It's imperative that we take care of Liebermann immediately.* 2 COUNT N In grammar, an **imperative** is a verb in the form that is typically used for giving instructions or making informal invitations. For example, in 'Turn left at the next crossroads' and 'Have another biscuit', 'turn' and 'have' are imperatives.

imperceptible /ɪmpəseptɪbə⁰l/. ADJ Something that is **imperceptible** is so small or slight that it exists or happens without being felt or noticed. *...an almost imperceptible sensation.* ♦ **imperceptibly** ADV *The room had grown imperceptibly warmer.*

imperfect /ɪmpɜːfɪ²kt/. 1 ADJ Something that is **imperfect** has faults. *We live in an imperfect society.* 2 SING N In grammar, the **imperfect** or the **imperfect tense** is used in describing continuous or repeated actions in the past. It is also called the 'past continuous'.

imperfection /ɪmpə⁵fekʃə⁰n/, **imperfections.** UNCOUNT N OR COUNT N An **imperfection** is a fault or weakness. *Americans do not tolerate such imperfections in themselves.*

imperfectly /ɪmpɜːfɪktli¹/. ADV If you do something **imperfectly,** you do not do it completely or satisfactorily. *...a world which we only imperfectly understand.*

imperial /ɪmpɪərɪəl/. 1 ATTRIB ADJ **Imperial** means belonging or relating to an empire, emperor, or empress. *...the decline of Britain as an imperial power... ...the Imperial Palace.* 2 ATTRIB ADJ The **imperial** system of measurement uses miles, feet, and inches, pounds and ounces, and gallons and pints.

imperialism /ɪmpɪərɪəlɪzə⁰m/. UNCOUNT N **Imperialism** is a system in which a rich and powerful country controls other countries. *...the struggle against imperialism.* ♦ **imperialist** /ɪmpɪərɪəlɪst/ ADJ OR COUNT N *...imperialist powers... ...rival imperialists.*

imperil /ɪmperɪ¹l/, **imperils, imperilling, imperilled;** spelled **imperiling** and **imperiled** in American English. VB WITH OBJ Something that **imperils** you puts you in danger; a formal use.

imperious /ɪmpɪərɪəs/. ADJ An **imperious** person is proud and expects to be obeyed; a formal use.

impersonal /ɪmpɜːsənə⁰l/. 1 ADJ An **impersonal** place or activity makes you feel that you are not important and do not matter. *...a vast, impersonal organization... ...dull, repetitive, impersonal work.* 2 ADJ **Impersonal** also means not concerned with any particular person. *...impersonal selection procedures.*

impersonate /ɪmpɜːsəneɪt/, **impersonates, impersonating, impersonated.** VB WITH OBJ If you **impersonate** someone, you pretend to be that person, either to deceive people or to entertain them. *I ought to be arrested for impersonating an officer.* ♦ **impersonation** /ɪmpɜːsəneɪʃə⁰n/ COUNT N OR UNCOUNT N *...his impersonation of a Russian prince... ...our powers of impersonation.*

impertinent /ɪmpɜːtɪnənt/. ADJ Someone who is being **impertinent** is not being polite or respectful. *It would be rather impertinent of me to express an opinion... ...impertinent questions.* ♦ **impertinence** /ɪmpɜːtɪnəns/ UNCOUNT N *They might be offended by such impertinence.*

impervious /ɪmpɜːvɪəs/. 1 ADJ If you are **impervious** to someone's actions, you are not affected by them. *They were impervious to any outside pressures.* 2 ADJ If something is **impervious** to water, water cannot pass through it.

impetuous /ɪmpetjʊəs/. ADJ Someone who is **impetuous** acts quickly and suddenly without thinking.

impetus /ɪmpɪ²təs/. UNCOUNT N WITH SUPP The **impetus** of something is the strong effect it has in causing something to happen. *The present conflict might provide fresh impetus for peace talks.*

impinge /ɪmpɪnd⁰ʒ/, **impinges, impinging, impinged.** VB WITH 'on' OR 'upon' Something that **impinges** on you has an effect on you, often by restricting the way that you can behave; a formal use. *Your political opinions will necessarily impinge on your public life.*

implacable /ɪmplækəbə⁰l/. ADJ Someone who is **implacable** has strong feelings of anger or dislike that you cannot change. *...our most implacable opponent... ...the implacable hatred that workers feel for their employers.*

implant, implants, implanting, implanted; pronounced /ɪmplɑːnt/ when it is a verb, and /ɪmplɑːnt/ when it is a noun. 1 VB WITH OBJ To **implant** something into a person's body means to put it there by means of an operation. 2 COUNT N An **implant** is something implanted into a person's body. *...hormone implants.*

implausible /ɪmplɔːzə¹bə⁰l/. ADJ Something that is **implausible** is not easy to believe, and unlikely to be true. *...a very implausible romantic thriller.*

implement, implements, implementing, implemented; pronounced /ɪmplɪ¹mə²nt/ when it is a verb and /ɪmplɪ¹mənt/ when it is a noun. 1 VB WITH OBJ If you **implement** a plan, system, or law, you carry it out. *...policies that they would like to see implemented.* ♦ **implementation** /ɪmplɪ¹mə²nteɪʃə⁰n/ UNCOUNT N *...the implementation of the desired reforms.* 2 COUNT N An **implement** is a tool or other piece of equipment. *...basic agricultural implements.*

implicate /ɪmplɪkeɪt/, **implicates, implicating, implicated.** VB WITH OBJ If you **implicate** someone in an unpleasant event or situation, you show that they were involved in it. *He was implicated in the murder of a teacher.*

implication /ɪmplɪkeɪʃə⁰n/, **implications.** COUNT N An **implication** is something suggested or implied by a situation, event, or statement. *Spencer began to query the political implications of Macaulay's statement.*

implicit /ɪmplɪsɪt/. 1 ADJ **Implicit** criticisms or attitudes are expressed in an indirect way. *...advertisements containing implicit racial prejudice.* ♦ **implicitly** ADV *Mr Biffen implicitly criticised the idea.* 2 ADJ If you have an **implicit** belief or faith in something, you believe it completely and have no doubts about it. ♦ **implicitly** ADV *I believe implicitly in the concept of Europe.*

implore /ɪmplɔː/, **implores, imploring, implored.** VB WITH OBJ AND TO-INF If you **implore** someone to do something, you beg them to do it; a formal use. *She implored me to come.*

imply /ɪmplaɪ/, **implies, implying, implied.** 1 REPORT VB If you **imply** that something is true, you suggest that it is true without actually saying so. *At one point she implied she would marry me... In Malta this gesture implies heavy sarcasm.* ♦ **implied** ADJ *...implied criticism.* 2 REPORT VB If a situation **implies** that something is the case, it makes it seem that it is the case. *These discoveries imply that the sea-bed is rich in fossil fuels.*

impolite /ɪmpəlaɪt/. ADJ **Impolite** behaviour is rude and offends people. *It was very impolite of him to ask.*

import, imports, importing, imported; pronounced /ɪmpɔːt/ when it is a verb and /ɪmpɔːt/ when it is a noun. 1 VB WITH OBJ When goods or services **are imported,** they are bought from another country and sent to your own country. *He tried to import orchids to England... ...imported sugar.* ♦ **importation** /ɪmpɔːteɪʃə⁰n/ UNCOUNT N *...the illegal importation of drugs into Britain.* 2 COUNT N **Imports** are products or raw materials bought from another country for use in your own country.

important /ɪmpɔːtənt/. 1 ADJ Something that is **important** is very significant, valuable, or necessary. *This is the most important part of the job... It is important to get on with your employer and his wife.* ♦ **importantly** ADV *The problems the Chinese face differ importantly from those facing Africa.* ♦ **importance** /ɪmpɔːtəns/ UNCOUNT N WITH SUPP *...the importance of mathematics to science... ...Stonehenge's historic importance.* 2 ADJ An **important** person has influence or power. *...the list of important people who are coming on state visits.* ♦ **importance** UNCOUNT N *Was he related to anyone of importance?*

importer /ɪmpɔːtə/, **importers.** COUNT N An **importer** is a person, country, or business that buys goods or services from another country for use in their own country.

impose /ɪmpəʊz/, **imposes, imposing, imposed.** 1 VB WITH OBJ If you **impose** something on people, you force them to accept it. *She was a harsh mother and imposed severe discipline on her children... ...the proposal to impose a 20p admission charge for museums.* ♦ **imposition** /ɪmpəzɪʃə⁰n/ UNCOUNT N *...the imposition of a wages freeze.* 2 VB If someone **imposes** on you, they expect you to do something for them which you do not want to do. *She would hate to feel that she was imposing on anyone.* ♦ **imposition** COUNT N *I'd be so grateful, though really it's an imposition.*

imposing /ɪmpəʊzɪŋ/. ADJ Someone or something that is **imposing** has an impressive appearance or manner. *Mrs Sabawala's house was large and imposing.*

impossible /ɪmpɒsə¹bə⁰l/. 1 ADJ Something that is **impossible** cannot be done, cannot happen, or cannot be believed. *It was an impossible task... Staying awake all night was virtually impossible.* ♦ **impossibly** SUBMOD *He had impossibly thin legs.* ♦ **impossibility** /ɪmpɒsəbɪlɪ¹ti¹/ UNCOUNT N *...the impossibility of change.* 2 ADJ You can say that a situation or person is **impossible** when they are very difficult to deal with. *They are in an impossible position on this matter... You're an impossible man to please.* ♦ **impossibly** SUBMOD *Flats make life impossibly restrictive for energetic young children.*

impostor /ɪmpɒstə/, **impostors;** also spelled **imposter.** COUNT N An **impostor** is someone who pretends to be someone else in order to get what they want.

impotent /ɪmpətənt/. 1 ADJ You say that someone is **impotent** when they have no power over people or events; a formal use. *Those who do not conform must be rendered impotent.* ♦ **impotence** /ɪmpətəns/ UNCOUNT N *...the inadequacies of planning law and the impotence of planners.* 2 ADJ If a man is **impotent,** he is unable to reach an orgasm when having sex. ♦ **impotence** UNCOUNT N

impound /ɪmpaʊnd/, **impounds, impounding, impounded.** VB WITH OBJ If policemen or other officials **impound** something that you own, they legally take possession of it; a formal use. *Security Police had come to our house and impounded all our belongings.*

impoverish /ɪmpɒvə⁰rɪʃ/, **impoverishes, impoverishing, impoverished.** VB WITH OBJ To **impoverish** someone or something means to make them poor. *They were impoverished by a prolonged spell of unemployment... ...an impoverished Third World country.* ♦ **impoverishment** /ɪmpɒvə⁰rɪʃmə²nt/ UNCOUNT N *...a period of very severe impoverishment.*

impracticable /ɪmpræktɪkəbə⁰l/. ADJ If a course of action is **impracticable,** it cannot be carried out. *It would be impracticable to ban all food additives.*

impractical /ɪmpræktɪkə⁰l/. ADJ An **impractical** idea or course of action is not sensible, realistic, or practical. *...a totally impractical view.*

imprecise /ɪmprɪsaɪs/. ADJ Something that is **imprecise** is not clear or accurate. *...imprecise data.*

impregnable /ɪmpregnəbə⁰l/. ADJ Something that is **impregnable** is so strong or solid that it cannot be broken into. *...an impregnable fortresses.*

impregnate /ɪmpregneɪt/, **impregnates, impregnating, impregnated.** VB WITH OBJ If you **impregnate** something with a substance, you make the substance pass into it and spread through it. *...paper that has been impregnated with chemicals.*

impresario /ɪmprɪ²sɑːrɪ¹əʊ/, **impresarios.** COUNT N An **impresario** is a person who arranges for plays, concerts, and musicals to be performed.

impress /ɪmprɛs/, **impresses, impressing, impressed.** 1 VB WITH OBJ If you **impress** someone, you make them admire and respect you. *I was hoping to impress my new boss with my diligence... I was greatly impressed by the pianist.* 2 VB WITH OBJ AND 'on' OR 'upon' If you **impress** something on someone, you make them understand the importance of it; a formal use. *She impressed on the Government the danger of making too many cuts.*

impression /ɪmprɛʃən/, **impressions.** 1 COUNT N Your **impression** of someone or something is the way they seem to you. *They give the impression of not working... I had the impression that he didn't trust me.* 2 COUNT N An **impression** is also an amusing imitation of a well-known person. *Have you seen her impressions of the TV newscasters?*
PHRASES • If you are **under the impression** that something is true, you believe it is true. *They were under the impression I had come to stay.* • If you **make an impression,** you have a strong effect on people, causing them to remember you. *She did not fail to make an impression.*

impressionable /ɪmprɛʃənəbəl/. ADJ Someone who is **impressionable** is easy to influence. *...an impressionable young girl.*

impressive /ɪmprɛsɪv/. ADJ Someone or something that is **impressive** impresses people. *The list of speakers was impressive.* ♦ **impressively** ADV *...an impressively large mansion.*

imprint, imprints, imprinting, imprinted; pronounced /ɪmprɪnt/ when it is a noun and /ɪmprɪnt/ when it is a verb. 1 COUNT N If something leaves an **imprint** on your mind or on a place, it has a strong effect on it. *These things have left a deep imprint on our thinking... The town still bears the imprint of its industrial origins.* 2 VB WITH OBJ If something **is imprinted** on your memory, you cannot forget it. *This sunset will be forever imprinted in my mind.* 3 COUNT N An **imprint** is a mark made by the pressure of an object on a surface. *In its centre was the imprint of his hand.* 4 VB WITH OBJ If an object **is imprinted** onto a surface, it is pressed hard onto the surface so that it leaves a mark. *...the hand imprinted in the sand.*

imprison /ɪmprɪzən/, **imprisons, imprisoning, imprisoned.** VB WITH OBJ To **imprison** someone means to lock them up in a prison. ♦ **imprisonment** /ɪmprɪzənmənt/ UNCOUNT N *They were sentenced to life imprisonment.*

improbable /ɪmprɒbəbəl/. ADJ Something that is **improbable** is unlikely to be true or to happen. *His explanation seems highly improbable.*

impromptu /ɪmprɒmptjuː/. ADJ An **impromptu** activity is not planned or organized. *I got drawn into a kind of impromptu party downstairs.*

improper /ɪmprɒpə/. 1 ADJ If you describe someone's behaviour as **improper,** you mean that it is rude or shocking. *Charlotte thought my mirth improper.* 2 ADJ **Improper** activities are illegal or dishonest. *...allegations of improper business dealings.* ♦ **improperly** ADV *There were charges that Hugel had improperly provided them with cash.* 3 ADJ **Improper** conditions or methods of treatment are not suitable or adequate. *...the cruel and improper treatment of cattle.* ♦ **improperly** ADV *Bottled milk, improperly handled, is a lethal carrier of disease.*

improve /ɪmpruːv/, **improves, improving, improved.** 1 ERG VB If something **improves** or is **improved,** it gets better. *The weather improved later in the day... These houses have been improved by the addition of bathrooms... Improved health and education are urgently needed.* ♦ **improvement** /ɪmpruːvmənt/ UNCOUNT N OR COUNT N *...the gradual improvement of relations between East and West... ...improvements in living conditions.* 2 ERG VB If you **improve** at a skill, you get better at it. *She went to the club to improve her tennis... His French was improving.* 3 VB WITH 'on' OR 'upon' If you **improve** on an achievement, you achieve a better standard or result than the previous one. *He thinks he's improving on my work.*

improvise /ɪmprəvaɪz/, **improvises, improvising, improvised.** 1 VB WITH OR WITHOUT OBJ When you **improvise,** you make something using whatever materials you have rather than the proper ones, or you carry out an activity without planning it in advance. *We had to improvise as we went along... The sisters helped me improvise a toilet.* ♦ **improvised** ADJ *Tanks were crossing the river on improvised bridges.* 2 VB WITH OR WITHOUT OBJ When actors or musicians **improvise,** they make up the words or music while they are performing. ♦ **improvisation** /ɪmprəvaɪzeɪʃən/ UNCOUNT N OR COUNT N *There was a good deal of improvisation... ...his improvisations on the organ.*

imprudent /ɪmpruːdənt/; a formal use. ADJ **Imprudent** behaviour is not sensible or careful. *It would be imprudent of you to make enemies.*

impudent /ɪmpjədənt/. ADJ Someone who is **impudent** behaves or speaks rudely or in a way that shows disrespect. *The impudent child extended her legs across my lap.*

impulse /ɪmpʌls/, **impulses.** 1 COUNT N An **impulse** is a sudden desire to do something. *I had a sudden impulse to turn around and walk out.* • If you do something **on impulse,** you do it suddenly without planning it. 2 COUNT N An **impulse** is also a short electrical signal sent along a wire or nerve or through the air.

impulsive /ɪmpʌlsɪv/. ADJ Someone who is **impulsive** does things suddenly without thinking about them first. *We must do nothing foolish or impulsive.* ♦ **impulsively** ADV *She kissed him impulsively.*

impunity /ɪmpjuːnɪti/. PHRASE If you do something wrong **with impunity,** you are not punished for it; a formal use. *Landlords were simply ignoring the law with impunity.*

impure /ɪmpjʊə/. 1 ADJ A substance that is **impure** is not of good quality because it has other substances mixed with it. 2 ADJ **Impure** thoughts and actions are concerned with sex and are regarded as sinful.

impurity /ɪmpjʊərɪti/, **impurities.** COUNT N **Impurities** are substances that are present in another substance, making it of a low quality. *There are traces of impurities in the gold.*

in /ɪn/. 1 PREP OR ADV Something that is **in** something else is enclosed by it or surrounded by it. *We put them away in a big box... We've just found a body in the water... She opened her bag and put her diary in.* 2 PREP If something is **in** a place, it is there. *I wanted to play in the garden... She locked herself in the bathroom... In Hamburg the girls split up... I could not sleep because of the pain in my feet.* 3 ADV If you are **in,** you are present at your home or place of work. *He's never in when I phone.* 4 ADV When someone comes **in,** they enter a room or building. *There was a knock at Howard's door. 'Come in,' he shouted... He had his meals brought in.* 5 ADV If a train, boat, or plane is **in** or has come **in,** it has arrived. *The train's not in yet.* 6 PREP Something that is **in** a window, especially a shop window, is just behind the window so that you can see it from outside. *How much is the hat in the window?* 7 PREP When you see something **in** a mirror, you see its reflection. 8 PREP Someone who is **in** a piece of clothing is wearing it. *Martin was in his pyjamas.* 9 PREP If something is **in** a book, film, play, or picture, you can read it or see it there. *She dies in the last act... In Chapter 7 this point is discussed in detail.* 10 PREP If you are **in** a play, race, or other activity, you are one of the people taking part. *She took part in a marathon.* 11 PREP If something happens **in** a particular year, month, or season, it happens during that time. *In 1872, Chicago was burned to the ground... It'll be warmer in the spring.* 12 PREP If you do something **in** a particular period of time, that is how long it takes you to do it. *I told him the money would be paid back in six months.* 13 PREP If something will happen **in** a particular length of time, it will happen after that length of time. *In another five minutes it'll be pitch dark.* 14 PREP If you are **in** a particular state or situation, that is your present state or situation. *We are in a position to advise our Indian friends.* 15 PREP You use **in** to mention the feeling or emotion that causes someone to behave in a particular way. *He shook his head in admiration... In his excitement, Billy had forgotten the letter.* 16 PREP You use **in** to specify a general subject or field of activity. *...recent advances in mathematics... He plans to make his career in music.* 17 PREP You use **in** to indicate how many people or things do something. *Students flocked to the SDP in considerable numbers.* 18 PREP You use **in** to indicate approximate ages or temperatures. For example, if someone is **in** their fifties, they are between 50 and 59 years old. If the temperature is **in** the seventies, it is between 70 and 79 degrees. *In her twenties and thirties she had had no difficulty in finding jobs.* 19 PREP You use **in** to indicate how something is expressed. *I need your complaints in writing... She spoke in a calm, friendly voice... They were speaking in French.* 20 PREP You use **in** to describe the arrangement or shape of something. *The students sit in a circle on the floor.* 21 PREP You use **in** to specify what something relates to. *It grew to eight metres in length... We need a change in direction.* 22 ADJ Something that is **in** is fashionable; an informal use. *Bright colours are in this year.* 23 ADV When the sea or tide comes **in,** the sea moves towards the shore rather than away from it.
PHRASES • You use **in that** to explain a statement you have just made. *He's a good listener in that he never interrupts you with thoughts of his own.* • If you say that someone **is in for** a shock or a surprise, you mean they are going to experience it. • If someone **has it in for** you, they dislike you and try to cause problems for you; an informal use. • If you are **in on** something, you are involved in it or know about it.

in.; The plural can be **in.** or **ins. In.** is a written abbreviation for 'inch'. *...6 x 4 ins.*

in-. PREFIX **In-** is added to words to form other words that have the opposite meaning. For example, something that is incorrect is not correct. *He was obviously insincere... 'No, Father,' she said, almost inaudibly.*

inability /ɪnəbɪlɪti/. UNCOUNT N WITH TO-INF Someone's **inability** to do something is the fact that they are unable to do it. *She despises her husband for his inability to work.*

inaccessible /ɪnəksɛsəbəl/. 1 ADJ An **inaccessible** place is impossible or very difficult to reach. *...the most inaccessible reaches of the jungle.* 2 ADJ If something such as music or art is **inaccessible,** it is hard for people to understand or appreciate; a formal use. *The music of Bartok is considered inaccessible by many people.*

inaccuracy /ɪnækjərəsi/, **inaccuracies.** 1 UNCOUNT N The **inaccuracy** of something is the fact that it is inaccurate. *...the inaccuracy of my estimates.* 2 COUNT N An **inaccuracy** is a statement that is inaccurate. *The report contained a number of inaccuracies.*

inaccurate /ɪnækjərɪt/. ADJ Something that is **inaccurate** is not correct in some way. *...a wildly inaccurate editorial.*

inaction /ɪnækʃən/. UNCOUNT N If you refer to someone's **inaction,** you mean that they are doing nothing. *We do not accept this as an excuse for government inaction.*

inactive /ɪnæktɪv/. ADJ A person, animal, or thing that is **inactive** is not doing anything. *Crocodiles are inactive for long periods.* ♦ **inactivity** /ɪnæktɪvɪti/ UNCOUNT N *...a time of inactivity.*

inadequacy /ɪnædɪkwəsi/, **inadequacies.** 1 UNCOUNT N The **inadequacy** of something is the fact that there is not enough of it or that it is not good enough. *...the inadequacy of education facilities in Britain.* 2 UNCOUNT N If someone has feelings of **inadequacy,** they feel they do not have the qualities necessary to do something or to cope with life. 3 COUNT N An **inadequacy** is a weakness or fault in a person or thing. *...the inadequacies of a superficial education.*

inadequate /ɪnædɪkwət/. 1 ADJ If something is **inadequate,** there is not enough of it or it is not good enough. *His income is inadequate to meet his basic needs... ...an inadequate lunch.* ♦ **inadequately** ADV *...inadequately heated accommodation.* 2 ADJ If someone feels **inadequate,** they feel that they do not have the qualities necessary to do something or to cope with life. *He makes me feel totally inadequate.*

inadvertently /ɪnədvɜːtəntli/. ADV If you do something **inadvertently,** you do it without intending to. *...a dog that has been kicked inadvertently by a friend.*

inadvisable /ɪnədvaɪzəbəl/. ADJ A course of action that is **inadvisable** is not sensible and should not be done. *It is inadvisable to plant lettuces too early.*

inane /ɪneɪn/. ADJ **Inane** remarks or actions are silly.

inanimate /ɪnænɪmət/. ADJ An **inanimate** object has no life.

inappropriate /ɪnəprəʊprɪət/. ADJ Something that is **inappropriate** is not suitable for a particular occasion. *...inappropriate clothes.*

inarticulate /ɪnɑːtɪkjələt/. ADJ If you are **inarticulate,** you cannot express yourself easily in speech.

inasmuch /ɪnəzmʌtʃ/; also spelled **in as much.** CONJ You use **inasmuch** as when you are giving the reason for something; a formal use. *This was important inasmuch as it showed just what human beings were capable of.*

inattentive /ɪnətɛntɪv/. ADJ Someone who is **inattentive** is not paying attention. *...children who are inattentive and doing poorly in school.*

inaudible /ɪnɔːdəbəl/. ADJ **Inaudible** means not loud enough to be heard. *Her voice became inaudible.*

inaugural /ɪnɔːgjərəl/. ATTRIB ADJ An **inaugural** meeting or speech is the first one of a new organization or leader. *...his inaugural address as President.*

inaugurate /ɪnɔːgjəreɪt/, **inaugurates, inaugurating, inaugurated.** 1 VB WITH OBJ When a new leader is **inaugurated,** they are established in their new position at an official ceremony. ♦ **inauguration** /ɪnɔːgjəreɪʃən/ UNCOUNT N *...the inauguration of a new President.* 2 VB WITH OBJ If you **inaugurate** a system or organization, you start it; a formal use.

inborn /ɪmbɔːn/. ADJ **Inborn** qualities are ones with which you are born. *...our inborn hatred for freaks and outcasts.*

inbuilt /ɪmbɪlt/. ADJ An **inbuilt** quality is one that someone or something has from the time they were born or produced. *The child has got an inbuilt feeling of inferiority.*

incalculable /ɪŋˈkælkjələbəl/. ADJ Something that is **incalculable** is so great that it cannot be estimated. *The loss to the race as a whole is incalculable.*

incantation /ɪŋkænteɪʃən/, **incantations.** COUNT N An **incantation** is a magic spell that is chanted or sung.

incapable /ɪŋˈkeɪpəbəl/. PRED ADJ WITH 'of' Someone who is **incapable** of doing something is unable to do it. *She is incapable of grasping what self-discipline means.*

incapacitate /ɪŋkəpæsɪteɪt/, **incapacitates, incapacitating, incapacitated.** VB WITH OBJ If you **are incapacitated** by something, it weakens you so much that you cannot do things; a formal use. *...those not yet incapacitated by seasickness.*

incapacity /ɪŋkəpæsɪti/. UNCOUNT N The **incapacity** of a person, society, or system is their inability to do something; a formal use. *...her incapacity to forgive herself.*

incarcerate /ɪŋˈkɑːsəreɪt/, **incarcerates, incarcerating, incarcerated.** VB WITH OBJ If someone **is incarcerated,** they are put in prison; a formal use. ♦ **incarceration** /ɪŋˈkɑːsəreɪʃən/ UNCOUNT N *...the incarceration of political dissenters.*

incarnation /ɪŋkɑːneɪʃən/, **incarnations.** COUNT N An **incarnation** is one of the lives that a person has, according to some religions.

incendiary /ɪnsendjəri/. ATTRIB ADJ **Incendiary** attacks or weapons involve setting fire to something. *...an incendiary bomb.*

incense, incenses, incensing, incensed; pronounced /ɪnsens/ when it is a noun and /ɪnsens/ when it is a verb. 1 UNCOUNT N **Incense** is a substance that is burned for its sweet smell, often during a religious ceremony. 2 VB WITH OBJ Something that **incenses** you makes you extremely angry; a formal use. *The proposed pay freeze has incensed the men.*

incentive /ɪnsentɪv/, **incentives.** COUNT N OR UNCOUNT N An **incentive** is something that encourages you to do something. *Money is being used as an incentive... He has no incentive to make permanent improvements.*

inception /ɪnsepʃən/. UNCOUNT N WITH POSS The **inception** of an institution or activity is its start; a formal use.

incessant /ɪnsesənt/. ADJ An **incessant** activity never stops. *...long centuries of almost incessant warfare.* ♦ **incessantly** ADV *She drank tea incessantly.*

incest /ɪnsest/. UNCOUNT N **Incest** is the crime of having sex with a close relative.

incestuous /ɪnsestjuəs/. 1 ADJ An **incestuous** relationship is one involving incest. 2 ADJ An **incestuous** group of people is a small group of people who all know each other well and do not associate with anyone outside the group.

inch /ɪntʃ/, **inches, inching, inched.** 1 COUNT N An **inch** is a unit of length, equal to approximately 2.54 centimetres. *Five inches of snow had fallen.* 2 ERG VB WITH ADJUNCT If you **inch** somewhere, you move there very slowly and carefully. *You can only enter the caves by inching through a narrow tunnel on your stomach... Howard inched the van forward.*

incidence /ɪnsɪdəns/. SING N WITH 'of' The **incidence** of something is how often it occurs. *There is a high incidence of heart disease among middle-aged men.*

incident /ɪnsɪdənt/, **incidents.** COUNT N An **incident** is an event, especially one involving something unpleasant; a formal use. *...a shooting incident.*

incidental /ɪnsɪdentəl/. ATTRIB ADJ Something that is **incidental** occurs in connection with something more important. *...incidental expenses.*

incidentally /ɪnsɪdentəli/. SENTENCE ADV You use **incidentally** when you add information or change the subject. *Incidentally, I suggest that you have the telephone moved to the sitting-room.*

incinerate /ɪnsɪnəreɪt/, **incinerates, incinerating, incinerated.** VB WITH OBJ If you **incinerate** something, you burn it completely; a formal use. *Tons of paper are incinerated every year.*

incinerator /ɪnsɪnəreɪtə/, **incinerators.** COUNT N An **incinerator** is a furnace for burning rubbish.

incipient /ɪnsɪpɪənt/. ATTRIB ADJ **Incipient** means starting to happen or appear; a formal use. *...incipient baldness.*

incision /ɪnsɪʒən/, **incisions.** COUNT N An **incision** is a careful cut made in something, for example by a surgeon; a formal use.

incisive /ɪnsaɪsɪv/. ADJ **Incisive** speech or writing is clear and forceful. *...an incisive critique of our society.*

incite /ɪnsaɪt/, **incites, inciting, incited.** VB WITH OBJ If you **incite** people to do something violent or to hate someone, you encourage them to do this. *...inciting people to acts of violence... He was accused of inciting violence.* ♦ **incitement** /ɪnsaɪtmənt/ UNCOUNT N *...incitement to murder.*

inclination /ɪŋklɪneɪʃən/, **inclinations.** COUNT N OR UNCOUNT N An **inclination** is a feeling that makes you want to act in a particular way. *Some parents have no time or inclination to play with their children.*

incline, inclines, inclining, inclined; a formal word, pronounced /ɪŋˈklaɪn/ when it is a noun and /ɪŋˈklaɪn/ when it is a verb. 1 COUNT N An **incline** is a slope. *They walked down a steep incline.* 2 VB WITH OBJ If you **incline** your head, you bend your neck so that your head is leaning forward.

inclined /ɪŋˈklaɪnd/. 1 PRED ADJ WITH TO-INF If you are **inclined** to behave in a particular way, you often behave in that way, or you want to do so. *My father was inclined to be very moody.* 2 PRED ADJ Someone who is mathematically or artistically **inclined** has a natural ability to do mathematics or art.

include /ɪŋˈkluːd/, **includes, including, included.** 1 VB WITH OBJ If one thing **includes** another, it has the other thing as one of its parts. *The four-man crew included one Briton... The proposals included the nationalization of major industries.* 2 VB WITH OBJ AND ADJUNCT If you **include** one thing in another, you make it part of the second thing. *Carpets and curtains are to be included in the purchase price.*

included /ɪŋˈkluːdɪd/. ADJ AFTER N You use **included** to emphasize that someone or something is part of a group. *All of us, myself included, had been totally committed to the project.*

including /ɪŋˈkluːdɪŋ/. PREP You use **including** when mentioning one or more members of a group. *Nine persons were injured, including two wounded by gunfire.*

inclusion /ɪŋˈkluːʒən/. UNCOUNT N The **inclusion** of one thing in another involves making it a part of the second thing. *...the inclusion of the Old Testament in the Christian Bible.*

inclusive /ɪŋˈkluːsɪv/. 1 ADJ An **inclusive** price includes payment for all parts of something or for a particular part. *All prices are inclusive of the return flights from London.* 2 ADJ AFTER N You use **inclusive** to indicate that the things mentioned are included in a series, as well as the things between them. *...ages 17 to 27 inclusive.*

incoherent /ɪŋˈkəʊhɪərənt/. ADJ If someone is **incoherent,** they are talking in an unclear way. *He was incoherent with joy.*

income /ɪŋˈkəm/, **incomes.** COUNT N A person's **income** is the money that they earn or receive.

incoming /ɪŋˈkʌmɪŋ/. 1 ATTRIB ADJ **Incoming** means coming in to a place. *...incoming passengers... ...incoming data.* 2 ATTRIB ADJ An **incoming** official or government has just been appointed or elected.

incomparable /ɪŋˈkɒmpərəbəl/. ADJ Something that is **incomparable** is very good or great in degree; a formal use. *...a movement of incomparable grace... ...a writer of incomparable prose.* ♦ **incomparably** SUBMOD *...an incomparably superior education.*

incompatible /ɪŋˈkəmpætəbəl/. ADJ Two things that are **incompatible** cannot exist or work together. *Their styles of life were incompatible... His actions are totally incompatible with the group's safety.*

incompetent /ɪŋˈkɒmpɪtənt/. ADJ Someone who is **incompetent** does their job badly. *Our secret services are completely incompetent.* ♦ **incompetence** /ɪŋˈkɒmpɪtəns/ UNCOUNT N *Graffman fired him for incompetence.*

incomplete /ɪŋˈkəmpliːt/. ADJ Something that is **incomplete** does not have all the parts that it should have or has not been finished. *...this short and incomplete account of my life.*

incomprehensible /ɪŋˈkɒmprɪhensəbəl/. ADJ Something that is **incomprehensible** is impossible to understand.

incomprehension /ɪŋˈkɒmprɪhenʃən/. UNCOUNT N **Incomprehension** is the state of being unable to understand something. *He went on staring in incomprehension.*

inconceivable /ɪŋˈkənsiːvəbəl/. ADJ If you describe something as **inconceivable,** you think it is impossible. *He found it inconceivable that Belov was insane.*

inconclusive /ɪŋˈkənkluːsɪv/. ADJ If something such as a discussion or experiment is **inconclusive,** it does not lead to any decision or result.

incongruous /ɪŋˈkɒŋgruːəs/. ADJ Something that is **incongruous** seems strange because it does not fit in with the rest of the situation. *He was an incongruous figure among the tourists.* ♦ **incongruously** ADV *...a fat lady, dressed incongruously in black satin.* ♦ **incongruity** /ɪŋˈkɒŋgruːɪti/ UNCOUNT N OR COUNT N *We were both conscious of the incongruity of the situation... ...looking for contradictions and incongruities.*

inconsequential /ɪŋˈkɒnsɪkwenʃəl/. ADJ Something that is **inconsequential** is not very important. *...some inconsequential conversation.*

inconsiderable /ɪŋˈkənsɪdərəbəl/. PHRASE If you describe something as **not inconsiderable,** you mean that it is large. *The country's not inconsiderable army was mobilized.*

inconsiderate /ɪŋˈkənsɪdərət/. ADJ **Inconsiderate** people do not care how their behaviour affects other people.

inconsistent /ɪŋˈkənsɪstənt/. 1 ADJ If people are **inconsistent,** they behave differently in similar situations; used showing disapproval. *The blame was laid on an inconsistent government... Some of your answers are rather inconsistent.* ♦ **inconsistency** /ɪŋˈkənsɪstənsi/ COUNT N OR UNCOUNT N *His life was full of inconsistencies... ...the complete inconsistency between the two views expressed by John.* 2 PRED ADJ WITH 'with' Something that is **inconsistent** with a particular set of ideas or values is not in accordance with them. *...a monarch whose behaviour they judged to be inconsistent with Hindu religious values.*

inconspicuous /ɪŋˈkənspɪkjuːəs/. ADJ Something that is **inconspicuous** is not at all noticeable. *I have asked the children to make themselves as inconspicuous as possible.*

incontinent /ɪŋˈkɒntɪnənt/. ADJ Someone who is **incontinent** is unable to control their bladder or bowels.

inconvenience /ɪŋˈkənviːnjəns, -viːnɪəns/, **inconveniences, inconveniencing, inconvenienced.** 1 UNCOUNT N OR COUNT N If something causes **inconvenience,** it causes problems or difficulties. *I'm very sorry to have caused so much inconvenience... You have to put up with these inconveniences as best you can.* 2 VB WITH OBJ If you **inconvenience** someone, you cause problems or difficulties for them.

inconvenient /ɪŋˈkənviːnjənt, -viːnɪənt/. ADJ Something that is **inconvenient** causes problems or difficulties for you. *I seem to have come at an inconvenient time.*

incorporate /ɪŋˈkɔːpəreɪt/, **incorporates, incorporating, incorporated.** 1 VB WITH OBJ AND 'into' OR 'in' If one thing **is incorporated** into another, it becomes a part of the second thing. *...legislation compelling manufacturers to incorporate safety features in all new cars.* ♦ **incorporation** /ɪŋˈkɔːpəreɪʃən/ UNCOUNT N *...the incorporation of Austria into the German Empire.* 2 VB WITH OBJ If one thing **incorporates** another, it includes the second thing as one of its parts. *These houses usually incorporated a long gallery.*

incorrect /ɪŋˈkərekt/. ADJ Something that is **incorrect** is wrong or untrue. *Sonny dismissed the information as incorrect... ...incorrect English.* ♦ **incorrectly** ADV *The problem has been incorrectly defined.*

incorrigible /ɪŋˈkɒrɪdʒəbəl/. ADJ Someone who is **incorrigible** has faults that will never change; a formal use. *...incorrigible criminals.*

incorruptible /ɪŋˈkərʌptəbəl/. ADJ Someone who is **incorruptible** cannot be bribed or persuaded to do things that they should not do.

increase, increases, increasing, increased; pronounced /ɪŋˈkriːs/ when it is a noun and /ɪŋˈkriːs/ when it is a verb. 1 ERG VB If something **increases,** it becomes larger in amount. *Crime has increased by three per cent in the past year... ...men seeking to increase their knowledge.* ♦ **increased** ADJ *...increased productivity.* ♦ **increasing** ADJ *Japanese industry is making increasing use of robots.* 2 COUNT N An **increase** is a rise in the number, level, or amount of something. *They demanded a sharp increase in wages.* 3 PHRASE If something is **on the increase,** it is becoming more frequent. *Crime is on the increase.*

increasingly /ɪŋˈkriːsɪŋli/. SUBMOD OR ADV You use **increasingly** to indicate that a situation or quality is becoming greater in intensity or more common. *It was becoming increasingly difficult to find jobs... Men increasingly find that they need more training.*

incredible /ɪŋˈkredəbəl/. 1 ADJ Something that is **incredible** is amazing or very difficult to believe. *It was an incredible experience... ...an incredible story.* ♦ **incredibly** SENTENCE ADV *Upstairs, incredibly, the beds were already made.* 2 ADJ **Incredible** also means very great in amount or degree. *They get an incredible amount of money.* ♦ **incredibly** SUBMOD *The water was incredibly hot.*

incredulous /ɪŋˈkredjələs/. ADJ If someone is **incredulous,** they cannot believe what they have just heard. *'You left her all alone?' He sounded incredulous.* ♦ **incredulously** ADV *I stared at him incredulously.* ♦ **incredulity** /ɪŋˈkrɪdjuːlɪti/ UNCOUNT N *I read the document with incredulity.*

increment /ɪŋˈkrəmənt/, **increments.** COUNT N An **increment** is an addition to something, especially a regular addition to someone's salary.

incriminate /ɪŋ1krɪmɪneɪt/, **incriminates, incriminating, incriminated.** VB WITH OBJ If something **incriminates** you, it indicates that you are the person responsible for a crime. *They raided his laboratory to seize any papers that might incriminate them.* ♦ **incriminating** ADJ *...incriminating evidence.*

incubate /ɪŋ1kjə4beɪt/, **incubates, incubating, incubated;** a technical word. 1 ERG VB When a bird **incubates** its eggs or when they **incubate,** it keeps them warm until they hatch. 2 VB The time that an infection or virus takes to **incubate** is the time that it takes to develop and affect someone.

incubator /ɪŋ1kjə4beɪtə/, **incubators.** COUNT N An **incubator** is a piece of hospital equipment in which a sick or weak newborn baby is kept.

inculcate /ɪŋ1kʌlkeɪt, ɪŋ1kʌlkeɪt/, **inculcates, inculcating, inculcated.** VB WITH OBJ AND 'in' OR 'into' If you **inculcate** an idea in someone, you teach it to them so that it becomes fixed in their mind; a formal use. *We want to inculcate the values of marriage and family life into our children.*

incumbent /ɪŋ1kʌmbənt/, **incumbents;** a formal word. 1 PRED ADJ If it is **incumbent** on you to do something, it is your duty to do it. 2 COUNT N An **incumbent** is the person who is holding a particular post. *...the new incumbent.*

incur /ɪŋ1kɜː/, **incurs, incurring, incurred.** VB WITH OBJ If you **incur** something, especially something unpleasant, it happens to you because of what you do; a formal use. *...the risk of incurring her displeasure... ...business expenses incurred outside the office.*

incurable /ɪŋ1kjʊərəbə0l/. 1 ADJ An **incurable** disease cannot be cured. *...incurable cancer.* 2 ATTRIB ADJ You can use **incurable** to describe people with a fixed attitude or habit. *...incurable optimists.*

incursion /ɪŋ1kɜːʃə0n/, **incursion.** COUNT N WITH SUPP An **incursion** is a small military invasion; a formal use. *...their incursion into Yugoslavia.*

indebted /ɪndetɪ2d/. 1 PRED ADJ WITH PREP 'to' If you are **indebted** to someone, you owe them gratitude for something. *I am indebted to Bob Walter for many of the ideas expressed here.* ♦ **indebtedness** UNCOUNT N *I readily acknowledge my indebtedness to my friends.* 2 PRED ADJ If you are **indebted,** you owe someone money; an American use. *His company became indebted to the bank.* ♦ **indebtedness** UNCOUNT N *Home ownership involves higher indebtedness than renting.*

indecent /ɪndiːsənt/. ADJ Something that is **indecent** is shocking, usually because it relates to sex or nakedness. *...indecent jokes.* ♦ **indecency** /ɪndiːsənsi1/ UNCOUNT N *...laws against public indecency.*

indecipherable /ɪndɪsaɪfə0rəbə0l/. ADJ If writing is **indecipherable,** you cannot read it; a formal use.

indecision /ɪndɪsɪʒə0n/. UNCOUNT N **Indecision** is uncertainty about what you should do.

indecisive /ɪndɪsaɪsɪv/. ADJ If you are **indecisive,** you find it difficult to make decisions.

indeed /ɪndiːd/. 1 SENTENCE ADV You use **indeed** to emphasize what you are saying. *'I think you knew him.'—'I did indeed.'... Thank you very much indeed.* 2 SENTENCE ADV You also use **indeed** when adding information which strengthens the point you have already made. *This act has failed to bring women's earnings up to the same level. Indeed the gulf is widening.* 3 SENTENCE ADV You can also use **indeed** to express anger or scorn; used in speech. *'She wants to go too.'—'Does she indeed!'*

indefatigable /ɪndi1fætɪgəbə0l/. ADJ People who are **indefatigable** never get tired of doing something; a formal use. *She was an indefatigable traveller.*

indefensible /ɪndi1fensəbə0l/. ADJ Statements, actions, or ideas that are **indefensible** are wrong and cannot be justified; a formal use. *He denounced the judge's savage attack as totally indefensible.*

indefinable /ɪndi1faɪnəbə0l/. ADJ A quality or feeling that is **indefinable** cannot easily be described.

indefinite /ɪndefɪnɪ1t/. 1 ADJ If something is **indefinite,** people have not decided when it will end. *...an indefinite strike.* 2 ADJ If something such as a plan is **indefinite,** it is not exact or clear. *Milner advised him not to answer so indefinite a proposal.*

indefinite article, indefinite articles. COUNT N In grammar, the words 'a' and 'an' are sometimes called **indefinite articles.** In this dictionary, 'a' and 'an' are called determiners.

indefinitely /ɪndefɪnɪ1tli1/. ADV If something will continue **indefinitely,** it will continue until there is a reason for it to change or end.

indelible /ɪndelɪbə0l/. 1 ADJ If a mark or stain is **indelible,** it cannot be removed or washed out. *His fingertips had turned an indelible black.* 2 ADJ **Indelible** memories will never be forgotten.

indentation /ɪndenteɪʃə0n/, **indentations.** COUNT N An **indentation** is a dent in the surface or edge of something; a formal use. *The high heels of her boots made little indentations in the carpet.*

independence /ɪndɪpendəns/. 1 UNCOUNT N If a country has **independence,** it is not ruled by any other country. *The country has had 24 years of independence.* 2 UNCOUNT N If you refer to someone's **independence,** you are referring to the fact that they do not rely on other people. *She shows great independence of mind.*

independent /ɪndɪpendənt/. 1 ADJ Something that is **independent** exists, happens, or acts separately from other people or things. *Two independent studies came to the same conclusions... ...20 clinics which are independent of the National Health Service.* ♦ **independently** ADV *Agriculture developed independently in many different parts of the globe.* 2 ADJ Someone who is **independent** does not rely on other people. *I became financially independent.*

indescribable /ɪndɪ2skraɪbəbə0l/. ADJ Something that is **indescribable** is too intense or extreme to be described. *The smell was indescribable.*

indestructible /ɪndɪ2strʌktə1bə0l/. ADJ Something that is **indestructible** cannot be destroyed.

indeterminate /ɪndi1tɜːmɪnət/. ADJ If something is **indeterminate,** you cannot say exactly what it is. *...a figure of indeterminate sex.*

index /ɪndeks/, **indexes** or **indices** /ɪndɪsiːz/. The plural is usually **indexes** for meanings 1 and 2, and **indices** for meaning 3. 1 COUNT N An **index** is an alphabetical list at the back of a book saying where particular things are referred to in the book. 2 COUNT N A card **index** is a set of cards with information on them, arranged in alphabetical order. 3 COUNT N An **index** is also a system by which changes in the value of something can be compared or measured. *...a 0.3 per cent rise in the wholesale prices index.*

index finger, index fingers. COUNT N Your **index finger** is next to your thumb.

Indian /ɪndi /, **Indians.** 1 ADJ **Indian** means belonging or relating to India. 2 COUNT N An **Indian** is a person who comes from India. 3 COUNT N An **Indian** is also someone descended from the people who lived in North, South, or Central America before Europeans arrived.

indicate /ɪndɪkeɪt/, **indicates, indicating, indicated.** 1 REPORT VB If something **indicates** a fact or situation, it shows that it exists. *These studies indicate that it's best to change your car every two years... This absurd action indicated the level of their intelligence.* 2 REPORT VB If you **indicate** a fact, you mention it in a rather indirect way. *As I have already indicated, there is now more competition for jobs than there used to be... I indicated that I had not seen enough of his work to be able to judge it.* 3 VB WITH OBJ If you **indicate** something to someone, you point to it. *She sat down in the armchair that Mrs Jones indicated.* 4 VB When a driver **indicates,** flashing lights on the car show which way he or she is going to turn.

indication /ɪndɪkeɪʃə0n/, **indications.** COUNT N OR UNCOUNT N An **indication** is a sign which gives you an idea of what someone feels, what is happening, or what is likely to happen. *The President gave a clear indication yesterday of his willingness to meet the visitors... There was no indication that he ever noticed my absence.*

indicative /ɪndɪkətɪv/. 1 PRED ADJ WITH 'of' If something is **indicative** of the existence or nature of something, it is a sign of it. *He regarded their action as indicative of their lack of courage.* 2 SING N If a verb is in the **indicative,** it is in the form used for making statements, as opposed to the imperative or interrogative forms.

indicator /ɪndɪkeɪtə/, **indicators.** 1 COUNT N WITH SUPP An **indicator** of something tells you whether it exists or what it is like; a formal use. *Price is not always an indicator of quality.* 2 COUNT N A car's **indicators** are the lights used to show when it is turning left or right.

indices /ɪndɪsiːz/. **Indices** is a plural of **index.**

indict /ɪndaɪt/, **indicts, indicting, indicted.** VB WITH OBJ When someone **is indicted** for a crime, they are officially charged with it; a formal use.

indictment /ɪndaɪtmənt/, **indictments.** 1 COUNT N WITH SUPP If you say that a fact or situation is an **indictment** of something, you mean that it shows how bad that thing is. *It is a striking indictment of our educational system that so many children cannot read or write.* 2 COUNT N OR UNCOUNT N An **indictment** is a criminal charge against someone; a formal use. *The indictment was read to the jury... Robbins is under indictment for fraud.*

indifferent /ɪndɪfə0rənt/. 1 ADJ If you are **indifferent** to something, you have no interest in it. *Children fail to progress if their parents seem indifferent to their success.* ♦ **indifferently** ADV *She looked at me indifferently as I pulled up a stool.* ♦ **indifference** /ɪndɪfə0rəns/ UNCOUNT N *...Aitken's indifference to criticism.* 2 ADJ **Indifferent** also means of a rather low standard. *He was an indifferent actor.*

indigenous /ɪndɪdʒɪnəs/. ADJ Something that is **indigenous** comes from the country in which it is found; a formal use. *...the indigenous population... The elephant is indigenous to India.*

indigestible /ɪndɪdʒestəbə0l/. ADJ Food that is **indigestible** cannot be digested easily.

indigestion /ɪndɪdʒestʃə0n/. UNCOUNT N **Indigestion** is pain that you get when you cannot digest food. *Food that is too fatty may cause indigestion.*

indignant /ɪndɪgnənt/. ADJ If you are **indignant,** you are shocked and angry. *Many taxpayers are indignant at what they regard as an illegal use of public funds.* ♦ **indignantly** ADV *'Why not?' cried Judy indignantly.*

indignation /ɪndɪgneɪʃə0n/. UNCOUNT N **Indignation** is shock and anger. *She seethed with indignation.*

indignity /ɪndɪgnɪ1ti1/, **indignities.** COUNT N OR UNCOUNT N An **indignity** is something that makes you feel embarrassed or humiliated. *He hated the rules and the petty indignities of prison life... ...the indignity of slavery.*

indigo /ɪndɪgəʊ/. ADJ Something that is **indigo** is dark purple. *...an indigo sky.*

indirect /ɪndaɪrekt/. 1 ADJ Something that is **indirect** is not done or caused directly, but by means of something or someone else. *A sudden increase in oil prices would have serious indirect effects.* ♦ **indirectly** ADV *I suppose I was indirectly responsible for the whole thing.* 2 ADJ An **indirect** route or journey does not use the shortest way between two places. 3 ADJ An **indirect** answer or reference does not directly mention the thing that is actually being talked about.

indirect object. See **object.**

indiscreet /ɪndɪskriːt/. ADJ If you are **indiscreet,** you talk about or do things openly when you should keep them secret. *...an indiscreet comment.*

indiscretion /ɪndɪskreʃə0n/, **indiscretions.** UNCOUNT N OR COUNT N **Indiscretion** is careless behaviour which is disapproved of. *How could she commit such an indiscretion?*

indiscriminate /ɪndɪskrɪmɪnɪ1t/. ADJ An **indiscriminate** action does not involve any careful choice. *Television watchers tend to be indiscriminate in their viewing habits.* ♦ **indiscriminately** ADV *He reads widely and indiscriminately.*

indispensable /ɪndɪspensəbə0l/. ADJ If something is **indispensable,** it is absolutely essential. *In my job, a telephone is indispensable.*

indisputable /ɪndɪspjuːtəbə0l/. ADJ If a fact is **indisputable,** it is obviously and definitely true. *We're going to have a very hard time. That's indisputable.* ♦ **indisputably** ADV *The book is indisputably a masterpiece.*

indistinct /ɪndɪstɪŋkt/. ADJ Something that is **indistinct** is unclear and difficult to see or hear. *His words were faint and often indistinct.*

indistinguishable /ɪndɪstɪŋgwɪʃəbə0l/. ADJ If two things are **indistinguishable** from each other, they are so similar that it is impossible to tell them apart.

individual /ɪndɪvɪdjʊ0əl/, **individuals.** 1 ATTRIB ADJ **Individual** means relating to one person or thing, rather than to a large group. *...individual tuition... We can identify each individual whale by its song.* ♦ **individually** ADV *Each fruit should be wrapped individually in paper.* 2 COUNT N An **individual** is a person. *...the freedom of the individual.*

individualist /ɪndɪvɪdjə4lɪst/, **individualists.** COUNT N If you are an **individualist,** you like to do things in your own way. *Academics are such individualists.* ♦ **individualistic** /ɪndɪvɪdjə4lɪstɪk/ ADJ *Lions are highly individualistic animals.*

individuality /ɪndɪvɪdjuːælɪ1ti1/. UNCOUNT N If something has **individuality,** it is different from all other things and is therefore interesting. *The advertisement lacks any individuality.*

indivisible /ɪndɪvɪzɪ1bə0l/. ADJ If something is **indivisible,** it cannot be divided into different parts. *...the ancient Greek belief that the atom is indivisible.*

indoctrinate /ɪndɒktrɪneɪt/, **indoctrinates, indoctrinating, indoctrinated.** VB WITH OBJ If you **indoctrinate** someone, you teach them a particular belief with the aim that they will not consider other beliefs; used showing disapproval. ♦ **indoctrination** /ɪndɒktrɪneɪʃə0n/ UNCOUNT N *It is difficult to overcome the early indoctrination of children.*

indolent /ɪndələnt/. ADJ Someone who is **indolent** is lazy; a formal use. *...an indolent smile.*

indomitable /ɪndɒmɪtəbə0l/. ADJ Someone who is **indomitable** never admits that they have been defeated; a formal use. *The boy had been kept alive by his indomitable spirit.*

indoor /ɪndɔː/. ATTRIB ADJ You use **indoor** to describe things inside a building rather than outside. *...indoor games such as table tennis.*

indoors /ɪndɔːz/. ADV If something happens **indoors**, it happens inside a building. *We'd better go indoors.*

induce /ɪndjuːs/, **induces, inducing, induced.** 1 VB WITH OBJ To **induce** a particular state or condition means to cause it. *...pills guaranteed to induce sleep.* 2 VB WITH OBJ AND TO-INF To **induce** someone to do something means to persuade or influence them to do it. *What on earth had induced her to marry a man like that?*

inducement /ɪndjuːsmə^{2}nt/, **inducements.** COUNT N An **inducement** is something which might persuade someone to do a particular thing. *These tax advantages provide the main inducement to become a home-owner.*

indulge /ɪndʌldʒ/, **indulges, indulging, indulged.** 1 VB WITH 'in', VB WITH OBJ, OR REFL VB If you **indulge** in something or **indulge** a hobby or interest, you allow yourself to have or do something that you enjoy. *Let us indulge in a little daydreaming... Jack had spent the previous three weeks indulging his passion for climbing... He indulged himself by smoking another cigarette.* 2 VB WITH OBJ If you **indulge** someone, you let them have or do whatever they want. *He was usually prepared to indulge his sister.*

indulgence /ɪndʌldʒəns/, **indulgences.** 1 COUNT N An **indulgence** is something pleasant that you allow yourself to do or have. *Smoking was his one indulgence.* 2 UNCOUNT N **Indulgence** is the act of indulging yourself or another person. *Simon listened to her with indulgence.*

indulgent /ɪndʌldʒənt/. ADJ If you are **indulgent,** you treat a person with special kindness. *...an indulgent father.* ♦ **indulgently** ADV *He smiled indulgently at her.*

industrial /ɪndʌstriəl/. 1 ATTRIB ADJ **Industrial** means relating to industry. *...industrial robots... ...industrial and technical change.* 2 ADJ An **industrial** city or country is one in which industry is important or highly developed.

industrial action. UNCOUNT N When a group of workers take **industrial action,** they stop working or take other action to protest about their pay or working conditions.

industrialism /ɪndʌstriəlɪzə^{0}m/. UNCOUNT N **Industrialism** is the state of having an economy based on industry.

industrialist /ɪndʌstriəlɪst/, **industrialists.** COUNT N An **industrialist** is a person who owns or controls large amounts of money or property in industry.

industrialize /ɪndʌstriəlaɪz/, **industrializes, industrializing, industrialized;** also spelled **industrialise.** ERG VB When a country **industrializes** or **is industrialized,** it develops a lot of industries. *...the funds needed to industrialize all the underdeveloped countries... ...the industrialized world.* ♦ **industrialization** /ɪndʌstriəlaɪzeɪʃə^{0}n/ UNCOUNT N *...the rising cost of industrialization.*

industrial relations. PLURAL N **Industrial relations** are the relationship between employers and workers.

industrious /ɪndʌstriəs/. ADJ Someone who is **industrious** works very hard; a formal use. *...an industrious student.*

industry /ɪndəstri^1/, **industries.** 1 UNCOUNT N **Industry** is the work and processes involved in making things in factories. *Japanese industry is making increasing use of robots.* 2 COUNT N An **industry** consists of all the people and the processes that are involved in manufacturing or producing a particular thing. *...the oil industry.* 3 UNCOUNT N **Industry** is also the quality of working very hard; a formal use.

inedible /ɪnedɪbə^{0}l/. ADJ Something that is **inedible** is poisonous or too nasty to eat.

ineffective /ɪnɪfektɪv/. ADJ Something that is **ineffective** has no effect.

ineffectual /ɪnɪfektʃu^{0}əl/. ADJ Something that is **ineffectual** does not do what it is supposed to do. *...ineffectual policies.* ♦ **ineffectually** ADV *...trying ineffectually to brush the mud off his jacket.*

inefficient /ɪnɪfɪʃənt/. ADJ A person, organization, system, or machine that is **inefficient** does not work in the most economical way. *...shutting down aging and inefficient refineries... ...inefficient farming.* ♦ **inefficiency** /ɪnɪfɪʃənsi^1/ UNCOUNT N *He criticised the inefficiency of public authorities.*

ineligible /ɪnelɪdʒə^{1}bə^{0}l/. ADJ If you are **ineligible** for something, you are not qualified for it or entitled to it; a formal use. *I am ineligible for unemployment benefit.*

inept /ɪnept/. ADJ Someone who is **inept** does something with a complete lack of skill. *...the government's inept handling of the crisis.*

ineptitude /ɪneptɪtjuːd/. UNCOUNT N **Ineptitude** is a complete lack of skill; a formal use. *...his record of political ineptitude.*

inequality /ɪnɪkwɒlɪ^{1}ti^1/, **inequalities.** UNCOUNT N OR COUNT N **Inequality** is a difference in wealth or opportunity between groups in a society. *...reform aimed at reducing inequality... We found great inequalities of opportunity.*

inert /ɪnɜːt/. ADJ Someone or something that is **inert** does not move at all and appears to be lifeless. *I carried her, still inert, up the stairs to her room.*

inertia /ɪnɜːʃɪ^{0}ə/. UNCOUNT N If you have a feeling of **inertia,** you feel very lazy and unwilling to do anything. *Though I wanted to go, I stayed from sheer inertia.*

inescapable /ɪnɪ^{2}skeɪpəbə^{0}l/. ADJ If something is **inescapable,** it cannot be avoided. *...an inescapable conclusion.*

inevitable /ɪnevɪtəbə^{0}l/. 1 ADJ If something is **inevitable,** it cannot be prevented or avoided. *If this policy continues, then violence is inevitable.* ♦ **inevitability** /ɪnevɪtəbɪlɪ^{1}ti^1/ UNCOUNT N *You must recognize the inevitability of change.* 2 SING N **The inevitable** is something that cannot be prevented or avoided. *I resigned myself to the inevitable.*

inevitably /ɪnevɪtəbli^1/. SENTENCE ADV If something **inevitably** happens or will happen, it is the only possible result. *A household of this size inevitably has problems.*

inexcusable /ɪnɪ^{2}kskjuːzəbə^{0}l/. ADJ Something that is **inexcusable** is too bad to be justified or tolerated. *...an inexcusable act of destruction.*

inexhaustible /ɪnɪ^{2}gzɔːstəbə^{0}l/. ADJ An **inexhaustible** supply of something is so great that it will never be used up. *His patience must be inexhaustible.*

inexorable /ɪneksə^{0}rəbə^{0}l/. ADJ Something that is **inexorable** cannot be prevented from continuing; a formal use. *...the inexorable rise in the cost of living.* ♦ **inexorably** ADV *These facts led inexorably to one conclusion.*

inexpensive /ɪnɪ^{2}kspensɪv/. ADJ Something that is **inexpensive** does not cost much. *...an inexpensive wine.*

inexperience /ɪnɪ^{2}kspɪəriəns/. UNCOUNT N If you refer to someone's **inexperience,** you are referring to the fact that they are inexperienced. *You're bound to make a few mistakes through inexperience.*

inexperienced /ɪnɪ^{2}kspɪəriənst/. ADJ If you are **inexperienced,** you have little or no experience of a particular activity. *...an inexperienced swimmer.*

inexplicable /ɪnɪ^{2}ksplɪkəbə^{0}l/. ADJ If something is **inexplicable,** you cannot explain it. *I still find this incident inexplicable.* ♦ **inexplicably** ADV *Anita had inexplicably disappeared.*

inextricably /ɪnɪ^{2}kstrɪkəbə^{0}li^1/. ADV If two or more things are **inextricably** linked, they cannot be separated. *Social and economic factors are inextricably linked.*

infallible /ɪnfælɪbə^{0}l/. ADJ Someone or something that is **infallible** is never wrong. *Doctors aren't infallible.*

infamous /ɪnfəməs/. ADJ **Infamous** people or things are well-known because of something bad. *How well I remember that infamous night.*

infancy /ɪnfənsi^1/. UNCOUNT N **Infancy** is the period in your life when you are a very young child. *The child died in infancy.*

infant /ɪnfənt/, **infants.** COUNT N An **infant** is a very young child or baby; a formal use.

infantile /ɪnfəntaɪl/. 1 ADJ You use **infantile** to describe the diseases or behaviour of very young children; a formal use. *...infantile paralysis.* 2 ADJ Someone who is **infantile** behaves in a foolish and childish way.

infantry /ɪnfəntri^1/. COLL N The **infantry** are the soldiers in an army who fight on foot.

infant school, infant schools. COUNT N An **infant school** is a school for children aged five to seven; a British use.

infatuated /ɪnfætjueɪtɪ^{2}d/. ADJ If you are **infatuated** with someone, you have a strong feeling of love for them that other people think is ridiculous. ♦ **infatuation** /ɪnfætjueɪʃə^{0}n/ COUNT N OR UNCOUNT N *This is not love but a foolish infatuation.*

infect /ɪnfekt/, **infects, infecting, infected.** VB WITH OBJ To **infect** people, animals, plants, or food means to cause them to suffer from germs or to carry germs. *Imported birds can infect their owners with an unpleasant illness.* ♦ **infected** ADJ *...a man limping on a badly infected leg.*

infection /ɪnfekʃə^{0}n/, **infections.** 1 COUNT N OR UNCOUNT N An **infection** is a disease caused by germs. *I had an ear infection... Radiation lessened bodily resistance to infection.* 2 UNCOUNT N **Infection** is the state of becoming infected. *There is little risk of infection.*

infectious /ɪnfekʃəs/. 1 ADJ If you have an **infectious** disease, people near you can catch it from you. 2 ADJ If a feeling is **infectious,** it spreads to other people. *Don't you find her enthusiasm infectious?*

infer /ɪnfɜː/, **infers, inferring, inferred.** REPORT VB If you **infer** something, you decide that it is true, on the basis of information you have; a formal use. *He can infer that if the battery is dead then the horn will not sound... As a result of this simple statement, I could infer a lot about his former wives.*

inference /ɪnfə^{0}rəns/, **inferences.** COUNT N An **inference** is a conclusion that you draw about something. *The inferences drawn from data have led to some major changes in our policy.*

inferior /ɪnfɪərɪə/, **inferiors.** 1 ADJ Someone or something that is **inferior** is not as good or important as other people or things. *Charlie, aged sixteen, felt inferior to lads of his own age... It was a cheap and inferior product.* ♦ **inferiority** /ɪnfɪərɪɒrɪti^1/ UNCOUNT N *...feelings of inferiority.* 2 COUNT N Your **inferiors** are people who have a lower position or status than you.

inferno /ɪnfɜːnəʊ/, **infernos.** COUNT N An **inferno** is a very large dangerous fire; a literary use.

infertile /ɪnfɜːtaɪl/. 1 ADJ Someone who is **infertile** cannot have children. *She learned she was infertile.* ♦ **infertility** /ɪnfɜːtɪlɪ^{1}ti^1/ UNCOUNT N *...an infertility clinic.* 2 ADJ **Infertile** soil is of poor quality, and so plants cannot grow well in it.

infested /ɪnfestɪ^{2}d/. PRED ADJ If a plant or area is **infested** with insects or other pests, there are lots of them on it or in it.

infidelity /ɪnfɪdelɪ^{1}ti^1/, **infidelities.** UNCOUNT N OR COUNT N **Infidelity** is the act of being unfaithful to your husband, wife, or lover.

infiltrate /ɪnfɪltreɪt/, **infiltrates, infiltrating, infiltrated.** VB WITH OBJ OR 'into' If people **infiltrate** an organization or **infiltrate** into it, they join it secretly in order to spy on it or influence it. *The organization was infiltrated by the police.* ♦ **infiltration** /ɪnfɪltreɪʃə^{0}n/ UNCOUNT N *...the infiltration of the party by extreme left-wing groups.*

infinite /ɪnfɪnə^{1}t/. ADJ Something that is **infinite** is extremely large in amount or degree, or has no limit. *Qualified doctors are found in an infinite variety of careers.* ♦ **infinitely** SUBMOD *The process of unloading had been infinitely easier than putting the stuff on.*

infinitesimal /ɪnfɪnɪtesɪmə^{0}l/. ADJ **Infinitesimal** means extremely small; a formal use. *The chances that the company will have any problems are infinitesimal.*

infinitive /ɪnfɪnɪ^{1}tɪv/, **infinitives.** COUNT N The **infinitive** of a verb is its base form or simplest form, such as 'do', 'take', and 'eat'. The infinitive can either be used on its own or with 'to' in front of it.

infinity /ɪnfɪnɪ^{1}ti^1/. 1 UNCOUNT N **Infinity** is a number that is larger than any other number and so can never be given an exact value. 2 UNCOUNT N **Infinity** is also a point that is further away than any other point and so can never be reached. *There was nothing but darkness stretching away to infinity.*

infirm /ɪnfɜːm/; a formal word. 1 ADJ A person who is **infirm** is weak or ill. *His grandfather was over eighty, infirm and totally blind.* ♦ **infirmity** /ɪnfɜːmɪ^{1}ti^1/ COUNT N OR UNCOUNT N *...physical infirmity or weakness... ...the infirmities of old age.* 2 PLURAL N **The infirm** are people who are infirm. *...the needs of the old and infirm.*

infirmary /ɪnfɜːmə^{0}ri^1/, **infirmaries.** COUNT N Some hospitals are called **infirmaries.**

inflamed /ɪnfleɪmd/. ADJ If part of your body is **inflamed,** it is red or swollen because of an infection or injury; a formal use.

inflammable /ɪnflæməbə^{0}l/. ADJ An **inflammable** material or chemical burns easily.

inflammation /ɪnfləmeɪʃə^{0}n/. UNCOUNT N OR SING N When **inflammation** occurs on a part of your body, that part becomes swollen and red. *...inflammation of the ears.*

inflatable /ɪnfleɪtəbə^{0}l/. ADJ An **inflatable** object can be filled with air. *...inflatable lifejackets.*

inflate /ɪnfleɪt/, **inflates, inflating, inflated.** ERG VB When you **inflate** something or when it **inflates,** it becomes bigger as it is filled with air or another gas. *...a rubber dinghy that took half a hour to inflate.* ♦ **inflated** ADJ *...the large inflated tyre they used as a raft.*

inflated /ɪnfleɪtɪ^{2}d/. 1 ADJ If you have an **inflated** opinion of yourself, you think you are much more important than you really are. *...his inflated self-image.* 2 ADJ An **inflated** price or salary is higher than is considered reasonable. *...food and clothing which had to be bought at inflated prices.*

inflation /ɪnfleɪʃə^{0}n/. UNCOUNT N **Inflation** is a general increase in the prices of goods and services in a country. *Chile has reduced its inflation in the past year from a hundred per cent to fifty.*

inflationary /ɪnfleɪʃənəºri¹/. ADJ An **inflationary** action or event causes inflation; a formal use. *...inflationary wage demands.*

inflect /ɪnflɛkt/, **inflects, inflecting, inflected.** VB If a word **inflects,** its ending or form changes in order to show its grammatical function or number. For example, 'makes', 'making', and 'made' are inflected forms of 'make'.

inflection /ɪnflɛkʃəºn/, **inflections;** also spelled **inflexion. 1** COUNT N OR UNCOUNT N An **inflection** is a change in the sound of your voice when you speak. *She spoke in a low voice, always without inflection.* **2** COUNT N OR UNCOUNT N An **inflection** is also a change in the form of a word that shows its grammatical function or number.

inflexible /ɪnflɛksɪbəºl/. ADJ Something that is **inflexible** cannot be altered. *Nursery schools have inflexible hours.*

inflexion /ɪnflɛkʃəºn/. See **inflection.**

inflict /ɪnflɪkt/, **inflicts, inflicting, inflicted.** VB WITH OBJ If you **inflict** something unpleasant on someone, you make them suffer it. *...the dreadful way she had inflicted her problems on him.*

influence /ɪnfluəns/, **influences, influencing, influenced. 1** UNCOUNT N **Influence** is power to affect people's actions. *Moscow retains some influence over their affairs... He was under the influence of friends who were highly conservative... ...the influence of religion on society.* **2** COUNT N WITH SUPP If you are an **influence** on people or things, you have an effect on them. *He was a bad influence on the children.* **3** VB WITH OBJ To **influence** a person, thing, or situation means to have an effect on the way that person acts or on what happens. *I didn't want him to influence me in my choice.*

influential /ɪnfluɛnʃəºl/. ADJ Someone who is **influential** has a lot of influence over people. *...a powerful and influential politician.*

influenza /ɪnfluɛnzə/. UNCOUNT N **Influenza** is flu; a formal use.

influx /ɪnflʌks/. SING N WITH SUPP An **influx** of people or things into a place is their steady arrival there in large numbers. *...a massive influx of refugees.*

inform /ɪnfɔːm/, **informs, informing, informed.** VB WITH OBJ AND 'of' OR REPORT VB If you **inform** someone of something, you tell them about it. *He intended to see Barbara to inform her of his objections... I informed her that I was unwell... 'They are late,' he informed her.* ● See also **informed.**

informal /ɪnfɔːməºl/. ADJ You use **informal** to describe behaviour and speech that is relaxed and casual rather than correct and serious. *...a relaxed and quite informal discussion.* ♦ **informally** ADV *...people talking informally together.* ♦ **informality** /ɪnfɔːmælɪ¹ti¹/ UNCOUNT N *...an atmosphere of informality.*

informant /ɪnfɔːmənt/, **informants.** COUNT N An **informant** is someone who gives another person a piece of information.

information /ɪnfəmeɪʃəºn/. UNCOUNT N If you have **information** about a particular thing, you know something about it. *I'm afraid I have no information on that... She provided me with a very interesting piece of information about his past.*

informative /ɪnfɔːmətɪv/. ADJ Something that is **informative** gives you useful information. *...an informative guidebook.*

informed /ɪnfɔːmd/. ATTRIB ADJ If you make an **informed** guess about something, you use your knowledge to decide what you think the answer should be.

informer /ɪnfɔːmə/, **informers.** COUNT N An **informer** is someone who tells the police that another person has done something wrong.

infra-red /ɪnfrə rɛd/. ADJ **Infra-red** light is below the colour red in the spectrum and cannot be seen. *...infra-red photography.*

infrequent /ɪnfriːkwənt/. ADJ If something is **infrequent,** it does not happen often. *...her sister's infrequent letters.* ♦ **infrequently** ADV *My parents were only able to visit us infrequently.*

infringe /ɪnfrɪnd z/, **infringes, infringing, infringed. 1** VB WITH OBJ If you **infringe** a law or an agreement, you break it; a formal use. *They occasionally infringe the law by parking near a junction.* ♦ **infringement** /ɪnfrɪndºʒmə²nt/ COUNT N OR UNCOUNT N *...small infringements of prison discipline.* **2** VB WITH OBJ OR 'on' If you **infringe** people's rights, you do not allow people the rights or freedom that they are entitled to. *They were citizens with legal rights, which were being infringed... We must fight them when they infringe on our children's right to freedom.* ♦ **infringement** COUNT N OR UNCOUNT N *The new law is an infringement on free speech.*

infuriate /ɪnfjʊəri¹eɪt/, **infuriates, infuriating, infuriated.** VB WITH OBJ If something or someone **infuriates** you, they make you extremely angry. *Old jeans and T-shirts infuriated him.*

infuriating /ɪnfjʊəri¹eɪtɪŋ/. ADJ **Infuriating** means extremely annoying. *...her infuriating habit of criticizing people all the time.*

-ing. SUFFIX **-ing** is added to verbs to form present participles or uncount nouns referring to activities. Present participles are often used as adjectives that describe a person or thing as doing something. Nouns and adjectives of this kind are often not defined but are treated with the related verbs. *I was walking along the road... Farming was something I really enjoyed... ...the dazzling sun.*

ingenious /ɪndʒiːnjəs, -nɪəs/. ADJ An **ingenious** idea, plan, or device is very clever. *...an ingenious method of forecasting economic trends.* ♦ **ingeniously** ADV *The hangers were ingeniously fixed to the wardrobe by pieces of wire.*

ingenuity /ɪndʒɪnjuː¹ɪ¹ti¹/. UNCOUNT N **Ingenuity** is skill at inventing things or at working out plans. *With a bit of ingenuity you can do almost anything.*

ingenuous /ɪndʒɛnjuːəs/. ADJ Someone who is **ingenuous** is innocent, trusting, and honest.

ingrained /ɪŋ¹greɪnd/. ADJ **Ingrained** habits and beliefs are difficult to change. *The belief that one should work hard is ingrained in our culture.*

ingratiate /ɪŋ¹greɪʃi¹eɪt/, **ingratiates, ingratiating, ingratiated.** REFL VB If you try to **ingratiate** yourself with other people, you try to make them like you; used showing disapproval. *They resented his knack for ingratiating himself with officers.* ♦ **ingratiating** ADJ *...an ingratiating smile.*

ingratitude /ɪŋ¹grætɪtjuːd/. UNCOUNT N **Ingratitude** is lack of gratitude for something that has been done for you. *I was shocked and enraged at such ingratitude.*

ingredient /ɪŋ¹griːdɪənt/, **ingredients.** COUNT N The **ingredients** of something that you cook or prepare are the different foods that you use. *Mix the ingredients to a soft dough.*

inhabit /ɪnhæbɪt/, **inhabits, inhabiting, inhabited.** VB WITH OBJ If a place or region **is inhabited,** people live there. *The town was a seaside resort, inhabited by fishermen and hoteliers.*

inhabitant /ɪnhæbɪtənt/, **inhabitants.** COUNT N The **inhabitants** of a place are the people who live there.

inhale /ɪnheɪl/, **inhales, inhaling, inhaled.** VB WITH OR WITHOUT OBJ When you **inhale,** you breathe in. *She put the cigarette between her lips and inhaled deeply... ...inhaling the scent of haymaking.*

inherent /ɪnhɪərənt, -hɛr-/. ADJ Characteristics that are **inherent** in something are a natural part of it. *...the dangers inherent in this kind of political system... ...my inherent laziness.* ♦ **inherently** ADV *Power stations are inherently inefficient.*

inherit /ɪnhɛrɪt/, **inherits, inheriting, inherited. 1** VB WITH OBJ If you **inherit** something such as a situation or attitude, you take it over from people who came before you. *They inherited a weak economy.* **2** VB WITH OBJ If you **inherit** money or property, you receive it from someone who has died. **3** VB WITH OBJ If you **inherit** a characteristic, you are born with it, because your parents or ancestors had it. *This kind of brain damage may be inherited.*

inheritance /ɪnhɛrɪtəºns/, **inheritances. 1** COUNT N OR UNCOUNT N An **inheritance** is money or property which you receive from someone who is dead. *He had no motive for depriving his son of the inheritance... ...the customs of inheritance in Asia.* **2** UNCOUNT N **Inheritance** is the fact of being born with characteristics which your parents or ancestors had. *To what extent does human nature depend on genetic inheritance?*

inheritor /ɪnhɛrɪtə/, **inheritors.** COUNT N WITH SUPP People who are the **inheritors** of something inherited it from people who came before them. *...the inheritors of a literary tradition.*

inhibit /ɪnhɪbɪt/, **inhibits, inhibiting, inhibited.** VB WITH OBJ If something **inhibits** growth or development, it prevents it or slows it down. *The drugs with which the animals are fed inhibit their development.*

inhibited /ɪnhɪbɪtɪ¹d/. ADJ If you are **inhibited,** you find it difficult to behave naturally and show your feelings. *Her severe upbringing had left her inhibited.*

inhibition /ɪnhºɪbɪʃəºn/, **inhibitions.** COUNT N OR UNCOUNT N **Inhibitions** are feelings of fear or embarrassment that make it difficult for you to behave naturally. *...a child who is free from inhibitions... She's prepared to argue without inhibition.*

inhospitable /ɪnhɒspɪtəbəºl/. **1** ADJ An **inhospitable** place is unpleasant to live in. *...inhospitable deserts.* **2** ADJ If you are **inhospitable,** you do not make people feel welcome when they visit you.

inhuman /ɪnhjuːmən/. **1** ADJ Behaviour that is **inhuman** is extremely cruel. *...barbarous and inhuman atrocities.* **2** ADJ Something that is **inhuman** is not human or does not seem human, and is strange or frightening. *Their faces looked inhuman, covered with scarlet and black paint.*

inhumane /ɪnhjuːmeɪn/. ADJ **Inhumane** treatment is extremely cruel.

inhumanity /ɪnhjuːmænɪ¹ti¹/. UNCOUNT N **Inhumanity** is cruelty or lack of feeling. *...man's inhumanity to man.*

inimical /ɪnɪmɪkəºl/. ADJ Conditions that are **inimical** to something make it hard for it to survive; a formal use. *The very nature of society is inimical to freedom.*

inimitable /ɪnɪmɪtəbəºl/. ADJ **Inimitable** is used to praise a special person or a special quality that someone has; a formal use. *The Welsh Rugby team have their own inimitable style.*

iniquitous /ɪnɪkwɪtəs/. ADJ **Iniquitous** means very bad and unfair; a formal use. *...this iniquitous policy.*

iniquity /ɪnɪkwɪ¹ti¹/, **iniquities.** COUNT N OR UNCOUNT N An **iniquity** is something that is wicked or unjust; a formal use. *We fought a revolution to put an end to such iniquities... ...Rose's iniquity and selfishness.*

initial /ɪnɪʃəºl/, **initials, initialling, initialled;** spelled **initialed** and **initialing** in American English. **1** ATTRIB ADJ You use **initial** to describe something that happens at the beginning of a process. *...the initial stages of learning English... My initial reaction was one of great relief.* **2** PLURAL N Your **initials** are the capital letters which begin each of your names, or begin your first names. **3** VB WITH OBJ When you **initial** a document, you write your initials on it to show that you have seen it or have officially approved it.

initially /ɪnɪʃəºli¹/. ADV **Initially** means in the early stages of a process. *I don't remember who initially conceived the idea.*

initiate, initiates, initiating, initiated; pronounced /ɪnɪʃi¹eɪt/ when it is a verb and /ɪnɪʃi¹ət/ when it is a noun. **1** VB WITH OBJ If you **initiate** something, you cause it to start. *We should initiate direct talks with the trades unions.* ♦ **initiation** /ɪnɪʃieɪʃəºn/ UNCOUNT N *...the initiation of a new revolutionary practice.* **2** VB WITH OBJ AND 'into' If you **initiate** someone into a group, you conduct a ceremony or teach them special things so that they become a member. *To understand, one must be initiated into great mysteries.* ♦ **initiation** UNCOUNT N *...an initiation ceremony.* **3** COUNT N An **initiate** is a person who has recently been allowed to join a particular group and who has been taught special things. *...an initiate into the world of politics.*

initiative /ɪnɪʃiºətɪv/, **initiatives. 1** COUNT N An **initiative** is an important act intended to solve a problem. *...launching various initiatives to tackle real or imagined problems.* **2** SING N If you have the **initiative,** you are in a stronger position than your opponents. *They had lost the initiative.* **3** UNCOUNT N If you have **initiative,** you are able to take action without needing other people to tell you what to do. *In special circumstances we have to use our initiative.* PHRASES ● If you do something **on your own initiative,** you do it without being told to do it by someone else. ● If you **take the initiative,** you are the first person to do something. *In Sweden employers have taken the initiative in promoting health insurance schemes.*

inject /ɪndʒɛkt/, **injects, injecting, injected. 1** VB WITH OBJ If you **inject** someone with a liquid, you use a syringe to get it into their body. *She injected a sleeping drug into my arm... Animals were injected with various doses.* ♦ **injection** /ɪndʒɛkʃəºn/ COUNT N *You had a smallpox injection when you were five.* **2** VB WITH OBJ AND 'into' If you **inject** something such as excitement or interest into a situation, you add it. *She was trying to inject some fun into the grim proceedings.* **3** VB WITH OBJ AND 'into' If you **inject** money into a business or organization, you provide it with more money. *Enormous sums of money are injected each year into teaching.* ♦ **injection** COUNT N WITH 'of' *...massive injections of commercial funds.*

injunction /ɪndʒʌŋkʃəºn/, **injunctions.** COUNT N An **injunction** is a court order which is issued to stop someone doing something. *We will apply to the courts for an injunction against the march.*

injure /ɪndʒə/, **injures, injuring, injured.** VB WITH OBJ OR REFL VB If you **injure** someone, you damage a part of their body. *She was not badly injured... Peter injured his right hand in an accident... I feared they might injure themselves.*

injury /ɪndʒəri¹/, **injuries.** COUNT N OR UNCOUNT N An **injury** is damage done to a person's body. *The earthquake caused many deaths and severe injuries... Louis received an injury to his head... He was weakened by illness and injury.*

injustice /ɪndʒʌstɪs/, **injustices. 1** UNCOUNT N OR COUNT N **Injustice** is a lack of fairness in a situation. *There's social injustice everywhere... He contemplated the injustices of life.* **2** PHRASE If you have **done**

someone **an injustice,** you have judged them too harshly.

ink /ɪŋk/, **inks.** MASS N **Ink** is the coloured liquid used for writing or printing. *Please write in ink.*

inkling /ɪŋklɪŋ/. PHRASE If you **have an inkling** of something, you suspect what it is or suspect that it is the case. *He had an inkling of what was going on... I had no inkling that she was interested in me.*

inky /ɪŋki1/. 1 ADJ **Inky** means very black or dark; a literary use. *...an inky sky.* 2 ADJ **Inky** also means covered in ink. *...an inky handkerchief.*

inland /ɪnlə3nd/. ADJ OR ADV **Inland** means away from the coast of a country. *The Sahara was once an inland sea... Donkeys bear goods inland to the towns and villages.*

in-laws. PLURAL N Your **in-laws** are the parents and close relatives of your husband or wife.

inlet /ɪnlə2t/, **inlets.** COUNT N An **inlet** is a narrow strip of water which goes from a sea or lake into the land.

inmate /ɪnmeɪt/, **inmates.** COUNT N The **inmates** of a prison or a psychiatric hospital are the people living there.

inn /ɪn/, **inns.** COUNT N An **inn** is a small hotel or a pub; an old-fashioned use. *...the Pilgrim's Inn.*

innate /ɪneɪt/. ADJ An **innate** quality or ability is one which a person is born with. *They believed intelligence was innate, and unlikely to change... ...an innate talent for music.* ♦ **innately** ADV *I don't think that anybody is innately good.*

inner /ɪnə/. 1 ATTRIB ADJ You use **inner** to describe something which is contained or enclosed inside something else. *There were several flats overlooking the inner courtyard.* 2 ATTRIB ADJ **Inner** feelings are feelings which you do not show to other people. *...his inner feelings of failure... ...inner doubts.*

inner city, inner cities. SING N OR PLURAL N You use **inner city** to refer to areas near the centre of a city where people live. *This is one of the most serious problems in the inner cities... ...inner-city children.*

innermost /ɪnəməʊst/. ATTRIB ADJ Your **innermost** thoughts and feelings are your most personal and secret ones; a literary use. *...her innermost wishes.*

innings /ɪnɪŋz/. **Innings** is the singular and plural. COUNT N An **innings** is a period in a game of cricket during which a particular player or team is batting.

innocent /ɪnəsənt/. 1 ADJ If someone is **innocent,** they are not guilty of a crime. *He was accused of a crime of violence of which he was innocent... ...the suffering that would be inflicted upon innocent people.* ♦ **innocence** /ɪnəsəns/ UNCOUNT N *He desperately protested his innocence.* 2 ADJ If you are **innocent,** you have no experience of the more complex or unpleasant aspects of life. *I was very young, and very innocent.* ♦ **innocence** UNCOUNT N *He had a peculiar air of childlike innocence.* 3 ADJ An **innocent** remark or action is not meant to offend people, although it may do so. *It was an innocent question.* ♦ **innocently** ADV *'What did I do wrong?' asked Howard, innocently.*

innocuous /ɪnɒkju:əs/. ADJ **Innocuous** means not at all harmful; a formal use. *Most of these substances are relatively innocuous.*

innovate /ɪnə6veɪt/, **innovates, innovating, innovated.** VB To **innovate** means to introduce changes and new ideas. *...the industry's capacity to respond swiftly to market changes and to innovate.* ♦ **innovator** /ɪnə6veɪtə/ COUNT N *The Pope thought of himself as an innovator.*

innovation /ɪnə6veɪʃə0n/, **innovations.** 1 COUNT N An **innovation** is a new thing or new method of doing something. *...a series of remarkable innovations in textile manufacturing... ...major innovations such as antibiotics.* 2 UNCOUNT N **Innovation** is the introduction of new things or new methods. *...a period of technological innovation.*

innovative /ɪnəvətɪv/. 1 ADJ Something that is **innovative** is new and original. *...their innovative campaign style... ...innovative ideas.* 2 ADJ An **innovative** person introduces changes and new ideas. *...a pioneering and innovative banker.*

innuendo /ɪnju:ɛndəʊ/, **innuendoes** or **innuendos.** UNCOUNT N OR COUNT N **Innuendo** is indirect reference to something rude or unpleasant. *...a campaign of innuendo and gossip... ...sexual innuendoes.*

innumerable /ɪnju:mə0rəbə0l/. ADJ **Innumerable** means too many to be counted. *The industrial age has brought innumerable benefits.*

inoculate /ɪnɒkjə4leɪt/, **inoculates, inoculating, inoculated.** VB WITH OBJ If you **are inoculated** against a disease, you are injected with a weak form of the disease to protect you against it. *A pedigree pup should have been inoculated against serious diseases.* ♦ **inoculation** /ɪnɒkjə4leɪʃə0n/ COUNT N OR UNCOUNT N *...inoculations against tetanus... ...prevention of disease by inoculation.*

inoffensive /ɪnəfɛnsɪv/. ADJ **Inoffensive** means harmless or not unpleasant. *...a nice, quiet, inoffensive little fellow.*

inordinate /ɪnɔ:dɪnɪ1t/. ADJ **Inordinate** means much greater than you would expect; a formal use. *Alan always spent an inordinate length of time in the bathroom.* ♦ **inordinately** SUBMOD *...an achievement of which I was inordinately proud.*

inorganic /ɪnɔ:gænɪk/. ADJ **Inorganic** substances are substances such as stone and metal that do not come from living things. *...inorganic fertilizers.*

input /ɪnpʊt/, **inputs.** 1 UNCOUNT N OR COUNT N **Input** consists of resources such as money, workers, or power that are given to something such as a machine or a project to make it work. *The project requires the input of more labour.* 2 UNCOUNT N **Input** is also information that is put into a computer.

inquest /ɪŋ1kwɛst/, **inquests.** COUNT N An **inquest** is an official inquiry into the cause of someone's death. *There have been demands from his family for an inquest.*

inquire /ɪŋ1kwaɪə/, **inquires, inquiring, inquired;** also spelled **enquire** /ɪ2ŋ1kwaɪə/. VB WITH ADJUNCT OR REPORT VB If you **inquire** about something, you ask for information about it; a formal use. *He went to enquire about the times of trains to Edinburgh... He inquired whether it was possible to leave his case at the station... 'What will it cost?' inquired Miss Musson.*

inquire after. PHR VB If you **inquire after** someone, you ask how they are. *She enquired after Mrs Carstair's daughter, who had just had a baby.*

inquire into. PHR VB If you **inquire into** something, you investigate it. *The police inquired into the deaths of two young girls.*

inquiring /ɪŋ1kwaɪərɪŋ/; also spelled **enquiring** /ɪ2ŋ1kwaɪərɪŋ/. 1 ATTRIB ADJ If you have an **inquiring** mind, you have a great interest in learning new things. 2 ADJ If you have an **inquiring** expression on your face, you show that you want to know something. *...the people's inquiring faces.* ♦ **inquiringly** ADV *I looked at her inquiringly.*

inquiry /ɪŋ1kwaɪəri1/, **inquiries;** also spelled **enquiry** /ɪ2ŋ1kwaɪəri1/, especially for meaning 1. 1 COUNT N An **inquiry** is a question which you ask in order to get information. *I shall make some enquiries.* 2 COUNT N An **inquiry** is also an official investigation. *Opposition MPs have called for a public inquiry.* 3 UNCOUNT N **Inquiry** is the process of asking about something to get information. *On further enquiry, I discovered that there had been nobody at home.*

inquisitive /ɪŋ1kwɪzɪ1tɪv/. ADJ An **inquisitive** person likes finding out about things, especially secret things. *He tried not to sound inquisitive.*

inroads /ɪnrəʊdz/. PLURAL N If one thing makes **inroads** into another, it starts affecting it or destroying it. *They are highly sensitive to any inroads upon their independence.*

insane /ɪnseɪn/. 1 ADJ Someone who is **insane** is mad. *Some went insane.* ♦ **insanity** /ɪnsænɪ1ti1/ UNCOUNT N *He saw the beginnings of insanity in her.* 2 ADJ You can also describe someone as **insane** when they behave foolishly. *You'd be insane to do that.* ♦ **insanely** SUBMOD *I must admit that I was insanely jealous.* ♦ **insanity** UNCOUNT N *I laughed at the insanity of it all.*

insatiable /ɪnseɪʃɪ0əbə0l/. ADJ An **insatiable** desire or greed is very great. *...an insatiable curiosity.*

inscribe /ɪnskraɪb/, **inscribes, inscribing, inscribed.** VB WITH OBJ AND ADJUNCT If words are **inscribed** on an object or if an object **is inscribed** with them, the words are written or carved on the object; a formal use. *The names of the dead were inscribed on the wall... ...a ring inscribed 'To My Darling'.*

inscription /ɪnskrɪpʃə0n/, **inscriptions.** COUNT N An **inscription** is words that are written or carved on something. *The inscription above the door was in English.*

inscrutable /ɪnskru:təbə0l/. ADJ Someone who is **inscrutable** does not show what they are really thinking. *The candidates are pretty inscrutable.*

insect /ɪnsɛkt/, **insects.** COUNT N An **insect** is a small creature with six legs and usually wings. Ants, flies, and butterflies are all insects.

insecticide /ɪnsɛktɪsaɪd/, **insecticides.** MASS N **Insecticide** is a chemical used to kill insects.

insecure /ɪnsɪkjʊə/. 1 ADJ If you feel **insecure,** you feel that you are not good enough or are not loved. *What had I done to make you so insecure and frightened?* ♦ **insecurity** /ɪnsɪ1kjʊərɪ1ti1/ UNCOUNT N *...feelings of insecurity.* 2 ADJ Something that is **insecure** is not safe or protected. *Their place in society is insecure.* ♦ **insecurity** UNCOUNT N *...financial insecurity.*

insensitive /ɪnsɛnsɪtɪv/. ADJ Someone who is **insensitive** is not aware of or sympathetic to other people's feelings. *...bad-mannered, loud, insensitive oafs... ...the insensitive attitude of the government.* ♦ **insensitivity** /ɪnsɛnsɪtɪvɪ1ti1/ UNCOUNT N *There were times when he showed a curious insensitivity.*

inseparable /ɪnsɛpə0rəbə0l/; a formal word. 1 ADJ If two things are **inseparable,** they cannot be considered separately. *Culture is inseparable from class... The social and ecological costs are inseparable.* 2 ADJ Friends who are **inseparable** are always together. *Soon they were inseparable.*

insert /ɪnsɜ:t/, **inserts, inserting, inserted.** 1 VB WITH OBJ If you **insert** an object into something, you put the object inside it. *He inserted the wooden peg into the hole.* 2 VB WITH OBJ If you **insert** a comment in a piece of writing or a speech, you include it. *The President inserted one unscripted item in his speech.*

inshore /ɪnʃɔ:/. ATTRIB ADJ OR ADV **Inshore** means in the sea but quite close to the land. *...inshore fishermen... These fish are not found inshore.*

inside /ɪnsaɪd/, **insides.** 1 PREP OR ADV Something or someone that is **inside** a place, container, or object is in it or surrounded by it. *Two minutes later we were inside the taxi... You left your lighter inside... It is a fruit with a seed inside.* Also ATTRIB ADJ *The door had no inside bolt.* 2 COUNT N The **inside** of something is the part or area that its sides surround or contain. *The inside of my mouth was dry... ...the inside of the castle.* 3 PLURAL N Your **insides** are your internal organs, especially your stomach; an informal use. *What we all need is a bit of food in our insides.* 4 ATTRIB ADJ On a wide road, the **inside** lanes are the ones closest to the edge of the road. 5 ADV You can also say that someone is **inside** when they are in prison; an informal use. 6 PHRASE If something such as a piece of clothing is **inside out,** the inside part has been turned so that it faces outwards.

insider /ɪnsaɪdə/, **insiders.** COUNT N An **insider** is someone who is involved in a situation and who knows more about it than other people. *According to one insider, the government is getting worried.*

insidious /ɪnsɪdi1əs/. ADJ Something that is **insidious** is unpleasant and develops gradually without being noticed. *The leaflets were a more insidious form of propaganda.*

insight /ɪnsaɪt/, **insights.** UNCOUNT N OR COUNT N **Insight** into a complex situation or problem is an understanding of it. *...a reading of insight, verve, and courage... ...interesting psychological insights.*

insignia /ɪnsɪgnɪə/. **Insignia** is the singular and plural. COUNT N An **insignia** is a badge or sign which shows that a person or object belongs to a particular organization. *...military insignia... ...a plane bearing the insignia of the Condor Legion.*

insignificance, /ɪnsɪgnɪfɪkəns/. UNCOUNT N **Insignificance** is the quality of being insignificant. *This emergency plunges all her other problems into insignificance.*

insignificant /ɪnsɪgnɪfɪkənt/. ADJ Something that is **insignificant** is not at all important. *Whatever I write seems so insignificant... ...an insignificant minority.*

insincere /ɪnsɪnsɪə/. ADJ Someone who is **insincere** pretends to have feelings that they do not have. *...people whose admiration is extravagant and often insincere.* ♦ **insincerity** /ɪnsɪnsɛrɪ1ti1/ UNCOUNT N *The young are quick to recognize insincerity.*

insinuate /ɪnsɪnju:eɪt/, **insinuates, insinuating, insinuated.** 1 REPORT VB If you **insinuate** that something is true, you hint in an unpleasant way that it is true. *He insinuated that my wife had betrayed my trust in her.* 2 REFL VB WITH 'into' If you **insinuate** yourself into a particular position, you manage to get yourself into that position; used showing disapproval. *He eventually insinuated himself into a key position in the Party.*

insipid /ɪnsɪpɪd/. 1 ADJ Someone or something that is **insipid** is dull and boring. *I used to find him insipid.* 2 ADJ **Insipid** food or drink has very little taste. *...gigantic insipid tomatoes, huge flavourless lettuces.*

insist /ɪnsɪst/, **insists, insisting, insisted.** 1 REPORT VB If you **insist** that something is true, you say it very firmly and refuse to change your mind. *She insisted that Jim must leave... 'But you know that she's innocent,' the girl insisted.* 2 VB WITH 'on' If you **insist** on something, you say that you must do it or have it. *He insisted on paying for the meal... We were right to insist on reform.*

insistence /ɪnsɪstəns/. UNCOUNT N Someone's **insistence** on something is the fact that they keep saying firmly that it must be done. *...my insistence on secrecy.*

insistent /ɪnsɪstənt/. 1 ADJ Someone who is **insistent** keeps saying firmly that something must be done. *...insistent demands that more should be done.* ♦ **insistently** ADV *No-one has spoken more insistently on the subject of education than her.* 2 ADJ If a noise or action is **insistent,** it continues for a long time and gets your attention. *...the insistent ringing of the* *telephone.* ♦ **insistently** ADV *I tugged insistently at his jacket.*

insofar as /ɪnsəfɑːr əz/. CONJ You use **insofar as** when giving the reason for something or when showing the extent of something; a formal use. *...contemptuous of the traditional culture, except insofar as it provided precious metals.*

insolent /ɪnsələnt/. ADJ An **insolent** person is very rude or impolite. *...an insolent remark.* ♦ **insolence** /ɪnsələns/ UNCOUNT N *I was taken to the headmistress for my insolence.*

insoluble /ɪnsɒljəbəl/. ADJ An **insoluble** problem cannot be solved.

insomnia /ɪnsɒmnɪə/. UNCOUNT N Someone who suffers from **insomnia** finds it difficult to sleep.

inspect /ɪnspekt/, **inspects, inspecting, inspected.** VB WITH OBJ If you **inspect** something, you examine it carefully. *She inspected his scalp for lice... The kitchens were now amongst the cleanest he had inspected.* ♦ **inspection** /ɪnspekʃən/ UNCOUNT N OR COUNT N *Closer inspection revealed crabs among the rocks... ...an inspection of the kitchen.*

inspector /ɪnspektə/, **inspectors.** 1 COUNT N An **inspector** is someone's whose job is to inspect things. *...the factory inspector... The inspector's report was released to the public.* 2 COUNT N An **inspector** is also an officer in the police force. *...Inspector Flint.*

inspiration /ɪnspɪreɪʃən/, **inspirations.** 1 UNCOUNT N **Inspiration** is a feeling of excitement and enthusiasm gained from new ideas. *I have derived inspiration from Freud.* 2 SING N WITH SUPP The **inspiration** for something such as a piece of work or a theory is the thing that provides the basic idea or example for it. *He became the inspiration for the comic strip character, Superman.* 3 UNCOUNT N If you get **inspiration,** you suddenly think of a good idea. *He paused, searching for inspiration.*

inspire /ɪnspaɪə/, **inspires, inspiring, inspired.** 1 VB WITH OBJ If someone or something **inspires** you, they make you want to do something by giving you new ideas and enthusiasm. *Not even Churchill could inspire the Party to reform... They were too gloomy to be inspired by his enthusiasm.* ♦ **inspired** ADJ *...works of inspired beauty.* 2 VB WITH OBJ Someone or something that **inspires** a particular emotion in people makes them feel this emotion. *...a man who inspired confidence in women.*

instability /ɪnstəbɪlɪti/, **instabilities.** UNCOUNT N OR COUNT N **Instability** is a lack of stability in a place, situation, or person. *Various signs of political instability began to appear... It was just one more sign of his instability.*

install /ɪnstɔːl/, **installs, installing, installed.** 1 VB WITH OBJ If you **install** a piece of equipment, you put or fit it so that it is ready for use. *We have just installed central heating.* 2 VB WITH OBJ If you **install** someone in an important job or position, you give them that job or position. *He installed a man named Briceland as head of the advertisement department.* 3 REFL VB WITH ADJUNCT If you **install** yourself in a place, you settle there. *By now he was installed at 7 New King Street.*

installation /ɪnstəleɪʃən/, **installations.** 1 COUNT N An **installation** is a place that contains equipment and machinery which are used for a particular purpose. *...North Sea oil and gas installations... ...missile installations.* 2 UNCOUNT N The **installation** of a piece of equipment involves putting it into place and making it ready for use. *...the installation of the colour TV.*

instalment /ɪnstɔːlmənt/, **instalments;** spelled **installment** in American English. 1 COUNT N If you pay for something in **instalments,** you pay small sums of money at regular intervals over a period of time. *I paid one hundred dollars in four monthly instalments.* 2 COUNT N If a story is published in **instalments,** part of it is published each day, week, or month. *...the first instalment of the story.*

instance /ɪnstəns/, **instances.** 1 PHRASE You use **for instance** when giving an example of the thing you are talking about. *I mean, for instance, a man like Tom... For instance, an electric fire is a relatively expensive method of heating a room.* 2 COUNT N An **instance** is a particular example of an event, situation, or person. *I do not think that in this instance the doctor was right... ...instances of government injustice.*

instant /ɪnstənt/, **instants.** 1 COUNT N An **instant** is an extremely short period of time. *Bal hesitated for an instant... It was all gone in a single instant.* 2 SING N WITH SUPP An **instant** is also the actual moment when something happened. *At that instant, an angry buzzing began.* 3 CONJ If you do something **the instant** something else happens, you do it as soon as it happens. *She must have dashed out the instant I grabbed the phone.* 4 ADJ You use **instant** to describe something that happens immediately. *Herschel did not have instant success.* ♦ **instantly** ADV *He was killed instantly.* 5 ADJ **Instant** food is food that you can prepare very quickly. *...instant coffee.*

instantaneous /ɪnstənteɪnɪəs/. ADJ Something that is **instantaneous** happens immediately and very quickly. *Death was instantaneous.* ♦ **instantaneously** ADV *The pain passed instantaneously.*

instead /ɪnsted/. PREP OR SENTENCE ADV If you do one thing **instead of** another or if you do it **instead,** you do the first thing rather than the second thing. *If you want to have your meal at seven o'clock instead of five o'clock, you can... He would have sat back, but instead his mind began to consider a more ambitious scheme.*

instep /ɪnstep/, **insteps.** COUNT N Your **instep** is the middle part of your foot, where it curves upwards.

instigate /ɪnstɪgeɪt/, **instigates, instigating, instigated.** VB WITH OBJ To **instigate** an event or situation means to cause it to happen; a formal use. *Further prosecutions were instigated privately.* ♦ **instigation** /ɪnstɪgeɪʃən/ UNCOUNT N *One husband, at the instigation of his wife, called the police.* ♦ **instigator** /ɪnstɪgeɪtə/ COUNT N *The instigator of the plot was Colonel Fletcher.*

instil /ɪnstɪl/, **instils, instilling, instilled;** spelled **instill, instills** in American English. VB WITH OBJ If you **instil** an idea or feeling into someone, you make them think it or feel it. *The presence of the guard was supposed to instil awe and fear in us.*

instinct /ɪnstɪŋkt/, **instincts.** 1 COUNT N OR UNCOUNT N An **instinct** is the natural tendency that a person has to behave or react in a particular way. *...a fundamental instinct for survival... She knew, by instinct, that he wouldn't come back... ...the maternal instinct.* 2 COUNT N If it is your **instinct** to do something, you feel that it is right to do it. *My first instinct was to resign.*

instinctive /ɪnstɪŋktɪv/. ADJ An **instinctive** feeling, idea, or action is one that you have or do without thinking. *Brody took an instinctive dislike to the man... My instinctive reaction was to take a couple of rapid steps backwards.* ♦ **instinctively** ADV *Charles instinctively understood I wanted to be alone.*

institute /ɪnstɪtjuːt/, **institutes, instituting, instituted.** 1 COUNT N An **institute** is an organization set up to do a particular type of work, especially research or teaching. *I visited a number of research institutes in Asia... ...the Massachusetts Institute of Technology.* 2 VB WITH OBJ If you **institute** a system, rule, or course of action, you start it; a formal use. *Mr Wilson was in Opposition when the scheme was instituted.*

institution /ɪnstɪtjuːʃən/, **institutions.** 1 COUNT N An **institution** is a custom or system that is an important or typical feature of a society. *...the institution of marriage.* 2 COUNT N An **institution** is also a large organization, such as a university, bank, or hospital. *These universities accept lower grades than the more prestigious institutions... He may end up in a mental institution... ...financial institutions.* ♦ **institutional** /ɪnstɪtjuːʃənəl, -ʃənəl/ ATTRIB ADJ *...institutional reform... The child has been in institutional care for many years.*

institutionalized /ɪnstɪtjuːʃənəlaɪzd/; also spelled **institutionalised.** 1 ADJ If someone is **institutionalized,** they have been living in an institution such as a hospital or a prison for so long that they find it hard to look after themselves. *...institutionalized children.* 2 ADJ If a custom or system becomes **institutionalized,** it becomes an important and typical part of the social system of a society. *...institutionalized religion.*

instruct /ɪnstrʌkt/, **instructs, instructing, instructed.** 1 VB WITH OBJ AND TO-INF OR REPORT VB If you **instruct** someone to do something, you tell them to do it; a formal use. *I've been instructed to take you to London... 'Breathe in,' he instructed her.* 2 VB WITH OBJ Someone who **instructs** people in a subject or skill teaches it to them.

instruction /ɪnstrʌkʃən/, **instructions.** 1 COUNT N An **instruction** is something that someone tells you to do. *She was only following the instructions of her supervisor.* 2 PLURAL N **Instructions** are clear and detailed information on how to do something. *Read the instructions before you switch on the engine.* 3 UNCOUNT N **Instruction** in a subject or skill is teaching that someone gives you about it.

instructive /ɪnstrʌktɪv/. ADJ Something that is **instructive** gives you useful information.

instructor /ɪnstrʌktə/, **instructors.** COUNT N An **instructor** is a teacher, especially of driving, skiing, or swimming. *...a Swiss ski instructor.*

instrument /ɪnstrəmənt/, **instruments.** 1 COUNT N An **instrument** is a tool or device that is used to do a particular task. *...surgical instruments... ...instruments of torture.* 2 COUNT N A musical **instrument** is an object such as a piano, guitar, or flute which you play in order to produce music. *...stringed instruments.* 3 COUNT N WITH SUPP Something that is an **instrument** for achieving a particular aim is used by people to achieve that aim; a formal use. *Incomes policy is a weak instrument for reducing inflation.*

instrumental /ɪnstrəmentəl/. 1 ADJ Someone or something that is **instrumental** in a process or event helps to make it happen. *The organization was instrumental in getting a ban on certain furs.* 2 ADJ **Instrumental** music is performed using musical instruments and not voices.

insubordination /ɪnsəbɔːdɪneɪʃən/. UNCOUNT N **Insubordination** is disobedient behaviour; a formal use. *...charges of insubordination.*

insubstantial /ɪnsəbstænʃəl/. ADJ **Insubstantial** things are not large, solid, or strong. *...slender and insubstantial structures.*

insufferable /ɪnsʌfərəbəl/. ADJ If someone or something is **insufferable,** they are very unpleasant or annoying. *He was becoming an insufferable pest with his stealing.*

insufficient /ɪnsəfɪʃənt/. ADJ Something that is **insufficient** is not enough for a particular purpose. *Insufficient research has been done... These steps will be insufficient to change our economic decline.* ♦ **insufficiently** ADV *My hand had proved insufficiently strong to open the door.*

insular /ɪnsjələ/. ADJ **Insular** people are unwilling to meet new people or to consider new ideas. *He lived a rather insular life.*

insulate /ɪnsjəleɪt/, **insulates, insulating, insulated.** 1 VB WITH OBJ If a material or substance **insulates** something, it keeps its temperature constant by covering it in a thick layer. *The function of a mammal's hair is to insulate the body.* 2 VB WITH OBJ If you **insulate** a person from harmful things, you protect them from those things; a formal use. *They could insulate the local population from these dangerous influences... ...in a sheltered, womb-like world, insulated against the events of life outside.* 3 VB WITH OBJ If you **insulate** an electrical device, you cover it with rubber or plastic to prevent electricity passing through it and giving the person using it an electric shock.

insulation /ɪnsjəleɪʃən/. UNCOUNT N **Insulation** is a thick layer of material used to keep something warm. *...a long roll of roof insulation.*

insult, insults, insulting, insulted; pronounced /ɪnsʌlt/ when it is a verb and /ɪnsʌlt/ when it is a noun. 1 VB WITH OBJ If you **insult** someone, you offend them by being rude to them. *You don't have to apologize to me. You didn't insult me... He feels deeply insulted.* ♦ **insulting** ADJ *He did use insulting language.* 2 COUNT N An **insult** is a rude remark or action which offends someone. *The older boys yelled out insults... I would take it as an insult if you left.*

insuperable /ɪnsjuːpərəbəl/. ADJ A problem that is **insuperable** cannot be solved; a formal use. *It would be an insuperable barrier to unity.*

insupportable /ɪnsəpɔːtəbəl/. ADJ If a remark or action is **insupportable** it is very unpleasant; a formal use. *Accusations of that kind are quite insupportable.*

insurance /ɪnʃʊərəns, -ʃɔː-/. 1 UNCOUNT N **Insurance** is an agreement in which you pay a fixed sum of money to a company, usually each year. Then, if you become ill or if your property is damaged or stolen, the company pays you a sum of money. *...private health insurance... ...insurance companies.* ● See also **national insurance.** 2 SING N If you do something as an **insurance** against something unpleasant, you do it in order to protect yourself in case the unpleasant thing happens. *They build up supplies as an insurance against drought.*

insure /ɪnʃʊə, -ʃɔː/, **insures, insuring, insured.** 1 REFL VB OR VB WITH OBJ If you **insure** yourself or your property, you pay money to an insurance company so that, if you become ill or if your property is damaged or stolen, the company will pay you a sum of money. *Insure your baggage before you leave home.* ♦ **insured** PRED ADJ *The house is not insured against fire.* 2 VB WITH 'against' If you **insure** against something unpleasant happening, you do something to protect yourself in case it happens. *In years of good rainfall they expand their stocks to insure against drought.* 3 See also **ensure.**

insurmountable /ɪnsəmaʊntəbəl/. ADJ An **insurmountable** problem cannot be solved; a formal use.

insurrection /ɪnsərekʃən/, **insurrections.** COUNT N OR UNCOUNT N An **insurrection** is violent action taken by a group of people against the rulers of their country. *...an armed insurrection... Such policies were intended to prevent insurrection.*

intact /ɪntækt/. ADJ Something that is **intact** is complete and has not been damaged or spoilt. *...the window remained intact... They are fighting to keep village life intact.*

intake /ɪnteɪk/, **intakes.** 1 UNCOUNT N WITH SUPP Your **intake** of food, drink, or air is the amount that you eat, drink, or breathe in, or the process of taking it into your body. *Nurses kept measuring her fluid intake.*

2 COUNT N WITH SUPP The people who are accepted into an institution or organization at a particular time are referred to as a particular **intake.** *...the army's huge emergency intake of soldiers.*

intangible /ɪntændʒɪbə^{0}l/. ADJ A quality or idea that is **intangible** is hard to define or explain.

integral /ɪntɪ^{2}grəl/. ADJ If something is an **integral** part of another thing, it is an essential part of it. *The Young Socialists were an integral feature of the Labour movement... The concept of loyalty is integral to the story.*

integrate /ɪntɪ^{2}greɪt/, **integrates, integrating, integrated. 1** ERG VB WITH 'into' OR RECIP VB If people **integrate** into a social group, they mix with people in that group. *...helping the individual integrate quickly into the community... ...ways of integrating handicapped children into ordinary schools... In theory, all schools should already be integrated.* ♦ **integrated** ATTRIB ADJ *...an integrated school for Protestants and Catholics.* ♦ **integration** /ɪntɪ^{2}greɪʃə^{0}n/ UNCOUNT N *He campaigned for the integration of immigrants into British society.* **2** VB WITH OBJ If you **integrate** things, you combine them so that they are closely linked or so that they form one thing. *The two regional railway systems were integrated.*

integrity /ɪntegrɪ^{1}ti^1/. UNCOUNT N **Integrity** is the quality of being honest and firm in your moral principles. *He was particularly respected for his integrity... ...a man of the highest integrity.*

intellect /ɪntə^{2}lekt/, **intellects. 1** UNCOUNT N OR COUNT N **Intellect** is the ability to think and to understand ideas and information. *...the intellect of modern man... ...the idea of computers with intellects.* **2** UNCOUNT N **Intellect** is also the quality of being very intelligent or clever. *...a family noted for its intellect.*

intellectual /ɪntə^{2}lektʃʊ^{0}əl/, **intellectuals. 1** ATTRIB ADJ **Intellectual** means involving a person's ability to think and to understand ideas and information. *...children in need of extra emotional or intellectual stimulation... ...his tremendous intellectual powers.* ♦ **intellectually** ADV *...an intellectually challenging occupation.* **2** COUNT N An **intellectual** is someone who spends a lot of time studying and thinking about complicated ideas. *...scholars and intellectuals.* Also ADJ *...an intellectual conversation.*

intelligence /ɪntelɪdʒəns/. **1** UNCOUNT N Someone's **intelligence** is their ability to understand and learn things. *...a person of average intelligence.* **2** UNCOUNT N **Intelligence** is the ability to think and understand instead of doing things by instinct or automatically. *Do hedgehogs have intelligence?... ...computer intelligence.* **3** UNCOUNT N **Intelligence** is also information gathered by the government about their country's enemies. *...American intelligence services.*

intelligent /ɪntelɪdʒənt/. **1** ADJ An **intelligent** person has the ability to understand and learn things well. *Jo is an intelligent student... ...a very intelligent question.* ♦ **intelligently** ADV *They dealt with that problem intelligently.* **2** ADJ An animal or computer that is **intelligent** has the ability to think and understand instead of doing things by instinct or automatically. *Computers can be intelligent.*

intelligible /ɪntelɪdʒəbə^{0}l/. ADJ Something that is **intelligible** can be understood. *Describe it in a way that would be intelligible to an outsider.*

intend /ɪntend/, **intends, intending, intended. 1** VB If you **intend** to do something, you have decided to do it or have planned to do it. *This is my job and I intend to do it... He had intended staying longer... He woke later than he had intended.* ♦ **intended** ATTRIB ADJ *What is the intended result?* **2** REPORT VB If you **intend** something to happen or to have a particular effect or function, you have planned that it should happen or should have that effect or function. *We never intended the scheme to be permanent... It is intended as a handbook, for frequent reference... It had been intended that a second group should be assembled.* **3** VB WITH OBJ Something that **is intended** for a particular person or purpose has been planned or made for that person or purpose. *The man had drunk what had been intended for me... They are not yet intended for use.*

intense /ɪntens/. **1** ADJ Something that is **intense** is very great in strength or degree. *The effects of the drug are intense and brief... ...the intense heat... The row caused her intense unhappiness.* ♦ **intensely** ADV *She had suffered intensely.* ♦ **intensity** /ɪntensɪ^{1}ti^1/ UNCOUNT N *The debates are renewed with great intensity.* **2** ADJ An **intense** person is serious all the time.

intensify /ɪntensɪfaɪ/, **intensifies, intensifying, intensified.** ERG VB If you **intensify** something or if it **intensifies,** it becomes greater in strength or degree. *In the late 1960s the pressures suddenly intensified... The search was intensified using dogs.* ♦ **intensified** ATTRIB ADJ *...intensified international competition.*

intensive /ɪntensɪv/. ADJ An **intensive** activity involves an increase in the concentration of energy or people on one particular task. *...the last intensive preparation for my exams.* ♦ **intensively** ADV *The land was developed very intensively in the mid 1930s.*

intensive care. UNCOUNT N **Intensive care** is extremely thorough care provided by hospitals for people who are very seriously ill.

intent /ɪntent/, **intents. 1** UNCOUNT N A person's **intent** is their intention to do something; a formal use. *The conference declared its intent to organize a national movement... They signed a declaration of intent.* **2** ADJ When you look **intent,** you show that you are paying great attention. *She was brushing her hair, intent on her face in the mirror.* ♦ **intently** ADV *I stood behind a parked van, watching intently.* **3** PRED ADJ WITH 'on' OR 'upon' If you are **intent** on doing something, you are determined to do it. *They were intent on keeping what they had.* **4** PHRASE You say **to all intents and purposes** to suggest that a situation is not exactly as you describe it but the effect is the same as if it were. *She was to all intents and purposes the infant's mother.*

intention /ɪntenʃə^{0}n/, **intentions.** COUNT N OR UNCOUNT N An **intention** is an idea or plan of what you are going to do. *He confirmed his intention to leave next April... She had no intention of spending the rest of her life working as a waitress.*

intentional /ɪntenʃə^{0}nəl, -ʃənə^{0}l/. ADJ Something that is **intentional** is deliberate. *...intentional misrepresentation.* ♦ **intentionally** ADV *I banged the door. Not intentionally.*

inter-. PREFIX **Inter-** is used to form adjectives that describe something as moving, existing, or happening between similar things or groups of people. For example, inter-governmental relations are relations between governments. *...inter-racial marriages.*

interact /ɪntərækt/, **interacts, interacting, interacted.** RECIP VB The way that two people or things **interact** is the way that they communicate or work in relation to each other. *The tidal currents interacted with the discharge from a river estuary... Mothers and babies interact in a very complex way.* ♦ **interaction** /ɪntərækʃə^{0}n/ UNCOUNT N OR COUNT N *There is a need for more interaction between staff and children... ...a method of encouraging the interaction of ideas.*

interactive /ɪntəræktɪv/. ADJ **Interactive** use of a computer is use in which the user and the computer communicate directly with each other by means of a keyboard and a screen; a technical use.

intercede /ɪntəsiːd/, **intercedes, interceding, interceded.** VB If you **intercede** with a person, you talk to them in order to try to end a disagreement that they have with another person; a formal use. *I had interceded for him with his employer.*

intercept /ɪntəsept/, **intercepts, intercepting, intercepted.** VB WITH OBJ If you **intercept** someone or something that is travelling from one place to another, you stop them.

intercession /ɪntəseʃə^{0}n/, **intercessions.** UNCOUNT N OR COUNT N **Intercession** is an act of trying to end a disagreement between two people; a formal use. *Through the intercession of a friend, my request was granted.*

interchange /ɪntətʃeɪnd^{0}ʒ/, **interchanges. 1** UNCOUNT N OR COUNT N WITH SUPP The **interchange** of things, people, or ideas is the exchange of things, people, or ideas. *...a regular forum for the interchange of information and ideas... ...interchange between the classes.* **2** COUNT N An **interchange** on a motorway is a junction where it meets another main road.

interchangeable /ɪntətʃeɪnd^{0}ʒəbə^{0}l/. ADJ Things that are **interchangeable** can be exchanged with each other without making any difference. *We tend to use these terms as if they were freely interchangeable.* ♦ **interchangeably** ADV *...the word 'fascist' was used interchangeably with the word 'racist'.*

intercom /ɪntəkɒm/, **intercoms.** COUNT N An **intercom** is a device like a small box with a microphone and loudspeaker which you use to talk to people in another room. *A voice on the intercom said, 'It's Mr Vaughan.'*

interconnect /ɪntəkənekt/, **interconnects, interconnecting, interconnected.** RECIP VB OR PASSIVE VB Things that **interconnect** or that **are interconnected** are connected with each other. *Monarch, court and government were all interconnected... This service must be able to interconnect with millions of others.*

intercontinental /ɪntəkɒntɪnentə^{0}l/. ADJ **Intercontinental** is used to describe something that exists or happens between continents. *...an intercontinental flight.*

intercourse /ɪntəkɔːs/. UNCOUNT N If people have **intercourse,** they have sex; a formal use.

interdependent /ɪntədɪ^{1}pendənt/. ADJ People or things that are **interdependent** all depend on each other. *Plants and animals are strongly interdependent.* ♦ **interdependence** /ɪntədɪ^{1}pendəns/ UNCOUNT N *...the interdependence of economies.*

interest /ɪntə^{0}rə^{2}st/, **interests, interesting, interested. 1** SING N OR UNCOUNT N If you have an **interest** in something, you want to learn or hear more about it. *None of them had the slightest interest in music... Brody was beginning to lose interest.* **2** COUNT N Your **interests** are the things that you enjoy doing. *He had two consuming interests: rowing and polo.* **3** VB WITH OBJ If something **interests** you, you want to learn more about it or to continue doing it. *Young men should always look for work which interests them.* **4** VB WITH OBJ If you **interest** someone in something, you persuade them to do it or to buy it. *Can I interest you in yet another horror movie?* **5** COUNT N If you have an **interest** in something being done, you want it to be done because you will benefit from it. *They had no interest in the overthrow of the established order... They would protect the interests of their members.* ● Something that is **in the interests** of a person or group will benefit them in some way. *It is not in the interests of any of us to have a weak government.* **6** PLURAL N Someone who has **interests** in a particular type of business owns companies or shares of this type. *...an industrialist with business interests in Germany.* **7** UNCOUNT N **Interest** is money that you receive if you have invested a sum of money, or money that you pay if you have borrowed money. *...the interest you pay on your mortgage... ...high interest rates.* **8** See also **vested interest.**

interested /ɪntə^{0}rə^{2}stɪ^{2}d/. **1** PRED ADJ If you are **interested** in something, you think it is important or worthwhile and you want to know more about it or want to develop it further. *I'm very interested in birds... He looked interested... My sister is interested in becoming a nurse.* **2** ATTRIB ADJ An **interested** party or group of people is affected by or involved in a particular event or situation. *We talked to scientists and other interested parties.*

interesting /ɪntə^{0}rə^{2}stɪŋ/. ADJ If you find something **interesting,** it attracts you or holds your attention. *That's a very interesting question... He was not very interesting to talk to.*

interestingly /ɪntə^{0}rə^{2}stɪŋli^1/. SENTENCE ADV You use **interestingly** to introduce a piece of information that you think is interesting and unexpected. *Interestingly enough, America is now dependent on Africa for oil imports.*

interfere /ɪntəfɪə/, **interferes, interfering, interfered. 1** VB If you **interfere** in a situation, you become involved in it although it does not really concern you; used showing disapproval. *My mother interferes in things... Don't interfere.* ♦ **interfering** ADJ *...an interfering old woman.* **2** VB Something that **interferes** with a situation, process, or activity has a damaging effect on it. *Child-bearing will not interfere with a career.*

interference /ɪntəfɪərəns/. **1** UNCOUNT N **Interference** is the act of interfering in something. *I wanted to do the thing on my own without outside interference or help... They didn't want any interference from their national government.* **2** UNCOUNT N When there is **interference,** a radio signal is affected by other radio waves so that it cannot be received properly.

interim /ɪntərɪm/. ATTRIB ADJ **Interim** describes things that are intended to be used until something permanent is arranged. *...a temporary or interim arrangement... ...an interim report.*

interior /ɪntɪərɪə/, **interiors. 1** COUNT N The **interior** of something is the inside part of it. *Very little is known about the deep interior of the earth... The castle has its interior well preserved.* Also ATTRIB ADJ *...an interior room without windows.* **2** ATTRIB ADJ An **interior** minister or political department deals with affairs in their own country.

interject /ɪntədʒekt/, **interjects, interjecting, interjected.** VB WITH OR WITHOUT OBJ If you **interject,** you say something when someone else is speaking; a formal use. *...if I may interject a word here... 'No, no,' interjected Schmidt.*

interjection /ɪntədʒekʃə^{0}n/, **interjections. 1** COUNT N An **interjection** is something you say when someone else is speaking; a formal use. *The bishop was prepared for this interjection.* **2** COUNT N In grammar, an **interjection** is a word or expression expressing a feeling of surprise, pain, or horror.

interlock /ɪntəlɒk/, **interlocks, interlocking, interlocked.** ERG VB OR RECIP VB Things that **interlock** with each other fit into each other and are firmly joined. *All the units interlock with one another rigidly... He interlocked his fingers... ...six or eight strong rods interlocked at right angles.*

interlude /ɪntəluːd/, **interludes.** COUNT N An **interlude** is a short period of time during which an activity or event stops. *After this interlude, the band started up again.*

intermarry /ɪntəmæri^1/, **intermarries, intermarrying, intermarried.** VB When people from different social, racial, or religious groups **intermarry,** they marry each other.

intermediary /ɪntəmiːdjəri^1/, **intermediaries.** COUNT N An **intermediary** is a person who passes messages between two people or groups. *He dealt through an intermediary with Beaverbrook himself.*

intermediate /ɪntəmiːdɪət/. 1 ATTRIB ADJ An **intermediate** stage is one that occurs between two other stages. *One group of animals developed into another by way of intermediate forms.* 2 ADJ **Intermediate** students are no longer beginners, but are not yet advanced. *...an English course, intermediate level, for adult students.*

interminable /ɪntɜːmɪnəbəl/. ADJ Something that is **interminable** continues for a very long time. *I was glad of company for this interminable flight.*

intermingle /ɪntəmɪŋgəl/, **intermingles, intermingling, intermingled.** RECIP VB When people or things **intermingle,** they mix with each other; a formal use. *The police intermingled with the crowds.*

intermission /ɪntəmɪʃən/, **intermissions.** COUNT N An **intermission** is an interval between two parts of a play or, in America, the interval in a play or a film.

intermittent /ɪntəmɪtənt/. ADJ Something that is **intermittent** happens occasionally rather than continuously. *I became aware of a faint, intermittent noise.* ♦ **intermittently** ADV *The magazine had been published intermittently since the war.*

intern /ɪntɜːn/, **interns, interning, interned.** VB WITH OBJ To **intern** someone means to put them in prison, for political reasons; a formal use.

internal /ɪntɜːnəl/. 1 ATTRIB ADJ You use **internal** to describe things that exist or happen inside a place, organization, or person. *Our internal human system uses about 100 watts of energy... ...an internal bank memorandum.* ♦ **internally** ADV *The house has been rebuilt internally.* 2 ATTRIB ADJ **Internal** also means relating to the political and commercial activities inside a country. *...the internal politics of France.* 3 ADJ **Internal** ideas or images exist in your mind; a formal use. *We have both external and internal values.*

international /ɪntənæʃənəl/. ADJ **International** means involving different countries. *...international affairs... ...an international agreement on nuclear waste.* ♦ **internationally** ADV *She's an internationally famous historian.*

internment /ɪntɜːnmə^{2}nt/. UNCOUNT N **Internment** is imprisonment for political reasons; a formal use.

interpersonal /ɪntəpɜːsənəl/. ATTRIB ADJ **Interpersonal** means relating to relationships between people. *...interpersonal relationships.*

interplay /ɪntəpleɪ/. UNCOUNT N The **interplay** between two or more things is the way that they react or work with each other; a formal use. *...the interplay between practical and theoretical constraints... ...the interplay of market forces.*

interpret /ɪntɜːprɪt/, **interprets, interpreting, interpreted.** 1 VB WITH OBJ If you **interpret** something in a particular way, you decide that this is its meaning or significance. *I'm not quite sure how to interpret that question... The election result is being interpreted as a serious setback for the government.* 2 VB WITH OR WITHOUT OBJ If you **interpret** what someone is saying, you translate it immediately into another language. *He interpreted the opening words of section 16... Paul had to interpret for us.*

interpretation /ɪntɜːprɪteɪʃən/, **interpretations.** 1 COUNT N OR UNCOUNT N An **interpretation** of something is an explanation of what it means. *This passage is open to a variety of interpretations.* 2 COUNT N OR UNCOUNT N A performer's **interpretation** of a piece of music or a dance is the particular way in which they choose to perform it. *Do you find his interpretation of Chopin satisfactory?*

interpreter /ɪntɜːprɪtə/, **interpreters.** COUNT N An **interpreter** is a person whose job is to translate what someone is saying into another language.

interrelate /ɪntəri^{1}leɪt/, **interrelates, interrelating, interrelated.** ERG VB If two or more things **interrelate** or **are interrelated,** there is a connection between them and they have an effect on one another; a formal use. *These courses interrelate in a variety of ways... All three factors are interrelated.*

interrogate /ɪntɛrəgeɪt/, **interrogates, interrogating, interrogated.** VB WITH OBJ If someone, especially a police officer or an army officer, **interrogates** you, they question you thoroughly for a long time, in order to get information from you. *They had been interrogated for 20 hours about political demonstrations.* ♦ **interrogation** /ɪntɛrəgeɪʃən/ COUNT N OR UNCOUNT N *Waddell had undergone a lengthy interrogation... We've had him under interrogation for 36 hours.*

interrogative /ɪntərɒgətɪv/, **interrogatives.** 1 ADJ An **interrogative** sentence is one that has the form of a question. For example, 'What is your name?' is **interrogative.** 2 COUNT N An **interrogative** is a word such as 'who', 'how', or 'why', which can be used to ask a question.

interrogator /ɪntɛrəgeɪtə/, **interrogators.** COUNT N An **interrogator** is a person, especially a police officer or an army officer, who questions someone thoroughly for a long time.

interrupt /ɪntərʌpt/, **interrupts, interrupting, interrupted.** 1 VB WITH OR WITHOUT OBJ If you **interrupt** someone who is speaking, you say or do something that causes them to stop. *Sorry to interrupt you... Don't interrupt.* 2 VB WITH OBJ If you **interrupt** an activity, you temporarily prevent it from continuing. *Bain had interrupted his holiday to go to Hamburg.*

interruption /ɪntərʌpʃən/, **interruptions.** 1 COUNT N An **interruption** is something which temporarily prevents an activity from continuing. *She hates interruptions when she's working.* 2 UNCOUNT N **Interruption** is the act of interrupting someone or something. *We should be safe from interruption.*

intersect /ɪntəsɛkt/, **intersects, intersecting, intersected.** 1 RECIP VB When roads **intersect,** they cross each other. *The highway intersected Main Street in a busy crossing.* 2 VB WITH OBJ If an area **is intersected** by roads or railways, they cross it and divide it into smaller areas. *The marshes were intersected by a maze of ditches.*

intersection /ɪntəsɛkʃən/, **intersections.** COUNT N An **intersection** is a place where roads cross each other. *...a city at the intersection of three motorways.*

interspersed /ɪntəspɜːst/. PRED ADJ WITH 'with' If something is **interspersed** with other things, these things occur at various points in it. *...shabby shops and houses interspersed with modern offices and banks... ...a story interspersed with long silences.*

interval /ɪntəvəl/, **intervals.** 1 COUNT N The **interval** between two events or dates is the period of time between them. *...the interval between supper and bedtime... ...after an interval of ten years.* 2 COUNT N At a play or concert, an **interval** is a break between two of the parts. *The audience were going out for the interval.*

PHRASES • If something happens **at intervals,** it happens several times, with gaps or pauses in between. *At intervals, the carriage was halted... They kept coming back at six-month intervals.* • If things are placed **at** particular **intervals,** there are spaces between them. *They were scattered through the forest, at varying intervals.*

intervene /ɪntəviːn/, **intervenes, intervening, intervened.** VB If you **intervene** in a situation, you become involved in it and try to change it. *Two officers intervened to stop their recording... The State may intervene in disputes between employers and workers.*

intervening /ɪntəviːnɪŋ/. ATTRIB ADJ An **intervening** period of time is one which separates two events or points in time. *What happened in the intervening years?*

intervention /ɪntəvɛnʃən/, **interventions.** 1 UNCOUNT N OR COUNT N **Intervention** is an attempt to change a situation by becoming involved in it. *He was against American intervention in the war... ...the interventions of government.* 2 COUNT N An **intervention** during a discussion is an interruption. *...the angry interventions of Lord Grant.*

interview /ɪntəvjuː/, **interviews, interviewing, interviewed.** 1 COUNT N OR UNCOUNT N An **interview** is a formal meeting at which someone is asked questions in order to find out if they are suitable for a job or a course of study. *I had an interview for a job on a newspaper... He was invited for interview at three universities.* 2 COUNT N An **interview** is also a conversation in which a journalist asks a famous person questions. *...a television interview.* 3 VB WITH OBJ When an employer **interviews** you, he or she asks you questions in order to find out whether you are suitable for a job. *I was once interviewed for a part in a film.* 4 VB WITH OBJ When a famous person **is interviewed,** a journalist asks them a series of questions. *Hopkins was interviewed by Wyndham for Queen magazine.* ♦ **interviewer** /ɪntəvjuːə/ COUNT N *Television interviewers were being too aggressive.*

interwoven /ɪntəwəʊvən/. ADJ If things are **interwoven,** they are joined together in a very close and complicated way. *Social and international unity have become interwoven.*

intestine /ɪntɛstɪn/, **intestines.** COUNT N Your **intestines** are the tubes in your body through which food from your stomach passes. *...pains in the intestine.* ♦ **intestinal** /ɪntɛstɪnəl/ ATTRIB ADJ *...intestinal infections.*

intimacy /ɪntɪ^{1}məsi^1/. UNCOUNT N When there is **intimacy** between people, they have a close relationship. *Never before had he known such intimacy with another person.*

intimate, intimates, intimating, intimated; pronounced /ɪntɪ^{1}mət/ when it is an adjective and /ɪntɪmeɪt/ when it is a verb. 1 ADJ If two people have an **intimate** relationship, they are very good friends. *...her best and most intimate friend.* ♦ **intimately** ADV *I don't know any girls intimately.* 2 ADJ **Intimate** also means personal and private. *...the most intimate details of their personal lives.* ♦ **intimately** ADV *...women talking intimately to other women.* 3 ADJ To be **intimate** with someone means to have a sexual relationship with them; an old-fashioned use. *He had been intimate with a number of women.* 4 ADJ An **intimate** connection is a very close one. *...its intimate bonds with government.* ♦ **intimately** ADV *These two questions are intimately linked.* 5 ATTRIB ADJ If you have an **intimate** knowledge of something, you know it in great detail. *...someone with an intimate knowledge of the station.* ♦ **intimately** ADV *He knew the contents of the files intimately.* 6 REPORT VB If you **intimate** that something is the case, you say it in an indirect way; a formal use. *Forbes intimated that he would prefer to do this later.*

intimation /ɪntɪmeɪʃən/, **intimations.** COUNT N WITH SUPP If you have an **intimation** of something, you feel that it exists or is true; a formal use. *For the first time I felt some intimation of danger... ...the first intimations of a new idea.*

intimidate /ɪntɪmɪdeɪt/, **intimidates, intimidating, intimidated.** VB WITH OBJ To **intimidate** someone means to frighten them, sometimes as a deliberate way of making them do something. *In 1972 his neighbours intimidated his family into leaving.* ♦ **intimidation** /ɪntɪmɪdeɪʃən/ UNCOUNT N *Young suffered imprisonment and intimidation.*

intimidated /ɪntɪmɪdeɪtɪ^{2}d/. ADJ If you are **intimidated** by someone, you are afraid of them and have no confidence in yourself. *Theo was intimidated by so many strangers.*

intimidating /ɪntɪmɪdeɪtɪŋ/. ADJ If something is **intimidating,** it causes you to feel afraid and to lose confidence in yourself. *The rooms were huge and intimidating.*

into /ɪntuː/. 1 PREP If you put one thing **into** another thing, you put the first thing inside the second thing. *Pour some water into a glass... He slipped the note into his pocket.* 2 PREP If you go **into** a place or vehicle, you go inside it. *He walked into a police station... They got into the car.* 3 PREP If one thing gets **into** another thing, the first thing enters the second thing and becomes part of it. *Drugs may get into the milk... ...Britain's entry into the Common Market.* 4 PREP If you bump or crash **into** something, you hit it accidentally. *I bumped into a chair.* 5 PREP If you get **into** a piece of clothing, you put it on. *She changed into her best dress.* 6 PREP To get **into** a particular state means to start being in that state. *The Labour Government came into power in 1974... The assembly was shocked into silence.* 7 PREP If something is changed **into** a new form or shape, it then has this new form or shape. *The bud develops into a flower... The play was made into a movie... I tore her letter into eight pieces.* 8 PREP An investigation **into** a subject or event is concerned with that subject or event. *...research into emotional problems... Some MPs demanded a full enquiry into the incident.*

intolerable /ɪntɒlərəbəl/. ADJ If something is **intolerable,** it is so bad that people cannot accept it. *...an intolerable dullness.* ♦ **intolerably** ADV *The days were still intolerably hot.*

intolerant /ɪntɒlərənt/. ADJ **Intolerant** people disapprove of behaviour and opinions that differ from their own. *He was intolerant of other people's weakness... We are giving support to intolerant regimes.* ♦ **intolerance** /ɪntɒlərəns/ UNCOUNT N *...religious intolerance.*

intonation /ɪntə^{6}neɪʃən/, **intonations.** COUNT N OR UNCOUNT N Your **intonation** is the way your voice rises and falls when you speak. *...their accents and intonations... ...the subtleties of middle-class intonation.*

intone /ɪntəʊn/, **intones, intoning, intoned.** VB WITH OBJ If you **intone** something, you say it in a slow and serious way, not allowing your voice to rise and fall very much; a literary use. *They intoned the afternoon prayers.*

intoxicated /ɪntɒksɪkeɪtɪ^{2}d/. 1 ADJ If someone is **intoxicated,** they are drunk; a formal use. 2 PRED ADJ If you are **intoxicated** by an event, idea, or feeling, it makes you behave in an extreme way. *Intoxicated by victory, he was dancing... They became intoxicated with pride.*

intoxicating /ɪntɒksɪkeɪtɪŋ/. 1 ADJ An **intoxicating** drink contains alcohol and can make you drunk. 2 ADJ

Something that is **intoxicating** causes you to be very excited and to behave in an uncontrolled or foolish way. *...her intoxicating beauty.*

intoxication /ɪntɒksɪkeɪʃə^{0}n/. 1 UNCOUNT N **Intoxication** is the state of being drunk. *They were in an advanced state of intoxication.* 2 UNCOUNT N **Intoxication** is also the state of being so excited that you behave in an uncontrolled or foolish way. *...the intoxication of success.*

intractable /ɪntræktəbə^{0}l/; a formal word. 1 ADJ **Intractable** people are stubborn and difficult to influence or control. *On one issue Luce was intractable.* 2 ADJ **Intractable** problems seem impossible to deal with. *Labour problems can be more intractable.*

intransigent /ɪntrænsɪdʒənt/. ADJ If someone is **intransigent,** they refuse to change their behaviour or opinions; a formal use showing disapproval. *...their intransigent attitude over our debts.* ♦ **intransigence** /ɪntrænsɪdʒəns/ UNCOUNT N WITH POSS *The party is forced into violence by the intransigence of its opponents.*

intransitive /ɪntrænsɪtɪv/. ADJ An **intransitive** verb does not have an object.

intrepid /ɪntrɛpɪd/. ADJ An **intrepid** person acts bravely, ignoring difficulties and danger; a literary use. *...the route of those intrepid explorers.*

intricacy /ɪntrɪkəsi^1/, **intricacies.** 1 PLURAL N The **intricacies** of a situation are its small details. *...the intricacies of American politics.* 2 UNCOUNT N The **intricacy** of something is the fact that it has many parts or details. *...the technical intricacy of modern industry.*

intricate /ɪntrɪkə^{1}t/. ADJ Something that is **intricate** has many small parts or details. *They were painted in intricate patterns... ...long, intricate discussions.* ♦ **intricately** ADV *...an intricately carved door.*

intrigue, intrigues, intriguing, intrigued; pronounced /ɪntri:g/ when it is a noun and /ɪntri:g/ when it is a verb. 1 UNCOUNT N OR COUNT N **Intrigue** is the making of secret plans that are intended to harm other people. *...a great deal of political intrigue... ...financial intrigues.* 2 VB WITH OBJ If something **intrigues** you, you are fascinated by it and curious about it. *The idea seemed to intrigue him.* ♦ **intrigued** PRED ADJ *Intrigued, I followed the instructions.* ♦ **intriguing** ADJ *That sounds most intriguing.*

intrinsic /ɪntrɪnsɪk/. ATTRIB ADJ The **intrinsic** qualities of something are its important and basic qualities; a formal use. *...the intrinsic idiocy of the plan... ...objects which have no intrinsic value.* ♦ **intrinsically** ADV *His material was intrinsically interesting.*

introduce /ɪntrə^{6}dju:s/, **introduces, introducing, introduced.** 1 VB WITH OBJ If you **introduce** one person to another, you tell them each other's name, so that they can get to know each other. *Hogan introduced him to Karl... At a party in Hollywood, I was introduced to Charlie Chaplin.* 2 VB WITH OBJ When someone **introduces** a television or radio programme, they tell you at the beginning what it will be about. 3 VB WITH OBJ To **introduce** something to a place or system means to take it or use it there for the first time. *Rabbits had been introduced into Australia by Europeans... Banks will soon introduce new savings plans.* 4 VB WITH OBJ AND PREP 'to' If you **introduce** someone to something, you cause them to have their first experience of it. *We introduced them to the new methods... He was first introduced to politics as a child.*

introduction /ɪntrə^{6}dʌkʃə^{0}n/, **introductions.** 1 UNCOUNT N WITH SUPP The **introduction** of something into a place or system is the occasion when it is taken or used there for the first time. *The Government saw the introduction of new technology as vital.* 2 SING N Your **introduction** to something is the occasion when you experience it for the first time. *This was my first real introduction to agriculture.* 3 COUNT N The **introduction** to a book or talk comes at the beginning and tells you what the rest of the book or talk is about. 4 COUNT N When you make an **introduction,** you tell two people each other's names so that they can get to know each other.

introductory /ɪntrə^{6}dʌktə^{0}ri^1/. ATTRIB ADJ **Introductory** remarks, books, or courses are intended to give you a general idea of a particular subject, often before more detailed information is given. *...a good introductory chapter on forests.*

introspection /ɪntrə^{6}spɛkʃə^{0}n/. UNCOUNT N **Introspection** is the examining of your own thoughts, ideas, and feelings.

introspective /ɪntrə^{6}spɛktɪv/. ADJ **Introspective** people spend a lot of time examining their own thoughts, ideas, and feelings. *The boy was downcast and introspective.*

introvert /ɪntrə^{6}vɜ:t/, **introverts.** COUNT N An **introvert** is a quiet, shy person. *...a bashful introvert.* ♦ **introverted** /ɪntrə^{6}vɜ:tr^{2}d/ ADJ *He was the most introverted boy in my school.*

intrude /ɪntru:d/, **intrudes, intruding, intruded.** 1 VB If you **intrude** on someone, you disturb them when they are in a private place or having a private conversation. *He felt that he couldn't intrude... I don't want to intrude on your family.* 2 VB WITH 'on' If something **intrudes** on your mood or your life, it disturbs it or has an unpleasant effect on it. *I shall not intrude on your grief.*

intruder /ɪntru:də/, **intruders.** COUNT N An **intruder** is a person who enters a place without permission. *An intruder had come into his home.*

intrusion /ɪntru:ʒə^{0}n/, **intrusions.** 1 COUNT N If someone disturbs you when you are in a private place or having a private conversation, you can describe their behaviour as an **intrusion.** *I must ask your pardon for this intrusion.* 2 COUNT N OR UNCOUNT N An **intrusion** is also something that affects your work or way of life in an unwelcome way. *...the bank's intrusions into Mr Wheeler's operations... Government could enforce the law with minimal intrusion.*

intrusive /ɪntru:sɪv/. ADJ If someone or something is **intrusive,** they disturb your mood or life in an unwelcome way. *...Gordon's intrusive interest in our religious activities.*

intuition /ɪntju:ɪʃə^{0}n/, **intuitions.** UNCOUNT N OR COUNT N If your **intuition** tells you that something is the case or if you have an **intuition** about it, you feel that it is the case although you have no evidence or proof. *My intuition told me to stay away... I've got an intuition that something is wrong... ...arguments based on intuition.*

intuitive /ɪntju:ɪtɪv/. ADJ **Intuitive** ideas or feelings tell you that something is the case although you have no evidence or proof. *...his intuitive understanding of nature.* ♦ **intuitively** ADV *I felt intuitively that they would not return.*

inundate /ɪnʌndeɪt/, **inundates, inundating, inundated.** VB WITH OBJ If you **are inundated** with things, you receive so many that you cannot deal with them all. *She was inundated with telephone calls.*

invade /ɪnveɪd/, **invades, invading, invaded.** 1 VB WITH OBJ To **invade** a country means to enter it by force with an army. *...Kennedy's secret plan to invade Cuba.* ♦ **invader** /ɪnveɪdə/ COUNT N *The invaders had been defeated.* 2 VB WITH OBJ When people or animals **invade** a place, they enter it in large numbers. *The town was invaded by reporters.*

invalid, invalids; pronounced /ɪnvəlɪd/ when it is a noun or modifier, and /ɪnvælɪd/ when it is an adjective. 1 COUNT N OR MOD An **invalid** is someone who is very ill or disabled and needs to be cared for by someone else. *The family treated her like an invalid... ...her invalid mother.* 2 ADJ If an argument, conclusion, or result is **invalid,** it is not correct. *The comparison is invalid.* ♦ **invalidity** UNCOUNT N *My experiments show the invalidity of his argument.* 3 ADJ If an official process, contract, or document is **invalid,** it is not legally acceptable. *The court ruled his election invalid.*

invalidate /ɪnvælɪdeɪt/, **invalidates, invalidating, invalidated;** a formal word. 1 VB WITH OBJ If something **invalidates** an argument, conclusion, or result, it proves that it is wrong. *Such exceptions do not invalidate the rule.* 2 VB WITH OBJ If something **invalidates** an official process, contract, or document, it makes it legally unacceptable. *The marriage would invalidate any earlier will.*

invaluable /ɪnvælju^{0}əbə^{0}l/. ADJ If someone or something is **invaluable,** they are extremely useful. *This experience proved invaluable later on.*

invariable /ɪnveərɪəbə^{0}l/. ADJ Something that is **invariable** always happens or never changes. *They followed an invariable routine.* ♦ **invariably** /ɪnveərɪəbli^1/ ADV *The conversation invariably returns to politics.*

invasion /ɪnveɪʒə^{0}n/, **invasions.** 1 COUNT N OR UNCOUNT N When there is an **invasion** of a country, an army enters it by force. *...the invasion of Europe by the Allies in 1944... It enabled us to remain free from invasion.* 2 UNCOUNT N WITH SUPP You can refer to the arrival of large numbers of things or people as an **invasion.** *...the invasion of Italian movies in the fifties.*

invent /ɪnvɛnt/, **invents, inventing, invented.** 1 VB WITH OBJ If you **invent** something, you are the first person to think of it or make it. *...the men who invented the sewing machine... He invented this phrase himself.* ♦ **inventor** /ɪnvɛntə/ COUNT N *...Cockerell, the inventor of the hovercraft.* 2 VB WITH OBJ If you **invent** a story or excuse, you try to persuade people that it is true when it is not. *...lies invented for a political purpose.*

invention /ɪnvɛnʃə^{0}n/, **inventions.** 1 COUNT N An **invention** is a machine or system that has been invented by someone. *Writing was the most revolutionary of all human inventions.* 2 COUNT N If you refer to someone's account of something as an **invention,** you mean that it is not true and that they have made it up. *The account was a deliberate and malicious invention.* 3 UNCOUNT N WITH SUPP When someone creates something that has never existed before, you can refer to this event as the **invention** of the thing. *...the invention of printing.* 4 UNCOUNT N **Invention** is also the ability to have clever and original ideas. *...his powers of invention.*

inventive /ɪnvɛntɪv/. ADJ An **inventive** person is good at inventing things or has clever and original ideas. *He is inventive in dealing with physical problems.* ♦ **inventiveness** UNCOUNT N *The musicians can play, even if they do lack inventiveness.*

inventory /ɪnvə^{2}ntri^1/, **inventories.** COUNT N An **inventory** is a written list of all the objects in a place.

inverse /ɪnvɜ:s/; a formal word. 1 ADJ If there is an **inverse** relationship between two things or amounts, one of them decreases as the other increases. *The time spent varies in inverse proportion to the amount of work done.* 2 SING N The **inverse** of something is its exact opposite. *It represents the inverse of everything I find worth preserving.* Also ATTRIB ADJ *The inverse case is also worth considering.*

inversion /ɪnvɜ:ʃə^{0}n/, **inversions.** COUNT N When there is an **inversion** of something, it is changed into its opposite; a formal use. *...this curious inversion of facts... ...an inversion of the expected order.*

invert /ɪnvɜ:t/, **inverts, inverting, inverted.** VB WITH OBJ If you **invert** something, you turn it upside down or back to front; a formal use. *The chairs are inverted on the tables.* ♦ **inverted** ADJ *It was shaped like an inverted cone.*

invertebrate /ɪnvɜ:tɪbreɪt, -brə^{1}t/, **invertebrates.** COUNT N An **invertebrate** is a creature without a spine, for example an insect, worm, or octopus.

inverted commas. PLURAL N **Inverted commas** are the punctuation marks (' ' or " ") that are used in writing to indicate where speech or a quotation begins and ends.

invest /ɪnvɛst/, **invests, investing, invested.** 1 VB WITH OR WITHOUT OBJ If you **invest** an amount of money, you pay it into a bank or buy shares with it, so that you will receive a profit. *...investing in stocks and shares... £20 million of public money had been invested.* ♦ **investor** /ɪnvɛstə/ COUNT N *The investor is entitled to a reasonable return on his money.* 2 VB WITH OR WITHOUT OBJ If you **invest** money, time, or energy in something, you use it to try and make the thing successful; a formal use. *They are willing to invest energy in a European disarmament campaign... They have failed to invest in job creation in the cities.* 3 VB WITH 'in' If you **invest** in something useful, you buy it because it will be cheaper or more efficient than something else over a period of time. *Good shoes are worth investing in even though they are expensive.* 4 VB WITH OBJ AND 'with' To **invest** someone with rights or responsibilities means to give them to them legally or officially; a formal use. *The law invests the shareholders alone with legal rights.*

investigate /ɪnvɛstɪgeɪt/, **investigates, investigating, investigated.** VB WITH OR WITHOUT OBJ If you **investigate** an event, situation, or person, you try to find out all the facts about them. *He had come to investigate a murder... I sent my men to investigate.*

investigation /ɪnvɛstɪgeɪʃə^{0}n/, **investigations.** COUNT N OR UNCOUNT N An **investigation** is a process in which you try to find out all the facts about an event, situation, or person. *...the results of their investigations... She was admitted to hospital for further investigation.*

investigative /ɪnvɛstɪgətɪv/. ATTRIB ADJ **Investigative** activities involve trying to find out all the facts about events, situations, or people; a formal use. *He was doing investigative work on Kennedy... ...investigative reporters.*

investigator /ɪnvɛstɪgeɪtə/, **investigators.** COUNT N An **investigator** is someone whose job is to investigate events, situations, or people. *Aircraft accident investigators got to the scene quickly.*

investment /ɪnvɛstmənt/, **investments.** 1 UNCOUNT N **Investment** is the activity of buying shares or of putting money into a bank account in order to obtain a profit. *We aim to encourage investment.* 2 COUNT N An **investment** is an amount of money that you put into a bank account or buy shares with. *...a better return on the investment.* 3 SING N You can refer to something useful that you buy as an **investment.** *The tractors proved a superb investment.*

invigilator /ɪnvɪdʒɪleɪtə/, **invigilators.** COUNT N An **invigilator** is someone who supervises the people taking an examination.

invigorating /ɪnvɪgəreɪtɪŋ/. ADJ Something that is **invigorating** makes you feel more energetic. *The air here is invigorating... ...an invigorating bath.*

invincible /ɪnvɪnsə^{1}bə^{0}l/. ADJ An **invincible** army or sports team is very powerful and difficult to defeat; a formal use. *They are invincible in battle.*

inviolable /ɪnvaɪələbə^{0}l/. ADJ If a law or principle is **inviolable,** you cannot or must not break it; a formal use. *Tradition was considered inviolable.*

invisible /ɪnvɪzə^{1}bə^{0}l/. 1 ADJ If something is **invisible,** you cannot see it, because it is hidden or because it is very small or faint. *Her legs were invisible beneath the table... ...hairs invisible to the naked eye.* ♦ **invisibility** /ɪnvɪzə^{1}bɪlɪ^{1}ti^1/ UNCOUNT N *The main advantage is the submarine's invisibility.* 2 ADJ In stories, **invisible** people or things cannot be seen by anyone.

invitation /ɪnvɪteɪʃə^{0}n/, **invitations.** 1 COUNT N An **invitation** is a written or spoken request to come to an event such as a party, a meal, or a meeting. *Cindy accepted invitations to cocktail parties... I had an invitation to go and talk to the cadets.* 2 COUNT N The card or paper on which an invitation is written is also called an **invitation.** *Jenny was waving the invitation.* 3 SING N WITH SUPP Behaviour that encourages you to do something can be referred to as an **invitation.** *Houses left unlocked are an open invitation to burglary.*

invite /ɪnvaɪt/, **invites, inviting, invited.** 1 VB WITH OBJ If you **invite** someone to a party or a meal, you ask them to come to it. *Leggett invited me for lunch at the hotel.* 2 VB WITH OBJ If you **are invited** to do something, you are formally asked to do it. *I was invited to attend future meetings... He was invited for interview.* 3 VB WITH OBJ To **invite** something such as confidence or disbelief means to cause people to have this attitude towards you; a formal use. *This kind of statement invites disbelief.* 4 VB WITH OBJ To **invite** danger or trouble means to make it more likely; a formal use. *To speak of it to others would invite danger.*

inviting /ɪnvaɪtɪŋ/. ADJ If you say that something is **inviting,** you mean it is attractive and desirable. *...large dark eyes, shy but inviting.* ♦ **invitingly** ADV *The packet of cigarettes lay invitingly open.*

invoice /ɪnvɔɪs/, **invoices.** COUNT N An **invoice** is an official document that lists the goods or services that you have received from a person or company and says how much money you owe them.

invoke /ɪnvəʊk/, **invokes, invoking, invoked;** a formal word. 1 VB WITH OBJ If you **invoke** a law, you use it to justify what you are doing. *The Government invoked the Emergency Powers Act.* 2 VB WITH OBJ To **invoke** feelings of a particular kind means to cause someone to feel them. *They tried to invoke popular enthusiasm for the war.*

involuntary /ɪnvɒləntə^{0}ri^1/. ADJ **Involuntary** actions are done without meaning to do them because people are unable to control themselves. *There were one or two involuntary exclamations.* ♦ **involuntarily** ADV *I shivered involuntarily.*

involve /ɪnvɒlv/, **involves, involving, involved.** 1 VB WITH OBJ OR -ING If an activity **involves** something, that thing is included or used in it. *Some of the experiments involve the equipment you've seen... Caring for a one-year-old involves changing nappies.* 2 VB WITH OBJ Something that **involves** you concerns or affects you. *Workers are never told about things which involve them.* 3 REFL VB If you **involve** yourself in something, you take part in it. *They involve themselves deeply in community affairs.* 4 VB WITH OBJ If you **involve** someone else in something, you get them to take part in it. *Did you have to involve me in this?*

involved /ɪnvɒlvd/. 1 PRED ADJ If you are **involved** in a situation or activity, you are taking part in it. *Should religious leaders get involved in politics?... ...the large number of people involved.* 2 PRED ADJ If you are deeply **involved** in something you are doing, you feel very strongly or enthusiastically about it. *I was deeply involved in my work... She became terribly involved with writing.* 3 PRED ADJ OR ADJ AFTER N The things **involved** in something such as a job or system are the things that are required in order to do it or understand it. *There is quite a lot of work involved... What is involved in making a television programme?... Explain the principles involved.* 4 ADJ If you describe a situation or activity as **involved,** you mean that it is very complicated. *We had long involved discussions.* 5 PRED ADJ If you are **involved** with another person, you are having a close relationship with them.

involvement /ɪnvɒlvmənt/. 1 UNCOUNT N Your **involvement** in something is the fact that you are taking part in it. *...parental involvement in schools... ...the active involvement of workers.* 2 UNCOUNT N **Involvement** is also the concern and enthusiasm that you feel about something. *...his deep involvement with socialism.*

invulnerable /ɪnvʌlnə^{0}rəbə^{0}l/. ADJ If someone or something is **invulnerable,** they cannot be harmed or damaged. *The nuclear submarine is almost invulnerable to attack.* ♦ **invulnerability** /ɪnvʌlnə^{0}rəbɪlɪ^{1}ti^1/ UNCOUNT N *Parents have a feeling of invulnerability.*

inward /ɪnwəd/, **inwards.** In normal British English, **inwards** is an adverb and **inward** is an adjective. In formal British English and in American English, **inward** is both an adjective and an adverb. 1 ATTRIB ADJ Your **inward** thoughts or feelings are the ones that you do not express or show to other people. *...my inward happiness.* ♦ **inwardly** ADV *I remained inwardly unconvinced.* 2 ADV If something moves or faces **inward** or **inwards,** it moves or faces towards the inside or centre of something. *The door swung inward... His cell faced inwards.*

iodine /aɪədi:n/. UNCOUNT N **Iodine** is a dark-coloured substance used in medicine and photography.

-ion, -ions. See **-ation.**

IOU /aɪ əʊ ju:/, **IOUs.** COUNT N An **IOU** is a written promise to pay back money that you have borrowed. **IOU** represents 'I owe you'. *He wrote out an IOU for five thousand dollars.*

IQ /aɪ kju:/, **IQs.** UNCOUNT N WITH SUPP Your **IQ** is your level of intelligence, measured by a special test. **IQ** is an abbreviation for 'intelligence quotient'. *He had an IQ of 50.*

irate /aɪreɪt/. ADJ If you are **irate,** you are very angry; a formal use. *The Bishop looked irate... ...irate customers... ...an irate letter.*

iris /aɪrɪs/, **irises.** 1 COUNT N The **iris** in your eye is the round coloured part. 2 COUNT N An **iris** is also a tall plant with long leaves and large purple, yellow, or white flowers.

Irish /aɪrɪʃ/. 1 ADJ **Irish** means belonging or relating to the Republic of Ireland, or to any part of Ireland. *...the Irish Prime Minister... She spoke with an Irish accent.* 2 PLURAL N The **Irish** are the people who come from Ireland. *The majority of the Irish accept these proposals.*

Irishman /aɪrɪʃmə^{3}n/, **Irishmen.** COUNT N An **Irishman** is a man who comes from Ireland.

Irishwoman /aɪrɪʃwʊmən/, **Irishwomen.** COUNT N An **Irishwoman** is a woman who comes from Ireland.

irk /ɜ:k/, **irks, irking, irked.** VB WITH OBJ If something **irks** you, it irritates or annoys you.

irksome /ɜ:ksəm/. ADJ If something is **irksome,** it irritates or annoys you.

iron /aɪən/, **irons, ironing, ironed.** 1 UNCOUNT N OR MOD **Iron** is a hard, dark metal used to make steel, and also to make objects such as gates and fences. Small amounts of iron occur in your blood and in food. *...a lump of iron... ...an iron bar... ...the iron and steel industries... Seaweed has a high iron content.* 2 COUNT N An **iron** is an electrical device with a heated flat metal base. You rub an iron over clothes to remove creases. *If it's cotton or linen, use a hot iron.* 3 VB WITH OBJ If you **iron** clothes, you remove the creases from them using an iron. *I can't iron shirts.* ♦ **ironing** UNCOUNT N *She's doing the ironing.* 4 ATTRIB ADJ You can use **iron** to describe the character or behaviour of someone who is very firm in their decisions and actions, or who can control their feelings well. *He was able to enforce his iron will... ...her iron composure.*

iron out. PHR VB If you **iron out** difficulties, you get rid of them; an informal use.

ironic /aɪrɒnɪk/. 1 ADJ An **ironic** remark or gesture is inappropriate in the situation in which it is made, and is intended as a joke or insult. *It was possible that his thanks were ironic.* 2 ADJ An **ironic** situation is strange or amusing because it is the opposite of what you expect. *It is ironic that the people who complain most loudly are the ones who do least to help.*

ironical /aɪrɒnɪkə^{0}l/. ADJ **Ironical** means the same as ironic.

ironically /aɪrɒnɪkə^{0}li^1/. 1 SENTENCE ADV You say **ironically** to draw attention to a situation which is strange or amusing, because it is the opposite of what you expect. *Ironically, the intelligence chief was the last person to hear the news.* 2 ADV If you say something **ironically,** you say it as a joke or insult, because it is an inappropriate thing to say in the particular situation. *'Do you want to search the apartment?' she enquired ironically.*

ironing board, ironing boards. COUNT N An **ironing board** is a long, narrow board covered with cloth, on which you iron clothes.

ironwork /aɪənwɜ:k/. UNCOUNT N You refer to iron objects or the iron parts of buildings as **ironwork.**

irony /aɪrəni^1/, **ironies.** 1 UNCOUNT N **Irony** is a way of speaking in which you say something which is inappropriate, as a joke or insult. *She said with slight irony, 'Bravo.'* 2 COUNT N OR UNCOUNT N The **irony** of a situation is an aspect of it which is strange or amusing, because it is the opposite of what you expect. *The irony is that many politicians agree with him... History has many ironies.*

irrational /ɪræʃə^{0}nəl, -ʃənə^{0}l/. ADJ **Irrational** feelings or behaviour are not based on logical reasons or thinking. *His anxiety was irrational... ...an irrational child.* ♦ **irrationally** ADV *They were accused of acting irrationally.* ♦ **irrationality** /ɪræʃə^{0}nælɪ^{1}ti^1/ UNCOUNT N *...the irrationality of contemporary economics.*

irreconcilable /ɪrekənsaɪləbə^{0}l/. 1 ADJ If two ideas are **irreconcilable,** they are so different from each other that it is impossible to believe or accept both of them; a formal use. *Their views had been irreconcilable from the beginning.* 2 ADJ An **irreconcilable** disagreement is so serious that it cannot be settled. *...an irreconcilable clash of loyalties.*

irrefutable /ɪrɪfju:təbə^{0}l/. ADJ An **irrefutable** statement cannot be shown to be incorrect; a formal use. *That is an opinion, not an irrefutable fact.*

irregular /ɪregjə^{4}lə/. 1 ADJ Something that is **irregular** is not smooth or straight, or does not form a regular pattern. *...its rough, irregular surface... ...dark, irregular markings on the photos.* ♦ **irregularly** ADV *...irregularly shaped fields.* 2 ADJ **Irregular** is also used to say that a series of events happens with different periods of time between them. *...feeding them at irregular intervals... The newspaper's appearance became increasingly irregular.* ♦ **irregularly** ADV *He went home, irregularly, at weekends.* ♦ **irregularity** /ɪregjə^{4}lærɪti^1/ COUNT N OR UNCOUNT N *These illnesses can be caused by irregularity in feeding... This is more likely to produce irregularities of heart rate.* 3 ADJ **Irregular** behaviour is unusual and not acceptable. *It isn't signed. This is irregular... ...a highly irregular request.* ♦ **irregularity** COUNT N *The report revealed a large number of irregularities.* 4 ADJ An **irregular** verb, noun, or adjective does not inflect in the same way as most other verbs, nouns, or adjectives in the language. 'Go' and 'be' are irregular verbs in English.

irrelevance /ɪreləvəns/. UNCOUNT N The **irrelevance** of something is the fact that it is not connected with what you are talking about or dealing with. *'By the way,' he added with apparent irrelevance, 'will you be locking it?'*

irrelevant /ɪreləvənt/. ADJ If something is **irrelevant,** it is not connected with what you are talking about or dealing with, and is therefore not important. *The book was full of irrelevant information... He felt that right and wrong were irrelevant to the situation.*

irreparable /ɪrepə^{0}rəbə^{0}l/. ADJ **Irreparable** damage is so severe that it cannot be repaired or put right; a formal use.

irreplaceable /ɪrɪpleɪsəbə^{0}l/. ADJ If things are **irreplaceable,** they are so special that they cannot be replaced if they are lost or destroyed.

irrepressible /ɪrɪpresɪ^{1}bə^{0}l/. ADJ **Irrepressible** people are lively, energetic, and cheerful. *Basil is irrepressible, funny, and affectionate.*

irresistible /ɪrɪzɪstəbə^{0}l/. 1 ADJ If your wish to do something is **irresistible,** you cannot prevent yourself doing it. *The urge to laugh was irresistible.* 2 ADJ If you describe someone or something as **irresistible,** you mean that they are very attractive. ♦ **irresistibly** SUBMOD *The songs are irresistibly catchy.* 3 ADJ An **irresistible** force cannot be stopped or controlled. *They put irresistible pressure upon the government.* ♦ **irresistibly** ADV *The waves take you irresistibly onwards.*

irresolute /ɪrezəlu:t/. ADJ If you are **irresolute,** you cannot decide what to do; a formal use.

irrespective /ɪrɪspektɪv/. PREP If something is true or happens **irrespective of** other things, those things do not affect it; a formal use. *They demanded equal pay irrespective of age or sex... ...available to all students, irrespective of where they live.*

irresponsible /ɪrɪspɒnsɪ^{1}bə^{0}l/. ADJ **Irresponsible** people do things without properly considering their possible consequences; used showing disapproval. *You've behaved like an irresponsible idiot... It would be irresponsible of me to encourage you.* ♦ **irresponsibly** ADV *...acting unfairly and irresponsibly.* ♦ **irresponsibility** /ɪrɪspɒnsɪbɪlɪ^{1}ti^1/ UNCOUNT N *...youthful irresponsibility.*

irretrievable /ɪrɪtri:vəbə^{0}l/. ADJ **Irretrievable** harm is so severe that it cannot be put right again; a formal use. *...the irretrievable damage done to the Earth.* ♦ **irretrievably** ADV *The war was irretrievably lost.*

irreverent /ɪrevə^{0}rənt/. ADJ If you are **irreverent,** you do not show respect for someone or something. *...rude and irreverent comments.*

irreversible /ɪrɪvɜ:sɪ^{1}bə^{0}l/. ADJ If a change is **irreversible,** the thing affected cannot be changed back to its original state. *The damage may be irreversible.*

irrevocable /ɪrevəkəbə^{0}l/. ADJ Actions or decisions that are **irrevocable** cannot be stopped or changed; a formal use. *The US has given its irrevocable commitment to the Russians.* ♦ **irrevocably** ADV *The world had changed irrevocably.*

irrigate /ɪrɪgeɪt/, **irrigates, irrigating, irrigated.** VB WITH OBJ To **irrigate** land means to supply it with water in order to help crops to grow. *A small pump will irrigate about an acre of land.* ♦ **irrigated** ADJ *...the irrigated areas of the Ganges plain.* ♦ **irrigation** /ɪrɪgeɪʃə^{0}n/ UNCOUNT N *...the area under irrigation... ...a complex irrigation system.*

irritable /ɪrɪtəbə^{0}l/. ADJ If you are **irritable,** you are easily annoyed. *Judy was feeling hot, tired, and irritable.* ♦ **irritably** ADV *'What do you want me to do?' she said irritably.* ♦ **irritability** /ɪrɪtəbɪl^{1}ti^1/ UNCOUNT N *...periods of irritability.*

irritant /ɪrɪtənt/, **irritants.** COUNT N If something keeps annoying you, you can refer to it as an **irritant;** a formal use. *Lack of national independence was a strong irritant.*

irritate /ɪrɪteɪt/, **irritates, irritating, irritated. 1** VB WITH OBJ If something **irritates** you, it keeps annoying you. *His style irritated some officials... Dixon, irritated by this question, said nothing.* ♦ **irritating** ADJ *...an irritating noise.* ♦ **irritatingly** SUBMOD *She was irritatingly slow.* **2** VB WITH OBJ If something **irritates** a part of your body, it causes it to itch or be sore. *The detergent can irritate sensitive feet.*

irritation /ɪrɪteɪʃə^{0}n/, **irritations. 1** UNCOUNT N **Irritation** is a feeling of annoyance about something that someone continues to do. *I began to feel the same irritation with all of them.* **2** COUNT N An **irritation** is something that keeps annoying you. *...the irritations of everyday existence.* **3** UNCOUNT N **Irritation** in a part of your body is a feeling of slight pain and discomfort there. *...eye irritation.*

is /ɪz/. **Is** is the third person singular of the present tense of **be.**

-ise, -ises, -ising, -ised. See **-ize.**

-ish. 1 SUFFIX **-ish** is added to adjectives to form other adjectives which indicate that something has a quality to a limited extent. For example, 'reddish' means slightly red. *He had a yellowish complexion... He was a biggish fellow.* **2** SUFFIX **-ish** is also added to nouns to form adjectives which indicate that someone or something has the qualities of a particular kind of thing or person. For example, someone who is childish behaves like a child. *She was a beautiful kittenish creature.*

Islam /ɪzlɑːm/. UNCOUNT N **Islam** is the religion of the Muslims, which teaches that there is only one God and that Mohammed is His prophet. ♦ **Islamic** /ɪzlæmɪk/ ATTRIB ADJ *...Islamic countries.*

island /aɪlənd/, **islands.** COUNT N An **island** is a piece of land that is completely surrounded by water. *There are pigs on the island... ...the Channel Islands.*

islander /aɪləndə/, **islanders.** COUNT N **Islanders** are people who live on an island. *The islanders had never seen a car... ...the Falkland Islanders.*

isle /aɪl/, **isles.** COUNT N **Isle** is used in the names of some islands. *...the Isle of Wight... ...the British Isles.*

-ism, -isms. 1 SUFFIX **-ism** is used to form nouns that refer to political or religious movements and beliefs. *...the emergence of nationalism... ...the importance of Hinduism as a unifying force.* **2** SUFFIX **-ism** is also used to form nouns that refer to attitudes or behaviour. *Clem's eyes gleamed with fanaticism... ...an opportunity for heroism.*

isn't /ɪzə^{0}nt/. **Isn't** is the usual spoken form of 'is not'. *It isn't dark... That's right, isn't it?*

isolate /aɪsəleɪt/, **isolates, isolating, isolated. 1** VB WITH OBJ OR REFL VB If something **isolates** you or if you **isolate** yourself, you become physically or socially separated from other people. *His wealth isolated him... They isolated themselves in order to build a new society.* **2** VB WITH OBJ To **isolate** a substance means to separate it from other substances so that it can be examined in detail; a technical use. *You can isolate genes and study how they work.* **3** VB WITH OBJ If you **isolate** a sick person or animal, you keep them apart from other people or animals, so that their illness does not spread.

isolated /aɪsəleɪtɪ^{2}d/. **1** ADJ An **isolated** place is a long way away from any town or village. *...an isolated farmhouse.* **2** ATTRIB ADJ An **isolated** example or incident is one that is rare and not part of a general pattern. *...a few isolated acts of violence.*

isolation /aɪsəleɪʃə^{0}n/. **1** UNCOUNT N **Isolation** is a state in which you feel separate from other people, because you live far away from them or because you do not have any friends. *...mothers living in isolation and poverty.* **2** PHRASE If something exists or happens **in isolation,** it exists or happens separately from other things of the same kind. *These questions can't be answered in isolation from each other.*

issue /ɪʃuː/, **issues, issuing, issued. 1** COUNT N An **issue** is an important problem or subject that people are discussing or arguing about. *I raised the issue with him... ...the issue of immigration.* **2** SING N If something is the **issue,** it is the thing you consider to be the most important part of a situation or discussion. *That's just not the issue... You cannot go on evading the issue.* **3** COUNT N An **issue** of a magazine or newspaper is a particular edition of it. *The article had appeared in the previous day's issue.* **4** VB WITH OBJ If someone **issues** a statement, they make it formally or publicly. *They issued a serious warning.* **5** VB WITH OBJ If you **are issued** with something or if it **is issued** to you, it is officially given it to you. *She was issued with travel documents... Radios were issued to the troops.* **6** VB WITH 'from' When something **issues** from a place, it comes out of it; a literary use. *...the smells issuing from the kitchen.*

PHRASES ● The thing **at issue** is the thing that is being argued about. *The point at issue is this.* ● If you **make an issue of** something, you make a fuss about it.

-ist, -ists. SUFFIX **-ist** is added to nouns, sometimes in place of '-ism', to form nouns and adjectives. The nouns refer to people who have particular beliefs or do a particular thing. For example, a pacifist believes in pacifism and a violinist plays the violin. These nouns and adjectives are often not defined but are treated with the related nouns. *...a nuclear physicist... ...imperialist sentiments.*

it /ɪt/. **It** is used as the subject of a verb or as the object of a verb or preposition. **1** PRON You use **it** to refer to an object, animal, or other thing that has already been mentioned or whose identity is known. *...a tray with glasses on it... The strike went on for a year before it was settled.* **2** PRON You also use **it** to refer to a situation or fact. *She was frightened, but tried not to show it... It was very pleasant at the Hochstadts... He found it hard to make friends.* **3** PRON You also use **it** when you are talking about the weather, the time, the date, or the day of the week. *It's hot... It's raining here... It is nearly one o'clock.* **4** PRON **It** also occurs in structures which are used to emphasize or draw attention to something. *It's my mother I'm worried about.*

Italian /ɪtæljən/, **Italians. 1** ADJ **Italian** means belonging or relating to Italy. **2** COUNT N An **Italian** is a person who comes from Italy. **3** UNCOUNT N **Italian** is the language spoken by people who live in Italy.

italics /ɪtælɪks/. PLURAL N **Italics** are letters printed so that they slope to the right. Italics are often used to emphasize a word or sentence. The examples in this dictionary are printed in italics.

itch /ɪtʃ/, **itches, itching, itched. 1** VB If you **itch** or if a part of your body **itches,** you have an unpleasant feeling on your skin that makes you want to scratch. *My toes are itching like mad.* **2** COUNT N An **itch** is an unpleasant feeling on your skin that makes you want to scratch. **3** VB WITH TO-INF If you **itch** to do something, you are very impatient to do it; an informal use. *I was itching to get away.*

it'd /ɪtə^{0}d/. **It'd** is a spoken form of 'it had', especially when 'had' is an auxiliary. **It'd** is also a spoken form of 'it would'. *It'd just been killed... If I went on the train, it'd be cheaper.*

item /aɪtəm/, **items.** COUNT N An **item** is one of a collection of objects, or one of a number of matters that you are dealing with. *...a list of household items... I had two items of business to attend to before lunch.*

itinerant /ɪ^{5}tɪnərənt/. ATTRIB ADJ **Itinerant** workers travel around a region, working for short periods in different places; a formal use.

itinerary /ɪ^{5}tɪnərəri^1/, **itineraries.** COUNT N An **itinerary** is a plan of a journey, including the route and the places that will be visited. *A detailed itinerary is supplied.*

it'll /ɪtə^{0}l/. **It'll** is a spoken form of 'it will'. *It'll be quite interesting.*

its /ɪts/. DET You use **its** to indicate that something belongs or relates to a thing, place, or animal that has just been mentioned or whose identity is known. *The creature lifted its head... The group held its first meeting last week.*

it's /ɪts/. **It's** is a spoken form of 'it is' or 'it has', especially when 'has' is an auxiliary verb. *It's very important... It's snowing... It's been nice talking to you.*

itself /ɪtself/. **1** REFL PRON You use **itself** as the object of a verb or preposition to refer to the same thing or animal that is mentioned as the subject of the clause, or as a previous object in the clause. *Britain must bring itself up to date... It wraps its furry tail around itself.* **2** REFL PRON You also use **itself** to emphasize the subject or object of a clause, and to make it clear what you are referring to. *The town itself was very small.* **3** PHRASE If you say that something has a particular quality **in itself,** you mean that it has this quality because of its own nature, regardless of any other factors. *The process is, in itself, an act of worship.*

-ity, -ities. SUFFIX **-ity** is added to adjectives to form nouns. These nouns usually refer to states, qualities, or behaviour. Nouns of this kind are often not defined but are treated with the related adjectives. *Their function is to give rigidity... About this there is unanimity among sociologists.*

I've /aɪv/. **I've** is the usual spoken form of 'I have', especially when 'have' is an auxiliary. *I've never met her... I've only been there once.*

ivory /aɪvə^{0}ri^1/. UNCOUNT N **Ivory** is the substance which forms the tusks of elephants. It is valuable, and is often used to make ornaments. *...the import of ivory... ...ivory chess sets.*

ivy /aɪvi^1/. UNCOUNT N **Ivy** is a plant that grows up walls and trees.

-ize, -izes, -izing, -ized; also spelled **-ise, -ises, -ising, -ised.** SUFFIX Verbs that can end in either '-ize' or '-ise' are dealt with in this dictionary as ending in '-ize'. Some verbs ending in **-ize** are derived from adjectives. These verbs describe processes by which things or people are changed to a particular state or condition. For example, when something is popularized, it is made popular. *Parliament finally legalized trade unions.*

Jj

jab /dʒæb/, **jabs, jabbing, jabbed. 1** VB WITH OBJ AND ADJUNCT If you **jab** something somewhere, you push it there with a quick, sudden movement. *She jabbed her knitting needles into a ball of wool... He jabbed his finger at me.* **2** COUNT N A **jab** is an injection of a substance into your blood to prevent illness; an informal British use.

jabber /dʒæbə/, **jabbers, jabbering, jabbered.** VB WITH OR WITHOUT OBJ Someone who **is jabbering** is talking very quickly and excitedly; an informal use. *She was jabbering in Italian to her husband.*

jack /dʒæk/, **jacks. 1** COUNT N A **jack** is a device for lifting a heavy object off the ground. **2** COUNT N A **jack** is also a playing card with a picture of a young man on it.

jacket /dʒækɪt/, **jackets. 1** COUNT N A **jacket** is a short coat. *...a tweed sports jacket.* ● See also **dinner jacket, lifejacket. 2** COUNT N The **jacket** of a baked potato is its skin. *...potatoes in their jackets.* **3** COUNT N The **jacket** of a book is the paper cover that protects it.

jackpot /dʒækpɒt/, **jackpots.** COUNT N The **jackpot** is the most valuable prize in a game or lottery.

jade /dʒeɪd/. UNCOUNT N **Jade** is a hard green stone used for making jewellery and ornaments.

jaded /dʒeɪdɪ^{2}d/. ADJ If you are **jaded,** you have no enthusiasm because you are tired and bored. *...jaded housewives who'd like to try something different.*

jagged /dʒægɪ^{2}d/. ADJ Something that is **jagged** has a rough, uneven shape with lots of sharp points. *...small pieces of jagged metal.*

jaguar /dʒægju^{4}ə/, **jaguars.** COUNT N A **jaguar** is a large member of the cat family with dark spots on its back.

jail /dʒeɪl/, **jails, jailing, jailed;** also spelled **gaol** in old-fashioned British English. **1** COUNT N OR UNCOUNT N A **jail** is a place where people are kept locked up, usually because they have been found guilty of a crime. *He went to jail for attempted robbery... ...a heavy jail sentence.* **2** VB WITH OBJ If someone **is jailed,** they are put into jail. *He was jailed for five years.*

jailer /dʒeɪlə/, **jailers;** also spelled **gaoler** in old-fashioned British English. COUNT N A **jailer** is a person in charge of a jail; an old-fashioned use.

jam /dʒæm/, **jams, jamming, jammed. 1** MASS N **Jam** is a food made by cooking fruit with sugar. You usually spread it on bread. *...pots of raspberry and blackcurrant jam.* **2** VB WITH OBJ AND ADJUNCT If you **jam** something somewhere, you push it there roughly. *Then he jammed his hat back on... Reporters jammed microphones in our faces.* **3** ERG VB If something **jams** or if you **jam** it, it becomes fixed in one position and cannot move freely or work properly. *The machines jammed and broke down... I jammed the window shut.* **4** VB WITH OBJ If a lot of things **are jammed** into a place, they are packed tightly together and can hardly move. *The town was jammed with traffic.* **5** COUNT N A **jam** is a situation where there are so many vehicles on a road that none of them can move. *There were traffic jams, and police clearing people away.* **6** COUNT N If you are in a **jam,** you are in a very difficult situation; an informal use. *He finds himself in exactly the same jam as his brother was in ten years before.* **7** VB WITH OBJ To **jam** a radio or electronic signal means to interfere with it and prevent it being received clearly.

jangle /dʒæŋgə^{0}l/, **jangles, jangling, jangled.** ERG VB If metal objects **jangle,** they make a ringing noise by hitting against each other. *I ran upstairs, the keys jangling in my pockets.* Also SING N *...the jangle of armour.*

janitor /dʒænɪtə/, **janitors.** COUNT N A **janitor** is a person whose job is to look after a building.

January /dʒænju^{0}əri^{1}/. UNCOUNT N **January** is the first month of the year in the Western calendar.

Japanese /dʒæpəniːz/. **Japanese** is the singular and plural of the noun. **1** ADJ **Japanese** means belonging or relating to Japan. **2** COUNT N A **Japanese** is a person who comes from Japan. **3** UNCOUNT N **Japanese** is the language spoken by people who live in Japan.

jar /dʒɑː/, **jars, jarring, jarred. 1** COUNT N A **jar** is a glass container with a lid that is used for storing food. **2** COUNT N You can use **jar** to refer to a jar and its contents, or to the contents only. *...a jar of peanut butter.* **3** VB If something **jars** on you, you find it unpleasant or annoying. *The harsh, metallic sound jarred on her... He had a way of speaking that jarred.* ♦ **jarring** ADJ *...a jarring office block.* **4** VB WITH OBJ If something **jars** you, it gives you an unpleasant shock. *He was evidently jarred by my appearance.* ♦ **jarring** ADJ *...a jarring experience.* **5** ERG VB If things **jar** or **are jarred,** they strike against each other with quite a lot of force. *The house shook and his bones were jarred.* Also COUNT N *Knocks and jars can cause weakness in the spine.*

jargon /dʒɑːgə^{0}n/. UNCOUNT N **Jargon** consists of words and expressions that are used in special or technical ways by particular groups of people. *...complex legal jargon.*

jaundice /dʒɔːndɪs/. UNCOUNT N **Jaundice** is an illness that makes your skin and eyes yellow.

jaundiced /dʒɔːndɪst/. ADJ A **jaundiced** attitude or view is pessimistic and not at all enthusiastic; a literary use. *He takes a rather jaundiced view of societies and clubs.*

jaunt /dʒɔːnt/, **jaunts.** COUNT N A **jaunt** is a short journey which you go on for pleasure.

jaunty /dʒɔːnti^{1}/. ADJ **Jaunty** means cheerful, full of confidence, and energetic. *He spoke suddenly in a jaunty tone... She adjusted her hat to a jaunty angle.*

javelin /dʒævə^{0}lɪn/, **javelins.** COUNT N A **javelin** is a long spear that is thrown in sports competitions.

jaw /dʒɔː/, **jaws. 1** COUNT N Your **jaw** is the part of your face below your mouth. Your jaw moves up and down when you eat. *His jaw dropped in surprise.* **2** COUNT N Your **jaw** is also one of the two bones in your head which your teeth are attached to. *...the upper jaw... The panther held a snake in its jaws.*

jazz /dʒæz/. UNCOUNT N **Jazz** is a style of music that has an exciting rhythm and is usually played with drums, saxophones, and trumpets.

jealous /dʒɛləs/. **1** ADJ If you are **jealous,** you feel anger or bitterness towards someone who has something that you would like to have. *I often felt jealous because David could go out when he wished... They may feel jealous of your success.* **2** ADJ If you are **jealous,** you feel that you must try to keep something that you have, because you think someone else might take it away from you. *She was a very jealous woman... He was jealous of his wife and suspected her of adultery.* ♦ **jealously** ADV *They were jealously guarding their independence.*

jealousy /dʒɛləsi^{1}/, **jealousies.** UNCOUNT N OR COUNT N **Jealousy** is the quality of being jealous. *Jimmie felt a surge of jealousy... He was good at talking me out of my suspicions and jealousies.*

jeans /dʒiːnz/. PLURAL N **Jeans** are casual trousers made of strong blue denim. *...a pair of jeans.*

jeep /dʒiːp/, **jeeps.** COUNT N A **jeep** is a small four-wheeled vehicle that can travel over rough ground. *A jeep pulled up and a marine jumped out.*

jeer /dʒɪə/, **jeers, jeering, jeered.** VB WITH OR WITHOUT OBJ If you **jeer** at someone, you say rude and insulting things to them. *Boys had jeered at him at school... He was jeered and booed as a traitor.* ♦ **jeering** ADJ *...the jeering crowd.*

jell /dʒɛl/. See **gel.**

jelly /dʒɛli^{1}/, **jellies. 1** MASS N **Jelly** is a clear food made from gelatine, fruit juice, and sugar, which is eaten as a dessert. **2** MASS N **Jelly** is also a kind of jam made by boiling fruit juice and sugar. *...slices of bread, smeared with butter and jelly.*

jellyfish /dʒɛli^{1}fɪʃ/. **Jellyfish** is the singular and plural. COUNT N A **jellyfish** is a sea creature with a clear soft body and tentacles which can sting you.

jeopardize /dʒɛpədaɪz/, **jeopardizes, jeopardizing, jeopardized;** also spelled **jeopardise.** VB WITH OBJ If you **jeopardize** a situation, you do something that may destroy or damage it. *This judgment may jeopardize his job... I didn't want to jeopardize my relationship with my new friend.*

jeopardy /dʒɛpədi^{1}/. PHRASE If someone or something is **in jeopardy,** they are in a dangerous situation. *She had placed herself in jeopardy in order to save my life... Their future is in jeopardy.*

jerk /dʒɜːk/, **jerks, jerking, jerked. 1** ERG VB If you **jerk** something, you pull it or move it suddenly and forcefully. *He jerked the boy savagely to his feet... The door of the van was jerked open... He jerked his head around to stare at me.* Also COUNT N *The man pulled the girl back with a jerk.* **2** VB WITH ADJUNCT If you **jerk** in a particular direction or in a particular way, you move with a very sudden and quick movement. *She jerked away from him... Jerking suddenly awake, he lay very still and listened.* **3** COUNT N If you call someone a **jerk,** you mean that they are very stupid; an offensive use.

jerky /dʒɜːki^{1}/. ADJ **Jerky** movements are very sudden and abrupt. *She lit a cigarette with quick, jerky movements.*

jersey /dʒɜːzi^{1}/, **jerseys. 1** COUNT N A **jersey** is a knitted garment that covers the upper part of your body and your arms. You pull it on over your head. *...her striped jersey.* **2** UNCOUNT N **Jersey** is a knitted fabric used to make clothing.

jest /dʒɛst/, **jests.** COUNT N A **jest** is an amusing comment or a joke; an old-fashioned use. ● If you say something **in jest,** you do not mean it seriously, but want to be amusing. *It was said half in jest.*

jet /dʒɛt/, **jets, jetting, jetted. 1** COUNT N A **jet** is a very fast aeroplane. *She woke just as the big jet from Hong Kong touched down.* **2** VB WITH ADJUNCT If you **jet** somewhere, you travel there in a fast aeroplane. **3** COUNT N A **jet** of water or gas is a strong, fast, thin stream of it. *He blew a jet of water into the air.* **4** UNCOUNT N **Jet** is a hard black stone that is used in jewellery.

jet engine, jet engines. COUNT N A **jet engine** is an engine, especially in an aeroplane, in which hot air and gases are pushed out at the back.

jetlag /dʒɛtlæg/. UNCOUNT N **Jetlag** is a feeling of confusion and tiredness that people experience after a long journey in an aeroplane. *With jet-lag still a problem, I almost fell asleep during the meeting.*

jettison /dʒɛtɪsə^{0}n, -zə^{0}n/, **jettisons, jettisoning, jettisoned.** VB WITH OBJ If you **jettison** something, you deliberately reject it or throw it away; a formal use. *...ideas too valuable, too sacred, to jettison.*

jetty /dʒɛti^{1}/, **jetties.** COUNT N A **jetty** is a wide stone wall or wooden platform at the edge of the sea or a river, where people can get on and off boats. *The boat was tied up alongside a crumbling limestone jetty.*

Jew /dʒuː/, **Jews.** COUNT N A **Jew** is a person who believes in and practises the religion of Judaism.

jewel /dʒuːə^{0}l/, **jewels.** COUNT N A **jewel** is a precious stone used to decorate valuable things that you wear, such as rings or necklaces. *She was wearing even more jewels than the Queen Mother!*

jewelled /dʒuːə^{0}ld/; spelled **jeweled** in American English. ATTRIB ADJ **Jewelled** items and ornaments are decorated with precious stones. *...a jewelled brooch.*

jeweller /dʒuːə^{0}lə/, **jewellers;** spelled **jeweler** in American English. **1** COUNT N A **jeweller** is a person who buys, sells, and repairs jewellery and watches. **2** COUNT N A **jeweller** or a **jeweller's** is a shop where jewellery and watches are bought, sold and repaired.

jewellery /dʒuːə^{0}lri^{1}/; spelled **jewelry** in American English. UNCOUNT N **Jewellery** consists of ornaments that people wear such as rings, bracelets, and necklaces. *She thought some of her jewellery was missing... ...a jewellery box.*

Jewess /dʒuːɪ^{2}s/, **Jewesses.** COUNT N A **Jewess** is a woman or girl who is Jewish; a formal use.

Jewish /dʒuːɪʃ/. ADJ **Jewish** means belonging or relating to the religion of Judaism or to its followers.

jibe /dʒaɪb/, **jibes;** also spelled **gibe.** COUNT N A **jibe** is a rude or insulting remark about someone. *He swallowed and tried to smile at the jibe.*

jiffy /dʒɪfi^{1}/. PHRASE If you say that you will do something **in a jiffy,** you mean that you will do it quickly and very soon; an informal use. *I'll be back in a jiffy.*

jig /dʒɪg/, **jigs.** COUNT N A **jig** is a lively folk dance, popular in the past among country people.

jigsaw /dʒɪgsɔː/, **jigsaws.** COUNT N A **jigsaw** or **jigsaw puzzle** is a game consisting of a picture on cardboard or wood that has been cut up, and which has to be put back together again.

jingle /dʒɪŋgə^{0}l/, **jingles, jingling, jingled. 1** ERG VB When something **jingles** or when you **jingle** it, it makes a gentle ringing noise, like small bells. *...waving her arms in the air so that her charm bracelet jingled.* Also SING N *I can hear the jingle of bracelets coming up behind me in the dark.* **2** COUNT N A **jingle** is a short and simple tune, often with words, used to advertise a product on radio or television.

jinx /dʒɪŋks/, **jinxes.** COUNT N A **jinx** is bad luck, or something that is thought to bring bad luck. *...Muck Hall: the farm with the jinx on it.*

jittery /dʒɪtə^{0}ri^{1}/. ADJ Someone who is **jittery** feels extremely nervous; an informal use.

job /dʒɒb/, **jobs. 1** COUNT N A **job** is the work that someone does to earn money. *Gladys finally got a good job as a secretary.* **2** COUNT N A **job** is also a particular task. *There are always plenty of jobs to be done round here... ...a repair job.* **3** COUNT N WITH POSS The **job** of a particular person or thing is their duty or function. *It's not their job to decide what ought to be the law.* **4** SING N If you say that you had a **job** doing something, you are emphasizing how difficult it was; an informal use.

PHRASES ● If you say that something is **just the job,** you mean that it is exactly what you wanted or needed; an informal use. ● **It's a good job:** see **good.**

jobless /dʒɒblɪ^{2}s/. ADJ Someone who is **jobless** does not have a job, but would like one. *During the depression millions were jobless and homeless.* Also PLURAL N *We have to do more for the poor and the jobless.*

jockey /dʒɒki^{1}/, **jockeys.** COUNT N A **jockey** is someone who rides a horse in a race.

jocular /dʒɒkjə^{4}lə/. **1** ADJ Someone who is **jocular** is cheerful and often makes jokes. *...a jocular English visitor.* **2** ADJ Something that is **jocular** is intended to make people laugh. *...a jocular remark.*

jodhpurs /dʒɒdpəz/. PLURAL N **Jodhpurs** are close-fitting trousers worn when riding a horse.

jog /dʒɒg/, **jogs, jogging, jogged. 1** VB If you **jog,** you run slowly, often as a form of exercise. *...people who jog or play squash.* ♦ **jogger** COUNT N *...a couple of track-suited joggers.* ♦ **jogging** UNCOUNT N *...the current enthusiasm for jogging.* **2** SING N A **jog** is a slow run. *I speeded up to a jog and moved up the road briskly.* **3** VB WITH OBJ If you **jog** something, you push or bump it slightly so that it shakes or moves. *Be careful not to jog the table.* **4** PHRASE If someone or something **jogs** your **memory,** they remind you of something. *He had demonstrated the sound to jog my memory.*

join /dʒɔɪn/, **joins, joining, joined. 1** VB WITH OBJ If one person or thing **joins** another, the two people or things come together. *He went for a walk before joining his brother for tea... The helicopter was quickly joined by a second.* **2** VB WITH OBJ If you **join** a queue, you go and stand at the end of it. *They went off to join the queue for coffee... The van joined the row of cars.* **3** RECIP VB If two roads or rivers **join,** or if one **joins** the other, they meet or come together at a particular point. *This road joins the motorway at junction 16.* **4** VB WITH OR WITHOUT OBJ If you **join** an organization, you become a member of it. *We both joined the Labour Party... I had decided to join.* **5** VB WITH OBJ If you **join** an activity, you become involved in it. *They were invited to join the feasting.* ● to **join forces:** see **force. 6** VB WITH OBJ To **join** two things means to connect them or fasten them together. *Draw a straight line joining these two points... The cities are joined by telecommunication links... Cut them down the middle and join the two outside edges together.* **7** COUNT N A **join** is a place where two things are fastened or fixed together. *The repair was done so well, you could hardly see the join.*

join in. PHR VB If you **join in** an activity, you become involved in it. *Parents should join in these discussions... He tries to join in.*

join up. PHR VB **1** If someone **joins up,** they become a member of the armed forces; a British use. *At eighteen, just before joining up and going abroad, I met Elizabeth.* **2** If you **join up** two things, you fasten or fix them together. *I used to join up all his paper clips in a long chain.*

joiner /dʒɔɪnə/, **joiners.** COUNT N A **joiner** is a person who makes wooden window frames, door frames, and doors; a British use.

joint /dʒɔɪnt/, **joints. 1** ATTRIB ADJ **Joint** means shared by or belonging to two or more people. *We have opened a joint account at the bank.* ♦ **jointly** ADV *It was built jointly by France and Germany.* **2** COUNT N A **joint** is a part of your body such as your elbow or knee where two bones meet and are able to move together. *He can feel the rheumatism in his joints... ...the joints of the fingers.* **3** COUNT N A **joint** is also a place where two things are fastened or fixed together. *Cracks appeared at the joints between the new plaster and the old.* **4** COUNT N A **joint** of meat is a fairly large piece of meat suitable for roasting. *...a joint of roast beef.* **5** COUNT N Some people refer to a cigarette which contains cannabis as a **joint;** an informal use.

joke /dʒəʊk/, **jokes, joking, joked. 1** COUNT N A **joke** is something that is said or done to make you laugh, for example a funny story. *Dave was telling me this joke about a penguin.* **2** VB If you **joke,** you tell funny stories or say things that are amusing and not serious. *Don't* *worry, I was only joking.* 3 SING N If you say that someone or something is a **joke,** you mean that they are ridiculous and not worthy of respect; an informal use. *His colleagues regard him as a joke.*

joker /dʒəʊkə/, **jokers.** 1 COUNT N Someone who is a **joker** likes making jokes or doing amusing things. 2 COUNT N The **joker** in a pack of cards is a card which does not belong to any of the four suits.

jokingly /dʒəʊkɪŋli^{1}/. ADV If you say or do something **jokingly,** you do it to amuse someone or without seriously meaning it. *My friend said jokingly that George had lost around two hundred pounds.*

jolly /dʒɒli^{1}/; an old-fashioned word. 1 ADJ A **jolly** person is happy and cheerful. *Buddy's mother was a jolly, easy-going woman.* 2 ADJ A **jolly** event is lively and enjoyable. 3 SUBMOD You can use **jolly** to emphasize something. *We provide a jolly good service, I think.* 4 ADV You can use **jolly well** to emphasize what you are saying, especially when you are annoyed or upset. *I'm jolly well not going to ring her up!*

jolt /dʒəʊlt/, **jolts, jolting, jolted.** 1 ERG VB If something **jolts** or if you **jolt** it, it moves suddenly and violently. *...enormous loads that jolted and swayed... She jolted his arm.* Also COUNT N *I came down slowly at first, but then with a jolt.* 2 VB WITH OBJ If you **are jolted** by something, it gives you an unpleasant surprise or shock. *I was jolted awake by a bright light.* Also SING N *The aim of Detention Centres is to give kids a jolt.*

jostle /dʒɒsə^{0}l/, **jostles, jostling, jostled.** VB WITH OR WITHOUT OBJ If people **jostle** or if they **jostle** each other, they bump against or push each other in a crowd. *Pedestrians jostled them on the pavement.*

jot /dʒɒt/, **jots, jotting, jotted.** VB WITH OBJ If you **jot** something down, you write it down in the form of a short informal note. *I asked you to jot down a few ideas... I jot odd notes in the back of the diary.*

journal /dʒɜːnə^{0}l/, **journals.** 1 COUNT N A **journal** is a magazine for people with a particular interest. *...a trade journal.* 2 COUNT N A **journal** is also an account which you write of your daily activities. *For nearly three months he had been keeping a journal.*

journalism /dʒɜːnə^{0}lɪzə^{0}m/. UNCOUNT N **Journalism** is the job of collecting, writing, and publishing news in newspapers and magazines and on television and radio. *Have you ever thought of going into journalism?*

journalist /dʒɜːnə^{0}lɪst/, **journalists.** COUNT N A **journalist** is a person who works on a newspaper or magazine and writes articles for it. *She worked as a journalist on The Times.* ♦ **journalistic** /dʒɜːnə^{0}lɪstɪk/ ATTRIB ADJ *I had no journalistic experience in Britain.*

journey /dʒɜːni^{1}/, **journeys, journeying, journeyed.** 1 COUNT N When you make a **journey,** you travel from one place to another. *He went on a journey to London.* 2 VB WITH ADJUNCT If you **journey** somewhere, you travel there; a literary use. *The nights became colder as they journeyed north.*

jovial /dʒəʊvɪəl/. ADJ A **jovial** person behaves in a cheerful and happy way. *He was a big, heavy, jovial man... a jovial smile.*

joy /dʒɔɪ/, **joys.** 1 UNCOUNT N **Joy** is a feeling of great happiness. *She shouted with joy when I told her she was free... His face showed his joy the moment he saw me.* 2 COUNT N WITH SUPP Something that is a **joy** makes you feel happy or gives you great pleasure. *She discovered the joy of writing.*

joyful /dʒɔɪfʊl/. 1 ADJ Something that is **joyful** causes happiness and pleasure. *I still felt sad even after you'd announced the joyful tidings.* 2 ADJ A **joyful** person is extremely happy. *The joyful parents named him Lexington.* ♦ **joyfully** ADV *We welcomed him joyfully to the club.*

joyless /dʒɔɪlɪ^{2}s/. ADJ **Joyless** means producing or experiencing no pleasure. *...years and years of joyless married life.*

JP, JPs. COUNT N A **JP** is a local magistrate in Britain. **JP** is an abbreviation for 'Justice of the Peace'.

jubilant /dʒuːbɪlənt/. ADJ If you are **jubilant,** you feel extremely happy and successful. *...a jubilant Labour Party Conference.*

jubilation /dʒuːbɪleɪʃə^{0}n/. UNCOUNT N **Jubilation** is a feeling of great happiness and success; a formal use. *There was a general air of jubilation.*

jubilee /dʒuːbɪliː, dʒuːbɪli^{1}/, **jubilees.** COUNT N A **jubilee** is a special anniversary of an event, especially the 25th or 50th anniversary. *...Queen Victoria's jubilee.*

Judaism /dʒuːdeɪɪzə^{0}m/. UNCOUNT N **Judaism** is the religion of the Jewish people, which is based on the Old Testament of the Bible and the Talmud or book of laws and traditions.

judge /dʒʌdʒ/, **judges, judging, judged.** 1 COUNT N A **judge** is the person in a court of law who decides how the law should be applied, for example how criminals should be punished. *Last week she appeared before a judge... Judge Arnason set Miss Davis free on bail.* 2 COUNT N WITH SUPP If someone is a good **judge** of something, they can understand it and make decisions about it. *He was a good judge of character.* 3 COUNT N A **judge** is also a person who chooses the winner of a competition. *The panel of judges consisted of a variety of famous people.* 4 VB WITH OR WITHOUT OBJ If you **judge** someone or something, you form an opinion about them based on the evidence or information that you have. *It's impossible to judge her age... He judged it wiser to put a stop to this quarrel... I'm not in a position to judge.* 5 VB WITH OBJ If you **judge** a competition, you decide who the winner is. *The competition was judged by the local mayor.*

judgement /dʒʌdʒmə^{2}nt/, **judgements;** also spelled **judgment.** 1 COUNT N A **judgement** is an opinion that you have or express after thinking carefully about something. *I shall make my own judgement on this matter when I see the results... In our judgment, her plan has definitely succeeded.* 2 COUNT N A **judgement** is also a decision made by a judge or by a court of law. *The final judgment will probably be made in court.* 3 COUNT N A **judgement** is also something unpleasant that happens to you and that is considered to be a punishment from God. *War is a judgement on us all for our sins.* 4 UNCOUNT N **Judgement** is the ability to make sensible guesses about a situation or sensible decisions about what to do. *My father did not permit me to question his judgement... ...an error of judgement.* 5 UNCOUNT N OR COUNT N **Judgement** is also the process of deciding how good something or someone is. *I have a great fear of judgment... During her career a scientist must survive many judgments.*

PHRASES ● If you **pass judgement** on something, you give your opinion about it, especially if you are making a criticism. ● If you **reserve judgement** about something, you do not give an opinion about it until you know more about it. ● If something is **against** your **better judgement,** you believe that it would be more sensible not to do it.

judicial /dʒuːdɪʃə^{0}l/; a formal word. 1 ATTRIB ADJ **Judicial** means relating to judgement in a court of law. *I would like to go through proper judicial procedures.* 2 ATTRIB ADJ **Judicial** also means showing or using judgement in thinking about something. *...examined with judicial care.*

judiciary /dʒuːdɪʃəri^{1}/. SING N The **judiciary** is the branch of authority in a country which is concerned with justice and the legal system.

judicious /dʒuːdɪʃəs/; a formal word. ADJ An action or decision that is **judicious** shows good judgement and sense. *They made judicious use of government incentives.* ♦ **judiciously** ADV *You put your case most judiciously.*

judo /dʒuːdəʊ/. UNCOUNT N **Judo** is a sport in which two people fight and try to throw each other to the ground.

jug /dʒʌg/, **jugs.** 1 COUNT N A **jug** is a container which is used for holding and pouring liquids. *...a big white jug full of beer... ...the milk jug.* 2 COUNT N You can use **jug** to refer to a jug and its contents, or to the contents only. *...a jug of water.*

juggernaut /dʒʌgənɔːt/, **juggernauts.** COUNT N A **juggernaut** is a very large lorry; a British use.

juggle /dʒʌgə^{0}l/, **juggles, juggling, juggled.** 1 VB WITH OR WITHOUT OBJ If you **juggle,** you entertain people by throwing things into the air, catching each one and throwing it up again so that there are several of them in the air at the same time. ♦ **juggler** /dʒʌglə/ COUNT N *...a juggler practising his act.* 2 VB WITH OBJ OR 'WITH' If you **juggle** numbers or ideas, or **juggle** with them, you rearrange them repeatedly in order to make them fit the pattern that you want them to. *Both of them juggle their working hours to be with the children... He was still juggling with figures.*

jugular /dʒʌgjə^{4}lə/, **jugulars.** COUNT N Your **jugular** or **jugular vein** is a large vein in your neck that carries blood from your head back to your heart.

juice /dʒuːs/, **juices.** 1 MASS N **Juice** is the liquid that can be obtained from a fruit or a plant. *...two glasses of pineapple juice.* 2 COUNT N OR UNCOUNT N The **juices** of a joint of meat are the liquid that comes out of it when you cook it. *...spooning the juices over the top of a leg of lamb.* 3 PLURAL N The **juices** in your stomach are the fluids that help you to digest food. *...digestive juices.*

juicy /dʒuːsi^{1}/, **juicier, juiciest.** 1 ADJ A fruit or other food that is **juicy** has a lot of juice in it. *...juicy, ripe tomatoes.* 2 ADJ **Juicy** also means interesting or exciting, or containing scandal; an informal use. *...juicy gossip.*

jukebox /dʒuːkbɒks/, **jukeboxes.** COUNT N A **jukebox** is a record player in pubs and bars. You put a coin in and choose the record that you want to hear.

July /dʒə^{4}laɪ/. UNCOUNT N **July** is the seventh month of the year in the Western calendar.

jumble /dʒʌmbə^{0}l/, **jumbles, jumbling, jumbled.** 1 SING N A **jumble** is a lot of different things that are all mixed together in a confused or untidy way. *...a chaotic jumble of motor vehicles of every description.* 2 VB WITH OBJ If you **jumble** things, or **jumble** them up, you mix them together so that they are not in the correct order. *The bits and pieces were jumbled up with a lot of stuff that would never be needed again.*

jumble sale, jumble sales. COUNT N A **jumble sale** is a sale of cheap second-hand goods, usually held to raise money for charity.

jumbo /dʒʌmbəʊ/, **jumbos.** 1 ATTRIB ADJ **Jumbo** means very large; used especially in advertising. *...jumbo steaks.* 2 COUNT N A **jumbo** or a **jumbo jet** is a very large jet aeroplane.

jump /dʒʌmp/, **jumps, jumping, jumped.** 1 VB When you **jump,** you push your feet against the ground and go into the air. *He jumped down from the terrace... The horse jumps over a small stream.* Also COUNT N *It was a spectacular jump.* 2 VB WITH ADJUNCT To **jump** also means to move quickly and suddenly. *Ralph jumped to his feet... He jumped up and went across to the large bookcase.* 3 VB WITH OBJ If you **jump** something such as a fence, you jump over it or across it. 4 VB If you **jump,** you make a sudden movement because you have just been frightened or surprised by something. *A sudden noise made me jump.* 5 VB If an amount or level **jumps,** it increases by a large amount in a short time. *The population jumped to nearly 10,000.* Also COUNT N *...a massive jump in expenditure.* 6 VB WITH OBJ If someone **jumps** a queue, they move to the front of it before it is their turn.

PHRASES ● If you **keep one jump ahead** of an opponent or rival, you manage always to be in a better position than they are. ● **to jump the gun:** see **gun.**

jump at. PHR VB If you **jump at** an offer or opportunity, you accept it eagerly as soon as it is offered to you. *He jumped at the idea.*

jumper /dʒʌmpə/, **jumpers.** COUNT N A **jumper** is a knitted garment that covers the upper part of your body and your arms. You pull it on over your head; a British use.

jumpy /dʒʌmpi^{1}/. ADJ If you are **jumpy,** you are nervous or worried about something; an informal use. *The very thought of it makes me feel slightly jumpy.*

junction /dʒʌŋkʃə^{0}n/, **junctions.** COUNT N A **junction** is a place where roads or railway lines join. *...the junction of Cortez Avenue and Main Street.*

juncture /dʒʌŋktʃə/. PHRASE At a particular **juncture** means at a particular time, especially when it is a very important point in a series of events; a formal use. *She knew that any move on her part at this juncture would be interpreted as a sign of weakness.*

June /dʒuːn/. UNCOUNT N **June** is the sixth month of the year in the Western calendar.

jungle /dʒʌŋgə^{0}l/, **jungles.** 1 COUNT N OR UNCOUNT N A **jungle** is a forest in a hot country where tall trees and other plants grow very closely together. *...the Amazon jungle... ...immense tracts of impenetrable jungle.* 2 SING N WITH SUPP You can refer to a situation in which progress is difficult or dangerous as a **jungle.** *...the jungle of real politics.*

junior /dʒuːnjə/, **juniors.** 1 ADJ Someone who is **junior** holds an unimportant position in an organization or profession. *We could give the job to somebody more junior.* Also COUNT N *Police officers later blamed their juniors.* 2 SING N WITH POSS If you are someone's **junior,** you are younger than they are. *...a man seventeen years her junior.*

junior school, junior schools. COUNT N OR UNCOUNT N A **junior school** in England or Wales is a school for children between the ages of about seven and eleven.

junk /dʒʌŋk/; an informal word. 1 UNCOUNT N **Junk** is an amount of old or useless things. *Look, get that junk off the table, will you!* 2 MOD **Junk** shops sell second-hand goods very cheaply. *We got most of our furniture from junk shops and jumble sales.*

junkie /dʒʌŋki^{1}/, **junkies.** COUNT N A **junkie** is a drug addict; an informal use. *You're turning into a junkie.*

jurisdiction /dʒʊə^{0}rɪsdɪkʃə^{0}n/. UNCOUNT N **Jurisdiction** is the power that a court of law or someone in authority has to carry out legal judgements or enforce laws. *The Governor had no jurisdiction over prices.*

juror /dʒʊərə/, **jurors.** COUNT N A **juror** is a member of a jury. *The jurors gave their verdict.*

jury /dʒʊəri^{1}/, **juries.** 1 COLL N A **jury** is a group of people in a court of law who listen to the facts about a crime and decide whether the person accused is guilty or not. *A jury would never convict on that evidence... ...trial by jury.* 2 COLL N A **jury** is also a group of people who choose the winner of a competition.

just /dʒʌst/. 1 ADV If you say that something has **just** happened, you mean that it happened a very short time ago. *I've just sold my car... She had only just moved in.* 2 ADV If you say that you are **just** doing something, you mean that you will finish doing it very soon. If you say that you are **just** going to do something, you mean that you will do it very soon. *I'm just making us some coffee... They were just about to leave.* **3** ADV You can also use **just** to emphasize that something happens or happened at exactly the moment you are talking about. *The telephone rang just as I was about to serve up the dinner... Judy didn't like to tell him just then.* **4** PHRASE **Just now** means now or a very short time ago. *Nasty weather we're having just now... She was here just now.* **5** CONVENTION You say **just a minute, just a moment,** or **just a second** when you are asking someone to wait for a short time. *'Have you got John's address?'—'Just a minute. I'll have a look.'* **6** ADV You also use **just** to indicate that something is not very important, interesting, difficult, or great. *It's just a story... It is not just a children's film... Just add boiling water.* **7** ADV **Just** is also used to indicate that you are talking about a small part or sample, not the whole of an amount. *These are just a few of the enquiries.* **8** ADV **Just** also indicates that what you are saying is the case, but only to a very small degree. *The heat was just bearable... He could only just hear them... It might just help.* **9** ADV You can use **just** to give emphasis to what you are saying. *I just know there's something wrong... Just listen to that noise.* **10** ADV **Just** also means exactly or precisely. *That's just what I wanted to hear... She was as fat as he was and just as unattractive.* **11** ADV If you say that someone is **just** the person, you mean that they are the right person. If something is **just** the thing, it is the right thing. *Sam would be just the person!... He knew just the place.* **12** ADV **Just** is also used in polite requests and interruptions. *Can I just use your lighter please?* **13** PHRASE You use **just about** to say that something is so close to a particular level or state that it can be regarded as having reached it. *She was just about his age... Everything is just about ready.* **14** ADJ Someone or something that is **just** is reasonable and fair. *...a just punishment... ...a just and civilised society.* ♦ **justly** ADV *I believe that I have acted justly.*

justice /dʒʌstɪs/, **justices. 1** UNCOUNT N **Justice** is fairness in the way that people are treated. *The concept of justice is very basic in human thought... ...economic justice.* **2** UNCOUNT N **Justice** is also the system that a country uses in order to make sure that people obey the law. *The courts are a very important part of our British system of justice.* **3** UNCOUNT N WITH SUPP The **justice** of a claim, argument, or cause is its quality of being reasonable and right. *They believe in the justice of their cause.* **4** COUNT N A **justice** is a judge; an American use.

PHRASES ● If a criminal **is brought to justice,** he or she is tried in a court of law and punished. ● If you **do justice to** something, you deal with it properly and completely. *I am the only man in Europe capable of doing it justice, of making a perfect job of it.*

Justice of the Peace, Justices of the Peace. COUNT N A **Justice of the Peace** is a local magistrate in Britain.

justifiable /dʒʌstɪfaɪəbəˀl/. ADJ An opinion, action, or fact that is **justifiable** is acceptable or correct because there is a good reason for it. *I hope this is a justifiable interpretation.* ♦ **justifiably** ADV *The Government is justifiably unpopular.*

justification /dʒʌstɪfɪkeɪʃəˀn/, **justifications.** COUNT N OR UNCOUNT N A **justification** for something is a good reason or explanation for it. *We all have justifications for what we do... There was no justification for higher interest rates.*

justified /dʒʌstɪfaɪd/. **1** PRED ADJ If you think that someone is **justified** in doing something, you think that they have good reasons for doing it. *I think he was quite justified in refusing to help her.* **2** ADJ An action that is **justified** is reasonable and acceptable. *In these circumstances, massive industrial action is justified and necessary.*

justify /dʒʌstɪfaɪ/, **justifies, justifying, justified.** VB WITH OBJ, REFL VB, OR VB WITH -ING If someone **justifies** an action or idea, they give a good reason why it is sensible or necessary. *The decision has been fully justified... I'm not going to try and justify myself... How did they justify putting that on a gallery wall?*

jut /dʒʌt/, **juts, jutting, jutted.** VB WITH ADJUNCT If something **juts** out, it sticks out above or beyond a surface. *A line of rocks jutted into the sea.*

juvenile /dʒuːvəˈnaɪl/, **juveniles. 1** ATTRIB ADJ **Juvenile** activity or behaviour involves young people who are not adults. *...the increase in juvenile crime.* **2** ADJ You can say that someone is **juvenile** when they are behaving in a silly way. *Mike has a somewhat juvenile sense of humour.* **3** COUNT N A **juvenile** is a child or young person who is not yet old enough to be regarded as an adult; a legal use. *17% of all crime in 1983 was committed by juveniles.*

juvenile delinquent, juvenile delinquents. COUNT N A **juvenile delinquent** is a young person who is guilty of committing crimes, especially vandalism or violence.

Kk

kaleidoscope /kəlaɪdəˢskəʊp/, **kaleidoscopes. 1** COUNT N A **kaleidoscope** is a tube that you hold in your hand. When you look through one end and turn the tube, you see a changing pattern of colours. **2** SING N WITH SUPP You can refer to any pattern of colours that keeps changing as a **kaleidoscope;** a literary use. *...in a kaleidoscope of colours, cars and lorries swept by.*

kangaroo /kæŋgəruː/, **kangaroos.** COUNT N A **kangaroo** is a large Australian animal which moves by jumping on its back legs. Female kangaroos carry their babies in a pouch on their stomachs.

karate /kərɑːti¹/. UNCOUNT N **Karate** is a sport in which people fight using their hands, elbows, feet, and legs.

kebab /kəˈbæb/, **kebabs.** COUNT N A **kebab** consists of small pieces of meat and vegetables that have been put on a thin rod and grilled.

keel /kiːl/, **keels, keeling, keeled.** PHRASE If something is **on an even keel,** it is working or proceeding smoothly and satisfactorily. *Most governments are able to keep their economies on an even keel.*

keel over. PHR VB If something or someone **keels over,** they fall over sideways. *One of the athletes suddenly keeled over.*

keen /kiːn/, **keener, keenest. 1** PRED ADJ If you are **keen** to do something, you want to do it very much. *Her solicitor was keener to talk than she was... He didn't seem all that keen on having it... He's not keen for Charlotte to know.* **2** ADJ You use **keen** to show that someone enjoys a particular sport or activity and does it a lot. *He was not a keen gardener... Boys are as keen on cooking as girls are.* **3** ADJ **Keen** people are enthusiastic and are interested in everything they do. *They were highly-motivated students, very keen.* **4** ADJ If you have a **keen** interest or desire, your interest or desire is very strong. *He took a keen interest in domestic affairs.* ♦ **keenly** ADV *I was keenly interested in outdoor activities.* **5** ADJ If you have **keen** sight or hearing, you can see or hear very well. *It takes a keen eye to spot them... ...keen powers of observation.* **6** ADJ A **keen** contest or competition is one in which the competitors are all trying very hard to win. *The competition for the first prize was keen.* ♦ **keenly** ADV *...a keenly contested football match.*

keenly /kiːnli¹/. ADV If you watch or listen **keenly,** you watch or listen with great concentration.

keep /kiːp/, **keeps, keeping, kept** /kɛpt/. **1** VB WITH OBJ AND ADJUNCT To **keep** someone or something in a particular state or place means to cause them to remain in that state or place. *They had been kept awake by nightingales... She kept her arm around her husband as she spoke... He bought a guard dog to keep out intruders... Sorry to keep you waiting.* **2** LINK VB If you **keep** in a particular state or place, you remain in that state or place. *They've got to hunt for food to keep alive... Keep in touch... They kept away from the forest.* ● If a sign says **'Keep Out',** it is warning you not to go somewhere. **3** VB WITH -ING If you **keep** doing something, or **keep** on doing it, you do it repeatedly or continually without stopping. *I keep making the same mistake... The men just kept walking... They kept on walking for a while in silence... I kept on getting up and staring out of the window.* **4** VB WITH OBJ If you **keep** something, you continue to have it. *Why didn't Daddy let me keep the ten dollars?... She would not be able to keep her job.* **5** VB WITH OBJ If you **keep** something in a particular place, it belongs in that place. *...the shelf where the butter and cheese were kept... Keep a spare key in your bag.* **6** VB WITH OBJ **Keep** is used with some nouns to indicate that someone continues to do something. For example, if you **keep** a grip on something, you continue to hold it or control it. *They would keep a look-out for him.* **7** VB WITH OBJ AND 'from' To **keep** someone or something from doing something means to prevent them from doing it. *She had to hold the boy tight, to keep him from falling.* **8** VB WITH OBJ If something **keeps** you, it makes you arrive somewhere later than expected. *Am I keeping you from your party?... What kept you?* **9** VB WITH OBJ When you **keep** something such as a promise or an appointment, you do what you said you would do. *Hearst kept his word.* **10** VB WITH OBJ AND 'from' If you **keep** something from someone, you do not tell them about it. *Why did you keep it from me?* **11** VB WITH OBJ If you **keep** a record of a series of events, you make a written record of it. *We keep a record of the noise levels.* **12** VB WITH OBJ People who **keep** animals own them and take care of them. *My dad kept chickens.* **13** SING N WITH POSS Your **keep** is the cost of food and other things that you need every day. *The grant includes £19 for your keep during the vacation.* **14** PHRASE If one thing is **in keeping** with another thing, it seems right or suitable with it. *Her white socks and brown shoes were not quite in keeping with her beautiful satin evening dress.* ● to **keep** your **head:** see **head.**

keep down. PHR VB If you **keep** a number or amount **down,** you do not allow it to increase. *The French are very concerned to keep costs down.*

keep off. PHR VB If you **keep** something **off,** you prevent it from reaching you and harming you. *They built a bamboo shelter to keep the rain off.*

keep on. PHR VB If someone **keeps on** about something, they talk about it a lot in an irritating way. *She kept on about the car.*

keep to. PHR VB **1** If you **keep to** a rule, plan, or agreement, you do as it says. *We must keep to the deadlines.* **2** If you **keep** something **to** a particular amount, you limit it to that amount. *Keep it to a minimum.*

keep up. PHR VB **1** If one person or thing **keeps up** with another, the first one moves, progresses, or increases as fast as the second. *I started to run, so that she had to hurry to keep up with me... Pensions were increased to keep up with the rise in prices.* **2** If you **keep up** with what is happening, you make sure that you know about it. *Even friends have trouble keeping up with each other's whereabouts.*

keeper /kiːpə/, **keepers.** COUNT N A **keeper** is a person who takes care of the animals in a zoo.

kennel /kɛnəˀl/, **kennels. 1** COUNT N A **kennel** is a small hut made for a dog to sleep in. **2** SING N A **kennels** is a place where people can leave their pet dogs when they go on holiday, or where dogs are bred.

kept /kɛpt/. **Kept** is the past tense and past participle of **keep.**

kerb /kɜːb/, **kerbs;** spelled **curb** in American English. COUNT N The **kerb** is the part of a pavement that is immediately next to the road. *The taxi pulled into the kerb... ...standing on the kerb.*

kernel /kɜːnəˀl/, **kernels.** COUNT N The **kernel** of a nut is the part inside the shell.

kerosene /kɛrəsiːn/. UNCOUNT N **Kerosene** is the same as paraffin; an American use.

ketchup /kɛtʃəp/. UNCOUNT N **Ketchup** is a thick, cold sauce made from tomatoes.

kettle /kɛtəˀl/, **kettles.** COUNT N A **kettle** is a covered container that you use for boiling water. It has a handle and a spout.

key /kiː/, **keys. 1** COUNT N A **key** is a specially shaped piece of metal which fits in a lock and is turned in order to open or lock a door, drawer, or suitcase. **2** COUNT N The **keys** of a typewriter, computer keyboard, or cash register are the buttons that you press in order to operate it. **3** COUNT N The **keys** of a piano or organ are the black and white bars that you press in order to play it. **4** COUNT N In music, a **key** is a scale of musical notes that starts at one particular note. *...the key of D.* **5** COUNT N The **key** to a map, diagram, or technical book is a list of the symbols and abbreviations used in it, and their meanings. **6** ATTRIB ADJ The **key** things or people in a group are the most important ones. *The country's key industries are coal, engineering, and transport... Unemployment was a key issue during the election campaign.* **7** COUNT N The **key** to a desirable situation or result is the way in which it can be achieved. *Education became the key to progress.*

keyboard /kiːbɔːd/, **keyboards. 1** COUNT N The **keyboard** of a typewriter or a computer terminal is the set of keys that you press in order to operate it. **2** COUNT N The **keyboard** of a piano or organ is the set of black and white keys that you press in order to play it. *She reached out her hands to the keyboard and began to play.*

keyhole /kiːhəʊl/, **keyholes.** COUNT N A **keyhole** is the hole in a lock that you put a key in.

key-ring, key-rings. COUNT N A **key-ring** is a ring which you use to keep your keys together.

kg. Kg is an abbreviation for 'kilogram'.

khaki /kɑːki¹/. ADJ Something that is **khaki** is yellowish-brown. *...khaki shorts... The boys looked smart in khaki and polished brass.*

kick /kɪk/, **kicks, kicking, kicked. 1** VB WITH OBJ If you **kick** someone or something, you hit them with your foot. *He protested violently, and threatened to kick me... We caught sight of Christopher, kicking a tin can down the High Street.* Also COUNT N *He gave him a good kick.* **2** VB If you **kick,** you move your feet violently or suddenly, for example when you are dancing or swimming. *Simon was floating in the water and kicking with his feet.* 3 PHRASE If someone **gets a kick** from something, they get pleasure or excitement from it; an informal use. *They loved debate, and got a kick out of court proceedings.* 4 VB WITH OBJ If you **kick** a habit, you stop having that habit; an informal use. *Leicester's supporters have never kicked the travelling habit.* 5 See also **free kick.**

kick off. PHR VB When you **kick off** an event or a discussion, you start it; an informal use. *They kicked off a two-month tour of the U.S. with a party in Washington.*

kick out. PHR VB If you **kick** someone **out,** you make them leave a place; an informal use. *He kicked me out... She kicked me out of the room.*

kick up. PHR VB If you **kick up** a fuss or a row, you get very annoyed or upset; an informal use. *When I told him, he kicked up a fuss.*

kick-off, kick-offs. UNCOUNT N OR COUNT N **Kick-off** or the **kick-off** is the time at which a football game starts. *Kick-off is at 2.30.*

kid /kɪd/, **kids, kidding, kidded.** 1 COUNT N You can refer to a child as a **kid**; an informal use. *...five-year-old kids... I can remember the feelings I had when I was a kid... ...his wife and kids.* 2 COUNT N Young people who are no longer children are sometimes referred to as **kids**; an informal American use. *GM's college kids pay only $1,200 tuition.* 3 VB If you **are kidding,** you are saying something that is not really true, as a joke; an informal use. *They're not sure whether I'm kidding or not... I'm not kidding, Jill. He could have taken it if he'd wanted.* ● You say **'No kidding'** to emphasize that you are serious or that something is true. *No kidding, Ginny, you look good.* 4 VB WITH OBJ If you **kid** someone, you tease them. *Tim's friends kidded him about his odd clothes.* 5 REFL VB If people **kid** themselves, they allow themselves to believe something that is not true. *They like to kid themselves they're keeping fit.* 6 COUNT N A **kid** is also a young goat.

kidnap /kɪdnæp/, **kidnaps, kidnapping, kidnapped.** 1 VB WITH OBJ If someone **kidnaps** you, they take you away by force, usually in order to demand money from your family or government. *He was kidnapped by terrorists just over a month ago.* ♦ **kidnapping** UNCOUNT N OR COUNT N *They charged me with murder and kidnapping... ...the kidnapping of a royal child.* ♦ **kidnapper** /kɪdnæpə/ COUNT N *I had given up all hope of tracing her kidnapper.* 2 UNCOUNT N **Kidnap** is the crime of kidnapping someone. *...the threat of kidnap or assassination... ...a kidnap victim.*

kidney /kɪdni^1/, **kidneys.** COUNT N Your **kidneys** are the two organs in your body that produce urine. *He had kidney trouble.*

kill /kɪl/, **kills, killing, killed.** 1 VB WITH OR WITHOUT OBJ OR REFL VB When someone or something **kills** a person, animal or plant, they cause the person, animal, or plant to die. *He had tried to kill himself five times... The sun had killed most of the plants... ...a desire to kill... Her mother was killed in a car crash.* 2 COUNT N The act of killing an animal after hunting it is referred to as the **kill.** *The hunters move in for the kill.* 3 VB WITH OBJ If something **kills** an activity, process, or feeling, it prevents it from continuing. *His behaviour outraged me and killed our friendship... These latest measures killed all hope of any relaxation of the system.*

PHRASES ● When you **kill time,** you so something unimportant or uninteresting while you are waiting. *He spent long hours keeping out of the way, killing time.* ● **to kill two birds with one stone:** see **bird.**

kill off. PHR VB If you **kill** something **off,** you completely destroy it. *This discovery killed off one of the last surviving romances about the place... The bacteria had been killed off.*

killer /kɪlə/, **killers.** 1 COUNT N A **killer** is a person who has killed someone. *He became a ruthless killer.* 2 COUNT N You can refer to anything that causes death as a **killer.** *The lion is one of the most efficient killers in the animal world... Heart disease is the major killer.*

killing /kɪlɪŋ/, **killings.** COUNT N A **killing** is an act in which one person deliberately kills another. *...a brutal killing.*

kiln /kɪln/, **kilns.** COUNT N A **kiln** is an oven used to bake pottery and bricks.

kilo /kiːləʊ/, **kilos.** COUNT N A **kilo** is the same as a kilogram.

kilogram /kɪlə^{6}græm/, **kilograms;** also spelled **kilogramme.** COUNT N A **kilogram** is a unit of weight equal to one thousand grams.

kilometre /kɪlə^{6}miːtə, kɪlɒmɪtə/, **kilometres;** spelled **kilometer** in American English. COUNT N A **kilometre** is a unit of distance equal to one thousand metres. *We could see rain falling about a kilometre away.*

kilt /kɪlt/, **kilts.** COUNT N A **kilt** is a short pleated skirt that is sometimes worn by Scotsmen. Kilts can also be worn by women and girls.

kin /kɪn/. UNCOUNT N Your **kin** are your relatives; an old-fashioned use. ● See also **next of kin.**

kind /kaɪnd/, **kinds; kinder, kindest.** 1 COUNT N OR UNCOUNT N WITH SUPP If you talk about a particular **kind** of thing, you are talking about one of the classes or sorts of that thing. *Was he carrying a weapon and, if so, what kind of weapon?... ...processes of an entirely new kind... These thoughts weren't the kind he could share with anyone.* 2 ADJ A **kind** person is gentle, caring, and helpful. *We were much kinder to one another after that night... It was kind of you to come.* ♦ **kindly** ADV *'You're not to blame yourself, Smithy,' Rick said kindly.*

PHRASES ● You use **kind of** to say that something can be roughly described in a particular way; an informal use. *He spoke in a kind of sad whisper.* ● **Kind of** is used to say that something is partly true; an informal American use. *I felt kind of sorry for him.* ● You use **of a kind** to say that something belongs to a particular class of things but that it is not really satisfactory. *A solution of a kind has been found to this problem.* ● Payment **in kind** is payment in the form of goods or services, rather than money.

kindergarten /kɪndəgɑːtə^{0}n/, **kindergartens.** COUNT N OR UNCOUNT N A **kindergarten** is a school for young children who are not old enough to go to a primary school.

kind-hearted. ADJ Someone who is **kind-hearted** is kind, loving, and gentle.

kindle /kɪndə^{0}l/, **kindles, kindling, kindled.** 1 VB WITH OBJ If something **kindles** an idea or feeling in you, it makes have that idea or feeling; a literary use. *...the aspirations kindled in us in early childhood.* 2 VB WITH OBJ If you **kindle** a fire, you light it.

kindly /kaɪndli^1/. 1 ATTRIB ADJ A **kindly** person is kind, caring, and sympathetic. *Being a kindly and reasonable man, he at once apologized.* ♦ **kindliness** UNCOUNT N *...the great virtues of humility and kindliness.* 2 ADV WITH INF If you ask someone to **kindly** do something, you are asking them in a way that shows your annoyance. *Kindly take your hand off my knee.* 3 See also **kind.**

PHRASES ● If someone **looks kindly** on something, they approve of it. *The White House will look more kindly on a robust economy.* ● If someone **does not take kindly to** something, they do not like it. *They are unlikely to take kindly to this suggestion.*

kindness /kaɪndnɪ^{2}s/, **kindnesses.** 1 COUNT N A **kindness** is a helpful or considerate act. *She thanked them both many times for all their kindnesses.* 2 UNCOUNT N **Kindness** is the quality of being gentle, caring, and helpful. *He treated his labourers with kindness and understanding.*

kindred /kɪndrɪ^{2}d/. ATTRIB ADJ Someone who is a **kindred** spirit has the same view of life that you have. *When I saw his work I recognized him as a kindred spirit.*

king /kɪŋ/, **kings.** 1 COUNT N OR TITLE A **king** is a man who is a member of the royal family of his country, and who is considered to be the head of that country. *...the King of Spain.* 2 COUNT N In chess, the **king** is the piece which each player must try to capture. 3 COUNT N A **king** is also a playing card with a picture of a king on it.

kingdom /kɪŋdəm/, **kingdoms.** 1 COUNT N A **kingdom** is a country or region that is ruled by a king or queen. 2 SING N WITH SUPP All the animals, birds, and insects in the world can be referred to together as the animal **kingdom.** All the plants can be referred to as the plant **kingdom.**

kinship /kɪnʃɪp/. 1 UNCOUNT N **Kinship** is the relationship between members of the same family; a formal use. *Their ties of kinship mean a lot to them.* 2 UNCOUNT N WITH SUPP If you feel **kinship** with someone, you feel close to them because you share their ideas or feelings; a literary use. *He felt a deep kinship with the other students.*

kiosk /kiːɒsk/, **kiosks.** COUNT N A **kiosk** is a small shop where sandwiches and newspapers are sold.

kipper /kɪpə/, **kippers.** COUNT N A **kipper** is a herring which has been preserved by being hung in smoke.

kiss /kɪs/, **kisses, kissing, kissed.** VB WITH OBJ OR RECIP VB If you **kiss** someone, you touch them with your lips to show affection or to greet them. *He opened his eyes when I kissed his cheek... I kissed her goodbye and drove away... They stopped and kissed.* Also COUNT N *Give me a kiss.*

kit /kɪt/, **kits.** 1 COUNT N WITH SUPP A **kit** is a group of items that are kept together because they are used for similar purposes. *...my first-aid kit... ...a tool kit.* 2 UNCOUNT N Your **kit** is the special clothing you use for a particular sport. *Have you brought your squash kit?* 3 COUNT N A **kit** is also a set of parts that can be put together in order to make something. *...a do-it-yourself radio kit.*

kitchen /kɪtʃɪn/, **kitchens.** COUNT N A **kitchen** is a room used for cooking and for jobs such as washing up.

kite /kaɪt/, **kites.** COUNT N A **kite** is an object consisting of a light frame covered with paper or cloth. It has a long string attached to it which you hold while the kite flies in the air.

kitten /kɪtə^{0}n/, **kittens.** COUNT N A **kitten** is a very young cat.

kitty /kɪti^1/, **kitties.** COUNT N A **kitty** is an amount of money consisting of contributions from several people, which is spent on things that they will share or use together. *After we paid the phone bill there was nothing left in the kitty.*

kiwi /kiːwi^1/, **kiwis.** COUNT N A **kiwi** is a type of bird that lives in New Zealand.

kiwi fruit, kiwi fruits. Kiwi fruit can also be the plural. COUNT N A **kiwi fruit** is a fruit with a brown hairy skin and green flesh.

km. Km is a written abbreviation for 'kilometres' or 'kilometre'. *My older sister lives about 10km from our village.*

knack /næk/. SING N If you have the **knack** of doing something, you are able to do it, although other people find it difficult. *He had the knack of balancing his pile of objects perfectly.*

knead /niːd/, **kneads, kneading, kneaded.** VB WITH OBJ When you **knead** dough, you press and squeeze it with your hands to make it smooth.

knee /niː/, **knees.** 1 COUNT N Your **knee** is the place where your leg bends. *Your knee's bleeding.* 2 COUNT N If something or someone is on your **knee,** they are resting or sitting on the upper part of your legs when you are sitting down. *She sat with Marcus by her side and Maria on her knee.* 3 PLURAL N If you are on your **knees,** you are kneeling. *Kurt threw himself on his knees... The woman got up off her knees.* 4 PHRASE If something **brings** a country **to its knees,** it almost destroys it. *The cost of the war would have brought the kingdom to its knees.*

kneecap /niːkæp/, **kneecaps.** COUNT N Your **kneecaps** are the bones at the front of your knees.

kneel /niːl/, **kneels, kneeling, knelt** /nɛlt/ or **kneeled.** 1 VB If you **are kneeling,** your legs are bent under you with your knees touching the ground and supporting the rest of your body. *Ralph was kneeling by the fire.* ♦ **kneeling** ATTRIB ADJ *The kneeling figure was Mary Darling.* 2 VB If you **kneel** or **kneel** down, you bend your legs and lower your body until your knees are on the ground. *Together they kneeled in prayer... I knelt down beside her.*

knew /njuː/. **Knew** is the past tense of **know.**

knickers /nɪkəz/. PLURAL N **Knickers** are a piece of underwear worn by women and girls which have holes for the legs and elastic around the top. *...a pair of knickers.*

knife /naɪf/, **knives** /naɪvz/; **knifes, knifing, knifed. Knives** is the plural of the noun. **Knifes** is the third person singular, present tense, of the verb. 1 COUNT N A **knife** is an object consisting of a sharp, flat piece of metal attached to a handle. You use a knife to cut things. *...knives and forks... ...men armed with knives... ...a knife blade.* 2 VB WITH OBJ To **knife** someone means to attack and injure them with a knife. *Rausenberger had been knifed and robbed near his home.* 3 See also **carving knife, penknife.**

knight /naɪt/, **knights, knighting, knighted.** 1 COUNT N In medieval times, a **knight** was a man of noble birth, who served his lord in battle. *...knights in armour.* 2 COUNT N In modern times, a **knight** is a man who has been given a knighthood. 3 COUNT N In chess, a **knight** is a piece shaped like a horse's head. 4 VB WITH OBJ If a man **is knighted,** he is given a knighthood. *He was knighted by Queen Anne in 1705.*

knighthood /naɪthʊd/, **knighthoods.** COUNT N A **knighthood** is a title given to a man in Britain for outstanding achievements or for service to his country. A man with a knighthood puts 'Sir' in front of his name.

knit /nɪt/, **knits, knitting, knitted.** 1 VB WITH OR WITHOUT OBJ When someone **knits** something, they make it from wool or a similar thread using knitting needles or a machine. *She wore a scarf that she had knitted... The old lady sat in her doorway and knitted.* ♦ **knitted** ADJ *...a knitted shawl.* 2 PHRASE If you **knit** your **brows,** you frown because you are angry or worried; a literary use. *He sat there knitting his brows and twisting his napkin.* 3 ADJ A group of people who are close **knit** or tightly **knit** feel closely linked to each other. *It's a very close-knit community... They live in tightly knit families.*

knitting needle, knitting needles. COUNT N **Knitting needles** are thin plastic or metal rods which you use when you are knitting.

knives /naɪvz/. **Knives** is the plural of **knife.**

knob /nɒb/, **knobs. 1** COUNT N A **knob** is a round handle on a door or drawer. *He turned the knob... ...polished brass knobs.* **2** COUNT N A **knob** is also a rounded lump on top of a stick or post. *Her umbrella is elegantly capped with a glass knob.* **3** COUNT N A round switch on a machine or device is also called a **knob.** *...the knobs on his tape recorder.*

knobbly /nɒbli^{i}/. ADJ Something that is **knobbly** is uneven with large lumps on it. *...knobbly old hands.*

knock /nɒk/, **knocks, knocking, knocked. 1** VB If you **knock** at a door or window, you hit it, usually several times, in order to attract someone's attention. *He knocked softly on the door.* Also COUNT N *There was a knock at the door.* **2** VB WITH OBJ If you **knock** something, you hit it roughly, so that it moves or falls over. *In the excitement he knocked over his chair... The glass had been knocked out from windows.* Also COUNT N *Knocks can cause weaknesses in the spine.* **3** VB WITH OBJ AND ADJUNCT OR COMPLEMENT If you **knock** someone down or **knock** them unconscious, you hit them so hard that they fall or become unconscious. *Dad knocked him to the floor... Rudolph had seen him knock Thomas unconscious with his fist.* **4** VB WITH OBJ If you **knock** someone or something, you criticize them; an informal use. *He was always knocking the performance of fellow-actors.*

knock about or **knock around.** PHR VB **1** If someone **is knocked about** or **knocked around,** they are hit several times; an informal use. *He did not like the thought of a woman being knocked about.* **2** Someone who **has knocked about** or **knocked around** has had experience in a lot of different places or situations; an informal use. *I'm a bachelor, I've knocked about the world a bit.*

knock back. PHR VB If you **knock back** a drink, you drink it quickly; an informal use.

knock down. PHR VB **1** If a vehicle **knocks** someone **down,** it hits them so that they are killed or injured. *He was knocked down by a bus.* **2** If you **knock down** a building, you deliberately destroy it or remove it. *I'd knock the wall down between the two rooms.*

knock off. PHR VB If someone **knocks** an amount **off** the price of something, they reduce the price by that amount. *He knocked £50 off the price, because it was scratched.*

knock out. PHR VB **1** If someone **knocks** you **out,** they make you unconscious by hitting you. *He hit me so hard he knocked me out.* **2** If a drug **knocks** you **out,** you become unconscious after taking it. *The tablet had knocked her out for four hours.* **3** If a person or team **is knocked out** of a competition, they are defeated in a game, so that they do not play any more games.

knocker /nɒkə/, **knockers.** COUNT N A **knocker** is a piece of metal attached to the door of a building, which you use to hit the door in order to attract the attention of the people inside.

knock-on. ATTRIB ADJ If something has a **knock-on** effect, it causes a series of events to happen, one after another. *We need to find a solution that doesn't have so many knock-on effects.*

knot /nɒt/, **knots, knotting, knotted. 1** COUNT N A **knot** is a place in a piece of string, rope, or cloth where one end has been passed through a loop and pulled tight. You tie a knot in order to join two things together or to keep something firmly in place. *He had tied a crude knot... The knot of her headscarf hung beneath her chin.* **2** VB WITH OBJ If you **knot** a piece of string, rope, or cloth, you pass one end of it through a loop and pull it tight. **3** VB WITH OBJ AND ADJUNCT If you **knot** one thing around another, you fasten them together using a knot. *He knotted a towel about his neck... I set off with the rope knotted round my waist.* **4** SING N A **knot** of people is a group of them standing very close together. *...watched by a knot of sightseers.* **5** COUNT N A **knot** is also a unit used for measuring the speed of ships and aircraft, equal to approximately 1.85 kilometres per hour. *...an underwater object moving at over 150 knots.*

know /nəʊ/, **knows, knowing, knew** /njuː/, **known. 1** REPORT VB If you **know** something, you have it correctly in your mind. *I don't know her address... I knew that she had recently graduated from law school... We knew what to expect... No one knew how to repair it... 'Will they come back?'—'I don't know.'* **2** VB WITH 'of' OR 'about' If you **know** of something or **know** about it, you have heard about it. *Many people did not even know of their existence... Claude knew about the killing.* **3** VB WITH OBJ If you **know** a language, you can understand it and speak it. *Shanti knew a few words of English.* **4** VB WITH 'about' OR OBJ If you **know** about a subject, you have studied it and have some knowledge of it. *They knew a lot about films... I don't know much about physics, I'm afraid.* **5** VB WITH OBJ If you **know** a person, place, or thing, you are familiar with them. *Do you know David?... He knew London well.* **6** See also **knowing, known.**

PHRASES ● If you **let** someone **know** about something, you tell them about it. *I'll find out about the car and let you know what happened.* ● If you **know better** than someone else, your ideas are more sensible or more correct than theirs. *The experts, who knew better, laughed at the idea.* ● If you say that someone ought to **know better,** you mean that they ought to behave in a more sensible and acceptable way. *Brian is old enough to know better.* ● If you say that someone **knows best,** you mean that they are always right about what should be done. *Parents always know best.* ● You say **'you know'** to emphasize something or to make your statement clearer. *You were very naughty, you know... You know, most of the time he seems like a fool... ...the old desk. You know, the one that's broken.* ● You say **'I know'** to indicate that you agree with what has just been said, or to indicate that you realize something is true. *'It's quite extraordinary.'—'I know.'... I get frightened in the night sometimes—it's silly, I know.* ● Someone who is **in the know** has information about something that only a few people have.

know-how. UNCOUNT N **Know-how** is knowledge about how to do scientific or technical things; an informal use. *They now had the facilities and know-how to produce advanced weapons.*

knowing /nəʊɪŋ/. ATTRIB ADJ A **knowing** gesture or remark shows that you understand something, even though it has not actually been mentioned directly. *This is usually greeted with deep sighs and knowing looks... ...a knowing smile.*

knowingly /nəʊɪŋli^{i}/. **1** ADV If you do something wrong **knowingly,** you are aware that it is wrong when you do it. *They knowingly broke laws that ban trade in rare reptiles.* **2** ADV If you look, smile, or wink **knowingly,** you do it in a way that shows that you understand something, even though it has not actually been mentioned directly. *The girls looked knowingly at each other.*

knowledge /nɒlɪdʒ/. **1** UNCOUNT N **Knowledge** is information and understanding about a subject, which someone has in their mind. *...advances in scientific knowledge... All knowledge comes to us through our senses... ...a knowledge of income-tax legislation.* **2** PHRASE If you say that something is true **to the best of** your **knowledge,** you mean that you think that it is true, although you are not completely sure. *...a play which to the best of my knowledge has never been performed in Britain.*

knowledgeable /nɒlɪdʒəbə^{0}l/. ADJ A **knowledgeable** person knows a lot about many different things or a lot about a particular subject. *He was surprisingly knowledgeable about what was going on in the theatre.*

known /nəʊn/. **1 Known** is the past participle of **know. 2** ADJ If something is **known** to people, they are aware of it and have information about it. *There's no known cure for a cold... ...the most dangerous substance known to man.* **3** PHRASE If you **let it be known** that something is the case, you make sure that people know it, without telling them directly; a formal use. *She let it be known that she wanted to leave China.* **4** See also **well-known.**

knuckle /nʌkə^{0}l/, **knuckles.** COUNT N Your **knuckles** are the rounded pieces of bone where your fingers join your hands, and where your fingers bend. *As he fell, he scraped the skin off his knuckles.*

Koran /kɔːrɑːn/. PROPER N The **Koran** is the sacred book on which the religion of Islam is based.

kosher /kəʊʃə/. ADJ **Kosher** food is approved of by the laws of Judaism.

Ll

l. l is a written abbreviation for 'litre'.

lab /læb/, **labs.** COUNT N A **lab** is a laboratory; an informal use. *Your X-rays have just come back from the lab.*

label /leɪbə^{0}l/, **labels, labelling, labelled;** spelled **labeling** and **labeled** in American English. **1** COUNT N A **label** is a piece of paper or plastic that is attached to an object to give information about it. *The bottles got wet and all the labels came off.* **2** VB WITH OBJ If you **label** something, you attach a label to it. *...the brown pot labelled 'Salt'.* **3** COUNT N WITH SUPP A **label** is also a word or phrase that people use to describe you; used showing disapproval. *He was not willing to accept the label of anarchist.* **4** VB WITH OBJ If people **label** you as something, they describe you or think of you in that way; used showing disapproval. *Once you are labelled as a secretary you will never become anything else.*

labor /leɪbə/. See **labour.**

laboratory /lə^{3}bɒrətə^{0}ri^{i}/, **laboratories. 1** COUNT N A **laboratory** is a building or room where scientific experiments and research are carried out. *The geologists took the samples back to the laboratory.* **2** COUNT N A **laboratory** in a school or university is a room containing scientific equipment where students are taught science subjects such as chemistry. ● See also **language laboratory.**

laborious /lə^{3}bɔːrɪəs/. ADJ A **laborious** task takes a lot of effort. *Clearing the forest is a laborious business.* ♦ **laboriously** ADV *...laboriously hand-written books.*

labour /leɪbə/, **labours, labouring, laboured;** spelled **labor** in American English. **1** UNCOUNT N OR COUNT N **Labour** is very hard work. *I really enjoy manual labour... ...a pleasant distraction from his political labours.* **2** VB WITH ADJUNCT If you **labour** at something, you do it with difficulty. *Tim had laboured over a letter to Gertrude.* ♦ **laboured** ADJ *McKellen's breathing was laboured.* **3** UNCOUNT N **Labour** is used to refer to the people who work in a country or industry. *...a shortage of skilled labour.* **4** UNCOUNT N **Labour** is also the work done by a group of workers. *They are threatening a withdrawal of labour in support of their claims.* **5** VB WITH 'under' If you **labour** under a delusion, you continue to believe something which is not true. *He laboured under the misapprehension that nobody liked him.* **6** VB WITH OBJ If you **labour** a point or an argument, you talk about it in great and unnecessary detail. *There is no need to labour the point.* **7** UNCOUNT N **Labour** is also the last stage of pregnancy, in which a woman gives birth to a baby. *She was in labour for seven hours.*

labourer /leɪbə^{0}rə/, **labourers.** COUNT N A **labourer** is a person who does a job which involves a lot of hard physical work. *...a farm labourer.*

labyrinth /læbə^{i}rɪnθ/, **labyrinths.** COUNT N A **labyrinth** is a complicated series of paths or passages, through which it is difficult to find your way. *He wandered through the labyrinths of the Old Town.*

lace /leɪs/, **laces, lacing, laced. 1** UNCOUNT N **Lace** is very delicate cloth which has a lot of holes in it. *...a white lace handkerchief.* **2** COUNT N **Laces** are pieces of cord or string that you put through holes along the two edges of something and tie in order to fasten them together. *...tying the laces of his shoes.*

lace up. PHR VB If you **lace** something **up,** you fasten it by pulling two ends of a lace tight and tying them together. *He bent and laced up his shoes.*

lack /læk/, **lacks, lacking, lacked. 1** SING N OR UNCOUNT N If there is a **lack** of something, there is not enough of it, or there is none at all. *I hated the lack of privacy in the dormitory... Lack of proper funding is making our job more difficult.* **2** VB WITH OBJ If you **lack** something, you do not have it. *They lack the confidence to make friends... The advertisement lacks any individuality.* **3** VB If you say that something **is lacking,** you mean that it does not exist, or there is not enough of it. *'What is lacking in this case,' he concluded, 'is a corpse.'* **4** VB WITH 'in' If someone or something **is lacking** in a particular quality, they do not have it or do not have enough of it. *Philip was not lacking in intelligence or ability.* **5** PHRASE If you say that there is **no lack of** something, you mean that there is a great deal of it, and perhaps more than you need. *There was no lack of schools to choose from.*

lacquer /lækə/, **lacquers. 1** MASS N **Lacquer** is a special type of paint which is put on wood or metal to protect it and make it shiny. *Why don't you spray it with lacquer?* **2** MASS N **Lacquer** is also a liquid which women put on their hair to hold it neatly in place.

lacquered /lækəd/. ADJ **Lacquered** wood or metal has been covered in lacquer. *...a lacquered box.*

lacy /leɪsi^{i}/. ADJ Something that is **lacy** is made from lace or has pieces of lace attached to it. *...a lacy dress.*

lad /læd/, **lads.** COUNT N A **lad** is a boy or young man. *He used to collect stamps when he was a lad.*

ladder /lædə/, **ladders.** COUNT N A **ladder** is a piece of equipment used for climbing up something such as a wall or a tree. It consists of two long pieces of wood, metal, or rope with steps fixed between them.

laden /leɪdə^{0}n/. ADJ If someone or something is **laden** with things, they are holding or have a lot of them; a literary use. *Ken arrived laden with presents... The trees were laden with fruit.*

ladle /leɪdə^{0}l/, **ladles, ladling, ladled. 1** COUNT N A **ladle** is a large, round, deep spoon with a long handle, used for serving soup or stew. **2** VB WITH OBJ If you **ladle** food such as soup or stew, you serve it using a ladle. *...ladling the soup into bowls.*

lady /leɪdi^{i}/, **ladies. 1** COUNT N You can use **lady** as a polite way of referring to a woman. *...a rich American lady... ...elderly ladies living on their own... ...a lady novelist.* **2** VOCATIVE You can say **'ladies'** when you are addressing a group of women. *Ladies, could I have your attention, please?... Good evening, ladies and gentlemen.* 3 COUNT N If you say that a woman is a **lady**, you mean that she behaves in a polite, dignified, and graceful way; an old-fashioned use. 4 TITLE **Lady** is a title used in front of the names of some women from the upper classes. *...Lady Diana Cooper.*

ladylike /leɪdi¹laɪk/. ADJ If you say that a woman or girl is **ladylike**, you mean that she behaves in a polite, dignified, and graceful way. *She took little ladylike sips of the cold drink.*

lag /læg/, **lags, lagging, lagged.** 1 VB If you **lag** behind someone or something, you move or progress more slowly than they do. *He set off at a brisk walk, Kate lagging behind... Britain's economic development must lag behind that of almost every other industrial nation.* 2 VB When something such as trade or investment **lags**, there is less of it than there was before. *Production lagged and unemployment rose.* 3 COUNT N WITH SUPP A time **lag** is a period of time between two related events. *There will be a one-year lag between the time I write this book and its publication.* 4 VB WITH OBJ If you **lag** a pipe, a water tank, or the inside of a roof, you cover it with a special material to prevent heat escaping from it.

lager /lɑːgə/, **lagers.** MASS N **Lager** is a kind of light beer.

lagoon /lə³guːn/, **lagoons.** COUNT N A **lagoon** is an area of calm sea water that is separated from the ocean by reefs or sand.

laid /leɪd/. **Laid** is the past tense and past participle of **lay.**

laid up. ADJ If you are **laid up**, you have to stay in bed because you are ill. *He had been laid up for five days with a bad cold.*

lain /leɪn/. **Lain** is the past participle of some meanings of **lie.**

lair /lɛə/, **lairs.** COUNT N A **lair** is a place where a wild animal lives, usually a place which is underground or well-hidden. *...animals that refuse to come out of their lairs.*

lake /leɪk/, **lakes.** COUNT N A **lake** is a large area of fresh water, surrounded by land.

lamb /læm/, **lambs.** 1 COUNT N A **lamb** is a young sheep. 2 UNCOUNT N **Lamb** is the flesh of a sheep or lamb eaten as food. *...roast lamb.*

lame /leɪm/. 1 ADJ A **lame** person cannot walk properly because an injury or illness has damaged one or both of their legs. *The illness left her permanently lame... ...a lame horse.* 2 ADJ A **lame** excuse, argument, or remark is poor or weak. *My lame excuse was that I had too much else to do.* ♦ **lamely** ADV *'I didn't recognize you,' Claude said lamely.*

lament /ləment/, **laments, lamenting, lamented.** REPORT VB If you **lament** something, you express your sadness or regret about it; a literary use. *He laments the changing pattern of life in the countryside... 'All the flour is wet!' lamented Miss Mutton.* Also COUNT N *'It's a dying industry,' is his lament.*

lamentable /ləmentəbə⁰l, læməntəbə⁰l/. ADJ If you describe something as **lamentable**, you mean that it is very unfortunate or disappointing; a formal use. *...the lamentable state of the industry in the Sixties.*

lamp /læmp/, **lamps.** COUNT N A **lamp** is a light that works by using electricity or by burning oil or gas. *She turned on the bedside lamp... ...the street lamp outside.*

lamp-post, lamp-posts. COUNT N A **lamp-post** is a tall metal or concrete pole beside a road with a light at the top.

lampshade /læmpʃeɪd/, **lampshades.** COUNT N A **lampshade** is a decorative covering over an electric light bulb which makes the light softer.

land /lænd/, **lands, landing, landed.** 1 UNCOUNT N **Land** is an area of ground. *It's good agricultural land... ...a piece of land.* 2 COUNT N WITH POSS If you refer to someone's **land** or **lands**, you mean an area of land which they own. 3 UNCOUNT N OR SING N **Land** or the **land** refers to the part of the world that is solid ground rather than sea or air. *We turned away from land and headed out to sea.* 4 COUNT N A particular **land** is a particular country; a literary use. *...a land where there is never any rain... Australia is the land of opportunities.* 5 VB If someone or something **lands** somewhere, they come down to the ground or in water after moving through the air. *The last man slipped and landed in the water... His plane lands at six-thirty.* 6 VB WITH OBJ To **land** people or goods somewhere means to unload them there at the end of a journey, especially a journey by ship. *...small ships sailing from Florida to land arms and combatants.* 7 ERG VB WITH ADJUNCT If you **land** in an unpleasant situation or if something **lands** you in it, you come to be in it; an informal use. *That would have landed him in jail.* 8 VB WITH OBJ AND 'with' If you **land** someone with something that causes difficulties, you cause them to have to deal with it; an informal use. *You landed us with that awful man.*

land up. PHR VB If you **land up** in a particular place or situation, you arrive in it after a long journey or at the end of a long series of events. *She landed up in Rome.*

landing /lændɪŋ/, **landings.** 1 COUNT N In a building, a **landing** is a flat area at the top of a staircase. 2 COUNT N OR UNCOUNT N When the pilot of an aircraft makes a **landing**, he brings the aircraft down to the ground. *We had to make an emergency landing.*

landlady /lændleɪdi¹/, **landladies.** 1 COUNT N A **landlady** is a woman who owns a house, flat, or room that other people live in, in return for rent. 2 COUNT N A woman who owns or runs a pub is also called a **landlady.**

landlocked /lændlɒkt/. ADJ A country that is **landlocked** is surrounded by other countries and has no sea coast.

landlord /lændlɔːd/, **landlords.** 1 COUNT N A **landlord** is a man who owns a house, flat, or room that other people live in, in return for payment of rent. 2 COUNT N A man who owns or runs a pub is also called a **landlord.**

landmark /lændmɑːk/, **landmarks.** 1 COUNT N A **landmark** is a noticeable building or feature of the land, which you can use to judge your position. *The Chamberlain tower is a landmark visible for miles.* 2 COUNT N You can also refer to an important stage in the development of something as a **landmark.** *The discovery of penicillin was a landmark in medicine.*

landscape /lændskeɪp/, **landscapes, landscaping, landscaped.** 1 COUNT N The **landscape** is everything that you can see when you look across an area of land, including hills, rivers, buildings, and trees. *...the beauty of the Welsh landscape.* 2 COUNT N A **landscape** is a painting of the countryside. *She painted landscapes and portraits.* 3 VB WITH OBJ If an area of land **is landscaped**, someone alters it to create a pleasing effect, for example by creating different levels and planting trees and bushes. *...landscaped grounds.*

landslide /lændslaɪd/, **landslides.** 1 COUNT N If an election is won by a **landslide**, it is won by a large number of votes. *Taylor should win by a landslide.* 2 COUNT N A **landslide** is also a large amount of earth and rocks falling down the side of a mountain. *The slightest noise might set off a landslide.*

lane /leɪn/, **lanes.** 1 COUNT N A **lane** is a narrow road in the country. 2 COUNT N Roads, race courses, and swimming pools are sometimes divided into **lanes.** These are parallel strips separated from each other by lines or ropes. *He changed lanes to make a left turn.*

language /læŋgwɪdʒ/, **languages.** 1 COUNT N A **language** is a system of sounds and written symbols used by the people of a particular country, area, or tribe to communicate with each other. *...the English language... I can speak six languages.* 2 UNCOUNT N **Language** is the ability to use words in order to communicate. *This research helps teachers to understand how children acquire language.* 3 UNCOUNT N WITH SUPP You can refer to the words used in connection with a particular subject as the **language** of that subject. *...the language of sociology.* 4 UNCOUNT N The **language** of a piece of writing or a speech is the style in which it is written or spoken. *I admire the directness of the language.* 5 UNCOUNT N OR COUNT N **Language** is also used to refer to other means of communication such as sign language, computer languages, and animal language.

language laboratory, language laboratories. COUNT N A **language laboratory** is a classroom equipped with tape recorders where people can improve their knowledge of foreign languages.

languid /læŋgwɪd/. ADJ Someone who is **languid** lacks interest and energy; a literary use.

languish /læŋgwɪʃ/, **languishes, languishing, languished.** VB You say that people **languish** when they are forced to remain and suffer in an unpleasant situation; a literary use. *A few people enjoyed rich lifestyles while the majority languished in poverty.*

lanky /læŋki¹/. ADJ Someone who is **lanky** is tall and thin and moves rather awkwardly. *Quentin was a lanky boy with long skinny legs.*

lantern /læntən/, **lanterns.** COUNT N A **lantern** is a lamp in a metal frame with glass sides.

lap /læp/, **laps, lapping, lapped.** 1 COUNT N WITH POSS Your **lap** is the flat area formed by your thighs when you are sitting down. *Her youngest child was asleep in her lap... He placed the baby on the woman's lap.* 2 COUNT N In a race, you say that a competitor has completed a **lap** when he or she has gone round the course once. 3 VB WITH OBJ If you **lap** another competitor in a race, you pass them while they are still on the previous lap. 4 VB WITH ADJUNCT When water **laps** against something, it touches it gently and makes a soft sound. *Waves lapped against the side of the boat.* 5 VB WITH OR WITHOUT OBJ When an animal **laps** a drink, it uses its tongue to flick the liquid into its mouth. *The cat was lapping at a saucer of milk.*

lap up. PHR VB 1 When an animal **laps up** a drink, it drinks it up very eagerly. 2 If someone **laps up** information or attention, they accept it eagerly, often when it is not really true or sincere. *It was a lie, but millions of newspaper readers lapped it up.*

lapel /lə³pel/, **lapels.** COUNT N The **lapels** of a jacket or coat are the two parts at the front that are folded back on each side and join the collar.

lapse /læps/, **lapses, lapsing, lapsed.** 1 COUNT N A **lapse** is a piece of bad behaviour by someone who usually behaves well. *I intended to make up for this lapse in manners at the next party.* 2 COUNT N WITH SUPP If you have a **lapse** of memory or a **lapse** of concentration, you forget to do something or fail to concentrate on something. 3 VB WITH 'into' If you **lapse** into a particular kind of behaviour, you start behaving that way. *He lapsed into an unhappy silence.* 4 SING N WITH SUPP A **lapse** of time is a period of time that is long enough for a situation to change. *After a certain lapse of time it would be safe for Daisy to return... He was not conscious of the time lapse.* 5 VB If a period of time **lapses**, it passes. *Hours lapsed between each phone call.* 6 VB If a situation, relationship, or legal contract **lapses**, it is allowed to end or to become invalid. *...traditions which had never lapsed.*

larch /lɑːtʃ/, **larches.** COUNT N A **larch** is a tree with needle-shaped leaves.

lard /lɑːd/. UNCOUNT N **Lard** is soft white fat obtained from pigs. It is used in cooking.

larder /lɑːdə/, **larders.** COUNT N A **larder** is a room or cupboard in which food is kept.

large /lɑːdʒ/, **larger, largest.** ADJ Something that is **large** is greater in size or amount than is usual or average. *...a large house... She made a very large amount of money.*

PHRASES ● You use **at large** to indicate that you are talking about most of the people mentioned. *There has been unrest in the country at large.* ● If you say that a dangerous person or animal is **at large**, you mean that they have escaped and have not yet been captured. ● You use **by and large** to indicate that a statement is mostly but not completely true. *By and large, they were free to do as they wished.*

largely /lɑːdʒli¹/. 1 ADV You use **largely** to say that a statement is mostly but not completely true. *The evidence shows them to be largely correct... Her work is largely confined to the cinema.* 2 ADV You also use **largely** to introduce the main reason for an event or situation. *We were there largely because of the girls... He was acquitted, largely on the evidence of a tape recording.*

large-scale. 1 ATTRIB ADJ A **large-scale** action or event happens over a wide area or involves a lot of people or things. *...large-scale forest fires... ...a large-scale farming operation.* 2 ATTRIB ADJ A **large-scale** map or diagram represents a small area of land or a building or machine on a scale that is large enough for small details to be shown.

lark /lɑːk/, **larks.** COUNT N A **lark** is a small brown bird that has a pleasant song.

larva /lɑːvə/, **larvae** /lɑːviː/. COUNT N A **larva** is an insect at the stage before it becomes an adult. Larvae look like short, fat worms.

lascivious /ləsɪvɪəs/. ADJ **Lascivious** people have a strong desire for sex.

laser /leɪzə/, **lasers.** COUNT N A **laser** is a narrow beam of concentrated light that is used especially for cutting very hard materials and in surgery. The machines which produce lasers are also called **lasers.** *A laser beam would cut into it... ...laser weapons.*

lash /læʃ/, **lashes, lashing, lashed.** 1 COUNT N Your **lashes** are the hairs that grow on the edge of your eyelids. 2 COUNT N A **lash** is the thin strip of leather at the end of a whip. *He gasped as the lash hit him.* 3 COUNT N A **lash** is also a blow with a whip on someone's back as a punishment. *...a public flogging of thirty-nine lashes.* 4 VB WITH OBJ If someone **lashes** you, they hit you with a whip. 5 VB WITH OBJ OR ADJUNCT If the wind or rain **lashes** something, it hits it violently; a literary use. *High winds lashed the branches of the elm.* 6 VB WITH OBJ If you **lash** one thing to another, you tie them firmly together. *We lashed our boats together.*

lash out. PHR VB 1 If you **lash out**, you try to hit someone with your hands or feet or with a weapon. *When cornered, they lash out with savage kicks.* 2 You can also say that someone **lashes out** when they criticize or scold people angrily. *Harris lashed out against the Committee.*

lass /læs/, **lasses.** COUNT N In some parts of Britain, a young woman or girl is referred to as a **lass.** *She'd worked on the farm as a lass.*

last /lɑːst/, **lasts, lasting, lasted.** 1 ADJ You use **last** to describe the most recent period of time, event, or thing. *I went to a party last night... ...the last four years... Thanks for your last letter.* 2 ADJ OR PRON The **last** thing or part is the one that comes at the end. *He missed the last bus... ...the last classroom along that passage... Hooper was the last to leave.* 3 ADJ OR PRON **Last** is also used to refer to the only thing or part that remains. *She removed the last traces of make-up... Otto drank the last of the brandy.* 4 ADJ OR PRON You can use **last** to emphasize that you do not want to do something or that something is unlikely to happen. *The last thing I want to do is offend you... I would be the last to suggest that.* 5 ADV If something **last** happened on a particular occasion, it has not happened since then. *They last saw their homeland nine years ago.* 6 ADV If something happens **last,** it happens after everything else. *He added the milk last.* 7 VB If something **lasts,** it continues to exist or happen. *His speech lasted for exactly fourteen minutes... Profits are as high as ever. It won't last.* 8 VB To **last** also means to remain in good condition. *A fresh pepper lasts about three weeks.* 9 VB WITH OR WITHOUT OBJ, WITH ADJUNCT If a quantity of something **lasts** for a period of time, there is enough of it for someone to use during that period. *A cheap box of toothpowder lasts two years... He had only £8 left to last him till he reached Bury.* 10 See also **lasting.**

PHRASES • If something has happened **at last** or **at long last,** it has happened after a long period of time. *At last Ralph stopped work and stood up... At long last I've found a girl that really loves me.* • You use **the last** to indicate that something did not happen or exist again after a particular time, or that it will never happen or exist again. *That was the last I ever saw of Northcliffe.* • You use expressions such as **to the last detail** or **to the last man** to emphasize that you are including every single thing or person. *The robbery was planned down to the last detail.*

lasting /lɑːstɪŋ/. ATTRIB ADJ Something that is **lasting** continues to exist or to be effective for a very long time. *This may provide a lasting solution to our problems... ...lasting friendships.*

lastly /lɑːstli[1]/. 1 SENTENCE ADV You use **lastly** when you want to make a final point that is connected with the ones you have already mentioned. *Lastly, I would like to ask you about your future plans.* 2 ADV You also use **lastly** when you are saying what happens after everything else in a series of actions or events. *Lastly he jabbed the knife into the trunk of the tree.*

last-minute. ATTRIB ADJ A **last-minute** action is done just before something else which is planned to happen at a fixed time. *...a last-minute attempt to stop the school being closed.*

latch /lætʃ/, **latches, latching, latched.** 1 COUNT N A **latch** is a fastening on a door or gate. It consists of a metal bar which is held in place to lock the door and which you lift in order to open the door. 2 VB WITH OBJ If you **latch** a door or gate, you fasten it by means of a latch. 3 PHRASE If a door with a lock that locks automatically is **on the latch,** the lock has been set so that it does not lock automatically when you shut the door. *He closed the door and left it on the latch in case Tom had forgotten his key.*

latch onto. PHR VB If you **latch onto** someone or something, you become very involved with them, because you are interested in them or find them useful; an informal use. *She latched onto someone with a family business.*

late /leɪt/, **later, latest.** 1 ADV OR ATTRIB ADJ **Late** means near the end of a period of time, a process, or a piece of work. *...late in 1952... Very late at night, I got a phone call... Decker arrived in late September... ...in the late afternoon... ...Picasso's late work.* 2 ADJ OR ADV If you are **late** for something or if you arrive **late,** you arrive after the time that was arranged. *I was ten minutes late for my appointment... I apologise for my late arrival... Etta arrived late.* 3 ADJ OR ADV You use **late** to describe things that happen after the normal time. *We had a late lunch at the hotel... ...if you get up late.* 4 ATTRIB ADJ You use **late** when you are talking about someone who is dead. *...the late Harry Truman.* 5 See also **later, latest.**

PHRASES • **As late as** means at a particular time or period that is surprisingly late. *Even as late as 1950 coal provided over 90% of our energy.* • If something happens **too late,** it is useless or ineffective because it happens after the proper or best time. *I realized my mistake too late... It's too late to change that now.*

lately /leɪtli[1]/. ADV **Lately** means recently. *John has seemed worried lately.*

latent /leɪtənt/. ADJ **Latent** is used to describe something which is hidden and not obvious at the moment, but which may develop further in the future. *Everyone has a latent mathematical ability.*

later /leɪtə/. 1 **Later** is the comparative of **late.** 2 ADV You use **later** or **later on** to refer to a time or situation that is after the one that you have been talking about or after the present one. *I returned four weeks later... Later on this evening, we shall have some music... See you later.* 3 ATTRIB ADJ You also use **later** to refer to the last part of someone's life. *This may cause illness in later life.*

lateral /lætə[0]rəl/. ATTRIB ADJ **Lateral** means relating to the sides of something, or moving in a sideways direction. *All of these primitive sea creatures had well developed lateral fins.*

latest /leɪtɪ[2]st/. 1 **Latest** is the superlative of **late.** 2 ADJ You use **latest** to describe something that is the most recent thing of its kind. *...the latest news... ...her latest book.* 3 PHRASE You use **at the latest** to emphasize that something must happen at or before a particular time. *Changes will become necessary by the autumn at the latest.*

lathe /leɪð/, **lathes.** COUNT N A **lathe** is a machine for shaping wood or metal. It works by turning the wood or metal against a tool which cuts it.

lather /lɑːðə/. SING N OR UNCOUNT N **Lather** is a white mass of bubbles which is produced by mixing soap or washing powder with water. *...a good lather.*

Latin /lætɪn/. 1 UNCOUNT N **Latin** is the language which the ancient Romans used to speak. 2 ADJ **Latin** is used to refer to people who come from the countries where French, Italian, Spanish, and Portuguese are spoken. *He had Latin blood.*

Latin American, Latin Americans. 1 ADJ **Latin American** means relating or belonging to the countries of South and Central America. *...Latin American countries.* 2 COUNT N A **Latin American** is someone who lives in or comes from South or Central America.

latitude /lætɪtjuːd/, **latitudes.** 1 COUNT N OR UNCOUNT N The **latitude** of a place is its distance to the north or south of the Equator: compare **longitude.** 2 UNCOUNT N **Latitude** is freedom to choose how to do something; a formal use. *She was given considerable latitude in how she spent the money.*

latrine /lətriːn/, **latrines.** COUNT N A **latrine** is a hole in the ground which is used as a toilet.

latter /lætə/. 1 SING N OR PLURAL N When two people or things have just been mentioned, you refer to the second one as the **latter.** *They were eating sandwiches and little iced cakes, (the latter obtained from Mrs Kaul's bakery).* Also ADJ *The novel was made into a film in 1943 and again in 1967: I prefer the latter version to the former.* 2 ADJ You use **latter** to describe the second part of a period of time. *By the latter half of July the total was well over two million.*

latter-day. ATTRIB ADJ **Latter-day** is used to describe a person or thing that is a modern equivalent of someone or something in the past. *...the latter-day martyr, Edith Cavell.*

latterly /lætəli[1]/. ADV **Latterly** means recently; a formal use. *I have found that latterly this rapport is getting less and less.*

lattice /lætɪs/, **lattices.** COUNT N A **lattice** is a pattern or structure made of strips which cross over each other diagonally leaving holes in between. *...a lattice of bamboo.*

laugh /lɑːf/, **laughs, laughing, laughed.** 1 VB When you **laugh,** you make the sound which shows that you are happy or amused. *He grinned, then started to laugh... The young men laughed at his jokes.* Also COUNT N *'Hurry up,' said Tony with a laugh.* 2 PHRASE If someone **has the last laugh,** they succeed after appearing to have been defeated. *Henry had outlived all the others to have the last laugh.*

laugh at. PHR VB If you **laugh at** someone or something, you mock them or make jokes about them. *I don't think it's nice to laugh at people's disabilities.*

laugh off. PHR VB If you **laugh off** a serious situation, you try to suggest that it is amusing and unimportant. *Northcliffe attempted to laugh the matter off.*

laughing stock. SING N If someone is a **laughing stock,** they have been made to seem ridiculous. *Arthur was the laughing stock of the neighbourhood.*

laughter /lɑːftə/. UNCOUNT N **Laughter** is the act of laughing, or the sound of people laughing. *Mr Evans heard laughter... We roared with laughter.*

launch /lɔːntʃ/, **launches, launching, launched.** 1 VB WITH OBJ When a ship **is launched,** it is put into water for the first time. 2 VB WITH OBJ To **launch** a rocket, missile, or satellite means to send it into the air or into space. *Soviet rockets launched more satellites into orbit.* Also COUNT N *They gave only a few minutes' warning of the missile launch.* 3 VB WITH OBJ To **launch** a large and important activity, for example a political movement or a military attack, means to start it. *The government has launched a massive literacy campaign.* 4 VB WITH OBJ If a company **launches** a new product, it starts to make it available to the public. *A magazine called 'The Week' was launched in January 1964.* Also COUNT N *We are already selling millions of copies just one year after the launch.* 5 COUNT N A **launch** is a large motorboat.

launch into. PHR VB If you **launch into** a speech, fight, or other activity, you start it enthusiastically.

launder /lɔːndə/, **launders, laundering, laundered.** VB WITH OBJ When you **launder** clothes, sheets, and towels, you wash and iron them; an old-fashioned use.

launderette /lɔːndə[0]ret/, **launderettes.** COUNT N A **launderette** is a shop where there are washing machines and dryers which you can pay to use.

laundry /lɔːndri[1]/, **laundries.** 1 UNCOUNT N OR SING N **Laundry** is clothes, sheets, and towels that are dirty and need to be washed, or which have just been washed. *The washing machine takes about two hours to do my laundry... ...laundry hung out to dry in the sun.* 2 COUNT N A **laundry** is a firm that washes and irons clothes, sheets, and towels for people. 3 COUNT N A **laundry** is also a room in a house or hotel where clothes, sheets, and towels are washed.

laurel /lɒrə[0]l/, **laurels.** 1 COUNT N A **laurel** is a small evergreen tree with shiny leaves. 2 PHRASE If you say that someone **is resting on** their **laurels,** you mean that they feel satisfied with what they have already achieved and are not making any more effort. *We have no cause to rest on our laurels.*

lava /lɑːvə/. UNCOUNT N **Lava** is the hot liquid rock that comes out of a volcano and becomes solid as it cools.

lavatory /lævətə[0]ri[1]/, **lavatories.** COUNT N A **lavatory** is a toilet.

lavender /lævɪ[1]ndə/. UNCOUNT N **Lavender** is a garden plant with sweet-smelling, bluish-purple flowers.

lavish /lævɪʃ/, **lavishes, lavishing, lavished.** 1 ADJ If you are **lavish** with your money or time, you are very generous in the way that you spend it for other people's benefit. *...the lavish hospitality of Indian princes.* ♦ **lavishly** ADV *Rich merchants lavishly entertained travelling tradesmen.* 2 VB WITH OBJ AND 'on' OR 'upon' If you **lavish** money, affection, or time on someone or something, you spend a lot of money on them or give them a lot of affection or attention. *He lavished presents on her.* 3 ADJ Something that is **lavish** is very large, or has an appearance of great wealth and extravagance. *The portions would be lavish.* ♦ **lavishly** ADV *The building has been lavishly restored to a fresh brilliance.*

law /lɔː/, **laws.** 1 SING N OR UNCOUNT N The **law** is a system of rules that a society or government develops in order to deal with business agreements, social relationships, and crime. *It's against the law to demonstrate here... She was caught breaking the law... Every company must by law submit accounts annually.* 2 UNCOUNT N WITH SUPP **Law** is used to refer to a particular branch of the law, for example company **law.** *The soldiers faced charges under military law.* 3 COUNT N A **law** is one of the rules in a system of law which deals with a particular type of agreement, relationship, or crime. *Many of the laws passed by Parliament are never enforced... ...immigration laws.* 4 COUNT N A **law** is also a rule or set of rules for good behaviour which seems right and important for moral, religious, or emotional reasons. *Children soon accept social laws.* 5 UNCOUNT N OR SING N **Law** or **the law** is all the professions which deal with advising people about the law, representing people in court, or giving decisions and punishments. *I was planning a career in law... There are curious parallels between medicine and the law... ...a New York law firm.* 6 PHRASE When someone **lays down the law,** they give other people orders because they think that they are right and the other people are wrong; used showing disapproval. 7 COUNT N WITH SUPP You also use **law** to refer to a natural process in which a particular event or thing always leads to a particular result. *...the laws of nature... The laws that govern the behaviour of light are universal.* 8 COUNT N WITH SUPP A scientific rule that explains natural processes is also called a **law.** *...the second law of heat distribution.*

law-abiding. ADJ A **law-abiding** person always obeys the law. *...respectable, law-abiding citizens.*

law and order. UNCOUNT N When there is **law and order** in a country, the laws are generally accepted and obeyed there. *There were periods of unrest and a breakdown of law and order.*

law court, law courts. COUNT N A **law court** is a place where legal matters are decided by a judge and jury or by a magistrate.

lawful /lɔːfʊl/. ADJ **Lawful** activities, organizations, and products are allowed by law; a formal use. *Use all lawful means to persuade employers.*

lawless /lɔːlɪ[2]s/. ADJ **Lawless** actions break the law; a formal use. *...the lawless activities of these gangs.* ♦ **lawlessness** UNCOUNT N *...our disapproval of lawlessness and violence.*

lawn /lɔːn/, **lawns.** COUNT N OR UNCOUNT N A **lawn** is an area of grass that is kept cut short. *I'm going to mow the lawn.*

lawnmower /lɔːnməʊə/, **lawnmowers.** COUNT N A **lawnmower** is a machine for cutting grass on lawns.

lawsuit /lɔːsuːt/, **lawsuits.** COUNT N A **lawsuit** is a case in a court of law which concerns a dispute between two people, rather than the prosecution of a criminal by the police; a formal use. *He had sought to bring a lawsuit against the airline.*

lawyer /lɔːjə, lɔɪə/, **lawyers.** COUNT N A **lawyer** is a person who is qualified to advise people about the law and represent them in court.

lax /læks/. ADJ If someone's behaviour or a system is **lax**, the rules are not being obeyed or standards are not being maintained. *Procedures are lax, discipline is weak.*

laxative /læksətɪv/, **laxatives.** COUNT N A **laxative** is a medicine that stops you being constipated.

lay /leɪ/, **lays, laying, laid** /leɪd/. **1 Lay** is the past tense of some meanings of **lie. 2** VB WITH OBJ AND ADJUNCT If you **lay** something somewhere, you place it there so that it rests there. *She laid the baby gently down on its bed... She laid a hand on his shoulder.* **3** VB WITH OBJ When you **lay** the table, you arrange the knives, forks, plates, and other things on a table before a meal. *I'm not laying a place at table for him.* **4** VB WITH OBJ If you **lay** something such as a carpet or a cable, you put it on the floor or in the ground in its proper position. *They're laying water pipes and electricity cables.* **5** VB WITH OR WITHOUT OBJ When a female bird or animal **lays** an egg, the egg comes out of its body. *She lays at night.* **6** VB WITH OBJ If you **lay** a trap, you hide a trap and set it in order to catch an animal. **7** VB WITH OBJ To **lay** a trap also means to deceive someone in order to catch them or get them to do what you want. *He walked right into the trap I had laid for him.* **8** VB WITH OBJ If you **lay** the basis for something, you make preparations for it in order to make sure that it will happen in the way you want it to. *Her new policy helped to lay the foundations of electoral success.* **9** VB WITH OBJ AND 'on' OR 'upon' If you **lay** something on someone, you cause them to be affected by it. *Women lay most of the blame on men... A curse has been laid on those who violated the tomb of the King.* **10** ATTRIB ADJ You use **lay** to describe people who are involved with a Christian church but are not members of the clergy, monks, or nuns. *...a lay preacher.* **11** ATTRIB ADJ You also use **lay** to describe someone who is not trained or qualified in a particular subject or activity. *The computer has become much more accessible to the lay person.*

PHRASES • If you **lay** someone **open to** criticism or attack, you do something which is likely to make people criticize or attack them. *That kind of behaviour can lay you open to the charge of wasting the company's time.* • If you **lay emphasis on** something, you emphasize it. • **to lay claim to:** see **claim.**

lay down. PHR VB **1** If rules or people in authority **lay down** what people must do, they tell people what they must do. *...the conditions laid down by the Department of Health.* • **to lay down the law:** see **law. 2** If someone **lays down** their **life** in a war or struggle, they are killed while fighting for something; a literary use.

lay into. PHR VB If you **lay into** someone, you start attacking them physically or criticizing them severely.

lay off. PHR VB **1** If workers **are laid off** by their employers, they are told to leave their jobs, usually because there is no more work for them to do. **2** If you tell someone to **lay off,** you are telling them to leave you alone; an informal use.

lay on. PHR VB If you **lay on** food, entertainment, or a service, you provide it. *We laid on a great show for them.*

lay out. PHR VB **1** If you **lay out** a group of things, you spread them out and arrange them. *Clothes, jewels, and ornaments were laid out on the ground.* **2** You can describe the design of a garden, building, or town by saying how it **is laid out.** *Their settlement is laid out traditionally as a small village.* **3** See also **layout.**

lay-by, lay-bys. COUNT N A **lay-by** is a short strip of road by the side of a main road, where cars can stop for a while. *Pull into the next lay-by.*

layer /leɪə/, **layers.** COUNT N A **layer** is a flat piece of something or a quantity of something that covers a surface or that is between two other things. *He wrapped each component in several layers of foam rubber... A fine layer of dust covered everything.*

layman /leɪmə[3]n/, **laymen.** COUNT N A **layman** is a person who is not qualified or experienced in a particular subject or activity. *...a task for industrial experts rather than for laymen.*

layout /leɪj[0]aʊt/, **layouts.** COUNT N WITH SUPP The **layout** of a garden, building, or piece of writing is the way in which the parts of it are arranged. *He knew the airport layout intimately.*

laze /leɪz/, **lazes, lazing, lazed.** VB If you **laze** somewhere or **laze** about, you relax and do nothing. *...lazing by the hotel pool.*

lazy /leɪzi[1]/, **lazier, laziest. 1** ADJ **Lazy** people try to avoid doing any work. *His maths teacher thought he was bright but lazy.* ♦ **laziness** UNCOUNT N *Only laziness prevented him from doing it.* **2** ATTRIB ADJ **Lazy** actions are done slowly without making very much effort. *She gave a lazy smile.* ♦ **lazily** ADV *Philip was lazily combing his hair.*

lb, lbs. lb can also be the plural. You use **lb** as a written abbreviation for 'pound' when you are mentioning the weight of something. *...a 2 lb bag of sugar... ...a fish weighing about 10 lbs.*

lead, leads, leading, led /led/. **Lead** is pronounced /liːd/ except in meanings 17 and 18, where it is pronounced /led/. **1** VB WITH OR WITHOUT OBJ If you **lead** someone somewhere, you go in front of them to show them the way. *He led a demonstration through the City... My mother takes me by the hand and leads me downstairs... Jenny was leading and I was at the back.* **2** VB WITH ADJUNCT If something such as a road, pipe, or wire **leads** somewhere, it goes there. *...the main street leading to the centre of the city.* **3** VB If a door or gate **leads** to a place, you can get to the place by going through it. *There was a gate on our left leading into a field.* **4** VB If you **are leading** in a race or competition, you are winning. **5** SING N If you are in the **lead** in a race or competition you are winning. *This win gave him the overall lead.* **6** VB WITH OR WITHOUT OBJ If you **lead** a group or organization, you are officially in charge of it. *The Labour Party was led by Wilson... He lacked any desire to lead.* **7** VB WITH OBJ If you **lead** an activity, you start it or guide it. *The rioting was led by students.* **8** COUNT N If you give a **lead,** you do something which is considered a good example to follow. *The European Community should give a lead... Other firms are now following the company's lead.* **9** VB WITH OBJ If you **lead** an exciting or dull life, your life is exciting or dull. *My friends seemed to be leading a much more exciting life.* **10** VB WITH PREP 'to' If one thing **leads** to another, it causes the second thing to happen. *...a drinking spree which had led to his court appearance.* **11** VB WITH OBJ AND TO-INF OR ADJUNCT If something **leads** you to do something, it influences or affects you so that you do that thing. *Recent evidence is leading historians to reassess that event... This led him to an obsession with art.* **12** COUNT N A dog's **lead** is a long, thin chain or piece of leather which you attach to the dog's collar so that you can keep it under control. **13** COUNT N A **lead** in a piece of electrical equipment is a piece of wire which supplies electricity to the equipment. **14** SING N The **lead** in a play or film is the most important role in it. *Richard was signed up to play the lead.* **15** ATTRIB ADJ The **lead** singer in a pop group is the one who sings the main tunes. **16** COUNT N A **lead** is also a piece of information which may help the police to solve a crime. **17** UNCOUNT N **Lead** is a soft, grey, heavy metal. **18** COUNT N The **lead** in a pencil is the centre part of it which makes a mark on paper. **19** See also **leading.**

PHRASES • If you **lead the way,** you go in front of someone in order to show them where to go. *I led the way to Andrew's cabin.* • If you **take the lead,** you start doing something before other people do. *France took the lead in the development of the airbus.*

lead up to. PHR VB **1** Events that **lead up to** a situation happen one after the other until that situation is reached. *...the chain of events that led up to her death.* **2** If you **lead up to** a particular subject in a conversation, you gradually guide the conversation to a point where you can introduce that subject. *Ever since you came in you've been leading up to this one question.*

leaden /ledə[0]n/; a literary word. **1** ADJ A **leaden** sky or sea is dark grey and has no movement of clouds or waves. **2** ADJ If your movements are **leaden,** you are moving slowly and heavily, because you are tired. *He took two leaden steps forward.* **3** ADJ A **leaden** conversation is very dull.

leader /liːdə/, **leaders. 1** COUNT N The **leader** of an organization or a group of people is the person who is in charge of it. *...the leader of the Labour Party.* **2** COUNT N The **leader** in a race or competition is the person who is winning at a particular time.

leadership /liːdəʃɪp/. **1** SING N You can refer to the people who are in charge of a group or organization as the **leadership.** *...the gap between the leadership and the men they represent.* **2** SING N The **leadership** is also the position or state of being in control of a group or organization. *...the election of Wilson to the leadership of the Labour Party... ...an independent group under the leadership of Jones.* **3** UNCOUNT N **Leadership** refers to the qualities that make someone a good leader. *...a task calling for energy and firm leadership.*

leading /liːdɪŋ/. **1** ATTRIB ADJ The **leading** people or things in a group are the most important ones. *A demand for change came from leading politicians.* **2** ATTRIB ADJ The **leading** role in a play or film is the main one. *...their leading lady, Yvonne Printemps.*

leaf /liːf/, **leaves** /liːvz/; **leafs, leafing, leafed. Leaves** is the plural of the noun. **Leafs** is the third person singular, present tense, of the phrasal verb. **1** COUNT N The **leaves** of a tree or plant are the parts that are flat, thin, and usually green. **2** PHRASE When trees are **in leaf,** they have leaves on their branches.

leaf through. PHR VB If you **leaf through** a book or newspaper, you turn the pages quickly without looking at them carefully.

leaflet /liːflɪ[2]t/, **leaflets, leafleting, leafleted. 1** COUNT N A **leaflet** is a little book or a piece of paper containing information about a particular subject. *The company produces a little leaflet called 'Protect your Pipes from Frost'.* **2** VB WITH OBJ If you **leaflet** a place, you distribute leaflets there. *All the local houses and shops had been leafleted.*

leafy /liːfi[1]/. **1** ADJ **Leafy** trees and plants have a lot of leaves. *...leafy green vegetables.* **2** ADJ You say that a place is **leafy** when there are a lot of trees and plants there. *...a leafy suburb.*

league /liːg/, **leagues. 1** COLL N A **league** is a group of people, clubs, or countries that have joined together for a particular purpose or because they share a common interest. *...the National Book League... ...the football league.* **2** PHRASE If you are **in league with** someone, you are working with them for a particular purpose, often secretly. *They are in league with the police.*

leak /liːk/, **leaks, leaking, leaked. 1** VB If a container or other object **leaks,** there is a hole or crack in it which lets liquid or gas escape. *The roof leaks... ...leaking drain pipes.* Also COUNT N *I fixed a small leak in the roof of her shed.* **2** VB When liquid or gas **leaks** through an object or **leaks** out of it, it escapes through a hole or crack in it. *The water was still slowly leaking out.* Also COUNT N *There's been a gas leak.* **3** VB WITH OBJ If someone **leaks** a piece of secret information, they let other people know about it. *He made sure the story was leaked to the media.* Also COUNT N *...the possibility of a security leak.*

leak out. PHR VB If information that you want to keep secret **leaks out,** it becomes known to other people.

leakage /liːkɪdʒ/, **leakages.** COUNT N If there is a **leakage** of liquid or gas, it escapes from a pipe or container through a hole or crack. *A leakage in the hydraulic system was diagnosed.*

leaky /liːki[1]/. ADJ Something that is **leaky** has holes or cracks in it which liquids or gases can escape through. *...a leaky roof.*

lean /liːn/, **leans, leaning, leaned** or **leant** /lent/. **1** VB WITH ADJUNCT When you **lean** in a particular direction, you bend your body in that direction. *He was sitting on the edge of his chair and leaning eagerly forwards... I leaned out of the window.* **2** VB WITH OR WITHOUT OBJ, WITH ADJUNCT If you **lean** on something, you rest against it so that it partly supports your weight. If you **lean** an object on something, you place the object so that its weight is partly supported by the thing it is resting against. *He leaned against a tree... He leaned the bike against a railing.* **3** VB WITH 'towards' If you **lean** towards a particular idea or action, you approve of it and behave in accordance with it. *...parents who naturally lean towards strictness.* **4** ADJ A **lean** person is thin but looks strong and fit. *...a lean, handsome man.* **5** ADJ **Lean** meat does not have very much fat. **6** ADJ A **lean** period of time is one in which people do not have very much food, money, or success. *In the lean years, crop failures are common.*

lean on or **lean upon.** PHR VB **1** If you **lean on** or **lean upon** someone, you try to influence them by threatening them. *They can lean on the administration by threatening to withhold their subscriptions.* **2** To **lean on** or **lean upon** someone also means to depend on them for support and encouragement.

leaning /liːnɪŋ/, **leanings.** COUNT N WITH SUPP If you have a **leaning** towards a particular belief or type of behaviour, you tend to have that belief or to behave in that way. *...their different political leanings.*

leap /liːp/, **leaps, leaping, leaped** /liːpt, lept/ or **leapt** /lept/. **1** VB WITH OR WITHOUT OBJ If you **leap** somewhere, you jump high in the air or jump a long distance. *Some monkeys can leap five metres from one tree to another... They leaped into the water.* Also COUNT N *She took a flying leap at the fence.* **2** VB WITH ADJUNCT To **leap** somewhere also means to move there suddenly and quickly. *She leapt into a taxi.* **3** VB WITH ADJUNCT You can say that things **leap** when they suddenly advance or increase by a large amount. *The number of computers in the world is leaping upwards daily.* Also COUNT N *...a leap in oil prices.*

leap at. PHR VB If you **leap at** a chance or opportunity, you accept it quickly and eagerly. *David would have leaped at the chance to go.*

leap year, leap years. COUNT N A **leap year** is a year in which there are 366 days instead of 365. There is a leap year every four years.

learn /lɜːn/, **learns, learning, learned** or **learnt** /lɜːnt/. **1** VB WITH OR WITHOUT OBJ If you **learn** something, you obtain knowledge or a skill through studying or training. *Children learn foreign languages very easily... The best way to learn is by practical experience... He had never learnt to read and write.* ♦ **learner** COUNT N *She is a very slow learner.* **2** VB WITH OBJ If you **learn** a poem, song, or the script of a play, you study or repeat the words so that you can remember them. *We have to learn the whole poem.* **3** VB WITH TO-INF If people **learn** to behave in a particular way, their attitudes gradually change and they start behaving that way. *If only these people could learn to live together.* **4** VB WITH 'of' OR REPORT VB If you **learn** of something, you find out about it. *They offered help as soon as they learnt of the accident... She was extremely upset to learn that he had died... ...the night when he learned the truth about Sam.*

learned /lɜːnɪ^{2}d/. **1** ADJ **Learned** people have gained a lot of knowledge by studying. *...the learned professions.* **2** ATTRIB ADJ **Learned** books or papers have been written by someone with a lot of academic knowledge. *...new ideas announced in learned journals.*

learning /lɜːnɪŋ/. UNCOUNT N **Learning** is knowledge that has been gained through studying. *...a man of learning.*

lease /liːs/, **leases, leasing, leased. 1** COUNT N A **lease** is a legal agreement under which someone pays money to use a building or piece of land for a period of time. *The house was let on a 99-year lease.* **2** VB WITH OBJ If you **lease** property from someone or if they **lease** it to you, they allow you to use it in return for money. *They leased a house at Cospoli... He had persuaded the local council to lease him a house.* **3** PHRASE If someone who seemed to be weak or failing has **a new lease of life,** they are now more lively or successful. *After her marriage it was as though she'd got a new lease of life.*

least /liːst/. **1** ADJ You use **least** to say that an amount of something is as small as it can be. *...the thinner animals, who had the least muscle over their bones.* **2** ADV You also use **least** to say that something is true to as small a degree or extent as is possible. *He came out when I least expected it... They're the ones who need it the least.* **3** SUBMOD You also use **least** to say that something has less of a particular quality than most other things of its kind. *...one of the smallest and least powerful of the African states.* **4** QUANTIF You can also use **least** to emphasize that a particular situation or thing is much less important or serious than other ones. *That was the least of her worries.*

PHRASES ● You use **at least** to say that the number or amount mentioned is the smallest that is likely, and that the actual number or amount may be greater. *He drank at least half a bottle of whisky a day... I must have slept twelve hours at least.* ● You also use **at least** to say that something is the minimum which should be done, although in fact you think that more than this ought to be done. *Go to see the administrator or at least write a letter.* ● You also use **at least** to indicate an advantage that exists in spite of the disadvantage or bad situation that has just been mentioned. *The process looks rather laborious but at least it is not dangerous.* ● You can use **at least** when you want to correct something that you have just said. *A couple of days ago I spotted my ex-wife; at least I thought I did, I wasn't sure.* ● You can use **in the least** and **the least bit** to emphasize a negative. *I don't mind in the least, I really don't... She wasn't the least bit jealous.* ● You can use **to say the least** to suggest that a situation is actually much more extreme or serious than you say it is. *...a development which will have, to say the least, intriguing effects.* ● You can use **not least** when giving an important example or reason. *...all western countries, not least the USA.* ● You can use **least of all** after a negative statement to emphasize that it applies especially to a particular person or thing. *Nobody seemed amused, least of all Jenny.*

leather /lɛðə/. UNCOUNT N OR MOD **Leather** is treated animal skin which is used for making shoes, clothes, bags, and furniture. *...leather jackets.*

leathery /lɛðəri^1/. ADJ If something has a **leathery** texture, it is tough, like leather. *The wrinkled, leathery face broke into a smile.*

leave /liːv/, **leaves, leaving, left** /lɛft/. **1** VB WITH OR WITHOUT OBJ When you **leave** a place, you go away from it. *They left the house to go for a walk after tea... My train leaves at 11.30.* **2** VB WITH OBJ If you **leave** a person or thing somewhere, they stay there when you go away. *Leaving Rita in a bar, I made for the town library... Leave your phone number with the secretary... I had left my raincoat in the restaurant.* **3** VB WITH OR WITHOUT OBJ If you **leave** a place or institution, you go away permanently from it. *She wanted to leave China altogether... What do you want to do when you leave school?... She told him she was going to leave her job... All they want to do is leave at 16 and get a job.* **4** VB WITH OBJ If someone **leaves** their husband or wife, they finish the relationship and stop living with him or her. *My husband had left me for another woman.* **5** VB WITH OBJ If you **leave** an amount of something, you do not use it, and so it remains available to be used later. *Leave some of the stew for the boys... I meant to leave myself with fifteen pounds a week.* ● See also **left. 6** VB WITH OBJ If something **leaves** a mark, effect, or impression, it causes that mark, effect, or impression to remain as a result. *I didn't want him to leave a trail of wet footprints... Does it leave a stain?* **7** VB WITH OBJ To **leave** someone or something in a particular state or position means to cause them to remain or be in that state or position. *Who left the gates open?... The result has left everybody dissatisfied... You are left with two alternatives... Leave a space between the fridge and the wall.* **8** VB WITH OBJ If you **leave** something to someone, you give them the responsibility for dealing with it. *He said the whole business should be left to the courts... Leave it with me, I'll fix it.* **9** VB WITH OBJ If you **leave** something until a particular time, you delay dealing with it. *Why do you always leave things to the last minute?* **10** VB WITH OBJ If you **leave** a particular subject, you stop talking about it and start discussing something else. *Let's leave the budget and go on to another question.* **11** VB WITH OBJ If you **leave** property or money to someone, you arrange for it to be given to them after you have died. *She did not leave a very large legacy.* **12** UNCOUNT N **Leave** is a period of time when you are on holiday from your job or absent for another reason. *He'd come over on leave from Northern Ireland... ...sick leave.* **13 Leaves** is also the plural form of **leaf.**

leave behind. PHR VB **1** If you **leave** someone or something **behind,** you go away permanently from them. *I hated having to leave behind all my friends.* **2** If you **leave** an object or a situation **behind,** it remains after you have left a place. *Millie had left her watch behind... ...leaving behind an unsolved mystery.*

leave off. PHR VB **1** If you **leave** someone or something **off** a list, you do not include them in that list. *Hopper was too important to be left off the guest list.* **2** PHRASE If you continue doing something **from where** you **left off,** you start doing it again at the point where you had previously stopped doing it. *He sat down at the piano again and started playing from where he left off.*

leave out. PHR VB If you **leave** a person or thing **out,** you do not include them in something. *One or two scenes in the play were left out.*

lecherous /lɛtʃərəs/. ADJ A **lecherous** man behaves towards women in a way which shows he is interested in them sexually; used showing disapproval.

lectern /lɛktə^{5}n/, **lecterns.** COUNT N A **lectern** is a high sloping desk on which someone puts their notes or a book when they are standing up and talking or reading to an audience.

lecture /lɛktʃə/, **lectures, lecturing, lectured. 1** COUNT N A **lecture** is a talk that someone gives in order to teach people about a particular subject. *...a series of lectures on literature.* **2** VB If you **lecture,** you give a lecture or series of lectures. *He lectured on Economic History at the University.* **3** VB WITH OBJ AND ADJUNCT If someone **lectures** you about something, they criticize you or tell you how you should behave. *I had always been lectured about not talking with my mouth full.* **4** COUNT N A **lecture** is also strong criticism that someone makes about something that they do not like. *He'll give her a lecture on her responsibilities.*

lecturer /lɛktʃərə/, **lecturers.** COUNT N A **lecturer** is a teacher at a university or college. *...a lecturer in sociology.*

lectureship /lɛktʃəʃɪp/, **lectureships.** COUNT N A **lectureship** is a position of lecturer at a university or college. *...a lectureship at Birmingham University.*

led /lɛd/. **Led** is the past tense and past participle of **lead.**

ledge /lɛdʒ/, **ledges. 1** COUNT N A **ledge** is a narrow, flat place in the side of a cliff or mountain. *Only a bird could get to that ledge.* **2** COUNT N A **ledge** is also a narrow shelf along the bottom edge of a window. *...students sitting on the window ledges.*

ledger /lɛdʒə/, **ledgers.** COUNT N A **ledger** is a book in which a company or organization writes down the amounts of money it spends and receives.

leek /liːk/, **leeks.** COUNT N A **leek** is a long thin vegetable which is white at one end and has long green leaves.

leer /lɪə/, **leers, leering, leered.** VB If someone **leers** at you, they smile in an unpleasant way, usually because they are sexually interested in you. *He leaned over and leered at them.* Also COUNT N *He was staring down with a leer on his face.*

left /lɛft/. **1 Left** is the past tense and past participle of **leave. 2** PRED ADJ OR ADV AFTER N If there is an amount of something **left** or **left over,** it remains after the rest has gone or been used. *I only had two pounds left... He drained what was left of his drink... We had a bit of time left over.* **3** UNCOUNT N OR SING N **Left** is one of two opposite directions, sides, or positions. In the word 'to', the 't' is to the left of the 'o'. *There was a gate on our left leading into a field... ...the third door to the left.* Also ADV OR ATTRIB ADJ *He turned left and began strolling down the street... In his left hand he clutched a book.* **4** SING N The **Left** is used to refer to the people or groups who support socialism rather than capitalism. *...the extreme left.*

left-hand. ATTRIB ADJ **Left-hand** refers to something which is on the left side. *She noted it down on the left-hand side of the page.*

left-handed. ADJ OR ADV **Left-handed** people use their left hand rather than their right hand for activities such as writing or throwing a ball. *...left-handed batsmen... They both play golf left-handed.*

leftist /lɛftɪst/, **leftists.** COUNT N Socialists and communists are sometimes referred to as **leftists.** Also ATTRIB ADJ *...extreme leftist activities.*

left-luggage office, left-luggage offices. COUNT N In a railway station or airport, you can pay to leave your luggage in a **left-luggage office;** a British use.

leftover /lɛftəuvə/, **leftovers. 1** PLURAL N The **leftovers** from a meal are the food that has not been eaten. *The dogs eat the leftovers.* **2** ATTRIB ADJ You use **leftover** to describe an amount of something that remains after the rest has been used. *...a bottle of leftover perfume.*

left-wing. 1 ADJ **Left-wing** people have political ideas that are close to socialism or communism. *...left-wing journalists.* **2** SING N The **left wing** of a political party consists of the members of it whose beliefs are closer to socialism or communism than those of its other members. *...the left wing of the Labour Party.*

left-winger, left-wingers. COUNT N A **left-winger** is a person whose political beliefs are close to socialism or communism, or closer to them than most of the other people in the same group or party.

leg /lɛg/, **legs. 1** COUNT N Your **legs** are the two long parts of your body between your hips and feet. **2** COUNT N The **legs** of an animal, bird, or insect are the thin parts of its body that it uses to stand on or to move across the ground. *...creatures with short legs and long tails.* **3** COUNT N WITH SUPP A **leg** of lamb or pork is a piece of meat from the thigh of a sheep, lamb, or pig. **4** COUNT N WITH SUPP The **legs** of a table or chair are the thin vertical parts that touch the floor. **5** COUNT N A **leg** of a long journey is one part of it. *They set off on the first leg of their 12,000 mile journey.*

PHRASES ● If someone **pulls** your **leg,** they tell you something untrue as a joke. *'You're pulling my leg.'—'No, it's true.'* ● If you say that someone **does not have a leg to stand on,** you mean that what they have done or said cannot be justified or proved. ● Something that is **on its last legs** is in a very bad condition and will soon stop working or break; an informal use.

legacy /lɛgəsi^1/, **legacies. 1** COUNT N A **legacy** is money or property which someone leaves to you when they die. *...a legacy of five thousand pounds.* **2** COUNT N WITH SUPP The **legacy** of an event or period of history is something which is a direct result of it and which continues to exist after it is over. *...a legacy of pre-war unemployment.*

legal /liːgə^{0}l/. **1** ATTRIB ADJ **Legal** is used to refer to things that relate to the law. *...the British legal system... ...a legal dispute.* ♦ **legally** ADV *Divorce could be made less legally complicated.* **2** ADJ An action or situation that is **legal** is allowed by law. *Capital punishment is legal in many countries.* ♦ **legally** ADV *...to make the contracts legally binding.*

legality /li^{1}gælɪ^{1}ti^1/. UNCOUNT N WITH SUPP The **legality** of an action or situation concerns whether or not it is allowed by law. *He disputed the legality of the invasion.*

legalize /liːgəlaɪz/, **legalizes, legalizing, legalized;** also spelled **legalise.** VB WITH OBJ If something **is legalized,** a law is passed that makes it legal.

legend /lɛdʒənd/, **legends. 1** COUNT N OR UNCOUNT N A **legend** is a very old story that may be based on real events. *...folk tales, legends, and myths... The original inhabitants, according to legend, were blacksmiths.* **2** COUNT N If you refer to someone as a **legend,** you mean that they are very famous and admired. *Brook has become something of a legend.*

legendary /lɛ̲dʒəndə^{0}ri^1/. 1 ADJ A **legendary** person or thing is very famous. *...one of his many legendary acts of courage.* 2 ADJ **Legendary** also means described in an old legend. *...the legendary king.*

legible /lɛ̲dʒə^{1}bə^{0}l/. ADJ **Legible** writing is clear enough to be read. *...a crumpled but still legible document.*

legion /li̲:dʒə^{0}n/, **legions.** 1 TITLE **Legion** is sometimes used in the names of large sections of an army. *...the Condor Legion.* 2 COUNT N A **legion** of people is a large number of them. *...legions of foreign visitors.* 3 PRED ADJ You can say that things are **legion** when there are many of them; a formal use. *Stories about him are legion.*

legislate /lɛ̲dʒɪsleɪt/, **legislates, legislating, legislated.** VB When a government **legislates,** it passes a new law; a formal use. *Parliament must eventually legislate against fox-hunting.*

legislation /lɛ̲dʒɪsleɪ̲ʃə^{0}n/. UNCOUNT N WITH SUPP **Legislation** consists of a law or laws passed by a government. *...tax legislation... ...the introduction of legislation to govern industrial relations.*

legislative /lɛ̲dʒɪslətɪv/. ATTRIB ADJ **Legislative** means involving or relating to the process of making and passing laws; a formal use. *The Government should consider further legislative reforms.*

legislator /lɛ̲dʒɪsleɪtə/, **legislators.** COUNT N A **legislator** is someone involved in making or passing laws; a formal use. *Many of the legislators who drafted the bill are landowners.*

legislature /lɛ̲dʒɪslətʃə/, **legislatures.** COUNT N The **legislature** of a state or country is the group of people with the power to make and pass laws; a formal use.

legitimacy /lɪ^{2}dʒɪtɪmɪ^{1}si^1/. UNCOUNT N The **legitimacy** of something is the fact that it is reasonable, acceptable, or legal. *...the legitimacy of our complaint.*

legitimate /lɪ^{2}dʒɪtɪmə^{1}t/. ADJ Something that is **legitimate** is reasonable or acceptable according to the law or to normal standards. *...a legitimate business transaction... Religious leaders have a legitimate reason to be concerned.*

leisure /lɛ̲ʒə/. 1 UNCOUNT N **Leisure** is time when you do not have to work and can do things that you enjoy. *Not everybody wants more leisure.* 2 PHRASE If you do something **at leisure** or **at** your **leisure,** you do it when you want to, without hurrying.

leisurely /lɛ̲ʒəli^1/. ADJ A **leisurely** action is done in a relaxed and unhurried way. *My wife went off for a leisurely walk round the gardens.* Also ADV *He strolled leisurely away from the bar.*

lemon /lɛ̲mə^{0}n/, **lemons.** COUNT N OR UNCOUNT N A **lemon** is a yellow citrus fruit with sour juice. *...slices of lemon.*

lemonade /lɛ̲məneɪ̲d/. UNCOUNT N **Lemonade** is a clear, sweet, fizzy drink.

lend /lɛ̲nd/, **lends, lending, lent** /lɛ̲nt/. 1 VB WITH OBJ AND OBJ, OR VB WITH OBJ AND PREP 'to' If you **lend** someone money or something that you own, you allow them to have or use it for a period of time. *I had to lend him a pound... She was reading a book I had lent her... ...lending money to Poland.* 2 VB WITH OBJ If you **lend** your support to a person or group, you support them. *He was there lending advice and support.* 3 VB WITH OBJ AND PREP 'to', OR VB WITH OBJ AND OBJ If something **lends** a particular quality to something else, it gives it that quality. *It would lend credibility to her arguments... ...lending the place a festive look.* 4 REFL VB WITH PREP 'to' If something **lends** itself to being dealt with or considered in a particular way, it is easy to deal with it or consider it in that way. *...problems which do not lend themselves to simple solutions.*

length /lɛ̲ŋk^{0}θ/, **lengths.** 1 COUNT N OR UNCOUNT N The **length** of something is the amount that it measures from one end to the other. *It grows to a length of three or four metres... The snake was a metre and a half in length.* 2 SING N If something happens or exists along the **length** of something, it happens or exists for the whole way along it. *They travelled the length of the island.* 3 COUNT N If you swim a **length** in a swimming pool, you swim from one end to the other. 4 COUNT N WITH SUPP A **length** of wood, string, cloth, or other material is a piece of it. *...a length of rope... ...a short length of steel chain.* 5 COUNT N OR UNCOUNT N The **length** of an event, activity, or situation is the time it lasts. *The length of the visit depends on you... It is foolish to expect to be happy for any length of time.* 6 UNCOUNT N The **length** of something is also its quality of being long. *I hope the length of this letter will make up for my not having written earlier.*

PHRASES • If someone does something **at length,** they do it after a long time or for a long time; used in written English. *There was another silence. At length Claire said, 'You mean you're not going?'... He spoke at some length about the press.* • If someone **goes to great lengths** to achieve something, they try very hard and perhaps do extreme things in order to achieve it.

lengthen /lɛ̲ŋk^{0}θən/, **lengthens, lengthening, lengthened.** ERG VB When something **lengthens** or **is lengthened,** it becomes longer. *The waiting lists are lengthening... The money has been spent on lengthening the runway.*

lengthy /lɛ̲ŋk^{0}θi^1/. ADJ Something that is **lengthy** lasts for a long time. *...lengthy explanations.*

lenient /li̲:nɪənt/. ADJ When someone in authority is **lenient,** they are not as strict or as severe as expected. *Fines were low and magistrates often too lenient.* ♦ **leniently** ADV *Offenders had been treated leniently by the judge.*

lens /lɛ̲nz/, **lenses.** COUNT N A **lens** is a thin, curved piece of glass or plastic which is part of something such as a camera, telescope, or pair of glasses. When you look through a lens, things appear larger, clearer, or smaller. • See also **contact lens.**

lent /lɛ̲nt/. 1 **Lent** is the past tense and past participle of **lend.** 2 UNCOUNT N In the Christian calendar, **Lent** is the period of forty days before Easter, during which some Christians give up doing something that they enjoy.

lentil /lɛ̲ntɪ^{1}l/, **lentils.** COUNT N **Lentils** are dried seeds taken from a particular plant which are cooked and eaten.

leopard /lɛ̲pəd/, **leopards.** COUNT N A **leopard** is a type of large, wild cat. Leopards have yellow fur and black spots, and live in Africa and Asia.

leper /lɛ̲pə/, **lepers.** COUNT N A **leper** is a person who has leprosy. *...a leper hospital.*

leprosy /lɛ̲prəsi^1/. UNCOUNT N **Leprosy** is a serious infectious disease that damages people's flesh.

lesbian /lɛ̲zbɪən/, **lesbians.** COUNT N A **lesbian** is a homosexual woman. Also ADJ *...lesbian activities.*

less /lɛ̲s/. 1 QUANTIF OR DET **Less** means not as much in amount or degree as before or as something else. *With practice it becomes less of an effort... We had less than three miles to go... Sixty per cent of them are aged 20 or less... A shower uses less water than a bath.* 2 SUBMOD **Less** also means not having as much of a quality as before or as something else. *From this time on, I felt less guilty... Fires occurred less frequently outside this area... ...the less developed countries.* 3 ADV If you do something **less** than before or **less** than someone else, you do it to a smaller extent or not as often. *You probably use them less than I do... The more I hear about him, the less I like him.* 4 PREP **Less** also means the same as minus. *He earns £200 a week, less tax.* 5 See also **lesser.**

PHRASES • You use **less and less** to say that something is becoming smaller all the time in degree or amount. *He found them less and less interesting... They had less and less to talk about.* • You use **less than** to say that something does not have a particular quality. For example, something that is **less than** perfect is not perfect. *It would have been less than fair.* • You can use **no less** as an emphatic way of expressing surprise or admiration at the importance of someone or something. *...the President of the United States, no less.* • You can use **no less than** before an amount to indicate that you think the amount is surprisingly large. *By 1880, there were no less than fifty-six coal mines... ...no less than 40 per cent of the material.* • **more or less:** see **more.**

-less. SUFFIX **-less** is added to nouns to form adjectives that indicate that someone or something does not have the thing that the noun refers to. *...landless peasants... ...meaningless sounds.*

lessen /lɛ̲sən/, **lessens, lessening, lessened.** ERG VB If something **lessens** or **is lessened,** it becomes smaller in amount or degree. *Their financial hardship has lessened... Separating the sick from the healthy lessens the risk of infection.* ♦ **lessening** UNCOUNT N WITH SUPP *...a lessening of his power.*

lesser /lɛ̲sə/. ADJ **Lesser** is used to indicate that something is smaller in degree, importance, or amount than another thing that is mentioned. *These customs are common in Czechoslovakia and to a lesser extent in Hungary and Romania... ...charges of attempted murder and lesser crimes.*

lesson /lɛ̲sən/, **lessons.** 1 COUNT N A **lesson** is a short period of time during which people are taught something. *...tennis lessons... ...a history lesson.* 2 COUNT N If an experience teaches you a **lesson,** it makes you realize the truth or realize what should be done. *This is a lesson that every generation has to learn.* 3 PHRASE If you **teach** someone **a lesson,** you punish them for something they have done, so that they do not do it again.

lest /lɛ̲st/. CONJ If you do something **lest** something unpleasant should happen, you do it to try to prevent the unpleasant thing from happening; a literary use. *I had to grab the iron rail at my side lest I slipped off.*

let /lɛ̲t/, **lets, letting.** **Let** is used in the present tense, and is the past tense and past participle. 1 VB WITH OBJ If you **let** something happen, you allow it to happen. *People here sit back and let everyone else do the work... She kept lifting handfuls of sand and letting it pour through her fingers.* 2 VB WITH OBJ If you **let** someone do something, you give them your permission to do it. *My parents wouldn't let me go out with boys.* 3 VB WITH OBJ AND ADJUNCT If you **let** someone in, out, or through, you make it possible for them to go there. *'I rang the bell,' Rudolph said, 'and your friend let me in.'... I asked him to stop the car and let me out.* 4 You use **let** when you are making a suggestion, recommendation, or request. *If she insists on going so early, let her take a taxi... Let me try and explain.* 5 You use **let's** or **let us** when you are making a suggestion. *Let's go... Let us give her one more chance.* 6 VB WITH OBJ If you **let** your house or land to someone, you allow them to use it in exchange for regular payments.

PHRASES • If you **let go** of someone or something, you stop holding them. *Let go of me.* • If you say that something is not the case, **let alone** something else, you mean that since the first thing is not the case, the second thing cannot be, because it is more difficult, complicated, or unusual. *I had never seen him, let alone spoken to him.*

let down. PHR VB 1 If you **let** someone **down,** you disappoint them, usually by not doing something that you said you would do. 2 If you **let down** something filled with air, such as a tyre, you allow air to escape from it.

let in. PHR VB If something **lets in** water or air, it has a hole or crack which allows the water or air to get into it. *My old boots had been letting in water.*

let in for. PHR VB If you wonder what you have **let** yourself **in for,** you think that you may be getting involved in something difficult or unpleasant; an informal use. *What have we let ourselves in for?*

let in on or **let into.** PHR VB If you **let** someone **in on** a secret or **let** someone **into** a secret, you tell it to them.

let off. PHR VB 1 If you **let** someone **off** a duty or task, you say that they do not have to do it. *We have been let off our homework.* 2 If you **let** someone **off,** you give them no punishment, or a less severe punishment than they expect. *He let me off with a reprimand.* 3 If you **let off** a gun or a bomb, you fire it or cause it to explode.

let on. PHR VB If you do not **let on** about something secret, you do not tell anyone about it.

let up. PHR VB If something **lets up,** it stops or becomes less. *Day followed day and still the heat did not let up.*

lethal /li̲:θə^{0}l/. ADJ Something that is **lethal** can kill people or animals. *The chemical is lethal to rats but safe for cattle... ...a lethal weapon.*

lethargic /lɪ^{2}θɑ̲:dʒɪk/. ADJ If you are **lethargic,** you have no energy or enthusiasm; a formal use.

lethargy /lɛ̲θədʒi^1/. UNCOUNT N **Lethargy** is a condition in which you have no energy or enthusiasm; a formal use. *He was determined to shake them out of their lethargy.*

let's /lɛ̲ts/. **Let's** is the usual spoken form of 'let us'.

letter /lɛ̲tə/, **letters.** 1 COUNT N When you write a **letter,** you write a message on paper and send it to someone. *Peter received a letter from his wife... They informed Victor by letter.* 2 COUNT N **Letters** are also written symbols which represent the sounds of a language.

letterbox /lɛ̲təbɒks/, **letterboxes.** 1 COUNT N A **letterbox** is a rectangular hole in a door through which letters are delivered. 2 COUNT N A **letterbox** is also a large metal container in the street into which you post letters.

lettering /lɛ̲tə^{0}rɪŋ/. UNCOUNT N WITH SUPP **Lettering** is writing, especially when you are describing the type of letters used. *Underneath it, in smaller lettering, was a name.*

lettuce /lɛ̲tɪs/, **lettuces.** COUNT N OR UNCOUNT N A **lettuce** is a plant with large green leaves that you eat in salads.

leukaemia /lu:ki̲:mɪə/; also spelled **leukemia.** UNCOUNT N **Leukaemia** is a serious illness which affects the blood.

level /lɛ̲və^{0}l/, **levels, levelling, levelled;** spelled **leveling** and **leveled** in American English. 1 COUNT N WITH SUPP A **level** is a point on a scale, for example a scale of amount, importance, or difficulty. *Mammals maintain their body temperature at a constant level... ...a high level of unemployment... ...an intermediate level English course.* 2 SING N The **level** of a lake or river, or the **level** of a liquid in a container, is the height of its surface. *The level of the lake continues to rise... Check the oil level and tyre pressure of your car regularly.* • See also **sea level.** 3 SING N WITH SUPP If one thing is at the **level** of another thing, it is at the same height. *He had a pile of books which reached to the level of his chin.* 4 PRED ADJ If one thing is **level** with another thing, it is at the same height. *He had his hands in front of him, level with his chest.* 5 PRED ADJ If something such as trade stays **level** with something else, it gets larger or smaller at the same rate. *Food production is going to keep level with population growth.* 6 ADV If you are going somewhere and you draw **level** with someone, you get closer to them until you are at their side. *Coming towards me was a man and when we drew level, I smiled.* 7 ADJ Something that is **level** is completely flat, with no part higher than any other. *The floor is quite level.* 8 VB WITH OBJ If you **level** an area of land, you make it flat. *...gardeners digging and levelling the ground.* 9 VB WITH OBJ If people **level** something such as a building or a wood, they knock it down completely so that there is nothing left. *Specially built tractors levelled more than 1,000 acres of forest.* 10 VB WITH OBJ If you **level** a criticism or accusation at or against someone, you criticize or accuse them. *...criticisms he has levelled against gangsters... Serious charges were levelled at television during the sixties.*

level off or **level out.** PHR VB 1 If something **levels off** or **levels out,** it stops increasing or decreasing. *Economic growth was starting to level off.* 2 When an aircraft **levels off** or **levels out,** it travels horizontally after it has been travelling upwards or downwards.

level crossing, level crossings. COUNT N A **level crossing** is a place where a railway line crosses a road at the same level; a British use.

level-headed. ADJ If you are **level-headed,** you act calmly in difficult situations.

lever /liːvə/, **levers.** 1 COUNT N A **lever** is a handle or bar that you pull or push to operate a piece of machinery. *...the gear lever.* 2 COUNT N A **lever** is also a bar, one end of which is placed under a heavy object so that when you press down on the other end you can move the object. 3 COUNT N A **lever** is also something that you can use as a means of getting someone to do something. *Industrial action may be threatened as a political lever.*

leverage /liːvə^{0}rɪdʒ/. 1 UNCOUNT N **Leverage** is the ability to influence people. *Relatively small groups can exert immense political leverage.* 2 UNCOUNT N **Leverage** is also the force that is applied to an object when a lever is used.

levy /levi^1/, **levies, levying, levied.** 1 COUNT N A **levy** is a sum of money that you pay in tax. 2 VB WITH OBJ When a government or organization **levies** a tax, it demands it from people.

liability /laɪəbɪlɪ^{1}ti^1/, **liabilities.** 1 COUNT N If someone or something is a **liability** they cause a lot of problems or embarrassment. *My car's a real liability.* 2 COUNT N A company's **liabilities** are the money that it owes; a technical use. *The company has had to undertake heavy liabilities.* 3 UNCOUNT N If you have **liability** for a debt or accident, you are legally responsible for it; a legal use.

liable /laɪəbə^{0}l/. 1 PRED ADJ WITH TO-INF Something that is **liable** to happen is very likely to happen. *The play is liable to give offence to many people.* 2 PRED ADJ WITH PREP 'to' If people or things are **liable** to something, they are likely to experience it; a formal use. *I was liable to sea-sickness.* 3 PRED ADJ If you are **liable** for a debt, you are legally responsible for it.

liaise /li^{1}eɪz/, **liaises, liaising, liaised.** RECIP VB When organizations or people **liaise,** they work together and keep each other informed. *Members can help by liaising with the press.*

liaison /li^{1}eɪzɒn/, **liaisons.** 1 UNCOUNT N **Liaison** is co-operation and communication between different organizations or between different sections of an organization. *...better liaison between the health and social services.* 2 COUNT N A **liaison** is a sexual relationship; a formal use which shows disapproval.

liar /laɪə/, **liars.** COUNT N A **liar** is someone who tells lies. *You're a liar.*

libel /laɪbə^{0}l/, **libels.** UNCOUNT N OR COUNT N **Libel** or a **libel** is something written which wrongly accuses someone of something, and which is therefore against the law. *Hinds brought an action for libel against him... This was a gigantic libel.*

libellous /laɪbə^{0}ləs/; spelled **libelous** in American English. ADJ If something written is **libellous,** it wrongly accuses someone of something, and is therefore against the law. *...libellous comments.*

liberal /lɪbə^{0}rəl/, **liberals.** 1 ADJ Someone who is **liberal** is tolerant of different behaviour or opinions. *My school was traditional, but more liberal than other public schools... ...a liberal democracy.* Also COUNT N *...a pair of enlightened liberals.* 2 ADJ **Liberal** also means giving, using, or taking a lot of something. *Could any man make a more liberal offer?* ♦ **liberally** ADV *Tim helped himself liberally to some more wine.*

liberalism /lɪbə^{0}rəlɪzə^{0}m/. UNCOUNT N **Liberalism** is the belief that people should have a lot of political and individual freedom.

liberalize /lɪbə^{0}rəlaɪz/, **liberalizes, liberalizing, liberalized;** also spelled **liberalise.** VB WITH OR WITHOUT OBJ When a country **liberalizes** its laws or its attitudes, it makes them less strict and allows more freedom. *There was a move to liberalize the state abortion laws.* ♦ **liberalization** /lɪbə^{0}rəlaɪzeɪʃə^{0}n/ UNCOUNT N *He called for the liberalization of the laws relating to immigration.*

liberate /lɪbəreɪt/, **liberates, liberating, liberated;** a formal word. 1 VB WITH OBJ To **liberate** people means to free them from prison or from an unpleasant situation. *He claimed that socialism alone could liberate black people... ...liberating people from poverty.* ♦ **liberation** /lɪbəreɪʃə^{0}n/ UNCOUNT N *...the women's liberation movement.* 2 VB WITH OBJ To **liberate** a place means to free it from the control of another country. *...the hero who liberated Cuba.* ♦ **liberation** UNCOUNT N *...wars of national liberation.*

liberated /lɪbəreɪtɪ^{2}d/. ADJ You say that people are **liberated** when they behave in a less restricted way than is traditional in their society.

liberty /lɪbəti^1/, **liberties;** a formal word. 1 UNCOUNT N OR PLURAL N **Liberty** is the freedom to choose how you want to live, without government interference. *...respect for individual liberty... ...increasing attacks on their liberties.* 2 UNCOUNT N **Liberty** is the freedom to go wherever you want. *...that fundamental aspect of imprisonment, the loss of liberty.*

PHRASES ● A criminal who is **at liberty** has not yet been caught, or has escaped from prison. *Only one important figure remains at liberty.* ● If you are not **at liberty** to do something, you are not allowed to do it.

librarian /laɪbreərɪən/, **librarians.** COUNT N A **librarian** is a person who is in charge of a library or who has been trained to do responsible work in a library.

library /laɪbrəri^1/, **libraries.** 1 COUNT N A **library** is a building where books and newspapers are kept for people to read. *... public libraries... ...a new extension to the library.* 2 COUNT N A **library** is also a private collection of books or records.

libretto /lɪbretəʊ/, **librettos** or **libretti.** COUNT N The **libretto** of an opera is the words that are sung in it.

lice /laɪs/. **Lice** is the plural of **louse.**

licence /laɪsəns/, **licences;** spelled **license** in American English. 1 COUNT N A **licence** is an official document which gives you permission to do, use, or own something. *...a driving licence.* 2 PHRASE If someone does something **under licence,** they do it by special permission from the authorities. 3 See also **off-licence.**

license /laɪsəns/, **licenses, licensing, licensed.** VB WITH OBJ To **license** a person, organization, or activity means to give official permission for the person or organization to do something or for the activity to happen. *The Royal College examines and licenses surgeons.* ♦ **licensing** ATTRIB ADJ *...a licensing authority.*

licensed /laɪsənst/. 1 ADJ If you are **licensed** to do something, you have official permission from a government or other authority to do it. *These men are licensed to carry firearms... ...a licensed pilot.* 2 ADJ If something that you own or use is **licensed,** you have official permission to own it or use it. *The car is licensed and insured.* 3 ADJ If a restaurant or hotel is **licensed,** it is allowed to sell alcoholic drinks.

lick /lɪk/, **licks, licking, licked.** VB WITH OBJ When you **lick** something, you move your tongue across its surface. *He licked the last of the egg off his knife... The cat was licking its paw.* Also COUNT N *...a few licks and nibbles.*

PHRASES ● If you **lick** your **lips,** you move your tongue across your lips, as you think eagerly about something. *She looked at the plate and licked her lips.* ● If you say that someone is **licking** their **wounds,** you mean that they are recovering after being defeated or humiliated.

licorice See **liquorice.**

lid /lɪd/, **lids.** 1 COUNT N A **lid** is the top which you open to reach inside a container. *She was opening and closing the lid of her tin.* 2 COUNT N Your **lids** are the same as your eyelids. *She looked round from under half-closed lids.*

lie /laɪ/. The forms **lie, lies, lying, lay** /leɪ/, **lain** /leɪn/ are used for the verb in meanings 1 to 6 and for the phrasal verbs. The forms **lie, lies, lying, lied** are used for the verb in meaning 8. **Lies** is also the plural form of the noun in meaning 7. 1 VB WITH ADJUNCT OR COMPLEMENT If you **are lying** somewhere, you are in a horizontal position and are not standing or sitting. *I lay there trying to remember what he looked like... Judy was lying flat on the bed.* 2 VB WITH ADJUNCT OR COMPLEMENT If an object **lies** in a particular place, it is in a flat position in that place. *...the folder lying open before him... The coffin lay undisturbed for centuries.* 3 VB WITH ADJUNCT If a place **lies** in a particular position, it is situated there. *The bridge lies beyond the docks.* 4 VB WITH ADJUNCT You use **lie** when you are mentioning the causes or the origins of something; a formal use. *The causes of this lie deep in the history of society.* 5 VB WITH ADJUNCT If something **lies** ahead, it is going to happen in the future. *Endless hours of pleasure lie before you... ...an unwelcome foretaste of what lay in store.* 6 VB WITH COMPLEMENT You can use **lie** to say what position someone is in during a competition. For example, if they **are lying** third, they are third. 7 COUNT N A **lie** is something that someone says which they know is untrue. *You're telling lies now.* 8 VB OR REPORT VB If someone **is lying,** they are saying something which they know is untrue. *You lied to me... 'Certainly not,' I lied.* 9 See also **lying.**

lie down. PHR VB 1 When you **lie down** you move into a horizontal position, usually in order to rest. *He lay down on the couch.* 2 PHRASE If you **take** unfair treatment **lying down,** you accept it without complaining or resisting; an informal use. *She was never one to take bullying lying down.*

lie with. PHR VB If the responsibility for something **lies with** you, it is your responsibility; a formal use. *Are you saying that the fault generally lies with the management?*

lie-in. SING N If you have a **lie-in,** you stay in bed later than usual in the morning; an informal use.

lieutenant, lieutenants; pronounced /leftenənt/ in British English and /luːtenənt/ in American English. COUNT N OR TITLE A **lieutenant** is a junior officer in the army or navy. *...Lieutenant Lawton.*

life /laɪf/, **lives** /laɪvz/. **Lives** is also the third person singular, present tense, of the verb 'live' and is then pronounced /lɪvz/. 1 UNCOUNT N **Life** is the quality which people, animals, and plants have when they are not dead and which objects and substances do not have. *...her last hours of life.* 2 UNCOUNT N **Life** is things which are alive. *Is there life on Jupiter?... ...plant life.* 3 COUNT N Someone's **life** is their state of being alive, or the period of time during which they are alive. *He nearly lost his life... People spend their lives worrying about money... I've had such a fascinating life.* 4 UNCOUNT N **Life** is also the events and experiences that happen to people. *Life is probably harder for women... I don't know what you want out of life.* 5 UNCOUNT N A person or place that is full of **life** is full of activity and excitement. 6 SING N The **life** of a machine, object, or substance is the period of time that it lasts for. *Using bleach shortens the life of any fabric.*

PHRASES ● If someone or something that has been inactive **comes to life,** they become active. *Their political movement came to life again.* ● If you **hold on** to something **for dear life,** you hold on very tightly; an informal use. *I held on to the ledge for dear life.* ● If you **live** your **own life,** you live in the way that you want to, without interference. *She was 18 after all, entitled to live her own life.* ● If someone **takes** a person's **life,** they kill that person; a formal use. *On the eve of his conviction, he took his own life.* to ● **risk life and limb:** see **limb.** ● See also **way of life.**

lifebelt /laɪfbelt/, **lifebelts.** COUNT N A **lifebelt** is a large ring used to keep a person afloat in water.

lifeboat /laɪfbəʊt/, **lifeboats.** 1 COUNT N A **lifeboat** is a boat which is sent out from a port or harbour to rescue people who are in danger at sea. 2 COUNT N A **lifeboat** is a small boat which is carried on a ship and which is used if the ship is in danger of sinking.

lifebuoy /laɪfbɔɪ/, **lifebuoys.** COUNT N A **lifebuoy** is the same as a lifebelt.

life-cycle, life-cycles. COUNT N The **life-cycle** of an animal or plant is the series of changes it passes through from the beginning of its life until its death. *...the life-cycle of the salmon.*

life expectancy, life expectancies. COUNT N OR UNCOUNT N The **life expectancy** of an animal or plant is the length of time that they are normally likely to live. *Women have a longer life expectancy than men.*

life form, life forms. COUNT N WITH SUPP A **life form** is any living thing. *Many of the deep-sea life forms feed directly on bacteria.*

lifeguard /laɪfgɑːd/, **lifeguards.** COUNT N A **lifeguard** is a person at a beach or swimming pool whose job is to rescue people who are in danger of drowning.

life imprisonment. UNCOUNT N When criminals are sentenced to **life imprisonment,** they are sentenced to stay in prison for the rest of their lives or for a very long time.

lifejacket /laɪfdʒækɪ^{1}t/, **lifejackets.** COUNT N A **lifejacket** is a sleeveless jacket which keeps you afloat in water.

lifeless /laɪflɪ²s/. 1 ADJ A person or animal that is **lifeless** is dead; a literary use. *...the lifeless body of Lieutenant Dowling.* 2 ADJ You use **lifeless** when you want to emphasize that an object is not a living thing. *...a lifeless chunk of rock.* 3 ADJ A **lifeless** place has nothing living or growing there. *...a time when the earth was completely lifeless.* 4 ADJ You can say that people or things are **lifeless** when you find them dull and not exciting. *...a lifeless voice.*

lifelike /laɪflaɪk/. ADJ Something that is **lifelike** looks real or alive. *...extremely lifelike computer-controlled robots.*

lifeline /laɪflaɪn/, **lifelines.** 1 COUNT N A **lifeline** is something of importance in helping people to survive, or in helping an activity to continue. *The household became my lifeline, my only link with the outside world... ...the oil lifeline of Western Europe.* 2 COUNT N A **lifeline** is also a rope which you throw to someone in danger of drowning.

lifelong /laɪflɒŋ/. ATTRIB ADJ **Lifelong** means existing or happening for the whole of a person's life. *...her friend and lifelong companion.*

life sentence, life sentences. COUNT N When criminals receive a **life sentence,** they are sentenced to stay in prison for the rest of their lives.

life-size. ADJ **Life-size** or **life-sized** paintings or models are the same size as the person or thing that they represent. *...a life-size statue.*

lifespan /laɪfspæn/, **lifespans.** 1 COUNT N WITH SUPP The **lifespan** of a person, animal, or plant is the period of time during which they are alive. *...the human lifespan.* 2 COUNT N WITH SUPP The **lifespan** of a product, organization, or idea is the period of time during which it exists or is used. *This job had a planned life-span of five years.*

life style, life styles. COUNT N WITH SUPP Your **life style** is the way you live, for example the things you normally do. *...this highly urban lifestyle.*

lifetime /laɪftaɪm/, **lifetimes.** 1 COUNT N A **lifetime** is the length of time that someone is alive. *I've seen a lot of changes in my lifetime.* 2 SING N WITH POSS The **lifetime** of something is the period of time that it lasts. *...during the lifetime of this parliament.*

lift /lɪft/, **lifts, lifting, lifted.** 1 VB WITH OBJ If you **lift** something, you move it to another position, usually upwards. *He lifted the glass to his mouth... She lifted her feet on to the settee... She lifted her eyes from the ground and fixed them on me.* 2 COUNT N A **lift** is a device like a large box which carries people from one floor to another in a building; a British use. *I took the lift to the eighth floor.* 3 COUNT N If you give someone a **lift,** you drive them in your car from one place to another. *She offered me a lift home.* 4 VB When fog or mist **lifts,** it disappears. *Around midday, the fog lifted.* 5 VB WITH OBJ If people in authority **lift** a law or rule, they end it. *He lifted the ban on the People's Party.*

lift-off, lift-offs. UNCOUNT N OR COUNT N **Lift-off** or a **lift-off** is the launching of a rocket into space.

ligament /lɪgəmə²nt/, **ligaments.** COUNT N A **ligament** is a band of strong tissue in your body, which connects bones. *He had torn a ligament in his knee.*

light /laɪt/, **lights, lighting, lit** /lɪt/; **lighter, lightest.** The form **lighted** is also used as the past tense and past participle, although **lit** is more usual. 1 UNCOUNT N **Light** is the brightness that lets you see things, and that comes from the sun, the moon, lamps, or fire. *We are dependent on the sun for heat and light... By the light of a torch, she began to read.* 2 COUNT N A **light** is anything that produces light, especially an electric bulb. *She went into her daughter's room and turned on the light.* 3 VB WITH OBJ A place or object that **is lit** by something has light shining in it or on it. *...a room lit by candles.* ♦ **lighted** ATTRIB ADJ *He looked up thoughtfully at the lighted windows.* 4 ADJ If a building or room is **light,** it has a lot of natural light in it. 5 PRED ADJ If it is **light outside,** it is daytime. 6 ADJ **Light** colours are very pale. *...light blue eyes.* 7 VB WITH OBJ If you **light** something, you make it start burning. *Light the gas fire if you feel chilly.* ♦ **lighted** ADJ *...a lighted candle.* 8 SING N If someone asks you for a **light,** they want a match or a cigarette lighter so they can start their cigarette burning. 9 SING N WITH SUPP If you see something in a particular **light,** you think about it in that way. *We were now seeing things in a different light.* 10 ADJ Something that is **light** does not weigh very much or is not very great in amount or intensity. *The bag was very light, as though there were nothing in it... A light rain was falling... The traffic on the highway was light that day.* ♦ **lightness** UNCOUNT N *...the extreme lightness of this particular shoe.* 11 ADJ **Light** work does not involve much physical effort. *He has grown much weaker and is now capable of only light work.* 12 ADJ Movements and actions that are **light** are graceful or gentle. *She runs up the stairs two at a time with her light graceful step.* ♦ **lightly** ADV *He kissed his wife lightly on the cheek.* ♦ **lightness** UNCOUNT N *For a heavy man he moves with surprising lightness and speed.* 13 ADJ **Light** books, plays, or pieces of music entertain you without making you think very deeply. *...light entertainment and comedy.* ● See also **lighting, lightly.**

PHRASES ● If you **set light to** something, you make it start burning. ● If a new piece of information **throws** or **casts light on** something, it makes it easier to understand. *His diaries throw a new light upon certain incidents.* ● If something **comes to light** or **is brought to light,** it becomes known. *It has come to light that he was lying.* ● **In the light of** something means considering it or taking it into account. *This development is significant in the light of what happened later.*

light up. PHR VB 1 If something **lights up** a place or object, it shines light on all of it. *The fire was still blazing, lighting up the sky.* 2 If your face or eyes **light up,** you suddenly look very happy. *His face lit up at the sight of Cynthia.* 3 If you **light up** a cigarette or pipe, you start smoking. *George lit up and puffed away for a while.*

light bulb, light bulbs. COUNT N A **light bulb** is the central glass part of an electric lamp which light shines from.

lighten /laɪtə⁰n/, **lightens, lightening, lightened.** 1 ERG VB When something **lightens** or **is lightened,** it becomes less dark. *After the rain stops, the sky lightens a little... Constant exposure to the sun had lightened my hair.* 2 VB WITH OBJ You also say that you **lighten** something when you make it less heavy. *They began to lighten their products in an effort to increase sales.* 3 VB If someone's face or expression **lightens,** it becomes more cheerful, happy, and relaxed. *Her whole expression lightened.*

lighter /laɪtə/, **lighters.** 1 COUNT N A **lighter** or a **cigarette lighter** is a small device for lighting cigarettes. 2 **Lighter** is the comparative of **light.**

light-headed. ADJ If you are **light-headed,** you feel dizzy and faint.

light-hearted. ADJ Someone or something that is **light-hearted** is cheerful and entertaining. *He was in a light-hearted mood... Let me finish with a slightly more light-hearted question.*

lighthouse /laɪthaus/, **lighthouses.** COUNT N A **lighthouse** is a tower near the sea which contains a powerful flashing lamp to guide ships or to warn them of danger.

light industry, light industries. UNCOUNT N OR COUNT N **Light industry** is industry in which only small items are made, for example household goods and clothes.

lighting /laɪtɪŋ/. UNCOUNT N The **lighting** in a place is the way that it is lit, or the quality of the light in it. *...artificial lighting... ...poorly designed street lighting.*

lightly /laɪtli¹/. ADV If you say that something is not done **lightly,** you mean that it is not done without serious thought. *This is not a charge to make lightly against the government... He knew it was not being said lightly.* ● See also **light.**

lightning /laɪtnɪŋ/. 1 UNCOUNT N **Lightning** is the bright flashes of light in the sky that you see during a thunderstorm. *...a flash of lightning... He was struck by lightning, and nearly died.* 2 ATTRIB ADJ **Lightning** describes things that happen very quickly or last for only a short time. *He drew his gun with lightning speed.*

lightweight /laɪtweɪt/. ADJ Something that is **lightweight** weighs less than most other things of the same type. *...a grey lightweight suit... ...lightweight cameras.*

light-year, light-years. 1 COUNT N A **light-year** is the distance that light travels in a year; a technical use. 2 COUNT N **Light-years** or a **light-year** means a very long time; an informal use. *Last Tuesday seemed light-years away already.*

likable /laɪkəbə⁰l/. See **likeable.**

like /laɪk/, **likes, liking, liked.** 1 PREP If one person or thing is **like** another, they have similar characteristics or behave in similar ways. *He looked like Clark Gable... She's very like her younger sister... The lake was like a bright blue mirror... She began to shake like a jelly.* 2 PREP If you ask someone what something is **like,** you are asking them to describe it. *What was Essex like?... What did they taste like?* 3 PREP **Like** can introduce an example of the thing that you have just mentioned. *You only get them in big countries, like Africa or India.* 4 PREP You can use **like** to say that something is true of a particular thing because it is true of all things of that kind. *There's no point in stirring up publicity about a foolish thing like this.* 5 PREP You can use **like** to say that someone is in the same situation as another person. *He, like everybody else, had worried about it.* 6 CONJ If you say that something is **like** you remembered it or **like** you imagined it, you mean that it is the way you remembered or imagined it; an informal use. *Is it like you remembered it?... It didn't work out quite like I intended it to.* 7 VB WITH OBJ, -ING, OR TO-INF If you **like** something, you find it pleasant or attractive, or you approve of it. *She's a nice girl, I like her... They didn't like what they saw... I like reading... Her folks like her to get in early.* 8 VB WITH OR WITHOUT OBJ, OR VB WITH TO-INF If you say that you would **like** something or would **like** to do something, you are expressing a wish or desire. *I'd like to marry him... Would you like some coffee?... He can stay here if he likes... I'd like you to come.* 9 See also **liking.**

PHRASES ● You say **'if you like'** when you are offering to do something for someone. *I'll drive, if you like.* ● You say **'and the like'** to indicate there are other similar things that can be included in what you are saying. *...the activities of ruthless mine owners and the like.* ● You say **'like this', 'like that',** or **'like so'** when you are showing someone how something is done. *Twist it round and put it on here, like that.* ● You can sometimes use **nothing like** instead of 'not' when you want to emphasize a negative statement. *The cast is nothing like as numerous as one might suppose.* ● You use **something like** to indicate that a number or quantity is an estimate, not an exact figure. *Something like ninety per cent of the crop was destroyed.*

-like. SUFFIX **-like** is added to nouns to form adjectives that describe something as similar to the thing referred to by the noun. *...a rock-like hump.*

likeable /laɪkəbə⁰l/; also spelled **likable.** ADJ If someone is **likeable,** they are pleasant and friendly. *...a very attractive and likeable young man.*

likelihood /laɪkli¹hʊd/. SING N The **likelihood** of something happening is the fact that it is likely to happen. *There is every likelihood that she will succeed... This increases the likelihood of an attack.*

likely /laɪkli¹/, **likelier, likeliest.** 1 ADJ If something is **likely,** it is probably true or will probably happen. *It seemed hardly likely that they would agree... What kind of change is likely?* 2 PRED ADJ WITH TO-INF If you are **likely** to do something, you will probably do it. *They were not likely to forget it.* 3 SENTENCE ADV **Very likely** or **most likely** means probably. *Most likely it will be a woman.* 4 ATTRIB ADJ You use **likely** to describe people who will probably be suitable for a particular purpose. *The local committee is always looking out for likely recruits.*

like-minded. ADJ People who are **like-minded** have similar opinions, or interests. *...Hubbard and his like-minded colleagues.*

liken /laɪkən/, **likens, likening, likened.** VB WITH OBJ AND PREP 'to' If you **liken** one thing to another thing, you say that they are similar. *It has a mildly nutty taste which has been likened to new potatoes.*

likeness /laɪknɪ²s/, **likenesses.** 1 SING N If one thing has a **likeness** to another, it is similar to it in appearance. *...a china dog that bore a likeness to his aunt.* 2 COUNT N WITH SUPP If a picture of someone is a good **likeness** of them, it looks very much like them.

likewise /laɪkwaɪz/. 1 SENTENCE ADV You use **likewise** when you are comparing two things and saying that they are similar. *In Yugoslavia there was a special local way of doing it, likewise in Italy.* 2 ADV If you do one thing, and someone else does **likewise,** they do the same thing. *He is relaxing and invites them to do likewise.*

liking /laɪkɪŋ/. SING N WITH SUPP If you have a **liking** for someone, you like them. *I took an enormous liking to Davies the moment I met him... She was developing a liking for Scotch.*

PHRASES ● If something is **to** your **liking,** you like it. *Did they find the temperature to their liking?* ● If something is too big or too fast **for** your **liking,** you would prefer it to be smaller or slower. *You are progressing too fast for his liking.*

lilac /laɪlək/, **lilacs.** 1 COUNT N OR UNCOUNT N A **lilac** is a small tree with pleasant-smelling flowers. *...lilac bushes in the garden.* 2 ADJ Something that is **lilac** in colour is pale pinkish-purple. *...her plain lilac dress.*

lilt /lɪlt/, **lilts.** COUNT N A **lilt** in someone's voice is its pleasant rising and falling sound. *There was something familiar in the lilt of her voice... ...his Irish lilt.*

lily /lɪli¹/, **lilies.** COUNT N A **lily** is a plant with large flowers that are often white.

limb /lɪm/, **limbs.** 1 COUNT N Your **limbs** are your arms and legs. *He was very tall with long limbs... We cough, yawn, and stretch our limbs.* 2 COUNT N The **limbs** of a tree are its branches; a literary use. *Thick smoke rose into the tree's upper limbs.*

PHRASES ● If someone has gone **out on a limb,** they have done or said something that is risky or extreme. ● If someone **risks life and limb,** they do something very dangerous.

limber /lɪmbə/, **limbers, limbering, limbered.**

limber up PHR VB If you **limber up,** you prepare for a sport by doing exercises. *We had no time to limber up on the practice range.*

limbo /lɪmbəʊ/. 1 UNCOUNT N If you are in **limbo,** you are in a situation where you do not know what will happen next and you have no control over things. *Refugees may remain in limbo for years.* 2 SING N The **limbo** is a West Indian dance in which you have to pass under a low bar while leaning backwards.

lime /laɪm/, **limes.** 1 COUNT N A **lime** is a small, round, citrus fruit with dark green skin. 2 COUNT N A **lime** is a large tree with pale green leaves, that is often planted in parks in towns and cities. *...the long avenue of limes.* 3 UNCOUNT N **Lime** or **lime juice** is a non-alcoholic drink that is made from the juice of limes. 4 UNCOUNT N OR MOD **Lime** is also a chemical substance which is used in cement, in whitewash, and as a fertilizer. *...a lime quarry.*

limelight /laɪmlaɪt/. SING N If someone is in the **limelight,** they are getting a lot of attention.

limestone /laɪmstəʊn/. UNCOUNT N **Limestone** is a white rock which is used for building and making cement.

limit /lɪmɪt/, **limits, limiting, limited.** 1 COUNT N A **limit** is the greatest amount, extent, or degree of something that is possible or allowed. *There is no limit to the risks they are prepared to take... The powers of the human brain are stretched to the limit... ...a motorist exceeding the speed limit.* 2 PLURAL N The **limits** of a situation are the facts involved in it which make only some actions or results possible. *...the problems of applying that system within the limits of a weekly, two-hour meeting.* 3 VB WITH OBJ If you **limit** something, you prevent it from becoming greater than a particular amount or degree. *Japanese exports would be limited to 1.68m vehicles.* 4 VB WITH OBJ OR REFL VB If someone or something **limits** you, or if you **limit** yourself, the number of things that you have or do is reduced. *Why should the people of this country limit me that way?... Will he limit himself to seeing that the enterprise is approved?* ♦ **limiting** ADJ *Many of these customs were narrow and limiting.* 5 VB WITH OBJ If something **is limited** to a particular place or group of people, it exists only in that place, or is had or done only by that group. *This problem is not limited to Sweden.*

PHRASES ● If a place is **off limits,** you are not allowed to go there. ● You say that someone **is the limit** when you are very annoyed with them; an informal use.

limitation /lɪmɪteɪʃəⁿn/, **limitations.** 1 UNCOUNT N **Limitation** is the control or reduction of something. *...the limitation of trade union power.* 2 PLURAL N If you talk about the **limitations** of someone or something, you mean that they can only do some things and not others, or that they can only achieve a fairly low degree of success or excellence. *It's important to know your own limitations... The technique has its limitations.* 3 COUNT N When there are **limitations** on something, it is not allowed to grow or extend beyond certain limits. *All limitations on earnings must cease.*

limited /lɪmɪtɪ²d/. 1 ADJ Something that is **limited** is rather small in amount or degree. *The choice was very limited... ...a painter of limited abilities.* 2 ADJ A **limited** company is one in which the shareholders are legally responsible for only a part of any money that it may owe if it goes bankrupt; a British use. *The Foundation had become a limited company... ...Hourmont Travel Limited.*

limitless /lɪmɪtlɪ²s/. ADJ You say that something is **limitless** when it is extremely large in amount or extent. *...the computer's limitless memory... ...our limitless fascination with toys and games.*

limp /lɪmp/, **limps, limping, limped.** 1 VB If you **limp,** you walk in an uneven way because one of your legs or feet is hurt. *He picked up his bag and limped back to the road... Two of the dogs were limping badly.* Also COUNT N *He walks with a limp... She had a slight limp.* 2 ADJ If someone is **limp,** they have no strength or energy and their body can be moved easily. *Her hand felt limp and damp.* ♦ **limply** ADV *The tiny baby lay limply on her arm.* 3 ADJ Something that is **limp** is soft and not stiff or firm. *...a dressing-gown of limp, shiny fabric.* ♦ **limply** ADV *The rope fell limply to the ground.*

line /laɪn/, **lines, lining, lined.** 1 COUNT N A **line** is a long, thin mark on a surface. *...a diagonal red line on the label... ...a straight line joining those two points.* 2 COUNT N The **lines** on someone's face are the wrinkles or creases in it. 3 COUNT N A **line** of people or things is a number of them that are arranged in a row. *...long lines of poplar trees... The men formed themselves into a line.* 4 COUNT N You can refer to a long piece of string or wire as a **line** when it is being used for a particular purpose. *...washing hanging on a line... The fish was heavy at the end of my line... ...a telephone line.* 5 COUNT N **Line** is also used to refer to a route along which people or things move or are sent. *Wireless waves travel in straight lines... All lines of communication had been cut... ...a long dripping tunnel under the railway line... They took the wrong line on the London Tube.* 6 COUNT N WITH SUPP You can use **line** to refer to the edge, outline, or shape of something. *...the firm, delicate lines of Paxton's buildings... ...the hard thin line of Lynn's mouth.* 7 COUNT N WITH SUPP **Line** also refers to the boundary between certain areas, things or types of people. *They were dropped by parachute behind enemy lines... The traditional social dividing lines are becoming blurred... She will be living below the poverty line.* 8 COUNT N A **line** is also one of the rows of words in a piece of writing or a remark said by an actor in a play or film. *I have read every line... She found it impossible to remember her lines.* 9 COUNT N WITH SUPP The **line** that someone takes on a problem or topic is their attitude or policy towards it. *...the official line of the Labour Party... The President takes a much harder line.* 10 SING N WITH POSS Your **line** of business, work or research is the kind of work or research that you do. *A man in my line of business has to take precautions... ...his particular line of research.* 11 COUNT N A **line** is also a type of product that a company makes or sells. *Unprofitable lines will be discontinued.* 12 SING N WITH SUPP A particular **line** of people or things is a series of them, all connected in some way, that has existed over a period of time. *...the long line of American Presidents.* 13 VB WITH OBJ If people or things **line** a road or room, they are present in large numbers along its edges or sides. *The streets were lined with cars.* 14 VB WITH OBJ If you **line** a container or a piece of clothing, you cover its inside surface with paper or cloth. *Line the cupboards and drawers with paper... ...a coffin lined with velvet.* 15 VB WITH OBJ If something **lines** a container or an area inside a person, animal, or plant, it forms a layer on the inside surface. *...tiny hairs lining the nose.* 16 See also **lined, lining,** and **front line, hard line, hot line.**

PHRASES ● If you are **in line for** something, you are likely to get it. *You are next in line for promotion.* ● If one person or group is **in line** with others, it is doing the same thing as the others. *Africa may bring itself in line with the rest of the world on this matter.* ● If something is done **in line** with a policy or guideline, it is done following that policy or guideline. ● If you keep someone **in line,** you make them behave in the way that they are supposed to. ● If you are **on line** when using a large computer, you type on a keyboard with a screen directly into the computer. ● If your job or reputation is **on the line,** you may lose it or harm it as a result of doing something brave or foolish. *I didn't dare fight and put my job on the line, so I went along with them.* ● If something happens **on** or **along** particular **lines,** it happens in that way. *The population is split along religious lines.* ● You use **on the lines of** and **along the lines of** when you are giving a general description of what someone has said or of what you want. *Driberg opened with a question on the lines of: 'What do you think about the present political situation?'* ● If someone is **on the right lines,** they are acting in a way that is sensible or likely to produce useful results. *Do his policies strike you as being on the right lines?* ● If someone is **out of line** or **steps out of line,** they do not behave in the way that they are supposed to. ● If you **draw the line** at a particular activity, you refuse to do it, because it is more than you are prepared to do. *There is a point at which they will have to draw the line.* ● If something happens somewhere **along the line,** it happens during a process or activity. *We slipped up somewhere along the line.* to ● **drop** someone **a line:** see **drop.** to ● **read between the lines:** see **read.**

line up. PHR VB 1 If people **line up** or if you **line** them **up,** they stand in a row or form a queue. *They lined us up and marched us off.* 2 If something **is lined up** for someone, it is arranged for them. *A formal farewell party was lined up.* 3 See also **line-up.**

linear /lɪniˈə/. 1 ADJ A **linear** process is one in which something progresses straight from one stage to another; a formal use. *...linear thinking... ...events occurring simultaneously rather than in a linear sequence.* 2 ADJ A **linear** shape consists of lines; a formal use.

lined /laɪnd/. 1 ADJ If someone's skin is **lined,** it has wrinkles on it. *Their faces are lined, immeasurably sad.* 2 ADJ **Lined** paper has lines printed across it. *He was writing on a lined pad.*

linen /lɪnɪn/. 1 UNCOUNT N **Linen** is a kind of cloth that is used, for example, for making tea-towels. *...a white linen suit.* 2 UNCOUNT N You can refer to tablecloths, sheets, and similar things as **linen.** *...bed linen.*

liner /laɪnə/, **liners.** 1 COUNT N A **liner** is a large passenger ship. 2 COUNT N WITH SUPP A bin **liner** is a plastic bag that you put inside a waste bin or dustbin.

linesman /laɪnzməˀn/, **linesmen.** COUNT N A **linesman** is an official in games such as football and tennis who watches the boundary lines and indicates when the ball goes outside them.

line-up, line-ups. COUNT N The **line-up** for a public event is the people who are going to take part in it; an informal use. *...the line-up for the next game.*

linger /lɪŋgə/, **lingers, lingering, lingered.** 1 VB If something **lingers,** it continues to exist for a long time. *The resentment and the longings lingered... This tradition apparently manages to linger on.* ♦ **lingering** ATTRIB ADJ *...a lingering sense of guilt.* 2 VB WITH ADJUNCT If you **linger** somewhere, you stay there for a longer time than is necessary, for example because you are enjoying yourself. *Davis lingered for a moment in the bar... ...lingering over their meals.*

lingerie /lɒnʒəri¹/. UNCOUNT N **Lingerie** is women's underwear and night-clothes; a formal use.

linguist /lɪŋgwɪst/, **linguists.** COUNT N A **linguist** is someone who can speak several languages.

linguistic /lɪŋgwɪstɪk/, **linguistics.** 1 UNCOUNT N **Linguistics** is the study of the way in which language works. 2 ADJ **Linguistic** studies or ideas relate to language or linguistics. *...linguistic development between the ages of nought and four.*

lining /laɪnɪŋ/, **linings.** COUNT N A **lining** is a material attached to the inside of something, for example in order to make it more slippery or to protect it. *...a white cloak with a scarlet lining.*

link /lɪŋk/, **links, linking, linked.** 1 VB WITH OBJ Two things **are linked** when there is a relationship between them. *...all that was known about how animal behaviour is linked to genes... Evidence has been offered linking the group to a series of bomb attacks.* 2 COUNT N A **link** is a relationship between two things. *There seems to be a link between the rising rate of unemployment and the rise in crime... We have very close links with industry.* 3 VB WITH OBJ Two places or objects **are linked** when there is a physical connection between them so that you can travel or communicate between them. *The television camera had been linked to a computer... ...a canal linking the Pacific and Atlantic oceans.* 4 COUNT N A **link** between two places is a physical connection between them. *They opened a rail link between the two towns... ...a telephone link between Washington and Moscow.* 5 VB WITH OBJ If you **link** two things, you join them loosely. *She linked her hand through the crook of his elbow.* 6 COUNT N A **link** of a chain is one of the rings in it.

link up. PHR VB If you **link up** two items or places, you connect them to each other. *This computer can be linked up to other computers.*

lino /laɪnəʊ/. UNCOUNT N **Lino** is the same as linoleum. *...a landing with cracked lino on the floor.*

linoleum /lɪnəʊlɪəm/. UNCOUNT N **Linoleum** is a floor covering with shiny surface; a formal use. *The linoleum felt cool and smooth against his bare feet.*

lion /laɪən/, **lions.** 1 COUNT N A **lion** is a large, wild member of the cat family found in Africa. Lions have yellowish fur, and male lions have long hair on their head and neck. 2 PHRASE If someone gets **the lion's share** of something, they get the largest part of it. *The lion's share of investment has gone to a few favoured companies.*

lip /lɪp/, **lips.** 1 COUNT N Your **lips** are the top and bottom edges of your mouth. *He had a freshly lit cigarette between his lips.* 2 PHRASE If you **keep a stiff upper lip,** you do not show any emotion, even though it is difficult not to.

lip-read, lip-reads, lip-reading. Lip-read is used in the present tense, and is the past tense and past participle. VB If someone can **lip-read,** they can understand what you are saying by watching your lips. Deaf people sometimes do this.

lip-service. PHRASE If someone **pays lip-service** to an idea, they pretend to be in favour of it, but they do not do anything to support it; used showing disapproval. *Our major political parties pay lip-service to the ideal of community participation.*

lipstick /lɪpstɪk/, **lipsticks.** MASS N **Lipstick** is a coloured substance which women put on their lips. *She was wearing lipstick and mascara.*

liqueur /lɪkjʊə/, **liqueurs.** MASS N A **liqueur** is a strong, sweet alcoholic drink, often drunk after a meal.

liquid /lɪkwɪd/, **liquids.** 1 MASS N A **liquid** is a substance such as water which is not solid and which can be poured. 2 ADJ Something that is **liquid** is in the form of a liquid rather than being solid or a gas. *...liquid polish.*

liquidate /lɪkwɪdeɪt/, **liquidates, liquidating, liquidated.** 1 VB WITH OBJ When someone **liquidates** people who are causing problems, they have them killed. *All his supporters were expelled, exiled, or liquidated.* 2 VB WITH OBJ When a company **is liquidated,** it is closed down; a technical use. *...if it permitted the* *industry to be liquidated because of the present glut of oil.* ♦ **liquidation** /lɪkwɪdeɪʃəⁿn/ UNCOUNT N *By April 1969, the group faced liquidation.*

liquor /lɪkə/, **liquors.** MASS N **Liquor** is strong alcoholic drink; an American use.

liquorice /lɪkərɪs, -ɪʃ/; also spelled **licorice.** UNCOUNT N **Liquorice** is a firm black substance with a strong taste used for making sweets.

lisp /lɪsp/, **lisps.** COUNT N Someone with a **lisp** pronounces the sounds 's' and 'z' as if they were 'th'. For example, they say 'thing' instead of 'sing'.

list /lɪst/, **lists, listing, listed.** 1 COUNT N A **list** is a set of things which are written down one below the other. *Look at your list of things to be mended... Find out all their names and make a list.* ● See also **short-list.** 2 VB WITH OBJ To **list** a set of things means to mention them all one after the other. *There was a label on each case listing its contents.* 3 VB WITH OBJ If something is **listed,** it is included as an item on a list. *He is still listed in the files by his code name, the Jackal.*

listen /lɪsəⁿn/, **listens, listening, listened.** 1 VB If you **listen** to someone who is talking or to a sound, you give your attention to the person or the sound. *Paul, are you listening?... Listen carefully to what he says... They listen to some music or read until I put them to bed.* 2 VB WITH 'for' If you **listen** for a sound, you keep alert, ready to hear it if it occurs. *She sat quite still, listening for her baby's cry.* 3 VB To **listen** to someone also means to believe them or accept their advice. *No one here will listen to you, not without proof... He refused to listen to reason.*

listen in. PHR VB If you **listen in** to a private conversation, you secretly listen to it.

listener /lɪsəⁿnə/, **listeners.** COUNT N People who listen to the radio are often referred to as **listeners.**

listless /lɪstlɪ³s/. ADJ If you are **listless,** you have no energy or enthusiasm. *She became listless and bored.*

lit /lɪt/. **Lit** is a past tense and past participle of **light.**

liter /li:tə/. See **litre.**

literacy /lɪtəⁿrəsi¹/. UNCOUNT N **Literacy** is the ability to read and write. *Mass literacy was only possible after the invention of printing.*

literal /lɪtəⁿrəl/. 1 ADJ The **literal** meaning of a word is its most basic meaning. *She was older than I was, and not only in the literal sense.* 2 ATTRIB ADJ A **literal** translation is one in which you translate each word separately, rather than expressing the meaning in a more natural way. *...a literal translation from the German.* 3 ADJ If you say that something is the **literal** truth, you are emphasizing that it is true.

literally /lɪtəⁿrəli¹/. 1 ADV You use **literally** to emphasize that what you are saying really is true, even though it seems surprising or exaggerated. *I have literally begged my son for help.* 2 ADV You also use **literally** to indicate that a word or expression is being used in its most basic sense. *They are people who have literally and spiritually left home.* 3 ADV If you translate a word or expression **literally,** you give its most basic meaning. *...a wati-pulka (literally 'big man').*

literary /lɪtəⁿrəri¹/. 1 ATTRIB ADJ **Literary** means connected with literature. *The text has some literary merit... ...literary critics.* 2 ADJ **Literary** words are rather unusual ones which are used to create a special effect in a poem, speech, or novel.

literate /lɪtəⁿrə¹t/. 1 ADJ Someone who is **literate** is able to read and write. *Only half the children in this class are literate.* 2 ADJ Someone who is highly **literate** is well educated and intelligent. *...the children of highly literate parents.*

literature /lɪtəⁿrətʃə/. 1 UNCOUNT N Novels, plays, and poetry are referred to as **literature.** *...a degree in English Literature.* 2 UNCOUNT N **Literature** is also printed information about something. *All major political parties print literature for hopeful candidates.*

litigation /lɪtɪgeɪʃəⁿn/. UNCOUNT N **Litigation** is the process of fighting or defending a case in a civil court of law; a formal use. *It was not unusual for the bank to be involved in litigation over failed companies.*

litre /li:tə/, **litres;** spelled **liter** in American English. 1 COUNT N A **litre** is a unit of volume for liquids and gases equal to a thousand cubic centimetres or approximately 1.76 pints. *...a litre of wine.* 2 COUNT N WITH SUPP You also use **litre** when talking about the capacity of a car engine. *...a 1.3 litre Vauxhall Astra.*

litter /lɪtə/, **litters, littering, littered.** 1 UNCOUNT N **Litter** is rubbish which is left lying around outside. *There were piles of litter in the streets.* 2 VB WITH OBJ If a number of things **litter** a place, they are scattered around in it. *Papers littered every surface... The floor was littered with ashtrays.* 3 COUNT N A **litter** is a group of animals born to the same mother at the same time. *It was the finest puppy in a litter of six.*

little /lɪtəⁿl/. For meanings 5 and 6, the comparative is **less** and the superlative is **least:** see the separate entries for these words. 1 ATTRIB ADJ **Little** things are small in size or short in length. *...a little table with a glass top... ...little groups of people... ...after he had walked for a little way... She lay awake a little while longer... ...a little chat.* 2 ADJ A **little** child is very young. *...two little girls... I often heard him do that when I was little.* 3 ATTRIB ADJ Your **little** sister or brother is younger than you are. 4 ATTRIB ADJ **Little** also means not important. *Don't bother me with little things like that... ...annoying little mishaps.* 5 QUANTIF OR DET You also use **little** to emphasize that there is only a small amount of something. *Little of the equipment was standardized... There is little to worry about... John and I had very little money left.* 6 ADV **Little** means not very often or to only a small extent. *Richardson interrupted very little... She seemed little changed.* 7 QUANTIF OR DET **A little** of something is a small amount of it. *The waiter poured a little of the wine into a glass... He spoke a little French.*

PHRASES ● **A little** or **a little bit** means to a small extent or degree. *He frowned a little... I felt a little uncomfortable... I thought he was a little bit afraid.* ● If something happens **little by little,** it happens gradually. *Then I learnt, little by little, the early history of her family.*

little finger, little fingers. COUNT N Your **little finger** is the smallest finger on your hand.

live, lives, living, lived. Live is pronounced /lɪv/ when it is a verb and /laɪv/ when it is an adjective or adverb. **Lives** is pronounced /lɪvz/ when it is a verb and /laɪvz/ when it is the plural of **life.** 1 VB WITH ADJUNCT If someone **lives** in a particular place, their home is there. *Where do you live?... I used to live in Grange Road.* 2 VB WITH ADJUNCT OR OBJ The way someone **lives** is the kind of life they have or the circumstances they are in. *We lived very simply... They are forced to live entirely artificial lives... We live in a technological society.* 3 VB To **live** means to be alive. *Women seem to live longer than men... She lost her will to live.* 4 ATTRIB ADJ **Live** animals or plants are alive, rather than being dead or artificial. *They grasp live snakes while dancing to bring rain.* 5 ADJ OR ADV A **live** television or radio programme is one in which an event is broadcast at the time that it happens. *...live pictures of a man walking on the moon... The concert will be broadcast live on Radio Three.* 6 ADJ OR ADV A **live** performance is one that is done in front of an audience. *...live theatre... I would like to perform live as much as possible.* 7 ADJ A **live** wire or piece of electrical equipment is directly connected to a source of electricity. 8 ADJ **Live** bullets, bombs, or missiles have not yet exploded or been fired. 9 PHRASE If you **live it up,** you have a very enjoyable and exciting time, for example by going to parties; an informal use. 10 **Lives** is the plural of **life.** 11 See also **living.**

live down. PHR VB If you cannot **live down** a mistake or failure, you cannot make people forget it. *If you were beaten by Jack, you'd never live it down.*

live in. PHR VB If someone **lives in,** they live in the place where they work or study. *The rest of the students tend to live in.*

live off. PHR VB If you **live off** a particular source of money, you get from it the money that you need. *They were living off welfare.*

live on. PHR VB 1 If you **live on** a particular amount of money, you have that amount of money to buy things. *I don't have enough to live on.* 2 If you **live on** a particular kind of food, it is the only kind you eat. *She lived on berries and wild herbs.* 3 If something **lives on,** it is remembered for a long time. *The Marilyn Monroe legend lives on in Hollywood.*

live up to. PHR VB If someone or something **lives up to** people's expectations, they are as good as they were expected to be. *She succeeded in living up to her extraordinary reputation.*

livelihood /laɪvlɪhʊd/, **livelihoods.** COUNT N OR UNCOUNT N Your **livelihood** is the job or the source of your income. *...their fear of losing their livelihood.*

lively /laɪvli¹/, **livelier, liveliest.** 1 ADJ **Lively** people are active, enthusiastic, and cheerful. *Four lively youngsters suddenly burst into the room.* 2 ADJ **Lively** also means interesting and exciting. *...a lively debate... ...a lively evening.* 3 ATTRIB ADJ You also use **lively** to describe a feeling which is strong and enthusiastic. *She took a lively interest in everything.*

liven /laɪvəⁿn/, **livens, livening, livened.**

liven up. PHR VB 1 If a place or event **livens up** or if you **liven it up,** it becomes more interesting and exciting. *There are lots of new shops and things. The place is really livening up.* 2 If people **liven up** or if something **livens** them **up,** they become more cheerful and energetic. *At least the incident livened her up.*

liver /lɪvə/, **livers.** 1 COUNT N Your **liver** is a large organ in your body which cleans your blood. 2 UNCOUNT N **Liver** is the liver of some animals, which is cooked and eaten.

livestock /laɪvstɒk/. UNCOUNT N OR PLURAL N Animals kept on a farm are referred to as **livestock.** *They encourage farmers to keep more livestock.*

livid /lɪvɪd/. 1 ADJ Someone who is **livid** is extremely angry; an informal use. *He said, 'No, you won't.' I was absolutely livid.* 2 ADJ Something that is **livid** is an unpleasant dark purple or greyish blue colour; a literary use. *...livid bruises.*

living /lɪvɪŋ/. 1 ADJ A **living** person or animal is alive. *I have no living relatives.* 2 SING N The work that you do for a **living** is the work that you do to earn the money that you need. *I never expected to earn my living as an artist... He made a modest living by painting.* 3 UNCOUNT N WITH SUPP You use **living** when talking about the quality of people's daily lives. *The quality of urban living has been damaged by excessive noise levels... ...the demand for better living standards.* 4 ATTRIB ADJ You also use **living** when talking about places where people relax when they are not working. *...the living quarters of the hotel staff... We are trying to improve living conditions at sea.* 5 **within living memory:** see **memory.** See also **cost of living, standard of living.**

living-room, living-rooms. COUNT N The **living-room** in a house is the room where people sit and relax.

lizard /lɪzəd/, **lizards.** COUNT N A **lizard** is a reptile with short legs and a long tail.

-'ll. SUFFIX **-'ll** is a short form of 'will' or 'shall' used in spoken English and informal written English. *He'll come back... That'll be all right.*

load /ləʊd/, **loads, loading, loaded.** 1 VB WITH OBJ If you **load** a vehicle or container or **load** things into it, you put things into it. *...when they came to load the van with their things... We started loading the pheasants into the sacks.* 2 COUNT N A **load** is something which is being carried. *We took up our heavy load and trudged back... Its load of minerals was dumped at sea.* 3 VB WITH OBJ When someone **loads** a gun, they put a bullet in it. 4 VB WITH OBJ When someone **loads** a camera, computer, or tape recorder or **loads** film or tape into it, they put film or tape into it. 5 QUANTIF **Loads** of something or a **load** of something means a lot of it; an informal use. *We talked about loads of things.*

loaded /ləʊdɪd/. 1 ADJ If something is **loaded** with things, it has a large number of them in it or on it. *...a truck loaded with bricks... ...waitresses with loaded trays.* 2 PRED ADJ If you say that someone is **loaded,** you mean that they have a lot of money; an informal use. 3 ADJ A **loaded** remark or question has more significance, meaning, or purpose than it appears to have.

loaf /ləʊf/, **loaves** /ləʊvz/. COUNT N A **loaf** of bread is bread in a shape that can be cut into slices.

loan /ləʊn/, **loans, loaning, loaned.** 1 COUNT N A **loan** is a sum of money that you borrow. *They found it impossible to get a bank loan.* 2 SING N If someone gives you a **loan** of something, you borrow it from them. *He asked for the loan of twelve dozen glasses.* 3 PHRASE If a book or picture is **on loan,** it has been borrowed. *Most of his books are on loan from the library.* 4 VB WITH OBJ AND PREP 'to', OR VB WITH OBJ AND OBJ If you **loan** something to someone, you lend it to them. *He never loaned his car to anybody... I'll loan you fifty dollars.*

loath /ləʊθ/; also spelled **loth.** PRED ADJ WITH TO-INF If you are **loath** to do something, you are unwilling to do it. *Governments have been loath to impose any sanctions.*

loathe /ləʊð/, **loathes, loathing, loathed.** VB WITH OBJ If you **loathe** something or someone, you dislike them very much. *I particularly loathed team games at school.*

loathing /ləʊðɪŋ/. UNCOUNT N **Loathing** is a feeling of great dislike. *He remembered his school days with loathing.*

loathsome /ləʊðsəm/. ADJ **Loathsome** means very unpleasant. *I hate the loathsome way you use other people.*

loaves /ləʊvz/. **Loaves** is the plural of **loaf.**

lob /lɒb/, **lobs, lobbing, lobbed.** 1 VB WITH OBJ If you **lob** something, you throw it high in the air. *She wrapped a piece of paper round a stone and lobbed it into the next garden.* 2 VB WITH OR WITHOUT OBJ If you **lob** the ball in tennis, you hit it high into the air so that it lands behind your opponent. *Miss Evert reached to lob a return of Miss Wade's.* Also COUNT N *...high lobs to the backhand corner.*

lobby /lɒbi¹/, **lobbies, lobbying, lobbied.** 1 COUNT N The **lobby** of a building is the main entrance area with corridors and staircases leading off it. *I rushed into the hotel lobby.* 2 COLL N WITH SUPP A **lobby** is also a group of people who try to persuade the government that something should be done. *...the anti-nuclear lobby.* 3 VB WITH OBJ OR ADJUNCT If you **lobby** a member of a government, you try to persuade them that a particular thing should be done. *He lobbied the Home Secretary and other members of parliament... ...lobbying for stricter controls on guns.*

lobe /ləʊb/, **lobes.** COUNT N The **lobe** of your ear is the soft part at the bottom.

lobster /lɒbstə/, **lobsters.** COUNT N A **lobster** is a sea creature with a hard shell, two large claws, and eight legs.

local /ləʊkəl/, **locals. 1** ATTRIB ADJ A **local** council is responsible for the government of a part of a country. *...local government.* ♦ **locally** ADV *Should housing policy be decided nationally or locally?* **2** ADJ **Local** means existing in or belonging to the area where you live or work. *...a picture in the local paper... Telephone your local police station.* ♦ **locally** ADV *Everything we used was bought locally.* **3** COUNT N You can refer to the people who live in a particular district as the **locals;** an informal use. *The locals view these road improvements with alarm.* **4** ADJ A **local** anaesthetic affects only one part of your body; a technical use.

locality /ləʊkælɪti/, **localities.** COUNT N A particular **locality** is an area of a country or city. *...the anxiety of people living in the same locality.*

localized /ləʊkəlaɪzd/; also spelled **localised.** ADJ Something that is **localized** exists or occurs only in one place. *...localized problems of erosion... ...a localized pain in the back of her head.*

locate /ləʊkeɪt/, **locates, locating, located. 1** VB WITH OBJ If you **locate** something or someone, you find them; a formal use. *If you do locate him, call me.* **2** PASSIVE VB WITH ADJUNCT If something **is located** in a particular place, it is in that place; a formal use. *The house was located in the heart of the city.*

location /ləʊkeɪʃən/, **locations. 1** COUNT N WITH SUPP A **location** is a place, especially the place where something happens or is situated. *Election officials ran out of ballot papers at six locations... The new job involves a new employer and a new location... ...the size and location of your office.* **2** PHRASE If a film is made **on location,** it is made away from a studio.

loch /lɒx/, **lochs.** COUNT N A **loch** is a large area of water in Scotland. *...Loch Lomond.*

lock /lɒk/, **locks, locking, locked. 1** VB WITH OBJ When you **lock** something, you fasten it by means of a key. *Lock the door after you leave.* ♦ **locked** ADJ *...the locked cupboard.* **2** VB WITH OBJ If you **lock** something in a cupboard, room, or drawer, you put it inside and lock the door or drawer. *He had locked all his papers in the safe... He locked them away in a drawer.* **3** ERG VB You say that something **locks** or **is locked** in a position when it moves into that position and is held firmly there. *Smoothly the rod locked into place.* **4** PASSIVE VB WITH ADJUNCT If people **are locked** in a fight or argument, they cannot stop fighting or arguing. *Rebel groups and government forces are locked in a fierce battle for control of the country.* **5** COUNT N The **lock** on something such as a door is the part which fastens it when you turn a key in it. *The key rattling in the lock startled me.* ● If something is **under lock and key,** it is in a locked room or container. *She would keep any sensitive documents under lock and key.* **6** COUNT N A **lock** on a canal is a section between barriers where the water level can be raised or lowered so that boats can move to a higher or lower section of the canal. **7** COUNT N A **lock** of hair is a small bunch of hairs; a literary use. *A lock of hair had fallen down over her eyes... He shook his black locks.*

lock up. PHR VB **1** If someone is **locked up,** they are put in prison or in a special psychiatric hospital. *The idea of being locked up in jail filled her with horror.* **2** When you **lock up,** you make sure that all the doors and windows of a building are properly closed or locked.

locker /lɒkə/, **lockers.** COUNT N A **locker** is a small cupboard for someone's personal belongings, for example in a changing room or railway station.

locket /lɒkɪt/, **lockets.** COUNT N A **locket** is a piece of jewellery containing something such as a picture which a woman wears on a chain round her neck.

locomotive /ləʊkəməʊtɪv/, **locomotives.** COUNT N A **locomotive** is a railway engine; a formal use.

locust /ləʊkəst/, **locusts.** COUNT N **Locusts** are insects that live in hot countries. They fly in large groups and eat crops.

lodge /lɒdʒ/, **lodges, lodging, lodged. 1** COUNT N A **lodge** is a small house at the entrance to the grounds of a large house. **2** COUNT N A **lodge** is also a hut where people stay on holiday. *They went to a shooting lodge in Scotland for the weekend.* **3** VB WITH ADJUNCT If you **lodge** in someone else's house for a period of time, you live there, usually paying rent. *He had arranged for me to lodge with his daughter.* **4** ERG VB WITH ADJUNCT If something **lodges** somewhere or **is lodged** there, it becomes stuck there. *The bullet had lodged a quarter of an inch from his spine... I had somehow got the bone lodged in my throat.* **5** VB WITH OBJ If you **lodge** a complaint, you formally make it; a formal use. *...the charges that had been lodged against them.*

lodger /lɒdʒə/, **lodgers.** COUNT N A **lodger** is a person who pays money to live in part of someone else's house. *She allowed her student lodgers a lot of freedom.*

lodging /lɒdʒɪŋ/, **lodgings. 1** UNCOUNT N If you are provided with **lodging,** you are provided with a place to stay for a period of time. *They were offered free lodging in first-class hotels.* **2** PLURAL N If you live in **lodgings,** you live in part of someone's house and pay them for this. *They have to find lodgings in the village.*

loft /lɒft/, **lofts.** COUNT N A **loft** is the space inside the roof of a house, often used for storing things.

lofty /lɒfti/. **1** ADJ Something that is **lofty** is very high; a literary use. *We explored lofty corridors.* **2** ADJ A **lofty** idea or aim is noble, important, and admirable; a literary use. *...trying to maintain a lofty principle... Such lofty goals justify any means.* **3** ADJ Someone who behaves in a **lofty** way behaves in a proud and rather unpleasant way; a formal use. *She hated his lofty manner.*

log /lɒg/, **logs, logging, logged. 1** COUNT N A **log** is a piece of a thick branch or of the trunk of a tree. *He threw another log on the fire.* **2** COUNT N A **log** is also an official written record of what happens each day, for example on board a ship. *The Controller entered this in his log.* **3** VB WITH OBJ If you **log** an event or fact, you record it officially in writing. *The death must be logged.*

log in or **log into.** PHR VB When someone **logs into** a computer system or **logs in,** they gain access to the system, usually by giving a special word or name that it will accept.

log on. PHR VB **Log on** means the same as log in.

log out. PHR VB When someone who is using a computer system **logs out,** they finish using the system.

loggerheads /lɒgəhedz/. PHRASE If people are **at loggerheads,** they disagree strongly with each other.

logic /lɒdʒɪk/. **1** UNCOUNT N **Logic** is a way of reasoning that involves a series of statements, each of which must be true if the statement before it is true. **2** UNCOUNT N WITH SUPP Different kinds of **logic** are different ways of thinking and reasoning. *Economic logic dictated the policy of centralization.*

logical /lɒdʒɪkəl/. **1** ADJ In a **logical** argument or analysis, each statement is true if the statement before it is true. *I made little attempt at logical argument.* ♦ **logically** ADV *Everything has to be logically analysed.* **2** ADJ A **logical** conclusion or result is the only one that can reasonably result. *There is only one logical conclusion... To him violence was a logical inevitability.* ♦ **logically** ADV *It follows logically that one of them is lying.* **3** ADJ A **logical** course of action seems reasonable or sensible in the circumstances. *Wouldn't it have been more logical for them to make the arrest downstairs?* ♦ **logically** SENTENCE ADV *Therefore, logically, he had to go.*

logistic /lədʒɪstɪk/, **logistics. 1** PLURAL N OR UNCOUNT N You can refer to the skilful organization of something complicated as the **logistics** of it; a formal use. *...the tiresome logistics of modern broadcasting.* **2** ATTRIB ADJ **Logistic** or **logistical** means relating to the organization of something complicated; a formal use. *...faced with daunting logistic and administrative problems.*

logo /ləʊgəʊ/, **logos.** COUNT N The **logo** of a company or organization is the special design that it puts on all its products and possessions. *You will be welcome at all hotels displaying our logo.*

loincloth /lɔɪnklɒθ/, **loincloths.** COUNT N A **loincloth** is a piece of cloth sometimes worn by men in hot countries to cover their sexual organs.

loins /lɔɪnz/. PLURAL N Someone's **loins** are the front part of their body between their waist and thighs, especially their sexual organs; a literary use.

loiter /lɔɪtə/, **loiters, loitering, loitered.** VB If you **loiter** somewhere, you remain there idly, without any real purpose. *Remember not to loiter on the way.*

loll /lɒl/, **lolls, lolling, lolled. 1** VB WITH ADJUNCT If you **loll** somewhere or **loll** about, you sit or lie in a very relaxed position. *The students lolled in the grass.* **2** VB If your head or tongue **lolls,** it hangs loosely. *...feeling so sleepy, head lolling, eyes closing... Her tongue lolled out, her eyes were rolled back.*

lollipop /lɒlipɒp/, **lollipops.** COUNT N A **lollipop** is a sweet on the end of a stick. *She was sitting on the front step sucking a lollipop.*

lolly /lɒli/, **lollies;** an informal word. **1** COUNT N A **lolly** is a piece of flavoured ice or ice cream on a stick. **2** COUNT N A **lolly** is also a lollipop.

lone /ləʊn/. ATTRIB ADJ A **lone** person or thing is alone or is the only one in a particular place; a literary use. *They saw ahead a lone figure walking towards them.*

lonely /ləʊnli/, **lonelier, loneliest. 1** ADJ Someone who is **lonely** is unhappy because they are alone. *...lonely widows.* ♦ **loneliness** UNCOUNT N *They suffer from isolation, poverty and loneliness.* **2** ADJ A **lonely** situation or period of time is one in which you feel alone and unhappy. *...that lonely night in Dakota.* **3** ADJ A **lonely** place is one where very few people come. *...lonely country roads.*

loner /ləʊnə/, **loners.** COUNT N A **loner** is a person who likes being alone.

lonesome /ləʊnsəm/. ADJ **Lonesome** means the same as lonely; an informal American use. *I get lonesome sometimes... ...a lonesome valley.*

long /lɒŋ/, **longer** /lɒŋgə/, **longest** /lɒŋgɪst/; **longs, longing, longed. 1** ADV **Long** means a great amount of time or for a great amount of time. *I haven't known her long... Sorry it took so long... Our oil won't last much longer... I had guessed long ago.* Also ADV OR ADJ AFTER N used in questions and statements about duration. *'How long have you been married?'—'Five years.'... His speeches are never less than two hours long.* **2** ADJ A **long** event or period of time lasts or takes a great amount of time. *There was a long pause... They are demanding longer holidays.* **3** ADJ Something that is **long** measures a great distance from one end to the other. *She had long dark hair... ...a long line of cars... ...long tables... We drove a long way the next day.* used in questions and statements about physical length. *How long is that side?... ...an area 3,000 feet long and 900 feet wide.* **4** ADJ A **long** book or other piece of writing contains a lot of words. *...an enormously long novel.* **5** VB WITH 'for' OR TO-INF If you **long** for something, you want it very much. *They longed for green trees and open spaces... They're longing to see you.* **6** See also **longing.**

PHRASES ● **For long** means for a great amount of time. *Men have been indoctrinated for too long... It didn't stay there for long.* ● You use **long** with 'all' and 'whole' to emphasize that something happens for the whole of a particular time. *We row all day long... They play the whole day long.* ● Something that **no longer** happens used to happen in the past but does not happen now. *We can no longer afford to live there... I couldn't stand it any longer.* ● **Before long** means soon. *They're bound to catch him before long.* ● If one thing is true **as long as** or **so long as** another thing is true, it is true only if the other thing is true. *We were all right as long as we kept our heads down.* ● You can say **'So long'** to say goodbye; an informal use.

long-distance. ATTRIB ADJ **Long-distance** travel or communication involves places that are far apart. *...long-distance phone calls.*

longevity /lɒndʒevɪti/. UNCOUNT N **Longevity** is long life; a formal use. *...improved health care resulting in increased longevity.*

longing /lɒŋɪŋ/, **longings.** COUNT N OR UNCOUNT N A **longing** is a rather sad feeling of wanting something very much. *People have a longing for normality... He gazed with longing and apprehension into the future.*

longingly /lɒŋɪŋli/. ADV If you think **longingly** about something, you think about it with a feeling of desire. *I began to think longingly of bed.*

longitude /lɒŋɪtjuːd/, **longitudes.** COUNT N OR UNCOUNT N The **longitude** of a place is its distance to the west or east of a line passing through Greenwich in England: compare **latitude.**

long jump. SING N The **long jump** is an athletics contest which involves jumping as far as you can from a marker which you run up to.

long-lasting. ADJ Something that is **long-lasting** lasts for a long time. *The failure of the dam is unlikely to have long-lasting environmental consequences.*

long-life. ATTRIB ADJ **Long-life** milk, fruit juice, and batteries are treated or made so that they last longer than ordinary kinds.

long-lost. ATTRIB ADJ **Long-lost** is used of someone or something that you have not seen for a long time. *She greeted me like a long-lost daughter.*

long-range. 1 ATTRIB ADJ A **long-range** piece of military equipment operates over long distances. *...a modern long-range strategic missile... ...long-range bombers.* **2** ATTRIB ADJ A **long-range** plan or prediction relates to a period extending a long time into the future. *...the necessity for long-range planning.*

long-sighted. ADJ If you are **long-sighted,** you cannot see things near you clearly, but you can see things a long way away.

long-standing. ADJ A **long-standing** situation has existed for a long time. *...a long-standing feud.*

long-suffering. ADJ Someone who is **long-suffering** patiently bears continual trouble or bad treatment. *...his noble, long-suffering wife.*

long-term. 1 ADJ **Long-term** things are intended to exist for a long time in the future. *...hopes for a long-term solution to the problem... I hesitated before making a long-term commitment.* 2 SING N When you talk about what happens in the **long term,** you are talking about what happens over a long period of time. *The results, in the long term, were successful.*

long-winded. ADJ If something that has been written or said is **long-winded,** it is boring because it is longer than necessary. *...long-winded prayers.*

loo /lu:/, **loos.** SING N OR COUNT N People sometimes refer to a toilet as the **loo;** an informal use.

look /lʊk/, **looks, looking, looked.** 1 VB If you **look** in a particular direction, you turn your eyes in that direction in order to see what is there. *She turned to look out of the window... They looked at each other... He blushed and looked away.* Also SING N *Take a good look... Did you have a look at the shop?* 2 VB WITH 'at' To **look** at something also means to read, examine, or consider it. *'I'd like to look at his medical history,' Percival said... Let's look at the implications of these changes.* Also SING N *Tony, I've had a look at that book you wrote.* 3 VB WITH 'at' If you **look** at a situation from a particular point of view, you judge it from that point of view. *If you're a Democrat, you look at things one way, and if you're a Republican you look at them very differently.* 4 VB WITH COMPLEMENT, 'as if', OR 'like' You use **look** to say how something seems to you. *The plan looks impressive enough on paper... Looks as if we're going to be late... It looks like a good book.* 5 COUNT N If you give someone a particular kind of **look,** you look at them in a way that shows what you are thinking. *Don't give me such severe looks. What have I done?* 6 VB WITH COMPLEMENT, 'as if', OR 'like' You use **look** when describing the appearance of someone or something. For example, if something **looks** nice, its appearance is nice. *You look very pale... He looked as if he hadn't slept very much... 'What does he look like?'—'Pale, thin, dark-haired.'* 7 SING N WITH SUPP If someone or something has a particular **look,** they have that appearance or expression. *He didn't have the look of a man who was thinking... There is a nervous look in their eyes.* 8 PLURAL N You refer to someone's **looks** when you are referring to how beautiful or handsome they are. *She had lost her looks... I didn't marry him for his looks.* 9 VB WITH ADJUNCT If a window, room, or building **looks** out onto something, it has a view of it. *The kitchen window looks out onto a yard.* 10 CONVENTION You say **'look'** or **'look here'** when you want someone to pay attention to what you are saying. *Look, Mrs Kintner, you've got it wrong.* 11 VB WITH 'at' You also use **look** with a word such as 'who' or 'what' or with 'at' to draw attention to something, for example when you are angry or surprised. *Now look what you've done... Goodness, look at the time. I promised I'd be home at six.*

look after. PHR VB 1 If you **look after** someone or something, you take care of them. *Your husband ought to be looking after the baby.* 2 If you **look after** something, you are responsible for it. *The duty of the local authority is to look after the interests of local people.*

look back. PHR VB If you **look back,** you think about things that happened in the past. *People can often look back and reflect on happy childhood memories.*

look down on. PHR VB If you **look down on** someone, you think that they are inferior. *Farm labourers used to be looked down on.*

look for. PHR VB If you **look for** someone or something, you try to find them. *I've been looking for you... She looked around for some paper... ...people looking for work.*

look forward to. PHR VB If you **are looking forward to** something, you want it to happen. *I'm quite looking forward to it... I look forward to seeing you.*

look into. PHR VB If you **look into** something, you find out about it. *A working party was set up to look into the problem.*

look on PHR VB 1 If you **look on** while something happens, you watch it. *His parents looked on with a triumphant smile.* 2 If you **look on** something as a particular thing, you think of it as that thing. *She looked on us as idiots.*

look out. PHR VB You say **'look out'** to warn someone of danger. *'Look out,' I said. 'There's something coming.'* • See also **lookout.**

look out for. PHR VB If you **look out for** something, you try to make sure that you notice it. *It's a film we shall look out for in the next couple of months.*

look round. PHR VB If you **look round** a place, you walk round it and look at the different parts of it. *Shall we look round the Cathedral this afternoon?*

look through. PHR VB If you **look through** something, you examine it to find what you are looking for. *He looked through the clothing on the bed.*

look to. PHR VB 1 If you **look to** someone for something such as help or advice, you hope that they will provide it. *Many people in the community will be looking to us for leadership.* 2 If you **look to** the future, you think about it. *Some New Englanders look to the future with a certain anxiety.*

look up. PHR VB 1 If you **look up** information, you find it out by looking in a book. *He looked up the meaning of 'legislation' in the dictionary.* 2 If you **look** someone **up,** you visit them after you have not seen them for a long time; an informal use. *It was such a fine day he thought he'd look me up.* 3 If a situation **is looking up,** it is improving; an informal use. *That summer, things began looking up.*

look upon. PHR VB If you **look upon** something as a particular thing, you think of it as that thing. *Houses are looked upon as investments.*

look up to. PHR VB If you **look up to** someone, you respect and admire them. *His younger brothers look up to him.*

look-in. SING N If you do not get a **look-in,** you do not get the chance to do something because too many other people are doing it; an informal use. *James talks so much that all the others barely get a look-in.*

lookout /lʊkaʊt/, **lookouts.** 1 COUNT N A **lookout** is a place from which you can see clearly in all directions. *...a lookout platform.* 2 COUNT N A **lookout** is also someone who is watching for danger. *Two of the burglars were tipped off by a lookout and escaped.* 3 PHRASE If you are **on the lookout** for something, you are watching out for it. *I'm on the lookout for a second-hand car.*

loom /lu:m/, **looms, looming, loomed.** 1 VB If something **looms** or **looms** up, it appears as a tall, unclear, and often frightening shape. *As you get closer they loom above you like icebergs.* 2 VB If a difficult event or situation **looms** or **looms** up, it will soon happen. *The next general election loomed.* 3 COUNT N A **loom** is a machine that is used for weaving thread into cloth.

loop /lu:p/, **loops, looping, looped.** 1 COUNT N A **loop** is a curved or circular shape in something long, such as a piece of string. *...loops of blue and pink ribbon.* 2 VB WITH OBJ If you **loop** a rope or string around an object, you tie a length of it in a loop around the object. *The king had pearls looped round his neck.* 3 VB If something **loops,** it goes in a circular direction, making the shape of a loop. *Birds loop and weave through the tall trees.*

loophole /lu:phəʊl/, **loopholes.** COUNT N A **loophole** in the law is a small mistake or omission which allows you to avoid doing something that the law intends you to do. *A number of obvious loopholes exist for tax avoidance.*

loose /lu:s/, **looser, loosest.** 1 ADJ Something that is **loose** is not firmly held or fixed in place. *The doorknob is loose and rattles... ...loose strands of wire... ...a few loose sheets of paper.* ♦ **loosely** ADV *Willie held the phone loosely.* 2 ADJ **Loose** clothes are rather large and do not fit closely. *...a loose cotton shirt.* ♦ **loosely** ADV *His black garments hung loosely from his powerful shoulders.* 3 ADJ When a woman's hair is **loose,** it is hanging freely rather than being tied back. *She shook her hair loose.* 4 PRED ADJ If people cut **loose** or are set **loose,** they become free from the influence or authority of other people. *The younger generation have tended to cut loose from the influence of class background.* 5 ADJ A **loose** organization or administration is not strictly controlled. *A loose grouping of 'radicals' was formed which met once a week... The country has a loose federal structure.*

PHRASES • If a dangerous person is **on the loose,** they are free. *A bandit leader was on the loose in the hills.* • If you are **at a loose end,** you are bored.

loosen /lu:sən/, **loosens, loosening, loosened.** 1 ERG VB If something **loosens,** or **is loosened,** it becomes undone or less tightly held in place. *The tyre on one of his wheels had loosened... The wind had loosened some leaves.* 2 VB WITH OBJ If you **loosen** something that is tied or fastened, you undo it slightly. *He took off his jacket and loosened his tie.*

loosen up. PHR VB If you **loosen up** or if something **loosens** you **up,** you become calmer and less worried; an informal use. *Her second drink loosened her up... As the day wore on he loosened up and became more chatty.*

loot /lu:t/, **loots, looting, looted.** 1 VB WITH OR WITHOUT OBJ When people **loot** shops or houses, they steal things from them during a battle or a riot. *Shops were looted and wrecked in London.* ♦ **looting** UNCOUNT N *There was widespread looting of stores and shops.* 2 UNCOUNT N **Loot** is stolen money or goods; an informal use. *He told his wife where the loot was hidden.*

lop /lɒp/, **lops, lopping, lopped.** VB WITH OBJ If you **lop** a tree, you cut off some of its branches.

lop off. PHR VB If you **lop** something **off,** you cut it off with a quick, strong stroke. *...a guillotine that probably lopped off many a head.*

lope /ləʊp/, **lopes, loping, loped.** VB WITH ADJUNCT When people or animals **lope,** they run in a relaxed way with long strides.

lopsided /lɒpsaɪdɪ^{2}d/. ADJ Something that is **lopsided** is uneven because its two sides are different from each other. *...a lopsided smile.*

lord /lɔ:d/, **lords.** 1 TITLE In Britain, **Lord** is the title used in front of the name of peers, judges, bishops, and officials of very high rank. *...Lord Harewood... ...the Lord Mayor of London... ...the Lord Chief Justice.* 2 COUNT N A **lord** is a man with a high rank in the British nobility. *...lords and ladies.* 3 PROPER N In the Christian church, people refer to God and to Jesus Christ as **Lord** or **The Lord.**

lore /lɔ:/. UNCOUNT N WITH SUPP The **lore** of a particular country or culture is the traditional stories and history of it. *...Jewish mystical lore.* • See also **folklore.**

lorry /lɒri^1/, **lorries.** COUNT N A **lorry** is a large vehicle used to transport goods by road; a British use.

lose /lu:z/, **loses, losing, lost** /lɒst/. 1 VB WITH OBJ If you **lose** something, you cannot find it. *You haven't lost the ticket, have you?... She's always losing her cigarette lighter... They lost their way in the woods.* 2 VB WITH OBJ You also say you **lose** something when you no longer have it, although you would like to have it. *I might lose my job... ...a complete list of all the goods lost in the fire... He lost the use of his legs.* 3 VB WITH OBJ If you **lose** a quality or characteristic, you have less of it than before. *He has lost a lot of weight... Brody was beginning to lose interest.* 4 VB WITH OBJ If you **lose** a relative or friend, they die. *I lost my father when I was nine.* 5 VB WITH OBJ If you **lose** an opportunity or **lose** time, you waste it. *Bill lost no time in telling everyone about his idea... He will lose his chances of promotion.* 6 VB WITH OBJ If a business **loses** money, it earns less than it spends. 7 VB WITH OBJ If a clock or watch **loses** time, it shows a time that is earlier than the real time. 8 VB WITH OR WITHOUT OBJ If you **lose** a competition or argument, someone does better than you and defeats you. *They expected to lose the election.* ♦ **losing** ATTRIB ADJ *He'd never played on a losing side.* 9 See also **lost.**

PHRASES • If you **have** something **to lose,** you may suffer if you do something unsuccessfully. *The price was too high and he had too much to lose... They had absolutely nothing to lose.* • If you **lose sight of** something, you can no longer see it. • to **lose face:** see **face.** • to **lose** your **head:** see **head.** • to **lose** your **temper:** see **temper.** • to **lose touch:** see **touch.**

lose out. PHR VB If you **lose out,** you suffer a loss or disadvantage. *They did not lose out in the struggle to keep up with inflation.*

loser /lu:zə/, **losers.** COUNT N The **loser** of a game, contest, or struggle is the person who is defeated. • **A good loser** is someone who accepts the fact that they have lost a game or contest, and **a bad loser** is someone who hates losing and complains a lot about it.

loss /lɒs/, **losses.** 1 UNCOUNT N **Loss** is the fact of no longer having something or of having less of it than before. *...temporary loss of vision... ...the loss of liberty... ...heat loss.* 2 UNCOUNT N OR COUNT N **Loss** of life occurs when people die. *The loss of life was appalling... Artillery fire caused heavy losses.* 3 UNCOUNT N WITH SUPP The **loss** of a relative or friend is their death. *...the loss of my daughter and husband.* 4 COUNT N OR UNCOUNT N If a business makes a **loss,** it earns less than it spends. *The company announced a huge loss for the first half of the year.*

PHRASES • If you are **at a loss,** you do not know what to do. *I was at a complete loss as to how I could lay my hands on the money.* • If you **cut** your **losses,** you stop doing what you were doing and accept defeat, in order to stop a bad situation becoming worse. *You ought to cut your losses and start again.* • If someone or something is a **dead loss,** they are completely useless or unsuccessful; an informal use.

lost /lɒst/. 1 **Lost** is the past tense and past participle of **lose.** 2 ADJ If you are **lost,** you do not know where you are or you are unable to find your way. *There was that time when we got lost in Dennington.* 3 ADJ If something is **lost,** you cannot find it. *Shopping lists on old envelopes tend to get lost.* 4 PRED ADJ WITH 'without' If you say that you would be **lost** without someone or something, you mean that you would be very unhappy without them. *I am lost without him.* 5 PRED ADJ WITH 'on' If advice or a comment is **lost** on someone, they do not understand it, or they ignore it. *The lesson was not lost on the committee.* 6 PHRASE If you tell someone to **get lost,** you tell them rudely to go away; an informal use.

lost property. UNCOUNT N **Lost property** consists of things that people have lost in a public place such as a railway station. *...a lost property office.*

lot /lɒt/, **lots.** 1 QUANTIF A **lot** of something or **lots** of it is a large amount of it. *We owed a lot of money... This is a subject that worries a lot of people... I feel that we have a lot to offer... ...a big house with lots of windows.* 2 SING N You can use the **lot** to refer to the whole of an amount; an informal use. *Wilks bet his last ten pounds and lost the lot.* 3 SING N WITH SUPP You can refer to a group of people as a particular **lot;** an informal use. *They were a rather arrogant boring lot.* 4 COUNT N You can refer to a set or group of things as a particular **lot.** *...two sets of cards, one lot written in blue, the other in red... I get two lots of everything.* 5 COUNT N A **lot** in an auction is one of the objects that is being sold. *Lot No 359 was a folder of 11 original sketches.* 6 See also **parking lot.**

PHRASES ● **A lot** means very much or very often. *The man in the photograph looked a lot like Mr Williams... The weather's a lot warmer there... He laughs a lot.* ● If people **draw lots** or **cast lots** to decide who will do something, each of them takes a piece of paper from a container. The person who takes the piece of paper that is different from the others is chosen.

loth /ləʊθ/. See **loath.**

lotion /ləʊʃə^{0}n/, **lotions.** MASS N A **lotion** is a liquid that you use on your skin or hair. *...a bottle of suntan lotion.*

lottery /lɒtə^{r}ri^{1}/, **lotteries.** 1 COUNT N A **lottery** is a type of gambling game in which people buy numbered tickets. Several numbers are then chosen, and the people who have those numbers on their tickets win a prize. *...a lottery ticket.* 2 SING N If you describe a contest as a **lottery,** you mean that the result depends entirely on luck or chance; used showing disapproval.

loud /laʊd/, **louder, loudest.** 1 ADJ OR ADV You say that a noise is **loud** when the level of sound is very high. *His voice was loud and savage... There was a loud explosion... He spoke louder.* ♦ **loudly** ADV *The audience laughed loudly.* 2 ADJ If someone is **loud** in their support or condemnation of something, they express their opinion forcefully. *Northcliffe's newspapers were loud in their condemnation of British sentimentality.* ♦ **loudly** ADV *Most people loudly allege that all this is just another excuse.* 3 ADJ A piece of clothing that is **loud** has very bright colours or a striking pattern; used showing disapproval. *...young men in loud shirts and jackets.* 4 PHRASE If you say something **out loud,** you say it, rather than just thinking it. *She was praying out loud... I laughed out loud at the thought.*

loud-mouthed /laʊdmaʊðd/. ADJ Someone who is **loud-mouthed** talks a lot in an unpleasant or offensive way. *...a loud-mouthed, hard-drinking actor.*

loudspeaker /laʊdspiːkə/, **loudspeakers.** COUNT N A **loudspeaker** is a device that makes your voice sound louder. *...an announcement over the loudspeaker.*

lounge /laʊnd^{0}ʒ/, **lounges, lounging, lounged.** 1 COUNT N A **lounge** is a room in a house or hotel where people sit and relax. 2 COUNT N A **lounge** at an airport is a large room where passengers wait. *...the arrivals lounge.* 3 COUNT N The **lounge** or **lounge bar** in a pub or hotel is a comfortably furnished bar; a British use. 4 VB If you **lounge** somewhere, you lie on something or lean against it lazily. *She lounged on the rug.*

lounge about or **lounge around.** PHR VB If you **lounge about** or **lounge around,** you spend your time in a relaxed and lazy way. *...people who were lounging about, apparently with nothing to do.*

louse /laʊs/, **lice** /laɪs/. COUNT N **Lice** are small insects that live on the bodies of people or animals.

lousy /laʊzi^{1}/; an informal word. 1 ADJ If you describe something as **lousy,** you mean that it is of very bad quality. *The hotels are lousy... ...a lousy hockey game.* 2 PRED ADJ If you feel **lousy,** you feel ill. *I feel really lousy tonight.*

lout /laʊt/, **louts.** COUNT N If you call a young man a **lout,** you mean that he behaves in an impolite or aggressive way. *...gangs of drunken louts.*

lovable /lʌvəbə^{0}l/. ADJ A **lovable** person is pleasant and easy to like. *...a mischievous but lovable child.*

love /lʌv/, **loves, loving, loved.** 1 VB WITH OBJ If you **love** someone, you feel romantically or sexually attracted to them, and they are very important to you. *I do not think I love him enough to marry him... 'I love you, Colin.'—'I love you too, Janet.'* 2 VB WITH OBJ You also say you **love** someone when you care for them very much. *...a little baby to love... They make us feel safe and secure, loved and wanted.* 3 VB WITH OBJ If you **love** something, you like it very much and feel that it is important. *They don't love their village in the way that their parents did... Sarah loves playing the flute.* 4 UNCOUNT N **Love** is a very strong feeling of affection or liking for someone or something. *Her love for him never wavered... You are not marrying for love... ...a man with a genuine love of literature.* 5 VB WITH OBJ OR TO-INF If you would **love** to do something, you very much want to do it. *I would love a photograph of Edith Evans... Posy said she'd love to stay.* 6 VOCATIVE Some people use **love** as an affectionate way of addressing someone; an informal use. *Thanks a lot, love.* 7 CONVENTION You can write **love** or **love from,** followed by your name, when you end an informal letter. *Hope you are all well at home. Love, Dan.* 8 In tennis, **love** is a score of zero. 9 See also **loving.**

PHRASES ● If you are **in love** with someone, you feel romantically or sexually attracted to them, and they are very important to you. *They are in love with each other and wish to marry.* ● If you **fall in love** with someone, you start to be in love with them. *I fell madly in love with Ellen the first time I saw her.* ● When two people **make love,** they have sex. ● If you have **a love-hate relationship** with someone or something, you have strong feelings of both love and hate towards them.

love affair, love affairs. COUNT N A **love affair** is a sexual relationship between two people who are not married to each other.

love life, love lives. COUNT N Someone's **love life** consists of their romantic and sexual relationships.

lovely /lʌvli^{1}/, **lovelier, loveliest.** 1 ADJ If you describe someone or something as **lovely,** you mean that it is very beautiful or that you like it very much. *'Doesn't she look lovely, Albert?' she whispered... To me Hong Kong was one of the loveliest places in the world... Lovely day, isn't it?... It was lovely to hear from you again.* ♦ **loveliness** UNCOUNT N *...a girl of film-star loveliness.* 2 ADJ You can describe someone as **lovely** when they are friendly, kind, and generous. *We've got lovely neighbours... She's the sweetest, loveliest person.*

love-making. UNCOUNT N **Love-making** refers to sexual activities that take place between two people.

lover /lʌvə/, **lovers.** 1 COUNT N Your **lover** is someone who you are having a sexual relationship with but are not married to. *Jenny and I were lovers.* 2 COUNT N You can refer to people as **lovers** when they are in love with each other; an old-fashioned use. *...young lovers.* 3 COUNT N WITH SUPP You can also use **lover** to refer to someone who enjoys a particular activity or subject. *...a music lover.*

loving /lʌvɪŋ/. 1 ADJ Someone who is **loving** feels or shows love to other people. *...a loving, beautiful wife.* ♦ **lovingly** ADV *For a moment she looked at her grandson lovingly.* 2 ATTRIB ADJ **Loving** actions are done with great enjoyment and care. *...tending the gardens with loving care.* ♦ **lovingly** ADV *The Society of Antiquaries have lovingly restored the building.*

low /ləʊ/, **lower, lowest; lows.** 1 ADJ Something that is **low** measures a short distance from the bottom to the top. *...a low brick wall... ...a low table... ...low hills.* 2 ADJ OR ADV You can also say something is **low** when it is close to the ground or close to the bottom of something. *She made a low curtsey... I asked him to fly low over the beach... She saw the scar low on his spine.* 3 ADJ OR ADV A dress or blouse that is described as **low** leaves a woman's neck and the top part of her chest bare. *...a low neckline... Her dress was cut low in front.* 4 ADJ **Low** means small in amount, value, or degree. *...workers on low incomes... ...low expectations... ...a low tar cigarette.* 5 ATTRIB ADJ You can use **low** with numbers to give an approximate amount. For example, if a number is 'in the low twenties', it is more than twenty but less than twenty-five. *The temperature is in the low eighties.* 6 PRED ADJ If a supply of something is **low,** you do not have much of it left. *We're a bit low on claret.* 7 ADJ If the quality or standard of something is **low,** it is bad. *...a low standard of living... ...low-grade material.* 8 ADJ **Low** is used to describe people who are near the bottom of a particular scale. *...a junior executive of a fairly low grade... ...the lowest 85 per cent of the working population.* 9 ADJ If you have a **low** opinion of someone, you disapprove of them or dislike them. 10 ADJ OR ADV You use **low** to describe people or actions which you disapprove of. *...mixing with low company... Well I'm not doing that. I haven't sunk that low.* 11 ADJ A **low** sound is deep. *...a long low note on the horn.* 12 ADJ OR ADV You can also describe a quiet sound as **low.** *Smithy spoke to him in a low and urgent voice... He turned the radio on low.* 13 ADJ A **low** light is dim rather than bright. 14 ADJ Someone who is feeling **low** is unhappy. 15 COUNT N WITH SUPP A **low** is the worst or smallest level that something has ever reached. *Output was at a record low.* 16 PHRASE If you **are lying low,** you are avoiding being seen in public; an informal use. *She'll have to lie low for a couple of years.*

lower /ləʊə/, **lowers, lowering, lowered.** 1 **Lower** is the comparative of **low.** 2 ATTRIB ADJ **Lower** is used to describe the bottom one of a pair of things, or the bottom part of something. *Thomas was lying in the lower bunk... Jane sucked at her lower lip... The bullet had penetrated the lower left corner of his back.* 3 ATTRIB ADJ You also use **lower** to describe people or things that are less important than similar people or things. *He could argue his case in the lower court... ...the lower levels of the organization.* 4 VB WITH OBJ If you **lower** something, you move it slowly downwards. *He lowered his glass... Lynn lowered herself into the water... She lowered her eyes and remained silent.* 5 VB WITH OBJ To **lower** an amount, value, or quality means to make it less. *The voting age was lowered to eighteen... Mexican hotels are lowering their rates sharply.* ♦ **lowering** SING N WITH SUPP *...the lowering of examination standards.* 6 VB WITH OBJ If you **lower** your voice, you speak more quietly.

lower class, lower classes. COUNT N The **lower classes** consist of the social class below the middle class. *I'm one of the lower classes and I'm proud of it... ...lower-class families.*

low-key. ADJ Something that is **low-key** is not obvious or intense. *The organization lent us support in its own low-key way.*

lowlands /ləʊlə^{3}ndz/. PLURAL N **Lowlands** are an area of flat, low land. *...the Scottish Lowlands.*

lowly /ləʊli^{1}/, **lowlier, lowliest.** ADJ Something that is **lowly** is low in rank, status, or importance. *...a lowly employee... ...his lowly social origins.*

low-paid. ADJ Workers who earn only a small amount of money are referred to as **low-paid.** *...low-paid workers... ...women in low paid jobs.*

low tide. UNCOUNT N At the coast, **low tide** is the time when the sea is at its lowest level. *The rocks are exposed at low tide.*

loyal /lɔɪəl/. ADJ A **loyal** person remains firm in their friendship or support for someone or something. *Most Tories remained loyal to the Government... ...a loyal friend.* ♦ **loyally** ADV *For thirty years she had served him loyally.*

loyalty /lɔɪəlti^{1}/, **loyalties.** 1 UNCOUNT N **Loyalty** is behaviour in which you stay firm in your friendship or support for someone or something. *I am convinced of your loyalty to the cause.* 2 COUNT N **Loyalties** are feelings of friendship, support, or duty. *...their loyalties to the church.*

lozenge /lɒzɪ^{2}ndʒ/, **lozenges.** COUNT N A **lozenge** is a tablet which you suck when you have a sore throat.

LP /ɛl piː/, **LPs.** COUNT N An **LP** is a record with about 25 minutes of music or speech on each side.

L-plate /ɛl pleɪt/, **L-plates.** COUNT N **L-plates** are small signs with an 'L' on them which you attach to a car when you are learning to drive.

LSD /ɛl ɛs diː/. UNCOUNT N **LSD** is a very powerful drug which causes hallucinations.

lubricate /luːbrɪkeɪt/, **lubricates, lubricating, lubricated.** VB WITH OBJ If you **lubricate** part of a machine, you put oil onto it to make it move smoothly. *The chain might need lubricating.* ♦ **lubrication** /luːbrɪkeɪʃə^{0}n/ UNCOUNT N *...the lubrication system of the engine.*

lucid /luːsɪd/; a formal word. 1 ADJ **Lucid** writing or speech is clear and easy to understand. *...a brief and lucid account.* ♦ **lucidly** ADV *Her ideas are very lucidly set out in his book.* ♦ **lucidity** /luːsɪdɪ^{1}ti^{1}/ UNCOUNT N *He expresses himself with quiet lucidity.* 2 ADJ When someone is **lucid,** they are able to think clearly again after being ill. *There was a ringing in my head, yet I was lucid.* ♦ **lucidity** UNCOUNT N *...in one of his moments of lucidity.*

luck /lʌk/. UNCOUNT N **Luck** or good **luck** is success that does not come from your own abilities or efforts. **Bad luck** is lack of success or bad things that happen to you, that have not been caused by yourself or other people. *I had some wonderful luck... He wished me luck... One spring we had a lot of bad luck.*

PHRASES ● If you say **'Bad luck'** or **'Hard luck'** to someone, you are expressing sympathy when something has gone badly for them. *Tough luck, Barrett. You played a great game.* ● You say **'Good luck'** or **'Best of luck'** to someone when you hope they will be successful. *Good luck to you, my boy... Best of luck with the exams.* ● If someone is **in luck,** they are lucky on a particular occasion. ● When someone **tries** their **luck** at something, they try to succeed at it. *He came to England to try his luck at a musical career.* ● You can add **with luck** to a statement to say that you hope a particular thing will happen; an informal use. *This one should work with a bit of luck... With any luck they might forget all about it.*

luckily /lʌkɪli^{1}/. SENTENCE ADV You add **luckily** to your statement to indicate that you are glad that something happened. *Luckily, Saturday was a fine day... Luckily for you, I happen to have the key.*

lucky /lʌki^{1}/, **luckier, luckiest.** 1 ADJ If someone is **lucky,** they have something that is very desirable. *I'm lucky in having an excellent teacher... He was the luckiest man in the world.* 2 ADJ A **lucky** person always has good luck. *Are you lucky at cards?* 3 ADJ If an event or situation is **lucky,** it had good effects or consequences, although it happened by chance. *It's lucky I'm here... It was lucky that I had cooked a big joint... ...a lucky guess.* **4** ADJ People describe something as **lucky** when they believe that it helps them to be successful. *...his lucky sweater.*

lucrative /luːkrətɪv/. ADJ A **lucrative** business or activity earns you a lot of money; a formal use. *It had been an exciting and lucrative business... ...the lucrative trade in tea and porcelain.*

ludicrous /luːdɪkrəs/. ADJ If something is **ludicrous,** it is extremely foolish, unreasonable, or unsuitable. *I had a ludicrous feeling of pride in him... ...one teacher for every 100 pupils, it was ludicrous.* ♦ **ludicrously** ADV *...a ludicrously low price.*

lug /lʌg/, **lugs, lugging, lugged.** VB WITH OBJ If you **lug** a heavy object, you carry it with difficulty; an informal use. *She lugged the suitcase out into the hallway.*

luggage /lʌgɪdʒ/. UNCOUNT N **Luggage** is the suitcases and bags that take when you travel. *They did not have much luggage.* ● See also **left luggage office.**

lugubrious /lə^{4}guːbriəs/. ADJ **Lugubrious** means sad and dull, and not lively; a formal use. *...a lugubrious face... ...lugubrious hymns.*

lukewarm /luːkwɔːm/. **1** ADJ Something that is **lukewarm** is only slightly warm. *...lukewarm water.* **2** ADJ If someone is **lukewarm,** they do not show much enthusiasm or interest. *...her parents' lukewarm response... He was lukewarm about the committee.*

lull /lʌl/, **lulls, lulling, lulled. 1** COUNT N A **lull** is a period of quiet or of little activity. *...a lull in the conversation... After a lull of several weeks, there has been a resumption of bombing.* **2** VB WITH OBJ If something **lulls** you, it causes you to feel sleepy, or calm because you feel safe and secure. *...lulling us into slumber... He had lulled me into thinking that I had won.*

lumber /lʌmbə/, **lumbers, lumbering, lumbered. 1** UNCOUNT N **Lumber** consists of wood that has been roughly cut up; an American use. *...piles of lumber... ...a lumber company.* **2** VB WITH ADJUNCT If someone **lumbers** around, they move slowly and clumsily. *He lumbered upstairs looking for the bathroom... Donkeys lumbered by.*

lumber with. PHR VB If you **are lumbered with** a task, you have to do it even though you do not want to. *Women are still lumbered with the cooking and cleaning.*

luminous /luːmɪnəs/. ADJ Something that is **luminous** shines or glows in the dark. *...the luminous hands of my watch.*

lump /lʌmp/, **lumps, lumping, lumped. 1** COUNT N A **lump** is a solid piece of something. *...lumps of clay... ...a lump of butter.* **2** COUNT N A **lump** on someone's body is a small, hard piece of flesh caused by an injury or an illness. *...a small lump, a little growth just above the right eye.* **3** COUNT N A **lump** of sugar is a small cube of it. *Black coffee, two lumps, please.* **4** VB WITH OBJ If you **lump** different people or things together, you consider them as a group. *'Don't lump me and Dave together,' he interrupted... The old rural counties were lumped together into new units.*

lump sum, lump sums. COUNT N A **lump sum** is a large amount of money that is given or received all at once. *He has been offered a tax-free lump sum of $4,000.*

lumpy /lʌmpi^1/, **lumpier, lumpiest.** ADJ Something that is **lumpy** contains lumps or is covered in lumps. *...sitting on his lumpy mattress... Her face tends to be puffy and lumpy.*

lunacy /luːnəsi^1/. UNCOUNT N **Lunacy** is very strange or foolish behaviour. *This comment would have seemed sheer lunacy to his ancestors... It would be lunacy to marry.*

lunar /luːnə/. ATTRIB ADJ **Lunar** means relating to the moon; a formal use. *...the lunar surface.*

lunatic /luːnətɪk/, **lunatics. 1** COUNT N If you describe someone as a **lunatic,** you mean that they behave in a stupid and annoying way; an informal use. *The man's a bloody lunatic.* **2** ADJ **Lunatic** behaviour is foolish and likely to be dangerous. *This Government's policies are lunatic.*

lunch /lʌnt^{0}ʃ/, **lunches, lunching, lunched. 1** UNCOUNT N OR COUNT N **Lunch** is a meal that you have in the middle of the day. *What did you have for lunch?... After lunch I went to see our doctor.* **2** VB When you **lunch,** you eat lunch; a formal use. *Why don't you two lunch with me tomorrow?*

luncheon /lʌnt^{0}ʃə^{0}n/, **luncheons.** COUNT N OR UNCOUNT N **Luncheon** is a formal meal in the middle of the day. *I had met him at a civic luncheon... I was planning something hot for luncheon.*

lunchtime /lʌnt^{0}ʃtaɪm/, **lunchtimes.** COUNT N OR UNCOUNT N **Lunchtime** is the time in the middle of the day when people have lunch. *She's going to see him at lunchtime... It's full most lunchtimes and evenings.*

lung /lʌŋ/, **lungs.** COUNT N Your **lungs** are the two organs inside your chest which you use for breathing. *She filled her lungs with smoke... ...lung cancer.*

lunge /lʌnd^{0}ʒ/, **lunges, lunging, lunged.** VB If you **lunge** in a particular direction, you move there suddenly and clumsily. *He lunged toward me.* Also SING N *When he makes a lunge at you, run.*

lurch /lɜːtʃ/, **lurches, lurching, lurched. 1** VB To **lurch** means to make a sudden, jerky movement. *He lurched and fell... The boat lurched ahead.* Also COUNT N *With a tremendous lurch he fell over me.* **2** VB WITH ADJUNCT If you **lurch** from one thing to another, you suddenly change your opinions or behaviour. *After lurching away from Socialism in 1976, they now seem to be lurching back.* **3** PHRASE If someone **leaves** you **in the lurch,** they stop helping you at a very difficult time; an informal use.

lure /lʊə/, **lures, luring, lured. 1** VB WITH OBJ To **lure** someone means to attract them and cause them to do something. *The price also lures students... Why else had Halliday come up, if not to lure me away?* **2** COUNT N WITH SUPP A **lure** is an attractive quality that something has. *Many economists have succumbed to the fatal lure of mathematics.*

lurid /lʊərɪd/. **1** ADJ Something that is **lurid** involves a lot of violence or sex; used showing disapproval. *...lurid stories about the war... ...lurid novels.* **2** ADJ **Lurid** things are very brightly coloured. *...lurid polyester skirts.* ♦ **luridly** ADV *...a luridly coloured advertisement.*

lurk /lɜːk/, **lurks, lurking, lurked. 1** VB To **lurk** somewhere means to wait there secretly. *Wild boars and wolves lurked near the isolated camp.* **2** VB If something such as a memory, suspicion, or danger **lurks,** it exists, but you are only slightly aware of it. *...outdated prejudices lurking in the minds of individuals.*

luscious /lʌʃəs/. **1** ADJ If something is **luscious,** it is extremely attractive. *She was looking luscious in faded overalls and a flannel shirt.* **2** ADJ **Luscious** fruit is juicy and delicious. *...a basket of luscious figs.*

lush /lʌʃ/, **lusher, lushest. 1** ADJ Fields or gardens that are **lush** have very healthy, thick grass or plants. *...a landscape of lush green meadows.* **2** ADJ Places or ways of life that are **lush** are rich and full of luxury. *...lush restaurants in London and Paris.*

lust /lʌst/, **lusts, lusting, lusted. 1** UNCOUNT N **Lust** is a feeling of strong sexual desire for someone; used showing disapproval. **2** COUNT N A **lust** for something is a very strong and eager desire to have it; used showing disapproval. *...the lust for power.*

lust after or **lust for.** PHR VB **1** If you **lust after** something or **lust for** it, you have a very strong desire to possess it. *They lusted after the gold of El Dorado.* **2** If you **lust after** someone or **lust for** them, you feel a very strong sexual desire for them.

lustful /lʌstfʊl/. ADJ **Lustful** means feeling or expressing strong sexual desire. *...lustful thoughts.*

lustre /lʌstə/; spelled **luster** in American English. UNCOUNT N **Lustre** is gentle shining light that is reflected from a surface; a literary use. *...the lustre of encrusted gold.*

lusty /lʌsti^1/, **lustier, lustiest.** ADJ **Lusty** means healthy and strong. *...a strong and lusty boy of whom any father could be proud.* ♦ **lustily** ADV *They stood waving their Union Jacks and singing lustily.*

luxuriant /lʌgzjʊərɪənt, lʌgʒ-/. **1** ADJ **Luxuriant** plants, trees, and gardens are large and healthy. *...luxuriant forests.* **2** ADJ **Luxuriant** hair is very thick and healthy. *...his pale lined face and luxuriant, flowing hair.*

luxuriate /lʌgzjʊərɪeɪt, lʌgʒ-/, **luxuriates, luxuriating, luxuriated.** VB If you **luxuriate** in something, you relax in it and enjoy it very much. *I luxuriated in my retirement.*

luxurious /lʌgzjʊərɪəs, lʌgʒ-/. **1** ADJ Something that is **luxurious** is very comfortable and expensive. *...big, luxurious cars.* ♦ **luxuriously** ADV *We lived luxuriously.* **2** ADJ **Luxurious** actions express great pleasure and comfort. *She took a deep luxurious breath.* ♦ **luxuriously** ADV *She stretched luxuriously.*

luxury /lʌkʃə^{0}ri^1/, **luxuries. 1** UNCOUNT N **Luxury** is very great comfort among beautiful and expensive surroundings. *We lived in great luxury... ...a life of ease and luxury.* **2** COUNT N A **luxury** is something expensive which is not necessary but which gives you pleasure. *Her mother provided her with clothes and little luxuries.* **3** SING N WITH SUPP A **luxury** is also a pleasure which you do not often experience. *Privacy was an unknown luxury.*

-ly. SUFFIX **-ly** is added to adjectives to form adverbs that indicate the manner or nature of an action. For example, 'rudely' means in a rude way. Adverbs of this kind are usually not defined but are treated with the related adjectives. *He walked slowly down the street... 'I was hoping you would,' Morris said mischievously.*

lying /laɪɪŋ/. **1 Lying** is the present participle of **lie. 2** ATTRIB ADJ A **lying** person is dishonest or deceitful. *...those lying journalists.* **3** UNCOUNT N **Lying** is the act of telling lies. *She's incapable of lying.*

lynch /lɪnt^{0}ʃ/, **lynchs, lynching, lynched.** VB WITH OBJ If someone **is lynched,** they are killed by an angry crowd of people. *At one point he was in danger of being lynched.*

lyric /lɪrɪk/, **lyrics. 1** ATTRIB ADJ **Lyric** poetry is written in a simple and direct style. **2** PLURAL N The **lyrics** of a song are its words.

lyrical /lɪrɪkə^{0}l/. **1** ADJ Something that is **lyrical** is poetic, musical, and romantic. *He tries to bring into his plays a special lyrical quality... ...a dreamy, lyrical study of the Covent Garden flower market.* **2** PRED ADJ If you are **lyrical** about something, you are very enthusiastic about it. *Ned was growing lyrical.*

Mm

m. m is a written abbreviation for 'metres' or 'metre'.

M.A. /ɛm eɪ/, **M.A.s.** COUNT N An **M.A.** is a higher degree in the arts or social sciences. **M.A.** is an abbreviation for 'Master of Arts'. *...an M.A. in Applied Linguistics.*

mac /mæk/, **macs.** COUNT N A **mac** is a mackintosh; an informal British use.

macabre /məkɑːbrə^0/. ADJ A **macabre** event or story is very strange and horrible. *...the macabre shooting.*

macaroni /mækərəʊni^1/. UNCOUNT N **Macaroni** is a kind of pasta made in the shape of short hollow tubes.

machete /məʃɛti^1/, **machetes.** COUNT N A **machete** is a large knife with a broad blade.

machine /məʃiːn/, **machines, machining, machined. 1** COUNT N A **machine** is a piece of equipment which uses electricity or an engine in order to do a particular kind of work. **2** VB WITH OBJ If you **machine** something, you make it or work on it using a machine. **3** SING N WITH SUPP You also use **machine** to refer to a well-controlled system or organization. *...the might of the enemy war machine... They had perfected their own propaganda machine.*

machine gun, machine guns. COUNT N A **machine gun** is a gun which fires a lot of bullets very quickly one after the other. *...bursts of machine-gun fire.*

machinery /məʃiːnə^{0}ri^1/. **1** UNCOUNT N **Machinery** is machines in general, or machines that are used in a factory. *Machinery is being introduced to save labour.* **2** UNCOUNT N WITH SUPP The **machinery** of a government or organization is the system that it uses to deal with things. *The party controls the state machinery.*

macho /mætʃəʊ/. ADJ A man who is **macho** behaves or dresses in an aggressively masculine way; an informal use which shows disapproval. *He emerged with a macho swagger.*

macintosh /mækɪntɒʃ/. See **mackintosh.**

mackerel /mækə^{0}rəl/. **Mackerel** is the singular and plural. COUNT N OR UNCOUNT N **Mackerel** are greeny-blue sea fish which are often caught and eaten. *...shoals of mackerel.*

mackintosh /mækɪntɒʃ/, **mackintoshes;** also spelled **macintosh.** COUNT N A **mackintosh** is a raincoat; an old-fashioned use.

mad /mæd/, **madder, maddest. 1** ADJ Someone who is **mad** has a mental illness which makes them behave in strange ways. *She was married to a man who'd gone mad.* ♦ **madness** UNCOUNT N *...the terrible madness that overtook the king.* **2** ADJ You describe someone as **mad** when they do or say things that you think are very foolish. *They think I am mad to live in such a place.* ♦ **madness** UNCOUNT N *It is madness for them to remain unarmed.* **3** ATTRIB ADJ You also use **mad** to describe wild, uncontrolled behaviour. *I was dashing around in the usual mad panic.* **4** PRED ADJ You can say that someone is **mad** when they are very angry; an informal use. *They're mad at me.* **5** PRED ADJ WITH 'about' If you are **mad** about something or someone, you like them very much indeed; an informal use. *For years he's been mad about opera.*

PHRASES ● If you say that someone **is driving** you **mad** or that they **will drive** you **mad,** you mean that they are annoying you very much. *These blinking kids will drive me mad.* ● If you do something **like mad,** you do it very energetically or enthusiastically; an informal use. *They were still arguing like mad.*

madam /mædə^{0}m/. VOCATIVE **Madam** is a formal and polite way of addressing a woman. 'Dear Madam' is often used at the beginning of letters. *Good evening, Madam.*

madden /mædən/, **maddens, maddening, maddened.** VB WITH OBJ If something **maddens** you, it makes you feel very angry or annoyed. *The colonel's calmness maddened Pluskat.* ♦ **maddening** ADJ *...a maddening clicking noise.*

made /meɪd/. **Made** is the past tense and past participle of **make.**

-made. SUFFIX **-made** is added to words such as 'factory', 'British', and 'machine' to form adjectives that indicate that something has been made or produced at a particular place or in a particular way. *It's factory-made... ...locally-made goods.*

madhouse /mædhaus/, **madhouses.** COUNT N You say that a place is a **madhouse** when it is full of noise and confusion.

madly /mædli^1/. 1 ADV If you do something **madly,** you do it in a fast, excited, or eager way. *We began rushing around madly in the dark.* 2 PHRASE If you are **madly in love** with someone, you love them very much in a romantic way. *I fell madly in love with Ellen the first time I ever saw her.*

madman /mædmən/, **madmen.** 1 COUNT N You can refer to a foolish or irresponsible person as a **madman.** *I have had enough trouble with that madman Smith.* 2 COUNT N A **madman** is also a man who is mad; an old-fashioned use. *They locked him up as a madman.*

magazine /mægəzi:n/, **magazines.** 1 COUNT N A **magazine** is a weekly or monthly publication which contains articles, stories, photographs and advertisements. *I got the recipe from a woman's magazine.* 2 COUNT N On radio or television, a **magazine** is a programme with interesting stories about people and events. *Newsbeat is the popular news magazine on Radio 1.*

maggot /mægət/, **maggots.** COUNT N A **maggot** is a tiny creature that looks like a very small worm. Maggots turn into flies.

magic /mædʒɪk/. 1 UNCOUNT N **Magic** is a special power that occurs in children's stories and that some people believe in. It can make apparently impossible things happen. *She was accused of inflicting bad fortune on them through evil magic.* Also ATTRIB ADJ *How fast the magic potion worked!* 2 UNCOUNT N **Magic** is also the art of performing tricks to entertain people, for example by seeming to make things appear and disappear. *He was in his bedroom practising magic tricks.* 3 UNCOUNT N The **magic** of something is a special quality that makes it seem wonderful and exciting. *...the magic of theatre... They need a bit of magic in their lives.* Also ADJ *...a truly magic moment.*

magical /mædʒɪkəl/. 1 ADJ Something that is **magical** uses or can produce magic. *I used to believe my mother had magical powers... ...a stream of magical water.* 2 ADJ You can also say that something is **magical** when it has a special mysterious quality that makes it seem wonderful and exciting. *The journey had lost all its magical quality.* ♦ **magically** ADV *The horizon was magically filling with ships.*

magician /mədʒɪʃən/, **magicians.** 1 COUNT N A **magician** is a person who performs tricks as a form of entertainment. *This process is very effectively used by stage magicians.* 2 COUNT N In fairy stories,a **magician** is a man who has magic powers.

magistrate /mædʒɪstreɪt/, **magistrates.** COUNT N A **magistrate** is an official who acts as a judge in a law court which deals with less serious crimes or disputes. *You'll have to appear before the magistrate... ...the magistrates' court.*

magnanimous /mægnænɪməs/. ADJ **Magnanimous** people are generous and forgiving, especially towards people they have beaten in a fight or contest. *We must encourage new regimes to be magnanimous towards their former oppressors.*

magnate /mægneɪt/, **magnates.** COUNT N WITH SUPP A **magnate** is someone who is very rich and powerful in business. *...a rich shipping magnate... ...a press magnate.*

magnet /mægnɪ^{1}t/, **magnets.** COUNT N A **magnet** is a piece of iron which attracts iron or steel towards it. *The pin was extracted with a magnet.*

magnetic /mægnetɪk/. 1 ADJ Something that is **magnetic** has the power of a magnet to attract iron or steel towards it. *He took a carving knife from a magnetic board on the wall.* 2 ATTRIB ADJ People who are described as **magnetic** have qualities which other people find attractive. *Without magnetic appeal, the politician is unlikely to succeed.*

magnetism /mægnɪ^{1}tɪzəm/. 1 UNCOUNT N **Magnetism** is a power that attracts some substances towards others. *...the forces of electricity and magnetism.* 2 UNCOUNT N Someone with **magnetism** has unusual and exciting qualities which people find attractive. *He had immense personal magnetism.*

magnification /mægnɪfɪkeɪʃən/, **magnifications.** 1 UNCOUNT N **Magnification** is the process of making something appear bigger than it actually is, as, for example, when you use a microscope. 2 UNCOUNT N OR COUNT N The **magnification** of a microscope, telescope, or pair of binoculars is the degree to which it can magnify things. *All the images, even under the highest magnification, were simply points of light.*

magnificent /mægnɪfɪsənt/. ADJ Something that is **magnificent** is extremely good, beautiful, or impressive. *It's a magnificent book... Her dress is magnificent.* ♦ **magnificence** /mægnɪfɪsəns/ UNCOUNT N *...the magnificence of the forest.* ♦ **magnificently** ADV *They performed magnificently.*

magnify /mægnɪfaɪ/, **magnifies, magnifying, magnified.** 1 VB WITH OBJ When a microscope or magnifying glass **magnifies** an object, it makes it appear bigger than it actually is. *The lenses magnified his eyes to the size of dinner plates.* 2 VB WITH OBJ To **magnify** something also means to make it seem more important than it actually is. *His fears have greatly magnified the true dangers.*

magnifying glass, magnifying glasses. COUNT N A **magnifying glass** is a piece of glass which makes objects appear bigger than they actually are.

magnitude /mægnɪtju:d/. UNCOUNT N The **magnitude** of something is its great size or importance. *They do not recognize the magnitude of the problem.*

magpie /mægpaɪ/, **magpies.** COUNT N A **magpie** is a black and white bird with a long tail.

mahogany /məhɒgəni^1/. UNCOUNT N **Mahogany** is a dark reddish-brown wood that is used to make furniture. *...a tall mahogany bookcase.*

maid /meɪd/, **maids.** COUNT N A **maid** is a female servant.

maiden /meɪdən/, **maidens.** 1 COUNT N A **maiden** is a young woman; a literary use. *Maidens performed graceful dances.* 2 ATTRIB ADJ The **maiden** voyage or flight of a ship or aeroplane is the first official journey that it makes.

maiden name, maiden names. COUNT N A married woman's **maiden name** is her surname before she got married and took her husband's surname.

mail /meɪl/, **mails, mailing, mailed.** 1 UNCOUNT N **Mail** is the letters and parcels that the post office delivers. *If there's anything urgent in the mail, I'll deal with it... Minnie was alone in the post office, sorting mail.* 2 SING N The **mail** is the system used by the post office for collecting and delivering letters and parcels. *Send it to me by mail.* 3 VB WITH OBJ If you **mail** something, you post it. *The books had to be mailed directly from the publisher.*

mailbag /meɪlbæg/, **mailbags.** COUNT N A **mailbag** is a large bag used by the post office for carrying letters and parcels.

mailbox /meɪlbɒks/, **mailboxes;** an American word. 1 COUNT N A **mailbox** is a box outside your house where letters are delivered. 2 COUNT N A **mailbox** is also a large container in the street where you post letters.

mail order. UNCOUNT N If you buy things by **mail order,** you chose them from a catalogue and they are sent to you by post. *The record is available by mail order... ...a mail-order firm.*

maim /meɪm/, **maims, maiming, maimed.** VB WITH OBJ To **maim** someone means to injure them so badly that part of their body is permanently damaged. *These people kill and maim innocent civilians.*

main /meɪn/, **mains.** 1 ATTRIB ADJ The **main** thing is the most important one. *What are the main reasons for going to university?... Mrs Foster hurried through the main entrance.* 2 PHRASE If something is true **in the main,** it is generally true, although there may be exceptions; a formal use. *The Worthingtons are in the main decent, friendly folk.* 3 COUNT N The **mains** are the pipes or wires which supply gas, water, or electricity to buildings, or which take sewage from them. *The radio we have at home plugs into the mains... You needn't turn off the mains water... A bulldozer had cut a gas main.*

main clause, main clauses. COUNT N In grammar, a **main clause** is a clause that can stand alone as a complete sentence.

mainframe /meɪnfreɪm/, **mainframes.** COUNT N A **mainframe** is a large computer which can be used by many people at the same time, and which can do very large or complicated tasks.

mainland /meɪnlənd/. SING N The **mainland** is the large main part of a country, in contrast to the islands around it. *The motorboat was waiting to ferry him back to the mainland.* Also ATTRIB ADJ *...the coast of mainland Greece.*

mainly /meɪnli^1/. ADV You use **mainly** to say that a statement is true in most cases or to a large extent. *The political groups have more power, mainly because of their larger numbers... I'll be concentrating mainly on French and German.*

main road, main roads. COUNT N A **main road** is a large important road that leads from one town or city to another. *We turned off the main road shortly after Alcester.*

mainstay /meɪnsteɪ/, **mainstays.** COUNT N WITH SUPP The **mainstay** of something is the most important part of it. *Homemade chocolate cookies were the mainstay of my diet.*

mainstream /meɪnstri:m/. SING N People or ideas that are part of the **mainstream** are regarded as normal and conventional. *We feel isolated from the mainstream of social life in the community.* Also ATTRIB ADJ *...mainstream education.*

maintain /meɪnteɪn/, **maintains, maintaining, maintained.** 1 VB WITH OBJ If you **maintain** something, you continue to have it, and do not let it stop or grow weaker. *I wanted to maintain my friendship with her... For twenty-five years they had failed to maintain law and order.* 2 VB WITH OBJ If you **maintain** something at a particular rate or level, you keep it at that rate or level. *One has to maintain the temperature at a very high level.* 3 VB WITH OBJ To **maintain** someone means to provide them with money and the things that they need. *I need the money to maintain me until I start a job.* 4 VB WITH OBJ If you **maintain** a building, vehicle, road, or machine, you keep it in good condition. *...the rising cost of maintaining the equipment.* 5 REPORT VB If you **maintain** that something is true, you state your opinion very strongly. *Mrs Camish always maintained that he had been a brilliant thinker.*

maintenance /meɪntɪnəns/. 1 UNCOUNT N The **maintenance** of a building, road, vehicle, or machine is the process of keeping it in good condition. *He learnt tractor maintenance.* 2 SING N The **maintenance** of a state or process consists of making sure that it continues. *...the maintenance of law and order... ...the maintenance of the same rate of expansion.* 3 UNCOUNT N **Maintenance** is also money that someone gives regularly to another person to pay for the things that they need; a British use.

maize /meɪz/. UNCOUNT N **Maize** is a tall plant which produces corn. The corn grows on long round parts called cobs. *...a field planted with maize.*

majestic /mədʒestɪk/. ADJ **Majestic** means very beautiful, dignified, and impressive. *...the majestic proportions of the great Pyramid... She looked majestic in her large, soft hat.* ♦ **majestically** ADV *Wet clouds, heavy with rain, moved majestically overhead.*

Majesty /mædʒɪ^{2}sti^1/, **Majesties.** TITLE **Your Majesty, Her Majesty,** or **Their Majesties** are used to address or refer to Kings or Queens. *...Her Majesty the Queen... Thank you, Your Majesty.*

major /meɪdʒə/, **majors, majoring, majored.** 1 ATTRIB ADJ You use **major** to describe something that is more important, serious, or significant than other things. *Finding a solicitor had been a major problem... One major factor was the revolution in communications.* 2 COUNT N OR TITLE A **major** is an army officer of medium rank. *...Major Burton-Cox.* 3 ADJ In European music, a **major** scale is one in which the third note is two tones higher than the first. *They're both in D major.* 4 VB WITH 'in' If you **major** in a particular subject, you study it as your main subject at university; an American use. *I decided to major in French.*

majority /mədʒɒrɪ^{1}ti^1/, **majorities.** 1 SING N The **majority** of people or things in a group is more than half of them. *...mass movements involving the overwhelming majority of the people.* ● If a group is **in a majority** or **in the majority,** they form more than half of a larger group. 2 COUNT N In an election, a **majority** is the difference between the number of votes gained by the winner and the number gained by the person or party that comes second. *Benn was returned by a majority of 15,479.*

make /meɪk/, **makes, making, made** /meɪd/. 1 VB WITH OBJ You use **make** to say that someone performs an action. For example, if someone **makes** a suggestion, they suggest something. *I made the wrong decision... He made the shortest speech I've ever heard... We have got to make a really serious effort... He had two phone calls to make.* 2 VB WITH OBJ AND INF If something **makes** you do something, it causes you to do it. If someone **makes** you do something, they force you to do it. *A sudden noise made Brody jump... Make him listen!... They were made to sit and wait.* 3 VB WITH OBJ AND COMPLEMENT OR 'into' You use **make** to say that someone or something is caused to be a particular thing or to have a particular quality. For example, if something **makes** someone happy, it causes them to be happy. *I'd like to make the world a better place... They're making the old kitchen into a little bedroom.* 4 VB WITH OBJ AND 'of' You use **make** to say how well or badly someone does something. For example, if you **make** a success of something, you do it well. *Let's not make a mess of this.* 5 VB WITH OBJ AND OBJ If you **make**

something, you produce it or construct it. *I like making cakes... ...the greatest film ever made... You can make petroleum out of coal... Martin, can you make us a drink?* 6 PASSIVE VB WITH 'of' OR 'from' If something **is made** of a particular substance, that substance was used to form or construct it. *The houses were made of brick... ...a flute made from bone.* 7 VB WITH OBJ If you **make** a sound, you produce it. *Try not to make so much noise.* 8 VB WITH COMPLEMENT You use **make** to say what two numbers add up to. For example, if two numbers **make** 12, they add up to 12. 9 VB WITH OBJ AND COMPLEMENT You use **make** to say what the time is, or to give the result of a calculation. For example, if you **make** it 4 o'clock, your watch says it is 4 o'clock. If you **make** the answer to a calculation 144, you calculate it to be 144. 10 VB WITH OBJ If you **make** money, you get it by working for it or by investing money. *He was making ninety dollars a week... She made a £200 profit.* 11 VB WITH COMPLEMENT You use **make** to say that someone or something is suitable for a particular task or role. For example, if someone would **make** a good secretary, they have the right qualities to be a good secretary. *Do garden tools make good gifts?* 12 VB WITH OBJ You can use **make** to say that a part or aspect of something is responsible for that thing's success. *Nicholson's acting really makes the film.* 13 VB WITH OBJ If you **make** a place, you manage to get there. *I made Ramsdale by dawn.* 14 VB WITH OBJ If you **make** friends or enemies, you cause people to become your friends or enemies. *Roger made a number of enemies... Karen made friends with several children.* 15 See also **making.** • **to make good:** see **good.** • **to make way:** see **way.**

make for. PHR VB If you **make for** a place, you move towards it. *We joined the crowd making for the exit.*

make of. PHR VB If you ask someone what they **make of** something, you want to know what their impression or opinion of it is. *He didn't know what to make of his new boss... Can you make anything of it?*

make off. PHR VB If you **make off,** you leave somewhere as quickly as possible. *The vehicle made off at once.*

make off with. PHR VB If you **make off with** something, you steal it. *Otto made off with the last of the brandy.*

make out. PHR VB 1 If you can **make** something **out,** you can see, hear, or understand it. *He could just make out the number plate of the car... She tried to make out what was being said.* 2 If you **make out** that something is the case, you try to cause people to believe it. *He's not really as hard as people make out.* 3 When you **make out** a cheque or receipt, you write all the necessary information on it.

make up. PHR VB 1 If a number of things **make up** something, they form it. *...the various groups which make up society... All substances are made up of molecules.* 2 If you **make up** a story, you invent it. 3 If you **make** yourself **up,** you put cosmetics on your face. ♦ **made up** ADJ *She had magnificent eyes, heavily made up.* • See also **make-up.** 4 If you **make up** an amount, you add to it so that it is as large as it should be. *Government would have to make up the difference out of its welfare budget.* 5 If two people **make up** or **make it up,** they become friends again after a quarrel. *He and Frank made it up.* 6 To **make up** for something that is lost or missing means to replace it or compensate for it. *If babies put on very little weight at first, eventually they will gain rapidly to make up for it.* 7 PHRASE If you **make it up to** someone for disappointing them, you do something for them to show how sorry you are.

make-believe. UNCOUNT N You refer to someone's behaviour as **make-believe** when they pretend that things are better or more exciting than they really are. *His whole life these days was a game of make-believe.*

maker /meɪkə/, **makers.** COUNT N WITH SUPP The **maker** of something is the person or company that makes it. *...film maker and critic, Iain Johnstone... The maker's label was carefully removed.*

makeshift /meɪkʃɪft/. ADJ **Makeshift** things are temporary and of poor quality. *...makeshift barricades... The accommodation was makeshift.*

make-up. 1 UNCOUNT N **Make-up** is coloured creams and powders which some people, especially women, put on their faces to make themselves look more attractive. *...eye make-up... She had a lot of make-up on.* 2 UNCOUNT N WITH SUPP The **make-up** of something is the different parts that it consists of, and the way these parts are arranged. *...the psychological make-up of primitive man.*

making /meɪkɪŋ/, **makings.** UNCOUNT N WITH SUPP The **making** of something is the act or process of producing it. *At the end of his life he turned to the making of beautiful books... People should be involved in all decision-making which affects them.*

PHRASES • If a problem is **of** your **own making,** you caused it: *The trouble here is of the President's own making.* • If something **is the making of** a person or thing, it is the reason that they are successful. *The description of Belfast is the making of the book.* • If you say that a person or thing has **the makings of** something, you mean that they seem likely to develop in that way. *She perceived that here might be the makings of the friendship that had so eluded her.*

maladjusted /mæləd͡ʒʌstr^{2}d/. ADJ **Maladjusted** children have psychological problems and behave in socially unacceptable ways.

malaise /mə^{3}leɪz/. UNCOUNT N **Malaise** is a state in which you feel dissatisfied or unhappy but do not know exactly what is wrong; a formal use. *Malaise had set in with the coming of the twentieth century.*

malaria /məlɛərɪə/. UNCOUNT N **Malaria** is a serious disease caught from mosquitoes which causes periods of fever.

male /meɪl/, **males.** 1 COUNT N A **male** is a person or animal that belongs to the sex that cannot have babies or lay eggs. *The males establish a breeding territory.* Also ADJ *...male hamsters.* 2 ATTRIB ADJ Something that is **male** concerns or affects men rather than women. *...male unemployment.*

male chauvinism. UNCOUNT N **Male chauvinism** is the belief which some men have that men are naturally better and more important than women. *This is clearly a symptom of the male chauvinism which prevails in our society.*

male chauvinist, male chauvinists. COUNT N A **male chauvinist** is a man who believes that men are naturally better and more important than women. *The men in my office are all blatant male chauvinists.* Also MOD *...a male chauvinist remark.*

malevolent /mə^{3}levələnt/. ADJ **Malevolent** people want to cause harm; a formal use. *These people seemed hard and malevolent.* ♦ **malevolence** /mə^{3}levələns/ UNCOUNT N *...the victims of his malevolence.*

malfunction /mælfʌŋkʃə^{0}n/, **malfunctions, malfunctioning, malfunctioned.** VB If a machine or a computer **malfunctions,** it fails to work properly. Also COUNT N *...a malfunction of the generator.*

malice /mælɪs/. UNCOUNT N **Malice** is a desire to harm people. *'So I notice,' he added with a touch of malice.*

malicious /məlɪʃəs/. ADJ **Malicious** talk or behaviour is intended to harm someone or their reputation.

malign /məlaɪn/, **maligns, maligning, maligned;** a formal word. 1 VB WITH OBJ If you **malign** someone, you say unpleasant and untrue things about them. *He had maligned both women.* 2 ADJ **Malign** behaviour is intended to harm someone. *His speeches are open to all sorts of malign interpretation.*

malignant /məlɪgnənt/. 1 ADJ **Malignant** behaviour is harmful and cruel. *...the consequence of a malignant plot.* 2 ADJ A **malignant** disease is uncontrollable and likely to cause death. *...a malignant growth.*

malinger /məlɪŋgə/, **malingers, malingering, malingered.** VB If you **are malingering,** you are pretending to be ill in order to avoid working. *I'm not malingering, really I'm not.*

mallet /mælɪ^{1}t/, **mallets.** COUNT N A **mallet** is a wooden hammer with a square head.

malnourished /mælnʌrɪʃt/. ADJ If someone is **malnourished,** they are physically weak because they have not eaten enough food. *The majority of the population is malnourished.*

malnutrition /mælnju:trɪʃə^{0}n/. UNCOUNT N **Malnutrition** is physical weakness caused by not eating enough food. *He is showing the first signs of malnutrition.*

malpractice /mælpræktɪs/, **malpractices.** UNCOUNT N OR COUNT N **Malpractice** is behaviour in which someone breaks the law or the rules of their profession in order to gain some personal advantage; a legal use. *A doctor who refused to give treatment is on trial for medical malpractice.*

malt /mɒlt/. UNCOUNT N **Malt** is a substance made from grain that is used to make some alcoholic drinks. *...a bottle of malt whisky.*

maltreat /mæltri:t/, **maltreats, maltreating, maltreated.** VB WITH OBJ If people or animals are **maltreated,** they are treated badly. *We do not intervene unless the children are being physically maltreated.*

mammal /mæmə^{0}l/, **mammals.** COUNT N **Mammals** are particular types of animals. Most female mammals give birth to babies rather than laying eggs, and feed their young with milk. Humans, dogs, lions, and whales are all mammals.

mammoth /mæməθ/, **mammoths.** 1 ATTRIB ADJ **Mammoth** means very large indeed. *...the immense foyer with its mammoth mirrors... ...a mammoth task.* 2 COUNT N **Mammoths** were animals like elephants with very long tusks and long hair. Mammoths no longer exist.

man /mæn/, **men** /men/; **mans, manning, manned.** **Men** is the plural of the noun. **Mans** is the third person singular, present tense, of the verb. 1 COUNT N A **man** is an adult male human being. *Larry was a handsome man in his early fifties.* 2 UNCOUNT N OR COUNT N Human beings in general are sometimes referred to as **man.** *Why does man seem to have more diseases than animals?... ...a deserted island where no man could live.* 3 PLURAL N The **men** in an army are the ordinary soldiers, rather than the officers. *In all, some 70,000 officers and men died.* 4 VB WITH OBJ To **man** a machine means to operate it. *They manned the phones all through the night.* 5 See also **manned.**

PHRASES • A **man-to-man** discussion is honest and open. • **the man in the street:** see **street.**

manage /mænɪd͡ʒ/, **manages, managing, managed.** 1 VB WITH OR WITHOUT OBJ If you **manage** to do something, you succeed in doing it. *How he managed to find us is beyond me... We'll manage it somehow... I'm sure you'll manage perfectly.* 2 VB WITH OBJ If someone **manages** an organization, business, or system, they are responsible for controlling it. *She manages a chain of pet shops.* 3 VB When people **manage,** they have an acceptable way of life, although they do not have much money. *I don't want charity. I can manage... I've always managed on a teacher's salary.*

manageable /mænɪd͡ʒəbə^{0}l/. ADJ Something that is **manageable** can be dealt with because it is not too big or complicated. *It is a perfectly manageable task.*

management /mænɪd͡ʒmənt/, **managements.** 1 UNCOUNT N The **management** of a business is the controlling and organizing of it. *She began to take over the management of the estate... It's a question of good management.* 2 UNCOUNT N OR COUNT N The people who control an organization are also called the **management.** *...communication between management and the workforce.*

manager /mænɪd͡ʒə/, **managers.** 1 COUNT N A **manager** is the person responsible for running an organization. *What you need is advice from your bank manager... ...the general manager of Philips Ltd in Singapore.* 2 COUNT N The **manager** of a pop star or other entertainer is the person who looks after the star's business interests. 3 COUNT N The **manager** of a sports team is the person responsible for organizing and training it.

manageress /mænɪd͡ʒəres/, **manageresses.** COUNT N A **manageress** is a woman who runs a shop or office. *...the manageress of a bookshop.*

managerial /mænɪd͡ʒɪərɪəl/. ATTRIB ADJ **Managerial** means relating to the work of a manager or manageress. *...technical and managerial skills.*

managing director, managing directors. COUNT N The **managing director** of a company is a director who is also responsible for the way that the company is managed.

mandate /mændeɪt/, **mandates;** a formal word. 1 COUNT N A government's **mandate** is the authority that it has to carry out particular policies as a result of winning an election. *The President will be able to claim that he has a mandate for the task that lies ahead.* 2 COUNT N A **mandate** is also a task that you are told to carry out. *My mandate is to find the best team.*

mandatory /mændətə^{0}rɪ^{1}/. ADJ If something is **mandatory,** a law states that it must be done. *The testing of cosmetics is not mandatory here.*

mane /meɪn/, **manes.** COUNT N A horse's or lion's **mane** is the long thick hair that grows from its neck.

maneuver /mənu:və/. See **manoeuvre.**

manfully /mænfʊlɪ^{1}/. ADV If someone does something **manfully,** they do it in a determined way; often used humorously. *I could see Simon manfully wielding a shovel.*

mangle /mæŋgə^{0}l/, **mangles, mangling, mangled.** VB WITH OBJ If something **is mangled,** it is crushed and twisted. *...the mangled cabs of overturned lorries.*

mango /mæŋgəʊ/, **mangoes** or **mangos.** COUNT N A **mango** is a large, sweet yellowish fruit which grows in hot countries.

mangy /meɪnd͡ʒɪ^{1}/. ADJ A **mangy** animal has lost a lot of its hair through disease. *...a mangy cat.*

manhandle /mænhændə^{0}l/, **manhandles, manhandling, manhandled.** VB WITH OBJ If you **manhandle** someone, you treat them very roughly. *He had been manhandled on the street by police.*

manhole /mænhəʊl/, **manholes.** COUNT N A **manhole** is a covered hole in the ground leading to a drain or sewer. *...an open manhole... ...manhole covers.*

manhood /mænhʊd/. UNCOUNT N **Manhood** is the state of being a man rather than a boy, or the period of a man's adult life. *...the dubious rewards of manhood... He had millions of dollars to play with in his early manhood.*

mania /meɪnɪə/, **manias. 1** COUNT N OR UNCOUNT N A **mania** for something is a strong liking for it. *She had a mania for cleanliness.* **2** UNCOUNT N A **mania** is also a mental illness. *...persecution mania.*

maniac /meɪnɪæk/, **maniacs.** COUNT N A **maniac** is a mad person who is violent and dangerous. *She was attacked by a maniac.*

manic /mænɪk/. ADJ You use **manic** to describe behaviour which is very energetic, because the person concerned is excited or anxious. *Weston finished his manic typing.*

manicure /mænɪkjʊə/, **manicures, manicuring, manicured.** VB WITH OBJ If you **manicure** your hands or nails, you care for them by softening the skin and cutting and polishing the nails. *She was sitting manicuring her nails.* Also COUNT N *His sister gave him a manicure once a month.*

manifest /mænɪfest/, **manifests, manifesting, manifested;** a formal word. **1** ADJ If something is **manifest,** it is obvious or can be easily seen. *...his manifest disapproval.* ♦ **manifestly** ADV *Hopper was manifestly too important to be left off the guest list.* **2** VB WITH OBJ OR REFL VB If you **manifest** something or if it **manifests** itself, people are made aware of it. *We should manifest our resistance... His inventiveness most often manifested itself as a skill in lying.*

manifestation /mænɪfesteɪʃ^{ə}n/, **manifestations.** COUNT N WITH SUPP A **manifestation** of something is a sign that it is happening or exists; a formal use. *...the first manifestations of the Computer Revolution.*

manifesto /mænɪfestəʊ/, **manifestos** or **manifestoes.** COUNT N A **manifesto** is a written statement in which a political party says what its aims and policies are. *...Shirley Williams' election manifesto.*

manifold /mænɪfəʊld/. ADJ Things that are **manifold** are of many different kinds; a literary use. *Her good works were manifold.*

manila /mənɪlə/; also spelled **manilla.** ATTRIB ADJ A **manila** envelope or folder is made from a strong brown paper. *...a stack of manila envelopes.*

manipulate /mə^{3}nɪpjə^{4}leɪt/, **manipulates, manipulating, manipulated. 1** VB WITH OBJ To **manipulate** people or events means to control or influence them to produce a particular result; often used showing disapproval. *Small children sometimes manipulate grown-ups.* ♦ **manipulation** /mə^{3}nɪpjə^{4}leɪʃ^{ə}n/ UNCOUNT N *...his unscrupulous manipulation of people.* **2** VB WITH OBJ If you **manipulate** a piece of equipment, you control it in a skilful way. *Lawrence manipulated the knobs on his tape recorder.* ♦ **manipulation** COUNT N *I had bent to watch the mechanic's manipulations.*

manipulative /mə^{3}nɪpjə^{4}lətɪv/. ADJ **Manipulative** behaviour is behaviour where one person skilfully causes another to act exactly in the way that he or she wants them to; used showing disapproval. *...the manipulative powers of the ruler.*

manipulator /mə^{3}nɪpjə^{4}leɪtə/, **manipulators.** COUNT N A **manipulator** is a person who skilfully controls events, systems, or people. *...the expert financial manipulator.*

mankind /mænkaɪnd/. UNCOUNT N You can refer to all human beings as **mankind** when you are considering them as a group. *You have performed a valuable service to mankind.*

manly /mænli^{1}/. ADJ **Manly** behaviour is typical of a man rather than a woman or boy; used showing approval. *He laughed a deep, manly laugh.*

man-made. ADJ Something that is **man-made** is made by people, rather than formed naturally. *...man-made fibres.*

manned /mænd/. ADJ A **manned** vehicle is controlled by people travelling in it. *They released special underwater manned vehicles.*

manner /mænə/, **manners. 1** SING N WITH SUPP The **manner** in which you do something is the way that you do it. *They filed the report in a routine manner... Their manner of rearing their young is extremely unusual.* **2** PLURAL N If you have good **manners,** you behave and speak very politely. *She had beautiful manners... His manners were charming.*

PHRASES ● **All manner of** things means things of many different kinds. *There were four canvas bags filled with all manner of tools.* ● You say **in a manner of speaking** to indicate that what you have just said is not absolutely or literally true, but is true in a general way. *If he hadn't been her boss, in a manner of speaking, she would have reported him to the police.*

mannered /mænəd/. ADJ If someone's speech or behaviour is **mannered,** it is very artificial, as if they were trying to impress people; a formal use that shows disapproval. *His conversation is a trifle mannered.*

mannerism /mænərɪz^{ə}m/, **mannerisms.** COUNT N Someone's **mannerisms** are gestures or ways of speaking which are typical of them. *As she grew older, her mannerisms became more pronounced.*

manoeuvre /mənuːvə/, **manoeuvres, manoeuvring, manoeuvred;** spelled **maneuver** in American English. **1** VB WITH OR WITHOUT OBJ If you **manoeuvre** something into or out of a place, you skilfully move it there. *She held the door open while I manoeuvred the suitcases into the back... Hooper started the car and manoeuvred out of the parking space.* Also COUNT N *Most people seem to manage this manoeuvre without causing havoc.* **2** COUNT N A **manoeuvre** is also something clever which you do in order to change a situation to your advantage. *These results have been achieved by a series of political manoeuvres.* **3** PHRASE If you have **no room for manoeuvre,** you do not have the opportunity to change your plans if it becomes necessary or desirable. **4** PLURAL N Military **manoeuvres** are training exercises which involve the movement of soldiers and equipment over a large area.

manor /mænə/, **manors.** COUNT N A **manor** is a large private house and land in the country.

manpower /mænpaʊə/. UNCOUNT N People refer to workers as **manpower** when considering them as a means of producing goods. *The country is in need of skilled manpower.*

mansion /mænʃ^{ə}n/, **mansions.** COUNT N A **mansion** is a very large house.

manslaughter /mænslɔːtə/. UNCOUNT N **Manslaughter** is the killing of a person by someone who may intend to injure them but does not intend to kill them; a legal use. *He was sentenced to two years for manslaughter.*

mantelpiece /mænt^{ə}lpiːs/, **mantelpieces;** also spelled **mantlepiece.** COUNT N A **mantelpiece** is a shelf over a fireplace.

manual /mænjʊ^{ə}l/, **manuals. 1** ADJ **Manual** work involves using physical strength rather than mental skills. **2** ATTRIB ADJ **Manual** also means operated by hand, rather than by electricity or by a motor. *...a manual system.* ♦ **manually** ADV *Such pumps can be operated manually.* **3** COUNT N A **manual** is a book which tells you how to do something. *The instruction manuals are printed in German.*

manufacture /mænjə^{4}fæktʃə/, **manufactures, manufacturing, manufactured. 1** VB WITH OBJ To **manufacture** things means to make them in a factory. *Many companies were manufacturing desk calculators... ...manufactured goods.* ♦ **manufacturing** UNCOUNT N *New England's economy is largely based on manufacturing, farming and tourism.* **2** UNCOUNT N The **manufacture** of something is the making of it in a factory. *...the manufacture and maintenance of vehicles.* **3** VB WITH OBJ If you **manufacture** information, you invent it. *She had manufactured the terrorist story to put everyone off.*

manufacturer /mænjə^{4}fæktʃ^{ə}rə/, **manufacturers.** COUNT N A **manufacturer** is a business that makes goods in large quantities, or the person who owns it. *...a furniture manufacturer.*

manure /mənjʊə/. UNCOUNT N **Manure** is animal faeces that is spread on the ground in order to improve the growth of plants.

manuscript /mænjə^{4}skrɪpt/, **manuscripts. 1** COUNT N A **manuscript** is the typed or handwritten version of a book before it is printed. **2** COUNT N A **manuscript** is also an old document that was written by hand before printing was invented. *...a medieval manuscript.*

many /meni^{1}/. The comparative is **more** and the superlative is **most:** see the separate entries for these words. **1** QUANTIF If there are **many** people or things, there are a lot of them. *Many people have been killed... ...the many brilliant speeches that had been made... Many of the old people were blind.* **2** QUANTIF You also use **many** in questions or statements about quantity. *How many children has she got?... I used to get a lot of sweets. As many as I liked.*

PHRASES ● You use **a good many** or **a great many** to refer to a very large number of things or people. *The information has proved useful to a great many people.* ● **many happy returns:** see **return.** ● **in so many words:** see **word.**

map /mæp/, **maps, mapping, mapped.** COUNT N A **map** is a drawing of an area as it would appear if you saw it from above, sometimes with special information on it. *On the map it is quite a brief strip of road.*

map out. PHR VB If you **map out** a plan or task, you work out how you will do it. *They met and mapped out their task.*

maple /meɪp^{ə}l/, **maples.** COUNT N A **maple** is a kind of tree. Its leaves have five points.

mar /mɑː/, **mars, marring, marred.** VB WITH OBJ To **mar** something means to spoil it; a formal use. *Graffiti marred the sides of buildings.*

marathon /mærəθ^{ə}n/, **marathons. 1** COUNT N A **marathon** is a race in which people run about 26 miles (about 42 km) along roads. *...the London Marathon.* **2** ATTRIB ADJ A **marathon** task takes a long time to do and is very tiring. *You need stamina to get through such a marathon production.*

marauder /mərɔːdə/, **marauders.** COUNT N **Marauders** are people who go around looking for something to steal or kill. *We were safe from marauders.*

marauding /mərɔːdɪŋ/. ATTRIB ADJ A **marauding** person or animal is one that goes around looking for something to steal or kill. *The countryside was being ravaged by marauding bands.*

marble /mɑːb^{ə}l/, **marbles. 1** UNCOUNT N **Marble** is a very hard rock used, for example, to make statues and fireplaces. *...a monument in black marble.* **2** UNCOUNT N **Marbles** is a children's game played with small glass balls. **3** COUNT N A **marble** is one of the small balls used by children in the game of marbles.

march /mɑːtʃ/, **marches, marching, marched. 1** UNCOUNT N **March** is the third month of the year in the western calendar. **2** VB When soldiers **march,** they walk with regular steps, as a group. *They marched through Norway.* Also COUNT N *We were woken in the middle of the night for a long march.* **3** VB When a large group of people **march,** they walk somewhere together in order to protest about something. *The crowds of demonstrators marched down the main street.* Also COUNT N *A million people took part in last year's march.* **4** VB WITH ADJUNCT If you **march** somewhere, you walk there quickly, for example because you are angry. *He marched out of the store.* **5** VB WITH OBJ AND ADJUNCT If you **march** someone somewhere, you force them to walk there with you by holding their arm. *He marched me out of the door.* **6** SING N WITH SUPP The **march** of something is its steady development or progress. *...the march of science.*

mare /meə/, **mares.** COUNT N A **mare** is an adult female horse.

margarine /mɑːdʒəriːn/. UNCOUNT N **Margarine** is a substance similar to butter that is made from vegetable oil and animal fats.

margin /mɑːdʒɪn/, **margins. 1** COUNT N If you win a contest by a large or small **margin,** you win it by a large or small amount. *They won by the small margin of five seats.* **2** COUNT N A **margin** of something is an extra amount which allows you more freedom in doing something. *What is the margin of safety?* **3** COUNT N The **margins** on a page are the blank spaces at each side. *They get a red tick in the margin to show that it's right.*

marginal /mɑːdʒɪnə^{ə}l/. **1** ADJ Something that is **marginal** is small and not very important. *The effect will be marginal... ...making marginal adjustments.* **2** ADJ A **marginal** seat or constituency is a political constituency where elections are won by a very small majority; a British use.

marginally /mɑːdʒɪnə^{ə}li^{1}/. SUBMOD **Marginally** means to only a small extent. *The prices of new houses are marginally higher than old houses.*

marijuana /mærɪh^{ə}ʊɑːnə/. UNCOUNT N **Marijuana** is an illegal drug which is smoked in cigarettes. *The room reeked of marijuana.*

marina /məriːnə/, **marinas.** COUNT N A **marina** is a small harbour for pleasure boats.

marinate /mærɪneɪt/, **marinates, marinating, marinated.** ERG VB If you **marinate** meat or fish or if it **marinates,** you soak it in vinegar, oil, and spices before cooking it, in order to flavour it.

marine /məriːn/, **marines. 1** COUNT N A **marine** is a soldier with the American Marine Corps or the British navy. **2** ATTRIB ADJ **Marine** is used to describe things relating to the sea. *...marine life... ...marine biology.*

marital /mærɪtə^{ə}l/. ATTRIB ADJ **Marital** means relating to marriage. *...marital problems.*

marital status. UNCOUNT N Your **marital status** is whether you are married, single, or divorced; a formal use.

maritime /mærɪtaɪm/. ATTRIB ADJ **Maritime** means relating to the sea and to ships; a formal use. *...the National Maritime Museum.*

mark /mɑːk/, **marks, marking, marked. 1** COUNT N A **mark** is a small stain or damaged area on a surface. *...grease marks... There seems to be a dirty mark on it.* **2** COUNT N A **mark** is also a number or letter which indicates your score in a test or examination. *You need 120 marks out of 200 to pass... ...anxious for good marks.* **3** COUNT N WITH SUPP When something reaches a particular **mark,** it reaches that stage. *Unemployment is well over the three million mark... Once past the halfway mark he found that he was running more easily.* **4** COUNT N WITH 'of' A **mark** of something is a sign or typical feature of it. *I took this smile as a mark of recognition... The scene bore all the marks of a country wedding.* **5** ERG VB If a substance **marks** a surface, it damages it and leaves a stain. *Vinegar, lemon juice, egg and salt can mark cutlery.* **6** VB WITH OBJ When a teacher **marks** a student's work, he or she decides how good it is and writes comments or a score on it. **7** VB WITH OBJ If you **mark** something, you put a written symbol or words on it. *...reports marked Top Secret... See that everything is marked with your initials.* 8 VB WITH OBJ If something **marks** a place or position, it shows where a particular thing is or was. *The area of burned clay marks the position of several Roman furnaces.* 9 VB WITH OBJ If an event **marks** a particular change or anniversary, it takes place at the time of that change or anniversary and draws attention to it. *The film marks a turning point in Allen's career... The concert is to mark the 75th Anniversary year of the composer's death.* 10 VB WITH OBJ AND 'as' Something that **marks** you as a particular type of person indicates that you are that type of person. *These signs marked him as a bachelor eager to wed.* 11 See also **marked, marking.**

PHRASES ● If you are **slow off the mark,** you respond to a situation slowly. If you are **quick off the mark,** you respond to a situation quickly. *Neighbours were always quick off the mark to ask him round when his wife was away.* ● If you **make** or **leave** your **mark** on something, you have an important influence on it. *...a scholar who has made his mark in history.* ● If something is **wide of the mark,** it is a long way from being correct. *His assessment of the situation might be rather wide of the mark.* ● If you **are marking time,** you are doing something boring or unimportant while you wait for something else to happen. *I've been marking time reading books.*

mark off. PHR VB If you **mark off** an item on a list, you indicate that it has been dealt with. *Each day was marked off with a neat X.*

marked /mɑːkt/. ADJ Something that is **marked** is very obvious and easily noticed. *He has shown marked improvements in spelling and writing.* ♦ **markedly** /mɑːkɪ^{2}dli^1/ SUBMOD OR ADV *Business in Nigeria is markedly different from that in Europe.*

marker /mɑːkə/, **markers.** COUNT N A **marker** is an object used to show the position of something. *The post served as a boundary marker.*

market /mɑːkɪt/, **markets, marketing, marketed.** 1 COUNT N A **market** is a place where goods or animals are sold by numbers of people. *These women sell fish in the markets... ...a cattle market... ...a market stall.* 2 COUNT N The **market** for a product is the number of people who want to buy it. *...the declining commercial vehicle market.* 3 VB WITH OBJ To **market** a product means to sell it in an organized way. *The felt-tip pen was first marketed by a Japanese firm.* ♦ **marketing** UNCOUNT N *...the importance of effective marketing.* 4 PHRASE If something is **on the market,** it is available for people to buy. *It's one of the slowest cars on the market... It's been on the market for three years.* 5 See also **black market.**

market place, market places. 1 SING N You can refer to the **market place** when talking about the buying and selling of products. *Its products must compete in the international market place.* 2 COUNT N A **market place** is a small area in a town where goods are sold. *Beggars crowded in every market-place.*

market research. UNCOUNT N **Market research** is research into what people want, need, and buy.

marking /mɑːkɪŋ/, **markings.** 1 COUNT N **Markings** are shapes or designs on the surface of something. *Look at the markings on the petals.* 2 UNCOUNT N When a teacher does some **marking,** he or she reads a student's work and writes comments or a score on it.

marksman /mɑːksmən/, **marksmen.** COUNT N A **marksman** is a person who can shoot very accurately.

marmalade /mɑːməleɪd/. MASS N **Marmalade** is a food like jam made from oranges or lemons.

maroon /məruːn/. ADJ Something that is **maroon** is a dark reddish-purple. *...a maroon jacket.*

marooned /məruːnd/. ADJ If you are **marooned** in a place, you cannot leave it. *...a story about a group of young boys marooned on a desert island.*

marquee /mɑːkiː/, **marquees.** COUNT N A **marquee** is a large tent which is used at an outdoor event.

marquis /mɑːkwɪs/, **marquises;** also spelled **marquess.** COUNT N A **marquis** is a male member of the nobility. *...the Marquis of Stafford.*

marriage /mærɪdʒ/, **marriages.** 1 COUNT N OR UNCOUNT N A **marriage** is the relationship between a husband and wife, or the state of being married. *It has been a happy marriage... ...in their early years of marriage.* 2 COUNT N OR UNCOUNT N A **marriage** is also the act of marrying someone. *Victoria's marriage to her cousin was not welcomed by her family... On marriage, she moves to her husband's family home.*

married /mærɪd/. 1 ADJ If you are **married,** you have a husband or wife. *She's married to an Englishman.* 2 PHRASE If you **get married,** you marry someone. 3 ATTRIB ADJ **Married** also means involving or relating to marriage. *...their early married life.*

marrow /mærəʊ/, **marrows.** 1 COUNT N OR UNCOUNT N A **marrow** is a long, thick, green vegetable with white flesh; a British use. 2 UNCOUNT N **Marrow** is the substance which is in the centre of human and animal bones. *...a bone marrow transplant.*

marry /mæri^1/, **marries, marrying, married.** 1 RECIP VB When a man and a woman **marry,** they become each other's husband and wife during a special ceremony. *They are in love with each other and wish to marry... I want to marry you.* 2 VB WITH OBJ When a clergyman or registrar **marries** two people, he or she is in charge of their marriage ceremony.

marsh /mɑːʃ/, **marshes.** COUNT N OR UNCOUNT N A **marsh** is a very wet, muddy area of land. *I went off into the marsh... ...a dense plantation bounded by marsh.*

marshal /mɑːʃə^{0}l/, **marshals, marshalling, marshalled;** spelled **marshaling** and **marshaled** in American English. 1 VB WITH OBJ If you **marshal** things or people, you gather them together and organize them. *He hesitated, marshalling his thoughts... Shipping was being marshalled into convoys.* 2 COUNT N A **marshal** is an official who helps to organize a public event. *If you undergo difficulties, please contact the nearest marshal.* 3 COUNT N In the United States, a **marshal** is a police officer who controls and organizes a particular district. 4 See also **field marshal.**

marshy /mɑːʃi^1/. ADJ **Marshy** land is covered in marshes. *...a stretch of marshy coastline.*

martial /mɑːʃəl/. ATTRIB ADJ **Martial** describes things that relate to soldiers or war; a formal use. *...martial music.* ● See also **court-martial.**

martial arts. PLURAL N The **martial arts** are the techniques of self-defence that come from the Far East, for example karate and judo.

martyr /mɑːtə/, **martyrs, martyred.** 1 COUNT N A **martyr** is someone who was killed because of their religious beliefs. *St Sebastian was a Christian martyr.* 2 PASSIVE VB If someone **was martyred,** they were killed because of their religious beliefs. *This is where St Peter was supposed to have been martyred.*

martyrdom /mɑːtədəm/. UNCOUNT N **Martyrdom** is the murder of someone because of their religious beliefs. *...the martyrdom of St Thomas.*

marvel /mɑːvə^{0}l/, **marvels, marvelling, marvelled;** spelled **marveling** and **marveled** in American English. 1 VB WITH 'at' OR REPORT VB If you **marvel** at something, it fills you with surprise or admiration. *Early travellers marvelled at the riches of Mali... We marvelled that so much could happen in such a short time.* 2 COUNT N A **marvel** is something that makes you feel great surprise or admiration. *Paestum is one of the marvels of Greek architecture... It's a marvel that I'm still alive.*

marvellous /mɑːvə^{0}ləs/; spelled **marvelous** in American English. ADJ If you say that people or things are **marvellous,** you mean that they are wonderful or excellent. *What a marvellous idea!* ♦ **marvellously** SUBMOD *I slept marvellously well.*

Marxism /mɑːksɪzə^{0}m/. UNCOUNT N **Marxism** is a political philosophy based on the writings of Karl Marx which stresses the importance of the struggle between different social classes. ♦ **Marxist** /mɑːksɪst/ ADJ OR COUNT N *...Marxist theory... The Marxists were forced to revise their plans.*

mascara /mæskɑːrə/. UNCOUNT N **Mascara** is a substance used to colour eyelashes.

mascot /mæskə^{7}t/, **mascots.** COUNT N A **mascot** is an animal or toy which is thought to bring good luck.

masculine /mæskjə^{4}lɪn/. ADJ **Masculine** characteristics or things relate to or are typical of men, rather than women. *I think it must have something to do with masculine pride.*

masculinity /mæskjə^{4}lɪnɪ^{1}ti^1/. UNCOUNT N **Masculinity** is the fact of being a man or having qualities considered typical of a man. *His masculinity was now in question.*

mash /mæʃ/, **mashes, mashing, mashed.** VB WITH OBJ If you **mash** vegetables, you crush them after cooking them. *Mash the lentils well.* ♦ **mashed** ADJ *...mashed potatoes.*

mask /mɑːsk/, **masks, masking, masked.** 1 COUNT N A **mask** is something which you wear over your face for protection or disguise. *The thieves were wearing masks... ...a surgical mask.* 2 VB WITH OBJ If you **mask** something, you hide it. *Her eyes were masked by huge, round sunglasses... They couldn't mask their disappointment.*

masked /mɑːskt/. ADJ Someone who is **masked** is wearing a mask. *Three armed and masked men suddenly burst in.*

masochism /mæsə^{6}kɪzə^{0}m/. UNCOUNT N **Masochism** involves getting pleasure from your own suffering.

masochist /mæsə^{6}kɪst/, **masochists.** COUNT N A **masochist** is someone who gets pleasure from their own suffering. *Unless you are a complete masochist, you are unlikely to derive much pleasure from the show.* ♦ **masochistic** /mæsə^{6}kɪstɪk/. ADJ *There are some actors with strong masochistic streaks who wish to hear only criticisms.*

mason /meɪsə^{0}n/, **masons.** COUNT N A **mason** is a person who makes things out of stone.

masonry /meɪsənri^1/. UNCOUNT N **Masonry** is the bricks or pieces of stone which form part of a wall or building. *Large chunks of masonry were beginning to fall.*

masquerade /mæskəreɪd/, **masquerades, masquerading, masqueraded.** VB If you **masquerade** as something, you pretend to be that thing. *He might try to masquerade as a policeman... He might be masquerading under an assumed name.*

mass /mæs/, **masses, massing, massed.** 1 COUNT N A **mass** of something is a large amount of it. *Bruce stuffed a mass of papers into his briefcase.* 2 COUNT N A **mass** is a large amount of a substance; a technical use. *...a mass of warm air laden with water vapour... ...the great land mass of Asia.* 3 QUANTIF **Masses** of something means a large amount of it; an informal use. *They've got simply masses of money.* 4 ATTRIB ADJ You use **mass** to describe something which involves a very large number of people. *...the power of mass communication... ...mass unemployment.* 5 PLURAL N The **masses** are the ordinary people in society. *We want to produce opera for the masses.* 6 VB When people or things **mass,** they gather together into a large crowd or group. *The students massed in Paris.* ♦ **massed** ATTRIB ADJ *...the massed groups of rival supporters.* 7 UNCOUNT N OR COUNT N The **mass** of an object is the amount of physical matter that it has; a technical use. *The velocity depends on the mass of the object.* 8 UNCOUNT N OR COUNT N In the Roman Catholic church, **Mass** is the ceremony in which people have bread and wine in remembrance of Christ's death and resurrection.

massacre /mæsəkə/, **massacres, massacring, massacred.** COUNT N OR UNCOUNT N A **massacre** is the killing of many people in a violent and cruel way. *...the massacre of a village.* Also VB WITH OBJ *The police had massacred crowds of people.*

massage /mæsɑːd^{0}ʒ/, **massages, massaging, massaged.** VB WITH OBJ If you **massage** someone, you rub their body to make them relax or to stop their muscles from hurting. *Could you massage the back of my neck?* Also UNCOUNT N OR COUNT N *We can relax our muscles by massage... Let me give you a massage.*

masse. See **en masse.**

massive /mæsɪv/. ADJ Something that is **massive** is extremely large in size, quantity, or extent. *He opened the massive oak front doors... ...a massive increase in oil prices.* ♦ **massively** ADV *We invested massively in West German machinery.*

mass media. COLL N The **mass media** are television, radio, and newspapers. *The mass media now play an increasing role in shaping our opinions.*

mass-produce, mass-produces, mass-producing, mass-produced. VB WITH OBJ When people **mass-produce** something, they make it in large quantities by repeating the same process many times. *...a vaccine which can be mass-produced cheaply.* ♦ **mass-produced** ADJ *...cheap mass-produced exports.*

mast /mɑːst/, **masts.** 1 COUNT N The **masts** of a boat are the tall upright poles that support its sails. 2 COUNT N A radio or television **mast** is a very tall pole that is used as an aerial to transmit sound or television pictures.

master /mɑːstə/, **masters, mastering, mastered.** 1 COUNT N A servant's **master** is the man he works for; an old-fashioned use. *Sometimes there was no dispute between a master and his slave.* 2 COUNT N A **master** is also a male teacher; a British use. *...the science master.* ● See also **headmaster.** 3 UNCOUNT N If you are **master** of a situation, you have control over it. *This was before man was total master of his environment.* 4 ATTRIB ADJ You use **master** to describe someone who is extremely skilled in a job or activity. *...master bakers.* 5 VB WITH OBJ If you **master** something, you manage to learn it or cope with it. *Slowly, one begins to master the complex skills involved... ...once we have mastered the basic problems.*

masterful /mɑːstəfʊl/. ADJ Someone who is **masterful** behaves in a way which shows that they can control people or situations. *His voice had become more masterful.*

masterly /mɑːstəli^1/. ADJ A **masterly** action is very skilful. *It was a masterly performance.*

Master of Arts, Masters of Arts. COUNT N A **Master of Arts** is a person with a higher degree in an arts or social science subject.

Master of Science, Masters of Science. COUNT N A **Master of Science** is a person with a higher degree in a science subject.

masterpiece /mɑːstəpiːs/, **masterpieces.** COUNT N A **masterpiece** is an extremely good painting, novel, film, or other work of art. *It is one of the great masterpieces of European art.*

mastery /mɑːstə^{0}ri^1/. **1** UNCOUNT N **Mastery** of a skill or art is excellence in it. *...his mastery of the language.* **2** UNCOUNT N **Mastery** is also complete power or control over something. *His sons were struggling to obtain mastery of the country.*

mat /mæt/, **mats. 1** COUNT N A **mat** is a small piece of cloth, card, or plastic which you put on a table to protect it. *She set his food on the mat before him... ...beer mats.* **2** COUNT N A **mat** is also a small piece of carpet or other thick material that you put on the floor. **3** See also **matt.**

match /mætʃ/, **matches, matching, matched. 1** COUNT N A **match** is an organized game of football, cricket, chess, or other sport. *...a football match.* **2** COUNT N A **match** is also a small wooden stick with a substance on one end that produces a flame when you pull or push it along the side of a matchbox. **3** RECIP VB If one thing **matches** another, the two things are similar. *The captain's feelings clearly matched my own... All her towels match.* ♦ **matching** ATTRIB ADJ *...a blue jacket with matching shirt.* **4** RECIP VB If you **match** one thing with another or **match** them up, you decide that one is suitable for the other, or that there is a connection between them. *All you have to do is correctly match the famous personalities with the towns they come from.* **5** VB WITH OBJ To **match** something means to be equal to it in speed, size, or quality. *They are trying to upgrade their cars to match the foreign competition... She walked at a pace that Morris's short legs could hardly match.* **6** PHRASE If something **is no match for** another thing, it is inferior to it. *A machine gun is no match for a tank.*

matchbox /mætʃbɒks/, **matchboxes.** COUNT N A **matchbox** is a small box that matches are sold in.

matched /mætʃt/. **1** ADJ If two people are well **matched,** they are suited to one another and are likely to have a successful relationship. *I thought we were perfectly matched.* **2** ADJ If two people or groups are well **matched,** they have the same strength or ability. *Government and rebel soldiers are evenly matched.*

mate /meɪt/, **mates, mating, mated. 1** COUNT N Your **mates** are your friends; an informal use. *He supposed his old mate Kowalski would be with them.* **2** COUNT N An animal's **mate** is its sexual partner. *The females are about half the size of their mates.* **3** RECIP VB When a male animal and a female animal **mate,** they have sex. *Male wild cats sometimes mate with domestic females.* ♦ **mating** ATTRIB ADJ *...the mating season.* **4** SING N The **mate** or **first mate** on a ship is the officer who is next in importance to the captain.

material /mətɪərɪəl/, **materials. 1** COUNT N OR UNCOUNT N A **material** is a solid substance. *...synthetic substitutes for natural materials... ...decaying material.* **2** MASS N **Material** is cloth. *The sleeping bags are made of acrylic material... ...delicate materials, like silk.* **3** PLURAL N **Materials** are the equipment or things that you need for a particular activity. *...writing materials... ...cleaning materials.* **4** UNCOUNT N Ideas or information that are used as a basis for a book, play, or film can be referred to as **material.** *She hoped to find material for some articles... They researched a lot of background material.* **5** ATTRIB ADJ **Material** things are related to possessions or money, rather than to more abstract things. *...the material comforts of life.* ♦ **materially** ADV *Children can gain materially and psychologically when both parents work.*

materialise /mətɪərɪəlaɪz/. See **materialize.**

materialism /mətɪərɪəlɪzə^{0}m/. UNCOUNT N **Materialism** is the attitude of people who think that money and possessions are the most important things in life. *They were determined to renounce the materialism of the society they had been brought up in.*

materialist /mətɪərɪəlɪst/, **materialists.** COUNT N A **materialist** is a person who thinks that money and possessions are the most important things in life. *He was an atheist and a materialist.* ♦ **materialistic** /mətɪərɪəlɪstɪk/ ADJ *This society has made people greedy and materialistic.*

materialize /mətɪərɪəlaɪz/, **materializes, materializing, materialized;** also spelled **materialise.** VB If a possible event **materializes,** it actually happens. *Fortunately, the attack did not materialize.*

maternal /mə^{3}tɜːnə^{0}l/. ADJ **Maternal** is used to describe things relating to a mother. *...maternal feelings.*

maternity /mə^{3}tɜːnɪ^{1}ti^1/. MOD **Maternity** is used to describe things relating to pregnancy and birth. *...maternity hospitals... ...maternity leave.*

math /mæθ/. UNCOUNT N **Math** is the same as mathematics; an American use.

mathematical /mæθəmætɪkə^{0}l/. ATTRIB ADJ **Mathematical** means relating to numbers and calculations. *...a mathematical formula.* ♦ **mathematically** ADV *...a mathematically provable law.*

mathematician /mæθəmətɪʃə^{0}n/, **mathematicians.** COUNT N A **mathematician** studies problems involving numbers and calculations.

mathematics /mæθəmætɪks/. UNCOUNT N **Mathematics** is a subject which involves the study of numbers, quantities, or shapes.

maths /mæθs/. UNCOUNT N **Maths** is the same as mathematics; a British use. *...a maths teacher.*

matinee /mætɪneɪ/, **matinees;** also spelled **matinée.** COUNT N A **matinee** is an afternoon performance of a play or showing of a film.

matrices /meɪtrɪsiːz/. **Matrices** is the plural of **matrix.**

matriculate /mə^{3}trɪkjə^{4}leɪt/, **matriculates, matriculating, matriculated.** VB If you **matriculate,** you formally register as a student at a university, having got the right qualifications; a technical use. ♦ **matriculation** /mə^{3}trɪkjə^{4}leɪʃə^{0}n/ UNCOUNT N *Work for a degree counts only from the date of matriculation.*

matrimony /mætrɪməni^1/. UNCOUNT N **Matrimony** is the state of being married; a formal use. *...a proposal of matrimony.* ♦ **matrimonial** /mætrɪməʊnɪəl/ ATTRIB ADJ *...matrimonial difficulties.*

matrix /meɪtrɪks/, **matrices** /meɪtrɪsiːz/. COUNT N WITH SUPP A **matrix** is the environment in which something such as a society develops and grows; a formal use. *Attitudes are formed in a matrix of psychological and social complications.*

matron /meɪtrən/, **matrons. 1** COUNT N In a hospital, the **matron** is a senior nurse. **2** COUNT N At a boarding school, the **matron** is a woman who looks after the health of the children.

matt /mæt/; also spelled **mat.** ADJ A **matt** surface is dull rather than shiny. *...matt black.*

matted /mætəd/. ADJ Something that is **matted** is twisted together untidily. *Their hair was matted.*

matter /mætə/, **matters, mattering, mattered. 1** COUNT N WITH SUPP A **matter** is a situation which you have to deal with. *It was a purely personal matter... She's very honest in money matters... This is a matter for the police.* **2** PLURAL N You use **matters** to refer to the situation that you are talking about. *The absence of electricity made matters worse.* **3** UNCOUNT N **Matter** is any substance; a formal use. *An atom is the smallest indivisible particle of matter... The termites feed on vegetable matter.* **4** UNCOUNT N WITH SUPP You can refer to books and magazines as reading **matter;** a formal use. **5** VB If something **matters** to you, it is important to you. *My family were all that mattered to me.* **6** VB If something does not **matter,** it is not important because it does not have an effect on the situation. *It does not matter which method you choose.*

PHRASES ● You say **'What's the matter?'** or **'Is anything the matter?'** when you think that someone has a problem and you want to know what it is. *What's the matter, Cynthia? You sound odd... What's the matter with your hand?* ● You use **no matter** in expressions such as 'no matter how' and 'no matter what' to indicate that something is true or happens in all circumstances. *I told him to report to me after the job was completed, no matter how late it was... They smiled continuously, no matter what was said.* ● If you do something **as a matter of** principle or policy, you do it for that reason. *Merchant banks recruit women as a matter of policy.* ● You use **matter** in expressions such as 'a matter of days' when you are drawing attention to how short a period of time is. *Within a matter of weeks she was crossing the Atlantic.* ● If you say that something is just **a matter of time,** you mean that it is certain to happen at some time in the future. *It appeared to be only a matter of time before they were caught.* ● If you say that something is just a **matter of** doing something, you mean it is easy and can be done just by doing that thing. *Skating's just a matter of practice.* ● You say **for that matter** to emphasize that a statement you have made about one thing is also true about another. *He's shaking with the cold. So am I, for that matter.* ● **as a matter of course:** see **course.** ● **as a matter of fact:** see **fact.**

matter-of-fact. ADJ Someone who is **matter-of-fact** is unemotional. *'I see,' she said, trying to seem matter-of-fact.*

matting /mætɪŋ/. UNCOUNT N **Matting** is a thick material woven from rope or straw, which is used as a floor covering. *...coconut matting.*

mattress /mætrə^{1}s/, **mattresses.** COUNT N A **mattress** is a large, flat pad which is put on a bed to make it comfortable.

mature /mətjʊə/, **matures, maturing, matured. 1** VB If someone **matures,** their personality and their emotional behaviour become more fully developed and controlled. *He had matured and quietened down considerably.* **2** ADJ **Mature** people behave in a sensible, well-balanced way. *She's in some ways mature and in some ways rather a child.* ♦ **maturity** /mətjʊərɪ^{1}ti^1, -tʃʊə-/ UNCOUNT N *I have long felt that you lacked maturity.* **3** VB To **mature** means to develop or to reach a state of complete development. *...the great casks where the wine matured.* **4** ADJ **Mature** means fully developed. *...mature plants.* ♦ **maturity** UNCOUNT N *Only half of the young birds may live to reach maturity.*

mature student, mature students. COUNT N In a British college or university, a **mature student** is a student who is over 25 years old.

maul /mɔːl/, **mauls, mauling, mauled.** VB WITH OBJ If someone **is mauled** by an animal, they are attacked and injured by it.

mausoleum /mɔːsəlɪəm/, **mausoleums.** COUNT N A **mausoleum** is a building containing the grave of someone famous or rich.

mauve /məʊv/. ADJ Something that is **mauve** is pale purple.

maverick /mævə^{0}rɪk/, **mavericks.** COUNT N A **maverick** is someone who thinks and acts in a very independent way; a literary use. Also ATTRIB ADJ *He is a self-confessed maverick Marxist.*

max. **max.** is a written abbreviation for 'maximum'. *...max. 17°C... The cost will be £90 max.*

maxim /mæksɪm/, **maxims.** COUNT N A **maxim** is a rule for sensible behaviour in the form of a short saying. *Instant action: that's my maxim.*

maximize /mæksɪmaɪz/, **maximizes, maximizing, maximized;** also spelled **maximise.** VB WITH OBJ To **maximize** something means to make it as great in amount or importance as you can. *The company's main objective is to maximize profits.*

maximum /mæksɪməm/. **1** ATTRIB ADJ The **maximum** amount of something is the largest amount possible. *They held the prisoner under maximum security conditions... Never exceed the maximum daily dosage of 150 mg.* **2** SING N The **maximum** is the largest amount possible. *Conscription should be limited to a maximum of six months' service.*

may /meɪ/. **1** MODAL If you say that something **may** happen or be true, you mean that it is possible. *We may be here a long time... You may be right... A gigantic meteorite may have wiped out the dinosaurs 65 million years ago... They struggle to cure diseases so that people may live longer.* **2** MODAL If someone **may** do something, they are allowed to do it. *If the verdict is unacceptable, the defendant may appeal... May I have a word with you, please?* **3** MODAL You can use **may** when saying that, although something is true, something contrasting is also true. *They may be seven thousand miles away but they know what's going on over here... Ingenious though these techniques may be, they can hardly be regarded as practical.* **4** MODAL You can also use **may** to express a wish that something will happen; a formal use. *Long may it continue.* **5** UNCOUNT N **May** is the fifth month of the year in the Western calendar.

maybe /meɪbiː/. **1** SENTENCE ADV You use **maybe** to indicate that something is possible, but you are not certain about it. *Maybe he'll be prime minister one day... Well, maybe you're right.* **2** SENTENCE ADV You also use **maybe** to show that a number is approximate. *There were maybe half a dozen men there... He's in his fifties, I'd say. Fifty-five, maybe.*

mayhem /meɪhem/. UNCOUNT N **Mayhem** is an uncontrolled and confused situation. *The kids began to create mayhem in the washrooms.*

mayonnaise /meɪəneɪz/. UNCOUNT N **Mayonnaise** is a pale, thick, uncooked sauce made from egg yolks and oil.

mayor /meə/, **mayors.** COUNT N The **mayor** of a town is the person who has been elected to lead and to represent it for a year.

mayoress /meərɪ^{2}s/, **mayoresses.** COUNT N A **mayoress** is the wife of a mayor.

maze /meɪz/, **mazes.** COUNT N A **maze** is a system of complicated passages which it is difficult to find your way through. *Some mice were trained to find their way through a simple maze.*

me /mi^1/. PRON **Me** is used as the object of a verb or preposition. A speaker or writer uses **me** to refer to himself or herself. *He told me about it... He looked at me reproachfully.*

meadow /medəʊ/, **meadows.** COUNT N A **meadow** is a field with grass and flowers growing in it.

meagre /miːgə/; spelled **meager** in American English. ADJ Something that is **meagre** is very small. *...a meagre crop of potatoes... ...his meagre wages.*

meal /miːl/, **meals.** COUNT N A **meal** is an occasion when people eat. It is also the food that they eat on that occasion. *...the evening meal... ...a simple meal of bread and cheese.*

mealtime /mi:ltaɪm/, **mealtimes.** COUNT N A **mealtime** is an occasion when you eat a meal. *I had a glass of juice three times a day at mealtimes.*

mean /mi:n/, **means, meaning, meant** /mɛnt/; **meaner, meanest. 1** VB WITH OBJ You ask what a word, expression, or gesture **means** when you want it to be explained to you. *What does 'imperialism' mean?... What is meant by the term 'mental activity'?* **2** REPORT VB What someone **means** is what they are referring to or intending to say. *But what do we mean by 'education'?... I know the guy you mean... I thought you meant you wanted to take your own car.* **3** VB WITH OBJ If something **means** a lot to you, it is important to you. *These were the friends who had meant most to her since childhood.* **4** REPORT VB If one thing **means** another, it shows that the second thing is true or makes it certain to happen. *A cut in taxes will mean a cut in government spending... Water running down the outside of a wall may mean that the gutters are blocked.* **5** VB WITH OBJ If you **mean** what you say, you are serious and not joking, exaggerating, or just being polite. *I'm going. I mean it... Anyone can program a computer. And I do mean anyone.* **6** VB WITH TO-INF If you **mean** to do something, you intend to do it. *I meant to ring you but I'm afraid I forgot... I'm sorry, I didn't mean to be rude.* **7** VB WITH OBJ AND TO-INF OR 'for' If something **is meant** to be a particular thing or **is meant** for a particular purpose, that is what you intended or planned. *Sorry, I'm not very good at drawing, but that's meant to be a cube... 'That hurts!'—'It's meant to!'... His smile was meant for me.* **8** PASSIVE VB WITH TO-INF If something **is meant** to happen or exist, it is strongly expected to happen or exist. *I found a road that wasn't meant to be there.* **9** PASSIVE VB WITH TO-INF You also use **meant** when you are talking about the reputation that something has. *They're meant to be excellent cars.* **10** COUNT N WITH SUPP A **means** of doing something is a method or thing which makes it possible. 'Means' is both the singular and plural. *Scientists are working to devise a means of storing this type of power... We have the means to kill people on a massive scale.* **11** PLURAL N You can refer to the money that someone has as their **means;** a formal use. *Sutcliffe has a house in Mayfair so he obviously has means.* **12** ADJ Someone who is **mean** is unwilling to spend much money or to use very much of a particular thing. *I used to be very mean about hot water.* ♦ **meanness** UNCOUNT N *These employers were famous for their meanness.* **13** ADJ If you are **mean** to someone, you are unkind to them. *She had apologized for being so mean to Rudolph.* ♦ **meanness** UNCOUNT N *...his meanness to his sisters.* **14** COUNT N In mathematics, the **mean** is the average of a set of numbers. *What you do first is to calculate the mean.*

PHRASES ● You say **'I mean'** when you are explaining something more clearly or justifying what you have said, or when you are correcting yourself. *If you haven't any climbing boots, you can borrow them. I mean dozens of people have got boots... This is Herbert, I mean Humbert.* ● If something is **a means to an end,** you do it only because it will help you to achieve what you want. ● If you do something **by means of** a particular method or object, you do it using that method or object. *The rig is anchored in place by means of steel cables.* ● You say **'by all means'** as a way of giving someone permission; a formal use. *By all means take a day's holiday.* ● **By no means** is used to emphasize that something is not true. *It is by no means certain that this is what he did.* ● You use **no mean** to emphasize that someone or something is especially good or remarkable; a formal use. *Sir George Gilbert Scott, himself no mean architect, approved the plans... Persuading John to come was no mean feat.*

meander /mi^{1}ændə/, **meanders, meandering, meandered. 1** VB If a river or road **meanders,** it has a lot of bends in it. *A stream meandered towards the sea.* **2** VB WITH ADJUNCT To **meander** also means to move slowly and indirectly. *We meandered along eating nuts and blackberries.*

meaning /mi:nɪŋ/, **meanings. 1** COUNT N OR UNCOUNT N The **meaning** of something is what it refers to or the idea that it expresses. *The word 'guide' is used with various meanings... The meaning of the remark was clear... I don't understand the meaning of Pollock's paintings.* **2** UNCOUNT N If something has **meaning** for you, it seems to be worthwhile and to have a real purpose. *We yearn for beauty, truth, and meaning in our lives.*

meaningful /mi:nɪŋfʊl/. **1** ADJ A **meaningful** sentence or event has a meaning that you can understand. *Nobody has ever explained electricity to me in a meaningful way.* **2** ADJ A **meaningful** look, expression, or remark is intended to express an attitude or opinion. *They exchanged meaningful glances.* ♦ **meaningfully** ADV *'Goodnight, and call again. Anytime,' Boon added meaningfully.* **3** ADJ Something that is **meaningful** is serious and important. *He felt the need to establish a more meaningful relationship with people... ...meaningful discussions.* ♦ **meaningfully** ADV *At least you'd be filling your time meaningfully.*

meaningless /mi:nɪŋlɪ^{2}s/. **1** ADJ Something that is **meaningless** has no meaning that you can understand. *These songs are largely meaningless.* **2** ADJ If your work or life is **meaningless,** you feel that it has no purpose and is not worthwhile.

meant /mɛnt/. **Meant** is the past tense and past participle of **mean.**

meantime /mi:ntaɪm/. PHRASE **In the meantime** means in the period of time between two events. *I will call Doctor Ford. In the meantime you must sleep.*

meanwhile /mi:nwaɪl/. **1** SENTENCE ADV **Meanwhile** means while something else is happening. *She ate an olive. Nick, meanwhile, was talking about Rose.* **2** SENTENCE ADV **Meanwhile** also means in the period of time between two events. *But meanwhile a number of steps will have to be taken.*

measles /mi:zə^{0}lz/. UNCOUNT N **Measles** is an infectious illness that gives you red spots on your skin. ● See also **German measles.**

measurable /mɛʒə^{0}rəbə^{0}l/. ADJ If something is **measurable,** it is large enough to be noticed or to be significant; a formal use. *Some measurable progress had been made.*

measure /mɛʒə/, **measures, measuring, measured. 1** VB WITH OBJ When you **measure** something, you find out how big or great it is, for example by using an instrument such as a ruler, thermometer, or set of scales. *He measured the diameter... The explosive force is measured in tons.* **2** VB WITH COMPLEMENT If something **measures** a particular distance, its length, width, or depth is that distance. *...slivers of glass measuring a few millimetres across... ...a square area measuring 900 metres.* **3** SING N You can use **measure** to refer to an amount or degree of something abstract; a formal use. *Everyone is entitled to some measure of protection... ...a large measure of public support.* **4** COUNT N A **measure** of an alcoholic drink such as brandy or whisky is an amount of it in a glass. *...a generous measure of cognac.* **5** SING N WITH 'of' If something is a **measure** of a particular thing, it shows how great or remarkable it is. *It is a measure of their achievement that the system has lasted so long.* **6** COUNT N **Measures** are also actions that are carried out by people in authority in order to achieve a particular result; a formal use. *Measures had been taken to limit the economic decline.* **7** PHRASE If something is done **for good measure,** it is done in addition to a number of other actions. *The waiter had taken away the plates, and, for good measure, had removed his glass.* **8** See also **tape measure.**

measure up. PHR VB Someone or something that **measures up** is as good as it is expected to be. *The repair failed to measure up to their standards.*

measured /mɛʒəd/. ADJ **Measured** behaviour is careful and deliberate; a literary use. *...walking at the same measured pace... ...his cool, measured speech.*

measurement /mɛʒəmə^{2}nt/, **measurements. 1** COUNT N A **measurement** is a result that you obtain by measuring something. *Check the measurements first... ...the exact measurements of the office.* **2** UNCOUNT N **Measurement** is the activity of measuring something. *...the first actual measurement of the speed of sound.* **3** PLURAL N Your **measurements** are the size of your chest, waist, hips, and other parts of your body.

meat /mi:t/, **meats.** MASS N **Meat** is the flesh of a dead animal that people cook and eat.

mechanic /mɪ^{2}kænɪk/, **mechanics. 1** COUNT N A **mechanic** is someone who mends and maintains machines and engines as a job. **2** PLURAL N You can refer to the way in which something works or is done as the **mechanics** of it. *...the mechanics of reading.*

mechanical /mɪ^{2}kænɪkə^{0}l/. **1** ADJ A **mechanical** device has moving parts and uses power in order to do a particular task. *They were using a mechanical shovel to clear up the streets.* ♦ **mechanically** ADV *The glass doors slid open mechanically as she approached them.* **2** ATTRIB ADJ Someone who has a **mechanical** mind understands how machines work. *...a given level of mechanical ability.* **3** ADJ A **mechanical** action is done automatically, without thinking about it. *...mindless and mechanical repetitions* ♦ **mechanically** ADV *'How are you?'—'Oh, fine, thanks,' said Philip mechanically.*

mechanism /mɛkənɪzə^{0}m/, **mechanisms. 1** COUNT N A **mechanism** is a part of a machine that does a particular task. *...a locking mechanism... ...steering mechanisms in cars.* **2** COUNT N WITH SUPP A **mechanism** is also a way of getting something done within a system. *There's no mechanism for changing the decision.* **3** COUNT N WITH SUPP **Mechanism** is used to refer to a part of your behaviour that is automatic. *...the defence mechanism of disbelief.*

mechanize /mɛkənaɪz/, **mechanizes, mechanizing, mechanized;** also spelled **mechanise.** VB WITH OBJ If a type of work **is mechanized,** it is done by machines. ♦ **mechanized** ADJ *Housework has become highly mechanised.* ♦ **mechanization** /mɛkənaɪzeɪʃə^{0}n/ UNCOUNT N *...the mechanisation of the postal service.*

medal /mɛdə^{0}l/, **medals.** COUNT N **Medals** are small metal discs that are given as awards for bravery or as prizes in sporting events. *He won six gold medals.*

medallion /mɪ^{2}dæljən/, **medallions.** COUNT N A **medallion** is a round metal disc which is worn as an ornament on a chain round a person's neck.

medallist /mɛdə^{0}lɪst/, **medallists.** COUNT N A **medallist** is a person who has won a medal in sport.

meddle /mɛdə^{0}l/, **meddles, meddling, meddled.** VB If you **meddle** in something, you try to influence or change it without being asked; used showing disapproval. *He's never wanted me to meddle in his affairs... I dared not meddle with my wife's plans.*

media /mi:dɪə/. **1** COLL N You can refer to television, radio, and newspapers as the **media.** *These problems have been exaggerated by the media.* **2** **Media** is a plural of **medium.**

mediaeval /mɛdɪi:və^{0}l/. See **medieval.**

mediate /mi:di^{1}eɪt/, **mediates, mediating, mediated.** VB If you **mediate** between two groups, you try to settle a dispute between them. *I mediated for him in a quarrel with his brother.* ♦ **mediator** /mi:di^{1}eɪtə/ COUNT N *Tom Hagen was busy trying to find a mediator satisfactory to both parties.*

medical /mɛdɪkə^{0}l/, **medicals. 1** ATTRIB ADJ **Medical** means relating to the treatment of illness and injuries and to the prevention of illness. *She had to undergo medical treatment... ...the medical care of babies.* **2** COUNT N A **medical** is a thorough examination of your body by a doctor. *They were all set to give him a medical.*

medication /mɛdɪkeɪʃə^{0}n/, **medications.** UNCOUNT N OR COUNT N **Medication** is medicine that is used to cure an illness. *The doctor can prescribe medication to relieve the symptoms... Don't forget your medication.*

medicinal /mɛdɪsɪnə^{0}l/. ADJ **Medicinal** substances are used to treat and cure illness. *...a medicinal herb.*

medicine /mɛdɪ^{0}sɪn/, **medicines. 1** MASS N A **medicine** is a substance that you drink or swallow in order to cure an illness. *...a medicine for his cold... ...cough medicines.* **2** UNCOUNT N **Medicine** is the treatment of illness and injuries by doctors and nurses. *...the professions of medicine and dentistry.*

medieval /mɛdɪi:və^{0}l/; also spelled **mediaeval.** ADJ **Medieval** things belong or relate to the period between about 1100 AD and about 1500 AD, especially in Europe. *...a medieval church.*

mediocre /mi:dɪəʊkə/. ADJ **Mediocre** things are of poor quality. *He spent much of his time reading mediocre paperbacks.* ♦ **mediocrity** /mi:dɪɒkrɪ^{1}ti^1 mɛd-/ UNCOUNT N *He was dismayed by the mediocrity of the people working with him.*

meditate /mɛdɪteɪt/, **meditates, meditating, meditated. 1** VB To **meditate** on something means to think about it carefully and deeply for a long time. *He was left alone to meditate on his sins.* ♦ **meditation** /mɛdɪteɪʃə^{0}n/ UNCOUNT N OR COUNT N *...the subject of my meditation... I hope we will not disturb your meditations.* **2** VB If you **meditate,** you remain in a calm, silent state for a period of time, often as part of a religious training or practice. *...meditating in the wilderness for seven days.* ♦ **meditation** UNCOUNT N *He was deeply interested in meditation and yoga.*

meditative /mɛdɪtətɪv/. ADJ **Meditative** means careful and thoughtful. *Daniel took a meditative sip of tea... We were both quiet and meditative.*

medium /mi:dɪəm/, **mediums** or **media.** The plural of the noun is **mediums** or **media** for meaning 3, and **mediums for meaning 4. 1** ADJ If something is of **medium** size, it is neither large nor small. *...a medium screwdriver... He was of medium height.* **2** ADJ If something is of a **medium** colour, it is neither light nor dark. *...medium brown.* **3** COUNT N A **medium** is the means that you use to communicate or express something; a formal use. *...sending messages through the medium of paper and printed word... ...the major broadcasting medium.* **4** COUNT N A **medium** is also a person who claims to communicate with people who are dead.

meek /mi:k/. ADJ A **meek** person is quiet or timid and does what other people say. *...his meek acceptance of insult.* ♦ **meekly** ADV *'I'm sorry dear,' Gretchen said meekly.*

meet /mi:t/, **meets, meeting, met** /mɛt/. **1** RECIP VB When two people **meet** for the first time, they happen to be in the same place and are introduced or get to know each other. *I met a Swedish girl on the train... They met each other at a party in London... Come and meet Tony and Rick.* **2** RECIP VB When two people arrange to **meet,** they arrange to go to the same place at the same time. *They met every day... Meet me under the clock.* **3** VB WITH OBJ If you **meet** someone who is travelling or if you **meet** their train, plane, or bus, you go to the station, airport, or bus stop in order to be there when they arrive. **4** VB When a group of people **meet,** they gather together for a purpose. *Teachers in Tokyo met to discuss our methods.* **5** VB WITH OBJ If something **meets** a need, requirement, or condition, it is satisfactory or sufficiently large to fulfil it. *His income is inadequate to meet his basic needs.* **6** VB WITH OBJ If you **meet** a problem or challenge, you deal satisfactorily with it. **7** VB WITH OBJ If you **meet** the cost of something, you provide the money for it. **8** VB WITH OBJ To **meet** a situation or attitude means to experience it. *Where had I met this kind of ignorance before?* **9** RECIP VB When one object **meets** another, it hits or touches it. *The heavy club met his head with a crack... Their fingers met.* **10** RECIP VB If your eyes **meet** someone else's, you both look at each other at the same time. *Their eyes meet, and they smile.* **11** RECIP VB The place where two areas or lines **meet** is the place where they are next to one another or join. *...where this road meets the one from Lairg... Parallel lines never meet.* **12** to **make ends meet:** see **end.** ● to **meet** someone **halfway:** see **halfway.**

meet up. PHR VB If you **meet up** with someone, you both go to the same place at the same time. *We planned to meet up with them in Florence.*

meet with. PHR VB **1** If you **meet with** someone, you have a meeting with them; an American use. *We can meet with the professor Monday night.* **2** If something **meets with** or **is met with** a particular reaction, people react to it in that way. *All appeals for aid meet with refusal... His approaches had been met with ill-concealed disdain.* **3** You can say that someone **meets with** success or failure when they are successful or unsuccessful.

meeting /mi:tɪŋ/, **meetings. 1** COUNT N A **meeting** is an event in which people discuss things and make decisions. *The committee will consider the proposal at its next meeting... I held a meeting that afternoon... ...a meeting of physicists.* **2** SING N You can refer to the people at a meeting as the **meeting.** *The meeting agreed with him.* **3** COUNT N A **meeting** is also an occasion when you meet someone. *...his first meeting with Alice.*

megaphone /mɛgəfəʊn/, **megaphones.** COUNT N A **megaphone** is a cone-shaped device for making your voice sound louder in the open air.

melancholy /mɛlənkɒli^1/; a literary word. **1** ADJ If you feel **melancholy,** you feel sad. *He became melancholy.* Also UNCOUNT N *...a touch of melancholy in his voice.* **2** ADJ Something that is **melancholy** makes you feel sad. *...melancholy music.*

mellow /mɛləʊ/, **mellows, mellowing, mellowed. 1** ADJ **Mellow** light is soft and golden. *...the mellow sunlight.* **2** ATTRIB ADJ **Mellow** stone or brick has a pleasant soft colour because it is old. **3** ADJ A **mellow** sound is smooth and pleasant to listen to. **4** ERG VB If someone **mellows,** they become more pleasant or relaxed. *He mellowed considerably as he got older... He says that age should have mellowed me.*

melodrama /mɛlə^{6}drɑ:mə/, **melodramas.** COUNT N OR UNCOUNT N A **melodrama** is a story or play in which there are a lot of exciting or sad events and in which people's emotions are very exaggerated.

melodramatic /mɛlə^{6}drəmætɪk/. ADJ If you are being **melodramatic,** you treat a situation as much more serious than it really is. *I think we're getting a bit too melodramatic.*

melody /mɛlədi^1/, **melodies.** COUNT N A **melody** is a tune; a literary use.

melon /mɛlən/, **melons.** COUNT N OR UNCOUNT N A **melon** is a large juicy fruit with a thick green or yellow skin.

melt /mɛlt/, **melts, melting, melted. 1** ERG VB When a solid substance **melts** or **is melted,** it changes to a liquid because of being heated. *The snow and ice had melted... Melt the margarine in a saucepan.* **2** VB If something **melts** or **melts** away, it gradually disappears. *Lynn's inhibitions melted... Their differences melted away.*

melt down. PHR VB If you **melt down** a metal or glass object, you heat it until it melts. *Railings were melted down for cannon.*

member /mɛmbə/, **members. 1** COUNT N WITH SUPP A **member** of a group is one of the people, animals, or things belonging to the group. *Babies usually have milder colds than older members of the family... ...junior members of staff... The weaver bird is a member of the sparrow family.* **2** COUNT N A **member** of an organization is a person who has joined it. *...members of trade unions.* **3** ATTRIB ADJ The states or countries that have joined an international organization are called the **member** states or countries. *All the member countries are under pressure to conform.* **4** COUNT N A **member** is also a Member of Parliament. *...John Parker, the Labour member for Dagenham.*

Member of Parliament, Members of Parliament. COUNT N A **Member of Parliament** is a person who has been elected to represent people in a country's parliament.

membership /mɛmbəʃɪp/, **memberships. 1** UNCOUNT N **Membership** is the fact or state of being a member of an organization. *Deacon was questioned about his membership of the Nationalist Party.* **2** COUNT N OR UNCOUNT N The **membership** of an organization is the people who belong to it. *Membership declined to half a million.*

membrane /mɛmbreɪn/, **membranes.** COUNT N A **membrane** is a thin piece of skin which connects or covers parts of a person's or animal's body; a formal use. *...the delicate membranes of the throat.*

memento /mɪ^{2}mɛntəʊ/, **mementos** or **mementoes.** COUNT N A **memento** is an object which you keep to remind you of a person or a special occasion. *...a memento of the singer's farewell concert.*

memo /mɛməʊ/, **memos.** COUNT N A **memo** is an official note from one person to another within the same organization. *He wrote a memo to the War Department asking for more soldiers.*

memoirs /mɛmwɑ:z/. PLURAL N If someone writes their **memoirs,** they write a book about their life.

memorable /mɛmə^{0}rəbə^{0}l/. ADJ **Memorable** things are likely to be remembered because they are special or unusual. *...a memorable train journey.*

memorandum /mɛmərændəm/, **memoranda** or **memorandums.** COUNT N A **memorandum** is a memo; a formal use.

memorial /mɪ^{2}mɔ:rɪəl/, **memorials. 1** COUNT N A **memorial** is a structure built in order to remind people of a famous person or event. *...a memorial to Queen Alexandra... ...a war memorial.* **2** ATTRIB ADJ A **memorial** event or prize is in honour of someone who has died, so that they will be remembered. *...funerals and memorial services.*

memorize /mɛməraɪz/, **memorizes, memorizing, memorized;** also spelled **memorise.** VB WITH OBJ If you **memorize** something, you learn it so that you can remember it exactly. *I was able to read a whole page and memorise it in under three minutes.*

memory /mɛmə^{0}ri^1/, **memories. 1** COUNT N Your **memory** is your ability to remember things *...people who have good memories... A few things stand out in my memory.* **2** COUNT N WITH SUPP A **memory** is something that you remember about the past. *My memories of a London childhood are happy ones.* **3** COUNT N A computer's **memory** is the capacity of the computer to store information.

PHRASES ● If you **lose** your **memory,** you forget things that you used to know. ● If you do something **from memory,** for example recite a poem or play a piece of music, you do it without looking at anything written or printed. ● If you do something **in memory of** someone who has died, you do it so that people will remember that person. ● If something has happened **within living memory,** there are people alive who can remember it happening. ● to **commit** something **to memory:** see **commit.**

men /mɛn/. **Men** is the plural of **man.**

menace /mɛnɪ^{1}s/, **menaces, menacing, menaced. 1** COUNT N Something or someone that is a **menace** is likely to cause serious harm. *These riots are a menace to democracy... ...the menace of totalitarianism.* **2** UNCOUNT N **Menace** is the quality of being threatening. *There was anger and menace in his eyes.* **3** VB WITH OBJ If someone or something **menaces** you, they threaten to harm you or are likely to do so. *We were menaced by drunks... ...the formidable threat that menaces Europe.* ♦ **menacing** ADJ *He advanced on me in a menacing fashion.* ♦ **menacingly** ADV *Joy scowled at him and waved her knife menacingly.*

mend /mɛnd/, **mends, mending, mended.** VB WITH OBJ If you **mend** something that is damaged or broken, you do something to it so that it works again or is whole or no longer damaged. *I mended some toys for her... He spent the evening mending socks.*

PHRASES ● If you are **on the mend,** you are recovering from an illness or an injury; an informal use. ● If someone **mends** their **ways,** they begin to behave better than they did before.

mending /mɛndɪŋ/. UNCOUNT N **Mending** is clothes that you have collected together to be mended. *...his mother's basket of mending.*

menial /mi:nɪəl/. ADJ **Menial** work is boring and tiring, and the people who do it have a low status. *...menial tasks.*

meningitis /mɛnɪndʒaɪtɪs/. UNCOUNT N **Meningitis** is a serious infectious illness which affects your brain and spinal cord.

menopause /mɛnə^{6}pɔ:z/. SING N OR UNCOUNT N The **menopause** is the time during which a woman stops menstruating, usually when she is about fifty.

menstrual /mɛnstrʊ^{0}əl/. ATTRIB ADJ **Menstrual** means relating to menstruation. *...the menstrual cycle.*

menstruate /mɛnstrʊeɪt/, **menstruates, menstruating, menstruated.** VB When a woman **menstruates,** blood flows from her womb. Women who are fertile menstruate once a month unless they are pregnant; a technical use. ♦ **menstruation** /mɛnstrʊeɪʃə^{0}n/ UNCOUNT N *...the onset of menstruation.*

menswear /mɛnzwɛə/. UNCOUNT N **Menswear** is clothing for men.

-ment, -ments. SUFFIX **-ment** is used to form nouns that refer to actions or states. When these nouns are formed directly from verbs, they are often not defined but are treated with the related verbs. *...the commencement of the flight... ...disillusionment with politics.*

mental /mɛntə^{0}l/. **1** ATTRIB ADJ **Mental** means relating to the process of thinking. *...mental effort... ...one's mental ability.* ♦ **mentally** ADV *She looked at the bouquets, mentally pricing the blooms.* **2** ATTRIB ADJ **Mental** also means relating to the health of a person's mind. *...mental illness.* ♦ **mentally** ADV *He was a sick man, mentally and physically.* **3** ATTRIB ADJ A **mental** act is one that involves only thinking and not physical action. *...mental arithmetic.* ♦ **mentally** ADV *They had all mentally worked out where it would appear.*

mental hospital, mental hospitals. COUNT N A **mental hospital** is a hospital for people who are suffering from mental illness.

mentality /mɛntælɪ^{1}ti^1/, **mentalities.** COUNT N WITH SUPP Your **mentality** is your attitudes or ways of thinking; often used showing disapproval. *She says I have a slave mentality.*

mention /mɛnʃə^{0}n/, **mentions, mentioning, mentioned. 1** REPORT VB If you **mention** something, you say something about it, usually briefly. *Penny decided not to mention her cold... I mentioned to Tom that I was thinking of going back to work.* **2** COUNT N OR UNCOUNT N A **mention** is a reference to something or someone. *My brother used to go purple in the face at the very mention of my name.* **3** PHRASE You use **not to mention** when adding something to a list in an emphatic way. *He's always travelling to Buenos Aires and Delhi, not to mention London and Paris.*

mentor /mɛntɔ:/, **mentors.** COUNT N Someone's **mentor** is a person who teaches them and gives them advice; a formal use. *...Harold, my mentor from my student days.*

menu /mɛnju:/, **menus.** COUNT N A **menu** is a list of the food that you can order to eat in a particular restaurant. *He ordered the most expensive items on the menu.*

MEP /ɛm i: pi:/, **MEPs.** COUNT N An **MEP** is a person who has been elected to the European Parliament. **MEP** is an abbreviation for 'Member of the European Parliament'.

mercenary /mɜ:sɪnə^{0}ri^1/, **mercenaries. 1** COUNT N A **mercenary** is someone who is paid to fight for countries or groups that they do not belong to. **2** ADJ Someone who is **mercenary** is interested only in the money they can get; used showing disapproval.

merchandise /mɜ:tʃəndaɪz/. UNCOUNT N **Merchandise** is goods that are sold. *I'd like to examine the merchandise.*

merchant /mɜ:tʃənt/, **merchants. 1** COUNT N A **merchant** is a person who buys or sells goods in large quantities, especially someone who imports and exports goods. *...a textile merchant.* **2** ATTRIB ADJ **Merchant** seamen or ships are involved in carrying goods for trade.

merciful /mɜ:si^{1}fʊl/. **1** ADJ If you describe an event or situation as **merciful,** you mean that it seems fortunate, especially because it stops someone suffering. *Death came as a merciful release.* ♦ **mercifully** ADV *In the end Mrs Paget mercifully died.* **2** ADJ A **merciful** person shows kindness and forgiveness to people who are in their power. *I begged him to be merciful.*

merciless /mɜ:si^{1}lɪ^{2}s/. ADJ A **merciless** person is very strict or cruel. *He had a reputation as a merciless foe of gambling.* ♦ **mercilessly** ADV *Unarmed peasants were beaten mercilessly.*

mercury /mɜ:kjə^{4}ri^1/. UNCOUNT N **Mercury** is a silver-coloured metal that exists as a liquid. It is used, for example, in thermometers.

mercy /mɜ:si^1/. **1** UNCOUNT N If you show **mercy** to someone, you do not punish them or treat them as severely as you could. *He pleaded for mercy.* **2** PHRASE If you are **at the mercy of** someone or something, they have complete power over you. *This action would leave them at the mercy of industrialised countries.*

mere /mɪə/, **merest. Merest** is used to give emphasis, rather than in comparisons. 1 ATTRIB ADJ **Mere** is used to say how unimportant, minor, or small something is. *They were mere puppets manipulated by men in search of power... He had found out only by the merest accident... In Tanganyika, a mere 2 per cent of the population lived in towns.* 2 ATTRIB ADJ You also use **mere** to refer to something very simple which has a surprisingly strong effect. *They feared the impact the mere presence of a political prisoner would have... The merest suggestion of marital infidelity enrages him.*

merely /mɪəli^1/. 1 ADV You use **merely** to emphasize that something is only what you say and not better, bigger, more important, or more exciting. *This is not genuine. It's merely a reproduction... We accept ideas like this merely because they have never been challenged.* 2 ADV You use **not merely** before the less important of two statements, as a way of emphasizing the more important statement. *Much of this new industry was not merely in India; it was Indian-owned.*

merge /mɜːdʒ/, **merges, merging, merged.** 1 ERG VB OR RECIP VB If one thing **merges** or **is merged** with another, they combine together to make a larger thing. *They advised their clients to merge with another company... The borough of Holborn was merged with St Pancras and Hampstead... The voices merged with one another.* 2 VB WITH 'into' If something **merges** into the darkness or the background, you can no longer see it clearly as a separate object. *They were painted so that they would merge into the landscape.*

merger /mɜːdʒə/, **mergers.** COUNT N When a **merger** takes place, two organizations join together. *...a merger between the two organizations.*

meringue /mə^{2}ræŋ/, **meringues.** COUNT N OR UNCOUNT N A **meringue** is a type of crisp, sweet food, made with sugar and egg white.

merit /mɛrɪt/, **merits, meriting, merited.** 1 UNCOUNT N If something has **merit,** it is good or worthwhile; a formal use. *...a work of high literary merit.* 2 COUNT N The **merits** of something are its advantages or good qualities. *...the relative merits of cinema and drama.* 3 PHRASE If you judge something **on** its **merits,** your opinion of it is based on its own qualities, rather than your personal feelings. *We endeavour to assess any case on its merits.* 4 VB WITH OBJ If something **merits** a particular treatment, it is good enough or important enough to be treated in this way; a formal use. *This experiment merits closer examination... It was not important enough to merit a special discussion.*

mermaid /mɜːmeɪd/, **mermaids.** COUNT N In children's stories, a **mermaid** is a woman with a fish's tail instead of legs, who lives in the sea.

merrily /mɛrɪli^1/. ADV You use **merrily** to say that something happens or is done without people thinking properly about it or about the problems involved. *Before you skip merrily on to the next page, pause.*

merriment /mɛrɪmə^{2}nt/. UNCOUNT N **Merriment** means laughter; an old-fashioned use. *She put a hand to her mouth to stifle her merriment.*

merry /mɛri^1/. 1 ADJ **Merry** means happy and cheerful; an old-fashioned use. *My in-laws, a merry band from Bath, had joined us... ...his merry blue eyes... ...merry music.* ♦ **merrily** ADV *Dr Mason laughed merrily.* 2 CONVENTION People say **Merry Christmas** to each other at Christmas time.

mesh /mɛʃ/, **meshes, meshing, meshed.** 1 UNCOUNT N **Mesh** is material like a net made from wire, thread, or plastic. *...a fence made of stout wire mesh.* 2 ERG VB If two things **mesh** or **are meshed,** they fit together closely.

mesmerize /mɛzməraɪz/, **mesmerizes, mesmerizing, mesmerized;** also spelled **mesmerise.** VB WITH OBJ If you **are mesmerized** by something, you are so interested in it or so attracted to it that you cannot think about anything else. *Blanche was mesmerized by his voice.*

mess /mɛs/, **messes, messing, messed.** 1 SING N OR UNCOUNT N You use **mess** to refer to something that is very untidy and dirty or disorganized. *I know the place is a mess, but make yourself at home... They went back to see how much mess they'd left behind... We cleared up the mess.* 2 COUNT N If a situation is a **mess,** it is full of problems and trouble. *My life is such a mess... It seemed a way out from the mess I'd got myself into.* 3 PHRASE If something is **in a mess,** it is untidy or disorganized. *Her hair was in a terrible mess... The US economy is now in a mess.* 4 COUNT N A **mess** is also a room or building in which members of the armed forces eat. *...a bomb attack on an officers' mess.*

mess about or **mess around.** PHR VB 1 If you are **messing about** or **messing around,** you do things without any particular purpose and without achieving anything; an informal use. *Some of the lads had been messing around when they should have been working.* 2 If you **mess about** or **mess around** with something, you interfere with it and make it worse. *She didn't want you coming and messing about with things.* 3 If you **mess** someone **about** or **around,** you continually change plans which affect them; an informal use.

mess up. PHR VB 1 If you **mess up** something that has been carefully made or done, you spoil it. *That will mess up the whole analysis.* 2 If you **mess up** a room, you make it untidy or dirty.

message /mɛsɪdʒ/, **messages.** 1 COUNT N A **message** is a piece of information or a request that you send to someone or leave for them. *Oh, there was a message. Professor Marvin rang. He'd like to meet you on Tuesday... He sent a message to Sir Ian Hamilton saying he was returning.* 2 COUNT N WITH SUPP A **message** is also the idea that someone tries to communicate to people, for example in a play or a speech. *The play's message is that in the end good and right always triumph.*

messenger /mɛsɪndʒə/, **messengers.** COUNT N A **messenger** is someone who takes a message to someone else or who takes messages regularly as their job. *By the time the messenger reached him, the damage had been done.*

Messrs /mɛsəz/. **Messrs** is the plural of 'Mr'. **Messrs** is used especially in the names of businesses. *Messrs Brant and Prout are dealers in hats.*

messy /mɛsi^1/; an informal word. 1 ADJ **Messy** means dirty or untidy. *...messy bits of food... I disliked the messy farmyard.* 2 ADJ A **messy** person or activity makes things dirty or untidy. *Sometimes I'm neat, sometimes I'm messy... I hate picnics; they're so messy.* 3 ADJ A **messy** situation is confused or complicated, and involves trouble for people. *Brown had been caught in a messy diplomatic dispute.*

met /mɛt/. **Met** is the past tense and past participle of **meet.**

metabolism /mɪ^{2}tæbəlɪzə^{0}m/, **metabolisms.** UNCOUNT N OR COUNT N Your **metabolism** is the chemical process in your body that causes food to be used for growth and energy; a technical use. *Some people's metabolism is more efficient than others.*

metal /mɛtə^{0}l/, **metals.** MASS N **Metal** is a hard substance such as iron, steel, copper, or lead. *It was made of glass and metal... ...a metal spoon.*

metallic /mɪ^{2}tælɪk/. 1 ADJ A **metallic** sound is like one piece of metal hitting another. *I heard the metallic click of a door handle.* 2 ADJ **Metallic** colours shine like metal. *Her hair was a metallic gold.* 3 ADJ **Metallic** things consist of metal; a technical use. *...metallic ores.*

metalwork /mɛtə^{0}lwɜːk/. UNCOUNT N **Metalwork** is the activity of making objects out of metal.

metamorphosis /mɛtəmɔːfəsɪs/, **metamorphoses** /mɛtəmɔːfəsiːz/. COUNT N OR UNCOUNT N When a **metamorphosis** occurs, a person or thing changes into something completely different; a formal use. *Science fiction may be undergoing a metamorphosis.*

metaphor /mɛtəfə^8/, **metaphors.** COUNT N OR UNCOUNT N A **metaphor** is a way of describing something by saying that it is something else which has the qualities that you are trying to describe. For example, if you want to say that someone is shy and timid, you might say that they are a mouse.

metaphorical /mɛtəfɒrɪkə^{0}l/. ADJ You use the word **metaphorical** to indicate that you are not using words with their ordinary meaning, but are describing something by means of an image or symbol. *I had sprouted metaphorical wings.* ♦ **metaphorically** ADV *I was speaking metaphorically.*

mete /miːt/, **metes, meting, meted.**

mete out PHR VB To **mete out** a punishment means to order that someone shall be punished in that way; a formal use. *Magistrates meted out fines of £1,000.*

meteor /miːtɪə^8/, **meteors.** COUNT N A **meteor** is a piece of rock or metal that burns very brightly when it enters the earth's atmosphere from space.

meteoric /miːtɪɒrɪk/. ADJ A **meteoric** rise to power or success happens very quickly. *He enjoyed a meteoric rise to power in Callaghan's government.*

meteorite /miːtɪəraɪt/, **meteorites.** COUNT N A **meteorite** is a large piece of rock or metal from space that has landed on the earth.

meteorological /miːtɪərəlɒdʒɪkə^{0}l/. ATTRIB ADJ **Meteorological** means relating to the weather or to weather forecasting; a technical use. *Meteorological conditions were reasonably good.*

meter /miːtə/, **meters.** 1 COUNT N A **meter** is a device that measures and records something such as the amount of gas or electricity that you have used. *Someone comes to read the gas and electricity meters.* 2 See also **metre.**

method /mɛθəd/, **methods.** COUNT N OR UNCOUNT N A **method** is a particular way of doing something. *...a change in the method of electing the party's leader... ...differences in method.*

methodical /mɪ^{2}θɒdɪkə^{0}l/. ADJ A **methodical** person does things carefully and in order. *With methodical thoroughness they demolished the prison.* ♦ **methodically** ADV *He worked quickly and methodically.*

meticulous /mɪ^{2}tɪkjə^{4}ləs/. ADJ A **meticulous** person does things very carefully and with great attention to detail. *He had prepared himself with meticulous care.* ♦ **meticulously** ADV *...meticulously folded newspapers.*

metre /miːtə/, **metres;** spelled **meter** in American English. COUNT N A **metre** is a unit of length equal to 100 centimetres. *The blue whale grows to over 30 metres long.*

metric /mɛtrɪk/. ATTRIB ADJ The **metric** system of measurement uses metres, grammes, and litres.

metro /mɛtrəʊ/, **metros.** COUNT N The **metro** is the underground railway system in some cities, for example in Paris.

metropolis /mɪ^{2}trɒpəlɪs/, **metropolises.** COUNT N A **metropolis** is a very large city; a formal use.

metropolitan /mɛtrəpɒlɪtə^{0}n/. ATTRIB ADJ **Metropolitan** means belonging to or typical of a large busy city. *...seven metropolitan districts in the Midlands.*

mew /mjuː/, **mews, mewing, mewed.** VB When a cat **mews,** it makes a soft high-pitched noise. *The cat was mewing for its supper.*

mg. mg is a written abbreviation for 'milligram' or 'milligrams'. *It contained 65mg of Vitamin C.*

miaow /mi^{1}aʊ/, **miaows, miaowing, miaowed.** COUNT N When a cat goes **'miaow',** it makes a short high-pitched sound. *That sounds like the miaow of a cat.* Also VB *There was a cat miaowing outside.*

mice /maɪs/. **Mice** is the plural of **mouse.**

mickey /mɪki^1/. PHRASE If you **take the mickey** out of someone, you make fun of them; an informal use.

micro /maɪkrəʊ/, **micros.** COUNT N A **micro** is a small computer.

micro-. PREFIX **Micro-** is used to form nouns that refer to a very small example of a particular type of thing. For example, a micro-organism is a very small organism such as a virus. *...diseases caused by micro-organisms... ...the invention of the microcassette.*

microbe /maɪkrəʊb/, **microbes.** COUNT N A **microbe** is a very small living thing, which you can only see with a microscope. *...the microbes in the human gut.*

microchip /maɪkrə^{6}tʃɪp/, **microchips.** COUNT N A **microchip** is a small piece of silicon inside a computer, on which electronic circuits are printed.

micro-computer, micro-computers. COUNT N A **micro-computer** is a small computer.

microcosm /maɪkrə^{6}kɒzə^{0}m/, **microcosms.** COUNT N A place or event that is a **microcosm** of a larger one has all the main features of the larger one and seems like a smaller version of it. *Bristol was a microcosm of urban England in the 1970s.*

microfiche /maɪkrə^{6}fiːʃ/, **microfiches.** COUNT N OR UNCOUNT N A **microfiche** is a small sheet of film on which information is stored in very small print. Microfiches are read on special machines which magnify them. *The Periodicals Catalogue is now on microfiche.*

microphone /maɪkrə^{6}fəʊn/, **microphones.** COUNT N A **microphone** is a device that is used to make sounds louder or to record them on a tape recorder.

microprocessor /maɪkrə^{6}prəʊsesə/, **microprocessors.** COUNT N A **microprocessor** is a microchip which can be programmed to do a large number of tasks or calculations.

microscope /maɪkrə^{6}skəʊp/, **microscopes.** COUNT N A **microscope** is an instrument which magnifies very small objects so that you can study them. *The slides are examined under the microscope.*

microscopic /maɪkrə^{6}skɒpɪk/. 1 ADJ Something that is **microscopic** is very small. *...microscopic forms of life.* 2 ADJ A **microscopic** examination of something is very detailed. *...a microscopic study of medieval customs.*

microwave /maɪkrə^{6}weɪv/, **microwaves.** COUNT N A **microwave** or a **microwave oven** is a cooker which cooks food very quickly by short-wave radiation rather than by heat.

mid-. PREFIX **Mid-** is used to form nouns or modifiers that refer to the middle part of a place or period of time. *...the Dyfi Valley in mid-Wales... ...studies published in the mid-1970s... ...the mid-morning sun.*

mid-air. UNCOUNT N If something happens in **mid-air,** it happens in the air rather than on the ground. *The bird turned in mid-air and darted away... ...a mid-air collision.*

midday /mɪddeɪ/. UNCOUNT N **Midday** is twelve o'clock in the middle of the day. *Just before midday the telephone rang... ...a midday meal.*

middle /mɪdəl/, **middles. 1** COUNT N The **middle** of something is the part that is farthest from its edges, ends, or outside surface. *In the middle of the lawn was a great cedar tree... He sat down in the middle of the front row... ...the white lines painted along the middle of the highway... Test the meat to see if it is cooked in the middle.* **2** ATTRIB ADJ The **middle** thing or person in a row or series is the one with an equal number of things or people on each side, or before it and after it. *...the middle button of her black leather coat... She was the middle child of the three.* **3** COUNT N Your **middle** is the front part of your body at your waist. *He had a large green towel wrapped round his middle.* **4** SING N The **middle** of an event or period of time is the part that comes after the first part and before the last part. *We landed at Canton in the middle of a torrential storm... ...the middle of December.* Also ATTRIB ADJ *He was in his middle thirties.* **5** PHRASE If you are **in the middle of** doing something, you are busy doing it. *I'm in the middle of washing up.* **6** ATTRIB ADJ The **middle** course or way is a moderate course of action that lies between two opposite and extreme courses. *Between Fascism or revolution there is a middle course.*

middle age. UNCOUNT N **Middle age** is the period in your life when you are between about 40 and 60 years old. *...a grave, courteous man in late middle age.*

middle-aged. ADJ **Middle-aged** people are between the ages of about 40 and 60. *...a middle-aged businessman.*

Middle Ages. PLURAL N In European history, the **Middle Ages** were the period between about 1100 AD and about 1500 AD.

middle class, middle classes. COUNT N The **middle classes** are the people in a society who are not working class or upper class, for example managers, doctors, and lawyers. *...the new Indian middle classes.* Also ADJ *...middle class families... Watson's upbringing was comfortably middle-class.*

Middle East. PROPER N **The Middle East** is a part of Asia. It includes Iran and all the countries in Asia that are to the west and south-west of Iran.

Middle Eastern. ATTRIB ADJ **Middle Eastern** means coming from or relating to the Middle East. *...Middle Eastern oil.*

middleman /mɪdəlmæn/, **middlemen.** COUNT N A **middleman** is someone who buys things from the people who produce them and sells them to other people at a profit.

middle name, middle names. COUNT N A person's **middle name** is a name that they have which comes between their first name and their surname.

middle-of-the-road. ADJ **Middle-of-the-road** politicians or opinions are moderate, not extreme. *...middle-of-the-road Labour MPs.*

middle school, middle schools. COUNT N A **middle school** is a state school in Britain that children go to between the ages of 8 or 9 and 12 or 13.

midge /mɪdʒ/, **midges.** COUNT N **Midges** are very small flying insects which can bite people.

midget /mɪdʒɪt/, **midgets.** COUNT N A **midget** is a very small person.

midnight /mɪdnaɪt/. UNCOUNT N **Midnight** is twelve o'clock in the middle of the night. *It was nearly midnight.*

midst /mɪdst/; a formal word.
PHRASES ● If you are **in the midst of** a group of people, you are among them or surrounded by them. *I found him in the midst of a group of his friends... We have in our midst two Nobel prize-winners.* ● If something happens **in the midst of** an event, it happens during that event. If you are **in the midst of** doing something, you are doing it at present. *In the midst of this humiliating scandal, news arrived of Mr Hodge's resignation... Brody was in the midst of swallowing a bite of egg salad sandwich.*

midsummer /mɪdsʌmə/. UNCOUNT N **Midsummer** is the period in the middle of the summer. *...a hot midsummer day.*

midway /mɪdweɪ/. **1** ADV If something is **midway** between two places, it is between them and the same distance from each of them. *St Germain is midway between Cherbourg and Granville.* **2** ADV If something happens **midway** through a period of time, it happens during the middle part of it. *She arrived midway through the afternoon.*

midwife /mɪdwaɪf/, **midwives.** COUNT N A **midwife** is a nurse who advises pregnant women and helps them to give birth.

might /maɪt/. **Might** is sometimes considered to be the past tense of **may,** but in this dictionary the two words are dealt with separately. **1** MODAL If you say that something **might** happen, you mean that it is possible that it will happen. If you say that something **might** be true, you mean that it is possible that it is true. *I might even lose my job... I might go to a concert tonight... Don't eat it. It might be a toadstool.* **2** MODAL If you say that something **might** have happened, you mean that it is possible that it happened. *He might well have said that. I just don't remember.* **3** MODAL You can also say that something **might** have happened when it was possible for it to have happened, although it did not in fact happen. *A lot of men died who might have been saved.* **4** MODAL You can use **might** in very polite and formal requests. *Might I inquire if you are the owner?... She asked the man's wife if she might borrow a pen.* **5** MODAL You can also use **might** when you are making suggestions. *The other thing you might find out is who owns the land.* **6** UNCOUNT N **Might** is power or strength; a literary use. *I tied the rope around the tree and heaved with all my might.*

mightily /maɪtɪli/. ADV **Mightily** means to a great extent or degree; an old-fashioned use. *Things have changed mightily since then.*

mightn't /maɪtənt/. **Mightn't** is a spoken form of 'might not'. *It mightn't be true at all.*

mighty /maɪti/, **mightier, mightiest. 1** ADJ **Mighty** means very large or powerful; a literary use. *...this mighty nation... ...two of Asia's mightiest rivers, the Ganges and the Brahmaputra... We're dealing with forces that are mightier than ourselves.* **2** SUBMOD **Mighty** also means very; an American use. *It's going to be mighty embarrassing.*

migraine /miːgreɪn, maɪ-/, **migraines.** UNCOUNT N OR COUNT N **Migraine** is a painful headache that makes you feel very ill. *Do you suffer from migraine?... The experience had brought on one of her migraines.*

migrant /maɪgrənt/, **migrants.** COUNT N A **migrant** is a person who moves from one place to another, especially in order to find work. *...migrants looking for a place to live... ...migrant workers.*

migrate /maɪgreɪt/, **migrates, migrating, migrated. 1** VB When people **migrate,** they move from one place to another, especially in order to find work. *Millions have migrated to the cities.* ♦ **migration** /maɪgreɪʃən/ UNCOUNT N OR COUNT N *Migration for work is accelerating in the Third World... ...the vast Greek migrations into Asia and Egypt.* **2** VB When birds or animals **migrate,** they go and live in a different area for part of the year, in order to breed or to find food. *Every spring they migrate towards the coast.* ♦ **migration** UNCOUNT N OR COUNT N *Swallows begin their migration south in early autumn... ...the migrations of the reindeer.*

mike /maɪk/, **mikes.** COUNT N A **mike** is a microphone; an informal use. *Is the mike turned on?*

mild /maɪld/, **milder, mildest. 1** ADJ Something that is **mild** is not strong and does not have any powerful effects. *...a mild detergent... A slight fever often accompanies a mild infection.* ♦ **mildly** ADV *The skin may become mildly infected.* **2** ADJ **Mild** people are gentle and do not get angry. *...my wife's mild nature.* ♦ **mildly** ADV *'No need to shout,' he said mildly.* ♦ **mildness** UNCOUNT N *The Colonel spoke with great mildness.* **3** ADJ **Mild** weather is less cold than usual. *The weather was comparatively mild through December.* **4** ADJ **Mild** also means not very great or extreme. *We looked at each other in mild astonishment.* ♦ **mildly** SUBMOD *It was mildly amusing.*

mildew /mɪldjuː/. UNCOUNT N **Mildew** is a soft white fungus that grows in warm and damp places.

mile /maɪl/, **miles.** COUNT N A **mile** is a unit of distance equal to 1760 yards or approximately 1.609 kilometres. *The island is 16 miles wide.*

mileage /maɪlɪdʒ/. UNCOUNT N **Mileage** refers to a distance that is travelled, measured in miles. *The approximate mileage for the journey is 200 miles.*

milestone /maɪlstəʊn/, **milestones.** COUNT N WITH SUPP A **milestone** is an important event in the history or development of something. *The conference was a milestone in the history of the party.*

milieu /miːljɜː/, **milieux** or **milieus.** COUNT N The **milieu** in which you live or work is the group of people that you live or work among; a formal use. *I was born in a social milieu where education was a luxury.*

militancy /mɪlɪtənsi/. UNCOUNT N **Militancy** is the behaviour and attitudes of people who are active in trying to bring about political change. *The League is well known for its militancy.*

militant /mɪlɪtənt/, **militants. 1** ADJ Someone who is **militant** is active in trying to bring about political change. *...militant trade unionists.* **2** COUNT N A **militant** is someone who is active in trying to bring about political change. *...a number of well-known militants.*

military /mɪlɪtəri/. **1** ATTRIB ADJ **Military** means relating to a country's armed forces. *...military leaders... ...direct military action.* **2** COLL N The **military** are the armed forces of a country, especially the officers of high rank. *The politicians and the military will do nothing.*

militia /mɪlɪʃə/, **militias.** COUNT N A **militia** is an organization that operates like an army but whose members are not professional soldiers. *...a building guarded by the local police and militia.*

milk /mɪlk/, **milks, milking, milked. 1** UNCOUNT N **Milk** is the white liquid produced by cows and goats, which people drink and make into butter, cheese, and yoghurt. *He only drinks milk in tea or coffee... ...a glass of milk.* ● See also **skimmed milk. 2** VB WITH OR WITHOUT OBJ When someone **milks** a cow or goat, they get milk from it by pulling its udders. *The men had milked the cows in the early morning.* ♦ **milking** UNCOUNT N *He used to help the farmer with his milking... I had to install milking equipment.* **3** UNCOUNT N **Milk** is also the white liquid from a woman's breasts which babies drink. **4** VB WITH OBJ If you **milk** a situation or place, you selfishly get as much benefit or profit as you can from it. *The island was milked by the invaders for five centuries.*

milkman /mɪlkmən/, **milkmen.** COUNT N A **milkman** is a person who delivers milk to people's homes.

milk-shake, milk-shakes. MASS N A **milk-shake** is a cold drink made by mixing milk with ice cream and a flavouring. *...a strawberry milkshake.*

milky /mɪlki/. **1** ADJ Something that is **milky** in colour is pale white. *...clouds of milky smoke.* **2** ADJ **Milky** food or drink contains a lot of milk. *We always had milky coffee at lunchtime.*

mill /mɪl/, **mills, milling, milled. 1** COUNT N A **mill** is a building where grain is crushed to make flour. *He sends his crop to a large mill instead of grinding it himself.* **2** COUNT N WITH SUPP A **mill** is also a factory used for making steel, wool, or cotton. *He had worked in a steel mill.* **3** See also **run-of-the-mill.**

mill about or **mill around.** PHR VB When a crowd of people **are milling about** or **are milling around,** they are moving around in a disorganized way. *Students and staff were milling about.*

millennium /mɪleniəm/, **millennia** or **millenniums.** COUNT N A **millennium** is a thousand years; a formal use. *...a landscape that had remained unchanged for millennia.*

milligram /mɪlɪgræm/, **milligrams;** also spelled **milligramme.** COUNT N A **milligram** is a unit of weight equal to one thousandth of a gram. *...0.3 milligrams of mercury.*

millilitre /mɪlɪliːtə/, **millilitres;** spelled **milliliter** in American English. COUNT N A **millilitre** is a unit of volume for liquids and gases, equal to one thousandth of a litre. *...45 millilitres of alcohol.*

millimetre /mɪlɪmiːtə/, **millimetres;** spelled **millimeter** in American English. COUNT N A **millimetre** is a unit of length equal to one tenth of a centimetre. *...a silicon chip less than a millimetre thick.*

million /mɪljən/, **millions. 1** A **million** is the number 1,000,000. *...30 million dollars.* **2** QUANTIF **Millions** is often used to mean an extremely large number. *...millions of mosquitoes... Her books still give pleasure to millions.*

millionaire /mɪljəneə/, **millionaires.** COUNT N A **millionaire** is a rich person who has property worth at least a million pounds or dollars.

millionth /mɪljənθ/, **millionths. 1** ADJ The **millionth** item in a series is the one you count as number one million. **2** COUNT N A **millionth** is one of a million equal parts of something. *...a millionth of a second.*

mime /maɪm/, **mimes, miming, mimed. 1** UNCOUNT N OR COUNT N **Mime** is the use of movements and gestures to express something or tell a story without using speech. *...the re-telling of legends in mime and song... He sought to improvise new mimes.* **2** VB WITH OR WITHOUT OBJ If you **mime** something, you describe or express it using mime rather than speech. *We were told he was miming the god Shiva coming down from heaven.*

mimic /mɪmɪk/, **mimics, mimicking, mimicked. 1** VB WITH OBJ If you **mimic** someone's actions or voice, you imitate them in an amusing or entertaining way. *I can mimic Cockney speech reasonably well.* **2** COUNT N A **mimic** is a person who is able to mimic people. *One of my brothers is a wonderful mimic.*

mimicry /mɪmɪkri/. UNCOUNT N **Mimicry** is the action of mimicking someone or something. *...his fine talent for mimicry.*

min. Min is a written abbreviation for 'minute' or 'minutes'. *...an easy 10 min run.*

mince /mɪns/, **minces, mincing, minced. 1** UNCOUNT N **Mince** is meat cut into very small pieces; a British use. *...the nutritional value of mince.* **2** VB WITH OBJ If you **mince** meat, you cut it into very small pieces. *Mince the lean meat finely.* ♦ **minced** ATTRIB ADJ *...minced beef.* **3** VB If you **mince,** you walk with quick small steps in an affected or effeminate way. *Off they minced to see the old lady.*

mind /maɪnd/, **minds, minding, minded. 1** COUNT N Your **mind** is your ability to think. If you say that something is in your **mind,** you mean that you are thinking about it. *...the evolution of the human mind... He could hear in his mind the wailings of the women.* **2** VB WITH OR WITHOUT OBJ If you say that you do not **mind** something, you mean that you are not annoyed or bothered by it. *I don't mind personal questions at all... I don't mind walking... Do you mind if I stay here?* **3** CONVENTION You say **mind** something to warn someone to be careful, so that they do not get hurt or cause damage. *Mind the ice on the step as you go... Mind my specs!* **4** VB WITH OBJ If you **mind** something such as a child, a shop, or luggage, you look after it for someone for a while. *My mother is minding the office.*

PHRASES • If something **takes** your **mind off** a problem, it helps you to forget about it for a while. • If something **comes to mind,** you think of it without making any effort. *I just pick up whatever groceries come to mind.* • If you tell someone to **bear** or **keep** something **in mind,** you are telling them to remember it because it is important or relevant. *Bear in mind that these are sixty-five-year-old men... It is important to keep in mind that these words are clues.* • If your **mind is on** something, you are thinking about it. *Her mind was not on the announcements she was making.* • If something is **on** your **mind,** you are worried about it and think about it a lot. • If you **have** something **in mind,** you intend to have it or do it. *It will be up to her to tell you what she has in mind.* • If you say you **have a good mind to** do something, you mean that you would like to do it, although you will probably not do it. *I've a good mind to punish you for behaving so badly.* • If you **put** your **mind to** something, you devote a lot of energy, effort, and attention to it. *You could get a job in London, if you put your mind to it.* • You use **to my mind** to indicate that you are giving your own opinion. *The worst part of air travel to my mind is the hanging around in airport lounges.* • If you have **an open mind,** you have not formed an opinion about a particular matter, and are waiting until you know all the facts. • When you **make** your **mind up,** you decide which of a number of possible things you will have or do. *We have to make up our minds quickly, or they'll go without us... My mind's made up.* • If you **change** your **mind,** you change a decision you have made or an opinion that you have had. *All of a sudden I changed my mind and decided not to go anywhere.* • If you are **in two minds** about something, you are uncertain whether or not to do it. *I was very much in two minds whether to apply for the Cambridge job.* • If you see something **in** your **mind's eye,** you imagine it and have a clear picture of it in your mind. *In her mind's eye, she had pictured herself in the new house.* • Your **state of mind** is your mental state at a particular time. *She was in a fairly disturbed state of mind.* • to **cross** your **mind:** see **cross.** • If you say that you **wouldn't mind** something, you mean that you would quite like it; an informal use. *I wouldn't mind a Renault myself.* • You say **never mind** to try and make someone feel better when they are upset or disappointed. • You also say **never mind** to indicate that something is not important, especially when someone is apologizing to you. *Some of their towels are soaking wet, but never mind.* • You use **mind you** when you are adding a further statement, especially one which contrasts with what you have just said. *Charles is fit and well. Not happy, mind you, just fit and well.* • to **mind** your **own business:** see **business.**

mindful /maɪndfʊl/. PRED ADJ If you are **mindful** of something, you remember it when taking action; a formal use. *Be mindful of the needs of others.*

mindless /maɪndlɪ^{2}s/. **1** ATTRIB ADJ **Mindless** actions are stupid and destructive. *...mindless violence... ...the mindless pollution of our cities.* **2** ADJ A **mindless** job or activity is so simple that you do not need to think about it. *...mindless routine tasks.*

mine /maɪn/, **mines, mining, mined. 1** PRON You use **mine** to indicate that something belongs or relates to you. *Margaret was a very old friend of mine... I took her hands in mine... He gave it to me, it's mine.* **2** COUNT N A **mine** is a place where people dig deep holes or tunnels in order to get out coal, diamonds, or gold. *...a coal mine.* **3** VB WITH OR WITHOUT OBJ To **mine** a substance such as coal or gold means to obtain it from the ground by digging deep holes and tunnels. *They mine their own coal and ore... ...mining for gold.* **4** COUNT N A **mine** is also a bomb hidden in the ground or floating on water which explodes when something touches it. **5** See also **mining.**

minefield /maɪnfiːld/, **minefields.** COUNT N A **minefield** is an area of land or water where explosive mines have been hidden.

miner /maɪnə/, **miners.** COUNT N A **miner** is a person who works underground in mines obtaining coal, diamonds, or gold. *My grandfather was a coal miner.*

mineral /mɪnə^{0}rəl/, **minerals.** COUNT N A **mineral** is a substance such as tin, salt, uranium, or coal that is formed naturally in rocks and in the earth. *...a continent exceptionally wealthy in minerals... ...rich mineral deposits.*

mineral water. UNCOUNT N **Mineral water** is water that comes out of the ground naturally and is often considered healthy to drink.

mingle /mɪŋgə^{0}l/, **mingles, mingling, mingled. 1** RECIP VB When things **mingle,** they become mixed together. *His cries mingled with theirs... Sand and dust mingled with the blood.* ♦ **mingled** ADJ *John watched her with mingled dismay and pleasure.* **2** VB If you **mingle,** you move among a group of people, chatting to different people. *Get out and mingle a bit... She invited me to drop in and mingle with the guests.*

mini-. PREFIX **Mini-** is added to nouns to form other nouns that refer to a smaller version of something. For example, a mini-computer is a computer which is smaller than a normal computer. *He was taken to school by minibus... ...the Chancellor's mini-budget.*

miniature /mɪnɪtʃə/, **miniatures. 1** ATTRIB ADJ A **miniature** thing is much smaller than other things of the same kind. *...tiny squares and miniature archways... They look like miniature sharks.* **2** PHRASE If you describe one thing as another thing **in miniature,** you mean that it is much smaller than the other thing, but is otherwise exactly the same. *It was an Austrian chalet in miniature.* **3** COUNT N A **miniature** is a very small detailed painting, often of a person. *I collect early English miniatures.*

miniaturize /mɪnɪtʃəraɪz/, **miniaturizes, miniaturizing, miniaturized;** also spelled **miniaturise.** VB WITH OBJ To **miniaturize** a machine means to produce a very small version of it. *We miniaturize spacecraft components.* ♦ **miniaturized** ATTRIB ADJ *...a miniaturized video recorder.*

minibus /mɪni^{1}bʌs/, **minibuses.** COUNT N A **minibus** is a van with seats in the back, which is used as a small bus. *We went to school by minibus.*

minimal /mɪnɪmə^{0}l/. ADJ Something that is **minimal** is very small in quantity or degree. *My knowledge of German was minimal.* ♦ **minimally** SUBMOD *His theories were only minimally more adequate than the ones they replaced.*

minimize /mɪnɪmaɪz/, **minimizes, minimizing, minimized;** also spelled **minimise. 1** VB WITH OBJ To **minimize** something means to keep it as small as possible. *Our aim must be to minimize the risks... Crop rotations will help to minimise disease.* **2** VB WITH OBJ To **minimize** something also means to make it seem smaller or less important than it really is. *He was careful to minimise his role in these proceedings.*

minimum /mɪnɪmə^{9}m/. **1** ATTRIB ADJ The **minimum** amount of something is the smallest that is possible. *...the minimum level of taxation... You need a minimum deposit of $20,000.* **2** SING N The **minimum** is the smallest amount of something that is possible. *Two hundred pounds is the bare minimum... Practise each day for a minimum of twenty minutes.*

mining /maɪnɪŋ/. UNCOUNT N **Mining** is the industry and activities connected with getting coal, diamonds, or other minerals from the ground. *...coal mining.*

minister /mɪnɪstə/, **ministers, ministering, ministered. 1** COUNT N A **minister** is a person in charge of a government department. *...the Minister for Scottish affairs.* • See also **Prime Minister. 2** COUNT N A **minister** in a church, especially a Protestant church, is a member of the clergy.

minister to. PHR VB If you **minister to** people or to their needs, you make sure that they have everything they need or want; a formal use.

ministerial /mɪnɪstɪərɪəl/. ATTRIB ADJ **Ministerial** means relating to a government minister or ministry. *We cannot afford a ministerial crisis.*

ministrations /mɪnɪstreɪʃə^{0}nz/. PLURAL N A person's **ministrations** are the things that they do to help or care for someone in a particular situation; a formal use. *I thanked him for his spiritual ministrations.*

ministry /mɪnɪstri^{1}/, **ministries. 1** COUNT N A **ministry** is a government department. *...the Ministry of Energy... The ministry will have no alternative but to cut its expenditure.* **2** COUNT N The **ministry** of a religious person is the work that they do according to their religious beliefs. *The central message of Christ's ministry was the concept of grace.* **3** SING N Members of the clergy belonging to some branches of the Christian church are referred to as the **ministry.** *Michael had intended to join the ministry.*

mink /mɪŋk/. UNCOUNT N **Mink** is a very expensive fur used to make coats or hats.

minor /maɪnə/, **minors. 1** ADJ You use **minor** to describe something that is not as important, serious, or significant as other things of the same sort. *The police were called to quell a minor disturbance... ...minor injuries... ...a rather minor artist.* **2** ADJ In European music, a **minor** scale is one in which the third note is three semitones higher than the first. *...Chopin's Scherzo in B flat minor.* **3** COUNT N A **minor** is a person who is still legally a child. In Britain, people are minors until they reach the age of eighteen.

minority /mɪ^{5}nɒrɪ^{1}ti^{1}/, **minorities. 1** SING N A **minority** of people or things in a group is less than half of the whole group. *Only a small minority of children get a chance to benefit from this system.* • If a group is **in a minority** or **in the minority,** they form less than half of a larger group. *Artistic people are in a tiny minority in this country.* **2** COUNT N A **minority** is a group of people of a particular race or religion who live in a place where most of the people are of a different race or religion. *...ethnic minorities.*

mint /mɪnt/, **mints, minting, minted. 1** UNCOUNT N **Mint** is a type of herb used in cooking. *...a sprig of mint... ...mint tea.* **2** COUNT N A **mint** is a sweet with a peppermint flavour. *...a packet of mints.* **3** SING N The place where a country's official coins are made is called its **mint.** *The Mint has decided to issue the new coins next year.* **4** VB WITH OBJ When coins or medals **are minted,** they are made in a mint. *One of the coins, dated 1693, was minted in Portuguese Africa.* **5** PHRASE If something is **in mint condition,** it is in very good condition, as if it was new.

minus /maɪnəs/. **1** PREP You use **minus** to show that one number is being subtracted from another, for example 'five minus three'. You represent this in figures as '5 - 3'. **2** ATTRIB ADJ **Minus** is also used to indicate that a number is less than zero. For example, a temperature of **minus** four is four degrees below zero. *Temperatures there are colder than minus 20°C.*

minuscule /mɪnəskjuːl/. ADJ Something that is **minuscule** is very small indeed. *He had to live in this minuscule room.*

minus sign, minus signs. COUNT N A **minus sign** is the sign (-) which is put between two numbers to show that the second number is being subtracted from the first one.

minute, minutes; pronounced /mɪnɪt/ when it is a noun and /maɪnjuːt/ when it is an adjective. **1** COUNT N A **minute** is one of the sixty equal parts of an hour. *Davis was ten minutes late... An accident had taken place only a few minutes before.* • See also **last-minute. 2** PLURAL N The **minutes** of a meeting are the written records of what is said or decided. *You must learn how to take minutes.* **3** ADJ Something that is **minute** is extremely small. *...minute amounts of fluoride... I had remembered in minute detail everything that had happened.*

PHRASES • **A minute** is often used to mean a short time. *Will you excuse me if I sit down for a minute?... Wait there a minute.* • If you do something **the minute** something else happens, you do it as soon as the other thing happens. *Ask for help the minute you're stuck.* • If you say that something must be done **this minute,** you mean that it must be done immediately. *She doesn't have to make a decision this minute.* • If you say that something will happen at **any minute,** you mean that it is likely to happen very soon. *Mrs Curry was going to cry any minute.* • If you do something **at the last minute,** you do it at the last possible time that it can be done. *Why do you always leave things to the last minute?*

minutely /maɪnjuːtli^{1}/. **1** ADV If you examine something **minutely,** you examine it very carefully, paying attention to small details. *She began examining it minutely from all angles.* **2** ADV **Minutely** also means very slightly. *His fingers trembled minutely.*

miracle /mɪrəkə^{0}l/, **miracles. 1** COUNT N A **miracle** is a surprising and fortunate event or discovery. *My father got a job. It was a miracle... ...the miracles of modern science.* **2** COUNT N A **miracle** is also a wonderful and surprising event believed to be caused by God. *Moses performed all the miracles in front of the people.*

miraculous /mɪrækjə^{4}ləs/. **1** ADJ **Miraculous** means very surprising and fortunate. *I had been expecting some miraculous change to occur.* ♦ **miraculously** ADV OR SENTENCE ADV *The door miraculously opened... It seemed, miraculously, that everyone was satisfied.* **2** ADJ **Miraculous** also means extremely beautiful. *...fossils of a near miraculous perfection.* **3** ADJ **Miraculous** is also used to describe wonderful events believed to be caused by God. *...the miraculous powers of the saint.*

mirage /mɪrɑːʒ/, **mirages. 1** COUNT N A **mirage** is an image which you see in the distance or in the air in very hot weather, but which does not actually exist. *...a mirage vibrating on the horizon.* **2** COUNT N A **mirage** is also something in the future that you look forward to, but that never actually happens. *The promised land turns out to be a mirage.*

mirror /mɪrə/, **mirrors, mirroring, mirrored.** 1 COUNT N A **mirror** is a flat piece of glass which reflects light, so that you can see yourself reflected in it. *She stared at herself in the mirror.* 2 VB WITH OBJ If you see something reflected in water, you can say that the water **mirrors** it; a literary use. *The clear water mirrored the blue sky.* 3 VB WITH OBJ To **mirror** something also means to have similar features to it and therefore to seem like a copy of it; a formal use. *In the country political allegiances mirrored existing divisions in society.*

mirth /mɜːθ/. UNCOUNT N **Mirth** is laughter; a literary use. *His anger gave place to mirth.*

mis-. PREFIX **Mis-** is used at the beginning of words to indicate that something is done badly or wrongly. For example, if you mismanage something, you manage it badly. *He had misjudged the situation... ...the misuse of psychiatry.*

misadventure /mɪsədvɛntʃə/, **misadventures.** COUNT N OR UNCOUNT N A **misadventure** is an unfortunate incident; a formal use. *...a funny story about a friend's misadventure... ...a verdict of death by misadventure.*

misapprehension /mɪsæpri1hɛnʃə0n/, **misapprehensions.** COUNT N OR UNCOUNT N A **misapprehension** is a wrong idea or impression. *I was still under a misapprehension as to the threat contained in the letter... It would give rise to immediate misapprehension.*

misbehave /mɪsbi1heɪv/, **misbehaves, misbehaving, misbehaved.** VB If someone, especially a child, **misbehaves,** they behave in an unacceptable way. *When children misbehave, their parents shouldn't become angry.*

misbehaviour /mɪsbi1heɪvjə/; spelled **misbehavior** in American English. UNCOUNT N **Misbehaviour** is behaviour that is not acceptable to other people.

miscalculate /mɪskælkjə4leɪt/, **miscalculates, miscalculating, miscalculated.** VB WITH OR WITHOUT OBJ If you **miscalculate,** you make a mistake in judging a situation. *I must have miscalculated... He badly miscalculated the response to his proposal.*

miscalculation /mɪskælkjə4leɪʃə0n/, **miscalculations.** COUNT N OR UNCOUNT N A **miscalculation** is a mistake in judging a situation. *These miscalculations had serious consequences... ...the risks of miscalculation.*

miscarriage /mɪskærɪdʒ/, **miscarriages.** COUNT N If a woman has a **miscarriage,** she gives birth to a foetus before it is properly formed and it dies.

miscarry /mɪskæri1/, **miscarries, miscarrying, miscarried.** 1 VB If a woman **miscarries,** she has a miscarriage. 2 VB If a plan **miscarries,** it goes wrong and fails. *Our scheme had miscarried.*

miscellaneous /mɪsəleɪnɪəs/. ADJ A **miscellaneous** group consists of people or things that are very different from each other. *...miscellaneous enemies of authority... ...a miscellaneous collection of tools.*

mischief /mɪstʃɪf/. 1 UNCOUNT N **Mischief** is eagerness to have fun, especially by embarrassing people or by playing tricks. *Her face was kind, her eyes full of mischief... There was about him an air of mischief.* 2 UNCOUNT N **Mischief** is also naughty behaviour by children. *He was old enough to get into mischief.*

mischievous /mɪstʃɪvəs/. 1 ADJ A **mischievous** person is eager to have fun, especially by embarrassing people or by playing tricks. *...a mischievous smile.* ♦ **mischievously** ADV *Kitty winked mischievously.* 2 ADJ A **mischievous** child is often naughty.

misconceived /mɪskə7nsiːvd/. ADJ A **misconceived** plan or method is the wrong one for a particular situation and is therefore not likely to succeed. *Their whole approach was misconceived.*

misconception /mɪskənsɛpʃə0n/, **misconceptions.** COUNT N A **misconception** is a wrong idea about something. *Another misconception is that cancer is infectious.*

misconduct /mɪskɒndʌkt/. UNCOUNT N **Misconduct** is bad or unacceptable behaviour, especially by a professional person. *They were victims of government misconduct.*

misdemeanour /mɪsdə1miːnə/, **misdemeanours;** spelled **misdemeanor** in American English. COUNT N A **misdemeanour** is an act that people consider to be shocking or unacceptable; a formal use. *They listened to accounts of his misdemeanours.*

miser /maɪzə/, **misers.** COUNT N A **miser** is a person who enjoys saving money and hates spending it; used showing disapproval. *She had married a miser.*

miserable /mɪzə0rəbə0l/. 1 ADJ If you are **miserable,** you are very unhappy. *Rudolph felt depressed and miserable... They all had miserable faces.* ♦ **miserably** ADV *He looked up miserably.* 2 ADJ A **miserable** place or situation makes you feel depressed. *Being without a grant is really miserable.* 3 ADJ You say the weather is **miserable** when it is raining or cold. *...a miserable Monday morning.*

miserly /maɪzəli1/. ADJ **Miserly** people are very mean and hate spending money. *...a miserly old lady.*

misery /mɪzə0ri1/, **miseries.** UNCOUNT N OR COUNT N **Misery** is great unhappiness. *I am ill with misery... ...the miseries of unemployment.*

misfire /mɪsfaɪə/, **misfires, misfiring, misfired.** VB If a plan **misfires,** it goes wrong. *The use of force in support of their demands had misfired.*

misfit /mɪsfɪt/, **misfits.** COUNT N A **misfit** is a person who is not easily accepted by other people, often because their behaviour is very different from everyone else's. *In such societies there have always been misfits.*

misfortune /mɪsfɔːtʃən/, **misfortunes.** COUNT N OR UNCOUNT N A **misfortune** is something undesirable that happens to you. *The violinist had the misfortune to turn over two pages at once... They had suffered their share of misfortune.*

misgiving /mɪsgɪvɪŋ/, **misgivings.** PLURAL N OR UNCOUNT N If you have **misgivings** about something, you are worried or unhappy about it. *The firm's collapse seemed to confirm their misgivings... I was filled with misgiving about the whole venture.*

misguided /mɪsgaɪdɪ2d/. ADJ **Misguided** opinions and attitudes are wrong, because they are based on wrong information or beliefs. *...Sir Terence's view was misguided... ...misguided idealism.*

mishap /mɪshæp/, **mishaps.** COUNT N OR UNCOUNT N A **mishap** is an unfortunate but not very serious event that happens to you. *Loss of your property and other mishaps can spoil your stay... Tell your mother you have arrived here without mishap.*

misinform /mɪsɪnfɔːm/, **misinforms, misinforming, misinformed.** VB WITH OBJ If you **are misinformed,** you are told something that is wrong or inaccurate. *Unfortunately we were misinformed about the purpose of the fund.*

misinformation /mɪsɪnfə8meɪʃə0n/. UNCOUNT N **Misinformation** is incorrect information which is deliberately given to people in order to deceive them. *...a piece of blatant misinformation.*

misinterpret /mɪsɪntɜːprɪt/, **misinterprets, misinterpreting, misinterpreted.** VB WITH OBJ If you **misinterpret** something, you understand it wrongly. *He saw the smile and misinterpreted it as friendliness.* ♦ **misinterpretation** /mɪsɪntɜːpri2teɪʃə0n/ UNCOUNT N *The new version was less open to misinterpretation.*

misjudge /mɪsdʒʌdʒ/, **misjudges, misjudging, misjudged.** VB WITH OBJ If you **misjudge** someone or something, you form an incorrect idea or opinion about them. *I had rather misjudged the timing.*

misjudgement /mɪsdʒʌdʒmə2nt/, **misjudgements;** also spelled **misjudgment.** COUNT N OR UNCOUNT N A **misjudgement** is the forming of an incorrect idea or opinion. *They were guilty of a serious misjudgement.*

mislay /mɪsleɪ/, **mislays, mislaying, mislaid.** VB WITH OBJ If you **have mislaid** something, you cannot remember where you have put it.

mislead /mɪsliːd/, **misleads, misleading, misled** /mɪslɛd/. VB WITH OBJ If you **mislead** someone, you make them believe something which is not true. *The public has been misled.* ♦ **misleading** ADJ *...misleading information.*

mismanage /mɪsmænɪdʒ/, **mismanages, mismanaging, mismanaged.** VB WITH OBJ To **mismanage** something means to manage it badly. *The local people thought that education was being mismanaged.* ♦ **mismanagement** /mɪsmænɪdʒmə2nt/ UNCOUNT N *...economic mismanagement.*

misplaced /mɪspleɪst/. ADJ A **misplaced** feeling or action is inappropriate, or is directed towards the wrong thing or person. *...misplaced loyalties.*

misprint /mɪsprɪnt/, **misprints.** COUNT N A **misprint** is a mistake in the way something is printed, for example a spelling mistake.

misread, misreads, misreading. Misread is used in the present tense, when it is pronounced /mɪsriːd/. It is also the past tense and past participle, when it is pronounced /mɪsrɛd/. 1 VB WITH OBJ If you **misread** a situation or someone's behaviour, you do not understand it properly. *Their behaviour was usually misread as indifference... He was unconsciously misreading their actions.* 2 VB WITH OBJ If you **misread** something that has been written or printed, you think it says something that it does not say. *She had misread a date in the Tour Book.*

misrepresent /mɪsrɛprə1zɛnt/, **misrepresents, misrepresenting, misrepresented.** VB WITH OBJ If you **misrepresent** someone, you give a wrong account of what they have said or written. *Witnesses claim to have been seriously misrepresented... He says that I have misrepresented his views.* ♦ **misrepresentation** /mɪsrɛpri2zɛnteɪʃə0n/. UNCOUNT N *All political policies are open to misrepresentation.*

miss /mɪs/, **misses, missing, missed.** 1 TITLE You use **Miss** in front of the name of a girl or unmarried woman. *Good morning, Miss Haynes.* 2 VB WITH OBJ If you **miss** something, you fail to notice it. *He doesn't miss much... You can't miss it, it's on the first floor.* 3 VB WITH OR WITHOUT OBJ If you **miss** when you are trying to hit something, you fail to hit it. *She had thrown her plate at his head and missed... He missed the ball at the first swipe.* 4 COUNT N A **miss** is a failure to hit something. *We had a few near misses in the first raid.* 5 VB WITH OBJ If you **miss** someone, you feel sad because they are no longer with you. If you **miss** something, you feel sad because you no longer have it or are no longer experiencing it. *The two boys miss their father a great deal... I knew I should miss living in the Transkei.* 6 VB WITH OBJ If you **miss** a chance or opportunity, you fail to take advantage of it. *It was a good opportunity which it would be a pity to miss.* 7 VB WITH OBJ If you **miss** a bus, plane, or train, you arrive too late to catch it. *She was going to miss her plane if her husband didn't hurry.* 8 VB WITH OBJ If you **miss** something such as a meeting, you do not go to it. *I couldn't miss a departmental meeting.* 9 PHRASE If you **give** something **a miss,** you decide not to do it or go to it; an informal use. *I'd advise you to give it a miss.* 10 See also **missing, hit and miss, hit or miss.**

miss out. PHR VB 1 If you **miss out** something or someone, you do not include them. *You can miss out a surprising number of words and still be understood.* 2 If you **miss out** on something interesting or useful, you do not become involved in it or get it, when other people do. *I miss out on all these kind of opportunities.*

misshapen /mɪsʃeɪpə0n/. ADJ Something that is **misshapen** does not have a normal or natural shape. *Her misshapen old fingers twitched at her beads.*

missile /mɪsaɪl/, **missiles.** 1 COUNT N A **missile** is a weapon that moves long distances through the air and explodes when it reaches its target. *...nuclear missiles.* 2 COUNT N Anything that is thrown as a weapon can be called a **missile.** *Demonstrators attacked police using sticks and assorted missiles.*

missing /mɪsɪŋ/. 1 ADJ If someone or something is **missing,** they are not where you expect them to be, and you cannot find them. *Some of her jewellery was missing... I want to report a missing person.* 2 ADJ If a part of something is **missing,** it has been removed and has not been replaced. *The car was a wreck, with all its wheels missing.*

mission /mɪʃə0n/, **missions.** 1 COUNT N A **mission** is an important task that you are given to do, especially one that involves travelling to another country. *...confidential missions to Berlin.* 2 COUNT N A **mission** is also a group of people who have been sent to a foreign country to carry out an official task. *He became head of the Ugandan mission.* 3 COUNT N A **mission** is also a special journey made by a military aeroplane or space rocket. *...a bombing mission.* 4 UNCOUNT N If you have a **mission,** there is something that you believe it is your duty to try to achieve. *...one of those girls who had a mission in life.* 5 COUNT N A **mission** is also the activity of a group of Christians who have been sent to a place to teach people about Christianity. *...evangelistic missions around Britain.*

missionary /mɪʃənə0ri1/, **missionaries.** COUNT N A **missionary** is a person who has been sent to a foreign country to teach people about his or her religion.

mist /mɪst/, **mists, misting, misted.** UNCOUNT N OR COUNT N **Mist** consists of many tiny drops of water in the air. When there is a mist, you cannot see very far. *Everything was shrouded in mist... ...the mists of early morning.*

mist over or **mist up.** PHR VB When a piece of glass **mists over** or **mists up,** it becomes covered with tiny drops of moisture, so that you cannot see through it easily. *His spectacles misted over.*

mistake /mɪsteɪk/, **mistakes, mistaking, mistook** /mɪstʊk/, **mistaken** /mɪsteɪkən/. 1 COUNT N If you make a **mistake,** you do something which you did not intend to do, or which produces a result that you do not want. *He had made a terrible mistake... We made the mistake of leaving our bedroom window open... ...a spelling mistake.* ● If you do something which you did not intend to do, you can say that you did it **by mistake.** *I opened the door into the library by mistake.* 2 VB WITH OBJ If you **mistake** something, you are wrong about it; a formal use. *At first he thought he had mistaken the address.* 3 VB WITH OBJ AND 'for' If you **mistake** one person or thing for another, you wrongly think that they are the other person or thing. *You mustn't mistake lack of formal education for lack of wisdom.*

mistaken /mɪsteɪkən/. 1 PRED ADJ If you are **mistaken** about something, you are wrong about it. *I told her she must be mistaken... How could she have been* *mistaken about a thing like this?... I had been mistaken in believing Nick was mad.* 2 ADJ A **mistaken** belief or opinion is incorrect. *The discovery of adrenalin came about through a mistaken impression.* ♦ **mistakenly** ADV *The parents may mistakenly believe that they are to blame for their child's illness.*

mister /mɪstə/. See **Mr.**

mistress /mɪstrɪ²s/, **mistresses.** 1 COUNT N A married man's **mistress** is a woman he is having a sexual relationship with, but who is not his wife. 2 COUNT N A **mistress** in a school is a female schoolteacher. *...the French mistress.*

mistrust /mɪstrʌst/, **mistrusts, mistrusting, mistrusted.** 1 UNCOUNT N **Mistrust** is the feeling that you have towards someone who you do not trust. *She gazed on me with a sudden fear and mistrust.* 2 VB WITH OBJ If you **mistrust** someone or something, you do not trust them. *Marshall deeply mistrusted Jefferson... The child soon learns to mistrust offers of affection.*

misty /mɪsti¹/. ADJ If it is **misty,** there is a lot of mist in the air. *The night was cold and misty.*

misunderstand /mɪsʌndəstænd/, **misunderstands, misunderstanding, misunderstood** /mɪsʌndəstʊd/. VB WITH OR WITHOUT OBJ If you **misunderstand** someone, you do not understand properly what they say or write. *She misunderstood my question.*

misunderstanding /mɪsʌndəstændɪŋ/, **misunderstandings.** 1 COUNT N OR UNCOUNT N A **misunderstanding** is a failure to understand something such as a situation or a person's remarks. *This was a minor misunderstanding which could be instantly cleared up... ...a source of suspicion and misunderstanding.* 2 COUNT N If two people have a **misunderstanding,** they have a disagreement or a slight quarrel. *They usually sort out their misunderstandings.*

misuse, misuses, misusing, misused; pronounced /mɪsjuːs/ when it is a noun and /mɪsjuːz/ when it is a verb. 1 UNCOUNT N OR COUNT N The **misuse** of something is incorrect, careless, or dishonest use of it. *...the misuse of company funds... She cared deeply about words, and hated their misuse.* 2 VB WITH OBJ If you **misuse** something, you use it incorrectly, carelessly, or dishonestly. *In some cases, pesticides are deliberately misused.*

mitigate /mɪtɪgeɪt/, **mitigates, mitigating, mitigated.** VB WITH OBJ To **mitigate** something means to make it less unpleasant, serious, or painful; a formal use. *They should endeavour to mitigate distress.*

mitigating /mɪtɪgeɪtɪŋ/. ATTRIB ADJ **Mitigating** circumstances are facts which make a crime less serious or more justifiable; a formal or legal use. *They may deny the offence or plead mitigating circumstances.*

mitten /mɪtə⁰n/, **mittens.** COUNT N **Mittens** are gloves which have one section that covers your thumb and another section for all your fingers.

mix /mɪks/, **mixes, mixing, mixed.** 1 ERG VB OR RECIP VB If you **mix** two substances, you stir or shake them together. *The mug had been used for mixing flour and water... They drink whisky mixed with beer... If you pour this liquid too fast, it will not mix.* 2 VB WITH OBJ If you **mix** something, you make it by stirring or shaking substances together. *He carefully mixed the cement.* 3 MASS N WITH SUPP A **mix** is a powder containing all the substances that you need in order to make something, to which you add liquid. *...cake mixes... She bought a packet of cement mix.* 4 COUNT N A **mix** is also two or more things combined together. *We should try and keep a broad mix of subjects in our schools... I find the mix of politics and literature very interesting.* 5 VB If you **mix** with other people, you meet them and talk to them at a social event. *He was making no effort to mix.*

mix up. PHR VB 1 If you **mix up** two things or people, you confuse them, so that you think that one of them is the other one. *People even mix us up and greet us by each other's names.* 2 See also **mixed up, mix-up.**

mixed /mɪkst/. 1 ATTRIB ADJ You use **mixed** to describe something which consists of different things of the same general kind. *...a mixed salad... He has mixed feelings towards his wife.* 2 ADJ **Mixed** also means involving people from two or more different races. *...a mixed marriage... He is of mixed parentage: half English, half Dutch.* 3 ADJ **Mixed** education or accommodation is intended for both males and females. *...a mixed school.*

mixed up. 1 ADJ If you are **mixed up,** you are confused. *I got mixed up and forgot which one I'd gone to first... Tim was in a strange mixed-up frame of mind.* 2 PRED ADJ If you are **mixed up** in a crime or a scandal, you are involved in it. *I wasn't mixed up in it myself.* 3 PRED ADJ If things get **mixed up,** they get out of order. *The letters had got too mixed up to be sorted out easily.*

mixer /mɪksə/, **mixers.** COUNT N WITH SUPP A **mixer** is a machine used for mixing things together. *...a food mixer... ...cement mixers.*

mixture /mɪkstʃə/, **mixtures.** 1 SING N A **mixture** of things consists of several different things together. *I swallowed a mixture of pills... She stared at the cold green soup in a mixture of disgust and hunger.* 2 COUNT N A **mixture** is a substance that consists of other substances which have been stirred or shaken together. *...a mixture of water and household bleach.*

mix-up, mix-ups. COUNT N A **mix-up** is a mistake in something that was planned; an informal use. *Due to some administrative mix-up the letters had not been sent.*

ml. 1 **ml** is a written abbreviation for 'millilitre' or 'millilitres'. *...180ml of water.* 2 **ml** is also a written abbreviation for 'mile' or 'miles'.

mm. **mm** is a written abbreviation for 'millimetre' or 'millimetres'. *...35mm film.*

moan /məʊn/, **moans, moaning, moaned.** 1 VB If you **moan,** you make a low, miserable cry because you are unhappy or in pain. *Otto moaned from the pain.* Also COUNT N *Each time she moved her leg she let out a moan.* 2 REPORT VB To **moan** also means to speak in a way which shows that you are very unhappy. *'What am I going to do?' she moaned.* 3 VB If you **moan** about something, you complain about it. *My brother's moaning about money again.*

moat /məʊt/, **moats.** COUNT N A **moat** is a deep, wide ditch dug round a hill or castle as a protection.

mob /mɒb/, **mobs, mobbing, mobbed.** 1 COUNT N A **mob** is a large, disorganized crowd of people. *The police faced a mob throwing bricks and petrol bombs.* 2 VB WITH OBJ If a crowd of people **mob** a person, they gather round the person and express their feelings in a disorderly way. *Pop stars are always moaning about being mobbed by their fans.*

mobile /məʊbaɪl/, **mobiles.** 1 ADJ Something or someone that is **mobile** is able to move or be moved easily. *Most antelopes are fully mobile as soon as they are born... The squadron was protected by a highly mobile air defence.* ♦ **mobility** /məʊbɪlɪ¹ti¹/ UNCOUNT N *Belongings take up space and restrict mobility.* 2 PRED ADJ If you are socially **mobile,** you are able to move to a different social class. *...socially mobile business leaders.* ♦ **mobility** UNCOUNT N *...growing affluence, opportunity, and social mobility.* 3 COUNT N A **mobile** is a light structure which hangs from a ceiling as a decoration and moves gently in air currents.

mobilize /məʊbɪlaɪz/, **mobilizes, mobilizing, mobilized;** also spelled **mobilise.** 1 VB WITH OBJ If you **mobilize** a group of people, you encourage them to do something. *The Trade Union Congress is prepared to mobilize the whole movement to defeat the bill.* ♦ **mobilization** /məʊbɪlaɪzeɪʃə⁰n/ UNCOUNT N *The building of the canal required the mobilization of large masses of labour.* 2 VB WITH OR WITHOUT OBJ If a country **mobilizes** or **mobilizes** its armed forces, it prepares for war; a formal use. *Reserves were mobilized.* ♦ **mobilization** UNCOUNT N *Defence chiefs urged mobilization at once.*

moccasin /mɒkəsɪn/, **moccasins.** COUNT N **Moccasins** are soft leather shoes with a raised seam at the front.

mock /mɒk/, **mocks, mocking, mocked.** 1 VB WITH OBJ If you **mock** someone, you say something unkind about them, or imitate them in an unkind way. *No child in this school would mock a stutterer... ...an unsympathetic teacher who had mocked her domestic ambitions.* ♦ **mocking** ADJ *...the boys' mocking laughter.* 2 ATTRIB ADJ You use **mock** to describe something which is not genuine. *Robert squealed in mock terror... ...mock battles.*

mockery /mɒkə⁰ri¹/. 1 UNCOUNT N **Mockery** is words, behaviour, or opinions that are unkind and scornful. *He had ignored Helen's mockery... There was a tone of mockery in his voice.* 2 SING N If you describe an event or situation as a **mockery,** you mean that it seems unsuccessful and worthless. *The examination was a mockery... The strikers were making a mockery of our efforts to build up employment.*

mock-up, mock-ups. COUNT N A **mock-up** of a structure is a model of it. *Here's a mock-up of the central section of the submarine.*

modal /məʊdə⁰l/, **modals.** COUNT N In grammar, a **modal** or a **modal verb** is a word such as 'can' or 'would' which is used in a verbal group and which expresses ideas such as possibility, intention, and necessity.

mode /məʊd/, **modes.** COUNT N WITH SUPP A **mode** of life or behaviour is a particular way of living or behaving; a formal use. *...conventionally acceptable modes of life... She always chose this mode of transport.*

model /mɒdə⁰l/, **models, modelling, modelled;** spelled **modeling, modeled** in American English. 1 COUNT N A **model** is a three-dimensional copy of an object, usually one that is smaller than the object. *...scale models of well known Navy ships... ...a model theatre.* 2 COUNT N WITH SUPP If a system is used as a **model,** people copy it in order to achieve similar results; a formal use. *This system seemed a relevant model for the new Africa.* 3 COUNT N WITH 'of' Something that is a **model** of clarity or a **model** of fairness, for example, is extremely clear or extremely fair. *She's a model of discretion.* 4 ATTRIB ADJ A **model** wife or a **model** teacher, for example, is an excellent wife or an excellent teacher. *They are model students.* 5 REFL VB WITH 'on' If you **model** yourself on someone, you copy the way that they do things, because you admire them. *The children have their parents on which to model themselves.* 6 COUNT N A particular **model** of a machine is a version of it. *The Granada is the most popular model.* 7 VB WITH OBJ If you **model** an object, you make it out of a substance such as clay. *...a statue of a boy that she had modelled in wax.* 8 COUNT N An artist's **model** is someone who poses for an artist. *She was one of Rossetti's favourite models.* 9 COUNT N A fashion **model** displays clothes by wearing them, as a job. 10 VB WITH OBJ If you **model** clothes, you display them by wearing them. *He models cardigans in knitting books.* ♦ **modelling** UNCOUNT N *She's not to do modelling while she's still at school.*

moderate, moderates, moderating, moderated; pronounced /mɒdərə¹t/ when it is an adjective or noun and /mɒdəreɪt/ when it is a verb. 1 ADJ **Moderate** political opinions or policies are not extreme and are concerned with slow or small changes. *...a woman with moderate views... The movement drew its support from moderate conservatives.* 2 COUNT N A **moderate** is a person whose political opinions and activities are not extreme. *The moderates have plenty to be anxious about.* 3 ADJ A **moderate** amount is neither large nor small. *The sun's rays, in moderate quantities, are important for health... ...her moderate income.* 4 ERG VB If you **moderate** something, it becomes less extreme or violent and more acceptable. *She had been given instructions to moderate her tone... The bad weather had moderated.*

moderately /mɒdərətli¹/. SUBMOD **Moderately** means to a medium degree. *Her handwriting was moderately good.*

moderation /mɒdəreɪʃə⁰n/. 1 UNCOUNT N **Moderation** is self-control and restraint. *He has not displayed the same moderation in his political behaviour as in his private life.* 2 PHRASE If you do something **in moderation,** you do not do it too much.

modern /mɒdə⁵n/. 1 ATTRIB ADJ **Modern** means relating to the present time. *The social problems in modern society are mounting.* 2 ADJ **Modern** things are new, or of a new kind. *...modern architecture... ...modern methods of production.* ♦ **modernity** /mə⁷dɜːnɪ¹ti¹/ UNCOUNT N *...industries half way between tradition and modernity.*

modernize /mɒdənaɪz/, **modernizes, modernizing, modernized;** also spelled **modernise.** VB WITH OBJ To **modernize** a system or a factory means to introduce new methods or equipment. *...a twenty year programme to modernise Britain's transport system.* ♦ **modernization** /mɒdənaɪzeɪʃə⁰n/ UNCOUNT N *...plans for modernisation of the Post Office.*

modern languages. PLURAL N If you study **modern languages,** you study modern European languages such as French, German, and Russian.

modest /mɒdɪ²st/. 1 ADJ Something that is **modest** is quite small in size or amount. *He moved from his hotel suite into a modest flat... ...a small theatre with a modest budget.* ♦ **modestly** ADV *He still gambled modestly.* 2 ADJ Someone who is **modest** does not talk much about their abilities, achievements, or possessions; used showing approval. *He's got a drawer full of medals but he's too modest to wear them.* ♦ **modestly** ADV *He talks quietly and modestly about his farm.* 3 ADJ You can also say that someone is **modest** when they are easily embarrassed by things such as nudity. ♦ **modestly** ADV *They slipped out of their garments modestly.*

modesty /mɒdɪ²sti¹/. 1 UNCOUNT N Someone who shows **modesty** does not talk much about their abilities, achievements, or possessions; used showing approval. 2 UNCOUNT N **Modesty** is also the fact of being easily embarrassed by things such as nudity.

modicum /mɒdɪkəm/. SING N A **modicum** of something is a small amount of it; a formal use. *...a designer with a modicum of good taste.*

modifier /mɒdɪfaɪə/, **modifiers.** COUNT N A **modifier** is a word which comes in front of a noun in a noun group.

modify /mɒdɪfaɪ/, **modifies, modifying, modified.** VB WITH OBJ If you **modify** something, you change it slightly, often in order to improve it. *The present Government has modified this approach.* ♦ **modifica-**

tion /mɒdɪfɪkeɪʃə^{0}n/ COUNT N OR UNCOUNT N *The engine was pulled apart for modifications... I said I thought the idea might need modification.*

module /mɒdju:l/, **modules.** COUNT N A **module** is a part of a spacecraft which can operate away from the spacecraft.

moist /mɔɪst/, **moister, moistest.** ADJ Something that is **moist** is slightly wet. *...moist black earth... His eyes grew moist.*

moisten /mɔɪsə^{0}n/, **moistens, moistening, moistened.** VB WITH OBJ If you **moisten** something, you make it slightly wet. *The girl moistened her lips.*

moisture /mɔɪstʃə/. UNCOUNT N **Moisture** is tiny drops of water that are present somewhere. *The kitchen's stone floor was shiny with moisture... Trees have enormous roots that can reach out for moisture far below the surface.*

molar /məʊlə/, **molars.** COUNT N Your **molars** are the large teeth at the side of your mouth.

mold /məʊld/. See **mould.**

moldy /məʊldi^1/. See **mouldy.**

mole /məʊl/, **moles.** 1 COUNT N A **mole** is a natural dark spot on someone's skin. 2 COUNT N A **mole** is also a small animal with black fur that lives underground. 3 COUNT N A member of an organization who secretly reveals confidential information to the press or to a rival organization is also called a **mole.** *There is some gossip in Westminster that there is a mole in the Thatcher cabinet.*

molecular /mə^{6}lekjə^{4}lə/. ATTRIB ADJ **Molecular** means relating to molecules. *...molecular biology.*

molecule /mɒlɪkju:l/, **molecules.** COUNT N A **molecule** is the smallest amount of a chemical substance which can exist. *The haemoglobin molecule contains only four atoms of iron.*

molehill /məʊlhɪl/, **molehills.** 1 COUNT N A **molehill** is a small pile of earth resulting from a mole digging a tunnel. 2 PHRASE If someone is **making a mountain out of a molehill,** they are treating an unimportant difficulty as if it were very serious.

molest /mə^{7}lest/, **molests, molesting, molested;** a formal word. 1 VB WITH OBJ Someone who **molests** children touches them in a sexual way. ♦ **molester** /mə^{7}lestə/ COUNT N *...child molesters.* 2 VB WITH OBJ If someone **molests** you, they threaten you or prevent you from doing something. *They feared they would be molested by the angry crowd.*

mollify /mɒlɪfaɪ/, **mollifies, mollifying, mollified.** VB WITH OBJ If you **mollify** someone, you make them less upset or angry; a formal use. *Mrs Pringle allowed herself to be mollified.* ♦ **mollified** PRED ADJ *She appeared slightly mollified.*

molt /məʊlt/. See **moult.**

molten /məʊltə^{0}n/. ADJ **Molten** rock or metal has been heated until it is a thick liquid. *...a great mass of molten rock.*

mom /mɒm/, **moms.** VOCATIVE OR COUNT N Someone's **mom** is their mother; an informal American use.

moment /məʊmə^{2}nt/, **moments.** COUNT N A **moment** is a very short period of time. *She hesitated for only a moment... A few moments later he heard footsteps... At that precise moment, Miss Pulteney came into the office... ...the moment of death.*

PHRASES ● A situation that exists **at the moment** exists now. *The biggest problem at the moment is unemployment.* ● If you do something at **the last moment,** you do it at the last possible time. *We escaped from Saigon at the last moment.* ● If you cannot do something **for the moment,** you cannot do it now, but you may be able to do it later. *I don't want to discuss this for the moment.* ● If something happens **the moment** something else happens, it happens as soon as the other thing happens. *The moment I saw this, it appealed to me.*

momentary /məʊməntə^{0}ri^1/. ADJ Something that is **momentary** lasts for only a very short time. *There was a momentary pause.* ♦ **momentarily** /məʊməntəərɪ^{1}li^1/ ADV *I had momentarily forgotten.*

momentous /mə^{6}mentəs/. ADJ A **momentous** event is very important. *There was no doubt it would be a momentous occasion.*

momentum /mə^{6}mentəm/. 1 UNCOUNT N **Momentum** is the ability that something has to keep developing. *It was necessary to crush the rebel movement before it had a chance to gather momentum.* 2 UNCOUNT N **Momentum** is also the ability that an object has to continue moving, because of its mass and speed. *...the momentum of the rocket.*

monarch /mɒnək/, **monarchs.** COUNT N A **monarch** is a king or queen who reigns over a country.

monarchist /mɒnəkɪst/, **monarchists.** COUNT N A **monarchist** is a person who believes that their country should have a monarch.

monarchy /mɒnəki^1/, **monarchies.** COUNT N A **monarchy** is a system in which a country has a king or queen. *We want to abolish the monarchy.*

monastery /mɒnəstri^1/, **monasteries.** COUNT N A **monastery** is a building in which monks live.

Monday /mʌndi^1/, **Mondays.** UNCOUNT N OR COUNT N **Monday** is the day after Sunday and before Tuesday.

monetary /mɒnɪ^{2}tə^{0}ri^1/. ATTRIB ADJ **Monetary** means relating to money, especially the money in a country; a formal use. *...monetary policy.*

money /mʌni^1/. UNCOUNT N **Money** is the coins or bank notes that you use to buy things, or the sum that you have in a bank account. *I spent all my money on sweets... They may not accept English money.*

PHRASES ● If you **make money,** you obtain money by earning it or by making a profit. *To make money you've got to take chances.* ● If you **get** your **money's worth,** you get good value for the money that you spend. *I always insist on getting my money's worth.*

mongrel /mʌŋgrəl/, **mongrels.** COUNT N A **mongrel** is a dog with parents of different breeds.

monitor /mɒnɪtə/, **monitors, monitoring, monitored.** 1 VB WITH OBJ If you **monitor** something, you regularly check its development or progress. *The child's progress is being monitored.* 2 COUNT N A **monitor** is a machine used to check or record things. *The patient was connected to the monitor.*

monk /mʌŋk/, **monks.** COUNT N A **monk** is a member of a male religious community.

monkey /mʌŋki^1/, **monkeys.** COUNT N A **monkey** is an animal with a long tail which lives in hot countries.

monogamous /mə^{7}nɒgəməs/. ADJ **Monogamous** means having only one husband, wife, or mate. *The birds are monogamous.*

monogamy /mə^{7}nɒgəmi^1/. UNCOUNT N **Monogamy** is the custom of being married to only one person at the same time. *Lifelong monogamy has other drawbacks.*

monolithic /mɒnə^{6}lɪθɪk/. ADJ A **monolithic** organization or system is very large and seems unlikely to change. *...the monolithic character of the main political parties.*

monologue /mɒnəlɒg/, **monologues.** COUNT N A **monologue** is a long speech by one person. *He went into a long monologue.*

monopolize /mə^{7}nɒpəlaɪz/, **monopolizes, monopolizing, monopolized;** also spelled **monopolise.** VB WITH OBJ To **monopolize** something means to control it completely and prevent other people having a share in it. *The Dutch wanted to monopolize the profitable spice trade from the East.*

monopoly /mə^{7}nɒpəli^1/, **monopolies.** COUNT N OR UNCOUNT N A **monopoly** is the control or possession of a particular thing by only one person or group. *I don't believe the medical profession has a monopoly on morality... ...the ending of the Communist Party's monopoly of power... Many local papers are prosperous because they enjoy a virtual monopoly.*

monosyllable /mɒnə^{6}sɪləbə^{0}l/, **monosyllables.** COUNT N If someone speaks in **monosyllables,** they speak using only very short words, for example 'yes' and 'no'. *He was answering only in monosyllables.*

monotone /mɒnətəʊn/. SING N A **monotone** is a sound which does not vary at all and is boring to listen to. *He droned on in a steady monotone.*

monotonous /mə^{7}nɒtənəs/. ADJ Something that is **monotonous** never changes and is boring. *...people who have monotonous jobs.*

monotony /mə^{7}nɒtəni^1/. UNCOUNT N The **monotony** of something is the fact that it never changes and is boring. *...the monotony of work on the assembly line.*

monsoon /mɒnsu:n/, **monsoons.** COUNT N The **monsoon** is the season of very heavy rain in Southern Asia. *Even during the monsoons the afternoons were warm and clear.*

monster /mɒnstə/, **monsters.** 1 COUNT N A **monster** is a large imaginary creature that is very frightening. *...hairy white monsters.* 2 ATTRIB ADJ **Monster** means extremely large. *...the monster Piccadilly Hotel.*

monstrosity /mɒnstrɒsɪ^{1}ti^1/, **monstrosities.** COUNT N A **monstrosity** is something that is large and extremely ugly. *...a monstrosity of a house.*

monstrous /mɒnstrəs/. 1 ADJ If you describe a situation or event as **monstrous,** you mean that it is very shocking or unfair. *The court's judgement was absolutely monstrous.* 2 ADJ Something that is **monstrous** is very large and rather ugly or shocking. *...a heavy man in a monstrous mustard-coloured sweater.*

month /mʌnθ/, **months.** 1 COUNT N A **month** is one of the twelve periods of time that a year is divided into, for example January or February. *It's happened three times this month... The pay will be five hundred pounds a month.* 2 COUNT N A **month** is also a period of about four weeks. *He was kidnapped just over a month ago.*

monthly /mʌnθli^1/. ATTRIB ADJ OR ADV You use **monthly** to describe something that happens every month. *...a monthly meeting... Our staff are paid monthly.*

monument /mɒnjə^{4}mə^{2}nt/, **monuments.** COUNT N A **monument** is a large stone structure built to remind people of a person or event. *...a monument to F D Roosevelt.*

monumental /mɒnjə^{4}mentə^{0}l/. 1 ATTRIB ADJ A **monumental** building or work of art is very large and impressive. *...the monumental facade of the Royal School.* 2 ADJ **Monumental** also means very great or extreme. *...a monumental hailstorm.*

moo /mu:/, **moos, mooing, mooed.** VB When a cow **moos,** it makes the noise that cows typically make.

mooch /mu:tʃ/, **mooches, mooching, mooched.** VB WITH ADJUNCT If you **mooch** about, you walk about slowly with no particular purpose; an informal use. *He mooched about the house in his pyjamas.*

mood /mu:d/, **moods.** 1 COUNT N Your **mood** is the state of your emotions at a particular time. *He was always in a good mood... I wasn't in the mood for helping.* 2 COUNT N If you are in a **mood,** you are angry and impatient. *When Chris was in one of his moods, he was unpleasant to everyone.* 3 SING N The **mood** of a group of people is their general feeling or attitude. *The debate took place amid a mood of growing political despair... The mood of this week's meeting has been one of cautious optimism.*

moody /mu:di^1/. 1 ADJ Someone who is **moody** is depressed and does not want to talk. *He's only moody because things aren't working out.* ♦ **moodily** ADV *She drank her coffee moodily.* 2 ADJ **Moody** people have feelings which change frequently. *He was moody and unpredictable.*

moon /mu:n/, **moons.** 1 SING N The **moon** is the object which appears in the sky at night as a circle or part of a circle. *...television pictures of a man walking on the moon.* 2 COUNT N A **moon** is a natural object that travels round a planet. *...Jupiter's four moons.*

moonlight /mu:nlaɪt/, **moonlights, moonlighting, moonlighted.** 1 UNCOUNT N **Moonlight** is the light that comes from the moon at night. *The field looked like water in the moonlight... Our meeting took place by moonlight.* 2 VB If you **moonlight,** you have a second job in addition to your main job, often without informing your main employers or the tax office. *She moonlighted as a waitress.*

moonlit /mu:nlɪt/. ADJ Something that is **moonlit** is lit by moonlight. *...a moonlit night.*

moor /mʊə, mɔ:/, **moors, mooring, moored.** 1 COUNT N A **moor** is a high area of open land covered mainly with rough grass and heather. *The mists had vanished from the moor... He used to go for long walks on the moors.* 2 VB WITH OBJ If a boat **is moored,** it is attached to the land with a rope. *Boats were moored on both sides of the river.*

mooring /mʊərɪŋ, mɔ:-/, **moorings.** COUNT N A **mooring** is a place on land where a boat can be tied. *During the storm, boats were torn from their moorings.*

moorland /mʊələ^{3}nd, mɔ:-/, **moorlands.** UNCOUNT N OR PLURAL N **Moorland** is land which consists of moors. *...the beauty of Britain's moorlands.*

moose /mu:s/. **Moose** is the singular and plural. COUNT N A **moose** is a large North American deer with flat antlers.

mop /mɒp/, **mops, mopping, mopped.** 1 COUNT N A **mop** is a tool for washing floors. It consists of a sponge or many pieces of string attached to a long handle. 2 VB WITH OBJ If you **mop** a floor, you clean it with a mop. 3 VB WITH OBJ If you **mop** a liquid from a surface or if you **mop** the surface, you wipe the surface with a dry cloth in order to remove the liquid. *He mopped the sweat from his face... Mop it with a tissue... He mopped his sweating brow.* 4 COUNT N A **mop** of hair is a large amount of loose or untidy hair. *...a coarse mop of black hair.*

mop up. PHR VB If you **mop up** a liquid, you remove it using a cloth or sponge. *Mother started mopping up the oil.*

mope /məʊp/, **mopes, moping, moped.** VB If you **mope,** you feel miserable and are not interested in anything. *He just sits about, moping in an armchair.*

moped /məʊped/, **mopeds.** COUNT N A **moped** is a small motorcycle.

moral /mɒrə^{0}l/, **morals.** 1 PLURAL N **Morals** are principles and beliefs concerning right and wrong behaviour. *Business morals nowadays are very low... Films like this are a danger to public morals.* 2 ATTRIB ADJ **Moral** means concerned with right or wrong behaviour. *I have noticed a fall in moral standards... It is our moral duty to stay.* ♦ **morally** SUBMOD *It is morally wrong not to do more to help the poor.* 3 ADJ Someone who is **moral** behaves in a way that they believe is right. *If parents are themselves honest and moral, their children will be too.* ♦ **morally** ADV *I try to live morally.* 4 ADJ If you give someone **moral** support, you encourage them in what they are doing by expressing approval. *I looked across to give moral support to my colleagues.* 5 SING N The **moral** of a story or event is what you learn from it about how you should or should not behave. *The moral is clear: you must never marry for money.*

morale /mɒrɑːl/. UNCOUNT N **Morale** is the amount of confidence and optimism that people have. *The morale of the men was good.*

moralise /mɒrəlaɪz/. See **moralize.**

moralist /mɒrəlɪst/, **moralists.** COUNT N A **moralist** is someone with strong ideas about right and wrong behaviour. *My grandfather was a stern moralist.*

moralistic /mɒrəlɪstɪk/. ADJ If you are **moralistic,** your ideas about right and wrong behaviour are extreme or are forced on other people. *She had rebuked David for his moralistic attitude.*

morality /mə^{7}rælɪ^{1}ti^1/, **moralities.** 1 UNCOUNT N OR COUNT N **Morality** is the belief that some behaviour is right and acceptable and that other behaviour is wrong. *...the decline in traditional morality... Conflicts must arise between the two moralities.* 2 UNCOUNT N The **morality** of something is how right or acceptable it is. *...arguments concerning the morality of taking part in a war.*

moralize /mɒrəlaɪz/, **moralizes, moralizing, moralized;** also spelled **moralise.** VB If someone **moralizes,** they tell people what they think is right or wrong; used showing disapproval. *...moralizing about the dangers of drink.*

morass /məræs/. SING N You use **morass** to refer to a situation that it is extremely complicated and confused. *These men are usually bogged down in a morass of paperwork.*

moratorium /mɒrətɔːrɪəm/, **moratoriums.** COUNT N If there is a **moratorium** on a particular activity, it is officially stopped for a period of time; a formal use. *The meeting did agree to extend the moratorium on the building of new warships.*

morbid /mɔːbɪd/. ADJ If someone or their behaviour is **morbid,** they have too great an interest in unpleasant things, especially in death. *It's morbid to dwell on cemeteries and suchlike... ...morbid imaginations.*

more /mɔː/. 1 DET OR QUANTIF **More** means a greater number or amount than before or than something else. *Do you spend more time teaching, or doing research?... Better management may enable one man to milk more cows... He saw more than 800 children dying of starvation... There are more of them seeking jobs than there are jobs available.* 2 ADV **More** also means to a greater extent. *The books that are true to life will attract them more... They were more amused than concerned.* 3 ADV If you do something some **more,** you continue doing it. *They talked a bit more... I apologized and thought no more about it... The employers don't want quality work any more.* 4 DET OR PRON **More** is also used to refer to an additional thing or amount. *In the next hour he found two more diamonds... Have some more coffee, Vicar... I wanted to find out more about her.* 5 SUBMOD **More** is used in front of adjectives or adverbs to form comparatives. *Your child's health is more important than the doctor's feelings... Next time, I will choose more carefully.*

PHRASES • If something is not the case **any more,** it has stopped being the case. *The employers don't want quality work any more... They're not here anymore... He did not feel like working any more.* • If something is **more than** a particular thing, it has greater value or importance than this thing. *It wasn't much more than a formality... This is more than a hunter's job.* • You can also use **more than** to emphasize that something is true to a greater degree than is necessary or than is said. *You'll have more than enough money for any equipment you need... This was a more than generous arrangement.* • If something is **more or less** true, it is true in a general way, but is not completely true. *Brian more or less implied that we were lying.* • You use **what's more** to introduce an additional piece of information which supports or emphasizes the point you are making. *What's more, he adds, there are no signs of a change.*

moreover /mɔːrəʊvə/. SENTENCE ADV **Moreover** is used to introduce a piece of information that adds to or supports the previous statement; a formal use. *They have accused the Government of corruption. Moreover, they have named names.*

morgue /mɔːg/, **morgues.** COUNT N A **morgue** is a building where dead bodies are kept before they are cremated or buried. *...the city morgue.*

morning /mɔːnɪŋ/, **mornings.** 1 COUNT N OR UNCOUNT N The **morning** is the part of a day between the time that people wake up and lunchtime. *She left after breakfast on Saturday morning... I was reading the morning paper.* 2 COUNT N The part of a day between midnight and noon is also called the **morning.** *She died in the very early hours of this morning... It was five o'clock in the morning.*

morning sickness. UNCOUNT N **Morning sickness** is a feeling of sickness that some women have when they are pregnant.

moron /mɔːrɒn/, **morons.** COUNT N If you describe someone as a **moron,** you mean that they are very stupid; an informal use.

moronic /mə^{8}rɒnɪk/. ADJ **Moronic** means very stupid; an informal use.

morose /mərəʊs/. ADJ Someone who is **morose** is miserable. *He was morose and silent.* ♦ **morosely** ADV *The man followed me morosely round the museum.*

morphine /mɔːfiːn/. UNCOUNT N **Morphine** is a drug used to relieve pain.

morsel /mɔːsə^{0}l/, **morsels.** COUNT N A **morsel** of something, especially food, is a very small piece of it.

mortal /mɔːtə^{0}l/, **mortals.** 1 ADJ When you describe people as **mortal,** you are referring to the fact that they have to die and cannot live forever. *Remember that you are mortal.* 2 COUNT N You can refer to ordinary people as **mortals** when contrasting them with someone very powerful or successful, often humorously. *He passed first time, something which we mortals couldn't manage.* 3 ATTRIB ADJ A **mortal** enemy or danger is one which may cause you severe harm. *They regard the police as their mortal enemies... We are all in mortal danger.* 4 ATTRIB ADJ If two people are involved in **mortal** combat, they are trying to kill each other. *They were locked in mortal combat.*

mortality /mɔːtælɪ^{1}ti^1/. 1 UNCOUNT N **Mortality** is the fact that all people must die. *...man contemplating his own mortality.* 2 UNCOUNT N The **mortality** in a particular place or situation is the number of people who die. *Infant mortality on the island has been reported at 200 per 1,000 births... ...variations in hospital mortality rates.*

mortally /mɔːtə^{0}li^1/. ADV Someone who is **mortally** wounded or **mortally** ill is going to die as a result of their wound or illness.

mortar /mɔːtə/, **mortars.** 1 COUNT N A **mortar** is a short cannon which fires missiles high into the air for a short distance. *We returned fire with mortars and machine-guns.* 2 UNCOUNT N **Mortar** is a mixture of sand, water, and cement which is used to hold bricks firmly together.

mortgage /mɔːgɪdʒ/, **mortgages, mortgaging, mortgaged.** 1 COUNT N A **mortgage** is a loan of money which you get from a bank or building society in order to buy a house. *We can't get a mortgage... ...mortgage repayments.* 2 VB WITH OBJ If you **mortgage** your house or land, you use it as a guarantee to a company in order to borrow money from them. *He will have to mortgage his land for a loan.*

mortify /mɔːtɪfaɪ/, **mortifies, mortifying, mortified.** VB WITH OBJ If you **are mortified,** you feel very offended, ashamed, or embarrassed. *She was deeply mortified at this rebuff.* ♦ **mortifying** ADJ *There were some mortifying setbacks.*

mortuary /mɔːtʃʊ^{0}əri^1/, **mortuaries.** COUNT N A **mortuary** is a room in a hospital where dead bodies are kept before they are buried or cremated.

mosaic /məʊzeɪɪk/, **mosaics.** COUNT N OR UNCOUNT N A **mosaic** is a design made of small pieces of coloured stone or glass set in concrete or plaster. *...a Roman mosaic... ...walls covered with mosaics.*

Moslem /mɒzlə^{0}m/. See **Muslim.**

mosque /mɒsk/, **mosques.** COUNT N A **mosque** is a building where Muslims go to worship.

mosquito /mə^{7}skiːtəʊ/, **mosquitoes** or **mosquitos.** COUNT N **Mosquitoes** are small flying insects which bite people in order to suck their blood.

moss /mɒs/, **mosses.** MASS N **Moss** is a very small soft green plant which grows on damp soil, or on wood or stone. *The bark was covered with moss... ...non-flowering plants such as mosses and fungi.*

mossy /mɒsi^1/. ADJ Something that is **mossy** is covered with moss. *...a flight of mossy stone steps.*

most /məʊst/. 1 QUANTIF OR DET **Most** of a group or amount means nearly all of it, or the majority of it. *I saw most of the early Shirley Temple films... He used to spend most of his time in the library... Most Arabic speakers understand Egyptian.* 2 ADJ OR PRON The **most** means a larger amount than anyone or anything else, or the largest amount possible. *This is the area that attracts the most attention... The most I could learn was that Lithgow had been sacked.* 3 ADV **Most** or the **most** means to a greater degree or extent than anything else. *What he most feared was being left alone... Which do you value most—wealth or health?... I liked him the most.* 4 SUBMOD **Most** is used in front of adjectives or adverbs to form superlatives. *It was one of the most important discoveries ever made... These are the works I respond to most strongly.* 5 SUBMOD You can use **most** to emphasize an adjective or adverb. For example, if you say that something is **most** interesting, you mean that it is very interesting; a formal use. *The trading results show a most encouraging trend... He always acted most graciously.*

PHRASES • You use **at most** when stating the maximum number that is possible or likely. *I only have fifteen minutes or twenty minutes at the most... There would be at most a hundred people listening.* • If you **make the most of** something, you get the maximum use or advantage from it. *Governments should face up to the situation and make the most of it.*

-most. SUFFIX **-most** is added to adjectives to form other adjectives that describe something as being further in a particular direction than other things of the same kind. For example, the northernmost part of a country is the part that is farthest to the north. *...the innermost room of the castle... ...the topmost branches of a tree.*

mostly /məʊstli^1/. ADV OR SENTENCE ADV **Mostly** is used to indicate that a statement is generally true, for example true about the majority of a group of things or people, or true most of the time. *The men at the party were mostly fairly young... A rattlesnake hunts mostly at night.*

motel /məʊtel/, **motels.** COUNT N A **motel** is a hotel intended for people who are travelling by car.

moth /mɒθ/, **moths.** COUNT N A **moth** is an insect like a butterfly, which usually flies about at night.

moth-eaten. ADJ **Moth-eaten** clothes look very old and ragged. *...moth-eaten sweaters and worn-out shoes.*

mother /mʌðə/, **mothers, mothering, mothered.** 1 COUNT N OR VOCATIVE Your **mother** is the woman who gave birth to you. *I always did everything my mother told me... You are looking wonderful, Mother.* 2 VB WITH OBJ The way that a mother **mothers** her children is the way that she looks after them and brings them up. *Female monkeys who were badly mothered became bad mothers themselves.* 3 VB WITH OBJ If someone **mothers** you, they treat you with great affection, and often spoil you. *Both the other senior typists tended to mother me.*

motherhood /mʌðəhʊd/. UNCOUNT N **Motherhood** is the state of being a mother. *...girls preparing for motherhood.*

mother-in-law, mothers-in-law. COUNT N Your **mother-in-law** is the mother of your husband or wife.

motherless /mʌðələ^{2}s/. ADJ You describe children as **motherless** when their mother has died or does not live with them.

motherly /mʌðəli^1/. ADJ A **motherly** woman is warm, kind, and protective. *...a plump, motherly woman.*

mother-of-pearl. UNCOUNT N **Mother-of-pearl** is the shining layer on the inside of some shells. It is used to make buttons or to decorate things.

mother-to-be, mothers-to-be. COUNT N A **mother-to-be** is a woman who is pregnant, especially for the first time.

mother-tongue, mother-tongues. COUNT N Your **mother-tongue** is the language you learnt from your parents when you were a child.

motif /məʊtiːf/, **motifs.** COUNT N A **motif** is a design used as a decoration. *There were white curtains with black and red motifs on them.*

motion /məʊʃə^{0}n/, **motions, motioning, motioned.** 1 UNCOUNT N **Motion** is continual movement. *The bed swayed with the motion of the ship... Just keep moving, stay in motion.* • See also **slow motion.** 2 COUNT N A **motion** is an action, gesture, or movement. *He made stabbing motions with his spear... With a quick motion of her hands, she did her hair up in a knot..* 3 COUNT N A **motion** in a meeting or debate is a proposal which is discussed and voted on. *He proposed the motion that 'the Public Schools of England should be abolished'.* 4 VB WITH OR WITHOUT OBJ If you **motion** to someone, you make a movement with your hand in order to show them what they should do. *Boylan motioned to Rudolph to sit down... He motioned Tom to follow him... He shook hands and motioned him to a seat.*

PHRASES • If you **go through the motions,** you say or do something that is expected of you, without being very sincere or serious about it. *Major Hawks went through the motions of advising me to quit.* • A process or event that is **in motion** is happening already. *The changes are already in motion.*

motionless /məʊʃə^{0}nlɪ^{2}s/. ADJ Someone or something that is **motionless** is not moving at all. *Rudolph sat motionless... ...queues of motionless cars.*

motivate /məʊtɪveɪt/, **motivates, motivating, motivated.** 1 VB WITH OBJ If you **are motivated** by something, especially an emotion, it causes you to behave in a particular way. *...people motivated by envy and the lust for power... My decision to make this trip was motivated by a desire to leave the country.* ♦ **motivation** /məʊtɪveɪʃə^{0}n/ COUNT N OR UNCOUNT N *There's a political motivation for these* *actions... What was the motivation to stay at school?* **2** VB WITH OBJ If you **motivate** someone, you make them feel determined to do something. *You have first got to motivate the children and then to teach them.* ♦ **motivated** ADJ *...highly motivated and enthusiastic people.* ♦ **motivation** UNCOUNT N *She insists her success is due to motivation rather than brilliance.*

motive /məʊtɪv/, **motives.** COUNT N Your **motive** for doing something is your reason for doing it. *I urge you to question his motives.*

motley /mɒtli^1/. ATTRIB ADJ A **motley** collection consists of people or things that are all different. *...a motley collection of hats and coats.*

motor /məʊtə/, **motors, motoring, motored. 1** COUNT N A **motor** is a part of a machine or vehicle that uses electricity or fuel to produce movement, so that the machine or vehicle can work. *He got into the car and started the motor... ...an electric motor.* **2** ATTRIB ADJ **Motor** means relating to vehicles with a petrol or diesel engine. *...the decline of the motor industry... ...a motor mechanic.* **3** VB If you **are motoring** somewhere, you are travelling there by car; an old-fashioned use. *They spent a week motoring through Italy.* ● See also **motoring.**

motorbike /məʊtəbaɪk/, **motorbikes.** COUNT N A **motorbike** is a motorcycle; an informal British use. *...youths riding up and down on powerful motorbikes.*

motorboat /məʊtəbəʊt/, **motorboats.** COUNT N A **motorboat** is a boat that is driven by a small engine.

motor car, motor cars. COUNT N A **motor car** is the same as a car; a formal use.

motorcycle /məʊtəsaɪkə^{ə}l/, **motorcycles.** COUNT N A **motorcycle** is a two-wheeled vehicle with an engine. *...cars and motorcycles for hire.*

motorcyclist /məʊtəsaɪklɪst/, **motorcyclists.** COUNT N A **motorcyclist** is someone who rides a motorcycle. *...police motorcyclists.*

motoring /məʊtə^{ə}rɪŋ/. ATTRIB ADJ **Motoring** means relating to cars and to driving. *...motoring offences.*

motorist /məʊtə^{ə}rɪst/, **motorists.** COUNT N A **motorist** is someone who drives a car.

motorized /məʊtə^{ə}raɪzd/; also spelled **motorised.** ADJ **Motorized** vehicles have engines. *...motorized transport.*

motorway /məʊtəweɪ/, **motorways.** COUNT N A **motorway** is a wide road specially built for fast travel over long distances; a British use.

mottled /mɒtə^{ə}ld/. ADJ Something that is **mottled** has areas of different colours. *...a mottled camouflage jacket.*

motto /mɒtəʊ/, **mottoes** or **mottos.** COUNT N A **motto** is a short sentence or phrase that expresses a rule for good or sensible behaviour. *...the school motto, 'To strive, to seek, to find.'*

mould /məʊld/, **moulds, moulding, moulded;** spelled **mold** in American English. **1** VB WITH OBJ To **mould** someone or something means to change or influence them over a period of time so that they develop in a particular way. *...the desire to mould the child into a disciplined creature... Television plays a dominant role in moulding public opinion.* **2** VB WITH OBJ If you **mould** plastic or clay, you make it into a particular shape. *...clay moulded into pots.* **3** COUNT N A **mould** is a container used to make something into a particular shape. You pour a liquid into the mould, and when it becomes solid you take it out. **4** MASS N **Mould** is a soft grey, green, or blue substance that sometimes forms on old food or on damp walls or clothes. *...nasty green mould... Peanuts, when they go bad, produce a mould.*

mouldy /məʊldi^1/; spelled **moldy** in American English. ADJ Something that is **mouldy** is covered with mould. *...mouldy fruit.*

moult /məʊlt/, **moults, moulting, moulted;** spelled **molt** in American English. VB When an animal or bird **moults,** it loses its coat or feathers so that a new coat or feathers can grow.

mound /maʊnd/, **mounds. 1** COUNT N A **mound** is a pile of earth like a very small hill. *...a large circular mound of earth... ...a few grass mounds.* **2** COUNT N A **mound** is also a large, untidy pile of things. *He lay in his bunk under a mound of blankets.*

mount /maʊnt/, **mounts, mounting, mounted. 1** VB WITH OBJ To **mount** a campaign or event means to organize it and make it take place. *No rescue operations could be mounted... We mounted an exhibition of recent books.* **2** VB If something **is mounting,** it is increasing. *Social problems in modern society are mounting... The temperature mounted rapidly.* ♦ **mounting** ATTRIB ADJ *...mounting unemployment.* **3** VB WITH OBJ To **mount** something means to go to the top of it; a formal use. *Walter mounted the steps and pressed the bell.* **4** VB WITH OR WITHOUT OBJ If you **mount** a horse, you climb on to its back. *The brothers watched as she mounted the mare.* ● See also **mounted. 5** VB WITH OBJ If you **mount** an object in a particular place, you fix it there. *The sword was mounted in a mahogany case.* **6 Mount** is used as part of the name of a mountain. *...Mount Erebus.* **7** PHRASE If you **mount a guard** over something, you get someone to guard it. If you **mount guard** over it, you guard it yourself. *Strong police guards were mounted at all hospitals... She had been asked to mount guard over a number of dogs.*

mount up. PHR VB If something **mounts up,** it increases. *The soil becomes more and more acidic as pollution mounts up.*

mountain /maʊntɪn/, **mountains. 1** COUNT N A **mountain** is a very high piece of land with steep sides. *...a pleasant hotel in the mountains... ...the Rocky Mountains... ...a mountain road.* **2** COUNT N A **mountain** of something is a very large amount of it. *...a mountain of rubble... ...mountains of letters.* **3** to **make a mountain out of a molehill:** see **molehill.**

mountaineer /maʊntɪnɪə/, **mountaineers.** COUNT N A **mountaineer** is a person who climbs mountains.

mountaineering /maʊntɪnɪərɪŋ/. UNCOUNT N **Mountaineering** is the activity of climbing mountains as a hobby or sport.

mountainous /maʊntɪnəs/. ADJ A **mountainous** area has a lot of mountains. *...mountainous country.*

mountainside /maʊntɪnsaɪd/, **mountainsides.** COUNT N A **mountainside** is one of the steep sides of a mountain. *...hurtling down the mountainside.*

mounted /maʊntɪ^{2}d/. ATTRIB ADJ **Mounted** police or soldiers ride horses when they are on duty.

mourn /mɔːn/, **mourns, mourning, mourned. 1** VB WITH OBJ OR 'for' If you **mourn** someone who has died or **mourn** for them, you are very sad and think about them a lot. *I remained to mourn him in Chicago... I shall always love Guy and mourn for him.* **2** VB WITH OBJ OR 'for' If you **mourn** something or **mourn** for it, you are very sad because you no longer have it. *I mourned for the loss of my beauty.*

mourner /mɔːnə/, **mourners.** COUNT N A **mourner** is a person who attends a funeral. *I went out into the garden to join the mourners.*

mournful /mɔːnfʊl/; a literary word. **1** ADJ If you are **mournful,** you are very sad. *Jefferson looked mournful.* ♦ **mournfully** ADV *He shook his head mournfully.* **2** ADJ A **mournful** sound seems very sad. *The little train kept up its mournful howl.*

mourning /mɔːnɪŋ/. **1** UNCOUNT N **Mourning** is behaviour in which you show sadness about a person's death. *Beards were shaved off as a sign of mourning.* **2** PHRASE If you are **in mourning,** you are wearing special clothes or behaving in a special way because a member of your family has died. *He was in mourning for his wife.*

mouse /maʊs/, **mice** /maɪs/. COUNT N A **mouse** is a small furry animal with a long tail. *The cat was there to keep the mice out of the kitchen.*

mousse /muːs/, **mousses.** MASS N **Mousse** is a sweet, light food made from eggs and cream.

moustache /məstɑːʃ/, **moustaches;** spelled **mustache** /mʌstæʃ/ in American English. COUNT N A man's **moustache** is the hair that grows on his upper lip. *...a tall man with a moustache.*

mouth, mouths, mouthing, mouthed. The noun is pronounced /maʊθ/ in the singular and /maʊðz/ in the plural. The verb is pronounced /maʊð/. **1** COUNT N Your **mouth** is your lips, or the space behind your lips where your teeth and tongue are. *She opened her mouth to say something, then closed it.* **2** COUNT N The **mouth** of a cave, hole, or bottle is its entrance or opening. *There was a vicious snarling in the mouth of the shelter.* **3** COUNT N The **mouth** of a river is the place where it flows into the sea. *We lived near the mouth of the Bashee River.* **4** REPORT VB If you **mouth** something, you form words with your lips without making any sound. *She mouthed the word no... Jane mouthed 'Water?'* **5 shut your mouth:** see **shut.** ● See also **hand-to-mouth, loud-mouthed, open-mouthed.**

mouthful /maʊθfʊl/, **mouthfuls.** COUNT N A **mouthful** of food or drink is an amount that you put or have in your mouth. *He took another mouthful of whisky... 'Don't you like me?' she asked between mouthfuls.*

mouth organ, mouth organs. COUNT N A **mouth organ** is a small musical instrument which you play by blowing and sucking air through it.

mouthpiece /maʊθpiːs/, **mouthpieces. 1** COUNT N The **mouthpiece** of a telephone is the part that you speak into. *She had her hand over the mouthpiece.* **2** COUNT N The **mouthpiece** of a musical instrument is the part that you blow into. **3** COUNT N The **mouthpiece** of a person or organization is the person who publicly states their opinions and policies. *He became the official mouthpiece of the leadership.*

movable /muːvəbə^{ə}l/; also spelled **moveable.** ADJ Something that is **movable** can be moved from one place to another. *...movable screens.*

move /muːv/, **moves, moving, moved. 1** ERG VB When you **move** something or when it **moves,** its position changes. *I'll have to move the car... The curtains behind began to move.* **2** VB When you **move,** you change your position or go to a different place. *I was so scared I couldn't move... He moved eagerly towards the door to welcome his visitors.* Also SING N *Neither she nor any of the others made a move.* **3** VB WITH OR WITHOUT OBJ If you **move** or if you **move** house, you go and live in a different house. *My parents moved from Hyde to Stepney.* Also COUNT N *I wrecked a good stereo on my last move.* **4** ERG VB If you **move** or **are moved** from one place or job to another, you go from one place or job to another. *Executives are being moved around from one company to another... He'd moved to the BBC from publishing.* Also COUNT N *Regular moves for junior executives are a company policy.* **5** VB WITH ADJUNCT If you **move** towards a particular state or opinion, you start to be in that state or have that opinion. *We are moving rapidly into the nuclear age.* Also SING N *This was the first step in his move away from the Labour party.* **6** VB If a situation **is moving,** it is developing or progressing. *Events now moved swiftly.* **7** VB WITH OBJ AND TO-INF If something **moves** you to do something, it causes you to do it; a formal use. *What has moved the President to take this step?* **8** VB WITH OBJ If something **moves** you, it causes you to feel a deep emotion, usually sadness or sympathy. *The whole incident had moved her profoundly.* ♦ **moved** ADJ *He was too moved to speak.* **9** VB WITH OBJ If you **move** a motion or amendment at a meeting, you propose it so that people can vote for or against it. **10** COUNT N A **move** is also an action that you take in order to achieve something. *Accepting this job was a very good move... For six days neither side made a move.* **11** COUNT N In a game such as chess, a **move** is the act of putting a counter or chess piece in a different position on the board. *Whose move is it?* **12** See also **moving.**

PHRASES ● If you are **on the move,** you are going from one place to another. *Billie Jean is constantly on the move.* ● If you tell someone to **get a move on,** you are telling them to hurry; an informal use.

move down. PHR VB If you **move down,** you go to a lower level, grade, or class. *When they fail their mathematics exams they move down a year.*

move in. PHR VB **1** If you **move in** somewhere, you begin to live in a different house or place. *He moved in with Mrs Camish.* **2** If soldiers or police **move in,** they go towards a place or person in order to attack them or deal with them. *They were under orders to move in from France.*

move off. PHR VB When vehicles or people **move off,** they start moving away from a place. *The gleaming fleet of cars prepared to move off.*

move on. PHR VB When you **move on,** you leave a place or activity and go somewhere else or do something else. *After three weeks in Hong Kong, we moved on to Japan... Can we move on to the second question?*

move out. PHR VB If you **move out,** you leave the house or place where you have been living, and go and live somewhere else.

move up. PHR VB If you **move up,** you go to a higher level, grade, or class. *The Vice-President should move up into the Presidency.*

moveable /muːvəbə^{ə}l/. See **movable.**

movement /muːvmə^{2}nt/, **movements. 1** UNCOUNT N OR COUNT N **Movement** involves changing position or going from one place to another. *He heard movement in the hut... ...the movement of oil cargoes... Tom lit a cigarette with quick, jerky movements.* **2** UNCOUNT N OR COUNT N **Movement** is also a gradual change in an attitude, opinion, or policy. *...the party's general leftward movement... There was a movement towards a revival of conscription.* **3** PLURAL N Your **movements** are everything which you do or plan to do during a period of time. *I don't know why you have any interest in my movements.* **4** COUNT N A **movement** is also a group of people who share the same beliefs, ideas, or aims. *...the Trade Union Movement... ...the successful movement to abolish child labour.* **5** COUNT N A **movement** in a piece of classical music is one of its major sections. *There is an immensely long first movement.*

movie /muːvi^1/, **movies. 1** COUNT N A **movie** is a cinema film. *...a war movie... I went to a movie.* **2** PLURAL N The cinema is sometimes called the **movies;** an American use.

moving /muːvɪŋ/. **1** ADJ Something that is **moving** causes you to feel a deep emotion, usually sadness or sympathy. *There is a moving account of his father's death.* ♦ **movingly** ADV *Her childhood is movingly described.* **2** ATTRIB ADJ A **moving** model or part of a machine is able to move. *These devices have no moving parts.*

mow /məʊ/, **mows, mowing, mowed** or **mown** /məʊn/. VB WITH OR WITHOUT OBJ If you **mow** an area of grass, you cut it using a lawnmower. *Everyone was mowing their lawns.*
mow down. PHR VB If a large number of people **are mown down,** they are all killed violently at one time. *Several children had strayed onto an airport runway and been mown down by a jet.*
mower /məʊə/, **mowers.** COUNT N A **mower** is a machine for cutting grass, corn, or wheat.
MP /ɛm piː/, **MPs.** COUNT N An **MP** is a person who has been elected to represent people in a country's parliament. **MP** is an abbreviation for 'Member of Parliament'. *...the MP for South East Bristol.*
mph /ɛm piː eɪtʃ/. **mph** is an abbreviation for 'miles per hour'. **mph** is used after a number to indicate speed. *These cars are reasonably economical at a steady 56 mph.*
Mr /mɪstə/. TITLE **Mr** is used before a man's name when you are speaking or referring to him. *...Mr Jenkins.*
Mrs /mɪsɪz/. TITLE **Mrs** is used before the name of a married woman when you are speaking or referring to her. *...Mrs Carstairs.*
Ms /məz/. TITLE **Ms** is used before the name of a single or married woman when you are speaking or referring to her. *...Ms Harman.*
M.Sc. /ɛm ɛs siː/, **M.Scs.** COUNT N An **M.Sc.** is a higher degree in a scientific subject. **M.Sc.** is an abbreviation for 'Master of Science'.
much /mʌtʃ/. For meanings 1, 2, and 4, the comparative is **more** and the superlative is **most:** see the separate entries for these words. **1** ADV You use **much** to emphasize that something is true to a great extent. *Myra and I are looking forward very much to the party... Now I feel much more confident.* **2** ADV If something does not happen **much,** it does not happen very often. *She doesn't talk about them much.* **3** ADV If two things are **much** the same, they are very similar. *The landscape was then much as it is today... The two poems convey much the same emotional tone.* **4** QUANTIF OR DET You also use **much** to refer to a large amount or proportion of something. *Much of the recent trouble has come from outside... There wasn't much to do... She had endured so much... We hadn't got much money.* **5** QUANTIF OR DET You also use **much** when you ask for or give information about an amount. *How much did he tell you?... He's done as much as I have... I doubt if she sees as much of him as you do... How much money have you got left?*
PHRASES ● If something is **not so much** one thing as another, it is more like the second thing than the first. *It was not so much an argument as a monologue.* ● If you say **so much for** a particular thing, you mean that it has not been successful or helpful. *So much for the experts and their learning.* ● **Nothing much** means an amount that is so small that it is not important. *There's nothing much left.* ● If a situation or action is **too much** for you, you cannot cope with it. *The long journey each day might prove too much for him.* ● If you describe something as **not much of a** particular type of thing, you mean that it is small or of poor quality. *It wasn't much of a garden.* ● You say **'I thought as much'** after you have just been told something that you had expected or guessed. ● **a bit much:** see **bit.** ● **not up to much:** see **up.**
muck /mʌk/, **mucks, mucking, mucked.** UNCOUNT N **Muck** is dirt or manure; an informal use. *There was muck everywhere... ...a muck heap.*
muck about or **muck around.** PHR VB If you **muck about** or **muck around,** you behave in a stupid way and waste time; an informal use. *She was mucking about with a jug of flowers on the table.*
muck out. PHR VB If you **muck out** a stable, pigsty, or cow shed, you clean it.
muck up. PHR VB If you **muck** something **up,** you do it very badly or fail when you try to do it; an informal use. *'How was the exam?'—'I mucked it up.'*
mucus /mjuːkəs/. UNCOUNT N **Mucus** is a liquid that is produced in some parts of your body, for example your nose; a formal use.
mud /mʌd/. UNCOUNT N **Mud** is a sticky mixture of earth and water. *She was covered in mud.*
muddle /mʌdə°l/, **muddles, muddling, muddled.** **1** COUNT N OR UNCOUNT N A **muddle** is a confused state or situation. *I have got into a muddle... ...the worsening muddle of her finances.* **2** VB WITH OBJ If you **muddle** things, you mix them up. *I wish you wouldn't muddle my books and drawings.* **3** VB WITH OBJ If you **muddle** someone, you confuse them. *Don't muddle her with too many suggestions.* ♦ **muddled** ADJ *I'm sorry. I'm getting muddled.*
muddle along. PHR VB If you **muddle along,** you live or exist without a proper plan or purpose in your life. *The church has lost its way, muddling along from Sunday to Sunday.*
muddle through. PHR VB If you **muddle through,** you manage to do something even though you do not really know how to do it properly. *The children are left to muddle through on their own.*
muddle up. PHR VB If you **muddle** things **up,** you get them mixed up or in the wrong order. *Later they may muddle up your names with those of your cousins.* ♦ **muddled up** ADJ *You've got the story muddled up.*
muddy /mʌdi^1/, **muddier, muddiest; muddies, muddying, muddied.** **1** ADJ Something that is **muddy** contains or is covered in mud. *...a muddy ditch... ...the muddy floor.* **2** ADJ A **muddy** colour is dull and brownish. *The landscape turns a mottled, muddy brown.* **3** VB WITH OBJ If you **muddy** a situation or issue, you make it harder to understand. *The issue has been muddied by allegations of bribery.*
mudguard /mʌdgɑːd/, **mudguards.** COUNT N The **mudguards** on a bicycle or other vehicle are the metal or plastic parts above the tyres, which stop the rider or vehicle from being splashed with mud.
muesli /mjuːzli^1/. UNCOUNT N **Muesli** is a mixture of nuts, dried fruit, and grains that you eat for breakfast with milk or yoghurt.
muffle /mʌfə°l/, **muffles, muffling, muffled.** VB WITH OBJ If something **muffles** a sound, it makes it quieter and more difficult to hear. *The snow muffled the sound of our footsteps.*
muffled /mʌfə°ld/. **1** ADJ A **muffled** sound is quiet, dull, or difficult to hear. *'I don't know,' he said in a muffled voice... ...a muffled explosion.* **2** PRED ADJ If you are **muffled** or **muffled** up, you are wearing thick, warm clothes which hide most of your body or face. *He was heavily muffled in a black overcoat... ...a boy muffled up in a blue scarf.*
mug /mʌg/, **mugs, mugging, mugged.** **1** COUNT N A **mug** is a large, deep cup with straight sides. *...a chipped mug.* **2** COUNT N You can use **mug** to refer to a mug and its contents, or to the contents only. *He sipped at his mug of coffee.* **3** VB WITH OBJ If someone **mugs** you, they attack you and steal your money; an informal use. *They lurk in dark side streets and mug passers-by.* ♦ **mugging** COUNT N OR UNCOUNT N *There has been a great increase in vandalism and muggings... ...the recent wave of mugging.* ♦ **mugger** /mʌgə/ COUNT N *Gangs of teenage muggers roam the streets.* **4** COUNT N If you call someone a **mug,** you mean that they are stupid and easily deceived; an informal use.
muggy /mʌgi^1/. ADJ **Muggy** weather is unpleasantly warm and damp.
mule /mjuːl/, **mules.** COUNT N A **mule** is an animal produced by a female horse and a male donkey.
mull /mʌl/, **mulls, mulling, mulled.**
mull over. PHR VB If you **mull** something **over,** you think about it for a long time before deciding what to do. *I sat there and tried to mull things over in my mind.*
multi-. PREFIX **Multi-** is used to form adjectives indicating that something has many things of a particular kind. *...a multi-storey car-park... ...a multi-coloured shirt.*
multilateral /mʌltɪlætə°rəl/. ADJ Something that is **multilateral** involves more than two different countries or groups of people. *...multilateral nuclear disarmament.*
multinational /mʌltɪnæʃə°nəl/, **multinationals.** **1** ADJ A **multinational** company has branches in many different countries. *Many of the West's large multinational companies have operations in Africa.* Also COUNT N *Trade in bananas is dominated by three huge food multinationals.* **2** ADJ **Multinational** also describes something that involves several different countries. *...the multinational forces deployed under the treaty.*
multiple /mʌltɪpə°l/. ATTRIB ADJ You use **multiple** to describe things that consist of many parts, involve many people, or have many uses. *...multiple locks on the doors... There have been several multiple collisions in fog this winter.*
multiple-choice. ADJ When you do a **multiple-choice** test, you have to choose the correct answer from several possible ones.
multiple sclerosis /mʌltɪpə°l sklərəʊsɪs/. UNCOUNT N **Multiple sclerosis** is a serious disease of the nervous system, which affects your ability to move.
multiplication /mʌltɪplɪkeɪʃə°n/. **1** UNCOUNT N **Multiplication** is the process of calculating the result of one number multiplied by another. **2** UNCOUNT N WITH SUPP The **multiplication** of things of a particular kind is a large increase in the number or amount of them. *...the multiplication of universities.*
multiplication sign, multiplication signs. COUNT N A **multiplication sign** is the sign (×) which is put between two numbers to show that they are being multiplied.
multiplicity /mʌltɪplɪsɪ^{1}ti^1/. SING N WITH 'of' A **multiplicity** of things is a large number or large variety of them; a formal use. *...the multiplicity of languages spoken in Africa.*
multiply /mʌltɪplaɪ/, **multiplies, multiplying, multiplied.** **1** ERG VB When something **multiplies** or **is multiplied,** it increases greatly in number or amount. *The shops began to multiply, eventually springing up in almost every town in the area.* **2** VB When animals **multiply,** they produce large numbers of young. *The creatures began to multiply very rapidly.* **3** VB WITH OBJ If you **multiply** one number by another, you calculate the total which you get when you add the number to itself a particular number of times. For example, 2 multiplied by 3 is equal to 2 plus 2 plus 2, which equals 6. *Multiply this figure by the number of years you have worked.*
multitude /mʌltɪtjuːd/, **multitudes.** COUNT N A **multitude** of things or people is a very large number of them; a formal use. *It didn't work out quite like I intended it to, for a multitude of reasons... 'We are keeping our options open,' he had told the assembled multitude.*
mum /mʌm/, **mums.** COUNT N OR VOCATIVE Your **mum** is your mother; an informal use. *My mum used to live here... I've been put in the special class, Mum.*
mumble /mʌmbə°l/, **mumbles, mumbling, mumbled.** VB OR REPORT VB If you **mumble,** you speak in a very quiet and indistinct way. *Stop mumbling... He took my hand and mumbled, 'Don't worry.'... I mumbled something about having an appointment.*
mummy /mʌmi^1/, **mummies.** **1** COUNT N OR VOCATIVE **Mummy** means mother; an informal word used especially by children; *Mummy put me on the train at Victoria.* **2** COUNT N A **mummy** is a dead body which was preserved long ago by being rubbed with oils and wrapped in cloth. *...a gilded Egyptian mummy case.*
mumps /mʌmps/. UNCOUNT N **Mumps** is a disease that causes a painful swelling of the glands in the neck.
munch /mʌntʃ/, **munches, munching, munched.** VB WITH OR WITHOUT OBJ If you **munch** food, you chew it steadily and thoroughly. *The father and son sat there, munching bread and butter.*
mundane /mʌndeɪn/. ADJ Something that is **mundane** is ordinary and not interesting. *...mundane tasks such as washing up.*
municipal /mjuːnɪsɪpə°l/. ATTRIB ADJ **Municipal** means associated with or belonging to a city or town that has its own local government. *...a big municipal housing scheme... ...the municipal gardens.*
munitions /mjuːnɪʃə°nz/. PLURAL N **Munitions** are bombs, guns, and other military supplies. *...munitions factories.*
mural /mjʊərəl/, **murals.** COUNT N A **mural** is a picture which is painted on a wall.
murder /mɜːdə/, **murders, murdering, murdered.** **1** UNCOUNT N OR COUNT N **Murder** is the crime of deliberately killing a person. *...attempted murder... ...the rising number of murders in San Francisco.* **2** VB WITH OR WITHOUT OBJ To **murder** someone means to commit the crime of killing them deliberately. *His father, mother, and sister were all murdered by the terrorists.* ♦ **murderer** COUNT N *I want to track down the murderers of my son.* **3** PHRASE If someone **gets away with murder,** they do whatever they like and nobody punishes them; an informal use.
murderous /mɜːdə°rəs/. **1** ADJ Someone who is **murderous** is likely to murder someone. *...murderous savages... The girl might have murderous tendencies.* **2** ADJ A **murderous** attack or other action results in the death of many people. *...murderous guerrilla raids.*
murky /mɜːki^1/. **1** ADJ **Murky** places are dark and rather unpleasant. *We looked out into the murky streets.* **2** ADJ **Murky** water is dark and dirty. *...murky ponds.* **3** ADJ **Murky** is also used to describe something that you suspect is dishonest or morally wrong; a literary use. *...murky goings-on in a local gallery.*
murmur /mɜːmə/, **murmurs, murmuring, murmured.** **1** VB OR REPORT VB If you **murmur** something, you say it very quietly. *'Darling,' she murmured... They murmured agreement.* **2** COUNT N A **murmur** is something that someone says which can hardly be heard. *There were murmurs of sympathy.* **3** SING N WITH SUPP A **murmur** is also a continuous, quiet, indistinct sound. *...the murmur of waves on a beach.*
muscle /mʌsə°l/, **muscles, muscling, muscled.** **1** COUNT N OR UNCOUNT N A **muscle** is a piece of flesh inside your body which is able to become smaller and to get bigger again. Your muscles enable you to move. *The boys couldn't help admiring their bulging muscles... Your mouth is mainly composed of muscle.* **2** UNCOUNT N If someone has **muscle,** they have power, which enables them to do something difficult; an informal use. *The campaign was valueless without the*

muscle of an organisation behind it.
muscle in. PHR VB If you **muscle in** on something, you force your way into a situation when you are not welcome. *They resent the way you are muscling in on their territory.*
muscular /mʌskjə^{4}lə/. 1 ATTRIB ADJ **Muscular** means involving or affecting your muscles. *Great muscular effort is needed... ...muscular pains.* 2 ADJ A **muscular** person has strong, firm muscles. *...a short but muscular man... ...his muscular arms.*
muscular dystrophy /mʌskjə^{4}lə dɪstrəfi^1/. UNCOUNT N **Muscular dystrophy** is a serious disease in which your muscles gradually weaken.
muse /mju:z/, **muses, musing, mused.** 1 VB OR REPORT VB If you **muse,** you think about something slowly or without a serious purpose; a literary use. *She lay musing for a while... 'I can't see him as a family man,' she mused.* 2 COUNT N A **muse** is an imaginary force which is believed to give people inspiration and creative ideas, especially for poetry or music; a formal use. *...the muse of music.*
museum /mju:zɪəm/, **museums.** COUNT N A **museum** is a building where interesting and valuable objects are kept and displayed to the public. *...classical sculpture in the British Museum.*
mush /mʌʃ/. UNCOUNT N OR SING N If you refer to a substance as **mush,** you mean that it is like a thick soft paste; an informal use. *He gulped down the tasteless mush.*
mushroom /mʌʃru^{4}m/, **mushrooms, mushrooming, mushroomed.** 1 COUNT N A **mushroom** is a fungus with a short stem and a round top. You can eat some kinds of mushrooms. *I liked helping to pick mushrooms.* 2 MOD A **mushroom** cloud is a large cloud of dust which rises into the sky after a nuclear explosion. 3 VB If something **mushrooms,** it grows or appears very quickly. *The organization quickly mushroomed into a mass movement.*
music /mju:zɪk/. 1 UNCOUNT N **Music** is the pattern of sounds performed by people singing or playing instruments. *...dance music... ...the music of Irving Berlin.* 2 UNCOUNT N **Music** is also the symbols written on paper that represent musical sounds. *Not one of them could read a note of music.*
musical /mju:zɪkə^{0}l/, **musicals.** 1 ATTRIB ADJ **Musical** describes things that are concerned with playing or studying music. *...a musical career... ...one of London's most important musical events.* ♦ **musically** ADV *There is a lot going on musically every night in London.* 2 ADJ Someone who is **musical** has a natural ability and interest in music. *He came from a musical family.* 3 ADJ **Musical** sounds are tuneful and pleasant. *A musical bell softly sounded somewhere in the passageway.* 4 COUNT N A **musical** is a play or film that uses singing and dancing in the story. *She appeared in the musical 'Oklahoma'.*
musical instrument, musical instruments. COUNT N A **musical instrument** is an object such as a piano, guitar, or violin which you play in order to produce music.
musician /mju:zɪʃə^{0}n/, **musicians.** COUNT N A **musician** is a person who plays a musical instrument as their job or hobby.
musk /mʌsk/. UNCOUNT N **Musk** is a substance with a strong, sweet smell which is used to make perfume.
Muslim /mʊzlɪm, mʌz-/, **Muslims;** also spelled **Moslem.** COUNT N A **Muslim** is a person who believes in Islam and lives according to its rules. *...a pious Muslim on his way to Mecca.* Also ADJ *...the medieval Muslim philosophers.*
muslin /mʌzlɪn/. UNCOUNT N **Muslin** is a very thin cotton material.
mussel /mʌsə^{0}l/, **mussels.** COUNT N A **mussel** is a kind of shellfish.
must /mʌst/. 1 MODAL If something **must** happen, it is very important or necessary that it happens. If something **must** not happen, it is very important or necessary that it does not happen. *Your family and children must always come first... You must learn to remain calm... You mustn't worry about me... Things must change.* 2 MODAL You also use **must** to express intentions or to make suggestions; an informal use. *I must come over and see you when he's away... You must play at the ship's concert... You must come and visit me.* 3 MODAL You ask why someone **must** do something when you are angry or upset about it and do not understand why they are doing it. *Why must she be so nasty to me?* 4 CONVENTION You say **'if you must'** when you cannot stop someone from doing something that you think is wrong or stupid. *Write and ask them yourself if you must.* 5 MODAL If you say that something **must** be true or **must** have happened, you mean that it is very likely to be the case. *You must be very fond of her... You must be Florrie Brown... We must have taken the wrong road.* 6 SING N If something is a **must,** it is absolutely necessary; an informal use. *Rubber gloves are a must if your skin is sensitive to washing powders.*
mustache /mʌstæʃ/. See **moustache.**
mustard /mʌstəd/. UNCOUNT N **Mustard** is a yellow or brown paste made from seeds which tastes spicy. *...a dash of French mustard.*
muster /mʌstə/, **musters, mustering, mustered.** 1 VB WITH OBJ If you **muster** something such as strength or energy, you gather as much as you can in order to do something. *I hit him with all the force I could muster... The group cannot muster sufficient working class support.* 2 ERG VB When soldiers **muster** or **are mustered,** they gather in one place in order to take action. *An enormous convoy mustered in the city.*
mustn't /mʌsə^{0}nt/. **Mustn't** is the usual spoken form of 'must not'.
must've /mʌstə^{0}v/. **Must've** is a spoken form of 'must have', when 'have' is an auxiliary verb.
musty /mʌsti^1/. ADJ Something that is **musty** smells stale and damp. *...musty old books.*
mutate /mju:teɪt/, **mutates, mutating, mutated.** VB If an animal or plant **mutates,** it develops different characteristics as the result of a change in its genes; a technical use. ♦ **mutated** ADJ *...a mutated flu virus.* ♦ **mutation** /mju:teɪʃə^{0}n/ COUNT N OR UNCOUNT N *The rate at which mutations occur is fairly regular.*
mute /mju:t/, **mutes, muting, muted.** 1 ADJ Someone who is **mute** does not speak; a formal use. *Sally was staring at him, mute and awestruck... Fanny clasped her hands in mute protest.* 2 VB WITH OBJ If you **mute** a noise or sound, you make it quieter; a formal use. *She had closed all the windows to mute the sounds from the town.* ♦ **muted** ADJ *People spoke in muted voices.*
muted /mju:tɪ^{2}d/. 1 ADJ **Muted** colours are soft and gentle. *...a muted colour scheme of cream and white.* 2 ADJ If a reaction is **muted,** it is not very strong. *On the whole, criticism was muted... ...muted enthusiasm.*
mutilate /mju:tɪleɪt/, **mutilates, mutilating, mutilated.** 1 VB WITH OBJ If someone **is mutilated,** their body is damaged very severely. *They tortured and mutilated their victims... Both bodies had been mutilated.* ♦ **mutilated** ADJ *...photos of mutilated bodies.* ♦ **mutilation** /mju:tɪleɪʃə^{0}n/ UNCOUNT N OR COUNT N *...the death or mutilation of innocent men and women... ...permanent mutilations of the skin.* 2 VB WITH OBJ If you **mutilate** something, you deliberately damage it and spoil it. *Almost every book had been mutilated.*
mutiny /mju:tɪni^1/, **mutinies.** COUNT N OR UNCOUNT N A **mutiny** is a rebellion by a group of people against a person in authority. *It's like a slave ship after a successful mutiny... Mutiny can lead to riot.*
mutter /mʌtə/, **mutters, muttering, muttered.** VB OR REPORT VB If you **mutter,** you speak very quietly so that you cannot easily be heard, often in a cross or unfriendly way. *Denis could be heard muttering to himself about my stupidity... 'Sorry,' he muttered.* Also SING N *...a quick low mutter.*
mutton /mʌtə^{0}n/. UNCOUNT N **Mutton** is meat from an adult sheep; an old-fashioned use. *...a leg of mutton.*
mutual /mju:tʃʊ^{0}əl/. 1 ADJ You use **mutual** to describe something that two or more people do to each other or for each other, or a feeling that they have towards each other. *They are in danger of mutual destruction... I didn't like him and I was sure the feeling was mutual.* 2 ADJ You also use **mutual** to describe something or someone which two people both have, or which several people all have. *They had discovered a mutual interest in rugby football... He sent a mutual friend to ask me.*
mutually /mju:tʃʊ^{0}əli^1/. 1 SUBMOD You use **mutually** when describing a situation in which two or more people feel the same way about each other. *He enjoyed a mutually respectful relationship with them.* 2 PHRASE If two things are **mutually exclusive** or **mutually contradictory,** they cannot both be true or both exist together. *The principles on which it is based are mutually contradictory.*
muzzle /mʌzə^{0}l/, **muzzles, muzzling, muzzled.** 1 COUNT N The **muzzle** of an animal such as a dog or a wolf is its nose and mouth. 2 COUNT N A **muzzle** is also a device that is put over a dog's nose and mouth so that it cannot bite people or bark. 3 VB WITH OBJ If you **muzzle** a dog, you put a muzzle over its nose and mouth. 4 COUNT N The **muzzle** of a gun is the end where the bullets come out when it is fired.
my /maɪ/. DET A speaker or writer uses **my** to indicate that something belongs or relates to himself or herself. *My name is Alan Jones... I closed my eyes.*
myopic /maɪɒpɪk/. ADJ Someone who is **myopic** cannot see distant things; a formal use.
myriad /mɪrɪəd/, **myriads.** COUNT N A **myriad** of people or things is a very large number of them; a literary use. *...a myriad of political action groups... ...myriads of tiny yellow flowers.* Also ADJ *...myriad pots of paint.*
myself /maɪself/. 1 REFL PRON A speaker or writer uses **myself** as the object of a verb or preposition in a clause where 'I' is the subject or 'me' is a previous object. *If you do not help me, I will kill myself... I was thoroughly ashamed of myself... I poured myself a small drink.* 2 REFL PRON **Myself** is also used to emphasize the subject or object of a clause. *I myself feel that Muriel Spark is very underrated... I find it a bit odd myself.* 3 REFL PRON A speaker or writer also uses **myself** in expressions such as 'I did it myself' in order to say that they did something without any help or interference from anyone else. *I dealt with it myself.*
mysterious /mɪstɪərɪəs/. 1 ADJ Something that is **mysterious** is strange and is not known about or understood. *Their grandson died of a mysterious illness... ...mysterious black boxes covered with wires.* ♦ **mysteriously** ADV *The American had mysteriously disappeared.* 2 ADJ If you are **mysterious** about something, you deliberately do not talk about it, usually because you want people to be curious about it. *Stop being so mysterious.* ♦ **mysteriously** ADV *They smiled mysteriously and said nothing.*
mystery /mɪstə^{0}ri^1/, **mysteries.** 1 COUNT N A **mystery** is something that is not understood or known about. *These two deaths have remained a mystery.* 2 UNCOUNT N WITH SUPP If you talk about the **mystery** of someone or something, you are talking about how difficult they are to understand or to know about. *The place continues to fascinate visitors, cloaked in its mystery... ...the mystery of God.* 3 ATTRIB ADJ A **mystery** person or thing is one whose identity or nature is not known. *...the mystery voice... ...a mystery tour.*
mystic /mɪstɪk/, **mystics.** 1 COUNT N A **mystic** is a person who practises or believes in religious mysticism. 2 ATTRIB ADJ **Mystic** means the same as mystical. *...a performer in a mystic rite.*
mystical /mɪstɪkə^{0}l/. ATTRIB ADJ Something that is **mystical** involves spiritual powers and influences that most people do not understand. *...religious and mystical experiences.*
mysticism /mɪstɪsɪzə^{0}m/. UNCOUNT N **Mysticism** is religious practice in which people search for truth, knowledge, and unity with God through meditation and prayer.
mystify /mɪstɪfaɪ/, **mystifies, mystifying, mystified.** VB WITH OBJ Something that **mystifies** you is impossible to explain or understand. *They say that they are mystified by the decision.* ♦ **mystified** ADJ *I felt a bit mystified.*
mystique /mɪsti:k/. UNCOUNT N **Mystique** is an atmosphere of mystery and importance or difficulty which is associated with a particular person or thing; a formal use. *...the mystique surrounding doctors.*
myth /mɪθ/, **myths.** 1 COUNT N A **myth** is an untrue belief or explanation. *...myths about the causes of cancer... ...the myth of love at first sight.* 2 COUNT N OR UNCOUNT N A **myth** is also a story which has been made up to explain natural events or to justify religious beliefs. *...Greek myths... ...queens in history, legend, and myth.*
mythical /mɪθɪkə^{0}l/. 1 ADJ Something that is **mythical** is imaginary and only exists in myths. *...mythical monsters.* 2 ADJ **Mythical** is also used to describe something which is untrue or does not exist. *They trekked out to the west coast in search of the mythical opportunities there.*
mythology /mɪθɒlədʒi^1/. 1 UNCOUNT N **Mythology** refers to stories that have been made up in the past to explain natural events or to justify religious beliefs. *Prometheus in Greek mythology brought fire to man.* ♦ **mythological** ATTRIB ADJ *Jupiter was the Roman mythological king of the heavens.* 2 UNCOUNT N You can also use **mythology** to refer to beliefs that people have about something which is not true. *...the whole mythology of national greatness.*

Nn

N. N is a written abbreviation for 'north'.
nadir /neɪdɪə, næ-/. SING N The **nadir** of something is its lowest point; a literary use. *The government was at the nadir of its unpopularity.*
nag /næg/, **nags, nagging, nagged.** 1 VB WITH OR WITHOUT OBJ If someone **nags** you, they keep complaining to you. *He used to nag me endlessly about money... ...having nagged for an invitation.* 2 VB WITH 'at' If a doubt or suspicion **nags** at you, it worries you a lot. *Something that she had said had been nagging at him.* ♦ **nagging** ATTRIB ADJ *She had a nagging sense of inadequacy.*

nail /neɪl/, **nails, nailing, nailed. 1** COUNT N A **nail** is a small piece of metal with a sharp end which you hit with a hammer in order to push it into something. *...the mirror that hung from a nail on the wall.* **2** VB WITH OBJ AND ADJUNCT If you **nail** something somewhere, you attach it there using a nail. *They nail plastic sheets over their windows... There were signs nailed to the trees.* **3** COUNT N Your **nails** are the thin hard areas covering the ends of your fingers and toes. *He keeps biting his nails.* **4** PHRASE If you say that someone has **hit the nail on the head,** you mean that what they have said is exactly right. **5** a **nail in** something's **coffin:** see **coffin.**

nail down. PHR VB If you **nail** something **down,** you fix it to the floor using nails.

nail up. PHR VB If you **nail** something **up,** you fix it to a vertical surface using nails. *...the warning notice that he had nailed up on the pole.*

naive /naɪ:v/; also spelled **naïve.** ADJ A **naive** person believes that things are much less difficult than they really are. *You're surely not so naive as to think that this will change anything.* ♦ **naively** ADV *They naively assume that things can only get better.*

naivety /naɪ:və^{0}ti^{1}/; also spelled **naïvety** or **naïveté** UNCOUNT N **Naivety** is behaviour which shows that a person thinks that things are much less difficult than they really are. *In this he showed political naivety.*

naked /neɪkɪ^{2}d/. **1** ADJ Someone who is **naked** is not wearing any clothes. *He was naked except for a pair of underpants... ...the men's naked bodies.* ♦ **nakedness** UNCOUNT N *They seized towels to hide their nakedness.* **2** ATTRIB ADJ You describe objects as **naked** when they are not covered. *...naked light bulbs... Never look for a gas leak with a naked flame.* **3** ATTRIB ADJ You use **naked** to describe behaviour or strong emotions which are not hidden in any way. *The home employment offered to housewives is naked exploitation... His face broke into an expression of naked anxiety.* **4** ATTRIB ADJ If you can see something with the **naked** eye, you can see it without using binoculars, a telescope, or a microscope.

name /neɪm/, **names, naming, named. 1** COUNT N The **name** of a person, thing, or place is the word or words that you use to identify them. *His name is Richard Arnason.* **2** VB WITH OBJ AND COMPLEMENT If you **name** someone or something, you give them a name. *She wanted to name the baby Colleen.* **3** VB WITH OBJ To **name** someone or something also means to identify them by saying their name. *...a Minister, whom he did not name... ...various flowers: roses, tulips and snapdragons, to name only a few.* ● See also **named. 4** VB WITH OBJ AND 'after' If you **name** someone or something after a person or thing, you give them the same name as that person or thing. *The College in Holborn is named after her.* **5** VB WITH OBJ If you **name** something, such as a date for a meeting or the price of something, you say what you want it to be. *He named a price he thought would scare me off.* **6** COUNT N You can refer to someone's reputation as their **name.** *Grey spoke out in public to clear Haldane's name... They were giving the country a bad name.* **7** COUNT N You can say that someone is a **name** when they have become famous. **8** See also **brand name, Christian name, maiden name.**

PHRASES ● If you mention someone **by name,** you say their name rather than referring to them indirectly. ● If you **call** someone **names,** you upset them by using unpleasant words to describe them. ● If something is registered **in your name,** it officially belongs to you or has been reserved for you. *The room was reserved in the name of Peters.* ● If you do something **in the name of** an ideal or a group of people, you do it because you believe in the ideal or represent the people. *The group claims to speak in the name of 'the simple people of the country'.* ● If you **make a name for yourself,** you become well-known and admired for something you have done. *George Eliot had already made a name for herself as a writer.*

named /neɪmd/. PRED ADJ When you say what a person, thing, or place is **named,** you give their name. *...a lecturer named Harold Levy.*

nameless /neɪmlɪ^{2}s/. ATTRIB ADJ You describe people and things as **nameless** when you do not know their name or when they have not been given a name. *...a new and nameless disease.*

namely /neɪmli^{1}/. SENTENCE ADV You use **namely** to introduce detailed information about what you have just said. *...three famous physicists, namely Simon, Kurte and Mendelsohn.*

namesake /neɪmseɪk/, **namesakes.** COUNT N WITH POSS Your **namesake** is someone with the same name as you.

nanny /næni^{1}/, **nannies.** COUNT N A **nanny** is a woman who is paid by parents to look after their children.

nap /næp/, **naps, napping, napped. 1** COUNT N A **nap** is a short sleep during the day. *It was time for her to take a nap.* **2** VB If you **nap,** you fall asleep for a short time during the day.

nape /neɪp/, **napes.** COUNT N The **nape** of your neck is the back of it.

napkin /næpkɪn/, **napkins.** COUNT N A **napkin** is a small piece of cloth or paper used to protect your clothes when you are eating.

nappy /næpi^{1}/, **nappies.** COUNT N A **nappy** is a piece of thick cloth or paper which is fastened round a baby's bottom in order to soak up its urine and faeces; a British use. *I seem to spend all day changing nappies.*

narcotic /nɑːkɒtɪk/, **narcotics.** COUNT N **Narcotics** are addictive drugs which make you sleepy and unable to feel pain.

narrate /nəreɪt/, **narrates, narrating, narrated.** VB WITH OBJ If you **narrate** a story, you tell it. *He narrated this tale with great effect.* ♦ **narration** /nəreɪʃə^{0}n/ UNCOUNT N *The richness of the novel comes from his narration.*

narrative /nærətɪv/, **narratives.** COUNT N A **narrative** is a story or an account of events. *...the narrative of her battle against depression.*

narrator /nə^{3}reɪtə/, **narrators.** COUNT N The **narrator** of a story is the person telling it.

narrow /nærəʊ/, **narrower, narrowest; narrows, narrowing, narrowed. 1** ADJ Something that is **narrow** has a very small distance from one side to the other. *We turned into a narrow lane... The stream became narrower.* ♦ **narrowness** UNCOUNT N *...the narrowness of the tunnels.* **2** VB If something **narrows,** it becomes less wide. *The river narrowed and curved sharply to the left.* **3** ERG VB If you **narrow** your eyes, or if your eyes **narrow,** you almost close them. *'I want you back here in five minutes,' he growled, narrowing his eyes.* **4** ADJ If someone's ideas or beliefs are **narrow,** they are concerned with only a few aspects of a situation and ignore other aspects. *I think you are taking too narrow a view.* ♦ **narrowness** UNCOUNT N *...the narrowness of the range of opinion represented.* **5** ERG VB If the difference between two things **narrows** or **is narrowed,** it becomes smaller. *The gap between the rich and the poor is narrowing.* ♦ **narrowing** UNCOUNT N WITH SUPP *...the narrowing of the individual's field of choice.* **6** ATTRIB ADJ If you have a **narrow** victory, you just succeed in winning. ♦ **narrowly** ADV *The motion was narrowly defeated.* **7** ATTRIB ADJ If you have a **narrow** escape, something unpleasant nearly happens to you. *...narrow misses.* ♦ **narrowly** ADV *He narrowly escaped being run over.*

narrow down. PHR VB If you **narrow** something **down,** you reduce it to a smaller number. *They had narrowed the choice down to a dozen sites.*

narrow-minded. ADJ If someone is **narrow-minded,** they are unwilling to consider new ideas or opinions. *How narrow-minded he had become... ...a narrow-minded approach to broadcasting.*

nasal /neɪzə^{0}l/. **1** ADJ You produce **nasal** sounds when air passes through your nose and mouth when you speak. *He spoke in a nasal voice... ...singing in a nasal tone.* **2** ATTRIB ADJ **Nasal** also means relating to your nose. *...nasal discharge.*

nasty /nɑːsti^{1}/, **nastier, nastiest. 1** ADJ Something that is **nasty** is very unpleasant. *This place has a nasty smell... I got a nasty feeling that I was being followed.* **2** ADJ You can also describe things as **nasty** when you think that they are unattractive or in bad taste. *It's a tacky, nasty little movie.* **3** ADJ A **nasty** problem or question is a difficult one. *This presented a nasty problem to Mayor Lindsay.* **4** ADJ You describe a disease or injury as **nasty** when it is serious or looks very unpleasant. *A nasty bruise rose where the handbag had landed.* **5** ADJ You describe someone's behaviour as **nasty** when they behave in an unkind and unpleasant way. *Why must she be so nasty to me?* ♦ **nastily** ADV *He was staring at them nastily.*

nation /neɪʃə^{0}n/, **nations. 1** COUNT N A **nation** is a country, together with its social and political structures. *...the great accomplishments of their nation.* **2** SING N The people who live in a country are sometimes referred to as the **nation.** *He appealed to the nation for self-restraint.*

national /næʃə^{0}nəl, -ʃənə^{0}l/, **nationals. 1** ADJ **National** means relating to the whole of a country, rather than to part of it. *It made the headlines in the national newspapers.* ♦ **nationally** ADV *Should housing policy be decided nationally or locally?* **2** ATTRIB ADJ **National** is also used to describe things that are typical of the people of a particular country. *Common sense is a national characteristic... ...national dress.* **3** COUNT N WITH SUPP A **national** of a country is a citizen of that country who is staying in a different country. *Much of the workforce was made up of foreign nationals... ...a German national.*

national anthem, national anthems. COUNT N A country's **national anthem** is its official song.

National Health Service. PROPER N In Britain, the **National Health Service** is a system providing free or cheap medical care for everyone.

national insurance. UNCOUNT N **National insurance** is the system by which a government collects money regularly from employers and employees so that money can be paid to people who are ill, unemployed, or retired.

nationalise /næʃə^{0}nəlaɪz/. See **nationalize.**

nationalism /næʃə^{0}nəlɪzə^{0}m/. **1** UNCOUNT N **Nationalism** is a desire for the political independence of a group of people who have the same religion, language, or culture. *...nineteenth-century Czech nationalism.* **2** UNCOUNT N **Nationalism** is also a great love for your country and the belief that it is better than other countries.

nationalist /næʃə^{0}nəlɪst/, **nationalists. 1** ATTRIB ADJ **Nationalist** ideas or movements are connected with attempts to obtain political independence for a particular group of people. *...the nationalist movements of French West Africa.* **2** COUNT N A **nationalist** is a person with nationalist beliefs. *...a great Indonesian nationalist.*

nationalistic /næʃə^{0}nəlɪstɪk/. ADJ Someone who is **nationalistic** is very proud of their country and believes that it is better than other countries. *...an attempt to arouse nationalistic passions.*

nationality /næʃə^{0}nælɪ^{1}ti^{1}/, **nationalities.** UNCOUNT N OR COUNT N Your **nationality** is the country you belong to. For example, someone with British **nationality** is legally a British citizen. *...an identity card proving Belgian nationality... ...scientists of different nationalities.*

nationalize /næʃə^{0}nəlaɪz/, **nationalizes, nationalizing, nationalized;** also spelled **nationalise.** VB WITH OBJ If a government **nationalizes** a private industry, the industry becomes owned by the state. *The revolutionary government has nationalized the mines.* ♦ **nationalized** ADJ *...nationalized industries.* ♦ **nationalization** /næʃə^{0}nəlaɪzeɪʃə^{0}n/ UNCOUNT N *He argued for nationalisation on grounds of efficiency.*

national park, national parks. COUNT N A **national park** is a large area of natural land protected by the government of a country.

national service. UNCOUNT N **National service** is a period of compulsory service in a country's armed forces.

nationwide /neɪʃə^{0}nwaɪd/. ATTRIB ADJ A **nationwide** activity happens in all parts of a country. *...a nationwide campaign to recruit women into trade unions.* Also ADV *She had lectured nationwide to various organizations.*

native /neɪtɪv/, **natives. 1** ATTRIB ADJ Your **native** country is the one where you were born. *She made her way home to her native Russia.* **2** COUNT N WITH SUPP A **native** of a country or region is someone who was born there. *...John Magee, a native of Northern Ireland.* Also ATTRIB ADJ *...native Britons.* **3** ATTRIB ADJ Your **native** language is the language that you learned to speak as a child. *He read a poem in his native Hungarian.* **4** ATTRIB ADJ A **native** speaker of a language is someone who has spoken that language since childhood, rather than learning it later. **5** ADJ Animals or plants that are **native** to a region grow there naturally and have not been brought there; a formal use. *These are the only lilies native to Great Britain.*

natural /nætʃə^{0}rə^{0}l/, **naturals. 1** ADJ If someone's behaviour is **natural,** it is the way people normally behave. *She's upset. It's natural, isn't it? Today's the funeral... It is natural for trade unions to adopt an aggressive posture.* **2** ADJ You also say that someone's behaviour is **natural** when they are not trying to hide anything. *...walking in a relaxed, natural manner... There was something not quite natural about her behaviour.* ♦ **naturalness** UNCOUNT N *I was impressed by their ease and naturalness.* **3** ATTRIB ADJ Someone with a **natural** ability was born with that ability. *He had a natural gift for making things work... Follow your own natural inclinations... She was a natural organizer.* **4** COUNT N If you describe someone as a **natural,** you mean that they were born with the ability to do something well; an informal use. *He is a great craftsman, a natural.* **5** ATTRIB ADJ **Natural** is used to describe things that exist in nature and were not caused by people. *...protection from natural disasters such as earthquakes.* **6** PHRASE If someone died of **natural causes,** they died because they were ill and not because they committed suicide or were killed. *The post-mortem showed that death was due to natural causes.* **7** ATTRIB ADJ Someone's **natural** mother or father is their real mother or father, rather than someone who has adopted them. *She claimed Prince Yousoupoff as her natural father.* **8** ADJ AFTER N A

natural note in music is not a sharp or a flat. *...B natural.*

natural history. UNCOUNT N **Natural history** is the study of animals, plants, and other living things.

naturalised /nætʃrəlaɪzd/. See **naturalized.**

naturalist /nætʃrəlɪst/, **naturalists.** COUNT N A **naturalist** is a person who studies plants, animals, and other living things.

naturalized /nætʃrəlaɪzd/; also spelled **naturalised.** ATTRIB ADJ A **naturalized** citizen has legally become a citizen of a country that they were not born in. *...a naturalized British subject.*

naturally /nætʃrəli1/. 1 SENTENCE ADV You use **naturally** to indicate that something is obvious and not surprising. *Dena was crying, so naturally Hannah was upset... 'Do you propose to take account of that?'—'Naturally.'* 2 ADV If one thing develops **naturally** from another, it develops as a normal result of it. *This leads us fairly naturally into what career advisers call careers counselling.* 3 ADV Something that happens or exists **naturally** happens or exists in nature and was not caused by people. *They tried to reproduce artificially what they had observed to happen naturally.* 4 ADV You say that someone is behaving **naturally** when they are not trying to hide anything or pretend in any way. *The children were too frightened to behave naturally.* 5 SUBMOD You can also use **naturally** to talk about qualities that people were born with, rather than those that were learned later. *...people who are naturally brilliant... She had a naturally cheerful and serene expression.* 6 PHRASE If something **comes naturally** to you, you can do it easily. *Politics came naturally to Tony.*

natural resources. PLURAL N **Natural resources** are all the land, forests, minerals, and sources of energy that occur naturally. *They plan to open up the region with its wealth of natural resources.*

nature /neɪtʃə/, **natures.** 1 UNCOUNT N **Nature** is all the animals, plants, and other things in the world that are not made by people, and all the events and processes that are not caused by people. *A sunset is one of the most beautiful sights in nature.* 2 UNCOUNT N WITH SUPP The **nature** of something is its basic quality or character. *...the unique nature of Elizabethan painting... Such a situation is by nature painful... These problems are political in nature.* 3 SING N WITH SUPP When you say that something is of a particular **nature,** you are saying what characteristic or quality it has. *They suffered injuries of a very serious nature.* 4 COUNT N WITH SUPP Someone's **nature** is their character, which they show by their behaviour. *Rob had a very sweet nature... ...a woman with a wildly passionate nature.* 5 See also **human nature.**

PHRASES • Someone's **better nature** is their feelings of kindness and helpfulness. • If a way of behaving is **second nature** to you, you behave like that without thinking because you have done it so often.

naughty /nɔːti1/. 1 ADJ You say that small children are **naughty** when they behave badly. *Don't be a naughty boy.* 2 ADJ **Naughty** books, pictures, or words are slightly rude or indecent. *...little boys who use naughty words... It's rather a naughty play.*

nausea /nɔːzɪə, -sɪə/. UNCOUNT N **Nausea** is a feeling of sickness and dizziness. *I cut into the meat and felt a sudden twinge of nausea.*

nauseate /nɔːzieɪt, -sɪ-/, **nauseates, nauseating, nauseated.** VB WITH OBJ If something **nauseates** you, it makes you feel as if you are going to vomit. *The thought of food nauseated him.* ♦ **nauseating** ADJ *...an nauseating candy bar.*

nautical /nɔːtɪkə0l/. ATTRIB ADJ **Nautical** people and things are involved with ships. *...a nautical uniform.*

naval /neɪvə0l/. ATTRIB ADJ **Naval** people and things belong to a country's navy. *...a French naval officer.*

navel /neɪvə0l/, **navels.** COUNT N Your **navel** is the small hollow in the middle of the front of your body.

navigate /nævɪgeɪt/, **navigates, navigating, navigated.** 1 VB WITH OR WITHOUT OBJ When someone **navigates,** they work out which direction a ship, plane, or car should go. *Sailors used to navigate by the stars.* ♦ **navigation** /nævɪgeɪʃə0n/ UNCOUNT N *You can't teach navigation in the middle of a storm.* 2 VB WITH OBJ If you **navigate** a dangerous place, you travel through it carefully. *Until then no ship had been large enough to navigate the Atlantic.*

navigator /nævɪgeɪtə/, **navigators.** COUNT N A **navigator** is someone who works out the direction in which a ship or plane should go.

navy /neɪvi1/, **navies.** 1 COLL N A country's **navy** is the part of its armed forces that fights at sea. *My father's in the Navy.* 2 ADJ Something that is **navy** or **navy-blue** is dark blue.

NB. You write **NB** to draw someone's attention to what you are going to write next. *Total cost: £500. NB. The following items are not included.*

-nd. SUFFIX **-nd** is added to most numbers written in figures and ending in 2 in order to form ordinal numbers. 2nd is pronounced the same as 'second'. *...2nd October 1957... ...42nd Street.*

NE. NE is a written abbreviation for 'north-east'.

near /nɪə/, **nearer, nearest; nears, nearing, neared.** 1 PREP, ADV, OR ADJ If something is **near** a place or thing or **near to** it, it is a short distance from it. *He stood near the door... I wish I lived nearer London... He pulled her nearer to him... I looked at the books nearest to where I stood.* 2 PREP If you are **near** a particular state or **near to** it, you have almost reached it. *Her father was angry, her mother near tears... I was very near to giving in to their demands.* 3 PREP OR ADV If two things are similar, you can say that they are **near** each other or **near to** each other. *Most views were fairly near the truth... He is the nearest we have to an English Leonardo da Vinci.* 4 ATTRIB ADJ Your **near** relatives are your closest relatives, for example your parents and grandparents. 5 PREP If something happens **near** a particular time or **near to** it, it happens just before or just after that time. *...near the beginning of the play.* 6 ADV If a time or event is **near,** it will happen very soon. *...as her wedding day drew near.* 7 ADJ OR ADV WITH ADJUNCT You can also use **near** to say that something almost has a particular quality or almost happens. *...a state of near chaos... ...our near catastrophic economic troubles.* 8 VB WITH OBJ If someone or something **is nearing** a particular place, stage, or point in time, they are approaching it. *As they neared the harbour, it began to rain... ...anybody nearing the age of retirement.*

PHRASES • The expressions **near enough** and **as near as makes no difference** mean that something is almost true; an informal use. *He paid £100, or as near as makes no difference.* • If something was **a near thing,** it was almost an accident or a disaster. *I lived—but it was a near thing.* • **nowhere near:** see **nowhere.**

nearby /nɪəbaɪ/. ADJ OR ADV **Nearby** things and places are only a short distance away. *...nearby towns... There was a river nearby.*

nearly /nɪəli1/. 1 ADV **Nearly** means not completely or not exactly. *It was nearly dark... I can nearly swim a mile... She was nearly as tall as he was.* 2 PHRASE You use **not nearly** to emphasize that something is not the case. For example, if something is 'not nearly big enough', it is much too small. *I haven't spent nearly long enough here... They don't have nearly so many foods to choose from as we do.*

neat /niːt/, **neater, neatest.** 1 ADJ Something that is **neat** is tidy and smart. *His clothes were neat... ...small, neat writing.* ♦ **neatly** ADV *Mother's clothes hung neatly in a row.* ♦ **neatness** UNCOUNT N *Their desks are models of neatness... I was pleased at the neatness of the stitches.* 2 ADJ Someone who is **neat** is careful and tidy in their appearance and behaviour. 3 ADJ If you drink an alcoholic drink **neat,** you drink it without anything added. *She takes her whisky neat... He gulped the neat brandy down in one draught.*

nebulous /nebjə4ləs/. ADJ **Nebulous** ideas are vague and not precise; a formal use. *I had a nebulous notion of a life after death.*

necessarily /nesɪ2sə0rɪ1li1, nesɪ2serɪ1li1/. 1 ADV If something is not **necessarily** the case, it is not always the case. *Fleas are not necessarily associated with dirt... Documentaries don't necessarily need interviewers.* 2 ADV If something **necessarily** happens in particular circumstances, it must happen in those circumstances; a formal use. *Growth has necessarily levelled off.*

necessary /nesə2sə0ri1/. 1 ADJ Something that is **necessary** is needed to get a particular result or effect. *Are we teaching undergraduates the necessary skills?... Make a soft dough, using a little more water if necessary... I don't want to stay longer than necessary.* 2 ADJ You can also say that something is **necessary** when it must happen in particular circumstances; a formal use. *There is no necessary connection between industrial democracy and productivity.*

necessitate /nɪ2sesɪ1teɪt/, **necessitates, necessitating, necessitated.** VB WITH OBJ OR -ING If something **necessitates** a particular course of action, it makes it necessary; a formal use. *The Government's action had necessitated a by-election... This job would necessitate working with his hands.*

necessity /nɪ2sesɪ1ti1/, **necessities.** 1 UNCOUNT N **Necessity** is the need to do something. *She went to work not out of choice but necessity.* 2 COUNT N **Necessities** are things that you must have to live. *They were supplied with all the necessities of life.*

neck /nek/, **necks.** 1 COUNT N Your **neck** is the part of your body which joins your head to the rest of your body. *She threw her arms around his neck... The cat had a blue collar round its neck.* 2 COUNT N The **neck** of a dress or shirt is the part which is round your neck or just below it. *...a dress with a lace neck... His shirt was open at the neck.* 3 COUNT N The **neck** of a bottle is the long narrow part at the top.

PHRASES • If you are **up to** your **neck** in problems, you are deeply involved in them. *You were up to your neck in trouble with the press.* • If someone is **breathing down** your **neck,** they are watching everything you do very carefully; an informal use. • If you **risk** your **neck,** you do something very dangerous to achieve something or to help someone. *I thanked him for risking his neck for me.* • If you **stick** your **neck out,** you do something that makes you likely to be criticized or harmed; an informal use. *Let someone else stick their neck out and take responsibility.* • **by the scruff of** your **neck:** see **scruff.**

necklace /neklɪ1s/, **necklaces.** COUNT N A **necklace** is a piece of jewellery, such as a chain or string of beads, which a woman wears round her neck.

necktie /nektaɪ/, **neckties.** COUNT N A **necktie** is the same as a tie; an American use.

née /neɪ/. **née** is used before a name to indicate that it was a woman's surname before she got married; a formal use. *...Jane Carmichael, née Byers.*

need /niːd/, **needs, needing, needed.** 1 VB WITH OBJ OR TO-INF If you **need** something, or **need** to do it, it is necessary for you to have it or to do it. *These animals need food throughout the winter... Children need to feel they matter to someone... Before we answer this question, we need to look briefly at the world environment.* 2 SEMI-MODAL If you say that something **need not** happen, or that someone **need not** do something, you are saying that there is no good reason for it to happen. *You needn't worry... It needn't cost very much... People died of diseases that need not have proved fatal.* 3 VB WITH OBJ, -ING, OR TO-INF If something **needs** a particular action or if an action **needs** doing, this action is necessary. *The shed needs a good clean out... Keep a list of all the jobs that need doing... The top rim needs to be cut off.* 4 COUNT N Your **needs** are the things you need for a satisfactory life. *She learned how to provide for her own needs.* 5 SING N A **need** is also a strong feeling that you must have or do something. *I began to feel the need of somewhere to retreat... She felt no need to speak.*

PHRASES • You use **if need be** to say that an action will be carried out if it is necessary. *She said she would stay with me for months and years if need be.* • If someone or something is **in need of** something, they need it. *I am badly in need of advice... The hospital was in need of decorating.* • People **in need** do not have enough money, or need help of some kind.

needle /niːdə0l/, **needles, needling, needled.** 1 COUNT N A **needle** is a small piece of polished metal with a hole at one end which is used for sewing. 2 COUNT N You can refer to knitting needles as **needles.** 3 COUNT N The **needle** in a record player is the small pointed instrument that touches the record and picks up the sound signals. 4 COUNT N A **needle** is also the sharp piece of metal which is attached to a syringe and used to give injections. 5 COUNT N On an instrument measuring speed, weight, or electricity, the **needle** is the thin piece of metal or plastic which moves backwards and forwards and shows the measurement. 6 COUNT N The **needles** of a fir or pine tree are its thin pointed leaves. *There was nothing on the ground except a thick layer of pine needles.* 7 VB WITH OBJ If someone **needles** you, they annoy you by criticizing you repeatedly; an informal use. *She was needling me about Doris.* 8 **a needle in a haystack:** see **haystack.** • See also **pins and needles.**

needless /niːdlɪ1s/. 1 ADJ Something that is **needless** is completely unnecessary. *It was a needless risk to run.* ♦ **needlessly** ADV *This may upset a mother needlessly.* 2 PHRASE You say **needless to say** to emphasize that what you are saying is obvious. *I left college in disgrace (needless to say without my Diploma).*

needlework /niːdə0lwɜːk/. 1 UNCOUNT N **Needlework** is sewing or embroidery that is done by hand. *...the basket in which she kept her needlework.* 2 UNCOUNT N **Needlework** is also the activity of sewing or embroidering. *The girls spend much time doing needlework.*

needn't /niːdə0nt/. **Needn't** is the usual spoken form of 'need not'.

needy /niːdi1/, **needier, neediest.** 1 ADJ A **needy** person is very poor. *...helping needy old people throughout the world... They are among the neediest children in Britain.* 2 PLURAL N Needy people are sometimes referred to as the **needy.** *It is important to serve everybody, not just the needy.*

negate /nɪ2geɪt/, **negates, negating, negated.** VB WITH OBJ If you **negate** something that someone has done, you cause it to have no value or effect; a formal use. *The denial of the importance of minorities negates all our efforts on their behalf.*

negative /nɛgətɪv/, **negatives.** 1 ADJ **Negative** is used to describe something with the answer 'no'. *We expected to receive a negative answer.* ♦ **negatively** ADV *The public responded negatively.* 2 PHRASE If an answer is **in the negative,** it is 'no'. *This question had been answered in the negative.* 3 ADJ If someone is **negative** or has a **negative** attitude, they consider only the bad aspects of a situation, rather than the good ones. *He was especially negative about my written work... No one else I met ever had such a negative view of Alice Springs.* 4 ADJ If a medical or other scientific test is **negative**, it shows that something has not happened or is not present. *...a negative pregnancy test.* 5 COUNT N A **negative** is the image that is first produced when you take a photograph. 6 ADJ A **negative** number is less than zero.

neglect /nɪ²glɛkt/, **neglects, neglecting, neglected.** 1 VB WITH OBJ If you **neglect** someone or something, you do not look after them properly. *...the farmer who neglects his crops.* ♦ **neglected** ADJ *The child looked neglected, scruffy and unloved.* 2 VB WITH TO-INF OR OBJ If you **neglect** to do something, you fail to do it. *I neglected to bring a gift... I feel I'm neglecting my duty.* 3 UNCOUNT N **Neglect** is failure to look after someone or something properly. *...estates suffering from vandalism and neglect.*

neglectful /nɪ²glɛktfʊl/. ADJ If someone is **neglectful** of someone or something, they do not look after them properly or give them the attention they deserve. *He had been neglectful of his duties... ...a neglectful father.*

negligee /nɛglɪʒeɪ/, **negligees;** also spelled **négligée.** COUNT N A woman's **negligee** is a dressing gown made of very thin material.

negligent /nɛglɪdʒənt/. ADJ When someone is **negligent,** they fail to do something that they should do. *He has to prove that he has not been negligent.* ♦ **negligently** ADV *They may act foolishly or negligently.* ♦ **negligence** /nɛglɪdʒəns/ UNCOUNT N *The chairman of the Party had been dismissed for negligence.*

negligible /nɛglɪdʒəbə⁰l/. ADJ Something that is **negligible** is so small or unimportant that it is not worth considering. *The cost in human life had been negligible.... This would have a negligible effect on the temperature.*

negotiable /nɪ²gəʊʃəbə⁰l/. ADJ Something that is **negotiable** can be changed or agreed by means of discussion. *The price is negotiable.*

negotiate /nɪ²gəʊʃieɪt/, **negotiates, negotiating, negotiated.** 1 VB WITH OBJ If you **negotiate** an agreement, you obtain it by discussing it with other people. *He negotiated a trade agreement with Brazil.* 2 VB If you **negotiate** for something, you try to obtain it by discussing it with other people. *Paul is negotiating for a job worth £18,000.* 3 VB WITH OBJ If you **negotiate** an obstacle, you succeed in moving around it. *Patrick is not sure whether he can negotiate the turn at the bottom.*

negotiation /nɪ²gəʊʃieɪʃə⁰n/, **negotiations.** COUNT N **Negotiations** are discussions that take place between people with different interests, in which they try to reach an agreement. *The early stages of their negotiations with the Government were unsuccessful.* Also UNCOUNT N *We need to allow more time for negotiation.*

negotiator /nɪ²gəʊʃieɪtə/, **negotiators.** COUNT N **Negotiators** are people who take part in negotiations in business, politics, or international affairs. *They acted as negotiators in all dealings with other villages.*

Negro /niːgrəʊ/, **Negroes.** COUNT N A **Negro** is someone with black skin. Some people find this word offensive.

neigh /neɪ/, **neighs, neighing, neighed.** VB When a horse **neighs,** it utters a loud sound.

neighbour /neɪbə/, **neighbours;** spelled **neighbor** in American English. 1 COUNT N Your **neighbours** are the people who live near you, especially the people who live next door to you. *Don't be afraid of what the neighbours will think.* 2 COUNT N WITH POSS Your **neighbour** is also the person who is standing or sitting next to you. *Rudolph turned his head towards his neighbour.* 3 COUNT N WITH POSS You can refer to something which is near or next to something else of the same kind as its **neighbour.** *The young plant risks being overshadowed by its neighbours.*

neighbourhood /neɪbəhʊd/, **neighbourhoods;** spelled **neighborhood** in American English. 1 COUNT N A **neighbourhood** is a part of a town where people live. *She'd just moved into the neighbourhood... ...a wealthy neighbourhood.* 2 PHRASE If something is **in the neighbourhood** of a place, it is near to it. *We were heading for a destination in the neighbourhood of the Lofoten Islands.*

neighbouring /neɪbə⁰rɪŋ/; spelled **neighboring** in American English. ATTRIB ADJ **Neighbouring** describes the places and things that are near to the place or thing that you are talking about. *Families came from neighbouring villages to look at her.*

neighbourly /neɪbəli¹/; spelled **neighborly** in American English. ADJ If people living near you are **neighbourly,** they are kind, friendly, and helpful. *That's a neighbourly thing to do.*

neither /naɪðə, niːðə/. 1 CONJ You use **neither** in front of the first of two or more words or expressions when you are saying that two or more things are not true or do not happen. The other things are introduced by 'nor'. *He spoke neither English nor French... She neither drinks, smokes, nor eats meat... The Englishman was neither gratified nor displeased.* 2 PRON OR DET You also use **neither** to refer to both of two things or people, when you are making a negative statement about both of them. *Neither of us was having any luck... Neither was suffering pain.* 3 CONJ If you say that one thing is not the case and **neither** is another, you mean that the second thing is also not the case. *'I don't normally drink at lunch.'—'Neither do I.'*

neolithic /niːəlɪθɪk/. ADJ **Neolithic** means relating to the period when people first started farming but still used stone weapons and tools. *...neolithic weapons.*

neon /niːɒn/. UNCOUNT N OR MOD **Neon** is a gas which exists in very small amounts in the atmosphere. It is used in glass tubes to make bright lights and signs.

neon light, neon lights. COUNT N OR UNCOUNT N **Neon lights** are bright electric lights that consists of a glass tube filled with neon. They are often used to light street signs.

nephew /nɛvjuː, nɛf-/, **nephews.** COUNT N Your **nephew** is the son of your sister or brother.

nerve /nɜːv/, **nerves.** 1 COUNT N A **nerve** is a long, thin fibre that transmits messages between your brain and other parts of your body. *...the optic nerves.* 2 PLURAL N If you talk about someone's **nerves,** you are referring to how able they are to remain calm and not become worried in a stressful situation. *Hoping to calm our nerves, we decided to spend the afternoon at the lake... She had strong nerves.* 3 UNCOUNT N **Nerve** is the courage you need to do something difficult or dangerous. *Nobody had the nerve to remind him that he was several hours late... His nerve began to crack.*

PHRASES ● If someone or something **gets on** your **nerves,** they annoy or irritate you very much; an informal use. *He got on my nerves tonight with his fishing stories.* ● If you say that someone **had a nerve** or **had the nerve** to do something, you mean that they made you angry by doing something rude or disrespectful; an informal use. *He had the nerve to say Fleet Street was corrupting me.*

nerve-racking. ADJ Something that is **nerve-racking** makes you tense and worried. *It was a nerve-racking period for us all.*

nervous /nɜːvəs/. 1 ADJ If you are **nervous,** you are worried and frightened, and show this in your behaviour. *Both actors were exceedingly nervous on the day of the performance.* ♦ **nervously** ADV *He laughed nervously.* ♦ **nervousness** UNCOUNT N *'Pa,' Rudolph began, trying to conquer his nervousness.* 2 ATTRIB ADJ A **nervous** person is very tense and easily upset. *She was a particularly nervous woman.* 3 PRED ADJ If you are **nervous** about something, you feel rather afraid or worried about it. *He's nervous of thieves in that little shop of his.* 4 ATTRIB ADJ A **nervous** illness or condition affects your mental state. *She had suffered a lot of nervous strain.*

nervous breakdown, nervous breakdowns. COUNT N A **nervous breakdown** is an illness in which someone suffers from deep depression and needs psychiatric treatment. *You'll give yourself a nervous breakdown going on working like this.*

nervous system, nervous systems. COUNT N Your **nervous system** is all the nerves in your body together with your brain and spinal cord, which control your movements and feelings.

nervous wreck, nervous wrecks. COUNT N If someone is a **nervous wreck,** they are extremely nervous or worried; an informal use. *I waited so long that by the time my turn came I was a nervous wreck.*

-ness, -nesses. SUFFIX **-ness** is added to adjectives to form nouns. These nouns usually refer to states, qualities, or behaviour. Nouns of this kind are usually not defined but are treated with the related adjectives. *The aim of life is happiness... ...the smallness of the school.*

nest /nɛst/, **nests, nesting, nested.** 1 COUNT N A **nest** is a place that birds, insects and other animals make to lay eggs in or give birth to their young in. *We had a wasp's nest in the roof.* 2 VB When a bird **nests** somewhere, it builds a nest and settles there to lay its eggs. *Hornbills nest in holes in trees.*

nestle /nɛsə⁰l/, **nestles, nestling, nestled.** 1 VB WITH ADJUNCT If you **nestle** somewhere, you move into a comfortable position, often by pressing against someone or something soft. *They nestled together on the sofa... ...nestling against his body.* 2 VB WITH ADJUNCT If a house or village **nestles** somewhere, it is in that place or position and seems safe or sheltered. *A village nestled in the hills to their right.*

net /nɛt/, **nets, netting, netted;** also spelled **nett** in British English for meanings 4 and 5. 1 UNCOUNT N **Net** is a cloth which you can see through. It is made of very fine threads woven together so that there are small spaces between them. *All the windows have net curtains.* ● See also **netting.** 2 COUNT N A **net** is a piece of netting of a particular shape which you use, for example, to protect something or to catch fish. **Nets** are also used to divide the two halves of a tennis or badminton court, or to form the back of a goal in football. *...a net to cover the plants... ...a butterfly trapped in a net.* 3 VB WITH OBJ If you **net** something, you manage to get it, often by using skill. *He was netting his largest fortune.* 4 ATTRIB ADJ OR ADJ AFTER N A **net** result or amount is one that is final, when everything necessary has been considered or included. *That gave him a net profit of just over 23%... The net result is a massive labour surplus... Last year he made a profit of £20,000 net.* 5 ATTRIB ADJ OR ADJ AFTER N The **net** weight of something is its weight without its container or wrapping. *If you look at the label, you'll see it says 450g net.*

netball /nɛtbɔːl/. UNCOUNT N **Netball** is a game played by two teams of seven players, usually women or girls. Each team tries to score goals by throwing a ball through a net which is at the top of a pole at each end of the court.

nett /nɛt/. See **net.**

netting /nɛtɪŋ/. UNCOUNT N **Netting** is material made of threads or metal wires woven or knotted together so that there are equal spaces between them. *...wire netting on the windows.*

nettle /nɛtə⁰l/, **nettles.** COUNT N A **nettle** is a wild plant with leaves that sting.

network /nɛtwɜːk/, **networks.** 1 COUNT N A **network** is a large number of roads, veins, or other things which look like lines, which cross each other or meet at many points. *...a network of tiny red veins running over her white skin... ...the network of back streets in the Latin Quarter.* 2 COUNT N A **network** is a large number of people or organizations that have a connection with each other and work together as a system. *...a network of clinics.* 3 COUNT N A radio or television **network** is a company or group of companies that usually broadcasts the same programmes at the same time in different parts of the country. *She gave an interview on a national television network.*

neurological /njʊərə⁶lɒdʒɪkə⁰l/. ATTRIB ADJ **Neurological** is used to describe things relating to the nervous system; a medical use. *...a progressive neurological disease.*

neurosis /njʊərəʊsɪs/, **neuroses** /njʊərəʊsiːz/. UNCOUNT N OR COUNT N **Neurosis** is a mental illness which causes people to have continual and unreasonable fears and worries. *Such problems can distort personality and lead to neurosis.*

neurotic /njʊərɒtɪk/. ADJ If someone is **neurotic,** they continually show a lot of unreasonable anxiety about something. *They are becoming neurotic about their careers.*

neutral /njuːtrə⁰l/. 1 ADJ A **neutral** country or person does not support either side in a disagreement or war. *Because I was neutral in the conflict I was a welcome visitor.* ♦ **neutrality** /njuːtrælɪti¹/ UNCOUNT N *We have a tradition of political neutrality.* 2 ADJ If someone is **neutral** or if something that they do is **neutral,** they do not show any emotions or opinions. *I waited, but her eyes were neutral... 'Look,' she said in a neutral voice.* 3 UNCOUNT N **Neutral** is the position between the gears of a vehicle, in which the gears are not connected to the engine. *I pushed the handle into neutral.* 4 ADJ The **neutral** wire in an electric plug is the wire that is not earth or live and that is needed to complete the electrical circuit.

neutralize /njuːtrəlaɪz/, **neutralizes, neutralizing, neutralized;** also spelled **neutralise.** VB WITH OBJ To **neutralize** something means to prevent it from having any effect or from working properly. *Their aim is to neutralize the Council's campaign.*

neutron /njuːtrɒn/, **neutrons.** COUNT N A **neutron** is an atomic particle that has no electrical charge.

never /nɛvə/. 1 ADV **Never** means at no time in the past or future. *I've never been to Europe... I shall never forget this day... I never eat breakfast on Sundays.* 2 ADV **Never** means not in any circumstances at all. *What is morally wrong can never be politically right.* 3 PHRASE **Never ever** is an emphatic expression for 'never'; an informal use. *She never ever wears a hat.* 4 ADV You use **never** with the simple past tense to mean 'did not'; an informal use. *My bus never ar-*

rived... Good gracious! I never knew that. ● **never mind:** see **mind.**

never-ending. ADJ If something is **never-ending,** it lasts a very long time, and seems as if it will never end. *...the never-ending flow of refugees.*

nevertheless /nɛvəðəlɛs/. SENTENCE ADV **Nevertheless** means in spite of what has just been said; a formal use. *She saw Clarissa immediately, but nevertheless pretended to look around for her.*

new /nju:/, **newer, newest; news. New** is an adjective and **news** is a noun. 1 ADJ Something that is **new** has been recently made or created, or is in the process of being made or created. *...smart new houses... ...a new type of bandage that stops minor bleeding almost immediately.* 2 ADJ You also use **new** to say that something has not been used or owned by anyone else. *There was another sign advertising new and used tractors... They cost over twenty dollars new.* 3 ATTRIB ADJ **New** also means different from what you have had, used, or experienced before. *Not long after that, he got a new job... The villagers were suspicious of anything new.* ♦ **newness** UNCOUNT N *...the newness and strangeness of her surroundings.* 4 ATTRIB ADJ You can describe something that has only recently been discovered as **new.** *In 1781 William Herschel discovered a new planet.* 5 ATTRIB ADJ A **new** period of time is just about to begin. *...on the eve of a new era... A new phase was about to start.* 6 ATTRIB ADJ **New** is also used to show that something has only just happened. For example, a **new** parent has only recently become a parent. *Thousands were there to hear the new party leader.* 7 PRED ADJ If you are **new** to a situation or place or if the situation or place is **new** to you, you have not experienced it or seen it before. *...a person who's new to the job of teaching... ...a part of England completely new to him.* 8 UNCOUNT N OR SING N **News** is information about a recent event or a recently changed situation. *I've got some good news for you... ...after receiving the news of my acceptance.* 9 UNCOUNT N OR SING N **News** is also information that is given in newspapers and on radio and television about recent events in the country or the world. *...a half hour of world and domestic news... It was on the news at 9.30.* ● See also **newly.**

newborn /nju:bɔ:n/. ADJ A **newborn** baby is one that has been born recently.

newcomer /nju:kʌmə/, **newcomers.** COUNT N A **newcomer** is a person who has recently arrived to live in a place, joined an organization, or started a job. *...newcomers to the neighbourhood.*

new-fangled. ATTRIB ADJ Older people sometimes describe new ideas or pieces of machinery as **new-fangled,** often when they think they are unnecessary or too complicated; an informal use. *...a new-fangled Japanese camera.*

new-found. ATTRIB ADJ A **new-found** quality, ability, or person is one that you have discovered recently. *...this new-found confidence.*

newly /nju:li^1/. ADV **Newly** is used before past participles to indicate that an action is very recent. *...the newly-married couple... ...her newly acquired food mixer.*

news agency, news agencies. COUNT N A **news agency** is an organization which collects news stories from all over the world and sells them to newspapers and television and radio stations.

newsagent /nju:zeɪdʒənt/, **newsagents.** COUNT N A **newsagent** or **newsagent's** is a shop which sells newspapers, magazines, and cigarettes.

newscaster /nju:zkɑ:stə/, **newscasters.** COUNT N A **newscaster** is a person who reads the news on television or radio.

newsflash /nju:zflæʃ/, **newsflashes.** COUNT N A **newsflash** is an interruption that is made to a radio or television programme to announce an important piece of news.

newsletter /nju:zlɛtə/, **newsletters.** COUNT N A **newsletter** is a printed sheet or small magazine containing information about an organization that is sent regularly to its members. *Members receive a newsletter three times a year.*

newsmen /nju:zmɛn/. PLURAL N **Newsmen** are reporters who work for newspapers, television, or radio; an American use. *Newsmen had been barred from the trial.*

newspaper /nju:speɪpə/, **newspapers.** 1 COUNT N A **newspaper** is a number of large sheets of folded paper on which news, articles, advertisements, and other information are printed. Some newspapers are produced every day from Monday to Saturday, and others once a week. *...a weekly newspaper... ...copies of France's leading daily newspaper Le Figaro.* 2 COUNT N A **newspaper** is also the organization that produces a newspaper. *I work for a newspaper.* 3 UNCOUNT N **Newspaper** consists of pieces of old newspapers, especially when they are being used for another purpose such as wrapping things up. *Wedge it with a wad of newspaper.*

newsprint /nju:zprɪnt/. UNCOUNT N **Newsprint** is the cheap paper on which newspapers are printed. *...bales of newsprint.*

newt /nju:t/, **newts.** COUNT N A **newt** is a small animal with a moist skin, short legs, and a long tail. Newts live partly on land and partly in water.

New Testament. PROPER N The **New Testament** is the part of the Bible that deals with the life of Jesus Christ and with Christianity in the early Church.

new wave, new waves. COUNT N A **new wave** is a movement in art, music, or film, which introduces new ideas instead of following traditional ones. *...the new wave of British music.*

New Year. UNCOUNT N OR SING N **New Year** or the **New Year** is the time when people celebrate the start of a year. *We had a marvellous time over New Year... Happy New Year!*

New Year's Day. UNCOUNT N **New Year's Day** is the first day of a year. In Western countries this is January 1st.

New Year's Eve. UNCOUNT N **New Year's Eve** is the last day of the year.

next /nɛkst/. 1 ADJ The **next** period of time, event, person, or thing is the one that comes immediately after the present one or after the one you have just mentioned. *The next five years are of vital importance... The next day, I left better prepared... I may vote for her at the next election... My next question is, 'What is art?'... What's next on the agenda?* 2 ADJ The **next** place or person is also the one nearest to you or the first one that you come to. *The telephone was ringing in the next room... Pull into the next lay-by.* 3 ADV The thing that happens **next** is the thing that happens immediately after something else. *The audience does not know what is going to happen next.* 4 ADV When you **next** do something, you do it for the first time since you last did it. *It was some years later when I next saw her.* 5 ADV You use **next** to say that something has more of a quality than all other things except one. For example, the thing that is **next** best is the one that is best except for one other thing. *The best kind of story is the one with a happy ending; the next best is the one with an unhappy ending.* 6 PREP If one thing is **next to** another thing, it is at the side of it. *She went and sat next to him... There was a bowl of goldfish next to the bed.*

PHRASES ● You use **after next** in expressions such as 'the week after next' to refer to a period of time after the next one. For example, when it is May, the month after next is July. *He had to go there the week after next.* ● You can also use **next to** to mean almost. *I knew next to nothing about him... The photographs were next to useless but they were all we had.* ● **next door:** see **door.**

next of kin. SING N Your **next of kin** are your closest relatives; a formal use. *The only next of kin seems to be a cousin in Droitwich.*

NHS /ɛn eɪtʃ ɛs/. PROPER N **NHS** is an abbreviation for 'National Health Service'.

nib /nɪb/, **nibs.** COUNT N The **nib** on a pen is the small pointed piece of metal at the end, where the ink comes out as you write.

nibble /nɪbə^{0}l/, **nibbles, nibbling, nibbled.** 1 VB WITH OR WITHOUT OBJ If you **nibble** something, or **nibble** at it, you eat it slowly by taking small bites out of it. *Just nibble a piece of bread... She nibbled at her food.* 2 VB WITH OR WITHOUT OBJ When a mouse or other small animal **nibbles** something, it takes small bites out of it quickly and repeatedly. *It was nibbling the end of a leaf.* 3 COUNT N A **nibble** is a gentle or quick bite of something.

nice /naɪs/, **nicer, nicest.** 1 ADJ If you say that something is **nice,** you mean that you find it enjoyable, pleasant, or attractive. *It would be nice to see you... Did you have a nice time at the party?... How nice you look.* ♦ **nicely** ADV *I always think Bessie dresses very nicely.* 2 ADJ If someone does or says something **nice,** they are being kind and thoughtful. *It's nice of you to say that... How nice of you to come.* 3 ADJ If someone is **nice,** they are friendly and pleasant. *He was a terribly nice man.* 4 PRED ADJ If you are **nice** to someone, you behave in a friendly, pleasant or polite way towards them. *I wish I'd been nicer to him.* ♦ **nicely** ADV *You may go if you ask nicely.*

nicely /naɪsli^1/. ADV Something that is happening or working **nicely** is working in a satisfactory way. *He thought he could manage quite nicely without them.*

nicety /naɪsɪti^1/, **niceties.** COUNT N **Niceties** are small details, especially concerning polite behaviour. *Here the niceties of etiquette must be observed.*

niche /ni:ʃ/, **niches.** 1 COUNT N A **niche** is a hollow area in a wall, or a natural hollow part in a cliff. *...the little statue of the saint in his niche near the pulpit.* 2 COUNT N If you say that you have found your **niche** in life, you mean that you have a job or position which is exactly right for you. *You can then find your own niche in public life.*

nick /nɪk/, **nicks, nicking, nicked.** 1 VB WITH OBJ OR REFL VB If you **nick** something, you make a small cut into the surface of it. *He shaved badly, nicking himself in a couple of places.* 2 COUNT N A **nick** is a small cut made in the surface of something. 3 VB WITH OBJ If someone **nicks** something, they steal it; an informal British use. *My typewriter had been nicked.* 4 PHRASE If something is achieved **in the nick of time,** it is achieved successfully, at the last possible moment; an informal use. *We got there in the nick of time.*

nickel /nɪkə^{0}l/, **nickels.** 1 UNCOUNT N **Nickel** is a silver-coloured metal that is used in making steel. 2 COUNT N A **nickel** is an American or Canadian coin worth five cents.

nickname /nɪkneɪm/, **nicknames, nicknaming, nicknamed.** 1 COUNT N A **nickname** is an informal name for someone. *...Graham Rathbone, whose nickname was Raffy.* 2 VB WITH OBJ AND COMPLEMENT If you **nickname** someone or something, you give them a nickname. *For a brief while, Mrs Thatcher was nicknamed 'Tina'.*

nicotine /nɪkəti:n/. UNCOUNT N **Nicotine** is an addictive substance in tobacco. *...teeth browned by nicotine.*

niece /ni:s/, **nieces.** COUNT N Your **niece** is the daughter of your sister or brother.

niggle /nɪgə^{0}l/, **niggles, niggling, niggled.** 1 VB WITH OR WITHOUT OBJ If something **niggles** you, it makes you worry slightly over a long time. *The question niggled at the back of his mind.* ♦ **niggling** ATTRIB ADJ *...little niggling doubts.* 2 COUNT N A **niggle** is a small worry that you keep thinking about.

night /naɪt/, **nights.** 1 COUNT N OR UNCOUNT N The **night** is the part of each period of twenty-four hours when it is dark outside, especially the time when most people are sleeping. *We walked for six days and six nights... He woke in the night with a dreadful pain.* 2 COUNT N OR UNCOUNT N You also use **night** to refer to the period of time between the end of the afternoon and the time when you go to bed. *I was out that night... I went on Saturday night.*

PHRASES ● If something happens **day and night** or **night and day,** it happens all the time without stopping. *They were being guarded night and day.* ● If you **have an early night,** you go to bed early. If you **have a late night,** you go to bed late.

nightcap /naɪtkæp/, **nightcaps.** COUNT N A **nightcap** is a drink that you have just before you go to bed.

nightclub /naɪtklʌb/, **nightclubs.** COUNT N A **nightclub** is a place where people go late in the evening to drink and to dance or see a show.

nightdress /naɪtdrɛs/, **nightdresses.** COUNT N A **nightdress** is a sort of dress that women or girls wear in bed.

nightfall /naɪtfɔ:l/. UNCOUNT N **Nightfall** is the time of day when it starts to get dark. *We wanted to get out before nightfall.*

nightgown /naɪtgaʊn/, **nightgowns.** COUNT N A **nightgown** is the same as a nightdress; an American or old-fashioned use.

nightie /naɪti^1/, **nighties.** COUNT N A **nightie** is a nightdress; an informal use.

nightingale /naɪtɪŋgeɪl/, **nightingales.** COUNT N A **nightingale** is a small brown European bird. The male nightingale is famous for singing beautifully at night.

nightlife /naɪtlaɪf/. UNCOUNT N **Nightlife** is the entertainment available at night in towns, such as nightclubs, theatres, and bars. *...the exotic nightlife of Montmartre.*

nightly /naɪtli^1/. ATTRIB ADJ OR ADV A **nightly** event happens every night. *My mother prayed nightly... I watched the nightly television news.*

nightmare /naɪtmɛə/, **nightmares.** 1 COUNT N A **nightmare** is a very frightening dream. *He rushed to her room when she had nightmares and comforted her.* 2 COUNT N A **nightmare** is also a very frightening or unpleasant situation or time. *The first day was a nightmare.*

nightmarish /naɪtmɛərɪʃ/. ADJ If you describe a situation as **nightmarish,** you mean that it is extremely frightening. *I had nightmarish visions of what could go wrong.*

night-time. UNCOUNT N **Night-time** is the part of the day between the time when it gets dark and the time when it gets light again. *Who would see smoke at night-time?*

nil /nɪl/. 1 NUMBER **Nil** means the same as nought; often used in scores of sports games. *Wales beat England three nil.* 2 UNCOUNT N If you say that the possibility of something happening is **nil,** you mean that it cannot happen. *You can reduce the danger to almost nil.*

nimble /nɪmbə^{0}l/, **nimbler, nimblest. 1** ADJ Someone who is **nimble** is able to move their fingers, hands, or legs quickly and easily. *By now, he was quite nimble on his wooden leg.* **2** ADJ Someone who has a **nimble** mind is very quick and clever in the way they think.

nine /naɪn/, **nines. Nine** is the number 9.

nineteen /naɪntiːn/, **nineteens. Nineteen** is the number 19.

nineteenth /naɪntiːnθ/. ADJ The **nineteenth** item in a series is the one that you count as number nineteen.

ninetieth /naɪntiɪ^{2}θ/. ADJ The **ninetieth** item in a series is the one that you count as number ninety.

ninety /naɪnti^1/, **nineties.** NUMBER **Ninety** is the number 90.

ninth /naɪnθ/, **ninths. 1** ADJ The **ninth** item in a series is the one that you count as number nine. *...the ninth floor of the Hotel.* **2** COUNT N A **ninth** is one of nine equal parts of something. *In exchange for this work they get one ninth of the crop.*

nip /nɪp/, **nips, nipping, nipped. 1** VB WITH ADJUNCT If you **nip** somewhere, usually somewhere nearby, you go there quickly or for a short time; an informal use. *I'll just nip out and post these letters.* **2** VB WITH OBJ If you **nip** someone, you pinch or bite them lightly. *The horse nipped me on the back of the head.*

nipple /nɪpə^{0}l/, **nipples.** COUNT N The **nipples** on your body are the two small pieces of slightly hard flesh on your chest. Babies suck milk through the nipples on their mothers' breasts.

nit /nɪt/, **nits.** COUNT N **Nits** are the eggs of a kind of louse that sometimes lives in people's hair. *The school doctor looks to see if you have nits in your hair.*

nitrate /naɪtreɪt/, **nitrates.** COUNT N OR UNCOUNT N A **nitrate** is a chemical compound that includes nitrogen and oxygen. Nitrates are used as fertilizers.

nitrogen /naɪtrədʒə^{1}n/. UNCOUNT N **Nitrogen** is a colourless element that has no smell and is usually found as a gas.

no /nəʊ/. **1** CONVENTION You use **no** to give a negative answer to a question, to say that something is not true, to refuse an offer, or to refuse permission. *'Did you see that programme last night?'—'No, I didn't.'... 'They go round kissing one another when they meet.'—'No they don't.'... 'Do you want a biscuit?'—'No thanks.'... 'Can I come too?'—'No.'* **2** CONVENTION You use **no** to say that you agree with a negative statement that someone else has made. *'It's not difficult, you see.'—'No, it must be quite easy when you know how.'* **3** CONVENTION You also use **no** to express shock or disappointment at something. *'Michael's fallen off his bike.'—'Oh no, not again.'* **4** SENTENCE ADV You use **no** as a way of introducing a correction to what you have just said. *...500 grams, no, a little less than that.* **5** DET **No** indicates that there is not even one thing of a particular kind or not even a small amount of a particular thing. For example, if someone has **no** job or **no** money, they do not have a job or do not have any money. *I do it all on my own. I have no help at all.* **6** DET You use **no** to emphasize that someone or something is not a particular kind of person or thing. For example, if you say that someone is **no** fool, you mean that they are definitely not a fool. *She is no friend of mine.* **7** SUBMOD You use **no** when emphasizing that something does not exceed a particular amount or number, or does not have more of a particular quality than something else. For example, something that is **no** bigger than a fingernail is not bigger than a fingernail. *The whole gun was no longer than eighteen inches... Winners will be notified by post no later than 31st August... ...a job that was no better than a common labourer's.* **8** DET **No** is also used, especially on notices, to say that a particular thing is forbidden. *No smoking... No talking once we're inside.* **9** PHRASE If you say **there is no** doing a particular thing, you mean that it is impossible to do that thing. *There's no arguing with my father.*

No., Nos. No. is a written abbreviation for 'number'. *He lives at No. 14 Sumatra Road.*

nobility /nəʊbɪlɪ^{1}ti^1/. **1** UNCOUNT N **Nobility** is the quality of being noble. *He had nobility in defeat... He followed his principles with nobility.* **2** COLL N The **nobility** of a society are all the people who have titles and high social rank.

noble /nəʊbə^{0}l/, **nobler, noblest; nobles. 1** ADJ Someone who is **noble** is honest, brave, and unselfish, and deserves admiration and respect. *Among them were some of the greatest and noblest men in our history... ...a man of noble character.* ♦ **nobly** ADV *She had nobly served the cause of Christianity.* **2** ADJ If someone is **noble** they belong to a high social class and have a title. *...young men of noble birth.* Also COUNT N *Every noble in the land wanted to marry the king's daughter.* **3** ADJ Something that is **noble** is very impressive in quality or appearance. *...an old man with a noble head and a bristling moustache.*

nobleman /nəʊbə^{0}lmə^{3}n/, **noblemen.** COUNT N A **nobleman** is a man who is a member of the nobility.

nobody /nəʊbə^{7}di^1/, **nobodies. 1** INDEF PRON **Nobody** means not a single person. *Nobody seems to notice... There was nobody on the bridge at all.* ● See also **no-one. 2** COUNT N If you say that someone is a **nobody,** you mean that they are not at all important. *Miss Watkins was a nobody; no family, no close friends.*

nocturnal /nɒktɜːnə^{0}l/. **1** ADJ **Nocturnal** events happen during the night. *...your nocturnal sightseeing tour of our city.* **2** ADJ An animal that is **nocturnal** is active mostly at night. *Their nocturnal habits make long-eared owls hard to see.*

nod /nɒd/, **nods, nodding, nodded. 1** VB WITH OR WITHOUT OBJ If you **nod,** you move your head down and up to show that you are answering 'yes' to a question, or to show agreement, understanding, or approval. *'Is it true?' She nodded... He nodded his head.* **2** VB WITH ADJUNCT To **nod** also means to bend your head once in a particular direction in order to indicate something. *'Ask him,' said Ringbaum, nodding towards Philip.* **3** VB WITH OR WITHOUT OBJ To **nod** also means to bend your head once, as a way of saying hello or goodbye. *I nodded to the ladies and sat down.* **4** COUNT N A **nod** is a quick movement of your head down and up. *From time to time, he gave him an encouraging nod.*

nod off. PHR VB If you **nod off,** you fall asleep, especially when you had not intended to; an informal use. *His remarks left delegates nodding off.*

nodule /nɒdju^{4}l/, **nodules.** COUNT N A **nodule** is a small round lump on something, often on the root of a plant. *...bacteria in the root nodules of beans.*

noise /nɔɪz/, **noises. 1** COUNT N A **noise** is a sound that someone or something makes. *A sudden noise made Brody jump.* **2** UNCOUNT N OR COUNT N **Noise** is a loud or unpleasant sound. *Try not to make so much noise... Our washing machine is making a terrible noise.*

noisy /nɔɪzi^1/, **noisier, noisiest. 1** ADJ Someone or something that is **noisy** makes a lot of loud or unpleasant noise. *The audience was large and noisy.* ♦ **noisily** ADV *My sister was crying noisily.* **2** ADJ A place that is **noisy** is full of loud or unpleasant noise. *They complained that Canton was hot and noisy.*

nomad /nəʊmæd/, **nomads.** COUNT N A **nomad** is a member of a tribe which travels from place to place rather than living in one place all the time.

nomadic /nəʊmædɪk/. ADJ **Nomadic** people travel from place to place rather than living in one place all the time. *These tribes have a nomadic way of life.*

nominal /nɒmɪnə^{0}l/. **1** ADJ You use **nominal** to describe a position or characteristic which something is supposed to have but which it does not have in reality. *We were directing the operation, though under the nominal leadership of a guerrilla general.* ♦ **nominally** ADV *Dad, nominally a Methodist, entered churches only for weddings and funerals.* **2** ATTRIB ADJ A **nominal** price or sum of money is very small in comparison with the real cost or value of the thing you are buying or selling. *At a nominal price, the settlers got the rest of the land.*

nominate /nɒmɪneɪt/, **nominates, nominating, nominated.** VB WITH OBJ If you **nominate** someone for a job, you suggest them as a candidate or formally choose them to hold that job. *I've been nominated for a Senior Lectureship... Trade unions nominate representatives to public bodies.*

nomination /nɒmɪneɪʃə^{0}n/, **nominations. 1** COUNT N A **nomination** is an official suggestion of someone as a candidate in an election or for a job. *...a list of nominations for senior lectureships.* **2** UNCOUNT N OR COUNT N The **nomination** of someone to a job or position is their appointment to the job or position. *...Judge O'Connor's nomination to the Supreme Court.*

nominee /nɒmɪniː/, **nominees.** COUNT N A **nominee** is someone who is nominated for something. *Dave is this year's nominee for the Exchange scheme.*

non-. 1 PREFIX **Non-** is used to form adjectives indicating that something does not have a particular quality or feature. For example, a non-nuclear war is a war fought without nuclear weapons. *...non-violent demonstrations... ...non-industrial societies.* **2** PREFIX **Non-** is also used to form nouns which refer to situations in which a particular kind of action is not taken, or to people who do not belong to a particular group *...a non-aggression pact... ...non-Christians.*

nonchalant /nɒnʃələnt/. ADJ Someone who is **nonchalant** behaves calmly and appears not to care much about things. *He tried to sound cheerful and nonchalant.* ♦ **nonchalantly** ADV *The officer waved a hand nonchalantly.* ♦ **nonchalance** /nɒnʃələns/ UNCOUNT N *The answers are given with such nonchalance.*

non-commissioned. ATTRIB ADJ A **non-commissioned** officer is person who holds a military rank such as sergeant or corporal and who has been appointed to this rank from the lower ranks, rather than being recruited as an officer.

noncommittal /nɒnkəmɪtə^{0}l/. ADJ If someone is **noncommittal,** they do not express their opinion or decision firmly. *I received a noncommittal letter in return.*

nonconformist /nɒnkənfɔːmɪst/, **nonconformists.** COUNT N A **nonconformist** is someone who behaves in an unusual or rebellious way. *...the persecution of nonconformists and minorities.* Also ADJ *I've got rather nonconformist ideas on this.*

nondescript /nɒndɪ^{2}skrɪpt/. ADJ Something that is **nondescript** is dull and uninteresting in appearance or design. *...a complex of nondescript buildings... The women were dressed in nondescript clothes.*

none /nʌn/. **1** PRON **None** means not a single thing or person, or not even a small amount of a particular thing. *None of these suggestions is very helpful... None of us were allowed to go... I have answered every single question. My opponent has answered none... 'You had no difficulty in finding it?'—'None at all.'* **2** PHRASE You use **none too** to mean 'not at all'; a formal use. *We're none too sure what we're arguing about... He hauled her none too gently to her feet.*

nonentity /nɒnentɪ^{1}ti^1/, **nonentities.** COUNT N If you refer to someone as a **nonentity,** you mean that they are not special or important in any way. *Grant came from a family of nonentities.*

nonetheless /nʌnðəles/. SENTENCE ADV **Nonetheless** means in spite of what has just been said; a formal use. *She couldn't act at all. Nonetheless she was a big box office attraction... It was not an impossible task, but they failed nonetheless.*

non-existent /nɒnɪ^{2}gzɪstənt/. ADJ Something that is **non-existent** does not exist in a place or does not exist at all. *Medical facilities are non-existent in most rural areas.*

non-fiction. UNCOUNT N **Non-fiction** is writing that gives information or describes real events, rather than telling a story. *...works of non-fiction... ...non-fiction books.*

no-nonsense. ATTRIB ADJ A **no-nonsense** person is firm and efficient. *I liked his no-nonsense approach to the whole matter.*

nonplussed /nɒnplʌst/. ADJ If you are **nonplussed** when something happens, you are surprised and unsure how to react. *'I've heard nothing about this,' he said, nonplussed.*

nonsense /nɒnsəns/. **1** UNCOUNT N You use **nonsense** to refer to words that do not mean anything. *You can confuse the computer program by typing in nonsense.* **2** UNCOUNT N OR CONVENTION If you say that something spoken or written is **nonsense,** you mean that it is untrue or silly. *A lot of nonsense is talked about the temperature of wine... Stop this nonsense, Louisa, for God's sake... 'I am her father.'—'Nonsense,' he said. 'You are not.'* **3** PHRASE To **make nonsense of** something means to make it seem ridiculous or pointless. *The rest of his policies made nonsense of his call for moderation.*

nonsensical /nɒnsensɪkə^{0}l/. ADJ Something that is **nonsensical** is stupid or ridiculous. *This attitude seemed nonsensical to the general public.*

non-smoker, non-smokers. COUNT N A **non-smoker** is someone who does not smoke. *For many years non-smokers were ridiculed for objecting to tobacco.*

non-starter, non-starters. COUNT N If you say that a plan or idea is a **non-starter,** you mean that it has no chance of success; an informal use. *Such a policy is really a complete non-starter.*

non-stop. ADJ OR ADV A **non-stop** activity continues without any pauses or breaks. *They keep up a non-stop conversation... Carter laughed non-stop for several minutes.*

non-violence. UNCOUNT N **Non-violence** is the use of peaceful methods to try to bring about change. *...my commitment to the principles of non-violence.*

non-violent. ADJ **Non-violent** methods of bringing about change do not involve hurting people or causing damage. *It is to be a peaceful, non-violent protest.*

noodles /nuːdə^{0}lz/. PLURAL N **Noodles** are long, thin pieces of pasta.

nook /nʊk/. PHRASE You use **every nook and cranny** to emphasize that you are talking about every part of a place. *Toddlers poke into every nook and cranny.*

noon /nuːn/. UNCOUNT N **Noon** is twelve o'clock in the middle of the day. *The visitor turned up at noon.*

no-one /nəʊ wʌn/. INDEF PRON **No-one** means not a single person. ● See also **nobody.** *They had seen no-one else all afternoon... Sorry, there's no-one here called Nikki.*

noose /nuːs/, **nooses.** COUNT N A **noose** is a loop at the end of a piece of rope, especially one used to hang someone.

nor /nɔː/. **1** CONJ You use **nor** after 'neither' to introduce the second thing that a negative statement applies to. *Neither Margaret nor John was there... My father could neither read nor write.* **2** CONJ You also use **nor** after a negative statement in order to add something else that the negative statement applies to. *Melanie was not to be found—not that day, nor the next day, nor the day after that... I could not afford to eat in restaurants and nor could anyone I knew.*

norm /nɔːm/, **norms. 1** COUNT N **Norms** are ways of behaving that are considered normal in a particular society. *...the conventional norms of polite European society.* **2** SING N If you say that a situation is the **norm,** you mean that it is usual and expected. *In Russia, working wives have been the norm for many years.*

normal /nɔːməl/. ADJ Something that is **normal** is usual and ordinary, and what people expect. *This is a perfectly normal baby.*

normality /nɔːmælɪti/. UNCOUNT N **Normality** is a situation in which everything is normal. *People have a longing for normality.*

normally /nɔːməli/. **1** ADV OR SENTENCE ADV If something **normally** happens, it is what usually happens. *Meetings are normally held three or four times a year... I don't normally drink at lunch.* **2** ADV If you do something **normally,** you do it in the usual or conventional way. *The important thing is that she's eating normally.*

north /nɔːθ/. **1** SING N The **north** is the direction on your left when you are looking towards the place where the sun rises. *The land to the north was low-lying.* **2** SING N The **north** of a place is the part which is towards the north. *...a man from somewhere in the north of England.* Also ATTRIB ADJ *...a flat in north London.* **3** ADV **North** means towards the north, or to the north of a place or thing. *They were heading north... It's 150 miles north of Salisbury.* **4** ATTRIB ADJ A **north** wind blows from the north.

north-east. 1 SING N The **north-east** is the direction halfway between north and east. *We attack from the north-east.* **2** SING N The **north-east** of a place is the part which is towards the north-east. *...the north-east of England.* Also ATTRIB ADJ *...north-east Brazil.* **3** ADV **North-east** means towards the north-east, or to the north-east of a place or thing. *Turn left and go north-east towards the station... It's a small town about fifteen kilometers north-east of Uppsala.* **4** ATTRIB ADJ A **north-east** wind blows from the north-east.

north-eastern. ATTRIB ADJ **North-eastern** means in or from the north-east of a region or country. *...floods in north-eastern India.*

northerly /nɔːðəli/. **1** ADJ **Northerly** means towards the north. *...the wet, northerly slopes... We proceeded along a more northerly route.* **2** ADJ A **northerly** wind blows from the north.

northern /nɔːðən/. ATTRIB ADJ **Northern** means in or from the north of a region or country. *...the high mountains of northern Japan... ...the Northern Hemisphere.*

northward /nɔːθwəd/ or **northwards. 1** ADV **Northward** or **northwards** means towards the north. *They had fled northwards towards Kurnal... Children were put on ponies and sent racing northward.* **2** ADJ **Northward** is used to describe things which are moving towards the north or which face towards the north. *...the northward drift of the massive Himalayan chain.*

north-west. 1 SING N The **north-west** is the direction halfway between north and west. *At the bridge the lake curves to the north-west.* **2** SING N The **north-west** of a place is the part which is towards the north-west. *...a hilly area in the north-west.* Also ATTRIB ADJ *...a Roman settlement in north-west England.* **3** ADV **North-west** means towards the north-west, or to the north-west of a place or thing. *Some 300 miles north-west of Kampala there is an abandoned village.* **4** ATTRIB ADJ A **north-west** wind blows from the north-west.

north-western. ADJ **North-western** means in or from the north-west of a region or country. *...a cattle station in North-western Australia.*

nose /nəʊz/, **noses, nosing, nosed. 1** COUNT N Your **nose** is the part of your face which you use for smelling. *Johnny punched me in the nose.* **2** COUNT N The **nose** of a plane is its front part.

PHRASES • If something is happening **under** your **nose,** it is happening in front of you and it should be obvious to you. *Cheating was going on under the teacher's nose.* • To **poke** your **nose into** something means to interfere in it; an informal use. *He had been sent to poke his nose into their business.* • If you **pay through the nose** for something, you pay a very high price for it; an informal use. *Country people have to pay through the nose for their goods.*

nose about or **nose around.** PHR VB If you **nose about** or **nose around,** you look around a place to see if you can find something interesting; an informal use. *He nosed about among the boilers... Stay outside the door and see that no one comes nosing around.*

nosey /nəʊzi/. See **nosy.**

nostalgia /nɒstældʒɪə/. UNCOUNT N **Nostalgia** is an affectionate feeling for things you have experienced in the past. *...nostalgia for the good old days.*

nostalgic /nɒstældʒɪk/. ADJ If you feel **nostalgic,** you think affectionately about experiences you have had in the past. *He was full of memories, nostalgic for the past.* ♦ **nostalgically** ADV *...talking nostalgically of the good old days.*

nostril /nɒstrɪl/, **nostrils.** COUNT N Your **nostrils** are the two openings at the end of your nose. *...with the smell of smoke in my nostrils.*

nosy /nəʊzi/, **nosier, nosiest;** also spelled **nosey.** ADJ Someone who is **nosy** tries to find out about things which do not concern them; used showing disapproval. *'Who was it?'—'Don't be so nosy.'*

not /nɒt/. You use **not** to make clauses or sentences negative. In speech, **not** is usually shortened to **-n't. 1** If the verb group contains an auxiliary or modal auxiliary, you put **not** between the auxiliary and the main verb. *I haven't tried to telephone him... She couldn't hear the orchestra properly.* **2** If the verb does not already have an auxiliary, you add 'do' in front of **not.** *I don't agree with everything he says... She did not answer.* **3** If the main verb is 'be', you use **not** without an auxiliary. *There wasn't enough room for everybody.* **4** When **not** is used with verbs such as 'think', 'want', and 'seem', the negative effect of **not** belongs to the clause or infinitive that follows the verb. For example, 'I don't think she's here' means 'I think she's not here'. *I don't want to talk about it... The book doesn't seem to be here.* **5** You use **not** in question tags after a positive statement. *That's a new one, isn't it?... You've seen this, haven't you?* **6** You use **not** in questions, for example when you are expressing surprise or annoyance. *Don't they realize it's against the law?* **7** You use **not** to represent the negative or opposite of a word, group, or clause that has just been used. *'Do you know how much it is?'—'I'm afraid not.'... They'd know if it was all right or not.* **8** You use **not** before 'all', 'every', or 'always' to say that there are exceptions to something that is generally true. *Not all scientists are honest... Not everyone agrees with me.*

PHRASES • You use the structure **not...but** when you are contrasting something that is untrue with something that is true. *We wept, not because we were frightened but because we were ashamed.* • You use **not that** to introduce a negative clause that decreases the importance of the previous statement. *Bob helped him. Not that it was difficult.* • **Not at all** is an emphatic way of saying 'No', when you are expressing a feeling or an opinion. *'Does that seem nonsense to you?'—'Not at all.'... 'Would you mind?'—'Not at all.'* • **Not at all** is also a fairly formal way of acknowledging thanks. *'Thanks.'—'Not at all.'* • **if not:** see **if.** • **nothing if not:** see **nothing.**

notable /nəʊtəbəl/. ADJ Something or someone that is **notable** is important or interesting. *With a few notable exceptions this trend has continued... Watermouth is notable for experimental forms of teaching.*

notably /nəʊtəbli/. ADV You use **notably** before mentioning the most important example of the thing you are talking about. *Some people, notably his business associates, had begun to distrust him.*

notation /nəʊteɪʃən/, **notations.** COUNT N A **notation** is a set of written symbols used in a system such as music or mathematics.

notch /nɒtʃ/, **notches.** COUNT N A **notch** is a small V-shaped cut in the surface or edge of something. *Carve notches at either end of a stick and wind the thread round them.*

note /nəʊt/, **notes, noting, noted. 1** COUNT N A **note** is a short letter. *She left a note saying she would see us again.* **2** COUNT N A **note** is also something that you write down to remind you about something. *I'll make a note of that... I took notes at the lecture.* **3** COUNT N In a book or article, a **note** is a short piece of additional information. *Yugoslavia is a different matter (see note on the Yugoslav situation, below).* **4** COUNT N In music, a **note** is a sound of a particular pitch, or a written symbol representing this sound. *The first notes of the concerto sounded softly in the room... Not one of them could read a note of music.* **5** COUNT N A **note** is also a banknote. *...a five pound note.* **6** SING N WITH SUPP You can use **note** to refer to a quality in someone's voice that shows how they feel. *There was a note of triumph in her voice.* **7** REPORT VB If you **note** a fact, you become aware of it. *He noted the minute change in her expression... Note that the report does not carry any form of official recommendation... His audience, I noted with regret, were looking bored.* • See also **noted.**

PHRASES • If you **take note** of something, you pay attention to it because you think it is important. *I had to start taking some note of political developments.* • If you **make a mental note** of something, you try to remember it, because it will be important or useful later. *He made a mental note to tell Lamin later who these men were.* • If you **compare notes** with someone, you talk to them and find out whether they have the same opinion, information, or experiences as yourself. *There are a few things we might compare notes on.*

note down. PHR VB If you **note** something **down,** you write it down so that you have a record of it. *I'll give you time to note down where to send them.*

notebook /nəʊtbʊk/, **notebooks.** COUNT N A **notebook** is a small book for writing notes in.

noted /nəʊtɪd/. ADJ Someone who is **noted** for something they do or have is well-known and admired for it; a formal use. *...a Scottish family noted for its intellect... ...a noted American writer.*

notepad /nəʊtpæd/, **notepads.** COUNT N A **notepad** is a pad of paper that you write notes on.

notepaper /nəʊtpeɪpə/. UNCOUNT N **Notepaper** is paper that you write letters on.

noteworthy /nəʊtwɜːði/. ADJ A **noteworthy** fact or event is interesting or significant; a formal word. *It was noteworthy that the Count was the only person there.*

nothing /nʌθɪŋ/. **1** INDEF PRON You use **nothing** when you are referring to an absence of things of a particular kind, for example objects, events, or ideas. *She shook the bottle over the glass; nothing came out... The man nodded but said nothing... There's nothing to worry about.* **2** INDEF PRON If you say that something is **nothing,** you mean that it is very unimportant. *'What's the matter with you?' Claud asked. 'It's nothing,' he gasped.*

PHRASES • **Nothing but** a particular thing means only that thing. *She could see nothing but his head... ...thirty years of nothing but war.* • You say **nothing of the sort** to emphasize a refusal or a negative statement. *You will do nothing of the sort... Nothing of the sort occurred.* • You say **nothing if not** to emphasize that someone or something has a lot of a quality. For example, if you say that someone is **nothing if not** considerate, you mean that they are very considerate; a formal use. • If you say that **there is nothing for it** but to do something, you mean that it is the only possible thing to do; a British use. *There was nothing for it now except to go straight ahead with the plan.* • **nothing like:** see **like.**

notice /nəʊtɪs/, **notices, noticing, noticed. 1** REPORT VB If you **notice** something, you become aware of it. *I suddenly noticed a friend in the front row... She noticed him scratching his head... She noticed that he was staring at her.* **2** COUNT N A **notice** is a written announcement in a place where everyone can read it. *At the main entrance, there was a large notice which said 'Visitors welcome at any time.'* **3** UNCOUNT N If you give **notice** of something that is going to happen, you warn people about it. *The union was to give 28 days' notice of strikes... She could have done it if she'd had a bit more notice.*

PHRASES • If you **take notice** of what someone says or does, you pay attention to it. *I hope the heads of schools will take notice of my comments.* • If you **take no notice** of someone, you ignore them. *Take no notice of him. He's always rude to people.* • If something **comes to** your **notice** or **is brought to** your **notice,** you become aware of it. *Many cases have come to my notice... We bring to the notice of the committee things that ought to be done.* • If something **escapes** your **notice,** you fail to notice it. *It did not escape her notice that he kept glancing at her.* • If something is done **at short notice** or **at a moment's notice,** you are told about it only a short time before it needs to be done. *It's going to be difficult to fix things at such short notice... It is there ready to be switched on at a moment's notice.* • If a situation will exist **until further notice,** it will continue until someone changes it. *The beaches are closed until further notice.* • If your employer **gives** you **notice,** he or she tells you that you must leave within a fixed period of time. *She had been given two weeks' notice at the Works.* • If you **hand in** your **notice,** you tell your employer that you intend to leave in a fixed period of time.

noticeable /nəʊtɪsəbəl/. ADJ Something that is **noticeable** is very obvious, so that it is easy to see or recognize. *It did not have any noticeable effect upon the rate of economic growth.* ♦ **noticeably** ADV *The air became noticeably cooler.*

noticeboard /nəʊtɪsbɔːd/, **noticeboards.** COUNT N A **noticeboard** is a board on a wall, which people pin notices to; a British use.

notification /nəʊtɪfɪkeɪʃᵊn/. UNCOUNT N If you are given **notification** of something, you are officially informed of it. *You will be sent notification of the results of your interview by post.*

notify /nəʊtɪfaɪ/, **notifies, notifying, notified.** VB WITH OBJ If you **notify** someone of something, you officially inform them of it. *The Housing Department is notified of all planning applications... He wrote to notify me that the cheque had arrived.*

notion /nəʊʃᵊn/, **notions.** COUNT N A **notion** is a belief or idea. *...the notion that the earth was flat... He had only the vaguest notion of what it was about.*

notoriety /nəʊtəraɪ^{1}ti^1/. UNCOUNT N To achieve **notoriety** means to become well known for something bad. *...terrorists who acquired international notoriety for the kidnapping of government figures.*

notorious /nə^{6}tɔːrɪəs/. ADJ Someone or something that is **notorious** is well known for something bad. *The area was notorious for murders... ...his notorious arrogance.* ♦ **notoriously** SUBMOD *Here, rainfall is notoriously variable and unreliable.*

notwithstanding /nɒtwɪθstændɪŋ, -wɪð-/. PREP If something is true **notwithstanding** something else, it is true in spite of that other thing; a formal use. *Computing remains a growth area in which, notwithstanding economic recessions, the outlook looks bright.*

nought /nɔːt/, **noughts. Nought** is the number 0.

noun /naʊn/, **nouns.** COUNT N In grammar, a **noun** is a word used to refer to a person, a thing, or an abstract idea such as a feeling or quality.

nourish /nʌrɪʃ/, **nourishes, nourishing, nourished.** 1 VB WITH OBJ To **nourish** people or animals means to provide them with food. *They had grown stronger now that they were better nourished.* 2 VB WITH OBJ If you **nourish** a feeling or belief, you keep feeling or believing it; a literary use. *She had nourished dreams of escape.*

nourishing /nʌrɪʃɪŋ/. ADJ **Nourishing** food makes you strong and healthy. *Ham sandwiches are nourishing and filling... ...a nourishing diet.*

nourishment /nʌrɪʃmə^{2}nt/. UNCOUNT N **Nourishment** is the food that people and animals need to grow and remain healthy. *The seeds are full of nourishment.*

novel /nɒvᵊl/, **novels.** 1 COUNT N A **novel** is a book that tells a story. *...a novel by Henry James.* 2 ADJ Something that is **novel** is unlike anything else that has been done or made before. *...a novel experience... ...novel teaching methods.*

novelist /nɒvᵊlɪst/, **novelists.** COUNT N A **novelist** is a person who writes novels.

novelty /nɒvᵊlti^1/, **novelties.** 1 UNCOUNT N **Novelty** is the quality of being different, new, and unusual. *He became interested because of the novelty of the problem.* 2 COUNT N A **novelty** is something that is new and therefore interesting. *The car was still a novelty at that time.* 3 COUNT N **Novelties** are cheap, unusual objects sold as gifts or souvenirs.

November /nəʊvembə/. UNCOUNT N **November** is the eleventh month of the year in the Western calendar.

novice /nɒvɪs/, **novices.** 1 COUNT N A **novice** is someone who is not experienced at the job or activity that they are doing. *He's still a novice as far as film acting is concerned... ...novice riders.* 2 COUNT N In a monastery or convent, a **novice** is a person who is preparing to become a monk or nun.

now /naʊ/. 1 ADV You use **now** to refer to the present time, often in contrast to the past or the future. *It is now just after one o'clock... She has three children now... Now is the time to find out... From now on, you are free to do what you like.* 2 CONJ You also use **now** or **now that** when you are talking about the effect of an event or change. *I like him a lot now he's older... Now that she's found him, she'll never let him go.* 3 ADV In stories, you can use **now** to contrast a situation with an earlier one. *They were walking more slowly now.* 4 SENTENCE ADV You can also use **now** in stories to add emphasis to a statement. *I ran downstairs. Now this was something the intruder had not expected.*

PHRASES ● If you say that something will happen **any day now** or **any time now,** you mean that it will happen very soon. *Any day now, the local authority is going to close it down.* ● If something happens **now and then, every now and then,** or **now and again,** it happens occasionally, but not often or regularly. *Every now and then there is a confrontation... I used to let him play with us now and again.*

nowadays /naʊədeɪz/. ADV **Nowadays** means at the present time, in contrast with the past. *Nowadays most babies in this country are born in a hospital... Why don't we ever see Jim nowadays?*

nowhere /nəʊweə/. ADV You use **nowhere** to say that there is no place where something can happen or did happen. *There was nowhere to hide... She had nowhere else to go... Nowhere have I seen any mention of this.*

PHRASES ● If you say that someone or something appears **from nowhere** or **out of nowhere,** you mean that they appear suddenly and unexpectedly. ● If you say that a place is **in the middle of nowhere,** you mean that it is a long way from other places; an informal use. *I spent hours waiting for a bus in the middle of nowhere.* ● If you say that you **are getting nowhere** or that something **is getting** you **nowhere,** you mean that you are not achieving anything or having any success. *Calling me names will get you nowhere.* ● You can use **nowhere near** instead of 'not' to emphasize that something is definitely not the case. *Lions are nowhere near as fast as cheetahs.*

noxious /nɒkʃəs/. ADJ A **noxious** gas or substance is harmful or poisonous; a formal use. *...a cloud of noxious paraffin vapour.*

nozzle /nɒzᵊl/, **nozzles.** COUNT N A **nozzle** is a narrow end piece fitted to a hose or pipe to control the flow of a liquid coming out of it. *The water shoots out of the nozzle in a powerful jet.*

nuance /njuːɑːns/, **nuances.** COUNT N OR UNCOUNT N A **nuance** is a slight difference in sound, appearance, feeling, or meaning. *He practised until he could imitate every nuance of Hall's speech.*

nuclear /njuːklɪə/. 1 ATTRIB ADJ **Nuclear** means relating to the nuclei of atoms, or to the energy produced when these nuclei are split or combined. *...nuclear physics... ...nuclear energy.* 2 ATTRIB ADJ **Nuclear** also means relating to weapons that explode by using the energy released by atoms. *...nuclear weapons... ...nuclear war.*

nuclear reactor, nuclear reactors. COUNT N A **nuclear reactor** is a machine which produces nuclear energy.

nucleus /njuːklɪəs/, **nuclei** /njuːklɪaɪ/. 1 COUNT N The **nucleus** of an atom or cell is the central part of it. *...hydrogen nuclei.* 2 COUNT N The most important people in a group can be referred to as its **nucleus.** *These people formed the nucleus of the American Vegetarian Movement.*

nude /njuːd/, **nudes.** 1 ADJ Someone who is **nude** is not wearing any clothes. *They lay nude on the beach.* ● Someone who is **in the nude** is nude. *He wanted to paint me in the nude.* 2 COUNT N A **nude** is a picture or statue of a nude person.

nudge /nʌdʒ/, **nudges, nudging, nudged.** 1 VB WITH OBJ If you **nudge** someone, you push them gently with your elbow, in order to draw their attention to something or to make them move. *The girls grinned and nudged each other.* 2 COUNT N If you give someone a **nudge,** you nudge them.

nudity /njuːdɪ^{1}ti^1/. UNCOUNT N **Nudity** is the state of wearing no clothes. *The boys treated nudity as a natural thing.*

nuisance /njuːsəns/, **nuisances.** COUNT N If you say that someone or something is a **nuisance,** you mean that they annoy you or cause you problems. *It was a nuisance for them to have all these visitors sitting around... I'm sorry to be such a nuisance.* ● If you **make a nuisance of** yourself, you behave in a way that annoys people.

numb /nʌm/, **numbs, numbing, numbed.** 1 ADJ If a part of your body is **numb,** you cannot feel anything there. *My shoulder was completely numb.* 2 ADJ If you are **numb** with shock or fear, you are so shocked or frightened that you cannot think clearly or feel any emotion. 3 VB WITH OBJ If a blow or cold weather **numbs** a part of your body, you can no longer feel anything in it. *A stone numbed his shoulder... Her fingers were numbed by the frost.* 4 VB WITH OBJ If an experience **numbs** you, you can no longer think clearly or feel any emotion. *We are numbed by repeated disappointments.*

number /nʌmbə/, **numbers, numbering, numbered.** 1 COUNT N A **number** is a word such as 'two', 'nine', or 'eleven', or a symbol such as 1, 3, or 47. You use numbers to say how many things you are referring to or where something comes in a series. *Your licence number is here... He lives at number 19 New King Street.* 2 COUNT N Someone's **number** is the series of digits that you dial when you telephone them. *Ring me tomorrow. Here's my number.* 3 COUNT N WITH SUPP You use **number** with words such as 'large' or 'small' to say approximately how many things or people there are. *...cities with large numbers of children in care... A surprising number of men never marry... They were produced in vast numbers.* ● **A number of** things means several things. *A number of people disagreed.* ● **Any number of** things means a lot of things. *The work can be done in any number of ways.* 4 VB WITH COMPLEMENT If a group of people or things **numbers** a particular amount, there are that many of them. *The force numbered almost a quarter of a million men.* 5 VB WITH OBJ If you **number** something, you give it a number in a series and write the number on it. *I haven't numbered the pages yet.*

number plate, number plates. COUNT N A vehicle's **number plates** are the signs on the front and back that show its registration number; a British use.

numeracy /njuːməᵊrəsi^1/. UNCOUNT N **Numeracy** is the ability to do arithmetic. *...numeracy problems.*

numeral /njuːməᵊrəl/, **numerals.** COUNT N A **numeral** is a symbol used to represent a number; a formal use. *My clock has Roman numerals.*

numerical /njuːmerɪkᵊl/. ADJ **Numerical** means expressed in numbers or relating to numbers. *...numerical data.* ♦ **numerically** ADV *...a numerically small group.*

numerous /njuːməᵊrəs/. 1 QUANTIF **Numerous** things or people means a lot of them. *We had numerous discussions on the meaning of communism... George was the only survivor of her numerous children.* 2 ADJ If people or things are **numerous,** there are a lot of them. *Small enterprises have become more numerous.*

nun /nʌn/, **nuns.** COUNT N A **nun** is a member of a female religious community.

nurse /nɜːs/, **nurses, nursing, nursed.** 1 COUNT N A **nurse** is a person whose job is to care for people who are ill. *...a trained nurse... Nurse Lorimer.* 2 VB WITH OBJ If you **nurse** someone, you care for them while they are ill. 3 See also **nursing.**

nursery /nɜːsəᵊri^1/, **nurseries.** 1 COUNT N A **nursery** is a place where very young children can be looked after while their parents are at work. 2 MOD **Nursery** education is the education of children who are between three and five years old. *We have a nursery school for forty children... ...the noise and bustle of a nursery class.* 3 COUNT N A **nursery** is also a place where plants are grown in order to be sold.

nursery rhyme, nursery rhymes. COUNT N A **nursery rhyme** is a poem or song for young children, especially one that is old or well-known.

nursing /nɜːsɪŋ/. 1 UNCOUNT N **Nursing** is the profession of looking after people who are ill. 2 ATTRIB ADJ A **nursing** mother feeds her baby with milk from her breasts.

nursing home, nursing homes. COUNT N A **nursing home** is a private hospital, especially one for old people.

nurture /nɜːtʃə/, **nurtures, nurturing, nurtured;** a formal word. 1 VB WITH OBJ If you **nurture** a young child or a young plant, you care for it while it is growing and developing. *...a mother's duty to nurture her children.* 2 VB WITH OBJ If you **nurture** plans, ideas, or people, you encourage their development and success. *After spending two years nurturing this project, Bains came to England.*

nut /nʌt/, **nuts.** 1 COUNT N **Nuts** grow on trees. They have hard shells and firm insides that can be eaten. 2 COUNT N A **nut** is also a small piece of metal with a hole in it which a bolt screws into. Nuts and bolts are used to fasten things together. *Take your spanner and tighten the nut.*

nutrient /njuːtrɪənt/, **nutrients.** COUNT N **Nutrients** are substances that help plants and animals to grow. *Excessive rainfall washes out valuable minerals and nutrients from the soil.*

nutrition /njuːtrɪʃᵊn/. UNCOUNT N **Nutrition** is the process of taking and absorbing nutrients from food. *...improvements in nutrition.* ♦ **nutritional** /njuːtrɪʃᵊnəl, -ʃənᵊl/ ATTRIB ADJ *...the nutritional value of steak.*

nutritious /njuːtrɪʃəs/. ADJ Food that is **nutritious** helps your body to be healthy.

nutshell /nʌtʃel/. PHRASE You use **in a nutshell** to indicate that you are saying something in the briefest way possible. *That, in a nutshell, is what we're trying to do here.*

nuzzle /nʌzᵊl/, **nuzzles, nuzzling, nuzzled.** VB WITH OBJ OR ADJUNCT If you **nuzzle** someone, you gently rub your nose and mouth against them, often to show affection. *'Ellen,' he said, nuzzling her neck... The dog began to nuzzle at his coat.*

NW. NW is a written abbreviation for 'north-west'.

nylon /naɪlɒn/. UNCOUNT N **Nylon** is a strong type of artificial cloth. *...nylon stockings.*

nymph /nɪmf/, **nymphs.** COUNT N In Greek and Roman mythology, **nymphs** were spirits of nature who took the form of young women.

Oo

oak /əʊk/, **oaks. 1** COUNT N An **oak** or an **oak tree** is a large tree. **2** UNCOUNT N **Oak** is the wood from oak trees, which is strong and hard. *...a square oak table.*

OAP /əʊ eɪ piː/, **OAPs.** COUNT N An **OAP** is a man over the age of 65 or a woman over the age of 60. **OAP** is an abbreviation for 'old-age pensioner'; a British use.

oar /ɔː/, **oars.** COUNT N **Oars** are long poles with flat ends which are used for rowing a boat.

oasis /əʊeɪsɪs/, **oases** /əʊeɪsiːz/. **1** COUNT N In a desert, an **oasis** is a small area where water and plants are found. **2** COUNT N You can refer to any pleasant place or situation as an **oasis** when it is surrounded by unpleasant ones. *The town was an oasis of prosperity in a desert of poverty.*

oat /əʊt/, **oats.** COUNT N **Oats** are a cereal crop or its grains, used for making porridge or feeding animals.

oath /əʊθ/, **oaths** /əʊðz/. **1** COUNT N An **oath** is a formal promise. *...an oath of allegiance.* ● If someone is **on oath** or **under oath,** they have made a promise to tell the truth in a court of law. **2** COUNT N An **oath** is also a swear-word; an old-fashioned use. *He was answered with a torrent of French oaths.*

oatmeal /əʊtmiːl/. **1** UNCOUNT N **Oatmeal** is a coarse flour made by crushing oats. *...oatmeal biscuits.* **2** ADJ Something that is **oatmeal** in colour is very pale creamy brown. *...an oatmeal coat.*

obedient /ə6biːdɪənt/. ADJ Someone who is **obedient** does what they are told to do. *She was an obedient little girl.* ♦ **obediently** ADV *'Try it,' Clem ordered. Obediently I picked up the cup.* ♦ **obedience** /ə6biːdɪəns/ UNCOUNT N *She failed to show proper obedience and respect to the elders.*

obese /əʊbiːs/. ADJ Someone who is **obese** is very fat; a formal use. ♦ **obesity** /ə6biːsɪ1ti1/ UNCOUNT N *Obesity is a health hazard.*

obey /ə6beɪ/, **obeys, obeying, obeyed.** VB WITH OR WITHOUT OBJ If you **obey** a person, a command, or an instruction, you do what you are told to do. *The troops were reluctant to obey orders... They obeyed me without question... Don't question anything, just obey!*

obituary /ə6bɪtjʊ0əri1/, **obituaries.** COUNT N An **obituary** is a piece of writing about someone who has just died. *I read Sewell's obituary in the Daily News.*

object, objects, objecting, objected; pronounced /ɒbdʒɪ2kt/ when it is a noun and /ə7bdʒɛkt/ when it is a verb. **1** COUNT N An **object** is anything that has a fixed shape and is not alive. *...the shabby, black object he was carrying... ...mats, bowls, and other objects.* **2** COUNT N Someone's **object** or the **object** of what they are doing is their aim or purpose. *The minder's object is to keep the child asleep... She would journey for months with the sole object of filming a rare creature.* **3** COUNT N The **object** of a feeling, a wish, or a kind of behaviour is the thing or person that it is directed towards. *She became an object of worship.* **4** COUNT N In grammar, the **object** of a clause is the noun group which refers to the person or thing that is affected by the action expressed by the verb. An **indirect object** is a second object used with verbs such as 'give', which refers to the person or thing that benefits from an action. Prepositions are also followed by objects. **5** VB OR REPORT VB If you **object** to something, you do not approve of it or you say that you do not approve of it. *This was exactly what he objected to in Christine... You may object that the system makes boys effeminate... The men objected and the women supported them.* ♦ **objector** /ə7bdʒɛktə/ COUNT N *...her refusal to listen to objectors.*

objection /ə7bdʒɛkʃə0n/, **objections. 1** COUNT N If you make or raise an **objection** to something, you say that you do not approve of it. *They raised objections to Seagram's bid... The objection that he had no experience was ignored.* **2** PHRASE If you **have no objection to** something, you do not disapprove of it. *He had no real objection to drinking.*

objectionable /ə7bdʒɛkʃə0nəbə0l/. ADJ Someone or something that is **objectionable** is offensive and unacceptable; a formal use. *...politicians whose views he found objectionable.*

objective /ə7bdʒɛktɪv/, **objectives. 1** COUNT N Your **objective** is what you are trying to achieve. *Mobil's primary objective is to win.* **2** ADJ **Objective** information is based on facts. *There is no objective evidence.* **3** ADJ If someone is **objective,** they base their opinions on facts, rather than on their feelings. *...a book on communism written by an astonishingly objective author.* ♦ **objectively** ADV *It was desirable to view these things objectively.* ♦ **objectivity** UNCOUNT N *Historians strive after objectivity.*

obligation /ɒblɪgeɪʃə0n/, **obligations.** COUNT N OR UNCOUNT N An **obligation** is a duty to do something. *He had to go home because of family obligations... We are under no obligation to give him what he wants.*

obligatory /ə7blɪgətə0ri1/. ADJ If something is **obligatory,** you must do it, because there is a rule or law about it. *It is not obligatory to answer.*

oblige /ə6blaɪdʒ/, **obliges, obliging, obliged. 1** VB WITH OBJ AND TO-INF If something **obliges** you to do something, it makes you feel that you must do it. *Politeness obliged me to go on with the conversation.* ♦ **obliged** PRED ADJ WITH TO-INF *I felt obliged to invite him into the parlour.* **2** VB WITH OR WITHOUT OBJ If you **oblige** someone, you help them by doing what they have asked you to do. *'Who did you ask?'—'Charlie. He's only too glad to oblige.'*

obliging /ə6blaɪdʒɪŋ/. ADJ Someone who is **obliging** is willing to do helpful things.

oblique /ə7bliːk/. **1** ADJ An **oblique** statement or comment is indirect and therefore difficult to understand. *...an oblique compliment.* **2** ADJ An **oblique** line is a sloping line.

obliterate /ə7blɪtəreɪt/, **obliterates, obliterating, obliterated.** VB WITH OBJ To **obliterate** something means to destroy it completely. *I watched bombs obliterate the villages.*

oblivion /ə7blɪvɪən/. **1** UNCOUNT N **Oblivion** is the state of not being aware of what is happening around you, because you are asleep, unconscious, or dead. *Cal still slept, deep in oblivion.* **2** UNCOUNT N **Oblivion** is the state of having been forgotten. *This art faded into oblivion years ago.*

oblivious /ə7blɪvɪəs/. PRED ADJ If you are **oblivious** of something, you are not aware of it. *She seemed oblivious of the attention she was drawing to herself... She remained oblivious to criticism.*

oblong /ɒblɒŋ/, **oblongs.** COUNT N An **oblong** is a shape with two long sides and two short sides at right angles to each other. *...a small oblong of silver.* Also ADJ *...an oblong table.*

obnoxious /ə7bnɒkʃəs/. ADJ Someone who is **obnoxious** is very unpleasant.

oboe /əʊbəʊ/, **oboes.** COUNT N An **oboe** is a woodwind instrument with a double reed in its mouthpiece.

obscene /ə7bsiːn/. ADJ Something that is **obscene** shocks and offends people, especially because it relates to sex. *...obscene pictures.*

obscenity /ə7bsɛnɪ1ti1/, **obscenities. 1** UNCOUNT N **Obscenity** is behaviour that relates to sex and shocks and offends people. *Existing laws on obscenity are to be tightened.* **2** COUNT N An **obscenity** is a very rude word or expression. *They started yelling obscenities.*

obscure /ə7bskjʊə/, **obscurer, obscurest; obscures, obscuring, obscured. 1** ADJ Something that is **obscure** is known by only a few people. *...experts in obscure subjects.* ♦ **obscurity** /ə7bskjʊərɪ1ti1/ UNCOUNT N *He has risen from obscurity to international fame.* **2** ADJ **Obscure** also means difficult to understand or see. *...obscure points of theology... He saw the hideous, obscure shape rise slowly to the surface.* ♦ **obscurity** UNCOUNT N *Dixon didn't mind the obscurity of the reference.* **3** VB WITH OBJ To **obscure** something means to make it difficult to understand, see, or hear. *Words that obscure the truth must be discarded... Some areas were obscured by fog.*

obsequious /ə7bsiːkwɪəs/. ADJ **Obsequious** people are too eager to help you or agree with you. *...obsequious shop assistants.*

observance /ə7bzɜːvəns/. UNCOUNT N WITH SUPP The **observance** of a law or custom is the practice of obeying or following it. *...observance of speed limits.*

observant /ə7bzɜːvənt/. ADJ Someone who is **observant** notices things that are not usually noticed.

observation /ɒbzəveɪʃə0n/, **observations. 1** UNCOUNT N **Observation** involves carefully watching someone or something. *...information gathered by observation or experiment... She was put under observation in a nursing home.* **2** COUNT N An **observation** is something that you have learned by seeing or watching something and thinking about it. *...clinical observations.* **3** COUNT N An **observation** is also a remark or comment. *We listened to Mama's tearful observations on the subject.* **4** UNCOUNT N **Observation** is also the ability to notice things that are not usually noticed. *...keen powers of observation.*

observatory /ə7bzɜːvətə0ri1/, **observatories.** COUNT N An **observatory** is a special building with telescopes that scientists use to study the sun, the moon, the planets, and the stars.

observe /ə7bzɜːv/, **observes, observing, observed. 1** VB WITH OBJ If you **observe** someone or something, you watch them carefully. *By observing your boss's moods, you will soon discover when to talk and when to keep quiet.* **2** VB WITH OBJ To **observe** someone or something also means to see or notice them; a formal use. *They observed a key in the bedroom door.* **3** REPORT VB You can use **observe** when you are quoting a remark or comment that someone has made; a formal use. *'People aren't interested in spiritual things,' observed the actress.* **4** VB WITH OBJ If you **observe** something such as a law or custom, you obey it or follow it.

observer /ə7bzɜːvə/, **observers. 1** COUNT N An **observer** is someone who studies the latest news about a situation. *...political observers.* **2** COUNT N An **observer** is also someone who sees or notices something. *A casual observer may get the wrong impression.*

obsess /ə7bsɛs/, **obsesses, obsessing, obsessed.** VB WITH OBJ If you **are obsessed** with something or something, you think about them all the time. *He became obsessed with a girl reporter.*

obsession /ə7bsɛʃə0n/, **obsessions.** COUNT N If you have an **obsession** about something, you think about it all the time or regard it as very important. *Taylor's fascination with bees developed into an obsession.*

obsessional /ə7bsɛʃə0nəl, -ʃənə0l/. ADJ **Obsessional** means the same as obsessive. *...an obsessional need to win.*

obsessive /ə7bsɛsɪv/. ADJ If someone's behaviour is **obsessive,** they cannot stop doing something or thinking about something. *Obsessive tidiness in the office is a bad sign.* ♦ **obsessively** ADV *At intervals, he obsessively read Conrad.*

obsolescence /ɒbsəlɛsəns/. UNCOUNT N **Obsolescence** is the state of being no longer needed because something newer or more efficient has been invented. *...an educational system whose obsolescence becomes more evident every day.*

obsolete /ɒbsəliːt/. ADJ Something that is **obsolete** is no longer needed because a better thing now exists. *The Falcon missile was now obsolete.*

obstacle /ɒbstəkə0l/, **obstacles.** COUNT N An **obstacle** is something which makes it difficult for you to go forward or do something. *Bats can sense obstacles in their path... ...the bureaucratic obstacles to getting her son over from Jamaica.*

obstetrician /ɒbstətrɪʃə0n/, **obstetricians.** COUNT N An **obstetrician** is a doctor who is specially trained to deal with pregnant women.

obstinacy /ɒbstɪnəsi1/. UNCOUNT N **Obstinacy** is obstinate behaviour. *...the obstinacy of the Transport Minister.*

obstinate /ɒbstɪnə1t/. ADJ Someone who is **obstinate** refuses to do what they do not want to do; used showing disapproval. *...an obstinate, rebellious child.*

obstruct /ə7bstrʌkt/, **obstructs, obstructing, obstructed. 1** VB WITH OBJ If something **obstructs** a road or path, it blocks it, so that people or vehicles cannot get past. *The crash obstructed the road for several hours.* **2** VB WITH OBJ If someone **obstructs** something such as justice or progress, they prevent it from happening or developing. *It is a crime for the President to obstruct justice.*

obstruction /ə7bstrʌkʃə0n/, **obstructions. 1** COUNT N An **obstruction** is something that blocks a road or path. *The obstructions could take weeks to clear.* **2** UNCOUNT N **Obstruction** is the act of deliberately preventing something from happening. *The unions faced legal obstruction.*

obstructive /ə7bstrʌktɪv/. ADJ Someone who is **obstructive** deliberately causes difficulties for other people.

obtain /ə7bteɪn/, **obtains, obtaining, obtained.** VB WITH OBJ If you **obtain** something, you get it or achieve it; a formal use. *She obtained her degree in 1951... These books can be obtained from the Public Library.*

obtainable /ə7bteɪnəbə0l/. ADJ Something that is **obtainable** can be obtained. *...the best cognac obtainable.*

obtrusive /ə7btruːsɪv/. ADJ Something that is **obtrusive** is noticeable in an unpleasant way. *Equally obtrusive was the graffiti that had started to appear.*

obvious /ɒbvɪəs/. ADJ If something is **obvious,** you can easily see it or understand it. *It was painfully obvious that I knew very little about it... ...obvious similarities.* ♦ **obviously** SENTENCE ADV OR ADV *Obviously I don't need to say how important this project is... The soldier was obviously badly hurt.*

occasion /əkeɪʒə0n/, **occasions, occasioning, occasioned. 1** COUNT N An **occasion** is a time when something happens. *I met him only on one occasion.* **2** COUNT N An **occasion** is also an important event, ceremony, or celebration. *They have the date fixed for the big occasion.* **3** SING N WITH SUPP OR UNCOUNT N WITH TO-INF An **occasion** for doing something is an opportunity for doing it; a formal use. *For the girls, nature study was an occasion for lazy walks and idle picnics... He had never had occasion to use his gun.* **4** PHRASE If something happens **on occasion** or **on occasions,** it happens sometimes, but not very often; a formal use.

You have on occasions surprised people. **5** VB WITH OBJ To **occasion** something means to cause it; a formal use. *...deaths occasioned by police activity.*

occasional /əkeɪʒ^{0}nəl, -ʒənə^{0}l/. ATTRIB ADJ **Occasional** means happening sometimes, but not regularly or often. *...an occasional trip as far as Aberdeen.* ♦ **occasionally** ADV *Friends visit them occasionally.*

occult /ɒkʌlt/. SING N The **occult** means supernatural or magical forces. *...enthusiasm for astrology and the occult.* Also ATTRIB ADJ *...the fantastic occult powers that he was said to possess.*

occupant /ɒkjə^{4}pənt/, **occupants.** COUNT N The **occupants** of a building or room are the people there. *The room's sole occupants were the boy and a dog.*

occupation /ɒkjə^{4}peɪʃə^{0}n/, **occupations. 1** COUNT N Your **occupation** is your job or profession. *...a poorly paid occupation.* **2** COUNT N An **occupation** is also something that you do for pleasure. *Riding was her favourite occupation.* **3** UNCOUNT N WITH SUPP The **occupation** of a country is its invasion and control by a foreign army. *...the French occupation of North Africa... Holland came under German occupation.*

occupational /ɒkjə^{4}peɪʃə^{0}nəl, -ʃənə^{0}l/. ATTRIB ADJ **Occupational** means relating to a person's job or profession. *...occupational hazards.*

occupier /ɒkjə^{4}paɪə/, **occupiers.** COUNT N The **occupier** of a house, flat, or piece of land is the person who lives or works there; a formal use. *The occupier of the premises has applied for planning permission.*

occupy /ɒkjə^{4}paɪ/, **occupies, occupying, occupied. 1** VB WITH OBJ The people who **occupy** a building are the people who live or work there. *Houses occupied by the aged must be centrally heated.* **2** PASSIVE VB If something such as a seat **is occupied,** someone is using it, so that it is not available for anyone else to use. **3** VB WITH OBJ When people **occupy** a place or a country, they move into it and gain control of it. *The students occupied the Administration Block.* **4** VB WITH OBJ If something **occupies** a particular place in a system, process, or plan, it has that place. *The demonstration occupies a central place in their campaign.* **5** REFL VB OR VB WITH OBJ If you **occupy** yourself in doing something, you are busy doing it. *They were occupying themselves in growing their own food... How do you occupy your time?* **6** VB WITH OBJ If something **occupies** you, it requires your efforts, attention, or time. *I'm occupied with official business.*

occur /ə^{7}kɜː/, **occurs, occurring, occurred. 1** VB When an event **occurs,** it happens. *The attack occurred six days ago.* **2** VB To **occur** also means to exist or be present. *Racism and sexism occur in all institutions.* **3** VB WITH PREP 'to' If a thought or idea **occurs** to you, you suddenly think of it or realize it. *It had never occurred to her that he might insist on paying.*

occurrence /ə^{7}kʌrəns/, **occurrences. 1** COUNT N An **occurrence** is something that happens; a formal use. *...weeks before the tragic occurrence.* **2** UNCOUNT N WITH SUPP The **occurrence** of something is the fact that it happens or exists. *We may reduce the occurrence of cancer by fifty per cent.*

ocean /əʊʃə^{0}n/, **oceans. 1** SING N The **ocean** is the sea; a literary use. *...in the depths of the ocean.* **2** COUNT N **Ocean** is part of the name of five very large areas of sea. *...the Atlantic Ocean.*

o'clock /əklɒk/. You use **o'clock** after numbers from one to twelve to refer to a time that is exactly at an hour, not before it or after it. *...at two o'clock in the morning.*

octagonal /ɒktægənə^{0}l/. ADJ Something that is **octagonal** has eight sides. *...the octagonal tower.*

octave /ɒktɪv/, **octaves.** COUNT N An **octave** is the musical interval between the first note and the eighth note of a scale.

October /ɒktəʊbə/. UNCOUNT N **October** is the tenth month of the year in the Western calendar.

octopus /ɒktəpəs/, **octopuses.** COUNT N An **octopus** is a sea creature with eight tentacles.

odd /ɒd/, **odder, oddest; odds. 1** ADJ If you say that someone or something is **odd,** you mean that they are strange or unusual. *There's something odd about its shape... It was odd that she still lived at home.* ♦ **oddly** ADV *The drug made him behave quite oddly... Marsha found the play oddly disappointing... Oddly enough, it was through him that I met Carson.* **2** ATTRIB ADJ **Odd** is used before a noun to indicate that the type or size of something is random or not important; an informal use. *You can add bones, the odd vegetable, and herbs... ...odd jobs.* **3** ATTRIB ADJ You say that two things are **odd** when they do not belong to the same set or pair. *...odd socks.* **4** ATTRIB ADJ **Odd** numbers, such as 3, 17, and 129, cannot be divided exactly by the number two. **5** ADV You use **odd** after a number to indicate that it is approximate; an informal use. *We first met twenty odd years ago.* **6** PLURAL N You refer to the probability of something happening as the **odds** that it will happen. *The odds are that they will succeed... The odds are against children learning in this environment.*

PHRASES ● In a group of people or things, the **odd** one **out** is the one that is different from all the others. *I was the odd one out; all my friends were in couples.* ● If you are **at odds** with someone, you are disagreeing or quarrelling with them. *She is at odds with her boss.* ● See also **odds and ends.**

oddity /ɒdɪti^{1}/, **oddities. 1** COUNT N An **oddity** is someone or something strange. *A career woman is still regarded as something of an oddity.* **2** UNCOUNT N The **oddity** of something is the fact that it is strange. *...the oddity of her behaviour.*

oddment /ɒdmə^{2}nt/, **oddments.** COUNT N **Oddments** are unimportant things of various kinds. *...old postcards and scraps, all sorts of oddments.*

odds and ends. PLURAL N You can refer to a disorganized group of things of various kinds as **odds and ends;** an informal use. *I had a trunk filled with various odds and ends that I would need for camping.*

odious /əʊdɪəs/. ADJ Someone or something that is **odious** is extremely unpleasant; a formal use.

odour /əʊdə/, **odours;** spelled **odor** in American English. COUNT N An **odour** is a smell; a formal use. *...the warm odour of freshly-baked scones.*

of /ə^{7}v/. **1** PREP You use **of** after nouns referring to quantities, groups, amounts, or containers to show what kind of thing or substance is involved. *...a collection of essays... ...25 gallons of hot water... ...a big piece of apple pie... ...a cup of tea.* **2** PREP You use **of** to indicate what group something belongs to or what thing a part belongs to. *...the first of his many historic meetings with Winston Churchill... Many of the students come from other countries... Some of her jewellery was missing... ...the corners of a triangle.* **3** PREP You use **of** to indicate who or what something belongs to or is connected with. *...the religious beliefs of the peasant communities... ...the size of the crowd... ...the Mayor of Moscow... Imagine a child of yours doing that.* **4** PREP You use **of** to indicate what something relates to or concerns. *...their hopes of a reconciliation... ...the cause of the infection... ...cancer of the stomach... ...a map of Sweden... ...the Department of Employment.* **5** PREP You use **of** with some verbs to indicate something else involved in the action, especially when the action involves thinking, having a quality, or removal. *I couldn't think of any practical alternatives... He reminded me of my brother... The towel smelled of lavender... His body was secretly disposed of.* **6** PREP You use **of** with some adjectives to indicate the thing that a feeling or quality relates to. *I'm frightened of machines... He is capable of doing much better... I'm not wholly devoid of imagination.* **7** PREP You use **of** to indicate a person or thing involved in an action, as the performer or the thing or person affected. For example, 'the kidnapping of a child' refers to an action affecting a child; 'the arrival of the next train' refers to an action performed by a train. *...protection of the environment... ...the failure of the talks.* **8** PREP You use **of** to indicate what someone creates, affects, or has a particular attitude towards. *...the organizers of the conference.* **9** PREP You also use **of** to indicate a characteristic or quality that something has. *...men of matchless honesty... She helped him to a gin and tonic of giant proportions.* **10** PREP You use **of** to indicate a person's age. *...a boy of nineteen.* **11** PREP You use **of** to indicate the material that forms something. *...a disc of steel.* **12** PREP You also use **of** to say exactly what something is. *...strong feelings of jealousy... ...gifts of olive oil... ...the village of Fairwater Green... ...a price increase of 2%.* **13** PREP You also use **of** when mentioning a date, to indicate what month a day occurs in. *...the 17th of June.* **14** PREP You use **of** in front of dates and periods of time to indicate when something happened. *...the recession of 1974-75... ...the great conflicts of the past ten years.* **15** PREP You use **of** after words referring to the time that an event occurred to indicate what the event was. *...on the day of his inauguration... ...at the time of the earthquake.* **16** PREP You also use **of** to say what illness caused someone's death. *She died of pneumonia.* **17** PREP You also use **of** to indicate the performer of an action when giving your opinion of it. *It was kind of her to take me in... That was nasty of him!*

off /ɒf/. **1** PREP OR ADV When something is taken **off** something else or when it moves or comes **off,** it is removed or it moves away so that it is no longer on the other thing. *He took his hand off her arm... He was wiping sweat off his face... The paint was peeling off... He took off his jacket.* **2** PREP OR ADV When you get **off** a bus, train, or plane, you get out of it. *The train stopped and people got off.* **3** ADV When you go **off,** you leave the place where you were. *He started the motor and drove off abruptly... When are you off to America?* **4** PREP If you keep **off** a street or piece of land, you do not go onto it. *I kept off the main roads.* **5** ADV WITH ADJUNCT OR -ING You can say that someone is **off** somewhere or **off** doing something when they are in a different place from yourself. *She's off in Florida at some labour conference.* **6** PREP If something is **off** a place, it is near it. *...two islands off the mainland of China... ...a hotel just off the Via Condotti.* **7** ADV If an area of land is walled **off** or fenced **off,** it has a wall or fence around it or in front of it. *The area surrounding the office had been cordoned off.* **8** ADV If you fight something **off** or keep it **off,** you make it go away or prevent it. *I could no longer ward off thoughts of my imprisonment.* **9** ADV If you have some time **off,** you do not go to work for a period of time. *I would love to have a year off.* ● If you are **off work,** you are not working because you are ill. **10** PRED ADJ OR ADV If something such as a machine or an electric light is **off,** it is not functioning. *Boylan switched off the headlights... He turned the radio off.* **11** PRED ADJ If an agreement or an arranged event is **off,** it has been cancelled. *I presume the deal is off.* **12** PRED ADJ If food or drink is **off,** it tastes and smells unpleasant because it is going bad. *The wine was off.* **13** PREP If you are **off** something, you have stopped using it or liking it; an informal use. *My father was off alcohol... He's gone off liberty.* **14** ADV If something is a long time **off,** it will not happen for a long time. *Control over the mind is not as far off as we think.* **15** PHRASE If you say that something happens **off and on,** you mean that it happens occasionally.

offal /ɒfə^{0}l/. UNCOUNT N **Offal** is the liver, kidneys, and other internal organs of animals, which are eaten by people or pets.

off-colour. PRED ADJ If you are **off-colour,** you are slightly ill. *He's been a bit off-colour for two days.*

offence /ə^{7}fɛns/, **offences;** spelled **offense** in American English. **1** COUNT N An **offence** is a crime; a formal use. *They were arrested for drug offences.* **2** UNCOUNT N If you give **offence,** you upset or embarrass someone. *The play is liable to give offence to many people.* **3** PHRASE If you **take offence,** you are upset by something that someone says or does. *He was always so quick to take offence.*

offend /ə^{7}fɛnd/, **offends, offending, offended. 1** VB WITH OBJ If you **offend** someone, you upset or embarrass them. *They are deeply offended by references to sex... I'm sorry if I offended you.* **2** VB WITH OBJ OR 'against' If something **offends** a law, rule, or principle, it breaks it; a formal use. *This process offends every known natural law... It would offend against her conventions.* **3** VB To **offend** also means to commit a crime; a formal use. *...criminals who offend again when they're released.* ♦ **offender** /ə^{7}fɛndə/ COUNT N *...the treatment of young offenders.*

offending /ə^{7}fɛndɪŋ/. ATTRIB ADJ You use **offending** to describe something that is causing a problem. *He tapped the offending bulge with a pencil.*

offense /ə^{7}fɛns/. See **offence.**

offensive /ə^{7}fɛnsɪv/, **offensives. 1** ADJ Something that is **offensive** upsets or embarrasses people because it is rude or insulting. *That was an extremely offensive remark.* ♦ **offensively** ADV *The examiners were often offensively rude.* **2** COUNT N An **offensive** is a strong attack. *...the enemy's air offensive... ...a propaganda offensive against the government.* Also ADJ *We took immediate offensive action.*

offer /ɒfə/, **offers, offering, offered. 1** VB WITH OBJ AND PREP 'to' OR VB WITH OBJ AND OBJ If you **offer** something to someone, you ask them if they would like to have it or to use it. *...an apple which he offered to his friend... I was offered a place at Harvard University... I'll offer you nine pounds for it.* **2** VB If you **offer** to do something, you say that you are willing to do it. *Gopal offered to take us to Mysore... 'We could take it for you,' offered Dolly.* **3** COUNT N If someone makes you an **offer,** they offer something to you or offer to do something for you. *She accepted the offer of a cigarette... ...Kirk's offer to take me to the clinic.* **4** VB WITH OBJ AND OBJ OR VB WITH OBJ If you **offer** someone information, advice, or praise, you give it to them. *...offering him advice about accommodation... They didn't ask Liebermann's name and Liebermann didn't offer it.* **5** VB WITH OBJ AND OBJ OR VB WITH OBJ If something **offers** a service, opportunity, or product, it provides it. *The new car plant offers the prospect of 5,000 jobs... ...the facilities and equipment offered by the playgroup.* **6** COUNT N WITH SUPP An **offer** in a shop is a specially low price for a product, or something extra that you get by buying the product. *...cut price offers... ...special offers.* **7** PHRASE If something is **on offer,** it is available to be used or bought. *...the weird and wonderful range of gear on offer.*

offering /ɒfə^{0}rɪŋ/, **offerings. 1** COUNT N You can refer to something that has been specially provided as an **offering.** *...last week's offerings of caviar and* *smoked salmon.* 2 COUNT N An **offering** is also something that is offered to a god as a sacrifice.

off-hand. 1 ADJ If someone behaves in an **off-hand** way, they are not friendly or polite, and show little interest. *...the off-hand contempt with which she treated most men.* 2 ADV OR SENTENCE ADV **Off-hand** means without needing to think very hard. *Off-hand, I can think of three examples.*

office /ɒfɪs/, **offices.** 1 COUNT N An **office** is a room or a part of a building where people work sitting at desks. *You didn't go to the office today?* 2 COUNT N An **office** is also a department of an organization, especially the government, where people deal with a particular kind of administrative work. *...your local education office... ...the tax office.* 3 COUNT N An **office** is also a small building or room where people can go for information, tickets, or a service of some kind. *...the ticket office... ...the enquiry office.* 4 UNCOUNT N Someone who holds **office** has an important job or a position of authority in government or in an organization. *The President of the BMA holds office for one year... ...Baldwin's second term of office as Premier.*

officer /ɒfɪsə/, **officers.** 1 COUNT N In the armed forces, an **officer** is a person in a position of authority. *...a retired army officer.* 2 COUNT N People with responsible positions in organizations, especially government organizations, are also referred to as **officers.** *...a Careers Officer... ...prison officers.* 3 COUNT N OR VOCATIVE Members of the police force are sometimes referred to as **officers.** *Inspector Darroway was the officer in charge of the investigation... Listen, Officer, why do you need all this information?*

official /əfɪʃəˡl/, **officials.** 1 ADJ Something that is **official** is approved by the government or by someone else in authority. *The official figures were published in January... Arabic is the official language of Morocco... ...the official opening of the new bridge.* ♦ **officially** ADV *The war officially ended the following year.* 2 ATTRIB ADJ **Official** is used to describe things which are done or used by people in authority as part of their job or position. *...an official visit to Tanzania... ...the Prime Minister's official residence.* 3 ATTRIB ADJ The **official** reason or explanation for a particular thing is something incorrect that people are told, because the truth is embarrassing. *Visiting his aunt was only the official motive.* ♦ **officially** SENTENCE ADV *Officially she shares a flat with some girlfriend.* 4 COUNT N An **official** is a person who holds a position of authority in an organization. *...government officials.*

officious /əfɪʃəs/. ADJ Someone who is **officious** is too eager to tell people what to do. *...officious interference by managers.*

offing /ɒfɪŋ/. PHRASE If you say that something is **in the offing,** you mean that it is likely to happen soon. *War was already in the offing.*

off-licence, off-licences. COUNT N An **off-licence** is a shop which sells alcoholic drinks; a British use.

offload /ɒfləʊd/, **offloads, offloading, offloaded.** VB WITH OBJ If you **offload** something that you do not want, you get rid of it, especially by giving it to someone else; an informal use.

off-peak. ATTRIB ADJ **Off-peak** things are available at a time when there is little demand for them, so that they are cheaper than usual. *...off-peak electricity.*

off-putting. ADJ You describe someone as **off-putting** when you find them rather unpleasant and do not want to know them better. *She has a rather off-putting manner.*

offset /ɒfset/, **offsets, offsetting. Offset** is used in the present tense and is the past tense and past participle. VB WITH OBJ If one thing **is offset** by another, its effect is reduced by the other thing, so there is no great advantage or disadvantage as a result. *They argued that their wage increases would be offset by higher prices.*

offshoot /ɒfʃuːt/, **offshoots.** COUNT N WITH SUPP If one thing is an **offshoot** of another thing, it has developed from the other thing. *Afrikaans is an offshoot of Dutch.*

offshore /ɒfʃɔː/. ADJ OR ADV Something that is **offshore** is situated in the sea near to the coast. *...offshore oil terminals... The boats waited offshore.*

offside /ɒfsaɪd/. 1 SING N The **offside** of a vehicle is the side farthest from the pavement when you are driving; a British use. *The mini had touched the offside of the truck with its nearside wing.* 2 ADJ OR ADV If a player in a game of football or hockey is **offside,** they have broken the rules by moving too far forward.

offspring /ɒfsprɪŋ/. **Offspring** is the singular and plural. COUNT N Your **offspring** are your children; a formal use. *How do parents pass genes on to their offspring?*

off-white. ADJ Something that is **off-white** is not pure white, but slightly grey or yellow. *...a tatty off-white dress.*

often /ɒfəˡn/. 1 ADV If something happens **often,** it happens many times or much of the time. *We often get very wet cold winters here... It's not often you meet someone who's really interested.* used in questions and statements about frequency. *How often do you need to weigh the baby?... John came as often as he could.* 2 PHRASE If you say that something happens **every so often,** you mean that it happens occasionally. *Every so often, she spends a weekend in London.*

ogre /əʊgə/, **ogres.** COUNT N An **ogre** is a character in fairy stories who is large, cruel, and frightening.

oh /əʊ/. 1 CONVENTION You use **oh** to introduce a response or a comment on something that has just been said. *'How's your brother then?'—'Oh, he's fine.'... 'I have a flat in London.'—'Oh yes, whereabouts?'* 2 CONVENTION You also use **oh** to express a feeling such as surprise, pain, annoyance, or joy. *'He wants to see you immediately,' I said. 'Oh!' she said. Her smile vanished.*

oil /ɔɪl/, **oils, oiling, oiled.** 1 UNCOUNT N **Oil** is a smooth, thick, sticky liquid used as a fuel and for lubricating machines. Oil is found underground. *...alternatives to coal and oil.* 2 VB WITH OBJ If you **oil** a machine, you put oil into it in order to make it work smoothly. *He has to oil and wind the clock.* 3 UNCOUNT N **Oil** is also a smooth, thick, sticky liquid made from plants or animals. Some oils are used for cooking. *...cooking oil... ...olive oil.* 4 PLURAL N **Oils** are oil paintings or oil paints. *...an exhibition of watercolours and oils by Turner... ...trying to capture the scene in oils.*

oilfield /ɔɪlfiːld/, **oilfields.** COUNT N An **oilfield** is an area of land or part of the seabed where oil is found and from which it is removed.

oil paint, oil paints. MASS N **Oil paint** is a thick paint used by artists. It is made from a coloured powder and an oil called linseed oil.

oil painting, oil paintings. COUNT N An **oil painting** is a painting that has been painted using oil paint.

oil slick, oil slicks. COUNT N An **oil slick** is a layer of oil that is floating on top of the sea or a lake because oil has accidentally come out of a ship or container.

oil well, oil wells. COUNT N An **oil well** is a hole which is drilled into the ground or the seabed in order to remove the oil which lies underground.

oily /ɔɪli¹/. 1 ADJ Something that is **oily** is covered with oil or contains oil. *...oily rags... ...oily fish.* 2 ADJ An **oily** substance looks or feels like oil. *There was an oily streak on her stocking.* 3 ADJ Someone who is **oily** is unpleasant because they flatter people or behave in an excessively polite way. *...an oily smile.*

ointment /ɔɪntməˡnt/, **ointments.** MASS N An **ointment** is a smooth thick substance that is put on sore skin or a wound to help it heal. *...eye ointments... ...a tube of sunburn ointment.*

okay /əʊkeɪ/; also spelled **OK;** an informal word. 1 ADJ OR ADV If you say that something is **okay,** you mean that it is acceptable. *I'll have another coffee and then I'll be going, if that's okay... She wanted to know if the trip was OK with the government... I asked Jenny how she thought it all went. 'Okay,' she said.* 2 PRED ADJ If you say that someone is **okay,** you mean that they are safe and well; an informal use. *'Where's Jane?'—'Just back there. She's okay. Just shocked.'* 3 CONVENTION You can say **okay** when you are agreeing to something or checking whether someone else understands or agrees. *'I'll be back at a quarter past one.'—'OK. I'll see you then.'... I'll be back in fifteen minutes. OK?* 4 CONVENTION You can also use **okay** to indicate to someone that you want to start talking about something else or doing something else. *Okay, do you mind if we speak a bit of German now?*

old /əʊld/, **older, oldest.** 1 ADJ Someone who is **old** has lived for many years. *...his old mother.* used in questions or statements about age. *She's about 50 years old... How old are you?... She was a couple of years older than me.* 2 PLURAL N You can refer to people who are old as **the old.** *...the particular needs of the old and infirm.* 3 ADJ Something that is **old** has existed for a long time, and is perhaps in bad condition. *...a massive old building of crumbling red brick... ...an old joke... ...wardrobes full of old clothes.* 4 ATTRIB ADJ **Old** is also used of things which are no longer used or which have been replaced by something else. *I was directed into the old dining room... ...his old job at the publishing company.* 5 ATTRIB ADJ If someone is an **old** friend of yours, they have been your friend for a long time. 6 ATTRIB ADJ You can use **old** to express affection or familiarity when talking to or about someone you know; an informal use. *I got a letter from good old Lewis.*

PHRASES ● **In the old days** means many years ago, before things changed. *Hong Kong was a shopper's paradise in the old days.* ● You use **any old** to emphasize that the quality or type of something is not important; an informal use. *Any old board will do.*

old-age pensioner, old-age pensioners. COUNT N An **old-age pensioner** is the same as an OAP.

old-fashioned. 1 ADJ Something that is **old-fashioned** is no longer considered appropriate in style or design, because it has been replaced by something more modern. *...old-fashioned plastic-rimmed glasses.* 2 ADJ If you are **old-fashioned,** your behaviour and beliefs are those which were common or accepted in the past, but are no longer common.

old hand, old hands. COUNT N An **old hand** is a person who is very skilled at something because they have a lot of experience. *...a few old hands in the press corps.*

old master, old masters. COUNT N An **old master** is a painting by a famous painter of the past.

Old Testament. PROPER N The **Old Testament** is the first part of the Bible.

old wives' tale, old wives' tales. COUNT N An **old wives' tale** is a traditional idea which is believed by many people but is usually incorrect.

O level, O levels. COUNT N An **O level** is an educational qualification in a particular subject which used to be taken by British schoolchildren at the age of 15 or 16. O levels were replaced by GCSEs in Britain in 1988.

olive /ɒlɪv/, **olives.** 1 COUNT N An **olive** is a small green or black fruit with a bitter taste. 2 ADJ Something that is **olive** or **olive green** is yellowish-green.

olive oil. UNCOUNT N **Olive oil** is oil obtained by pressing olives. It is put on salads or used for cooking.

-ological. SUFFIX **-ological** is used to replace '-ology' at the end of nouns in order to form adjectives that describe something as relating to a particular science or subject. Adjectives of this kind are not usually defined but are treated with the related nouns. *...a geological survey... ...the Zoological Society.*

-ologist, -ologists. SUFFIX **-ologist** is used to replace '-ology' at the end of nouns in order to form other nouns that refer to people concerned with a particular science or subject. Nouns of this kind are not usually defined but are treated with the nouns ending in '-ology'. *...a well known anthropologist... ...amateur geologists.*

Olympic /əlɪmpɪk/. ATTRIB ADJ **Olympic** means relating to the Olympic Games. *...an Olympic finalist.*

Olympic Games. PLURAL N The **Olympic Games** or the **Olympics** are a set of international sports competitions which take place every four years, each time in a different country.

omelette /ɒmlɪ²t/, **omelettes;** spelled **omelet** in American English. COUNT N An **omelette** is a food made by beating eggs and cooking them in a flat pan.

omen /əʊmə²n/, **omens.** COUNT N An **omen** is something that is thought to indicate what is going to happen in the future. *An eclipse of the sun is the worst of bad omens.*

ominous /ɒmɪnəs/. ADJ Something that is **ominous** is worrying or frightening because it makes you think that something unpleasant is going to happen. *There was an ominous silence.* ♦ **ominously** ADV *Black clouds were piling up ominously.*

omission /ə⁶mɪʃəˡn/, **omissions.** COUNT N OR UNCOUNT N An **omission** is the act of not including something or not doing something. *The reports were full of errors and omissions... ...the omission of women from these studies.*

omit /ə⁶mɪt/, **omits, omitting, omitted.** 1 VB WITH OBJ If you **omit** something, you do not include it. *Two groups were omitted from the survey—the old and women.* 2 VB WITH TO-INF If you **omit** to do something, you do not do it; a formal use. *He omitted to say whether the men were armed.*

omnipotent /ɒmnɪpətənt/. ADJ Someone or something that is **omnipotent** has complete power over things or people; a formal use. *...an omnipotent central committee... ...an omnipotent and perfect deity.*

omniscient /ɒmnɪsɪənt/. ADJ Someone who is **omniscient** knows or seems to know everything; a formal use. *...faith in an omniscient God.*

omnivorous /ɒmnɪvərəs/. ADJ An **omnivorous** person or animal eats both meat and plants; a technical use. *...an omnivorous diet.*

on /ɒn/. 1 PREP If you are standing or resting **on** something, it is underneath you and is supporting your weight. *They were sitting on chairs... ...a cow grazing on a hill... Put the tray on the bed, please.* 2 PREP If you are **on** a bus, train, or plane, you are travelling in it. *Afterwards they got on a bus and went to the cinema.* 3 PREP If something is **on** a surface or object, it is stuck to it or attached to it. *...the posters on the walls... ...the light on the ceiling... ...the buttons on a shirt.* 4 PREP If there is something **on** a piece of paper, it has been written or printed there. *...the table on the back page of the book... She wrote it down on a piece of paper.* 5 ADV When you put **on** a piece of clothing, you place it over a part of your body in order to wear it. *She put her shoes on... She had her coat on.* 6 PREP You can say that you have something **on** you if you are carrying it in your pocket or in a bag. **7** PREP If a building is **on** a road, it is next to it. *The house is on Pacific Avenue.* **8** PREP You can use **on** when mentioning the area of land where someone works or lives. For example, someone can work **on** a farm or a building site, or live **on** a housing estate. **9** PREP If you hurt yourself **on** something, you hurt yourself by accidentally hitting it with a part of your body. *He cut himself on the gatepost.* **10** PREP If something happens **on** a particular day or date, that is when it happens. *...on the first day of term... ...on Thursday night... Caro was born on April 10th.* **11** PREP You use **on** when mentioning an event that was followed by another one. For example, if something happened **on** someone's return, it happened just after they returned. *'It's so unfair,' Clarissa said on her return... On being called 'young lady', she laughed.* **12** PREP If something is done **on** an instrument, machine, or system, it is done using that instrument, machine, or system. *...waltzes played on the violin... His first film was shown on television yesterday... They work on a rota system.* **13** ADV If something such as a machine or an electric light is **on,** it is functioning. *A tap had been left on.* **14** PREP Books, discussions, remarks, or thoughts **on** a particular subject are concerned with that subject. *...books on philosophy, art, and religion... They occasionally commented on how good her work was... ...brooding on the events that had taken place.* **15** PREP If something affects you, you can say that it has an effect **on** you. *The effect on the environment could be considerable.* **16** PREP Taxes or profits that are obtained from something are referred to as taxes or profits **on** it. *...a new sales tax on luxury goods... Profits on books will be down... You pay interest on your mortgage.* **17** PREP To spend money **on** something means to buy it or to pay for repairs to it. *...the amount of money he spent on clothes... Why waste money on them?* **18** PREP To spend time **on** something means to spend time doing it or making it. *I spent a lot of time on this picture.* **19** PREP You use **on** with some verbs when mentioning something else involved in the action, especially when the action involves attacking, relying, or using. *The dog turned on her and bit her... Never rely on your memory... Beveridge's calculations were all based on 1938 prices.* **20** ADV You use **on** to indicate that someone or something continues, progresses, or moves forward. *I read on... He urged them on as they charged up Sayer Street.* **21** PREP If you are **on** a council or committee, you are a member of it. **22** PREP Someone who is **on** a drug or who lives **on** a particular kind of food regularly consumes it. *She was on pills of various kinds.* **23** PREP If you are **on** a particular kind of income, that is the kind of income you have. *...people on a low income.* **24** ADV If an event is **on,** it is happening. *The war was on then... What's on at the Odeon?* **25** PREP When you pay for something that someone else receives, you can say that it is **on** you; an informal use. *The drinks were always on him.* **26** ADV If you say that someone goes **on** at you or **on** about something, you mean they are talking to you in an irritating or boring way; an informal use. *He's always on at me about the way I dress... He's always on about yoga... What are you on about?*

PHRASES • If something happens **on and off,** it happens occasionally. • If you **have a lot on,** you are very busy. If you **do not have much on,** you are not busy; an informal use. • **and so on:** see **so.**

once /wʌns/. **1** ADV If something happens **once,** it happens one time only, or one time within a particular period of time. *I've been out with him once, that's all... Some trees only bear fruit once every twenty-five years.* **2** ADV If something was **once** true, it was true at some time in the past, but is no longer true. *Texas was once ruled by Mexico.* **3** CONJ If something happens **once** another thing has happened, it happens immediately afterwards. *Once inside her flat, she glanced at the clock.*

PHRASES • If you do something **at once,** you do it immediately. *I knew at once that something was wrong.* • If several things happen **at once** or **all at once,** they all happen at the same time. *Everybody is talking at once.* • If something happens **once again** or **once more,** it happens again. *She wanted to see him once more before she died... Companies are once again queueing to join the scheme.* • If you have done something **once or twice,** you have done it a few times, but not very often. *She had been to London once or twice before.* • If something happens **once in a while,** it happens occasionally. *Once in a while she'd give me some lilacs to take home.* • If you say that something happened **for once,** you are emphasizing that it does not usually happen. *For once Castle went without his lunch.* • If something happens **once and for all,** it happens completely or finally. *They had to be defeated once and for all.* • **Once upon a time** is used at the beginning of a children's story to indicate that the events in it are supposed to have taken place a long time ago.

oncoming /ɒnkʌmɪŋ/. ATTRIB ADJ **Oncoming** means moving towards you. *...oncoming traffic.*

one /wʌn/, **ones. 1 One** is the number 1. *...one hundred miles... Of these four suggestions, only one is correct... The two friends share one job... The road goes from one side of the town to the other.* **2** PRON You also use **one** to refer to a particular thing or person. *These trousers aren't as tight as the other ones... ...buying old houses and building new ones... Oh, that's a difficult one to answer, isn't it?* **3** DET You can use **one** when referring to a time in the past or the future. For example, if you say that you did something **one** day, you mean that you did it on a day in the past. If you say that you will do something **one** day, you mean that you will do it on a day in the future. *One evening, I had a visit from Henry Cox... One day you and I must have a long talk together.* **4** PRON A speaker or writer uses **one** to refer to people in general; a formal use. *One can eat well here... The law should guard one against this sort of thing.*

PHRASES • **One or two** means a very few. *One or two of the girls help in the kitchen.* • If you are or have **one up on** someone, you have an advantage over them; an informal use. • **A hundred and one** or **a thousand and one** means a great many. *There must be a thousand and one books of this sort on the market.* • **one another:** see **another.**

onerous /ɒnərəs, əʊ-/. ADJ **Onerous** work is difficult and unpleasant; a formal use. *...the onerous duties of postal delivery.*

one's /wʌnz/. **1** DET **One's** is used to indicate that something belongs or relates to people in general; a formal use. *Naturally, one wanted only the best for one's children.* **2 One's** is also a spoken form of 'one is' or 'one has', especially when 'has' is an auxiliary verb; a formal use. *One's never quite sure exactly how things are going to turn out... One's got to pay for it.*

oneself /wəⁿnsɛlf/. **1** REFL PRON A speaker or writer uses **oneself** as the object of a verb or preposition in a clause where 'one' is the subject or a previous object. *One must keep such interests to oneself.* **2** REFL PRON **Oneself** is also used to emphasize the subject or object of a clause. *Others might find odd what one finds perfectly normal oneself.*

one-sided. 1 ADJ In a **one-sided** activity or relationship, one of the people involved does much more than the other. *...one-sided conversations.* **2** ADJ A **one-sided** argument or report is not acceptable because it only considers some of the relevant facts. *The report is one-sided in its interpretation of the evidence.*

one-time. ATTRIB ADJ You use **one-time** to indicate that someone used to have a particular job, position, or role. *...Fred Dunn, a onetime farm worker.*

one-to-one. ATTRIB ADJ In a **one-to-one** relationship, you deal with only one other person. *...one-to-one tuition.*

one-way. 1 ATTRIB ADJ **One-way** streets are streets along which vehicles can drive in only one direction. **2** ATTRIB ADJ A **one-way** ticket is one which you can use to travel to a place, but not to travel back again. *...a one-way ticket to Jersey.*

ongoing /ɒngəʊɪŋ/. ATTRIB ADJ An **ongoing** situation is continuing to happen. *...an ongoing economic crisis.*

onion /ʌnjən/, **onions.** COUNT N OR UNCOUNT N An **onion** is a small, round vegetable. It is white with a brown skin, and has a strong smell and taste.

onlooker /ɒnlʊkə/, **onlookers.** COUNT N An **onlooker** is someone who is watching an event. *She blew a kiss to the shivering onlookers.*

only /əʊnli¹/. In written English, 'only' is usually placed immediately before the word it qualifies. In spoken English, you can use stress to indicate what 'only' qualifies, so its position is not so important. **1** ADV You use **only** to indicate the one thing that is involved or that happens in a particular situation. *He read only paperbacks... I'm only interested in facts... Only Mother knows... The video is to be used for teaching purposes only.* **2** ATTRIB ADJ If you talk about the **only** thing involved in a particular situation, you mean that there are no others. *I was the only one smoking... It was the only way out.* **3** ATTRIB ADJ An **only** child has no brothers or sisters. **4** ADV You can use **only** to emphasize that something is unimportant or small. *It was only a squirrel... I was only joking... We only paid £26.* **5** ADV You can use **only** to emphasize how recently something happened. *I've only just arrived.* **6** ADV You can also use **only** to emphasize a wish or hope. *I only wish I had the money.* **7** CONJ You can use **only** to add a comment which slightly changes or corrects what you have just said; an informal use. *Snake is just like chicken, only tougher.* **8** CONJ You can use **only** to introduce the reason why something is not done; an informal use. *'That's what I'm trying to do,' said Mrs Oliver, 'only I can't get near enough.'* **9** ADV WITH TO-INF You can use **only** before an infinitive to introduce an event which happens immediately after the previous one, and which is rather surprising or unfortunate. *He broke off, only to resume almost at once... I had tried this years before, only to receive a polite refusal.* **10** SUBMOD You can use **only** to emphasize that you think a course of action or type of behaviour is reasonable in a particular situation. *It is only natural that she will have mixed feelings about your promotion.*

PHRASES • You say that one thing will happen **only if** another thing happens when you want to indicate that it will not happen unless the other thing happens. *These snakes only attack if they feel cornered or threatened.* • You say that something is **only just** the case to emphasize that it is very nearly not the case. *He could only just hear them... The heat was only just bearable.* • You use **not only** to introduce the first of two linked statements when the second is even more surprising or extreme than the first. *Chimpanzees not only use tools but make them.* • If you say that someone **has only** to do one thing in order to achieve or prove another, you are emphasizing how easily or quickly it can be done. *You've only got to read the newspapers to see what can happen to hitch-hikers.* • You use **only too** to emphasize that something happens to a greater extent than is expected or wanted. *He is only too pleased to help... She remembered that night only too clearly.* • **if only:** see **if.**

onset /ɒnsɛt/. SING N The **onset** of something unpleasant is the beginning of it. *...the onset of war.*

onslaught /ɒnslɔːt/, **onslaughts.** COUNT N WITH SUPP An **onslaught** is a violent attack. *...a co-ordinated onslaught on enemy airfields.*

onto /ɒntu/; also spelled **on to. 1** PREP If someone or something moves **onto** an object or is put **onto** it, the object is then underneath them and supporting them. *I got onto the bed... She spooned a portion of potato onto his plate... I ran out onto the porch.* **2** PREP When you get **onto** a bus, train, or plane, you get into it. **3** PREP If you fasten one thing **onto** another, you fasten the first thing to the second one. *I bent a pin and tied it onto a piece of string.* **4** PREP If you hold **onto** something, you hold it firmly. *...clinging onto his shirt.* **5** PREP If people who are talking get **onto** a different subject, they begin talking about it. *Let's move onto another question.*

onward /ɒnwəd/, **onwards.** In normal British English, **onwards** is an adverb and **onward** is an adjective. In formal British English and in American English, **onward** is both an adjective and an adverb. **1** ADV If something happens from a particular time **onwards** or **onward,** it begins to happen at that time and continues to happen. *From 1968 onwards the situation began to change... From that time onward he had never spoken to her again.* **2** ADV OR ATTRIB ADJ If someone or something moves **onwards** or **onward,** they continue travelling or moving forward. *We travelled from China to India, and onwards to East Africa... ...the onward motion of the boat.* **3** ADV OR ATTRIB ADJ You can say that things move **onwards** or **onward** when they continue to develop or progress. *...this onward march of the Labour movement.*

ooze /uːz/, **oozes, oozing, oozed. 1** ERG VB When a thick, sticky liquid **oozes** from an object or when the object **oozes** it, the liquid flows slowly from the object. *...blood oozing from his wounds... His sandals oozed black slime.* **2** VB WITH OBJ OR 'with' If someone **oozes** a quality or feeling, they show it very strongly, often when they do not really feel it. *His letter, oozing remorse, appeared in all the newspapers... Her voice oozed with politeness.*

opal /əʊpəᵊl/, **opals.** COUNT N An **opal** is a white semi-precious stone.

opaque /əʊpeɪk/. **1** ADJ If an object or substance is **opaque,** you cannot see through it. *...the opaque windows of the jail... ...the opaque water.* **2** ADJ **Opaque** also means difficult to understand; a formal use.

open /əʊpəᵊn/, **opens, opening, opened. 1** ERG VB When you **open** something such as a door or the lid of a box, or when it **opens,** you move it so that it no longer covers a hole or gap. *Elizabeth opened the door and went in... The door opened almost before Brody had finished knocking.* Also ADJ *...the open window.* **2** VB WITH OBJ When you **open** a cupboard, container, or letter, you move, remove, or cut part of it so that you can take out what is inside. *Open the tool-box... I opened a can of beans.* Also ADJ *He tore open the envelope.* **3** VB WITH OBJ When you **open** a book, you move its covers apart in order to read or write on the pages inside. *He opened the book at random.* Also ADJ *...the open Bible.* **4** ERG VB When you **open** your mouth, or when it **opens,** you move your lips and teeth apart. *She opened her mouth to say something, then closed it.* Also ADJ *Angelica looked at me with her mouth open.* **5** ERG VB When you **open** your eyes, or when they **open,** you move your eyelids upwards so that you can see. *She opened her eyes and looked at me.* Also ADJ *...lying with his eyes wide open.* **6** ADJ If you have an **open** mind or are **open** to ideas or suggestions, you are prepared to consider any ideas or suggestions. **7** ADJ An **open** person is honest and does not try to hide anything. *They looked at her with open curiosity.* ♦ **openness** UNCOUNT N *...their relaxed openness.* **8** PRED ADJ WITH PREP 'to' If you say that a person, idea, or system is **open** to something such as criticism or blame, you mean they could be treated in the way indicated. *The proposals were certainly open to criticism.* **9** ERG VB When a shop, office, or public building **opens** or **is opened,** its doors are unlocked and the people in it start working. *When does the library open?* Also ADJ *The Tate Gallery is open 10 a.m.—6 p.m.* **10** VB WITH OBJ When someone important **opens** a building or a public area, they declare officially in a public ceremony that it is ready to be used or to start operating. Also PRED ADJ *Lord Shawcross declared the hotel open.* ♦ **opening** UNCOUNT N WITH SUPP *...the opening of the new theatre.* **11** VB When an event such as a conference or a play **opens,** it begins to take place or to be performed. *The UN General Assembly opens in New York later this month.* ♦ **opening** UNCOUNT N *...the opening of 'Nicholas Nickleby' on Broadway.* **12** VB WITH OBJ The person who **opens** an event is the first to speak or do something. *Senator Denton opened the hearing by reminding us of our duty.* **13** VB WITH OBJ If you **open** an account with a bank, you begin to use their services by giving them some of your money to look after or invest. **14** VB WITH ADJUNCT If a room or door **opens** into or onto a place, you can go straight to that place from the room or through the door. *These rooms have doors opening directly onto the garden.* **15** VB When flowers **open,** their petals spread out. **16** ADJ If an item of clothing is **open,** it is not fastened. *...an open black raincoat... ...an open-necked shirt.* **17** ATTRIB ADJ An **open** area of land or sea is a large area with few things such as buildings or islands in it. *The road stretched across open country.* ♦ **openness** UNCOUNT N *...the openness of Vincent Square.* **18** ATTRIB ADJ You can use **open** to describe something that is not covered or enclosed. *...an open car... Never dry clothes in front of an open fire.* **19** PRED ADJ WITH PREP 'to' If a course of action is **open** to you, it is possible for you to do it. *We should use the opportunities now open to us.* **20** ADJ An **open** meeting, competition, or invitation is one which anyone can take part in or accept. *Most Council meetings are open to the public... ...the Women's Open Golf Championship.* **21** ADJ If you describe a situation or topic as **open,** you mean that no decision has been made about it yet. *I let joining the Party remain an open question... They had left their options open.* **22** See also **opening, openly.**

PHRASES ● If you do something **in the open,** you do it out of doors. *The children enjoyed sleeping out in the open.* ● If a situation is brought out **into the open,** people are told about it and it is no longer a secret.

open up. PHR VB **1** When an opportunity **opens up** or **is opened up,** it is given to you. *All sorts of possibilities began to open up.* **2** If a place **opens up** or **is opened up,** people can then get to it or trade with it more easily. *Brunel opened up the West.* **3** When someone **opens up** a building or **opens up,** they unlock the door so that people can get in.

open air. SING N If you are in the **open air,** you are outside. *Dry clothes in the open air, if possible... ...open-air swimming pools.*

open-ended. ADJ An **open-ended** discussion or activity is started without the intention of achieving a particular decision or result.

opening /əʊpənɪŋ/, **openings. 1** ATTRIB ADJ The **opening** item or part of something is the first one. *...his opening remarks.* **2** SING N The **opening** of a book or film is the first part of it. *The main characters are established in the opening of the book.* **3** COUNT N An **opening** is a hole or empty space through which things can pass. *We slid through the opening into the field.* **4** COUNT N An **opening** is also an opportunity to do something. *Charlotte herself provided me with an opening.* **5** See also **open.**

openly /əʊpənli/. ADV If you do something **openly,** you do it without trying to hide anything. *His mother wept openly.*

open-minded. ADJ Someone who is **open-minded** is willing to listen to other people's ideas and consider them. *...an intelligent, open-minded man... ...an open-minded approach to new techniques.*

open-mouthed. ADJ If someone is looking **open-mouthed** at something, their mouth is open because they are very surprised. *She was staring open-mouthed at a picture of her father.*

opera /ɒpərə/, **operas.** COUNT N OR UNCOUNT N An **opera** is a musical entertainment. It is like a play, but most of the words are sung. *...choruses from Verdi's operas... ...a book on Italian opera.*

operate /ɒpəreɪt/, **operates, operating, operated. 1** ERG VB If a business or organization **operates** in a place, it carries out its work there. *...the multinational companies which operate in their country... He operates an Afghan news service.* ♦ **operation** UNCOUNT N *...our first year of operation.* **2** VB The way that something **operates** is the way that it works or has an effect. *We discussed how language operates... ...the way calculators operated.* **3** ERG VB When you **operate** a machine or device, you make it work. *...how to operate the safety equipment.* ♦ **operation** UNCOUNT N *...instructions for the operation of machinery.* **4** VB When surgeons **operate** on a patient, they cut open the patient's body in order to remove, replace, or repair a diseased or damaged part. *They operated but it was too late... His knees have been operated on three times.*

operatic /ɒpərætɪk/. ADJ **Operatic** means relating to opera. *...the local operatic society.*

operating theatre, operating theatres. COUNT N An **operating theatre** is a room in a hospital where surgeons carry out operations.

operation /ɒpəreɪʃən/, **operations. 1** COUNT N An **operation** is a planned activity that involves many complicated actions. *...military operations in Europe... ...a rescue operation.* **2** COUNT N Businesses or companies are sometimes referred to as **operations.** *...Multiponics, a large-scale farming operation.* **3** COUNT N If a patient has an **operation,** a surgeon cuts open the patient's body in order to remove, replace, or repair a diseased or damaged part. *Her mother was about to undergo a major operation... ...heart operations.* **4** PHRASE If something is **in operation,** it is working or being used. *...gas drilling rigs in operation in the USA... The plans were put into operation at once.* **5** See also **operate.**

operational /ɒpəreɪʃənəl, -ʃənəl/. **1** ADJ A machine or piece of equipment that is **operational** is working or able to be used. *...fifty operational warships... The system is not yet operational.* **2** ATTRIB ADJ **Operational** actions or difficulties occur while a plan or system is being carried out. *...operational positions.*

operative /ɒpərətɪv/, **operatives. 1** ADJ Something that is **operative** is working or having an effect. *The scheme was fully operative by 1975.* **2** COUNT N An **operative** is a worker; a formal use. *...each operative on a production line.*

operator /ɒpəreɪtə/, **operators. 1** COUNT N An **operator** is a person who works at a telephone exchange or on the switchboard of an office or hotel. *He dialled the operator... ...telephone operators.* **2** COUNT N WITH SUPP An **operator** is also someone who is employed to operate or control a machine. *...computer operators.* **3** COUNT N WITH SUPP An **operator** is also someone who runs a business. *...tour operators... ...casino operators.*

opinion /əpɪnjən/, **opinions. 1** COUNT N Your **opinion** of something is what you think about it. *The students were eager to express their opinions... Information of this nature was valuable, in his opinion... We have a high opinion of you.* **2** PHRASE If someone **is of the opinion** that something is the case, they think that it is the case; a formal use. *He is of the opinion that money is not important.* **3** UNCOUNT N You can refer to the beliefs or views that people have as **opinion.** *...changes in public opinion... Difficulties arise where there's a difference of opinion.*

opinionated /əpɪnjəneɪtɪd/. ADJ Someone who is **opinionated** has firm opinions and refuses to accept that they may be wrong; used showing disapproval. *...this inexperienced but opinionated newcomer.*

opinion poll, opinion polls. COUNT N An **opinion poll** involves asking people for their opinion on a particular subject, especially one concerning politics.

opium /əʊpɪəm/. UNCOUNT N **Opium** is a drug made from the seeds of a type of poppy. Opium is illegal in many countries.

opponent /əpəʊnənt/, **opponents. 1** COUNT N A politician's **opponents** are other politicians who belong to a different party or have different aims or policies. *...their political opponents.* **2** COUNT N In a game, your **opponent** is the person who is playing against you. *He beat his opponent three sets to love.* **3** COUNT N The **opponents** of an idea or policy do not agree with it. *...a leading opponent of the budget cuts.*

opportune /ɒpətjuːn/. ADJ **Opportune** means happening at a convenient time; a formal use. *It was most opportune that Mrs Davenport should arrive... The call came at an opportune moment.*

opportunism /ɒpətjuːnɪzəm/. UNCOUNT N If you refer to someone's behaviour as **opportunism,** you mean that they take advantage of any opportunity that occurs in order to gain money or power; a formal use that shows disapproval. *...a piece of cheap, cynical opportunism.* ♦ **opportunist** /ɒpətjuːnɪst/ COUNT N *...the intrigues of a business opportunist.* ♦ **opportunistic** /ɒpətjuːnɪstɪk/ ADJ *...an opportunistic foreign policy.*

opportunity /ɒpətjuːnɪti/, **opportunities.** COUNT N OR UNCOUNT N An **opportunity** is a situation in which it is possible for you to do something that you want to do. *It will give you an opportunity to meet all kinds of people... They would return to power at the first opportunity... ...equality of opportunity.*

oppose /əpəʊz/, **opposes, opposing, opposed.** VB WITH OBJ If you **oppose** someone or **oppose** what they want to do, you disagree with what they want to do and try to prevent them from doing it. *My father opposed my wish to become a sculptor.*

opposed /əpəʊzd/. **1** PRED ADJ If you are **opposed** to something, you disagree with it or disapprove of it. *They were violently opposed to the idea... I am opposed to capital punishment.* **2** ADJ You say that two ideas or systems are **opposed** when they are opposite to each other or very different from each other. *...two bitterly opposed schools of socialist thought... ...a strategy which is diametrically opposed to that of the previous government.* **3** PHRASE You use **as opposed to** when you want to make it clear that you are talking about a particular thing and not something else. *There's a need for technical colleges as opposed to universities.*

opposing /əpəʊzɪŋ/. ATTRIB ADJ **Opposing** ideas or tendencies are totally different from each other. *We held opposing points of view.*

opposite /ɒpəzɪt, -sɪt/, **opposites. 1** PREP OR ADV If one thing is **opposite** another, it is facing it. *The hotel is opposite a railway station... Lynn was sitting opposite him.* **2** ADJ The **opposite** side or part of something is the one that is farthest away from you. *...on the opposite side of the street.* **3** ATTRIB ADJ **Opposite** is used to describe things of the same kind which are as different as possible in a particular way. For example, north and south are opposite directions, and winning and losing are opposite results in a game. *I wanted to impress them but probably had the opposite effect... Paul turned and walked in the opposite direction.* **4** COUNT N If two things of the same kind are completely different in a particular way, you can say that one is the **opposite** of the other. *My interpretation was the absolute opposite of Olivier's... My brother is just the opposite. He loves sport.*

opposition /ɒpəzɪʃən/. **1** UNCOUNT N When there is **opposition** to a plan or proposal, people disapprove of it and try to prevent it being carried out. *It was only built after much opposition from the planners.* **2** COLL N The **opposition** refers to the politicians or political parties that form part of a country's parliament but are not in the government. *...the leader of the Opposition... ...two new opposition parties.* **3** COLL N The **opposition** is also the people who are against you in an argument or sports event. *The opposition consisted of chiefs and elders... One player broke through the opposition's defence.*

oppress /əprɛs/, **oppresses, oppressing, oppressed. 1** VB WITH OBJ To **oppress** someone means to treat them cruelly or unfairly. *...institutions that oppress women.* ♦ **oppressed** ADJ *...the sufferings of oppressed people everywhere.* ♦ **oppressor** /əprɛsə/ COUNT N *They didn't have the will to stand up against their foreign oppressors.* **2** VB WITH OBJ If something **oppresses** you, it makes you feel depressed and uncomfortable. *Somehow the room oppressed him.*

oppression /əprɛʃən/. **1** UNCOUNT N **Oppression** is the cruel or unfair treatment of a group of people. *...the oppression of the weak and defenceless.* **2** UNCOUNT N **Oppression** is also a feeling of depression, especially one caused by a place or situation. *Passing the place, my sense of oppression increased.*

oppressive /əprɛsɪv/. **1** ADJ You say that the weather is **oppressive** when it is hot and humid. *...the oppressive heat of the plains.* ♦ **oppressively** SUBMOD *The room was oppressively hot.* **2** ADJ An **oppressive** situation makes you feel depressed or uncomfortable. *The silence became oppressive.* **3** ADJ **Oppressive** laws, societies, and customs treat people cruelly and unfairly. *...an oppressive bureaucracy.*

opt /ɒpt/, **opts, opting, opted.** VB WITH 'for' OR TO-INF If you **opt** for something, you choose it. If you **opt** to do something, you choose to do it. *My father left the choice of career to me, and I opted for law... ...those who opt to cooperate with the regime.*

opt out. PHR VB If you **opt out** of something, you choose not to be involved in it. *He tried to opt out of political decision-making.*

optical /ɒptɪkə^{0}l/. 1 ATTRIB ADJ **Optical** instruments, devices, or processes involve or relate to vision or light. *...an optical microscope.* 2 ATTRIB ADJ **Optical** means relating to the way that things appear to people. *...an optical illusion.*

optician /ɒptɪʃə^{0}n/, **opticians.** COUNT N An **optician** is someone whose job involves testing people's eyesight or providing glasses and contact lenses.

optimism /ɒptɪmɪzə^{0}m/. UNCOUNT N **Optimism** is the feeling of being hopeful about the future. *I felt cheerful and full of optimism.* ♦ **optimist** /ɒptɪmɪst/ COUNT N *I'm an optimist by nature.*

optimistic /ɒptɪmɪstɪk/. ADJ Someone who is **optimistic** is hopeful about the future. *...an optimistic estimate.* ♦ **optimistically** ADV *It might work, she thought optimistically.*

optimum /ɒptɪməm/. ATTRIB ADJ **Optimum** means the best that is possible; a formal use. *The optimum feeding time is around dawn.*

option /ɒpʃə^{0}n/, **options.** 1 COUNT N An **option** is a choice between one or more things. *He had, I would say, two options... ...the option of another referendum.* 2 SING N If you have the **option** to do something, you can choose whether to do it or not. *He was given the option: give them up or lose your job... ...mothers who have no option but to work.*

optional /ɒpʃə^{0}nəl, -ʃənə^{0}l/. ADJ If something is **optional,** you can choose whether or not you do it or have it. *Games are optional at this school.*

opulent /ɒpjə^{4}lənt/. ADJ **Opulent** things look grand and expensive; a formal use. *...the magnificently opulent marble altar.* ♦ **opulence** /ɒpjə^{4}ləns/ UNCOUNT N *His eyes had never beheld such opulence.*

or /ɔː, ə/. 1 CONJ You use **or** to link alternatives. *Do you want your drink up there or do you want to come down for it?... Have you any brothers or sisters?* 2 CONJ **Or** is used to give a second alternative, when the first alternative is introduced by 'either' or 'whether'. *Most aircraft accidents occur at either take-off or landing... He didn't know whether to laugh or cry.* 3 CONJ **Or** is also used between two numbers to indicate that you are giving an approximate amount. *You are supposed to polish your car three or four times a year.* 4 CONJ You also use **or** to introduce a comment which corrects or modifies what you have just said. *The company is paying the rent or at least contributing to it.* 5 CONJ You use **or** when you are telling someone what will happen if they do not follow your instructions or advice. *Don't put anything plastic in the oven or it will probably start melting.* 6 CONJ You can also use **or** to introduce an explanation or justification for what you have just said. *He can't be that bad, can he, or they wouldn't have allowed him home.* 7 **or else:** see **else.** ● **or other:** see **other.** ● **or so:** see **so.**

-or, -ors. SUFFIX **-or** is added to some verbs to form nouns referring to people who do a particular thing. For example, a supervisor is someone who supervises people. Nouns of this kind are sometimes not defined but are treated with the related verbs. *He worked as a translator... ...the conquerors of Peru.*

oral /ɔːrəl/, **orals.** 1 ATTRIB ADJ **Oral** is used to describe things that involve speaking rather than writing. *...an oral test in German.* ♦ **orally** ADV *The candidate will be examined orally.* 2 COUNT N An **oral** is an oral test or examination. *The oral follows a written paper.* 3 ADJ **Oral** medicines are ones that you swallow. *...an oral vaccine.* ♦ **orally** ADV *...a pill taken orally.*

orange /ɒrɪndʒ/, **oranges.** 1 ADJ Something that is **orange** is of a colour between red and yellow. *...an orange silk scarf.* 2 COUNT N An **orange** is a round orange fruit that is juicy and sweet.

orator /ɒrətə/, **orators.** COUNT N An **orator** is someone who is skilled at making speeches; a formal use. *He is a marvellous orator.*

oratory /ɒrətə^{0}ri^1/. UNCOUNT N **Oratory** is the art of making formal speeches; a formal use. *He roused the troops with his oratory.*

orbit /ɔːbɪt/, **orbits, orbiting, orbited.** 1 COUNT N OR UNCOUNT N An **orbit** is the curved path followed by an object going round a planet, a moon, or the sun. *...the orbit of Mercury... How much does it cost to put a satellite into orbit?* 2 VB WITH OR WITHOUT OBJ If something such as a satellite **orbits** a planet, a moon, or the sun, it goes round and round it. *...the first American astronaut to orbit in space.*

orbital /ɔːbɪtə^{0}l/. ATTRIB ADJ An **orbital** road goes all the way round a large city.

orchard /ɔːtʃəd/, **orchards.** COUNT N An **orchard** is an area of land on which fruit trees are grown.

orchestra /ɔːkɪ^{2}strə/, **orchestras.** COUNT N An **orchestra** is a large group of musicians who play a variety of different instruments together.

orchestral /ɔːkestrə^{0}l/. ATTRIB ADJ **Orchestral** means consisting of or relating to the music played by an orchestra. *...Mozart's orchestral pieces.*

orchestrate /ɔːkɪ^{2}streɪt/, **orchestrates, orchestrating, orchestrated.** 1 VB WITH OBJ If you **orchestrate** something, you organize it very carefully in order to produce a particular result or situation. *He personally orchestrated that entire evening.* ♦ **orchestrated** ATTRIB ADJ *...a brilliantly orchestrated campaign of persuasion and protest.* 2 VB WITH OBJ If you **orchestrate** a piece of music, you rewrite it so that it can be played by an orchestra.

orchid /ɔːkɪd/, **orchids.** COUNT N An **orchid** is a plant with beautiful and unusual flowers.

ordain /ɔːdeɪn/, **ordains, ordaining, ordained.** 1 VB WITH OBJ When someone **is ordained,** they are made a member of the clergy in a religious ceremony. *When I was first ordained, I served as a hospital chaplain.* 2 REPORT VB If someone in authority **ordains** something, they order that it shall happen; a formal use. *Lady Sackville ordained complete discretion... The law ordained that she should be executed.*

ordeal /ɔːdiːl/, **ordeals.** COUNT N An **ordeal** is an extremely unpleasant and difficult experience. *He described the rest of his terrible ordeal.*

order /ɔːdə/, **orders, ordering, ordered.** 1 COUNT N If someone in authority gives you an **order,** they tell you to do something. *George went away to carry out this order... An official inquiry was set up on the orders of the Minister of Health.* 2 VB WITH OBJ OR REPORT VB If someone in authority **orders** people to do something or **orders** something to be done, they tell people to do it. *He ordered me to fetch the books... Sherman ordered an investigation into her husband's death... The Captain ordered the ship's masts to be cut down... 'Sit down!' he ordered... The prime minister ordered that they be taken to prison.* 3 COUNT N An **order** is something that you ask to be brought or sent to you, and that you are going to pay for. *A waiter came to take their order... We will continue to deal with overseas orders.* 4 VB WITH OR WITHOUT OBJ When you **order** something that you are going to pay for, you ask for it to be brought or sent to you. *She ordered an extra delivery of coal... I'll order now.* 5 UNCOUNT N If a set of things are arranged or done in a particular **order,** one thing is put first or done first, another thing second, another thing third, and so on. *The names are not in alphabetical order.* 6 UNCOUNT N **Order** is the situation that exists when everything is in the correct place or is done at the correct time. *I felt it would create some order in our lives... Gretchen combed her hair into some sort of order.* 7 UNCOUNT N **Order** is also the situation that exists when people live together peacefully rather than fighting or causing trouble. *...the task of restoring order.* 8 SING N WITH SUPP When people talk about a particular **order,** they mean the way society is organized at a particular time. *They don't accept the existing order.* 9 COUNT N An **order** is also a group of monks or nuns who live according to certain rules. 10 SING N WITH SUPP If you refer to something of a particular **order,** you mean something of a particular quality, amount, or degree; a formal use. *...a thinker of the highest order.*

PHRASES ● If you do something **in order to** achieve a particular thing, you do it because you want to achieve that thing. *He had to hurry in order to reach the next place on his schedule... Rose trod with care, in order not to spread the dirt... They are learning English in order that they can study engineering.* ● If you are **under orders** to do something, you have been told to do it by someone in authority. ● Something that is **on order** at a shop has been asked for but has not yet been supplied. ● If a set of things are done, arranged, or dealt with **in order,** they are done, arranged, or dealt with according to the correct sequence. ● If you **keep order** or **keep** people **in order,** you prevent people from behaving in an excited or violent way. ● A machine or device that is **in working order** is functioning properly and is not broken. *...cars in good working order.* ● A machine or device that is **out of order** is broken and does not work. ● You use **in the order of** or **of the order of** when giving an approximate figure; a formal use. *Britain's contribution is something in the order of 5 per cent.* ● **a tall order:** see **tall.** ● See also **law and order, mail order, postal order, standing order.**

order about or **order around.** PHR VB If you **order** someone **about** or **order** them **around,** you always tell them what to do, in an unsympathetic way.

ordered /ɔːdəd/. ADJ An **ordered** society or system is well organized or arranged. *In Mrs Kaul's house everything was well ordered.*

orderly /ɔːdəli^1/, **orderlies.** 1 ADJ Something that is **orderly** is well organized or arranged. *...a system of orderly government.* ♦ **orderliness** UNCOUNT N *We pride ourselves on the orderliness of our way of life.* 2 COUNT N An **orderly** is an untrained hospital attendant. *I sat at the end of the ward with the orderly.*

ordinal /ɔːdɪnə^{0}l/, **ordinals.** COUNT N An **ordinal** is a number such as 'third' or 'forty-fifth' which tells you what position something has in an ordered group of things.

ordinarily /ɔːdɪ^{1}nerɪli^1/. ADV OR SENTENCE ADV If something **ordinarily** happens, it usually happens. *This room was ordinarily used by the doctor... Ordinarily, of course, we would use the telephone.*

ordinary /ɔːdɪ^{1}nri^1/. 1 ADJ Something that is **ordinary** is not special or different in any way. *...ordinary everyday objects... What do ordinary people really think about universities?... She is likeable enough, but very ordinary.* 2 PHRASE Something that is **out of the ordinary** is unusual or different. *I'd like to bring her something a little out of the ordinary.*

ordination /ɔːdɪneɪʃə^{0}n/, **ordinations.** COUNT N OR UNCOUNT N When someone's **ordination** takes place, they are made a member of the Christian clergy in a special ceremony. *...the ordination of women.*

ore /ɔː/, **ores.** MASS N **Ore** is rock or earth from which metal can be obtained. *...iron ore.*

organ /ɔːgən/, **organs.** 1 COUNT N An **organ** is a part of your body that has a particular purpose or function, for example your heart or your lungs. *Children's bones and organs are very sensitive to radiation.* 2 COUNT N An **organ** is also a large musical instrument with pipes of different lengths through which air is forced. You play the organ rather like a piano. ♦ **organist** /ɔːgənɪst/ COUNT N *He is a very fine organist.* 3 COUNT N WITH SUPP You refer to a newspaper as an **organ** of a particular organization when the organization uses it as a means of giving information or influencing people. *They decided to close the newspaper and launch it again as a government organ.*

organic /ɔːgænɪk/. 1 ADJ Something that is **organic** is produced by or found in plants or animals. *The rocks were carefully searched for organic remains.* 2 ATTRIB ADJ **Organic** gardening or farming uses only natural animal and plant products and does not use artificial fertilizers or pesticides. ♦ **organically** ADV *...organically grown vegetables.*

organisation /ɔːgənaɪzeɪʃə^{0}n/. See **organization.**

organisational /ɔːgənaɪzeɪʃə^{0}nəl, -ʃənə^{0}l/. See **organizational.**

organise /ɔːgənaɪz/. See **organize.**

organism /ɔːgənɪzə^{0}m/, **organisms.** COUNT N An **organism** is an animal or plant, especially one that is so small that you cannot see it without a microscope. *These creatures are descended from simpler organisms like corals.*

organization /ɔːgənaɪzeɪʃə^{0}n/, **organizations;** also spelled **organisation.** 1 COUNT N An **organization** is a group of people who do something together regularly in an organized way. Businesses and clubs are organizations. *...student organizations... ...the World Health Organisation.* 2 UNCOUNT N The **organization** of a system is the way in which its different parts are related and how they work together. *There has been a total change in the organization of society.* 3 UNCOUNT N The **organization** of an activity or public event involves making all the arrangements for it. *I don't want to get involved in the actual organisation of things.*

organizational /ɔːgənaɪzeɪʃə^{0}nəl, -ʃənə^{0}l/; also spelled **organisational.** 1 ATTRIB ADJ **Organizational** means relating to the way that things are planned and arranged. *...an organizational genius named Alfred P. Sloan.* 2 ATTRIB ADJ **Organizational** also means relating to organizations. *The group has no political or organisational links with the terrorists.*

organize /ɔːgənaɪz/, **organizes, organizing, organized;** also spelled **organise.** 1 VB WITH OBJ If you **organize** an activity or event, you make all the arrangements for it. *We organized a concert in the village hall.* ♦ **organizer** COUNT N *...the organizers of the conference.* 2 VB WITH OBJ If you **organize** things, you put them into order. *He's better able now to organise his thoughts... Papers are organized in enormous filing cabinets.* 3 VB When workers or employees **organize,** they form themselves into a group such as a trade union in order to have more power. *Their poverty prevents them from organizing effectively to improve their wages.*

organized /ɔːgənaɪzd/; also spelled **organised.** 1 ATTRIB ADJ **Organized** activities are planned and controlled. *...an organized holiday... ...organized crime.* 2 ADJ People who are **organized** work in an efficient and effective way. *How organised you are!*

orgasm /ɔːgæzə^{0}m/, **orgasms.** COUNT N An **orgasm** is the moment of greatest pleasure and excitement during sexual activity.

orgy /ɔːdʒi^1/, **orgies.** 1 COUNT N An **orgy** is a party in which people behave in a very uncontrolled way. *...a drunken orgy.* 2 COUNT N WITH SUPP You can refer to a period of intense and extreme activity as an **orgy** of that activity. *...an orgy of destruction.*

orient /ɔ:rɪənt/, **orients, orienting, oriented.** REFL VB If you **orient** yourself to a new situation, you learn about it and prepare to deal with it; a formal use. *The raw newcomer has to orient himself.* ● See also **oriented.**

oriental /ɔ:rɪentəl/. ADJ Something that is **oriental** comes from or is associated with eastern and south-eastern Asia. *...Oriental philosophy... ...her oriental features.*

orientate /ɔ:rɪenteɪt/, **orientates, orientating, orientated.** REFL VB When you **orientate** yourself, you discover where you are by looking at a map, or by searching for familiar places or objects.

orientated /ɔ:rɪenteɪtɪd/. ADJ **Orientated** means the same as oriented. *...an industry orientated towards quick, easy profits.*

orientation /ɔ:rɪenteɪʃən/. UNCOUNT N WITH SUPP You can refer to the activities and aims of an organization as its **orientation.** *...the party's revolutionary orientation.*

oriented /ɔ:rɪentɪd/. ADJ You use **oriented** to indicate what someone or something is interested in or concerned with. For example, if someone is politically **oriented,** they are interested in politics. *...a society oriented towards information.*

origin /ɒrɪdʒɪn/, **origins. 1** COUNT N OR UNCOUNT N You can refer to the beginning or cause of something as its **origin** or its **origins.** *The unrest has its origins in economic problems... ...the origin of the universe... ...a word of recent origin.* **2** COUNT N OR UNCOUNT N When you talk about a person's **origin** or **origins,** you are referring to the country, race, or social class of their parents or ancestors. *...a woman of Pakistani origin... His origins were humble.*

original /ərɪdʒɪnəl/, **originals. 1** ATTRIB ADJ You use **original** to refer to the characteristics that something had when it first existed. *They will restore the house to its original state... The original idea came from Dr Ball.* ♦ **originally** ADV *It was originally a toy factory.* **2** COUNT N You refer to a work of art or a document as an **original** when it is genuine and not a copy. *The original is in the British Museum.* Also ADJ *...working on original documents.* **3** ADJ An **original** piece of writing or music was written recently and has not been published or performed before. *...her first collection of short stories, some original, some reprinted.* **4** ADJ If you describe someone, their ideas, or their work as **original,** you mean that they are very imaginative and clever. *...a daring and original idea.* ♦ **originality** /ərɪdʒɪnælɪti/ UNCOUNT N *...a sculptor of genius and great originality.*

originate /ərɪdʒɪneɪt/, **originates, originating, originated.** VB If something **originated** at a particular time or in a particular place, it began to happen or exist at that time or in that place. *These beliefs originated in the 19th century.*

originator /ərɪdʒɪneɪtə/, **originators.** COUNT N The **originator** of something such as an idea or scheme is the person who first thought of it or began it. *The originator of the idea was a young professor.*

ornament /ɔ:nəmənt/, **ornaments. 1** COUNT N An **ornament** is a small object that you display in your home because it is attractive. *...painted china ornaments.* **2** UNCOUNT N **Ornament** refers to decorations and designs on a building or piece of furniture. *...different styles of ornament.*

ornamental /ɔ:nəmentəl/. ADJ Something that is **ornamental** is intended to be attractive rather than useful. *...an ornamental pond.*

ornate /ɔ:neɪt/. ADJ Something that is **ornate** has a lot of decoration on it. *...ornate necklaces.*

ornithology /ɔ:nɪθɒlədʒi/. UNCOUNT N **Ornithology** is the study of birds; a formal use. *I've taken up ornithology.*

orphan /ɔ:fən/, **orphans, orphaned. 1** COUNT N An **orphan** is a child whose parents are dead. *She became an orphan at twelve.* **2** PASSIVE VB If a child **is orphaned,** its parents die. *We adopted the twins when they were orphaned.*

orphanage /ɔ:fənɪdʒ/, **orphanages.** COUNT N An **orphanage** is a place where orphans are looked after.

orthodox /ɔ:θədɒks/. **1** ATTRIB ADJ **Orthodox** beliefs, methods, or systems are the ones that most people have or use. *...orthodox medicine.* **2** ADJ People who are **orthodox** believe in the older and more traditional ideas of their religion or political party. *...Orthodox Jews... ...a fairly orthodox socialist.*

orthodoxy /ɔ:θədɒksi/, **orthodoxies. 1** COUNT N An **orthodoxy** is an accepted view about something. *...the prevailing orthodoxy on this problem.* **2** UNCOUNT N WITH SUPP **Orthodoxy** is traditional and accepted beliefs. *...Islamic orthodoxy... ...Marxist orthodoxy.* **3** UNCOUNT N **Orthodoxy** is the degree to which a person believes in and supports the ideas of their religion or political party. *...the rigid orthodoxy of Mr Mzali.*

oscillate /ɒsɪleɪt/, **oscillates, oscillating, oscillated;** a formal word. **1** VB If something **oscillates,** it moves repeatedly from one position to another and back again. *Its wings oscillate up and down.* **2** VB WITH 'between' If you **oscillate** between two moods, attitudes, or types of behaviour, you keep changing from one to the other and back again. *His mood oscillated between co-operation and aggression.*

ostensible /ɒstensɪbəl/. ATTRIB ADJ **Ostensible** is used to refer to things that seem or are said to be the case, but which you think are probably not the case; a formal use. *...the ostensible purpose of his excursion.* ♦ **ostensibly** ADV *Rose left the room, ostensibly to explain about dinner to the cook.*

ostentation /ɒstenteɪʃən/. UNCOUNT N You say that someone's behaviour is **ostentation** when they do things in order to impress other people with their wealth or importance; a formal use. *More than two telephones is pure ostentation.*

ostentatious /ɒstenteɪʃəs/; a formal word. **1** ADJ Something that is **ostentatious** is very expensive and is intended to impress people. *...a magnificent and ostentatious palace.* **2** ADJ People who are **ostentatious** try to impress other people with their wealth or importance. ♦ **ostentatiously** ADV *They were never ostentatiously dressed.* **3** ADJ An **ostentatious** action is done in an exaggerated way in order to attract people's attention. *...an ostentatious gesture.* ♦ **ostentatiously** ADV *...ostentatiously smiling.*

ostracize /ɒstrəsaɪz/, **ostracizes, ostracizing, ostracized;** also spelled **ostracise.** VB WITH OBJ If you **are ostracized,** people deliberately behave in an unfriendly way towards you and do not allow you to take part in their social activities; a formal use. *Their children were ostracized by teachers and pupils alike.*

ostrich /ɒstrɪtʃ/, **ostriches.** COUNT N An **ostrich** is a large African bird that cannot fly.

other /ʌðə/, **others.** When **other** is used after the determiner 'an', it is written as one word. See **another. 1** ATTRIB ADJ OR PRON **Other** people or things are not the people or things that you have just mentioned or have just been talking about, but are different things. *There were some other people in the compartment... There was no other way to do it... Results in other countries are impressive... Some projects are shorter than others.* **2** ATTRIB ADJ OR PRON When you have mentioned the first of two things, you refer to the second one as the **other** one. *He had his papers in one hand, his hat in the other... They have two daughters, one a baby, the other a girl of twelve.* **3** ATTRIB ADJ OR PLURAL N The **other** people or things in a group are the rest of them. *...the other members of the class... I shall wait until the others come back.* **4** ATTRIB ADJ OR PLURAL N You refer to **other** people or **others** when you are talking about people in general, but not including yourself. *One ought not to inflict one's problems on other people... Working for others can be most fulfilling.* **5** ATTRIB ADJ You use **other** with words such as 'day' or 'week' when you want to say that something happened recently but you are not saying exactly when. *I saw Davis the other day.*

PHRASES ● You use **other than** after a negative in order to introduce an exception to what you have said, or to introduce something that is the only thing possible in the situation. *She never discussed it with anyone other than Derek... There's no choice other than to reopen his case.* ● You use **every other** when talking about the intervals at which something occurs. For example, if something happens **every other** day, it could happen on the 1st, 3rd, 5th, etc of a particular month. *Their local committees are usually held every other month.* ● You say **or other** after words such as 'some', 'something', or 'somehow' in order to show that you are not being precise about the information you are giving. *For some reason or other your name was omitted... Somehow or other, he reached the Alps.* ● You use **one or other** to refer to one or more things or people in a group, when it does not matter which one is thought of or chosen. *One or other current must be altered.* ● **each other:** see **each.** ● **in other words:** see **word.**

otherwise /ʌðəwaɪz/. **1** SENTENCE ADV You use **otherwise** after stating a situation or fact, to say what the result or consequence would be if this situation or fact was not the case. *It's perfectly harmless, otherwise I wouldn't have done it.* **2** SENTENCE ADV OR SUBMOD You use **otherwise** when stating the general condition or quality of something after you have mentioned an exception to this general condition or quality. *The cement is slightly cracked but otherwise in good condition... That was a sudden outbreak in an otherwise blameless career.* **3** ADV **Otherwise** also means in a different way; a formal use. *Stiff and formal, the man was incapable of acting otherwise.*

otter /ɒtə/, **otters.** COUNT N An **otter** is a small animal with a long tail. Otters swim well and eat fish.

ought /ɔ:t/. **1** MODAL If you say that someone **ought** to do something, or **ought** to have done it, you mean that it is the right thing to do, or that it would have been the right thing to do. *She ought to see the doctor... 'I don't care,' he said. 'Well, you ought to,' she said... I ought to have said yes... I ought not to have come here.* **2** MODAL If you say that something **ought** to be true, you mean that you expect it to be true. *It ought to be quite easy... He ought to be out of jail by now.*

oughtn't /ɔ:tənt/. **Oughtn't** is a spoken form of 'ought not'.

ounce /aʊns/, **ounces. 1** COUNT N An **ounce** is a unit of weight equal to approximately 28.35 grams. *...an ounce of tobacco... The baby gains 6 to 8 ounces a week.* ● See also **fluid ounce. 2** SING N You can also refer to a very small amount of a quality or characteristic as an **ounce;** an informal use. *...using every ounce of strength he possessed... ...anyone with an ounce of intelligence.*

our /aʊə/. DET A speaker or writer uses **our** to refer to something that belongs or relates to a group of people which includes himself or herself. *...our children... This could change our lives.*

ours /aʊəz/. PRON A speaker or writer uses **ours** to refer to something that belongs or relates to a group of people which includes himself or herself. *It is a very different country from ours.*

ourselves /aʊəselvz/. **1** REFL PRON A speaker or writer uses **ourselves** as the object of a verb or preposition in a clause where 'we' is the subject or 'us' is a previous object. *We almost made ourselves ill... In 1968 we built ourselves a new surgery.* **2** REFL PRON **Ourselves** is also used to emphasize the subject or object of a clause. *In teaching, we ourselves have to do a lot of learning.* **3** REFL PRON A speaker or writer also uses **ourselves** in expressions such as 'we did it ourselves' in order to say that a group of people which included himself or herself did something without any help or interference from anyone else.

oust /aʊst/, **ousts, ousting, ousted.** VB WITH OBJ If you **oust** someone from a job or a place, you force them to leave it. *...the coup which ousted the President.*

out /aʊt/. **1** ADV When you go **out** of a place or get **out** of something such as a vehicle, you leave it, so that you are no longer inside it. *She rushed out of the house... She's just got out of bed.* **2** ADV If you are **out,** you are not at home or not at your usual place of work. *He came when I was out... Joe is out looking for her.* **3** ADV If you look **out** of a window, you look through it at things that are outside. *She stared out at the rain... I was standing looking out over the view.* **4** ADV You can use **out** to indicate that something is happening outside a building rather than inside it. *Many people were sleeping out... It's hot out.* **5** ADV If you take something **out** of a container or place, you remove it from the container or place. *She opened a box and took out a cigarette... He got out a book and read.* **6** ADV To keep someone or something **out** of a place means to stop them going into it. *It's designed to keep out intruders.* **7** ADV If a light or fire is **out,** it is no longer shining or burning. *The lights went out... He helped to put the fire out.* **8** PRED ADJ If flowers are **out,** their petals have opened. *The daffodils were out.* **9** PRED ADJ If workers are **out,** they are on strike; an informal use. *The men stayed out for nearly a month.* **10** PRED ADJ If you say that a proposal or suggestion is **out,** you mean that it is unacceptable; an informal use. *That's right out, I'm afraid.* **11** PRED ADJ If a particular fashion or method is **out,** it is no longer fashionable; an informal use. *Romance is making a comeback. Reality is out.* **12** ADV When the sea or tide goes **out,** the sea moves away from the shore. **13** PRED ADJ If a calculation or measurement is **out,** it is incorrect. *It's only a couple of degrees out.* **14** PRED ADJ If someone is **out** to do something, they intend to do it; an informal use. *They're out to use your house as a free hotel.* **15** PREP You use **out of** to say what causes someone to do something. For example, if you do something **out of** pity, you do it because you pity someone. *He wrote that review out of pure spite.* **16** PREP If you get pleasure or an advantage **out of** something, you get it because you were involved in that thing. **17** PREP If you are **out of** something, you no longer have any of it. *We're out of paper.* **18** PREP If something is made **out of** a particular material, it is made from it. *You can make petroleum out of coal.*

out-. PREFIX **Out-** is used to form verbs that describe one person doing something better than another. For example, if you can outswim someone, you can swim farther or faster than they can. *She managed to outrun them.*

out-and-out. ATTRIB ADJ You use **out-and-out** to emphasize that someone or something has all the characteristics of a particular type of person or thing. *He's an out-and-out villain... ...an out-and-out triumph.*

outback /aʊtbæk/. SING N The parts of Australia where very few people live are referred to as the **outback.**

outbreak /aʊtbreɪk/, **outbreaks.** COUNT N WITH SUPP An **outbreak** of something unpleasant is a sudden occurrence of it. *...the outbreak of war... ...outbreaks of disease.*

outburst /aʊtbɜːst/, **outbursts. 1** COUNT N An **outburst** is a sudden and strong expression of anger. *I apologize for my outburst just now.* **2** COUNT N WITH SUPP An **outburst** of violent activity is a sudden period of it. *There followed an outburst of shooting.*

outcast /aʊtkɑːst/, **outcasts.** COUNT N An **outcast** is someone who is rejected by a group of people. *They are treated as outcasts.*

outcome /aʊtkʌm/, **outcomes.** COUNT N The **outcome** of an action or process is the result of it. *Nobody dared predict the outcome of the election.*

outcrop /aʊtkrɒp/, **outcrops.** COUNT N An **outcrop** is a large area of rock sticking out of the ground. *...a massive outcrop of granite.*

outcry /aʊtkraɪ/, **outcries.** COUNT N An **outcry** is a strong reaction of disapproval or anger by many people. *The experiments continued, despite the public outcry against them.*

outdated /aʊtdeɪtɪ²d/. ADJ Something that is **outdated** is old-fashioned and no longer useful. *...outdated methods of management.*

outdo /aʊtduː/, **outdoes, outdoing, outdid** /aʊtdɪd/, **outdone** /aʊtdʌn/. VB WITH OBJ If you **outdo** someone, you are more successful than they are at a particular activity. *A heavy person can outdo a lighter one in such jobs.*

outdoor /aʊtdɔː/. ATTRIB ADJ **Outdoor** activities or clothes take place or are used in the open air, rather than in a building. *...outdoor work... He was fully dressed in his outdoor clothes.*

outdoors /aʊtdɔːz/. ADV If something exists or happens **outdoors,** it exists or happens in the open air, rather than in a building. *School classes were held outdoors... Let them go outdoors and play.*

outer /aʊtə/. ATTRIB ADJ The **outer** parts of something are the parts which contain or enclose the other parts, and which are farthest from the centre. *Peel off the outer plastic cover of the flex.*

outermost /aʊtəməʊst/. ATTRIB ADJ The **outermost** thing in a group of things is the one that is farthest from the centre. *...the outermost wall.*

outer space. UNCOUNT N **Outer space** refers to the area outside the Earth's atmosphere.

outfit /aʊtfɪt/, **outfits. 1** COUNT N An **outfit** is a set of clothes. *I can't afford a new evening outfit.* **2** COUNT N You can refer to an organization as an **outfit;** an informal use. *I joined this outfit hoping to go abroad... ...a couple of guys from a security outfit.*

outgoing /aʊtgəʊɪŋ/, **outgoings. 1** ATTRIB ADJ You use **outgoing** to describe someone or something that is leaving a place or position. *...the outgoing president in his last days of office... ...outgoing mail... ...incoming and outgoing passengers.* **2** ADJ An **outgoing** person is very friendly and likes meeting people. *Adler was an outgoing, sociable kind of man.* **3** PLURAL N Your **outgoings** are the amounts of money which you spend. *Try to reduce as many outgoings as possible.*

outgrow /aʊtgrəʊ/, **outgrows, outgrowing, outgrew** /aʊtgruː/, **outgrown** /aʊtgrəʊn/. VB WITH OBJ If you **outgrow** a piece of clothing, you get bigger and can no longer wear it. *Small children outgrow their shoes at a fast rate.*

outhouse /aʊthaʊs/, **outhouses.** COUNT N An **outhouse** is a small building attached to a house or in its garden.

outing /aʊtɪŋ/, **outings.** COUNT N An **outing** is an occasion on which you leave your house, school, or place of work, usually for an enjoyable activity. *...family outings on the River Thames.*

outlast /aʊtlɑːst/, **outlasts, outlasting, outlasted.** VB WITH OBJ If one thing **outlasts** another, it lives or exists longer than the other thing. *Even those trees would outlast him... She had not yet outlasted her usefulness.*

outlaw /aʊtlɔː/, **outlaws, outlawing, outlawed. 1** VB WITH OBJ When something **is outlawed,** it is made illegal. *...legislation which will outlaw this system... The use of poison gas was outlawed.* **2** COUNT N An **outlaw** is a criminal who is hiding from the authorities; an old-fashioned use. *...a band of outlaws.*

outlay /aʊtleɪ/, **outlays.** COUNT N An **outlay** is an amount of money that is invested in a project or business; a formal use. *...an initial outlay for clothing and books... ...a total outlay of £72,550.*

outlet /aʊtlɪ²t/, **outlets. 1** COUNT N An **outlet** is an activity which allows you to express your feelings or ideas. *They can find no outlet for their grievances... Competitiveness can find an outlet in sport.* **2** COUNT N An **outlet** is also a hole or pipe through which water or air can flow away. *...the sewage outlet.*

outline /aʊtlaɪn/, **outlines, outlining, outlined. 1** VB WITH OBJ If you **outline** an idea or plan, you explain it in a general way. *I outlined my reasons.* **2** SING N An **outline** is a general explanation or description of something. *...a brief outline of European art.* **3** VB WITH OBJ You say that an object **is outlined** when you can see its general shape because there is a light behind it. *He was clearly outlined in the light of a lamp.* **4** SING N An **outline** of something is also its general shape, especially when it cannot be clearly seen. *He saw the outline of a house against the sky.*

outlive /aʊtlɪv/, **outlives, outliving, outlived.** VB WITH OBJ If one person or a thing **outlives** another, they are still alive or still exist after the second person or thing has died or no longer exists. *Olivia outlived Pepita by eighteen years... The organization had outlived its usefulness.*

outlook /aʊtlʊk/. **1** UNCOUNT N WITH SUPP Your **outlook** is your general attitude towards life. *My whole outlook had changed... They are European in outlook.* **2** SING N WITH SUPP The **outlook** of a situation is the way it is likely to develop. *The economic outlook is bright.*

outlying /aʊtlaɪɪŋ/. ATTRIB ADJ **Outlying** places are far away from the main cities of a country. *...teachers from outlying villages.*

outmoded /aʊtməʊdɪ²d/. ADJ Something that is **outmoded** is old-fashioned and no longer useful. *...outmoded techniques.*

outnumber /aʊtnʌmbə/, **outnumbers, outnumbering, outnumbered.** VB WITH OBJ If one group of people or things **outnumbers** another, it has more people or things in it than the other group. *The men outnumbered the women by four to one.*

out of date. ADJ Something that is **out of date** is old-fashioned and no longer useful. *It wasn't published until 1972, by which time it was out of date... This is rather an out-of-date concept.*

out of doors. ADV **Out of doors** means outside a building rather than inside it. *Hunting dogs should be kept out of doors... We sat out-of-doors beneath the trees.*

out-of-the-way. ADJ **Out-of-the-way** places are not often visited. *Our expeditions have been to some out-of-the-way places.*

out of work. ADJ Someone who is **out of work** does not have a job. *...out-of-work actors.*

out-patient, out-patients. COUNT N An **out-patient** is someone who receives treatment at a hospital but does not stay there overnight. *The psychiatrists dealt with her as an out-patient... ...an out-patient clinic.*

outpost /aʊtpəʊst/, **outposts.** COUNT N An **outpost** is a small settlement in a foreign country or in a distant area. *...a trading outpost.*

outpouring /aʊtpɔːrɪŋ/, **outpourings. 1** COUNT N WITH SUPP An **outpouring** of something is a large amount of it that is produced very rapidly. *...a prolific outpouring of ideas and energy... ...an outpouring of wild rumours.* **2** PLURAL N WITH SUPP **Outpourings** are strong feelings that are expressed in an uncontrolled way. *...the hysterical outpourings of fanatics.*

output /aʊtpʊt/, **outputs. 1** UNCOUNT N OR COUNT N You use **output** to refer to the amount of something that a person or thing produces. *The party maintains a constant output of pamphlets... Their total industrial output grew at an annual rate of 7%.* **2** UNCOUNT N OR COUNT N The **output** of a computer is the information that it displays on a screen or prints on paper as a result of a particular program.

outrage /aʊtreɪdʒ/, **outrages, outraging, outraged. 1** VB WITH OBJ If something **outrages** you, it makes you extremely shocked and angry. *The idea outraged me... One woman was outraged by this response.* ♦ **outraged** ADJ *...the expression of outraged dignity on his face.* **2** UNCOUNT N **Outrage** is a strong feeling of anger and shock. *Benn shared this sense of outrage.* **3** COUNT N An **outrage** is an act or event which people find very shocking. *There have been more reports of bomb outrages in Falmouth.*

outrageous /aʊtreɪdʒəs/. ADJ If something is **outrageous,** it is very shocking. *She used to say some outrageous things... ...outrageous crimes.* ♦ **outrageously** ADV *He was behaving outrageously.*

outright /aʊtraɪt/. **1** ATTRIB ADJ OR ADV You use **outright** to describe actions and behaviour that are open and direct, rather than indirect. *...an outright refusal... If I ask outright I get nowhere.* **2** ATTRIB ADJ OR ADV **Outright** also means complete and total. *...an outright victory.* ● If someone **is killed outright,** they die immediately.

outset /aʊtset/. PHRASE If something happens **at the outset** of an event, process, or period of time, it happens at the very beginning of it. If something happens **from the outset,** it happens from the beginning onwards. *You should explain this to him at the outset... The police had participated from the outset.*

outside /aʊtsaɪd/, **outsides. 1** COUNT N OR ATTRIB ADJ The **outside** of a container or building is the part which surrounds or encloses the rest of it. *...the outside of the bottle... Examine the property closely from the outside... ...a wooden shed that stood against the outside wall.* **2** ADV, PREP, OR ATTRIB ADJ If you are **outside** a building, place, or country, you are not in it. *Let's go outside... It was dark outside... He's on the landing outside... ...a small village just outside Birmingham... ...an outside lavatory.* **3** ADJ When you talk about the **outside** world, you are referring to things that happen or exist in places other than your own home or community. *They don't want to go out into the outside world.* **4** ATTRIB ADJ On a wide road, the **outside** lanes are the ones which are closest to its centre. **5** PREP OR ATTRIB ADJ People or things that are **outside** a group, range, or organization are not included in it. *The bill was supported by a mass movement outside Parliament... The pipeline was outside his range of responsibility... Since 1974, no outside body has questioned the advice.* **6** PREP Something that happens **outside** a particular period of time does not happen during that time. *You'll have to do it outside office hours.*

outsider /aʊtsaɪdə/, **outsiders.** COUNT N An **outsider** is someone who is not involved in a particular group, or is not accepted by that group. *...an independent committee of seven outsiders... ...the sense of being out of place, of being an outsider.*

outsize /aʊtsaɪz/. ATTRIB ADJ **Outsize** or **outsized** things are much larger than usual. *...a blonde with outsize spectacles... ...an outsized envelope.*

outskirts /aʊtskɜːts/. PLURAL N The **outskirts** of a city or town are the parts that are farthest from its centre. *The garage was on the outskirts of town.*

outspoken /aʊtspəʊkən/. ADJ If you are **outspoken,** you give your opinions about things openly, even if they shock people. *You are younger and more outspoken than they are... ...clear, outspoken statements.*

outstanding /aʊtstændɪŋ/. **1** ADJ If you describe a person or their work as **outstanding,** you mean that they are very good. *She would never be an outstanding actress... His war record was outstanding.* ♦ **outstandingly** SUBMOD *...an outstandingly successful director.* **2** ATTRIB ADJ **Outstanding** also means very obvious or important. *There are significant exceptions, of which oil is the outstanding example.* **3** ADJ Money that is **outstanding** is still owed to someone. *There is fifty pounds outstanding... ...£280 in outstanding fines.*

outstretched /aʊtstretʃt/. ADJ If your arms or hands are **outstretched,** they are stretched out as far as possible. *...balancing himself with outstretched arms... He sat there, hand outstretched in greeting.*

outstrip /aʊtstrɪp/, **outstrips, outstripping, outstripped.** VB WITH OBJ If one thing **outstrips** another, it becomes larger in amount or more successful than the second thing. *His wealth far outstripped Northcliffe's.*

outward /aʊtwəd/, **outwards.** In normal British English, **outwards** is an adverb and **outward** is an adjective. In formal British English and in American English, **outward** is both an adjective and an adverb. **1** ADV If something moves or faces **outwards** or **outward,** it moves or faces away from the place you are in or the place you are talking about. *He swam outwards into the bay... The door opened outwards.* **2** ATTRIB ADJ OR ADV An **outward** journey is a journey that you make away from a place that you are intending to return to later. *It was time to begin the outward trek... Our journey outwards was delayed at the airport.* **3** ATTRIB ADJ The **outward** feelings or qualities are the ones people appear to have, rather than the ones they actually have. *I said it with what I hoped was outward calm.* ♦ **outwardly** ADV *He is seething, but outwardly he remains composed.* **4** ATTRIB ADJ The **outward** features of something are the ones that you can see from the outside. *...the outward and visible signs of the disease.*

outweigh /aʊtweɪ/, **outweighs, outweighing, outweighed.** VB WITH OBJ If you say that the advantages of something **outweigh** the disadvantages, you mean that the advantages are more important than the disadvantages; a formal use. *The benefits from the medicine outweigh the risks of treatment.*

outwit /aʊtwɪt/, **outwits, outwitting, outwitted.** VB WITH OBJ If you **outwit** someone, you cleverly defeat them or gain an advantage over them. *They managed to outwit Bill and get inside.*

outworn /aʊtwɔːn/. ADJ An **outworn** idea or method is old-fashioned and no longer useful; a formal use.

oval /əʊvəˡl/, **ovals.** COUNT N An **oval** is a round shape which is similar to a circle, but is wider in one direction than the other. *...an oval mirror.*

ovary /əʊvəᵊri/, **ovaries.** COUNT N A woman's **ovaries** are the two organs in her body that produce eggs; a technical use.

ovation /əᵘveɪʃəᵊn/, **ovations.** COUNT N An **ovation** is a long burst of applause; a formal use. *...a speech that won him a long, standing ovation.*

oven /ʌvəᵊn/, **ovens.** COUNT N An **oven** is a cooker or part of a cooker that is like a box with a door. You cook food inside an oven.

over /əʊvə/. 1 PREP If one thing is **over** another thing, it is directly above it, either resting on it, or with a space between them. *I had reached the little bridge over the stream... ...the monument over the west door... Leave it to dry over the back of the sofa.* 2 PREP You can also say that one thing is **over** another when the first thing covers the second. *Place a piece of blotting paper over the stain... Students were spraying paint over each other.* 3 PREP If you look or talk **over** an object, you look or talk across the top of it. *The ponies would come and look over the wall... She was watching him over the rim of her cup.* 4 PREP If you look **over** a piece of writing or a group of things, you quickly look at all the writing or all the things. *He ran his eye over one particular paragraph.* 5 PREP If a window has a view **over** a piece of land, you can see the land through the window. *The windows look out over a park.* 6 ADV If you go **over** to a place, you go there. *The doctor walked over to the door... I've got some friends coming over tonight... Liz, come over here.* 7 PREP OR ADV WITH PREP If someone or something goes **over** a boundary of some kind, such as a river or bridge, or if they go **over** an area of land, they cross it and get to the other side. *His pen moved rapidly over the paper... ...on the way back over the Channel... Castle stepped over the dog... They throw their rubbish over the fence into the neighbour's garden.* 8 PREP OR ADV WITH PREP You can use **over** to indicate a particular position or place away from you. *Eastwards over the Severn lie the hills... Mr Stryker was standing over by the window.* 9 ADV OR PREP If you lean **over,** you bend your body in a particular direction. *Pat leaned over and picked it up... He crouched over a typewriter.* 10 ADV If something rolls **over** or is turned **over,** its position changes so that it is facing in another direction. *He flicked over the page... She tipped the pan over.* 11 PREP OR ADV If something is **over** a particular amount or measurement it is more than that amount or measurement. *They paid out over 3 million pounds... ...people aged 80 or over... She did it for over a week.* 12 ADV If an activity is **over** or all **over,** it is completely finished. *Rodin's search was over... Why worry her when it's all over?* 13 PREP If someone has control or influence **over** other people, they are able to control or influence them. *...his authority over them.* 14 PREP You also use **over** to indicate the cause of a disagreement or feeling. *...disagreements over administrative policies... They were always quarrelling over women.* 15 PREP If something happens **over** a period of time, it happens during that time. *He'd had flu over Christmas... ...a process developed over many decades.*

PHRASES • **All over** a place means in every part of it. *I've been all over Austria... They come from all over the world.* • **Over there** means in a place away from you, or in another country. **Over here** means near you, or in the country you are in. *Who's the woman over there?... Are you over here on a trip?* • If you say that something is happening **all over again,** you mean that it is happening again, and that it is tiring, boring, or unpleasant. *The whole thing began all over again.* • If you say that something happened **over and over** or **over and over again,** you mean that it happened many times. *Over and over, the same stories kept cropping up... I read it over and over again.*

over-. PREFIX **Over-** is used to form words that indicate that a quality exists or an action is done to too great an extent. For example, if you say that someone is being over-cautious, you mean that they are being too cautious. *...an over-confident young man... ...the attempt of some shop assistant to overcharge her.*

overall, overalls; pronounced /əʊvərᵊɔːl/ when it is an adjective or adverb and /əʊvərᵊɔːl/ when it is a noun. 1 ATTRIB ADJ You use **overall** to indicate that you are talking about a situation in general or about the whole of something. *...the overall pattern of his life... The overall impression was of a smoky industrial city.* Also SENTENCE ADV *Overall, imports account for half of our stock.* 2 PLURAL N **Overalls** are a piece of clothing that combine trousers and a jacket which you wear over your clothes to protect them while you are working. 3 COUNT N An **overall** is a type of coat that you wear over your clothes to protect them while you are working.

overawe /əʊvərɔː/, **overawes, overawing, overawed.** VB WITH OBJ If you **are overawed** by something, you are very impressed by it and a little afraid of it. *Don't be overawed by what the experts say.*

overbalance /əʊvəbæləns/, **overbalances, overbalancing, overbalanced.** VB If you **overbalance,** you fall over because you are not in a steady position. *He flung an arm in the direction of the church and nearly overbalanced.*

overbearing /əʊvəbeərɪŋ/. ADJ An **overbearing** person tries to make other people do what he or she wants in an unpleasant and forceful way. *...her jealous, overbearing mother-in-law.*

overboard /əʊvəbɔːd/. ADV If you fall **overboard,** you fall over the side of a ship into the water. *He had to hang on to avoid being washed overboard.*

overcame /əʊvəkeɪm/. **Overcame** is the past tense of **overcome.**

overcast /əʊvəkɑːst/. ADJ If it is **overcast,** there are a lot of clouds in the sky. *It was a warm day, but overcast.*

overcoat /əʊvəkəʊt/, **overcoats.** COUNT N An **overcoat** is a thick, warm coat.

overcome /əʊvəkʌm/, **overcomes, overcoming, overcame** /əʊvəkeɪm/. **Overcome** is used in the present tense and is the past participle. 1 VB WITH OBJ If you **overcome** a problem or a feeling, you successfully deal with it or control it. *I was still trying to overcome my fear of the dark... We tried to overcome their objections to the plan.* 2 VB WITH OBJ If you **are overcome** by a feeling, you feel it very strongly. *I was overcome by a sense of failure... He was overcome with astonishment.*

overcrowded /əʊvəkraʊdᵊd/. ADJ If a place is **overcrowded,** there are too many things or people in it. *...overcrowded cities.*

overcrowding /əʊvəkraʊdɪŋ/. UNCOUNT N If there is **overcrowding** in a place, there is not enough room for all the people living there. *There is serious overcrowding in our prisons.*

overdo /əʊvəduː/, **overdoes** /əʊvədʌz/, **overdoing, overdid** /əʊvədɪd/, **overdone** /əʊvədʌn/. 1 VB WITH OBJ If someone **overdoes** something, they behave in an exaggerated way. *Wish them luck, but don't overdo it or they may become suspicious.* 2 VB WITH OBJ If you **overdo** an activity, you try to do more than you can physically manage. *Don't overdo it. It's very hot in the sun.*

overdone /əʊvədʌn/. PRED ADJ If food is **overdone,** it has been cooked for too long.

overdose /əʊvədəʊs/, **overdoses.** COUNT N If someone takes an **overdose,** they take more of a drug than it is safe to do, and may lose consciousness and die. *Alice took an overdose after a row with her mother.*

overdraft /əʊvədrɑːft/, **overdrafts.** COUNT N An **overdraft** is an arrangement with a bank that allows you to spend more money than you have in your account. *She asked for a fifty-pound overdraft.*

overdue /əʊvədjuː/. 1 ADJ If a person, bus, or train is **overdue,** they are late in arriving somewhere. *They're half an hour overdue. I wish they'd come.* 2 ADJ If a change or an event is **overdue,** it should have happened before the present time. *Reform in all these areas is long overdue.* 3 ADJ If something borrowed or due to be paid is **overdue,** it is now later than the date when it should have been returned or paid. *The rent on his apartment was three weeks overdue... ...overdue library books.*

overestimate /əʊvərᵊestɪmeɪt/, **overestimates, overestimating, overestimated.** VB WITH OBJ If you **overestimate** someone or something, you think that they are better, bigger, or more important than they really are. *We greatly overestimated the time this would take... Her confidence drained away and he knew he had overestimated her.*

overflow, overflows, overflowing, overflowed; pronounced /əʊvəfləʊ/ when it is a verb and /əʊvəfləʊ/ when it is a noun. 1 VB OR ERG VB If a liquid or a river **overflows,** it flows over the edges of the container it is in or the place where it is. *He was careful to see that the jar did not overflow... Rivers often overflow their banks.* 2 VB WITH 'with' If something **is overflowing** with things, it is too full of them. *The table was overflowing with clothes.* 3 VB If someone **is overflowing** with a feeling, they are experiencing it very strongly and show this in their behaviour. *...a nurse overflowing with love.* 4 COUNT N An **overflow** is a hole or pipe through which liquid can flow out of a container when it gets too full. *...the sink overflow... ...overflow pipes.*

overgrown /əʊvəgrəʊn/. ADJ If a place is **overgrown,** it is thickly covered with plants because it has not been looked after. *...a large house, overgrown with brambles... ...the overgrown path.*

overhang /əʊvəhæŋ/, **overhangs, overhanging, overhung** /əʊvəhʌŋ/. VB WITH OR WITHOUT OBJ If one thing **overhangs** another, it sticks out sideways above it. *...a tree which overhung the lake... ...the shadow of an overhanging rock... ...wet clothes overhang the tub.*

overhaul /əʊvəhɔːl/, **overhauls, overhauling, overhauled.** 1 VB WITH OBJ If you **overhaul** a piece of equipment, you clean and check it, and repair it if necessary. *The engines were overhauled before our departure.* 2 VB WITH OBJ If you **overhaul** a system or method, you examine it carefully and change it in order to improve it. *The company needs to overhaul its techniques and methods.* Also COUNT N *...a major overhaul of the country's educational system.*

overhead, overheads; pronounced /əʊvəhed/ when it is an adverb, /əʊvəhed/ when it is an adjective, and /əʊvəhedz/ when it is a noun. 1 ADV OR ATTRIB ADJ If something is **overhead,** it is above you or above the place you are talking about. *Seagulls were circling overhead... The guard switched on an overhead light.* 2 PLURAL N The **overheads** of a business are its regular and essential expenses. *...reducing expenditure on overheads.*

overhear /əʊvəhɪə/, **overhears, overhearing, overheard** /əʊvəhɜːd/. VB WITH OBJ If you **overhear** someone, you hear what they are saying when they are not talking to you and do not know that you are listening. *Judy overheard him telling the children about it... I was too far away to overhear their conversation.*

overheat /əʊvəhiːt/, **overheats, overheating, overheated.** ERG VB If a machine **overheats,** it becomes hotter than it should, usually because there is a fault in it. *The appliances might overheat and catch fire.*

overhung /əʊvəhʌŋ/. **Overhung** is the past tense and past participle of **overhang.**

overjoyed /əʊvədʒɔɪd/. PRED ADJ If you are **overjoyed,** you are extremely pleased about something. *Francis was overjoyed to see him... They were overjoyed at this treatment.*

overland /əʊvəlænd/. ADJ OR ADV An **overland** journey is made across land rather than by ship or aeroplane. *You travelled overland to India?*

overlap, overlaps, overlapping, overlapped; pronounced /əʊvəlæp/ when it is a verb and /əʊvəlæp/ when it is a noun. 1 RECIP VB If one thing **overlaps** another, one part of it covers a part of the other thing. *The circles overlap... A quilt must overlap the sides of the bed.* 2 RECIP VB If two ideas or activities **overlap,** they involve some of the same subjects, people, or periods of time. *The two theories obviously overlap... The work of the inspectors overlaps with that of the internal auditors... We worked overlapping shifts so there were always two of us on duty.* Also UNCOUNT N OR COUNT N *There is no overlap between our material and that of Lipset.*

overload /əʊvələʊd/, **overloads, overloading, overloaded.** 1 VB WITH OBJ If a vehicle **is overloaded,** there is not enough room for the things or people in it. *...little boats overloaded with desperate people.* 2 VB WITH OBJ If you **overload** an electrical system, you use too many appliances and damage it. *Your fuse has blown because you have overloaded the circuit.* 3 VB WITH OBJ If you **overload** someone with work or problems, you give them more than they can manage. *Medical services were overloaded with casualties.*

overlook /əʊvəlʊk/, **overlooks, overlooking, overlooked.** 1 VB WITH OBJ If a building or window **overlooks** a place, you can see the place from the building or window. *...a room which overlooked the garden.* 2 VB WITH OBJ If you **overlook** a fact or problem, you ignore it, do not notice it, or do not realize its importance. *They overlook the enormous risks involved.* 3 VB WITH OBJ If you **overlook** someone's faults or bad behaviour, you forgive them and do not criticize them.

overnight /əʊvənaɪt/. 1 ADV OR ATTRIB ADJ **Overnight** means during all of the night. *Soak the raisins overnight in water... ...an overnight stay.* 2 ATTRIB ADJ **Overnight** cases or clothes are ones that you take when you go and stay somewhere for one or two nights. *He packed a little overnight bag.* 3 ADV You say that something happens **overnight** when it happens quickly and unexpectedly. *The colonel became a hero overnight... You can't expect these problems to be solved overnight.*

overpopulation /əʊvəpɒpjəˈleɪʃəᵊn/. UNCOUNT N If there is **overpopulation** in a place, there are too many people living there. *...poverty and overpopulation.*

overpower /əʊvəpaʊə/, **overpowers, overpowering, overpowered.** 1 VB WITH OBJ If you **overpower** someone, you seize them despite their struggles because you are stronger than they are. *They easily overpowered her and dragged her inside.* 2 VB WITH OBJ If an emotion or sensation **overpowers** you, it affects you very strongly. *Occasionally this desire overpowers me and leads me to be cruel.* ♦ **overpowering** ADJ *...an overpowering feeling of failure.*

overran /əʊvəræn/. **Overran** is the past tense of **overrun.**

overrate /əʊvəreɪt/, **overrates, overrating, overrated.** VB WITH OBJ If you **overrate** something, you think it is better or more important than it really is. *They overrate the extent of political freedom in England.* ♦ **overrated** ADJ *They feel that maths is somewhat overrated as a school subject.*

override /əʊvəraɪd/, **overrides, overriding, overrode** /əʊvərəʊd/, **overridden** /əʊvərɪdən/. 1 VB WITH OBJ If something **overrides** other things, it is more important than these things. *The day-to-day struggle for survival overrode all other things.* 2 VB WITH OBJ If you **override** a person or their decisions, you cancel their decisions because you have more authority than they have. *Will they dare override what the people decide?*

overriding /əʊvəraɪdɪŋ/. ATTRIB ADJ **Overriding** means more important than anything else. *The overriding need in the world is to promote peace.*

overrule /əʊvəruːl/, **overrules, overruling, overruled.** VB WITH OBJ If someone in authority **overrules** a person or their decisions, they officially decide that their decisions are incorrect or not valid. *The judgement was overruled by the Supreme Court... Frank was overruled by the planners in Berlin.*

overrun /əʊvərʌn/, **overruns, overrunning, overran** /əʊvəræn/. **Overrun** is used in the present tense and is the past participle. 1 VB WITH OBJ If an army **overruns** a country, it succeeds in occupying it quickly. *The north was overrun by the advancing troops.* 2 VB WITH OBJ If a place **is overrun** with animals or plants, there are too many of them there. *The city is overrun by rodents.* 3 VB WITH OR WITHOUT OBJ If an event or meeting **overruns,** it continues for a longer time than it should have. *I think we've overrun our time, haven't we?*

oversaw /əʊvəsɔː/. **Oversaw** is the past tense of **oversee.**

overseas /əʊvəsiːz/. 1 ATTRIB ADJ OR ADV You use **overseas** to describe things that happen or exist in countries that you must cross the sea to get to. *There is a vast overseas market for our goods... Roughly 4 million Americans travel overseas each year.* 2 ATTRIB ADJ An **overseas** student or visitor comes from a foreign country that you must cross the sea to get to.

oversee /əʊvəsiː/, **oversees, overseeing, oversaw** /əʊvəsɔː/, **overseen** /əʊvəsiːn/. VB WITH OBJ If someone in authority **oversees** a job or an activity, they make sure that it is done properly. *We need a guy to oversee our operations in Guyana.*

overshadow /əʊvəʃædəʊ/, **overshadows, overshadowing, overshadowed.** 1 VB WITH OBJ If a building, tree, or large structure **overshadows** another, it stands near it and is taller than it. *...the elm trees overshadowing the school.* 2 VB WITH OBJ To **be overshadowed** by someone or something means to be less successful, important, or impressive than them. *She was sometimes overshadowed by the more talkative members.*

overshoot /əʊvəʃuːt/, **overshoots, overshooting, overshot** /əʊvəʃɒt/. VB WITH OR WITHOUT OBJ If you **overshoot** a place that you want to get to, you go past it by mistake. *Natalie's glider overshot the landing zone and crashed into a field.*

oversight /əʊvəsaɪt/, **oversights.** COUNT N OR UNCOUNT N An **oversight** is something which you should have done but did not. *My oversight was in not remembering to inform the authorities.*

oversimplify /əʊvəsɪmplɪfaɪ/, **oversimplifies, oversimplifying, oversimplified.** VB WITH OBJ If you **oversimplify** something, you explain it so simply that what you say is no longer true or reasonable. *We may have oversimplified the discussion by ignoring this.* ♦ **oversimplified** ADJ *...an oversimplified view of the world.*

oversize /əʊvəsaɪz/. ADJ **Oversize** or **oversized** things are too big, or bigger than usual. *...a girl in an oversize pair of slacks... ...an oversized tent.*

oversleep /əʊvəsliːp/, **oversleeps, oversleeping, overslept** /əʊvəslept/. VB If you **oversleep,** you sleep longer than you intended to. *Some mornings I oversleep and miss breakfast.*

overstate /əʊvəsteɪt/, **overstates, overstating, overstated.** VB WITH OBJ If you **overstate** something, you describe it in a way that exaggerates its importance or a quality that it has. *Its effect on history cannot be overstated.*

overstep /əʊvəstep/, **oversteps, overstepping, overstepped.** PHRASE If you **overstep the mark,** you behave in an unacceptable way. *Last week he overstepped the mark and there will be trouble.*

overt /əʊvɜːt/. ADJ An **overt** action or attitude is done or shown in an open and obvious way. *...overt hostility... ...overt acts of violence.* ♦ **overtly** ADV *His jokes got more overtly malicious.*

overtake /əʊvəteɪk/, **overtakes, overtaking, overtook** /əʊvətʊk/, **overtaken** /əʊvəteɪkən/. 1 VB WITH OR WITHOUT OBJ If you **overtake** a moving vehicle or person, you pass them because you are moving faster than they are. *The truck had overtaken us... ...people waiting to overtake.* 2 VB WITH OBJ If an event **overtakes** you, it happens unexpectedly or suddenly. *...all the changes that have overtaken Shetland recently.*

overthrow, overthrows, overthrowing, overthrew /əʊvəθruː/, **overthrown** /əʊvəθrəʊn/; **overthrow** is pronounced /əʊvəθrəʊ/ when it is a verb and /əʊvəθrəʊ/ when it is a noun. 1 VB WITH OBJ When a government or a leader **is overthrown,** they are removed by force. *He was arrested for attempting to overthrow the regime.* Also COUNT N *...the overthrow of the dictator.* 2 VB WITH OBJ If an idea, value or standard **is overthrown,** it is replaced by another one. *Laws are openly violated, standards of behaviour are overthrown.*

overtime /əʊvətaɪm/. UNCOUNT N **Overtime** is time that you spend at your job in addition to your normal working hours. *He had been putting in overtime whenever he could.*

overtone /əʊvətəʊn/, **overtones.** COUNT N If something has **overtones** of a quality, it has a small amount of that quality but does not openly express it. *The play has heavy political overtones... ...a pleasure that carried no overtones of fear.*

overtook /əʊvətʊk/. **Overtook** is the past tense of **overtake.**

overture /əʊvətjʊə/, **overtures.** 1 COUNT N An **overture** is a piece of music used as the introduction to an opera or play. *...Elgar's 'Cockaigne' Overture.* 2 PLURAL N If you make **overtures** to someone, you behave in a friendly or romantic way towards them. *Mrs Thorne had made overtures of friendship... He feared they would reject his overtures.*

overturn /əʊvətɜːn/, **overturns, overturning, overturned.** 1 ERG VB If something **overturns** or if you **overturn** it, it turns upside down or on its side. *She overturned the chairs and hurled the cushions about... His car crashed into a tree and overturned.* 2 VB WITH OBJ If someone with more authority than you **overturns** your decision, they change it. *If they persist in their attitude he can't overturn their decision.* 3 VB WITH OBJ To **overturn** a government or system means to remove or destroy it. *The unrest might have overturned the military rulers.*

overview /əʊvəvjuː/, **overviews.** COUNT N An **overview** of a situation is a general understanding or description of it. *...a short report giving a useful overview of recent developments.*

overweight /əʊvəweɪt/. ADJ Someone who is **overweight** is too fat. *Nearly half the people in this country are overweight... ...an overweight schoolgirl.*

overwhelm /əʊvəwelm/, **overwhelms, overwhelming, overwhelmed.** 1 VB WITH OBJ If you **are overwhelmed** by a feeling or event, it affects you very strongly. *He was overwhelmed by the intensity of her love... The horror of it all had overwhelmed me.* 2 VB WITH OBJ If a group of people **overwhelm** a place or another group, they gain control of them. *Their mission was to seize the bridges and overwhelm the garrison.*

overwhelming /əʊvəwelmɪŋ/. 1 ADJ Something that is **overwhelming** affects you very strongly. *...an overwhelming sense of powerlessness.* ♦ **overwhelmingly** ADV *They had been overwhelmingly appreciative.* 2 ADJ You can use **overwhelming** to emphasize that one part of something is much greater than the rest of it. *An overwhelming majority of people are in favour of this plan.* ♦ **overwhelmingly** SUBMOD *It is still an overwhelmingly rural country.*

overwork /əʊvəwɜːk/, **overworks, overworking, overworked.** 1 ERG VB If you **are overworking** or **are overworked,** you are working too hard. *You look tired. Have you been overworking?... They were overworked and poorly paid.* Also UNCOUNT N *...a body made weak through undernourishment and overwork.* 2 VB WITH OBJ If you **overwork** something, you use it too much. *Farmers have overworked the soil.* ♦ **overworked** ADJ *'Crisis' has become one of the most overworked words of modern politics.*

overwrought /əʊvərɔːt/. ADJ Someone who is **overwrought** is upset and uncontrolled in their behaviour.

owe /əʊ/, **owes, owing, owed.** 1 VB WITH OBJ OR VB WITH OBJ AND OBJ If you **owe** money to someone, they have lent it to you and you have not yet paid it back. *I still owe you seven pounds... I paid Gower what I owed him.* 2 VB WITH OBJ AND PREP 'to' If you **owe** a quality or ability to someone or something, they are responsible for your having it. *She owed her technique entirely to his teaching.* 3 VB WITH OBJ AND OBJ OR VB WITH OBJ AND PREP 'to' If you say that you **owe** gratitude, respect, or loyalty to someone, you mean that they deserve it from you; a formal use. *We owe you our thanks, Dr Marlowe... Neither he nor Melanie owe me any explanation.* 4 PREP You use **owing to** to introduce the reason for something. *I missed my flight owing to a traffic hold-up.*

owl /aʊl/, **owls.** COUNT N An **owl** is a bird with large eyes which hunts small animals at night.

own /əʊn/, **owns, owning, owned.** 1 ATTRIB ADJ You use **own** to emphasize that something belongs to or is typical of the person or thing mentioned. *She'd killed her own children... Each city has its own peculiarities.* Also PRON *His background was similar to my own.* 2 ADJ You also use **own** to emphasize that someone does something without any help. *They are expected to make their own beds.* Also PRON *I said 'What about lunch?' and he said, 'Oh, get your own.'* 3 VB WITH OBJ If you **own** something, it is your property. *...a huge old house owned by an Irish doctor.*

PHRASES ● When you are **on your own,** you are alone. *She lived on her own... ...sitting on his own.* ● If you do something **on your own,** you do it without any help. *We want to write a book on our own.* ● If you **get** your **own back,** you harm or trick someone who has harmed or tricked you; an informal use. *At last he was getting his own back.* ● **to hold your own:** see **hold.**

own up. PHR VB If you **own up** to something wrong that you have done, you admit that you did it. *They don't want to own up to this.*

owner /əʊnə/, **owners.** COUNT N The **owner** of something is the person to whom it belongs. *The average car owner drives 10,000 miles per year.*

ownership /əʊnəʃɪp/. UNCOUNT N **Ownership** is the state of owning something. *...public ownership of land... ...the desire for home ownership.*

ox /ɒks/, **oxen** /ɒksən/. COUNT N An **ox** is a castrated bull. *...a plough pulled by two oxen.*

oxygen /ɒksɪdʒən/. UNCOUNT N **Oxygen** is a colourless gas in the air which is needed by all living things.

oyster /ɔɪstə/, **oysters.** COUNT N An **oyster** is a large, flat shellfish. Some oysters can be eaten and others produce pearls.

oz. oz is a written abbreviation for 'ounce' or 'ounces'.

ozone /əʊzəʊn/. UNCOUNT N **Ozone** is a form of oxygen. There is a layer of ozone high above the earth's surface.

Pp

p /piː/. 1 **p** is an abbreviation for 'pence' or 'penny'. *It's only 10p... ...a 50p piece.* 2 You write **p.** in front of a number as an abbreviation for 'page'. The plural form is 'pp.' *See p. 72... ...Tables I and II on pp. 40-43.*

pace /peɪs/, **paces, pacing, paced.** 1 UNCOUNT N The **pace** of something is the speed at which it happens or is done. *...the pace of change... The sale resumed at a brisk pace.* 2 SING N Your **pace** is the speed at which you walk. *He proceeds at a leisurely pace... He quickened his pace.* 3 COUNT N A **pace** is the distance you move when you take one step. *He took two quick paces forward... He stopped when he was a few paces away.* 4 VB WITH OBJ OR ADJUNCT If you **pace** up and down, you keep walking up and down, because you are anxious or impatient. *Harold paced nervously up and down the platform... She paced the room angrily.*

PHRASES ● To **keep pace** with something that is changing means to change quickly in response to it. *Earnings have not kept pace with inflation.* ● If you do something **at your own pace,** you do it at a speed that is comfortable for you.

pacifism /pæsɪfɪzəm/. UNCOUNT N **Pacifism** is the belief that war and violence are always wrong. ♦ **pacifist** /pæsɪfɪst/ COUNT N *I was accused of being a pacifist.*

pacify /pæsɪfaɪ/, **pacifies, pacifying, pacified.** VB WITH OBJ If you **pacify** someone who is angry or upset, you succeed in making them calm. *The manager was trying hard to pacify our clients.*

pack /pæk/, **packs, packing, packed.** 1 VB WITH OR WITHOUT OBJ When you **pack,** you put your belongings into a bag, because you are leaving. *He went into the bedroom to pack... He packed his bags and left.* ♦ **packing** UNCOUNT N *Have you started your packing?* 2 VB WITH OBJ When goods **are packed,** they are put into containers or parcels so that they can be transported. *...the wooden boxes in which the eggs were packed.* 3 ERG VB If people or things **are packed** into a place, there are so many of them that the place is full. *About 300 of us were packed into a half-built mansion... Thirty thousand people packed into the stadium to hear him.* 4 COUNT N A **pack** is a rucksack. *He pulled a plastic bag out of his pack.* 5 COUNT N A **pack** of things is a packet of them; an American use. *...a pack of* *cigarettes.* 6 COUNT N A **pack** of playing cards is a complete set of them. 7 COUNT N A **pack** of wolves or dogs is a group of them hunting together. 8 See also **packed, packing case.**

pack in. PHR VB If you **pack** something **in,** you stop doing it; an informal British use. *It's a good job. I don't think he'd pack it in.*

pack off. PHR VB If you **pack** someone **off** somewhere, you send them there; an informal use. *They pack their sons off to boarding school.*

pack up. PHR VB If you **pack up** your belongings, you put them in a case or bag, because you are leaving. *We packed up the things I had accumulated... Once term finishes we all pack up and go home.*

package /pækɪdʒ/, **packages, packaging, packaged.** 1 COUNT N A **package** is a small parcel. *...a small package wrapped in tissue paper.* 2 VB WITH OBJ When something **is packaged,** it is put into packets to be sold. *The cereal is packaged in plain boxes.* 3 COUNT N WITH SUPP A **package** is also a set of proposals that must be accepted or rejected as a whole. *...the announcement of a fresh package of spending cuts... They offered a package worth sixty million dollars.*

package holiday, package holidays. COUNT N A **package holiday** or a **package tour** is a holiday arranged by a travel company in which your travel and accommodation are booked for you.

packaging /pækɪdʒɪŋ/. UNCOUNT N The paper or box that something is sold in is called its **packaging.**

packed /pækt/. 1 ADJ A **packed** place is very crowded. *The theatre was packed... ...a packed courtroom.* 2 PRED ADJ Something that is **packed** with things contains a very large number of them. *The book is packed full of information.*

packet /pækɪt/, **packets.** 1 COUNT N A **packet** is a small box, bag, or envelope in which a quantity of something is sold. *Check the washing instructions on the packet.* 2 COUNT N You can use **packet** to refer to a packet and its contents, or to the contents only. *...a packet of cigarettes... ...a packet of crisps.*

packing case, packing cases. COUNT N A **packing case** is a large wooden box in which things are stored or taken somewhere.

pact /pækt/, **pacts.** COUNT N A **pact** is a formal agreement between two or more governments to do a particular thing or to help each other. *A pact was signed banning all military activity.*

pad /pæd/, **pads.** 1 COUNT N A **pad** is a thick, flat piece of a material such as cloth or foam rubber. Pads are used, for example, to clean things or for protection. *...a cotton wool pad soaked in antiseptic... Elbow pads and knee pads are essential on a skateboard.* 2 COUNT N A **pad** is also a number of pieces of paper fixed together along one side, so that each piece can be torn off when it has been used. *He took a pad and pencil from his pocket.* 3 COUNT N A helicopter **pad** is an area of flat, hard ground where helicopters can land and take off. 4 COUNT N A cat's or dog's **pads** are the soft parts on the bottom of its paws.

padded /pædɪ^{2}d/. ADJ Something that is **padded** has soft material on it or inside it which makes it less hard, protects it, or gives it a different shape. *The steering wheel is padded with real leather.*

padding /pædɪŋ/. UNCOUNT N **Padding** is soft material on the outside or inside of something which makes it less hard, protects it, or gives it a different shape. *...a jacket with padding at the shoulders.*

paddle /pædə^{0}l/, **paddles, paddling, paddled.** 1 COUNT N A **paddle** is a short pole with a wide, flat part at one end or at both ends, which you use as an oar to move a small boat through water. 2 VB When people **paddle,** they walk or stand in shallow water at the edge of the sea, for pleasure. *It was too cold for paddling.*

paddock /pædək/, **paddocks.** 1 COUNT N A **paddock** is a small field where horses are kept. 2 COUNT N At a race course, the **paddock** is the place where the horses walk about before each race.

paddy /pædi^1/, **paddies.** COUNT N A **paddy** or **paddy field** is a flooded field that is used for growing rice.

padlock /pædlɒk/, **padlocks.** COUNT N A **padlock** is a lock with a U-shaped bar attached to it. One end of this bar is released when the padlock is unlocked.

paediatrician /piːdɪətrɪʃə^{0}n/, **paediatricians;** also spelled **pediatrician.** COUNT N A **paediatrician** is a doctor who specializes in treating sick children.

pagan /peɪgə^{0}n/, **pagans.** 1 ADJ **Pagan** is used to describe religious beliefs and practices that do not belong to any of the main religions of the world. *...an ancient pagan festival... ...pagan gods.* 2 COUNT N A **pagan** is a person who has pagan beliefs or takes part in pagan practices.

page /peɪdʒ/, **pages.** 1 COUNT N A **page** is a side of one of the pieces of paper in a book, magazine, or newspaper. *The story appeared on the front page of the Daily Mail... For details of pensions, see page 16.* 2 COUNT N The **pages** of a book, magazine, or newspaper are the pieces of paper it consists of.

pageant /pædʒənt/, **pageants.** COUNT N A **pageant** is a show, often performed out of doors, which is made up of historical or literary scenes.

pageantry /pædʒəntri^1/. UNCOUNT N You can refer to grand and colourful ceremonies as **pageantry.** *The week was crammed with festivities and pageantry.*

paid /peɪd/. 1 **Paid** is the past tense and past participle of **pay.** 2 ADJ If you are well **paid,** you receive a lot of money for your work. If you are badly **paid,** you do not receive much money for it. *Secretaries are pretty well paid these days... ...low paid jobs.* 3 ATTRIB ADJ If you have **paid** holiday, you receive your pay even when you are on holiday.

pail /peɪl/, **pails.** COUNT N A **pail** is a bucket made of metal or wood; an old-fashioned use.

pain /peɪn/, **pains, paining, pained.** 1 UNCOUNT N OR COUNT N **Pain** is an unpleasant feeling in a part of your body caused by illness or an injury. *He was in pain... She complained of severe pains in her chest.* 2 UNCOUNT N **Pain** is also the unhappiness that you feel when something very upsetting happens. *...the pain of realizing that she had failed.* 3 VB WITH OBJ If something **pains** you, it makes you feel upset or unhappy. *It pained him that his father talked like that.*

PHRASES ● If you say that someone is **a pain or a pain in the neck,** you mean they are very annoying or irritating; an informal use. ● If you **take pains** to do something, you try hard to do it successfully. *She took great pains to conceal this from her parents... She always took great pains with her make-up.*

pained /peɪnd/. ADJ Someone who looks or sounds **pained** seems upset or offended. *She raised her eyebrows and looked pained... ...a pained expression.*

painful /peɪnfʊl/. 1 ADJ If a part of your body is **painful,** it hurts. *My back is so painful that I cannot stand upright any more.* 2 ADJ You say that things are **painful** when they cause you physical pain. *My boots are still painful... ...a long and painful illness.* ♦ **painfully** ADV *She struck him, quite painfully, with the ruler.* 3 ADJ A **painful** experience is upsetting or difficult. *...the painful process of growing up... It was painful to admit that I was wrong.* ♦ **painfully** SUBMOD *I was always painfully aware of my shortcomings.*

painless /peɪnlɪ^{2}s/. 1 ADJ When something is **painless,** it does not cause physical pain. *...painless childbirth.* ♦ **painlessly** ADV *My tooth came out quite painlessly.* 2 ADJ A **painless** way of achieving something does not involve much trouble. *...the painless way to learn German.* ♦ **painlessly** ADV *Industrialization in western countries was achieved painlessly.*

painstaking /peɪnsteɪkɪŋ/. ADJ Someone who is **painstaking** does things extremely thoroughly. *The picture had been cleaned with painstaking care.* ♦ **painstakingly** ADV *He painstakingly records details of every race.*

paint /peɪnt/, **paints, painting, painted.** 1 MASS N **Paint** is a coloured liquid that you put on a wall or other surface with a brush. *...a tin of pink paint... ...non-drip paints.* 2 MASS N **Paint** is also a coloured liquid or thick paste used to make a picture. *...tubes of oil paint.* 3 VB WITH OR WITHOUT OBJ When you **paint** something or **paint** a picture of it, you make a picture of it using paint. *Whistler painted his mother in a rocking chair... Hopper painted in a 'realist' style.* 4 VB WITH OBJ When you **paint** a wall or other surface, you cover it with paint. *The rooms were painted green.*

paintbrush /peɪntbrʌʃ/, **paintbrushes.** COUNT N A **paintbrush** is a brush which you use for putting paint onto something.

painter /peɪntə/, **painters.** 1 COUNT N A **painter** is an artist who paints pictures. *...a landscape painter.* 2 COUNT N A **painter** is also someone whose job is painting parts of buildings.

painting /peɪntɪŋ/, **paintings.** 1 COUNT N A **painting** is a picture produced using paint. *...a painting of a horse.* 2 UNCOUNT N **Painting** is the activity of painting pictures. *...the unique nature of Elizabethan painting.*

paintwork /peɪntwɜːk/. UNCOUNT N The **paintwork** of a building or vehicle is the paint on it. *Use warm water and detergent to wash paintwork.*

pair /pɛə/, **pairs, pairing, paired.** 1 COUNT N You refer to two things as a **pair** when they are the same size and shape and are intended to be used together. *...a pair of boots... Dragonflies have two pairs of wings.* 2 COUNT N You also use **pair** when you are referring to certain objects which have two main parts of the same size and shape. *...a pair of trousers... ...a pair of scissors.* 3 COLL N You can refer to two people as a **pair** when they are standing or walking together or when they have some kind of relationship with each other. *They'd always been a devoted pair.* 4 See also **au pair.**

pair off. PHR VB When people **pair off** or **are paired off,** they become grouped in pairs. *People are paired off according to their level of competence.*

pajamas /pədʒɑːməz/. See **pyjamas.**

pal /pæl/, **pals.** COUNT N Your **pal** is your friend; an old-fashioned, informal use. *Is he a pal of yours?*

palace /pælɪs/, **palaces.** COUNT N A **palace** is a very large, grand house, especially one which is the home of a king, queen, or president. *...Buckingham Palace.*

palatable /pælətəbə^{0}l/; a formal word. 1 ADJ If you describe food or drink as **palatable,** you mean that it tastes quite pleasant. *The food looked quite palatable.* 2 ADJ If you describe something such as an idea as **palatable,** you mean that it is easy to accept. *The truth is not always palatable.*

palate /pælə^{1}t/, **palates.** 1 COUNT N Your **palate** is the top part of the inside of your mouth. 2 COUNT N You can also refer to someone's ability to judge good food and wine as their **palate.** *All that junk food must have ruined my palate.*

palatial /pəleɪʃə^{0}l/. ADJ If a house is **palatial,** it is large and splendid.

pale /peɪl/, **paler, palest.** 1 ADJ Something that is **pale** is not strong or bright in colour. *He had on a pale blue shirt... The house is built of pale stone.* 2 ADJ If someone looks **pale,** their face is a lighter colour than usual, because they are ill, frightened, or shocked. *You look awfully pale: are you all right?* ♦ **paleness** UNCOUNT N *Symptoms are unusual paleness and tiredness.*

pall /pɔːl/, **palls, palling, palled.** 1 VB If something **palls,** it becomes less interesting or less enjoyable. *George's jokes were beginning to pall.* 2 COUNT N WITH SUPP A **pall** of smoke is a thick cloud of it; a literary use. *A pall of smoke hung over the entire area.*

pallid /pælɪd/. ADJ **Pallid** means unnaturally pale; a literary use. *...his pallid face.*

pallor /pælə/. SING N Someone's **pallor** is an unhealthy paleness in their face; a literary use. *I was struck by her pallor.*

palm /pɑːm/, **palms.** 1 COUNT N A **palm** or **palm tree** is a tree with long leaves at the top and no branches. Palms grow in hot countries. *He sat in the shade beneath the palms.* 2 COUNT N WITH POSS The **palm** of your hand is the flat surface which your fingers can bend towards. *She placed the money in his palm.*

palpable /pælpəbə^{0}l/. ADJ Something that is **palpable** is very obvious; a formal use. *...a palpable lie.*

paltry /pɔːltri^1/. ATTRIB ADJ A **paltry** sum of money is surprisingly small; a literary use. *The deal cost him a paltry £100.*

pamper /pæmpə/, **pampers, pampering, pampered.** VB WITH OBJ If you **pamper** someone, you treat them too kindly and do too much for them. *His mother pampered him.*

pamphlet /pæmflɪ^{2}t/, **pamphlets.** COUNT N A **pamphlet** is a very thin book with a paper cover, which gives information about something.

pan /pæn/, **pans.** COUNT N A **pan** is a round metal container with a long handle, which is used for cooking things, usually on top of a cooker.

panacea /pænəsɪə/, **panaceas.** COUNT N A **panacea** is something that is supposed to be a cure for any problem or illness. *...an obsession with technology as a panacea for life's ills.*

panache /pənæʃ, -nɑːʃ/. UNCOUNT N If you do something with **panache,** you do it in a confident and stylish way. *He made his final speech with more panache than ever before.*

pancake /pænkeɪk/, **pancakes.** COUNT N A **pancake** is a thin, flat, circular piece of cooked batter. Pancakes are usually folded and eaten hot with a sweet or savoury filling.

panda /pændə/, **pandas.** COUNT N A **panda** or **giant panda** is a large animal with black and white fur which lives in China.

pandemonium /pændə'məʊnɪəm/. UNCOUNT N If there is **pandemonium** in a place, the people there are behaving in a confused and noisy way. *When the spectators heard about this, pandemonium broke loose.*

pander /pændə/, **panders, pandering, pandered.** VB WITH PREP 'to' If you **pander** to someone, you do everything they want; used showing disapproval. *They pander to their children's slightest whim.*

pane /peɪn/, **panes.** COUNT N A **pane** is a flat sheet of glass in a window or door.

panel /pænə^{0}l/, **panels.** 1 COLL N A **panel** is a small group of people who are chosen to do something, for example to discuss something in public or to make a decision. *...questions answered by a panel of experts.* 2 COUNT N A **panel** is also a flat, rectangular piece of wood or other material that forms part of a larger object such as a door. *There were glass panels in the front door.* 3 COUNT N WITH SUPP A control **panel** or instrument **panel** is a board containing switches and controls. *The instrument panel is just forward of the wheel.*

panelled /pænə^{0}ld/; spelled **paneled** in American English. ADJ A **panelled** room has decorative wooden panels covering its walls. *His office was panelled in dark wood.*

panelling /pænə^{0}lɪŋ/; spelled **paneling** in American English. UNCOUNT N **Panelling** consists of boards or strips of wood covering a wall inside a building.

pang /pæŋ/, **pangs.** COUNT N WITH SUPP A **pang** is a sudden, strong feeling, for example of sadness or pain. *She felt a sudden pang of regret... ...hunger pangs.*

panic /pænɪk/, **panics, panicking, panicked.** 1 UNCOUNT N **Panic** is a strong feeling of anxiety or fear that makes you act without thinking carefully. *Sandy was close to panic.* 2 COUNT N A **panic** is a situation in which there is panic. *We don't want to start a panic.* 3 VB If you **panic,** you become anxious or afraid, and act without thinking carefully. *She panicked as his hand closed on her wrist.*

panic-stricken. ADJ Someone who is **panic-stricken** is so anxious or afraid that they are acting without thinking carefully. *...a panic-stricken crowd.*

panorama /pænərɑːmə/, **panoramas.** COUNT N A **panorama** is a view in which you can see a long way over a wide area of land. *...every bend in the road revealing fresh panoramas of empty beaches.* ♦ **panoramic** /pænəræmɪk/ ADJ *...a panoramic view.*

pant /pænt/, **pants, panting, panted.** 1 PLURAL N **Pants** are a piece of underwear with two holes to put your legs through and elastic around the top. *...a pair of pants.* 2 PLURAL N In America, trousers are referred to as **pants.** *He fumbled in his pants pocket for his whistle.* 3 VB If you **pant,** you breathe quickly and loudly, because you have been doing something energetic. *We lugged the branch along, panting and puffing.*

panther /pænθə/, **panthers.** COUNT N A **panther** is a large wild animal that belongs to the cat family. Panthers are usually black.

panties /pæntɪz/. PLURAL N **Panties** are pants worn by women or girls.

pantomime /pæntə^{6}maɪm/, **pantomimes.** COUNT N A **pantomime** is a funny musical play for children. Pantomimes are usually performed at Christmas.

pantry /pæntri^1/, **pantries.** COUNT N A **pantry** is a small room where food is kept.

papal /peɪpə^{0}l/. ATTRIB ADJ **Papal** is used to describe things relating to the Pope. *...a papal election.*

paper /peɪpə/, **papers, papering, papered.** 1 UNCOUNT N OR MOD **Paper** is a material that you write on or wrap things with. The pages of this book are made of paper. *Rudolph picked up the piece of paper and gave it to her... ...a paper bag.* 2 COUNT N A **paper** is a newspaper. *I read about the riots in the papers.* 3 PLURAL N **Papers** are sheets of paper with information on them. *He consulted the papers on his knee.* 4 PLURAL N Your **papers** are your official documents, for example your passport or identity card. *One of the men had no papers.* 5 COUNT N A **paper** is also part of a written examination. *He failed the history paper.* 6 COUNT N A **paper** is also a long essay on an academic subject. *...a paper on linguistics and literary criticism.* 7 PHRASE If you put your thoughts down **on paper,** you write them down. *He had put his suggestions down on paper.* 8 VB WITH OBJ If you **paper** a wall, you put wallpaper on it. *The lounge was papered and painted.*

paperback /peɪpəbæk/, **paperbacks.** COUNT N A **paperback** is a book with a paper cover. *From then on he read only paperbacks.* ● If a book is available **in paperback,** you can buy a paperback copy of it.

paper clip, paper clips. COUNT N A **paper clip** is a small piece of bent wire used to fasten papers together.

paperweight /peɪpəweɪt/, **paperweights.** COUNT N A **paperweight** is a small, heavy object placed on papers to prevent them from being blown away.

paperwork /peɪpəwɜːk/. UNCOUNT N **Paperwork** is the routine part of a job which involves dealing with letters, reports, and records.

par /pɑː/. PHRASE If one thing is **on a par** with another, the two things are equally good or equally bad. *Forcing a child to learn is on a par with forcing a man to adopt a religion.*

parable /pærəbə^{0}l/, **parables.** COUNT N A **parable** is a short story which makes a moral or religious point.

parachute /pærəʃuːt/, **parachutes.** COUNT N A **parachute** is a device which enables you to float to the ground from an aircraft. It consists of a large circle of thin cloth attached to your body by strings.

parade /pəreɪd/, **parades, parading, paraded.** 1 COUNT N A **parade** is a line of people or vehicles moving together, for example through the streets of a town, to celebrate a special event. *When the war was over there was a parade in London.* 2 ERG VB WITH ADJUNCT When people **parade,** they march or walk together in a formal group. *The army paraded round the square... The captured criminals were paraded in chains through the streets.* 3 PHRASE When soldiers are **on parade,** they are standing or marching together on a formal occasion. 4 VB WITH OBJ If you **parade** something, you show it to people in order to impress them. *She seldom paraded this knowledge.*

paradise /pærədaɪs/. 1 PROPER N According to some religions, **Paradise** is a wonderful place where good people go after they die. 2 UNCOUNT N OR SING N You can refer to a place or situation that seems perfect as **paradise.** *'That must have been interesting.'—'For me it was paradise.'... ...the palm-fringed paradise of Mauritius.*

paradox /pærədɒks/, **paradoxes.** COUNT N You describe a situation as a **paradox** when it involves two facts which you would not expect to be both true. *It was crowded and yet at the same time peaceful. This was a paradox she often remarked on.*

paradoxical /pærədɒksɪkə^{0}l/. ADJ A **paradoxical** situation involves two facts which you would not expect to be both true. *It's paradoxical that the loneliest people live in the most crowded places.* ♦ **paradoxically** /pærədɒksɪkə^{0}li^1/ SENTENCE ADV *Paradoxically, he represented both escape and safety.*

paraffin /pærəfɪn/. UNCOUNT N **Paraffin** is a strong-smelling liquid which is used as a fuel in heaters and lamps.

paragon /pærəgə^{0}n/, **paragons.** COUNT N If you describe someone as a **paragon,** you mean that their behaviour is perfect. *He was a paragon of honesty.*

paragraph /pærəgrɑːf/, **paragraphs.** COUNT N A **paragraph** is a section of a piece of writing. A paragraph always begins on a new line.

parallel /pærəlel/, **parallels, paralleling, paralleled;** also spelled **parallelling, parallelled** in British English. 1 COUNT N A **parallel** is something that is very similar to something else, but exists or happens in a different place or at a different time. *It is not difficult to find a living parallel for these prehistoric creatures... ...a book which has no parallel in the English language.* 2 COUNT N If there are **parallels** between two things, they are similar in some ways. *There are curious parallels between medicine and law... His career and attitudes have interesting parallels with Potter's.* 3 VB WITH OBJ If something **parallels** something else, it is as good as that thing, or it is similar to it. *...computers with intellects paralleling Man's.* 4 ADJ If two lines or two long objects are **parallel,** they are the same distance apart all along their length. *The boys were marching in two parallel lines... Vanderhoff Street ran parallel to Broadway.*

paralyse /pærəlaɪz/, **paralyses, paralysing, paralysed;** spelled **paralyze** in American English. 1 VB WITH OBJ If something **paralyses** you, it causes you to have no feeling in your body, and to be unable to move. *A stroke paralysed half his face.* ♦ **paralysed** ADJ *...a person paralysed from the neck down.* 2 VB WITH OBJ If people, places, or organizations are **paralysed** by something, they are unable to act or function properly. *Great cities are paralysed by strikes and power failures.*

paralysis /pərælə^{1}sɪs/. UNCOUNT N **Paralysis** is the loss of feeling in your body and the inability to move. *One drop of this poison would be enough to induce paralysis and blindness.*

parameter /pəræmə^{1}tə/, **parameters.** COUNT N **Parameters** are factors or limits which affect the way something can be done or made; a formal use. *It is necessary to be aware of all the parameters that have a bearing on the design process.*

paramilitary /pærəmɪlɪtə^{0}ri^1/. ATTRIB ADJ A **paramilitary** organization behaves like an army but is not the official army of a country. *...a paramilitary terrorist group.*

paramount /pærəmaʊnt/. ADJ Something that is **paramount** is more important than anything else. *The interests of the child are paramount.*

paranoia /pærənɔɪə/. UNCOUNT N Someone who suffers from **paranoia** wrongly believes that other people are trying to harm them.

paranoid /pærənɔɪd/. ADJ **Paranoid** people are suspicious, distrustful, and afraid of other people. *You're getting paranoid.*

parapet /pærəpɪ^{2}t/, **parapets.** COUNT N A **parapet** is a low wall along the edge of a bridge, roof, or balcony.

paraphernalia /pærəfəneɪlɪə/. UNCOUNT N You can refer to a large number of belongings or pieces of equipment as **paraphernalia.** *The girls gathered together their hockey sticks, satchels, and other paraphernalia.*

paraphrase /pærəfreɪz/, **paraphrases, paraphrasing, paraphrased.** 1 COUNT N A **paraphrase** of something written or spoken is the same thing expressed in a different way. *This article was a close paraphrase of Dixon's own original article.* 2 VB WITH OBJ If you **paraphrase** someone, you express what they have said or written in a different way. *We must, to paraphrase Socrates, bring out the knowledge that people have inside them.*

parasite /pærəsaɪt/, **parasites.** 1 COUNT N A **parasite** is a small animal or plant that lives on or inside a larger animal or plant. ♦ **parasitic** /pærəsɪtɪk/ ADJ *...tiny parasitic insects.* 2 COUNT N If you call someone a **parasite,** you mean that they get money or other things from people without doing anything in return.

parasol /pærəsɒl/, **parasols.** COUNT N A **parasol** is an umbrella that provides shade from the sun.

paratroops /pærətruːps/. The form **paratroop** is used before a noun. PLURAL N **Paratroops** are soldiers who are dropped by parachute. *...elite paratroops in their red berets... ...paratroop attacks.*

parcel /pɑːsə^{0}l/, **parcels.** COUNT N A **parcel** is something wrapped in paper. *He started undoing a little parcel tied with string... Charities sent parcels of clothes.* ● **part and parcel:** see **part.**

parched /pɑːtʃt/. 1 ADJ If the ground is **parched,** it is very dry, because there has been no rain. *...the parched plains of India.* 2 ADJ If your mouth, throat, or lips are **parched,** they are unpleasantly dry. 3 PRED ADJ If you are **parched,** you are very thirsty; an informal use.

parchment /pɑːtʃmə^{2}nt/. UNCOUNT N In former times, **parchment** was the skin of a sheep or goat used for writing on.

pardon /pɑːdə^{0}n/, **pardons, pardoning, pardoned.** 1 CONVENTION You say **'Pardon?'** when you want someone to repeat what they have just said. *'How old is she?'—'Pardon?'—'I said how old is she?'* 2 CONVENTION You say **'I beg your pardon'** to apologize for making a mistake. *It is treated in the sentence as a noun—I beg your pardon—as an adjective.* 3 VB WITH OBJ If you **pardon** someone, you forgive them for something bad they have done, or do not punish them. *I hope that poor fellow may be pardoned for whatever crime he has committed.*

parent /peərənt/, **parents.** COUNT N Your **parents** are your father and mother. *Her parents are well-off... ...the bond between parents and children.* ♦ **parental** /pərentə^{0}l/ ATTRIB ADJ *...lack of parental control.*

parenthood /peərənthʊd/. UNCOUNT N **Parenthood** is the state of being a parent. *...the responsibility of parenthood.*

parish /pærɪʃ/, **parishes.** 1 COUNT N OR MOD A **parish** is the area served by an Anglican or Catholic church. *...the parish of St Mark's, Sambourne Fishley... ...the parish church.* 2 COUNT N OR MOD A **parish** is also a small country area with its own elected council. *Stroud parish has a population of 20,000... ...a parish councillor.*

parishioner /pərɪʃənə/, **parishioners.** COUNT N A clergyman's **parishioners** are the people in his parish.

parity /pærɪ^{1}ti^1/. UNCOUNT N If there is **parity** between two things, they are equal; a formal use. *...the theoretical parity in powers between the two Houses of Parliament.*

park /pɑːk/, **parks, parking, parked.** 1 COUNT N A **park** is a public area of land with grass and trees where people go to relax and enjoy themselves. *She took her children for a walk in the park... ...Hyde Park.* 2 COUNT N In Britain, a **park** is also a private area of grass and trees around a large country house. 3 VB WITH OR WITHOUT OBJ When you **park** a vehicle, you drive it into a position where it can be left. *She parked in front of the library.* ♦ **parked** ADJ *We could see the lights of a parked car.* 4 See also **car park, national park.**

parking lot, parking lots. COUNT N A **parking lot** is the same as a car park; an American use.

parkland /pɑːklə^{3}nd/. UNCOUNT N **Parkland** is land with grass and trees on it, especially around a country house. *...twenty-five acres of parkland.*

parliament /pɑːlə^{1}mə^{2}nt/, **parliaments.** COUNT N OR UNCOUNT N The **parliament** of a country is the group of people who make or change its laws. *...the creation of Welsh and Scottish parliaments... He was the second farm-worker to get into Parliament.* ● See also **Member of Parliament.**

parliamentary /pɑːlə^{1}mentə^{0}ri^1/. ATTRIB ADJ **Parliamentary** means relating to the parliament of a country. *...the start of each parliamentary session.*

parlour /pɑːlə/, **parlours;** spelled **parlor** in American English. COUNT N A **parlour** is a sitting-room; an old-fashioned use.

parochial /pə^{3}rəʊkɪəl/. ADJ Someone who is **parochial** is too concerned with their own local affairs and interests. *This is a narrow and parochial view.*

parody /pærədi^1/, **parodies.** COUNT N OR UNCOUNT N A **parody** is an amusing imitation of the style of an author or of a familiar situation. *...a parody of American life... ...real modern verse, not parody.*

parole /pərəʊl/. UNCOUNT N When prisoners are given **parole,** they are released before their sentence is due to end, on condition that they behave well. ● Prisoners who are **on parole** have been given parole.

paroxysm /pærəksɪzə^{0}m/, **paroxysms.** COUNT N WITH 'of' A **paroxysm** of anger or jealousy is a very strong feeling of it. *In a sudden paroxysm of rage, Wilt hurled the vase across the room.*

parquet /pɑːkeɪ/. UNCOUNT N OR MOD **Parquet** is a floor covering made of small rectangular blocks of wood fitted together. *...the highly polished parquet floor.*

parrot /pærət/, **parrots, parroting, parroted.** 1 COUNT N A **parrot** is a tropical bird with a curved beak and brightly-coloured or grey feathers. Parrots can be kept as pets and sometimes copy what people say. 2 VB WITH OBJ If you **parrot** what someone else has said, you repeat it without really understanding what it means. 3 PHRASE If you repeat something **parrot fashion,** you do it accurately but without really understanding what it means.

parry /pæri^1/, **parries, parrying, parried.** 1 VB WITH OBJ OR 'with' If you **parry** an argument or question, you cleverly avoid dealing with it or answering it. *He parried the arguments put to him by saying that he could not comment until the report was published... Instead of answering he parried with another question.* 2 VB WITH OR WITHOUT OBJ If you **parry** a blow, you push aside your attacker's arm or weapon so that you are not hurt.

parsley /pɑːsli^1/. UNCOUNT N **Parsley** is a small plant with curly leaves used for flavouring or decorating savoury food.

parsnip /pɑːsnɪp/, **parsnips.** COUNT N OR UNCOUNT N A **parsnip** is a long, thick, pale cream vegetable that grows under the ground.

parson /pɑːsə^{0}n/, **parsons.** COUNT N A **parson** is a vicar or other clergyman; an old-fashioned use.

part /pɑːt/, **parts, parting, parted.** 1 COUNT N OR UNCOUNT N If one thing is a **part** of another thing or **part** of it, the first thing is one of the pieces, sections, or elements that the second thing consists of. *The head is the most sensitive part of the body... I don't know this part of London very well... The first part of that statement is a lie... Economic measures must form part of any solution to this crisis.* 2 COUNT N A **part** in a play or film is one of the roles in it. *She plays the part of the witch.* 3 SING N Your **part** in something that happens is your involvement in it. *He was arrested for his part in the demonstrations.* 4 ERG VB If things which are touching **part** or **are parted,** they move away from each other. *Ralph's lips parted in a delighted smile... Rudolph parted the curtains.* 5 VB WITH OBJ If your hair **is parted,** it is combed in two different directions so that there is a straight line across your head. 6 RECIP VB When two people **part,** they leave each other; a formal use. *A year ago they had parted for ever... I parted from them on excellent terms.* 7 See also **parting, partly.**

PHRASES ● If you **take part** in an activity, you are one of the people involved in it. *I asked her if she'd take part in a discussion about the uprising.* ● If you **play a** large or important **part** in something, you are very involved in it and have an important effect on what happens. *Men should play a bigger part in children's upbringing.* ● You can refer to what someone feels or does as a feeling or action **on** their **part;** a formal use. *I consider this a gross oversight on your part.* ● **For the most part** means mostly. *The forest is, for the most part, dark and wet.* ● **In part** means partly. *The improvement was brought about in part by the Trade Union Movement.* ● If you say that one thing is **part and parcel** of another, you are emphasizing that it is involved or included in it. *These things are part and parcel of my everyday life.* ● If something happened for **the best part** or **the better part** of a period of time, it happened for most of that time. *The men stayed for the best part of a year.*

part with. PHR VB If you **part with** something that you would prefer to keep, you give it or sell it to someone else. *She didn't want to part with the money.*

partial /pɑːʃə^{0}l/. 1 ADJ A **partial** thing, state, or quality is not complete or whole. *I could give it only partial support... ...a partial solution.* 2 PRED ADJ If you are **partial** to something, you like it very much; an old-fashioned use. *The vicar is very partial to roast pheasant.*

partially /pɑːʃə^{0}li^1/. ADV **Partially** means to some extent, but not completely. *...a horse partially hidden by the trees.*

participant /pɑːtɪsɪpənt/, **participants.** COUNT N Someone who is a **participant** in an activity takes part in it. *She was a willing participant in these campaigns.*

participate /pɑːtɪsɪpeɪt/, **participates, participating, participated.** VB If you **participate** in an activity, you take part in it. *We asked high school students to participate in an anti-drugs campaign.* ♦ **participation** /pɑːtɪsɪpeɪʃə^{0}n/ UNCOUNT N *The success of the festival depended upon the participation of the whole community.*

participle /pɑːtɪsɪpə^{0}l/, **participles.** COUNT N In grammar, a **participle** is a form of a verb that can be used in compound tenses of the verb. English verbs have a past participle, which usually ends in '-ed', and a present participle, which ends in '-ing'.

particle /pɑːtɪkə^{0}l/, **particles.** COUNT N A **particle** of something is a very small piece or amount of it. *...particles of metal... ...food particles.*

particular /pətɪkjə^{4}lə/, **particulars.** 1 ATTRIB ADJ If you refer to a **particular** thing, you are referring only to that thing, rather than to other things of that type. *Let me ask you about one particular artist... She wasn't, at that particular moment, watching the cat at all.* 2 ATTRIB ADJ If a person or thing has a **particular** quality or possession, it belongs only to them. *It is important to discuss a child's particular problems and interests... Each species has its own particular place on the reef.* 3 PHRASE You use **in particular** to indicate that what you are saying applies especially to one thing or person. *Joan Greenwood in particular I thought was wonderful... ...Africans, and in particular African women.* 4 ATTRIB ADJ You can use **particular** to emphasize that something is greater or more intense than usual. *The shortage of airfields gave particular concern.* 5 PLURAL N **Particulars** are facts or details; a formal use. *Renshaw jotted down a few particulars in his notebook.* 6 PRED ADJ Someone who is **particular** has very high standards and is not easily satisfied. *They're quite particular about their personnel.*

particularly /pətɪkjə^{4}ləli^1/. 1 ADV You use **particularly** to indicate that what you are saying applies especially to one thing or situation. *It was hard for children, particularly when they were ill... He was challenged by the workers, particularly Gibson.* 2 SUBMOD **Particularly** also means more than usually or normally. *She was looking particularly attractive today... This is not particularly difficult to do.*

parting /pɑːtɪŋ/, **partings.** 1 UNCOUNT N OR COUNT N **Parting** is an occasion when one person leaves another. *She felt unable to bear the strain of parting... George said no more until their final parting.* 2 COUNT N The **parting** in someone's hair is the line running along their head where their hair has been combed in opposite directions.

partisan /pɑːtɪzæn/, **partisans.** 1 ADJ Someone who is **partisan** strongly supports a particular person or cause; a formal use. *There are real dangers in a partisan Civil Service.* 2 COUNT N Someone who is a **partisan** of someone else supports them; a formal use. *He was a partisan of General Jackson.* 3 COUNT N **Partisans** are people who get together to fight enemy soldiers who are occupying their country. *...those who fought in the hills as partisans.*

partition /pɑːtɪʃə^{0}n/, **partitions, partitioning, partitioned.** 1 COUNT N A **partition** is a wall or screen separating one part of a room or vehicle from another. *David tapped on the glass partition and the car stopped.* 2 VB WITH OBJ If you **partition** a room, you separate one part of it from another by means of a partition. *They had partitioned the inside into offices.* 3 VB WITH OBJ To **partition** a country means to divide it into two or more independent countries. *One plan involved partitioning the country.* Also UNCOUNT N *...the partition of India in 1947.*

partly /pɑːtli^1/. ADV **Partly** means to some extent, but not completely. *The brass handles are partly obscured by white paint... This is partly a political and partly a legal question.*

partner /pɑːtnə/, **partners.** 1 COUNT N Your **partner** is the person you are married to or are having a sexual relationship with. *A marriage is likely to last if you and your partner are similar in personality.* 2 COUNT N Your **partner** in a game or dance is the person you are playing or dancing with. 3 COUNT N The **partners** in a business are the people who share the ownership of it. *She was a partner in a firm of solicitors.*

partnership /pɑːtnəʃɪp/, **partnerships.** UNCOUNT N OR COUNT N **Partnership** is a relationship in which two or more people or organizations work together in an equal and co-operative way. *Our aim is to establish a working partnership with the teachers.*

part of speech, parts of speech. COUNT N A **part of speech** is a grammatical class of word, for example noun, adjective, or verb.

partridge /pɑːtrɪdʒ/, **partridges.** COUNT N A **partridge** is a wild bird with a round body and a short tail.

part-time. ADJ If someone is a **part-time** worker or has a **part-time** job, they work for only a part of each day or week. *We employ five part-time receptionists.* Also ADV *40 per cent of women work part-time.*

party /pɑːti^1/, **parties.** 1 COUNT N A **party** is a social event at which people enjoy themselves doing things such as eating, drinking, dancing, talking, or playing games. *...a birthday party... They gave a farewell party for her.* ● See also **garden party.** 2 COUNT N A political **party** is an organization that tries to get its members elected to government. *He's a member of the Labour Party.* 3 COUNT N A **party** of people is a group of them doing something together, for example travelling. *...a party of Americans on a tour... ...rescue parties.* 4 COUNT N WITH SUPP One of the people involved in a legal agreement or dispute can be referred to as a particular **party;** a formal use. *...the guilty party.* ● See also **third party.** 5 PHRASE If you **are a party to** an action or agreement, you are involved in it, and are therefore partly responsible for it. *They wouldn't be a party to such a ridiculous enterprise.*

pass /pɑːs/, **passes, passing, passed.** 1 VB WITH OR WITHOUT OBJ To **pass** someone or something means to go past them. *We passed the New Hotel... Please let us pass... I was just passing by and I saw your car.* 2 VB WITH ADJUNCT To **pass** in a particular direction means to move or go in that direction. *They passed through an arched gateway... The pipe passed under the city sewer.* 3 VB WITH OBJ AND ADJUNCT If you **pass** something such as a rope through, over, or round something, you put one end of it through, over, or round that thing. *Pass the string under the hook.* 4 VB WITH OBJ OR VB WITH OBJ AND OBJ If you **pass** an object to someone, you give it to them. *Pass the sugar, please... She passed me her glass.* 5 VB WITH PREP 'to' If something **passes** from one person to another, the second person then has it instead of the first. *Her property passes to her next of kin.* 6 VB When a period of time **passes,** it happens and finishes. *The time seems to have passed so quickly... The crisis passed.* 7 VB WITH OBJ AND ADJUNCT OR -ING If you **pass** a period of time in a particular way, you spend it in that way. *Men pass their lives farming their small plots of land.* 8 VB WITH OBJ OR ERG VB If someone or something **passes** a test or **is passed,** they are considered to be of an acceptable standard. *I passed my driving test in Holland... You have to get 120 marks out of 200 to pass... This drug has been passed by the US Food and Drug Administration.* 9 VB WITH OBJ When people in authority **pass** a new law or a proposal, they formally agree to it or approve it. *Many of the laws passed by Parliament are never enforced.* 10 PHRASE When a judge **passes sentence** on someone, he or she says what their punishment will be. 11 VB WITH 'for' OR 'as' To **pass** for or as a particular thing means to be accepted as that thing, in spite of not having all the right qualities. *...that brief period that passes for summer in those regions... A strip of space 4 feet wide passed as a kitchen.* 12 VB WITH ADJUNCT OR ADJ If something **passes** without comment or reaction or **passes** unnoticed, nobody comments on it, reacts to it, or notices it. *Social change was so slow that it passed unnoticed.* 13 COUNT N A **pass** in an examination or test is a successful result in it. *She got a grade A pass in physics.* 14 COUNT N A **pass** is also a document that allows you to do something. *I have a pass to go from New York to East Hampton.* 15 COUNT N A **pass** in a mountainous area is a narrow way between two mountains. *...the Khyber Pass.* 16 **to pass judgement:** see **judgement.** ● **to pass the time:** see **time.** ● **to pass water:** see **water.** ● See also **passing.**

pass around. PHR VB See **pass round.**

pass away. PHR VB If someone has **passed away,** they have died; an old-fashioned use.

pass off. PHR VB If you **pass** one thing **off** as another, you convince people that it is that other thing. *The man who made the cabinet passed it off as an antique.*

pass on. PHR VB If you **pass on** something that you have been given, you give it to someone else. *He handed a sheet to Lee to pass on to me.*

pass out. PHR VB If you **pass out,** you faint or collapse.

pass over. PHR VB If you **pass over** a topic in a conversation, you do not discuss it. *He passed over the events of that week.*

pass round or **pass around.** PHR VB If a group of people **pass** something **round** or **pass it around,** they each take it and then give it to the next person. *Pass the matches round.*

pass up. PHR VB If you **pass up** an opportunity, you do not take advantage of it. *I wouldn't have passed up the chance for a million dollars.*

passable /pɑːsəbə^{0}l/. 1 ADJ Something that is **passable** is satisfactory in quality. *...some passable small restaurants.* 2 PRED ADJ If a road or path is **passable,** it is not completely blocked. *Many of these roads are not passable in bad weather.*

passage /pæsɪdʒ/, **passages.** 1 COUNT N A **passage** is a long, narrow space between walls or fences connecting one room or place with another. *At the end of the narrow passage was a bathroom... We went along a little passage to the garden.* 2 COUNT N A **passage** in a book, speech, or piece of music is a section of it. *The flute and oboe have long solo passages.* 3 UNCOUNT N The **passage** of someone or something is their movement or progress from one place or stage to another. *The wind of the train's passage ruffled his hair... ...the moment of passage from one state to the next.* 4 COUNT N A **passage** is also a journey by ship. *The passage across to Belfast was very rough.*

passageway /pæsɪdʒweɪ/, **passageways.** COUNT N A **passageway** is a long, narrow space between walls or fences connecting one room or place with another.

passenger /pæsɪndʒə/, **passengers.** COUNT N A **passenger** is a person who is travelling in a vehicle, aircraft, or ship but is not controlling it. *The ferry service handles 400 passengers a week.*

passer-by /pɑːsə baɪ/, **passers-by.** COUNT N A **passer-by** is a person who is walking past someone or something. *One of the boys stopped a passer-by and asked him to phone an ambulance.*

passing /pɑːsɪŋ/. 1 ATTRIB ADJ **Passing** feelings, activities, or fashions last for only a short period of time. *...the passing whims of her mother.* 2 PHRASE If you mention something **in passing,** you mention it briefly while you are talking or writing about something else. *We can note, in passing, the rapid expansion of private security organisations.*

passion /pæʃən/, **passions.** 1 UNCOUNT N OR PLURAL N **Passion** is a very strong emotional feeling, often of sexual attraction. *I felt such extraordinary passion for this girl... ...their attempt to arouse nationalistic passions.* 2 COUNT N WITH SUPP If you have a **passion** for something, you like it very much. *She had developed a passion for gardens... Biology is their great passion.*

passionate /pæʃənə^{1}t/. ADJ A **passionate** person has very strong feelings. *...a passionate social reformer... ...passionate love.* ♦ **passionately** ADV *People care deeply and passionately about this issue.*

passive /pæsɪv/, **passives.** 1 ADJ Someone who is **passive** does not react or show their feelings when things are said or done to them. *She was so enraged that she could remain passive no longer.* ♦ **passively** ADV *They accept passively every law that is passed.* 2 COUNT N In grammar, the **passive** consists of a verb group made up of the auxiliary verb 'be' and the past participle of a main verb. For example, in 'She was asked to wait', the verb 'ask' is in the passive.

Passover /pɑːsəʊvə/. UNCOUNT N **Passover** is a Jewish festival that begins in late March or early April and lasts for eight days.

passport /pɑːspɔːt/, **passports.** 1 COUNT N A **passport** is an official document containing your name, photograph, and personal details, which you need to show when you enter or leave a country. *My husband has a British passport.* 2 COUNT N WITH SUPP If you say that something is a **passport** to something that you want, you mean that it enables you to get it. *The right contacts were the only passports to success.*

password /pɑːswɜːd/, **passwords.** COUNT N A **password** is a secret word or phrase that enables you to enter a place or use a computer system.

past /pɑːst/. 1 SING N The **past** is the period of time before the present, and the things that happened in that period. *He was highly praised in the past as head of the National Security Agency... ...the traditional values of the past... He never discussed his past.* 2 ATTRIB ADJ You use **past** to describe things that happened or existed before the present time. *He refused to answer questions about his past business dealings... They criticised past Governments for spending £3,500m on military aid.* 3 ATTRIB ADJ You use **past** to describe a period of time immediately before the present time. *I've spent the past eight years at sea.* 4 PREP OR ADV You use **past** when you are telling the time. For example, if it is twenty **past** six, it is twenty minutes after six o'clock. *It's ten past eleven... It's quarter past.* 5 PREP OR ADV If you go **past** something, you go near it and then continue moving in a straight line until you are away from it. *He drove straight past me... People ran past laughing.* 6 PREP If something is **past** a place, it is situated on the other side of it. *Past Doctor Ford's surgery was the grocer's.* 7 PHRASE If you say that someone is **past it,** you mean that they no longer have the skill or energy to do something; an informal use.

pasta /pæstə/. UNCOUNT N **Pasta** is a type of food made from a mixture of flour, eggs, and water that is formed into different shapes. Spaghetti and macaroni are types of pasta.

paste /peɪst/, **pastes, pasting, pasted.** 1 UNCOUNT N OR COUNT N **Paste** is a soft, often sticky mixture of a substance and a liquid, which can be spread easily. *Mix together the flour and the water to form a paste.* 2 VB WITH OBJ AND ADJUNCT If you **paste** something on a surface, you stick it to the surface with glue. *The children were busy pasting gold stars on a chart.*

pastel /pæstəl/. ATTRIB ADJ **Pastel** colours are pale. *...pastel shades of pink, blue, and brown.*

pasteurized /pɑːstjəraɪzd/. ADJ **Pasteurized** milk or cream has had bacteria removed from it by means of a special heating process.

pastime /pɑːstaɪm/, **pastimes.** COUNT N A **pastime** is something that you do in your spare time because you enjoy it. *...leisurely pastimes, like gardening, woodwork, music and toy-making.*

pastor /pɑːstə/, **pastors.** COUNT N A **pastor** is a member of the clergy in some Protestant churches.

pastoral /pɑːstərəl/. 1 ATTRIB ADJ The **pastoral** activities of clergy relate to the general needs of people, rather than just their religious needs. *...a pastoral visit.* 2 ATTRIB ADJ **Pastoral** also means relating to peaceful country life. *...a pastoral scene with little lambs and yellow flowers.*

past participle, past participles. COUNT N In grammar, the **past participle** of a verb is a form which usually ends in '-ed' or '-en'. It is used to form perfect tenses and passives.

pastry /peɪstri^{1}/, **pastries.** 1 MASS N **Pastry** is a food made of flour, fat, and water mixed into a dough and then rolled flat. It is used for making pies and flans. 2 COUNT N A **pastry** is a small cake made with sweet pastry.

past tense. SING N In grammar, the **past tense** is used to refer to things that happened or existed before the time when you are speaking or writing.

pasture /pɑːstʃə/, **pastures.** UNCOUNT N OR COUNT N **Pasture** is an area of grass on which farm animals graze. *...five acres of pasture... ...the lush green pastures of Ireland.*

pasty /peɪsti^{1}/. ADJ If you look **pasty,** you look pale and unhealthy.

pat /pæt/, **pats, patting, patted.** VB WITH OBJ If you **pat** something, you hit it lightly with your hand held flat. *He patted the tree trunk softly.* Also COUNT N *...a friendly pat on the shoulder.*

patch /pætʃ/, **patches, patching, patched.** 1 COUNT N A **patch** is a piece of material used to cover a hole in something. *I mended holes in the sheets by sewing on square patches.* 2 VB WITH OBJ If you **patch** something that has a hole in it, you mend it by fixing a patch over the hole. *They patched the leaking roof... Anne sat by the fire, patching a pair of jeans.* 3 COUNT N An eye **patch** is a small piece of material which you wear to cover an injured eye. 4 COUNT N WITH SUPP A **patch** on a surface is a part of it which is different in appearance from the area around it. *...the damp patch at the corner of the ceiling... ...patches of snow.* 5 COUNT N WITH SUPP You can use **patch** to refer to a period in the life or existence of someone or something. *The country was going through a bad patch.*

patch up. PHR VB 1 If you **patch up** something which is damaged, you mend it. *They have to patch up the mud walls that the rains have battered.* 2 If you **patch up** a quarrel with someone, you end it. *They tried to patch things up.*

patchwork /pætʃwɜːk/. ATTRIB ADJ A **patchwork** quilt or dress has been made by sewing together small pieces of material of different colours.

patchy /pætʃi^{1}/. 1 ADJ Something that is **patchy** is not spread evenly, but exists in different quantities in different places. *If you dye clothes in too small a pan, the colour will be patchy.* 2 ADJ If you describe information or knowledge as **patchy,** you mean that it is incomplete. *The evidence is a bit patchy.*

pâté /pæteɪ/, **pâtés.** MASS N **Pâté** is meat, fish, or vegetables mashed into a fairly soft mass. It is usually spread on bread or toast.

patent /peɪtənt/, **patents, patenting, patented;** also pronounced /pætənt/ in meanings 1 and 2. 1 COUNT N A **patent** is an official right to be the only person or company to make and sell a new product. *The first English patent for a typewriter was issued in 1714.* 2 VB WITH OBJ If you **patent** something, you obtain a patent for it. *I never attempted to patent the idea.* 3 ATTRIB ADJ **Patent** means obvious; a formal use. *This is patent nonsense... ...the patent honesty of Butler.* ♦ **patently** ADV *Anne was patently annoyed.* 4 UNCOUNT N **Patent** or **patent leather** is leather or plastic with a shiny surface. *...a pair of black patent leather shoes.*

paternal /pətɜːnəl/. ATTRIB ADJ **Paternal** is used to describe things relating to a father. *...lack of paternal love... ...our paternal grandmother.*

path /pɑːθ/, **paths.** 1 COUNT N A **path** is a strip of ground that people walk along to get somewhere. *He went up the path to his front door.* 2 COUNT N WITH POSS Your **path** is the space ahead of you as you move along. *On arrival he found his path barred... It moves forward killing anything in its path.* 3 COUNT N WITH POSS The **path** of something is the line which it moves along in a particular direction. *The flight path of the 747 carried it directly overhead.* 4 COUNT N WITH SUPP A **path** that you take is a particular course of action or way of doing something. *He saw public ownership as one of many paths to achieving a socialist society.*

pathetic /pəθetɪk/. 1 ADJ Someone or something that is **pathetic** is sad and weak or helpless, and makes you feel pity and sadness. *It was pathetic to see a man to whom reading meant so much become almost totally blind.* ♦ **pathetically** ADV *He looked pathetically defenceless.* 2 ADJ You can also describe someone or something as **pathetic** when they are so bad or weak that they make you feel impatient or angry. *Our efforts so far have been rather pathetic.*

pathological /pæθəlɒdʒɪkəl/. 1 ADJ You use **pathological** to describe people who cannot help behaving in an extreme way, or their feelings. *...a pathological liar... ...a pathological fear of being late.* 2 ATTRIB ADJ **Pathological** also means relating to pathology or diseases; a medical use. *...pathological changes in the nervous system.*

pathology /pəθɒlədʒi^{1}/. UNCOUNT N **Pathology** is the study of diseases and illnesses; a medical use.

pathos /peɪθɒs/. UNCOUNT N **Pathos** is a quality in a situation that makes people feel sadness and pity; a formal use. *...the pathos of his situation... ...a scene of real pathos.*

pathway /pɑːθweɪ/, **pathways.** COUNT N A **pathway** is a path which you can walk along or a route which you can take. *Marsha could make out a possible pathway through the wire.*

patience /peɪʃəns/. 1 UNCOUNT N If you have **patience,** you are able to stay calm and not get annoyed, for example when you are waiting for something. *Paul was waiting his turn with patience... I've lost all patience with him and his excuses.* 2 PHRASE If you **try** someone's **patience,** you annoy them so much that it is very difficult for them to stay calm. *I tried her patience to the limit.* 3 UNCOUNT N **Patience** is also a card game for only one player.

patient /peɪʃənt/, **patients.** 1 ADJ If you are **patient,** you are able to stay calm and not get annoyed, for example when you are waiting for something. *He was very patient with me.* ♦ **patiently** ADV *James waited patiently for her to finish.* 2 COUNT N A **patient** is a person who is receiving medical treatment, or who is registered with a particular doctor. *...a consultant who treats kidney patients.*

patio /pætiəʊ/, **patios.** COUNT N A **patio** is an area of paving close to a house, where people can sit in chairs. *She was sitting in a deck chair on the patio.*

patriot /pætrɪət, peɪt-/, **patriots.** COUNT N Someone who is a **patriot** loves their country and feels very loyal towards it.

patriotic /pætrɪɒtɪk, peɪt-/. ADJ Someone who is **patriotic** loves their country and feels very loyal towards it. *...a patriotic song.*

patriotism /pætrɪətɪzəm, peɪt-/. UNCOUNT N **Patriotism** is love for your country and loyalty towards it.

patrol /pətrəʊl/, **patrols, patrolling, patrolled.** 1 VB WITH OBJ OR ADJUNCT When soldiers, police, or guards **patrol** an area or building, they move around it in order to make sure that there is no trouble there. *I saw men patrolling the streets with rifles on their backs... ...the policeman who is patrolling in a dangerous area.* Also COUNT N *An entire platoon was ambushed during a patrol... The police came in a black patrol car.* 2 PHRASE People who are **on patrol** are patrolling an area. *Two policemen on patrol saw the boy running away.* 3 COUNT N A **patrol** is a group of soldiers or vehicles that are patrolling an area.

patron /peɪtrən/, **patrons.** 1 COUNT N A **patron** is a person who supports and gives money to artists, writers, or musicians. *...a patron of the arts.* 2 COUNT N The **patron** of a charity, group, or campaign is an important person who is interested in it and who allows his or her name to be used for publicity. *Our Chamber Music Society has the Lord Mayor as its patron.* 3 COUNT N The **patrons** of a particular shop, pub, or other place are its customers; a formal use. *Patrons are requested to wear neat attire.*

patronage /pætrənɪdʒ/. UNCOUNT N **Patronage** is the support and money given by someone to a person or a group such as a charity. *...public patronage of the arts.*

patronize /pætrənaɪz/, **patronizes, patronizing, patronized;** also spelled **patronise.** 1 VB WITH OBJ If someone **patronizes** you, they speak or behave towards you in a way which seems friendly, but which shows that they think they are superior to you; used showing disapproval. *Don't patronize me!* ♦ **patronizing** /pætrənaɪzɪŋ/ ADJ *...a patronizing attitude.* 2 VB WITH OBJ If you **patronize** a shop, pub, or other place, you are one of its customers; a formal use.

patron saint, patron saints. COUNT N WITH SUPP The **patron saint** of a place or a group of people is a saint who is believed to give them special help and protection. *...St Hubert, patron saint of hunters.*

patter /pætə/, **patters, pattering, pattered.** 1 VB WITH ADJUNCT If something **patters** on a surface, it makes light tapping sounds as it hits it. *Spots of rain pattered on the window... I heard her feet pattering about upstairs.* Also SING N *They heard a patter of paws as the dog came to meet them.* **2** COUNT N The **patter** of an entertainer or salesman is the series of things that they learn in advance and say quickly. *He gave the usual patter about watertight boxes.*

pattern /pætə^{0}n/, **patterns. 1** COUNT N A **pattern** is a particular way in which something is usually done. *Over the next few months their work pattern changed... ...behaviour patterns.* **2** COUNT N A **pattern** is also a decorative design of repeated shapes. *Jack was drawing a pattern in the sand with his forefinger.* **3** COUNT N A **pattern** is also a diagram or shape that you can use as a guide when you are making something such as a model or a piece of clothing.

patterned /pætə^{0}nd/. ADJ Something that is **patterned** is covered with a pattern or design. *...patterned carpets.*

paunch /pɔ:ntʃ/, **paunches.** COUNT N If a man has a **paunch,** he has a fat stomach.

pauper /pɔ:pə/, **paupers.** COUNT N A **pauper** is a very poor person; an old-fashioned use.

pause /pɔ:z/, **pauses, pausing, paused.** VB If you **pause** while you are speaking or doing something, you stop for a short time. *He paused and then went on in a low voice... He does not pause for breath until he reaches the top floor.* Also COUNT N *She continued after a pause.*

pave /peɪv/, **paves, paving, paved. 1** VB WITH OBJ When an area of ground **is paved,** it is covered with blocks of stone or concrete. *...a steep causeway paved with slabs of granite.* **2** PHRASE If one thing **paves the way** for another, it creates a situation in which the other thing is able to happen. *His work paved the way for Burkitt's theories.*

pavement /peɪvmə^{2}nt/, **pavements.** COUNT N A **pavement** is a path with a hard surface by the side of a road. *He was standing on the pavement.*

pavilion /pəvɪljən/, **pavilions.** COUNT N A **pavilion** is a building on the edge of a sports field where players can change their clothes and wash; a British use.

paving stone, paving stones. COUNT N **Paving stones** are flat pieces of stone, usually square or rectangular, that are used for making pavements.

paw /pɔ:/, **paws, pawing, pawed. 1** COUNT N The **paws** of an animal such as a cat, dog, or bear are its feet. *...a black cat with white paws.* **2** VB WITH OBJ OR 'at' If an animal **paws** something, it draws its paw or hoof over it. *...bulls pawing the earth... The dog pawed at the door again.*

pawn /pɔ:n/, **pawns, pawning, pawned. 1** VB WITH OBJ If you **pawn** something that you own, you leave it with a pawnbroker, who gives you money for it and who can sell it if you do not pay back the money before a certain time. *Brian didn't have a watch—he had pawned it some years ago.* **2** COUNT N In chess, a **pawn** is the smallest and least valuable playing piece. **3** COUNT N If you refer to someone as a **pawn,** you mean that another person is using them for his or her own advantage. *We are simply pawns in the hands of larger powers.*

pawnbroker /pɔ:nbrəʊkə/, **pawnbrokers.** COUNT N A **pawnbroker** is a person who will lend you money if you give them something that you own. The pawnbroker can sell that thing if you do not pay back the money before a certain time.

pay /peɪ/, **pays, paying, paid** /peɪd/. **1** VB WITH OR WITHOUT OBJ When you **pay** someone an amount of money for something they have given you or done for you, you give them that amount of money. *He had paid £5,000 for the boat... Pay me five pounds... He paid his bill and left... I'll pay by cheque.* **2** VB WITH OR WITHOUT OBJ When your employers **pay** you, they give you your wages or salary. *She was being paid sixty dollars a week... The company pays well.* **3** UNCOUNT N Someone's **pay** is the money that they receive as their wages or salary. *She lost three weeks' pay... ...a pay rise of £20 a week.* **4** VB WITH OBJ OR ADJUNCT If a job, deal, or investment **pays** a particular amount, it brings you that amount of money. *A day's work pays £2,500... She complained about her job and how poorly it paid.* **5** VB If a course of action **pays,** it results in some advantage or benefit for you. *It pays to keep on the right side of your boss.* **6** VB WITH OR WITHOUT OBJ If you **pay** for something that you do or have, you suffer as a result. *He paid dearly for his mistake... The men paid with their lives... You failed, and you must pay the penalty.* **7** VB WITH OBJ You use **pay** with some nouns to indicate that something is given or done. *It would be nice if you paid me a visit... I paid little attention to what I heard... It was probably the greatest compliment I could have paid her.* **8** PHRASE If you **pay** your **way,** you pay for things that you need rather than letting other people pay for them. **9** See also **paid.**

pay back. PHR VB **1** If you **pay back** money that you have borrowed from someone, you give them an equal amount at a later time. *I'll pay you back next week.* **2** If you **pay** someone **back** for doing something unpleasant to you, you make them suffer in some way.

pay off. PHR VB **1** If you **pay off** a debt, you give someone all the money that you owe them. *He had used the firm's money to pay off gambling debts.* **2** If an action **pays off,** it is successful. *It was a risk and it paid off.* **3** See also **payoff.**

pay out. PHR VB If you **pay out** money, usually a large amount, you spend it on a particular thing. *He had paid out good money to educate Julie.*

pay up. PHR VB If you **pay up,** you give someone the money that you owe them.

payable /peɪəbə^{0}l/. **1** PRED ADJ If an amount of money is **payable,** it has to be paid or it can be paid. *The interest payable on these loans was vast.* **2** PRED ADJ WITH PREP 'to' If a cheque is made **payable** to you, it has your name written on it to indicate that you are the person who will receive the money. *Cheques should be made payable to Trans Euro Travel Ltd.*

payment /peɪmə^{2}nt/, **payments. 1** UNCOUNT N **Payment** is the act of paying money to someone or of being paid. *Was the payment of rent optional?... When can I expect payment?* **2** COUNT N A **payment** is an amount of money that is paid to someone. *Some said that social security payments were too high.*

payoff /peɪɒf/, **payoffs.** COUNT N A **payoff** is an advantage or benefit that results from an action. *Some carry out research and hope that there could be a practical pay-off.*

payroll /peɪrəʊl/, **payrolls.** COUNT N If you are on an organization's **payroll,** you are employed and paid by that organization.

PC /pi: si:/, **PCs. 1** TITLE In Britain, **PC** is used in front of the name of a male police officer of the lowest rank. *...PC Cooper.* **2** COUNT N A **PC** is also a small computer. It is an abbreviation for 'personal computer'.

pea /pi:/, **peas.** COUNT N **Peas** are small, round, green seeds eaten as a vegetable.

peace /pi:s/. **1** UNCOUNT N **Peace** is a state of undisturbed quiet and calm. *Go away and leave us in peace... He returned to the peace of his village.* **2** UNCOUNT N When a country is at **peace,** it is not involved in a war. *Their activities threaten world peace... ...peace negotiations.* **3** UNCOUNT N If there is **peace** among a group of people, they live or work together in a friendly way and do not quarrel. *She had done it for the sake of peace in the family.*

peaceful /pi:sfʊl/. **1** ADJ A **peaceful** place or time is quiet, calm, and undisturbed. *...peaceful parks and gardens... It was a peaceful Christmas.* ♦ **peacefully** ADV *They lived there peacefully, happily.* **2** ADJ Someone who feels or looks **peaceful** is calm and not at all worried. *He looked peaceful as he lay there.* ♦ **peacefully** ADV *That night he slept peacefully.* **3** ADJ **Peaceful** people are not violent and try to avoid quarrelling or fighting with other people. *...the most peaceful nation on earth... ...peaceful demonstrations.*

peach /pi:tʃ/, **peaches.** COUNT N A **peach** is a soft, round, juicy fruit with sweet yellow flesh and pinky-yellow skin.

peacock /pi:kɒk/, **peacocks.** COUNT N A **peacock** is a large bird. The male has a very long tail with large blue and green spots which it can spread out like a fan.

peak /pi:k/, **peaks, peaking, peaked. 1** COUNT N The **peak** of a process or activity is the point at which it is greatest, most successful, or most fully developed. *They were trained to a peak of physical fitness... Computer technology has not yet reached its peak.* **2** VB When someone or something **peaks,** they reach their highest value or highest level of success. *The annual workload peaks at harvest time.* **3** ATTRIB ADJ The **peak** level or value of something is its highest level or value. *...the peak voltage... ...a peak output of 165 cars per day.* **4** COUNT N A **peak** is a mountain, or the top of a mountain. *It is one of the highest peaks in the Alps.* **5** COUNT N The **peak** of a cap is the part at the front that sticks out above your eyes.

peaked /pi:kt/. ATTRIB ADJ A **peaked** cap has a part at the front that sticks out above your eyes.

peal /pi:l/, **peals, pealing, pealed. 1** VB When bells **peal,** they ring one after the other, making a musical sound. *Nearby church bells pealed across the quiet city.* Also COUNT N *The peals can be overwhelming for people living nearby.* **2** COUNT N WITH SUPP A **peal** of laughter or thunder consists of a long, loud series of sounds. *...bursting into peals of laughter.*

peanut /pi:nʌt/, **peanuts.** COUNT N **Peanuts** are small nuts often eaten as a snack, especially when they are roasted and salted.

pear /peə/, **pears.** COUNT N A **pear** is a juicy fruit which is narrow at the top and wider at the bottom. It has white flesh and green or yellow skin.

pearl /pɜ:l/, **pearls.** COUNT N A **pearl** is a hard, shiny, white ball which grows inside the shell of an oyster. Pearls are used for making jewellery. *She was wearing a string of pearls.* ● See also **mother-of-pearl.**

pearly /pɜ:li^1/. ADJ Something that is **pearly** shines softly like a pearl. *...pearly teeth.*

peasant /pezə^{0}nt/, **peasants.** COUNT N A **peasant** is a person who works on the land, especially in a poor country.

peasantry /pezə^{0}ntri^1/. COLL N The peasants in a country can be referred to as the **peasantry;** an old-fashioned use.

peat /pi:t/. UNCOUNT N **Peat** is dark decaying plant material which is found in some cool, wet regions. Peat is added to soil to improve it or is used as fuel.

pebble /pebə^{0}l/, **pebbles.** COUNT N A **pebble** is a smooth, round stone. *...the pebbles on the beach.*

peck /pek/, **pecks, pecking, pecked. 1** VB WITH OBJ OR ADJUNCT If a bird **pecks** something, it moves its beak forward quickly and bites at it. *...a plump brown hen, pecking around for grains of corn.* Also SING N *It hopped over and made a quick peck at the ground.* **2** VB WITH OBJ If you **peck** someone on the cheek, you give them a quick, light kiss. *She pecked his cheek.* Also SING N *She gave him a peck on the cheek.*

peculiar /pɪ^{2}kju:lɪə/. **1** ADJ Someone or something that is **peculiar** is strange and sometimes rather unpleasant. *He was wearing a peculiar suit... She gave him a peculiar look.* ♦ **peculiarly** ADV *Molly is behaving rather peculiarly these days.* **2** PRED ADJ If you feel **peculiar,** you feel slightly ill or dizzy. *Seeing blood makes me feel a bit peculiar inside.* **3** PRED ADJ If something is **peculiar** to a particular thing or person, it belongs or relates only to that thing or person. *...the style of decoration peculiar to the late 1920s.* ♦ **peculiarly** ADV *It's an idiom that people recognise as peculiarly English.*

peculiarity /pɪ^{2}kju:lɪærɪ^{1}ti^1/, **peculiarities. 1** COUNT N A **peculiarity** that someone or something has is an individual characteristic or habit, especially an unusual one. *Each city has its own peculiarities, its own history and character.* **2** UNCOUNT N **Peculiarity** is the quality of being strange and sometimes rather unpleasant. *...the peculiarity of his eyes.*

pedal /pedə^{0}l/, **pedals, pedalling, pedalled;** spelled **pedaling** and **pedaled** in American English. **1** COUNT N The **pedals** on a bicycle are the two parts that you push with your feet in order to make the bicycle move. **2** VB WITH OR WITHOUT OBJ When you **pedal** a bicycle, you push the pedals around with your feet to make it move. *His legs were aching from pedalling too fast.* **3** COUNT N A **pedal** is also a lever that you press with your foot in order to control a car or machine.

pedantic /pɪ^{2}dæntɪk/. ADJ Someone who is **pedantic** is too concerned with unimportant details or traditional rules. *...a fussy and pedantic middle-aged clerk.*

peddle /pedə^{0}l/, **peddles, peddling, peddled. 1** VB WITH OBJ Someone who **peddles** drugs sells them illegally. **2** VB WITH OBJ If someone **peddles** an idea or piece of information, they try hard to get people to accept it. *...those who peddled this solution.*

peddler /pedlə/, **peddlers.** COUNT N A drug **peddler** is a person who sells drugs illegally.

pedestal /pedɪ^{2}stə^{0}l/, **pedestals.** COUNT N A **pedestal** is the base on which a statue or a column stands.

pedestrian /pɪ^{2}destrɪən/, **pedestrians. 1** COUNT N A **pedestrian** is a person who is walking in a town. *Pedestrians jostled them on the pavement.* **2** ADJ Someone or something that is **pedestrian** is dull and ordinary; a formal use.

pedestrian crossing, pedestrian crossings. COUNT N A **pedestrian crossing** is a place where pedestrians can cross a street safely.

pediatrician /pi:dɪətrɪʃə^{0}n/. See **paediatrician.**

pedigree /pedɪgri:/, **pedigrees. 1** ATTRIB ADJ A **pedigree** animal is descended from animals which have all been of a particular breed and is therefore considered to be of good quality. *...a pedigree cat.* **2** COUNT N If a dog, cat, or other animal has a **pedigree,** its ancestors are known and recorded. *...fine dogs with pedigrees.* **3** COUNT N WITH SUPP Someone's **pedigree** is their background or ancestry. *He had a criminal pedigree.*

peek /pi:k/, **peeks, peeking, peeked.** VB If you **peek** at something or someone, you have a quick look at them, often secretly; an informal use. *He peeked through the door.* Also SING N *I took a peek at the list.*

peel /pi:l/, **peels, peeling, peeled. 1** UNCOUNT N The **peel** of a fruit such as a lemon or apple is its skin. *...grated lemon peel.* **2** VB WITH OBJ When you **peel** fruit or vegetables, you remove their skins. *I found Jane peeling potatoes.* **3** VB WITH OBJ AND ADJUNCT If you **peel** something off a surface, you pull it off gently in one piece. *I peeled some moss off the wood... Peel off the outer plastic cover.* **4** VB If paint **is peeling** off a surface or if the surface **is peeling,** the paint is coming off. *The paint was peeling off the woodwork... ...peeling yellow walls.* 5 VB If you **are peeling,** small pieces of skin are coming off your body, usually because you are sunburnt. *Her nose was peeling.*

peelings /piːlɪŋz/. PLURAL N Potato **peelings** are pieces of skin peeled from potatoes.

peep /piːp/, **peeps, peeping, peeped. 1** VB If you **peep** at something, you have a quick look at it, often secretly. *They crept up to the glass doors and peeped inside.* Also SING N *I was allowed in to have a peep at the painting.* **2** VB WITH ADJUNCT If something **peeps** out from somewhere, a small part of it is visible; a literary use. *The sun was just peeping over the horizon.*

peer /pɪə/, **peers, peering, peered. 1** VB WITH ADJUNCT If you **peer** at something, you look at it very hard, usually because it is difficult to see clearly. *He peered at his reflection... Howard sat peering through the windscreen.* **2** COUNT N A **peer** is a member of the nobility. **3** PLURAL N Your **peers** are people of the same age or status as you; a formal use. *...comparing students with their peers outside university.*

peerage /pɪərɪdʒ/, **peerages. 1** COUNT N If someone has a **peerage,** they are a noble or peer. *...an heir to a peerage.* **2** SING N The nobles or peers of a country are referred to as the **peerage.** *...his elevation to the peerage.*

peer group, peer groups. COUNT N Your **peer group** is the group of people who are of the same age or status as yourself; a technical use.

peg /pɛg/, **pegs, pegging, pegged. 1** COUNT N A **peg** is a small hook or knob on a wall or door which is used for hanging things on. *He takes his coat from the peg.* **2** COUNT N A clothes **peg** is a wooden or plastic object used to attach washing to a clothes line. **3** VB WITH OBJ AND ADJUNCT If you **peg** clothes on a washing line, you fix them there with pegs.

pejorative /pədʒɒrətɪv/. ADJ A **pejorative** word or expression expresses criticism; a formal use.

pelican /pɛlɪkən/, **pelicans.** COUNT N A **pelican** is a large water bird. It catches fish and keeps them in the lower part of its beak.

pellet /pɛlɪ^{2}t/, **pellets.** COUNT N A **pellet** is a small ball of paper, mud, lead, or other material. *...a pellet of mud... ...shotgun pellets.*

pelt /pɛlt/, **pelts, pelting, pelted. 1** VB WITH OBJ AND 'with' If you **pelt** someone with things, you throw things at them. *He was pelted with eggs.* **2** VB If it **is pelting** with rain or if the rain **is pelting** down, it is raining very hard; an informal use.

pelvis /pɛlvɪs/, **pelvises.** COUNT N Your **pelvis** is the wide, curved group of bones at the level of your hips.

pen /pɛn/, **pens, penning, penned. 1** COUNT N A **pen** is a long thin object which you use to write in ink. **2** VB WITH OBJ If someone **pens** a letter, article, or book, they write it; a literary use. *Infuriated, he penned a blistering reply.* **3** COUNT N A **pen** is also a small fenced area in which farm animals are kept for a short time. **4** VB WITH OBJ If people or animals **are penned** somewhere or **are penned up,** they are forced to remain in a very small area. *...the boredom of endless hours penned up in a hot and dusty railway carriage.*

penal /piːnə^{0}l/. ATTRIB ADJ **Penal** means relating to the punishment of criminals. *...the British penal system.*

penalize /piːnəlaɪz/, **penalizes, penalizing, penalized;** also spelled **penalise.** VB WITH OBJ If someone **is penalized** for something, they are made to suffer some disadvantage because of it. *It would be unfair to penalise those without a job.*

penalty /pɛnə^{0}lti^1/, **penalties. 1** COUNT N A **penalty** is a punishment that someone is given for doing something which is against a law or rule. *There are now stiffer penalties for drunken drivers.* **2** COUNT N In sport, a **penalty** is a chance to score a goal without being prevented by other players. A penalty is given when a member of the other team commits a foul near the goal.

penance /pɛnəns/. UNCOUNT N If you do **penance** for something wrong that you have done, you do something that you find unpleasant to show you are sorry. *As penance for his condescension, he forced himself to be pleasant to them.*

pence /pɛns/. **Pence** is a plural form of **penny.**

pencil /pɛnsə^{0}l/, **pencils, pencilling, pencilled. 1** COUNT N A **pencil** is a thin wooden rod with graphite down the centre which is used for writing or drawing. **2** VB WITH OBJ If you **pencil** something, you write it using a pencil. *He pencilled his initials at the end.*

pendant /pɛndənt/, **pendants.** COUNT N A **pendant** is an ornament on a chain worn round your neck.

pending /pɛndɪŋ/; a formal word. **1** ADJ Something that is **pending** is going to happen or be dealt with soon. *He knew my examination was pending... ...a pending lawsuit.* **2** PREP If something is done **pending** a future event, it is done before that event happens, when the situation may change. *An interim government is to be set up, pending elections.*

pendulum /pɛndjə^{4}ləm/, **pendulums. 1** COUNT N The **pendulum** of a clock is a rod with a weight at the end which swings from side to side in order to make the clock work. **2** SING N People use the word **pendulum** as a way of talking about regular changes in a situation or in people's opinions. *...the pendulum of fashion.*

penetrate /pɛnɪtreɪt/, **penetrates, penetrating, penetrated. 1** VB WITH OBJ OR ADJUNCT If someone or something **penetrates** an area, they succeed in getting into it or through it. *They penetrated into territory where no man had ever gone before... The sun was not high enough yet to penetrate the thick foliage overhead.* ♦ **penetration** /pɛnɪtreɪʃə^{0}n/ UNCOUNT N *...the penetration of hostile defences.* **2** VB WITH OBJ If someone **penetrates** an enemy group, they succeed in joining it in order to get information or cause trouble.

penetrating /pɛnɪtreɪtɪŋ/. **1** ADJ A **penetrating** sound is loud and clear. *...his penetrating voice.* **2** ADJ Something that is **penetrating** shows deep understanding. *...a penetrating question.*

pen-friend, pen-friends. COUNT N A **pen-friend** is someone whom you write to regularly, although the two of you may never have met.

penguin /pɛŋgwɪn/, **penguins.** COUNT N A **penguin** is a black and white bird found mainly in the Antarctic. Penguins cannot fly.

penicillin /pɛnɪsɪlɪn/. UNCOUNT N **Penicillin** is an antibiotic.

peninsula /pɪ^{2}nɪnsjə^{4}lə/, **peninsulas.** COUNT N A **peninsula** is an area of land almost surrounded by water.

penis /piːnɪs/, **penises.** COUNT N A man's **penis** is the part of his body that he uses when urinating and when having sex.

penitent /pɛnɪtənt/. ADJ Someone who is **penitent** is very sorry for doing something wrong; a literary use.

penitentiary /pɛnɪtɛnʃə^{0}ri^1/, **penitentiaries.** COUNT N A **penitentiary** is a prison; an American use.

penknife /pɛnnaɪf/, **penknives.** COUNT N A **penknife** is a small knife with a blade that folds back into the handle.

penniless /pɛnɪlɪ^{2}s/. ADJ Someone who is **penniless** has hardly any money.

penny /pɛni^1/, **pennies** or **pence** /pɛns/. The plural is **pennies** for meaning 1 and **pence** for meaning 2. **1** COUNT N A **penny** is a British coin worth one hundredth of a pound. **2** COUNT N A **penny** is also the amount of money that a penny is worth. *...a ten pence coin... They only cost a few pence.*

pension /pɛnʃə^{0}n/, **pensions.** COUNT N A **pension** is a regular sum of money paid to someone who is old, retired, widowed, or disabled. *...an old age pension.*

pensioner /pɛnʃənə/, **pensioners.** COUNT N A **pensioner** is a person who receives a pension, especially an old or retired person.

pensive /pɛnsɪv/. ADJ Someone who is **pensive** is thinking deeply about something. *Jefferson looked pensive. 'What's wrong?' asked Tyler.*

penthouse /pɛnthaʊs/, **penthouses.** COUNT N OR MOD A **penthouse** or a **penthouse** apartment or suite is a luxurious set of rooms at the top of a tall building.

pent-up /pɛnt ʌp/. ADJ **Pent-up** emotions or energies have been held back and not expressed or released. *...pent-up frustrations.*

penultimate /pɪ^{2}nʌltɪ^{1}mə^{1}t/. ADJ The **penultimate** thing in a series is the last but one; a formal use. *...the penultimate paragraph of the letter.*

people /piːpə^{0}l/, **peoples, peopling, peopled. 1** PLURAL N **People** are men, women, and children. *There were 120 people at the lecture.* **2** PLURAL N The **people** are ordinary men and women, as opposed to the upper classes or the government. *Power to the people!* **3** COUNT N A **people** consists of all the men, women, and children of a particular country or race. *...the beliefs of various peoples across the world.* **4** VB WITH OBJ If a place **is peopled** by a particular group of people, those people live there. *...Istanbul, now peopled by 4 million Turks.*

pepper /pɛpə/, **peppers, peppering, peppered. 1** UNCOUNT N **Pepper** is a hot-tasting powder used to flavour food. *...salt and pepper.* **2** COUNT N A **pepper** is a hollow green or red vegetable. *...a salad of green peppers.* **3** VB WITH OBJ If something **is peppered** with small objects, they hit it or are scattered over it. *I felt my fingers being peppered with small, hot fragments.*

peppermint /pɛpəmɪnt/, **peppermints. 1** UNCOUNT N **Peppermint** is a strong flavouring that makes your mouth feel cold. *...peppermint candy.* **2** COUNT N A **peppermint** is a peppermint-flavoured sweet.

pep talk /pɛp tɔːk/, **pep talks.** COUNT N A **pep talk** is a speech intended to encourage a group of people to make more effort; an informal use.

per /pɜː/. PREP You use **per** to express rates and ratios. For example, if something costs £50 **per** year, you must pay £50 each year for it. If a vehicle is travelling at 40 miles **per** hour, it travels 40 miles each hour. *...an income of less than £1000 per person.*

per annum /pɜː ænəm/. ADV A particular amount **per annum** means that amount each year. *It costs £125 per annum.*

perceive /pəsiːv/, **perceives, perceiving, perceived. 1** REPORT VB If you **perceive** something, especially something that is not obvious, you see, notice, or realize it. *Many insects can perceive colours that are invisible to us... They failed to perceive that this was what I objected to.* **2** VB WITH OBJ AND ADJUNCT If you **perceive** someone or something as being or doing a particular thing, that is what you think their nature or effect is. *It is important that the president be perceived as moving the country forward... ...the truth as I perceive it.*

per cent /pəsɛnt/. PHRASE You use **per cent** to talk about fractions. For example, if an amount is 10 **per cent** of a larger amount, it is equal to 10 hundredths of the larger amount. **Per cent** is often written %. *45 per cent of Americans were against it.*

percentage /pəsɛntɪdʒ/, **percentages.** COUNT N A **percentage** is a fraction expressed as a particular number of hundredths. *...areas with a high percentage of immigrants.*

perceptible /pəsɛptɪbə^{0}l/. ADJ Something that is **perceptible** can only just be seen. *There was a barely perceptible flicker of light.*

perception /pəsɛpʃə^{0}n/, **perceptions. 1** UNCOUNT N Someone who has **perception** realizes or notices things that are not obvious. *...a person of extraordinary perception.* **2** COUNT N A **perception** is an opinion that you have about someone or something. *My perception of her had changed.* **3** UNCOUNT N **Perception** is the recognition of things by using your senses, especially the sense of sight. *...visual perception.*

perceptive /pəsɛptɪv/. ADJ Someone who is **perceptive** realizes or notices things that are not obvious. *...a perceptive critic.*

perch /pɜːtʃ/, **perches, perching, perched. 1** VB WITH ADJUNCT If you **perch** on a wall or table, you sit on the edge of it. *Dr Quilty perched on the corner of his desk.* **2** ERG VB WITH ADJUNCT If you **perch** one thing on another, you put it on the top or edge, so that it looks as if it might fall off. *He would take out his spectacles and perch them on the end of his nose... The building perches precariously within a few feet of a sudden drop.* **3** VB When a bird **perches** on a branch or a wall, it stands there. **4** COUNT N A **perch** is a short rod for a tame bird to stand on.

percussion /pəkʌʃə^{0}n/. MOD OR UNCOUNT N **Percussion** instruments are musical instruments that you hit, such as drums and cymbals. *We had Dailey on percussion, and Flannery on the clarinet.*

peremptory /pərɛmptə^{0}ri^1/. ADJ Someone who does something in a **peremptory** way shows that they expect to be obeyed immediately; a formal use. *Our conversation was interrupted by a peremptory thudding at the door.*

perennial /pɪ^{2}rɛnɪəl/. ADJ A **perennial** situation is one that keeps occurring or that never ends. *...perennial problems... ...a perennial feature of British politics.*

perfect, perfects, perfecting, perfected; pronounced /pɜːfɪ^{2}kt/ when it is an adjective or noun, and /pəfɛkt/ when it is a verb. **1** ADJ Something that is **perfect** is as good as it can possibly be. *She speaks perfect English... I've got the perfect solution.* ♦ **perfectly** ADV *The plan worked perfectly.* **2** ATTRIB ADJ You can use **perfect** for emphasis. *They may be perfect strangers... I have a perfect right to be here.* ♦ **perfectly** SUBMOD *It's a perfectly reasonable question... I knew perfectly well it was a trap.* **3** VB WITH OBJ If you **perfect** something, you make it as good as it can possibly be. *She hoped to perfect her technique.* **4** ATTRIB ADJ OR SING N In grammar, the **perfect** tenses of a verb are the tenses formed with the auxiliary 'have' and the past participle of the verb. The present **perfect** uses the present tense of 'have' and the past **perfect** uses the past tense of 'have'.

perfection /pəfɛkʃə^{0}n/. UNCOUNT N **Perfection** is the quality of being perfect. *...gardens of incredible perfection.*

perfectionist /pəfɛkʃənɪst/, **perfectionists.** COUNT N Someone who is a **perfectionist** refuses to do or accept anything that is not perfect.

perforated /pɜːfəreɪtɪd/. ADJ Something that is **perforated** has had a number of small holes made in it. *...a perforated steel plate.*

perform /pəfɔːm/, **performs, performing, performed. 1** VB WITH OBJ To **perform** a task, action, or service means to do it. *About 200 heart operations a year are performed at the Brook Hospital... Their* *organization performs a vital service.* 2 VB WITH ADJUNCT If something **performs** well or badly, it works or functions well or badly. *...the difficulty of finding a rifle which will perform satisfactorily under those conditions.* 3 VB WITH OR WITHOUT OBJ If you **perform** a play, a piece of music, or a dance, you do it in front of an audience. *He performed for them a dance of his native Samoa... We had to perform on stage.* ♦ **performer** /pəfɔ:mə/ COUNT N *Good comic performers are in big demand.*

performance /pəfɔ:məns/, **performances.** 1 COUNT N A **performance** is the acting of a play, or a piece of work done by an actor or musician. *...an amateur performance of 'Macbeth'.* 2 UNCOUNT N Your **performance** is how well you do something. *...Britain's poor economic performance... ...after a disappointing performance in the semi-final.* 3 SING N The **performance** of a task or action is the doing of it. *...the performance of his Presidential duties.*

perfume /pɜ:fju^{4}m/, **perfumes.** 1 MASS N **Perfume** is a pleasant-smelling liquid which you put on your body. *...a bottle of perfume... ...an expensive perfume.* 2 COUNT N A **perfume** is a pleasant smell. *The familiar perfumes of wild flowers filled her nostrils.*

perfumed /pɜ:fju^{4}md/. ADJ Something that is **perfumed** has a pleasant smell. *...the perfumed air.*

perfunctory /pəfʌŋktə^{0}ri^1/. ADJ A **perfunctory** action is done quickly and carelessly; a formal use. *Max gave his wife a perfunctory kiss.*

perhaps /pəhæps/. SENTENCE ADV You use **perhaps** to indicate that you are not sure whether something is true, possible, or likely. *Perhaps Andrew is right after all... Perhaps I'll come. Perhaps not... There are perhaps fifty women here.*

peril /perɪl/, **perils.** UNCOUNT N OR COUNT N **Peril** is great danger; a literary use. *They placed themselves in great peril by openly opposing him... ...the perils of being a fugitive.*

perilous /perɪləs/. ADJ Something that is **perilous** is very dangerous; a literary use. *The perilous journey was over.* ♦ **perilously** SUBMOD OR ADV *It came perilously close to destruction.*

perimeter /pərɪmɪtə/, **perimeters.** COUNT N OR MOD The **perimeter** of an area of land is its outer edge or boundary. *...the perimeter of the clearing... ...dog patrols around the perimeter fence.*

period /pɪərɪəd/, **periods.** 1 COUNT N A particular **period** is a particular length of time. *...over a period of several months... ...a short period of time... ...long periods of rain... ...in the Edwardian period.* 2 ATTRIB ADJ **Period** costumes, objects, and houses were made at an earlier time in history, or look as if they were made then. *...period furniture.* 3 COUNT N A woman's **period** is the bleeding from her womb that happens each month. 4 COUNT N A **period** is also a full stop.

periodic /pɪəri^{1}ɒdɪk/. ATTRIB ADJ A **periodic** event or situation happens occasionally, at fairly regular intervals. *...periodic droughts.*

periodical /pɪəri^{1}ɒdɪkə^{0}l/, **periodicals.** 1 COUNT N A **periodical** is a magazine, especially a serious or academic one. 2 ATTRIB ADJ **Periodical** means the same as periodic. *These mood shifts are periodical and recurring.* ♦ **periodically** /pɪəri^{1}ɒdɪkə^{0}li^1/ ADV *We met them periodically during the summer break.*

peripheral /pərɪfə^{0}rəl/; a formal word. 1 ADJ A **peripheral** thing or part of something is not very important compared with other things or parts. *...the peripheral features of religion.* 2 ADJ **Peripheral** also means on or relating to the edge of an area. *This gives greater peripheral vision.*

periphery /pərɪfəri^1/, **peripheries.** COUNT N The **periphery** of an area is the edge of it; a formal use. *The cost of land on the periphery of Calcutta went up.*

periscope /perɪskəʊp/, **periscopes.** COUNT N A **periscope** is a vertical tube through which people in a submarine can see above the surface of the water.

perish /perɪʃ/, **perishes, perishing, perished.** 1 VB To **perish** means to die or be destroyed; a literary use. *All the passengers and crew members perished... The old religion is perishing.* 2 VB If rubber **perishes,** it starts to fall to pieces.

perishable /perɪʃəbə^{0}l/. ADJ **Perishable** foods go rotten quite quickly.

perjury /pɜ:dʒəri^1/. UNCOUNT N If someone who is giving evidence in a court of law commits **perjury,** they lie; a legal use. *She was charged with perjury.*

perk /pɜ:k/, **perks.** COUNT N A **perk** is something extra that employees get in addition to their salaries; an informal use. *There are nice perks too, such as help with your mortgage.*

permanent /pɜ:mənənt/. ADJ Something that is **permanent** lasts for ever or is present all the time. *Some drugs taken in large quantities cause permanent brain damage... ...the only permanent water supply.* ♦ **permanently** ADV *The doors were kept permanently locked.* ♦ **permanence** /pɜ:mənəns/ UNCOUNT N *People have a need for permanence.*

permeate /pɜ:mieɪt/, **permeates, permeating, permeated;** a formal word. 1 VB WITH OBJ If an idea or attitude **permeates** something, it affects every part of it. *...the extent to which secrecy permeates every part of our society.* 2 VB WITH OBJ OR 'through' If a liquid, smell, or flavour **permeates** something, it spreads through it. *Damp can easily permeate the wood... Chemicals may permeate through the soil into rivers.*

permissible /pəmɪsəbə^{0}l/. ADJ Something that is **permissible** is allowed; a formal use. *...the maximum permissible levels of radiation.*

permission /pəmɪʃə^{0}n/. UNCOUNT N If you give someone **permission** to do something, you say that they are allowed to do it. *I have permission to tell you... He refused permission for Biddle to enter Britain... You can't go without permission.*

permissive /pəmɪsɪv/. ADJ A **permissive** society allows things which other people disapprove of, especially freedom in sexual behaviour. *...the frequency of divorce within the permissive society.* ♦ **permissiveness** UNCOUNT N *...sexual permissiveness.*

permit, permits, permitting, permitted; pronounced /pəmɪt/ when it is a verb, and /pɜ:mɪt/ when it is a noun. 1 VB WITH OBJ If you **permit** something, you allow it; a formal use. *Visits are permitted only once a month... Her father would not permit her to eat sweets... The doctor has permitted him only two meals a day.* 2 VB WITH OR WITHOUT OBJ If something **permits** a particular thing, it makes it possible for that thing to happen; a formal use. *Had time permitted, we would have stayed longer... The timetable permits teams only a few weeks for preparation.* 3 COUNT N A **permit** is an official document which says that you may do something. *She could not get in without a permit... ...work permits.*

permutation /pɜ:mju:teɪʃə^{0}n/, **permutations.** COUNT N A **permutation** is one of the ways in which a number of things can be arranged; a formal use. *The possible permutations were endless.*

pernicious /pənɪʃəs/. ADJ Something that is **pernicious** is very harmful; a literary use. *This had a pernicious influence on countless generations.*

perpendicular /pɜ:pə^{2}ndɪkjə^{4}lə/. ADJ Something that is **perpendicular** points straight up, rather than sloping; a formal use. *...the perpendicular cliff-face.*

perpetrate /pɜ:pɪ^{2}treɪt/, **perpetrates, perpetrating, perpetrated.** VB WITH OBJ If someone **perpetrates** a crime, they do it; a formal use. *...a fraud perpetrated by lawyers.* ♦ **perpetrator** /pɜ:pɪ^{2}treɪtə/ COUNT N *...the perpetrator of the crime.*

perpetual /pəpetju^{0}əl/. ATTRIB ADJ A **perpetual** situation never ends or changes; a formal use. *These bats live in deep caves in perpetual darkness... She had me in perpetual fear.* ♦ **perpetually** ADV *The younger children seemed to be perpetually hungry.*

perpetuate /pəpetju:eɪt/, **perpetuates, perpetuating, perpetuated.** VB WITH OBJ If someone or something **perpetuates** a situation or belief, they cause it to continue; a formal use. *...an education system that perpetuates inequality.*

perplexed /pəplekst/. ADJ If you are **perplexed,** you are puzzled or do not know what to do. *She frowned a little, as if perplexed.*

perplexing /pəpleksɪŋ/. ADJ If something is **perplexing,** you do not understand it or do not know how to deal with it. *...a perplexing and difficult problem.*

perplexity /pəpleksɪ^{1}ti^1/. UNCOUNT N **Perplexity** is the state of being perplexed. *She looked at us in some perplexity.*

persecute /pɜ:sɪkju:t/, **persecutes, persecuting, persecuted.** VB WITH OBJ If someone **persecutes** you, they treat you cruelly and unfairly over a long period of time. *Members of these sects are ruthlessly persecuted.* ♦ **persecution** /pɜ:sɪkju:ʃə^{0}n/ UNCOUNT N *...the persecution of minorities.*

perseverance /pɜ:sɪvɪərəns/. UNCOUNT N **Perseverance** is the fact of continuing with something difficult, rather than giving up. *I underestimated his perseverance.*

persevere /pɜ:sɪvɪə/, **perseveres, persevering, persevered.** VB If you **persevere** with something difficult, you continue doing it and do not give up. *Confidence is needed both to start and to persevere.*

persist /pəsɪst/, **persists, persisting, persisted.** 1 VB If something undesirable **persists,** it continues to exist. *Political differences still persist... The pain persisted until the morning.* 2 VB If you **persist** in doing something, you continue to do it, even though it is difficult or other people oppose you. *People still persist in thinking that standards are going down... He persisted with his policy of conciliation... 'And what,' persisted Casson, 'is to prevent us?'*

persistent /pəsɪstənt/. 1 ADJ Something that is **persistent** continues to exist or happen for a long time. *How do you get rid of a persistent nasty smell?* ♦ **persistently** ADV *...persistently rattling window frames.* ♦ **persistence** /pəsɪstəns/ UNCOUNT N *Because of the persistence of the depression, I saw my doctor.* 2 ADJ Someone who is **persistent** continues trying to do something, even though it is difficult or other people oppose them. *I think you have to be persistent if people say no to you.* ♦ **persistently** ADV *...policemen who tried persistently to force their way into his house.* ♦ **persistence** UNCOUNT N *In the end our persistence was rewarded.*

person /pɜ:sə^{0}n/, **persons. Persons** is only used in formal or legal language. 'People' is normally used instead to refer to more than one person: see **people.** 1 COUNT N A **person** is a man or a woman. *I want to see the person responsible for accounts... She was a charming person.* 2 COUNT N WITH SUPP In grammar, the first **person** means the speaker, or the speaker and someone else, the second **person** means the person or people being spoken to, and the third **person** means someone or something else.

PHRASES ● If you do something **in person,** you do it yourself rather than letting someone else do it for you. *He wished he had gone to the house in person.* ● If you hear or see someone **in person,** you hear or see them directly, rather than on radio or television.

personage /pɜ:sə^{0}nɪdʒ/, **personages.** COUNT N A **personage** is a famous or important person; a formal use. *...a distinguished personage.*

personal /pɜ:sə^{0}nəl/. 1 ATTRIB ADJ A **personal** opinion, quality, or thing belongs or relates to a particular person. *My personal view is that he should resign... ...his personal belongings.* 2 ATTRIB ADJ If you give something your **personal** attention, you deal with it yourself rather than letting someone else deal with it. *The book was translated under the personal supervision of the author.* 3 ADJ **Personal** matters relate to your feelings, relationships, and health. *...the most intimate details of their personal lives... ...personal problems.* 4 ADJ **Personal** comments refer to someone's appearance or character in an offensive way. *I think we're getting too personal.*

personal assistant, personal assistants. COUNT N A **personal assistant** is a person who does secretarial and administrative work for someone.

personality /pɜ:sənæli^{1}ti^1/, **personalities.** 1 COUNT N WITH SUPP OR UNCOUNT N Your **personality** is your whole character and nature. *He has a wonderful personality... He was no judge of personality.* 2 COUNT N You can refer to a famous entertainer, broadcaster, or sports player as a **personality.** *...a television personality.*

personalized /pɜ:sə^{0}nəlaɪzd/; also spelled **personalised.** 1 ADJ A **personalized** object has its owner's initials or name on it. *...personalized pens.* 2 ADJ A **personalized** service is designed for one particular person. *...personalized counseling services.*

personally /pɜ:sə^{0}nəli^1/. 1 SENTENCE ADV You use **personally** to emphasize that you are giving your own opinion. *Well, personally, I feel that this is very difficult.* 2 ADV If you do something **personally,** you do it yourself rather than letting someone else do it. *Since then I have undertaken all the enquiries personally.* 3 ADV Something that affects you **personally** affects you rather than other people. *I wasn't referring to you personally... It would be unjust for him to bear personally the great expenses involved.*

personal pronoun, personal pronouns. COUNT N In grammar, **personal pronouns** refer to the speaker, the person or people being spoken to, or other people or things which have already been mentioned.

personify /pə^{5}sɒnɪfaɪ/, **personifies, personifying, personified.** VB WITH OBJ If someone **personifies** a particular quality, they seem to have that quality to a very large degree. *He seemed to personify the evil that was in the world.*

personnel /pɜ:sənel/. PLURAL N The **personnel** of an organization are the people who work for it; a formal use. *We've advertised for extra security personnel.*

perspective /pəspektɪv/, **perspectives.** 1 COUNT N A **perspective** is a particular way of thinking about something. *He wanted to leave the country in order to get a better perspective on things.* 2 PHRASE If you get something **in perspective** or **into perspective,** you judge its real importance by considering it in relation to other things. *It will help to put in perspective the vast gulf that separates existing groups.* 3 UNCOUNT N In art, **perspective** is a method by which things in the background of a picture are made to look further away than things in the foreground.

perspiration /pɜ:spə^{r}reɪʃə^{0}n/. UNCOUNT N **Perspiration** is the liquid which comes out onto your skin when you are hot or frightened; a formal use. *There were beads of perspiration on his upper lip.*

perspire /pəspaɪə/, **perspires, perspiring, perspired.** VB When you **perspire,** a liquid comes out onto your skin; a formal use. *Hot and perspiring, John toiled up the dusty ascent.*

persuade /pəsweɪd/, **persuades, persuading, persuaded. 1** VB WITH OBJ If someone or something **persuades** you to do a particular thing, they cause you to do it by giving you a good reason for doing it. *Marsha was trying to persuade Posy to change her mind... ...as the threat of unemployment persuades workers to moderate their pay demands.* **2** VB WITH OBJ If someone **persuades** you that something is true, they say things that eventually make you believe that it is true. *We worked hard to persuade them that we were genuinely interested... Persuade him of your seriousness about this.* ♦ **persuaded** PRED ADJ *Few of them are persuaded of the benefits of the shop.*

persuasion /pəsweɪʒə^{0}n/, **persuasions. 1** UNCOUNT N **Persuasion** is the act of persuading someone to do something or to believe that something is true. *They didn't need much persuasion.* **2** COUNT N WITH SUPP If you are of a particular **persuasion,** you have a particular set of beliefs; a formal use. *...people of different political persuasions.*

persuasive /pəsweɪsɪv/. ADJ Someone or something that is **persuasive** is likely to persuade you to do or believe a particular thing. *...a very persuasive argument.*

pertain /pəteɪn/, **pertains, pertaining, pertained.** VB WITH PREP 'to' Something that **pertains** to something else belongs or relates to it; a formal use. *...documents pertaining to the suspects.*

pertinent /pɜːtɪnənt/. ADJ Something that is **pertinent** is relevant; a formal use. *I asked him a lot of pertinent questions about the original production.*

perturbed /pətɜːbd/. PRED ADJ Someone who is **perturbed** is worried; a formal use. *She was perturbed about a rash which had come out on her face.*

peruse /pəruːz/, **peruses, perusing, perused.** VB WITH OBJ If you **peruse** a piece of writing, you read it; a formal use. *Having perused its contents, he flung down the paper.*

pervade /pə^{5}veɪd/, **pervades, pervading, pervaded.** VB WITH OBJ Something that **pervades** a place or thing is present or noticed throughout it; a formal use. *An atmosphere of contentment pervades the school.*

pervasive /pə^{5}veɪsɪv/. ADJ Something that is **pervasive** is present or noticed throughout a place or thing; a formal use. *...the Church's all-pervasive influence.*

perverse /pəvɜːs/. ADJ Someone who is **perverse** deliberately does things that are unreasonable. *He takes a perverse delight in irritating people.* ♦ **perversely** ADV *They persisted, perversely, in trying to grow grain.*

perversion /pəvɜːʃə^{0}n/, **perversions. 1** COUNT N OR UNCOUNT N A **perversion** is a sexual desire or action that is considered abnormal and unacceptable. **2** UNCOUNT N OR COUNT N The **perversion** of something is the changing of it so that it is no longer what it should be. *...the systematic perversion of the truth... It is a perversion of the local authorities' role.*

perversity /pəvɜːsɪ^{1}ti^1/. UNCOUNT N Someone who shows **perversity** deliberately does things that are unreasonable. *...her perversity as a child.*

pervert, perverts, perverting, perverted; pronounced /pəvɜːt/ when it is a verb, and /pɜːvɜːt/ when it is a noun. **1** VB WITH OBJ If you **pervert** something, for example a process or society, you interfere with it so that it is not what it used to be or should be; a formal use. *Traditional ceremonies were perverted into meaningless rituals.* **2** COUNT N A **pervert** is a person whose behaviour, especially sexual behaviour, is abnormal or unacceptable.

perverted /pəvɜːtɪ^{2}d/. **1** ADJ Someone who is **perverted** has abnormal behaviour or ideas, especially sexual ones. **2** ADJ Something that is **perverted** is wrong, unnatural, or harmful. *...a perverted form of love.*

pessimism /pesɪmɪzə^{0}m/. UNCOUNT N **Pessimism** is the belief that bad things are going to happen. *His pessimism was unjustified.* ♦ **pessimist** /pesɪmɪst/ COUNT N *Pessimists tell us that the family is doomed.*

pessimistic /pesɪmɪstɪk/. ADJ Someone who is **pessimistic** thinks that bad things are going to happen. *Success now seemed very remote and Bernard felt pessimistic.*

pest /pest/, **pests. 1** COUNT N A **pest** is an insect or small animal which damages crops or food supplies. **2** COUNT N Someone who is a **pest** keeps bothering you; an informal use.

pester /pestə/, **pesters, pestering, pestered.** VB WITH OBJ If you **pester** someone, you keep bothering them or asking them to do something. *Desiree had been pestering him to take her to Europe.*

pesticide /pestɪsaɪd/, **pesticides.** MASS N **Pesticides** are chemicals which farmers put on their crops to kill harmful insects.

pet /pet/, **pets, petting, petted. 1** COUNT N OR MOD A **pet** is an animal that you keep in your home to give you company and pleasure. *It is against the rules to keep pets... ...his pet dog.* **2** ATTRIB ADJ Someone's **pet** theory or subject is one that they particularly support or like. *We were listening to a gardener with his pet theories.* **3** VB WITH OBJ If you **pet** a person or animal, you pat or stroke them affectionately.

petal /petə^{0}l/, **petals.** COUNT N The **petals** of a flower are the thin coloured outer parts. *...rose petals.*

peter /piːtə/, **peters, petering, petered.**

peter out. PHR VB If something **peters out,** it gradually comes to an end. *The tracks petered out a mile later.*

petition /pɪ^{2}tɪʃə^{0}n/, **petitions, petitioning, petitioned. 1** COUNT N A **petition** is a document signed by a lot of people which asks for some official action to be taken. *He presented a petition signed by 10,357 electors.* **2** COUNT N A **petition** is also an application to a court of law for some specific legal action to be taken; a legal use. *She has filed a petition for divorce.* **3** VB WITH OR WITHOUT OBJ If you **petition** someone in authority, you make a formal request to them; a formal use. *It is my duty to petition the court to declare this action illegal.*

petrified /petrɪfaɪd/. ADJ If you are **petrified,** you are extremely frightened.

petrol /petrəl/. UNCOUNT N **Petrol** is a liquid used as a fuel for motor vehicles; a British use.

petroleum /pə^{2}trəʊlɪəm/. UNCOUNT N **Petroleum** is oil which is found underground or under the sea bed. Petrol and paraffin are obtained from petroleum.

petrol station, petrol stations. COUNT N A **petrol station** is a garage where petrol is sold and put into vehicles; a British use.

petticoat /peti^{1}kəʊt/, **petticoats.** COUNT N A **petticoat** is an item of women's underwear like a thin skirt.

petty /peti^1/. **1** ADJ **Petty** things are small and unimportant. *...petty details... ...petty problems.* **2** ADJ If someone is **petty,** they care too much about unimportant things and are perhaps selfish and unkind. *...petty jealousies.*

petty cash. UNCOUNT N **Petty cash** is money kept in an office for making small payments.

petulant /petjə^{4}lənt/. ADJ Someone who is **petulant** is angry and upset in a childish way; used showing disapproval. *With a petulant snarl, I pushed the door.*

pew /pjuː/, **pews.** COUNT N A **pew** is a long wooden seat for people in church.

pewter /pjuːtə/. UNCOUNT N **Pewter** is a grey metal made by mixing tin and lead. *...pewter plates.*

pH /piː eɪtʃ/. SING N The **pH** of a solution indicates whether it is an acid or alkali. A pH of less than 7 indicates that it is an acid, and a pH of more than 7 indicates that it is an alkali.

phantom /fæntə^{0}m/, **phantoms;** a literary word. **1** COUNT N A **phantom** is a ghost. **2** ATTRIB ADJ You use **phantom** to describe something which you think you see or hear but which is not real. *...a phantom presence.*

pharmaceutical /fɑːməsjuːtɪkə^{0}l/, **pharmaceuticals. 1** ATTRIB ADJ **Pharmaceutical** means connected with the industrial production of medicines and medical products. *...the world's largest pharmaceutical company.* **2** PLURAL N **Pharmaceuticals** are medicines. *...the sale of pharmaceuticals.*

pharmacist /fɑːməsɪst/, **pharmacists.** COUNT N A **pharmacist** is a person who is qualified to prepare and sell medicines.

pharmacy /fɑːməsi^1/, **pharmacies.** COUNT N A **pharmacy** is a shop where medicines are sold.

phase /feɪz/, **phases, phasing, phased. 1** COUNT N A **phase** is a particular stage in a process or in the development of something. *We have moved into a new phase in European history... ...cameras set to record every phase of the eclipse.* **2** VB WITH OBJ If you **phase** a change over a period of time, you cause it to happen in stages. *The reduction in nuclear weapons would be phased over ten years.*

phase in. PHR VB If you **phase in** something new, you introduce it gradually. *...a plan to phase in equal pay.*

phase out. PHR VB If you **phase** something **out,** you gradually stop using it. *This type of weapon was now being finally phased out.*

Ph.D. /piː eɪtʃ diː/, **Ph.D.s.** COUNT N A **Ph.D.** is a degree awarded to people who have done advanced research.

pheasant /fezə^{0}nt/, **pheasants. Pheasant** can also be the plural. COUNT N A **pheasant** is a bird with a long tail, sometimes shot for sport and then eaten.

phenomenal /fɪ^{2}nɒmɪnə^{0}l/. ADJ Something that is **phenomenal** is extraordinarily great or good. *It was a phenomenal success.*

phenomenon /fɪ^{2}nɒmɪnən/, **phenomena** /fɪ^{2}nɒmɪnə/. COUNT N A **phenomenon** is something that is observed to happen or exist. *...animals and plants and other natural phenomena... Is this concern about energy a recent phenomenon?*

philanthropist /fɪlænθrəpɪst/, **philanthropists.** COUNT N A **philanthropist** is someone who freely gives money to people who need it. *...wealthy philanthropists.*

philistine /fɪlɪstaɪn/, **philistines.** COUNT N Someone who is a **philistine** does not admire or recognize good art, music, or literature. *What does a little philistine like you know about it?* Also ADJ *He raged at a philistine public.*

philosopher /fɪlɒsəfə/, **philosophers.** COUNT N A **philosopher** is a person who creates or studies theories about basic things such as the nature of existence or how people should live. *...the Greek philosopher Thales.*

philosophic /fɪləsɒfɪk/. ADJ **Philosophic** means the same as philosophical.

philosophical /fɪləsɒfɪkə^{0}l/. **1** ATTRIB ADJ **Philosophical** means concerned with or relating to philosophy. *They used to have long philosophical conversations.* **2** ADJ Someone who is **philosophical** does not get upset when disappointing or disturbing things happen. *He was a placid boy with a philosophical approach to life.* ♦ **philosophically** ADV *He accepted their conclusion philosophically.*

philosophy /fɪlɒsəfi^1/, **philosophies. 1** UNCOUNT N **Philosophy** is the study or creation of theories about basic things such as the nature of existence or how people should live. *...an expert on Eastern philosophy.* **2** COUNT N WITH SUPP A **philosophy** is a particular set of theories or beliefs. *...the political philosophies of the West... ...new philosophies of child rearing.*

phlegm /flem/. UNCOUNT N **Phlegm** is the thick yellowish substance that develops in your throat when you have a cold.

phlegmatic /flegmætɪk/. ADJ Someone who is **phlegmatic** stays calm even when upsetting or exciting things happen; a formal use. *He was a phlegmatic, rather unemotional man.*

phobia /fəʊbɪə/, **phobias.** COUNT N A **phobia** is an irrational fear or hatred of something. *I've got a phobia about spiders.*

phone /fəʊn/, **phones, phoning, phoned. 1** SING N The **phone** is an electrical system used to talk to someone in another place, by dialling a number on a piece of equipment and speaking into it. *Most of the work is carried out over the phone.* Also ADJ *I must go and make a phone call.* **2** COUNT N A **phone** is the piece of equipment that you use when you talk to someone by phone. *I'm scared to answer the phone... The phone rang.* **3** VB WITH OR WITHOUT OBJ When you **phone** someone, you dial their phone number and speak to them by phone. *I went to phone Jenny... Harland phoned to tell me what time the bus was due.*

PHRASES • If you are **on the phone,** you are speaking to someone by phone. *I spent an hour on the phone trying to sort things out.* • You also say that you are **on the phone** when you have a phone in your home. *Are you on the phone?*

phone book, phone books. COUNT N A **phone book** is a book containing an alphabetical list of the names, addresses, and telephone numbers of the people in a town or area.

phone booth, phone booths. COUNT N A **phone booth** is a place in a public building where there is a telephone that can be used by the public.

phone box, phone boxes. COUNT N A **phone box** is a small shelter in the street in which there is a public telephone; a British use.

phone-in, phone-ins. COUNT N A **phone-in** is a radio programme in which people telephone with questions or opinions and their calls are broadcast.

phonetic /fə^{6}netɪk/, **phonetics;** a technical word. **1** UNCOUNT N **Phonetics** is the study of speech sounds. **2** ATTRIB ADJ **Phonetic** means relating to the sound of a word or to the sounds that are used in languages. *...phonetic spelling.*

phoney /fəʊni^1/, **phoneys;** an informal word, also spelled **phony. 1** ADJ Something that is **phoney** is false. *He gave a phony name and address... She put on a phoney English accent.* **2** ADJ Someone who is **phoney** is insincere or pretentious. *He thought all grown-ups were phony... ...your phoney manners.* Also COUNT N *I suddenly realized what a phoney he is.*

phosphate /fɒsfeɪt/, **phosphates.** COUNT N OR UNCOUNT N A **phosphate** is a chemical compound that contains phosphorus. Phosphates are used in fertilizers.

photo /fəʊtəʊ/, **photos.** COUNT N A **photo** is the same as a photograph; an informal use. *I took a magnificent photo of him.*

photocopier /fəʊtə^{6}kɒpɪə/, **photocopiers.** COUNT N A **photocopier** is a machine which quickly copies documents by photographing them.

photocopy /fəʊtə^{6}kɒpi^1/, **photocopies, photocopying, photocopied. 1** COUNT N A **photocopy** is a copy of a document made using a photocopier. 2 VB WITH OBJ If you **photocopy** a document, you make a copy of it using a photocopier.

photogenic /fəʊtədʒenɪk/. ADJ Someone who is **photogenic** looks attractive in photographs. *Photogenic girls were sought for a series of adverts.*

photograph /fəʊtəgrɑːf, -græf/, **photographs, photographing, photographed.** 1 COUNT N A **photograph** is a picture that is made using a camera. *They contacted the police after seeing his photograph in a newspaper.* 2 VB WITH OBJ When you **photograph** someone or something, you use a camera to obtain a picture of them. *She photographed the pigeons in Trafalgar Square.*

photographer /fətɒgrəfə/, **photographers.** COUNT N A **photographer** is someone who takes photographs, especially as their job.

photographic /fəʊtəgræfɪk/. 1 ATTRIB ADJ **Photographic** means connected with photographs or photography. *...expensive photographic equipment.* 2 ATTRIB ADJ If you have a **photographic** memory, you can remember things in great detail after seeing them once.

photography /fətɒgrəfi[1]/. UNCOUNT N **Photography** is the skill, job, or process of producing photographs. *Fox-Talbot was a pioneer of photography.*

phrasal verb /freɪzəl vɜːb/, **phrasal verbs.** COUNT N A **phrasal verb** is a combination of a verb and an adverb or preposition, used together to have a particular meaning. 'Give up' and 'set out' are phrasal verbs.

phrase /freɪz/, **phrases, phrasing, phrased.** 1 COUNT N A **phrase** is a short group of words that are used as a unit and whose meaning is not obvious from the words contained in it. *People still use the phrase 'doctor's orders'.* 2 VB WITH OBJ AND ADJUNCT If you **phrase** something in a particular way, you express it in words in that way. *The moment I'd said it, I could see that I'd phrased it wrong.*

PHRASES ● A **turn of phrase** is a particular way of expressing something in words. *You have a nice turn of phrase.*

phrase book, phrase books. COUNT N A **phrase book** is a book for travellers with lists of useful words and expressions in a foreign language, together with the translation of each word or expression.

phraseology /freɪziɒlədʒi[1]/. UNCOUNT N WITH SUPP If something is expressed using a particular **phraseology**, it is expressed in words and expressions of that type; a formal use. *...the sort of phraseology used by some journalists.*

physical /fɪzɪkə[0]l/. 1 ATTRIB ADJ **Physical** qualities, actions, or things are connected with a person's body, rather than with their mind. *All his physical and emotional needs would be attended to.* ♦ **physically** ADV *He looked physically fit... She didn't attract me physically.* 2 ATTRIB ADJ **Physical** also refers to things that can be touched or seen, especially with regard to their size or shape. *...the physical characteristics of the earth... ...the physical size of a computer.* 3 ADJ You can refer to things connected with the laws of physics as **physical**. *...basic physical laws.*

physician /fɪzɪʃə[0]n/, **physicians.** COUNT N A **physician** is a doctor; an American use.

physicist /fɪzɪsɪst/, **physicists.** COUNT N A **physicist** is a person who studies physics. *...a well-known nuclear physicist.*

physics /fɪzɪks/. UNCOUNT N **Physics** is the scientific study of forces and qualities such as heat, light, sound, pressure, gravity, and electricity. *According to our present ideas of physics, nothing can travel faster than light... ...nuclear physics.*

physiology /fɪziɒlədʒi[1]/. 1 UNCOUNT N **Physiology** is the scientific study of how people, animals, and plants function. 2 SING N WITH POSS The **physiology** of an animal or plant is the way that it functions. *He was interested in the physiology of bulls.* ♦ **physiological** /fɪziəlɒdʒɪkə[0]l/ ADJ *...physiological changes.*

physiotherapist /fɪziəʊθerəpɪst/, **physiotherapists.** COUNT N A **physiotherapist** is a person whose job is doing physiotherapy.

physiotherapy /fɪziəʊθerəpi[1]/. UNCOUNT N **Physiotherapy** is medical treatment given to people who cannot move a part of their body and involves exercise, massage, or heat treatment.

physique /fɪziːk/, **physiques.** COUNT N OR UNCOUNT N Someone's **physique** is the shape and size of their body. *...a good-looking lad with a fine physique.*

pi /paɪ/. **Pi** is a number, approximately 3.142, which is equal to the circumference of a circle divided by its diameter. It is usually represented by the Greek letter π.

pianist /pɪənɪst/, **pianists.** COUNT N A **pianist** is a person who plays the piano.

piano /pi'ænəʊ/, **pianos.** COUNT N A **piano** is a large musical instrument with a row of black and white keys. You strike the keys with your fingers in order to make a sound. *I play the piano.* ● See also **grand piano.**

pick /pɪk/, **picks, picking, picked.** 1 VB WITH OBJ If you **pick** a particular person or thing, you choose that one. *Next time let's pick somebody else... I could not have picked a better way to travel.* 2 VB WITH OBJ When you **pick** flowers, fruit, or leaves, you break them off the plant and collect them. *...the woods where we picked blackberries.* 3 VB WITH OBJ AND ADJUNCT If you **pick** something from a place, or **pick** it up, you remove it from there with your fingers. *He picked his blazer off a chair... She picked a cigarette from her box and lit it.* 4 VB WITH OBJ If you **pick** an argument with someone, you deliberately cause one. *He had ceased to pick quarrels with her.* 5 VB WITH OBJ If someone **picks** a lock, they open it without using a key, for example by using a piece of wire.

PHRASES ● If you **pick** your **way** across an area, you walk across it carefully, avoiding any obstacles. *He began to pick his way over the rocks.* ● to **pick** someone's **brains**: see **brain.** ● to **pick holes in** something: see **hole.** ● to **pick** someone's **pocket**: see **pocket.** ● See also **hand-picked.**

pick at. PHR VB If you **pick at** the food you are eating, you eat only very small amounts of it. *Laing was picking morosely at his salad.*

pick on. PHR VB If you **pick on** someone, you criticize them unfairly or are unkind to them; an informal use. *Why are you always picking on me?*

pick out. PHR VB If you **pick out** someone or something, you recognize them when it is difficult to see them. *Ralph picked out Jack easily, even at that distance.*

pick up. PHR VB 1 When you **pick** an object **up**, you lift it up. *He stooped down to pick up the two pebbles.* 2 When you **pick up** something or someone, you collect them from somewhere. *I might get my brother to come and pick me up.* 3 If someone **is picked up** by the police, they are arrested. *I don't want you to be picked up for drunkenness.* 4 If you **pick up** a skill or an idea, you acquire it without effort; an informal use. *Did you pick up any Swedish?... I may pick up a couple of useful ideas for my book.* 5 If you **pick up** someone you do not know, you talk to them and try to start a sexual relationship with them; an informal use. *I doubt whether Tony ever picked up a woman in his life.* 6 If a piece of equipment **picks up** a signal or sound, it receives it or detects it. *It was easier to pick up Radio Luxembourg than the Light Programme.* 7 If trade or the economy of a country **picks up,** it improves. *The economy is picking up.*

picket /pɪkɪt/, **pickets, picketing, picketed.** 1 VB WITH OR WITHOUT OBJ When a group of workers who are on strike **picket** a place of work, they stand outside it as a protest and to persuade other workers to join a strike. *The plan was to picket docks and power stations.* Also COUNT N *...the historic picket at Saltley coke depot.* 2 COUNT N **Pickets** are people who are picketing a place of work. *We could hear the chanting of the pickets.*

pickle /pɪkə[0]l/, **pickles, pickling, pickled.** 1 COUNT N OR UNCOUNT N **Pickles** are vegetables or fruit which have been kept in vinegar or salt water for a long time to give them a strong, sharp taste. *...a jar of pickles.* 2 VB WITH OBJ When you **pickle** food, you preserve it by keeping it in vinegar or salt water. *To pickle herring, soak the fish in salted water.*

pickpocket /pɪkpɒkɪt/, **pickpockets.** COUNT N A **pickpocket** is a person who steals things from people's pockets or handbags.

picnic /pɪknɪk/, **picnics, picnicking, picnicked.** COUNT N When people have a **picnic,** they eat a meal in the open air. *They often went on picnics.* Also VB *The woods might be full of people picnicking.* ♦ **picnicker** COUNT N *In October, picnickers were unlikely.*

pictorial /pɪktɔːrɪəl/. **Pictorial** means relating to or using pictures. *...pictorial conventions... ...pictorial skills.*

picture /pɪktʃə/, **pictures, picturing, pictured.** 1 COUNT N A **picture** is a drawing or painting. *...the most important picture Picasso ever painted... He picked up a book to look at the pictures.* 2 COUNT N A **picture** is also a photograph. *We all had our pictures taken.* 3 VB WITH OBJ If someone or something **is pictured** in a newspaper or magazine, they appear in a photograph in it. *Murray was pictured in The Times.* 4 COUNT N You can refer to the image you see on a television screen as a **picture.** *We have all seen television news pictures of their forces in action.* 5 COUNT N You can also refer to a film as a **picture.** *We worked together in the last picture I made.* 6 PLURAL N In Britain, the **pictures** refers to the cinema. *She met him at the pictures.* 7 COUNT N If you have a **picture** of something, you have an idea or impression of it in your mind. *A picture flashed through Kunta's mind of the panther springing at him... They can get quite a distorted picture of what's going on.* Also VB WITH OBJ *He could picture all too easily the consequences of being caught.* 8 COUNT N If you give a **picture** of what something is like, you describe it. *Mr Hamilton gives a most interesting picture of Monty's family background.* 9 SING N When you refer to the **picture** in a particular place, you are referring to the situation there. *In Nigeria, the picture appears to be different.* 10 PHRASE If you **put** someone **in the picture,** you give them the details of a situation. *Let me put you in the picture about the situation there.*

picturesque /pɪktʃəresk/. ADJ A **picturesque** place is attractive, interesting, and unspoiled. *...a small hotel overlooking the picturesque fishing harbour of Zeebrugge.*

pie /paɪ/, **pies.** COUNT N OR UNCOUNT N A **pie** consists of meat, vegetables, or fruit, baked in pastry. *...chicken pie... ...a piece of apple pie.*

piece /piːs/, **pieces, piecing, pieced.** 1 COUNT N A **piece** of something is a portion, part, or section of it. *He came back dragging a great big piece of a tree... She cut the cake and gave me a piece... He tore both letters into small pieces.* 2 COUNT N A **piece** of something is also an individual item of it. *The only piece of clothing she bought was a jumper... ...the most important piece of apparatus.* 3 SING N You use **piece** to refer to an individual group of facts or an individual action or product. *...a valuable piece of information... ...a thoughtful piece of research... ...this piece of advice.* 4 COUNT N A **piece** is also something that is written or created, such as an article, work of art, or musical composition. *...a thoughtful piece about President Roosevelt... It was a classic piece called Forever Is For Us.* 5 COUNT N WITH SUPP You can refer to specific coins as **pieces.** For example, a 10p **piece** is a coin that is worth 10p. *...a lighter that was no bigger than a 50p piece.* 6 COUNT N In a board game, the **pieces** are the objects which you move around the board.

PHRASES ● If someone or something is still **in one piece** after a dangerous experience, they are not damaged or hurt. ● If you **go to pieces,** you lose control of yourself because you are nervous or upset; an informal use. ● If someone **tears** you **to pieces** or **pulls** your work **to pieces,** they criticize you or your work very severely; an informal use. ● **a piece of cake:** see **cake.**

piece together. PHR VB 1 If you **piece together** the truth about something, you gradually discover it. *She had not yet been able to piece together exactly what had happened.* 2 If you **piece** something **together,** you gradually make it complete by joining its parts together. *She pieced together the torn-up drawing.*

piecemeal /piːsmiːl/. ADJ OR ADV A **piecemeal** process happens gradually, usually at irregular intervals. *...the piecemeal accumulation of land... Films are financed piecemeal; the distributor doles out money little by little.*

piecework /piːswɜːk/. UNCOUNT N If you do **piecework,** you are paid for the amount of work you do rather than the length of time you work.

pier /pɪə/, **piers.** COUNT N A **pier** is a large structure which sticks out into the sea and which people can walk along.

pierce /pɪəs/, **pierces, piercing, pierced.** VB WITH OBJ OR ADJUNCT If you **pierce** something with a sharp object, the object goes into it and makes a hole. *When the snake's fangs pierce its victim's flesh, the venom is injected... The pointed end of the stick pierced through its throat into its mouth.*

piercing /pɪəsɪŋ/. 1 ADJ A **piercing** sound is high-pitched and sharp in an unpleasant way. *I was jolted out of my exhaustion by piercing screams.* 2 ADJ Someone with **piercing eyes** has bright eyes which seem to look at you very intensely. *He had piercing blue eyes.* 3 ADJ A **piercing** wind is very cold.

piety /paɪɪ'ti[1]/. UNCOUNT N **Piety** is strong religious belief, or religious behaviour. *...men of true piety.*

pig /pɪg/, **pigs.** 1 COUNT N A **pig** is a farm animal with a pinkish skin which is kept for meat. 2 COUNT N If you call someone a **pig,** you mean that you think they are greedy, unkind, or unpleasant in some way; an informal use that some people find offensive. 3 PHRASE If you **make a pig of** yourself, you eat too much; an informal use that shows disapproval.

pigeon /pɪdʒɪn/, **pigeons.** COUNT N A **pigeon** is a grey bird which is often seen in towns.

pigeon-hole, pigeon-holes. COUNT N A **pigeon-hole** is one of the sections in a frame on a wall where letters and messages can be left. *Howard strolled over to the rows of pigeon-holes to collect his mail.*

piggyback /pɪgi'bæk/, **piggybacks.** COUNT N If you give someone a **piggyback,** you carry them high on your back, supporting them under their knees.

piglet /pɪglɪ't/, **piglets.** COUNT N A **piglet** is a young pig.

pigment /pɪgmə^{2}nt/, **pigments.** COUNT N OR UNCOUNT N A **pigment** is a substance that gives something a particular colour; a formal use. *It forms part of the red pigment of blood... I persisted with brush, pigment, and canvas.*

pigsty /pɪgstaɪ/, **pigsties.** COUNT N A **pigsty** is a hut with a yard where pigs are kept.

pigtail /pɪgteɪl/, **pigtails.** COUNT N A **pigtail** is a length of plaited hair. *...a girl with a blonde pigtail down her back.*

pike /paɪk/. **Pike** is the singular and the plural. COUNT N A **pike** is a large river fish that catches other fish.

pile /paɪl/, **piles, piling, piled. 1** COUNT N A **pile** of things is a quantity of them lying on top of one another. *There in front of me was a great pile of old tin cans... ...a pile of sand... He lifted a pile of books from the bedside table.* **2** VB WITH OBJ AND ADJUNCT If you **pile** a quantity of things somewhere, you put them there so that they form a pile. *Brody picked up the heap of papers and piled them on top of a radiator... Her hair was piled high on her head.* **3** VB WITH OBJ If a surface **is piled** with things, it is covered with piles of them. *His desk was piled with papers.* **4** COUNT N A **pile** or **piles** of something is a large amount of it; an informal use. *He's got an enormous pile of money stashed away.* **5** VB WITH ADJUNCT If people **pile** into or out of a place, they all get into it or out of it in a disorganized way. *The troops piled into the coaches.* **6** PLURAL N **Piles** are painful swellings that appear in the veins inside a person's anus. **7** UNCOUNT N The **pile** of a carpet is its soft surface, which consists of lots of little threads standing on end. *...a luxurious deep pile carpet.*

pile up. PHR VB **1** If you **pile** things **up**, you gather them together in a pile. *Her hair had been piled up on top of her head... The papers she was meant to be reading piled up on her desk.* **2** If things **pile up**, more and more of them happen or are acquired. *All these disasters piled up on the unfortunate villagers... Last year the company piled up losses totalling £4 billion.*

pile-up, pile-ups. COUNT N A **pile-up** is a road accident involving several vehicles.

pilgrim /pɪlgrɪm/, **pilgrims.** COUNT N A **pilgrim** is a person who makes a journey to a holy place.

pilgrimage /pɪlgrɪmɪdʒ/, **pilgrimages.** COUNT N OR UNCOUNT N A **pilgrimage** is a journey that someone makes to a holy place. *She made the pilgrimage to Lourdes... ...a place of pilgrimage.*

pill /pɪl/, **pills. 1** COUNT N A **pill** is a small, round mass of medicine that you swallow. *I took a sleeping pill.* **2** SING N The **pill** is a type of drug that women can take regularly to prevent pregnancy. *I'm not on the pill.*

pillar /pɪlə/, **pillars. 1** COUNT N A **pillar** is a tall, narrow, solid structure, used to support part of a building. *I fell asleep leaning against a pillar on someone's porch.* **2** COUNT N WITH SUPP Someone who is a **pillar** of a particular group is an active and important member of it. *I thought you had to be a pillar of the community to foster children... ...pillars of society.*

pillar box, pillar boxes. COUNT N A **pillar box** is a red box in the street in which you put letters for collection; an old-fashioned British use.

pilloried /pɪləri^{1}d/. PRED ADJ If someone is **pilloried,** they are criticized severely and in public; a formal use. *He was pilloried and his resignation demanded.*

pillow /pɪləʊ/, **pillows.** COUNT N A **pillow** is a rectangular cushion which you rest your head on when you are in bed.

pillowcase /pɪlə^{6}keɪs/, **pillowcases.** COUNT N A **pillowcase** is a cover for a pillow.

pilot /paɪlət/, **pilots, piloting, piloted. 1** COUNT N A **pilot** is a person who is trained to fly an aircraft. **2** VB WITH OBJ When someone **pilots** an aircraft, they act as its pilot. **3** VB WITH OBJ If you **pilot** a new law or scheme, you introduce it. *He was keen to see through the Bill which John Silkin was piloting.* **4** ATTRIB ADJ A **pilot** study is a small test of a scheme or product to see if it will be successful. *This year we are trying a pilot scheme whereby the university leases one or two houses for students.*

pimp /pɪmp/, **pimps.** COUNT N A **pimp** is a man who finds clients for prostitutes and takes a large part of their earnings; an informal use.

pimple /pɪmpə^{0}l/, **pimples.** COUNT N **Pimples** are small red spots, especially on your face.

pin /pɪn/, **pins, pinning, pinned. 1** COUNT N A **pin** is a very small, thin, pointed piece of metal which is used to fasten pieces of cloth together. ● See also **drawing pin, safety pin. 2** VB WITH OBJ AND ADJUNCT If you **pin** something somewhere, you fasten it there with a pin, a drawing pin, or a safety pin. *She wore a white rose pinned to her blouse.* **3** VB WITH OBJ AND ADJUNCT If someone **pins** you in a particular position, they hold you down firmly so that you cannot move. *His strong arms were around me, pinning me down.* **4** VB WITH OBJ AND 'on' OR 'upon' If someone **pins** the blame for something on you, they say that you did it or caused it; an informal use. *You can't pin that on me.* **5** VB WITH OBJ AND 'on' OR 'upon' If you **pin** your hopes on something, you rely on it to be successful. *He pinned his hopes on the prospect of a split in the opposition party.*

pin down. PHR VB **1** If you try to **pin down** something which is hard to describe, you try to say exactly what it is or what it is like. *The courts have found obscenity impossible to pin down as a punishable offence.* **2** If you **pin** someone **down,** you force them to make a definite statement. *He was anxious to pin the Minister down to some definite commitment.*

pin up. PHR VB **1** If you **pin up** a poster or a notice, you pin it to a wall. **2** If you **pin up** part of a piece of clothing, you pin the bottom of it to a higher position. *The hem was pinned up.* **3** See also **pin-up.**

pinafore /pɪnəfɔː/, **pinafores.** COUNT N A **pinafore** is a type of sleeveless dress that can be worn over a blouse or sweater, or over another dress to protect it.

pincer /pɪnsə/, **pincers. 1** PLURAL N **Pincers** are a tool consisting of two pieces of metal that are hinged in the middle. Pincers are used for gripping things tightly. *...a pair of pincers.* **2** COUNT N The **pincers** of a crab or a lobster are its front claws.

pinch /pɪntʃ/, **pinches, pinching, pinched. 1** VB WITH OBJ If you **pinch** someone, you squeeze a part of their body between your thumb and first finger. *Dr. Hochstadt pinched Judy's cheek as she passed.* Also COUNT N *She gave my wrist a little pinch.* **2** SING N A **pinch** of something is the amount of it that you can hold between your thumb and your first finger. *Season with salt and a pinch of cinnamon.* **3** VB WITH OBJ If someone **pinches** something, they steal it; an informal use. *I pinched fourpence from the box.*

PHRASES ● **At a pinch** means if absolutely necessary and if there is no alternative; an informal use. *At a pinch the new doctor would do.* ● If you **are feeling the pinch,** you do not have as much money as you used to, and cannot buy all the things that you want. *The big fashion establishments have been feeling the pinch lately.* ● to **take** something **with a pinch of salt:** see **salt.**

pine /paɪn/, **pines, pining, pined. 1** COUNT N A **pine** or a **pine tree** is a tall evergreen tree with long thin leaves and a fresh smell. **2** UNCOUNT N **Pine** is the pale-coloured wood of pine trees, which is used for making furniture. **3** VB WITH 'for' OR TO-INF If you **are pining** for something, you feel sad because you cannot have it. *Helen pines for you... Most of them were pining to be recognized and admitted as citizens.*

pineapple /paɪnæpə^{0}l/, **pineapples.** COUNT N OR UNCOUNT N A **pineapple** is a large oval fruit with sweet juicy flesh and a thick, brownish, knobbly skin. *...a slice of pineapple.*

ping /pɪŋ/, **pings, pinging, pinged.** COUNT N A **ping** is a short, high-pitched, metallic sound. *There is a loud ping from the alarm clock.* Also VB *The bell pings; the lift doors open.*

ping-pong /pɪŋ pɒŋ/. UNCOUNT N **Ping-pong** is the game of table tennis.

pink /pɪŋk/, **pinker, pinkest; 1** ADJ Something that is **pink** is of a colour between red and white. *...the white and pink blossom of orchard apples.* **2** ADJ If you go **pink,** your face goes slightly red because you are embarrassed or angry. *He went very pink, and looked away.*

pinkish /pɪŋkɪʃ/. ADJ **Pinkish** means slightly pink. *...a faint pinkish glow.*

pinnacle /pɪnəkə^{0}l/, **pinnacles. 1** COUNT N A **pinnacle** is a tall pointed piece of a building or a rock. *...the pinnacles of St John's Church... ...the white pinnacles of the distant mountains.* **2** COUNT N WITH SUPP The **pinnacle** of something is the best or highest level of it. *These newspapers were regarded as the pinnacle of journalism.*

pinpoint /pɪnpɔɪnt/, **pinpoints, pinpointing, pinpointed. 1** VB WITH OBJ If you **pinpoint** something, you discover or explain exactly what it is. *In their book, Jackson and Marsden pinpointed the difference.* **2** VB WITH OBJ If you **pinpoint** the position of something, you indicate its exact position. *'Just here,' he said, pinpointing it on the map.*

pins and needles. PLURAL N If you get **pins and needles,** you feel sharp tingling pains for a while because you have been in an awkward or uncomfortable position.

pin-stripe. ATTRIB ADJ **Pin-stripe** cloth or **pin-striped** cloth has very narrow vertical stripes. *He wore a pin-stripe suit.*

pint /paɪnt/, **pints. 1** COUNT N In Britain, a **pint** is a unit of volume for liquids equal to one-eighth of an imperial gallon or approximately 568 cubic centimetres. *...one pint of milk.* **2** COUNT N In America, a **pint** is a unit of volume for liquids equal to one-eighth of an American gallon or approximately 473 cubic centimetres. **3** COUNT N A **pint** is also a pint of beer. *He likes having a couple of pints with his lunch.*

pin-up, pin-ups. COUNT N A **pin-up** is a picture of an attractive woman or man. *...pin-ups of film stars.*

pioneer /paɪənɪə/, **pioneers, pioneering, pioneered. 1** COUNT N A **pioneer** in a particular activity is one of the first people to be involved in it and develop it. *He was a pioneer of photography.* **2** VB WITH OBJ Someone who **pioneers** a new activity, invention, or process is one of the first people to do it. *...a hospital which pioneered open heart surgery in this country.* ♦ **pioneering** ATTRIB ADJ *...a pioneering and innovative banker.* **3** COUNT N A **pioneer** is also one of the first people to live or farm in a particular place.

pious /paɪəs/. ADJ A **pious** person is very religious and moral.

pip /pɪp/, **pips. 1** COUNT N A **pip** is one of the small hard seeds in a fruit such as an apple, orange, or pear. **2** COUNT N The **pips** on the radio are a series of short, high-pitched sounds that are used as a time signal.

pipe /paɪp/, **pipes, piping, piped. 1** COUNT N A **pipe** is a long, round, hollow object through which a liquid or gas can flow. *...hot water pipes.* **2** VB WITH OBJ To **pipe** a liquid or gas somewhere means to transfer it from one place to another through a pipe. *Hot water is piped to all the rooms.* **3** COUNT N A **pipe** is also an object which is used for smoking tobacco. It consists of a hollow cup-shaped bowl for holding the tobacco, and a tube through which you inhale the smoke. *He was sitting in his armchair, smoking a pipe and reading the paper.* **4** See also **piping, piping hot.**

piped music. UNCOUNT N **Piped music** is music which is played through loudspeakers in public places.

pipe dream, pipe dreams. COUNT N A **pipe dream** is a hope or plan which you know will never really happen.

pipeline /paɪplaɪn/, **pipelines. 1** COUNT N A **pipeline** is a large pipe used for carrying oil or gas over a long distance. **2** PHRASE If something is **in the pipeline,** it is already planned or begun. *More improvements were in the pipeline.*

piper /paɪpə/, **pipers.** COUNT N A **piper** is a musician who plays the bagpipes.

piping /paɪpɪŋ/. **1** UNCOUNT N **Piping** is lengths of pipe or tube made from metal or plastic. *...a length of steel piping.* **2** ATTRIB ADJ A **piping** voice is high-pitched voice and shrill; used in written English. *In a piping voice she ordered me to sit down.*

piping hot. ADJ Food or water that is **piping hot** is very hot. *...mugs of piping hot coffee.*

piquant /piːkənt, -kɑːnt/. ADJ Something that is **piquant** is interesting and exciting; a formal word. *...a piquant face with large appealing dark-blue eyes.* ♦ **piquancy** UNCOUNT N *Argument adds piquancy to the contest.*

pique /piːk/. UNCOUNT N **Pique** is the feeling of resentment you have when your pride is hurt. *He withdrew from the contest in a fit of pique.*

piracy /paɪrə^{1}sɪ/. **1** UNCOUNT N **Piracy** was robbery carried out by pirates. **2** UNCOUNT N You can also refer to the illegal copying of electronic, recorded, or printed material as **piracy.** *...software piracy.*

pirate /paɪrə^{1}t/, **pirates, pirating, pirated. 1** COUNT N **Pirates** were sailors who attacked and robbed other ships. **2** VB WITH OBJ Someone who **pirates** electronic, recorded, or printed material copies and sells it illegally. *New advertisers were pirating his paintings.* ♦ **pirated** ADJ *There were a lot of pirated editions.*

pirouette /pɪruɛt/, **pirouettes.** COUNT N In ballet, a **pirouette** is a fast turn of the dancer's body done on the toes or the ball of the foot.

pistol /pɪstə^{0}l/, **pistols.** COUNT N A **pistol** is a small hand gun.

piston /pɪstə^{0}n/, **pistons.** COUNT N A **piston** is a cylinder or metal disc in an engine. Pistons slide up and down inside tubes to make parts of the engine move.

pit /pɪt/, **pits, pitting, pitted. 1** COUNT N A **pit** is a hole in the ground. *The pit was stacked with ammunition.* **2** COUNT N A **pit** is also a small, shallow hole in the surface of something. *...scratches and pits on the enamel.* **3** COUNT N You can refer to a coal mine as a **pit.** *...the men coming home from the pit.* **4** PLURAL N In motor racing, the **pits** are the areas where drivers stop for fuel and repairs during races. **5** See also **pitted.**

PHRASES ● If you have a feeling **in the pit of your stomach,** you have an unpleasant feeling inside your body because you are afraid or anxious. ● If you describe someone or something as **the pits,** you mean that they are the worst of their kind; an informal use. *That first week is the pits, isn't it?* ● If you **pit** your **wits against** someone, you compete with them in a test of knowledge or intelligence.

pitch /pɪtʃ/, **pitches, pitching, pitched. 1** COUNT N A **pitch** is an area of ground that is marked out and used for playing a game such as football, cricket, or hockey. 2 VB WITH OBJ If you **pitch** something somewhere, you throw it forcefully but aiming carefully. *He was pitching a penny at a crack in the sidewalk.* 3 VB WITH ADJUNCT If someone or something **pitches** to the ground, they suddenly fall forwards. *He suddenly pitched headlong to the ground.* 4 UNCOUNT N The **pitch** of a sound is how high or low it is. *Her voice dropped to a lower pitch.* 5 SING N WITH SUPP If something reaches a high **pitch,** it reaches a high level or degree. *Excitement is now at fever pitch... Her frustration mounted to such a pitch of anger that she could no longer keep silent.* 6 VB WITH OBJ AND ADJUNCT If you **pitch** something at a particular level, you set it at that level. *Her lectures are pitched directly at the level of the students.* 7 VB WITH OBJ To **pitch** a tent means to erect it.

pitch in. PHR VB If you **pitch in,** you join in an activity; an informal use. *They will be expected to pitch in and make their own beds.*

pitch-black. ADJ If a place or the night is **pitch-black,** it is completely dark.

pitched battle, pitched battles. COUNT N A **pitched battle** is a very fierce, violent fight. *Police fought a pitched battle with about 40 youths.*

pitcher /pɪtʃə/, **pitchers;** an American word. 1 COUNT N A **pitcher** is a jug. *...a pitcher of water.* 2 COUNT N In baseball, the **pitcher** is the person who throws the ball to the person who is batting.

piteous /pɪtɪəs/. ADJ Something that is **piteous** is so sad that you feel great pity; a literary use. *There were piteous sounds of suffering and pain.*

pitfall /pɪtfɔːl/, **pitfalls.** COUNT N The **pitfalls** of a particular activity or situation are the things that may go wrong or may cause problems later. *...the pitfalls of pursuing such a drastic policy.*

pith /pɪθ/. UNCOUNT N The **pith** of a citrus fruit such as an orange is the white substance underneath the peel.

pithy /pɪθi¹/. ADJ A **pithy** comment or piece of writing is short, direct, and memorable. *...pithy, ironic observations... ...pithy working-class humour.*

pitiable /pɪtɪəbə⁰l/. ADJ Someone who is **pitiable** is in such a sad or weak situation that you feel pity for them. *She was in a pitiable plight.*

pitiful /pɪtɪfʊl/. ADJ Someone or something that is **pitiful** is so sad, weak, or small that you feel pity for them. *...his thin, bony legs and his pitiful arms... ...the pitiful sound of a human being in pain.* ♦ **pitifully** ADV *He looks pitifully thin.*

pitiless /pɪtɪlɪ³s/. ADJ Someone or something that is **pitiless** shows no feelings of pity or mercy. *His face was cool and pitiless.*

pittance /pɪtə⁰ns/. SING N If you receive a **pittance,** you receive only a very small amount of money. *They are tired of working for a pittance.*

pitted /pɪtɪ²d/. ADJ If the surface of something is **pitted,** it is covered with a lot of small, shallow holes. *The walls were pitted with bullet holes.*

pity /pɪti¹/, **pities, pitying, pitied.** 1 UNCOUNT N If you feel **pity** for someone, you feel very sorry for them. 2 VB WITH OBJ If you **pity** someone, you feel very sorry for them. *She pitied him with her whole heart.* 3 SING N You say that it is a **pity** that something is the case when you are expressing disappointment or regret. *It will be a terrible pity if this should happen.* 4 PHRASE If you **take pity on** someone, you feel sorry for them and help them. *A man who spoke English took pity on us and it was all sorted out.*

pivot /pɪvət/, **pivots, pivoting, pivoted.** 1 COUNT N A **pivot** is the pin or central point on which something balances or turns. *The compass needle swung round on its pivot.* 2 VB To **pivot** means to balance or turn on a central point. *Michael stopped, pivoted and walked back in.* 3 COUNT N The **pivot** in a situation is the most important thing around which everything else is based or arranged. *Their daughter was the pivot of their lives.*

pizza /piːtsə/, **pizzas.** COUNT N OR UNCOUNT N A **pizza** is a flat piece of dough covered with tomatoes, cheese, and other savoury food, which is baked in an oven. *...a plate of pizza.*

placard /plækɑːd/, **placards.** COUNT N A **placard** is a large notice that is carried in a march or demonstration.

placate /plə³keɪt/, **placates, placating, placated.** VB WITH OBJ If you **placate** someone, you try to stop them feeling angry or resentful by doing things that will please them. *...the desire of politicians to placate the public.*

place /pleɪs/, **places, placing, placed.** 1 COUNT N A **place** is any point, building, area, town, or country. *The cellar was a very dark place... ...photographs of places taken during his travels abroad... ...a meeting place... We were looking for a good place to camp.* 2 COUNT N WITH SUPP You can refer to the position where something belongs as its **place.** *She put the book back in its place on the shelf.* 3 SING N **Place** can be used after 'any', 'no', 'some', or 'every' to mean 'anywhere', 'nowhere', 'somewhere', or 'everywhere'; an informal American use. *You are not going any place... He had no place else to go.* 4 COUNT N Your **place** is the house or flat where you live; an informal use. *What sort of place do they have?* 5 COUNT N Your **place** at a table or in a classroom, for example, is a seat that is intended for you to use or that you normally use. *Mrs Kaul had to leave her place and go to the back of the room.* 6 COUNT N A **place** at a table is also a space with a knife, fork, and other things arranged on it, so that one person can sit down and eat. *Every day 12 places are laid for dinner.* 7 COUNT N If you have a **place** on a committee or at a college, for example, you are a member of the committee or are accepted by the college as a student. *I got a place at a teachers' training college... Harper failed to win a place on the committee.* 8 COUNT N WITH SUPP Your **place** in a society, system, or situation is your position or role in relation to other people. *...Britain's place in the world... Frank felt it was not his place to raise any objection... The demonstration occupies a central place in their political campaign.* 9 PASSIVE VB If someone **is** well **placed,** they have a lot of advantages or resources. *As for finance, we're better placed than people think.* 10 COUNT N Your **place** in a competition or on a scale is your position at the end of the competition or on the scale. First place is the winning or top position. *The US leapt from sixth place to second.* 11 COUNT N WITH POSS Your **place** in a book or speech is the point that you have reached in it. *He lost his place in his notes.* 12 VB WITH OBJ AND ADJUNCT If you **place** something somewhere, you put it there neatly or carefully. *She placed the music on the piano and sat down... Chairs had been placed in rows all down the room.* 13 VB WITH OBJ AND 'on' OR 'upon' If you **place** responsibility, pressure, or a restriction on someone, you cause them to have it or be affected by it. If you place emphasis or blame on something, you emphasize or blame it. *The responsibility placed upon us is too heavy to bear... Vita is placing most of the blame on her mother... The New Left placed much emphasis on the role of culture.* 14 VB WITH OBJ If you **place** an order for goods or an advert in a newspaper, for example, you ask a company to send you the goods or you ask the newspaper to publish the advert. 15 VB WITH OBJ If you cannot **place** someone, you cannot remember exactly who they are or where you have met them before. *She was looking at me as if she could not quite place me.* 16 COUNT N If you say how many decimal **places** there are in a number, you are saying how many numbers there are to the right of the decimal point.

PHRASES ● If something is **in place,** it is in its correct or usual position. If it is **out of place,** it is not in its correct or usual position. *He held the handle in place while the glue set... She was slightly out of breath but not one hair was out of place.* ● You say **in the first place** when you are talking about the beginning of a situation. *Nobody can remember what was agreed in the first place.* ● You say **in the first place** and **in the second place** to introduce the first and second in a series of points. *...information that, in the first place, would have been very difficult for me to obtain and, in the second place, would have been useless anyhow.* ● When something **takes place,** it happens. *The next attack took place four hours later... The talks will take place in Vienna.* ● If one thing is used **in place of** another, or if it **takes the place of** the other thing, it replaces the other thing. *This task is carried out by robots in place of human workers.* ● If you **put** someone **in** their **place,** you show them that they are less important or clever than they think they are; an informal use.

placement /pleɪsmə²nt/, **placements.** 1 UNCOUNT N WITH SUPP The **placement** of something is the act of putting it in a particular place. *I spent a week directing the placement of the boulders.* 2 COUNT N If someone gets a **placement,** they get a job for a period of time which will give them experience in the work they are training for. *Amongst other placements, he spent some months at the Children's Hospital.*

placid /plæsɪd/. ADJ A **placid** person is calm and not easily excited. *He was a placid boy with a philosophical approach to life.*

plague /pleɪg/, **plagues, plaguing, plagued.** 1 COUNT N OR UNCOUNT N A **plague** is a very infectious disease that spreads quickly and kills large numbers of people. 2 COUNT N WITH 'of' A **plague** of unpleasant things is a large number of them that arrive or happen at the same time. *...a plague of locusts.* 3 VB WITH OBJ If unpleasant things **plague** you, they keep happening and cause you a lot of trouble. *The system is plagued by technical faults... He suffered severe back injuries, which plague him to this day.* 4 VB WITH OBJ If you **plague** someone, you keep bothering them or asking them for something. *The readers were urged to plague their MP with letters of protest.*

plaice /pleɪs/. **Plaice** is the singular and plural. COUNT N OR UNCOUNT N A **plaice** is a kind of flat sea fish.

plain /pleɪn/, **plains; plainer, plainest.** 1 ATTRIB ADJ A **plain** object or surface is entirely in one colour and has no pattern, design, or writing on it. *They are set against a plain background with carefully controlled lighting.* 2 ADJ **Plain** things are very simple in style. *She felt ashamed of her plain dress... I enjoy good plain food; nothing fancy.* 3 ADJ If a fact, situation or statement is **plain,** it is easy to recognize or understand. *It was plain that Eddie wanted to get back to sleep... ...a plain statement of fact.* 4 ATTRIB ADJ OR SUBMOD **Plain** can be used for emphasis before a noun or an adjective. *Petty is the wrong word. It's plain meanness... Logical judgment can also be just plain wrong.* 5 ADJ A **plain** woman or girl is not at all beautiful. *...a plain plump girl with pigtails.* 6 COUNT N A **plain** is a large, flat area of land with very few trees on it. *...vast plains covered in yellow grasses.*

plain-clothes. ATTRIB ADJ **Plain-clothes** police officers wear ordinary clothes instead of a uniform. *...a plain-clothes detective.*

plainly /pleɪnli¹/. 1 SENTENCE ADV If something is **plainly** the case, it is obviously the case. *He was plainly angry.* 2 ADV If you can see, hear, or smell something **plainly,** you can see, hear, or smell it easily. *You could see the oysters quite plainly, lying all over the sea-bed.* 3 ADV If you say something **plainly,** it is easy to understand and cannot be mistaken. *The judge said that quite plainly.*

plaintiff /pleɪntɪf/, **plaintiffs.** COUNT N A **plaintiff** is a person who brings a legal case against someone; a legal use.

plaintive /pleɪntɪv/. ADJ A **plaintive** sound or voice is sad and high-pitched. *...a plaintive wail.*

plait /plæt/, **plaits, plaiting, plaited.** 1 VB WITH OBJ If you **plait** three or more lengths of hair or rope together, you twist them over and under each other to make one thick length. *Her thick brown hair was plaited in a single braid down her back... ...long ropes of plaited rushes.* 2 COUNT N A **plait** is a length of hair that has been plaited. *...her long gold plaits.*

plan /plæn/, **plans, planning, planned.** 1 COUNT N A **plan** is a method of achieving something that you have worked out carefully in advance. *I told them of my plan... ...a plan to give women more power.* 2 VB WITH OBJ OR 'for' If you **plan** what you are going to do, you decide in detail what you are going to do. *At breakfast I planned my day... We must plan for the future.* 3 VB WITH TO-INF OR OBJ If you **plan** to do something, you intend to do it. *What do you plan to do after college?... I was planning a career in law.* ♦ **planned** ADJ *...news of the planned sale of 50,000 acres of state forests.* 4 PLURAL N If you have **plans,** you are intending to do a particular thing. *The gales forced him to change his plans.* 5 VB WITH OBJ When you **plan** something that you are going to make, build, or create, you decide what the main parts of it will be and how they will be arranged. *How do you plan a book?... ...the art of planning gardens.* 6 COUNT N A **plan** of something that is going to be built or made is a detailed diagram or drawing of it. *...the plan and overall design of the building... Make a neat plan of your new home.* 7 PHRASE A **plan of action** or a **plan of campaign** is a series of actions that you have decided to take in order to achieve something. *His plan of campaign is to cycle into town and collect the money personally.* 8 See also **planning.**

plan on. PHR VB If you **plan on** doing something, you intend to do it. *I plan on staying in London.*

plane /pleɪn/, **planes.** 1 COUNT N A **plane** is a vehicle with wings and engines which can fly. *We bought the cigarettes on the plane... We went by plane.* 2 COUNT N A **plane** is also a flat surface; a technical use. *...an elaborate structure of coloured planes.* 3 COUNT N WITH SUPP You can refer to a particular level of something as a particular **plane;** a literary use. *She tried to lift the conversation onto a more elevated plane.* 4 COUNT N A **plane** is also a tool that has a flat bottom with a sharp blade in it. You move the plane over a piece of wood to remove thin pieces of its surface.

planet /plænɪ¹t/, **planets.** COUNT N A **planet** is a large, round object in space that moves around a star. The Earth is a planet. *...the orbit of the planet Mars.*

planetary /plænɪ¹tə⁰ri¹/. ATTRIB ADJ **Planetary** means relating to or belonging to planets. *...the planetary exploration programme.*

plank /plæŋk/, **planks.** COUNT N A **plank** is a long rectangular piece of wood.

planner /plænə/, **planners.** 1 COUNT N The **planners** in local government are the people who decide how land should be used and what new buildings should be built. *...architects and planners.* 2 COUNT N A **planner** is a person who works out in detail what is going to be done in the future. *...TV programme planners.*

planning /plænɪŋ/. 1 UNCOUNT N **Planning** is the process of deciding in detail how to do something before you actually start to do it. *The project is still in the planning stage.* 2 UNCOUNT N **Planning** is also control by the local government of the way that land is used and of what new buildings are built. *...the concrete deserts created by modern planning at its worst.* 3 See also **family planning.**

plant /plɑːnt/, **plants, planting, planted.** 1 COUNT N A **plant** is a living thing that grows in the earth and has a stem, leaves, and roots. *...a tall banana plant.* 2 VB WITH OBJ When you **plant** a seed, plant, or young tree, you put it into the ground to grow. *Each autumn we planted primroses in the garden.* 3 VB WITH OBJ When someone **plants** land with a particular type of plant or crop, they put plants or seeds into the land to grow. *...small front gardens planted with rose trees.* 4 COUNT N A **plant** is also a factory or a place where power is generated. *...the re-opening of a nuclear plant after an accident.* 5 UNCOUNT N **Plant** is large machinery used in industrial processes; a technical use. *The company plans to spend nearly £1 billion on new plant and equipment.* 6 VB WITH OBJ AND ADJUNCT If you **plant** something somewhere, you put it there. *I planted my deckchair beside hers... They had planted the bomb beneath the house.* 7 VB WITH OBJ If you **plant** something such as a weapon or drugs on someone, you put it amongst their belongings so that they will be wrongly accused of a crime. *I'm convinced the evidence was planted in John's flat.*

plantation /plɑːnteɪʃə⁰n/, **plantations.** 1 COUNT N A **plantation** is a large piece of land, where crops such as cotton, tea, or sugar are grown. *...rubber plantations.* 2 COUNT N A **plantation** is also a large number of trees planted together. *...conifer plantations.*

plaque /plæk, plɑːk/, **plaques.** 1 COUNT N A **plaque** is a flat piece of metal or wood, which is fixed to a wall or monument in memory of a person or event. *...a memorial plaque at the crematorium... A plaque marks the site of Chippendale's workshops.* 2 UNCOUNT N **Plaque** is a substance that forms on the surface of your teeth. It consists of saliva, bacteria, and food.

plasma /plæzmə/. UNCOUNT N **Plasma** is the clear fluid part of blood.

plaster /plɑːstə/, **plasters, plastering, plastered.** 1 UNCOUNT N **Plaster** is a smooth paste made of sand, lime, and water, used to cover walls and ceilings inside buildings. *The walls were in a dreadful condition—the plaster was peeling off.* 2 VB WITH OBJ If you **plaster** a wall or ceiling, you cover it with a layer of plaster. *...a wall that was poorly plastered.* 3 COUNT N A **plaster** is a strip of sticky material with a small pad, used for covering small cuts or sores on your body. 4 PHRASE If your leg or arm is **in plaster,** it has a plaster cast on it to protect a broken bone.

plaster cast, plaster casts. COUNT N A **plaster cast** is a hard case made of plaster of Paris, used for protecting broken bones by keeping part of the body rigid.

plastered /plɑːstəd/. 1 PRED ADJ WITH PREP 'to' If something is **plastered** to a surface, it is sticking to the surface. *His wet hair was plastered to his forehead.* 2 PRED ADJ WITH 'with' If a surface is **plastered** with something, it is covered with it. *Her back was thickly plastered with suntan oil... The walls of his tiny shop were plastered with pictures of actors.*

plaster of Paris /plɑːstər əv pærɪs/. UNCOUNT N **Plaster of Paris** is a type of plaster made from a white powder and water which is used to make plaster casts.

plastic /plæstɪk/, **plastics.** UNCOUNT N OR COUNT N **Plastic** is a light material produced by a chemical process. It can be moulded when soft and used to make objects. *The roofs are covered in winter by sheets of plastic... What's special about this new type of plastic?* Also ADJ *...a plastic bag.*

plastic surgery. UNCOUNT N **Plastic surgery** is the practice of performing operations to repair damaged skin, or to improve people's appearance by changing their features. *One of the survivors needed plastic surgery.*

plate /pleɪt/, **plates, plating, plated.** 1 COUNT N A **plate** is a round or oval flat dish used to hold food. *He looked at the food on his plate.* 2 COUNT N You can use **plate** to refer to a plate and its contents, or to the contents only. *She pushed her plate of boiled fish away... He greedily ate up a plate of food that he did not want.* 3 COUNT N A **plate** is also a flat piece of metal, especially on machinery or a building. *We got into the cellar through a round hole covered by a metal plate.* 4 UNCOUNT N **Plate** consists of dishes, bowls, and cups made of silver or gold. *We would prefer church plate and other treasures to be stored in bank vaults.* 5 VB WITH OBJ Metal that **is plated** is covered with a thin layer of gold or silver. Also ADJ *...gold-plated brooches.* 6 COUNT N A **plate** in a book is a picture or photograph which takes up a whole page. 7 COUNT N A dental **plate** is a piece of shaped plastic with a set of false teeth attached to it. 8 PHRASE If you **have a lot on** your **plate,** you have a lot of work to do or a lot of things to deal with; an informal use. 9 See also **number plate.**

plateau /plætəʊ/, **plateaus** or **plateaux.** 1 COUNT N A **plateau** is a large area of high, flat land. 2 SING N If an activity or process has reached a **plateau,** it has reached a stage where there is no further change or development. *The US space programme seemed to have reached a plateau of development.*

plate glass. UNCOUNT N **Plate glass** is thick glass made in large, flat pieces, used to make large windows and doors. *...a new plate-glass window.*

platform /plætfɔːm/, **platforms.** 1 COUNT N A **platform** is a flat raised structure, on which someone or something can stand. *The speaker mounted the platform... ...loading platforms.* 2 COUNT N A **platform** in a railway station is the area beside the rails where you wait for or get off a train. *Jordache paced nervously up and down the platform.* 3 COUNT N If someone has a **platform,** they have an opportunity to tell people what they think or want. *It provides a platform for the consumer's viewpoint.* 4 COUNT N WITH SUPP The **platform** of a political party is what they say they will do if they are elected. *He campaigned on a socialist platform.*

platinum /plætɪnəm/. 1 UNCOUNT N **Platinum** is a valuable, silvery-grey metal often used for making jewellery. 2 ADJ **Platinum** hair is very fair, almost white. *...a platinum blonde.*

platitude /plætɪtjuːd/, **platitudes.** COUNT N A **platitude** is a statement considered to be meaningless because it has been made many times before in similar situations; a formal use. *...empty platitudes about democracy.*

platonic /plətɒnɪk/. ADJ **Platonic** relationships or feelings do not involve sex. *Her interest in him was entirely platonic.*

platoon /plətuːn/, **platoons.** COLL N A **platoon** is a small group of soldiers commanded by a lieutenant. *In his platoon he had thirty-two men.*

platter /plætə/, **platters.** COUNT N A **platter** is a large serving dish; an old-fashioned use.

plausible /plɔːzə¹bə⁰l/. ADJ An explanation that is **plausible** seems likely to be true or valid. *Such a theory seems very plausible... ...a plausible answer.*

play /pleɪ/, **plays, playing, played.** 1 VB When children **play,** they spend time with their toys or taking part in games. *The kids went off to play on the swings... I played with the children all day.* 2 VB WITH OR WITHOUT OBJ When you **play** a sport, game, or match, you take part in it. *Do you play chess?... I used to play for the village cricket team.* 3 VB WITH OBJ OR 'against' When one person or team **plays** another, they compete against them in a sport or game. *I saw Australia play against England at Lords.* 4 VB WITH OBJ If you **play** a joke or a trick on someone, you deceive or surprise them in a way that you think is funny, but may annoy them. *I presumed someone was playing a rather silly joke.* 5 VB WITH COMPLEMENT You can use **play** to say how someone behaves. For example, if someone **plays** the innocent, they pretend to be innocent; an informal use. *Don't you play the wise old professor with me, Franz.* 6 COUNT N A **play** is a piece of writing performed in a theatre, on the radio, or on television. *Wesker has written four major plays since then.* 7 VB WITH OBJ OR ADJUNCT If an actor **plays** a character in a play or film, he or she performs the part of that character. *Brutus was played by James Mason... I was asked to play in a revival of 'Ghosts'.* 8 VB WITH OR WITHOUT OBJ If you **play** a musical instrument or **play** a tune on it, you produce music from it. *Out on the balcony, a man stood playing a trombone... Doesn't he play beautifully?... The child played him a tune.* 9 VB WITH OBJ If you **play** a record or tape, you listen to it. *I'll play you the tape.*

PHRASES • If something or someone **plays a part** or **plays a role** in a situation, they are involved in it and have an effect on it. *Examinations seem to play a large part in education.* • If someone **plays it safe,** they do not take risks. *Should I play it safe and follow the judge's order?* • If you **play for time,** you try to delay something happening, so that you can prepare for it or prevent it from happening. *She was playing for time, half hoping that he would forget all about it.*

play along. PHR VB If you **play along** with a person you agree with them and do what they want, even though you are not sure whether they are right. *I'll play along with them for the moment.*

play at. PHR VB 1 If you **play at** an activity, you do it without effort or seriousness. *They played at being huntsmen.* 2 CONVENTION If you ask **what** someone **is playing at,** you are angry because you think that they are doing something stupid or wrong; an informal use. *What do you think you're playing at?*

play back. PHR VB When you **play back** a tape or film, you listen to the sounds or watch the pictures after recording them.

play down. PHR VB If you **play down** something, you try to make people think that it is less important than it really is. *He played down his recent promotion.*

play off against. PHR VB If you **play** people **off against** each other, you make them compete or argue, so that you gain some advantage. *Annie played one parent off against the other.*

play on. PHR VB If you **play on** or **play upon** people's weaknesses or faults, you deliberately use them in order to achieve what you want. *He used to play on their prejudices and their fears... He found himself in a position to play upon the fears of his colleagues.*

play up. PHR VB 1 If something such as a machine or a part of your body **is playing up** or **is playing** you **up,** it is not working properly. *Our phone is playing up again... Is your leg still playing you up?* 2 When children **are playing up,** they are being naughty and are difficult to control; an informal use.

play upon. PHR VB See **play on.**

playboy /pleɪbɔɪ/, **playboys.** COUNT N A **playboy** is a rich man who spends most of his time enjoying himself.

player /pleɪə/, **players.** 1 COUNT N A **player** in a sport or game is a person who takes part. 2 COUNT N You can refer to a musician as a **player.** For example, a piano **player** is someone who plays the piano. *He's one of the most original guitar players in jazz.* 3 See also **record player.**

playful /pleɪfʊl/. 1 ADJ Someone who is **playful** is friendly and jokes a lot. *She gave Philip's hand a little playful squeeze.* ♦ **playfully** ADV *Elaine kissed Harold playfully on the cheek.* 2 ADJ An animal that is **playful** is lively and friendly. *...a playful kitten.*

playground /pleɪgraʊnd/, **playgrounds.** COUNT N A **playground** is a piece of land where children can play.

playgroup /pleɪgruːp/, **playgroups.** COUNT N OR UNCOUNT N A **playgroup** is an informal kind of school for very young children where they learn by playing.

playing card, playing cards. COUNT N **Playing cards** are thin pieces of card with numbers and pictures on them that are used to play various games. *...a pack of playing cards.*

playing field, playing fields. COUNT N A **playing field** is a large area of grass where people play games such as hockey and football.

playmate /pleɪmeɪt/, **playmates.** COUNT N A child's **playmates** are other children who often play with him or her. *My playmates were my cousins.*

playoff /pleɪɒf/, **playoffs.** COUNT N A **playoff** is an extra game played to decide the winner of a sports competition when two or more people have got the same score.

plaything /pleɪθɪŋ/, **playthings.** COUNT N A **plaything** is a toy that a child plays with; a formal use. *I used to get them new playthings to keep them quiet.*

playtime /pleɪtaɪm/. UNCOUNT N **Playtime** is a period of time between lessons at school when children can play outside.

playwright /pleɪraɪt/, **playwrights.** COUNT N A **playwright** is a person who writes plays.

plc /piː ɛl siː/. **plc** is an abbreviation for 'public limited company'. It is used after the name of a company whose shares can be bought by the public. *...National Westminster Bank plc.*

plea /pliː/, **pleas.** 1 COUNT N A **plea** is an intense, emotional request for something. *She at last responded to his pleas for help.* 2 COUNT N In a court of law, a **plea** is the answer which someone gives when they say whether they are guilty or not; a legal use. *I agreed to enter a plea of guilty.*

plead /pliːd/, **pleads, pleading, pleaded.** 1 VB WITH ADJUNCT OR REPORT VB If you **plead** with someone to do something, you ask them in an intense, emotional way to do it. *He was pleading with her to control herself... 'Take me with you,' he pleaded.* 2 VB WITH OBJ OR ADJUNCT If someone, especially a lawyer, **pleads** someone else's case or cause, they speak in support or defence of that person; a formal use. *Of course his mother does her best to plead his case... Who will plead for us?* 3 REPORT VB If you **plead** a particular thing, you give it as your reason or excuse for not doing something. *I pleaded that I felt ill.* 4 VB When someone charged with a crime **pleads** in a court of law, they officially state that they are guilty or not guilty of the crime. *'How do you plead?'—'Not guilty.'*

pleading /pliːdɪŋ/, **pleadings.** 1 ATTRIB ADJ A **pleading** expression or gesture shows that you want something very much. *Then he saw his brother's pleading expression and his heart softened.* 2 UNCOUNT N OR PLURAL N **Pleading** is asking someone in an intense, emotional way to do something. *After days of tearful pleading and sulking, she stayed... It was hard to resist his daughter's pleadings.*

pleasant /plɛzə°nt/, **pleasanter, pleasantest. 1** ADJ Something that is **pleasant** is enjoyable or attractive. *...a pleasant chat... It was pleasant to sit under the apple tree.* ♦ **pleasantly** ADV *I was pleasantly surprised... ...a pleasantly nutty taste.* **2** ADJ Someone who is **pleasant** is friendly and likeable. *They were pleasant lads.* ♦ **pleasantly** ADV *'Please come in,' she said pleasantly.*

pleasantry /plɛzə°ntrɪ¹/, **pleasantries.** COUNT N **Pleasantries** are casual, friendly remarks which you say in order to be polite; a formal use. *We stood exchanging a few pleasantries.*

please /pliːz/, **pleases, pleasing, pleased. 1** CONVENTION You say **please** to show politeness when you ask someone to do something or ask them for something. *'Follow me, please,' the guide said... Could I speak to Sue, please?* **2** CONVENTION You use **please** when you are accepting something politely. *'Do you want some milk?'—'Yes please.'* **3** VB WITH OR WITHOUT OBJ If someone or something **pleases** you, they make you feel happy and satisfied. *He seemed eager to please... Neither idea pleased me.* **4** VB WITH OR WITHOUT OBJ You use **please** in 'as she pleases' and 'whatever you please' to indicate that someone can do or have whatever they want. *Judy had a right to come and go as she pleased... He can get anyone he pleases to work with him.* **5** CONVENTION You say **'please yourself'** to indicate that you do not mind or care whether the person you are talking to does a particular thing or not; an informal use. *'Do you mind if I wait?' I asked. Melanie shrugged: 'Please yourself.'*

pleased /pliːzd/. **1** PRED ADJ If you are **pleased**, you are happy about something or satisfied with it. *She seemed very pleased that he had come... He was pleased with my progress.* **2** CONVENTION You say **'Pleased to meet you'** as a polite way of greeting someone you are meeting for the first time.

pleasing /pliːzɪŋ/. ADJ Something that is **pleasing** gives you pleasure and satisfaction; a formal use. *...a pleasing piece of news... It has a pleasing smell.*

pleasurable /plɛʒə°rəbə°l/. ADJ Something that is **pleasurable** is pleasant and enjoyable; a formal use. *...a pleasurable sensation.*

pleasure /plɛʒə/, **pleasures. 1** UNCOUNT N **Pleasure** is a feeling of happiness, satisfaction, or enjoyment. *McPherson could scarcely conceal his pleasure at my resignation... I'd travel a thousand miles just for the pleasure of meeting you.* **2** UNCOUNT N **Pleasure** is also the activity of enjoying yourself rather than working. *She is a disciplined creature who will put duty before pleasure.* **3** COUNT N A **pleasure** is an activity or experience that you find very enjoyable and satisfying. *...the pleasures of choral singing.* PHRASES ● You can say **'It's a pleasure'** or **'My pleasure'** as a polite way of replying to someone who has just thanked you for doing something. *'Thank you for talking to us about your research.'—'It's a pleasure.'* ● You can say **'With pleasure'** as a polite way of saying that you are very willing to do something; a formal use. *'Could you help?'—'With pleasure.'*

pleat /pliːt/, **pleats.** COUNT N A **pleat** in a piece of clothing is a permanent fold made in the cloth.

pleated /pliːtɪd/. ADJ A **pleated** piece of clothing has pleats in it. *...a brown pleated skirt.*

pledge /plɛdʒ/, **pledges, pledging, pledged. 1** COUNT N A **pledge** is a solemn promise to do something. *The Government should fulfil its 1979 Manifesto pledge... He gave a pledge to handle the affair in a friendly manner.* **2** VB WITH OBJ OR TO-INF, OR REPORT VB If you **pledge** something, you promise solemnly that you will do it or give it. *They will pledge $1 million to fund the project... The government pledged to reduce the level of imports... He has pledged that the ban will be lifted after two years.* **3** REFL VB If you **pledge** yourself to something, you promise to follow a particular course of action or to support a particular person, group, or idea. *The new organization pledged itself to the revolutionary overthrow of the dictator.*

plentiful /plɛntɪfʊl/. ADJ Something that is **plentiful** exists in large amounts. *Food became more plentiful each day.*

plenty /plɛntɪ¹/. QUANTIF If there is **plenty** of something, there is a large amount of it. If there are **plenty** of things, there is a large number of them. *We've got plenty of time... There are always plenty of jobs.*

pliable /plaɪəbə°l/. **1** ADJ If something is **pliable**, it bends easily without breaking. *...a soft and pliable material.* **2** ADJ Someone who is **pliable** can be easily influenced and controlled.

pliers /plaɪəz/. PLURAL N **Pliers** are a tool used for holding or pulling out things such as nails, or for bending or cutting wire. *Use a pair of pliers.*

plight /plaɪt/. SING N WITH POSS Someone's **plight** is the difficult or dangerous situation that they are in; a formal use. *...the plight of the mentally handicapped... He had heard of my plight through an acquaintance.*

plimsoll /plɪmsəl/, **plimsolls.** COUNT N **Plimsolls** are shoes made of canvas with flat rubber soles worn for sports and leisure.

plod /plɒd/, **plods, plodding, plodded. 1** VB If someone **plods** along, they walk slowly and heavily. *He plodded along the road.* **2** VB WITH ADJUNCT If someone **plods** on or **plods** along with a job, they work slowly and without enthusiasm. *He plodded on in the Board of Trade.*

plonk /plɒŋk/, **plonks, plonking, plonked.** VB WITH OBJ AND ADJUNCT If you **plonk** something in a place, you put it or drop it there heavily and carelessly; an informal use. *Bottles of beer were plonked on the wooden table... ...plonking himself down in the middle.*

plop /plɒp/, **plops, plopping, plopped. 1** COUNT N A **plop** is a soft gentle sound, like the sound made by something light dropping into water. *My hat landed with a plop in the bucket.* **2** VB WITH ADJUNCT If something **plops** into a liquid, it drops into it with a soft gentle sound. *Great big tears plopped into her soup.*

plot /plɒt/, **plots, plotting, plotted. 1** COUNT N A **plot** is a secret plan by a group of people to do something illegal or wrong. *Another plot to assassinate the General was uncovered.* **2** VB WITH OR WITHOUT OBJ If people **plot** something or **plot** to do something, they plan secretly to do it. *He was always plotting strikes... They were accused of plotting to assassinate the President... Anyone convicted of plotting against the king will be executed.* **3** COUNT N The **plot** of a film, novel, or play is the story and the way in which it develops. *They were having some difficulty in following the plot.* **4** COUNT N A **plot** is a small piece of land. *His land is split up into several widely scattered plots.* **5** VB WITH OBJ When someone **plots** the position or course of a plane or ship, they mark it on a map or chart. *They plotted the new positions of each vessel.* **6** VB WITH OBJ When you are drawing a graph, you **plot** the points on it by marking them at the correct places to form the graph.

plough /plaʊ/, **ploughs, ploughing, ploughed;** spelled **plow** in American English. **1** COUNT N A **plough** is a large farming tool with sharp blades that is pulled across the soil to turn it over, usually before seeds are planted. **2** VB WITH OR WITHOUT OBJ When someone **ploughs** an area of land, they turn over the soil using a plough. *A small tractor can plough an acre in six to nine hours.* **3** VB WITH ADJUNCT If you **plough** on or **plough** through a task, you continue moving or trying to complete it, although it needs a lot of effort; an informal use. *The fighters ploughed on to their destination airfields.* **4** VB WITH 'into' If one thing **ploughs** into another, it crashes into it. *The car wavered crazily before ploughing into the bank.* **5** VB WITH OBJ If someone **ploughs** money into a business, they invest large sums of money in it. *...the huge sums of money which were ploughed into computing.*

plough up. PHR VB If an area of grassland **is ploughed up,** the soil is turned over using a plough.

plow /plaʊ/. See **plough.**

ploy /plɔɪ/, **ploys.** COUNT N A **ploy** is a way of behaving that you have planned carefully in order to get something you want. *This headache was clearly a delaying ploy.*

pluck /plʌk/, **plucks, plucking, plucked. 1** VB WITH OBJ If you **pluck** something from somewhere, you take hold of it and pull it with a sharp movement; a literary use. *He plucked a tomato and offered it to Hilda... He laughed and plucked the paper from my hand.* **2** VB WITH OBJ If you **pluck** a chicken or other dead bird, you pull its feathers out to prepare it for cooking. **3** VB WITH OBJ OR ADJUNCT If you **pluck** a guitar or other stringed musical instrument, you use your fingers to pull the strings and let them go, so that they make a sound. **4** PHRASE If you **pluck up the courage** to do something frightening, you make an effort to be brave enough to do it. *I eventually plucked up enough courage to go in.*

plug /plʌg/, **plugs, plugging, plugged. 1** COUNT N A **plug** is a small plastic object with metal pieces which fit into the holes in a socket and connect a piece of electrical equipment to the electricity supply. *This lamp doesn't have a plug.* **2** COUNT N A **plug** is also a socket in the wall of a room that is a source of electricity; an informal use. *...electricity from a plug in the garage.* **3** COUNT N A **plug** is also a thick, circular piece of rubber or plastic used to block the hole in a bath or sink when it is filled with water. **4** VB WITH OBJ If you **plug** a hole, you block it with something. *Have you plugged all the leaks?* **5** VB WITH OBJ If someone **plugs** a book or film, they praise it to encourage people to buy it or see it; an informal use. *The radio stations are plugging the record like mad.* Also COUNT N

Can I quickly give our new show a plug?

plug in. PHR VB If you **plug in** a piece of electrical equipment, you push its plug into an electric socket. *I plugged in the kettle.*

plughole /plʌghəʊl/, **plugholes.** COUNT N A **plughole** is a hole in a bath or sink which allows the water to flow away.

plum /plʌm/, **plums. 1** COUNT N A **plum** is a small, sweet fruit with a smooth red or yellow skin and a stone in the middle. **2** ATTRIB ADJ A **plum** job is a very good job that a lot of people would like.

plumage /pluːmɪdʒ/. UNCOUNT N A bird's **plumage** is all its feathers. *Its plumage had turned grey.*

plumb /plʌm/, **plumbs, plumbing, plumbed.** PHRASE If someone **plumbs the depths** of an unpleasant emotion, they experience it to an extreme degree. *The story shows how she plumbs the depths of humiliation.*

plumber /plʌmə/, **plumbers.** COUNT N A **plumber** is a person who connects and repairs things such as water and drainage pipes, baths, and toilets. *The plumbers came to mend the pipes.*

plumbing /plʌmɪŋ/. **1** UNCOUNT N The **plumbing** in a building consists of the water and drainage pipes, baths, and toilets. *Will it need new wiring and plumbing?* **2** UNCOUNT N **Plumbing** is the work of connecting and repairing water and drainage pipes, baths, and toilets. *...minor plumbing repairs.*

plume /pluːm/, **plumes. 1** COUNT N A **plume** is a large, often brightly coloured bird's feather; a formal use. *...an ostrich plume.* **2** COUNT N WITH 'of' A **plume** of smoke is a small column of it rising into the air. *The last plume of blue smoke curled away.*

plummet /plʌmɪt/, **plummets, plummeting, plummeted. 1** VB WITH ADJUNCT If something **plummets** downwards, it falls very quickly. *The explosion sent the aircraft plummeting towards the sea.* **2** VB If an amount, rate, or price **plummets,** it decreases quickly and suddenly. *The price of paper plummeted.*

plump /plʌmp/, **plumper, plumpest; plumps, plumping, plumped.** ADJ Someone who is **plump** is rather fat. *...a plump, red-faced man.*

plump for. PHR VB If you **plump for** someone or something, you choose them after hesitating and thinking. *She plumped for the eclair.*

plunder /plʌndə/, **plunders, plundering, plundered. 1** VB WITH OR WITHOUT OBJ If someone **plunders** a place or **plunders** things from a place, they steal things from it; a literary use. *Imperialist governments plunder the weaker nations... Instead he chose to plunder and kill.* **2** UNCOUNT N OR SING N **Plunder** is the activity of stealing property from people or places, or the property that is stolen. *...the savage burning and plunder of the commercial centre of town... He escaped with his plunder.*

plunge /plʌndʒ/, **plunges, plunging, plunged. 1** VB WITH ADJUNCT If something **plunges** in a particular direction, it falls in that direction. *The car plunged into the river... They plunged into the pool together.* Also SING N *They were relying on the plunge into icy waters to kill me.* **2** VB WITH OBJ AND ADJUNCT If you **plunge** an object into something, you push it quickly or violently into it. *She plunged her hands into her coat pockets... He plunged the knife into her breast.* **3** ERG VB WITH ADJUNCT To **plunge** someone or something into a state means to cause them suddenly to be in that state. *The hall was plunged into darkness... ...the danger of plunging society into chaos and anarchy.* **4** VB WITH 'into' If you **plunge** into an activity, you suddenly get very involved in it. *She plunged bravely into the debate.* **5** VB If an amount or rate **plunges,** it decreases quickly and suddenly. *Sales have plunged by 24%.* **6** PHRASE If you **take the plunge,** you decide to do something that you consider difficult or risky. *Take the plunge and start your own firm.*

pluperfect /pluːpɜːfɪkt/. SING N In grammar, the **pluperfect** is the tense of a verb describing actions that were completed before another event in the past happened. In English it is formed using 'had' followed by the past participle of the verb, as in the sentences 'I had gone by then' and 'She'd eaten them before I arrived'.

plural /plʊərəl/, **plurals. 1** COUNT N OR ADJ In grammar, **plural** is the term used for a noun, pronoun, determiner, or verb when it refers to two or more people, things, or groups. *Use the first person plural... The singular is 'louse' and the plural form is 'lice'.* **2** ATTRIB ADJ **Plural** also means consisting of more than one person or thing or different kinds of people or things; a formal use. *We need a plural system of education.*

plus /plʌs/. **1** PREP You use **plus** to show that one number is being added to another, for example, 'five plus three'. You represent this in figures as '5+3'. **2** ADJ AFTER N You use **plus** to show that the actual number or quantity is greater than the one mentioned. *...my 25* *years plus as a police officer... They take the exams at 13 plus.* **3** PREP OR CONJ You can also use **plus** to add an item to one or more that you have already mentioned. *Now five people, plus Val, are missing... He wore strange scarves and beads, plus he was English.*

plush /plʌʃ/. ADJ Something that is **plush** is smart, comfortable, and expensive. *...his plush car with reclining seats.*

plus sign, plus signs. COUNT N A **plus sign** is the sign (+) which is put between two numbers to show that the second number is being added to the first one.

plutonium /plu:təʊnɪəm/. UNCOUNT N **Plutonium** is a radioactive element used especially as a fuel in nuclear power stations.

ply /plaɪ/, **plies, plying, plied. 1** VB WITH OBJ AND 'with' If you **ply** someone with food or drink, you keep giving them more of it. *Dolly plied me with sweets.* **2** VB WITH OBJ AND 'with' If you **ply** someone with questions, you keep asking them questions. *I plied him with questions about his novel.* **3** N AFTER NUMBER **Ply** is the thickness of wool, thread, or rope measured by the number of strands it is made from. *...four-ply wool.*

plywood /plaɪwʊd/. UNCOUNT N OR MOD **Plywood** consists of several thin layers of wood stuck together to make a board. *...the flimsy plywood door.*

p.m. /pi: ɛm/. **p.m.** after a number indicates that the number refers to a particular time between noon and midnight.

PM /pi: ɛm/. PROPER N **PM** is an abbreviation for 'Prime Minister'; an informal use. *...the PM's speech to the conference.*

pneumatic /nju:mætɪk/. ATTRIB ADJ A **pneumatic** drill is operated by compressed air and is very powerful.

pneumonia /nju:məʊnɪə/. UNCOUNT N **Pneumonia** is a serious disease which affects your lungs and makes breathing difficult. *She nearly died of pneumonia.*

PO /pi: əʊ/. **PO** is an abbreviation for 'Post Office'.

poach /pəʊtʃ/, **poaches, poaching, poached. 1** VB WITH OR WITHOUT OBJ If someone **poaches** animals, they illegally catch them on someone else's property. *He had been poaching deer.* **2** VB WITH OBJ If someone **poaches** an idea, they dishonestly use the idea. *The design had even been poached by manufacturers of washing powder.* **3** VB WITH OBJ If you **poach** food such as fish or eggs, you cook it gently in boiling water or milk. *...poached eggs and beans... ...poached salmon.*

poacher /pəʊtʃə/, **poachers.** COUNT N A **poacher** is someone who illegally catches animals on someone else's property.

PO Box. PO Box is used followed by a number as part of an address. The Post Office keeps the letters for collection by the customer. *...PO Box 48.*

pocket /pɒkɪt/, **pockets, pocketing, pocketed. 1** COUNT N A **pocket** is a small bag or pouch that forms part of a piece of clothing. *She put her hand in her coat pocket.* **2** VB WITH OBJ If you **pocket** something, you put it in your pocket. *I locked the door and pocketed the key.* **3** VB WITH OBJ You can say that someone who steals something **pockets** it; an informal use. *...servants who pocketed household funds for their own use.* **4** MOD You use **pocket** to describe something that is small enough to fit into a pocket. *...a pocket calculator.* **5** COUNT N A **pocket** of something is a small area of it. *We sat in the pocket of warmth by the fire.*
PHRASES • If someone **picks** your **pocket,** they steal something from it. • If you are **out of pocket,** you have less money than you should have, usually because you have paid for something for someone else.

pocketbook /pɒkɪtbʊk/, **pocketbooks. 1** COUNT N A **pocketbook** is a small book or notebook. **2** COUNT N A **pocketbook** is also a wallet or small case used for carrying money and papers; an American use.

pocket money. UNCOUNT N **Pocket money** is money which parents give their children each week.

pod /pɒd/, **pods.** COUNT N A **pod** is a seed container that grows on some plants such as peas or beans.

poem /pəʊɪm/, **poems.** COUNT N A **poem** is a piece of writing in which the words are chosen for their beauty and sound and are carefully arranged, often in short lines which rhyme.

poet /pəʊɪt/, **poets.** COUNT N A **poet** is a person who writes poems. *...the Soviet poet, Yevtushenko.*

poetic /pəʊɛtɪk/. **1** ADJ Something that is **poetic** is very beautiful, expressive, and sensitive. *...a poetic and beautiful picture of the landscape.* **2** ATTRIB ADJ **Poetic** also means relating to poetry. *...a poetic tradition older than writing.*

poetry /pəʊɪtri^1/. UNCOUNT N **Poetry** is poems, considered as a form of literature. *...a book of poetry... ...poetry recitals.*

poignant /pɔɪnjənt/. ADJ Something that is **poignant** makes you feel very sad. *His cry of protest is still poignant today.* ♦ **poignancy** /pɔɪnjənsi^1/ UNCOUNT N *It was a moment of extraordinary poignancy.*

point /pɔɪnt/, **points, pointing, pointed. 1** COUNT N A **point** is something that you say which expresses a particular fact, idea, or opinion. *We had a long argument on this point... I want to make several quick points... Let me tell you a little story to illustrate my point.* **2** COUNT N If you say that someone has a **point,** you mean that you accept that what they have said is worth considering. *You've got a point there.* **3** SING N The **point** of what you are saying or discussing is the most important part that provides a reason or explanation for the rest. *The point was that Dick could not walk... You've all missed the point... I may as well come straight to the point.* **4** COUNT N WITH SUPP A **point** is also a detail, aspect, or quality of something or someone. *The two books have some interesting points in common... Your strong points are your speed and accuracy.* **5** SING N You use **point** in expressions such as 'I don't see the point of it', 'What's the point', and 'There's no point' in order to say that a particular action has no purpose or would not be useful. *I didn't see the point of boring you with all this... There was not much point in thinking about it.* **6** COUNT N WITH SUPP A **point** is also a particular place or position where something happens. *We were nearing the point where the lane curved round to the right... The circle passes through those two points.* **7** COUNT N WITH SUPP The **points** of a compass are the marks on it that show the directions, especially North, South, East, and West. **8** COUNT N The **point** of something such as a pin, needle, or knife is the thin, sharp end of it. *...tapping with the point of the pencil at a place on the diagram.* **9** COUNT N On a railway track, the **points** are the levers and rails which enable a train to move from one track to another. **10** COUNT N The decimal **point** in a number is the dot that separates the whole numbers from the fractions. *...four point eight.* **11** SING N WITH SUPP You also use **point** to refer to a particular time or moment, or a particular stage in the development of something. *At one point, I was dreadfully rude... The strikers brought the economy to crisis point... I exercised to the point of exhaustion.* **12** COUNT N In some sports, competitions, and games, a **point** is one of the single marks that are added together to give the total score. *The panel of judges gave him the highest points.* **13** COUNT N A **point** is also an electric socket. *The room has a wash-basin and an electric-shaver point.* **14** VB WITH OR WITHOUT OBJ If you **point** at something, you hold out your finger or an object such as a stick to show someone where it is or to make them notice it. *'Over there,' she said and pointed to the door... He pointed a finger at my friend and hissed with rage.* **15** VB WITH OBJ AND ADJUNCT If you **point** something at someone, you aim the tip or end of it towards them. *I had actually pointed a gun at someone.* **16** VB WITH ADJUNCT If something **points** to a place or **points** in a particular direction, it shows where that place is or faces in that direction. *...a street sign that pointed down towards the cemetery... One of its toes pointed backwards.* **17** VB WITH PREP 'to' If something **points** to a particular situation, it suggests that the situation exists or is likely to occur. *This activity points to the likelihood that an armed revolution is imminent.*
PHRASES • If something is **beside the point,** it is not relevant to the subject that you are discussing. • If you **make a point of** doing something, you do it in a very deliberate or obvious way. *I made a special point of being sociable.* • If something is true **up to a point,** it is partly, but not completely, true. *He is right, but only up to a point.* • to **be a case in point:** see **case.** • **in point of fact:** see **fact.** • to **point the finger at** someone: see **finger.** • **a sore point:** see **sore.** • See also **focal point, vantage point.**

point out. PHR VB **1** If you **point out** an object or place, you make people look at it or show them where it is. *On car journeys we all used to shout and point out lovely places along the way.* **2** If you **point out** a fact or mistake, you tell someone about it. *Mr Merritt pointed this problem out to you the other day... She pointed out that he was wrong.*

point-blank. 1 ADV OR ATTRIB ADJ If you say something **point-blank,** you say it very directly, without explaining or apologizing. *She asked him point-blank if I was with him on Saturday... ...a point-blank refusal to discuss the matter.* **2** ADV OR ATTRIB ADJ To shoot someone or something **point-blank** means to shoot them when the gun is touching them or extremely close to them. *He shot him in the brain, point-blank... ...shooting at point-blank range.*

pointed /pɔɪntɪ^{2}d/. **1** ADJ Something that is **pointed** has a point at one end. *His daughter has a pointed nose... ...pointed trees.* **2** ADJ **Pointed** comments or behaviour express criticism or warning in an obvious and often unpleasant way. *Etta gave a pointed look in their direction... She made two pointed comments.* ♦ **pointedly** ADV *'How old is he?' Freya asked pointedly.*

pointer /pɔɪntə/, **pointers. 1** COUNT N A **pointer** is a piece of advice or information which helps you to understand a situation or solve a problem. *...a list of things that seemed to be pointers to the truth of what happened.* **2** COUNT N A **pointer** is also a long, thin stick that you use to point at things such as charts. **3** COUNT N The **pointer** on a measuring instrument is the long, thin piece of metal that points to the numbers.

pointless /pɔɪntlɪ^{2}s/. ADJ Something that is **pointless** has no sense or purpose. *...pointless violence... It was pointless to protest.* ♦ **pointlessly** ADV *He had pointlessly hurt her.*

point of view, points of view. 1 COUNT N Your **point of view** is your opinion about something or your attitude towards it. *We understand your point of view.* **2** PHRASE If you consider something **from a** particular **point of view,** you are using one aspect of a situation to judge the situation. *From the commercial point of view, they have little to lose.*

poise /pɔɪz/. UNCOUNT N If you behave with **poise,** you behave in a calm and dignified manner. *She received me with incredible poise for one so young.*

poised /pɔɪzd/. **1** PRED ADJ If a part of your body is **poised,** it is completely still but ready to move at any moment. *I saw her hand poised to strike.* **2** PRED ADJ If you are **poised** to do something, you are ready to take action at any moment. *His party seems poised to return to power... ...powerful military forces, poised for invasion.* **3** PRED ADJ If you are **poised,** you are calm and dignified. *She was poised and diplomatic on the telephone.*

poison /pɔɪzə^{0}n/, **poisons, poisoning, poisoned. 1** MASS N **Poison** is a substance that harms or kills people or animals if they swallow or absorb it. *It was deadly poison and if he drank it he'd die.* **2** VB WITH OBJ If someone **poisons** another person, they kill the person or make them ill by means of poison. *He had been poisoned with strychnine.* ♦ **poisoning** UNCOUNT N *The poisoning had not been accidental.* **3** VB WITH OBJ If you **are poisoned** by a substance, it makes you very ill. *You can be poisoned by agricultural and industrial wastes.* ♦ **poisoning** UNCOUNT N *...food poisoning.* **4** VB WITH OBJ If something such as food or the atmosphere **is poisoned,** it has poison or other harmful substances added to it. *Soil and water are being poisoned.* ♦ **poisoned** ADJ *...a poisoned whisky bottle.*

poisonous /pɔɪzə^{0}nəs/. **1** ADJ **Poisonous** substances will kill you or make you ill if you swallow or absorb them. *...a poisonous plant.* **2** ADJ A **poisonous** animal produces a poison that will kill you or make you ill if the animal bites you. *...poisonous snakes.*

poke /pəʊk/, **pokes, poking, poked. 1** VB WITH OBJ If you **poke** someone or something, you quickly push them with your finger or a sharp object. *People poked the students with their umbrellas... Ralph began to poke little holes in the sand.* Also COUNT N *Len gave him an affectionate poke.* **2** VB WITH OBJ AND ADJUNCT If you **poke** one thing into another, you push the first thing into the second thing. *Never poke scissors into an electric socket.* **3** VB WITH ADJUNCT If something **pokes** out of or through another thing, you can see part of it appearing from behind or underneath the other thing. *...cotton wool poking out of his ear... Blades of grass poked up between the paving stones.* **4** VB WITH OBJ AND ADJUNCT If you **poke** your head through an opening, you push it through, often so that you can see something more easily. *The driver slowed down and poked his head out of the window.*

poke about or **poke around.** PHR VB If you **poke about** or **poke around** for something, you search for it, usually by moving lots of objects around; an informal use. *He was lying flat on his stomach, poking around under the bed with his arm.*

poke at. PHR VB If you **poke at** something, you make lots of little pushing movements at it with a sharp object. *The chef poked at his little pile of ashes.*

poker /pəʊkə/, **pokers. 1** UNCOUNT N **Poker** is a card game that people play, usually in order to win money. **2** COUNT N A **poker** is a metal bar which you use to move coal or wood in a fire so that air can circulate.

polar /pəʊlə/. ATTRIB ADJ **Polar** refers to the area around the North and South Poles. *...the melting of the polar ice caps.*

polar bear, polar bears. COUNT N A **polar bear** is a large white bear which lives near the North Pole.

polarize /pəʊləraɪz/, **polarizes, polarizing, polarized;** also spelled **polarise.** ERG VB If people **are polarized,** they form into two separate groups with opposite opinions or positions. *In Britain the political debate is polarized between two major parties... Do we now polarize into two groups?* ♦ **polarization** /pəʊləraɪzeɪʃə^{0}n/ UNCOUNT N *...a growing polarisation between rich and poor countries.*

pole /pəʊl/, **poles.** 1 COUNT N A **pole** is a long, thin piece of wood or metal, used especially for supporting things. *...tent poles... ...telegraph poles.* 2 COUNT N WITH SUPP The earth's **poles** are the two opposite ends of its axis. 3 PHRASE If you say that two people are **poles apart,** you mean that they have completely different beliefs and opinions. *Politically they were poles apart.*

pole vault, pole vaults. COUNT N A **pole vault** is a very high jump which athletes make over a high bar, using a long, flexible pole to help lift themselves up.

police /pə0liːs/, **polices, policing, policed.** 1 PLURAL N The **police** are the official organization that is responsible for making sure that people obey the law, or the people who are members of this organization. *The police were called... 280 people were arrested and 117 police injured.* 2 VB WITH OBJ To **police** a place means to preserve law and order in it by means of the police or the army. *It is impossible to police such a vast area.*

police force, police forces. COUNT N A **police force** is the police organization in a particular country or area.

policeman /pə0liːsmə3n/, **policemen** /pə0liːsmə2n/. COUNT N A **policeman** is a man who is a member of the police force.

police officer, police officers. COUNT N A **police officer** is a policeman or policewoman.

police station, police stations. COUNT N A **police station** is the local office of the police force in a particular area.

policewoman /pə0liːswʊmən/, **policewomen** /pə0liːswɪmɪn/. COUNT N A **policewoman** is a woman who is a member of the police force.

policy /pɒlɪsi1/, **policies.** 1 COUNT N OR UNCOUNT N A **policy** is a set of plans that is used as a basis for making decisions, especially in politics, economics, or business. *They oppose Conservative policies... ...economic and foreign policy.* 2 COUNT N An insurance **policy** is a document which shows the agreement that you have made with an insurance company. *...a life assurance policy... This service is free to policy holders.*

polio /pəʊliəʊ/. UNCOUNT N **Polio** is a serious infectious disease which often causes paralysis.

polish /pɒlɪʃ/, **polishes, polishing, polished.** 1 UNCOUNT N **Polish** is a substance that you put on the surface of something to clean it and make it shine. *Use wax polish on wooden furniture... ...shoe polish.* 2 VB WITH OBJ If you **polish** something, you put polish on it. *Leather needs polishing with good quality cream.* ♦ **polished** ADJ *She slipped on the polished wooden floor.* 3 VB WITH OBJ To **polish** something also means to rub it with a cloth to make it shine. *I polished my glasses with a handkerchief.*

polished /pɒlɪʃt/. 1 ADJ Someone who is **polished** shows confidence and sophistication. *He had the most polished, sophisticated manner.* 2 ADJ If you describe an ability or skill as **polished,** you mean that it is of a very high standard. *My German was not very polished... ...polished actors.*

polite /pəlaɪt/, **politer, politest.** ADJ A **polite** person has good manners and is not rude to other people. *He was very polite to his superiors... ...a polite refusal.* ♦ **politely** ADV *He thanked me politely.* ♦ **politeness** UNCOUNT N *I do expect reasonable politeness.*

political /pəlɪtɪkə0l/. 1 ADJ **Political** means relating to politics. *...the major political parties... ...demands for political and religious freedom.* ♦ **politically** ADV *...a country which is politically stable.* 2 ADJ A **political** person is interested in politics and holds strong beliefs about it. *He was always very political.*

politician /pɒlɪtɪʃə0n/, **politicians.** COUNT N A **politician** is a person whose job is in politics, especially a member of parliament. *...Labour and Tory politicians.*

politics /pɒlɪtɪks/. 1 UNCOUNT N OR PLURAL N **Politics** is the actions or activities which people use to achieve power in a country, society, or organization. *...local politics... ...office politics... Politics has no place in our church.* 2 PLURAL N Your **politics** are your beliefs about how a country ought to be governed. *Her politics could be described as radical.*

poll /pəʊl/, **polls.** 1 COUNT N A **poll** is a survey in which people are asked their opinions about something. *Last year the polls gave the President a 10 to 15 point lead.* • See also **opinion poll.** 2 PLURAL N The **polls** are a political election. *The party won a convincing victory at the polls.*

pollen /pɒlən/. UNCOUNT N **Pollen** is a fine powder which flowers produce in order to fertilize other flowers of the same species.

pollutant /pəluːtənt/, **pollutants.** COUNT N A **pollutant** is a substance that pollutes the environment. *The main pollutants in this country are sulphur dioxide and smoke.*

pollute /pəluːt/, **pollutes, polluting, polluted.** VB WITH OBJ To **pollute** the water, air, or atmosphere means to make it dirty and dangerous to use or live in. *Our water supply is becoming polluted with nitrates.*

pollution /pəluːʃə0n/. 1 UNCOUNT N **Pollution** is the process of polluting the water, air, or atmosphere. *...changes in the climate due to pollution of the atmosphere by industrial waste.* 2 UNCOUNT N **Pollution** is also the unpleasant substances that pollute the water, air, or atmosphere. *They didn't seem to notice the pollution and the noise.*

polo /pəʊləʊ/. UNCOUNT N **Polo** is a game played between two teams of players. The players ride horses and use wooden hammers with long handles to hit a ball.

polo-necked /pəʊləʊ nekt/. ATTRIB ADJ A **polo-necked** sweater has a thick fold of material at the top which covers most of a person's neck.

polyester /pɒli1estə/. UNCOUNT N **Polyester** is a type of cloth used especially to make clothes.

polygamy /pəlɪgəmi1/. UNCOUNT N **Polygamy** is the custom of having more than one wife at the same time.

polystyrene /pɒli1staɪriːn/. UNCOUNT N **Polystyrene** is a very light, plastic substance used especially to make containers or as insulating material.

polytechnic /pɒli1teknɪk/, **polytechnics.** COUNT N A **polytechnic** is a college in Britain where you can go to study after leaving school. *...a course in drama at Manchester Polytechnic.*

polythene /pɒli1θiːn/. UNCOUNT N **Polythene** is a type of plastic made into thin sheets or bags and used especially to keep food fresh.

pomp /pɒmp/. UNCOUNT N **Pomp** is the use of a lot of ceremony, fine clothes, and decorations, especially on a special occasion. *...coming ashore with pomp and ceremony.*

pompous /pɒmpəs/. 1 ADJ Someone who is **pompous** behaves in a very serious way because they think they are more important than they really are; used showing disapproval. *...a pompous and conceited old fool... ...a pompous document of over 500 pages.* ♦ **pomposity** /pɒmpɒsɪ1ti1/ UNCOUNT N *They were annoyed by my pomposity.* 2 ADJ A **pompous** building or ceremony is very grand and elaborate. *...a pompous celebration.*

pond /pɒnd/, **ponds.** COUNT N A **pond** is a small area of water that is smaller than a lake. *...an ornamental pond in the garden.*

ponder /pɒndə/, **ponders, pondering, pondered.** VB WITH OR WITHOUT OBJ If you **ponder,** you think about something carefully; a literary use. *I pondered the ethics of the situation... Mary pondered upon the meaning of life.*

ponderous /pɒndə0rəs/; a literary word. 1 ADJ **Ponderous** speech or writing is dull and serious. *He spoke in a slow, ponderous way.* ♦ **ponderously** ADV *She nodded ponderously.* 2 ADJ A **ponderous** object is large and heavy. *...ponderous royal tombs.* 3 ADJ A **ponderous** action is slow or clumsy. *...taking a ponderous swing at the ball.* ♦ **ponderously** ADV *Slowly, ponderously, the vehicle shifted a few inches.*

pony /pəʊni1/, **ponies.** COUNT N A **pony** is a type of small horse. *Two girls rode up on small ponies.*

ponytail /pəʊni1teɪl/, **ponytails.** COUNT N If someone has their hair in a **ponytail,** it is tied up at the back so that it hangs down like a tail.

poodle /puːdə0l/, **poodles.** COUNT N A **poodle** is a type of dog with thick curly hair.

pool /puːl/, **pools, pooling, pooled.** 1 COUNT N A **pool** is a small area of still water. *...long stretches of sand with rocks and pools.* 2 COUNT N A **pool** is also a swimming pool. *She went swimming in the hotel pool.* 3 COUNT N WITH 'of' A **pool** of liquid or light is a small area of it. *...a pool of blood... A spotlight threw a pool of violet light onto the stage.* 4 COUNT N WITH SUPP A **pool** of people, money, or things is a number of them that are used or shared by several people or organizations. *...a pool of agricultural workers... ...car pools.* 5 VB WITH OBJ If people **pool** their money, knowledge, or equipment, they allow it to be used or shared by all of them. *We pooled our money, bought a van, and travelled.* 6 UNCOUNT N **Pool** is a game. Players use long, thin sticks to hit coloured balls into holes around the edges of a table. *...a pool table.* 7 PLURAL N If you do the **pools,** you take part in a gambling competition in which people try to win money by guessing correctly the results of football matches; a British use. *They won £300,000 on the Pools.*

poor /pʊə, pɔː/, **poorer, poorest.** 1 ADJ Someone who is **poor** has very little money or few possessions. *I was a student then, and very poor... ...a poor family... He was now one thousand pounds poorer.* 2 PLURAL N The **poor** are poor people. *The children of the poor are more likely to get diseases.* 3 ADJ A **poor** country or area is inhabited by people with very little money or few possessions. *...aid to the poorer countries... ...a shop in a poor part of Stratford.* 4 ATTRIB ADJ You use **poor** to express sympathy for someone. *Poor old Dennis, he can't do a thing right.* 5 ADJ If you describe something as **poor,** you mean that it is of a low quality or standard. *...books in a very poor condition... The pay was poor... In spite of poor health, I was able to continue working.* ♦ **poorly** ADV *...poorly designed equipment.* 6 ATTRIB ADJ You also use **poor** to describe someone who is not very skilful in a particular activity. *She was a very poor swimmer.* ♦ **poorly** ADV *I spoke Spanish so poorly.* 7 PRED ADJ WITH 'in' If something is **poor** in a particular quality or substance, it contains very little of the quality or substance. *The water was poor in oxygen.*

poorly /pʊəli1, pɔː-/. PRED ADJ If someone is **poorly,** they are ill; an informal British use. *Your brother's had an operation and he's quite poorly.*

pop /pɒp/, **pops, popping, popped.** 1 UNCOUNT N OR MOD **Pop** is modern music that usually has a strong rhythm and uses electronic equipment. *...pop music... ...pop concerts.* 2 MASS N You can refer to fizzy drinks such as lemonade as **pop;** an informal use. 3 **Pop** is used to represent a short sharp sound, for example the sound made by bursting a balloon or by pulling a cork out of a bottle. *The cork came out with a loud pop.* 4 VB If something **pops,** it makes a short sharp sound. *The cork popped and flew out of the bottle.* 5 VB If your eyes **pop,** you look very surprised or excited; an informal use. *His mouth hung open and his eyes popped.* 6 VB WITH OBJ AND ADJUNCT If you **pop** something somewhere, you put it there; an informal use. *He popped a piece of gum into his mouth... I popped a note through her letter box.* 7 VB WITH ADJUNCT If you **pop** somewhere, you go there; an informal use. *Why don't you pop in for a coffee... I'm just popping out for a haircut.*

pop up. PHR VB If someone or something **pops up,** they appear in a place or situation unexpectedly. *He's one of those rare types who pops up every so often.*

popcorn /pɒpkɔːn/. UNCOUNT N **Popcorn** is grains of maize that have been heated until they burst and become large and light.

Pope /pəʊp/, **Popes.** COUNT N OR TITLE The **Pope** is the head of the Catholic Church. *...Pope John Paul II.*

poplar /pɒplə/, **poplars.** COUNT N A **poplar** is a type of tall, thin tree.

poppy /pɒpi1/, **poppies.** COUNT N A **poppy** is a plant with large, delicate, red flowers.

populace /pɒpjə4lə1s/. SING N The **populace** of a country is its people; a formal use. *They represented only a fraction of the general populace.*

popular /pɒpjə4lə/. 1 ADJ Someone or something that is **popular** is liked or enjoyed by a lot of people. *He has always been popular among Conservatives... Swimming is very popular with all ages.* ♦ **popularity** /pɒpjə4lærɪ1ti1/ UNCOUNT N *...the popularity of science fiction films.* 2 ATTRIB ADJ **Popular** ideas or attitudes are held or approved of by most people. *Contrary to popular belief, science does not offer us certainties... ...the popular image of feminism.* 3 ATTRIB ADJ **Popular** newspapers and television programmes are aimed at ordinary people and not at specialists in a particular subject. *The popular press is obsessed with the Royal Family.* 4 ATTRIB ADJ **Popular** is used to describe political activities which involve everyone, and not just members of political parties; a formal use. *...popular democracy.*

popularize /pɒpjə4ləraɪz/, **popularizes, popularizing, popularized;** also spelled **popularise.** 1 VB WITH OBJ To **popularize** something means to make a lot of people interested in it and able to enjoy it. *Television has done a great deal to popularize snooker.* 2 VB WITH OBJ To **popularize** an academic subject or idea means to make it more easily understandable to ordinary people; a formal use. *Scientific notions soon become inaccurate when they are popularized.*

popularly /pɒpjə4ləli1/. 1 ADV You use **popularly** to indicate that a name is used by most people, although it is not the official one. *This theory was popularly called the Big Bang.* 2 ADV You also use **popularly** to indicate that an idea is believed by most people, although it may not be true. *It is popularly believed that eating carrots makes you see better in the dark.*

populate /pɒpjə4leɪt/, **populates, populating, populated.** VB WITH OBJ If an area **is populated** by people or animals, those people or animals live there. *The town is heavily populated by immigrants... ...the rabbits that thickly populated the area.* ♦ **populated** ADJ *...the densely populated countryside.*

population /pɒpjə4leɪʃə0n/, **populations.** 1 COUNT N OR UNCOUNT N The **population** of a place is all the people who live in it. *The country is unable to feed its population... Kandahar has a population of 230,000... ...the increase in population.* 2 COUNT N WITH SUPP You also use **population** to refer to all the people or animals of a particular type in a place. *...a prison population of 44,000.*

porcelain /pɔːsə^{0}lɪ^{3}n/. UNCOUNT N **Porcelain** is a hard, shiny substance made by heating clay. It is used to make cups, plates, and ornaments. *...antique pottery and porcelain.*

porch /pɔːtʃ/, **porches.** 1 COUNT N A **porch** is a sheltered area at the entrance to a building. It has a roof and sometimes walls. *...a big house with a glass porch.* 2 COUNT N A **porch** is also a raised platform built along the outside wall of a house and often covered with a roof; an American use.

porcupine /pɔːkjə^{4}paɪn/, **porcupines.** COUNT N A **porcupine** is an animal with many long, thin, spines on its back.

pore /pɔː/, **pores, poring, pored.** 1 COUNT N The **pores** in your skin or on the surface of a plant are very small holes which allow moisture to pass through. *...the pores round his nose... ...mushrooms with minute yellow pores.* 2 COUNT N **Pores** in rocks or soil are tiny gaps or cracks. *...water trapped in pores in rocks.*

pore over. PHR VB If you **pore over** a book or information, you look at it and study it very carefully. *We pored over our maps.*

pork /pɔːk/. UNCOUNT N **Pork** is meat from a pig, usually fresh and not smoked or salted. *...pork chops.*

porn /pɔːn/. UNCOUNT N **Porn** is pornography; an informal use. *...porn shops.*

pornography /pɔːnɒgrəfi^1/. UNCOUNT N **Pornography** refers to books, magazines, and films that are designed to cause sexual excitement by showing naked people and sexual acts. *...pornography in the cinema.* ♦ **pornographic** /pɔːnəgræfɪk/ ADJ *...pornographic films and magazines.*

porous /pɔːrəs/. ADJ Something that is **porous** has many small holes in it, which water and air can pass through. *The volcanic rocks are porous.*

porpoise /pɔːpəs/, **porpoises.** COUNT N A **porpoise** is a sea animal that looks similar to a dolphin.

porridge /pɒrɪdʒ/. UNCOUNT N **Porridge** is a thick, sticky food made from oats cooked in water.

port /pɔːt/, **ports.** 1 COUNT N A **port** is a town by the sea or on a river, which has a harbour. *...a fishing port... It is the major port on this coastline.* 2 COUNT N A **port** is also a harbour area with docks and warehouses, where ships load or unload goods or passengers. 3 ATTRIB ADJ The **port** side of a ship is the left side when you are facing the front. 4 MASS N **Port** is a type of strong, sweet red wine. *...a glass of port.*

portable /pɔːtəbə^{0}l/. ADJ A **portable** machine or device is designed to be easily carried. *...a little portable TV... ...portable typewriters.*

portal /pɔːtə^{0}l/, **portals.** COUNT N A **portal** is a large, impressive entrance to a building; a literary use. *...villas with huge marble portals.*

portent /pɔːtent/, **portents.** COUNT N A **portent** is something that indicates what is likely to happen in the future; a formal use. *Are dreams a portent of things to come?*

porter /pɔːtə/, **porters.** 1 COUNT N A **porter** is a person whose job is to be in charge of the entrance of a building such as a hotel. *...a hotel porter.* 2 COUNT N A **porter** is also a person whose job is to carry things, for example at a railway station. *...railway porters.*

portfolio /pɔːtfəʊliəʊ/, **portfolios.** 1 COUNT N A **portfolio** is a thin, flat case for carrying papers or drawings. 2 COUNT N A **portfolio** is also a set of drawings or paintings that represent an artist's work. *...a portfolio of photographs.*

porthole /pɔːthəʊl/, **portholes.** COUNT N A **porthole** is a small round window in a ship or aircraft.

portico /pɔːtɪkəʊ/, **porticos** or **porticoes.** COUNT N A **portico** is a large, covered area at the entrance to a building, with pillars supporting the roof; a formal use.

portion /pɔːʃə^{0}n/, **portions.** 1 COUNT N A **portion** of something is a part of it. *Divide the cake into eight portions... A large portion of this money would come to her.* 2 COUNT N A **portion** is the amount of food that is given to one person at a meal. *...a small portion.*

portly /pɔːtli^1/. ADJ **Portly** people are rather fat; an old-fashioned use. *...portly middle-aged gentlemen.*

portrait /pɔːtrɪ^{3}t/, **portraits.** COUNT N A **portrait** is a painting, drawing, or photograph of a person. *...the portrait of George Washington.*

portray /pɔːtreɪ/, **portrays, portraying, portrayed.** 1 VB WITH OBJ When an actor or actress **portrays** someone, he or she plays that person in a play or film. *In her final sketch she portrayed a temperamental countess.* 2 VB WITH OBJ AND ADJUNCT To **portray** someone or something in a particular way means to represent them in that way, for example in a book or film. *Advertising tends to portray women in a very traditional role.*

portrayal /pɔːtreɪəl/, **portrayals.** COUNT N A **portrayal** of someone is a representation of them in a play, film, or book. *...his portrayal of Willy Loman in 'Death of a Salesman'.*

Portuguese /pɔːtjə^{4}giːz/. 1 ADJ **Portuguese** means belonging or relating to Portugal. *...the great Portuguese navigators.* 2 UNCOUNT N **Portuguese** is the language spoken in Portugal, Brazil, Angola, and Mozambique.

pose /pəʊz/, **poses, posing, posed.** 1 VB If you **pose** for a photograph or painting, you stay in a particular position so that someone can photograph or paint you. *The bride and groom posed for the photograph.* 2 COUNT N WITH SUPP Your **pose** is the way you stand, sit, or lie when you are being painted or photographed. *...hundreds of photographs in various poses.* 3 VB If someone **is posing,** they are behaving in an exaggerated way because they want people to admire them. *You're always posing.* 4 VB WITH 'as' If you **pose** as someone, you pretend to be that person. *...an agent posing as a telephone engineer.* 5 VB WITH OBJ If something **poses** a problem or danger, it is the cause of it; a formal use. *He posed a serious threat to their authority.* 6 VB WITH OBJ If you **pose** a question, you ask it; a formal use. *This brings me back to the question you posed earlier.*

posh /pɒʃ/; an informal word. 1 ADJ **Posh** means smart, fashionable, and expensive. *She had stayed in posh hotels.* 2 ADJ If you describe a person as **posh,** you mean that they belong to a high social class. *...your posh friends.*

position /pəzɪʃə^{0}n/, **positions, positioning, positioned.** 1 COUNT N OR UNCOUNT N The **position** of someone or something is the place where they are. *They tell the time by the position of the sun... He had shifted position from the front to the back of the room.* ● If someone or something is **in position,** they are in their correct or usual place. *By 8.05 the groups were in position.* 2 COUNT N WITH SUPP When someone or something is in a particular **position,** they are sitting, lying, or arranged in that way. *I helped her to a sitting position... Hold it in an upright position.* 3 VB WITH OBJ OR REFL VB If you **position** something somewhere, you put it there. *Mel positioned his car alongside the foreman's... The boy positioned himself near the door.* 4 COUNT N WITH SUPP Your **position** in society is your status in it. *Women hold a strong position in Aboriginal society... ...people in positions of power and influence.* 5 COUNT N Someone's **position** in a company or organization is their job; a formal use. *...top management positions... Thorn lost his position as steward.* 6 COUNT N WITH SUPP Your **position** in a race or competition is your place among the winners, or your place at some time during the event. 7 COUNT N WITH SUPP You can describe your situation at a particular time by saying that you are in a particular **position.** *It puts me in a rather difficult position... You are in the fortunate position of having no responsibilities.* 8 COUNT N WITH SUPP Your **position** on a particular matter is your attitude towards it; a formal use. *What is their position on the proposed sale of aircraft?*

positive /pɒzɪtɪv/. 1 PRED ADJ If you are **positive** about something, you are completely sure about it. *He was positive that he had seen it in the newspaper.* 2 ADJ People who are **positive** are hopeful and confident. *I began to feel more positive... ...positive feelings about life.* 3 ADJ A **positive** response shows agreement, approval, or encouragement. *Public response was positive.* 4 ATTRIB ADJ **Positive** evidence gives definite proof of something. *I was looking for some positive evidence that Barney came to the flat.* 5 ADJ If a scientific test is **positive,** it shows that something has happened or is present. *...a positive pregnancy test.* 6 ADJ A **positive** number is greater than zero. 7 ATTRIB ADJ You can use **positive** to emphasize that something is the case. *Life in a town brings positive advantages to children.*

positively /pɒzɪtɪvli^1/. ADV OR SENTENCE ADV You use **positively** to emphasize that something is the case. *Her friends had been positively abusive... It's quite positively the last time that you'll see me.*

possess /pəzes/, **possesses, possessing, possessed;** a formal word. 1 VB WITH OBJ If you **possess** something, you have it or own it. *How I longed to possess a suit like that... They were found guilty of possessing petrol bombs.* 2 VB WITH OBJ To **possess** a quality, ability, or feature means to have it. *He possessed the qualities of a war leader... For hundreds of years London possessed only one bridge.*

possession /pəzeʃə^{0}n/, **possessions.** 1 UNCOUNT N The **possession** of something is the fact of having it or owning it. *Freedom depended on the possession of land... The possession of a degree does not guarantee you a job.* 2 PHRASE If something is **in your possession,** or if you are **in possession** of it, you have it; a formal use. *I had in my possession a portion of the money... The document came into the possession of the Daily Mail... MacDonald has been in possession of the letter for some weeks.* 3 COUNT N Your **possessions** are the things that you own or have with you. *He had few possessions... Check your possessions on arrival.*

possessive /pəzesɪv/, **possessives.** 1 ADJ Someone who is **possessive** about another person wants all that person's love and attention. *She was very possessive about Rod.* ♦ **possessiveness** UNCOUNT N *...a child's possessiveness towards its mother.* 2 ADJ When people are **possessive** about things that they own, they do not like other people to use them. *I am possessive about my car.* 3 COUNT N OR ADJ In grammar, the **possessive** is the form of a noun or pronoun used to indicate possession. For example 'George's', 'his', and 'mine' are possessives.

possessor /pəzesə/, **possessors.** COUNT N The **possessor** of something is the person who has it or owns it; a formal use.

possibility /pɒsɪbɪlɪ^{1}ti^1/, **possibilities.** COUNT N If there is a **possibility** of something happening or being true, it might happen or might be true. *I considered the possibility of joining the Communist Party... We must accept the possibility that we might be wrong.*

possible /pɒsɪbə^{0}l/. 1 ADJ If it is **possible** to do something, it can be done. *It is possible for us to measure his progress... They are doing everything possible to take care of you... Whenever possible, loads were flown in... 'When do you want to go?'—'This weekend, if possible.'* 2 ADJ If you do something as soon as **possible,** you do it as soon as you can. If you get as much as **possible** of something, you get as much as you can. *Go as soon as possible... I like to know as much as possible about my patients... He sat as far away from the others as possible.* 3 ADJ You use **possible** with superlative adjectives to emphasize that something has more of a quality than anything else of its kind. *We provide the best possible accommodation for our students... ...the harshest possible conditions.* 4 ADJ If it is **possible** that something is true or correct, it might be true or correct. *It is possible that he said these things.* 5 ADJ A **possible** event is one that might happen. *His staff warned him of the possible consequences.* 6 ATTRIB ADJ If you describe someone as, for example, a **possible** Prime Minister, you mean that he or she may become the Prime Minister. *America and Russia were both possible financiers of the dam.*

possibly /pɒsɪbli^1/. 1 SENTENCE ADV You use **possibly** to indicate that you are not sure whether something is true or will happen. *Television is possibly to blame for this... We could possibly get some money by going to my parents.* 2 ADV You use **possibly** to emphasize that you are surprised or puzzled. *How could it possibly accomplish anything?... I wondered what he could possibly be doing it for.* 3 ADV You use **possibly** in front of a modal to emphasize that something is done as well or as soon as it can be done. *He will do everything he possibly can to aid you... I have made myself as comfortable as I possibly can... He planned to come back as soon as he possibly could.* 4 ADV You use **possibly** with a negative modal to emphasize that something cannot happen or cannot be done. *I can't possibly stay in all the weekend... Nobody could possibly tell the difference.*

post /pəʊst/, **posts, posting, posted.** 1 SING N The **post** is the system by which letters and parcels are collected and delivered; a British use. *There is a cheque for you in the post... Winners will be notified by post.* ♦ **postal** /pəʊstə^{0}l/ ATTRIB ADJ *...increases in postal charges... ...the postal service.* 2 UNCOUNT N You can refer to letters and parcels delivered to you as your **post.** *There is some post for you... Rose was reluctant to answer her post.* 3 VB WITH OBJ If you **post** a letter or parcel, you send it to someone by putting it in a post-box or by taking it to a post office. *I'm going to post a letter... I'll be glad to post you details.* 4 PHRASE If you **keep** someone **posted,** you keep them informed about something. *David promised to keep them posted.* 5 COUNT N A **post** is an upright pole fixed into the ground. *A dog sat chained to a post.* 6 COUNT N A **post** in an organization is a job or official position in it; a formal use. *She is well qualified for the post.* 7 VB WITH OBJ AND ADJUNCT If you **are posted** somewhere, you are sent there by the organization you work for. *I have been posted to Paris.* 8 See also **posting.**

post-. PREFIX **Post-** is used to form words that describe something as taking place after a particular date or event. *...the post-1918 period... ...a post-election survey.*

postage /pəʊstɪdʒ/. UNCOUNT N **Postage** is the money that you pay for sending letters and parcels by post. *Send 25p extra for postage and packing.*

postage stamp, postage stamps. COUNT N A **postage stamp** is a small piece of paper that you have to buy and stick on an envelope or parcel before you post it; a formal use.

postal order, postal orders. COUNT N A **postal order** is a piece of paper representing a sum of money which you buy at a post office and send to someone as a way of sending money by post; a British use.

post-box, post-boxes. COUNT N A **post-box** is a metal box with a hole in it in which you post letters.

postcard /pəʊstkɑːd/, **postcards.** COUNT N A **postcard** is a piece of card, often with a picture on one side, which you can write on and post to someone without using an envelope.

postcode /pəʊstkəʊd/, **postcodes.** COUNT N Your **postcode** is a short sequence of numbers and letters at the end of your address, which helps the post office to sort the mail; a British use.

poster /pəʊstə/, **posters.** COUNT N A **poster** is a large notice, advertisement, or picture that you stick on a wall or noticeboard. *...cinema posters.*

posterity /pɒstɛrɪ^{1}ti^{1}/. UNCOUNT N You can refer to everyone who will be alive in the future as **posterity;** a formal use. *This fine building should be preserved for posterity.*

postgraduate /pəʊstgrædjuːət/, **postgraduates.** COUNT N A **postgraduate** is a student with a first degree who is studying or doing research at a more advanced level. Also ATTRIB ADJ *...postgraduate students... Many students go on and do postgraduate work.*

posthumous /pɒstjə^{4}məs/. ADJ **Posthumous** is used to describe something that happens after someone's death; a formal use. *...a posthumous award for bravery.*

posting /pəʊstɪŋ/, **postings.** COUNT N A **posting** is a job that you are given which involves going to a different town or country. *I've been given an overseas posting to Japan.*

postman /pəʊstmə^{3}n/, **postmen.** COUNT N A **postman** is a man whose job is to collect and deliver letters and parcels that are sent by post.

postmark /pəʊstmɑːk/, **postmarks.** COUNT N A **postmark** is a mark printed on letters and parcels at a post office. It shows the time and place at which they are posted.

postmaster /pəʊstmɑːstə/, **postmasters.** COUNT N A **postmaster** is a man in charge of a post office; an old-fashioned use.

postmistress /pəʊstmɪstrɪ^{2}s/, **postmistresses.** COUNT N A **postmistress** is a woman in charge of a post office; an old-fashioned use.

post-mortem /pəʊst mɔːtəm/, **post-mortems.** COUNT N A **post-mortem** is a medical examination of a dead person's body to find out how they died.

post office, post offices. 1 SING N The **Post Office** is the national organization responsible for postal services. 2 COUNT N A **post office** is a building where you can buy stamps, post letters and parcels, and use other services provided by the national postal service.

postpone /pə^{6}st^{0}pəʊn/, **postpones, postponing, postponed.** VB WITH OBJ If you **postpone** an event, you arrange for it to take place later. *Could you postpone your departure for five minutes?... The flight had been postponed until eleven o'clock.* ♦ **postponement** /pə^{6}st^{0}pəʊnmə^{2}nt/ UNCOUNT N *...the postponement of the wedding.*

postscript /pəʊstskrɪpt/, **postscripts.** COUNT N A **postscript** is a message written at the end of a letter after you have signed your name. You write 'PS' in front of it.

posture /pɒstʃə/, **postures.** 1 UNCOUNT N Your **posture** is the position or manner in which you stand or sit. *...his stiff, upright posture.* 2 COUNT N WITH SUPP A **posture** is also an attitude. *They are trying to adopt a more co-operative posture.*

post-war. ATTRIB ADJ **Post-war** is used to describe things that happen, exist, or are made in the period immediately after a war. *...a post-war building... ...the post-war era.*

posy /pəʊzi^{1}/, **posies.** COUNT N A **posy** is a small bunch of flowers.

pot /pɒt/, **pots, potting, potted.** 1 COUNT N A **pot** is a deep, round container used for cooking, or a round container for paint or some other thick liquid. *...clay pots... ...old paint pots.* 2 COUNT N You can use **pot** to refer to a pot and its contents, or to the contents only. *...a pot of cream.* 3 COUNT N You can also use **pot** to refer to a teapot or coffee pot, with or without its contents, or to the contents only. *I'll go and make a fresh pot of tea.* 4 VB WITH OBJ If you **pot** a plant, you put it into a flowerpot filled with earth, so that it can grow there. 5 See also **potted, chimney pot.**

potato /pəteɪtəʊ/, **potatoes.** COUNT N OR UNCOUNT N A **potato** is a round white vegetable with a brown or red skin. Potatoes grow underground. *...baked potatoes.*

potent /pəʊtə^{0}nt/. 1 ADJ Something that is **potent** is effective and powerful. *Potent new weapons will shortly be available... ...a potent argument.* ♦ **potency** /pəʊtə^{0}nsi^{1}/ UNCOUNT N *Princess Ida's spell lost its potency.* 2 ADJ A man who is **potent** is capable of having sex. *In early adulthood you are at your most potent.* ♦ **potency** UNCOUNT N *...sexual potency.*

potential /pətɛnʃə^{0}l/. 1 ATTRIB ADJ You use **potential** to describe something as capable of becoming a particular kind of thing. *All 92 countries are customers or potential customers of the United States... ...potential sources of food production.* ♦ **potentially** SUBMOD *Electricity is potentially dangerous.* 2 SING N Your **potential** is the range of abilities which you are capable of having. *Many children do not achieve their potential.* 3 UNCOUNT N If something has **potential,** it is capable of being useful or successful in the future. *The land has great strategic potential.*

potentiality /pətɛnʃɪælɪ^{1}ti^{1}/, **potentialities.** PLURAL N OR UNCOUNT N If something has **potentialities** or **potentiality,** it is capable of being used or developed; a formal use. *...the potentialities of motoring and flight... ...the realization of human potentiality.*

potion /pəʊʃə^{0}n/, **potions.** COUNT N A **potion** is a drink containing medicine, poison, or something that is supposed to have magic powers. *...love potions.*

potted /pɒtɪ^{2}d/. 1 ATTRIB ADJ **Potted** meat or fish has been cooked and put into a small sealed container. *...potted shrimps.* 2 ATTRIB ADJ A **potted** biography or history contains the main facts in a simplified form. *...potted character studies of famous authors.*

potter /pɒtə/, **potters, pottering, pottered.** COUNT N A **potter** is someone who makes pottery.

potter about. PHR VB If you **potter about** or **potter around,** you pass the time in an unhurried way, doing pleasant things; a British use. *He loved to potter around in the garden.*

pottery /pɒtə^{0}ri^{1}/. 1 UNCOUNT N **Pottery** is pots, dishes, and other objects made from clay. *...a sale of antique pottery.* 2 UNCOUNT N **Pottery** is also the craft or activity of making pottery. *My hobbies are pottery and basket-weaving.*

potty /pɒti^{1}/, **potties.** 1 COUNT N A **potty** is a deep bowl which a small child uses as a toilet. 2 ADJ Someone who is **potty** is crazy or foolish; an informal use. *They thought she was potty... I think it's a potty idea.*

pouch /paʊtʃ/, **pouches.** 1 COUNT N A **pouch** is a flexible container like a small bag. *...a tobacco pouch.* 2 COUNT N A kangaroo's **pouch** is a pocket of skin on its stomach in which its baby grows.

poultry /pəʊltri^{1}/. 1 PLURAL N You can refer to chickens, ducks, and other birds kept for their eggs and meat as **poultry.** *They keep poultry.* 2 UNCOUNT N You can also refer to the meat of these birds as **poultry.** *They sell a wide range of cooked, frozen and fresh poultry.*

pounce /paʊns/, **pounces, pouncing, pounced.** 1 VB When an animal or bird **pounces** on something, it leaps on it and grabs it. *He had seen leopards pouncing on young baboons.* 2 VB If you **pounce** on something such as a mistake, you draw attention to it. *Local politicians are quick to pounce on any trouble.*

pound /paʊnd/, **pounds, pounding, pounded.** 1 COUNT N A **pound** is a unit of money in Britain, equal to one hundred pence. Many other countries use a unit of money called a **pound.** *I was paid fifty pounds a week.* 2 COUNT N A **pound** is also a unit of weight equal to 16 ounces or approximately 0.454 kilograms. *...one pound of rice... He weighs about 140 pounds.* 3 VB WITH OBJ OR ADJUNCT If you **pound** something or **pound** on it, you hit it loudly and repeatedly with your fists. *In frustration she would pound the dining-room table... They began pounding on the walls.* ♦ **pounding** UNCOUNT N *The pounding of the drums grew louder.* 4 VB WITH OBJ To **pound** something also means to crush it into a paste or powder, or into very small pieces. *The women of the village pounded grain in their mortars.* 5 VB If your heart **is pounding,** it is beating with a strong, fast rhythm. *My heart pounded with joy.* ♦ **pounding** UNCOUNT N *I felt only the pounding of my heart.*

pour /pɔː/, **pours, pouring, poured.** 1 VB WITH OBJ If you **pour** a liquid or other substance, you make it flow steadily out of a container by holding the container at an angle. *The waiter poured the wine into her glass... ...a machine that poured grain into sacks.* 2 VB WITH OBJ If you **pour** someone a drink, you fill a cup or glass with it so that they can drink it. *He poured Ellen a glass of wine... She poured a drink for herself.* 3 VB WITH ADJUNCT When a liquid or other substance **pours** somewhere, it flows there quickly and in large quantities. *The rain poured through a hole in the roof.* 4 VB When it **is pouring,** it is raining heavily. *In London it poured all the time... It was absolutely pouring with rain.* ♦ **pouring** ATTRIB ADJ *Don't go out in the pouring rain.* 5 VB WITH ADJUNCT When people **pour** into a place, they go into it in large numbers. *Refugees are now pouring into this country.* 6 VB WITH OBJ AND 'into' When someone **pours** money into an activity or organization, they spend a lot of money on it.

pour out. PHR VB If you **pour out** a drink, you fill a cup or glass with it. *Castle poured out two glasses of whisky.*

pout /paʊt/, **pouts, pouting, pouted.** VB If you **pout,** you stick out your lips as a way of showing that you are annoyed. *She tossed back her hair and pouted.* ♦ **pouting** ADJ *...a pouting blonde.*

poverty /pɒvəti^{1}/. UNCOUNT N **Poverty** is the state of being very poor. *There are thousands living in poverty.*

poverty-stricken. ADJ **Poverty-stricken** people or places are extremely poor. *...this small poverty-stricken town.*

powder /paʊdə/, **powders, powdering, powdered.** 1 MASS N **Powder** consists of many tiny particles of a solid substance. *Their bones turn to powder... ...washing powders.* 2 REFL VB OR VB WITH OBJ If you **powder** yourself, you cover parts of your body with scented powder. *She lightly powdered her face.*

powdered /paʊdəd/. ATTRIB ADJ A **powdered** substance is in the form of a powder. *...powdered milk.*

power /paʊə/, **powers, powering, powered.** 1 UNCOUNT N Someone who has **power** has control over people and activities. *...his yearning for power... It gave the President too much power.* 2 UNCOUNT N WITH SUPP Your **power** to do something is your ability to do it. *They lose the power to walk... They did not have the power of speech.* 3 COUNT N OR UNCOUNT N WITH SUPP If someone in authority has the **power** to do something, they have the legal right to do it. *The Government curbed the Lords' powers... ...the court's power to punish young offenders.* 4 UNCOUNT N WITH SUPP The **power** of something is its physical strength. *I underestimated the power of the explosion.* 5 UNCOUNT N **Power** is energy obtained, for example, by burning fuel or by using the wind or the sun. *...steam power... ...a cheap source of power.* 6 UNCOUNT N Electricity is often referred to as **power.** *...a power failure.* 7 VB WITH OBJ To **power** a machine means to provide the energy that makes it work. *Its radar equipment was powered by a nuclear reactor.*

PHRASES ● To **come to power** means to take charge of a country's affairs. If someone is **in power,** they are in charge of a country's affairs. *The Wilson Government came to power in 1964... The Tories were in power at the time.* ● If something is **within** or **in** your **power,** you are able to do it. *It may not be within their power to help... I did everything in my power to console her.*

powerful /paʊəfʊl/. 1 ADJ A **powerful** person or organization is able to control or influence people and events. *They organize themselves into powerful and effective trade unions... ...the most powerful government in western Europe.* 2 ADJ If someone's body is **powerful,** it is physically strong. *He had broad shoulders and powerful arms.* ♦ **powerfully** ADV *They were young, powerfully built men.* 3 ADJ A **powerful** smell is strong and unpleasant. *...the powerful odour of horse manure.* ♦ **powerfully** ADV *...a room smelling powerfully of cats.* 4 ADJ A **powerful** voice is loud and easily heard. 5 ADJ A **powerful** speech or work of art has a strong effect on people's feelings. *He produced a series of extraordinarily powerful paintings.*

powerless /paʊəlɪ^{2}s/. 1 ADJ Someone who is **powerless** is unable to control or influence events. *Without the support of the party, the Cabinet is powerless.* ♦ **powerlessness** UNCOUNT N *She experienced an overwhelming sense of powerlessness.* 2 PRED ADJ WITH TO-INF If you are **powerless** to do something, you are unable to do it. *I stood there watching, feeling powerless to help.*

power station, power stations. COUNT N A **power station** is a place where electricity is generated.

pp. pp. is the plural of **p.**

practicable /præktɪkəbə^{0}l/. ADJ If a task or plan is **practicable,** it is capable of being carried out; a formal use.

practical /præktɪkə^{0}l/, **practicals.** 1 ATTRIB ADJ **Practical** means involving real situations, rather than ideas and theories. *The Party faces practical difficulties of organization and finance... Practical experience of broadcasting would be valuable.* 2 ADJ **Practical** people deal with problems sensibly and effectively. 3 ADJ **Practical** ideas and methods are able to be carried out successfully. *Their ideas are too opposed to our way of thinking to be considered practical... How long will it be before nuclear fusion becomes practical?* 4 ADJ **Practical** clothes and things in your house are useful rather than fashionable or attractive. *Ceramic tiles are very hard on the feet, though practical.* 5 COUNT N A **practical** is an examination or lesson in which you make things or do experiments rather than simply write.

practicality /præktɪkælɪti^{1}/, **practicalities.** PLURAL N The **practicalities** of a situation are the aspects of it which are concerned with real events rather than with ideas or theories. *He turned out to know very little about the practicalities of teaching.*

practical joke, practical jokes. COUNT N A **practical joke** is a trick that is intended to make someone look ridiculous.

practically /præktɪkə^{0}li^1/. ADV **Practically** means almost. *The town was practically deserted... He knew practically no English.*

practice /præktɪs/, **practices.** 1 COUNT N You can refer to something that people do regularly as a **practice.** *Benn began the practice of holding regular meetings... ...the ancient Japanese practice of binding the feet from birth.* 2 UNCOUNT N WITH SUPP People's religious activities are referred to as the **practice** of their religion. *...the practice of the Christian religion.* 3 UNCOUNT N **Practice** is regular training or exercise in something. *I help them with their music practice... Skating's just a matter of practice.* 4 COUNT N A doctor's or lawyer's **practice** is his or her business, often shared with other doctors or lawyers. *...a doctor with a private practice.*

PHRASES ● If you **put** an idea or method **into practice,** you make use of it. *He had not yet attempted to put his principles into practice... I'm not sure how effective these methods will be when put into practice.* ● What happens **in practice** is what actually happens, in contrast to what is supposed to happen. *In practice, he exerted little influence over the others... What it means in practice is that he does twice the work for half the money.* ● If you are **out of practice** at doing something, you have not done it recently.

practise /præktɪs/, **practises, practising, practised;** spelled **practice, practices, practicing, practiced** in American English. 1 VB WITH OR WITHOUT OBJ If you **practise** something, you keep doing it regularly in order to do it better. *I played the piece I had been practising for months... The baseball team was practising in the park.* 2 VB WITH OBJ To **practise** something such as a custom, craft, or religion means to take part in the activities associated with it. *These crafts were practised by many early cultures... They have managed to practise their religion for years.* 3 VB WITH OBJ Someone who **practises** medicine or law works as a doctor or lawyer. *He's in Hull practising medicine now.* ♦ **practising** ATTRIB ADJ *...a practising doctor.*

practised /præktɪst/. ADJ Someone who is **practised** at something is good at it because they have had a lot of experience of it. *A practised burglar rarely leaves any trace of his presence.*

practitioner /præktɪʃə^{0}nə/, **practitioners.** COUNT N Doctors are sometimes referred to as **practitioners;** a formal use.

pragmatic /prægmætɪk/. ADJ A **pragmatic** way of dealing with something is based on practical considerations, rather than theoretical ones. *He argued the case for increased state intervention on wholly pragmatic grounds.*

prairie /preəri^1/, **prairies.** COUNT N OR UNCOUNT N A **prairie** is a large area of flat, grassy land in North America. *...days of travel across the prairies... ...acres of rolling prairie.*

praise /preɪz/, **praises, praising, praised.** 1 VB WITH OBJ If you **praise** someone or something, you express approval for their achievements or qualities. *Sylvia had a stern father who never praised her... They praised his speech for its clarity and humour.* 2 UNCOUNT N **Praise** is what you say or write about someone when you are praising them. *Three entrants were singled out for special praise... She finds it hard to give praise.* 3 PHRASE To **sing** someone's **praises** means to praise them in an enthusiastic way.

pram /præm/, **prams.** COUNT N A **pram** is a vehicle like a baby's cot on wheels, which you push along when you want to take a small baby somewhere.

prance /prɑːns/, **prances, prancing, pranced.** 1 VB WITH ADJUNCT If someone **prances** around, they walk with exaggerated movements. 2 VB When a horse **prances,** it moves with quick, high steps.

prank /præŋk/, **pranks.** COUNT N A **prank** is a childish trick; an old-fashioned use. *...a boyish prank.*

prawn /prɔːn/, **prawns.** COUNT N A **prawn** is a small shellfish, similar to a shrimp.

pray /preɪ/, **prays, praying, prayed.** VB When people **pray,** they speak to God in order to give thanks or to ask for help. *He kneeled down and prayed to Allah... She prayed that God would send her strength.*

prayer /preə/, **prayers.** 1 UNCOUNT N **Prayer** is the activity of praying to God. *Her eyes were shut and her lips were moving in prayer.* 2 PHRASE When people **say** their **prayers,** they pray. 3 COUNT N A **prayer** is the words that someone says when they pray. *I made a brief prayer for her recovery.*

pre-. PREFIX **Pre-** is used to form words that describe something as taking place before a particular date or event. *...pre-1914 Europe... ...the pre-Christmas period.*

preach /priːtʃ/, **preaches, preaching, preached.** 1 VB WITH OR WITHOUT OBJ When a member of the clergy **preaches,** he or she gives a talk on a religious or moral subject as part of a church service. *The chaplain preached to a packed church.* 2 VB WITH OBJ To **preach** a set of ideas means to try to persuade people to accept them. *He used to go round the villages preaching Socialism.*

preacher /priːtʃə/, **preachers.** COUNT N A **preacher** is a person, usually a member of the clergy, who preaches sermons as part of a church service.

preamble /priːæmbə^{0}l/, **preambles.** COUNT N OR UNCOUNT N A **preamble** is an introduction to something you say or write; a formal use. *...an intensely long preamble... Philip said quickly without preamble, 'Somebody shot your father.'*

precarious /pri^{1}keərɪəs/. 1 ADJ If your situation is **precarious,** you might fail at any time in what you are doing. *The management was in a precarious position.* ♦ **precariously** ADV *I found myself living, somewhat precariously, from one assignment to another.* 2 ADJ If something is **precarious,** it is not securely held in place and seems likely to fall. *...precarious piles of books.* ♦ **precariously** ADV *I sat precariously on the roof of the cabin.*

precaution /pri^{1}kɔːʃə^{0}n/, **precautions.** COUNT N A **precaution** is an action intended to prevent something dangerous or unpleasant from happening. *I had taken the precaution of swallowing two sea sickness tablets... ...fire precautions.*

precautionary /pri^{1}kɔːʃənə^{0}ri^1/. ADJ **Precautionary** actions are intended to prevent something dangerous or unpleasant from happening. *Precautionary measures were unnecessary.*

precede /pri^{1}siːd/, **precedes, preceding, preceded;** a formal word. 1 VB WITH OBJ If one event or period of time **precedes** another, it happens before it. *...the drop in temperature that precedes a heavy thunderstorm... The children's dinner was preceded by games.* ♦ **preceding** ATTRIB ADJ *...the activities we discussed in the preceding chapter.* 2 VB WITH OBJ If you **precede** someone somewhere, you go in front of them. *She preceded him across the hallway... We were preceded by a huge man called Teddy Brown.*

precedence /presɪdəns/. PHRASE If one thing **takes precedence** over another, the first thing is regarded as more important than the second one; a formal use. *The peaceful ordering of society takes precedence over every other consideration.*

precedent /presɪdənt/, **precedents;** a formal word. 1 COUNT N If an action or decision is regarded as a **precedent,** people refer to it as a reason for taking a similar action or decision at a later time. *The Supreme Court had already set a precedent.* 2 COUNT N OR UNCOUNT N If there has been a **precedent** for something, something similar to it has happened before. *There was no precedent for the riots... He broke with precedent by making his maiden speech on a controversial subject.*

precept /priːsept/, **precepts.** COUNT N A **precept** is a general rule that helps you to decide how you should behave in particular circumstances; a formal use. *...precepts of tolerance and forgiveness.*

precinct /priːsɪŋkt/, **precincts.** 1 COUNT N In Britain, a **precinct** is a specially built shopping area in the centre of a town, in which cars are not allowed. 2 COUNT N In the United States, a **precinct** is a part of a city which has its own police force and fire service. *...police at work patrolling the 12th precinct.* 3 PLURAL N The **precincts** of an institution are its buildings and land; a formal use. *Gambling is prohibited within the precincts of the University.*

precious /preʃəs/. 1 ADJ If you say that something such as time is **precious,** you mean that it is valuable and should not be wasted. *They have lost precious working time... The one resource more precious than any other was land.* 2 ADJ **Precious** objects and materials are worth a lot of money because they are rare. *...precious metals.* 3 ADJ If a possession is **precious** to you, you regard it as important and do not want to lose it. *I imagine he treasures that letter as one of the precious mementoes of his Presidency.* 4 ATTRIB ADJ People sometimes use **precious** to express their dislike for things which other people think are important; an informal use. *I'm sick and tired of your precious brother-in-law.* 5 ADJ If you describe someone as **precious,** you mean that they behave in a formal and unnatural way. *...that rather precious young man... He has a slightly precious prose style.* 6 PHRASE **Precious little** of something means very little of it. *There's precious little they can learn from us.*

precious stone, precious stones. COUNT N **Precious stones** are valuable stones such as diamonds, rubies, and sapphires that are used for making jewellery.

precipice /presɪpɪs/, **precipices.** COUNT N A **precipice** is a very steep cliff on a mountain; a literary use.

precipitate /prɪ^{1}sɪpɪteɪt/, **precipitates, precipitating, precipitated.** VB WITH OBJ If something **precipitates** a new event or situation, it causes it to happen suddenly; a formal use. *This would precipitate an economic crisis.*

precipitous /prɪ^{1}sɪpɪtəs/. ADJ **Precipitous** means very steep; a formal use. *...precipitous hillsides.*

precise /pri^{1}saɪs/. 1 ATTRIB ADJ You use **precise** to emphasize that you are describing something correctly and exactly. *At that precise moment we were interrupted by the telephone... The precise nature of the disease has not yet been established.* ♦ **precisely** SENTENCE ADV *He was furious, precisely because he had not been consulted.* 2 ADJ Something that is **precise** is exact and accurate. *Mr Jones gave him precise instructions... The timing had to be very precise.* ♦ **precisely** ADV *He made the knots precisely, losing no time.*

precision /pri^{1}sɪʒə^{0}n/. UNCOUNT N If you do something with **precision,** you do it exactly as it should be done. *He had established a reputation for unfailing precision in his job.*

preclude /pri^{1}kluːd/, **precludes, precluding, precluded.** VB WITH OBJ If something **precludes** an event or action, it prevents it from happening; a formal use. *This should not preclude a search for a better hypothesis.*

precocious /pri^{1}kəʊʃəs/. ADJ **Precocious** children do or say things that seem very advanced for their age. *I have a brilliant, precocious pupil in my class.*

preconceived /priːkənsiːvd/. ATTRIB ADJ If you have **preconceived** ideas about something, you have already formed an opinion about it before you have had enough information or experience. *...getting away from preconceived notions.*

preconception /priːkə^{7}nsepʃə^{0}n/, **preconceptions.** COUNT N Your **preconceptions** about something are beliefs formed about it before you have had enough information or experience. *He tries to deny information that challenges his preconceptions.*

precondition /priːkə^{7}ndɪʃə^{0}n/, **preconditions.** COUNT N If one thing is a **precondition** for another, it must happen or be done before the second thing can happen; a formal use. *Economic growth was regarded as the precondition for greater equality... Protection of the environment is a precondition of a healthy society.*

precursor /pri^{1}kɜːsə/, **precursors.** COUNT N A **precursor** of something is a similar thing that happened or existed before; a formal use. *...the precursors of man.*

predator /predətə/, **predators.** COUNT N A **predator** is an animal that kills and eats other animals. *The whiting is a major predator on smaller fish.*

predatory /predətə^{0}ri^1/. ATTRIB ADJ **Predatory** animals kill and eat other animals.

predecessor /priːdɪsesə/, **predecessors.** 1 COUNT N WITH POSS Someone's **predecessor** is the person who had their job or role before them. *She wasn't being paid the same wage as her predecessor.* 2 COUNT N WITH POSS The **predecessor** of an object or machine is the object or machine that it replaced. *The latest model is more refined than its predecessor.*

predestined /priːdestɪnd/. ADJ If you say something was **predestined** to happen, you mean that it could not have been prevented because it had already been decided by God or by fate. *I was predestined to be a slave.*

predetermined /priːdɪtɜːmɪnd/. ADJ If something is **predetermined,** its form or nature was decided by previous events or by people rather than by chance; a formal use. *He believes that we're all genetically predetermined.*

predicament /pri^{1}dɪkəmə^{2}nt/, **predicaments.** COUNT N WITH SUPP If you are in a **predicament,** you are in a difficult situation. *We are in a worse predicament than ever.*

predict /pri^{1}dɪkt/, **predicts, predicting, predicted.** REPORT VB If you **predict** an event, you say that it will happen. *He predicted a brilliant future for the child... The government predicts that the region will draw 500,000 tourists a year.*

predictable /pri^{1}dɪktəbə^{0}l/. ADJ Something that is **predictable** can be known about in advance. *The outcome is not always predictable.* ♦ **predictably** SENTENCE ADV OR ADV *Predictably, the affair went hopelessly wrong... ...situations where everyone behaves predictably.* ♦ **predictability** /prə^{1}dɪktəbɪl^{1}ti^1/ UNCOUNT N *It happened month by month, with boring predictability.*

prediction /pri^{1}dɪkʃə^{0}n/, **predictions.** COUNT N OR UNCOUNT N If you make a **prediction,** you say what you think will happen. *...a prediction of the likely outcome of the next election... ...methods of prediction.*

predispose /priːdɪspəʊz/, **predisposes, predisposing, predisposed.** VB WITH OBJ AND TO-INF If something **predisposes** you to think or behave in a particular way, it makes it likely that you will think or behave in that way; a formal use. *Their experiences predisposed them to accept extremist policies.* ♦ **predisposed** PRED ADJ WITH TO-INF *She was predisposed to be critical.*

predominance /pri[1]dɒmɪnəns/. UNCOUNT N If there is a **predominance** of one type of person or thing, there are many more of that type than any other; a formal use. *...the predominance of businessmen in the party's ranks.*

predominant /pri[1]dɒmɪnənt/. ADJ If something is **predominant,** it is more important or noticeable than other things of the same kind; a formal use. *Italian opera became predominant at the end of the 17th century... The predominant mood among policy-makers is one of despair.* ♦ **predominantly** /pri[1]dɒmɪnəntli[1]/ ADV *The debates were predominantly about international affairs.*

predominate /pri[1]dɒmɪneɪt/, **predominates, predominating, predominated.** VB If one type of person or thing **predominates** in a group, there are more of that type than any other; a formal use. *In most churches, women predominate in the congregations.*

pre-eminent /priːɛmɪnə[2]nt/. ADJ The **pre-eminent** person in a group is the most important or powerful one; a formal use. *For the next thirty years Bryce was the pre-eminent figure in Canadian economic policy.* ♦ **pre-eminence** /priː ɛmɪnəns/ UNCOUNT N *No one disputed his claim to pre-eminence.*

preen /priːn/, **preens, preening, preened.** 1 REFL VB When people **preen** themselves, they spend time making themselves look neat and attractive. *He preened himself in front of the mirror.* 2 VB WITH OR WITHOUT OBJ When birds **preen** their feathers, they clean and arrange them with their beaks. *A peacock pecked and preened on the lawn.*

prefabricated /pri[1]fæbrɪkeɪtɪ[2]d/. ATTRIB ADJ **Prefabricated** buildings are built from large parts which can be easily put together.

preface /prɛfɪ[1]s/, **prefaces, prefacing, prefaced.** 1 COUNT N A **preface** is an introduction at the beginning of a book. 2 VB WITH OBJ AND 'with' OR 'by' If you **preface** an action or speech with something else, you do or say this other thing first; a formal use. *Each girl prefaced her remarks with 'sorry'.*

prefect /priːfɛkt/, **prefects.** COUNT N A **prefect** is an older pupil at a British school who has special duties.

prefer /pri[1]fɜː/, **prefers, preferring, preferred.** VB WITH OR WITHOUT OBJ If you **prefer** one thing to another, you like the first thing better. *I prefer Barber to his deputy... They prefer to suffer deprivation rather than claim legal aid... The Head Master prefers them to act plays they have written themselves.*

preferable /prɛfə[0]rəbə[0]l/. ADJ If one thing is **preferable** to another, it is more desirable or suitable. *Gradual change is preferable to sudden, large-scale change... Many people find this method immensely preferable.* ♦ **preferably** SENTENCE ADV *Clean the car from the top, preferably with a hose and warm water.*

preference /prɛfə[0]rəns/, **preferences.** 1 COUNT N OR UNCOUNT N If you have a **preference** for something, you would like to have or do it rather than something else. *Each of us has personal preferences for certain types of entertainment... I took the non-stop flight to London, in preference to the two-stage journey via New York.* 2 UNCOUNT N If you give **preference** to someone, you choose them rather than someone else. *Preference was given to those who had overseas experience.*

preferential /prɛfərɛnʃəl/. ATTRIB ADJ If you get **preferential** treatment, you are treated better than other people. *Disabled people at work should have preferential treatment.*

prefix /priːfɪks/, **prefixes.** COUNT N A **prefix** is a letter or group of letters added to the beginning of a word in order to make a new word with a different meaning.

pregnancy /prɛgnənsi[1]/, **pregnancies.** UNCOUNT N OR COUNT N **Pregnancy** is the condition of being pregnant, or the period of time during which a female is pregnant. *The breasts enlarge during pregnancy... She has had fifteen pregnancies.*

pregnant /prɛgnənt/. ADJ If a woman or female animal is **pregnant,** a baby is developing in her body. *She was three months pregnant... My mother was pregnant with me at the time.*

prehistoric /priːhɪstɒrɪk/. ATTRIB ADJ **Prehistoric** people and things existed before information was written down. *...prehistoric cooking pots.*

prejudice /prɛdʒʊdɪs/, **prejudices.** 1 UNCOUNT N OR COUNT N **Prejudice** is an unreasonable dislike of someone or something. *...racial prejudice... Barber was a man of strong prejudices.* 2 UNCOUNT N If you show **prejudice** in favour of someone, you treat them better than other people. *There was some regrettable prejudice in favour of middle class children.*

prejudiced /prɛdʒʊdɪst/. ADJ A person who is **prejudiced** against someone has an unreasonable dislike of them. A person who is **prejudiced** in favour of someone has an unreasonable preference for them. *People were prejudiced against her... We all know how difficult it is to reason with a prejudiced person.*

preliminary /pri[1]lɪmɪnə[0]ri[1]/, **preliminaries.** ATTRIB ADJ **Preliminary** activities or discussions take place in preparation for an event before it starts. *...preliminary arrangements.* Also COUNT N *He spent a long time on polite preliminaries.*

prelude /prɛljuːd/, **preludes.** COUNT N You describe an event as a **prelude** to a more important event when it happens before it and acts as an introduction to it. *This speech has been hailed by his friends as the prelude to his return to office.*

premature /prɛmətjʊə/. 1 ADJ Something that is **premature** happens too early or earlier than expected. *This disease produces premature ageing... ...the premature departure of the visitors.* ♦ **prematurely** ADV *The warden retired prematurely with a nervous disorder.* 2 ADJ A **premature** baby is born before the date when it was due to be born.

premeditated /pri[1]mɛdɪteɪtɪ[2]d/. ADJ A **premeditated** action is planned or thought about before it is done. *...a premeditated act of murder.*

premier /prɛmjə/, **premiers.** 1 COUNT N OR TITLE The leader of a government can be referred to as the **premier.** *...the French premier... ...Premier Francisco Pinto Balsemao.* 2 ATTRIB ADJ **Premier** is used to describe something that is considered to be the best or most important thing of its kind. *The article referred to Hull as Europe's premier port.*

premiere /prɛmɪɛə, prɛmɪə/, **premieres.** COUNT N The **premiere** of a new play or film is its first public performance. *The film had its world premiere at San Sebastian.*

premiership /prɛmjəʃɪp/. UNCOUNT N OR SING N **Premiership** is the position of being the leader of a government. *He should never have been considered for the premiership.*

premise /prɛmɪs/, **premises.** 1 PLURAL N The **premises** of a business are all the buildings and land that it occupies. *In 1971 the firm moved to new premises in Bethnal Green.* 2 COUNT N A **premise** is something that you suppose is true and therefore use as a basis for an idea; a formal use. *I'm questioning whether the whole premise is correct.*

premium /priːmɪəm/, **premiums.** 1 COUNT N A **premium** is an extra sum of money which is paid in addition to the normal cost of something. *Investors were willing to pay a premium for companies that offered such a potential for growth.* 2 COUNT N A **premium** is also a sum of money that you pay regularly to an insurance company for an insurance policy. *...tax relief on life insurance premiums.*

premonition /prɛmənɪʃə[0]n/, **premonitions.** COUNT N A **premonition** is a feeling that something unpleasant is going to happen. *He had a sudden terrible premonition that she had run away.*

prenatal /priːneɪtə[0]l/. ATTRIB ADJ **Prenatal** things relate to the medical care of pregnant women. *...prenatal classes for expectant mothers.*

preoccupation /priːɒkjə[4]peɪʃə[0]n/, **preoccupations.** COUNT N OR UNCOUNT N If you have a **preoccupation** with something, you cannot stop thinking about. *Top jobs should be your next preoccupation... He was capable of total preoccupation.*

preoccupy /priːɒkjə[4]paɪ/, **preoccupies, preoccupying, preoccupied.** VB WITH OBJ If something **preoccupies** you, you think about it a lot. *This is a question which increasingly preoccupies me.* ♦ **preoccupied** ADJ *His wife becomes more and more preoccupied with the children.*

preparation /prɛpəreɪʃə[0]n/, **preparations.** 1 UNCOUNT N The **preparation** of something is the activity of getting it ready. *Benn was involved in the preparation of Labour's manifesto... ...food preparation.* 2 PLURAL N **Preparations** are the arrangements that are made for a future event. *He'll have to make preparations for the funeral.* 3 COUNT N A **preparation** is a mixture that has been prepared for use as food, medicine, or a cosmetic; a formal use.

preparatory /prə[2]pærətə[0]ri[1]/. ATTRIB ADJ **Preparatory** actions are done as a preparation for something else; a formal use. *...a preparatory report... ...preparatory language courses.*

preparatory school, preparatory schools. COUNT N OR UNCOUNT N A **preparatory school** is the same as a prep school; a formal use.

prepare /pri[1]pɛə/, **prepares, preparing, prepared.** 1 VB WITH OBJ If you **prepare** something, you make it ready for something that is going to happen. *A room has been prepared for you... Schools have to prepare children for life in the community.* 2 VB WITH OR WITHOUT OBJ OR REFL VB If you **prepare** for an event, action, or situation, you get ready for it. *The guests prepared for their departure... Prepare yourself for a shock... I was not really prepared for her fits of boredom.* 3 VB WITH OBJ When you **prepare** food, you get it ready to be eaten. *He had spent all morning preparing the meal.*

prepared /pri[1]pɛəd/. 1 PRED ADJ WITH TO-INF If you are **prepared** to do something, you are willing to do it. *I'm prepared to say I was wrong... Many countries seem prepared to consider nuclear energy.* 2 PRED ADJ If you are **prepared** for something that may happen, you are ready for it. *Be prepared for power cuts by buying lots of candles.* 3 ADJ Something that is **prepared** has been done or made beforehand. *He read out a prepared statement.*

preposition /prɛpəzɪʃə[0]n/, **prepositions.** COUNT N A **preposition** is a word such as 'by', 'for', 'into', or 'with', which is always followed by a noun group or a clause built around the '-ing' form of a verb. ♦ **prepositional** /prɛpəzɪʃə[0]nəl/ ATTRIB ADJ *...prepositional phrases.*

preposterous /pri[1]pɒstə[0]rəs/. ADJ If something is **preposterous,** it is extremely unreasonable and foolish. *...a preposterous idea.*

prep school, prep schools. COUNT N OR UNCOUNT N A **prep school** is a private school in Britain for children up to 11 or 13.

prerequisite /priːrɛkwɪzɪt/, **prerequisites.** COUNT N If one thing is a **prerequisite** for another, it must happen or exist before the second thing is possible; a formal use. *Confidence is a prerequisite for mastering other skills.*

prerogative /pri[1]rɒgətɪv/, **prerogatives.** COUNT N Something that is the **prerogative** of a particular person or group is a privilege or right that only they have; a formal use. *...luxuries which were considered the prerogative of the rich.*

prescribe /pri[1]skraɪb/, **prescribes, prescribing, prescribed.** 1 VB WITH OBJ If a doctor **prescribes** treatment, he or she states what medicine or treatment a patient should have. *Her doctor prescribed a sedative.* 2 VB WITH OBJ If someone **prescribes** an action or duty, they state formally that it must be done; a formal use. *The factory laws prescribed a heavy fine for contravention of this rule.*

prescription /pri[1]skrɪpʃə[0]n/, **prescriptions.** 1 COUNT N A **prescription** is a medicine which a doctor has told you to take, or the form on which the doctor has written the details of that medicine. *...a prescription for sleeping tablets.* 2 PHRASE A medicine that is available **on prescription** is available from a chemist if you have a prescription for it.

presence /prɛzəns/. 1 UNCOUNT N WITH POSS Someone's **presence** in a place is the fact that they are there. *He tried to justify his presence in Belfast... He had to cope with the presence of her family.* 2 PHRASE If you are **in** someone's **presence,** you are in the same place as they are. *I felt comfortable in her presence... Haldane repeated his statement in the presence of the chairman.* 3 UNCOUNT N If someone has **presence,** they have an impressive physical appearance and manner. *He had tremendous physical presence.*

presence of mind. UNCOUNT N **Presence of mind** is the ability to act quickly and sensibly in a difficult situation. *Richard had the presence of mind to step forward and pick it up.*

present, presents, presenting, presented; pronounced /prɛzənt/ when it is an adjective or noun, and /pri[1]zɛnt/ when it is a verb. 1 ATTRIB ADJ You use **present** to describe people and things that exist now, rather than in the past or the future. *The present chairperson is a woman... Economic planning cannot succeed in present conditions.* 2 SING N The **present** is the period of time that is taking place now and the things that are happening now. *We have to come to terms with the present.* 3 PRED ADJ If someone is **present** at an event, they are there. *He had been present at the dance... There was a photographer present.* 4 COUNT N A **present** is something that you give to someone, for example for their birthday or for Christmas. *I gave him an atlas as a birthday present.* 5 REFL VB WITH ADJUNCT If you **present** yourself somewhere, you announce that you have arrived; a formal use. *The next morning I presented myself at their offices.* 6 VB WITH OBJ If you **present** someone to an important person, you officially introduce them; a formal use. *May I present Mr Rudolph Wallace.* 7 VB WITH OBJ If you **present** someone with something, you formally give it to them. *He presented her with a signed copy of his book... One of his constituents presented a petition to Parliament.* 8 VB WITH OBJ Something that **presents** a difficulty or a challenge causes or provides it. *The tornado presented the island with severe problems.* 9 VB WITH OBJ If you **present** information, you give it to people. *...a way of*

presenting new material... Our teachers were trying to present us with an accurate picture of history. **10** VB WITH OBJ AND ADJUNCT If you **present** someone or something in a particular way, you describe them in that way. *Her lawyer wanted to present her in the most favourable light... They present the British as the colonialist oppressor.* **11** VB WITH OBJ Someone who **presents** a programme on television or radio introduces each part of it or each person on it. *...'University Link', compiled and presented by Dr Brian Smith.* ♦ **presenter** /pri^{1}zentə/ COUNT N *Her strong point is that she's a very good presenter.*
PHRASES ● If something is happening **at present,** it is happening now. *He is at present serving a life sentence.* ● If a situation exists **for the present,** it exists now but is likely to change. *For the present she continues with the antibiotics.* ● **The present day** is the period of history that is taking place now. *This tradition has continued till the present day.*

presentable /pri^{1}zentəbə^{0}l/. ADJ If someone or something is **presentable,** they are quite attractive and suitable for other people to see. *She looked quite presentable... ...some of his more presentable pictures.*

presentation /prezənteɪʃə^{0}n/, **presentations. 1** UNCOUNT N The **presentation** of information is the process of making it available to people. *...the collection and presentation of statistical data.* **2** UNCOUNT N **Presentation** is the appearance of something and the impression that it gives. *Presentation is very important in cooking.* **3** COUNT N A **presentation** is a formal event at which someone is given something such as a prize. *I said I would not be able to attend the presentation.* **4** COUNT N WITH SUPP A **presentation** is also something such as a play or a lecture that is presented before an audience; a formal use. *Darwin was urged to deliver a presentation on the subject.*

present-day. ATTRIB ADJ You use **present-day** to describe people and things that exist now. *...present-day Japanese children... ...social conditions in present-day India.*

presently /prezəntli^1/. **1** ADV You use **presently** to indicate that something happened quite a short time after something you have just mentioned. *Presently I got the whole story.* **2** ADV If you say that something will happen **presently,** you mean that it will happen quite soon. *He will be here presently.* **3** ADV If something is **presently** happening, it is happening now. *...the oil rigs that are presently in operation.*

present participle, present participles. COUNT N The **present participle** of an English verb is the form that ends in '-ing'. It is used to form continuous tenses, and to form adjectives and nouns from a verb.

present tense. SING N In grammar, the **present tense** of a verb is used mainly to talk about things that happen or exist at the time of speaking or writing.

preservative /pri^{1}zɜːvətɪv/, **preservatives.** MASS N A **preservative** is a chemical that is added to substances to prevent them from decaying. *This yoghurt is free from artificial preservatives.*

preserve /pri^{1}zɜːv/, **preserves, preserving, preserved. 1** VB WITH OBJ If you **preserve** a situation or condition, you make sure that it stays as it is. *We are interested in preserving world peace... I stood there, determined to preserve my dignity.* ♦ **preservation** /prezəveɪʃə^{0}n/ UNCOUNT N *...the preservation of democracy.* **2** VB WITH OBJ If you **preserve** something, you take action to save it or protect it. *...a big house which had been preserved as a museum.* **3** VB WITH OBJ If you **preserve** food, you treat it in a way that prevents it from decaying. *Deep freezing is the simplest way of preserving food.* **4** MASS N **Preserves** are foods such as jam or chutney that are made by cooking fruit with sugar to preserve the fruit.

preside /pri^{1}zaɪd/, **presides, presiding, presided.** VB If you **preside** over a formal meeting or event, you are in charge or act as the chairperson; a formal use.

presidency /prezɪdənsi^1/. SING N The **presidency** is the position of being the president of a country. *He is to be nominated for the presidency.*

president /prezɪdənt/, **presidents. 1** COUNT N OR TITLE In a country without a king or queen, the official leader is often called the **president.** Some presidents are elected. *The French president arrived in the United States this week... ...the assassination of President Kennedy.* **2** COUNT N The **president** of an organization is the person with the highest position in it. *...the former President of the Royal Academy.*

presidential /prezɪdenʃə^{0}l/. ATTRIB ADJ **Presidential** activities or things relate or belong to a president. *...the next presidential election.*

press /pres/, **presses, pressing, pressed. 1** VB WITH OBJ AND ADJUNCT If you **press** one thing against another, you push the first thing against the second. *Stroganov pressed his hand to his heart... The animal presses itself against a tree trunk.* **2** VB WITH OBJ If you **press** a button or switch, you push it with your finger. *Mrs Carstairs pressed an electric bell.* Also COUNT N *All this can be called up at the press of a button.* **3** VB WITH OR WITHOUT OBJ If you **press** on something or **press** it, you push it with your hand or foot. *She pressed down upon the velvet cloth... ...pressing the mattress with his fingers.* **4** VB WITH OBJ If you **press** clothes, you iron them. *He always pressed his trousers before wearing them.* **5** VB WITH 'for' If you **press** for something, you try hard to persuade someone to give it to you. *He pressed for full public ownership.* **6** VB WITH OBJ If you **press** someone, you try hard to persuade them to do or say something. *He pressed me to have a cup of coffee with him.* **7** VB WITH OBJ WITH 'on' OR 'upon' If you **press** something on someone, you insist that they take it. *His aunt was pressing upon him cups of tea and cookies.* **8** VB WITH OBJ If you **press** charges against someone, you make an official accusation which has to be decided in a court of law. *They decided against pressing charges.* **9** COLL N The **Press** refers to newspapers, or to the journalists who write them. *...an amusing story in the press... I got to know a lot of the American press.* **10** COUNT N A printing **press** is a machine used for printing books, newspapers, and leaflets. **11** See also **pressed, pressing.**
press on. PHR VB If you **press on,** you continue doing something in spite of difficulties. *They courageously pressed on with their vital repair work.*

press conference, press conferences. COUNT N A **press conference** is a meeting held by a famous or important person in which they answer questions asked by journalists.

pressed /prest/. PRED ADJ If you are **pressed** for money or **pressed** for time, you do not have enough money or time. *He was always pressed for money.*

pressing /presɪŋ/. ADJ Something that is **pressing** needs to be dealt with immediately. *...a pressing appointment with the doctor.*

pressure /preʃə/, **pressures, pressuring, pressured. 1** UNCOUNT N **Pressure** is the force produced when you press hard on something. *He disliked the pressure of her hand... It bent when pressure was put upon it.* **2** UNCOUNT N WITH SUPP **Pressure** is also the force that a quantity of gas or liquid has on a surface that it touches. *I'll just check the tyre pressure.* **3** UNCOUNT N If someone puts **pressure** on you, they try to persuade you to do something. *For a long time he's been trying to put pressure on us to go... They were under pressure from feminists.* **4** VB WITH OBJ If you **pressure** someone to do something, you try forcefully to persuade them to do it. *The children are not pressured to eat... Some young people are pressured into staying on at school.* **5** UNCOUNT N OR PLURAL N If you feel **pressure,** you feel that you have too much to do and not enough time to do it. *We do our best work under pressure... ...the pressures of public life.* **6** See also **blood pressure.**

pressure group, pressure groups. COUNT N A **pressure group** is an organization that campaigns to change a law. *There followed six years of campaigning by pressure groups.*

pressurize /preʃəraɪz/, **pressurizes, pressurizing, pressurized;** also spelled **pressurise.** VB WITH OBJ If you **pressurize** someone to do something, you try hard to persuade them to do it. *It was a move designed to pressurise workers to return earlier.*

pressurized /preʃəraɪzd/; also spelled **pressurised.** ADJ In a **pressurized** container or area, the pressure inside is different from the pressure outside. *...the pressurized cabin of a Boeing 707.*

prestige /prestiːʒ/. UNCOUNT N If you have **prestige,** other people admire you because of your position or the quality of your work. *...a job with some prestige attached to it.*

prestigious /prestɪdʒɪ^{0}əs/. ADJ Something that is **prestigious** is important and admired. *...one of the most prestigious universities in the country.*

presumably /pri^{1}zjuːməbli^1/. SENTENCE ADV If you say that something is **presumably** the case, you mean that you think it is the case, although you are not certain. *Presumably they're a bit more expensive... The bomb was presumably intended to go off while the meeting was in progress.*

presume /pri^{1}zjuːm/, **presumes, presuming, presumed. 1** REPORT VB OR VB If you **presume** that something is the case, you think that it is the case, although you are not certain. *If you do not come, I shall presume the deal is off... You are married, I presume?* **2** VB WITH OBJ AND TO-INF OR COMPLEMENT If something **is presumed** to be the case, people believe that it is the case, although they are not certain. *...Larry Burrows, missing and presumed dead since 1971... He is presumed to be living in Spain.*

presumption /pri^{1}zʌmpʃə^{0}n/, **presumptions.** COUNT N A **presumption** is something that is believed to be true. *...based on the presumption that heaven exists.*

presumptuous /pri^{1}zʌmptjuəs/. ADJ If someone's behaviour is **presumptuous,** they do things that they have no right to do. *It is dangerous and presumptuous to interfere between parents and children.*

presuppose /priːsəpəuz/, **presupposes, presupposing, presupposed.** REPORT VB If one thing **presupposes** another, the first thing cannot be true or exist unless the second is true or exists; a formal use. *The myth of the Ascension presupposes there is a Heaven.*

pretence /pri^{1}tens/, **pretences;** spelled **pretense** in American English. **1** COUNT N OR UNCOUNT N A **pretence** is behaviour that is intended to make people believe something that is not true. *She leapt up with a pretence of eagerness... The industry has abandoned any pretence of restraint.* **2** PHRASE If you do something **under false pretences,** you do it when people do not know the truth about you and your intentions. *I felt that I was taking money under false pretences.*

pretend /pri^{1}tend/, **pretends, pretending, pretended.** REPORT VB OR VB WITH TO-INF If you **pretend** that something is the case, you try to make people believe that it is the case, although it is not. *Her father tried to pretend that nothing unusual had happened... He pretended to fall over.*

pretension /pri^{1}tenʃə^{0}n/, **pretensions.** UNCOUNT N OR PLURAL N Someone with **pretensions** pretends that they are more important than they really are. *He is evidently a person of some social pretension... He has pretensions to greatness.*

pretentious /pri^{1}tenʃəs/. ADJ Someone or something that is **pretentious** tries to appear more important or significant than they really are. *...one of the most pretentious films of all time.*

pretext /priːtekst/, **pretexts.** COUNT N A **pretext** is a reason which you pretend has caused you to do something. *The Government invented a 'plot' as a pretext for arresting opposition leaders.*

pretty /prɪti^1/, **prettier, prettiest. 1** ADJ **Pretty** means attractive in a delicate way. *Who's that pretty little girl?... The wallpaper was very pretty, covered in roses.* **2** SUBMOD You can use **pretty** before an adjective or adverb to mean 'quite' or 'rather'; an informal use. *I thought it was pretty good... I'm pretty certain she enjoys it.* **3** PHRASE **Pretty much** or **pretty well** means 'almost'; an informal use. *I felt pretty much the same... She hated pretty well all of them.*

prevail /pri^{1}veɪl/, **prevails, prevailing, prevailed. 1** VB WITH ADJUNCT If a custom or belief **prevails** at a particular place or time, it is normal at that place or time. *...the traditions that have prevailed in Britain since the 17th century.* ♦ **prevailing** ATTRIB ADJ *The prevailing view shifted still further.* **2** VB If a proposal or a principle **prevails,** it gains influence or is accepted. *In the end, common sense prevailed... Political arguments had prevailed over economic sense.*

prevalent /prevələnt/. ADJ A condition or belief that is **prevalent** is very common. *...one theory prevalent among scientists.* ♦ **prevalence** /prevələns/ SING N *...the prevalence of snobbery in Britain.*

prevaricate /pri^{1}værɪkeɪt/, **prevaricates, prevaricating, prevaricated.** VB If you **prevaricate,** you avoid giving a direct, truthful answer or a firm decision. *The doctors prevaricated, arguing the need for additional tests.*

prevent /pri^{1}vent/, **prevents, preventing, prevented.** VB WITH OBJ If you **prevent** something, you stop it happening or being done. *My only idea was to prevent him from speaking... It was not enough to prevent war... ...a layer of fat beneath the skin that prevents their body heat from escaping.*

preventative /pri^{1}ventətɪv/. ATTRIB ADJ **Preventative** means the same as preventive.

prevention /pri^{1}venʃə^{0}n/. UNCOUNT N **Prevention** is action that prevents something from happening. *...the prevention of cruelty to animals... ...fire prevention.*

preventive /pri^{1}ventɪv/. ATTRIB ADJ **Preventive** actions are intended to help prevent things such as disease or crime. *Preventive measures are essential... ...preventive medicine.*

preview /priːvjuː/, **previews.** COUNT N A **preview** of a film or exhibition is an opportunity to see it before it opens publicly. *Welcome to the press preview of the Seyer Street exhibition.*

previous /priːvɪəs/. ATTRIB ADJ A **previous** event or thing is one that occurred before the one you are talking about. *...children from a previous marriage... They had arrived the previous night.*

previously /priːvjəsli^1/. **1** ADV **Previously** means at some time before the period that you are talking about. *He was previously British consul in Atlanta.* **2** ADV You can use **previously** to say how much earlier one event was than another. *They had retired ten years previously.*

pre-war /priː wɔː/. ATTRIB ADJ **Pre-war** things existed before a war, especially the 1939-45 war in Europe. *...the pre-war telephone network.*

prey /preɪ/, **preys, preying, preyed.** UNCOUNT N WITH POSS The creatures that an animal hunts and eats are called its **prey.** *The mole seeks its prey entirely underground.*

prey on. PHR VB **1** If one animal **preys on** another, it lives by catching and eating the second animal. *The amphibians were hunters, preying on worms and insects.* **2** PHRASE If something **preys on** your **mind,** you cannot stop worrying about it. *Barton agreed, but the decision preyed on his mind.*

price /praɪs/, **prices, pricing, priced. 1** COUNT N OR UNCOUNT N The **price** of something is the amount of money that you must pay to buy it. *The price of firewood has risen steeply... Petrol will continue to drop in price.* **2** SING N WITH SUPP The **price** that you pay for something is an unpleasant thing that you have to do in order to get it. *This was the price that had to be paid for progress... This is a small price to pay for freedom.* **3** VB WITH OBJ If something **is priced** at a particular amount, it costs that amount. *The least expensive will be priced at £7,000... ...reasonably priced accommodation.* **4** See also **cut-price.**

priceless /praɪslɪ²s/. **1** ADJ Something that is **priceless** is worth a lot of money. *...a beautiful priceless sapphire.* **2** ADJ You can also describe a quality or characteristic as **priceless** when it is extremely useful. *This priceless asset has enabled him to win innumerable tournaments.*

prick /prɪk/, **pricks, pricking, pricked. 1** VB WITH OBJ If you **prick** something, you make a small hole in it with a sharp object such as a pin. *Prick the apples all over, using the prongs of a fork... He pricked himself with the needle.* **2** VB WITH OBJ If something sharp **pricks** you, it sticks into your skin. *Sharp thorns pricked his knees.* Also COUNT N *...the sharp pricks as the pellets struck his hands.* **3** ERG VB If an animal **pricks** its ears, or **pricks** its ears up, its ears suddenly point straight up because it has heard a noise. *He would prick his ears and whine at the sound of my voice... When a dog hears a strange noise, his ears prick and his head turns.* **4** VB WITH OBJ If you **prick** your ears up, you suddenly listen eagerly when you hear something interesting or important. *...an argument that made mathematicians all over the world prick up their ears.*

prickle /prɪkəᵒl/, **prickles, prickling, prickled. 1** COUNT N **Prickles** are small, sharp points that stick out from leaves or the stalks of plants. **2** VB If your skin **prickles,** it feels as if a lot of small, sharp points are being stuck into it. *The shirt I was wearing made my skin prickle... My skin prickled with fear.* Also COUNT N *I felt a prickle of pleasure.*

prickly /prɪkli¹/. **1** ADJ A **prickly** plant has a lot of sharp points sticking out from it. *...prickly thorn bushes.* **2** ADJ Someone who is **prickly** loses their temper very easily. *...a prickly and tiresome man.*

pride /praɪd/, **prides, priding, prided. 1** UNCOUNT N **Pride** is a feeling of satisfaction which you have because you or people close to you have done something good or possess something good. *His mother looked at him with affection and pride... She pointed with pride to the fine horses she had trained.* **2** UNCOUNT N **Pride** is also a sense of dignity and self-respect. *My pride did not allow me to complain too often... Pride alone prevented her from giving up.* **3** UNCOUNT N You can also refer to a feeling of being superior to other people as **pride.** *...a show of masculine pride.* **4** REFL VB WITH 'on' If you **pride** yourself on a quality or skill, you are very proud of having it. *Mrs Hochstadt prided herself on her intelligence.*

PHRASES ● If you **take pride** in something that you have or do, you feel pleased and happy because of it. *I take great pride in the success of my children.* ● If you **swallow** your **pride,** you decide that you must do something that you are rather ashamed to do. *He swallowed his pride and accepted the money.* ● If something in a group has **pride of place,** it is the most important thing there. *Musical compositions take pride of place in the festivities.*

priest /priːst/, **priests. 1** COUNT N A **priest** is a member of the clergy in the Catholic or Orthodox church, and in some Protestant churches. **2** COUNT N A **priest** is also a man in many non-Christian religions with particular duties and responsibilities in a place where people worship. *...a Buddhist priest.*

priestess /priːstɛs/, **priestesses.** COUNT N A **priestess** is a woman in a non-Christian religion with particular duties and responsibilities in a place where people worship.

priestly /priːstli¹/. ATTRIB ADJ **Priestly** refers to things belonging or relating to a priest. *...priestly duties.*

prig /prɪg/, **prigs.** COUNT N A **prig** is someone who is irritating because they behave very correctly and disapprove of other people's behaviour.

prim /prɪm/. ADJ Someone who is **prim** is easily shocked by anything rude or improper; often used showing disapproval. *...a prim, severe woman.* ♦ **primly** ADV *His sister sat primly with her legs together.*

prima donna /priːmə dɒnə/, **prima donnas. 1** COUNT N A **prima donna** is the main female singer in an opera. **2** COUNT N If you describe someone as a **prima donna,** you mean that they are difficult to deal with because their moods change suddenly. *Bob was a prima donna who played heartily at office politics.*

primaeval /praɪmiːvəᵒl/. See **primeval.**

primarily /praɪmərəli¹/. ADV You use **primarily** to indicate the most important feature of something or reason for something. *These linguists were concerned primarily with the structure of languages.*

primary /praɪməri¹/, **primaries. 1** ADJ The **primary** one of a group of things is the most important one. *One of Europe's primary requirements was minerals... She gets her primary satisfaction from her career.* **2** ATTRIB ADJ **Primary** education or a **primary** school is for pupils between the ages of 5 and 11 in Britain. **3** COUNT N A **primary** is an election in an American state in which people vote for someone to become a candidate for a political office.

primate /praɪmeɪt, -mɪ¹t/, **primates.** COUNT N A **primate** is a member of the group of mammals which includes humans, monkeys, and apes.

prime /praɪm/, **primes, priming, primed. 1** ATTRIB ADJ You use **prime** to describe something that is most important in a situation. *What was said was of prime importance... Maths is no longer a prime requirement for a career in accountancy.* **2** ATTRIB ADJ **Prime** is also used to describe something that is of the best possible quality. *He wants his herd delivered in prime condition.* **3** ATTRIB ADJ A **prime** example of something is a typical example of it. *...a prime example of the power of the press.* **4** SING N WITH POSS Your **prime** is the stage in your life when you are most active or most successful. *I had been a good player in my prime.* **5** VB WITH OBJ If you **prime** someone about something, you prepare them by giving them information about something. *I had primed him for this meeting.*

Prime Minister, Prime Ministers. PROPER N OR COUNT N The leader of the government in some countries such as Britain is called the **Prime Minister.**

primeval /praɪmiːvəᵒl/; also spelled **primaeval.** ATTRIB ADJ **Primeval** is used to describe things belonging or relating to a very early historical period. *...primeval forests... ...our primeval ancestors.*

primitive /prɪmɪtɪv/. **1** ADJ In **primitive** societies, people live in a simple way, usually without industries or a writing system. *...primitive tribes.* **2** ADJ Something that is **primitive** is of an early type and is therefore not well developed. *...primitive insect-eating mammals... ...primitive microprocessors.* **3** ADJ If you describe something as **primitive,** you mean that it is very basic or old-fashioned. *The sleeping accommodation is somewhat primitive.*

primrose /prɪmrəʊz/, **primroses.** COUNT N A **primrose** is a wild plant with pale yellow flowers.

prince /prɪns/, **princes.** COUNT N OR TITLE A **prince** is a male member of a royal family, especially the son of a king or queen. *...Prince Charles.*

princess /prɪnsɛs/, **princesses.** COUNT N OR TITLE A **princess** is a female member of a royal family, especially the daughter of a king or queen or the wife of a prince. *...Princess Mary.*

principal /prɪnsɪpəᵒl/, **principals. 1** ATTRIB ADJ The **principal** person or thing is the main or most important one. *...the principal character in James Bernard Fagan's play.* **2** COUNT N The **principal** of a school or college is the person in charge of it.

principality /prɪnsɪpæli¹ti¹/, **principalities.** COUNT N A **principality** is a country that is ruled by a prince.

principally /prɪnsɪpəᵒli¹/. ADV **Principally** means more than anything else. *He dealt principally with Ethiopia... ...a protein which occurs principally in wheat.*

principle /prɪnsɪpəᵒl/, **principles. 1** COUNT N OR UNCOUNT N A **principle** is a belief that you have about the way you should behave. *...a man of high principles... Our party remains a party of principle.* **2** COUNT N WITH SUPP A **principle** is also a general rule or scientific law about how something happens or works. *...the principles of formal logic... ...the principle of acceleration.*

PHRASES ● If you do something **on principle,** you do it because of your beliefs. *I had to vote for him, of course, on principle.* ● If you agree with something **in principle,** you agree with the idea but may be unable or unwilling to support it in practice. *We are willing, in principle, to look afresh at the 1921 constitution.*

principled /prɪnsɪpəᵒld/. ADJ **Principled** behaviour is based on moral principles. *...the principled stand we have taken on matters of contemporary concern.*

print /prɪnt/, **prints, printing, printed. 1** VB WITH OBJ If someone **prints** a book, newspaper, or leaflet, they produce it in large quantities by a mechanical process. *I asked him for an estimate to print a weekly paper for me.* ♦ **printing** UNCOUNT N *...the invention of printing.* **2** VB WITH OBJ If someone **prints** a speech or a piece of writing, they include it in a newspaper or magazine. *The paper printed a story about Margaret Thatcher.* **3** UNCOUNT N The letters and numbers on a page of a book or newspaper are the **print.** *The print is rather poor.* **4** COUNT N A **print** is a photograph or a photographed copy of a painting. *...simple black and white prints.* **5** VB WITH OBJ If you **print** a pattern on cloth, you reproduce it on the cloth using dye and special equipment. *...a pattern which is printed onto the fabric by hand.* **6** COUNT N **Prints** are footprints or fingerprints. *His feet left prints in the soft soil.* **7** VB WITH OR WITHOUT OBJ If you **print,** you write in letters that are not joined together. *As long as you print clearly, you don't have to type... There was an envelope on her desk with her name printed on it.*

PHRASES ● If something appears **in print,** it appears in a book or newspaper. *He admitted it in print.* ● If a book is **out of print,** it is no longer available.

print out. PHR VB When information from a computer **is printed out,** it is reproduced on paper.

printer /prɪntə/, **printers. 1** COUNT N A **printer** is a person or firm that prints books, newspapers, or leaflets. **2** COUNT N A **printer** is also a machine used for printing information from a computer.

printout /prɪntaʊt/, **printouts.** COUNT N OR UNCOUNT N A **printout** is a piece of paper on which information from a computer has been printed.

prior /praɪə/; a formal word. **1** PREP If something happens **prior to** a particular time or event, it happens before it. *It occurred in Dallas, just prior to President Kennedy's assassination.* **2** ATTRIB ADJ You use **prior** to describe something that has happened or been planned earlier. *No prior knowledge should be required... I have a prior engagement.* **3** ATTRIB ADJ A **prior** claim or duty is more important than other claims or duties. *He feels a prior obligation to his job as a journalist.*

priority /praɪɒri¹ti¹/, **priorities. 1** COUNT N WITH SUPP Something that is a **priority** must be done or dealt with as soon as possible. *Getting food was the main priority... Factories seemed to be China's highest priority.* Also ATTRIB ADJ *The waiting list contains a thousand priority cases.* **2** PLURAL N Someone's **priorities** are the tasks or things they consider to be the most important. *We must find out the priorities of the public... He had his priorities right.* **3** UNCOUNT N If someone or something has **priority** over other things, they are considered to be more important than other things and are therefore dealt with first. *These children are given priority when day nursery places are allocated.*

prise /praɪz/, **prises, prising, prised;** also spelled **prize.** VB WITH OBJ AND ADJUNCT If you **prise** one thing away from another, you use force to remove it from the other thing. *He prised the lid off a tin of paint.*

prism /prɪzəᵒm/, **prisms.** COUNT N A **prism** is an object made of clear glass with straight sides. When light passes through it, the light waves separate and form a rainbow.

prison /prɪzəᵒn/, **prisons.** COUNT N OR UNCOUNT N A **prison** is a building where criminals are kept. *I had never before been inside a prison... He was sent to prison for two years.*

prisoner /prɪzəᵒnə/, **prisoners.** COUNT N A **prisoner** is a person who is kept in a prison as a punishment or because they have been captured by an enemy.

privacy /praɪvəsi¹, prɪvəsi¹/. UNCOUNT N **Privacy** is the fact of being alone so that you can do things without being seen or disturbed. *...the privacy of your own home... Take it home and read it in privacy.*

private /praɪvə¹t/, **privates. 1** ADJ If something is **private,** it is for the use of one person or group only, rather than for the general public. *All rooms have got private bath and WC... ...private property.* **2** ATTRIB ADJ **Private** discussions take place between a small group of people and are kept secret from others. *...a private interview.* ♦ **privately** ADV *The notion was discussed privately between the two men at lunch.* **3** ATTRIB ADJ **Private** activities and belongings are connected with your personal life rather than with your work or business. *She never spoke about her private life.* **4** ATTRIB ADJ Your **private** thoughts are personal and you do not discuss them with other people. *He was* *engaged in a private quest of his own.* ♦ **privately** ADV *Privately Ben felt close to despair.* **5** ADJ A **private** place is quiet and secluded. *...a private place of meditation.* **6** ADJ A **private** person is very quiet and does not share their thoughts and feelings with other people. *Away from the glare of publicity he becomes an intensely private man.* **7** ATTRIB ADJ **Private** is used to describe services or industries that are owned by an individual person or group, rather than being controlled by the state. *...private education... ...private health insurance.* ♦ **privately** ADV *...privately owned firms.* **8** COUNT N OR TITLE A **private** is a soldier of the lowest rank.

privation /praɪveɪʃə^{0}n/, **privations.** UNCOUNT N OR COUNT N If you suffer **privation** you are deprived of things that you need; a formal use. *Life was riddled with privation... ...the privations of frontier life.*

privatize /praɪvətaɪz/, **privatizes, privatizing, privatized;** also spelled **privatise.** VB WITH OBJ If an organization that is owned by the state **is privatized,** the government sells it to a private individual or group. *The nuclear industry was to be privatized.* ♦ **privatization** /praɪvətaɪzeɪʃə^{0}n/ UNCOUNT N *...the privatisation of the telephone service.*

privilege /prɪvɪ^{0}lɪdʒ/, **privileges.** COUNT N OR UNCOUNT N A **privilege** is a special right or advantage that puts one person or group in a better position than other people. *The children would resent any special privileges given to the staff... ...the power and privilege which they had once enjoyed.* ♦ **privileged** ADJ *It was expensive and available only to the privileged few.*

privy /prɪvi^1/. PRED ADJ WITH PREP 'to' If you are **privy** to something secret, you know about it; a formal use. *Very few of them were privy to the details of the conspiracy.*

prize /praɪz/, **prizes, prizing, prized. 1** COUNT N A **prize** is something of value, such as money or a trophy, that is given to the winner of a game, competition, or contest. *I entered two competitions and won prizes... ...Nobel Prize winners.* **2** ATTRIB ADJ You use **prize** to describe things that are of a very high quality. *...prize carnations.* **3** VB WITH OBJ Something that **is prized** is wanted and admired because it is of good quality. *These fish are highly prized for their excellent flavour.* **4** See also **prise.**

pro /prəʊ/, **pros. 1** COUNT N A **pro** is the same as a professional; an informal use. *He's a pro and I'm only an amateur.* **2** PHRASE **The pros and cons** of something are its advantages and disadvantages.

pro-. PREFIX **Pro-** is used to form adjectives that describe people as supporting something such as a group of people or a practice. *...the pro-nuclear lobby.*

probability /prɒbəbɪlɪ^{1}ti^1/, **probabilities. 1** COUNT N OR UNCOUNT N The **probability** of something happening is how likely it is to happen, sometimes expressed as a fraction or a percentage. *Many people prefer mathematical probabilities to inspired guesses... ...a triumph of determination against all probability.* **2** COUNT N OR UNCOUNT N The **probability** that something will happen is the fact that it is very likely to happen. *The real source of his gloom was the probability that Kathy would not come... The probability is that they will find themselves in debt.*

probable /prɒbəbə^{0}l/. ADJ Something that is **probable** is very likely to be true or likely to happen. *It seems very probable that they are descended from a single ancestor... The Belgians face a probable general election this autumn.*

probably /prɒbəbli^1/. SENTENCE ADV If something is **probably** the case, it is very likely to be the case. *He probably kept your examination papers... The owner is probably a salesman.*

probation /prə^{6}beɪʃə^{0}n/. **1** UNCOUNT N If a criminal is on **probation,** they are not sent to prison but instead have to report regularly to the official in charge of their case. *I wondered whether Daniel would be let off on probation.* **2** UNCOUNT N **Probation** is a period of time during which someone's work is assessed before they are given a permanent job. *Probation is more or less a formality.*

probation officer, probation officers. COUNT N A **probation officer** is a person whose job is to supervise and help people who have committed crimes but who are not serving a prison sentence for them.

probe /prəʊb/, **probes, probing, probed.** VB WITH OR WITHOUT OBJ If you **probe,** you try to find out about something by asking questions. *She had learnt not to probe too far... ...to probe the mysteries of the universe.* Also COUNT N *...a probe into suspected drug dealing in Florida.*

problem /prɒbləm/, **problems. 1** COUNT N A **problem** is an unsatisfactory situation that causes difficulties for people. *They have financial problems... ...to help solve the problem of racism.* **2** COUNT N A **problem** is also a puzzle that requires logical thought or mathematics to solve it. *...the development of problem-solving programs.*

problematic /prɒbləmætɪk/. ADJ Something that is **problematic** involves problems and difficulties; a formal use. *...the problematic nature of the relationship.*

problematical /prɒbləmætɪkə^{0}l/. ADJ **Problematical** means the same as problematic; a formal use.

procedure /prə^{6}siːdʒə/, **procedures.** COUNT N OR UNCOUNT N A **procedure** is a way of doing something, especially the usual or correct way. *...the proper procedure to be followed in decision-making... This was not standard procedure.*

proceed, proceeds, proceeding, proceeded; pronounced /prə^{6}siːd/ when it is a verb and /prəʊsiːdz/ when it is a noun. **1** VB WITH TO-INF If you **proceed** to do something, you do it after doing something else. *He proceeded to explain.* **2** VB If you **proceed** with a course of action, you continue with it; a formal use. *It is necessary to examine this claim before we proceed any further.* **3** VB If an activity, process, or event **proceeds,** it continues as planned; a formal use. *Preparations were proceeding on schedule.* **4** VB If you **proceed** in a particular direction, you go in that direction; a formal use. *...as we were proceeding along Chiswick High Street.* **5** PLURAL N The **proceeds** of an event or activity are the money that has been obtained from it. *The proceeds will be given away to a deserving charity.*

proceedings /prə^{6}siːdɪŋz/; a formal word. **1** PLURAL N You can refer to an organized series of events that happen in a place as the **proceedings.** *Millions of people watched the proceedings on television.* **2** PLURAL N Legal **proceedings** are legal action taken against someone. *I shall institute proceedings against you for unfair dismissal.*

process /prəʊsɛs/, **processes, processing, processed. 1** COUNT N A **process** is a series of actions or events which have a particular result. *It has been a long process getting this information... ...industrial processes.* **2** VB WITH OBJ When raw materials or foods **are processed,** they are treated in a chemical or industrial process. *...chemically processed food.* **3** VB WITH OBJ To **process** information means to deal with it. *Ten computers are processing the data... Your application will take a few weeks to process.* • See also **word processing.**

PHRASES • If you **are in the process of** doing something, you are doing it. *She is still in the painful process of growing up.* • If you are doing something and you do something else **in the process,** you do the second thing as a result of doing the first thing. *I got him out, but overbalanced in the process and fell.*

procession /prə^{6}sɛʃə^{0}n/, **processions.** COUNT N A **procession** is a group of people who are walking, riding, or driving in a line as part of a public event. *Lady Branwell led the procession through the village.*

proclaim /prə^{6}kleɪm/, **proclaims, proclaiming, proclaimed.** REPORT VB To **proclaim** something means to announce it; a formal use. *The Government proclaimed a state of emergency... ...a signpost that proclaimed that it was only 108 miles to Rock Springs.*

proclamation /prɒkləmeɪʃə^{0}n/, **proclamations.** COUNT N A **proclamation** is a public announcement about something important. *The king issued a proclamation outlawing the rebels.*

procreation /prəʊkrieɪʃə^{0}n/. UNCOUNT N **Procreation** is the producing of babies or young; a formal use. *...the natural process of procreation.*

procure /prəkjʊə/, **procures, procuring, procured.** VB WITH OBJ If you **procure** something, you obtain it; a formal use. *It would be necessary to procure more grain.*

prod /prɒd/, **prods, prodding, prodded. 1** VB WITH OBJ If you **prod** someone or something, you give them a quick push with your finger or with a pointed object. *She prodded a bean with her fork.* Also COUNT N *Mrs Travers gave her a prod.* **2** VB WITH OBJ AND ADJUNCT If you **prod** someone into doing something, you remind them or urge them to do it. *...companies who prod the ministry into action every now and again.*

prodigal /prɒdɪgə^{0}l/. ADJ If you describe someone as a **prodigal** son or daughter, you mean that they left their family but have now returned; a literary use.

prodigious /prədɪdʒəs/. ADJ Something that is **prodigious** is amazingly great; a formal use. *...prodigious amounts of food.*

produce, produces, producing, produced; pronounced /prədjuːs/ when it is a verb, and /prɒdjuːs/ when it is a noun. **1** VB WITH OBJ To **produce** something means to make it, create it, or cause it. *This drug has produced terrible effects on children... ...factories producing electrical goods... Parents are responsible for the offspring they produce.* **2** VB WITH OBJ If you **produce** evidence or an argument, you show it or explain it to people. *He produces no evidence for his belief.* **3** VB WITH OBJ If you **produce** an object from somewhere, you bring it out so that it can be seen. *Poirot produced the letter from his pocket.* **4** VB WITH OBJ If someone **produces** a play, film, programme, or record, they organize it and decide how it should be done. *The film was directed, written and produced by Mel Brooks.* **5** UNCOUNT N **Produce** is food or other things grown in large quantities to be sold. *They go to market to buy supplies and sell their produce.*

producer /prədjuːsə/, **producers. 1** COUNT N A **producer** is a person whose job is organizing plays, films, programmes, or records. *...a TV producer.* **2** COUNT N WITH SUPP A **producer** of a food or material is a company or country that grows or provides a large amount of it. *The Soviet Union is the world's leading crude oil producer... ...producers of consumer goods.*

product /prɒdʌkt/, **products. 1** COUNT N A **product** is something that a company makes. *...car-cleaning products.* **2** COUNT N WITH SUPP Something or someone that is a **product** of a particular situation or process has resulted from that situation or process. *The uniformity of the dancers was the product of hours of training... She is a product of the 1970s.*

production /prədʌkʃə^{0}n/, **productions. 1** UNCOUNT N **Production** is the process of manufacturing or growing something in large quantities, or the amount of goods manufactured or grown. *...more efficient methods of production... Industrial production has fallen by 20% over two years.* **2** UNCOUNT N WITH SUPP The **production** of something is its creation. *...the production of electricity.* **3** COUNT N A **production** is a particular performed version of a play, opera, or other show. *...Peter Hall's production of The Tempest.*

production line, production lines. COUNT N A **production line** is a system in a factory whereby the products pass from one section to another until they are finished. *...cars coming off the production line.*

productive /prədʌktɪv/. **1** ADJ Something or someone that is **productive** produces a lot of goods or does a lot of work. *Agriculture and industry both grew more productive.* **2** ADJ If a meeting or a relationship is **productive,** good or useful things happen as a result of it. *...a productive friendship.*

productivity /prɒdə^{6}ktɪvɪ^{1}ti^1/. UNCOUNT N **Productivity** is the rate at which goods are produced, or the amount of goods produced by each worker. *...increases in agricultural productivity.*

Prof. /prɒf/. **Prof.** is a written or informal abbreviation for 'professor'. *...Prof. Brewer.*

profane /prəfeɪn/. ADJ **Profane** means showing disrespect for religion or religious things. *...profane acts.*

profess /prə^{6}fɛs/, **professes, professing, professed.** VB WITH TO-INF OR OBJ If you **profess** to do or have something, you claim that you do it or have it; a formal use. *Nell didn't like her, or professed not to... Many have professed disgust at the use of such weapons.*

profession /prə^{6}fɛʃə^{0}n/, **professions. 1** COUNT N A **profession** is a type of job that requires advanced education or training. *She decided on law or journalism as her profession.* **2** COLL N You use **profession** to refer to all the people who have the same profession. *The medical profession are doing a difficult job.*

professional /prə^{6}fɛʃə^{0}nəl, -ʃənə^{0}l/, **professionals. 1** ATTRIB ADJ **Professional** means relating to the work of someone qualified for a particular job. *I sought professional advice.* ♦ **professionally** ADV *They are professionally qualified.* **2** ATTRIB ADJ You use **professional** to describe people who do a particular thing to earn money rather than as a hobby. *...a professional athlete.* ♦ **professionally** ADV *...someone who's never acted professionally.* **3** ATTRIB ADJ **Professional** people have jobs that require advanced education or training. *The flat is ideal for the professional single person.* **4** ADJ A **professional** piece of work is of a high standard. *He had typed the whole scheme out in a very professional manner.* **5** COUNT N A **professional** is someone who does something to earn money rather than as a hobby. *He has 17 championship victories as a professional plus two amateur titles.* **6** COUNT N A **professional** is also someone who has a job that requires special training and has a fairly high status. *...nurses, doctors, social workers, and other professionals.*

professionalism /prə^{6}fɛʃə^{0}nəlɪzə^{0}m/. UNCOUNT N **Professionalism** is skill at doing a job. *The paper was produced with incredible professionalism.*

professor /prəfɛsə/, **professors. 1** COUNT N OR TITLE A **professor** in a British university is the most senior teacher in a department. *...the Professor of English at Strathclyde University... ...Professor Cole.* **2** COUNT N A **professor** in an American or Canadian university or college is a teacher there.

proffer /prɒfə/, **proffers, proffering, proffered.** VB WITH OBJ If you **proffer** something to someone, you offer it to them; a formal use. *He put down his luggage* *and proffered his passport... She had already proffered her resignation.*

proficient /prəfɪʃənt/. ADJ If you are **proficient** in something, you can do it well. *They were all proficient in needlework... ...a proficient swimmer.* ♦ **proficiency** /prəfɪʃənsi^1/ UNCOUNT N *...your proficiency in English.*

profile /prəufaɪl/, **profiles.** 1 COUNT N Your **profile** is the outline of your face seen from the side. *She glanced at his haughty profile.* 2 COUNT N A **profile** of someone is a short article or programme describing their life and character. *She wanted to write profiles of the founders of the Party.* 3 PHRASE If you **keep a low profile,** you avoid doing things that will make people notice you. *Keep a low profile until you have had time to settle in.*

profit /prɒfɪt/, **profits, profiting, profited.** 1 COUNT N OR UNCOUNT N A **profit** is an amount of money that you gain when you are paid more for something than it cost you. *The company made a profit of 113 per cent... The profits are used to buy more equipment... He wants to make as much profit as he can.* 2 VB WITH 'from' OR 'by' If you **profit** from something, you benefit or gain from it; a formal use. *I profited from his advice... They had profited by their experience.*

profitable /prɒfɪtəbə^{0}l/. 1 ADJ A **profitable** organization or practice makes a profit. *The farm is a highly profitable business... It was more profitable to export the crops.* ♦ **profitably** ADV *Can the motor vehicle industry operate profitably?* ♦ **profitability** UNCOUNT N *...a decline in the profitability of public transport.* 2 ADJ Something that is **profitable** results in some benefit for you. *He certainly made profitable use of the lessons he had learnt.* ♦ **profitably** ADV *There was little I could profitably do sitting at my desk.*

profound /prə^{6}faund/. 1 ADJ You use **profound** to emphasize the great degree or intensity of something. *The war was to have a profound effect on all our lives.* ♦ **profoundly** ADV *I found the film profoundly moving.* 2 ADJ A **profound** idea or work shows great intellectual understanding. *...a very profound question.*

profuse /prə^{6}fjuːs/. ADJ **Profuse** is used to indicate that a quantity of something is very large; a formal use. *There were profuse apologies for its absence.* ♦ **profusely** ADV *He was bleeding profusely.*

profusion /prə^{6}fjuːʒə^{0}n/. SING N OR UNCOUNT N If there is a **profusion** of something or if it occurs in **profusion,** there is a very large quantity of it; a formal use. *...a garden filled with a profusion of flowering shrubs... Daffodils grow in enormous profusion under the trees.*

prognosis /prɒgnəusɪs/, **prognoses** /prɒgnəusiːz/. COUNT N A **prognosis** is a prediction about the future of someone or something, especially a patient; a formal use. *It was a serious heart defect; the prognosis was poor, even with treatment.*

program /prəugræm/, **programs, programming, programmed.** 1 COUNT N A **program** is a set of instructions that a computer follows. 2 VB WITH OBJ When you **program** a computer, you give it a set of instructions to make it able to perform a particular task. *Can computers be programmed to hold intelligent conversations?* ♦ **programming** UNCOUNT N *...computer programming.* 3 **Program** is also the American spelling for **programme.**

programme /prəugræm/, **programmes, programming, programmed;** spelled **program** in American English. 1 COUNT N A **programme** is a series of actions or events that are planned to be done. *...a programme of modernization... They have embarked on an ambitious energy programme.* 2 COUNT N A television or radio **programme** is something that is broadcast on television or radio. *...the last programme in our series on education... ...gardening programmes.* 3 COUNT N A theatre or concert **programme** is a booklet giving information about the play or concert you are attending. 4 VB WITH OBJ When you **programme** a machine or system, you set its controls so that it will work in a particular way. *The radiators are programmed to come on at six every morning.*

programmer /prəugræmə/, **programmers.** COUNT N A computer **programmer** is a person whose job involves writing programs for computers.

progress, progresses, progressing, progressed; pronounced /prəugrɛs/ when it is a noun, and /prə^{6}grɛs/ when it is a verb. 1 UNCOUNT N **Progress** is the process of gradually improving or getting nearer to achieving or completing something. *She is making good progress with her German... ...technological progress.* 2 SING N The **progress** of an activity is the way in which it develops. *He followed the progress of hostilities with impatience.* 3 PHRASE If something is **in progress,** it is happening. *The battle was still in progress.* 4 VB To **progress** means to improve or to become more advanced or higher in rank. *You're not progressing quickly enough... Technology did not progress any further for centuries.* 5 VB To **progress** also means to continue. *My impressions changed as the trip progressed.* 6 VB WITH PREP 'to' If you **progress** to something new, better, or more advanced, you start doing it or having it. *From there we progressed to a discussion on politics.*

progression /prə^{6}grɛʃə^{0}n/, **progressions.** COUNT N WITH SUPP A **progression** is a gradual development from one state to another; a formal use. *The progression from one extreme to the other is gradual.*

progressive /prə^{6}grɛsɪv/. 1 ADJ Someone who is **progressive** has modern ideas. *Some young parents are eager to be progressive.* 2 ADJ A **progressive** change happens gradually. *...the progressive industrialization of our society.* ♦ **progressively** ADV *It became progressively easier to see.*

prohibit /prə^{6}hɪbɪt/, **prohibits, prohibiting, prohibited.** VB WITH OBJ If someone **prohibits** something, they forbid it or make it illegal. *She believes that nuclear weapons should be totally prohibited... The country has a law prohibiting employees from striking.* ♦ **prohibition** UNCOUNT N OR COUNT N *...the prohibition of strikes... ...a prohibition on nuclear weapons.*

prohibitive /prə^{6}hɪbɪtɪv/. ADJ If the cost of something is **prohibitive,** it is so high that you cannot afford it. *...the prohibitive price of domestic labour.*

project, projects, projecting, projected; pronounced /prɒdʒɛkt/ when it is a noun, and /prə^{6}dʒɛkt/ when it is a verb. 1 COUNT N A **project** is a large-scale attempt to do something. *...the cancellation of the Blue Streak Missile project.* 2 COUNT N A **project** is also a detailed study of a subject by a pupil or student. 3 VB WITH OBJ If something **is projected,** it is planned or expected. *There were demonstrations against the projected visit... The population of Calcutta is projected to rise to seventy million people.* 4 VB WITH OBJ If you **project** a film or picture onto a screen or wall, you make it appear there. *The images were projected on a screen.* 5 VB WITH OBJ The way that someone or something **is projected** is the way that they are made to seem. *He had projected himself as a reformer.* 6 VB If something **projects,** it sticks out beyond a surface or edge; a formal use. *He could see the end of a spear projecting over the rock.*

projection /prədʒɛkʃə^{0}n/, **projections.** 1 COUNT N A **projection** is an estimate of a future amount. *The company made projections of sales of 3000 aircraft.* 2 COUNT N A **projection** is also a part of something that sticks out; a formal use. *...the projection on the mantelpiece.*

projector /prədʒɛktə/, **projectors.** COUNT N A **projector** is a machine that projects films or slides onto a screen or wall.

proletarian /prəulɪtɛərɪən/. ATTRIB ADJ **Proletarian** means relating to the proletariat; a technical use. *...the proletarian masses.*

proletariat /prəulɪtɛərɪət/. COLL N You can refer to working-class people, especially industrial workers, as the **proletariat;** a technical use.

proliferate /prə^{6}lɪfəreɪt/, **proliferates, proliferating, proliferated.** VB If things **proliferate,** they quickly increase in number; a formal use. *Polytechnics proliferated all over the country.* ♦ **proliferation** /prə^{6}lɪfəreɪʃə^{0}n/ UNCOUNT N *We can prevent the proliferation of nuclear weaponry.*

prolific /prə^{6}lɪfɪk/. ADJ A **prolific** writer, artist, or composer produces a large number of works.

prolong /prə^{6}lɒŋ/, **prolongs, prolonging, prolonged.** VB WITH OBJ To **prolong** something means to make it last longer. *All the time people are seeking to prolong life.*

prolonged /prə^{6}lɒŋd/. ADJ A **prolonged** event or situation continues for a long time. *...a prolonged period of uncertainty.*

promenade /prɒmənɑːd/, **promenades.** COUNT N At a seaside town, the **promenade** is a road or path next to the sea.

prominent /prɒmɪnənt/. 1 ADJ Someone who is **prominent** is important. *...US Senators and other prominent American personalities.* ♦ **prominence** /prɒmɪnəns/ UNCOUNT N *Alan Travers had risen to prominence in his wife's organisation.* 2 ADJ Something that is **prominent** is very noticeable. *There were two prominent landmarks.* ♦ **prominently** ADV *...a large photograph prominently displayed in her front room.*

promiscuous /prəmɪskjuəs/. ADJ Someone who is **promiscuous** has sex with many different people; used showing disapproval. *...when young people engage in promiscuous behaviour.* ♦ **promiscuity** /prɒmɪskjuː^{1}ɪti^1/ UNCOUNT N *...sexual promiscuity.*

promise /prɒmɪs/, **promises, promising, promised.** 1 REPORT VB WITH OBJ, REPORT VB, OR VB WITH TO-INF If you **promise** that you will do something, you say that you will definitely do it. *Promise me you'll go... 'I won't fail you,' he promised... I promised to take the children to the fair.* 2 VB WITH OBJ AND OBJ If you **promise** someone something, you tell them that you will definitely give it to them or make sure that they have it. *I promised him a canary for his birthday.* 3 COUNT N A **promise** is a statement which you make to someone in which you say that you will definitely do something or give them something. *They tried to break the promises made in negotiations... They fulfilled their promise to revive trade.* 4 VB WITH TO-INF If a situation or event **promises** to have a particular quality, it shows signs that it will have that quality. *The debate promises to be lively.* 5 UNCOUNT N If someone or something shows **promise,** they seem likely to be very good or successful. *She showed considerable promise as a tennis player.*

promising /prɒmɪsɪŋ/. ADJ Someone or something that is **promising** seems likely to be very good or successful. *...a most promising new actress... The menu looked promising.*

promote /prəməut/, **promotes, promoting, promoted.** 1 VB WITH OBJ If people **promote** something, they try to make it happen, increase, or become more popular. *The government could do more to promote economic growth... The new town was vigorously promoted as an ideal place to settle.* ♦ **promotion** UNCOUNT N *There are government controls on the promotion of cigarettes.* 2 VB WITH OBJ If someone **is promoted,** they are given a more important job. *He had recently been promoted to captain.* ♦ **promotion** UNCOUNT N *What are your chances of promotion?*

promoter /prəməutə/, **promoters.** 1 COUNT N A **promoter** is a person who helps organize and finance a public event. *...concert promoters.* 2 COUNT N The **promoter** of something tries to make it become popular. *She was a tireless promoter of new causes.*

prompt /prɒmp^{0}t/, **prompts, prompting, prompted.** 1 VB WITH OBJ If something **prompts** someone to do something, it makes them decide to do it. *The Times article prompted him to call a meeting... My choice was prompted by a number of considerations.* 2 VB WITH OR WITHOUT OBJ If you **prompt** someone when they stop speaking, you encourage or help them to continue. *'Yes?' Morris prompted, after a pause.* 3 ADJ A **prompt** action is done without any delay. *...a prompt reply... She requires prompt medical attention.*

prompting /prɒmp^{0}tɪŋ/, **promptings.** UNCOUNT N OR COUNT N **Prompting** is reminding or urging. *She did it without any prompting... ...Mummy's constant promptings to be 'a nice, clever, boy like your brother'.*

promptly /prɒmp^{0}tli^1/. 1 ADV If you do something **promptly,** you do it immediately. *He slapped her and she promptly burst into tears.* 2 ADV **Promptly** also means at exactly the time that has been arranged. *I arrived at the gates promptly at six o'clock.*

prone /prəun/. 1 PRED ADJ If you are **prone** to something, you have a tendency to be affected by it or to do it. *He was prone to indigestion... They were prone to argue.* 2 ADJ If you are lying **prone,** you are lying flat, facing downwards; a formal use.

prong /prɒŋ/, **prongs.** COUNT N The **prongs** of a fork are the long, thin pointed parts.

pronoun /prəunaun/, **pronouns.** COUNT N In grammar, a **pronoun** is a word which is used instead of a noun group to refer to someone or something. 'He', 'she', 'them', and 'something' are pronouns.

pronounce /prənauns/, **pronounces, pronouncing, pronounced.** 1 VB WITH OBJ To **pronounce** a word means to say it. *I can't pronounce his name... ...the town of Ixtlan, pronounced East-lon.* 2 VB WITH OBJ AND COMPLEMENT If you **pronounce** something to be true, you formally state that it is true; a formal use. *The victim was pronounced dead on arrival at the hospital.* 3 REPORT VB If someone **pronounces** a verdict or opinion on something, they formally give their verdict or opinion; a formal use. *'Are the people ready to pronounce their verdict?'—'Guilty.'... 'Not bad,' he pronounced.*

pronounced /prənaunst/. ADJ Something that is **pronounced** is very noticeable. *He spoke with a pronounced English accent.*

pronouncement /prənaunsmə^{1}nt/, **pronouncements.** COUNT N A **pronouncement** is a formal or official statement. *...official pronouncements made by politicians.*

pronunciation /prənʌnsieɪʃə^{0}n/, **pronunciations.** UNCOUNT N OR COUNT N The **pronunciation** of a word or language is the way in which it is pronounced. *...the recommended American pronunciation... He tried to correct Francois's pronunciation.*

proof /pruːf/, **proofs.** UNCOUNT N OR COUNT N **Proof** is a fact or a piece of evidence which shows that something is true or exists. *Do you have any proof of that allegation?... He hadn't any proof that Davis had not died.*

-proof. SUFFIX **-proof** is added to nouns to form adjectives which indicate that something cannot be damaged by a particular thing or person. *This build-*

ing's supposed to be earthquake-proof... Can these containers be made vandal-proof?

prop /prɒp/, **props, propping, propped. 1** VB WITH OBJ AND ADJUNCT If you **prop** an object on something, you place it so that it is supported by that thing. *She propped her chin on her hand... His gun lay propped against the wall.* **2** COUNT N A **prop** is a stick or other object used to support something. *We need a clothes prop for the washing line.* **3** COUNT N The **props** in a play or film are the objects and furniture used in it. *The sets, props, and costumes were all ready.*

prop up. PHR VB **1** To **prop** something **up** means to support it in an upright or raised position. *His feet were propped up on the coffee table... ...timbers used to prop a building up during alterations.* **2** If one organization or group **props up** another, it helps the other one to survive. *The Government does not intend to prop up declining industries.*

propaganda /prɒpəgændə/. UNCOUNT N **Propaganda** is information, often inaccurate information, which an organization publishes or broadcasts in order to influence people. *...a campaign of anti-British propaganda.*

propagandist /prɒpəgændɪst/, **propagandists.** COUNT N A **propagandist** is a person who tries to persuade people to support a particular idea or group; often used showing disapproval.

propagate /prɒpəgeɪt/, **propagates, propagating, propagated. 1** VB WITH OBJ If people **propagate** an idea or some information, they spread it; a formal use. *The group is doing what it can to propagate the rumour.* **2** VB WITH OBJ If you **propagate** plants, you grow more of them from the original ones; a technical use.

propel /prə^{6}pel/, **propels, propelling, propelled.** VB WITH OBJ To **propel** something means to cause it to move along. *The bullet is propelled out of the chamber.*

propeller /prə^{6}pelə/, **propellers.** COUNT N A **propeller** on a boat or aircraft is a device with blades which is turned by the engine, causing the boat or aircraft to move.

propensity /prəpensɪ^{1}ti^1/, **propensities.** COUNT N WITH SUPP If you have a **propensity** to behave in a particular way, you have a natural tendency to do this; a formal use. *There was no evidence of any propensity to act violently towards others... ...the patient's propensity for socially dangerous behaviour.*

proper /prɒpə/. **1** ATTRIB ADJ You use **proper** to describe things that you consider to be real and satisfactory. *He's never had a proper job... Lack of proper funding is making our job more difficult.* **2** ATTRIB ADJ The **proper** thing is the one that is correct or most suitable. *Everything was in its proper place... What's the proper word for those things?* **3** ADJ AFTER N You can add **proper** after a word that refers to a place to emphasize that you are referring to the main or central part of the place. *By the time I got to the village proper everyone was out to meet me.*

properly /prɒpəli^1/. ADV If something is done **properly**, it is done correctly and satisfactorily. *We must see that the children are properly fed... The reviewers aren't doing their job properly.*

proper noun, proper nouns. COUNT N In grammar, a **proper noun** is a noun which refers to a particular person, place, or institution. Proper nouns begin with a capital letter.

property /prɒpəti^1/, **properties. 1** UNCOUNT N Someone's **property** is all the things that belong to them, or something that belongs to them. *Their job is to protect private property.* **2** COUNT N A **property** is a building and the land belonging to it; a formal use. *He arranged to rent the property.* **3** COUNT N The **properties** of a substance or object are the ways in which it behaves in particular conditions.

prophecy /prɒfɪsi^1/, **prophecies.** COUNT N OR UNCOUNT N A **prophecy** is a statement in which someone says what they believe will happen. *The prophecy was fulfilled... ...a plausible bit of prophecy.*

prophesy /prɒfɪsaɪ/, **prophesies, prophesying, prophesied.** REPORT VB If you **prophesy** something, you say that you believe it will happen. *He prophesied a violent uprising... He has prophesied that the State will be destroyed.*

prophet /prɒfɪt/, **prophets.** COUNT N A **prophet** is a person believed to be chosen by God to say the things that God wants to tell people.

prophetic /prə^{6}fetɪk/. ADJ If something was **prophetic,** it described or suggested something that did happen later. *...more than fifty years after she wrote those prophetic words.*

proponent /prə^{6}pəʊnənt/, **proponents.** COUNT N A **proponent** of a particular idea or course of action actively supports it; a formal use. *...the proponents of conservation.*

proportion /prəpɔːʃə^{0}n/, **proportions. 1** COUNT N A **proportion** of an amount or group is a part of it. *Courts are now sending a smaller proportion of offenders to prison.* **2** COUNT N WITH SUPP The **proportion** of one part of a group is its size in relation to the whole group or to another part of it. *The proportion of workers to employers was large... Usually men outnumber women, but we have about equal proportions at Sussex.* **3** PLURAL N WITH SUPP You can refer to the size of something as its **proportions.** *...a gin and tonic of giant proportions.*

PHRASES ● If one thing is small or large **in proportion** to another thing, it is small or large when you compare it with the other thing. *Babies have big heads in proportion to their bodies.* ● If something is **out of all proportion** to something else, it is far greater or more serious than it should be. *Every small event was magnified out of all proportion to its importance.* ● If someone has a **sense of proportion,** they know what is really important and what is not.

proportional /prəpɔːʃə^{0}nəl, -ʃənə^{0}l/. ADJ If one amount is **proportional** to another, it always remains the same fraction of the other. *As a rule the suicide rates are proportional to the size of the city.*

proportionate /prəpɔːʃə^{0}nə^{1}t/. ADJ **Proportionate** means the same as proportional. *After a run, your recovery time is proportionate to your fitness.* ♦ **proportionately** ADV *Britain spent proportionately more on research than its competitors.*

proposal /prəpəʊzə^{0}l/, **proposals. 1** COUNT N A **proposal** is a suggestion or plan. *There is controversy about a proposal to build a new nuclear power station... ...proposals for cheaper flights to the United States.* **2** COUNT N A **proposal** is also a request that someone makes to another person to marry them. *...the second proposal of marriage which she received.*

propose /prəpəʊz/, **proposes, proposing, proposed. 1** REPORT VB If you **propose** a plan or idea, you suggest it. *He proposed a bargain... I proposed that the culprits should be fined.* ♦ **proposed** ATTRIB ADJ *...the proposed alliance.* **2** VB WITH TO-INF If you **propose** to do something, you intend to do it. *I do not propose to discuss this matter.* **3** VB WITH OBJ If someone **proposes** a motion in a debate, they introduce it and say why they agree with it. *Webb proposed the motion 'That this House has no confidence in the Government'.* **4** VB WITH OBJ If you **propose** a toast to someone or something, you ask people to drink a toast to them. **5** VB If you **propose** to someone, you ask them to marry you. *He had known her for two years before he proposed.*

proposition /prɒpəzɪʃə^{0}n/, **propositions. 1** COUNT N A **proposition** is a statement expressing a theory or opinion. *I had plenty of evidence to support the proposition that man was basically selfish.* **2** COUNT N A **proposition** is also an offer or suggestion. *He came to me one day with an extraordinary proposition.*

proprietary /prə^{6}praɪətə^{0}ri^1/. ATTRIB ADJ **Proprietary** substances are ones sold under a trade name; a formal use. *...a proprietary dry cleaner.*

proprietor /prə^{6}praɪətə/, **proprietors.** COUNT N The **proprietor** of a hotel, shop, or newspaper is the person who owns it.

propriety /prə^{6}praɪəti^1/. UNCOUNT N **Propriety** is the quality of being socially or morally acceptable; a formal use. *I doubt the propriety of receiving a lady this late at night.*

prosaic /prəʊzeɪɪk/. ADJ Something that is **prosaic** is dull and uninteresting. *...a prosaic existence.*

prose /prəʊz/. UNCOUNT N **Prose** is ordinary written language, in contrast to poetry.

prosecute /prɒsɪkjuːt/, **prosecutes, prosecuting, prosecuted.** VB WITH OR WITHOUT OBJ If someone **is prosecuted,** they are charged with a crime and put on trial. *He was prosecuted for drunken driving.*

prosecution /prɒsɪkjuːʃə^{0}n/, **prosecutions. 1** UNCOUNT N OR COUNT N **Prosecution** is the action of charging someone with a crime and putting them on trial. *He could face criminal prosecution... The Smiths brought a prosecution against the organizers.* **2** SING N The lawyers who try to prove that a person on trial is guilty are called the **prosecution.** *Today he will be questioned by the prosecution.*

prosecutor /prɒsɪkjuːtə/, **prosecutors.** COUNT N A **prosecutor** is a lawyer or official who brings charges against someone or tries to prove in a trial that they are guilty; an American use.

prospect, prospects, prospecting, prospected; pronounced /prɒspekt/ when it is a noun, and /prə^{7}spekt/ when it is a verb. **1** COUNT N OR UNCOUNT N A **prospect** is a possibility or a possible event. *She did not relish the prospect of climbing another flight of stairs... ...the prospects for peace... There was little prospect of significant military aid.* **2** PLURAL N Someone's **prospects** are their chances of being successful. *Success or failure here would be crucial to his future prospects.* **3** VB If people **prospect** for a substance such as oil or gold, they look for it in the ground or under the sea.

prospective /prə^{7}spektɪv/. ATTRIB ADJ You use **prospective** to describe a person who wants to be the thing mentioned. *...prospective students.*

prospectus /prə^{7}spektəs/, **prospectuses.** COUNT N A **prospectus** is a document produced by a college, school, or company which gives details about it.

prosper /prɒspə/, **prospers, prospering, prospered.** VB If people or businesses **prosper,** they are successful and do well financially.

prosperity /prɒsperɪ^{1}ti^1/. UNCOUNT N **Prosperity** is a condition in which a person or community is doing well financially. *...a period of wealth and prosperity.*

prosperous /prɒspə^{0}rəs/. ADJ Someone who is **prosperous** is wealthy and successful.

prostitute /prɒstɪtjuːt/, **prostitutes.** COUNT N A **prostitute** is a person, usually a woman, who has sex with men in exchange for money.

prostitution /prɒstɪtjuːʃə^{0}n/. UNCOUNT N **Prostitution** involves having sex in exchange for money.

prostrate, prostrates, prostrating, prostrated; pronounced /prɒstreɪt/ when it is a verb, and /prɒstreɪt/ when it is an adjective. **1** REFL VB If you **prostrate** yourself, you lie flat on the ground with your face downwards. *I wanted to throw my arms about him, prostrate myself before him.* **2** ADJ If you are **prostrate,** you are lying flat on the ground with your face downwards. *...the prostrate figure of Mr Green.*

protagonist /prə^{6}tægənɪst/, **protagonists;** a formal word. **1** COUNT N A **protagonist** of an idea or movement is a supporter of it. *She was a vehement protagonist of sexual equality.* **2** COUNT N A **protagonist** in a play or event is one of the main people in it.

protect /prə^{6}tekt/, **protects, protecting, protected.** VB WITH OBJ To **protect** someone or something means to prevent them from being harmed or damaged. *She had his umbrella to protect her from the rain... Babies are protected against diseases like measles by their mothers' milk.* ♦ **protector** /prə^{6}tektə/ COUNT N *...ecologists and protectors of wildlife.*

protection /prə^{6}tekʃə^{0}n/. UNCOUNT N If something gives **protection** against something unpleasant, it prevents people or things from being harmed or damaged by it. *The mud walls of these huts offer little protection against rats... We need protection from the sun's rays.*

protective /prə^{6}tektɪv/. **1** ATTRIB ADJ A **protective** object or action is intended to protect something or someone from harm. *...protective clothing and equipment.* **2** ADJ If someone is **protective** towards you, they show a strong desire to keep you safe. *She felt very protective towards her sister.*

protégé /prɒtɪʒeɪ/, **protégés;** also spelled **protégée** when referring to a woman. COUNT N WITH POSS Someone's **protégé** is a person that they help and guide over a period of time. *She was a painter and a protégée of Duncan Grant.*

protein /prəʊtiːn/, **proteins.** COUNT N OR UNCOUNT N **Protein** is a substance that is found, for example, in meat, eggs, and milk and that is needed for growth.

protest, protests, protesting, protested; pronounced /prətest/ when it is a verb, and /prəʊtest/ when it is a noun. **1** VB If you **protest** about something, you say or show publicly that you do not approve of it. *Labour MPs took to the streets to protest against government economic policy... ...a group protesting at official inaction.* ♦ **protester** /prətestə/ COUNT N *The protesters surrendered to the police after about an hour.* **2** REPORT VB If you **protest** that something is the case, you insist that it is the case, when other people think that it may not be. *They protested that they had never heard of him... 'You're wrong,' I protested... The mother protested her innocence.* **3** COUNT N OR UNCOUNT N A **protest** is the act of saying or showing publicly that you do not approve of something. *They joined in the protests against the government's proposals... There was a wave of student riots, in protest at university conditions.*

Protestant /prɒtɪ^{2}stənt/, **Protestants.** COUNT N A **Protestant** is a member of one of the Christian churches which separated from the Catholic church in the sixteenth century. *...bringing Catholics and Protestants together... ...Protestant clergymen.*

protestation /prɒtesteɪʃə^{0}n, prɒ/, **protestations.** COUNT N A **protestation** is a strong declaration; a formal use. *...his protestations of innocence.*

protocol /prəʊtəkɒl/. UNCOUNT N **Protocol** is a system of rules about the correct way to act in formal situations. *She was ignorant of protocol.*

proton /prəʊtɒn/, **protons.** COUNT N A **proton** is an atomic particle that has an electrical charge.

prototype /prəʊtə^{6}taɪp/, **prototypes.** COUNT N A **prototype** is the first model that is made of something new. *Funds for testing of the prototypes ran out.*

protracted /prə^{6}trækti^{2}d/. ADJ Something that is **protracted** lasts longer than usual. *...after a protracted lunch.*

protrude /prə^{6}tru:d/, **protrudes, protruding, protruded.** VB If something **protrudes** from somewhere, it sticks out; a formal use. *He tripped over a pair of boots protruding from under the table.*

proud /praʊd/, **prouder, proudest. 1** ADJ If you feel **proud,** you feel pleasure and satisfaction at something that you own, have done, or are connected with. *They seemed proud of what they had accomplished... It makes me proud to be an American.* ♦ **proudly** ADV *He was grinning proudly, delighted with his achievement.* **2** ADJ Someone who is **proud** has dignity and self-respect. *He was a poor but very proud old man.* **3** ADJ You also use **proud** to describe someone who feels that they are superior to other people. *She was too proud to apologize.*

prove /pru:v/, **proves, proving, proved, proven** /pru:və^{0}n/. The past participle can be **proved** or **proven. 1** REPORT VB OR VB WITH OBJ AND COMPLEMENT To **prove** that something is true means to show definitely that it is true. *He was able to prove that he was an American... He is going to have to prove his innocence... She has to be proved wrong.* ♦ **proven** ATTRIB ADJ *This man is a proven liar.* **2** VB WITH TO-INF OR COMPLEMENT If someone or something **proves** to have a particular quality, they are found to have that quality. *I proved to be hopeless as a teacher... This information has proved useful.*

proverb /prɒvɜ:b/, **proverbs.** COUNT N A **proverb** is a short sentence that people often quote, which gives advice or comments on life. *...the old Jewish proverb 'A man is not a man until he has a son.'*

proverbial /prəvɜ:biəl/. ATTRIB ADJ You use **proverbial** to emphasize that what you are saying is part of a proverb or well-known expression. *It is rather like looking for the needle in the proverbial haystack.*

provide /prəvaɪd/, **provides, providing, provided.** VB WITH OBJ If you **provide** something that someone needs or wants, you give it to them or make it available to them. *Most animals provide food for their young... The government cannot provide all young people with a job.*

provide for. PHR VB **1** If you **provide for** someone, you give them the things that they need. *Parents are expected to provide for their children.* **2** If you **provide for** a possible future event, you make arrangements to deal with it; a formal use. *Should the law provide for these cases?*

provided /prəvaɪdɪ^{2}d/. CONJ If something will happen **provided** or **providing** that something else happens, the first thing will happen only if the second thing also happens. *Children were permitted into the hall, provided they sat at the back... It would be pleasant living in Glasgow providing you were living in a nice flat.*

providence /prɒvɪdəns/. UNCOUNT N **Providence** is God, or a force which is believed to arrange the things that happen to us; a literary use. *The money lender proposed that they let providence decide the matter.*

providing /prəvaɪdɪŋ/. See **provided.**

province /prɒvɪns/, **provinces. 1** COUNT N A **province** is a large section of a country, with its own administration. *...rallies in Zimbabwe's five provinces.* **2** PLURAL N The **provinces** are the parts of a country outside the area of the capital. *...teenage life in the provinces.*

provincial /prəvɪnʃə^{0}l/. **1** ATTRIB ADJ **Provincial** means connected with the parts of a country outside the capital. *...provincial newspapers... ...provincial towns.* **2** ADJ Someone or something that is **provincial** is narrow-minded or unsophisticated.

provision /prəvɪʒə^{0}n/, **provisions. 1** UNCOUNT N The **provision** of something is the act of giving it or making it available. *...helping needy people by the provision of food, clothing, and shelter... ...the provision of credit.* **2** UNCOUNT N If you make **provision** for a future need, you make arrangements to ensure that it is dealt with. *She did not make any provision for her children.* **3** COUNT N A **provision** in an agreement or law is an arrangement included in it. *The Government had still to agree on the provisions of the Bill.* **4** PLURAL N **Provisions** are supplies of food. *We set out with enough provisions for the long trip.*

provisional /prəvɪʒə^{0}nəl, -ʒənə^{0}l/. ADJ Something that is **provisional** may be changed in the future. *...a provisional government... ...a provisional diagnosis of schizophrenia.*

proviso /prəvaɪzəʊ/, **provisos.** COUNT N A **proviso** is a condition in an agreement. *At last she consented, with the proviso that he should repay her as soon as he could.*

provocation /prɒvəkeɪʃə^{0}n/, **provocations.** UNCOUNT N OR COUNT N **Provocation** is a deliberate attempt to make someone react angrily. *They must not react to this provocation... She has a tantrum at the least provocation.*

provocative /prəvɒkətɪv/. **1** ADJ Something that is **provocative** is intended to make people react angrily. *He wrote a provocative article on 'Anti-racialism'.* **2** ADJ **Provocative** behaviour is intended to make someone feel sexual desire. *...a provocative dance.*

provoke /prəvəʊk/, **provokes, provoking, provoked. 1** VB WITH OBJ If you **provoke** someone, you deliberately annoy them and try to make them behave in an aggressive way. *Ray was trying to provoke them into fighting.* **2** VB WITH OBJ If something **provokes** a violent or unpleasant reaction, it causes it. *The petition provoked a storm of criticism.*

prowess /praʊɪ^{2}s/. UNCOUNT N Someone's **prowess** is their great ability at doing something; a formal use. *There are legends about his prowess as a jockey.*

prowl /praʊl/, **prowls, prowling, prowled.** VB WITH ADJUNCT OR OBJ When animals or people **prowl** around, they move around quietly, for example when they are hunting. *I found four foxes prowling round my flock one night... Gangs of youths prowl the streets.*

proximity /prɒksɪmɪ^{1}ti^{1}/. UNCOUNT N WITH SUPP **Proximity** is the fact of being near something or someone; a formal use. *...the town's proximity to the northern cape of Japan.*

proxy /prɒksi^{1}/. PHRASE If you do something **by proxy,** you arrange for someone else to do it for you. *...the urge to commit homicide by proxy.*

prude /pru:d/, **prudes.** COUNT N Someone who is a **prude** is easily shocked by things relating to nudity or sex; used showing disapproval.

prudent /pru:dənt/. ADJ Someone who is **prudent** is sensible and careful. *He now considered it prudent to carry a revolver.* ♦ **prudently** ADV *Fanny prudently resolved to keep silent.* ♦ **prudence** /pru:dəns/ UNCOUNT N *Her eagerness had overcome her prudence.*

prune /pru:n/, **prunes, pruning, pruned. 1** COUNT N A **prune** is a dried plum. **2** VB WITH OBJ When you **prune** a tree or bush, you cut off some of the branches. *He went to prune the roses.*

pry /praɪ/, **pries, prying, pried.** VB When someone **pries,** they try to find out about someone else's private affairs. *Don't go prying into my affairs or you'll get hurt.*

PS /pi: es/. You write **PS** to introduce a further message at the end of a letter after you have signed it. *With love from us both, Dad. PS Mum asks me to remind you to bring back her duvet.*

psalm /sɑ:m/, **psalms.** COUNT N The **Psalms** are the 150 songs, poems, and prayers which together form the Book of Psalms in the Bible.

pseudonym /sju:dənɪm/, **pseudonyms.** COUNT N A **pseudonym** is a name used by a writer instead of his or her real name. *Many journalists wrote under pseudonyms.*

psyche /saɪki^{1}/, **psyches.** COUNT N Your **psyche** is your mind and your deepest feelings and attitudes. *It is easy to understand how a person's psyche can be damaged by such experiences.*

psychiatric /saɪkiætrɪk/. ATTRIB ADJ **Psychiatric** means relating to psychiatry or involving mental illness. *...a psychiatric hospital... ...a mother with psychiatric problems.*

psychiatrist /saɪkaɪətrɪst/, **psychiatrists.** COUNT N A **psychiatrist** is a doctor who treats people suffering from mental illness.

psychiatry /saɪkaɪətri^{1}/. UNCOUNT N **Psychiatry** is the branch of medicine concerned with the treatment of mental illness.

psychic /saɪkɪk/. **1** ADJ Someone who is **psychic** has unusual mental powers, such as being able to read the minds of other people or to see into the future. **2** ADJ **Psychic** means relating to the mind rather than the body; a formal use. *Most of the psychic damage to a child is done in the first five years of its life.*

psychoanalysis /saɪkəʊənælɪsɪs/. UNCOUNT N **Psychoanalysis** is the method of treating someone who is mentally ill by asking them about their feelings and their past in order to discover what may be causing their condition.

psychoanalyst /saɪkəʊænəlɪst/, **psychoanalysts.** COUNT N A **psychoanalyst** uses psychoanalysis to treat people who are mentally ill.

psychological /saɪkə^{6}lɒdʒɪkəl/. **1** ADJ **Psychological** means concerned with people's minds and thoughts. *Are there important psychological differences between the two sexes?* ♦ **psychologically** ADV *She was tough, both physically and psychologically.* **2** ATTRIB ADJ **Psychological** also means relating to psychology. *...psychological tests.*

psychology /saɪkɒlədʒi^{1}/. **1** UNCOUNT N **Psychology** is the scientific study of the human mind and the reasons for people's behaviour. ♦ **psychologist** /saɪkɒlədʒɪst/ COUNT N *...child psychologists.* **2** SING N If you refer to someone's **psychology,** you mean the kind of mind that they have, which makes them think or behave in a particular way. *...the psychology of the travelling salesman.*

psychopath /saɪkə^{6}pæθ/, **psychopaths.** COUNT N A **psychopath** is someone who is insane and does violent things, such as killing people.

psychotherapy /saɪkəʊθerəpi^{1}/. UNCOUNT N **Psychotherapy** is the use of psychological methods to treat people who are mentally ill, rather than physical methods such as drugs or surgery. *Psychotherapy has helped me enormously.* ♦ **psychotherapist** /saɪkəʊθerəpɪst/ COUNT N *...a psychotherapist who has treated many suicidal young women.*

psychotic /saɪkɒtɪk/. ADJ Someone who is **psychotic** has a severe mental illness; a medical use. *...a psychotic patient.*

pt, pts. pt is a written abbreviation for 'pint'. The plural is either 'pt' or 'pts'. *...1 pt warm water.*

PTO /pi: ti: əʊ/. **PTO** is a written abbreviation for 'please turn over'. You write it at the bottom of a page to indicate that there is more writing on the other side.

pub /pʌb/, **pubs.** COUNT N A **pub** is a building where people can have drinks, especially alcoholic drinks, and talk to their friends.

puberty /pju:bəti^{1}/. UNCOUNT N **Puberty** is the stage in someone's life when they start to change physically from a child to an adult. *...a boy who has reached the age of puberty.*

public /pʌblɪk/. **1** COLL N You can refer to people in general as the **public.** *All members of the public are welcome... The gardens are open to the public.* **2** ATTRIB ADJ **Public** means relating to all the people in a country or community. *The politicians have to respond to public opinion... These fumes are a hazard to public health.* **3** ATTRIB ADJ **Public** spending is money spent by a government to provide services for its people. *The government is reducing public spending.* **4** ATTRIB ADJ **Public** buildings and services are provided for everyone to use. *Both of these books can be obtained from the Public Library... ...public transport.* **5** ATTRIB ADJ A **public** figure or a person in **public** life is known about by many people. *...famous and highly respected public figures... Well-known people from all sections of public life gave the scheme their support.* **6** ATTRIB ADJ **Public** statements, actions, and events are made or done in such a way that everyone can see them or be aware of them. *No public announcement had yet been made... ...public meetings.* ♦ **publicly** ADV *I am going to say what I think of him openly and publicly.* **7** PHRASE If you say or do something **in public,** you say or do it when a group of other people are present. *He repeated in public what he had said in private.* **8** PRED ADJ If a fact is made **public,** it becomes known to everyone rather than being kept secret. *The cause of death was not made public.* **9** ADJ A **public** place is one where people can go about freely and where you can easily be seen and heard. *This is a very public place. Can we talk somewhere else?*

publican /pʌblɪkən/, **publicans.** COUNT N A **publican** is a person who owns or manages a pub; a formal British use.

publication /pʌblɪkeɪʃə^{0}n/, **publications. 1** UNCOUNT N The **publication** of a book or magazine is the act of printing it and making it available. *Several of her articles have already been accepted for publication.* **2** COUNT N A **publication** is a book, magazine, or article that has been published.

public convenience, public conveniences. COUNT N A **public convenience** is a toilet provided in a public place for anyone to use; a British use.

public house, public houses. COUNT N A **public house** is the same as a pub; a British use.

publicise /pʌblɪsaɪz/. See **publicize.**

publicist /pʌblɪsɪst/, **publicists.** COUNT N A **publicist** is a person who publicizes things, especially as part of a job in advertising or journalism.

publicity /pʌblɪsɪ^{1}ti^{1}/. **1** UNCOUNT N **Publicity** is advertising, information, or actions intended to attract the public's attention to someone or something. *There was some advance publicity for the book.* **2** UNCOUNT N When newspapers and television pay a lot of attention to something, you can say that it is receiving **publicity.** *Feminism has attracted a lot of publicity.*

publicize /pʌblɪsaɪz/, **publicizes, publicizing, publicized;** also spelled **publicise.** VB WITH OBJ If you **publicize** a fact or event, you make it widely known to the public. *His programme for reform was well publicised in his newspapers.*

public relations. 1 UNCOUNT N **Public relations** is the part of an organization's work that is concerned with obtaining the public's approval for what it does. *Public relations is a function of management... ...running a large public relations department.* **2** PLURAL N **Public relations** is also the state of the relationship between an organization and the public. *It's good for public relations.*

public school, public schools. 1 COUNT N OR UNCOUNT N In Britain, a **public school** is a private school that provides secondary education and that parents have to pay special fees for. 2 COUNT N OR UNCOUNT N In the USA, Australia, and some other countries, a **public school** is a school that is supported financially by the government.

publish /pʌblɪʃ/, **publishes, publishing, published.** 1 VB WITH OBJ When a company **publishes** a book or magazine, it prints copies of it, which are sent to shops and sold. *The Collins Cobuild dictionary was published in 1987.* 2 VB WITH OBJ When a piece of writing or information **is published** in a newspaper, magazine, or document, it is included and printed there. *The Times would never publish any letter I sent in.* 3 VB WITH OBJ If someone **publishes** a book or an article that they have written, they arrange to have it published. *He has published quite a lot of articles.*

publisher /pʌblɪʃə/, **publishers.** COUNT N A **publisher** is a person or company that publishes books. *The publishers of the book are Collins.*

publishing /pʌblɪʃɪŋ/. UNCOUNT N **Publishing** is the business of publishing books.

pucker /pʌkə/, **puckers, puckering, puckered.** ERG VB When a part of your face **puckers** or **is puckered,** it becomes wrinkled because you are frowning or trying not to cry. *His face puckered, the tears leapt from his eyes.*

pudding /pʊdɪŋ/, **puddings.** 1 COUNT N OR UNCOUNT N A **pudding** is a cooked sweet food made with flour, fat, and eggs, and usually served hot. *They want vanilla pudding.* 2 UNCOUNT N Some people refer to the sweet course of a meal as the **pudding;** an informal British use. *Can they have second helpings of pudding?*

puddle /pʌdəºl/, **puddles.** COUNT N A **puddle** is a small, shallow pool of liquid on the ground. *The road was filled with puddles from the rain... ...a puddle of blood.*

puff /pʌf/, **puffs, puffing, puffed.** 1 VB WITH OR WITHOUT OBJ If someone **puffs** a cigarette or pipe, or if they **puff** at it, they smoke it. *He puffed his pipe for several moments... She puffed on the cigarette.* Also COUNT N *She raised the cigarette to her lips, intending to take a puff.* 2 VB If you **are puffing,** you are breathing loudly and quickly because you are out of breath after a lot of physical effort. *We lugged the branch underneath, panting and puffing.* Also COUNT N *Her breath came in puffs and gasps.* 3 COUNT N A **puff** of air or smoke is a small amount of it that is blown out from somewhere.

puff out. PHR VB To **puff** something **out** means to make it larger and rounder by filling it with air. *Their chests were puffed out like angry swans... They puffed out their cheeks.*

puffed /pʌft/. 1 PRED ADJ If a part of your body is **puffed** or **puffed up,** it is swollen because of an injury. *...his scarred, puffed face... Her left eye is all puffed up.* 2 PRED ADJ If you are **puffed** or **puffed out,** you are breathing with difficulty because you have been using a lot of energy; an informal use. *By the time I got to the top I was pretty well puffed out.*

puffy /pʌfi^1/. ADJ Something that is **puffy** has a round, swollen appearance. *One eye was a slit in his puffy cheek.*

pull /pʊl/, **pulls, pulling, pulled.** 1 VB WITH OR WITHOUT OBJ When you **pull** something, you hold it firmly and move it towards you. *She pulled Paul's hair so hard that he yelled... I shut my eyes when I pulled the trigger... He hoisted the rope over the branch and pulled with all his strength.* 2 VB WITH OBJ When a vehicle, animal, or person **pulls** a cart or piece of machinery, they are attached to it or hold it, so that it moves along behind them when they move forward. 3 VB WITH OBJ AND ADJUNCT If you **pull** a part of your body in a particular direction, you move it forcefully in that direction. *'Let go of me,' she said, and pulled her arm savagely out of his grasp.* 4 REFL VB WITH ADJUNCT If you **pull** yourself out of a place, you hold onto something and use effort to move your body out of the place. *Ralph pulled himself out of the water.* 5 VB WITH OBJ When you **pull** a curtain or blind, you move it across a window in order to cover or uncover it. *She closed the window and pulled the blind.* 6 VB WITH OBJ AND ADJUNCT If you **pull** something apart or **pull** it to pieces, you break it or take it apart without much care. *If you pull apart one of the calculators, you won't get it back together again... Try and stop the cat pulling the Christmas tree to bits.* 7 VB WITH OBJ To **pull** people means to attract their support or interest; an informal use. *He was interested in the number of voters she would pull.* 8 VB WITH OBJ If you **pull** a muscle, you injure it by stretching it.

pull apart. PHR VB If you **pull** people or animals **apart** when they are fighting, you separate them using force. *I rushed in and tried to pull the dogs apart.*

pull at. PHR VB If you **pull at** something, you hold it and move it towards you and then let it go again. *'Come home now, Jim,' she said, pulling at his sleeve.*

pull away. PHR VB 1 When a vehicle **pulls away,** it starts moving forward. *As the lights changed, I pulled away.* 2 If you **pull away** from someone who is holding you, you suddenly move away from them. *He tried to kiss her, but she pulled away fiercely.*

pull down. PHR VB When a building **is pulled down,** it is deliberately destroyed, often in order to build a new one. *Why did they pull those houses down?*

pull in. PHR VB When a vehicle **pulls in** somewhere, it stops there. *The London train pulled in to the station.*

pull off. PHR VB 1 When you **pull off** your clothes, you take them off quickly. *He pulled off his shirt.* 2 If someone has succeeded in doing something very difficult, you can say that they **have pulled** it **off;** an informal use.

pull on. PHR VB When you **pull on** your clothes, you put them on quickly. *He started to pull on his shorts.*

pull out. PHR VB 1 When a vehicle **pulls out** from a place, it moves out of the place. *The train pulled out of the station.* 2 If you **pull out** of an activity or agreement, you decide not to continue it. *You pay a 10% deposit which you lose if you pull out before completion... He pulled his party out of the coalition.* 3 If an army **pulls out** of a place, it leaves it. *Troops had begun to pull out of the area... The Prime Minister intended to pull them out soon.*

pull over. PHR VB When a vehicle **pulls over,** it moves closer to the side of the road. *Pull over, Oliver. Stop the car.*

pull through. PHR VB If you **pull through** a serious illness or if the doctor **pulls** you **through,** you recover from it. *I think she'll pull through.*

pull together. PHR VB 1 If people **pull together,** they co-operate with each other. *We all pulled together during the war.* 2 If someone tells you to **pull** yourself **together** when you are upset or angry, they are telling you to control your feelings.

pull up. PHR VB 1 When a vehicle **pulls up,** it slows down and stops. *The rain stopped as we pulled up at the hotel.* 2 If you **pull up** a chair, you move it closer to something or someone. *I pulled up a chair and sat down to watch the news.*

pulley /pʊli^1/, **pulleys.** COUNT N A **pulley** is a device used for lifting or lowering heavy weights. It consists of a wheel with a hollow rim which is fixed above the ground. You pass a rope over the rim, attach one end of the rope to the weight, and pull or gradually release the other end.

pullover /pʊləʊvə/, **pullovers.** COUNT N A **pullover** is a woollen piece of clothing that covers the upper part of your body and your arms.

pulp /pʌlp/. UNCOUNT N OR SING N If something is turned into **pulp,** it is crushed or beaten until it is soft, smooth, and moist. *We squashed the berries into a pulp... ...wood pulp.*

pulpit /pʊlpɪt/, **pulpits.** COUNT N A **pulpit** is a small raised platform in a church with a rail or barrier around it, where a member of the clergy stands to preach.

pulsate /pʌlseɪt/, **pulsates, pulsating, pulsated.** VB If something **pulsates,** it moves in and out or shakes with strong, regular movements. *The creature has no heart, only a number of pulsating arteries.*

pulse /pʌls/, **pulses, pulsing, pulsed.** 1 COUNT N Your **pulse** is the regular beating of blood through your body, which you can feel when you touch particular parts of your body, especially your wrist. *Her pulse started to race.* • When a doctor or nurse **takes** your **pulse,** he or she finds out the speed of your heartbeat by feeling the pulse in your wrist. 2 COUNT N Some seeds which can be cooked and eaten are called **pulses,** for example the seeds of peas, beans, and lentils. 3 VB If something **pulses,** it moves or shakes with strong, regular movements. *...a soft rhythmic pulsing sound.*

pulverize /pʌlvəraɪz/, **pulverizes, pulverizing, pulverized;** also spelled **pulverise.** VB WITH OBJ To **pulverize** something means to crush it. *The processes involved pulverising the nuts.*

pummel /pʌməºl/, **pummels, pummelling, pummelled;** spelled **pummeling, pummeled** in American English. VB WITH OBJ If you **pummel** someone or something, you hit them repeatedly with your fists.

pump /pʌmp/, **pumps, pumping, pumped.** 1 COUNT N A **pump** is a machine or device used to force a liquid or gas to flow in a particular direction. 2 COUNT N A **pump** is also a device for bringing water to the surface from below the ground. Pumps often have handles that you push in order to force the water upwards. *We scrubbed ourselves under the pump.* 3 COUNT N A **pump** is also a device that you use to force air into something, especially into the tyre of a vehicle. *...a bicycle pump.* 4 COUNT N A petrol **pump** is a machine with a hose attached to it from which you can fill a car with petrol. 5 COUNT N **Pumps** are canvas shoes with flat rubber soles which people wear for sports and leisure. 6 VB WITH OBJ AND ADJUNCT To **pump** a liquid or gas in a particular direction means to force it to flow in that direction, using a pump. *We can use the electricity to pump water back into a dam or a reservoir.* 7 VB WITH OBJ To **pump** water, oil, or gas means to get a supply of it from below the ground, using a pump. *John went to a cast-iron pump and started pumping water to drink.* 8 VB WITH OBJ If you **pump** something such as a tyre or if you **pump** it up, you fill it with air. 9 VB WITH OBJ AND 'into' If you **pump** money or energy into something, you put a lot of money or energy into it; an informal use. *Most governments have pumped all available funds into large-scale modern technological projects.* 10 VB WITH OBJ If you **pump** someone about something, you keep asking them questions in order to get information; an informal use. *I pumped him discreetly about his past.*

pumpkin /pʌmpºkɪn/, **pumpkins.** COUNT N OR UNCOUNT N A **pumpkin** is a large, round, orange vegetable with a thick skin.

pun /pʌn/, **puns.** COUNT N A **pun** is a clever and amusing use of words which have more than one meaning, or which have the same sound, so that what you say has two different meanings.

punch /pʌntʃ/, **punches, punching, punched.** 1 VB WITH OBJ If you **punch** someone, you hit them hard with your fist. *Boylan punched him hard on the nose... I was punched in the stomach.* Also COUNT N *...aiming a slow punch at my jaw.* 2 COUNT N A **punch** is a tool used for making holes in something. *He made a small hole in the belt with a leather punch.* 3 VB WITH OBJ If you **punch** holes in something, you make holes in it by pushing or pressing it with something sharp. *Edward was punching holes in a can.* 4 MASS N **Punch** is a drink usually made from wine or spirits mixed with sugar, fruit, and spices. *...hot rum punch.*

punctual /pʌŋktjʊºəl/. PRED ADJ If you are **punctual,** you arrive or do something at the arranged time. *I expect my guests to be punctual for breakfast.* ♦ **punctually** ADV *Mary arrived punctually at ten o'clock.*

punctuate /pʌŋktjʊeɪt/, **punctuates, punctuating, punctuated;** a formal word. VB WITH OBJ If an activity **is punctuated** by something, it is regularly interrupted by it. *The old lady's words were punctuated by noise from outside.*

punctuation /pʌŋktjʊeɪʃəºn/. UNCOUNT N **Punctuation** is the system of marks such as full stops, commas, and question marks that you use in writing to divide words into sentences and clauses.

punctuation mark, punctuation marks. COUNT N A **punctuation mark** is a sign such as a full stop, comma, or question mark.

puncture /pʌŋktʃə/, **punctures, puncturing, punctured.** 1 COUNT N A **puncture** is a small hole in a car or bicycle tyre that has been made by a sharp object. *One of the wheels has a puncture.* 2 VB WITH OBJ To **puncture** something means to make a small hole in it.

pundit /pʌndɪt/, **pundits.** COUNT N A **pundit** is a person who knows a lot about a subject and is asked to give information or opinions about it.

pungent /pʌnd3ənt/. 1 ADJ Something that is **pungent** has a strong, unpleasant smell or taste. *The pungent, choking smell of sulphur filled the air.* 2 ADJ **Pungent** speech or writing is direct, powerful, and often critical; a formal use.

punish /pʌnɪʃ/, **punishes, punishing, punished.** 1 VB WITH OBJ To **punish** someone means to make them suffer in some way because they have done something wrong. *They discovered his crime and punished him for it.* 2 VB WITH OBJ To **punish** a crime means to punish anyone who commits that crime. *They punished adultery with death.*

punishing /pʌnɪʃɪŋ/. ATTRIB ADJ A **punishing** experience makes you very weak or helpless. *The purpose was to inflict a punishing defeat on the enemy.*

punishment /pʌnɪʃmə^{2}nt/, **punishments.** 1 UNCOUNT N **Punishment** is the act of punishing someone. *Punishment and prison sentences cannot reform the hardened criminal.* 2 COUNT N A **punishment** is a particular way of punishing someone. *He maintained that the only true punishment for murder was death.* 3 UNCOUNT N **Punishment** is also severe physical treatment of any kind. *The crew were in no condition to withstand any further punishment from the sea.* 4 See also **capital punishment, corporal punishment.**

punitive /pju:nɪ^{1}tɪv/. ADJ **Punitive** actions are intended to punish people; a formal use. *We will take no punitive action against those who have broken the rules.*

punt /pʌnt/, **punts.** COUNT N A **punt** is a long boat with a flat bottom. You move the boat along by standing at one end and pushing a long pole down against the bottom of the river.

punter /pʌntə/, **punters;** an informal British word. **1** COUNT N A **punter** is a person who bets money on horse races. **2** COUNT N People sometimes refer to their customers or clients as the **punters.**

puny /pju:ni[1]/. ADJ **Puny** means very small or weak. *...a puny old man... ...her puny efforts.*

pup /pʌp/, **pups.** COUNT N A **pup** is a young dog. Some other young animals are also called **pups.** *...a cocker spaniel pup... ...a seal pup.*

pupil /pju:pɪ[0]l/, **pupils. 1** COUNT N The **pupils** of a school are the children who go to it. *...a school with more than 1300 pupils.* **2** COUNT N WITH POSS A **pupil** of a painter, musician, or other expert is someone who studies with them to learn their skills. **3** COUNT N The **pupils** of your eyes are the small, round, black holes in the centre of them.

puppet /pʌpɪt/, **puppets. 1** COUNT N A **puppet** is a doll that you can move, either by pulling strings which are attached to it, or by putting your hand inside its body and moving your fingers. **2** COUNT N You can refer to people or countries as **puppets** when their actions are controlled by more powerful people or countries, although they may appear to be independent. *...puppet governments.*

puppy /pʌpi[1]/, **puppies.** COUNT N A **puppy** is a young dog.

purchase /pɜ:tʃə[1]s/, **purchases, purchasing, purchased;** a formal word. **1** VB WITH OBJ When you **purchase** something, you buy it. *He sold the house he had purchased only two years before.* ♦ **purchaser** /pɜ:tʃə[1]sə/ COUNT N *...purchasers of paintings.* **2** UNCOUNT N **Purchase** is the act of buying something. *We need to know the exact day of purchase.* **3** COUNT N A **purchase** is something that you buy. *Among his purchases were several books.*

pure /pjʊə/, **purer, purest. 1** ATTRIB ADJ **Pure** means not mixed with anything else or not spoiled by anything. *...a dress of pure silk... ...pure white.* ♦ **purity** /pjʊərɪti[1]/ UNCOUNT N *...their claim to ideological purity.* **2** ADJ Something that is **pure** is clean, healthy, and does not contain any harmful substances. *...the pure, dry desert air.* ♦ **purity** UNCOUNT N *...the importance of purity in the water supply.* **3** ADJ People who are **pure** have not done anything bad or sinful; a literary use. *...pure in mind and body.* ♦ **purity** UNCOUNT N *...the forces of virtue and purity.* **4** ADJ A **pure** sound is clear and pleasant to hear. *The singer's voice remained pure and clear throughout the evening.* **5** ATTRIB ADJ **Pure** science or research is concerned only with theory and not with how this theory can be used in practical ways. *...pure maths... ...chemistry, both pure and applied.* **6** ATTRIB ADJ **Pure** also means complete and total. *I came on the idea by pure chance... ...pure bliss.*

purely /pjʊəli[1]/. **1** ADV **Purely** means involving only one feature or characteristic and not including anything else. *...something purely practical like mending a washing machine... There's nothing personal in this. Purely a routine check.* **2** PHRASE You use **purely and simply** to emphasize that a particular thing is the only thing involved. *It is done through ignorance purely and simply.*

purgatory /pɜ:gətə[0]ri[1]/. **1** PROPER N **Purgatory** is the place where Roman Catholics believe the spirits of dead people are sent to suffer for their sins before they can go to heaven. **2** UNCOUNT N You can refer to a very unpleasant experience as **purgatory.** *It was a sort of purgatory that had to be endured.*

purge /pɜ:dʒ/, **purges, purging, purged. 1** VB WITH OBJ To **purge** an organization of its unacceptable members means to remove them from it. You can also talk about **purging** people from an organization. *...to purge the government of Latimer's supporters... They had done their best to purge extremists from the party.* Also COUNT N *They discovered that there were infiltrators inside the party. A purge began.* **2** VB WITH OBJ OR REFL VB When you **purge** something of undesirable things, you get rid of them. *I tried desperately to purge myself of these dangerous desires.*

purify /pjʊərɪfaɪ/, **purifies, purifying, purified.** VB WITH OBJ If you **purify** a substance, you make it pure by removing any harmful, dirty, or inferior substances from it. *...specially purified water.*

purist /pjʊərɪst/, **purists.** COUNT N A **purist** is a person who believes in absolute correctness. *Musical purists were outraged at this innovation.*

puritan /pjʊərɪtə[0]n/, **puritans.** COUNT N You refer to someone as a **puritan** when they live according to strict moral or religious principles, especially by avoiding physical pleasures. *...an austere old puritan.* Also ADJ *...puritan morality.*

puritanical /pjʊərɪtænɪkə[0]l/. ADJ Someone who is **puritanical** behaves according to strict moral or religious principles, especially by avoiding physical pleasures. *...a puritanical distaste for alcohol.*

purple /pɜ:pə[0]l/. ADJ Something that is **purple** is reddish-blue.

purport /pə[5]pɔ:t/, **purports, purporting, purported.** VB WITH TO-INF If something **purports** to do or be a particular thing, it is claimed to do or be that thing; a formal use. *...advertisements for cosmetics purporting to delay the development of wrinkles.*

purpose /pɜ:pəs/, **purposes. 1** COUNT N The **purpose** of something is the reason for which it is made or done. *The purpose of the meeting was to discuss the committee's report... The buildings are now used as a prison, but they weren't built for that purpose.* **2** COUNT N Your **purpose** is the thing that you want to achieve. *Her only purpose in life was to get rich.* **3** UNCOUNT N **Purpose** is the feeling of having a definite aim and of being determined to achieve it. *She has given them a sense of purpose.*

PHRASES • If you do something **on purpose,** you do it deliberately. *He had gone there on purpose, to see what happened.* • You use the phrase **for all practical purposes** to suggest that a situation is not exactly as you describe it but the effect is the same as if it were. *The rest are now, for all practical purposes, useless.* • If you say that an action was done **to no purpose,** you mean that it achieved nothing. If you say that it was done **to good purpose,** you mean that it achieved something. *He used his past experience to good purpose.* • **to all intents and purposes:** see **intent.**

purpose-built. ADJ A **purpose-built** building has been specially designed and built for a particular use. *...a purpose-built nursery school.*

purposeful /pɜ:pəsfʊl/. ADJ If someone is **purposeful,** they show that they have a definite aim and a strong desire to achieve it. *They were striving to bring about change in a purposeful way.* ♦ **purposefully** ADV *She began walking slowly but purposefully towards the bridge.*

purposely /pɜ:pəsli[1]/. ADV If you do something **purposely,** you do it deliberately. *She purposely sat in the outside seat.*

purr /pɜ:/, **purrs, purring, purred. 1** VB When a cat **purrs,** it makes a low vibrating sound with its throat because it is contented. **2** VB When an engine or machine **purrs,** it makes a quiet, continuous, vibrating sound. *I heard cars purr in the distance.* Also SING N *I could hear the gentle purr of a movie projector.*

purse /pɜ:s/, **purses, pursing, pursed. 1** COUNT N A **purse** is a very small bag that people, especially women, keep their money in; a British use. *She began hunting in her purse for some coins.* **2** COUNT N A **purse** is also the same as a handbag; an American use. *She strolled along, swinging her old white purse.* **3** VB WITH OBJ If you **purse** your lips, you move them into a small, rounded shape. *He pursed his lips in distaste.*

purser /pɜ:sə/, **pursers.** COUNT N The **purser** on a ship is an officer who deals with the accounts and official papers. On a passenger ship, the purser is also responsible for the welfare of the passengers.

pursue /pəsj[0]u:/, **pursues, pursuing, pursued;** a formal word. **1** VB WITH OBJ If you **pursue** an activity, interest, or plan, you do it or carry it out. *Lyttleton pursued a policy of peace and order... His wealth enabled him to pursue his passionate interest in art.* **2** VB WITH OBJ If you **pursue** a particular aim or result, you make efforts to achieve it, often over a long period of time. *Economic growth must not be pursued at the expense of environmental pollution.* **3** VB WITH OBJ If you **pursue** a particular topic, you try to find out more about it. *I don't want to pursue that question now.* **4** VB WITH OBJ If you **pursue** someone or something, you follow them, usually in order to catch them. *The police pursued the wrong car.* ♦ **pursuer** /pəsj[0]u:ə/ COUNT N *He managed to give his pursuers the slip.*

pursuit /pəsj[0]u:t/, **pursuits;** a formal word. **1** UNCOUNT N WITH 'of' Your **pursuit** of something that you want consists of your attempts at achieving it. *...the pursuit of happiness... How far should any of us go in pursuit of what we want?* **2** UNCOUNT N WITH 'of' The **pursuit** of an activity, interest, or plan consists of all the things that you do when you are carrying it out. *...some of the risks inherent in the pursuit of these policies.* **3** UNCOUNT N The **pursuit** of someone or something is the act of chasing them. *...a gamekeeper in pursuit of a poacher.* • If you are **in hot pursuit** of someone, you are chasing after them with great determination. *He started running—with all the others in hot pursuit.* **4** COUNT N **Pursuits** are activities, especially ones that you do for enjoyment. *Games like chess are rather intellectual pursuits.*

pus /pʌs/. UNCOUNT N **Pus** is a thick yellowish liquid that forms in wounds when they are infected.

push /pʊʃ/, **pushes, pushing, pushed. 1** VB WITH OR WITHOUT OBJ When you **push** something, you press it with force, often in order to move it. *She pushed the button that locked the door... I pushed open the door... Castle pushed his bicycle up King's Road.* Also COUNT N *The gate slid open at the push of a button.* **2** VB WITH OR WITHOUT OBJ, WITH ADJUNCT If you **push** through things that are blocking your way or **push** your way through them, you use force in order to be able to move past them. *Ralph pushed between them to get a better view... I pushed my way through the people.* **3** VB WITH OBJ AND ADJUNCT To **push** a value or amount up or down means to cause it to increase or decrease. *The oil boom will push the inflation rate up to higher levels.* **4** VB WITH OBJ If you **push** someone into doing something, you urge or force them to do it; an informal use. *No one pushed me into this; I decided to do it of my own accord... The government was pushed to desperate extremes.* **5** VB WITH 'for' If you **push** for something, you try very hard to achieve it. *He is pushing for secret balloting in Party elections.* Also SING N *India led the non-aligned nations in a push for sanctions.* **6** VB WITH OBJ To **push** something also means to try to increase its popularity or to attract people to it; an informal use. *...huge adverts pushing slimming drugs.* **7** VB WITH OBJ When someone **pushes** drugs, they sell them illegally; an informal use. ♦ **pusher** /pʊʃə/ COUNT N *...professional dope pushers.* **8** PHRASE If someone **gives** you **the push,** they say they no longer want you; an informal British use. *Another forty workers have been given the push.* **9** See also **pushed.**

push ahead. PHR VB If you **push ahead** with something, you continue with it. *They have pushed ahead with an optimistic development strategy.*

push around. PHR VB If someone **pushes** you **around,** they give you orders in a rude and insulting way. *We're not going to let them push us around.*

push in. PHR VB When someone **pushes in,** they come into a queue in front of other people; used showing disapproval. *Felicity pushed in next to Howard.*

push off. PHR VB When you **push off,** you leave a place; an informal use. *Push off. You're not wanted.*

push on. PHR VB When you **push on,** you continue travelling somewhere or doing something.

push over. PHR VB If you **push** someone or something **over,** you push them so that they fall onto the ground. *The children were pushing each other over on the sand.*

push through. PHR VB If you **push through** a proposal, you succeed in getting it accepted, often with difficulty. *I'll see that the scheme is pushed through at the earliest date.*

pushchair /pʊʃtʃeə/, **pushchairs.** COUNT N A **pushchair** is a small chair on wheels, in which a small child can sit and be wheeled around; a British use.

pushed /pʊʃt/. PRED ADJ If you are **pushed** for time, you do not have very much time in which to do things; an informal use.

pussy /pʊsi[1]/, **pussies.** COUNT N You can refer to a cat as a **pussy** or a **pussy cat;** an informal use.

put /pʊt/, **puts, putting. Put** is used in the present tense and is the past tense and past participle. **1** VB WITH OBJ AND ADJUNCT When you **put** something in a particular place or position, you move it into that place or position. *She put her hand on his arm... I put her suitcase on the table... Marsha put her cup down... The women put a garland round her neck.* **2** VB WITH OBJ AND ADJUNCT If you **put** someone somewhere, you cause them to go there and to stay there. *They had to put him into an asylum... I have to put the kids to bed.* **3** VB WITH OBJ When you **put** an idea or remark in a particular way, you express it in that way. *They cannot put their feelings into words... To put it briefly, the man is mad and may become dangerous.* **4** VB WITH OBJ When you **put** a question or suggestion to someone, you ask them the question or make the suggestion. *I put this question to Dr Leslie Cook... I put it to him that, in fact, he was losing a good worker.* **5** VB WITH OBJ AND ADJUNCT To **put** a person or thing in a particular state or situation means to cause them to be in that state or situation. *It puts me in a rather difficult position... The company closed several months ago, putting 120 people out of a job... This would put the party into power.* **6** VB WITH OBJ AND 'on' OR 'upon' To **put** something on people or things means to cause them to have it or be affected by it. *It puts a tremendous responsibility on us... We put pressure on our children to learn to read... ...a plan to put a tax on children's clothes.* **7** VB WITH OBJ If you **put** written information somewhere, you write or type it there. *Put all the details on the card... For 'profession' he put down simply 'business man'.* **8** to **stay put:** see **stay.**

put across. PHR VB When you **put** something **across** or **put it over,** you succeed in describing or explaining it to someone. *You need the skill to put your ideas across... It has always been very difficult for her to put*

over her own thoughts.
put aside. PHR VB If you **put** something **aside,** you keep it to be dealt with or used at a later time. *Your best plan is to put aside funds to cover these bills.*
put at. PHR VB If the cost, age, or value of something **is put at** a particular amount, it is estimated to be that amount. *The pipeline's cost is now put at 2.7 billion pounds.*
put away. PHR VB **1** If you **put** something **away,** you put it into the place where it is normally kept. *Right—put your books away.* **2** If someone **is put away,** they are sent to prison or to a mental hospital; an informal use. *The doctor wanted to have him put away.*
put back. PHR VB To **put** something **back** means to delay or postpone it. *The meeting's been put back till Monday... This will put production back at least a month.*
put by. PHR VB If you **put** money **by,** you keep it so that you can use it at a later time. *I've got a bit put by.*
put down. PHR VB **1** When soldiers, police, or the government **put down** a riot or rebellion, they stop it by using force. *These riots were put down by the local police.* **2** If you **put** someone **down,** you criticize them or make them appear foolish; an informal use. *...her infuriating habit of putting people down in small ways.* ● See also **put-down. 3** When an animal **is put down,** it is killed because it is dangerous or very ill. *We had to have the cat put down.*
put down to. PHR VB If you **put** something **down to** a particular thing, you believe that it is caused by that thing. *I put it down to arthritis.*
put forward. PHR VB If you **put forward** something or someone, you suggest that they should be considered or chosen for a particular purpose or job. *They rejected every proposal put forward.*
put in. PHR VB **1** If you **put in** an amount of time or effort doing something, you spend that time or effort doing it. *I put in fifteen hours of work daily... You've put in a lot of work.* **2** If you **put in** a request or **put in** for something, you make a formal request or application for it. *I put in a request for an interview... After the gamekeeper died, Father put in for his job.* **3** to **put in a word** for someone: see **word.**
put into. PHR VB **1** If you **put** time, strength, or energy **into** an activity, you use it in doing that activity. *She put all her energy into tidying the place up.* **2** If you **put** money **into** a business or project, you invest the money in it. *Capitalists are encouraged to put their wealth into productive enterprises.*
put off. PHR VB **1** If you **put** something **off,** you delay doing it. *Don't put it off till tomorrow.* **2** If you **put** someone **off,** you cause them to stop trying to get or do what they had planned. *Nothing would put her off once she had made up her mind.* **3** To **put** someone **off** something means to cause them to dislike it. *I had seen enough to put me off farm work.*
put on. PHR VB **1** When you **put on** a piece of clothing, you place it on your body in order to wear it. *I put on my jacket.* **2** When people **put on** a show, exhibition, or service, they perform it, arrange it, or organize it. *A French company has put on 'Peter Grimes'... They're putting on a special train service.* **3** If someone **puts on** weight, they become heavier. *She had put on over a stone since I last saw her.* **4** If you **put on** a piece of equipment or a device, you make it start working. *He put on the light... She put the radio on.* **5** If you **put on** a record, tape, or video, you place it on a record player or in a tape machine so you can listen to it or watch it. **6** If you **put** food **on,** you begin to cook it. *She often forgets to put the dinner on before she goes to collect the children.* **7** If you **put on** a way of behaving, you behave in a way that is not natural to you or that does not express your real feelings. *She put on that look of not caring... I don't see why you have to put on a phoney English accent.*
put out. PHR VB **1** If you **put out** an announcement or story, you make it known to a lot of people. *He put out a statement denouncing the commission's conclusions.* **2** If you **put out** something that is burning, you make it stop burning. *He helped to put the fire out.* **3** If you **put out** an electric light, you make it stop shining by pressing a switch. *She put out the light.* **4** If you **put out** things that will be needed, you place them somewhere ready to be used. *I put clean clothes out for you on the bed.* **5** If you **put out** your hand, you move it forward, away from your body, often in order to greet someone. *I walked over to one young woman and put out my hand.* **6** If you **are put out** by something, you are rather annoyed or upset by it. *I was somewhat put out when the audience laughed loudly.* **7** If you **put** yourself **out** for someone, you do something for them even though it requires a lot of effort or causes you problems. *He was putting himself out to please her.*
put over. PHR VB See **put across.**
put through. PHR VB **1** When someone **puts through** a telephone call or a caller, they make the connection that allows the caller to speak to the person they are phoning. *'Data Room, please.'—'I'll put you through.'* **2** If someone **puts** you **through** an unpleasant experience, they make you experience it. *I'm sorry to put you through this again.*
put together. PHR VB **1** If you **put** something **together,** you join its different parts to each other so that it can be used. *He started to put his fishing rod together.* **2** If you **put** an event **together,** you organize or arrange it. *The agency has put together the biggest ever campaign for a new car.* **3** PHRASE You say that one person or thing is better or greater than a group of other people or things **put together** when you are emphasizing how much better or greater they are. *He is smarter than all your colonels put together.*
put up. PHR VB **1** If people **put up** a wall or a building, they construct it. *We shall have to put up a fence.* **2** If you **put up** something such as an umbrella or hood, you unfold it or raise it so that it covers you. **3** If you **put up** a poster or notice, you fix it to a wall or board. **4** If you **put up** resistance to something, you resist it. *America has put up so much resistance to Concorde... We had put up a fierce struggle.* **5** If you **put up** the money for something, you provide the money that is needed to pay for it. *The National Council for the Arts put up half the cost.* **6** To **put up** the price of something means to cause it to increase. *This is what happens when they put up prices too far.* **7** If someone **puts** you **up,** you stay at their home. *I offered to put him up for the night.*
put up to. PHR VB If you **put** someone **up to** something wrong or foolish, you encourage them to do it. *Julie herself had probably put them up to it.*
put up with. PHR VB If you **put up with** something, you tolerate or accept it, even though you find it unpleasant or unsatisfactory. *The natives have to put up with gaping tourists... I can't think why I put up with it.*
put-down, put-downs. COUNT N A **put-down** is a remark or action which makes someone appear foolish; an informal use. *The ultimate put-down is to be given a pat on the head.*
putty /pʌti^1/. UNCOUNT N **Putty** is a stiff paste used to fix glass panes into frames and to fill cracks or holes.
puzzle /pʌzə^{0}l/, **puzzles, puzzling, puzzled. 1** VB WITH OBJ If something **puzzles** you, it makes you feel confused because you do not understand it. *There was one sentence which puzzled me deeply.* ♦ **puzzling** ADJ *I find this rather puzzling.* **2** VB WITH ADJUNCT If you **puzzle** over something, you try hard to think of the answer or the explanation for it. *Astronomers had puzzled over these white ovals for some time.* **3** COUNT N A **puzzle** is a question, game, or toy which you have to think about carefully in order to answer it correctly or put it together properly. **4** SING N You can describe anything that is hard to understand as a **puzzle.** *The motives of the film-makers remain a puzzle.*
puzzle out. PHR VB If you **puzzle out** a problem, you find the answer to it by thinking hard about it. *She sat down and tried to puzzle out the reports.*
puzzled /pʌzə^{0}ld/. ADJ If you are **puzzled,** you are confused because you do not understand something.
puzzlement /pʌzə^{0}lmənt/. UNCOUNT N **Puzzlement** is confusion that you feel when you do not understand something. *I looked at him in puzzlement.*
pyjamas /pədʒ ɑːməz/; spelled **pajamas** in American English. The forms **pyjama** and **pajama** are used in front of another noun. PLURAL N A pair of **pyjamas** consists of loose trousers and a loose jacket that people, especially men, wear in bed. *...pyjama trousers.*
pylon /paɪlə^{7}n/, **pylons.** COUNT N **Pylons** are tall metal structures which hold electric cables high above the ground so that electricity can be transmitted over long distances.
pyramid /pɪrəmɪd/, **pyramids.** COUNT N A **pyramid** is a three-dimensional shape with a flat base and flat triangular sides which slope upwards to a point.
python /paɪθə^{7}n/, **pythons.** COUNT N A **python** is a large snake that kills animals by squeezing them with its body.

Qq

quack /kwæk/, **quacks, quacking, quacked.** VB When a duck **quacks,** it makes the noise that ducks typically make.
quadruped /kwɒdrupɛd/, **quadrupeds.** COUNT N A **quadruped** is any animal with four legs; a formal use.
quadruple /kwɒdrʊpə^{0}l/, **quadruples, quadrupling, quadrupled.** VB When an amount or number **quadruples,** it becomes four times as large. *Wheat production has almost quadrupled.*
quail /kweɪl/, **quails. Quail** can also be the plural. COUNT N A **quail** is a small bird which is often shot and eaten.
quaint /kweɪnt/. ADJ Something that is **quaint** is attractive because it is unusual and rather old-fashioned. *...a quaint fishing village.*
quake /kweɪk/, **quakes, quaking, quaked. 1** VB If you **quake,** you tremble or shake because you are afraid. *I stood there quaking with fear.* **2** COUNT N A **quake** is the same as an earthquake; an informal use.
qualification /kwɒlɪfɪkeɪʃə^{0}n/, **qualifications. 1** COUNT N Your **qualifications** are the examinations that you have passed. *I haven't got any qualifications in English Literature.* **2** COUNT N The **qualifications** needed for a particular activity or task are the qualities and skills that you need in order to do it. *One of the qualifications you need in advertising is a fertile mind.* **3** COUNT N OR UNCOUNT N A **qualification** is also something that you add to a statement to make it less strong or less generalized. *Two qualifications need to be made... Few praised him without qualification.*
qualified /kwɒlɪfaɪd/. **1** ADJ Someone who is **qualified** has passed the examinations that they need in order to work in a particular profession. *...a qualified doctor.* **2** PRED ADJ If you are **qualified** to do something, you have the qualities, knowledge, or skills necessary to do it. *She did not feel qualified to discuss it.* **3** ADJ **Qualified** agreement or praise is not total and suggests that you have doubts. *The reaction was one of qualified praise.*
qualify /kwɒlɪfaɪ/, **qualifies, qualifying, qualified. 1** VB When someone **qualifies,** they pass the examinations that they need to pass in order to work in a particular profession. *I was thirty-three before I qualified as a doctor.* ♦ **qualification** UNCOUNT N *Even after qualification, jobs were hard to find.* **2** VB WITH OBJ If you **qualify** a statement, you add a detail or explanation to it to make it less strong or less generalized. *If I said that Warsaw was grim and grey, that statement has to be qualified.* **3** VB If someone **qualifies** for something, they have the right to have it. *By working all their lives, people qualify automatically for their pensions.* **4** VB If you **qualify** in a competition, you are successful in one part of it and go on to the next stage. *He worked all season to qualify for the match.*
qualitative /kwɒlɪtətɪv, -teɪt-/. ATTRIB ADJ **Qualitative** means relating to the quality of something. *...qualitative improvements... ...a qualitative change.*
quality /kwɒlɪ^{1}ti^1/, **qualities. 1** UNCOUNT N The **quality** of something is how good or bad it is. *The quality of the photograph was poor.* Also ADJ *...good quality paper.* **2** UNCOUNT N Something of **quality** is of a high standard. *...a programme of quality.* Also ADJ *The employers don't want quality work any more.* **3** COUNT N Your **qualities** are your characteristics. *...the qualities they look for in a teacher.* **4** COUNT N The **qualities** of a substance or object are its physical characteristics. *The skin on the baby's face had a pearly translucent quality.*
qualm /kwɑːm/, **qualms.** COUNT N If you have **qualms** about what you are doing, you are worried that it may not be right.
quandary /kwɒndə^{0}ri^1/, **quandaries.** COUNT N If you are in a **quandary,** you cannot decide what to do.
quantitative /kwɒntɪtətɪv, -teɪt-/. ADJ **Quantitative** means relating to the size or amount of something. *...a quantitative assessment of the effectiveness of our investment.*
quantity /kwɒntɪ^{1}ti^1/, **quantities. 1** COUNT N A **quantity** of something is an amount that you can measure or count. *You only need a very small quantity... ...a quantity of leaves... Natural gas was discovered in large quantities beneath the North Sea.* **2** UNCOUNT N **Quantity** is the amount of something that there is; often used in contrast to its quality. *The food supply has grown less, in quantity and quality.*
PHRASES ● Things that are produced **in quantity** are produced in large amounts. ● You can say that someone or something is an **unknown quantity** when you do not know anything about them. *To Shanti the outside world was a totally unknown quantity.*
quantum /kwɒntə^{0}m/. MOD **Quantum** is used to describe theories in physics and mathematics which are concerned with atomic particles; a technical use. *...quantum mechanics.*
quarantine /kwɒrəntiːn/. UNCOUNT N If a person or animal is in **quarantine,** they are kept separate from other people or animals in case they have an infectious disease.
quarrel /kwɒrə^{0}l/, **quarrels, quarrelling, quarrelled;** spelled **quarreling, quarreled** in American

English. 1 COUNT N A **quarrel** is an angry argument between two or more people. *I don't think we should enter into a family quarrel... There wasn't any evidence of quarrels between them.* 2 RECIP VB When two or more people **quarrel,** they have an angry argument. *They quarrelled quite often... I don't want to quarrel with you.* 3 SING N If you say that you have no **quarrel** with something, you mean that you do not object to it. *I wouldn't have any quarrel with this proposal myself.*

quarrelsome /kwɒrəlsəm/. ADJ People who are **quarrelsome** are always having angry arguments.

quarry /kwɒri¹/, **quarries, quarrying, quarried.** 1 COUNT N A **quarry** is a place where large quantities of stone, slate, or minerals are dug out of the ground. 2 VB WITH OBJ To **quarry** a stone or mineral means to remove it from a quarry by digging, drilling, or blasting. *Limestone has been quarried for centuries.* 3 COUNT N A person's or animal's **quarry** is the animal that they are hunting. The plural is also 'quarry'; a formal use. *Move slowly, or you will startle your quarry.*

quarter /kwɔːtə/, **quarters.** 1 COUNT N A **quarter** is one of four equal parts of something. *...a quarter of a century... ...an hour and a quarter.* Also ATTRIB ADJ *...the quarter century following the Second World War.* 2 UNCOUNT N OR SING N If it is a **quarter** to a particular hour, it is fifteen minutes before that hour. If it is a **quarter** past a particular hour, it is fifteen minutes past that hour. *It's quarter to five... We're due at Janet's at quarter past eleven... ...a quarter past three in the afternoon.* 3 COUNT N A **quarter** is also a period of three months. *In the last quarter of 1980 inflation rose by 1%.* 4 COUNT N In the United States and Canada, a **quarter** is a coin worth 25 cents. 5 COUNT N You can refer to the area in a town where a particular group of people live or work as a particular **quarter.** *...the Black quarters of New York, Detroit or Washington.* 6 COUNT N WITH SUPP When you refer to the feeling or reaction in certain **quarters** or from a particular **quarter,** you are referring rather vaguely to the feeling or reaction of a particular person or group. *Male prejudice still exists in certain quarters.* 7 PLURAL N You can refer to the room or rooms provided for a person such as a soldier to live in as that person's **quarters.** *...servants' quarters.* 8 PHRASE If you see someone **at close quarters,** you see them from a place that is very close to them.

quarter-final /kwɔːtəfaɪnəᵒl/, **quarter-finals.** COUNT N A **quarter-final** is one of the four matches in a competition which decides which four players or teams will compete in the semi-final.

quarterly /kwɔːtəli¹/. ADV AFTER VB OR ATTRIB ADJ If something happens **quarterly,** it happens regularly four times a year, at intervals of three months. *We meet quarterly... ...a quarterly conference.*

quartet /kwɔːtet/, **quartets.** 1 COUNT N A **quartet** is a group of four people who play musical instruments or sing together. 2 COUNT N A **quartet** is also a piece of music for four instruments or four singers.

quartz /kwɔːts/. UNCOUNT N **Quartz** is a kind of hard, shiny crystal, used in making electronic equipment and very accurate watches and clocks.

quash /kwɒʃ/, **quashes, quashing, quashed.** VB WITH OBJ If someone in authority **quashes** a decision or judgement, they officially reject it and it is no longer legally valid. *Their prison sentences were quashed.*

quasi- /kweɪzaɪ/. PREFIX **quasi-** is used to form adjectives and nouns that describe something as being very like something else, without actually being that thing. *...a quasi-religious experience... They have turned their countries into quasi-republics.*

quaver /kweɪvə/, **quavers, quavering, quavered.** REPORT VB OR VB If someone's voice **quavers,** it sounds unsteady, for example because they are nervous or uncertain. *'Am I safe?' he quavered.*

quay /kiː/, **quays.** COUNT N A **quay** is a long platform beside the sea or a river where boats can be tied up and loaded or unloaded.

queasy /kwiːzi¹/. ADJ If you feel **queasy,** you feel rather sick. *She felt a little queasy on the boat.*

queen /kwiːn/, **queens.** 1 COUNT N OR TITLE A **queen** is a woman who rules a country as its monarch, or a woman who is married to a king. *...Queen Victoria.* 2 COUNT N A **queen** or a **queen bee** is a large female bee which lays eggs. 3 COUNT N In chess, the **queen** is the most powerful piece, which can be moved in any direction. 4 COUNT N A **queen** is also a playing card with a picture of a queen on it. *...the queen of spades.*

queer /kwɪə/, **queerer, queerest.** ADJ **Queer** means strange or peculiar. *...a queer sensation.*

quell /kwel/, **quells, quelling, quelled.** 1 VB WITH OBJ To **quell** opposition or violent behaviour means to stop it by using persuasion or force. *The police had been called in to quell a minor disturbance.* 2 VB WITH OBJ If you **quell** feelings such as fear or grief, you stop yourself having these feelings. *I was trying to quell a growing unease.*

quench /kwentʃ/, **quenches, quenching, quenched.** VB WITH OBJ You **quench** your thirst when you are thirsty by having a drink.

querulous /kwerjᵒʊləs/. ADJ Someone who is **querulous** often complains about things; a formal use.

query /kwɪəri¹/, **queries, querying, queried.** 1 COUNT N OR UNCOUNT N A **query** is a question about a particular point. *If you have any queries, please don't hesitate to write... The assistant accepted my cheque without query.* 2 REPORT VB You can use **query** to say that someone asks a question. *'How much do I owe you?' I queried.* 3 VB WITH OBJ If you **query** something, you ask about it because you are not sure if it is correct. *Your expenses have been queried by the tax man.*

quest /kwest/, **quests.** COUNT N A **quest** is a long and difficult search for something; a literary use. *...the quest for truth.*

question /kwestʃəᵒn/, **questions, questioning, questioned.** 1 COUNT N A **question** is something which you say or write in order to ask about a particular matter. *Jill began to ask Fred a lot of questions about his childhood... A panel of experts will answer questions on education.* 2 VB WITH OBJ If you **question** someone, you ask them a lot of questions about something. *I started questioning her about Jane and Anthony.* 3 VB WITH OBJ If you **question** something, you express your doubts about whether it is true, reasonable, or worthwhile. *No one ever questioned the necessity of the visit.* 4 UNCOUNT N WITH SUPP If there is **question** about a particular matter, there is doubt or uncertainty about it. *There has been some question as to whether or not the President will resign.* 5 COUNT N WITH SUPP A **question** is also a problem or point which needs to be discussed. *His resignation raised the question of his successor... There is another side to the missile question.* 6 COUNT N In an examination, a **question** is a problem which is set in order to test your knowledge or ability. *You have to answer four questions in two hours.*

PHRASES • If something is **beyond question,** there is no doubt at all about it. *She knew beyond question that I was a person who could be trusted.* • If you **call** something **into question,** you express serious doubts about it. *Are you calling my professional competence into question?* • If something is **open to question,** it is not yet certain and people may disagree about it. • If something is **out of the question,** it is impossible. *She knew that a holiday this year was out of the question.* • If **there is no question** of something, it is impossible. *With so much happening there was no question of getting a full night's sleep.* • If you do something **without question,** you do it without arguing or asking why it is necessary. • The time, place, or thing **in question** is the time, place, or thing you have just been talking about. *Did James have dinner with you on the night in question?*

questionable /kwestʃənəbəᵒl/. ADJ If something is **questionable,** it may be wrong or unsuitable. *...questionable projects like convention centres.*

question mark, question marks. COUNT N A **question mark** is the punctuation mark (?).

questionnaire /kwᵒestʃəneə/, **questionnaires.** COUNT N A **questionnaire** is a written list of questions which are answered by a number of people in order to provide information for a report or survey.

queue /kjuː/, **queues, queueing** or **queuing, queued.** 1 COUNT N A **queue** is a line of people or vehicles that are waiting for something. *She was in the queue for coffee.* 2 VB When people **queue** or **queue** up, they stand in a line waiting for something. *They had queued for hours to get in... People were queueing up for his autograph.*

quibble /kwɪbəᵒl/, **quibbles, quibbling, quibbled.** 1 VB When people **quibble,** they argue about a small matter which is not important. 2 COUNT N A **quibble** is a minor objection to something.

quick /kwɪk/, **quicker, quickest.** 1 ADJ **Quick** means moving or doing things with great speed. *She was precise and quick in her movements... Her hands were quick and strong.* ♦ **quickly** ADV *I walked quickly up the passage.* 2 ADJ Something that is **quick** takes or lasts only a short time. *Let's just have a quick look at that... ...a quick visit.* ♦ **quickly** ADV *They embraced quickly.* 3 ADJ **Quick** also means happening with very little delay. *You're likely to get a quicker reply if you telephone... John was quick to help him.* ♦ **quickly** ADV *She wants to get the whole thing over with as quickly as possible.* 4 **quick off the mark:** see **mark.** • **quick on the uptake:** see **uptake.**

quicken /kwɪkəᵒn/, **quickens, quickening, quickened.** ERG VB If something **quickens** or **is quickened,** it moves at a greater speed. *This thought made him quicken his pace.*

quicksand /kwɪksænd/. UNCOUNT N **Quicksand** is deep, wet sand that you sink into when you try to walk on it.

quid /kwɪd/. **Quid** is also the plural. COUNT N A **quid** is a pound in money. an informal use.

quiet /kwaɪət/, **quieter, quietest; quiets, quieting, quieted.** 1 ADJ Something or someone that is **quiet** makes only a small amount of noise. *Bal said in a quiet voice, 'I have resigned.'... The music had gone very quiet.* ♦ **quietly** ADV *'I'm going to do it,' I said quietly.* 2 ADJ If a place is **quiet,** there is very little noise there. *It was very quiet in there; you could just hear the wind moving the trees.* ♦ **quietness** UNCOUNT N *Winter brings a strange quietness to the seashore.* 3 ADJ You also say that a place is **quiet** when nothing exciting or important happens there. *The village is so quiet now.* 4 UNCOUNT N **Quiet** is silence. *Ralph was on his feet too, shouting for quiet.* 5 PRED ADJ If you are **quiet,** you do not say anything. *Be quiet and listen.* ♦ **quietly** ADV *We lay quietly.* 6 ADJ You describe activities as **quiet** when they happen in secret or in such a way that people do not notice. *The funeral was as quiet as the marriage had been.* 7 ADJ You describe colours or clothes as **quiet** when they are not bright or noticeable.

PHRASES • If something is done **on the quiet,** it is done secretly, or so that people do not notice. • If you **keep quiet** about something, you do not say anything about it. *You must keep quiet about what you saw.*

quiet down. PHR VB To **quiet down** means to become less noisy, less active, or calmer; an American use.

quieten /kwaɪətəᵒn/, **quietens, quietening, quietened.** VB WITH OBJ If you **quieten** someone, you make them become less noisy.

quieten down. PHR VB To **quieten down** means to become less noisy, less active, or calmer; a British use. *Things are quietening down.*

quill /kwɪl/, **quills.** 1 COUNT N A **quill** is a pen made from a bird's feather. 2 COUNT N A bird's **quills** are the large, stiff feathers on its wings and tail. 3 COUNT N A porcupine's **quills** are the long, stiff, sharp points on its body.

quilt /kwɪlt/, **quilts.** COUNT N A **quilt** is a bed covering filled with feathers or other warm, soft material.

quilted /kwɪltɪ²d/. ADJ **Quilted** clothes or coverings consist of two layers of fabric with a layer of thick material between them. *...a quilted jacket.*

quinine /kwɪniːn/. UNCOUNT N **Quinine** is a drug used to treat fevers such as malaria.

quip /kwɪp/, **quips.** COUNT N A **quip** is an amusing or clever remark; an old-fashioned use.

quirk /kwɜːk/, **quirks.** 1 COUNT N A **quirk** is a habit or aspect of a person's character which is odd or unusual. 2 COUNT N A **quirk** is also a strange occurrence that is difficult to explain. *By one of those strange quirks of fate, both had died within a few days of each other.*

quit /kwɪt/, **quits, quitting. Quit** is used in the present tense, and is the past tense and past participle. 1 VB WITH OR WITHOUT OBJ If you **quit** doing something, you stop doing it; mainly used in American English. *Jack wants to quit smoking... A week later he quit.* 2 PHRASE If people who are arguing or fighting **call it quits,** they agree to stop their argument or fight; an informal use. *We decided to call it quits.*

quite /kwaɪt/. 1 SUBMOD OR ADV You use **quite** to indicate that something is the case to a fairly great extent but not to a very great extent. *He was quite young... I could save quite a lot of money... He calls quite often... I quite enjoy looking round museums.* 2 SUBMOD OR ADV You also use **quite** to emphasize that something is completely the case or very much the case. *I stood quite still... Oh I quite agree... Quite frankly, I'm too miserable to care.* 3 ADV You use **quite** after a negative to reduce the force of the negative, and to express uncertainty or politeness. *It's not quite big enough... I didn't quite understand what it was all about... I don't know quite where to go.* 4 PHRASE You use **quite a** to emphasize that something is unusual, impressive, or significant. *It was quite a sight... They have quite a problem.* 5 CONVENTION You can say **'quite'** to express your agreement with someone; a formal use. *'It does a lot for public relations.'—'Quite.'*

quiver /kwɪvə/, **quivers, quivering, quivered.** VB If something **quivers,** it shakes or trembles. *His fingers quivered uncontrollably.* Also SING N *Her whole body gave a slight quiver.*

quiz /kwɪz/, **quizzes.** COUNT N A **quiz** is a game or competition in which someone tests your knowledge by asking you questions. *...musical quizzes on TV.*

quizzical /kwɪzɪkəᵒl/. ADJ If you give someone a **quizzical** look, you look at them with a slight smile, because you are suspicious of their behaviour or amused by it.

quota /kwəʊtə/, **quotas.** COUNT N A **quota** is a quantity of something that has been limited or is officially allowed. *...an import quota of 1.6m cars... ...a daily food quota.*

quotation /kwəʊteɪʃə^{0}n/, **quotations.** 1 COUNT N A **quotation** is a sentence or phrase from a book, poem, or play. *...a quotation from a novel by Somerset Maugham.* 2 COUNT N When someone gives you a **quotation,** they tell you how much they will charge to do a particular piece of work. *They submitted quotations and agreed prices.*

quotation mark, quotation marks. COUNT N **Quotation marks** are punctuation marks used in writing to show where speech or a quotation begins and ends. They are usually written or printed as ' and '.

quote /kwəʊt/, **quotes, quoting, quoted.** 1 VB WITH OR WITHOUT OBJ If you **quote** someone or something, you repeat the exact words that they have written or said. *He was quoted in the paper as saying: 'This strike is evil.'... She quoted the Chinese proverb about candles... ...quoting from a book he'd read.* 2 VB WITH OBJ If you **quote** something such as a law or a fact, you state it because it supports what you are saying. *They quote figures to compare the costs of adult education in different countries.* 3 COUNT N A **quote** from a book, poem, or play is a sentence or phrase from it. *...a quote from the Bible.* 4 COUNT N A **quote** for a piece of work is the price that someone says they will charge you to do the work. *Get a quote from a caterer for a big party.* 5 PLURAL N **Quotes** are the same as quotation marks; an informal use.

Rr

rabbi /ræbaɪ/, **rabbis.** COUNT N A **rabbi** is a Jewish religious leader.

rabbit /ræbɪt/, **rabbits.** COUNT N A **rabbit** is a small furry animal with long ears. Rabbits live in holes in the ground.

rabble /ræbə^{0}l/. SING N A **rabble** is a crowd of noisy, disorderly people. *...a rabble of boys and girls of all ages.*

rabid /ræbɪd, reɪ-/. 1 ATTRIB ADJ You use **rabid** to describe someone who has very strong and unreasonable opinions. *...a rabid feminist.* 2 ADJ A **rabid** animal is infected with rabies. *...a rabid dog.*

rabies /reɪbi^{1}z/. UNCOUNT N **Rabies** is a serious infectious disease which causes people and animals to go mad and die.

race /reɪs/, **races, racing, raced.** 1 COUNT N A **race** is a competition to see who is the fastest, for example in running or driving. *She came second in the race... The race is run through the streets of London.* 2 SING N WITH SUPP A **race** for power or control is a situation in which people compete for power or control. *The race for the White House is now on... ...the arms race.* 3 VB WITH OBJ OR ADJUNCT If you **race** someone or **race** against them, you compete with them in a race. *They would often race one another to the bus stop... She has raced against some of the best runners in the country.* ♦ **racing** UNCOUNT N *...motor racing... ...a racing car.* 4 VB WITH ADJUNCT If you **race** somewhere, you go there as quickly as possible. *She raced down the stairs... We had to race across London to get the train.* 5 VB If your heart **races,** it beats very quickly. *His heart raced as he saw the plane coming in to land.* 6 COUNT N OR UNCOUNT N A **race** is also one of the major groups which human beings can be divided into according to their physical features, such as their skin colour. *...discrimination on the grounds of colour or race.*

PHRASES ● If you describe a situation as **a race against time,** you mean you have to work very fast to get something done. ● See also **human race, rat race.**

racecourse /reɪskɔːs/, **racecourses.** COUNT N A **racecourse** is a track on which horses race; a British use.

racehorse /reɪshɔːs/, **racehorses.** COUNT N A **racehorse** is a horse that is trained to run in races.

race relations. PLURAL N **Race relations** are the ways in which people of different races behave towards each other. *...efforts to improve race relations.*

racial /reɪʃə^{0}l/. ADJ **Racial** describes things relating to people's race. *...racial prejudice... ...racial harmony.* ♦ **racially** ADV *...children of racially mixed parentage.*

racialism /reɪʃəlɪzə^{0}m/. UNCOUNT N **Racialism** is the same as **racism.**

racism /reɪsɪzə^{0}m/. UNCOUNT N **Racism** is the belief that people of particular races are inferior to others, and behaviour which is a result of this belief; used showing disapproval. *...subtle forms of racism... ...a struggle against racism.* ♦ **racist** /reɪsɪst/ COUNT N OR ADJ *He's a racist and a sexist... ...racist posters.*

rack /ræk/, **racks, racking, racked;** the verb is also spelled **wrack** in American English. 1 COUNT N A **rack** is a piece of equipment used for holding things. *He rinsed the plates and put them on the rack to drain.* 2 VB WITH OBJ If someone **is racked** by something, it causes them great suffering or pain; a literary use. *She stood there, racked by indecision, and began to cry.* 3 PHRASE If you **rack** your **brains,** you try very hard to think of something; an informal use.

racket /rækɪt/, **rackets;** also spelled **racquet** in meaning 3. 1 SING N A **racket** is a loud unpleasant noise. *...the non-stop racket that a healthy baby makes.* 2 COUNT N You can refer to an illegal activity used to make money as a **racket.** *He was involved in an insurance racket.* 3 COUNT N A **racket** is also a bat in the shape of an oval with strings across it which is used in games such as tennis and badminton.

racy /reɪsi^1/. ADJ **Racy** writing or behaviour is lively, amusing, and slightly shocking. *...a racy, romantic historical novel.*

radar /reɪdɑː/. UNCOUNT N **Radar** is a way of discovering the position or speed of things that cannot be seen, using radio signals. *His speed was checked by radar.*

radiance /reɪdɪəns/. 1 UNCOUNT N **Radiance** is great happiness which is shown in someone's face. *...the radiance of her features... Hilary lost a little of her radiance.* 2 UNCOUNT N **Radiance** is also a glowing light shining from something. *The candle's light threw a faint radiance on the sleeping girl.*

radiant /reɪdɪənt/. 1 ADJ Someone who is **radiant** is so happy that their joy shows in their face. *Charlotte, you look radiant.* 2 ADJ Something that is **radiant** glows brightly. *...a morning of radiant light.*

radiate /reɪdi^{1}eɪt/, **radiates, radiating, radiated.** 1 VB If things **radiate** from a place, they form a pattern that spreads out like lines drawn from the centre of a circle. *...roads that radiated before us... Rods radiate outwards from the centre.* 2 VB WITH OBJ OR 'from' If you **radiate** an emotion or quality or if it **radiates** from you, people can see it very clearly in your face and in your behaviour. *There was a tenderness that radiated from her.*

radiation /reɪdi^{1}eɪʃə^{0}n/. 1 UNCOUNT N **Radiation** is very small particles of a radioactive substance that can cause illness and death. *Those exposed to a very large amount of radiation experience internal bleeding.* 2 UNCOUNT N **Radiation** is also energy that comes from a particular source. *...heat radiation.*

radiator /reɪdɪeɪtə/, **radiators.** 1 COUNT N A **radiator** is a hollow metal device which is connected to a central heating system and used to heat a room. 2 COUNT N A car **radiator** is the part of the engine which is used to cool the engine.

radical /rædɪkə^{0}l/, **radicals.** 1 COUNT N A **radical** is someone who believes that there should be great changes in society and tries to bring about these changes. *...a new group of radicals who turned against the established social order.* Also ADJ *The League had become too radical.* 2 ADJ **Radical** also refers to things that relate to the basic nature of something. *...a radical disagreement over fundamentals.* ♦ **radically** ADV *Attitudes towards education will have to change radically.*

radii /reɪdɪaɪ/. **Radii** is the plural of **radius.**

radio /reɪdɪəʊ/, **radios, radioing, radioed.** 1 UNCOUNT N **Radio** is a system of sending sound over a distance using electrical signals. *...radio waves... We managed to establish radio communication with them.* 2 SING N OR UNCOUNT N You refer to the broadcasting of programmes for the public to listen to as **radio.** *...one of those plays that are the stuff of radio... ...a local radio station.* 3 COUNT N A **radio** is also the piece of equipment used to listen to radio programmes. *She switched on the radio.* 4 VB WITH OR WITHOUT OBJ If you **radio** someone, you send a message to them by radio. *I had radioed Rick and arranged to have a car waiting for me... The captain had radioed ahead and the security guards were waiting.*

radioactive /reɪdɪəʊæktɪv/. ADJ Something that is **radioactive** contains a substance that produces energy in the form of powerful and harmful rays. *...radioactive waste.*

radioactivity /reɪdɪəʊæktɪvɪ^{1}ti^1/. UNCOUNT N **Radioactivity** is radioactive energy. *...a serious leak of radioactivity.*

radiography /reɪdɪɒgrəfi^1/. UNCOUNT N **Radiography** is the process of taking X-rays.

radiology /reɪdɪɒləʤi^1/. UNCOUNT N **Radiology** is the branch of medical science that uses radioactivity.

radiotherapy /reɪdɪəʊθerəpi^1/. UNCOUNT N **Radiotherapy** is the treatment of diseases such as cancer using radiation.

radish /rædɪʃ/, **radishes.** COUNT N A **radish** is a small red or white root vegetable which is eaten raw.

radius /reɪdɪəs/, **radii** /reɪdɪaɪ/. 1 COUNT N The **radius** of a circle is the distance from its centre to its outside edge. 2 SING N WITH SUPP **Radius** also refers to the distance in any direction from a particular point. *The missile landed within a half-mile radius of its target.*

RAF /ɑː aɪ ef, ræf/. **RAF** is a written abbreviation for 'Royal Air Force', the air force of the United Kingdom.

raffle /ræfə^{0}l/, **raffles.** COUNT N A **raffle** is a competition in which you buy numbered tickets. If your ticket is chosen, you win a prize. *...organizing a raffle.*

raft /rɑːft/, **rafts.** COUNT N A **raft** is a floating platform made from large pieces of wood tied together.

rafter /rɑːftə/, **rafters.** COUNT N **Rafters** are the sloping pieces of wood that support a roof.

rag /ræg/, **rags.** 1 COUNT N OR UNCOUNT N A **rag** is a piece of old cloth which you can use to clean or wipe things. *Wiping his hands on a rag, he went out to the car... ...a crumpled piece of rag.* 2 PLURAL N **Rags** are old, torn clothes. *They were thin and hungry, dressed in rags.* 3 COUNT N People refer to a newspaper as a **rag** when they do not have a high opinion of it; an informal use. *...the local rag.*

rage /reɪʤ/, **rages, raging, raged.** 1 UNCOUNT N OR COUNT N **Rage** is strong, uncontrollable anger. *She was trembling with rage... I stormed out of the room in a rage.* 2 VB OR REPORT VB If you **rage** about something, you speak or think very angrily about it. *'How do you mean, you can't tell me?' he raged.* 3 VB If something **rages,** it continues with great force or violence. *There was a monsoon raging outside... The debate raged throughout the whole day.* 4 PHRASE If something is **all the rage,** it is very popular and fashionable; an informal use.

ragged /rægɪd/. ADJ **Ragged** things or people are old, untidy, and in bad condition. *...ragged cotton garments... ...a ragged, skinny man of about fifty.*

raging /reɪʤɪŋ/. ATTRIB ADJ **Raging** feelings or desires are very intense and severe. *...a raging thirst.*

raid /reɪd/, **raids, raiding, raided.** VB WITH OBJ When soldiers, the police, or criminals **raid** a place, they enter it by force to attack it, or to look for someone or something. *Blanco's supporters are still raiding villages along the border... Their headquarters in London were raided by the police.* Also COUNT N *...police raids... ...a series of bank raids.*

raider /reɪdə/, **raiders.** COUNT N **Raiders** are people who take part in a raid.

rail /reɪl/, **rails.** 1 COUNT N A **rail** is a horizontal bar which is fixed to something and used as a fence or as a support for hanging things on. *Holding on to the rail with one hand, he pulled himself up... ...picture rails... ...a towel rail.* 2 COUNT N The steel bars which trains run on are called **rails.** 3 UNCOUNT N If you travel or send something by **rail,** you travel or send it in a train. *I usually go by rail... ...rail travel.*

railing /reɪlɪŋ/, **railings.** COUNT N A **railing** is a fence made from metal bars. *I peered through the railings into the courtyard.*

railroad /reɪlrəʊd/, **railroads.** COUNT N A **railroad** is the same as a railway; an American use.

railway /reɪlweɪ/, **railways;** a British word. 1 COUNT N A **railway** is a route along which trains travel on steel rails. *...the railway to Addis Ababa... ...the early days of railways.* 2 COUNT N A **railway** is also a company or organization that operates railway routes. *...the Great Western Railway.*

railway line, railway lines. 1 COUNT N A **railway line** is a route along which trains travel on steel rails. *...the railway line from London to Brighton.* 2 COUNT N A **railway line** is also the steel rails on which trains travel. *... a body found in the undergrowth near a railway line.*

rain /reɪn/, **rains, raining, rained.** 1 UNCOUNT N **Rain** is water that falls from the clouds in small drops. *You can't go home in this rain... A light rain had begun to fall.* 2 VB When rain falls, you can say that it is **raining.** *It had started to rain.* 3 VB WITH ADJUNCT OR OBJ If something **rains** from above, or **rains** down, it falls rapidly in large quantities. *Ash rained from the sky... ...raining down arrows from both sides.*

rain off. PHR VB If a sports match **is rained off,** it cannot take place because of the rain.

rainbow /reɪnbəʊ/, **rainbows.** COUNT N A **rainbow** is the arch of different colours that you sometimes see in the sky when it is raining.

raincoat /reɪnkəʊt/, **raincoats.** COUNT N A **raincoat** is a waterproof coat.

raindrop /reɪndrɒp/, **raindrops.** COUNT N A **raindrop** is a single drop of rain.

rainfall /reɪnfɔːl/. UNCOUNT N **Rainfall** is the amount of rain that falls in a place during a particular period of time. *...the average monthly rainfall of London.*

rainforest /reɪnfɒrɪst/, **rainforests.** COUNT N OR UNCOUNT N A **rainforest** is a thick forest of tall trees found in tropical areas where there is a lot of rain. *...100 hectares of virgin rainforest.*

rainstorm /reɪnstɔːm/, **rainstorms.** COUNT N A **rainstorm** is a heavy fall of rain.

rainwater /reɪnwɔːtə/. UNCOUNT N **Rainwater** is rain that has been stored in a tank or bucket.

rainy /reɪni^1/. 1 ADJ If it is **rainy,** it is raining a lot. *Most tropical areas have rainy and dry seasons... ...a rainy Sunday afternoon.* 2 PHRASE If you are saving something **for a rainy day,** you are saving it until a time when you might need it. *They put part of the money in the bank for a rainy day.*

raise /reɪz/, **raises, raising, raised.** 1 VB WITH OBJ If you **raise** something, you move it to a higher position. *He tried to raise the window, but the sash cord was broken... She raised her eyebrows in surprise.* ♦ **raised** ADJ *He stood on a raised platform.* 2 VB WITH OBJ If you **raise** the rate or level of something, you increase it. *The maximum speed was raised to seventy miles per hour.* 3 VB WITH OBJ To **raise** the standard of something means to improve it. *Putting teachers in day nurseries would raise standards.* 4 VB WITH OBJ If you **raise** your voice, you speak more loudly. 5 COUNT N A **raise** is an increase in your wages or salary; an American use. 6 VB WITH OBJ To **raise** money for a charity or a cause means to get people to donate money towards it. *He raised £300 to finance it.* 7 VB WITH OBJ To **raise** a child means to look after it until it is grown up. *It was no place to raise a child.* 8 VB WITH OBJ To **raise** a particular type of animal or crop means to breed the animal or grow the crop. *He moved to Petaluma to raise chickens.* 9 VB WITH OBJ If you **raise** a subject, objection, or question, you mention it or bring it to someone's attention. *You would have to raise that with Mr Gerran personally.*

raisin /reɪzə^{0}n/, **raisins.** COUNT N **Raisins** are dried grapes.

rake /reɪk/, **rakes, raking, raked.** 1 COUNT N A **rake** is a garden tool consisting of a row of metal teeth attached to a long handle. 2 VB WITH OBJ To **rake** leaves or soil means to use a rake to gather the leaves or make the soil smooth. *Jeremy had raked the fallen leaves into a pile... The field had been raked.*

rake in. PHR VB If someone **is raking in** money, they are earning a lot of it fairly easily; an informal use.

rake up. PHR VB If you **rake up** something unpleasant or embarrassing from the past, you remind someone of it.

rally /ræli^1/, **rallies, rallying, rallied.** 1 COUNT N A **rally** is a large public meeting held in support of something such as a political party. *...a big anti-government rally in Hyde Park.* 2 COUNT N A **rally** is also a competition in which vehicles are driven over public roads. 3 ERG VB When people **rally** to something, they unite to support it. *She believed that the voters would rally to the Conservatives... They made a final effort to rally their supporters.* 4 VB When a sick person **rallies,** they become stronger again.

rally round. PHR VB When people **rally round,** they work as a group in order to support someone at a difficult time.

ram /ræm/, **rams, ramming, rammed.** 1 VB WITH OBJ If one vehicle **rams** another, it crashes into it with a lot of force. *The ship had been rammed by a British destroyer.* 2 VB WITH OBJ AND ADJUNCT If you **ram** something somewhere, you push it there with great force. *I rammed the bolt back across the door.* 3 COUNT N A **ram** is an adult male sheep.

Ramadan /ræmədæn/. UNCOUNT N **Ramadan** is the ninth month of the Muslim year, during which Muslims fast from sunrise to sunset.

ramble /ræmbə^{0}l/, **rambles, rambling, rambled.** 1 COUNT N A **ramble** is a long walk in the countryside. *We were out on a country ramble.* Also VB WITH ADJUNCT *...rambling over the Yorkshire hills.* 2 VB When someone **rambles,** they talk for a long time in a confused way. *He often rambled and said strange things.*

rambling /ræmblɪŋ/. 1 ADJ A **rambling** building is big and old with an irregular shape. *We bought a rambling old house near the village.* 2 ADJ **Rambling** speech or writing is very long and confused. *She wrote me a long rambling letter.*

ramification /ræmɪfɪkeɪʃə^{0}n/, **ramifications.** COUNT N The **ramifications** of a decision, idea, or plan are all its consequences and effects, especially ones which were not obvious at first; a formal use. *Not many people actually understand the ramifications of these guidelines.*

ramp /ræmp/, **ramps.** COUNT N A **ramp** is a sloping surface between two places that are at different levels. *It was driven up a ramp and straight on to the train.*

rampage /ræmpeɪdʒ/, **rampages, rampaging, rampaged.** 1 VB When people or animals **rampage,** they rush about in a wild or violent way, causing damage or destruction. *...elephants rampaging through the bush.* 2 PHRASE If people **go on the rampage,** they rush about in a wild or violent way. *A section of the crowd broke loose and went on the rampage.*

rampant /ræmpənt/. ADJ If a crime, feeling, or disease is **rampant,** it is growing or spreading in an uncontrolled way. *..the abuses now rampant in the American legal system.*

ramshackle /ræmʃækə^{0}l/. ATTRIB ADJ A **ramshackle** building is badly made or in a very bad condition. *...a ramshackle cottage.*

ran /ræn/. **Ran** is the past tense of **run.**

ranch /rɑːntʃ/, **ranches.** COUNT N A **ranch** is a large farm, especially one used for raising farm animals.

rancid /rænsɪd/. ADJ If butter, bacon, or other fatty foods are **rancid,** they have gone bad and taste unpleasant.

rancour /ræŋkə/; spelled **rancor** in American English. UNCOUNT N **Rancour** is a feeling of deep and bitter hatred; a formal use. *He was shaken by rage and rancour.*

random /rændə^{0}m/. 1 ADJ Something that is done in a **random** way is done without a definite plan or pattern. *The way the books were arranged seemed completely random... ...a random selection.* 2 PHRASE If something is done **at random,** it is done without a definite plan or pattern. *He opened the book at random... I let my thoughts come at random.*

randy /rændi^1/. ADJ Someone who is **randy** is eager to have sexual intercourse; an informal British use.

rang /ræŋ/. **Rang** is the past tense of some meanings of **ring.**

range /reɪnʒ/, **ranges, ranging, ranged.** 1 COUNT N WITH SUPP The **range** of something is the maximum area within which it can reach things or detect things. *What is the range of their transmitters?... ...medium range ballistic missiles.* 2 SING N WITH SUPP A **range** of things is a number of different things of the same general kind. *...a wide range of electrical goods... ...the range of research activities in the university.* 3 COUNT N WITH SUPP A **range** is the complete group that is included between two points on a scale of measurement or quality. *The age range is from six months to forty-seven years.* 4 VB WITH ADJUNCT When things **range** between two points or **range** from one point to another, they vary within these points on a scale of measurement or quality. *Their politics ranged from liberal to radical... They were offered increases ranging from £6.71 to £16.31 a week.* 5 VB WITH ADJUNCT If a piece of writing or speech **ranges** over a group of topics, it includes all those topics. *The book ranges historically as far back as the Renaissance... The conversation ranged widely.* 6 COUNT N WITH SUPP A **range** of mountains or hills is a line of them. 7 COUNT N A rifle **range** or a firing **range** is a place where people can practise shooting at targets.

PHRASES • If something is **within range,** it is near enough to be reached or detected. If it is **out of range,** it is too far away to be reached or detected. *We managed to keep out of range.* • If you shoot something **at close range,** you are very close to it when you shoot it.

ranger /reɪndʒə/, **rangers.** COUNT N A **ranger** is a person whose job is to look after a forest or park.

rank /ræŋk/, **ranks, ranking, ranked.** 1 COUNT N OR UNCOUNT N Someone's **rank** is their position or grade in an organization. *She achieved the rank of professor at the age of 31... He wasn't getting the salary to which he was entitled by rank.* 2 ERG VB When you say what something **ranks,** you state its position on a scale. *The island ranks as one of the poorest of the whole region... They are ranked according to the quality of things they make.* 3 PLURAL N The **ranks** are the ordinary members of an organization, especially of the armed forces. *...a senior officer who had risen from the ranks.* 4 PLURAL N WITH SUPP When you become a member of a large group of people, you can say that you are joining its **ranks.** *...the growing ranks of the unemployed.* 5 ATTRIB ADJ You use **rank** to describe a very bad or undesirable quality; a formal use. *...rank corruption... ...rank favouritism.* 6 ADJ You can describe something with a strong and unpleasant smell as **rank;** a formal use.

PHRASES • If someone **pulls rank,** they make unfair use of the authority that they have in an organization. • When the members of a group **close ranks,** they support each other in a united way to oppose any attack or criticism; used showing disapproval.

rank and file. COLL N The **rank and file** are the ordinary members of an organization rather than the leaders or officers. *...political differences between the leadership and the rank and file.*

ransack /rænsæk/, **ransacks, ransacking, ransacked.** VB WITH OBJ If you **ransack** a building or a room, you disturb everything in it and leave it in a mess, because you are looking for something. *Detectives ransacked the house.*

ransom /rænsə^{0}m/, **ransoms.** 1 COUNT N A **ransom** is an amount of money that is demanded for the release of a kidnapped person. *The family paid a ransom of £50,000 for the child's release.* 2 PHRASE If someone **holds** you **to ransom,** they keep you as a prisoner until money is paid for you to be set free.

rant /rænt/, **rants, ranting, ranted.** VB If someone **rants,** they talk in a loud, excited, and angry way. *He would rant like this till she could not bear it any more.*

rap /ræp/, **raps, rapping, rapped.** 1 VB WITH OR WITHOUT OBJ, WITH ADJUNCT If you **rap** on something or if you **rap** it, you hit it with a series of quick blows. *He rapped on the table and called for silence.* 2 COUNT N A **rap** is a quick hit or knock against something. *A light rap sounded at the door.*

PHRASES • If you receive **a rap over the knuckles,** you receive a warning or criticism. • If you **take the rap,** you are blamed or punished for something, even if it is not your fault; an informal use. *Lloyd will have to take the rap.*

rap out. PHR VB If you **rap out** an order or a question, you say it quickly and sharply. *'Is that the truth?' he suddenly rapped out.*

rapacious /rəpeɪʃəs/. ADJ A **rapacious** person is extremely greedy for money; a formal use. *...rapacious businessmen.*

rape /reɪp/, **rapes, raping, raped.** VB WITH OBJ When a man **rapes** a woman, he forces her to have sex with him against her will. *...an organization to help women who have been raped.* Also UNCOUNT N OR COUNT N *She had to testify to his attempts at rape... ...the riots, rapes, and muggings in our streets and parks.*

rapid /ræpɪd/, **rapids.** 1 ADJ Something that is **rapid** happens or moves very quickly. *...a time of rapid economic growth... He took a few rapid steps towards the beach.* ♦ **rapidly** ADV *The situation had rapidly deteriorated.* ♦ **rapidity** /rəpɪdɪ^{1}ti^1/ UNCOUNT N *The film shows the rapidity of the changes in this area of medicine.* 2 PLURAL N **Rapids** are parts of a river where the water moves very fast.

rapist /reɪpɪst/, **rapists.** COUNT N A **rapist** is a man who has raped a woman.

rapport /ræpɔː/. UNCOUNT N **Rapport** is a feeling of understanding and sympathy which two or more people share. *There is insufficient rapport between hospitals and family doctors.*

rapt /ræpt/. ADJ Someone who is **rapt** is so interested or fascinated by something that they cannot stop thinking about it. *Claud was staring at me, rapt... My audience listened in rapt silence.*

rapture /ræptʃə/, **raptures.** UNCOUNT N OR PLURAL N **Rapture** is an overpowering feeling of delight; a literary use. *...his face shining with rapture... ...the first raptures of their honeymoon.*

rapturous /ræptʃərəs/. ADJ A **rapturous** feeling or reaction is one of great happiness or enthusiasm. *...a rapturous reception from their supporters.*

rare /reə/, **rarer, rarest.** 1 ADJ Something that is **rare** is not common or does not happen very often, and is therefore interesting, valuable, or unusual. *Diane's hobby is collecting rare books... Cases of smallpox are extremely rare.* 2 ADJ **Rare** meat is very lightly cooked.

rarely /reəli^1/. ADV **Rarely** means not very often. *We rarely quarrel.*

rarity /reərɪ^{1}ti^1/, **rarities.** 1 COUNT N A **rarity** is something that is interesting or valuable because it is so unusual. *Blue marble was a rarity anywhere.* 2 UNCOUNT N The **rarity** of something is the fact that it is very uncommon. *Many animals are endangered by their rarity and beauty.*

rash /ræʃ/, **rashes.** 1 ADJ If you or your behaviour is **rash,** you do foolish things because you act without thinking carefully first. *Don't do anything rash... Some rash promises were made.* ♦ **rashly** ADV *I'm not a man who does things rashly.* 2 COUNT N A **rash** is an area of red spots on your skin which appear when you are ill or have an allergy. *...a man with a rash on one side of his neck.* 3 SING N A **rash** of events is a large number of them that all happen within a short period of time. *No one wishes to see a rash of strikes.*

rasher /ræʃə/, **rashers.** COUNT N A **rasher** of bacon is a thin slice of it.

rasp /rɑːsp/, **rasps, rasping, rasped.** VB To **rasp** means to make a harsh unpleasant sound. *Crickets rasped loudly... ...a dry rasping voice.* Also SING N *...the rasp of sandpaper on wood.*

raspberry /rɑːzbə^{0}ri^1/, **raspberries.** COUNT N A **raspberry** is a small, soft, red fruit that grows on bushes. *...raspberry jam.*

rat /ræt/, **rats.** 1 COUNT N A **rat** is an animal with a long tail which looks like a large mouse. 2 COUNT N You call someone a **rat** when you are angry with them because they have done something unpleasant; an informal use.

rate /reɪt/, **rates, rating, rated.** 1 COUNT N WITH SUPP The **rate** at which something happens is the speed or frequency with which it happens. *...the rapid rate of change which the industrial world is facing... The divorce rate is fantastically high... ...a rising rate of unemployment.* 2 COUNT N The **rate** of taxation or interest is its level, expressed as a percentage. *This money is taxed at the rate of 59%... ...a good rate of interest.* 3 PLURAL N Until 1990, **rates** were a local tax in Britain which was paid by people who owned buildings or who rented unfurnished buildings. 4 VB WITH OR WITHOUT OBJ You use **rate** to talk about your opinion of someone or something. For example, if someone **is rated** as brilliant, people consider them to be brilliant. *She was a self-taught geologist, rated as one of the best... Leontiev rated socialism highly... On a scale of one to ten, it probably rated about number seven.* 5 See also **rating.**

PHRASES ● If you say that **at this rate** something will happen, you mean that it will happen if the present situation continues. *At this rate we'll be millionaires by Christmas!* ● You use **at any rate** to indicate that the important thing is what you are going to say now and not what has just been said. *I don't think there's been an edition since 1977; at any rate that's the one I'll be referring to.*

ratepayer /reɪtpeɪə/, **ratepayers.** COUNT N In Britain, a **ratepayer** was a person who had to pay rates.

rather /rɑːðə/. 1 ADV OR SUBMOD You use **rather** to say politely that something is the case to a slight extent. *I'm rather puzzled by this question... He looked rather pathetic standing in the rain outside... I rather think it was three hundred and fifty pounds.* 2 ADV OR SUBMOD You also use **rather** to say that something is true to a large or surprising extent. *The company thought I did rather well.* 3 PHRASE If you say that you **would rather** do a particular thing, you mean that you would prefer to do that thing. *'What was all that about?'—'I'm sorry, I'd rather not say.'* 4 PREP OR CONJ You use **rather than** to introduce a statement saying what is not done, to contrast this with a statement saying what actually is done. *I have used familiar English names rather than scientific Latin ones.* 5 SENTENCE ADV You also use **rather** to introduce a correction or contrast to what you have just said. *This was no matter for congratulation, but rather a matter for vengeance.*

ratify /rætɪfaɪ/, **ratifies, ratifying, ratified.** VB WITH OBJ When people **ratify** a written agreement or document, they give their formal approval to it, usually by signing it; a formal use. *Over 90 countries ratified an agreement to ban the use of these chemicals.* ♦ **ratification** /rætɪfɪkeɪʃəⁿn/ UNCOUNT N *On each occasion, American objections prevented ratification of the proposals.*

rating /reɪtɪŋ/, **ratings.** 1 COUNT N A **rating** is a score or assessment based on how much of a particular quality something has. *...jobs which are assigned a low rating on the economic scale.* 2 PLURAL N The **ratings** are the statistics published each week which show how many people watch each television programme. *The ratings are a disaster and the reviews are worse.*

ratio /reɪʃɪəʊ/, **ratios.** COUNT N A **ratio** is a relationship between two numbers, amounts, or measurements, which shows how much greater one is than the other. For example, if there are two boys and six girls in a room, the ratio of boys to girls is one to three. *...a high teacher/pupil ratio... ...a ratio of one tutor to five students.*

ration /ræʃəⁿn/, **rations, rationing, rationed.** 1 COUNT N When something is scarce, your **ration** of it is the amount that you are allowed to have. *...monthly meat rations.* 2 VB WITH OBJ When something **is rationed,** you are only allowed to have a limited amount of it. *Meat, flour and sugar were all rationed.* ♦ **rationing** UNCOUNT N *...food and petrol rationing during the war.* 3 PLURAL N **Rations** are the food which is supplied to a soldier or a member of an expedition each day. *They had two days' rations.*

rational /ræʃəⁿnəl, -ʃənəⁿl/. ADJ A **rational** person is able to make decisions and judgements based on reason rather than emotion. *Let's talk about this like two rational people... Panic destroys rational thought.* ♦ **rationally** ADV *Let's discuss this rationally.* ♦ **rationality** /ræʃənælɪ¹ti¹/ UNCOUNT N *The debate soon lost all semblance of rationality.*

rationale /ræʃənɑːl/. SING N The **rationale** for a course of action, practice, or belief is the set of reasons on which it is based. *We discussed the rationale for taking city kids into the country.*

rationalism /ræʃəⁿnəlɪzəⁿm/. UNCOUNT N **Rationalism** is the belief that your life should be based on reason and not on emotions or religious beliefs. ♦ **rationalist** /ræʃəⁿnəlɪst/ COUNT N *Lavrov was a thorough rationalist.*

rationalize /ræʃəⁿnəlaɪz/, **rationalizes, rationalizing, rationalized;** also spelled **rationalise.** 1 VB WITH OBJ If you **rationalize** something that you are unhappy or unsure about, you think of reasons to justify it or explain it. *I rationalise my decision by saying that I need the money.* ♦ **rationalization** /ræʃəⁿnəlaɪzeɪʃəⁿn/ COUNT N OR UNCOUNT N *They devise elaborate rationalizations for their behaviour... ...periodic attempts at rationalization.* 2 VB WITH OBJ When a company, system, or industry **is rationalized,** it is made more efficient, especially by getting rid of staff and equipment. ♦ **rationalization** /ræʃəⁿnəlaɪzeɪʃəⁿn/ UNCOUNT N *...the continuing rationalization of the armed forces.*

rat race. SING N If you describe a situation as a **rat race,** you mean that the people in it are all competing fiercely with each other; used showing disapproval. *I was determined to get out of the rat race.*

rattle /rætəⁿl/, **rattles, rattling, rattled.** 1 ERG VB When something **rattles** or **is rattled,** it makes a series of short, regular knocking sounds because it is being shaken or it is hitting against something hard. *A cold November wind rattled the windows.* Also COUNT N *The rattle of the engine became louder.* 2 COUNT N A **rattle** is a baby's toy with loose bits inside which make a noise when the baby shakes it. 3 VB WITH OBJ If something **rattles** you, it makes you worried or annoyed. *His questions obviously rattled her.*

rattle off. PHR VB If you **rattle** something **off,** you say it or do it quickly and without much effort. *She rattled off a few names that I tried to write down.*

rattlesnake /rætəⁿlsneɪk/, **rattlesnakes.** COUNT N A **rattlesnake** is a poisonous American snake.

raucous /rɔːkəs/. ADJ A **raucous** voice is loud and harsh. *...raucous laughter.*

ravage /rævɪdʒ/, **ravages, ravaging, ravaged.** 1 VB WITH OBJ To **ravage** something means to harm or damage it so that it is almost destroyed. *...the diseases which ravage Aboriginal populations... ...a country ravaged by war.* 2 PLURAL N The **ravages** of the weather, time, or war are the bad effects these things have. *...the ravages of rain and sun.*

rave /reɪv/, **raves, raving, raved.** 1 VB If someone **raves,** they talk in an excited and uncontrolled way. *He started raving about the horror and brutality of war.* 2 VB WITH 'about' OR REPORT VB If you **rave** about something, you speak or write about it with great enthusiasm; an informal use. *People were raving about his fantastic course... One newspaper raved: 'the most exciting play I have ever seen.'* 3 COUNT N A **rave** notice or review is a very enthusiastic one; an informal use. *Stoppard's new play has received rave reviews.* 4 See also **raving.**

raven /reɪvəⁿn/, **ravens.** 1 COUNT N A **raven** is a large black bird with a deep harsh call. 2 ATTRIB ADJ **Raven** hair is shiny and black. *...a raven-haired girl.*

ravenous /rævənəs/. ADJ If you are **ravenous,** you are very hungry indeed. *Most infants have a ravenous appetite.*

ravine /rəviːn/, **ravines.** COUNT N A **ravine** is a very deep, narrow valley with steep sides.

raving /reɪvɪŋ/. ADJ If you describe someone as **raving** or **raving mad,** you mean they are completely mad; an informal use. *You're all raving lunatics... He went raving mad.*

ravish /rævɪʃ/, **ravishes, ravishing, ravished.** VB WITH OBJ If you **are ravished** by something that is very beautiful, it gives you great pleasure and delight; a literary use. *...ravished by the beauty of the language.*

ravishing /rævɪʃɪŋ/. ADJ Someone or something that is **ravishing** is very beautiful. *...a ravishing blonde.*

raw /rɔː/. 1 ADJ **Raw** food is uncooked. *...a piece of raw meat... ...a raw carrot.* 2 ATTRIB ADJ A **raw** substance is in its natural state before being processed. *...exports of raw cotton... ...raw rubber from Malaysia.* 3 ADJ If a part of your body is **raw,** it is sore because the skin has been damaged. *Every boy's feet had big raw blisters on them.* 4 ADJ If you describe someone as **raw,** you mean that they are too inexperienced to know how to behave properly. *He's just a raw kid.* 5 PHRASE If you have been given **a raw deal,** you have been treated unfairly; an informal use.

raw material, raw materials. COUNT N OR UNCOUNT N **Raw materials** are the natural substances used to make something, for example in an industrial process. *...coal, oil, gas, and other raw materials.*

ray /reɪ/, **rays.** 1 COUNT N A **ray** is a beam of heat or light. *...the rays of the sun... ...ultraviolet rays.* 2 SING N A **ray** of hope or comfort is a small amount that makes a bad situation seem better.

rayon /reɪɒn/. UNCOUNT N **Rayon** is a smooth fabric made from cotton, wool, or synthetic fibres.

raze /reɪz/, **razes, razing, razed.** VB WITH OBJ If people **raze** a building, town, or forest, they completely destroy it. *Many villages were razed to the ground.*

razor /reɪzə/, **razors.** COUNT N A **razor** is a tool used for shaving. *...an electric razor.*

razor blade, razor blades. COUNT N A **razor blade** is a small, thin, sharp piece of metal that you fix to a razor and use for shaving.

Rd. Rd is a written abbreviation for 'road'. *...49 St Johns Rd.*

-rd. SUFFIX **-rd** is added to most numbers written in figures and ending in 3 in order to form ordinal numbers. 3rd is pronounced the same as 'third'. *...3rd November 1972.*

re-. PREFIX **Re-** is used to form verbs and nouns that refer to the repeating of an action or process. For example, to re-read something means to read it again.

-'re. SUFFIX **-'re** is a short form of 'are' used in spoken English and informal written English. *You're quite right... What're you waiting for?*

reach /riːtʃ/, **reaches, reaching, reached.** 1 VB WITH OBJ When you **reach** a place, you arrive there. *It was dark by the time I reached their house... It took three days for the letter to reach me.* 2 VB WITH OR WITHOUT OBJ, WITH ADJUNCT If you **reach** in a particular direction, you stretch out your arm to do something or to get something. *He reached into his inside pocket and produced a pen... I reached out my hand to touch him.* 3 VB WITH OR WITHOUT OBJ If you say that you can **reach** something, you mean that you can touch it by stretching out your arm and hand. *I can't reach that shelf unless I stand on a chair... I can just reach.* 4 VB WITH OBJ You can say that you **reach** someone when you succeed in contacting them by telephone. *Where can I reach you?* 5 VB WITH OBJ OR ADJUNCT If someone or something **reaches** a place, level, or stage, they get as far or as high as that place, level, or condition. *When the water reached his waist, he had to start swimming... Rumours of an enemy invasion began to reach the capital... Unemployment has reached a very high level.* 6 VB WITH OBJ When people **reach** an agreement, decision, or result, they succeed in achieving it. *They managed to reach an agreement on rates of pay.* 7 PLURAL N WITH SUPP The upper or lower **reaches** of a place are the upper or lower parts of it. *...the upper reaches of the Amazon.*

react /ri¹ækt/, **reacts, reacting, reacted.** 1 VB When you **react** to something that has happened to you, you behave in a particular way because of it. *She tends to react strongly if he lights a cigarette.* 2 VB WITH 'against' If you **react** against the way other people behave, you deliberately behave in a different way. *They reacted against the formality of their predecessors.* 3 VB When someone **reacts** to a drug, they are made ill by it. *Her skin reacted to it.* 4 RECIP VB When one chemical substance **reacts** with another, it combines with it chemically to form another substance.

reaction /ri¹ækʃəⁿn/, **reactions.** 1 COUNT N OR UNCOUNT N WITH SUPP Your **reaction** to something is what you feel, say, or do because of it. *My immediate reaction was one of revulsion.* 2 COUNT N WITH 'against' A **reaction** against something is a way of behaving or doing something that is deliberately different from what has been done before. *My work has never been a reaction against Abstract Expressionism.* 3 COUNT N WITH 'against' If there is a **reaction** against something, it becomes unpopular. *This led to a reaction against public expenditure.* 4 PLURAL N You refer to your ability to move quickly in response to something, for example when you are in danger, as your **reactions.** *...a computer game designed to time their reactions.* 5 COUNT N A chemical **reaction** is a process in which two substances combine together chemically to form another substance.

reactionary /ri¹ækʃənəⁿri¹/, **reactionaries.** ADJ Someone who is **reactionary** tries to prevent social or political changes; used showing disapproval. *...reactionary forces.* Also COUNT N *...political reactionaries.*

reactor /ri¹æktə/, **reactors.** COUNT N A **reactor** is the same as a nuclear reactor.

read, reads, reading. Read is used in the present tense, when it is pronounced /riːd/, and is also the past tense and past participle, when it is pronounced /red/. 1 VB WITH OR WITHOUT OBJ When you **read** something that is written down, you look at written words or symbols and understand them. *Have you read that article?... I remember reading about it in the paper... I have never been able to read music.* 2 VB WITH OBJ OR PREP 'to' To **read** or **read** something out means to say written words aloud. *Could you just read out this next paragraph?... Shall I read to you?* 3 VB WITH ADJUNCT If you refer to how a piece of writing **reads,** you are referring to its style. *It read like a translation from the Latin.* 4 VB WITH COMPLEMENT You can use **read** to say what is written somewhere. For example, if a notice **reads** 'Exit', the word 'Exit' is written on it. 5 VB WITH OBJ If you **read** someone's moods or mind, you guess their feelings or thoughts. *He so often reads my thoughts.* 6 VB WITH OBJ When you **read** a meter or gauge, you look at it and record the figure on it. 7 VB WITH COMPLEMENT If a measuring device **reads** a particular amount, it shows that amount. *The thermometers are reading 108 degrees in the shade.* 8 VB WITH OBJ If you **read** a subject at university, you study it. 9 See also **reading.**

PHRASES • If you **read between the lines,** you understand what someone really means, even though they do not say it openly. • If a book or magazine is **a good read,** it is very enjoyable to read.

read into. PHR VB If you **read** a meaning **into** something, you think it is there although it may not be.

read up on. PHR VB If you **read up on** a subject, you read a lot about it so that you become informed on it.

readable /riːdəbəˀl/. ADJ A book or article that is **readable** is interesting and worth reading.

reader /riːdə/, **readers.** COUNT N A **reader** of a book, newspaper, or magazine is a person who reads it. *The paper is gathering one thousand new readers a week.*

readership /riːdəʃɪp/. SING N WITH SUPP The **readership** of a book, newspaper, or magazine is all the people who read it. *...a readership of about ten million people.*

readily /rɛdɪliˡ/. 1 ADV If you do something **readily,** you do it in a way which shows that you are willing to do it. *He readily accepted an invitation to dinner.* 2 ADV You also use **readily** to say that something can be done or obtained quickly and easily. *Personal computers are readily available these days.*

readiness /rɛdɪnɪ²s/. 1 UNCOUNT N **Readiness** is the state of being prepared for something. *He faces it with calm readiness and resolute determination.* 2 UNCOUNT N WITH TO-INF Your **readiness** to do something is your willingness to do it. *I restated our readiness to resume negotiations.*

reading /riːdɪŋ/, **readings.** 1 UNCOUNT N **Reading** is the activity of reading books. *I don't do a lot of reading.* 2 COUNT N WITH SUPP A poetry **reading** is an entertainment in which poetry is read to an audience. 3 COUNT N The **reading** on a meter or gauge is the figure or measurement that it shows.

readjust /riːədʒʌst/, **readjusts, readjusting, readjusted.** 1 VB OR REFL VB If you **readjust** or **readjust** yourself, you adapt to a new situation. *It is difficult to readjust to changing environments... The applicants readjust themselves to meet the availability of university places.* 2 VB WITH OBJ If you **readjust** something, you alter the position it is in. *He readjusted the saddle before getting on.*

readjustment /riːədʒʌstmə²nt/, **readjustments.** 1 UNCOUNT N OR COUNT N **Readjustment** is adapting to a new situation. *...a period of readjustment... The launch requires great readjustments on all sides.* 2 COUNT N OR UNCOUNT N A **readjustment** to something is an alteration to its controls so that it functions in a different way. *Most schools now face a readjustment of their timetables.*

ready /rɛdiˡ/, **readies, readying, readied.** 1 PRED ADJ If someone or something is **ready,** they have prepared themselves or have been prepared for something, or they now have the right qualities for something. *You're nowhere near ready for such a job... Lunch is ready... Their crops would soon be ready for harvesting.* 2 PRED ADJ WITH TO-INF If you are **ready** to do something, you are willing to do it or are about to do it. *...couples who are ready to move house in order to get work... I was ready to cry.* 3 PRED ADJ WITH 'for' If you are **ready** for something, you need it or want it. *We were all ready for sleep.* 4 ATTRIB ADJ You use **ready** to describe things that are able to appear or be used quickly and easily. *...ready cash.* 5 VB WITH OBJ OR REFL VB When you **ready** something, you prepare it for a particular purpose; a formal use. *The satellite would be readied with all possible haste.*

ready-made. 1 ATTRIB ADJ OR ADV If something that you buy is **ready-made,** you can use it immediately. *...ready-made products such as baked beans... You can buy your greenhouse ready-made.* 2 ADJ If you have a **ready-made** reply to a question, you can answer it immediately. *He had no ready-made answers.*

reaffirm /riːəfɜːm/, **reaffirms, reaffirming, reaffirmed.** REPORT VB If you **reaffirm** something, you state it again; a formal use. *The ministers reaffirmed their intention not to surrender... She reaffirmed that the laws would be changed.*

real /rɪəl/. 1 ADJ Something that is **real** actually exists and is not imagined, invented, or theoretical. *You must know the difference between what's real and make-believe... ...real or imagined feelings of inferiority.* 2 ADJ **Real** also means genuine and not artificial or an imitation. *...real leather... ...fancy chocolates, with real liqueurs inside.* 3 ATTRIB ADJ You also use **real** to say that something has all the characteristics or qualities that such a thing typically has. *...the only real accident that I've ever had... I used to tell him he wasn't a real Christian.* 4 ATTRIB ADJ **Real** can also mean that something is the true or original thing of its kind. *That is the real reason for the muddle... My real home is in Tshabo.* 5 SUBMOD **Real** is sometimes used instead of 'very'; an American use. *You and I must have lunch together real soon.*

PHRASES • If something is **for real,** it is actually happening or being done; an informal use. *It was done. I was on my own. For real.* • You use **in real terms** to talk about the actual value or cost of something. For example, if your salary rises by 5% but prices rise by 10%, your salary has fallen **in real terms.**

real estate. UNCOUNT N **Real estate** is property in the form of buildings and land; an American use. *He acquired a bit of real estate... ...real estate agents.*

realise /rɪəlaɪz/. See **realize.**

realism /rɪəlɪzəˀm/. 1 UNCOUNT N When people show **realism** in their behaviour, they recognize and accept the true nature of a situation and try to deal with it in a practical way. *He marvelled at his father's lack of realism.* 2 UNCOUNT N In painting, novels, and films, **realism** is the representing of things and people in a way that is like real life.

realist /rɪəlɪst/, **realists.** COUNT N A **realist** is someone who accepts the true nature of a situation and tries to deal with it practically. *I am a realist and know that all this cannot last.*

realistic /rɪəlɪstɪk/. 1 ADJ If you are **realistic** about a situation, you recognize and accept its true nature and try to deal with it practically. *They were more realistic about its long term commercial prospects... ...a realistic attempt to solve problems.* ♦ **realistically** ADV *She accepted the position realistically.* 2 ADJ A **realistic** painting, story, or film represents real life. *...a 19th century realistic novel.*

reality /riˡælɪˡtiˡ/, **realities.** 1 UNCOUNT N **Reality** is the real nature of everything, rather than the way someone imagines it to be. *He is out of touch with reality.* 2 COUNT N WITH SUPP The **reality** of a situation is the truth about it, especially when it is unpleasant. *...the harsh reality of daily life.* 3 COUNT N OR UNCOUNT N If something becomes a **reality,** it actually exists or is actually happening. *It is often hard to distinguish fantasy from reality... Day-dreams had become realities.* 4 PHRASE You can use **in reality** to state the real nature of something, when it contrasts with something that is incorrect or imaginary. *They imagined that they made the rules but, in reality, they were mere puppets.*

realize /rɪəlaɪz/, **realizes, realizing, realized;** also spelled **realise.** 1 REPORT VB If you **realize** something, you become aware of it. *She realized the significance of what he was trying to do... I realized that this man wasn't going to hurt me.* ♦ **realization** /rɪəlaɪzeɪʃəˀn/ UNCOUNT N *This realization was shattering for all of us.* 2 VB WITH OBJ When someone **realizes** a design or an idea, they put it into a physical form, for example by painting a picture or building a machine; a formal use. *No design is too sophisticated for him to realize.* 3 VB WITH OBJ If your hopes, desires, or fears **are realized,** the things that you hope for, desire, or fear actually happen; a formal use. *My worst fears were realized.* ♦ **realization** UNCOUNT N *...the realization of a lifelong dream.*

really /rɪəliˡ/. 1 ADV OR SUBMOD You can use **really** to emphasize what you are saying. *I really ought to go... It was really good.* 2 ADV You use **really** to mention the real facts about something, as opposed to something that is incorrect. *I want to know what really happened... He's not really going for a bath; he's going to sit in the garden.* 3 ADV People use **really** in questions when they want you to answer 'no'; used in speech. *Do you really think they bother to listen to us?... Is there really anything new to say about him?* 4 ADV You can add **really** to negative statements to avoid seeming impolite. *I'm not really in favour of that... 'Any more problems?'—'Not really, no.'* 5 CONVENTION You can say **'Really?'** to express great interest, surprise, or disbelief. *'It was quite close to the airport.'—'Really?'... 'Inflation's dropped faster than it did under Labour.'—'Has it really?'*

realm /rɛlm/, **realms;** a formal word. 1 COUNT N WITH SUPP You can refer to any area of activity or thought as a **realm.** *Changes would not be confined to the technical realm... ...the realm of imagination rather than historical fact.* 2 COUNT N A **realm** is also a country with a king or queen. *...the established church of the realm.*

reap /riːp/, **reaps, reaping, reaped.** 1 VB WITH OBJ When people **reap** a crop such as corn, they cut and gather it. 2 VB WITH OBJ If you **reap** benefits or rewards, you obtain them by working hard. *One day we will reap the full benefits of North Sea oil.*

reappear /riːəpɪə/, **reappears, reappearing, reappeared.** VB When people or things **reappear,** you can see them again, because they have returned from another place or because they are being used again. *The waiter reappeared with a loaded tray... From time to time 'gypsy' clothes reappear as a fashion.* ♦ **reappearance** /riːəpɪərəns/ UNCOUNT N *He wanted to know the reason for my sudden reappearance.*

reappraisal /riːəpreɪzəˀl/, **reappraisals.** COUNT N OR UNCOUNT N A **reappraisal** of something such as a policy is the process of thinking carefully about it and deciding whether or not to change it; a formal use. *...a reappraisal of U.S. policy toward South Asia.*

rear /rɪə/, **rears, rearing, reared.** 1 SING N The **rear** of something such as a building or vehicle is the part at the back of it. *He walked toward the rear of the house.* Also ATTRIB ADJ *I got out and examined the right rear wheel.* 2 SING N If you are at the **rear** of a queue or line of people, you are the last person in it. 3 VB WITH OBJ If you **rear** children, you bring them up until they are old enough to look after themselves. *Geraldo has adopted and reared four children.* 4 VB When a horse **rears** or **rears** up, it stands on its hind legs.

PHRASES • If you **bring up the rear,** you are the last person in a moving line of people. • If something unpleasant **rears** its **ugly head,** it happens or appears. *Jealousy might so easily have reared its ugly head.*

rearrange /riːəreɪndʒ/, **rearranges, rearranging, rearranged.** VB WITH OBJ If you **rearrange** something, you organize or arrange it in a different way. *She rearranged the furniture.* ♦ **rearrangement** /riːəreɪndʒmə²nt/, COUNT N OR UNCOUNT N *...the rearrangement of the examination system.*

reason /riːzəˀn/, **reasons, reasoning, reasoned.** 1 COUNT N The **reason** for something is the fact or situation which explains why it happens or exists. *I asked the reason for the decision.* 2 UNCOUNT N You use **reason** to say that you believe or feel something and that there are definite reasons why you believe it or feel it. *I have reason to believe that you are concealing something... I'm getting annoyed, and with reason.* 3 UNCOUNT N **Reason** is also the ability people have to think and make judgements. *He had to rely less on reason than on the rousing of emotion.* 4 PHRASE If you get someone to **listen to reason,** you persuade them to listen to sensible arguments and be influenced by them. *The man refused to listen to reason.* 5 REPORT VB If you **reason** that something is the case, you decide after careful thought that it is the case. *Copernicus reasoned that the earth revolved around the sun.* 6 See also **reasoned, reasoning.**

reason with. PHR VB If you **reason with** someone, you try to convince them of something using logical arguments.

reasonable /riːzəˀnəbəˀl/. 1 ADJ If someone is being **reasonable,** they are behaving in a fair and sensible way. *I can't do that, Morris. Be reasonable.* ♦ **reasonableness** UNCOUNT N *The landlords responded with great reasonableness.* 2 ADJ If a decision or explanation is **reasonable,** there are good reasons for thinking that it is correct. *There was no reasonable explanation for her decision... It was quite reasonable to suppose that he wanted the money too.* 3 ADJ A **reasonable** amount of something is a fairly large amount. *...a reasonable amount of luck... A reasonable number of students are involved.* 4 ADJ If the price of something is **reasonable,** it is fair and not too high.

reasonably /riːzəˀnəbliˡ/. 1 SUBMOD If something is **reasonably** large or **reasonably** good, it is fairly large or fairly good. *I'm reasonably broad across the shoulders... ...a reasonably well-known writer.* 2 ADV If someone is behaving **reasonably,** they are behaving in a fair and sensible way.

reasoned /riːzəˀnd/. ATTRIB ADJ A **reasoned** argument or explanation is based on sensible reasons, rather than on feelings. *We must counter their propaganda with reasoned argument.*

reasoning /riːzəˀnɪŋ/. UNCOUNT N **Reasoning** is the process by which you reach a conclusion after considering all the facts. *I'm puzzled by his reasoning.*

reassemble /riːəsɛmbəˀl/, **reassembles, reassembling, reassembled.** VB WITH OBJ If you **reassemble** something, you put it back together after it has been taken apart. *He reassembled an entire engine.*

reassert /riːəsɜːt/, **reasserts, reasserting, reasserted.** 1 VB WITH OBJ If you **reassert** your power or authority, you make it clear that you have it again. *He made efforts to reassert his authority over them.* 2 REFL VB If an idea or habit **reasserts** itself, it becomes noticeable again. *The urge to survive reasserted itself.*

reassess /riːəsɛs/, **reassesses, reassessing, reassessed.** VB WITH OBJ If you **reassess** something, you consider it and decide whether it still has the same value or importance as you thought previously. *He was reassessing his political position.*

reassurance /riːəʃʊərəns/, **reassurances.** COUNT N OR UNCOUNT N **Reassurances** are things you say to stop someone worrying. *Reassurances were given that investigations would proceed... She wants reassurance, that is all.*

reassure /riːəʃʊə/, **reassures, reassuring, reassured.** VB WITH OBJ If you **reassure** someone, you say or do things to stop them worrying. *I was trying to reassure her that things weren't as bad as she thought.* ♦ **reassuring** ADJ *The woman smiled at him in a reassuring manner.* ♦ **reassuringly** ADV *She looked at me reassuringly.*

rebate /riːbeɪt/, **rebates.** COUNT N A **rebate** is an amount of money which is paid back to you because you have paid too much tax or rent.

rebel, rebels, rebelling, rebelled; pronounced /rɛbəᵒl/ when it is a noun, and /rɪ¹bɛl/ when it is a verb. 1 COUNT N **Rebels** are people who are fighting against their own country's army in order to change the political system. 2 VB When people **rebel,** they fight against their own country's army in order to change the political system. *The Duke of Monmouth rebelled against James II in 1685.* 3 COUNT N You also describe someone as a **rebel** when they behave differently from other people, having rejected their society's values. 4 VB You can say that someone **rebels** when they behave differently from other people because they have rejected their society's or parents' values. *...adolescents who rebel and demand freedom and independence.*

rebellion /rɪ¹bɛljən/, **rebellions.** 1 COUNT N OR UNCOUNT N A **rebellion** is a violent, organized action by a large group of people who are trying to change their country's political system. 2 COUNT N OR UNCOUNT N Opposition to the leaders of an organization can also be referred to as a **rebellion.** *He faces a growing rebellion from the left wing of his party... Hradilek was charged with incitement to rebellion.*

rebellious /rɪ¹bɛljəs/. ADJ A **rebellious** person does not do what someone in authority wants them to do. *...an obstinate, rebellious child with a violent temper.*

rebirth /riːbɜːθ/. SING N WITH SUPP The **rebirth** of something such as a political movement that was popular or important in the past is the fact that it becomes popular or important again. *...the rebirth of nationalism.*

rebuff /rɪ¹bʌf/, **rebuffs, rebuffing, rebuffed.** VB WITH OBJ If you **rebuff** someone's suggestion or advice, you respond in an unfriendly way and refuse to accept it. *He tried to question the girl and got rebuffed.* Also COUNT N *Her rebuff had hurt him.*

rebuild /riːbɪld/, **rebuilds, rebuilding, rebuilt** /riːbɪlt/. 1 VB WITH OBJ When a town or building **is rebuilt,** it is built again after it has been damaged or destroyed. 2 VB WITH OBJ When an organization **is rebuilt,** it is developed again after it has stopped or become ineffective. *...help him to rebuild his nation's shattered economy.*

rebuke /rɪ¹bjuːk/, **rebukes, rebuking, rebuked.** VB WITH OBJ If you **rebuke** someone, you speak severely to them because they have said or done something that you do not approve of. *She often rebuked David for his authoritarian attitude.* Also COUNT N OR UNCOUNT N *He received a stern rebuke from his superiors... The team now returns to face rebuke from the athlete's association.*

recall /rɪ¹kɔːl/, **recalls, recalling, recalled.** 1 REPORT VB OR VB WITH -ING When you **recall** something, you remember it. *I recalled that my blankets had been taken away... 'I ran outside to look for my children,' recalled Miriam... I started to recall the years after the War... Deirdre recalled seeing a poster on his wall.* 2 VB WITH OBJ If you **are recalled** to a place, you are ordered to return there. *Eighteen months ago they recalled him to Mozambique.*

recapture /riːkæptʃə/, **recaptures, recapturing, recaptured.** 1 VB WITH OBJ When you **recapture** a pleasant feeling, you experience it again. *She failed to recapture her earlier mood.* 2 VB WITH OBJ When soldiers **recapture** a place, they capture it from the people who had taken it from them. Also SING N *...the recapture of the lost territories.* 3 VB WITH OBJ When animals or prisoners **are recaptured,** they are caught after they have escaped.

recede /rɪ¹siːd/, **recedes, receding, receded.** 1 VB If something **recedes,** it moves away into the distance. *Now and then cars passed me, their tail-lights receding.* 2 VB You also say that something **recedes** when it decreases in clarity, brightness, or amount. *Already the memory was receding... The floods caused by two days of storms receded over the weekend.*

receipt /rɪ¹siːt/, **receipts.** 1 COUNT N A **receipt** is a piece of paper that confirms that money or goods have been received. *Give students a written receipt for each payment.* 2 PLURAL N Money received in a shop or a theatre is often referred to as the **receipts.** *The receipts from admission fees fell sharply.* 3 UNCOUNT N The **receipt** of something is the act of receiving it; a formal use. *You have to sign here and acknowledge receipt.*

receive /rɪ¹siːv/, **receives, receiving, received.** 1 VB WITH OBJ When you **receive** something, someone gives it to you, or it arrives after it has been sent to you. *Did they receive money for their work?... Northcliffe received a letter from his brother.* 2 VB WITH OBJ You can use **receive** to say that certain kinds of thing happen to you. *...the criticism he received in England... She received a tremendous ovation.* 3 VB WITH OBJ When you **receive** a visitor or guest, you welcome them; a formal use. *Fass received Lieber in his office.* 4 VB WITH OBJ AND ADJUNCT If something **is received** in a particular way, people react to it in that way. *Her latest novel has been very well received.*

received /rɪ¹siːvd/. ATTRIB ADJ The **received** opinion or method is the one that is generally accepted as correct; a formal use. *...received ideas... ...received religion.*

receiver /rɪ¹siːvə/, **receivers.** 1 COUNT N A **receiver** is the part of a telephone that you hold near to your ear and speak into. *He replaced the receiver.* 2 COUNT N A **receiver** is also a radio or television set.

recent /riːsənt/. ADJ A **recent** event or period of time happened a short while ago. *...their recent trip to Africa... Few sights have become more familiar in recent times.*

recently /riːsəntli¹/. ADV If something happened **recently,** it happened only a short time ago. *Recently, I lectured to seven hundred Swedes... The problem has been ignored until very recently.*

receptacle /rɪ¹sɛptəkəᵒl/, **receptacles.** COUNT N A **receptacle** is an object which you use to put or keep things in; a formal use. *Please put your cigarette ends into the receptacle provided.*

reception /rɪ¹sɛpʃəᵒn/, **receptions.** 1 UNCOUNT N In a hotel, office, or hospital, **reception** is the place where reservations, appointments, and enquiries are dealt with. *...the reception desk.* 2 COUNT N A **reception** is a formal party which is given to welcome someone or to celebrate a special event. *The reception was held in the Albany.* 3 COUNT N WITH SUPP If something or someone has a particular kind of **reception,** that is the way people react to them. *I wrote to George about the enthusiastic reception of his book... Butler received a hostile reception in Bristol.* 4 SING N The **reception** of guests is the act of formally welcoming them; a formal use. *...a room which was kept for the reception of visitors.* 5 UNCOUNT N If you get good **reception** from your radio or television, the sound or picture is clear. *Radio reception kept fading.*

receptionist /rɪ¹sɛpʃənɪst/, **receptionists.** COUNT N The **receptionist** in a hotel, office, or doctor's surgery is the person whose job is to deal with people when they first arrive, to answer the telephone, and to arrange reservations or appointments.

receptive /rɪ¹sɛptɪv/. ADJ A **receptive** person is willing to consider and accept new ideas and suggestions. *America has proved more receptive to Anna Freud's ideas.*

recess, recesses; pronounced /rɪ¹sɛs/ for meaning 1 and /riːsɛs/ for meanings 2 and 3. 1 UNCOUNT N OR COUNT N A **recess** is a holiday period between the sessions of a committee or parliament. *The committee is going into recess for a couple of weeks.* 2 COUNT N In a room, a **recess** is a small area created when one part of a wall is built farther back than the rest. *...the arched window recess.* 3 COUNT N WITH SUPP The **recesses** of something are its deep or hidden parts. *I pushed the problem down into the dim recesses of my mind.*

recession /rɪ¹sɛʃəᵒn/, **recessions.** COUNT N OR UNCOUNT N A **recession** is a period when the economy of a country is not very successful. *...new prosperity and Britain's emergence from the recession.*

recipe /rɛsɪpi¹/, **recipes.** 1 COUNT N A **recipe** is a list of ingredients and a set of instructions telling you how to cook something. *...a recipe for beetroot soup.* 2 SING N WITH 'for' If something is a **recipe** for disaster or a **recipe** for success, you mean that it is likely to result in disaster or success.

recipient /rɪ²sɪpɪənt/, **recipients.** COUNT N The **recipient** of something is the person who receives it; a formal use. *...letters kept by the recipients.*

reciprocal /rɪ²sɪprəkəᵒl/. ADJ **Reciprocal** actions or arrangements involve two people or groups who do the same thing to each other or who agree to help each other in a similar way; a formal use. *Their social security system is linked to Britain's by a reciprocal agreement.*

reciprocate /rɪ²sɪprəkeɪt/, **reciprocates, reciprocating, reciprocated.** VB WITH OR WITHOUT OBJ If you **reciprocate** someone's feelings or behaviour towards you, you share the same feelings or behave the in same way towards them; a formal use. *This hostile attitude is reciprocated by potential employers... Maybe one day it will occur to you to reciprocate.*

recital /rɪ¹saɪtəᵒl/, **recitals.** COUNT N A **recital** is a solo performance of music or poetry. *She had been asked to give a piano recital.*

recite /rɪ¹saɪt/, **recites, reciting, recited.** VB WITH OBJ If you **recite** a piece of writing, you read or say it aloud, often after you have learned it. *She recited a speech from 'As You Like It'... Mrs Zapp recited a catalogue of her husband's sins.*

reckless /rɛklɪ²s/. ADJ A **reckless** person shows a lack of care about danger or about the results of their actions. *I don't like the way he drives. He's reckless... They denounced the government for its reckless squandering of public funds.* ♦ **recklessly** ADV *He accelerated recklessly round a blind corner.*

reckon /rɛkəᵒn/, **reckons, reckoning, reckoned.** 1 REPORT VB If you **reckon** that something is true, you think it is true; an informal use. *She reckoned that there was a risk... What do you reckon?* 2 VB WITH OBJ AND TO-INF If something **is reckoned** to be true, people generally think that it is true. *About 40 per cent of the country is reckoned to be illiterate.* 3 VB WITH OR WITHOUT OBJ When you **reckon** an amount, you calculate it. *The number of days lost through unemployment can be reckoned at 146 million.*

reckon on. PHR VB If you **reckon on** something, you feel certain that it will happen and you make your plans accordingly. *He reckoned on a large reward if he succeeded.*

reckon with. PHR VB If you had not **reckoned with** something, you had not expected it and so were not ready for it.

reckoning /rɛkəᵒnɪŋ/, **reckonings.** COUNT N OR UNCOUNT N A **reckoning** is the same as a calculation. *It's only a rough reckoning... By his own reckoning, he had taken five hours to get there.*

reclaim /rɪ¹kleɪm/, **reclaims, reclaiming, reclaimed.** 1 VB WITH OBJ If you **reclaim** something that you have lost or had taken away from you, you succeed in getting it back. *You must present this ticket when you reclaim your luggage.* 2 VB WITH OBJ When people **reclaim** land, they make it suitable for use by draining or irrigating it. *Lowland bogs have been reclaimed.* ♦ **reclaimed** ADJ *...reclaimed land.*

recline /rɪ¹klaɪn/, **reclines, reclining, reclined.** VB If you **recline,** you sit or lie with the upper part of your body supported at an angle; a formal use. *She was reclining comfortably in her chair.*

reclining /rɪ¹klaɪnɪŋ/. ATTRIB ADJ A **reclining** chair or seat is designed so that you can lie down or sit with the upper part of your body supported at an angle.

recluse /rɪ¹kluːs/, **recluses.** COUNT N A **recluse** is a person who lives alone and deliberately avoids other people.

recognise /rɛkəgᵒnaɪz/. See **recognize.**

recognition /rɛkəgᵒnɪʃəᵒn/. 1 UNCOUNT N **Recognition** is the experience of recognizing someone or something. *She walked past me without so much as a glance of recognition.* 2 UNCOUNT N WITH SUPP When there is **recognition** of something, people realize or accept that it exists or that it is true. *There has been insufficient recognition of the magnitude of the problem.* 3 PHRASE If something is done **in recognition of** someone's achievements, it is done as a way of showing official appreciation of them. *He was awarded a knighthood in recognition of his great contribution to the British cinema.*

recognizable /rɛkəgᵒnaɪzəbəᵒl/; also spelled **recognisable.** ADJ Something that is **recognizable** is easy to recognize or identify. *...a recognizable voice... ...an old statue barely recognisable as Charles II.*

recognize /rɛkəgᵒnaɪz/, **recognizes, recognizing, recognized;** also spelled **recognise.** 1 VB WITH OBJ AND 'as' If you **recognize** someone or something, you know who or what they are, because you have seen or heard them before or because they have been described to you. *The postmistress recognised her as Mrs Pennington's daughter... They are trained to recognize the symptoms of radiation-sickness.* 2 VB WITH OBJ AND 'as' OR REPORT VB You also say that you **recognize** something when you realize or accept that it exists or that it is true. *Governments are beginning to recognize the problem... We recognise this as a genuine need... They refused to recognise that a wrong decision had been made.* 3 VB WITH OBJ You say that something **is recognized** when it is officially accepted or approved. *Are qualifications gained in Britain recognized in other European countries?... The new regime was at once recognized by China.* ♦ **recognized** ADJ *There are several recognized techniques for dealing with this.* 4 VB WITH OBJ When an achievement **is recognized,** people officially show their appreciation of it. *The nation recognized her efforts by making a monument.*

recoil /rɪ1kɔɪl/, **recoils, recoiling, recoiled.** 1 VB If you **recoil** from something, you feel afraid or disgusted by it. *He recoiled in horror from the savagery which he witnessed... Parents may recoil at this kind of behaviour.* 2 VB You also say that someone **recoils** when they move part of their body away from something because it gives them an unpleasant feeling. *When he touched the man's arm, he recoiled in horror, for it was cold and rigid.*

recollect /rɛkəlɛkt/, **recollects, recollecting, recollected.** REPORT VB If you **recollect** something, you remember it. *He was unable to recollect the names... He does not recollect how long they were in the house.*

recollection /rɛkəlɛkʃə0n/, **recollections.** COUNT N OR UNCOUNT N If you have a **recollection** of something, you remember it. *I have a vivid recollection of the house where I was born... ...a flash of recollection.*

recommend /rɛkəmɛnd/, **recommends, recommending, recommended.** 1 VB WITH OBJ If someone **recommends** something to you, they suggest that you should have it or use it, because it is good or useful. *...a fine novel which I'd strongly recommend... Perhaps you could recommend me a solicitor.* 2 VB WITH OBJ OR REPORT VB If you **recommend** an action, you suggest that it should be done. *The Harveys do not recommend other couples to have families of this size... Mr Tebbit recommends cycling as a good form of exercise... The Committee recommended that shareholders should vote against the offer.*

recommendation /rɛkəmɛndeɪʃə0n/, **recommendations.** 1 COUNT N OR UNCOUNT N If you make a **recommendation,** you suggest that someone should have something or use something, because it is good or useful. *The best way to find a gardener is through personal recommendation.* 2 COUNT N A **recommendation** is also advice about the best thing to do. *...recommendations for training.*

reconcile /rɛkə7nsaɪl/, **reconciles, reconciling, reconciled.** 1 VB WITH OBJ If you **reconcile** two opposing beliefs, you find a way in which both of them can be held by the same person at the same time. *I asked how he would reconcile apartheid with Christianity.* 2 VB WITH OBJ If you **are reconciled** with someone, you become friendly with them again after a disagreement. *They had been reconciled with their families.* ♦ **reconciliation** /rɛkə7nsɪli1eɪʃə0n/ UNCOUNT N *...hopes of reconciliation in Western Europe.* 3 REFL VB If you **reconcile** yourself to an unpleasant situation, you accept it. *He told them to reconcile themselves to their misery on earth.* ♦ **reconciled** PRED ADJ WITH PREP 'to' *After a while he grew reconciled to the situation.*

reconnaissance /rɪ2kɒnɪ1səns/. UNCOUNT N **Reconnaissance** is the process of obtaining military information about a place using soldiers, planes, or satellites. *They decided to step up reconnaissance of enemy naval movements.*

reconsider /riːkə7nsɪdə/, **reconsiders, reconsidering, reconsidered.** VB WITH OR WITHOUT OBJ If you **reconsider** a decision or method, you think about it and try to decide whether it should be changed. *He asked me to reconsider my decision... I asked them to reconsider but they refused.* ♦ **reconsideration** /riːkə7nsɪdəreɪʃə0n/ UNCOUNT N *This would allow time for reconsideration.*

reconstruct /riːkə7nstrʌkt/, **reconstructs, reconstructing, reconstructed.** 1 VB WITH OBJ If you **reconstruct** a building that has been destroyed or badly damaged, you build it again. 2 VB WITH OBJ When a system or policy **is reconstructed,** it is replaced with one that works differently. *...an attempt to reconstruct race relations policy.* 3 VB WITH OBJ If you **reconstruct** a past event, you obtain a complete description of it by combining a lot of small pieces of information.

reconstruction /riːkə7nstrʌkʃə0n/. 1 UNCOUNT N **Reconstruction** is the process of making a country normal again after a war, for example by replacing buildings that have been damaged or destroyed. *...the reconstruction of post-war Britain.* 2 UNCOUNT N When the **reconstruction** of a building takes place, it is built again after it has been damaged or destroyed.

record, records, recording, recorded; pronounced /rɛkɔːd/ when it is a noun or adjective and /rɪ1kɔːd/ when it is a verb. 1 COUNT N If you keep a **record** of something, you keep a written account of it or store information about it in a computer. *Keep a record of any repair bills... ...medical records.* 2 VB WITH OBJ If you **record** something, you write it down, film it, or put it into a computer so that it can be referred to later. *All the details could be recorded on a computer... Their every action was recorded by concealed cameras.* 3 COUNT N A **record** is a round, flat piece of black plastic on which sound, especially music, is stored. You listen to the sound by playing the record on a record player. 4 VB WITH OBJ When music or speech **is recorded,** it is put onto a tape or a record, so that it can be heard again later. 5 COUNT N A **record** is also the shortest time or the longest distance that has ever been achieved in a particular sport. *He held the record for the mile.* 6 ATTRIB ADJ You use **record** to say that something is higher, lower, or better than has ever been achieved before. *Unemployment was at a record high.* 7 COUNT N WITH SUPP Your **record** is all the facts that are known about your achievements or character. *Mr Gerran has a very distinguished record.* 8 See also **recording, track record.**

PHRASES • If something you say is **off the record,** it is not official and not intended to be published or made known. • If you **set** or **put the record straight,** you show that something which has been regarded as true is in fact not true. *Harold Begbie wrote a book to put the record straight.*

recorded delivery. UNCOUNT N If you send a letter or parcel by **recorded delivery,** you receive an official note telling you that it has been sent. When the letter or parcel arrives, the person who receives it has to sign to say they have received it; a British use.

recorder /rɪ1kɔːdə/, **recorders.** 1 COUNT N You can refer to a cassette recorder, a tape recorder, or a video recorder as a **recorder.** 2 COUNT N A **recorder** is also a hollow musical instrument that you play by blowing down one end and covering a series of holes with your fingers.

recording /rɪ1kɔːdɪŋ/, **recordings.** 1 COUNT N A **recording** of something is a record, tape, or video of it. 2 UNCOUNT N **Recording** is the process of making records, tapes, or videos. *...a recording engineer.*

record player, record players. COUNT N A **record player** is a machine on which you play records.

recount, recounts, recounting, recounted; pronounced /rɪ1kaʊnt/ when it is a verb and /riːkaʊnt/ when it is a noun. 1 VB WITH OBJ If you **recount** a story or event, you tell it to people; a formal use. *I let Henry recount the incident in his own words.* 2 COUNT N A **recount** is a second count of votes in an election when the result is very close. *I'm demanding a recount.*

recourse /rɪ1kɔːs/. UNCOUNT N If you have **recourse** to something, you use it to help you in a difficult situation; a formal use. *We need never have recourse to violence.*

recover /rɪ1kʌvə/, **recovers, recovering, recovered.** 1 VB When you **recover** from an illness or an injury, you become well again. *...a wound from which he did not recover... It was weeks before he fully recovered.* ♦ **recovered** PRED ADJ *Stay at home until you are fully recovered.* 2 VB If you **recover** from an unhappy or unpleasant experience, you stop being upset by it. *They took a long time to recover from this shock.* 3 VB WITH OBJ If you **recover** something that has been lost or stolen, you get it back. *I would do my best to recover these documents... They recovered her body from the old mine-shaft.* 4 VB WITH OBJ If you **recover** your former mental or physical state or **recover** the ability to do something, you get it back. *He died without recovering consciousness... He was beginning to recover the use of his voice.*

recovery /rɪ1kʌvə0ri1/, **recoveries.** 1 SING N If a sick person makes a **recovery,** he or she becomes well again. *He made a good recovery from his stroke... The shock of the operation delayed his recovery.* 2 UNCOUNT N OR COUNT N When there is a **recovery** in a country's economy, it improves after being in a bad state. *His advisers insisted that economic recovery was in sight... ...last minute recoveries despite two decades of steady decline.* 3 UNCOUNT N The **recovery** of something that was lost or stolen is the fact of getting it back; a formal use. *...the recovery of the treasure.* 4 UNCOUNT N The **recovery** of someone's physical or mental state is their return to this state; a formal use. *The news was sufficient to bring about the recovery of his equanimity.*

recreate /riːkri1eɪt/, **recreates, recreating, recreated.** VB WITH OBJ If you **recreate** something, you succeed in making it happen or exist again. *The opportunity could not be recreated.*

recreation /rɛkri1eɪʃə0n/, **recreations.** UNCOUNT N OR COUNT N **Recreation** consists of things that you do to exercise your body or mind when you are not working or studying. *Sport and recreation have always been part of university life... The library was reserved for quieter recreations.* ♦ **recreational** /rɛkri1eɪʃənə0l/ ADJ *...recreational facilities.*

recrimination /rɪ2krɪmɪneɪʃə0n/, **recriminations.** PLURAL N OR UNCOUNT N **Recriminations** are accusations that two people or groups make about each other. *There will be recriminations, no doubt... ...prolonged bouts of recrimination.*

recruit /rɪ1kruːt/, **recruits, recruiting, recruited.** 1 VB WITH OR WITHOUT OBJ If you **recruit** people for an organization, you get them to do join it or work for it. *I am recruiting for the Union.* ♦ **recruiting** UNCOUNT N *Other organizations reported sharp rises in recruiting.* 2 COUNT N A **recruit** is a person who has recently joined an organization or army. *He joined the firm as a young recruit more than thirty years ago.* 3 VB WITH OBJ If you **recruit** someone for a particular purpose, you get them to do something for you. *Men from the villages were recruited to carry stores.*

recruitment /rɪ1kruːtmə2nt/. UNCOUNT N When **recruitment** takes place, people are persuaded to join an organization or an army. *...the mass recruitment of volunteer teachers.*

rectangle /rɛktæŋgə0l/, **rectangles.** COUNT N A **rectangle** is a shape with four sides whose angles are all right angles. Each side of a rectangle is the same length as the one opposite to it.

rectangular /rɛktæŋgjə4lə/. ADJ Something that is **rectangular** is shaped like a rectangle. *...a rectangular flower-bed.*

rectify /rɛktɪfaɪ/, **rectifies, rectifying, rectified.** VB WITH OBJ If you **rectify** something that is damaged or that is causing problems, you change it so that it becomes correct or satisfactory. *The tenant will be held responsible for rectifying any damage... Armed forces were sent in to rectify the situation.*

rector /rɛktə/, **rectors.** COUNT N A **rector** is a Church of England priest in charge of a parish.

rectory /rɛktə0ri1/, **rectories.** COUNT N A **rectory** is a house in which a rector and his family live.

rectum /rɛktəm/, **rectums.** COUNT N Your **rectum** is the bottom end of the tube down which waste food passes out of your body; a medical word.

recuperate /ri1kj0uːpəreɪt/, **recuperates, recuperating, recuperated.** VB If you **recuperate,** you recover your health or strength after you have been ill or injured; a formal use. *I was recuperating from an accident in the gym.*

recur /rɪ1kɜː/, **recurs, recurring, recurred.** VB If something **recurs,** it happens again, either once or many times. *It was probable that the same circumstances would now recur... It was a phrase that was to recur again and again.*

recurrence /rɪ1kʌrəns/, **recurrences.** COUNT N OR UNCOUNT N If there is a **recurrence** of something, it happens again; a formal use. *There were minor recurrences of her eye trouble.*

recurrent /rɪ1kʌrənt/. ATTRIB ADJ **Recurrent** means the same as recurring; a formal use.

recurring /rɪ1kɜːrɪŋ/. ATTRIB ADJ **Recurring** things happen many times. *Food scarcity will be a recurring problem in the future.*

recycle /riːsaɪkə0l/, **recycles, recycling, recycled.** VB WITH OBJ If you **recycle** things that have already been used, such as bottles or sheets of paper, you process them so that they can be used again. *Plastic bottles can easily be recycled.* ♦ **recycled** ADJ *...recycled paper.*

red /rɛd/, **redder, reddest; reds.** 1 ADJ Something that is **red** is the colour of blood or of a ripe tomato. *...a bunch of red roses.* 2 ADJ If someone goes **red,** their face becomes redder than normal, because they are embarrassed or angry. 3 ADJ **Red** hair is between red and brown in colour. 4 COUNT N If you call someone a **red,** you mean that they support left-wing ideas such as communism; used showing disapproval.

PHRASES • If you are **in the red,** you have spent more money than you have in your account and therefore you owe money to the bank; an informal use. • If you **see red,** you become very angry.

reddish /rɛdɪʃ/. ADJ Something that is **reddish** is slightly red.

redeem /rɪ1diːm/, **redeems, redeeming, redeemed.** 1 VB WITH OBJ When something **redeems** a bad thing or situation, it prevents it from being completely bad. *Swallow was doing his best to redeem what could be a disastrous dinner.* ♦ **redeeming** ATTRIB ADJ *...a book with no redeeming qualities.* 2 REFL VB If you **redeem** yourself, you do something that gives people a good opinion of you again after you have behaved badly. *He was trying to redeem himself for his earlier failure.* 3 VB WITH OBJ If you **redeem** something, you get it back from someone by repaying them money that you have borrowed from them; a technical use. *They came to redeem their jewellery.*

redemption /rɪ1dɛmp0ʃə0n/. UNCOUNT N **Redemption** is freedom from the consequences of sin and evil which Christians believe was made possible by Christ's death.

redevelopment /riːdi1vɛləpmə2nt/. UNCOUNT N When **redevelopment** takes place, old buildings in a part of a town are replaced by new ones. *The area is undergoing redevelopment.*

red herring, red herrings. COUNT N A **red herring** is something which is irrelevant and takes people's attention away from important things. *They were using the issue as a red herring.*

red-hot. 1 ADJ Something that is **red-hot** is too hot to touch. 2 ADJ People or situations that are **red-hot** are full of very strong feelings; an informal use. *...a red-hot revolutionary... ...red-hot patriotism.*

redistribute /riːdɪstrɪbjuːt/, **redistributes, redistributing, redistributed.** VB WITH OBJ When money or goods **are redistributed,** they are shared among people or organizations in a different way from the way that they were previously shared. *Money would be redistributed from the traditional arts institutions.* ♦ **redistribution** /riːdɪstrɪbjuːʃən/ UNCOUNT N *We do not envisage any redistribution of wealth and power.*

redouble /riːdʌbəl/, **redoubles, redoubling, redoubled.** VB WITH OBJ If you **redouble** your efforts, you try much harder to achieve something. *She redoubled her efforts to attract his curiosity.*

redress, redresses, redressing, redressed; pronounced /rɪˈdrɛs/ when it is a verb and /rɪˈdrɛs/ or /riːdrɛs/ when it is a noun. 1 VB WITH OBJ If you **redress** something such as a wrong or a grievance, you do something to correct it or to improve things for the person who has been badly treated; a formal use. *He did all that he could to redress these wrongs.* 2 UNCOUNT N **Redress** is compensation for something wrong that has been done; a formal use. *Your claims for redress may yet succeed.* 3 PHRASE If you **redress the balance** between two unequal things, you make them equal again. *We were refused the pay increase needed to redress the balance.*

red tape. UNCOUNT N You refer to official rules and procedures as **red tape** when they seem unnecessary and cause delay.

reduce /rɪˈdjuːs/, **reduces, reducing, reduced.** 1 VB WITH OBJ If you **reduce** something, you make it smaller. *They have promised to reduce public expenditure... The work-force would have to be reduced from 13,000 to 7,500.* ♦ **reduced** ADJ *...a reduced rate of production.* 2 VB WITH OBJ AND PREP 'to' If you say that someone **is reduced** to a weaker or inferior state, you mean that they change to this state as a result of something that happens to them. *He was reduced to tears... Her mother was reduced to infantile dependence.* 3 VB WITH OBJ AND PREP 'to' If someone **is reduced** to doing something, they have to do it, although it is unpleasant or humiliating. *They are reduced to begging in the streets.*

reduction /rɪˈdʌkʃən/, **reductions.** UNCOUNT N OR COUNT N When there is a **reduction** in something, it is made smaller. *The unions will be demanding a reduction in working hours... They're talking about arms reduction all over Europe.*

redundancy /rɪˈdʌndənsi/, **redundancies.** 1 COUNT N When there are **redundancies,** an organization dismisses some of its employees because their jobs are no longer necessary or because the organization can no longer afford to pay them. *The trade unions accepted 3500 redundancies.* 2 UNCOUNT N **Redundancy** is the state of no longer having a job because you have been made redundant. *The possibility of redundancy was present in their minds.*

redundant /rɪˈdʌndənt/. 1 ADJ If you are made **redundant,** you lose your job because it is no longer necessary or because your employer cannot afford to keep paying you. *Alumetal Ltd will be making 250 workers redundant next year.* 2 ADJ Something that is **redundant** is no longer needed because it has been replaced by something else. *...skills which have been made redundant by technological advance.*

reed /riːd/, **reeds.** COUNT N OR UNCOUNT N **Reeds** are tall plants that grow in shallow water or wet ground.

reef /riːf/, **reefs.** COUNT N A **reef** is a long line of rocks or sand lying close to the surface of the sea.

reek /riːk/, **reeks, reeking, reeked.** 1 VB If someone or something **reeks** of a particular thing, they smell very strongly of it. *...reeking of brandy.* 2 SING N WITH SUPP A **reek** of something is a strong, unpleasant smell of it. *...the sickening reek of blood.*

reel /riːl/, **reels, reeling, reeled.** 1 COUNT N A **reel** is a cylindrical object around which you wrap something such as thread or cinema film. *...a reel of white string.* 2 COUNT N The **reel** on a fishing rod is a round device used to control the length of the fishing line. 3 VB When someone **reels** somewhere, they move there unsteadily as if they were going to fall. *I reeled back into the room.* 4 VB If your brain or your mind **is reeling,** you are very confused because you have too much to think about.

reel off. PHR VB If you **reel off** information, you repeat it from memory quickly and easily.

re-elect, re-elects, re-electing, re-elected. VB WITH OBJ When someone such as an MP or a trade union official **is re-elected,** they win a new election and are therefore able to continue in their position as MP or union official. *I was re-elected with a majority of over 4,300... The Council re-elected him President.* ♦ **re-election** UNCOUNT N *He stood for re-election.*

re-examine, re-examines, re-examining, re-examined. VB WITH OBJ If you **re-examine** your ideas or beliefs, you think about them carefully because you are no longer sure if they are correct. *This forced researchers to re-examine their assumptions about man's early evolution.* ♦ **re-examination** COUNT N OR UNCOUNT N *...a re-examination of the purposes of education in modern Britain... ...a book that brings you to attentive and reflective re-examination.*

ref /rɛf/, **refs.** COUNT N A **ref** is a referee; an informal use.

ref. Ref. is an abbreviation for 'reference' that is written in front of a code at the top of business letters so that the letter can be filed. *Ref. ESB/33593/64.*

refectory /rɪfɛktəri/, **refectories.** COUNT N In a university or a monastery, the **refectory** is the dining hall.

refer /rɪˈfɜː/, **refers, referring, referred.** 1 VB WITH PREP 'to' If you **refer to** a particular subject or person, you talk about them or mention them. *In his letters he rarely referred to political events... I am not allowed to describe the officers or refer to them by name.* 2 VB WITH PREP 'to' AND 'as' If you **refer** to someone or something by a particular name, you call them this name. *This kind of art is often referred to as 'minimal art'.* 3 VB WITH PREP 'to' If a word or expression **refers** to something, it is used as a name for it. *In the 18th century, 'antique' referred specifically to Greek and Roman antiquities.* 4 VB WITH PREP 'to' If you **refer to** a book or other source of information, you look at it in order to find something out. *She could make a new dish without referring to a cookery book.* 5 VB WITH OBJ If you **refer** a task or problem to a person or an organization, you formally request that they deal with it. *She referred the matter to the European Court of Justice.*

referee /rɛfəriː/, **referees.** COUNT N The **referee** is the official who controls a game such as football or boxing.

reference /rɛfərəns/, **references.** 1 UNCOUNT N OR COUNT N If you make a **reference** to someone or something, you talk about them or mention them; a formal use. *...the person to whom Philip had made such contemptuous reference... There is no further reference to him in her diary.* 2 UNCOUNT N **Reference** is also the act of referring to someone or something for information. *They acted without reference to the police committee.* 3 COUNT N A **reference** is also something such as a number or a name that tells you where you can obtain information. *...the two page references that I gave you.* 4 MOD You look at **reference** books or visit a **reference** library in order to obtain information. *...a valuable reference document.* 5 PHRASE You use **'with reference to'** to indicate who or what you are referring to; a formal use. *Dear Sir, With reference to your recent communication, the matter is being dealt with.* 6 COUNT N If someone gives you a **reference** when you are applying for a job, they write a letter describing your character and abilities.

referendum /rɛfərɛndəm/, **referenda** /rɛfərɛndə/ or **referendums.** COUNT N A **referendum** is a vote in which all the people in a country are asked whether they agree or disagree with a particular policy.

refill /riːfɪl/, **refills, refilling, refilled.** VB WITH OBJ If you **refill** something, you fill it again after it has been emptied. *Sue refilled Jennifer's glass.*

refine /rɪˈfaɪn/, **refines, refining, refined.** 1 VB WITH OBJ When a substance **is refined,** it is made pure by the removal of other substances from it. *...men who tested and refined gold.* ♦ **refining** UNCOUNT N *...the refining of petroleum.* 2 VB WITH OBJ If you **refine** something such as a theory or an idea, you improve it by making small alterations to it. *I used these meetings to refine my ideas.*

refined /rɪˈfaɪnd/. 1 ADJ **Refined** people are polite and well-mannered. *...a thin, refined man in a bow tie.* 2 ADJ A machine or process that is **refined** has been carefully developed and is therefore very efficient. *The new model was larger, faster, and more refined than its predecessor.* 3 ADJ A **refined** substance has been made pure by having other substances removed from it. *...refined oil.*

refinement /rɪˈfaɪnmənt/, **refinements.** 1 COUNT N OR UNCOUNT N **Refinements** are small alterations that you make to something in order to improve it. *...refinements of the system.* 2 UNCOUNT N **Refinement** is politeness and good manners; a formal use. *Mr Willet's tone changed to one of genteel refinement.*

refinery /rɪˈfaɪnəri/, **refineries.** COUNT N A **refinery** is a factory where substances such as oil or sugar are refined. *...oil refineries.*

reflect /rɪˈflɛkt/, **reflects, reflecting, reflected.** 1 VB WITH OBJ If something **reflects** someone's attitude or a situation, it indicates that the attitude or situation exists. *The choice of school reflected Dad's hopes for us.* 2 VB WITH OBJ When something **reflects** light or heat, the light or heat is sent back from it and does not pass through it. *Unlike a normal fabric, it reflects heat back into the room.* 3 VB WITH OBJ When something **is reflected** in a mirror or in water, you can see its image in the mirror or water. *I saw street lamps mistily reflected in black water.* 4 VB When you **reflect** on something or **reflect** over it, you think deeply about it. *Rodin reflected long over Casson's argument.* 5 REPORT VB If you **reflect** that something is the case, you know it is the case and think about it. *Well, I reflected, I couldn't say I hadn't been warned.*

reflection /rɪˈflɛkʃən/, **reflections.** 1 COUNT N WITH 'of' A **reflection** of a person's attitude or a situation indicates that the attitude or situation exists. *Their behaviour was a reflection of their very different personalities.* 2 SING N WITH 'on' OR 'upon' A **reflection** is also a situation or event which has the effect of making people aware of a particular aspect of someone or something. *This is a very sad reflection on the state of the Labour Party.* 3 COUNT N A **reflection** is an image that you can see in a mirror or in water. *She was standing there looking at her reflection in the mirror.* 4 UNCOUNT N **Reflection** is the process by which light and heat are sent back from a surface and do not pass through it; a technical use. 5 UNCOUNT N OR COUNT N **Reflection** is thought. You can refer to your thoughts about something as your **reflections.** *'You ought to take it,' she said, after a moment's reflection... Furious flashes of light jolted me out of my reflections.*

reflective /rɪˈflɛktɪv/. ADJ If you are **reflective,** you are thinking deeply about something. *He studied the statement in the same reflective way he always studied things... There was a long reflective silence.* ♦ **reflectively** ADV *Barney scratched his chin reflectively.*

reflex /riːflɛks/, **reflexes.** 1 COUNT N A **reflex** or a **reflex** action is a sudden, uncontrollable movement made by a part of your body as a result of pressure or a blow. *...the reflex that makes the baby kick.* 2 PLURAL N If you have good **reflexes,** you can respond quickly to an unexpected event, for example while you are driving a car. *She had incredible reflexes.*

reflexive pronoun /rɪˈflɛksɪv prəʊnaʊn/, **reflexive pronouns.** COUNT N In grammar, a **reflexive pronoun** is one which you use as the object of a verb or preposition when you are referring back to someone who has already been mentioned as the subject of the clause. For example, in the sentence 'you'll just have to do it yourself', the reflexive pronoun 'yourself' refers back to 'you'.

reflexive verb /rɪˈflɛksɪv vɜːb/, **reflexive verbs.** COUNT N In grammar, a **reflexive verb** is a transitive verb which describes actions in which the subject and the object are the same. The object is always a reflexive pronoun. For example in the sentence 'She introduced herself', the object of the verb, 'herself', refers to the subject of the verb, 'she'.

reform /rɪˈfɔːm/, **reforms, reforming, reformed.** 1 UNCOUNT N OR COUNT N **Reform** consists of changes and improvements to a law, social system, or institution. *He called for the reform of the divorce laws... ...the task of carrying through the necessary reforms.* 2 VB WITH OBJ To **reform** something such as a law, a social system, or an institution means to improve it by making changes. *...proposals to reform the Labour Party.* 3 ERG VB When someone **reforms,** they stop doing something that society does not approve of. *You have had every chance to reform... Prison sentences cannot reform the criminal.* ♦ **reformed** ADJ *...a reformed alcoholic.*

reformer /rɪˈfɔːmə/, **reformers.** COUNT N A **reformer** is someone who tries to improve laws or social conditions.

refrain /rɪˈfreɪn/, **refrains, refraining, refrained.** 1 VB If you **refrain** from doing something, you deliberately do not do it; a formal use. *I carefully refrained from looking at him.* 2 COUNT N A **refrain** is a short, simple part of a song which you repeat several times.

refresh /rɪˈfrɛʃ/, **refreshes, refreshing, refreshed.** 1 VB WITH OBJ If something **refreshes** you when you are hot or tired, it makes you feel cooler or more energetic. *I hoped that sleep would refresh me.* ♦ **refreshed** ADJ *...feeling positively refreshed.* 2 PHRASE If someone **refreshes** your **memory,** they tell you something you have forgotten.

refreshing /rɪˈfrɛʃɪŋ/. 1 ADJ If something is **refreshing,** it is pleasantly different from what you are used to. *It was a refreshing change for her to meet a woman executive.* 2 ADJ A **refreshing** bath or drink makes you feel better after you have been uncomfortably tired or hot.

refreshment /rɪˈfrɛʃmənt/, **refreshments.** PLURAL N **Refreshments** are drinks and small amounts of food that are provided, for example, during a meeting or journey.

refrigerator /rɪ¹frɪdʒəreɪtə/, **refrigerators.** COUNT N A **refrigerator** is a large container which is kept cool inside, usually by electricity, so that the food and drink in it stays fresh.

refuge /rɛfju:dʒ/, **refuges.** 1 UNCOUNT N When you take **refuge,** you try to protect yourself from unhappiness or an unpleasant situation by behaving or thinking in a particular way. *He seeks refuge in silence.* 2 COUNT N To take **refuge** also means to try and avoid physical harm by hiding somewhere. *Whole families had taken refuge down the tunnels.* 3 COUNT N A **refuge** is a place where you go for safety and protection. *A small cave was the only refuge from the cold.*

refugee /rɛfju⁴dʒi:/, **refugees.** COUNT N **Refugees** are people who have been forced to leave their country because there is a war there or because of their political or religious beliefs.

refund, refunds, refunding, refunded; pronounced /ri:fʌnd/ when it is a noun and /rɪfʌnd/ when it is a verb. 1 COUNT N A **refund** is a sum of money which is returned to you, for example because you have paid too much for goods, or have returned them to a shop. 2 VB WITH OBJ If you **refund** money to someone, you return it to them, for example because they have paid you too much for something.

refusal /rɪ¹fju:zə⁰l/, **refusals.** UNCOUNT N OR COUNT N A **refusal** is when someone says firmly or shows that they will not do, allow, or accept something. *...this refusal of a gift offered to us... I made many applications and had many refusals.*

refuse, refuses, refusing, refused; pronounced /rɪfju:z/ when it is a verb, and /rɛfju:s/ or /rɛfju:z/ when it is a noun. 1 VB If you **refuse** to do something, you deliberately do not do it, or say firmly that you will not do it. *He refused to accept this advice... Their bosses refuse to allow them any responsibility.* 2 VB WITH OBJ If someone **refuses** you something, they do not allow you to have it. *Only the president could refuse him a loan... The Council refused permission for them to live together.* 3 VB WITH OBJ If you **refuse** something that is offered to you, you do not accept it. *I offered him wine but he refused it.* 4 UNCOUNT N **Refuse** consists of the rubbish and unwanted thing in a house, shop, or factory, that are regularly thrown away; a formal use. *...a dump for refuse... ...refuse collection.*

refute /rɪ¹fju:t/, **refutes, refuting, refuted.** VB WITH OBJ If you **refute** something such as a theory or argument, you prove that it is wrong; a formal use.

regain /rɪ¹geɪn/, **regains, regaining, regained.** VB WITH OBJ If you **regain** something that you have lost, you get it back again. *He might be able to regain his old job.*

regal /ri:gə⁰l/. ADJ Something that is **regal** is very impressive. *...a regal staircase leading into a vast reception hall.*

regale /rɪ¹geɪl/, **regales, regaling, regaled.** VB WITH OBJ AND 'with' If someone **regales** you with stories or jokes, they tell you a lot of them, whether you want to hear them or not.

regard /rɪ¹gɑ:d/, **regards, regarding, regarded.** 1 VB WITH OBJ OR REFL VB If you **regard** someone or something as being a particular thing or as having a particular quality, you believe that they are that thing or have that quality. *I regard it as one of my masterpieces... She now regarded herself as a woman.* 2 VB WITH OBJ If you **regard** something or someone with a particular feeling, you have that feeling about them. *He is regarded with some suspicion by the country's leaders.* 3 UNCOUNT N If you have a high **regard** for someone, you have a lot of respect for them. *I have a high regard for Mike... My regard for him grew day by day.* 4 PLURAL N **Regards** is used in expressions like 'best regards' and 'with warm regards' as a way of expressing friendly feelings towards someone. *Give my regards to your daughter.* 5 PHRASE Some people say **as regards, with regard to,** or **in regard to** when indicating what they are referring to; a formal use. *As regards the car, I put an advertisement in the paper... With regard to the gas fire, we hardly use it... My upbringing was fairly strict in regard to obedience and truthfulness.*

regarding /rɪ¹gɑ:dɪŋ/. PREP You can use **regarding** to indicate what you are referring to. *There was always some question regarding education.*

regardless /rɪ¹gɑ:dlɪ²s/. 1 PHRASE If something happens **regardless of** something else, it happens in spite of it. *If they are determined to strike, they will do so regardless of what the law says.* 2 ADV If someone did something **regardless,** they did it even though there were problems that could have stopped them. *Mrs Hochstadt walked on regardless.*

reggae /rɛgeɪ/. UNCOUNT N **Reggae** is a kind of West Indian popular music with a very strong beat.

regime /reɪʒi:m/, **regimes;** also spelled **régime.** COUNT N A **regime** is a government. *...the corrupt regime that had ruled since 1921.*

regiment /rɛdʒɪmə²nt/, **regiments.** COUNT N A **regiment** is a large group of soldiers commanded by a colonel.

regimental /rɛdʒɪmɛntə⁰l/. ATTRIB ADJ **Regimental** means belonging to a particular regiment. *...the regimental commander.*

regimented /rɛdʒɪmɛntɪ²d/. ADJ Something that is **regimented** is very strictly controlled; used showing disapproval. *...the tightly regimented life of the prison.*

region /ri:dʒən/, **regions.** 1 COUNT N A **region** is an area of a country or of the world. *The country has nine autonomous regions... ...desert regions.* 2 PHRASE You say **in the region of** to indicate that you are mentioning an approximate amount. *Temperatures would be in the region of 500 degrees centigrade.*

regional /ri:dʒə⁰nəl, -dʒənə⁰l/. ADJ **Regional** organizations and activities relate to a particular area of a country. *...regional health authorities.*

register /rɛdʒɪstə/, **registers, registering, registered.** 1 COUNT N A **register** is an official list or record. *...the register of births, marriages, and deaths.* 2 VB If you **register** for something, you put your name on an official list. *You must register for work at the employment agency... They're coming to register as students on the English course.* ♦ **registered** ADJ *...a registered drug addict.* 3 VB WITH OBJ If you **register** something, you cause information about it to be recorded on an official list. *One of the cars was registered in my name.* 4 ERG VB When an amount **registers** or **is registered,** it is shown on a scale or measuring instrument. *The inflation index registered a modest 7.8% annual rate.* 5 VB WITH OBJ If you **register** a feeling or opinion that you have, you make it clear to other people. *He stared at me for a moment, his face registering disbelief.*

registrar /rɛdʒɪstrɑ:/, **registrars.** 1 COUNT N A **registrar** is a person whose job is to keep official records, especially of births, marriages, and deaths. 2 COUNT N A **registrar** is also a senior administrative official in a college or university.

registration /rɛdʒɪstreɪʃə⁰n/. UNCOUNT N The **registration** of something is the recording of it in an official list. *...a certificate of registration of death.*

registration number, registration numbers. COUNT N The **registration number** of a car or other vehicle is the series of letters and numbers shown at the front and back.

registry /rɛdʒɪstri¹/, **registries.** COUNT N A **registry** is a place where official records are kept.

registry office, registry offices. COUNT N A **registry office** is a place where births, marriages, and deaths are officially recorded, and where people can get married.

regress /rɪ¹grɛs/, **regresses, regressing, regressed.** VB If someone or something **regresses,** they return to a worse condition; a formal use. *Since 1976 many rivers have regressed from being clean to being grossly polluted.* ♦ **regression** /rɪ¹grɛʃə⁰n/ UNCOUNT N *...moral and social regression.*

regressive /rɪ¹grɛsɪv/. ADJ Something that is **regressive** involves a return to a worse condition; a formal use. *This fee has been criticized as a regressive tax.*

regret /rɪ¹grɛt/, **regrets, regretting, regretted.** 1 REPORT VB OR VB WITH -ING If you **regret** something that you have done, you wish that you had not done it. *I immediately regretted my decision... It made me regret that I had left home... Afterwards he regretted having spoken to them.* Also UNCOUNT N OR PLURAL N *...pangs of regret... Linda has no regrets at having become a banker.* 2 REPORT VB You can say that you **regret** something as a polite way of saying that you are sorry about it; a formal use. *London Transport regrets any inconvenience caused by these delays... The Prime Minister regrets that he is unable to reconsider your case.* Also UNCOUNT N *We informed them with regret of our decision.* 3 PHRASE You can use expressions such as **'I regret to say'** or **'I regret to inform you'** to show that you are sorry about something; a formal use. *The food and service, I regret to say, were disappointing.*

regretful /rɪ¹grɛtfʊl/. ADJ If you are **regretful,** you feel sorry about something. *Michael gave me a sad regretful smile.* ♦ **regretfully** ADV *He shook his head regretfully.*

regrettable /rɪ¹grɛtəbə⁰l/. ADJ Something that is **regrettable** is unfortunate and undesirable. *His tiredness caused him to make a regrettable error.* ♦ **regrettably** SUBMOD OR SENTENCE ADV *Regrettably few of them have gone to university... Regrettably, it is not an easy plant to grow in this country.*

regroup /ri:gru:p/, **regroups, regrouping, regrouped.** VB When soldiers **regroup,** they form an organized group again, in order to continue fighting.

regular /rɛgjə⁴lə/, **regulars.** 1 ADJ **Regular** things happen at equal intervals, or involve things happening at equal intervals. *They give regular Sunday afternoon concerts... You need to take regular exercise... The doctor examined the baby at regular intervals.* ♦ **regularly** ADV *The members meet regularly in one another's homes.* 2 ADJ **Regular** is also used to describe events that happen often. *...one of the regular bombings.* ♦ **regularly** ADV *Children are regularly abandoned.* 3 ATTRIB ADJ **Regular** is also used to describe people who often go to a place. *...our regular customers.* Also COUNT N *He's one of the regulars at the village pub.* 4 ATTRIB ADJ Your **regular** way of doing something is your normal way of doing it. *It's past his regular bedtime... You can get in touch with a psychiatrist through your regular doctor.* 5 ADJ If an object is **regular,** it has parts of equal size or is symmetrical and well-balanced in appearance. *His face was sun-tanned, with regular features... ...a regular shape.* 6 ADJ A **regular** verb, noun, or adjective inflects in the same way as most other verbs, nouns, or adjectives in the language.

regularity /rɛgjə⁴lærɪ¹ti¹/, **regularities.** 1 UNCOUNT N If something happens with **regularity,** it happens often. *The same exam questions cropped up with unfailing regularity.* 2 COUNT N **Regularities** are similar features which you notice in several different things and which may have the same cause or explanation. *...regularities in nature.*

regulate /rɛgjə⁴leɪt/, **regulates, regulating, regulated.** 1 VB WITH OBJ To **regulate** an activity or process means to control it, usually by means of rules. *The Government has a responsibility to regulate this kind of technology.* 2 VB WITH OBJ If you **regulate** a machine or device, you adjust it to control the way it operates.

regulation /rɛgjə⁴leɪʃə⁰n/, **regulations.** 1 COUNT N **Regulations** are rules made by a government or other authority. *There are specific regulations governing these types of machines.* Also ATTRIB ADJ *He had the short regulation haircut of a policeman.* 2 UNCOUNT N **Regulation** is the controlling of an activity or process, usually by means of rules. *...strict regulation over toxic waste disposal.*

regurgitate /rɪ¹gɜ:dʒɪteɪt/, **regurgitates, regurgitating, regurgitated.** VB WITH OBJ If you **regurgitate** food, you bring it back up from your stomach; a formal use.

rehabilitate /ri:h⁰əbɪlɪteɪt/, **rehabilitates, rehabilitating, rehabilitated.** VB WITH OBJ To **rehabilitate** someone who has been ill or in prison means to help them to live a normal life again. *He used exercise programmes to rehabilitate heart-attack victims.* ♦ **rehabilitation** /ri:h⁰əbɪlɪteɪʃə⁰n/ UNCOUNT N *...the rehabilitation of drug addicts.*

rehearsal /rɪ¹hɜ:sə⁰l/, **rehearsals.** COUNT N OR UNCOUNT N A **rehearsal** of a play, dance, or piece of music is a practice of it. *I develop a part during rehearsals with the company... In rehearsal he was meticulous and efficient.*

rehearse /rɪ¹hɜ:s/, **rehearses, rehearsing, rehearsed.** VB WITH OR WITHOUT OBJ When people **rehearse** a play, dance, or piece of music, they practise it. *The actors began to rehearse a few scenes... Stay and hear the orchestra rehearse.*

rehouse /ri:haʊz/, **rehouses, rehousing, rehoused.** VB WITH OBJ If someone **is rehoused,** they are provided with a different house to live in.

reign /reɪn/, **reigns, reigning, reigned.** 1 VB You can say that something **reigns** when it is the strongest or most noticeable feature of a situation or period of time; a literary use. *In the kitchen, chaos reigned.* 2 VB When a king or queen **reigns,** he or she is the leader of the country. *The emperor Chia Ching reigned from 1522 to 1566.* 3 COUNT N WITH POSS The **reign** of a king or queen is the period during which he or she is the leader of the country. *...George III's long reign.*

reimburse /ri:ɪmbɜ:s/, **reimburses, reimbursing, reimbursed.** VB WITH OBJ If you **reimburse** someone for something, you pay them back the money that they have spent or lost; a formal use. *I promised to reimburse her for the damage to her car.*

rein /reɪn/, **reins.** PLURAL N **Reins** are the leather straps attached to a horse's bridle which are used for controlling the horse. *He pulled at the reins.*

PHRASES ● If you **give free rein** to someone, or to your feelings or thoughts, you give them a lot of freedom. *They were encouraged to give free rein to their feelings.* ● If you **keep a tight rein on** someone, you control them firmly.

reincarnation /ri:ɪŋ¹kɑ:neɪʃə⁰n/, **reincarnations.** 1 UNCOUNT N If people believe in **reincarnation,** they believe that people are born as other people or animals after they die. 2 COUNT N A **reincarnation** is a person or animal who is believed to be a dead person born again. ...*reincarnations of their ancestors.*

reindeer /reɪndɪə/. **Reindeer** is the singular and plural. COUNT N A **reindeer** is a deer with large antlers that lives in northern areas of Europe, Asia, and America.

reinforce /riːɪnfɔːs/, **reinforces, reinforcing, reinforced.** 1 VB WITH OBJ If something **reinforces** a feeling, situation, or process, it strengthens it. *This sort of experience reinforces their feelings of worthlessness.* 2 VB WITH OBJ If something **reinforces** an idea or point of view, it provides more evidence or support for it. *This report reinforces practically everything that has been said.* 3 VB WITH OBJ To **reinforce** an object means to make it stronger or harder. *I had not thought of reinforcing the handles with leather.* ♦ **reinforced** ADJ ...*reinforced concrete.*

reinforcement /riːɪnfɔːsmənt/, **reinforcements.** 1 PLURAL N **Reinforcements** are soldiers who are sent to join an army in order to make it stronger. 2 UNCOUNT N **Reinforcement** is the strengthening of something. ...*the reinforcement of existing systems.*

reinstate /riːɪnsteɪt/, **reinstates, reinstating, reinstated.** 1 VB WITH OBJ If you **reinstate** someone, you give them back a job which had been taken from them. 2 VB WITH OBJ To **reinstate** something means to make it exist again; a formal use. *The trip reinstated my faith in myself.*

reiterate /riːɪtəreɪt/, **reiterates, reiterating, reiterated.** REPORT VB If you **reiterate** something, you say it again; a formal use. *He reiterated this advice several more times during the meeting.*

reject, rejects, rejecting, rejected; pronounced /rɪˈdʒɛkt/ when it is a verb and /riːdʒɛkt/ when it is a noun. 1 VB WITH OBJ If you **reject** something such as a proposal or request, you do not accept it or agree to it. *I rejected his offer... The amendment was rejected by 207 votes to 143.* ♦ **rejection** /riːdʒɛkʃən/ UNCOUNT N OR COUNT N ...*his rejection of repeated requests for military action.* 2 VB WITH OBJ If you **reject** a belief or a political system, you decide that you do not believe in it or want to support it. *It was hard for me to reject my family's religious beliefs.* ♦ **rejection** SING N OR UNCOUNT N *There is a rejection of conventional social values... ...rejection of racial discrimination.* 3 VB WITH OBJ If an employer **rejects** a person who has applied for a job, he or she does not offer that person the job. ♦ **rejection** UNCOUNT N OR COUNT N ...*in the face of repeated rejection... ...a succession of rejections.* 4 COUNT N A **reject** is a product that is not sold, or is sold cheaply, because there is something wrong with it.

rejoice /rɪˈdʒɔɪs/, **rejoices, rejoicing, rejoiced.** VB If you **rejoice**, you are very pleased about something; a literary use. *All his friends gathered to rejoice in his freedom.*

rejuvenate /rɪˈdʒuːvɪneɪt/, **rejuvenates, rejuvenating, rejuvenated.** 1 VB WITH OBJ If something **rejuvenates** you, it makes you feel or look young again. 2 VB WITH OBJ If you **rejuvenate** an organization or system, you make it more lively and more efficient. *He resolved to rejuvenate the party.*

relapse, relapses, relapsing, relapsed; pronounced /rɪˈlæps/ when it is a verb and /rɪlæps/ or /riːlæps/ when it is a noun. 1 VB If someone **relapses** into undesirable behaviour, they start to behave that way again. *She relapsed into depression.* Also COUNT N ...*her relapses into alcoholism.* 2 COUNT N If a sick person has a **relapse**, their health suddenly gets worse after it had been improving.

relate /rɪˈleɪt/, **relates, relating, related.** 1 VB WITH PREP 'to' If something **relates** to a particular subject, it concerns that subject. *I want to ask you a question that relates to electricity... ...information relating to national security.* 2 RECIP VB The way that two things **relate** is the sort of connection between them. *Let us examine the way that the words in a sentence relate to each other... How the two agreements related is unimportant.* 3 VB WITH OBJ If you **relate** one thing to another, you see or say what connection there is between them. *It enables students to relate their theory to the real world.* 4 RECIP VB The way that people **relate** is the way that they communicate with each other and behave towards each other. *Children need to learn to relate to other children.* 5 VB WITH OBJ If you **relate** a story, you tell it; a literary use. *Davis related the experience of three Cuban girls.*

related /rɪˈleɪtɪd/. 1 ADJ If things are **related**, there is a connection between them. ...*two important and closely related questions... Physics is closely related to mathematics.* 2 PRED ADJ People who are **related** belong to the same family. ...*four people closely related to each other.*

relation /rɪˈleɪʃən/, **relations.** 1 PHRASE You use **in relation to** when you are comparing one thing with another, to introduce the second thing. *Wages are very low in relation to the cost of living.* 2 UNCOUNT N The **relation** of one thing to another is the connection between them. *She argued that literature has no relation to reality.* 3 COUNT N Your **relations** are the members of your family. *I was a distant relation of her husband.* 4 PLURAL N WITH SUPP **Relations** between people or groups are contacts between them and the way they behave towards each other. *The unions should have close relations with management.*

relationship /rɪˈleɪʃənʃɪp/, **relationships.** 1 COUNT N WITH SUPP The **relationship** between two people or groups is the way they feel and behave towards each other. *Pakistan's relationship with India has changed dramatically.* 2 COUNT N A **relationship** is also a close friendship between two people, especially one involving romantic or sexual feelings. 3 COUNT N The **relationship** between two things is the way in which they are connected. *What is the relationship between language and thought?*

relative /rɛlətɪv/, **relatives.** 1 ATTRIB ADJ You use **relative** to indicate that your description of something applies when a comparison is made with other things. *The head of the department is a relative newcomer... He chose to return to the relative peace of his childhood village.* ♦ **relatively** SUBMOD *A relatively small number of people disagreed.* 2 ATTRIB ADJ You also use **relative** when you are referring to a comparison of the size or nature of two things. *There was a discussion on the relative naval strengths of the two countries.* 3 PRED ADJ If you say that something is **relative**, you mean that it needs to be considered and judged in relation to other things; a formal use. *All human values are relative.* 4 PHRASE **Relative to** something means in comparison with it; a formal use. *There is a shortage of labour relative to the demand for it.* 5 COUNT N Your **relatives** are the members of your family.

relative clause, relative clauses. COUNT N In grammar, a **relative clause** is a subordinate clause relating to a noun group, which is introduced by a relative pronoun such as 'who', or by 'when' or 'where'.

relative pronoun, relative pronouns. COUNT N In grammar, a **relative pronoun** is a pronoun such as 'who' that is used to introduce a relative clause.

relax /rɪˈlæks/, **relaxes, relaxing, relaxed.** 1 ERG VB If you **relax** or if something **relaxes** you, you feel calmer and less worried or tense. *He saw that nothing was wrong, and relaxed... Running relaxes you.* ♦ **relaxed** ADJ ...*a relaxed and informal discussion.* ♦ **relaxing** ADJ *It is a delightful, relaxing place for a holiday.* 2 VB When your body or a part of it **relaxes**, it becomes less stiff, firm, or tense. *All his facial muscles relaxed.* 3 ERG VB If you **relax** your grip on something or if your grip **relaxes**, you hold the thing less tightly than before. 4 VB WITH OBJ If you **relax** a rule, you make it less strict.

relaxation /riːlækseɪʃən/. UNCOUNT N **Relaxation** refers to ways of spending time that are pleasant and restful. *It is so necessary for the mother to have some rest and relaxation.*

relay, relays, relaying, relayed; pronounced /riːleɪ/ for meanings 1, 2, and 3, and /rɪˈleɪ/ for meaning 4. 1 COUNT N A **relay** or a **relay race** is a race between teams in which each member of the team runs or swims one section of the race. 2 PHRASE If people do something **in relays**, they do it in small groups at different times. *The children at our school have to be fed in two relays.* 3 VB WITH OBJ To **relay** television or radio signals means to send them on or broadcast them. *The Sunday Concert will be relayed live on Radio Three.* 4 VB WITH OBJ If you **relay** something that has been said to you, you repeat it to another person. *McKenzie relayed the question to me.*

release /rɪˈliːs/, **releases, releasing, released.** 1 VB WITH OBJ To **release** someone means to set them free. *They had just been released from prison... This failure released him from any obligation to take further exams.* Also UNCOUNT N *Nearly a year after his release he was still unable to sleep properly.* 2 VB WITH OBJ To **release** something means to make it available or issue it; a formal use. ...*in a statement released at 8 a.m... Last week they released their latest album, 'Cloudland'.* 3 VB WITH OBJ If something such as gas or water **is released,** it is let out of an enclosed space. ...*releasing radioactivity into the environment.* 4 VB WITH OBJ If you **release** something, you stop holding it; a formal use. *He quickly released her hand.* 5 VB WITH OBJ If you **release** a catch or brake, you move it so that it stops holding something. 6 COUNT N WITH SUPP A press **release** or publicity **release** is an official written statement that is given to reporters. 7 COUNT N A new **release** is a new record or video that has just become available for people to buy.

relegate /rɛləgeɪt/, **relegates, relegating, relegated.** VB WITH OBJ If you **relegate** someone or something, you give them a less important position or status. *The management had relegated Mr Pelker to the role of part-time consultant.*

relent /rɪˈlɛnt/, **relents, relenting, relented.** VB If you **relent,** you allow someone to do something that you did not allow them to do before. *Sometimes our parents would relent and permit us to meet.*

relentless /rɪˈlɛntləs/; a literary word. 1 ADJ Something that is **relentless** never stops or never becomes less intense. ...*the relentless beating of the sun on the roofs.* ♦ **relentlessly** ADV *The chase relentlessly continues.* 2 ADJ Someone who is **relentless** is determined to do something and refuses to give up. *He could be a relentless enemy.* ♦ **relentlessly** ADV ...*a relentlessly ambitious politician.*

relevant /rɛləvənt/. 1 ADJ If something is **relevant,** it is connected with what you are talking or writing about. *This is not strictly relevant to what I'll be saying.* ♦ **relevance** /rɛləvəns/ UNCOUNT N *She did not understand the relevance of his remarks.* 2 ATTRIB ADJ The **relevant** thing of a particular kind is the one that is appropriate. *They are made to conform with the relevant British Standards.*

reliable /rɪˈlaɪəbəl/. 1 ADJ People or things that are **reliable** can be trusted to work well or to behave in the way that you want them to. *She is a charming and reliable person... The diesel engine is long-lasting and extremely reliable.* ♦ **reliably** ADV *They worked reliably under battle conditions.* ♦ **reliability** /rɪˈlaɪəbɪlɪti/ UNCOUNT N *These machines have always been noted for reliability.* 2 ADJ **Reliable** information is very likely to be correct. ...*information from a reliable source.* ♦ **reliably** ADV *We are reliably informed that her new record will be released in the autumn.*

reliance /rɪˈlaɪəns/. UNCOUNT N **Reliance** on someone or something is the state of needing them in order to live or work properly. ...*the student's reliance on the teacher... ...complete reliance on drugs.*

relic /rɛlɪk/, **relics.** 1 COUNT N Something that is a **relic** has survived from an earlier time. ...*a museum with relics of great explorers.* 2 COUNT N In a church, a **relic** is part of the body of a saint, or an object associated with a saint.

relief /rɪˈliːf/. 1 UNCOUNT N OR SING N If you feel **relief,** you feel glad because something unpleasant has not happened or has stopped. *I breathed a sigh of relief... To my relief, he found the suggestion acceptable... It was such a relief to be free of disguises and pretence.* 2 UNCOUNT N **Relief** is also money, food, or clothing that is provided for people who are very poor or hungry. *She outlined what was being done to provide relief.*

relieve /rɪˈliːv/, **relieves, relieving, relieved.** 1 VB WITH OBJ If something **relieves** an unpleasant feeling, it makes it less unpleasant. *The passengers in the plane swallow to relieve the pressure on their eardrums.* 2 VB WITH OBJ AND 'of' If someone or something **relieves** you of an unpleasant feeling or a difficulty, they take it away from you. *The news relieved him of some of his embarrassment.*

relieved /rɪˈliːvd/. ADJ If you are **relieved,** you feel glad because something unpleasant has not happened or has stopped. *I am relieved to hear that this isn't true.*

religion /rɪˈlɪdʒən/, **religions.** UNCOUNT N OR COUNT N **Religion** is belief in a god or gods and the activities connected with this belief. *The school placed strong emphasis on religion... ...the Christian religion.*

religious /rɪˈlɪdʒəs/. 1 ATTRIB ADJ You use **religious** to describe things connected with religion. *All religious activities were suppressed.* 2 ADJ Someone who is **religious** has a strong belief in a god or gods.

relinquish /rɪˈlɪŋkwɪʃ/, **relinquishes, relinquishing, relinquished.** VB WITH OBJ If you **relinquish** something such as authority or responsibility, you give it up; a formal use. *She relinquished the editorship of the newspaper.*

relish /rɛlɪʃ/, **relishes, relishing, relished.** 1 VB WITH OBJ If you **relish** something, you get a lot of enjoyment from it. *He relishes the challenge of competition.* Also UNCOUNT N *In his book he exposed with relish all the evils of our present day.* 2 VB WITH OBJ If you **relish** the idea or prospect of something, you are looking forward to that thing very much. *She didn't relish the idea of going on her own.*

relive /riːlɪv/, **relives, reliving, relived.** VB WITH OBJ If you **relive** something that has happened to you in the past, you remember it and imagine that you are experiencing it again.

relocate /riːləukeɪt/, **relocates, relocating, relocated.** ERG VB If people or businesses **are relocated,** they move to a different place. *They relocated me in another building... Semi-skilled workers find themselves compelled to relocate.* ♦ **relocation** /riːləukeɪʃən/ UNCOUNT N *Priority must be given to the relocation of industry.*

reluctant /rɪ'lʌktənt/. ADJ If you are **reluctant** to do something, you are unwilling to do it. *He is reluctant to be photographed.* ♦ **reluctantly** ADV *A wage increase of 21% was reluctantly conceded.* ♦ **reluctance** /rɪ'lʌktəns/ UNCOUNT N *...the reluctance of the banks to allow credit.*

rely /rɪ'laɪ/, **relies, relying, relied.** 1 VB WITH 'on' OR 'upon' If you **rely** on someone or something, you need them in order to live or work properly. *Some industries rely heavily on government for finance.* 2 VB WITH 'on' OR 'upon' If you can **rely** on someone to work well or behave as you want them to, you can trust them to do this. *One could always rely on him to be polite.*

remade /ri:meɪd/. **Remade** is the past tense and past participle of **remake.**

remain /rɪ'meɪn/, **remains, remaining, remained.** 1 LINK VB To **remain** in a particular state means to stay in that state and not change. *Oliver remained silent... He remained standing... The results of these experiments remain a secret.* 2 VB If you **remain** in a place, you stay there and do not move away. *I was allowed to remain at home.* 3 VB If something **remains,** it still exists. *Even today remnants of this practice remain... The fact remains that they mean to destroy us.* ♦ **remaining** ATTRIB ADJ *...the demise of her last remaining relatives.* 4 VB WITH TO-INF If something **remains** to be done, it has not yet been done. *One hazard remained to be overcome... It remains to be seen what the long term effects will be.* 5 PLURAL N The **remains** of something are the parts of it that are left after most of it has been taken away or destroyed. *The remains of the meat sat on the kitchen table... They discovered the remains of a huge dinosaur.* 6 PLURAL N **Remains** are objects and parts of buildings from an earlier period of history, usually found in the ground. *...Roman remains.*

remainder /rɪ'meɪndə/. COLL N The **remainder** of something is the part of it that remains after the other parts have gone or been dealt with. *She went to Brighton where she lived for the remainder of her life... I will pay you a hundred pounds deposit and the remainder on delivery.*

remake /ri:meɪk/, **remakes, remaking, remade** /ri:meɪd/. VB WITH OBJ If you **remake** something, you make it again, especially in a better way. *Ask what the price is for remaking old mattresses.*

remand /rɪ'mɑ:nd/, **remands, remanding, remanded.** 1 VB WITH OBJ If someone accused of a crime **is remanded** by a judge, they are ordered to come back for their trial at a later date. 2 PHRASE If someone is **on remand,** they have appeared in court and are waiting for their trial to take place.

remark /rɪ'mɑ:k/, **remarks, remarking, remarked.** 1 REPORT VB OR VB WITH 'on' If you **remark** that something is the case, you say that it is the case. *He remarked that the lighting was not very good... His friends remarked on his failure to arrive.* 2 COUNT N A **remark** is something that you say, often in a casual way. *At school some of the children used to make unkind remarks about my clothes.*

remarkable /rɪ'mɑ:kəbəl/. ADJ Someone or something that is **remarkable** is very impressive or unusual. *He prepared the dinner with remarkable speed and efficiency.* ♦ **remarkably** SUBMOD OR SENTENCE ADV *He has recovered from the accident remarkably well.*

remedial /rɪ'mi:dɪəl/. ATTRIB ADJ **Remedial** activities are intended to improve something; a formal use. *...remedial exercises for handicapped children.*

remedy /rɛmɪ'di'/, **remedies, remedying, remedied.** 1 COUNT N A **remedy** is a successful way of dealing with a problem. *...a drastic remedy for lawlessness and disorder.* 2 COUNT N A **remedy** is also something that is intended to stop illness or pain. *Home-made remedies can often lessen the pain.* 3 VB WITH OBJ If you **remedy** something that is wrong or harmful, you correct it. *Technicians laboriously tried to find and remedy faults.*

remember /rɪ'mɛmbə/, **remembers, remembering, remembered.** 1 VB OR REPORT VB If you **remember** people or events from the past, your mind still has an impression of them and you are able to think about them. *He remembered the man well... I remember him falling down the steps... I remembered that the shop was on the way to Muswell Hill.* 2 VB OR REPORT VB If you can **remember** something, you are able to bring it back into your mind by making an effort to do so. *I'm trying to remember the things I have to do... There was something else, but she could not remember what it was.* 3 VB WITH TO-INF If you **remember** to do something, you think of it and do it at the right time. *Remember to go to the bank.* 4 VB WITH OBJ AND PREP 'to' If you ask someone to **remember** you to a person who you have not seen for a long time, you are asking them to pass your greetings to that person. *Remember me to your Grandma.*

remembrance /rɪ'mɛmbrəns/. UNCOUNT N If you do something in **remembrance** of a dead person, you do it as a way of showing that you remember them and respect them; a formal use. *We stood in silence for two minutes in remembrance of the dead.*

remind /rɪ'maɪnd/, **reminds, reminding, reminded.** 1 VB WITH OBJ If someone **reminds** you about a fact or event that you already know about, they deliberately say something which makes you think about it. *She had to remind him that he had a wife... Miss Lemon reminded him of two appointments... Remind me to speak to you about Davis.* 2 VB WITH OBJ AND 'of' If someone or something **reminds** you of another person or thing, they are similar to the other person or thing and they make you think about them. *Your son reminds me of you at his age.*

reminder /rɪ'maɪndə/, **reminders.** 1 COUNT N If one thing is a **reminder** of another, the first thing makes you think about the second. *Seeing her again was a painful reminder of how different things had been five years ago.* 2 COUNT N A **reminder** is also a letter that is sent to tell you that you have not done something such as pay a bill or return library books.

reminisce /rɛmɪnɪs/, **reminisces, reminiscing, reminisced.** VB If you **reminisce** about something from your past, you write or talk about it; a formal use. *He reminisced about the 'old days'.*

reminiscence /rɛmɪnɪsəns/, **reminiscences.** COUNT N Someone's **reminiscences** are things which they remember from the past, and which they talk or write about.

reminiscent /rɛmɪnɪsənt/. PRED ADJ If one thing is **reminiscent** of another, the first thing reminds you of the second; a formal use. *There was a sweet smell, vaguely reminiscent of coffee.*

remission /rɪ'mɪʃən/. UNCOUNT N If someone in prison gets **remission,** their prison sentence is reduced, usually because they have behaved well. *I got four months' remission for good conduct.*

remnant /rɛmnənt/, **remnants.** COUNT N A **remnant** of something is a small part of it that is left when the main part has disappeared or been destroyed. *Even today remnants of this practice remain.*

remorse /rɪ'mɔ:s/. UNCOUNT N **Remorse** is a strong feeling of sorrow about something wrong that you have done; a formal use. *I had been filled with remorse over hurting her.*

remote /rɪ'məʊt/, **remoter, remotest.** 1 ADJ **Remote** areas are far away from places where people live. 2 ADJ If something happened in the **remote** past, it happened a very long time ago. 3 PRED ADJ If something is **remote** from ordinary people or life, it is very different. *His stories are too remote from everyday life.* 4 ADJ If someone is **remote,** they are not friendly and do not get closely involved with other people. *She was a silent girl, cool and remote.* ♦ **remoteness** UNCOUNT N *He criticised the remoteness of public authorities.* 5 ADJ If the possibility of something happening is **remote,** it is very unlikely that it will happen.

remote control. UNCOUNT N **Remote control** is a system of controlling a machine or vehicle from a distance by using radio or electronic signals. *The missile is guided by remote control.*

remotely /rɪ'məʊtli'/. SUBMOD You use **remotely** to emphasize a negative statement. *Agreement did not seem remotely possible at the time... I've never seen anything remotely like it.*

removal /rɪ'mu:vəl/. 1 UNCOUNT N The **removal** of something is the act of removing it. *He consented to the removal of the flags.* 2 MOD A **removal** company transports furniture from one building to another, for example when people move house. *...removal men.*

remove /rɪ'mu:v/, **removes, removing, removed.** 1 VB WITH OBJ If you **remove** something from a place, you take it away. *The servants came in to remove the cups... He removed his hand from the man's collar.* 2 VB WITH OBJ When you **remove** clothing, you take it off. *Will you remove your shoes before you go in, please?* 3 VB WITH OBJ If you **remove** a stain from something, you treat it with a chemical or wash it and make the stain disappear. 4 VB WITH OBJ When you **remove** something undesirable, you get rid of it. *Instant publication would have removed suspicion.*

removed /rɪ'mu:vd/. PRED ADJ If an idea or situation is far **removed** from something, it is very different from it. *His ideas on foreign policy were far removed from those of the Government.*

renaissance /rə'neɪsəns/. SING N When there is a **renaissance,** there is a revival of interest in a particular type of activity, especially in the arts. *...the renaissance of the British theatre in the late 1950s.*

rename /ri:neɪm/, **renames, renaming, renamed.** VB WITH OBJ If you **rename** something, you give it a different name. *Mr Haq has taken over the Carousel Cafe and renamed it The Pearl of India.*

render /rɛndə/, **renders, rendering, rendered;** a formal word. 1 VB WITH OBJ AND COMPLEMENT You can use **render** to say that someone or something is changed. For example, if you **render** something harmless, you make it harmless. *Frank was rendered speechless by her reply.* 2 VB WITH OBJ AND OBJ OR VB WITH OBJ AND PREP 'to' If you **render** someone help or assistance, you help them. *Dr Lister Smith rendered vital first aid to Commander Bond.*

rendering /rɛndərɪŋ/, **renderings.** COUNT N Someone's **rendering** of a play, poem, or piece of music is the way they perform it; a formal use. *...a rendering of the hymn 'Onward Christian Soldiers'.*

rendezvous /rɒndeɪvu:/. **Rendezvous** is the singular and plural; the plural is pronounced /rɒndeɪvu:z/. 1 COUNT N A **rendezvous** is a meeting, often a secret one, that you have arranged with someone for a particular time and place. *We made a dawn rendezvous.* 2 COUNT N A **rendezvous** is also a place where you have arranged to meet someone. *I met him at a secret rendezvous outside the city.*

renegade /rɛnɪgeɪd/, **renegades.** COUNT N A **renegade** is a person who abandons their former group and joins an opposing or different group; a formal use. *He was a traitor and renegade... ...renegade supporters of the deposed king.*

renew /rɪ'nju:/, **renews, renewing, renewed.** 1 VB WITH OBJ If you **renew** an activity or relationship, you begin it again. *She at once renewed her attack on Judy... I hoped that we might renew our friendship.* ♦ **renewed** ATTRIB ADJ *...renewed efforts to recruit more members.* 2 VB WITH OBJ When you **renew** something such as a licence or a contract, you extend the period of time for which it is valid. 3 VB WITH OBJ If something that has been destroyed or lost **is renewed,** it comes again or is replaced. *My strength was renewed.* ♦ **renewed** ATTRIB ADJ *He looked at me with renewed interest.*

renewable /rɪ'nju:əbəl/. ADJ A **renewable** source of energy is one which is naturally replaced when it is used, rather than being destroyed. *Wind power is another renewable source of electricity.*

renewal /rɪ'nju:əl/, **renewals.** 1 SING N OR UNCOUNT N If there is a **renewal** of an activity, it starts again. *Renewal of hostility with neighbouring countries seemed likely.* 2 UNCOUNT N OR COUNT N The **renewal** of a document such as a licence or a contract is an official extension of the time for which it remains valid. *Some licences need yearly renewal.*

renounce /rɪ'naʊns/, **renounces, renouncing, renounced.** VB WITH OBJ If you **renounce** a belief or a way of behaving, you decide to stop having that belief or behaving in that way; a formal use. *We have renounced the use of force to settle our disputes.*

renovate /rɛnəveɪt/, **renovates, renovating, renovated.** VB WITH OBJ If someone **renovates** an old building or machine, they repair it and get it back into good condition. *The house had been renovated three years earlier.*

renown /rɪ'naʊn/. UNCOUNT N **Renown** is fame; a literary use. *His renown as a soldier spread.*

renowned /rɪ'naʊnd/. ADJ Someone who is **renowned** is famous or well-known. *The locals are renowned for their hospitality.*

rent /rɛnt/, **rents, renting, rented.** 1 VB WITH OBJ If you **rent** something, you regularly pay its owner a sum of money for using it. *They rented a villa not far from Rome... He rented a colour TV soon after moving in.* ♦ **rented** ADJ *...a rented flat.* 2 SING N OR UNCOUNT N **Rent** is the amount of money that you pay regularly for the use of a house, flat, or piece of land. *He made enough money to pay the rent.*

rent out. PHR VB If you **rent out** something such as a room or a car, you allow it to be used in return for payment.

rental /rɛntəl/. 1 ATTRIB ADJ **Rental** means connected with the renting out of goods. *...a computer rental service.* 2 SING N The **rental** is the amount of money that you have to pay when you rent something such as a television or a car. *The quarterly rental will be £35.*

renunciation /rɪnʌnsieɪʃən/. UNCOUNT N The **renunciation** of a belief or way of behaving is a decision to stop having that belief or behaving in that way; a formal use. *...the renunciation of revolution.*

reorganize /ri'ɔ:gənaɪz/, **reorganizes, reorganizing, reorganized;** also spelled **reorganise.** VB WITH OR WITHOUT OBJ If you **reorganize** something, you organize it in a new way. *The manufacturers were reorganising the soap industry.* ♦ **reorganization** /ri:ɔ:gənaɪzeɪʃən/ UNCOUNT N OR COUNT N *...the reorganization of the health system.*

rep /rɛp/, **reps.** COUNT N A **rep** is a person who travels round selling their company's products or services to other companies or to shops; an informal use. *...a sales rep.*

repaid /rɪ^{1}peɪd/. **Repaid** is the past tense and past participle of **repay.**

repair /rɪ^{1}pɛə/, **repairs, repairing, repaired.** 1 COUNT N OR UNCOUNT N A **repair** is something that you do to mend an item that is damaged or is not working properly. *He had left his car for repairs in the garage... The chairs are in need of repair.* 2 VB WITH OBJ If you **repair** something that is damaged or is not working properly, you mend it. *No one knew how to repair the engine.* 3 PHRASE If something such as a building is **in good repair,** it is in good condition. If it is **in bad repair,** it is in bad condition; a formal use. 4 VB WITH OBJ If you **repair** an undesirable action or situation, you do something to correct it; a formal use. *I'll repair the omission.*

repatriate /riːpætri^{1}eɪt/, **repatriates, repatriating, repatriated.** VB WITH OBJ If someone **is repatriated,** they are sent back to their own country. ♦ **repatriation** /riːpætri^{1}eɪʃə^{0}n/ UNCOUNT N *...emergency repatriation flights for tourists.*

repay /rɪ^{1}peɪ/, **repays, repaying, repaid** /rɪ^{1}peɪd/. 1 VB WITH OBJ If you **repay** money, you give it back to the person you borrowed it from or took it from. *He plans to repay most of that debt... He ordered the President to repay the money to the State.* 2 VB WITH OBJ If you **repay** a favour that someone did for you, you do something or give them something in return. *We hope we can repay you for the pleasure you have given us.*

repayment /rɪ^{1}peɪmə^{2}nt/, **repayments.** 1 COUNT N **Repayments** are amounts of money which you pay at regular intervals to a person or organization in order to repay a debt over a period of time. 2 UNCOUNT N The **repayment** of money is the process of paying it back to the person you owe it to. *...repayment of international debts.*

repeal /rɪ^{1}piːl/, **repeals, repealing, repealed.** VB WITH OBJ If the government **repeals** a law, it officially ends it; a legal use. *Nine countries repealed their anti-discrimination laws last year.* Also UNCOUNT N *...a campaign for the repeal of incomes legislation.*

repeat /rɪ^{1}piːt/, **repeats, repeating, repeated.** 1 REPORT VB If you **repeat** something, you say or write it again. *Haldane repeated his statement in the presence of the Prime Minister... 'We need half a million dollars,' Monty kept repeating. 'Half a million dollars.'* 2 VB WITH OBJ If you **repeat** something that someone else has said or written, you say or write the same thing. *Ballin repeated what he had been told by Haldane.* 3 REFL VB If you **repeat** yourself, you say something which you have said before, without meaning to. *People tend to repeat themselves a lot in conversation.* 4 VB WITH OBJ If you **repeat** an action, you do it again. *I decided not to repeat the mistake of my first marriage.* 5 VB WITH OBJ If a television or radio programme **is repeated,** it is broadcast again. 6 COUNT N A **repeat** is something which is done again or which happens again. *They're all old films or repeats... He didn't want a repeat of yesterday's scene with Hooper... ...a repeat performance.*

repeated /rɪ^{1}piːtɪ^{2}d/. ATTRIB ADJ **Repeated** actions or events are ones which happen many times. *After repeated attempts, the manager finally managed to call the police.*

repeatedly /rɪ^{1}piːtɪdli^1/. ADV If you do something **repeatedly,** you do it many times. *The child learns to read by seeing the words repeatedly.*

repel /rɪ^{1}pɛl/, **repels, repelling, repelled.** VB WITH OBJ If something **repels** you, you find it horrible and disgusting. *Any deformity frightened and repelled her.*

repellent /rɪ^{1}pɛlənt/, **repellents.** 1 ADJ If you find something **repellent,** you find it horrible and disgusting; a formal use. *The idea of eating meat has become repellent to me.* 2 MASS N A **repellent** is a chemical which is used to keep insects or other creatures away. *...a bottle of insect repellent.*

repent /rɪ^{1}pɛnt/, **repents, repenting, repented.** VB If you **repent,** you feel sorry for doing something bad; a formal use. *He may repent of his sins.* ♦ **repentance** /rɪ^{1}pɛntəns/ UNCOUNT N *...the need for repentance.*

repercussions /riːpəkʌʃə^{0}nz/. PLURAL N The **repercussions** of an event are the effects that it has at a later time; a formal use. *What happened had enormous repercussions on my family.*

repertoire /rɛpətwɑː/. SING N WITH SUPP A performer's **repertoire** is all the pieces of music or parts in plays he or she has learned and can perform. *It was wonderful to be able to extend my song repertoire.*

repertory /rɛpətə^{0}ri^1/. UNCOUNT N **Repertory** is the practice of performing a small number of plays in a theatre during a period, using the same actors in every play; a technical use.

repetition /rɛpɪtɪʃə^{0}n/, **repetitions.** COUNT N OR UNCOUNT N If there is a **repetition** of something that has happened before, it happens again. *He didn't want a repetition of the scene with his mother.*

repetitious /rɛpɪtɪʃəs/. ADJ **Repetitious** means the same as repetitive. *...repetitious jobs.*

repetitive /rɪ^{1}pɛtɪtɪv/. ADJ Something that is **repetitive** contains unnecessary repetition, and is therefore boring. *His job consists of dull, repetitive work.*

replace /rɪ^{1}pleɪs/, **replaces, replacing, replaced.** 1 VB WITH OBJ When one thing or person **replaces** another, the first one takes the place of the second one. *Thomas bought a new sweater to replace the one he lost.* 2 VB WITH OBJ If you **replace** something that is damaged, lost, or old-fashioned, you get a new thing which will perform the same function. *The books that have been stolen will have to be replaced... The airline is currently replacing its DC10s with Boeing 747s.* 3 VB WITH OBJ To **replace** something also means to put it back in the place where it was before. *She replaced the receiver.*

replacement /rɪ^{1}pleɪsmə^{2}nt/, **replacements.** 1 UNCOUNT N The **replacement** of someone or something happens when they are replaced by another person or thing. *...the replacement of steam by diesel.* 2 COUNT N A **replacement** for someone or something is another person or thing that takes their place. *The Colonel's replacement was due any day now.*

replay, replays, replaying, replayed; pronounced /riːpleɪ/ when it is a verb and /riːpleɪ/ when it is a noun. 1 VB WITH OBJ If two sports teams **replay** a match in a competition, they play it again because the previous match between them was a draw. *The match will be replayed on Saturday.* Also COUNT N *Who won the replay?* 2 VB WITH OBJ If you **replay** something that you have recorded on tape or film, you play it in order to listen to it or look at it.

replenish /rɪ^{1}plɛnɪʃ/, **replenishes, replenishing, replenished.** VB WITH OBJ To **replenish** something means to make it full or complete again by adding a quantity of a substance that has gone; a formal use. *We have to import an extra 4 million tons of wheat to replenish our reserves... Mr Jones replenished his glass.*

replica /rɛplɪkə/, **replicas.** COUNT N A **replica** of a statue, machine, or building is an accurate copy of it.

reply /rɪ^{1}plaɪ/, **replies, replying, replied.** 1 REPORT VB When you **reply** to something that someone has said or written to you, you say or write something as an answer. *He gave me no chance to reply to his question... 'Did you have a nice journey?'—'Yes,' Jenny replied... I sent you a letter, and you never replied.* 2 COUNT N A **reply** is something that you say or write when you reply to someone. *He called 'Sarah', but there was no reply... I received about a dozen replies to my enquiry.* 3 PHRASE If you say or do something **in reply** to what someone else has said or done, you say or do it as a response to them. *I have nothing to say in reply to your question.*

report /rɪ^{1}pɔːt/, **reports, reporting, reported.** 1 REPORT VB If you **report** something that has happened, you tell people about it. *Accidents must be reported to the police within twenty-four hours... The papers reported that Southern England was 'paralysed' by snow.* 2 VB WITH OBJ If someone **reports** you to a person in authority, they tell the person about something wrong that you have done. *You should have reported them to the police.* 3 VB If you **report** to a person or place, you go to them and say that you are ready to start work. *The next morning he reported for duty at Jack Starke's office... I told him to report to me after the job was completed.* 4 COUNT N A **report** is a written or spoken account of an event or situation. *When you get back, write a report on the visit... So far, there have been no reports of bomb attacks in the area.* 5 COUNT N A school **report** is a written account of how well or badly a pupil has done during the term that has just finished; a British use.

reportedly /rɪ^{1}pɔːtɪdli^1/. ADV If something is **reportedly** true, someone has said that it is true; a formal use. *He has reportedly instructed his family not to interfere if he tries to kill himself.*

reported speech. UNCOUNT N **Reported speech** gives an account of something that someone has said, but without quoting their actual words. **Reported speech** is usually introduced by a verb such as 'say' or 'tell' followed by 'that'.

reporter /rɪ^{1}pɔːtə/, **reporters.** COUNT N A **reporter** is someone who writes news articles or broadcasts news reports. *...a reporter from a Chicago newspaper.*

repose /rɪ^{1}pəʊz/. UNCOUNT N **Repose** is a state in which you are resting and feel calm; a literary use. *Her face was lovely in repose.*

repository /rɪ^{1}pɒzɪtə^{0}ri^1/, **repositories.** COUNT N WITH SUPP A **repository** is a place where something is kept safely; a formal use. *The Foreign Office was regarded as the repository of all relevant information.*

reprehensible /rɛprɪhɛnsə^{1}bə^{0}l/. ADJ **Reprehensible** behaviour is morally wrong; a formal use.

represent /rɛprɪ^{2}zɛnt/, **represents, representing, represented.** 1 VB WITH OBJ If someone **represents** you, they act on your behalf, for example in a court of law or in parliament. *...lawyers representing relatives of the victims... Thirty one nations are now represented at the Disarmament Conference.* 2 VB WITH OBJ If a sign or symbol **represents** something, it is accepted as meaning that thing. *The word 'love' was represented by a small heart.* 3 VB WITH OBJ If you **represent** something in a particular way, you describe it in that way. *The evacuation of our forces was represented as a triumphant success.*

representation /rɛprɪ^{2}zɛnteɪʃə^{0}n/, **representations.** 1 UNCOUNT N **Representation** is the state of being represented by someone, for example in a parliament or on a committee. *They're campaigning for student representation on the university's governing bodies.* 2 COUNT N You can describe a picture or statue of someone as a **representation** of them; a formal use. *...crude representations of angels.* 3 PLURAL N **Representations** are formal requests, complaints, or statements made to a government or other official group. *...representations made by a group of local residents.*

representative /rɛprɪ^{2}zɛntətɪv/, **representatives.** 1 COUNT N A **representative** is a person who acts on behalf of another person or group of people. *The Consumer Congress is made up of representatives of a wide range of organizations... ...union representatives.* 2 ATTRIB ADJ A **representative** group acts on behalf of a larger group. *The government consists of two representative assemblies.* 3 ADJ If something is **representative** of a group, it is typical of that group. *...a representative cross-section of the public.*

repress /rɪ^{1}prɛs/, **represses, repressing, repressed.** 1 VB WITH OBJ If you **repress** a feeling, you succeed in not having it or not showing it. *It was all I could do to repress my laughter.* 2 VB WITH OBJ To **repress** a group of people means to restrict their freedom and control them by force. *The officers would help to repress their own people.*

repressed /rɪ^{1}prɛst/. 1 ADJ **Repressed** people try to stop themselves having natural feelings and desires, especially sexual ones. *In her next film she played a repressed governess.* 2 ADJ A person's **repressed** feelings are the ones they do not allow themselves to have. *...the child's repressed hate of his mother.*

repression /rɪ^{1}prɛʃə^{0}n/. UNCOUNT N **Repression** is the use of force to restrict and control a group of people. *They wanted to fight all forms of injustice and repression.*

repressive /rɪ^{1}prɛsɪv/. ADJ **Repressive** governments use force and unjust laws to restrict and control their people. *...a repressive society.*

reprieve /rɪ^{1}priːv/, **reprieves, reprieving, reprieved.** 1 VB WITH OBJ If someone who has been sentenced to death **is reprieved,** their sentence is changed and they are not executed. 2 COUNT N A **reprieve** is an official order cancelling a death sentence. 3 COUNT N A **reprieve** is also an unexpected delay before something unpleasant happens. *The finding of oil represents a colossal reprieve for the islanders.*

reprimand /rɛprɪmɑːnd/, **reprimands, reprimanding, reprimanded.** VB WITH OBJ If someone in authority **reprimands** you, they tell you officially that you have done something wrong. *He was called to the office of a superior to be reprimanded.* Also COUNT N *...a gentle reprimand.*

reprint, reprints, reprinting, reprinted; pronounced /riːprɪnt/ when it is a verb and /riːprɪnt/ when it is a noun. 1 VB WITH OBJ When a book **is reprinted,** further copies of it are printed after all the other ones have been sold. 2 COUNT N A **reprint** is a copy of a book which has been reprinted.

reprisal /rɪ^{1}praɪzə^{0}l/, **reprisals.** COUNT N OR UNCOUNT N **Reprisals** are violent actions taken by a group of people against another group who have harmed them. *They engaged in brutal reprisals against those who had fought them... ...threats of reprisal.*

reproach /rɪ^{1}prəʊtʃ/, **reproaches, reproaching, reproached;** a formal word. 1 UNCOUNT N OR COUNT N If you express **reproach,** you indicate to someone that you are sad and disappointed about something they have done. *She was still staring at him in shocked and silent reproach... She responded submissively to his reproaches.* 2 VB WITH OBJ OR REFL VB If you **reproach** someone, you tell them sadly they have done something wrong. *He used to reproach her mother for not being nice enough to her... He had bitterly reproached himself for his complacency.*

reproachful /rɪ^{1}prəʊtʃfʊl/. ADJ **Reproachful** looks or remarks show sadness and disappointment about something that someone has done. *They kept sending* *us reproachful messages.* ♦ **reproachfully** ADV *Morris looked at her reproachfully.*

reproduce /ri:prədju:s/, **reproduces, reproducing, reproduced.** 1 VB WITH OBJ If you **reproduce** something, you produce a copy of it. *This painting has never been reproduced anywhere.* 2 VB OR REFL VB When people, animals, or plants **reproduce** or **reproduce** themselves, they produce more of their own species. *Bacteria reproduce by splitting into two.*

reproduction /ri:prədʌkʃə0n/, **reproductions.** 1 COUNT N A **reproduction** is a modern copy of a painting or piece of furniture. *...reproductions of Impressionist paintings.* 2 UNCOUNT N The **reproduction** of sound, art, or writing is the copying of it. *The Controller has no objection to the reproduction of the Report.* 3 UNCOUNT N **Reproduction** is the process by which living things produce more of their own species. *...plant reproduction.*

reproductive /ri:prədʌktɪv/. ATTRIB ADJ **Reproductive** means relating to the reproduction of living things. *...a worm's digestive and reproductive systems.*

reproof /rɪ1pru:f/, **reproofs.** COUNT N OR UNCOUNT N A **reproof** is something that you say to someone to show that you disapprove of what they have done; a formal use. *This reproof was ignored... Discipline and reproof are out of fashion.*

reprove /rɪ1pru:v/, **reproves, reproving, reproved.** VB WITH OBJ If you **reprove** someone, you tell them that they have behaved wrongly or foolishly; a formal use. *He constantly reproved Sonny for his outbursts of temper.* ♦ **reproving** ADJ *She received a reproving look from her Aunt Agnes.*

reptile /rɛptaɪl/, **reptiles.** COUNT N A **reptile** is a scaly animal which lays eggs. Snakes, lizards, and crocodiles are reptiles.

republic /rɪ1pʌblɪk/, **republics.** COUNT N A **republic** is a country which has a president and is governed by elected representatives. *Cuba became an independent republic... ...the Republic of Ireland.*

repudiate /rɪ1pju:dieɪt/, **repudiates, repudiating, repudiated.** VB WITH OBJ If you **repudiate** something, you say that you will not accept it or have anything to do with it; a formal use. *He repudiated the authority of the Church.* ♦ **repudiation** /rɪ1pju:dɪeɪʃə0n/ UNCOUNT N *...his repudiation of the evidence.*

repugnant /rɪ1pʌgnənt/. ADJ If something is **repugnant** to you, you think it is horrible and disgusting; a formal use. *The majority of British people find this sort of souvenir repugnant.*

repulsion /rɪ1pʌlʃə0n/. UNCOUNT N **Repulsion** is a strong feeling of dislike and disgust; a formal use. *She shivered with repulsion.*

repulsive /rɪ1pʌlsɪv/. ADJ **Repulsive** means horrible and disgusting. *It's a repulsive idea... His behaviour was absolutely repulsive.*

reputable /rɛpjə4təbə0l/. ADJ A **reputable** company or person is known to be good and reliable. *All reputable companies give a guarantee.*

reputation /rɛpjə4teɪʃə0n/, **reputations.** COUNT N Your **reputation** is the opinion that people have of you. *She had a reputation as a very good writer... ...his reputation for integrity.*

reputed /rɪ1pju:tɪ2d/. ADJ If something is **reputed** to be true or to exist, some people say that it is true or that it exists. *The buildings were reputed to be haunted... ...their reputed beauty.* ♦ **reputedly** ADV *...events that reputedly took place thousands of years ago.*

request /rɪ1kwɛst/, **requests, requesting, requested.** 1 VB WITH OBJ To **request** something means to ask for it formally. *The President requested an emergency session of the United Nations... Visitors are requested not to pick the flowers.* 2 COUNT N If you make a **request** for something, you ask for it. *I made repeated requests for money.*

PHRASES • If something is done **on request,** it is done when you ask for it. *A booklet on this subject will be sent on request.* • If you do something **at** someone's **request,** you do it because they ask you to.

require /rɪ1kwaɪə/, **requires, requiring, required;** a formal word. 1 VB WITH OBJ To **require** something means to need it. *Is there anything you require?... Parliamentary approval would be required for it.* 2 VB WITH OBJ If you **are required** to do something, you have to do it, for example because of a rule or law. *All the boys were required to study religion... He was doing what was required of him.* ♦ **required** ADJ *Check that the machines meet required standards.*

requirement /rɪ1kwaɪəmə2nt/, **requirements.** 1 COUNT N A **requirement** is something that you must have or do in order to do what you want. *Maths is no longer the most important requirement for a career in accounting.* 2 COUNT N Your **requirements** are the things that you need. *Mexico imported half her grain requirements in 1940.*

requisite /rɛkwɪzɪt/. ATTRIB ADJ **Requisite** means necessary for a particular purpose; a formal use. *They needed time to establish the requisite number of prisons.*

requisition /rɛkwɪzɪʃə0n/, **requisitions, requisitioning, requisitioned.** VB WITH OBJ When people, especially soldiers, **requisition** something, they take it for their own use. *Transport was being requisitioned by the army.*

rescue /rɛskju:/, **rescues, rescuing, rescued.** 1 VB WITH OBJ If you **rescue** someone, you get them out of a dangerous or difficult situation. *He was rescued from the sinking aircraft by a passing ship... The Cabinet decided not to rescue the company.* ♦ **rescuer** COUNT N *The man's shouts could not be heard by the rescuers.* 2 UNCOUNT N OR COUNT N **Rescue** is help which gets someone out of a dangerous or difficult situation. *Rescue was at hand... The coastguard may be working on as many as 20 rescues at any one time.* 3 PHRASE If you **come to** someone's **rescue,** you help them when they are in danger or difficulty.

research /rɪ1sɜ:tʃ/, **researches, researching, researched.** 1 UNCOUNT N OR PLURAL N **Research** is work that involves studying something and trying to discover facts about it. *...scientific research... Soon after, Faraday began his researches into electricity.* 2 VB WITH OR WITHOUT OBJ If you **research** something, you try to discover facts about it. *The historical background to the play had been very carefully researched... I spent some time researching abroad.* ♦ **researcher** COUNT N *...a team of researchers.*

resemblance /rɪ1zɛmbləns/. SING N OR UNCOUNT N If there is a **resemblance** between two people or things, they are similar to each other. *She bore a striking resemblance to his wife.*

resemble /rɪ1zɛmbə0l/, **resembles, resembling, resembled.** VB WITH OBJ If one thing or person **resembles** another, they are similar to each other. *The situation closely resembles that of Europe in 1940.*

resent /rɪ1zɛnt/, **resents, resenting, resented.** VB WITH OBJ If you **resent** something, you feel bitter and angry about it. *I resented his attitude... They resent being treated as common criminals.*

resentful /rɪ1zɛntfʊl/. ADJ If you are **resentful,** you feel resentment. *He was resentful at the way he had been treated.*

resentment /rɪ1zɛntmə2nt/. UNCOUNT N **Resentment** is a feeling of bitterness and anger. *He was filled with resentment... I felt no resentment against Keith.*

reservation /rɛzəveɪʃə0n/, **reservations.** 1 COUNT N OR UNCOUNT N If you have **reservations** about something, you are not sure that it is entirely good or right. *I have reservations about the desirability of such a change... They accepted the plan without reservation.* 2 COUNT N If you make a **reservation,** you arrange for something such as a table in a restaurant or a room in a hotel to be kept for you. *I will make the reservation for seven thirty.*

reserve /rɪ1zɜ:v/, **reserves, reserving, reserved.** 1 VB WITH OBJ If something **is reserved** for a particular person or purpose, it is kept specially for that person or purpose. *The garden is reserved for those who work in the museum... St Faith's Chapel is reserved for private prayer.* 2 COUNT N A **reserve** is a supply of something that is available for use when needed. *We have large coal reserves... He was able to draw on vast reserves of talent and enthusiasm.* 3 PHRASE If you have something **in reserve,** you have it available for use. *I kept some tranquillizers in reserve in case I became agitated.* 4 COUNT N In sport, a **reserve** is someone who is available to play in a team if one of the members cannot play. 5 COUNT N A nature **reserve** is an area of land where animals, birds, and plants are officially protected. 6 UNCOUNT N If someone shows **reserve,** they keep their feelings hidden. *His tone had lost the cautious reserve it had previously had.*

reserved /rɪ1zɜ:vd/. ADJ Someone who is **reserved** keeps their feelings hidden. *He is reserved and cautious, never making a swift decision.*

reservoir /rɛzəvwɑ:/, **reservoirs.** COUNT N A **reservoir** is a lake used for storing water before it is supplied to people.

reside /rɪ1zaɪd/, **resides, residing, resided.** VB If a quality **resides** in something, it is in that thing; a formal use. *Real power now resides in the workshop... The value of his sculptures resides in their simplicity.*

residence /rɛzɪdəns/, **residences;** a formal word. 1 COUNT N Someone's **residence** is their house. *...the Prime Minister's official residence.* 2 UNCOUNT N Your place of **residence** is the place where you live. 3 See also **hall of residence.**

PHRASES • If you **take up residence** somewhere, you start living there. • If someone is **in residence** in a place, they are living there.

resident /rɛzɪdənt/, **residents.** 1 COUNT N The **residents** of an area are the people who live there. *The local residents complained.* 2 ADJ Someone who is **resident** in a country or town lives there; a formal use. *...students resident in England.* 3 ADJ **Resident** is used to describe people who live in the place where they work. *...a resident chaplain.*

residential /rɛzɪdɛnʃə0l/. 1 ATTRIB ADJ A **residential** area contains houses rather than offices or factories. *...fashionable residential suburbs.* 2 ATTRIB ADJ A **residential** institution is one where you can live while you are studying or being cared for there. *...residential colleges.*

residual /rɪ2zɪdjʊ0əl/. ATTRIB ADJ **Residual** is used to describe what remains of something when most of it has gone; a formal use. *...the residual prejudices of the past.*

residue /rɛzɪdju:/, **residues.** COUNT N A **residue** of something is a small amount that remains after most of it has gone; a formal use. *Residues of pesticides can build up in the soil.*

resign /rɪ1zaɪn/, **resigns, resigning, resigned.** 1 VB If you **resign** from a job or position, you formally announce that you are leaving it. *She resigned from the Government... Lloyd George was threatening to resign.* 2 REFL VB WITH PREP 'to' If you **resign** yourself to an unpleasant situation or fact, you accept it because you cannot change it. *You're a widow now, Mrs Pearl. I think you must resign yourself to that fact.*

resignation /rɛzɪgneɪʃə0n/, **resignations.** 1 COUNT N OR UNCOUNT N Your **resignation** is a formal statement of your intention to leave a job or position. *Mr McPherson has accepted my resignation... ...her letter of resignation.* 2 UNCOUNT N **Resignation** is the acceptance of an unpleasant situation or fact because you cannot change it. *She spoke with quiet resignation.*

resigned /rɪ1zaɪnd/. ADJ If you are **resigned** to an unpleasant situation or fact, you accept it because you cannot change it. *They feel resigned to losing their money.* ♦ **resignedly** /rɪ1zaɪnədli1/ ADV *'He will come,' said Joe resignedly.*

resilient /rɪ1zɪljənt/. ADJ People who are **resilient** are able to recover quickly from unpleasant things that happen to them. *He's bright, resilient, and ambitious.* ♦ **resilience** /rɪ1zɪljəns/ UNCOUNT N *The chairman has shown remarkable resilience.*

resin /rɛzɪn/, **resins.** 1 MASS N **Resin** is a sticky substance produced by some trees. 2 MASS N **Resin** is also a chemically produced substance used to make plastics.

resist /rɪ1zɪst/, **resists, resisting, resisted.** 1 VB WITH OBJ If you **resist** something such as a change, you refuse to accept it and try to prevent it. *Our trade union has resisted the introduction of automation.* 2 VB WITH OBJ To **resist** an attack means to fight back. *Any attack will be resisted with force if necessary.* 3 VB WITH OBJ OR -ING If you **resist** the temptation to do something, you do not do it. *I resisted the temptation to get very drunk... I can't resist teasing him.*

resistance /rɪ1zɪstəns/. 1 UNCOUNT N **Resistance** to something such as a change or a new idea is a refusal to accept it. *There will be fierce resistance if this is attempted... ...resistance to bureaucratic controls.* 2 UNCOUNT N When there is **resistance** to an attack, people fight back. *The advancing army met with no resistance.*

resistant /rɪ1zɪstənt/; a formal word. 1 PRED ADJ People who are **resistant** to something are opposed to it and want to prevent it. *They are extremely resistant to change.* 2 ADJ If something is **resistant** to something else, it is not harmed by it. *This type of plastic is highly resistant to steam.*

resolute /rɛzəlj0u:t/. ADJ Someone who is **resolute** refuses to change their mind or to give up a course of action; a formal use. *We urged him to be resolute... ...their resolute refusal to make any real concessions.* ♦ **resolutely** ADV *She had resolutely refused to speak to me.*

resolution /rɛzəlj0u:ʃə0n/, **resolutions.** 1 COUNT N A **resolution** is a formal decision taken at a meeting by means of a vote. *Congress passed a resolution accepting his services.* 2 COUNT N If you make a **resolution** to do something, you decide to try hard to do it. *I'm always making resolutions, like giving up smoking.* 3 UNCOUNT N **Resolution** is determination to do something or not do something. *A note of resolution entered his voice.* 4 UNCOUNT N The **resolution** of a problem or difficulty is the solving of it; a formal use. *I longed for the resolution of the agonizing dilemma.*

resolve /rɪ1zɒlv/, **resolves, resolving, resolved;** a formal word. 1 VB WITH TO-INF OR REPORT VB If you **resolve** to do something, you make a firm decision to do it. *I resolved to tell the truth... He had already resolved that Kitchener should be appointed.* 2 UNCOUNT N **Resolve** is determination to do something. *We must be firm in our resolve to oppose them.* 3 VB WITH OBJ To **resolve** a problem, argument, or difficulty means to deal with it successfully. *The Cabinet met to resolve the crisis.*

resonant /rezənənt/. ADJ **Resonant** sounds are deep and strong. *She could hear her father's resonant voice.* ♦ **resonance** /rezənəns/ UNCOUNT N *His voice took on a new resonance.*

resort /rɪ'zɔːt/, **resorts, resorting, resorted.** 1 VB WITH PREP 'to' If you **resort** to methods that you disapprove of, you use them because you cannot see any other way of achieving what you want. *They had not so far chosen to resort to violence.* 2 PHRASE If you do something **as a last resort,** you do it to solve a problem after trying all other ways of solving it. *As a last resort he went to the British Library.* 3 COUNT N A **resort** is a place where many people spend their holidays. *...a seaside resort.*

resound /rɪ'zaʊnd/, **resounds, resounding, resounded;** a literary word. 1 VB When a noise **resounds,** it is heard loudly and clearly. *His steps resounded in the courtyard.* 2 VB If a place **resounds** with noise, it is filled with it. *The room began to resound with that powerful voice.*

resounding /rɪ'zaʊndɪŋ/. 1 ATTRIB ADJ A **resounding** noise is loud and echoing. *The tile sprang from the wall with a resounding crack.* 2 ATTRIB ADJ A **resounding** success is a very great success.

resource /rɪ'zɔːs, -sɔːs/, **resources.** COUNT N The **resources** of a country, organization, or person are the things they have and can use. *...Britain's energy resources... Julius had invested all his resources in a restaurant.*

resourceful /rɪ'zɔːsfʊl, -sɔːs-/. ADJ Someone who is **resourceful** is good at finding ways of dealing with problems. *...an able, resourceful politician.* ♦ **resourcefulness** UNCOUNT N *They faced misfortune with resourcefulness and courage.*

respect /rɪspekt/, **respects, respecting, respected.** 1 VB WITH OBJ If you **respect** someone, you have a good opinion of their character or ideas. *He was particularly respected for his integrity.* ♦ **respected** ADJ *...a highly respected scholar.* 2 UNCOUNT N Your **respect** for someone is your good opinion of them. *I had an enormous respect and admiration for him... It is up to you to gain her respect.* 3 VB WITH OBJ If you **respect** someone's wishes, rights, or customs, you avoid doing things that they would dislike or regard as wrong. *She respected his need for peace and quiet... We must respect the practices of cultures different from our own.* 4 UNCOUNT N If you show **respect** for someone's wishes, rights, or customs, you avoid doing anything they would dislike or regard as wrong. *...respect for the rights of the minority.*

PHRASES ● You say **with respect** when you are politely disagreeing with someone; a formal use. *But Mr Hume, with respect, that wouldn't work.* ● You say **with respect to** to indicate what something relates to; a formal use. *He informed me about my rights with respect to the forthcoming extradition.* ● You say **in this respect** to indicate that what you are saying applies to the thing you have just mentioned. *We are lagging behind in this respect.* ● **In many respects** means in many different ways. *He is different from the people around him in many respects.*

respectable /rɪ'spektəbəl/. 1 ADJ Someone or something that is **respectable** is approved of by society and considered to be morally correct. *...a respectable businessman... ...young people from respectable homes.* ♦ **respectability** /rɪ'spektəbɪlɪti/ UNCOUNT N *...a statesman of great eminence and respectability.* 2 ADJ **Respectable** also means adequate or acceptable. *He had begun to earn a very respectable income.*

respectful /rɪ'spektfʊl/. ADJ If you are **respectful,** you show respect for someone. *The woman kept a respectful silence.* ♦ **respectfully** ADV *He expected them to stand respectfully when he entered the room.*

respective /rɪ'spektɪv/. ATTRIB ADJ **Respective** means relating separately to the people you have just mentioned. *He drove them both to their respective homes.*

respectively /rɪ'spektɪvli/. ADV **Respectively** means in the same order as the items you have just mentioned. *Harvard University and MIT are respectively the fourth and fifth largest employers in the area.*

respiration /respəreɪʃən/. UNCOUNT N Your **respiration** is your breathing; a medical use.

respiratory /respərətri/. ATTRIB ADJ **Respiratory** means relating to breathing; a medical use. *...respiratory infections.*

respite /respɪt/. UNCOUNT N A **respite** is a short period of rest from something unpleasant; a formal use. *She was interrogated without respite for twenty-four hours.*

resplendent /rɪ'splendənt/. ADJ If someone is **resplendent,** their appearance is very impressive; a formal use. *Miss Jackson, resplendent in a new red suit, watched the ceremony.*

respond /rɪ'spɒnd/, **responds, responding, responded.** VB When you **respond** to something that is done or said, you react by doing or saying something yourself. *The crowd waved and the liner responded with a blast on its siren... The government has responded to pressure by moving towards reform.*

response /rɪ'spɒns/, **responses.** 1 COUNT N Your **response** to an event, action, or statement is what you do or say as a reaction or reply to it. *The Government's response to the riots was firm.* 2 PHRASE If you do or say something **in response** to an event, action, or statement, you do it or say it as a reaction or reply to it. *Will waved his hand in response.*

responsibility /rɪ'spɒnsəbɪlɪti/, **responsibilities.** 1 UNCOUNT N If you have **responsibility** for something or if it is your **responsibility,** it is your duty to deal with it and make decisions relating to it. *She took over the responsibility for the project.* 2 UNCOUNT N If you accept **responsibility** for something that has happened, you agree that you were to blame for it. *I made a mistake and I will assume responsibility for it.* 3 COUNT N Your **responsibilities** are the duties that you have because of your job or position. *...the responsibilities of citizenship.* 4 COUNT N If you have a **responsibility** to someone, you have a duty to help them or to look after them. *I presume you take your responsibility to your students seriously?*

responsible /rɪ'spɒnsəbəl/. 1 PRED ADJ If you are **responsible** for something, it is your job or duty to deal with it. *...the minister responsible for civil defence.* 2 PRED ADJ If you are **responsible** for something bad that has happened, it is your fault. *I hold you personally responsible for all this.* 3 PRED ADJ If you are **responsible** to a person or group, you are controlled by them and have to report to them about what you have done. *We're responsible to a development committee.* 4 ADJ **Responsible** people behave properly without needing to be controlled by anyone else. *...responsible members of the local community.* ♦ **responsibly** ADV *You are doing your job conscientiously and responsibly.* 5 ATTRIB ADJ **Responsible** jobs involve making important decisions or carrying out important actions.

responsive /rɪ'spɒnsɪv/. PRED ADJ If you are **responsive** to things that happen, you take notice of them and react in an appropriate way. *Broadcasters should be responsive to public opinion.*

rest /rest/, **rests, resting, rested.** 1 SING N The **rest** of something is all that remains of it. *He spent the rest of his life in prison.* 2 SING N When you have been talking about one member of a group of things or people, you can refer to all the other members as the **rest.** *It was just another grave like all the rest... The rest of us were allowed to go home.* 3 VB WITH OR WITHOUT OBJ If you **rest,** you do not do anything active for a period of time. *Go back to bed and rest... Stop to relax and rest your muscles.* 4 UNCOUNT N OR COUNT N If you get some **rest** or have a **rest,** you sit or lie without doing anything active. *Try to get some rest... They wanted a rest.* 5 VB WITH 'on' OR 'upon' If something such as an idea **rests** on a particular thing, it depends on that thing; a formal use. *I believe that the future of civilisation rests on that decision.* 6 VB WITH 'with' If a responsibility or duty **rests** with you, you have that responsibility or duty; a formal use. *Final authority on all matters rests with him.* 7 ERG VB WITH ADJUNCT If something **rests** somewhere, its weight is supported there. *He let her shoulders rest against his knees... ...a tub with a wide edge to rest your arm on.* 8 VB WITH 'on' OR 'upon' If your eyes **rest** on something, you stop looking round you and look at that thing; a literary use. *Her eyes travelled slowly upward and rested on his hands.* 9 COUNT N A **rest** is also an object used to support something. *...a head rest.*

PHRASES ● When a moving object **comes to rest,** it stops. ● If you **put** or **set** someone's **mind at rest,** you say something that stops them worrying.

restaurant /restərɒnt, -rɒŋ/, **restaurants.** COUNT N A **restaurant** is a place where you can buy and eat a meal. *...a splendid Hungarian restaurant.*

rested /restɪd/. ADJ If you feel **rested,** you feel less tired because you have had a rest.

restful /restfʊl/. ADJ Something that is **restful** helps you to feel calm and relaxed. *The lighting is restful.*

restive /restɪv/. ADJ If you are **restive,** you are impatient, bored, or dissatisfied; a formal use. *The crew were restive and mutinous.*

restless /restlɪs/. 1 ADJ If you are **restless,** you are bored or dissatisfied, and want to do something else. *I knew that within a fortnight I should feel restless again.* ♦ **restlessness** UNCOUNT N *They are showing some signs of restlessness.* 2 ADJ You also say that someone is **restless** when they keep moving around, because they find it difficult to stay still. *She was restless and fidgety.* ♦ **restlessly** ADV *He walked restlessly around the room.*

restore /rɪ'stɔː/, **restores, restoring, restored.** 1 VB WITH OBJ To **restore** something means to cause it to exist again. *...the task of restoring order.* ♦ **restoration** /restəreɪʃən/ UNCOUNT N *...the restoration of law and order.* 2 VB WITH OBJ AND PREP 'to' To **restore** someone or something to a previous state or condition means to cause them to return to that state or condition. *The Tories were restored to power.* 3 VB WITH OBJ When someone **restores** an old building, painting, or piece of furniture, they repair and clean it, so that it returns to its original condition. ♦ **restoration** UNCOUNT N *...the restoration of ancient halls and manors.* 4 VB WITH OBJ If you **restore** something that was lost or stolen to someone, you return it to them; a formal use.

restrain /rɪ'streɪn/, **restrains, restraining, restrained.** 1 VB WITH OBJ OR REFL VB To **restrain** someone means to stop them doing what they were going to do. *She raised a finger as if to restrain Morris from speaking... He had been unable to restrain himself from telling Gertrude.* 2 VB WITH OBJ To **restrain** something that is growing or increasing means to prevent it from getting too large. *...the efforts of governments to restrain inflation.*

restrained /rɪ'streɪnd/. ADJ **Restrained** means calm and unemotional. *He was polite and restrained.*

restraint /rɪ'streɪnt/, **restraints.** 1 COUNT N OR UNCOUNT N **Restraints** are rules or conditions that limit or restrict someone or something. *The king suffered few restraints on his freedom of action... ...an agreed policy of income and price restraint.* 2 UNCOUNT N **Restraint** is calm, controlled, and unemotional behaviour. *'Dear me,' he said with splendid restraint.*

restrict /rɪ'strɪkt/, **restricts, restricting, restricted.** 1 VB WITH OBJ If you **restrict** something, you put a limit on it to stop it becoming too large. *A third possibility would be to restrict wage increases.* ♦ **restricted** ADJ *...the restricted field of vision provided by the camera.* 2 VB WITH OBJ OR REFL VB To **restrict** people or animals means to limit their movements or actions. *Some manufacturers were not prepared to restrict themselves voluntarily.* 3 VB WITH OBJ AND PREP 'to' If you **restrict** someone's activities to one thing, they can only do or deal with that thing. *The State should restrict its activities to the maintenance of law and order... I will restrict myself to countries where English is the main language.* 4 VB WITH OBJ AND PREP 'to' If something **is restricted** to a particular group, only that group can have it or do it. *Membership is restricted to men.*

restricted /rɪ'strɪktɪd/. 1 ADJ A **restricted** number of things is quite small or limited. *The range of choices is not as restricted as this.* 2 ADJ **Restricted** documents can only be read by people who have special permission.

restriction /rɪ'strɪkʃən/, **restrictions.** 1 COUNT N OR UNCOUNT N A **restriction** is an official rule that limits what you can do or that limits the amount or size of something. *The government placed restrictions on sales of weapons... There is no restriction on filming in the area.* 2 COUNT N You can refer to anything that limits what you can do as a **restriction.** *...small salaries which placed restrictions on our social life.*

restrictive /rɪ'strɪktɪv/. ADJ Something that is **restrictive** makes it difficult for you to do what you want to. *...teenagers eager to escape restrictive home environments.*

restructure /riːstrʌktʃə/, **restructures, restructuring, restructured.** VB WITH OBJ To **restructure** an organization or system means to change the way it is organized. *...proposals for restructuring the industry.*

result /rɪzʌlt/, **results, resulting, resulted.** 1 COUNT N A **result** is something that happens or exists because of something else that has happened. *I nearly missed the flight as a result of going to Havana... Twice he followed his own advice, with disastrous results.* 2 VB WITH 'in' If something **results** in a particular situation or event, it causes that situation or event to happen. *The use of such techniques could result in disastrous ecological changes.* 3 VB If something **results** from a particular event or action, it is caused by that event or action. *Four-fifths of the damage resulted from bombing.* 4 COUNT N A **result** is also the situation that exists at the end of a contest. *...the result of the Warrington by-election... ...football results.* 5 COUNT N A **result** is also the number that you get when you do a calculation. *The result should be calculated to three decimal places.* 6 COUNT N Your **results** are the marks or grades that you get for examinations. *You need good A-level results.*

resultant /rɪzʌltənt/. ATTRIB ADJ **Resultant** means caused by the event just mentioned; a formal use. *The resultant improvement in health totally justified the treatment.*

resume /rɪ1zj0u:m/, **resumes, resuming, resumed;** a formal word. 1 ERG VB If you **resume** an activity or if it **resumes,** it begins again. *She was ready to resume her duties... The music would stop at intervals, then resume after a while.* 2 VB WITH OBJ If you **resume** your former place or position, you return to it. *He resumed his seat.*

resumption /rɪ1zʌmp0ʃə0n/. UNCOUNT N When there is a **resumption** of an activity, it begins again; a formal use. *...a quick resumption of arms negotiations.*

resurgence /rɪ1sɜ:dʒəns/. UNCOUNT N If there is a **resurgence** of an attitude or activity, it reappears and grows; a formal use. *There has been a resurgence of small scale guerrilla activity.*

resurrect /rɛzərɛkt/, **resurrects, resurrecting, resurrected.** VB WITH OBJ When you **resurrect** something that has ended, you cause it to exist again. *There is not the remotest possibility of the government ever resurrecting the Maplin project.*

resurrection /rɛzərɛkʃə0n/. 1 UNCOUNT N The **resurrection** of something that had ended is the act of making it exist again. *...a resurrection of the Jazz Festival.* 2 PROPER N In Christian belief, the **Resurrection** is the event in which Jesus Christ became alive again three days after he was killed.

resuscitate /rɪ1sʌsɪteɪt/, **resuscitates, resuscitating, resuscitated.** VB WITH OBJ If you **resuscitate** someone who has lost consciousness, you cause them to become conscious again; a formal use.

retail /ri:teɪl/. MOD **Retail** is the activity of selling goods to the public. *We have opened a retail department... The original retail price was $80.*

retailer /ri:teɪlə/, **retailers.** COUNT N A **retailer** is a person or business that sells goods to the public.

retain /rɪ1teɪn/, **retains, retaining, retained;** a formal word. 1 VB WITH OBJ If you **retain** something, you keep it. *We are fighting to retain some independence.* 2 VB WITH OBJ If an object or substance **retains** heat or a liquid, it continues to contain it. *Water retains heat much longer than air.*

retaliate /rɪ1tælieɪt/, **retaliates, retaliating, retaliated.** VB If you **retaliate** when someone harms you, you harm them in return. *...the ability to retaliate during an attack... They retaliated by changing the venue for the meeting.* ♦ **retaliation** /rɪ1tælieɪʃə0n/ UNCOUNT N *It was agreed that immediate retaliation was necessary.*

retaliatory /rɪ1tæljətə0ri1/. ADJ If you take **retaliatory** action, you try to harm someone who has harmed you; a formal use.

retarded /rɪ1tɑ:dɪ2d/. ADJ **Retarded** people are less advanced mentally than most people of their age. *Her younger daughter was mentally retarded.*

retch /rɛtʃ/, **retches, retching, retched.** VB If you **retch,** your stomach moves as if you are vomiting.

retention /rɪ1tɛnʃə0n/. UNCOUNT N The **retention** of something is the keeping of it; a formal use. *They voted in favour of the retention of capital punishment.*

rethink /ri:θɪŋk/, **rethinks, rethinking, rethought.** VB WITH OR WITHOUT OBJ If you **rethink** something such as a plan or a policy, you think about it and change it. *This forced us to rethink all of our plans.*

reticent /rɛtɪsənt/. ADJ If you are **reticent** about something, you do not talk about it. *She was always extremely reticent about her colleagues.* ♦ **reticence** /rɛtɪsəns/ UNCOUNT N *...her reticence about her personal life.*

retire /rɪ1taɪə/, **retires, retiring, retired.** 1 VB When older people **retire,** they leave their job and stop working. *Women, unlike men, retire at sixty... They had decided to retire from farming.* 2 VB To **retire** also means to go to bed; a formal use. *She retired early with a good book.*

retired /rɪ1taɪəd/. ADJ A **retired** person is an older person who has left his or her job and has stopped working. *...a retired Army officer.*

retirement /rɪ1taɪəmə2nt/. 1 UNCOUNT N **Retirement** is the time when a worker retires. *Since my retirement, I have felt more energetic.* 2 UNCOUNT N **Retirement** is also the period in a person's life after they have retired. *...the house that he had bought for his retirement.*

retiring /rɪ1taɪərɪŋ/. ADJ Someone who is **retiring** is shy and avoids meeting other people. *She was a shy, retiring girl.*

retort /rɪ1tɔ:t/, **retorts, retorting, retorted.** REPORT VB To **retort** means to reply angrily; used in written English. *Lady Sackville retorted that if they came, she would leave.* Also COUNT N *...a sharp retort.*

retrace /ri:treɪs/, **retraces, retracing, retraced.** VB WITH OBJ If you **retrace** your steps or **retrace** your way, you return to where you started from using the same route. *Stella retraced her steps toward the entrance.*

retract /rɪ1trækt/, **retracts, retracting, retracted;** a formal word. 1 VB WITH OBJ If you **retract** something that you have said or written, you say publicly that you did not mean it. *At his trial, he retracted his confession.* 2 ERG VB If a part of a machine **retracts,** it can be moved inwards so that it no longer sticks out.

retreat /rɪ1tri:t/, **retreats, retreating, retreated.** 1 VB If you **retreat** from someone or something, you move away from them; a literary use. *Betsy and I retreated to the edge of the field.* 2 VB When an army **retreats,** it moves away from an enemy in order to avoid fighting. *They retreated a few kilometres.* Also COUNT N OR UNCOUNT N *...the retreat of Napoleon's army... They can be starved into retreat.* 3 COUNT N A **retreat** is a quiet place where you go to rest or to do something in private. *They met at a woodland retreat.*

retribution /rɛtrɪbju:ʃə0n/. UNCOUNT N **Retribution** is punishment for a crime; a literary use. *...the fear of retribution.*

retrieval /rɪ1tri:və0l/. UNCOUNT N The **retrieval** of information from a computer is the process of getting it back. *...data retrieval.*

retrieve /rɪ1tri:v/, **retrieves, retrieving, retrieved;** a formal word. 1 VB WITH OBJ If you **retrieve** something, you get it back from the place where you left it. *I ran back to my room and retrieved my bag.* 2 VB WITH OBJ If you **retrieve** a situation, you bring it back into a more acceptable state.

retrograde /rɛtrə6greɪd/. ADJ You describe an action as **retrograde** when you think that it makes a situation worse rather than better; a formal use. *The move was held to be an economically retrograde step.*

retrospect /rɛtrə6spɛkt/. PHRASE When you consider something **in retrospect,** you think about it at a later time. *In retrospect, what I had done was clearly unjustifiable.*

retrospective /rɛtrə6spɛktɪv/. ADJ **Retrospective** feelings or opinions concern things that happened in the past; a formal use. *...a retrospective view of what went wrong.*

return /rɪ1tɜ:n/, **returns, returning, returned.** 1 VB When you **return** to a place, you go back there. *He returned home several hours later... Her husband left for work one morning and did not return.* 2 UNCOUNT N WITH POSS Your **return** is your arrival back at a place. *On his return Haldane reported to the Cabinet.* 3 VB WITH OBJ If you **return** something that you have taken or borrowed, you put it back or give it back. *We returned the books to the shelf... He borrowed my best suit and didn't return it.* 4 UNCOUNT N You can refer to the giving back of something as its **return.** *Greece will be offered the return of these treasures as a goodwill gift.* 5 VB WITH OBJ If you **return** something such as a smile, you smile back at the person who has smiled at you. If you **return** someone's feelings, you feel the same way towards them as they feel towards you. *He didn't return their greetings... She was looking for somebody to return her affection.* 6 VB If a feeling or situation **returns,** it happens again. *If the pain returns, the treatment is repeated... After nine months, the rains returned.* 7 SING N WITH SUPP You can refer to the reappearance of a feeling or situation as its **return.** *...the return of better times.* 8 VB WITH PREP 'to' If you **return** to a subject, you start talking about it again. If you **return** to an activity, you start doing it again. *We shall return to this theme in Chapter 7... After lunch, Edward returned to his gardening.* 9 VB WITH PREP 'to' If you **return** to a state you were in before, you start being in that state again. *...the groans of wounded men returning to consciousness.* 10 SING N WITH PREP 'to' You can refer to a change back to a former state as a **return** to that state. *He referred to the Party's hopes for a return to power.* 11 VB WITH OBJ When a judge or jury **returns** a verdict, they announce whether a person is guilty or not; a legal use. 12 COUNT N A **return** or a **return ticket** is a ticket that allows you to travel to a place and then back again. *...a return ticket to Vienna.* 13 COUNT N OR UNCOUNT N The **return** on an investment is the profit you get from it. *Companies seek higher returns by investing in other corporations.*

PHRASES ● If you do something **in return** for what someone has done for you, you do it because of what they did. *They had nothing to give in return.* ● You say **'many happy returns'** to wish someone a happy birthday. ● If you have reached **the point of no return,** you have to continue with what you are doing and it is too late to stop.

reunion /ri1ju:njə0n/, **reunions.** COUNT N A **reunion** is a party attended by members of the same family, school, or other group who have not seen each other for a long time. *...a family reunion.*

reunite /ri:ju:naɪt/, **reunites, reuniting, reunited.** 1 VB WITH OBJ If you **are reunited** with your family or friends, you meet them again after being separated from them. *It won't be long before you are reunited with your family.* 2 VB WITH OBJ To **reunite** a divided organization or country means to cause it to be united again. *He worked to reunite the Labour movement.*

rev /rɛv/, **revs, revving, revved.** ERG VB When you **rev** the engine of a stationary vehicle or **rev** it up, you increase the engine speed by pressing the accelerator. *He revved the motor and then roared off... I heard the sound of an engine revving up.*

Rev or **Revd. Rev** and **Revd** are written abbreviations for 'Reverend'. *...the Rev David Drew.*

reveal /rɪ1vi:l/, **reveals, revealing, revealed.** 1 REPORT VB To **reveal** something means to make people aware of it. *They were not ready to reveal any details of the arrest... A newspaper had once revealed that he'd wanted to marry his cousin.* 2 VB WITH OBJ If you **reveal** something that has been out of sight, you uncover it so that people can see it. *She drew the curtains aside to reveal beautiful gardens.*

revealing /rɪ1vi:lɪŋ/. 1 ADJ A **revealing** action or statement tells you something that you were not aware of. *He had nothing very revealing to say.* 2 ADJ **Revealing** clothes show a lot of your body.

revel /rɛvə0l/, **revels, revelling, revelled;** spelled **reveling, reveled** in American English. VB If you **revel** in a situation or experience, you enjoy it very much. *She seemed to revel in her success.*

revelation /rɛvəleɪʃə0n/, **revelations.** 1 COUNT N **Revelations** are interesting facts that are made known to people. *His book offers no illuminating personal revelations.* 2 SING N If an experience is a **revelation** to you, it makes you aware of something that you did not know before. *The whole episode was a revelation to him of how poor the family had been.*

revelry /rɛvə0lri1/. UNCOUNT N **Revelry** is noisy and often drunken enjoyment; an old-fashioned use.

revenge /rɪ1vɛndʒ/, **revenges, revenging, revenged.** 1 UNCOUNT N **Revenge** involves hurting someone who has hurt you. *They had taken their revenge by blowing up his house.* 2 REFL VB If you **revenge** yourself on someone who has hurt you, you hurt them in return; a formal use. *She will revenge herself on those who helped him to escape.*

revenue /rɛvɪ2nju:/, **revenues.** UNCOUNT N OR PLURAL N **Revenue** is the money that a government or organization receives from people. *A recession would reduce government tax revenues... The editor was concerned at the drop in advertising revenue.*

reverberate /rɪ1vɜ:bəreɪt/, **reverberates, reverberating, reverberated.** VB When a loud sound **reverberates,** it echoes through a place; a literary use.

revere /rɪ1vɪə/, **reveres, revering, revered.** VB WITH OBJ If you **revere** someone, you respect and admire them greatly; a formal use. *...her dead mother, whose memory she revered.* ♦ **revered** ADJ *He was a revered figure with a national reputation.*

reverence /rɛvə0rəns/. UNCOUNT N **Reverence** is a feeling of great respect for someone or something. *The sect teaches reverence for all life.*

Reverend /rɛvə0rənd/. **Reverend** is a title used before the name of a member of the clergy. *...the Reverend John Lamb.*

reverent /rɛvə0rənt/. ADJ If your behaviour is **reverent,** you show great respect for someone or something. *We filed past the tomb in a reverent manner.* ♦ **reverently** ADV *She laid the book reverently on the desk.*

reversal /rɪ1vɜ:sə0l/, **reversals.** COUNT N When there is a **reversal** of a process or policy, it is changed to the opposite process or policy. *Fortunately there was a reversal of this tendency.*

reverse /rɪ1vɜ:s/, **reverses, reversing, reversed.** 1 VB WITH OBJ To **reverse** a process, decision, or policy means to change it to its opposite. *The farmers want to see this trend reversed... The party reversed its decision and agreed to the change.* 2 VB WITH OBJ If you **reverse** the order of a set of things, you arrange them in the opposite order, so that the first thing comes last. 3 VB WITH OBJ If you **reverse** the positions or functions of two things, you change them so that each thing has the position or function that the other one had. *In this play the traditional sex roles are reversed.* 4 ERG VB When you **reverse** a car, you drive it backwards. *The street was so narrow that cars which entered it had to reverse out again.* 5 UNCOUNT N If your car is in **reverse,** you have changed gear so that you can drive it backwards. *I threw the truck into reverse.* 6 ATTRIB ADJ **Reverse** means opposite to what has just been described. *In the past ten years I think we've seen the reverse process.* 7 SING N The **reverse** is the opposite of what has just been mentioned. *You may think we have been making a profit. In fact the reverse is true.* 8 PHRASE If you **reverse the charges** when you make a telephone call, the person you are calling receives the bill; a British use.

reversion /rɪ1vɜ:ʃə0n/. UNCOUNT N WITH PREP 'to' **Reversion** to a former state, system, or kind of behaviour is a change back to it; a formal use. *...this reversion to pre-scientific attitudes.*

revert /rɪ1vɜːt/, **reverts, reverting, reverted.** VB WITH PREP 'to' When people or things **revert** to a former state, system, or type of behaviour, they go back to it; a formal use. *He was reverting rapidly to adolescence... Areas cleared for farming sometimes revert to forest later.*

review /rɪ1vjuː/, **reviews, reviewing, reviewed.** 1 COUNT N A **review** is an article in a newspaper or magazine, or an item on television or radio, in which someone gives their opinion of something such as a new book or play. *...a review of Lord Harewood's autobiography... ...book reviews.* 2 COUNT N OR UNCOUNT N When there is a **review** of a situation or system, it is formally examined in order to decide whether changes are needed. *...a review of public expenditure.* 3 VB WITH OBJ When a situation or system **is reviewed,** it is formally examined in order to decide whether changes are needed. *By law, state pensions must be reviewed once a year.* 4 PHRASE When something **comes up for review,** the time arrives for it to be formally examined to see whether changes are needed. When it is **under review,** it is being examined in this way. 5 VB WITH OBJ If you **review** a situation, you consider it carefully. 6 VB WITH OBJ When someone **reviews** something such as a new book or play, they write an article or give a talk on television or radio in which they express their opinion of it. ♦ **reviewer** COUNT N *Reviewers loved the book.*

revise /rɪ1vaɪz/, **revises, revising, revised.** 1 VB WITH OBJ If you **revise** something, you alter it in order to make it better or more correct. *The judges may revise their selection process.* 2 VB WITH OR WITHOUT OBJ When you **revise** for an examination, you read things again in order to learn them thoroughly. *I've been revising for the last three days... I was revising Dickens last night.*

revision /rɪ1vɪʒə0n/, **revisions.** 1 COUNT N OR UNCOUNT N When there is a **revision** of something, it is altered in order to improve it. *They're discussing a complete revision of the timetable... The Shops Act is in need of revision.* 2 UNCOUNT N When you do **revision,** you read things again in order to learn them for an examination. *I've got to do some revision.*

revitalize /riːvaɪtəlaɪz/, **revitalizes, revitalizing, revitalized;** also spelled **revitalise.** VB WITH OBJ To **revitalize** something means to make it more active or lively. *...its plan to revitalise the economy.*

revival /rɪ1vaɪvə0l/, **revivals.** UNCOUNT N OR COUNT N When there is a **revival** of something, it becomes active again. *Inflation may start to rise with the revival of trade... a revival of interest in the supernatural.*

revive /rɪ1vaɪv/, **revives, reviving, revived.** 1 ERG VB When something such as a feeling or a practice **revives** or **is revived,** it becomes active or successful again. *My spirits revived as we drove out into the countryside... They failed to fulfil their promises to revive the economy.* 2 ERG VB When you **revive** someone who has fainted, they become conscious again. *They had difficulty in reviving him... He slowly began to revive.*

revoke /rɪ1vəʊk/, **revokes, revoking, revoked.** VB WITH OBJ When someone in authority **revokes** something such as an order, they cancel it; a formal use.

revolt /rɪ1vəʊlt/, **revolts, revolting, revolted.** 1 COUNT N OR UNCOUNT N A **revolt** is a violent attempt by a group of people to change their country's political system. *...the Peasants' Revolt of 1381... The settlers rose in revolt.* 2 VB When people **revolt,** they use violence to try to change a country's political system. *Large sections of the army revolted against the civil government.*

revolting /rɪ1vəʊltɪŋ/. ADJ **Revolting** means horrible and disgusting. *The smell was quite revolting.*

revolution /rɛvəlj0uːʃə0n/, **revolutions.** 1 COUNT N OR UNCOUNT N A **revolution** is a successful attempt by a large group of people to change their country's political system using force. *...the fiftieth anniversary of the Russian revolution... France seemed to be on the verge of revolution.* 2 COUNT N A **revolution** is also an important change in a particular area of human activity. *...the Industrial Revolution... ...the revolution in communications.*

revolutionary /rɛvəlj0uːʃənə0ri1/, **revolutionaries.** 1 ADJ **Revolutionary** activities are intended to cause a political revolution. *They had fled as a result of their revolutionary activities.* 2 COUNT N A **revolutionary** is a person who tries to cause a revolution or takes part in one. 3 ADJ **Revolutionary** ideas and developments involve great changes in the way something is done or made. *...a revolutionary change in the way cars are manufactured.*

revolutionize /rɛvəlj0uːʃənaɪz/, **revolutionizes, revolutionizing, revolutionized;** also spelled **revolutionise.** VB WITH OBJ When something **revolutionizes** an activity, it causes great changes in the way it is done. *Our ideas will revolutionize the film industry.*

revolve /rɪ1vɒlv/, **revolves, revolving, revolved.** 1 VB WITH 'round' OR 'around' If you say that someone's life **revolves** around something, you mean that it is the main feature of their life. *Rural life revolved around agriculture.* 2 VB WITH 'round' OR 'around' If a discussion **revolves** around a particular topic, it is mainly about that topic. *The discussion revolved round three topics.* 3 VB When something **revolves,** it moves or turns in a circle around a central point or line. *...the discovery that the earth revolved around the sun.* ♦ **revolving** ATTRIB ADJ *They were watering the ground with big revolving sprinklers.*

revolver /rɪ1vɒlvə/, **revolvers.** COUNT N A **revolver** is a kind of gun that you hold in your hand.

revolving door, revolving doors. COUNT N A **revolving door** consists of four glass doors which turn together around a vertical post.

revulsion /rɪ1vʌlʃə0n/. UNCOUNT N **Revulsion** is a strong feeling of disgust or disapproval. *Germ warfare has always been regarded with revulsion.*

reward /rɪ1wɔːd/, **rewards, rewarding, rewarded.** 1 COUNT N OR UNCOUNT N A **reward** is something that you are given because you have done something useful or good. *...a reward for outstanding service... They work with no thought of reward.* 2 VB WITH OBJ To **reward** someone means to give them something because they have done something useful or good. *People should be rewarded for special effort... They rewarded the winners with gifts of fruit and flowers.*

rewarding /rɪ1wɔːdɪŋ/. ADJ Something that is **rewarding** gives you a lot of satisfaction. *...rewarding jobs.*

rewrite /riːraɪt/, **rewrites, rewriting, rewrote** /riːrəʊt/, **rewritten** /riːrɪtə0n/. VB WITH OBJ If you **rewrite** a piece of writing, you write it in a different way in order to improve it.

rhetoric /rɛtərɪk/. UNCOUNT N **Rhetoric** is speech or writing that is meant to convince and impress people; often used showing disapproval.

rhetorical /rɪ2tɒrɪkə0l/. 1 ADJ A **rhetorical** question is used in order to make a statement rather than to get an answer. 2 ADJ **Rhetorical** language is intended to be grand and impressive.

rheumatic /ruːmætɪk/. 1 ADJ **Rheumatic** pains are caused by rheumatism. 2 ADJ Someone who is **rheumatic** suffers from rheumatism.

rheumatism /ruːmətɪzə0m/. UNCOUNT N **Rheumatism** is an illness that makes your joints or muscles stiff and painful.

rhino /raɪnəʊ/, **rhinos.** COUNT N A **rhino** is the same as a rhinoceros.

rhinoceros /raɪnɒsə0rəs/, **rhinoceroses.** COUNT N A **rhinoceros** is a large African or Asian animal with one or two horns on its nose.

rhubarb /ruːbɑːb/. UNCOUNT N **Rhubarb** is a plant with long red stems which can be cooked and eaten.

rhyme /raɪm/, **rhymes, rhyming, rhymed.** 1 RECIP VB If one word **rhymes** with another or if two words **rhyme,** they have a very similar sound. *She called him Guppy, to rhyme with puppy.* 2 COUNT N A **rhyme** is a word which rhymes with another word. *...two words he could not find a rhyme for.* 3 COUNT N A **rhyme** is also a short poem with rhyming words at the ends of its lines. *...children's games and rhymes.* ● See also **nursery rhyme.** 4 UNCOUNT N **Rhyme** is the use of rhyming words as a technique in poetry. *She had a gift for rhythm and rhyme.*

rhythm /rɪðə0m/, **rhythms.** 1 COUNT N OR UNCOUNT N A **rhythm** is a regular movement or beat. *...the rhythm of the drums... J J Cale uses rhythm for the opposite effect in his music.* 2 COUNT N A **rhythm** is also a regular pattern of changes, for example changes in the seasons or the tides.

rhythmic /rɪðmɪk/. ADJ If a movement or sound is **rhythmic,** it is repeated at regular intervals, forming a regular pattern or beat. *The machine made a soft rhythmic sound.* ♦ **rhythmically** ADV *The cradle rocked rhythmically to and fro.*

rib /rɪb/, **ribs.** COUNT N Your **ribs** are the curved bones that go from your backbone to your chest.

ribbon /rɪbə0n/, **ribbons.** 1 COUNT N OR UNCOUNT N A **ribbon** is a long, narrow piece of cloth used for fastening things or for decoration. 2 COUNT N OR UNCOUNT N A typewriter **ribbon** is the long, narrow piece of cloth containing ink that is used in a typewriter to make typed letters visible.

rice /raɪs/. UNCOUNT N **Rice** is a food consisting of white or brown grains which you cook and eat. The plant from which rice is taken is also called **rice.**

rich /rɪtʃ/, **richer, richest; riches.** 1 ADJ A **rich** person has a lot of money or valuable possessions. *She was extremely rich... Our father was a very rich man.* 2 PLURAL N **Riches** are valuable possessions or large amounts of money. 3 PRED ADJ WITH 'in' If something is **rich** in a desirable substance or quality, it has a lot of it. *The sea bed is rich in buried minerals... The story is rich in comic and dramatic detail.* ♦ **richness** UNCOUNT N *...the richness of Asian culture.* 4 ATTRIB ADJ A **rich** deposit of a mineral or other substance consists of a large amount of it. 5 ADJ **Rich** food contains a lot of fat or oil. *He was prone to indigestion after rich restaurant meals.* 6 ADJ If a place has a **rich** history, its history is very interesting. *The town has a rich social history.*

richly /rɪtʃli1/. 1 ADV You use **richly** to say that someone deserves or has been given something valuable for what they have done. *It was a richly deserved honour... I had seldom been so richly rewarded.* 2 ADV You also use **richly** to say that a place or thing has a large amount of elaborate or valuable things. *These libraries are richly equipped with games and books... ...the richly carved wooden screen.*

rickety /rɪkɪ1ti1/. ADJ A **rickety** building or piece of furniture is likely to collapse or break.

rickshaw /rɪkʃɔː/, **rickshaws.** COUNT N A **rickshaw** is a cart, often pulled by hand, that is used in parts of Asia for carrying passengers.

ricochet /rɪkəʃeɪ, rɪkəʃɛt/, **ricochets, ricocheting, ricocheted.** VB When a bullet **ricochets,** it hits a surface and bounces away from it. *Reporters were injured by bullets ricocheting off the hotel.*

rid /rɪd/, **rids, ridding. Rid** is used in the present tense, and is the past tense and past participle. 1 PHRASE When you **get rid of** something or someone that is unwanted, you take action so that you no longer have them. *She bathed thoroughly to get rid of the last traces of make-up... We had to get rid of the director.* 2 VB WITH OBJ AND 'of' If you **rid** a place or yourself of something unpleasant or annoying, you take action so that it no longer exists, or no longer affects you; a formal use. *We must rid the country of this wickedness... He had rid himself of his illusions.* 3 PRED ADJ WITH 'of' If you are **rid** of someone or something unpleasant or annoying, they are no longer with you or affecting you. *Eric was glad to be rid of him.*

ridden /rɪdə0n/. **Ridden** is the past participle of **ride.**

riddle /rɪdə0l/, **riddles.** 1 COUNT N A **riddle** is a puzzle in which you ask a question that seems to be nonsense but which has a clever or amusing answer, for example 'When is a door not a door? When it's ajar'. 2 COUNT N You can describe something that is puzzling as a **riddle.** *I was trying to solve the perplexing riddle of how to help my people.*

riddled /rɪdə0ld/. 1 PRED ADJ WITH 'with' If something is **riddled** with holes, it is full of them. 2 PRED ADJ WITH 'with' If something is **riddled** with undesirable qualities or features, it is full of them. *...cities riddled with corruption.*

ride /raɪd/, **rides, riding, rode** /rəʊd/, **ridden** /rɪdə0n/. 1 VB WITH OR WITHOUT OBJ When you **ride** a horse, you sit on it and control its movements. *Every morning he used to ride his mare across the fields... I rode in the Grand National.* 2 VB WITH OBJ OR ADJUNCT When you **ride** a bicycle or a motorcycle you control it and travel along on it. *He rode round the campus on a bicycle.* 3 VB WITH ADJUNCT When you **ride** in a vehicle such as a car, you travel in it. *That afternoon he rode in a jeep to the village.* 4 COUNT N A **ride** is a journey on a horse or bicycle, or in a vehicle. *...the bus ride to Worcester.* 5 PHRASE If someone **has taken** you **for a ride,** they have deceived or cheated you; an informal use.

rider /raɪdə/, **riders.** COUNT N A **rider** is someone who is riding a horse, a bicycle, or a motorcycle.

ridge /rɪdʒ/, **ridges.** 1 COUNT N A **ridge** is a long, narrow piece of raised land. *We drove up a hillside and finally stopped on a high ridge.* 2 COUNT N A **ridge** is also a raised line on a flat surface. *He was counting the ridges in the wet sand.*

ridicule /rɪdɪkjuːl/, **ridicules, ridiculing, ridiculed.** VB WITH OBJ If you **ridicule** someone, you make fun of them in an unkind way. *He is liable to be teased and ridiculed.* Also UNCOUNT N *His prophecy was greeted with a good deal of ridicule.*

ridiculous /rɪdɪkjə4ləs/. ADJ Something that is **ridiculous** is very foolish. *It would be ridiculous to pretend that there were no difficulties... They charge you a ridiculous price.* ♦ **ridiculously** SUBMOD *He let out his house at a ridiculously low rent.*

rife /raɪf/. PRED ADJ If something bad or unpleasant is **rife,** it is very common; a formal use. *Bribery and corruption in the government service were rife.*

rifle /raɪfə0l/, **rifles, rifling, rifled.** 1 COUNT N A **rifle** is a gun with a long barrel. 2 VB WITH OBJ When someone **rifles** a place, they steal everything they want from it. *He rifled the dead man's wallet.* 3 VB WITH 'through' If you **rifle** through things, you make a quick search among them. *The doctor rifled through the papers.*

rift /rɪft/, **rifts.** 1 COUNT N A **rift** between people is a serious quarrel that makes them stop being friends. 2 COUNT N A **rift** is also a split that appears in the ground. *The Jemez Mountains face Santa Fe across the rift.*

rig /rɪg/, **rigs, rigging, rigged.** 1 VB WITH OBJ If someone **rigs** an election, a job appointment, or a game, they dishonestly arrange it so that they achieve the result that they want. 2 COUNT N A **rig** is a large structure that is used when extracting oil or gas from the ground or the sea bed. *...an oil rig.*

rig up. PHR VB If you **rig** something **up,** you make it and fix it in place using any available materials. *He had rigged up a listening device.*

rigging /rɪgɪŋ/. UNCOUNT N The ropes which support a ship's masts and sails are referred to as the **rigging.**

right /raɪt/, **rights, righting, righted.** 1 ADJ OR ADV If something is **right,** it is correct and in accordance with the facts. *You get full marks for getting the right answer... You are French, is that right?... I hope I'm pronouncing the name right.* 2 PRED ADJ If someone is **right** about something, they are correct in what they say or think about it. *Lally was right about the repairs which the cottage needed.* ♦ **rightly** ADV *The arts are, as Geoffrey rightly said, underfinanced.* 3 ADJ If something such as a choice, action, or decision is the **right** one, it is the best or most suitable one. *I thought it was the right thing to do... Clare is obviously the right person to talk to about it.* 4 PRED ADJ If a situation isn't **right,** there is something unsatisfactory about it. *She sensed that things weren't right between us.* 5 PRED ADJ If someone is **right** to do something, they are morally justified in doing it. *We were right to insist on certain reforms... I don't think it's right to leave children alone in a house.* ♦ **rightly** ADV *Many people are rightly indignant.* 6 UNCOUNT N **Right** is used to refer to actions that are considered to be morally good and acceptable. *One must have some principles, some sense of right and wrong.* 7 ATTRIB ADJ If you refer to the **right** people or places, you are referring to people and places that are socially admired. *He knew all the right people.* 8 ATTRIB ADJ The **right** side of a piece of material is the side that is intended to be seen when it is made into clothes or furnishings. 9 SENTENCE ADV You say **'Right'** in order to attract someone's attention. *Right, open your mouth, let's have a look.* 10 COUNT N If you have a **right** to do or have something, you are morally or legally entitled to do it or have it. *...the right to strike... They will fight for their rights.* 11 UNCOUNT N OR SING N **Right** is one of two opposite directions, sides, or positions. In the word 'to', the 'o' is to the right of the 't'. *On my left was Tony Heard and on my right Allister Sparks.* Also ADV OR ATTRIB ADJ *Turn right off Broadway into Caxton Street... Her right hand was covered in blood.* 12 COLL N The **Right** is used to refer to the people or groups who support capitalism and conservatism rather than socialism. 13 ADV WITH ADJUNCT **Right** is used to emphasize the precise place, distance, or length of time that you are talking about. *Our hotel was right on the beach... Stay right here... We took the lift right down to the basement.* 14 ATTRIB ADJ **Right** is also used to emphasize a noun referring to something bad; an informal use. *They've made a right mess of that, haven't they?* 15 ADV WITH ADJUNCT **Right** also means immediately. *I'll be right back... The Music Hall is going to close down right after Easter.* 16 REFL VB If something that has fallen over **rights** itself, it returns to its normal position. *The ship righted itself.* 17 VB WITH OBJ To **right** a wrong means to correct it or compensate for it.

PHRASES ● If you **get** something **right,** you do it correctly. *Get the spelling right this time.* ● **Right away** means immediately. *He had written down a list of things to do right away.* ● If you are **in the right,** what you are doing is morally or legally correct. ● If something should be the case **by rights,** it should be the case, but it is not. *I should by rights speak German—my mother's German—but I only know a few words.* ● If you have a position, title, or claim to something **in** your **own right,** you have it because of what you are yourself rather than because of other people. *He had emerged as a leader in his own right.* ● **to serve** someone **right:** see **serve.** ● **on the right side of** someone: see **side.** ● See also **all right.**

right angle, right angles. 1 COUNT N A **right angle** is an angle of 90°. 2 PHRASE If two things are **at right angles,** they form an angle of 90° where they touch. *...four corridors at right angles to each other.*

righteous /raɪtʃəs/. ADJ **Righteous** people behave in a way that is morally good and admirable; a formal use. *...righteous anger.* ♦ **righteousness** UNCOUNT N *Some of us strive for righteousness.*

rightful /raɪtful/. ATTRIB ADJ Someone's **rightful** possession, place, or role is one which they have a legal or moral right to have; a formal use. *They had been deprived of their rightful share of the property.*

right-hand. ATTRIB ADJ **Right-hand** refers to something which is on the right side. *...a biggish house on the right-hand side of the road.*

right-handed. ADJ **Right-handed** people use their right hand rather than their left hand for activities such as writing or throwing a ball.

right of way, rights of way. 1 UNCOUNT N When a car or other vehicle has **right of way,** other traffic must stop for it at a junction or roundabout. 2 COUNT N A **right of way** is a public path across private land.

right-wing. 1 ADJ **Right-wing** people support conservatism and capitalism. *...the election of a right-wing government... They are very right-wing.* 2 SING N The **right wing** of a political party consists of the members who are most strongly in favour of conservatism and capitalism.

right-winger, right-wingers. COUNT N A **right-winger** is a person whose political beliefs are closer to conservatism and capitalism than those of other people in the same party.

rigid /rɪdʒɪd/. 1 ADJ **Rigid** laws or systems cannot be changed or varied, and are therefore considered to be rather severe. *Some mothers resented the rigid controls.* ♦ **rigidity** /rɪdʒɪdɪti/ UNCOUNT N *...the rigidity of Victorian marriage.* 2 ADJ A **rigid** person cannot or will not change their attitudes, opinions, or behaviour; used showing disapproval. *...the rigid attitude of the Foreign Secretary.* 3 ADJ A **rigid** substance or object is stiff and does not bend easily. *...with permed hair in rigid waves.* ♦ **rigidity** UNCOUNT N *The function of bones is largely to give rigidity.*

rigidly /rɪdʒɪdli/. 1 ADV If you stay **rigidly** in one position, you do not move. *I looked rigidly ahead... My features stayed rigidly fixed in the same expression.* 2 ADV If you do something **rigidly,** you do it in a strict way with no possibility of variation or change. *These suggestions must not be interpreted too rigidly.*

rigorous /rɪgərəs/. ADJ **Rigorous** is used to describe things that are done or carried out thoroughly. *...rigorous controls.* ♦ **rigorously** ADV *These methods have been rigorously tested over many years.*

rigours /rɪgəz/; spelled **rigors** in American English. PLURAL N The **rigours** of a situation or way of life are the features that make it unpleasant; a formal use. *...the rigours of a city winter.*

rim /rɪm/, **rims.** COUNT N The **rim** of a container or round object is its top edge or its outside edge. *...the rim of his glass... Muller's glasses had gold rims.*

rind /raɪnd/, **rinds.** 1 COUNT N OR UNCOUNT N The **rind** of a fruit such as a lemon is its thick outer skin. *...fruit with tough rinds... ...grated lemon rind.* 2 COUNT N OR UNCOUNT N The **rind** of cheese or bacon is the hard outer edge.

ring /rɪŋ/, **rings, ringing, rang** /ræŋ/, **rung** /rʌŋ/. For meanings 9 and 10, the past tense and past participle is **ringed.** 1 VB WITH OR WITHOUT OBJ If you **ring** someone, you phone them. *You must ring the hospital at once... He may ring again.* 2 ERG VB When you **ring** a bell or when a bell **rings,** it makes a sound. *In the distance a church bell was ringing... He had to ring the bell several times.* 3 COUNT N A **ring** is the sound made by a bell. *There was a ring at the door.* 4 VB If a place **rings** with a sound, the sound there is very loud; a literary use. *The barn rang with the cries of geese and turkeys.* 5 SING N You can use **ring** after an adjective to say that something that is mentioned seems to you to have a particular quality. *The books he mentioned had a familiar ring about them... The name had an unpleasant ring to it.* 6 COUNT N A **ring** is also a small circle of metal worn on your finger as an ornament or to show that you are married. 7 COUNT N An object or group of things with the shape of a circle can be referred to as a **ring.** *They formed a ring round him... ...a ring of excited faces.* 8 COUNT N The **ring** is the enclosed space with seats round it where a boxing match, show jumping contest, or circus performance takes place. 9 VB WITH OBJ If you **ring** something, you draw a circle round it. *I got a map and ringed all the likely villages.* 10 PASSIVE VB If a place is **ringed** with something, it is surrounded by that thing. *...a valley ringed with mountains.* 11 COUNT N A **ring** is also a group of people who do something illegal together, such as selling drugs or controlling the sale of art or antiques. *...a large drug ring operating in the area.*

PHRASES ● If you **give** someone **a ring,** you phone them; an informal use. *Give me a ring if you need me.* ● If a statement **rings true,** it seems likely to be true. *The bishop's answers so often ring true.*

ring back. PHR VB If someone phones you and you **ring** them **back,** you then phone them. *He asked if you'd ring him back when you got in.*

ring off. PHR VB If you **ring off** when you are using the phone, you put down your receiver.

ring up. PHR VB If you **ring** someone **up,** you phone them.

ringing /rɪŋɪŋ/. ATTRIB ADJ A **ringing** sound can be heard very clearly. *...clear ringing tones.*

ringleader /rɪŋli:də/, **ringleaders.** COUNT N The **ringleader** of a group of people who are causing trouble is the person who is leading them.

ring road, ring roads. COUNT N A **ring road** is a road that goes round the edge of a town and avoids the city centre.

rink /rɪŋk/, **rinks.** COUNT N A **rink** is a large area, usually indoors, where people go to skate. *There's a good ice rink in Leeds.*

rinse /rɪns/, **rinses, rinsing, rinsed.** 1 VB WITH OBJ When you **rinse** something, you wash it without using soap. *He rinsed his hands under the tap.* Also COUNT N *Just give these a quick rinse.* 2 VB WITH OBJ If you **rinse** your mouth or **rinse** it out, you wash it with a mouthful of liquid.

riot /raɪət/, **riots, rioting, rioted.** 1 COUNT N When there is a **riot,** a crowd of people behave violently in a public place. *In May 1968 there was a wave of student riots.* 2 VB When people **riot,** they behave violently in a public place. *If food prices are put up too far, the people will riot.* ♦ **rioter** COUNT N *Courts dealt with rioters quickly and harshly.*

riotous /raɪətəs/. 1 ATTRIB ADJ **Riotous** behaviour is violent and uncontrolled; a formal use. *...a riotous mob... He was found guilty of riotous behaviour.* 2 ADJ You can also describe people's behaviour as **riotous** when they do things very enthusiastically. *Both children would come rushing out in a riotous welcome.*

rip /rɪp/, **rips, ripping, ripped.** 1 ERG VB When something **rips** or **is ripped,** it is torn violently. *The canvas bags had ripped... The poster had been ripped to pieces.* 2 VB WITH OBJ AND ADJUNCT If you **rip** something away, you remove it quickly and violently. *I ripped the phone from her hand... He ripped his shirt off.* 3 COUNT N A **rip** is a long cut or split in something made of cloth or paper. *...the rip in the book.*

rip off. PHR VB If someone **rips** you **off,** they cheat you by charging too much for goods or services; an informal use. *The local shopkeepers were all trying to rip off the tourists.*

rip up. PHR VB If you **rip** something **up,** you tear it into small pieces.

ripe /raɪp/, **riper, ripest.** 1 ADJ **Ripe** fruit or grain is fully grown and ready to be harvested or eaten. *The pears are heavy and ripe.* 2 PRED ADJ WITH 'for' If something is **ripe** for a change, it is ready for it. *Our people are ripe for freedom... The nation was ripe for collapse.*

PHRASES ● If you say **the time is ripe,** you mean that a suitable time has arrived for something to happen. *The time was ripe to break his silence.* ● If someone lives to a **ripe old age,** they live to be very old.

ripen /raɪpən/, **ripens, ripening, ripened.** ERG VB When crops **ripen** or when the sun **ripens** them, they become ripe. *...fields of ripening wheat.*

ripple /rɪpəl/, **ripples, rippling, rippled.** 1 COUNT N **Ripples** are little waves on the surface of water caused by the wind or by an object dropping into the water. *...sending out patterns of ripples.* 2 ERG VB When the surface of an area of water **ripples,** a number of little waves appear on it. *...the pond rippling where the wind ruffled through the grass... A gentle breeze rippled the surface of the sea.* 3 SING N WITH 'of' A **ripple** of laughter or applause is a short, quiet burst of it. *...a ripple of amused applause.*

rise /raɪz/, **rises, rising, rose** /rəʊz/, **risen** /rɪzən/. 1 VB If something **rises** or **rises** up, it moves upwards. *Clouds of birds rose from the tree-tops... He could see the smoke from his bonfire rising up in a white column.* 2 VB When you **rise,** you stand up; a formal use. *Dr Willoughby rose to greet him.* 3 VB To **rise** also means to get out of bed. *They had risen at dawn.* 4 VB When the sun or moon **rises,** it appears from below the horizon. 5 VB If land **rises,** it slopes upwards. *He followed Jack towards the castle where the ground rose slightly.* ♦ **rising** ATTRIB ADJ *The house was built on rising ground.* 6 VB If a sound **rises,** it becomes louder or higher. *His voice rose to a shriek.* 7 VB If a sound **rises** from a group of people, it comes from them. *A loud gasp rose from the boys.* 8 VB If an amount **rises,** it increases. *Prices rose by more than 10%... The temperature began to rise.* ♦ **rising** ADJ *...the rising rate of inflation.* 9 COUNT N WITH SUPP A **rise** in the amount of something is an increase in it. *...the rise in crime... ...price rises... ...a pay rise of about £20 a week.* 10 VB WITH PREP 'to' If you **rise** to a challenge or remark, you respond to it, rather than ignoring it. 11 VB When the people in a country **rise** up, they start fighting the people in authority there. *The settlers rose in revolt.* ♦ **rising** COUNT N *...a big peasant rising.* 12 VB WITH ADJUNCT If someone **rises** to a higher

position or status, they become more important, successful, or powerful. *Bergson rose rapidly to fame.* **13** SING N Someone's **rise** is the process by which they become more important, successful, or powerful. *...the decline of the Liberal Party and the rise of Labour... ...his rise to fame.*
PHRASES ● If something **gives rise to** an event or situation, it causes it. *This breakthrough could give rise to ethical problems.*
rise above. PHR VB If you **rise above** a problem, you do not allow it to affect you. *She was in continual pain, but rose above it.*

risk /rɪsk/, **risks, risking, risked. 1** COUNT N OR UNCOUNT N If there is a **risk** of something unpleasant, there is a possibility that it will happen. *There is very little risk of infection... ...the risk that their men might disappear without trace.* **2** SING N If something is a **risk**, it might have dangerous or unpleasant results. *Such a response would be an irrational risk... Your television is a fire risk if left plugged in overnight.* **3** VB WITH OBJ OR -ING If you **risk** something unpleasant, you do something knowing that the unpleasant thing might happen as a result. *They were willing to risk losing their jobs.* **4** VB WITH OBJ OR -ING If you **risk** an action, you do it, even though you know that it might have undesirable consequences. *If you have an expensive rug, don't risk washing it yourself.* **5** VB WITH OBJ If you **risk** someone's life, you put them in a dangerous position. *She had risked her life to help save mine.*
PHRASES ● To be **at risk** means to be in a situation where something unpleasant or dangerous might happen. *You're putting my career at risk.* ● If you are doing something **at your own risk,** it will be your own responsibility if you are harmed. ● If you **run the risk** of doing or experiencing something undesirable or dangerous, you do something knowing that this thing might happen as a result. *We run the risk of confusing the voters.* ● If you **take a risk,** you do something which you know might be dangerous. *I am taking a tremendous risk.*

risky /rɪski^{1}/, **riskier, riskiest.** ADJ If an activity or action is **risky,** it is dangerous or likely to fail. *The whole thing has become too risky.*

rite /raɪt/, **rites.** COUNT N A **rite** is a traditional ceremony carried out by a particular group. *...the rite of circumcision... ...fertility rites.*

ritual /rɪtju^{0}əl/, **rituals. 1** COUNT N OR UNCOUNT N A **ritual** is a series of actions which are traditionally carried out in a particular situation. *Our society has many rituals of greeting, farewell, and celebration.* **2** ATTRIB ADJ **Ritual** activities happen as part of a ritual or tradition. *...the practice of ritual murder.*

rival /raɪvə^{0}l/, **rivals, rivalling, rivalled;** spelled **rivaling, rivaled** in American English. **1** COUNT N Your **rival** is someone who you are competing with. *His newspaper outstripped its rivals in circulation.* Also ATTRIB ADJ *Fighting broke out between rival groups.* **2** VB WITH OBJ If one thing **rivals** another, they are both of the same standard or quality. *Of all the flowers in the garden few can rival the lily.*

rivalry /raɪvəlri^{1}/, **rivalries.** COUNT N OR UNCOUNT N **Rivalry** is active competition between people. *...the intense rivalries between groups and personalities... Burr's rivalry with Hamilton began in those days.*

river /rɪvə/, **rivers.** COUNT N A **river** is a large amount of fresh water flowing continuously in a long line across land.

riverside /rɪvəsaɪd/. SING N The **riverside** is the area of land by the banks of a river.

rivet /rɪvɪt/, **rivets, riveting, riveted. 1** VB WITH OBJ If you **are riveted** by something, it fascinates you. *I was riveted by his presentation.* ♦ **riveting** ADJ *...a riveting television documentary.* **2** COUNT N A **rivet** is a type of bolt used for holding pieces of metal together.

RN /ɑː ɛn/. **RN** is a written abbreviation for 'Royal Navy', the navy of the United Kingdom.

road /rəʊd/, **roads.** COUNT N A **road** is a long piece of hard ground built between two places so that people can drive or ride easily from one place to the other. *...the road from Belfast to Londonderry... The ruins were accessible by road... ...Tottenham Court Road.*

roadblock /rəʊdblɒk/, **roadblocks.** COUNT N A **roadblock** is a barrier which is put across a road to prevent people or traffic going along the road.

roadside /rəʊdsaɪd/, **roadsides.** COUNT N The **roadside** is the area at the edge of a road.

roam /rəʊm/, **roams, roaming, roamed.** VB WITH OBJ OR ADJUNCT If you **roam** an area or **roam** around it, you wander around it without having a particular purpose. *He roamed the streets at night... They roam over the hills and plains.*

roar /rɔː/, **roars, roaring, roared. 1** VB If something **roars,** it makes a very loud noise. *The wind roared in the forest.* Also SING N *I could hear the roar of traffic outside.* **2** VB OR REPORT VB If someone **roars,** they shout very loudly. *'Forward with the Revolution,' the crowd roared back.* **3** VB When a lion **roars,** it makes the loud sound typical of a lion. Also COUNT N *The lion let out one of its roars.*

roaring /rɔːrɪŋ/. **1** ATTRIB ADJ **Roaring** means making a very loud noise. *...the roaring traffic.* **2** ATTRIB ADJ A **roaring** fire is one which is very hot with large flames. **3** ATTRIB ADJ If something is a **roaring** success, it is very successful indeed.

roast /rəʊst/, **roasts, roasting, roasted. 1** ERG VB When you **roast** meat or other food, you cook it by dry heat in an oven or over a fire. *You can make peanut butter by roasting the nuts for twenty minutes... The stake burnt more quickly than the pig roasted.* Also ATTRIB ADJ *...roast beef.* **2** COUNT N OR UNCOUNT N A **roast** is a piece of meat that has been roasted. *...taking the roast out of the oven... ...a thick slab of roast.*

rob /rɒb/, **robs, robbing, robbed. 1** VB WITH OBJ If someone **robs** you, they steal something from you. *The only way I can get the money is to rob a few banks... He tried to rob her of her share.* ♦ **robber** /rɒbə/ COUNT N *...bank robbers.* **2** VB WITH OBJ AND 'of' If you **rob** someone of something that they should have, you take it away from them. *You robbed me of my moment of glory.*

robbery /rɒbə^{0}ri^{1}/, **robberies.** UNCOUNT N OR COUNT N **Robbery** is the crime of stealing money or property, often by using force or threats. *He was arrested on charges of armed robbery... ...if he had committed the robbery.*

robe /rəʊb/, **robes.** COUNT N A **robe** is a loose piece of clothing which reaches the ground; a formal use. *...ceremonial robes.*

robin /rɒbɪn/, **robins.** COUNT N A **robin** is a small brown bird with a red breast.

robot /rəʊbɒt/, **robots.** COUNT N A **robot** is a machine which moves and performs certain tasks automatically. *Industry is making increasing use of robots.*

robust /rə^{6}bʌst, rəʊbə^{9}st/. ADJ Someone or something that is **robust** is strong and healthy. *She has four robust daughters... The once robust economy now lies in ruins.*

rock /rɒk/, **rocks, rocking, rocked. 1** UNCOUNT N **Rock** is the hard substance which the earth is made of. *Large masses of rock are constantly falling into the sea.* **2** COUNT N A **rock** is a piece of stone sticking out of the ground or the sea, or that has broken away from a mountain or cliff. *I sat down on a rock.* **3** ERG VB When something **rocks,** it moves slowly and regularly backwards and forwards or from side to side. *She sat there, rocking gently... Our parents cuddle and hug us, and rock us gently back and forth.* **4** VB WITH OBJ If something **rocks** people, it shocks and horrifies them; used in written English. *France was rocked by an outbreak of violent crime.* **5** UNCOUNT N **Rock** or **rock music** is loud music with a strong beat that is played and sung by a small group of people using a variety of instruments including guitars and drums. *...a rock concert.* **6** UNCOUNT N **Rock** is also a sweet made in long, hard sticks which are sold at tourist places.
PHRASES ● If an alcoholic drink is **on the rocks,** it is served with ice. *...whisky on the rocks.* ● If a relationship is **on the rocks,** it is unsuccessful and is likely to end soon. ● **rock the boat:** see **boat.**

rock and roll. UNCOUNT N **Rock and roll** is a kind of music developed in the 1950s which has a strong beat and is played by small groups.

rocket /rɒkɪt/, **rockets, rocketing, rocketed. 1** COUNT N A **rocket** is a space vehicle shaped like a long tube. *...a space rocket.* **2** COUNT N A **rocket** is also a missile containing explosive that is powered by burning gas. *...anti-tank rockets.* **3** VB If prices or profits **rocket,** they increase very quickly and suddenly; an informal use. *Land sales rocketed.*

rocky /rɒki^{1}/. ADJ A **rocky** place is covered with rocks. *She drives carefully up the rocky lane.*

rod /rɒd/, **rods.** COUNT N A **rod** is a long, thin, metal or wooden bar. *The aluminium rod that held the seats broke.*

rode /rəʊd/. **Rode** is the past tense of **ride.**

rodent /rəʊdənt/, **rodents.** COUNT N A **rodent** is a small mammal with sharp front teeth. Rats, mice, and squirrels are rodents. *Some of the crop may be eaten up by insects or rodents.*

roe /rəʊ/. UNCOUNT N **Roe** is the eggs or sperm of a fish, which is eaten as food.

rogue /rəʊg/, **rogues.** COUNT N A **rogue** is a man who behaves in a dishonest way; an old-fashioned use.

role /rəʊl/, **roles. 1** COUNT N WITH SUPP Your **role** is your position and function in a situation or society. *What is the role of the University in modern society?... He had played a major role in the formation of the United Nations.* **2** COUNT N A **role** is one of the characters that an actor or singer plays in a film, play, or opera. *She played the leading role in The Winter's Tale.*

roll /rəʊl/, **rolls, rolling, rolled. 1** ERG VB When something **rolls,** it moves along a surface, turning over many times. *The bucket rolled and clattered down the path... He rolled a boulder down the slope.* **2** VB WITH ADJUNCT When vehicles **roll** along, they move along. *Trucks with loudspeakers rolled through the streets.* **3** VB WITH ADJUNCT If drops of liquid **roll** down a surface, they move quickly down it. *He stood in a corner with tears rolling down his face.* **4** VB WITH OBJ AND ADJUNCT If you **roll** something into a cylinder or a ball, or **roll** it up, you form it into a cylinder or a ball by wrapping it several times around itself or by shaping it between your hands. *She went on sorting the socks, rolling them into neat little bundles... The mattress was rolled up.* ♦ **rolled** ATTRIB ADJ *...a rolled newspaper... ...a rolled umbrella.* **5** COUNT N A **roll** of paper or cloth is a long piece of it that has been wrapped many times around itself or around a tube. *...a roll of film.* **6** COUNT N A **roll** is a small circular loaf of bread. **7** COUNT N WITH SUPP A **roll** is also an official list of people's names. *...the roll of members.* **8** COUNT N A **roll** of drums is a long, rumbling sound made by drums. **9** See also **rolling, rock and roll, sausage roll, toilet roll.**
PHRASES ● If something is several things **rolled into one,** it combines the main features of those things. *A good musical is a new play, a new opera and a new ballet all rolled into one.* ● **to start the ball rolling:** see **ball.**
roll in. PHR VB If money or profits **are rolling in,** they are being received in large quantities; an informal use.
roll over. PHR VB If someone who is lying down **rolls over,** they move so that a different part of them is facing upwards.

roll-call, roll-calls. COUNT N If you take a **roll-call,** you check which of the members of a group are present by reading their names out.

roller /rəʊlə/, **rollers. 1** COUNT N A **roller** is a cylinder that turns round in a machine or device. *She pulled the sheet of paper out of the roller.* **2** COUNT N **Rollers** are hollow tubes that women use in their hair to make it curly.

roller-skate, roller-skates, roller-skating, roller-skated. 1 COUNT N **Roller-skates** are shoes with four small wheels on the bottom. **2** VB If you **roller-skate,** you move over a flat surface wearing roller-skates.

rolling /rəʊlɪŋ/. **1** ATTRIB ADJ **Rolling** hills are small with gentle slopes that extend a long way into the distance. *...the rolling countryside west of Detroit.* **2** ATTRIB ADJ A **rolling** walk is slow and swaying, usually because the person is drunk or very fat.

rolling pin, rolling pins. COUNT N A **rolling pin** is a cylinder that you roll over pastry to make it flat.

Roman Catholic /rəʊmən kæθə^{0}lɪk/, **Roman Catholics.** COUNT N A **Roman Catholic** is the same as a Catholic.

Roman Catholicism /rəʊmən kəθɒlɪsɪzə^{0}m/. UNCOUNT N **Roman Catholicism** is the same as Catholicism.

romance /rəʊmæns, rəmæns/, **romances. 1** COUNT N OR UNCOUNT N A **romance** is a relationship in which two people love each other. *...a wartime romance... Young people are re-discovering romance and passion.* **2** UNCOUNT N **Romance** is the pleasure and excitement of doing something new or exciting. *There is romance to be found in life on the river.* **3** COUNT N A **romance** is also a novel about a love affair. *...historical romances.*

Roman numeral /rəʊmən njuːmə^{0}rəl/, **Roman numerals.** COUNT N **Roman numerals** are the letters used by the Romans to write numbers. For example, I, IV, XL, and C are used to represent 1, 4, 40, and 100.

romantic /rə^{6}mæntɪk/, **romantics. 1** ADJ A **romantic** person has a lot of unrealistic ideas, especially about love. *She's as romantic as a child of sixteen.* Also COUNT N *Cedric's a great romantic.* **2** ATTRIB ADJ **Romantic** means connected with sexual love. *No woman needs a romantic attachment.* **3** ATTRIB ADJ A **romantic** play, film, or story describes or represents a love affair. *...a charming romantic comedy starring Audrey Hepburn.* **4** ADJ Something that is **romantic** is beautiful in a way that strongly affects your feelings. *...a romantic moonlight ride.* ♦ **romantically** ADV *Her long hair was spread romantically over the pillow.*

romanticism /rə^{6}mæntɪsɪzə^{0}m/. UNCOUNT N **Romanticism** is thoughts and feelings which are idealistic and romantic, rather than realistic.

romanticize /rə^{6}mæntɪsaɪz/, **romanticizes, romanticizing, romanticized;** also spelled **romanticise.** VB WITH OBJ If you **romanticize** someone or something, you imagine them to be better than they really are. *Perhaps he romanticized the onward march of the people somewhat.*

romp /rɒmp/, **romps, romping, romped.** VB When children **romp** around, they play and move around in a noisy, happy way. *They romped with their dogs.*

roof /ruːf/, **roofs** /ruːvz, ruːfs/. **1** COUNT N The **roof** of a building or car is the covering on top of it. *...a slate* *roof... I fixed a leak in the roof of her shed.* 2 COUNT N The **roof** of your mouth or of a cave is the highest part of it.

PHRASES ● If you have a **roof over your head,** you have somewhere to live. *She was without money and with no real roof over her head.* ● If someone **hits the roof,** they are very angry indeed; an informal use.

roofed /ru:ft/. ADJ You can use **roofed** to say what kind of roof a building has. *...houses roofed with reddish-brown tiles... ...red-roofed farmhouses.*

rooftop /ru:ftɒp/, **rooftops.** COUNT N **Rooftops** are the outside parts of roofs. *...a view over the roof-tops.*

rook /rʊk/, **rooks.** 1 COUNT N A **rook** is a large black bird. 2 COUNT N In chess, a **rook** is a piece which can move forwards, backwards, or sideways. A **rook** is also called a **castle.**

room /ru:m/, **rooms.** 1 COUNT N A **room** is one of the separate sections in a building, which has its own walls, ceiling, floor, and door. *The room contained a couch and a glass cabinet.* 2 UNCOUNT N If there is **room** for something, there is enough space for it. *There wasn't enough room for everybody.* 3 UNCOUNT N If there is **room** for a particular kind of behaviour, people are able to behave in that way. *There ought to be room for differences of opinion... There is room for much more research.*

roommate /ru:mmeɪt/, **roommates.** COUNT N Your **roommate** is the person who you share a rented room with.

roomy /ru:mi^1/, **roomier, roomiest.** ADJ A **roomy** place has plenty of space. *...a ground floor apartment which was roomy but sparsely furnished.*

roost /ru:st/, **roosts, roosting, roosted.** 1 COUNT N A **roost** is a place where birds rest or build nests. *The gulls were returning to their roosts among the rocks.* 2 VB When birds **roost,** they settle in somewhere for the night. *The chickens roost there all winter.*

rooster /ru:stə/, **roosters.** COUNT N A **rooster** is an adult male chicken; an American use.

root /ru:t/, **roots, rooting, rooted.** 1 COUNT N The **roots** of a plant are the parts that grow underground. *These trees have large, spreading roots.* 2 COUNT N The **root** of a hair or tooth is the part beneath the skin. *They pulled her hair out by the roots.* 3 PLURAL N Your **roots** are the place or culture that you or your family grew up in, which you have now left. *People are searching again for their roots.* 4 COUNT N The **root** of something is its original cause or basis. *Perhaps the root of the tragedy was here.* Also ATTRIB ADJ *...the root causes of poverty.* 5 VB WITH ADJUNCT If you **root** through things, you search through them thoroughly. *Meadows rooted around in his bag and pulled out a map.* 6 See also **grass roots, square root.**

PHRASES ● To **take root** means to start to grow or develop. *The seedlings of bushes and trees might take root there... ...the ideas that were to take root in a new land.* ● If you **put down roots** somewhere, you become connected with it, for example by taking part in activities there.

root out. PHR VB If you **root** someone or something **out,** you find them and remove them from a place. *He's in there somewhere. Let's go and root him out.*

rooted /ru:tɪ^{1}d/. 1 PRED ADJ If one thing is **rooted** in another, it is strongly influenced by that thing or has developed from it. *...attitudes deeply rooted in history.* 2 ADJ A **rooted** opinion is a firm one that is unlikely to change. *He had a rooted objection to British drivers.* ● See also **deep-rooted.**

rope /rəʊp/, **ropes, roping, roped.** 1 COUNT N OR UNCOUNT N A **rope** is a long piece of very thick string, made by twisting together several thinner pieces of string or several bunches of fibres. *They should be tied together with a rope... ...a piece of rope.* 2 VB WITH OBJ AND ADJUNCT If you **rope** one thing to another, you tie them together with a rope. *The wagons were roped together.* 3 PHRASE If you **know the ropes,** you know how something should be done in a particular place; an informal use.

rope in. PHR VB If you **rope** someone **in** to do something, you persuade them to help you; an informal use.

rosary /rəʊzəri^1/, **rosaries.** COUNT N A **rosary** is a string of beads that Catholics and Hindus use in praying.

rose /rəʊz/, **roses.** 1 COUNT N A **rose** is a flower which has a pleasant smell and grows on a bush with thorns. 2 **Rose** is also the past tense of **rise.**

rosé /rəʊzeɪ/. UNCOUNT N **Rosé** is pink wine.

rosette /rəʊzet/, **rosettes.** COUNT N A **rosette** is a large, circular badge made from coloured ribbons which is worn as a prize or to show support for a sports team or political party.

roster /rɒstə/, **rosters.** COUNT N A **roster** is a list of people who take turns to do a particular job.

rostrum /rɒstrəm/, **rostrums** or **rostra** /rɒstrə/. COUNT N A **rostrum** is a raised platform on which someone stands when they are speaking to an audience or conducting an orchestra.

rosy /rəʊzi^1/. 1 ADJ Something that is **rosy** is pink. *...her bright eyes and rosy cheeks.* 2 ADJ If a situation seems **rosy,** it seems likely to be good. *...a rosy future.*

rot /rɒt/, **rots, rotting, rotted.** 1 ERG VB When food, wood, or other substances **rot,** they change and fall apart. *Her teeth were rotting... ...the smell of rotting vegetables... Bleach might rot the fibres.* Also UNCOUNT N *Destroy any bulbs with rot and buy healthy ones.* 2 PHRASE If you say that **the rot is setting in,** you mean that a situation is beginning to get worse and that nothing can prevent this from happening.

rot away. PHR VB When something made of a natural material **rots away,** it changes until none of it remains. *The shack rotted away.*

rota /rəʊtə/, **rotas.** COUNT N A **rota** is a list of people who take turns to do a particular job.

rotary /rəʊtə^{0}ri^1/. ATTRIB ADJ **Rotary** means involving movement in a circular direction. *...a rotary mower.*

rotate /rəʊteɪt/, **rotates, rotating, rotated.** 1 ERG VB When something **rotates,** it turns with a circular movement. *...two drums rotating in opposite directions... He rotated the camera.* ♦ **rotation** /rəʊteɪʃə^{0}n/ UNCOUNT N OR COUNT N *...the earth's rotation... ...the rotations of the ceiling fan.* 2 VB WITH OBJ If you **rotate** a group of things or people, you use each of them in turn, and then begin with the first one again. *Weeds and diseases are controlled by rotating the crops.* ♦ **rotation** UNCOUNT N OR COUNT N *She did everything in strict rotation... Crop rotations will help to minimize disease.*

rotor /rəʊtə/, **rotors.** COUNT N The **rotors** or **rotor blades** of a helicopter are the four long pieces of metal on top of it which go round and lift it off the ground.

rotten /rɒtə^{0}n/. 1 ADJ If food, wood, or other substances are **rotten,** they have become bad or fallen apart, so that they can no longer be used. *...rotten eggs.* 2 ADJ If you say that something is **rotten,** you mean that it is bad, unpleasant, or unfair; an informal use. *...a rotten novel... They're having a rotten deal.* 3 PRED ADJ If you feel **rotten,** you feel ill; an informal use.

rough /rʌf/, **rougher, roughest; roughs, roughing, roughed.** 1 ADJ If a surface is **rough,** it is uneven and not smooth. *...rough roads... By now the sea was really rough.* ♦ **roughness** UNCOUNT N *Roughness of the skin can be caused by bad diet.* 2 ADJ If someone is having a **rough** time, they are experiencing something difficult or unpleasant. 3 ADJ A **rough** calculation, description, or drawing is approximate rather than exact or detailed. *Multiply the weekly amount by fifty-two to get the rough annual cost... ...a rough outline of the proposals.* ♦ **roughly** ADV *...a woman of roughly her own age... Could you tell us roughly what is required?* 4 ADJ You can say that something is **rough** when it is not well made. *...a rough shelter of branches and leaves.* ♦ **roughly** ADV *The pieces were then roughly cobbled together.* 5 ADJ You say that people are **rough** when they use too much force. *...complaints of rough handling.* ♦ **roughly** ADV *He shoved the boy roughly aside.* 6 ADJ If a town or district is **rough,** there is a lot of crime or violence there. *...one of the roughest towns in America.* 7 PHRASE When people **sleep rough,** they sleep out of doors, usually because they have no home.

roulette /ru:let/. UNCOUNT N **Roulette** is a gambling game in which a ball is dropped onto a revolving wheel with numbered holes in it. The players bet on which hole the ball will end up in.

round /raʊnd/, **rounder, roundest; rounds, rounding, rounded.** The form **around** can be used instead of **round** when it is a preposition or an adverb. 1 ADJ Something that is **round** is shaped like a ball or a circle. *...heavy round stones... Shanti had a round face.* 2 ADJ **Round** also means curved. *...the round bulge of the girl's belly.* 3 PREP OR ADV If something or a group of things is **round** or **around** something else, it is situated on every side of it. *She was wearing a scarf round her head... We were sitting round a table eating and drinking... There was a wall all the way round.* 4 PREP OR ADV If one thing moves **round** or **around** another, the first thing keeps moving in a circle, with the second thing at the centre of the circle. *The earth moves round the sun.* 5 ADV If you turn or look **round** or **around,** you turn so that you are facing in a different direction. *He swung round and faced the window.* 6 PHRASE If something is going **round and round,** it is spinning or moving in circles. *A swallow flew frantically round and round.* 7 PREP OR ADV If you go **round** or **around** something, you move in a curve past it. *They sailed round the Cape... The boys had disappeared around a corner.* 8 PREP If something happens or exists in many parts of a place, you can say that it happens or exists **round** or **around** that place. *Think of what's happening politically round the world.* 9 PREP OR ADV If you go **round** or **around** a place, you go to several different parts of it. *I wandered around the orchard.* 10 ADV When someone comes **round,** they visit you. *I'd like to ask him round for dinner.* 11 VB WITH OBJ When you **round** something, you move in a curve past it. *...as he rounded the corner at the top of the stairs.* 12 COUNT N WITH SUPP A **round** of events is a series of connected events that is part of a longer series. *Turkey is eager for a further round of talks.* 13 COUNT N When people such as doctors go on their **rounds,** they make a series of visits as part of their job. 14 COUNT N A **round** of a competition is a set of games or turns within it. 15 COUNT N A **round** of golf is one game. 16 COUNT N In a boxing match, a **round** is one of the periods during which the boxers fight. 17 COUNT N If you buy a **round** of drinks, you buy a drink for each member of the group of people that you are with. 18 COUNT N A **round** of ammunition is the bullet or bullets that are released when a gun is fired.

round up. PHR VB If you **round up** animals or people, you gather them together. *They had rounded up people at gunpoint.* ● See also **roundup.**

roundabout /raʊndəbaʊt/, **roundabouts.** 1 COUNT N In a fair or playground, a **roundabout** is a large, circular platform with seats which goes round and round; a British use. 2 COUNT N A **roundabout** is also a circle at a place where several roads meet. You drive round it until you come to the road that you want; a British use. 3 ADJ If you do something in a **roundabout** way, you do not do it in the simplest or most direct way. *They drove back to Glasgow by a long roundabout route... He told me this in a rather gentle, roundabout way.*

rounded /raʊndɪ^{2}d/. ADJ Something that is **rounded** is curved rather than pointed or sharp. *Its teeth are small and rounded.*

roundly /raʊndli^1/. ADV If you say something **roundly,** you say it very forcefully. *Britain was roundly condemned for selling arms to the rebels.*

round-the-clock. ATTRIB ADJ **Round-the-clock** activities happen all day and all night. *...keeping the hotel under round-the-clock surveillance.* Also ADV *Factories are working round the clock.*

round trip, round trips. COUNT N If you make a **round trip,** you travel to a place and then back again.

roundup /raʊndʌp/, **roundups.** COUNT N On television or radio, a **roundup** of news is a summary of it. *...the news followed by the sports roundup.*

rouse /raʊz/, **rouses, rousing, roused.** 1 VB WITH OBJ If you **rouse** someone, you wake them up; a formal use. 2 REFL VB If you **rouse** yourself to do something, you make yourself get up and do it. *He roused himself to talk to Christine.* 3 VB WITH OBJ If something **rouses** you, it makes you very emotional or excited. *He roused the troops with his oratory.* ♦ **rousing** ADJ *...a rousing cheer.* 4 VB WITH OBJ If something **rouses** an emotion in you, it causes you to feel it. *The proposal roused fears among the public.*

rout /raʊt/, **routs, routing, routed.** VB WITH OBJ If an army or a sports team **routs** its opponents, it defeats them completely and easily. *Spain could not muster sufficient resources to rout the Cubans.* Also COUNT N OR UNCOUNT N *The retreat turned into a rout... The terrified army fled in rout.*

route /ru:t/, **routes, routing, routed.** 1 COUNT N A **route** is a way from one place to another. *I took the route through Beechwood... ...the main route out of London to the west.* ● See also **en route.** 2 COUNT N WITH SUPP You can refer to a way of achieving something as a **route.** *Another route is by active participation in a trade union.* 3 VB WITH OBJ When vehicles **are routed** past a place or through it, they are made to travel past it or through it. *Flights were being routed around the trouble area.*

routine /ru:ti:n/, **routines.** 1 ADJ **Routine** activities are done regularly as a normal part of your job, rather than for a special reason. *...a routine check.* ♦ **routinely** ADV *This information is routinely collected and published.* 2 COUNT N OR UNCOUNT N A **routine** is the set of things you usually do. *...his daily routine... Davis's death has upset our routine.*

rove /rəʊv/, **roves, roving, roved.** VB WITH OBJ OR ADJUNCT Someone who **roves** an area wanders around it; a literary use. *...the thugs who rove the streets at night... ...his old habits of roving round the rubbish tips.*

row, rows, rowing, rowed; pronounced /rəʊ/ for meanings 1 to 3, and /raʊ/ for meanings 4 and 5. 1 COUNT N A **row** of things or people is a number of them arranged in a line. *...a large hall filled with rows of desks... They were standing neatly in a row.* 2 PHRASE If the same thing happens several times **in a row,** it happens that number of times without interruption. *He was elected president three times in a row.* 3 VB WITH OR WITHOUT OBJ When you **row** a boat, you make it move through the water by using oars. *We rowed slowly towards the centre of the river.* Also SING N ...*a row on the lake.* **4** COUNT N A **row** is a quarrel or argument. *They were always having terrible rows.* **5** COUNT N If you say that someone is making a **row,** you mean that they are making a loud, unpleasant noise.

rowdy /raʊdi^1/. ADJ People who are **rowdy** are noisy, rough, and likely to cause trouble.

rowing /rəʊɪŋ/. UNCOUNT N **Rowing** is a sport in which people or teams race against each other in special rowing boats. ...*a rowing club.*

rowing boat /rəʊɪŋ bəʊt/, **rowing boats.** COUNT N A **rowing boat** is a small boat that you move through the water by using oars; a British use.

royal /rɔɪəl/. **1** ATTRIB ADJ **Royal** means related or belonging to a king, a queen, or a member of their family. ...*the royal family... ...the royal wedding.* **2** ATTRIB ADJ **Royal** is used in the names of organizations that are officially appointed or supported by a member of a royal family. ...*the Royal Navy.*

royal blue. ADJ Something that is **royal blue** is deep blue.

Royal Highness, Royal Highnesses. TITLE **Your Royal Highness, His** or **Her Royal Highness,** or **Their Royal Highnesses** are used to address or refer to members of royal families who are not kings or queens. ...*Her Royal Highness Princess Alexandra.*

royalist /rɔɪəlɪst/, **royalists.** COUNT N A **royalist** is someone who thinks it is right that their country should have a royal family.

royalty /rɔɪəlti^1/, **royalties. 1** UNCOUNT N The members of a royal family are sometimes referred to as **royalty.** ...*an official visit by royalty.* **2** COUNT N **Royalties** are payments made to authors and musicians which are linked to the sales of their books or records, or to performance of their works. ...*all the royalties from my next play.*

RSVP /ɑːr ɛs viː piː/. CONVENTION **RSVP** means 'please reply'. It is written at the end of invitations.

rub /rʌb/, **rubs, rubbing, rubbed. 1** VB WITH OBJ OR ADJUNCT If you **rub** something, you move your hand or a cloth backwards and forwards over it while pressing firmly. *He groaned and rubbed his eyes... He rubbed at his throat.* **2** VB WITH OBJ AND ADJUNCT If you **rub** a part of your body against a surface, you move it backwards and forwards while pressing it against the surface. *She rubbed her cheek against my temple.* **3** VB WITH OBJ AND ADJUNCT If you **rub** a substance onto a surface, you spread it over the surface using your hand. *The ointment he rubbed into the wound made it feel better.* **4** ERG VB If two things **rub** together or if you **rub** them together, they move backwards and forwards, pressing against each other. *He rubbed his hands and laughed.*

PHRASES ● If someone draws attention to something that involves you and that you find embarrassing or unpleasant, you can say that they **are rubbing it in;** an informal use. *'How old are you? Forty?'—'All right, no need to rub it in.'* ● **to rub salt into** someone's **wounds:** see **salt.** ● **to rub shoulders with** someone: see **shoulder.**

rub off on. PHR VB If someone's habits or characteristics **rub off on** you, you develop the same habits or characteristics after spending time with them; an informal use. *They hoped that some of his prowess might rub off on them.*

rub out. PHR VB If you **rub out** something written on paper or on a blackboard, you remove it by rubbing it with a rubber or a cloth.

rubber /rʌbə/, **rubbers. 1** UNCOUNT N **Rubber** is a strong, waterproof, elastic substance made from the sap of a tropical tree or produced chemically. ...*a rubber ball... ...rubber gloves.* **2** COUNT N A **rubber** is a small piece of rubber used for rubbing out writing.

rubber band, rubber bands. COUNT N A **rubber band** is a thin circle of rubber that you put around things to hold them together.

rubbery /rʌbə^{0}ri^1/. ADJ Something that is **rubbery** is soft or elastic like rubber. ...*a long, rubbery piece of seaweed.*

rubbish /rʌbɪʃ/. **1** UNCOUNT N **Rubbish** consists of unwanted things or waste material. *That old shed is full of rubbish... ...a rubbish dump.* **2** UNCOUNT N You can refer to something as **rubbish** when you think that it is of very poor quality. *There is so much rubbish on TV.* **3** UNCOUNT N OR CONVENTION You can describe an idea or a statement as **rubbish** if you think that it is foolish or wrong; an informal use. *Don't talk rubbish... 'I suppose he has a right to be angry.'—'Rubbish.'*

rubble /rʌbə^{0}l/. UNCOUNT N **Rubble** consists of the bricks or pieces of stone or concrete which result when a building is destroyed. *Every building was reduced to rubble.*

ruby /ruːbi^1/, **rubies.** COUNT N A **ruby** is a dark red jewel.

rucksack /rʌksæk/, **rucksacks.** COUNT N A **rucksack** is a bag, often on a frame, used for carrying things on your back, for example when you are climbing.

rudder /rʌdə/, **rudders.** COUNT N A **rudder** is a vertical piece of wood or metal at the back of a boat or plane which is moved to make the boat or plane turn.

ruddy /rʌdi^1/. ADJ Something that is **ruddy** is reddish; a literary use. ...*a square ruddy face.*

rude /ruːd/, **ruder, rudest. 1** ADJ If someone is **rude,** they behave in a way that is not polite. *I was rather rude to a young nurse... It's rude to stare... ...rude remarks.* ♦ **rudely** ADV *They commented rudely on my appearance.* ♦ **rudeness** UNCOUNT N *He seemed not to notice their rudeness.* **2** ADJ **Rude** words and behaviour are likely to embarrass or offend people, because they relate to sex or other bodily functions. ...*a rude gesture... ...a rude joke.* **3** ATTRIB ADJ **Rude** is also used to describe events that are unexpected and unpleasant. ...*a rude awakening to the realization that he had been robbed.* ♦ **rudely** ADV *My belief in the future was rudely shattered.*

rudimentary /ruːdɪmɛntə^{0}ri^1/. ADJ Something that is **rudimentary** is very basic and undeveloped or incomplete; a formal use. ...*rudimentary knowledge.*

rudiments /ruːdɪmə^{2}nts/. PLURAL N When you learn the **rudiments** of something, you learn only the simplest and most important things about it.

rue /ruː/, **rues, ruing, rued.** VB WITH OBJ If you **rue** something that you have done, you are sorry that you did it, because it has had unpleasant results; a literary use. *I had ample cause to rue that decision.*

rueful /ruːfʊl/. ADJ If someone is **rueful,** they feel or express regret or sorrow in a quiet and gentle way; a literary use. *She managed a rueful little smile.* ♦ **ruefully** ADV *She smiled ruefully.*

ruffian /rʌfɪən/, **ruffians.** COUNT N A **ruffian** is a man who behaves violently and is involved in crime; an old-fashioned use.

ruffle /rʌfə^{0}l/, **ruffles, ruffling, ruffled. 1** VB WITH OBJ If you **ruffle** someone's hair, you move your hand quickly and fairly roughly over their head as a way of showing affection. **2** COUNT N **Ruffles** are small, decorative folds of material.

ruffled /rʌfə^{0}ld/. **1** ADJ Something that is **ruffled** is no longer smooth or neat. ...*the ruffled bedclothes.* **2** ADJ **Ruffled** clothes are decorated with small folds of material. ...*a ruffled white blouse.* **3** ADJ If someone is **ruffled,** they are confused or annoyed. *'Why don't you come back later?' said Alex, mildly ruffled.*

rug /rʌg/, **rugs. 1** COUNT N A **rug** is a piece of thick or furry material that you put on the floor. **2** COUNT N A **rug** is also a small blanket which you use to cover your shoulders or your knees.

rugby /rʌgbi^1/. UNCOUNT N **Rugby** is a game played by two teams, who try to get an oval ball to their opponents' end of the pitch.

rugged /rʌgɪ^{2}d/; a literary word. **1** ADJ A **rugged** area of land is rocky and uneven. *The coastline is wild and rugged.* **2** ADJ A man who is **rugged** has strong, rough features. *He was rugged and handsome.*

rugger /rʌgə/. UNCOUNT N **Rugger** is the same as rugby; an informal use.

ruin /ruːɪn/, **ruins, ruining, ruined. 1** VB WITH OBJ To **ruin** something means to severely harm, damage, or spoil it. *You are ruining your health... India's textile industry was ruined.* **2** COUNT N A **ruin** is a building that has been partly destroyed. *It was splendid once, but it is a ruin now... ...the ruins of an old tower.* **3** COUNT N The **ruins** of something are the parts of it that remain after it has been severely damaged or weakened. *The Progressive Party was founded on the ruins of our Federal Party.* **4** PHRASE If something is **in ruins,** it has been completely or almost completely destroyed. *The castle, partly in ruins, stands on a crag... Their once robust economy lies in ruins.* **5** VB WITH OBJ To **ruin** someone means to cause them to no longer have any money. *The contract would certainly have ruined him.* **6** UNCOUNT N **Ruin** is the state of no longer having any money. *Crow was heading for ruin.*

ruined /ruːɪnd/. ATTRIB ADJ A **ruined** building has been badly damaged or has fallen apart from disuse.

ruinous /ruːɪnəs/. ADJ If something that you are paying for is **ruinous,** it costs far more money than you can afford. ...*the ruinous expense of a funeral.*

rule /ruːl/, **rules, ruling, ruled. 1** COUNT N **Rules** are instructions that tell you what you are allowed to do and what you are not allowed to do. ...*the rules of chess... It is against the rules to keep pets... If she breaks the rules, she will be punished.* **2** SING N If something is the **rule,** it is the normal state of affairs. *Short haircuts became the rule.* **3** VB WITH OBJ OR 'over' When someone **rules** a country, they control its affairs. ...*states ruled by kings... At this time Denmark ruled over Southern Sweden.* Also UNCOUNT N WITH SUPP ...*the days of British rule.* **4** VB WITH ADJUNCT OR REPORT VB When someone in authority **rules** on a particular matter, they give an official decision about it; a formal use. *I was asked to rule on the case of a British seaman... The Supreme Court ruled that there was no federal offence involved.* **5** See also **ruling, ground rules, work-to-rule.**

PHRASES ● If you say that a particular thing happens **as a rule,** you mean that it usually happens. *Doctors are not as a rule trained in child rearing.* ● If someone in authority **bends the rules,** they allow you to do something, even though it is against the rules.

rule out. PHR VB **1** If you **rule out** an idea or course of action, you reject it because it is impossible or unsuitable. **2** If one thing **rules out** another, it prevents it from happening or from being possible. *The radio was on, effectively ruling out conversation.*

ruler /ruːlə/, **rulers. 1** COUNT N A **ruler** is a person who rules a country. *Caesar was then ruler of Persia.* **2** COUNT N A **ruler** is also a long, flat object with straight edges marked in inches or centimetres, used for measuring things or drawing straight lines.

ruling /ruːlɪŋ/, **rulings. 1** ATTRIB ADJ The **ruling** group of people in an organization or country is the group that controls its affairs. ...*the Church's ruling body.* **2** COUNT N A **ruling** is an official decision made by a judge or court. *The judge gave his ruling.*

rum /rʌm/. UNCOUNT N **Rum** is an alcoholic drink made from sugar cane juice.

rumble /rʌmbə^{0}l/, **rumbles, rumbling, rumbled.** VB If something **rumbles,** it makes a low, continuous noise, often while moving slowly. ...*the rumbling noise of barrels being rolled down the ramp.* Also COUNT N ...*a menacing rumble of distant thunder.*

rumbling /rʌmblɪŋ/, **rumblings. 1** COUNT N A **rumbling** is a low, continuous noise. ...*the rumbling of thunder.* **2** COUNT N **Rumblings** are signs that a bad situation is developing. ...*rumblings of discontent.*

ruminate /ruːmɪneɪt/, **ruminates, ruminating, ruminated.** VB If you **ruminate** about something, you think about it very carefully; a formal use.

rummage /rʌmɪdʒ/, **rummages, rummaging, rummaged.** VB WITH ADJUNCT If you **rummage** somewhere, you search for something there by moving things in a careless way. *He rummaged around in his drawer.*

rumour /ruːmə/, **rumours, rumoured;** spelled **rumor** in American English. **1** COUNT N A **rumour** is a piece of information that may or may not be true, but that people are talking about. *There's a rumour that Mangel is coming here to speak... ...rumours of street fighting and violence.* **2** PASSIVE VB If something **is rumoured** to be true, people are suggesting that it is true, but they do not know for certain. *He was rumored to be living in Detroit... It was rumoured that the body had been removed.*

rump /rʌmp/, **rumps.** COUNT N An animal's **rump** is its rear end.

rumple /rʌmpə^{0}l/, **rumples, rumpling, rumpled.** VB WITH OBJ If you **rumple** something, you cause it to be untidy or creased. *He rumpled her hair.* ♦ **rumpled** ADJ ...*a rumpled grey suit.*

rumpus /rʌmpəs/. SING N A **rumpus** is a lot of noise or argument. *They caused a rumpus in the House of Commons.*

run /rʌn/, **runs, running, ran** /ræn/. **Run** is used in the present tense and is the past participle. **1** VB WITH OR WITHOUT OBJ When you **run,** you move quickly, leaving the ground during each stride. *I ran downstairs to open the door... He ran the mile in just over four minutes.* **2** COUNT N When you have a **run,** you run. *We had to go for a cross-country run every weekend... He found himself breaking into a run.* **3** VB WITH ADJUNCT You say that something long, such as a road, **runs** in a particular direction when you are describing its course or position. *The reef runs parallel to the coast.* **4** VB WITH OBJ AND ADJUNCT If you **run** an object or your hand over something, you move the object or your hand over it. *She ran her finger down a list of names.* **5** VB WITH ADJUNCT If someone **runs** in an election, they take part as a candidate; an American use. *He ran for Governor.* **6** VB WITH OBJ If you **run** an organization or an activity, you are in charge of it or you organize it. *She ran the office as a captain runs a ship... We run a course for local teachers.* **7** VB WITH OBJ If you **run** an experiment, computer program, or tape, you start it and let it continue. *Check everything and run the whole test again.* **8** VB WITH OBJ If you **run** a car or piece of equipment, you have it and use it. *A freezer doesn't cost much to run.* **9** VB When a machine **is running,** it is switched on and operating. *The engine was running.* **10** ERG VB WITH ADJUNCT If you **run** a machine on or off a particular source of energy, you use that source to make it work. *You can run the entire system off a mains plug... The heater ran on half-price electricity.* **11** VB If a train or bus **runs** somewhere, it travels on a regular route at set times. *No buses have been* *running in the town for the past week.* 12 VB WITH OBJ AND ADJUNCT If you **run** someone somewhere in a car, you drive them there. *Would you mind running me to the station?* 13 VB WITH ADJUNCT If a liquid **runs** in a particular direction, it flows in that direction. *Tears were running down his face... The river ran past our house.* 14 VB WITH OBJ If you **run** water or if you **run** a tap, you cause water to flow from the tap. *She was running hot water into the tub... Run my bath now!* 15 VB If the colour in a piece of clothing **runs,** it comes out when the clothing is washed. 16 VB WITH ADJUNCT If a play, event, or legal contract **runs** for a particular period of time, it lasts for that period of time. *'Chu-Chin-Chow' ran for years... The monsoons had six weeks more to run.* 17 COUNT N WITH SUPP In the theatre, a **run** is the period of time during which performances of a play are given. *The play ended its six-week run at the Regent.* 18 COUNT N WITH SUPP A **run** of success or failure is a series of successes or failures. *Leeds United had a run of wins in December.* 19 COUNT N In cricket or baseball, a **run** is a score of one, which is made by players running between marked places on the pitch after hitting the ball. *They had beaten England by seventeen runs.* 20 See also **running, trial run.**

PHRASES • If someone is **on the run,** they are trying to escape or hide from someone such as the police or an enemy. • If you **make a run for it** or if you **run for it,** you go somewhere quickly in order to escape from something. *It was still raining hard, but we made a run for it... We'll just have to run for it.* • If you talk about what will happen **in the long run,** you are saying what you think will happen over a long period of time in the future. If you talk about what will happen **in the short run,** you are saying what you think will happen in the near future. *Their policy would prove very costly in the long run.* • If someone or something **is running late,** they have taken more time than had been planned. • If a river or well **runs dry,** it ceases to have any water in it. • If people's feelings **are running high,** they are very angry, concerned, or excited. *Public indignation was running high.* • to **make your blood run cold:** see **blood.** • to **run its course:** see **course.** • to **run** someone or something **to ground:** see **ground.** • to **run the risk:** see **risk.** • to **run wild:** see **wild.**

run across. PHR VB If you **run across** someone, you meet them unexpectedly.

run away. PHR VB 1 If you **run away** from a place, you leave it because you are unhappy there. *He had run away from home at the age of thirteen.* 2 See also **runaway.**

run away with. PHR VB If you let your emotions **run away with** you, you fail to control them. *They did not allow their enthusiasm to run away with them.*

run down. PHR VB 1 If you **run down** people or things, you criticize them strongly. *She was not used to people running down their own families.* 2 See also **run-down.**

run into. PHR VB 1 If you **run into** problems or difficulties, you unexpectedly begin to experience them. *The firm ran into foreign exchange problems.* 2 If you **run into** someone, you meet them unexpectedly. 3 If a vehicle **runs into** something, it accidentally hits it. 4 You use **run into** to say that something costs a lot of money. *...exports running into billions of dollars.*

run off. PHR VB 1 If you **run off** with someone, you secretly go away with them in order to live with them or marry them. *His wife ran off with another man.* 2 If you **run off** copies of a piece of writing, you produce them using a machine.

run out. PHR VB 1 If you **run out** of something or if it **runs out,** you have no more of it left. *We were rapidly running out of money... Time is running out fast.* • to **run out of steam:** see **steam.** 2 When a legal document **runs out,** it stops being valid. *My passport's run out.*

run over. PHR VB If a vehicle **runs over** someone or something, it knocks them down. *Rosamund nearly got run over last night.*

run through. PHR VB 1 If you **run through** something, you rehearse it or practise it. *You could hear the performers running through the whole programme in the background.* 2 If you **run through** a list of items, you read or mention all the items quickly. 3 See also **run-through.**

run up. PHR VB 1 If someone **runs up** bills or debts, they acquire them by buying a lot of things or borrowing money. 2 See also **run-up.**

run up against. PHR VB If you **run up against** problems, you suddenly begin to experience them.

runaway /rʌnəweɪ/. 1 ATTRIB ADJ You use **runaway** to describe someone who has left their home secretly. *...a runaway slave.* 2 ATTRIB ADJ A **runaway** vehicle is moving and its driver has lost control of it. *...a runaway bulldozer.* 3 ATTRIB ADJ You also use **runaway** to describe situations which happen unexpectedly and cannot be controlled. *...the runaway success of 'Nicholas Nickleby'.*

run-down. 1 PRED ADJ If someone is **run-down,** they are tired or ill; an informal use. 2 ADJ A **run-down** building or organization is in very poor condition. *...two small rooms in a run-down building... ...run-down public services.* 3 SING N If you give someone the **run-down** on a situation or subject, you tell them the important facts about it; an informal use.

rung /rʌŋ/, **rungs.** 1 **Rung** is the past participle of some meanings of **ring.** 2 COUNT N The **rungs** of a ladder are the wooden or metal bars that form the steps. 3 COUNT N WITH SUPP If you reach a particular **rung** in an organization, you reach that level in it. *...the lower rungs of management.*

runner /rʌnə/, **runners.** 1 COUNT N A **runner** is a person who runs, especially for sport or pleasure. *...a long-distance runner... Not being a fast runner, I was glad I was close to the hall.* 2 COUNT N WITH SUPP A drugs **runner** or gun **runner** is someone who illegally takes drugs or guns into a country. 3 COUNT N **Runners** are thin strips of wood or metal underneath something which help it to move smoothly. *...sledge runners.*

runner bean, runner beans. COUNT N **Runner beans** are the long green pods of a climbing plant which are eaten as a vegetable.

runner-up, runners-up. COUNT N A **runner-up** is someone who finishes in second place in a race or competition. *He was runner-up in the Amateur Squash Championships in 1933.*

running /rʌnɪŋ/. 1 UNCOUNT N **Running** is the activity of running, especially as a sport. 2 UNCOUNT N WITH SUPP The **running** of something such as a business is the managing or organizing of it. *...the day-to-day running of the school.* 3 ATTRIB ADJ You use **running** to describe things that are continuous. *...a running commentary.* 4 ADJ AFTER N You also use **running** when saying that something has happened repeatedly. For example, if something has happened every day for three days, you can say that it has happened for three days **running** or that it has happened for the third day **running.** *For three days running he had left the sandwiches at home.* 5 ATTRIB ADJ **Running** water is flowing rather than standing still. *...the sound of running water.*

PHRASES • If someone **makes the running** in a situation, they are more active than the other people involved. *Women made all the running in demands for change.* • If someone is **in the running** for something, they have a good chance of winning or obtaining it. If they are **out of the running,** they have no chance of winning or obtaining it. *He's still in the running for the leadership of the Labour Party.*

runny /rʌni^{1}/. 1 ADJ Something that is **runny** is more liquid than usual or than was intended. *They had runny eggs for breakfast.* 2 ADJ If someone's nose or eyes are **runny,** liquid is flowing from them.

run-of-the-mill. ADJ A **run-of-the-mill** person or thing is very ordinary, with no special features.

run-through, run-throughs. COUNT N A **run-through** of a play or event is a rehearsal or practice for it.

run-up. SING N The **run-up** to an event is the period of time just before it. *...the run-up to the election.*

runway /rʌnweɪ/, **runways.** COUNT N A **runway** is a long strip of ground with a hard surface which is used by aeroplanes when they are taking off or landing.

rupture /rʌptʃə/, **ruptures, rupturing, ruptured.** 1 ERG VB OR REFL VB If you **rupture** a part of your body, it tears or bursts open. *An abscess had ruptured... ...the Mayor's ruptured appendix... He ruptured himself playing football.* 2 COUNT N A **rupture** is a severe injury in which a part of your body tears or bursts open. 3 COUNT N When there is a **rupture** between people, their relationship ends; a formal use.

rural /rʊərəl/. ATTRIB ADJ **Rural** means relating to country areas as opposed to large towns. *...small rural schools... ...rural poverty.*

ruse /ruːz/, **ruses.** COUNT N A **ruse** is an action which is intended to deceive someone; a formal use. *The offer was just a ruse to gain time.*

rush /rʌʃ/, **rushes, rushing, rushed.** 1 VB To **rush** somewhere means to go there quickly. *When they saw us, they rushed forward... Please don't rush off... The water rushed in over the top of his boots.* Also SING N *There was a little rush of air.* 2 VB WITH TO-INF OR PREP 'to' When people **rush** to do something, they do it without delay, because they are very eager to do it. *People were rushing to buy the newspaper... Her friends rushed to her aid.* 3 VB WITH OBJ If you **rush** something, you do it in a hurry. *I rushed my lunch.* ♦ **rushed** ATTRIB ADJ *It'll be a bit of a rushed job, I'm afraid.* 4 VB WITH OBJ AND ADJUNCT If you **rush** someone or something to a place, you take them there quickly. *Barnett was rushed to hospital with a broken back.* 5 VB WITH OBJ If you **rush** someone into doing something, you make them do it without allowing them enough time to think about it. *Do not be rushed into parting with goods before taking legal advice.* 6 PHRASE If there is **no rush** to do something, there is no need to do it quickly. *There is no rush to fill the vacancy... I'm not in any rush.* 7 SING N WITH SUPP If there is a **rush** for something or a **rush** to do something, there is a sudden increase in people's attempts to get it or do it. *There had been a rush for tickets... ...a rush to find the treasure.* 8 SING N If you experience a **rush** of a feeling, you suddenly experience it very strongly. *She felt a rush of pity for the boy.* 9 COUNT N **Rushes** are plants that grow near water and have long, thin stems.

rush into. PHR VB If you **rush into** a situation, you get involved in it without thinking about it carefully.

rush-hour. SING N The **rush-hour** is one of the periods of the day when most people are travelling to or from work. *I had to start in the morning rush-hour.*

Russian /rʌʃə^{0}n/, **Russians.** 1 ADJ **Russian** means belonging or relating to Russia. *...Russian dancers.* 2 COUNT N A **Russian** is a person who comes from Russia. 3 UNCOUNT N **Russian** is the official language of Russia.

rust /rʌst/, **rusts, rusting, rusted.** 1 UNCOUNT N **Rust** is a brown substance that forms on iron or steel when it comes into contact with water. 2 VB When a metal object **rusts,** it becomes covered in rust.

rustic /rʌstɪk/. ATTRIB ADJ **Rustic** things are simple, in a way that is typical of places far away from large cities; a formal use. *...rustic comfort and good food... ...rustic benches.*

rustle /rʌsə^{0}l/, **rustles, rustling, rustled.** 1 ERG VB When something **rustles** or when you **rustle** it, it makes soft sounds as it moves. *They could hear mice rustling about... He rustled his papers.* ♦ **rustling** COUNT N OR UNCOUNT N *Jim heard some furtive rustlings among the bushes.* 2 COUNT N OR UNCOUNT N A **rustle** is a soft sound made by something moving gently. *She heard a rustle behind her and turned... ...the rustle of chocolate wrappers.*

rusty /rʌsti^{1}/. 1 ADJ Something that is **rusty** is affected by rust. *...a heap of rusty tins.* 2 ADJ If someone's skill or knowledge is **rusty,** it is not as good as it was before, because they have not used it for a long time. *My German's pretty rusty.*

rut /rʌt/, **ruts.** 1 COUNT N A **rut** is a deep, narrow mark made in the ground by the wheels of vehicles. *We bumped over the ruts.* 2 COUNT N If someone is in a **rut,** they have become fixed in their way of thinking and doing things, and find it difficult to change.

ruthless /ruːθlɪ^{2}s/. ADJ Someone who is **ruthless** is very harsh or determined, and will do anything that is necessary to achieve their aim. *Political power was in the hands of a few ruthless men... ...a ruthless investigation.* ♦ **ruthlessly** ADV *Napoleon acted swiftly and ruthlessly.* ♦ **ruthlessness** UNCOUNT N *He often operated with extreme ruthlessness.*

rye /raɪ/. UNCOUNT N **Rye** is a type of grass that is grown in cold countries for animals to eat, and for making some types of bread and whisky.

Ss

S. S is a written abbreviation for 'south'.

-s; also spelled **-es.** 1 SUFFIX **-s** and **-es** are added to nouns to form plurals. *...dogs, cats, and rabbits... ...ancient palaces... ...profits and losses.* 2 SUFFIX **-s** and **-es** are added to verbs to form the third person singular of the present tense. *The lift stops at the fifth floor... He realizes what he has done... He pushes the button.*

-'s. 1 SUFFIX **-'s** is added to singular nouns or names, and plural nouns that do not end in 's', to form possessives. With a plural noun ending in 's', you form the possessive by just adding '. *...Ralph's voice... The girl's name was Pam... ...women's rights... ...students' interests.* 2 SUFFIX **-'s** is a short form of 'is' or 'has' used in spoken English and informal written English, especially when 'has' is an auxiliary verb. *It's fantastic... She's gone home.* 3 SUFFIX **-'s** is added to letters, numbers, and abbreviations to form plurals. *...a row of q's... ...the 1870's.*

Sabbath /sæbəθ/. PROPER N The **Sabbath** is the day of the week when members of some religious groups, especially Jews and Christians, do not work.

sabotage /sæbətɑːʒ/, **sabotages, sabotaging, sabotaged.** 1 VB WITH OBJ If something **is sabotaged,** it is deliberately damaged or destroyed. *The power station had been sabotaged by anti-government guerrillas.*

Also UNCOUNT N *...widespread sabotage and the disruption of rail communications.* 2 VB WITH OBJ If you **sabotage** a plan or activity, you deliberately prevent it from being successful. *I don't wish to be accused of sabotaging the President's programme.*

saccharine /sækəraɪn, -riːn/; also spelled **saccharin.** UNCOUNT N **Saccharine** is a sweet chemical substance, sometimes used instead of sugar.

sachet /sæʃeɪ/, **sachets.** COUNT N A **sachet** is a small closed plastic or paper packet, containing a small quantity of something.

sack /sæk/, **sacks, sacking, sacked.** 1 COUNT N A **sack** is a large bag made of rough material. Sacks are used to carry or store goods. *...sacks of flour.* 2 VB WITH OBJ If your employers **sack** you from your job, they get rid of you. *Three railwaymen were sacked because they would not join a union.* 3 PHRASE If you **get the sack** or **are given the sack,** your employer sacks you.

sacking /sækɪŋ/. UNCOUNT N **Sacking** is rough woven material that is used to make sacks.

sacrament /sækrəmə^{3}nt/, **sacraments.** COUNT N A **sacrament** is an important Christian religious ceremony such as communion, baptism, or marriage.

sacred /seɪkrɪ^{2}d/. 1 ADJ Something that is **sacred** is believed to be holy. *They entered the sacred mosque.* 2 ADJ **Sacred** also means connected with religion or used in religious ceremonies. *...sacred music.* 3 ADJ You can describe something as **sacred** when you regard it as too important to be changed or interfered with. *In their search for a good news story, nothing was sacred.*

sacrifice /sækrɪfaɪs/, **sacrifices, sacrificing, sacrificed.** 1 VB WITH OBJ To **sacrifice** an animal means to kill it as an offering to God or to a god. *White animals were sacrificed by white-robed priests.* Also COUNT N OR UNCOUNT N *...a ritual sacrifice... ...human sacrifice.* 2 VB WITH OBJ If you **sacrifice** something valuable or important, you give it up, often in order to do something for another person. *...women who have sacrificed career and marriage to care for elderly relatives.* Also COUNT N OR UNCOUNT N *...a mother's sacrifices for her children... ...a story of bravery and sacrifice.*

sacrificial /sækrɪfɪʃə^{0}l/. ATTRIB ADJ **Sacrificial** means connected with or used in a religious sacrifice. *...sacrificial victims.*

sacrilege /sækrɪlɪdʒ/. UNCOUNT N **Sacrilege** is disrespectful behaviour towards something holy or towards something that should be respected.

sacrilegious /sækrɪlɪdʒəs/. ADJ If your behaviour is **sacrilegious,** you show disrespect towards something holy or towards something that should be respected. *It would have been sacrilegious to speak.*

sacrosanct /sækrə^{6}sæŋkt/. ADJ Something that is **sacrosanct** is considered to be so important or special that it must not be criticized or changed. *He seems to think there's something sacrosanct about his annual fishing trip.*

sad /sæd/, **sadder, saddest.** 1 ADJ If you are **sad,** you are not happy, usually because something has happened that you do not like. *She looked sad... He was sad to see her go... ...a sad face.* ♦ **sadly** ADV *He shook his head sadly.* ♦ **sadness** UNCOUNT N *The news filled him with sadness.* 2 ADJ Something that is **sad** makes you feel sad. *She told Susan there was some sad news for her.* ♦ **sadness** UNCOUNT N *...the indescribable sadness of those final pages.* 3 ATTRIB ADJ You also use **sad** to describe an unfortunate situation. *The sad fact is that full employment may never be regained.* ♦ **sadly** ADV OR SENTENCE ADV *One aspect of education today has been sadly neglected... Sadly, we don't appear to have much chance of getting the contract.*

sadden /sædə^{0}n/, **saddens, saddening, saddened.** VB WITH OBJ If something **saddens** you, it makes you feel sad. *I'm saddened by the fact that so many people died for nothing.*

saddle /sædə^{0}l/, **saddles, saddling, saddled.** 1 COUNT N A **saddle** is a leather seat that you sit on when you ride a horse or other animal. *Jennifer swung herself into the saddle.* 2 COUNT N A **saddle** is also a seat on a bicycle or motorcycle. 3 VB WITH OBJ If you **saddle** a horse or pony, you put a saddle on it.

saddle up. PHR VB If you **saddle up,** you put a saddle on a horse or pony. *I saddled up and rode off... He went out to saddle up his horse.*

saddle with. PHR VB If you **saddle** someone **with** a problem or responsibility, you put them in a position where they have to deal with it. *The last thing I want is to saddle myself with a second mortgage.*

sadism /seɪdɪzə^{0}m, sæ-/. UNCOUNT N **Sadism** is behaviour in which a person gets pleasure from hurting other people and making them suffer. *He teased her with malicious sadism.* ♦ **sadist** /sədɪst/ COUNT N *...sadists and bullies.* ♦ **sadistic** /sədɪstɪk/ ADJ *...scenes of sadistic cruelty.*

s.a.e. /ɛs eɪ iː/, **s.a.e.s.** COUNT N An **s.a.e.** is an envelope on which you have stuck a stamp and written your own name and address. You send it to someone so that they can send you something back in it. **s.a.e.** is an abbreviation for 'stamped addressed envelope'.

safari /səfɑːri^1/, **safaris.** COUNT N A **safari** is an expedition for hunting or observing wild animals, especially in East Africa.

safe /seɪf/, **safer, safest; safes.** 1 ADJ Something that is **safe** does not cause harm or danger. *This powder is not safe for babies... It isn't safe to swim here... Keep your passport in a safe place.* ♦ **safely** ADV *Most food can safely be frozen for months.* 2 PRED ADJ If you are **safe,** you are not in any danger. *We're safe now. They've gone... They were safe from attack.* 3 ATTRIB ADJ A **safe** journey or arrival is one in which you arrive somewhere without being harmed. *...the safe delivery of essential equipment.* ♦ **safely** ADV *I sent a telegram to my mother saying I had arrived safely.* 4 ADJ If it is **safe** to say something, you can say it with little risk of being wrong. *These practices, it is safe to say, are no longer common.* ♦ **safely** ADV *These creatures, we can safely say, have been dead a long time.* 5 PRED ADJ If a secret is **safe** with you, you will not tell it to anyone. *They knew their secrets would be safe with him.* 6 COUNT N A **safe** is a strong metal cupboard with special locks, in which you keep money, jewellery, and other valuable things.

PHRASES ● You say that someone is **safe and sound** when they are unharmed after being in danger. *I'm glad to see you home safe and sound.* ● If you **play safe,** you do not take unnecessary risks. *Play safe and always wear goggles.* ● If someone or something is **in safe hands,** they are being looked after by a reliable person and will not be harmed. *Don't worry, she's in safe hands at the hospital.*

safeguard /seɪfgɑːd/, **safeguards, safeguarding, safeguarded.** 1 VB WITH OBJ To **safeguard** something means to prevent it from being harmed. *They have to fight to safeguard their future.* 2 COUNT N A **safeguard** is a law or rule that is intended to prevent something from happening. *This clause was inserted as a safeguard against possible exploitation.*

safety /seɪfti^1/. 1 UNCOUNT N **Safety** is the state of being safe from harm or danger. *He was assured of his daughter's safety... They swam to the safety of a small, rocky island.* 2 UNCOUNT N If you are concerned about the **safety** of something, you are concerned that it might be harmful or dangerous. *People worry about the safety of nuclear energy.* 3 MOD **Safety** features or measures are intended to make something less dangerous. *Every car will come with built-in safety features.*

safety belt, safety belts. COUNT N A **safety belt** is a strap that you fasten across your body for safety when travelling in a car or aeroplane.

safety catch, safety catches. COUNT N The **safety catch** on a gun is a device that stops you firing the gun accidentally.

safety net, safety nets. COUNT N In a circus, a **safety net** is a large net that is placed below performers on a high wire or trapeze in order to catch them and prevent them being injured if they fall off.

safety pin, safety pins. COUNT N A **safety pin** is a bent metal pin, used for fastening things together. The point of the pin has a cover.

safety-valve, safety-valves. 1 COUNT N A **safety-valve** is a piece of equipment in a machine that allows liquids or gases to escape when the pressure inside the machine becomes too great. 2 SING N You can use **safety-valve** to refer to something that allows you to express strong feelings without harming other people. *...a safety-valve for the harmless release of rebellious feelings.*

sag /sæg/, **sags, sagging, sagged.** VB When something **sags,** it hangs down loosely or sinks downwards in the middle. *The bed sagged in the middle.*

saga /sɑːgə/, **sagas.** COUNT N A **saga** is a long story, account, or sequence of events. *...a saga of my efforts to replace him.*

sage /seɪdʒ/, **sages;** a literary word. 1 COUNT N A **sage** is a person who is regarded as being wise. *...the great sages buried in the city.* 2 ADJ A **sage** person is wise and knowledgeable, usually because they are old and have had a lot of experience.

said /sɛd/. **Said** is the past tense and past participle of **say.**

sail /seɪl/, **sails, sailing, sailed.** 1 COUNT N A **sail** is a large piece of material attached to the mast of a boat. The wind blows against the sail and moves the boat along. *...the white sails of the yacht.* 2 VB WITH OR WITHOUT OBJ To **sail** a boat means to make it move across water using its sails. *I spent two weeks swimming and sailing in New Hampshire.* 3 VB When a ship **sails,** it moves over the sea. *The ship sailed down the east coast of South America.* 4 PHRASE When a ship **sets sail,** it leaves a port. 5 VB WITH ADJUNCT If someone or something **sails** somewhere, they move there steadily and fairly quickly. *I watched the ball as it went sailing over the bushes.*

sail through. PHR VB If you **sail through** a difficult situation or experience, you deal with it easily and successfully. *She was expecting to sail through her exams.*

sailing /seɪlɪŋ/, **sailings.** 1 COUNT N A **sailing** is a voyage made by a ship carrying passengers. *...regular sailings from Portsmouth.* 2 UNCOUNT N **Sailing** is the activity or sport of sailing boats. *...the traditional Royal sailing week in August.*

sailor /seɪlə/, **sailors.** COUNT N A **sailor** is a person who works on a ship as a member of its crew. *He had been a sailor in the Italian navy.*

saint /seɪnt/, **saints.** COUNT N OR TITLE A **saint** is a dead person who is officially recognized and honoured by the Christian church because his or her life was a perfect example of the way Christians should live. *...the church of Saint Francis.*

saintly /seɪntli^1/. ADJ A **saintly** person behaves in a very good or holy way.

sake /seɪk/, **sakes.**

PHRASES ● If you do something **for the sake of** a particular thing, you do it for that purpose or in order to achieve that result. *I usually check from time to time, just for safety's sake... Let us assume, for the sake of argument, that the level of unemployment does not fall.* ● If you do something **for its own sake,** you do it because you enjoy it, and not for any other reason. *I'm studying the subject for its own sake.* ● When you do something **for** someone's **sake,** you do it in order to help them. *We moved out to the country for the children's sake.* ● Some people say **for God's sake** or **for heaven's sake** in order to express annoyance or impatience, or to add force to a question or request.

salad /sæləd/, **salads.** MASS N A **salad** is a mixture of uncooked vegetables, eaten as part of a meal.

salami /səlɑːmi^1/. UNCOUNT N **Salami** is a type of sausage made from chopped meat and spices.

salaried /sælərɪd/. ADJ **Salaried** people receive a salary from their job.

salary /sæləri^1/, **salaries.** COUNT N OR UNCOUNT N A **salary** is the money that someone is paid for their job each month, especially when they have a professional job. *She earns a high salary as an accountant... ...the difference in salary between an instructor and a lecturer.*

sale /seɪl/, **sales.** 1 SING N The **sale** of goods is the selling of them for money. *...new laws to control the sale of guns.* 2 PLURAL N The **sales** of a product are the quantity that is sold. *Car sales are 5 per cent down... Sales of the magazine are declining.* 3 PLURAL N The part of a company that deals with **sales** deals with selling the company's products. *...a sales executive.* 4 COUNT N A **sale** is an occasion when a shop sells things at less than their normal price. *They're having a clearance sale.* 5 COUNT N A **sale** is also an event at which goods are sold to the person who offers the highest price. *...the quarterly cattle sale.*

PHRASES ● If something is **for sale** or **up for sale,** its owner is trying to sell it. *Their house is up for sale.* ● Products that are **on sale** can be bought in shops. *The only English newspaper on sale was the Morning Star.* ● See also **jumble sale.**

salesman /seɪlzmə^{3}n/, **salesmen.** COUNT N A **salesman** is a man whose job is selling things, especially directly to shops or other businesses.

salient /seɪlɪənt/. ADJ The **salient** points or facts of a situation are the most important and relevant ones; a formal use.

saline /seɪlaɪn/. ATTRIB ADJ A **saline** substance or liquid contains salt; a formal use.

saliva /səlaɪvə/. UNCOUNT N **Saliva** is the watery liquid that forms in your mouth.

sallow /sæləʊ/. ADJ If someone is **sallow,** their skin has a pale yellowish colour and looks unhealthy.

salmon /sæmən/. **Salmon** is the singular and plural. COUNT N OR UNCOUNT N A **salmon** is a large silver-coloured fish.

salmonella /sælmənɛlə/. UNCOUNT N **Salmonella** is a kind of bacteria which can cause severe food poisoning.

salon /sælɒn/, **salons.** 1 COUNT N A **salon** is a place where hairdressers work. *...a hairdressing salon.* 2 COUNT N A **salon** is also a shop where smart, expensive clothes are sold. *She is dressed by Dior, whose salon is located across the street.*

saloon /səluːn/, **saloons.** 1 COUNT N A **saloon** is a car with seats for four or more people, a fixed roof, and a boot that is separated from the rear seats. 2 COUNT N In the United States, a **saloon** is a place where alcoholic drinks are sold and drunk. 3 COUNT N In Britain, the **saloon** or **saloon bar** in a pub or hotel is a comfortable bar where the drinks are more expensive than in the other bars.

salt /sɒlt/, **salts, salting, salted.** 1 UNCOUNT N **Salt** is a substance in the form of white powder or crystals, used to improve the flavour of food or to preserve it. **Salt** occurs naturally in sea water. 2 VB WITH OBJ When you **salt** food, you add salt to it. *The potatoes should be lightly salted.*

PHRASES • If something **rubs salt into** your **wounds,** it makes the unpleasant situation that you are in even worse, often by reminding you of your failures or faults. • If you **take** something **with a pinch of salt,** you do not believe that it is completely accurate or true; an informal use.

salt cellar, salt cellars. COUNT N A **salt cellar** is a small container for salt, used at mealtimes.

salty /sɒlti^{1}/, **saltier, saltiest.** ADJ **Salty** things contain salt or taste of salt. *...salty water.*

salutary /sæljə^{4}tə^{0}ri^{1}/. ADJ A **salutary** experience is good for you, even though it may seem difficult or unpleasant; a formal use. *The defeat was a deserved punishment, but also a salutary shock.*

salute /səluːt/, **salutes, saluting, saluted.** 1 VB WITH OR WITHOUT OBJ If you **salute** someone, you greet them or show your respect with a formal sign. Soldiers salute officers by raising their right hand so that their fingers touch their forehead. *He stood as if he were saluting the flag.* Also COUNT N *He greeted King Edward VIII with the customary salute.* 2 VB WITH OBJ To **salute** a person or an achievement means to publicly show or state your admiration for them. *...festivals in Spain that salute the independence of the Spanish character.* Also COUNT N *...a salute to America.*

salvage /sælvɪdʒ/, **salvages, salvaging, salvaged.** 1 VB WITH OBJ When you **salvage** things, you manage to save them, for example from a ship that has sunk, or from a building that has been destroyed. *...a finely decorated window salvaged from an old chemist's shop.* 2 UNCOUNT N The **salvage** from wrecked ships or destroyed buildings consists of the things that are saved from them. *The insurers are entitled to take the wreck as salvage... ...a salvage operation.* 3 VB WITH OBJ If you **salvage** something from a difficult situation, you manage to get something useful from it so that it is not a complete failure. *They were salvaging what they could from the present unhappy state of affairs.*

salvation /sælveɪʃə^{0}n/. 1 UNCOUNT N In Christianity, the **salvation** of a person is the fact that Christ has saved them from evil. 2 UNCOUNT N The **salvation** of someone or something is the act of saving them from harm. *The country's salvation was of immense importance.* 3 SING N WITH POSS If someone or something is your **salvation,** they are responsible for saving you from harm or from an unpleasant situation. *Small industries will be the salvation of many areas now in decline... Their children were their only salvation.*

same /seɪm/. 1 ATTRIB ADJ OR PRON If two things are the **same** or if one thing is the **same** as another, the two are exactly like each other in some way. *They both wore the same overcoats... He did exactly the same as John did.* 2 ATTRIB ADJ If two things have the **same** quality, they both have that quality. *He and Tom were exactly the same age... It was the same colour as the wall.* 3 ATTRIB ADJ You use **same** to indicate that you are referring to only one thing, and not to different ones. *We come from the same place... It was possible to work while watching TV at the same time.* 4 PRON OR ATTRIB ADJ Something that is still the **same** has not changed in any way. *The village stayed the same... He will never be the same again... It wouldn't improve me, I'd be the same person I was before I saw it.* 5 ATTRIB ADJ OR PRON You also use **same** to refer to something that has already been mentioned. *For the same reason, the United States lodged a formal protest... It's the same with teenage fashions.*

PHRASES • You say **all the same** or **just the same** to indicate that a situation or your opinion has not changed, in spite of what has happened or been said. *She knew he wasn't listening, but she went on all the same... All the same, the courses are very popular.* • **thanks all the same:** see **thanks.**

sameness /seɪmnɪ^{2}s/. UNCOUNT N The **sameness** of something is its lack of variety. *I was struck by the sameness of clothing among the villagers.*

sample /sɑːmpə^{0}l/, **samples, sampling, sampled.** 1 COUNT N A **sample** of a substance or product is a small quantity of it that shows you what it is like. *...free samples of shampoo.* 2 COUNT N A **sample** of a substance is also a small amount of it that is examined and analysed scientifically. *I'll take water samples here and in East Hampton.* 3 COUNT N A **sample** of people or things is a number of them chosen out of a larger group and then used in tests or used to provide information about the whole group. *...a random sample of 10,000 adult civilians.* 4 VB WITH OBJ If you **sample** food or drink, you taste a small amount of it in order to find out if you like it. *Next he sampled the roast beef.* 5 VB WITH OBJ If you **sample** a place or situation, you experience it for a short time in order to find out about it. *They can learn the language and sample the British way of life.*

sanatorium /sænətɔːrɪəm/, **sanatoriums** or **sanatoria** /sænətɔːrɪə/; spelled **sanitarium** /sænɪtɛərɪəm/ in American English. COUNT N A **sanatorium** is an institution that provides medical treatment and rest for people who have been ill for a long time.

sanctify /sæŋktɪfaɪ/, **sanctifies, sanctifying, sanctified.** 1 VB WITH OBJ If the Church or a holy person **sanctifies** something, they officially bless it or approve of it. *St Francis wanted to sanctify poverty, not to abolish it.* 2 VB WITH OBJ If someone **sanctifies** an idea, practice, or situation, they approve of it, support it, and want it to stay the same. *...to protect and sanctify the power that was so ruthlessly being used.*

sanction /sæŋk^{0}ʃə^{0}n/, **sanctions, sanctioning, sanctioned.** 1 VB WITH OBJ If someone in authority **sanctions** an action or practice, they officially approve of it and allow it to be done. *...the law of 1856 which sanctioned the remarriage of widows.* Also UNCOUNT N WITH SUPP *Some months later our proposal was given official sanction.* 2 COUNT N A **sanction** is a severe course of action which is intended to make people obey the law. *The ultimate sanction of the government is the withdrawal of funds.* 3 PLURAL N **Sanctions** are measures taken by countries to restrict trade and official contact with a country that has broken international law. *The UN would impose economic sanctions against the offending nation.*

sanctity /sæŋk^{0}tɪ^{1}ti^{1}/. UNCOUNT N If you talk about the **sanctity** of something, you mean that it is important and should be respected. *...the sanctity of human life.*

sanctuary /sæŋk^{0}tj^{0}ʊəri^{1}/, **sanctuaries.** 1 COUNT N OR UNCOUNT N A **sanctuary** is a place of safety. *It was Clement's island and his sanctuary... This would give him sanctuary in the British Embassy.* 2 COUNT N A wildlife **sanctuary** is a place where birds or animals are protected and allowed to live freely.

sand /sænd/, **sands, sanding, sanded.** 1 UNCOUNT N **Sand** is a powder-like substance that consists of extremely small pieces of stone. Most deserts and beaches are made of sand. *The children played in the sand at the water's edge... ...grains of sand.* 2 PLURAL N **Sands** are a large area of sand, for example a beach or desert. *...miles of empty sands.* 3 VB WITH OBJ If you **sand** an object, you rub sandpaper over it in order to make it smooth or clean. *A scratched item of furniture can be professionally sanded.*

sandal /sændəl/, **sandals.** COUNT N **Sandals** are light shoes that have straps instead of a solid part over the top of your foot.

sandpaper /sændpeɪpə/. UNCOUNT N **Sandpaper** is strong paper that has a coating of sand on it. It is used for rubbing surfaces to make them smoother.

sandstone /sændstəun/. UNCOUNT N **Sandstone** is a type of rock. *...a long sandstone cliff.*

sandstorm /sændstɔːm/, **sandstorms.** COUNT N A **sandstorm** is a strong wind in a desert area, which creates large moving clouds of sand.

sandwich /sænwɪdʒ, -wɪtʃ/, **sandwiches, sandwiched.** 1 COUNT N A **sandwich** consists of two slices of bread with a layer of food such as cheese or meat between them. *...a bacon, lettuce, and tomato sandwich.* 2 PASSIVE VB WITH ADJUNCT When something **is sandwiched** between two other things, it is in a narrow space between them. *Wooden shacks are sandwiched between modern blocks of flats.*

sandwich course, sandwich courses. COUNT N A **sandwich course** is an educational course in which you have periods of study in between periods of work in industry or business; a British use.

sandy /sændi^{1}/. 1 ADJ A **sandy** area is covered with sand. *...the long sandy beach.* 2 ADJ **Sandy** hair is light orange-brown.

sane /seɪn/, **saner, sanest.** 1 ADJ Someone who is **sane** is able to think and behave normally and reasonably, and is not mentally ill. *She appeared to be completely sane.* 2 ADJ If you describe an action or idea as **sane,** you mean that it is reasonable and sensible. *It is the only sane thing to do.*

sang /sæŋ/. **Sang** is the past tense of **sing.**

sanitarium /sænɪtɛərɪəm/. See **sanatorium.**

sanitary /sænɪtə^{0}ri^{1}/. 1 ADJ If you say that a place is not **sanitary,** you mean that it is not very clean. *...a small and not very sanitary café in Soho.* 2 ATTRIB ADJ **Sanitary** also means concerned with keeping things clean and hygienic. *Sanitary conditions in the hospitals had deteriorated rapidly... ...a sanitary inspector.*

sanitary napkin, sanitary napkins. COUNT N A **sanitary napkin** is the same as a sanitary towel; an American use.

sanitary towel, sanitary towels. COUNT N A **sanitary towel** is a pad of thick soft material which women wear when they have periods.

sanitation /sænɪteɪʃə^{0}n/. UNCOUNT N **Sanitation** is the process of keeping places clean and hygienic, especially by providing a sewage system and a clean water supply. *...the lack of sanitation and adequate health care.*

sanity /sænɪ'ti^{1}/. 1 UNCOUNT N A person's **sanity** is their ability to think and behave normally and reasonably. *...doubts about Wilt's sanity.* 2 UNCOUNT N **Sanity** is also the quality of having a purpose and a regular pattern, rather than being confusing and worrying. *They give some point and sanity to daily life.*

sank /sæŋk/. **Sank** is the past tense of **sink.**

Santa Claus /sæntə klɔːz/. PROPER N **Santa Claus** is another name for Father Christmas.

sap /sæp/, **saps, sapping, sapped.** 1 VB WITH OBJ If something **saps** your strength or confidence, it gradually weakens or destroys it over a period of time. *The constant tension at work was sapping my energy.* 2 UNCOUNT N **Sap** is the watery liquid in plants and trees. *The sap was rising in the maples.*

sapling /sæplɪŋ/, **saplings.** COUNT N A **sapling** is a young tree.

sapphire /sæfaɪə/, **sapphires.** COUNT N A **sapphire** is a blue precious stone.

sarcasm /sɑːkæzə^{0}m/. UNCOUNT N **Sarcasm** is speech or writing which is intended to mock or insult someone in an unpleasant way and which often involves irony. *'Oh yeah,' said Jenny with broad sarcasm, 'I notice how you hate getting paid.'*

sarcastic /sɑːkæstɪk/. ADJ If you are **sarcastic,** you mock or insult someone in an unpleasant way, often using irony. *She seemed her usual sarcastic self at dinner... ...a sarcastic smile.* ♦ **sarcastically** ADV *Brady became the seventh player to be cautioned for sarcastically applauding the referee.*

sardine /sɑːdiːn/, **sardines.** COUNT N A **sardine** is a small sea fish. *...tins of sardines.*

sardonic /sɑːdɒnɪk/. ADJ A **sardonic** person is mocking or scornful in their behaviour. *...a sardonic young man who never joined in the fun... ...a sardonic chuckle.* ♦ **sardonically** ADV *She smiled sardonically.*

sari /sɑːri^{1}/, **saris.** COUNT N A **sari** is a piece of clothing worn especially by Indian women. It consists of a long piece of thin material that is wrapped around the body.

sartorial /sɑːtɔːrɪəl/. ATTRIB ADJ **Sartorial** means relating to clothes and to the way they are made or worn; a formal use. *People's sartorial habits have changed.*

sash /sæʃ/, **sashes.** COUNT N A **sash** is a long piece of cloth which people wear round their waist or over one shoulder, especially with formal or official clothes.

sash window, sash windows. COUNT N A **sash window** is a window which consists of two frames placed one above the other. The window can be opened by sliding one frame over the other.

sat /sæt/. **Sat** is the past tense and past participle of **sit.**

Satan /seɪtə^{0}n/. PROPER N **Satan** is the Devil, considered to be the chief opponent of God.

satanic /sətænɪk/. ADJ Something that is **satanic** is considered to be caused by or influenced by Satan.

satchel /sætʃə^{0}l/, **satchels.** COUNT N A **satchel** is a bag with a long strap that schoolchildren use for carrying books.

sated /seɪtɪ^{2}d/. ADJ If you are **sated** with something, you have had more of it than you can enjoy; a formal use. *They were sated with fresh air and hard exercise.*

satellite /sætəlaɪt/, **satellites.** 1 COUNT N A **satellite** is an object which has been sent into space in order to collect information or to be part of a communications system. *...communications satellites... The pictures were transmitted by satellite.* 2 COUNT N A **satellite** is also a natural object in space that moves round a planet or star. 3 MOD **Satellite** countries and organizations have no real power of their own, but are dependent on a larger and more powerful country or organization.

satin /sætɪn/. UNCOUNT N **Satin** is a smooth and shiny type of cloth. *The bride was dressed in white satin.*

satire /sætaɪə/, **satires.** 1 UNCOUNT N **Satire** is humour and exaggeration that is used to show how foolish or wrong something is. *...exquisite touches of irony and satire.* 2 COUNT N A **satire** is a play or piece of writing that uses satire to criticize something. *...a brilliant political satire... ...a satire on existing society.*

satirical /sətɪrɪkə^{0}l/. ADJ **Satirical** drawings or writings use satire to criticize something. *...satirical cartoons... ...a satirical fortnightly magazine.*

satisfaction /sætɪsfækʃə^{0}n/. 1 UNCOUNT N **Satisfaction** is the pleasure you feel when you do something that you wanted or needed to do. *She read what she had written with satisfaction... ...a sigh which ex-*

pressed her satisfaction at being there... ...a sense of satisfaction. 2 UNCOUNT N If you get **satisfaction** from someone, you get money or an apology from them because of some harm or injustice which has been done to you. *Consumers who have been unable to get satisfaction from their local branch should write direct to the Chairman.* 3 PHRASE If something is done **to** your **satisfaction,** you are happy with the way it has been done. *Every detail was worked out to everyone's satisfaction.*

satisfactory /sætɪsfæktə^{0}ri^{1}/. ADJ If something is **satisfactory,** it is acceptable to you or fulfils a particular need or purpose. *His doctor described his general state of health as fairly satisfactory... The arrangement sounded satisfactory.* ♦ **satisfactorily** ADV *She was not recovering satisfactorily.*

satisfied /sætɪsfaɪd/. 1 ADJ If you are **satisfied** with something, you are pleased because you have got what you wanted. *He was well satisfied with the success of the aircraft... ...satisfied customers who had bought the car.* 2 PRED ADJ If you are **satisfied** that something is true or has been done properly, you are convinced about this after checking it. *We can be satisfied that we've missed nothing important.*

satisfy /sætɪsfaɪ/, **satisfies, satisfying, satisfied.** 1 VB WITH OBJ If someone or something **satisfies** you, they give you enough of what you want to make you pleased or contented. *More frequent feeding will usually help to satisfy a baby... He had not even been able to satisfy her simple needs.* 2 VB WITH OBJ OR REFL VB If someone **satisfies** you that something is true or has been done properly, they convince you by giving you more information or by showing you what has been done. *He would need to satisfy the authorities that he had paid tax for the previous three years... I glanced around, satisfied myself that the last diner had left, and turned off the lights.* 3 VB WITH OBJ If you **satisfy** the requirements for something, you are good enough or suitable to fulfil these requirements. *There is some doubt whether they can satisfy our entrance requirements.*

satisfying /sætɪsfaɪɪŋ/. ADJ Something that is **satisfying** gives you a feeling of pleasure and fulfilment. *There's nothing more satisfying than doing the work you love.*

saturate /sætʃəreɪt/, **saturates, saturating, saturated.** 1 VB WITH OBJ If a place **is saturated** with things, it is so full of those things that no more can be added. *The next morning, teams saturated the community with literature about the attack.* ♦ **saturation** /sætʃəreɪʃə^{0}n/ UNCOUNT N *Even when the market reaches saturation, the process doesn't stop.* 2 VB WITH OBJ If someone or something **is saturated,** they become extremely wet. *Philip was totally saturated.*

Saturday /sætədi^{1}/, **Saturdays.** UNCOUNT N OR COUNT N **Saturday** is the day after Friday and before Sunday.

sauce /sɔːs/, **sauces.** MASS N A **sauce** is a thick liquid which is served with other food. *...tomato sauce... Make a sauce to go with the fish.*

saucepan /sɔːspən/, **saucepans.** COUNT N A **saucepan** is a deep metal cooking pot, usually with a long handle and a lid.

saucer /sɔːsə/, **saucers.** COUNT N A **saucer** is a small curved plate on which you stand a cup. *...her best cup and saucer.* ● See also **flying saucer.**

saucy /sɔːsi^{1}/. ADJ Someone who is **saucy** is rather cheeky in a light-hearted, amusing way; an informal use. *Don't be saucy with me.*

sauna /sɔːnə/, **saunas.** 1 COUNT N A **sauna** is a hot steam bath. 2 COUNT N A **sauna** is also the room or building where you have a sauna.

saunter /sɔːntə/, **saunters, sauntering, sauntered.** VB WITH ADJUNCT If you **saunter** somewhere, you walk there in a slow, casual way. *He sauntered up and down, looking at the shops and the people.*

sausage /sɒsɪdʒ/, **sausages.** 1 UNCOUNT N **Sausage** is finely minced meat which is mixed with other ingredients and put into a thin casing like a tube. *We lunched on garlic sausage and bread.* 2 COUNT N A **sausage** is a tube-shaped piece of minced meat. *...bacon, eggs, and sausages for breakfast.*

sausage roll, sausage rolls. COUNT N A **sausage roll** is a small amount of sausage or minced meat which is covered with pastry and cooked.

savage /sævɪdʒ/, **savages, savaging, savaged.** 1 ADJ Something that is **savage** is extremely fierce or violent. *...two weeks of savage rioting.* ♦ **savagely** ADV *The dog began to bark savagely.* 2 ADJ **Savage** remarks and actions are cruel and nasty. *...savage remarks about the futility of life.* ♦ **savagely** ADV *...the report he has so savagely denounced.* 3 COUNT N If you call someone a **savage,** you mean that they are cruel, violent, or uncivilized. 4 VB WITH OBJ If a dog **savages** you, it attacks you violently. 5 VB WITH OBJ If you **savage** someone or **savage** something they have done, you criticize them severely. *An opposition spokesman savaged the Government's housing programme.*

savagery /sævɪdʒri^{1}/. UNCOUNT N **Savagery** is cruel and violent behaviour. *...the savagery of the attack.*

save /seɪv/, **saves, saving, saved.** 1 VB WITH OBJ If you **save** someone or something, you help them to avoid harm or to escape from a dangerous or unpleasant situation. *An artificial heart could save his life... She saved him from drowning.* 2 VB WITH OR WITHOUT OBJ If you **save** money or if you **save** it up, you gradually collect it by spending less than you get, often in order to buy something you want. *They had managed to save enough to buy a house... She told him that she was saving with a building society... It took me a year to save up for a new coat.* 3 VB WITH OR WITHOUT OBJ If you **save** time or money, you prevent the loss or waste of it. *The manufacturers save money on promotion... This measure would save the government £185 million... It's an attempt to save on labour costs.* 4 VB WITH OBJ If you **save** something, you keep it because it will be needed later. *Always save business letters, bills, and receipts... Will you save him a place at your table?* 5 VB WITH OBJ OR -ING If someone or something **saves** you from doing something, they do it for you or change the situation so that you do not have to do it. *Well, that saves me from denying it... You could save yourself a lot of work if you used a computer... Using electronic circuit boards saves wiring up thousands of individual transistors.* 6 VB WITH OBJ If a goalkeeper **saves** a shot, they prevent the ball from going into the goal. *The shot was saved by Buller, who returned to Liverpool last week after three seasons with Barcelona.* Also COUNT N *He made a brilliant save.* 7 PREP You can use **save** or **save for** to introduce an exception to your main statement; a formal use. *No visitors are allowed save in the most exceptional cases... The stage was empty save for a few pieces of furniture.*

saving /seɪvɪŋ/, **savings.** 1 COUNT N A **saving** is a reduction in the amount of time or money that is used or needed. *...a very great saving in cost... The new management had achieved even bigger savings.* 2 PLURAL N Your **savings** are the money that you have saved, especially in a bank or a building society. *She drew out all her savings... ...a savings account.*

saviour /seɪvjə/, **saviours.** 1 COUNT N A **saviour** is a person who saves people from danger. *Many people regarded Churchill as the saviour of the country.* 2 PROPER N In Christianity, the **Saviour** is Jesus Christ.

savour /seɪvə/, **savours, savouring, savoured;** spelled **savor** in American English. 1 VB WITH OBJ If you **savour** food or drink, you eat or drink it slowly in order to taste its full flavour and to enjoy it properly. *Meadows took a bite of meat, savoured it, and said, 'Fantastic.'* 2 VB WITH OBJ If you **savour** an experience, you take great pleasure and delight in it, enjoying it as much as you can. *He leaned back into his seat, savouring the comfort.*

savoury /seɪvə^{0}ri^{1}/; spelled **savory** in American English. 1 ADJ **Savoury** food has a salty or spicy flavour rather than a sweet one. 2 ADJ Something that is not very **savoury** is not very pleasant or morally acceptable. *...the less savoury episodes in her past.*

saw /sɔː/, **saws, sawing, sawed, sawn** /sɔːn/. 1 **Saw** is the past tense of **see.** 2 COUNT N A **saw** is a tool for cutting wood, which has a blade with sharp teeth along one edge. 3 VB WITH OBJ If you **saw** something, you cut it with a saw. *I started sawing the branches off the main trunk.*

sawdust /sɔːdʌst/. UNCOUNT N **Sawdust** is the very fine fragments of wood which are produced when you saw wood.

saxophone /sæksəfəʊn/, **saxophones.** COUNT N A **saxophone** is a musical wind instrument. It is made of metal in a curved shape, and is often played in jazz bands.

say /seɪ/, **says** /sez/, **saying** /seɪɪŋ/, **said** /sed/. 1 REPORT VB When you **say** something, you speak words. *'Please come in,' she said... He said it was an accident... He had said nothing to me about his meeting.* 2 REPORT VB You use **say** to introduce an opinion or comment. *I just want to say how pleased I am to be here... One thing you have to say about Americans: they love drama.* 3 REPORT VB If you **say** something in a letter or a book, for example, you express it in writing. *She wrote to say she wanted to meet me in London... There were stickers all over the crate saying: 'Glass—Handle with Care'.* 4 REPORT VB If something such as a clock or map **says** a particular thing, it gives you information when you look at it. *The clock says that it is six o'clock... The road was not where the map said it should be.* 5 REPORT VB To **say** something about a person, situation, or thing means to reveal something about them. *The title says it all... Their glances seemed to be saying something about their relationship.* 6 You can use **say** when you mention something as an example or when you mention an approximate amount or time. *Compare, say, a Michelangelo painting with a Van Gogh... ...in the next, say, ten years.* 7 SING N If you have a **say** in something, you have the right to give your opinion and influence decisions. *People want a much greater say in how the country should be governed.*

PHRASES ● If you **say** something **to** yourself, you think it without speaking it aloud. *I began to say to myself, 'What about becoming an actor?'* ● You use expressions such as **just say** and **let's say** when you want to discuss something that might possibly happen or be true. *Just say you found treasure in your garden. Would you sell it?* ● You use **to say the least** to suggest that a situation is actually much more serious, shocking, or extreme than you say it is. *She lacked tact (to say the least) in expressing her views.* ● You use **that is to say** to indicate that you are about to express the same idea more clearly; a formal use. *The Romans left Britain in 410 AD—that is to say, England was under Roman rule for nearly 500 years.* ● You use **to say nothing of** when you add something which gives even more strength to the point you are making. *The effort required is immense, to say nothing of the cost.* ● If something **goes without saying,** it is obvious or is bound to be true. *It goes without saying that I am grateful for all your help.* ● If something **has a lot to be said for it,** it has a lot of good qualities. ● If you **have** your **say,** you give your opinion.

saying /seɪɪŋ/, **sayings.** COUNT N A **saying** is a traditional sentence that people often say and that gives advice or information about life. *There is a saying that 'man shall not live by bread alone'.*

scab /skæb/, **scabs.** COUNT N A **scab** is a hard, dry covering that forms over the surface of a wound. *A great scab had formed on his right knee.*

scaffold /skæfə^{6}ld/, **scaffolds.** COUNT N A **scaffold** is a platform on which criminals used to be executed. *Guy Fawkes died on the scaffold.*

scaffolding /skæfə^{6}ldɪŋ/. UNCOUNT N **Scaffolding** is a temporary framework of poles and boards, used by workmen while they are constructing, repairing, or painting the outside walls of a tall building.

scald /skɔːld/, **scalds, scalding, scalded.** 1 REFL VB OR VB WITH OBJ If you **scald** yourself, you burn yourself with very hot liquid or steam. *When it was cool enough not to scald my lips, I swallowed the coffee and asked for more.* 2 COUNT N A **scald** is a burn caused by very hot liquid or steam.

scalding /skɔːldɪŋ/. ADJ Something that is **scalding** is very hot. *...scalding coffee.*

scale /skeɪl/, **scales, scaling, scaled.** 1 SING N WITH SUPP If you refer to the **scale** of something, you are referring to its size, especially when it is big. *The scale of change is so enormous... ...the sheer scale of the United States.* 2 UNCOUNT N You use **scale** in expressions such as 'large scale' and 'on a small scale' when you are indicating the size, extent, or degree of one thing as compared to other similar things. *The district grew peas on a large scale... The plan was never very grand in scale... ...small scale methods of getting energy.* 3 COUNT N A **scale** is a set of levels or numbers which are used in a particular system of measuring things or comparing things. *...the scale by which we measure the severity of earthquakes... ...a temperature scale... ...the pay scale.* 4 COUNT N OR UNCOUNT N The **scale** of a map, plan, or model is the relationship between its measurements and those of the thing in the real world that it represents. *...a map with a scale of 1:50,000.* ● If a map, plan, or model is **to scale,** it is accurately drawn or made according to the scale being used. 5 COUNT N A **scale** is also a sequence of musical notes that are played or sung in an upward or downward order. *...the scale of C.* 6 COUNT N The **scales** of fish or reptiles are the small, flat pieces of hard skin that cover their bodies. 7 PLURAL N **Scales** are a piece of equipment for weighing things. *...a pair of scales.* 8 VB WITH OBJ If you **scale** something high or steep, you climb up or over it. *She scaled the barrier like a Commando.*

scale down. PHR VB If something **is scaled down,** it has been made smaller in size or amount than it used to be. *The operations were scaled down.*

scalloped /skɒləpt, skæl-/. ATTRIB ADJ **Scalloped** objects are decorated with a series of small curves along the edges. *...a blue and green scalloped design.*

scalp /skælp/, **scalps.** COUNT N Your **scalp** is the skin under the hair on your head. *...rubbing his sore scalp.*

scalpel /skælpə^{0}l/, **scalpels.** COUNT N A **scalpel** is a knife with a short, thin, sharp blade. Scalpels are used by surgeons during operations.

scaly /skeɪli^{1}/. ADJ Something that is **scaly** is covered in small, stiff patches of hard skin.

scamper /skæmpə/, **scampers, scampering, scampered.** VB WITH ADJUNCT When children or small animals **scamper** somewhere, they move with small, quick, bouncing steps. *The squirrels scamper along the twigs.*

scan /skæn/, **scans, scanning, scanned.** 1 VB WITH OBJ When you **scan** an area, group of things, or piece of writing, you look at it carefully, usually because you are looking for something in particular. *Anxiously Carol scanned their faces to see who she might know... ...lifeguards scanning the sea for shark fins.* 2 VB WITH OBJ If a machine **scans** something, it examines it quickly, for example by moving a beam of light or X-rays over it. *The reconnaissance plane's job was to scan the oceans with its radar.* Also COUNT N *A liver scan was performed.*

scandal /skændə^{0}l/, **scandals.** 1 COUNT N A **scandal** is a situation or event that a lot of people think is shocking and immoral. *We can't afford another scandal in the firm.* 2 UNCOUNT N **Scandal** is talk about people's shocking and immoral behaviour. *Someone must have been spreading scandal.* 3 SING N You can refer to something as a **scandal** when you are angry about it. *The defences were a scandal.*

scandalize /skændə^{0}laɪz/, **scandalizes, scandalizing, scandalized;** also spelled **scandalise.** VB WITH OBJ If you **are scandalized,** you are shocked and offended. *He was uncertain whether to laugh or be scandalized.*

scandalous /skændə^{0}ləs/. 1 ADJ Something that is **scandalous** is considered immoral and shocking. *There were some scandalous stories about her.* 2 ADJ You can describe something as **scandalous** when it makes you very angry. *It is scandalous that the public should be treated in this way.* ♦ **scandalously** SUBMOD *...schemes offering scandalously large tax advantages.*

scanner /skænə/, **scanners.** COUNT N A **scanner** is a machine which is used to examine things, for example by moving a beam of light or X-rays over them. Scanners are used in places such as hospitals, airports, and research laboratories.

scant /skænt/. ATTRIB ADJ If something receives **scant** attention, it receives less attention than you think it should do. *The campaign was conducted with scant regard for truth.*

scanty /skænti^1/, **scantier, scantiest.** ADJ You describe something as **scanty** when it is smaller in quantity or size than you think it should be. *...a rather scanty but enthusiastic audience.*

scapegoat /skeɪpgəʊt/, **scapegoats.** COUNT N If someone is made a **scapegoat,** they are blamed for something, although it may not be their fault, because other people are very angry about it.

scar /skɑː/, **scars, scarring, scarred.** 1 COUNT N A **scar** is a mark on the skin which is left after a wound has healed. *There was a scar on her arm.* 2 VB WITH OBJ If your skin **is scarred,** it is badly marked as a result of a wound. *They will be scarred for life.* 3 VB WITH OBJ If an object **is scarred,** it is damaged and there are ugly marks on it. *...the scarred tree trunk.* 4 COUNT N A **scar** is also a permanent effect on someone's mind that results from an unpleasant experience. *...the scars of poverty.* 5 VB WITH OBJ If an unpleasant experience **scars** you, it has a permanent effect on you, and influences the way you think and behave. *...the violence of the attack that scarred my mind.*

scarce /skɛəs/, **scarcer, scarcest.** ADJ If something is **scarce,** there is not much of it. *...an environment where water is scarce.*

scarcely /skɛəsli^1/. 1 ADV You use **scarcely** to say that something is only just true. *I can scarcely remember what we ate... They were scarcely ever apart... ...a very young man, scarcely more than a boy.* 2 ADV You can use **scarcely** in an ironic way to emphasize that something is certainly not true. *There could scarcely be a less promising environment for children.* 3 ADV If you say **scarcely** had one thing happened when something else happened, you mean that the first event was followed immediately by the second. *Scarcely had the car drawn to a halt when armed police surrounded it.*

scarcity /skɛəsɪ^{1}ti^1/. UNCOUNT N If there is a **scarcity** of something, there is not enough of it; a formal use. *...the scarcity of food.*

scare /skɛə/, **scares, scaring, scared.** 1 VB WITH OBJ When people or things **scare** you, they frighten you. *I didn't mean to scare you.* 2 COUNT N If something gives you a **scare,** it frightens you. *That night I had an even worse scare.* 3 COUNT N If there is a **scare** about something, a lot of people are worried or frightened by it. *Since none of the fragments picked up was radioactive the scare died down... ...a rabies scare.*

scare away or **scare off.** PHR VB If you **scare** animals or people **away** or **scare** them **off,** you frighten them so that they go away. *The least shadow or movement would scare the fish away.*

scarecrow /skɛəkrəʊ/, **scarecrows.** COUNT N A **scarecrow** is an object in the shape of a person. It is put in a field to frighten birds away from crops.

scared /skɛəd/. 1 PRED ADJ If you are **scared** of someone or something, you are frightened of them. *Everybody's scared of him... He was terribly scared... She was too shocked and scared to move.* 2 PRED ADJ If you are **scared** that something unpleasant might happen, you are nervous and worried because you think that it might happen. *I'm scared that these will turn out to be the wrong ones... They're scared of making a fool of themselves.*

scarf /skɑːf/, **scarfs** or **scarves** /skɑːvz/. COUNT N A **scarf** is a piece of cloth that you wear round your neck or head, usually to keep yourself warm.

scarlet /skɑːlə^{1}t/. ADJ Something that is **scarlet** is bright red. *...a scarlet handkerchief.*

scarlet fever. UNCOUNT N **Scarlet fever** is an infectious disease that gives you a sore throat, high temperature, and red rash.

scarves /skɑːvz/. **Scarves** is a plural of **scarf.**

scary /skɛəri^1/. ADJ **Scary** things are rather frightening; an informal use. *It was a scary moment.*

scathing /skeɪðɪŋ/. ADJ If you are **scathing** about something, you criticize it harshly and scornfully. *Miss Jackson was scathing about our efforts... ...a rather scathing article about lady novelists.*

scatter /skætə/, **scatters, scattering, scattered.** 1 VB WITH OBJ If you **scatter** things over an area, you throw or drop them so that they spread all over the area. *Parrots scatter their food about and make a mess... The papers had been scattered all over the floor.* 2 VB If a group of people **scatter,** they suddenly separate and move in different directions. *The boys scattered, squealing in horror.*

scattered /skætəd/. 1 ADJ Things that are **scattered** are spread over an area and are a long way from each other. *We drove over the debris scattered across the streets... The old people could not visit their scattered families.* 2 PRED ADJ WITH 'with' If something is **scattered** with a lot of small things, they are spread all over it. *Her hair was scattered with pollen.*

scattering /skætə^{0}rɪŋ/. SING N A **scattering** of things is a small number of them spread over a large area; a literary use. *...the blue night sky with its scattering of stars.*

scavenge /skævɪndʒ/, **scavenges, scavenging, scavenged.** VB WITH OR WITHOUT OBJ If someone **scavenges** for food or other things or **scavenges** things, they collect them by searching among waste and unwanted objects. *I had no resources at all, except what I could scavenge or beg.* ♦ **scavenger** COUNT N *...a scavenger living from the dustbins.*

scenario /sɪnɑːrɪəʊ/, **scenarios.** 1 COUNT N If you talk about a likely or possible **scenario,** you are talking about the way in which a situation may develop. *The death of democracy becomes quite a likely scenario.* 2 COUNT N The **scenario** of a film is a piece of writing that gives an outline of the story; a technical use.

scene /siːn/, **scenes.** 1 COUNT N A **scene** is one of the parts of a play, film, or book in which a series of events happen in the same place. *...the balcony scene from 'Romeo and Juliet'... It was like some scene from a Victorian novel.* 2 COUNT N WITH SUPP Paintings and drawings of places are sometimes called **scenes.** *...the harbour scenes that he drew as a teenager.* 3 COUNT N WITH SUPP You can describe something that you see as a **scene** of a particular kind. *The moon rose over a scene of extraordinary destruction... ...a scene of domestic tranquillity.* 4 COUNT N The **scene** of an accident or crime is the place where it happened. 5 SING N WITH SUPP You can refer to an area of activity as a particular **scene.** *...the business scene... ...the German political scene.* 6 COUNT N If you make a **scene,** you embarrass people by publicly showing your anger about something. *There was a scene, and Father called Christopher a liar.*

PHRASES ● If something is done **behind the scenes,** it is done secretly. *Officials working behind the scenes urged them to avoid further confrontation.* ● If you **set the scene** for someone, you tell them what they need to know in order to understand what is going to happen next.

scenery /siːnə^{0}ri^1/. 1 SING N OR UNCOUNT N You can refer to everything you see around you as the **scenery,** especially when you are in the countryside. *As we neared the border the scenery became lush and spectacular.* 2 SING N OR UNCOUNT N In a theatre, the **scenery** is the painted cloth and boards at the back of the stage. *Who designed the scenery?... The production uses a minimum of scenery.*

scenic /siːnɪk/. ADJ A **scenic** place or route is attractive and has nice views. *The island has a scenic coastline... ...a scenic railway.*

scent /sɛnt/, **scents, scenting, scented.** 1 COUNT N A **scent** is a pleasant smell. *...the overpowering scent of English garden flowers.* 2 MASS N **Scent** is a liquid that women put on their skin to make themselves smell nice. *She walked in smelling of French scent.* 3 COUNT N OR UNCOUNT N An animal's **scent** is the smell that it gives off. *The queen bee produces a scent which attracts the other bees... They mark their territories with scent from glands in their groin.* 4 VB WITH OBJ When an animal **scents** something, it becomes aware of it by smelling it. *...when it scents its prey.*

scented /sɛntɪ^{2}d/. ADJ Something that is **scented** has a pleasant smell. *...scented soap... ...a sweet-scented variety of rose.*

sceptic /skɛptɪk/, **sceptics;** spelled **skeptic** in American English. COUNT N A **sceptic** is a person who has doubts about things that other people believe.

sceptical /skɛptɪkə^{0}l/; spelled **skeptical** in American English. ADJ If you are **sceptical** about something, you have doubts about it. *Robert's father was sceptical about hypnotism... Mrs Swallow gave a sceptical grunt.*

scepticism /skɛptɪsɪzə^{0}m/; spelled **skepticism** in American English. UNCOUNT N **Scepticism** is great doubt about something. *There was widespread scepticism about these proposals.*

schedule /ʃɛdju^{4}l/, **schedules, scheduling, scheduled;** also pronounced /skɛdju^{4}l/, especially in American English. 1 COUNT N A **schedule** is a plan that gives a list of events or tasks, together with the times at which each thing should happen or be done. *...the next place on his busy schedule... ...the daily schedule of classes.* 2 VB WITH OBJ If something **is scheduled** to happen at a particular time, arrangements have been made for it to happen then. *He was scheduled to leave Plymouth yesterday... A meeting had been scheduled for that day.* 3 COUNT N A **schedule** is also a written list of things, for example a list of prices, details, or conditions; a formal use.

PHRASES ● If something happens **ahead of schedule,** it happens earlier than the time planned. *We arrived several hours ahead of schedule.* ● If you are **behind schedule,** you are doing things later than the times planned. ● If something happens **on schedule,** it happens at the time planned. *Simon showed up right on schedule.* ● If something is done **to schedule** or **according to schedule,** it is done at the times that were planned in advance. *The operations have been carried out according to schedule.*

scheme /skiːm/, **schemes, scheming, schemed.** 1 COUNT N A **scheme** is a plan or arrangement, especially one produced by a government or other organization. *...the State pension scheme... ...a scheme to build 63 houses... ...some scheme for perfecting the world.* 2 VB When people **scheme,** they make secret plans; used showing disapproval. *He schemed against her... She schemed on her daughter's behalf.* ♦ **scheming** ATTRIB ADJ *...a ruthless, scheming man.* 3 PHRASE **The scheme of things** is the way that everything in the world seems to be organized. *Man needed to understand his place in the scheme of things.*

schizophrenia /skɪtsə^{4}friːnɪə/. UNCOUNT N **Schizophrenia** is a serious mental illness that prevents people from relating their thoughts and feelings to what is happening around them.

schizophrenic /skɪtsə^{4}frɛnɪk/, **schizophrenics.** COUNT N A **schizophrenic** is a person who is suffering from schizophrenia. *...a paranoid schizophrenic.* Also ADJ *...a schizophrenic patient.*

scholar /skɒlə/, **scholars.** 1 COUNT N A **scholar** is a person who studies an academic subject and knows a lot about it. *...Benjamin Jowett, the theologian and Greek scholar.* 2 COUNT N A **scholar** is also a pupil or student who has a scholarship. *...an Eton scholar.*

scholarly /skɒləli^1/. ADJ A **scholarly** person spends a lot of time studying and knows a lot about academic subjects.

scholarship /skɒləʃɪp/, **scholarships.** 1 COUNT N If you get a **scholarship** to a school or university, you get money for your studies from the school or university or some other organization. *I applied for a scholarship to study philosophy at Oxford.* 2 UNCOUNT N **Scholarship** is serious academic study and the knowledge that is obtained from it. *...the Islamic tradition of scholarship.*

scholastic /skə^{7}læstɪk/. ATTRIB ADJ Your **scholastic** ability is your ability to study and learn things at school; a formal use. *He was more involved in sports than in scholastic achievements.*

school /skuːl/, **schools.** 1 UNCOUNT N OR COUNT N **School** or a **school** is a place where children are educated. *I went to school here... He was doing badly at school... ...the school holidays... ...a school with more than 1300 pupils.* 2 COUNT N OR UNCOUNT N WITH SUPP University departments and colleges are sometimes called **schools.** *I went to an art school... She had recently graduated from law school.* 3 UNCOUNT N In America, university is often referred to as **school;** an informal use. 4 PHRASE A **school of thought** is a theory or opinion shared by a group of people. *One school of* *thought argues that the enterprise should be abandoned... There seemed to be two schools of thought.* **5** COUNT N A **school** of dolphins is a large group of them. **6** See also **schooling.**

schoolboy /skuːlbɔɪ/, **schoolboys.** COUNT N A **schoolboy** is a boy who goes to school.

schoolchild /skuːltʃaɪld/, **schoolchildren.** COUNT N **Schoolchildren** are children who go to school.

schooldays /skuːldeɪz/. PLURAL N Your **schooldays** are the period of your life when you are at school.

schoolgirl /skuːlgɜːl/, **schoolgirls.** COUNT N A **schoolgirl** is a girl who goes to school.

schooling /skuːlɪŋ/. UNCOUNT N Your **schooling** is the education that you receive at school. *Many of the workers had no schooling at all.*

schoolmaster /skuːlmɑːstə/, **schoolmasters.** COUNT N A **schoolmaster** is a man who teaches children in a school; an old-fashioned use.

schoolmistress /skuːlmɪstrɪ²s/, **schoolmistresses.** COUNT N A **schoolmistress** is a woman who teaches children in a school; an old-fashioned use. *...the village schoolmistress.*

schoolroom /skuːlru⁴m/, **schoolrooms.** COUNT N A **schoolroom** is a classroom, especially when it is the only classroom in a small school; an old-fashioned use.

schoolteacher /skuːltiːtʃə/, **schoolteachers.** COUNT N A **schoolteacher** is a teacher in a school.

science /saɪəns/, **sciences. 1** UNCOUNT N **Science** is the study of the nature and behaviour of natural things and the knowledge that we obtain about them. *...the importance of mathematics to science... Why don't many girls go into science?* **2** COUNT N A **science** is a particular branch of science, for example physics or biology. **3** See also **social science.**

science fiction. UNCOUNT N **Science fiction** consists of stories and films about events that take place in the future or in other parts of the universe.

scientific /saɪəntɪfɪk/. **1** ADJ **Scientific** is used to describe things that relate to science or to a particular science. *...scientific research... ...scientific instruments.* ♦ **scientifically** ADV *...a scientifically advanced civilization.* **2** ADJ If you do something in a **scientific** way, you do it systematically, using experiments or tests. *...a scientific study of a language.* ♦ **scientifically** ADV *Our relationship to apes has been confirmed scientifically.*

scientist /saɪəntɪst/, **scientists.** COUNT N A **scientist** is an expert who does work in one of the sciences. *...a distinguished medical scientist.*

scissors /sɪzəz/. PLURAL N **Scissors** are a small tool with two sharp blades which are screwed together. You use scissors for cutting things such as paper and cloth. *She took a pair of scissors and cut his hair.*

scoff /skɒf/, **scoffs, scoffing, scoffed.** VB OR REPORT VB If you **scoff,** you speak in a scornful, mocking way about something. *They scoff at the idea that he will retire next year... 'Women's movement!' they scoffed. 'There isn't one.'*

scold /skəʊld/, **scolds, scolding, scolded.** VB WITH OBJ If you **scold** someone, you speak angrily to them because they have done something wrong. *He scolded his daughter for keeping them waiting.*

scone /skəʊn, skɒn/, **scones.** COUNT N **Scones** are small cakes made from flour and fat. They are usually eaten with butter.

scoop /skuːp/, **scoops, scooping, scooped. 1** VB WITH OBJ If you **scoop** something up, you put your hands under it and lift it in a quick movement. *The boys began to scoop up handfuls of water.* **2** VB WITH OBJ To **scoop** something up also means to pick it up with something such as a spoon. *He scooped some instant coffee into a cup.* **3** COUNT N A **scoop** is an object like a large spoon which is used for picking up a quantity of a food such as ice cream or flour. **4** COUNT N A **scoop** is also an exciting news story which is reported in one newspaper before it appears anywhere else. *He got all the big scoops for the paper.*

scoop out. PHR VB If you **scoop** part of something **out,** you remove it using a spoon or other tool. *Scoop out the flesh of the melon with a teaspoon.*

scooter /skuːtə/, **scooters.** COUNT N A **scooter** is a small, lightweight motorcycle with a low seat.

scope /skəʊp/. **1** UNCOUNT N If there is **scope** for a particular kind of behaviour, you have the opportunity to act in this way. *There is not much scope for originality.* **2** UNCOUNT N The **scope** of an activity or piece of work is the area which it deals with or includes. *Lack of time limited the scope of the course... It seemed out of place in a book so limited in scope.*

scorch /skɔːtʃ/, **scorches, scorching, scorched.** VB WITH OBJ If something **is scorched,** it is burned slightly or damaged by heat. *I once scorched a beautiful pink suit while ironing it... The lawn was scorched and the soil was baked hard.*

scorching /skɔːtʃɪŋ/. ADJ **Scorching** weather is very hot; an informal use. *...a scorching day.*

score /skɔː/, **scores, scoring, scored. 1** VB WITH OR WITHOUT OBJ If someone **scores** in a game, they get a goal, run, or point. *Barnes scored from a distance of twenty feet... Fowler scored 83.* **2** COUNT N The **score** in a game is the number of goals, runs, or points obtained by the teams or players. *'What's the score?'—'2-0.'* **3** VB WITH OBJ If you **score** a success, victory, or hit, you are successful in what you are doing. *The Liberals have scored a dramatic victory in this by-election.* **4** VB WITH ADJUNCT OR OBJ If you **score** over someone or **score** a point, you gain an advantage over them or defeat them in some way. *The Government was anxious to score over the opposition in the education debate... Gareth grinned, as if he had scored an important point.* **5** PLURAL N **Scores** of things means a large number of them. *We received scores of letters.* **6** VB WITH OBJ If something sharp **scores** a surface, it cuts a line into it; a formal use. *Each stone is scored with very thin grooves.* **7** COUNT N The **score** of a piece of music is the written version of it. **8** PHRASE **On this score** or **on that score** means in relation to the thing already mentioned; a formal use. *There was no need for concern on that score.*

scorn /skɔːn/, **scorns, scorning, scorned. 1** UNCOUNT N If you treat someone or something with **scorn,** you show contempt for them. *This suggestion was greeted with scorn... She had nothing but scorn for those who got themselves into debt.* **2** VB WITH OBJ If you **scorn** someone or something, you feel or show contempt for them. *She scorned the girls who worshipped football heroes... What is now admired as art was then scorned as vulgar extravagance.* **3** VB WITH OBJ If you **scorn** something, you refuse to accept it because you think it is not good enough or suitable for you; a formal use. *Although his hearing was not good, he scorned a deaf aid.*

scornful /skɔːnfʊl/. ADJ If you are **scornful,** you show contempt for someone or something. *She is openly scornful of the idea that girls are weaker than men... ...scornful laughter.* ♦ **scornfully** ADV *She looked at him scornfully.*

scorpion /skɔːpɪən/, **scorpions.** COUNT N A **scorpion** is a small tropical animal that has a long tail with a poisonous sting on the end.

Scot /skɒt/, **Scots. 1** COUNT N A **Scot** is a person who comes from Scotland. **2** UNCOUNT N **Scots** is a dialect of the English language that is spoken in Scotland. *He speaks broad Scots.* **3** ATTRIB ADJ **Scots** also means the same as Scottish. *He spoke with a Scots accent.*

scotch /skɒtʃ/, **scotches. 1** UNCOUNT N **Scotch** or **scotch whisky** is whisky made in Scotland. *...a bottle of Scotch.* **2** COUNT N A **scotch** is a glass of scotch. *He fixed two more scotches.*

Scotsman /skɒtsmə³n/, **Scotsmen.** COUNT N A **Scotsman** is a man who comes from Scotland.

Scotswoman /skɒtswʊmən/, **Scotswomen.** COUNT N A **Scotswoman** is a woman who comes from Scotland.

Scottish /skɒtɪʃ/. ADJ **Scottish** means belonging or relating to Scotland. *...the Scottish mountains... ...the Scottish legal system.*

scoundrel /skaʊndrə⁰l/, **scoundrels.** COUNT N A **scoundrel** is someone who cheats and deceives people; an old-fashioned use.

scour /skaʊə/, **scours, scouring, scoured.** VB WITH OBJ If you **scour** a place for something, you make a thorough search there for it. *Traders were scouring the villages for family treasures.*

scourge /skɜːdʒ/. SING N When something causes a lot of trouble or suffering to a group of people, you can refer to it as a **scourge.** *Smallpox was the scourge of the Western world.*

scout /skaʊt/, **scouts, scouting, scouted. 1** COUNT N A **scout** or a **boy scout** is a member of the Scout Association which encourages boys to become disciplined and to learn practical skills. *He joined the boy scouts.* **2** COUNT N A **scout** is also a person who is sent somewhere to find out the position of an enemy army. *The scouts reported that the enemy was advancing.* **3** VB WITH ADJUNCT If you **scout** around for something, you search for it in different places. *We'll scout around to see if anyone is here.*

scowl /skaʊl/, **scowls, scowling, scowled.** VB If you **scowl,** you frown because you are angry. *I scowled at him.* Also COUNT N *Her grin changed to a scowl.*

scrabble /skræbə⁰l/, **scrabbles, scrabbling, scrabbled. 1** VB WITH ADJUNCT If you **scrabble** at something, you scrape at it with your fingers or feet. *I hung there, scrabbling with my feet to find a foothold.* **2** VB WITH ADJUNCT If you **scrabble** around, you move your hands about in order to find something that you cannot see. *I scrabbled around on the floor and eventually found my ring... She scrabbled in her handbag.*

scramble /skræmbə⁰l/, **scrambles, scrambling, scrambled. 1** VB If you **scramble** over rough or difficult ground, you move quickly over it using your hands to help you. *John scrambled up the bank.* **2** VB WITH ADJUNCT To **scramble** also means to move somewhere in a hurried, undignified way. *He scrambled to his feet... Sightseers had scrambled for the best position.* **3** SING N If there is a **scramble** for something, people rush to get it. *There may be a world-wide scramble for oil.*

scrambled egg, scrambled eggs. UNCOUNT N OR PLURAL N **Scrambled egg** or **scrambled eggs** is a dish made of eggs and milk, and cooked in a pan.

scrap /skræp/, **scraps, scrapping, scrapped. 1** COUNT N A **scrap** of something is a very small piece or amount of it. *He found a scrap of paper and a pencil... ...a rug made of scraps of old clothes... ...scraps of information.* **2** PLURAL N **Scraps** are pieces of unwanted food which are thrown away or given to animals. *...a tame puppy, begging for scraps.* **3** VB WITH OBJ If you **scrap** something, you get rid of it or cancel it. *The existing system should be completely scrapped... Plans have now been scrapped for four nuclear power stations.* **4** UNCOUNT N **Scrap** or **scrap metal** is metal from old or damaged machinery or cars. *All he could do was sell it for scrap.* **5** COUNT N A **scrap** is also a fight; an informal use.

scrapbook /skræpbʊk/, **scrapbooks.** COUNT N A **scrapbook** is a book with blank pages where people stick things such as pictures or newspaper articles.

scrape /skreɪp/, **scrapes, scraping, scraped. 1** VB WITH OBJ AND ADJUNCT If you **scrape** something from a surface or **scrape** it off, you remove it by pulling a knife or other object over it. *She scraped the mud off her boots.* **2** VB WITH OBJ If you **scrape** something, you remove its skin or surface by pulling a knife over it. *The nuts can be eaten raw once they have been scraped.* **3** VB WITH OBJ If you **scrape** one thing against another, you rub the first thing against the second, causing slight damage. *He scraped his hand painfully on a rock.* **4** VB WITH OR WITHOUT OBJ If something **scrapes** something else or **scrapes** against it, it rubs against it and damages it slightly or makes a harsh noise. *In winter, the branches tapped and scraped the glass... His beard scraped against her skin.* Also SING N *...the clink and scrape of knives and forks.*

scrape through. PHR VB If you **scrape through** an examination, you just succeed in passing it.

scrape together or **scrape up.** PHR VB If you **scrape together** or **scrape up** an amount of money or a number of things, you succeed in obtaining them with difficulty. *He scraped up the money to start a restaurant.*

scratch /skrætʃ/, **scratches, scratching, scratched. 1** VB WITH OBJ If a sharp object **scratches** you, it rubs against your skin, cutting you slightly. *I got scratched by a rose bush... His knees were scratched by thorns.* **2** VB WITH OBJ If you **scratch** an object, you accidentally make small cuts on it. **3** COUNT N **Scratches** on someone or something are small cuts or marks. *You're not going to die. It's only a scratch... White shoe polish can hide scratches on white woodwork.* **4** VB WITH OR WITHOUT OBJ OR REFL VB If you **scratch** a part of your body or **scratch** yourself, you rub your fingernails against your skin because it is itching. *The cook began scratching the rash on his neck... We are scratching because we itch... Jackson was sleepily scratching himself.*

PHRASES ● If you say that someone **is scratching** their **head,** you mean that they are thinking hard and trying to solve a problem. ● If you do something **from scratch,** you do it without making use of anything that has been done before. *Now we have to start again from scratch.* ● If something is **not up to scratch,** it is not good enough. *My Economics isn't likely to be up to scratch.*

scrawl /skrɔːl/, **scrawls, scrawling, scrawled. 1** VB WITH OBJ If you **scrawl** something, you write it carelessly and untidily. *Someone had scrawled 'What does it all mean?' across the cover.* **2** COUNT N **Scrawl** is writing that looks careless and untidy. *I did my best to write neatly instead of with my usual scrawl.*

scrawny /skrɔːni¹/, **scrawnier, scrawniest.** ADJ A **scrawny** person or animal is unpleasantly thin and bony. *...a scrawny youth... ...scrawny cattle.*

scream /skriːm/, **screams, screaming, screamed. 1** VB When someone **screams,** they make a loud, high-pitched cry, usually because they are in pain or frightened. *Kunta screamed as a whip struck his back.* Also COUNT N *He was awakened by the sound of screams.* **2** REPORT VB If you **scream** something, you shout it in a loud, high-pitched voice. *'Get out of there,' I screamed... She stood there screaming abuse at me.* **3** SING N If someone is a **scream,** they are very funny; an informal use. *Do you know Sheila? She's a scream.*

screech /skriːtʃ/, **screeches, screeching, screeched. 1** VB When a person or an animal **screeches,** they make an unpleasant, loud, high-pitched cry. *The parrots screeched in the trees... 'You'll be sorry you did that!' she screeched.* Also COUNT N *The parrot gave a loud screech.* 2 VB If a vehicle **screeches,** its tyres make an unpleasant high-pitched noise on the road. *The bus came screeching to a stop.* Also SING N *I heard a screech of tyres.*

screen /skri:n/, **screens, screening, screened.** 1 COUNT N A **screen** is the flat, vertical surface of a television or computer or in the cinema on which pictures or words are shown. *A picture would flash onto the screen... ...the television screen.* 2 SING N The films that are shown in cinemas are sometimes referred to as the **screen.** *...Greta Garbo and other stars of the screen.* 3 VB WITH OBJ When a film or a television programme **is screened,** it is shown in the cinema or broadcast on television. *They tried to prevent the programme being screened.* ♦ **screening** UNCOUNT N OR COUNT N *...the screening of information programmes... There was an attempt to stop the screening.* 4 COUNT N A **screen** is also a vertical panel that is used to separate different parts of a room or to keep cold air away from a part of it. *He got up and walked behind the screen.* 5 VB WITH OBJ If you **screen** someone, you stand in front of them or place something in front of them, in order to prevent them from being seen or hurt. *I moved in front of her trying to screen her.* 6 VB WITH OBJ When an organization **screens** people, they investigate them to make sure that they are not likely to be dangerous or disloyal. *The Secret Service screens several hundred people every week.* 7 VB WITH OBJ To **screen** people for a disease means to examine them to make sure that they do not have it. *...a study of women who were screened for breast cancer.* ♦ **screening** UNCOUNT N OR COUNT N *...plans to set targets for screening... ...a screening at a London medical centre.*

screen off. PHR VB If you **screen off** part of a room, you make it into a separate area, using a screen.

screw /skru:/, **screws, screwing, screwed.** 1 COUNT N A **screw** is a small, sharp piece of metal with a spiral groove, which is used to fix one thing to another. 2 ERG VB WITH ADJUNCT If you **screw** something to something else, you fix it there by means of a screw or screws. *I'm going to screw some handles onto the bathroom cabinet... The curtains are attached to special clips which screw to the window-frame.* 3 ERG VB WITH ADJUNCT To **screw** something also means to fasten or fix it by twisting it round and round. *He screwed the lid tightly onto the top of the jar... ...hollow tubes which screw together.*

screw up. PHR VB 1 If you **screw up** your face or something flexible, you twist it or squeeze it so that it no longer has its natural shape. *She screwed up her eyes as she faced the sun... She screwed up the paper and tossed it in the bin.* 2 If you **screw up** a plan or situation, you cause it to fail; an informal use.

screwdriver /skru:draɪvə/, **screwdrivers.** COUNT N A **screwdriver** is a tool for fixing screws into place.

scribble /skrɪbə^{0}l/, **scribbles, scribbling, scribbled.** 1 VB WITH OR WITHOUT OBJ If you **scribble** something, you write it quickly and untidily. *She was scribbling a letter to her mother... We were scribbling away furiously.* 2 VB WITH ADJUNCT To **scribble** also means to make meaningless marks or untidy drawings using a pencil or pen. *Someone's scribbled all over the wall.* 3 UNCOUNT N OR COUNT N **Scribble** or a **scribble** is something that has been written or drawn quickly and untidily. *She was looking at my scribble, trying to work out what it said... There are scribbles on the lift wall.*

script /skrɪpt/, **scripts.** 1 COUNT N The **script** of a play, film, or television programme is the written version of it. *You can't have good acting without a decent script.* 2 COUNT N OR UNCOUNT N A **script** is a particular system of writing. *...the Arabic script.*

scripture /skrɪptʃə/, **scriptures.** UNCOUNT N OR COUNT N You use **scripture** or **scriptures** to refer to writings that are regarded as sacred in a particular religion. *The scripture says, 'Man cannot live on bread alone.'... They invoked Hindu scripture to justify their position.*

scroll /skrəʊl/, **scrolls.** COUNT N A **scroll** is a long roll of paper, parchment, or other material with writing on it. *...an ancient Chinese scroll.*

scrounge /skraʊnd^{0}ʒ/, **scrounges, scrounging, scrounged.** VB WITH OR WITHOUT OBJ If you **scrounge** something such as food or money, you get it by asking someone for it, rather than by buying it or earning it; an informal use. *He had come over to scrounge a few cans of food... She was always scrounging.*

scrub /skrʌb/, **scrubs, scrubbing, scrubbed.** 1 VB WITH OBJ If you **scrub** something, you rub it hard in order to clean it, using a stiff brush and water. *They scrub the kitchen floor every day... He scrubbed his hands at the sink.* Also SING N *That floor needs a good scrub.* 2 VB WITH OBJ AND ADJUNCT If you **scrub** dirt off something, you remove it by rubbing hard. *There was a stain on the collar and he tried to scrub it off.* 3 UNCOUNT N **Scrub** consists of low trees and bushes in an area that has very little rain. *The country is flat, grassy, and covered in scrub.*

scruff /skrʌf/. PHRASE If someone holds you **by the scruff of your neck,** they hold the back of your neck or collar.

scruffy /skrʌfi^1/, **scruffier, scruffiest.** ADJ Someone or something that is **scruffy** is dirty and untidy. *We looked scruffy... ...scruffy trousers.*

scrum /skrʌm/, **scrums.** COUNT N In the game of rugby, a **scrum** is a formation in which players form a tight group and push against each other with their heads down in an attempt to get the ball.

scruples /skru:pə^{0}lz/. PLURAL N **Scruples** are moral principles that make you unwilling to do something that seems wrong. *He had no scruples about borrowing money... ...religious scruples.*

scrupulous /skru:pjə^{4}ləs/. 1 ADJ A **scrupulous** person or organization takes great care to do what is fair, honest, or morally right. *The paper was not entirely scrupulous in setting out its assumptions.* ♦ **scrupulously** ADV *...the pressure on manufacturers to behave scrupulously.* 2 ADJ **Scrupulous** also means thorough, exact, and careful about details. *They pay scrupulous attention to style.* ♦ **scrupulously** ADV *Everything was scrupulously clean.*

scrutinize /skru:tɪnaɪz/, **scrutinizes, scrutinizing, scrutinized;** also spelled **scrutinise.** VB WITH OBJ If you **scrutinize** something, you examine it very carefully. *Bank examiners scrutinized the books of 600 financial institutions... He began to scrutinize the faces in the compartment.*

scrutiny /skru:tɪni^1/. UNCOUNT N If something is under **scrutiny,** it is being studied or observed very carefully. *At these visits the whole college comes under scrutiny... ...close scrutiny by explosives experts.*

scuff /skʌf/, **scuffs, scuffing, scuffed.** VB WITH OBJ If you **scuff** your feet, you drag them along the ground when you walk.

scuffed /skʌft/. ADJ **Scuffed** shoes have been damaged by being scraped against things. *...a man in a baggy suit and scuffed shoes.*

scuffle /skʌfə^{0}l/, **scuffles.** COUNT N A **scuffle** is a short fight or struggle. *Two policemen were injured in the scuffle.*

scullery /skʌləri^1/, **sculleries.** COUNT N A **scullery** is a small room next to a kitchen where washing is done; an old-fashioned use.

sculptor /skʌlptə/, **sculptors.** COUNT N A **sculptor** is someone who makes sculptures.

sculpture /skʌlptʃə/, **sculptures.** 1 COUNT N OR UNCOUNT N A **sculpture** is a work of art that is produced by carving or shaping stone, wood, or clay. *...Aztec sculptures... ...an exhibition of 20th century sculpture.* 2 UNCOUNT N **Sculpture** is the art of making sculptures. *The college offers classes in sculpture.*

sculptured /skʌlptʃəd/. ADJ **Sculptured** objects have been carved or shaped from something. *...sculptured heads of civic dignitaries.*

scum /skʌm/. SING N OR UNCOUNT N **Scum** is a layer of an unpleasant-looking substance on the surface of a liquid. *There was green scum over the pond.*

scurry /skʌri^1/, **scurries, scurrying, scurried.** VB WITH ADJUNCT To **scurry** somewhere means to run there quickly, like a small animal that is frightened. *A mouse scurried across the floor... Everyone scurried for cover.*

scuttle /skʌtə^{0}l/, **scuttles, scuttling, scuttled.** VB WITH ADJUNCT To **scuttle** somewhere means to run there with short, quick steps. *A porcupine scuttled across the road.*

scythe /saɪð/, **scythes.** COUNT N A **scythe** is a tool with a long handle and a long curved blade, used for cutting grass or grain.

SE. SE is a written abbreviation for 'south-east'.

sea /si:/, **seas.** 1 COUNT N OR UNCOUNT N The **sea** is the salty water that covers much of the earth's surface. *I watched the children running into the sea... ...a wrecked ship at the bottom of the sea... ...calm seas... ...a bit of blue sea.* 2 COUNT N A **sea** is a large area of salty water. It can be part of an ocean or be surrounded by land. *...the North Sea... ...the Caspian Sea.* 3 SING N WITH SUPP A **sea** of people or things is a very large number of them; a literary use. *...a sea of white faces... ...a sea of troubles.*

PHRASES ● **At sea** means on or under the sea, far away from land. *...a storm at sea... Submarines can stay at sea for weeks.* ● If someone is **at sea,** they are in a state of confusion. ● If you travel or send something **by sea,** you travel or you send it in a ship.

seabed /si:bed/. SING N The **seabed** is the ground under the sea. *...pipelines on the sea-bed.*

seafood /si:fu:d/. UNCOUNT N **Seafood** refers to shellfish and other sea creatures that you can eat.

seagull /si:gʌl/, **seagulls.** COUNT N A **seagull** is a type of bird that lives near the sea.

seal /si:l/, **seals, sealing, sealed.** 1 COUNT N A **seal** is an official mark on a document which shows that it is genuine. 2 COUNT N A **seal** is also something fixed to a container or letter that must be broken before it can be opened. *I noticed that the seals of the packet had been broken.* 3 VB WITH OBJ If you **seal** an envelope, you stick down the flap. *Mrs Slesers sealed the envelopes and left them on her desk.* ♦ **sealed** ADJ *He took a sealed envelope from the folder on his desk.* 4 VB WITH OBJ If you **seal** an opening, you fill or cover it to prevent air, gas, or a liquid getting in or out. *Small cracks can be sealed with this compound... ...a thin tube sealed at one end.* 5 PHRASE If someone **gives** something their **seal of approval,** they say officially that they approve of it. 6 COUNT N A **seal** is also a large, shiny animal without legs, which eats fish and lives partly on land and partly in the sea.

seal off. PHR VB If you **seal** a place **off,** you block all the entrances so that nobody can get in or out.

sea level. UNCOUNT N If you are at **sea level,** you are at the same level as the surface of the sea. *...land below sea level.*

seam /si:m/, **seams.** 1 COUNT N A **seam** is a line of stitches joining two pieces of cloth together. 2 COUNT N A **seam** of coal is a long, narrow layer of it beneath the ground. 3 PHRASE If something is **bursting at the seams,** it is very full.

seaman /si:mə^{3}n/, **seamen.** COUNT N A **seaman** is a sailor.

séance /seɪɑ:ns/, **séances;** also spelled **seance.** COUNT N A **séance** is a meeting in which people try to speak to people who are dead.

search /sɜ:tʃ/, **searches, searching, searched.** 1 VB WITH ADJUNCT OR OBJ If you **search** for something, you look carefully for it. If you **search** a place, you look carefully for something there. *He glanced around the room, searching for a place to sit... He searched through a drawer and eventually found the photo... I searched the city for a room.* 2 VB WITH OBJ If the police **search** you, they examine your clothing for hidden objects. *We were stopped by the police and searched.* 3 COUNT N A **search** is an attempt to find something by looking for it carefully. *I found the keys after a long search... ...the search for oil.* ● If you go **in search** of something, you try to find it. *We went round the town in search of a place to stay.*

searching /sɜ:tʃɪŋ/. ADJ A **searching** question or look is intended to discover the truth about something. *...the searching questions of the Social Security officials... He gave the girl a quick, searching look.*

search party, **search parties.** COUNT N A **search party** is an organized group of people who are looking for someone.

searing /sɪərɪŋ/. 1 ATTRIB ADJ A **searing** pain is very sharp. *He felt a searing pain in his left arm.* 2 ATTRIB ADJ A **searing** speech or piece of writing is very critical. *...a searing exposure of modern America.*

seashore /si:ʃɔ:/, **seashores.** COUNT N The **seashore** is the part of a coast where the land slopes down into the sea. *...a walk along the seashore.*

seasick /si:sɪk/. ADJ If you are **seasick** when you are in a boat, the movement of the boat causes you to vomit or feel sick. *He felt seasick.* ♦ **seasickness** UNCOUNT N *He suffers from seasickness.*

seaside /si:saɪd/. SING N The **seaside** is an area next to the sea. *We spent the weekend at the seaside... ...a seaside resort.*

season /si:zə^{0}n/, **seasons, seasoning, seasoned.** 1 COUNT N The **seasons** are the periods into which a year is divided, because there is different weather in each period. *Autumn is my favourite season... Most tropical areas have rainy and dry seasons.* 2 COUNT N WITH SUPP A **season** is also the period during each year when something usually happens. *When does the football season end?... ...the holiday season.* 3 COUNT N WITH SUPP A **season** of films is several of them shown as a series because they are connected in some way. *...a season of Clint Eastwood movies.* 4 VB WITH OBJ If you **season** food, you add salt, pepper, or spices to it. *...tuna fish seasoned with salt.*

PHRASES ● If fruit or vegetables are **in season,** it is the time of year when they are ready for eating and are widely available. ● If you go to a place **out of season,** you go there when it is not the busy holiday period.

seasonal /si:zənə^{0}l/. ADJ Something that is **seasonal** happens during one particular time of the year. *People found seasonal work on farms.*

seasoned /si:zə^{0}nd/. ATTRIB ADJ **Seasoned** means having a lot of experience of something. For example, a **seasoned** traveller is someone who has travelled a lot. *...seasoned troops.*

seasoning /si:zə^{0}nɪŋ/. UNCOUNT N **Seasoning** is salt, pepper, or spices that are added to food.

season ticket, season tickets. COUNT N A **season ticket** is a ticket that you can use repeatedly over a certain period without having to pay each time. *...a monthly season ticket... This entrance is reserved for season ticket holders.*

seat /siːt/, **seats, seating, seated. 1** COUNT N A **seat** is an object that you can sit on, for example a chair. *Roger sat down carefully, using the edge of the crate as a seat... ...the back seat of the car... I rang the theatre to see if I could get seats for the show... Come in, take a seat.* **2** COUNT N The **seat** of a chair is the part that you sit on. **3** REFL VB If you **seat** yourself somewhere, you sit down. *'Thank you,' she said, seating herself on the sofa.* ♦ **seated** PRED ADJ *General Tomkins was seated behind his desk.* **4** VB WITH OBJ A building or vehicle that **seats** a particular number of people has enough seats for that number. *The hall seats four hundred.* **5** COUNT N When someone is elected to parliament, you can say that they or their party have won a **seat.** *The Nationalists failed to win a single seat.* **6** PHRASE If you **take a back seat,** you allow other people to have all the power and to make all the decisions.

seat-belt, seat-belts. COUNT N A **seat-belt** is a strap that you fasten across your body for safety when travelling in a car or aeroplane.

seating /siːtɪŋ/. UNCOUNT N The **seating** in a place is the seats there. *The plastic seating was uncomfortable.*

seaweed /siːwiːd/, **seaweeds.** MASS N **Seaweed** is a plant that grows in the sea.

secluded /sɪ[1]kluːdɪ[2]d/. ADJ A **secluded** place is quiet, private, and undisturbed. *...secluded beaches.*

seclusion /sɪ[1]kluːʒə[0]n/. UNCOUNT N If you are living in **seclusion,** you are in a quiet place away from other people. *She was reared in seclusion.*

second, seconds, seconding, seconded; pronounced /sekənd/, except for meaning 6, when it is pronounced /sɪ[2]kɒnd/. **1** COUNT N A **second** is one of the sixty parts that a minute is divided into. *The rocket was rising at the rate of 300 feet per second... She looked at me for a few seconds.* **2** COUNT N A **second** or **seconds** is also used to mean a very short time. *Could I see your book for a second?... In seconds the building had gone up in flames.* **3** ADJ The **second** item in a series is the one that you count as number two. *...his father's second marriage... ...the second of February.* **4** COUNT N **Seconds** are goods that are sold cheaply because they are slightly faulty. **5** VB WITH OBJ If you **second** a proposal in a meeting or debate, you formally agree with it so that it can then be discussed or voted on. *I seconded Gene's nomination.* **6** VB WITH OBJ If you **are seconded** somewhere, you are moved there temporarily in order to do special duties. *He was for a time seconded to the army.* **7 second nature:** see **nature.**

PHRASES ● If something is **second only to** something else, the other thing is the only one that is better than it. *San Francisco is second only to New York as the tourist city of the States.* ● If you experience something **at second hand,** you are told about it by other people rather than experiencing it yourself. *I knew nothing about Judith except what I'd heard at second hand.* ● See also **second-hand.**

secondary /sekəndə[0]ri[1]/. **1** ADJ **Secondary** means less important than something else. *Many older people still believe that men's careers come first and women's careers are secondary.* **2** ATTRIB ADJ In Britain, **secondary** education is for pupils between the ages of 11 and 18.

secondary school, secondary schools. COUNT N OR UNCOUNT N In Britain, a **secondary school** is a school for pupils between the ages of 11 and 18.

second-best. ADJ OR SING N Something that is **second-best** is not as good as the best thing of its kind but is better than all the other things of that kind. *...businessmen in their second-best suits... Hiring professionals is impractical, so as a second-best, we will use unpaid amateurs.*

second-class. 1 ATTRIB ADJ **Second-class** things are regarded as less valuable or less important than others of the same kind. *There can be no second-class citizens in a free society.* **2** MOD A **second-class** ticket allows you to travel in the ordinary accommodation on a train, aircraft, or ship. *...a second-class carriage.* **3** ADJ OR ADV **Second-class** postage is a cheaper and slower type of postage. **4** ATTRIB ADJ A **second-class** degree is a good or average university degree.

second cousin, second cousins. COUNT N Your **second cousins** are the children of your parents' cousins.

second-hand. 1 ADJ OR ADV Something that is **second-hand** has been owned by someone else. *...second-hand clothing... ...a book he bought second-hand.* **2** ATTRIB ADJ A **second-hand** shop sells second-hand goods. **3** ADV OR ADJ If you hear a story **second-hand,** you hear it from someone who has heard it from someone else. *I heard about it secondhand... ...a second-hand report.*

second language. SING N Someone's **second language** is a language which is not their native language but which they use at work or at school. *...learners of English as a second language.*

secondly /sekəndli[1]/. SENTENCE ADV You say **secondly** when you want to make a second point or give a second reason for something. *Firstly, the energy already exists in the ground. Secondly, there's plenty of it.*

second-rate. ADJ Something that is **second-rate** is of poor quality. *...second-rate ideas... ...second-rate students.*

second thoughts. PLURAL N If you have **second thoughts** about a decision, you have doubts and begin to wonder if it was wise. ● You say **on second thoughts** when you suddenly change your mind about something. *Tell me more about America. No, on second thoughts, tell me more about your family.*

secrecy /siːkrɪsi[1]/. UNCOUNT N **Secrecy** is the fact or state of keeping something secret. *She stressed the necessity of absolute secrecy... The operation was conducted in secrecy.*

secret /siːkrɪt/, **secrets. 1** ADJ Something that is **secret** is known about by only a small number of people, and is not told or shown to anyone else. *The letter was marked 'secret'... ...secret negotiations.* ♦ **secretly** ADV *Their work had to be done secretly.* **2** ATTRIB ADJ You use **secret** to describe someone who does something that they do not tell other people about. *She had become a secret drinker.* ♦ **secretly** ADV OR SENTENCE ADV *He secretly hoped I would one day change my mind... Secretly, perhaps, some of them were also a little scared.* **3** PHRASE If you do something **in secret,** you do it without anyone else knowing. *I arranged to meet him in secret... He'll manufacture it in secret.* **4** COUNT N A **secret** is a fact that is known by only a small number of people, and is not told to anyone else. *The results of these experiments remain a secret... I'll tell you a secret.* **5** SING N If a way of behaving is the **secret** of achieving something, it is the best way or the only way to achieve it. *Think big! This is the secret of success.*

secret agent, secret agents. COUNT N A **secret agent** is a person employed by a government to find out the secrets of other governments.

secretarial /sekrəteərɪəl/. ATTRIB ADJ **Secretarial** work is the work of a secretary. *...secretarial staff.*

secretariat /sekrəteərɪət/, **secretariats.** COUNT N A **secretariat** is a department responsible for the administration of an international political organization. *...a senior member of the U.N. Secretariat.*

secretary /sekrətə[0]ri[1]/, **secretaries. 1** COUNT N A **secretary** is a person whose job is to type letters, answer phone calls and do other office work. **2** COUNT N The **secretary** of a club is the person whose job involves keeping records and writing letters. *If you want to join the cricket club, write to the secretary.* **3** COUNT N WITH SUPP **Secretary** is also the title of ministers who are in charge of major government departments. *...one of the best Foreign Secretaries since the war.*

secrete /sɪ[1]kriːt/, **secretes, secreting, secreted. 1** VB WITH OBJ If part of a plant or animal **secretes** a liquid, it produces it. *The skin pores enlarge and secrete more oil.* ♦ **secretion** /sɪ[1]kriːʃə[0]n/ UNCOUNT N *Hormone secretion is controlled by the pituitary gland.* **2** VB WITH OBJ If you **secrete** something somewhere, you hide it there; a formal use. *...clothes that she had secreted in her basket.*

secretive /siːkrɪtɪv, sɪ[1]kriːtɪv/. ADJ If you are **secretive,** you keep your feelings, or intentions hidden from other people. *She's very secretive about money matters.*

secret service, secret services. COUNT N A country's **secret service** is a government department that is responsible for the security of a country, and whose job is to find out enemy secrets and to prevent its own government's secrets from being discovered.

sect /sekt/, **sects.** COUNT N A **sect** is a group of people that has separated from a larger group and has a particular set of religious or political beliefs. *...an extremist Protestant sect.*

sectarian /sekteərɪən/. **1** ATTRIB ADJ **Sectarian** means resulting from the differences between sects; a formal use. *The conference had collapsed in sectarian squabbles.* **2** ADJ Someone who is **sectarian** strongly supports a particular sect; a formal use. *This group is frequently attacked as sectarian and fanatical.*

section /sekʃə[0]n/, **sections.** COUNT N A **section** of something is one of the parts that it is divided into. *...the first-class section of the train... I passed the written exam but failed the oral section.* ● See also **cross-section.**

sector /sektə/, **sectors.** COUNT N A **sector** of something, especially a country's economy, is a particular part of it. *...the manufacturing sector... ...resistance from all sectors of the Black community.*

secular /sekjə[4]lə/. ADJ You use **secular** to describe things that have no connection with religion. *...secular education... The choir sings both sacred and secular music.*

secure /sɪ[2]kjʊə/, **secures, securing, secured. 1** VB WITH OBJ If you **secure** something, you get it after a lot of effort; a formal use. *He secured only 526 votes... I did everything possible to secure him a posting.* **2** VB WITH OBJ If you **secure** a place, you make it safe from harm or attack; a formal use. *They endeavoured to secure the bridge from the threat of attack.* **3** ADJ If a building is **secure,** it is tightly locked or well protected. *Try and make your house as secure as you can.* **4** VB WITH OBJ If you **secure** an object, you fasten it firmly to another object. *A plastic box was secured to the wall by screws.* **5** ADJ If an object is **secure,** it is fixed firmly in position. *Check that the leads to the battery are in good condition and secure.* ♦ **securely** ADV *The chain seemed to be securely fastened.* **6** ADJ If a position or power is **secure,** it is safe and certain not to be lost. *You've got a secure job.* ♦ **securely** ADV *The strike was securely under the union's control.* **7** ADJ If you feel **secure,** you feel safe and happy and are not worried about life. *We feel financially secure.*

security /sɪ[2]kjʊərɪ[1]ti[1]/, **securities. 1** UNCOUNT N **Security** refers to all the precautions that are taken to protect a place. *...a threat to national security... Security forces were patrolling the streets.* **2** UNCOUNT N **Security** is legal protection against possible harm or loss. *He hasn't got security of employment... The tenants are exploited and have no security of tenure.* **3** UNCOUNT N A feeling of **security** is a feeling of being safe. *Children count on their parents for love and security.* **4** COUNT N **Securities** are stocks, shares, bonds, or other certificates bought as an investment; a technical use. **5** See also **social security.**

sedate /sɪ[2]deɪt/, **sedates, sedating, sedated. 1** ADJ A **sedate** person is quiet, calm, and rather dignified. *Irene was graver and more sedate.* ♦ **sedately** ADV *He walked sedately down the lane.* **2** VB WITH OBJ If you **are sedated,** you are given a drug to calm you or to make you sleep.

sedation /sɪ[2]deɪʃə[0]n/. UNCOUNT N **Sedation** is the use of drugs in order to calm someone or to make them sleep. *Freddie was still under sedation.*

sedative /sedətɪv/, **sedatives.** COUNT N A **sedative** is a drug that calms you or makes you sleep. *Dolly had taken a sedative.*

sedentary /sedəntə[0]ri[1]/. ADJ A **sedentary** occupation or way of life involves a lot of sitting down and not much exercise.

sediment /sedɪmə[2]nt/, **sediments.** UNCOUNT N OR COUNT N **Sediment** is solid material that settles at the bottom of a liquid.

seduce /sɪ[1]djuːs/, **seduces, seducing, seduced. 1** VB WITH OBJ If something **seduces** you, it is so attractive that it tempts you to do something that you would not normally approve of. *He was seduced into saying that he would do it.* **2** VB WITH OBJ If someone **seduces** another person, they persuade that person to have sex with them. *He used to seduce all the maids.* ♦ **seduction** /sɪ[1]dʌkʃə[0]n/ COUNT N OR UNCOUNT N *The girl's seduction is an important part of the story... ...a subtle form of seduction.*

seductive /sɪ[1]dʌktɪv/. **1** ADJ Something that is **seductive** is very attractive or tempting. *These are seductive arguments.* **2** ADJ A **seductive** person is sexually attractive. ♦ **seductively** ADV

see /siː/, **sees, seeing, saw** /sɔː/, **seen** /siːn/. **1** VB WITH OR WITHOUT OBJ When you **see** something, you notice it using your eyes, or you look at it. *I saw him glance at his watch... He went to India to see the Taj Mahal... Did you see 'The Doctor's Dilemma' on telly last night?... Some animals have the ability to see in very dim light.* **2** VB WITH OBJ If you go to **see** someone, you visit them or meet them. *Perhaps she did not wish to come and see me... It would be a good idea for you to see a doctor for a checkup.* **3** VB WITH OBJ AND ADJUNCT If you **see** someone to a particular place, you accompany them to make sure that they get there safely. *I went down to see her safely to her car.* **4** REPORT VB If you **see** that something is true or exists, you realise that it is true or exists, by carefully observing it or thinking about it. *Etta could see that he wasn't listening... She begins to see that she has a choice.* **5** REPORT VB If you **see** what someone means or **see** why something happened, you understand what they mean or understand why it happened. *'Yes,' she said. 'I see what you mean.'... I can see why Mr Smith is worried... Somebody got killed and I don't see how.* **6** REPORT VB If you say that you will **see** what is happening or what the situation is, you mean you intend to find out. *I'd better go and see what he wants... I must phone her up and see if she can come tonight.* 7 REPORT VB If you **see** that something is done, you make sure that it is done. *See that everything is marked with your initials.* 8 VB WITH OBJ If you **see** a situation or someone's behaviour in a particular way, you regard it in that way. *I did not see his determination as a defect... The problem, as I see it, is not advice but direct help.* 9 VB WITH OBJ If a person or a period of time **sees** a particular change or event, the change or event takes place while that person is alive or during that period of time. *In recent times we have seen a huge split develop between rich and poor nations... How would you like to see education changed?* 10 VB WITH OBJ If you **see** something happening in the future, you imagine it, or predict that it will happen. *She saw herself seated behind the cash register, smiling... Can you see women going into combat carrying forty-pound guns?* 11 VB WITH OBJ **See** is used in books to indicate to readers where they should look for more information. *Reference to this problem is made elsewhere (see Chapter 14).*

PHRASES ● If you say that you will **see if** you can do something, you mean that you will try to do it. *See if you can find my birthday book somewhere.* ● When someone asks you for help, if you say that you will **see what you can do,** you mean that you will try to help them. ● People say **'I'll see'** or **'We'll see'** to indicate that they do not intend to make a decision immediately, and will decide later. *'Will you write to me?' she asked. 'I'll see,' he said.* ● People say **'let me see'** or **'let's see'** when they are trying to remember something, or are trying to find something. *I think I've got her name somewhere. Now let me see.* ● You say **' I see '** to indicate that you understand what someone is telling you. *'Humbert is Dolly's real father.'—'I see.'* ● You can use **'seeing that'** or **'seeing as'** to introduce the reason for what you are doing or saying; an informal use. *Seeing that you're the guest on this little trip, you can decide where we're going.* ● **'See you'** and **'see you later'** are informal ways of saying goodbye when you expect to meet again soon.

see about. PHR VB 1 When you **see about** something, you arrange for it to be done or provided. *Rudolph went into the station to see about Thomas's ticket.* 2 CONVENTION If someone says that they will do something, and you say **'We'll see about that',** you mean that you intend to prevent them from doing it.

see in. PHR VB If you ask what someone **sees in** a particular person, you want to know what they find attractive about that person. *'What can she see in him?'*

see through. PHR VB If you **see through** someone or **see through** what they are doing, you realize what their intentions are, even though they are trying to hide them. *She had learned to see through him... The jailers saw through my scheme.*

see to. PHR VB If you **see to** something that needs attention, you deal with it. *Don't you worry about that. I'll see to that... He went out to see to the chickens.*

seed /siːd/, **seeds.** 1 COUNT N OR UNCOUNT N A **seed** is the small, hard part of a plant from which a new plant grows. *...sunflower seeds... ...a packet of seed.* 2 PLURAL N WITH SUPP The **seeds** of something are its beginnings or origins; a literary use. *The seeds of doubt had been sown.*

seedling /siːdlɪŋ/, **seedlings.** COUNT N A **seedling** is a young plant grown from a seed.

seedy /siːdiˡ/. ADJ A **seedy** person or place is untidy, shabby, and unpleasant. *...a seedy character with a cigarette between his lips... ...a seedy and rundown photographer's studio.*

seek /siːk/, **seeks, seeking, sought** /sɔːt/; a formal word. 1 VB WITH OBJ OR 'for' If you **are seeking** something, you are trying to find and obtain it. *Thousands of people were seeking food and shelter... I was seeking the help of someone who spoke French... Books are eagerly sought for and sold on the streets.* 2 VB WITH TO-INF If you **seek** to do something, you try to do it. *Power stations are seeking to reduce their use of oil.*

seek out. PHR VB If you **seek out** someone or something, you keep looking for them until you find them.

seem /siːm/, **seems, seeming, seemed.** 1 LINK VB OR VB WITH TO-INF If someone or something **seems** to have a particular quality or attitude, they give the impression of having that quality or attitude. *Even minor problems seem important... It seemed like a good idea... You seem to be very interested.* 2 VB WITH TO-INF, LINK VB, OR REPORT VB If something **seems** to be the case, you get the impression that it is the case. *There don't seem to be many people here today... It seemed as though I had known them for a long time... Berger's thesis seems right... It seemed that everybody smoked cigarettes.* 3 VB WITH TO-INF OR LINK VB You use **seem** to indicate that you are not completely certain that what you are saying is correct. *The experiments seem to prove that sugar is not good for you... For the time being, Thatcher seems politically secure.* 4 LINK VB OR REPORT VB You also use **seem** when you are giving your opinion or asking someone else's opinion. *Does that seem nonsense to you?... It did seem to me that she was far too romantic... That would seem a sensible thing to do... There don't seem to be many people on campus today.* 5 VB WITH TO-INF If you say that you cannot **seem** to do something, you mean that you have tried to do it and are unable to do it. *I can't seem to get to sleep.*

seeming /siːmɪŋ/. ATTRIB ADJ Someone's **seeming** willingness or **seeming** interest means that they appear to be willing or interested, but you are not sure; a formal use. *...his seeming willingness to participate.* ♦ **seemingly** SUBMOD OR SENTENCE ADV *...their seemingly limitless resources... Seemingly they don't have any problems.*

seen /siːn/. **Seen** is the past participle of **see.**

seep /siːp/, **seeps, seeping, seeped.** VB WITH ADJUNCT If a liquid or gas **seeps** through something, it passes through it very slowly. *I used to lie awake at night watching the rain seep through the cracks.*

seethe /siːð/, **seethes, seething, seethed.** 1 VB If you **are seething,** you are angry but do not express your feelings. *I seethed with secret rage... By now David was seething.* 2 VB WITH 'with' If a place **is seething** with people there are a lot of them moving about. *The streets of London seethed with a marching, cheering crowd.* ♦ **seething** ATTRIB ADJ *...a seething mass of maggots.*

segment /sɛgməˡnt/, **segments.** 1 COUNT N A **segment** of something is one part of it. *I did show her a segment of the eight-page letter.* 2 COUNT N A **segment** of an orange or grapefruit is one of the sections into which it can easily be divided.

segregate /sɛgrɪgeɪt/, **segregates, segregating, segregated.** VB WITH OBJ To **segregate** two groups or types of things means to keep them apart. *They tried to segregate pedestrians and vehicles.*

segregated /sɛgrɪgeɪtɪˡd/. ADJ A **segregated** group of people is kept apart from other people belonging to a different sex, race, or religion. *He refused to play before segregated audiences.*

segregation /sɛgrɪgeɪʃəⁿn/. UNCOUNT N **Segregation** is the practice of keeping apart people of different sexes, races, or religions groups.

seize /siːz/, **seizes, seizing, seized.** 1 VB WITH OBJ If you **seize** something, you take hold of it quickly and firmly. *I seized him by the collar.* 2 VB WITH OBJ When a group of people **seize** a place they take control of it quickly and suddenly, using force. *The airfield had been seized by US troops.* 3 VB WITH OBJ When someone **is seized,** they are arrested or captured. *A university professor was seized on Wednesday by three armed men.* 4 VB WITH OBJ If you **seize** an opportunity, you take advantage of it, and do something that you want to do. *Derrick seized the chance and went to Spain.*

seize on or **seize upon.** PHR VB If you **seize on** something or **seize upon** it, you show great interest in it, often because it is useful to you. *This was one of the points that I seized upon with some force... ...seizing on it as an excuse for a rest period.*

seize up. PHR VB 1 If a part of your body **seizes up,** it suddenly becomes too painful to move, because you have strained it. *Your back may seize up.* 2 If an engine **seizes up,** it stops working, because of overheating or lack of oil.

seize upon. PHR VB See **seize on.**

seizure /siːʒə/, **seizures.** 1 COUNT N If there is a **seizure** of power in a place, a group of people suddenly take control of the place, using force. *...the seizure of factories by the workers.* 2 UNCOUNT N If someone has a **seizure,** they have a heart attack or an epileptic fit.

seldom /sɛldəⁿm/. ADV If something **seldom** happens, it happens only occasionally; a formal use. *It seldom rains there.*

select /sɪˡlɛkt/, **selects, selecting, selected.** 1 VB WITH OBJ If you **select** something, you choose it. *They select books that seem to them important.* ♦ **selected** ATTRIB ADJ *We were shown carefully selected places during our visit.* 2 ADJ **Select** means considered to be among the best of its kind. *They are members of a select band of professional athletes.*

selection /sɪˡlɛkʃəⁿn/, **selections.** 1 UNCOUNT N **Selection** is the act of selecting of one or more things from a group. *She stood little chance of selection.* 2 COUNT N A **selection** of people or things is a set of them chosen from a larger group. *The orchestra was playing a selection of tunes from the Merry Widow.* 3 SING N The **selection** of goods in a shop is the range of goods available. *...London's largest selection of office furniture.*

selective /sɪˡlɛktɪv/. 1 ATTRIB ADJ A **selective** process involves choosing particular people or things. *...the selective education of the most talented children.* ♦ **selectively** ADV *Trees are felled selectively.* 2 ADJ When someone is **selective,** they choose things carefully. *They are particularly selective in their television watching.* ♦ **selectively** ADV *A film crew was selectively filming broken windows of shops owned by white people.*

self /sɛlf/, **selves** /sɛlvz/. COUNT N WITH POSS Your **self** is your basic personality or nature. *By evening she was her normal self again.*

self-. PREFIX **Self-** is used to form adjectives and nouns that describe something that people or things do to themselves. *...a self-locking door... ...self-improvement... ...self-pity.*

self-assured. ADJ Someone who is **self-assured** shows confidence in what they say and do. *His comments were firm and self-assured.*

self-centred. ADJ Someone who is **self-centred** is only concerned with their own wants and needs. *He was much too self-centred to notice her.*

self-confident. ADJ Someone who is **self-confident** behaves confidently because they feel sure of their abilities or worth. *She was remarkably self-confident for her age.* ♦ **self-confidence** UNCOUNT N *We began to lose our self-confidence.*

self-conscious. ADJ Someone who is **self-conscious** is easily embarrassed and worried about what other people think of them. *I stood there, feeling self-conscious. Was my hair out of place?*

self-contained. 1 ADJ Something that is **self-contained** is complete and separate and does not need help or resources from outside. *...a society of immense power, self-contained and well organized.* 2 ADJ A **self-contained** flat has all its own facilities including a kitchen and bathroom.

self-control. UNCOUNT N Your **self-control** is your ability to control your feelings and appear calm, even when you feel angry or afraid. *He lost his self-control and cried aloud.*

self-defence. 1 UNCOUNT N **Self-defence** is the use of violence or special physical skills to protect yourself against someone who attacks you. *He had struck her in self-defence.* 2 PHRASE If you say something **in self-defence,** you give reasons for your behaviour to someone who thinks you have behaved wrongly. *'I didn't want to go anyway,' he grumbled in self-defence.*

self-employed. ADJ If you are **self-employed,** you organize your own work, pay, and taxes, rather than being employed by someone who pays you regularly. *...a self-employed builder and decorator.*

self-esteem. UNCOUNT N If you have **self-esteem,** you feel that you are a good, worthwhile person, and so you behave confidently. *He wanted to regain his self-esteem.*

self-evident. ADJ A fact or situation that is **self-evident** is so obvious that there is no need for proof or explanation. *The answers to moral problems are not self-evident.*

self-government. UNCOUNT N **Self-government** is government of a country by its own people rather than by others. *In Parliament he called for the democratic self-government of the colonies.*

self-imposed. ADJ A **self-imposed** task or responsibility is one that you have deliberately accepted for yourself. *...troubles that were largely self-imposed.*

self-indulgent. ADJ If you are **self-indulgent,** you allow yourself to have or do things that you enjoy very much. *We are, by and large, idle, self-indulgent and lacking in public spirit.* ♦ **self-indulgence** UNCOUNT N *Temptations to self-indulgence should be resisted.*

self-interest. UNCOUNT N **Self-interest** is the attitude of always wanting to do what is best for yourself. *Are they influenced by duty or self-interest?*

selfish /sɛlfɪʃ/. ADJ If you are **selfish,** you care only about yourself, and not about other people. *...a totally selfish attitude... How mean and selfish you are!* ♦ **selfishly** ADV *Why is he acting so selfishly?* ♦ **selfishness** UNCOUNT N *He felt ashamed of his selfishness.*

selfless /sɛlflɪˡs/. ADJ A **selfless** person considers other people's needs rather than their own. *It was impossible to repay years of selfless devotion.*

self-made. ATTRIB ADJ **Self-made** people have become successful and rich through their own efforts. *My father was a self-made man.*

self-respect. UNCOUNT N **Self-respect** is a feeling of confidence and pride in your own ability and worth. *Billy needs to have his self-respect restored.*

self-righteous. ADJ Someone who is **self-righteous** is convinced that they are right in their beliefs and attitudes and that other people are wrong. *...self-righteous indignation.* ♦ **self-righteousness** UNCOUNT N *...a strong note of self-righteousness in his voice.*

self-sacrifice. UNCOUNT N **Self-sacrifice** is the giving up of what you want so that other people can have what they need. *The children's education demanded effort and self-sacrifice.*

self-satisfied. ADJ If someone is **self-satisfied,** they are so pleased about their achievements or their situation that they do not feel there is any need to do anything more; used showing disapproval.

self-service. ADJ A **self-service** shop, restaurant, or garage is one where you serve yourself.

self-sufficient. ADJ If a country or group is **self-sufficient,** it is able to produce or make everything that it needs. *This country is self-sufficient in energy supplies.*

sell /sɛl/, **sells, selling, sold** /səʊld/. 1 VB WITH OBJ AND OBJ If you **sell** something, you let someone have it in return for money. *I hope to sell the house for £60,000... He is going to sell me his car.* 2 VB WITH OBJ If a shop **sells** a particular thing, it has it available for people to buy. *Do you sell flowers?* 3 VB WITH 'for' OR 'at' If something **sells** for a particular price, it is offered for sale at that price. *These little books sell for 95p each... ...a pocket calculator selling at the same price.* 4 VB If something **sells,** it is bought in fairly large quantities. *Their revolutionary jet did not sell well.* 5 VB WITH OBJ Something that **sells** a product makes people want to buy the product. *Scandal and gossip is what sells newspapers.*

sell out. PHR VB 1 If a shop **is sold out** of something or **has sold out** of it, it has sold it all and there is none left. *They've sold out of bread.* 2 If a performance of a play, film, or other entertainment **is sold out,** all the tickets have been sold.

seller /sɛlə/, **sellers.** COUNT N A **seller** is a person or business that sells something. *Umbrella sellers went out of business.* ● See also **best-seller.**

selves /sɛlvz/. **Selves** is the plural of **self.**

semblance /sɛmbləns/. SING N WITH 'of' If there is a **semblance** of a particular condition or quality, it appears to exist, even though this may be a false impression; a formal use. *By this time some semblance of order had been established.*

semen /siːmɛn/. UNCOUNT N **Semen** is the liquid containing sperm produced by the sex organs of men.

semi-. PREFIX **Semi-** is used to form adjectives and nouns that describe someone or something as being partly, but not completely, in a particular state. *...semi-skilled workers... We sat in the semi-darkness.*

semicircle /sɛmiˈsɜːkəᵒl/, **semicircles.** COUNT N A **semicircle** is one half of a circle. *We sat in a big semicircle round Hunter's desk.*

semi-colon, semi-colons. COUNT N A **semi-colon** is the sign (;).

semi-detached. ADJ A **semi-detached** house is a house joined to another house on one side by a shared wall. *...his small semi-detached house in King's Road.* Also SING N *They have a small semi-detached.*

semi-final, semi-finals. COUNT N A **semi-final** is one of the two matches in a competition played to decide who will compete in the final.

semi-modal, semi-modals. COUNT N The **semi-modals** are the verbs 'dare', 'need', and 'used to'. They can be used like the modal verbs, in which case they do not inflect and are followed by the base form of the verb. 'Dare', and 'need' can also be used as ordinary verbs.

seminar /sɛmɪnɑː/, **seminars.** COUNT N A **seminar** is a class at a university in which the teacher and a small group of students discuss a topic.

semi-precious. ATTRIB ADJ **Semi-precious** stones are stones such as opals and turquoises that are used in jewellery. They are less valuable than precious stones such as diamonds and sapphires.

semitone /sɛmiˈtəʊn/, **semitones.** COUNT N A **semitone** is the smallest interval between two notes in Western music. Twelve semitones are equal to one octave.

SEN /ɛs iː ɛn/, **SEN's.** COUNT N An **SEN** is a nurse who has successfully completed a two-year practical course in nursing in the United Kingdom. **SEN** is an abbreviation for 'State Enrolled Nurse'.

Senate /sɛnɪᵗt/. PROPER N The **Senate** is the smaller and more important of the two councils in the government of some countries, such as the United States of America. *This proposal was approved by both the House and the Senate.*

senator /sɛnətə/, **senators.** COUNT N A **senator** is a member of a Senate. *...Senator Edward Kennedy.*

send /sɛnd/, **sends, sending, sent** /sɛnt/. 1 VB WITH OBJ OR VB WITH OBJ AND OBJ When you **send** something to someone, you arrange for it to be taken and delivered to them, for example by post. *I drafted a letter and sent it to the President... Send it round in the morning... I promised I would send her the money.* ♦ **sender** /sɛndə/ COUNT N *The sender's name and address should be written on the back.* 2 VB WITH OBJ If you **send** a radio signal or message, you cause it to go to a place by means of radio waves. *Marconi succeeded in sending a signal across the Atlantic.* 3 VB WITH OBJ If you **send** someone somewhere, you arrange for them to go there or stay there. *The doctor sent me to a specialist... Could you send someone round to help?... His parents couldn't afford to send him to university.* 4 VB WITH OBJ AND ADJUNCT OR -ING If something **sends** things or people in a particular direction, it causes them to move in that direction. *The stubble was burning in the fields, sending wisps of black smoke into the air... The noise sent them racing towards the bush.*

send for. PHR VB 1 If you **send for** someone, you ask them to come and see you, by sending them a message. *She sent for a doctor... We'd better send for the police.* 2 If you **send for** something or **send off for** it, you write and ask for it to be sent to you. *Send for the nomination forms before it's too late... I'll send off for them next week.*

send off. PHR VB If you **send off** a letter or parcel, you send it somewhere by post. *You fill in both parts of the form, then send it off.*

send off for. PHR VB See **send for.**

senile /siːnaɪl/. ADJ If old people become **senile,** they become confused and are unable to look after themselves. *The old lady was now half blind and nearly senile.* ♦ **senility** /sənɪlɪˈti/ UNCOUNT N *Sheila became increasingly affected by senility.*

senior /siːnjə/, **seniors.** 1 ADJ The **senior** people in an organization have the highest and most important jobs in it. *...senior officers... ...a senior member of staff.* Also COUNT N *His seniors, however, were not amused.* 2 SING N WITH POSS Someone who is your **senior** is older than you are. *She was at least fifteen years his senior.*

senior citizen, senior citizens. COUNT N A **senior citizen** is a person who is old enough to receive an old-age pension. *...free bus travel for senior citizens.*

seniority /siːniˈɒrɪˈti/. UNCOUNT N A person's **seniority** in an organization is their degree of importance and power compared to other people. *The report listed their names in order of seniority.*

sensation /sɛnseɪʃəᵒn/, **sensations.** 1 COUNT N A **sensation** is a physical feeling. *It produces a mild burning sensation in the mouth.* 2 COUNT N You can use **sensation** to refer to the general feeling caused by a particular experience. *It was a strange sensation to return to the school again after so long.* 3 COUNT N If an event or situation is a **sensation,** it causes great excitement or interest. *The discovery was hailed as the scientific sensation of the century.*

sensational /sɛnseɪʃəᵒnəl, -ʃənəᵒl/. 1 ADJ Something that is **sensational** is remarkable and causes great excitement and interest. *...the most sensational result of any election since the war.* 2 ADJ You can describe something as **sensational** when you think that it is extremely good. *That was a sensational evening.*

sense /sɛns/, **senses, sensing, sensed.** 1 COUNT N Your **senses** are the physical abilities of sight, smell, hearing, touch, and taste. *They all have an excellent sense of smell.* 2 REPORT VB If you **sense** something, you become aware of it, although it is not very obvious. *Doctors often sense uneasiness in people... He sensed that she did not want to talk to him.* 3 SING N WITH 'of' If you have a **sense** of guilt or shame, for example, you feel guilty or ashamed. *I was overcome by a sense of failure.* 4 SING N WITH 'of' If you have a **sense** of something such as duty or justice, you can recognize it and you believe that it is important. *She has a strong sense of justice.* 5 SING N WITH SUPP Someone who has a **sense** of timing or style, for example, has a natural ability for timing or style. *A good sense of timing is important for an actor... He hasn't got much dress sense.* 6 UNCOUNT N **Sense** is the ability to make good judgements and to behave sensibly. *She had the good sense to realize that the plan would never work.* ● See also **common sense.** 7 COUNT N A **sense** of a word or expression is one of its possible meanings. *I don't like the Washington climate—in all senses of the word.*

PHRASES ● If something **makes sense** or you can **make sense** of it, you can understand it. *I looked at the page but the words made no sense... You had to read it six times to make any sense of it.* ● If a course of action **makes sense,** it seems sensible. *Under these conditions it made sense to adopt labour-saving methods.* ● If someone **has come to** their **senses** or **has been brought to** their **senses,** they have stopped being foolish and are being sensible again. ● If you say that something is true **in a sense,** you mean that it is partly true. *In a sense, I still love him.*

senseless /sɛnslɪ²s/. 1 ADJ A **senseless** action seems to have no meaning or purpose. *It was a senseless thing to do.* 2 ADJ If someone is **senseless,** they are unconscious. *A heavy blow with a club knocked him senseless.*

sense of humour. 1 SING N Someone who has a **sense of humour** often finds things amusing, rather than being serious all the time. *He lacked any sense of humour.* 2 UNCOUNT N Someone's **sense of humour** is the way that they are amused by certain things but not by others. *I see your sense of humour hasn't changed.*

sensibility /sɛnsɪbɪlɪˈti/, **sensibilities.** UNCOUNT N OR COUNT N Someone's **sensibility** is their ability to experience deep feelings; a formal use. *...a writer of high sensibility and intelligence.*

sensible /sɛnsɪbəᵒl/. ADJ A **sensible** person is able to make good decisions and judgements based on reason. *It seemed sensible to move to a bigger house... ...sensible decisions.* ♦ **sensibly** ADV *They sensibly concluded that this wouldn't be a good idea.*

sensitive /sɛnsɪtɪv/. 1 ADJ If you are **sensitive** to other people's problems and feelings, you understand and are aware of them. *We're trying to make people more sensitive to the difficulties faced by working mothers.* ♦ **sensitively** ADV *...this well acted, sensitively directed play.* ♦ **sensitivity** /sɛnsɪtɪvɪˈti/ UNCOUNT N *Her remarks showed a lack of sensitivity.* 2 ADJ If you are **sensitive** about something, it worries or upsets you. *You really must stop being so sensitive about your accent... He's very sensitive to criticism.* 3 ADJ A **sensitive** subject or issue needs to be dealt with carefully because it is likely to cause disagreement or make people upset. *This is one of the most sensitive issues that the government faces.* 4 ADJ Something that is **sensitive** to a physical force, substance, or condition is easily affected or harmed by it. *Children's bones are very sensitive to radiation... ...people with sensitive skin.* ♦ **sensitivity** UNCOUNT N *...the sensitivity of the lining of the nasal cavity.* 5 ADJ A **sensitive** piece of scientific equipment is capable of measuring or recording very small changes. *...highly sensitive electronic cameras.*

sensor /sɛnsə/, **sensors.** COUNT N A **sensor** is an instrument which reacts to certain physical conditions or impressions such as heat or light, and which is used to provide information. *...when the sensors in the engine detect a fire.*

sensory /sɛnsəᵒri/. ATTRIB ADJ **Sensory** means relating to the physical senses; a formal use. *With these two highly developed sensory organs it hunts at night for insects.*

sensual /sɛnsjʊᵒəl/. 1 ADJ A **sensual** person shows or suggests a great liking for physical pleasures, especially sexual pleasures. *...an extravagantly sensual woman.* ♦ **sensuality** /sɛnsjʊælɪˈti/ UNCOUNT N *Her body shone through the cloth with sheer sensuality.* 2 ADJ Something that is **sensual** gives pleasure to your physical senses rather than to your mind. *...the subtle, sensual rhythms of the drums.* ♦ **sensuality** UNCOUNT N *...African gardens of strangeness and sensuality.*

sensuous /sɛnsjuᵒəs/. ADJ Something that is **sensuous** gives pleasure to the mind or body through the senses. *...fresh peaches, sweet, cool, and sensuous.* ♦ **sensuously** ADV *Her fingers sensuously stroked his neck.*

sent /sɛnt/. **Sent** is the past tense and past participle of **send.**

sentence /sɛntəns/, **sentences, sentencing, sentenced.** 1 COUNT N A **sentence** is a group of words which, when they are written down, begin with a capital letter and end with a full stop. *...the opening sentence of the report... He put the phone down before she could finish the sentence.* 2 COUNT N OR UNCOUNT N In a law court, a **sentence** is the punishment that a person receives after they have been found guilty. *He is serving a life sentence for murder... ...offenders who misbehave during their sentence.* 3 VB WITH OBJ When judges **sentence** someone, they state in court what their punishment will be. *Griffiths was sentenced to four years' imprisonment.*

sentiment /sɛntɪməᵊnt/, **sentiments.** 1 UNCOUNT N OR COUNT N A **sentiment** is an attitude, feeling, or opinion. *...anti-imperialist sentiment... These sentiments were generally echoed by other speakers at the meeting.* 2 UNCOUNT N **Sentiment** is an emotion such as tenderness, romance, or sadness, which influences a person's behaviour. *I'm worried that you might be doing it out of sentiment. Out of affection for me.*

sentimental /sɛntɪmɛntəᵒl/. 1 ADJ A **sentimental** person or thing feels or arouses emotions such as tenderness, romance, or sadness. *...sentimental songs... People have become sentimental about the passing of ways and customs.* ♦ **sentimentality** /sɛntɪmɛntælɪˈti/ UNCOUNT N *...her sentimentality about animals.* 2 ADJ **Sentimental** means relating to a person's emotions. *The ring had been her mother's and she wore it for sentimental reasons.* ♦ **sentimen-**

tally ADV *He had become sentimentally attached to a student.*

sentry /sɛntri1/, **sentries.** COUNT N A **sentry** is a soldier who guards a camp or a building. *...look-out posts where sentries kept watch.*

separate, separates, separating, separated; pronounced /sɛpəᵊrə1t/ when it is an adjective and /sɛpəreɪt/ when it is a verb. **1** ADJ If one thing is **separate** from another, the two things are apart and are not connected. *Rosa had remained separate from us, asking for a room by herself... Two masses can be kept separate inside the bomb casing.* ♦ **separately** ADV *What we achieve together is more important than what we can do separately.* **2** ADJ **Separate** things are individual and distinct from each other. *The sunlight caught each tiny separate hair and made it shine.* ♦ **separately** ADV *Wash each pile separately.* **3** RECIP VB If you **separate** people, things or ideas, you keep them apart or consider them individually. *In any angry discussion he would separate the opponents and soothe them... It is important to separate learning English orally from learning English by reading books.* **4** VB WITH OBJ A detail that **separates** one thing from another thing shows that the two things are different from each other. *Higher living standards separate the older generation from their children.* **5** RECIP VB If an object, period of time, or distance **separates** two people or things, it exists between them and prevents them from having contact with each other. *A fence at the back of the garden separated us from the neighbours... ...the Great Lakes separating Canada from America.* **6** VB WITH OBJ If you **separate** a group of things or if you **separate** them out, you divide them so that each different part becomes separate. *Most schools decide to separate out their pupils into different groups according to age.* **7** RECIP VB If a group of people or things **separate,** they move away from each other after being together or connected for a time. *They talked by the gate, unwilling to separate... The two pipes separated from each other.* **8** VB If a married couple **separate,** they decide to live apart.

separated /sɛpəreɪtɪ2d/. PRED ADJ Someone who is **separated** from their wife or husband lives apart from them, but is not divorced. *My wife and I are separated.*

separation /sɛpəreɪʃᵊn/, **separations.** **1** UNCOUNT N The **separation** of two or more people or things is their movement away from each other or their state of being kept apart. *...the separation of infant from mother.* **2** COUNT N OR UNCOUNT N A **separation** between two or more people is a period of time that they spend apart from each other. *Children recover remarkably quickly from a brief separation from their parents... The Muslim minority are seeking separation from Georgia.* **3** COUNT N OR UNCOUNT N If a married couple have a **separation,** they decide to live apart. *Last night we talked about a separation... ...marital disruption, caused by separation.*

September /sɛptɛmbə/. UNCOUNT N **September** is the ninth month of the year in the Western calendar.

septic /sɛptɪk/. ADJ If a wound becomes **septic,** it becomes infected.

sequel /siːkwəᵊl/, **sequels.** **1** COUNT N The **sequel** to a book or film is another one which continues the story. *He starred in 'The Godfather' and in its sequel, 'The Godfather II'.* **2** COUNT N The **sequel** to an event is something that happened after it or because of it. *There was an amusing sequel to this incident.*

sequence /siːkwəᵊns/, **sequences.** **1** COUNT N WITH SUPP A **sequence** of events or things is a number of them that come one after another in a particular order. *...the strange sequence of events that led up to the murder.* **2** COUNT N OR UNCOUNT N A particular **sequence** is the order in which things happen or are arranged. *The paintings are exhibited in a chronological sequence... These recordings are in sequence and continuous.* **3** COUNT N A film **sequence** is a short part of a film. *What did you think of that ghastly sequence at the end?*

sequin /siːkwɪn/, **sequins.** COUNT N **Sequins** are small, shiny discs that are sewn on clothes to decorate them.

serene /sɪ2riːn/. ADJ **Serene** means calm and quiet. *She had a naturally cheerful and serene expression... ...a serene mountain landscape.* ♦ **serenely** ADV *Her blue eyes gazed serenely into space.* ♦ **serenity** /sɪ2rɛnɪ1ti1/ UNCOUNT N *I was moved by her serenity and confidence.*

sergeant /sɑːdʒənt/, **sergeants.** **1** COUNT N OR TITLE A **sergeant** is a non-commissioned officer of middle rank in the army or air force. **2** COUNT N A police **sergeant** is a police officer of the next to lowest rank.

sergeant major, **sergeant majors.** COUNT N OR TITLE A **sergeant major** is a non-commissioned army officer of the highest rank.

serial /sɪərɪəl/, **serials.** COUNT N A **serial** is a story which is broadcast or published in a number of parts over a period of time. *...a television serial.*

serialize /sɪərɪəlaɪz/, **serializes, serializing, serialized;** also spelled **serialise.** VB WITH OBJ If a book **is serialized,** it is broadcast or published in a number of parts.

serial number, **serial numbers.** COUNT N The **serial number** of an object is the number on it which identifies it. *...the serial number of the cheque card.*

series /sɪəri1z/. **Series** is the singular and plural. **1** COUNT N A **series** of things or events is a number of them that come one after the other. *He was arrested in connection with a series of armed bank robberies... ...a series of lectures on American politics.* **2** COUNT N A radio or television **series** is a set of related programmes with the same title. *...a new 6 week series on Europe.*

serious /sɪərɪəs/. **1** ADJ **Serious** problems or situations are very bad and cause people to be worried. *Bad housing is one of the most serious problems in the inner cities... ...a serious illness.* ♦ **seriously** ADV *She was seriously ill.* ♦ **seriousness** UNCOUNT N *...the seriousness of the problem.* **2** ADJ **Serious** matters are important and deserve careful consideration. *It's time to get down to the serious business of the meeting... She is a serious candidate for the presidency.* **3** ATTRIB ADJ **Serious** work or consideration of something involves thinking about things deeply because they are important. *The programme is a forum for serious political discussion... ...a serious newspaper.* **4** ADJ If you are **serious** about something, you are sincere about it, and not joking. *You can't be serious!... I knew that he was serious about the struggle.* ♦ **seriously** ADV *I'm seriously thinking of retiring.* ♦ **seriousness** UNCOUNT N *I see no reason, in all seriousness, why women should not become priests.* **5** ADJ **Serious** people are thoughtful, quiet, and slightly humourless. *She was a rather serious girl.* ♦ **seriously** ADV *He talked very seriously and solemnly about theoretical matters.*

seriously /sɪərɪəsli1/. **1** SENTENCE ADV You say **seriously** to indicate that you really mean what you say, or to ask someone else if they really mean what they have said. *What I do think is important, quite seriously, is that people should know the facts... You haven't seriously locked the door?* **2** PHRASE If you **take** someone or something **seriously,** you believe that they are important and deserve attention. *His work was not taken seriously.*

sermon /sɜːmən/, **sermons.** COUNT N A **sermon** is a talk on a religious or moral subject given during a church service. *The vicar preached a sermon on the importance of humility.*

serpent /sɜːpənt/, **serpents.** COUNT N A **serpent** is a snake; a literary use.

serrated /sɪ2reɪtɪ2d/. ATTRIB ADJ A **serrated** object has a row of V-shaped points along the edge, like a saw. *...serrated scissors.*

serum /sɪərəᵊm/, **serums.** COUNT N OR UNCOUNT N A **serum** is a liquid that is injected into someone's blood to protect them against a poison or disease. *This serum was most effective against snake poison... ...an antidote of serum.*

servant /sɜːvəᵊnt/, **servants.** COUNT N A **servant** is someone who is employed to work in another person's house, for example as a cleaner or a gardener. ● See also **civil servant.**

serve /sɜːv/, **serves, serving, served.** **1** VB WITH OBJ OR ADJUNCT If you **serve** your country, an organization, or a person, you do useful work for them. *For over thirty years, she has served the company loyally and well... He served with the army in France.* **2** VB WITH ADJUNCT, TO-INF, OR OBJ If something **serves** as a particular thing or **serves** a particular purpose, that is its use or function. *There was a long, grey building that served as a cafeteria... His refusal to answer only serves to increase our suspicions... I failed to see what purpose this could serve.* **3** VB WITH OBJ If something **serves** people or an area, it provides them with something that they need. *There were five water taps to serve all thirty camps... ...work which will serve the community.* **4** VB WITH OBJ If you **serve** people or if you **serve** food and drink, you give people food and drink. *When everybody had been served, the meal began... I served the children their meal.* **5** VB WITH OR WITHOUT OBJ The person who **serves** you in a shop is the person who you buy the goods from. *Are you being served?... She spent six months serving in a shop.* **6** VB WITH OBJ When a court **serves** a legal order on someone or **serves** them with it, it sends the order to them; a legal use. **7** VB WITH OBJ If you **serve** a prison sentence, you spend a period of time in jail. *He is now serving a life sentence in an Italian jail.* **8** VB WITH OR WITHOUT OBJ When you **serve** in tennis, you throw the ball up and hit it to start play. *It's my turn to serve.* Also COUNT N *Her second serve went into the net.* **9** PHRASE If you say it **serves** someone **right** when something unpleasant happens to them, you mean that it is their own fault and you have no sympathy for them. **10** See also **serving.**

serve out or **serve up.** PHR VB If you **serve out** food or **serve it up,** you give it to people as a meal. *Army kitchens serve up better fare than some hotels do.*

service /sɜːvɪs/, **services, servicing, serviced.** **1** COUNT N WITH SUPP A **service** is an organization or system that provides something for the public. *I think the train service is better than it used to be... ...the postal service.* **2** COUNT N WITH SUPP Some government organizations are called **services.** *...the diplomatic service.* **3** COUNT N WITH SUPP A **service** is also a job that an organization or business can do for you. *The fee for this service is £6.* **4** PLURAL N The **services** are the army, navy, and air force. *Young people are being encouraged to join the services.* **5** PLURAL N WITH POSS Your **services** are the work that you can do for people. *They will be very happy to give their services free of charge.* **6** UNCOUNT N **Service** is the state or activity of working for a particular person or organization. *Conscription would be limited to a maximum of six months' service.* **7** UNCOUNT N **Service** is also the process of being served in a shop or restaurant. *He hammered the table for immediate service.* **8** UNCOUNT N If a machine or vehicle is in **service,** it is being used or is able to be used. If it is out of **service,** it cannot be used. *Most of the vehicles had been withdrawn from service.* **9** VB WITH OBJ To **service** a machine or vehicle means to examine, adjust, and clean it so that it will keep working efficiently and safely. *Gas appliances should be serviced regularly.* Also COUNT N *The car needs a service.* **10** COUNT N A **service** is also a religious ceremony, especially a Christian one. *...the Sunday evening service.* **11** COUNT N A dinner **service** or a tea **service** is a complete set of dishes, plates, and other crockery. **12** COUNT N A **services** is a place on a motorway where there is a garage, restaurant, shop, and toilets. The plural is also 'services'. **13** See also **Civil Service, National Health Service, national service.**

serviceable /sɜːvɪsəbəᵊl/. ADJ Something that is **serviceable** performs its function effectively; a formal use. *I wore serviceable boots.*

service charge. SING N A **service charge** is an amount added to your restaurant bill to pay for the work of the waiter or waitress.

servile /sɜːvaɪl/. ADJ A **servile** person is too eager to do things for someone and shows them too much respect; a formal use that shows disapproval.

serving /sɜːvɪŋ/, **servings.** **1** COUNT N A **serving** is an amount of food given to one person at a meal. *His mother was spooning out servings of tuna fish casserole.* **2** ATTRIB ADJ A **serving** spoon or dish is used for serving food.

session /sɛʃᵊn/, **sessions.** **1** COUNT N A **session** is a meeting of an official group. *...an emergency session of the United Nations Security Council.* **2** COUNT N A **session** is also a period during which the meetings of an official group are regularly held. *...the government's programme for the 1966-67 parliamentary session.* **3** COUNT N A **session** of a particular activity is a period of that activity. *...a tough bargaining session.*

set /sɛt/, **sets, setting.** **Set** is used in the present tense, and is the past tense and past participle. **1** COUNT N WITH SUPP A **set** of things is a number of things that are considered as a group. *...a set of encyclopaedias... ...a chess set... We soon encountered a new set of problems.* **2** VB WITH OBJ AND ADJUNCT If you **set** something somewhere, you put it there, especially in a careful or deliberate way. *He filled the kettle and set it on the stove.* **3** PASSIVE VB WITH ADJUNCT If something **is set** in a particular place or position, it is in that place or position. *The house is set back from the road... His eyes were set close together.* **4** VB WITH OBJ AND 'into' OR 'in' If something **is set** into a surface, it is fixed there and does not stick out. *There was one tiny window set into the stone wall... ...nine large panels set in a rich framework.* **5** VB WITH OBJ AND ADJUNCT, ADJ, OR -ING You can use **set** to say that a person or thing causes something to happen. *Let me set your mind at rest... One prisoner had been set free... Two further pieces of information set me questioning it all again.* **6** VB When the sun **sets,** it goes below the horizon. **7** VB WITH OBJ To **set** a trap means to prepare it. **8** VB WITH OBJ If you **set** the table, you put the plates and cutlery on it ready for a meal. **9** VB WITH OBJ If you **set** a clock or control, you adjust it to a particular point or level. *His alarm clock was set for four a.m.* **10** VB WITH OBJ If you **set** a time, price, or level, you decide what it will be. *They haven't set a date for the wedding... The government set a minimum price of £1.15.* **11** ATTRIB ADJ You use **set** to describe something which is fixed and does not change. *We paid a set amount for the* *course... Her day usually followed a set pattern.* 12 VB WITH OBJ If you **set** a precedent, standard, or example, you establish it for other people to copy or try to achieve. *Try and set the younger children a good example... They tended to follow the trend set by the other banks.* 13 VB WITH OBJ If someone **sets** you some work or **sets** a target, they say that you must do the work or reach the target. *Let me set you a little problem... It set a target for economic growth.* 14 PRED ADJ If you are **set** to do something, you are ready or likely to do it. *The left-wing seem set to do very well in the general election.* 15 PRED ADJ WITH 'on' If you are **set** on doing something, you are determined to do it. *She is set on regaining her title.* 16 VB When glue, jelly, or cement **sets,** it becomes firm. *The cement had set hard.* 17 VB WITH OBJ AND PREP 'to' If someone **sets** a poem to music, they write music for it. 18 COUNT N A television **set** is a television. *We have a TV set in the living room.* 19 COUNT N The **set** for a play or film is the scenery or furniture. 20 VB WITH OBJ AND ADJUNCT If a play, film, or story **is set** at a particular time or in a particular place, the events in it take place at that time or in that place. *The play is set in a small Midlands village.* 21 COUNT N In tennis, a **set** is one of the groups of six or more games that form part of a match. 22 See also **setting.** ● **to set fire to** something: see **fire.** ● **to set foot:** see **foot.** ● **to set your heart on** something: see **heart.** ● **to set sail:** see **sail.** ● **to set the stage for:** see **stage.**

set about. PHR VB If you **set about** doing something, you start doing it. *The next morning they set about cleaning the house.*

set against. PHR VB To **set** one person **against** another means to cause them to become enemies or rivals.

set apart. PHR VB If a characteristic **sets** you **apart** from other people, it makes you noticeably different from the others. *His exceptional height set him apart from the rest of the men.*

set aside. PHR VB 1 If you **set** something **aside** for a special use or purpose, you keep it available for that use or purpose. *Try and set aside time to do some mending jobs.* 2 If you **set aside** a belief, principle, or feeling, you decide that you will not be influenced by it. *We must try and set aside our past hostilities.*

set back. PHR VB 1 To **set** someone or something **back** means to delay them. *This has set back the whole programme of nuclear power in America.* 2 If something **sets** you **back** a large amount of money, it costs you that much money; an informal use. 3 See also **setback.**

set down. PHR VB If you **set down** your thoughts or experiences, you write them down. *They were asked to set down a summary of their views.*

set in. PHR VB If something unpleasant **sets in,** it begins and seems likely to continue or develop. *A feeling of anti-climax set in... It must be treated quickly before infection sets in.*

set off. PHR VB 1 When you **set off,** you start a journey. *He set off on a trip to Mexico.* 2 If something **sets off** an event or a series of events, it causes it to start.

set on. PHR VB To **set** animals **on** someone means to cause the animals to attack them. *We were afraid they might set the dogs on us.*

set out. PHR VB 1 When you **set out,** you start a journey. *They set out for Cuba.* 2 If you **set out** to do something, you start trying to do it. *They had failed in what they had set out to do.* 3 If you **set** things **out,** you arrange or display them. *There were plenty of chairs set out for the guests.* 4 If you **set out** facts or opinions, you state them in a clear, organized way. *Darwin set out his theory in 'The Origin of Species'.*

set up. PHR VB 1 If you **set** something **up,** you make the necessary preparations for it. *It took a long time to set up the experiment... The government were setting up an inquiry into the affair... An anti-terrorist squad was set up.* ♦ **setting up** SING N *...the setting up of a Northern Seas Environmental Control Agency.* 2 If you **set up** a structure, you place it or build it somewhere. *A fund was launched to set up a monument in memory of the dead men.* 3 If you **set up** somewhere, you establish yourself in a new home or business. *She left her parents' home and set up on her own... He used the money to set himself up in business.* 4 If someone **sets** you **up,** they make it seem that you have done something wrong when you have not; an informal use. 5 See also **set-up.**

setback /setbæk/, **setbacks.** COUNT N A **setback** is an event that delays you or makes your position worse than before. *The by-election result is a serious setback for the government.*

settee /seti:/, **settees.** COUNT N A **settee** is a long comfortable seat with a back and arms, for two or three people.

setting /setɪŋ/, **settings.** 1 COUNT N WITH SUPP The **setting** for something is its surroundings or the circumstances in which it takes place. *The castle provided the perfect setting for a horror story... Children should be cared for in a home setting.* 2 COUNT N The **settings** on a machine are the different positions to which the controls can be adjusted. *Set the control to the coldest setting.*

settle /setə^{0}l/, **settles, settling, settled.** 1 VB WITH OBJ To **settle** an argument means to put an end to it. *The strike went on for over a year before it was finally settled.* 2 VB WITH OBJ If something **is settled,** it has all been decided and arranged. *Good, well, that's settled then.* 3 VB WITH OBJ If you **settle** a bill, you pay it. 4 VB WITH ADJUNCT When people **settle** somewhere, they start living there permanently. *He had settled in England.* 5 REFL VB OR VB WITH ADJUNCT If you **settle** yourself somewhere or **settle** somewhere, you sit down and make yourself comfortable. *He settled himself beside her in the car... Casson took off his raincoat and settled before the fire.* 6 VB If something **settles,** it sinks slowly down and becomes still. *The dust was settling... The hull of the boat slowly settled in the mud.* 7 VB WITH ADJUNCT When birds or insects **settle** on something, they land on it from above. *...flies and other insects that settle on plants growing on the banks.*

settle down. PHR VB 1 If you **settle down** to something, you prepare to do it and concentrate on it. *...before they settle down to university work... He had settled down to watch a sports programme.* 2 When someone **settles down,** they start living a quiet life in one place, especially when they get married or buy a house. *You should get a job and settle down.* 3 If people who are upset or noisy **settle down,** they become calm or quiet.

settle for. PHR VB If you **settle for** something, you choose or accept it, especially when it is not what you really want but there is nothing else available. *When in doubt he settled for hamburgers.*

settle in. PHR VB If you **are settling in,** you are getting used to living in a new place or doing a new job. *And how are you settling in, Mr Swallow?*

settle on. PHR VB If you **settle on** a particular thing, you choose it after considering other possible choices. *Have you settled on a name for him yet?*

settle up. PHR VB When you **settle up,** you pay a bill.

settled /setə^{0}ld/. 1 ADJ If you have a **settled** way of life, you stay in one place rather than travelling around. *It's time Humboldt led a more dignified settled life.* 2 ADJ A **settled** system stays the same all the time. *...an easy, rich, peaceful and settled social order.* 3 ADJ If you feel **settled,** you have been living or working in a place long enough to feel comfortable.

settlement /setə^{0}lmə^{2}nt/, **settlements.** 1 COUNT N A **settlement** is an official agreement between two sides who have been involved in a conflict. *The chance for a peaceful political settlement has disappeared... ...enormous wage settlements.* 2 COUNT N A **settlement** is also a place where people have come to live and built homes. *He lives in the jungle, in a settlement by a river.*

settler /setlə/, **settlers.** COUNT N **Settlers** are people who go to live in a new country. *The first white settlers in South Africa were Dutch.*

set-up, set-ups. COUNT N A particular **set-up** is a particular system or way of organizing something; an informal use. *I've only been here a couple of days and I don't quite know the set-up.*

seven /sevə^{0}n/, **sevens. Seven** is the number 7.

seventeen /sevə^{0}nti:n/. **Seventeen** is the number 17.

seventeenth /sevə^{0}nti:nθ/. ADJ The **seventeenth** item in a series is the one that you count as number seventeen.

seventh /sevə^{0}nθ/, **sevenths.** 1 ADJ The **seventh** item in a series is the one that you count as number seven. 2 COUNT N A **seventh** is one of seven equal parts of something.

seventieth /sevə^{0}ntɪɪθ/. ADJ The **seventieth** item in a series is the one that you count as number seventy.

seventy /sevə^{0}nti^{1}/, **seventies. Seventy** is the number 70.

sever /sevə/, **severs, severing, severed.** 1 VB WITH OBJ To **sever** something means to cut right through it or cut it off. *A bulldozer had severed a gas pipe... The boy's legs were severed at the hip.* 2 VB WITH OBJ If you **sever** a relationship or connection with someone, you end it completely. *She had to sever all ties with her parents.*

several /sevə^{0}rəl/. 1 QUANTIF You use **several** to refer to a fairly small number of people or things, when the exact number is not important. *He returned home several hours later.* 2 QUANTIF You also use **several** to refer to a number of people or things, when the number itself is not very large, but in a particular situation represents quite a lot. *Several hundred people were killed... Several of us are married and have children.*

severe /sɪ^{2}vɪə/, **severer, severest.** 1 ADJ You use **severe** to describe something that is very bad or undesirable. *The blast caused severe damage... ...a severe shortage of food.* ♦ **severely** ADV *A fire had severely damaged the school.* ♦ **severity** /sɪ^{2}verɪti^{1}/ UNCOUNT N *...the severity of the world-wide recession.* 2 ADJ A **severe** person is stern and rather harsh. *I hope the magistrate has not been too severe with him... ...her severe upbringing.* ♦ **severely** ADV *They were severely punished.* ♦ **severity** UNCOUNT N *...prison sentences of excessive severity.*

sew /səʊ/, **sews, sewing, sewed, sewn** /səʊn/. VB WITH OR WITHOUT OBJ When you sew things together, you join them using a needle and thread. *...sewing buttons onto one of my shirts... They teach the children to cook, sew, or knit.*

sewage /su:ɪdʒ/. UNCOUNT N **Sewage** is waste matter from homes and factories, which flows away through sewers.

sewer /su:ə/, **sewers.** COUNT N A **sewer** is a large underground channel that carries waste matter and rain water away.

sewing /səʊɪŋ/. 1 UNCOUNT N **Sewing** is the activity of making or mending things using a needle and thread. 2 UNCOUNT N **Sewing** is also things that are being sewn. *My aunt put aside her sewing.*

sewn /səʊn/. **Sewn** is the past participle of **sew.**

sex /seks/, **sexes.** 1 COUNT N The **sexes** are the two groups, male and female, into which people and animals are divided. *...people of both sexes... ...a member of the opposite sex.* 2 UNCOUNT N The **sex** of a person or animal is their characteristic of being either male or female. *...tests to ascertain the sex of the baby before it was born... ...to prevent discrimination on the grounds of sex.* 3 UNCOUNT N **Sex** is the physical activity by which people and animals can produce young. ● If two people **have sex,** they perform the physical act of sex.

sexism /seksɪzə^{0}m/. UNCOUNT N **Sexism** is discrimination against the members of one sex, usually women; used showing disapproval.

sexist /seksɪst/, **sexists.** 1 ADJ Something that is **sexist** involves sexism. *...sexist attitudes.* 2 COUNT N A **sexist** is a person, usually a man, who has sexist attitudes.

sexual /seksjʊ^{0}əl/. 1 ADJ **Sexual** feelings or activities are connected with the act of sex or with desire for sex. *...sexual attraction... They were not having a sexual relationship.* ♦ **sexually** ADV *I find her sexually attractive.* 2 ATTRIB ADJ **Sexual** also means relating to the differences between men and women. *...campaigning for non-discrimination and sexual equality.* 3 ATTRIB ADJ **Sexual** is also used to refer to the biological process by which people and animals produce young. *...sexual reproduction.*

sexual intercourse. UNCOUNT N **Sexual intercourse** is the physical act of sex between a man and a woman; a formal use.

sexuality /seksjʊælɪ^{1}ti^{1}/. UNCOUNT N A person's **sexuality** is their ability to experience sexual feelings.

sexy /seksi^{1}/, **sexier, sexiest.** ADJ **Sexy** means sexually exciting or sexually attractive. *...her sexy brown eyes.*

sh /ʃ/. CONVENTION **Sh** is a noise that you make to tell someone to be quiet. *Sh! The boys are in bed.*

shabby /ʃæbi^{1}/, **shabbier, shabbiest.** 1 ADJ Something that is **shabby** looks old and is in bad condition. *...his shabby clothes.* 2 ADJ A **shabby** person is wearing old, worn clothes. *...shabby children in the streets.* 3 ADJ **Shabby** behaviour is unfair or unacceptable. *...a series of shabby compromises.*

shack /ʃæk/, **shacks.** COUNT N A **shack** is a small hut built from bits of wood or metal.

shackle /ʃækə^{0}l/, **shackles, shackling, shackled.** 1 PLURAL N **Shackles** are two metal rings joined by a chain which are fastened around someone's wrists or ankles to prevent them from moving or escaping. 2 VB WITH OBJ To **shackle** someone means to put shackles on them. *The guards shackled his wrists and ankles.* 3 PLURAL N **Shackles** are also circumstances that prevent you from doing what you want to do; a literary use. *There are a few who have managed to throw off the shackles of the past.* 4 VB WITH OBJ If you **are shackled** by something, it prevents you from doing what you want to do; a literary use. *He is shackled by domestic responsibilities.*

shade /ʃeɪd/, **shades, shading, shaded.** 1 UNCOUNT N OR SING N **Shade** is an area of darkness and coolness which the sun cannot reach. *There are no trees or bushes to give shade... The air is cool in the shade... ...the shade of a large oak tree.* 2 VB WITH OBJ If a place **is shaded** by something, that thing prevents light from falling on it. *The broad walks are shaded by chestnut trees.* 3 COUNT N A **shade** is a lampshade. *...a lamp with a thick silk shade.* 4 COUNT N The **shades** of a particular colour are its different forms. For example, emerald green and olive green are shades of green. *...jackets in shades of pink, blue, and brown.* **5** COUNT N WITH SUPP The **shades** of something abstract are its different forms, especially when they are only slightly different from each other. *The phrase has many shades of meaning... ...various shades of socialist opinion.* **6** VB WITH 'into' When one thing **shades** into another, there is no clear division between them. *...reds shading into pinks.*

shadow /ʃædəʊ/, **shadows. 1** COUNT N A **shadow** is a dark shape made when something prevents light from reaching a surface. *...a car parked in the shadow of a tree.* **2** UNCOUNT N **Shadow** is darkness caused by light not reaching a place. *The whole canyon is in shadow.* **3** ATTRIB ADJ In Britain, the **Shadow** Cabinet consists of the leaders of the main opposition party. Each Shadow Cabinet member takes a special interest in matters of a particular kind. *He is Shadow Secretary for Trade and Industry.*

shadowy /ʃædəʊi^1/. **1** ADJ A **shadowy** place is dark and full of shadows. *...a shadowy alcove.* **2** ATTRIB ADJ A **shadowy** figure or shape is difficult to see because the weather is dark or misty. *...the shadowy musicians in the background.* **3** ADJ You describe people and activities as **shadowy** when very little is known about them. *...the shadowy world of espionage.*

shady /ʃeɪdi^1/. **1** ADJ A **shady** place is sheltered from the sun by buildings or trees. *We found a shady spot in the park to have a rest.* **2** ADJ **Shady** trees produce a lot of shade. **3** ADJ **Shady** people and activities are slightly dishonest; an informal use. *...shady dealings.*

shaft /ʃɑːft/, **shafts. 1** COUNT N A **shaft** is a vertical passage, for example for a lift. *...the lift shaft.* **2** COUNT N A **shaft** in a machine is a rod that turns round and round to transfer movement in the machine. *...the drive shaft.* **3** COUNT N A **shaft** of light is a beam of light.

shaggy /ʃægi^1/. ADJ **Shaggy** hair or fur is long and untidy. *...his shaggy, unkempt beard... ...shaggy sheep.*

shake /ʃeɪk/, **shakes, shaking, shook** /ʃʊk/, **shaken** /ʃeɪk^{ə}n/. **1** VB WITH OBJ If you **shake** someone or something, you move them quickly backwards and forwards or up and down. *He awakened to find himself being shaken roughly by his father... The wind shook white petals from the tree.* Also COUNT N *She gave her skirts a vigorous shake.* **2** VB If something **shakes,** it moves from side to side or up and down with quick, small movements. *The earth shook and the sky darkened... He was shaking with laughter.* **3** VB If your voice **is shaking,** you cannot control it because you are nervous or angry. *His eyes were wild and his voice shook.* **4** VB WITH OBJ If something **shakes** you, it makes you feel shocked and upset. *My mother's death had shaken him dreadfully.* ♦ **shaken** ADJ *I was badly shaken. I had never had a crash before.*
PHRASES ● If you **shake hands** with someone or **shake** their **hand,** you hold their right hand in your own when you are meeting them, saying goodbye, congratulating them, or showing friendship. *Elijah and I shook hands and said good night... Someone shook my hand.* ● If you **shake** your **head,** you move it from side to side in order to say 'no'.

shake off. PHR VB If you **shake off** someone or something that you do not want, you manage to get away from them or get rid of them. *It had taken Franklin several hours to shake off the police.*

shake-up, shake-ups. COUNT N A **shake-up** is a major set of changes in an organization or system. *Many were eager for a shake-up in the two-party system.*

shaky /ʃeɪki^1/, **shakier, shakiest. 1** ADJ If you are **shaky,** you are shaking or feeling weak because you are frightened, shocked, or ill. *I was nervous and a bit shaky.* ♦ **shakily** ADV *The man stood up shakily.* **2** ADJ Something that is described as **shaky** is rather weak or not very good. *After a shaky start the orchestra grew more confident... ...a company with very shaky financial prospects.*

shall /ʃə^{3}l/. The usual spoken form of 'shall not' is 'shan't'. **1** MODAL You use **shall** when you are referring to something that you intend to do or that will happen to you in the future. *I shall get angry in a moment... I shan't let you go... We probably shan't sleep much.* **2** MODAL If you say that something **shall** happen, you are saying that it must happen and therefore it will happen; a formal use. *It must be done and therefore it shall be done... You're here to enjoy yourself, and enjoy yourself you shall... No more drink shall be drunk tonight.* **3** MODAL You use **shall** in questions when you are asking for advice. *Whatever shall I do?... Where shall we go for our drink?* **4** MODAL You also use **shall** in questions when you are making a suggestion. *Shall I shut the door?... Shall we go and see a film?... We'll go forward a little more, shall we?*

shallow /ʃæləʊ/, **shallower, shallowest; shallows. 1** ADJ A **shallow** hole, container, or layer of something measures only a short distance from the top to the bottom. *...a shallow bowl... ...shallow water.* **2** ADJ A **shallow** person, idea, or activity does not show or involve serious or careful thought; used showing disapproval. *I was too young and shallow to understand love... This kind of life is shallow and trivial.* **3** ADJ If your breathing is **shallow,** you take only a small amount of air into your lungs at each breath. **4** PLURAL N The **shallows** are the shallow part of an area of water. *Thousands of little fish swim in the shallows.*

sham /ʃæm/, **shams.** COUNT N Something that is a **sham** is not what it seems to be; used showing disapproval. *Their independence is a sham.* Also ATTRIB ADJ *...a sham fight.*

shambles /ʃæmb^{ə}lz/. SING N If a place, event, or situation is a **shambles,** everything is in disorder; an informal use. *The rehearsal was a shambles.*

shame /ʃeɪm/, **shames, shaming, shamed. 1** UNCOUNT N **Shame** is an uncomfortable feeling that you have when you know that you have done something wrong or embarrassing, or when you know that someone close to you has. *The memory fills me with shame... Simon lowered his face in shame.* **2** UNCOUNT N If someone brings **shame** on you, they make other people lose their respect for you. *Don't bring shame on the family.* **3** VB WITH OBJ If something **shames** you, it causes you to feel shame. *It shamed him to know that his father had behaved in such a way.* **4** VB WITH OBJ AND ADJUNCT If you **shame** someone into doing something, you force them to do it by making them feel ashamed not to. *Father was shamed into helping them.* **5** SING N If you say that something is **a shame,** you mean that you are sorry or sad about it. *It's a shame he didn't come too... What a shame. Never mind... It's a shame to waste all this food.*

shameful /ʃeɪmfʊl/. ADJ **Shameful** behaviour is so bad that the people who behave in that way ought to be ashamed. *It shows a shameful lack of concern.* ♦ **shamefully** ADV *The government have shamefully neglected this area.*

shameless /ʃeɪmlɪ^{2}s/. ADJ Someone who is **shameless** behaves very badly, but is not ashamed of their behaviour. *She is shameless!* ♦ **shamelessly** ADV *Matty flatters me shamelessly.*

shampoo /ʃæmpuː/, **shampoos.** MASS N **Shampoo** is a soapy liquid that you use for washing your hair.

shan't /ʃɑːnt/. **Shan't** is the usual spoken form of 'shall not'.

shanty town /ʃænti^1 taʊn/, **shanty towns.** COUNT N A **shanty town** is a large collection of rough huts which people live in.

shape /ʃeɪp/, **shapes, shaping, shaped. 1** COUNT N OR UNCOUNT N The **shape** of something is the form or pattern of its outline, for example whether it is round or square. *Bear Island is triangular in shape... You can spin-dry this sweater and it will still retain its shape... ...a huge animal the size and shape of a rhinoceros.* **2** COUNT N A **shape** is something which has a definite form, for example a circle, square, or triangle. *...patterns created from geometric shapes.* **3** COUNT N A **shape** is also an object or person that you cannot see clearly. *One could just distinguish a slim shape in a short white dress.* **4** SING N WITH POSS The **shape** of something such as a plan or organization is its structure and size. *...developments which may alter the future course and shape of industry.* **5** VB WITH OBJ If you **shape** an object, you cause it to have a particular shape. *He began to shape the dough into rolls.* **6** VB WITH OBJ To **shape** a thing or activity means to cause it to develop in a particular way. *It was the Greeks who shaped the thinking of Western man.*
PHRASES ● If someone or something is **in good shape,** they are in a good condition or state of health. ● You use **in the shape of** before mentioning exactly what you are referring to, after referring to it in a general way. *He was convinced that the end of the world was at hand in the shape of a nuclear holocaust.*

shape up. PHR VB The way that someone or something **is shaping up** is the way that they are developing. *The new recruits are shaping up quite well.*

shaped /ʃeɪpt/. ADJ Something that is **shaped** in a particular way has the shape indicated. *...a chair shaped like a saddle... ...weirdly shaped trees.*

-shaped. SUFFIX **-shaped** is added to nouns to form adjectives that describe the shape of an object. *...an egg-shaped face... ...a star-shaped card.*

shapeless /ʃeɪplɪ^{2}s/. ADJ Something that is **shapeless** does not have a definite or attractive shape. *...shapeless pyjamas.*

shapely /ʃeɪpli^1/. ADJ A **shapely** person has an attractive figure. *She had a slim waist and shapely legs.*

share /ʃɛə/, **shares, sharing, shared. 1** RECIP VB If you **share** something with another person, you both use it, do it, or experience it. *Ralph went upstairs to the room he shared with his brother... Let's share the petrol costs... Both partners share in rearing their family.* **2** VB WITH OBJ If you **share** a thought or piece of news with someone, you tell them about it. *He was so excited about his idea that he felt he had to share it with someone.* **3** RECIP VB If two people or things **share** a particular quality, characteristic, or idea, they both have it. *I share your concern... This was a taste which he shared with Guy.* **4** SING N If you have or do a **share** of something, you have or do part of it. *...a campaign for parents to have a share in discussing school policy... An increasing share of the work is handed over to computers.* **5** COUNT N The **shares** of a company are the equal parts into which its ownership is divided. People can buy shares in a company as an investment. *The firm's shares jumped 10p to 114p.*

share out. PHR VB If you **share** something **out,** you give each person in a group an equal or fair part of it.

shareholder /ʃɛəhəʊldə/, **shareholders.** COUNT N A **shareholder** is a person who owns shares in a company.

shark /ʃɑːk/, **sharks.** COUNT N **Sharks** are very large fish with sharp teeth that sometimes attack people.

sharp /ʃɑːp/, **sharper, sharpest; sharps. 1** ADJ A **sharp** object has a very thin edge or a very pointed end and so it can easily cut or pierce things. *Cut it away with a sharp knife... ...small, sharp teeth.* **2** ADJ A **sharp** picture, outline, or distinction is clear and easy to see or understand. *...sharp, fresh footprints in the snow... We try to draw a sharp dividing line between Civil Service and Government.* ♦ **sharply** ADV *His clothes contrast sharply with Gaspar's.* **3** ADJ Someone who is **sharp** is quick to notice, hear, or understand things. *You've got to be sharp to get ahead... His sharp eyes would never miss it.* **4** ADJ A **sharp** change is sudden and very big. *...sharp food-price increases.* ♦ **sharply** ADV *Sales of the car have risen sharply in recent weeks.* **5** ADJ A **sharp** action or movement is quick and firm. *She received a sharp clout on the head... With his finger and thumb he gave it a sharp turn.* ♦ **sharply** ADV *Both birds turned their heads sharply at the sound.* **6** ADJ If someone says something in a **sharp** way, they say it suddenly and rather firmly or angrily. *A sharp order came through his headphones.* ♦ **sharply** ADV *'Don't talk nonsense,' she said sharply.* **7** ADJ A **sharp** sound is very short, sudden, and quite loud. *...the sharp crack of a twig.* **8** ADJ **Sharp** pain or cold hurts a lot. *His blistered foot at that moment caused him a sharp pang.* **9** ADJ Food that has a **sharp** taste is slightly sour and refreshing. *...the sharp, pure taste of gooseberries.* **10** ADV If something happens at a certain time **sharp,** it happens at exactly that time. *His train came in at eight sharp.* **11** COUNT N OR ADJ AFTER N In music, a **sharp** is the note a semitone higher than the note described by the same letter. It is usually represented by the symbol (113) after the letter. *...C sharp.* **12** ADV OR ADJ If a musical note is played or sung **sharp,** it is slightly higher in pitch than it should be.

sharpen /ʃɑːp^{ə}n/, **sharpens, sharpening, sharpened. 1** VB WITH OBJ If you **sharpen** an object, you make its edge very thin or you make its end pointed. *Roger sharpened a stick at both ends.* **2** ERG VB If your senses or abilities **sharpen** or **are sharpened,** you become quicker at thinking or at noticing things. *His eyes and instincts sharpened as he saw the fort in the distance... Generations of urban living had sharpened their wits.* **3** ERG VB If your voice **sharpens,** you begin to speak more angrily and quickly. *'Who told you?' Her voice had sharpened a little... Fear and urgency sharpened Sarah's voice.* **4** ERG VB If something **sharpens** disagreements or differences between people, it makes them greater; a formal use. *This sharpened the conflict between them... Tension in society has increased and sharpened.*

sharpener /ʃɑːp^{ə}nə/, **sharpeners.** COUNT N A pencil **sharpener** is a device for sharpening pencils.

shatter /ʃætə/, **shatters, shattering, shattered. 1** ERG VB If something **shatters,** it breaks into a lot of small pieces. *The vase fell from her hand and shattered on the floor... I shattered the glass.* **2** VB WITH OBJ If something **shatters** your beliefs or hopes, it destroys them. **3** PASSIVE VB If someone **is shattered** by an event, it shocks and upsets them. *My father was shattered by the news.*

shattered /ʃætəd/. **1** PRED ADJ If you are **shattered,** you are shocked and upset. *When Harris died, Dean was shattered.* **2** PRED ADJ You can also say that you are **shattered** when you are very tired; an informal use. *I'm shattered after a day's work.*

shattering /ʃætə^{r}rɪŋ/. ADJ Something that is **shattering** shocks and upsets you, or makes you very tired. *...a shattering experience.*

shave /ʃeɪv/, **shaves, shaving, shaved. 1** VB When a man **shaves,** he cuts hair from his face using a razor. *When he had shaved and dressed, he went down to the kitchen.* Also COUNT N *He had a shave and a bath.*

2 VB WITH OBJ When someone **shaves** a part of their body, they cut all the hair from it using a razor. 3 PHRASE If something was a **close shave,** there was nearly an accident or a disaster but it was avoided; an old-fashioned use.

shaven /ʃeɪvə^{0}n/. ADJ If a part of someone's body is **shaven,** it has been shaved. *His hair was very short, the back of his neck shaven.* ● See also **clean-shaven.**

shaver /ʃeɪvə/, **shavers.** COUNT N A **shaver** is an electric tool used for shaving hair.

shaving /ʃeɪvɪŋ/, **shavings.** 1 MOD You use **shaving** to describe things that people use when they shave. *...a shaving brush.* 2 COUNT N **Shavings** are small, very thin pieces cut from something such as wood.

shawl /ʃɔːl/, **shawls.** COUNT N A **shawl** is a large piece of woollen cloth worn over a woman's shoulders or head, or wrapped around a baby to keep it warm.

she /ʃiː/. **She** is used as the subject of a verb. 1 PRON You use **she** to refer to a woman or girl who has already been mentioned, or whose identity is known. *'So long,' Mary said as she passed Miss Saunders... Ask her if she can do something with them.* 2 PRON You can use **she** to refer to a nation. *Britain is a poor nation now, and she would do well to remember this.* 3 PRON You can also use **she** to refer to a ship, car, or other vehicle. *She does 0 to 60 in 10 seconds.*

sheaf /ʃiːf/, **sheaves** /ʃiːvz/. 1 COUNT N A **sheaf** of papers is a bundle of them. *...a thick sheaf of letters.* 2 COUNT N A **sheaf** of corn is a bundle of ripe corn plants tied together.

shear /ʃɪə/, **shears, shearing, sheared, shorn** /ʃɔːn/. The past participle can be **sheared** or **shorn.** 1 VB WITH OBJ To **shear** a sheep means to cut off its wool. 2 PLURAL N A pair of **shears** is a garden tool like a large pair of scissors. 3 See also **shorn.**

sheath /ʃiːθ/, **sheaths.** 1 COUNT N A **sheath** is a covering for the blade of a knife. 2 COUNT N A **sheath** is also a rubber covering for a man's penis that is used as a contraceptive.

sheathe /ʃiːð/, **sheathes, sheathing, sheathed.** VB WITH OBJ When you **sheathe** a knife, you put it in its sheath.

sheaves /ʃiːvz/. **Sheaves** is the plural of **sheaf.**

shed /ʃed/, **sheds, shedding. Shed** is used in the present tense, and is the past tense and past participle. 1 COUNT N A **shed** is a small building used for storing things. *...the coal shed.* 2 VB WITH OBJ When an animal **sheds** hair or skin, some of its hair or skin drops off. When a tree **sheds** its leaves, its leaves fall off in the autumn. 3 VB WITH OBJ To **shed** something also means to get rid of it; a literary use. *I shed all my restraint.* 4 VB WITH OBJ If a lorry **sheds** its load, the goods it is carrying fall onto the road.

PHRASES ● To **shed tears** means to cry. ● To **shed blood** means to kill people in a violent way. ● If something **sheds light on** a problem, it makes it easier to understand.

she'd /ʃiːd/. **She'd** is the usual spoken form of 'she had', especially when 'had' is an auxiliary verb. **She'd** is also a spoken form of 'she would'. *It was too late. She'd done it... She said she'd come by train.*

sheen /ʃiːn/. SING N WITH SUPP If the surface of something has a **sheen,** it has a smooth and gentle brightness. *...beautiful, long hair with a silky sheen.*

sheep /ʃiːp/. **Sheep** is the singular and plural. COUNT N A **sheep** is a farm animal with a thick woolly coat. Sheep are kept for their wool or meat. *...a flock of sheep.* ● See also **black sheep.**

sheepish /ʃiːpɪʃ/. ADJ If you look **sheepish,** you look embarrassed because you feel foolish. *He gave me a sheepish grin.* ♦ **sheepishly** ADV *Jo looked up at his father sheepishly.*

sheer /ʃɪə/. 1 ATTRIB ADJ **Sheer** means not mixed with anything else; often used for emphasis. *The eighth floor of the hotel was sheer luxury... Many of the audience walked out through sheer boredom.* 2 ADJ A **sheer** cliff or drop is completely vertical. *...a gorge with sheer rock sides.* 3 ADJ **Sheer** is used to describe silk or other material which is very thin and delicate.

sheet /ʃiːt/, **sheets.** 1 COUNT N A **sheet** is a large rectangular piece of cloth, used with blankets or a duvet on a bed. 2 COUNT N A **sheet** of paper is a rectangular piece of it. *He handed a typewritten sheet to Karen.* 3 COUNT N A **sheet** of glass, metal, or wood is a large, flat, thin piece of it.

sheikh /ʃeɪk/, **sheikhs;** also spelled **sheik.** COUNT N A **sheikh** is an Arab chief or ruler.

shelf /ʃelf/, **shelves** /ʃelvz/. COUNT N A **shelf** is a flat piece of wood, metal, or glass fixed to a wall or inside a cupboard. Shelves are used for keeping things on. *There were a lot of books on the shelves.*

shell /ʃel/, **shells, shelling, shelled.** 1 COUNT N The **shell** of an egg or nut is the hard covering which surrounds it. *...coconut shells.* 2 COUNT N The **shell** of a tortoise, snail, or crab is the hard, protective covering on its back. 3 COUNT N A **shell** is also a hard covering surrounding a small, soft sea creature; also used of the covering without the creature in it. *...a handkerchief full of shells which my sister had collected... ...oyster shells.* 4 VB WITH OBJ If you **shell** peas or nuts, you remove their covering. 5 COUNT N You can refer to the frame of a building as a **shell.** *...the burned-out shell that had once been their home.* 6 COUNT N A **shell** is also a metal container filled with explosives that is fired from a large gun. *Arnold had his leg smashed when a shell hit the truck he was driving.* 7 VB WITH OBJ To **shell** a place means to fire explosive shells at it. *They continued to shell towns on the northern coast.*

she'll /ʃiːl/. **She'll** is the usual spoken form of 'she will'. *I hope she'll be all right.*

shellfish /ʃelfɪʃ/. **Shellfish** is the singular and plural. COUNT N A **shellfish** is a small creature with a shell that lives in the sea.

shelter /ʃeltə/, **shelters, sheltering, sheltered.** 1 COUNT N A **shelter** is a small building or covered place constructed to protect people from bad weather or danger. 2 UNCOUNT N If a place provides **shelter,** it provides protection from bad weather or danger. *He found shelter in caves... We waited in the shelter of the trees.* 3 VB If you **shelter** in a place, you stay there and are protected from bad weather or danger. *It is natural to shelter from a storm.* 4 VB WITH OBJ If a place or thing is **sheltered** by something, it is protected by it from wind and rain. *This wide alley is sheltered by plane trees.* 5 VB WITH OBJ If you **shelter** someone, you hide them when people are looking for them. *Some villagers are prepared to shelter wanted men.*

sheltered /ʃeltəd/. 1 ADJ A **sheltered** place is protected from wind and rain. *I lay down in the warmest and most sheltered spot I could find.* 2 ADJ If you have a **sheltered** life, you do not experience things which other people experience, especially unpleasant things. *We lived a sheltered life in our Irish village.* 3 ATTRIB ADJ **Sheltered** accommodation is designed for old or handicapped people. It allows them to be independent but also provides care when they need it. *...a sheltered housing scheme.*

shelve /ʃelv/, **shelves, shelving, shelved.** 1 VB WITH OBJ If you **shelve** a plan, you decide not to continue with it for a while. *The project seems to have been shelved for the moment.* 2 **Shelves** is the plural of **shelf.**

shelving /ʃelvɪŋ/. UNCOUNT N **Shelving** is a set of shelves. *...layers of glass shelving.*

shepherd /ʃepəd/, **shepherds, shepherding, shepherded.** 1 COUNT N A **shepherd** is a person whose job is to look after sheep. 2 VB WITH OBJ If you **shepherd** someone somewhere, you accompany them there to make sure that they go to the right place. *I shepherded them towards the lobby.*

sheriff /ʃerɪf/, **sheriffs.** COUNT N In the United States, a **sheriff** is a person who is elected to make sure that the law is obeyed in a particular county.

sherry /ʃeri^{1}/, **sherries.** MASS N **Sherry** is a strong alcoholic drink made from grapes. It is usually drunk before a meal.

she's /ʃiːz/. **She's** is the usual spoken form of 'she is', especially when 'has' is an auxiliary verb. *She's Swedish... She's gone back to Montrose.*

shield /ʃiːld/, **shields, shielding, shielded.** 1 COUNT N A **shield** is a large piece of metal or leather which soldiers used to carry to protect their bodies while they were fighting. 2 VB WITH OBJ To **shield** someone from danger means to protect them by being between them and the danger. *Her parasol was propped up behind her to shield her from the sun.*

shift /ʃɪft/, **shifts, shifting, shifted.** 1 ERG VB If you **shift** something somewhere, you move it there. *He shifted the chair closer to the bed... Muller's eyes shifted to the telephone.* 2 COUNT N WITH SUPP A **shift** in a situation or in someone's opinion is a slight change. *You may detect a shift of emphasis... ...a radical shift in public opinion.* 3 ERG VB If a situation or opinion **shifts,** it changes slightly. *The talk shifted to our neighbour's land... ...shifting the balance of financial control.* 4 COUNT N A **shift** is also one of the set periods of time during which people work, for example in a factory. *He had chosen the midnight to 8 shift.*

shifty /ʃɪfti^{1}/. ADJ Someone who looks **shifty** gives the impression of being deceitful. *...a man with small shifty eyes.*

shilling /ʃɪlɪŋ/, **shillings.** COUNT N A **shilling** was a unit of money equivalent to 5p which was used in Britain until 1971.

shimmer /ʃɪmə/, **shimmers, shimmering, shimmered.** VB If something **shimmers,** it shines with a faint, unsteady light. *I sat looking at the sea shimmering in the moonlight.*

shin /ʃɪn/, **shins, shinning, shinned.** COUNT N Your **shin** is the front part of your leg between your knee and ankle.

shin up. PHR VB If you **shin up** a tree or a pole, you climb it quickly and easily. *I shinned up a lamp post to get a better view.*

shine /ʃaɪn/, **shines, shining, shone** /ʃɒn/. 1 VB When the sun or a light **shines,** it gives out bright light. 2 VB WITH OBJ If you **shine** a torch or lamp somewhere, you point its light there. *I asked him to shine the headlight on the door.* 3 VB Something that **shines** is very bright, usually because it is reflecting light. ♦ **shining** ADJ *...rows of shining glasses.* 4 VB If someone's eyes **shine,** they look very happy and excited. 5 VB Someone who **shines** at a skill or activity does it very well. *He shines at amateur theatricals.*

shingle /ʃɪŋgə^{0}l/. UNCOUNT N **Shingle** consists of small stones on the shore of a sea or river. *The beach is a mixture of sand and shingle.*

shiny /ʃaɪni^{1}/. ADJ **Shiny** things are bright and reflect light. *...shiny black shoes... ...shiny cars.*

ship /ʃɪp/, **ships, shipping, shipped.** 1 COUNT N A **ship** is a large boat which carries passengers or cargo. *The ship was due to sail the following morning... They were sent home by ship.* 2 VB WITH OBJ If people or things **are shipped** somewhere, they are sent there by ship or by some other means of transport. *They had their luggage shipped to Nigeria.*

shipping /ʃɪpɪŋ/. UNCOUNT N **Shipping** refers to a particular group of ships. *Nearly a fifth of the shipping had been sunk.*

shipwreck /ʃɪprek/, **shipwrecks, shipwrecked.** 1 COUNT N When there is a **shipwreck,** a ship is destroyed in an accident at sea. *The whole family perished in a shipwreck.* 2 COUNT N A **shipwreck** is also a ship which has been destroyed in a shipwreck. *Treasure has sometimes been found in shipwrecks.* 3 PASSIVE VB When someone **is shipwrecked,** their ship is destroyed but they survive and reach land. *He was shipwrecked off the lonely island of Iona.*

shipyard /ʃɪpjɑːd/, **shipyards.** COUNT N A **shipyard** is a place where ships are built and repaired.

shirk /ʃɜːk/, **shirks, shirking, shirked.** VB WITH OR WITHOUT OBJ If someone **shirks** a job or task, they avoid doing it; used showing disapproval. *It was a job everyone shirked whenever possible... He worked as he had always done, never shirking and never complaining.*

shirt /ʃɜːt/, **shirts.** COUNT N A **shirt** is a piece of clothing worn on the upper part of your body. Shirts usually have a collar, sleeves, and buttons down the front.

shirtsleeves /ʃɜːtsliːvz/. PHRASE If a man is **in** his **shirtsleeves,** he is wearing a shirt but not a jacket. *I lay on the bed in my shirtsleeves.*

shiver /ʃɪvə/, **shivers, shivering, shivered.** VB When you **shiver,** your body shakes slightly because you are cold or frightened. *I stood shivering with cold on the doorstep.* Also COUNT N *I could not repress a shiver whenever I thought of him.*

shoal /ʃəʊl/, **shoals.** COUNT N A **shoal** of fish is a large group of them swimming together.

shock /ʃɒk/, **shocks, shocking, shocked.** 1 COUNT N If you have a **shock,** you suddenly have an unpleasant or surprising experience. *She got such a shock that she dropped the milk... I recovered gradually from the shock of her death... It was a shock to discover that they were English.* 2 UNCOUNT N **Shock** is a person's emotional and physical condition when something frightening or upsetting has happened to them. *Numb with shock, she stood watching as they took his body away.* 3 UNCOUNT N In medicine, **shock** is a serious physical condition in which your blood cannot circulate properly, for example because you have had a bad injury. *She was taken to hospital suffering from shock.* 4 COUNT N OR UNCOUNT N A **shock** is also a slight movement in something when it is hit by something else. *This padding should absorb any sudden shocks.* 5 VB WITH OBJ If something **shocks** you, it makes you feel very upset. *She was deeply shocked by her husband's death.* 6 VB WITH OR WITHOUT OBJ You can also say that something **shocks** you when it upsets or offends you because you think it is rude or morally wrong. *Are you easily shocked?* ♦ **shocked** ADJ *Don't look so shocked.* 7 COUNT N A **shock** of hair is a thick mass of it; a literary use. *He was tall and handsome with a shock of hair falling over his forehead.*

shocking /ʃɒkɪŋ/. 1 ADJ Something that is **shocking** makes people upset or angry, because they think it is morally wrong. *It was shocking how badly paid these young girls were... ...the most shocking book of its time.* 2 ADJ **Shocking** also means very bad; an informal use. *The paintwork was really shocking... I'm shocking at spelling.*

shod /ʃɒd/. **Shod** is the past tense and past participle of **shoe.**

shoddy /ʃɒdi^{1}/. ADJ Something that is **shoddy** has been done or made carelessly or badly. *It is up to the teacher not to accept shoddy work... ...shoddy goods.*

shoe /ʃuː/, **shoes, shoeing, shod** /ʃɒd/. 1 COUNT N Shoes are objects worn on your feet, usually over socks or stockings. Shoes cover most of your foot but not your ankle. *She needs a new pair of shoes.* 2 VB WITH OBJ To **shoe** a horse means to fix horseshoes onto its hooves.

shoelace /ʃuːleɪs/, **shoelaces.** COUNT N **Shoelaces** are long, narrow cords used to fasten shoes. *He stopped to tie up his shoelace.*

shoestring /ʃuːstrɪŋ/. PHRASE If something is done **on a shoestring**, it is done using very little money. *...budgeting for a family on a shoestring.*

shone /ʃɒn/. **Shone** is the past tense and past participle of **shine.**

shoo /ʃuː/, **shoos, shooing, shooed.** 1 VB WITH OBJ AND ADJUNCT If you **shoo** an animal or a person somewhere, you make them go there by waving your hands or arms at them. *She shooed the birds in the direction of the open window.* 2 CONVENTION You say **'Shoo!'** to an animal to make it go away.

shook /ʃʊk/. **Shook** is the past tense of **shake.**

shoot /ʃuːt/, **shoots, shooting, shot** /ʃɒt/. 1 VB To **shoot** means to fire a bullet from a gun. *We were told to shoot first and ask questions later.* 2 VB WITH OBJ OR REFL VB To **shoot** a person or animal means to kill or injure them by firing a gun at them. *He shot his wife and then shot himself.* 3 VB WITH OBJ If you **shoot** an arrow, you fire it from a bow. 4 ERG VB WITH ADJUNCT To **shoot** in a particular direction means to move in that direction quickly and suddenly. *She shot back into the room... He shot out his hand and stopped the child from falling.* 5 VB WITH OBJ AND ADJUNCT If you **shoot** a glance at someone, you look at them quickly and briefly; a literary use. *He shot a suspicious glare at me.* 6 VB WITH OBJ When a film **is shot,** it is photographed using film cameras. *Most of the film was shot in Spain.* 7 COUNT N A **shoot** is also a plant that is beginning to grow, or a new part growing from a plant or tree. *A few tender shoots had started to appear.* 8 See also **shot.** ● to **shoot on sight:** see **sight.**

shoot down. PHR VB If someone **shoots down** an aeroplane or helicopter, they make it fall to the ground by hitting it with a bullet or missile.

shoot up. PHR VB If something **shoots up,** it grows or increases very quickly. *The inflation rate shot up from 30% to 48%.*

shooting /ʃuːtɪŋ/, **shootings.** 1 COUNT N When there is a **shooting,** someone is killed or injured by being shot with a gun. *The police arrived fifteen minutes after the shooting.* 2 UNCOUNT N **Shooting** is the sport of hunting birds or animals with a gun; a British use.

shop /ʃɒp/, **shops, shopping, shopped.** 1 COUNT N A **shop** is a building or part of a building where things are sold. *Two customers came into the shop... ...a shoe shop.* 2 VB When you **shop,** you go to shops and buy things. *We allow the older girls to shop in the village without an escort... They went shopping after lunch.* ♦ **shopper** COUNT N *The city centre was crowded with shoppers.* 3 COUNT N WITH SUPP A **shop** is also a place where a particular kind of thing is made. *...metalwork shops.* 4 See also **shopping.**

shop around. PHR VB If you **shop around,** you go to different shops and compare prices and quality before buying something.

shop assistant, shop assistants. COUNT N A **shop assistant** is a person who works in a shop selling things to customers.

shop floor. SING N The **shop floor** refers to all the workers in a factory, especially in contrast to the management. *There should be participation in decisions made on the shop floor.*

shopkeeper /ʃɒpkiːpə/, **shopkeepers.** COUNT N A **shopkeeper** is a person who owns a small shop.

shoplifting /ʃɒplɪftɪŋ/. UNCOUNT N **Shoplifting** is stealing from a shop by walking round the shop and hiding things in your bag or clothes.

shopping /ʃɒpɪŋ/. UNCOUNT N Your **shopping** consists of things that you have just bought from shops. *She put her shopping away in the kitchen.*

shopping centre, shopping centres. COUNT N A **shopping centre** is an area in a town where a lot of shops have been built close together.

shop-soiled. ADJ **Shop-soiled** goods are slightly dirty or damaged, and are therefore sold at a lower price; a British use.

shop steward, shop stewards. COUNT N A **shop steward** is a trade union member who has been elected to represent other members.

shore /ʃɔː/, **shores, shoring, shored.** 1 COUNT N The **shore** of a sea, lake, or wide river is the land along the edge of it. *We could see the trees on the other shore.* 2 PHRASE Someone who is **on shore** is on the land rather than on a ship.

shore up. PHR VB If you **shore up** something which is becoming weak, you strengthen it. *Action is needed to shore up economic links with American suppliers.*

shoreline /ʃɔːlaɪn/, **shorelines.** COUNT N The **shoreline** is the edge of a sea, lake, or wide river.

shorn /ʃɔːn/. 1 ADJ **Shorn** grass or hair has been cut very short. *...shorn blades of grass... ...his shorn head.* 2 **Shorn** is also a past participle of **shear.**

short /ʃɔːt/, **shorter, shortest; shorts.** 1 ADJ If something lasts for a **short** time, it does not last very long. *...a short holiday... He uttered a short cry of surprise.* 2 ADJ **Short** speeches, letters, or books do not have many words or pages. *She spoke in short sentences.* 3 ADJ A **short** person is not as tall as most people. *...a short, fat man.* 4 ADJ A **short** object measures only a small amount from one end to the other. *Her hair was cut short... ...a short flight of steps.* 5 PRED ADJ WITH 'with' If you are **short** with someone, you speak impatiently and crossly to them. 6 ADJ If you have a **short** temper, you get angry easily. 7 PLURAL N **Shorts** are trousers with short legs. 8 PRED ADJ If you are **short** of something or if it is **short,** you do not have enough of it. *We're dreadfully short of staff at present... When money is short, we stick to a very careful budget.*

PHRASES ● If something is **short of** a place or amount, it has not quite reached it. *He drove up the hill and stopped the car just short of the summit... He was only a year short of fifty.* ● If something **is cut short,** it is stopped before it has finished. *The war cut short his education.* ● If you **stop short** or if something **stops** you **short,** you suddenly stop what you are doing, for example because something has surprised you. *The soldier took a few steps and then stopped short... His disapproval stopped her short.* ● If someone **stops short of** doing something, they nearly do it but do not actually do it. *He just stopped short of calling her a murderer.* ● If you are called something **for short,** it is a short version of your name. You can also say that a short version of your name is **short for** your name. *Her name was Madeleine but Celia always called her 'Maddy' for short... People usually call me 'Ferdy'. It's short for 'Ferdinand'.* ● You use the expression **in short** when you are summarizing what you have just said. *I was packing, arranging the trip, cleaning the house, and saying countless goodbyes. In short, it was a hectic week.* ● **at short notice:** see **notice.** ● **in short supply:** see **supply.**

shortage /ʃɔːtɪdʒ/, **shortages.** COUNT N If there is a **shortage** of something, there is not enough of it. *...a world shortage of fuel... ...the housing shortage.*

short-circuit, short-circuits. COUNT N If there is a **short-circuit** in an electrical system, there is a wrong connection or a damaged wire, so that electricity travels along the wrong route and damages the system or device.

shortcoming /ʃɔːtkʌmɪŋ/, **shortcomings.** COUNT N Someone's **shortcomings** are their faults or weaknesses. *You've got to realize your own shortcomings.*

short cut, short cuts. 1 COUNT N A **short cut** is a quicker way of getting somewhere. *Will you show me that short cut to Wirral Hill?* 2 COUNT N A **short cut** is also a quicker way of achieving something. *Short cuts at this stage can be costly.*

shorten /ʃɔːtəⁿn/, **shortens, shortening, shortened.** 1 VB WITH OBJ If you **shorten** an event or the length of time that something lasts, it does not last as long as it would otherwise have done. *The colonel had a plan to shorten the war.* 2 ERG VB If an object **shortens** or if you **shorten** it, it becomes smaller in length. *The back muscles contract and shorten as your leg lifts... She wondered if she could have the sleeves shortened.*

shortfall /ʃɔːtfɔːl/, **shortfalls.** COUNT N If there is a **shortfall** of something, there is not enough of it. *...a shortfall of energy supplies seems likely.*

shorthand /ʃɔːthᵒænd/. UNCOUNT N **Shorthand** is a quick way of writing which uses signs to represent words or syllables.

short-list, short-lists, short-listing, short-listed. 1 COUNT N If someone or something is on a **short-list** for a job or prize, they are one of a small group chosen from a larger group. The small group is judged again and a final decision is made about which of them is the best. 2 VB WITH OBJ If someone or something **is short-listed,** they are put on a short-list. *Her novel has been short-listed for the Booker Prize.*

short-lived. ADJ Something that is **short-lived** does not last very long. *His joy and relief were short-lived.*

shortly /ʃɔːtliⁱ/. 1 ADV If something is going to happen **shortly,** it is going to happen soon. If something happened **shortly** after something else, it happened soon after it. *She's going to London shortly... She died in an accident shortly afterwards... Shortly before dawn he had an idea.* 2 ADV If you speak to someone **shortly,** you speak in a cross or impatient way. *'You ought to be in bed,' I said shortly.*

short-sighted. 1 ADJ If you are **short-sighted,** you cannot see things properly when they are far away. 2 ADJ A **short-sighted** decision does not take account of the way things may develop in the future. *Until this short-sighted policy is reversed we shall never make any progress.*

short-tempered. ADJ **Short-tempered** people get angry very easily.

short-term. ADJ **Short-term** means happening or lasting for only a short time. *A few short-term advantages have been achieved... The artificial heart is designed only for short-term use.*

short-wave. MOD **Short-wave** is a range of radio waves used for broadcasting. *The only communication with the mainland was by short-wave radio.*

shot /ʃɒt/, **shots.** 1 **Shot** is the past tense and past participle of **shoot.** 2 COUNT N If you fire a **shot,** you fire a gun once. *One of them fired several shots at Ward.* 3 COUNT N Someone who is a good **shot** can shoot well. *He's an excellent shot.* 4 COUNT N In sport, a **shot** is the act of kicking or hitting a ball, especially in an attempt to score. *Try to hit the green with your first shot... Oh, good shot.* 5 COUNT N A **shot** is also a photograph. *I got some great shots of you.* 6 COUNT N A **shot** of a drug is an injection of it. *The doctor gave her a shot of Librium.*

PHRASES ● If you **have a shot** at something, you try to do it; an informal use. *We must have a shot at saying how large or small it is.* ● If you do something **like a shot,** you do it without any delay; an informal use. *I told him to bring her at once. He was off like a shot.*

shotgun /ʃɒtgʌn/, **shotguns.** COUNT N A **shotgun** is a gun used for shooting birds and animals which fires a lot of small metal balls at one time.

should /ʃəᵈd/. **Should** is sometimes considered to be the past tense of **shall,** but in this dictionary the two words are dealt with separately. 1 MODAL If you say that something **should** happen, you mean that it will probably happen. *We should be there by dinner time... There shouldn't be any difficulties.* 2 MODAL You also say that something **should** happen when you are saying what you think is morally right. *Crimes should be punished... These birds shouldn't be in a cage.* 3 MODAL You use **should** in questions when you are asking for advice, permission, or information. *Where should I meet you tonight?... Should I turn the light on?* 4 MODAL You also use **should** when you are giving advice; an informal use. *If you have anything really confidential I should install a safe... I shouldn't bother to copy these down.* 5 MODAL If you say that something **should have** happened, you mean that it did not happen, although it was expected to happen. *Muskie should have won by a huge margin.* 6 MODAL If you say that something **should have** happened by now, you mean that it has probably happened by now. *Dear Mom, you should have heard by now that I'm O.K.* 7 MODAL If you say that you **should** think something is true, you mean that you think it is true but you are not sure. *I should think it was about twelve years ago... He weighs, I should say, about 140 pounds.* 8 MODAL You use **should** to say politely that you would like to have something or do something. *I should like a large cutlet, please... I should like to say something about my new novel.* 9 MODAL You use **should** in 'that' clauses after some verbs and adjectives. *It was arranged that Celia should come to Switzerland.* 10 MODAL Some people use **should** in conditional clauses when they are talking about things that might happen; a formal or old-fashioned use. *If we should be seen arriving together, they would get suspicious... Should you have an accident, synthetic quilts are quite easy to wash.*

shoulder /ʃəʊldə/, **shoulders, shouldering, shouldered.** 1 COUNT N Your **shoulders** are the two parts of your body between your neck and the tops of your arms. *Sally patted me on the shoulder.* 2 VB WITH OBJ If you **shoulder** something heavy, you put it across one of your shoulders so that you can carry it more easily. *He shouldered his bundle again and set off.* 3 VB WITH OBJ If you **shoulder** the responsibility or blame for something, you accept it. *The government is expected to shoulder the responsibility for financing the project.* 4 PLURAL N You can say that a person's problems or responsibilities are on that person's **shoulders;** a literary use. *The burden of decision is placed on the shoulders of the individual.* 5 PHRASE If you **rub shoulders with** famous people, you meet them and talk to them; an informal use. 6 COUNT N OR UNCOUNT N A **shoulder** is also a joint of meat from the upper part of the front leg of an animal. *...a shoulder of lamb.*

shoulder blade, shoulder blades. COUNT N Your **shoulder blades** are the two large, flat, triangular bones in the upper part of your back, below your shoulders.

shouldn't /ʃʊdənt/. **Shouldn't** is the usual spoken form of 'should not'.

should've /ʃʊdəv/. **Should've** is the usual spoken form of 'should have', especially when 'have' is an auxiliary verb.

shout /ʃaʊt/, **shouts, shouting, shouted. 1** COUNT N A **shout** is a loud call or cry. *Excited shouts and laughter could be heard from the garden.* **2** VB OR REPORT VB If you **shout,** you speak as loudly as you can, so that you can be heard a long way away. *The children on the sand were shouting with excitement... 'Stop it!' he shouted.*

shout down. PHR VB To **shout** someone **down** means to prevent them from being heard by shouting at them. *Mr Healey was shouted down at a meeting in Birmingham.*

shove /ʃʌv/, **shoves, shoving, shoved.** VB WITH OBJ AND ADJUNCT If you **shove** someone or something, you give them a hard push. *He shoved the man through the door.* Also COUNT N *I gave him a shove in the direction of the street.*

shovel /ʃʌvə^{0}l/, **shovels, shovelling, shovelled;** spelled **shoveling, shoveled** in American English. **1** COUNT N A **shovel** is a tool like a spade, used for lifting and moving earth, coal, or snow. **2** VB WITH OBJ If you **shovel** earth, coal, or snow, you lift and move it with a shovel. *She helped us shovel the snow off the front path.* **3** VB WITH OBJ AND ADJUNCT If you **shovel** something somewhere, you push a lot of it there quickly. *They were shovelling food into their mouths.*

show /ʃəʊ/, **shows, showing, showed, shown** /ʃəʊn/. **1** REPORT VB If something **shows** that a state of affairs exists, it proves it or makes people aware of it. *The post-mortem shows that death was due to natural causes... These figures show an 8.5 per cent increase in exports.* **2** VB WITH OBJ If a picture **shows** something, it represents it. *The painting shows four athletes bathing.* **3** VB WITH OBJ If you **show** something to someone, you give it to them, take them to it, or point to it, so that they can see it. *Fetch that lovely drawing and show it to the vicar... I showed William what I had written... She showed me where to park the car.* **4** VB WITH OBJ AND ADJUNCT If you **show** someone to a room or seat, you lead them to it. *I was shown into a large apartment.* **5** VB WITH OR WITHOUT OBJ If you **show** someone how to do something, you do it yourself so that they can watch and learn how to do it. *The woman took the gun and showed how the cylinder slotted into the barrel... Show us a card game.* **6** ERG VB If something **shows,** it is visible or noticeable. *The stitching is so fine that it doesn't show at all... He had a strange fierce way of grinning that showed his teeth... Come out from there and show yourself.* **7** VB WITH OBJ If something **shows** a quality or characteristic, you can see that it has it. *Prices began to show some signs of decline in 1974... The sketch shows a lot of talent.* **8** REPORT VB If you **show** a particular attitude towards someone or something, people can see that you have it from the way you behave. *I had been taught to show respect towards my elders... This is a way in which Britain can show a readiness to help... He dared not show that he was pleased.* **9** COUNT N When you make a **show** or put on a **show** of having a feeling or attitude, you try to make people think that you have it. *...those who had made open shows of defiance... She put on a good show of looking interested.* **10** COUNT N A **show** is an entertainment at the theatre or on television consisting of several items. **11** VB WITH OBJ When a film or television programme **is shown,** it appears in a cinema or is broadcast on television. *One evening the school showed a cowboy film.* **12** COUNT N A **show** is also an exhibition. *...a flower show.*

PHRASES • If something is **on show,** it has been put in a place where it can be seen by the public. *The photographs are on show at the Museum until October.* • When something is done **for show,** it is done just to give a good impression. • What you **have to show for** your efforts is what you have achieved. *Rodin's search was over and what he had to show for it was three slim dossiers.* • A **show of hands** is a method of voting in which people raise their hands to be counted.

show off. PHR VB **1** When someone **shows off,** they try to impress people. **2** If you **show off** something that you own, you show it to a lot of people because you are proud of it. *He was eager to show off the new car.* **3** See also **show-off.**

show round. PHR VB If you **show** someone **round** a place, you go round it with them, pointing out its interesting features.

show up. PHR VB **1** To **show up** means to arrive; an informal use. *He showed up at ten o'clock the next morning.* **2** If someone who is with you **shows you up,** they behave in public in a way that embarrasses you.

show business. UNCOUNT N **Show business** is the entertainment industry of film, theatre, and television.

showcase /ʃəʊkeɪs/, **showcases.** COUNT N A **showcase** is a glass container with valuable objects inside.

showdown /ʃəʊdaʊn/, **showdowns.** COUNT N A **showdown** is a big argument or conflict which is intended to settle a dispute. *It's time for a showdown with your boss.*

shower /ʃaʊə/, **showers, showering, showered. 1** COUNT N A **shower** is a device which sprays you with water so that you can wash yourself. **2** COUNT N If you have a **shower,** you wash yourself by standing under a shower. *A hot shower and a change of clothes would be wonderful.* **3** COUNT N A **shower** is also a short period of light rain. *...a week of scattered showers.* **4** COUNT N You can refer to a lot of small objects that are falling as a **shower.** *...a shower of falling leaves.* **5** VB WITH OBJ AND ADJUNCT If you **are showered** with a lot of small objects, they are scattered onto you from above. *Suddenly the lid came off and showered him with flakes of rust.* **6** VB WITH OBJ AND ADJUNCT If you **shower** someone with presents or kisses, you give them a lot of them. *They showered each other with gifts at Christmas.*

show jumping. UNCOUNT N **Show jumping** is a sport in which horses are ridden in competitions to demonstrate their skill in jumping over walls and fences.

shown /ʃəʊn/. **Shown** is the past participle of **show.**

show-off, show-offs. COUNT N A **show-off** is someone who shows their skills or abilities in an obvious way in order to impress people; an informal use.

showroom /ʃəʊru^{4}m/, **showrooms.** COUNT N A **showroom** is a shop in which goods such as cars, furniture, or electrical appliances are displayed for sale. *The new model will be in the showrooms in a fortnight's time.*

showy /ʃəʊi^1/. ADJ Something that is **showy** is very noticeable because it is large, colourful, or bright. *...a showy bracelet and earrings.*

shrank /ʃræŋk/. **Shrank** is the past tense of **shrink.**

shrapnel /ʃræpnə^{0}l/. UNCOUNT N **Shrapnel** consists of small pieces of metal scattered from exploding bombs and shells. *...a piece of shrapnel.*

shred /ʃred/, **shreds, shredding, shredded. 1** VB WITH OBJ If you **shred** something such as food or paper, you cut or tear it into very small pieces. **2** COUNT N A **shred** of material is a small, narrow piece of it. *She took the letter and ripped it to shreds.*

shrew /ʃru:/, **shrews.** COUNT N A **shrew** is an animal like a small mouse with a pointed nose.

shrewd /ʃru:d/, **shrewder, shrewdest.** ADJ **Shrewd** people are able to understand and judge situations quickly. *He is a shrewd and sometimes ruthless adversary.* ♦ **shrewdly** ADV *She looked at him shrewdly.*

shriek /ʃri:k/, **shrieks, shrieking, shrieked.** VB If you **shriek,** you give a sudden loud scream. *She shrieked in alarm.* Also COUNT N *...a shriek of laughter.*

shrill /ʃrɪl/, **shriller, shrillest.** ADJ A **shrill** sound is high-pitched, piercing, and unpleasant to listen to. *The boys broke into shrill, excited cheering.* ♦ **shrilly** ADV *Lewis whistled shrilly.*

shrimp /ʃrɪmp/, **shrimps.** COUNT N A **shrimp** is a small shellfish with a long tail and many legs.

shrine /ʃraɪn/, **shrines.** COUNT N A **shrine** is a holy place associated with a sacred person or object. *...the shrine of St Foy.*

shrink /ʃrɪŋk/, **shrinks, shrinking, shrank** /ʃræŋk/, **shrunk** /ʃrʌŋk/. **1** ERG VB When cloth **shrinks,** it becomes smaller as a result of being washed. **2** VB WITH ADJUNCT If you **shrink** away from something, you move away because you are frightened or horrified by it. *The boys shrank away in horror.* **3** VB WITH 'from' If you **shrink** from doing something, you are reluctant to do it because you find it unpleasant. *He shrank from giving Francis a direct answer.*

shrivel /ʃrɪvə^{0}l/, **shrivels, shrivelling, shrivelled;** spelled **shriveling, shriveled** in American English. ERG VB When something **shrivels** or **shrivels** up, it becomes dry and wrinkled. *Every year we have a long dry season that shrivels and scorches plants... The seedlings had shrivelled up in the hot sun.*

shroud /ʃraʊd/, **shrouds, shrouding, shrouded. 1** COUNT N A **shroud** is a cloth used for wrapping a dead body. **2** VB WITH OBJ If something **is shrouded** in darkness or fog, it is hidden by it; a literary use. *Everything was shrouded in mist.* **3** VB WITH OBJ If something **is shrouded** in mystery, very little is known about it.

shrub /ʃrʌb/, **shrubs.** COUNT N A **shrub** is a plant like a small tree with several stems instead of a trunk.

shrubbery /ʃrʌbə^{0}ri^1/, **shrubberies.** COUNT N OR UNCOUNT N In a garden, a **shrubbery** is an area where there are a lot of shrubs.

shrug /ʃrʌg/, **shrugs, shrugging, shrugged.** VB WITH OR WITHOUT OBJ If you **shrug** your shoulders, you raise them to show that you are not interested in something or that you do not know or care about it. *'Do you mind if I wait?' I asked. Melanie shrugged. 'Please yourself.'* Also COUNT N *The man nodded with a faint shrug of his shoulders.*

shrug off. PHR VB If you **shrug** something **off,** you treat it as not important or serious. *The chairman shrugs off any criticism that their methods are not legal.*

shrunk /ʃrʌŋk/. **Shrunk** is the past participle of **shrink.**

shrunken /ʃrʌŋkə^{0}n/. ADJ Something that is **shrunken** has become smaller. *...a shrunken old man.*

shudder /ʃʌdə/, **shudders, shuddering, shuddered. 1** VB If you **shudder,** you tremble with fear or disgust. *Robert shuddered with fear... The smell made her shudder.* Also COUNT N *Max looked round him with a shudder.* **2** VB If something such as a machine **shudders,** it shakes violently. *The tank braked and shuddered to a violent halt.*

shuffle /ʃʌfə^{0}l/, **shuffles, shuffling, shuffled. 1** VB If you **shuffle** somewhere, you walk without lifting your feet properly. *He shuffled out of the room.* Also SING N *We recognized him by his distinctive walk, a kind of shuffle.* **2** VB WITH OR WITHOUT OBJ If you **shuffle** when you are sitting or standing, you move your bottom or your feet about, because you are uncomfortable or embarrassed. *I was shuffling in my seat... I shuffled my feet and mumbled.* **3** VB WITH OBJ If you **shuffle** a pack of cards, you mix them up before you begin a game.

shun /ʃʌn/, **shuns, shunning, shunned.** VB WITH OBJ If you **shun** someone or something, you deliberately avoid them. *These people shun publicity.*

shunt /ʃʌnt/, **shunts, shunting, shunted.** VB WITH OBJ If you **shunt** objects or people somewhere, you move them to a different place; an informal use. *...the sound of heavy desks being shunted across the room.*

shut /ʃʌt/, **shuts, shutting. Shut** is used in the present tense, and is the past tense and past participle. **1** ERG VB If you **shut** something, you close it. *I shut the door quietly... He goes in and the door shuts behind him.* Also PRED ADJ *The windows were all shut.* **2** VB WITH OBJ If you **shut** your eyes, you lower your eyelids so that you cannot see. *Mrs Kaul shut her eyes for a moment.* Also PRED ADJ *He lay with his eyes shut.* **3** VB WITH OBJ If you **shut** your mouth, you place your lips close together. *Mr Boggis opened his mouth, then quickly shut it again.* **4** ERG VB When a shop or other business **shuts,** it is closed and you cannot go into it until it opens again. *'What time do the shops shut?'—'Half past five.'... The troops forced merchants to shut their shops.* Also PRED ADJ *I'm afraid all the pubs will be shut.*

shut away. PHR VB If you **shut** something **away,** you keep it in a place where people cannot see it. *We have a small number of books which are shut away.*

shut down. PHR VB **1** If a factory or business **is shut down,** it closes and stops working. *His department was shut down for lack of funds... That year my grandfather had to shut down the forge.* **2** See also **shutdown.**

shut out. PHR VB **1** If you **shut** someone or something **out,** you prevent them from getting into a place. *They had covered the holes to shut out the water.* **2** If you **shut out** a thought or a feeling, you stop yourself thinking about it or feeling it. *She found it impossible to shut out the pain.*

shut up. PHR VB **1** If you **shut up,** you stop talking. *Shut up and listen.* **2** If someone **shuts** you **up,** they prevent you from talking; an informal use. *Turn the television on. That usually shuts them up.*

shutdown /ʃʌtdaʊn/, **shutdowns.** COUNT N A **shutdown** is the closing of a factory, shop, or other business. *...temporary shutdowns.*

shutter /ʃʌtə/, **shutters. 1** COUNT N **Shutters** are wooden or metal covers fitted to a window. *...an old brick house with green shutters.* **2** COUNT N The **shutter** in a camera is the part which opens to allow light through the lens when a photograph is taken.

shuttered /ʃʌtəd/. ADJ A **shuttered** window has its shutters closed. *All doors were locked and the windows closed and shuttered.*

shuttle /ʃʌtə^{0}l/, **shuttles. 1** ATTRIB ADJ A **shuttle** service is an air, bus, or train service which makes frequent journeys between two places. **2** COUNT N A **shuttle** is a plane used in a shuttle service. *He caught the nine o'clock shuttle to New York.*

shy /ʃaɪ/, **shyer, shyest; shies, shying, shied. 1** ADJ A **shy** person is nervous and uncomfortable with other people. *I've always been a bit shy... ...a shy smile.* ♦ **shyly** ADV *She smiled shyly at him.* ♦ **shyness** UNCOUNT N *I tried to overcome my shyness.* **2** PRED ADJ WITH 'of' If you are **shy** of doing something, you are unwilling to do it because you are afraid of what might happen. *Don't be shy of telling them what you think.* **3** VB When a horse **shies,** it moves suddenly because it is frightened. **4** See also **work-shy.**

Siamese twins /saɪəmi:z twɪnz/. PLURAL N **Siamese twins** are twins who are joined by a part of their bodies at birth.

sibling /sɪblɪŋ/, **siblings.** COUNT N Your **siblings** are your brothers and sisters; a formal use.

sick /sɪk/, **sicker, sickest. 1** ADJ If you are **sick,** you are ill. **2** PRED ADJ If you feel **sick,** you feel ill in your stomach, and food that you have eaten is likely to be sent out through your mouth. *Flying always makes me feel sick.* **3** PRED ADJ WITH 'of' If you are **sick** of something, you are annoyed or bored by it and want it to stop. *We're sick of sitting around waiting for something to happen.* **4** ADJ A **sick** story or joke deals with death or suffering in an unpleasantly frivolous way. *She made a rather sick joke.*
PHRASES ● If you **are sick,** food that you have eaten is sent out through your mouth. *I think I'm going to be sick.* ● If something **makes** you **sick,** it makes you feel angry or disgusted. *It makes me sick the way they waste our money.* ● If you are **worried sick,** you are extremely worried; an informal use. *He was worried sick that the factory might close.*

sicken /sɪkəⁿn/, **sickens, sickening, sickened.** VB WITH OBJ If something **sickens** you, it makes you feel disgusted. *The young officers were sickened by the greed of their generals.* ♦ **sickening** ADJ *The food smelled sickening.*

sickle /sɪkəⁿl/, **sickles.** COUNT N A **sickle** is a tool with a short handle and a curved blade that is used for cutting grass and grain crops.

sickly /sɪkli¹/, **sicklier, sickliest. 1** ADJ A **sickly** person is weak and often ill. *He was a sickly and ineffective man.* **2** ADJ **Sickly** things are unpleasant to smell or look at. *...a musty, sickly smell.*

sickness /sɪknɪ²s/, **sicknesses. 1** UNCOUNT N **Sickness** is the state of being ill or unhealthy. *...people who are not working because of sickness or unemployment... ...radiation sickness.* **2** UNCOUNT N **Sickness** is also a condition in which you feel ill in your stomach and in which food that you have eaten is sent out through your mouth. *The disease causes sickness and diarrhoea.* **3** COUNT N A **sickness** is particular disease. *The nuns at the convent attend to small sicknesses.* **4** See also **morning sickness.**

side /saɪd/, **sides, siding, sided. 1** COUNT N The **side** of something is a position to the left or right of it. *A taxi bumped into us from the side... Standing on either side of him were two younger men... I sat down by her side.* **2** COUNT N Something that is on one **side** of a boundary or barrier is in one of the two areas that the boundary or barrier separates. *We were told of threatening developments on the other side of the border.* **3** COUNT N Your **sides** are the parts of your body from your armpits down to your hips. *She lay on her side with her back to me.* **4** COUNT N The **sides** of an object are the outside surfaces that are not the top or the bottom. *The box opens on this side... Hogan walked round to the side of the car and unlocked the door... She was kneeling by the side of the bed.* Also ATTRIB ADJ *Smithy left the side door open.* **5** COUNT N The **sides** of an area or surface are its two halves or its edges. *Blood was streaming from one side of her face... ...the wrong side of the road... A hedge surrounds my garden on three sides.* **6** COUNT N The **sides** of something flat, such as a piece of paper, are its two flat surfaces. *What does the leaflet say on the other side?* **7** COUNT N The **sides** of a hill or valley are the sloping parts between its top and bottom. *We were driving up the side of a mountain.* **8** ATTRIB ADJ A **side** road is a less important road leading off an important one. *I slipped away down a side street.* **9** COUNT N You can call the two groups of people involved in an argument, war, or game the two **sides** of that argument, war, or game. *The argument was settled to the satisfaction of both sides.* **10** COUNT N The two **sides** of an argument are the opposing points of view. *She only ever hears his side of things.* **11** COUNT N A particular **side** of something is one aspect of it. *The producers wanted to emphasize the political side of the play... There is something distasteful about this side of her character.* **12** COUNT N The two **sides** of your family are your mother's family and your father's family. *My grandparents on my father's side were both Polish.*
PHRASES ● If you put something **to one side,** you keep it separate from other things, so that you can deal with it later. ● If two people are **side by side,** they are next to each other. ● If someone stays **at your side** or **by your side,** they stay near you and support or comfort you. *He wanted to live forever by her side.* ● If you **take sides** or **take** someone's **side,** you support someone who is involved in an argument. *I wouldn't want anyone to take my side against Tom.* ● If you are **on** someone's **side,** you are supporting them in an argument or a war. *Whose side are you on?* ● If you do something **on the side,** you do it in addition to your main work. *If the farm prospers, we could start a little business on the side.* ● You can use **side** to give your opinion about the size or quality of something. For example, if something is **on the large side,** it is slightly too large. *The food is excellent though on the expensive side.* ● If you keep **on the right side of**

someone, you try to please them and avoid annoying them. ● to **err on the side of** something: see **err.**
side with. PHR VB If you **side with** someone, you support them in an argument. *The daughters sided with their mothers.*

sideboard /saɪdbɔːd/, **sideboards.** COUNT N A **sideboard** is a long, low cupboard, in which plates and glasses are kept.

side-effect, side-effects. 1 COUNT N The **side-effects** of a drug are the effects it has on you in addition to its function of curing illness or pain. *This type of aspirin can have appalling side-effects.* **2** COUNT N The **side-effects** of a situation are the things that happen in addition to the main consequences, without being planned. *One side-effect of the crisis could be that she loses her job.*

sidelight /saɪdlaɪt/, **sidelights.** COUNT N The **sidelights** on a vehicle are the small lights at the front.

sideline /saɪdlaɪn/, **sidelines. 1** COUNT N A **sideline** is an extra job you do in addition to your main job. *Fishing is both a relaxing hobby and a money-producing sideline.* **2** COUNT N The **sidelines** of a tennis court or football pitch are the lines marking the long sides. **3** PLURAL N If you are on the **sidelines** in a situation, you are not involved in it; a literary use. *I prefer to stand on the sidelines and watch.*

sidelong /saɪdlɒŋ/. ADV OR ATTRIB ADJ If you look at someone **sidelong** or if you give them **sidelong** looks, you look at them out of the corner of your eyes. *Ralph looked at him sidelong and said nothing... Terry and I exchanged sidelong glances.*

sidestep /saɪdstep/, **sidesteps, sidestepping, sidestepped.** VB WITH OBJ If you **sidestep** a problem, you avoid dealing with it. *...a book that does not sidestep essential questions.*

sidetracked /saɪdtrækt/. PASSIVE VB If you are **sidetracked,** you forget what you are supposed to be doing and start doing something else. *I told him how I'd been sidetracked by Mr Starke.*

sidewalk /saɪdwɔːk/, **sidewalks.** COUNT N A **sidewalk** is the same as a pavement; an American use.

sideways /saɪdweɪz/. ADV OR ATTRIB ADJ **Sideways** means from or to the side of something or someone. *Flames blew out sideways from the fire... ...a sideways glance.*

siding /saɪdɪŋ/, **sidings.** COUNT N A **siding** is a short railway track beside the main tracks for engines and carriages which are not being used.

sidle /saɪdəⁿl/, **sidles, sidling, sidled.** VB WITH ADJUNCT If you **sidle** somewhere, you walk there cautiously, as if you do not want to be noticed. *She stammered some apology as she sidled towards the door.*

siege /siːdʒ/, **sieges.** COUNT N OR UNCOUNT N A **siege** is a military or police operation in which an army or police force surrounds a place in order to force the people to come out. *...the siege of Mafeking... He had been in London to report on the Embassy siege.*

siesta /si¹ˈestə/, **siestas.** COUNT N OR UNCOUNT N A **siesta** is a short sleep that people have in the early afternoon in hot countries.

sieve /sɪv/, **sieves, sieving, sieved. 1** COUNT N A **sieve** is a tool consisting of a metal or plastic ring with a wire net attached. It is used for separating liquids from solids or larger pieces of something from smaller pieces. **2** VB WITH OBJ When you **sieve** a liquid or powder-like substance, you put it through a sieve. *Sieve the flour into a basin to remove all the lumps.*

sift /sɪft/, **sifts, sifting, sifted. 1** VB WITH OBJ If you **sift** a powder-like substance such as flour or sand, you put it through a sieve to remove large lumps. *Always sift icing sugar through a fine sieve.* **2** VB WITH 'through' OR OBJ If you **sift** through something such as evidence, you examine it thoroughly. *There are archives and documents to be sifted through... He was accustomed to sifting evidence.*

sigh /saɪ/, **sighs, sighing, sighed.** VB When you **sigh,** you let out a deep breath. *She sighed and shook her head sadly... Sighing with relief, she took the money.* Also COUNT N *With a sigh, he rose and walked away.*

sight /saɪt/, **sights, sighting, sighted. 1** UNCOUNT N **Sight** is the ability to see. *Her sight is failing.* **2** SING N OR COUNT N WITH SUPP A **sight** is something that you see, or the act of seeing it. *This was the most encouraging sight I'd seen all day... It was an awe-inspiring sight... He was reduced to tears at the sight of the hundreds of dead bodies.* **3** PLURAL N The **sights** are interesting places that are often visited by tourists. *...the sights of London.* **4** VB WITH OBJ If you **sight** someone or something, you see them briefly or suddenly. *The missing woman has been sighted in the Birmingham area.*
PHRASES ● If one thing is **a sight** better or **a sight** worse than a similar thing, it is very much better or very much worse; an informal use. *It's a damn sight better than most of the places we've stayed in.* ● If something is **in sight,** you can see it. If it is **out of**

sight, you cannot see it. *As soon as the car was out of sight, we relaxed.* ● If you **catch sight of** someone, you see them suddenly or briefly. *She caught sight of her mother.* ● If you **know** someone **by sight,** you can recognize them when you see them, but you have never spoken to them. ● If someone is ordered to **shoot on sight,** they have to shoot someone as soon as they see them. *They used to shoot on sight in those days.* ● If a result or a decision is **in sight,** it is likely to happen soon. *It seemed that an end to his agony was in sight.* ● If you **lose sight of** an important feature or detail, you no longer pay attention to it because you are worrying about less important things. *We mustn't get so bogged down by detail that we lose sight of our main objectives.* ● If you **set** your **sights on** something, you are determined to have it. *We have set our sights on a bigger house.*

sighted /saɪtɪ²d/. **1** ADJ People who are **sighted** are not blind. *...if you are blind or poorly sighted... ...partially sighted children.* **2** See also **far-sighted, long-sighted, short-sighted.**

sighting /saɪtɪŋ/, **sightings.** COUNT N A **sighting** of something is an occasion on which it is seen. *There had been four reports of shark sightings.*

sight-read, sight-reads, sight-reading. Sight-read is used in the present tense, and is the past tense and past participle. VB WITH OR WITHOUT OBJ Someone who can **sight-read** can read musical symbols and convert them into notes when they see them.

sightseeing /saɪtsiːɪŋ/. UNCOUNT N If you go **sightseeing,** you travel around visiting the interesting places that tourists usually visit.

sightseer /saɪtsiːə/, **sightseers.** COUNT N A **sightseer** is someone who is travelling around and visiting places of interest. *...a large crowd of sightseers.*

sign /saɪn/, **signs, signing, signed. 1** COUNT N A **sign** is a mark or shape with a particular meaning, for example in mathematics or music. *...a minus sign.* **2** COUNT N A **sign** is a movement of your arms, hands, or head which is intended to have a particular meaning. *Through signs she communicated that she wanted the women to hide.* **3** COUNT N A **sign** is also a piece of wood, metal, or plastic with words or pictures on it, giving information or instructions. *The exit sign is marked with an arrow... A sign saying 'Women's Centre' hung over the door.* **4** COUNT N WITH 'of' If there is a **sign** of something, there is evidence that it exists. *How pleasant to see a sign of summer once again... The Englishman showed no signs of his annoyance... His sores had begun to show signs of healing.* **5** VB WITH OR WITHOUT OBJ If you **sign** a document, you put your signature on it. *Sign your name in the book... Sign here to acknowledge receipt.*
sign away. PHR VB If you **sign** something **away,** you sign official documents to say that you no longer have a right to it. *Chiefs were encouraged to sign away land that appeared to be unoccupied.*
sign for. PHR VB If you **sign for** something, you officially state that you have received or accepted it, by signing a form. *When signing for any parcel, always add 'not inspected'.*
sign in. PHR VB If you **sign in,** you indicate that you have arrived at a hotel or club by signing a book or form. *They signed in at the reception desk.*
sign on. PHR VB **1** If you **sign on** for a job or course, or **sign up** for it, you officially agree to do it by signing a contract or form. *He signed on the next morning with the RAF... You could sign on for a course in word processing... He signed up as a painter on the Federal Art Project.* **2** If you **sign on,** you officially state that you are unemployed, so that you can receive money from the government in order to live; a British use.
sign out. PHR VB If you **sign out,** you indicate that you have left a hotel or club by signing a book or form.
sign up. PHR VB See **sign on 1.**

signal /sɪgnəⁿl/, **signals, signalling, signalled;** spelled **signaling** and **signaled** in American English. **1** COUNT N A **signal** is a gesture, sound, or action which is intended to send a particular message. *My signal will be three knocks.* **2** VB OR REPORT VB If you **signal** something or if you **signal** to someone, you make a gesture or sound in order to give someone a particular message. *Don signalled his permission... Signal the driver to move off... ...a parent signalling to a child in the distance... The helpers signalled that all was ready.* **3** REPORT VB If something **signals** an event, it suggests that the event is happening or likely to happen. *This decision seemed to signal a switch in the paper's editorial policy... ...the crisis signalling that the final moment was near.* Also COUNT N WITH SUPP *This was the first signal that an attack was brewing.* **4** COUNT N A **signal** is also a piece of equipment beside a railway, which tells train drivers whether to stop. **5** COUNT N A **signal** is also a series of sound or light waves which carry information. *Marconi finally succeeded in sending a signal across the Atlantic.*

signal box, signal boxes. COUNT N A **signal box** is a small building near a railway containing the switches used to control the signals.

signatory /sɪgnətə^{r}ri^1/, **signatories.** COUNT N The **signatories** of an official document are the people who sign it; a formal use. *...a signatory to the North Atlantic Treaty.*

signature /sɪgnə^{1}tʃə/, **signatures.** COUNT N Your **signature** is your name, when you write it in your own characteristic way. *He underlined his signature with a little flourish.*

signature tune, signature tunes. COUNT N A **signature tune** is the tune which is always played at the beginning or end of a particular television or radio programme.

significance /sɪgnɪfɪkəns/. UNCOUNT N The **significance** of something is its importance. *A year later I found out the true significance of the name.*

significant /sɪgnɪfɪkənt/. 1 ATTRIB ADJ A **significant** amount is a large amount. *Lack of insulation can result in a significant amount of heat being lost.* ♦ **significantly** ADV *Prices were significantly reduced.* 2 ADJ Something that is **significant** is important or has a special meaning. *The incident was very significant... ...a significant discovery... With a significant look at her husband, Mrs Hochstadt went out.* ♦ **significantly** ADV OR SENTENCE ADV *He cleared his throat significantly a few times... Significantly, there was no reference to Iran.*

signify /sɪgnɪfaɪ/, **signifies, signifying, signified.** REPORT VB A sign, symbol, or gesture that **signifies** something has a particular meaning. *Leggett gave a long wheeze, to signify disgust... Short pips signify that the phone is engaged.*

signpost /saɪnpəʊst/, **signposts.** COUNT N A **signpost** is a sign beside a road with information on it such as the name of a town and how far away it is.

Sikh /si:k/, **Sikhs.** COUNT N A **Sikh** is a person who believes in the Indian religion of Sikhism. Also ADJ *...a Sikh name.*

Sikhism /si:kɪzm/. UNCOUNT N **Sikhism** is an Indian religion which teaches that there is only one God.

silence /saɪləns/, **silences, silencing, silenced.** 1 UNCOUNT N OR COUNT N If there is **silence,** it is completely quiet. *We walked on in silence... There was a shocked silence.* 2 UNCOUNT N WITH SUPP Someone's **silence** about something is their refusal to tell people anything about it. *Levy's silence on the subject was unnerving.* 3 VB WITH OBJ If you **silence** someone or something, you stop them speaking or making a noise. *Rodin silenced him with a gesture... Butler's firm speech failed to silence opposition.*

silencer /saɪlənsə/, **silencers.** COUNT N A **silencer** is a device on a car exhaust or a gun which makes it quieter.

silent /saɪlənt/. 1 ADJ Someone who is **silent** is not speaking. *The woman was silent for a moment.* ♦ **silently** ADV *We finished breakfast silently.* 2 ADJ A **silent** person does not talk to people very much. *She was a silent girl, cool and aloof.* 3 PRED ADJ If you are **silent** about something, you do not tell people about it. *He remained absolutely silent on his plans for using the money.* 4 ADJ Something that is **silent** makes no sound. *The guns have fallen silent.* ♦ **silently** ADV *It appeared suddenly and silently out of the dusk.* 5 ATTRIB ADJ A **silent** film has no sound or speech. *In 1924 I did my first silent film.*

silhouette /sɪlu:ɛt/, **silhouettes.** COUNT N A **silhouette** is the outline of a dark shape against a bright light or pale background. *The figure turned towards the sunrise, a tiny silhouette.*

silhouetted /sɪlu:ɛt^{2}d/. PRED ADJ If something is **silhouetted** against a background, it can be seen as a silhouette. *...hills silhouetted against a pale blue sky.*

silicon /sɪlɪkən/. UNCOUNT N **Silicon** is an element used to make parts of computers and other electronic equipment. *...tiny silicon chips.*

silk /sɪlk/, **silks.** MASS N **Silk** is a very smooth, fine cloth made from a substance produced by a kind of moth. *...a white silk scarf.*

silken /sɪlkə^{0}n/. ADJ You use **silken** to describe things that are smooth and soft; a literary use. *...silken hair.*

silky /sɪlki^1/. ADJ Something that is **silky** is smooth and soft. *...fine silky skin.*

sill /sɪl/, **sills.** COUNT N A **sill** is a ledge at the bottom of a window. *She sat with one elbow resting on the sill of the open window... ...the window sill.*

silly /sɪli^1/, **sillier, silliest.** ADJ Someone who is being **silly** is behaving in a foolish or childish way. *You're a silly little boy... It was a silly thing to say.*

silt /sɪlt/, **silts, silting, silted.** UNCOUNT N **Silt** is fine sand or mud which is carried along by a river. *The problem is keeping the harbours free of silt.*

silt up. PHR VB If a river or lake **silts up,** it becomes blocked with silt.

silver /sɪlvə/. 1 UNCOUNT N **Silver** is a valuable greyish-white metal used for making jewellery and ornaments. *...a little box made of solid silver.* 2 UNCOUNT N **Silver** is also coins that look like silver. *...leaving five pounds in silver in case somebody needed change.* 3 UNCOUNT N In a house, the **silver** is things made from silver, for example cutlery. *The silver sparkled in the candlelight.* 4 ADJ Something that is **silver** in colour is greyish-white. *...sparkling silver paint... ...a tall old man with long silver hair.*

silver medal, silver medals. COUNT N A **silver medal** is a medal made of silver which is awarded as second prize in a contest or competition.

silver-plated. ADJ Something that is **silver-plated** is covered with a thin layer of silver.

silvery /sɪlvə^{0}ri^1/. ADJ Something that is **silvery** looks like silver. *...a silvery dress.*

similar /sɪmɪlə/. ADJ If one thing is **similar** to another, they have features that are the same or are like each other. *My problems are very similar to yours... The four restaurants were all serving similar food at similar prices.*

similarity /sɪmɪlærɪ^{1}ti^1/, **similarities.** UNCOUNT N OR COUNT N If there is a **similarity** between two or more things, they share some features that are the same. *...the similarities and differences between British and American English... Many species have close similarities with one another.*

similarly /sɪmɪləli^1/. ADV OR SENTENCE ADV You use **similarly** to say that one thing is similar to another that you have just mentioned. *Other guests sat under similarly striped umbrellas... Similarly, savings certificates should be registered with the Post Office.*

simile /sɪmɪli^1/, **similes.** COUNT N A **simile** is an expression which describes one person or thing as being similar to another. For example, the sentences 'She runs like a deer' and 'He's as white as a sheet' are similes.

simmer /sɪmə/, **simmers, simmering, simmered.** ERG VB When you **simmer** food, you cook it by keeping it just below boiling point. *Simmer the beans for four hours until tender.*

simmer down. PHR VB If you **simmer down,** you stop being angry; an informal use. *I thought the trip might give me time to simmer down.*

simper /sɪmpə/, **simpers, simpering, simpered.** VB When someone **simpers,** they smile in a rather silly way. *The maid lowered her chin and simpered.* Also SING N *'Thank you, doctor,' she said with a simper.*

simple /sɪmpə^{0}l/, **simpler, simplest.** 1 ADJ If something is **simple,** it is easy to understand or do. *The point I am making is a very simple one... ...a very simple calculator... The solution is very simple... It's a simple operation, you can do it in a lunch hour.* 2 ADJ **Simple** things are plain and not elaborate in style. *...a tall woman in a simple brown dress.* 3 ADJ A **simple** way of life is uncomplicated and fairly basic. *Nature, the simple life, that's what I need... They are only simple farmers.* 4 ATTRIB ADJ You use **simple** to emphasize that the thing you are mentioning is the only important one. *Simple fear of death is often what turns people to religion.*

simple-minded. 1 ADJ A **simple-minded** person interprets things in a way that is too simple, because they do not understand how complicated things are. *...the simple-minded view that people have of robots.* 2 ADJ You can also refer to someone who is mentally slow or confused as **simple-minded.** *She became frail, simple-minded, and returned to her youth.*

simplicity /sɪmplɪsɪ^{1}ti^1/. 1 UNCOUNT N The **simplicity** of something is the fact that it is uncomplicated and can be understood easily. *The advantage of the idea was its simplicity.* 2 UNCOUNT N If there is **simplicity** in the way that someone does something, they do it in a simple and attractive way. *He dressed with elegant simplicity.*

simplification /sɪmplɪfɪkeɪʃə^{0}n/, **simplifications.** COUNT N OR UNCOUNT N A **simplification** is the thing that you produce when you make something simpler. *I see this proposal as a long overdue simplification.*

simplify /sɪmplɪfaɪ/, **simplifies, simplifying, simplified.** VB WITH OBJ If you **simplify** something, you make it easier to understand or do. *The subject is immensely complex, and hard to simplify.* ♦ **simplified** ADJ *...a simplified version of the model.*

simplistic /sɪmplɪstɪk/. ADJ A **simplistic** view or interpretation makes something seem much less complicated than it really is. *...a rather simplistic analysis of the situation.*

simply /sɪmpli^1/. 1 ADV You use **simply** to emphasize that something consists of only one thing, happens for only one reason, or is done in only one way. *The job of a caterpillar is simply to eat... It's simply a question of hard work.* 2 ADV You also use **simply** to emphasize what you are saying. *I simply can't believe it.* 3 ADV If you say or write something **simply,** you do it in a way that makes it easy to understand or without giving unnecessary details. *'His life is finished,' he said simply.*

simulate /sɪmjə^{4}leɪt/, **simulates, simulating, simulated.** VB WITH OBJ To **simulate** something means to pretend to do it or to produce something like it. *We used this trick in the Army to simulate illness... Bomb tests can be simulated on computers... The wood is carved to simulate hair.*

simulation /sɪmjə^{4}leɪʃə^{0}n/, **simulations.** 1 UNCOUNT N OR COUNT N **Simulation** is the process or result of simulating something. *Her remark had been greeted with a simulation of diffidence... The viewer was unable to distinguish reality from simulation.* 2 COUNT N OR UNCOUNT N A **simulation** is also an attempt to solve a problem by representing it mathematically, often using a computer; a technical use. *Computer modelling and simulation have been used as an aid to battle tactics.*

simultaneous /sɪmə^{4}lteɪnɪəs/. ADJ **Simultaneous** things or events happen or exist at the same time. *...the simultaneous failure of all the lifts in the building.* ♦ **simultaneously** ADV *His fear and his hate grew simultaneously.*

sin /sɪn/, **sins, sinning, sinned.** 1 UNCOUNT N OR COUNT N **Sin** is behaviour which is considered to be very bad and immoral. *They believed they were being punished for their sins... They had no sense of sin.* 2 VB If you **sin,** you do something that is believed to be very bad and immoral. *You have sinned against the Lord.* ♦ **sinner** COUNT N *Christ is inviting sinners to repentance.*

since /sɪns/. 1 PREP, CONJ, OR ADV If something has happened **since** a particular time or event, it has happened from then until the present time. *I've been wearing glasses since I was three... I came here in 1972 and I have lived here ever since... I've been here since twelve o'clock.* 2 ADV **Since** also means at some time after a particular time or event in the past. *He used to be an art student. He has since become a lawyer.* 3 CONJ You use **since** to introduce a reason. *Aircraft noise is a problem here since we're close to Heathrow Airport... Since it was Saturday, he stayed in bed an extra hour.*

sincere /sɪnsɪə/. ADJ If you are **sincere,** you really mean the things you say. *He was decent, sincere, a good man... The apology was sincere.* ♦ **sincerity** /sɪnsɛrɪ^{1}ti^1/ UNCOUNT N *The Head Master is a man of deep conviction and sincerity.*

sincerely /sɪnsɪəli^1/. 1 ADV If you say or feel something **sincerely,** you really mean it or feel it. *'I owe you an awful lot,' I said sincerely... He loves you very sincerely.* 2 CONVENTION You write **Yours sincerely** before your signature at the end of a formal letter.

sinew /sɪnju:/, **sinews.** COUNT N OR UNCOUNT N A **sinew** is a cord in your body that connects a muscle to a bone.

sinewy /sɪnju:i^1/. ADJ A **sinewy** person has a lean body with strong muscles. *...his sinewy brown arm... She was a tall, sinewy type.*

sinful /sɪnfʊl/. ADJ Someone or something that is **sinful** is considered to be wicked or immoral. *Good women have always saved sinful men in stories... She believed that eye-shadow was sinful.*

sing /sɪŋ/, **sings, singing, sang** /sæŋ/, **sung** /sʌŋ/. 1 VB WITH OR WITHOUT OBJ If you **sing,** you make musical sounds with your voice, usually producing words that fit a tune. *I started to sing... The song is sung by Romy Blakeley.* 2 VB When birds or insects **sing,** they make pleasant sounds. *I could hear birds singing in the trees.* 3 PHRASE If you **sing** someone's **praises,** you enthusiastically praise them. *I understand that he's now singing the praises of Mcleod.*

singe /sɪndʒ/, **singes, singeing, singed.** ERG VB If you **singe** something, you burn it very slightly so that it changes colour but does not catch fire.

singer /sɪŋə/, **singers.** COUNT N A **singer** is a person who sings, especially as part of their job.

singing /sɪŋɪŋ/. 1 UNCOUNT N **Singing** is the activity of making musical sounds with your voice. *The dancing and singing ended at midnight.* 2 UNCOUNT N **Singing** is also the art of being a singer. *...singing lessons.* 3 UNCOUNT N The pleasant sounds made by birds can be referred to as **singing.** *...the singing of the blackbirds.*

single /sɪŋgə^{0}l/, **singles, singling, singled.** 1 ATTRIB ADJ A **single** thing is only one, and not more. *We heard a single shot... I just couldn't think of a single thing to say.* 2 ATTRIB ADJ You use **single** when considering something on its own and separately from the other things like it. *This is the most important single invention since the wheel... We went to the house every single day for six months.* 3 ADJ If you are **single,** you are not married. 4 ADJ A **single** bed or room is intended for one person. 5 ADJ A **single** ticket is for a journey from one place to another but not back again; a British use. *How much is the single fare to London?* Also COUNT N *A single to Edinburgh, please.* **6** COUNT N A **single** is also a small gramophone record which has one short song on each side. **7** UNCOUNT N **Singles** is a game of tennis or badminton for only two players. *The high serve is used a lot in singles.* **8 in single figures:** see **figure.**

single out. PHR VB If you **single** someone **out,** you choose them from a group for special attention or treatment. *Three other people were singled out for special praise.*

single-handed. ADV If you do something **single-handed,** you do it without any help. *He had rescued the girl single-handed.*

single-minded. ADJ A **single-minded** person has only one aim and is determined to achieve it. *...the single-minded pursuit of wealth.*

singly /sɪŋgli[1]/. ADV If people do something **singly,** they do it on their own or one by one. *The children came out singly or in small groups.*

singular /sɪŋgjə[4]lə/. **1** SING N OR ADJ In grammar, **singular** is the term used for a noun, pronoun, determiner, or verb when it refers to only one person, thing, or group. *The singular of 'lice' is 'louse'... What is the singular form of 'media'?* **2** ADJ Something that is **singular** is unusual and remarkable; a formal use. *...a lady of singular beauty.*

singularly /sɪŋgjə[4]ləli[1]/. SUBMOD **Singularly** means to a remarkable or extraordinary degree; a formal use. *Then we did some singularly boring experiments.*

sinister /sɪnɪstə/. ADJ Something that is **sinister** seems evil or harmful. *...a rather sinister figure walking behind the bushes.*

sink /sɪŋk/, **sinks, sinking, sank** /sæŋk/, **sunk** /sʌŋk/. **1** COUNT N A **sink** is a basin with taps that supply water, usually in a kitchen or a bathroom. **2** VB If something **sinks,** it moves slowly downwards, especially below the surface of water. *The boat sank to the bottom of the lake... The sun had just sunk below the horizon.* **3** VB WITH OBJ If people **sink** a ship, they attack it and cause it to sink. **4** VB WITH ADJUNCT If you **sink** back or down, you move into a lower position. *She sank back in her chair and sipped her drink.* **5** VB WITH ADJUNCT If an amount or value **sinks,** it decreases by a large amount. *Wages have sunk so low in relation to the cost of living.* **6** VB If your voice **sinks,** it becomes quieter or lower; a literary use. **7** VB WITH 'into' If you **sink** into an unpleasant or less active state, you pass gradually into it. *My father sank further into debt... I sank into a deep sleep.* **8** VB If your heart **sinks,** you become depressed. *His heart sank at the thought that the exams were a week away.* **9** ERG VB WITH 'into' If you **sink** something sharp into something solid, you make it go deeply into it. *He sank his teeth into the apple.* **10** See also **sunken.**

sink in. PHR VB When a statement or fact **sinks in,** you understand and realize it. *It took a moment or two for her words to sink in.*

sinuous /sɪnjuəs/. ADJ Something that is **sinuous** moves with smooth twists and turns, like a snake; a literary use. *Women danced sinuous dances in the middle of the room.*

sinus /saɪnəs/, **sinuses.** COUNT N Your **sinuses** are the spaces in the bones of your skull just behind your nose.

sip /sɪp/, **sips, sipping, sipped.** VB WITH OBJ If you **sip** a drink, you drink a small amount at a time. *The guests were sipping their drinks.* Also COUNT N *She took another sip from her glass... ...sips of water.*

siphon /saɪfə[0]n/, **siphons, siphoning, siphoned;** also spelled **syphon. 1** VB WITH OBJ If you **siphon** a liquid or **siphon** it off, you draw it out of a container through a tube by using atmospheric pressure. *Claude siphoned off a little petrol from his father's car.* **2** COUNT N A **siphon** is a tube used for siphoning liquid.

sir /sɜː/. **1** VOCATIVE People sometimes call a man **sir** when they are being formal and polite. 'Dear Sir' is often used at the beginning of official letters addressed to men. *What would you like, sir?* **2** TITLE **Sir** is the title used in front of the name of a knight or baronet. *...Sir John Hargreaves.*

siren /saɪərə[0]n/, **sirens.** COUNT N A **siren** is a warning device which makes a long, loud, wailing noise. *...the distant wail of police sirens.*

sister /sɪstə/, **sisters. 1** COUNT N Your **sister** is a girl or woman who has the same parents as you. *Have you got any brothers and sisters?* ● See also **half-sister. 2** COUNT N A **sister** is a female member of a religious order. **3** COUNT N A senior female nurse who supervises a hospital ward is also called a **sister;** a British use. **4** COUNT N A woman sometimes refers to other women as her **sisters** when she shares the same beliefs or aims. *They would go to Paris and stay with feminist sisters there.* **5** COUNT N WITH POSS The **sister** of something is another, related thing of the same type. *The city shows every sign of outgrowing its sister.* Also ATTRIB ADJ *Her sister ship was sunk by a torpedo.*

sister-in-law, sisters-in-law. COUNT N Your **sister-in-law** is the sister of your husband or wife, or the woman who is married to your brother or to your wife's or husband's brother.

sisterly /sɪstəli[1]/. ATTRIB ADJ A woman's **sisterly** feelings are her feelings of warmth and affection towards her sister or brother.

sit /sɪt/, **sits, sitting, sat** /sæt/. **1** VB If you **are sitting** somewhere, your weight is supported by your buttocks rather than your feet. *She was sitting on the edge of the bed.* **2** VB When you **sit,** you lower your body until you are sitting on something. *He came into the room and sat in his usual chair.* **3** VB WITH OBJ If you **sit** an examination, you take it; a British use. **4** VB WITH 'on' If you **sit** on a committee, you are a member of it. *Representatives of the workers should sit on the board of directors.* **5** VB When a parliament, law court, or other official body **sits,** it officially carries out its work; a formal use. *Visitors are only allowed in on days when the Houses are not sitting.* **6** VB WITH ADJUNCT If a building or other object **sits** in a particular place, it is in that place; a literary use. *The little parish church sits cosily in the middle of the village.* **7** See also **sitting, baby-sit.**

PHRASES ● If you **sit tight,** you remain where you are and do not take any action. *All they have to do is sit tight until the Republic recognises their claims.* ● to **sit on the fence:** see **fence.**

sit back. PHR VB If you **sit back,** you relax and do not become involved in a situation; an informal use. *He believes he has the right to sit back while others do the hard work.*

sit down. PHR VB When you **sit down** or **sit** yourself **down,** you lower your body until you are sitting on something. *He sat down on the edge of the bed.*

sit in on. PHR VB If you **sit in on** a meeting you are present at it but do not take part. *I was allowed to sit in on the deliberations of the board.*

sit out. PHR VB If you **sit** something **out,** you wait for it to finish, without taking any action. *They would retire to their caves to sit out the winter.*

sit up. PHR VB **1** If you **sit up,** you bring yourself into a sitting position when you have been leaning back or lying down. *She sat up in bed when she saw him coming.* **2** If you **sit up** all night, you do not go to bed. *Sometimes I sit up reading until three or four in the morning.*

site /saɪt/, **sites, siting, sited. 1** COUNT N A **site** is a piece of ground used for a particular purpose. *...dusty building sites... ...the site of the murder of the little princes in 1483.* **2** VB WITH OBJ AND ADJUNCT If something **is sited** in a particular place or position, it is placed there. *They refused to have cruise missiles sited on their soil.*

sit-in, sit-ins. COUNT N A **sit-in** is a protest in which people sit in a public place and refuse to be moved.

sitting /sɪtɪŋ/, **sittings. 1** COUNT N A **sitting** is one of the times when a meal is served, when there is not enough space for everyone to eat at the same time. *The first sitting for breakfast is at 7.30.* **2** COUNT N A **sitting** is also an occasion when an official body, such as a parliament or law court, has a meeting. *...the first sitting of the Senate since the election.*

sitting-room, sitting-rooms. COUNT N A **sitting-room** is a room in a house where people sit and relax.

situated /sɪtjueɪtɪ[2]d/. PRED ADJ If something is **situated** somewhere, it is in a particular place or position. *The control centre is situated many miles away... Their flat was most conveniently situated.*

situation /sɪtjʊeɪʃə[0]n/, **situations. 1** COUNT N You use the word **situation** to refer generally to what is happening at a particular place and time. *The situation was beginning to frighten me... It's an impossible situation... ...the economic situation.* **2** COUNT N Your **situation** refers to your circumstances and the things that are happening to you. *He knew a lot about my father's situation... ...the seriousness of his situation.* **3** COUNT N The **situation** of a building or town is its surroundings; a formal use. *The city is in a beautiful situation.* **4** PHRASE The **Situations Vacant** column in a newspaper is a list of jobs that are being advertised.

situation comedy, situation comedies. COUNT N OR UNCOUNT N A **situation comedy** is a television or radio comedy series in which the same characters are shown in everyday, amusing situations.

six /sɪks/, **sixes. Six** is the number 6.

sixteen /sɪkstiːn/. **Sixteen** is the number 16.

sixteenth /sɪkstiːnθ/. ADJ The **sixteenth** item in a series is the one that you count as number sixteen.

sixth /sɪksθ/, **sixths. 1** ADJ The **sixth** item in a series is the one that you count as number six. **2** COUNT N A **sixth** is one of six equal parts of something.

sixth form, sixth forms. COUNT N The **sixth form** in a British school is the classes that pupils go into at the age of sixteen to study for 'A' Levels. *What subjects are you taking in the sixth form?*

sixtieth /sɪkstɪ[2]əθ/. ADJ The **sixtieth** item in a series is the one that you count as number sixty.

sixty /sɪksti[1]/, **sixties. Sixty** is the number 60.

sizable /saɪzəbə[0]l/. See **sizeable.**

size /saɪz/, **sizes, sizing, sized. 1** UNCOUNT N The **size** of something is how big or small it is. *The company doubled its size in nine years... We saw butterflies the size of birds... ...a block of ice one cubic foot in size.* **2** UNCOUNT N The **size** of something is also the fact that it is very large. *The Grand was the only hotel of any size in the town... The world overwhelms us by its sheer size.* **3** COUNT N A **size** is one of a series of graded measurements, especially for things such as clothes or shoes. *What size do you take?... ...a jacket three sizes too big.*

size up. PHR VB If you **size up** a person or situation, you carefully look at the person or think about the situation, so that you can decide how to act; an informal use. *...people sizing each other up as if for a fight.*

sizeable /saɪzəbə[0]l/; also spelled **sizable.** ADJ **Sizeable** means fairly large. *...a sizeable sum of money... ...a sizeable number of students.*

sizzle /sɪzə[0]l/, **sizzles, sizzling, sizzled.** VB If something **sizzles,** it makes a hissing sound like the sound made by frying food. *The steak and kidney pudding sizzled deliciously on the stove.*

skate /skeɪt/, **skates, skating, skated. 1** COUNT N A **skate** is an ice-skate or roller-skate. **2** VB To **skate** means to move over ice or a flat surface wearing skates. *...skating across the frozen pond.* ♦ **skating** UNCOUNT N *There is skating in the winter.* **3** VB WITH ADJUNCT If you **skate** round or over a difficult subject, you avoid it. *He skated round the subject once or twice... The book skates over the technicalities.*

skateboard /skeɪtbɔːd/, **skateboards.** COUNT N A **skateboard** is a narrow board on wheels, which people stand on and ride for pleasure.

skein /skeɪn/, **skeins.** COUNT N A **skein** is a loosely coiled length of thread, especially wool or silk. *...a skein of wool.*

skeletal /skelɪ[2]tə[0]l/. **1** ATTRIB ADJ **Skeletal** means relating to skeletons. *...skeletal remains... ...their skeletal structure.* **2** ADJ A **skeletal** person is extremely thin. *...harrowing photographs of skeletal children.*

skeleton /skelɪ[2]tə[0]n/, **skeletons. 1** COUNT N Your **skeleton** is the framework of bones in your body. *...the skeleton of a gigantic whale.* **2** PHRASE If someone has **a skeleton in the cupboard,** they are keeping secret something that is scandalous or embarrassing. **3** MOD A **skeleton** staff is the smallest number of staff necessary to run an organization.

skeptic /skeptɪk/. See **sceptic.**

skeptical /skeptɪkə[0]l/. See **sceptical.**

sketch /sketʃ/, **sketches, sketching, sketched. 1** COUNT N A **sketch** is a quick, rough drawing. *...a rough sketch.* **2** VB WITH OR WITHOUT OBJ If you **sketch** something, you make a quick, rough drawing of it. *I sometimes sketched her... She began to sketch on a piece of paper.* **3** COUNT N A **sketch** of a situation or incident is a brief description of it. *...a brief sketch of the school's early history.* **4** VB WITH OBJ If you **sketch** a situation or incident, you give a brief description of it. *His rise to power is briefly sketched in the first two chapters.* **5** COUNT N A **sketch** is also a short humorous piece of acting, usually forming part of a comedy show. *I loved the sketch about the dead parrot.*

sketchy /sketʃi[1]/, **sketchier, sketchiest.** ADJ Something that is **sketchy** does not have many details. *...his sketchy lecture notes... I had only the sketchiest notion of what it was all about.*

skewer /skjuːə/, **skewers, skewering, skewered. 1** COUNT N A **skewer** is a long metal pin which is used to hold pieces of food together during cooking. **2** VB WITH OBJ If you **skewer** something, you push a long, thin, pointed object through it. *They skewered bits of meat on branches and held them in the flames.*

ski /skiː/, **skis, skiing, skied. 1** COUNT N **Skis** are long, flat, narrow pieces of wood, metal, or plastic that are fastened to boots so that you can move easily over snow. *...a pair of skis.* **2** VB When people **ski,** they move over snow on skis. ♦ **skiing** UNCOUNT N *They go skiing every winter.* **3** MOD **Ski** is used to refer to things that are concerned with skiing. *...ski boots... ...a Swiss ski instructor... ...a ski resort.*

skid /skɪd/, **skids, skidding, skidded.** VB If a vehicle **skids,** it slides sideways or forwards in an uncontrolled way, for example because the road is wet or icy. *He slammed on his brakes and skidded into a wall... We skidded to a halt.* Also COUNT N *The car went into a skid.*

skilful /skɪlfʊl/; spelled **skillful** in American English. ADJ Someone who is **skilful** at something does it very well. *The girl had grown more skilful with the* *sewing-machine... ...a skilful hunter... ...skilful manoeuvres.* ♦ **skilfully** ADV *...a skilfully organized campaign.*

skill /skɪl/, **skills.** 1 UNCOUNT N **Skill** is the knowledge and ability that enables you to do something well. *The carving shows remarkable technical skill.* 2 COUNT N A **skill** is a type of work or craft which requires special training and knowledge. *...the skills of painting and drawing... ...learning new skills.*

skilled /skɪld/. 1 ADJ Someone who is **skilled** has the knowledge and ability to do something well. *...hand-made items produced by skilled craftsmen.* 2 ATTRIB ADJ **Skilled** work can only be done by people who have had some training.

skillful /skɪlfʊl/. See **skilful.**

skim /skɪm/, **skims, skimming, skimmed.** 1 VB WITH OBJ AND ADJUNCT If you **skim** something from the surface of a liquid, you remove it. *Skim off the cream.* 2 VB WITH OBJ If something **skims** a surface, it moves quickly along just above it. *The birds swoop in a breathtaking arc to skim the pond.* 3 VB WITH OBJ OR 'through' If you **skim** a piece of writing, you read through it quickly. *I thought I would skim through a few of the letters.*

skimmed milk. UNCOUNT N **Skimmed milk** is milk from which the cream has been removed.

skimp /skɪmp/, **skimps, skimping, skimped.** VB WITH OR WITHOUT OBJ If you **skimp** on something, you use less time, money, or material for it than you really need. *Don't skimp on stair carpet... When people get harassed work is skimped or rushed.*

skimpy /skɪmpi[1]/. ADJ **Skimpy** means too small in size or quantity. *...little girls in skimpy cotton frocks.*

skin /skɪn/, **skins, skinning, skinned.** 1 UNCOUNT N OR COUNT N Your **skin** is the natural covering of your body. *They had light skin and blue eyes... The poison may be absorbed through the skin... The Lapps of Scandinavia have fair skins.* 2 COUNT N OR UNCOUNT N An animal **skin** is skin with fur on it which has been removed from a dead animal. *...fox skins... A few coats hung in the closet, one of leopard skin.* 3 COUNT N OR UNCOUNT N The **skin** of a type of food is its outer layer or covering. *Cook the potatoes quickly with their skins on... ...sausage skins.* 4 COUNT N OR UNCOUNT N If a **skin** forms on the surface of a liquid, a fairly solid layer forms on it. *The custard had a thick skin on it.* 5 VB WITH OBJ If you **skin** a dead animal, you remove its skin. *The boys skinned and cleaned the day's game.* 6 VB WITH OBJ If you **skin** part of your body, you accidentally scrape some of the skin off. *She skinned her knee.* 7 PHRASE If you do something **by the skin of your teeth,** you only just manage to do it.

skinny /skɪni[1]/. ADJ A **skinny** person is very thin; an informal use. *He's tall and skinny.*

skin-tight. ADJ **Skin-tight** clothes fit very tightly.

skip /skɪp/, **skips, skipping, skipped.** 1 VB If you **skip** along, you move along with a series of little jumps from one foot to the other. *He skipped around the room.* Also COUNT N *...taking little skips as they walked.* 2 VB When someone **skips,** they jump up and down over a rope which they or other people are holding at each end and turning round and round. *Three energetic little girls were skipping in the playground.* 3 VB WITH OBJ If you **skip** something that you usually do, you deliberately do not do it; an informal use. *I could skip every lecture for a month and still graduate... I decided to skip lunch.* 4 COUNT N A **skip** is a large metal container for holding rubbish and old bricks; a British use. *Debris was being loaded into skips.*

skipper /skɪpə/, **skippers.** COUNT N The **skipper** of a boat or of a sports team is its captain; an informal use.

skirmish /skɜːmɪʃ/, **skirmishes.** COUNT N A **skirmish** is a short battle which is not part of a planned war strategy. *...a bitter skirmish in the half light of dawn.*

skirt /skɜːt/, **skirts, skirting, skirted.** 1 COUNT N A **skirt** is a piece of clothing worn by women and girls. It fastens at the waist and hangs down around the legs. *...a very short skirt.* 2 VB WITH OBJ Something that **skirts** an area is situated around the edge of it. *...the path which skirted the house.* 3 VB WITH OBJ, 'round', OR 'around' If you **skirt** something, you go around the edge of it. *As I walked through the lobby, I had to skirt a group of ladies... They skirted round a bus.* 4 VB WITH OBJ If you **skirt** a problem or question, you avoid dealing with it. *The President has skirted the issue.*

skittles /skɪtə[0]lz/. UNCOUNT N **Skittles** is a game in which players try to knock down wooden objects called skittles by rolling a ball at them.

skulk /skʌlk/, **skulks, skulking, skulked.** VB WITH ADJUNCT If you **skulk** somewhere, you stay there quietly because you do not want to be seen. *There were half a dozen foxes skulking in the undergrowth.*

skull /skʌl/, **skulls.** COUNT N Your **skull** is the bony part of your head which encloses your brain. *He had two broken ribs and a fractured skull.*

skunk /skʌŋk/, **skunks.** COUNT N A **skunk** is a small black and white animal which gives off an unpleasant smell if it is frightened.

sky /skaɪ/, **skies.** SING N, OR COUNT N WITH SUPP The **sky** is the space around the earth which you can see when you stand outside and look upwards. *There were little white clouds high in the blue sky... ...the night skies of London.*

sky-high. 1 ADV OR ADJ If prices or wages go **sky-high,** they reach a very high level. *Land value has gone sky-high... ...sky-high property prices.* 2 PHRASE If you **blow** something **sky-high,** you destroy it completely. *His argument has just been blown sky-high.*

skylight /skaɪlaɪt/, **skylights.** COUNT N A **skylight** is a window in a roof.

skyline /skaɪlaɪn/, **skylines.** COUNT N The **skyline** is the line where the sky meets buildings or the land. *...the impressive Manhattan skyline.*

skyscraper /skaɪskreɪpə/, **skyscrapers.** COUNT N A **skyscraper** is a very tall building in a city.

slab /slæb/, **slabs.** COUNT N A **slab** of something is a thick, flat piece of it. *...a great slab of rock... ...a concrete slab... ...a slab of cheese.*

slack /slæk/, **slacker, slackest; slacks.** 1 ADJ **Slack** means loose and not firmly stretched or tightly in position. *...a slack rope... ...his slack and wrinkled skin.* 2 UNCOUNT N The **slack** in a rope is the part that hangs loose. 3 ADJ A **slack** period is one in which there is not much activity. *Very few hotels offered work for the slack season.* 4 ADJ If you are **slack** in your work, you do not do it properly. *Security's got a bit slack.* 5 PLURAL N **Slacks** are casual trousers; an old-fashioned use. *...a pair of golfing slacks.*

slacken /slækə[0]n/, **slackens, slackening, slackened.** 1 ERG VB If something **slackens** or if you **slacken** it, it becomes slower, less active, or less intense. *The rain began to slacken... She slackened her pace.* 2 ERG VB If your grip or your body **slackens** or if you **slacken** it, it becomes looser or more relaxed. *The grip on Casson's right wrist did not slacken... Slacken your legs and slowly lie back.*

slacken off. PHR VB If something **slackens off,** it becomes slower, less active, or less intense. *The Depression slackened off and prosperity returned.*

slag heap, slag heaps. COUNT N A **slag heap** is a hill made of waste materials from mines and factories.

slain /sleɪn/. **Slain** is the past participle of **slay.**

slam /slæm/, **slams, slamming, slammed.** 1 ERG VB If you **slam** a door or window or if it **slams,** it shuts noisily and with great force. *She went out, slamming the door behind her... I waited for the gate behind me to slam shut.* 2 VB WITH OBJ AND ADJUNCT If you **slam** something down, you put it there quickly and with great force. *He slammed the money on the table.*

slander /slɑːndə/, **slanders, slandering, slandered.** 1 COUNT N OR UNCOUNT N A **slander** is an untrue spoken statement about someone which is intended to damage their reputation. *I'll sue her for slander.* 2 VB WITH OBJ If someone **slanders** you, they make untrue spoken statements about you in order to damage your reputation. *She slandered him behind his back.*

slang /slæŋ/. UNCOUNT N Words, expressions, and meanings which are very informal are referred to as **slang.** *...military slang.* Also ATTRIB ADJ *'Porridge' is a slang term for 'prison'.*

slant /slɑːnt/, **slants, slanting, slanted.** 1 VB Something that **slants** is sloping, rather than horizontal or vertical. *The old wooden floor slanted a little.* ♦ **slanting** ATTRIB ADJ *...her slanting eyes.* 2 SING N A **slant** is a slanting position. *For some reason the shelf was set on a slant.* 3 VB WITH OBJ If news or information **is slanted,** it is presented in a way that shows favour towards a particular group or opinion. *Burger's report was obviously slanted.* 4 SING N WITH SUPP A particular **slant** on a subject is a particular way of thinking about it, especially one that is biased or prejudiced. *...a leftist political slant.*

slap /slæp/, **slaps, slapping, slapped.** 1 VB WITH OBJ If you **slap** someone, you hit them with the palm of your hand. *He slapped her across the face... I slapped her hand.* Also COUNT N *Give him a slap if he is too much of a pest.* 2 VB WITH OBJ If you **slap** someone on the back, you hit them in a friendly manner on their back. *I slapped him on the back and wished him the best of luck.* Also COUNT N *...a hefty slap on the back.* 3 VB WITH OBJ AND ADJUNCT If you **slap** something onto a surface, you put it there quickly and carelessly, often with a lot of force. *All you have to do is slap a bit of Sellotape across it... He slapped the report down on the table.*

slapstick /slæpstɪk/. UNCOUNT N **Slapstick** is a simple type of comedy in which the actors behave in a rough and foolish way.

slash /slæʃ/, **slashes, slashing, slashed.** 1 VB WITH OBJ If you **slash** something, you make a long, deep cut in it. *Jack's face had been slashed with broken glass.* 2 VB If you **slash** at something, you quickly hit at it with something. *...slashing at each other with their swords.* 3 VB WITH OBJ To **slash** money or time means to reduce it greatly; an informal use. *...a plan to slash taxes.* 4 COUNT N OR UNCOUNT N A **slash** is a diagonal line that separates letters, words, or numbers. For example, you say the number 340/21/K as 'Three four zero, slash two one, slash K'; used in speech.

slat /slæt/, **slats.** COUNT N **Slats** are the narrow pieces of wood, metal, or plastic in things such as Venetian blinds or cupboard doors.

slate /sleɪt/, **slates.** 1 UNCOUNT N **Slate** is a dark grey rock that can be easily split into thin layers. Slate is often used for covering roofs. 2 COUNT N **Slates** are the small flat pieces of slate used for covering roofs.

slatted /slætɪ[2]d/. ADJ Something that is **slatted** is made with slats. *...white slatted Venetian blinds.*

slaughter /slɔːtə/, **slaughters, slaughtering, slaughtered.** 1 VB WITH OBJ To **slaughter** a large number of people means to kill them in a way that is cruel, unjust, or unnecessary. *Opponents of the regime were systematically slaughtered.* 2 UNCOUNT N **Slaughter** is the cruel, unjust, or unnecessary killing of large numbers of people. *...the needless annual slaughter on our roads.* 3 VB WITH OBJ To **slaughter** animals such as cows and sheep means to kill them for their meat. *...a freshly slaughtered bullock.* 4 UNCOUNT N **Slaughter** is also the killing of animals for their meat. *...animals going away to slaughter.*

slaughterhouse /slɔːtəhaʊs/, **slaughterhouses.** COUNT N A **slaughterhouse** is a place where animals are killed for their meat.

slave /sleɪv/, **slaves, slaving, slaved.** 1 COUNT N A **slave** is a person who is owned by another person and has to work for that person. *...a story about a slave who escapes and becomes a free man.* 2 COUNT N WITH SUPP If you are a **slave** to something, you are very strongly influenced or controlled by it. *He's just become a slave to possessions and money.* 3 VB If you **slave** for someone, you work very hard for them. *Why am I slaving away, running a house and family single-handed?*

slavery /sleɪvə[0]ri[1]/. 1 UNCOUNT N **Slavery** is the system by which people are owned by other people as slaves. *...the abolition of slavery.* 2 UNCOUNT N WITH SUPP You also use **slavery** to refer to the state of not being free because you have to work very hard or because you are strongly influenced by something. *I had at last been freed from the slavery of a 9 to 5 job.*

slavish /sleɪvɪʃ/. 1 ADJ You use **slavish** to describe things that copy or imitate something exactly, without any attempt to be original. *...a slavish adherence to things of the past.* ♦ **slavishly** ADV *I don't expect you to slavishly copy this.* 2 ADJ You also use **slavish** to describe someone who always obeys other people; used showing disapproval. *...a slavish figure, down on her knees polishing the floor.*

slay /sleɪ/, **slays, slaying, slew** /slj[0]uː/, **slain** /sleɪn/. VB WITH OBJ To **slay** someone means to kill them; a literary use. *Two visitors were brutally slain yesterday.*

sleazy /sliːzi[1]/. ADJ A **sleazy** place looks dirty and badly cared for, and not respectable. *...a sleazy cafe.*

sledge /sledʒ/, **sledges.** COUNT N A **sledge** is a vehicle which can slide over snow.

sledgehammer /sledʒhæmə/, **sledgehammers.** COUNT N A **sledgehammer** is a large, heavy hammer with a long handle.

sleek /sliːk/, **sleeker, sleekest.** 1 ADJ **Sleek** hair or fur is smooth and shiny. *...her sleek black hair.* 2 ADJ A **sleek** person looks stylish and wealthy; usually used showing disapproval. *They were fat and sleek and too pleased with themselves.* 3 ADJ A **sleek** vehicle or animal has a smooth, graceful shape. *...sleek, black cars.*

sleep /sliːp/, **sleeps, sleeping, slept** /slept/. 1 UNCOUNT N **Sleep** is the natural state of rest in which your eyes are closed and your mind and body are inactive and unconscious. *I haven't been getting enough sleep recently... Now go to sleep and stop worrying.* 2 VB When you **sleep,** you rest in a state of sleep. *She slept till ten in the morning... He was so excited he could hardly sleep.* ♦ **sleeping** ATTRIB ADJ *I glanced down at the sleeping figure.* 3 SING N A **sleep** is a period of sleeping. *You'll feel better if you have a little sleep.* 4 VB WITH OBJ If a house **sleeps** a particular number of people, it has beds for that number. *Each apartment sleeps up to five adults.* 5 VB WITH ADJUNCT If two people **are sleeping** together, they are having a sexual relationship.

PHRASES ● If a part of your body **goes to sleep,** you lose the sense of feeling in it. *His foot had gone to sleep.* ● If a sick or injured animal is **put to sleep,** it is painlessly killed. *Sheba had to be put to sleep.*

sleep around. PHR VB If someone **sleeps around,** they have sex with several different people during a period of time; an informal use.

sleep off. PHR VB If you **sleep off** the effects of too much food or alcohol, you recover from them by sleeping. *We went back to our room to sleep it off.*

sleep through. PHR VB If you **sleep through** a noise, it does not wake you up. *The girl slept through everything.*

sleeper /sliːpə/, **sleepers.** 1 COUNT N WITH SUPP Someone who is a light **sleeper** is easily woken up. Someone who is a sound or deep **sleeper** is not easily woken up. 2 COUNT N A **sleeper** is a bed on a train. *I booked a first-class sleeper.* 3 COUNT N A train with beds for passengers is also called a **sleeper.** *I usually go up to London on the sleeper.* 4 COUNT N Railway **sleepers** are the large, heavy beams that support the rails of a railway track; a British use.

sleeping bag, sleeping bags. COUNT N A **sleeping bag** is a large, warm bag for sleeping in, especially when you are camping.

sleeping pill, sleeping pills. COUNT N A **sleeping pill** or a **sleeping tablet** is a pill that you can take to help you sleep.

sleepless /sliːplə^{2}s/. 1 ADJ A **sleepless** night is one during which you do not sleep. *He'd had a sleepless night.* 2 ADJ If you are **sleepless,** you cannot sleep. *Late in the night, sleepless and troubled, he went for a walk.* ♦ **sleeplessness** UNCOUNT N *I began to suffer from sleeplessness.*

sleepwalk /sliːpwɔːk/, **sleepwalks, sleepwalking, sleepwalked.** VB If someone is **sleepwalking,** they are walking around while they are asleep. *She must have been sleepwalking.*

sleepy /sliːpi^1/, **sleepier, sleepiest.** 1 ADJ If you are **sleepy,** you feel tired and ready to go to sleep. *She suddenly started to feel very sleepy... ...a sleepy yawn.* ♦ **sleepily** ADV *'Where have you been?' Rudolph asked sleepily.* 2 ATTRIB ADJ A **sleepy** place is very quiet and does not have much excitement. *...sleepy villages.*

sleet /sliːt/, **sleeting.** 1 UNCOUNT N **Sleet** is partly frozen rain. *An icy sleet was beginning to fall.* 2 VB If it **is sleeting,** sleet is falling. *It started to sleet.*

sleeve /sliːv/, **sleeves.** 1 COUNT N The **sleeves** of a garment are the parts that cover your arms. *...a yellow dress with short sleeves.* 2 COUNT N A record **sleeve** is the stiff envelope in which a gramophone record is kept. 3 PHRASE If you **have** something **up** your **sleeve,** you have an idea or plan which you have not told anyone about. *She thought the old man had some clever trick up his sleeve.*

sleeveless /sliːvlə^{2}s/. ATTRIB ADJ A **sleeveless** garment has no sleeves. *...a blue sleeveless dress.*

sleigh /sleɪ/, **sleighs.** COUNT N A **sleigh** is a vehicle which can slide over snow.

slender /slendə/. 1 ADJ A **slender** person is thin and graceful in an attractive way. *...the girl's slender waist... She crossed her slender legs.* 2 ADJ You use **slender** to describe something that is small in amount or degree when you would like it to be greater. *With such slender resources they cannot hope to achieve their aims... ...slender prospects of promotion.*

slept /slept/. **Slept** is the past tense and past participle of **sleep.**

slew /slj^{0}uː/. **Slew** is the past tense of **slay.**

slice /slaɪs/, **slices, slicing, sliced.** 1 COUNT N A **slice** is a piece of food that has been cut from a larger piece. *She cut him three large slices of bread... ...slices of chicken pie.* 2 VB WITH OBJ If you **slice** food, you cut it into thin pieces. *I saw her slicing an apple.* 3 COUNT N A **slice** of something is a part of it. *Rents provided a large slice of his income.* 4 VB WITH OBJ OR 'through' To **slice** or **slice** through something means to cut or move through it quickly, like a knife. *They sliced the air with their knives... The shark's fin sliced through the water.*

slick /slɪk/, **slicks.** 1 ADJ A **slick** book or film seems well-made and attractive, but has little quality or sincerity; used showing disapproval. *Some people thought the broadcasts too slick.* 2 ADJ A **slick** person speaks easily and is persuasive, but is not sincere; used showing disapproval. *...a slick businessman.* 3 ADJ A **slick** action is done quickly and smoothly, without obvious effort. *...a relay race round London, with slick baton-changing.* 4 COUNT N A **slick** is also an oil slick.

slide /slaɪd/, **slides, sliding, slid** /slɪd/. 1 ERG VB When something **slides** or when you **slide** it, it moves smoothly over or against something else. *The gate slid open at the push of a button... She slid the key into the keyhole.* 2 VB To **slide** somewhere means to move there smoothly and quietly. *An elderly lady slid into the seat... The black Mercedes slid away.* 3 VB WITH ADJUNCT If you **slide** into a particular attitude, you change to it gradually, without trying to stop yourself. *He felt himself sliding into obsession.* 4 COUNT N A **slide** is a small piece of photographic film which can be projected onto a screen so that you can see the picture. *...colour slides showing rice fields in Bangkok.* 5 COUNT N A **slide** is also a piece of glass on which you put something that you want to examine through a microscope. 6 COUNT N A **slide** in a playground is a structure that has a steep slope for children to slide down. 7 COUNT N A **slide** is also a hair slide.

slight /slaɪt/, **slighter, slightest; slights, slighting, slighted.** 1 ADJ Something that is **slight** is very small in degree or quantity. *He had a slight German accent... ...after a slight hesitation... I haven't the slightest idea what you're talking about.* ♦ **slightly** ADV *White wine should be slightly chilled.* ● You use **in the slightest** to emphasize a negative statement. *My tennis hadn't improved in the slightest.* 2 ADJ Someone who is **slight** has a slim and delicate body. *I watched her slight figure cross the street.* 3 VB WITH OBJ If you **slight** someone, you insult them by treating them as if they were unimportant. *His fear of being slighted made him avoid people.* Also COUNT N *It was a slight on a past award-winner, Stevenson.*

slim /slɪm/, **slimmer, slimmest; slims, slimming, slimmed.** 1 ADJ Someone who is **slim** has a thin, attractive, well-shaped body. *...a tall, slim girl with long, straight hair.* 2 VB If you **are slimming,** you try to make yourself thinner and lighter by eating less food or healthier food, or by taking exercise. *I may be slimming but I've no intentions of starving myself.* ♦ **slimmer** COUNT N *...clubs for slimmers.* 3 ADJ A **slim** object is thinner than usual. *...a slim book.* 4 ADJ If the chance of something happening is **slim,** it is unlikely to happen. *The chance of American intervention is slim.*

slime /slaɪm/. UNCOUNT N **Slime** is a thick, slippery substance which covers a surface or comes from the bodies of animals such as snails. *There was a green slime around the edges of the tub... ...a trail of slime.*

slimy /slaɪmi^1/. ADJ Something that is **slimy** is covered in slime. *...a slimy pond.*

sling /slɪŋ/, **slings, slinging, slung** /slʌŋ/. 1 VB WITH OBJ AND ADJUNCT If you **sling** something somewhere, you throw it there. *She slung the book across the room.* 2 VB WITH OBJ AND ADJUNCT If you **sling** something over your shoulder or over a chair, for example, you put it there quickly and carelessly so that it hangs down. *Patrick gets his bag and slings it over his shoulder.* ♦ **slung** PRED ADJ *His few bits of clothing were slung over a string on the wall.* 3 VB WITH OBJ AND ADJUNCT If you **sling** something such as a rope between two points, you attach it so that it hangs loosely between them. ♦ **slung** PRED ADJ *Pieces of meat were hanging to dry over a rope slung on the wall.* 4 COUNT N A **sling** is an object made of ropes, straps, or cloth that is used for carrying things. *Mothers carry their babies around with them in slings.* 5 COUNT N A **sling** is also a piece of cloth which is tied around someone's neck to support an injured arm. *His arm was in a sling.*

slink /slɪŋk/, **slinks, slinking, slunk** /slʌŋk/. VB WITH ADJUNCT If you **slink** somewhere, you move there in a slow and secretive way because you do not want to be seen. *I slunk away to my room, to brood.*

slip /slɪp/, **slips, slipping, slipped.** 1 VB If you **slip,** you accidentally slide and lose your balance. *I slipped on the snow and sprained my ankle.* 2 VB If something **slips,** it slides out of place. *She pulled up her sock which had slipped down... It slipped from his fingers and fell with a bump.* 3 VB WITH ADJUNCT If you **slip** somewhere, you go there quickly and quietly. *I hope we can slip away before she notices.* 4 VB WITH OBJ AND ADJUNCT If you **slip** something somewhere, you put it there quickly and quietly. *He slipped it quickly into his pocket.* 5 VB WITH OR WITHOUT OBJ, WITH ADJUNCT You use **slip** to show that someone puts their clothes on or takes them off quickly and easily. *I slipped into my pyjamas... He slipped on his shoes and went out... She slipped off her dress.* 6 COUNT N A **slip** is a small mistake. *I must have made a slip somewhere.* 7 COUNT N A **slip** of paper is a small piece of paper.

PHRASES ● If something **slips** your **mind,** you forget about it. ● If you **give** someone **the slip,** you succeed in escaping from them; an informal use. ● **slip of the tongue:** see **tongue.**

slip up. PHR VB If you **slip up,** you make a mistake. *We must have slipped up somewhere.* ● See also **slip-up.**

slipped disc, slipped discs. COUNT N If you have a **slipped disc,** one of the discs in your spine has moved out of its proper position.

slipper /slɪpə/, **slippers.** COUNT N **Slippers** are soft shoes that you wear in the house.

slippery /slɪpə^{0}ri^1/. ADJ Something that is **slippery** is smooth, wet, or greasy and is therefore difficult to hold or walk on. *The soap was smooth and slippery... ...a slippery pavement.*

slip-up, slip-ups. COUNT N A **slip-up** is a small or unimportant mistake; an informal use.

slit /slɪt/, **slits, slitting. Slit** is used in the present tense, and is the past tense and past participle. 1 VB WITH OBJ If you **slit** something, you make a long narrow cut in it. *She got a knife and slit the envelope... He slit open the packet with his thumb nail.* 2 COUNT N A **slit** is a long narrow cut. *We make a tiny slit in it with a razor blade.* 3 COUNT N A **slit** is also a long narrow opening in something. *...neon light came through the slits in the blind.*

slither /slɪðə/, **slithers, slithering, slithered.** VB If you **slither** somewhere, you slide along, often in an uncontrolled way. *We slithered down the steep slope.*

sliver /slɪvə/, **slivers.** COUNT N A **sliver** of something is a small thin piece of it. *...a sliver of soap.*

slobber /slɒbə/, **slobbers, slobbering, slobbered.** VB If someone **slobbers,** they let liquid fall from their mouth, like babies do.

slog /slɒg/, **slogs, slogging, slogged;** an informal word. 1 VB WITH ADJUNCT If you **slog** at something, you work hard and steadily at it. *The children are slogging away at revision.* Also SING N *...the hard slog of trying to get views changed.* 2 VB WITH ADJUNCT If you **slog** somewhere, you make a long and tiring journey there. *...slogging through the snow.* Also SING N *...his long slog home.*

slogan /sləʊgə^{0}n/, **slogans.** COUNT N **Slogans** are short, easily-remembered phrases, often used in advertising or by politicians.

slop /slɒp/, **slops, slopping, slopped.** ERG VB If liquid **slops** or if you **slop** it, it spills over the edge of a container in a messy way. *We carried the buckets, slopping water, back to the kitchen.*

slope /sləʊp/, **slopes, sloping, sloped.** 1 COUNT N A **slope** is a flat surface that is at an angle, so that one end is higher than the other. *She rode up a grassy slope.* 2 VB If a surface **slopes,** it is at an angle, so that one end is higher than the other. *The roof sloped down at the back.* ♦ **sloping** ATTRIB ADJ *...gently sloping hills.* 3 VB If something **slopes,** it leans to the right or to the left rather than being upright. ♦ **sloping** ATTRIB ADJ *...sloping handwriting.* 4 SING N WITH SUPP The **slope** of something is the angle at which it slopes. *...a slope of ten degrees.*

sloppy /slɒpi^1/. ADJ Something that is **sloppy** is messy and careless; an informal use. *...sloppy workmanship.*

slosh /slɒʃ/, **sloshes, sloshing, sloshed.** ERG VB If a liquid **sloshes** or if you **slosh** it, it splashes or moves around in a messy way. *The whiskey sloshed over from his glass on to his hand... They sat out on the decks laughing and sloshing water everywhere.*

slot /slɒt/, **slots, slotting, slotted.** 1 COUNT N A **slot** is a narrow opening in a machine or container, for example a hole that you put coins in to make a machine work. *He put money in the slot and the music started again.* 2 ERG VB WITH 'in' OR 'into' When something **slots** into something else or when you **slot** it in, you put it into a space where it fits. *The cylinder just slots into the barrel... I slotted my money in.* 3 COUNT N A **slot** is also a place in a schedule, scheme, or organization. *Students get only two slots in the week for private study.*

sloth /sləʊθ/. UNCOUNT N **Sloth** is laziness; a formal use.

slot machine, slot machines. COUNT N A **slot machine** is a machine from which you can get food, drink, or cigarettes or on which you can gamble. You work it by putting coins into a slot in the machine.

slouch /slaʊtʃ/, **slouches, slouching, slouched.** VB If you **slouch,** you have your shoulders and head drooping down. *Many children slouch because of lack of self-confidence.*

slovenly /slʌvənli^1/. ADJ A **slovenly** person is careless, untidy, or inefficient. *His appearance was even more slovenly than usual.*

slow /sləʊ/, **slower, slowest; slows, slowing, slowed.** 1 ADJ **Slow** means moving, acting, or happening without very much speed. *His movements were all deliberate and slow... They have slow reflexes... ...slow changes in the family structure.* Also ADV *You're going too slow.* ♦ **slowly** ADV *He nodded slowly and walked very sadly out of the door* ♦ **slowness** UNCOUNT N *Time passed with agonizing slowness.* 2 ERG VB If something **slows** or if you **slow** it, it starts to move or happen more slowly. *He slowed to a walk... ...ways of slowing population growth.* 3 PRED ADJ A **slow** person is not very clever. 4 PRED ADJ If an activity, place, or story is **slow,** it is not very busy or exciting. *Business will be slow in the shop for another hour.* 5 PRED ADJ If a clock or watch is **slow,** it shows a time that is earlier than the correct time. *That clock's half an hour slow.*

slow down. PHR VB 1 If something **slows down** or if you **slow** it **down,** it starts to move or happen more slowly. *Economic growth has slowed down dramatically... Harold slowed the car down.* 2 If someone **slows down,** they become less active. *He needs to slow down a little or he'll get an ulcer.*

slow up. PHR VB If something **slows up** or if you **slow** it **up,** it starts to move or happen more slowly. *She* *slowed up a little... The extra weight would have slowed me up considerably.*

slow motion. UNCOUNT N **Slow motion** is movement which is much slower than normal, especially in a film or on television. *I dreamt I was falling off a cliff in slow motion.* Also ADJ *...slow-motion film of people talking.*

sludge /slʌdʒ/. UNCOUNT N **Sludge** is thick mud. *I was covered in sludge and weeds.*

slug /slʌg/, **slugs. 1** COUNT N A **slug** is a small, slow-moving creature with a long, slimy body, like a snail without a shell. **2** COUNT N A **slug** is also a bullet; an informal American use.

sluggish /slʌgɪʃ/. ADJ Something that is **sluggish** moves or works much more slowly than normal. *I feel very sluggish... ...black sluggish waters.*

slum /slʌm/, **slums.** COUNT N A **slum** is an area of a city where living conditions are very bad. *I grew up in a slum... ...children from a slum area.*

slumber /slʌmbə/, **slumbers, slumbering, slumbered;** a literary word. **1** UNCOUNT N OR COUNT N **Slumber** is sleep. *She fell into profound and dreamless slumber... Roused from his slumbers, O'Shea departed.* **2** VB If you **slumber,** you sleep. *One old man slumbered over his newspaper.*

slump /slʌmp/, **slumps, slumping, slumped. 1** VB If something such as the value of something **slumps,** it falls suddenly and by a large amount. *Profits last year slumped from $40 million to $26 million.* Also COUNT N *...the continuing slump in oil demand.* **2** COUNT N A **slump** is also a time when there is a lot of unemployment and poverty. *The slump set in during the summer of 1921.* **3** VB WITH ADJUNCT If you **slump** somewhere, you fall or sit down there heavily. *Sarah slumped against the wall.*

slung /slʌŋ/. **Slung** is the past tense and past participle of **sling.**

slunk /slʌŋk/. **Slunk** is the past tense and past participle of **slink.**

slur /slɜː/, **slurs, slurring, slurred. 1** COUNT N A **slur** is an insulting remark which could damage someone's reputation. *He got angry whenever anyone cast the slightest slur on the regiment.* **2** ERG VB If you **slur** your speech or if it **slurs,** you do not pronounce your words clearly, often because you are drunk. *'I'll sing for you,' he said, his voice slurring so that he could barely be understood.* ♦ **slurred** ADJ *His words were slurred and his breath smelled of wine.*

slush /slʌʃ/. UNCOUNT N **Slush** is snow which has begun to melt.

sly /slaɪ/, **slyer** or **slier, slyest** or **sliest. 1** ADJ A **sly** look, expression, or remark shows that you know something that other people do not know. *...a slow sly smile.* ♦ **slyly** ADV *She glanced slyly at Madeleine.* **2** ADJ A **sly** person is clever at deceiving people. *They are suspicious and wary and sly.*

smack /smæk/, **smacks, smacking, smacked. 1** VB WITH OBJ If you **smack** someone, you hit them with your hand. *He smacked her on the bottom.* Also COUNT N *I gave him a smack in the face.* **2** VB WITH OBJ AND ADJUNCT If you **smack** something somewhere, you put it or throw it there so that it makes a loud, sharp noise. *He laughed, smacking the flat of his hand on the steering wheel.* Also SING N *She gave out the books, dropping them with a satisfying smack on each desk.* **3** VB WITH 'of' If something **smacks** of something else, it reminds you of it or is like it; a formal use. *Any literature other than romantic novels smacked to her of school.*

small /smɔːl/, **smaller, smallest. 1** ADJ Someone or something that is **small** is not large in physical size. *She was rather small in stature... The male is smaller than the female... This is the smallest church in England.* ♦ **smallness** UNCOUNT N *The smallness of the courtroom exaggerated its height.* **2** ADJ A **small** group or amount consists of only a few things or of not much of something. *...small families... ...a relatively small number of people... ...a small amount of milk.* **3** ADJ A **small** child is a very young child. *She had two small children.* **4** ADJ You also use **small** to describe something that is not significant or great in degree. *Certain small changes resulted from my report... ...a matter of small importance.*

PHRASES ● The **small of** your **back** is the narrow part of your back where it curves inwards slightly. ● **the small hours:** see **hour.** ● **small wonder:** see **wonder.**

small ad, small ads. COUNT N A **small ad** in a newspaper is a short advertisement in which you can advertise something such as an object for sale or a room to let.

small change. UNCOUNT N **Small change** is coins of low value. *I need some small change to make a phone call.*

small fry. UNCOUNT N **Small fry** is used to refer to people who are considered unimportant.

smallish /smɔːlɪʃ/. ADJ **Smallish** means fairly small. *He was a smallish man.*

smallpox /smɔːlpɒks/. UNCOUNT N **Smallpox** is a serious infectious disease that causes a high fever and a rash.

small-scale. ATTRIB ADJ A **small-scale** activity or organization is limited in extent. *...small-scale industry.*

small talk. UNCOUNT N **Small talk** is conversation at social occasions about unimportant things. *We stood around making small talk.*

smart /smɑːt/, **smarter, smartest; smarts, smarting, smarted. 1** ADJ A **smart** person is pleasantly neat and clean in appearance. *The boys looked smart in their school uniforms.* ♦ **smartly** ADV *...a smartly dressed executive.* **2** ADJ **Smart** also means clever; an American use. *She's one of the smartest students in the whole school... ...a smart idea.* **3** ADJ A **smart** place or event is connected with wealthy and fashionable people. *We met at a very smart lunch party.* **4** ATTRIB ADJ A **smart** movement or action is sharp and quick; a literary use. *...the smart crack of a whip... ...moving along at a smart trot.* ♦ **smartly** ADV *Grabbing the bottle, she hit him smartly on the head.* **5** VB If a part of your body or a wound **smarts,** you feel a sharp stinging pain in it. *His eyes smarted from the smoke of the fire.* **6** VB If you **are smarting** from criticism or unkind remarks, you are feeling upset about it. *Brody smarted under Quint's derision.*

smarten /smɑːtəⁿn/, **smartens, smartening, smartened.**

smarten up. PHR VB If you **smarten** something **up,** you make it look neater and tidier. *The New Electric Cinema has been smartened up.*

smash /smæʃ/, **smashes, smashing, smashed. 1** VB WITH OBJ If you **smash** something, you break it into many pieces by hitting, throwing, or dropping it. *Some windows have been smashed... I nearly smashed the TV set.* **2** VB If something **smashes,** it breaks into many pieces when it falls and hits the ground. *A plate dropped from his fingers and smashed on the kitchen floor.* **3** VB WITH OR WITHOUT OBJ, WITH ADJUNCT If you **smash** through something such as a wall, you go through it by breaking it. *The police smashed their way into eleven homes.* **4** ERG VB WITH ADJUNCT If something **smashes** or **is smashed** against something solid, it moves with great force against it. *The waves smashed onto the shore... The sea smashed the boat against the rocks.* **5** VB WITH OBJ If people **smash** something such as a political system, they deliberately ruin it. *We are interested in transforming the system rather than smashing it.* **6** SING N OR MOD A play or film that is a **smash** or a **smash** hit is very successful and popular. *The show was a smash hit in London and New York.*

smash up. PHR VB If you **smash** something **up,** you completely destroy it by breaking it into many pieces. *He started smashing up all the furniture.*

smashing /smæʃɪŋ/. ADJ If you say something is **smashing,** you mean that you like it very much; an informal use. *We had a smashing time.*

smattering /smætəⁿrɪŋ/. SING N A **smattering** of knowledge or information is a very small amount of it. *Jane spoke Spanish, and a smattering of Greek.*

smear /smɪə/, **smears, smearing, smeared. 1** COUNT N A **smear** is a dirty or greasy mark caused by something rubbing against a surface. *...a smear of blue paint.* **2** VB WITH OBJ To **smear** something means to make dirty or greasy marks on it. *Soot smeared our faces... The windows were all smeared.* **3** VB WITH OBJ AND ADJUNCT If you **smear** a surface with a substance or **smear** the substance onto the surface, you spread a layer of the substance over the surface. *Smear the baking tin with butter... She smeared this blood onto a slide.* **4** COUNT N A **smear** is also an unpleasant and untrue rumour or accusation that is intended to damage someone's reputation. *Party leaders denounced the allegation as a right-wing smear.*

smell /smel/, **smells, smelling, smelled** or **smelt** /smelt/. **1** COUNT N The **smell** of something is a quality it has which you become aware of through your nose. *What's that smell?... ...the smell of fresh bread... The air had a sweet smell... ...cooking smells.* **2** VB If something **smells,** it has a quality which you become aware of through your nose. *The room smelled of cigars... Our kitchen smelt like a rubber factory... The papers smelt musty and stale... Dinner smells good.* **3** VB WITH OBJ If you **smell** something, you become aware of it through your nose. *Don't strike a match if you smell gas.* **4** VB WITH OBJ To **smell** something also means to put your nose near it and breathe in, in order to discover its smell. *She picked up the soap and smelled it.* **5** UNCOUNT N **Smell** is the ability that your nose has to detect things. *They all have an excellent sense of smell.* **6** VB WITH OBJ If you **smell** something such as danger, you feel instinctively that it is likely to happen. *He's shrewd and can smell a successful project.* ● If you **smell a rat,** you become suspicious that there is something wrong.

smelly /smeli¹/. ADJ Something that is **smelly** has an unpleasant smell. *...some rather smelly cheese.*

smile /smaɪl/, **smiles, smiling, smiled. 1** VB When you **smile,** the corners of your mouth curve outwards and slightly upwards, for example because you are pleased or amused. *Hooper smiled and leaned back in his chair... The girl was smiling at me.* **2** COUNT N A **smile** is the expression that you have on your face when you smile. *Barber welcomed me with a smile... ...a mocking, unpleasant smile.* **3** REPORT VB If you **smile** something, you express or say it with a smile. *She smiled her approval... 'That remains to be seen,' smiled Mrs Barrett.*

smirk /smɜːk/, **smirks, smirking, smirked.** VB If you **smirk,** you smile in an unpleasant way. *'That's where you're wrong,' Ellen said, smirking.* Also COUNT N *Mark detected a smirk on the clerk's face.*

smock /smɒk/, **smocks.** COUNT N A **smock** is a loose garment, often worn over other clothes to protect them.

smog /smɒg/. UNCOUNT N **Smog** is a mixture of fog and smoke which occurs in some industrial cities. *Black smog reduced visibility to about fifty yards.*

smoke /sməʊk/, **smokes, smoking, smoked. 1** UNCOUNT N **Smoke** consists of gas and small bits of solid material that are sent into the air when something burns. *The room was full of smoke... ...cigarette smoke.* **2** VB If something **is smoking,** smoke is coming from it. *Down below in the valleys the chimneys were smoking.* **3** VB WITH OR WITHOUT OBJ When someone **smokes** a cigarette, cigar, or pipe, they suck smoke from it into their mouth and blow it out again. *He sat and smoked and stared out of the window.* **4** VB If you **smoke,** you regularly smoke cigarettes, cigars, or a pipe. *Do you smoke?* ♦ **smoker** COUNT N *...a pipe smoker.* **5** VB WITH OBJ To **smoke** fish or meat means to hang it over burning wood so that the smoke will preserve and flavour it. ♦ **smoked** ATTRIB ADJ *...smoked salmon.*

smokeless /sməʊklɪ²s/. ATTRIB ADJ **Smokeless** fuel burns without producing smoke.

smoking /sməʊkɪŋ/. **1** UNCOUNT N **Smoking** is the act or habit of smoking cigarettes, cigars, or a pipe. *Does smoking cause cancer?... I'm trying to give up smoking.* **2** ATTRIB ADJ A **smoking** section or compartment is intended for smokers. *Do you want to go in the smoking or non-smoking section?*

smoky /sməʊki¹/. **1** ADJ A **smoky** place has a lot of smoke in the air. *...a smoky industrial scene of the 1930's.* **2** ATTRIB ADJ You can also use **smoky** to describe something that reminds you of smoke. *...a smoky-blue scarf... ...the smoky twilight.*

smolder /sməʊldə/. See **smoulder.**

smooth /smuːð/, **smoother, smoothest; smooths, smoothing, smoothed. 1** ADJ A **smooth** surface has no roughness or holes. *Your skin looks so smooth... The boulders were so smooth and slippery I couldn't get a grip.* ♦ **smoothness** UNCOUNT N *...the smoothness of his skin.* **2** ADJ A **smooth** liquid or mixture has no lumps in it. *...a smooth paste.* **3** VB WITH OBJ If you **smooth** something, or **smooth** it out, you move your hands over its surface to make it smooth and flat. *Don't iron pyjamas. Just smooth and fold them... He turned his head and smoothed back the hair over one temple.* **4** ADJ A **smooth** movement or process happens or is done evenly and steadily with no sudden changes or breaks. *He walked with a long, smooth stride.* ♦ **smoothly** ADV *The snake glides smoothly towards it.* **5** ADJ **Smooth** also means successful and without problems. *Cooperation is essential if you are going to lead a smooth existence in the office.* ♦ **smoothly** ADV *Life is running smoothly for them.* **6** ADJ A **smooth** man is extremely smart, confident, and polite, in an unpleasant way.

smooth over. PHR VB If you **smooth over** a problem or difficulty, you make it less serious and easier to deal with, especially by talking to the people concerned. *I tried to smooth over the awkwardness of this first meeting.*

smother /smʌðə/, **smothers, smothering, smothered. 1** VB WITH OBJ If you **smother** a fire, you cover it with something in order to put it out. *She grabbed a blanket to smother the flames.* **2** VB WITH OBJ To **smother** someone means to kill them by covering their face so that they cannot breathe. **3** VB WITH OBJ To **smother** someone also means to give them too much love and protection. *She should love them without smothering them with attention.* **4** PASSIVE VB If something **is smothered** with things, it is completely covered with them. *The pear tree was smothered in ivy.*

smoulder /sməʊldə/, **smoulders, smouldering, smouldered;** spelled **smolder** in American English.

VB If something **smoulders,** it burns slowly, producing smoke but not flames. *The ruins are still smouldering.*

smudge /smʌdʒ/, **smudges, smudging, smudged.** 1 COUNT N A **smudge** is a dirty or blurred mark. *The wallpaper had smudges all over it.* 2 VB WITH OBJ If you **smudge** something, you make it dirty or messy by touching it. *Her cheeks were smudged with tears.*

smug /smʌg/. ADJ Someone who is **smug** is very pleased with how good or clever they are; used showing disapproval. *...looks of smug satisfaction.* ♦ **smugly** ADV *'I know all that,' I said smugly.*

smuggle /smʌgəl/, **smuggles, smuggling, smuggled.** VB WITH OBJ If someone **smuggles** things or people into a place or out of it, they take them there illegally or secretly. *She smuggled these diamond bracelets out... ...smuggling refugees into the country.* ♦ **smuggler** /smʌglə/ COUNT N *...drug smugglers.*

snack /snæk/, **snacks.** COUNT N A **snack** is a small, quick meal, or something eaten between meals.

snack bar, snack bars. COUNT N A **snack bar** is a place where you can buy small meals such as sandwiches, and also drinks.

snag /snæg/, **snags, snagging, snagged.** 1 COUNT N A **snag** is a small problem or disadvantage. *It cleans very effectively. The only snag is that it dissolves plastics.* 2 VB WITH OBJ AND ADJUNCT If you **snag** part of your clothing on a sharp or rough object, it gets caught on it and tears. *I snagged my skirt on a bramble.*

snail /sneɪl/, **snails.** COUNT N A **snail** is a small, slimy, slow-moving animal with a spiral-shaped shell.

snake /sneɪk/, **snakes, snaking, snaked.** 1 COUNT N A **snake** is a long, thin reptile with no legs. *He was bitten by a poisonous snake.* 2 VB WITH ADJUNCT Something that **snakes** along goes along in a series of curves; a literary use. *The procession snaked round the houses.*

snap /snæp/, **snaps, snapping, snapped.** 1 ERG VB If something **snaps,** it breaks suddenly, usually with a sharp sound. *The rope snapped... One of those kicks could snap you in half like a dry twig.* Also SING N *The snap of a twig broke the silence.* 2 ERG VB WITH ADJUNCT If something **snaps** into position, it moves quickly into position, with a sharp sound. *The jaws snapped shut around her arm... She snapped the silver chain around her neck.* Also SING N *The trap closes with a sudden snap.* 3 PHRASE If you **snap** your **fingers,** you make a sharp sound by moving your middle finger quickly across your thumb. 4 VB If an animal **snaps** at you, it shuts its jaws quickly near you. *The dogs ran snapping and barking at his heels.* 5 VB WITH 'at' OR REPORT VB If someone **snaps** at you, they speak to you in a sharp, unfriendly way. *'Don't do that!' she snapped.* 6 ATTRIB ADJ A **snap** decision or action is taken suddenly, without careful thought. *The snap reaction of the press was to welcome the change.* 7 COUNT N A **snap** is a photograph that is taken quickly and casually; an informal use.

snap up. PHR VB If you **snap** something **up,** you buy it quickly; an informal use. *All these houses were snapped up as soon as they were offered for sale.*

snapshot /snæpʃɒt/, **snapshots.** COUNT N A **snapshot** is a photograph that is taken quickly and casually. *...family snapshots.*

snare /snɛə/, **snares.** COUNT N A **snare** is a trap for catching birds or small animals. *...a rabbit snare.*

snarl /snɑːl/, **snarls, snarling, snarled.** VB When an animal **snarls,** it makes a fierce, rough sound and shows its teeth. *...dogs snarling and snapping at the heels of sheep.* Also COUNT N *The leopard gave a snarl of fury.*

snatch /snætʃ/, **snatches, snatching, snatched.** 1 VB WITH OBJ OR 'at' If you **snatch** something, you take it or pull it away quickly. *He snatched the letter from the man's hand... He remembered snatching at his gun.* 2 VB WITH OBJ If you **snatch** a small amount of time or an opportunity, you quickly make use of it. *I packed, then snatched four hours' sleep... I snatched the opportunity to tell them that I was leaving.* 3 COUNT N A **snatch** of a conversation or a song is a very small piece of it.

sneak /sniːk/, **sneaks, sneaking, sneaked.** 1 VB WITH ADJUNCT If you **sneak** somewhere, you go there quietly, trying to avoid being seen or heard. *I didn't notice Bob sneaking up behind me.* 2 VB WITH OBJ AND ADJUNCT If you **sneak** something somewhere, you take it there secretly. *Eugene would sneak food down to his room.* 3 VB WITH OBJ AND ADJUNCT If you **sneak** a look at someone or something, you secretly have a quick look at them. 4 ATTRIB ADJ A **sneak** preview of something is an unofficial opportunity to look at it before it is officially shown to the public. *We were shown his latest masterpiece in a sneak preview.*

sneaker /sniːkə/, **sneakers.** COUNT N **Sneakers** are casual shoes with rubber soles.

sneaking /sniːkɪŋ/. ATTRIB ADJ A **sneaking** feeling is a slight or vague feeling, especially one that you are unwilling to have. *I have a sneaking suspicion you're right... ...a sneaking admiration for his commercialism.*

sneaky /sniːki[1]/. ADJ Someone who is **sneaky** does things secretly rather than openly; an informal use which shows disapproval. *I had a sneaky glimpse at the list.*

sneer /snɪə/, **sneers, sneering, sneered.** VB WITH 'at' OR REPORT VB If you **sneer** at someone or something, you express your contempt for them. *She was afraid he would sneer at the idea... 'We could certainly get cheaper estimates,' sneered Casson.* Also COUNT N *'Oh yes,' said McFee, a sneer flitting over his face.*

sneeze /sniːz/, **sneezes, sneezing, sneezed.** VB When you **sneeze,** you suddenly take in your breath and then blow it down your nose noisily. *He sneezed violently.* Also COUNT N *...the coughs and sneezes.*

snide /snaɪd/. ADJ A **snide** comment or remark criticizes someone nastily, often in an indirect way.

sniff /snɪf/, **sniffs, sniffing, sniffed.** 1 VB When you **sniff,** you breathe in air noisily through your nose, for example when you have a cold, or are trying not to cry, or in order to show disapproval. *Felicity said, sniffing, 'When will you see me again?'* Also COUNT N *The classroom rang with coughs, sniffs, and sneezes.* 2 VB WITH OBJ OR 'at' If you **sniff** something, you smell it by sniffing. *'What a revolting smell,' he said, sniffing the air... The dog sniffed at Marsha's bags.* Also COUNT N *He took a cautious sniff.*

snigger /snɪgə/, **sniggers, sniggering, sniggered.** VB If you **snigger,** you laugh quietly and in a disrespectful way. *What are you sniggering at?* Also COUNT N *His sniggers became uncontrollable.*

snip /snɪp/, **snips, snipping, snipped.** VB WITH OR WITHOUT OBJ If you **snip** off part of something, you cut it off with scissors or shears in a single quick action. *...snipping off the last two inches of his hair... Brian snipped energetically at the hedge.*

snipe /snaɪp/, **snipes, sniping, sniped.** 1 VB If someone **snipes** at you, they criticize you. *The unions are an easy target to snipe at.* 2 VB To **snipe** at someone also means to shoot at them from a hidden position. *Just then someone started sniping at us.* ♦ **sniper** /snaɪpə/ COUNT N *...a sniper's bullet.*

snippet /snɪpɪt/, **snippets.** COUNT N A **snippet** of information or news is a small piece of it.

snivel /snɪvəl/, **snivels, snivelling, snivelled;** spelled **sniveling, sniveled** in American English. VB If someone **is snivelling,** they are crying and sniffing in an irritating way.

snob /snɒb/, **snobs;** a word used showing disapproval. 1 COUNT N A **snob** is someone who admires upper-class people and despises lower-class people. 2 COUNT N WITH SUPP An intellectual **snob** is someone who believes that they are superior to other people because of their intelligence or taste.

snobbery /snɒbəri[1]/. UNCOUNT N **Snobbery** is the attitude of a snob; used showing disapproval. *Social snobbery reached a peak in the last century.*

snobbish /snɒbɪʃ/. ADJ Someone who is **snobbish** is too proud of their social status, intelligence, or taste; used showing disapproval.

snooker /snuːkə/. UNCOUNT N **Snooker** is a game in which two players use long sticks called cues to hit a white ball across a special table so that it knocks coloured balls into pockets at the side of the table.

snoop /snuːp/, **snoops, snooping, snooped.** VB Someone who **is snooping** is secretly looking round a place in order to find out things.

snooty /snuːti[1]/. ADJ Someone who is **snooty** behaves as if they are superior to other people; used showing disapproval. *I got a very snooty letter from them rejecting my application.*

snooze /snuːz/, **snoozes, snoozing, snoozed.** VB When you **snooze** you have a short, light sleep during the day; an informal use. *I lay on the sofa, snoozing.* Also SING N *I've just had a nice snooze.*

snore /snɔː/, **snores, snoring, snored.** VB When someone who is asleep **snores,** they make a loud noise each time they breathe. *He snored loudly on the camp-bed.* Also COUNT N *I could hear heavy snores coming from the bedroom.*

snort /snɔːt/, **snorts, snorting, snorted.** VB When people or animals **snort,** they breathe air noisily out through their noses. People snort in order to express disapproval or amusement. *The pigs grunted and snorted... My sister snorted with laughter.* Also COUNT N *Clarissa gave a snort of disgust.*

snout /snaʊt/, **snouts.** COUNT N The **snout** of an animal such as a pig is its long nose.

snow /snəʊ/, **snows, snowing, snowed.** 1 UNCOUNT N **Snow** is the soft white bits of frozen water that fall from the sky in cold weather. *Outside the snow lay thick on the ground.* Also PLURAL N *...driving down from the snows of the Alps.* 2 VB When it **snows,** snow falls from the sky. *It was snowing quite heavily.* ● See also **snowed in, snowed under.**

snowball /snəʊbɔːl/, **snowballs, snowballing, snowballed.** 1 COUNT N A **snowball** is a ball of snow. *...children throwing snowballs.* 2 VB If something such as a campaign **snowballs,** it rapidly increases and grows.

snowbound /snəʊbaʊnd/. ADJ If people or vehicles are **snowbound,** they cannot go anywhere because of heavy snow.

snowdrift /snəʊdrɪft/, **snowdrifts.** COUNT N A **snowdrift** is a deep pile of snow formed by the wind.

snowdrop /snəʊdrɒp/, **snowdrops.** COUNT N A **snowdrop** is a small white flower which appears in the early spring.

snowed in. PRED ADJ If you are **snowed in** or **snowed up,** you cannot go anywhere because of heavy snow.

snowed under. PRED ADJ If you are **snowed under,** you have too much work to deal with. *At present we are snowed under with work.*

snowed up. See **snowed in.**

snowflake /snəʊfleɪk/, **snowflakes.** COUNT N A **snowflake** is one of the soft, white bits of frozen water that fall as snow.

snowman /snəʊmæn/, **snowmen.** COUNT N A **snowman** is a mass of snow formed roughly into the shape of a person.

snowplough /snəʊplaʊ/, **snowploughs;** spelled **snowplow** in American English. COUNT N A **snowplough** is a vehicle used to push snow off roads or railway lines.

snowy /snəʊi[1]/. ADJ Something that is **snowy** has a lot of snow. *...two high snowy peaks.*

snub /snʌb/, **snubs, snubbing, snubbed.** VB WITH OBJ If you **snub** someone, you insult them by ignoring them or by behaving rudely. *Both she and her husband were snubbed by the intellectuals they knew.* Also COUNT N *But George was impervious to snubs.*

snuff /snʌf/. UNCOUNT N **Snuff** is powdered tobacco which people take by sniffing it up their nose. *My father used to take snuff.*

snug /snʌg/. 1 ADJ If you are **snug,** you feel warm and comfortable. *We lit a big fire which made us feel very snug and safe.* 2 ADJ A **snug** place is small but warm and comfortable. *It was warm and dry in his snug studio.* 3 ADJ If something is a **snug** fit, it fits tightly. *...snug overcoats.* ♦ **snugly** ADV *The metal box fitted snugly into the bottom.*

snuggle /snʌgəl/, **snuggles, snuggling, snuggled.** VB WITH ADJUNCT If you **snuggle** somewhere, you settle yourself into a warm, comfortable position, especially by moving closer to another person. *He turned over to snuggle close to her.*

so /səʊ/. 1 ADV You use **so** when you are referring back to something that has just been mentioned. *Do you enjoy romantic films? If so, you should watch the film on ITV tonight... 'Is there anything else you want to tell me about?'—'I don't think so.'... The issue is unresolved, and will remain so until the next SDP Congress.* 2 SENTENCE ADV If one person or thing does something and **so** does another one, the other one does it too. *Etta laughed heartily and so did he... His shoes are brightly polished; so is his briefcase.* 3 CONJ You use **so** and **so that** to introduce the result of the situation you have just mentioned. *He speaks very little English, so I talked to him through an interpreter... The door was open, so that anyone passing could look in.* 4 CONJ You use **so that** and **so as** to introduce the reason for doing the thing you have just mentioned. *He has to earn lots of money so that he can buy his children nice food and clothes... They went on foot, so as not to be heard.* 5 SENTENCE ADV You can use **so** in a discussion or talk when you are checking something, summarizing something, or moving on to a new stage. *So it wasn't just an accident?... And so for now, goodnight... So what are the advantages of nuclear energy?* 6 ADV You can also use **so** when you are saying that something is done or arranged in the way that you describe. *They have the eyes so located as to give a wide field of vision... The others are moving right to left, like so.* 7 ADV You can also use **so** to describe or emphasize the degree or extent of something. *I'm so glad you could come... Don't go so fast... The engine was so hot the air around it shimmered.* 8 ADV You can use **so** before words such as 'much' and 'many' to indicate that there is a limit to something. *We will only pay so much, no more.*

PHRASES ● You use **and so on** or **and so forth** at the end of a list to indicate that there are other items that you could also mention. *You can program a computer to paint, play chess and so on.* ● You use **or so** when you are giving an approximate amount. *We arrived a month or so ago.* ● You use the structures **as...so** and **just as...so** to indicate that two events or situations are alike in some way. *Just as one gesture can have* *many different meanings, so many different gestures can have the same meaning.* ● You use the structures **not so much** and **not so much...as** to say that something is one kind of thing rather than another kind. *...a cry not so much of pain as of amazement.* ● You say **'So?'** and **'So what?'** to indicate that you think that what someone has said is unimportant; an informal use. *'Someone will see us.'—'So what?'* ● **ever so:** see **ever.** ● **so far:** see **far.** ● **so long, so long as:** see **long.** ● **so much for:** see **much.** ● **every so often:** see **often.** ● **so there:** see **there.**

soak /səʊk/, **soaks, soaking, soaked.** 1 ERG VB When you **soak** something, you put it into a liquid and leave it there. *Soak the material for several hours in cold water... 'Can I help you with the dishes?'—'Oh, I'll just leave them to soak.'* 2 VB WITH OBJ When a liquid **soaks** something, it makes it very wet. *A stream of water came in and soaked both sleeping bags.* 3 VB WITH ADJUNCT When a liquid **soaks** through something, it passes through it. *The blood had soaked through the handkerchief.*

soak up. PHR VB When a soft or dry substance **soaks up** a liquid, the liquid goes into the substance. *The soil soaked up a huge volume of water.*

soaked /səʊkt/. PRED ADJ If someone or something gets **soaked,** they get extremely wet. *It was pouring down and we all got soaked.*

soaking /səʊkɪŋ/. ADJ If something is **soaking** or **soaking wet,** it is very wet. *My boots were soaking wet inside.*

so-and-so. UNCOUNT N You use **so-and-so** instead of a name or word when talking generally rather than giving a specific example; an informal use. *What happens is that somebody will phone me and say, 'Mrs So-and-So would like a visit.'*

soap /səʊp/, **soaps, soaping, soaped.** 1 MASS N **Soap** is a substance used with water for washing. *...a bar of yellow soap.* 2 REFL VB If you **soap** yourself, you rub soap on your body to wash yourself. 3 COUNT N A **soap** is a soap opera.

soap opera, soap operas. COUNT N A **soap opera** is a television drama serial about the daily lives of a group of people.

soapy /səʊpi¹/. ADJ Something that is **soapy** is full of soap or covered with soap. *Wash your brushes in warm soapy water.*

soar /sɔː/, **soars, soaring, soared.** 1 VB If an amount **soars,** it quickly increases by a large amount. *Property prices have soared.* 2 VB If something **soars** into the air, it goes quickly upwards. *Flames were soaring into the sky.* 3 VB WITH ADJUNCT Trees or buildings that **soar** upwards are very tall. *Great trees soar above to cut out most of the light... ..the soaring spire of St Patrick's.*

sob /sɒb/, **sobs, sobbing, sobbed.** 1 VB When someone **sobs,** they cry noisily. *She was sobbing bitterly.* ♦ **sobbing** UNCOUNT N *The sobbing began again.* 2 COUNT N A **sob** is one of the noises that you make when you are crying. *...gasping, choking sobs.*

sober /səʊbə/, **sobers, sobering, sobered.** 1 ADJ When you are **sober,** you are not drunk. *Rudolph knew he had to stay sober to drive home.* 2 ADJ A **sober** person is serious and thoughtful. *...sober and sensible attitudes.* ♦ **soberly** ADV *'That's true,' Andy said soberly.* 3 ATTRIB ADJ **Sober** colours and clothes are plain and rather dull. *...a pair of sober black walking shoes.* ♦ **soberly** ADV *...a soberly dressed office employee.*

sober up. PHR VB When someone **sobers up,** they become sober after being drunk.

so-called. ATTRIB ADJ You use **so-called** in front of a word to indicate that you think that the word is incorrect or misleading. *...her so-called friends... Why did the so-called Agricultural Revolution occur?*

soccer /sɒkə/. UNCOUNT N **Soccer** is football; a British use.

sociable /səʊʃəbə⁰l/. ADJ **Sociable** people enjoy meeting and talking to other people. *Adler was an outgoing, sociable kind of man.* ♦ **sociability** /səʊʃəbɪlɪ¹ti¹/ UNCOUNT N *There was no doubt about his sociability.*

social /səʊʃə⁰l/. 1 ATTRIB ADJ **Social** means relating to society. *...demands for modernisation and social change... ...children from different social backgrounds.* ♦ **socially** ADV *They must behave in a way which will be socially acceptable.* 2 ADJ **Social** activities are leisure activities that involve meeting other people, as opposed to activities related to work. *We've met at social and business functions... ...their circle of social contacts.* ♦ **socially** ADV *...the only people my father ever visited socially.*

socialism /səʊʃəlɪzə⁰m/. UNCOUNT N **Socialism** is the belief that the state should own industries on behalf of the people and that everyone should be equal. ♦ **socialist** /səʊʃəlɪst/ ADJ OR COUNT N *...the French Socialist Party... ...disillusionment among radicals and socialists.*

socialize /səʊʃəlaɪz/, **socializes, socializing, socialized;** also spelled **socialise.** VB If you **socialize,** you meet other people socially. *I socialized with the philosophy students.*

social life, social lives. COUNT N Your **social life** consists of ways in which you spend time with your friends and acquaintances.

social science, social sciences. 1 UNCOUNT N **Social science** is the scientific study of society. 2 COUNT N The **social sciences** are the various branches of social science. *Economics is the oldest of the social sciences.*

social security. UNCOUNT N **Social security** is a system by which the government pays money regularly to people who have no income or only a very small income.

social services. PLURAL N **Social services** are services provided by a local authority to help people who have social and financial problems.

social work. UNCOUNT N **Social work** involves giving help and advice to people with serious financial problems or family problems.

social worker, social workers. COUNT N A **social worker** is a person whose job is to do social work.

society /səsaɪəti¹/, **societies.** 1 UNCOUNT N OR COUNT N You can refer to the people in a country as its **society.** *...society's attitude towards the elderly... We live in a multi-racial society.* 2 COUNT N A **society** is an organization for people who have the same interest or aim. *...the Royal Horticultural Society.*

sociology /səʊsɪɒləd͡ʒi¹/. UNCOUNT N **Sociology** is the study of human societies. *...sociology students.* ♦ **sociological** /səʊsɪəlɒd͡ʒɪkə⁰l/ ATTRIB ADJ *...sociological studies of criminals.* ♦ **sociologist** /səʊsɪɒləd͡ʒɪst/ COUNT N *This is what sociologists have been saying for years.*

sock /sɒk/, **socks.** COUNT N **Socks** are pieces of clothing which cover your foot and ankle and are worn inside shoes. *...a pair of light-blue wool socks.*

socket /sɒkɪt/, **sockets.** 1 COUNT N A **socket** is a place on a wall or on a piece of electrical equipment into which you can put a plug or bulb. 2 COUNT N You can refer to any hollow part or opening in a structure which another part fits into as a **socket.** *...deep eye sockets.*

soda /səʊdə/. UNCOUNT N **Soda** or **soda water** is fizzy water used for mixing with alcoholic drinks or fruit juice. *...a whisky and soda.*

sodden /sɒdə⁰n/. ADJ Something that is **sodden** is extremely wet. *My coat was sodden from the rain.*

sofa /səʊfə/, **sofas.** COUNT N A **sofa** is a long, comfortable seat with a back and arms, which two or three people can sit on.

soft /sɒft/, **softer, softest.** 1 ADJ Something that is **soft** changes shape easily when you press it and is not hard or stiff. *...a soft bed... His feet left prints in the soft soil... ...soft black fur.* ♦ **softness** UNCOUNT N *...the softness of her arms.* 2 ADJ **Soft** also means very gentle, with no force. *...a soft breeze.* ♦ **softly** ADV *Mike softly placed his hand on her shoulder.* 3 ADJ A **soft** sound or voice is quiet and not harsh. *She had a soft South German accent.* ♦ **softly** ADV *'Listen,' she said softly.* 4 ADJ A **soft** light or colour is pleasant and restful, not bright. *...the soft glow of the evening light... ...walls in soft pink stone.* 5 ADJ Someone who is **soft** is kind, and perhaps not strict or severe enough. *...the 'soft' approach to juvenile offenders.* 6 ADJ **Soft** drugs are illegal drugs which are not considered to be very strong or harmful. 7 PHRASE If you **have a soft spot for** someone, you are especially fond of them.

soft drink, soft drinks. COUNT N A **soft drink** is a non-alcoholic drink such as lemonade or fruit juice.

soften /sɒfə⁰n/, **softens, softening, softened.** 1 ERG VB If something **is softened,** it becomes less hard, stiff, or firm. *Fry the onions for about 10 minutes to soften them... I'm waiting for the ice-cream to soften.* 2 VB WITH OBJ If something **softens** a shock or a damaging effect, it makes it seem less severe. *He had alcohol to soften the blow.* 3 ERG VB If you **soften,** you become more sympathetic and less hostile. *She gradually softened towards me... I refused to be softened.*

soften up. PHR VB If you **soften** someone **up,** you put them into a good mood before asking them to do something; an informal use.

soft-hearted. ADJ Someone who is **soft-hearted** is sympathetic and kind.

soft-spoken. ADJ Someone who is **soft-spoken** has a quiet, gentle voice.

software /sɒftweə/. UNCOUNT N Computer programs are referred to as **software.**

soggy /sɒgi¹/. ADJ Something that is **soggy** is unpleasantly wet. *...soggy biscuits.*

soil /sɔɪl/, **soils, soiling, soiled.** 1 UNCOUNT N **Soil** is the substance on the land surface of the earth in which plants grow. *The soil here is very fertile.* 2 UNCOUNT N WITH SUPP You can use **soil** to refer to a country's territory. *...if no foreign armies had invaded Russian soil.* 3 VB WITH OBJ If you **soil** something, you make it dirty; a formal use.

solace /sɒlə¹s/; a formal word. 1 UNCOUNT N **Solace** is a feeling of comfort that makes you feel less sad. *He began to find solace in the Bible.* 2 SING N If something is a **solace** to you, it makes you feel less sad. *Her poetry has always been a solace to me.*

solar /səʊlə/. ATTRIB ADJ **Solar** means relating to the sun. *...solar eclipses... ...the potential of solar energy.*

solar system. PROPER N The **solar system** is the sun and all the planets that go round it.

sold /səʊld/. **Sold** is the past tense and past participle of **sell.**

soldier /səʊld͡ʒə/, **soldiers.** COUNT N A **soldier** is a person in an army.

sole /səʊl/, **soles.** 1 ATTRIB ADJ The **sole** thing or person of a particular type is the only one of that type. *In some families, the woman is the sole wage earner... They went with the sole purpose of making a nuisance of themselves.* 2 ATTRIB ADJ If you have **sole** charge or ownership of something, you are the only person in charge of it or who owns it. *She has the sole responsibility for bringing up the child.* 3 COUNT N The **sole** of your foot or of a shoe or sock is the underneath surface of it. 4 COUNT N OR UNCOUNT N A **sole** is a kind of flat fish that you can eat. The plural is also 'sole'.

solely /səʊlli¹/. ADV If something involves **solely** one thing, it involves only this thing and no others. *This is solely a matter of money.*

solemn /sɒləm/. 1 ADJ Someone or something that is **solemn** is very serious rather than cheerful or humorous. *...solemn and mournful music.* ♦ **solemnly** ADV *Ralph nodded solemnly.* ♦ **solemnity** /sə⁷lɛmnɪ¹ti¹/ UNCOUNT N *...the solemnity of the occasion.* 2 ATTRIB ADJ A **solemn** promise or agreement is formal and sincere. *The government has solemn commitments and must honour them.* ♦ **solemnly** ADV *Jacob solemnly vowed to keep this promise.*

solicit /səlɪsɪt/, **solicits, soliciting, solicited.** 1 VB WITH OBJ If you **solicit** money, help, or an opinion from someone, you ask them for it; a formal use. *Roy solicited aid from a number of influential members.* 2 VB When prostitutes **solicit,** they offer to have sex with people in return for money. ♦ **soliciting** UNCOUNT N *She's been fined £35 for soliciting.*

solicitor /səlɪsɪtə/, **solicitors.** COUNT N A **solicitor** is a lawyer who gives legal advice and prepares legal documents and cases.

solicitous /səlɪsɪtəs/. ADJ Someone who is **solicitous** shows anxious concern for someone; a formal use. *The hotel personnel could not have been more solicitous.* ♦ **solicitously** ADV *'Now, Mr Gerran, you must take it easy,' I said solicitously.*

solicitude /səlɪsɪtjuːd/. UNCOUNT N **Solicitude** is anxious concern for someone; a formal use. *I was moved by their genuine kindness and solicitude for Karin.*

solid /sɒlɪd/, **solids.** 1 ADJ A **solid** substance or object is hard or firm, rather than being a liquid or a gas. *The basic choice is gas, electricity, or solid fuel... Even the sea around them is frozen solid.* 2 COUNT N A **solid** is a substance that is hard or firm. *You must at least know whether it's a solid or a liquid or a gas.* 3 ADJ A **solid** object or mass does not have a space inside it, or any holes or gaps in it. *...a solid-tyred bus... The car park was packed solid.* 4 ATTRIB ADJ An object made of **solid** gold or **solid** oak, for example, is made of gold or oak all the way through. 5 ADJ A **solid** structure is strong and is not likely to collapse or fall over. *...solid Victorian houses.* ♦ **solidly** ADV *...large houses built solidly of wooden planks.* ♦ **solidity** /səlɪdɪ¹ti¹/ UNCOUNT N *...their appearance of massive solidity.* 6 ADJ A **solid** citizen is respectable and reliable. *She regarded them as solid, good, dull people.* ♦ **solidly** ADV *...a solidly respectable family.* 7 ADJ If something is **solid,** it is reliable, strong, and large in amount. *...a veteran British Council worker, with solid experience in Asia and Africa... Solid evidence is needed.* ♦ **solidly** ADV *They are solidly behind the proposal.* ♦ **solidity** UNCOUNT N *...giving an added strength and solidity to the state.* 8 ATTRIB ADJ OR ADJ AFTER N If you do something for a **solid** period of time, you do it without any pause or interruption throughout that time. *I waited a solid hour... I read for two hours solid.* ♦ **solidly** ADV *If you work for ten weeks solidly you might stand more of a chance.*

solidarity /sɒlɪdærɪ¹ti¹/. UNCOUNT N If a group of people show **solidarity,** they show complete unity and support for each other. *...working-class solidarity.*

solidify /səlɪdɪfaɪ/, **solidifies, solidifying, solidified.** VB When a liquid **solidifies,** it changes into a solid.

solitary /sɒlɪtə⁰ri¹/. 1 ATTRIB ADJ A **solitary** activity is one that you do alone. *He formed the habit of taking long solitary walks.* 2 ADJ A person or animal that is **solitary** spends a lot of time alone. *Tigers are solitary creatures.* 3 ATTRIB ADJ A **solitary** person or object is alone and has no others nearby. *Madeleine walked over to the solitary figure.*

solitary confinement. UNCOUNT N A prisoner who is in **solitary confinement** is being kept alone, away from all other prisoners.

solitude /sɒlɪtju:d/. UNCOUNT N **Solitude** is the state of being alone. *One can study far better in solitude.*

solo /səʊləʊ/, **solos.** 1 COUNT N A **solo** is a piece of music played or sung by one person. *...a clarinet solo by Donizetti.* 2 ATTRIB ADJ A **solo** performance or activity is done by one person. *...a solo flight.* Also ADV *...the boat in which he sailed solo round the world.*

soloist /səʊləʊɪst/, **soloists.** COUNT N A **soloist** is a person who plays a musical instrument alone or sings alone.

soluble /sɒljə⁴bə⁰l/. ADJ A **soluble** substance will dissolve in a liquid. *The powder is soluble in water.*

solution /səlu:ʃə⁰n/, **solutions.** 1 COUNT N A **solution** is a way of dealing with or removing a difficulty. *It's a very neat little solution to our problem.* 2 COUNT N The **solution** to a riddle or a puzzle is the answer. *...the crossword solution.* 3 COUNT N A **solution** is also a liquid in which a solid substance has been dissolved; a technical use. *...a solution of detergent and water.*

solve /sɒlv/, **solves, solving, solved.** VB WITH OBJ If you **solve** a problem or a question, you find a solution or an answer to it. *...the failure of successive Government policies to solve Britain's economic problems... ...solving crossword puzzles.*

solvent /sɒlvənt/, **solvents.** 1 ADJ If a person or a company is **solvent,** they have enough money to pay all their debts; a formal use. 2 COUNT N OR UNCOUNT N A **solvent** is a liquid that can dissolve other substances; a technical use. *...rubber solvents... ...grease solvent.*

sombre /sɒmbə/; a literary word, spelled **somber** in American English. 1 ADJ **Sombre** colours and places are dark and dull. *...two women dressed in sombre black.* 2 ADJ If someone is **sombre,** they are serious, sad, or pessimistic. *Mr Morris took a more sombre view.*

some /sʌm/. 1 DET OR PRON You use **some** to refer to an unspecified amount of something or to a number of people or things. *She had a piece of pie and some coffee... I've got some friends coming over... 'You'll need graph paper.'—'Yeah, I've got some at home.'* 2 DET You also use **some** to emphasize that an amount or number is fairly large. *They were having some difficulty in following the plot... I did not meet her again for some years.* 3 QUANTIF OR DET **Some** is also used to refer to part of an amount or group. *She took some of the meat out... Some sports are very dangerous.* 4 DET If you refer to **some** person or thing, you are referring to that person or thing vaguely, without stating precisely which one you mean. *We found it lying in some ditch in the middle of the desert... At some stage in your career you may need my help.* 5 **Some** is also used to mean approximately; a formal use. *...a single layer of stone, some four metres thick.*

somebody /sʌmbə⁷di¹/. See **someone.**

some day. ADV **Some day** or **someday** means at a vague date in the future. *I'd like to see it some day.*

somehow /sʌmhaʊ/. 1 ADV You use **somehow** to indicate that you do not know how something was done or will be done. *...a boy who'd somehow broken his thumb... We'll manage somehow.* 2 SENTENCE ADV You also use **somehow** to indicate that you do not know the reason for something. *Somehow it didn't seem important to him any more.*

someone /sʌmwə⁰n/. INDEF PRON You use **someone** or **somebody** to refer to a person without saying exactly who you mean. *There's someone coming upstairs... It belongs to somebody else.*

someplace /sʌmpleɪs/. ADV **Someplace** means the same as somewhere; an informal American use. *Why don't you boys go and sit someplace else?*

somersault /sʌməsɒ:lt/, **somersaults.** COUNT N A **somersault** is a movement in which you bring your legs right over your head, in the air or with your hands on the ground. *My sister turned a somersault.*

something /sʌmθɪŋ/. 1 INDEF PRON You use **something** to refer in a vague way to anything that is not a person, for example an object, action, or quality. *Hendricks saw something ahead of him... Something terrible has happened.* 2 INDEF PRON If what you have or what has been done is **something,** it is useful, even if only in a small way. *Of course I've got my savings now, that's something.*

PHRASES • If you say that a person or thing is **something of** a particular thing, you mean that they are that thing to a limited extent. *It is something of a mystery.* • If you say that **there is something in** an idea or suggestion, you mean that it is quite good. *I believe there is something in having ballots in trade unions.* • **something like:** see **like.**

sometime /sʌmtaɪm/. 1 ADV **Sometime** means at a vague or unspecified time in the future or the past. *Can I come and see you sometime?... He saw Frieda Maloney sometime last week.* 2 ATTRIB ADJ You can also use **sometime** to indicate what job a person used to have; a formal use. *...Sir Alfred Munnings, sometime President of the Royal Academy.*

sometimes /sʌmtaɪmz/. ADV You use **sometimes** to say that something happens on some occasions. *Sometimes they just come for a term, sometimes six months.*

somewhat /sʌmwɒt/. ADV OR SUBMOD **Somewhat** means to a moderate extent or degree; a formal use. *...a fine, though somewhat daunting, director... Communication has altered things somewhat.*

somewhere /sʌmweə/. 1 ADV You use **somewhere** to refer to a place without saying exactly where you mean. *They lived somewhere near Bournemouth... There's an ashtray somewhere.* 2 ADV You also use **somewhere** when giving an approximate amount, number, or time. *This part of the church was built somewhere around 700 AD... ...somewhere between 55,000 and 60,000 men.* 3 PHRASE If you **are getting somewhere,** you are making progress.

son /sʌn/, **sons.** COUNT N Your **son** is your male child. *Don Culver is the son of an engineer.*

sonar /səʊnɑ:/. UNCOUNT N OR MOD **Sonar** is equipment on a ship which can calculate the depth of the sea or the position of an underwater object using sound waves. *...sonar apparatus.*

sonata /sənɑ:tə/, **sonatas.** COUNT N A **sonata** is a piece of classical music written for the piano or for a piano and one other instrument.

song /sɒŋ/, **songs.** 1 COUNT N OR UNCOUNT N A **song** consists of words and music sung together. *...a love song... We all burst into song.* 2 COUNT N OR UNCOUNT N A bird's **song** is the pleasant, musical sounds that it makes.

son-in-law, sons-in-law. COUNT N Your **son-in-law** is the husband of your daughter.

sonnet /sɒnɪt/, **sonnets.** COUNT N A **sonnet** is a poem with 14 lines, in which some lines rhyme with others according to fixed patterns.

soon /su:n/, **sooner, soonest.** ADV If something is going to happen **soon,** it will happen in a short time. If something happened **soon** after a particular time or event, it happened a short time after it. *It will soon be Christmas... He rented a TV soon after moving into his apartment... Contact the police as soon as possible... I swore I'd get out soonest.*

PHRASES • You say **the sooner the better** when you think something should be done as soon as possible. *The sooner we get out the better.* • If you say that something will happen **sooner or later,** you mean that it will certainly happen, even though it might take a long time. *If you do not look after it carefully, sooner or later your car will fall to bits.* • If you say that something will happen **as soon as** something else happens, you mean that it will happen immediately after the other thing. *As soon as we get the tickets we'll send them to you.* • If you say that **no sooner** did one thing happen **than** another thing happened, you mean that the second thing happened immediately after the first. *No sooner had he closed his eyes than he fell asleep.* • If you say that you **would sooner** do something, you mean that you would prefer to do it. *I would sooner read than watch television.*

soot /sʊt/. UNCOUNT N **Soot** is black powder which collects on the inside of chimneys.

soothe /su:ð/, **soothes, soothing, soothed.** 1 VB WITH OBJ If you **soothe** someone who is angry or upset, you make them calmer. *He tried to soothe her by making conversation.* ♦ **soothing** ADJ *...soothing music... ...a few soothing words.* 2 VB WITH OBJ Something that **soothes** pain makes it less severe. *...cream she put on to soothe her sunburn.*

sooty /sʊti¹/. ADJ Something that is **sooty** is covered with soot. *...his sooty hands.*

sophisticated /səfɪstɪkeɪtɪ²d/. 1 ADJ A **sophisticated** person knows about culture, fashion, and other matters that are considered socially important. *...a glossy magazine for today's sophisticated woman... ...a sophisticated lifestyle.* 2 ADJ A **sophisticated** machine or device has advanced features which others do not have. *These planes are among the most sophisticated aircraft now being manufactured.*

sophistication /səfɪstɪkeɪʃə⁰n/. UNCOUNT N **Sophistication** is the quality of being sophisticated. *The management prided itself on its sophistication.*

soprano /səprɑ:nəʊ/, **sopranos.** COUNT N A **soprano** is a woman, girl, or boy with a high singing voice.

sordid /sɔ:dɪd/. ADJ You say that something is **sordid** when it involves dishonest or immoral behaviour. *...a rather sordid affair.*

sore /sɔ:/, **sores.** 1 ADJ If part of your body is **sore,** it causes you pain and discomfort. *Her throat was so sore she could not talk.* 2 COUNT N A **sore** is a painful place on your body where the skin is infected. 3 PRED ADJ If you are **sore** about something, you are angry and upset about it; an American use. *Nobody believed him, and this made him sore as hell.* 4 PHRASE If something is **a sore point** with you, you do not like to talk about it because it makes you angry or upset.

sorely /sɔ:li¹/. ADV **Sorely** means greatly; a literary word. *They were sorely in need of rest.*

sorrow /sɒrəʊ/, **sorrows.** 1 UNCOUNT N **Sorrow** is a feeling of deep sadness. *She wrote to express her sorrow at the tragic death of their son.* 2 COUNT N **Sorrows** are events or situations that cause sorrow. *...the sorrows that life brings.*

sorrowful /sɒrə⁶fʊl/. ADJ **Sorrowful** means very sad; a literary use. *They kept giving me sorrowful looks.*

sorry /sɒri¹/, **sorrier, sorriest.** 1 CONVENTION OR PRED ADJ You say **'Sorry'** or **'I'm sorry'** as a way of apologizing for something you have done. *'You're giving me a headache with all that noise.'—'Sorry.'... Sorry about the coffee on your bedspread... I'm sorry I'm late... I'm sorry if I worried you.* 2 CONVENTION OR PRED ADJ You use **sorry** when you are saying that you cannot help someone or when you are giving them bad news. *I'm sorry but there's no-one here called Nikki... I'm sorry to say that the experiment has failed.* 3 CONVENTION You also say **sorry** when you have not heard what someone has said and you want them to repeat it. *'Have you seen the guide book anywhere?'—'Sorry?'—'Seen the guide book?'* 4 PRED ADJ If you are **sorry** about a situation, you feel sadness, disappointment, or regret about it. *He was sorry he had agreed to stay.* 5 PRED ADJ WITH 'for' If you are **sorry** for someone who is unhappy or in an unpleasant situation, you feel sympathy for them. *I knew they were having a rough time and I felt sorry for them.* 6 ATTRIB ADJ You also use **sorry** to describe people and things that are in a bad state; a formal use. *'We are in a sorry state,' she lamented.*

sort /sɔ:t/, **sorts, sorting, sorted.** 1 COUNT N WITH SUPP A particular **sort** of something is one of its different kinds or types. *'What sort of iron did she get?'—'A steam iron.'... ...a rock plant of some sort... There were five different sorts of biscuits.* 2 VB WITH OBJ OR ADJUNCT If you **sort** things, you arrange them into groups. *Minnie was in the office, sorting mail... They had got mixed up and needed to be sorted into three sets.*

PHRASES • You use **sort of** when you want to say that something can roughly be described in a particular way; an informal use. *She was wearing a sort of velvet dress.* • You use **of sorts** to indicate that something is not of very good quality. *...cleaning a carpet of sorts... Farlow was a lawyer of sorts.* • If you feel **out of sorts,** you feel slightly unwell or discontented.

sort out. PHR VB 1 If you **sort out** a group of things, you organize or tidy them. *It took a while to sort out all our luggage.* 2 If you **sort out** a problem, you deal with it and find a solution to it.

SOS /es əʊ es/. SING N An **SOS** is a signal which indicates to other people that you are in danger and need help quickly. *...an SOS from a private plane.*

so-so. ADJ OR ADV If you say that something is **so-so,** you mean that it is neither good nor bad, but of average quality; an informal use.

sought /sɔ:t/. **Sought** is the past tense and past participle of **seek.**

soul /səʊl/, **souls.** 1 COUNT N A person's **soul** is the spiritual part of them which is believed to continue existing after their body is dead. *They said a prayer for the souls of the men who had been drowned.* 2 COUNT N Your **soul** is also your mind, character, thoughts, and feelings. *His soul was in turmoil.* 3 SING N WITH SUPP A person can be referred to as a particular kind of **soul;** an old-fashioned use. *She was a kind soul... Poor soul!* 4 SING N You use **soul** in negative statements to mean nobody at all. *When I first went there I didn't know a single soul... I swear I will never tell a soul.* 5 UNCOUNT N **Soul** is a type of pop music performed mainly by black American musicians. *...a new soul band from Chicago.*

soul-destroying. ADJ **Soul-destroying** activities are boring and depressing. *The job has its soul-destroying aspects.*

sound /saʊnd/, **sounds, sounding, sounded; sounder, soundest.** 1 COUNT N A **sound** is a particular thing that you hear. *He heard the sound of footsteps in the hall... He opened the door without a sound.* 2 UNCOUNT N **Sound** is everything that can be heard. *Sound travels better in water than in air.* 3 ERG VB When something such as a horn **sounds,** it makes a noise. *A car passed* him at top speed, sounding its horn. 4 VB WITH COMPLEMENT OR 'like' When you are describing a noise, you can talk about the way it **sounds.** *The rustling of the woman's dress sounded alarmingly loud... Her footsteps sounded like pistol shots.* 5 LINK VB When you talk about the way someone **sounds,** you are describing the impression you have of them when they speak. *'Ah,' Piper said. He sounded a little discouraged... You know, you sound just like an insurance salesman.* 6 LINK VB You can also give your impression of something you have just read or heard about by talking about the way it **sounds.** *'They've got a small farm down in Devon.'—'That sounds nice.'... It sounds to me as though he's just doing it to be awkward.* 7 SING N The **sound** of something that you have heard about is the impression you get of it. *I don't like the sound of linguistics.* 8 ADJ If something is **sound,** it is in good condition or healthy. *My heart is basically sound.* 9 ADJ If something such as advice is **sound,** it is reliable and sensible. 10 PHRASE If you are **sound asleep,** you are sleeping deeply. 11 **safe and sound:** see **safe.**

sound out. PHR VB If you **sound** someone **out,** you question them to find out their opinion.

sound effect, sound effects. COUNT N **Sound effects** are sounds created artificially to make a play more realistic.

soundly /saʊndli^1/. ADV If you sleep **soundly,** you sleep deeply and do not wake.

soundproof /saʊnd^{0}pru:f/. ADJ A **soundproof** room has been constructed so that sound cannot get in or out.

soundtrack /saʊnd^{0}træk/, **soundtracks.** COUNT N The **soundtrack** of a film is its sound, speech, and music.

soup /su:p/, **soups.** MASS N **Soup** is liquid food made by cooking meat, fish, or vegetables in water.

sour /saʊə/, **sours, souring, soured.** 1 ADJ Something that is **sour** has a sharp taste like the taste of a lemon or an apple that is not ripe. *Add enough sugar to keep it from tasting sour.* 2 ADJ **Sour** milk has an unpleasant taste because it is no longer fresh. 3 ADJ **Sour** people are bad-tempered and unfriendly. *I received a sour look every time I passed her house.* 4 PHRASE If something **goes sour** or **turns sour,** it becomes less enjoyable or less satisfactory. *The evening had turned sour.* 5 ERG VB If a friendship or attitude **sours** or if something **sours** it, it becomes less friendly or hopeful. *Detente has soured... These latest cuts might sour relations between the government and the military.*

source /sɔ:s/, **sources.** 1 COUNT N The **source** of something is the person, place, or thing which you get it from. *...one of the world's main sources of uranium... Candidates are required to publish the sources of their campaign funds.* 2 COUNT N The **source** of a difficulty is its cause. *They're trying to trace the source of the trouble.* 3 COUNT N A **source** of information is a person or book that provides it. *Western diplomatic sources confirmed reports of fighting in the capital... The story was based on information from a 'reliable source'.* 4 SING N The **source** of a river or stream is the place where it begins. *We are following the creek to its source.*

south /saʊθ/. 1 SING N The **south** is the direction on your right when you are looking towards the place where the sun rises. *...a place in the hills to the south of the little town.* 2 SING N The **south** of a place is the part which is towards the south. *...the South of France.* Also ATTRIB ADJ *...South Wales.* 3 ADV **South** means towards the south, or to the south of a place or thing. *I travelled south by bus through Philadelphia... I was living in a house just south of Market Street.* 4 ATTRIB ADJ A **south** wind blows from the south.

south-east. 1 SING N The **south-east** is the direction halfway between south and east. *To the south-east there is a plantation.* 2 SING N The **south-east** of a place is the part which is towards the south-east. *...the south-east of England.* Also ATTRIB ADJ *...south-east London.* 3 ADV **South-east** means towards the south-east, or to the south-east of a place or thing. *If we proceed south-east we come to Eaton Place.* 4 ATTRIB ADJ A **south-east** wind blows from the south-east.

south-eastern. ATTRIB ADJ **South-eastern** means in or from the south-east of a region or country.

southerly /sʌðəli^1/. 1 ADJ **Southerly** means towards the south. *They headed in a southerly direction... ...the most southerly tip of Bear Island.* 2 ADJ A **southerly** wind blows from the south.

southern /sʌðə^{5}n/. ATTRIB ADJ **Southern** means in or from the south of a region or country. *...the southern edge of the Sahara.*

southward /saʊθwəd/ or **southwards.** 1 ADV **Southward** or **southwards** means towards the south. *A level expanse of low-lying country extended southward.* 2 ADJ **Southward** is used to describe things which are moving towards the south or which face towards the south. *The shore was badly eaten away on its southward side.*

south-west. 1 SING N The **south-west** is the direction halfway between south and west. *To the south-west lay the city.* 2 SING N The **south-west** of a place is the part which is towards the south-west. *...the south-west of England.* Also ATTRIB ADJ *...the Conservative Party agent for South-west Staffordshire.* 3 ADV **South-west** means towards the south-west, or to the south-west of a place or thing. *It flows south-west to the Atlantic Ocean.* 4 ATTRIB ADJ A **south-west** wind blows from the south-west.

south-western. ADJ **South-western** means in or from the south-west of a region or country.

souvenir /su:vənɪə, su:vənɪə/, **souvenirs.** COUNT N A **souvenir** is something which you buy or keep to remind you of a holiday, place, or event. *He kept a spoon as a souvenir of his journey.*

sovereign /sɒvrɪn/, **sovereigns.** 1 COUNT N A **sovereign** is a king, queen, or other royal ruler. 2 ATTRIB ADJ A **sovereign** state or country is not under the authority of any other country. 3 ADJ **Sovereign** is used to describe someone who has the highest power in a country; a formal use. *Parliament is sovereign... He will be given sovereign powers.*

sovereignty /sɒvrə^{1}nti^1/. UNCOUNT N **Sovereignty** is the power that a country has to govern itself or to govern other countries. *...a threat to national sovereignty... ...sovereignty over Africa.*

sow, sows, sowing, sowed, sown /səʊn/; **sow** is pronounced /səʊ/ when it is a verb and /saʊ/ when it is a noun. 1 VB WITH OBJ If you **sow** seeds or **sow** an area of land with seeds, you plant the seeds in the ground. *You can sow winter wheat in October... The land was cleared of weeds and sown with grass.* 2 VB WITH OBJ If you **sow** an undesirable feeling among people, you cause them to have it; a literary use. *She attacked those who sow dismay and division in the party... ...sowing doubt and uncertainty.* 3 COUNT N A **sow** is an adult female pig.

soya /sɔɪj^{0}ə/. MOD **Soya** flour, butter, or other food is made from soya beans.

soya bean, soya beans. COUNT N **Soya beans** are a type of bean that can be eaten or used to make flour, oil, or soy sauce.

soy sauce /sɔɪ sɔ:s/. UNCOUNT N **Soy sauce** is a dark brown liquid flavouring made from soya beans.

spa /spɑ:/, **spas.** COUNT N A **spa** is a place where water with minerals in it bubbles out of the ground. People drink the water or bathe in it to improve their health.

space /speɪs/, **spaces, spacing, spaced.** 1 UNCOUNT N **Space** is the area that is empty or available in a building or container. *There was just enough space for a bed... Belongings take up space... ...the luggage space at the back of the car.* 2 UNCOUNT N **Space** is also the area outside the Earth's atmosphere. *...the first human being to travel in space... ...space research.* 3 COUNT N A **space** is a gap or empty place. *The door had spaces at the top and bottom... ...an open space in the jungle... We spent half an hour looking for a parking space.* 4 SING N WITH 'of' A **space** of time is a period of time. *It happened three times in the space of five months... He should arrive in a very short space of time.* 5 VB WITH OBJ If you **space** a series of things or **space** them out, you arrange them so that they have gaps between them. *The lines were spaced well apart... These books should have large print well spaced out on the page.*

spacecraft /speɪskrɑ:ft/. **Spacecraft** is the singular and plural. COUNT N A **spacecraft** is a rocket or other vehicle that can travel in space.

spaceship /speɪsʃɪp/, **spaceships.** COUNT N A **spaceship** is the same as a spacecraft.

spacious /speɪʃəs/. ADJ A **spacious** building or vehicle is large and has plenty of room in it. *...a spacious dining-room.*

spade /speɪd/, **spades.** 1 COUNT N A **spade** is a tool used for digging, with a flat metal blade and a long handle. 2 UNCOUNT N **Spades** is one of the four suits in a pack of playing cards. 3 COUNT N A **spade** is also one of the thirteen playing cards in the suit of spades.

spaghetti /spəgeti^1/. UNCOUNT N **Spaghetti** is a type of pasta. It looks like long pieces of string and is usually served with a sauce.

span /spæn/, **spans, spanning, spanned.** 1 COUNT N A **span** is a period of time. *...the forty-year span from 1913 to 1953... ...in the short span that man has been on earth.* 2 VB WITH OBJ If something **spans** a period of time, it lasts throughout that time. *At 79, Dame Flora can look back at a career spanning more than half a century.* 3 COUNT N The **span** of something is its total length. *Some eagles have a wing span of one and a half metres.* 4 VB WITH OBJ A bridge that **spans** a river or valley stretches right across it. *...a long lake spanned by a high, arching iron bridge.*

spangled /spæŋgə^{0}ld/. ADJ Something that is **spangled** is covered with small sparkling objects. *...spangled headdresses... ...the star-spangled night sky.*

spaniel /spænjəl/, **spaniels.** COUNT N A **spaniel** is a type of dog with long drooping ears.

Spanish /spænɪʃ/. 1 ADJ **Spanish** means belonging or relating to Spain. *...the Spanish government... ...a Spanish port.* 2 UNCOUNT N **Spanish** is the language spoken in Spain, and in many countries in South and Central America. 3 PLURAL N The **Spanish** are the people who come from Spain.

spank /spæŋk/, **spanks, spanking, spanked.** VB WITH OBJ If you **spank** a child, you punish it by hitting its bottom several times with your hand.

spanner /spænə/, **spanners.** COUNT N A **spanner** is a metal tool with a specially shaped end that you use for tightening a nut.

spare /speə/, **spares, sparing, spared.** 1 ADJ You use **spare** to describe an extra object that is like the ones you are using, but that you do not need yet. *Keep a spare fuse handy by the fuse box... Take a spare shirt.* 2 COUNT N You can refer to an extra object that you do not yet need as a **spare.** *There are some spares at the back if anyone wants more.* 3 ADJ You can also use **spare** to describe something that is not being used by anyone, and is therefore available for you to use. *We found a spare parking meter.* 4 VB WITH OBJ If you **spare** something for a particular purpose, you make it available for that purpose. *I got to my feet, thanking him for sparing time to see me... More land is needed to grow food and less can be spared to graze cattle.* 5 VB WITH OBJ When a person or place is not harmed by a danger, you can say that they **are spared.** *Thank God we were spared... The great cities of the Rhineland had not been spared.* 6 VB WITH OBJ AND OBJ If you **spare** someone an unpleasant experience, you prevent them from having it. *At least I am spared the shame of the children knowing.* PHRASES • If you have time or money **to spare,** you have some extra time or money which you do not need for anything in particular. *He often had money to spare nowadays... She caught her plane with a few minutes to spare.* • If you **spare no expense** in doing something, you do it as well as possible, without trying to save money. *The Agency has spared no expense with the system for storage.*

spare parts. PLURAL N **Spare parts** are parts that you buy separately to replace old or broken parts in a piece of equipment. *The tractors are out of order and there are no spare parts to get them working again.*

sparing /speərɪŋ/. PRED ADJ If you are **sparing** with something, you use it or give it only in very small quantities. *She was sparing with heat and light.* ♦ **sparingly** ADV *Use hot water sparingly.*

spark /spɑ:k/, **sparks, sparking, sparked.** 1 COUNT N A **spark** is a tiny, bright piece of burning material that flies up from a fire. *The fire sent smoke and sparks over the top of the fence.* 2 COUNT N A **spark** is also a flash of light caused by electricity. 3 SING N A **spark** of feeling is a small but noticeable amount of it. *A faint spark of pleasure came into his eyes.* 4 VB WITH OBJ If one thing **sparks** another or **sparks** it off, it causes it to start happening. *The crisis was sparked by the assassination of the duke... The letter sparked off a friendship between the two men.*

sparkle /spɑ:kə^{0}l/, **sparkles, sparkling, sparkled.** VB If something **sparkles,** it shines with a lot of small points of light. *They looked down to the sea, sparkling in the sun... The lawn was sparkling with frost.* Also UNCOUNT N *Her eyes had lost their sparkle.*

sparkling /spɑ:klɪŋ/. ADJ **Sparkling** things shine brightly. *...a sparkling necklace... ...sparkling eyes.*

spark plug, spark plugs. COUNT N A **spark plug** is a device in the engine of a motor vehicle, which produces electric sparks to ignite the fuel.

sparrow /spærəʊ/, **sparrows.** COUNT N A **sparrow** is a very common small brown bird.

sparse /spɑ:s/. ADJ If something is **sparse,** there is very little of it. *The population was sparse... ...his sparse white hair... ...the sparse rainfall.* ♦ **sparsely** ADV *...a sparsely populated region... ...his sparsely furnished room.*

spartan /spɑ:tə^{0}n/. ADJ A **spartan** way of life is very simple with no luxuries. *...the spartan lives of the islanders.*

spasm /spæzə^{0}m/, **spasms.** 1 COUNT N OR UNCOUNT N A **spasm** is a sudden tightening of your muscles. *Spasms shook her lungs and chest... This may leave the muscle in spasm.* 2 SING N WITH 'of' You can refer to an unpleasant feeling which lasts for a short time as a **spasm** of that feeling. *...a spasm of anger.*

spasmodic /spæzmɒdɪk/. ADJ Something that is **spasmodic** happens for short periods of time at irregular intervals. *The survivors suffer spasmodic bouts of illness.* ♦ **spasmodically** ADV *The orchestra continued to play spasmodically.*

spastic /spæstɪk/. ADJ Someone who is **spastic** is born with a disability which makes it difficult for them to control their muscles.

spat /spæt/. **Spat** is the past tense and past participle of **spit.**

spate /speɪt/. SING N A **spate** of things is a lot of them happening or appearing within a short period of time. *The incident caused another spate of protests... ...a spate of new books.*

spatial /speɪʃə[0]l/. ATTRIB ADJ **Spatial** is used to describe things relating to size, area, or position; a formal use. *...spatial perception.*

spatter /spætə/, **spatters, spattering, spattered.** VB WITH OBJ To **spatter** a surface or **spatter** a liquid over it means to cover the surface with small drops. *Beer spattered the bedspread... He picked up his spoon so hurriedly that it spattered milk over his cardigan.*

spawn /spɔːn/, **spawns, spawning, spawned.** 1 UNCOUNT N **Spawn** is a jelly-like substance containing the eggs of fish or frogs. 2 VB When fish or frogs **spawn,** they lay eggs. 3 VB WITH OBJ To **spawn** something means to cause it to happen or be created; a literary use. *Poverty had spawned numerous religious movements.*

speak /spiːk/, **speaks, speaking, spoke** /spəʊk/, **spoken** /spəʊkə[0]n/. 1 VB When you **speak,** you use your voice to say words. *She spoke with an Irish accent... Mary turned her head to speak to him... He hadn't been able to speak of what had happened.* ♦ **spoken** ADJ *...a robot capable of understanding spoken commands.* 2 VB WITH OBJ If you **speak** a foreign language, you know it and can use it. *They spoke fluent English.* 3 VB WITH ADV If you **speak** well or badly of someone, you say good or bad things about them. *The students spoke highly of their history lecturer.*

PHRASES ● You say **so to speak** to indicate that what you are saying is not literally true. *He goes to work early; before the office is awake, so to speak.* ● You use expressions such as **generally speaking** and **technically speaking** to indicate the kind of statement you are making. *America is still, generally speaking, the most technologically advanced country... Roughly speaking, there are two possibilities.* ● You say **speaking of** to introduce a new topic suggested by a word or expression that has just been used. *It's nice to have an admirer who gives nothing away. Speaking of giving away, I have brought you a present.* ● **Nobody to speak of** or **nothing to speak of** means hardly anyone or anything, or only unimportant people or things. *'Did you find anything?'—'No, nothing to speak of.'* ● People who are not **on speaking terms** never speak to each other. ● If you **speak** your **mind** about something, you say exactly what you think. ● If something **speaks for itself,** its meaning or qualities are obvious and do not need to be explained or pointed out.

speak for. PHR VB If you **speak for** a group of people, you give their opinion on their behalf. *I'm only speaking for myself, not for my colleagues.*

speak out. PHR VB If you **speak out** in favour of something or against something, you say publicly that you think it is a good thing or a bad thing. *He spoke out against racial discrimination many times.*

speak up. PHR VB If you ask someone to **speak up,** you are asking them to speak more loudly.

speaker /spiːkə/, **speakers.** 1 COUNT N You can refer to someone who is speaking as the **speaker.** *...the gap between the speaker and the listener.* 2 COUNT N A **speaker** is also a person who makes a speech. *The chairman got up to introduce the speaker.* 3 COUNT N WITH SUPP A **speaker** of a particular language is someone who can speak that language. *Some sounds are very difficult for French speakers of English.* 4 COUNT N A **speaker** is also the piece of equipment, for example on a radio or hi-fi, through which the sound comes out.

spear /spɪə/, **spears, spearing, speared.** 1 COUNT N A **spear** is a weapon consisting of a long pole with a sharp point. 2 VB WITH OBJ If you **spear** something, you push a pointed object into it. *Lally took her fork and speared an oyster from its shell.*

spearhead /spɪəhɛd/, **spearheads, spearheading, spearheaded.** VB WITH OBJ To **spearhead** a campaign means to lead it; a literary use. *Mrs Gandhi's son Sanjay spearheaded a 'moral crusade' against slums.*

special /spɛʃə[0]l/. 1 ADJ Something that is **special** is unusual, and is better or more important than other things of the same kind. *...china that was reserved for special occasions... Is there anything special you would like for dinner, dear?* 2 ATTRIB ADJ You also use **special** to describe someone or something that has a particular function or purpose. *He was a special adviser to Mrs Judith Hart at the Ministry... ...special schools for maladjusted children.* 3 ATTRIB ADJ You also use **special** to describe something that relates to one particular person, group, or place. *He spoke his own special variety of German... Hospital food seldom caters for the special needs of the aged.*

specialise /spɛʃəlaɪz/. See **specialize.**

specialist /spɛʃəlɪst/, **specialists.** COUNT N A **specialist** is a person who has a particular skill or knows a lot about a particular subject. *...an eye specialist... She is a specialist in Eastern European affairs.* Also ATTRIB ADJ *...a specialist teacher of mathematics.*

speciality /spɛʃiæli[1]ti[1]/, **specialities.** 1 COUNT N Someone's **speciality** is the kind of work they do best or the subject they know most about. *Work with children is their speciality... They enjoy talking about their own specialities.* 2 COUNT N WITH SUPP A **speciality** of a place is something that is very well made there. *Chocolate gateau was a speciality of the Café de Rome.*

specialize /spɛʃəlaɪz/, **specializes, specializing, specialized;** also spelled **specialise.** VB If you **specialize** in something, you concentrate on doing, making, or supplying it. *...a shop specializing in camping equipment.* ♦ **specialization** /spɛʃəlaɪzeɪʃə[0]n/ UNCOUNT N *...the increasing specialization of working life.*

specialized /spɛʃəlaɪzd/; also spelled **specialised.** ADJ Someone or something that is **specialized** is trained or developed for a particular purpose. *...highly specialized staff... ...radar and specialised television systems.*

specially /spɛʃəli[1]/. 1 ADV If something has been done **specially** for a particular person or purpose, it has been done only for that person or purpose. *...free hotels run by the state specially for tourists... The rules were specially designed to protect travellers.* 2 SUBMOD You use **specially** with an adjective to emphasize a quality; an informal use. *...a pub where the beer was specially good.*

specialty /spɛʃəlti[1]/, **specialties.** COUNT N A **specialty** is the same as a speciality; an American use.

species /spiːʃiːz/. **Species** is the singular and plural. COUNT N A **species** is a class of plants or animals whose members have the same main characteristics and are able to breed with each other. *There are two hundred and fifty species of shark.*

specific /spɪ[2]sɪfɪk/, **specifics.** 1 ATTRIB ADJ You use **specific** to emphasize that you are talking about a particular thing or subject. *Education should not be restricted to any one specific age group... On certain specific issues there may be changes of emphasis.* 2 ADJ If a description is **specific,** it is precise and exact. *It was a tooth, a tiger-shark tooth, to be more specific.* 3 PRED ADJ Something that is **specific** to a particular thing is connected with that thing only. *It's the program that's specific to this problem.* 4 PLURAL N The **specifics** of a subject are its details. *Let us focus on the specifics of Bengal's life.*

specifically /spɪ[2]sɪfɪkə[0]li[1]/. 1 ADV You use **specifically** to emphasize that a subject is being considered separately from other subjects. *It is Christianity with which we are specifically concerned.* 2 ADV You also use **specifically** to indicate that you are stating or describing something precisely. *...the peasant rising in the West of France, in Brittany specifically.*

specification /spɛsɪfɪkeɪʃə[0]n/, **specifications.** COUNT N The **specifications** for something are necessary requirements for making it. *...ships built to merchant ship specifications.*

specify /spɛsɪfaɪ/, **specifies, specifying, specified.** REPORT VB If you **specify** something, you state it precisely. *The report specified seven areas where the Government had a responsibility... The landlord can specify that rent be paid in cash.*

specimen /spɛsɪmɪ[2]n/, **specimens.** COUNT N A **specimen** of something is an example or small amount of it which gives an idea of the whole. *The fins of fossil specimens are carefully dissected.*

speck /spɛk/, **specks.** COUNT N A **speck** is a very small stain or mark, or a small piece of a powder-like substance. *There was a speck of blood on his collar... ...a tiny speck of dust.*

speckled /spɛkə[0]ld/. ADJ A **speckled** object or animal is covered with small marks or spots. *...a speckled sweater... ...speckled fish.*

spectacle /spɛktəkə[0]l/, **spectacles.** 1 PLURAL N Someone's **spectacles** are their glasses; a formal use. *She carried a spare pair of spectacles in her pocket.* 2 COUNT N A **spectacle** is a strange or interesting sight or scene. *She stood at the head of the stairs and surveyed the spectacle.* 3 COUNT N A **spectacle** is also an impressive event or performance. *...a seven-hour spectacle consisting of songs, comedy acts, and acrobatics.*

spectacular /spɛktækjə[4]lə/, **spectaculars.** 1 ADJ Something that is **spectacular** is very impressive. *The most spectacular of these extraordinary fossils can be seen in the museum... It was a spectacular jump.* 2 COUNT N WITH SUPP A **spectacular** is a grand and impressive show or performance. *They are to hold a fashion spectacular on Friday with 100 models.*

spectator /spɛkteɪtə/, **spectators.** COUNT N A **spectator** is a person who watches something, especially a sporting event. *The spectators rose to their feet to pay tribute to an outstanding performance.*

spectre /spɛktə/, **spectres;** spelled **specter** in American English. 1 COUNT N A **spectre** is a ghost. 2 SING N You can also refer to a frightening image or idea as a **spectre;** a literary use. *...the spectre of another world war.*

spectrum /spɛktrəm/. 1 SING N The **spectrum** is the range of different colours produced when light passes through a prism or through a drop of water. 2 SING N WITH SUPP A **spectrum** of opinions or emotions is a wide range of them. *They have support at both ends of the political spectrum.*

speculate /spɛkjə[4]leɪt/, **speculates, speculating, speculated.** 1 VB OR REPORT VB If you **speculate** about something, you guess about its nature or identity. *It is natural for us to speculate about the reasons for their visits... Industry sources speculated that the least expensive model will be priced at £7000.* ♦ **speculation** /spɛkjə[4]leɪʃə[0]n/ UNCOUNT N *The papers are full of speculation about who is likely to be the next prime minister.* 2 VB When people **speculate** financially, they buy property or shares in the hope of being able to sell them at a profit.

speculative /spɛkjə[4]lətɪv/. ADJ **Speculative** statements are based on guesses rather than knowledge. *Budgets and profit forecasts were equally speculative.*

speculator /spɛkjə[4]leɪtə/, **speculators.** COUNT N A **speculator** is a person who speculates financially.

sped /spɛd/. **Sped** is a past tense and past participle of **speed.**

speech /spiːtʃ/, **speeches.** 1 UNCOUNT N **Speech** is spoken language, the act of speaking, or the ability to speak. *...communication through writing and speech... In ordinary speech we often shorten the word 'cannot' to 'can't'... She was so shocked that she lost her powers of speech.* 2 COUNT N A **speech** is a formal talk given to an audience. *Mr Macmillan made a speech on the importance of education.* 3 COUNT N A **speech** is also a group of lines spoken by a character in a play. *She recited a speech from 'As You Like It'.* 4 UNCOUNT N WITH SUPP The **speech** of a particular place is the language or dialect spoken there. *He can mimic Cockney speech quite well.*

speechless /spiːtʃlɪ[2]s/. ADJ If you are **speechless,** you are temporarily unable to speak, because something has shocked you. *She was speechless with astonishment.*

speed /spiːd/, **speeds, speeding, sped** /spɛd/. For the phrasal verb, the past tense and past participle is **speeded.** 1 UNCOUNT N OR COUNT N The **speed** of something is the rate at which it moves, happens, or is done. *I drove at great speed to West Bank... ...capable of reaching speeds of over 110kph... None of us grows at the same speed.* 2 UNCOUNT N **Speed** is very fast movement. *The car is travelling at speed.* 3 VB WITH ADJUNCT To **speed** somewhere means to move or travel there quickly. *They sped along Main Street towards the highway.* 4 VB A motorist who **is speeding** is driving a vehicle faster than the legal speed limit.

speed up. PHR VB When something **speeds up,** it moves, happens, or is done more quickly. *They're way ahead of us. Speed up!... Warmth speeds up chemical reactions.*

speed limit, speed limits. COUNT N The **speed limit** on a road is the maximum speed at which you can legally drive on it.

speedometer /spi[1]dɒmɪtə/, **speedometers.** COUNT N A **speedometer** is an instrument in a vehicle which shows how fast the vehicle is moving.

speedy /spiːdi[1]/. ADJ A **speedy** action happens or is done very quickly. *A speedy settlement of the strike is essential.* ♦ **speedily** ADV *Such doubts were now speedily removed.*

spell /spɛl/, **spells, spelling, spelled** or **spelt** /spɛlt/. 1 VB WITH OBJ When you **spell** a word, you write or speak each letter in the word in the correct order. *'Qatar'—'How do you spell that?'—'Q-A-T-A-R'... Ninety per cent of the words were spelt wrong.* 2 VB WITH COMPLEMENT If something **spells** a particular result, it suggests that this will be the result. *Nuclear conflict would spell the end of life as we know it... Any discussion of politics would spell disaster.* 3 COUNT N A **spell** of an activity or type of weather is a short period of it. *She had a spell as editor... ...a spell of good summer weather.* 4 COUNT N In children's stories, a **spell** is a sequence of words used to perform magic. *The spell of the wicked fairy was broken.*

spell out. PHR VB If you **spell** something **out,** you explain it in detail. *Let me try and spell out what I mean by that.*

spellbound /spelbaund/. ADJ If you are **spellbound,** you are so fascinated by something that you cannot think about anything else. *We were all spellbound as we listened to her.*

spelling /spelɪŋ/, **spellings.** 1 COUNT N The **spelling** of a word is the correct sequence of letters in it. 2 UNCOUNT N If you are good at **spelling,** you can spell words in the correct way. *I'm terrible at spelling.*

spend /spend/, **spends, spending, spent** /spent/. 1 VB WITH OBJ When you **spend** money, you use it to pay for things. *We always spend a lot of money on parties... The buildings need a lot of money spent on them.* 2 VB WITH OBJ AND ADJUNCT OR -ING If you **spend** a period of time somewhere, you are there during that time. If you **spend** a period of time doing something, you are doing it during that time. *He spent most of his time in the library... She woke early, meaning to spend all day writing.*

spending /spendɪŋ/. UNCOUNT N **Spending** refers to the amount of money paid for public services by a government or other organization. *Departments must reduce their spending by £35 million before July 1st.*

spent /spent/. ADJ **Spent** is used to describe things that have already been used and cannot be used again. *...spent matches.*

sperm /spɜːm/, **sperms. Sperm** can also be the plural. COUNT N A **sperm** is a cell produced in the sex organs of a male animal which can enter a female animal's egg and fertilize it.

spew /spjuː/, **spews, spewing, spewed.** ERG VB When things **spew** from a place, they come out in large quantities. *Factories spewed dense dirty smoke.*

sphere /sfɪə/, **spheres.** 1 COUNT N A **sphere** is a round three-dimensional shape like a ball. 2 COUNT N WITH SUPP A **sphere** of activity or interest is a particular area of it. *He works in the sphere of race relations.*

spherical /sferɪkəºl/. ADJ Something that is **spherical** is shaped like a sphere.

spice /spaɪs/, **spices, spicing, spiced.** 1 COUNT N OR UNCOUNT N **Spice** is a powder used to flavour food, for example pepper or ginger. It is made from seeds, bark, or roots. 2 VB WITH OBJ When you **spice** food, you add spice to it. *Take the peas and butter and spice them with nutmeg... The soup was heavily spiced.*

spicy /spaɪsi¹/. ADJ **Spicy** food is strongly flavoured with spices. *...a spicy sauce.*

spider /spaɪdə/, **spiders.** COUNT N A **spider** is a small creature with eight legs. Most spiders make webs.

spidery /spaɪdəri¹/. ATTRIB ADJ **Spidery** handwriting consists of thin, angular lines and is hard to read.

spike /spaɪk/, **spikes.** 1 COUNT N A **spike** is a long piece of metal with a sharp point. *...a wall topped with spikes.* 2 COUNT N Any long, pointed object can be referred to as a **spike.** *The plant bears spikes of greenish flowers.*

spiked /spaɪkt/. ADJ **Spiked** things have spikes or a spike on them. *...a spiked fence... ...spiked shoes.*

spiky /spaɪki¹/. ATTRIB ADJ Something that is **spiky** has sharp points. *...a tiny man with spiky hair... The shrub has spiky green leaves.*

spill /spɪl/, **spills, spilling, spilled** or **spilt** /spɪlt/. 1 ERG VB If you **spill** a liquid, it accidentally flows over the edge of its container. *She carried the bucket without spilling a drop... Make sure the water doesn't spill over the floor.* 2 VB WITH ADJUNCT If people or things **spill** out of a place, they come out in large numbers. *Crowds started spilling out of bars.*

spin /spɪn/, **spins, spinning, spun** /spʌn/. 1 ERG VB If something **spins,** it turns quickly around a central point. *The football went spinning into the canal... He spun the chair round to face the desk.* 2 VB If your head **is spinning,** you feel dizzy or confused. *His head was spinning from wine and liqueurs.* 3 VB WITH OR WITHOUT OBJ When people **spin,** they make thread by twisting together pieces of fibre using a device or machine. *His wife was spinning wool.*

spin out. PHR VB If you **spin** something **out,** you make it last longer than it otherwise would. *I might be able to spin my talk out to three-quarters of an hour.*

spinach /spɪnɪdʒ, -ɪtʃ/. UNCOUNT N **Spinach** is a vegetable with large green leaves.

spinal /spaɪnəºl/. ATTRIB ADJ **Spinal** means relating to your spine. *...a spinal injury.*

spinal cord, spinal cords. COUNT N Your **spinal cord** is a bundle of nerves inside your spine which connects your brain to nerves in all parts of your body.

spindly /spɪndli¹/. ADJ Something that is **spindly** is long, thin, and weak. *...spindly legs... ...spindly trees.*

spin drier, spin driers; also spelled **spin dryer.** COUNT N A **spin drier** is a machine used to spin washing to get the water out.

spine /spaɪn/, **spines.** 1 COUNT N Your **spine** is the row of bones down your back. 2 COUNT N **Spines** are long, sharp points on an animal's body or on a plant. *...a cactus with red spines.*

spineless /spaɪnlɪ²s/. ADJ Someone who is **spineless** is cowardly.

spin-off, spin-offs. COUNT N A **spin-off** is something useful that unexpectedly results from an activity. *The search for knowledge frequently has beneficial spin-offs for mankind.*

spinster /spɪnstə/, **spinsters.** COUNT N A **spinster** is a woman who has never been married; an old-fashioned, formal use.

spiral /spaɪərəºl/, **spirals, spiralling, spiralled;** spelled **spiraling** and **spiraled** in American English. 1 COUNT N A **spiral** is a curved shape which winds round and round, with each curve above or outside the previous one. Also ATTRIB ADJ *...a spiral staircase.* 2 VB WITH ADJUNCT If something **spirals,** it moves up or down in a spiral curve. *A small bird shot up, spiralling into the sky.* 3 VB If an amount or level **spirals,** it rises quickly. *Military budgets had continued to spiral.* Also SING N *...a wage and price spiral.* 4 VB WITH ADJUNCT If an amount or level **spirals** downwards, it falls quickly. *Costs started to spiral downwards.* Also SING N WITH SUPP *Industry entered a spiral of decline.*

spire /spaɪə/, **spires.** COUNT N The **spire** of a church is a tall cone-shaped structure on top of a tower.

spirit /spɪrɪt/, **spirits, spiriting, spirited.** 1 SING N Your **spirit** is the part of you that is not physical and that is connected with your deepest thoughts and feelings. *Fulfilment must be sought through the spirit, not the body or the mind.* 2 COUNT N The **spirit** of a dead person is a non-physical part of them that is believed to remain alive after their death. 3 COUNT N A **spirit** is also a supernatural being. *The charm is worn to ward off evil spirits.* 4 UNCOUNT N **Spirit** is enthusiasm, energy, and self-confidence. *...a performance full of spirit and originality.* 5 SING N WITH SUPP You can use **spirit** to refer to a particular attitude. *He made the proposal in a spirit of rebellion.* 6 PLURAL N WITH SUPP You can refer to your **spirits** when saying how happy or unhappy you are. For example, if your spirits are high, you are happy. *The children lifted my spirits with their laughter.* 7 SING N The **spirit** of a law or an agreement is the way that it was intended to be interpreted or applied. *I think we'd be breaking the spirit of the agreement if we went ahead.* 8 PLURAL N **Spirits** are strong alcoholic drinks such as whisky and gin. 9 VB WITH OBJ AND ADJUNCT If you **spirit** someone out of or into a place, you get them out or in quickly and secretly. *Somehow the Action Service had spirited him across the frontier.*

spirited /spɪrɪtɪ¹d/. ADJ A **spirited** action shows energy and courage. *Despite spirited resistance by Republican forces, the town fell to the Nationalists.*

spiritual /spɪrɪtʃuºəl/. ADJ **Spiritual** means relating to people's deepest thoughts and beliefs, rather than to their bodies and physical surroundings. *...people's pursuit of material ends to the neglect of their spiritual needs.* ♦ **spiritually** ADV *...a spiritually sick society.* ♦ **spirituality** /spɪrɪtjuælɪ¹ti¹/ UNCOUNT N *...the decline of spirituality in our time.*

spit /spɪt/, **spits, spitting, spat** /spæt/. **Spit** is used as the past tense in American English. 1 UNCOUNT N **Spit** is the watery liquid produced in your mouth. 2 VB When people **spit,** they force an amount of spit out of their mouth. *The driver spat contemptuously.* 3 VB WITH OBJ If you **spit** liquid or food somewhere, you force a small amount of it out of your mouth. *If I don't like it I can always spit it out.* 4 COUNT N A **spit** is a rod which is pushed through a piece of meat so that it can be hung over an open fire and cooked. 5 PHRASE If someone is **the spitting image of** another person, they look very like that other person. *She was the spitting image of his mother.*

spite /spaɪt/. UNCOUNT N **Spite** is the desire to hurt or upset someone. *He wrote that review out of pure spite.*

PHRASES ● If you do something nasty **to spite** someone, you do it deliberately in order to hurt or upset them. *They are being controversial to spite us.* ● You use **in spite of** to introduce information which makes your previous or next statement seem surprising. *In spite of poor health, my father was always cheerful.* ● If you do something **in spite of** yourself, you do it although you did not really intend to or expect to. *Jane became edgy in spite of herself.*

spiteful /spaɪtful/. ADJ Someone who is **spiteful** does nasty things to people they dislike. *Thomas could be so spiteful to his little brother.*

spittle /spɪtəºl/. UNCOUNT N **Spittle** is the watery liquid produced in your mouth; an old-fashioned use.

splash /splæʃ/, **splashes, splashing, splashed.** 1 VB WITH ADJUNCT OR OBJ If you **splash** around in water, you disturb the water in a violent and noisy way, so that it flies up. *Ralph started to run, splashing through the shallow water... They proceeded to hurl themselves about, splashing everybody within sight.* 2 ERG VB WITH ADJUNCT OR VB WITH OBJ If a liquid **splashes** on something, it scatters in a lot of small drops over it. *Drenching spray splashed over the deck... He stopped at a fountain to splash water over his face... They flinched as the cold rain splashed them.* 3 COUNT N A **splash** is the sound made when something hits water. *She disappeared into the water with a splash.* 4 COUNT N A **splash** of a liquid is a small quantity of it that has been spilt on something. *He wiped away the splash of gasoline on the near fender.* 5 COUNT N A **splash** of colour is an area of a bright colour. *A large bouquet of tulips made a brilliant splash of yellow on the table.*

splash out. PHR VB If you **splash out** on a luxury, you buy it even though it costs a lot of money; an informal use. *We splashed out on a colour television.*

splatter /splætə/, **splatters, splattering, splattered.** ERG VB WITH ADJUNCT OR VB WITH OBJ If a thick wet substance **is splattered** on something or **splatters** it, it is splashed or thrown over it. *Food was splattered all over the kitchen walls... She was wearing an apron splattered with blood.*

splay /spleɪ/, **splays, splaying, splayed.** ERG VB If two or more things **are splayed** or **splay out,** their ends are spread out away from each other. *He pressed the mattress with splayed fingers... The brush's bristles were beginning to splay out.*

splendid /splendɪd/. 1 ADJ Something that is **splendid** is excellent. *I think it's a splendid idea.* ♦ **splendidly** ADV *She was caring for him splendidly.* 2 ADJ A **splendid** building or work of art is magnificent and impressive. *In the middle of Hull stands a splendid Victorian building.* ♦ **splendidly** ADV *...a splendidly furnished room.*

splendour /splendə/, **splendours;** spelled **splendor** in American English. 1 UNCOUNT N The **splendour** of something is its magnificent and impressive appearance. *...the splendour of Hyde Park Hotel... The room was decorated with great splendour.* 2 PLURAL N The **splendours** of something are its beautiful and impressive features. *...the Elizabethan splendours of Watermouth Hall.*

splint /splɪnt/, **splints.** COUNT N A **splint** is a long piece of wood or metal fastened to a broken arm or leg to keep it still.

splinter /splɪntə/, **splinters, splintering, splintered.** 1 COUNT N A **splinter** is a very thin, sharp piece of wood or glass which has broken off from a larger piece. *...splinters of coloured glass... Sue was worried about splinters in her bare feet.* 2 ERG VB If something **splinters,** it breaks into thin, sharp pieces. *When feeding dogs, avoid chicken, rabbit or fish bones, which can splinter... ...splintered wood.* 3 ATTRIB ADJ A **splinter** group is a group of people who have broken away from a larger organization.

split /splɪt/, **splits, splitting. Split** is used in the present tense, and is the past tense and past participle. 1 ERG VB If something **splits** or **is split,** it is divided into two or more parts, or a crack or tear appears in it. *Three people died when their car split in two after hitting a tree... It was a very poor quality wood which had already split in many places.* Also ADJ *Eric fingered his split lip.* 2 COUNT N A **split** is a long crack or tear. *There's a split down the page of the atlas.* 3 ERG VB If an organization **splits** or **is split,** one group of members disagrees strongly with the other members. *The council split down the middle over the issue... The government is split on how to deal with the situation.* 4 COUNT N A **split** in an organization is a disagreement between its members. *The last thing he wanted was a split in the party.* 5 SING N A **split** between two things is a division or difference between them. *...the split between reality and the perception of it.* 6 VB WITH OBJ If two or more people **split** something, they share it between them. *The profits are to be split fifty-fifty between the two of them.* 7 to **split hairs:** see **hair.**

split up. PHR VB 1 If two people **split up,** they end their relationship or marriage. *After he split up with his wife he went to Arizona.* 2 If a group of people **split up,** they go away in different directions. *In Hamburg the girls split up.* 3 If you **split** something **up,** you divide it into a number of separate sections. *You achieve more by splitting them up into groups.*

split second. SING N A **split second** is a very short period of time. *For a split second nothing happened... She has to make split-second decisions.*

splitting /splɪtɪŋ/. ATTRIB ADJ A **splitting** headache is a very severe one.

splutter /splʌtə/, **splutters, spluttering, spluttered.** 1 VB OR REPORT VB If someone **splutters,** they make spitting sounds and have difficulty speaking clearly. *The fumes make you cough and splutter... 'I know them. They're my friends,' I was spluttering.* Also COUNT N *'Of course not,' she said with a splutter of mirth.* 2 VB If something **splutters,** it makes a series of short, sharp sounds. *...the roaring and spluttering of motorbikes.*

spoil /spɔɪl/, **spoils, spoiling, spoiled** or **spoilt** /spɔɪlt/. **1** VB WITH OBJ If you **spoil** something, you prevent it from being successful or satisfactory. *She shouted at him for spoiling her lovely evening.* **2** VB WITH OBJ If you **spoil** children, you give them everything they want, which has a bad effect on their character. **3** VB WITH OBJ OR REFL VB If you **spoil** someone, you give them something nice as a treat. **4** PLURAL N **Spoils** are things that people get as a result of winning a battle or of doing something else successfully; a literary use. *...the spoils of war.*

spoke /spəʊk/, **spokes. 1 Spoke** is the past tense of **speak. 2** COUNT N The **spokes** of a wheel are the bars that connect the outer ring to the centre.

spoken /spəʊkə^{0}n/. **Spoken** is the past participle of **speak.**

spokesman /spəʊksmə^{3}n/, **spokesmen.** COUNT N A **spokesman** is a male spokesperson.

spokesperson /spəʊkspɜːsə^{0}n/, **spokespersons.** COUNT N A **spokesperson** is a person who speaks as the representative of a group. *...the spokesperson for the delegation.*

spokeswoman /spəʊkswʊmən/, **spokeswomen.** COUNT N A **spokeswoman** is a female spokesperson.

sponge /spʌndʒ/, **sponges, sponging, sponged. 1** COUNT N OR UNCOUNT N A **sponge** is a piece of a squashy, absorbent substance with lots of holes in it, used for cleaning things or washing your body. *Wipe the surface with a clean sponge... ...a sponge mop.* **2** VB WITH OBJ If you **sponge** something, you wipe it with a wet sponge. **3** COUNT N OR UNCOUNT N A **sponge** is also a light cake or pudding. *...baked apple with a layer of sponge on top.*

sponge off or **sponge on.** PHR VB Someone who **sponges off** other people or **sponges on** other people regularly gets money from them without giving anything in return; an informal use showing disapproval. *He sponged on his friends.*

spongy /spʌndʒi^1/. ADJ Something that is **spongy** is soft and squashy. *...spongy bread.*

sponsor /spɒnsə/, **sponsors, sponsoring, sponsored. 1** VB WITH OBJ If an organization **sponsors** an event or someone's training, it pays some or all of the expenses connected with it. *The conference was sponsored by the Guardian.* **2** VB WITH OBJ If you **sponsor** someone who is doing something to raise money for charity, you agree to give them a sum of money for the charity if they succeed in doing it. *Would you mind sponsoring me in this swim for cancer research?... ...a sponsored walk.* **3** VB WITH OBJ If you **sponsor** a proposal, you officially put it forward and support it. *Two Liberal MPs sponsored the Bill.* **4** COUNT N A **sponsor** is a person or organization that sponsors something or someone.

sponsorship /spɒnsəʃɪp/. UNCOUNT N **Sponsorship** is financial support given by a sponsor. *...industrial sponsorship of the arts.*

spontaneity /spɒntəniːɪ^{1}ti^1, -neɪ-/. UNCOUNT N **Spontaneity** is spontaneous, natural behaviour. *...a child's spontaneity.*

spontaneous /spɒnteɪnɪəs/. **1** ADJ **Spontaneous** acts are not planned or arranged, but are done because someone suddenly wants to do them. *...a spontaneous display of friendship and affection.* ♦ **spontaneously** ADV *Flo and I decided spontaneously to board a train for Geneva.* **2** ADJ A **spontaneous** event happens because of processes within something, rather than being caused by things outside it. *...spontaneous explosions.* ♦ **spontaneously** ADV *The fuel ignites spontaneously from the heat created by the compression.*

spooky /spuːki^1/. ADJ A **spooky** place has a strange, frightening atmosphere; an informal use.

spool /spuːl/, **spools.** COUNT N A **spool** is a round object onto which thread, tape, or film can be wound.

spoon /spuːn/, **spoons, spooning, spooned. 1** COUNT N A **spoon** is an object used for eating, stirring, and serving food. It is shaped like a small shallow bowl with a long handle. *...a knife, fork, and spoon.* **2** COUNT N You can use **spoon** to refer to the amount of a substance that a spoon can hold. *He takes six spoons of sugar in his tea.* **3** VB WITH OBJ If you **spoon** food somewhere, you put it there using a spoon. *He spooned the vegetables onto the plates.*

spoonful /spuːnfʊl/, **spoonfuls.** COUNT N A **spoonful** of a substance is the amount that a spoon can hold. *She put a spoonful of milk in each of the two cups.*

sporadic /spə^{7}rædɪk/. ADJ **Sporadic** events happen at irregular intervals. *Sporadic attacks continued throughout the night.* ♦ **sporadically** ADV *Most families watch television sporadically.*

spore /spɔː/, **spores.** COUNT N **Spores** are cells produced by bacteria and non-flowering plants such as fungi which develop into new bacteria or plants; a technical use.

sport /spɔːt/, **sports, sporting, sported. 1** UNCOUNT N OR COUNT N **Sports** are games and other competitive activities which need physical effort and skill. *My favourite sport is football... I was bad at sport.* **2** VB WITH OBJ If you **sport** something noticeable or unusual, you wear it. *One of them even sported an earring.*

sporting /spɔːtɪŋ/. ATTRIB ADJ **Sporting** means relating to sport or used for sport. *It was his 29th international sporting event.*

sports car, sports cars. COUNT N A **sports car** is a low, fast car, usually for only two people.

sports jacket, sports jackets. COUNT N A **sports jacket** is a man's jacket, usually made of tweed.

sportsman /spɔːtsmə^{3}n/, **sportsmen.** COUNT N A **sportsman** is a man who takes part in sports.

sportswoman /spɔːtswʊmən/, **sportswomen.** COUNT N A **sportswoman** is a woman who takes part in sports.

spot /spɒt/, **spots, spotting, spotted. 1** COUNT N **Spots** are small, round, coloured areas on a surface. *She was wearing a white blouse with red spots.* **2** COUNT N **Spots** on a person's skin are small lumps or marks. *Their bites leave itching red spots on the skin.* **3** COUNT N A **spot** of a substance is a small amount of it. *I felt a few spots of rain.* **4** SING N A **spot** of something is a small amount of it; an informal use. *What about a spot of lunch?* **5** COUNT N You can refer to a particular place as a **spot.** *It's a lovely spot for a picnic... Four brass plates in the floor mark the spot where the throne stood.* **6** VB WITH OBJ If you **spot** something, you notice it. *I spotted you standing by your car at the gas station.* **7** See also **blind spot, spotted.**

PHRASES ● If you are **on the spot,** you are at the actual place where something is happening. *Certain decisions had to be taken by the man on the spot.* ● If you do something **on the spot,** you do it immediately. *They dismissed him on the spot.* ● If you **put** someone **on the spot,** you put them in a difficult situation. ● to **have a soft spot for** someone: see **soft.**

spot check, spot checks. COUNT N A **spot check** is a random inspection of one of a group of things.

spotless /spɒtlɪ^{2}s/. ADJ Something that is **spotless** is perfectly clean. *...a spotless white shirt.*

spotlight /spɒtlaɪt/, **spotlights.** COUNT N A **spotlight** is a powerful light, often in a theatre, which can be directed so that it lights up a small area.

spotted /spɒtɪ^{2}d/. ADJ Something that is **spotted** has a pattern of spots on it. *...a red and white spotted handkerchief.*

spotty /spɒti^1/. ADJ Someone who is **spotty** has spots or pimples on their skin, especially on their face.

spouse /spaʊs, spaʊz/, **spouses.** COUNT N Someone's **spouse** is the person they are married to; a formal use. *They receive free membership for themselves and their spouses.*

spout /spaʊt/, **spouts, spouting, spouted. 1** ERG VB When liquid or flame **spouts** out of something, it comes out fast in a long stream. *...jets of water spouting up from the basins below... Their tanks came on in hordes, spouting flames.* **2** VB WITH OBJ If someone **spouts** something that they have learned, they speak without stopping or thinking. *You were always spouting some theory to us.* **3** COUNT N The **spout** of a kettle or teapot is the tube that the liquid comes out of.

sprain /spreɪn/, **sprains, spraining, sprained. 1** VB WITH OBJ If you **sprain** your ankle or wrist, you accidentally damage it by twisting it, for example when you fall. **2** COUNT N A **sprain** is the injury caused by spraining a joint.

sprang /spræŋ/. **Sprang** is the past tense of **spring.**

sprawl /sprɔːl/, **sprawls, sprawling, sprawled. 1** VB If you **sprawl** somewhere, you sit or lie down with your legs and arms spread out in a careless way. *Segal sprawled out on the couch.* ♦ **sprawled** PRED ADJ *He lay sprawled in the chair.* **2** VB WITH ADJUNCT A place that **sprawls** covers a large area of land. *The village sprawls along the coastline... ...a sprawling city.* **3** UNCOUNT N WITH SUPP You can use **sprawl** to refer to an area where a city has expanded in an uncontrolled way. *...London's urban sprawl.*

spray /spreɪ/, **sprays, spraying, sprayed. 1** UNCOUNT N **Spray** is a lot of small drops of water which are being splashed or forced into the air. *Drenching spray splashed over the deck.* **2** VB WITH OBJ If you **spray** something with a liquid, you cover it with drops of the liquid, for example using a hose or an aerosol. *Spray the shelves with insecticide... He sprayed a little eau-de-cologne over himself.* **3** MASS N A **spray** is a liquid kept under pressure in a container, which you can force out in very small drops. *...chemical sprays... ...hair spray.* **4** COUNT N A **spray** is also a piece of equipment for spraying water or another liquid on something. **5** COUNT N A **spray** of flowers or leaves is a number of them on one stem or branch. *...great sprays of lilies.*

spread /spred/, **spreads, spreading. Spread** is used in the present tense, and is the past tense and past participle. **1** VB WITH OBJ If you **spread** something, you arrange it over a surface, so that all of it can be seen or used easily. *He took the envelope, tipped it open and spread the contents on the table.* **2** VB WITH OBJ If you **spread** your hands, arms, or legs, you move them far apart. *He just shrugged and spread his hands.* **3** VB WITH OBJ If you **spread** a substance on a surface, you put a thin layer of the substance over the surface. *Liz was spreading marmalade on a piece of toast... I love biscuits spread with butter.* **4** MASS N A **spread** is a soft food which is put on bread. *...cheese spread.* **5** ERG VB If something **spreads,** it gradually reaches or affects a larger area or more people. *A stain was spreading on the bathroom ceiling... News of the wreck spread quickly... Disease might be spread very easily.* **6** SING N The **spread** of something is its increasing presence or occurrence. *Girls have benefited more than boys from the spread of higher education.* **7** ERG VB WITH 'over' If something **spreads** over a period of time, it takes place over that period. *The breeding season is spread over five months.* **8** SING N A **spread** of ideas, interests, or other things is a wide variety of them. *The IBA wants to have a broad spread of opinion represented on its board.*

spread out. PHR VB **1** If people, animals, or vehicles **spread out** or **are spread out,** they are far apart. *They followed him and spread out, nervously, in the forest... My family were spread out all over the countryside.* **2** If you **spread** something **out,** you arrange it over a surface, so that all of it can be seen or used easily. *I removed the tool kit and spread it out on the seat.*

spread-eagled /spred iːgə^{0}ld/. ADJ Someone who is **spread-eagled** somewhere is lying with their arms and legs spread out.

spree /spriː/, **sprees.** COUNT N If you go on a **spree,** you spend time away from home doing something that you enjoy. *Tim was away on a shopping spree.*

sprig /sprɪg/, **sprigs.** COUNT N A **sprig** of a plant is a small piece of stem with leaves on it. *...a sprig of holly.*

sprightly /spraɪtli^1/. ADJ Someone, especially an old person, who is **sprightly** is lively and active.

spring /sprɪŋ/, **springs, springing, sprang** /spræŋ/, **sprung** /sprʌŋ/. In American English **sprung** is sometimes used as the past tense. **1** UNCOUNT N OR COUNT N **Spring** is the season between winter and summer. In the spring the weather starts to get warmer. *...the first day of spring... He left in the spring of 1956.* **2** COUNT N A **spring** is a coil of wire which returns to its original shape after it is pressed or pulled. **3** COUNT N A **spring** is also a place where water comes up through the ground. **4** VB When a person or animal **springs,** they move suddenly upwards or forwards. *She sprang to her feet and faced him... The panther crouched, ready to spring.* **5** VB WITH ADJUNCT If something **springs** in a particular direction, it moves suddenly and quickly. *Hands sprang up... The door of the safe had sprung open.* **6** VB WITH ADJUNCT If one thing **springs** from another, the first thing is the result of the second. *These problems spring from different causes.* **7** VB WITH OBJ If you **spring** some news or an event on someone, you do not tell them about it in advance. **8** PHRASE If a boat, container, or roof **springs a leak,** a hole or crack appears in it and it starts leaking.

spring up. PHR VB If something **springs up,** it suddenly appears or comes into existence. *Computer stores are springing up all over the place.*

springboard /sprɪŋbɔːd/, **springboards. 1** COUNT N WITH SUPP If something is a **springboard** for an action or enterprise, it makes it possible for the action or enterprise to begin. *The campaign might well be the springboard for the launching of a new party.* **2** COUNT N A **springboard** is also a flexible board which you jump on before performing a dive or a gymnastic movement.

spring-cleaning. UNCOUNT N When you do **spring-cleaning,** you clean your home very thoroughly.

springtime /sprɪŋtaɪm/. UNCOUNT N **Springtime** is the period of time during which spring lasts.

springy /sprɪŋi^1/. ADJ If something is **springy,** it returns quickly to its original shape after you press it. *...a springy mattress... The grass was short and springy.*

sprinkle /sprɪŋkə^{0}l/, **sprinkles, sprinkling, sprinkled.** VB WITH OBJ If you **sprinkle** a liquid or powder over something, you scatter it over it. *Sprinkle the oil over the courgettes... She sprinkled the cakes with sugar.*

sprinkler /sprɪŋklə/, **sprinklers.** COUNT N A **sprinkler** is a device used to spray water, in order to water lawns or put out fires in buildings.

sprinkling /sprɪ́ŋklɪŋ/. sɪɴɢ ɴ A **sprinkling** of things is a small quantity of them spread over a large area. ...*a sprinkling of sightseers outside the palace.*

sprint /sprɪnt/, **sprints, sprinting, sprinted. 1** ᴄᴏᴜɴᴛ ɴ A **sprint** is a short fast race. ...*a 100 metre sprint.* **2** ᴠʙ If you **sprint**, you run as fast as you can over a short distance. *She sprinted to her car.* Also sɪɴɢ ɴ *Bessie had suddenly broken into a sprint.*

sprinter /sprɪ́ntə/, **sprinters.** ᴄᴏᴜɴᴛ ɴ A **sprinter** is a person who takes part in short, fast races.

sprout /spraʊt/, **sprouts, sprouting, sprouted. 1** ᴇʀɢ ᴠʙ ᴏʀ ᴠʙ When plants or vegetables **sprout** new shoots or leaves, they produce them. *The seeds soon sprouted... Greenery sprouted between the white gravestones.* **2** ᴄᴏᴜɴᴛ ɴ **Sprouts** or **Brussels sprouts** are vegetables like very small cabbages.

spruce /spruːs/. ᴀᴅᴊ Someone who is **spruce** is very neat and smart.

sprung /sprʌŋ/. **Sprung** is the past participle of **spring.**

spry /spraɪ/. ᴀᴅᴊ An old person who is **spry** is lively and active.

spud /spʌd/, **spuds.** ᴄᴏᴜɴᴛ ɴ **Spuds** are potatoes; an informal use.

spun /spʌn/. **Spun** is the past tense and past participle of **spin.**

spur /spɜː/, **spurs, spurring, spurred. 1** ᴠʙ ᴡɪᴛʜ ᴏʙᴊ If something **spurs** you to do something, it encourages you to do it. *Martin's job either spurred the others to do something themselves... Companies might spur one another on.* **2** ᴠʙ ᴡɪᴛʜ ᴏʙᴊ If something **spurs** a change or event, it makes it happen faster or sooner. ...*a period of extremely rapid growth, spurred by the advent of the microprocessor.* **3** sɪɴɢ ɴ Something that acts as a **spur** encourages someone to do something or makes something happen faster or sooner. *International competition was a spur to modernisation.* **4** ᴘʜʀᴀsᴇ If you do something **on the spur of the moment,** you do it suddenly, without planning it beforehand. *I just took the bus on the spur of the moment.* **5** ᴄᴏᴜɴᴛ ɴ **Spurs** are sharp metal points attached to the heels of a rider's boots and used to make the horse go faster.

spurious /spjʊ́əriəs/. ᴀᴅᴊ Something that is **spurious** is not genuine or real; a formal use. ...*the spurious attractions of modernity.*

spurn /spɜːn/, **spurns, spurning, spurned.** ᴠʙ ᴡɪᴛʜ ᴏʙᴊ If you **spurn** something, you refuse to accept it; a formal use. *You spurned my friendship.*

spurt /spɜːt/, **spurts, spurting, spurted. 1** ᴇʀɢ ᴠʙ When a liquid or flame **spurts** out of something, it comes out quickly in a thin, powerful stream. ...*a blow that sent blood spurting from his mouth... My arm began to spurt blood.* Also ᴄᴏᴜɴᴛ ɴ ...*a small, clear spurt of flame.* **2** ᴄᴏᴜɴᴛ ɴ A **spurt** of activity or emotion is a sudden, brief period of it. *Her feelings varied from tenderness to sudden spurts of genuine love.* **3** ᴠʙ If you **spurt** somewhere, you suddenly increase your speed for a short while. *With Claude driving they spurted through back streets.*

sputter /spʌ́tə/, **sputters, sputtering, sputtered.** ᴠʙ If something **sputters**, it makes soft hissing and popping sounds. *The engine began sputtering.*

spy /spaɪ/, **spies, spying, spied. 1** ᴄᴏᴜɴᴛ ɴ A **spy** is a person whose job is to find out secret information about another country or organization. *A member of his staff was discovered to be a foreign spy.* **2** ᴠʙ Someone who **spies** for a country or organization tries to find out secret information about another country or organization. *He was convicted of spying for Russia.* **3** ᴠʙ ᴡɪᴛʜ 'on' If you **spy** on someone, you watch them secretly. ...*girls spying on their unfaithful lovers.* **4** ᴠʙ ᴡɪᴛʜ ᴏʙᴊ If you **spy** something, you notice it; a literary use. *Suddenly Quint spied a shark.*

sq. You write **sq** as a written abbreviation for 'square' when giving the measurement of an area. ...*280,000 sq ft of space.*

squabble /skwɒ́bəl/, **squabbles, squabbling, squabbled.** ᴠʙ When people **squabble**, they quarrel about something unimportant. *They're always squabbling over details.* Also ᴄᴏᴜɴᴛ ɴ ...*squabbles between the children.*

squad /skwɒd/, **squads. 1** ᴄᴏᴜɴᴛ ɴ ᴡɪᴛʜ sᴜᴘᴘ A **squad** is a section of a police force that is responsible for dealing with a particular type of crime. ...*the drugs squad.* **2** ᴄᴏᴜɴᴛ ɴ A **squad** of soldiers is a small group of them.

squad car, squad cars. ᴄᴏᴜɴᴛ ɴ A **squad car** is a car used by the police.

squadron /skwɒ́drən/, **squadrons.** ᴄᴏᴜɴᴛ ɴ A **squadron** is a section of one of the armed forces, especially the air force. ...*a squadron of fighter planes.*

squalid /skwɒ́lɪd/. **1** ᴀᴅᴊ A **squalid** place is dirty, untidy, and in bad condition. ...*our small, squalid flat.* **2** ᴀᴅᴊ **Squalid** activities are unpleasant and often

dishonest. *They're involved in a rather squalid battle as to who controls the party.*

squall /skwɔːl/, **squalls.** ᴄᴏᴜɴᴛ ɴ A **squall** is a brief, violent storm.

squalor /skwɒ́lə/. ᴜɴᴄᴏᴜɴᴛ ɴ You can refer to squalid conditions or surroundings as **squalor.** ...*poor people living in conditions of squalor.*

squander /skwɒ́ndə/, **squanders, squandering, squandered.** ᴠʙ ᴡɪᴛʜ ᴏʙᴊ If you **squander** resources, you use them in a wasteful way. *He squandered large quantities of cash on overpriced clothes.*

square /skweə/, **squares, squaring, squared. 1** ᴄᴏᴜɴᴛ ɴ A **square** is a shape with four sides of the same length and four corners that are all right angles. **2** ᴀᴅᴊ If something that is **square** has a shape similar to a square. *The post office was a small, square building... He had a square ruddy face.* **3** ᴄᴏᴜɴᴛ ɴ In a town or city, a **square** is a flat open place, often in the shape of a square. ...*Trafalgar Square.* **4** ᴀᴛᴛʀɪʙ ᴀᴅᴊ **Square** is used in front of units of length to form units of area such as 'square metre' and 'square inch'. ...*hundreds of square miles of pine forest.* **5** ᴀᴅᴊ ᴀғᴛᴇʀ ɴ **Square** is also used after units of length when you are giving the length of each side of something square. ...*a silicon chip less than a centimetre square.* **6** ᴠʙ ᴡɪᴛʜ ᴏʙᴊ If you **square** a number, you multiply it by itself. For example, 3 squared is 3 x 3, or 9. You usually write 3 squared as 3^2. **7** ᴄᴏᴜɴᴛ ɴ The **square** of a number is another number that is produced by multiplying the first number by itself. For example, the square of 2 is 4. **8** ᴇʀɢ ᴠʙ ᴡɪᴛʜ 'with' If two different situations or things **square** with each other, they can be accepted together or seem compatible. *His interpretation is unlikely to square with the Committee's guidelines... How do you square being a Lord with being a Marxist?* **9** ᴄᴏᴜɴᴛ ɴ A **square** meal is a large and satisfying one. *He had gone without a square meal for nearly three days.* **10** ᴘʜʀᴀsᴇ If you are **back to square one,** you have to start dealing with something from the beginning again; an informal use. *If he says 'No', you are back to square one.*

squarely /skwéəli/. **1** ᴀᴅᴠ **Squarely** means directly and in the middle, rather than indirectly or at an angle. *The television mast fell squarely onto a Methodist chapel.* **2** ᴀᴅᴠ If you face something **squarely**, you face it directly, without trying to avoid it. *This difficulty will have to be squarely faced.*

square root, square roots. ᴄᴏᴜɴᴛ ɴ The **square root** of a number is another number which produces the first number when it is multiplied by itself. For example, 4 is a square root of 16.

squash /skwɒʃ/, **squashes, squashing, squashed. 1** ᴠʙ ᴡɪᴛʜ ᴏʙᴊ If you **squash** something, you press it, so that it becomes flat or loses its shape. ...*squashed paper cups.* **2** ᴜɴᴄᴏᴜɴᴛ ɴ **Squash** is a game in which two players hit a small rubber ball against the walls of a court using rackets. **3** ᴍᴀss ɴ **Squash** is also a drink made from fruit juice, sugar, and water; a British use. ...*lemon squash.*

squashy /skwɒ́ʃi/. ᴀᴅᴊ Something that is **squashy** is soft and can be squashed easily. ...*squashy tomatoes.*

squat /skwɒt/, **squats, squatting, squatted. 1** ᴠʙ ᴡɪᴛʜ ᴀᴅᴊᴜɴᴄᴛ If you **squat** down, you crouch, balancing on your feet with your legs bent. *He told the boys to squat in a semicircle around him.* **2** ᴀᴅᴊ Something that is **squat** is short and wide. ...*squat wooden churches.* **3** ᴠʙ A person who **squats** in an unused building lives there without having a legal right to do so. *We were squatting in an empty house.* ◆ **squatter** /skwɒ́tə/. ᴄᴏᴜɴᴛ ɴ ...*the subject of squatters' rights.*

squawk /skwɔːk/, **squawks, squawking, squawked.** ᴠʙ When a bird **squawks**, it makes a loud sharp noise. *Scrawny chickens ran squawking around the village.* Also ᴄᴏᴜɴᴛ ɴ ...*the sad squawks of the peacocks.*

squeak /skwiːk/, **squeaks, squeaking, squeaked.** ᴠʙ If something **squeaks**, it makes a short, high-pitched sound. *A door squeaked open nearby.* Also ᴄᴏᴜɴᴛ ɴ *She let out a squeak.*

squeaky /skwiːki/. ᴀᴅᴊ Something that is **squeaky** makes squeaking noises. ...*a squeaky iron gate... a high, squeaky voice.*

squeal /skwiːl/, **squeals, squealing, squealed.** ᴠʙ If someone or something **squeals**, they make a long, high-pitched sound. *The boys scattered, squealing in horror.* Also ᴄᴏᴜɴᴛ ɴ *There was a squeal of brakes.*

squeamish /skwiːmɪʃ/. ᴀᴅᴊ If you are **squeamish**, you are easily upset by unpleasant sights or situations.

squeeze /skwiːz/, **squeezes, squeezing, squeezed. 1** ᴠʙ ᴡɪᴛʜ ᴏʙᴊ When you **squeeze** something soft or flexible, you press it firmly from two sides. *The children were squeezing the packets to find out what was inside.* Also ᴄᴏᴜɴᴛ ɴ *He gave her hand a squeeze.* **2** ᴠʙ ᴡɪᴛʜ ᴏʙᴊ ᴀɴᴅ ᴀᴅᴊᴜɴᴄᴛ When you **squeeze** a liquid or a soft substance out of an object, you get it out by pressing it. *Squeeze all the water out of the cloth.* **3** ᴠʙ ᴡɪᴛʜ ᴀᴅᴊᴜɴᴄᴛ If you **squeeze** through or into

a small space, you manage to get through it or into it. *We squeezed under the wire... The inhabitants have to squeeze into a tiny area of living space.* **4** sɪɴɢ ɴ If getting a number of people into a small space is a **squeeze**, it is only just possible; an informal use. *We all got in the lift but it was a bit of a squeeze.*

squelch /skwɛltʃ/, **squelches, squelching, squelched.** ᴠʙ To **squelch** means to make a wet, sucking sound. *I squelched along by the water's edge.*

squid /skwɪd/, **squids. Squid** can also be the plural. ᴄᴏᴜɴᴛ ɴ A **squid** is a sea creature with a soft body and many tentacles.

squint /skwɪnt/, **squints, squinting, squinted. 1** ᴠʙ If you **squint** at something, you look at it with your eyes partly closed. *I squinted up at the sky.* **2** ᴄᴏᴜɴᴛ ɴ If someone has a **squint**, their eyes are looking in different directions.

squire /skwaɪə/, **squires.** ᴄᴏᴜɴᴛ ɴ In former times, the **squire** of an English village was the man who owned most of the land in it.

squirm /skwɜːm/, **squirms, squirming, squirmed.** ᴠʙ If you **squirm**, you wriggle, because you are nervous or uncomfortable.

squirrel /skwɪ́rəl/, **squirrels.** ᴄᴏᴜɴᴛ ɴ A **squirrel** is a small furry animal with a long bushy tail which climbs trees.

squirt /skwɜːt/, **squirts, squirting, squirted.** ᴇʀɢ ᴠʙ ᴏʀ ᴠʙ ᴡɪᴛʜ ᴏʙᴊ If you **squirt** a liquid somewhere, the liquid comes out of a narrow opening in a thin fast stream. *Squirt a little oil into the keyhole... Water squirted out of a hole in the pipe... One woman was squirting windows with water.*

SRN /ɛs ɑː ɛn/, **SRNs.** ᴄᴏᴜɴᴛ ɴ An **SRN** is a fully qualified nurse in the United Kingdom. **SRN** is an abbreviation for 'State Registered Nurse'.

St. The plural for meaning 2 is **SS. 1 St** is a written abbreviation for 'Street'. ...*22 Harley St, London W1.* **2 St** is also a written abbreviation for 'Saint'. ...*St Anselm.... SS Peter and Paul.*

-st. sᴜғғɪx **-st** is added to most numbers written in figures and ending in 1 to form ordinal numbers. 1st is pronounced the same as 'first'. ...*1st April 1982... 21st Street.*

stab /stæb/, **stabs, stabbing, stabbed. 1** ᴠʙ ᴡɪᴛʜ ᴏʙᴊ If someone **stabs** you, they push a knife into your body. *A man was stabbed to death as he left a London library.* **2** ᴠʙ ᴡɪᴛʜ ᴏʙᴊ ᴏʀ ᴀᴅᴊᴜɴᴄᴛ If you **stab** something or **stab** at it, you push at it with your finger or with something pointed. *He stabbed the air with his index finger... She was typing in a fury, her fingers stabbing at the keys.* **3** ᴄᴏᴜɴᴛ ɴ If you have a **stab** at something, you try to do it; an informal use. *I'd like to have a stab at tap dancing.* **4** sɪɴɢ ɴ ᴡɪᴛʜ 'of' You can refer to a sudden feeling as a **stab** of that feeling; a literary use. *Kitty felt a stab of dismay.*

stabbing /stǽbɪŋ/, **stabbings. 1** ᴄᴏᴜɴᴛ ɴ A **stabbing** is an incident in which someone stabs someone else. **2** ᴀᴛᴛʀɪʙ ᴀᴅᴊ A **stabbing** pain is a sudden sharp pain.

stabilize /stéɪbɪlaɪz/, **stabilizes, stabilizing, stabilized;** also spelled **stabilise.** ᴇʀɢ ᴠʙ If something **stabilizes** or is **stabilized**, it becomes stable. *Eventually your weight will stabilise... The family is one of the great stabilizing elements in society.*

stable /stéɪbəl/, **stables. 1** ᴀᴅᴊ If something is **stable**, it is not likely to change or come to an end suddenly. *Oil prices are stable for the first time in years... a stable marriage.* ◆ **stability** /stəbɪ́lɪti/. ᴜɴᴄᴏᴜɴᴛ ɴ ...*a period of economic growth and stability.* **2** ᴀᴅᴊ If an object is **stable**, it is not likely to move or fall. *A typist's chair should be stable.* **3** ᴄᴏᴜɴᴛ ɴ A **stable** is a building in which horses are kept.

staccato /stəkɑ́ːtəʊ/. ᴀᴛᴛʀɪʙ ᴀᴅᴊ A **staccato** noise consists of a series of short, sharp, separate sounds; a literary use. ...*the man's staccato Berlin accent.*

stack /stæk/, **stacks, stacking, stacked. 1** ᴄᴏᴜɴᴛ ɴ A **stack** of things is a neat pile of them. *On the sideboard was a stack of plates.* **2** ᴠʙ ᴡɪᴛʜ ᴏʙᴊ If you **stack** a number of things, you arrange them in neat piles. *I started stacking the chairs... We stacked up the plates and carried them to the sink.* **3** ᴘᴀssɪᴠᴇ ᴠʙ If a place or surface is **stacked** with objects, it is filled with piles of them. *The shed was stacked with old boxes.* **4** ǫᴜᴀɴᴛɪғ **Stacks** of something means a lot of it; an informal use. *They've got stacks of money.*

stadium /stéɪdɪəm/, **stadiums.** ᴄᴏᴜɴᴛ ɴ A **stadium** is a large sports ground with rows of seats all round it. ...*football stadiums.*

staff /stɑːf/, **staffs, staffed. 1** ᴄᴏʟʟ ɴ The **staff** of an organization are the people who work for it. *She was invited to join the staff of the BBC... There are two students to every member of staff... They have already agreed to cut their staffs.* **2** ᴘᴀssɪᴠᴇ ᴠʙ If an organization is **staffed** by particular people, they are the people who work for it. *It was staffed and run by engineers.*

staffing /stɑːfɪŋ/. UNCOUNT N **Staffing** refers to the number of workers employed to work somewhere. *...inadequate staffing.*

stag /stæg/, **stags.** COUNT N A **stag** is an adult male deer.

stage /steɪdʒ/, **stages, staging, staged. 1** COUNT N A **stage** is a part of a process or activity. *In the early stages of learning to read, a child will usually need a lot of help... ...at this stage in my life... ...the first stage of an 800 mile expedition.* **2** COUNT N In a theatre, the **stage** is the raised platform where actors or entertainers perform. *She stood alone on the enormous stage.* **3** SING N You can refer to acting and the production of plays in a theatre as the **stage.** *She retired from the stage some years ago.* **4** VB WITH OBJ If someone **stages** a play or other show, they present a performance of it. **5** VB WITH OBJ If you **stage** an event or ceremony, you organize it. *The women staged a demonstration.* **6** PHRASE To **set the stage** for something means to make preparations so that it can happen.

stage-manage, stage-manages, stage-managing, stage-managed. VB WITH OBJ If an event **is stage-managed,** it is carefully organized and controlled by someone, rather than happening spontaneously.

stagger /stægə/, **staggers, staggering, staggered. 1** VB If you **stagger,** you walk very unsteadily, for example because you are ill. *I staggered to the nearest chair.* **2** VB WITH OBJ If something **staggers** you, it surprises you very much. *This fact staggered me.* ♦ **staggered** ADJ *We were staggered to learn they would not be returning.* ♦ **staggering** ADJ *Its estimated cost has climbed to a staggering £35 billion.* **3** VB WITH OBJ If people's holidays or hours of work **are staggered,** they are arranged so that they do not all happen at the same time.

stagnant /stægnənt/. **1** ADJ If something such as a business or society is **stagnant,** there is little activity or change; used showing disapproval. *...stagnant economies.* **2** ADJ **Stagnant** water is not flowing or fresh, and is dirty and unhealthy.

stagnate /stægneɪt, stægneɪt/, **stagnates, stagnating, stagnated.** VB If something such as a business or society **stagnates,** it becomes inactive or does not change; used showing disapproval. *The economy stagnated as a result of these tax measures.* ♦ **stagnation** /stægneɪʃəⁿn/ UNCOUNT N *...industrial stagnation.*

staid /steɪd/. ADJ A **staid** person is serious, dull, and rather old-fashioned.

stain /steɪn/, **stains, staining, stained. 1** COUNT N A **stain** is a mark on something that is difficult to remove. *...grease stains.* **2** VB WITH OBJ If a liquid **stains** something, the thing becomes coloured or marked by the liquid. *...the pink spots staining my new blue jacket.* ♦ **stained** ADJ *...a little man with stained teeth... His shirt was stained with blood.*

stained glass. UNCOUNT N **Stained glass** consists of pieces of coloured glass fixed together to make decorative windows or other objects. *...Victorian stained-glass windows.*

stainless steel /steɪnlɪˢs stiːl/. UNCOUNT N **Stainless steel** is a metal made from steel and chromium which does not rust. *...a stainless steel sink.*

stair /steə/, **stairs. 1** PLURAL N **Stairs** are a set of steps inside a building. *He ran up the stairs... ...another flight of stairs.* **2** COUNT N A **stair** is one of the steps in a set of stairs. *Not a stair creaked as she made her way downstairs.*

staircase /steəkeɪs/, **staircases.** COUNT N A **staircase** is a set of stairs inside a house.

stairway /steəweɪ/, **stairways.** COUNT N A **stairway** is a set of steps, inside or outside a building.

stake /steɪk/, **stakes, staking, staked. 1** PHRASE If something is **at stake,** it is being risked and might be lost or damaged. *There's a great deal of money at stake... His political life is at stake.* **2** PLURAL N The **stakes** involved in a risky action or a contest are the things that can be gained or lost. *I'm playing for high stakes.* **3** VB WITH OBJ If you **stake** something such as your money or your reputation on the result of something, you risk your money or reputation on it. *He staked his reputation as a prophet on this assertion.* **4** COUNT N If you have a **stake** in something, its success matters to you, for example because you own part of it. *...a substantial stake in the British textile industry.* **5** PLURAL N WITH SUPP You can use **stakes** to refer to something that is considered as a contest. *...the Presidential stakes... This gives you an advantage in the promotion stakes.* **6** COUNT N A **stake** is a pointed wooden post. *His boat was fastened by a chain to a stake in the ground.* **7** PHRASE If you **stake a claim,** you say that you have a right to something. *Each group had staked its claim to its own territory.*

stale /steɪl/. **1** ADJ **Stale** food or air is old and no longer fresh. *...stale bread.* **2** ADJ If you feel **stale,** you have no new ideas and are bored.

stalemate /steɪlmeɪt/. UNCOUNT N **Stalemate** is a situation in which neither side in an argument or contest can win. *The coalition ended the political stalemate caused by the election.*

stalk /stɔːk/, **stalks, stalking, stalked. 1** COUNT N The **stalk** of a flower, leaf, or fruit is the thin part that joins it to the plant or tree. **2** VB WITH OBJ If you **stalk** a person or a wild animal, you follow them quietly and secretly in order to catch them or observe them. *He moved like a tiger stalking its prey.* **3** VB WITH ADJUNCT If you **stalk** somewhere, you walk in a stiff, proud, or angry way. *She stalked into the living room.*

stall /stɔːl/, **stalls, stalling, stalled. 1** COUNT N A **stall** is a large table with goods for sale or leaflets on it. *...a market stall.* **2** PLURAL N The **stalls** in a theatre or concert hall are the seats on the ground floor in front of the stage. **3** ERG VB When a vehicle **stalls** or when you accidentally **stall** it, the engine stops suddenly. **4** VB If you **stall,** you try to avoid doing something until later. *'Well?' she said. Tom grinned at her, stalling for time.* **5** VB WITH OBJ If you **stall** someone, you prevent them from doing something until later. *Perhaps I can stall him till Thursday or Friday.*

stallion /stæljən/, **stallions.** COUNT N A **stallion** is a male horse.

stalwart /stɔːlwət/, **stalwarts.** ADJ A **stalwart** worker or supporter of an organization is loyal and hardworking. *...the stalwart Somerset cricketer, Bill Andrews.* Also COUNT N *They were all Government stalwarts.*

stamina /stæmɪnə/. UNCOUNT N **Stamina** is the physical or mental energy needed to do a tiring activity for a long time.

stammer /stæmə/, **stammers, stammering, stammered. 1** VB OR REPORT VB If you **stammer,** you speak with difficulty, hesitating and repeating words or sounds. *'But...but...that's impossible,' the youth stammered.* **2** COUNT N Someone who has a **stammer** tends to stammer when they speak.

stamp /stæmp/, **stamps, stamping, stamped. 1** COUNT N A **stamp** or a **postage stamp** is a small piece of gummed paper which you stick on an envelope or parcel before you post it, to show that you have paid the appropriate fee. **2** COUNT N A **stamp** is also a small block of wood or metal with words or a design on it. You press it onto an inky pad and then onto a document in order to produce a mark on the document. The mark is also called a **stamp.** *They had German passports with Brazilian entrance stamps.* **3** VB WITH OBJ If you **stamp** a mark or word on an object, you press the mark or word onto the object using a stamp or other device. *Articles that conform with the relevant British Standards are stamped with a kite-shaped mark... Unless pots are stamped 'ovenproof' assume they are not.* **4** SING N WITH SUPP If something bears the **stamp** of a particular quality or person, it clearly has that quality or was done by that person. *His work hardly bore the stamp of maturity.* **5** VB WITH OBJ If you **stamp** your foot, you put your foot down very hard on the ground because you are angry. *'Damn you, Edward!' she shouted, stamping her foot.* **6** VB WITH 'on' If you **stamp** on something, you put your foot down on it very hard. *I stamped heavily on her foot and muttered, 'Shut up.'*

stamp out. PHR VB If you **stamp** something **out,** you put an end to it. *They are determined to stamp out political extremism.*

stamped /stæmpt/. ADJ A **stamped** envelope or parcel has a stamp stuck on it.

stampede /stæmpiːd/, **stampedes, stampeding, stampeded. 1** ERG VB When a group of animals **stampede** or **are stampeded,** they run in a wild, uncontrolled way. **2** COUNT N When there is a **stampede,** a group of animals or people run in a wild, uncontrolled way. *...a stampede of elephants... Her foot got trodden on in the general stampede to the exit.*

stance /stæns, stɑːns/, **stances. 1** COUNT N WITH SUPP Your **stance** on a particular matter is your attitude to it. *...his rigid stance on non-violence.* **2** COUNT N Your **stance** is also the way that you are standing; a formal use. *He altered his stance slightly and leaned against a tree.*

stand /stænd/, **stands, standing, stood** /stʊd/. **1** VB When you **are standing,** your body is upright, your legs are straight, and your weight is supported by your feet. *She was standing at the bus stop... I stood very still, hoping they wouldn't see me.* **2** VB When you **stand,** you change your position so that you are standing, rather than sitting; a formal use. *One by one, he asked each graduate to stand.* **3** VB WITH ADJUNCT If you **stand** aside or **stand** back, you move to a different place a short distance away. *Miss Darke told the girls to stand aside... He stood back and surveyed his handiwork.* **4** VB If something **stands** somewhere, it is in an upright position in that place. *In the middle of the town stands a splendid Victorian building... Only one of the houses is still standing.* **5** VB WITH OBJ AND ADJUNCT If you **stand** something somewhere, you put it there in an upright position. *He stood the bottle on the bench beside him.* **6** VB If a decision or offer **stands,** it is still valid. *Fifty years later, this Supreme Court ruling still stands.* **7** VB WITH ADJUNCT OR COMPLEMENT You can use **stand** instead of 'is' to describe the state or condition of something. *His real intentions now stand revealed... They are dissatisfied with the law as it stands.* **8** VB WITH OBJ If something can **stand** a situation or a test, it is good enough or strong enough to cope with it. *The economy couldn't stand another rise in interest rates... Her arguments could hardly stand close inspection.* **9** VB WITH OBJ If you cannot **stand** something, it irritates you so that you cannot tolerate it. *He kept on nagging until I couldn't stand it any longer... She can't stand children.* **10** VB WITH TO-INF If you **stand** to gain or lose something, you are likely to gain or lose it. *Other groups stand to make a profit out of it... Few people are yet aware of how much we stand to lose by this agreement.* **11** VB If you **stand** in an election, you are a candidate in it. *She was invited to stand as the Liberal candidate... He has stood for Parliament 21 times.* **12** COUNT N WITH SUPP A **stand** is a small shop or stall. *...a hamburger stand... ...an information stand.* **13** COUNT N A **stand** is also an object or piece of furniture that is designed for holding a particular kind of thing. *...an umbrella stand... ...a music stand.* **14** See also **standing.**

PHRASES ● If you ask someone **how** or **where** they **stand,** you are asking them for their opinion or attitude on a particular situation. *There was never any doubt about where he stood on the racial issue.* ● If you **take a stand** or **make a stand,** you resist attempts to defeat you or to make you change your mind. *It's an important issue and you must be prepared to take a stand on it.* ● If you say that **it stands to reason** that something is true or possible, you mean that it is obvious; an informal use. *If they keep doing that, it stands to reason that the police are going to get suspicious.* ● When someone **stands trial,** they are tried in a court of law. *He has come back to stand trial on a murder charge.* ● When a witness **takes the stand** in a court of law, he or she answers questions; an American use. *Hearne had not yet taken the stand.* ● **to stand on your own two feet:** see **foot.** ● **to stand your ground:** see **ground.**

stand at. PHR VB If something that can be measured **stands at** a particular level, it is at that level. *Unemployment in North Wales now stands at 38%.*

stand by. PHR VB **1** If you **stand by,** you are ready to help or take action if it becomes necessary. *Stand by with lots of water in case a fire breaks out.* **2** If you **stand by** and let something bad happen, you do not do anything to stop it. *We cannot stand by and watch while our allies are attacked.* **3** If you **stand by** someone, you support them when they are in trouble. *If they try to make you resign, we'll stand by you.* **4** If you **stand by** an earlier decision or agreement, you keep to it. *I said I would do it and I stand by my promise.* **5** See also **standby.**

stand down. PHR VB If someone **stands down,** they resign. *She was prepared to stand down in favour of a younger candidate.*

stand for. PHR VB **1** If a letter **stands for** a particular word, it is an abbreviation for that word. *T.E.C. stands for Technical Education Certificate.* **2** The ideas or attitudes that someone or something **stands for** are the ones that they support or represent. *I disagreed fundamentally with what the party stood for.* **3** If you will not **stand for** something, you will not tolerate it. *The Army would not stand for it much longer.*

stand in. PHR VB **1** If you **stand in** for someone, you take their place or do their job. *He was standing in for his younger brother... You will stand in for me, John?* **2** See also **stand-in.**

stand out. PHR VB **1** If something **stands out,** it can be seen very clearly. *The name on the van stood out clearly.* **2** If an issue or achievement **stands out,** it is much better or more important than other, similar things. *One issue stood out as especially important... One article in this collection stands out from all the others.*

stand up. PHR VB **1** When you **stand up,** you change your position so that you are standing, rather than sitting. *I put down my glass and stood up.* **2** If something **stands up** to rough treatment, it is not damaged or harmed by it. *This carpet stands up to the wear and tear of continual use.* **3** If you **stand up** to someone, you defend yourself against their attacks or demands. *Maybe if I stood up to him, he'd back down.* **4** If you **stand up** for someone or something that is being criticized, you defend them. *...people who stood up for human rights... I'm glad to see that he's standing up for himself.* **5** If something such as a claim or a piece of evidence **stands up,** it is accepted as true or satisfactory. *The prosecution had no evidence which would stand up in a court of law.* **6** If you **are stood up** by a boyfriend or girlfriend, they fail to keep an arrangement to meet you; an informal use.

standard /stændəd/, **standards. 1** COUNT N OR UNCOUNT N WITH SUPP A **standard** is a level of quality or achievement. *The acting ability of the pupils is of a high standard... You're way below the standard required... By any standard the work was good.* **2** COUNT N **Standards** are moral principles which affect people's behaviour. *There has been a corruption of moral standards.* **3** ADJ You use **standard** to describe things which are usual and normal, and considered to be correct. *There is a standard procedure for recording drugs given to patients.* **4** ATTRIB ADJ A **standard** work or text on a particular subject is one which is widely read and often recommended. *This is the standard work on British moths.*

standardize /stændədaɪz/, **standardizes, standardizing, standardized;** also spelled **standardise.** VB WITH OBJ To **standardize** things means to change them so that they share the same features. *Some people have criticized television for standardizing speech, habits, and tastes.* ♦ **standardized** ADJ *Equipment is going to become more standardized.*

standard of living, standards of living. COUNT N Your **standard of living** is the level of comfort and wealth which you have. *There will have to be an adjustment to a lower standard of living.*

standby /stænd^{0}baɪ/, **standbys. 1** COUNT N A **standby** is something that is always ready to be used if it is needed. *Eggs are a great standby in the kitchen.* **2** MOD A **standby** ticket for the theatre or a plane journey is a cheap ticket that you can sometimes buy just before the performance starts or the plane leaves.

stand-in, stand-ins. COUNT N A **stand-in** is a person who takes someone else's place because the other person is ill or away.

standing /stændɪŋ/. **1** ATTRIB ADJ You use **standing** to describe something which is permanently in existence. *...a standing committee... This is a standing joke amongst psychologists.* **2** UNCOUNT N WITH SUPP Someone's **standing** is their status or reputation; a formal use. *She was an economist of considerable standing.*

standing order, standing orders. COUNT N A **standing order** is an instruction to your bank to pay someone a fixed amount of money regularly. *I pay their allowance by standing order.*

standpoint /stændpɔɪnt/, **standpoints.** COUNT N WITH SUPP Your **standpoint** is your attitude or opinion about something. *Up to now, we have only discussed the issue from a western standpoint.*

standstill /stændstɪl/. SING N If movement or an activity comes to a **standstill,** it stops completely. *The traffic had come to a standstill... The negotiations are at a standstill.*

stank /stæŋk/. **Stank** is the past tense of **stink.**

staple /steɪpə^{0}l/, **staples, stapling, stapled. 1** COUNT N **Staples** are small pieces of wire used for holding sheets of paper together. They are pushed through the paper using a special device called a stapler. **2** VB WITH OBJ AND ADJUNCT If you **staple** something, you fix it in place using staples. *The letter was stapled to the other documents in the file.* **3** ATTRIB ADJ A **staple** meal or food is one that forms a basic part of your everyday diet. *...the dry bread which is their staple diet.*

star /stɑː/, **stars, starring, starred. 1** COUNT N A **star** is a large ball of burning gas in space. You can see stars on clear nights as small points of light. **2** COUNT N You can refer to a shape or an object as a **star** when it has four, five, or more points sticking out of it in a regular pattern. *...little star-shaped flowers.* **3** COUNT N **Stars** are star-shaped marks printed against the name of something to indicate its quality. *...a four-star hotel.* **4** COUNT N Famous actors, musicians, and sports players are often referred to as **stars.** *...film stars.* **5** VB If an actor or actress **stars** in a play or film, they have one of the most important parts in it. *She'll be starring in a new play by Alan Bleasdale.* **6** VB WITH OBJ If a play or film **stars** a famous actor or actress, they have one of the most important parts in it. *The last version of the movie starred John Garfield and Lana Turner.* **7** PLURAL N The horoscope in a newspaper or magazine is sometimes referred to as the **stars;** an informal use. *What do the stars say for today?*

starboard /stɑːbə^{8}d/. ATTRIB ADJ The **starboard** side of a ship is the right side when you are facing the front.

starch /stɑːtʃ/, **starches. 1** UNCOUNT N **Starch** is a substance used for stiffening cloth. **2** MASS N **Starch** is also a carbohydrate found in foods such as bread, potatoes, and rice. *Cut down on the starches.*

starched /stɑːtʃt/. ADJ **Starched** garments have been stiffened using starch. *They wore starched caps and white gloves.*

stare /steə/, **stares, staring, stared.** VB If you **stare** at something, you look at it for a long time. *He stared at us in disbelief... She sat there quietly, staring out of the window.* Also COUNT N *...a dreamy stare.*

starfish /stɑːfɪʃ/. **Starfish** is the singular and plural. COUNT N A **starfish** is a flat, star-shaped creature with five arms that lives in the sea.

stark /stɑːk/, **starker, starkest. 1** ADJ Something that is **stark** is very bare and plain. *...the stark black rocks and deserted beaches... The names were written in stark black print.* **2** ATTRIB ADJ **Stark** means harsh and unpleasant. *Those are the stark facts of the matter... ...grim stark poverty.* **3** PHRASE Someone who is **stark naked** is completely naked.

starlight /stɑːlaɪt/. UNCOUNT N **Starlight** is the light that comes from the stars at night. *I enjoyed the view of the bay in the starlight.*

starling /stɑːlɪŋ/, **starlings.** COUNT N A **starling** is a very common European bird with greenish-black feathers.

starry /stɑːri^1/. ATTRIB ADJ A **starry** night or sky is full of stars. *It was a cold, starry night.*

starry-eyed. ADJ If you are **starry-eyed,** you are so unrealistic about things that you do not see how they really are. *We were all starry-eyed about visiting London.*

start /stɑːt/, **starts, starting, started. 1** VB WITH OR WITHOUT OBJ If you **start** to do something, you do something you were not doing before. *Ralph started to run... He started laughing... My father started work when he was ten... Now we have to start again.* Also SING N *We've not made a bad start.* **2** VB WITH ADJUNCT You use **start** to say what someone's first job was. For example, if their first job was that of a porter, you can say that they **started** as a porter. **3** ERG VB When something **starts** it takes place from a particular time. *The meeting starts at 7... We didn't want to start a panic.* Also COUNT N *...the start of negotiations.* **4** VB WITH OBJ If you **start** a business or organization, you create it or cause it to begin. *He scraped up the money to start a restaurant.* **5** ERG VB If you **start** an engine or car, it begins to work. *They have to push it to start it... The engine just wouldn't start.* **6** VB If you **start,** your body jerks because you are surprised or frightened. *I sat down so quietly that she started.* Also COUNT N *He awakened with a start.*

PHRASES ● You use **for a start** to introduce the first of a number of things that you are about to say. *We can't afford this house for a start.* ● See also **head start.** ● **in fits and starts:** see **fit.**

start off. PHR VB **1** You can use **start off** to say what someone's first job was. For example, if their first job was that of a taxi driver, you can say that they **started off** as a taxi driver. **2** If you **start off** by doing something, you do it as the first part of an activity. *I started off by showing a slide of the diseased cell.* **3** To **start** something **off** means to cause it to start. *I know what started it all off.*

start on. PHR VB If you **start on** something that needs to be done, you begin doing it. *She put the forks in a neat pile and started on the knives.*

start out. PHR VB **1** If someone or something **starts out** as a particular thing, they are that thing at the beginning although they change later. *These areas started out as the private lands of settlers.* **2** If you **start out** doing something, you do it at the beginning of an activity. *You started out by saying that this was the weapon they used.*

start up. PHR VB **1** If you **start up** something such as a new business, you create it or cause it to start. *She wanted to start up a little country pub.* **2** If you **start up** an engine or car, you make it start to work. *The driver started up the car.*

starter /stɑːtə/, **starters. 1** COUNT N A **starter** is a small quantity of food served as the first course of a meal. **2** COUNT N The **starter** of a car is a device that starts the engine.

starting point, starting points. COUNT N Your **starting point** on a journey is the place from which you start. *This is a good starting point for a car tour.*

startle /stɑːtə^{0}l/, **startles, startling, startled.** VB WITH OBJ If something sudden **startles** you, it surprises and frightens you. *Goodness, you startled me—I thought you were in the garden.* ♦ **startled** ADJ *We laughed at the startled expressions on their faces.*

startling /stɑːtlɪŋ/. ADJ Something that is **startling** is so unexpected that people are surprised by it. *The results were quite startling—a 77% increase in six months.*

starvation /stɑːveɪʃə^{0}n/. UNCOUNT N **Starvation** is extreme suffering or death, caused by lack of food. *Thousands of people die from starvation every year.*

starve /stɑːv/, **starves, starving, starved. 1** VB If people **are starving,** they are suffering from a serious lack of food and are likely to die. *People are starving because of inefficient farming methods.* **2** VB WITH OBJ OR REFL VB To **starve** someone means to not give them any food. *You should starve him for twelve hours... Ten men starved themselves to death in prison last year.* **3** VB If you say that you **are starving,** you mean that you are very hungry; an informal use. *I've got to have something to eat. I'm starving.* **4** VB WITH OBJ AND 'of' If you **are starved** of something you need, you are suffering because you are not getting enough of it. *They seem to be starved of attention from adults... The plant was starved of light and died.*

stash /stæʃ/, **stashes, stashing, stashed.** VB WITH OBJ AND ADJUNCT If you **stash** something valuable somewhere, you store it there to keep it safe; an informal use. *They had all that money stashed away in the loft.*

state /steɪt/, **states, stating, stated. 1** REPORT VB If you **state** something, you say or write it, especially in a formal way. *The government have stated quite categorically that we're going to see changes... The police were called, but the man refused to state his business... He stated, 'I have passed the stage where such things matter.'* **2** COUNT N WITH SUPP The **state** of someone or something refers to what they are like or what they are experiencing. *They are very concerned about the state of the churchyard... She seemed in a very queer and nervous state... People wandered about in a state of shock.* **3** COUNT N Countries or large areas of countries are often referred to as **states.** *The Latin American states maintained their independence... ...a one-party state... Haryana and Punjab were the fastest-developing states in India.* **4** SING N You can refer to the government of a country as the **state.** *...the conflict between the freedom of the individual and the security of the state.* **5** MOD A **state** occasion is a formal one involving the head of a country. *...the state visit of a European monarch.*

PHRASES ● If you are **in a state,** you feel upset and nervous; an informal use. *He used to get into an awful state as exams approached.* ● If someone **is not in a fit state** to do something, they are too upset or ill to do it. *The parent is in no fit state to help the children.* ● See also **head of state, welfare state.**

stately /steɪtli^1/. ADJ **Stately** things are impressive and dignified. *...strong and stately towers.*

statement /steɪtmə^{2}nt/, **statements. 1** COUNT N A **statement** is something that you say or write, especially when you give facts or information formally. *I could not deny the truth of this statement... Soon afterwards he made his first public statement about the affair.* **2** COUNT N A **statement** is also a printed document showing all the money paid into and taken out of a bank or building society account.

state of affairs. SING N A **state of affairs** is the general situation and circumstances connected with someone or something. *What our present state of affairs demands is a firm leader.*

state of mind, states of mind. COUNT N Your **state of mind** is your mood at a particular time. *My sister was in a happier state of mind.*

statesman /steɪtsmə^{3}n/, **statesmen.** COUNT N A **statesman** is an important, experienced, and famous politician.

static /stætɪk/. **1** ADJ Something that is **static** does not move or change. *...a series of static images... ...the static quality in all village life.* **2** UNCOUNT N **Static** or **static electricity** is electricity which is caused by friction and which collects in things such as your body or metal objects. **3** UNCOUNT N If there is **static** on the radio or television, you hear loud crackling noises.

station /steɪʃə^{0}n/, **stations, stationing, stationed. 1** COUNT N A **station** is a building by a railway line where a train stops. **2** COUNT N WITH SUPP A bus **station** or coach **station** is a place where buses or coaches start a journey. **3** COUNT N A radio **station** is the particular frequency used by a radio company to broadcast programmes. *The radio was tuned permanently to his favourite station.* **4** VB WITH OBJ AND ADJUNCT If people **are stationed** somewhere, they are sent there to do a job or to work for a period of time. *Two guards were stationed at the top of the stairs... ...the British forces stationed in Germany.* **5** See also **fire station, gas station, petrol station, police station.**

stationary /steɪʃənə^{0}ri^1/. ADJ Something that is **stationary** is not moving. *...a stationary boat... The vehicle remained stationary.*

stationer /steɪʃənə/, **stationers.** COUNT N A **stationer** is a person who sells paper, envelopes, and writing equipment.

stationery /steɪʃənə^{0}ri^1/. UNCOUNT N **Stationery** is paper, envelopes, and writing equipment.

stationmaster /steɪʃə^{0}nmɑːstə/, **stationmasters.** COUNT N A **stationmaster** is the person in charge of a railway station.

station wagon, station wagons. COUNT N A **station wagon** is the same as an estate car; an American use.

statistic /stətɪstɪk/, **statistics. 1** COUNT N **Statistics** are facts obtained from analysing information that is expressed in numbers. ...*divorce statistics.* 2 UNCOUNT N **Statistics** is a branch of mathematics concerned with the study of information that is expressed in numbers. *I teach statistics.*

statistical /stətɪstɪkəˀl/. ADJ **Statistical** means relating to the use of statistics. *Statistical techniques are regularly employed.* ♦ **statistically** ADV *Statistically you have a one in six chance of succeeding.*

statue /stætjuː/, **statues.** COUNT N A **statue** is a large stone or metal sculpture of a person or an animal. ...*a bronze statue of Charles I.*

statuette /stætjuɛt/, **statuettes.** COUNT N A **statuette** is a very small statue. ...*a statuette of a little girl.*

stature /stætʃə/. 1 UNCOUNT N Someone's **stature** is their height and general size. *She was rather small in stature.* 2 UNCOUNT N Someone's **stature** is also their importance and reputation. *I can't tell you how pleased we are to have someone of your stature here.*

status /steɪtəs/. 1 UNCOUNT N Your **status** is your position in society, and the importance you have for other people. ...*the changing status of women... He came in search of wealth, status, and power.* 2 UNCOUNT N WITH SUPP **Status** is also an official classification which gives a person, organization, or country certain rights or advantages. *They appeared to have dropped their demand for status as political prisoners.*

status quo /steɪtəs kwəʊ/. SING N The **status quo** is the situation that exists at a particular time; a formal use.

status symbol, status symbols. COUNT N A **status symbol** is something that someone has and that shows their prestige and importance in society. *A personal chauffeur is undoubtedly a status symbol.*

statute /stætjuːt/, **statutes.** COUNT N A **statute** is a formal rule or law. *There have been more than twenty statutes governing what can be published in newspapers.*

statutory /stætjətəˀriˀ/. ADJ **Statutory** means consisting of, or done because of, formal rules or laws; a formal use. ...*the IBA's statutory code of advertising standards.*

staunch /stɔːntʃ/, **staunchest; staunches, staunching, staunched.** 1 ADJ A **staunch** supporter is a very loyal one. *Both are staunch supporters of Manchester United... ...Benny's staunchest ally.* 2 VB WITH OBJ If you **staunch** blood, you stop it from flowing out of a wound; a formal use. *Sophia staunched the blood with a cloth.*

stave /steɪv/, **staves, staving, staved.**

stave off. PHR VB If you **stave** something **off,** you delay it happening. *They want to stave off any attempt to intervene.*

stay /steɪ/, **stays, staying, stayed.** 1 VB WITH ADJUNCT If you **stay** somewhere, you continue to be there and do not move away. *Fewer women these days stay at home to look after their children.* 2 VB WITH ADJUNCT If you **stay** in a hotel or at someone's house, you live there for a short time. *She was staying in a hotel as I was.* Also COUNT N *We were good friends throughout my stay in Germany.* 3 LINK VB If someone or something **stays** in a particular condition or situation, they continue to be in it. *Last night I stayed awake until the whole house was sleeping... We'll work till eight if it stays light.* 4 VB WITH ADJUNCT If you **stay** away from a place, you avoid it. *This town is unsafe: stay away from here.* 5 VB WITH ADJUNCT If you **stay** out of something, you do not get involved in it. *We try to stay out of politics.* 6 PHRASE If you **stay put,** you remain somewhere. *Those kinds of people stay put in one job all their lives.*

stay in. PHR VB If you **stay in,** you remain at home and do not go out. *We ought to have stayed in tonight.*

stay on. PHR VB If you **stay on** somewhere, you remain there. *He had stayed on to have a drink.*

stay out. PHR VB 1 If you **stay out,** you remain away from home. *She stayed out all night.* 2 If workers **stay out,** they remain on strike. *The men stayed out for nearly a year.*

stay up. PHR VB If you **stay up,** you remain out of bed at a later time than normal. *Willie liked to eat out in restaurants and stay up late.*

stead /stɛd/. PHRASE If something will **stand you in good stead,** it will be useful to you in the future. *My school theatrical performances stood me in good stead in later years.*

steadfast /stɛdfəst, -fɑːst/. ADJ If you are **steadfast** in your beliefs or opinions, you are convinced that they are right and you refuse to change them; used showing approval. *The refugees remained steadfast... ...steadfast loyalty.* ♦ **steadfastly** ADV *Her father has steadfastly refused to take part in such activities.*

steady /stɛdiˀ/, **steadier, steadiest; steadies, steadying, steadied.** 1 ADJ Something that is **steady** continues or develops gradually without any interruptions or sudden changes. ...*a steady rise in prices...*

These vehicles are reasonably economical at a steady 56 mph. ♦ **steadily** ADV *Unemployment has risen steadily.* 2 ADJ If an object is **steady,** it is firm and does not move about. *His hand was not quite steady.* 3 ADJ A **steady** look or voice is calm and controlled. *Her voice was faint but steady.* ♦ **steadily** ADV *Foster looked steadily at me for some moments.* 4 ADJ **Steady** work is certain to continue for a long time. *My son has a steady job.* 5 ADJ A **steady** person is sensible and reliable. *I like Simon very much—he's a very steady boy.* 6 ERG VB When you **steady** something, you stop it shaking or moving about. *His elbows were resting on his knees to steady the binoculars... The boat moved slightly, then steadied.* 7 REFL VB When you **steady** yourself, you control and calm yourself. *He drew a deep breath to steady himself.*

steak /steɪk/, **steaks.** 1 MASS N **Steak** is beef without much fat on it. 2 COUNT N A fish **steak** is a large piece of fish. ...*four halibut steaks.*

steal /stiːl/, **steals, stealing, stole** /stəʊl/, **stolen** /stəʊləˀn/. 1 VB WITH OR WITHOUT OBJ If you **steal** something, you take it away from someone without their permission and without intending to return it. *He stole knives and a gun.* ♦ **stealing** UNCOUNT N *He had been expelled from his previous school for stealing.* ♦ **stolen** ADJ ...*stolen credit cards.* 2 VB WITH ADJUNCT If you **steal** somewhere, you move there quietly and cautiously; a literary use. *Simon came stealing out of the shadows.*

stealth /stɛlθ/. UNCOUNT N If you do something with **stealth,** you do it in a slow, quiet, and secretive way. *Sometimes tigers rely on stealth, creeping towards their victims.*

stealthy /stɛlθiˀ/, **stealthier, stealthiest.** ADJ **Stealthy** actions or movements are performed in a slow, quiet, and secretive way. *I managed to get there by a series of stealthy movements.* ♦ **stealthily** ADV *I heard my landlady creeping stealthily up to my door.*

steam /stiːm/, **steams, steaming, steamed.** 1 UNCOUNT N **Steam** is the hot mist formed when water boils. *The room was filled with steam... Steam hissed between the blocks of lava.* 2 ATTRIB ADJ **Steam** vehicles and machines are powered by steam. *The first steam locomotive was introduced in 1825.* 3 VB If something **steams,** it gives off steam. *The kettle was steaming away on the stove... Lynn brought her a steaming cup of tea.* 4 VB WITH ADJUNCT If you **steam** food, you cook it in steam rather than in water. ...*steamed rice.*

PHRASES ● If you **let off steam,** you get rid of your energy or anger by behaving noisily or violently; an informal use. ● If you **run out of steam,** you stop doing something because you are very tired; an informal use.

steam up. PHR VB 1 PHRASE If you are **steamed up** about something, you are very annoyed about it; an informal use. *What was she getting so steamed up about?* 2 When glass **steams up,** it becomes covered with steam or mist. *Her spectacles had steamed up and she couldn't see.*

steamer /stiːmə/, **steamers.** COUNT N A **steamer** is a ship that is powered by steam.

steamroller /stiːmrəʊlə/, **steamrollers.** COUNT N A **steamroller** is a large, heavy vehicle with wide solid wheels which is used to flatten road surfaces.

steamy /stiːmiˀ/, **steamier, steamiest.** ADJ A **steamy** place is hot and humid, usually because it is full of steam. ...*a steamy and noisy kitchen.*

steel /stiːl/, **steels, steeling, steeled.** 1 UNCOUNT N **Steel** is a strong metal made mainly from iron which is used for making many things, for example bridges, buildings, vehicles, and cutlery. ...*a modern tower made of concrete and steel.* ● See also **stainless steel.** 2 REFL VB If you **steel** yourself, you prepare to deal with something unpleasant. *You had better steel yourself for a shock.*

steel band, steel bands. COUNT N A **steel band** is a band of people who play music on special metal drums.

steelworker /stiːlwɜːkə/, **steelworkers.** COUNT N A **steelworker** is a person who works in a steelworks.

steelworks /stiːlwɜːks/. **Steelworks** is the singular and plural. COUNT N A **steelworks** is a factory where steel is made.

steely /stiːliˀ/. 1 ADJ You use **steely** to describe something that has a hard, greyish colour. *The blue sky had changed to a steely grey.* 2 ATTRIB ADJ **Steely** is also used to describe someone who is hard, strong, and determined. *There was shy modesty behind that steely determination.*

steep /stiːp/, **steeper, steepest.** 1 ADJ A **steep** slope forms a large angle with the horizontal, and is difficult to go up. *He reached the steepest part of the mountain.* ♦ **steeply** ADV ...*mountains rising steeply on three sides.* 2 ADJ A **steep** increase is a very big increase. *There's likely to be a steep increase in*

unemployment. ♦ **steeply** ADV *The costs of public services have risen steeply.* 3 PRED ADJ If the price of something is a bit **steep,** it is expensive; an informal use. *Your fees are pretty steep.*

steeped /stiːpt/. PRED ADJ WITH 'in' If a place or person is **steeped** in a quality or characteristic, they are deeply influenced by it. *The house is centuries old and steeped in history.*

steeple /stiːpəˀl/, **steeples.** COUNT N A **steeple** is a tall pointed structure on the top of a church tower.

steer /stɪə/, **steers, steering, steered.** 1 ERG VB OR VB When you **steer** a car, boat, or plane, you control it so that it goes in the correct direction. *He steered the car through the broad entrance... The freighter steered out of Santiago Bay that evening... I was trying to steer.* 2 VB WITH OBJ If you **steer** someone in a particular direction, you guide them there. *He steered me to a table and sat me down in a chair.*

steering wheel, steering wheels. COUNT N The **steering wheel** in a car or lorry is the wheel held by the driver when they are driving.

stem /stɛm/, **stems, stemming, stemmed.** 1 COUNT N The **stem** of a plant is the long, thin, central part of it which is above the ground and which the leaves are joined to. 2 COUNT N The **stem** of a glass or vase is the long thin part of it connecting the bowl to the base. 3 COUNT N The **stem** of a pipe is the long part of it through which smoke is sucked. 4 VB WITH OBJ If you **stem** something that is spreading from one place to another, you stop it spreading. ...*stemming the flow of illegal drugs.* 5 VB WITH 'from' If a condition or problem **stems** from a particular situation, it started originally because of this situation. *Their aggressiveness stemmed from fear.*

stench /stɛntʃ/, **stenches.** COUNT N A **stench** is a strong, unpleasant smell. ...*the unmistakable stench of rotting eggs.*

stencil /stɛnsəˀl/, **stencils, stencilling, stencilled.** spelled **stenciling, stenciled** in American English. 1 COUNT N A **stencil** is a piece of paper, plastic, or metal with a design cut out of it. You place the stencil on a surface and create a design by putting ink or paint over the cut area. 2 VB WITH OR WITHOUT OBJ If you **stencil** letters or designs, you print them using a stencil. ...*large dustbins bearing the stencilled word LITTER.*

step /stɛp/, **steps, stepping, stepped.** 1 COUNT N A **step** is the movement made by lifting your foot and putting it down in a different place. *She took a step back... I walked on with quick steps.* 2 VB WITH ADJUNCT If you **step** on something, you put your foot on it. *He had stepped on a thorn.* 3 VB WITH ADJUNCT If you **step** in a particular direction, you move in that direction. *Step over the wire... Tom stepped back.* 4 COUNT N A **step** is also one of a series of stages, or a single action taken for a particular purpose. *Today's announcement is a step in the right direction... Simmel carried this idea one step further.* 5 COUNT N A **step** is also a raised flat surface, often one of a series, on which you put your feet in order to walk up or down to a different level. *She was sitting on the top step... ...a flight of steps.*

PHRASES ● If someone tells you to **watch your step,** they are warning you to be more careful about your behaviour so that you don't get into trouble. *I'm cleverer than you are, so watch your step.* ● If you do something **step by step,** you do it by progressing gradually from one stage to the next. *The proof is set out, step by step, on page 6.* ● If a group of people are walking **in step,** they are moving their feet forward at exactly the same time as each other. ...*a party of boys marching in step.*

step aside. PHR VB See **step down.**

step back. PHR VB If you **step back,** you think about a situation in a fresh and detached way. *It is tempting to step back and ask whether it is worth all the trouble.*

step down. PHR VB If you **step down** or **step aside,** you resign from an important job or position. *He stepped down last month because of illness.*

step in. PHR VB If you **step in,** you start to help in a difficult situation. *She really appreciates the way you stepped in and saw to things.*

step up. PHR VB If you **step up** something, you increase it. *The government is stepping up its efforts.*

stepbrother /stɛpbrʌðə/, **stepbrothers.** COUNT N Your **stepbrother** is the son of your stepfather or stepmother.

stepchild /stɛptʃaɪld/, **stepchildren.** COUNT N Your **stepchild** is the child of your husband or wife by an earlier marriage.

stepdaughter /stɛpdɔːtə/, **stepdaughters.** COUNT N Your **stepdaughter** is the daughter of your husband or wife by an earlier marriage.

stepfather /stɛpfɑːðə/, **stepfathers.** COUNT N Your **stepfather** is the man who has married your mother after the death or divorce of your father.

stepladder /stɛplædə/, **stepladders.** COUNT N A **stepladder** is a ladder consisting of two sloping parts that are hinged together at the top so that it will stand up on its own.

stepmother /stɛpmʌðə/, **stepmothers.** COUNT N Your **stepmother** is the woman who has married your father after the death or divorce of your mother.

stepping stone, stepping stones. 1 COUNT N A **stepping stone** is a job or event that helps you to make progress. *That film was a big stepping-stone in my career.* 2 COUNT N **Stepping stones** are a line of stones which you can walk on in order to cross a shallow stream or river.

stepsister /stɛpsɪstə/, **stepsisters.** COUNT N Your **stepsister** is the daughter of your stepfather or stepmother.

stepson /stɛpsʌn/, **stepsons.** COUNT N Your **stepson** is the son of your husband or wife by an earlier marriage.

stereo /stɛri¹əʊ/, **stereos.** 1 ADJ OR UNCOUNT N **Stereo** is used to describe a record or a system of playing music in which the sound is directed through two different speakers. *...buying stereo equipment... It sounds much better in stereo.* 2 COUNT N A **stereo** is a hi-fi or record player with two speakers; an informal use. *He turned on the stereo.*

stereotype /stɛri¹ə⁶taɪp/, **stereotypes, stereotyping, stereotyped.** 1 COUNT N A **stereotype** is a fixed general image or set of characteristics that are considered to represent a particular type of person or thing. *The song perpetuates two racist stereotypes.* 2 VB WITH OBJ If you **stereotype** someone, you form a fixed general idea of them and assume that they will behave in a particular way. *These images confine women to stereotyped roles.*

sterile /stɛraɪl/. 1 ADJ Something that is **sterile** is completely clean and free of germs. *...rolls of sterile bandage.* 2 ADJ A **sterile** person or animal is unable to have or produce babies. *He had learnt early in his marriage that he was sterile.* ♦ **sterility** /stə²rɪlɪti¹/ UNCOUNT N *...physical degeneration leading to sterility.* 3 ADJ A **sterile** situation is lacking in energy and new ideas. *The meeting degenerated into a sterile debate.* ♦ **sterility** UNCOUNT N *...the ugly sterility of urban life.*

sterilize /stɛrɪ¹laɪz/, **sterilizes, sterilizing, sterilized;** also spelled **sterilise.** 1 VB WITH OBJ If you **sterilize** a thing or place, you make it completely clean and free from germs. *All nearby brickwork must be sterilized with a blowlamp.* 2 VB WITH OBJ If a person or an animal **is sterilized,** they have an operation that makes it impossible for them to have or produce babies. *By 1950, 16 per cent of women over twenty had been sterilized.* ♦ **sterilization** /stɛrɪ¹laɪzeɪʃ⁰n/ UNCOUNT N *...compulsory sterilization for parents of more than two children.*

sterling /stɜːlɪŋ/. UNCOUNT N OR ADJ **Sterling** is the money system of Great Britain. *Sterling has once again become one of the stronger currencies... ...a hundred and fifty pounds sterling.*

stern /stɜːn/, **sterner, sternest; sterns.** 1 ADJ A **stern** person is very serious and strict. *Sylvia had a stern father who never praised her.* ♦ **sternly** ADV *He walked over and said to him sternly, 'Give that to me'.* 2 COUNT N The **stern** of a boat is the back part of it. *She seated herself in the stern.*

stethoscope /stɛθəskəʊp/, **stethoscopes.** COUNT N A **stethoscope** is an instrument that a doctor uses to listen to your heart and breathing. It consists of a hollow tube with ear pieces connected to a small disc.

stew /stjuː/, **stews, stewing, stewed.** 1 MASS N A **stew** is a meal made by cooking meat and vegetables in liquid at a low temperature. *We've got lamb stew tonight.* 2 VB WITH OBJ If you **stew** meat, vegetables, or fruit, you cook them slowly in liquid in a closed dish. *...stewed fruit.*

steward /stjʊəd/, **stewards.** 1 COUNT N A **steward** is a man whose job is to look after passengers on a ship, plane, or train. 2 COUNT N A **steward** is also someone who helps to organize a race, march, or other public event. See also **shop steward.**

stewardess /stjʊədɛs/, **stewardesses.** COUNT N A **stewardess** is a woman whose job is to look after passengers on a ship, plane, or train.

stick /stɪk/, **sticks, sticking, stuck** /stʌk/. 1 COUNT N A **stick** is a long, thin piece of wood, for example dead wood from a tree. *I gathered some sticks to start the fire.* 2 COUNT N A **stick** of something is a long thin piece of it. *...sticks of dynamite.* 3 ERG VB WITH ADJUNCT If you **stick** a pointed object in something, you push it in. *He stuck the knife right in... He stuck a cigar in his mouth.* 4 VB WITH OBJ AND ADJUNCT If you **stick** one thing to another, you fix them together using glue or sticky tape. *They went round sticking posters on walls... Someone has stuck a label on the crate.* 5 VB If something **sticks** somewhere, it becomes attached or fixed in one position and cannot be moved. *...sand that sticks to your hair and skin... If your zip sticks, it might be because a thread has caught in it.* 6 VB If something **sticks** in your mind, you remember it for a long time. *One lecture stuck in my mind.* 7 VB WITH OBJ AND ADJUNCT If you **stick** something somewhere, you put it there in a rather casual way; an informal use. *She closed the bag and stuck it back on the shelf.* 8 See also **stuck.**

PHRASES ● If you **stick it** in a difficult situation, or if you **stick at it,** or **stick it out,** you do not leave or give up; an informal use. *I don't know how I've stuck it. It's been hell... You must stick at it if you want to succeed... I stuck it out as long as I could.* ● If someone **gets the wrong end of the stick,** they completely misunderstand something; an informal use. ● to **stick** your **neck out:** see **neck.**

stick around. PHR VB If you **stick around,** you stay where you are; an informal use. *I'll stick around and keep an eye on the food.*

stick by. PHR VB If you **stick by** someone, you continue to help or support them. *...a good commanding officer who stuck by his men when they got into trouble.*

stick out. PHR VB 1 If something **sticks out,** it extends beyond something else. *There was a little chimney sticking out of the roof.* 2 If you **stick** something **out,** you make it appear from inside or behind something else. *Lally stuck her head out of a window... Lynn stuck out her tongue.* 3 You can also say that something **sticks out** when it is very noticeable. *His accent made him stick out.*

stick out for. PHR VB If you **stick out for** something you want, you keep demanding it and do not accept anything different or less. *He stuck out for twice the usual salary, and got it.*

stick to. PHR VB 1 If you **stick to** something, you stay close to it or with it and do not change to something else. *I went over the hill instead of sticking to the river... They are sticking to their present policy.* 2 If you **stick to** a promise or agreement, you do what you said you would do. *They stuck to the bargain.*

stick up. PHR VB 1 If you **stick up** a picture or a notice, you fix it to a wall. *We have a painting stuck up on the wall.* 2 If something long **sticks up,** it points upwards. *These plants stick up vertically from the seabed.*

stick up for. PHR VB If you **stick up for** someone or something, you support or defend them forcefully. *He thanked his father for sticking up for him... I was too scared to stick up for my rights.*

stick with. PHR VB If you **stick with** someone or something, you stay with them and do not change to something else. *Stick with me and you'll be okay... I stuck with my staple diet: brown rice.*

sticker /stɪkə/, **stickers.** COUNT N A **sticker** is a small piece of paper or plastic, with writing or a picture on it, which you can stick onto a surface. *They sell stickers and badges... On the rear window was a sticker saying 'Save the Whales'.*

sticking plaster. UNCOUNT N **Sticking plaster** is material that you can stick over a cut or blister to protect it.

sticky /stɪki¹/. 1 ADJ Something that is **sticky** is covered with a substance that can stick to other things and leave unpleasant marks. *Her hands were sticky from the ice cream... ...a sticky bottle of fruit juice.* 2 ADJ **Sticky** paper has glue on one side so that you can stick it to surfaces. *...sticky labels.* 3 ADJ **Sticky** weather is unpleasantly hot and damp. *...a hot, sticky, July afternoon.* 4 ADJ A **sticky** situation is difficult or embarrassing; an informal use.

stiff /stɪf/, **stiffer, stiffest.** 1 ADJ Something that is **stiff** is firm and does not bend easily. *Use a stiff brush... ...stiff brown paper.* 2 ADJ If a drawer or door is **stiff,** it does not move as easily as it should. *...a stiff latch.* 3 ADJ If you are **stiff,** your muscles or joints ache when you move. *My arms were stiff.* ♦ **stiffness** UNCOUNT N *She complained of stiffness in her knees.* 4 ADJ **Stiff** behaviour is rather formal and not relaxed. *...a stiff smile... The letter was stiff and formal.* ♦ **stiffly** ADV *'No, I haven't,' Rudolph said stiffly.* ♦ **stiffness** UNCOUNT N *Their stiffness and self-consciousness soon disappeared.* 5 ADJ **Stiff** also means difficult or severe. *Competition is so stiff that he'll be lucky to get a place at all... ...stiffer penalties for drunken drivers.* 6 ATTRIB ADJ A **stiff** drink contains a large amount of strong alcohol. *Morris fixed himself a stiff drink.* 7 ADJ A **stiff** breeze is one which is blowing quite strongly. 8 ADV If you are bored **stiff,** worried **stiff,** or scared **stiff,** you are extremely bored, worried, or scared; an informal use. *The subject bores them stiff... We were scared stiff of meeting him.*

stiffen /stɪfᵊn/, **stiffens, stiffening, stiffened.** 1 VB If you **stiffen,** you stop moving and become very tense, for example because you are afraid or angry. *Tom suddenly stiffened with alarm... Her whole body stiffened.* 2 VB If your muscles or joints **stiffen,** they become difficult to bend or move. *You are unlikely to be troubled with stiffening joints.* 3 ERG VB If attitudes or behaviour **stiffen,** they become stronger or more severe, and less flexible. *Resistance stiffened even further last week... You will only stiffen his resolve.* 4 VB WITH OBJ When something such as cloth **is stiffened,** it is made firm. ♦ **stiffened** ADJ *...a dress of stiffened satin.*

stifle /staɪfᵊl/, **stifles, stifling, stifled.** 1 VB WITH OBJ If someone **stifles** something, they stop it from starting or continuing. *An authoritarian leadership stifled internal debate... She placed a hand over her mouth to stifle a shriek of laughter.* 2 VB WITH OBJ If the air or the atmosphere **stifles** you, it makes you feel as if you cannot breathe properly. *She was stifled by its scent.*

stifling /staɪflɪŋ/. ADJ If the air or atmosphere is **stifling,** it is so hot that you feel as if you cannot breathe properly. *It was stifling inside... ...a stifling night.*

stigma /stɪgmə/. SING N OR UNCOUNT N If something has a **stigma** attached to it, people consider it to be unacceptable or a disgrace. *...the stigma of failure... The stigma attached to mental illness will be removed in future years.*

stile /staɪl/, **stiles.** COUNT N A **stile** is a step on either side of a fence or wall that enables you to climb over.

still /stɪl/, **stiller, stillest; stills.** 1 ADV If a situation that existed previously **still** exists, it has continued and exists at the present time. *She still lives in London... She was still beautiful... I was still a schoolboy.* 2 ADV If something that has not yet happened could **still** happen, it is possible that it will happen. *She could still change her mind... There is still a chance that a few might survive.* 3 ADV You use **still** to emphasize that something remains the case or is true. *Whatever they have done, they are still your parents... There are ten weeks still to go... I've still got three left.* 4 SENTENCE ADV You also use **still** when dismissing a problem or difficulty as not really worth worrying about. *...and that made me miss the last bus. Still, that's life, isn't it?* 5 ADV You can use **still** with 'better' or 'more' to indicate that something has even more of a quality than something else. *How about some Bach to begin with? Or, better still, Vivaldi.* 6 PRED ADJ OR ADV If you stay **still,** you stay in the same position without moving. *We had to keep still for about four minutes... Stand still!* 7 ADJ If something is **still,** there is no movement or activity there. *...the still water of the lagoon... Around them the forest was very still.* ♦ **stillness** UNCOUNT N *The stillness of the fields was broken by the sound of a gunshot.*

stillborn /stɪlbɔːn/. ADJ A **stillborn** baby is dead when it is born.

stilted /stɪltɪ²d/. ADJ **Stilted** conversation or behaviour is very formal and unnatural. *After some stilted efforts at conversation, he gave up and left.*

stilts /stɪlts/. 1 PLURAL N **Stilts** are long pieces of wood or metal used to support some buildings. *Thatched huts were raised high above the paddy fields on stilts.* 2 PLURAL N **Stilts** are also two long pieces of wood that circus clowns stand on in order to walk high up above the ground. *He is walking on stilts.*

stimulant /stɪmjə⁴lənt/, **stimulants.** COUNT N A **stimulant** is a drug that increases your heart rate and makes you less likely to sleep. *...coffee in which the drug caffeine acts as a stimulant.*

stimulate /stɪmjə⁴leɪt/, **stimulates, stimulating, stimulated.** 1 VB WITH OBJ To **stimulate** something means to encourage it to begin or develop further. *Rising prices will stimulate demands for higher incomes... An outsider who may stimulate new ideas.* 2 VB WITH OBJ If something **stimulates** you, it makes you feel full of ideas and enthusiasm. *The art course stimulated me.* ♦ **stimulating** ADJ *...a conversation which I found both stimulating and exciting.* ♦ **stimulation** /stɪmjə⁴leɪʃᵊn/ UNCOUNT N *I find great intellectual stimulation in these surroundings.* 3 VB WITH OBJ If something **stimulates** a part of a person's body, it causes it to move or function automatically; a technical use. *The optical system of the eye stimulates cells in the retina.*

stimulus /stɪmjə⁴ləs/, **stimuli** /stɪmjə⁴laɪ/. 1 COUNT N If something acts as a **stimulus,** it makes a process develop further or more quickly. *There would not have been the same stimulus to mechanize production so rapidly.* 2 UNCOUNT N **Stimulus** is something which causes people to feel energetic and enthusiastic. *...all the stimulus and excitement that battle brought.* 3 COUNT N A **stimulus** is something that causes a part of a person's body to move or function automatically; a technical use.

sting /stɪŋ/, **stings, stinging, stung** /stʌŋ/. 1 VB WITH OR WITHOUT OBJ If an insect, animal, or plant **stings** you, it causes you to feel a sharp pain by pricking your skin, usually with poison. *Bees do not normally sting* *without being provoked.* 2 COUNT N The **sting** of an insect or animal is the part that stings you. *They paralyse their victims with their stings.* 3 ERG VB If a part of your body **stings,** you feel a sharp pain there. *My eyes were stinging... The fire smoked glumly and stung our eyes.* Also SING N *...the sting of ashes in his eyes.* 4 VB WITH OBJ If someone's remarks **sting** you, they upset and annoy you. *I wondered why I'd said it, knowing it would really sting him.* ♦ **stinging** ADJ *He made a stinging attack on Taverne.* 5 PHRASE If something **takes the sting out** of a situation, it makes it less painful or unpleasant. *He smiled to take the sting out of his words.*

stingy /stɪndʒi^1/. ADJ A **stingy** person is very mean; an informal use. *The government was stingy and his salary was miserable.*

stink /stɪŋk/, **stinks, stinking, stank** /stæŋk/, **stunk** /stʌŋk/. 1 VB Something that **stinks** smells extremely unpleasant. *The butcher's shop stank in hot weather... ...a foul, stinking lavatory.* Also SING N *...the stink of vomit.* 2 VB If a place or situation **stinks,** it is extremely bad or unpleasant; an informal use. *'What do you think of the town?'—'I think it stinks.'*

stinking /stɪŋkɪŋ/. ATTRIB ADJ You use **stinking** to describe something that is extremely unpleasant; an informal use. *I've got a stinking cold... You couldn't hide anything in this stinking little town.*

stint /stɪnt/, **stints.** COUNT N WITH SUPP A **stint** is a period of time spent doing a particular job or activity. *I arrived at the University for a three month stint as a lecturer.*

stipulate /stɪpjə^{4}leɪt/, **stipulates, stipulating, stipulated.** REPORT VB If you **stipulate** that something must be done, you say clearly that it must be done; a formal use. *The document stipulated nine criteria as the basis for any reform.*

stir /stɜː/, **stirs, stirring, stirred.** 1 VB WITH OBJ When you **stir** a liquid, you mix it inside a container using something such as a spoon. *The tourist was stirring his coffee and gazing at the buildings.* 2 VB If you **stir,** you move slightly, for example because you are uncomfortable. *The boys stirred uneasily... Etta didn't stir, pretending to be asleep.* 3 VB WITH OBJ If the wind **stirs** an object, it moves it gently. *A stray breath of wind stirred the stillness of the robes.* 4 REFL VB If you **stir** yourself, you move in order to do something. *Finally, one of the males stirred himself and took a step forward.* 5 VB WITH OBJ If something **stirs** you, it makes you react with a strong emotion because it is very beautiful or moving. *There was a particular passage which always stirred him profoundly.* 6 SING N If an event causes a **stir,** it causes great excitement, shock, or anger. *Her speech created a huge stir.* 7 VB If a particular mood, feeling, or idea **stirs** in someone, they begin to feel it or think about it. *The debate was reopened and a new mood was stirring... Something seemed to stir within her.*

stir up. PHR VB 1 If something **stirs up** dust or mud, it causes it to move around. *Some gentle winds stirred up the dust.* 2 If you **stir up** trouble or **stir up** a feeling, you cause trouble or cause people to have the feeling. *...a rally called to stir up popular support for nuclear disarmament.*

stirring /stɜːrɪŋ/, **stirrings.** 1 ADJ Something that is **stirring** makes people very excited or enthusiastic. *...one of the most stirring shots of the whole film... They must have been stirring times.* 2 COUNT N When there is a **stirring** of emotion, people begin to feel it. *There was a slight stirring of interest among them... ...the first stirrings of student protest.*

stirrup /stɪrəp/, **stirrups.** COUNT N **Stirrups** are the two metal loops attached to a horse's saddle which the rider places his or her feet in.

stitch /stɪtʃ/, **stitches, stitching, stitched.** 1 VB WITH OR WITHOUT OBJ When you **stitch** pieces of material together, you join them using a needle and thread. *They were cut out and stitched together... She picked up her embroidery and started stitching.* 2 COUNT N A **stitch** is one of the short pieces of thread that can be seen on a piece of material that has been stitched. *...the little stitches in the canvas she was embroidering.* 3 VB WITH OBJ When doctors **stitch** a wound or **stitch** it up, they use a special needle and thread to tie the skin together. *The doctor who stitched it should have another look at it tomorrow.* 4 COUNT N A **stitch** is also a piece of thread that has been used to stitch a wound. *His wound required five stitches.* 5 SING N If you have a **stitch,** you feel a sharp pain at the side of your stomach, usually after running fast or laughing a lot. *I began to have a bad stitch.* 6 PHRASE If you are **in stitches,** you cannot stop laughing; an informal use.

stock /stɒk/, **stocks, stocking, stocked.** 1 COUNT N OR UNCOUNT N **Stocks** are shares in the ownership of a company, or investments on which a fixed amount of interest will be paid. *...heavy bidding for oil company stocks... ...buying big blocks of stock.* 2 VB WITH OBJ A shop that **stocks** particular goods keeps a supply of them to sell. *Several shops in London stock large fittings.* 3 UNCOUNT N A shop's **stock** is the total amount of goods which it has available to sell. *...selling a week's worth of stock in a single day.* 4 VB WITH OBJ If you **stock** a shelf or cupboard, you fill it with food or other things. *I found part-time work, stocking shelves in supermarkets... His locker was always stocked with screws.* 5 COUNT N WITH SUPP A **stock** of things is a supply of them. *Keep a stock of fuses... They want to conserve coal stocks during the miners' strike.* 6 UNCOUNT N The **stock** that a person or animal comes from is the type of people or animals from which they are descended. *They were of European stock... He came from sturdy, peasant stock.* 7 PLURAL N Animals kept on a farm are referred to as **stock.** *...a sale of dairy stock.* 8 MASS N **Stock** is a liquid made by boiling meat, bones, or vegetables in water. 9 ATTRIB ADJ A **stock** expression or way of doing something is one that is commonly used. *'Wild and wanton' was a stock phrase of the time.*

PHRASES ● If goods are **in stock** in a shop, they are available to be sold. If they are **out of stock,** they have all been sold. ● If you **take stock,** you pause and think about a situation before deciding what to do next. ● See also **laughing stock.**

stock up. PHR VB If you **stock up** with something, you buy a supply of it. *Stock up with groceries and canned foods.*

stockbroker /stɒkbrəʊkə/, **stockbrokers.** COUNT N A **stockbroker** is a person whose job is to buy and sell stocks and shares for people.

stock exchange, stock exchanges. COUNT N A **stock exchange** is a place where people buy and sell stocks and shares. *...the Tokyo Stock Exchange.*

stocking /stɒkɪŋ/, **stockings.** COUNT N **Stockings** are long garments that cover a woman's legs. They are held up by suspenders. *...a woman in a flowered skirt and black stockings and shoes.*

stockinged /stɒkɪŋd/. PHRASE Someone who is in their **stockinged feet** is wearing socks, tights, or stockings, but no shoes.

stock market, stock markets. COUNT N The **stock market** is the business organization and activity involved in buying and selling stocks and shares. *Prices have risen sharply on the stock market.*

stockpile /stɒkpaɪl/, **stockpiles, stockpiling, stockpiled.** 1 VB WITH OBJ If people **stockpile** things, they store large quantities of them for future use. *...a nation that stockpiled reserves of food.* 2 COUNT N A **stockpile** is a large store of something. *...a stockpile of nuclear weapons.*

stocktaking /stɒkteɪkɪŋ/. UNCOUNT N **Stocktaking** is the activity of counting and checking all the goods that a shop or business has.

stocky /stɒki^1/, **stockier, stockiest.** ADJ **Stocky** people are rather short, but look strong and solid. *...a short, stocky man with dark hair.*

stodgy /stɒdʒi^1/; an informal word. 1 ADJ **Stodgy** food is very solid and makes you feel very full. *...a stodgy meal.* 2 ADJ **Stodgy** also means dull and uninteresting. *His friend Beale was stodgy and solemn.*

stoic /stəʊɪk/ or **stoical** /stəʊɪkə^{0}l/. ADJ If you behave in a **stoic** or **stoical** way, you accept difficulties and suffering without complaining or getting upset; a formal use. *I admired her stoic patience... He knew how brave and stoical they had to be.* ♦ **stoically** ADV *Accept your punishment stoically.*

stoicism /stəʊɪsɪzə^{0}m/. UNCOUNT N **Stoicism** is stoical behaviour; a formal use. *He endured this treatment with stoicism.*

stoke /stəʊk/, **stokes, stoking, stoked.** 1 VB WITH OBJ If you **stoke** a fire or **stoke** it up, you put more fuel onto it. *Willet was stoking up the stove again.* 2 VB WITH OBJ To **stoke** or **stoke** up an emotion or conflict means to make it stronger or worse. *Similar schemes will only stoke the conflict... He stoked up their disgust.*

stole /stəʊl/. **Stole** is the past tense of **steal.**

stolen /stəʊlə^{0}n/. **Stolen** is the past participle of **steal.**

stolid /stɒlɪd/. ADJ **Stolid** people do not show much emotion. *He was slow to move, stolid, and dependable.*

stomach /stʌmək/, **stomachs, stomaching, stomached.** 1 COUNT N Your **stomach** is the organ inside your body where food is digested. *Foxes have small stomachs... His stomach was rumbling.* 2 COUNT N You can also refer to the front part of your body below your waist as your **stomach.** *He lay down on his stomach.* 3 VB WITH OBJ If you cannot **stomach** something, you strongly dislike it and cannot accept it. *Rothermere was unable to stomach the idea.*

stomach-ache, stomach-aches. COUNT N OR UNCOUNT N If you have a **stomach-ache,** you have a pain in your stomach.

stomp /stɒmp/, **stomps, stomping, stomped.** VB WITH ADJUNCT If you **stomp** around, you walk with heavy steps, often because you are angry. *I stomped back to the hotel.*

stone /stəʊn/, **stones, stoning, stoned.** 1 UNCOUNT N **Stone** is a hard, solid substance found in the ground and often used for building. *The bits of stone are joined together with cement... ...the little stone bridge... ...a low stone wall.* 2 COUNT N A **stone** is a small piece of rock. *Roger picked up a stone and threw it at Henry.* 3 COUNT N The **stone** in a fruit such as a peach or plum is the large seed in the middle. *...plum stones.* 4 VB WITH OBJ To **stone** someone or something means to throw stones at them. *They took the man outside and stoned him to death... Rioters had been stoning the Embassy.* 5 COUNT N A **stone** is also a unit of weight equal to 14 pounds or approximately 6.35 kilograms. The plural form is 'stone' or 'stones'. *She weighed twelve stone.*

PHRASES ● If one place is **a stone's throw** from another, the places are close together. *They live within a stone's throw of the school.* ● **to kill two birds with one stone:** see **bird.** ● See also **cornerstone, paving stone, precious stone, stepping stone.**

Stone Age. PROPER N The **Stone Age** is the earliest known period of human history, when people used tools and weapons made of stone.

stone-cold. ADJ Something that is **stone-cold** is very cold indeed. *...cups of stone-cold coffee.*

stoned /stəʊnd/. ADJ Someone who is **stoned** is affected by drugs or very drunk; an informal use.

stone deaf. ADJ Someone who is **stone deaf** is completely deaf.

stonework /stəʊnwɜːk/. UNCOUNT N **Stonework** is objects or parts of a building that are made of stone. *...figures carved into the stonework.*

stony /stəʊni^1/. 1 ADJ **Stony** ground is rough and contains a lot of stones. *...a stony plain between low, barren hills.* 2 ADJ If someone's expression or behaviour is **stony,** they show no friendliness or sympathy. *She turned a stony face on Lucas... Her voice was stony... The announcement was received in stony silence.*

stood /stʊd/. **Stood** is the past tense and past participle of **stand.**

stooge /stuːdʒ/, **stooges.** COUNT N A **stooge** is someone who is used by another person to do unpleasant or dishonest tasks; an informal use. *With the help of his stooges, he awarded contracts to favoured firms.*

stool /stuːl/, **stools.** COUNT N A **stool** is a seat with legs but no back or arms. *He was sitting on a stool.*

stoop /stuːp/, **stoops, stooping, stooped.** 1 VB If you **stoop,** you stand or walk with your shoulders bent forwards. *If your ironing board is too low you have to stoop over it.* Also SING N *He walks with a stoop.* 2 VB If you **stoop** or **stoop** down, you bend your body forwards and downwards. *She stooped to feel the carpet... Bert stooped down and arranged them in a row.* 3 VB WITH PREP 'to' OR TO-INF If you **stoop** to doing something, you lower your usual standards of behaviour in order to do it; used showing disapproval. *Only once did he stoop to the tactics of his opponents... ...never stooping to indulge the audience.*

stop /stɒp/, **stops, stopping, stopped.** 1 VB WITH OR WITHOUT OBJ If you **stop** doing something, you no longer do it. *She stopped work to have her baby... Stop it! You're hurting!... She put the key in the keyhole, began turning it, and then she stopped... We all stopped talking... He couldn't stop crying.* 2 VB WITH OBJ If you **stop** something, you prevent it from happening or continuing. *You're trying to stop my trip to London... How do I stop a tap dripping?... Nothing was going to stop Sandy from being a writer.* 3 VB If an activity or process **stops,** it comes to an end. *The music stopped abruptly... They were waiting for the rain to stop.* 4 ERG VB If a machine or device **stops** or if you **stop** it, it no longer works or it is switched off. *My watch has stopped... Stop the recording now.* 5 ERG VB When people or things that are moving **stop** or **are stopped,** they no longer move. *He followed them for a few yards, and then stopped... The train stopped at Watford... Stop people in Oxford Street and ask them to answer these questions... Stop the car and let me out.* 6 SING N If something that is moving comes to a **stop,** it no longer moves. *The elevator came to a stop on the main floor... Harris brought the plane to a stop.* 7 COUNT N A **stop** is a place where buses or trains regularly stop so that people can get on and off. *We'll get off at the next stop.* 8 VB If you **stop** somewhere on a journey, or **stop** off there, you stay there for a short while before continuing. *On my way home I stopped at the shop... I stopped off in London.* 9 COUNT N A **stop** during a journey is a time or place at which you stop. *The first stop was a hotel outside Paris.* 10 VB WITH OBJ If you **stop** someone's pay or a cheque, you prevent the money from being paid.

PHRASES ● If you **put a stop to** something, you prevent

it from happening or continuing. *We must put a stop to all this nonsense.* ● to **stop short:** see **short.**

stopgap /stɒpgæp/, **stopgaps.** COUNT N A **stopgap** is something that serves a purpose for a short time, but is replaced as soon as possible. *It can be used as a stopgap with patients who have lost a lot of blood.*

stopover /stɒpəʊvə/, **stopovers.** COUNT N A **stopover** is a short stay in a place between parts of a journey. *...a five-week tour abroad with a three-day stopover in the United States.*

stoppage /stɒpɪdʒ/, **stoppages.** COUNT N When there is a **stoppage,** people stop working because of a disagreement with their employers. *The stoppage had the full support of both unions.*

stopper /stɒpə/, **stoppers.** COUNT N A **stopper** is a piece of glass, plastic, or cork that fits into the top of a bottle or jar. *I put the stopper in the bottle.*

stopwatch /stɒpwɒtʃ/, **stopwatches.** COUNT N A **stopwatch** is a watch that can be started and stopped by pressing buttons to time the length of a race or event.

storage /stɔːrɪdʒ/. 1 UNCOUNT N **Storage** is the keeping of something in a special place until it is needed. *A quarter of the crop may be lost in storage... You haven't got much storage space.* 2 UNCOUNT N **Storage** is also the process of storing data in a computer. *...information storage and retrieval systems.*

store /stɔː/, **stores, storing, stored.** 1 COUNT N A **store** is a shop, especially a large one. *...a health-food store.* ● See also **chain store.** 2 VB WITH OBJ When you **store** things, you leave them somewhere until they are needed. *The tool kit is stored under the seat... ...storing water for use in the dry season... ...storing and transmitting electricity.* 3 VB WITH OBJ When you **store** information, you keep it in your memory, a file, or a computer. *...stored as images in the minds of people... ...pocket calculators which can store telephone numbers.* 4 COUNT N A **store** is also a supply of something that you keep somewhere until you need it. *...the village's store of grain... ...emergency stores of food and medical equipment.* 5 COUNT N OR UNCOUNT N A **store** is also a place where things are kept while they are not being used. *...weapon stores in which nuclear warheads were kept... Goods in store will be insured for loss or damage.*

PHRASES ● Something that is **in store** for you is going to happen to you in the future. *You never know what the next few months have got in store.* ● If you **set great store** on or by something, you think that it is extremely important or necessary. *He set the greatest store on carrying out his decision.*

store up. PHR VB If you **store** something **up,** you keep it until you think that the time is right to use it. *She had some sausage carefully stored up for the occasion.*

store-room, store-rooms. COUNT N A **store-room** is a room where you keep things until you need them.

storey /stɔːri¹/, **storeys;** spelled **story, stories** in American English. COUNT N The **storeys** of a building are its different floors or levels. *The house was three storeys high... ...a multi-storey car park.*

stork /stɔːk/, **storks.** COUNT N A **stork** is a large bird with a long beak and long legs, which lives near water.

storm /stɔːm/, **storms, storming, stormed.** 1 COUNT N A **storm** is very bad weather, with heavy rain, strong winds, and often thunder and lightning. *Wait until the storm passes over.* 2 COUNT N A **storm** is also an angry or excited reaction from a large number of people. *The decision provoked a storm of criticism from Conservative MPs... ...the storm of applause.* 3 VB WITH ADJUNCT If you **storm** into or out of a place, you enter or leave it quickly and noisily, because you are angry. *I stormed into the room in a rage.* 4 REPORT VB OR VB To **storm** means to say something very loudly and angrily; a literary use. *'You misled us,' the professor stormed... No matter how I pleaded or stormed, I could never make her understand.* 5 VB WITH OBJ OR ADJUNCT If people **storm** a place, they attack it. *The mob stormed the church... The infantry stormed through the walls of the Imperial Palace.*

stormy /stɔːmi¹/, **stormier, stormiest.** 1 ADJ If the weather is **stormy,** there is a strong wind and heavy rain. *...that stormy autumn evening.* 2 ADJ A **stormy** situation involves a lot of angry argument or criticism. *There was a stormy debate over it... ...the stormy relations between George and his mother.*

story /stɔːri¹/, **stories.** 1 COUNT N A **story** is a description of imaginary people and events, which is written or told in order to entertain people. *Tell me a story... ...a story about a foolish hunter... ...ghost stories.* 2 COUNT N A **story** is also a description or account of things that have happened. *The story of the firm begins in 1820... ...her life story.* ● **tall story:** see **tall.** 3 See also **storey.**

stout /staʊt/, **stouter, stoutest.** 1 ADJ A **stout** person is rather fat. *...a short, stout man.* 2 ADJ Something that is **stout** is thick and strong. *He broke a stout branch from a bush... ...stout black shoes.* 3 ATTRIB ADJ **Stout** actions or beliefs are firm and strong. *...the stoutest possible resistance.* ♦ **stoutly** ADV *Chris stoutly denied Eva's accusations.*

stove /stəʊv/, **stoves.** COUNT N A **stove** is a piece of equipment for heating a room or cooking. *...a gas stove... She left the sausages on the stove.*

stow /stəʊ/, **stows, stowing, stowed.** VB WITH OBJ AND ADJUNCT If you **stow** something somewhere or **stow** it **away,** you put it carefully somewhere until it is needed. *She stowed the bags in two baskets... His baggage was safely stowed away in the plane.*

stowaway /stəʊəweɪ/, **stowaways.** COUNT N A **stowaway** is a person who hides in a ship, plane, or other vehicle in order to make a journey without paying.

straddle /strædə⁰l/, **straddles, straddling, straddled.** 1 VB WITH OBJ If you **straddle** something, you sit or stand with one leg on each side of it. *He straddled a chair and began fiddling with the keys.* 2 VB WITH OBJ If something **straddles** a place, it crosses it or links different parts of it together. *A viaduct straddles the river Wye... ...a communications net that straddles the globe.*

straggle /strægə⁰l/, **straggles, straggling, straggled.** 1 VB If people **straggle** somewhere, they move there slowly in irregular, disorganized groups. *The players straggled across the field.* 2 VB WITH ADJUNCT When things **straggle** over an area, they cover it untidily. *The shacks straggle along the dirt road... ...her hair straggling down over her eyes.*

straggly /strægli¹/. ADJ Something that is **straggly** grows or spreads out in different directions, in an untidy way. *...a few straggly trees... ...a straggly beard.*

straight /streɪt/, **straighter, straightest.** 1 ADJ OR ADV If something is **straight,** it continues in the same direction and does not bend or curve. *...a straight line... ...a long straight road... I saw the car coming straight at me... She was staring straight ahead.* 2 ADJ OR ADV A **straight** position is one that is upright or level, rather than sloping or bent. *Keep your knees bent and your back straight... Check that all the pictures hang straight.* 3 ADV WITH ADJUNCT If you go **straight** to a place, you go there immediately. *The doctor told me to go straight to bed.* 4 ADJ If you are **straight** with someone, you speak to them honestly and frankly. *I just want a straight answer to the question.* 5 ATTRIB ADJ A **straight** choice or a **straight** fight involves only two people or things. *The voters have a straight choice between the two candidates.*

PHRASES ● If you **get** something **straight,** you make sure that you understand it properly; an informal use. ● If someone who was a criminal **is going straight,** they are no longer involved in crime. ● If you **keep a straight face,** you manage not to laugh.

straight away /streɪt əweɪ/. ADV If you do something **straight away,** you do it immediately. *You might not recognize it straight away... We went to work straightaway.*

straighten /streɪtə⁰n/, **straightens, straightening, straightened.** 1 VB WITH OBJ If you **straighten** something, you make it tidy or put it in its proper position. *I'll just straighten the bed... Straightening his tie, he knocked on the door.* 2 VB If you are bending and you then **straighten** or **straighten** up, you make your body straight and upright. *The man straightened and looked him in the face... He straightens up, combs his hair, and walks into the meeting.*

straighten out. PHR VB If you **straighten out** a confused situation, you succeed in dealing with it or getting it properly organized. *It'll take six weeks to get things straightened out.*

straightforward /streɪtfɔːwəd/. 1 ADJ Something that is **straightforward** is easy to do or understand. *...a very straightforward set of instructions in simple English.* 2 ADJ If your behaviour is **straightforward,** you are honest and frank. *...the only Senator to speak with straightforward contempt.*

strain /streɪn/, **strains, straining, strained.** 1 UNCOUNT N OR COUNT N If there is a **strain** on something, it has to hold more or do more than normal, and may therefore break or become inefficient. *The additional supports will help to take some of the strain off the original structure... Civil defence forces were under heavy strain... This policy puts a greater strain on the economic system than it can bear.* 2 UNCOUNT N OR COUNT N **Strain** is a state of worry and tension. *Many people doing this sort of job suffer from strain... ...severe mental strains.* 3 UNCOUNT N **Strain** is also a muscle injury. *...back strain.* 4 COUNT N WITH SUPP A **strain** of a plant is a variety of it. *...high-yielding strains of wheat.* 5 PLURAL N WITH SUPP If you hear **strains** of music, you hear music being played; a literary use. *The strains of Chopin drifted in from the music room.* 6 VB WITH OBJ To **strain** something means to use it beyond normal or reasonable limits. *The oil-price increases have strained the resources of the poorer countries.* 7 VB WITH OR WITHOUT OBJ If you **strain** to do something, you make a great effort to do it. *He was straining to hear what the speaker was saying... He strained his eyes to catch a glimpse of the President.* 8 VB WITH OBJ If you **strain** a muscle, you injure it by using it suddenly or too much. 9 VB WITH OBJ When you **strain** food, you pour the liquid off it. *I'll just strain the potatoes.*

strained /streɪnd/. 1 ADJ If you are **strained,** you are worried and nervous. *She looked strained and tired... Her voice was strained.* 2 ADJ If relations between people are **strained,** they are unfriendly and do not trust each other. *Relations between the two families had become increasingly strained.*

strait /streɪt/, **straits.** 1 COUNT N You can refer to a narrow strip of sea which joins two large areas of sea as a **strait** or the **straits.** *...the Strait of Hormuz... ...the Straits of Gibraltar.* 2 PLURAL N WITH SUPP You use **straits** to say that someone is in a difficult situation. *The family was in difficult straits... The company was now in dire financial straits.*

strait jacket, strait jackets. COUNT N A **strait jacket** is a special jacket used to tie the arms of a violent person tightly around his or her body.

strand /strænd/, **strands.** 1 COUNT N A **strand** of thread, wire, or hair is a single piece of it. *...a strand of silk... Make sure that there are no loose strands of wire... A strand of hair fell over her eyes.* 2 COUNT N A **strand** of a situation or idea is a part of it. *...these two strands of industrial policy... Several strands in Kate's life seemed to be pulled together.*

stranded /strændɪ²d/. ADJ If someone or something is **stranded** somewhere, they are stuck and cannot leave. *The boat was stranded in the mud... ...the stranded holidaymakers.*

strange /streɪnd⁰ʒ/, **stranger, strangest.** 1 ADJ **Strange** means unusual or unexpected. *I had a strange dream last night... It was strange to hear her voice again... Her husband had become strange and distant.* ♦ **strangeness** UNCOUNT N *I was overwhelmed with a sense of strangeness.* 2 ADJ A **strange** person or place is one that you do not know. *I don't like strange people coming into my house... Never get in a strange car.*

strangely /streɪnd⁰ʒli¹/. 1 ADV OR SUBMOD You use **strangely** to indicate that an action or quality is unusual or unexpected. *They had acted strangely as he went by... He answered in a strangely calm voice.* 2 SENTENCE ADV You use **strangely** or **strangely enough** to emphasize that what you are saying is surprising. *It has, strangely, only recently been discovered... 'Are students interested in religion these days?'—'Strangely enough, they are.'*

stranger /streɪnd⁰ʒə/, **strangers.** 1 COUNT N A **stranger** is someone you have not met before. *Antonio was a stranger to all of us.* 2 COUNT N Someone who is a **stranger** in a place has not been there before. Someone who is a stranger to a situation has not experienced it before. *They are strangers in the village and lost their way in the fog... I was a stranger to this kind of gathering.*

strangle /stræŋgə⁰l/, **strangles, strangling, strangled.** 1 VB WITH OBJ To **strangle** someone means to kill them by squeezing their throat. *He was strangled in his bed.* 2 VB WITH OBJ To **strangle** something means to prevent it from developing. *Such policies were strangling economic development.*

strangled /stræŋgə⁰ld/. ATTRIB ADJ A **strangled** sound is unclear and muffled. *...a strangled cry of amazement.*

stranglehold /stræŋgə⁰lhəʊld/, **strangleholds.** COUNT N To have a **stranglehold** on something means to have control over it and prevent it from developing. *The unions have a stranglehold on the country.*

strap /stræp/, **straps, strapping, strapped.** 1 COUNT N A **strap** is a narrow piece of leather or cloth, used to carry things or fasten them together. *I undid the straps, and opened the case... ...high-heeled shoes, with straps above the ankle.* 2 VB WITH OBJ AND ADJUNCT If you **strap** something somewhere, you fasten it there with a strap. *Children should be strapped into a special car seat... He straps on his watch.*

strapping /stræpɪŋ/. ADJ A **strapping** person is tall, strong, and healthy-looking. *...a strapping boy of eighteen.*

strata /strɑːtə/. **Strata** is the plural of **stratum.**

stratagem /strætə¹dʒəm/, **stratagems.** COUNT N A **stratagem** is a plan or tactic. *...a cunning stratagem to quieten the rebellious peasants.*

strategic /strətiːdʒɪk/. 1 ADJ A **strategic** plan or action is intended to achieve something. *I took up a strategic position near the exit.* 2 ADJ **Strategic** weapons and policies are part of a country's defence system. ...*strategic nuclear weapons... His country had made the same strategic error.* ♦ **strategically** ADV *The islands were strategically important to Venice.*

strategist /strætəˈdʒɪst/, **strategists.** COUNT N A **strategist** is someone who is skilled in planning the best way to achieve something, especially in war.

strategy /strætəˈdʒi¹/, **strategies. 1** COUNT N A **strategy** is a plan. *...Britain's defence strategy... He adopted a strategy of massive deflation.* **2** UNCOUNT N **Strategy** is the art of planning the best way to achieve something, especially in war. *...a major exercise in military strategy... ...the debate over strategy.*

stratum /strɑːtəm/, **strata** /strɑːtə/. **1** COUNT N A **stratum** of society is a group of people in it who are similar in their education, income, or social class; a formal use. *Our military leaders have always been drawn from the upper strata of society.* **2** COUNT N The **strata** in the earth's surface are the different layers of rock; a technical use. *...the underlying rock strata.*

straw /strɔː/, **straws. 1** UNCOUNT N **Straw** is the dried, yellowish stalks from crops such as wheat or barley. *The eggs were packed in straw.* **2** COUNT N A **straw** is a thin tube of paper or plastic, which you drink through. *Fiona was drinking a milk shake through a straw.* **3** PHRASE If something is **the last straw,** it is the latest in a series of bad events, and makes you feel that you cannot bear any more.

strawberry /strɔːbəˈri¹/, **strawberries.** COUNT N A **strawberry** is a small red fruit with tiny seeds in its skin.

stray /streɪ/, **strays, straying, strayed. 1** VB If people or animals **stray,** they wander away from where they should be. *Children had strayed on to an airport runway... I hoped my animals wouldn't stray too far.* **2** ATTRIB ADJ A **stray** animal has wandered away from its owner's home. *...stray cats.* **3** VB If your thoughts **stray,** you stop concentrating on a particular thing. *He let his thoughts stray for five minutes... He does not stray from facts.* **4** ATTRIB ADJ **Stray** things have become separated from other similar things. *A hen was pecking around for stray grains of corn.*

streak /striːk/, **streaks, streaking, streaked. 1** COUNT N A **streak** is a long mark on something. *The table was smeared with streaks of paint... Her hair had a grey streak in it.* **2** VB WITH OBJ If something **is streaked** with a colour, it has lines of the colour in it. *His moustache was streaked with grey... The sun is streaking the sea with long lines of gold.* **3** COUNT N WITH SUPP If someone has a particular **streak,** they have a particular quality in their character. *Children have a streak of cruelty... ...the possessive streak in her.* **4** VB WITH ADJUNCT To **streak** somewhere means to move there very quickly. *The fish streaked away.*

stream /striːm/, **streams, streaming, streamed. 1** COUNT N A **stream** is a small, narrow river. *He led us along the bank of the stream.* **2** COUNT N You can refer to a steady flow of people or things as a **stream.** *A steady stream of workers left the factory... ...a stream of smoke... The stream of insults continues.* ● See also **bloodstream. 3** VB WITH ADJUNCT If people, vehicles, or liquids **stream** somewhere, large numbers or amounts of them move there in a steady flow. *The doors opened and the audience began to stream out... The cars are streaming by at sixty miles an hour... She stood in the doorway, tears streaming down her face.* **4** VB WITH ADJUNCT When light **streams** into a place, it shines into it strongly. *The sun was streaming in through the windows.* **5** COUNT N WITH SUPP A **stream** in a school is a group of children of the same age and ability who are taught together. *...pupils in the top streams.* **6** VB WITH OBJ To **stream** pupils means to teach them in groups according to their ability.

streamer /striːmə/, **streamers.** COUNT N A **streamer** is a long narrow strip of coloured paper used as a decoration.

streamline /striːmlaɪn/, **streamlines, streamlining, streamlined. 1** VB WITH OBJ To **streamline** a vehicle or object means to improve its shape so that it moves more quickly and efficiently. ♦ **streamlined** ADJ *Their new cars have lighter and more streamlined bodywork.* **2** VB WITH OBJ To **streamline** an organization or process means to make it more efficient by removing parts of it. *He aimed to streamline the Post Office... ...an attempt to streamline timber production.*

street /striːt/, **streets. 1** COUNT N A **street** is a road in a town or village, usually with buildings along it. *The two men walked slowly down the street... She lives in Seyer Street.* **2** COUNT N You can use **street** when talking about activities that happen out of doors in a town. *We've got to keep youngsters off the streets... We don't usually embrace friends in the street... ...street theatre.* **3** See also **high street.**

PHRASES ● If you talk about **the man in the street,** you mean ordinary people in general. *The man in the street was unlikely ever to have seen a ghost.* ● If a subject or activity is **right up** your **street,** you are very interested in it or know a lot about it; an informal use.

streetcar /striːtkɑː/, **streetcars.** COUNT N A **streetcar** is a tram; an American use. *He caught the next streetcar home.*

strength /streŋθ/, **strengths. 1** UNCOUNT N Your **strength** is your physical energy and ability. *...recovering their strength before trying again... He pulled with all his strength.* **2** UNCOUNT N **Strength** is also courage or determination. *With unshakable strength of character she stayed on after the crisis... This gave us the strength to resist further temptation.* **3** UNCOUNT N You can also refer to power or influence as **strength.** *...the enormous strength and influence of the unions.* **4** COUNT N OR UNCOUNT N Your **strengths** are your good qualities and abilities. *Each firm has its particular strengths and weaknesses.* **5** UNCOUNT N The **strength** of an object is its ability to withstand rough treatment or heavy weights. **6** UNCOUNT N The **strength** of a feeling or opinion is the degree to which people have it. *The Government had clearly underestimated the strength of popular feeling.* **7** UNCOUNT N The **strength** of an opinion, argument, or story is the extent to which it is likely to be true. *He continued to deny it, despite the growing strength of the argument.* **8** UNCOUNT N The **strength** of a relationship is its degree of closeness. *This leads to bonds of deceptive strength being formed with the company.* **9** UNCOUNT N The **strength** of a group of people is the total number of people in it. *Their forces were growing in strength.*

PHRASES ● If people or organizations **go from strength to strength,** they gradually become more successful. ● If you act **on the strength of** a fact or situation, this provides the basis or reason for your action. *The Cabinet agreed to a grant of £4m on the strength of the Company's projections of sales.*

strengthen /streŋθəⁿn/, **strengthens, strengthening, strengthened. 1** VB WITH OBJ If a number of people **strengthen** a group, they make it more powerful by joining it. *The new peers will strengthen the Labour Party in the Upper House.* **2** VB WITH OBJ If something **strengthens** an argument or opinion, it provides more reasons or evidence to support it. *The uncertainty about the railways strengthened the argument for planning.* **3** ERG VB If a feeling or attitude **strengthens** or **is strengthened,** it becomes more intense and has greater influence. *During the prolonged depression of the seventies, racialism strengthened... ...countless little cruelties that only strengthened my resolve not to give in.* **4** VB WITH OBJ If a relationship **is strengthened,** it becomes closer. *We want to strengthen our ties with the United States.* **5** VB WITH OBJ If something **strengthens** you, it increases your courage and determination. *It is designed to strengthen you against the hostile world.* **6** VB WITH OBJ If something **strengthens** an object, it makes it able to withstand rough treatment or heavy weights. *...struts designed to strengthen the wings of aeroplanes.*

strenuous /strenjuːəs/. ADJ A **strenuous** action or activity involves a lot of effort or energy. *Alf made strenuous efforts to improve his reading... ...a strenuous twenty minute walk.* ♦ **strenuously** ADV *He strenuously denied that his airline was in any danger.*

stress /stres/, **stresses, stressing, stressed. 1** REPORT VB If you **stress** a point, you emphasize it because you think it is important. *I ought to stress that this was not a trial but an enquiry... He stressed the importance of better public relations.* Also UNCOUNT N WITH 'on' *...this stress on community values.* **2** UNCOUNT N OR COUNT N If you feel or are under **stress,** you feel tense and worried about something. *...parents under stress... ...the stress of examinations... Too many stresses are being placed on the family.* **3** COUNT N OR UNCOUNT N **Stresses** are strong physical pressures applied to an object. *Earthquakes can result from stresses in the earth's crust... It has stood up to tests under extreme heat and stress.* **4** UNCOUNT N **Stress** is emphasis that you put on a word or part of a word when you say it, so that it sounds slightly louder. **5** VB WITH OBJ If you **stress** a word or part of a word when you say it, you put emphasis on it. *You should stress the second syllable in 'computer'.*

stressful /stresfʊl/. ADJ A **stressful** situation or experience causes someone to feel stress. *Life with several children is hard and stressful.*

stretch /stretʃ/, **stretches, stretching, stretched. 1** VB WITH ADJUNCT Something that **stretches** over an area or distance extends over it. *...the belt of flat land which stretches from the capital up to York.* **2** COUNT N WITH SUPP A **stretch** of land or water is an area of it. **3** VB WITH OR WITHOUT OBJ When you **stretch,** you hold your arms or legs out straight and tighten your muscles. *I just grunted and stretched my limbs... Thomas yawned and stretched.* **4** COUNT N A **stretch** of time is a period of time. *Any job carries with it daily stretches of boredom.* **5** ERG VB When something soft or elastic **stretches** or **is stretched,** it is pulled until it becomes very tight. *Nylon stretches... The skin of her face was stretched very tightly over the bones.* **6** ATTRIB ADJ **Stretch** material can be stretched. *...stretch covers on armchairs.* **7** VB WITH OBJ If someone's money or resources **are stretched,** they have hardly enough for their needs. *The nation's resources were already stretched to their limits.* **8** VB WITH OBJ If a job or task **stretches** you, it makes you use all your energy or skills. **9** PHRASE If you say that something is not true or possible **by any stretch of the imagination,** you are emphasizing that you think it is completely untrue or absolutely impossible. *It could by no stretch of the imagination be seen as a victory.*

stretch out. PHR VB **1** If you **stretch out** or if you **stretch** yourself **out** somewhere, you lie there with your legs and body in a straight line. *I just want to stretch out in my own bed.* **2** If you **stretch out** a part of your body, you hold it out straight. *He stretched out a thin arm and took our hands.*

stretcher /stretʃə/, **stretchers.** COUNT N A **stretcher** is a long piece of canvas with a pole along each side, used to carry an injured person.

strew /struː/, **strews, strewing, strewed, strewn** /struːn/. **1** VB WITH OBJ If things **are strewn** somewhere, they are scattered there untidily. *His clothes were strewn all over the room.* **2** VB WITH OBJ If things **strew** a place, they lie scattered there. *Books and cushions strewed the floor... The carpet is strewn with broken glass.*

stricken /strɪkəⁿn/. ADJ If someone is **stricken** by something unpleasant, they are severely affected by it. *Madeleine was stricken by fear... Stricken with arthritis, she lay in bed for many years.*

strict /strɪkt/, **stricter, strictest. 1** ADJ A **strict** person does not tolerate impolite or disobedient behaviour. *Parents were strict in Victorian times... ...a school with strict discipline.* ♦ **strictly** ADV *The curfew was strictly enforced.* **2** ADJ A **strict** rule or order must be obeyed absolutely. *Strict instructions were issued... The Opposition demanded stricter control of prices.* ♦ **strictly** ADV *This is strictly confidential.* **3** ATTRIB ADJ The **strict** meaning of something is its precise meaning. *He may not be lying in the strict sense of the word, but he has not told the whole truth.* ♦ **strictly** SUBMOD *That's not strictly true.* **4** ATTRIB ADJ You use **strict** to describe someone who never does things that are against their beliefs. For example, a strict vegetarian never eats meat.

strictly /strɪktli¹/. **1** ADV WITH 'for' If something is **strictly** for a particular thing or person, it is to be used or done only by them. *The discussion was strictly for members.* **2** SENTENCE ADV You say **strictly speaking** to correct a statement or add more precise information. *Paul's a friend of mine. Well, strictly speaking my sister's friend.*

stride /straɪd/, **strides, striding, strode** /strəʊd/, **stridden** /strɪdəⁿn/. **1** VB If you **stride** somewhere, you walk there with quick, long steps. *Louisa watched him striding across the lawn... He was striding out of the entrance.* **2** COUNT N A **stride** is a long step which you take when you are walking or running. *...the length of each stride.* **3** SING N A **stride** is also a way of walking with long steps. *She walked ahead with her purposeful stride.* **4** COUNT N If you make **strides** in something that you are doing, you make rapid progress in it. *On the question of pay, giant strides have been made.* **5** PHRASE If you **take** a difficult situation **in** your **stride,** you deal with it calmly and easily. *She takes examinations in her stride.*

strident /straɪdənt/. **1** ADJ A **strident** sound is loud and unpleasant. *His voice was strident and triumphant.* **2** ADJ If someone is **strident,** they state their feelings or opinions very strongly; used showing disapproval. *...strident Marxists... ...a strident demand for rearmament.*

strife /straɪf/. UNCOUNT N **Strife** is strong disagreement or fighting; a formal use. *...family strife.*

strike /straɪk/, **strikes, striking, struck** /strʌk/. **1** COUNT N When there is a **strike,** workers stop working for a period of time, to try to get better pay or conditions. *...the miners' strike.* **2** VB If workers **strike,** they stop working for a period of time, to try to get better pay or conditions. *Airline pilots are threatening to strike.* **3** COUNT N WITH SUPP A hunger **strike** is a refusal to eat anything as a protest. A rent **strike** is a refusal to pay your rent. **4** VB WITH OBJ If you **strike** someone or something, you deliberately hit them; a literary use. *He struck the ball beautifully.* **5** VB WITH OBJ OR ADJUNCT If something **strikes** something else or **strikes** against it, it hits it. *The house was struck by lightning... The trawler struck against the jetty.* **6** VB WITH OR WITHOUT OBJ If an illness or disaster **strikes,** it suddenly happens. *...the earthquake that struck Japan last Tuesday... When disaster strikes, you need sympathy and practical advice.* **7** VB To

strike means to attack someone or something quickly and violently. *Raising herself slightly, the snake strikes.* Also COUNT N *The Air Force carried out air strikes as a result of the information received.* **8** VB WITH OBJ If an idea or thought **strikes** you, it comes into your mind suddenly. *It struck him how foolish his behaviour had been.* **9** VB WITH OBJ If something **strikes** you in a particular way, it gives you a particular impression. *Gertie strikes me as a very silly girl... How did London strike you?* **10** PASSIVE VB If you **are struck** by something, you are very impressed by it. *He had been struck by what he saw.* **11** VB WITH OR WITHOUT OBJ When a clock **strikes,** its bells make a sound to indicate what the time is. *The church clock struck eleven.* **12** VB WITH OBJ If you **strike** a bargain or deal with someone, you come to an agreement. *The council hoped to strike a deal that would give it more power.* **13** VB WITH OBJ If you **strike** a match, you make it produce a flame. *He struck a match and put it to his pipe.* **14** VB WITH OBJ If someone **strikes** oil or gold, they discover it in the ground as a result of mining or drilling. **15** See also **striking.**

PHRASES ● Workers who are **on strike** are refusing to work. *I would never go on strike for more money.* ● If something that someone says **strikes a** particular **note,** it produces a particular impression or atmosphere. *His words struck a slightly false note for me.* ● To **strike a balance** means to do something that is halfway between two extremes. ● If something **strikes fear** or **strikes terror** into people, it causes them to be suddenly very frightened. *The tanks struck terror into the hearts of the peasants.* ● If you **are struck dumb** or **are struck blind,** you suddenly become unable to speak or see. *We were struck dumb with horror.*

strike down. PHR VB To **strike** someone **down** means to kill or severely harm them. *Kennedy was struck down by an assassin's bullet.*

strike off. PHR VB If a doctor or lawyer **is struck off,** their name is removed from the official register and they are not allowed to practise their profession.

strike out. PHR VB **1** If you **strike out** somewhere, you set out in a particular direction. *He struck out for the village of Tracy.* **2** To **strike out** also means to begin to do something different on your own. *He decided to strike out on his own.*

strike up. PHR VB **1** When you **strike up** a conversation or friendship, you begin it. *Alice and I struck up a friendship immediately.* **2** When musicians **strike up,** they begin to play. *The band had just struck up Ellington's 'Satin Doll'.*

striker /straɪkə/, **strikers. 1** COUNT N **Strikers** are people who are on strike. **2** COUNT N In football, a **striker** is a player whose main function is to attack and score goals, rather than defend.

striking /straɪkɪŋ/. **1** ADJ Something that is **striking** is very noticeable or unusual. *The most striking thing about Piccadilly Circus is the statue of Eros in the centre.* ♦ **strikingly** SUBMOD *The two women appeared strikingly different.* **2** ADJ A **striking** person is very attractive. *...a striking redhead.* ♦ **strikingly** SUBMOD *...a strikingly beautiful child.*

string /strɪŋ/, **strings, stringing, strung** /strʌŋ/. **1** UNCOUNT N OR COUNT N **String** is thin rope made of twisted threads. *...a ball of string... ...a bunch of balloons on a string.* **2** COUNT N A **string** of things is a number of them on the same piece of thread or wire. *...a string of beads round her neck.* **3** COUNT N You can refer to a row or series of similar things as a **string.** *...a string of islands... ...the latest in a string of hotel disasters.* **4** COUNT N The **strings** on a musical instrument are the tightly-stretched lengths of wire or nylon which vibrate to produce notes. **5** PLURAL N The section of an orchestra which consists of stringed instruments is called the **strings.**

PHRASES ● If you **pull strings** to get something done, you use your influence to get it done; often used showing disapproval. ● If something is offered to you with **no strings attached,** it is offered without any special conditions.

string out. PHR VB If things are **strung out** somewhere, they are spread out in a long line. *...small towns strung out along the dirt roads.*

string together. PHR VB If you **string** things **together,** you make them into one thing by adding them to each other, one at a time. *I strung together some rhymes to amuse her.*

stringed /strɪŋd[1]/. ATTRIB ADJ A **stringed** instrument is one with strings, such a guitar.

stringent /strɪndʒənt/. ADJ **Stringent** laws, rules, or conditions are severe or are strictly controlled; a formal use. *His budget proposal is even more stringent than the President's... These requirements are often very stringent.*

stringy /strɪŋi[1]/. **1** ADJ **Stringy** food is tough and difficult to chew. **2** ADJ **Stringy** hair is thin and rough.

strip /strɪp/, **strips, stripping, stripped. 1** COUNT N A **strip** of something is a long, narrow piece of it. *...a thin strip of paper... There was only a narrow strip of beach.* **2** VB If you **strip,** you take off your clothes. **3** VB WITH OBJ To **strip** someone or something means to remove their clothes or covering. *Before the ship sailed they were stripped and searched... The wind stripped the tree of all its leaves.* **4** VB WITH OBJ AND ADJUNCT To **strip** property or rights from someone means to take them away from that person. *She was stripped of all her property and possessions... They were stripping away my remaining pension rights.* **5** COUNT N A comic **strip** is a series of drawings which tell a story, often with the words spoken by the characters written on them. **6** PHRASE If you **tear a strip off** someone or if you **tear** them **off a strip,** you scold them severely; an informal use.

strip off. PHR VB To **strip off** clothing means to remove it. *Casson stripped off his raincoat.*

stripe /straɪp/, **stripes. 1** COUNT N **Stripes** are long, thin lines, usually of different colours. *...a shirt with blue and white stripes.* **2** COUNT N **Stripes** are also narrow bands of material sewn onto a uniform to indicate someone's rank. *...a red uniform with sergeant's stripes.*

striped /straɪpt/. ADJ If something is **striped,** it has stripes on it. *...striped trousers.*

strip lighting. UNCOUNT N **Strip lighting** is a method of lighting which uses long tubes rather than light bulbs.

strive /straɪv/, **strives, striving, strove** /strəʊv/, **striven** /strɪvə[0]n/. VB WITH 'for' OR TO-INF If you **strive** for something or **strive** to do something, you make a great effort to get or do it; a formal use. *They strove to give the impression that they were leaving... They have striven for freedom for many years.*

strode /strəʊd/. **Strode** is the past tense of **stride.**

stroke /strəʊk/, **strokes, stroking, stroked. 1** VB WITH OBJ If you **stroke** someone or something, you move your hand slowly and gently over them. *She put out a hand and stroked the cat... He stroked her hair affectionately.* **2** COUNT N A **stroke** is a sudden and severe illness which affects your brain, and which often kills people or causes them to be paralysed in one side of their body. *She had a stroke and was unable to walk again.* **3** COUNT N The **strokes** of a pen or brush are the movements or marks you make with it when you are writing or painting. *She began to paint with bold, defiant strokes.* **4** COUNT N When you are swimming or rowing, your **strokes** are the repeated movements you make with your arms or the oars. *She swam with steady strokes.* **5** COUNT N A swimming **stroke** is a particular style or method of swimming. **6** COUNT N The **strokes** of a clock are the sounds that indicate each hour. *At the twelfth stroke, we welcomed in the New Year.* **7** SING N WITH SUPP A **stroke** of luck is something lucky that suddenly happens. A **stroke** of genius is a sudden idea or inspiration. *Then it came, my stroke of great good fortune... Her idea was a stroke of genius.*

PHRASES ● If something happens **at a stroke** or **in one stroke,** it happens suddenly and completely because of one single action. *He was determined at a stroke to remove those distinctions.* ● Someone **who does not do a stroke** of work is very lazy; an informal use.

stroll /strəʊl/, **strolls, strolling, strolled.** VB WITH ADJUNCT If you **stroll** somewhere, you walk in a slow, relaxed way. *They strolled along the beach.* Also COUNT N *She decided to take a stroll in the garden.*

strong /strɒŋ/, **stronger, strongest. 1** ADJ A **strong** person has powerful muscles. *His strong arms were around me, pinning me down.* **2** ADJ **Strong** also means very confident and not easily influenced or worried by other people. *I felt very strong in the knowledge of my own innocence... ...a strong personality.* **3** ADJ **Strong** objects are not easily broken. *...steel cylinders strong enough to survive even a nuclear catastrophe.* ♦ **strongly** ADV *...strongly constructed buildings.* **4** ADJ **Strong** also means great in degree or intensity. *The strong possibility is that he will be told tomorrow... ...the strong wind... They still spoke with a strong German accent.* ♦ **strongly** ADV *His mother will strongly influence his choice of a wife.* **5** ADJ If you have **strong** views on something or express your views using **strong** words, you have very definite views or express them in a very definite way. *There is strong criticism of certain aspects of the case... He has condemned the present sit-in by students in strong terms.* ♦ **strongly** ADV *I feel very strongly about drugs... I would strongly advise you against such an action.* **6** ADJ **Strong** action is firm and severe. *They introduced a strong anti-inflation programme.* **7** ADJ **Strong** arguments for something are supported by a lot of evidence. *There is a strong case for an Act of Parliament.* **8** ADJ A **strong** group is large or powerful. *It was essential to build a strong organization.* **9** ADJ You use **strong** to say how many people there are in a group. For example, a group that is twenty **strong** has twenty people in it. **10** ATTRIB ADJ Your **strong** points are the things you are good at. *Maths was always his strong subject.* **11** ATTRIB ADJ A **strong** competitor or candidate is likely to do well. **12** ADJ A **strong** relationship is firm and likely to last. *Links with the trade unions were strong.* **13** ADJ **Strong** industries, economies, or currencies are financially successful. *Sterling has once again become one of the stronger currencies.* **14** ADJ **Strong** drinks, chemicals, or drugs contain a lot of a particular substance. *She made him a cup of tea so strong that he could not drink it... ...a strong household bleach.* **15** PHRASE If someone or something is still **going strong,** they are still living or working well after a long time.

stronghold /strɒŋhəʊld/, **strongholds.** COUNT N WITH SUPP If a place is a **stronghold** of an attitude or belief, many people there have this attitude or belief. *It is a solid Labour stronghold.*

strove /strəʊv/. **Strove** is the past tense of **strive.**

struck /strʌk/. **Struck** is the past tense and past participle of **strike.**

structural /strʌktʃə[0]rəl/. ADJ **Structural** is used to describe an aspect of the structure of something. *...structural faults in the walls... ...structural damage.*

structure /strʌktʃə/, **structures, structuring, structured. 1** UNCOUNT N OR COUNT N The **structure** of something is the way in which it is made, built, or organized. *She analysed the structure of its skull in great detail... The whole structure of the film was rather simplistic... The class structures of England and America are quite different.* **2** COUNT N A **structure** is something that has been built or constructed. *We visited the Children's Palace, a great sprawling structure.* **3** UNCOUNT N A system or activity that has **structure** is well organized and efficient. *She loved the sense of structure, organization and enthusiasm.* **4** VB WITH OBJ If you **structure** something, you arrange it in an organized pattern or system. *They structure their communication to meet the needs of the client.*

struggle /strʌgə[0]l/, **struggles, struggling, struggled. 1** VB If you **struggle** to do something difficult, you try hard to do it. *They struggle to build a more democratic society... ...a nationalist movement that has had to struggle for independence.* Also COUNT N *...the day-to-day struggle for survival.* **2** VB If you **struggle** when you are being held, you try hard to get free. *She struggled in his embrace.* **3** RECIP VB If two people **struggle** with each other, they fight. *We struggled for the gun... I had to struggle with men I could not even see.* Also COUNT N *There was a moment's struggle and the gun fell to the ground.* **4** VB WITH TO-INF OR ADJUNCT If you **struggle** to move yourself, you manage to do it with great difficulty. *He struggled to his feet... He struggled forward for about half a mile.* **5** SING N An activity that is a **struggle** is difficult and takes a lot of effort. *Reading was a struggle for him.*

strum /strʌm/, **strums, strumming, strummed.** VB WITH OR WITHOUT OBJ If you **strum** a guitar, you play it by moving fingers quickly up and down across the strings. *The guitar player started strumming softly.*

strung /strʌŋ/. **Strung** is the past tense and past participle of **string.**

strut /strʌt/, **struts, strutting, strutted. 1** VB Someone who **struts** walks in a proud way, with their head high and their chest out. *Eddie turned around and strutted back to them... ...a peacock strutting on the lawn.* **2** COUNT N A **strut** is a piece of wood or metal which strengthens or supports a building or structure.

stub /stʌb/, **stubs, stubbing, stubbed. 1** COUNT N WITH SUPP The **stub** of a cigarette or a pencil is the short piece which remains when the rest has been used. *...an ashtray full of old cigarette stubs.* **2** COUNT N The **stub** of a cheque or ticket is the small part that you keep. **3** VB WITH OBJ If you **stub** your toe, you hurt it by accidentally kicking something. *I stubbed my toe against a stone.*

stub out. PHR VB When someone **stubs out** a cigarette, they put it out by pressing it against something hard.

stubble /stʌbə[0]l/. **1** UNCOUNT N **Stubble** is the short stalks which remain after corn or wheat has been harvested. *The stubble was burning on the harvested fields.* **2** UNCOUNT N **Stubble** is also the very short hairs on a man's face when he has not shaved recently.

stubborn /stʌbə[0]n/. **1** ADJ A **stubborn** person is determined to do what they want and refuses to change their mind. *Our son is stubborn and rebellious... ...his stubborn determination.* ♦ **stubbornly** ADV *'It was an accident,' he said stubbornly, 'and that's that.'* **2** ADJ A **stubborn** stain is difficult to remove. *Remove stubborn marks on tiles with a wire brush.*

stubby /stʌbi[1]/. ADJ A **stubby** object is short and thick. *His stubby fingers were strong and mobile.*

stuck /stʌk/. 1 **Stuck** is the past tense and past participle of **stick.** 2 PRED ADJ If something is **stuck** in a particular position, it is fixed there and cannot move. *The lift seems to be stuck between the second and third floors.* 3 PRED ADJ If you are **stuck** when you are trying to do something, you cannot continue because it is too difficult. *Ask for help the minute you're stuck.* 4 PRED ADJ If you are **stuck** in a place or unpleasant situation, you cannot get away from it. *The boss rang to explain that he was stuck in Milan.*

stud /stʌd/, **studs.** 1 COUNT N A **stud** is a small piece of metal attached to a surface. *...black leather with gold studs.* 2 UNCOUNT N Male horses or other animals that are kept for **stud** are kept for breeding. *I'm not going to race him, I'm going to put him to stud.*

studded /stʌdɪ^{2}d/. ADJ Something that is **studded** is decorated with studs or things that look like studs. *...enamel bracelets studded with precious stones.*

student /stjuːdənt/, **students.** 1 COUNT N A **student** is a person who is studying at a university or college, or in America, someone who is studying in a secondary school. *...a part-time student at King's College, London.* ● See also **mature student.** 2 COUNT N WITH 'of' A **student** of a particular subject is trying to learn about it. *It is our treatment of old people which most shocks students of our culture.*

studied /stʌdɪd/. 1 ATTRIB ADJ A **studied** action has been carefully planned and is not spontaneous or natural. *With studied casualness he mentioned his departure to Hilary.* 2 See also **study.**

studio /stjuːdɪəʊ/, **studios.** 1 COUNT N A **studio** is a room where a painter or photographer works. 2 COUNT N A **studio** is a room where radio or television programmes, records, or films are made. *...the big recording studio in Maida Vale.*

studious /stjuːdɪəs/. ADJ A **studious** person spends a lot of time reading and studying.

studiously /stjuːdɪəsli^1/. ADV If you do something **studiously,** you do it carefully and deliberately. *The Colonel studiously examined his folders.*

study /stʌdi^1/, **studies, studying, studied.** 1 VB WITH OR WITHOUT OBJ If you **study** a subject, you spend time learning about it. *He studied chemistry at university... They are both studying for A levels.* 2 UNCOUNT N **Study** is the activity of studying a subject. *There are no rooms specifically set aside for quiet study.* 3 PLURAL N **Studies** are subjects which are studied. *...the School of European Studies.* 4 VB WITH OBJ If you **study** something, you look at it or watch it carefully. *He looked at her hard, studying her face... I studied a map.* 5 COUNT N A **study** of a subject is a piece of research on it. *She has made a close study of drinking habits.* 6 COUNT N A **study** by an artist is a drawing done in preparation for a larger picture. 7 COUNT N A **study** in a house is a room used for reading, writing, and studying. 8 See also **studied.**

stuff /stʌf/, **stuffs, stuffing, stuffed.** 1 UNCOUNT N You can refer to a substance or a group of things as **stuff.** *What's that stuff in the bucket?... Quite a lot of stuff had been stolen... She was reading the travel stuff in the colour supplement.* 2 VB WITH OBJ AND ADJUNCT If you **stuff** something somewhere, you push it there quickly and roughly. *Willie gathered up the bills and stuffed them carelessly into his pocket.* 3 VB WITH OBJ If a place or container **is stuffed** with things, it is full of them. *The cupboard was stuffed with old fishing tackle.* ♦ **stuffed** ADJ *He'd got a big rucksack, stuffed with notes, on his back.* 4 REFL VB OR VB WITH OBJ If you **stuff** yourself, you eat a lot of food; an informal use. *Karin was stuffing herself with eggs and toast... I was stuffing my face with ice-cream.* 5 VB WITH OBJ If you **stuff** a bird or a vegetable, you put a mixture of food inside it before cooking it. 6 VB WITH OBJ If a dead animal **is stuffed,** it is filled with material so that it can be preserved and displayed. ♦ **stuffed** ADJ *...a stuffed parrot.*

stuffing /stʌfɪŋ/. 1 MASS N **Stuffing** is a mixture of food that is put inside a bird or a vegetable before it is cooked. *We had chicken with stuffing and new potatoes.* 2 UNCOUNT N **Stuffing** is also material that is put inside pillows, cushions, or toys, to fill them and make them firm.

stuffy /stʌfi^1/. 1 ADJ **Stuffy** people or institutions are formal and old-fashioned; an informal use. 2 ADJ If a place is **stuffy,** it is unpleasantly warm and there is not enough fresh air. *...a stuffy room.*

stultify /stʌltɪfaɪ/, **stultifies, stultifying, stultified.** VB WITH OBJ If something **stultifies** you, it is so boring that it destroys your interest; a formal use. *The regular use of calculators can stultify a child's capacity to do mental arithmetic.* ♦ **stultifying** ADJ *...the stultifying rituals of court procedure.*

stumble /stʌmbə^{0}l/, **stumbles, stumbling, stumbled.** 1 VB If you **stumble,** you nearly fall while walking or running. *The man was drunk and he stumbled on the bottom step.* 2 VB If you **stumble** while speaking, you make a mistake, and have to pause and say it again. *She stumbled over the foreign words.*

stumble across or **stumble on.** PHR VB If you **stumble across** something or **stumble on** it, you discover it unexpectedly. *In the course of their search they may stumble across something quite different... Sir Alexander Fleming stumbled on his great discovery of penicillin by accident.*

stumbling block, stumbling blocks. COUNT N A **stumbling block** is a problem which stops you from achieving something. *Perhaps the biggest stumbling block to disarmament is the deterrent theory.*

stump /stʌmp/, **stumps, stumping, stumped.** 1 COUNT N A **stump** is a small part of something that remains when the rest of it has been removed or broken off. *We left him sitting on the stump of an old oak tree.* 2 COUNT N The **stumps** in cricket are the three upright wooden sticks that form the wicket. 3 VB WITH OBJ If a question or problem **stumps** you, you cannot think of a solution to it. *...the question that has stumped philosophers since the beginning of time.* 4 VB WITH ADJUNCT If you **stump** somewhere, you walk there angrily with heavy steps. *She stumped back into the house.*

stump up. PHR VB If you **stump up** a sum of money, you pay the money that is required for something, often reluctantly; an informal use. *The government is being asked to stump up the balance.*

stumpy /stʌmpi^1/. ADJ **Stumpy** things are short and thick. *...a short stumpy tail.*

stun /stʌn/, **stuns, stunning, stunned.** 1 VB WITH OBJ If you **are stunned,** you are very shocked by something. *We were all stunned by the news.* ♦ **stunned** ADJ *I sat in stunned silence.* 2 VB WITH OBJ If a blow on the head **stuns** you, it makes you unconscious or confused and unsteady. *He was stunned by a blow from the rifle.* 3 See also **stunning.**

stung /stʌŋ/. **Stung** is the past tense and past participle of **sting.**

stunk /stʌŋk/. **Stunk** is the past participle of **stink.**

stunning /stʌnɪŋ/. 1 ADJ Something that is **stunning** is very beautiful, attractive, or impressive. *The film is visually stunning... Her dress was simply stunning.* 2 ADJ Something that is **stunning** is also so unusual or unexpected that people are astonished by it. *...a stunning victory in the general election.*

stunt /stʌnt/, **stunts, stunting, stunted.** 1 COUNT N A **stunt** is something that someone does to get publicity. *Climbing up the church tower was a fine publicity stunt.* 2 COUNT N A **stunt** is also a dangerous and exciting action that someone does in a film. *Steve McQueen did most of his own stunts.* 3 VB WITH OBJ To **stunt** the growth or development of something means to prevent it from growing or developing as it should. *These insecticides can stunt plant growth.* ♦ **stunted** ADJ *...old, stunted thorn trees.*

stupefied /stjuːpɪfaɪd/. 1 ADJ If you are **stupefied,** you feel so tired or bored that you are unable to think clearly. *I felt stupefied by the heavy meal.* 2 ADJ If you are **stupefied,** you are very surprised. *He was too stupefied to answer her.*

stupendous /stjuːpɛndəs/. ADJ Something **stupendous** is extremely large or impressive. *The roar of the explosion was stupendous.*

stupid /stjuːpɪd/, **stupider, stupidest.** 1 ADJ A **stupid** person shows a lack of good judgement or intelligence and is not at all sensible. *I have been extremely stupid... ...a stupid question.* ♦ **stupidly** ADV *I once stupidly asked him why he smiled so often.* 2 ADJ You say that something is **stupid** to indicate that you do not like it or that it annoys you; an informal use. *I hate these stupid black shoes.*

stupidity /stjuːpɪdɪ^{1}ti^1/, **stupidities.** 1 COUNT N OR UNCOUNT N **Stupidity** is behaviour that is not at all sensible. *I used to find her occasional stupidities amusing... He is paying a big price for his stupidity.* 2 UNCOUNT N **Stupidity** is the quality of being stupid. *...the stupidity of their error.*

stupor /stjuːpə/, **stupors.** COUNT N Someone who is in a **stupor** is almost unconscious. *He collapsed in a drunken stupor.*

sturdy /stɜːdi^1/, **sturdier, sturdiest.** ADJ Something **sturdy** looks strong and unlikely to be easily damaged. *...sturdy oak tables.* ♦ **sturdily** ADV *...a sturdily built little boy.*

stutter /stʌtə/, **stutters, stuttering, stuttered.** 1 VB OR REPORT VB If you **stutter,** you have difficulty saying a word. *'I...I want to do it,' she stuttered.* 2 COUNT N Someone who has a **stutter** tends to stutter when they speak.

sty /staɪ/, **sties.** COUNT N A **sty** is a pigsty.

style /staɪl/, **styles, styling, styled.** 1 COUNT N WITH SUPP The **style** of something is the general way it is done or presented. *Some people find our leisurely style of decision-making rather frustrating... ...western styles of education.* 2 COUNT N OR UNCOUNT N WITH SUPP Someone's **style** is all their general attitudes and usual ways of behaving. *...a consciously national style... In characteristic style, he peered over his glasses.* 3 UNCOUNT N Someone or something that has **style** is smart and elegant. *Both were rather short and plump, but they had style... Here you can eat in style.* 4 UNCOUNT N OR COUNT N The **style** of a product is its design. *These pants come in several styles... The clothes I wore weren't different in style or appearance from those of the other children.* 5 VB WITH OBJ If you **style** clothing or someone's hair, you design the clothing or do their hair. *Her hair was styled in a short cropped pony tail.* ● to **cramp** someone's **style:** see **cramp.** ● See also **hairstyle.**

stylish /staɪlɪʃ/. ADJ Someone or something that is **stylish** is smart, elegant, and fashionable. *...the stylish Swiss resort of Gstaad.*

stylistic /staɪlɪstɪk/. ATTRIB ADJ **Stylistic** describes things relating to the methods and techniques used in creating a piece of writing, music, or art. *Such work lacks any development of stylistic features.*

stylized /staɪlaɪzd/; also spelled **stylised.** ADJ Something that is **stylized** uses various artistic or literary conventions in order to create an effect, instead of being natural, spontaneous, or true to life. *...a stylised picture of a Japanese garden... In the past, acting performances were usually highly stylized.*

suave /swɑːv/. ADJ Someone who is **suave** is charming and polite. *...a suave young man.*

sub-. PREFIX **Sub-** is used to form nouns that refer to the parts into which something is divided. *...subsection 1(b) of the report... ...the sub-groups of society.*

subconscious /sʌbkɒnʃəs/. 1 SING N Your **subconscious** is the part of your mind that can influence you even though you are not aware of it. *The knowledge was there somewhere in the depths of his subconscious.* 2 ADJ Something that is **subconscious** happens or exists in your subconscious. *...a subconscious desire to punish himself.* ♦ **subconsciously** ADV *...a fictional character with whom millions could subconsciously identify.*

subcontract, /sʌbkə^{7}ntrækt/, **subcontracts, subcontracting, subcontracted.** VB WITH OBJ If one firm **subcontracts** a part of its work to another firm, it pays the second firm to do that part. *They had subcontracted some of the work to an electrician.*

subculture /sʌbkʌltʃə/, **subcultures.** COUNT N A **subculture** is the ideas, art, and way of life of a particular group within a society. *...the posters and poetry of the hippie subculture.*

subdivide /sʌbdɪvaɪd/, **subdivides, subdividing, subdivided.** VB WITH OBJ If something **is subdivided,** it is made into several smaller areas, parts, or sections. *Our office was subdivided into departments.*

subdivision /sʌbdɪvɪʒə^{0}n/, **subdivisions.** COUNT N A **subdivision** is an area or section which is a part of a larger area or section.

subdue /səbdjuː/, **subdues, subduing, subdued.** 1 VB WITH OBJ If soldiers **subdue** a group of people, they bring them under control using force. *Troops were sent to subdue the rebels.* 2 VB WITH OBJ If something **subdues** your feelings, it makes them less strong. *This thought subdued my delight at the news.*

subdued /səbdjuːd/. 1 ADJ Someone who is **subdued** is quiet, often because they are sad. *They were subdued and silent.* 2 ADJ **Subdued** feelings, sounds, lights, or colours are not very noticeable. *The assembly murmured in subdued agreement.*

subject, subjects, subjecting, subjected; pronounced /sʌbdʒɪ^{2}kt/ when it is a noun, adjective, or preposition, and /səbdʒɛkt/ when it is a verb. 1 COUNT N The **subject** of a conversation, letter, or book is the thing that is being discussed or written about. *I don't have any strong views on the subject... However much you try to change the subject, the conversation invariably returns to politics.* 2 COUNT N In grammar, the **subject** of a clause is the noun group which refers to the person or thing that does the action expressed by the verb. 3 COUNT N A **subject** is also something such as chemistry, history, or English, studied in schools, colleges, and universities. *Maths was my best subject at school.* 4 COUNT N The **subjects** of a country are the people who live there; a formal use. *...British subjects.* 5 ATTRIB ADJ **Subject** people are controlled by a government or ruler. **Subject** countries are controlled by another country. *...freedom for the subject peoples of the world.* 6 PRED ADJ WITH PREP 'to' If you are **subject** to something, you are affected, or likely to be affected, by it. *Your profit will be subject to tax... He is highly strung and, therefore, subject to heart attacks.* 7 PREP If one thing will happen **subject to** another, it will happen only if the other thing happens. *The property will be sold subject to the following conditions.* 8 VB WITH OBJ AND PREP 'to' If you **subject** someone to something unpleasant, you make them experience it. *He was subjected to the harshest possible punishment.*

subjective /səbdʒɛktɪv/. ADJ Something that is **subjective** is influenced by personal opinions and feelings. *He knew his arguments were subjective, based on intuition.*

subject matter. UNCOUNT N The **subject matter** of a conversation, book, or film is the thing, person, or idea that is being discussed, written about, or shown.

subjugate /sʌbdʒə⁴geɪt/, **subjugates, subjugating, subjugated;** a formal word. 1 VB WITH OBJ If someone **subjugates** a group of people, they take complete control of them, especially by defeating them in a war. *They wondered where Hitler would turn when he had subjugated Europe.* ♦ **subjugation** /sʌbdʒə⁴geɪʃə⁰n/ UNCOUNT N *These people are resisting attempted subjugation by armed minorities.* 2 VB WITH OBJ If your wishes **are subjugated** to something, they are treated as less important than that thing. *She has subjugated her own desires to those of her husband.*

sublime /səblaɪm/. ADJ Something that is **sublime** has a wonderful quality that affects you deeply; a literary use. *...the author of this sublime document.*

subliminal /səblɪmɪnə⁰l/. ADJ Something that is **subliminal** affects your mind without your being aware of it. *...subliminal advertising.*

sub-machine gun, sub-machine guns. COUNT N A **sub-machine gun** is a light, portable machine gun.

submarine /sʌbməriːn/, **submarines.** COUNT N A **submarine** is a ship that can travel below the surface of the sea.

submerge /səbmɜːdʒ/, **submerges, submerging, submerged.** 1 ERG VB If something **submerges** or **is submerged,** it goes below the surface of the water. *The alligator showed its snout before submerging.* ♦ **submerged** ADJ *...a line of submerged rocks.* 2 REFL VB WITH 'in' If you **submerge** yourself in an activity, you give all your attention to it. *He submerged himself in company reports.*

submission /səbmɪʃə⁰n/. 1 UNCOUNT N **Submission** is a state in which people are forced to accept the control of someone else. *The trade unions were brought into submission.* 2 UNCOUNT N The **submission** of a proposal or application is the act of sending it to someone, so they can decide whether to accept it; a formal use. *...the submission of these plans to the local authority.*

submissive /səbmɪsɪv/. ADJ If you are **submissive,** you are quiet and obedient. *She became submissive and subservient.*

submit /səbmɪt/, **submits, submitting, submitted;** a formal word. 1 VB If you **submit** to something, you accept it, because you are not powerful enough to resist it. *They were forced to submit to military discipline.* 2 VB WITH OBJ If you **submit** a proposal or application to someone, you send it to them so they can decide whether to accept it. *I submitted my resignation.*

subnormal /sʌbnɔːmə⁰l/. ADJ If someone is **subnormal,** they have less ability or intelligence than a normal person of their age.

subordinate, subordinates, subordinating, subordinated; pronounced /səbɔːdɪnə¹t/ when it is a noun or adjective, and /səbɔːdɪneɪt/ when it is a verb. 1 COUNT N WITH POSS If someone is your **subordinate,** they have a less important position than you in the organization that you both work for. *He humiliated his senior staff before their subordinates.* 2 ADJ If one thing is **subordinate** to another, it is less important than the other thing; a formal use. *All other questions are subordinate to this one.* 3 VB WITH OBJ AND PREP 'to' If you **subordinate** one thing to another, you treat it as less important than the other thing; a formal use. *To keep his job, he subordinated his own interests to the objectives of the company.*

subordinate clause, subordinate clauses. COUNT N A **subordinate clause** is a clause which begins with a subordinating conjunction such as 'because' and which must be used with a main clause.

subscribe /səbskraɪb/, **subscribes, subscribing, subscribed.** 1 VB If you **subscribe** to an opinion or belief, you have this opinion or belief. *The rest of us do not subscribe to this theory.* 2 VB If you **subscribe** to a magazine or a newspaper, you pay to receive copies of it regularly. *I started subscribing to a morning newspaper.* 3 VB WITH OR WITHOUT OBJ, WITH ADJUNCT If you **subscribe** money to a charity or a campaign, you send money to it regularly. *They subscribed to local charities.*

subscriber /səbskraɪbə/, **subscribers.** 1 COUNT N The **subscribers** of a magazine or newspaper are the people who pay to receive copies of it regularly. 2 COUNT N **Subscribers** to a service are the people who pay to receive the service. *...telephone subscribers.* 3 COUNT N The **subscribers** to a charity or campaign are the people who support it by sending money regularly to it.

subscription /səbskrɪpʃə⁰n/, **subscriptions.** COUNT N A **subscription** is an amount of money that you pay regularly to belong to an organization or to receive copies of a magazine or newspaper. *...my first year's subscription to the National Union of Agricultural Workers... ...magazine subscriptions.*

subsequent /sʌbsɪkwənt/. ATTRIB ADJ **Subsequent** describes something that happens or exists at a later time than something else. *Subsequent research has produced even better results.* ♦ **subsequently** ADV *Brooke was arrested and subsequently sentenced to five years' imprisonment.*

subservient /səbsɜːvɪənt/. 1 ADJ If you are **subservient,** you do whatever someone wants you to do. *She was subservient and eager to please.* ♦ **subservience** /səbsɜːvɪəns/ UNCOUNT N *How long would they keep us in subservience?* 2 PRED ADJ WITH PREP 'to' If one thing is **subservient** to another, it is treated as less important than the other thing. *Economic systems became subservient to social objectives.*

subside /səbsaɪd/, **subsides, subsiding, subsided.** 1 VB If a feeling or sound **subsides,** it becomes less intense or quieter.. *She stopped and waited until the pain subsided... His voice subsided to a mutter.* 2 VB If water **subsides** or if the ground **subsides,** it sinks to a lower level. *The flooded river was subsiding rapidly.*

subsidence /səbsaɪdəns, sʌbsɪdəns/. UNCOUNT N When there is **subsidence,** the ground sinks to a lower level.

subsidiary /səbsɪdjəri¹/, **subsidiaries.** 1 ADJ If something is **subsidiary,** it is less important than something else with which it is connected. *The Department offers a course in Opera Studies as a subsidiary subject... I tried to discuss this and some subsidiary questions.* 2 COUNT N A **subsidiary** is a company which is part of a larger company. *The British company is a subsidiary of Racal Electronics.*

subsidize /sʌbsɪdaɪz/, **subsidizes, subsidizing, subsidized;** also spelled **subsidise.** VB WITH OBJ If a government **subsidizes** a public service or an industry, they pay part of its costs. *In this country the State subsidizes education.* ♦ **subsidized** ADJ *...subsidized housing.*

subsidy /sʌbsɪdi¹/, **subsidies.** COUNT N OR UNCOUNT N A **subsidy** is money paid by a government to help a company or to pay for a public service.

subsist /səbsɪst/, **subsists, subsisting, subsisted.** VB If you **subsist,** you only have just enough food to stay alive. *In some places, the settlers were subsisting on potato peelings.*

subsistence /səbsɪstəns/. UNCOUNT N **Subsistence** is the condition of only having just enough food to stay alive. *They do not have access to sufficient land for subsistence... ...living at subsistence level.*

substance /sʌbstəns/, **substances.** 1 COUNT N A **substance** is a solid, powder, or liquid. *He discovered a substance called phosphotase... We try to remove the harmful substances from cigarettes.* 2 UNCOUNT N You use **substance** to refer to something that you can touch, rather than something that you can only see, hear, or imagine. *They had no more substance than shadows.* 3 SING N The **substance** of what someone says is the main thing that they are trying to say. *The substance of their talk is condensed into a paragraph.* 4 UNCOUNT N **Substance** is also the quality of being important or significant. *There isn't anything of real substance in her book.*

substandard /sʌbstændəd/. ADJ Something **substandard** is of an unacceptably low standard. *...substandard housing.*

substantial /səbstænʃə⁰l/. 1 ADJ **Substantial** means very large in amount or degree. *She will receive a substantial amount of money... Many factories suffered substantial damage.* 2 ADJ A **substantial** building is large and strongly built.

substantially /səbstænʃəli¹/. 1 ADV If something increases or decreases **substantially,** it increases or decreases by a large amount. *The price may go up quite substantially.* 2 SUBMOD If something is **substantially** true, it is generally or mostly true. *Steed always maintained that the story was substantially true.*

substantiate /səbstænʃɪeɪt/, **substantiates, substantiating, substantiated.** VB WITH OBJ To **substantiate** a statement or a story means to supply evidence proving that it is true; a formal use. *Your report might be difficult to substantiate.*

substitute /sʌbstɪtjuːt/, **substitutes, substituting, substituted.** 1 VB WITH OBJ If you **substitute** one thing for another, you use it instead of the other thing. *Force was substituted for argument.* ♦ **substitution** /sʌbstɪtjuːʃə⁰n/ UNCOUNT N OR COUNT N *...the substitution of local goods for those previously imported... Some of these substitutions were successful.* 2 COUNT N A **substitute** is something that you have or use instead of something else. *Their dog was a substitute for the children they never had.*

subsume /səbsjuːm/, **subsumes, subsuming, subsumed.** VB WITH OBJ If something **is subsumed** within a larger group, it is included within it, rather than being considered as something separate; a formal use.

subterfuge /sʌbtəfjuːdʒ/, **subterfuges.** COUNT N OR UNCOUNT N A **subterfuge** is a trick or a dishonest way of getting what you want. *Resistance will be possible only through cheating, subterfuge and sabotage.*

subterranean /sʌbtəreɪnɪən/. ATTRIB ADJ A **subterranean** river or tunnel is underground; a formal use. *...winding subterranean passages.*

subtitles /sʌbtaɪtə⁰lz/. PLURAL N **Subtitles** are the translation or dialogue that is provided at the bottom of a screen, for example during a foreign film. *...an Italian film with English subtitles... ...with subtitles for the hard of hearing.*

subtle /sʌtə⁰l/, **subtler, subtlest.** 1 ADJ Something **subtle** is not immediately obvious or noticeable. *His whole attitude had undergone a subtle change.* ♦ **subtly** ADV *The tastes are subtly different.* 2 ADJ Someone **subtle** uses indirect and clever methods to achieve something. *You must be more subtle... My plan was subtler.* ♦ **subtly** ADV *He subtly criticized me.*

subtlety /sʌtə⁰lti¹/, **subtleties.** 1 COUNT N A **subtlety** is a very small detail or difference which is difficult to notice. *...the subtleties of English intonation.* 2 UNCOUNT N **Subtlety** is the quality of not being immediately obvious or noticeable. *In your cooking remember that subtlety is everything.* 3 UNCOUNT N **Subtlety** is also the ability to use indirect and clever methods to achieve something. *...their subtlety of mind.*

subtract /səbtrækt/, **subtracts, subtracting, subtracted.** VB WITH OBJ If you **subtract** one number from another, you take the first number away from the second. For example, if you subtract 3 from 5, you get 2. ♦ **subtraction** /səbtrækʃə⁰n/ UNCOUNT N OR COUNT N *...simple techniques for handling subtraction.*

subtropical /sʌbtrɒpɪkə⁰l/. ATTRIB ADJ **Subtropical** describes things relating to the areas of the world that lie between the tropical and temperate regions. *...subtropical forests.*

suburb /sʌbɜːb/, **suburbs.** COUNT N A **suburb** or the **suburbs** of a city is an area of it which is away from the centre. *...people who live in the suburbs.*

suburban /səbɜːbə⁰n/. 1 ADJ **Suburban** means relating to a suburb. *...suburban areas.* 2 ADJ Something **suburban** is dull, conventional, and not exciting at all. *...a suburban lifestyle.*

suburbia /səbɜːbɪə/. UNCOUNT N **Suburbia** refers to suburbs considered as a whole. *...the gardens of London suburbia.*

subversion /səbvɜːʃə⁰n/. UNCOUNT N **Subversion** is the attempt to weaken or destroy a political system or government; a formal use.

subversive /səbvɜːsɪv/, **subversives;** a formal word. 1 ADJ Something **subversive** is intended to weaken or destroy a political system or government. *...subversive literature.* 2 COUNT N **Subversives** are people who attempt to weaken or destroy a political system or government.

subvert /səbvɜːt/, **subverts, subverting, subverted.** VB WITH OBJ To **subvert** something means to destroy its power and influence; a formal use. *Conflict and division subvert the foundations of society.*

subway /sʌbweɪ/, **subways.** 1 COUNT N A **subway** is a passage for pedestrians underneath a busy road. 2 COUNT N In American English a **subway** is an underground railway. *...a subway station.*

succeed /səksiːd/, **succeeds, succeeding, succeeded.** 1 VB If you **succeed** in doing something, you manage to do it. *I succeeded in getting the job.* 2 VB If something **succeeds,** it has the result that is intended or works in a satisfactory way. *Nobody expected that strike to succeed.* 3 VB Someone who **succeeds** gains a high position in what they do, for example in business. *She is eager to succeed.* 4 VB WITH OR WITHOUT OBJ If you **succeed** another person, you are the next person to have their job or position. *Somebody's got to succeed Murray as editor... Elizabeth succeeded to the throne in 1952.* 5 VB WITH OBJ If one thing **succeeds** another, it comes after it in time. *The first demand would be succeeded by others.* ♦ **succeeding** ATTRIB ADJ *In the succeeding months, little was heard about him.*

success /səksɛs/, **successes.** 1 UNCOUNT N **Success** is the achievement of something that you have been trying to do. *His attempt to shoot the president came very close to success.* 2 UNCOUNT N OR COUNT N Someone or something that has achieved **success** has reached an important position or made a lot of money. *Confidence is the key to success... His next film—'Jaws'—was a tremendous success.*

successful /səksɛsfʊl/. 1 ADJ Something **successful** achieves what it was intended to achieve, or is popular or makes a lot of money. *...a successful* *attempt to land on the moon... ...a very successful film.* ♦ **successfully** ADV *The operation had been completed successfully.* 2 ADJ Someone who is **successful** in their job or career achieves a high position. *...a successful writer.*

succession /səkseʃə^{0}n/, **successions.** 1 COUNT N WITH 'of' A **succession** of things is a number of them occurring one after the other. *My life is a succession of failures.* 2 UNCOUNT N **Succession** is the act or right of being the next person to have a particular job or position. *...his succession to the peerage.* 3 PHRASE If something happens for a number of weeks or years **in succession,** it happens in each of those weeks or years, without a break. *Vita went to Florence for the third year in succession.*

successive /səksesɪv/. ATTRIB ADJ **Successive** means happening or existing one after another, without a break. *On two successive Saturdays, the car broke down.*

successor /səksesə/, **successors.** COUNT N Someone's **successor** is the person who takes their job after they have left. *Who will be Brearley's successor?*

succinct /səksɪŋkt/. ADJ Something that is **succinct** expresses facts or ideas clearly and in few words. *...an accurate and succinct account of their policies.* ♦ **succinctly** ADV *She puts the case very succinctly.*

succulent /sʌkjə^{4}lənt/. ADJ **Succulent** food is juicy and delicious. *...a succulent mango.*

succumb /səkʌm/, **succumbs, succumbing, succumbed.** VB If you **succumb** to persuasion or desire, you are unable to resist it. *He finally succumbed to the temptation to have another drink.*

such /sʌtʃ/. 1 PREDET, DET, OR PRON You use **such** to refer to the person or thing you have just mentioned or to something similar. *They lasted for hundreds of thousands of years. On a human time scale, such a period seems an eternity... The nobility held tournaments, but peasants had no time to spare for such frivolity... I don't believe in magic, there is no such thing... We have been asked to consider alternatives. Many such have been proposed in the last few years.* 2 PREDET OR DET You also use **such** to emphasize the degree or extent of something. *It was such a lovely day... It was strange that such elegant creatures made such ugly sounds.*

PHRASES ● You use **such as** or **such...as** to introduce one or more examples of something. *...a game of chance such as roulette... ...such things as pork pies, sausage rolls, and plum cake.* ● You use **such...that** or **such...as** when saying what the result or consequence of something is. *They have to charge in such a way that they don't make a loss... She got such a shock that she dropped the milk-can.* ● You use **such as it is** to indicate that something is not very good, important, or useful. *Dinner's on the table, such as it is.* ● You use **as such** to indicate that you are considering something by itself without considering related things or issues. *He is not terribly interested in politics as such.* ● You use **such and such** to refer to something without being specific. *John always tells me that I have not taken such and such into account.*

suchlike /sʌtʃlaɪk/. DET OR PRON You use **suchlike** to refer to other things like the ones already mentioned. *...artichokes, smoked fish, and suchlike delicacies... ...mills, threshing machines and such like.*

suck /sʌk/, **sucks, sucking, sucked.** 1 VB WITH OBJ OR ADJUNCT If you **suck** something, you hold it in your mouth and pull at it with your cheeks and tongue, usually to get liquid out of it. *The baby went on sucking the bottle.* 2 VB WITH OBJ AND ADJUNCT If something **sucks** an object or liquid somewhere, it draws it there with a powerful force. *The water is sucked upwards through the roots.*

sucker /sʌkə/, **suckers.** 1 COUNT N If you call someone a **sucker,** you mean that it is easy to cheat or fool them; an informal use. 2 COUNT N **Suckers** are pads on the bodies of some animals and insects which they use to stick to a surface.

suckle /sʌkə^{0}l/, **suckles, suckling, suckled.** ERG VB When a mother **suckles** her baby or when a baby **suckles,** the mother feeds it with milk from her breast.

suction /sʌkʃə^{0}n/. 1 UNCOUNT N **Suction** is the force involved when liquids, gases, or other substances are drawn from one space to another. *The draining process was assisted by suction.* 2 UNCOUNT N **Suction** is also the process by which two surfaces stick together when the air between them is removed. *...stuck on to the bath by suction pads.*

sudden /sʌdə^{0}n/. 1 ADJ Something that is **sudden** happens quickly and unexpectedly. *...a sudden drop in the temperature.* ♦ **suddenly** ADV OR SENTENCE ADV *Suddenly, the door opened and in walked the boss.* ♦ **suddenness** UNCOUNT N *...surprised by the suddenness of the attack.* 2 PHRASE If something happens **all of a sudden,** it happens so quickly and unexpectedly that you are surprised by it.

suds /sʌdz/. PLURAL N **Suds** are the bubbles produced when soap is mixed with water.

sue /suː/, **sues, suing, sued.** VB WITH OR WITHOUT OBJ If you **sue** someone, you start a legal case against them to claim money from them because they have harmed you in some way. *He couldn't sue them for wrongful arrest... He let it be known that he would sue.*

suede /sweɪd/. UNCOUNT N **Suede** is thin, soft leather with a slightly rough surface. *...boots of light brown suede... ...a suede jacket.*

suffer /sʌfə/, **suffers, suffering, suffered.** 1 VB WITH OR WITHOUT OBJ If someone **suffers** pain or an illness, they are badly affected by it. *She was suffering violent abdominal pains... Seventy-five percent of its population suffers from malnutrition.* ♦ **sufferer** COUNT N WITH SUPP *...sufferers of chronic disease.* 2 VB WITH OR WITHOUT OBJ If you **suffer,** you are badly affected by an unfavourable event or situation. *We were warned to support the government or suffer the consequences... They would be the first to suffer if these proposals were ever carried out.* 3 VB If something **suffers,** it becomes worse in quality or condition as a result of neglect or an unfavourable situation. *I'm not surprised that your studies are suffering.*

suffering /sʌfə^{0}rɪŋ/, **sufferings.** UNCOUNT N OR COUNT N **Suffering** is serious pain which someone feels in their body or their mind. *This would cause great hardship and suffering... This might alleviate their sufferings.*

suffice /səfaɪs/, **suffices, sufficing, sufficed.** VB If something **suffices,** it is enough to achieve a purpose or to fulfil a need; a formal use.

sufficiency /səfɪʃənsi^1/. SING N If there is a **sufficiency** of something, there is enough of it; a formal use. *We had 600 jet fighters and a sufficiency of airfields to support them.*

sufficient /səfɪʃənt/. ADJ If something is **sufficient** for a particular purpose, there is as much of it as is necessary. *Japan had a reserve of oil sufficient for its needs.* ♦ **sufficiently** ADV *He had not insured the house sufficiently.*

suffix /sʌfɪks/, **suffixes.** COUNT N A **suffix** is a letter or group of letters added to the end of a word in order to make a new word with different grammar or with a different meaning.

suffocate /sʌfəkeɪt/, **suffocates, suffocating, suffocated.** ERG VB If someone **suffocates** or if something **suffocates** them, they die because there is no air for them to breathe. *Sir, we are suffocating. We must surrender... The smoke and fumes almost suffocated me.* ♦ **suffocation** /sʌfəkeɪʃə^{0}n/ UNCOUNT N *Many slaves died of heat and suffocation.*

suffrage /sʌfrɪdʒ/. UNCOUNT N **Suffrage** is the right that people have to vote for a government or national leader. *...universal adult suffrage.*

sugar /ʃʊgə/, **sugars.** MASS N **Sugar** is a sweet substance, often in the form of white crystals, used to sweeten food and drink. *I take my coffee black with no sugar.*

sugar beet. UNCOUNT N **Sugar beet** is a plant cultivated for the sugar obtained from its root.

sugar cane. UNCOUNT N **Sugar cane** is a tall tropical plant with thick stems from which sugar is obtained.

suggest /sədʒest/, **suggests, suggesting, suggested.** 1 REPORT VB If you **suggest** something, you put forward a plan or idea for someone to consider. *We have to suggest a list of possible topics for next term's seminars... Can you suggest somewhere for a short holiday?... I'm not suggesting that the accident was your fault.* 2 REPORT VB If one thing **suggests** another, it implies it or makes you think that it is the case. *His expression suggested pleasure at the fact that I had come... The forecasts suggest that there will be higher unemployment.*

suggestion /sədʒestʃə^{0}n/, **suggestions.** 1 COUNT N A **suggestion** is an idea or plan put forward for people to think about. *I made a few suggestions about how we could spend the afternoon.* 2 SING N WITH 'of' If there is a **suggestion** of something, there is a slight sign of it. *He replied to her question with the merest suggestion of a smile.* 3 UNCOUNT N **Suggestion is** the fact of giving people a particular idea by associating it with other ideas. *Such is the power of suggestion that within two minutes the patient is asleep.*

suggestive /sədʒestɪv/. 1 PRED ADJ WITH 'of' If one thing is **suggestive** of another, it gives a hint of it or reminds you of it. *His behaviour was suggestive of a cultured man.* 2 ADJ **Suggestive** remarks cause people to think about sex.

suicidal /sj^{0}uːɪsaɪdə^{0}l/. 1 ADJ People who are **suicidal** want to kill themselves. 2 ADJ **Suicidal** behaviour is so dangerous that it is likely to result in death. *...a suicidal attack.*

suicide /sj^{0}uːɪsaɪd/, **suicides.** 1 UNCOUNT N OR COUNT N People who commit **suicide** deliberately kill themselves. *The founder of British India, Clive, committed suicide in 1774... ...a worsening crisis of neglect, suicide, and crime.* 2 UNCOUNT N You also say that people commit **suicide** when they deliberately do something which ruins their career or position in society. *People had told me it was suicide to admit my mistake.*

suit /sj^{0}uːt/, **suits, suiting, suited.** 1 COUNT N A man's **suit** consists of a matching jacket, trousers, and sometimes a waistcoat. *He arrived at the office in a suit and tie.* 2 COUNT N A woman's **suit** consists of a matching jacket and skirt. *She wore a black suit and a tiny black hat.* 3 COUNT N A **suit** can also be a piece of clothing worn for a particular activity. *She was wearing a short robe over her bathing suit.* 4 VB WITH OBJ If a piece of clothing or a particular style or colour **suits** you, it makes you look attractive. *That coat really suits you.* 5 VB WITH OBJ If you say that something **suits** you, you mean that it is convenient, acceptable or appropriate for you. *Would Monday suit you?... All this suits my purpose very well... A job where I was indoors all day wouldn't suit me.* 6 REFL VB If you **suit** yourself, you do something just because you want to do it, without considering other people. *They have been running their businesses to suit themselves.* 7 COUNT N In a court of law, a **suit** is a legal action taken by one person against another. 8 COUNT N A **suit** is also one of the four types of card in a set of playing cards. These are hearts, diamonds, clubs, and spades. 9 PHRASE If people **follow suit,** they do what someone else has just done. *He bowed his head. Mother and Jenny followed suit.*

suitable /sj^{0}uːtəbə^{0}l/. ADJ Someone or something that is **suitable** for a particular purpose or occasion is right or acceptable for it. *These flats are not really suitable for families with children... ...a list of names of suitable people.* ♦ **suitability** /sj^{0}uːtəbɪlɪ^{1}ti^1/ UNCOUNT N *...the candidate's intellectual ability and suitability for admission.* ♦ **suitably** ADV *See that you are suitably dressed for the weather.*

suitcase /sj^{0}uːtkeɪs/, **suitcases.** COUNT N A **suitcase** is a case for carrying clothes when you are travelling.

suite /swiːt/, **suites.** 1 COUNT N A **suite** is a set of rooms in a hotel. *They always stayed in a suite at the Ritz.* 2 COUNT N A **suite** is also a set of matching furniture for a sitting-room or bathroom. *...a three-piece suite for the lounge.*

suited /sj^{0}uːtɪ^{2}d/. 1 PRED ADJ If something is **suited** to a particular purpose or person, it is right or appropriate for them. *They preferred to join clubs more suited to their tastes... He considered himself ideally suited for the job.* 2 PRED ADJ If a couple is well **suited,** they are likely to have a successful relationship because they have similar personalities and interests.

suitor /sj^{0}uːtə/, **suitors.** COUNT N A woman's **suitor** is a man who wants to marry her; an old-fashioned use. *She had many suitors.*

sulfur /sʌlfə/. See **sulphur.**

sulk /sʌlk/, **sulks, sulking, sulked.** VB If you **sulk,** you are silent and bad-tempered for a while because you are annoyed. *He sulked and behaved badly for weeks after I refused.* Also COUNT N *I thought you were in one of your sulks.*

sulky /sʌlki^1/. ADJ A **sulky** person is bad-tempered and silent because they are annoyed about something. *Sam glowered at him in sulky silence.* ♦ **sulkily** ADV *'I don't want anything,' the boy answered sulkily.*

sullen /sʌlən/. ADJ A **sullen** person is bad-tempered and does not speak much. *...a sullen look in Ned's eyes.* ♦ **sullenly** ADV *'So what?' Thomas said sullenly.*

sulphur /sʌlfə/; spelled **sulfur** in American English. UNCOUNT N **Sulphur** is a yellow substance with a strong unpleasant smell.

sultan /sʌltə^{0}n/, **sultans.** COUNT N A **sultan** is a ruler in some Muslim countries.

sultry /sʌltri^1/. 1 ADJ **Sultry** weather is unpleasantly hot and humid. 2 ADJ A **sultry** woman is attractive in a way that suggests hidden passion.

sum /sʌm/, **sums, summing, summed.** 1 COUNT N A **sum** of money is an amount of it. *...the staggering sum of 212,000 million pounds... Manufacturers spend huge sums of money on advertising their product.* 2 COUNT N A **sum** is a simple calculation in arithmetic. *He couldn't do his sums.* ● See also **lump sum.**

sum up. PHR VB 1 If you **sum up** or **sum** something **up,** you briefly describe the main features of something. *My mood could be summed up by the single word 'boredom'... To sum up: within our society there still exist rampant inequalities.* 2 See also **summing up.**

summarize /sʌməraɪz/, **summarizes, summarizing, summarized;** also spelled **summarise.** VB WITH OR WITHOUT OBJ If you **summarize** something, you give a brief description of its main points. *The seven catego-*

ries can be briefly summarized as follows... To summarize, she is intuitive and decisive.

summary /sʌməri[1]/, **summaries. 1** COUNT N A **summary** is a short account of something giving the main points but not the details. *Here is a summary of the plot.* **2** ATTRIB ADJ **Summary** actions are done without delay when something else should have been done first or done instead. *...mass arrests and summary executions.* ♦ **summarily** ADV *He summarily dismissed our problem as unimportant.*

summer /sʌmə/, **summers.** COUNT N OR UNCOUNT N **Summer** is the season between spring and autumn. In summer the weather is usually warm or hot. *I am going to Greece this summer... ...summer holidays.*

summer school, summer schools. COUNT N OR UNCOUNT N A **summer school** is an educational course on a particular subject that is run during the summer.

summertime /sʌmətaɪm/. UNCOUNT N **Summertime** is the period of time during which summer lasts.

summing up, summings up. COUNT N In a court of law, the **summing up** is a summary of all the evidence that has been presented at the trial.

summit /sʌmɪt/, **summits. 1** COUNT N A **summit** is a meeting between the leaders of different countries to discuss important matters. *Western leaders are gathering for this week's Ottawa summit... ...a summit meeting.* **2** COUNT N The **summit** of a mountain is the top of it.

summon /sʌmən/, **summons, summoning, summoned.** VB WITH OBJ If you **summon** someone, you order them to come to you. *He summoned his secretary... He was summoned to report on the accident.*

summon up. PHR VB If you **summon up** your strength or courage, you make a great effort to be strong or brave. *He eventually summoned up the courage to ask them if Melanie was all right... ...if you can't summon up enough energy to get up early.*

summons /sʌmənz/, **summonses, summonsing, summonsed. 1** COUNT N A **summons** is an order to come and see someone. *I waited in my office for a summons from the boss.* **2** COUNT N A **summons** is also an official order to appear in court. **3** VB WITH OBJ If someone **is summonsed,** they are officially ordered to appear in court.

sumptuous /sʌmptjʊəs/. ADJ Something that is **sumptuous** is magnificent and obviously expensive. *...sumptuous furnishings.*

sun /sʌn/, **suns, sunning, sunned. 1** SING N The **sun** is the ball of fire in the sky that the Earth goes round, and that gives us heat and light. **2** UNCOUNT N OR SING N WITH SUPP You also refer to the light and heat that reach us from the sun as **sun.** *You need plenty of sun and fresh air... We all sat in the sun.* **3** REFL VB If you **sun** yourself, you sit or lie where the sun shines on you. *He spent Saturday sunning himself on the beach.*

sunbathe /sʌnbeɪθ/, **sunbathes, sunbathing, sunbathed.** VB When people **sunbathe,** they sit or lie in a place where the sun shines on them, in order to get a suntan. *I spent my afternoons sunbathing.*

sunburn /sʌnbɜːn/. UNCOUNT N If someone has **sunburn,** their skin is red and sore because they have spent too much time in the sun.

sunburnt /sʌnbɜːnt/; also spelled **sunburned. 1** ADJ Someone who is **sunburnt** has sore red skin because they have spent too much time in the sun. *His neck was badly sunburnt.* **2** ADJ You can also describe someone as **sunburnt** when they have very brown skin because they have spent a lot of time in the sunshine. *Carlo was handsomely sunburned.*

Sunday /sʌndi[1]/, **Sundays.** UNCOUNT N OR COUNT N **Sunday** is the day after Saturday and before Monday.

sundial /sʌndaɪəl/, **sundials.** COUNT N A **sundial** is a device used for telling the time. It consists of a pointer which casts a shadow on a flat base which is marked with the hours.

sundown /sʌndaʊn/. UNCOUNT N **Sundown** is the same as sunset; an American use. *It was about an hour before sundown.*

sundry /sʌndri[1]/. **1** ATTRIB ADJ If you refer to **sundry** things or people, you mean several things or people of various sorts; a formal use. *...stools, wicker mats, food bowls, and sundry other objects.* **2** PHRASE **All and sundry** means everyone; an informal use. *She was fondly known to all and sundry as 'Little Madge'.*

sunflower /sʌnflaʊə/, **sunflowers.** COUNT N A **sunflower** is a tall plant with large yellow flowers.

sung /sʌŋ/. **Sung** is the past participle of **sing.**

sunglasses /sʌnglɑːsɪz/. PLURAL N **Sunglasses** are spectacles with dark lenses to protect your eyes from bright sunlight.

sunk /sʌŋk/. **Sunk** is the past participle of **sink.**

sunken /sʌŋkə°n/. **1** ATTRIB ADJ **Sunken** is used to describe things that have sunk to the bottom of a large expanse of water. *...the remains of a sunken battleship.* **2** ATTRIB ADJ A **sunken** object or area is built below the level of the surrounding area. *...a sunken garden.* **3** ADJ **Sunken** cheeks or eyes or a **sunken** chest curve inwards and make a person look thin and unwell.

sunlight /sʌnlaɪt/. UNCOUNT N **Sunlight** is the light that comes from the sun. *The sea sparkled in the brilliant sunlight.*

sunlit /sʌnlɪt/. ADJ **Sunlit** places are brightly lit by the sun. *...the sunlit slopes of the valley.*

sunny /sʌni[1]/, **sunnier, sunniest. 1** ADJ When it is **sunny,** the sun is shining. **2** ADJ **Sunny** places are brightly lit by the sun. *...a lovely sunny region of green hills and valleys.*

sunrise /sʌnraɪz/, **sunrises. 1** UNCOUNT N **Sunrise** is the time in the morning when the sun first appears. *They left their camp at sunrise.* **2** COUNT N OR UNCOUNT N A **sunrise** is the colours and light that you see in the sky when the sun first appears. *...the beautiful sunrise over the sea.*

sunset /sʌnsɛt/, **sunsets. 1** UNCOUNT N **Sunset** is the time in the evening when the sun disappears. *We'll leave just before sunset.* **2** COUNT N OR UNCOUNT N A **sunset** is the colours and light that you see in the sky when the sun disappears in the evening. *You must see some beautiful sunsets here.*

sunshine /sʌnʃaɪn/. UNCOUNT N **Sunshine** is the light that comes from the sun. *Families were scattered along the beach enjoying the sunshine.*

sunstroke /sʌnstrəʊk/. UNCOUNT N **Sunstroke** is an illness caused by spending too much time in the sunshine.

suntan /sʌntæn/, **suntans.** COUNT N If you have a **suntan,** the sun has turned your skin darker than usual.

sun-tanned /sʌntænd/. ADJ If you are **sun-tanned,** your skin is darker than usual because you have spent time in the hot sunshine. *You look sort of sun-tanned.*

super /sj°uːpə/. **1** ADJ **Super** means very nice or good; an informal use. *I've got a super secretary.* **2** ATTRIB ADJ **Super** is also used to describe things that are larger or better than similar things. *...new super warships.*

superb /sj°ʊpɜːb/. ADJ If something is **superb,** it is very good indeed. *The children's library is superb.* ♦ **superbly** ADV *...a small but superbly equipped workshop.*

supercilious /sj°uːpəsɪlɪəs/. ADJ **Supercilious** people are scornful of other people and think that they are superior to them; used showing disapproval. *...a slow supercilious smile.*

superficial /sj°uːpəfɪʃə°l/. **1** ADJ Something that is **superficial** involves only the most obvious or general aspects of something. *...a superficial knowledge of linguistics... The new scheme has superficial similarities with the old one.* ♦ **superficially** ADV OR SENTENCE ADV *Superficially it looks rather harmless.* **2** ADJ **Superficial** people do not care very deeply about anything serious or important. **3** ADJ **Superficial** wounds are not very deep or severe.

superfluous /sj°uːpɜːfluəs/. ADJ Something that is **superfluous** is unnecessary or is no longer needed. *Certain parts of our religion have become superfluous... Maps were superfluous with Eddie around.*

superhuman /sj°uːpəhjuːmən/. ADJ If you describe a quality that someone has as **superhuman,** you mean that it is greater than that of ordinary people. *You must have superhuman strength... I controlled myself with a superhuman effort.*

superimpose /sj°uːpə°rɪmpəʊz/, **superimposes, superimposing, superimposed.** VB WITH OBJ If one image **is superimposed** on another, the first one is on top of the second. *Three photos were superimposed one on top of the other.*

superintendent /sj°uːpə°rɪntɛndənt/, **superintendents. 1** COUNT N A **superintendent** in the police force is an officer above the rank of inspector. **2** COUNT N A **superintendent** is a person who is responsible for a particular thing or department.

superior /sj°uːpɪərɪə/, **superiors. 1** ADJ To be **superior** to something or someone means to be better than them. *I secretly feel superior to him... The school prided itself upon its policy of providing a superior education.* ♦ **superiority** /sj°uːpɪərɪɒrɪ[1]ti[1]/ UNCOUNT N *...the great superiority of Hoyland over younger abstract painters.* **2** ADJ A person in an organization who is **superior** to someone else has more authority than them. *These matters are better left to someone superior to you.* Also COUNT N *He was called to the office of a superior to be reprimanded.* **3** ADJ Someone who is **superior** behaves in a way which shows that they believe they are better than other people. *'You wouldn't understand,' Clarissa said in a superior way.*

superlative /sj°uːpɜːlətɪv/, **superlatives.** COUNT N In grammar, a **superlative** is the form of an adjective which indicates that the person or object being described has more of a particular quality or character than anyone or anything else.

supermarket /sj°uːpəmɑːkɪt/, **supermarkets.** COUNT N A **supermarket** is a large shop selling all kinds of food and household goods. You select the food and goods yourself and pay for them before leaving.

supernatural /sj°uːpənætʃrəl/. **1** ADJ **Supernatural** creatures, forces, and events are believed by some people to exist or happen, although they are impossible according to scientific laws. *...witchcraft, the supernatural power to cure or control.* **2** SING N Supernatural things and events are referred to as the **supernatural.** *Do you believe in the supernatural?*

superpower /sj°uːpəpaʊə/, **superpowers.** COUNT N A **superpower** is a very powerful country. In the past, when people talked about 'the superpowers', they usually meant the USA and the former USSR.

supersede /sj°uːpəsiːd/, **supersedes, superseding, superseded.** VB WITH OBJ If one thing **supersedes** another thing that is older, it replaces it. *Steam locomotives were superseded by diesel... New ways of thinking superseded older ones.*

supersonic /sj°uːpəsɒnɪk/. ADJ **Supersonic** aircraft travel faster than the speed of sound.

superstition /sj°uːpəstɪʃə°n/, **superstitions.** UNCOUNT N OR COUNT N **Superstition** is belief in things that are not real or possible, for example magic. *They were peasants filled with ignorance and superstition... ...old prejudices and superstitions.*

superstitious /sj°uːpəstɪʃəs/. ADJ People who are **superstitious** believe in things that are not real or possible, for example magic. *...a superstitious man with an unnatural fear of the dark.*

supervise /sj°uːpəvaɪz/, **supervises, supervising, supervised.** VB WITH OR WITHOUT OBJ If you **supervise** a person or the activity they are doing, you make sure that they behave properly. *Miss Young had three netball games to supervise... One evening, when there were no staff to supervise her, she walked out of the hospital.* ♦ **supervision** /sj°uːpəvɪʒə°n/ UNCOUNT N *They are under the supervision of social workers.*

supervisor /sj°uːpəvaɪzə/, **supervisors.** COUNT N A **supervisor** is a person who supervises workers or students. *The maintenance supervisor dispatched a crew to repair the damage.*

supper /sʌpə/, **suppers.** UNCOUNT N OR COUNT N **Supper** is a meal eaten in the early part of the evening or one eaten just before you go to bed at night. *He insisted on staying for supper... ...tea, talks and a working supper.*

supplant /səplɑːnt/, **supplants, supplanting, supplanted.** VB WITH OBJ To **supplant** something or someone means to take their place; a formal use. *Electric cars may one day supplant petrol-driven ones... He began his campaign to supplant Gaitskell as party leader.*

supple /sʌpə°l/. ADJ Someone or something that is **supple** moves and bends easily. *She had once been slim and supple... The leather straps were supple with use.*

supplement /sʌplɪmə[2]nt/, **supplements, supplementing, supplemented. 1** VB WITH OBJ If you **supplement** something, you add something to it in order to make it more adequate. *They had to get a job to supplement the family income... I supplemented my diet with vitamin pills.* Also COUNT N *They will sometimes eat fish as a supplement to their natural diet.* **2** COUNT N A magazine or newspaper **supplement** is a separate part of a magazine or newspaper.

supplementary /sʌplɪmɛntə°ri[1]/. ATTRIB ADJ **Supplementary** is used to describe something that is added to another thing in order to make it more adequate. *You can claim a supplementary pension... They asked if I was on supplementary benefit.*

supplier /sə°plaɪə/, **suppliers.** COUNT N A **supplier** is a person or firm that provides you with goods or equipment. *...textile suppliers.*

supply /səplaɪ/, **supplies, supplying, supplied. 1** VB WITH OBJ If you **supply** someone with something, you provide them with it. *I can supply you with food and drink... Germany is supplying the steel for the new pipeline.* **2** COUNT N A **supply** of something is an amount of it which is available for use. *Bill had his own supply of whisky... Most houses now have lavatories and a hot water supply.* **3** PLURAL N **Supplies** are food, equipment, and other things needed by a group of people, for example by an army or people going on an expedition. *The plane had been ferrying military supplies over the border.* **4** UNCOUNT N **Supply** is the fact of goods and services being produced and made available. *Economic stability can be reached if supply and demand are balanced.* **5** PHRASE If something is **in short supply,** there is very little of it available.

support /sə°pɔːt/, **supports, supporting, supported. 1** VB WITH OBJ If you **support** someone or their aims, you agree with them and try to help them to succeed. *A lot of building workers supported the campaign...*

His work colleagues refused to support him. Also UNCOUNT N *The party declared its support for the campaign.* **2** VB WITH OBJ If you **support** a sports team, you want them to win and perhaps watch their games regularly. ♦ **supporter** /səpɔːtə/ COUNT N WITH SUPP *He's an Everton supporter.* **3** UNCOUNT N If you give **support** to someone during a difficult time, you are kind to them and help them. *They find it hard to give their children emotional support.* **4** VB WITH OBJ If something **supports** an object, it is underneath it and holding it up. *...the steel girders that supported the walkway.* **5** COUNT N A **support** is something that supports something else. *Most large scale buildings now have steel supports.* **6** REFL VB If you **support** yourself, you prevent yourself from falling by holding onto something. *I clung to the outside edge of the door to support myself.* Also UNCOUNT N *She was standing behind the ladder and holding on to it for support.* **7** UNCOUNT N Financial **support** is money provided to enable a firm or organization to continue. *These industries were dependent on state support.* **8** VB WITH OBJ If you **support** someone, you provide them with money or the things that they need. *He has a wife and three children to support.* **9** VB WITH OBJ If a fact **supports** a statement or a theory, it helps to show that it is true or correct. *There was simply no visible evidence to support such a theory.* Also UNCOUNT N *Scholars have found little support for this interpretation.*

supportive /səpɔːtɪv/. ADJ If you are **supportive**, you are kind and helpful to someone at a difficult time.

suppose /səpəʊz/, **supposes, supposing, supposed.** **1** REPORT VB OR VB WITH OBJ If you **suppose** that something is true, you think that it is likely to be true. *He supposed that MPs were unaware of the danger... The situation was even worse than was supposed... They'd supposed it to be sabotage.* **2** CONJ You use **suppose** or **supposing** when you are considering a possible situation or action and trying to think what effects it would have. *Suppose we don't say a word, and somebody else finds out about it... Supposing something should go wrong, what would you do then?* **3** PHRASE You say **I suppose** to show that you are not certain or enthusiastic about something. *I suppose he wasn't trying hard enough... I don't suppose you would be prepared to stay in Edinburgh?... 'So it was worth doing?'—'I suppose so.'*

supposed; pronounced /səpəʊzd/ for meaning 1 and /səpəʊzd/ or /səpəʊsd/ for meanings 2, 3, and 4. **1** ATTRIB ADJ You use **supposed** to express doubt about a way of describing someone or something that is generally believed. *...his supposed ancestor, the pirate Henry Morgan... ...the supposed benefits of a progressive welfare state.* ♦ **supposedly** ADV *...a robot supposedly capable of understanding spoken commands.* **2** PRED ADJ WITH TO-INF If something is **supposed** to be done, it should be done because of a rule, instruction, or custom. *You are supposed to report it to the police as soon as possible... I'm not supposed to talk to you about this.* **3** PRED ADJ WITH TO-INF If something is **supposed** to happen, it is planned or intended to happen, but often does not. *I was supposed to go last summer... A machine at the entrance is supposed to check the tickets.* **4** PRED ADJ WITH TO-INF If something is **supposed** to be true, people generally think that it is true. *They are supposed to be the best in London... The hill was supposed to be haunted by a ghost.*

supposition /sʌpəzɪʃən/, **suppositions.** COUNT N A **supposition** is an idea or statement which is thought or assumed to be true; a formal use. *The supposition is that the infiltrators knew the raids were to take place.*

suppress /səprɛs/, **suppresses, suppressing, suppressed.** **1** VB WITH OBJ If an army or government **suppresses** an activity, they prevent it from continuing. *The army soon suppressed the revolt.* ♦ **suppression** /səprɛʃən/ UNCOUNT N *...the suppression of freedom.* **2** VB WITH OBJ If someone **suppresses** a piece of information, they prevent it from becoming known. *The committee's report has been suppressed.* ♦ **suppression** UNCOUNT N *...the deliberate suppression of information.* **3** VB WITH OBJ If you **suppress** your feelings, you prevent yourself from expressing them. *Suppressing her annoyance, she smiled at him... She was struggling to suppress her sobs.* ♦ **suppression** UNCOUNT N *...the polite suppression of a yawn.*

supremacy /sjʊprɛməsi/. UNCOUNT N If one group of people has **supremacy** over another group, they are more powerful than the second group. *Their political supremacy continued.*

supreme /sjuːpriːm/. **1** ATTRIB ADJ **Supreme** is used in a title to indicate that a person or group is at the highest level of an organization. *The Supreme Commander ordered their release... ...the Supreme Court.* **2** ADJ You also use **supreme** to emphasize the greatness of something. *...one of this century's supreme achievements... ...tasks of supreme importance.* ♦ **supremely** SUBMOD *...a supremely important moment.*

sure /ʃʊə, ʃɔː/, **surer, surest.** **1** PRED ADJ If you are **sure** about something, you are certain that it is true and have no doubts about it. *I'm sure she's right... I'm not quite sure but I think it's half past five... The only thing we're sure about is that it's a boy... Are you sure you won't have another drink?* **2** PRED ADJ WITH 'of' If you are **sure** of yourself, you are very confident about your abilities or opinions. **3** PRED ADJ WITH 'of' If someone is **sure** of getting something, they are certain to get it. *We can be sure of success... You could not always be sure of winning.* **4** PRED ADJ WITH TO-INF If something is **sure** to happen, it will certainly happen. *He was sure to see her again... We're sure to get a place.* **5** ADJ **Sure** is used to describe a method or system which is reliable or accurate. *Wood dust beneath a piece of furniture is a sure sign of woodworm... She had a sure grasp of the subject.* **6** CONVENTION **Sure** is an informal way of saying 'yes'. *'Can I go with you?'—'Sure.'* **7** ADV You can also use **sure** to emphasize what you are saying; an informal American use. *He sure is cute... You sure do have an interesting job.*

PHRASES • If you **make sure** about something, you check it or take action to see that it is done. *He glanced over his shoulder to make sure that there was nobody listening.* • If you say that something is **for sure** or that you know it **for sure,** you mean that it is definitely true or will definitely happen; an informal use. *One thing was for sure, there was nothing wrong with Allen's eyesight.* • You say **sure enough** to confirm that something is really true. *'The baby's crying,' she said. Sure enough, a yelling noise was coming from upstairs.*

surely /ʃʊəli, ʃɔː-/. **1** SENTENCE ADV You use **surely** to emphasize that you think something is true, and often to express surprise that other people do not agree. *He surely knew the danger... She was surely one of the rarest women of our time... You don't mind that surely?* **2** PHRASE If something is happening **slowly but surely,** it is happening gradually and cannot be stopped. *Slowly but surely we're becoming a computer-centred society.*

surf /sɜːf/. UNCOUNT N The **surf** is the mass of white foam formed by waves as they fall on the shore. *We watched the children play in the surf.*

surface /sɜːfɪs/, **surfaces, surfacing, surfaced.** **1** COUNT N The **surface** of something is the top part of it or the outside of it. *A gentle breeze rippled the surface of the sea... ...holes in the road surface.* **2** COUNT N The **surface** of a situation is what can be seen easily rather than what is not immediately obvious. *His job was not as enviable as it appeared on the surface... This dispute first came to the surface in 1962... You don't have to look far to encounter the tensions beneath the surface.* **3** VB If someone or something under water **surfaces,** they come up to the surface of the water. *Bobby surfaced twenty feet in front of the boat.*

surfeit /sɜːfɪt/. SING N If there is a **surfeit** of something, there is too much of it; a formal use. *Recently there has been a surfeit of cricket on the television.*

surfing /sɜːfɪŋ/. UNCOUNT N **Surfing** is the sport or activity of riding on top of a big wave while standing or lying on a special board.

surge /sɜːdʒ/, **surges, surging, surged.** **1** COUNT N A **surge** is a sudden great increase in something. *A surge of activity spread through the party... ...a surge in sales of Waugh's novels.* **2** VB WITH ADJUNCT If an emotion or sensation **surges** in you, you feel it suddenly and powerfully; a literary use. *Hope surged in Peter... Relief surged through him.* Also COUNT N *She felt a surge of affection for him... ...a surge of jealousy.* **3** VB WITH ADJUNCT If people or vehicles **surge** forward, they move forward suddenly in a mass. *When the doors were flung open, a crowd surged in.* ♦ **surging** ATTRIB ADJ *...surging crowds of demonstrators.* **4** VB If water **surges,** it moves forward suddenly and powerfully. *...the tides surging over the rocks.*

surgeon /sɜːdʒən/, **surgeons.** COUNT N A **surgeon** is a doctor who performs surgery. *...a brain surgeon.*

surgery /sɜːdʒəri/, **surgeries.** **1** UNCOUNT N **Surgery** is medical treatment which involves cutting open a person's body in order to repair or remove a diseased or damaged part. *He has had major abdominal surgery.* **2** COUNT N A **surgery** is the room or house where a doctor or dentist works; a British use. **3** COUNT N OR UNCOUNT N A doctor's **surgery** is also the period of time each day when he or she sees patients at the surgery; a British use. *I'll be in for morning surgery at ten.* **4** See also **plastic surgery.**

surgical /sɜːdʒɪkəl/. ATTRIB ADJ **Surgical** means relating to surgery. *...surgical instruments... Some people can have their vision restored by a surgical operation.* ♦ **surgically** ADV *The cataract can then be removed surgically.*

surly /sɜːli/. ADJ A **surly** person is rude and bad-tempered. *His voice was surly.*

surmise /səmaɪz/, **surmises, surmising, surmised.** REPORT VB If you **surmise** that something is true, you guess that it is true, although it may not be; a formal use. *The last question, Turing surmised, was the key one.*

surmount /səmaʊnt/, **surmounts, surmounting, surmounted.** **1** VB WITH OBJ If you **surmount** a difficulty, you deal successfully with it. *She managed to surmount this obstacle.* **2** VB WITH OBJ If something **is surmounted** by a particular thing, that thing is on top of it; a formal use. *The column is surmounted by a statue.*

surname /sɜːneɪm/, **surnames.** COUNT N Your **surname** is the name that you share with other members of your family. *'What's your surname?'—'Barker.'*

surpass /səpɑːs/, **surpasses, surpassing, surpassed.** VB WITH OBJ To **surpass** someone or something means to be better than them, to do better than them, or to have more of a particular quality than them; a formal use. *The women were able to equal or surpass the men who worked beside them... In my opinion the jewel is surpassed in beauty by the other ornaments.*

surplus /sɜːpləs/, **surpluses.** COUNT N OR UNCOUNT N If there is a **surplus** of something, there is more than is needed. *...the recent worldwide surplus of crude oil... In this continent there is a vast surplus of workers.* Also ADJ *...surplus grain.*

surprise /səpraɪz/, **surprises, surprising, surprised.** **1** COUNT N A **surprise** is an unexpected event. *This ruling came as a surprise to everyone... 'Why don't you tell me?'—'Because I want it to be a surprise.'* Also MOD *...a surprise attack.* **2** UNCOUNT N **Surprise** is the feeling that you have when something unexpected happens. *Boylan looked at her in surprise... To my surprise, he nodded and agreed.* **3** VB WITH OBJ If something **surprises** you, you did not expect it. *I surprised everyone by gobbling an enormous lunch... It would not surprise me if he ends up in jail.* **4** VB WITH OBJ If you **surprise** someone, you attack them or find them when they are not expecting it. *They were surprised by a unit of US marines during the night... She feared her parents would return and surprise them.*

surprised /səpraɪzd/. ADJ If you are **surprised** by something, you have a feeling of surprise, because it is unexpected or unusual. *The twins were very surprised to see Ralph... I was surprised at the number of bicycles.*

surprising /səpraɪzɪŋ/. ADJ Something that is **surprising** is unexpected or unusual and makes you feel surprised. *He leapt out of the car with surprising agility... It was surprising how much money she managed to earn.* ♦ **surprisingly** SUBMOD OR SENTENCE ADV *It was surprisingly cheap... Not surprisingly the proposal met with hostile reactions.*

surreal /sərɪəl/. ADJ **Surreal** means the same as surrealistic.

surrealist /sərɪəlɪst/. ATTRIB ADJ **Surrealist** paintings show strange objects or strange combinations of objects.

surrealistic /sərɪəlɪstɪk/. ADJ A situation that is **surrealistic** is very strange and like a dream. *The search had a kind of mad, surrealistic quality.*

surrender /sərɛndə/, **surrenders, surrendering, surrendered.** **1** VB If you **surrender,** you stop fighting or resisting someone and agree that you have been beaten. *All the British forces surrendered... The protesters surrendered to the police after about an hour.* Also UNCOUNT N *They tried to starve us into surrender.* **2** VB If you **surrender** to a force, temptation, or feeling, you allow it to gain control over you. *...surrendering to a sense of apathy.* **3** VB WITH OBJ If you **surrender** something, you let someone else have it. *The United States would never surrender this territory.* Also UNCOUNT N *...the surrender of liberties.*

surreptitious /sʌrəptɪʃəs/. ADJ A **surreptitious** action is done secretly. *He began paying surreptitious visits to betting shops.* ♦ **surreptitiously** ADV *Rudolph looked surreptitiously at his watch.*

surrogate /sʌrəgeɪt, -gət/, **surrogates.** ATTRIB ADJ You use **surrogate** to describe a person or thing that acts as a substitute for someone or something else; a formal use. *Uncle Paul has become a surrogate father to me.* Also COUNT N *...a surrogate for another person.*

surround /səraʊnd/, **surrounds, surrounding, surrounded.** **1** VB WITH OBJ If one thing **surrounds** another, it is situated all round it. *Muscles surround blood vessels in the body... The house was surrounded by high walls.* **2** VB WITH OBJ If people **surround** a person or place, they position themselves all the way round them. *Don't get near him. Just surround him and keep him there.* **3** VB WITH OBJ If problems or dangers

surround something, there are problems or dangers associated with it. *...the dangers which surround us... ...the uncertainty surrounding the future of the railways.* 4 REFL VB WITH 'with' If you **surround** yourself with things, you make sure that you have a lot of them near you all the time. *Get involved in social activities and surround yourself with friends.*

surrounding /səraundɪŋ/, **surroundings.** 1 ATTRIB ADJ You use **surrounding** to describe the area which is all around a particular place. *Foxes started coming in from the surrounding countryside... ...the roofs of the surrounding buildings.* 2 PLURAL N You can refer to the place where you live or where you are as your **surroundings.** *We used to live in nice surroundings.*

surveillance /səveɪləns/. UNCOUNT N **Surveillance** is the careful watching of someone, especially by the police or army; a formal use. *Everyone we knew was under surveillance.*

survey, surveys, surveying, surveyed; pronounced /səveɪ/ when it is a verb and /sɜːveɪ/ when it is a noun. 1 VB WITH OBJ If you **survey** something, you look carefully at the whole of it; a formal use. *She stepped back and surveyed her work.* 2 VB WITH OBJ To **survey** a building or piece of land means to examine it carefully in order to make a report or a plan of its structure and features. 3 COUNT N A **survey** is a detailed investigation of something, for example people's behaviour or opinions. *...a national survey of eye diseases among children.* 4 COUNT N A **survey** is also an examination of land or a house in order to report on its condition and features.

surveyor /səveɪə/, **surveyors.** COUNT N A **surveyor** is a person whose job is to survey houses or land.

survival /səvaɪvəl/, **survivals.** 1 UNCOUNT N **Survival** is the fact of continuing to live or exist in spite of great danger or difficulty. *What are their chances of survival?... ...the day-to-day struggle for survival.* 2 COUNT N Something that is a **survival** from an earlier time has continued to exist from that time; a formal use. *The royal house is full of survivals from many centuries.*

survive /səvaɪv/, **survives, surviving, survived.** 1 VB WITH OR WITHOUT OBJ If someone **survives,** they continue to live or exist in spite of great danger or difficulty. *Four of his brothers died: the fifth survived... Very few people survived the immediate effects of the explosion.* 2 VB WITH OBJ If you **survive** someone, you continue to live after they have died. *She will probably survive me by many years.* 3 VB WITH OR WITHOUT OBJ If something **survives,** it continues to exist. *I doubt whether the National Health Service will survive to the end of the century... The project survived three changes of government.* 4 VB WITH OR WITHOUT OBJ If you **survive** a difficult experience, you manage to cope with it and do not let it affect you badly. *She survived the divorce pretty well... You have to make difficult decisions to survive in business.*

survivor /səvaɪvə/, **survivors.** 1 COUNT N A **survivor** of a disaster is someone who continues to live in spite of coming close to death. *I talked to one of the survivors of the crash.* 2 COUNT N Someone who is a **survivor** is able to carry on with their life in spite of difficult experiences. *...one of life's survivors.*

susceptible /səseptɪbəl/. 1 PRED ADJ If you are **susceptible** to something, you are likely to be influenced by it. *We are all susceptible to advertising.* 2 ADJ If you are **susceptible** to a disease or injury, you are likely to be affected by it. *Many people were lightly dressed and therefore susceptible to burns.*

suspect, suspects, suspecting, suspected; pronounced /səspekt/ when it is a verb, and /sʌspekt/ when it is a noun or adjective. 1 REPORT VB If you **suspect** that something is the case, you think that it is likely to be true. *People suspected that a secret deal had been made... He suspected murder.* 2 VB WITH OBJ If you **suspect** something, you doubt if it can be trusted or is reliable. *I had many reasons for suspecting this approach.* 3 VB WITH OBJ If you **suspect** someone of a crime, you think that they are guilty of it. *He was suspected of treason.* 4 COUNT N A **suspect** is a person who is thought to be guilty of a crime. *Last week police finally had a suspect for the murder.* 5 ADJ If something is **suspect,** it cannot be trusted or regarded as genuine. *My friendliness was viewed as suspect by some people.*

suspend /səspend/, **suspends, suspending, suspended.** 1 VB WITH OBJ AND ADJUNCT If something **is suspended** from a high place, it is hanging from that place. *A model aeroplane was suspended above the stage.* 2 VB WITH OBJ If you **suspend** something, you delay or stop it for a while. *The builders suspended their work.* 3 VB WITH OBJ If someone **is suspended** from their job, they are told not to do it for a period of time, usually as a punishment. *The people involved in the incident have been suspended from their duties.*

suspender /səspendə/, **suspenders.** COUNT N **Suspenders** are fastenings which hang down from a belt and hold up a woman's stockings.

suspense /səspens/. 1 UNCOUNT N **Suspense** is a state of excitement or anxiety about something that is going to happen soon. *I try to add an element of suspense and mystery to my novels.* 2 PHRASE If you keep someone **in suspense,** you delay telling them something that they are eager to know about. *I did not leave him in suspense, but quickly informed him that he had passed.*

suspension /səspenʃən/, **suspensions.** 1 UNCOUNT N The **suspension** of something is the act of delaying or stopping it for a while. *...the suspension of all social security payments.* 2 UNCOUNT N OR COUNT N Someone's **suspension** is their removal from a job for a period of time, usually as a punishment. *If he is found guilty, he could face suspension from duty... ...suspensions without pay.* 3 UNCOUNT N A vehicle's **suspension** consists of the springs and other devices, which give a smooth ride over bumps in the road.

suspension bridge, suspension bridges. COUNT N A **suspension bridge** is a bridge supported from above by cables.

suspicion /səspɪʃən/, **suspicions.** 1 UNCOUNT N OR COUNT N **Suspicion** is the feeling that someone should not be trusted or that something is wrong. *Derek shared Lynn's suspicion of Michael... I had aroused his suspicions last week.* 2 PHRASE If someone is **under suspicion,** they are suspected of being guilty of something such as a crime. 3 COUNT N A **suspicion** is a feeling that something is probably true or is likely to happen. *Investigators have strong suspicions of a clandestine trade.*

suspicious /səspɪʃəs/. 1 ADJ If you are **suspicious** of someone, you do not trust them. *The policeman on duty became suspicious of the youth... He shot a suspicious glance at me.* ♦ **suspiciously** ADV *'Why are you laughing?' Rachel asked suspiciously.* 2 ADJ **Suspicious** things make you think that something is wrong with a situation. *There were suspicious circumstances about his death... Several suspicious aircraft were spotted.* ♦ **suspiciously** SUBMOD *The lump was suspiciously big.*

sustain /səsteɪn/, **sustains, sustaining, sustained.** 1 VB WITH OBJ If you **sustain** something, you continue it or maintain it for a period of time. *They do not have enough money to sustain a strike... The problem was how to sustain public interest.* ♦ **sustained** ADJ *The enemy mounted a sustained attack on the castle.* 2 VB WITH OBJ If food or drink **sustains** you, it gives you energy and strength; a formal use. *They had nothing to sustain them all day except two cups of coffee.* 3 VB WITH OBJ If something **sustains** you, it supports you by giving you help, strength, or encouragement. *It is his belief in God that sustains him.*

sustenance /sʌstənəns/. UNCOUNT N **Sustenance** is food and drink which helps to keep you strong and healthy; a formal use. *We derive our sustenance from the land.*

SW. SW is a written abbreviation for 'south-west'.

swab /swɒb/, **swabs.** COUNT N A **swab** is a small piece of cotton wool used for cleaning a wound.

swagger /swægə/, **swaggers, swaggering, swaggered.** VB If you **swagger,** you walk in a proud way, holding your body upright and swinging your hips. *She swaggered back to her place by the window.* Also SING N *Bernard left the room with a swagger.*

swallow /swɒləʊ/, **swallows, swallowing, swallowed.** 1 VB WITH OBJ If you **swallow** something, you cause it to go from your mouth down into your stomach. *He swallowed more pills.* Also COUNT N *Breen took a swallow of brandy.* 2 VB If you **swallow,** you make a movement in your throat as if you are swallowing something, often because you are nervous or frightened. *He swallowed and closed his eyes.* 3 VB WITH OBJ If someone **swallows** a story or a statement, they believe it completely. *I sometimes think that crowds will swallow whole any political speech whatsoever.* 4 VB WITH OBJ If you **swallow** an insult or unkind remark, you accept it and do not protest. *She swallowed the sarcasm and got on with her work.* ● to **swallow** your **pride:** see **pride.** 5 COUNT N A **swallow** is also a small bird with pointed wings and a forked tail.

swam /swæm/. **Swam** is the past tense of **swim.**

swamp /swɒmp/, **swamps, swamping, swamped.** 1 COUNT N OR UNCOUNT N A **swamp** is an area of wet land with wild plants growing in it. *This area is full of small islands and swamps... It smelled like rotten swamp.* 2 VB WITH OBJ If something **swamps** a place or object, it fills it with water. *Sudden heavy seas swamped the ship.* 3 VB WITH OBJ If you **are swamped** by things, you have more of them than you can deal with. *We've been swamped with applicants.*

swan /swɒn/, **swans.** COUNT N A **swan** is a large white bird with a long neck that lives on rivers and lakes.

swap /swɒp/, **swaps, swapping, swapped;** also spelled **swop.** 1 VB WITH OBJ When you **swap** something with someone, you give it to them and receive something else in exchange. *He swapped a dozen goats for a female calf.* Also COUNT N *Let's do a swap.* 2 VB WITH OBJ AND 'for' If you **swap** one thing for another, you remove the first thing and replace it with the second. *I swapped my cap for a large black waterproof hat.* 3 VB WITH OBJ When you **swap** stories or opinions with someone, you tell each other stories or give each other your opinions. *They swap amusing stories about the place.*

swarm /swɔːm/, **swarms, swarming, swarmed.** 1 COUNT N A **swarm** of bees or other insects is a large group of them flying together. *The showers brought swarms of flying insects to torment them.* 2 VB When bees or other insects **swarm,** they move or fly in a large group. 3 VB WITH ADJUNCT When people **swarm** somewhere, they move there quickly in a large group. *They swarmed across the bridge.* 4 COUNT N A **swarm** of people is a large group of them moving about quickly. *She left amid a swarm of photographers.* 5 VB WITH 'with' If a place **is swarming** with people, it is full of people moving about in a busy way. *The White House garden was swarming with security men.*

swarthy /swɔːðɪ/. ADJ A **swarthy** person has a dark complexion.

swat /swɒt/, **swats, swatting, swatted.** VB WITH OBJ If you **swat** an insect, you hit it with a quick, swinging movement.

swathe /sweɪð/, **swathes;** a literary word. 1 COUNT N A **swathe** is a long strip of cloth, especially one that is wrapped round someone or something. *...balconies strewn with swathes of silk.* 2 COUNT N A **swathe** of land is a long strip of land that is different from the land on either side of it. *...new roads cutting swathes through our countryside.*

swathed /sweɪðd/. PRED ADJ WITH 'in' If someone is **swathed** in cloth, they are completely wrapped in it; a literary use. *She was swathed in bandages.*

sway /sweɪ/, **sways, swaying, swayed.** 1 VB When people or things **sway,** they lean or swing slowly from one side to the other. *She sang and swayed from side to side... ...trees swaying in the wind.* 2 VB WITH OBJ If you **are swayed** by something that you hear or read, it influences you. *Do not be swayed by glamorous advertisements.* 3 UNCOUNT N If you are under the **sway** of someone or something, they have great influence over you; a literary use. *Laing was coming increasingly under the sway of new ideas.* ● If someone or something **holds sway,** they have great power or influence; a literary use. *The beliefs which now hold sway may one day be rejected.*

swear /sweə/, **swears, swearing, swore** /swɔː/, **sworn** /swɔːn/. 1 VB If someone **swears,** they use rude or blasphemous language. *Glenys leant out of the car window and swore at the other driver.* 2 VB WITH TO-INF OR REPORT VB If you **swear** to do something, you solemnly promise that you will do it. *Will you swear not to run away and vanish?... I swear I will never tell anyone.* 3 REPORT VB OR VB WITH PREP 'to' If you **swear** that something is true or if you **swear** to it, you say very firmly that it is true. *I swear that he never consulted me... ...thousands of experts who would swear to its impossibility.* 4 See also **sworn.**

swear by. PHR VB If you **swear by** a particular thing, you believe that it is especially effective or reliable; an informal use. *He swears by my herbal tea to make him sleep.*

swear in. PHR VB When someone **is sworn in,** they solemnly promise to fulfil the duties of a new job or appointment. *The jury was sworn in on May 4.*

swear-word, swear-words. COUNT N A **swear-word** is a word which is considered rude or blasphemous.

sweat /swet/, **sweats, sweating, sweated.** 1 UNCOUNT N **Sweat** is the salty, colourless liquid which comes through your skin when you are hot, ill, or afraid. *Jack paused, wiping the sweat from his face.* 2 VB When you **sweat,** sweat comes through your skin. *I lay and sweated in bed.* 3 PHRASE If someone is **in a sweat** or **in a cold sweat,** they are sweating a lot, especially because they are afraid or ill. *He awoke trembling and in a cold sweat.*

sweater /swetə/, **sweaters.** COUNT N A **sweater** is a warm knitted piece of clothing which covers the upper part of your body and your arms.

sweatshirt /swetʃɜːt/, **sweatshirts.** COUNT N A **sweatshirt** is a piece of casual clothing, usually made from thick cotton, which covers the upper part of your body and your arms.

sweaty /swetɪ/. 1 ADJ A **sweaty** place or activity makes you sweat because it is hot or tiring. *...the sweaty march along the blazing beach.* 2 ADJ If your clothing or body is **sweaty,** it is soaked or covered with sweat. *...students in sweaty sports shirts.*

sweep /swiːp/, **sweeps, sweeping, swept** /swɛpt/. 1 VB WITH OBJ If you **sweep** an area of ground, you push dirt or rubbish off it with a broom. *I must sweep the kitchen floor... He swept away the broken glass.* 2 VB WITH OBJ AND ADJUNCT If you **sweep** things off a surface, you push them off with a quick, smooth movement of your arm. *He went into the study and swept some books and papers off the couch.* 3 VB WITH ADJUNCT To **sweep** also means to move quickly in a smooth line or curve. *He stared out at the traffic sweeping along the road... The dog was flung aside by the panther's sweeping paw.* Also COUNT N *With a great sweep of the arm he flung the whole handful high in the air.* 4 VB WITH OBJ AND ADJUNCT If a strong force **sweeps** you along, it moves you quickly along. *She was swept out to sea by the currents.* 5 VB WITH OBJ OR ADJUNCT If ideas, beliefs, or statements **sweep** a place, they spread quickly through it. *...the camping craze that is currently sweeping America... Change sweeps through the highly industrialized countries.* 6 VB WITH OBJ AND ADJUNCT To **sweep** something away means to remove it quickly and completely. *The matter was soon swept from his mind... ...sweeping away restrictions on publication.* 7 VB WITH OBJ If your gaze or a light **sweeps** an area, it moves over it. *We began rushing around in the dark, sweeping the ground with our flashlights.* 8 PHRASE If you **sweep** something **under the carpet**, you try to prevent people from hearing about it, usually because you are rather ashamed of it. 9 See also **chimney sweep.**

sweep up. PHR VB If you **sweep up** dirt or rubbish, you push it together with a brush and then remove it.

sweeping /swiːpɪŋ/. 1 ATTRIB ADJ A **sweeping** curve is long, wide, and stretched out. *...a place where the stream made a sweeping curve.* 2 ADJ A **sweeping** statement or generalization is a general one that is made without considering facts or details carefully; used showing disapproval. *It is too easy to make sweeping generalizations about someone else's problems.* 3 ATTRIB ADJ **Sweeping** effects or consequences are great or serious. *...sweeping public expenditure cuts.*

sweet /swiːt/, **sweeter, sweetest; sweets.** 1 ADJ Food or drink that is **sweet** contains a lot of sugar. *...a cup of sweet tea.* 2 COUNT N **Sweets** are sweet things such as toffees, chocolates, or mints; a British use. 3 COUNT N A **sweet** is a dessert; a British use. *We get soup and a main meal and a sweet.* 4 ADJ A feeling or experience that is **sweet** gives you great pleasure and satisfaction. *However sweet love is, when it goes there is always bitterness.* ♦ **sweetness** UNCOUNT N *...the sweetness of freedom.* 5 ADJ A **sweet** smell is pleasant and fragrant. *...the sweet smell of ripe blackberry bushes.* 6 ADJ A **sweet** sound is pleasant, smooth, and gentle. *...the sweet song of the skylark.* ♦ **sweetly** ADV *...a piper who played sweetly on his pipes.* 7 ADJ Someone who is **sweet** is pleasant, kind, and gentle towards other people. *My grandparents were very sweet to me.* 8 ADJ You can also describe someone or something as **sweet** when you think that they are attractive and delightful, especially in a rather sentimental way. *Oh! Look at that kitten! How sweet!* ♦ **sweetly** ADV *She remembered him sitting so sweetly on the cot, looking up at her.*

sweet corn. UNCOUNT N **Sweet corn** is the yellow seeds of the maize plant, which are eaten as a vegetable.

sweeten /swiːtə^{o}n/, **sweetens, sweetening, sweetened.** VB WITH OBJ If you **sweeten** food or drink, you add sugar, honey, or another sweet substance to it.

sweetener /swiːtə^{o}nə/, **sweeteners.** MASS N A **sweetener** is an artificial substance that can be used instead of sugar.

sweetheart /swiːthɑːt/, **sweethearts.** 1 VOCATIVE You call someone **sweetheart** if you are very fond of them. 2 COUNT N Your **sweetheart** is your boyfriend or girlfriend. *He married his childhood sweetheart.*

swell /swɛl/, **swells, swelling, swelled, swollen** /swəʊlə^{o}n/. The past participle can be **swelled** or **swollen.** 1 VB If something **swells** or **swells** up, it becomes larger and rounder than normal. *A mosquito had bitten her and her arm had swollen up... The insect inflates her lungs so that they swell into her abdomen.* ♦ **swollen** ADJ *Her fingers were badly swollen with arthritis.* 2 ERG VB If an amount **swells,** it increases. *It took another twenty years for the population to swell to twice its size... The army had its ranks swollen by new recruits.* 3 VB If feelings or sounds **swell,** they suddenly get stronger or louder; a literary use. *The murmur swelled and then died away.* 4 COUNT N A **swell** is the regular movement of waves up and down in the sea. *...the gentle swell of the ocean.*

swelling /swɛlɪŋ/, **swellings.** COUNT N OR UNCOUNT N A **swelling** is a raised, curved patch on your body which appears as a result of an injury or an illness. *He had a painful swelling on his neck... ...if there is swelling or redness.*

sweltering /swɛltə^{o}rɪŋ/. ADJ If the weather is **sweltering,** it is very hot.

swept /swɛpt/. **Swept** is the past tense and past participle of **sweep.**

swerve /swɜːv/, **swerves, swerving, swerved.** VB If a vehicle or other moving thing **swerves,** it suddenly changes direction, often in order to avoid colliding with something else. *The car swerved off the road and into the river... I swerved to avoid a lorry.*

swift /swɪft/, **swifter, swiftest; swifts.** 1 ADJ If something is **swift,** it happens or moves very quickly. *I made a swift and complete recovery... ...a swift stream.* ♦ **swiftly** ADV *He walked swiftly down the dark street.* ♦ **swiftness** UNCOUNT N *...stunned by the swiftness of the assault.* 2 COUNT N A **swift** is a small bird with crescent-shaped wings.

swig /swɪg/, **swigs, swigging, swigged.** VB WITH OBJ If you **swig** a drink, you drink it from a bottle or cup quickly and in large amounts; an informal use. *When her back was turned I swigged two cupfuls from the tub.* Also COUNT N *She took a swig of brandy.*

swim /swɪm/, **swims, swimming, swam** /swæm/, **swum** /swʌm/. 1 VB When you **swim,** you move through water by making movements with your arms and legs. *The children are learning to swim... We managed to swim ashore.* Also SING N *Let's go for a swim.* 2 VB If objects seem to you to **swim,** they seem to be moving backwards and forwards, usually because you are ill. *The room swam and darkened before his eyes.* 3 VB If your head **is swimming,** you feel dizzy.

swimmer /swɪmə/, **swimmers.** COUNT N A **swimmer** is someone who can swim or who is swimming. *Are they good swimmers?*

swimming /swɪmɪŋ/. UNCOUNT N **Swimming** is the activity of swimming. *Her father encouraged her to take up swimming again.*

swimming bath, swimming baths. COUNT N A **swimming bath** is a public swimming pool, especially an indoor one; a British use.

swimming pool, swimming pools. COUNT N A **swimming pool** is a large hole that is built and filled with water so that people can swim in it.

swimming trunks. PLURAL N **Swimming trunks** are shorts that a man wears when he goes swimming.

swimsuit /swɪmsj^{o}uːt/, **swimsuits.** COUNT N A **swimsuit** is a tight-fitting piece of clothing that a woman wears when she goes swimming.

swindle /swɪndə^{o}l/, **swindles, swindling, swindled.** VB WITH OBJ If someone **swindles** you, they deceive you in order to get money or something valuable from you. *I'm sure they swindled you out of that money.* Also COUNT N *I'm afraid we have been the victims of a monumental swindle.*

swindler /swɪndlə/, **swindlers.** COUNT N A **swindler** is someone who swindles people.

swing /swɪŋ/, **swings, swinging, swung** /swʌŋ/. 1 ERG VB If something **swings** or if you **swing** it, it moves repeatedly backwards and forwards or from side to side, from a fixed point. *The chandelier started to swing... He sat there swinging his legs.* Also SING N *She walked with an exaggerated swing of the hips.* 2 ERG VB WITH ADJUNCT If something **swings** in a particular direction, it moves in that direction with a smooth, curving movement. *I pushed the door and it swung open... Boylan swung the bag on to the back seat.* Also COUNT N *...a grand, impatient swing of his arm.* 3 ERG VB WITH ADJUNCT If a person or vehicle **swings** in a particular direction, they turn suddenly in that direction. *I swing quickly around... He swung his car out of the side road.* 4 VB WITH OR WITHOUT OBJ, WITH ADJUNCT If you **swing** at someone or something, you try to hit them. *I swung at him and hit him forcefully... The soldier swung a slow, heavy right hand at Tom.* 5 COUNT N A **swing** is a seat hanging by two ropes or chains from a metal frame or tree. You can sit on it and move forwards and backwards through the air. 6 COUNT N WITH SUPP A **swing** in people's opinions or attitudes is a significant change in them. *There was a 16.2% swing to the Social Democrats.* 7 VB WITH ADJUNCT If something such as public opinion or a balance of power **swings** in a particular direction, it changes. *The balance of power had swung decisively in favour of the moderates.*

PHRASES ● If something is **in full swing,** it is operating fully and is no longer in its early stages. ● If you **get into the swing** of something, you become involved in it and enjoy what you are doing; an informal use.

swipe /swaɪp/, **swipes, swiping, swiped.** VB WITH 'at' If you **swipe** at something, you try to hit it, making a swinging movement with your arm. *The batsman swiped at the ball and missed it.* Also SING N *She took a casual swipe at the nettles.*

swirl /swɜːl/, **swirls, swirling, swirled.** ERG VB WITH ADJUNCT If something **swirls,** it moves round and round quickly. *Dust swirled in small circles around me... He swirled his drink round his glass.*

swish /swɪʃ/, **swishes, swishing, swished.** ERG VB If something **swishes** or if you **swish** it, it moves quickly through the air, making a soft sound. *The curtains swished open... ...swishing his long black tail.* Also SING N *...the swish of a horse's tail.*

switch /swɪtʃ/, **switches, switching, switched.** 1 COUNT N A **switch** is a small control for an electrical device which you use to operate the device. *...electric light switches... Somebody pressed the wrong switch.* 2 VB WITH OR WITHOUT OBJ If you **switch** to something different, for example to a different task or subject of conversation, you change to it from what you were doing or saying before. *I would like now to switch to quite a different topic... He switched his attention back to the magazine.* Also COUNT N *...a switch in policy.* 3 VB WITH OBJ If you **switch** two things, you replace one with the other. *The plane switched loads and took off.*

switch off. PHR VB 1 If you **switch off** a light or other electrical device, you stop it working by pressing a switch. *He switched the radio off.* 2 If you **switch off,** you stop paying attention to something; an informal use. *I just switched off after the first speech.*

switch on. PHR VB If you **switch on** a light or other electrical device, you make it start working by pressing a switch. *He switched on the TV.*

switchboard /swɪtʃbɔːd/, **switchboards.** COUNT N The **switchboard** in an organization is a central place where all the telephone calls are received.

swivel /swɪvə^{o}l/, **swivels, swivelling, swivelled;** spelled **swiveling** and **swiveled** in American English. ERG VB If something **swivels** or **is swivelled,** it turns around a central point so that it is facing in a different direction. *I swivelled right round in my chair... Mellors slowly swivelled his chair round.*

swollen /swəʊlə^{o}n/. **Swollen** is a past participle of **swell.**

swoon /swuːn/, **swoons, swooning, swooned.** VB If you **swoon,** you almost faint as a result of strong emotion or shock; a literary use.

swoop /swuːp/, **swoops, swooping, swooped.** 1 VB When a bird or aeroplane **swoops,** it suddenly moves downwards through the air in a smooth, curving movement. *We saw a distant eagle swoop down from the sky.* Also COUNT N *The swallow made a dazzling swoop through the air.* 2 VB WITH ADJUNCT If soldiers or police **swoop** on a place, they move towards it suddenly and quickly in order to attack it or to arrest someone. *British troops swooped down twice in dawn raids.* Also COUNT N *The police made a swoop on the headquarters.*

swop /swɒp/. See **swap.**

sword /sɔːd/, **swords.** COUNT N A **sword** is a weapon with a handle and a long blade.

swore /swɔː/. **Swore** is the past tense of **swear.**

sworn /swɔːn/. 1 **Sworn** is the past participle of **swear.** 2 ATTRIB ADJ If you make a **sworn** statement or declaration, you swear that everything that you have said in it is true. *The American made a sworn statement to the police.*

swum /swʌm/. **Swum** is the past participle of **swim.**

swung /swʌŋ/. **Swung** is the past tense and past participle of **swing.**

syllable /sɪləbə^{o}l/, **syllables.** COUNT N A **syllable** is a part of a word that contains a single vowel-sound and that is pronounced as a unit. For example, 'book' has one syllable, and 'reading' has two syllables.

syllabus /sɪləbəs/, **syllabuses.** COUNT N You can refer to the subjects studied in a particular course as the **syllabus.** *They've got to cover a very wide syllabus.*

symbol /sɪmbə^{o}l/, **symbols.** 1 COUNT N WITH SUPP A **symbol** of something is a shape, design, or other thing that is used to represent it. *Picasso painted a red circle as a symbol of the Revolution... ...a peace symbol.* 2 COUNT N Something that is a **symbol** of a society or aspect of life seems to represent it because it is typical of it. *Perhaps the most glittering symbol of the new Britain was London's Post Office Tower.* 3 COUNT N A **symbol** for an item, for example in a calculation or formula, is a number, letter, or shape that represents the item. *I use my own symbol for 'approximately'.*

symbolic /sɪmbɒlɪk/. 1 ADJ A thing that is **symbolic** of someone or something is regarded or used as a symbol of them. *The crescent moon is symbolic of Allah... ...gold, with its rich symbolic significance.* ♦ **symbolically** ADV *To put on someone else's clothes is symbolically to take on their personality.* 2 ADJ **Symbolic** is also used to describe things involving or relating to symbols. *...a symbolic play.*

symbolism /sɪmbəlɪzəᵐ/. UNCOUNT N **Symbolism** is the use of symbols in order to represent something. *...messages conveyed by symbolism in the architecture.*

symbolize /sɪmbəlaɪz/, **symbolizes, symbolizing, symbolized**; also spelled **symbolise**. VB WITH OBJ If one thing **symbolizes** another, it is used or regarded as a symbol of it. *...a dancer in a flame-red robe symbolizing the sun.*

symmetrical /sɪmetrɪkəᵈl/. ADJ Something that is **symmetrical** has two halves which are exactly the same, except that one half is like a reflection of the other half. *...pleasingly symmetrical designs.* ♦ **symmetrically** ADV *Smaller rooms were arranged symmetrically to either side.*

symmetry /sɪmɪ�²trɪ¹/. UNCOUNT N Something that has **symmetry** is symmetrical in shape or design. *...the symmetry of the Square.*

sympathetic /sɪmpəθetɪk/. 1 ADJ If you are **sympathetic** to someone who has had a misfortune, you are kind to them and show that you understand their feelings. *My boyfriend was very sympathetic and it did make me feel better.* ♦ **sympathetically** ADV *She put a hand sympathetically on his arm.* 2 PRED ADJ If you are **sympathetic** to a proposal or action, you approve of it and are willing to support it. *He is sympathetic to our cause.* 3 ADJ You describe someone as **sympathetic** when you like them and approve of the way that they behave. *I found him a very sympathetic character.*

sympathize /sɪmpəθaɪz/, **sympathizes, sympathizing, sympathized**; also spelled **sympathise**. 1 VB If you **sympathize** with someone who has had a misfortune, you show that you are sorry for them. *I sympathized with her and tried to help.* 2 VB WITH 'with' If you **sympathize** with someone's feelings, you understand them and are not critical. *I can sympathize with your hesitations.* 3 VB WITH 'with' If you **sympathize** with a proposal or action, you approve of it and are willing to support it. *Everyone sympathised with the anti-colonial cause.*

sympathizer /sɪmpəθaɪzə/, **sympathizers**; also spelled **sympathiser**. COUNT N The **sympathizers** of an organization or cause are the people who support it. *White was an ardent Communist sympathiser.*

sympathy /sɪmpəθi¹/, **sympathies**. 1 UNCOUNT N If you have **sympathy** for someone who has had a misfortune, you are sorry for them, and show this in your behaviour. *People feel immediate sympathy for a man left alone with his children.* 2 UNCOUNT N WITH 'with' If you have **sympathy** with someone's ideas or opinions, you agree with them. *On that point I'm in sympathy with Mr McCabe.* 3 PLURAL N Your **sympathies** are your feelings of approval and support for a particular proposal or action. *He knows I have strong left-wing sympathies.* 4 PHRASE If you take some action **in sympathy** with someone, you do it to show that you support them. *They were carrying out a hunger strike in sympathy with mine.*

symphony /sɪmfəni¹/, **symphonies**. COUNT N A **symphony** is a piece of music for an orchestra, usually in four parts called movements.

symptom /sɪmptəm/, **symptoms**. 1 COUNT N A **symptom** of an illness is something wrong with your body that is a sign of the illness. *The first symptom of a cold is often a sore throat.* 2 COUNT N A **symptom** of a bad situation is something that happens which is considered to be a sign of this situation. *Migration is a symptom of rural poverty.*

symptomatic /sɪmptəmætɪk/. PRED ADJ If one thing is **symptomatic** of another, it is a sign of it; a formal use. *The irritation seems symptomatic of something deeper.*

synagogue /sɪnəgɒg/, **synagogues**. COUNT N A **synagogue** is a building where Jewish people meet to worship or to study their religion.

synchronize /sɪŋkrənaɪz/, **synchronizes, synchronizing, synchronized**; also spelled **synchronise**. 1 RECIP VB If two people **synchronize** something that they do, they do it at the same time and speed as each other. *They frequently synchronize their movements as they talk... The rhythm was not synchronized with the pictures.* 2 RECIP VB If you **synchronize** two watches or clocks, you adjust them so that they say exactly the same time. *His watch has been accurately synchronized with the church clock.*

syndicate /sɪndɪkəˈt/, **syndicates**. COUNT N A **syndicate** is an association of people or organizations that is formed for business purposes or to carry out a project. *...a syndicate of German industrialists.*

syndrome /sɪndrəʊm/, **syndromes**. 1 COUNT N WITH SUPP A **syndrome** is a medical condition that is characterized by a particular group of symptoms. 2 COUNT N WITH SUPP You also use **syndrome** to refer to an undesirable condition that is characterized by a

particular type of activity or behaviour. *...the capitalist syndrome of growth, profits, competition.*

synonym /sɪnənɪm/, **synonyms**. COUNT N A **synonym** is a word or expression which means the same as another one. *'Totalitarian' is not a synonym for 'communist'.*

synonymous /sɪnɒnɪməs/. 1 ADJ **Synonymous** words or expressions have the same meaning as each other. 2 PRED ADJ If one thing is **synonymous** with another, the two things are closely associated with each other so that the first suggests the second. *Socialism became to him synonymous with peace.*

syntax /sɪntæks/. UNCOUNT N **Syntax** is the grammatical arrangement of words in a language or the grammatical rules in a language; a technical use.

synthesis /sɪnθə¹sɪs/, **syntheses** /sɪnθə¹siːz/. 1 COUNT N A **synthesis** of different ideas or styles is a mixture or combination of these ideas or styles; a formal use. *...a synthesis of Jewish theology and Greek philosophy.* 2 UNCOUNT N The **synthesis** of a substance is the production of it by means of chemical or biological reactions; a technical use. *We need sunlight for the synthesis of vitamin D.*

synthesize /sɪnθɪsaɪz/, **synthesizes, synthesizing, synthesized**; also spelled **synthesise**. 1 VB WITH OBJ If you **synthesize** a substance, you produce it by means of chemical or biological reactions; a technical use. *...proteins which the body is unable to synthesise for itself.* 2 VB WITH OBJ If you **synthesize** different ideas, facts, or experiences, you combine them to develop a single idea or impression; a formal use. *They synthesise their experience into principles and theories.*

synthetic /sɪnθetɪk/. ADJ A **synthetic** material is made from chemicals or artificial substances rather than from natural ones. *...synthetic fibres.*

syphilis /sɪfɪlɪs/. UNCOUNT N **Syphilis** is a type of venereal disease.

syphon /saɪfəᵉn/, **syphons**. See **siphon**.

syringe /sɪrɪndʒ³/, **sɪrɪndʒ³/**, **syringes**. COUNT N A **syringe** is a small tube with a fine hollow needle or pointed end. Syringes are used, for example, to inject drugs into a person's body or to take blood samples from them.

syrup /sɪrəp/, **syrups**. MASS N **Syrup** is a sweet liquid made with sugar and water, often with a flavouring. *...waffles with maple syrup.*

system /sɪstəᵉm/, **systems**. 1 COUNT N A **system** is a way of organizing or doing something in which you follow a fixed plan or set of rules. *They have developed a remarkably efficient system for gathering food.* 2 COUNT N A **system** is also a particular set of rules, especially one in mathematics or science which is used to count or measure things. *...Egyptian or Roman number systems.* 3 COUNT N WITH SUPP You use **system** to refer to a whole institution or aspect of society that is organized in a particular way. *There's a difference between the Scottish legal system and the English one... ...the need to modernise Britain's transport system.* 4 SING N People sometimes refer to the government or administration of a country as the **system**. *...the revolutionary overthrow of the system.* 5 COUNT N WITH SUPP You also use **system** to refer to a set of equipment, parts, or devices, for example a hi-fi or computer, or the set of pipes or wiring which supplies water, heat, or electricity. *They stole the stereo system and the television set... Have you thought of installing your own central heating system?* 6 COUNT N WITH SUPP A **system** in your body is a set of organs or other parts that together perform a particular function. *...a diagram of the digestive system.*

systematic /sɪstəmætɪk/. ADJ Activity or behaviour that is **systematic** follows a fixed plan, so that things are done in an efficient way. *These skills are developed in a formal and systematic way.* ♦ **systematically** ADV *I wish they'd organise themselves more systematically.*

Tt

tab /tæb/, **tabs**. 1 COUNT N A **tab** is a small piece of cloth or paper attached to something. *It had the maker's name on a small cloth tab inside.* 2 PHRASE If you **keep tabs on** someone, you make sure that you always know where they are and what they are doing; an informal use.

table /teɪbəᵉl/, **tables, tabling, tabled**. 1 COUNT N A **table** is a piece of furniture with a flat top that you put things on or sit at. 2 COUNT N A **table** is also a set of facts or figures arranged in columns or rows on a piece of paper. 3 PHRASE If you **turn the tables on**

someone who is causing you problems, you change the situation so that you cause problems for them instead. 4 VB WITH OBJ If you **table** a proposal, you say formally that you want it to be discussed at a meeting. *...parliamentary questions tabled by Frank Field.*

tablecloth /teɪbəᵉlklɒθ/, **tablecloths**. COUNT N A **tablecloth** is a cloth used to cover a table.

tablespoon /teɪbəᵉlspuːn/, **tablespoons**. 1 COUNT N A **tablespoon** is a large spoon used for serving food. 2 COUNT N You can use **tablespoon** to refer to the amount that a tablespoon contains. *Use 1 tablespoon of vinegar to 1 pint of warm water.*

tablespoonful /teɪbəᵉlspuːnful/, **tablespoonfuls** or **tablespoonsful**. COUNT N A **tablespoonful** is the amount that a tablespoon contains. *...two level tablespoonfuls of sugar.*

tablet /tæblɪ¹t/, **tablets**. 1 COUNT N A **tablet** is a small, hard piece of medicine, which you swallow. *Take three tablets after each meal.* 2 COUNT N A **tablet** is also a flat piece of stone with words cut into it; a formal use. *There is a tablet in memory of those who died.*

table tennis. UNCOUNT N **Table tennis** is a game in which two or four people use bats to hit a small, light ball over a low net across a table.

tabloid /tæblɔɪd/, **tabloids**. COUNT N A **tabloid** is a newspaper with small pages and short articles.

taboo /təbuː/, **taboos**. 1 COUNT N A **taboo** is a social rule that some words, subjects, or actions must be avoided because they are embarrassing or offensive. *...the old taboo on kissing in public.* Also ADJ *Money is no longer a taboo subject.* 2 COUNT N A **taboo** is also a religious rule forbidding people to do something. *Tribal taboos forbade the Mandinkas to eat monkeys and baboons.*

tacit /tæsɪt/. ADJ **Tacit** means understood or implied without actually being said; a formal use. *They had by tacit agreement not renewed the contract.* ♦ **tacitly** ADV *Is she tacitly admitting that her place is in the home?*

taciturn /tæsɪtɜːn/. ADJ Someone who is **taciturn** does not talk very much and so seems unfriendly or depressed; a formal word.

tack /tæk/, **tacks, tacking, tacked**. 1 COUNT N A **tack** is a short nail with a broad, flat head. 2 VB WITH OBJ If you **tack** something to a surface, you nail it there with tacks. *Gretchen had tacked some travel posters on the wall.* 3 UNCOUNT N If you change **tack** or try a different **tack**, you try using a different method from the one you were using before. *They didn't seem convinced so I tried another tack.* 4 to **get down to brass tacks**: see **brass**.

tack on. PHR VB If you tack something **on** to something else, you add it in an unsatisfactory way. *They've tacked a couple of new clauses on to the end of the contract.*

tackle /tækəᵉl/, **tackles, tackling, tackled**. 1 VB WITH OBJ If you **tackle** a difficult task, you start dealing with it in a determined way. *...a means of tackling the growing housing problem.* 2 VB WITH OBJ If you **tackle** someone in a game such as football, you try to take the ball away from them. *He was tackled before he had a chance to shoot.* Also COUNT N *The tackle looked fair but a free kick was awarded.* 3 VB WITH OBJ If you **tackle** someone about a matter, you talk to them about it in order to get something changed or done. *He tackled me about several editorials I had written.* 4 UNCOUNT N **Tackle** is the equipment that you need for an activity, especially fishing. *...fishing tackle.*

tacky /tæki¹/. ADJ Something that is **tacky** is badly made and unpleasant; an informal use. *...tacky jewellery.*

tact /tækt/. UNCOUNT N **Tact** is behaviour in which you are careful to avoid upsetting or offending people. *I tried to behave with the utmost tact.*

tactful /tæktful/. ADJ If you are **tactful**, you are careful not to upset or offend people. *The tactful thing would have been not to say anything.* ♦ **tactfully** ADV *The topic was tactfully dropped.*

tactic /tæktɪk/, **tactics**. COUNT N **Tactics** are the methods that you use to achieve what you want. *They use delaying tactics.*

tactical /tæktɪkəᵉl/. 1 ADJ A **tactical** action is intended to gain an advantage in the future, rather than immediately. *This was simply a tactical move by De Gaulle.* 2 ATTRIB ADJ **Tactical** weapons are used over fairly short distances. 3 ATTRIB ADJ **Tactical** also means relating to tactics. *...a tactical error.*

tactile /tæktaɪl/. ADJ **Tactile** means relating to the sense of touch; a formal use. *...the tactile qualities of the physical world.*

tactless /tæktlɪ²s/. ADJ If someone is **tactless**, they behave in a way that is likely to upset or offend people. *I suppose it was rather tactless of me to ask.*

tadpole /tædpəʊl/, **tadpoles.** COUNT N **Tadpoles** are small, black, water creatures which grow into frogs or toads.

tag /tæg/, **tags, tagging, tagged.** COUNT N A **tag** is a label which is tied to an object. *...a price tag.*

tag along. PHR VB If you **tag along** with someone, you go with them, especially when they have not asked you to. *Our sisters always wanted to tag along.*

tail /teɪl/, **tails, tailing, tailed. 1** COUNT N The **tail** of an animal, bird, or fish is the part extending beyond the end of its body. *The dog was wagging his tail.* **2** COUNT N You can use **tail** to refer to the end or back of something, especially something long and thin. *...the stairway descending from the tail of the plane... ...the tail of the queue.* **3** VB WITH OBJ If you **tail** someone, you follow them in order to find out where they go and what they do; an informal use. *All day he was tailed by police cars.* **4** ADV If you toss a coin and it comes down **tails,** you can see the side of it that does not have a person's head on it. **5** to not **make head nor tail** of something: see **head.**

tail off. PHR VB If something **tails off,** it gradually becomes less, and perhaps ends completely. *The rains tail off in September.*

tailor /teɪlə/, **tailors.** COUNT N A **tailor** is a person who makes clothes, especially for men.

tailored /teɪləd/. **1** ATTRIB ADJ **Tailored** clothes are made to fit close to your body. **2** ADJ If something is **tailored** for a particular purpose, it is specially designed for that purpose. *...factories and equipment tailored to meet the needs of the 20th century.*

tailor-made. ADJ Something that is **tailor-made** for a person or purpose is very suitable or was specially designed for them. *Both the play and the role were tailor-made for her.*

taint /teɪnt/, **taints, tainting, tainted;** a formal word. **1** VB WITH OBJ If you **taint** something, you spoil it by adding an undesirable quality to it. *He feared that this would taint the scheme with some element of commercialism.* ♦ **tainted** ADJ *The report was heavily tainted with racism.* **2** SING N WITH SUPP A **taint** is an undesirable quality in something which spoils it. *His career was never free of the taint of corruption.*

take /teɪk/, **takes, taking, took** /tʊk/, **taken** /teɪkə^{ə}n/. **1** VB WITH OBJ You can use **take** to say that someone performs an action. For example, if you say that someone **takes** a look at something, you mean that they look at it. *She took a shower... He formed the habit of taking long, solitary walks... Certain decisions had to be taken... I took a magnificent photo of him.* **2** VB WITH OBJ If you **take** a particular attitude or view, you have it. *The public was beginning to take a positive interest in defence.* **3** VB WITH OBJ If something **takes** a certain amount of time, you need that amount of time in order to do it. *How long will it take?... It may take them several weeks to get back.* **4** VB WITH OBJ If something **takes** a particular quality or thing, it requires it. *It took a lot of courage to admit his mistake.* **5** VB WITH OBJ If you **take** something, you put your hand round it and hold it. *Let me take your coat... She took the menu from him.* **6** VB WITH OBJ If you **take** something from one place to another, you carry it there. *She gave me some books to take home.* **7** VB WITH OBJ If you **take** someone somewhere, you drive them or lead them there. *It's his turn to take the children to school.* **8** VB WITH OBJ If someone **takes** something that belongs to you, they steal it. *A pick-pocket took Barry's wallet.* **9** VB WITH OBJ If soldiers or terrorists **take** people or places, they capture them. *We took the village without a shot being fired.* **10** VB WITH OBJ If someone **takes** office or **takes** power, they start being in control of something. *He asked me to take charge.* **11** VB WITH OBJ If you **take** something that is offered to you, you accept it. *She took a job in publishing.* **12** VB WITH OBJ If you **take** someone's advice or orders, you do what they say you should do. *They have to take instructions from her.* **13** VB WITH OBJ If you **take** pills, medicine, or drugs, you swallow them. *I took a couple of aspirins.* **14** VB WITH OBJ If you **take** a road or route, you travel along it. *He took the road southwards into the hills.* **15** VB WITH OBJ If you cannot **take** something unpleasant, you cannot bear it. *I can't take any more... Ordinary people find his arrogance hard to take.* **16** VB WITH OBJ AND ADJUNCT If you **take** an event or piece of news well or badly, you react to it well or badly. **17** VB WITH OBJ AND ADJUNCT If you **take** what someone says in a particular way, you interpret it in that way. *They took what I said as a kind of rebuke.* **18** VB WITH OBJ If you **take** students for a subject, you give them lessons in it. **19** VB WITH OBJ If you **take** a person's temperature or pulse, you measure it. **20** VB WITH OBJ If you **take** a particular size in shoes or clothes, you wear that size. **21** VB WITH OBJ You use **take** in the imperative to introduce an example that you want to be considered. *Some men change the world. Take Albert Einstein, for instance.* **22** PHRASE You can say **'I take it'** to check that the person you are talking to knows or understands something. *I take it you know what a stethoscope is?*

take aback. PHR VB If you **are taken aback,** you are surprised or shocked. *I was a bit taken aback by this sudden reversal.*

take after. PHR VB If you **take after** someone in your family, you look or behave like them. *You don't take after your sister.*

take apart. PHR VB If you **take** something **apart,** you separate it into its different parts. *We encouraged them to explore, invent, take things apart, and put them together.*

take away. PHR VB If you **take away** one number or amount from another, you subtract it or deduct it. For example, if you take 3 away from 5, you get 2. ● See also **takeaway.**

take back. PHR VB **1** If you **take** something **back,** you return it. *Don't forget to take your books back to the library.* **2** If you **take back** something that you said, you admit that it was wrong. *I'm going to have to take back all those things I said about you.*

take down. PHR VB **1** When people **take down** a structure, they separate it into pieces and remove it. *The scaffolding won't be taken down until next year.* **2** If you **take down** what someone is saying, you write it down. *She began to take down the message.*

take in. PHR VB **1** If someone **is taken in,** they are deceived. *I wasn't going to be taken in by sentimentality.* **2** If you **take in** information, you understand it when you hear it or read it. *People never take in new facts very easily when they're unhappy.*

take off. PHR VB **1** When an aeroplane **takes off,** it leaves the ground and starts flying. ● See also **takeoff. 2** If you **take off** something that you are wearing, you move it off your body. *He took off his glasses and blinked.* **3** If you **take** time **off,** you do not go to work. *She's taken the day off.*

take on. PHR VB **1** If you **take on** a job or responsibility, you accept it. *She takes on more work than is good for her.* **2** If something **takes on** a new quality, it begins to have that quality. *His voice took on a new note of uncertainty.* **3** If you **take** someone **on,** you start employing them. *They took me on because I was a good mathematician.* **4** If you **take on** someone more powerful than you, you fight them or compete against them. *British Leyland plans to take on the competition at home and abroad.*

take out. PHR VB If you **take** someone **out,** you take them to an enjoyable place, and you pay for both of you. *He offered to take her out for a meal.*

take out on. PHR VB If you **take** your unhappiness or anger **out on** someone, you behave in an unpleasant way towards them, even though it is not their fault that you feel upset. *She took out most of her unhappiness on her husband.*

take over. PHR VB **1** To **take over** something such as a company or country means to gain control of it. *The agency tried to take over another company.* ● See also **takeover. 2** If you **take over** a job or if you **take over,** you start doing the job after someone else has stopped doing it. *They want me to take over as editor when Harold leaves.*

take to. PHR VB **1** If you **take to** someone or something, you like them immediately. *We asked him if the Russians would take to golf.* **2** If you **take to** doing something, you begin to do it regularly. *He took to wearing black leather jackets.*

take up. PHR VB **1** If you **take up** an activity or job, you start doing it. *I thought I'd take up fishing... My assistant left to take up another post.* **2** If you **take up** an activity that was interrupted, you continue doing it from the point where it had stopped. *Sam took up the story.* **3** If you **take up** an idea or suggestion, you discuss it further. *The committee is expected to take up the question of government grants.* **4** If something **takes up** an amount of time, space, or effort, it uses that amount. *I won't take up any more of your time.*

take up on. PHR VB If you **take** someone **up on** an offer that they have made, you accept their offer. *I didn't expect her to take me up on my invitation so soon.*

take upon. PHR VB If you **take** it **upon** yourself to do something, you do it even though it is not your duty. *She took it upon herself to turn round and say 'Sh'.*

takeaway /teɪkəweɪ/, **takeaways;** a British word. **1** COUNT N A **takeaway** is a shop or restaurant which sells hot cooked food to be eaten elsewhere. **2** COUNT N A **takeaway** is also a hot cooked meal sold to be eaten elsewhere. *I fancy an Indian takeaway.*

taken /teɪkə^{ə}n/. **1 Taken** is the past participle of **take. 2** PRED ADJ If you are **taken** with something, you find it attractive and interesting. *Philip had been rather taken with the idea.*

takeoff /teɪkɒf/, **takeoffs.** UNCOUNT N OR COUNT N **Takeoff** is the beginning of a flight, when an aircraft leaves the ground. *...fifty minutes after takeoff.*

takeover /teɪkəʊvə/, **takeovers. 1** COUNT N OR UNCOUNT N A **takeover** occurs when someone buys enough shares in a company to gain control of it. *The trend towards takeovers has intensified... ...another oil company ripe for takeover.* **2** COUNT N OR UNCOUNT N When someone takes control of a country by force, this is also described as a **takeover.** *He may be ousted by a military takeover.*

taker /teɪkə/, **takers.** COUNT N If there are no **takers** or few **takers** for an offer or challenge, hardly anyone is willing to accept it. *Recruiters are already trying to get volunteers. No takers so far.*

takings /teɪkɪŋz/. PLURAL N The **takings** are the money that a shop, theatre, or cinema gets from selling its goods or tickets.

talcum powder /tælkəm paʊdə/. UNCOUNT N **Talcum powder** is a soft, perfumed powder which people put on their bodies.

tale /teɪl/, **tales. 1** COUNT N A **tale** is a story, especially one involving adventure or magic. **2** COUNT N You can refer to an account of an interesting real event as a **tale.** *Everyone had some tale to tell about the very cold winter.* **3** See also **old wives' tale.**

talent /tælə^{ə}nt/, **talents.** UNCOUNT N OR COUNT N **Talent** is the natural ability to do something well. *Your work shows a lot of talent... Rudolph had a talent for music.*

talented /tæləntɪ^{2}d/. ADJ Someone who is **talented** has a natural ability to do something well. *...a young and very talented writer.*

talisman /tælɪzmən/, **talismans.** COUNT N A **talisman** is an object which you believe has magic powers to protect you or bring you luck; a formal use.

talk /tɔːk/, **talks, talking, talked. 1** VB When you **talk,** you say things to someone. *They talked about old times... He was the only one in the family she could talk to.* Also COUNT N OR UNCOUNT N *I must have a long talk with him... There was a lot of talk about his divorce.* **2** VB WITH OBJ If you **talk** politics or sport, for example, you discuss it. *Let's talk a little business, shall we?* **3** VB If you **talk** on or about something, you make an informal speech about it. *I talked yesterday about the history of the project.* Also COUNT N *I used to give the staff a talk on psychology every week.* **4** PLURAL N **Talks** are formal discussions, especially between two countries or two sides in a dispute. *...peace talks.* **5** PHRASE You use **talking of** to introduce a new topic that is connected with something just mentioned. *Talking of girls, has anyone seen Sylvia Wicks recently?* **6** See also **small talk.**

talk down to. PHR VB If someone **talks down to** you, they talk to you in a way that shows that they think they are cleverer or more important than you.

talk into. PHR VB If you **talk** someone **into** doing something, you persuade them to do it. *She talked me into taking a week's holiday.*

talk out of. PHR VB If you **talk** someone **out of** doing something, you persuade them not to do it. *He tried to talk me out of buying such a big car.*

talk over. PHR VB If you **talk** something **over,** you discuss it with someone. *I agreed to go home and talk things over with my father.*

talkative /tɔːkətɪv/. ADJ Someone who is **talkative** talks a lot.

tall /tɔːl/, **taller, tallest.** ADJ Someone or something that is **tall** is above average height. *He was a tall, dark man... ...a tall cypress tree.* Also ADJ OR ADJ AFTER N used in questions and statements about height. *How tall is he?... ...a six-foot tall fifteen-year-old.*

PHRASES ● If you say that a task is **a tall order,** you mean that it will be difficult to do. ● If you describe someone's account of an event as a **tall story,** you mean that you find it difficult to believe.

tally /tæli^{1}/, **tallies, tallying, tallied. 1** COUNT N A **tally** is an informal record of amounts which you keep adding to as an activity progresses. *Can you keep a tally of your own marks, please?* **2** RECIP VB If numbers or statements **tally,** they are the same as each other. *We've checked their stories and they don't quite tally... The amount she mentioned failed to tally with the figure shown in the records.*

talon /tælən/, **talons.** COUNT N The **talons** of a bird of prey are its hooked claws.

tambourine /tæmbəriːn/, **tambourines.** COUNT N A **tambourine** is a musical instrument which you shake or hit. It consists of a skin on a circular frame with pieces of metal around the edge which clash together.

tame /teɪm/, **tamer, tamest; tames, taming, tamed. 1** ADJ A **tame** animal or bird is not afraid of people and is not violent towards them. *...a tame monkey.* **2** ADJ **Tame** people do what they are told to do without questioning it; used showing disapproval. *...a tame victim.* ♦ **tamely** ADV *These measures are unlikely to be accepted as tamely as the government hopes.* **3** ADJ You describe an activity as **tame** when you think that it is uninteresting because it does not involve any excitement. *It sounded like a rather tame party.* **4** VB

WITH OBJ If you **tame** wild animals or uncontrolled people or things, you bring them under control.

tamper /tæmpə/, **tampers, tampering, tampered.**
tamper with. PHR VB If you **tamper with** something, you do something to it, and perhaps damage it, when you have no right to do so. *He claimed that his briefcase had been tampered with.*

tampon /tæmpɒn/, **tampons.** COUNT N A **tampon** is a firm piece of cotton wool that a woman puts inside herself to absorb menstrual blood.

tan /tæn/. 1 SING N If you have a **tan,** your skin has become darker than usual because you have been in the sun. *She had a beautiful golden tan.* 2 ADJ Something that is **tan** is pale brown or golden. *...tan shoes.*

tandem /tændəm/, **tandems.** 1 COUNT N A **tandem** is a bicycle designed for two riders. 2 PHRASE If two people do something **in tandem,** they do it working together. *...a new play we had written in tandem.*

tang /tæŋ/. SING N A **tang** is a strong, sharp smell or taste. *...the tang of an expensive perfume.*

tangent /tændʒənt/. PHRASE If you **go off at a tangent,** you start talking about something that is not directly connected with what you were talking about before.

tangible /tændʒəbəl/. ADJ Something that is **tangible** can be easily seen, felt, or noticed. *Politicians always want tangible results.*

tangle /tæŋgəl/, **tangles, tangling, tangled.** 1 COUNT N A **tangle** is a mass of things such as string or hair twisted together untidily. *...an impenetrable tangle of creepers and trees.* 2 PASSIVE VB Something that **is tangled** is twisted together untidily. *The wires got all tangled... ...her tangled hair.* 3 PASSIVE VB If you **are tangled** in something such as ropes or **are tangled** up in them, you are caught or trapped in them. *His leg got tangled in a harpoon line.*
tangle with. PHR VB If you **tangle with** someone, you get involved in a fight or quarrel with them.

tank /tæŋk/, **tanks.** 1 COUNT N A **tank** is a large container for holding liquid or gas. *...a petrol tank... ...the cold water tank... ...a tank of tropical fish.* 2 COUNT N A **tank** is also a military vehicle covered with armour and equipped with guns or rockets.

tankard /tæŋkəd/, **tankards.** COUNT N A **tankard** is a large metal beer mug.

tanker /tæŋkə/, **tankers.** COUNT N A **tanker** is a ship or truck used for transporting large quantities of gas or liquid. *...an oil tanker.*

tanned /tænd/. ADJ If you are **tanned,** your skin is darker than usual because you have been in the sun.

tantalize /tæntəlaɪz/, **tantalizes, tantalizing, tantalized;** also spelled **tantalise.** VB WITH OBJ If something or someone **tantalizes** you, they make you feel hopeful and excited, and then do not allow you to have what you want.

tantalizing /tæntəlaɪzɪŋ/; also spelled **tantalising.** ADJ Something that is **tantalizing** is very attractive and tempting, especially because you know that it is not possible to have it. *This raises the tantalizing possibility that there may be life on other stars.* ♦ **tantalizingly** ADV *Sometimes a new idea may be tantalizingly close.*

tantamount /tæntəmaunt/. PRED ADJ If you say that something is **tantamount** to something else, you mean that it is almost the same; a formal use. *His statement was tantamount to an admission.*

tantrum /tæntrəm/, **tantrums.** COUNT N A **tantrum** is a noisy outburst of bad temper, especially by a child.

tap /tæp/, **taps, tapping, tapped.** 1 COUNT N A **tap** is a device that you turn in order to control the flow of a liquid or gas from a pipe or container. *Turn on the hot tap.* 2 VB WITH OBJ OR ADJUNCT If you **tap** something or **tap** on it, you hit it lightly with your fingers or with something else. *It will come loose if you tap it with a hammer... She tapped on the glass partition.* Also COUNT N *I heard a soft tap at the front door.* 3 VB WITH OBJ If you **tap** a resource, you make use of it. *...a new way of tapping the sun's energy.*

tape /teɪp/, **tapes, taping, taped.** 1 UNCOUNT N **Tape** is a narrow plastic strip covered with a magnetic substance. It is used to record sounds, pictures, and computer information. *...a conversation recorded on tape.* 2 COUNT N A **tape** is a cassette or spool with magnetic tape wound round it. *His manager persuaded him to make a tape of the song.* 3 VB WITH OBJ If you **tape** music, sounds, or television pictures, you record them using a tape recorder or a video recorder. 4 COUNT N OR UNCOUNT N A **tape** is also a strip of cloth used to tie things together or to identify who a piece of clothing belongs to. *...three metres of white tape... ...name tapes.* 5 UNCOUNT N **Tape** is also a sticky strip of plastic used for sticking things together. *...a bit of adhesive tape.* 6 VB WITH OBJ AND ADJUNCT If you **tape** one thing to another, you attach it using sticky tape. 7 See also **red tape, videotape.**

tape measure, tape measures. COUNT N A **tape measure** is a strip of plastic or cloth marked with centimetres or inches, which is used for measuring.

taper /teɪpə/, **tapers, tapering, tapered.** VB Something that **tapers** gradually becomes thinner at one end. *Eventually the gallery tapered to a long, narrow corridor.* ♦ **tapered** ADJ *The trousers should have tapered legs.* ♦ **tapering** ADJ *...long tapering fingers.*
taper off. PHR VB If something **tapers off,** it gradually becomes much smaller. *The economic boom tapered off.*

tape recorder, tape recorders. COUNT N A **tape recorder** is a machine used for recording and playing tapes of music and other sounds.

tape recording, tape recordings. COUNT N A **tape recording** is a recording of sounds that has been made on tape.

tapestry /tæpɪstri/, **tapestries.** COUNT N OR UNCOUNT N A **tapestry** is a piece of heavy cloth with a picture or pattern sewn on it. *They're experts in stretching and framing tapestry.*

tar /tɑː/. UNCOUNT N **Tar** is a thick, black, sticky substance used in making roads.

target /tɑːgɪt/, **targets, targeting, targeted.** 1 COUNT N A **target** is something that you are is trying to hit with a missile, arrow, or bullet. *The station was an easy target for an air attack... My first two shots missed the target.* 2 COUNT N Someone or something that is being criticized can also be described as a **target.** *He has become the target of furious criticism.* 3 COUNT N A **target** is also a result that you are trying to achieve. *It set a target for economic growth in excess of 4% a year.* ● If you are **on target,** you are making good progress and are likely to achieve the result you want. *The latest sales figures are on target.* 4 VB WITH OBJ If you **target** a particular group of people or **target** something at them, you try to appeal to or affect those people. *...targeting markets such as mature drivers and women under thirty... The scheme is targeted at salaried workers.*

tariff /tærɪf/, **tariffs.** COUNT N A **tariff** is a tax on goods coming into a country.

tarmac /tɑːmæk/. 1 UNCOUNT N **Tarmac** is a material used for making road surfaces. It consists of crushed stones mixed with tar; a trademark. 2 SING N You can refer to any area with a tarmac surface as the **tarmac.** *He went out onto the tarmac where the jet was waiting.*

tarnish /tɑːnɪʃ/, **tarnishes, tarnishing, tarnished.** 1 ERG VB If metal **tarnishes,** it becomes stained and loses its brightness. *Chrome doesn't tarnish easily... The damp atmosphere tends to tarnish the brass taps.* ♦ **tarnished** ADJ *...a photo in a tarnished silver frame.* 2 VB WITH OBJ If something **tarnishes** your reputation, it damages it and causes people to lose their respect for you. *...a trial that tarnished the names of many intellectuals.* ♦ **tarnished** ADJ *...an attempt to restore some of their tarnished popularity.*

tarpaulin /tɑːpɔːlɪn/, **tarpaulins.** COUNT N A **tarpaulin** is a sheet of heavy, waterproof material that is used as a protective cover.

tarred /tɑːd/. ADJ A **tarred** road has a surface of tar.

tart /tɑːt/, **tarts.** 1 COUNT N OR UNCOUNT N A **tart** is a shallow pastry case with a sweet filling. *...jam tarts... Have another slice of tart.* 2 ADJ A **tart** remark is unpleasant and rather cruel; a written use. *She spoke with tart contempt.* ♦ **tartly** ADV *She tartly pointed out that he owed her some money.*

tartan /tɑːtən/. ADJ **Tartan** cloth, which mainly comes from Scotland, has different coloured stripes crossing each other. *...a tartan rug.*

task /tɑːsk/, **tasks.** COUNT N A **task** is a piece of work that must be done. *Computers can be applied to a wide range of tasks.*

tassel /tæsəl/, **tassels.** COUNT N A **tassel** is a bunch of threads attached to something as a decoration. *...the tassels on their cloaks.*

taste /teɪst/, **tastes, tasting, tasted.** 1 UNCOUNT N Your sense of **taste** is your ability to recognize the flavour of things with your tongue. 2 SING N The **taste** of something is the flavour that it has, for example whether it is sweet or salty. *The soup was peppered and spiced to improve the taste.* 3 VB WITH ADJUNCT OR COMPLEMENT You use **taste** to say that something has a particular flavour. *The tea tasted faintly of bitter almonds... Tinned tomatoes taste delicious.* 4 VB WITH OBJ If you can **taste** something that you are eating or drinking, you are aware of its flavour. *Roger chewed and swallowed so fast that he hardly tasted the meat.* 5 VB WITH OBJ If you **taste** food or drink, you try a small amount to see what its taste is like. *He insisted on pouring the wine for a guest to taste.* 6 SING N If you have a **taste** of food or drink, you try a small amount to see what its taste is like. *I opened one of the bottles and had a taste of the contents.* 7 SING N If you have a **taste** for something, you enjoy it. *He had not lost the taste for power.* 8 SING N If you have a **taste** of a state or activity, you experience it for a short time. *The child may already have had a taste of street life.* 9 UNCOUNT N A person's **taste** is their liking for some things and dislike of others. *She has very good taste in clothes... Her novels are too violent for my taste.* 10 PHRASE If something is **in bad taste,** it is rather offensive. If it is **in good taste,** it is not offensive. *That remark was in rather poor taste.*

tasteful /teɪstful/. ADJ Something that is **tasteful** is attractive and elegant. *The bedroom was simple but tasteful.* ♦ **tastefully** ADV *Their house was tastefully furnished.*

tasteless /teɪstlɪs/. 1 ADJ Something that is **tasteless** is vulgar and unattractive. *...tasteless ornaments.* 2 ADJ A **tasteless** remark or joke is rather offensive. 3 ADJ **Tasteless** food has very little flavour and is therefore unpleasant. *...cold, tasteless pizzas.*

tasty /teɪsti/, **tastier, tastiest.** ADJ **Tasty** food has a fairly strong, often savoury flavour which you find pleasant. *...tasty sauces.*

tattered /tætəd/. ADJ **Tattered** clothing or paper is torn or crumpled.

tatters /tætəz/. PHRASE Clothes that are **in tatters** are badly torn.

tattoo /tætuː/, **tattoos, tattooing, tattooed.** 1 VB WITH OBJ If someone **tattoos** you, they draw a design on your skin by pricking little holes and filling them with coloured dye. *He had tattooed the name 'Marlene' on his upper arm.* ♦ **tattooed** ADJ *...a tattooed sailor.* 2 COUNT N A **tattoo** is a design tattooed on someone's body. 3 COUNT N If you beat a **tattoo,** you hit something quickly and repeatedly. *He beat a frantic tattoo with his hands on the door.* 4 COUNT N A **tattoo** is also a public military display of exercises and music.

tatty /tæti/. ADJ Something that is **tatty** is in bad condition; an informal use. *...a tatty old skirt.*

taught /tɔːt/. **Taught** is the past tense and past participle of **teach.**

taunt /tɔːnt/, **taunts, taunting, taunted.** VB WITH OBJ If you **taunt** someone, you speak offensively to them about their weaknesses or failures in order to upset or annoy them. *...street marchers taunting the police.* Also COUNT N *The children had to put up with taunts like 'You haven't got a Dad.'*

taut /tɔːt/. ADJ Something that is **taut** is stretched very tight. *...a taut wire.*

tavern /tævən/, **taverns.** COUNT N A **tavern** is a pub; an old-fashioned use.

tax /tæks/, **taxes, taxing, taxed.** 1 UNCOUNT N OR COUNT N **Tax** is an amount of money that you have to pay to the government so that it can pay for public services. *...income tax... ...a tax on pensions.* 2 VB WITH OBJ If a sum of money or type of goods **is taxed,** you have to pay some money to the government when you get it. *Any money earned over that level is taxed at the rate of 59%... Crops were taxed very heavily.* 3 VB WITH OBJ If a person or company **is taxed,** they have to pay a part of their income or profits to the government. 4 See also **taxing.**

taxable /tæksəbəl/. ADJ If something is **taxable,** you have to pay tax on it. *...taxable income.*

taxation /tækseɪʃən/. 1 UNCOUNT N **Taxation** is the taxing of things by a government. 2 UNCOUNT N **Taxation** is also the amount that people have to pay in taxes. *The government is hoping to reduce taxation.*

tax-free. ADJ If goods or services are **tax-free,** you do not have to pay tax on them.

taxi /tæksi/, **taxis, taxiing, taxied.** 1 COUNT N A **taxi** is a car whose driver is paid by people to take them where they want to go. 2 VB When an aircraft **taxis,** it moves slowly along the runway before taking off or after landing. *The Boeing taxied down the runway.*

taxing /tæksɪŋ/. ADJ A **taxing** task requires a lot of mental or physical effort.

taxpayer /tækspeɪə/, **taxpayers.** COUNT N **Taxpayers** are people who pay a percentage of their income to the government as tax.

TB /tiː biː/. **TB** is an abbreviation for 'tuberculosis'.

tea /tiː/, **teas.** 1 MASS N **Tea** is a drink made with hot water and the chopped, dried leaves of a particular bush. *She went into the kitchen to make a fresh pot of tea... Two teas, please.* 2 UNCOUNT N **Tea** is also the chopped, dried leaves that you use to make tea. *...a packet of tea.* 3 MASS N WITH SUPP Other drinks made with hot water and leaves or flowers are also called **tea.** *...mint tea.* 4 UNCOUNT N OR COUNT N **Tea** is also a light meal eaten in the afternoon, or a meal eaten in the early evening. *Mr Evans is coming to tea.*

tea bag, tea bags. COUNT N A **tea bag** is a small paper bag with tea leaves in it which is put into hot water to make tea.

teach /tiːtʃ/, **teaches, teaching, taught** /tɔːt/. 1 VB WITH OBJ If you **teach** someone something, you give them instructions so that they know about it or know how to do it. *Mother taught me how to read... Boylan* *had taught him to drive.* **2** VB WITH OBJ If you **teach** someone to think or behave in a particular way, you persuade them to think or behave in that way. *We've been taught to believe in the wisdom of those who govern us... Boys are often taught that they mustn't show their feelings.* **3** VB WITH OR WITHOUT OBJ If you **teach,** your job is to help students to learn about something at a school, college, or university. *I taught history for many years.*

teacher /ti:tʃə/, **teachers.** COUNT N A **teacher** is someone who teaches, especially at a school. *...a French teacher.*

teaching /ti:tʃɪŋ/, **teachings. 1** UNCOUNT N **Teaching** is the work that a teacher does. *...the professions of medicine, dentistry, and teaching.* **2** PLURAL N The **teachings** of a religious or political thinker are the ideas that he or she teaches to other people. *His teachings still exert a strong influence.*

teacup /ti:kʌp/, **teacups.** COUNT N A **teacup** is a cup that you drink tea from.

teak /ti:k/. UNCOUNT N **Teak** is a very hard wood.

team /ti:m/, **teams, teaming, teamed. 1** COLL N A **team** is a group of people who play together against another group in a sport or game. *...the New Zealand rugby team.* **2** COLL N You can refer to any group of people who work together as a **team.** *...a team of scientists.*

team up. PHR VB If you **team up** with someone, you join them so that you can do something together. *He teamed up with a friend and set up a business doing interior decorating.*

teamwork /ti:mwɜ:k/. UNCOUNT N **Teamwork** is action in which a group of people work together effectively. *Teamwork was even more important in the later stages of the project.*

tea party, tea parties. COUNT N A **tea party** is a social event in the afternoon at which people have tea, sandwiches, and cakes.

teapot /ti:pɒt/, **teapots.** COUNT N A **teapot** is a container with a lid, a handle, and a spout, used for making and serving tea.

tear, tears, tearing, tore /tɔ:/, **torn** /tɔ:n/. **Tear** is pronounced /tɪə/ for meaning 1, and /tɛə/ for the other meanings. **1** COUNT N **Tears** are the drops of liquid that come out of your eyes when you cry. *Tears were streaming down her face.* • If someone is **in tears,** they are crying. *She rushed out of the room, in tears... When Curzon heard the news, he burst into tears.* **2** ERG VB If you **tear** something made of cloth or paper, you pull it so that a hole appears in it or pull it to pieces. *He tore both letters into small pieces... I tugged at the sleeve to get it free. It tore.* ♦ **torn** ADJ *...my torn sweater.* **3** COUNT N A **tear** in something made of cloth is a hole that has been made in it. *There was a triangular tear at the knee of his trousers.* • See also **wear and tear. 4** PHRASE If you **tear** something **open,** you open it by tearing it. *He tore open the envelope.* **5** VB WITH OBJ AND ADJUNCT To **tear** something from somewhere means to remove it violently. *She tore several sheets out of the book... Boats were torn from their moorings by the storm.* **6** VB WITH ADJUNCT If you **tear** somewhere, you move very quickly. *They tore down the street after the dog.* **7** PASSIVE VB If you **are torn** between two or more things, you cannot decide which one to choose, and this makes you feel unhappy.

tear apart. PHR VB **1** If you **tear** something **apart,** you pull it into pieces violently. *I tore the parcel apart.* **2** If something **tears** an organization or country **apart,** it causes great quarrels or disturbances. *...a crisis which threatens to tear society apart.*

tear at. PHR VB If you **tear at** something, you violently try to pull pieces off it. *The boys tore at the meat like wolves.*

tear away. PHR VB If you **tear** yourself **away** from a place, you come away very unwillingly. *Mourners often find it difficult to tear themselves away from the grave.*

tear down. PHR VB If you **tear down** a building, you destroy it. *It is often cheaper to tear down the buildings than to modify them.*

tear off. PHR VB If you **tear** your clothes **off,** you take them off quickly in a rough way.

tear up. PHR VB If you **tear up** a piece of paper, you pull it into a lot of small pieces.

tearful /tɪəfʊl/. ADJ Someone who is **tearful** is crying or is about to cry.

tear gas /tɪə gæs/. UNCOUNT N **Tear gas** is a gas that causes your eyes to sting and fill with tears. It is used by the police to control violent crowds.

tease /ti:z/, **teases, teasing, teased.** VB WITH OR WITHOUT OBJ If you **tease** someone, you deliberately embarrass them or make fun of them, because this amuses you. *She teased him about his girlfriends... 'Ah hah,' the old man teased, 'perhaps you already have a child?'*

tea shop, tea shops. COUNT N A **tea shop** is a small restaurant or café where tea, coffee, cakes, and light meals are served; a British use.

teaspoon /ti:spu:n/, **teaspoons. 1** COUNT N A **teaspoon** is a small spoon. **2** COUNT N A **teaspoon** of food or liquid is the amount that a teaspoon will hold. *Add one teaspoon of salt.*

teaspoonful /ti:spu:nfʊl/, **teaspoonfuls** or **teaspoonsful.** COUNT N A **teaspoonful** is the amount that a teaspoon will hold. *...two teaspoonfuls of sugar.*

tea strainer /ti: streɪnə/, **tea strainers.** COUNT N A **tea strainer** is a metal or plastic object with small holes in it, used to stop tea leaves going into the cup when you are pouring tea.

teat /ti:t/, **teats. 1** COUNT N A **teat** is a nipple on the chest or stomach of a female animal from which its babies suck milk. *...tiny naked pink creatures clinging to the teats with their mouths.* **2** COUNT N A **teat** is also a piece of rubber shaped like a teat and fitted to a baby's feeding bottle. *The baby grabbed the teat and began to suck.*

teatime /ti:taɪm/. UNCOUNT N **Teatime** is the time in the afternoon when people have tea; a British use. *At teatime there was much excited chatter around the table.*

tea-towel, tea-towels. COUNT N A **tea-towel** is a cloth used for drying dishes and cutlery; a British use.

tech /tɛk/, **techs.** COUNT N A **tech** is the same as a technical college; an informal British use.

technical /tɛknɪkəᵒl/. **1** ADJ **Technical** means involving machines, processes, and materials used in industry, transport, and communications. *...scientific and technical knowledge.* **2** ADJ You also use **technical** to describe the practical skills and methods used to do an activity such as an art, a craft, or a sport. *...wood carving of remarkable technical skill.* **3** ATTRIB ADJ **Technical** language involves using special words to describe the details of a specialized activity.

technical college, technical colleges. COUNT N A **technical college** is a college in Britain where you can study subjects, usually as part of the qualifications and training required for a particular job.

technicality /tɛknɪkælɪ¹ti¹/, **technicalities. 1** PLURAL N The **technicalities** of a process or activity are the detailed methods used to do it. **2** COUNT N A **technicality** is a point that is based on a strict interpretation of a law or a set of rules. *On a technicality, the judge dismissed the case.*

technically /tɛknɪkəᵒli¹/. **1** SENTENCE ADV If something is **technically** true or possible, it is true or possible according to the facts, laws, or rules but may not be important or relevant in a particular situation. *He was technically in breach of contract... The electric car is technically feasible.* **2** ADV You use **technically** when discussing the practical skills and methods used to do an art, a craft, or a sport. *Pollock was certainly a skilful artist technically.*

technician /tɛknɪʃəᵒn/, **technicians.** COUNT N A **technician** is someone whose job involves skilled practical work with scientific equipment in a laboratory.

technique /tɛkni:k/, **techniques. 1** COUNT N A **technique** is a particular method of doing something. *...the techniques of film-making.* **2** UNCOUNT N **Technique** is skill and ability in an artistic, sporting, or other practical activity that is developed through training and practice. *She owed her technique entirely to his teaching.*

technological /tɛknəᶿlɒdʒɪkəᵒl/. ATTRIB ADJ **Technological** means relating to technology. *...modern scientific and technological knowledge.* ♦ **technologically** ADV *...the world's most technologically advanced nations.*

technology /tɛknɒlədʒi¹/, **technologies. 1** UNCOUNT N **Technology** is the activity or study of using scientific knowledge for practical purposes. *...advances in technology and science.* ♦ **technologist** /tɛknɒlədʒɪst/ COUNT N *...a small group of distinguished scientists and technologists.* **2** COUNT N OR UNCOUNT N WITH SUPP A **technology** is a particular area of activity that requires scientific methods and knowledge. *...computer technology.*

teddy /tɛdi¹/, **teddies.** COUNT N A **teddy** or a **teddy bear** is a soft toy that looks like a bear.

tedious /ti:dɪəs/. ADJ **Tedious** things are boring and last for a long time. *The arguments were tedious and complicated... ...remarkably tedious work.*

tedium /ti:dɪəm/. UNCOUNT N The **tedium** of a situation is its quality of being boring and seeming to last for a long time; a formal use. *...a cricket match of unspeakable tedium.*

teem /ti:m/, **teems, teeming, teemed.** VB WITH 'with' If a place **is teeming** with people, there are a lot of people moving around in it. *...a large, busy capital teeming with people.* ♦ **teeming** ATTRIB ADJ *She walked home through the teeming streets.*

teenage /ti:neɪdʒ/. **1** ATTRIB ADJ **Teenage** people are aged between thirteen and nineteen. *...a divorced woman with two teenage children.* **2** ATTRIB ADJ **Teenage** fashions and activities are typical of young people aged between thirteen and nineteen or are suitable for them. *...the teenage culture of pop music.*

teenager /ti:neɪdʒə/, **teenagers.** COUNT N A **teenager** is someone between thirteen and nineteen years of age. *Two teenagers died in separate accidents.*

teens /ti:nz/. PLURAL N Your **teens** are the period of your life when you are between thirteen and nineteen years old. *She was young, maybe still in her teens.*

teeter /ti:tə/, **teeters, teetering, teetered. 1** VB If someone or something **teeters,** they seem about to fall over. *I hovered and teetered on the edge of the cliff.* **2** VB WITH 'on' **Teeter** is also used in expressions like ' **teeter** on the brink' and ' **teeter** on the edge' to describe situations which are very close to becoming disastrous. *British theatre is teetering on the brink of ruin.*

teeth /ti:θ/. **Teeth** is the plural of **tooth.**

teethe /ti:ð/, **teethes, teething, teethed.** VB When babies **are teething,** their teeth are starting to appear, usually causing them pain.

teething troubles. PLURAL N **Teething troubles** are difficulties which arise at the beginning of a project or when something is new. *They had terrible teething troubles with the steering on the new model.*

teetotaller /ti:təʊtəᵒlə/, **teetotallers.** COUNT N A **teetotaller** is someone who never drinks alcohol.

TEFL /tɛfəᵒl/. UNCOUNT N **TEFL** is the teaching of English to people whose first language is not English. **TEFL** is an abbreviation for 'teaching English as a foreign language'.

telecommunications /tɛlɪkəmju:nɪkeɪʃəᵒnz/. UNCOUNT N **Telecommunications** is the science and activity of sending signals and messages over long distances using electronic equipment.

telegram /tɛlɪgræm/, **telegrams.** COUNT N A **telegram** is a message that is sent by telegraph and then printed and delivered. *I sent a telegram to my mother saying I had arrived safely.*

telegraph /tɛlɪgræf, -grɑ:f/, **telegraphs, telegraphing, telegraphed. 1** SING N The **telegraph** is a system of sending messages over long distances by means of electrical or radio signals. **2** VB WITH OR WITHOUT OBJ If you **telegraph** someone, you send them a message by telegraph. *Harold telegraphed him in France.*

telepathic /tɛlɪpæθɪk/. ADJ If someone claims to be **telepathic** they say they can communicate directly with other people using only their minds.

telepathy /tɪ²lɛpəθi¹/. UNCOUNT N **Telepathy** is direct communication between people's minds. *We are particularly interested in phenomena such as telepathy.*

telephone /tɛlɪfəʊn/, **telephones, telephoning, telephoned. 1** UNCOUNT N OR SING N The **telephone** is an electrical system used to talk to someone in another place by dialling a number on a piece of equipment and speaking into it. *Reports came in by telephone... I have to make a telephone call.* **2** COUNT N A **telephone** is the piece of equipment used to talk to someone by telephone. *He put down the telephone.* **3** VB WITH OR WITHOUT OBJ If you **telephone** someone, you dial their telephone number and speak to them by telephone; a formal use. *Brody telephoned to thank her.*

telephone book, telephone books. COUNT N A **telephone book** is a book containing an alphabetical list of names, addresses, and telephone numbers of the people in a town or area.

telephone booth, telephone booths. COUNT N A **telephone booth** is a place in a public building where there is a telephone that can be used by the public; a British use.

telephone box, telephone boxes. COUNT N A **telephone box** is a small shelter in the street in which there is a public telephone; a British use.

telephone directory, telephone directories. COUNT N A **telephone directory** is the same as a telephone book.

telephone exchange, telephone exchanges. COUNT N A **telephone exchange** is a building where the telephone lines are connected when someone in the area makes or receives a telephone call.

telephone number, telephone numbers. COUNT N Your **telephone number** is the number that other people dial when they want to talk to you on the telephone. *He gave her his telephone number.*

telephonist /tɪ²lɛfənɪst/, **telephonists.** COUNT N A **telephonist** is someone who works in a telephone exchange; a British use.

telescope /tɛlɪskəʊp/, **telescopes.** COUNT N A **telescope** is a long instrument shaped like a tube which has lenses which make distant things appear larger and nearer. *They peered at the targets through the telescope.*

telescopic /tɛlɪskɒpɪk/. 1 ATTRIB ADJ **Telescopic** instruments and lenses make things seem larger and nearer. *...a 400 mm telescopic lens.* 2 ATTRIB ADJ A **telescopic** device has sections that fit or slide into each other so that it can be made shorter when it is not in use. *I pulled out the telescopic aerial to its fullest extent.*

televise /tɛlɪvaɪz/, **televises, televising, televised.** VB WITH OBJ If an event **is televised,** it is filmed and shown on television. *The ceremony would be televised nationally.*

television /tɛlɪvɪʒəⁿn/, **televisions.** 1 COUNT N A **television** or a **television set** is a piece of electrical equipment consisting of a box with a glass screen on which you can watch programmes with pictures and sounds. *I turned on the television to watch the news.* 2 UNCOUNT N **Television** is the system of sending pictures and sounds by electrical signals over a distance so that people can receive them on a television set. *...television pictures transmitted from a camera on the other side of the world.* 3 UNCOUNT N **Television** also refers to all the programmes that are broadcast and that you can watch on a television set. *The boys were watching television.* 4 UNCOUNT N The business or industry concerned with making and broadcasting programmes is also called **television.** *...the most exciting job in television.*

telex /tɛlɛks/, **telexes, telexing, telexed.** 1 UNCOUNT N **Telex** is an international system of sending written messages. The message is typed on a machine in one place and is immediately printed out by a machine in another place. 2 COUNT N A **telex** is a machine that sends and receives telex messages, or the message that is sent by the machine. *He burst in with an urgent telex.* 3 VB WITH OBJ If you **telex** a message, you send it by a telex machine. *The file on this man had been telexed to Paris.*

tell /tɛl/, **tells, telling, told** /təʊld/. 1 REPORT VB WITH OBJ, OR VB WITH OBJ If someone **tells** you something, they give you information in words. *John refused to tell me her name... He told me that he was a farmer... 'We told a lot of lies,' said Bill.* 2 REPORT VB WITH OBJ If something **tells** you something, it reveals a fact to you or indicates what you should do. *The design of the computer tells us nothing about such things... Every movement they make tells you that they are tired.* 3 VB WITH OBJ If you **tell** someone to do something, you order, instruct, or advise them to do it. *Just do as you're told... My uncle smiled and told me not to worry... I told her that what she needs is a good long book.* 4 VB WITH OBJ If you can **tell** what is happening or what is true, you are able to judge correctly what is happening or what is true. *You can't tell the difference between truth and fiction... I couldn't tell what they were thinking... So far as we can tell, it is still in perfect condition.* 5 VB If an unpleasant or tiring experience begins to **tell,** it begins to have a serious effect. *The strain was beginning to tell... All these late nights were beginning to tell on my health.*

PHRASES • If you say **'Time will tell',** you mean that the truth about something will not be known until some time in the future.

tell apart. PHR VB If you can **tell** similar people or things **apart,** you are able to recognize the differences between them.

tell off. PHR VB If you **tell** someone **off,** you speak to them angrily or seriously because they have done something wrong. *We don't want to get told off, do we?* ♦ **telling-off** SING N *When she got back she would give him such a telling-off about that doll.*

telling /tɛlɪŋ/. ADJ If something that you say is **telling,** it is very important, relevant, or significant. *The lawyer made a brief, telling speech to the magistrate... He let slip a particularly telling remark.*

telltale /tɛlteɪl/. ADJ A **telltale** sign reveals information about something that is meant to be secret. *I was beginning to recognize the first tell-tale signs of panic.*

telly /tɛli¹/, **tellies.** COUNT N OR UNCOUNT N A **telly** is the same as a television; an informal use. *Dad was half asleep in front of a flickering telly... Did you see it on telly last night?*

temerity /tɪ²mɛrɪ¹ti¹/. UNCOUNT N WITH SUPP If someone has the **temerity** to do something, they do it even though it upsets or annoys other people; a formal use. *He had the temerity to suggest that a few of us should leave.*

temp /tɛmp/, **temps.** COUNT N A **temp** is a secretary who is employed by an agency to work for short periods of time in different offices.

temper /tɛmpə/, **tempers, tempering, tempered.** 1 COUNT N OR UNCOUNT N Your **temper** is the tendency you have to become angry or to stay calm. *He had a most violent temper.* 2 COUNT N OR UNCOUNT N WITH SUPP Your **temper** is also your general mood. *She might come home in a better temper.* 3 VB WITH OBJ To **temper** something means to make it less extreme or more acceptable; a formal use. *Our delight was tempered by surprise.*

PHRASES • If you are **in a temper,** you are extremely angry and cannot control yourself. *One day the man attacked me in a temper.* • If you **lose** your **temper,** you become very angry. *She suddenly lost her temper and left the room.*

temperament /tɛmpəⁿrəmə²nt/, **temperaments.** UNCOUNT N OR COUNT N Your **temperament** is your character, which you show in your usual way of behaving towards people or reacting in situations. *They were gamblers by temperament... He had a cheerful temperament.*

temperamental /tɛmpəⁿrəmɛntəⁿl/. 1 ADJ A **temperamental** person has moods that change often and suddenly. *...a temperamental Polish actress.* 2 ADJ **Temperamental** features relate to the temperament a person has. *Temperamental differences exist between them.* ♦ **temperamentally** ADV *My father wasn't temperamentally suited for business.*

temperance /tɛmpəⁿrəns/. UNCOUNT N **Temperance** is the habit of not drinking alcohol because you believe that it is dangerous or morally wrong. *She didn't need temperance lectures from me.*

temperate /tɛmpəⁿrə¹t/. ADJ A **temperate** place has weather that is never extremely hot or extremely cold. *...the temperate woodlands of Tasmania.*

temperature /tɛmprə¹tʃə/, **temperatures.** 1 COUNT N OR UNCOUNT N The **temperature** of something is how hot or cold it is. *...a sudden drop in temperature... ...a temperature of 10°C.* 2 COUNT N Your **temperature** is the temperature of your body.

PHRASES • If someone **takes** your **temperature,** they use a thermometer to measure your temperature. • If you **have a temperature** or **are running a temperature,** your temperature is higher than it usually is and you feel ill.

tempestuous /tɛmpɛstjʊəs/. ADJ Something or someone that is **tempestuous** is full of strong emotions. *...a tempestuous love affair.*

temple /tɛmpəⁿl/, **temples.** 1 COUNT N A **temple** is a building used for the worship of a god in some religions. 2 COUNT N Your **temples** are the flat parts on each side of your forehead.

tempo /tɛmpəʊ/, **tempos.** 1 SING N OR UNCOUNT N The **tempo** of an event is the speed at which it happens; a formal use. *Events had been moving at an equally dramatic tempo... ...the tempo of everyday life.* 2 UNCOUNT N OR COUNT N The **tempo** of a piece of music is the speed at which it is played; a technical use. *Fluctuations of tempo are possible in a romantic piece... ...the light-footed tempos of the Magic Flute.*

temporary /tɛmpəⁿrəri¹/. ADJ Something that is **temporary** lasts for only a short time. *...my temporary absence from the saloon... ...temporary jobs.* ♦ **temporarily** ADV *She is temporarily in charge.*

tempt /tɛmpᵒt/, **tempts, tempting, tempted.** VB WITH OBJ If you **tempt** someone, you try to persuade them to do a particular thing by offering them something. *The building societies are offering higher rates of interest to tempt new savers.*

temptation /tɛmpᵒteɪʃəⁿn/, **temptations.** 1 UNCOUNT N **Temptation** is the state you are in when you want to do or have something, although you know it might be wrong or harmful. *He had the strength to resist further temptation.* 2 COUNT N A **temptation** is something that you want to do or have, although you know it might be wrong or harmful. *...the temptations to which he was continually exposed.*

tempting /tɛmpᵒtɪŋ/. ADJ Something that is **tempting** makes you want to do or have something, although you know it might be wrong or harmful. *...an extremely tempting price.*

ten /tɛn/, **tens. Ten** is the number 10.

tenacious /tɪ²neɪʃəs/. ADJ A **tenacious** person is very determined and does not give up easily. *They kept a tenacious grip on their possessions.* ♦ **tenacity** /tɪnæsɪ¹ti¹/ UNCOUNT N *We respect their tenacity and courage.*

tenancy /tɛnənsi¹/, **tenancies.** UNCOUNT N OR COUNT N **Tenancy** is the renting of land or property belonging to someone else. *Once they took up the tenancy they couldn't be evicted... ...a three-year tenancy.*

tenant /tɛnənt/, **tenants.** COUNT N A **tenant** is someone who pays rent for the place they live in, or for land or buildings that they use.

tend /tɛnd/, **tends, tending, tended.** 1 VB WITH TO-INF If something **tends** to happen, it happens usually or often. *I tend to wake up early in the morning.* 2 VB WITH OBJ If you **tend** someone or something, you look after them carefully; a formal use. *She'd tended four very sick men... ...a young man who tended his crops well.*

tendency /tɛndənsi¹/, **tendencies.** 1 COUNT N WITH SUPP If there is a **tendency** for something, it starts happening more often or increases in intensity. *There is a growing tendency for people to opt out... ...a permanent tendency towards inflation.* 2 COUNT N WITH SUPP If you have a particular **tendency,** you are likely to behave in that way. *I have a tendency to tease... The girl might have murderous tendencies.*

tender /tɛndə/, **tenderest; tenders, tendering, tendered.** 1 ADJ A **tender** person expresses gentle and caring feelings. *He gave her a tender smile.* ♦ **tenderly** ADV *She cradled the baby tenderly.* ♦ **tenderness** UNCOUNT N *I have a feeling of great tenderness for you.* 2 ATTRIB ADJ If someone is at a **tender** age, they are young and inexperienced. 3 ADJ **Tender** meat is soft and easy to cut or chew. 4 ADJ If a part of your body is **tender,** it hurts when you touch it. *...the tender, swollen side of his jaw.* 5 COUNT N A **tender** is a formal offer to supply goods or do a job for a particular price; a technical use. *Tenders are to be submitted on 15 December at 10 a.m.* 6 VB WITH OBJ If you **tender** a suggestion, an apology, or your resignation, you formally make it or offer it; a formal use.

tendon /tɛndəⁿn/, **tendons.** COUNT N A **tendon** is a strong cord of tissue in your body joining a muscle to a bone.

tendril /tɛndrɪⁿl/, **tendrils.** COUNT N **Tendrils** are short, thin stems which grow on some plants and attach themselves to walls or other plants.

tenement /tɛnəmənt/, **tenements.** COUNT N A **tenement** is a large building divided into a lot of flats.

tenet /tɛnɪ¹t/, **tenets.** COUNT N The **tenets** of a theory or belief are the principles on which it is based; a formal use. *...one of the central tenets of capitalism.*

tennis /tɛnɪs/. UNCOUNT N **Tennis** is a game played by two or four players on a rectangular court in which a ball is hit over a central net by players using rackets. *They've gone to play tennis in the park... ...a tennis court.*

tenor /tɛnə/, **tenors.** 1 COUNT N A **tenor** is a male singer with a fairly high voice. *...'Roses of Picardy' sung by an Irish tenor.* Also ADJ *...his pleasant tenor voice.* 2 ATTRIB ADJ A **tenor** musical instrument has a range of notes of fairly low pitch. 3 SING N WITH SUPP The **tenor** of something is the general meaning or mood that it expresses; a formal use. *The whole tenor of his work was socialist.*

tense /tɛns/, **tenser, tensest; tenses, tensing, tensed.** 1 ADJ If you are **tense,** you are worried and nervous, and cannot relax. *They began to grow tense over the likelihood of a long delay.* 2 ERG VB OR VB If you **tense,** or if your muscles **tense,** your muscles become tight and stiff. *The man on the terrace tensed slightly... 'What are you talking about?' I asked, the skin of my cheek-bones tensing up... He tensed his jaw muscles in fear.* Also ADJ *Your neck is tense.* 3 ADJ A **tense** situation or period of time is one that makes people anxious. *...a long, tense silence... The situation was very tense; anything might happen.* 4 COUNT N OR UNCOUNT N The **tense** of a verb is the form which shows whether you are referring to past, present, or future time.

tension /tɛnʃəⁿn/, **tensions.** 1 UNCOUNT N OR PLURAL N **Tension** is a feeling of fear or nervousness produced before a difficult, dangerous, or important event. *...the tension between the two countries... Family tensions are increasing.* 2 UNCOUNT N The **tension** in a rope or wire is how tightly it is stretched. *The loss of tension in the cables is a problem.*

tent /tɛnt/, **tents.** COUNT N A **tent** is a shelter made of canvas or nylon and held up by poles and ropes. You sleep in a **tent** when you are camping. *She pitched her tent in a field.*

tentacle /tɛntəkəⁿl/, **tentacles.** COUNT N The **tentacles** of an animal such as an octopus are the long, thin parts that it uses to feel and hold things, to catch food, and to move.

tentative /tɛntətɪv/. ADJ If you are **tentative,** you act or speak slowly and carefully because you are uncertain or afraid. *Each step he took was slightly tentative.* ♦ **tentatively** ADV *He smiled tentatively.*

tenth /tɛnθ/, **tenths.** 1 ADJ The **tenth** item in a series is the one that you count as number ten. 2 COUNT N A **tenth** is one of ten equal parts of something.

tenuous /tɛnjʊəs/. ADJ If an idea, connection, or reason is **tenuous,** it is so slight or weak that it may not really exist or may easily cease to exist. *...tenuous evidence... Their links with the school were tenuous.*

tenure /tɛnjʊᵒə/. 1 UNCOUNT N **Tenure** is the legal right to live in a place or to use land or buildings for a period of time. *They get tenure under the Rent Act.* 2 UNCOUNT N **Tenure** is also the period of time during which someone holds an important job. *...the first week of his tenure of the Home Office.*

tepid /tɛpɪd/. 1 ADJ A **tepid** liquid is slightly warm. *...drinking tepid coffee.* 2 ADJ A **tepid** feeling or reaction lacks enthusiasm. *Tepid applause greeted her efforts.*

term /tɜːm/, **terms, terming, termed.** 1 COUNT N A **term** is a word or expression used in relation to a particular subject. *He asked them what they understood by the term 'radical'... 'Habeas corpus' is a legal term.* **2** VB WITH OBJ AND COMPLEMENT You can use **term** to say what something is called. *...recent breakthroughs in what might be termed 'birth technology'.* **3** COUNT N OR UNCOUNT N A **term** is one of the periods of time that each year is divided into at a school or college. *...the spring term... It was the first week of term.* **4** COUNT N WITH SUPP The period of time during which someone does a particular job or activity is also called a **term.** *...Baldwin's second term of office as Premier... ...a long prison term.* **5** PLURAL N The **terms** of an agreement or arrangement are the conditions that have been accepted by the people involved in it. *We will not accept these terms.*

PHRASES ● If you talk about something **in** particular **terms** or **in terms of** a particular thing, you are specifying which aspect of it you are discussing. *Life is going to be a little easier in economic terms... In Marxist terms, nationalism of this kind cannot last... These losses are not to be explained in terms of what happened last week.* ● If you say you are **thinking in terms of** doing something or **talking in terms of** doing it, you mean that you are considering it. *You should be thinking in terms of paying off your debts.* ● If you talk about 'the **long term**' or 'the **short term**', you are talking about what will happen over a long or short period of time. *Such a policy would be economically disastrous in the long term... These are only short-term solutions.* ● If you **come to terms with** something difficult or unpleasant, you learn to accept it. *He has come to terms with death.* ● If two people are treated **on the same terms** or **on equal terms,** they are treated in the same way. ● If two people are **on good terms** or **on friendly terms,** they are friendly towards each other. *You need to be on friendly terms with him.* ● **on speaking terms:** see **speak.** ● **contradiction in terms:** see **contradiction.**

terminal /tɜːmɪnəºl/, **terminals. 1** ADJ A **terminal** illness or disease causes death gradually and is incurable. **2** COUNT N A **terminal** is a place where vehicles, passengers, or goods begin or end a journey. *...a bus terminal.* **3** COUNT N A computer **terminal** is a piece of equipment consisting of a keyboard and a screen that is used for putting information into a computer or for getting information from it. *...terminals giving access to larger computers.*

terminate /tɜːmɪneɪt/, **terminates, terminating, terminated;** a formal word. **1** ERG VB When you **terminate** something it ends completely. *I thought that he would terminate the discussion then and there... We are confident that the case will terminate with two words: 'Not guilty'.* ♦ **termination** /tɜːmɪneɪʃəºn/ UNCOUNT N *...the termination of their romance.* **2** VB WITH ADJUNCT When a train or bus **terminates** somewhere, it ends its journey there.

terminology /tɜːmɪnɒlədʒiˡ/, **terminologies.** MASS N The **terminology** of a subject is the set of special words and expressions used in connection with it. *...conflicting terminologies... ...using Marxist terminology.*

terminus /tɜːmɪnəs/, **terminuses.** COUNT N A **terminus** is a place where trains or buses begin or end their journeys. *He had waited near the terminus until the last bus had come in.*

termite /tɜːmaɪt/, **termites.** COUNT N **Termites** are small white insects that eat wood.

terrace /terəˡs/, **terraces. 1** COUNT N A **terrace** is a row of similar houses joined together by their side walls; a British use. *...a house in a fashionable terrace.* **2** COUNT N A **terrace** is also a flat area of stone or grass next to a building, where people can sit or eat meals. *He wandered out onto the terrace.* **3** COUNT N A flat area of ground built like steps on a hillside where crops are grown is also called a **terrace.** *...the landscape with its terraces of vines and olives.* **4** PLURAL N The **terraces** at a football ground are wide steps where some spectators stand. *...on the terraces of football clubs.*

terraced /terəˡst/. **1** ADJ In Britain, a **terraced** house is one of a row of similar houses joined together by their side walls. **2** ADJ A **terraced** hillside has flat areas of ground like steps built on it so that people can grow crops there. *...the forests and terraced vineyards.*

terrain /tereɪn/. UNCOUNT N WITH SUPP The **terrain** in an area is the type of land there. *The terrain was bare and flat.*

terrapin /terəpɪn/, **terrapins.** COUNT N A **terrapin** is a small turtle.

terrible /terəˡbəºl/. **1** ADJ A **terrible** experience or situation is very serious and unpleasant. *...a terrible accident.* **2** ADJ If you feel **terrible,** you feel ill or feel a very strong and unpleasant emotion. *...a terrible sense of guilt.* **3** ADJ If something is **terrible,** it is very bad or poor quality. *I've had a terrible day at the office... The food was terrible.*

terribly /terəˡbliˡ/. SUBMOD You use **terribly** to emphasize the extent or degree of something; an informal use. *I'm terribly sorry.*

terrier /terɪə/, **terriers.** COUNT N A **terrier** is a type of small dog.

terrific /tərɪfɪk/. **1** ADJ If you say that something is **terrific,** you mean that you are very pleased with it or that you like it a lot; an informal use. *Our new carpet looks terrific.* **2** ATTRIB ADJ **Terrific** also means very great in amount, degree, or intensity. *...a terrific thunderstorm... ...a terrific amount of money.*

terrify /terɪfaɪ/, **terrifies, terrifying, terrified.** VB WITH OBJ If something **terrifies** you, it makes you feel extremely frightened. *Rats terrify me.* ♦ **terrifying** ADJ *The most terrifying aspect of nuclear bombing is radiation.* ♦ **terrified** ADJ *My sister was too terrified to cry.*

territorial /terɪtɔːrɪəl/. ATTRIB ADJ **Territorial** means concerned with the ownership of a particular area of land or water. *...territorial boundaries.*

territory /terɪtəºriˡ/, **territories. 1** UNCOUNT N OR COUNT N The **territory** of a country is the land that it controls. *This meeting is to be held on neutral territory.* **2** UNCOUNT N WITH SUPP **Territory** is land that has a particular character. *We were passing through mountainous territory.* **3** UNCOUNT N WITH SUPP You can use **territory** to refer to an area of knowledge or experience. *All this is familiar territory to readers of her recent novels.*

terror /terə/. UNCOUNT N **Terror** is very great fear. *She awakened in terror as the flaming roof came crashing down.*

terrorise /terəraɪz/. See **terrorize.**

terrorism /terərɪzəºm/. UNCOUNT N **Terrorism** is the use of violence for political reasons. *These measures failed to bring acts of terrorism to an end.* ♦ **terrorist** /terərɪst/ COUNT N *They have given aid to terrorists... ...terrorist activities.*

terrorize /terəraɪz/, **terrorizes, terrorizing, terrorized;** also spelled **terrorise.** VB WITH OBJ If someone **terrorizes** you, they frighten you by threatening you. *Lee was a bully who terrorized us all.*

terse /tɜːs/, **terser, tersest.** ADJ A **terse** comment or statement is brief and unfriendly. *I received a terse and unsympathetic reply.*

TESL /tesəºl/. UNCOUNT N **TESL** is the teaching of English to people whose first language is not English. **TESL** is an abbreviation for 'teaching English as a second language'.

test /test/, **tests, testing, tested. 1** VB WITH OBJ When you **test** something, you try using it in order to find out what it is, what condition it is in, or how well it works. *The BBC in Scotland wanted to test the range of their transmitters... A number of new techniques were tested.* Also COUNT N *...an underground nuclear test.* **2** VB WITH OBJ If you **test** someone, you ask them questions to find out how much they know about something. *I will test you on your knowledge of French.* Also COUNT N *...a mathematics test.* **3** COUNT N If an event or situation is a **test** of a person or thing, it reveals their qualities or effectiveness. *...the first major test of the President's policies.* **4** COUNT N A medical **test** is an examination of a part of your body in order to check the state of your health. *...a blood test.*

PHRASES ● If you **put** something **to the test,** you try using it to see how useful or effective it is. *The idea is being put to the test in a theatre in Paris.*

testament /testəməˡnt/, **testaments. 1** COUNT N If one thing is a **testament** to another thing, it shows that the other thing exists or is true; a formal use. *The building is a testament to their success.* **2** See also **Old Testament, New Testament.**

test case, test cases. COUNT N A **test case** is a legal case which becomes an example for deciding other, similar cases.

testicle /testɪkəºl/, **testicles.** COUNT N A man's **testicles** are the two sex glands that produce sperm.

testify /testɪfaɪ/, **testifies, testifying, testified;** a formal word. **1** VB OR REPORT VB When someone **testifies,** they make a formal statement in a court of law. *None of the victims would appear in court to testify against him... Witnesses testify to his attempts at rape... One man testified that he had seen me with Jonathan.* **2** VB If something **testifies** to an idea, it shows that the idea is likely to be true. *All kinds of human experience testify to the close link between love and fear.*

testimonial /testɪməʊnɪəl/, **testimonials.** COUNT N A **testimonial** is a statement made by someone in authority saying how good someone or something is.

testimony /testɪməniˡ/, **testimonies. 1** UNCOUNT N OR COUNT N **Testimony** is a formal statement that someone makes in a court of law. *Three women backed up her testimony... Philip gave testimony against his own brother.* **2** UNCOUNT N WITH PREP 'to' If one thing is a **testimony** to another, it shows that the second thing exists or is true; a formal use. *This is spectacular testimony to the computer's creative powers.*

Test match, Test matches. COUNT N A **Test match** is a cricket or rugby match that is one of a series played between the same two countries.

test tube, test tubes. COUNT N A **test tube** is a small glass container used in chemical experiments.

test-tube baby, test-tube babies. COUNT N A **test-tube baby** is a baby that develops from an egg that is fertilized outside the mother's body and then replaced in her womb.

tetanus /tetəºnəs/. UNCOUNT N **Tetanus** is a serious and painful disease caused by germs getting into wounds.

tether /teðə/, **tethers, tethering, tethered. 1** VB WITH OBJ If you **tether** an animal, you tie it to a post. **2** PHRASE If you are **at the end of** your **tether,** you are so tired or unhappy that you cannot cope with your problems.

text /tekst/, **texts. 1** SING N The **text** of a book is the main written part of it, rather than the introduction, pictures, or index. **2** UNCOUNT N OR COUNT N **Text** is any written material. *These machines have the capacity to 'read' printed text... Herr Kohl produced the text of his statement.* **3** COUNT N A **text** is a book or other piece of writing connected with an academic subject. *...a text on Oriental philosophy.*

textbook /tekstbʊk/, **textbooks.** COUNT N A **textbook** is a book about a particular subject that is intended for students to use. *...a history textbook.*

textile /tekstaɪl/, **textiles. 1** COUNT N A **textile** is a woven cloth or fabric. **2** PLURAL N **Textiles** are the industries concerned with making cloth. *There are more people employed in textiles than in computers.*

texture /tekstʃə/, **textures.** UNCOUNT N OR COUNT N The **texture** of something is the way that it feels when you touch it. *...the slightly rough texture of the cloth.*

-th. SUFFIX **-th** is added to numbers written in figures and ending in 4, 5, 6, 7, 8, 9, 0, 11, 12, or 13 in order to form ordinal numbers. These numbers are pronounced as if they were written as words. For example, 7th is pronounced the same as 'seventh'.

than; usually pronounced /ðən/, but pronounced /ðæn/ when you are emphasizing it. **1** PREP OR CONJ You use **than** to link two parts of a comparison. *You've got more money than me... We talked for more than an hour... ...temperatures lower than 25 degrees... She was fatter than when he last saw her.* **2** PREP OR CONJ You also use **than** in order to link two parts of a contrast. *He chose the stairs rather than the lift... I would sooner read than watch television.*

thank /θæŋk/, **thanks, thanking, thanked. 1** CONVENTION You say **thanks** or **thank you** to express your gratitude when someone does something for you or gives you something. *Many thanks for your long and interesting letter... 'What'll you have, Castle? A whisky?'—'A small one, thank you.'* **2** VB WITH OBJ When you **thank** someone, you express your gratitude to them for something. *He thanked me for bringing the books.* **3** PLURAL N When you express your **thanks** to someone, you express your gratitude to them for something. *He sent a letter of thanks to Haldane.*

PHRASES ● You say **thank God, thank goodness** or **thank heavens** when you are very relieved about something. *Thank goodness it only lasts an hour.* ● If one thing happens **thanks to** another thing or a person, that thing or person caused it to happen. *Thanks to him I began to learn to trust my feelings... The building became very well known, thanks to detective films.* ● You say **'Thanks all the same'** when you are thanking someone for an offer that you are refusing. *'Do you want a lift?'—'No, but thanks all the same.'*

thankful /θæŋkfʊl/. PRED ADJ When you are **thankful,** you feel happy and relieved that something has happened. *We were thankful that it was all over.*

thankfully /θæŋkfəˡliˡ/. **1** ADV If you do something **thankfully,** you do it feeling happy and relieved that something is the case or that something has happened. *We sat down thankfully... 'It wasn't like that with Tony,' Alice said, thankfully.* **2** SENTENCE ADV You also use **thankfully** to express approval and relief about a statement that you are making. *Thankfully, the memory of it soon faded.*

thankless /θæŋklɪ²s/. ATTRIB ADJ A **thankless** job or task is one which is hard work and is which is not appreciated by other people. *She used to take on thankless jobs like running school dances.*

Thanksgiving /θæŋksgɪvɪŋ/. UNCOUNT N **Thanksgiving** or **Thanksgiving Day** is a public holiday in the United States and Canada in the autumn.

that /ðæt/, **those** /ðəʊz/. **That** can also be pronounced /ðəˡt/ for meanings 3 and 4. **1** DET OR PRON

You use **that** or **those** to refer to things or people already mentioned or known about. *That old woman saved my life... Not all crimes are committed for those reasons... 'Did you see him?'—'No.'—'That's a pity.'* 2 PRON OR DET You can use **those** to refer to people or things you are going to give details about. *I want to thank those of you who've offered to help... The scheme was set up to help those concerned with the teaching of reading.* 3 CONJ You use **that** after some verbs, nouns, and adjectives to introduce a clause. *She suggested that I telephoned you... He was motivated by the conviction that these tendencies would increase... It is important that you should know precisely what is needed.* 4 PRON You also use **that** to introduce a relative clause. *...the gate that opened onto the lake... For dessert there was ice cream that Mum had made.* 5 SUBMOD If something is not **that** bad or not **that** funny, it is not as bad or as funny as other people think. *It isn't quite that bad.*

PHRASES • You use **that is** or **that is to say** to give further details about something. *It deals with matters of social policy; that is to say, everything from housing to education.* • You use **that's that** to say there is nothing more you can do or say about a particular matter. *It was an accident, and that's that... The Ravenscrofts refused and that was that.* • **this and that:** see **this.**

thatched /θætʃt/. ATTRIB ADJ A **thatched** house has a roof made of straw or reeds. *...a three-hundred-year old thatched cottage.*

that's /ðæts/. **That's** is a spoken form of 'that is'.

thaw /θɔː/, **thaws, thawing, thawed.** 1 ERG VB When ice or snow **thaws,** it melts. *The snow soon thawed and they all went out for a walk... The ice was thawed by the warm wind.* 2 COUNT N A **thaw** is a period of warmer weather when the snow and ice melts. *A thaw had set in and the streets were slushy.* 3 VB WITH OBJ When you **thaw** frozen food, you leave it in a place where it can warm up so that it is ready for use. *Unwrap the pastry and then thaw it overnight.* 4 ERG VB When unfriendly people or unfriendly relationships **thaw,** they start to be more friendly. *The Vatican indicated that it might be thawing and accepting the critics' argument... A similar invitation thawed Jimmy Carter in 1979.*

the; usually pronounced /ðə/ before a consonant and /ði^1/ before a vowel, but pronounced /ðiː/ when you are emphasizing it. 1 DET You use **the** in front of a noun in order to indicate that you are referring to a person or thing that is known about or has just been mentioned, or when you are going to give more details about them. *The sea was really rough... ...Her Majesty the Queen... He said that she ought to see the doctor... They continued walking on the opposite pavement.* 2 DET You can also use **the** in front of a singular noun to refer to all people or things of that type. *The koala bear is a medium-sized creature that lives in trees.* 3 DET You can use **the** in front of a plural form of a surname to refer to a couple or to a whole family who have that surname. *...some friends of hers called the Hochstadts.* 4 DET You use **the** in front of an adjective to make it a noun referring to someone or something described by this adjective. *...the British and the French... The wounded were given first aid.* 5 DET You can use **the** in front of numbers which refer to dates or decades. *...Tuesday, May the thirteenth... ...Stockholm during the thirties.* 6 DET You use **the** in front of two comparative adjectives or adverbs to describe how one amount or quality changes in relation to another. *The more I hear about him, the less I like him... The longer we look at it the more interesting we find it.*

theatre /θɪətə/, **theatres;** spelled **theater** in American English. 1 COUNT N A **theatre** is a building with a stage on which plays and other entertainments are performed. *Her mother never went to the theatre.* 2 SING N You can use the **theatre** to refer to work in the theatre such as acting or writing plays. *She was only really happy when she was working in the theatre.* 3 COUNT N In a hospital, a **theatre** is the same as an operating theatre.

theatrical /θi^{1}ætrɪkə^{0}l/. 1 ATTRIB ADJ A **theatrical** event or production is one that is performed in a theatre. *...posters advertising theatrical productions.* 2 ATTRIB ADJ You can use **theatrical** to describe behaviour that is exaggerated, unnatural, and done deliberately for effect. *Jack moved forward with theatrical caution.*

theft /θeft/, **thefts.** COUNT N OR UNCOUNT N **Theft** is the act or crime of stealing. *He reported the theft of his passport... ...the drop in petty crime and theft.*

their /ðeə/. 1 DET You use **their** to indicate that something belongs or relates to people or things that have just been mentioned or whose identity is known. *...the car companies and their workers... Don't hope to change anyone or their attitudes.* 2 DET You also use **their** to refer to people with titles. *Their Lordships were already late for dinner.*

theirs /ðeəz/. PRON You use **theirs** to indicate that something belongs or relates to people or things that have just been mentioned or whose identity is known. *It was his fault, not theirs... They were off to visit a friend of theirs.*

them /ðem, ðəm/. **Them** is used as the object of a verb or preposition 1 PRON You use **them** to refer to people or things that have just been mentioned or whose identity is known. *He took off his glasses and put them in his pocket... I think some of them may attempt to take an overdose.* 2 PRON You can use **them** instead of 'him' or 'her' to refer to a person whose sex is not known or not stated. Some people consider this use to be incorrect. *If anyone phones, tell them I'm out.*

theme /θiːm/, **themes.** 1 COUNT N A **theme** in a discussion or lecture is a main idea or subject in it. *...organised public meetings on the theme: 'Law not War'.* 2 COUNT N A **theme** in an artist's or writer's work is an idea that is developed or repeated in it. *The main theme of the play was clear.* 3 COUNT N In music, a **theme** is a short simple tune on which a piece of music is based. *...variations on a theme.* 4 COUNT N A **theme** is also a tune that is played at the beginning and end of a television or radio programme.

themselves /ðə^{2}mselvz/. 1 REFL PRON You use **themselves** as the object of a verb or preposition when it refers to the same people or things as the subject of the clause or a previous object in the clause. *They are trying to educate themselves... They had ceased to think of themselves as rebels.* 2 REFL PRON You also use **themselves** to emphasize the subject or object of a clause, and to make it clear who or what you are referring to. *Let's turn to the books themselves... ...a cultural preference on the part of the Chinese themselves.* 3 REFL PRON If people do something **themselves,** they do it without any help or interference from anyone else. *They must settle it themselves and get their own solutions.*

then /ðen/. 1 ADV **Then** means at a particular time in the past or in the future. *I didn't have it then... The situation's changed since then... I'm going to see him at lunchtime. He's busy till then.* 2 ADV You use **then** to say that one thing happens or comes after another. *He went to the village school, then to the grammar school, and then to the university... You go right, then left.* 3 SENTENCE ADV You use **then** in conversation to link your statement to what has just been said. *'Are you a student?'—'No, I'm not'—'What do you do then?'* 4 SENTENCE ADV You also use **then** to introduce a summary or conclusion to what you have just said, or to end a conversation. *Democracy, then, is a form of government... If any questions do occur to you, then don't hesitate to write... Well, that's settled, then... Bye then.* 5 SENTENCE ADV You also use **then** after words like 'now', 'well', and 'okay', to emphasize what you are about to say. *Now then, it's time you went to bed.* 6 SENTENCE ADV You use **then** at the beginning of a sentence or after 'and' or 'but' to introduce an extra piece of information. *Then there could be a tax problem... Iron would do the job much better. But then you can't weld iron so easily.* 7 **now and then:** see **now.** • **there and then:** see **there.**

thence /ðens/. ADV **Thence** means from the place that has just been mentioned; a formal, old-fashioned use. *He hitched south towards Italy, and thence into France.*

theologian /θɪələʊdʒɪən/, **theologians.** COUNT N A **theologian** is someone who studies religion and God.

theology /θi^{1}ɒlədʒi^1/. UNCOUNT N **Theology** is the study of religion and God. *...a diploma in theology.* ♦ **theological** /θɪəlɒdʒɪkə^{0}l/ ADJ *...a theological college.*

theorem /θɪərə^{0}m/, **theorems.** COUNT N A **theorem** is a statement in mathematics that can be logically proved to be true. *...the theorem of Pythagoras... ...a book about the attempts to prove Fermat's last theorem.*

theoretical /θɪəretɪkə^{0}l/. ATTRIB ADJ **Theoretical** means based on or concerning the ideas and abstract principles of a subject, rather than the practical aspects of it. *...theoretical ideas which, in practice, may not work.*

theoretically /θɪəretɪkə^{0}li^1/. SENTENCE ADV You use **theoretically** to say that although something is supposed to happen or to be the case, it may not in fact happen or be the case. *Laws still theoretically controlled the availability of alcohol... It was theoretically possible to get permission from the council.*

theorize /θɪəraɪz/, **theorizes, theorizing, theorized;** also spelled **theorise.** VB If you **theorize** about something, you develop ideas about it to try and explain it. *...people who theorize about teaching.*

theory /θɪəri^1/, **theories.** 1 COUNT N A **theory** is an idea or set of ideas intended to explain something. *...Darwin's theory of evolution.* 2 UNCOUNT N **Theory** is the set of rules, principles, or ideas that a practical method or skill is based on. *...Marxist economic theory... ...the theory and practice of inoculation.* 3 PHRASE You use **in theory** to say that although something is supposed to happen or to be the case, it may not in fact happen or be the case. *In theory all British citizens are eligible for this.*

therapeutic /θerəpjuːtɪk/. 1 ADJ If something is **therapeutic,** it helps you to feel happier and more relaxed. *All that fresh air is very therapeutic.* 2 ADJ **Therapeutic** treatment is designed to treat a disease or to improve a person's health.

therapist /θerəpɪst/, **therapists.** COUNT N A **therapist** is a person skilled in a particular type of therapy. *...a speech therapist.*

therapy /θerəpi^1/. UNCOUNT N **Therapy** is the treatment of mental or physical illness, often without the use of drugs or operations. *...a short course of heat therapy.*

there /ðeə/. 1 PRON You use **there** as the subject of the verb 'be' to say that something exists or does not exist, or to draw attention to it. *There was a new cushion on one of the settees... There must be a reason.* 2 PRON You use **there** in front of some intransitive verbs to emphasize the meaning. The subject of the verb is placed after the verb; a formal use. *Beside them there curls up a twist of blue smoke... There still remains the point about creativity.* 3 ADV If something is **there,** it exists or is available. *We talked about reality, about whether things are really there... The play group is there for the children of staff and students.* 4 ADV You use **there** to refer to a place that has already been mentioned. *I must get home. Bill's there on his own.* 5 ADV You say **there** to indicate a place that you are pointing to or looking at. *'Over there,' she said and pointed to the door... Where's the ball? Oh, there it is.* 6 ADV You use **there** when speaking on the telephone to ask if someone is available to speak to you. *Is Veronica there, please?* 7 ADV You use **there** to refer to a point that someone has made in a conversation. *Could I interrupt you just there?... You're right there Howard.* 8 ADV You also use **there** to refer to a stage reached in an activity or process. *I'll write to the headmaster and then take the matter from there.*

PHRASES • If someone is **not all there,** they are stupid or not mentally alert; an informal use. • If something happens **there and then** or **then and there,** it happens immediately. *He terminated the discussion then and there.* • You say **'There you are'** or **'There you go'** when accepting an unsatisfactory situation. *It wasn't a very good reason for refusing, but there you are.* • You also use **'There you are'** or **'There you go'** to emphasize that something proves you right. *There you are, Mabel! What did I tell you?* • You also say **'There you are'** or **'There you go'** when you are giving something to someone. *'There you are', he said, handing the screws to me.* • You can add **'so there'** to what you are saying to show that you will not change your mind about a decision you have made; an informal use. *Well, I won't apologize, so there.*

thereabouts /ðeərəbaʊts/. PHRASE You can add **or thereabouts** after a number to indicate that it is approximate. *It was in 1982 or thereabouts.*

thereafter /ðeərɑːftə/. ADV **Thereafter** means after the event or date mentioned; a formal use. *We first met in 1966 and I saw him quite often thereafter.*

thereby /ðeəbaɪ/. SENTENCE ADV **Thereby** means as an inevitable result of the event or action mentioned; a formal use. *The President had lied and thereby obstructed justice.*

therefore /ðeəfɔː/. SENTENCE ADV You use **therefore** to introduce a conclusion. *The new car is smaller and therefore cheaper.* perciò

therein /ðeərɪn/. ADV **Therein** means in the place just mentioned or because of the situation just mentioned; a formal use. *...the lakes and the fish therein... He was not a snob, you see. And therein lay his downfall.*

thereupon /ðeərəpɒn/. ADV **Thereupon** means immediately after an event and usually as a result of it; a formal use. *I flung a few copies of the report in his lap, which thereupon fell to the floor.*

thermal /θɜːmə^{0}l/. 1 ATTRIB ADJ **Thermal** means relating to heat or caused by heat. *...the thermal efficiency of an engine... ...thermal energy.* 2 ATTRIB ADJ **Thermal** clothes are specially designed to keep you warm. *...thermal underwear.*

thermometer /θəmɒmɪtə/, **thermometers.** COUNT N A **thermometer** is an instrument for measuring the temperature of a room or of a person's body. *The thermometer reads 92 degrees.*

Thermos /θɜːməs/, **Thermoses.** COUNT N A **Thermos** or a **Thermos flask** is a container used to keep drinks at a constant temperature; a trademark.

thermostat /θɜːməstæt/, **thermostats.** COUNT N A **thermostat** is a device used to keep the temperature of a car engine or a house at a particular level.

thesaurus /θɪ²sɔːrəs/, **thesauruses.** COUNT N A **thesaurus** is a reference book in which words with similar meanings are grouped together.

these /ðiːz/. **These** is the plural of **this.**

thesis /θiːsɪs/, **theses** /θiːsiːz/. 1 COUNT N A **thesis** is an idea or theory expressed as a statement and discussed in a logical way. *It is my thesis that Australia underwent fundamental changes in the 1920s.* 2 COUNT N A **thesis** is also a long piece of writing, based on original research, that is done as part of a university degree. *She is writing a thesis on Jane Austen.*

they /ðeɪ/. **They** is used as the subject of a verb. 1 PRON You use **they** to refer to people or things that have just been mentioned or whose identity is known. *All universities have chancellors. They are always rather senior people.* 2 PRON You also use **they** to refer to people in general, or to a group of people whose identity is not actually stated. *Isn't that what they call love.* 3 PRON You can use **they** instead of 'he' or 'she' to refer to a person whose sex is not known or not stated. Some people consider this use to be incorrect. *Nearly everybody thinks they're middle class... I was going to stay with a friend, but they were ill.*

they'd /ðeɪd/. **They'd** is the usual spoken form of 'they had', especially when 'had' is an auxiliary verb. **They'd** is also a spoken form of 'they would'. *They said they'd read it all before... I wish they'd publish more books like this.*

they'll /ðeɪə⁰l/. **They'll** is the usual spoken form of 'they will'. *They'll probably sell it cheaper.*

they're /ðɛə, ðeɪə/. **They're** is the usual spoken form of 'they are'. *They're not interested.*

they've /ðeɪv/. **They've** is the usual spoken form of 'they have', especially when 'have' is an auxiliary verb. *They've been studying very hard.*

thick /θɪk/, **thicker, thickest.** 1 ADJ OR ADV If something is **thick**, there is a large distance between its two opposite surfaces. *We were separated by thick concrete walls... Last winter the snow lay thick on the ground.* ♦ **thickly** ADV *She buttered my bread thickly.* 2 ADJ If something that consists of several things is **thick**, the things in it are present in large quantities. *She had a lot of thick black hair... They were on the edge of the thick forest... She came out of the thickest part of the crowd.* ♦ **thickly** ADV *Plants and trees grew thickly on both sides of the river.* 3 ADJ You use **thick** to say how wide or deep something is. *The tree was one foot thick at the base.* ♦ **thickness** UNCOUNT N *Insert a new wire of the same thickness and wind it round the screws.* 4 ADJ **Thick** liquids contain very little water and do not flow easily. *The chef has made the sauce too thick... ...thick cream.* 5 ADJ **Thick** smoke or fog is difficult to see through. *The fog seemed to be getting thicker.* 6 ADJ If someone's voice is **thick**, they are not speaking clearly, for example because they are ill, upset, or drunk. *His voice sounded blurred and thick.* ♦ **thickly** ADV *'Let's get out of here,' Tom said thickly.* 7 ADJ If you say that someone is **thick**, you mean that they are stupid; an informal use. *They were too thick to notice it.*

PHRASES ● If things happen **thick and fast**, they happen very quickly and in large numbers. *More discoveries followed thick and fast.* ● To be **thick with** something means to be full of it or be covered with it. *The air was thick with butterflies... The windows were thick with grime.* ● If you are **in the thick of** an activity or situation, you are very involved in it. *It won't be long before Amanda is in the thick of O levels.* ● If you do something **through thick and thin**, you do it even though the conditions or circumstances are very bad. *She stayed with her husband through thick and thin.*

thicken /θɪkə⁰n/, **thickens, thickening, thickened.** 1 VB If something **thickens**, it becomes more closely grouped together or denser than it was before. *Here the vegetation thickens into a jungle... By noon the cloud layer had thickened.* 2 ERG VB When you **thicken** a liquid you make it stiffer and more solid. *You can use flour to thicken sauces... After a while the mixture thickens.*

thicket /θɪkɪt/, **thickets.** COUNT N A **thicket** is a small group of trees or bushes growing closely together.

thickset /θɪksɛt/. ADJ A **thickset** person is broad and heavy. *...a big, thickset man with heavy shoulders.*

thick-skinned. ADJ A **thick-skinned** person is not easily hurt by what other people say to them.

thief /θiːf/, **thieves.** COUNT N A **thief** is a person who steals something from another person, especially without using violence. *...jewel thieves.*

thieving /θiːvɪŋ/. ATTRIB ADJ **Thieving** means involved in stealing things. *...those thieving village kids.*

thigh /θaɪ/, **thighs.** COUNT N Your **thighs** are the top parts of your legs, between your knees and your hips. *I walked the last six miles in water up to my thighs.*

thimble /θɪmbə⁰l/, **thimbles.** COUNT N A **thimble** is a small metal or plastic object, used to protect your finger when you are sewing.

thin /θɪn/, **thinner, thinnest; thins, thinning, thinned.** 1 ADJ If something is **thin**, there is a small distance between its two opposite surfaces. *...their tall, thin house... ...thin cotton cloth.* ♦ **thinly** ADV *...fresh, thinly cut bread.* 2 ADJ A **thin** person or animal has very little fat on their body. *Angela was dreadfully thin.* 3 ADJ **Thin** liquids contain a lot of water. *The liquid was thin and greyish brown.* 4 ADJ A crowd of people that is **thin** has very few people in it. *The crowd seemed suddenly thinner.* ♦ **thinly** ADV *...a thinly populated region.* 5 VB If your hair **is thinning** you are beginning to go bald.

PHRASES ● If people or things are **thin on the ground**, there are not very many of them and so they are hard to find. *Good new plays are still rather thin on the ground.* ● to disappear **into thin air**: see **air.**

thin down. PHR VB When you **thin** a liquid **down**, you add more water or other liquid to it. *The paint has been thinned down too much.*

thing /θɪŋ/, **things.** 1 COUNT N WITH SUPP You use **thing** as a substitute for another word when you do not want to be more precise, when you are referring to something that has already been mentioned, or when you are going to give more details about it. *He needed a few things so we went to the store to purchase them... It's silly to train a group of people just to do one thing... A terrible thing happened to me on my way to work... The fourth drawer holds family things such as photographs and letters.* 2 COUNT N A **thing** is a physical object, rather than plants, animals, or human beings. *He's only interested in things and not people.* 3 PLURAL N WITH POSS Your **things** are your clothes or possessions. *She changed into her bathing things... I like my own things around me: my photos and books.* 4 PLURAL N **Things** refers to life in general and the way it affects you. *Things are going very well for us at the moment.* 5 COUNT N WITH SUPP You can call a person or an animal a **thing** when you are expressing your feelings towards them. *She was very cold, poor thing.*

PHRASES ● You can say **'The thing is'** to introduce an explanation or opinion relating to something that has just been said; used in speech. *I can't come on Thursday. The thing is, I've already arranged to do something on Thursday.* ● You say **for one thing** when you give only one reason for something, but want to indicate that there are other reasons. *I prefer badminton to squash. It's not so tiring for one thing.* ● If you say **it is just one of those things**, you mean that you cannot explain why something happens. ● If you **have a thing** about someone or something, or **make a thing** about them, you have very strong feelings about them and think they are important; an informal use. *I've got a thing about drinking... He made a big thing of not eating chilli.*

think /θɪŋk/, **thinks, thinking, thought** /θɔːt/. 1 REPORT VB OR VB If you **think** that something is the case, you have the opinion that it is the case. *I think a woman has as much right to work as a man... At first I thought he was asleep... She thought of Deirdre simply as an old chum... She's cleverer than I thought.* 2 VB WITH 'about' When you **think** about something, you consider it. *That ought to make us think about how we can make a safer product.* 3 VB WITH 'of' When you **think** of something or someone, you remember them or they come into your mind. *I can never think of her name... He can think of no reason for going... ...a method which had never been thought of before.* 4 VB WITH 'of' OR 'about' To **think** of someone also means to show consideration for them. *It was very kind of you to think of him... You never think about anybody but yourself!* 5 VB WITH ADJUNCT If you **think** a lot of someone or something, you admire them. *She thinks a lot of you... I didn't think much of his letter.* 6 REPORT VB When you **are thinking** something, you are concentrating your attention on it. *I lay there thinking how funny it was.* 7 VB WITH 'of' OR 'about' If you **are thinking** of doing something, you are considering doing it. *Is he still thinking of going away to Italy for a month?* 8 See also **thinking, thought.**

PHRASES ● You can say **'I think'** to sound less forceful or rude. *I think I ought to go... I think that you will find my figures are correct... Thank you, I don't think I will.* ● If you were intending to do something but **think better of it**, you decide not to do it. *She was on the point of waking Ben again, but then thought better of it.* ● If you say that someone would **think nothing** of doing something difficult or strange, you mean that they would do it and not think that it was difficult or strange at all. *We would think nothing of walking six miles just to post a letter.* ● **come to think of it**: see **come.** ● to **think the world of** someone: see **world.**

think back. PHR VB If you **think back**, you remember things that happened in the past. *I'm thinking back to my own experience as a teacher.*

think over. PHR VB If you **think** something **over**, you consider it carefully before making a decision. *I wanted to think over one or two business problems.*

think through. PHR VB If you **think** a problem or situation **through**, you consider it thoroughly. *I haven't really thought the whole business through.*

think up. PHR VB If you **think up** something clever or unusual, you create it in your mind. *...a new financial agreement he had thought up.*

thinker /θɪŋkə/, **thinkers.** COUNT N A **thinker** is someone who is famous for their ideas.

thinking /θɪŋkɪŋ/. 1 UNCOUNT N **Thinking** is the activity of using your brain to consider a problem or to create an idea. *That requires a great deal of serious thinking.* 2 UNCOUNT N WITH SUPP The general ideas or opinions of a person or group can be referred to as their **thinking.** *We are so alike in our thinking.* 3 See also **wishful thinking.**

third /θɜːd/, **thirds.** 1 ADJ The **third** item in a series is the one that you count as number three. *This room was on the third floor.* 2 COUNT N A **third** is one of three equal parts of something. *It covers a third of the world's surface.*

third party, third parties. 1 COUNT N A **third party** is someone who is not one of the two main people or groups involved in a business or legal matter, but who becomes involved in a minor way. *A third party from outside the village was brought in as a witness.* 2 ADJ If you have **third-party** insurance and cause an accident, your insurance company will pay money only to other people who are hurt or whose property is damaged, and not to you.

third-rate. ADJ Something that is **third-rate** is of an extremely poor quality or standard. *...the seedy world of third-rate theatricals.*

Third World. PROPER N The poorer countries of Africa, Asia, and South America are sometimes referred to as the **Third World.** *I had seen a good deal of the Third World before I visited Calcutta.*

thirst /θɜːst/. 1 SING N If you have a **thirst**, you feel a need to drink something. *She had a terrible thirst.* 2 UNCOUNT N **Thirst** is the condition of not having enough to drink. *She was dying of thirst.* 3 SING N WITH 'for' A **thirst** for something is a very strong desire for it; a literary use. *...his thirst for knowledge.*

thirsty /θɜːsti¹/. 1 ADJ If you are **thirsty**, you feel the need to drink something. *Have you got any water? I'm thirsty.* 2 ATTRIB ADJ **Thirsty** is used to describe activities that make you thirsty. *Gardening is really thirsty work.*

thirteen /θɜːtiːn/. **Thirteen** is the number 13. *He hadn't appeared in a film for thirteen years.*

thirteenth /θɜːtiːnθ/. ADJ The **thirteenth** item in a series is the one that you count as number thirteen.

thirtieth /θɜːti¹ə¹θ/. ADJ The **thirtieth** item in a series is the one that you count as number thirty.

thirty /θɜːti¹/, **thirties. Thirty** is the number 30. *...thirty years of marriage.*

this /ðɪs/, **these** /ðiːz/. 1 DET OR PRON You use **this** to refer to a person or thing that has been mentioned, to someone or something that is present, or to something that is happening. *This was a sad end to her career... So, for all these reasons, my advice is to be very, very careful... This is Desiree, my father's second wife... Get these kids out of here... 'My God,' I said. 'This is awful.'* 2 DET In informal speech, people use **this** to introduce a person or thing into a story. *I stopped at a junction and this bowler-hatted gent comes up.* 3 DET You use **this** to refer to the present time. *Could I make an appointment to see the doctor this morning please?* 4 DET **This** means 'next' when you use it with words such as 'Friday' or 'summer'. *Let's fix a time. This Sunday. Four o'clock.* 5 PHRASE You can refer to a variety of things as **this and that.** *'What have you been up to ?'—'This and that.'*

thistle /θɪsə⁰l/, **thistles.** COUNT N A **thistle** is a wild plant with prickly leaves and purple flowers.

thong /θɒŋ/, **thongs.** COUNT N A **thong** is a long, thin strip of leather, plastic, or rubber.

thorn /θɔːn/, **thorns.** COUNT N **Thorns** are the sharp points on some plants and trees, for example on a rose bush. *He stepped on a sharp thorn.*

thorny /θɔːni¹/. 1 ADJ A **thorny** plant or tree is covered with thorns. 2 ADJ A **thorny** problem or question is difficult to deal with.

thorough /θʌrə/. 1 ADJ A **thorough** action is done very completely. *...a thorough search.* ♦ **thoroughly** ADV *They had not studied the language thoroughly.* ♦ **thoroughness** UNCOUNT N *...the thoroughness of the training programme.* 2 ADJ People who are **thorough**

do things in a careful and methodical way. *He is enormously thorough and full of inspiration.* ♦ **thoroughness** UNCOUNT N *The President was impressed by his speed and thoroughness.* 3 ATTRIB ADJ You can use **thorough** for emphasis. *I'd enjoy giving him a thorough beating.* ♦ **thoroughly** ADV *...a thoroughly unreasonable person... Yes, I thoroughly agree.*

thoroughfare /θʌrəfɛə/, **thoroughfares.** COUNT N A **thoroughfare** is a main road in a town or city; a formal use. *We went back towards the main thoroughfare.*

those /ðəʊz/. **Those** is the plural of **that.**

though /ðəʊ/. 1 CONJ OR SENTENCE ADV You use **though** to introduce a fact or comment which contrasts with something else that is being said, or makes it seem surprising. *She wore a fur coat, even though it was a very hot day... Though he hadn't stopped working all day, he wasn't tired... 'It's not very useful.'—'It's pretty, though, isn't it?'* 2 **as though:** see **as.**

thought /θɔːt/, **thoughts.** 1 **Thought** is the past tense and past participle of **think.** 2 COUNT N A **thought** is an idea in your mind. *I had vague thoughts of emigrating.* 3 UNCOUNT N **Thought** is the activity of thinking. *She frowned as though deep in thought... After giving our predicament some thought, he said he had a proposal.* 4 UNCOUNT N WITH SUPP You can refer to a set of ideas as a particular type of **thought.** *...two schools of socialist thought.* 5 PLURAL N Your **thoughts** are the ideas in your mind when you are thinking about something. *They walked back, each deep in his own private thoughts... His mind was empty except for thoughts of her.* 6 PLURAL N Your **thoughts** on something are your opinions on it. *Rothermere disclosed his thoughts on Britain.* 7 See also **second thoughts.**

thoughtful /θɔːtfʊl/. 1 ADJ If you are **thoughtful,** you are quiet because you are thinking about something. *He looked thoughtful for a moment.* ♦ **thoughtfully** ADV *Tom closed the book thoughtfully.* 2 ADJ A **thoughtful** person remembers what other people want or need, and is kind and helpful. *I thanked him for his thoughtful gesture.* ♦ **thoughtfully** ADV *The book thoughtfully provides a clue on how to do this.*

thoughtless /θɔːtlɪ²s/. ADJ **Thoughtless** people forget or ignore what other people want, need, or feel. *I had to scold Vita severely for being so thoughtless.* ♦ **thoughtlessly** ADV *Traditional sources of employment are thoughtlessly destroyed.*

thousand /θaʊzənd/, **thousands.** 1 A **thousand** is the number 1,000. *...an annual income of twenty thousand dollars.* 2 QUANTIF **Thousands** is often used to mean a very large number. *I've told him thousands of times.* 3 **a thousand and one:** see **one.**

thousandth /θaʊzənθ/, **thousandths.** 1 ADJ The **thousandth** item in a series is the one you count as number one thousand. 2 COUNT N A **thousandth** is one of a thousand equal parts of something. *...a thousandth of a second.*

thrash /θræʃ/, **thrashes, thrashing, thrashed.** 1 VB WITH OBJ If someone **thrashes** you, they hit you several times. *We were thrashed a lot at school.* ♦ **thrashing** COUNT N *He got a thrashing from his father.* 2 VB WITH OBJ If someone **thrashes** you in a game or contest, they defeat you completely; an informal use. ♦ **thrashing** COUNT N *...the thrashing our team got at Southampton.*

thrash around. PHR VB If you **thrash around,** you twist and turn your body quickly and violently. *The boy was thrashing around, trying to get free.*

thrash out. PHR VB When people **thrash out** something such as a policy, they discuss it until they agree on an acceptable form of it. *...an agreement that we had already thrashed out.*

thread /θrɛd/, **threads, threading, threaded.** 1 COUNT N OR UNCOUNT N A **thread** is a long, thin piece of cotton, silk, nylon, or wool. Thread is used in sewing. 2 COUNT N The **thread** on something such as a screw or the top of a container is the raised spiral line around it. 3 COUNT N The **thread** in an argument or story is the idea or theme that connects the different parts together. *He had lost his thread and didn't know what to say next.* 4 VB WITH OBJ When you **thread** a needle, you put a piece of thread through the hole at the end. 5 PHRASE If you **thread your way** through a group of people or things, you go through the gaps between them. *We turned and threaded our way through the fairground.*

threadbare /θrɛdbɛə/. ADJ **Threadbare** clothes and carpets are old and have become thin. *O'Shea's suit was baggy and threadbare.*

threat /θrɛt/, **threats.** 1 COUNT N OR UNCOUNT N If someone makes a **threat,** they say that they will harm you, especially if you do not do what they want. *We mustn't give in to threats... Under threat of death, he confessed.* 2 SING N You can refer to anything that seems likely to harm you as a **threat.** *I was becoming a real threat to his plans... ...the threat of flooding.*

threaten /θrɛtəⁿn/, **threatens, threatening, threatened.** 1 VB WITH TO-INF OR OBJ If you **threaten** to do something that will harm someone, you warn them that you will do it. *He threatened to resign... They were threatened with imprisonment.* 2 VB WITH OBJ If something **threatens** people or things, it is likely to harm them. *He said that the war threatened the peace of the whole world... The whole country is threatened with starvation.* 3 VB WITH TO-INF If something **threatens** to do something unpleasant, it seems likely to do it. *The riots threatened to get out of hand.*

threatening /θrɛtəⁿnɪŋ/. ADJ Something or someone that is **threatening** seems likely to cause harm. *...a threatening environment... He became angry and threatening.* ♦ **threateningly** ADV *He advanced threateningly on the boy.*

three /θriː/, **threes. Three** is the number 3.

three-dimensional /θriː dəmɛnʃəⁿnəl, -ʃənəⁿl/. ADJ A **three-dimensional** object is solid rather than flat. *...a three-dimensional model of the theatre.*

three-quarters. QUANTIF **Three-quarters** of something is a half of it plus a quarter of it. *Three-quarters of the world's surface is covered by water... ...one and three-quarter hours.* Also ADV *The tank is three-quarters full.*

thresh /θrɛʃ/, **threshes, threshing, threshed.** VB WITH OBJ When people **thresh** corn, wheat, or rice, they beat it in order to separate the grains from the rest of it.

threshold /θrɛʃhⁿəʊld/, **thresholds.** 1 COUNT N The **threshold** of a building or room is the floor in the doorway, or the doorway itself; a formal use. *Madame stood on the threshold... Morris had never crossed the threshold of a public house before.* 2 PHRASE If you are **on the threshold of** something, you are about to experience it; a formal use. *He was on the threshold of public life.*

threw /θruː/. **Threw** is the past tense of **throw.**

thrift /θrɪft/. UNCOUNT N **Thrift** is the practice of being thrifty.

thrifty /θrɪftiˡ/, **thriftier, thriftiest.** ADJ Someone who is **thrifty** saves money and does not waste things. *She was a thrifty housekeeper.*

thrill /θrɪl/, **thrills, thrilling, thrilled.** 1 COUNT N If something gives you a **thrill,** it gives you a sudden feeling of excitement or pleasure. *The sound of the bell sent a thrill of anticipation through her... The thrill for me was finding the rare specimens.* 2 VB WITH OBJ If something **thrills** you, it gives you a thrill. *It's a sight that never fails to thrill me.*

thrilled /θrɪld/. PRED ADJ If you are **thrilled** about something, you are pleased and excited about it. *I was thrilled to be sitting next to such a distinguished author.*

thriller /θrɪlə/, **thrillers.** COUNT N A **thriller** is a book, film, or play that tells an exciting story about dangerous, frightening, or mysterious events. *...a spy thriller.*

thrilling /θrɪlɪŋ/. ADJ Something that is **thrilling** is very exciting and enjoyable. *...a thrilling adventure... She gave a thrilling performance.*

thrive /θraɪv/, **thrives, thriving, thrived.** VB When people or things **thrive,** they are healthy, happy, or successful. *Are you the type of person who thrives on activity?... My business was thriving.* ♦ **thriving** ADJ *...a thriving community.*

throat /θrəʊt/, **throats.** 1 COUNT N Your **throat** is the back of your mouth and the top part of the tubes inside your neck. *His throat was so dry that he could hardly swallow.* 2 COUNT N Your **throat** is also the front part of your neck. *He grabbed the man by the throat.*

PHRASES ● If two people or groups are **at each other's throats,** they are quarrelling or fighting. ● If you **ram** or **force** something **down** someone's **throat,** you keep mentioning it in order to make them accept it or believe it. *They have this viewpoint rammed down their throats every day.* ● to **clear** your **throat:** see **clear.**

throb /θrɒb/, **throbs, throbbing, throbbed.** 1 VB If a part of your body **throbs,** you feel a series of strong beats there. *His head was throbbing.* 2 VB You say that something **throbs** when it vibrates and makes a loud, rhythmic noise. *The drums seemed to throb in his ears.* Also COUNT N *...the throb of the engine.*

throes /θrəʊz/. PHRASE If you are busy doing something, you can say that you are **in the throes of** it. *The British Army was in the throes of reorganization.*

throne /θrəʊn/, **thrones.** 1 COUNT N A **throne** is a special chair used by a king or queen on important occasions. 2 SING N The position of being king or queen is sometimes referred to as the **throne.** *...when Queen Victoria was on the throne... ...the heir to the throne.*

throng /θrɒŋ/, **throngs, thronging, thronged;** a literary word. 1 COUNT N A **throng** is a large crowd of people. *A patient throng was waiting in silence.* 2 VB WITH ADJUNCT OR OBJ When people **throng** somewhere, they go there in great numbers. *Mourners thronged to the funeral... The lane was thronged with shoppers.*

throttle /θrɒtəⁿl/, **throttles, throttling, throttled.** VB WITH OBJ To **throttle** someone means to kill them by holding them tightly by the throat so that they cannot breathe.

through /θruː/. 1 PREP OR ADV To move **through** a hole or opening means to move directly from one side of it to the other. *Go straight through that door and then turn right... No one can get their hand through.* 2 PREP OR ADV If you cut **through** something such as a rope, you cut it into two pieces. *The fish must have chewed right through it... It went through like a knife through butter.* 3 PREP OR ADV If you move **through** a place or area, you move across it or in it. *We drove through London... We decided to drive straight through to Birmingham.* 4 PREP OR ADV If something goes into the middle of an object and comes out of the other side, you can say that it passes **through** the object. *...a hat with a feather stuck through it.* 5 PREP If you can see, hear, or feel something **through** a particular thing, that thing is between you and the thing you can see, hear, or feel. *Lonnie gazed out through a side window... I can hear John snoring right through the partition... She could feel the gravel through the soles of her slippers.* 6 PREP OR ADV If something happens **through** a period of time, it happens from the beginning until the end. *I wished that I could stay through the winter... We had no rain from March right through to October.* 7 PREP If you go **through** an experience, it happens to you. *He didn't want to go through all that divorce business again.* 8 PREP If you live **through** a historical event, it takes place while you are alive. *He lived through the decline of the Liberal Party.* 9 PRED ADJ If you are **through** with something, you no longer do it, use it, or want to be involved with it. *He was through with seminars and tutorials.* 10 PREP If something happens because of something else, you can say that it happens **through** it. *Many people have difficulty in walking, for example through age or frailty... They were opposed to change through violence.* 11 PREP If you go **through** or look **through** a lot of things, you deal with them one after another. *I wanted to read through as much information as possible... She was sorting through a pile of socks.*

PHRASES ● You use expressions such as **halfway through** and **all the way through** to indicate to what extent an action or task is completed. *Harris tried to stop the operation halfway through... I do not think she ever saw a play right through.* ● **Through and through** means thoroughly or completely. *Those boards are rotten through and through.*

throughout /θruːaʊt/. 1 PREP OR ADV If something happens **throughout** an event or period of time, it happens during the whole of it. *This dream recurred throughout her life... We co-operated throughout with trade unionists.* 2 PREP OR ADV If something happens or exists **throughout** a place, it happens or exists in all parts of it. *The pictures can be transmitted by satellite throughout the world... The house was carpeted throughout.*

throw /θrəʊ/, **throws, throwing, threw** /θruː/, **thrown** /θrəʊn/. 1 VB WITH OBJ If you **throw** an object that you are holding, you move your hand quickly and let go of the object, so that it moves through the air. *Roger picked up a stone and threw it at Henry.* 2 VB WITH OBJ AND ADJUNCT To **throw** something into a place or position means to cause it to fall there. *Tom undressed in the dark, throwing his clothes carelessly over a chair... The train braked violently, throwing everyone to the floor.* 3 VB WITH OBJ AND ADJUNCT If you **throw** a part of your body somewhere, you move it there suddenly and with a lot of force. *She threw her arms around his neck... He threw himself on his bed.* 4 VB WITH OBJ If a horse **throws** its rider, it makes the rider fall off. 5 VB WITH OBJ AND ADJUNCT To **throw** someone into an unpleasant situation means to suddenly cause them to be in that situation. *The thought of being late would throw her into a state of panic... The Depression had thrown almost everybody out of work.* 6 VB WITH OBJ AND ADJUNCT If something **throws** light or shadow on something else, it causes that thing to have light or shadow on it. *A spotlight threw a pool of violet light onto the stage.* 7 REFL VB OR VB WITH OBJ, WITH 'into' If you **throw** yourself into an activity, you become involved in it actively and enthusiastically. *Mrs Kaul threw herself into her work heart and soul... Many women throw all of their energies into a career.* 8 VB WITH OBJ If someone **throws** a fit or tantrum, they suddenly start to behave in an uncontrolled way. *She threw a fit of hysterics.* 9 VB WITH OBJ If something such as a remark or an experience **throws** you, it confuses you because it is unexpected; an informal use. *It was the fact that she was married that threw me.* 10 **a stone's throw:** see **stone.** ● to **throw light on** something: see **light.**

throw away. PHR VB 1 If you **throw away** something you do not want, you get rid of it. *She likes to keep things, even old things, rather than throw them away.* 2 If you **throw away** something good that you have, you waste it. *They threw away their advantage.*

throw in. PHR VB If the person who is selling you something **throws in** something else, they give you the extra thing and only ask you to pay for the first one.

throw out. PHR VB 1 If you **throw** something **out,** you get rid of it. *The broken cooking pots were thrown out.* 2 If you **throw** someone **out,** you force them to leave. *Her parents threw her out when they found she was pregnant.*

throw up. PHR VB To **throw up** means to vomit; an informal use.

throwback /θrəʊbæk/, **throwbacks.** COUNT N If something is a **throwback,** it is like something that existed a long time ago. *His sentiments were a throwback to the old colonial days.*

thrown /θrəʊn/. **Thrown** is the past participle of **throw.**

thrush /θrʌʃ/, **thrushes.** COUNT N A **thrush** is a small brown bird with a speckled chest.

thrust /θrʌst/, **thrusts, thrusting. Thrust** is used in the present tense, and is the past tense and past participle. 1 VB WITH OBJ AND ADJUNCT If you **thrust** something somewhere, you push or move it there quickly with a lot of force. *The captain thrust his hands into his pockets.* 2 COUNT N A **thrust** is a sudden forceful movement. *...repeated sword thrusts.*

thrust upon. PHR VB If you **thrust** something **upon** someone, you force them to have it. *The new religion was thrust upon the population by force.*

thud /θʌd/, **thuds, thudding, thudded.** 1 COUNT N A **thud** is a dull sound, usually made by a solid, heavy object hitting something soft. *He fell on the floor with a thud.* 2 VB If something **thuds** somewhere, it makes a dull sound, usually by hitting something else. *The mail bags thudded onto the platform.*

thug /θʌg/, **thugs.** COUNT N A **thug** is a very rough and violent person. *...a gang of thugs.*

thumb /θʌm/, **thumbs, thumbing, thumbed.** 1 COUNT N Your **thumb** is the short, thick digit on the side of your hand next to your first finger. 2 VB WITH OBJ If you **thumb** a lift, you stand next to a road and stick out your thumb until a driver stops and gives you a lift.

thumb through. PHR VB If you **thumb through** a book or magazine, you turn the pages quickly rather than reading each page carefully.

thumbnail /θʌmneɪl/, **thumbnails.** 1 COUNT N Your **thumbnail** is the nail on your thumb. 2 ATTRIB ADJ A **thumbnail** sketch or account is a very brief one.

thump /θʌmp/, **thumps, thumping, thumped.** 1 VB WITH OBJ If you **thump** someone or something, you hit them with your fist. *I'll thump you, if you don't get out... She thumped the table.* Also COUNT N *Ralph pushed between them and got a thump on the chest.* 2 VB If something **thumps** somewhere, it makes a loud, dull sound by hitting something else. *Feet thumped up the stairs... Two rockets thumped into the ground.* Also COUNT N *He sat down with a thump.* 3 VB When your heart **thumps,** it beats strongly and quickly. *My heart was thumping with happiness.*

thunder /θʌndə/, **thunders, thundering, thundered.** 1 UNCOUNT N **Thunder** is the loud noise that you hear in the sky after a flash of lightning. *...a clap of thunder.* 2 VB When it **thunders,** you hear thunder in the sky. 3 UNCOUNT N WITH 'of' The **thunder** of something such as traffic is the loud, deep noise it makes. *...the thunder of five hundred war drums.* 4 VB If something **thunders,** it makes a loud continuous noise.

thunderbolt /θʌndəbəʊlt/, **thunderbolts.** COUNT N A **thunderbolt** is a flash of lightning, accompanied by thunder, which strikes something such as a building or a tree.

thunderous /θʌndərəs/. ADJ A **thunderous** noise is very loud and deep. *The tree fell with a thunderous crash... ...thunderous applause.*

thunderstorm /θʌndəstɔːm/, **thunderstorms.** COUNT N A **thunderstorm** is a storm in which there is thunder and lightning.

Thursday /θɜːzdi[1]/, **Thursdays.** UNCOUNT N OR COUNT N **Thursday** is the day after Wednesday and before Friday.

thus /ðʌs/; a formal word. 1 SENTENCE ADV You use **thus** to introduce the consequence or conclusion of something that you have just said. *They are down to their last 2,000 pounds and thus qualify for social security benefits.* 2 ADV If you say that something is **thus** or happens **thus,** you mean that it is or happens in the way you are describing. *She lay down. Her eyelids closed. It was thus that Robert saw her... Thus encouraged, Lexington walked through the gate.*

thwart /θwɔːt/, **thwarts, thwarting, thwarted.** VB WITH OBJ If you **thwart** someone or **thwart** their plans, you prevent them from doing or getting what they want; a formal use. *She had never tried to thwart him in any way... His hopes were thwarted by Taylor.*

thyme /taɪm/. UNCOUNT N **Thyme** is a type of herb used in cooking.

tic /tɪk/, **tics.** COUNT N If someone has a **tic,** a part of their face or body keeps moving suddenly and they cannot control it. *She developed a tic in her neck.*

tick /tɪk/, **ticks, ticking, ticked.** 1 COUNT N A **tick** is a written mark 013. You use it to show that something is correct or has been dealt with. *There was a red tick in the margin.* 2 VB WITH OBJ If you **tick** something that is written on a piece of paper, you put a tick next to it. 3 VB When a clock or watch **ticks,** it makes a regular series of short sounds as it works. *I could hear my wristwatch ticking away.* ♦ **ticking** UNCOUNT N *She could hear a faint ticking.* 4 COUNT N The **tick** of a clock or watch is the series of short sounds it makes when it is working. *The clock in the kitchen had a noisy tick.* 5 VB If you talk about what makes someone **tick,** you are talking about the reasons for their character and behaviour. *What makes Patrick tick?*

tick by. PHR VB If you say that the seconds, minutes, or hours **ticked by,** you are emphasizing that time was passing. *The seconds ticked by and still they heard no explosion.*

tick off. PHR VB 1 If you **tick off** an item on a list, you put a tick by it to show that it has been dealt with. 2 If you **tick** someone **off,** you speak to them angrily because they have done something wrong; an informal use. *David had ticked her off for being careless.*

tick over. PHR VB Something that **is ticking over** is working or operating steadily but not as hard or as well as it can do. *...enough to keep the essential processes ticking over for a few months.*

ticket /tɪkɪt/, **tickets.** COUNT N A **ticket** is an official piece of paper or card which shows that you have paid for a journey or have paid to enter a place of entertainment. *...bus tickets... I'd like a return ticket to Vienna, please... She bought two tickets for the opera.* ● See also **season ticket.**

tickle /tɪkəl/, **tickles, tickling, tickled.** 1 VB WITH OBJ When you **tickle** someone, you move your fingers lightly over their body, often in order to make them laugh. *Babies want to be tickled and hugged.* 2 VB WITH OR WITHOUT OBJ If something **tickles,** it causes an irritating feeling by lightly touching a part of your body. *He flicked away a strand of hair that was tickling Ellen's nose.* 3 VB WITH OBJ If a fact or a situation **tickles** you, it amuses you or gives you pleasure.

ticklish /tɪklɪʃ/. 1 ADJ A **ticklish** problem or situation needs to be dealt with carefully. *It was a ticklish moment in the discussion.* 2 ADJ If someone is **ticklish,** you can make them laugh easily by tickling them.

tidal wave, tidal waves. COUNT N A **tidal wave** is a very large wave, often caused by an earthquake, that flows over the land and destroys things.

tide /taɪd/, **tides, tiding, tided.** 1 SING N OR UNCOUNT N WITH SUPP **The tide** is the regular change in the level of the sea on the shore. When it is at its highest level, you say that the tide is in. When it is at its lowest level, you say that the tide is out. *The tide was coming in.* ♦ **tidal** /taɪdəl/ ATTRIB ADJ *...tidal estuaries.* ● See also **high tide, low tide.** 2 SING N WITH 'of' The **tide** of opinion or fashion is what the majority of people think or do at a particular time. *He's always gone against the tide of fashion.*

tide over. PHR VB If something will **tide** you **over,** it will help you through a difficult time. *I only want to borrow enough to tide me over till Monday.*

tidings /taɪdɪŋz/. PLURAL N WITH SUPP **Tidings** are news; a formal use. *He told her the good tidings.*

tidy /taɪdi[1]/, **tidier, tidiest; tidies, tidying, tidied.** 1 ADJ Something that is **tidy** is neat and arranged in an orderly way. *It is difficult to keep a house tidy... ...a tidy desk.* ♦ **tidiness** UNCOUNT N *...his parents' concern with tidiness.* 2 ADJ **Tidy** people keep their things tidy. *I wish you were a little bit tidier!* 3 VB WITH OBJ When you **tidy** a place, you make it neat by putting things in their proper places. *You can't tidy a bedroom until you've made the beds.* 4 ATTRIB ADJ A **tidy** amount of money is a fairly large amount of it; an informal use. *He managed to make quite a tidy income every year.*

tidy away. PHR VB When you **tidy** something **away,** you put it in a cupboard or drawer so that it is not in the way. *Someone had tidied my papers away.*

tidy up. PHR VB When you **tidy up** or **tidy** a place **up,** you put things back in their proper places so that everything is neat. *I made the beds and tidied up.*

tie /taɪ/, **ties, tying, tied.** 1 VB WITH OBJ AND ADJUNCT If you tie one thing to another, you fasten it using string or rope. *...one of those labels you tie onto the handle of your suitcase.* 2 VB WITH OBJ AND ADJUNCT If you **tie** a piece of string round something or **tie** something with string, you put string round it and fasten the ends together. *...a little dog which had a ribbon tied round its neck... ...a parcel tied with string.* 3 VB WITH OBJ When you **tie** your shoelaces, you fasten the ends together in a bow. *He was still tying his laces.* 4 COUNT N A **tie** is a long, narrow piece of cloth worn under someone's shirt collar and tied in a knot at the front. *He took off his jacket and loosened his tie.* ● See also **bow tie.** 5 PASSIVE VB WITH PREP 'to' Something that **is tied** to something else is closely linked to it. *The course I chose wasn't tied to a particular academic discipline.* 6 COUNT N **Ties** are the connections you have with people or a place. *Family ties are often very strong... They want to loosen their ties with Britain.* 7 RECIP VB If you **tie** with someone in a competition or a game, you have the same number of points or the same degree of success. *Two actresses tied for the Best Actress award.* Also COUNT N *In the event of a tie, the winner will be the contestant who took the shortest time.*

tie up. PHR VB 1 When you **tie** something **up,** you fasten string or rope round it so that it is secure. *Clarissa came in, carrying some canvases tied up in brown paper.* 2 If you **tie up** an animal, you fasten it to a fixed object with a piece of rope so that it cannot run away. 3 When you **tie up** your shoelaces, you fasten them in a bow. 4 If someone **ties** you **up,** they fasten ropes around you so that you cannot escape. 5 Something that **is tied up** with something else is closely linked with it. *It's all tied up with the attempt to build a new spire for the cathedral.*

tied up. PRED ADJ If you are **tied up,** you are busy; an informal use. *I'm tied up right now, can you call me back later?*

tier /tɪə/, **tiers.** COUNT N A **tier** is one of a series of layers or levels that form part of a structure. *The theatre had semicircular tiers of seats.*

tiger /taɪgə/, **tigers.** COUNT N A **tiger** is a large, fierce animal belonging to the cat family. Tigers are orange with black stripes.

tight /taɪt/, **tighter, tightest; tights.** 1 ADJ **Tight** clothes or shoes fit closely to your body or feet. *He was wearing tight cream-coloured trousers.* ♦ **tightly** ADV *...a tightly fitting suit.* 2 ADV If you hold something **tight** or **tightly,** you hold it firmly. *Ann was clutching the letter tight in her hand... They clung together very tightly.* 3 ADJ Something that is **tight** is firmly fastened, and difficult to move. *...a tight knot.* ♦ **tightly** ADV *He screwed the caps tightly onto the bottles.* 4 ADV Something that is shut **tight** is shut very firmly. *He closed his eyes tight.* 5 ADJ Skin, cloth, or string that is stretched **tight** is stretched or pulled so that it is smooth or straight. ♦ **tightly** ADV *The skin on his face was drawn back tightly like stretched leather.* 6 ADJ You use **tight** to describe things that are very close together. *They stood in a tight group.* ♦ **tightly** ADV *...houses tightly packed together.* 7 ADJ A **tight** schedule or budget allows very little time or money for something. 8 ADJ **Tight** controls are very strict. *Security has become visibly tighter over the last year.* ♦ **tightly** ADV *...a society which is very tightly controlled.* 9 PLURAL N **Tights** are a piece of clothing made of thin material that fits closely round a woman's hips, legs, and feet. 10 **to keep a tight rein on** someone: see **rein.** ● **to sit tight:** see **sit.**

tighten /taɪtən/, **tightens, tightening, tightened.** 1 ERG VB If you **tighten** your hold on something, you hold it more firmly. *He tightened his grip on the spear... His fingers tightened around his rifle.* 2 ERG VB If you **tighten** a rope or chain, you stretch or pull it until it is straight. *The chain tightened and the pig's leg was pulled back.* 3 VB WITH OBJ To **tighten** controls means to make them stricter. *The authorities tightened security around the embassy.*

tighten up. PHR VB To **tighten up** a rule means to make it stricter. *Regulations on the testing of drugs have been tightened up.*

tightrope /taɪtrəʊp/, **tightropes.** COUNT N A **tightrope** is a piece of rope which is stretched between two poles and on which an acrobat balances and performs tricks.

tile /taɪl/, **tiles.** COUNT N **Tiles** are small, flat, square objects used to cover floors, walls, or roofs. *...polystyrene ceiling tiles... ...brick houses roofed in reddish-brown tiles.*

tiled /taɪld/. ADJ A **tiled** surface is covered with tiles. *...footsteps on the tiled floor... ...with red tiled roofs.*

till /tɪl/, **tills.** 1 PREP OR CONJ **Till** means the same as until. *He wrote from morning till night... Wait till I come back.* 2 COUNT N A **till** is a drawer or box in a shop where money is kept, usually as part of a machine called a cash register.

tilt /tɪlt/, **tilts, tilting, tilted.** ERG VB If you **tilt** an object, you change its position so that one end or side is higher than the other. *He tilted the flask and two or* *three drops trickled out... Let your head gently tilt forwards.* Also COUNT N *He indicated, with a tilt of his head, a girl nearby.*

timber /tɪmbə/. UNCOUNT N **Timber** is wood used for building houses and making furniture. *Most of the region's timber is imported from the south.*

time /taɪm/, **times, timing, timed. 1** UNCOUNT N **Time** is what we measure in hours, days, and years. *...a period of time... Time passed, and finally he fell asleep again.* **2** COUNT N You use **time** to refer to a specific point in time, which can be stated in hours and minutes and is shown on clocks. *What's the time?... Ask the times of planes from Rome to Vienna.* **3** UNCOUNT N OR SING N You also use **time** to refer to the period of time that someone spends doing something. *How do you find time to write these books?... She spends most of her time sunbathing... It would take a long time to discuss.* **4** COUNT N You use **time** to refer to an individual point in time, when you are describing what is happening then. *He blushed each time she spoke to him... Ask for something different next time... There were times when I didn't know what to do.* **5** COUNT N You use **time** after numbers to say how often something happens. *Ray and I play squash three times a week... The telephone rang a second time.* **6** COUNT N OR UNCOUNT N WITH SUPP You also use **time** to refer to a stage in someone's life, or to a period of time in history. *...during my time in Toronto... ...the time of the Roman Empire... ...one of the great unsolved mysteries of our time... ...the history of modern times.* **7** SING N If something happens for a **time,** it happens for a fairly long period of time. *It's nice to be in London for a time... It became clear after a time that he was very ill.* **8** PLURAL N You also use **time** after numbers when you are saying how much bigger, smaller, better, or worse one thing is compared to another. *It would cost me ten times as much... It has become three times as difficult as it used to be.* **9** You use **times** in arithmetic to link numbers or amounts that are multiplied together. *5 times 50—that's 250.* **10** VB WITH OBJ If you **time** something for a particular time, you plan that it should happen at that time. *Their disruption was timed for 9.20.* **11** VB WITH OBJ If you **time** an action or activity, you measure how long it lasts. *This was repeated at intervals which he timed on his watch.* **12** See also **timing.**

PHRASES ● If you are **in time** for something, you are not late. ● If you are **in good time,** you are earlier than necessary. ● If you arrive **on time,** you arrive at the correct time. ● If a situation existed **at one time,** it existed in the past. ● If something happens **at times,** it happens occasionally. ● You use **at a time** when saying how many things or people are involved in one instance of something. *He used to abandon his work for many months at a time... There was only room for one person at a time.* ● You use **at the same time** to introduce a statement that contrasts with the previous statement. *It made us cautious but at the same time it made us willing to take a risk.* ● If you say it is **about time** that something was done, you are saying firmly that it should be done. *It's about time that Parliament concentrated on unemployment.* ● If someone is **ahead of** their **time,** they have an idea long before other people start thinking in the same way. ● Someone who is **behind the times** is old-fashioned. ● If you do something **for the time being,** you do it until something else can be arranged. *For the time being, we ought to stay with him.* ● If you do something **from time to time,** you do it occasionally. ● If something will happen **in time,** it will happen eventually. ● If something will happen **in** a week's **time** or **in** a month's **time,** it will happen after one week or one month. ● When you talk about how well a watch or clock **keeps time,** you are talking about how accurately it measures time. *This has kept perfect time since I got it back.* ● If you **have no time for** someone or something, you do not like them or approve of them. ● If you **make good time** on a journey, you complete the journey more quickly than you expected. ● If you do something to **pass the time,** you do it because you are bored or are waiting for something, and not because you really want to. ● If something will **take time,** it will be achieved slowly. ● If you **take** your **time** doing something, you do it slowly. ● If something happens **time after time** or **time and again,** it happens often. ● If you say **'Time is worth ten thousand words',** you mean that it is more useful to give people your time and practical assistance, rather than just talking to them and expressing sympathy.

time-honoured. ATTRIB ADJ A **time-honoured** way of doing something has been used for a very long time. *...a time-honoured practice.*

timeless /taɪmlɪ[2]s/. ADJ Something which is **timeless** is so good or beautiful that it cannot be affected by changes in society or fashion; a formal use. *His art has something universal, something timeless about it.*

time limit, time limits. COUNT N A **time limit** is a period of time during which a particular task must be completed. *I had set myself a time limit of two years.*

timely /taɪmli[1]/. ADJ Something that is **timely** happens at just the right time. *...the timely arrival of reinforcements.*

time scale, time scales. COUNT N The **time scale** of an event is the length of time during which it happens. *...the time scale of technological development.*

timetable /taɪmteɪbə[0]l/, **timetables. 1** COUNT N A **timetable** is a schedule of the times when activities or jobs should be done. **2** COUNT N A **timetable** is also a list of the times when trains, boats, buses, or aeroplanes arrive and depart.

timid /tɪmɪd/. ADJ **Timid** people are shy and have no courage or self-confidence. *...a timid young girl... ...a timid smile.* ♦ **timidly** ADV *I left the car and timidly rang the doorbell.* ♦ **timidity** /tɪmɪdɪ[1]ti[1]/ UNCOUNT N *He had a terrible time in overcoming his timidity.*

timing /taɪmɪŋ/. **1** UNCOUNT N Someone's **timing** is their skill in judging the right moment at which to do something. *She displayed perfect timing and control.* **2** UNCOUNT N When people decide about the **timing** of an event, they decide when it will happen. *They met to consider the timing of elections.*

tin /tɪn/, **tins. 1** UNCOUNT N **Tin** is a soft metal that is the same colour as silver. **2** COUNT N A **tin** is a metal container which is filled with food and sealed in order to preserve the food; a British use. **3** COUNT N A **tin** is also a small metal container with a lid. *...the biscuit tin.* **4** COUNT N You can use **tin** to refer to a tin and its contents, or to the contents only. *...a tin of sardines... You've upset a tin of paint on the carpet.*

tinge /tɪndʒ/, **tinges.** COUNT N WITH SUPP A **tinge** of a colour or a feeling is a small amount of it. *The sky had a greenish tinge... ...a tinge of envy.*

tinged /tɪndʒd/. PRED ADJ WITH 'with' If something is **tinged** with a colour or a feeling, it has a small amount of that colour or feeling in it. *Her eyes were slightly tinged with red... ...joy tinged with bitterness.*

tingle /tɪŋg[0]əl/, **tingles, tingling, tingled. 1** VB When a part of your body **tingles,** you feel a slight prickling feeling there. *The side of my face was still tingling from the blow she'd given me.* ♦ **tingling** UNCOUNT N *...a sharp tingling in her fingers.* **2** VB If you **tingle** with excitement or shock, you feel it very strongly. *Kunta felt himself tingle with that extra strength that fear brings.*

tinker /tɪŋkə/, **tinkers, tinkering, tinkered.** VB If you **tinker** with something, you make a lot of small adjustments to it in order to repair or improve it. *He's still tinkering with the motor.*

tinkle /tɪŋkə[0]l/, **tinkles, tinkling, tinkled.** VB If something **tinkles,** it makes a sound like a small bell ringing. *He slammed the door so violently that the sherry-glasses tinkled on their tray.* Also COUNT N *The telephone gave a tinkle.*

tinned /tɪnd/. ADJ **Tinned** food has been preserved by being sealed in a tin. *...tinned peas.*

tinny /tɪni[1]/. ADJ A **tinny** sound has an unpleasant high-pitched quality. *...the tinny voice coming over the radio.*

tin-opener /tɪn əʊpə[0]nə/, **tin-openers.** COUNT N A **tin-opener** is a tool used for opening tins of food.

tinsel /tɪnsəl/. UNCOUNT N **Tinsel** consists of small strips of shiny paper attached to long pieces of thread. It is used to decorate rooms at Christmas.

tint /tɪnt/, **tints, tinted, tinting. 1** COUNT N A **tint** is a small amount of a colour. *His eyes had a yellow tint.* **2** VB WITH OBJ If you **tint** your hair, you change its colour by adding a weak dye to it. *He acquired a preparation for tinting his hair chestnut brown.*

tinted /tɪntɪ[1]d/. ADJ **Tinted** glass is slightly coloured. *He glanced through the tinted rear window.*

tiny /taɪni[1]/, **tinier, tiniest.** ADJ Something that is **tiny** is extremely small. *...a tiny little room.*

-tion, -tions. See **-ation.**

tip /tɪp/, **tips, tipping, tipped. 1** COUNT N The **tip** of something long and thin is the end of it. *He was hanging by his finger tips from a window frame... ...the tips of branches.* **2** VB WITH OBJ AND ADJUNCT If you **tip** an object, you move it so that it is no longer horizontal or upright. *He tipped his soup bowl towards himself.* **3** VB WITH OBJ AND ADJUNCT If you **tip** something somewhere, you pour it there quickly and carelessly. *He tipped the contents of the rucksack out on to the floor.* **4** COUNT N A **tip** is a place where rubbish is dumped; a British use. **5** COUNT N If you give someone such as a waiter or a taxi driver a **tip,** you give them some money to thank them for their services. *The woman gave me a dollar tip.* **6** VB WITH OBJ If you **tip** someone, you give them money as a tip. *I tipped the chauffeur.* **7** COUNT N A **tip** is also a useful piece of advice or information. *He consulted books by well-known tennis players for tips on basic techniques.* **8** PHRASE If you say that something is **the tip of the iceberg,** you mean that it is only a very small part of a much larger problem.

tip off. PHR VB If you **tip** someone **off,** you give them information or a warning, often privately or secretly. *The burglars were tipped off by a lookout and escaped.*

tip over. PHR VB If you **tip** something **over** or if it **tips over,** it falls over or turns over. *She tipped the pan over and a dozen fish flopped out.*

tip-off, tip-offs. COUNT N A **tip-off** is a piece of information or a warning that you give to someone, often privately or secretly. *The building was evacuated as the result of a tip-off.*

tipped /tɪpt/. ADJ Something that is **tipped** with a substance has that substance on its tip. *...arrows tipped with poison.*

tipsy /tɪpsi[1]/. ADJ If you are **tipsy,** you are slightly drunk; an informal use.

tiptoe /tɪptəʊ/, **tiptoes, tiptoeing, tiptoed. 1** VB If you **tiptoe** somewhere, you walk there very quietly on your toes. *He knocked softly on the door and tiptoed into the room.* **2** PHRASE If you stand or walk **on tiptoe,** you stand or walk on your toes.

tirade /taɪreɪd/, **tirades.** COUNT N A **tirade** is a long, angry speech criticizing someone or something; a formal use.

tire /taɪə/, **tires, tiring, tired. 1** ERG VB If something **tires** you, it makes you use a lot of energy, so that you want to rest or sleep. *The run did not seem to tire them at all... The other men began to tire.* ♦ **tiring** ADJ *We should have an early night after such a tiring day.* **2** VB WITH 'of' If you **tire** of something, you become bored with it. *He tired of my questions.* **3** See also **tyre.**

tire out. PHR VB If something **tires** you **out,** it makes you exhausted.

tired /taɪəd/. **1** ADJ If you are **tired,** you want to rest or sleep. *I'm sure you must be tired after cycling all that distance.* ♦ **tiredness** UNCOUNT N *Tiredness overwhelmed me.* **2** PRED ADJ If you are **tired** of something, you are bored with it. *Judy was tired of quarrelling with him.*

tireless /taɪəlɪ[2]s/. ADJ Someone who is **tireless** has a lot of energy and never seems to need a rest. *Both of them were tireless workers.*

tiresome /taɪəsəm/. ADJ Someone or something that is **tiresome** makes you feel irritated or bored. *...a tiresome problem.*

tissue /tɪsju:, tɪʃu:/, **tissues. 1** MASS N In animals and plants, **tissue** consists of cells that are similar in appearance and function. *...scar tissue... ...living tissues.* **2** UNCOUNT N **Tissue** or **tissue paper** is thin paper used for wrapping things that are easily damaged. **3** COUNT N A **tissue** is a small, square piece of soft paper that you use as a handkerchief.

titbit /tɪtbɪt/, **titbits.** COUNT N A **titbit** is a small, tasty piece of food. *...a dog begging for titbits.*

titillate /tɪtɪleɪt/, **titillates, titillating, titillated.** VB WITH OR WITHOUT OBJ If something **titillates** someone, it pleases and excites them, especially in a sexual way. *...various other bits of scandal designed to titillate.*

title /taɪtə[0]l/, **titles. 1** COUNT N The **title** of a book, play, or piece of music is its name. **2** COUNT N Someone's **title** is a word such as 'Lord' or 'Mrs' that is used before their name to show their status. **3** COUNT N A **title** in a sports competition is the position of champion. *We had beaten Cornell and taken the title.*

titled /taɪtə[0]ld/. ADJ A **titled** person has a title such as 'Lord' or 'Lady' which shows their high social rank.

titter /tɪtə/, **titters, tittering, tittered.** VB If you **titter,** you laugh in a way that shows that you are nervous or embarrassed.

to /tə, tu:/. **1** PREP You use **to** when indicating the place that someone or something is moving towards or pointing at. *I'm going with her to Australia... He was pointing to an oil tanker somewhere on the horizon.* **2** PREP You use **to** when indicating where something is tied or attached, or what it is touching. *I was planning to tie him to a tree... He clutched the parcel to his chest.* **3** PREP You use **to** when indicating the position of something. For example, if something is **to** your left, it is nearer your left side than your right. *To one side, he could see the block of luxury flats.* **4** PREP You use **to** when indicating who or what an action or a feeling is directed towards. *He showed the letter to Barbara... We don't do repairs to farm machines... They were sympathetic to his ideas.* **5** PREP You use **to** when indicating someone's reaction to something. *To his surprise he was offered both jobs.* **6** PREP You use **to** when indicating the person whose opinion you are stating. *To me it didn't seem necessary.* **7** PREP You use **to** when indicating the state that someone or something gradually starts to be in. *It had turned to dust over the years... ...her rise to fame.*

8 PREP You use **to** when indicating the last thing in a range of things. *Breakfast was from 9 to 10... The job will take anything from two to five weeks.* **9** PREP You use **to** when you are stating a time. For example, 'five to eight' means five minutes before eight o'clock. **10** PREP You use **to** in ratios and rates. *My car does 35 miles to the gallon.* **11** PREP You use **to** when indicating that something happens at the same time as something else, perhaps as a reaction. *To a chorus of laughter the President left the room.* **12** ADV If you push a door **to,** you close it but do not shut it completely. **13** PHRASE If someone moves **to and fro,** they move repeatedly from one place to another and back again. *All day, he rushed to and fro between his living quarters and his place of work.* **14** You use **to** with an infinitive when indicating the purpose of an action. *People would stroll down the path to admire the garden.* **15** You also use **to** with an infinitive when commenting on your attitude or intention in making a statement. *To be honest, we knew he was there... To sum up, the law must be changed.* **16** You also use **to** with an infinitive in various other constructions when talking about an action or state. *...the first person to climb Everest... He was too proud to apologize... They were lovely to watch... Some of us have got work to do... She looked up to find Tony standing there.*

toad /təʊd/, **toads.** COUNT N A **toad** is an animal like a frog, but with a drier skin.

toadstool /təʊdstu:l/, **toadstools.** COUNT N A **toadstool** is a type of poisonous fungus.

toast /təʊst/, **toasts, toasting, toasted. 1** UNCOUNT N **Toast** is slices of bread heated until they are brown and crisp. *...a piece of toast.* **2** VB WITH OBJ When you **toast** bread, you heat it so that it becomes brown and crisp. **3** COUNT N When you drink a **toast** to someone, you wish them success or good health, and then drink some alcoholic drink. *Harold raised his glass in a toast: 'Welcome!'* **4** VB WITH OBJ When you **toast** someone, you drink a toast to them.

toaster /təʊstə/, **toasters.** COUNT N A **toaster** is a piece of electric equipment used to toast bread.

tobacco /təbækəʊ/. UNCOUNT N **Tobacco** is the dried leaves of a particular plant which people smoke in pipes, cigars, and cigarettes.

tobacconist /təbækənɪst/, **tobacconists.** COUNT N A **tobacconist** or **tobacconist's** is a shop where things such as tobacco, cigarettes, and cigars are sold.

toboggan /təbɒgən/, **toboggans.** COUNT N A **toboggan** is a small vehicle that slides over snow.

today /tədeɪ/. **1** ADV OR UNCOUNT N **Today** means the day on which you are speaking or writing. *I had a letter today from my solicitor... Today is Thursday.* **2** ADV OR UNCOUNT N You can refer to the present period of history as **today.** *Today we are threatened on all sides by financial crises... ...the America of today and the America of thirty years ago.*

toddle /tɒdə^{0}l/, **toddles, toddling, toddled.** VB When a child **toddles,** it walks unsteadily with short, quick steps. *His grandson was toddling around in the garden.*

toddler /tɒdlə/, **toddlers.** COUNT N A **toddler** is a small child who has just learned to walk.

toe /təʊ/, **toes, toeing, toed. 1** COUNT N Your **toes** are the five movable parts at the end of each foot. **2** COUNT N The **toe** of a shoe or sock is the part that covers the end of your foot. *Maria's shoes had holes in the toes.* **3** PHRASE If you **toe the line,** you behave in the way that people in authority expect you to.

toenail /təʊneɪl/, **toenails.** COUNT N Your **toenails** are the hard coverings on the ends of your toes.

toffee /tɒfi^1/, **toffees.** COUNT N OR UNCOUNT N A **toffee** is a sweet made by boiling sugar and butter together with water. *...a chunk of toffee.*

together /təgeðə/. **1** ADV If people do something **together,** they do it with each other. *They flew back to London together... You all work together as a team.* **2** ADV If two things happen **together,** they happen at the same time. *The reports will have to be seen and judged together before we decide.* **3** ADV If things are joined or fixed **together,** they are joined or fixed to each other. *Her hands were clasped tightly together.* **4** ADV If things or people are **together,** they are next to each other. *The fossils are packed densely together in display cases.* **5** ADV You use **together** when considering the total amount that two or more things spend, produce, or are worth. *The two companies together spend more on research than the whole of the rest of the industry.* **6** PREP **Together with** something means as well as that thing. *Lee handed over the key to his room, together with some forms and leaflets.*

toil /tɔɪl/, **toils, toiling, toiled.** VB When people **toil,** they work hard doing unpleasant or tiring tasks; a formal use. *...factories where men toiled all through the night.* Also UNCOUNT N *The wealth of industrial society could only come from the toil of the masses.*

toilet /tɔɪlɪ^{2}t/, **toilets. 1** COUNT N A **toilet** is a large bowl connected to the drains which you use when you want to get rid of urine or faeces from your body. **2** COUNT N A **toilet** is also a small room containing a toilet.

toilet paper. UNCOUNT N **Toilet paper** is paper that you use to clean yourself after getting rid of urine or faeces from your body.

toiletries /tɔɪlɪ^{2}trɪz/. PLURAL N **Toiletries** are things that you use when cleaning or taking care of your body, such as soap and toothpaste.

toilet roll, toilet rolls. COUNT N A **toilet roll** is a long strip of toilet paper wound around a cardboard tube.

token /təʊkə^{0}n/, **tokens. 1** COUNT N A **token** is a piece of paper or card which is bought as a present and can be exchanged for goods. *...a book token.* **2** COUNT N **Tokens** are also round, flat pieces of metal that are sometimes used instead of money. **3** COUNT N If you give something to someone as a **token** of your feelings for them, you give it as a way of expressing those feelings; a formal use. *He gave her a gold brooch as a token of his esteem.* **4** ATTRIB ADJ You use **token** of things or actions which show your intentions or feelings but are small or unimportant. *...token resistance.* **5** PHRASE You use **by the same token** to introduce a statement that you think is true for the same reasons that were given for a previous statement. *We make people mentally old by retiring them, and we may even by the same token make them physically old.*

told /təʊld/. **Told** is the past tense and past participle of **tell.**

tolerable /tɒlə^{0}rəbə^{0}l/. ADJ If something is **tolerable,** it is acceptable or bearable, but not pleasant or good. *I was given a tolerable meal.*

tolerant /tɒlərənt/. ADJ If you are **tolerant,** you let other people say and do what they like, even if you do not agree with it or approve of it. *I think I've become more tolerant of other people's attitudes.* ♦ **tolerance** /tɒlərəns/ UNCOUNT N *I remember him for his humour and tolerance.*

tolerate /tɒləreɪt/, **tolerates, tolerating, tolerated. 1** VB WITH OBJ If you **tolerate** things that you do not agree with or approve of, you allow them to exist or happen. *They happily tolerated the existence of opinions contrary to their own.* **2** VB WITH OBJ If you can **tolerate** something unsatisfactory or unpleasant, you are able to accept it. *They couldn't tolerate the noise.*

toll /təʊl/, **tolls, tolling, tolled. 1** COUNT N WITH SUPP The death **toll** in an accident is the number of people who have died in it. *By Wednesday the death toll had risen to more than 40.* **2** PHRASE If something **takes a toll** or **takes its toll,** it has the effect of causing suffering. *The walking was beginning to take its toll on all of us.* **3** COUNT N A **toll** is a sum of money that you have to pay in order to use a particular bridge or road. **4** ERG VB When someone **tolls** a bell or when it **tolls,** they ring it slowly and repeatedly, often as a sign that someone has died.

tomato /təmɑ:təʊ/, **tomatoes.** COUNT N A **tomato** is a small, soft, red fruit that is used in cooking or eaten raw.

tomb /tu:m/, **tombs.** COUNT N A **tomb** is a stone structure containing the body of a dead person.

tomboy /tɒmbɔɪ/, **tomboys.** COUNT N A **tomboy** is a young girl who likes rough activities.

tombstone /tu:mstəʊn/, **tombstones.** COUNT N A **tombstone** is a large, flat piece of stone on someone's grave, with their name written on it.

tomorrow /təmɒrəʊ/. **1** ADV OR UNCOUNT N **Tomorrow** means the day after today. *They're coming tomorrow... Tomorrow's concert has been cancelled.* **2** ADV OR UNCOUNT N You can refer to the future, especially the near future, as **tomorrow.** *They live today as millions more will live tomorrow... One of the big tasks of today and tomorrow is the investigation of repressed sexual energy.*

ton /tʌn/, **tons. 1** COUNT N A **ton** is a unit of weight equal to 2240 pounds in Britain and 2000 pounds in the United States. *...ten million tons of coal.* **2** COUNT N A **ton** is also the same as a tonne. **3** PLURAL N **Tons** of something means a lot of it; an informal British use. *I've got tons of paper to draw on.*

tone /təʊn/, **tones, toning, toned. 1** COUNT N WITH SUPP Someone's **tone** is a quality in their voice which shows what they are feeling or thinking. *'Very good,' he said in an encouraging tone... Her tone was defiant.* **2** COUNT N A **tone** is one of the sounds that you hear when you are using a telephone, for example the sound that tells you that a number is engaged. *I'm getting the ringing tone, but there doesn't appear to be anyone at home.* **3** UNCOUNT N The **tone** of a musical instrument or a singer's voice is the kind of sound it has. *I wish I had a piano with a better tone.* **4** UNCOUNT N The **tone** of a piece of writing is its style and the feelings expressed in it. *I was greatly offended by the tone of the article.* **5** COUNT N OR UNCOUNT N A **tone** is also one of the lighter, darker, or brighter shades of the same colour. *...the tones of the sky... You need a blue that is darker in tone.* **6** PHRASE To **lower the tone** of a place or conversation means to make it less respectable. *He said the new people had lowered the tone of the neighbourhood.*

tone down. PHR VB If you **tone down** something that you have written, you make it less forceful, severe, or offensive. *He advised me to tone down my letter.*

tone-deaf. ADJ Someone who is **tone-deaf** cannot sing in tune or recognize different tunes.

tongs /tɒŋz/. PLURAL N **Tongs** consist of two long pieces of metal joined together at one end. You press the pieces together in order to pick up an object.

tongue /tʌŋ/, **tongues. 1** COUNT N Your **tongue** is the soft movable part inside your mouth that you use for tasting, licking, and speaking. **2** COUNT N A **tongue** is a language; a literary use. *I answered her in her own tongue.* **3** UNCOUNT N **Tongue** is the cooked tongue of an ox.

PHRASES ● If you **hold** your **tongue,** you do not say anything. ● **A slip of the tongue** is a small mistake that you make when you are speaking.

tongue-in-cheek. ADJ A **tongue-in-cheek** remark is made as a joke, and is not serious or sincere.

tongue-tied. ADJ If you are **tongue-tied,** you are unable to say anything because you feel shy or nervous.

tonic /tɒnɪk/, **tonics. 1** MASS N **Tonic** or **tonic water** is a colourless, fizzy drink that has a slightly bitter flavour. *...a gin and tonic.* **2** MASS N A **tonic** is a medicine that makes you feel stronger, healthier, and less tired. **3** COUNT N You can refer to anything that makes you feel stronger or more cheerful as a **tonic.** *It was a tonic to talk to her.*

tonight /tənaɪt/. ADV OR UNCOUNT N **Tonight** means the evening or night that will come at the end of today. *I think I'll go to bed early tonight... In tonight's programme we shall be explaining its history.*

tonnage /tʌnɪdʒ/. **1** UNCOUNT N The **tonnage** of a ship is its size or the amount of cargo that it can carry; a technical use. **2** UNCOUNT N The **tonnage** of something is the amount of it that there is, measured in tons. *...the total tonnage of TNT used during the last war.*

tonne /tʌn/, **tonnes.** COUNT N A **tonne** is a unit of weight equal to 1000 kilograms.

tonsil /tɒns^{0}əl/, **tonsils.** COUNT N Your **tonsils** are the two small, soft lumps at the back of your mouth.

tonsillitis /tɒnsɪ^{1}laɪtɪ^{1}s/. UNCOUNT N **Tonsillitis** is a painful swelling of your tonsils caused by an infection.

too /tu:/. **1** SENTENCE ADV You use **too** after mentioning another person, thing, or aspect that a previous statement applies to or includes. *I'm on your side. Seibert is too... There were carrots too.* **2** SUBMOD You also use **too** to indicate that there is more of a thing or quality than is desirable or acceptable. *Avoid using too much water... Don't leave it in too warm a place.* **3** PHRASE You use **all too** or **only too** to emphasize that something happens to a greater degree than is pleasant or desirable. *I can remember only too well the disasters that followed... The suspicions had proved all too true.* **4** SUBMOD You can use **too** to make a negative opinion politer or more cautious. *He wasn't too keen on it.* **5 too bad:** see **bad.** ● **none too:** see **none.**

took /tʊk/. **Took** is the past tense of **take.**

tool /tu:l/, **tools.** COUNT N A **tool** is any instrument or simple piece of equipment, for example a hammer or a knife, that you hold in your hands and use to do a particular kind of work.

toot /tu:t/, **toots, tooting, tooted.** ERG VB If you **toot** your car horn, you make it produce a short sound or series of sounds. *A car horn tooted.* Also COUNT N *'Look,' she said and gave a toot on the horn.*

tooth /tu:θ/, **teeth** /ti:θ/. **1** COUNT N Your **teeth** are the hard, white objects in your mouth that you use for biting and chewing. **2** COUNT N The **teeth** of a comb, saw, or zip are the parts that stick out in a row. **3** to **grit your teeth:** see **grit.** ● **by the skin of** your **teeth:** see **skin.**

toothache /tu:θeɪk/. UNCOUNT N **Toothache** is pain in one of your teeth.

toothbrush /tu:θbrʌʃ/, **toothbrushes.** COUNT N A **toothbrush** is a small brush used for cleaning your teeth.

toothless /tu:θlɪ^{2}s/. ADJ If someone is **toothless,** they have no teeth.

toothpaste /tu:θpeɪst/, **toothpastes.** MASS N **Toothpaste** is a thick substance which you use to clean your teeth.

toothpick /tu:θpɪk/, **toothpicks.** COUNT N A **toothpick** is a small stick which you use to remove food from between your teeth.

top /tɒp/, **tops, topping, topped. 1** COUNT N WITH SUPP The **top** of something is its highest point, part, or surface. *...at the top of the steps... He filled his glass to* *the top.* 2 ATTRIB ADJ The **top** thing of a series of things is the highest one. *...a room on the top floor.* 3 SING N The **top** of a street is one end of it. *...a new building at the top of Victoria Street.* 4 SING N The **top** of an organization or scale of measurement is its highest level or point. *Officials at the top make the decisions.* Also ATTRIB ADJ *...top executives... The vehicle's top speed is about 100.* 5 COUNT N The **top** of a bottle, jar, or tube is its cap or lid. *He unscrewed the top and put the bottle to his mouth.* 6 COUNT N A **top** is a piece of clothing worn on the upper half of a woman's body. 7 COUNT N A **top** is also a toy shaped like a cone that can spin on its pointed end. 8 VB WITH OBJ If someone **tops** a poll or popularity chart, they do better than anyone else in it. 9 VB WITH OBJ If something **tops** a particular amount, it becomes greater than that amount. *US investments topped fifty million dollars.* 10 See also **topped**.

PHRASES • Something that is **on top** of something else is on its highest part. *...a tower with a little flag on top.* • **On top of** other things means in addition to them. *You don't want to give the poor man ulcers on top of all the problems he's already got.* • If you are **on top of** a task, you are dealing with it successfully. • When something **gets on top of** you, it makes you feel depressed because you cannot cope with it. *You may find the housework is getting on top of you.* • If something is **over the top**, it is unacceptable because it is too extreme. • **off the top of** your **head:** see **head.** • **at the top of** your **voice:** see **voice.**

top up. PHR VB If you **top up** a container, you fill it again when it has been partly emptied. *The radiator will have to be topped up because of evaporation.*

top hat, top hats. COUNT N A **top hat** is a tall hat with a narrow brim that men wear on very formal occasions.

topic /tɒpɪk/, **topics.** COUNT N A **topic** is a particular subject that you write about or discuss. *The main topic of conversation was food.*

topical /tɒpɪkə⁰l/. ADJ **Topical** means relating to events that are happening at the time when you are speaking or writing. *They used to discuss topical issues.*

topless /tɒplɪ²s/. ADJ When a woman is **topless,** she has no clothing covering her breasts.

topmost /tɒpməʊst/. ATTRIB ADJ The **topmost** thing in a group of things is the one that is highest or nearest the top. *...the topmost branches of the lime trees.*

topped /tɒpt/. PRED ADJ WITH ADJUNCT If something is **topped** by or with another thing, the other thing is on top of it. *...a heap of stones topped by a wooden cross.*

topple /tɒpə⁰l/, **topples, toppling, toppled.** 1 VB If something **topples,** it becomes unsteady and falls over. *She looked at the tree nervously, as if expecting it to topple over.* 2 VB WITH OBJ To **topple** a government or leader means to cause them to lose power. *His regime was toppled in a coup.*

top-secret. ADJ Something that is **top-secret** is intended to be kept completely secret. *...a top-secret experiment.*

torch /tɔːtʃ/, **torches.** 1 COUNT N A **torch** is a small electric light which you carry in your hand. 2 COUNT N In former times, a **torch** was a stick with burning material at the end, used to provide light.

tore /tɔː/. **Tore** is the past tense of **tear.**

torment, torments, tormenting, tormented; pronounced /tɔːmə²nt/ when it is a noun, and /tɔːmɛnt/ when it is a verb. 1 UNCOUNT N **Torment** is extreme pain or unhappiness. *...the scream of a man dying in torment.* 2 COUNT N A **torment** is something that causes extreme pain or unhappiness. *The boredom became a worse torment than the cold.* 3 VB WITH OBJ To **torment** someone means to make them very unhappy. *She is forever tormenting and teasing Tom... He was tormented by his desire to see her again.*

tormentor /tɔːmɛntə/, **tormentors.** COUNT N Someone's **tormentor** is a person who deliberately causes them pain or unhappiness.

torn /tɔːn/. **Torn** is the past participle of **tear.**

tornado /tɔːneɪdəʊ/, **tornadoes** or **tornados.** COUNT N A **tornado** is a violent storm with strong circular winds.

torpedo /tɔːpiːdəʊ/, **torpedoes, torpedoing, torpedoed.** 1 COUNT N A **torpedo** is a bomb shaped like a tube that travels underwater. 2 VB WITH OBJ If a ship is **torpedoed,** it is hit, and usually sunk, by a torpedo.

torrent /tɒrənt/, **torrents.** 1 COUNT N When a lot of water is falling very rapidly, you can say that it is falling in **torrents.** *The rain suddenly burst upon us in torrents.* 2 COUNT N WITH SUPP A **torrent** of speech is a lot of it directed continuously at someone. *He was answered with a torrent of oaths.*

torrential /tə⁷rɛnʃə⁰l/. ATTRIB ADJ **Torrential** rain pours down very rapidly in great quantities.

torso /tɔːsəʊ/, **torsos.** COUNT N Your **torso** is the main part of your body, excluding your head, arms, and legs; a formal use.

tortoise /tɔːtəs/, **tortoises.** COUNT N A **tortoise** is an animal with a shell into which it can pull its head and legs for protection. Tortoises move very slowly.

tortuous /tɔːtjʊəs/; a formal word. 1 ADJ A **tortuous** road or route is full of bends and twists. 2 ADJ A **tortuous** process or piece of writing is long and complicated.

torture /tɔːtʃə/, **tortures, torturing, tortured.** 1 VB WITH OBJ To **torture** someone means to deliberately cause them great pain in order to punish them or get information from them. 2 UNCOUNT N OR COUNT N **Torture** is the practice of torturing people. *...the constant threat of death and torture... Here floggings and tortures were carried out.*

toss /tɒs/, **tosses, tossing, tossed.** 1 VB WITH OBJ If you **toss** something somewhere, you throw it there lightly and carelessly. *He took the bag and tossed it into some nearby bushes.* 2 VB WITH OR WITHOUT OBJ If you **toss** a coin, you decide something by throwing the coin into the air and guessing which side will be facing upwards after it falls. *They used the penny to toss for the first round of drinks.* Also COUNT N *Business deals were clinched by the toss of a coin.* 3 VB WITH OBJ If you **toss** your head, you move it suddenly backwards. *'No,' she said, tossing her head in disgust.* Also COUNT N *She gave a toss of her head.* 4 ERG VB If something or someone **tosses,** they move repeatedly from side to side. *I tossed and turned all night... Ships were tossed at sea.*

tot /tɒt/, **tots, totting, totted.** 1 COUNT N A **tot** is a very young child; an informal use. *...tiny tots.* 2 COUNT N A **tot** of whisky or rum is a small amount of it in a glass.

tot up. PHR VB If you **tot up** numbers, you add them together. *The machine totted up your score.*

total /təʊtə⁰l/, **totals, totalling, totalled.** 1 COUNT N A **total** is the number that you get when you add several numbers together. *The factory employed a total of forty workers.* Also ATTRIB ADJ *...the total number of students on campus.* 2 PHRASE If there are a number of things **in total,** there are that many of them altogether. *...a force containing in total over half a million men.* 3 VB WITH COMPLEMENT If several numbers **total** a certain figure, that is the figure you get when all the numbers are added together. *Conoco's 1980 revenues totalled £18.3 billion.* 4 ADJ **Total** means complete. *...total secrecy.* ♦ **totally** SUBMOD OR ADV *He became almost totally blind... I totally disagree.*

totalitarian /təʊtælɪtɛəriən/. ADJ A **totalitarian** political system is one in which one political party controls everything and does not allow any other parties to exist.

totality /təʊtælɪ¹ti¹/. UNCOUNT N The **totality** of something is the whole of it; a formal use. *...the totality of life.*

totter /tɒtə/, **totters, tottering, tottered.** VB When someone **totters,** they walk in an unsteady way. *I tottered back to my bed.*

touch /tʌtʃ/, **touches, touching, touched.** 1 VB WITH OBJ If you **touch** something, you gently put your fingers or hand on it. *The metal is so hot I can't touch it.* Also SING N *He remembered the touch of her hand.* 2 RECIP VB When two things **touch,** their surfaces come into contact with one another. *Make sure that the wires are not touching... My feet touched the ground.* 3 UNCOUNT N Your sense of **touch** is your ability to tell what something is like when you feel it with your hands. *The skin was slightly waxy to the touch.* 4 PASSIVE VB If you **are touched** by something, it makes you feel sad, sympathetic, or grateful. *I was touched by his thoughtfulness.* 5 COUNT N WITH SUPP A **touch** is a detail which is added to something to improve it. *The final touches were put to their report.* • See also **finishing touches.** 6 SING N WITH SUPP A **touch** of something is a very small amount of it. *There was a touch of frost this morning.*

PHRASES • If you get **in touch** with someone or keep **in touch** with them, you write to them or telephone them. *Please drop in when you can. I'd like to keep in touch.* • If you **lose touch** with someone, you gradually stop writing, phoning, or visiting each other. • If you are **in touch** with a subject or situation, you know the latest information about it. If you are **out of touch** with it, your knowledge of it is out of date. *I'm a bit out of touch with new developments.* • If you say that something is **touch and go,** you mean that you are uncertain whether it will happen or succeed.

touch down. PHR VB When an aircraft **touches down,** it lands.

touch on. PHR VB If you **touch on** something, you mention it briefly. *...the topic which I touched on at the beginning of this chapter.*

touching /tʌtʃɪŋ/. ADJ Something that is **touching** makes you feel sad or sympathetic. *...their touching faith in the power of education.*

touchy /tʌtʃi¹/, **touchier, touchiest.** 1 ADJ **Touchy** people are easily upset or irritated. *Most young parents are touchy about criticism.* 2 ADJ A **touchy** subject is one that needs to be dealt with carefully, because it might upset or offend people.

tough /tʌf/, **tougher, toughest.** 1 ADJ Someone who is **tough** has a strong character and is able to tolerate a lot of pain or hardship. *...a tough reporter.* 2 ADJ A **tough** substance is strong, and difficult to break or cut. *Some plastics are as tough as metal.* 3 ADJ A **tough** task, problem, or way of life is difficult or full of hardship. *The toughest problem is theft.* 4 ADJ **Tough** policies or actions are strict and firm. *We are convinced that her tough economic policies will succeed.*

toughen /tʌfə⁰n/, **toughens, toughening, toughened.** 1 VB WITH OBJ To **toughen** something means to make it stronger so that it will not break easily. ♦ **toughened** ADJ *...the use of toughened glass in windscreens.* 2 VB WITH OBJ If an experience **toughens** you, it makes you stronger and more independent in character. *She had been toughened by Guy's death.*

tour /tʊə, tɔː/, **tours, touring, toured.** 1 COUNT N A **tour** is a long journey during which you visit several places. *...a five-month tour of the Far East.* 2 COUNT N A **tour** is also a short trip round a city or an interesting building. *...guided tours.* 3 VB WITH OBJ If you **tour** an area, you go round it visiting places. *He spent his vacation touring the highlands of Scotland.*

tourism /tʊərɪzə⁰m, tɔː-/. UNCOUNT N **Tourism** consists of the activities of people visiting a place on holiday, and the providing of services for these people.

tourist /tʊərɪst, tɔː-/, **tourists.** COUNT N A **tourist** is a person who is visiting a place for pleasure and interest. *She showed a party of tourists round.*

tournament /tʊənəmə²nt, tɔː-/, **tournaments.** COUNT N A **tournament** is a sports competition in which the winners of each match play further matches, until just one person or team is left. *...a table tennis tournament.*

tousled /taʊzə⁰ld/. ADJ **Tousled** hair is untidy.

tout /taʊt/, **touts, touting, touted;** an informal word. 1 VB WITH OBJ If someone **touts** something, they try to sell it. *...an exporter touting a range of plastic toys.* 2 VB WITH 'for' If someone **touts** for business or custom, they try to obtain it. *...porters touting for loads at a railway station.* 3 COUNT N A **tout** is someone who sells things such as tickets informally and at high prices.

tow /təʊ/, **tows, towing, towed.** 1 VB WITH OBJ If one vehicle **tows** another, the first vehicle pulls the second along behind it. *...a lorry towing a trailer of hay.* Also SING N *If you can't get a tow, you'll have to walk.* 2 PHRASE If you have someone **in tow,** they are with you because you are looking after them; an informal use. *He arrived with his children in tow.*

towards /təwɔːdz/ or **toward.** 1 PREP If you move, look, or point **towards** something or someone, you move, look, or point in their direction. *He saw his mother running towards him.* 2 PREP If people move **towards** a particular situation, that situation becomes likely to happen. *We are drifting towards disaster... There is a tendency towards inflation.* 3 PREP If you have a particular attitude **towards** something or someone, you feel like that about them. *He felt very friendly towards them.* 4 PREP If you give money **towards** something, you give it to help pay for that thing. *They may give you something towards your housing costs.* 5 PREP **Towards** the end of a period of time means just before its end. *I went to London towards the end of 1977.* 6 PREP **Towards** a part of a place means near to that part. *He was sitting towards the back of the room.*

towel /taʊəl/, **towels.** COUNT N A **towel** is a piece of thick, soft cloth that you use to dry yourself with.

tower /taʊə/, **towers, towering, towered.** 1 COUNT N A **tower** is a tall, narrow building, or a tall part of a building such as a castle or church. 2 VB WITH ADJUNCT Someone or something that **towers** over other people or things is a lot taller than they are; a literary use. *Jane stood up, towering over him.*

tower block, tower blocks. COUNT N A **tower block** is a tall building divided into flats or offices; a British use.

towering /taʊərɪŋ/. ATTRIB ADJ A **towering** building, tree, or mountain is very tall and impressive; a literary use.

town /taʊn/, **towns.** 1 COUNT N A **town** is a place with many streets and buildings where people live and work. 2 UNCOUNT N People sometimes refer to the town they live in as **town.** *We packed our stuff and left town.*

town hall, town halls. COUNT N The **town hall** in a town is a large building owned and used by the town council, often as its headquarters.

township /taʊnʃɪp/, **townships.** COUNT N A **township** is a town in South Africa where only black people or coloured people are allowed to live.

toxic /tɒksɪk/. ADJ A **toxic** substance is poisonous; a formal use. *...toxic chemicals.*

toy /tɔɪ/, **toys, toying, toyed.** COUNT N OR MOD A **toy** is an object for children to play with. *...a toy car.*

toy with. PHR VB 1 If you **toy with** an idea, you consider it casually, without making any decisions about it. 2 If you **toy with** an object, you keep moving it slightly while thinking about something.

trace /treɪs/, **traces, tracing, traced.** 1 VB WITH OBJ If you **trace** something, you find it after looking for it. *They were trying to trace her missing husband.* 2 VB WITH OBJ If you **trace** the development of something, you find out or describe how it developed. *...attempting to trace the evolution of man.* 3 VB WITH OBJ If you **trace** a drawing or map, you copy it by covering it with a piece of transparent paper and drawing over the lines underneath. 4 COUNT N A **trace** is a sign which shows that someone or something has been in a place. *No trace was found of either the bag or its contents.* ● If someone disappears **without trace,** there is no sign of where they have gone. 5 COUNT N A **trace** of something is a very small amount of it. *...traces of the paint.*

track /træk/, **tracks, tracking, tracked.** 1 COUNT N A **track** is a narrow road or path. *...a dusty mountain track.* 2 COUNT N A **track** is also a piece of ground which horses, cars, or athletes race around. 3 COUNT N A railway **track** consists of the rails that a train travels along. 4 PLURAL N **Tracks** are footprints or other marks left on the ground by a person or animal. 5 VB WITH OBJ If you **track** animals or people, you follow their footprints or other signs that they have left behind them. 6 COUNT N A **track** on a record or tape is one of the songs or pieces of music on it.
PHRASES ● A place that is **off the beaten track** is in a quiet and isolated area. ● If you **keep track of** things or people, you pay attention to them so that you know where they are or what is happening. If you **lose track of** them, you no longer know where they are or what is happening. *We would never be able to keep track of the luggage on such a long journey.* ● If you are **on the right track,** you are thinking in a way that is likely to give you the right answer to a question or problem.

track down. PHR VB If you **track down** someone or something, you find them by searching for them. *They lost all hope of tracking down the submarine.*

track record, track records. COUNT N WITH SUPP The **track record** of a person or a company consists of their past achievements or failures.

tracksuit /træksj^{0}u:t/, **tracksuits.** COUNT N A **tracksuit** is a loose, warm suit consisting of trousers and a top, worn mainly when exercising.

tract /trækt/, **tracts.** 1 COUNT N A **tract** of land is a large area of it; a formal use. *...immense tracts of impenetrable jungle.* 2 COUNT N A **tract** is a short article making a religious, moral, or political point.

tractor /træktə/, **tractors.** COUNT N A **tractor** is a farm vehicle with large rear wheels that is used for pulling machinery.

trade /treɪd/, **trades, trading, traded.** 1 UNCOUNT N **Trade** is the activity of buying, selling, or exchanging goods or services. *France is heavily dependent on foreign trade... ...the antique trade.* 2 VB When people, firms, or countries **trade,** they buy, sell, or exchange goods or services. *They specialized in trading with China.* 3 COUNT N Someone's **trade** is the kind of work that they do, especially when it requires special training in practical skills. *...the trade of blacksmith.*

trade in. PHR VB If you **trade in** something you own, such as your car or TV set, you give it to a dealer when you buy a new one so that you get a reduction on the price. *You might trade the car in for a smaller one.*

trademark /treɪdmɑ:k/, **trademarks.** COUNT N A **trademark** is a name or symbol that a company uses on its products and that cannot legally be used by another company.

trader /treɪdə/, **traders.** COUNT N A **trader** is a person who trades, especially in a foreign country. *...a whisky trader.*

tradesman /treɪdzmə^{3}n/, **tradesmen.** COUNT N A **tradesman** is a person who sells goods, especially one who owns and runs a shop.

trade union, trade unions. The form **trades union** is also used. COUNT N A **trade union** is an organization of workers that tries to improve the pay and working conditions of its members.

trade unionist, trade unionists. COUNT N A **trade unionist** is an active member of a trade union.

tradition /trə^{3}dɪʃə^{0}n/, **traditions.** COUNT N OR UNCOUNT N A **tradition** is a custom or belief that has existed for a long time. *...Britain's long tradition of political independence... We must have respect for tradition.*

traditional /trə^{3}dɪʃə^{0}nəl, -ʃənə^{0}l/. ADJ **Traditional** customs or beliefs have existed for a long time. *The bride is dressed in traditional costume.* ♦ **traditionally** ADV *The dry season was traditionally a time of inactivity.*

traffic /træfɪk/, **traffics, trafficking, trafficked.** 1 UNCOUNT N **Traffic** refers to all the vehicles that are moving along a road. *...rush-hour traffic.* 2 UNCOUNT N WITH SUPP **Traffic** in something such as drugs is an illegal trade in them. *...illegal traffic in protected animals.* 3 VB WITH 'in' Someone who **traffics** in drugs or other goods buys and sells them illegally.

traffic jam, traffic jams. COUNT N A **traffic jam** is a long line of vehicles that cannot move because the road is blocked.

traffic light, traffic lights. COUNT N **Traffic lights** are the coloured lights at road junctions which control the flow of traffic.

traffic warden, traffic wardens. COUNT N A **traffic warden** is a person whose job is to make sure that cars are parked legally.

tragedy /trædʒɪ'di^1/, **tragedies.** 1 COUNT N OR UNCOUNT N A **tragedy** is an extremely sad event or situation. *The change of flight plans was the principal cause of the tragedy... When tensions are so high, tragedy is inevitable.* 2 COUNT N OR UNCOUNT N **Tragedy** is a type of literature, especially drama, that is serious and sad and often ends with the death of the main character. *She acted brilliantly in Greek tragedy... ...an Elizabethan tragedy.*

tragic /trædʒɪk/. 1 ADJ Something that is **tragic** is very sad. *...the tragic death of his elder brother Michael.* ♦ **tragically** ADV *He was tragically killed in a car crash.* 2 ATTRIB ADJ **Tragic** is also used to refer to tragedy as a form of literature. *...Scott Fitzgerald's tragic novel 'Tender is the Night'.*

trail /treɪl/, **trails, trailing, trailed.** 1 COUNT N A **trail** is a rough path across open country or through forests. *They trudged along the seemingly endless trail.* 2 COUNT N A **trail** is a series of marks or other signs left by someone or something as they move along. *She didn't want him to leave a trail of wet footprints all over the house.* 3 PHRASE If you are **on the trail of** a person or animal, you are trying to find them. 4 ERG VB If you **trail** something or if it **trails,** it moves along, hanging down loosely. *She trails the fingers of her right hand through the water... She went out with her dress trailing behind her on the floor.* 5 VB WITH ADJUNCT If someone **trails** along, they move slowly, without any energy or enthusiasm, often following someone else. *I used to trail around after him like a small child.*

trail away or **trail off.** PHR VB If a speaker's voice **trails away** or **trails off,** it gradually becomes more hesitant until it stops completely. *'I have an appointment that's very...' His voice trailed off unconvincingly.*

trailer /treɪlə/, **trailers.** 1 COUNT N A **trailer** is a small vehicle which can be loaded with things and pulled behind a car. 2 COUNT N A **trailer** is also a long vehicle which people use as a home or office and which can be pulled behind a car; an American use. 3 COUNT N A **trailer** for a film or television programme is a set of short extracts which are shown or broadcast to advertise it.

train /treɪn/, **trains, training, trained.** 1 COUNT N A **train** is a number of carriages or trucks pulled by an engine along a railway line. *I caught a train to Oxford... We are going by train... ...the train journey to Leeds.* 2 PHRASE A **train of thought** is a connected series of thoughts. *I felt annoyed with her for interrupting my train of thought.* 3 VB WITH OBJ If you **train** a person or animal to do something, you teach them how to do it. *The police are trained to keep calm.* ♦ **trained** ADJ *...a trained nurse.* 4 VB If you **train** as something, you learn how to do a particular job. *She started to train as a nurse.* 5 ERG VB If you **train** for an activity such as a race, you prepare for it by doing exercises and eating special foods. *He was training for the marathon.* 6 See also **training.**

trainee /treɪni:/, **trainees.** COUNT N A **trainee** is someone who is being taught how to do a job. *The trainees are shown around each of the departments... ...a trainee chef.*

trainer /treɪnə/, **trainers.** 1 COUNT N A **trainer** is a person who trains people or animals. 2 COUNT N **Trainers** are special shoes worn for running.

training /treɪnɪŋ/. 1 UNCOUNT N **Training** for a particular job involves learning the skills needed for the job. *...giving people training in computer programming.* 2 UNCOUNT N **Training** also involves doing exercises and eating special foods in preparation for an activity such as a race.

traipse /treɪps/, **traipses, traipsing, traipsed.** VB WITH ADJUNCT If you **traipse** somewhere, you walk there slowly and wearily; an informal use. *For eighteen weeks we traipsed around southern England.*

trait /treɪt^0/, **traits.** COUNT N WITH SUPP A **trait** is a characteristic or tendency. *Certain personality traits had made her unpopular.*

traitor /treɪtə/, **traitors.** COUNT N A **traitor** is someone who betrays their country or the group which they belong to. *He was denounced as a traitor to France.*

tram /træm/, **trams.** COUNT N A **tram** is an electric vehicle which travels on rails along a street.

tramp /træmp/, **tramps, tramping, tramped.** 1 COUNT N A **tramp** is a person with no permanent home or job who gets money by doing occasional work or by begging. 2 VB WITH ADJUNCT OR OBJ If you **tramp** somewhere, you walk with slow, heavy footsteps. *She tramped slowly up the beach... ...tramping the streets all day as a postman.*

trample /træmpə^{0}l/, **tramples, trampling, trampled.** 1 VB WITH ADJUNCT OR OBJ If you **trample** on something, you tread heavily on it and damage it. *...trampling through the undergrowth... They had trampled his lovely rose garden.* 2 VB WITH 'on' If you **trample** on someone or on their rights or feelings, you behave towards them in a cruel or unjust way.

trampoline /træmpə^{0}li^{1}n/, **trampolines.** COUNT N A **trampoline** is a piece of apparatus on which you do acrobatic jumps. It consists of a large piece of strong cloth held by springs in a frame.

trance /trɑ:ns/, **trances.** COUNT N A **trance** is a mental state in which you appear to be asleep, but you can see and hear things and respond to commands. *She used to go into a trance and talk to the spirits.*

tranquil /træŋkwɪl/. ADJ **Tranquil** means calm and peaceful; a literary use. *...this tranquil island.* ♦ **tranquillity** /træŋkwɪlɪti^1/ UNCOUNT N *...a time of political tranquillity.*

tranquillize /træŋkwɪlaɪz/, **tranquillizes, tranquillizing, tranquillized;** also spelled **tranquillise** and, in American English, **tranquilize.** VB WITH OBJ If people or animals **are tranquillized,** they are given a drug to make them become calm, sleepy, or unconscious.

tranquillizer /træŋkwɪlaɪzə/, **tranquillizers;** also spelled **tranquilliser** and, in American English, **tranquilizer.** COUNT N A **tranquillizer** is a drug that makes people feel less anxious or nervous.

trans-. PREFIX **Trans-** is used to form adjectives that describe something that goes or exists from one side of a place to the other. *...the Trans-Siberian Railway.*

transaction /trænzækʃə^{0}n/, **transactions.** COUNT N A **transaction** is a business deal.

transatlantic /trænzə^{3}tlæntɪk/. 1 ATTRIB ADJ **Transatlantic** journeys or communications involve travelling or communicating across the Atlantic Ocean. *...a transatlantic phone call... ...regular transatlantic crossings.* 2 ATTRIB ADJ **Transatlantic** is also used by Europeans to describe things in the USA, and by Americans to describe things in Europe. *...transatlantic holidays.*

transcend /trænsend/, **transcends, transcending, transcended.** VB WITH OBJ If one thing **transcends** another, it is not limited by the other thing; a formal use. *...a vital national issue that transcended party loyalties.*

transcribe /trænskraɪb/, **transcribes, transcribing, transcribed.** VB WITH OBJ If you **transcribe** something that is spoken or written, you write it down, copy it, or change it into a different form of writing. *He transcribed recordings of schoolchildren.*

transcript /trænskrɪpt/, **transcripts.** COUNT N A **transcript** of something that is spoken is a written copy of it. *...transcripts of tapes.*

transfer, transfers, transferring, transferred; pronounced /trænsfɜ:/ when it is a verb and /trænsfɜ:/ when it is a noun. 1 VB WITH OBJ If you **transfer** something from one place or person to another, you move it. *Ten thousand pounds has been transferred into your account... He transferred the trout to a plate... Ravenscroft transferred his affections to his secretary.* Also UNCOUNT N OR COUNT N *...the electronic transfer of money... ...a transfer of public funds.* 2 ERG VB If you **are transferred** to a different place or job, you move to a different place or job within the same organization. *What branch did you say you would like to transfer to?* Also COUNT N OR UNCOUNT N *He had applied for a transfer to the north... He resisted his transfer to the political section.*

transfixed /trænsfɪkst/. PRED ADJ If you are **transfixed** by something, you are so impressed, fascinated, or frightened by it that you cannot move; a literary use. *I stood transfixed with terror.*

transform /trænsfɔ:m/, **transforms, transforming, transformed.** VB WITH OBJ If something **is transformed,** it is changed completely. *An area of pasture land can be transformed into a barren landscape in two or three years... They claimed to be able to transform the lives of millions of people.* ♦ **transformation** /trænsfəmeɪʃə^{0}n/ COUNT N OR UNCOUNT N *After a few months, the creature undergoes a transformation... ...the social and political transformation of society.*

transfusion /trænsfju:ʒə^{0}n/, **transfusions.** COUNT N When a patient is given a blood **transfusion,** blood is put into his or her body.

transient /trænzi^{1}ənt/. ADJ Something that is **transient** does not last very long; a formal use. *...his bored wife's transient affair with a poet.* ♦ **transience** /trænzi^{1}əns/ UNCOUNT N *...the transience of human ties.*

transistor /trænzɪstə/, **transistors.** 1 COUNT N A **transistor** is a small electronic device in something such as a television or a radio. It is used for amplification and switching. 2 COUNT N A **transistor** or **transistor radio** is a small portable radio.

transit /trænzɪt/. 1 PHRASE People or things that are **in transit** are travelling or being taken from one place to another. *The tablets had been lost in transit.* 2 ATTRIB ADJ A **transit** area or building is a place where people wait or where goods are kept between different stages of a journey. *...the transit lounge.*

transition /trænzɪʃə^{0}n/, **transitions.** COUNT N OR UNCOUNT N A **transition** is a change from one form or state to another. *...a transition from misery to happiness... The area is now in a state of transition.*

transitional /trænzɪʃə^{0}nəl, -ʃənə^{0}l/. ADJ A **transitional** period or stage is one during which something changes from one form or state to another. *...a transitional period of civil war.*

transitive /trænzɪtɪv/. ADJ A **transitive** verb has an object.

transitory /trænzɪtə^{0}ri^1/. ADJ If something is **transitory,** it lasts for only a short time. *Love is transitory, but art is eternal.*

translate /trænsleɪt, trænz-/, **translates, translating, translated.** 1 VB WITH OR WITHOUT OBJ If you **translate** something that someone has said or written, you say it or write it in a different language. *My books have been translated into many languages.* 2 VB WITH OBJ AND 'into' To **translate** one thing into another means to convert it into something else. *He started to translate into action the dreams of African unity.*

translation /trænsleɪʃə^{0}n, trænz-/, **translations.** COUNT N A **translation** is a piece of writing or speech that has been translated from a different language. *...a new translation of the Bible.*

translator /trænsleɪtə, trænz-/, **translators.** COUNT N A **translator** is a person whose job involves translating writing or speech from one language to another.

translucent /trænzlu:sə^{0}nt/. ADJ If something is **translucent,** light passes through it, so that it seems to glow; a literary use. *The leaves of the beeches are translucent in the setting sun.*

transmission /trænzmɪʃə^{0}n/, **transmissions.** 1 UNCOUNT N The **transmission** of something involves passing it or sending it to a different place or person. *...data transmission... ...the transmission of diseases.* 2 UNCOUNT N The **transmission** of television or radio programmes is the broadcasting of them. *...a unique film record that was destroyed after transmission.* 3 COUNT N A **transmission** is a broadcast. *Millions would have heard that transmission.*

transmit /trænzmɪt/, **transmits, transmitting, transmitted.** 1 VB WITH OBJ When a message or electronic signal **is transmitted,** it is sent by radio waves. *The material was transmitted by satellite throughout the world.* 2 VB WITH OBJ To **transmit** something to a different place or person means to pass or send it to the place or person; a formal use. *...a disease that is sometimes transmitted to humans.*

transmitter /trænzmɪtə/, **transmitters.** COUNT N A **transmitter** is a piece of equipment used for sending radio signals or for broadcasting programmes.

transparency /trænspærənsi^1/, **transparencies.** 1 COUNT N A **transparency** is a small piece of photographic film in a frame which can be projected onto a screen. 2 UNCOUNT N **Transparency** is the quality that an object or substance has if you can see through it. *The crystal lost its transparency.*

transparent /trænspærənt/. 1 ADJ If an object or substance is **transparent,** you can see through it. *...a transparent plastic lid.* 2 ADJ If something such as a feeling is **transparent,** it is easily understood or recognized. *We wanted our goals to be transparent.* ♦ **transparently** SUBMOD *...an attitude that was transparently false.*

transpire /trænspaɪə/, **transpires, transpiring, transpired;** a formal word. 1 VB When it **transpires** that something is the case, people discover that it is the case. *It finally transpired that he was a special investigator for the CIA.* 2 VB When something **transpires,** it happens. *Nobody knows what transpired at the meeting.*

transplant, transplants, transplanting, transplanted; pronounced /trænsplɑ:nt/ when it is a noun and /trænsplɑ:nt/ when it is a verb. 1 COUNT N OR UNCOUNT N A **transplant** is a surgical operation in which a part of a person's body is replaced because it is diseased. *...kidney transplants... ...allegations of a trade in human organs for transplant.* Also VB WITH OBJ *Doctors hope to transplant a human heart into the patient within the next few days.* 2 ERG VB When something **is transplanted,** it is moved to a different place. *...how an established technology can be transplanted to another region.*

transport, transports, transporting, transported; pronounced /trænspɔ:t/ when it is a noun and /trænspɔ:t/ when it is a verb. 1 UNCOUNT N Vehicles that you travel in are referred to as **transport.** *It is easier if you have your own transport... Why can't he use public transport?* 2 UNCOUNT N **Transport** involves moving goods or people from one place to another. *The essential means of transport for heavy equipment remained the railway... ...high transport costs.* 3 VB WITH OBJ When goods or people **are transported** from one place to another, they are moved there. *The goods were transported to East Africa.*

transportation /trænspɔ:teɪʃə^{0}n/. UNCOUNT N **Transportation** is the same as transport; an American use. *The food is ready for transportation.*

trap /træp/, **traps, trapping, trapped.** 1 COUNT N A **trap** is a device or hole that is intended to catch animals or birds. *...an otter trap.* 2 COUNT N A **trap** is also a trick intended to catch or deceive someone. *I knew perfectly well it was a trap.* 3 VB WITH OBJ To **trap** animals means to catch them using traps. 4 VB WITH OBJ If you **trap** someone, you trick them so that they do or say something which they did not want to. *This wasn't the first time we had been trapped into a situation like this.* 5 VB WITH OBJ If you **are trapped** in an unpleasant place or situation, you cannot escape from it. *I can't get up, I'm trapped here... Many women are trapped in loveless marriages.* 6 COUNT N WITH SUPP A **trap** is also an unpleasant situation that you cannot easily escape from. *To break out of the poverty trap they need help from the government.* 7 See also **booby-trap.**

trapdoor /træpdɔ:/, **trapdoors.** COUNT N A **trapdoor** is a small horizontal door in a floor, ceiling, or stage.

trapeze /trəpi:z/, **trapezes.** COUNT N A **trapeze** is a bar of wood or metal hanging from two ropes on which acrobats and gymnasts swing and perform skilful movements.

trappings /træpɪŋz/. PLURAL N The **trappings** of a particular rank, position, or state are the things that you acquire as a result of having it. *...the trappings of power that have surrounded him since he took office.*

trash /træʃ/. 1 UNCOUNT N **Trash** is rubbish; an American use. *The yards were filled with trash.* 2 UNCOUNT N If you think a book or film is of very poor quality, you can refer to it as **trash;** an informal use. *I've told you not to read that trash.*

trashcan /træʃkæn/, **trashcans.** COUNT N A **trashcan** is a dustbin; an American use.

trauma /trɔ:mə/, **traumas.** 1 COUNT N A **trauma** is a very upsetting experience. *...the trauma of having their parents arrested.* 2 UNCOUNT N **Trauma** is great stress and unhappiness. *This would impose unnecessary trauma and suffering.*

traumatic /trɔ:mætɪk/. ADJ A **traumatic** experience is very upsetting. *...the traumatic ordeal of facing a firing squad.*

travel /trævə^{0}l/, **travels, travelling, travelled;** spelled **traveling** and **traveled** in American English. 1 VB WITH OR WITHOUT OBJ When you **travel,** you go from one place to another. *I travelled sixty miles to buy those books... I travelled to work by train.* 2 UNCOUNT N **Travel** is the act of travelling. *...air travel.* 3 PLURAL N WITH POSS Someone's **travels** are the journeys they make to places a long way from their home. *...his extensive travels abroad.* 4 VB WITH ADJUNCT When something reaches one place from another, you say that it **travels** there. *Sound travels better in water... News travels fast.*

travel agency, travel agencies. COUNT N A **travel agency** is a business which makes arrangements for people's holidays and journeys.

travel agent, travel agents. COUNT N A **travel agent** is someone who works in a travel agency.

traveller /trævə^{0}lə/, **travellers;** spelled **traveler** in American English. COUNT N A **traveller** is a person who is making a journey or who travels a lot.

traveller's cheque, traveller's cheques; spelled **traveler's check** in American English. COUNT N **Traveller's cheques** are cheques that you can exchange for local currency when you are abroad.

traverse /trævɜ:s, trə^{3}vɜ:s/, **traverses, traversing, traversed.** VB WITH OBJ If you **traverse** an area of land or water, you cross it; a formal use. *I traversed the rest of the slope at a run.*

travesty /trævəsti^1/, **travesties.** COUNT N A **travesty** of something is a very bad representation of it. *His account of my essay was a travesty... ...the travesties of justice played out in their courts.*

trawler /trɔ:lə/, **trawlers.** COUNT N A **trawler** is a fishing boat from which fish are caught in large nets.

tray /treɪ/, **trays.** COUNT N A **tray** is a flat object with raised edges which is used for carrying food or drinks.

treacherous /tretʃərəs/. 1 ADJ A **treacherous** person is likely to betray you. *...my treacherous fellow travellers.* 2 ADJ If the ground or the sea is **treacherous,** it is dangerous and unpredictable.

treachery /tretʃəri^1/. UNCOUNT N If someone betrays their country or betrays a person who trusts them, you describe their action as **treachery.** *He could not believe that Clemenza was guilty of treachery.*

treacle /tri:kə^{0}l/. UNCOUNT N **Treacle** is a sweet, sticky liquid used in making cakes and puddings.

tread /tred/, **treads, treading, trod** /trɒd/, **trodden** /trɒdə^{0}n/. 1 VB WITH ADJUNCT If you **tread** on something, you step on it. *Don't tread on the flowers.* 2 VB WITH OBJ AND ADJUNCT If you **tread** something into the ground or into a carpet, you step on it and crush it in. *Damp chips had been trodden into the carpet.* 3 VB WITH ADJUNCT If you **tread** in a particular way, you walk in that way. *She trod heavily out of the room.* 4 SING N WITH SUPP Someone's **tread** is the sound they make with their feet as they walk. *They could hear his heavy limping tread.* 5 VB WITH ADJUNCT If you **tread** carefully, you behave cautiously. *The government was treading warily.* 6 COUNT N The **tread** of a tyre or shoe is the pattern of ridges on it that stops it slipping.

treason /tri:zə^{0}n/. UNCOUNT N **Treason** is the crime of betraying your country.

treasure /treʒə/, **treasures, treasuring, treasured.** 1 UNCOUNT N **Treasure** is a collection of gold, silver, or jewels, especially one that has been hidden. *...buried treasure.* 2 COUNT N **Treasures** are valuable works of art. *...the sale of art treasures.* 3 VB WITH OBJ If you **treasure** something that you have, you regard it as precious. *...one of the memories which they would treasure.* ♦ **treasured** ATTRIB ADJ *...my most treasured possessions.*

treasurer /treʒərə/, **treasurers.** COUNT N The **treasurer** of an organization is the person in charge of its finances and accounts.

treasury /treʒəri^1/. PROPER N The **Treasury** is the government department in Britain and some other countries that deals with the country's finances. *The Treasury was opposed in principle to the proposals... ...a former Treasury official.*

treat /tri:t/, **treats, treating, treated.** 1 VB WITH OBJ AND ADJUNCT If you **treat** someone or something in a particular way, you behave towards them or deal with them in that way. *Their parents continue to treat them as children... Electricity is potentially dangerous, so treat it with respect.* 2 VB WITH OBJ When a doctor **treats** a patient or an illness, he or she tries to make the patient well again. *...a way to treat cancer.* 3 VB WITH OBJ If something such as wood or cloth **is treated,** a special substance is put on it to protect it or give it special properties. *New timber should be treated with a preservative.* 4 COUNT N If you give someone a **treat,** you buy or arrange something special for them which they will enjoy. *Granny took us for tea at Lyons Corner House as a special treat.* Also REFL VB OR VB WITH OBJ *Treat yourself to a new pair of shoes... I was treated to lunch by the vice-president.*

treatment /tri:tmə^{0}nt/, **treatments.** 1 UNCOUNT N OR COUNT N Medical **treatment** consists of all the things done to make a sick person well again. *...free dental treatment... I tried every treatment the doctor suggested.* 2 UNCOUNT N Your **treatment** of someone is the way you behave towards them or deal with them. *Their treatment of women is unspeakable... I didn't want special treatment.*

treaty /tri:ti^1/, **treaties.** COUNT N A **treaty** is a written agreement between countries. *The Government has signed a treaty with Moscow.*

treble /trebə^{0}l/, **trebles, trebling, trebled.** ERG VB If something **trebles** or **is trebled,** it becomes three times greater in number or amount. *The population has nearly trebled since 1950.*

tree /tri:/, **trees.** COUNT N A **tree** is a tall plant with a hard trunk, branches, and leaves. ● See also **Christmas tree, family tree.**

trek /trek/, **treks, trekking, trekked.** VB WITH ADJUNCT If you **trek** somewhere, you go on a long and difficult journey there, especially on foot. *They trekked for three days along the banks of the Zambezi.* Also COUNT N *We set off on a four hour trek.*

trellis /trelɪs/, **trellises.** COUNT N A **trellis** is a frame which supports climbing plants.

tremble /trembə[0]l/, **trembles, trembling, trembled. 1** VB If you **tremble,** you shake slightly, because you are frightened or cold. *...trembling with fear.* **2** VB If something **trembles,** it shakes slightly. *The wind made the branches shake and tremble.*

tremendous /trɪ[2]mendəs/. **1** ADJ **Tremendous** means very large or impressive. *They cost a tremendous amount of money... The play became a tremendous hit.* ♦ **tremendously** ADV *She envied and admired Judy tremendously.* **2** ADJ You also describe something as **tremendous** when it is very good or pleasing. *The holiday was tremendous.*

tremor /tremə/, **tremors. 1** COUNT N A **tremor** is a shaking of your body or voice which you cannot control. *...a tremor of pleasure... Burton detected a tremor in her voice.* **2** COUNT N A **tremor** is also a small earthquake.

tremulous /tremjə[4]ləs/. ADJ A **tremulous** smile or voice is unsteady; a literary use. *Jack's voice went on, tremulous yet determined.*

trench /trentʃ/, **trenches.** COUNT N A **trench** is a long, narrow channel dug in the ground.

trend /trend/, **trends.** COUNT N A **trend** is a change towards something different. *There is a trend towards equal opportunities for men and women.*

trendy /trendi[1]/, **trendier, trendiest.** ADJ **Trendy** means fashionable; an informal use. *...trendy clothes.*

trepidation /trepɪdeɪʃə[0]n/. UNCOUNT N **Trepidation** is fear or anxiety; a formal use. *We approached with trepidation.*

trespass /trespəs/, **trespasses, trespassing, trespassed.** VB If you **trespass** on someone's land, you go onto it without their permission. *...signs saying 'No trespassing'.* ♦ **trespasser** COUNT N *Trespassers will be prosecuted.*

trial /traɪəl/, **trials. 1** COUNT N OR UNCOUNT N A **trial** is the legal process in which a judge and jury listen to evidence and decide whether a person is guilty of a crime. *She won't get a fair trial... Huey was awaiting trial for murder.* ● **to stand trial:** see **stand. 2** COUNT N A **trial** is also an experiment in which you test something. *We've completed a number of fairly successful trials with laboratory animals.* **3** COUNT N WITH SUPP Someone's **trials** are the unpleasant things that they experience. *...the trials of pregnancy.*
PHRASES ● If someone is **on trial,** they are being tried in a court of law. *We don't intend to put him on trial.* ● If something is **on trial,** it is being tested or closely examined. *The Parliamentary system is on trial.* ● If you do something by **trial and error,** you try different ways of doing it until you find a good one.

trial run, trial runs. COUNT N A **trial run** is a first attempt at doing something, to make sure that you can do it properly.

triangle /traɪæŋgə[0]l/, **triangles.** COUNT N A **triangle** is a shape with three straight sides.

triangular /traɪæŋgjə[4]lə/. ADJ Something that is **triangular** is in the shape of a triangle. *I punched two triangular holes in the tin.*

tribal /traɪbə[0]l/. ATTRIB ADJ **Tribal** describes things relating or belonging to tribes. *...tribal leaders.*

tribe /traɪb/, **tribes.** COUNT N A **tribe** is a small group of people with the same language and customs. *Mr Otunnu is a member of the Acholi tribe.*

tribesman /traɪbzmə[3]n/, **tribesmen.** COUNT N A **tribesman** is a man who belongs to a tribe.

tribulation /trɪbjə[4]leɪʃə[0]n/, **tribulations.** UNCOUNT N OR PLURAL N **Tribulation** is trouble or suffering; a formal use. *Life is uncertain and full of tribulation... ...after many trials and tribulations during the war.*

tribunal /traɪbjuːnə[0]l/, **tribunals.** COLL N A **tribunal** is a special court or committee that is appointed to deal with particular problems. *An industrial tribunal was hearing cases of unfair dismissal.*

tributary /trɪbjə[4]tə[0]ri[1]/, **tributaries.** COUNT N The **tributaries** of a large river are the smaller rivers that flow into it. *...the Neander River, a tributary of the Rhine.*

tribute /trɪbjuːt/, **tributes. 1** COUNT N OR UNCOUNT N A **tribute** is something that you say or do to show your admiration and respect for someone. *She accepted the tribute graciously... Asquith paid tribute to his personal qualities.* **2** SING N If one thing is a **tribute** to another, it is the result of the other thing and shows how good it is. *The fact that I survived is a tribute to the indestructibility of the human body.*

trick /trɪk/, **tricks, tricking, tricked. 1** VB WITH OBJ If someone **tricks** you, they deceive you, often in order to make you do something. *He realized that the visitors had tricked him... She felt she had been tricked into marriage.* **2** COUNT N A **trick** is an action that is intended to deceive someone. *They played a dirty trick on us.* **3** COUNT N A **trick** is also a clever way of doing something. *An old campers' trick is to use three thin blankets instead of one thick one.* **4** ATTRIB ADJ A **trick** question is one where the obvious answer is in fact wrong, or one which is intended to make you accidentally reveal something. **5** ATTRIB ADJ **Trick** devices and methods are intended to deceive people for entertainment. *...trick photography.* **6** PHRASE If something **does the trick,** it achieves what you wanted; an informal use. **7** See also **conjuring trick.**

trickery /trɪkəri[1]/. UNCOUNT N **Trickery** is deception. *The old man suspected trickery.*

trickle /trɪkə[0]l/, **trickles, trickling, trickled. 1** VB If a liquid **trickles** somewhere, it flows slowly in a thin stream. *The tears were beginning to trickle down her cheeks.* **2** VB WITH ADJUNCT If people or things **trickle** somewhere, they move there slowly in small groups or amounts. *The coach parties began trickling back to the car park.* **3** COUNT N A **trickle** of liquid is a thin, slow stream of it. *...a thin trickle of blood.* **4** COUNT N A **trickle** of people or things is a small number or quantity of them. *A trickle of people were still coming.*

tricky /trɪki[1]/, **trickier, trickiest.** ADJ A **tricky** task or problem is difficult to deal with.

tricycle /traɪsɪkə[0]l/, **tricycles.** COUNT N A **tricycle** is a vehicle similar to a bicycle but with two wheels at the back instead of one.

tried /traɪd/. **Tried** is the past tense and past participle of **try.**

trifle /traɪfə[0]l/, **trifles, trifling, trifled. 1** ADV A **trifle** means a little; a formal use. *She was a trifle breathless.* **2** COUNT N **Trifles** are things that are not considered important or valuable. *They worry over trifles.* **3** COUNT N OR UNCOUNT N A **trifle** is a cold pudding made of layers of sponge cake, fruit, jelly, and custard.

trifle with. PHR VB If you **trifle with** someone or something, you do not treat them seriously. *Mitchell was not someone to be trifled with.*

trifling /traɪflɪŋ/. ADJ A **trifling** matter is small and unimportant.

trigger /trɪgə/, **triggers, triggering, triggered. 1** COUNT N The **trigger** of a gun is the small lever which you pull to fire it. **2** VB WITH OBJ If something **triggers** an event or **triggers** it off, it causes it to happen.

trillion /trɪljən/. A **trillion** is a million million.

trilogy /trɪlədʒi[1]/, **trilogies.** COUNT N A **trilogy** is a series of three books, plays, or films with the same characters or subject.

trim /trɪm/, **trimmer, trimmest; trims, trimming, trimmed. 1** ADJ Something that is **trim** is neat, tidy, and attractive. *...the trim lawns and trees of suburbia.* **2** ADJ If someone has a **trim** figure, they are slim. *...a trim, balding man in his early sixties.* **3** VB WITH OBJ If you **trim** something, you cut off small amounts of it to make it look neater. *The grass needed trimming.* Also SING N *My hair needs a trim.* **4** VB WITH OBJ If a garment **is trimmed** with things such as ribbons, they are added to the edge as decorations. ♦ **trimmed** PRED ADJ WITH 'with' *...a hat trimmed with ribbons.*

trimming /trɪmɪŋ/, **trimmings. 1** MASS N OR PLURAL N The **trimming** or **trimmings** on a garment are extra parts added for decoration. *...a pink nightdress with nylon lace trimmings.* **2** PLURAL N **Trimmings** are also nice things that can be added to something or included in something. *Tonight it was turkey with all the trimmings.*

trinket /trɪŋkɪt/, **trinkets.** COUNT N A **trinket** is a cheap ornament or piece of jewellery.

trio /triːəʊ/, **trios.** COUNT N A **trio** is a group of three people, especially musicians or singers. *...a trio of journalists... ...the Pump Room Trio.*

trip /trɪp/, **trips, tripping, tripped. 1** COUNT N A **trip** is a journey that you make to a place and back again. *Morris decided to take a trip to London... ...executives on business trips abroad.* **2** VB If you **trip** when you are walking, you knock your foot against something and fall over or nearly fall over. *She tripped over a stone.* **3** VB WITH OBJ If you **trip** someone who is walking or **trip** them up, you put your foot or something else in front of them so that they knock their own foot against it and fall. *Somebody thrust out a foot and tripped him... She tripped up the steward as he passed.* **4** COUNT N A **trip** is also an unreal experience caused by taking drugs; an informal use. **5** See also **round trip.**

tripartite /traɪpɑːtaɪt/. ATTRIB ADJ **Tripartite** means having three parts or involving three groups of people; a formal use. *...the tripartite system of education... The unions called for tripartite talks.*

tripe /traɪp/. UNCOUNT N **Tripe** is the stomach of a pig, cow, or ox, which is eaten as food.

triple /trɪpə[0]l/, **triples, tripling, tripled. 1** ATTRIB ADJ **Triple** means consisting of three things or parts. *...a triple alliance... ...a breath-taking triple somersault.* **2** ERG VB If something **triples** or **is tripled,** it becomes three times greater in size or number. *In three years the company had tripled its sales.*

triplet /trɪplɪ[2]t/, **triplets.** COUNT N **Triplets** are three children born at the same time to the same mother.

tripod /traɪpɒd/, **tripods.** COUNT N A **tripod** is a stand with three legs, used to support something such as a camera or telescope.

trite /traɪt/. ADJ **Trite** ideas, remarks, and stories are dull and not original. *...trite films.*

triumph /traɪəmf/, **triumphs, triumphing, triumphed. 1** COUNT N A **triumph** is a great success or achievement. *The election result was a personal triumph for the party leader... This machine is a triumph of advanced technology.* **2** UNCOUNT N **Triumph** is a feeling of great satisfaction when you win or achieve something. *I saw a gleam of triumph in his eye.* **3** VB If you **triumph,** you win a victory or succeed in overcoming something. *She learned to triumph over her disabilities.*

triumphant /traɪʌmfənt/. ADJ If you are **triumphant,** you feel very happy because you have won a victory or achieved something. *...triumphant soldiers... ...a triumphant smile.* ♦ **triumphantly** ADV *Robert was looking at me triumphantly.*

trivia /trɪvɪə/. UNCOUNT N If you refer to things as **trivia,** you mean that they are unimportant. *She takes a childish delight in remembering trivia.*

trivial /trɪvɪəl/. ADJ **Trivial** means unimportant. *All those little details of organization seemed trivial.*

triviality /trɪvɪælɪ[1]ti[1]/, **trivialities. 1** PLURAL N **Trivialities** are unimportant things. *...the daily trivialities which seem so important to men.* **2** UNCOUNT N The **triviality** of something is the fact that it is unimportant. *...conversations of unbelievable triviality.*

trod /trɒd/. **Trod** is the past tense of **tread.**

trodden /trɒdə[0]n/. **Trodden** is the past participle of **tread.**

trolley /trɒli[1]/, **trolleys. 1** COUNT N A **trolley** is a small cart that you use to carry things, for example shopping or luggage. *...supermarket trolleys.* **2** COUNT N A **trolley** is also a small table on wheels on which food and drinks can be carried. *The room-service boy wheeled the trolley in.* **3** COUNT N A **trolley** is also a tram; an American use.

trombone /trɒmbəʊn/, **trombones.** COUNT N A **trombone** is a brass musical instrument which you play by blowing into it and sliding part of it backwards and forwards.

troop /truːp/, **troops, trooping, trooped. 1** PLURAL N **Troops** are soldiers. *They have more than 11,000 troops in Northern Ireland... ...reports on troop movements.* **2** COUNT N A **troop** of people or animals is a group of them. *...a troop of monkeys.* **3** VB WITH ADJUNCT If people **troop** somewhere, they walk there in a group. *The twelve men trooped downstairs.*

trophy /trəʊfi[1]/, **trophies.** COUNT N A **trophy** is a prize, for example a cup or shield, given to the winner of a competition.

tropical /trɒpɪkə[0]l/. ATTRIB ADJ **Tropical** means belonging to or typical of the tropics. *...tropical rain forests.*

tropics /trɒpɪks/. PLURAL N The **tropics** are the hottest parts of the world, near the equator.

trot /trɒt/, **trots, trotting, trotted. 1** VB When an animal such as a horse **trots,** it moves fairly fast, lifting its feet quite high off the ground. *He made the beast turn aside and trot away.* Also SING N *She urged her pony into an energetic trot.* **2** VB WITH ADJUNCT If you **trot** somewhere, you move fairly fast, taking small quick steps. *We trotted along behind him.* **3** PHRASE If several things happen **on the trot,** they happen one after the other, without a break; an informal use. *Try not to miss two lessons on the trot.*

trot out. PHR VB If you **trot out** old ideas or pieces of information, you repeat them in a boring way. *They trot out all the old reasons for their failure.*

trouble /trʌbə[0]l/, **troubles, troubling, troubled. 1** UNCOUNT N If you have **trouble** doing something, you have difficulties or problems doing it. *You shouldn't have any trouble locating them... This would save everyone a lot of trouble.* **2** SING N If you say that one aspect of a situation is the **trouble,** you mean that it is the aspect which is causing problems or making the situation unsatisfactory. *It's getting a bit expensive now, that's the trouble... The trouble with you is that you've forgotten what it's like to be young.* **3** PLURAL N Your **troubles** are your problems. *She thought that all her troubles were over.* **4** UNCOUNT N WITH SUPP You use **trouble** to say that you have something wrong with a part of your body. For example, if you have something wrong with your back, you can say that you have back **trouble. 5** UNCOUNT N If there is **trouble,** people are quarrelling or fighting. *He's the sort of person who always makes trouble.* **6** VB WITH OBJ If something **troubles** you, it makes you feel worried. *What's troubling you?* ♦ **troubling** ADJ *It was a new*

and troubling thought.
PHRASES • If you are **in trouble,** you have a serious problem. *Frank was still in deep financial trouble.* • You also say that someone is **in trouble** when they have broken a rule or law and are likely to be punished. *...if a child is in trouble with the police... I don't want to get you into trouble.* • If you **take the trouble** to do something, you do it although it requires some time or effort.
troubled /trʌbəºld/. ADJ A **troubled** person has many worries or problems. *He was deeply troubled.*
troublemaker /trʌbəºlmeɪkə/, **troublemakers.** COUNT N A **troublemaker** is someone who causes trouble. *The trouble-makers are a tiny minority.*
troublesome /trʌbəºlsəm/. ADJ Someone or something that is **troublesome** causes problems. *...troublesome tenants.*
trough /trɒf/, **troughs.** COUNT N A **trough** is a long container from which farm animals drink or eat.
troupe /truːp/, **troupes.** COLL N A **troupe** is a group of actors, singers, or dancers who work together.
trousers /traʊzəz/. The form **trouser** is used in front of another noun. PLURAL N **Trousers** are a piece of clothing that covers your body from the waist downwards, and covers each leg separately. *...a pair of black trousers... He slid it gently into his trouser pocket.*
trout /traʊt/. **Trout** is the singular and plural. COUNT N OR UNCOUNT N A **trout** is a kind of fish that lives in rivers and freshwater lakes.
trowel /traʊəl/, **trowels.** 1 COUNT N A **trowel** is a small garden tool with a curved, pointed blade used for weeding and planting. 2 COUNT N A **trowel** is also a small tool with a flat blade shaped like a diamond that is used for spreading cement.
truancy /truːənsi¹/. UNCOUNT N When children stay away from school without permission, you describe their behaviour as **truancy.** *The longer the period of truancy, the harder it becomes to return to school.*
truant /truːənt/, **truants.** COUNT N A **truant** is a child who stays away from school without permission. *His elder brother had been a habitual truant.* • If children **play truant,** they stay away from school without permission. *In my last year I played truant a lot.*
truce /truːs/, **truces.** COUNT N A **truce** is an agreement between two people or groups to stop fighting for a short time.
truck /trʌk/, **trucks.** 1 COUNT N A **truck** is a lorry. *...a rusty old truck... ...a truck driver.* 2 COUNT N A **truck** is also an open vehicle used for carrying goods on a railway.
trudge /trʌdʒ/, **trudges, trudging, trudged.** VB WITH ADJUNCT If you **trudge** somewhere, you walk there with slow, heavy steps. *Michael trudged up the hill.* Also SING N *They set off for the long trudge home.*
true /truː/, **truer, truest.** 1 ADJ A **true** story or statement is based on facts and is not invented or imagined. *The story about the murder is true... Unfortunately it was true about Sylvie.* 2 ATTRIB ADJ **True** also means genuine or typical. *She smiled with true amusement... ...true democracy... He's a true American, in every respect.*
PHRASES • If a dream, wish, or prediction **comes true,** it actually happens. • If you are **true to** your **word,** you do what you had promised to do.
truly /truːli¹/. 1 ADV **Truly** means completely and genuinely. *He was now truly American... He alone truly appreciates it.* 2 SENTENCE ADV You can use **truly** to emphasize that what you are saying is true. *And truly, coming home was the nicest part of the trip.* 3 SUBMOD **Truly** also means to a very great degree; a formal use. *He possessed a truly remarkable talent.*
PHRASES • You can write **yours truly** before your signature at the end of a formal letter. *Yours truly, Desmond Burton-Cox.* • **well and truly:** see **well.**
trump /trʌmp/, **trumps.** 1 PLURAL N In a game of cards, **trumps** is the suit with the highest value. 2 PHRASE Your **trump card** is the most powerful thing that you can use or do to gain an advantage. *Spain has at last produced her trump card and sent on the field of battle her most deadly weapon.*
trumpet /trʌmpɪt/, **trumpets.** 1 COUNT N A **trumpet** is a brass wind instrument with three buttons that you press to get different notes. 2 PHRASE If you **blow** your **own trumpet,** you boast about something; an informal expression. *I'm not blowing my own trumpet, but I do all the top jobs.*
trumpeter /trʌmpɪtə/, **trumpeters.** COUNT N A **trumpeter** is someone who plays a trumpet.
truncheon /trʌntºʃəºn/, **truncheons.** COUNT N A **truncheon** is a short, thick stick used by British policemen as a weapon.
trundle /trʌndəºl/, **trundles, trundling, trundled.** 1 VB WITH ADJUNCT If a vehicle **trundles** somewhere, it moves there slowly. 2 VB WITH OBJ AND ADJUNCT If you **trundle** something somewhere, you move or roll it along slowly. *She saw him trundling the push chair along in the nearby park.*
trunk /trʌŋk/, **trunks.** 1 COUNT N The **trunk** of a tree is the large main stem from which the branches grow. 2 COUNT N Your **trunk** is the central part of your body. 3 COUNT N An elephant's **trunk** is its long nose. 4 COUNT N A **trunk** is also a large, strong case or box used for storing things or for taking on a journey. 5 COUNT N The **trunk** of a car is a covered space at the back or front that is used for luggage; an American use.
trust /trʌst/, **trusts, trusting, trusted.** 1 VB WITH OBJ If you **trust** someone, you believe that they are honest and will not deliberately do anything to harm you. *Everybody liked and trusted him.* Also UNCOUNT N *Adam could feel his father's trust in him.* 2 VB WITH OBJ AND TO-INF If you **trust** someone to do something, you believe that they will do it. *She didn't trust anyone to look after her child properly.* 3 VB WITH OBJ AND 'with' If you **trust** someone with something, you allow them to look after it or deal with it. *Next year I hope the company will trust me with a bigger budget.* 4 VB WITH OBJ If you do not **trust** something, you feel that it is not safe or reliable. *I don't trust fancy gimmicks in cars... He wanted to get up and walk, but he didn't trust his legs.* 5 VB WITH OBJ If you **trust** someone's judgement or advice, you believe that it is good or right. *Trust your own instincts... She seems to trust his advice.* 6 REPORT VB If you say you **trust** that something is true, you mean that you hope and expect that it is true; an old-fashioned use. *They will give you a good pension, I trust?* 7 UNCOUNT N **Trust** is also responsibility that you are given to deal with important, valuable, or secret things. *The judge took the view that to betray a position of trust in such a manner was disgraceful.* 8 COUNT N A **trust** is a financial arrangement in which an organization keeps and invests money for someone. *...a lifetime interest trust.*
trustee /trʌstiː/, **trustees.** COUNT N A **trustee** is someone with legal control of money or property that is kept or invested for another person. *Her request for money was turned down by the trustees.*
trusting /trʌstɪŋ/. ADJ A **trusting** person believes that people are honest and sincere and do not intend to harm them. *Judy had an open and trusting nature.*
trustworthy /trʌstwɜːði¹/. ADJ A **trustworthy** person is reliable and responsible. *He was an experienced and trustworthy travelling companion.*
truth /truːθ/, **truths.** 1 SING N **The truth** is all the facts about something, rather than things that are imagined or invented. *He learned the truth about Sam... He's probably telling the truth.* 2 UNCOUNT N If you say that there is **truth** in a statement or story, you mean that it is true, or partly true. *There is an element of truth in this... I could not deny the truth of this statement.* 3 COUNT N A **truth** is an idea or principle that is generally accepted to be true. *It's a book that contains important truths... ...a universal truth.*
truthful /truːθfʊl/. 1 ADJ A **truthful** person is honest and tells the truth. *Many patients are more truthful when they talk to the computer than when they talk to the doctor.* ♦ **truthfully** ADV *If I ask him a question he will answer it as truthfully as he can.* 2 ADJ A **truthful** statement or account is true rather than invented. *He gave a truthful answer.*
try /traɪ/, **tries, trying, tried.** 1 VB If you **try** to do something, you make an effort to do it. *My sister tried to cheer me up... They tried but failed... I tried hard not to think about it... Try and finish that by next Friday.* Also COUNT N *After a few tries they gave up... It's certainly worth a try.* 2 VB WITH 'for' If you **try** for something, you make an effort to get it or achieve it. *The school advised Mr Denby to let his son try for university.* 3 VB WITH OBJ If you **try** something, you use it or do it in order to find out how useful, effective, or enjoyable it is. *I tried a different approach to the problem... Have you ever tried painting?* Also COUNT N *We can give it a try and see how it looks.* 4 VB WITH OBJ If you **try** a particular place or person, you go to that place or person because you think they may be able to provide you with what you want. *We tried two or three hotels, but they were full.* 5 VB WITH OBJ When a person **is tried,** he or she appears in a law court and is found innocent or guilty after the judge and jury have heard the evidence. *A youth was tried in the criminal courts for stealing.* 6 to **try** your **hand** at something: see **hand.** • to **try** your **luck** at something: see **luck.**
try on. PHR VB If you **try on** a piece of clothing, you put it on to see if it suits you. *She tried on her new dress.*
try out. PHR VB If you **try** something **out,** you test it in order to find out how useful or effective it is. *Oxford is trying out an idea to help working parents.*
trying /traɪɪŋ/. ADJ Something or someone that is **trying** is difficult to deal with and makes you feel impatient or annoyed. *It had been a most trying experience for them.*
T-shirt, T-shirts. COUNT N A **T-shirt** is a cotton shirt with short sleeves and no collar or buttons.
tub /tʌb/, **tubs.** 1 COUNT N A **tub** is a wide, circular container. *...a tub big enough to hold eighteen gallons.* 2 COUNT N A **tub** is also a bath; an American use.
tuba /tjuːbə/, **tubas.** COUNT N A **tuba** is a very large brass musical instrument that can produce very low notes.
tube /tjuːb/, **tubes.** 1 COUNT N A **tube** is a long, hollow object through which air or a liquid passes. *...a rubber tube fixed to the tap... ...breathing tubes.* 2 COUNT N A **tube** of paste is a long, thin container which you squeeze in order to force the paste out. *...a tube of toothpaste.* 3 SING N The **Tube** is the underground railway system in London. *When I come by Tube it takes about an hour.*
tuberculosis /tjʊbɜːkjəⁱləʊsɪs/. UNCOUNT N **Tuberculosis** is a serious infectious disease that affects the lungs.
tubing /tjuːbɪŋ/. UNCOUNT N **Tubing** is a material such as plastic or rubber made into tubes. *The cooling system runs through 300 feet of copper tubing.*
tuck /tʌk/, **tucks, tucking, tucked.** 1 VB WITH OBJ AND ADJUNCT If you **tuck** one piece of clothing into another, you push the loose ends of the first piece inside the other piece. *I sat up and tucked my shirt into my shorts.* 2 VB WITH OBJ AND ADJUNCT If you **tuck** something somewhere, you put it there so that it is safe or comfortable. *He tucked the shell under his arm.*
tuck away. PHR VB 1 If you **tuck** something **away,** you store it in a safe place. *She had a bit of money tucked away.* 2 If something **is tucked away,** it is in a quiet place where very few people go. *The parish church is tucked away behind the cathedral.*
tuck in. PHR VB 1 If you **tuck** someone **in,** you make them comfortable in bed by pushing the loose ends of the blankets under the mattress. *He was asleep before I tucked him in.* 2 If you **tuck in** your shirt or blouse, you put the loose ends of it inside your trousers or skirt. 3 If you **tuck in,** you eat something with a lot of pleasure; an informal use. *She was happily tucking into whatever dishes were put in front of her.*
Tuesday /tjuːzdi¹/, **Tuesdays.** UNCOUNT N OR COUNT N **Tuesday** is the day after Monday and before Wednesday.
tuft /tʌft/, **tufts.** COUNT N A **tuft** of hair or grass is a bunch of it growing closely together. *Her tiny head was covered with tufts of fair hair.*
tug /tʌg/, **tugs, tugging, tugged.** 1 VB WITH OBJ OR 'at' If you **tug** something or **tug** at it, you give it a quick pull. *He tugged at the handle, and it came off in his hand.* Also COUNT N *Tom felt a tug at his sleeve.* 2 COUNT N A **tug** is a small, powerful boat used to pull large ships.
tuition /tjuːɪʃəºn/. UNCOUNT N **Tuition** is the teaching of a subject, especially to one person or to a small group. *...private tuition.*
tulip /tjuːlɪp/, **tulips.** COUNT N A **tulip** is a garden flower shaped like an upside down bell.
tumble /tʌmbəºl/, **tumbles, tumbling, tumbled.** 1 VB If you **tumble,** you fall. *She pushed him and sent him tumbling downstairs.* Also COUNT N *She suffered a tumble running after her kite.* 2 VB If water **tumbles,** it flows quickly over an uneven surface so that it splashes a lot. *He could hear the water tumbling over the rocks.*
tumble dryer, tumble dryers; also spelled **tumble drier.** COUNT N A **tumble dryer** is an electric machine that dries washing using hot air.
tumbler /tʌmblə/, **tumblers.** COUNT N A **tumbler** is a drinking glass with straight sides.
tummy /tʌmi¹/, **tummies.** COUNT N Your **tummy** is your stomach; an informal use. *...tummy upsets.*
tumour /tjuːmə/, **tumours;** spelled **tumor** in American English. COUNT N A **tumour** is a mass of diseased or abnormal cells that has grown in a person's or animal's body. *He was suffering from a brain tumour.*
tumult /tjuːməºlt/. SING N A **tumult** is a lot of noise caused by a crowd of people; a literary use. *A tumult of shots and yells could be heard... Presently the tumult died down.*
tumultuous /tjuːmʌltjʊəs/. ATTRIB ADJ A **tumultuous** event is very noisy, because people are happy or excited; a literary use. *When the war was over, there was a tumultuous parade in London.*
tuna /tjuːnə/. **Tuna** is the singular and plural. UNCOUNT N OR COUNT N **Tuna** or **tuna fish** are large fish that live in warm seas and are caught for food.
tune /tjuːn/, **tunes, tuning, tuned.** 1 COUNT N A **tune** is a series of musical notes that is pleasing or memorable. A tune sometimes occurs repeatedly in a piece of music. *The orchestra was playing a selection of tunes from The Merry Widow.* 2 VB WITH OBJ When someone **tunes** a musical instrument, they adjust it so that it produces the right notes. 3 VB WITH OBJ When someone **tunes** an engine or machine, they adjust it so that it works well. *I told her the car needed tuning.*

4 VB WITH OBJ OR PREP 'to' If your radio or television **is tuned** to a particular broadcasting station, you are listening to or watching the programmes on that station. *Stay tuned to Radio Desland for a further announcement.*
PHRASES ● If a musical instrument is **in tune,** it produces the right notes exactly. ● If you are **in tune** with a group of people, you are in agreement or sympathy with them. *His ideas are in tune with the spirit of his age.* ● If you **change** your **tune,** you say or do something different from what you previously said or did. *He soon changed his tune and started working as hard as the others.* ● **To the tune of** a particular amount means to the extent of that amount; a formal use. *The university subsidises its students to the tune of £100,000 a year.*
tune in. PHR VB If you **tune in** to a radio station, you adjust your radio so that you can listen to it. *He turned the dial and tuned in to Radio Paris.*
tune up. PHR VB When a group of musicians **tune up,** they adjust their instruments so that they produce the right notes. *The orchestra was tuning up for its regular Sunday afternoon broadcast.*
tuneful /tjuːnfʊl/. ADJ A **tuneful** piece of music has pleasant tunes.
tunic /tjuːnɪk/, **tunics.** COUNT N A **tunic** is a sleeveless garment covering the top part of your body.
tunnel /tʌnə^{0}l/, **tunnels.** COUNT N A **tunnel** is a long underground passage. *Suddenly the train roared into a tunnel and everything was black.*
turban /tɜːbə^{6}n/, **turbans.** COUNT N A **turban** is a covering for the head consisting of a long piece of cloth which is wrapped around a man's head. Turbans are worn by Hindu, Muslim, and Sikh men.
turbine /tɜːbɪ^{5}n/, **turbines.** COUNT N A **turbine** is a machine or engine which produces power using a stream of air, gas, water, or steam to turn a wheel.
turbulent /tɜːbjə^{4}lənt/. 1 ADJ A **turbulent** period of time is one in which there is a lot of change and confusion. *...a period of fierce and turbulent struggle.* ♦ **turbulence** /tɜːbjə^{4}ləns/ UNCOUNT N *...periods of social turbulence.* 2 ADJ **Turbulent** water or air contains currents which change direction suddenly. *...in the midst of turbulent seas and clashing rocks.* ♦ **turbulence** SING N *The turbulence caused the plane to turn over.*
turf /tɜːf/, **turfs, turfing, turfed.** UNCOUNT N **Turf** is short, thick, even grass. *He was busy levelling the ground and laying turf.*
turf out. PHR VB If you **turf** someone **out,** you force them to leave; an informal use. *She was turfed out of her flat.*
turkey /tɜːki^1/, **turkeys.** 1 COUNT N A **turkey** is a large bird that is kept on a farm for its meat. 2 UNCOUNT N **Turkey** is the meat of a turkey.
Turkish /tɜːkɪʃ/. 1 ADJ **Turkish** means belonging or relating to Turkey. 2 UNCOUNT N **Turkish** is the language spoken by people who live in Turkey.
turmoil /tɜːmɔɪl/. UNCOUNT N **Turmoil** is a state of confusion, disorder, or great anxiety. *...his emotional turmoil... The city was in turmoil.*
turn /tɜːn/, **turns, turning, turned.** 1 VB WITH OR WITHOUT OBJ When you **turn** or **turn** your head, you move your body or head so that you are facing in a different direction. *She turned and walked away... They kept turning round to smile at friends.* Also COUNT N *He made a smart military turn, clicking his heels.* 2 ERG VB When you **turn** something or when it **turns,** it moves and faces in a different direction, or keeps changing the direction it faces in. *He turned the handle and pushed open the door... The wheels started to turn.* Also COUNT N *...with an agile turn of the wrist.* 3 ERG VB When you **turn** in a particular direction or **turn** a corner, you change the direction in which you are moving. *You come over a bridge and turn sharply to the right.* Also COUNT N *The cars were waiting to make the turn into the campus.* 4 VB WITH PREP 'to' If you **turn** to a particular page in a book, you find that page. 5 ERG VB WITH PREP 'to' If you **turn** your attention or thoughts to someone or something, you start thinking about them or discussing them. *I wonder if we can turn our attention to something you mentioned earlier... His thoughts turned to Calcutta.* 6 VB WITH ADJUNCT If you **turn** to someone for help or advice, you ask them for it. *She'd turned to him for help.* 7 ERG VB WITH ADJUNCT To **turn** into something means to become it. *If you apply more heat, the water turns into steam... Soon her glee turned to fear... My hair has turned completely grey.* 8 COUNT N WITH SUPP A **turn** is also a change in the way that something is happening or being done. *In that year things took a sharp turn for the worse... Employers are not happy about this turn of events.* 9 COUNT N If it is your **turn** to do something, you now have the right, chance, or duty to do it, after other people have done it. *It is his turn to take the children to school... ...waiting his turn.* 10 See also **turning.**
PHRASES ● **A good turn** is something you do to help someone. ● You use **in turn** to refer to people, things, or actions that are in a sequence one after the other. *She went round the ward, talking to each woman in turn... It became in turn a stable, a chapel, and a theatre.* ● If people **take turns** or **take it in turns,** they do something one after the other. *You can take turns paying... They took turns at the same typewriter.* ● **to turn** your **back on** someone or something: see **back.** ● **to turn the tables on** someone: see **table.**
turn against. PHR VB If someone **turns against** you, they start to dislike or disapprove of you. *They might at any time turn against their masters.*
turn away. PHR VB If you **turn** someone **away,** you reject them or send them away. *The college has been forced to turn away 300 prospective students.*
turn back. PHR VB 1 If you **turn back** when travelling somewhere, you stop and begin going back to your starting place. *The snow started to fall, so we turned back.* 2 If you **turn** someone **back,** you stop them travelling any farther and make them return. *A lot of the convoys had been turned back at the border.*
turn down. PHR VB 1 If you **turn down** a request or offer, you refuse or reject it. *I was invited to be foreman but I turned it down.* 2 If you **turn down** something such as a radio or a heater, you reduce the amount of sound or heat being produced. *If you are hot you can turn the heating down.*
turn off. PHR VB 1 If you **turn off** a road, you start going along a different road leading from it. *They turned off the main road.* ● See also **turn-off.** 2 If you **turn off** something such as a device or machine, you adjust the controls so that it stops working. *We couldn't turn the heat off... She turned off the tap.*
turn on. PHR VB 1 If you **turn on** a machine or device, you adjust the controls so that it starts working. *Shall I turn the fire on?... She turned on the shower.* 2 To **turn** someone **on** means to attract them and make them sexually excited; an informal use. 3 If someone **turns on** you, they attack you or speak angrily to you. *She turned on the men. 'How can you treat your daughters like this!'*
turn out. PHR VB 1 If something **turns out** a particular way, it happens in that way. *Nothing ever turned out right... The transaction turned out badly.* 2 If something **turns out** to be a particular thing, it is discovered to be that thing. *The Marvins' house turned out to be an old converted barn.* 3 If you **turn out** a light or a gas fire, you adjust the controls so that it stops working. 4 If a business or other organization **turns out** something, it produces it. *Salford was turning out the type of graduate they wanted.* 5 If you **turn** someone **out,** you force them to leave. *...a woman who had been turned out of the community 20 years before.* 6 If you **turn out** a container, you empty it. *Come on everyone, turn out your pockets!* 7 If people **turn out** for an event or activity, they go and take part in it or watch it. *Voters turned out in extraordinary numbers for the election.*
turn over. PHR VB 1 If you **turn** something **over** in your mind, you think carefully about it. *Going home that night, Dr Renshaw turned over the facts of the case.* 2 If you **turn** something **over** to someone, you officially give it to them. *He had refused to turn over funds that belonged to Potter.* 3 See also **turnover.**
turn up. PHR VB 1 If someone or something **turns up,** they arrive, appear, or are discovered somewhere. *He turned up at rehearsal the next day looking awful... You must be willing to take a job as soon as one turns up.* 2 If you **turn up** a machine or device you adjust the controls so that it produces more heat, light, or sound. *Turn the volume control up.*
turned out. ADJ WITH SUPP You use **turned out** to describe how a person is dressed. *...attractive girls, well turned out and smart.*
turning /tɜːnɪŋ/, **turnings.** COUNT N A **turning** is a road leading away from another road. *It's the next turning on the left.*
turning point, turning points. COUNT N A **turning point** is a time at which an event or change occurs which greatly affects the future of a person or thing. *The turning point for the business came in 1974 when I bought the computer... It proved to be a turning point in his life.*
turnip /tɜːnɪp/, **turnips.** COUNT N A **turnip** is a round vegetable with a green and white skin.
turn-off, turn-offs. COUNT N A **turn-off** is a road leading away from another road.
turnout /tɜːnaʊt/, **turnouts.** COUNT N The **turnout** at an event is the number of people who go to it. *There was a very large turnout at the trial.*
turnover /tɜːnəʊvə/. 1 UNCOUNT N The **turnover** of people in an organization is the rate at which people leave and are replaced. 2 UNCOUNT N The **turnover** of a company is the value of goods or services sold during a particular period of time. *Annual turnover is about £9,000 million.*
turntable /tɜːnteɪbə^{0}l/, **turntables.** COUNT N A **turntable** is the flat, round part of a record player on which the record is put.
turpentine /tɜːpəntaɪn/. UNCOUNT N **Turpentine** is a colourless liquid used for cleaning paint off brushes.
turquoise /tɜːkwɔɪz, -kwɑːz/, **turquoises.** 1 ADJ Something that is **turquoise** is a colour between blue and green. *...the warm turquoise sea.* 2 UNCOUNT N OR COUNT N **Turquoise** is a semi-precious stone which is a colour between blue and green.
turret /tʌrɪt/, **turrets.** COUNT N A **turret** is a small, narrow tower on top of a larger tower or other building.
turtle /tɜːtə^{0}l/, **turtles.** COUNT N A **turtle** is a large reptile with a thick shell which lives in the sea.
tusk /tʌsk/, **tusks.** COUNT N The **tusks** of an elephant, wild boar, or walrus are its two very long, curved, pointed teeth.
tussle /tʌsə^{0}l/, **tussles, tussling, tussled.** COUNT N A **tussle** is a struggle or argument between two people. *He was still smarting from the tussle over the bottle.* Also RECIP VB *...directors tussling about levels of authority.*
tutor /tjuːtə/, **tutors, tutoring, tutored.** 1 COUNT N A **tutor** is a teacher at a British university or college. 2 COUNT N A **tutor** is also someone who privately teaches one pupil or a very small group of pupils. 3 VB WITH OR WITHOUT OBJ If someone **tutors** a person or subject, they teach that person or subject. *Next year I want to tutor A level maths.*
tutorial /tjuːtɔːrɪəl/, **tutorials.** COUNT N A **tutorial** is a regular meeting for a tutor and a small group of students.
tuxedo /tʌksiːdəʊ/, **tuxedos.** COUNT N A **tuxedo** is a black or white jacket worn for formal social events; an American use.
TV /tiː viː/, **TVs.** 1 UNCOUNT N **TV** is television. *I've just been watching a film on TV.* 2 COUNT N A **TV** is a television set. *Nicola turned on the TV.*
twang /twæŋ/, **twangs, twanging, twanged.** COUNT N A **twang** is a sound like the one made by pulling and then releasing a tight wire. *...the twang of tennis balls bouncing off tightly-strung rackets.* Also ERG VB *He was sitting twanging a guitar... The bed springs twanged.*
tweed /twiːd/. UNCOUNT N **Tweed** is a type of thick woollen cloth.
tweezers /twiːzəz/. PLURAL N **Tweezers** are a small tool consisting of two joined narrow strips of metal. Tweezers are used for pulling out hairs and picking up small objects.
twelfth /twelf^{0}θ/. ADJ The **twelfth** item in a series is the one that you count as number twelve.
twelve /twelv/. **Twelve** is the number 12.
twentieth /twenti^{1}ə^{1}θ/. ADJ The **twentieth** item in a series is the one that you count as number twenty.
twenty /twenti^1/, **twenties. Twenty** is the number 20.
twice /twaɪs/. 1 ADV Something that happens **twice** happens two times. *I knocked on the door twice.* 2 ADV OR PREDET If one thing is **twice** as big or old as another thing, it is two times as big or old as the other thing. *This is twice as common in France as in England... He's twice my size.* 3 **once or twice:** see **once.**
twiddle /twɪdə^{0}l/, **twiddles, twiddling, twiddled.** VB WITH OBJ OR 'with' If you **twiddle** something or **twiddle** with it, you twist it or turn it using your fingers. *Ella sat twiddling her long, dark hair... Frank twiddled with the knobs of the radio.*
twig /twɪg/, **twigs.** COUNT N A **twig** is a very small, thin branch of a tree or bush.
twilight /twaɪlaɪt/. UNCOUNT N **Twilight** is the time after sunset when it is just getting dark. *We wandered around the temple until twilight.*
twin /twɪn/, **twins.** 1 COUNT N If two people are **twins,** they have the same mother and were born on the same day. ● See also **identical twin.** 2 MOD You use **twin** to describe a pair of similar things that are close together. *...the twin turrets of Tower Bridge.*
twine /twaɪn/, **twines, twining, twined.** 1 UNCOUNT N **Twine** is strong, smooth string. *...a ball of twine.* 2 VB WITH OBJ AND ADJUNCT If you **twine** one thing round another, you twist or wind the first thing around the second. *...twining the rope around his legs.*
twinge /twɪndʒ/, **twinges.** COUNT N If you feel a **twinge** of an unpleasant emotion or pain, you feel this emotion or pain for a short time. *...a twinge of fear... I feel a twinge in my back now and again.*
twinkle /twɪŋkə^{0}l/, **twinkles, twinkling, twinkled.** 1 VB If a star or a light **twinkles,** it shines with an unsteady light. *He could see lights twinkling through the haze of rain.* 2 VB If your eyes **twinkle,** they show that you are amused or excited. Also SING N *She noticed a twinkle in his eye at the suggestion.*

twirl /twɜːl/, **twirls, twirling, twirled. 1** ERG VB When you **twirl** something, you make it spin round and round. *She twirled her parasol.* **2** VB If you **twirl,** you spin round and round, for example when you are dancing. *He twirled round on his toes.*

twist /twɪst/, **twists, twisting, twisted. 1** ERG VB When you **twist** something, you turn one end of it in one direction while turning the other end in the opposite direction. *Never twist or wring woollen garments.* Also COUNT N *He gave one short twist to its neck.* **2** VB When something **twists,** it moves or bends into a strange shape. *Her features twisted into a stare of disgusted incredulity.* ♦ **twisted** ADJ *Hundreds of people were trapped under the twisted steel girders.* **3** VB To **twist** also means to move in a circular direction. *She twisted round on the couch to watch him.* **4** VB WITH OBJ If you **twist** your ankle or wrist, you injure it by turning it too sharply or in an unusual direction. **5** VB If a road or river **twists,** it has a lot of sharp bends. *The road began to twist up past the lower slopes of a pine forest.* **6** VB WITH OBJ If you **twist** what someone has said, you repeat it in a way that changes its meaning. *You're twisting my words around.* **7** COUNT N A **twist** is also the shape of something that has been twisted. *...a shell with a spiral twist.* **8** COUNT N A **twist** in a story or film is an unexpected development. *There was an odd twist to the plot.*

PHRASES ● If you **twist** someone's **arm,** you persuade them to do something; an informal use. ● If you can **twist** someone **round** your **little finger,** you can persuade them to do anything; an informal use.

twisted /twɪstɪ²d/. ADJ If someone's mind or behaviour is **twisted,** it is unpleasantly abnormal. *He has become bitter and twisted.*

twitch /twɪtʃ/, **twitches, twitching, twitched. 1** VB If you **twitch,** you make little jerky movements which you cannot control. *Ralph felt his lips twitch... She trembled and twitched as I touched her.* Also COUNT N *...twitches of the muscles.* **2** ERG VB If you **twitch** something, you give it a little jerk in order to move it. *She twitched the curtain into place.*

twitter /twɪtə/, **twitters, twittering, twittered.** VB When birds **twitter,** they make a lot of short, high-pitched sounds.

two /tuː/, **twos. Two** is the number 2.

two-dimensional /tuː dəmɛnʃə⁰nəl, -ʃənə⁰l/. ADJ Something that is **two-dimensional** is flat and in two dimensions only.

two-way. ATTRIB ADJ **Two-way** means moving or working in two opposite directions. *...a two-way channel of communication... ...two-way radio.*

tycoon /taɪkuːn/, **tycoons.** COUNT N A **tycoon** is a person who is successful in business and so has become rich and powerful. *...a newspaper tycoon.*

type /taɪp/, **types, typing, typed. 1** COUNT N WITH SUPP A **type** of something is a class of it whose members have particular features in common. *...several different types of accounts... They usually test your blood type during pregnancy.* **2** COUNT N WITH SUPP If you refer to a particular thing as a **type,** you are thinking of it in relation to other things that have similar qualities. *How much longer can you do this type of work?... ...simple problems of this type.* **3** COUNT N WITH SUPP A particular **type** of person has a particular appearance or quality. *He was good-looking, if you like the strong, dark type.* **4** VB WITH OR WITHOUT OBJ If you **type** something, you use a typewriter or word processor to write it. *I typed the reply.* ♦ **typing** UNCOUNT N *I had to do some typing for her.* **5** VB WITH OBJ If you **type** information into a computer or word processor, you put it in by pressing the keys. *The letter was typed into a word processor.*

type up. PHR VB If you **type up** your a handwritten text, you produce a typed form of it. *After thinking about it, she typed it up, then we both read it.*

typewriter /taɪpraɪtə/, **typewriters.** COUNT N A **typewriter** is a machine with keys which are pressed in order to print letters, numbers, or other characters onto paper.

typewritten /taɪprɪtə⁰n/. ADJ Something that is **typewritten** has been typed on a typewriter or word processor.

typhoid /taɪfɔɪd/. UNCOUNT N **Typhoid** is a very serious infectious disease that produces fever.

typhoon /taɪfuːn/, **typhoons.** COUNT N A **typhoon** is a very violent tropical storm.

typical /tɪpɪkə⁰l/. ADJ Something that is **typical** of a particular thing or way of behaving shows the most usual characteristics of that thing or behaviour. *It was typical tropical weather... Louisa is typical of many young women who attempt suicide.*

typically /tɪpɪkə⁰li¹/. **1** SENTENCE ADV You use **typically** to say that something usually happens in the way that you are describing it. *She typically handles less than a dozen accounts at a time.* **2** SUBMOD You also use **typically** to say that something shows all the most usual characteristics of a particular type of thing. *...this group of typically American students.*

typify /tɪpɪfaɪ/, **typifies, typifying, typified.** VB WITH OBJ To **typify** something means to be a typical example of it. *He typified the old Liberalism.*

typist /taɪpɪst/, **typists.** COUNT N A **typist** is someone whose job is typing.

tyrannical /tɪræ̱nɪkə⁰l/. ADJ A **tyrannical** ruler, government, or organization acts cruelly and unjustly towards the people they control.

tyranny /tɪrəni¹/. UNCOUNT N **Tyranny** is cruel and unjust rule by a person or small group of people who have power over everyone else in their country or state. *They came here to escape political tyranny.*

tyrant /taɪrənt/, **tyrants.** COUNT N A **tyrant** is a ruler who uses his or her power cruelly and unjustly.

tyre /taɪə/, **tyres;** spelled **tire** in American English. COUNT N A **tyre** is a thick ring of rubber filled with air and fitted round the wheel of a vehicle.

Uu

ubiquitous /juːbɪkwɪtəs/. ADJ Something that is **ubiquitous** seems to be everywhere; a formal use. *...the ubiquitous white dust of Athens.*

udder /ʌdə/, **udders.** COUNT N A cow's **udder** is the organ that hangs below its body and produces milk.

UFO /juː ɛf əʊ, juːfəʊ/, **UFOs.** COUNT N A **UFO** is a strange object seen in the sky or landing on earth which some people believe to be a spaceship from another planet. **UFO** is an abbreviation for 'unidentified flying object'.

ugly /ʌgli¹/, **uglier, ugliest. 1** ADJ Someone or something **ugly** is very unattractive in appearance. *She really was frightfully ugly... This is the ugliest dress I've ever worn.* ♦ **ugliness** UNCOUNT N *...the architectural ugliness of the place.* **2** ADJ An **ugly** situation is very unpleasant, and often involves violence. *A couple of ugly incidents occurred, and one man was killed.*

UK /juː keɪ/. PROPER N The **UK** consists of Great Britain and Northern Ireland. **UK** is an abbreviation for 'United Kingdom'.

ulcer /ʌlsə/, **ulcers.** COUNT N An **ulcer** is a sore area on your skin or inside your body, which sometimes bleeds. *...stomach ulcers.*

ulterior /ʌltɪərɪə/. ATTRIB ADJ If someone has an **ulterior** motive for doing something, they have a hidden reason for it. *I assure you there was no ulterior motive in my suggestion.*

ultimate /ʌltɪmə¹t/. **1** ATTRIB ADJ You use **ultimate** to describe the final result of a long series of events. *He knew this action was necessary for the ultimate success of the revolution.* **2** ATTRIB ADJ You also use **ultimate** to describe the most important or powerful thing of a particular kind. *Parliament retains the ultimate authority to dismiss the government... ...the ultimate goal.* **3** PHRASE **The ultimate in** something is the best or most advanced thing of its kind. *...the ultimate in luxury.*

ultimately /ʌltɪmə¹tli¹/. **1** ADV **Ultimately** means finally, after a long series of events. *Elections ultimately produced a Communist victory.* **2** SENTENCE ADV You also use **ultimately** to emphasize that what you are saying is the most important point in a discussion. *Ultimately, the problems are not scientific but moral... Isn't it ultimately the fault of the universities?*

ultimatum /ʌltɪmeɪtəm/, **ultimatums.** COUNT N An **ultimatum** is a warning that unless someone acts in a particular way, you will take action against them; a formal use. *Belgium rejected the ultimatum and war was declared.*

ultra-. PREFIX **Ultra-** is used to form adjectives that describe someone or something as having a quality to an extreme degree. *...ultra-sophisticated equipment... ...an ultra-modern building.*

ultraviolet /ʌltrəvaɪələ²t/. ATTRIB ADJ **Ultraviolet** light or radiation causes your skin to darken after you have been in sunlight. *...the ultraviolet rays of the sun.*

umbilical cord /ʌmbɪlɪkə⁰l kɔːd/, **umbilical cords.** COUNT N The **umbilical cord** is the tube connecting an unborn baby to its mother, through which it receives oxygen and nutrients.

umbrella /ʌmbrɛlə/, **umbrellas. 1** COUNT N An **umbrella** is an object which you use to protect yourself from the rain or hot sun. It consists of a long stick with a folding frame covered in cloth. *Put your umbrella up. It's going to rain.* **2** ATTRIB ADJ **Umbrella** describes a single organization or idea that includes a lot of different organizations or ideas. *Corn is an umbrella word for wheat, barley and oats.*

umpire /ʌmpaɪə/, **umpires, umpiring, umpired. 1** COUNT N In games, the **umpire** is the person whose job is to make sure the game is played fairly and the rules are not broken. *The umpires declared that play should start.* **2** VB WITH OBJ If you **umpire** a game, you are the umpire.

UN /juː ɛn/. PROPER N The **UN** is an organization which most countries in the world belong to, and which tries to encourage international peace, co-operation, and friendship. **UN** is an abbreviation for 'United Nations'.

un-. PREFIX **un-** is added to words to form words which have the opposite meaning or refer to a reverse process. For example, if something is unavailable, it is not available. If you untie a knot, you reverse the process of tying it. *...an uncomfortable chair... She may unintentionally have caused suffering... He regretted his unkindness... He unlocked the door.*

unabated /ʌnəbeɪtɪ²d/. ADJ If something continues **unabated,** it continues without any reduction in intensity or amount. *The war at sea continued unabated... They continued with unabated enthusiasm.*

unable /ʌneɪbə⁰l/. PRED ADJ WITH TO-INF If you are **unable** to do something, you cannot do it, for example because you do not have the necessary skill. *Many people were unable to read or write... He was unable to sleep at night because of his anxiety.*

unacceptable /ʌnə³ksɛptəbə⁰l/. ADJ If something is **unacceptable,** you strongly disapprove of it and feel you cannot allow it to continue. *That sort of behaviour was completely unacceptable.* ♦ **unacceptably** ADV *Their standard of performance has been unacceptably poor on several recent occasions.*

unaccompanied /ʌnəkʌmpənɪd/. **1** ADJ If you are **unaccompanied,** you are alone. *I wouldn't leave him for a moment unaccompanied.* **2** ADJ An **unaccompanied** song is written to be sung by singers alone, without musical instruments.

unaccountable /ʌnəkaʊntəbə⁰l/; a formal word. **1** ADJ Something that is **unaccountable** does not seem to have any sensible explanation. *For some unaccountable reason, I put the letter in the wrong envelope.* ♦ **unaccountably** ADV OR SENTENCE ADV *Elaine felt unaccountably shy.* **2** PRED ADJ If you are **unaccountable,** you do not have to justify your actions to anyone. *Many of our important decision-makers are unaccountable to the public.*

unaccustomed /ʌnəkʌstəmd/. **1** PRED ADJ WITH PREP 'to' If you are **unaccustomed** to something, you are not used to it. *They were unaccustomed to wearing suits and ties.* **2** ATTRIB ADJ If someone's behaviour or experiences is **unaccustomed,** they do not usually behave like this or have experiences of this kind. *Judy cried with unaccustomed vehemence, 'Yes, I know!'... ...his unaccustomed and unwelcome leisure time.*

unadulterated /ʌnədʌltəreɪtɪ²d/. **1** ADJ Something that is **unadulterated** is completely pure with nothing added to it. *...unadulterated spring water.* **2** ATTRIB ADJ You can also use **unadulterated** to emphasize a quality, especially a bad quality. *It was going to be unadulterated misery from now on.*

unaffected /ʌnə³fɛktɪ²d/. **1** PRED ADJ Something that is **unaffected** by a particular thing is not changed in any way by it. *Jobs have been largely unaffected by automation... This acid is unaffected by heat.* **2** ADJ Someone who is **unaffected** is natural and genuine in their behaviour. *He was simple and unaffected.*

unaided /ʌneɪdɪ²d/. ADJ If you do something **unaided,** you do it without help. *The baby was sitting up unaided... ...men who have arrived at the top by their own unaided efforts.*

unalterable /ʌnɒltə⁰rəbə⁰l, ʌnɔːl- /. ADJ Something that is **unalterable** cannot be changed. *...an unalterable decision.*

unaltered /ʌnɒltəd, ʌnɔːl-/. ADJ Something that is **unaltered** has not been changed. *The Great Hall survives relatively unaltered.*

unambiguous /ʌnæmbɪgju⁴əs/. ADJ An **unambiguous** statement has only one meaning. *The rules are quite unambiguous.*

unanimous /juːnæ̱nɪməs/. ADJ When a group of people are **unanimous,** they all agree about something. *We reached unanimous agreement.* ♦ **unanimously** ADV *The union voted unanimously to boycott foreign imports.* ♦ **unanimity** /juːnə³nɪmɪ¹ti¹/ UNCOUNT N *About this there is unanimity among the sociologists.*

unannounced /ʌnənaʊnst/. ADJ If an event is **unannounced,** it happens unexpectedly, without any warning. *Forgive me for this unannounced intrusion... Churchill arrived unannounced.*

unanswered /ʌnɑːnsəd/. ADJ Something that is **unanswered** has not been answered. *...unanswered letters.*

unarmed /ʌnɑːmd/. ADJ If you are **unarmed,** you are not carrying any weapons. *They were shooting unarmed peasants... He walked alone and unarmed.*

unashamed /ʌnəʃeɪmd/. ATTRIB ADJ If someone behaves in an **unashamed** way, they openly do things that other people find shocking. *...their unashamed pursuit of money.*

unassuming /ʌnəsjuːmɪŋ/. ADJ An **unassuming** person is modest and quiet.

unattached /ʌnətætʃt/. ADJ An **unattached** person is not married and is not having a steady relationship. *A lot of unattached women seem to be very happy.*

unattended /ʌnətendɪd/. ADJ When people or things are **unattended,** they are not being watched or looked after. *Most of the casualties were lying unattended... ...unattended baggage.*

unattractive /ʌnətræktɪv/. 1 ADJ **Unattractive** people and things are unpleasant in their appearance or behaviour. *He was physically unattractive... ...unattractive dwellings.* 2 ADJ If something such as an idea or proposal is **unattractive,** people do not like it and do not want to be involved with it. *Being unemployed is a most unattractive prospect.*

unavoidable /ʌnəvɔɪdəbᵊl/. ADJ If something is **unavoidable,** it cannot be avoided or prevented. *This delay was unavoidable.*

unaware /ʌnəweə/. PRED ADJ If you are **unaware** of something, you do not know about it. *She seemed quite unaware of the other people sitting around her... I was unaware that he had any complaints.*

unawares /ʌnəweəz/. PHRASE If something **catches** you **unawares** or **takes** you **unawares,** it happens when you are not expecting it. *It's a change like this that catches you unawares.*

unbalanced /ʌmbælənst/. 1 ADJ If someone is **unbalanced,** they are slightly mad. *The strain of the past few days has made you mentally unbalanced.* 2 ADJ An **unbalanced** account of something is unfair or inaccurate because it emphasizes some things and ignores others. *She complained that the magazine had published an unbalanced report.*

unbearable /ʌmbeərəbᵊl/. ADJ Something that is **unbearable** is so unpleasant, painful, or upsetting that you feel unable to accept it or deal with it. *The heat was unbearable... I found it unbearable to be the centre of attention.* ♦ **unbearably** SUBMOD *It was unbearably painful.*

unbeatable /ʌmbiːtəbᵊl/. ADJ Something that is **unbeatable** is considered the best thing of its kind. *The food here is absolutely unbeatable.*

unbelievable /ʌmbiliːvəbᵊl/. 1 ADJ You say that something is **unbelievable** when it is extremely good, large, or surprising. *They work with unbelievable speed... I went to her house in Henley: it was unbelievable.* 2 ADJ If an idea or theory is **unbelievable,** it is so unlikely or so illogical that you cannot believe it. *There are many unbelievable aspects to this theory.*

unbelievably /ʌmbiliːvəbli/. 1 SENTENCE ADV You use **unbelievably** to indicate that the event or situation you are describing is very surprising. *Unbelievably, the door in the wall opened.* 2 SUBMOD You also use **unbelievably** to emphasize that something is extremely good, large, or surprising. *He has been unbelievably successful.*

unbeliever /ʌmbiliːvə/, **unbelievers.** COUNT N People are referred to as **unbelievers** when they do not believe in a particular religion.

unborn /ʌmbɔːn/. ADJ An **unborn** child has not yet been born and is still inside its mother's womb.

unbroken /ʌmbrəʊkᵊn/. ADJ If something is **unbroken,** it is continuous or complete. *The silence continued, unbroken.*

unbutton /ʌmbʌtᵊn/, **unbuttons, unbuttoning, unbuttoned.** VB WITH OBJ When you **unbutton** something, you unfasten the buttons on it. *He unbuttoned his coat.*

uncalled-for /ʌŋkɔːld fɔː/. ADJ An **uncalled-for** remark is unkind or unfair and should not have been made. *That last remark was uncalled-for.*

uncanny /ʌŋkæni/. ADJ If something is **uncanny,** it is strange and hard to explain. *The owl strikes at its prey with uncanny accuracy... The silence was uncanny.*

unceasing /ʌnsiːsɪŋ/. ADJ If something is **unceasing,** it continues without stopping. *The noise of the traffic was loud and unceasing.*

unceremoniously /ʌnserəməʊniəsli/. ADV If you do something **unceremoniously,** you do it suddenly and rudely. *The door was unceremoniously pushed open.*

uncertain /ʌnsɜːtən/. 1 ADJ If you are **uncertain** about something, you do not know what to do. *She hesitated, uncertain whether to continue.* ♦ **uncertainly** ADV *They looked at each other uncertainly.* 2 ADJ If something in the future is **uncertain,** nobody knows what will happen. *The outcome of his case was uncertain.* 3 ADJ If the cause of something is **uncertain,** nobody knows what caused it. *The cause of death remains uncertain.*

uncertainty /ʌnsɜːtənti/, **uncertainties.** 1 UNCOUNT N When there is **uncertainty,** people do not know what will happen or what they should do. *...the continued uncertainty about the future of the aircraft industry.* 2 COUNT N **Uncertainties** are things, especially future events, which nobody is certain about. *The industry is still plagued by economic uncertainties.*

unchallenged /ʌntʃæləndʒd/. ADJ When something is **unchallenged,** people accept it without questioning whether it is right or wrong. *His authority was secure and unchallenged... Her decisions on these matters went unchallenged.*

unchanged /ʌntʃeɪndʒd/. ADJ Something that is **unchanged** has stayed the same during a period of time. *The process remains unchanged... My orders are unchanged.*

uncharacteristic /ʌŋkærəktərɪstɪk/. ADJ **Uncharacteristic** behaviour is not typical. *He jumped out of the car with uncharacteristic agility.*

unchecked /ʌntʃekt/. ADJ If something undesirable is **unchecked,** it keeps growing without anyone trying to stop it. *...unchecked military expansion... Such horrors could not be allowed to continue unchecked.*

uncivilized /ʌnsɪvɪlaɪzd/; also spelled **uncivilised.** ADJ **Uncivilized** behaviour is unacceptable, for example because it is cruel or rude. *The conditions in which we keep them are uncivilized and inhumane.*

uncle /ʌŋkᵊl/, **uncles.** COUNT N Your **uncle** is the brother of your mother or father, or the husband of your aunt. *...Uncle Harold.*

unclean /ʌŋkliːn/. 1 ADJ Something that is **unclean** is dirty and likely to cause disease. *A major cause of illness in the Third World is unclean water.* 2 ADJ People sometimes use **unclean** to describe practices which are unacceptable according to their religion. *Pigs are considered unclean and must not be eaten.*

unclear /ʌŋklɪə/. PRED ADJ If something is **unclear** or if you are **unclear** about it, it is not obvious or is so confusing that you cannot understand it properly. *The reasons for this remained unclear... I'm still very unclear about what he has actually done.*

uncomfortable /ʌŋkʌmftəbᵊl/. 1 ADJ If you are **uncomfortable,** you are not physically relaxed, and feel slight pain or discomfort. *I was cramped and uncomfortable in the back seat.* ♦ **uncomfortably** ADV *...sitting uncomfortably on the rock... My shirt was uncomfortably tight.* 2 ADJ **Uncomfortable** also means slightly worried or embarrassed and not relaxed. *Her presence made him uncomfortable.* ♦ **uncomfortably** ADV *She smiled across the room at him uncomfortably.* 3 ADJ If a piece of furniture is **uncomfortable,** you do not feel comfortable when you are using it. *They were sitting on uncomfortable chairs.*

uncommitted /ʌŋkəmɪtɪd/. ADJ If you are **uncommitted,** you do not support either side in a dispute. *...their uncommitted position in the war.*

uncommon /ʌŋkɒmən/. 1 ADJ If something is **uncommon,** it does not happen often, or it is not often seen. *Frost and snow are not uncommon during these months... ...uncommon birds.* 2 ATTRIB ADJ You also use **uncommon** to describe a quality that is unusually large in degree. *...a general of uncommon intelligence and subtlety.* ♦ **uncommonly** SUBMOD *Marcus was uncommonly gifted.*

uncommunicative /ʌŋkəmjuːnɪkətɪv/. ADJ An **uncommunicative** person is unwilling to talk to people, express opinions, or give information. *Roger, uncommunicative by nature, said nothing.*

uncomplicated /ʌŋkɒmplɪkeɪtɪd/. ADJ **Uncomplicated** things are simple and straightforward. *The play had an uncomplicated plot.*

uncomprehending /ʌŋkɒmprɪhendɪŋ/. ADJ If someone is **uncomprehending,** they do not understand what is said or done. *Bonasera turned to his uncomprehending wife and explained.*

uncompromising /ʌŋkɒmprəmaɪzɪŋ/. ADJ **Uncompromising** people are determined not to change their opinions or aims in any way. *...an uncompromising opponent of the Great War... ...an uncompromising commitment to the equality of all races.*

unconcerned /ʌŋkənsɜːnd/. ADJ If someone is **unconcerned** about something, they are not interested in it or not worried about it. *You seem remarkably unconcerned.*

unconditional /ʌŋkəndɪʃᵊnəl, -ʃənᵊl/. ADJ Something that is **unconditional** has no conditions or limitations attached to it. *...unconditional surrender... They offered unconditional support.* ♦ **unconditionally** ADV *The laws had to be obeyed unconditionally.*

unconfirmed /ʌŋkənfɜːmd/. ADJ If a report or rumour is **unconfirmed,** there is not yet any definite proof that it is true.

unconnected /ʌŋkənektɪd/. ADJ If one thing is **unconnected** with another, the two things are not related to each other in any way. *The two incidents were unconnected.*

unconscious /ʌŋkɒnʃəs/. 1 ADJ Someone who is **unconscious** is in a state similar to sleep, as a result of a shock, accident, or injury. *The blow knocked him unconscious... She lay unconscious on the table.* ♦ **unconsciousness** UNCOUNT N *He dropped back into unconsciousness.* 2 PRED ADJ If you are **unconscious** of something that has been said or done, you are not aware of it. *Dekker seemed totally unconscious of the insult.* 3 ADJ If feelings or attitudes are **unconscious,** you are not aware of them, but they show in the way that you behave. *...unconscious feelings of envy.* ♦ **unconsciously** ADV *They can't help resenting the baby unconsciously.* 4 SING N Your **unconscious** is the part of your mind which contains feelings and ideas that you do not know about or cannot control. *...images retrieved from the unconscious.*

unconstitutional /ʌŋkɒnstɪtjuːʃᵊnəl, -ʃənᵊl/. ADJ Something that is **unconstitutional** is against the rules of an organization or political system. *...unconstitutional strikes.*

uncontrollable /ʌŋkəntrəʊləbᵊl/. ADJ If something such as an emotion is **uncontrollable,** you can do nothing to prevent it or control it. *...the sudden uncontrollable note of fear in her voice.* ♦ **uncontrollably** ADV *He found himself giggling quite uncontrollably.*

uncontrolled /ʌŋkəntrəʊld/. 1 ADJ If someone's behaviour is **uncontrolled,** they do not try to stop it or make it less extreme. *He was letting out loud uncontrolled shrieks.* 2 ADJ If a situation or activity is **uncontrolled,** nobody is responsible for controlling it and preventing it from becoming harmful. *...uncontrolled building development.*

unconventional /ʌŋkənvenʃᵊnəl, -ʃənᵊl/. ADJ If someone is **unconventional,** they do not behave in the same way as most other people in their society. *...an unconventional clergyman... ...her unconventional dress.*

unconvincing /ʌŋkənvɪnsɪŋ/. ADJ If arguments or reasons are **unconvincing,** you do not believe that they are true or valid. *...an unconvincing excuse.*

uncooked /ʌŋkʊkt/. ADJ **Uncooked** meat or other food has not yet been cooked. *There were three uncooked chops on the kitchen table.*

uncooperative /ʌŋkəʊɒpəᵊrətɪv/; also spelled **unco-operative.** ADJ If someone is **uncooperative,** they make no effort at all to help other people. *He is deliberately being uncooperative.*

uncork /ʌŋkɔːk/, **uncorks, uncorking, uncorked.** VB WITH OBJ When you **uncork** a bottle, you pull the cork out of it.

uncount noun /ʌŋkaʊnt naʊn/, **uncount nouns.** COUNT N In grammar, an **uncount noun** is a noun which has only one form and refers to a general kind of thing rather than to an individual item.

uncouth /ʌŋkuːθ/. ADJ Someone who is **uncouth** has bad manners and behaves in an unpleasant way. *...an uncouth soldier... ...her uncouth behaviour.*

uncover /ʌŋkʌvə/, **uncovers, uncovering, uncovered.** 1 VB WITH OBJ If you **uncover** something secret, you find out about it. *...helping to uncover illegal activity... Another plot to assassinate General de Gaulle was uncovered.* 2 VB WITH OBJ To **uncover** something also means to remove a cover from it. *She uncovered her face.*

uncovered /ʌŋkʌvəd/. ADJ Something that is **uncovered** does not have a cover over it. *...uncovered food.*

uncritical /ʌŋkrɪtɪkᵊl/. ADJ If you are **uncritical,** you are unable or unwilling to judge whether or something is good or bad. *...uncritical acceptance of traditional values... ...an uncritical audience.*

undaunted /ʌndɔːntɪd/. ADJ If you are **undaunted,** you are not discouraged by disappointing things that have happened; a formal use. *Undaunted by his first setbacks, he decided to try once more.*

undecided /ʌndɪsaɪdɪd/. ADJ If you are **undecided** about something, you have not yet made a decision about it. *She was still undecided whether she would or would not return home.*

undemanding /ʌndɪmɑːndɪŋ/. 1 ADJ An **undemanding** job is not difficult or not hard work. *The pay was adequate, the job undemanding.* 2 ADJ Someone who is **undemanding** is easy to be with and does not ask other people to do a lot for them. *...an undemanding husband.*

undemocratic /ʌndeməkrætɪk/. ADJ In an **undemocratic** system, decisions are made by a small number of powerful people, rather than by all the people who are affected.

undeniable /ʌndɪnaɪəbᵊl/. ADJ Something that is **undeniable** is certainly true. *The evidence is undeni-*

able. ♦ **undeniably** SUBMOD *He was a tall, dark, and undeniably handsome man.*

under /ʌndə/. 1 PREP If something is **under** something else, it is directly below or beneath it. *There was a cask of beer under the bench... He had no shirt on under his thin jumper... We squeezed under the wire and into the garden.* 2 PREP If something happens **under** particular circumstances or conditions, it happens when those circumstances or conditions exist. *He travelled under difficult circumstances... The family cannot cope under stress.* 3 PREP If something happens **under** a law or system, it happens because that law or system says that it must happen. *Equal pay for men and women is guaranteed under English law.* 4 PREP If something happens **under** a particular person or government, it happens when that person or government is in power. *...China under Chairman Mao.* 5 PREP If you study or work **under** a particular person, that person is your teacher or boss. *He studied under Benton... He has a large number of executives under him.* 6 PREP If someone uses a different name as an author, you can say that they write **under** that name. *He wrote an anti-war novel under an assumed name.* 7 PREP If something is **under** an amount or number, it is less than that amount or number. *Expenditure this year should be just under 15 billion pounds... Tickets cost 50p for children under 16.*

under-. PREFIX **Under-** is used to form words that indicate that something is not being provided to a sufficient extent, or has not happened to a sufficient extent. *The hospitals were seriously under-financed... ...under-ripe fruit.*

underclothes /ʌndəkləʊðz/. PLURAL N **Underclothes** are clothes such as a vest, bra, or pants that people wear under their other clothes.

undercover /ʌndəkʌvə/. ATTRIB ADJ **Undercover** work involves secretly obtaining information for the government or the police. *...police on undercover duty... ...undercover agents.*

undercurrent /ʌndəkʌrənt/, **undercurrents.** COUNT N If there is an **undercurrent** of a feeling, the feeling exists in a weak form, and may become powerful later. *He was aware of an increasing undercurrent of unease in his mind.*

undercut /ʌndəkʌt/, **undercuts, undercutting. Undercut** is used in the present tense, and is the past tense and past participle. 1 VB WITH OBJ To **undercut** someone or **undercut** their prices means to sell a product more cheaply than they do. *The large-scale producer can usually undercut smaller competitors.* 2 VB WITH OBJ If something **undercuts** your attempts to achieve something, it prevents them from being effective. *The delay would surely undercut efforts to force modernization.*

underdeveloped /ʌndədɪ^{2}veləpt/. ADJ An **underdeveloped** country does not have modern industries and usually has a low standard of living. *...the problem of underdeveloped rural areas.*

underdog /ʌndədɒg/. SING N The **underdog** in a competition or situation is the person who seems least likely to succeed or win. *She took up the cause of the underdog.*

underemployed /ʌndərɪmplɔɪd/. ADJ If someone is **underemployed,** they do not have enough work to do.

underestimate /ʌndərestɪmeɪt/, **underestimates, underestimating, underestimated.** 1 REPORT VB If you **underestimate** something, you do not realize how large it is or will be. *The Americans underestimated the power of the explosion... It was easy to underestimate what she had endured.* 2 VB WITH OBJ If you **underestimate** someone, you do not realize what they are capable of doing. *He had underestimated Muller.*

underfed /ʌndəfed/. ADJ People who are **underfed** do not get enough food to eat. *Underfed children are more likely to catch diseases.*

underfoot /ʌndəfʊt/. 1 ADJ AFTER N, OR ADV You describe something as **underfoot** when you are standing or walking on it. *The grass underfoot was short and springy... The ground was hardening underfoot.* 2 ADV If you trample or crush something **underfoot,** you spoil or destroy it by treading on it. *The banner was accidentally trampled underfoot.*

undergo /ʌndəgəʊ/, **undergoes, undergoing, underwent** /ʌndəwent/, **undergone** /ʌndəgɒn/. VB WITH OBJ If you **undergo** something necessary or unpleasant, it happens to you. *Her mother was about to undergo a major operation.*

undergraduate /ʌndəgrædjuə^{1}t/, **undergraduates.** COUNT N An **undergraduate** is a student at a university or college who is studying for his or her first degree. *...a Cambridge undergraduate.* Also ATTRIB ADJ *...an undergraduate degree.*

underground; pronounced /ʌndəgraʊnd/ when it is an adverb, and /ʌndəgraʊnd/ when it is an adjective or noun. 1 ADJ OR ADV Something that is **underground** is below the surface of the ground. *...an underground car park... The larvae hatch and make their way underground.* 2 ATTRIB ADJ **Underground** activities take place secretly in a country where political opposition is not allowed, and are directed against the government. *...an underground newspaper.* 3 UNCOUNT N The **Underground** is a railway system in which electric trains travel underground in tunnels; a British use. *We went by Underground to Trafalgar Square.*

undergrowth /ʌndəgrəʊθ/. UNCOUNT N In a forest or jungle, the **undergrowth** consists of bushes and plants growing close together under the trees. *She went crashing through the undergrowth.*

underhand /ʌndəhænd/. ADJ **Underhand** actions are secret and dishonest. *Did they ever do anything which you regarded as underhand?*

underlie /ʌndəlaɪ/, **underlies, underlying, underlay** /ʌndəleɪ/, **underlain** /ʌndəleɪn/. VB WITH OBJ If something **underlies** a situation, it is the cause or basis of it. *The social problems underlying these crises are unsolved.*

underline /ʌndəlaɪn/, **underlines, underlining, underlined.** 1 VB WITH OBJ If something **underlines** a feeling or problem, it emphasizes its importance. *An article in the Lancet underlined the same problem.* 2 VB WITH OBJ If you **underline** a word or sentence, you draw a line underneath it. *He underlined his signature with a little flourish.*

underlying /ʌndəlaɪɪŋ/. ATTRIB ADJ **Underlying** features are important but not obvious. *There are underlying similarities between all human beings... The underlying theme of the novel is very serious.*

undermine /ʌndəmaɪn/, **undermines, undermining, undermined.** VB WITH OBJ To **undermine** a feeling or a system means to make it less certain or less secure. *Public confidence in the company had now been completely undermined... They resented measures which undermined their authority.*

underneath /ʌndəni:θ/. 1 PREP OR ADV If one thing is **underneath** another, it is directly below or beneath it. *The dog was underneath the table... There was a portrait with an inscription underneath.* 2 ATTRIB ADJ OR ADV The **underneath** part of something is the part which normally touches or faces the ground. *The underneath part felt damp... I lifted the dog's foot and checked the soft pad underneath.* Also SING N *The underneath of the car was covered with rust.* 3 ADV OR PREP You use **underneath** when talking about feelings and emotions that people do not show in their behaviour. *Underneath, most of us are shy... I seem confident, but underneath it all I'm terribly nervous.*

undernourished /ʌndənʌrɪʃt/. ADJ An **undernourished** person is weak and unhealthy because they have not been eating enough food. *He was badly undernourished.*

underpaid /ʌndəpeɪd/. ADJ People who are **underpaid** are not paid enough money for the job that they do. *...a great mass of underpaid workers.*

underpants /ʌndəpænts/. PLURAL N **Underpants** are a piece of clothing worn by men and boys under their trousers.

underprivileged /ʌndəprɪvɪ^{0}lɪdʒd/. ADJ **Underprivileged** people have less money and fewer opportunities than other people. *...an underprivileged family.*

underrate /ʌndəreɪt/, **underrates, underrating, underrated.** VB WITH OBJ If you **underrate** someone, you do not recognize how clever or able they are. *He soon discovered that he had underrated Lucy... Frank had underrated Sir James's knowledge of Africa.*

underside /ʌndəsaɪd/, **undersides.** COUNT N The **underside** of something is the part which normally faces towards the ground. *He turned the rifle over and examined the underside.*

understand /ʌndəstænd/, **understands, understanding, understood** /ʌndəstʊd/. 1 VB OR REPORT VB If you **understand** someone or **understand** what they are saying, you know what they mean. *She understood him perfectly... I don't understand what you mean.* 2 VB WITH OBJ To **understand** someone also means to know why they behave in the way that they do. *His wife doesn't understand him.* 3 REPORT VB If you **understand** what is happening or why it is happening, you know what is happening or why it is happening. *I don't understand why the engine isn't working.* 4 REPORT VB If you say that you **understand** that something is the case, you mean that you have been told that it is the case; a formal use. *I understand she has several aunts.* 5 VB WITH OBJ If you **understand** a language, you know what someone is saying when they are speaking that language. *I don't understand English.* 6 PHRASE If you **make** yourself **understood,** you get someone to understand what you are telling them.

understandable /ʌndəstændəbə^{0}l/. ADJ If you say that someone's behaviour is **understandable,** you mean that they have reacted to a situation in a natural way. *His reaction was perfectly understandable.* ♦ **understandably** SENTENCE ADV *Understandably, he was frightened.*

understanding /ʌndəstændɪŋ/, **understandings.** 1 UNCOUNT N If you have an **understanding** of something, you know how it works or what it means. *I doubt whether he had any real understanding of Shakespeare... The job requires an understanding of Spanish.* 2 ADJ If you are **understanding** towards someone, you are kind and forgiving. *I have always thought you were an understanding person.* 3 UNCOUNT N If there is **understanding** between people, they are friendly towards each other and trust each other. *What is needed is greater understanding between management and workers.* 4 COUNT N An **understanding** is an informal agreement about something. *Tacit understandings had been reached.* 5 PHRASE If you agree to do something **on the understanding that** something else will be done, you do it because you have been told that the other thing will be done. *I signed the contract on the understanding that delivery would be this week.*

understate /ʌndəsteɪt/, **understates, understating, understated.** VB WITH OBJ If you **understate** something, you suggest that it is less important than it really is. *They understate the magnitude of the problem.*

understatement /ʌndəsteɪtmə^{2}nt/, **understatements.** COUNT N OR UNCOUNT N An **understatement** is a statement which does not fully express the extent to which something is true. *To say it's been good is quite an understatement... That sounds like typical British understatement.*

understood /ʌndəstʊd/. **Understood** is the past tense and past participle of **understand.**

understudy /ʌndəstʌdi^1/, **understudies.** COUNT N An actor's or actress's **understudy** is a person who has learned their part in a play and can act the part if the actor or actress is ill.

undertake /ʌndəteɪk/, **undertakes, undertaking, undertook** /ʌndətʊk/, **undertaken** /ʌndəteɪkə^{0}n/; a formal word. 1 VB WITH OBJ When you **undertake** a task or job, you start doing it and accept responsibility for it. *Reluctantly, he undertook the mission.* 2 VB WITH TO-INF If you **undertake** to do something, you promise that you will do it. *They have undertaken to accept the offer.*

undertaker /ʌndəteɪkə/, **undertakers.** COUNT N An **undertaker** is a person whose job is to deal with the bodies of people who have died and to arrange funerals.

undertaking /ʌndəteɪkɪŋ/, **undertakings;** a formal word. 1 COUNT N An **undertaking** is a task or job. *...a complex and expensive undertaking.* 2 COUNT N If you give an **undertaking** to do something, you formally promise to do it. *Jenkins gave an undertaking not to stand again for election.*

undertone /ʌndətəʊn/, **undertones.** 1 COUNT N If you say something in an **undertone,** you say it very quietly. *Marcus said in an undertone, 'It doesn't matter, Lucas.'* 2 COUNT N WITH SUPP If something has **undertones** of a particular kind, it suggests ideas or attitudes of this kind without expressing them directly. *The custom had religious undertones.*

undertook /ʌndətʊk/. **Undertook** is the past tense of **undertake.**

undervalue /ʌndəvælju:/, **undervalues, undervaluing, undervalued.** VB WITH OBJ If you **undervalue** something, you fail to recognize how valuable or important it is. *We tend to overvalue money and undervalue art.*

underwater /ʌndəwɔ:tə/. ADV OR ATTRIB ADJ **Underwater** means below the surface of the sea, a river, or a lake. *She swam underwater... ...underwater exploration.*

underway /ʌndəweɪ/. PRED ADJ If an activity is **underway,** it has started. *Preparations for the trial were underway.*

underwear /ʌndəweə/. UNCOUNT N **Underwear** is clothing such as a vest, bra, or pants that people wear under their other clothes.

underwent /ʌndəwent/. **Underwent** is the past tense of **undergo.**

underworld /ʌndəwɜ:ld/. SING N The **underworld** is organized crime and the people involved in it. *...professional thugs from the underworld.*

undesirable /ʌndi^{1}zaɪərəbə^{0}l/. ADJ If something is **undesirable,** you disapprove of it and think it will have harmful effects. *These cuts in education are very undesirable.*

undetected /ʌndi^{1}tektɪ^{2}d/. 1 ADJ If you are **undetected,** people do not notice you or recognize you. *It was important to my safety that I should remain* *undetected.* 2 ADV If you do something **undetected,** people do not notice you doing it. *I don't see any way I could get her out undetected.*

undeveloped /ʌndiˈvɛləpt/. ADJ **Undeveloped** countries are not industrialized and do not use modern methods of farming.

undid /ʌndɪd/. **Undid** is the past tense of **undo.**

undignified /ʌndɪgnɪfaɪd/. ADJ **Undignified** behaviour is foolish and embarrassing. *They had a somewhat undignified argument.*

undiscovered /ʌndɪskʌvəd/. ADJ If something is **undiscovered,** it has not been discovered or noticed. *These authors were undiscovered geniuses.*

undisguised /ʌndɪsgaɪzd/. ADJ **Undisguised** feelings are shown openly, and are not hidden. *He looked at her with undisguised admiration.*

undisputed /ʌndɪspjuːtɪ^{2}d/. 1 ADJ If something is **undisputed,** everyone accepts that it exists or is true. *...her undisputed good looks... The facts are undisputed.* 2 ADJ If someone is the **undisputed** leader of a group of people, everyone accepts that they are the leader. *Mao became undisputed leader in China.*

undistinguished /ʌndɪstɪŋgwɪʃt/. ADJ Something that is **undistinguished** has no especially good qualities or features. *His political career had been undistinguished.*

undisturbed /ʌndɪstɜːbd/. 1 ADJ A place that is **undisturbed** is peaceful and has not been affected by changes that have happened in other places. *The village is still very undisturbed.* 2 PRED ADJ If you are **undisturbed** in something that you are doing, you continue doing it and are not affected by anything else that is happening. *The children pursued their studies undisturbed by the many visitors.*

undivided /ʌndɪvaɪdɪ^{2}d/. ATTRIB ADJ If you give something your **undivided** attention, you concentrate on it fully. *I was listening with undivided attention.*

undo /ʌnduː/, **undoes** /ʌndʌz/, **undoing** /ʌnduːɪŋ/, **undid** /ʌndɪd/, **undone** /ʌndʌn/. 1 VB WITH OBJ If you **undo** something that is closed, tied, or held together in some way, you open it or loosen it so that its parts separate or so that you can remove what is inside. *...undoing a newspaper parcel tied with string... He bent down and undid the laces of his shoes.* 2 VB WITH OBJ If you **undo** something useful that has been done, you prevent it from being effective. *He appeared to be undoing all their patient work.*

undoing /ʌnduːɪŋ/. UNCOUNT N If something is your **undoing,** it is the cause of your failure; a formal use. *Stress can be the undoing of so many fine players.*

undone /ʌndʌn/. PRED ADJ Something that is **undone** is no longer tied or fastened. *His bow tie had come undone.*

undoubted /ʌndaʊtɪ^{2}d/. ADJ You use **undoubted** to emphasize that something exists or is true. *...her undoubted acting ability.* ♦ **undoubtedly** SENTENCE ADV *A chauffeur is undoubtedly a status symbol.*

undreamed of /ʌndriːmd ɒv/ or **undreamt of** /ʌndrɛmt ɒv/. ADJ Something that is **undreamed of** is much better, worse, or more unusual than you thought was possible. *...undreamed-of luxury.*

undress /ʌndrɛs/, **undresses, undressing, undressed.** 1 VB When you **undress,** you take off your clothes. 2 VB WITH OBJ If you **undress** someone, you take off their clothes.

undressed /ʌndrɛst/. PRED ADJ If you are **undressed,** you are wearing no clothes or very few clothes. *He took ages getting undressed.*

undue /ʌndjuː/. ATTRIB ADJ **Undue** means greater or more extreme than is reasonable; a formal use. *She was reprimanded for putting undue pressure on her clients.*

undulate /ʌndjə^{4}leɪt/, **undulates, undulating, undulated.** VB Something that **undulates** has gentle curves or slopes, or moves gently and slowly up and down; a formal use. *The road undulates through pleasant scenery.*

unduly /ʌndjuːli^1/. ADV OR SUBMOD You use **unduly** to say that something is done to an unnecessary extent. *This would not have surprised Morris unduly... This attitude seemed to me unduly fussy.*

unearned /ʌnɜːnd/. ADJ **Unearned** income is money that you gain from property, investment, etc rather than money that you earn from a job. *...a tax on unearned income.*

unearth /ʌnɜːθ/, **unearths, unearthing, unearthed.** VB WITH OBJ If you **unearth** something that is hidden or secret, you discover it. *The dossier was unearthed along with many others.*

unearthly /ʌnɜːθli^1/. ADJ **Unearthly** means strange and unnatural. *The light was unearthly.*

unease /ʌniːz/. UNCOUNT N If you have a feeling of **unease,** you feel that something is wrong and you are anxious about it. *'He'll be alright,' I said to myself, trying to quell a growing unease.*

uneasy /ʌniːzi^1/. ADJ If you are **uneasy,** you feel anxious that something may be wrong or that there may be danger. *She had an uneasy feeling that they were following her... I felt increasingly uneasy about my answer.* ♦ **uneasily** ADV *Philip blushed and laughed uneasily.* ♦ **uneasiness** UNCOUNT N *Pat's uneasiness grew as each minute passed.*

uneconomic /ʌniːkənɒmɪk, ʌnɛkə-/. ADJ Something that is **uneconomic** does not make a profit, or uses money in an inefficient way. *...uneconomic coal mines... ...a one-teacher school is uneconomic.*

uneducated /ʌnɛdʒə^{4}keɪtɪ^{2}d/. ADJ Someone who is **uneducated** has not received much education.

unemotional /ʌnɪməʊʃə^{0}nəl, -ʃənə^{0}l/. ADJ Someone who is **unemotional** does not show any feelings. *He was cold and unemotional.*

unemployed /ʌnɪ^{2}mplɔɪd/. 1 ADJ Someone who is **unemployed** does not have a job. *The government ought to create more jobs for unemployed young people.* 2 PLURAL N People who want to work but cannot get a job are often referred to as the **unemployed.** *...the problem of the unemployed.*

unemployment /ʌnɪ^{2}mplɔɪmə^{2}nt/. UNCOUNT N You say that there is **unemployment** in a place when many people there cannot get jobs. *The government is concerned about the level of unemployment in Scotland.*

unending /ʌnɛndɪŋ/. ADJ You say that something is **unending** when it has continued for a long time and seems as though it will never stop. *...the unending debate about tobacco.*

unenviable /ʌnɛnvɪəbə^{0}l/. ATTRIB ADJ An **unenviable** situation is one that you would not like to be in, because it is difficult or unpleasant. *...the unenviable task of phoning the parents of the dead child.*

unequal /ʌniːkwəl/. 1 ADJ An **unequal** system is unfair because it treats people in different ways. *...the unequal distribution of wealth.* 2 ADJ **Unequal** things are different in size or amount. *Her feet are of unequal sizes.*

unequivocal /ʌnɪkwɪvəkə^{0}l/. ADJ An **unequivocal** statement can only be understood in one way; a formal use. *The reply was unequivocal.* ♦ **unequivocally** ADV *They have stated unequivocally what they stand for.*

unethical /ʌnɛθɪkə^{0}l/. ADJ **Unethical** behaviour is morally wrong; a formal use. *He was accused of unethical conduct.*

uneven /ʌniːvə^{0}n/. 1 ADJ Something that is **uneven** is not regular or consistent. *...uneven teeth... It was an uneven but inspired performance.* 2 ADJ An **uneven** surface is not level or smooth. *She stumbled on the uneven ground.*

uneventful /ʌnɪvɛntfʊl/. ADJ If a period of time is **uneventful,** nothing interesting or important happens during it. *The day was quiet and uneventful.*

unexpected /ʌnɪ^{2}kspɛktɪ^{2}d/. ADJ Something that is **unexpected** surprises you because you were not expecting it to happen. *My hostess greeted me with unexpected warmth.* ♦ **unexpectedly** ADV *She died quite unexpectedly.*

unfailing /ʌnfeɪlɪŋ/. ADJ **Unfailing** qualities or attitudes stay the same and never get weaker; a formal use. *I could never have carried on without the unfailing support of the teaching staff.*

unfair /ʌnfɛə/. ADJ Something that is **unfair** is not right or not just. *It would be quite unfair to expose him to publicity... I knew I was being unfair to him.* ♦ **unfairly** ADV *Workers who have been unfairly dismissed may claim compensation.*

unfaithful /ʌnfeɪθfʊl/. ADJ If someone is **unfaithful** to their lover or to the person they are married to, they have a sexual relationship with someone else.

unfamiliar /ʌnfəmɪlɪə/. ADJ If something is **unfamiliar** to you or if you are **unfamiliar** with it, you have not seen or heard it before. *This name may be unfamiliar to most of you... ...a person unfamiliar with the French railway system.*

unfashionable /ʌnfæʃə^{0}nəbə^{0}l/. ADJ If something is **unfashionable,** it is not fashionable or popular. *His ideas were unfashionable among his colleagues... The place was quiet and unfashionable.*

unfasten /ʌnfɑːsə^{0}n/, **unfastens, unfastening, unfastened.** VB WITH OBJ If you **unfasten** a piece of clothing or something such as a seat belt, you undo its buttons, hooks, or straps. *He unfastened the buttons of his shirt.*

unfavourable /ʌnfeɪvə^{0}rəbə^{0}l/; spelled **unfavorable** in American English. 1 ADJ **Unfavourable** conditions or circumstances cause problems and reduce the chance of success. *...unfavourable weather conditions.* 2 ADJ If you have an **unfavourable** opinion of something, you do not like it. *He had formed an unfavourable opinion of my work.*

unfeeling /ʌnfiːlɪŋ/. ADJ Someone who is **unfeeling** is not sympathetic towards people who are suffering or unhappy. *...unfeeling journalists.*

unfettered /ʌnfɛtəd/. ADJ **Unfettered** activities are not restricted in any way; a formal use. *...the right of free speech, unfettered by the party system.*

unfinished /ʌnfɪnɪʃt/. ADJ If something is **unfinished,** it has not been completed. *The unfinished building grew rusty and dilapidated.*

unfit /ʌnfɪt/. 1 ADJ If you are **unfit,** your body is not in good condition because you have not been taking regular exercise. 2 PRED ADJ If someone or something is **unfit** for a particular purpose, they are not suitable or not of a good enough quality. *This meat is unfit for human consumption... Adams is clearly unfit to hold an administrative post.*

unfold /ʌnfəʊld/, **unfolds, unfolding, unfolded.** 1 VB When a situation **unfolds,** it develops and becomes known or understood. *The great invasion plan was beginning to unfold.* 2 VB WITH OBJ If you **unfold** your plans or intentions, you tell someone about them. 3 ERG VB If you **unfold** something which has been folded, you open it so that it becomes flat. *She thrust a small piece of paper at me. I unfolded it... The older woman's hands unfolded.*

unforeseen /ʌnfə^{8}siːn/. ADJ An **unforeseen** event happens unexpectedly. *This was an unforeseen complication.*

unforgettable /ʌnfəgɛtəbə^{0}l/. ADJ If something is **unforgettable,** it is so good or so bad that you are unlikely to forget it. *...an unforgettable experience.*

unforgivable /ʌnfəgɪvəbə^{0}l/. ADJ An **unforgivable** act is so bad or cruel that it can never be forgiven or justified. *...an unforgivable error in judgement.*

unfortunate /ʌnfɔːtʃə^{4}nə^{1}t/. 1 ADJ Someone who is **unfortunate** is unlucky. *We will do our utmost to help these unfortunate people.* 2 ADJ If you say that something that has happened is **unfortunate,** you mean that it is a pity that it happened. *It is rather unfortunate that the Prime Minister should have said this... ...one of those unfortunate conversations.*

unfortunately /ʌnfɔːtʃə^{4}nə^{1}tli^1/. SENTENCE ADV You use **unfortunately** to express regret about what you are saying. *'Will you be here in the morning?'—'No, unfortunately I won't.'*

unfounded /ʌnfaʊndɪ^{2}d/. ADJ You say that a belief is **unfounded** when it is not based on facts or evidence. *Our worst fears have proved unfounded.*

unfriendly /ʌnfrɛndli^1/. ADJ Someone who is **unfriendly** does not behave in a friendly way. *...a cold, unfriendly stare.*

unfulfilled /ʌnfʊlfɪld/. ADJ You say that a hope is **unfulfilled** when the thing that you hoped for has not happened. *...an unfulfilled wish.*

unfurnished /ʌnfɜːnɪʃt/. ADJ If you rent an **unfurnished** flat or house, no furniture is provided by the owner.

ungainly /ʌngeɪnli^1/. ADJ **Ungainly** people move in an awkward or clumsy way.

ungrateful /ʌngreɪtfʊl/. ADJ If someone is **ungrateful,** they do not show gratitude for something that has been given to them or done for them. *I hope I don't sound ungrateful.*

unhappily /ʌnhæpɪli^1/. 1 ADV If you do something **unhappily,** you are not happy or contented while you do it. *He trudged unhappily towards the house.* 2 SENTENCE ADV You use **unhappily** to express regret about what you are saying. *Unhappily, George had died by the time Ralph got to America.*

unhappy /ʌnhæpi^1/, **unhappier, unhappiest.** 1 ADJ If you are **unhappy,** you are sad and depressed. *She looked unhappy... I had an unhappy time at school.* ♦ **unhappiness** UNCOUNT N *The quarrel caused her intense unhappiness.* 2 PRED ADJ WITH ADJUNCT If you are **unhappy** about something, you are not pleased about it or not satisfied with it. *The residents of the area are unhappy about the noise.* 3 ATTRIB ADJ If you describe a situation as an **unhappy** one, you are expressing regret about it. *This unhappy state of affairs would not exist if Ministers acted in a responsible way.*

unharmed /ʌnhɑːmd/. ADJ If someone who has been attacked or involved in an accident is **unharmed,** they are not injured. *The four men managed to escape unharmed.*

unhealthy /ʌnhɛlθi^1/. 1 ADJ Something that is **unhealthy** is likely to cause illness. *This is probably the most unhealthy place in the world.* 2 ADJ **Unhealthy** people are often ill.

unheard of /ʌnhɜːd ɒv/. 1 ADJ You say that an event or situation is **unheard of** when it never happens. *Contracts and written agreements are quite unheard of.* 2 ADJ You also say that an event is **unheard of** when it happens for the first time and is very surprising or shocking. *This is an unheard of outrage.*

unheeded /ʌnhiːdɪ^{2}d/. PRED ADJ If something goes **unheeded**, it is ignored. *Their appeals for help went unheeded.*

unhelpful /ʌnhɛlpfʊl/. ADJ You say that someone is **unhelpful** when they do nothing to help you. *He came barging into the kitchen with unhelpful suggestions.*

unhesitatingly /ʌnhɛzɪteɪtɪŋli^1/. ADV If you do something **unhesitatingly**, you do it immediately, because you are sure that it is the right thing to do. *She had unhesitatingly gone straight to the police.*

unhinged /ʌnhɪnd^{0}ʒd/. ADJ You say that someone is **unhinged** when they have become mentally ill; an informal use. *According to Morris, Gordon Masters is quite unhinged.*

unholy /ʌnhəʊli^1/. ADJ Something that is **unholy** is considered to be wicked or sinful. *I discovered the unholy pleasures of gossip and malice.*

unhurried /ʌnhʌrɪd/. ADJ **Unhurried** actions are done in a slow and relaxed way. *He proceeded up the stairs at his usual unhurried pace.* ♦ **unhurriedly** ADV *She walked unhurriedly out of the building.*

unhurt /ʌnhɜːt/. PRED ADJ If someone who has been attacked or involved in an accident is **unhurt**, they are not injured. *Two men crawled out unhurt.*

unidentified /ʌnaɪdɛntɪfaɪd/. ADJ You say that someone or something is **unidentified** when nobody knows who or what they are. *...an unidentified Scottish merchant... ...unidentified flying objects.*

unification /juːnɪfɪkeɪʃə^{0}n/. UNCOUNT N **Unification** is the process by which two or more countries join together and become one country. *...the unification of Italy.*

uniform /juːnɪfɔːm/, **uniforms.** 1 COUNT N OR UNCOUNT N A **uniform** is a special set of clothes which some people, for example soldiers or the police, wear at work, and which some children wear at school. *...a man in the uniform of a captain in the Air Force... She wasn't in uniform.* ♦ **uniformed** ATTRIB ADJ *...uniformed policemen.* 2 ADJ If something is **uniform**, it does not vary, but is even and regular throughout. *...a structure of uniform width.* ♦ **uniformly** ADV *The weather throughout the region was uniformly good.*

uniformity /juːnɪfɔːmɪti^1/. UNCOUNT N **Uniformity** is a state in which every part of something looks or is the same as every other part. *...the dreary uniformity of the housing estate.*

unify /juːnɪfaɪ/, **unifies, unifying, unified.** VB WITH OBJ If you **unify** a number of things or people, you join or bring them together. *Smaller tribes are unified into larger societies.* ♦ **unified** ADJ *...a unified labour movement.* ♦ **unifying** ADJ *...the importance of Hinduism as a unifying cultural force.*

unilateral /juːnɪlætə^{0}rəl/. ATTRIB ADJ A **unilateral** decision or action is made or done by only one of the groups involved in a particular situation. *We will take unilateral action... ...unilateral disarmament.*

unimaginable /ʌnɪmædʒɪnəbə^{0}l/. ADJ Something that is **unimaginable** is difficult to imagine or understand properly, because it is not part of people's normal experience. *...the unimaginable vastness of space... ...experiments carried out under unimaginable conditions.*

unimaginative /ʌnɪmædʒɪnətɪv/. ADJ You say that people are **unimaginative** when they do not use their imagination enough in what they do. *...unimaginative teachers... ...unimaginative projects.*

unimportant /ʌnɪmpɔːtənt/. ADJ If something is **unimportant**, it has very little significance or importance. *...a relatively unimportant feature of the system.*

unimpressive /ʌnɪmprɛsɪv/. ADJ You say that someone or something is **unimpressive** when they seem to have no good or interesting qualities. *Barney's wife was an unimpressive little woman.*

uninhabitable /ʌnɪnhæbɪtəbə^{0}l/. ADJ An **uninhabitable** place is one where it is impossible for people to live. *Worldwide pollution threatens to make the planet uninhabitable.*

uninhabited /ʌnɪnhæbɪtɪ^{2}d/. ADJ An **uninhabited** place is one where nobody lives. *...an uninhabited island.*

uninhibited /ʌnɪnhɪbɪtɪ^{2}d/. ADJ **Uninhibited** people behave freely and naturally and do not hide their feelings. *...a sound of uninhibited laughter.*

uninitiated /ʌnɪnɪʃieɪtɪ^{2}d/. PLURAL N You can refer to the people who have no knowledge or experience of something as the **uninitiated**. *For the uninitiated, may I say that golf is one game that demands patience and concentration.*

unintelligible /ʌnɪntɛlɪdʒə^{1}bə^{0}l/. ADJ Something that is **unintelligible** is impossible to understand. *He answered in words unintelligible to her.*

unintended /ʌnɪntɛndɪ^{2}d/. ADJ If something that happens is **unintended**, it was not planned to happen. *...the unintended consequences of advertising.*

unintentional /ʌnɪntɛnʃə^{0}nəl, -ʃənə^{0}l/. ADJ Something that is **unintentional** is not done deliberately, but happens by accident. *...unintentional damage.*

uninterested /ʌnɪntə^{0}rɪ^{2}stɪ^{2}d/. ADJ If you are **uninterested** in something, you are not interested in it. *Lionel was uninterested in the house.*

uninteresting /ʌnɪntə^{0}rɪ^{2}stɪŋ/. ADJ Something that is **uninteresting** is dull and boring. *He found her uninteresting as a person.*

uninterrupted /ʌnɪntərʌptɪ^{2}d/. ADJ If something is **uninterrupted**, it continues without any breaks or interruptions. *Lynn did some uninterrupted reading.*

uninvited /ʌnɪnvaɪtɪ^{2}d/. ADJ You use **uninvited** to describe a person who arrives somewhere or does something without being asked. *...uninvited guests... Henry sat down uninvited.*

union /juːnjən/, **unions.** 1 COUNT N A **union** is a workers' organization that tries to improve such things as the pay and working conditions of its members. *...Mr Ray Buckton, leader of the train drivers' union.* 2 UNCOUNT N When the **union** of two or more things takes place, they are joined together and become one thing; a formal use. *We are working for the union of the two countries.*

unique /juːniːk/. 1 ADJ If something is **unique**, it is the only thing of its kind. *...that unique human ability, speech.* ♦ **uniqueness** UNCOUNT N *...the uniqueness of the individual.* 2 PRED ADJ WITH PREP 'to' If something is **unique** to one thing or person, it concerns or belongs only to that thing or person. *These problems are not unique to nuclear power.* 3 ADJ Some people use **unique** to mean very unusual and special. *It was a unique and exquisite performance.* ♦ **uniquely** SUBMOD *He had a fine singing voice, uniquely gentle and deep.*

unison /juːnɪsən, -zən/. PHRASE If a group of people do something **in unison**, they all do it together at the same time. *'All of us,' they said in unison.*

unit /juːnɪt/, **units.** 1 COUNT N If you consider something as a **unit**, you consider it as a single, complete thing. *...the decline of the family as a self-sufficient unit.* 2 COUNT N A **unit** of measurement is a fixed, standard length, quantity, or weight. The metre, the litre, and the gram are all units.

unite /juːnaɪt/, **unites, uniting, united.** ERG VB When a group of people or things **unite**, they join together to form one thing. *They must unite to combat the enemy... This measure would unite all the provinces into a single state.*

united /juːnaɪtɪ^{2}d/. 1 ADJ When people are **united** about something, they agree about it and act together. *They were united in their dislike of authority.* 2 ADJ **United** is used to describe a country which has been formed from two or more countries or states. *Some people want a united Ireland... ...the United States.*

United Kingdom. PROPER N **The United Kingdom** is the official name for Great Britain and Northern Ireland.

unity /juːnɪ^{1}ti^1/. UNCOUNT N When there is **unity**, people are in agreement and act together for a particular purpose. *He failed to preserve his party's unity... They are discussing church unity.*

universal /juːnɪvɜːsə^{0}l/. 1 ADJ Something that is **universal** relates to everyone in the world or to everyone in a particular group or society. *They touched on various topics of universal interest.* ♦ **universally** ADV *This explanation is not yet universally accepted.* 2 ADJ You also say that something is **universal** when it relates to every part of the world or universe. *...the threat of universal extinction.*

universe /juːnɪvɜːs/. SING N The **universe** is the whole of space, including all the stars and planets. *They thought the earth was the centre of the universe.*

university /juːnɪvɜːsɪ^{1}ti^1/, **universities.** COUNT N OR UNCOUNT N A **university** is an institution where students study for degrees and where academic research is done. *...Norwich University... Her one aim in life is to go to university.*

unjust /ʌndʒʌst/. ADJ An **unjust** action, system, or law is morally wrong because it treats a person or group badly in a way that they do not deserve. *...a thoroughly unjust society.* ♦ **unjustly** ADV *...schoolmates who had unjustly accused him of bullying.*

unjustifiable /ʌndʒʌstɪfaɪəbə^{0}l/. ADJ You say that an action which harms someone is **unjustifiable** when there is no good reason for doing it. *What I had done was clearly unjustifiable.*

unjustified /ʌndʒʌstɪfaɪd/. ADJ You say that a belief or action is **unjustified** when there is no good reason for having it or doing it. *It was an unjustified attack.*

unkempt /ʌŋ^{1}kɛmpt/. ADJ Something that is **unkempt** is untidy and not looked after carefully. *He had a shaggy, unkempt beard.*

unkind /ʌŋ^{1}kaɪnd/, **unkinder, unkindest.** ADJ Someone who is **unkind** behaves towards you in an unpleasant and rather cruel way. *Why are you so unkind to me?... ...a silly and unkind remark.*

unknown /ʌnnəʊn/. 1 ADJ If someone or something is **unknown**, people do not know about them, or do not know who or what they are. *...this man Boris, whose real name is unknown to me... She wouldn't be alone with an unknown male visitor.* 2 SING N You can refer to the things that people do not know about as the **unknown**. *...fear of the unknown.*

unlawful /ʌnlɔːfə^{4}l/. ADJ Something that is **unlawful** is not legal; a formal use. *...unlawful activities.*

unleash /ʌnliːʃ/, **unleashes, unleashing, unleashed.** VB WITH OBJ To **unleash** a powerful or violent force means to release it; a formal use. *Strong feelings had been unleashed in me by the news of the bomb.*

unless /ʌnlɛs/. CONJ You use **unless** to introduce the only circumstances in which something does not happen or is not true. *He phoned me to say that unless the paper stopped my articles he would withdraw his advertisements... I couldn't get a grant unless I had five years' teaching experience.*

unlike /ʌnlaɪk/. 1 PREP If one thing is **unlike** another thing, the two things have different features from each other. *Rodin was unlike his predecessor in every way.* 2 PREP You can use **unlike** to contrast two people, things, or situations, and to show how they are different. *Mrs Hochstadt, unlike Etta, was a careful shopper.* 3 PREP If you describe something that someone has done as **unlike** them, you mean that it is not typical of their normal behaviour. *It was unlike her to mention it.*

unlikely /ʌnlaɪkli^1/. 1 ADJ If something is **unlikely** to happen or **unlikely** to be true, it will probably not happen, or it is probably not true. *The dispute is unlikely to be settled for a long time... It is unlikely that you will get your own office.* 2 ATTRIB ADJ You also use **unlikely** to describe an actual situation or event that seems very strange because it is so unexpected. *Brody was startled by the unlikely sight of Hendricks in a bathing suit.*

unlimited /ʌnlɪmɪtɪ^{2}d/. ADJ You say that something is **unlimited** when you can have as much of it as you want. *...unlimited travel... They were given unlimited amounts of food.*

unlit /ʌnlɪt/. 1 ADJ An **unlit** fire or cigarette has not yet been lit. 2 ADJ An **unlit** street or building is dark because there are no lights switched on in it.

unload /ʌnləʊd/, **unloads, unloading, unloaded.** VB WITH OR WITHOUT OBJ To **unload** goods from a vehicle means to remove them. *We began to unload the bricks from Philip's car.*

unlock /ʌnlɒk/, **unlocks, unlocking, unlocked.** VB WITH OBJ If you **unlock** something such as a door or a container, you open it using a key. *He unlocked the drawer and took out the money.*

unlocked /ʌnlɒkt/. ADJ An **unlocked** door has not been locked. *The door was always unlocked.*

unlucky /ʌnlʌki^1/. 1 ADJ Someone who is **unlucky** has bad luck. *I was unlucky enough to miss the final episode... She had been unlucky in love.* 2 ADJ If something is **unlucky**, it is thought to cause bad luck. *13 is a very unlucky number.*

unmade /ʌm^{1}meɪd/. ADJ An **unmade** bed has not had the bedclothes neatly arranged after it was last slept in.

unmanageable /ʌm^{1}mænɪdʒəbə^{0}l/. ADJ If something is **unmanageable**, it is difficult to use or deal with, usually because it is too big. *The complete encyclopaedia is quite unmanageable.*

unmanned /ʌm^{1}mænd/. ADJ **Unmanned** aircraft or spacecraft do not carry people in them.

unmarked /ʌm^{1}mɑːkt/. 1 ADJ Something that is **unmarked** has no marks of damage or injury on it. *His face was unmarked.* 2 ADJ An **unmarked** object has no signs on it to identify it. *...unmarked police cars.*

unmarried /ʌm^{1}mærɪd/. ADJ Someone who is **unmarried** is not married. *...an unmarried mother.*

unmentionable /ʌm^{1}mɛnʃənəbə^{0}l/. ADJ Something that is **unmentionable** is too embarrassing or unpleasant to talk about. *He's had all kinds of unmentionable operations.*

unmistakable /ʌm^{1}mɪsteɪkəbə^{0}l/; also spelled **unmistakeable.** ADJ If something is **unmistakable**, it is so obvious that you cannot be wrong about it. *...the unmistakable stench of rotting eggs.* ♦ **unmistakably** ADV OR SENTENCE ADV *He was unmistakably of Italian descent.*

unmitigated /ʌm^{1}mɪtɪgeɪtɪ^{2}d/. ATTRIB ADJ You use **unmitigated** to say that a bad situation or quality is totally and completely bad; a formal use. *...several days' unmitigated hell... ...his unmitigated selfishness.*

unmoved /ʌm^{1}muːvd/. PRED ADJ If you are **unmoved** by something, you are not emotionally affected by it. *No one can remain unmoved by this music.*

unnamed /ʌnneɪmd/. ADJ If someone or something is **unnamed,** their name is not mentioned. *...an unnamed ministry spokesman.*

unnatural /ʌnnætʃə0rəl/. 1 ADJ If something is **unnatural,** it is strange and rather frightening, because it is different from what you normally expect. *...the house's unnatural silence.* ♦ **unnaturally** ADV *Her arms felt unnaturally hot.* 2 ADJ **Unnatural** behaviour seems artificial and not typical. *Her voice was a little strained, a little unnatural.*

unnecessary /ʌnnɛsə1sə0ri1/. ADJ Something that is **unnecessary** is not necessary. *The reason behind this is to avoid unnecessary expenses.* ♦ **unnecessarily** ADV *Some parents worry unnecessarily about their children.*

unnerve /ʌnnɜ:v/, **unnerves, unnerving, unnerved.** VB WITH OBJ If something **unnerves** you, it frightens or startles you. *His touch unnerved her.* ♦ **unnerving** /ʌnnɜ:vɪŋ/ ADJ *This kind of experience can be quite unnerving.*

unnoticed /ʌnnəʊtɪst/. PRED ADJ If something happens or passes **unnoticed,** it is not seen or noticed by anyone. *We tried to get into the room unnoticed... He hoped his departure had passed unnoticed.*

unobserved /ʌnə7bzɜ:vd/. ADJ If you do something **unobserved,** you do it without being seen by anyone. *She was able to slip past the guard unobserved.*

unobtrusive /ʌnə7btru:sɪv/. ADJ Something that is **unobtrusive** does not draw attention to itself; a formal use. ♦ **unobtrusively** ADV *Unobtrusively, Ginny tried to close the drawer.*

unoccupied /ʌnɒkjə4paɪd/. ADJ If a place is **unoccupied,** there is nobody in it. *The house was left unoccupied for fifteen years.*

unofficial /ʌnəfɪʃə0l/. ADJ An **unofficial** action is not authorized, approved, or organized by a person in authority. *...an unofficial strike... You will be sent unofficial notification of the results.*

unorthodox /ʌnɔ:θədɒks/. ADJ **Unorthodox** behaviour, beliefs, or customs are unusual and not generally accepted.

unpack /ʌm1pæk/, **unpacks, unpacking, unpacked.** VB WITH OR WITHOUT OBJ When you **unpack** a suitcase, bag, or box, you take everything out of it. *He began to unpack his briefcase... I'll leave you now so that you can unpack.*

unpaid /ʌm1peɪd/. 1 ADJ If you are **unpaid,** you do a job without receiving any money for it. *Carol was Pat's unpaid teacher.* 2 ADJ **Unpaid** work or leave is work or leave that you do not get paid for. *...unpaid overtime.* 3 ADJ If something such as rent or a bill is **unpaid,** it has not yet been paid.

unpalatable /ʌm1pælə1təbə0l/; a formal word. 1 ADJ **Unpalatable** food is so unpleasant that you can hardly eat it. *...an unpalatable breakfast.* 2 ADJ An **unpalatable** idea is one that you find unpleasant and difficult to accept. *...the unpalatable truth.*

unparalleled /ʌm1pærəlɛld/. ADJ If something is **unparalleled,** it is bigger or better than anything else of its kind. *Our specialist library is unparalleled.*

unpleasant /ʌm1plɛzənt/. 1 ADJ If something is **unpleasant,** it gives you bad feelings, for example by making you feel upset or uncomfortable. *The only work available is dirty, unpleasant and dangerous... The smell was unpleasant.* ♦ **unpleasantly** ADV *The rain dripped unpleasantly.* 2 ADJ An **unpleasant** person is unfriendly and rude. *Their son is even more ill-tempered, difficult, and unpleasant.* ♦ **unpleasantly** ADV *He laughed unpleasantly.*

unplug /ʌm1plʌg/, **unplugs, unplugging, unplugged.** VB WITH OBJ If you **unplug** a piece of electrical equipment, you take its plug out of the socket.

unpopular /ʌm1pɒpjə4lə/. ADJ Something or someone that is **unpopular** is disliked by most people. *The war was unpopular... ...an unpopular minister.*

unprecedented /ʌm1prɛsɪdɛntɪ2d/. ADJ If something is **unprecedented,** it has never happened before, or is the best or largest of its kind so far; a formal use. *...a period of unprecedented wealth.*

unpredictable /ʌm1prɪdɪktəbə0l/. ADJ If someone or something is **unpredictable,** you never know how they will behave or what effects they will have. *She was totally unpredictable... Poisons are notoriously unpredictable.*

unprepared /ʌm1prɪpɛəd/. ADJ If you are **unprepared** for something, you are not ready for it, and are therefore surprised or at a disadvantage when it happens. *We were pushed into battle unprepared.*

unproductive /ʌm1prədʌktɪv/. ADJ Something that is **unproductive** does not produce anything useful. *Their land is unproductive.*

unprofitable /ʌm1prɒfɪtəbə0l/. ADJ **Unprofitable** things do not make any profit or do not make enough profit. *Agriculture remained unprofitable... ...unprofitable business contracts.*

unprovoked /ʌm1prəvəʊkt/. ADJ If you make an **unprovoked** attack, you attack someone who has not harmed you in any way. *...casual and unprovoked violence.*

unqualified /ʌnkwɒlɪfaɪd/. 1 ADJ If you are **unqualified,** you do not have any qualifications, or do not have the right qualifications for a particular job. *...an unqualified childminder.* 2 ATTRIB ADJ **Unqualified** also means total and complete. *The party was an unqualified disaster.*

unquestionable /ʌnkwɛstʃənəbə0l/. ADJ Something that is **unquestionable** is so obviously true or real that nobody can doubt it. *His courage and commitment are unquestionable.* ♦ **unquestionably** SENTENCE ADV *The visit to Greenland was unquestionably the highlight of the voyage.*

unquestioned /ʌnkwɛstʃənd/. ADJ Something that is **unquestioned** is accepted by everyone, without anyone doubting or disagreeing. *...a system in which obedience and fortitude were unquestioned virtues.*

unquestioning /ʌnkwɛstʃənɪŋ/. ADJ You use **unquestioning** to describe beliefs or attitudes that people have without thinking closely about them or doubting them in any way. *You were chosen because of your unquestioning obedience.*

unravel /ʌnrævəl/, **unravels, unravelling, unravelled;** spelled **unraveling, unraveled** in American English. 1 ERG VB If you **unravel** something that is knotted or twisted, or if it **unravels,** it becomes undone. *Her knitting was starting to unravel.* 2 VB WITH OBJ If you **unravel** a mystery or puzzle, you work out the answer to it. *...factors which only the experts could unravel.*

unreal /ʌnrɪəl/. ADJ If something is **unreal,** it is so strange that you find it difficult to believe. *This conversation is getting more and more unreal.*

unrealistic /ʌnrɪəlɪstɪk/. ADJ If you are **unrealistic** or have **unrealistic** ideas, you do not recognize the truth about a situation or do not deal with it in a practical way. *This demand proved unrealistic... ...unrealistic expectations.*

unreasonable /ʌnri:znəbə0l/. 1 ADJ People who are **unreasonable** are difficult to deal with because they behave in an unfair or illogical way. *We think he is being unreasonable.* 2 ADJ An **unreasonable** decision or action seems unfair and difficult to justify. *The request didn't seem unreasonable.*

unrecognizable /ʌnrɛkəg0naɪzəbə0l/; also spelled **unrecognisable.** ADJ Something that is **unrecognizable** is impossible to recognize or identify. *His voice was almost unrecognizable.*

unrecognized /ʌnrɛkəg0naɪzd/; also spelled **unrecognised.** 1 ADJ If someone or something is **unrecognized,** they are not recognized or are not known about. *Unrecognized by any of the women, he entered the house... There was another consequence, at that time almost unrecognised.* 2 ADJ If you or your achievements or qualities are **unrecognized,** you have not been properly appreciated or acknowledged by other people for what you have done. *It is a disgrace that such talent should go unrecognised.*

unrelated /ʌnri1leɪtɪ2d/. ADJ Things which are **unrelated** have no connection with each other. *...a series of unrelated incidents... New issues may arise, unrelated to the original ones.*

unrelenting /ʌnri1lɛntɪŋ/. ADJ If your behaviour is **unrelenting,** you continue to do something in a determined way, often without caring whether you hurt or embarrass other people. *...the unrelenting pursuit of growth and industrial expansion.*

unreliable /ʌnri1laɪəbə0l/. ADJ If people, machines, or methods are **unreliable,** you cannot trust them or rely on them. *Godwin was a thoroughly unreliable man... ...an unreliable second-hand car.*

unremarkable /ʌnri1mɑ:kəbə0l/. ADJ If you say that something is **unremarkable,** you mean that it is not beautiful, interesting, or exciting. *The view is unremarkable.*

unremitting /ʌnri1mɪtɪŋ/. ADJ Something that is **unremitting** continues without stopping; a formal use. *...their unremitting efforts to get him into college.*

unrepentant /ʌnri1pɛntənt/. ADJ If you are **unrepentant,** you are not ashamed of your beliefs or actions. *...an unrepentant believer in free enterprise.*

unresolved /ʌnri1zɒlvd/. ADJ If a problem or difficulty is **unresolved,** no satisfactory solution has been found to it; a formal use. *Several major technological problems remained unresolved.*

unrest /ʌnrɛst/. UNCOUNT N If there is **unrest,** people are angry and dissatisfied. *...the causes of industrial unrest.*

unrestricted /ʌnri1strɪktɪ2d/. ADJ If something is **unrestricted,** it is not limited by any laws or rules. *...the unrestricted dumping of waste.*

unrivalled /ʌnraɪvəld/. ADJ If something is **unrivalled,** it is better than anything else of the same kind. *...an unrivalled collection of modern art.*

unroll /ʌnrəʊl/, **unrolls, unrolling, unrolled.** ERG VB If you **unroll** something such as a roll of paper or a roll of cloth, you open it up so that it is flat. *Someone unrolled a map of America... ...with long streamers of cloth unrolling behind them.*

unruffled /ʌnrʌfəld/. ADJ If you are **unruffled,** you are calm and not affected by surprising or frightening events. *She remained singularly unruffled when confronted with my discovery.*

unruly /ʌnru:li1/. 1 ADJ **Unruly** people are difficult to control or organize. *...unruly children.* 2 ADJ **Unruly** hair is difficult to keep tidy.

unsafe /ʌnseɪf/. 1 ADJ If something is **unsafe,** it is dangerous. *The house was declared unsafe for habitation.* 2 PRED ADJ If you are **unsafe,** you are in danger of being harmed. *I feel very unsafe.*

unsatisfactory /ʌnsætɪsfæktə0ri1/. ADJ Something that is **unsatisfactory** is not good enough to be acceptable. *I had an unsatisfactory discussion with him about my job.*

unsavoury /ʌnseɪvə0ri1/; spelled **unsavory** in American English. ADJ You describe people, places, and things as **unsavoury** when you find them unpleasant. *Parts of Birmingham are pretty unsavoury.*

unscathed /ʌnskeɪðd/. PRED ADJ If you are **unscathed** after a dangerous experience, you have not been injured or harmed by it. *We all escaped unscathed.*

unscheduled /ʌnʃɛdju:ld, ʌnskɛd-/. ADJ An **unscheduled** event is not planned, but happens unexpectedly or because someone changes their plans. *He was about to make an unscheduled announcement.*

unscrew /ʌnskru:/, **unscrews, unscrewing, unscrewed.** VB WITH OBJ If you **unscrew** something, you remove it by turning it, or by removing the screws that fasten it to something else. *He unscrewed the top and put the bottle to his mouth... The mirrors had been unscrewed and removed.*

unscrupulous /ʌnskru:pjə4ləs/. ADJ **Unscrupulous** people are prepared to act dishonestly to get what they want.

unseemly /ʌnsi:mli1/. ADJ **Unseemly** behaviour is not polite or not suitable for a particular occasion; an old-fashioned use. *...an unseemly public squabble.*

unseen /ʌnsi:n/. ADJ You use **unseen** to describe things that you cannot see. *A large unseen orchestra was playing jazzy rhythms.*

unselfish /ʌnsɛlfɪʃ/. ADJ If you are **unselfish,** you think about other people's wishes and needs rather than your own. *He was a brave and unselfish man... ...her unselfish devotion to her children.*

unsettled /ʌnsɛtə0ld/. 1 ADJ In an **unsettled** situation, there is a lot of uncertainty about what will happen. *...in the early days of 1968, when everything was unsettled.* 2 PRED ADJ If you are **unsettled,** you cannot concentrate on anything, because you are worried. *I felt pretty unsettled all that week.*

unsettling /ʌnsɛtlɪŋ/. ADJ An **unsettling** experience causes you to feel nervous or worried. *Swift change is extremely uncomfortable and unsettling.*

unshakable /ʌnʃeɪkəbə0l/; also spelled **unshakeable.** ADJ **Unshakable** beliefs are so strong that they cannot be destroyed or altered. *...her unshakable faith in progress.*

unshaven /ʌnʃeɪvə0n/. ADJ If a man is **unshaven,** he has not shaved recently and there are short hairs on his face and chin. *...his unshaven face.*

unsightly /ʌnsaɪtli1/. ADJ If something is **unsightly,** it is unattractive to look at. *His skin was covered with unsightly blotches.*

unskilled /ʌnskɪld/. ADJ **Unskilled** workers do work that does not require special training. *...unskilled labourers... They are all in low-paid, unskilled jobs.*

unsolicited /ʌnsəlɪsɪtɪ2d/. ADJ Something that is **unsolicited** is given without being asked for; a formal use. *She was given much unsolicited advice.*

unsolved /ʌnsɒlvd/. ADJ An **unsolved** problem or mystery has never been solved.

unsophisticated /ʌnsəfɪstɪkeɪtɪ2d/. 1 ADJ **Unsophisticated** people do not have wide experience or knowledge, and have simple tastes. *It is easy to write because the readers are relatively unsophisticated.* 2 ADJ An **unsophisticated** method or device is very simple. *These forecasts are based on rather unsophisticated economic analyses.*

unsound /ʌnsaʊnd/. 1 ADJ If a conclusion or method is **unsound,** it is based on ideas that are wrong. *These procedures are economically unsound.* 2 ADJ An **unsound** building or other structure is in poor condition and is likely to collapse.

unspeakable /ʌnspi:kəbə0l/. ADJ If something is **unspeakable,** it is extremely unpleasant. *Their treatment of women is unspeakable.*

unspecified /ʌnspɛsɪfaɪd/. ADJ You say that something is **unspecified** when you are not told exactly what it is. *She was dying of some unspecified disease.*

unspoiled /ʌnspɔɪld/; also spelled **unspoilt** /ʌnspɔɪlt/. ADJ If something is **unspoiled,** it has not been damaged or harmed. *The wine's flavour was unspoiled... ...areas of unspoiled countryside.*

unspoken /ʌnspəʊkə^{0}n/. ADJ If your thoughts, wishes, or feelings are **unspoken,** you do not tell other people about them. *I was full of unspoken fears.*

unstable /ʌnsteɪbə^{0}l/. 1 ADJ If a situation is **unstable,** it is likely to change suddenly. *...the unstable political situation.* 2 ADJ **Unstable** objects are likely to move or fall. *...the unstable cliffs.* 3 ADJ If people are **unstable,** their emotions and behaviour keep changing because their minds are disturbed or upset. *He was a neurotic and unstable man.*

unsteady /ʌnstɛdi^1/. 1 ADJ If you are **unsteady,** you have difficulty standing or walking. *She seemed unsteady on her feet.* ♦ **unsteadily** ADV *He rose unsteadily to his feet.* 2 ADJ If your hands are **unsteady,** you have difficulty controlling them. *Stephen poured two brandies with an unsteady hand.* 3 ADJ **Unsteady** objects are not held, fixed, or balanced securely. *She was balancing three boxes in an unsteady pile.*

unstructured /ʌnstrʌktʃəd/. ADJ If an activity is **unstructured,** it is not organized in a complete or detailed way. *...an unstructured but effective method of education.*

unstuck /ʌnstʌk/.
PHRASES ● If something **comes unstuck,** it becomes separated from the thing that it was attached to. *Some of the posters regularly came unstuck.* ● If a plan or system **comes unstuck,** it fails; an informal use. ● If someone **comes unstuck,** they fail badly with what they are trying to achieve; an informal use. *I always knew he'd come unstuck somewhere.*

unsubstantiated /ʌnsəbstænʃɪeɪtɪ^{2}d/. ADJ An **unsubstantiated** statement or story has not been proved true.

unsuccessful /ʌnsəksɛsfʊl/. ADJ If you are **unsuccessful,** you do not succeed in what you are trying to do. *Tom tried to hypnotize me but he was unsuccessful... ...an unsuccessful attempt to kill him.* ♦ **unsuccessfully** ADV *I tried unsuccessfully to talk to him.*

unsuitable /ʌnsuːtəbə^{0}l/. ADJ Someone or something that is **unsuitable** for a particular purpose or situation does not have the right qualities for it. *...areas that are entirely unsuitable for agriculture.* ♦ **unsuitably** ADV *She was most unsuitably dressed.*

unsuited /ʌnsj^{0}uːtɪ^{2}d/. ADJ Someone or something that is **unsuited** to a particular situation, place, or task, does not have the right qualities for it. *...vehicles that are clearly unsuited for use in the desert.*

unsure /ʌnʃʊə/. 1 ADJ If you are **unsure** of yourself, you lack confidence. *His demands made the boy nervous and unsure of himself.* 2 ADJ If you are **unsure** about something, you feel uncertain about it. *She took a step back, unsure of his reaction.*

unsuspected /ʌnsəspɛktɪ^{2}d/. ADJ If something is **unsuspected,** people are not aware of it. *As the project developed, unsuspected difficulties came to light.*

unsuspecting /ʌnsəspɛktɪŋ/. ADJ Someone who is **unsuspecting** is not aware of what is happening or going to happen. *...a survey conducted on 763 unsuspecting male students.*

unsympathetic /ʌnsɪmpəθɛtɪk/. ADJ If you are **unsympathetic,** you are not kind or helpful to a person in difficulties. *Posy had been utterly unsympathetic... ...an unsympathetic reply.*

untangle /ʌntæŋgə^{0}l/, **untangles, untangling, untangled.** VB WITH OBJ If you **untangle** something such as string when it is twisted together, you undo the knots in it and straighten it. *He untangled the cable.*

untapped /ʌntæpt/. ADJ An **untapped** supply of something has not yet been used. *...Britain's vast untapped reserves of coal.*

untenable /ʌntɛnəbə^{0}l/. ADJ An **untenable** argument, theory, or position cannot be defended successfully against criticism or attack; a formal use.

unthinkable /ʌnθɪŋkəbə^{0}l/. ADJ If something is **unthinkable,** it is so shocking or awful that you cannot imagine it happening or being true. *War was unthinkable.*

unthinking /ʌnθɪŋkɪŋ/. ADJ Someone who is **unthinking** does not think carefully about the effects of their behaviour. *Our society seems to be rushing ahead, unthinking, into ever greater mechanisation.*

untidy /ʌntaɪdi^1/, **untidier, untidiest.** 1 ADJ Something that is **untidy** is messy and disordered, and not neatly arranged. *The living-room was untidier than usual.* ♦ **untidily** ADV *It had been unwrapped and untidily tossed onto the floor.* 2 ADJ An **untidy** person leaves things in an untidy state. *She is so careless and untidy.*

untie /ʌntaɪ/, **unties, untying, untied.** VB WITH OBJ If you **untie** someone or something, you remove the string or rope that has been tied round them by undoing the knots. *He quickly untied the captives... She tried to untie the knot.*

untied /ʌntaɪd/. ADJ Something such as a tie, shoelace, or ribbon that is **untied** has its ends loose rather than tied together in a bow or knot.

until /ʌntɪl/. 1 PREP OR CONJ If something happens **until** a particular time, it happens before that time and stops at that time. *We went on duty at six in the evening and worked until 2 a.m... You can get free prescriptions until you are 16.* 2 PREP OR CONJ If something does not happen **until** a particular time, it does not happen before that time and only happens after it. *They didn't find her until the next day... Women did not gain the vote until after the First World War.*

unto /ʌntuː/. PREP In old-fashioned English, **unto** is sometimes used instead of the preposition 'to'; *Do unto others as you would have them do unto you.*

untold /ʌntəʊld/. ATTRIB ADJ You use **untold** to emphasize how great something is, especially something unpleasant; a formal use. *The war brought untold suffering upon the population.*

untouched /ʌntʌtʃt/. 1 ADJ Something that is **untouched** has not been changed, moved, or damaged in any way. *The island has been untouched by tourism.* 2 ADJ If a meal is **untouched,** none of it has been eaten. *She sent back her breakfast tray untouched.*

untoward /ʌntəwɔːd/. ADJ You use **untoward** to describe something that happens unexpectedly and causes difficulties; a formal use. *Nothing untoward had happened.*

untrained /ʌntreɪnd/. ADJ Someone who is **untrained** has had no education in the skills that they need for a particular job or activity. *...untrained assistants.*

untreated /ʌntriːtɪ^{2}d/. 1 ADJ If an injury or illness is left **untreated,** it is not given medical treatment. 2 ADJ Harmful materials or chemicals that are **untreated** have not been made safe.

untroubled /ʌntrʌbə^{0}ld/. PRED ADJ If you are **untroubled** by something, you are not affected or worried by it.

untrue /ʌntruː/. 1 ADJ Something that is **untrue** is not true. *The story was probably untrue.* 2 PRED ADJ If someone is **untrue** to you, they are unfaithful to you or lie to you; a literary use.

untruth /ʌntruːθ/, **untruths** /ʌntruːðz/. COUNT N An **untruth** is a lie; a formal use. *I hesitated rather than tell a deliberate untruth.*

unused; pronounced /ʌnjuːzd/ in meaning 1 and /ʌnjuːst/ in meaning 2. 1 ADJ Something that is **unused** has not been used. *...a pile of unused fuel.* 2 PRED ADJ WITH PREP 'to' If you are **unused** to something, you have not often done it or experienced it. *She was unused to hardship.*

unusual /ʌnjuːʒʊ^{0}əl/. ADJ If something is **unusual,** it does not often happen or is not often found. *He had an unusual name... It was not unusual for me to come home at two or three in the morning.*

unusually /ʌnjuːʒʊ^{0}əli^1/. 1 SUBMOD You use **unusually** to say that something is bigger than usual or has more of a quality than usual. *...a clump of weed that seemed unusually large... October has been unusually wet and cold.* 2 SENTENCE ADV You also use **unusually** to say that something is not what normally happens. *The service charge, unusually, is 10 per cent.*

unveil /ʌnveɪl/, **unveils, unveiling, unveiled.** 1 VB WITH OBJ When someone **unveils** something such as a new statue or painting, they draw back a curtain which is covering it, in a special ceremony. 2 VB WITH OBJ If you **unveil** something that has been a secret, you make it known; a formal use. *The plan was unveiled with approval from the Minister.*

unwanted /ʌnwɒntɪ^{2}d/. ADJ You say that something is **unwanted** when a particular person does not want it, or when nobody wants it. *...the appalling suffering caused by unwanted pregnancies... She was starting to feel unwanted.*

unwarranted /ʌnwɒrəntɪ^{2}d/. ADJ Something that is **unwarranted** is not justified or deserved; a formal use. *It was a totally unwarranted waste of money.*

unwary /ʌnwɛəri^1/. ADJ Someone who is **unwary** is not cautious, and is likely to be harmed or deceived. *...the shrieks of unwary animals taken by surprise.*

unwelcome /ʌnwɛlkə^{0}m/. 1 ADJ An **unwelcome** experience is one that you do not like and did not want. *...unwelcome publicity... The move from London was entirely unwelcome to her.* 2 ADJ If a visitor is **unwelcome,** you did not want them to come. *...an unwelcome guest.*

unwell /ʌnwɛl/. PRED ADJ If you are **unwell,** you are ill. *He complained of feeling unwell.*

unwieldy /ʌnwiːldi^1/. 1 ADJ An **unwieldy** object is difficult to move or carry because it is big or heavy. 2 ADJ An **unwieldy** system does not work well because it is too large or is badly organized. *...the country's unwieldy banking system.*

unwilling /ʌnwɪlɪŋ/. ADJ If you are **unwilling** to do something, you do not want to do it. *She was unwilling to go out.* ♦ **unwillingly** ADV *He submitted unwillingly to his mother.* ♦ **unwillingness** UNCOUNT N *...their unwillingness to discuss common problems.*

unwind /ʌnwaɪnd/, **unwinds, unwinding, unwound** /ʌnwaʊnd/. 1 VB When you **unwind** after working hard, you relax. *Reading is a good way to unwind.* 2 VB WITH OBJ If you **unwind** something that is wrapped round something else, you undo it or straighten it out.

unwise /ʌnwaɪz/. ADJ Something that is **unwise** is foolish. *It would be very unwise for the boy to marry her... ...an unwise choice.*

unwitting /ʌnwɪtɪŋ/. ATTRIB ADJ An **unwitting** person does something or becomes involved in something without realizing what is really happening; a formal use. *I became the unwitting instrument of that unscrupulous man.* ♦ **unwittingly** ADV *Sometimes we ourselves unwittingly invite trouble.*

unworkable /ʌnwɜːkəbə^{0}l/. ADJ If an idea or plan is **unworkable,** it cannot succeed. *His proposals for reform of the Trades Unions are unworkable.*

unworldly /ʌnwɜːldli^1/. ADJ Someone who is **unworldly** is not interested in having a lot of money or possessions; a formal use.

unworthy /ʌnwɜːði^1/. ADJ If someone is **unworthy** of something, they do not deserve it; a formal use. *I felt I was unworthy of her love.*

unwound /ʌnwaʊnd/. **Unwound** is the past tense and past participle of **unwind.**

unwrap /ʌnræp/, **unwraps, unwrapping, unwrapped.** VB WITH OBJ When you **unwrap** something, you take off the paper or covering that is around it. *I started to unwrap my sandwiches.*

unwritten /ʌnrɪtə^{0}n/. ADJ **Unwritten** things have not been printed or written down. *...unwritten laws.*

unzip /ʌnzɪp/, **unzips, unzipping, unzipped.** VB WITH OBJ When you **unzip** something which is fastened by a zip, you unfasten it.

up /ʌp/. 1 PREP OR ADV **Up** means towards a higher place, or in a higher place. *I carried my suitcase up the stairs behind her... Bill put up his hand... ...comfortable houses up in the hills.* 2 ADV If someone stands **up,** they move so that they are standing. *She scrambled up from the floor... She helped Henry up from the bench.* 3 ADV WITH ADJUNCT **Up** also means in the north or towards the north. *We're having brilliant sunshine up here.* 4 PREP OR ADV If you go **up** a road, you go along it. *We walked up the road together... There's a cafe just a hundred yards further up.* 5 PREP If you go **up** a river, you go along it towards its source. *...a voyage up the Nile.* 6 ADV WITH ADJUNCT You also use **up** to show that something is close to something else, or moves closer to it. *It's only when you get right up to them that you realise what they are... Ferdinand ran up to his father-in-law.* 7 PRED ADJ If you are **up,** you are not in bed. *They were up early.* 8 ADV If an amount goes **up,** it increases. *...when interest rates go up.* 9 PRED ADJ If a period of time is **up,** it has come to an end. *When the six weeks were up, everybody was sad that she had to leave.* 10 ADV WITH PREP If someone or something is **up** for election, review, or examination, they are about to be considered or judged. *One of my colleagues comes up for election next week.*

PHRASES ● If you move **up and down,** you move repeatedly in one direction and then in the opposite direction. *I was so happy I jumped up and down... He started pacing up and down the office.* ● If you have **ups and downs,** you experience a mixture of good things and bad things. ● If you say that something **is up,** you mean that something is wrong or that something worrying is happening; an informal use. *What's up, Myra? You look sad.* ● If you are **up against** something, you have a difficult situation or problem to deal with. ● You use **up to** to say how large something can be. *They might be up to a metre wide.* ● You also use **up to** to say what level something has reached. *The work isn't up to the standard I require.* ● If you say that something is **not up to much,** you mean that it is of poor quality; an informal use. ● If you do not feel **up to** doing something, you do not feel well enough to do it; an informal use. ● If you say that someone is **up to** something, you mean that they are secretly doing something that they should not be; an informal use. ● If you say that it is **up to** someone to do a particular thing, you mean that it is their responsibility to do it. *It is up to the teacher not to accept shoddy work.* ● If something happens **up to** or **up until** a particular time, it happens until that time. *Up until the early sixties there was no shortage.*

upbringing /ʌpbrɪŋɪŋ/. UNCOUNT N Your **upbringing** is the way your parents treat you and the things that they teach you. *...a strict upbringing.*

update /ʌpdeɪt/, **updates, updating, updated.** VB WITH OBJ If you **update** something, you make it more modern, usually by adding newer parts to it. *The information will need updating from time to time.*

upend /ʌpɛnd/, **upends, upending, upended.** VB WITH OBJ If something **is upended,** it is turned upside down.

upgrade /ʌpgreɪd/, **upgrades, upgrading, upgraded.** VB WITH OBJ To **upgrade** something means to change it so that it is more important or better. *We need to upgrade the pay and status of doctors.*

upheaval /ʌphiːvə^{0}l/, **upheavals.** COUNT N OR UNCOUNT N An **upheaval** is a big change which causes a lot of trouble and confusion. *Great upheavals were taking place in the States... They have brought social upheaval and conflict into the country.*

upheld /ʌphɛld/. **Upheld** is the past tense and past participle of **uphold.**

uphill /ʌphɪl/. 1 ADV If you go **uphill,** you go up a slope. *She ran furiously uphill... ...the effort of pushing the cart uphill.* 2 ATTRIB ADJ An **uphill** task requires a great deal of effort and determination. *This is hard, uphill work.*

uphold /ʌphəʊld/, **upholds, upholding, upheld** /ʌphɛld/. VB WITH OBJ If you **uphold** a law, principle, or decision, you support and maintain it. *He had sworn to uphold the law... His conviction was upheld on appeal.*

upholstered /ʌphɒlstəd/. ADJ **Upholstered** chairs and sofas have a soft covering that makes them comfortable. *...two chairs, upholstered in leather.*

upholstery /ʌphəʊlstə^{0}ri^{1}/. UNCOUNT N **Upholstery** is the soft covering on chairs and sofas that makes them comfortable.

upkeep /ʌpkiːp/. UNCOUNT N The **upkeep** of a building is the continual process of keeping it in good condition.

upland /ʌplə^{3}nd/, **uplands.** 1 ATTRIB ADJ **Upland** places are situated on high hills or high land. *They move with their flocks to upland pastures.* 2 PLURAL N **Uplands** are areas of high land. *...the chalk uplands of Wiltshire.*

uplifting /ʌplɪftɪŋ/. ADJ If something is **uplifting,** it makes you feel cheerful and happy. *...uplifting literature.*

upmarket /ʌpmɑːkɪt/. ADJ **Upmarket** places and goods are visited or bought by people who have sophisticated and expensive tastes; an informal use.

upon /əpɒn/. 1 PREP If one thing is **upon** another, it is on it; a formal use. *She was sitting with a cat upon her knee... He lay down upon the grass.* 2 PREP You use **upon** when mentioning an event that is followed immediately by another. *Upon entering the cabin, she sat down.* 3 PREP You also use **upon** between two occurrences of the same noun in order to say that there are large numbers of the thing mentioned. *We drove through mile upon mile of brick villas... ...row upon row of red roofs.* 4 PREP If an event is **upon** you, it is just about to happen. *Suddenly the concert was upon us with me totally unprepared.*

upper /ʌpə/, **uppers.** 1 ATTRIB ADJ You use **upper** to describe something that is above something else, usually the top one of a pair of things. *I pulled down a book from an upper shelf.* 2 ATTRIB ADJ The **upper** part of something is the higher part. *Dark glasses masked the upper half of his face.* 3 PHRASE If you have **the upper hand** in a situation, you have more power than the other people involved and can make decisions about what happens. 4 COUNT N The **upper** of a shoe is the top part of it, which is attached to the sole.

upper class, upper classes. COUNT N The **upper classes** are the people who belong to the social class above the middle class. *The upper classes still send their children to Eton... ...upper-class families.*

upper lip, upper lips. COUNT N Your **upper lip** is the part of your face between your mouth and your nose. • to **keep a stiff upper lip:** see **lip.**

uppermost /ʌpəməʊst/. 1 ADJ You say that something is **uppermost** when it is higher than the rest of a particular thing, or when it is the highest thing in a group. *He was pointing with the whole of his hand, thumb uppermost... He gently examined the uppermost leaves.* 2 PRED ADJ If something is **uppermost** in a situation, it is the most important thing in that situation. *Political motives were uppermost... There were two thoughts uppermost in my mind.*

upright /ʌpraɪt/. 1 ADJ OR ADV If you are **upright,** you are sitting or standing with your back straight. *I cannot stand upright any more... He sat bolt upright.* 2 ADJ An **upright** chair has a straight back and no arms. 3 ADJ **Upright** people are careful to behave in a way that is moral and socially acceptable.

uprising /ʌpraɪzɪŋ/, **uprisings.** COUNT N When there is an **uprising,** a group of people start fighting against the people who are in power in their country.

uproar /ʌprɔː/. SING N OR UNCOUNT N If there is **uproar,** there is a lot of shouting and noise because people are angry or upset. *She could hear the uproar in the prisoners' coaches... Soon all was uproar.*

uproot /ʌpruːt/, **uproots, uprooting, uprooted.** 1 REFL VB OR VB WITH OBJ If you **uproot** yourself or if you **are uprooted,** you leave or are made to leave a place where you have lived for a long time. *People were uprooted and rehoused.* 2 VB WITH OBJ To **uproot** a tree means to pull it out of the ground. *Windows were smashed and large trees uprooted.*

upset, upsets, upsetting. Upset is used in the present tense of the verb, and is the past tense and past participle; pronounced /ʌpsɛt/ when it is an adjective used after a verb or when it is a verb, and /ʌpsɛt/ when it is an adjective used in front of a noun or when it is a noun. 1 PRED ADJ If you are **upset,** you are unhappy or disappointed because something unpleasant has happened. *I'm dreadfully upset about it all... They were upset by the poverty they saw.* 2 VB WITH OBJ If something **upsets** you, it makes you feel worried or unhappy. *I didn't mean to upset you.* ♦ **upsetting** ADJ *It was a very upsetting experience.* 3 VB WITH OBJ To **upset** something such as a procedure means to cause it to go wrong. *Davis's death has upset the routine.* 4 VB WITH OBJ To **upset** something also means to turn it over accidentally. *He almost upset the canoe.* 5 COUNT N A stomach **upset** is a slight illness in your stomach caused by an infection or by something that you have eaten. Also ADJ *I've got an upset stomach.*

upshot /ʌpʃɒt/. SING N The **upshot** of a series of events or discussions is the final result; a formal use. *The upshot was that the agreement had to be renegotiated.*

upside down. 1 PRED ADJ OR ADV If something is **upside down,** it has been turned round so that the part that is usually lowest is above the part that is usually highest. *You are holding it upside down... They were hanging upside down.* 2 ADV If you turn a place **upside down,** you move everything around or make it untidy. *I've turned the house upside down, but I still can't find his watch.*

upstage /ʌpsteɪdʒ/, **upstages, upstaging, upstaged.** VB WITH OBJ If someone **upstages** you, they draw attention away from you by being more attractive or interesting. *He seems to be attempting to upstage the Prime Minister.*

upstairs /ʌpstɛəz/. 1 ADV If you go **upstairs** in a building, you go up to a higher floor. *I ran back upstairs.* 2 ADV If something or someone is **upstairs** in a building, they are on an upper floor. *Upstairs, there were three little bedrooms.* 3 SING N The **upstairs** of a building is its upper floor or floors; an informal use. *They had to rent out the upstairs to make the mortgage payments.* 4 ATTRIB ADJ An **upstairs** room or object is situated on an upper floor of a building. *Neighbours watched from their upstairs windows.*

upstart /ʌpstɑːt/, **upstarts.** COUNT N You refer to someone as an **upstart** when they behave as if they are important, but you think they are too new in a place or job to be treated as important.

upstream /ʌpstriːm/. ADV Something that is moving **upstream** is moving along a river towards the source of the river. *He was making his way upstream.*

upsurge /ʌpsɜːdʒ/. SING N If there is an **upsurge** in something, there is a sudden, large increase in it; a formal use. *...a massive upsurge of social unrest.*

uptake /ʌpteɪk/. PHRASE If someone is **quick on the uptake,** they understand things quickly. If someone is **slow on the uptake,** they have difficulty understanding simple or obvious things; an informal use.

uptight /ʌptaɪt/. ADJ Someone who is **uptight** is tense or annoyed about something but is not saying so directly; an informal use.

up-to-date. 1 ADJ If something is **up-to-date,** it is the newest thing of its kind. *...a fleet of up-to-date lorries.* 2 ADJ If you are **up-to-date** about something, you have the latest information about it.

uptown /ʌptaʊn/. ADV OR ADJ If you go **uptown,** you go away from the centre of a city towards an outer part; an American use. *He walked uptown... She met him at his apartment uptown.*

upturn /ʌptɜːn/, **upturns.** COUNT N If there is an **upturn** in something, it starts to improve. *The economy is experiencing an upturn.*

upturned /ʌptɜːnd/. 1 ADJ If something is **upturned,** it points upwards. *She had a small upturned nose.* 2 ADJ **Upturned** also means upside down. *She sat on an upturned bucket.*

upward /ʌpwəd/, **upwards.** In normal British English, **upwards** is an adverb and **upward** is an adjective. In formal British English and in American English, **upward** is both an adjective and an adverb. 1 ADV If you move or look **upwards** or **upward,** you move or look up towards a higher place. *He happened to look upwards.* Also ATTRIB ADJ *He would steal upward glances at the clock.* 2 ADV If an amount or rate moves **upwards** or **upward,** it increases. *The world urban population is rocketing upward at a rate of 6.5 per cent per year.* 3 PREP **Upwards of** or **upward of** a particular number means more than that number. *The cyclone killed upwards of 200,000 people.*

uranium /jʊreɪnɪəm/. UNCOUNT N **Uranium** is a radioactive metal that is used to produce nuclear energy and weapons.

urban /ɜːbən/. ATTRIB ADJ **Urban** means belonging or relating to a town or city. *...urban unemployment.*

urbane /ɜːbeɪn/. ADJ Someone who is **urbane** is well-mannered, relaxed, and appears comfortable in social situations; a formal use. *The professor was an urbane little man.*

urbanized /ɜːbənaɪzd/; also spelled **urbanised.** PASSIVE VB When an area **is urbanized,** a lot of buildings, industries, and businesses are built or developed there. *...highly urbanized and industrialized areas.* ♦ **urbanization** /ɜːbənaɪzeɪʃə^{0}n/ UNCOUNT N *...the urbanization of farmland.*

urchin /ɜːtʃɪn/, **urchins.** COUNT N You can refer to a young child who is dirty and poorly dressed as an **urchin;** an old-fashioned use.

urge /ɜːdʒ/, **urges, urging, urged.** 1 COUNT N If you have an **urge** to do or have something, you have a strong wish to do or have it. *They have a strong urge to communicate... ...our insane urge for greater and greater material wealth.* 2 REPORT VB If you **urge** someone to do something, you try hard to persuade them to do it. *I urged him to take a year off to study drawing... 'At least stay for Christmas,' Pam urged... She urged that I should support the girls.* 3 VB WITH OBJ If you **urge** a course of action, you strongly advise that it should be taken; a formal use. *US officials urged restraint.*

urgent /ɜːdʒənt/. 1 ADJ Something that is **urgent** needs to be dealt with as soon as possible. *Most of the motorway network is in urgent need of repair... ...urgent messages.* ♦ **urgently** ADV *Improved health and education are urgently needed.* ♦ **urgency** /ɜːdʒənsi^{1}/ UNCOUNT N *...matters of the greatest urgency.* 2 ADJ If you speak in an **urgent** way, you show that you are anxious for people to notice something or do something. *She spoke to him in a low and urgent voice.* ♦ **urgently** ADV *'Do you see it?' he demanded urgently.* ♦ **urgency** UNCOUNT N *There was a note of urgency in his voice.*

urinal /jʊraɪnə^{0}l, jʊərɪnə^{0}l/, **urinals.** COUNT N A **urinal** is a bowl or trough fixed to the wall of men's public lavatories for men to urinate in.

urinate /jʊərɪneɪt/, **urinates, urinating, urinated.** VB When you **urinate,** you get rid of urine from your body; a formal use.

urine /jʊərɪn/. UNCOUNT N **Urine** is the liquid that you get rid of from your body when you go to the toilet.

urn /ɜːn/, **urns.** 1 COUNT N An **urn** is a decorated container that is used to hold the ashes of a person who has been cremated. 2 COUNT N A tea **urn** is a container used for making a large quantity of tea and for keeping it warm.

us /ʌs, əs/. PRON **Us** is used as the object of a verb or preposition. A speaker or writer uses **us** to refer to a group of people which includes himself or herself. *Why didn't you tell us?... There wasn't room for us all.*

usable /juːzəbə^{0}l/. ADJ If something is **usable,** it is in a condition which makes it possible to use it. *He told me which wells were usable along the road.*

usage /juːsɪdʒ, -zɪdʒ/, **usages.** 1 UNCOUNT N **Usage** is the way in which words are actually used in particular contexts, especially with regard to their meanings. *...a guide to English usage.* 2 COUNT N A **usage** is a meaning that a word has or a way in which it can be used. 3 UNCOUNT N **Usage** is also the degree to which something is used or the way in which it is used. *...the environmental effects of energy usage.*

use, uses, using, used; pronounced /juːz/ when it is a verb and /juːs/ when it is a noun. 1 VB WITH OBJ If you **use** a particular thing, you do something with it in order to do a job or to achieve something. *Use pins to keep it in place... He wants to use the phone... No violence was used.* 2 VB WITH OBJ If you **use** a particular word or expression, you say or write it. *It's a phrase I once heard him use in a sermon.* 3 VB WITH OBJ If you **use** people, you make them do things for you, without caring about them. *For the first time he felt used.* 4 UNCOUNT N The **use** of something is the act or fact of using it. *...the large-scale use of fertilisers and insecticides... ...a pamphlet for use in schools.* 5 SING N If you have the **use** of something, you have the ability or permission to use it. *He lost the use of his legs... I've got the use of the car this evening.* 6 COUNT N OR UNCOUNT N If something has a **use** or if you have a **use** for it, there is a purpose for which it can be used. *He might later have a use for it... Possibly I could find*

some use for these drawers. 7 COUNT N WITH SUPP A **use** of a word is a way of using it so that it has a particular meaning. *He brooded on her use of the word 'important'.*
PHRASES ● If you **make use of** something, you do something with it in order to do a job or to achieve something. *Industry is making increasing use of robots.* ● If a device, machine, or technique is **in use,** it is being used regularly by people. If it has gone **out of use,** it is no longer used regularly. *Within the next decade industrial robots will be in widespread use.* ● If something is **of use,** it is useful. If it is **no use** , it is not at all useful. *I don't know whether any of these things will be any use to you.* ● You say **it's no use** doing something or **what's the use** of doing something as a way of saying that the action is pointless and will not achieve anything. *It is no use arguing with you... There's no use having regrets.*
use up. PHR VB If you **use up** a supply of something, you finish it so that none of it is left. *He used up all the coins he had.*
used; pronounced /ju:st/ in meanings 1 and 2, and /ju:zd/ in meanings 3 and 4. 1 SEMI-MODAL WITH TO-INF If something **used** to be done or **used** to be the case, it was done regularly in the past or was the case in the past. *They used to send me a card at Christmas time... I used to be very mean.* 2 PHRASE If you **are used to** something, you are familiar with it because you have done or seen it often. If you **get used to** something, you become familiar with it. *San Diego was not used to such demonstrations... We are used to working together... After a few days, I got used to it all.* 3 ATTRIB ADJ A **used** handkerchief, towel, or glass is dirty because it has been used. 4 ATTRIB ADJ A **used** car is not new but has already had an owner.
useful /ju:sfʊl/. 1 ADJ If something is **useful,** you can use it to do something or to help you. *She gave us some useful information.* ♦ **usefulness** UNCOUNT N *...the usefulness of the computer.* 2 ADJ If you are being **useful,** you are doing things that help other people. *Make yourself useful and fry up some bacon.* ♦ **usefully** ADV *His time could be more usefully spent.* 3 PHRASE If a possession or skill **comes in useful,** you are able to use it on a particular occasion; an informal use.
useless /ju:slɪ^{2}s/. 1 ADJ If something is **useless,** you cannot use it. *Land is useless without labour.* 2 ADJ If a course of action is **useless,** it does not achieve anything. *I realized it was useless to pursue the subject.* 3 ADJ If someone is **useless** at something, they are no good at it; an informal use. *I was always useless at maths.*
user /ju:zə/, **users.** COUNT N WITH SUPP The **users** of a product, machine, service, or place are the people who use it. *...vehicle users... ...electricity users.*
usher /ʌʃə/, **ushers, ushering, ushered.** 1 VB WITH OBJ AND ADJUNCT If you **usher** someone somewhere, you show them where they should go, often by going with them. *The hostess ushered me into the room.* 2 COUNT N An **usher** is a person who shows people where to sit, for example at a wedding or concert.
usual /ju:ʒʊ^{0}əl/. 1 ADJ **Usual** is used to describe the thing that happens most often, or that is done or used most often, in a particular situation. *He asked the usual questions... He sat in his usual chair... She got up earlier than usual.* 2 PHRASE You use **as usual** to indicate that you are describing something that normally happens or that is normally the case. *As usual, he spent the night at home... She had to try and carry on as usual.*
usually /ju:ʒʊ^{0}əli^1/. 1 ADV OR SENTENCE ADV If something **usually** happens, it is the thing that most often happens in a particular situation. *She usually found it easy to go to sleep at night.* 2 SUBMOD You use **more than usually** to say that something shows even more of a particular quality than it normally does. *They had shown themselves to be more than usually gullible.*
usurp /ju:zɜ:p/, **usurps, usurping, usurped.** VB WITH OBJ If you **usurp** a title or position, you take it from someone when you have no right to; a formal use.
utensil /ju:tɛnsə^{0}l/, **utensils.** COUNT N **Utensils** are tools or other objects that you use when you are cooking or doing other tasks in your home; a formal use. *The kitchen had no cooker and no proper cooking utensils.*
uterus /ju:tərəs/, **uteruses.** COUNT N A woman's **uterus** is her womb; a medical use.
utilise /ju:tɪlaɪz/. See **utilize.**
utilitarian /ju:tɪlɪtɛəriən/; a formal word. 1 ADJ Something that is **utilitarian** is intended to produce benefit for the greatest number of people possible. 2 ADJ **Utilitarian** objects and buildings are designed to be useful rather than beautiful.
utility /ju:tɪlɪ^{1}ti^1/, **utilities.** 1 UNCOUNT N The **utility** of something is its usefulness. *...the utility and potential of computers.* 2 COUNT N A **utility** is an important service such as water, electricity, or gas that is provided for everyone. *...the development of roads and public utilities in the area.*
utilize /ju:tɪlaɪz/, **utilizes, utilizing, utilized;** also spelled **utilise.** VB WITH OBJ If you **utilize** something, you use it; a formal use. *He thought it impossible to utilize atomic energy.* ♦ **utilization** /ju:tɪlaɪzeɪʃə^{0}n/ UNCOUNT N *...the utilization of things like wind energy and wave-power.*
utmost /ʌtməʊst/. 1 ATTRIB ADJ You use **utmost** to emphasize the quality that you are mentioning. *Learning is of the utmost importance... He had the utmost respect for his children.* 2 SING N If something is done to the **utmost,** it is done to the greatest extent possible. *We will do our utmost to help.*
Utopia /ju:təʊpiə/, **Utopias.** COUNT N OR UNCOUNT N A **Utopia** is a perfect social system in which everyone is satisfied and happy. *Every so often someone invents a new Utopia... ...visions of Utopia.*
utopian /ju:təʊpiən/. ADJ You use **utopian** to refer to the idea of a perfect social system in which everyone is satisfied and happy. *...this utopian dream.*
utter /ʌtə/, **utters, uttering, uttered.** 1 VB WITH OBJ When you **utter** sounds or words, you say them. *Sam opened his mouth, then quickly shut it again without uttering a sound.* 2 ATTRIB ADJ You use **utter** to emphasize something such as a quality or state. *To my utter amazement I was made managing director... Judith is a complete and utter fool.* ♦ **utterly** SUBMOD OR ADV *I am utterly convinced of your loyalty... She was trying to look like a young lady but failing utterly.*
utterance /ʌtə^{0}rəns/, **utterances.** COUNT N An **utterance** is something expressed in speech or writing, such as a word or a sentence; a formal use. *The children watched and copied every act and utterance of the older men.*
U-turn /ju: tɜ:n/, **U-turns.** 1 COUNT N When a vehicle does a **U-turn,** it turns through a half circle and faces or moves in the opposite direction. 2 COUNT N When a government does a **U-turn,** it abandons a policy and does something completely different.

Vv

vacancy /veɪkənsi^1/, **vacancies.** 1 COUNT N A **vacancy** is a job or position which has not been filled. *...an unexpected vacancy in the Department.* 2 COUNT N If there are **vacancies** at a hotel, some of the rooms are available for people to stay in.
vacant /veɪkənt/. 1 ADJ If something is **vacant,** it is not being used by anyone. *I sat down in a vacant chair.* 2 ADJ If a job or position is **vacant,** it has not yet been filled. *They keep a list of all vacant jobs in the area.* 3 ADJ A **vacant** look suggests that someone does not understand or that they are not very intelligent. *She looked round with a rather vacant expression.*
vacate /vəkeɪt/, **vacates, vacating, vacated.** VB WITH OBJ If you **vacate** a place or a job, you leave it and make it available for other people. *He ordered her to vacate her apartment... I got the job Allister was vacating.*
vacation /vəkeɪʃə^{0}n/, **vacations.** 1 COUNT N A **vacation** is a period of the year when universities or colleges are officially closed. *I've a lot of reading to do over the vacation... ...the summer vacation.* 2 COUNT N OR UNCOUNT N A **vacation** is also a holiday; an American use. *Harold used to take a vacation at that time... She plans to go on vacation for most of August.*
vaccinate /væksɪneɪt/, **vaccinates, vaccinating, vaccinated.** VB WITH OBJ If you **are vaccinated** against a disease, you are given an injection to prevent you from getting it. *Most of them were vaccinated against hepatitis.* ♦ **vaccination** /væksɪneɪʃə^{0}n/ UNCOUNT N OR COUNT N *...vaccination against smallpox.*
vaccine /væksi:n/, **vaccines.** COUNT N OR UNCOUNT N A **vaccine** is a substance containing the germs that cause a disease which is given to people to prevent them getting the disease. *...the measles vaccine... ...polio vaccine.*
vacillate /væsɪleɪt/, **vacillates, vacillating, vacillated.** VB If you **vacillate** between two alternatives or choices, you keep changing your mind; a formal use. *He vacillated between periods of creative fever and nervous exhaustion.*
vacuum /vækju^{0}əm/, **vacuums.** 1 COUNT N A **vacuum** is a space that contains no air or other gas. 2 COUNT N If someone or something creates a **vacuum,** they leave a place or position which then needs to be filled by someone or something else. *Rival groups would seek to fill the power vacuum that the departing British would leave.*
vacuum cleaner, vacuum cleaners. COUNT N A **vacuum cleaner** is an electric machine which sucks up dust and dirt from carpets.
vagina /vədʒaɪnə/, **vaginas.** COUNT N A woman's **vagina** is the passage connecting her outer sex organs to her womb.
vagrant /veɪgrənt/, **vagrants.** COUNT N A **vagrant** is a person who moves from place to place and has no regular home or job.
vague /veɪg/, **vaguer, vaguest.** 1 ADJ If something is **vague,** it is not explained, expressed, or experienced clearly. *The terms of the agreement were left deliberately vague... ...vague instructions... I realized with a vague feeling of surprise that he had gone... ...a vague recollection.* ♦ **vaguely** ADV *I vaguely remember their house.* 2 PRED ADJ If you are **vague** about something, you avoid telling people about it. *They were vague and evasive about their backgrounds.* 3 ADJ A **vague** shape is not clear or easy to see. *It appeared in vague form at first and then in sharper outline.*
vain /veɪn/. 1 PHRASE If you do something **in vain,** you do not succeed in achieving what you intend. *We tried in vain to discover what had happened... Your son didn't die in vain.* 2 ATTRIB ADJ A **vain** attempt or action is not successful. *...the teacher's vain plea for silence.* ♦ **vainly** ADV *She vainly attempted to open the door.* 3 ADJ A **vain** person is extremely proud of their beauty, intelligence, or other good qualities; used showing disapproval. *...a vain young aristocrat.*
vale /veɪl/, **vales.** COUNT N A **vale** is a valley; a literary use.
valentine /væləntaɪn/, **valentines.** COUNT N A **valentine** or a **valentine card** is a card that you send to someone you love on St Valentine's Day.
valet /vælɪt, væleɪ/, **valets.** COUNT N A **valet** is a male servant who looks after his male employer by doing things such as caring for his clothes.
valiant /væljənt/. ADJ **Valiant** means very brave. *...a valiant attempt to rescue the struggling victim.*
valid /vælɪd/. 1 ADJ Something that is **valid** is based on sound reasoning. *This is a valid argument against economic growth... This was the real reason, and it was a valid reason.* ♦ **validity** /vəlɪdɪti^1/ UNCOUNT N *We should question the validity of those figures.* 2 ADJ If a ticket or document is **valid,** it can be used and will be accepted by people in authority. *It's valid for six months from the date of issue.*
validate /vælɪdeɪt/, **validates, validating, validated.** VB WITH OBJ If something **validates** a statement or claim, it proves that it is true or correct. *Their remarkable achievement seems to validate Bomberg's claim.*
Valium /væliəm/. UNCOUNT N **Valium** is a drug which is given to people to calm their nerves; a trademark.
valley /væli^1/, **valleys.** COUNT N A **valley** is a long, narrow area of land between hills, often with a river flowing through it.
valuable /vælju^{0}əbə^{0}l/, **valuables.** 1 ADJ **Valuable** help or advice is very useful. *They could also give valuable help.* 2 ADJ **Valuable** objects such as paintings or jewellery are worth a lot of money. *She collected vintage cars and built up a valuable stamp collection.* Also PLURAL N *They were robbed of money and valuables at gunpoint.*
valuation /væljʊeɪʃə^{0}n/, **valuations.** 1 COUNT N OR UNCOUNT N A **valuation** is a judgement about how much money something is worth. *The land's valuation was £6,000.* 2 COUNT N OR UNCOUNT N A **valuation** is also a judgement about how good or bad something is. *...his rather low valuation of the novel.*
value /vælju:/, **values, valuing, valued.** 1 UNCOUNT N The **value** of something such as a quality or a method is its importance or usefulness. *Everyone realizes the value of sincerity... It should have novelty value, if nothing else.* 2 UNCOUNT N OR COUNT N The **value** of something you can own is the amount of money that it is worth. *What will happen to the value of my property?* 3 PLURAL N The **values** of a person or group are their moral principles and beliefs. *...the traditional values of civility and moderation... They have different values from the families they serve.* 4 VB WITH OBJ If you **value** something, you think that it is important and you appreciate it. *Which do you value most—wealth or health?* ♦ **valued** ADJ *...one of our valued customers.* 5 VB WITH OBJ When experts **value** something, they decide how much money it is worth. *The table silver was valued at £20,000.*
PHRASES ● Something that is **good value** or **value for money** is worth the money it costs. *The set lunch is good value at £5.95.* ● Something that is **of value** is useful or important. *Nothing of value can be said about this matter.* ● If you put **a high value** on something, you think that it is very important. *He places a high value on educating his children.* ● If you **take a remark or action at face value,** you accept it

without thinking what its real meaning or purpose might be. *She took the praise at face value.*

valueless /vǽljuːl²s/. ADJ Something that is **valueless** is not effective or useful. *...involvement in valueless activities.*

valve /vǽlv/, **valves**. 1 COUNT N A **valve** is a part attached to a pipe or a tube which controls the flow of a gas or liquid. *...a radiator valve.* 2 See also **safety-valve**.

vampire /vǽmpaɪə/, **vampires**. COUNT N In horror stories, **vampires** are people who come out of their graves at night and suck the blood of living people.

van /vǽn/, **vans**. COUNT N A **van** is a vehicle like a large car or small lorry that is used for carrying goods.

vandal /vǽndə²l/, **vandals**. COUNT N A **vandal** is someone who deliberately damages things, especially public property. *The phone box is attacked by vandals from time to time.*

vandalise /vǽndəlaɪz/. See **vandalize**.

vandalism /vǽndəlɪzə²m/. UNCOUNT N **Vandalism** is the deliberate damaging of things, especially public property. *These housing estates suffer from widespread vandalism.*

vandalize /vǽndəlaɪz/, **vandalizes**, **vandalizing**, **vandalized**; also spelled **vandalise**. VB WITH OBJ If someone **vandalizes** something, they damage it on purpose. *All our telephones were vandalized.*

vanguard /vǽngɑːd/. SING N If someone is in the **vanguard** of something such as a revolution or an area of research, they are involved in the most advanced part of it. *They are in the vanguard of technological advance.*

vanilla /vənɪlə/. UNCOUNT N **Vanilla** is a flavouring used in ice cream and other sweet food. *...vanilla ice-cream... ...vanilla fudge.*

vanish /vǽnɪʃ/, **vanishes**, **vanishing**, **vanished**. VB If something **vanishes**, it disappears suddenly or ceases to exist altogether. *The car had vanished from sight... Madeleine vanished without trace... ...laws to protect vanishing American species.*

vanity /vǽnɪ²tɪ/. UNCOUNT N **Vanity** is a feeling of pride about your appearance or abilities; used showing disapproval. *He refused to wear glasses. It was sheer vanity.*

vanquish /vǽnkwɪʃ/, **vanquishes**, **vanquishing**, **vanquished**. VB WITH OBJ If you are **vanquished**, you are defeated completely in a battle or a competition; a literary use. *All their enemies were vanquished.*

vantage point /vɑːntɪdʒ pɔɪnt/, **vantage points**. COUNT N A **vantage point** is a place from which you can see a lot of things. *From the vantage point on the hill, Port Philip shimmered beneath them.*

vapour /veɪpə/; spelled **vapor** in American English. UNCOUNT N **Vapour** is a mass of tiny drops of water or other liquids in the air, which appear as a mist. *...water vapour... ...a little cloud of exhaust vapour.*

variability /veəri²əbɪlɪ²tɪ/. UNCOUNT N The **variability** of something is the range of different forms that it can take. *...the enormous variability you get in speech sounds.*

variable /veəri²əbəl/, **variables**. 1 ADJ Something that is **variable** is likely to change at any time. *In the tropics, rainfall is notoriously variable.* 2 COUNT N A **variable** is a factor in a situation that can change. *How long your shoes will last depends on a lot of variables, such as how much you weigh, how far you walk, and so on.* 3 COUNT N In mathematics, a **variable** is an expression that can have any one of a set of values; a technical use.

variance /veəri²əns/. PHRASE If one thing is **at variance** with another, the two things seem to contradict each other; a formal use. *Nothing in the story was at variance with what he understood to be true.*

variant /veəri²ənt/, **variants**. COUNT N A **variant** of something has a different form from the usual one. *This American bird is a variant of the English buzzard.* Also ATTRIB ADJ *...a variant form of the basic action.*

variation /veəri²eɪʃə²n/, **variations**. 1 COUNT N A **variation** on something is the same thing presented in a different form. *...the same programme with only nightly variations... His books are all variations on a basic theme.* 2 COUNT N OR UNCOUNT N A **variation** is also a change in a level, amount, or quantity. *The Boards have learned how to cope with a large variation in demand for electricity... Plants were observed for variation in flowering dates.*

varicose veins /vǽrɪkə²s veɪnz/. PLURAL N **Varicose veins** are swollen and painful veins in a person's legs which sometimes need to be operated on.

varied /veərɪd/. 1 **Varied** is the past tense and past participle of **vary**. 2 ADJ Something that is **varied** consists of things of different types, sizes, or qualities. *The work of a JP is very varied.*

variety /vəraɪ¹tɪ/, **varieties**. 1 UNCOUNT N If something has **variety**, it consists of things which are different from each other. *Those are the holiday brochures that give you the most variety.* 2 SING N If you have a **variety** of things, you have a number of different kinds of them. *The college library had a wide variety of books.* 2 COUNT N A **variety** of something is a type of it. *...three varieties of whisky.* 4 UNCOUNT N **Variety** is a type of entertainment including many different kinds of acts in the same show. *...a high-quality variety show.*

various /veərɪəs/. 1 ATTRIB ADJ If you say that there are **various** things, you mean there are several different things of the type mentioned. *There were various questions he wanted to ask... ...various bits of information... The birth had been delayed for various reasons.* 2 PRED ADJ If a number of things are described as **various**, they are very different from one another. *His excuses are many and various.*

variously /veərɪəslɪ¹/. ADV **Variously** is used to introduce a number of different ways in which something is described. *He married a Japanese lady who was variously described as a painter and a film maker.*

varnish /vɑːnɪʃ/, **varnishes**, **varnishing**, **varnished**. 1 MASS N **Varnish** is an oily liquid which is painted onto wood to give it a hard, clear, shiny surface. 2 SING N The **varnish** on an object is the hard, clear, shiny surface that it has when it has been painted with varnish. *The varnish was slightly chipped.* 3 VB WITH OBJ If you **varnish** something, you paint it with varnish. *He has varnished the table.*

vary /veərɪ¹/, **varies**, **varying**, **varied**. 1 VB If things **vary**, they change or are different in size, amount, or degree. *The fees vary a lot... The screens will vary in size depending upon what one wants... The colour of the fruit varies with age.* ◆ **varying** ATTRIB ADJ *Its members have widely varying views on foreign policy.* 2 VB WITH OBJ If you **vary** something that you do, you keep changing the way that you do it. *He took special care to vary his daily routine.* 3 See also **varied**.

vase /vɑːz/, **vases**. COUNT N A **vase** is a jar, usually made of glass or pottery which is used for holding cut or dried flowers or as an ornament.

vasectomy /vəˈsektəmɪ/, **vasectomies**. COUNT N OR UNCOUNT N A **vasectomy** is a surgical operation to sterilize a man.

vast /vɑːst/. ADJ Something that is **vast** is extremely large. *...a vast organization... ...the roads that they're building at vast expense.*

vastly /vɑːstlɪ¹/. SUBMOD **Vastly** means very much or to a very large extent. *Management of the factory could be vastly improved.*

vat /vǽt/, **vats**. COUNT N A **vat** is a large barrel or tank for storing liquids. *...a vat of water.*

VAT /viː eɪ tiː, vǽt/. UNCOUNT N **VAT** is a tax that is added to the price of goods or services.

vault /vɔːlt/, **vaults**, **vaulting**, **vaulted**. 1 COUNT N A **vault** is a secure room where money and other valuable things can be kept safely. *The money was deposited in the vaults of a firm of solicitors.* 2 COUNT N The **vault** of a church or cemetery is the place where people are buried. 3 COUNT N A **vault** is also an arched roof or ceiling. 4 VB WITH OBJ OR ADJUNCT If you **vault** something or **vault** over it, you jump over it, putting one or both of your hands on it. *They vaulted effortlessly over the wall.*

VD /viː diː/. **VD** is an abbreviation for venereal disease.

VDU /viː diː juː/, **VDUs**. COUNT N A **VDU** is a machine with a screen which is used to display information from a computer. **VDU** is an abbreviation for 'visual display unit'.

veal /viːl/. UNCOUNT N **Veal** is meat from a calf.

veer /vɪə/, **veers**, **veering**, **veered**. VB WITH ADJUNCT If something that is moving **veers** in a particular direction, it suddenly starts moving in that direction. *He veered away from a tree... The plane seemed to veer off to one side.*

vegetable /vedʒɪ²təbə²l/, **vegetables**. 1 COUNT N **Vegetables** are plants such as cabbages, potatoes, and onions which you can cook and eat. 2 UNCOUNT N **Vegetable** is used to refer to plants in general. *...vegetable matter.*

vegetarian /vedʒɪteərɪən/, **vegetarians**. COUNT N A **vegetarian** is someone who does not eat meat or fish. *...a strict vegetarian.* Also ADJ *...a vegetarian diet.*

vegetate /vedʒɪteɪt/, **vegetates**, **vegetating**, **vegetated**. VB If you **vegetate**, you have a very boring life with little to interest you. *Many elderly folk vegetate and die in loneliness.*

vegetation /vedʒɪteɪʃə²n/. UNCOUNT N **Vegetation** is plant life in general. *The forest floor is not rich in vegetation.*

vehemence /viːə¹məns/. UNCOUNT N **Vehemence** is intense and violent emotion, especially anger. *...the hate and vehemence in Hubert's eyes.*

vehement /viːə¹mənt/. ADJ Someone who is **vehement** has strong feelings or opinions and expresses them forcefully. *They are vehement in their praises of the new system.* ◆ **vehemently** ADV *They were arguing vehemently.*

vehicle /viːɪkə²l/, **vehicles**. 1 COUNT N A **vehicle** is a machine with an engine such as a car or bus that carries people or things from place to place. *We saw a vehicle travelling across the bridge.* 2 COUNT N A **vehicle** is also something that is used to achieve a particular purpose; a formal use. *They saw education as a vehicle of liberation... They support the Labour Party as a vehicle for socialism.*

veil /veɪl/, **veils**. 1 COUNT N A **veil** is a piece of thin, soft cloth that women sometimes wear over their heads. 2 SING N WITH 'of' You can refer to something that conceals something else as a **veil**; a literary use. *Everything was wrapped in a veil of evening light... The research centre shrouded its communications with every possible veil of secrecy.*

veiled /veɪld/. ATTRIB ADJ A **veiled** comment is expressed in a disguised form rather than directly and openly *...thinly veiled criticism... ...veiled threats.*

vein /veɪn/, **veins**. 1 COUNT N Your **veins** are the tubes in your body through which your blood flows. ◆ See also **varicose veins**. 2 COUNT N The **veins** on a leaf are the thin lines on it. 3 COUNT N WITH SUPP A **vein** of a metal or mineral is a layer of it in rock. *...the world's richest vein of copper.* 4 UNCOUNT N WITH SUPP Something that is written or spoken in a particular **vein** is written or spoken in that style or mood. *The letter continued in this vein for several pages.*

velocity /vɪ¹lɒsɪ¹tɪ¹/, **velocities**. UNCOUNT N OR COUNT N **Velocity** is the speed at which something moves; a technical use. *...the velocity of light.*

velvet /velvɪt/. UNCOUNT N **Velvet** is soft material with a thick layer of short, cut threads on one side. *...velvet curtains.*

velvety /velvɪ¹tɪ¹/. ADJ Something that is **velvety** is soft to touch and has the appearance of velvet. *The spider has a velvety black body.*

vendetta /vendetə/, **vendettas**. COUNT N A **vendetta** is a long-lasting, bitter quarrel between people in which they attempt to harm each other. *He conducted a vendetta against Haldane behind the scenes.*

vending machine /vendɪŋ məʃiːn/, **vending machines**. COUNT N A **vending machine** is a machine from which you can get things such as cigarettes, chocolate, or coffee by putting in money and pressing a button.

vendor /vendə⁸/, **vendors**. 1 COUNT N A **vendor** is someone who sells things such as newspapers, cigarettes, or hamburgers from a small stall or cart. *...cigarette vendors.* 2 COUNT N The **vendor** of a house or piece of land is the person who owns it and is selling it; a technical use.

veneer /vɪ¹nɪə/. 1 SING N Behaviour that hides someone's real feelings or character is called a **veneer**. *He hides his values beneath a veneer of scientific objectivity.* 2 UNCOUNT N **Veneer** is a thin layer of wood or plastic which is used to improve the appearance of something. *...a table whose veneer had come loose.*

venerable /venə²rəbə²l/. ADJ **Venerable** people are people who are entitled to respect because they are old and wise; a formal use. *...the venerable head of the house.*

venereal disease /vəˈnɪərɪəl dɪziːz/, **venereal diseases**. COUNT N OR UNCOUNT N A **venereal disease** is a disease that is passed on by having sex.

Venetian blind /vəniːʃə²n blaɪnd/, **Venetian blinds**. COUNT N A **Venetian blind** is a window blind made of thin horizontal strips which can be adjusted to let in more or less light.

vengeance /vendʒəns/. 1 UNCOUNT N **Vengeance** is the act of killing, injuring, or harming someone because they have harmed you; a formal use. *I want vengeance for the deaths of my parents and sisters.* 2 PHRASE If something happens **with a vengeance**, it happens to a much greater extent than was expected. *He now broke the rules with a vengeance.*

vengeful /vendʒful/. ADJ If you are **vengeful**, you feel a great desire for revenge; a literary use.

venison /venɪ²zən, -sən/. UNCOUNT N **Venison** is meat from a deer.

venom /venəm/. 1 UNCOUNT N **Venom** is a feeling of great bitterness or anger towards someone. *'What a filthy trick,' she said with unexpected venom.* 2 UNCOUNT N The **venom** of a snake, scorpion, or spider is the poison that it injects into you when it bites or stings you.

venomous /venəməs/. 1 ADJ A **venomous** snake, scorpion, or spider uses poison to attack its enemy or prey. **2** ADJ **Venomous** behaviour shows great bitterness or anger. ...*venomous glances.*

vent /vɛnt/, **vents, venting, vented. 1** COUNT N A **vent** is a hole in something through which air can come in and smoke, gas, or smells can go out. ...*the air vents of the bunkers.* **2** VB WITH OBJ If you **vent** your feelings, you express them forcefully; a formal use. *He vented his rage on Bernard.*

ventilate /vɛntɪleɪt/, **ventilates, ventilating, ventilated.** VB WITH OBJ To **ventilate** a room or building means to allow fresh air to get into it. *The air becomes thick if it is not ventilated by fans.* ♦ **ventilated** ADJ ...*badly ventilated houses.* ♦ **ventilation** /vɛntɪleɪʃ°n/ UNCOUNT N The only ventilation was through a small door at the back.

ventilator /vɛntɪleɪtə/, **ventilators.** COUNT N A **ventilator** is a device which lets fresh air into a room or building and lets stale air out.

venture /vɛntʃə/, **ventures, venturing, ventured. 1** COUNT N A **venture** is something new, exciting, and difficult which involves the risk of failure. ...*an interesting scientific venture... The number of successful new business ventures is dwindling.* **2** VB WITH ADJUNCT If you **venture** into an activity, you do something that involves the risk of failure because it is new and different. *I might actually venture into advertising if I had enough money.* **3** REPORT VB OR VB WITH TO-INF If you **venture** an opinion, you say it cautiously and hesitantly because you are afraid it might be foolish or wrong. *'I'd make a good husband,' he ventured... No one has ventured to suggest why this should be.* **4** VB WITH ADJUNCT If you **venture** somewhere you go there, although it might be dangerous. *He wouldn't venture far from his mother's door.*

venue /vɛnjuː/, **venues.** COUNT N The **venue** for an event or activity is the place where it will happen; a formal use.

veranda /vərændə/, **verandas;** also spelled **verandah.** COUNT N A **veranda** is a platform with a roof along the outside wall of a house.

verb /vɜːb/, **verbs.** COUNT N In grammar, a **verb** is a word which you use with a subject to say what someone or something does, or what happens to them.

verbal /vɜːb°l/. **1** ADJ You use **verbal** to describe things connected with words and their use. *It was a contest in verbal skills.* **2** ADJ **Verbal** refers to things that are spoken rather than written. ...*a succession of verbal attacks on the chairman.* ♦ **verbally** ADV *I will communicate your views verbally.* **3** ADJ **Verbal** also describes something that relates to verbs. ...*the structure of verbal groups in English.*

verbatim /vɜːbeɪtɪm/. ADV OR ADJ If you repeat something **verbatim,** you use exactly the same words as were used originally; a formal use. *The rules for last year's contest were reprinted verbatim... It was almost a verbatim quotation of the article.*

verdict /vɜːdɪkt/, **verdicts. 1** COUNT N In a law court, a **verdict** is the decision whether a prisoner is guilty or not guilty. *The jury gave a verdict of not guilty.* **2** COUNT N Your **verdict** on something is your opinion of it, after thinking about it. *The critics hated the film, but the public verdict was favourable.*

verge /vɜːdʒ/, **verges, verging, verged. 1** PHRASE If you are **on the verge** of something, you are about to do it or it is about to happen. *The unions are on the verge of settling their latest pay dispute... ...people living on the verge of starvation.* **2** COUNT N The **verge** of a road is a narrow strip of grass at the side. ...*a grass verge.*

verge on or **verge upon** PHR VB Something that **verges on** or **verges upon** something else is almost the same as it. *I had a feeling of distrust verging on panic. ...direct action verging on violence.*

verify /vɛrɪfaɪ/, **verifies, verifying, verified.** VB WITH OBJ If you **verify** something, you check or confirm that it is true. ...*evidence that could be tested and verified... I was asked to verify or deny this suggestion.* ♦ **verification** /vɛrɪfɪkeɪʃ°n/ UNCOUNT N *Any hypothesis must depend for its verification on observable evidence.*

veritable /vɛrɪtəb°l/. ATTRIB ADJ You use **veritable** when you are exaggerating, often humorously, in order to emphasize a feature that something has. *His toilet flushed like a veritable Niagara.*

vermin /vɜːmɪn/. PLURAL N **Vermin** are small animals such as rats and mice, which can carry diseases. *Wild cats are treated as vermin, and are poisoned.*

vernacular /vənækjʊlə/, **vernaculars.** COUNT N The **vernacular** of a country or region is the language most widely spoken there. *'Who is it?' asked Ash in the vernacular.*

versatile /vɜːsətaɪl/. **1** ADJ A **versatile** person has many different skills. *He's the most versatile of actors.* **2** ADJ **Versatile** tool, machine, or material can be used for many different purposes. ...*this extremely versatile new kitchen machine.*

verse /vɜːs/, **verses. 1** UNCOUNT N **Verse** is writing arranged in lines with a rhythm which often rhymes at the end. *She used to write plays in verse.* **2** COUNT N A **verse** is one of the parts into which a poem, a song, or a chapter of the Bible is divided.

versed /vɜːst/. PHRASE If you **are versed in** something, you know a lot about it; a formal use. *She is well versed in French history.*

version /vɜːʃ°n, -ʒ°n/, **versions. 1** COUNT N WITH SUPP A **version** of something is a form of it in which some details are different from earlier or later forms. *She asked a different version of the question... ...the 1939 film version of 'Wuthering Heights'.* **2** COUNT N WITH SUPP Someone's **version** of an event is their description of what happened. *Each of the women had a different version of what actually happened.*

versus /vɜːsəs/. **1** PREP You use **versus** to say that two ideas or things are opposed. ...*the problem of determinism versus freedom.* **2** PREP **Versus** is also used to say that two people or teams are competing against each other in a sporting event. *The big match tonight is England versus Spain.*

vertebra /vɜːtɪbrə/, **vertebrae** /vɜːtɪbriː/. COUNT N Your **vertebrae** are the small bones in your spine.

vertebrate /vɜːtɪbreɪt, -brə't/, **vertebrates.** COUNT N A **vertebrate** is a creature such as a mammal or bird which has a backbone; a technical use.

vertical /vɜːtɪk°l/. ADJ Something that is **vertical** stands or points straight upwards. *The monument consists of a horizontal slab supported by two vertical pillars... A vertical line divides the page into two halves.* ♦ **vertically** ADV *The human brain is divided vertically down the middle into two hemispheres.*

vertigo /vɜːtɪgəʊ/. UNCOUNT N **Vertigo** is a feeling of dizziness, especially caused by looking down from a high place. *Looking out of the window gives him vertigo.*

very /vɛrɪ¹/. **1** SUBMOD You use **very** in front of adverbs or adjectives in order to emphasize them. ...*a very small child... Think very carefully... I liked it very much.* **2** ATTRIB ADJ You use **very** with nouns to emphasize a point in space or time. *I walked up to the very top... We were there from the very beginning.* **3** ATTRIB ADJ You also use **very** with nouns to emphasize that something is exactly right or exactly the same as something else. *The very man I've been looking for!... Those are the very words he used.*
PHRASES ● You say **very much so** as an emphatic way of saying 'yes'. *'Did your father resist this?'—'Very much so.'* ● You can say **very well** when you agree to do something; a formal use. *'Mr Brown wants to see you.'—'Very well. I'll be along in a moment.'*

vessel /vɛs°l/, **vessels. 1** COUNT N A **vessel** is a large ship; a formal use. ...*fishing vessels.* **2** COUNT N A **vessel** is also a bowl or other container for liquid; a literary use. ...*sacred vessels.* **3** See also **blood vessel.**

vest /vɛst/, **vests. 1** COUNT N A **vest** is a piece of underwear which is worn to keep the top part of your body warm; a British use. **2** COUNT N A **vest** is also a waistcoat; an American use.

vested /vɛstɪ²d/. PRED ADJ WITH 'in' Something that is **vested** in someone is given to them as a right or responsibility; a formal use. ...*the authority vested in him by the State of Massachusetts.*

vested interest, vested interests. 1 COUNT N If you have a **vested interest** in something, you have a strong reason for acting in a particular way to protect your own money, power, or reputation. *They have vested interests in farming and forestry... They share a common vested interest in a strong modern army.*

vestige /vɛstɪdʒ/, **vestiges.** COUNT N If there is no **vestige** of something, there is not even a small part of it left; a formal use. ...*a country without any vestige of political freedom.*

vet /vɛt/, **vets, vetting, vetted. 1** COUNT N A **vet** is someone who is qualified to treat sick or injured animals; a British use. *Get your kitten checked by the vet.* **2** VB WITH OBJ When someone or something **is vetted,** they are carefully checked to make sure that they are acceptable; a British use. *His speeches were vetted... He was thoroughly vetted.* ♦ **vetting** UNCOUNT N *He wanted to tighten the security vetting of civil servants.*

veteran /vɛtə°rən/, **veterans. 1** COUNT N A **veteran** is someone who has served in the armed forces of their country, especially during a war. ...*a World War Two veteran.* **2** COUNT N A **veteran** is also someone who has been involved in a particular activity for a long time. ...*a veteran of the civil rights movement.*

veterinarian /vɛtə°rɪnɛərɪən/, **veterinarians.** COUNT N A **veterinarian** is someone who is qualified to treat sick or injured animals; an American use.

veterinary /vɛtə°rɪnə°rɪ¹/. ATTRIB ADJ **Veterinary** refers to the medical treatment of animals. *They had a veterinary practice in Perth.*

veterinary surgeon, veterinary surgeons. COUNT N A **veterinary surgeon** is the same as a vet; a formal British use.

veto /viːtəʊ/, **vetoes, vetoing, vetoed. 1** VB WITH OBJ If someone in authority **vetoes** something, they forbid it. *The government vetoed this proposal.* Also COUNT N *The rest of the committee could not accept the veto.* **2** UNCOUNT N **Veto** is the right that someone in authority has to forbid something. ...*the Sovereign's power of veto.*

vex /vɛks/, **vexes, vexing, vexed.** VB WITH OBJ If something **vexes** you, it makes you feel annoyed; a formal use. *It vexed her to be ignored like this.*

vexed /vɛkst/. **1** ADJ If you are **vexed,** you are annoyed and slightly puzzled. *Feeling vexed, I spoke up for myself.* **2** ATTRIB ADJ A **vexed** problem or question is very difficult and causes people a lot of trouble. *This leads to the vexed issue of priorities.*

via /vaɪə, viːə/. **1** PREP If you go to one place **via** another, you go through the second place to your destination. ...*a ticket to Washington via Frankfurt and New York.* **2** PREP **Via** also means done or achieved using a particular thing or person. ...*the transmission of television pictures via satellite... It was so kind of you to send that message via Toby.*

viable /vaɪəb°l/. ADJ Something that is **viable** is capable of doing what it is intended to do. ...*viable alternatives to petrol... ...a viable project.* ♦ **viability** /vaɪəbɪlɪ'tɪ¹/ UNCOUNT N ...*the commercial viability of the new product.*

viaduct /vaɪədʌkt/, **viaducts.** COUNT N A **viaduct** is a long, high bridge that carries a road or railway across a valley.

vibrant /vaɪbrənt/. **1** ADJ Something or someone that is **vibrant** is full of life, energy, and enthusiasm. *His vibrant talk fascinated and excited me... ...the vibrant tones of Richard Burton.* **2** ADJ **Vibrant** colours are very bright. ...*a flower bed vibrant with red tulips.*

vibrate /vaɪbreɪt/, **vibrates, vibrating, vibrated.** VB When something **vibrates,** it shakes with a slight, very quick movement. *The foundation of the city began to rumble and vibrate.* ♦ **vibration** /vaɪbreɪʃ°n/ COUNT N OR UNCOUNT N *Your fingers feel the vibration on the violin string.*

vicar /vɪkə/, **vicars.** COUNT N A **vicar** is a priest in the Church of England.

vicarage /vɪkərɪdʒ/, **vicarages.** COUNT N A **vicarage** is a house in which a vicar lives.

vicarious /vɪkɛərɪəs, vaɪ-/. ATTRIB ADJ A **vicarious** pleasure or feeling is one that you experience by watching, listening to, or reading about other people doing something, rather than by doing it yourself. ...*a vicarious sense of power and adventure.*

vice /vaɪs/, **vices;** spelled **vise** in American English in meaning 3. **1** COUNT N A **vice** is a moral fault in someone's character or behaviour. ...*human vices such as greed and envy... Her one small vice was smoking.* **2** UNCOUNT N **Vice** is the criminal activities connected with pornography, prostitution, drugs, or gambling. ...*a campaign against vice and violence... ...strict vice laws.* **3** COUNT N A **vice** is also a tool that you use to hold an object tightly while you work on it.

vice-chancellor, vice-chancellors. COUNT N The **vice-chancellor** is the head of academic and administrative matters in British Universities.

vice versa /vaɪsə vɜːsə/. PHRASE **Vice versa** is used to indicate that the reverse of what you have said is also true. For example, 'Women may bring their husbands with them, and vice versa' means that men may also bring their wives with them.

vicinity /vɪsɪnɪ'tɪ¹/. SING N If something is in the **vicinity** of a place, it is in the nearby area. *The hotels in the vicinity of the campus were cheap and shabby.*

vicious /vɪʃəs/. ADJ Someone or something that is **vicious** is cruel and violent. ...*a vicious killer.* ♦ **viciously** ADV *He twisted her wrist viciously.*

vicious circle. SING N A **vicious circle** is a situation in which a difficulty causes a new difficulty which then causes the original difficulty to occur again. *Punishment always forms a vicious circle.*

victim /vɪktɪm/, **victims.** COUNT N A **victim** is someone who has been hurt or killed by someone or something. *Most of the victims were shot in the back while trying to run away... ...a rape victim.*

victimize /vɪktɪmaɪz/, **victimizes, victimizing, victimized;** also spelled **victimise.** VB WITH OBJ If someone **is victimized,** they are deliberately treated unfairly. *Management insisted that she was not being victimized.* ♦ **victimization** /vɪktɪmaɪzeɪʃ°n/ UNCOUNT N *There must be no victimization of workers.*

victor /vɪktə/, **victors.** COUNT N The **victor** in a contest or battle is the person who wins; an old-fashioned use. *...the victor of Waterloo... He emerged as the victor over Mulder.*

Victorian /vɪktɔːrɪən/. 1 ADJ **Victorian** describes things that were made in Britain when Victoria was the Queen, between 1837-1901. *...Victorian architecture.* 2 ADJ You say that someone is **Victorian** when they believe in strict discipline and morals. *His parents were very Victorian and very domineering.*

victorious /vɪktɔːrɪəs/. ADJ Someone who is **victorious** has won a victory, especially in a war.

victory /vɪktə^{0}ri^{1}/, **victories.** COUNT N OR UNCOUNT N A **victory** is a success in a war or a competition. *In A.D. 636, an Arab army won a famous victory over a much larger Persian force... Nobody believed he had any chance of victory.*

video /vɪdɪəʊ/, **videos, videoing, videoed.** 1 UNCOUNT N **Video** is the recording and showing of films and events, using a video recorder, video tapes, and a television set. *I know that you use video for teaching these students.* 2 COUNT N A **video** is a video recorder. *Turn off the video.* 3 COUNT N A **video** is also a film or television programme recorded on video tape for people to watch on a television set. *I've seen this video before.* 4 VB WITH OBJ If you **video** something, you record it on magnetic tape, either by using a television camera and recording the actual events, or by using a video to record a television programme as it is being transmitted, in order to watch it later.

video recorder, video recorders. COUNT N A **video recorder** is a machine that can record and play video tapes on a television set.

videotape, /vɪdɪəʊteɪp/, **videotapes.** UNCOUNT N OR COUNT N **Videotape** is magnetic tape that is used to record pictures or films which you can then play back and watch on a television set. *It's all down on videotape, you see... They saw the videotapes of Mr Frost's interviews.*

vie /vaɪ/, **vies, vying, vied.** RECIP VB If you **vie** with someone, you try hard to do something sooner or better than they do; a formal use. *The artists vied for the prime sites... ...vying with each other to express their disgust.*

view /vjuː/, **views, viewing, viewed.** 1 COUNT N Your **view** on a particular subject is your opinion about it. *I've changed my view on this issue... He was sent to jail for his political views.* 2 SING N WITH SUPP Your **view** of something is your attitude to it and the way you understand it. *She has a view of life which is deeply corrupt... He tends to take a wider, more overall view of things.* 3 VB WITH OBJ AND ADJUNCT If you **view** something in a particular way, you think of it in that way. *Their missiles are viewed as a defensive and deterrent force.* 4 COUNT N The **view** from a particular place is everything you can see from it. *From the top there is a fine view.* 5 SING N WITH SUPP If you have a **view** of something, you can see it. *The driver blocked his view.* 6 VB WITH OBJ If you **view** something, you look at it; a formal use. *...a drop of water from a pond, viewed through a microscope.*

PHRASES ● You use **in my view** to emphasize that you are stating your opinion. *In my view, we have a long way to go before we have a United States of Europe.* ● If you **take the view that** something is true, your opinion is that it is true. ● You use **in view of** to specify the main fact or event that causes you to do, say, or think something. *In view of the fact that all the other members of the group are going, I think you should go too.* ● If you do something **with a view to** a particular result, you do it to achieve that result. *We have exchanged letters with a view to meeting to discuss these problems.* ● If something is **in view,** you can see it from where you are. *We crept around the cage to keep the monkey in view.* ● If something is **on view,** it is being exhibited in public. *The Turner exhibition is on view at the Tate Gallery.* ● See also **point of view.**

viewer /vjuːə/, **viewers.** COUNT N A **viewer** is someone who watches television.

viewpoint /vjuːpɔɪnt/, **viewpoints.** 1 COUNT N WITH SUPP Someone's **viewpoint** is the way that they think about things in general or about a particular thing. *I cannot make sense of it from my particular viewpoint as a Christian minister.* 2 COUNT N A **viewpoint** is also a place from which you can get a good view of something.

vigil /vɪdʒɪl/, **vigils.** COUNT N A **vigil** is a period of time when you remain quietly in a place, especially at night, for example because you are praying or are making a political protest. *Last weekend a nun on a hunger strike held a vigil at the United Nations.*

vigilant /vɪdʒɪlənt/. ADJ If you are **vigilant,** you are careful and try to notice any danger or trouble that there might be; a formal use. *This evening, I had to be especially vigilant.* ♦ **vigilance** /vɪdʒɪləns/ UNCOUNT N *Constant vigilance is required from all of us.*

vigilante /vɪdʒɪlænti^{1}/, **vigilantes.** COUNT N **Vigilantes** are people who organize themselves into an unofficial group to protect their community and to catch and punish criminals.

vigorous /vɪgərəs/. 1 ADJ A **vigorous** action is done with a lot of energy and enthusiasm. *Mary gave her skirt a vigorous shake... ...a vigorous campaign.* ♦ **vigorously** ADV *Chomsky defended this view very vigorously.* 2 ADJ Someone who is **vigorous** is healthy and full of energy. *...an elderly but vigorous man.*

vigour /vɪgə/; spelled **vigor** in American English. UNCOUNT N **Vigour** is energy and enthusiasm. *These problems were discussed with great vigour.*

vile /vaɪl/, **viler, vilest.** ADJ If something is **vile,** it is very unpleasant or disgusting. *...England's vile weather... ...her vile language.*

villa /vɪlə/, **villas.** COUNT N A **villa** is a house, especially one that is used for holidays in Mediterranean countries.

village /vɪlɪdʒ/, **villages.** COUNT N A **village** consists of a group of houses, together with other buildings such as a church and school, in a country area. *...an Austrian village... ...the village school.*

villager /vɪlɪdʒə/, **villagers.** COUNT N **Villagers** are people who live in a village. *The villagers were suspicious of anything new.*

villain /vɪlən/, **villains.** COUNT N A **villain** is someone who deliberately harms other people or breaks the law; an old-fashioned use. *A villain named Thomson broke into the premises.*

villainous /vɪlənəs/. ADJ Someone who is **villainous** is very bad and willing to harm other people or break the law. *...villainous or wicked characters.*

vindicate /vɪndɪkeɪt/, **vindicates, vindicating, vindicated.** VB WITH OBJ When someone **is vindicated,** their ideas or actions are proved to be correct; a formal use. *Benn was decisively vindicated at the polls, receiving 23,275 votes to 10,231.* ♦ **vindication** /vɪndɪkeɪʃə^{0}n/ COUNT N OR UNCOUNT N *These changes to the law were widely regarded as a vindication of his long campaign... She took this as triumphant vindication of the effectiveness of the device.*

vindictive /vɪndɪktɪv/. ADJ Someone who is **vindictive** tries deliberately to hurt someone, often for revenge. *...a vindictive and violent man.*

vine /vaɪn/, **vines.** COUNT N A **vine** is a climbing or trailing plant, especially one which produces grapes.

vinegar /vɪnɪgə/. UNCOUNT N **Vinegar** is a sharp-tasting liquid, usually made from sour wine or malt.

vineyard /vɪnjəd/, **vineyards.** COUNT N A **vineyard** is an area of land where grape vines are grown to produce wine. *...the vineyards of Bordeaux.*

vintage /vɪntɪdʒ/. 1 ATTRIB ADJ **Vintage** wine is quality wine of a particular year that has been stored for several years to improve its quality. *...vintage port.* 2 ATTRIB ADJ **Vintage** describes something which is old but which is respected or admired because it is the best or most typical of its kind. *...vintage cars.*

vinyl /vaɪnɪ^{0}l/. UNCOUNT N **Vinyl** is a strong plastic used for making things such as furniture and floor coverings. *...white vinyl chairs.*

viola /vi^{1}əʊlə/, **violas.** COUNT N A **viola** is a musical instrument which looks like a violin but is slightly larger.

violate /vaɪəleɪt/, **violates, violating, violated.** 1 VB WITH OBJ If you **violate** an agreement, law, or promise, you break it. *He is violating his contract.* ♦ **violation** /vaɪəleɪʃə^{0}n/ UNCOUNT N OR COUNT N *They blockaded the Suez Canal in violation of international agreements... ...violations of the Constitution.* 2 VB WITH OBJ If you **violate** someone's privacy or peace, you disturb it; a formal use. *The calm of the press lounge was suddenly violated.* 3 VB WITH OBJ If someone **violates** a holy place, they treat it with disrespect or violence. *...a curse on those who violated the tomb of the king.* ♦ **violation** UNCOUNT N OR COUNT N *...the violation of our homes... The disaster aroused suspicions of negligence and violations.*

violence /vaɪələns/. 1 UNCOUNT N **Violence** is behaviour which is intended to injure or kill people. *...threats of terrorist violence... ...acts of violence... ...robbery with violence.* 2 UNCOUNT N If you do something with **violence,** you use a lot of energy in doing it, often because you are angry. *He flung open the door with unnecessary violence.*

violent /vaɪələnt/. 1 ADJ If someone is **violent,** they try to injure or kill people, for example by hitting or kicking them or using guns or bombs. *People in this society are prepared to be violent... ...violent clashes with the police.* ♦ **violently** ADV *They have come into conflict, sometimes violently.* 2 ADJ A **violent** event happens suddenly and with great force. *...a violent explosion... ...the constant threat of violent death.* ♦ **violently** ADV *The train braked violently.* 3 ADJ Something that is **violent** is said, done, or felt with great force and energy. *At times the argument grew violent... He had a violent urge to create.* ♦ **violently** ADV *They violently disagreed with their Commander-in-Chief.* 4 ATTRIB ADJ **Violent** colours are unpleasantly bright. *...a shirt of violent red.*

violet /vaɪəlɪ^{2}t/, **violets.** 1 COUNT N A **violet** is a small purple or white flower that blooms in the spring. 2 ADJ Something that is **violet** in colour is bluish-purple.

violin /vaɪəlɪn/, **violins.** COUNT N A **violin** is a musical instrument with four strings stretched over a shaped hollow box. You hold a violin under your chin and play it with a bow.

violinist /vaɪəlɪnɪst/, **violinists.** COUNT N A **violinist** is someone who plays the violin.

VIP /viː aɪ piː/, **VIPs.** COUNT N A **VIP** is someone who is given better treatment than ordinary people because he or she is famous, or important. **VIP** is an abbreviation for 'very important person'. *...a private lounge for VIPs.*

viper /vaɪpə/, **vipers.** COUNT N A **viper** is a small poisonous snake found mainly in Europe.

virgin /vɜːdʒɪn/, **virgins.** 1 COUNT N A **virgin** is someone who has never had sex. *...the girls they marry should be virgins.* ♦ **virginity** /və^{5}dʒɪnɪ^{1}ti^{1}/ UNCOUNT N *His sister had lost her virginity many years before.* 2 ADJ Something that is **virgin** is fresh and clean, and its appearance shows that it has never been used. *There were piles and piles of books, all virgin, all untouched.* 3 ATTRIB ADJ **Virgin** land has not been explored, cultivated, or spoiled by people. *...opening up virgin territory... ...virgin rain forest.*

virginal /vɜːdʒɪnəl/. ADJ Someone who is **virginal** is young and innocent, and has had no experience of sex. *The men have decreed that their women must be pure, virginal, innocent.*

virile /vɪraɪl/. ADJ A **virile** man has the qualities that a man is traditionally expected to have, such as strength and sexuality. *...virile young male actors.* ♦ **virility** /vɪrɪlɪti^{1}/ UNCOUNT N *The macho male wishes to prove his virility.*

virtual /vɜːtʃʊ^{0}əl/. ATTRIB ADJ **Virtual** means that something has all the characteristics of a particular thing, but is not formally recognized as being that thing. *The peasants remain in a state of virtual slavery... ...a virtual revolution in organization.*

virtually /vɜːtʃʊ^{0}əli^{1}/. ADV **Virtually** means that something is so nearly true that for most purposes it can be regarded as being true. *They are virtually impossible to detect... He virtually lived in his office... This opinion was held by virtually all the experts.*

virtue /vɜːtjuː, -tʃuː/, **virtues.** 1 UNCOUNT N **Virtue** is thinking and doing what is right, and avoiding what is wrong. *We accept certain principles of religion and traditional virtue.* 2 COUNT N A **virtue** is a good quality or way of behaving. *Charity is the greatest of Christian virtues.* 3 COUNT N OR UNCOUNT N A **virtue** of something is an advantage that it has. *...the virtues of female independence... There is no virtue in taking this action.* 4 PHRASE You use **by virtue of** to explain why something happens or is true; a formal use. *He was an object of interest simply by virtue of being British.*

virtuoso /vɜːtjuəʊzəʊ, -səʊ/, **virtuosos** or **virtuosi** /vɜːtjuəʊzi^{1}/. COUNT N A **virtuoso** is someone who is exceptionally good at playing a musical instrument. *He was a virtuoso of the jazz guitar.*

virtuous /vɜːtʃʊəs, -tjʊəs/. ADJ **Virtuous** behaviour is morally correct. *People who lead virtuous lives in this world are assured of paradise in the next.*

virulent /vɪrʊlənt/. 1 ADJ **Virulent** feelings or actions are extremely bitter and hostile; a formal use. *They were the objects of special hatred and virulent attack.* ♦ **virulently** ADV *Fighting broke out again much more virulently.* 2 ADJ A **virulent** disease or poison is extremely powerful and dangerous; a formal use. *...a virulent virus.*

virus /vaɪrəs/, **viruses.** COUNT N A **virus** is a germ that can cause disease. *She had a flu virus.*

visa /viːzə/, **visas.** COUNT N A **visa** is an official stamp put in your passport which allows you to enter a particular country. *The visa may be granted by the embassy.*

vis-à-vis /viːz æ viː/. PREP You use **vis-à-vis** when you are considering one thing in comparison with another; a formal use. *One solution would be for us to lower our exchange rate vis-à-vis other countries.*

viscount /vaɪkaʊnt/, **viscounts.** COUNT N OR TITLE A **viscount** is a British nobleman who is below an earl and above a baron in rank.

viscountess /vaɪkaʊntɪ^{2}s/, **viscountesses.** COUNT N OR TITLE A **viscountess** is either the wife of a viscount or a woman who holds the same rank as a viscount.

vise /vaɪs/. See **vice.**

visibility /vɪzɪbɪlɪ^{1}ti^{1}/. UNCOUNT N **Visibility** means how far or how clearly you can see in particular weather conditions. *Visibility was excellent that day.*

visible /vɪzɪbəºl/. 1 ADJ If an object is **visible,** it can be seen. *These tiny creatures are hardly visible to the naked eye... It was just visible from the beach.* 2 ADJ **Visible** changes can be noticed or recognized. *The results are visible... ...a period of little visible advance.* ♦ **visibly** ADV *She was visibly nervous.*

vision /vɪʒəºn/, **visions.** 1 COUNT N If you have a **vision** of a possible situation, you have a mental picture of it, in which you imagine how things might be different from the way they are now. *...fighting for the vision of the new China... I had nightmarish visions of what could go wrong.* 2 UNCOUNT N **Vision** is the ability to see clearly. *...children with poor vision.*

visionary /vɪʒənəºri¹/, **visionaries.** COUNT N A **visionary** is someone who has visions about how things might be different in the future. *...left-wing visionaries.* Also ADJ *...the visionary imagination.*

visit /vɪzɪt/, **visits, visiting, visited.** 1 VB WITH OR WITHOUT OBJ If you **visit** someone, you go to see them and spend time with them. *She visited some of her relatives for a few days... You might need to visit a solicitor... My aunt and uncle did visit once.* Also COUNT N *It would be nice if you paid me a visit.* 2 VB WITH OR WITHOUT OBJ If you **visit** a place, you go to see it. *This is the best museum we've visited... 'Do you live here?'—'No, we're just visiting.'* Also COUNT N *...a brief visit to the U.S.*

visitor /vɪzɪtə/, **visitors.** COUNT N A **visitor** is someone who is visiting a person or place. *Marsha was a frequent visitor to our house.*

visor /vaɪzə/, **visors.** COUNT N A **visor** is a movable part of a helmet which can be pulled down to protect a person's eyes or face.

vista /vɪstə/, **vistas.** 1 COUNT N WITH SUPP A **vista** is the view from a particular place, especially a long view rather than a wide one; a literary use. *He could see through the tall windows a vista of green fields.* 2 COUNT N WITH SUPP A **vista** also refers to a range of exciting or worrying new ideas and possibilities; a literary use. *...a whole new vista of troubles for me.*

visual /vɪʒuəl, -zju-/. ADJ **Visual** means relating to sight. *...visual jokes... ...exhibitions in the visual arts.* ♦ **visually** SENTENCE ADV OR ADV *Visually, it is a very exciting film... The island is visually stunning.*

visual aid, visual aids. COUNT N **Visual aids** are things you can look at, such as films, maps, or slides, to help you understand, or to remember information.

visualize /vɪʒuºəlaɪz/, **visualizes, visualizing, visualized;** also spelled **visualise.** VB WITH OBJ If you **visualize** something, you form a mental picture of it. *He found he could visualize her face quite clearly.*

vital /vaɪtəºl/. 1 ADJ Something that is **vital** is necessary or very important. *It is vital to keep an accurate record of every transaction... ...vital repair work.* ♦ **vitally** SUBMOD *The way we choose to bring up children is vitally important.* 2 ADJ People or organizations that are **vital** are energetic, exciting, and full of life. *The Chinese were trusting, open, and vital... We want to have a modern vital parliament.*

vitality /vaɪtælɪ¹ti¹/. UNCOUNT N People who have **vitality** are energetic and lively. *...the vitality and eagerness of a normal toddler.*

vitamin /vɪtəmɪn/, **vitamins.** COUNT N **Vitamins** are organic substances in food which you need in order to remain healthy. *She needs extra vitamins and protein... One tiny berry contained more vitamin C than an orange.*

viva /vaɪvə/, **vivas.** COUNT N A **viva** is an oral examination, especially in a university.

vivacious /vɪveɪʃəs/. ADJ Someone who is **vivacious** is lively, exciting, and attractive. *She was young and vivacious.*

vivacity /vɪvæsɪ¹ti¹/. UNCOUNT N **Vivacity** is the quality of being lively in an attractive and exciting way; a formal use. *...a man of great charm and vivacity.*

vivid /vɪvɪd/. 1 ADJ Something that is **vivid** is very bright in colour. *...a vivid green lawn.* ♦ **vividly** ADV *...vividly coloured birds.* 2 ADJ **Vivid** memories or descriptions are very clear and detailed. *I have a vivid memory of an excursion with my grandmother... She gave a vivid account of her travels.* ♦ **vividly** ADV *'You remember Captain van Donck?'—'Oh, yes. Vividly.'*

vivisection /vɪvɪsɛkʃəºn/. UNCOUNT N **Vivisection** is the practice of using living animals for scientific experiments.

vocabulary /vəºkæbjə⁴ləri¹/, **vocabularies.** 1 COUNT N OR UNCOUNT N Your **vocabulary** is the total number of words you know in a particular language. *...improvements in intelligence, vocabulary, and motivation... By the age of five, a child has a vocabulary of over 2,000 words.* 2 SING N The **vocabulary** of a language is all the words in it. *New words are constantly coming into use and then dropping out of the vocabulary.*

vocal /vəʊkəºl/. 1 ADJ You say that people are **vocal** when they speak loudly and with feeling about something. *The members had been quite vocal on issues of academic freedom.* 2 ATTRIB ADJ **Vocal** means involving the use of the human voice, especially in singing. *She amazed her audiences with her superb vocal range.*

vocal cords; also spelled **vocal chords.** PLURAL N Your **vocal cords** are the part of your throat which can be made to vibrate when you breathe out, making the sounds you use for speaking.

vocation /vəʊkeɪʃəºn/, **vocations.** COUNT N OR UNCOUNT N A **vocation** is a strong wish to do a particular job, especially one which involves serving other people. *Medicine is my vocation... By vocation I'm not a politician.*

vocational /vəʊkeɪʃəºnəl, -ʃənəºl/. ADJ **Vocational** describes the skills needed for a particular job or profession. *...a college that does technical and vocational training.*

vociferous /vəºsɪfərəs/. ADJ Someone who is **vociferous** speaks very loudly, because they want their views to be heard; a formal use. *They were supported by a vociferous group in the actors' union.*

vodka /vɒdkə/, **vodkas.** MASS N **Vodka** is a strong, clear alcoholic drink.

vogue /vəʊg/. 1 SING N If something is the **vogue,** it is very popular and fashionable. *Flowery carpets became the vogue.* 2 PHRASE Something that is **in vogue** is very popular and fashionable. *At that time after-shave was not in vogue in France.*

voice /vɔɪs/, **voices, voicing, voiced.** 1 COUNT N When someone speaks, you hear their **voice.** *He recognized me by my voice... 'I suppose we'd better go,' said John in a low voice.* 2 COUNT N You use **voice** to refer to someone's opinion on a particular topic and what they say about it. *Numerous voices were raised against the idea... The only dissenting voice was Mr Foot's.* 3 SING N If you have a **voice** in something, you have the right to express an opinion on it. *Students should have a voice in determining the way universities develop.* 4 VB WITH OBJ If you **voice** an opinion or an emotion, you say what you think or feel. *The African delegates voiced their anger.* 5 SING N In grammar, if a verb is in the active **voice,** the person who performs the action is the subject of the verb. If a verb is in the passive **voice,** the thing or person affected by the action is the subject of the verb.

PHRASES • If you **raise** your **voice,** you speak more loudly. If you **lower** your **voice,** you speak more quietly. • If someone tells you to **keep** your **voice down,** they want you to speak more quietly. • If you say something **at the top of** your **voice,** you say it as loudly as possible. *'I am drenched,' she declared at the top of her voice.*

void /vɔɪd/, **voids.** 1 COUNT N A **void** is a situation or state of affairs which seems empty because it has no interest, excitement, or value; a literary use. *Tending her mother had filled the void for a time.* 2 COUNT N A **void** is also a big hole or space; a literary use. *He looked down into the gaping void at his feet.* 3 PRED ADJ Something that is **void** has no official value or authority; a technical use.

volatile /vɒlətaɪl/. ADJ Something or someone that is **volatile** is liable to change suddenly and unexpectedly. *The situation in Lebanon was 'tense, dangerous and volatile'... He was a very clever, volatile actor.*

volcanic /vɒlkænɪk/. ADJ A place or region that is **volcanic** has a lot of volcanoes or was created by volcanoes. *The islands are volcanic.*

volcano /vɒlkeɪnəʊ/, **volcanoes.** COUNT N A **volcano** is a mountain which hot melted rock, gas, steam, and ash sometimes burst out of, coming from inside the earth. *Six other volcanoes were still erupting.*

volition /vəºlɪʃəºn/. PHRASE If you do something **of** your **own volition,** you do it because you have decided for yourself that you will do it; a formal use. *She didn't go down there of her own volition.*

volley /vɒli¹/, **volleys.** COUNT N A **volley** of shots or gunfire is a lot of shots fired at the same time. *...a volley of automatic rifle fire.*

volleyball /vɒli¹bɔːl/. UNCOUNT N **Volleyball** is a game in which two teams hit a large ball with their hands, backwards and forwards over a high net. If you allow the ball to touch the ground, your team loses a point.

volt /vəʊlt/, **volts.** COUNT N A **volt** is a unit of measurement of electrical potential.

voltage /vəʊltɪdʒ/, **voltages.** UNCOUNT N OR COUNT N The **voltage** of an electrical current is its force measured in volts.

voluble /vɒljəbəºl/. ADJ Someone who is **voluble** talks a lot with great energy; a formal use. *He became very voluble and told her everything.*

volume /vɒljuːm/, **volumes.** 1 COUNT N A **volume** is one of a series of books. *It was published in three volumes.* 2 SING N The **volume** of something is the amount of space that it contains or occupies. *The gas expanded to nine times its original volume.* 3 SING N The **volume** of something is also the amount of it that there is. *The volume of work is incredible... ...the growing volume of imports.* 4 UNCOUNT N The **volume** of a radio, TV, or record player is the amount of sound that it produces. *She turned up the volume... Black Flag play rock music at excruciatingly high volume.*

voluminous /vəljºuːmɪnəs/. ADJ **Voluminous** means very large in size or quantity; a formal use. *...a voluminous skirt... I took voluminous notes.*

voluntary /vɒləntəºri¹/. 1 ADJ **Voluntary** describes actions that you choose to do, rather than have been forced to do. *Attendance at the parade was voluntary... He went into voluntary exile.* ♦ **voluntarily** ADV *They were said to have left their land voluntarily.* 2 ADJ **Voluntary** work is done by people who are not paid for it. *I do voluntary home tuition.*

volunteer /vɒləntɪə/, **volunteers, volunteering, volunteered.** 1 COUNT N A **volunteer** is someone who does work for which they are not paid. *Teaching literacy to adults using volunteers began in 1963.* Also MOD *...volunteer work at the hospital.* 2 COUNT N A **volunteer** is also someone who chooses to join the armed forces, especially in wartime, as opposed to someone who is forced to join by law. *Many Australians fought as volunteers on the Allied side.* 3 VB WITH OR WITHOUT OBJ If you **volunteer** to do something, you offer to do it, rather than being forced to do it. *He volunteered to do whatever he could for them... ...an extra payment to those who volunteer for redundancy.* 4 REPORT VB If you **volunteer** information, you give it without being asked; a formal use. *I volunteered no explanation for our visit... 'It's all fascinating and intriguing,' Maria volunteered.*

voluptuous /vəlʌptjuəs/. ADJ A **voluptuous** woman has large breasts and hips and is considered to be sexually desirable; a formal use.

vomit /vɒmɪt/, **vomits, vomiting, vomited.** 1 VB WITH OR WITHOUT OBJ If you **vomit,** food and drink comes back up from your stomach and out through your mouth. 2 UNCOUNT N **Vomit** is partly digested food and drink that has come back up from someone's stomach and out through their mouth.

voracious /vəºreɪʃəs/. ADJ If you say that someone is **voracious** or that they have a **voracious** appetite for something, you mean that they want a lot of it; a literary use. *...voracious readers of detective stories... ...the Duke's voracious capacity for food.*

vote /vəʊt/, **votes, voting, voted.** 1 COUNT N Your **vote** is your choice in an election or at a meeting where decisions are taken. *...an increase in votes for the Conservative Party... He will get my vote.* 2 COUNT N When a group of people have a **vote** or take a **vote,** they make a decision by allowing each person in the group to say what they would prefer. *Let's have a vote.* 3 SING N In an election, the **vote** is the total number of people who have indicated their choice. *They captured 13 per cent of the vote.* 4 VB WITH OR WITHOUT OBJ When you **vote,** you make your choice in an election or at a meeting, by writing on a piece of paper or by raising your hand. *They voted to continue the strike.* 5 SING N People have the **vote** when they have the legal right to indicate in an election who they would like to represent them as their government. *Women have had the vote for over fifty years.*

vote of thanks, votes of thanks. COUNT N A **vote of thanks** is an official speech in which the speaker formally thanks a person for doing something. *The chairman will be proposing the vote of thanks.*

voter /vəʊtə/, **voters.** COUNT N A **voter** is someone who has the legal right to vote in an election. *Many of Britain's voters are looking for new answers.*

vouch /vaʊtʃ/, **vouches, vouching, vouched.**

vouch for PHR VB 1 If you say that you can or will **vouch for** someone, you mean that you can guarantee their good behaviour or support. *He said that he could vouch for your discretion... I was vouched for by the Tattaglia family.* 2 If you say that you can **vouch for** something, you mean that you have evidence from your own personal experience that it is true or correct. *I can vouch for the accuracy of my information.*

voucher /vaʊtʃə/, **vouchers.** COUNT N A **voucher** is a piece of paper that can be used instead of money to pay for something. *...meal vouchers worth 15p each.*

vow /vaʊ/, **vows, vowing, vowed.** 1 VB WITH TO-INF OR REPORT VB If you **vow** to do something, you make a solemn promise to do it. *He vowed never to let it happen again... He vowed that he would ride at my side.* 2 COUNT N A **vow** is a solemn promise. *She made a vow to give up smoking.*

vowel /vaʊəl/, **vowels.** COUNT N A **vowel** is a sound such as the ones represented by the letters 'a' or 'o', which you pronounce with your mouth open. Most words are pronounced with a combination of consonants and vowels.

voyage /vɔɪɪdʒ/, **voyages.** COUNT N A **voyage** is a long journey on a ship or in a spacecraft. *...the long sea voyage from London to Bombay.*

voyager /vɔɪɪdʒə/, **voyagers.** COUNT N A **voyager** is someone who goes on a voyage, especially a difficult or dangerous one. *...early ocean voyagers.*

vs. vs. is a written abbreviation for 'versus'. *The first match is England vs. South America.*

vulgar /vʌlgə/. ADJ **Vulgar** means socially unacceptable or offensive. *...vulgar remarks.* ♦ **vulgarity** /vʌlgærɪti/ UNCOUNT N *...the vulgarity of his speech.*

vulnerable /vʌlnərəbəl/. ADJ A **vulnerable** person is weak and easily hurt physically or emotionally. *Elderly people, living alone, are especially vulnerable... Lack of employment outside the home tends to make women vulnerable to depression.* ♦ **vulnerability** /vʌlnərəbɪlɪti/ UNCOUNT N *...Britain's extreme vulnerability to attack.*

vulture /vʌltʃə/, **vultures.** COUNT N **Vultures** are large birds which live in hot countries and eat the flesh of dead animals.

vying /vaɪɪŋ/. **Vying** is the present participle of **vie**.

Ww

W. W is a written abbreviation for 'west'.

wad /wɒd/, **wads.** COUNT N A **wad** of something such as papers or banknotes is a thick bundle of them. *She handed over a wad of forms.*

waddle /wɒdəl/, **waddles, waddling, waddled.** VB When fat people or ducks **waddle,** they walk with short, quick steps, swaying slightly from side to side.

wade /weɪd/, **wades, wading, waded.** VB If you **wade** through water, you walk through it. *The children waded out into the lake.*

wade through. PHR VB If you **wade through** a difficult book or document, you spend a lot of time and effort reading it. *Each evening, he had to wade through columns of Parliamentary reports.*

wafer /weɪfə/, **wafers.** COUNT N A **wafer** is a thin, crisp biscuit, often eaten with ice cream.

waffle /wɒfəl/, **waffles, waffling, waffled.** 1 VB If you **waffle,** you talk or write a lot without saying anything clear or important. *He's still waffling away about economic recovery.* Also UNCOUNT N *I don't want waffle, I want the real figures.* 2 COUNT N A **waffle** is a type of thick pancake.

waft /wɑːft, wɒft/, **wafts, wafting, wafted.** ERG VB WITH ADJUNCT If a sound or scent **wafts** or **is wafted** through the air, it moves gently through the air. *A scent of lemon wafted up from the gardens below... ...the aromatic oils that are wafted upwards.*

wag /wæg/, **wags, wagging, wagged.** ERG VB When a dog **wags** its tail or when its tail **wags,** its tail moves repeatedly from side to side.

wage /weɪdʒ/, **wages, waging, waged.** 1 PLURAL N OR COUNT N Someone's **wages** are the money they are paid each week for working, especially when they have a manual or unskilled job. *My wages had not increased for two years... ...the problems of families bringing up children on a low wage.* 2 VB WITH OBJ To **wage** a campaign or war means to start it and carry it on over a period of time; a formal use. *...the fierce struggle that had been waged against racism.*

wager /weɪdʒə/, **wagers.** COUNT N A **wager** is a bet; an old-fashioned use. *...wagers on who will win the World Series.*

waggle /wægəl/, **waggles, waggling, waggled.** ERG VB If you **waggle** something or if it **waggles,** it moves up and down or from side to side with short, quick movements. *He waggled his eyebrows.*

wagon /wægən/, **wagons;** also spelled **waggon** in British English. 1 COUNT N A **wagon** is a strong vehicle with four wheels which is used for carrying heavy loads, and which is usually pulled by a horse or tractor. 2 COUNT N **Wagons** are also large containers on wheels pulled by a railway engine; a British use. *The cattle go by rail in wagons.*

wail /weɪl/, **wails, wailing, wailed.** VB To **wail** means to cry loudly. *One of the children began to wail... 'Come and help me, someone!' wailed Crabby.* Also COUNT N *I could hear the wail of a baby next door.*

waist /weɪst/, **waists.** COUNT N Your **waist** is the middle part of your body, above your hips. *She tied an apron around her waist.*

waistband /weɪstbænd/, **waistbands.** COUNT N A **waistband** is a narrow piece of material sewn on to the waist of a skirt, pair of trousers, or other garment to strengthen it.

waistcoat /weɪstkəʊt/, **waistcoats.** COUNT N A **waistcoat** is a sleeveless piece of clothing with buttons, usually worn over a shirt.

waistline /weɪstlaɪn/, **waistlines.** COUNT N Your **waistline** is your waist measurement. *...a lady with a large waistline.*

wait /weɪt/, **waits, waiting, waited.** 1 VB If you **wait,** you spend some time, usually doing very little, before something happens. *He waited patiently for her... She had been waiting in the queue to buy some stamps... Wait until we sit down... Don't keep him waiting about in the hotel.* ♦ **waiting** ATTRIB ADJ *There was a waiting period of one month.* 2 COUNT N A **wait** is a period of time in which you do very little, before something happens. *There was a long wait.* 3 VB If something is **waiting** for you, it is ready for you to use or do. *I have a lot of work waiting.* 4 VB If you say that something **can wait,** you mean that can be dealt with later. *The dishes can wait.* 5 VB WITH ADJUNCT If you **wait on** people in a restaurant, you serve them food.

PHRASES • If you **can't wait** to do something, you are very excited about it and eager to do it. *He couldn't wait to tell Judy.* • You say **'you wait'** to someone to threaten or warn them. *You wait! You'll find Robinson isn't as gentle as he seems.* • If you **wait on** someone **hand and foot,** you are always doing things for them, even if they could do the things themselves; usually used showing disapproval.

wait up. PHR VB If you **wait up,** you do not go to bed, because you are expecting someone to return home late at night. *She said that you shouldn't bother to wait up for her.*

waiter /weɪtə/, **waiters.** COUNT N A **waiter** is a man who serves food and drink in a restaurant.

waiting list, waiting lists. COUNT N A **waiting list** is a list of people who have asked for something which cannot be given to them immediately, for example medical treatment or a job, and who must therefore wait until it is available. *He's on the waiting list for a council house.*

waiting-room, waiting-rooms. COUNT N A **waiting-room** is a room in a place such as a railway station or a doctor's surgery, where people can sit and wait.

waitress /weɪtrɪs/, **waitresses.** COUNT N A **waitress** is a woman who serves food and drink in a restaurant.

waive /weɪv/, **waives, waiving, waived.** VB WITH OBJ If someone **waives** a rule, they decide not to enforce it; a formal use. *Rules about proper dress may be waived.*

wake /weɪk/, **wakes, waking, woke** /wəʊk/, **woken** /wəʊkən/. The form **waked** is also used for the past tense and past participle in American English. ERG VB When you **wake** or **are woken,** you become conscious again after being asleep. *I sometimes wake at four in the morning... He woke me early.*

PHRASES • Your **waking hours** are the times when you are awake rather than asleep. *I spend most of my waking hours in the library.* • If you leave something **in your wake,** you leave it behind you as you go. *They left trails of sweet papers in their wake.* • If one thing follows **in the wake of** another, it happens after the other thing is over, often as a result of it. *Famine came in the wake of disastrous floods.*

wake up. PHR VB 1 When you **wake up** or **are woken up,** you become conscious again after being asleep. *Ralph, wake up!... I woke them up again.* 2 If you **wake up** to a dangerous situation, you become aware of it. *The West began to wake up to the danger it faced.*

waken /weɪkən/, **wakens, wakening, wakened.** ERG VB When you **waken** or **are wakened,** you wake; a literary use.

walk /wɔːk/, **walks, walking, walked.** 1 VB WITH OR WITHOUT OBJ When you **walk,** you move along by putting one foot in front of the other on the ground. *Most children learn to walk when they are about one... We walked along in silence... He could walk the streets and fear nothing.* 2 SING N A **walk** is the action of walking rather than running. *He slowed down to a walk.* 3 COUNT N A **walk** is also a journey or outing made by walking. *He went out for a long walk... The station is a three minute walk from the park.* 4 COUNT N Your **walk** is the way you walk. *He came in with his distinctive walk.* 5 VB WITH OBJ AND ADJUNCT If you **walk** someone somewhere, you walk there with them. *He walked her home.* 6 See also **walking.**

walk away with. PHR VB If you **walk away with** something such as a prize, you win it; an informal use.

walk off with. PHR VB 1 If someone **walks off with** something that does not belong to them, they take it without permission; an informal use. *Who's walked off with my pen?* 2 If you **walk off with** something such as a prize, you win it very easily; an informal use. *She'll walk off with a first class degree.*

walk out. PHR VB 1 If you **walk out** of a meeting, performance, or unpleasant situation, you leave it suddenly, usually to show that you are angry. *Most of the audience walked out after the first half hour... He walked out of his job.* 2 If workers **walk out,** they go on strike. • See also **walkout.**

walk out on. PHR VB If you **walk out on** someone, you leave them suddenly. *His girlfriend walked out on him.*

walker /wɔːkə/, **walkers.** COUNT N A **walker** is a person who walks, especially in the countryside for pleasure. *The woods are heavily visited by walkers.*

walkie-talkie /wɔːki tɔːki/, **walkie-talkies.** COUNT N A **walkie-talkie** is a small portable radio used for sending and receiving messages. *There were hundreds of policemen around with walkie-talkies.*

walking /wɔːkɪŋ/. UNCOUNT N **Walking** is the activity of going for walks in the country. *Walking and mountaineering are very popular here... ...a walking holiday.*

walking stick, walking sticks. COUNT N A **walking stick** is a long wooden stick which a person can lean on while walking.

Walkman /wɔːkmən/, **Walkmans.** COUNT N A **Walkman** is a small cassette player with very light headphones, which people carry around so that they can listen to music while they are doing something or going somewhere; a trademark.

walk of life, walks of life. COUNT N The **walk of life** that you come from is the position that you have in society and the kind of job you have. *Members of this club come from many different walks of life.*

walkout /wɔːkaʊt/, **walkouts.** COUNT N A **walkout** is a strike. *The pay deal ended the 43-day-old walkout.*

walkway /wɔːkweɪ/, **walkways.** COUNT N A **walkway** is a path or passage in a built-up area, especially one which is raised above the ground.

wall /wɔːl/, **walls.** 1 COUNT N A **wall** is one of the vertical sides of a building or room. *There was a picture on the wall.* 2 COUNT N A **wall** is also a long narrow vertical structure made of stone or brick that surrounds or divides an area of land. *We crouched behind the wall and waited.* 3 COUNT N WITH SUPP The **wall** of something hollow is its side. *...the cell walls of plants.*

walled /wɔːld/. ADJ A **walled** area of land is surrounded by a wall. *...the old walled city of Jerusalem.*

wallet /wɒlɪt/, **wallets.** COUNT N A **wallet** is a small, flat case made of leather or plastic, in which you keep banknotes and other small things such as credit cards.

wallop /wɒləp/, **wallops, walloping, walloped.** VB WITH OBJ To **wallop** someone means to hit them very hard; an informal use. *His mother would have walloped him if she'd known.*

wallow /wɒləʊ/, **wallows, wallowing, wallowed.** 1 VB WITH 'in' If you **wallow** in an unpleasant situation or feeling, you allow it to continue longer than is reasonable or necessary. *At first I just wanted to wallow in misery... Her mother was wallowing in widowhood.* 2 VB When an animal **wallows** in mud or water, it lies or rolls about in it slowly.

wallpaper /wɔːlpeɪpə/, **wallpapers.** MASS N **Wallpaper** is thick coloured or patterned paper that is used to decorate the walls of rooms.

walnut /wɔːlnʌt/, **walnuts.** COUNT N A **walnut** is a nut with a distinctive, wrinkled shape.

walrus /wɔːlrəs, wɒl-/, **walruses.** COUNT N A **walrus** is an animal like a large seal which lives in the sea. It has long whiskers and two tusks pointing downwards.

waltz /wɔːls/, **waltzes, waltzing, waltzed.** 1 COUNT N A **waltz** is a piece of music with a rhythm of three beats in each bar, which people can dance to. 2 COUNT N A **waltz** is also a dance which people do to waltz music. 3 RECIP VB When two people **waltz,** they dance a waltz together. *I dreamt of going to Hollywood to waltz with Ginger Rogers.* 4 VB WITH ADJUNCT If you **waltz** into a place, you enter in a quick, confident way that makes other people notice you; an informal use. *She waltzed across to Helen and sat down beside her.*

wan /wɒn/. ADJ Someone who is **wan** looks pale and tired; a literary use. *...a wan smile.*

wand /wɒnd/, **wands.** COUNT N A **wand** is a long, thin rod that magicians wave when they are performing tricks and magic.

wander /wɒndə/, **wanders, wandering, wandered.** 1 VB WITH ADJUNCT OR OBJ If you **wander** around, you walk around in a casual way. *We wandered round the little harbour town... A man was found wandering in the hills... The children wandered the streets after school.* 2 VB If your mind **wanders** or your thoughts **wander,** you stop concentrating on something and start thinking about other things. *When she was alone, she would let her mind wander... My thoughts kept wandering back to that night.*

wane /weɪn/, **wanes, waning, waned.** 1 VB If a condition, attitude, or emotion **wanes,** it becomes weaker, often disappearing completely in the end. *Her enthusiasm for Harold was beginning to wane...*

The influence of this group waned considerably. ● to **wax and wane:** see **wax. 2** PHRASE If a condition, attitude, or emotion is **on the wane,** it is becoming weaker. *They could claim that pollution for the first time was on the wane.*

wangle /wæŋgəl/, **wangles, wangling, wangled.** VB WITH OBJ If you **wangle** something that you want, you manage to get it by being clever or persuasive; an informal use. *He always managed to wangle the easy jobs.*

want /wɒnt/, **wants, wanting, wanted. 1** VB WITH OBJ OR TO-INF If you **want** something, you feel a desire to have it or a need for it. *Do you want a cup of coffee?... All they want is a holiday... I want to be an actress... I didn't want him to go.* **2** VB WITH -ING If something **wants** doing, there is a need for it to be done. *We've got a couple of jobs that want doing in the garden.* **3** VB WITH TO-INF If you tell someone that they **want** to do a particular thing, you are advising them to do it. *You want to book your holiday early this year.* **4** VB WITH OBJ If someone **is wanted,** the police are searching for them. *He is wanted for the crimes of murder and kidnapping.* **5** SING N WITH 'of' A **want** of something is a lack of it; a formal use. *They had to confess their complete want of foresight.* **6** PHRASE If you do something **for want of** something else, you do it because the other thing is not available or not possible; a formal use. *For want of anything better to do, he continued to read.*

wanting /wɒntɪŋ/. PRED ADJ If you find something **wanting** or if it proves **wanting,** it is not as good as you think it should be; a formal use. *He judged the nation and found it wanting.*

wanton /wɒntən/. ADJ A **wanton** action deliberately causes harm, damage, or waste without any reason; a formal use. *...senseless and wanton cruelty.*

war /wɔː/, **wars. 1** COUNT N OR UNCOUNT N A **war** is a period of fighting between countries. *They fought in the war against Britain... There are no winners in nuclear war... England and Germany were at war.* **2** COUNT N OR UNCOUNT N You also use **war** to refer to competition between groups of people, or a campaign against a particular thing. *...a trade war.* **3** See also **civil war, cold war.**
PHRASES ● If a country **goes to war,** it starts fighting a war. ● If someone **has been in the wars,** they have been injured, for example in a fight or accident; an informal use.

warble /wɔːbəl/, **warbles, warbling, warbled.** VB WITH OR WITHOUT OBJ When a bird **warbles,** it sings pleasantly; a literary use.

ward /wɔːd/, **wards, warding, warded. 1** COUNT N A **ward** is a room in a hospital which has beds for several people, often people who need similar treatment. *She stayed five days in the emergency ward for observation.* **2** COUNT N A **ward** is also a district which forms part of a political constituency or local council; a British use. **3** COUNT N A **ward** is a child who is officially put in the care of an adult because his or her parents are dead. A **ward of court** is a child who is in the care of a court of law because he or she needs protection.

ward off. PHR VB If you **ward off** a danger or illness, you do something to prevent it from affecting you or harming you. *He wears a copper bracelet to ward off rheumatism.*

-ward. SUFFIX **-ward** and **-wards** are added to nouns referring to places or directions to form adverbs or adjectives which indicate the direction in which something is moving or facing. *He was gazing skyward... He led the group homewards... ...the westward trail.*

warden /wɔːdən/, **wardens. 1** COUNT N WITH SUPP A **warden** is an official who makes sure that certain laws are being obeyed. *...traffic wardens... ...game wardens.* **2** COUNT N A **warden** is also a person in charge of a building or institution such as a youth hostel. **3** COUNT N The **warden** of a prison is the person in charge of it; an American use.

warder /wɔːdə/, **warders.** COUNT N A **warder** is a person who is in charge of prisoners.

wardrobe /wɔːdrəub/, **wardrobes. 1** COUNT N A **wardrobe** is a tall cupboard in which hang your clothes. **2** COUNT N Someone's **wardrobe** is all of their clothes. *He was familiar with her entire wardrobe.*

-wards. See **-ward.**

ware /wɛə/, **wares. 1** UNCOUNT N WITH SUPP You use **ware** to refer to objects that are made of a particular substance, such as glass or china, or things that are used for a particular domestic purpose, such as cooking. *...glass ware... ...kitchen ware.* **2** PLURAL N Someone's **wares** are the things that they sell, usually in the street or in a market; an old-fashioned use. *The market traders began to sell their wares at half-price.*

warehouse /wɛəhaus/, **warehouses.** COUNT N A **warehouse** is a large building where raw materials or manufactured goods are stored.

warfare /wɔːfɛə/. UNCOUNT N **Warfare** is the activity of fighting a war; a formal use. *They are anxious to prevent this conflict from erupting into open warfare.*

warhead /wɔːhɛd/, **warheads.** COUNT N A **warhead** is the front end of a bomb or missile, where the explosives are. *...missiles with nuclear warheads.*

warlike /wɔːlaɪk/. ADJ People who are **warlike** seem aggressive and eager to start a war; a formal use. *...a warlike leader... ...a warlike nation.*

warm /wɔːm/, **warmer, warmest; warms, warming, warmed. 1** ADJ Something that is **warm** has some heat but not enough to be hot. *...a bowl of warm water... ...a warm summer evening.* **2** VB WITH OBJ OR REFL VB If you **warm** a part of your body, you put it near a fire or heater so that it stops feeling cold. *I warmed my hand on the radiator... Come and warm yourself in front of the fire.* **3** ADJ **Warm** clothes and blankets are made of a material such as wool which protects you from the cold. *...a pair of nice warm socks.* ♦ **warmly** ADV *I'll see that Chris dresses warmly.* **4** ADJ A **warm** person is friendly and affectionate. *She had a warm, generous heart... He was given a warm welcome.* ♦ **warmly** ADV *He shook Tony warmly by the hand.* **5** VB WITH PREP 'to' If you **warm** to a person, you become fonder of them. If you **warm** to an idea, you become more interested in it. *This makes you warm to Meadows... He warmed to the prospect of a new job.*

warm up. PHR VB **1** If you **warm** something **up** or if it **warms up,** it gets hotter. *Start warming up the soup now... When the weather warmed up mosquitoes began swarming.* **2** If you **warm up** for an event such as a race, you prepare yourself for it by doing exercises or by practising just before it starts. ● See also **warm-up. 3** When a machine or engine **warms up,** it becomes ready for use a little while after being switched on or started.

warm-blooded. ADJ An animal that is **warm-blooded,** for example a bird or a mammal, has a relatively high body temperature which remains constant and does not change according to the surrounding temperature.

warm-hearted. ADJ A **warm-hearted** person is friendly and affectionate.

warmonger /wɔːmʌŋgə/, **warmongers.** COUNT N A **warmonger** is a person, for example a politician or a newspaper editor, who encourages people to start a war or to prepare for one.

warmongering /wɔːmʌŋgərɪŋ/. UNCOUNT N **Warmongering** is behaviour in which someone encourages people to start a war or to prepare for one.

warmth /wɔːmθ/. **1** UNCOUNT N **Warmth** is a moderate amount of heat that something has, for example enough heat to make you feel comfortable. *...the warmth of the sun... We huddled together for warmth.* **2** UNCOUNT N **Warmth** is also friendly and affectionate behaviour. *...my uncle's warmth and affection... 'How do you do, sir?' she said, without warmth.*

warm-up, warm-ups. COUNT N A **warm-up** is preparation that you do just before an event such as a race, for example exercises or practising.

warn /wɔːn/, **warns, warning, warned. 1** VB WITH OBJ If you **warn** someone about a possible danger or problem, you tell them about it so that they are aware of it. *The least I can do is warn them that there is a danger... I did warn you of possible failure... I warn you it's going to be expensive.* **2** VB WITH OBJ If you **warn** someone not to do something, you advise them not to do it in order to avoid possible danger or punishment. *I warned him not to lose his temper with her... I'm warning you, if you do that again there'll be trouble.*

warn off. PHR VB If you **warn** someone **off,** you tell them to go away or to stop doing something because of possible danger or punishment. *Intruders are warned off by the sound.*

warning /wɔːnɪŋ/, **warnings. 1** COUNT N OR UNCOUNT N A **warning** is something which is said or written to tell people of a possible danger, problem, or other unpleasant thing that might happen. *The hospital issued warnings about drugs to be avoided... Dad gave a final warning to them not to look directly at the sun... Mary left her husband without any warning.* **2** ATTRIB ADJ **Warning** actions or signs give a warning. *Watch out for the warning signs of depression like insomnia.*

warp /wɔːp/, **warps, warping, warped. 1** ERG VB If something **warps** or **is warped,** it becomes damaged by bending or curving, often because of the effect of heat or water. *The cabinet doors began to warp soon after they were installed.* ♦ **warped** ADJ *The wooden balconies were warped and weatherbeaten.* **2** VB WITH OBJ If something **warps** someone's character, it influences them and makes them abnormal or bad. *...a man whose whole character was warped by being bullied.* **3** COUNT N A **warp** in time or space is an imaginary break or sudden change in the normal experience of time or space. *There's a kind of time warp in his education.*

warrant /wɒrənt/, **warrants, warranting, warranted. 1** VB WITH OBJ If something **warrants** a particular action, it makes the action seem necessary; a formal use. *The case warrants further investigation.* **2** COUNT N A **warrant** is an official document signed by a judge or magistrate, which gives the police special permission to do something such as arrest someone or search their house.

warren /wɒrən/, **warrens.** COUNT N A **warren** is a group of holes in the ground connected by tunnels, which rabbits live in.

warrior /wɒrɪə/, **warriors.** COUNT N **Warriors** were soldiers or experienced fighting men in former times; a literary use. *...stories of ancient kings, warriors and great battles.*

warship /wɔːʃɪp/, **warships.** COUNT N A **warship** is a ship with guns that is used for fighting in wars.

wart /wɔːt/, **warts.** COUNT N A **wart** is a small, hard piece of skin which can grow on someone's face or hands. *...a large woman with a wart on her nose.*

wartime /wɔːtaɪm/. UNCOUNT N **Wartime** is a period of time when there is a war. *...the disruption of the environment in wartime... ...wartime memories.*

wary /wɛəri/. ADJ If you are **wary** of something, you are cautious about it, for example because it is a new experience or because there may be dangers or problems. *People are understandably wary of the new government.* ♦ **warily** ADV *She was watching Stuart warily.*

was /wəz/. **Was** is the first and third person singular of the past tense of **be.**

wash /wɒʃ/, **washes, washing, washed. 1** VB WITH OBJ If you **wash** something, you clean it using water and soap. *...the clatter of dishes being washed and put away... She washes and irons his clothes.* Also COUNT N *Give it a good wash.* **2** SING N The **wash** is all the clothes that are washed together at one time. *...the average weekly wash.* **3** VB WITH OR WITHOUT OBJ If you **wash** or if you **wash** part of your body, you clean part of your body using soap and water. *I'll have to wash... First wash your hands.* Also COUNT N *He was having a wash.* **4** VB WITH ADJUNCT If a liquid **washes** somewhere, it flows there. *The surf washed over her ankles.* **5** ERG VB WITH ADJUNCT If something carried by a liquid **is washed** or **washes** in a particular direction, it is carried there. *The body was washed ashore in Norway... Soil from the mountains washes down in the rivers.* **6** PHRASE If you say that you **wash your hands of** something, you mean that you refuse to be involved with it any longer or to accept responsibility for it. **7** See also **washing.**

wash away. PHR VB If floods **wash away** buildings, they destroy them and carry them away.

wash down. PHR VB If you **wash down** food, you drink something after you have eaten it or while you are eating it. *...a mash of overcooked rice, washed down with the local wine.*

wash out. PHR VB **1** If you **wash** a stain or colour **out** of something, you manage to remove it using water and soap. **2** If you **wash out** a container, you wash the inside of it.

wash up. PHR VB **1** If you **wash up,** you wash the pans, plates, cups, and cutlery which have been used in cooking and eating a meal. **2** To **wash up** also means to clean part of your body with soap and water, especially your hands and face; an American use. **3** If something **is washed up** on a piece of land, it is carried there by a river or the sea. *His body was washed up under the bridge at Dakao.* **4** See also **washing-up.**

washable /wɒʃəbəl/. ADJ **Washable** clothes or materials can be washed without being damaged. *Acrylic blankets are warm and washable.*

washbasin /wɒʃbeɪsən/, **washbasins.** COUNT N A **washbasin** is a large basin for washing your hands and face, usually fixed to a wall and with taps for hot and cold water.

washer /wɒʃə/, **washers.** COUNT N A **washer** is a thin, flat ring of metal or plastic, which is placed over a bolt before the nut is screwed on, in order to make a tighter connection.

washing /wɒʃɪŋ/. UNCOUNT N **Washing** is clothes, sheets, and towels that need to be washed, or have just been washed. *Her husband comes home at weekends bringing his washing with him... There was nowhere to hang washing.*

washing machine, washing machines. COUNT N A **washing machine** is a machine that washes clothes. *...a fully automatic washing machine.*

washing powder, **washing powders.** MASS N **Washing powder** is powdered detergent that you use to wash clothes.

washing-up. UNCOUNT N If you do the **washing-up,** you wash the pans, plates, cups, and cutlery which have been used in cooking and eating a meal.

washing-up liquid, **washing-up liquids.** MASS N **Washing-up liquid** is thick, soapy liquid which you add to hot water to clean dirty dishes after a meal.

washroom /wɒʃru:^{4}m/, **washrooms.** COUNT N A **washroom** is a room with toilets and washing facilities in a large building such as a factory.

wasn't /wɒzə^{0}nt/. **Wasn't** is the usual spoken form of 'was not'. *I wasn't ready for it... He was first, wasn't he?*

wasp /wɒsp/, **wasps.** COUNT N A **wasp** is a small insect with yellow and black stripes across its body.

wastage /weɪstɪdʒ/. UNCOUNT N **Wastage** of something is a waste of it; a formal use. *The Government is to blame for this serious wastage of talent.*

waste /weɪst/, **wastes, wasting, wasted.** 1 VB WITH OBJ If you **waste** time, money, or energy, you use it on something that is not important or necessary. *You're wasting your time... ...fear of wasting money on a new idea.* 2 VB WITH OBJ If you **waste** an opportunity, you do not take advantage of it. 3 SING N If you say that an action or activity is a **waste** of time, money, or energy, you mean that it involves using it when it is not important or necessary. *It's probably a waste of time... It's a waste of money hiring skis.* 4 UNCOUNT N **Waste** is the use of money or other resources on things that do not need it. *A committee was set up to avoid future waste of public money.* 5 UNCOUNT N **Waste** is also material which has been used and is no longer wanted, for example because the useful part has been removed. *The river was thick with industrial waste.* Also ATTRIB ADJ *...waste paper.* 6 ATTRIB ADJ **Waste** land is not used or looked after by anyone, and so is covered by wild plants and rubbish. *The car was found abandoned on waste ground near Leeds.* 7 PLURAL N **Wastes** are large areas of land in which there are very few people, plants, or animals; a formal use. *...the endless wastes of the desert.*

waste away. PHR VB If someone **wastes away,** they become thin and weak because they are ill or worried and are not eating properly.

wasted /weɪstɪ^{2}d/. ADJ A **wasted** action is one that is unnecessary. *It was a wasted journey.*

wasteful /weɪstfʊl/. ADJ A **wasteful** action causes waste, because it uses resources in a careless or inefficient way. *...the wasteful use of scarce resources.*

wasteland /weɪstlænd/, **wastelands.** COUNT N OR UNCOUNT N A **wasteland** is an area of land which is of no use because it is infertile or has been misused. *The highways cross endless wastelands.*

wastepaper basket, **wastepaper baskets.** COUNT N The **wastepaper basket** or **wastepaper bin** in a room is the container where you put waste paper and other rubbish. *He crumpled the note and tossed it into the wastepaper basket.*

watch /wɒtʃ/, **watches, watching, watched.** 1 COUNT N A **watch** is a small clock which you wear on a strap on your wrist. *My watch has stopped.* 2 VB WITH OR WITHOUT OBJ If you **watch** someone or something, you look at them for a period of time, and pay attention to what is happening. *I'm just watching television... When did you last watch a football match?... Watch me, Grandma... A policeman stood watching.* ♦ **watcher** /wɒtʃə/ COUNT N *Their behaviour baffled the watchers in the house.* 3 VB WITH OBJ To **watch** someone also means to follow them secretly or spy on them. *Liebermann's going to be watched from now on.* 4 VB WITH OBJ OR ADJUNCT If you **watch** a situation, you pay attention to it or you are aware of it. *She sits back and just watches a situation develop... Many companies have watched helplessly as their stock prices fell.*

PHRASES ● If someone **keeps watch,** they look around all the time, for example while other people are asleep, so that they can warn them of danger. *A woman kept watch at the gate.* ● You say **'watch it'** to warn someone to be careful; an informal use.

watch out. PHR VB If you **watch out,** you are very careful because something unpleasant might happen to you. *If you don't watch out, he might stick a knife into you.*

watch over. PHR VB If you **watch over** someone or something, you care for them. *The wives took turns to watch over the children.*

watchband /wɒtʃbænd/, **watchbands.** COUNT N A **watchband** is a watchstrap; an American use.

watchdog /wɒtʃdɒg/, **watchdogs.** COUNT N You use **watchdog** to refer to a person or committee whose job is to make sure that companies do not act illegally or irresponsibly. *They established the Atomic Energy Commission to act as a watchdog.*

watchful /wɒtʃfʊl/. ADJ Someone who is **watchful** is careful to notice everything that is happening. *He spent his days under the watchful eyes of his grandmother.*

watchstrap /wɒtʃstræp/, **watchstraps.** COUNT N A **watchstrap** is a piece of leather, plastic, or metal which is attached to a watch so that you can wear it round your wrist.

water /wɔːtə/, **waters, watering, watered.** 1 UNCOUNT N **Water** is the clear, colourless liquid that has no taste or smell and that is necessary for all plant and animal life. *...a drink of water... Mammals can't breathe under water.* 2 UNCOUNT N OR PLURAL N You use **water** or **waters** to refer to a large amount or area of water, for example a lake or sea. *The children played at the water's edge... ...the black waters of the Thames.* 3 PLURAL N WITH SUPP A country's **waters** consist of the area of sea near it which is regarded as belonging to it. *The ship was in British waters.* 4 VB WITH OBJ If you **water** plants, you pour water into the soil to help them to grow. 5 VB If your eyes **water,** you have tears in them because they are hurting. *The onions made his eyes water.* 6 VB If your mouth **waters,** it produces more saliva, usually because you can smell or see some appetizing food. *This should make your mouth water.*

PHRASES ● When you **pass water,** you urinate. ● If you say that an event is **water under the bridge,** you mean that it has happened and cannot now be changed, so there is no point in worrying about it any more.

water down. PHR VB 1 If you **water down** food or drink, you add water to it to make it weaker. *The milk had been watered down.* 2 If a speech or plan is **watered down,** it is made less forceful. *The whole article had been watered down.*

watercolour /wɔːtəkʌlə/, **watercolours;** spelled **watercolor** in American English. 1 PLURAL N **Watercolours** are coloured paints which you mix with water to use. 2 COUNT N A **watercolour** is a picture which has been painted using watercolours. *...an exhibition of watercolours.*

watercress /wɔːtəkres/. UNCOUNT N **Watercress** is a small plant with white flowers which grows in streams and pools. Its leaves taste hot and are eaten raw in salads.

waterfall /wɔːtəfɔːl/, **waterfalls.** COUNT N A **waterfall** is water that flows over the edge of a steep cliff and falls to the ground below.

waterfront /wɔːtəfrʌnt/, **waterfronts.** COUNT N A **waterfront** is a street or piece of land which is next to an area of water, for example a river or the sea. *...a warehouse on the waterfront.*

waterhole /wɔːtəhəʊl/, **waterholes.** COUNT N A **waterhole** is a pool in a desert or other dry area where animals can find water to drink.

watering can, **watering cans.** COUNT N A **watering can** is a container with a long spout which is used to water plants.

waterlogged /wɔːtəlɒgd/. ADJ **Waterlogged** ground is very wet and cannot soak up the water on it.

watermelon /wɔːtəmelən/, **watermelons.** COUNT N A **watermelon** is a large, round fruit with green skin, pink flesh, and black seeds.

waterproof /wɔːtəpruːf/. ADJ Something that is **waterproof** does not let water pass through it. *...a pair of waterproof trousers.*

watershed /wɔːtəʃed/, **watersheds.** COUNT N A **watershed** is an event or time which marks the beginning of a new stage in something. *The Vietnam war was one of the great watersheds of modern history.*

waterside /wɔːtəsaɪd/. SING N The **waterside** is an area of land near a river, canal, or lake. *I drove down to the waterside.*

water-skiing. UNCOUNT N **Water-skiing** is a sport in which you are pulled along on water by a boat, while wearing flat boards under your feet which enable you to stand.

watertight /wɔːtətaɪt/. 1 ADJ A **watertight** container or door does not allow water to get into it or past it because it is tightly sealed. 2 ADJ A **watertight** agreement, argument, or explanation has been put together so carefully that nobody can find a fault in it.

waterway /wɔːtəweɪ/, **waterways.** COUNT N A **waterway** is a canal, river, or narrow channel of sea which boats can sail along.

watery /wɔːtə^{0}ri^{1}/. 1 ADJ Something that is **watery** is weak or pale. *...a watery smile... ...a watery April sun.* 2 ADJ Food or drink that is **watery** contains a lot of water. *...watery cabbage.*

watt /wɒt/, **watts.** COUNT N A **watt** is a unit of measurement of electrical power. *...a 60 watt bulb.*

wave /weɪv/, **waves, waving, waved.** 1 VB WITH OR WITHOUT OBJ If you **wave** or **wave** your hand, you move your hand from side to side in the air, usually to say hello or goodbye. *His mother waved to him.* Also COUNT N *Jack gave his usual cheery wave.* 2 VB WITH OBJ AND ADJUNCT If you **wave** someone away or **wave** them on, you make a movement with your hand to tell them where to go. *He waves on the traffic... I was waved through.* 3 VB WITH OBJ If you **wave** something, you hold it up and move it rapidly from side to side. *All along the route, people applauded and waved flags at them.* 4 COUNT N A **wave** is a raised mass of water on the sea or a lake, caused by the wind or the tide. *...the line of white foam where the waves broke on the beach.* ● See also **tidal wave.** 5 COUNT N If someone's hair has **waves,** it has curves in it. 6 COUNT N WITH SUPP **Wave** is used to refer to the way in which things such as sound, light, and radio signals travel, or the way in which the force of an explosion or earthquake spreads. *Radar employs radio waves whereas sonar uses sound waves... ...the shock wave from a one megaton bomb.* 7 UNCOUNT N WITH SUPP **Wave** is used in the expressions 'long wave', 'medium wave', and 'short wave' to refer to a range of radio waves used for broadcasting. 8 COUNT N WITH SUPP A **wave** of sympathy, alarm, or panic is a steady increase in that feeling which spreads through a person or group of people. *In the general wave of panic, nobody thought of phoning for an ambulance.* 9 COUNT N WITH SUPP You also use **wave** to refer to a sudden increase in a particular activity or type of behaviour. *In Paris in May 1968 there was a massive wave of student riots... ...a crime wave.* ● See also **new wave.**

waveband /weɪvbænd/, **wavebands.** COUNT N A **waveband** is a group of radio waves of similar length which are used for radio transmission.

wavelength /weɪvleŋkθ/, **wavelengths.** 1 COUNT N A **wavelength** is the size of radio wave which a particular radio station uses to broadcast its programmes. 2 PHRASE If two people are **on the same wavelength,** they share the same attitudes and get on well with each other.

waver /weɪvə/, **wavers, wavering, wavered.** 1 VB If you **waver,** your beliefs or intentions become less firm. *Meehan has never wavered in his assertions of innocence... He felt his determination waver.* 2 VB If something **wavers,** it moves or changes slightly. *I looked into his eyes. They didn't waver.*

wavy /weɪvi^{1}/. ADJ Something that is **wavy** has curves in it. *He had wavy grey hair.*

wax /wæks/, **waxes, waxing, waxed.** 1 UNCOUNT N **Wax** is a solid, slightly shiny substance made of fat or oil which is used to make candles and polish. It goes soft and melts when it is heated. 2 PHRASE If something **waxes and wanes,** it first increases and then decreases over a period of time; a literary use. *The popularity of the film stars waxed and waned.*

waxwork /wækswɜːk/, **waxworks.** COUNT N A **waxwork** is a model of a famous person, made out of wax.

waxy /wæksi^{1}/. ADJ Something that is **waxy** looks or feels like wax. *...waxy blossoms.*

way /weɪ/, **ways.** 1 COUNT N WITH SUPP A **way** of doing something is a thing or series of things that you do to achieve a particular result. *...different ways of cooking fish... The only way to stop an accident is to remove the risk.* 2 SING N WITH SUPP You can refer to the **way** that an action is done to indicate the quality that it has. *He smiles in a superior way... He hated the way she talked.* 3 PLURAL N WITH SUPP The **ways** of a particular person or group of people are their customs or their usual behaviour. *...the difficulty of changing one's ways.* 4 COUNT N WITH SUPP You say that something is the case in the **way** stated when you are referring to an aspect of something or the effect that something has. *Breast feeding is valuable in a number of ways... The job was changing me in a way that I had not expected.* 5 SING N WITH SUPP The **way** you feel about something is your attitude to it or your opinion about it. *Do you still feel the same way?* 6 SING N WITH SUPP When you mention the **way** that something happens, you are mentioning the fact that it happens. *Do you remember the way the boat leaked?* 7 SING N WITH 'with' If you have a **way** with people or things of a particular type, you are very skilful at dealing with them. *...a village boy who had a way with horses.* 8 SING N The **way** to a particular place is the route that you must take in order to get there. *A man asked me the way to Tower Bridge.* 9 SING N WITH SUPP If you go or look a particular **way,** you go or look in that direction. *Will you come this way, please?... I waved but she was looking the other way.* 10 SING N WITH SUPP If something is the right **way** up or the right **way** round, it is facing in the right direction. 11 SING N If someone or something is in the **way,** they prevent you from moving freely or from seeing clearly. *Get out of my way.* 12 SING N In a building, the **way in** is the entrance and the **way out** is the exit. 13 SING N WITH POSS You use **way** in expressions such as 'push your way somewhere' or 'work your way somewhere' which refer to movement or progress that is difficult or slow, or takes a long time. *You can't force your way into somebody's house... He started to work his way through the back copies of 'The Times'.* **14** SING N You use **way** in expressions such as 'a long way' and 'a little way' to say how far away something is. *We're a long way away from Cuba.* **15** SING N You use **way** in expressions such as 'all the way' and 'most of the way' which refer to a particular amount of a journey or distance. *They drove all the way back without a word.* **16** ADV You use **way** with adjuncts to emphasize that something is a great distance away, or is very much below or above a particular level or amount; an informal use. *They're way ahead of us... You're way below the standard required.*

PHRASES ● If you **lose** your **way,** you get lost and do not know which direction to go in order to get to your destination. ● When you **make** your **way** somewhere, you walk or travel there. *I made my way back to my seat.* ● If one person or thing **makes way** for another, the other person or thing takes their place. *Slums have been cleared to make way for new high-rise apartments.* ● If you say that something **goes a long way** towards doing a particular thing, you mean that it helps to achieve that thing. *Goodwill and cooperation can go a long way towards smoothing your way to the top.* ● **On the way** or **on** your **way** means in the course of your journey. *Lynn was on her way home.* ● If you **go out of** your **way** to do something, you make a special effort to do it. *He didn't really go out of his way to help me.* ● If you **keep out of** someone's **way,** you avoid them. ● When something **is out of the way,** it is over or you have dealt with it. *We'll be all right once this meeting is out of the way.* ● If an activity or plan is **under way,** it has begun and is now taking place. *Formal negotiations are under way.* ● If you **get** or **have** your **way,** or if you **have everything your own way,** what you want to happen happens. *If Baker has his way, the money will be paid to you.* ● You say to someone **'You can't have it both ways'** to remind them that they have to choose between two things and cannot do or have them both. ● If you say that someone or something **has a way** of doing a particular thing, you mean that they commonly do it. *Ex-wives have a way of reappearing.* ● You say **by the way** when you add something, especially something that you have just thought of. *By the way, this visit of Muller's is strictly secret.* ● If you do something **by way of** a particular thing, you do it as that thing; a formal use. *I'm going to sketch in a bit of the background by way of introduction.* ● You use **in a way** to indicate that your statement is true to some extent or in one respect. *In a way, these officers were prisoners themselves.* ● You use **in a big way** and **in a small way** to suggest the scale or importance of an activity. *They are going into the arms business in a big way.* ● You use **in the way of** to specify exactly what you are talking about. *He received very little in the way of wages.*

waylay /weɪleɪ/, **waylays, waylaying, waylaid** /weɪleɪd/. VB WITH OBJ If you **waylay** someone, you stop them when they are going somewhere, in order to talk to them.

way of life, ways of life. COUNT N Someone's **way of life** consists of their habits and daily activities. *...the British way of life.*

wayside /weɪsaɪd/. **1** SING N The **wayside** is the side of the road; an old-fashioned use. *Broken-down buses may frequently be seen by the wayside... ...travellers who buy food from wayside stalls.* **2** PHRASE If someone or something **falls by the wayside,** they fail or become forgotten. *We must care for the weak who would otherwise fall by the wayside.*

wayward /weɪwəd/. ADJ Someone who is **wayward** does not behave sensibly and is difficult to control; a literary use. *...wayward children.*

wc, wc's; also written **WC.** COUNT N A **wc** is a toilet.

we /wiː/. PRON **We** is used as the subject of a verb. A speaker or writer uses **we** to refer to a group of people which includes himself or herself. *We could hear the birds singing.*

weak /wiːk/, **weaker, weakest. 1** ADJ Someone who feels **weak** does not have very much strength or energy. *He was weak from hunger.* ♦ **weakly** ADV *She sat down, rather weakly.* ♦ **weakness** UNCOUNT N *...his worsening pain and physical weakness.* **2** ADJ Something that is **weak** is not strong or good, and is likely to break or fail. *A fuse is a deliberately weak link in an electrical system... ...a weak excuse.* ♦ **weakness** UNCOUNT N OR COUNT N *...the weakness of their economy... This would exploit a known weakness on the enemy's Eastern Front.* **3** ADJ Someone who is **weak** is easily influenced by other people. *...incompetent and weak leadership.* ♦ **weakness** UNCOUNT N *...his apparent weakness under pressure.* **4** ADJ A **weak** response to something is made without enthusiasm or emphasis. *He managed a weak smile.* ♦ **weakly** ADV *I argued weakly against these conclusions.* **5** ADJ Someone or something that is **weak** on a particular subject does not have much ability or information relating to it. *The book was weak on fact and documentation.* **6** ADJ **Weak** drinks are made using a lot of water and therefore do not have a strong taste. *...weak tea.* **7** ADJ **Weak** sounds or lights are very faint.

weaken /wiːkəⁿn/, **weakens, weakening, weakened. 1** ERG VB To **weaken** something means to make it less strong or less powerful. *Her armed forces had been weakened by the restriction on equipment supplies... ...weakening traditions.* **2** VB If someone **weakens,** they become less certain about a decision they have made. *Do you think she's beginning to weaken?* **3** VB WITH OBJ If something **weakens** you, it causes you to lose some of your physical strength. *I was weakened by my exertions.*

weakling /wiːklɪŋ/, **weaklings.** COUNT N Someone who is a **weakling** is physically weak.

weakness /wiːknɪs/, **weaknesses.** COUNT N If you have a **weakness** for something, you like it very much, although this is perhaps surprising or undesirable. *He had a weakness for sweets.* ● See also **weak.**

wealth /welθ/. **1** UNCOUNT N **Wealth** is a large amount of money or property owned by someone, or the possession of it. *She was a woman of considerable wealth... It was a period of wealth and prosperity.* **2** SING N WITH 'of' A **wealth** of something means a very large amount of it; a formal use. *...ordinary people, who have a tremendous wealth of experience.*

wealthy /welθiˡ/, **wealthier, wealthiest.** ADJ Someone who is **wealthy** has a large amount of money or property.

wean /wiːn/, **weans, weaning, weaned.** VB WITH OBJ When a mother **weans** her baby, she stops feeding it with milk from her breast and starts giving it other food.

weapon /wepən/, **weapons.** COUNT N A **weapon** is an object which is used to kill or hurt people in a fight or war. *...nuclear weapons.*

wear /weə/, **wears, wearing, wore** /wɔː/, **worn** /wɔːn/. **1** VB WITH OBJ The clothes you **are wearing** are the clothes on your body. *She was wearing a T-shirt and jeans... ...a girl who wore spectacles.* **2** VB WITH OBJ AND ADJUNCT If you **wear** your hair in a particular way, it is cut or arranged in that way. *His face was framed by his curly hair which he wore too long.* **3** UNCOUNT N WITH SUPP You can refer to clothes that are suitable for a particular time or occasion as a particular kind of **wear.** *...evening wear.* **4** VB If something **wears,** it becomes thinner or weaker from constant use. *Move the carpet up or down as it starts to wear.* **5** UNCOUNT N **Wear** is the use that clothes or other things have over a period of time, which causes damage to them. *...when your sheets are showing signs of wear.* **6** PHRASE If something **is wearing thin,** it is becoming weaker. *His patience was clearly wearing thin.* **7** See also **wearing, worn.**

wear away. PHR VB If something **wears away** or **is worn away,** it becomes thin and eventually disappears because it is touched a lot. *The grass was worn away where the children used to play.*

wear down. PHR VB If you **wear** people **down,** you weaken them by repeatedly doing something or asking them to do something. *We tried to wear them down gradually and make them agree.*

wear off. PHR VB If a feeling such as pain **wears off,** it slowly disappears. *By the next afternoon the shock had worn off.*

wear out. PHR VB When something **wears out** or **is worn out,** it is used so much that it becomes thin or weak and cannot be used any more. *His shoes keep wearing out.* ● See also **worn-out.**

wear and tear. UNCOUNT N **Wear and tear** is the damage caused to something during normal use.

wearing /weərɪŋ/. ADJ An activity that is **wearing** makes you feel very tired. *...a very wearing and demanding job.*

weary /wɪəriˡ/, **wearies, wearying, wearied;** a literary use. **1** ADJ If you are **weary,** you are very tired. *...a weary sigh.* ♦ **wearily** ADV *The farmers trudged wearily to the nearest stream.* ♦ **weariness** UNCOUNT N *There were lines of weariness around her eyes.* **2** VB WITH 'of' If you **weary** of something, you become bored with it or tired of it. *He is beginning to weary of sitting still.*

weather /weðə/, **weathers, weathering, weathered. 1** SING N OR UNCOUNT N The **weather** is the condition of the atmosphere in an area at a particular time, for example, whether it is raining, hot, or windy. *The weather was good for the time of year... The tractors couldn't be used in wet weather.* **2** VB If something such as rock or wood **weathers,** it changes colour or shape as a result of the effects of wind, sun, rain, or frost. **3** VB WITH OBJ If you **weather** a difficult time, you survive it. *Anyone who weathers the first four years seems to be all right.*

PHRASES ● If someone **is making heavy weather** of a task, they are doing it in an inefficient way and making it seem more difficult than it really is. ● If you feel **under the weather,** you feel slightly ill.

weatherbeaten /weðəbiːtəⁿn/. ADJ If your face is **weatherbeaten,** it is rough, wrinkled, and brown or red because you have spent a lot of time outside.

weather-vane, weather-vanes. COUNT N A **weather-vane** is a metal object on the roof of a building which turns and shows which way the wind is blowing.

weave /wiːv/, **weaves, weaving, wove** /wəʊv/, **woven** /wəʊvəⁿn/. **1** VB WITH OR WITHOUT OBJ If you **weave** cloth, you make it by crossing threads over and under each other using a machine called a loom. *If you want to learn to weave, you must get somebody to teach you... ...woven fabrics.* ♦ **weaver** /wiːvə/ COUNT N *He had worked as a silk weaver.* **2** COUNT N WITH SUPP The **weave** of a cloth is the way in which the threads are arranged. *...a tight, firm weave.* **3** VB WITH OR WITHOUT OBJ, WITH ADJUNCT If you **weave** your way somewhere, you move between and around things as you go there. *He weaves his way through the crowd... She wove through the guests, smiling brightly.*

web /web/, **webs. 1** COUNT N A **web** is a fine net that a spider makes from a sticky substance produced in its body. **2** COUNT N WITH SUPP You can use **web** to refer to a complicated pattern, structure, or set of things; a literary use. *...the complex web of reasons.*

webbed /webd/. ADJ Water birds with **webbed** feet have skin connecting their toes.

we'd /wiːd/. **We'd** is the usual spoken form of 'we had', especially when 'had' is an auxiliary verb. **We'd** is also a spoken form of 'we would. *We'd done a good job... We'd have given them five if they'd asked.*

wedded /wedɪˡd/. PRED ADJ WITH PREP 'to' If you are **wedded** to an idea or system, you support it very strongly; a formal use. *...a party wedded to unrestricted free enterprise.*

wedding /wedɪŋ/, **weddings.** COUNT N A **wedding** is a marriage ceremony.

wedge /wedʒ/, **wedges, wedging, wedged. 1** VB WITH OBJ If you **wedge** something such as a door or window, you keep it firmly in position by forcing something between it and the surface next to it. *Open the door wide and wedge it with a wad of newspaper.* **2** VB WITH OBJ AND ADJUNCT If you **wedge** something somewhere, you put it there so that it fits tightly. *Captain Imrie wedged himself more deeply into his chair.* **3** COUNT N A **wedge** is an object with one pointed edge and one thick edge, for example one that you put under a door to keep it firmly in position.

PHRASES ● If you **drive a wedge** between people or groups, you cause bad feelings between them in order to weaken their relationship. ● If you describe something as **the thin end of the wedge,** you mean that it appears to be unimportant, but is actually the beginning of a harmful development.

Wednesday /wenzdɪˡ/, **Wednesdays.** UNCOUNT N OR COUNT N **Wednesday** is the day after Tuesday and before Thursday.

wee /wiː/. ATTRIB ADJ **Wee** means small or little; a Scottish use. *Can I ask you just one wee question?*

weed /wiːd/, **weeds, weeding, weeded. 1** COUNT N A **weed** is a wild plant growing where it is not wanted, for example in a garden. **2** VB WITH OR WITHOUT OBJ If you **weed** a place, you remove the weeds from it. *I had weeded the garden... Go and ask that man who's weeding there.* **3** COUNT N If you call someone a **weed,** you mean that they are cowardly and physically weak; an informal British use.

weed out. PHR VB If you **weed out** things that are not wanted in a group, you get rid of them. *Natural selection had weeded out the weakest.*

weedy /wiːdiˡ/. **1** ADJ A place that is **weedy** is full of weeds. *...the long weedy path.* **2** ADJ If you describe someone as **weedy,** you mean that they are thin and physically weak; an informal British use.

week /wiːk/, **weeks. 1** COUNT N OR UNCOUNT N A **week** is a period of seven days, especially one beginning on a Sunday or Monday. *He died in an explosion a few weeks ago... I bought them last week.* **2** COUNT N WITH SUPP Your working **week** is the hours that you spend at work during a week. *I work a thirty-five hour week.* **3** SING N The **week** means the days in a week apart from Saturday and Sunday. *She never goes out during the week.* **4** You use **week** in expressions such as 'a week on Monday', 'a week next Tuesday', and 'tomorrow week' to mean exactly one week after the day that you mention. *'When is it to open?'—'Monday week.'... It's due a week tomorrow.* **5** You use **week** in expressions such as 'a week last Monday' and 'a week ago this Tuesday' to mean exactly one week before the day that you mention. *She died a week last Thursday.*

weekday /wiːkdeɪ/, **weekdays.** COUNT N A **weekday** is any day of the week except Saturday and Sunday.

weekend /wiːkɛnd/, **weekends.** COUNT N A **weekend** is Saturday and Sunday. *I spent the weekend at home.*

weekly /wiːkli¹/, **weeklies. 1** ADJ **Weekly** is used to describe something that happens or appears once a week. *...a weekly newspaper... ...a weekly payment of seven shillings.* Also ADV *Several groups meet weekly.* **2** COUNT N A **weekly** is a newspaper or magazine that is published once a week.

weep /wiːp/, **weeps, weeping, wept** /wɛpt/. VB When someone **weeps,** they cry; a literary use. *The girl was weeping as she kissed him goodbye.* Also SING N *They had a little weep together.*

weigh /weɪ/, **weighs, weighing, weighed. 1** VB WITH COMPLEMENT If something **weighs** a particular amount, that is how heavy it is. *It weighs ten tons.* **2** VB WITH OBJ If you **weigh** something, you measure how heavy it is, using scales. *She was weighing a parcel.*

weigh down. PHR VB **1** If you **are weighed down** by something, you are carrying a lot of it and it is very heavy. *He was weighed down with weapons and equipment.* **2** If you **are weighed down** by a difficulty, it is making you very worried.

weigh on or **weigh upon.** PHR VB If a problem **weighs on** you or **weighs upon** you, it makes you worry. *Her absence began to weigh upon me.*

weigh up. PHR VB **1** If you **weigh up** a situation, you carefully consider the different factors involved before making a decision. *You have to weigh up in your mind whether to punish him or not.* **2** If you **weigh** someone **up,** you consider them and form an opinion of them.

weight /weɪt/, **weights, weighting, weighted. 1** COUNT N OR UNCOUNT N The **weight** of something is how heavy it is, which you can measure in units such as kilos or pounds. *The weight of the load is too great... It was 25 metres long and 30 tons in weight.* **2** COUNT N A **weight** is a metal object which weighs a known amount. Weights are used with some sets of scales to weigh things. **3** COUNT N You can refer to a heavy object as a **weight.** *I'm not allowed to carry heavy weights any more.* **4** VB WITH OBJ If you **weight** something or **weight** it down, you put something heavy on it or in it, often so that it cannot move easily. *...a plastic sheet weighted down with straw bales.* **5** SING N WITH 'of' The **weight** of something is its great amount or power, which makes it difficult to contradict or oppose. *They had the weight of official support behind them.* **6** SING N If you feel a **weight** of some kind on you, you have a worrying problem or responsibility. *Without a producer, the weight of responsibility fell upon me.*

PHRASES • If you **pull your weight,** you work as hard as the other people involved in the same task or activity. • See also **dead weight.**

weighted /weɪtɪ²d/. PRED ADJ WITH ADJUNCT A system that is **weighted** in favour of a person or group is organized so that this person or group has an advantage. *The law is weighted in favour of landlords... Higher education there is weighted towards the arts.*

weightless /weɪtlɪ²s/. ADJ Something that is **weightless** seems to have very little weight or no weight at all. *These creatures may have been virtually weightless in water.*

weightlifting /weɪtlɪftɪŋ/. UNCOUNT N **Weightlifting** is a sport in which the competitor who can lift the heaviest weight wins.

weighty /weɪti¹/, **weightier, weightiest.** ADJ **Weighty** matters are serious or important. *Weightier things get dealt with immediately.*

weir /wɪə/, **weirs.** COUNT N A **weir** is a low dam built across a river to control the flow of water.

weird /wɪəd/, **weirder, weirdest.** ADJ **Weird** means strange and peculiar. *...odd religions and weird cults.* ♦ **weirdly** ADV *...weirdly shaped trees.*

welcome /wɛlkəm/, **welcomes, welcoming, welcomed. 1** VB WITH OBJ If you **welcome** someone, you greet them in a friendly way when they arrive. *He moved eagerly towards the door to welcome his visitor.* Also COUNT N *I was given a warm welcome by the President.* **2** CONVENTION You can say **'Welcome'** to someone who has just arrived. *Welcome to Peking... Welcome back.* **3** ADJ If someone is **welcome** in a place, people are pleased when they come there. *All members of the public are welcome.* **4** PRED ADJ WITH TO-INF If you tell someone that they are **welcome** to do something, you are encouraging them to do it. *You will always be welcome to come back.* **5** VB WITH OBJ If you **welcome** something new, you approve of it and support it. *I warmly welcomed his proposal.* **6** ADJ If something that happens or occurs is **welcome,** you are pleased about it or approve of it. *This is a welcome development.*

PHRASES • If you **make** someone **welcome,** you make them feel happy and accepted when they arrive in a new place. • You can acknowledge someone's thanks by saying **'You're welcome'.** *'Thank you for the beautiful scarf.'—'You're welcome. I'm glad you like it.'*

welcoming /wɛlkəmɪŋ/. ADJ Someone who is **welcoming** is friendly to you when you arrive in a place. *She gave him a welcoming smile.*

weld /wɛld/, **welds, welding, welded. 1** VB WITH OBJ If you **weld** two pieces of metal together, you join them by heating their edges and putting them together so that they cool and harden into one piece. **2** COUNT N A **weld** is a join where two pieces of metal have been welded together.

welfare /wɛlfɛə/. **1** UNCOUNT N WITH POSS The **welfare** of a person or group is their health, comfort, and prosperity. *I would devote my life to the child's welfare.* **2** MOD **Welfare** services are provided to help with people's living conditions and financial problems. *...welfare workers.* **3** UNCOUNT N **Welfare** is money paid by the government to people who are poor, ill, or unemployed; an American use. *They were living off welfare.*

welfare state. SING N The **welfare state** is a system in which the government uses money from taxes to provide free social services such as health care and education.

well /wɛl/, **wells, welling, welled.** When it is an adverb, the comparative is **better** and the superlative is **best:** see the separate entries for these words. **1** CONVENTION You say **'Well'** when you are about to say something else, especially when you are hesitating or trying to make your statement less strong, or when you are about to correct a statement. *'Is that right?'—'Well, I think so.'... I suppose you want to know if I've changed my mind. Well, I haven't... Well, thank you Jim for talking to us about your work... Well, thank God for that... It took me years, well months at least, to realise that he'd actually lied to me.* **2** ADV If you do something **well,** you do it to a high standard. *She speaks French well... He handled it well.* **3** ADV **Well** also means thoroughly or to a very great extent. *You say you don't know this man very well?... They were on the brink of war, but they were well prepared.* Also ADV used in questions and statements about degree. *I don't know how well Dennis knew him.* **4** ADV You use **well** to give emphasis to some adjuncts and to a few adjectives. *They stood well back from the heat... Actors are well aware of this problem.* **5** ADV If you say that something may **well** happen, you mean that it is likely to happen. *Your eyesight may well improve.* **6** ADJ If you are **well,** you are healthy. *They told me you weren't well.* **7** COUNT N A **well** is a hole in the ground from which a supply of water is extracted. **8** COUNT N You can also refer to an oil well as a **well.**

PHRASES • If things **are going well** or **all is well,** things are satisfactory. *Things went well for John until the First World War.* • If someone **is well out of** a situation, it is a good thing that they are no longer involved in it. • If you say that something that has happened **is just as well,** you mean that it is fortunate that it happened. *He didn't have to speak very often, which was just as well as he was a man who liked to keep words to himself.* • If one thing is involved **as well as** another, the first thing is involved in addition to the second. *Women, as well as men, have a fundamental right to work.* • If one thing is involved and another thing is involved **as well,** the second thing is also involved. *He needs to develop his reading further, and his writing as well.* • If you say that you **may as well** or **might as well** do something, you mean that you will do it although you feel slightly reluctant. *I may as well admit that I knew the answer all along.* • You use **well and truly** to emphasize that something is definitely the case; an informal use. *So the Space Age had now well and truly begun.* • You say **'oh well'** to indicate that you accept that a situation cannot be changed, although you are not happy about it. *Oh well, you wouldn't understand.* • **would do well to** do something: see **do.** • **very well:** see **very.** • See also **well done.**

well up. PHR VB If tears **well up** in your eyes, they come to the surface.

we'll /wiːl/. **We'll** is the usual spoken form of 'we shall' or 'we will'. *Come on, then, we'll have to hurry.*

well-balanced. ADJ Someone who is **well-balanced** is sensible and does not have emotional problems.

well-behaved. ADJ A child who is **well-behaved** behaves in a way that adults like and think is correct.

well-being. UNCOUNT N Someone's **well-being** is their health and happiness. *This new physical fitness will produce a general feeling of well-being.*

well-bred. ADJ Someone who is **well-bred** has good manners.

well-built. ADJ Someone, especially a man, who is **well-built** is strong and muscular.

well done. 1 CONVENTION You say **'Well done'** to indicate that you are pleased that someone has got something right or done something good. **2** ADJ If something that you have cooked, especially meat, is **well done,** it has been cooked thoroughly.

well-dressed. ADJ Someone who is **well-dressed** is wearing smart or elegant clothes.

well-established. ADJ If something is **well-established,** it has existed for a long time and is successful. *Senegal already has a well-established film industry.*

well-fed. ADJ Someone who is **well-fed** gets enough good food regularly.

well-founded. ADJ If an idea, opinion, or feeling is **well-founded,** it is based on facts. *These warnings proved well-founded.*

well-groomed. ADJ Someone who is **well-groomed** is neat and tidy in appearance; an old-fashioned use.

well-informed. ADJ Someone who is **well-informed** knows a lot about something or about things in general.

wellington /wɛlɪŋtən/, **wellingtons.** COUNT N **Wellingtons** or **wellington boots** are long rubber boots which you wear to keep your feet dry.

well-intentioned. ADJ If someone is **well-intentioned,** they are trying to be helpful or kind, but are unsuccessful or cause unfortunate results.

well-known. ADJ Something or someone that is **well-known** is famous or familiar. *...his two well-known books on modern art.*

well-mannered. ADJ Someone who is **well-mannered** is polite and has good manners.

well-meaning. ADJ Someone who is **well-meaning** tries to be helpful or kind, but is often unsuccessful. *Some well-meaning parents are too fussy about food.*

well-off. 1 ADJ Someone who is **well-off** is fairly rich. *A lot of the students were quite well-off.* **2** PHRASE If you say that someone **doesn't know when** they **are well off,** you are criticizing them for not appreciating how fortunate they are; an informal use.

well-read. ADJ Someone who is **well-read** has read a lot of books and has learnt a lot from them.

well-spoken. ADJ Someone who is **well-spoken** speaks in a polite, correct way.

well-to-do. ADJ Someone who is **well-to-do** is rich; an old-fashioned use.

well-wisher /wɛlwɪʃə/, **well-wishers.** COUNT N A **well-wisher** is someone who tells you that they hope you will be successful in what you are doing. *Hundreds of telegrams arrived from well-wishers.*

well-worn. 1 ADJ A **well-worn** expression or remark has been used so often that it is boring. *...a well-worn joke.* **2** ADJ A **well-worn** object or piece of clothing has been used so much that it looks old and untidy.

Welsh /wɛlʃ/. **1** ADJ **Welsh** means belonging or relating to Wales. **2** UNCOUNT N **Welsh** is a language spoken in Wales. **3** PLURAL N The **Welsh** are the people who come from Wales.

Welshman /wɛlʃmə³n/, **Welshmen.** COUNT N A **Welshman** is a man who comes from Wales.

Welshwoman /wɛlʃwʊmən/, **Welshwomen.** COUNT N A **Welshwoman** is a woman who comes from Wales.

welter /wɛltə/. SING N A **welter** of things is a large number of them; a literary use. *...the daily welter of details and little problems.*

wend /wɛnd/, **wends, wending, wended.** PHRASE If you **wend** your **way** in a particular direction, you go there slowly; a literary use. *We watched them wend their leisurely way up and down the street.*

went /wɛnt/. **Went** is the past tense of **go.**

wept /wɛpt/. **Wept** is the past tense and past participle of **weep.**

were /wɔ, wɜː/. **1 Were** is the plural and the second person singular of the past tense of **be. 2** AUX OR VB WITH COMPLEMENT **Were** is sometimes used instead of 'was' in conditional clauses or wishes; a formal use. *He wished he were taking a bath... He treated me as if I were crazy.* • **as it were:** see **as.**

we're /wɪə/. **We're** is the usual spoken form of 'we are'. *We're all here.*

weren't /wɜːnt/. **Weren't** is the usual spoken form of 'were not'. *We weren't asleep.*

west /wɛst/. **1** SING N The **west** is the direction in which you look to see the sun set. *The next settlement is two hundred miles to the west.* **2** SING N The **west** of a place is the part which is towards the west. *...the west of Ireland.* Also ATTRIB ADJ *...West Africa.* **3** ADV **West** means towards the west, or to the west of a place or thing. *...an English friend who had never been West.* **4** ATTRIB ADJ A **west** wind blows from the west. **5** SING N **The West** is also used to refer to the United States, Canada, and the countries of Western and Southern Europe.

westerly /wɛstəli¹/. 1 ADJ **Westerly** means towards the west. *The harbour has a westerly outlook.* 2 ADJ A **westerly** wind blows from the west.

western /wɛstə⁵n/, **westerns.** 1 ATTRIB ADJ **Western** means in or from the west of a region or country. *...Western Nigeria.* 2 ATTRIB ADJ **Western** also means coming from or associated with the societies of Europe and North America. *...the impact of western technology.* 3 COUNT N A **western** is a film or book about life in the west of America in the nineteenth century.

westerner /wɛstənə/, **westerners.** COUNT N A **westerner** is a person who was born in or lives in the West.

westernize /wɛstənaɪz/, **westernizes, westernizing, westernized;** also spelled **westernise.** VB WITH OBJ If a society or system **is westernized,** ideas and behaviour which are common in Europe and North America are introduced into it.

westward /wɛstwəd/ or **westwards.** 1 ADV **Westward** or **westwards** means towards the west. *The reef stretches westwards from the tip of Florida.* 2 ATTRIB ADJ **Westward** is used to describe things which are moving towards the west or which face towards the west. *...the westward expansion of the city.*

wet /wɛt/, **wetter, wettest; wets, wetting, wetted.** The past tense and past participle can be **wet** or **wetted.** 1 ADJ If something is **wet,** it is covered in water or another liquid. *The grass is wet... His face was wet with perspiration.* 2 ADJ If the weather is **wet,** it is raining. *Take a raincoat if it's wet.* 3 ADJ If something such as paint, ink, or cement is **wet,** it is not yet dry or solid. 4 ADJ If you say that someone is **wet,** you mean that they lack confidence, energy, or enthusiasm; an informal use. 5 VB WITH OBJ To **wet** something means to cause it to have water or another liquid on it. *Uncle Ted wet his lips... A column of spray wetted them.* 6 VB WITH OBJ OR REFL VB If people, especially children, **wet** their beds or clothes or **wet** themselves, they urinate in their beds or clothes because they cannot control their bladder.

we've /wiːv/. **We've** is the usual spoken form of 'we have', especially when 'have' is an auxiliary verb. *We've had a very interesting discussion.*

whack /wæk/, **whacks, whacking, whacked.** VB WITH OBJ If you **whack** someone or something, you hit them hard.

whale /weɪl/, **whales.** COUNT N A **whale** is a very large sea mammal.

whaling /weɪlɪŋ/. UNCOUNT N **Whaling** is the activity of hunting and killing whales.

wharf /wɔːf/, **wharves.** COUNT N A **wharf** is a platform by a river or the sea, where ships can be tied up.

what /wɒt/. 1 PRON OR DET You use **what** in questions when you are asking for information. *What is your name?... What time is it?* 2 PRON OR DET You also use **what** to introduce reported questions and reported statements. *I asked her what had happened... I don't know what to do... We didn't know what bus to get.* 3 PRON You use **what** at the beginning of a relative clause which is used as a subject, object, or complement. *A computer can only do what you have programmed it to do... What he really needs is a nice cup of tea.* 4 DET OR PRON You use **what** to indicate that you are talking about the whole of an amount. *I've spent what money I had... It took what I could give.* 5 PREDET OR DET You use **what** in exclamations to express your opinion of something. *What a pity... What rubbish!* 6 CONVENTION Some people say **'What?'** when they want you to repeat something because they did not hear it properly. 'What' is not as polite as 'pardon' or 'sorry'. *'Do you want another coffee?'—'What?'—'Do you want another coffee?'* 7 CONVENTION You can say **'What'** to express surprise or disbelief. *'Could I see you?'—'What, right this minute?'*

PHRASES • You use **what about** when you are making a suggestion or offer. *What about some lunch, Colonel?* • You use **what if** at the beginning of a question about the consequences of something, especially something undesirable. *What if I miss the train?* • You say **what with** to introduce the reasons for a situation, especially an undesirable one. *What with paying for lunch and the theatre tickets, I'm very short of cash.* • You can refer to someone as **what's his name** or **what's her name** when you cannot remember their name; an informal use. *You're like what's his name.* • **what's more:** see **more.**

whatever /wɒ³tɛvə/. 1 PRON OR DET You use **whatever** to refer to anything or everything of a particular type. *He volunteered to do whatever he could... She had to rely on whatever books were lying around.* 2 PRON OR DET You also use **whatever** to refer to things of a particular type when you cannot be specific about their precise nature. *Whatever the reason, Rudolph was glad that she had come back... She gave us a bowl of chilli, whatever that is.* 3 PHRASE You say **or whatever** to refer generally to something of the same kind as the thing you have just mentioned; an informal use. *You plug it into a computer or whatever and it does the rest.* 4 CONJ You also use **whatever** to say that something is the case in all circumstances. *I have to bring my family back whatever happens.* 5 ADV You also use **whatever** after a noun group to emphasize a negative statement. *There is no scientific evidence whatever to support such a view... He knew nothing whatever about it.* 6 PRON **Whatever** is used in questions when you want to sound surprised. *Whatever is the matter?*

what's /wɒts/. **What's** is the usual spoken form of 'what is' or 'what has', especially when 'has' is an auxiliary verb. *What's your name?... What's going on?... What's happened?*

whatsoever /wɒtsəʊɛvə/. ADV You use **whatsoever** after a noun group in order to emphasize a negative statement. *I don't think there's any evidence of that whatsoever.*

wheat /wiːt/. UNCOUNT N **Wheat** is a cereal plant which is ground into flour to make bread.

wheedle /wiːdə⁰l/, **wheedles, wheedling, wheedled.** 1 VB WITH OR WITHOUT OBJ If you **wheedle** someone into doing something, you gently and cleverly persuade them to do it. *They tried to wheedle her into leaving the house.* 2 VB WITH OBJ AND ADJUNCT If you **wheedle** something out of someone, you persuade them to give it you. *She wheedled money out of him.*

wheel /wiːl/, **wheels, wheeling, wheeled.** 1 COUNT N A **wheel** is a circular object which turns round on a rod attached to its centre. Wheels are fixed underneath vehicles so that they can move along. *The train started, its wheels squealing against the metal tracks.* 2 COUNT N A **wheel** is also a steering wheel. *Howard sits behind the wheel.* 3 VB WITH OBJ If you **wheel** something such as a bicycle or cart, you push it along. *My father was wheeling his bicycle up the hill... The equipment had to be wheeled around on a large trolley.* 4 VB If someone or something **wheels,** they move round in the shape of a circle or part of a circle. *The sky becomes filled with birds wheeling back and forth... The plane banked and wheeled... I wheeled around and shook her hand.*

wheelbarrow /wiːlbærəʊ/, **wheelbarrows.** COUNT N A **wheelbarrow** is a small, open cart with one wheel and handles that is used for carrying things in the garden.

wheelchair /wiːltʃɛə/, **wheelchairs.** COUNT N A **wheelchair** is a chair with wheels that sick or disabled people use in order to move about.

wheeze /wiːz/, **wheezes, wheezing, wheezed.** VB If you **wheeze,** you breathe with difficulty, making a hissing or whistling sound. *Coughing and wheezing, he climbed up the last few steps.* Also COUNT N *All this was said very slowly, between wheezes.*

when /wɛn/. 1 ADV You use **when** to ask questions about the time at which things happen. *'I have to go to Germany.'—'When?'—'Now.'... When did you arrive?... When are you getting married?* 2 CONJ You also use **when** in reported questions and reported statements about the time at which something happens. *He didn't know when he was coming back... Ask her when the trouble first started.* 3 CONJ OR PRON **When** is also used to introduce a clause which specifies or refers to the time at which something happens. *He left school when he was eleven... When I have free time, I always spend it fishing... Do you remember that time when Adrian phoned up from Tunbridge?* 4 CONJ You also use **when** to introduce the reason for an opinion, comment, or question. *How can I get a job when I can't even read or write?* 5 CONJ You also use **when** at the beginning of a subordinate clause to make a statement that makes your previous statement seem surprising. *You describe this policy as rigid and inflexible, when in fact it has been extremely flexible.*

whence /wɛns/. ADV OR CONJ **Whence** means from where; an old-fashioned use. *He returned hastily to the United States, whence he originally came.*

whenever /wɛnɛvə/. CONJ You use **whenever** to refer to any time or every time that something happens or is true. *Come and see me whenever you feel depressed... I avoided conflict whenever possible.*

where /wɛə/. 1 ADV You use **where** to ask questions about the place something is in, or is coming from or going to. *Where's Jane?... Where are you going?* 2 CONJ OR PRON You also use **where** to specify or refer to the place in which something is situated or happens. *I think I know where we are... How did you know where to find me?... She walked over to where Madeleine stood.* 3 CONJ, PRON, OR ADV You also use **where** when you are referring to or asking about a situation, a stage in something, or an aspect of something. *Bryan wouldn't know where to start... ...a situation where unemployment is three million and rising fast... This is where I profoundly disagree with you.* 4 CONJ **Where** is used to introduce a clause which contrasts with what is said in the main clause. *Sometimes a teacher will be listened to, where a parent might not.*

whereabouts /wɛərəbaʊts/. 1 PLURAL N WITH POSS If you refer to the **whereabouts** of a person or thing, you mean the place where that person or thing is. *I will not give anyone my whereabouts... We have discovered the whereabouts of one of the paintings.* 2 ADV You use **whereabouts** in questions when you are asking precisely where something is. *Whereabouts are you going in Yugoslavia?*

whereas /wɛəræz/. CONJ You use **whereas** to introduce a comment which contrasts with what is said in the main clause. *Humans are capable of error whereas the computer is not.*

whereby /wɛəbaɪ/. PRON A system or action **whereby** something happens is one that makes that thing happen; a formal use. *...a system whereby we work more overtime than any other country.*

wherein /wɛərɪn/; an old-fashioned word. 1 PRON **Wherein** means in which place. *...the box wherein she kept her wool.* 2 ADV OR CONJ **Wherein** also means in which part or respect. *Wherein lay her greatness?*

whereupon /wɛərəpɒn/. CONJ You use **whereupon** to say that one thing happens immediately after another thing and usually as a result of it; a formal use. *His department was shut down, whereupon he returned to Calcutta.*

wherever /wɛərɛvə/. 1 CONJ You use **wherever** to say that something is true or happens in any place or situation. *Wherever he was, he was happy... They have tried to restore the house wherever possible to its original state.* 2 CONJ You also use **wherever** to indicate that you do not know where a place or person is. *'Where does she live?'—'Alten, wherever that is.'*

whet /wɛt/, **whets, whetting, whetted.** PHRASE If you **whet** someone's **appetite** for something, you increase their desire for it. *The tutor at the college had whetted her appetite for more work.*

whether /wɛðə/. 1 CONJ You use **whether** to talk about a choice or doubt between two or more alternatives. *I can't tell whether she loves me or she hates me... I wasn't sure whether I liked it or not.* 2 CONJ You also use **whether** to say that something is true in any of the circumstances you mention. *He's going to buy a house whether he gets married or not.*

which /wɪtʃ/. 1 DET OR PRON You use **which** to ask questions when there are two or more possible answers or alternatives. *Which department do you want?... Which is her room?* 2 DET OR PRON You also use **which** to refer to a choice between two or more possible answers or alternatives. *I don't know which country he played for... The book says one thing and you say another. I don't know which to believe.* 3 PRON You also use **which** at the beginning of a relative clause that specifies the thing you are talking about or that gives more information about it. *...the awful conditions which exist in British prisons... We sat on the carpet, which was pale green.* 4 PRON OR DET You also use **which** to refer back to what has just been said. *It takes me an hour from door to door, which is not bad... I enjoy these dinners, unless I have to make a speech, in which case I worry throughout the meal.*

whichever /wɪtʃɛvə/. 1 DET OR PRON You use **whichever** to indicate that it does not matter which of the possible alternatives happens or is chosen. *The United States would be safe whichever side won... Then they have lunch, have a chat, have a sleep, whichever they like, up in the lounge.* 2 DET OR PRON You also use **whichever** to specify which of a number of possibilities is the right one or the one you mean. *Use whichever soap powder is recommended by the manufacturer... Use whichever of the forms is appropriate.*

whiff /wɪf/. 1 SING N WITH 'of' If there is a **whiff** of something, there is a faint smell of it. *...a little whiff of perfume as she passed.* 2 SING N WITH 'of' A **whiff** of a particular feeling or type of behaviour is a slight sign of it. *...a whiff of rebellion... ...the first whiff of danger.*

while /waɪl/, **whiles, whiling, whiled.** 1 CONJ If one thing happens **while** another thing is happening, the two things happen at the same time. *He stayed with me while Dad talked with Dr Leon... They wanted a place to stay while in Paris.* 2 CONJ You also use **while** to introduce a clause which contrasts with the other part of the sentence. *Fred gambled his money away while Julia spent hers all on dresses... While I have some sympathy for these fellows, I think they went too far.* 3 SING N A **while** is a period of time. *They talked for a short while... After a while, my eyes became accustomed to the darkness.* 4 **once in a while:** see **once.** • to be **worth** your **while:** see **worth.**

while away. PHR VB If you **while away** the time in a particular way, you spend time in that way because you are waiting for something or because you have nothing else to do. *How about whiling away the time by telling me a story?*

whilst /waɪlst/. CONJ **Whilst** means the same as while. *I didn't want to live at home whilst I was at university... Whilst these cars are economical at a steady 56 mph, they perform badly in traffic.*

whim /wɪm/, **whims.** COUNT N OR UNCOUNT N A **whim** is a sudden desire to do or have something without any particular reason. *She might go, or might not, as the whim took her... ...his tendency to change his mind at whim.*

whimper /wɪmpə/, **whimpers, whimpering, whimpered. 1** VB If children or animals **whimper,** they make little, low, unhappy sounds. *You don't have to feed the baby the minute she whimpers.* Also COUNT N *I was listening for a cry or a whimper from upstairs.* **2** REPORT VB If someone **whimpers** something, they say it in an unhappy or frightened way. *'I want to go home,' she whimpered.*

whimsical /wɪmzɪkəl/. ADJ Something that is **whimsical** is unusual and slightly playful, and is done for no particular reason. *...a whimsical smile... ...whimsical images of birds and beasts.*

whine /waɪn/, **whines, whining, whined. 1** VB To **whines** means to make a long, high-pitched noise, especially one which sounds sad or unpleasant. *His dog was whining in pain... The clattering and whining elevator began to move slowly upwards.* Also COUNT N *...the whine of the police sirens.* **2** VB If someone **whines** about something, they complain about it in an annoying way. *My father never whined about his work.*

whip /wɪp/, **whips, whipping, whipped. 1** COUNT N A **whip** is a piece of leather or rope fastened to a handle which is used for hitting people or animals. *He was lashed with whips.* **2** VB WITH OBJ If you **whip** a person or animal, you hit them with a whip. *I saw him whipping his mules.* ♦ **whipping** COUNT N *He could not possibly have endured a whipping.* **3** VB WITH OBJ If the wind **whips** something, it strikes it sharply. *The wind whipped my face.* **4** VB WITH OBJ AND ADJUNCT If you **whip** something out or off, you take it out or remove it very quickly and suddenly. *Glenn whipped off the mask to reveal his identity.* **5** VB WITH OBJ If you **whip** cream or eggs, you stir them very quickly to make them thick and frothy. ♦ **whipped** ADJ *...fruit flan with whipped cream.*

whip up. PHR VB If you **whip up** a strong emotion, you deliberately make people feel that emotion. *The interview whipped up the Americans into a frenzy of rage.*

whir /wɜː/. See **whirr.**

whirl /wɜːl/, **whirls, whirling, whirled. 1** ERG VB When something **whirls** or when you **whirl** it round, it turns round very fast. *...the whirling blades of a helicopter.* Also SING N *...a whirl of dust.* **2** COUNT N WITH SUPP You can refer to a lot of intense activity as a **whirl** of activity. *We flung ourselves into the mad whirl of pleasure.*

whirlpool /wɜːlpuːl/, **whirlpools.** COUNT N A **whirlpool** is a small area in a river or sea where the water is moving quickly round and round, so that objects floating near it are pulled into its centre.

whirlwind /wɜːlwɪnd/, **whirlwinds. 1** COUNT N A **whirlwind** is a tall column of air which spins round and round very fast. **2** ATTRIB ADJ A **whirlwind** event happens much more quickly than normal. *...a whirlwind romance.*

whirr /wɜː/, **whirrs, whirring, whirred;** also spelled **whir.** VB When something **whirrs,** it makes a series of low sounds so fast that they seem to be continuous. *Fans whirred on the ceiling... ...insects whirring and buzzing through the air.* Also COUNT N *...the whirr of an engine.*

whisk /wɪsk/, **whisks, whisking, whisked. 1** VB WITH OBJ AND ADJUNCT If you **whisk** someone or something somewhere, you take them there quickly. *I was whisked into hospital with fierce abdominal pains.* **2** VB WITH OBJ If you **whisk** eggs or cream, you stir air into them very fast. *Whisk the egg whites until stiff.* **3** COUNT N A **whisk** is a kitchen tool used for whisking eggs or cream.

whisker /wɪskə/, **whiskers. 1** COUNT N The **whiskers** of an animal such as a cat or mouse are the long, stiff hairs growing near its mouth. **2** PLURAL N You can refer to the hair on a man's face, especially on the sides of his face, as his **whiskers.** *He tugged at his side whiskers.*

whisky /wɪski/, **whiskies;** spelled **whiskey** in American English and Irish English. MASS N **Whisky** is a strong alcoholic drink made from barley or rye. *...Scotch whisky.*

whisper /wɪspə/, **whispers, whispering, whispered.** REPORT VB OR VB When you **whisper** something, you say it very quietly, using only your breath and not your throat. *'Follow me,' Claude whispered. 'And keep quiet.'... When we were washing I whispered the news to my sister... Why are you whispering?* Also COUNT N *Hooper lowered his voice to a whisper... We spoke in whispers.*

whistle /wɪsəl/, **whistles, whistling, whistled. 1** VB WITH OR WITHOUT OBJ When you **whistle,** you make a sound by forcing your breath out between your lips. *He walked home whistling cheerfully... I was whistling little bits of the song.* Also COUNT N *Sean let out a low whistle of surprise.* **2** VB If something **whistles,** it makes a loud, high sound. *The bullets whistled past his head... The train whistled as it approached the tunnel.* **3** COUNT N A **whistle** is a small metal tube which you blow to produce a loud sound and attract someone's attention. *The guard blew his whistle and waved his green flag.*

white /waɪt/, **whiter, whitest; whites. 1** ADJ Something that is **white** is the colour of snow or milk. *There were little white clouds high in the blue sky... A woman dressed in white came up to me.* **2** ADJ Someone who is **white** has a pale skin and is of European origin. *They had never seen a white person before.* Also COUNT N *The race riots had been caused by whites attacking blacks.* **3** ADJ If someone goes **white,** their hair becomes white as they get older. *My grandfather went white at the age of fifty.* **4** PRED ADJ If you go **white,** you become very pale because you are afraid or shocked. *My sister went white with rage.* **5** ADJ **White** coffee contains milk or cream. **6** ADJ **White** wine is wine of a pale yellowish colour. **7** COUNT N The **white** of an egg is the transparent liquid surrounding the yolk. **8** COUNT N The **white** of someone's eye is the white part of their eyeball.

white-collar. ATTRIB ADJ **White-collar** workers work in offices rather than doing manual work.

white elephant. SING N If something is a **white elephant,** it is a waste of money because it is completely useless. *The new naval base has proved to be a white elephant.*

white-hot /waɪt hɒt/. ADJ If something is **white-hot,** it is extremely hot. *...the white-hot centre of the bonfire.*

whiten /waɪtən/, **whitens, whitening, whitened.** ERG VB WITH ADJUNCT When something **whitens** or when you **whiten** it, it becomes whiter or paler in colour. *Use very mild bleach to whiten white nylon.*

whitewash /waɪtwɒʃ/. **1** UNCOUNT N **Whitewash** is a mixture of chalk and water used for painting walls white. **2** UNCOUNT N OR SING N **Whitewash** is also an attempt to hide the unpleasant facts about something. *...the refusal to accept official whitewash in police enquiries.*

whiting /waɪtɪŋ/. **Whiting** is the singular and plural. COUNT N A **whiting** is a kind of sea fish.

whittle /wɪtəl/, **whittles, whittling, whittled.**

whittle away or **whittle down.** PHR VB To **whittle** something **away** or to **whittle** it **down** means to make it smaller or less effective. *This may whittle away our liberties... Profits are whittled down by the ever-rising cost of energy.*

whizz /wɪz/, **whizzes, whizzing, whizzed;** an informal word, also spelled **whiz. 1** VB WITH ADJUNCT If you **whizz** somewhere, you move there very fast. *We just stood there with the cars whizzing by.* **2** COUNT N If you are a **whizz** at something, you are very good at it. *He might be a whizz at electronics.*

whizz-kid /wɪz kɪd/, **whizz-kids;** also spelled **whiz-kid.** COUNT N A **whizz-kid** is someone who is very good at their job and achieves success quickly; an informal use. *...a multi-millionaire insurance whizz-kid.*

who /huː/. **Who** is used as the subject or object of a verb. ● See also **whom, whose. 1** PRON You use **who** when asking questions about someone's name or identity. *Who are you?... Who are you going to invite?* **2** PRON You also use **who** in reported questions and reported statements about someone's name or identity. *She didn't know who I was.* **3** PRON You also use **who** at the beginning of a relative clause that specifies the person you are talking about. *If you can't do it, we'll find someone who can... Joe, who was always early, was there already.*

who'd /huːd/. **Who'd** is the usual spoken form of 'who had', especially when 'had' is an auxiliary verb. **Who'd** is also a spoken form of 'who would'. *It was the little girl who'd come to play with her that afternoon... I don't think he's the sort of young man who'd be thinking of marriage.*

whoever /huːevə/. **1** PRON You use **whoever** to refer to the person who does something, when their identity does not matter or is not known. *If death occurs at home, whoever discovers the body should contact the family doctor... Whoever answered the telephone was a very charming woman.* **2** CONJ You also use **whoever** to indicate that the actual identity of the person who does something will not affect a situation. *Whoever wins the war, there will be little peace... Whoever you vote for, prices will go on rising.* **3** PRON You also use **whoever** in questions as an emphatic way of saying 'who'. *Whoever could that be at this time of night?*

whole /həʊl/. **1** SING N If you refer to the **whole** of something, you mean all of it. *...the whole of Europe... ...the whole of July.* Also ATTRIB ADJ *They're the best in the whole world... I've never told this to anyone else in my whole life.* **2** SING N A **whole** is a single thing containing several different parts. *The earth's weather system is an integrated whole.* **3** PRED ADJ If something is **whole,** it is not broken or damaged; a formal use. *Fortunately, the plates were still whole.* **4** ADV **Whole** means in one piece. For example, if you swallow something **whole,** you do not bite it into smaller bits. *The snake can swallow a small rat whole.* **5** SUBMOD OR ADJ You also use **whole** to emphasize what you are saying; an informal use. *...a whole new way of life... Charles was a whole lot nicer than I had expected.*

PHRASES ● If you refer to something **as a whole,** you are referring to it generally and as a single unit. *Is that just in India, or in the world as a whole?* ● You say **on the whole** to indicate that what you are saying is only true in general and may not be true in every case. *On the whole he is a very difficult character.*

wholefood /həʊlfuːd/, **wholefoods.** PLURAL N OR UNCOUNT N **Wholefoods** are foods which do not contain additives or artificial ingredients. *Wholefoods and fresh fruit are essential in your diet... ...a wholefood shop.*

wholehearted /həʊlhɑːtɪd/. ADJ If you support something in a **wholehearted** way, you support it enthusiastically and completely. *He had the wholehearted backing of the younger members.* ♦ **wholeheartedly** ADV *I agree wholeheartedly.*

wholemeal /həʊlmiːl/. ATTRIB ADJ **Wholemeal** flour or bread is made from the complete grain of the wheat plant, including the husk.

wholeness /həʊlnɪs/. UNCOUNT N **Wholeness** is the quality of being complete or a single unit and not divided into parts; a literary use. *...a sense of the wholeness of life.*

wholesale /həʊlseɪl/. **1** ATTRIB ADJ OR ADV You use **wholesale** to refer to the activity of buying and selling goods cheaply in large quantities and then selling them again. *...a sharp rise in wholesale prices... Stein got the food for me wholesale.* ♦ **wholesaler** COUNT N *...a jewellery wholesaler.* **2** ATTRIB ADJ OR ADV You also use **wholesale** to describe something undesirable or unpleasant that is done to an excessive extent. *Wholesale slaughter was carried out in the name of progress.*

wholesome /həʊlsəm/. **1** ADJ Something that is **wholesome** is good and morally acceptable. *Young people enter marriage nowadays with a much more wholesome attitude.* **2** ADJ **Wholesome** food is good for you.

wholewheat /həʊlwiːt/. ATTRIB ADJ **Wholewheat** means the same as wholemeal; an American use. *Wholewheat spaghetti takes slightly longer to cook.*

who'll /huːl/. **Who'll** is a spoken form of 'who will' or 'who shall'. *Who'll believe him?*

wholly /həʊlli/. ADV **Wholly** means completely. *The idea was not a wholly new one... ...people whom we could not wholly trust.*

whom /huːm/. **Whom** is used in formal or written English instead of 'who' when it is the object of a verb or preposition. **1** PRON You use **whom** in questions, indirect questions, and other structures to refer to someone whose name or identity is unknown. *'I'm a reporter.'—'Oh yes? For whom?'... Whom do you suggest I should ask?* **2** PRON You also use **whom** at the beginning of a relative clause in which you specify the person you are talking about or give more information about them. *She was engaged to a sailor named Raikes, whom she had met at Dartmouth.*

whoop /wuːp/, **whoops, whooping, whooped.** VB If you **whoop,** you shout loudly in a very happy or excited way; used in written English. *Eddie whooped with delight.* Also COUNT N *There were whoops of approval by the bar customers.*

whooping cough /huːpɪŋ kɒf/. UNCOUNT N **Whooping cough** is a serious infectious disease which causes people to cough and make a loud noise when they breathe in.

whoosh /wʊʃ/, **whooshes, whooshing, whooshed.** VB WITH ADJUNCT If something **whooshes** somewhere, it moves there quickly or suddenly; an informal use. *Thousands of rockets whooshed over our heads.* Also SING N *The train came in with a whoosh of dust.*

whore /hɔː/, **whores.** COUNT N If someone calls a woman a **whore,** they mean that they consider her sexual behaviour to be immoral or unacceptable; an old-fashioned offensive word.

who's /huːz/. **Who's** is the usual spoken form of 'who is' or 'who has', especially when 'has' is an auxiliary verb. *'Edward drove me up.'—'Who's Edward?'... ...an American author who's settled in London.*

whose /hu:z/. 1 PRON You use **whose** at the beginning of a relative clause to indicate that something belongs to or is associated with the person or thing mentioned in the previous clause. *...a woman whose husband had deserted her.* 2 DET OR PRON You also use **whose** in questions, reported questions, and other structures in which you ask about or refer to the person that something belongs to or is associated with. *Whose fault is it?*

who've /hu:v/. **Who've** is the usual spoken form of 'who have,' especially when 'have' is an auxiliary verb. *...people who've gone to universities.*

why /waɪ/. 1 ADV You use **why** when asking questions about the reason for something. *'I had to say no.'—'Why?'... Why did you do it, Martin?* 2 CONJ You also use **why** at the beginning of a clause in which you talk about the reason for something. *He wondered why she had come... I did not know why, but I was afraid... There are several good reasons why I have a freezer.* 3 ADV You use **why** with 'not' to introduce a suggestion in the form of a question. *Why don't we all go?*

wick /wɪk/, **wicks.** 1 COUNT N The **wick** of a candle is the piece of string in it which burns when it is lit. 2 COUNT N The **wick** of a paraffin lamp or cigarette lighter is the part which supplies the fuel to the flame when it is lit. *It's very hard to turn the wick up and down.*

wicked /wɪkɪ²d/. 1 ADJ Someone or something that is **wicked** is very bad in a way that is deliberately harmful to people. *It was clear to him that he had done something wicked.* ♦ **wickedness** UNCOUNT N *...the wickedness of his crime.* 2 ADJ **Wicked** also means mischievous in a way that you find attractive or enjoyable. *He had a wicked grin... ...the wicked wit of the cartoonist.* ♦ **wickedly** ADV *She smiled wickedly.*

wicker /wɪkə/. UNCOUNT N A **wicker** basket, chair, or mat is made of wickerwork.

wickerwork /wɪkəwɜ:k/. UNCOUNT N **Wickerwork** is a material made by weaving twigs, canes, or reeds together. **Wickerwork** is used to make furniture. *...wickerwork armchairs.*

wicket /wɪkɪt/, **wickets.** COUNT N In cricket, a **wicket** is a set of three upright sticks with small sticks on top of them at which the ball is bowled. You also use **wicket** to refer to the area of grass between two wickets on a cricket pitch.

wide /waɪd/, **wider, widest.** 1 ADJ Something that is **wide** measures a large distance from one side to the other. *...a wide bed... She looked across the wide, flat meadow... ...a wide grin.* ♦ **widely** ADV *'That's all right,' she said, smiling widely.* 2 ADJ **Wide** is used in questions and statements about the distance something measures from one side or edge to the other. *The bay is about six miles wide... How wide is the bed?* 3 ADV If you open or spread something **wide,** you open or spread it to its fullest extent. *Rudolph always opened the window wide at night... He left his office door wide open.* 4 ADJ If your eyes are **wide** or **wide open,** they are more open than usual, because you are surprised or frightened. *She sat looking up at me, her eyes wide with pleasure.* 5 ADJ A **wide** variety, range, or selection includes a lot of different things. *The college library had a wide variety of books.* ♦ **widely** ADV *Over the next twelve years, he travelled widely.* 6 ADJ You also use **wide** when describing something which is believed or known by many people. *The event received wide publicity in the press.* ♦ **widely** ADV *Your views on education are already widely known.* 7 ADJ A **wide** difference or gap between two things is a large one. *The gap between the poor and the rich is very wide indeed.* ♦ **widely** ADV *Customs vary widely from one area to another.* 8 ADJ **Wide** is used to describe something relating to the most important or general parts of a situation. *...the wider context of world events.* 9 PRED ADJ A **wide** shot or punch does not hit its target. 10 **far and wide:** see **far.** • **wide of the mark:** see **mark.**

wide-awake. PRED ADJ If you are **wide-awake,** you are completely awake.

wide-eyed. 1 ADJ If someone is **wide-eyed,** their eyes are more open than usual. *Her face seemed frozen in an expression of wide-eyed alarm.* 2 ADJ If you describe someone as **wide-eyed,** you mean that they seem inexperienced, and perhaps lack common sense. *Part of me was still a wide-eyed American.*

widen /waɪdə⁰n/, **widens, widening, widened.** 1 ERG VB If something **widens,** it becomes bigger from one side or edge to the other. *Below Wapping, the river widens... Sandy stared at me, his eyes widening... The original trail had been widened.* 2 ERG VB You can also say that something **widens** when it becomes greater in range, size, or variety or affects a larger number of people or things. *The gap between the rich and poor regions widened... Labour had to widen its appeal if it was to win the election... They could widen their experience by going on a course.*

wide-ranging. ADJ If something is **wide-ranging,** it includes or deals with a great variety of different things. *...a wide-ranging interview... This attack carried wide-ranging implications for the police.*

widespread /waɪdspred/. ADJ If something is **widespread,** it exists or happens over a large area, or to a very great extent. *These housing estates suffer from widespread vandalism and neglect.*

widow /wɪdəʊ/, **widows.** COUNT N A **widow** is a woman whose husband has died.

widowed /wɪdəʊd/. ADJ If someone is **widowed,** their husband or wife has died.

widower /wɪdəʊə/, **widowers.** COUNT N A **widower** is a man whose wife has died.

widowhood /wɪdəʊhʊd/. UNCOUNT N **Widowhood** is the state of being a widow. *The shock of widowhood weakens resistance to illness.*

width /wɪdθ/. UNCOUNT N The **width** of something is the distance that it measures from one side to the other. *The area was just over a thousand yards in width... ...the width of a man's hand.*

wield /wi:ld/, **wields, wielding, wielded;** a literary word. 1 VB WITH OBJ If you **wield** a weapon, you carry it and use it. *They surrounded the Embassy, wielding sticks.* 2 VB WITH OBJ If someone **wields** power, they have it and are able to use it.

wife /waɪf/, **wives** /waɪvz/. COUNT N A man's **wife** is the woman that he is married to. • See also **old wives' tale.**

wig /wɪg/, **wigs.** COUNT N A **wig** is a mass of false hair which is worn on your head.

wiggle /wɪgə⁰l/, **wiggles, wiggling, wiggled.** 1 ERG VB If you **wiggle** something, you move it around with small, quick movements. *They wiggle their hips to the sound of pop music... Can you wiggle your ears?* Also COUNT N *Give the wire a quick wiggle.* 2 COUNT N A **wiggle** is a line with a lot of little bumps or curves in it. *He drew the sea as a series of wiggles.*

wild /waɪld/, **wilder, wildest; wilds.** 1 ATTRIB ADJ **Wild** animals and plants live or grow in natural surroundings and are not looked after by people. *...wild pigs... He lived on berries and wild herbs.* 2 ADJ **Wild** land is natural and not cultivated. *...the wilder parts of Scotland.* 3 PLURAL N The **wilds** are remote areas, far away from towns. *...the wilds of Australia.* 4 ADJ **Wild** is used to describe the weather or the sea when it is very stormy. *...a wild night in February.* 5 ADJ **Wild** behaviour is uncontrolled, excited, or energetic. *The audience went wild... The men were wild with excitement.* ♦ **wildly** ADV *The spectators applauded wildly.* 6 ADJ A **wild** idea, plan, or guess is unusual and made without much thought. *Childhood is full of wild hopes and dreams.* ♦ **wildly** ADV OR SUBMOD *I was guessing wildly... ...wildly impractical ideas.*

PHRASES • Animals living **in the wild** live in a free and natural state. *They couldn't survive in the wild.* • If something **runs wild,** it behaves in a natural or free way. *Early in the morning, dogs run wild in the park.* • If you **are not wild about** something, you do not like it very much; an informal use. *I'm not wild about the wallpaper.* • If something is **beyond** your **wildest dreams,** it is far better than you believed possible. *He's paying them a salary beyond their wildest dreams.*

wilderness /wɪldənɪ²s/, **wildernesses.** 1 COUNT N A **wilderness** is an area of natural land which is not cultivated. *...the arctic wilderness... The garden's turned into a wilderness.* 2 PHRASE If a politician spends time **in the wilderness,** he or she is not in an influential position in politics for that time. *He is enjoying a revival after four years in the wilderness.*

wildlife /waɪldlaɪf/. UNCOUNT N You can refer to animals that live in the wild as **wildlife.** *These chemicals would destroy crops and all wildlife.*

wiles /waɪlz/. PLURAL N **Wiles** are clever tricks used to persuade people to do something; a formal use. *You seem familiar with the wiles of children.*

wilful /wɪlfʊl/. 1 ATTRIB ADJ **Wilful** actions or attitudes are done or expressed deliberately, especially with the intention of hurting someone. *...wilful destruction.* ♦ **wilfully** ADV *She had wilfully betrayed him to his father.* 2 ADJ A **wilful** person is obstinate and determined to get what they want. *She was a wilful child.*

will /wɪl/, **wills, willing, willed.** The usual spoken form of 'will not' is 'won't'. 1 MODAL If you say that something **will** happen, you mean that it is going to happen in the future. *Inflation is rising and will continue to rise... Perhaps this time it won't rain... Perhaps when I am fifty I will have forgotten.* 2 MODAL If you say that you **will** do something, you mean that you intend to do it or that it is acceptable to you. *I will never betray you... People won't admit that they can't read.* 3 MODAL You can use **will** when making offers, invitations, or requests. *Will you have a whisky, Doctor?... Will you do me a favour?... Will you shut up!* 4 MODAL You can also use **will** to say that someone or something is able to do something. *This will cure anything... The car won't go.* 5 MODAL You also use **will** to say that you are assuming or guessing that something is true, because it is likely, or because it is normally the case. *You will probably already be a member of a union... You will already have gathered that I don't like her... The bonus will usually be paid automatically.* 6 UNCOUNT N OR COUNT N **Will** is the determination to do something. *He lacked will and ambition... Their marriage became a fierce battle of wills.* • See also **free will.** 7 SING N WITH POSS If something is the **will** of a person or group of people with power or authority, they want it to happen; a formal use. *I must abide by the will of the people... It is the will of Allah.* 8 VB WITH OBJ AND TO-INF If you **will** something to happen, you try to make it happen using mental rather than physical effort. *I willed my trembling legs to walk straight.* 9 PHRASE If you can do something **at will,** you can do it whenever you want. *Chang told us that we could wander around at will.* 10 COUNT N A **will** is a legal document stating what you want to happen to your money and property when you die. *Has Des made a will?*

willing /wɪlɪŋ/. 1 PRED ADJ If you are **willing** to do something, you will do it if someone wants you to. *I was still willing to marry her.* ♦ **willingly** ADV *Many liberties were given up quite willingly during the war.* ♦ **willingness** UNCOUNT N *You need initiative and a willingness to work.* 2 ADJ If you describe someone as **willing,** you mean that they are eager and enthusiastic. *...a class of willing students.*

willow /wɪləʊ/, **willows.** COUNT N A **willow** is a tree with long, narrow leaves.

will-power. UNCOUNT N If you do something by **will-power,** you succeed in doing it because you are very determined to do it. *She stayed calm by sheer will-power.*

willy-nilly /wɪli¹ nɪli¹/. ADV If something happens to you **willy-nilly,** it happens whether you like it or not. *All of them were taken willy-nilly on a guided tour of the town.*

wilt /wɪlt/, **wilts, wilting, wilted.** VB If a plant **wilts,** it gradually bends downwards and becomes weak, because it needs more water or is dying.

wily /waɪli¹/, **wilier, wiliest.** ADJ **Wily** people are clever and cunning. *...a wily diplomat.*

win /wɪn/, **wins, winning, won** /wʌn/. 1 VB WITH OR WITHOUT OBJ If you **win** a fight, game, or argument, you defeat your opponent. *Their side was winning... Aren't you interested in who's winning the war?* Also COUNT N *...another win for our team.* 2 VB WITH OR WITHOUT OBJ To **win** an election or competition means to do better than anyone else involved. *The results showed that Labour had not won.* 3 VB WITH OBJ If you **win** a prize or medal, you get it because you have been very successful at something. *Mum has just won a microwave cooker in a competition.* 4 VB WITH OBJ If you **win** someone's approval or support, you succeed in getting it. *...the party's failure to win mass support among the working class.* 5 See also **winning.**

win over or **win round.** PHR VB If you **win** someone **over** or **win** them **round,** you persuade them to support you or agree with you.

wince /wɪns/, **winces, wincing, winced.** VB When you **wince,** the muscles of your face tighten suddenly because you are in pain or have experienced something unpleasant. *The pressure made her wince with pain.* Also COUNT N *His smile soon changed to a wince.*

winch /wɪntʃ/, **winches, winching, winched.** 1 COUNT N A **winch** is a machine for lifting heavy objects. It consists of a cylinder around which a rope or chain is wound. 2 VB WITH OBJ AND ADJUNCT If you **winch** an object or person somewhere, you lift or lower them using a winch.

wind, winds, winding, wound /waʊnd/. **Wind** is pronounced /wɪnd/ for meanings 1 to 5 and /waɪnd/ for meanings 6 to 8 and the phrasal verb. For meaning 3 the past tense and past participle is **winded.** 1 COUNT N OR UNCOUNT N A **wind** is a current of air moving across the earth's surface. *...poppies fluttering in the wind... There was a fierce wind blowing.* 2 SING N WITH POSS Your **wind** is your ability to breathe easily. *I had to stop and regain my wind.* 3 VB WITH OBJ If you **are winded** by something such as a blow, you have difficulty breathing for a short time. 4 ADJ A **wind** instrument is an instrument such as a trumpet or a flute that you play by blowing into it or across it. *...wind players.* 5 PHRASE If you **get wind of** something, you hear about it; an informal use. *He somehow got wind of the party and managed to get himself invited.* 6 VB WITH ADJUNCT If a road or river **winds** somewhere, it goes there with a lot of bends in it. *The river winds* *through the town.* ♦ **winding** ADJ *...the winding road leading to the Castle.* 7 VB WITH OBJ AND ADJUNCT When you **wind** something round something else, you wrap it round it several times. 8 VB WITH OBJ When you **wind** a clock or watch, you make it operate by turning a knob, key, or handle.

wind up. PHR VB When an activity or a business **is wound up,** it is finished or closed down. *Four years later the company was wound up.*

windfall /wɪndfɔːl/, **windfalls.** COUNT N A **windfall** is a sum of money that you receive unexpectedly. *He had a windfall from the football pools.*

windmill /wɪnd^{0}mɪl/, **windmills.** COUNT N A **windmill** is a tall building with sails which turn as the wind blows, creating power which is used to crush grain.

window /wɪndəʊ/, **windows.** COUNT N A **window** is a space in a wall or roof or in a vehicle, usually with glass in it. *The kitchen windows were wide open.*

window-box, window-boxes. COUNT N A **window-box** is a long, narrow container on a window-sill in which plants are grown.

window-pane, window-panes. COUNT N A **window-pane** is a piece of glass in the window of a building.

window-sill, window-sills. COUNT N A **window-sill** is a ledge along the bottom of a window, either inside or outside a building. *Pots of herbs stood on the window-sill.*

windpipe /wɪndpaɪp/, **windpipes.** COUNT N Your **windpipe** is the tube in your body that carries air into your lungs when you breathe.

windscreen /wɪndskriːn/, **windscreens.** COUNT N The **windscreen** of a car or other vehicle is the glass window at the front which the driver looks through; a British use.

windscreen wiper, windscreen wipers. COUNT N A **windscreen wiper** is a device which wipes rain from a vehicle's windscreen; a British use.

windshield /wɪndʃiːld/, **windshields.** COUNT N A **windshield** is a windscreen; an American use.

windsurfer /wɪndsɜːfə/, **windsurfers.** 1 COUNT N A **windsurfer** is a long, narrow board with a sail attached, which you stand on in the sea or on a lake and which is blown along by the wind. 2 COUNT N A **windsurfer** is also a person riding on a windsurfer.

windsurfing /wɪndsɜːfɪŋ/. UNCOUNT N **Windsurfing** is the sport of riding on a windsurfer.

windswept /wɪndswɛpt/; a literary word. 1 ADJ A **windswept** place is exposed to strong winds. *...a beautiful windswept hillside.* 2 ADJ Someone who looks **windswept** has untidy hair because they have been out in the wind.

windy /wɪndi^{1}/, **windier, windiest.** ADJ If it is **windy,** the wind is blowing a lot. *The winter was cold, wet, and windy.*

wine /waɪn/, **wines.** MASS N **Wine** is an alcoholic drink, usually made from grapes. There are two main kinds, called red wine and white wine.

wing /wɪŋ/, **wings.** 1 COUNT N The **wings** of a bird or insect are the parts of its body that it uses for flying. 2 COUNT N The **wings** of an aeroplane are the long, flat parts at each side which support it while it is flying. 3 COUNT N A **wing** of a building is a smaller part which sticks out from the main part. *...the west wing of the museum.* 4 COUNT N WITH SUPP A **wing** of an organization is a group within it which has a particular function or beliefs. *...the political wing of the IRA.* 5 COUNT N The **wings** of a car are the parts around the wheels; a British use. 6 See also **left-wing, right-wing.**

winged /wɪŋd/. ATTRIB ADJ **Winged** means having wings. *...winged creatures... ...a winged statue.*

winger /wɪŋə/, **wingers.** COUNT N In football or hockey, a **winger** is an attacking player who plays mainly on the far left or far right of the pitch.

wink /wɪŋk/, **winks, winking, winked.** 1 VB When you **wink,** you close one eye briefly, usually as a signal that something is a joke. *Uncle John winked at me across the table.* Also COUNT N *'What a hostess!' said Clarissa with a big wink at George.* 2 PHRASE If you **don't sleep a wink,** you stay awake and do not sleep at all; an informal use. *I never slept a wink that night.*

winner /wɪnə/, **winners.** COUNT N The **winner** of a prize, race, or competition is the person who wins it. *He was a worthy winner of the Nobel Prize.*

winning /wɪnɪŋ/, **winnings.** 1 ATTRIB ADJ The **winning** competitor, team, or entry in a competition is the one that has won. 2 ATTRIB ADJ **Winning** is also used to describe actions or qualities that please people and make them feel friendly towards you; a literary use. *His chief asset is his winning smile.* 3 PLURAL N You refer to money that you win in a competition or by gambling as your **winnings.**

winter /wɪntə/, **winters.** UNCOUNT N OR COUNT N **Winter** is the season between autumn and spring. In winter the weather is cold. *It was a terrible winter... ...a dark winter's night.*

wintry /wɪntri^{1}/. ADJ Something that is **wintry** has features that are typical of winter. *...one wintry day early in March.*

wipe /waɪp/, **wipes, wiping, wiped.** 1 VB WITH OBJ If you **wipe** something, you rub its surface to remove dirt or liquid from it. *He wiped his mouth with the back of his hand.* Also COUNT N *Give the table a wipe.* 2 VB WITH OBJ AND ADJUNCT If you **wipe** dirt or liquid from something, you remove it, for example by using a cloth or your hand. *She wiped the tears from her eyes.*

wipe out. PHR VB To **wipe out** a place or group of people means to destroy it completely. *Epidemics wiped out the local population.*

wire /waɪə/, **wires, wiring, wired.** 1 COUNT N OR UNCOUNT N A **wire** is a long, thin piece of metal used to fasten or connect things. *You can mend it with a length of wire... ...overhead lights suspended from wires.* 2 COUNT N A **wire** is also a telegram; an American use. 3 VB WITH OBJ If you **wire** a person, you send them a telegram; an American use. *I wired Renata yesterday and asked her to marry me.* 4 See also **barbed wire.**

wire up PHR VB If you **wire** something **up,** you connect it to something else with electrical wires so that electricity can pass between them. *...electrical fittings wired up to the mains.*

wireless /waɪəlɪ^{2}s/, **wirelesses.** COUNT N A **wireless** is a radio; an old-fashioned use.

wiring /waɪərɪŋ/. UNCOUNT N The **wiring** in a building is the system of wires that supply electricity to the rooms. *Will the cottage need new wiring?*

wiry /waɪəri^{1}/. 1 ADJ Someone who is **wiry** is thin but has strong muscles. *...a short, wiry man.* 2 ADJ Something that is **wiry** is stiff and rough to touch. *...her wiry, black hair.*

wisdom /wɪzdə^{0}m/. 1 UNCOUNT N **Wisdom** is the ability to use your experience and knowledge to make sensible decisions and judgements. *She spoke with authority as well as wisdom.* 2 SING N If you talk about the **wisdom** of an action or decision, you are talking about how sensible it is. *Doubts were expressed about the wisdom of the visit.*

wise /waɪz/, **wiser, wisest.** 1 ADJ **Wise** people are able to use their experience and knowledge to make sensible decisions and judgements. *He's a very wise man... Hugh made the wisest decision of all.* ♦ **wisely** ADV *You have chosen wisely.* 2 PHRASE If someone is **no wiser** or **none the wiser** after an explanation or event, they have failed to understand it, or are not fully aware of what happened. *No one outside would be any the wiser.*

wish /wɪʃ/, **wishes, wishing, wished.** 1 COUNT N A **wish** is a desire for something. *She told me of her wish to leave the convent.* 2 VB If you **wish** to do something, you want to do it; a formal use. *They are in love and wish to marry.* 3 REPORT VB If you **wish** that something were the case, you would like it to be the case, even though it is impossible or unlikely. *I often wish that I were really wealthy.* 4 VB WITH OBJ AND OBJ If you **wish** someone something such as good luck, you tell them that you hope they will have it. *They wished each other luck before the exam... ...wishing him happy birthday.* 5 PLURAL N When you send someone your good **wishes,** you are indicating that you hope they will be happy or successful. 6 CONVENTION You use **wishes** in expressions such as 'best wishes' or 'with all good wishes' at the end of informal letters, before you sign your name.

wishful thinking /wɪʃfəl θɪŋkɪŋ/. UNCOUNT N If a hope or wish is **wishful thinking,** it is unlikely to be fulfilled. *It is wishful thinking to assume that the generals will agree to this.*

wisp /wɪsp/, **wisps.** 1 COUNT N A **wisp** of hair is a thin, untidy bunch of it. *A wisp of grey hair stuck out from under her hat.* 2 COUNT N A **wisp** of smoke or cloud is a long, thin amount of it.

wispy /wɪspi^{1}/. ADJ **Wispy** hair is thin and grows in small, untidy bunches.

wistful /wɪstful/. ADJ If someone is **wistful,** they are sad because they want something and know they cannot have it. *She had a last wistful look round the flat.* ♦ **wistfully** ADV *'Guy doesn't want to see me,' said Manfred wistfully.*

wit /wɪt/, **wits.** 1 UNCOUNT N **Wit** is the ability to use words or ideas in an amusing and clever way. *The girl laughed at his wit... ...the wit of the cartoonist.* 2 PLURAL N You can refer to someone's ability to think quickly in a difficult situation as their **wits.** *Her only chance was to use her wits to bluff the enemy.*

PHRASES ● If you **have** or **keep your wits about** you, you are alert and ready to act in a difficult situation. *In this part of the city you have to keep your wits about you all the time.* ● If something frightens you **out of your wits,** it frightens you very much indeed. ● If you are **at your wits' end,** you have so many problems or difficulties that you do not know what to do next. ● to **pit** your **wits against** someone: see **pit.**

witch /wɪtʃ/, **witches.** COUNT N A **witch** is a woman who is believed to have magic powers, especially evil ones.

witchcraft /wɪtʃkrɑːft/. UNCOUNT N **Witchcraft** is the use of magic powers, especially evil ones.

witch doctor, witch doctors. COUNT N A **witch doctor** is a person in some societies, especially in Africa, who is thought to have magic powers.

witch-hunt, witch-hunts. COUNT N A **witch-hunt** is a search for people who are thought to be responsible for things that have gone wrong, in order to punish them. Often the victims of witch-hunts are innocent people.

with /wɪð, wɪθ/. 1 PREP If one thing or person is **with** another, they are together in one place. *I stayed with her until dusk.* 2 PREP If you do something **with** someone else, you do it together. *Boys do not generally play with girls... I discussed it with Phil.* 3 PREP If you fight or argue **with** someone, you oppose them. *...a naval war with France... Judy was tired of quarrelling with Bal.* 4 PREP If you do something **with** a particular tool or object, you do it using that tool or object. *Clean mirrors with a mop... He brushed back his hair with his hand.* 5 PREP You use **with** when you mention a feature, characteristic, or possession that someone or something has. *...an old man with a beard... ...an old house with steep stairs and dark corridors.* 6 PREP Something that is filled or covered **with** things has those things in it or on it. *The building is decorated with bright banners.* 7 PREP You use **with** to indicate the manner in which someone does something, or the feeling they have when they do it. *Their fossils were studied with great care... Jordache looked over at his son with genuine surprise.* 8 PREP You also use **with** to indicate the feeling that makes someone behave in a particular way. *This experience leaves him quaking with fear.* 9 PREP You can use **with** to indicate the thing that your statement relates to. *Don't be inflexible with shopping... There was a particular problem with claims for maternity allowance.* 10 PREP You can also use **with** to say that something happens at the same time as something else. *He didn't have the courage to put his hat on with Perkins watching him... With advancing age, reactions become slower.* 11 PREP You use **with** to introduce a factor that affects something and so is relevant to what you are saying. *With all the traffic jams, it wouldn't be economic.*

withdraw /wɪðdrɔː/, **withdraws, withdrawing, withdrew** /wɪðdruː/, **withdrawn** /wɪðdrɔːn/; a formal word. 1 VB WITH OBJ If you **withdraw** something from a place, you remove it or take it away. *She withdrew the key from the door... You must present your cheque card when you withdraw any money.* 2 VB If you **withdraw** to another room, you go there. *He withdrew to his office to count the money.* 3 ERG VB When troops **withdraw,** they leave the place where they are fighting or where they are based. *We could see the force withdrawing... They are willing to withdraw some troops.* 4 VB WITH OR WITHOUT OBJ If you **withdraw** from an activity, you stop taking part in it. *Marsha withdrew from the argument.* 5 VB WITH OBJ If you **withdraw** a remark or statement you have made, you say that you want people to ignore it. *I want to withdraw a statement I made earlier on.*

withdrawal /wɪðdrɔːəl/, **withdrawals;** a formal word. 1 UNCOUNT N OR COUNT N The **withdrawal** of something is the act or process of removing it or taking it away. *They are trying to negotiate the withdrawal of 20,000 troops... ...the withdrawal of public services.* 2 UNCOUNT N **Withdrawal** from an activity or organization is a refusal to continue taking part in it. *...withdrawal from the Common Market.* 3 UNCOUNT N **Withdrawal** is behaviour in which someone shows that they do not want to communicate with other people. 4 COUNT N A **withdrawal** is an amount of money that you take from your bank account. *It is not the bank's policy to deduct interest on withdrawals.*

withdrawn /wɪðdrɔːn/. 1 **Withdrawn** is the past participle of **withdraw.** 2 ADJ Someone who is **withdrawn** is quiet and shy. *The isolated life made them withdrawn.*

withdrew /wɪðdruː/. **Withdrew** is the past tense of **withdraw.**

wither /wɪðə/, **withers, withering, withered.** 1 VB When something **withers** or **withers** away, it becomes weaker until it no longer exists. *Links with the outside community withered.* 2 ERG VB If a plant **withers,** it shrinks, dries up, and dies. *The leaves had withered and fallen.*

withered /wɪðəd/. 1 ADJ A **withered** plant has shrunk, dried up, and died. *...a pot of withered roses.* 2 ADJ If you describe an old person as **withered,** you mean that their skin has become wrinkled and dry. *...a withered old lady... ...her withered fingers.*

withering /wɪðəᵒrɪŋ/. ADJ If someone gives you a **withering** look, they look at you in a way that makes you feel ashamed or stupid. *Scylla gave him a withering glare.*

withhold /wɪðhəʊld/, **withholds, withholding, withheld** /wɪðhɛld/. VB WITH OBJ If you **withhold** something that someone wants, you do not let them have it; a formal use. *His salary was withheld... I decided to withhold the information till later.*

within /wɪðɪn/. 1 PREP OR ADV **Within** something means inside it. *The prisoners demanded the freedom to congregate within the prison... There were sounds of protest within.* 2 PREP OR ADV If you have a feeling, you can say that it is **within** you; a literary use. *A mounting wave of dislike and anger rose within me... ...the hatred he felt within.* 3 PREP If something is **within** a particular limit, it does not go beyond that limit. *We must ask the schools to keep within their budget.* 4 PREP If you are **within** a particular distance of a place, you are less than that distance from it. *They were within fifty miles of Chicago.* 5 PREP If something is **within** sight, **within** earshot, or **within** reach, you can see it, hear it, or reach it. *They finally came within sight of the gates.* 6 PREP **Within** a particular length of time means before that length of time has passed. *Within minutes I was called to his office.*

without /wɪðaʊt/. 1 PREP If a person or thing is **without** something, they do not have it. *...city slums without lights, roads or water... She was without an ambition in the world.* 2 CONJ OR PREP If you do one thing **without** doing another, you do not do the second thing. *They drove into town without talking to each other... 'No,' she said, without explanation.* 3 PREP If you do something **without** a particular feeling, you do not have that feeling when you do it. *They greeted him without enthusiasm.* 4 PREP If one thing happens **without** another thing happening, the other thing does not happen. *The rest of the press conference passed without incident... I knocked twice, without reply.* 5 PREP If you do something **without** someone, you do not have their company or help when you do it. *You can go without me... Her husband felt he couldn't face life without her.*

withstand /wɪðstænd/, **withstands, withstanding, withstood** /wɪðstʊd/. VB WITH OBJ To **withstand** a force or action means to survive it or not to give in to it; a formal use. *They have to make the walls strong enough to withstand high winds... He was in no condition to withstand any further punishment.*

witness /wɪtnɪ¹s/, **witnesses, witnessing, witnessed.** 1 COUNT N A **witness** to an event is a person who saw it. *Witnesses to the murder told what they had seen.* 2 VB WITH OBJ If you **witness** something, you see it happen; a formal use. *At least fifteen people witnessed the attack.* 3 COUNT N A **witness** is someone who appears in a court of law to say what they know about a crime or other event. *Other witnesses were called to give evidence.* 4 COUNT N A **witness** is also someone who writes their name on a document that you have signed, to confirm that it really is your signature. 5 VB WITH OBJ If someone **witnesses** your signature, they write their name after it, to confirm that it really is your signature. *Now everything is signed and witnessed.*

PHRASES • If you **are witness to** something, you see it happen; a formal use. *This was the first time I was witness to one of his rages.* • If one thing **bears witness to** another, the first thing shows that the second thing exists or happened; a formal use. *This lack of action bears witness to a complacency which has survived two World Wars.*

witness-box, witness-boxes. COUNT N In a court of law, the **witness-box** is the place where people stand or sit when they give evidence.

witticism /wɪtɪsɪzəᵒm/, **witticisms.** COUNT N A **witticism** is a witty remark or joke. *Don smiled at this witticism.*

witty /wɪti¹/, **wittier, wittiest.** ADJ **Witty** means amusing in a clever way. *He found her charming and witty... ...a witty play.*

wives /waɪvz/. **Wives** is the plural of **wife.**

wizard /wɪzəd/, **wizards.** COUNT N A **wizard** is a man in a fairy story who has magic powers.

wizened /wɪzənd/. ADJ A **wizened** person is old and has wrinkled skin; a literary use. *Mr Solomon was a wizened little man with frizzy grey hair.*

wobble /wɒbəᵒl/, **wobbles, wobbling, wobbled.** VB If something **wobbles,** it makes small movements from side to side, because it is loose or unsteady. *My legs were wobbling under me.*

wobbly /wɒbli¹/. ADJ If something is **wobbly,** it is unstable and likely to move from side to side; an informal use. *...a wobbly bed... My legs still feel weak and wobbly.*

woe /wəʊ/, **woes;** a literary or old-fashioned use. 1 UNCOUNT N **Woe** is great unhappiness or sorrow. *...an exclamation of woe.* 2 PLURAL N You can refer to someone's problems or misfortunes as their **woes.** *They listened sympathetically to his woes.*

woeful /wəʊfʊl/; a literary word. 1 ADJ **Woeful** means very sad. *...the lovers' long and woeful farewell.* ♦ **woefully** ADV *She announced woefully, 'I've lost my job.'* 2 ADJ You also use **woeful** to emphasize how bad something is. *His work displays a woeful lack of imagination.* ♦ **woefully** SUBMOD *The quantities were woefully inadequate.*

woke /wəʊk/. **Woke** is the past tense of **wake.**

woken /wəʊkəᵒn/. **Woken** is the past participle of **wake.**

wolf /wʊlf/, **wolves** /wʊlvz/; **wolfs, wolfing, wolfed. Wolves** is the plural of the noun. **Wolfs** is the third person singular, present tense, of the verb. 1 COUNT N A **wolf** is a wild animal that looks like a large dog and kills and eats other animals. 2 VB WITH OBJ If you **wolf** food or **wolf** it down, you eat it quickly and greedily; an informal use.

woman /wʊmən/, **women** /wɪmɪn/. COUNT N A **woman** is an adult female human being. *...an old woman... There were men and women working in the fields.* Also MOD *We had one woman teacher.*

womanhood /wʊmənhʊd/. UNCOUNT N **Womanhood** is the state of being a woman rather than a girl, or the period of a woman's adult life. *...the threshold of womanhood... ...the years of her womanhood.*

womanly /wʊmənli¹/. ADJ **Womanly** behaviour is typical of a woman rather than a man or a girl; used showing approval. *...the womanly virtues of gentleness and compassion.*

womb /wu:m/, **wombs.** COUNT N A woman's **womb** is the part inside her body where a baby grows before it is born.

women /wɪmɪn/. **Women** is the plural of **woman.**

won /wʌn/. **Won** is the past tense and past participle of **win.**

wonder /wʌndə/, **wonders, wondering, wondered.** 1 VB OR REPORT VB If you **wonder** about something, you think about it and try to guess or understand more about it. *I keep wondering and worrying about what you said... I wonder what she'll look like... I am beginning to wonder why we ever invited them.* 2 VB WITH 'at' If you **wonder** at something, you are surprised and amazed about it. *I wondered at her strength.* 3 SING N If you say that it is a **wonder** that something happened, you mean it is very surprising. *It was a wonder that she managed to come.* 4 UNCOUNT N **Wonder** is a feeling of surprise and amazement. *...exclamations of wonder.* 5 COUNT N A **wonder** is something remarkable that people admire. *...the wonders of modern technology.*

PHRASES • You say **no wonder, little wonder,** or **small wonder** to indicate that you are not surprised by something. *Little wonder that today we are in such a mess... 'Anyway, he didn't win.'—'No wonder.'* • If something **works wonders** or **does wonders,** it has a very good effect. *A whisky at the end of the day will sometimes work wonders... The doctors have done wonders for your leg.*

wonderful /wʌndəfʊl/. 1 ADJ You describe an experience as **wonderful** when it makes you very happy and pleased. *It was wonderful to be able to walk again.* 2 ADJ You can show your admiration for something by saying that it is **wonderful.** *I think the heart transplant is a wonderful thing.*

wonderfully /wʌndəfʊli¹/. SUBMOD You use **wonderfully** to emphasize how good something is. *Both plays are wonderfully funny... She was always wonderfully kind to me.*

wonderment /wʌndəmə²nt/. UNCOUNT N **Wonderment** is a feeling of amazement and admiration; a literary use. *I stood shaking my head in wonderment.*

wont /wəʊnt/. PRED ADJ WITH TO-INF If someone is **wont** to do something, they do it regularly as a habit; an old-fashioned use. *They were wont to take long walks in the evening.*

won't /wəʊnt/. **Won't** is the usual spoken form of 'will not'.

woo /wu:/, **woos, wooing, wooed.** 1 VB WITH OBJ If you **woo** people, you try to get them to help or support you; a literary use. *She hoped to woo the working-class voters of Warrington.* 2 VB WITH OBJ When a man **woos** a woman, he tries to make himself attractive to her, because he wants to marry her; an old-fashioned use.

wood /wʊd/, **woods.** 1 MASS N **Wood** is the material which forms the trunks and branches of trees. *We gathered wood for the fire.* 2 COUNT N A **wood** is a large area of trees growing near each other. *...the big wood where the pheasants lived.* 3 PLURAL N You can refer to a large wood as the **woods.** *They walked through the woods.*

wooded /wʊdɪ¹d/. ADJ A **wooded** area is covered in trees. *...a narrow wooded valley.*

wooden /wʊdəᵒn/. ADJ A **wooden** object is made of wood. *...a wooden box.*

woodland /wʊdlə³nd/, **woodlands.** UNCOUNT N OR COUNT N **Woodland** is land covered with trees. *...a patch of woodland in Malaysia... The boundaries of many woodlands have not changed for hundreds of years.*

woodpecker /wʊdpɛkə/, **woodpeckers.** COUNT N A **woodpecker** is a bird with a long sharp beak, which makes holes in tree trunks in order to eat insects.

woodwind /wʊdwɪnd/. ADJ A **woodwind** instrument is a musical instrument such as a clarinet or flute that you play by blowing into it or across it. Many woodwind instruments are made of wood.

woodwork /wʊdwɜ:k/. 1 UNCOUNT N You can refer to the doors and other wooden parts of a house as the **woodwork.** *The paint was peeling from the woodwork.* 2 UNCOUNT N **Woodwork** is also the activity or skill of making things out of wood.

woodworm /wʊdwɜ:m/. **Woodworm** is the singular and plural. COUNT N **Woodworm** are the larvae of a particular type of beetle, which make holes in wood by feeding on it.

woody /wʊdi¹/. 1 ADJ **Woody** plants have very hard stems. 2 ADJ A **woody** area has a lot of trees in it. *...a farm set amid woody valleys.*

wool /wʊl/, **wools.** 1 MASS N **Wool** is the hair that grows on sheep and on some other animals. 2 MASS N **Wool** is also a material made from animals' wool. It is used for making clothes, blankets, and carpets. 3 PHRASE To **pull the wool over** someone's **eyes** means to deliberately deceive them in order to have an advantage over them. 4 See also **cotton wool.**

woollen /wʊlən/; spelled **woolen** in American English. ATTRIB ADJ **Woollen** clothes are made from wool, or from a mixture of wool and artificial fibres. *...a woollen scarf.*

woolly /wʊli²/, **woollier, woolliest; woollies;** spelled **wooly** in American English. 1 ADJ Something that is **woolly** is made of wool or looks like wool. *...a woolly cap.* 2 COUNT N A **woolly** is a woollen piece of clothing, especially a pullover; an informal use. *She wore a long woolly with a belt.* 3 ADJ If you describe people or their thoughts as **woolly,** you mean that their ideas are very unclear. *They cannot afford to be vague and woolly with their messages.*

word /wɜ:d/, **words, wording, worded.** 1 COUNT N A **word** is a single unit of language in writing or speech. In English, a word has a space on either side of it when it is written. Some words have more than one meaning. 2 COUNT N If you have a **word** or a few **words** with someone, you have a short conversation with them; an informal use. *May I have a word with you please?* 3 SING N A **word** of advice or warning is a short piece of advice or warning. 4 SING N If you cannot hear, understand, or believe a **word** of what someone is saying, you cannot hear, understand, or believe it at all. *I did not understand one word of what she'd said.* 5 UNCOUNT N OR SING N You can use **word** to mean news. *The young man brought them word of her visit... The word got out that he was leaving.* 6 SING N WITH POSS If you give your **word,** you promise to do something. *I give you my word I won't ask him... I apologized for having doubted his word.* 7 VB WITH OBJ When you **word** something in a particular way, you express it that way. *How would one word such an announcement?* ♦ **worded** ADJ *He wrote a strongly worded report to the Secretary of the Interior.*

PHRASES • If you repeat something **word for word,** you repeat it exactly as it was originally said or written. • If you have **the last word** in an argument, you make the comment that finishes it and defeats the other person. • If you **put in a good word** for someone, you speak favourably about them to a person who has influence. • You say **in a word** to indicate that you are summarizing what you have just been saying. *The house is roomy, cool in summer, and in a word comfortable.* • If you **have words with** someone, you have an argument with them. • You say **in other words** when introducing a simpler or clearer explanation of something that has just been said. *Is there a cheaper solution? In other words, can you make a cheaper device?* • If you say something **in your own words,** you say it in your own way, without copying or repeating what someone else has said. *He was asked to tell the story in his own words.* • If you say that something was not said **in so many words,** you mean that it was said indirectly, but that you are giving its real meaning. *This is what he claims, only he does not state it in so many words.*

wording /wɜ:dɪŋ/. UNCOUNT N The **wording** of a piece of writing or a speech is the way it is expressed. *For a full hour he argued over the wording of the editorial.*

word processing. UNCOUNT N **Word processing** is the work of producing documents, letters, and other printed material using a word processor.

word processor /wɜːd prəʊsɛsə/, **word processors.** COUNT N A **word processor** is an electronic machine which has a keyboard and a screen like a computer terminal, but which is used as a typewriter to produce documents, letters, and other printed material.

wordy /wɜːdi[1]/. ADJ Something that is **wordy** uses too many words. *...this very wordy book on biology.*

wore /wɔː/. **Wore** is the past tense of **wear.**

work /wɜːk/, **works, working, worked.** **1** VB People who **work** have a job which they are paid to do. *He was working in a bank... Some of my salesmen formerly worked for a rival firm.* **2** UNCOUNT N People who have **work** or are in **work** have a job. *...people who can't find work... ...the numbers out of work.* **3** VB When you **work,** you do the tasks which your job involves, or a task that needs to be done. *I watched the people working at the weaving looms... She works hard at keeping herself fit... He has been working all season on his game... I used to work a ten-hour day.* **4** UNCOUNT N **Work** is also the tasks which your job involves, or any tasks which need to be done. *I've got some work to do... I finish work at 3... A housewife's work can take ten or twelve hours a day.* **5** UNCOUNT N Something produced as a result of an activity, job, or area of research is also called **work.** *That's an absolutely fascinating piece of work... There has been considerable work done in America on this subject.* **6** VB WITH OBJ If you **work** the land, you cultivate it. *...peasants working the land.* **7** VB WITH OBJ If you **work** a machine or piece of equipment, you use it or control it. *...the boy who worked the milking machine.* **8** VB If a machine or piece of equipment **works,** it operates and performs its function. *The traffic lights weren't working properly.* **9** VB If an idea, method, or system **works,** it is successful. *That kind of democracy will never work.* **10** VB WITH ADJUNCT If something **works** against you, it causes problems for you. If something **works** in your favour, it helps you. *The apathy of the opposition is working in his favour.* **11** VB WITH 'on' If you **work** on an assumption or idea, you make decisions based on it. **12** VB WITH ADJUNCT OR COMPLEMENT If something **works** into a particular position, it gradually moves into that position. *The ropes had worked loose.* **13** VB WITH OBJ AND ADJUNCT If you **work** your way somewhere, you move there with difficulty. *I worked my way slowly out of the marsh.* **14** COUNT N WITH SUPP A **work** is something such as a painting, book, or piece of music. *...a large volume containing all of Chopin's works... ...the collected works of Proust.* **15** COLL N A **works** is a place where something is made or produced by an industrial process. *...the gas works.* **16** See also **working, social work.**

PHRASES • If you **have** your **work cut out** to do something, it is very difficult for you to do it. *We'll have our work cut out to finish on time.* • If workers **work to rule,** they stop doing extra work and just do the minimum that is required of them; a British use. *The delivery men are working to rule.* • See also **work-to-rule.**

work into. PHR VB If you **work** yourself **into** a state of being upset or angry, you make yourself become upset or angry. *She worked herself into a rage.*

work off. PHR VB If you **work off** a feeling, you overcome it by doing something energetic or violent. *We should all be able to work off our stress physically.*

work out. PHR VB **1** If you **work out** a solution to a problem or mystery, you find the solution or calculate it. *We are always hoping that a more peaceful solution can be worked out... Now you can work out the area of the triangle.* **2** If something **works out** at a particular amount, it is calculated to be that amount. *Petrol prices here work out at around £1.15 a gallon.* **3** If a situation **works out** in a particular way, it happens or progresses in that way. *It's funny how life worked out... Things worked out well with Marian.* **4** If you **work out,** you do physical exercises to make your body fit and strong. *She worked out in a ballet class three hours a week.* **5** See also **workout.**

work up. PHR VB **1** If you **work** yourself **up,** you gradually make yourself very upset or angry about something. *She worked herself up into a frenzy.* **2** If you **work up** a feeling, you gradually start to have it. *I can hardly work up enough energy to go to the shops... She went for a run to work up an appetite.* **3** See also **worked up.**

work up to. PHR VB If you **work up to** a particular amount or level, you gradually increase or improve what you are doing until you reach that amount or level. *Start slowly and work up to a faster time.*

workable /wɜːkəbə[0]l/. ADJ Something that is **workable** can operate efficiently or can be used for a particular purpose. *This doesn't seem to be a workable solution.*

worked up. PRED ADJ If you are **worked up** about something, you are upset or angry about it. *Why are you so worked up over that editorial?*

worker /wɜːkə/, **workers.** **1** COUNT N A **worker** is a person employed in an industry or business who has no responsibility for managing it. *The dispute affected relations between management and workers.* **2** COUNT N WITH SUPP You can use **worker** to say how well or badly someone works. *My husband was a hard worker.* **3** COUNT N A **worker** is also someone who does a particular kind of job. *...American research workers.* • See also **social worker.**

workforce /wɜːkfɔːs/. SING N WITH SUPP The **workforce** is all the people who work in a particular place, industry or organization. *Asia's workforce will expand by 60 per cent.*

working /wɜːkɪŋ/, **workings.** **1** ATTRIB ADJ **Working** people have jobs which they are paid to do. *...children with working mothers.* **2** ATTRIB ADJ Your **working** life is the period of your life in which you have a job, or are of a suitable age to have a job. *Most of these people spend their entire working lives at General Motors.* **3** ATTRIB ADJ **Working** is used to refer to things connected with your job. *We want to achieve better working conditions for all women... I didn't bring any working clothes... The unions will demand a reduction in working hours.* **4** ATTRIB ADJ A **working** knowledge of something such as a foreign language is a reasonable knowledge of it that enables you to use it effectively. *In the first week I picked up a tolerable working knowledge of Spanish.* **5** PLURAL N WITH SUPP The **workings** of a piece of equipment, an organization, or a system are the ways in which it operates. **6** **in working order:** see **order.**

working class, working classes. COUNT N The **working class** or **working classes** are the people in a society who do not own much property and whose work involves physical and practical skills rather than intellectual ones. *...the urban working class.*

workload /wɜːkləʊd/, **workloads.** COUNT N WITH SUPP Your **workload** is the amount of work that you have to do. *I have a terrible workload this year.*

workman /wɜːkmə[3]n/, **workmen.** COUNT N A **workman** is a man whose job involves working with his hands, for example building houses or plumbing.

workmanship /wɜːkmə[3]nʃɪp/. UNCOUNT N **Workmanship** is the skill with which something is made. *...good materials and sound workmanship.*

work of art, works of art. **1** COUNT N A **work of art** is a painting or piece of sculpture of high quality. *Some of the world's greatest works of art are on display here.* **2** COUNT N You can refer to something that has been skilfully produced as a **work of art.** *His own papers were works of art on which he laboured with loving care.*

workout /wɜːkaʊt/, **workouts.** COUNT N A **workout** is a period of physical exercise or training.

workplace /wɜːkpleɪs/, **workplaces.** COUNT N Your **workplace** is the place where you work. *Their houses were workplaces as well as dwellings.*

workshop /wɜːkʃɒp/, **workshops.** **1** COUNT N A **workshop** is a room or building containing tools or machinery for making or repairing things. *...a small engineering workshop.* **2** COUNT N A **workshop** on a particular subject is a period of discussion and practical work on that subject by a group of people. *...a theatre workshop... ...a workshop on child care.*

work-shy. ADJ A **work-shy** person is lazy and does not want a job.

work-to-rule. SING N A **work-to-rule** is a protest in which workers stop doing extra work and just do the minimum that is required of them; a British use.

world /wɜːld/, **worlds.** **1** SING N The **world** is the planet that we live on. *He attempted to sail round the world... ...the growth in world population.* **2** MOD **World** is used to describe someone or something that is one of the best or most important of its kind. *This book is a world classic... ...a world famous physicist.* **3** COUNT N WITH SUPP Someone's **world** is their life, experiences, and the relationships they have with other people. *Look, Howard, we're in different worlds now... They were letting me into their world.* **4** COUNT N WITH SUPP A particular **world** is a field of activity, and the people involved in it. *They are well-known names in the film world... ...the world of art.* **5** SING N You can refer to the state of being alive as this **world** and to a state of existence after death as the next **world.** **6** COUNT N WITH SUPP You can refer to a group of living things as the animal **world,** the plant **world,** or the insect **world.** **7** COUNT N You can refer to another planet as a **world.** *...an alien world.*

PHRASES • You can use **in the world** with superlatives to emphasize that the thing you are talking about is the most important, significant, or extreme of its kind. *To them housework was the most important activity in the world... ...the simplest job in the world.* • **The world over** means throughout the world. • If someone has or wants **the best of both worlds,** they have or want all the benefits from two different situations, without the disadvantages. • If you **think the world of** someone or something, you admire them very much. • If something **does** you **the world of good,** it makes you feel better; an informal use. *A bit of fresh air will do you the world of good.* • If **there is a world of difference** between two things, they are very different from each other.

worldly /wɜːldli[1]/. **1** ADJ **Worldly** refers to things relating to the ordinary activities of life, rather than to spiritual things. *Coleridge had experienced a conversion and put aside worldly things.* **2** ATTRIB ADJ You can refer to someone's possessions as their **worldly** goods or possessions; a literary use. **3** ADJ Someone who is **worldly** is experienced, practical, and knowledgeable about life.

world war, world wars. COUNT N OR UNCOUNT N A **world war** is a war involving countries from all over the world. *...the First World War.*

worldwide /wɜːldwaɪd/. ADJ OR ADV **Worldwide** means happening throughout the world. *...in 1930, during the world-wide economic depression... This move made headlines worldwide last year.*

worm /wɜːm/, **worms, worming, wormed.** **1** COUNT N A **worm** is a small thin animal without bones or legs which lives in the soil. **2** PLURAL N If animals or people have **worms,** worms are living as parasites in their intestines. *...a dog with worms.* **3** PHRASE If you **worm** your **way** somewhere, you move there slowly and with difficulty. *He wormed his way forward.*

worm out. PHR VB If you **worm** information **out** of someone, you gradually persuade them to give you it. *The truth had been wormed out of him by his lawyers.*

worn /wɔːn/. **1** **Worn** is the past participle of **wear.** **2** ADJ **Worn** things are damaged or thin because they are old and have been used a lot. *...the worn carpet.* **3** ADJ Someone who is **worn** looks old and tired.

worn-out. **1** ADJ **Worn-out** things are too old, damaged, or thin from use to be used any more. *...a worn-out sofa.* **2** ADJ If you are **worn-out,** you are extremely tired.

worry /wʌri[1]/, **worries, worrying, worried.** **1** VB OR REPORT VB If you **worry,** you keep thinking about a problem or about something unpleasant that might happen. *Don't worry, Andrew, you can do it... People worry about the safety of nuclear energy... I worried that when I got back he wouldn't be there.* **2** VB WITH OBJ If someone or something **worries** you, they cause you to worry. *Terry was worried by the challenge... It worried him to think that Sylvie was alone.* ♦ **worried** ADJ *People are becoming increasingly worried about pollution... I was worried that she'd say no.* **3** VB WITH OBJ If you **worry** someone about a problem, you disturb or upset them by telling them about it. *Why worry her when it's all over?* **4** COUNT N OR UNCOUNT N **Worries** are feelings of anxiety and unhappiness caused by a problem or by thinking about something unpleasant that might happen. *I don't have any worries... My only worry was that my aunt would be upset... Bad housing is their main source of worry.*

worrying /wʌri[1]ɪŋ/. ADJ Something that is **worrying** causes you a lot of worry. *...a very worrying situation... She asked me a worrying question.*

worse /wɜːs/. **1** ADJ **Worse** is the comparative of **bad.** *I have even worse news for you... The noise is getting worse.* **2** ADV **Worse** is also the comparative of **badly.** *Some people ski worse than others.* **3** ADJ If someone who is ill gets **worse,** they become more ill. *You'll get worse if you don't take this medicine.*

PHRASES • If someone or something is **none the worse** for something, they are not harmed by it. *The children had gone to bed very late but they were none the worse for it.* • If something happens **for the worse,** the situation becomes more unpleasant or difficult. *There were constant changes, usually for the worse.*

worsen /wɜːsən/, **worsens, worsening, worsened.** ERG VB If a situation **worsens,** it becomes more difficult, unpleasant, or unacceptable. *The weather steadily worsened... Economic sanctions would only worsen the situation.*

worse off. **1** PRED ADJ Someone who is **worse off** has less money than before or less than someone else. *This budget would leave taxpayers far worse off... There are lots of people worse off than us.* **2** PRED ADJ To be **worse off** also means to be in a more unpleasant situation than before or than someone else. *You believe the world to be worse off because of Kennedy's death.*

worship /wɜːʃɪp/, **worships, worshipping, worshipped;** spelled **worshiping, worshiped** in American English. **1** VB WITH OR WITHOUT OBJ If you **worship** a god, you show your respect to the god, for example by saying prayers. *I knelt down and worshipped the Lord.* Also UNCOUNT N *...places of worship.* **2** VB WITH OBJ If you **worship** someone or something, you love them or admire them very much. *Vita worshipped her father.* Also UNCOUNT N *She became an object of worship.* **3** TITLE **Your Worship** and **His Worship** are respectful ways of addressing or referring to a magistrate or a mayor; a British use.

worshipper /wɜ:ʃɪpə/, **worshippers;** spelled **worshiper** in American English. COUNT N A **worshipper** is someone who believes in and worships a god. *...shoes left by worshippers who had gone into the mosque.*

worst /wɜ:st/. **1** ADJ **Worst** is the superlative of **bad.** *...the worst thing which ever happened to me... The worst is over.* **2** ADV **Worst** is also the superlative of **badly.** *...the worst affected areas.*

PHRASES ● You use **at worst** when considering a situation in the most unfavourable or most pessimistic way. *At worst they are looked upon as an irritation... He was described as forceful at best, ruthless at worst.* ● If you say that something might happen **if the worst comes to the worst,** you mean that it might happen if the situation develops in the most unfavourable way. *If the worst comes to the worst I'll have to sell the house.*

worth /wɜ:θ/. **1** PREP If something is **worth** an amount of money, it can be sold for that amount or has that value. *...a two-bedroom house worth 50,000 pounds.* **2** UNCOUNT N You use **worth** to indicate that the value of something is equal to a particular amount of money. For example, fifty dollars' **worth** of equipment can be bought for fifty dollars. **3** UNCOUNT N OR PRED ADJ Someone's **worth** is their value, usefulness, or importance; a formal use. *This job has robbed me of all worth... No man can say what another man is worth.* **4** UNCOUNT N You can use **worth** to say how long something will last. For example, a week's **worth** of food is the amount of food that will last you for a week. **5** PREP You use **worth** to say that something is so enjoyable or useful that it is a good thing to do or have. *This film's really worth seeing... The building is well worth a visit... They're expensive, but they're worth it.* **6** PHRASE If an action or activity is **worth** your **while,** it will be helpful or useful to you. *It will be well worth your while to track down these treasures.*

worthless /wɜ:θlɪ²s/. ADJ Something or someone that is **worthless** is of no real use or value. *The goods are often worthless by the time they arrive... This made the treaty worthless... His brother is a worthless fool.*

worthwhile /wɜ:θwaɪl/. ADJ If something is **worthwhile,** it is enjoyable or useful, and worth the time, money, or effort spent on it. *A visit to Dorset will always be worthwhile.*

worthy /wɜ:ði¹/, **worthier, worthiest.** ADJ Someone or something that is **worthy** of respect, support, or admiration deserves it because of their qualities or abilities; a literary use. *Their cause is worthy of our continued support... He was a worthy winner.*

would /wə⁴d/. **Would** is sometimes considered to be the past form of **will,** but in this dictionary the two words are dealt with separately. **1** MODAL If someone said or thought that something **would** happen, they said or thought that it was going to happen. *I felt confident that everything would be all right... He made me promise that I would never break the law.* **2** MODAL You use **would** when you are referring to the result or effect of a possible situation. *If you can help me I would be very grateful... Without them life would not be the same.* **3** MODAL If you say that you **would** do something, you mean you are willing to do it. *Some men would do more for a dog than they would for a wife... Though we were as rude as possible, she wouldn't go.* **4** MODAL If you **would** like to do or have something, you want to do it or have it. *Posy said she'd love to stay... Would you like a drink?* **5** MODAL You use **would** in polite questions and requests. *Would you tell her that Adrian phoned?... Put the light on, Bryan, would you?* **6** MODAL You say that someone **would** do something when it is or was typical of them. *'Of course you would say that,' says Miss Callendar... 'He's backed out of it.'—'He would.'... I used to meet her and she would say 'Can't stop. I must get home.'* **7** MODAL You use **would** or **would have** to express your opinion about something that you think is true, or was true in the past. *I would think that in our climate we might have a few problems... I would have thought that his chief asset was his enthusiasm... We had a discussion on jazz, but you wouldn't remember that... She wouldn't have noticed. She was too far away.* **8** MODAL If you talk about what **would have** happened if a possible event had occurred, you are talking about the result or effect of that event. *If the bosses had known that he voted Liberal, he would have got the sack.* **9** MODAL If you say that someone **would have** liked or preferred something, you mean that they wanted to do it or have it but were unable to. *I would have liked a year more.*

would-be. ATTRIB ADJ You use **would-be** to describe what someone wants to do or become. For example, if someone is a **would-be** writer, they want to become a writer.

wouldn't /wʊdə⁰nt/. **Wouldn't** is the usual spoken form of 'would not'. *It wouldn't be safe.*

would've /wʊdəv/. **Would've** is a spoken form of 'would have', especially when 'have' is an auxiliary verb. *It would've meant leaving home.*

wound, wounds, wounding, wounded; pronounced /wu:nd/ for meanings 1, 2, and 3, and /waʊnd/ for meaning 4. **1** COUNT N A **wound** is a cut in part your body, especially one caused by a weapon or a sharp instrument. *He died from his wounds nine days after the shooting... The wound on his face was burning.* **2** VB WITH OBJ If someone **wounds** you, they damage your body using a weapon. *He had been badly wounded in the fighting.* **3** VB WITH OBJ If you **are wounded** by what someone says or does, you feel hurt and upset; a literary use. *She had been grievously wounded by his words.* **4 Wound** is also the past tense and past participle of most senses of the verb **wind.**

wove /wəʊv/. **Wove** is the past tense of **weave.**

woven /wəʊvə⁰n/. **Woven** is the past participle of **weave.**

WPC /dʌbə⁰lju: pi: si:/, **WPCs.** TITLE In Britain, **WPC** is used in front of the name of a female police officer of the lowest rank. *...WPC Williams.*

wrack /ræk/. See **rack.**

wrangle /ræŋgə⁰l/, **wrangles, wrangling, wrangled.** RECIP VB If you **wrangle** with someone, you argue with them angrily, often about something unimportant. *They wrangled over what to do next.* Also COUNT N *We avoided wrangles and got down to business.*

wrap /ræp/, **wraps, wrapping, wrapped. 1** VB WITH OBJ If you **wrap** something, you fold paper or cloth tightly round it to cover it. *I wrapped the ring in my handkerchief... The book was wrapped in brown paper... A handkerchief was wrapped around his left hand.* **2** VB WITH OBJ AND 'round' OR 'around' If you **wrap** your arms or fingers around something, you put them tightly around it. *He wrapped his arms around me.* **3** See also **wrapping.**

wrap up. PHR VB **1** If you **wrap** something **up,** you fold paper or cloth tightly around it to cover it. *Could you wrap the vase up?* **2** If you **wrap up,** you put warm clothes on. *Wrap up well. It's a cold night tonight.* **3** If you **wrap up** a job or an agreement, you complete it in a satisfactory way; an informal use. *The whole deal was wrapped up in a matter of days.*

wrapped up. PRED ADJ WITH 'in' If you are **wrapped up** in a person or thing, you are giving them a lot of attention; an informal use. *He was always wrapped up in his work... All the household are completely wrapped up in the baby.*

wrapper /ræpə/, **wrappers.** COUNT N A **wrapper** is a piece of paper, plastic, or foil which covers and protects something that you buy.

wrapping /ræpɪŋ/, **wrappings.** COUNT N OR UNCOUNT N A **wrapping** is a piece of paper or plastic used to cover and protect something. *He picked up the bottle and tore off its paper wrapping.*

wrapping paper. UNCOUNT N **Wrapping paper** is special pretty paper used for wrapping presents.

wrath /rɒθ/. UNCOUNT N **Wrath** is great anger; a literary use.

wreak /ri:k/, **wreaks, wreaking, wreaked;** a literary word. **1** VB WITH OBJ If something **wreaks** havoc or damage, it causes it. *These chemicals can wreak havoc on crops.* **2** VB WITH OBJ If you **wreak** revenge or vengeance on someone, you do something to harm them, because they have harmed you.

wreath /ri:θ/, **wreaths.** COUNT N A **wreath** is a ring of flowers and leaves which is put onto a grave as a sign of remembrance for the dead person.

wreathed /ri:ðd/. PRED ADJ WITH 'in' To be **wreathed** in something means to be surrounded by it; a literary use. *The sun was wreathed in mist.*

wreck /rɛk/, **wrecks, wrecking, wrecked. 1** VB WITH OBJ If someone **wrecks** something, they break it or spoil it in some way. *I wrecked a good stereo by not following the instructions properly... I'm sorry if I wrecked your weekend.* ♦ **wrecked** ADJ *Piles of wrecked cars took up most of the space.* **2** VB WITH OBJ If a ship **is wrecked,** it is damaged so much that it sinks. *...Spanish vessels that had been wrecked off the North American coast.* **3** COUNT N A **wreck** is a plane, car, or ship which has been destroyed in an accident. *All around were the wrecks of previous crashes... The seabed where the wreck lies is level and rocky.* **4** COUNT N If someone is a **wreck,** they are very unhealthy or exhausted; an informal use. *If you work like this you'll end up a wreck.* ● See also **nervous wreck.**

wreckage /rɛkɪdʒ/. UNCOUNT N When a plane, car, or building has been destroyed, you can refer to what remains as the **wreckage.** *Experts arrived to examine the wreckage of a cargo plane.*

wren /rɛn/, **wrens.** COUNT N A **wren** is a type of very small brown bird.

wrench /rɛntʃ/, **wrenches, wrenching, wrenched. 1** VB WITH OBJ If you **wrench** something that is fixed into a particular position, you pull or twist it violently. *He was trying to wrench my button off... I wrenched the door open.* **2** VB WITH OBJ If you **wrench** a limb or one of your joints, you twist it and injure it. **3** VB WITH OBJ AND ADJUNCT If you **wrench** your eyes or mind away from something, you make a great effort to stop looking at it or thinking about it. *I tried to wrench my gaze away from the appalling sight.* **4** SING N If leaving someone or something is a **wrench,** you feel very sad about it. **5** COUNT N A **wrench** is an adjustable metal tool used for tightening or loosening nuts and bolts.

wrest /rɛst/, **wrests, wresting, wrested.** VB WITH OBJ AND ADJUNCT If you **wrest** something away from someone, you take it from them by pulling it violently; a literary use. *He wrested the knife from her.*

wrestle /rɛsə⁰l/, **wrestles, wrestling, wrestled. 1** RECIP VB If you **wrestle** with someone, you fight them by forcing them into painful positions or throwing them to the ground, rather than by hitting them. *John wrestled with the intruder... The males wrestle and fight.* **2** VB WITH 'with' When you **wrestle** with a problem, you try to deal with it. *For decades, mathematicians have wrestled with this problem.*

wrestler /rɛslə/, **wrestlers.** COUNT N A **wrestler** is someone who wrestles as a sport.

wrestling /rɛslɪŋ/. UNCOUNT N **Wrestling** is a sport in which two people wrestle and try to throw each other to the ground.

wretch /rɛtʃ/, **wretches.** COUNT N A **wretch** is someone who is wicked or unfortunate; an old-fashioned use. *...the wretch who shot the President... The poor wretch groaned.*

wretched /rɛtʃɪ²d/. **1** ADJ Someone who is **wretched** is very unhappy or unfortunate; a formal use. *She spent the day in her room lying down and feeling wretched.* **2** ATTRIB ADJ You use **wretched** to describe something or someone that you dislike or feel angry with; an informal use. *I had to drag the wretched animal all the way... I hate this wretched system.*

wriggle /rɪgə⁰l/, **wriggles, wriggling, wriggled. 1** VB WITH OR WITHOUT OBJ If you **wriggle** a part of your body, you twist and turn it with quick movements. *The children were wriggling in anticipation... She wriggled her toes.* **2** VB WITH OR WITHOUT OBJ, WITH ADJUNCT If you **wriggle** somewhere, you move there by twisting and turning your body. *We had to wriggle under the fence.*

wriggle out of. PHR VB If you **wriggle out of** doing something that you do not want to do, you manage to avoid doing it; an informal use. *I can't wriggle out of accompanying my parents to Europe.*

wring /rɪŋ/, **wrings, wringing, wrung** /rʌŋ/. **1** VB WITH OBJ When you **wring** a wet cloth or **wring** it out, you squeeze the water out of it by twisting it strongly. **2** VB WITH OBJ When someone **wrings** their hands, they hold them together and twist and turn them because they are very worried or upset; a literary use. *He looked dazed and wrung his hands.* **3** VB WITH OBJ If someone **wrings** a bird's neck, they kill the bird by twisting its neck.

wrinkle /rɪŋkə⁰l/, **wrinkles, wrinkling, wrinkled. 1** COUNT N **Wrinkles** are lines which form on someone's face as they grow old. *His small eyes were surrounded by many wrinkles.* ♦ **wrinkled** ADJ *...a very old woman with a wrinkled face.* **2** ERG VB If something **wrinkles,** it gets folds or lines in it. *Clean the surface well or the paint might wrinkle and peel... He's always telling me that the sun will wrinkle my skin.* ♦ **wrinkled** ADJ *She looked to make sure her dress wasn't wrinkled.* **3** VB WITH OBJ When you **wrinkle** your nose or forehead, you tighten the muscles in your face so that the skin folds. *He wrinkled his nose. 'What an awful smell.'*

wrist /rɪst/, **wrists.** COUNT N Your **wrist** is the part of your body between your hand and arm which bends when you move your hand.

wristwatch /rɪstwɒtʃ/, **wristwatches.** COUNT N A **wristwatch** is a watch with a strap which you wear round your wrist.

writ /rɪt/, **writs.** COUNT N A **writ** is a legal document that orders a person to do a particular thing.

write /raɪt/, **writes, writing, wrote** /rəʊt/, **written** /rɪtə⁰n/. **1** VB WITH OR WITHOUT OBJ When you **write** something or **write** it down, you use a pen or pencil to produce words, letters, or numbers on a surface. *I'm learning to read and write... Write the appropriate letter on the label... I wrote down what the boy said.*

2 VB WITH OBJ If you **write** something such as a book, a poem, or a piece of music, you create it and record it on paper. *I have been asked to write a biography of Dylan Thomas.* 3 VB Someone who **writes** creates books, stories, or articles, usually for publication. *She writes on anthropology.* 4 VB WITH OR WITHOUT OBJ When you **write** to someone or **write** them a letter, you give them information, ask them something, or express your feelings in a letter. *I've written to invite him here... She wrote me a letter from Singapore... She wrote a note to the chief of police.* 5 VB WITH OBJ When you **write** something such as a cheque or a receipt, or **write** it out, you put the necessary information on it and sign it. *I remember writing a cheque for £100... I'll write you a prescription... I went to write out the death certificate.* 6 See also **writing, written.**

write in. PHR VB If you **write in** to an organization, you send them a letter. *People have been phoning and writing in asking for advice.*

write into. PHR VB If a rule or detail **is written into** a contract or agreement, it is included in it when the contract or agreement is made. *The new arrangements have been written into the agreement.*

write off. PHR VB 1 If you **write off** to a company or organization, you send them a letter asking for something. *I was writing off to various places asking about work opportunities.* 2 If you **write off** an amount of money you have lost, you accept that you will never get it back. *I've written off that hundred pounds.* 3 If you **write off** a plan or project, you accept that it will not be successful and you do not continue with it. 4 If you **write** someone **off,** you decide that they are unimportant or useless. *You will be written off as a hysterical woman.*

write up. PHR VB If you **write up** something that has been done or said, you record it on paper in a neat and complete form. *These are notes that you are going to write up afterwards... The results were written up into a report.* ● See also **write-up.**

write-off, write-offs. COUNT N If a vehicle is a **write-off,** it is so badly damaged in an accident that it is not worth repairing. *Their car was a write-off.*

writer /raɪtə/, **writers.** 1 COUNT N A **writer** is a person whose job is writing books, stories, or articles. *...the writer and critic, Hilary Spurling.* 2 COUNT N WITH SUPP The **writer** of a particular article, story, or other piece of writing is the person who wrote it. *I arranged an appointment with the writer of the letter.*

write-up, write-ups. COUNT N A **write-up** is an article in a newspaper or magazine, in which someone gives their opinion of a play or a new product.

writhe /raɪð/, **writhes, writhing, writhed.** VB If you **writhe,** you twist and turn your body violently backwards and forwards, usually because you are in great pain. *He writhed in agony.*

writing /raɪtɪŋ/, **writings.** 1 UNCOUNT N **Writing** is something that has been written or printed. *Put the papers face down so that the writing cannot be seen... You must get the offer in writing.* 2 UNCOUNT N You can refer to any piece of written work as **writing,** especially when you are considering the style of language used in it. *...some brilliant and very witty writing.* 3 UNCOUNT N **Writing** is also the activity of writing, especially writing books for money. *I hate writing and I'm not very good at it.* 4 PLURAL N An author's **writings** are all the things that he or she has written. *His political writings remind me of those of Sartre.*

written /rɪtəⁿn/. 1 **Written** is the past participle of **write.** 2 ADJ A **written** test or piece of work is one which involves writing rather than doing an experiment or giving spoken answers. 3 ATTRIB ADJ A **written** agreement, rule, or law has been officially written down. *I will send written confirmation.*

wrong /rɒŋ/, **wrongs, wronging, wronged.** 1 PRED ADJ If there is something **wrong,** there is something unsatisfactory about the situation or thing that you are talking about. *The front door was unlocked—something was wrong... I asked what was wrong... There was nothing wrong with his eyesight.* 2 ADJ OR ADV **Wrong** means not correct or not suitable. *I'm afraid I'll make the wrong decision... Her name was spelt wrong.* ♦ **wrongly** ADV *Many of us choose wrongly.* 3 PRED ADJ If you are **wrong** about something, what you say or think about it is not correct. *We had to admit the possibility that we might be wrong.* ♦ **wrongly** ADV *She supposed, wrongly, that the other two agreed with her.* 4 ADJ If something that you do is **wrong,** it is bad or immoral. *You were wrong to speak to the newspapers first.* 5 UNCOUNT N **Wrong** is used to refer to actions that are bad or immoral. *Any good parent feels strongly about right and wrong.* 6 COUNT N A **wrong** is an unjust action or situation. *In a democracy wrongs should be righted by the vote and not by violence.* 7 VB WITH OBJ If someone **wrongs** you, they treat you in an unfair or unjust way; a literary use. 8 ATTRIB ADJ The **wrong** side of a piece of cloth or paper is the side which is intended to face inwards or downwards and not be seen.

PHRASES ● If you **get** something **wrong,** you make a mistake. *I think she got his name wrong.* ● If you **go wrong,** you make a mistake. *Where did I go wrong?* ● If something **goes wrong,** it stops working or is no longer successful. *Computers do go wrong... Their relationship went wrong after the birth of their child.* ● If you are **in the wrong,** what you are doing is immoral or illegal.

wrongful /rɒŋfʊl/. ATTRIB ADJ A **wrongful** act is one regarded as illegal, immoral, or unfair; a formal use. *...the wrongful imprisonment of Napoleon.* ♦ **wrongfully** ADV *The workers were wrongfully dismissed.*

wrote /rəʊt/. **Wrote** is the past tense of **write.**

wrought /rɔːt/. 1 VB WITH OBJ If something **has wrought** a change, it has caused it; a literary use. *That moment had wrought a profound change in him.* 2 ATTRIB ADJ **Wrought** metal has been made into a particular shape, usually a decorative one. *...wrought silver... ...a wrought iron gate.*

wrung /rʌŋ/. **Wrung** is the past tense and past participle of **wring.**

wry /raɪ/. 1 ADJ If someone has a **wry** expression, it shows that they find a bad or difficult situation slightly amusing or ironic. *He came out with a wry smile on his face... She said this with a wry glance at me.* ♦ **wryly** ADV *My friend smiled wryly when he saw me.* 2 ADJ A **wry** remark or piece of writing refers to a bad or difficult situation in an amusing or ironic way. *On receipt of his insurance claim, there were some wry comments... ...his direct style of writing and wry humour.*

Xx

xenophobia /zenəfəʊbɪə/. UNCOUNT N **Xenophobia** is fear or strong dislike of people from other countries; a formal use.

Xmas /krɪsməs, eksməs/. UNCOUNT N **Xmas** is the same as Christmas; an informal use.

X-ray /eks reɪ/, **X-rays, X-raying, X-rayed.** 1 COUNT N An **X-ray** is a stream of radiation that can pass through some solid materials. X-rays are used by doctors to examine the bones or organs inside your body. *He agreed to go for an X-ray to see if the bone was broken.* 2 COUNT N An **X-ray** is also a picture made by sending X-rays through your body. *The chest X-ray showed enlargement of the heart.* 3 VB WITH OBJ If a doctor **X-rays** you, he or she takes a picture of the inside of your body using an X-ray machine.

-y. SUFFIX **-y** is added to nouns, especially ones referring to substances, to form adjectives which indicate that something is like something else, or is full of it or covered in it. *...spongy bread... ...her inky, chalky hand.*

yacht /jɒt/, **yachts.** COUNT N A **yacht** is a boat with sails or a motor, used for racing or for pleasure trips.

yam /jæm/, **yams.** COUNT N A **yam** is a root vegetable which grows in tropical regions. It is similar to a potato in appearance and texture.

yank /jæŋk/, **yanks, yanking, yanked.** 1 COUNT N A **Yank** is a person from the United States of America; an informal British use that is offensive. 2 VB WITH OBJ If you **yank** something, you pull it suddenly with a lot of force; an informal use. *Glenn yanked out the sore tooth.*

Yankee /jæŋki¹/, **Yankees.** COUNT N A **Yankee** is the same as a Yank; an offensive use.

yap /jæp/, **yaps, yapping, yapped.** VB If a dog **yaps,** it barks a lot with a high-pitched sound.

yard /jɑːd/, **yards.** 1 COUNT N A **yard** is a unit of length equal to 36 inches or approximately 91.4 centimetres. 2 COUNT N A **yard** is also a flat area of concrete or stone that is next to a building and often has a wall around it. *...a tiny cramped house without even a back yard.* 3 COUNT N You can refer to a large area where a particular type of work is done as a **yard.** *...a ship repair yard.*

yardstick /jɑːdstɪk/, **yardsticks.** COUNT N WITH SUPP If you use someone or something as a **yardstick,** you use them as a standard for comparison when you are judging other people or things. *She was a yardstick against which I could measure what I had achieved.*

yarn /jɑːn/, **yarns.** 1 MASS N **Yarn** is thread that is used for knitting or making cloth. 2 COUNT N A **yarn** is a story that someone tells, often a true story with invented details which make it more interesting; an informal use.

yawn /jɔːn/, **yawns, yawning, yawned.** 1 VB When you **yawn,** you open your mouth wide and breathe in more air than usual. You often yawn when you are tired or bored. *I yawned all through the concert.* Also COUNT N *She stifled a yawn.* 2 VB A gap or opening that **yawns** is large and wide, and often frightening; a literary use. *A great gap yawned between the rocks.* ♦ **yawning** ATTRIB ADJ *...yawning craters.*

yd, yds. COUNT N **yd** is a written abbreviation for 'yard'. The plural is either 'yds' or 'yd'. *The reel holds 400 yds of line.*

yeah /jeə/. CONVENTION **Yeah** means the same as yes; an informal use.

year /jɪə/, **years.** 1 COUNT N A **year** is a period of 365 or 366 days, beginning on the first day of January and ending on the last day of December. *...at the end of next year... ...in the year 2000.* 2 COUNT N A **year** is also a period of about twelve months. *...a hundred years ago... For seven years I was a designer.* 3 COUNT N A school **year** is the period of time in each twelve months when the school is open and students are studying there. 4 COUNT N WITH SUPP A financial or business **year** is an exact period of twelve months which businesses or institutions use as a basis for organizing their finances. *...the final account at the end of each trading year.* 5 PLURAL N You can use **years** to emphasize that you are referring to a very long time. *They've known each other for years and years.* 6 PHRASE If you do something **all year round** or **all the year round,** you do it all the time. *They grow crops all the year round.* 7 See also **leap year, New Year.**

yearly /jɪəli¹/. 1 ATTRIB ADJ OR ADV You use **yearly** to describe something that happens once a year or every year. *...a yearly meeting... Interest is paid yearly.* 2 ATTRIB ADJ OR ADV You also use **yearly** to describe something such as an amount that relates to a period of one year. *...the yearly income of workers... ...infections that hit thousands of babies yearly.*

yearn /jɜːn/, **yearns, yearning, yearned.** VB WITH 'for' OR TO-INF If you **yearn** for something, you want it very much; a literary use. *He passionately yearned for happiness... She yearned to go back to the south.*

yearning /jɜːnɪŋ/, **yearnings.** COUNT N OR UNCOUNT N A **yearning** is a strong desire for something. *...to satisfy the yearnings of the workers... Both sides were tense with yearning.*

-year-old, -year-olds. SUFFIX **-year-old** is added to numbers to form adjectives and nouns that indicate the age of people or things. *...a fifteen-year-old boy... ...a class of 4-year-olds.*

yeast /jiːst/. MASS N **Yeast** is a fungus which is used to make bread rise, and to make alcoholic drinks.

yell /jel/, **yells, yelling, yelled.** 1 VB OR REPORT VB If you **yell,** you shout loudly, usually because you are excited, angry, or in pain. *I yelled at Richard to hang on... 'Speed up!' he yelled to the driver.* 2 COUNT N A **yell** is a loud shout given by someone who is afraid or in pain. *I heard a yell from inside the house.*

yellow /jeləʊ/, **yellows, yellowing, yellowed.** 1 ADJ Something that is **yellow** is the colour of lemons or egg yolks. *...a bright yellow hat.* 2 ERG VB When something **yellows** or **is yellowed,** it becomes yellow, often because it is old. *...a photograph of her, yellowed with age.*

yellow fever. UNCOUNT N **Yellow fever** is a serious infectious disease that is found in tropical countries.

yellowish /jeləʊɪʃ/. ADJ Something that is **yellowish** is slightly yellow. *...a soft yellowish glow.*

yelp /jelp/, **yelps, yelping, yelped.** VB When people or animals **yelp,** they give a sudden short cry, often because of fear or pain. *He yelped in pain.* Also COUNT N *I gave a little yelp and fled upstairs.*

yen /jen/. SING N If you have a **yen** to do something, you have a strong desire to do it. *Nicholas has a yen to hike through Canada.*

yes /jes/. 1 CONVENTION You use **yes** when you are agreeing with someone, saying that something is true, or accepting something. *'Did you enjoy it?'—'Yes.'... 'Do you want some coffee?'—'Yes please.'... 'It was a beautiful day.'—'It was nice, yes.'* 2 CONVENTION You can use **yes** in a conversation to encourage someone to continue speaking. *'I miss the country very much.'—'Yes?'—'And yet, I would hate to give up my job here.'* 3 CONVENTION You can also use **yes** when contradicting something. *'Nowadays you don't learn any basic principles in maths.'—'Oh, yes you do.'*

yesterday /jestədi³/. 1 ADV **Yesterday** means the day before today. *It was hot yesterday... Yesterday morning there were more than 500 boats on the lake.* 2 ADV **Yesterday** can also mean the past, especially the recent past. *The worker of today is different from the worker of yesterday.*

yet /jet/. 1 ADV If something has not happened **yet,** it has not happened up to the present time. *I haven't made up my mind yet... It isn't dark yet... Have you* *had your lunch yet?* 2 ADV If something should not be done **yet,** it should not be done now but at a later time. *Loosen nuts with a spanner but don't take them off yet.* 3 ADV You also use **yet** to say that there is still a possibility that something will happen. *The figures may yet be revised again... There is hope for me yet.* 4 ADV You use **yet** after an expression referring to a period of time, when you want to say how much longer a situation will continue. *He's going to be around for a long while yet... It will not be dark for half an hour yet.* 5 ADV WITH TO-INF If you have **yet** to do something, you have not done it but may do it in the future. If something is **yet** to happen, it has not happened but may happen in the future.. *I have yet to meet a man I can trust... A whole range of issues had yet to be resolved.* 6 CONJ You also use **yet** to introduce a fact which seems rather surprising in relation to the thing you have just mentioned. *Everything around him was blown to pieces, yet the minister escaped without a scratch... ...a firm yet gentle hand.* 7 ADV You can also use **yet** to emphasize a comparative or a word that refers to an increase or repetition. *I am sorry to bring up the subject of money yet again... The queues are likely to grow longer yet.*

yield /jiːld/, **yields, yielding, yielded.** 1 VB If you **yield** to someone or something, you stop resisting them; a formal use. *He was yielding to public pressure.* 2 VB WITH OBJ If you **yield** something that you have control of or responsibility for, you allow someone else to have control or responsibility. *He will not yield even a limited measure of editorial control.* 3 VB If something **yields,** it breaks or moves because of force or pressure on it. *Any lock will yield to brute force.* 4 VB WITH OBJ If an investigation or discussion **yields** a particular result or information, it produces it. *Talks between the two sides yielded no results.* 5 VB WITH OBJ If an area of land or a number of animals **yields** a particular amount of food, this amount is produced by the land or the animals. *0.23 acres yields only 200 pounds of rice.* 6 COUNT N A **yield** is an amount of food produced on an area of land or by a number of animals. *They have a far better yield than any farm round here.* 7 VB WITH OBJ If a tax or investment **yields** an amount of money or profit, you get this money or profit from it.

yoga /jəʊgə/. UNCOUNT N **Yoga** is a type of exercise in which you move your body into various positions in order to become more fit or flexible, to improve your breathing, and to relax your mind.

yoghurt /jɒgət/; also spelled **yoghourt** or **yogurt.** MASS N **Yoghurt** is a slightly sour, thick liquid made by adding bacteria to milk.

yoke /jəʊk/, **yokes.** 1 SING N WITH SUPP If people are suffering under a **yoke** of a particular kind, they are in a difficult or unhappy state, such as being governed by a severe leader; a literary use. *...a war against the yoke of tyranny.* 2 COUNT N A **yoke** is a long piece of wood which is tied across the necks of two animals such as oxen, in order to make them walk close together when they are pulling a plough.

yolk /jəʊk/, **yolks.** COUNT N OR UNCOUNT N The **yolk** of an egg is the yellow part in the middle.

yonder /jɒndə/. ADV **Yonder** means over there; an old-fashioned use. *They came galloping over that hill yonder.*

you /juː/. **You** is used as the subject of a verb or as the object of a verb or preposition. It can refer to one or more people. 1 PRON A speaker or writer uses **you** to refer to the person or people that he or she is speaking to. *What do you think?* 2 PRON **You** is also used to refer to people in general rather than to a particular person or group. *You can get freezers with security locks.*

you'd /juːd/. **You'd** is the usual spoken form of 'you had', especially when 'had' is an auxiliary verb. **You'd** is also a spoken form of 'you would'. *If you'd asked me that ten years ago, I'd have said yes... You'd be surprised how easy it is.*

you'll /juːl/. **You'll** is the usual spoken form of 'you will'. *You'll have to get a job.*

young /jʌŋ/, **younger** /jʌŋgə/, **youngest** /jʌŋgərst/. 1 ADJ A **young** person, animal, or plant has not lived or existed for long and is not yet mature. *Julia has two young boys... She was three years younger than me... The young seedlings grow very rapidly.* 2 ATTRIB ADJ You also use **young** to describe the time when a person was young. *I was fond of dancing in my younger days.* 3 PLURAL N The **young** of an animal are its babies. *When the young first hatch, they are naked.*

youngish /jʌŋgɪʃ/. ADJ Someone who is **youngish** is fairly young in appearance, behaviour, or age. *...a youngish man with blond hair.*

youngster /jʌŋkstə/, **youngsters.** COUNT N A **youngster** is a young person or child. *I don't know what the youngsters of today think.*

your /jɔː, jʊə/. 1 DET A speaker or writer uses **your** to indicate that something belongs or relates to the person or people that he or she is speaking to. *Where's your father?... ...your books.* 2 DET **Your** is also used to indicate that something belongs or relates to people in general rather than to a particular person or group. *You can't use your own name in a novel.* 3 DET **Your** is also used in some titles when addressing people with that title. *...your Majesty.*

you're /jɔː, jʊə/. **You're** is the usual spoken form of 'you are'. *You're quite right.*

yours /jɔːz, jʊəz/. 1 PRON A speaker or writer uses **yours** to refer to something that belongs or relates to the person or people that he or she is speaking to. *Our swimming pool isn't as deep as yours... A student of yours came to see me.* 2 CONVENTION People write **Yours, Yours sincerely,** or **Yours faithfully** at the end of a letter before they sign their name.

yourself /jəsɛlf/, **yourselves.** 1 REFL PRON A speaker or writer uses **yourself** as the object of a verb or preposition in a clause where 'you' is the subject or a previous object, or in a clause which consists of a command. *Would you call yourself a Marxist?... Help yourselves to sandwiches... Tell me about yourself.* 2 REFL PRON **Yourself** is also used to emphasize the subject or object of a clause. *You yourself said it's only a routine check.* 3 REFL PRON If you do something **yourself,** you do it without any help or interference from anyone else. *Did you make these cakes yourself?*

youth /juːθ/, **youths** /juːðz/. 1 UNCOUNT N Someone's **youth** is the period of their life when they are a child, before they are a fully mature adult. *We change and learn from youth to old age... He had visited Calcutta in his youth.* 2 UNCOUNT N **Youth** is the quality or state of being young and perhaps immature or inexperienced. *...marvelling at his freshness and apparent youth.* 3 COUNT N A **youth** is a boy or a young man, especially a teenager. *...two youths in leather jackets.* 4 PLURAL N The **youth** are young people considered as a group. *...unemployment among the youth of this country.*

youthful /juːθfʊl/. 1 ADJ Someone who is **youthful** is young, lively, and full of energy. *...youthful dancers.* 2 ADJ **Youthful** also means having qualities or characteristics that are typical of young people. *Despite her age she still had a youthful body.*

youth hostel, youth hostels. COUNT N A **youth hostel** is a place where young people can stay cheaply when they are travelling around.

you've /juːv/. **You've** is the usual spoken form of 'you have', especially when 'have' is an auxiliary verb. *You've been very lucky.*

yr, yrs. COUNT N **Yr** is a written abbreviation for 'year'. The plural is either 'yrs' or 'yr'. *...children aged 3-11 yrs.*

yuppie /jʌpi/, **yuppies.** COUNT N **Yuppies** are young middle class people who earn a lot of money and spend it on expensive possessions and activities.

zany /zeɪni/. ADJ **Zany** means strange and amusing. *...zany ideas.*

zeal /ziːl/. UNCOUNT N **Zeal** is great enthusiasm, especially in connection with work, religion, or politics; a formal use. *...revolutionary zeal.*

zealot /zɛlət/, **zealots.** COUNT N A **zealot** is a person who acts with extreme zeal, especially because of political or religious ideals; a formal use.

zealous /zɛləs/. ADJ A **zealous** person spends a lot of time or energy in supporting something, especially a political or religious ideal; a formal use.

zebra /zɛbrə, ziː-/, **zebras.** COUNT N A **zebra** is an African wild horse which has black and white stripes.

zebra crossing, zebra crossings. COUNT N In Britain, a **zebra crossing** is a place where the road is marked with black and white stripes. Vehicles must stop there to let people cross the road.

zenith /zɛnɪθ/. SING N The **zenith** of something is the time when it is most successful or powerful; a literary use. *...Greek civilization at its zenith... ...at the zenith of his career.*

zero /zɪərəʊ/, **zeros** or **zeroes, zeroing, zeroed.** 1 **Zero** is the number 0. *This scale goes from zero to forty.* 2 UNCOUNT N **Zero** is also freezing point, 0°C. *It was fourteen below zero when they woke up.* 3 ADJ You can use **zero** to say that there is none at all of the thing mentioned. *Its running costs were zero... We drove in zero visibility.*

zero in on. PHR VB 1 To **zero in on** a target means to aim at it or move towards it. *The missile zeroed in on the tank.* 2 If you **zero in on** a problem or subject, you give it your full attention.

zest /zɛst/; a literary word. 1 UNCOUNT N **Zest** is a feeling of pleasure and enthusiasm. *The children were full of life and zest.* 2 UNCOUNT N **Zest** is also a quality in an activity or situation which you find exciting. *Some of the zest had gone out of his life.*

zigzag /zɪgzæg/, **zigzags, zigzagging, zigzagged.** 1 COUNT N A **zigzag** is a line with a series of angles in it, like a continuous series of 'W's. *Suddenly there was a flash and a zigzag of forked lightning.* 2 VB WITH ADJUNCT To **zigzag** means to move forward by going at an angle first to one side and then to the other. *We zigzagged laboriously up the track.*

zinc /zɪŋk/. UNCOUNT N **Zinc** is a grey metal which is used to make other metals or to cover other metals such as iron to stop them rusting.

zip /zɪp/, **zips, zipping, zipped.** 1 COUNT N A **zip** is a device used on clothes and bags to close them. It consists of two rows of metal or plastic teeth that you pull together in order to keep things closed; a British use. 2 VB WITH OBJ When you **zip** something, you close it using a zip.

zip up. PHR VB When you **zip up** something such as a piece of clothing, you fasten it using a zip. *She zipped up the dress with difficulty.*

zip code, zip codes. COUNT N A **zip code** is a combination of letters and numbers that are part of an address; an American use.

zipper /zɪpə/, **zippers.** COUNT N A **zipper** is a zip.

zodiac /zəʊdiæk/. SING N The **zodiac** is a diagram used by astrologers to represent the positions of the planets and stars. It is divided into 12 sections, each with a special name and symbol.

zone /zəʊn/, **zones.** COUNT N WITH SUPP A **zone** is an area that has particular features or characteristics. *...the war zone... ...a nuclear-free zone.*

zoo /zuː/, **zoos.** COUNT N A **zoo** is a park where live animals are kept so that people can look at them.

zoology /zuːɒlədʒi/. UNCOUNT N **Zoology** is the scientific study of animals. *His lifelong interest was zoology.* ♦ **zoologist** /zuːɒlədʒɪst/ COUNT N *...university zoologists.* ♦ **zoological** /zuːəlɒdʒɪkəl/ ATTRIB ADJ *...zoological specimens.*

zoom /zuːm/, **zooms, zooming, zoomed;** an informal word. 1 VB If you **zoom** somewhere, you go there very quickly. *They zoomed down to Folkestone on their bikes.* 2 VB If prices or sales **zoom,** they increase rapidly. *Sales had zoomed to 33 million.*

Unit 1 Clause and sentence structure

Main points

- Simple sentences have one clause.
- Clauses usually consist of a noun group as the subject, and a verb group.
- Clauses can also have another noun group as the object or complement.
- Clauses can have an adverbial, also called an adjunct.
- Changing the order of the words in a clause can change its meaning.
- Compound sentences consist of two or more main clauses. Complex sentences always include a subordinate clause, as well as one or more main clauses.

1 A simple sentence has one clause, beginning with a noun group called the subject. The subject is the person or thing that the sentence is about. This is followed by a verb group, which tells you what the subject is doing, or describes the subject's situation.

I waited.
The girl screamed.

2 The verb group may be followed by another noun group, which is called the object. The object is the person or thing affected by the action or situation.

He opened <u>the car door</u>.
She married <u>a young engineer</u>.

After link verbs like 'be', 'become', 'feel', and 'seem', the verb group may be followed by a noun group or an adjective, called a complement. The complement tells you more about the subject.

She was <u>a doctor</u>.
He was <u>angry</u>.

3 The verb group, the object, or the complement can be followed by an adverb or a prepositional phrase, called an adverbial. The adverbial tells you more about the action or situation, for example how, when, or where it happens. Adverbials are also called adjuncts.

They shouted <u>loudly</u>.
She won the competition <u>last week</u>.
He was a policeman <u>in Birmingham</u>.

4 The word order of a clause is different when the clause is a statement, a question, or a command.

<u>He speaks</u> English very well. (statement)
<u>Did she win</u> at the Olympics? (question)
<u>Stop</u> her. (command)

Note that the subject is omitted in commands, so the verb comes first.

5 A compound sentence has two or more main clauses: that is, clauses which are equally important. You join them with 'and', 'but', or 'or'.

He met Jane at the station <u>and</u> went shopping.
I wanted to go <u>but</u> I felt too ill.
You can come now <u>or</u> you can meet us there later.

Note that the order of the two clauses can change the meaning of the sentence.

He went shopping <u>and</u> met Jane at the station.

If the subject of both clauses is the same, you usually omit the subject in the second clause.

I wanted to go <u>but felt</u> too ill.

6 A complex sentence contains a subordinate clause and at least one main clause. A subordinate clause gives information about a main clause, and is introduced by a conjunction such as 'because', 'if', 'that', or a 'wh'-word. Subordinate clauses can come before, after, or inside the main clause.

<u>When he stopped</u>, no one said anything.
<u>If you want</u>, I'll teach you.

They were going by car <u>because it was more comfortable</u>.
I told him <u>that nothing was going to happen to me</u>.

The car <u>that I drove</u> was a Ford.
The man <u>who came into the room</u> was small.

Unit 2 The noun group

Main points

- Noun groups can be the subject, object, or complement of a verb, or the object of a preposition.
- Noun groups can be nouns on their own, but often include other words such as determiners, numbers, and adjectives.
- Noun groups can also be pronouns.
- Singular noun groups take singular verbs, plural noun groups take plural verbs.

1 Noun groups are used to say which people or things you are talking about. They can be the subject or object of a verb.

Strawberries are very expensive now.
Keith likes strawberries.

A noun group can also be the complement of a link verb such as 'be', 'become', 'feel', or 'seem'.

She became champion in 1964.
He seemed a nice man.

A noun group can be used after a preposition, and is often called the object of the preposition.

I saw him in town.
She was very ill for six months.

2 A noun group can be a noun on its own, but it often includes other words. A noun group can have a determiner such as 'the' or 'a'. You put determiners at the beginning of the noun group.

The girls were not in the house.
He was eating an apple.

3 A noun group can include an adjective. You usually put the adjective in front of the noun.

He was using blue ink.
I like living in a big city.

Sometimes you can use another noun in front of the noun.

I like chocolate cake.
She wanted a job in the oil industry.

A noun with 's (apostrophe s) is used in front of another noun to show who or what something belongs to or is connected with.

I held Sheila's hand very tightly.
He pressed a button on the ship's radio.

4 A noun group can also have an adverbial, a relative clause, or a 'to'-infinitive clause after it, which makes it more precise.

I spoke to a girl in a dark grey dress.
She wrote to the man who employed me.
I was trying to think of a way to stop him.

A common adverbial used after a noun is a prepositional phrase beginning with 'of'.

He tied the rope to a large block of stone.
The front door of the house was wide open.
I hated the idea of leaving him alone.

Participles and some adjectives can also be used after a noun. See Units 19 and 29.

She pointed to the three cards lying on the table.
He is the only man available.

5 Numbers come after determiners and before adjectives.

I had to pay a thousand dollars.
Three tall men came out of the shed.

6 A noun group can also be a pronoun. You often use a pronoun when you are referring back to a person or thing that you have already mentioned.

I've got two boys, and they both enjoy playing football.

You also use a pronoun when you do not know who the person or thing is, or do not want to be precise.

Someone is coming to mend it tomorrow.

7 A noun group can refer to one or more people or things. Many nouns have a singular form referring to one person or thing, and a plural form referring to more than one person or thing. See Unit 4.

My dog never bites people.
She likes dogs.

Similarly, different pronouns are used in the singular and in the plural.

I am going home now.
We want more money.

When a singular noun group is the subject, it takes a singular verb. When a plural noun group is the subject, it takes a plural verb.

His son plays football for the school.
Her letters are always very short.

Unit 3 The verb group

Main points

- In a clause, the verb group usually comes after the subject and always has a main verb.
- The main verb has several different forms.
- Verb groups can also include one or two auxiliaries, or a modal, or a modal and one or two auxiliaries.
- The verb group changes in negative clauses and questions.
- Some verb groups are followed by an adverbial, a complement, an object, or two objects.

1 The verb group in a clause is used to say what is happening in an action or situation. You usually put the verb group immediately after the subject. The verb group always includes a main verb.

I waited.
They killed the elephants.

2 Regular verbs have four forms: the base form, the third person singular form of the present simple, the '-ing' form or present participle, and the '-ed' form used for the past simple and for the past participle.

ask	⇨ asks	⇨ asking	⇨ asked
try	⇨ tries	⇨ trying	⇨ tried
reach	⇨ reaches	⇨ reaching	⇨ reached
dance	⇨ dances	⇨ dancing	⇨ danced
dip	⇨ dips	⇨ dipping	⇨ dipped

Irregular verbs may have three forms, four forms, or five forms. Note that 'be' has eight forms.

cost	⇨ costs	⇨ costing		
think	⇨ thinks	⇨ thinking	⇨ thought	
swim	⇨ swims	⇨ swimming	⇨ swam	⇨ swum
be	⇨ am / is / are	⇨ being	⇨ was / were	⇨ been

See the Appendix for details of verb forms.

3 The main verb can have one or two auxiliaries in front of it.

I had met him in Zermatt.
The car was being repaired.

The main verb can have a modal in front of it.

You can go now.
I would like to ask you a question.

The main verb can have a modal and one or two auxiliaries in front of it.

I could have spent the whole year on it.
She would have been delighted to see you.

4 In negative clauses, you have to use a modal or auxiliary and put 'not' after the first word of the verb group.

He does not speak English very well.
I was not smiling.
It could not have been wrong.

Note that you often use short forms rather than 'not'.

I didn't know that.
He couldn't see it.

5 In 'yes/no' questions, you have to put an auxiliary or modal first, then the subject, then the rest of the verb group.

Did you meet George?
Couldn't you have been a bit quieter?

In 'wh'-questions, you put the 'wh'-word first. If the 'wh'-word is the subject, you put the verb group next.

Which came first?
Who could have done it?

If the 'wh'-word is the object or an adverbial, you must use an auxiliary or modal next, then the subject, then the rest of the verb group.

What did you do?
Where could she be going?

6 Some verb groups have an object or two objects after them. See Units 72 and 73.

He closed the door.
She sends you her love.

Verb groups involving link verbs, such as 'be', have a complement after them. See Unit 80.

They were sailors.
She felt happy.

Some verb groups have an adverbial after them.

We walked through the park.
She put the letter on the table.

Unit 4 Count nouns

Main points

- Count nouns have two forms, singular and plural.
- They can be used with numbers.
- Singular count nouns always take a determiner.
- Plural count nouns do not need a determiner.
- Singular count nouns take a singular verb and plural count nouns take a plural verb.

In English, some things are thought of as individual items that can be counted directly. The nouns which refer to these countable things are called count nouns. Most nouns in English are count nouns. See Unit 6 for information on uncount nouns.

1 Count nouns have two forms. The singular form refers to one thing or person.

...a book... ...the teacher.

The plural form refers to more than one thing or person.

...books... ...some teachers.

2 You add '-s' to form the plural of most nouns.

book ⇨ books	school ⇨ schools

You add '-es' to nouns ending in '-ss', '-ch', '-s', '-sh', or '-x'.

class ⇨ classes	watch ⇨ watches
gas ⇨ gases	dish ⇨ dishes
fox ⇨ foxes	

Some nouns ending in '-o' add '-s', and some add '-es'.

photo ⇨ photos	piano ⇨ pianos
hero ⇨ heroes	potato ⇨ potatoes

Nouns ending in a consonant and '-y' change to '-ies'.

country ⇨ countries	lady ⇨ ladies
party ⇨ parties	victory ⇨ victories

Nouns ending in a vowel and '-y' add an '-s'.

boy ⇨ boys	day ⇨ days
key ⇨ keys	valley ⇨ valleys

Some common nouns have irregular plurals.

child ⇨ children	foot	⇨ feet
man ⇨ men	mouse	⇨ mice
tooth ⇨ teeth	woman	⇨ women

WARNING: Some nouns that end in '-s' are uncount nouns, for example 'athletics' and 'physics'. See Unit 6.

3 Count nouns can be used with numbers.

...one table... ...two cats... ...three hundred pounds.

4 Singular count nouns cannot be used alone, but always take a determiner such as 'a', 'another', 'every', or 'the'.

We've killed a pig.
He was eating another apple.
She had read every book on the subject.
I parked the car over there.

5 Plural count nouns can be used with or without a determiner. They do not take a determiner when they refer to things or people in general.

Does the hotel have large rooms?
The film is not suitable for children.

Plural count nouns do take a determiner when they refer precisely to particular things or people.

Our computers are very expensive.
These cakes are delicious.

See Unit 11 for more information on determiners.

6 When a count noun is the subject of a verb, a singular count noun takes a singular verb.

My son likes playing football.
The address on the letter was wrong.

A plural count noun takes a plural verb.

Bigger cars cost more.
I thought more people were coming.

See also Unit 5 on collective nouns.

Unit 5 Singular, plural, and collective nouns

Main points

- Singular nouns are used only in the singular, always with a determiner.
- Plural nouns are used only in the plural, some with a determiner.
- Collective nouns can be used with singular or plural verbs.

1 Some nouns are used in particular meanings in the singular with a determiner, like count nouns, but are not used in the plural with that meaning. They are often called 'singular nouns'.
Some of these nouns are normally used with 'the' because they refer to things that are unique.

air	daytime	moon	sky
country	end	past	sun
countryside	future	sea	wind
dark	ground	seaside	world

The sun was shining.
I am scared of the dark.

Other singular nouns are normally used with 'a' because they refer to things that we usually talk about one at a time.

bath	go	ride	snooze
chance	jog	run	start
drink	move	shower	walk
fight	rest	smoke	wash

I went upstairs and had a wash.
Why don't we go outside for a smoke?

2 Some nouns are used in particular meanings in the plural with or without determiners, like count nouns, but are not used in the singular with that meaning. They are often called 'plural nouns'.

His clothes looked terribly dirty.
Troops are being sent in today.

Some of these nouns are always used with determiners.

activities	feelings	pictures	travels
authorities	likes	sights	

I went to the pictures with Tina.
You hurt his feelings.

Some are usually used without determiners.

airs	goods	riches
expenses	refreshments	

Refreshments are available inside.
They have agreed to pay for travel and expenses.

WARNING: 'Police' is a plural noun, but does not end in '-s'.

The police were informed immediately.

3 A small group of plural nouns refer to single items that have two linked parts. They refer to things that people wear or tools that people use.

glasses	pyjamas	~	scales
jeans	shorts	binoculars	scissors
knickers	tights	pincers	shears
pants	trousers	pliers	tweezers

She was wearing brown trousers.
These scissors are sharp.

You can use 'a pair of' to make it clear you are talking about one item, or a number with 'pairs of' when you are talking about several items.

I was sent out to buy a pair of scissors.
Liza had given me three pairs of jeans.

Note that you also use 'a pair of' with words such as 'gloves', 'shoes', and 'socks' that you often talk about in twos.

4 With some nouns that refer to a group of people or things, the same form can be used with singular or plural verbs, because you can think of the group as a unit or as individuals. Similarly, you can use singular or plural pronouns to refer back to them. These nouns are often called 'collective nouns'.

army	enemy	group	staff
audience	family	herd	team
committee	flock	navy	~
company	gang	press	data
crew	government	public	media

Our little group is complete again.
The largest group are the boys.
Our family isn't poor any more.
My family are perfectly normal.

The names of many organizations and sports teams are also collective nouns, but are normally used with plural verbs in spoken English.

The BBC is showing the programme on Saturday.
The BBC are planning to use the new satellite.
Liverpool is leading 1-0.
Liverpool are attacking again.

Unit 6 Uncount nouns

Main points

- Uncount nouns have only one form, and take a singular verb.
- They are not used with 'a', or with numbers.
- Some nouns can be both uncount nouns and count nouns.

1 English speakers think that some things cannot be counted directly. The nouns which refer to these uncountable things are called uncount nouns. Uncount nouns often refer to:

substances:	coal food ice iron rice steel water
human qualities:	courage cruelty honesty patience
feelings:	anger happiness joy pride relief respect
activities:	aid help sleep travel work
abstract ideas:	beauty death freedom fun life luck

The donkey needed food and water.
Soon, they lost patience and sent me to Durban.
I was greeted with shouts of joy.
All prices include travel to and from London.
We talked for hours about freedom.

See Unit 4 for information on count nouns.

2 Uncount nouns have only one form. They do not have a plural form.

I needed help with my homework.
The children had great fun playing with the puppets.

WARNING: Some nouns which are uncount nouns in English have plurals in other languages.

advice	homework	machinery
baggage	information	money
equipment	knowledge	news
furniture	luggage	traffic

We want to spend more money on roads.
Soldiers carried so much equipment that they were barely able to move.

3 Some uncount nouns end in '-s' and therefore look like plural count nouns. They usually refer to:

subjects of study:	mathematics physics
activities:	athletics gymnastics
games:	cards darts
illnesses:	measles mumps

Mathematics is too difficult for me.
Measles is in most cases a harmless illness.

4 When an uncount noun is the subject of a verb, it takes a singular verb.

Electricity is dangerous.
Intelligence develops very slowly in these children.
Food was very expensive in those days.

5 Uncount nouns are not used with 'a'.

They resent having to pay money to people like me.
My father started work when he was ten.

Uncount nouns are used with 'the' when they refer to something that is specified or known.

I am interested in the education of young children.
She buried the money that Hilary had given her.
I liked the music, but the words were boring.

6 Uncount nouns are not used with numbers. However, you can often refer to a quantity of something which is expressed by an uncount noun by using a word like 'some'. See Unit 11.

Please buy some bread when you go to town.
Let me give you some advice.

Some uncount nouns that refer to food or drink can be count nouns when they refer to quantities of the food or drink.

Do you like coffee? (uncount)
We asked for two coffees. (count)

Uncount nouns are often used with expressions such as 'a loaf of', 'packets of', or 'a piece of', to talk about a quantity or an item. 'A bit of' is common in spoken English.

I bought two loaves of bread yesterday.
He gave me a very good piece of advice.
They own a bit of land near Cambridge.

7 Some nouns are uncount nouns when they refer to something in general and count nouns when they refer to a particular instance of something.

Victory was now assured. (uncount)
In 1960, the party won a convincing victory. (count)

Unit 7 Personal pronouns

Main points

- You use personal pronouns to refer back to something or someone that has already been mentioned.
- You also use personal pronouns to refer to people and things directly.
- There are two sets of personal pronouns: subject pronouns and object pronouns.
- You can use 'you' and 'they' to refer to people in general.

1 When something or someone has already been mentioned, you refer to them again by using a pronoun.

John took the book and opened it.
He rang Mary and invited her to dinner.
'Have you been to London?' — 'Yes, it was very crowded.'
My father is fat — he weighs over fifteen stone.

In English, 'he' and 'she' normally refer to people, occasionally to animals, but very rarely to things.

2 You use a pronoun to refer directly to people or things that are present or are involved in the situation you are in.

Where shall we meet, Sally?
I do the washing; he does the cooking; we share the washing-up.
Send us a card so we'll know where you are.

3 There are two sets of personal pronouns, subject pronouns and object pronouns. You use subject pronouns as the subject of a verb.

I	you	he	she	it	we	they

Note that 'you' is used for the singular and plural form.

We are going there later.
I don't know what to do.

4 You use object pronouns as the direct or indirect object of a verb.

me	you	him	her	it	us	them

Note that 'you' is used for the singular and plural form.

The nurse washed me with cold water.
The ball hit her in the face.
John showed him the book.
Can you give me some more cake?

Note that, in modern English, you use object pronouns rather than subject pronouns after the verb 'be'.

'Who is it?' — 'It's me.'
There was only John, Baz, and me in the room.

You also use object pronouns as the object of a preposition.

We were all sitting in a cafe with him.
Did you give it to them?

5 You can use 'you' and 'they' to talk about people in general.

You have to drive on the other side of the road on the continent.
They say she's very clever.

6 You can use 'it' as an impersonal subject in general statements which refer to the time, the date, or the weather. See Unit 86.

'What time is it?' — 'It's half past three.'
It is January 19th.
It is rainy and cold.

You can also use 'it' as the subject or object in general statements about a situation.

It is too far to walk.
I like it here. Can we stay a bit longer?

7 A singular pronoun usually refers back to a singular noun group, and a plural pronoun to a plural noun group. However, you can use plural pronouns to refer back to:

- indefinite pronouns, even though they are always followed by a singular verb

If anybody comes, tell them I'm not in.

- collective nouns, even when you have used a singular verb

His family was waiting in the next room, but they had not yet been informed.

Unit 8 This, that, these, those, one, ones

Main points

- You use the demonstrative pronouns 'this', 'that', 'these', and 'those' when you are pointing to physical objects or identifying people.
- You use 'one' or 'ones' instead of a noun that has been mentioned or is known.

1 You use the demonstrative pronouns 'this', 'that', 'these', and 'those' when you are pointing to physical objects. 'This' and 'these' refer to things near you, 'that' and 'those' refer to things farther away.

This is a list of rules.
'I brought you these'. Adam held out a bag of grapes.
That looks interesting.
Those are mine.

You can also use 'this', 'that', 'these', and 'those' as determiners in front of nouns. See Unit 11.

This book was a present from my mother.
When did you buy that hat?

2 You use 'this', 'that', 'these', and 'those' when you are identifying or introducing people, or asking who they are.

Who's this?
These are my children, Susan and Paul.
Was that Patrick on the phone?

3 You use 'this', 'that', 'these', and 'those' to refer back to things that have already been mentioned.

That was an interesting word you used just now.
More money is being pumped into the education system, and we assume this will continue.
'Let's go to the cinema.' — 'That's a good idea'.
These are not easy questions to answer.

You also use 'this' and 'these' to refer forward to things you are going to mention.

This is what I want to say: it wasn't my idea.
These are the topics we will be looking at next week: how the accident happened, whether it could have been avoided, and who was to blame.

This is the important point: you must never see her again.

4 You use 'one' or 'ones' instead of a noun that has already been mentioned or is known in the situation, usually when you are adding information or contrasting two things of the same kind.

My car is the blue one.
Don't you have one with buttons instead of a zip?
Are the new curtains longer than the old ones?

You can use 'which one' or 'which ones' in questions.

Which one do you prefer?
Which ones were damaged?

You can say 'this one', 'that one', 'these ones', and 'those ones'.

I like this one better.
We'll have those ones, thank you.

You can use 'each one' or 'one each', but note that there is a difference in meaning. In the following examples, 'each one' means 'each brother' but 'one each' means 'one for each child'.

I've got three brothers and each one lives in a different country.
I bought the children one each.

5 In formal English, people sometimes use 'one' to refer to people in general.

One has to think of the practical side of things.
One never knows what to say in such situations.

6 There are several other types of pronoun, which are dealt with in other units.
See Unit 27 for information on possessive pronouns.
See Unit 51 for information on 'who', 'whom', 'whose', 'which', and 'what' as interrogative pronouns.
See Units 97 and 98 for information on 'that', 'which', 'who', 'whom', and 'whose' as relative pronouns.
Most determiners, except 'the', 'a', 'an', 'every', 'no', and the possessives, are also pronouns. See Units 15 to 18.

Unit 9 Reflexive pronouns

Main points

- Reflexive pronouns can be direct or indirect objects.
- Most transitive verbs can take a reflexive pronoun as object.
- Reflexive pronouns can be the object of a preposition.
- Reflexive pronouns can emphasize a noun or pronoun.

1 The reflexive pronouns are:

> **singular:** myself yourself himself herself itself
> **plural:** ourselves yourselves themselves

Note that, unlike 'you' and 'your', there are two forms for the second person: 'yourself' in the singular and 'yourselves' in the plural.

2 You use reflexive pronouns as the direct or indirect object of the verb when you want to say that the object is the same person or thing as the subject of the verb in the same clause.
For example, 'John taught himself' means that John did the teaching and was also the person who was taught, and 'Ann poured herself a drink' means that Ann did the pouring and was also the person that the drink was poured for.

She stretched herself out on the sofa.
The men formed themselves into a line.
He should give himself more time.

Note that although the subject 'you' is omitted in imperatives, you can still use 'yourself' or 'yourselves'.

Here's the money, go and buy yourself an ice cream.

3 Most transitive verbs can take a reflexive pronoun.

I blame myself for not paying attention.
He introduced himself to me.

> WARNING: Verbs which describe actions that people normally do to themselves do not take reflexive pronouns in English, although they do in some other languages.

I usually shave before breakfast.
She washed very quickly and rushed downstairs.

See Unit 74 for more information.

4 You use a reflexive pronoun as the object of a preposition when the object of the preposition refers to the same person or thing as the subject of the verb in the same clause.

I was thoroughly ashamed of myself.
They are making fools of themselves.
Tell me about yourself.

Note that you use personal pronouns, not reflexive pronouns, when referring to places and after 'with' meaning 'accompanied by'.

You should have your notes in front of you.
He would have to bring Judy with him.

5 You use reflexive pronouns after nouns or pronouns to emphasize the person or thing that you are referring to.

The town itself was so small that it didn't have a bank.
I myself have never read the book.

6 You use a reflexive pronoun at the end of a clause to emphasize that someone did something without any help from anyone else.

She had printed the card herself.
I'll take it down to the police station myself.
Did you make these yourself?

7 You use reflexive pronouns with 'by' to say:

- that someone does something without any help from other people

…when babies start eating their meals by themselves.
She was certain she could manage by herself.

- that someone is alone

He went off to sit by himself.
I was there for about six months by myself.

You can also use 'on my own', 'on your own', and so on, to say that someone is alone or does something without any help.

We were in the park on our own.
They managed to reach the village on their own.

You can use 'all' for emphasis.

Did you put those shelves up all by yourself?
We can't solve this problem all on our own.

> WARNING: 'One another' and 'each other' are not reflexive pronouns.

See Unit 75 for more information on 'one another' and 'each other'.

Unit 10 Indefinite pronouns

Main points

- Indefinite pronouns refer to people or things without saying exactly who or what they are.
- When an indefinite pronoun is the subject, it always takes a singular verb.
- You often use a plural pronoun to refer back to an indefinite pronoun.

1 The indefinite pronouns are:

anybody	everybody	nobody	somebody
anyone	everyone	no one	someone
anything	everything	nothing	something

Note that 'no one' is written as two words, or sometimes with a hyphen: 'no-one'.

2 You use indefinite pronouns when you want to refer to people or things without saying exactly who or what they are. The pronouns ending in '-body' and '-one' refer to people, and those ending in '-thing' refer to things.

I was there for over an hour before _anybody_ came.
It had to be _someone_ with a car.
Jane said _nothing_ for a moment.

3 When an indefinite pronoun is the subject, it always takes a singular verb, even when it refers to more than one person or thing.

Everyone knows that.
Everything was fine.
Is anybody there?

When you refer back to indefinite pronouns, you use plural pronouns or possessives, and a plural verb.

Ask _anyone_. They 'll tell you.
Has _everyone_ eaten as much as _they_ want?
You can't tell _somebody_ why _they_'ve failed.
WARNING: Some speakers prefer to use singular pronouns. They prefer to say 'You can't tell somebody why he or she has failed'.

4 You can add apostrophe s ('s) to indefinite pronouns that refer to people.
She was given a room in _someone's_ studio.
That was _nobody's_ business but mine.

WARNING: You do not usually add apostrophe s ('s) to indefinite pronouns that refer to things. You do not say 'something's value', you say 'the value of something'.

5 You use indefinite pronouns beginning with 'some-' in:

- affirmative clauses

Somebody shouted.
I want to introduce you to _someone_.

- questions expecting the answer 'yes'

Would you like _something_ to drink?
Can you get _someone_ to do it?

6 You use indefinite pronouns beginning with 'any-':

- as the subject or object in statements

dichiarazioni
IF ANYBODY COMES, TELL THEM I'M NOT IN.
Anyone knows that you need a licence.
You still haven't told me _anything_.
I haven't given _anyone_ their presents yet.

You do not use them as the subject of a negative statement. You do not say 'Anybody can't come in'.

- in both affirmative and negative questions

Does _anybody_ agree with me?
Won't _anyone_ help me?

7 If you use an indefinite pronoun beginning with 'no-', you must not use another negative word in the same clause. You do not say 'There wasn't nothing'.

There was _nothing_ you could do.
Nobody left, nobody went away.

8 You use the indefinite adverbs 'anywhere', 'everywhere', 'nowhere', and 'somewhere' to talk about places in a general way. 'Nowhere' makes a clause negative.

I thought I'd seen you _somewhere_.
No-one can find Howard or Barbara _anywhere_.
There was _nowhere_ to hide.
marsouelle

9 You can use 'else' after indefinite pronouns and adverbs to refer to people, things, or places other than those that have been mentioned.

Everyone else is downstairs.
I don't like it here. Let's go _somewhere else_.

Unit 11 Determiners

Main points

- Determiners are used at the beginning of noun groups.
- You use specific determiners when people know exactly which things or people you are talking about.
- You use general determiners to talk about people or things without saying exactly who or what they are.

1 When you use a determiner, you put it at the beginning of a noun group, in front of numbers or adjectives.

I met the two Swedish girls in London.
Our main bedroom is through that door.
Have you got another red card?
Several young boys were waiting outside.

2 When the people or things that you are talking about have already been mentioned, or the people you are talking to know exactly which ones you mean, you use a specific determiner.

The man began to run towards the boy.
Young people don't like these operas.
Her face was very red.

The specific determiners are:

the definite article: the
demonstratives: this that these those
possessives: my your his her its our their

Note that 'your' is used both for the singular and plural possessive.
See Unit 8 for 'this', 'that', 'these', and 'those' as pronouns.

3 When you are mentioning people or things for the first time, or talking about them generally without saying exactly which ones you mean, you use a general determiner.

There was a man in the lift.
We went to an art exhibition.
You can stop at any time you like.
There were several reasons for this.

The general determiners are:

a	both	few	more	other
all	each	fewer	most	several
an	either	less	much	some
another	enough	little	neither	
any	every	many	no	

4 Each general determiner is used with particular types of noun. You use some general determiners with:

- singular count nouns

a	another	each	every	no
an	any		either	neither

I got a postcard from Susan.
Any big tin container will do.
He opened another shop last month.

- plural count nouns

all	enough	many	no	some
any	few	more	other	
both	fewer	most	several	

There were few doctors available.
He spoke many different languages.
Several projects had to be postponed.

- uncount nouns

all	enough	little	most	no
any	less	more	much	some

There was little applause.
We need more information
He did not speak much English.

WARNING: The following general determiners can never be used with uncount nouns.

a	both	every	neither
an	each	few	several
another	either	many	

5 Most of the determiners are also pronouns, except 'the', 'a', 'an', 'every', 'no' and the possessives.

I saw several in the woods last night.
Have you got any that I could borrow?
There is enough for all of us.

You use 'one' as a pronoun instead of 'a' or 'an', 'none' instead of 'no', and 'each' instead of 'every'.

Have you got one?
There are none left.
Each has a separate box and number.

Unit 12 Main uses of 'the'

Main points

- You can use 'the' in front of any noun.
- You use 'the' when the person you are talking to knows which person or thing you mean.
- You use 'the' when you are referring back to someone or something.
- You use 'the' when you are specifying which person or thing you are talking about.
- You use 'the' when you are referring to something that is unique.
- You use 'the' when you want to use one thing as an example to say something about all things of the same type.

1 'The' is called the definite article, and is the commonest determiner. You use 'the' when the person you are talking to knows which person or thing you mean. You can use 'the' in front of any noun, whether it is a singular count noun, an uncount noun, or a plural count noun.

She dropped the can.
I remembered the fun I had with them.
The girls were not at home.

2 You use 'the' with a noun when you are referring back to someone or something that has already been mentioned.

I called for a waiter... ...The waiter with a moustache came.
I have bought a house in Wales... ...The house is in an agricultural area.

3 You use 'the' with a noun and a qualifier, such as a prepositional phrase or a relative clause, when you are specifying which person or thing you are talking about.

I've no idea about the geography of Scotland.
The book that I recommended now costs over three pounds.

4 You use 'the' with a noun when you are referring to something of which there is only one in the world.

They all sat in the sun.
We have landed men on the moon.
The sky was a brilliant blue.

You also use 'the' when you are referring to something of which there is only one in a particular place.

Mrs Robertson heard that the church had been bombed.
He decided to put some words on the blackboard.

5 You can use 'the' with a singular count noun when you want to make a general statement about all things of that type. For example, if you say 'The whale is the largest mammal in the world', you mean all whales, not one particular whale.

The computer allows us to deal with a lot of data very quickly.
My father's favourite flower is the rose.

6 You can use 'the' with a singular count noun when you are referring to a system or service. For example, you can use 'the phone' to refer to a telephone system and 'the bus' to refer to a bus service.

I don't like using the phone.
How long does it take on the train?

7 You can use 'the' with the name of a musical instrument when you are talking about someone's ability to play the instrument.

'You play the guitar, I see,' said Simon.
Geoff plays the piano very well.

Unit 13 Other uses of 'the'

Main points

- You do not normally use 'the' with proper nouns referring to people. You do use 'the' with many proper nouns referring to geographical places.
- You use 'the' with some adjectives to talk about groups of people.

1 You do not normally use 'the' with proper nouns that are people's names. However, if you are talking about a family, you can say 'the Browns'.
You use 'the' with some titles, such as 'the Queen of England', and with the names of some organizations, buildings, newspapers, and works of art.

... *the United Nations*... ... *the Taj Mahal*...
... *the Times*... ... *the Mona Lisa*.

2 You do use 'the' with some proper nouns referring to geographical places.

... *the Bay of Biscay*... ... *the Suez Canal*.
... *the Arabian Gulf*... ... *the Pacific Ocean*.

You use 'the' with countries whose names include words such as 'kingdom', 'republic', 'states', or 'union'.

... *the United Kingdom*... ... *the Soviet Union*.

You use 'the' with countries that have plural nouns as their names.

... *the Netherlands*... ... *the Philippines*.

Note that you do not use 'the' with countries that have singular nouns as their names, such as 'China', 'Italy', or 'Turkey'.
You use 'the' with names of mountain ranges and groups of islands.

... *the Alps*... ... *the Himalayas*.
... *the Bahamas*... ... *the Canaries*.

Note that you do not use 'the' with the names of individual mountains such as 'Everest' or 'Etna', or the names of individual islands such as 'Sicily', 'Minorca', or 'Bali'.
You use 'the' with regions of the world, or regions of a country that include 'north', 'south', 'east', or 'west'.

... *the Middle East*... ... *the Far East*.
... *the north of England*... ... *the west of Ireland*.

Note that there are some exceptions.

... *North America*... ... *South-East Asia*... ... *East Anglia*.

You do not use 'the' with 'northern', 'southern', 'eastern', or 'western' and a singular name.

... *northern England*... ... *western Africa*.

You use 'the' with the names of areas of water such as seas, oceans, rivers, canals, gulfs, and straits.

... *the Mediterranean Sea*... ... *the Atlantic Ocean*.
... *the river Ganges*... ... *the Panama Canal*.
... *the Gulf of Mexico*... ... *the straits of Gibraltar*.

Note that you do not use 'the' with lakes.

... *Lake Geneva*... ... *Lake Superior*.

Note that you do not use 'the' with continents, cities, streets, or addresses.

... *Asia*... ... *Tokyo*... ... *Oxford Street*... ... *15 Park Street*.

3 You use 'the' with adjectives such as 'rich', 'poor', 'young', 'old', and 'unemployed' to talk about a general group of people. You do not need a noun.

Only the rich could afford his firm's products.
They were discussing the problem of the unemployed.

When you use 'the' with an adjective as the subject of a verb, you use a plural verb.

In the cities the poor are as badly off as they were in the villages.

4 You use 'the' with some nationality adjectives to talk about the people who live in a country.

They will be increasingly dependent on the support of the French.
The Spanish claimed that the money had not been paid.

With other nationalities, you use a plural noun.

... *Germans*... ... *the Americans*.

When you use 'the' with a nationality adjective as the subject of a verb, you use a plural verb.

The British are worried.

5 You use 'the' with superlatives.

He was the cleverest man I ever knew.
He was the youngest.
His shoulders hurt the worst.
It was the most exciting summer of their lives.

Unit 14 'A' and 'an'

Main points

- You only use 'a' or 'an' with singular count nouns.
- You use 'a' or 'an' to talk about a person or thing for the first time.

1 You only use 'a' or 'an' with singular count nouns. 'A' and 'an' are called the indefinite article.

I got a postcard from Susan.
He was eating an apple.

Remember that you use 'a' in front of a word that begins with a consonant sound even if the first letter is a vowel, for example 'a piece, a university, a European language'. You use 'an' in front of a word that begins with a vowel sound even if the first letter is a consonant, for example 'an exercise, an idea, an honest man'.

2 You use 'a' or 'an' when you are talking about a person or thing for the first time.

She picked up a book.
After weeks of looking, we eventually bought a house.
A colleague and I got some money to do research on rats.

Note that the second time you refer to the same person or thing, you use 'the'.

She picked up a book... ... The book was lying on the table.
After weeks of looking, we eventually bought a house... ... The house was in a small village.

3 After the verb 'be' or another link verb, you can use 'a' or 'an' with an adjective and a noun to give more information about someone or something.

His brother was a sensitive child.
He seemed a worried man.
It was a really beautiful house.

You can also use 'a' or 'an' with a noun followed by a qualifier. such as a prepositional phrase or a relative clause. when you want to give more information about someone or something.

The information was contained in an article on biology.
I chose a picture that reminded me of my own country.

4 You use 'a' or 'an' after the verb 'be' or another link verb when you are saying what someone is or what job they have

He became a school teacher.
She is a model and an artist.

5 You use 'a' or 'an' to mean 'one' with some numbers. You can use 'a' or 'an' with nouns that refer to whole numbers, fractions, money, weights, or measures.

a hundred	a quarter	a pound	a kilo
a thousand	a half	a dollar	a litre

6 You do not use 'a' or 'an' with uncount nouns or plural count nouns. You do not need to use a determiner at all with plural count nouns, but you can use the determiners 'any', 'a few', 'many', 'several', or 'some'.

I love dogs.
Do you have any dogs?
Many adults don't listen to children.
I have some children like that in my class.

Note that if you do not use a determiner with a plural count noun, you are often making a general statement about people or things of that type. For example. if you say 'I love dogs', you mean all dogs. However, if you say 'There are eggs in the kitchen', you mean there are some eggs. If you do use a determiner, you mean a number of people or things but not all of them, without saying exactly how many.

I have some friends coming for dinner.
He has bought some plants for the house.
I have some important things to tell them.

Unit 15 All, most, no, none

Main points

- You use 'all' with plural count nouns and uncount nouns. You use 'all' to talk about every person or thing in the world, or in the group you are talking about.
- You use 'most' with plural count nouns and uncount nouns. You use 'most' to talk about nearly all of a number of people or things, or nearly all of a quantity of something.
- You use 'no' with singular and plural count nouns and uncount nouns. You use 'no' to say that something does not exist or is not present.

1 You use 'all' with plural count nouns and uncount nouns to talk about every person or thing in the world or in the group that you are talking about.

All children should complete the primary course.
All important decisions were taken by the government.
He soon lost all hope of becoming a rock star.
All luggage will be searched.

2 You use 'most' with plural count nouns and uncount nouns to talk about nearly all of a number of people or things, or nearly all of a quantity of something.

The method was suitable for most purposes.
Most good drivers stop at zebra crossings.
Most milk is still delivered to people's houses.
He ignored most advice, and did what he thought best.

3 You use 'no' with singular count nouns, plural count nouns, and uncount nouns to say that something does not exist or is not present.

There was no chair for me to sit on.
They had no immediate plans to change house.
No money was available for the operation.

Note that if there is another word in the clause that makes it negative, you use 'any', not 'no'.

It hasn't made any difference.
He will never do any work for me again.

4 'All' and 'most' are also pronouns, so you can say 'all of' and 'most of'. 'No' is not a pronoun, so you must say 'none of'.

He spent all of the money on a new car.
Most of my friends live in London.
None of those farmers had ever driven a tractor.

Note that you use 'all of', 'most of', and 'none of' with an object pronoun.

All of us were sleeping.
I had seen most of them before.
None of them came to the party.

Note that if the clause is already negative, you use 'any of', not 'none of'.

I hadn't eaten any of the biscuits.

When 'none of' is followed by a plural noun or pronoun, the verb is usually plural, but can be singular.

None of us are the same.
None of them has lasted very long.

5 You can use 'all the' with a plural count noun or an uncount noun. There is no difference in meaning between 'all the' and 'all of the'.

All the girls think it's great.
All the best jokes came at the end of the programme.
Thank you for all the help you gave me.

WARNING: You cannot say 'most the' or 'none the'. You must say 'most of the' or 'none of the'.

6 You can use 'all' after a noun or pronoun to emphasize that the noun or pronoun refers to everyone or everything that has been mentioned or is involved. Note that you can use 'all' to emphasize the subject or the object.

The band all live together in the same house.
I enjoyed it all.

Unit 16 Both, either, neither

Main points

- You use 'both', 'either', and 'neither' to talk about two people or things that have been mentioned or are known to the hearer.
- You use 'both' with plural nouns, and 'either' and 'neither' with singular nouns.
- You use 'both of', 'either of', and 'neither of' with plural nouns or pronouns.

1 You use 'both', 'either', and 'neither' when you are saying something about two people or things that have been mentioned, or are known to the person you are talking to.

There were excellent performances from both actresses.
Denis held his cocoa in both hands.
No argument could move either man from this decision.
Neither report mentioned the Americans.

2 You use 'both' when you think of the two people or things as a group. You use 'both' with a plural noun.

Both children were happy with their presents.
Both policies make good sense.

3 You use 'either' when you think of the two people or things as individuals. You use 'either' with a singular noun.

Either way is acceptable.
She could not see either man.

4 You use 'neither' when you are thinking of the two people or things as individuals and you are making a negative statement about them. You use 'neither' with a singular noun.

In reality, neither party was enthusiastic.
Neither man knew what he was doing.

5 You can use 'both' with a specific determiner such as 'the', 'these', or 'my'.

Both the young men agreed to come.
Both these books have been recommended to us.
Both her parents were dead.

WARNING: You cannot use 'either' or 'neither' with a specific determiner.

6 You can use 'both of', 'either of', or 'neither of' with a plural noun or pronoun. Note that when 'both of', 'either of', and 'neither of' are followed by a noun rather than a pronoun, you must use a specific determiner such as 'the', 'these', or 'her' before the noun.

Both of these restaurants are excellent.
Either of them could have done the job.
Neither of our boys was involved.

Note that 'neither of' is normally used with a singular verb but it can be used with a plural verb.

Neither of us was having any luck.
Neither of the children were there.

7 Remember that you can also use 'both', 'either', and 'neither' as conjunctions. You use 'both...and' to give two alternatives and say that each of them is possible or true.

I am looking for opportunities both in this country and abroad.
Both I and my wife were surprised to see you there.

You use 'either...or' to give two alternatives and say that only one of them is possible or true.

You can have either fruit or ice cream.
I was expecting you either today or tomorrow.
You either love him or hate him.

You also use 'neither...nor' to give two alternatives and say that each of them is not possible or is not true.

Neither Margaret nor John was there.
He did it neither quickly nor well.

Unit 17 Much, little, many, few, more, less, fewer

Main points

- You use 'much' and 'little' with uncount nouns to talk about a quantity of something.
- You use 'many' and 'few' with plural nouns to talk about a number of people or things.
- You use 'much' in negative sentences and questions, and 'a lot of' or 'plenty of' rather than 'much' in affirmative sentences.
- You use 'more' and 'less' with uncount nouns, and 'more' and 'fewer' with plural count nouns.

1 You use 'much' to talk about a large quantity of something, and 'little' to talk about a small quantity of something. You only use 'much' and 'little' with uncount nouns.

I haven't got much time.
We've made little progress.

2 You use 'many' to talk about a large number of people or things, and 'few' to talk about a small number of people or things. You can only use 'many' and 'few' with plural count nouns.

He wrote many novels.
There were few visitors to our house.

3 You normally use 'much' in negative sentences and questions.

He did not speak much English.
Why haven't I given much attention to this problem?

In affirmative sentences you do not use 'much', you use 'a lot of', 'lots of', or 'plenty of' instead. You can use them with both uncount nouns and plural nouns.

He demanded a lot of attention.
I make a lot of mistakes.
They spent lots of time on the project.
He remembered a large room with lots of windows.
I've got plenty of money.
There are always plenty of jobs to be done.

Note that you can use 'so much' and 'too much' in affirmative sentences.

She spends so much time here.
There is too much chance of error.

4 You use 'so much' to emphasize that a large quantity of something is involved.

I have so much work to do.
They have so much money and we have so little.

You use 'too much' and 'too many' to say that the quantity of something, or the number of people or things, is larger than is reasonable or necessary.

He has too much work.
Too many people still smoke.

You use 'very many' to emphasize that a large number of people or things are involved.

Very many old people live alone.

Note that 'very much' is used with nouns and verbs.

There isn't very much time.
I liked it very much.

5 You use 'few' and 'little' to emphasize that only a small quantity of something or a small number of people or things are involved. They can be used with 'very' for greater emphasis.

The town has few monuments.
I have little time for anything but work.
Very few cars had reversing lights.
I had very little money left.

Note that 'a few' and 'a little' just indicate that a quantity or number is small.

He spread a little honey on a slice of bread.
I usually do a few jobs for him in the house.

6 You use 'more' with uncount nouns and plural count nouns to refer to a quantity of something or a number of people or things that is greater than another quantity or number.

His visit might do more harm than good.
He does more hours than I do.

You use 'less' with uncount nouns to refer to an amount of something that is smaller than another amount.

The poor have less access to education.
This machinery uses less energy.

You use 'fewer', or 'less' in informal English, with plural nouns to refer to a number of people or things that is smaller than another number.

There are fewer trees here.
They have sold less computers this year.

Unit 18 Some, any, another, other, each, every

Main points

- You use 'some' to talk about a quantity or number without being precise.
- You use 'any' to talk about a quantity or number that may or may not exist.
- You use 'another', or 'another' and a number, to talk about additional people or things.
- You use 'each' and 'every' to talk about all the members of a group of people or things.

1 You use 'some' with uncount nouns and plural nouns to talk about a quantity of something or a number of people or things without being precise.

I have left some food for you in the fridge.
Some trains are running late.

You normally use 'some' in affirmative sentences.

There's some chocolate cake over there.
I had some good ideas.

You use 'some' in questions when you expect the answer to be 'yes', for example in offers or requests.

Would you like some coffee?
Could you give me some examples?

You can use 'some' with a singular noun when you do not know which person or thing is involved, or you think it does not matter.

Some man phoned, but didn't leave his number.
Is there some problem?

2 You use 'any' in front of plural and uncount nouns to talk about a quantity of something that may or may not exist. You normally use 'any' in questions and negative sentences.

Are there any jobs men can do but women can't?
It hasn't made any difference.

You use 'any' with a singular noun to emphasize that it does not matter which person or thing is involved.

Any container will do.

You can use 'no' with an affirmative verb instead of 'not any'.

There weren't any tomatoes left.
There were no tomatoes left.

You can also use 'not' and 'any', or 'no', with a comparative.

Her house wasn't any better than ours.
Her house was no better than ours.

3 You use 'another' with singular nouns to talk about an additional person or thing.

Could I have another cup of coffee?
He opened another shop last month.

You can also use 'another' with a number and a plural noun to talk about more people or things.

Another four years passed before we met again.
I've got another three books to read.

You use 'other' with plural nouns and 'the other' with singular or plural nouns.

I've got other things to think about.
The other man has gone.
The other European countries have beaten us.

4 You use 'each' or 'every' with a singular noun to talk about all the members of a group of people or things. You use 'each' when you are thinking about the members as individuals, and 'every' when you are making a general statement about all of them.

Each county is subdivided into several districts.
Each applicant has five choices.
Every child would have milk every day.
She spoke to every person at that party.

You can modify 'every' but not 'each'.

He spoke to them nearly every day.
We went out almost every evening.

5 You can use 'some of', 'any of', or 'each of', and a noun group to talk about a number of people or things in a group of people or things.

Some of the information has already been analysed.
It was more expensive than any of the other magazines.
He gave each of us advice about our present goals.

You can use 'each of' and a plural noun group but 'every' must be followed by 'one of'.

Each of the drawings is different.
Every one of them is given a financial target.

Note that you can also use 'each' with 'one of'.

This view of poverty influences each one of us.

Unit 19 Position of adjectives

Main points

- There are two main positions for adjectives: in front of a noun, or as the complement of a link verb.
- Most adjectives can be used in either of these positions, but some adjectives can only be used in one.

1 Most adjectives can be used in a noun group, after determiners and numbers if there are any, in front of the noun.

He had a beautiful smile.
She bought a loaf of white bread.
There was no clear evidence.

2 Most adjectives can also be used after a link verb such as 'be', 'become', or 'feel'.

I'm cold.
I felt angry.
Nobody seemed amused.

3 Some adjectives are normally used only after a link verb.

afraid	asleep	due	ready	unable
alive	aware	glad	sorry	well
alone	content	ill	sure	

For example, you can say 'She was glad', but you do not talk about 'a glad woman'.

I wanted to be alone.
We were getting ready for bed.
I'm not quite sure.
He didn't know whether to feel glad or sorry.

4 Some adjectives are normally used only in front of a noun.

eastern	~	existing	neighbouring
northern	atomic	indoor	occasional
southern	countless	introductory	outdoor
western	digital	maximum	

For example, you talk about 'an atomic bomb', but you do not say 'The bomb was atomic'.

He sent countless letters to the newspapers.
This book includes a good introductory chapter on forests.

5 When you use an adjective to emphasize a strong feeling or opinion, it always comes in front of a noun.

absolute	outright	pure	true
complete	perfect	real	utter
entire	positive	total	

Some of it was absolute rubbish.
He made me feel like a complete idiot.

6 Some adjectives that describe size or age can come after a noun group consisting of a number or determiner and a noun that indicates the unit of measurement.

deep	long	tall	wide
high	old	thick	

He was about six feet tall.
The water was several metres deep.
The baby is nine months old.

Note that you do not say 'two pounds heavy', you say 'two pounds in weight'.

7 A few adjectives are used alone after a noun.

designate	elect	galore	incarnate

She was now the president elect.
There are empty houses galore.

8 A few adjectives have a different meaning depending on whether they come in front of or after a noun.

concerned	involved	present	proper	responsible

For example, 'the concerned mother' means a mother who is worried, but 'the mother concerned' means the mother who has been mentioned.

It's one of those incredibly involved stories.
The people involved are all doctors.

I'm worried about the present situation.
Of the 18 people present, I knew only one.

Her parents were trying to act in a responsible manner.
We do not know the person responsible for his death.

Unit 20 Order of adjectives

Main points

- You put opinion adjectives in front of descriptive adjectives.
- You put general opinion adjectives in front of specific opinion adjectives.
- You can sometimes vary the order of adjectives.
- If you use two or more descriptive adjectives, you put them in a particular order.
- If you use a noun in front of another noun, you put any adjectives in front of the first noun.

1 You often want to add more information to a noun than you can with one adjective, so you need to use two or more adjectives. In theory, you can use the adjectives in any order, depending on the quality you want to emphasize. In practice, however, there is a normal order.
When you use two or more adjectives in front of a noun, you usually put an adjective that expresses your opinion in front of an adjective that just describes something.

You live in a nice big house.
He is a naughty little boy.
She was wearing a beautiful pink suit.

2 When you use more than one adjective to express your opinion, an adjective with a more general meaning such as 'good', 'bad', 'nice', or 'lovely' usually comes before an adjective with a more specific meaning such as 'comfortable', 'clean', or 'dirty'.

I sat in a lovely comfortable armchair in the corner.
He put on a nice clean shirt.
It was a horrible dirty room.

3 You can use adjectives to describe various qualities of people or things. For example, you might want to indicate their size, their shape, or the country they come from.
Descriptive adjectives belong to six main types, but you are unlikely ever to use all six types in the same noun group. If you did, you would normally put them in the following order:

size	shape	age	colour	nationality	material

This means that if you want to use an 'age' adjective and a 'nationality' adjective, you put the 'age' adjective first.

We met some young Chinese girls.

Similarly, a 'shape' adjective normally comes before a 'colour' adjective.

He had round black eyes.

Other combinations of adjectives follow the same order. Note that 'material' means any substance, not only cloth.

There was a large round wooden table in the room.
The man was carrying a small black plastic bag.

4 You usually put comparative and superlative adjectives in front of other adjectives.

Some of the better English actors have gone to live in Hollywood.
These are the highest monthly figures on record.

5 When you use a noun in front of another noun, you never put adjectives between them. You put any adjectives in front of the first noun.

He works in the French film industry.
He receives a large weekly cash payment.

6 When you use two adjectives as the complement of a link verb, you use a conjunction such as 'and' to link them. With three or more adjectives, you link the last two with a conjunction, and put commas after the others.

The day was hot and dusty.
The room was large but square.
The house was old, damp and smelly.
We felt hot, tired and thirsty.

Unit 21 Adjectives with prepositions

Main points

- Some adjectives used after link verbs can be used alone or followed by a prepositional phrase.
- Some adjectives must be followed by particular prepositions.
- Some adjectives can be followed by different prepositions to introduce different types of information.

1 When you use an adjective after a link verb, you can often use the adjective on its own or followed by a prepositional phrase. See Unit 22 for other patterns.

He was afraid.
He was afraid of his enemies.

2 Some adjectives cannot be used alone after a link verb. If they are followed by a prepositional phrase, it must have a particular preposition:

aware of	unaware of	fond of
accustomed to	unaccustomed to	used to

I've always been terribly fond of you.
He is unaccustomed to the heat.

3 Some adjectives can be used alone, or followed by a particular preposition:
- used alone, or with 'of' to specify the cause of a feeling

afraid	critical	jealous	suspicious
ashamed	envious	proud	terrified
convinced	frightened	scared	tired

They may feel jealous of your success.
I was terrified of her.

- used alone, or with 'of' to specify the person who has a quality

brave	good	polite	thoughtful
careless	intelligent	sensible	unkind
clever	kind	silly	unreasonable
generous	nice	stupid	wrong

That was clever of you!
I turned the job down, which was stupid of me.

- used alone or with 'to', usually referring to:

similarity: close equal identical related similar
marriage: married engaged
loyalty: dedicated devoted loyal
rank: junior senior

My problems are very similar to yours.
He was dedicated to his job.

- used alone, or followed by 'with' to specify the cause of a feeling

bored	displeased	impatient	pleased
content	dissatisfied	impressed	satisfied

I could never be bored with football.
He was pleased with her.

- used alone or with 'at', usually referring to:

strong reactions: amazed astonished shocked surprised
ability: bad excellent good hopeless useless

He was shocked at the hatred they had shown.
She had always been good at languages.

- used alone, or with 'for' to specify the person or thing that quality relates to

common	essential	possible	unusual
difficult	important	unnecessary	usual
easy	necessary		

It's difficult for young people on their own.
It was unusual for them to go away at the weekend.

4 Some adjectives can be used alone, or used with different prepositions.
- used alone, with an impersonal subject and 'of' and the subject of the action, or with a personal subject and 'to' and the object of the action

cruel	good	nasty	rude
friendly	kind	nice	unfriendly
generous	mean	polite	unkind

It was rude of him to leave so suddenly.
She was rude to him for no reason.

- used alone, with 'about' to specify a thing or 'with' to specify a person

angry	delighted	fed up	happy
annoyed	disappointed	furious	upset

She was still angry about the result.
They're getting pretty fed up with him.

Unit 22 Adjectives with 'to'-infinitive or 'that'-clauses

Main points

- Adjectives used after link verbs are often followed by 'to'-infinitive clauses or 'that'-clauses.
- Some adjectives are always followed by 'to'-infinitive clauses.
- You often use 'to'-infinitive clauses or 'that'-clauses after adjectives to express feelings or opinions.
- You often use 'to'-infinitive clauses after adjectives when the subject is impersonal 'it'.

1 After link verbs, you often use adjectives that describe how someone feels about an action or situation. With some adjectives, you can add a 'to'-infinitive clause or a 'that'-clause to say what the action or situation is.

afraid	disappointed	happy	sad
anxious	frightened	pleased	surprised
ashamed	glad	proud	unhappy

If the subject is the same in both clauses, you usually use a 'to'-infinitive clause. If the subject is different, you must use a 'that'-clause.

I was happy to see them again.
He was happy that they were coming to the party.

You often use a 'to'-infinitive clause when talking about future time in relation to the main clause.

I am afraid to go home.
He was anxious to leave before it got dark.

You often use a 'that'-clause when talking about present or past time in relation to the main clause.

He was anxious that the passport was missing.
They were afraid that I might have talked to the police.

2 You often use 'sorry' with a 'that'-clause. Note that 'that' is often omitted.

I'm very sorry that I can't join you.
I'm sorry I'm so late.

3 Some adjectives are not usually used alone, but have a 'to'-infinitive clause after them to say what action or situation the adjective relates to.

able	due	likely	unlikely
apt	inclined	prepared	unwilling
bound	liable	ready	willing

They were unable to help her.
They were not likely to forget it.
I am willing to try.
I'm prepared to say I was wrong.

4 When you want to express an opinion about someone or something, you often use an adjective followed by a 'to'-infinitive clause.

difficult	easy	impossible	possible	right	wrong

She had been easy to deceive.
The windows will be almost impossible to open.
Am I wrong to stay here?

Note that in the first two examples, the subject of the main clause is the object of the 'to'-infinitive clause. In the third example, the subject is the same in both clauses.

5 With some adjectives, you use a 'that'-clause to express an opinion about someone or something.

awful	extraordinary	important	sad
bad	funny	interesting	true
essential	good	obvious	

I was sad that people had reacted in this way.
It is extraordinary that we should ever have met!

6 You can also use adjectives with 'to'-infinitive clauses after 'it' as the impersonal subject. You use the preposition 'of' or 'for' to indicate the person or thing that the adjective relates to.

It was easy to find the path.
It was good of John to help me.
It was difficult for her to find a job.

See Unit 86 for 'it' as impersonal subject.
See Unit 21 for more information about adjectives followed by 'of' or 'for'.

Unit 23 Adjectives ending in '-ing' or '-ed'

Main points

- Many adjectives ending in '-ing' describe the effect that something has on someone's feelings.
- Some adjectives ending in '-ing' describe a process or state that continues over a period of time.
- Many adjectives ending in '-ed' describe people's feelings.

1 You use many '-ing' adjectives to describe the effect that something has on your feelings, or on the feelings of people in general. For example, if you talk about 'a surprising number', you mean that the number surprises you.

alarming	charming	embarrassing	surprising
amazing	confusing	exciting	terrifying
annoying	convincing	frightening	tiring
astonishing	depressing	interesting	welcoming
boring	disappointing	shocking	worrying

He lives in a charming house just outside the town.
She always has a warm welcoming smile.

Most '-ing' adjectives have a related transitive verb. See Unit 72 for information on transitive verbs.

2 You use some '-ing' adjectives to describe something that continues over a period of time.

ageing	decreasing	existing	living
booming	dying	increasing	remaining

Britain is an ageing society.
Increasing prices are making food very expensive.

These adjectives have related intransitive verbs. See Unit 72 for information on intransitive verbs.

3 Many '-ed' adjectives describe people's feelings. They have the same form as the past participle of a transitive verb and have a passive meaning. For example, 'a frightened person' is a person who has been frightened by something.

alarmed	delighted	frightened	surprised
amused	depressed	interested	tired
astonished	disappointed	satisfied	troubled
bored	excited	shocked	worried

She looks alarmed about something.
A bored student complained to his teacher.
She had big blue frightened eyes.

Note that the past participles of irregular verbs do not end in '-ed', but can be used as adjectives. See the Appendix for a list of irregular past participles.

The bird had a broken wing.
His coat was dirty and torn.

4 Like other adjectives, '-ing' and '-ed' adjectives can be:
- used in front of a noun

They still show amazing loyalty to their parents.
This is the most terrifying tale ever written.
I was thanked by the satisfied customer.
The worried authorities cancelled the match.

- used after link verbs

It's amazing what they can do.
The present situation is terrifying.
He felt satisfied with all the work he had done.
My husband was worried.

- modified by adverbials such as 'quite', 'really', and 'very'

The film was quite boring.
There is nothing very surprising in this.
She was quite astonished at his behaviour.
He was a very disappointed young man.

- used in the comparative and superlative

His argument was more convincing than mine.
He became even more depressed after she died.
This is one of the most boring books I've ever read.
She was the most interested in going to the cinema.

5 A small number of '-ed' adjectives are normally only used after link verbs such as 'be', 'become', or 'feel'. They are related to transitive verbs, and are often followed by a prepositional phrase, a 'to'-infinitive clause, or a 'that'-clause.

convinced	interested	prepared	tired
delighted	involved	scared	touched
finished	pleased	thrilled	

The Brazilians are pleased with the results.
He was always prepared to account for his actions.
She was scared that they would find her.

Unit 24 Comparatives and superlatives: forms

Main points

- You add '-er' for the comparative and '-est' for the superlative of one-syllable adjectives and adverbs.
- You use '-er' and '-est' with some two-syllable adjectives.
- You use 'more' for the comparative and 'most' for the superlative of most two-syllable adjectives, all longer adjectives, and adverbs ending in '-ly'.
- Some common adjectives and adverbs have irregular forms.

1 You add '-er' for the comparative form and '-est' for the superlative form of one-syllable adjectives and adverbs. If they end in '-e', you add '-r' and '-st'.

| cheap ⇨ cheaper ⇨ cheapest |
| safe ⇨ safer ⇨ safest |

cold	light	rough	young	large
fast	poor	small	~	nice
hard	quick	weak	close	wide

They worked _harder_.
I've found a _nicer_ hotel.

If they end in a single vowel and consonant (except '-w'), you double the consonant.

| big ⇨ bigger ⇨ biggest |

| fat | hot | sad | thin | wet |

The day grew _hotter_.
Henry was the _biggest_ of them.

2 With two-syllable adjectives ending in a consonant followed by '-y', you change the '-y' to '-i' and add '-er' and '-est'.

| happy ⇨ happier ⇨ happiest |

| angry | dirty | friendly | heavy | silly |
| busy | easy | funny | lucky | tiny |

It couldn't be _easier_.
That is the _funniest_ bit of the film.

3 You use 'more' for the comparative and 'most' for the superlative of most two-syllable adjectives, all longer adjectives, and adverbs ending in '-ly'.

careful	⇨ more careful	⇨ most careful
beautiful	⇨ more beautiful	⇨ most beautiful
seriously	⇨ more seriously	⇨ most seriously

Be _more careful_ next time.
They are the _most beautiful_ gardens in the world.
It affected Clive _most seriously._

Note that for 'early' as an adjective or adverb, you use 'earlier' and 'earliest', not 'more' and 'most'.

4 With some common two-syllable adjectives and adverbs, you can either add '-er' and '-est', or use 'more' and 'most'.

| common | gentle | likely | pleasant | simple |
| cruel | handsome | narrow | polite | stupid |

Note that 'clever' and 'quiet' only add '-er' and '-est'.

It was _quieter_ outside.
He was the _cleverest_ man I ever met.

5 You normally use 'the' with superlative adjectives in front of nouns, but you can omit 'the' after a link verb.

It was _the happiest_ day of my life.
It was one of _the most important_ discoveries.
I was _happiest_ when I was on my own.

WARNING When 'most' is used without 'the' in front of adjectives and adverbs, it often means almost the same as 'very'.

This book was _most interesting._
I object _most strongly._

6 A few common adjectives and adverbs have irregular comparative and superlative forms.

good/well ⇨ better	⇨ best
bad/badly ⇨ worse	⇨ worst
far	⇨ farther/further	⇨ farthest/furthest
old	⇨ older/elder	⇨ oldest/eldest

She would ask him when she knew him _better._
She sat near the _furthest_ window.

Note that you use 'elder' or 'eldest' to say which brother, sister, or child in a family you mean.

Our _eldest_ daughter couldn't come.

Unit 25 Comparatives and superlatives: uses

Main points

- Comparative adjectives are used to compare people or things.
- Superlative adjectives are used to say that one person or thing has more of a quality than others in a group or others of that kind.
- Comparative adverbs are used in the same way as adjectives.

1 You use comparative adjectives to compare one person or thing with another, or with the same person or thing at another time. After a comparative adjective, you often use 'than'.

She was much older than me.
I am happier than I have ever been.

2 You use a superlative to say that one person or thing has more of a quality than others in a group or others of that kind.

Tokyo is Japan's largest city.
He was the tallest person there.

3 You can use comparative and superlative adjectives in front of a noun.

I was a better writer than he was.
He had more important things to do.
It was the quickest route from Rome to Naples.

You can also use comparative and superlative adjectives after link verbs.

My brother is younger than me.
He feels more content now.
The sergeant was the tallest.
This book was the most interesting.

4 You can use adverbs of degree in front of comparative adjectives.

a bit	a great/good deal	a lot	rather
far	a little	much	slightly

This car's a bit more expensive.
Now I feel a great deal more confident.
It's a rather more complicated story than that.

You can also use adverbs of degree such as 'by far', 'easily', 'much', or 'quite' in front of 'the' and superlative adjectives.

It was by far the worst hospital I had ever seen.
She was easily the most intelligent person in the class.

Note that you can put 'very' between 'the' and a superlative adjective ending in '-est'.

It was of the very highest quality.

5 When you want to say that one situation depends on another, you can use 'the' and a comparative followed by 'the' and another comparative.

The smaller it is, the cheaper it is to post.
The larger the organisation is, the greater the problem of administration becomes.

When you want to say that something increases or decreases, you can use two comparatives linked by 'and'.

It's getting harder and harder to find a job.
Cars are becoming more and more expensive.

6 After a superlative adjective, you can use a prepositional phrase to specify the group you are talking about.

Henry was the biggest of them.
These cakes are probably the best in the world.
He was the most dangerous man in the country.

7 You use the same structures in comparisons using adverbs as those given for adjectives:

- 'than' after comparative adverbs

Prices have been rising faster than incomes.

- 'the' and a comparative adverb followed by 'the' and another comparative adverb

The quicker we finish, the sooner we will go home.

- two comparative adverbs linked by 'and'

He sounded worse and worse.
He drove faster and faster till we told him to stop.

Unit 26 Other ways of comparing things

Words like: as ... as, the same (as), like

Main points

- You use 'as...as...' to compare people or things.
- You can also compare people or things by using 'the same (as)'.
- You can also compare people or things by using a link verb and a phrase beginning with 'like'.

1 You use 'as...as...' to compare people or things that are similar in some way. You use 'as' and an adjective or adverb, followed by 'as' and a noun group, an adverbial, or a clause.

You're as bad as your sister.
The airport was as crowded as ever.
I am as good as she is.
Let us examine it as carefully as we can.

2 You can make a negative comparison using 'not as...as...' or 'not so...as...'.

The food wasn't as good as yesterday.
They are not as clever as they appear to be.
He is not so old as I thought.

3 You can use the adverbs 'almost', 'just', 'nearly', or 'quite' in front of 'as...as...'.

He was almost as fast as his brother.
Mary was just as pale as before.
She was nearly as tall as he was.

In a negative comparison, you can use 'not nearly' or 'not quite' before 'as...as...'.

This is not nearly as complicated as it sounds.
The hotel was not quite as good as they expected.

4 When you want to say that one thing is very similar to something else, you can use 'the same as' followed by a noun group, an adverbial, or a clause.

Your bag is the same as mine.
I said the same as always.
She looked the same as she did yesterday.

If people or things are very similar or identical, you can also say that they are 'the same'.

Teenage fashions are the same all over the world.
The initial stage of learning English is the same for many students.

You can use some adverbs in front of 'the same as' or 'the same'.

almost	just		much	roughly
exactly	more or less		nearly	virtually

He did exactly the same as John did.
You two look almost the same.

You can use 'the same' in front of a noun group, with or without 'as' after the noun group.

They reached almost the same height.
It was painted the same colour as the wall.

5 You can also compare people or things by using a link verb such as 'be', 'feel', 'look', or 'seem' and a phrase beginning with 'like'.

It was like a dream.
He still feels like a child.
He looked like an actor.
The houses seemed like mansions.

You can use some adverbs in front of 'like'.

a bit	exactly	least	more	quite	somewhat
a little	just	less	most	rather	very

He looks just like a baby.
Of all his children, she was the one most like me.

6 If the noun group after 'as' or 'like' in any of these structures is a pronoun, you use an object pronoun or possessive pronoun.

Jane was as clever as him.
His car is the same as mine.

7 You can also use 'less' and 'least' to make comparisons with the opposite meaning to 'more' and 'most'.

They were less fortunate than us.
He was the least skilled of the workers.
We see him less frequently than we used to.

Unit 27 Possession

Main points

- Possessives and possessive pronouns are used to say that one person or thing belongs to another or is connected with another.
- You use apostrophe s ('s) to say who something belongs to.
- You use phrases with 'of' to say that one person or thing belongs to another or is connected with another.

1 You use possessives to say that a person or thing belongs to another person or thing or is connected with them. The possessives are sometimes called 'possessive adjectives'.

| my | your | his | her | its | our | their |

Note that 'your' is both singular and plural.

I'd been waiting a long time to park my car.
They took off their shoes.

WARNING: The possessive 'its' is not spelled with an apostrophe. The form 'it's' with an apostrophe is the short form for 'it is' or 'it has'.

2 You put numbers and adjectives after the possessive and in front of the noun.

Their two small children were playing outside.
She got a bicycle on her sixth birthday.

3 You use a possessive pronoun when you want to refer to a person or thing and to say who that person or thing belongs to or is connected with. The possessive pronouns are:

| mine | yours | his | hers | ours | theirs |

Note that 'yours' is both singular and plural.

Is that coffee yours or mine?
It was his fault, not theirs.

WARNING: There is no possessive pronoun 'its'.

4 You can also say who or what something belongs to or is connected with by using a noun with apostrophe s ('s). For example, if John owns a motorbike, you can refer to it as 'John's motorbike'.

Sylvia put her hand on John's arm.
I like the car's design.

You add apostrophe s ('s) to singular nouns and irregular plural nouns, usually referring to people rather than things.

I wore a pair of my sister's boots.
Children's birthday parties can be boring.

With plural nouns ending in '-s' you only add the apostrophe (').

It is not his parents' problem.

You add apostrophe s ('s) to people's names, even when they end in '-s'.

Could you give me Charles's address?

Note that when you use two or more names linked by 'and', you put the apostrophe s ('s) after the last name.

They have bought Sue and Tim's car.

5 When you want to refer to someone's home, or to some common shops and places of work, you can use apostrophe s ('s) after a name or noun on its own.

He's round at David's. (home)
I bought it at the chemist's. (shop)
She must go to the doctor's. (place)

6 You can also use apostrophe s ('s) with some expressions of time to identify something, or to say how much time is involved.

Did you see the cartoon in yesterday's newspaper?
They have four weeks' holiday per year.

7 You can use a prepositional phrase beginning with 'of' to say that one person or thing belongs to or is connected with another.

She is the mother of the boy who lives next door.
Ellen aimlessly turned the pages of her magazine.

After 'of' you can use a possessive pronoun, or a noun or name with apostrophe s ('s).

He was an old friend of mine.
That word was a favourite of your father's.
She's a friend of Stephen's.

8 You can add 'own' after a possessive, or a noun or name with apostrophe s ('s), for emphasis.

My own view is that there are no serious problems.
The professor's own answer may be unacceptable.

Unit 28 Nouns with prepositions

Main points

- 'Of' can be used to add many different types of information, 'with' is used to specify a quality or possession.
- Some nouns are always followed by particular prepositions.

1 You can give more information about a noun by adding a prepositional phrase after it.

Four men on holiday were in the car.
A sound behind him made him turn.

2 You often use the preposition 'of' after a noun to add various kinds of information. For example, you can use 'of' to indicate:

- what something is made of or consists of

...a wall of stone.
A feeling of panic was rising in him.

- what the subject matter of speech, writing, or a picture is

She gave a brief account of her interview.
There was a picture of them both in the paper.

- what a person or thing belongs to or is connected with

She was the daughter of the village priest.
The boys sat on the floor of the living room.

- what qualities a person or thing has

She was a woman of energy and ambition.
They faced problems of great complexity.

3 After nouns referring to actions, you use 'of' to indicate the subject or object of the action.

...the arrival of the police.
...the destruction of their city.

After nouns referring to people who perform an action, you use 'of' to say what the action involves or is aimed at.

...supporters of the hunger strike.
...a student of English.

Note that you often use two nouns, rather than a noun and a prepositional phrase. For example, you say 'bank robbers', not 'robbers of the bank'.

4 After nouns referring to measurement, you use 'of' to give the exact figure.

...an average annual temperature of 20 degrees.
...a speed of 25 kilometres an hour.

You can use 'of' after a noun to give someone's age.

Jonathan was a child of seven when it happened.

5 You use 'with' after a noun to say that a person or thing has a particular quality, feature, or possession.

...a girl with red hair.
...the man with the gun.

Note that you use 'in' after a noun to say what someone is wearing.

...a grey-haired man in a raincoat.
...the man in dark glasses.

6 Some nouns are usually followed by a particular preposition. Here are some examples of:

- nouns followed by 'to'

alternative	attitude	invitation	relevance
answer	devotion	reaction	resistance
approach	introduction	reference	return

This was my first real introduction to Africa.

- nouns followed by 'for'

admiration	need	responsibility	taste
desire	reason	search	thirst
dislike	respect	substitute	

Their need for money is growing fast.

- nouns followed by 'on'

agreement	attack	comment	effect	tax

She had a dreadful effect on me.

- nouns followed by 'with' or 'between'

connection	contact	link	relationship

His illness had some connection with his diet.

- nouns followed by 'in'

decrease	difficulty	fall	increase	rise

They demanded a large increase in wages.

Unit 29 Nouns with '-ing', '-ed', or 'to'-infinitive clauses

Main points

- Nouns are followed by '-ing' clauses that say what a person or thing is doing.
- Nouns are followed by '-ed' clauses that show that a person or thing has been affected or caused by an action.
- Nouns are followed by 'to'-infinitive clauses that indicate the aim, purpose, or necessity of something, or that give extra information.

1 You can often give more information about a noun, or an indefinite pronoun such as 'someone' or 'something', by adding a clause beginning with an '-ing' form, an '-ed' form, or a 'to'-infinitive.

He gestured towards the box lying on the table.
I think the idea suggested by Tim is the best one.
She wanted someone to talk to.

2 You use an '-ing' clause after a noun to say what someone or something is doing or was doing at a particular time.
The young girl sitting opposite him was his daughter.
Most of the people strolling in the park were teenagers.

3 You can also use an '-ing' clause after a noun to say what a person or thing does generally, rather than at a particular time.
Problems facing parents should be discussed.
The men working there were not very friendly.

4 You often use an '-ing' clause after a noun which is the object of a verb of perception, such as 'see', 'hear', or 'feel'. See also Unit 84.
Suddenly we saw Amy walking down the path.
He heard a distant voice shouting.

5 You use an '-ed' clause after a noun to show that someone or something has been affected or caused by an action.

He was the new minister appointed by the President.
The man injured in the accident was taken to hospital.

Remember that not all verbs have regular '-ed' forms.

A story written by a young girl won the competition.
She was wearing a dress bought in Paris.

6 You use a 'to'-infinitive clause after a noun to indicate the aim of an action or the purpose of physical object.

We arranged a meeting to discuss the new rules.
He had nothing to write with.

You also use a 'to'-infinitive clause after a noun to say that something needs to be done.

I gave him several things to mend.
'What's this?'—'A list of things to remember.'

7 You use a 'to'-infinitive clause after a noun group that includes an ordinal number, a superlative, or a word like 'next', 'last', or 'only'.

She was the first woman to be elected to the council.
Mr Holmes was the oldest person to be chosen.
The only person to speak was James.

8 You use a 'to'-infinitive clause after abstract nouns to give more specific information about them.

All it takes is a willingness to learn.
He'd lost the ability to communicate with people.

The following abstract nouns are often followed by a 'to'-infinitive clause:

ability	desire	need	willingness
attempt	failure	opportunity	
chance	inability	unwillingness	

Note that the verbs or adjectives which are related to these nouns can also be followed by a 'to'-infinitive clause. For example, you can say 'I attempted to find them', and 'He was willing to learn'.
See Unit 30 for information on nouns that are related to reporting verbs and can be followed by a 'to'-infinitive clause.

Unit 30 Other ways of adding to a noun group

Main points

- Some adjectives can be used after nouns.
- You can use relative clauses after nouns.
- Adverbials of place and time can come after nouns.
- A noun can be followed by another noun group.
- You can use 'that'-clauses after some nouns.

1 You can use some adjectives after a noun to give more information about it, but the adjectives are usually followed by a prepositional phrase, a 'to'-infinitive clause, or an adverbial.

This is a warning to people eager for a quick profit.
These are the weapons likely to be used.
For a list of the facilities available here, ask the secretary.
You must talk to the people concerned.

See Unit 19 for more information on adjectives used after nouns.

2 When you want to give more precise information about the person or thing you are talking about, you can use a defining relative clause after the noun.

The man who had done it was arrested.
There are a lot of things that are wrong.
Nearly all the people I used to know have gone.

Note that you can also use defining relative clauses after indefinite pronouns such as 'someone' or 'something'.

I'm talking about somebody who is really ill.

See Unit 97 for more information on defining relative clauses.

3 You can use an adverbial of place or time after a noun.

People everywhere are becoming more selfish.
This is a reflection of life today.

4 You can add a second noun group after a noun. The second noun group gives you more precise information about the first noun.

Her mother, a Canadian, died when she was six.

Note that the second noun group is separated by commas from the rest of the clause.

5 Nouns such as 'advice', 'hope', and 'wish', which refer to what someone says or thinks, can be followed by a 'that'-clause. Here are some examples:

advice	claim	feeling	threat
agreement	conclusion	hope	warning
belief	decision	promise	wish

It is my firm belief that more women should stand for Parliament.
I had a feeling that no-one thought I was good enough.

Note that all these nouns are related to reporting verbs, which also take a 'that'-clause. For example, 'information' is related to 'inform', and 'decision' is related to 'decide'.
Some of these nouns can also be followed by a 'to'-infinitive clause.

agreement	hope	promise	warning
decision	order	threat	wish

The decision to go had not been an easy one.
I reminded Barnaby of his promise to buy his son a horse.

6 A few other nouns can be followed by a 'that'-clause.

advantage	effect	idea	opinion
confidence	evidence	impression	possibility
danger	fact	news	view

He didn't want her to get the idea that he was rich.
I had no evidence that Jed was the killer.
He couldn't believe the news that his house had just burned down.

Note that when a noun group is the object of a verb, it may be followed by different structures. See Units 81 to 84 for more information.

Unit 31 Adverbials

Main points

- Adverbials are usually adverbs, adverb phrases, or prepositional phrases.
- Adverbials of manner, place, and time are used to say how, where, or when something happens.
- Adverbials usually come after the verb, or after the object if there is one.
- The usual order of adverbials is manner, then place, then time.

1 An adverbial is often one word, an adverb.

Sit there _quietly_, and listen to this music.

However, an adverbial can also be a group of words:
- an adverb phrase

He did not play _well enough_ to win.

- a prepositional phrase

The children were playing _in the park_.

- a noun group, usually a time expression

Come and see me _next week_.

2 You use an adverbial of manner to describe the way in which something happens or is done.

They looked _anxiously_ at each other.
She listened _with great patience_ as he told his story.

You use an adverbial of place to say where something happens.

A plane flew _overhead_.
No birds or animals came _near the body_.

You use an adverbial of time to say when something happens.

She will be here _soon_.
He was born _on 3 April 1925_.

3 You normally put adverbials of manner, place, and time after the main verb.

She sang _beautifully_.
The book was lying _on the table_.
The car broke down _yesterday_.

If the verb has an object, you put the adverbial after the object.

I did learn to play a few tunes _very badly_.
Thomas made his decision _immediately_.
He took the glasses _to the kitchen_.

If you are using more than one of these adverbials in a clause, the usual order is _manner_, then _place_, then _time_.

They were sitting _quite happily in the car_. (manner, place)
She spoke _very well at the village hall last night_. (manner, place, time)

4 You usually put adverbials of frequency, probability, and duration in front of the main verb.

She _occasionally comes_ to my house.
You have _very probably heard_ the news by now.
They had _already given_ me the money.

A few adverbs of degree also usually come in front of the main verb.

She _really enjoyed_ the party.

5 When you want to focus on an adverbial, you can do this by putting it in a different place in the clause:

- you can put an adverbial at the beginning of a clause, usually for emphasis

Slowly, he opened his eyes.
In September I travelled to California.
Next to the coffee machine stood _a pile of cups_.

Note that after adverbials of place, as in the last example, the verb can come in front of the subject.

- you can sometimes put adverbs and adverb phrases in front of the main verb for emphasis, but not prepositional phrases or noun groups

He _deliberately_ chose it because it was cheap.
I _very much_ wanted to go with them.

- you can change the order of adverbials of manner, place, and time when you want to change the emphasis

They were sitting _in the car quite happily_. (place, manner)
At the meeting last night_, she spoke _very well_. (place, time, manner)

Unit 32 Adverbials of manner

Main points

- Most adverbs of manner are formed by adding '-ly' to an adjective, but sometimes other spelling changes are needed.
- You cannot form adverbs from adjectives that end in '-ly'.
- Some adverbs have the same form as adjectives.
- You do not use adverbs after link verbs, you use adjectives.
- Adverbials of manner are sometimes prepositional phrases or noun groups.

1 Adverbs of manner are often formed by adding '-ly' to an adjective.

Adjectives	Adverbs
bad	⇨ badly
beautiful	⇨ beautifully
careful	⇨ carefully
quick	⇨ quickly
quiet	⇨ quietly
soft	⇨ softly

2 Adverbs formed in this way usually have a similar meaning to the adjective.

She is as clever as she is beautiful.
He talked so politely and danced so beautifully.

'We must not talk. We must be quiet,' said Sita.
She wanted to sit quietly, to relax.

3 There are sometimes changes in spelling when an adverb is formed from an adjective.

	Adjectives	Adverbs
'-le' changes to '-ly':	gentle	⇨ gently
'-y' changes to '-ily':	easy	⇨ easily
'-ic' changes to '-ically':	automatic	⇨ automatically
'-ue' changes to '-uly':	true	⇨ truly
'-ll' changes to '-lly':	full	⇨ fully

Note that 'public' changes to 'publicly', not 'publically'.

WARNING: You cannot form adverbs from adjectives that already end in '-ly'. For example, you cannot say 'He smiled at me friendlily'. You can

sometimes use a prepositional phrase instead: 'He smiled at me in a friendly way'.

4 Some adverbs of manner have the same form as adjectives and have similar meanings, for example 'fast', 'hard', and 'late'.

I've always been interested in fast cars. (adjective)
The driver was driving too fast. (adverb)

Note that 'hardly' and 'lately' are not adverbs of manner and have different meanings from the adjectives 'hard' and 'late'.

It was a hard decision to make.
I hardly had any time to talk to her.

The train was late as usual.
Have you seen John lately?

5 The adverb of manner related to the adjective 'good' is 'well'.

He is a good dancer.
He dances well.

Note that 'well' can sometimes be an adjective when it refers to someone's health.

'How are you?'—'I am very well, thank you.'

6 You do not use adverbs after link verbs such as 'be', 'become', 'feel', 'get', 'look', and 'seem'. You use an adjective after these verbs. For example, you do not say 'Sue felt happily'. You say 'Sue felt happy'. See Unit 80 for more information on link verbs.

7 You do not often use prepositional phrases or noun groups as adverbials of manner. However, you occasionally need to use them, for example when there is no adverb form available. The prepositional phrases and noun groups usually include a noun such as 'way', 'fashion', or 'manner', or a noun that refers to someone's voice.

She asked me in such a nice manner that I couldn't refuse.
He did it the right way.
They spoke in angry tones.

Prepositional phrases with 'like' are also used as adverbials of manner.

I slept like a baby.
He drove like a madman.

Unit 33 Adverbials of time

Main points

- Adverbials of time can be time expressions such as 'last night'.
- Adverbials of time can be prepositional phrases with 'at', 'in', or 'on'.
- 'For' refers to a period of time in the past, present, or future.
- 'Since' refers to a point in past time.

1 You use adverbials of time to say when something happens. You often use noun groups called time expressions as adverbials of time.

yesterday	last year	the day after tomorrow
today	next Saturday	last night
tomorrow	next week	the other day

Note that you do not use the prepositions 'at', 'in', or 'on' with time expressions.

One of my children wrote to me today.
So, you're coming back next week?

You often use time expressions with verbs in the present tense to talk about the future.

The plane leaves tomorrow morning.
They're coming next week.

2 You can use prepositional phrases as adverbials of time:

- 'at' is used with:

clock times: at eight o'clock, at three fifteen
religious festivals: at Christmas, at Easter
mealtimes: at breakfast, at lunchtimes
specific periods: at night, at the weekend, at weekends, at half-term

- 'in' is used with:

seasons: in autumn, in the spring
years and centuries: in 1985, in the year 2000, in the nineteenth century
months: in July, in December
parts of the day: in the morning, in the evenings

Note that you also use 'in' to say that something will happen during or after a period of time in the future.

I think we'll find out in the next few days.

- 'on' is used with:

days: on Monday, on Tuesday morning, on Sunday evenings
special days: on Christmas Day, on my birthday, on his wedding anniversary
dates: on the twentieth of July, on June 21st

3 You use 'for' with verbs in any tense to say how long something continues to happen.

He is in Italy for a month.
I remained silent for a long time.
I will be in London for three months.

> WARNING: You do not use 'during' to say how long something continues to happen. You cannot say 'I went there during three weeks'.

4 You use 'since' with a verb in the present perfect or past perfect tense to say when something started to happen.

Marilyn has lived in Paris since 1984.
I had eaten nothing since breakfast.

5 You can use many other prepositional phrases as adverbials of time. You use:

- 'during' and 'over' for a period of time in which something happens

I saw him twice during the summer holidays.
Will you stay in Edinburgh over Christmas?

- 'from...to/till/until' and 'between...and' for the beginning and end of a period of time

The building is closed from April to May.
She worked from four o'clock till ten o'clock.
Can you take the test between now and June?

- 'by' when you mean 'not later than'

By eleven o'clock, Brody was back in his office.
Can we get this finished by tomorrow?

- 'before' and 'after'

I saw him before the match.
She left the house after ten o'clock.

'Since', 'till', 'until', 'after', and 'before' can also be conjunctions with time clauses. See Unit 90.

I've been wearing glasses since I was three.

You use the adverb 'ago' with the past simple to say how long before the time of speaking something happened. You always put 'ago' after the period of time.

We saw him about a month ago.
John's wife died five years ago.

> WARNING: You do not use 'ago' with the present perfect tense. You cannot say 'We have gone to Spain two years ago'.

Unit 34 Adverbials of frequency and probability

Words like: always, ever, never, perhaps, possibly, probably

Main points

- Adverbials of frequency are used to say how often something happens.
- Adverbials of probability are used to say how sure you are about something.
- These adverbials usually come before the main verb, but they come after 'be' as a main verb.

1 You use adverbials of frequency to say how often something happens.

a lot	frequently	normally	rarely
always	hardly ever	occasionally	sometimes
ever	never	often	usually

We often swam in the sea.
She never comes to my parties.

2 You use adverbials of probability to say how sure you are about something.

certainly	maybe	perhaps	probably
definitely	obviously	possibly	really

I definitely saw her yesterday.
The driver probably knows the quickest route.

3 You usually put adverbials of frequency and probability before the main verb and after an auxiliary or a modal.

He sometimes works downstairs in the kitchen.
You are definitely wasting your time.
I have never had such a horrible meal!
I shall never forget this day.

Note that you usually put them after 'be' as a main verb.

He is always careful with his money.
You are probably right.

'Perhaps' usually comes at the beginning of the sentence.

Perhaps the beaches are cleaner in the north.
Perhaps you need a membership card to get in.

'A lot' always comes after the main verb.

I go swimming a lot in the summer.

4 'Never' is a negative adverb.

She never goes abroad.
I've never been to Europe.

You normally use 'ever' in questions, negative sentences, and 'if'-clauses.

Have you ever been to a football match?
Don't ever do that again!
If you ever need anything, just call me.

Note that you can sometimes use 'ever' in affirmative sentences, for example after a superlative.

She is the best dancer I have ever seen.

You use 'hardly ever' in affirmative sentences to mean almost never.

We hardly ever meet.

The bus is always late.

Perhaps it has broken down.

It's probably stuck in traffic.

Unit 35 Adverbials of duration - already, still, yet

Main points

- 'Already' is used to say that something has happened earlier than expected.
- 'Still' is used to say that something continues to happen until a particular time.
- 'Yet' is used to say that something has not happened before a particular time.
- 'Any longer', 'any more', 'no longer', and 'no more' are used to say that something has stopped happening.

1 You use adverbials of duration to say that an event or situation is continuing, stopping, or is not happening at the moment.

She still lives in London.
I couldn't stand it any more.
It isn't dark yet.

2 You use 'already' to say that something has happened sooner than it was expected to happen. You put 'already' in front of the main verb.

He had already bought the cups and saucers.
I've already seen them.
The guests were already coming in.

You put 'already' after 'be' as a main verb.

Julie was already in bed.

You can also use 'already' to emphasize that something is the case, for example when someone else does not know or is not sure.

I am already aware of that problem.

You do not normally use 'already' in negative statements, but you can use it in negative 'if'-clauses.

Show it to him if he hasn't already seen it.

You can put 'already' at the beginning or end of a clause for emphasis.

Already he was calculating the profit he could make.
I've done it already.

3 You use 'still' to say that a situation continues to exist up to a particular time in the past, present, or future. You put 'still' in front of the main verb.

We were still waiting for the election results.
My family still live in India.
You will still get tickets, if you hurry.

You put 'still' after 'be' as a main verb.

Martin's mother died, but his father is still alive.

You can use 'still' after the subject and before the verb group in negative sentences to express surprise or impatience.

You still haven't given us the keys.
He still didn't say a word.
It was after midnight, and he still wouldn't leave.

Remember that you can use 'still' at the beginning of a clause with a similar meaning to 'after all' or 'nevertheless'.

Still, he is my brother, so I'll have to help him.
Still, it's not too bad. We didn't lose all the money.

4 You use 'yet' at the end of negative sentences and questions to say that something has not happened or had not happened up to a particular time, but is or was expected to happen later.

We haven't got the tickets yet.
Have you joined the swimming club yet?
They hadn't seen the baby yet.

Remember that 'yet' can also be used at the beginning of a clause with a similar meaning to 'but'.

I don't miss her, yet I do often wonder where she went.
They know they won't win. Yet they keep on trying.

5 You use 'any longer' and 'any more' at the end of negative clauses to say that a past situation has ended and does not exist now or will not exist in the future.

I wanted the job, but I couldn't wait any longer.
He's not going to play any more.

In formal English, you can use an affirmative clause with 'no longer' and 'no more'. You can put them at the end of the clause, or in front of the main verb.

He could stand the pain no more.
He no longer wanted to buy it.

Unit 36 Adverbials of degree

Main points

- Adverbs of degree usually modify verbs.
- Some adverbs of degree can modify adjectives, other adverbs, or clauses.

1 You use adverbs of degree to modify verbs. They make the verb stronger or weaker.

I totally disagree.
I can nearly swim.

2 Some adverbs can come in front of a main verb, after a main verb, or after the object if there is one.

badly	greatly	strongly
completely	seriously	totally

Mr Brooke strongly criticized the Bank of England.
I disagree completely with John Taylor.
That argument doesn't convince me totally.

Some adverbs are mostly used in front of the verb.

almost	largely	nearly	really	quite

He almost crashed into a lorry.

Note that 'really' is used at the beginning of a clause to express surprise, and at the end of a clause as an adverb of manner.

Really, I didn't know that!
He wanted it really, but he was too shy to ask.

'A lot' and 'very much' come after the main verb if there is no object, or after the object.

She helped a lot.
We liked him very much.

'Very much' can come after the subject and in front of verbs like 'want', 'prefer', and 'enjoy'.

I very much wanted to take it with me.

3 Some adverbs of degree go in front of adjectives or other adverbs and modify them.

awfully	fairly	quite	really
extremely	pretty	rather	very

...a fairly large office, with filing space.

Note that you can use 'rather' before or after 'a' or 'an' followed by an adjective and a noun.

Seaford is rather a pleasant town.
He told me a rather long and complicated story.

When 'quite' means 'fairly', you put it in front of 'a' or 'an' followed by an adjective and a noun.

My father gave me quite a large sum of money.

However, when 'quite' means 'extremely', you can put it after 'a'. You can say 'a quite enormous sum'.

4 You use some adverbs of degree to modify clauses and prepositional phrases.

entirely	just	largely	mainly	partly	simply

Are you saying that simply because I am here?
I don't think it's worth going just for a day.

5 You use 'so' and 'such' to emphasize a quality that someone or something has. 'So' can be followed by an adjective, an adverb, or a noun group beginning with 'many', 'much', 'few', or 'little'.

John is so interesting to talk to.
Science is changing so rapidly.
I want to do so many different things.

'Such' is followed by a singular noun group with 'a', or a plural noun group.

There was such a noise we couldn't hear.
They said such nasty things about you.

WARNING: 'So' is never followed by a singular noun group with 'a' or a plural noun group.

6 You use 'too' when you mean 'more than is necessary' or 'more than is good'. You can use 'too' before adjectives and adverbs, and before 'many', 'much', 'few', or 'little'.

The prices in that shop are too high.
I've been paying too much tax.

You use 'enough' after adjectives and adverbs.

I waited until my daughter was old enough to read.
He didn't work quickly enough.

Note that 'enough' is also a determiner.

We've got enough money to buy that car now.

7 You use emphasizing adverbs to modify adjectives such as 'astonishing', 'furious', and 'wonderful', which express extreme qualities.

absolutely	entirely	purely	really	totally
completely	perfectly	quite	simply	utterly

I think he's absolutely wonderful.

Unit 37 Prepositions of place and direction

Words like: above, below, down, from, to, towards, up

Main points

- You normally use prepositional phrases to say where a person or thing is, or the direction they are moving in.
- You can also use adverbs and adverb phrases for place and direction.
- Many words are both prepositions and adverbs.

1 You use prepositions to talk about the place where someone or something is. Prepositions are always followed by a noun group, which is called the object of the preposition.

above	below	in	opposite	through
among	beneath	inside	outside	under
at	beside	near	over	underneath
behind	between	on	round	

He stood near the door.
Two minutes later we were safely inside the taxi.

Note that some prepositions consist of more than one word.

in between	in front of	next to	on top of

There was a man standing in front of me.
The books were piled on top of each other.

2 You can also use prepositions to talk about the direction that someone or something is moving in, or the place that someone or something is moving towards.

across	into	past	to
along	onto	round	towards
back to	out of	through	up
down			

They dived into the water.
She turned and rushed out of the room.

3 Many prepositions can be used both for place and direction.

The bank is just across the High Street. (place)
I walked across the room. (direction)

We live in the house over the road. (place)
I stole his keys and escaped over the wall. (direction)

4 You can also use adverbs and adverb phrases for place and direction.

abroad	here	underground	everywhere
away	indoors	upstairs	nowhere
downstairs	outdoors	~	somewhere
downwards	there	anywhere	

Sheila was here a moment ago.
Can't you go upstairs and turn the bedroom light off?

Note that a few noun groups can also be used as adverbials of place or direction.

Steve lives next door at number 23.
I thought we went the other way last time.

5 Many words can be used as prepositions and as adverbs, with no difference in meaning. Remember that prepositions have noun groups as objects, but adverbs do not.

Did he fall down the stairs?
Please do sit down.
I looked underneath the bed, but the box had gone!
Always put a sheet of paper underneath.

Unit 38 Prepositions of place - at, in, on

Main points

- You use 'at' to talk about a place as a point.
- You use 'in' to talk about a place as an area.
- You use 'on' to talk about a place as a surface.

1 You use 'at' when you are thinking of a place as a point in space.

She waited at the bus stop for over twenty minutes.
'Where were you last night?' - 'At Mick's house.'

2 You also use 'at' with words such as 'back', 'bottom', 'end', 'front', and 'top' to talk about the different parts of a place.

Mrs Castle was waiting at the bottom of the stairs.
They escaped by a window at the back of the house.
I saw a taxi at the end of the street.

You use 'at' with public places and institutions. Note that you also say 'at home' and 'at work'.

I have to be at the station by ten o'clock.
We landed at a small airport.
A friend of mine is at Training College.
She wanted to stay at home.

You say 'at the corner' or 'on the corner' when you are talking about streets.

The car was parked at the corner of the street.
There's a telephone box on the corner.

You say 'in the corner' when you are talking about a room.

She put the chair in the corner of the room.

3 You use 'in' when you are talking about a place as an area. You use 'in' with:

- a country or geographical region

When I was in Spain, it was terribly cold.
A thousand homes in the east of Scotland suffered power cuts.

- a city, town, or village

I've been teaching at a college in London.

- a building when you are talking about people or things inside it

They were sitting having dinner in the restaurant.

You also use 'in' with containers of any kind when talking about things inside them.

She kept the cards in a little box.

4 Compare the use of 'at' and 'in' in these examples.

I had a hard day at the office. ('at' emphasizes the office as a public place or institution)

I left my coat behind in the office. ('in' emphasizes the office as a building)

There's a good film at the cinema. ('at' emphasizes the cinema as a public place)

It was very cold in the cinema. ('in' emphasizes the cinema as a building.)

5 When talking about addresses, you use 'at' when you give the house number, and 'in' when you just give the name of the street.

They used to live at 5, Weston Road.
She got a job in Oxford Street.

Note that American English uses 'on': 'He lived on Penn Street.'
You use 'at' when you are talking about someone's house.

I'll see you at Fred's house.

6 You use 'on' when you are talking about a place as a surface. You can also use 'on top of'.

I sat down on the sofa.
She put her keys on top of the television.

You also use 'on' when you are thinking of a place as a point on a line, such as a road, a railway line, a river, or a coastline.

Scrabster is on the north coast.
Oxford is on the A34 between Birmingham and London.

See Unit 33 for information on 'at', 'in', and 'on' in adverbials of time.

Unit 39 Prepositions with forms of transport

Phrases like: by bus, in a car, on the plane, off the train

Main points

- You can use 'by' with most forms of transport.
- You use 'in', 'into', and 'out of' with cars.
- You normally use 'on', 'onto', and 'off' with other forms of transport.

1 When you talk about the type of vehicle or transport you use to travel somewhere, you use 'by'.

by bus	by car	by plane	by train
by bicycle	by coach		

She had come by car with her husband and her four children.
I left Walsall in the afternoon and went by bus and train to Nottingham.

WARNING: If you want to say you walk somewhere, you say you go 'on foot'. You do not say 'by foot'.

Marie decided to continue on foot.

2 You use 'in', 'into', and 'out of' when you are talking about cars, vans, lorries, taxis, and ambulances.

I followed them in my car.
The carpets had to be collected in a van.
Mr Ward happened to be getting into his lorry.
She was carried out of the ambulance and up the steps.

3 You use 'on', 'onto', and 'off' when you are talking about other forms of transport, such as buses, coaches, trains, ships, and planes.

Why don't you come on the train with me to New York?
Peter Hurd was already on the plane from California. The last thing he wanted was to spend ten days on a boat with Hooper.
He jumped back onto the old bus, now nearly empty.
Mr Bixby stepped off the train and walked quickly to the exit.

You can use 'in', 'into', and 'out of' with these other forms of transport, usually when you are focusing on the physical position or movement of the person, rather than stating what form of transport they are using.

The passengers in the plane were beginning to panic.
He got back into the train quickly, before Batt could stop him.
We jumped out of the bus and ran into the nearest shop.

Unit 40 Auxiliary verbs - be, have, do

Main points

- The auxiliaries 'be', 'have', and 'do' are used in forming tenses, negatives, and questions.
- The auxiliary 'be' is used in forming the continuous tenses and the passive.
- The auxiliary 'have' is used in forming the perfect tenses.
- The auxiliary 'do' is used in making negative and question forms from sentences that have a verb in a simple tense.

1 The auxiliary verbs are 'be', 'have', and 'do'. They are used with a main verb to form tenses, negatives, and questions.

He is planning to get married soon.
I haven't seen Peter since last night.
Which doctor do you want to see?

2 'Be' as an auxiliary is used:

● with the '-ing' form of the main verb to form continuous tenses

He is living in Germany.
They were going to phone you.

● with the past participle of the main verb to form the passive

These cars are made in Japan.
The walls of her flat were covered with posters.

3 You use 'have' as an auxiliary with the past participle to form the perfect tenses.

I have changed my mind.
I wish you had met Guy.

The present perfect continuous, the past perfect continuous, and the perfect tenses in the passive, are formed using both 'have' and 'be'.

He has been working very hard recently.
She did not know how long she had been lying there.
The guest-room window has been mended.
They had been taught by a young teacher.

4 'Be' and 'have' are also used as auxiliaries in negative sentences and questions in continuous and perfect tenses, and in the passive.

He isn't going.
Hasn't she seen it yet?
Was it written in English?

You use 'do' as an auxiliary to make negative and question forms from sentences that have a verb in the present simple or past simple.

He doesn't think he can come to the party.
Do you like her new haircut?
She didn't buy the house.
Didn't he get the job?

Note that you can use 'do' as a main verb with the auxiliary 'do'.

He didn't do his homework.
Do they do the work themselves?

You can also use the auxiliary 'do' with 'have' as a main verb.

He doesn't have any money.
Does anyone have a question?

You only use 'do' in affirmative sentences for emphasis or contrast.

I do feel sorry for Roger.

WARNING: You never use the auxiliary 'do' with 'be' except in the imperative.

Don't be stupid!
Do be a good boy and sit still.

5 Some grammars include modals among the auxiliary verbs. When there is a modal in the verb group, it is always the first word in the verb group, and comes before the auxiliaries 'be' and 'have'.

She might be going to Switzerland for Christmas.
I would have liked to have seen her.

Note that you never use the auxiliary 'do' with a modal. See Units 59–71 for more information on modals.

Unit 41 The present tenses

Main points

- There are four present tenses - present simple, present continuous, present perfect, and present perfect continuous.
- All the present tenses are used to refer to a time which includes the present.
- Present tenses can also be used for predictions made in the present about future events.

1 There are four tenses which begin with a verb in the present tense. They are the present simple, the present continuous, the present perfect, and the present perfect continuous. These are the present tenses.

2 The present simple and the present continuous are used with reference to present time. If you are talking about the general present, or about a regular or habitual action, you use the present simple.

George lives in Birmingham.
They often phone my mother in London.

If you are talking about something in the present situation, you use the present continuous.

He's playing tennis at the University.
I'm cooking the dinner.

The present continuous is often used to refer to a temporary situation.

She's living in a flat at present.

3 You use the present perfect or the present perfect continuous when you are concerned with the present effects of something which happened at a time in the past, or which started in the past but is still continuing.

Have you seen the film at the Odeon?
We've been waiting here since before two o'clock.

4 If you are talking about something which is scheduled or timetabled to happen in the future, you can use the present simple tense.

The next train leaves at two fifteen in the morning.
It's Tuesday tomorrow.

5 If you are talking about something which has been arranged for the future, you can use the present continuous. When you use the present continuous like this, there is nearly always a time adverbial like 'tomorrow', 'next week', or 'later' in the clause.

We're going on holiday with my parents this year.
The Browns are having a party next week.

6 It is only in main clauses that the choice of tense can be related to a particular time. In subordinate clauses, for example in 'if'-clauses, time clauses, and defining relative clauses, present tenses often refer to a future time in relation to the time in the main clause.

You can go at five if you have finished.
Let's have a drink before we start.
We'll save some food for anyone who arrives late.

7 The present simple tense normally has no auxiliary verb, but questions and negative sentences are formed with the auxiliary 'do'.

Do you live round here?
Does your husband do most of the cooking?
They don't often phone during the week.
She doesn't like being late if she can help it.

Unit 42 The past tenses

Main points

- There are four past tenses - past simple, past continuous, past perfect, and past perfect continuous.
- All the past tenses are used to refer to past time.
- The past tenses are often used as polite forms.
- The past tenses have special meanings in conditional clauses and when referring to imaginary situations.

1 There are four tenses which begin with a verb in the past tense. They are the past simple, the past continuous, the past perfect, and the past perfect continuous. These are the past tenses. They are used to refer to past time, and also to refer to imaginary situations, and to express politeness.

2 The past simple and the past continuous are used with reference to past time. You use the past simple for events which happened in the past.

I woke up early and got out of bed.

If you are talking about the general past, or about regular or habitual actions in the past, you also use the past simple.

She lived just outside London.
We often saw his dog sitting outside his house.

If you are talking about something which continued to happen before and after a particular time in the past, you use the past continuous.

They were sitting in the kitchen, when they heard the explosion.
Jack arrived while the children were having their bath.

The past continuous is often used to refer to a temporary situation.

He was working at home at the time.
Bill was using my office until I came back from America.

3 You use the past perfect and past perfect continuous tenses when you are talking about the past and you are concerned with something which

happened at an earlier time, or which had started at an earlier time but was still continuing.

I had heard it was a good film so we decided to go and see it.
It was getting late. I had been waiting there since two o'clock.

4 You sometimes use a past tense rather than a present tense when you want to be more polite. For example, in the following pairs of sentences, the second one is more polite.

Do you want to see me now?
Did you want to see me now?

I wonder if you can help me.
I was wondering if you could help me.

5 The past tenses have special meanings in conditional clauses and when referring to hypothetical and imaginary situations, for example after 'I wish' or 'What if …?'. You use the past simple and past continuous for something that you think is unlikely to happen.

If they saw the mess, they would be very angry.
We would tell you if we were selling the house.

You use the past perfect and past perfect continuous when you are talking about something which could have happened in the past, but which did not actually happen.

If I had known that you were coming, I would have told Jim.
They wouldn't have gone to bed if they had been expecting you to arrive.

Unit 43 The continuous tenses

Main points

- Continuous tenses describe actions which continue to happen before and after a particular time.
- Continuous tenses can also indicate duration and change.

1 You use a continuous tense to indicate that an action continues to happen before and after a particular time, without stopping. You use the present continuous for actions which continue to happen before and after the moment of speaking.

I'm looking at the photographs my brother sent me.
They're having a meeting.

2 When you are talking about two actions in the present tense, you use the present continuous for an action that continues to happen before and after another action that interrupts it. You use the present simple for the other action.

The phone always rings when I'm having a bath.
Friends always talk to me when I'm trying to study.

3 When you are talking about the past, you use the past continuous for actions that continued to happen before and after another action, or before and after a particular time. This is often called the 'interrupted past'. You use the past simple for the other action.

He was watching television when the doorbell rang.
It was 6 o'clock. The train was nearing London.

WARNING: If two things happened one after another, you use two verbs in the past simple tense.

As soon as he saw me, he waved.

4 You can use continuous forms with modals in all their usual meanings. See Units 59 to 71 for more information on modals.

What could he be thinking of?
They might be telling lies.

5 You use continuous tenses to express duration, when you want to emphasize how long something has been happening or will happen for.

We had been living in Athens for five years.
They'll be staying with us for a couple of weeks.
He has been building up the business all his life.
By 1992, he will have been working for ten years.

Note that you do not have to use continuous tenses for duration.

We had lived in Africa for five years.
He worked for us for ten years.

6 You use continuous tenses to describe a state or situation that is temporary.

I'm living in London at the moment.
He'll be working nights next week.
She's spending the summer in Europe.

7 You use continuous tenses to show that something is changing, developing, or progressing.

Her English was improving.
The children are growing up quickly.
The video industry has been developing rapidly.

8 As a general rule, verbs which refer to actions that require a deliberate effort can be used in continuous tenses, verbs which refer to actions that do not require a deliberate effort are not used in continuous tenses.

I think it's going to rain. ('think' = 'believe'. Believing does not require deliberate effort)
Please be quiet. I'm thinking . ('think' = 'try to solve a problem'. Trying to solve a problem does require deliberate effort)

However, many verbs are not normally used in the continuous tenses. These include verbs that refer to thinking, liking and disliking, appearance, possession, and perception.
See Unit 45 for lists of these verbs.

Unit 44 The perfect tenses

Main points

- You use the present perfect to relate the past to the present.
- You use the past perfect to talk about a situation that occurred before a particular time in the past.

1 You use the present perfect tense when you are concerned with the present effects of something which happened at an indefinite time in the past.

I'm afraid I've forgotten my book.
Have you heard from Jill recently?

Sometimes, the present effects are important because the events are very recent.

Karen has just passed her exams.

You also use the present perfect when you are thinking of a time which started in the past and is still continuing.

Have you really lived here for ten years?
He has worked here since 1987.

You also use the present perfect in time clauses, when you are talking about something which will be done at some time in the future.

Tell me when you have finished.
I'll write to you as soon as I have heard from Jenny.

2 When you want to emphasize the fact that a recent event continued to happen for some time, you use the present perfect continuous.

She's been crying.
I've been working hard all day.

3 You use the past perfect tense when you are looking back from a point in past time, and you are concerned with the effects of something which happened at an earlier time in the past.

I apologized because I had forgotten my book.
He felt much happier once he had found a new job.
They would have come if we had invited them.

You also use the past perfect when you are thinking of a time which had started earlier in the past but was still continuing.

I was about twenty. I had been studying French for a couple of years.
He hated games and had always managed to avoid children's parties.

4 You use the future perfect tense when you are looking back from a point in the future and you are talking about something which will have happened at a time between now and that future point.

In another two years, you will have left school.
Take these tablets, and in twenty-four hours the pain will have gone.

You also use the future perfect when you are looking back from the present and guessing that an action will be finished.

I'm sure they will have arrived home by now.
It's too late to ring Don. He will have left the house by now.

5 You can also use other modals with 'have', when you are looking back from a point in time at something which you think may have happened at an earlier time.

I might have finished work by then.
He should have arrived in Paris by the time we phone.

For more information on modals with 'have', see Units 59 to 71.

Unit 45 Talking about the present

Main points

- For the general present, general truths, and habitual actions, you use the present simple.
- For something which is happening now, or for temporary situations, you use the present continuous.

---

1 If you are talking about the present in general, you normally use the present simple tense. You use the present simple for talking about the general present including the present moment.

My dad works in Saudi Arabia.
He lives in the French Alps near the Swiss border.

2 If you are talking about general truths, you use the present simple.

Water boils at 100 degrees centigrade.
Love makes the world go round.
The bus takes longer than the train.

3 If you are talking about regular or habitual actions, you use the present simple.

Do you eat meat?
I get up early and eat my breakfast in bed.
I pay the milkman on Fridays.

4 If you are talking about something which is regarded as temporary, you use the present continuous.

Do you know if she's still playing tennis these days?
I'm working as a British Council officer.

5 If you are talking about something which is happening now, you normally use the present continuous tense.

We're having a meeting. Come and join in.
Wait a moment. I'm listening to the news.

6 There are a number of verbs which are used in the present simple tense even when you are talking about the present moment. These verbs are not normally used in the present continuous or the other continuous tenses. These verbs usually refer to:

> **thinking:** believe forget imagine know realize recognize suppose think understand want wish
> **liking and disliking:** admire dislike hate like love prefer
> **appearance:** appear look like resemble seem
> **possession:** belong to contain have include own possess
> **perception:** hear see smell taste
> **being:** be consist of exist

I believe he was not to blame.
She hates going to parties.
Our neighbours have two cars.

Note that you normally use verbs of perception with the modal 'can', rather than using the present simple tense.

I can smell gas.

Some other common verbs are not normally used in the present continuous or the other continuous tenses.

> concern fit involve mean surprise
> deserve interest matter satisfy

What do you mean?

WARNING: Some of the verbs listed above can be used in continuous tenses in other meanings. For example, 'have' referring to possession is not used in continuous tenses. You do not say 'I am having a car'. But note the following examples.

We're having a party tomorrow.
He's having problems with his car.
She's having a shower.

Unit 46 Talking about the past

Main points

- For actions, situations, or regular events in the past, you use the past simple. For regular events in the past, you can also use 'would' or 'used to'.
- For events that happened before and after a time in the past, and for temporary situations, you use the past continuous.
- For present effects of past situations, you use the present perfect, and for past effects of earlier events you use the past perfect.
- For future in the past, you use 'would', 'was / were going to', or the past continuous.

1 When you want to talk about an event that occurred at a particular time in the past, you use the past simple.

The Prime Minister flew into New York yesterday.
The new term started last week.

You also use the past simple to talk about a situation that existed over a period of time in the past.

We spent most of our time at home last winter.
They earned their money quickly that year.

2 When you want to talk about something which took place regularly in the past, you use the past simple.

They went for picnics most weekends.
We usually spent the winter at Aunt Meg's house.

WARNING: The past simple always refers to a time in the past. A time reference is necessary to say what time in the past you are referring to. The time reference can be established in an earlier sentence or by another speaker, but it must be established.

When you want to talk about something which occurred regularly in the past, you can use 'would' or 'used to' instead of the past simple.

We would normally spend the winter in Miami.
People used to believe that the world was flat.

WARNING: You do not normally use 'would' with this meaning with verbs which are not used in the continuous tenses. For a list of these verbs, see Unit 45.

3 When you want to talk about something which continued to happen before and after a given time in the past, you use the past continuous.

I hurt myself when I was mending my bike.
It was midnight. She was driving home.

You also use the past continuous to talk about a temporary state of affairs in the past.

Our team were losing 2-1 at the time.
We were staying with friends in Italy.

For more information on continuous tenses, see Unit 43.

4 When you are concerned with the present effects or future effects of something which happened at an indefinite time in the past, you use the present perfect.

I'm afraid I've forgotten my book, so I don't know.
He's broken his leg, so he won't be able to come.

You also use the present perfect when you are thinking of a time which started in the past and still continues.

Have you ever stolen anything? (= at any time up to the present)
He has been here since six o'clock. (= and he is still here)

5 When you are looking back from a point in past time, and you are concerned with the effects of something which happened at an earlier time in the past, you use the past perfect.

I apologized because I had left my wallet at home.
They would have come if we had invited them.

6 When you want to talk about the future from a point of view in past time, you can use 'would', 'was / were going to', or the past continuous.

He thought to himself how wonderful it would taste.
Her daughter was going to do the cooking.
Mike was taking his test the week after.

Unit 47 Reporting the past

Main points

- A report structure is used to report what people say or think.
- You use the present tense of the reporting verb when you are reporting something that someone says or thinks at the time you are speaking.
- You often use past tenses in report structures because a reported clause usually reports something that was said or believed in the past.

1 You use a report structure to report what people say or think. A report structure consists of two parts. One part is the reporting clause, which contains the reporting verb.

I told him nothing was going to happen to me.
I agreed that he should do it.

The other part is the reported clause.

He felt that he had to do something.
Henry said he wanted to go home.

See Units 88 and 89 for more information on report structures.

2 For the verb in the reporting clause, you choose a tense that is appropriate at the time you are speaking.
Because reports are usually about something that was said or believed in the past, both the reporting verb and the verb in the reported clause are often in a past tense.

Mrs Kaur announced that the lecture had begun.
At the time, we thought that he was mad.

3 Although you normally use past tenses in reports about the past, you can use a present tense in the reported clause if what you are saying is important in the present, for example:

- because you want to emphasize that it is still true

Did you tell him that this young woman is looking for a job?

- because you want to give advice or a warning, or make a suggestion for the present or future

I told you they have this class on Friday afternoon, so you should have come a bit earlier.

4 You use a present tense for the reporting verb when you are reporting:

- what someone says or thinks at the time you are speaking

She says she wants to see you this afternoon.
I think there's something wrong.

Note that, as in the last example, it may be your own thoughts that you are reporting.

- what someone often says

He says that no one understands him.

- what someone has said in the past, if what they said is still true

My doctor says it's nothing to worry about.

5 If you are predicting what people will say or think, you use a future tense for the reporting verb.

No doubt he will claim that his car broke down.
They will think we are making a fuss.

6 You very rarely try to report the exact words of a statement. You usually give a summary of what was said. For example, John might say:

'I tried to phone you about six times yesterday. I let the phone ring for ages but there was no answer. I couldn't get through at all so I finally gave up.'

You would probably report this as:

John said he tried to phone several times yesterday, but he couldn't get through.

7 When you are telling a story of your own, or one that you have heard from someone else, direct speech simply becomes part of the narrative.
In this extract a taxi driver picks up a passenger:

'What part of London are you headed for?' I asked him. 'I'm going to Epsom for the races. It's Derby day today.' 'So it is,' I said. 'I wish I were going with you. I love betting on horses.'

You might report this as part of the narrative without reporting verbs:

My passenger was going to Epsom to see the Derby, and I wanted to go with him.

Unit 48 Talking about the future using 'will' and 'going to'

Main points

- When you are making predictions about the future or talking about future intentions, you can use either 'will' or 'going to'.
- For promises and offers relating to the future, you use 'will'.
- For future events based on arrangements, you use the future continuous.
- For events that will happen before a time in the future, you use the future perfect.

1 You cannot talk about the future with as much certainty as you can about the present or the past. You are usually talking about what you think might happen or what you intend to happen. This is why you often use modals. Although most modals can be used with future reference, you most often use the modal 'will' to talk about the future.

Nancy will arrange it.
When will I see them?

2 When you are making predictions about the future that are based on general beliefs, opinions, or attitudes, you use 'will'.

The weather tomorrow will be warm and sunny.
I'm sure you will enjoy your visit to the zoo.

This use of 'will' is common in sentences with conditional clauses.

You'll be late, if you don't hurry.

When you are using facts or events in the present situation as evidence for a prediction, you can use 'going to'.

It's going to rain. (I can see black clouds)
I'm going to be late. (I have missed my train)

3 When you are talking about your own intentions, you use 'will' or 'going to'.

I'll ring you tonight.
I'm going to stay at home today.

When you are saying what someone else has decided to do, you use 'going to'.

They're going to have a party.

WARNING: You do not normally use 'going to' with the verb 'go'. You usually just say 'I'm going' rather than 'I'm going to go'.

'What are you going to do this weekend?' - 'I'm going to the cinema.'

When you are announcing a decision you have just made or are about to make, you use 'will'.

I'm tired. I think I'll go to bed.

4 In promises and offers relating to the future, you often use 'will' with the meaning 'be willing to'.

I'll do what I can.
I'll help with the washing-up.

Note that you can use 'will' with this meaning in an 'if'-clause.

I'll put you through, if you'll hang on for a minute. (= if you are willing to hang on for a minute)

WARNING: Remember that you do not normally use 'will' in 'if'-clauses. See Unit 91 for more information on 'if'-clauses.

If you do that, you will be wasting your time.
The children will call out if they think he is wrong.

5 When you want to say that something will happen because arrangements have been made, you use the future continuous tense.

I'll be seeing them when I've finished with you.
I'll be waiting for you outside.
She'll be appearing at the Royal Festival Hall.

6 When you want to talk about something that has not happened yet but will happen before a particular time in the future, you use the future perfect tense.

By the time we phone he'll already have started.
By 1992, he will have worked for twelve years.

Unit 49 Talking about the future using present tenses

Main points

- When you are talking about the future in relation to official timetables or the calendar, you use the present simple.
- When talking about people's plans and arrangements for the future, you use the present continuous.
- In 'if'-clauses, time clauses, and defining relative clauses, you can use the present simple to refer to the future.

1 When you are talking about something in the future which is based on an official timetable or calendar, you use the present simple tense. You usually put a time adverbial in these sentences.

My last train leaves Euston at 11.30.
The UN General Assembly opens in New York this month.
Our next lesson is on Thursday.
We set off early tomorrow morning in Ken's car.

2 In statements about fixed dates, you normally use the present simple.

Tomorrow is Tuesday.
It's my birthday next month.
Monday is the seventeenth of July.

3 When you want to talk about people's plans or arrangements for the future, you use the present continuous tense.

I'm meeting Bill next week.
They're getting married in June.

4 You often talk about the future using the present tense of verbs such as 'hope', 'expect', 'intend', and 'want' with a 'to'-infinitive clause, especially when you want to indicate your uncertainty about what will actually happen.

We hope to see you soon.
Bill expects to be back at work tomorrow.

After the verb 'hope', you often use the present simple to refer to the future.

I hope you enjoy your holiday.

5 In subordinate clauses, the relationship between tense and time are different. In 'if'-clauses and time clauses, you normally use the present simple for future reference.

If he comes, I'll let you know.
Please start when you are ready.
We won't start until everyone arrives.
Lock the door after you finally leave.

6 In defining relative clauses, you normally use the present simple, not 'will', to refer to the future.

Any decision that you make will need her approval.
Give my love to any friends you meet.
There is a silver cup for the runner who finishes first.

7 If you want to show that a condition has to be the case before an action can be carried out, you use the present perfect for future events.

We won't start until everyone has arrived.
I'll let you know when I have arranged everything.

Unit 50 Questions

Main points

- In most questions the first verb comes before the subject.
- 'Yes/no'-questions begin with an auxiliary or a modal.
- 'Wh'-questions begin with a 'wh'-word.

1 Questions which can be answered 'yes' or 'no' are called 'yes/no'-questions.

'Are you ready?' - *'Yes.'*
'Have you read this magazine?' - *'No.'*

If the verb group has more than one word, the first word comes at the beginning of the sentence, before the subject. The rest of the verb group comes after the subject.

Is he coming?
Can John swim?
Will you have finished by lunchtime?
Couldn't you have been a bit quieter?
Has he been working?

2 If the verb group consists of only a main verb, you use the auxiliary 'do', 'does', or 'did' at the beginning of the sentence, before the subject. After the subject you use the base form of the verb.

Do the British take sport seriously?
Does that sound like anyone you know?
Did he go to the fair?

Note that when the main verb is 'do', you still have to add 'do', 'does', or 'did' before the subject.

Do they do the work themselves?
Did you do an 'O' Level in German?

3 If the main verb is 'have', you usually put 'do', 'does', or 'did' before the subject.

Does anyone have a question?
Did you have a good flight?

When 'have' means 'own' or 'possess', you can put it before the subject, without using 'do', 'does', or 'did', but this is less common.

Has he any idea what it's like?

4 If the main verb is the present simple or past simple of 'be', you put the verb at the beginning of the sentence, before the subject.

Are you ready?
Was it lonely without us?

5 When you want someone to give you more information than just 'yes' or 'no', you ask a 'wh'-question, which begins with a 'wh'-word:

what	where	who	whose	~
when	which	whom	why	how

Note that 'whom' is only used in formal English.

6 When a 'wh'-word is the subject of a question, the 'wh'-word comes first, then the verb group. You do not add 'do', 'does', or 'did' as an auxiliary.

What happened?
Which is the best restaurant?
Who could have done it?

7 When a 'wh'-word is the object of a verb or preposition, the 'wh'-word comes first, then you follow the rules for 'yes/no'-questions, adding 'do', 'does', or 'did' where necessary.

How many are there?
Which do you like best?

If there is a preposition, it comes at the end. However, you always put the preposition before 'whom'.

What's this for?
With whom were you talking?

Note that you follow the same rules as for 'wh'-words as objects when the question begins with 'when', 'where', 'why', or 'how'.

When would you be coming down?
Why did you do it?
Where did you get that from?

8 You can also use 'what', 'which', 'whose', 'how many', and 'how much' with a noun.

Whose idea was it?
How much money have we got in the bank?

You can use 'which', 'how many', and 'how much' with 'of' and a noun group.

Which of the suggested answers was the correct one?
How many of them bothered to come?

See Unit 51 for more information on 'wh'-words.

Unit 51 'Wh'-words

Main points

- You use 'who', 'whom', and 'whose' to ask about people, and 'which' to ask about people or things.
- You use 'what' to ask about things, and 'what for' to ask about reasons and purposes.
- You use 'how' to ask about the way something happens.
- You use 'when' to ask about times, 'why' to ask about reasons, and 'where' to ask about places and directions.

1 You use 'who', 'whom', or 'whose' in questions about people. 'Who' is used to ask questions about the subject or object of the verb, or about the object of a preposition.

Who discovered this?
Who did he marry?
Who did you dance with?

In formal English, 'whom' is used as the object of a verb or preposition. The preposition always comes in front of 'whom'.

Whom did you see?
For whom were they supposed to do it?

You use 'whose' to ask which person something belongs to or is related to. 'Whose' can be the subject or the object.

Whose is nearer?
Whose did you prefer, hers or mine?

2 You use 'which' to ask about one person or thing, out of a number of people or things. 'Which' can be the subject or object.

Which is your son?
Which does she want?

3 You use 'what' to ask about things, for example about actions and events. 'What' can be the subject or object.

What has happened to him?
What is he selling?
What will you talk about?

You use 'what...for' to ask about the reason for an action, or the purpose of an object.

What are you going there for?
What are those lights for?

4 You use 'how' to ask about the way in which something happens or is done.

How did you know we were coming?
How are you going to get home?

You also use 'how' to ask about the way a person or thing feels or looks.

'How are you?' - 'Well, how do I look?'

5 'How' is also used:

- with adjectives to ask about the degree of a quality that someone or something has

How good are you at Maths?
How hot shall I make the curry?

- with adjectives such as 'big', 'old', and 'far' to ask about size, age, and distance

How old are your children?
How far is it to Montreal from here?

Note that you do not normally use 'How small', 'How young', or 'How near'.

- with adverbs such as 'long' and 'often' to ask about time, or 'well' to ask about abilities

How long have you lived here?
How well can you read?

- with 'many' and 'much' to ask about the number or amount of something

How many were there?
How much did he tell you?

6 You use 'when' to ask about points in time or periods of time, 'why' to ask about the reason for an action, and 'where' to ask about place and direction.

When are you coming home?
When were you in London?
Why are you here?
Where is the station?
Where are you going?

You can also ask about direction using 'which direction...in' or 'which way'.

Which direction did he go in?
Which way did he go?

Unit 52 Question tags: forms

Main points:

- You add a question tag to a statement to turn it into a question.
- A question tag consists of a verb and a pronoun. The verb in a question tag is always an auxiliary, a modal, or a form of the main verb 'be'.
- With a positive statement, you usually use a negative question tag containing a short form ending in '-n't'.
- With a negative statement, you always use a positive question tag.

1 A question tag is a short phrase that is added to the end of a statement to turn it into a 'yes/no'-question. You use question tags when you want to ask someone to confirm or disagree with what you are saying, or when you want to sound more polite. Question tags are rarely used in formal written English.

He's very friendly, isn't he?
You haven't seen it before, have you?

2 You form a question tag by using an auxiliary, a modal, or a form of the main verb 'be', followed by a pronoun. The pronoun refers to the subject of the statement.

David's school is quite nice, isn't it?
She made a remarkable recovery, didn't she?

3 If the statement contains an auxiliary or modal, the same auxiliary or modal is used in the question tag.

Jill's coming tomorrow, isn't she?
You didn't know I was an artist, did you?
You've never been to Benidorm, have you?
You will stay in touch, won't you?

4 If the statement does not contain an auxiliary, a modal, or 'be' as a main verb, you use 'do', 'does', or 'did' in the question tag.

You like it here, don't you?
Sally still works there, doesn't she?
He played for Ireland, didn't he?

5 If the statement contains the present simple or past simple of 'be' as a main verb, the same form of the verb 'be' is used in the question tag.

It is quite warm, isn't it?
They were really rude, weren't they?

6 If the statement contains the simple present or simple past of 'have' as a main verb, you usually use 'do', 'does', or 'did' in the question tag.

He has a problem, doesn't he?

You can also use the same form of 'have' in the question tag, but this is not very common.

She has a large house, hasn't she?

7 With a positive statement you normally use a negative question tag, formed by adding '-n't' to the verb.

You like Ralph a lot, don't you?
They are beautiful, aren't they?

Note that the negative question tag with 'I' is 'aren't'.

I'm a fool, aren't I?

8 With a negative statement you always use a positive question tag.

It doesn't work, does it?
You won't tell anyone else, will you?

Unit 53 Question tags: uses

Main points

- You can use negative statements with positive question tags to make requests.
- You use positive statements with positive question tags to show reactions.
- You use some question tags to make imperatives more polite.

1 You can use a negative statement and a positive question tag to ask people for things, or to ask for help or information.

You wouldn't sell it to me, would you?
You won't tell anyone else this, will you?

2 When you want to show your reaction to what someone has just said, for example by expressing interest, surprise, doubt, or anger, you use a positive statement with a positive question tag.

You've been to North America before, have you?
You fell on your back, did you?
I borrowed your car last night. - Oh, you did, did you?

3 When you use an imperative, you can be more polite by adding one of the following question tags.

will you	won't you	would you

See that she gets safely back, won't you?
Look at that, would you?

When you use a negative imperative, you can only use 'will you' as a question tag.

Don't tell Howard, will you?

'Will you' and 'won't you' can also be used to emphasize anger or impatience. 'Can't you' is also used in this way.

Oh, hurry up, will you!
For goodness sake be quiet, can't you!

4 You use the question tag 'shall we' when you make a suggestion using 'let's'.

Let's forget it, shall we?

You use the question tag 'shall I' after 'I'll'.

I'll tell you, shall I?

5 You use 'they' in question tags after 'anybody', 'anyone', 'everybody', 'everyone', 'nobody', 'no one', 'somebody', or 'someone'.

Everyone will be leaving on Friday, won't they?
Nobody had bothered to plant new ones, had they?

You use 'it' in question tags after 'anything', 'everything', 'nothing', or 'something'.

Nothing matters now, does it?
Something should be done, shouldn't it?

You use 'there' in question tags after 'there is', 'there are', 'there was', or 'there were'.

There's a new course out now, isn't there?

6 When you are replying to a question tag, your answer refers to the statement, not the question tag.

If you want to confirm a positive statement, you say 'yes'. For example, if you have finished a piece of work and someone says to you 'You've finished that, haven't you?', the answer is 'yes'.

'It became stronger, didn't it?' - 'Yes, it did.'

If you want to disagree with a positive statement, you say 'no'. For example, if you have not finished your work and someone says 'You've finished that, haven't you?', the answer is 'no'.

You've just seen a performance of the play, haven't you? - No, not yet.

If you want to confirm a negative statement, you say 'no'. For example, if you have not finished your work and someone says 'You haven't finished that, have you?', the answer is 'no'.

'You didn't know that, did you?' - 'No.'

If you want to disagree with a negative statement, you say 'yes'. For example, if you have finished a piece of work and someone says 'You haven't finished that, have you?', the answer is 'yes'.

'You haven't been there, have you?' - 'Yes, I have.'

Unit 54 Indirect and reported questions

Main points

- You use indirect questions to ask for information or help.
- You use reported questions to talk about a question that someone else has asked.
- In indirect and reported questions, the subject of the question comes before the verb.
- You use 'if' or 'whether' in indirect and reported 'yes/no'-questions.

1 When you ask someone for information, you can use an indirect question beginning with a phrase such as 'Could you tell me..' or 'Do you know..'.

Could you tell me how far it is to the bank?
Do you know where Jane is?

2 When you want to ask someone politely to do something, you can use an indirect question after 'I wonder'.

I wonder if you can help me.

You also use 'I wonder' followed by an indirect question to indicate what you are thinking about.

I wonder what she'll look like.
I wonder which hotel it was.

3 When you are talking about a question that someone has asked, you use a reported question.

She asked me why I was so late.
He wanted to know where I was going.
I demanded to know what was going on.
I asked her if I could help her.
I asked her whether there was anything wrong.

In formal and written English, 'enquire' (also spelled 'inquire') is often used instead of 'ask'.

Wilkie had enquired if she did a lot of acting.
He inquired whether he could see her.

4 In indirect and reported questions, the subject of the question comes before the verb, just as it does in affirmative sentences.

Do you know where Jane is?
I wonder if you can help me.
She asked me why I was late.

5 You do not normally use the auxiliary 'do' in indirect or reported questions.

Can you remember when they open on Sundays?
I wonder what he feels about it.
She asked him if his parents spoke French.

The auxiliary 'do' can be used in indirect or reported questions, but only for emphasis, or to make a contrast with something that has already been said. It is not put before the subject as in direct questions.

She asked me whether I really did mean it.
I told him I didn't like classical music. He asked me what kind of music I did like.

6 You use 'if' or 'whether' to introduce indirect and reported 'yes/no'-questions.

I wonder if you'd give the children a bath?
I am writing to ask whether you would care to come and visit us.

'Whether' is used especially when there is a choice of possibilities.

I was asked whether I wanted to stay at a hotel or at his home.
They asked whether Tim was or was not in the team.

Note that you can put 'or not' immediately after 'whether', but not immediately after 'if'.

The police didn't ask whether or not they were in.

7 When you are reporting a question, the verb in the reported clause is often in a past tense. This is because you are often talking about the past when you are reporting someone else's words.

She asked me why I was so late.
Pat asked him if she had hurt him.

However, you can use a present or future tense if the question you are reporting relates to the present or future.

Mark was asking if you're enjoying your new job.
They asked if you'll be there tomorrow night.

See Units 47, 88, and 89 for more information on reporting.

Unit 55 Short answers

Main points

- A short answer uses an auxiliary, a modal, or the main verb 'be'.
- A short answer can be in the form of a statement or a question.

1 Short answers are very common in spoken English. For example, when someone asks you a 'yes/no'-question, you can give a short answer by using a pronoun with an auxiliary, modal, or the main verb 'be'. You usually put 'yes' or 'no' before the short answer.

'Does she still want to come?' — 'Yes, she does.'
'Can you imagine what it might feel like?' — 'No, I can't.'
'Are you married?' — 'I am.'

Note that a short answer such as 'Yes, I will' is more polite or friendly than just 'Yes', or than repeating all the words used in the question. People often repeat all the words used in the question when they feel angry or impatient.

'Will you have finished by lunchtime?' — 'Yes, I will have finished by lunchtime.'

2 You can also use short answers to agree or disagree with what someone says.

'You don't like Joan?' — 'No, I don't.'
'I'm not coming with you.' — 'Yes, you are.'

If the statement that you are commenting on does not contain an auxiliary, modal, or the main verb 'be', you use a form of 'do' in the short answer.

'He never comes on time.' — 'Oh yes he does.'

3 You often reply to what has been said by using a short question.

'He's not in Japan now.' — 'Oh, isn't he?'
'He gets free meals.' — 'Does he?'

Note that questions like these are not always asked to get information, but are often used to express your reaction to what has been said, for example to show interest or surprise.

'Dad doesn't help me at all.' — 'Doesn't he? Why not?'
'Penny has been climbing before.' — 'Oh, has she? When was that?'

4 If you want to show that you definitely agree with a positive statement that someone has just made, you can use a negative short question.

'Well, that was very nice.' — 'Yes, wasn't it?'

5 When you want to ask for more information, you can use a 'wh'-word on its own or with a noun as a short answer.

'He saw a snake.' — 'Where?'
'He knew my cousin.' — 'Which cousin?'

You can also use 'Which' one' and 'Which ones'.

'Can you pass me the cup?' — 'Which one?'

6 Sometimes a statement about one person also applies to another person. When this is the case, you can use a short answer with 'so' for positive statements, and with 'neither' or 'nor' for negative statements, using the same verb that was used in the statement.
You use 'so', 'neither', or 'nor' with an auxiliary, modal, or the main verb 'be'. The verb comes before the subject.

'You were different then.' — 'So were you.'
'I don't normally drink at lunch.' — 'Neither do I.'
'I can't do it.' — 'Nor can I.'

You can use 'not either' instead of 'neither', in which case the verb comes after the subject.

'He doesn't understand.' — 'We don't either.'

7 You often use 'so' in short answers after verbs such as 'think', 'hope', 'expect', 'imagine', and 'suppose', when you think that the answer to the question is 'yes'.

'You'll be home at six?' — 'I hope so.'
'So it was worth doing?' — 'I suppose so.'

You use 'I'm afraid so' when you are sorry that the answer is 'yes'.

'Is it raining?' — 'I'm afraid so.'

With 'suppose', 'think', 'imagine', or 'expect' in short answers, you also form negatives with 'so'.

'Will I see you again?' — 'I don't suppose so.'
'Is Barry Knight a golfer?' — 'No, I don't think so.'

However, you say 'I hope not' and 'I'm afraid not'.

'It isn't empty, is it?' — 'I hope not.'

Unit 56 The imperative and 'let'

Main points

- The imperative is the same as the base form of a verb.
- You form a negative imperative with 'do not', 'don't', or 'never'.
- You use the imperative to ask or tell someone to do something, or to give advice, warnings, or instructions on how to do something.
- You use 'let' when you are offering to do something, making suggestions, or telling someone to do something.

1 The imperative is the same as the base form of a verb. You do not use a pronoun in front of it.

Come to my place.
Start when you hear the bell.

2 You form a negative imperative by putting 'do not', 'don't', or 'never' in front of the verb.

Do not write in this book.
Don't go so fast.
Never open the front door to strangers.

3 You use the imperative when you are:

● asking or telling someone to do something

Pass the salt.
Hurry up!

● giving someone advice or a warning

Mind your head.
Take care!

● giving someone instructions on how to do something

Put this bit over here, so it fits into that hole.
Turn right off Broadway into Caxton Street.

4 When you want to make an imperative more polite or more emphatic, you can put 'do' in front of it.

Do have a chocolate biscuit.
Do stop crying.
Do be careful.

5 The imperative is also used in written instructions on how to do something, for example on notices and packets of food, and in books.

To report faults, dial 6666.
Store in a dry place.
Fry the chopped onion and pepper in the oil.

Note that written instructions usually have to be short. This means that words such as 'the' are often omitted.

Wear rubber gloves. Turn off switch. Wipe bulb.

Written imperatives are also used to give warnings.

Reduce speed now.

6 You use 'let me' followed by the base form of a verb when you are offering to do something for someone.

Let me take your coat.
Let me give you a few details.

7 You use 'let's' followed by the base form of a verb when you are suggesting what you and someone else should do.

Let's go outside.
Let's look at our map.

Note that the form 'let us' is only used in formal or written English.

Let us consider a very simple example.

You put 'do' before 'let's' when you are very keen to do something.

Do let's get a taxi.

The negative of 'let's' is 'let's not' or 'don't let's'.

Let's not talk about that.
Don't let's actually write it in the book.

8 You use 'let' followed by a noun group and the base form of a verb when you are telling someone to do something or to allow someone else to do it.

Let me see it.
Let Philip have a look at it.

Unit 57 Negative sentences with 'not'

Main points

- 'Not' is often shortened to '-n't' and added to some verbs.
- You put 'not' after the first verb in the verb group, or you use a short form.

1 In spoken and in informal written English, 'not' is often shortened to '-n't' and added to an auxiliary, a modal, or a form of the main verb 'be'.

I haven't heard from her recently.
I wasn't angry.

Here is a list of short forms.

isn't	haven't	doesn't	mightn't	won't
aren't	hasn't	didn't	mustn't	wouldn't
wasn't	hadn't	~	oughtn't	~
weren't	~	can't	shan't	daren't
~	don't	couldn't	shouldn't	needn't

If the verb is already shortened, you cannot add '-n't'.

It's not easy.
I've not had time.

You cannot add '-n't' to 'am'. You use 'I'm not'.

I'm not excited.

2 If the verb group has more than one word, you put 'not' after the first word, or you use a short form.

I was not smiling.
He hadn't attended many meetings.
They might not notice.
I haven't been playing football recently.

3 If the sentence only contains a main verb other than 'be', you use the auxiliary 'do'.
You use 'do not', 'does not', 'did not', or a short form, followed by the base form of the main verb.

They do not need to talk.
He does not speak English very well.
I didn't know that.

Note that if the main verb is 'do', you still use a form of 'do' as an auxiliary.

They didn't do anything about it.

4 If the main verb is the present or past simple of 'be', you put 'not' immediately after it, or you use a short form.

It is not difficult to understand.
It's not the same, is it?
He wasn't a bad actor actually.

5 If the main verb is 'have', you usually use a form of 'do' as an auxiliary.

They don't have any money.

You can also use a short form, or you can put 'not' after the verb but this is not very common.

He hadn't enough money.

6 You can put 'not' in front of an '-ing' form or a 'to'-infinitive.

We stood there, not knowing what to do.
Try not to worry.

7 In negative questions, you use a short form.

Why didn't she win at the Olympics?
Hasn't he put on weight?
Aren't you bored?

8 You can use a negative question:

- to express your feelings, for example to show that you are surprised or disappointed

Hasn't he done it yet?

- in exclamations

Isn't the weather awful!

- when you think you know something and you just want someone to agree with you

'Aren't you Joanne's brother?' - 'Yes, I am.'

9 Note the meaning of 'yes' and 'no' in answers to negative questions.

'Isn't Tracey going to get a bit bored in Birmingham?'
— 'Yes.' (She is going to get bored.)
— 'No.' (She is not going to get bored.)

Unit 58 Negative words

Main points

- A negative sentence contains a negative word.
- You do not normally use two negative words in the same clause.

1 Negative statements contain a negative word.

not	none	no one	~
never	~	nothing	neither
no	nobody	nowhere	nor

See Unit 57 for negative statements using 'not'.

2 You use 'never' to say that something was not the case at any time, or will not be the case at any time.
If the verb group has more than one word, you put 'never' after the first word.

I've never had such a horrible meal.
He could never trust her again.

3 If the only verb in the sentence is the present simple or past simple of any main verb except 'be', you put 'never' before the verb.

She never goes abroad.
He never went to university.

If the only verb in the sentence is the present simple or past simple of the main verb 'be', you normally put 'never' after the verb.

He's never late.
There were never any people in the house.

You can also use 'never' at the beginning of an imperative sentence.

Never walk alone late at night.

4 You use 'no' before a noun to say that something does not exist or is not available.

He has given no reason for his decision.
The island has no trees at all.

Note that if there is another negative word in the clause, you use 'any', not 'no'.

It won't do any good.

5 You use 'none' or 'none of' to say that there is not even one thing or person, or not even a small amount of something.

You can't go to a college here because there are none in this area.
'Where's the coffee?' - 'There's none left.'
None of us understood the play.

See Unit 15 for more information on 'none' and 'none of'.

6 You also use 'nobody', 'no one', 'nothing', and 'nowhere' in negative statements.
You use 'nobody' or 'no one' to talk about people.

Nobody in her house knows any English.
No one knew.

'No one' can also be written 'no-one'.

There's no-one here.

You use 'nothing' to talk about things.

There's nothing you can do.

You use 'nowhere' to talk about places.

There's almost nowhere left to go.

See Unit 10 for more information about these words.

7 You do not normally use two negative words in the same clause. For example, you do not say 'Nobody could see nothing'. You say 'Nobody could see anything'.
You use 'anything', 'anyone', 'anybody', and 'anywhere' instead of 'nothing, 'no one', 'nobody', and 'nowhere' when the clause already contains a negative word.

No-one can find Howard or Barbara anywhere.
I could never discuss anything with them.

8 The only negative words that are often used together in the same clause are 'neither' and 'nor'.
You use 'neither' and 'nor' together to say that two alternatives are not possible, not likely, or not true.

Neither Margaret nor John was there.
They had neither food nor money.

Unit 59 Introduction to modals

can, could, may, might, must, ought, shall, should, will, would

Main points

- Modals are always the first word in a verb group.
- All modals except for 'ought' are followed by the base form of a verb.
- 'Ought' is followed by a 'to'-infinitive.
- Modals have only one form.

Modals can be used for various different purposes. These are explained in Units 60-71.

1 Modals are always the first word in a verb group. All modals except for 'ought' are followed by the base form of a verb.

I must leave fairly soon.
I think it will look rather nice.
Things might have been so different.
People may be watching.

2 'Ought' is always followed by a 'to'-infinitive.

She ought to go straight back to England.
Sam ought to have realized how dangerous it was.
You ought to be doing this.

3 Modals have only one form. There is no '-s' form for the third person singular of the present tense, and there are no '-ing' or '-ed' forms.

There's nothing I can do about it.
I'm sure he can do it.

4 Modals do not normally indicate the time when something happens. There are, however, a few exceptions.
'Shall' and 'will' often indicate a future event or situation.

I shall do what you suggested.
He will not return for many hours.

'Could' is used as the past form of 'can' to express ability. 'Would' is used as the past form of 'will' to express the future.

When I was young, I could run for miles.
He remembered that he would see his mother the next day.

5 In spoken English and informal written English, 'shall' and 'will' are shortened to '-'ll', and 'would' to '-'d', and added to a pronoun.

I'll see you tomorrow.
I hope you'll agree.
Posy said she'd love to stay.

'Shall', 'will', and 'would' are never shortened if they come at the end of a sentence.

Paul said he would come, and I hope he will.

In spoken English, you can also add '-'ll' and '-'d' to nouns.

My car'll be outside.
The headmaster'd be furious.

WARNING: Remember that '-d' is also the short form of the auxiliary 'had'.

I'd heard it many times.

Unit 60 Modals - negatives and questions

Main points

- You use negative words with modals to make negative clauses.
- Modals go in front of the subject in questions.
- You never use two modals together.

1 To make a clause negative, you put a negative word immediately after the modal.

You must not worry.
I can never remember his name.
He ought not to have done that.

'Can not' is always written as one word, 'cannot'.

I cannot go back.

However, if 'can' is followed by 'not only', 'can' and 'not' are not joined.

We can not only book your flight for you, but also advise you about hotels.

2 In spoken English and informal written English, 'not' is often shortened to '-n't' and added to the modal. The following modals are often shortened in this way:

could not	⇨ couldn't
should not	⇨ shouldn't
must not	⇨ mustn't
would not	⇨ wouldn't

We couldn't leave the farm.
You mustn't talk about Ron like that.

Note the following irregular short forms:

shall not	⇨ shan't
will not	⇨ won't
cannot	⇨ can't

I shan't let you go.
Won't you change your mind?
We can't stop now.

'Might not' and 'ought not' are sometimes shortened to 'mightn't' and 'oughtn't'.
Note that 'may not' is very rarely shortened to 'mayn't' in modern English.

3 To make a question, you put the modal in front of the subject.

Could you give me an example?
Will you be coming in later?
Shall I shut the door?

Modals are also used in question tags. See Units 52 and 53 for more information.

4 You never use two modals together. For example, you cannot say 'He will can come'. Instead you can say 'He will be able to come'.

I shall have to go.
Your husband might have to give up work.

5 Instead of using modals, you can often use other verbs and expressions to make requests, offers, or suggestions, to express wishes or intentions, or to show that you are being polite.
For example, 'be able to' is used instead of 'can', 'be likely to' is used instead of 'might', and 'have to' is used instead of 'must'.

All members are able to claim expenses.
I think that we are likely to see more of this.

These expressions are also used after modals.

I really thought I wouldn't be able to visit you this week.

6 'Dare' and 'need' sometimes behave like modals.
See Unit 84 for information on 'dare' and Units 70 and 83 for information on 'need'.

Unit 61 Can, could, may, might - possibility

Main points

- You use 'can' to say that something is possible.
- You use 'could', 'might', and 'may' to indicate that you are not certain whether something is possible, but you think it is.

1 When you want to say that something is possible, you use 'can'.

Cooking can be a real pleasure.
In some cases this can cause difficulty.

You use 'cannot' or 'can't' to say that something is not possible.

This cannot be the answer.
You can't be serious.

2 When you want to indicate that you are not certain whether something is possible, but you think it is, you use 'could', 'might', or 'may'. There is no important difference in meaning between these modals, but 'may' is slightly more formal.

That could be one reason.
He might come.
They may help us.

You can also use 'might not' or 'may not' in this way.

He might not be in England at all.
They may not get a house with central heating.

Note that 'could not' normally refers to ability in the past. See Unit 63.

3 When there is a possibility that something happened in the past, but you are not certain if it actually happened, you use 'could have', 'may have', or 'might have', followed by a past participle.

It could have been tomato soup.
You may have noticed this advertisement.

You can also use 'might not have' or 'may not have' in this way.

He might not have seen me.
They may not have done it.

You use 'could not have' when you want to indicate that it is not possible that something happened.

He didn't have a boat, so he couldn't have rowed away.
It couldn't have been wrong.

You also use 'could have' to say that there was a possibility of something happening in the past, but it did not happen.

It could have been awful. (But it wasn't awful.)
You could have got a job last year. (But you didn't get a job.)

4 You also use 'might have' or 'could have' followed by a past participle to say that if a particular thing had happened, then there was a possibility of something else happening.

She said it might have been all right, if the weather had been good. (But the weather wasn't good, so it wasn't all right.)
If I'd been there, I could have helped you. (But I wasn't there, so I couldn't help you.)

5 'Be able to', 'not be able to', and 'be unable to' are sometimes used instead of 'can' and 'cannot', for example after another modal, or when you want to use a 'to'-infinitive, an '-ing' form, or a past participle.

When will I be able to pick them up?
He had been unable to get a ticket.

6 You use 'used to be able to' to say that something was possible in the past, but is not possible now.

Everyone used to be able to have free eye tests.
You used to be able to buy cigarettes in packs of five.

7 Note that you also use 'could' followed by a negative word and the comparative form of an adjective to emphasize a quality that someone or something has. For example, if you say 'I couldn't be happier', you mean that you are very happy indeed and cannot imagine being happier than you are now.

You couldn't be more wrong.
He could hardly have felt more ashamed of himself.

Unit 62 Cannot, can't, must, ought, should, will - probability and certainty

Main points

- You use 'must', 'ought', 'should', or 'will' to express probability or certainty.
- You use 'cannot' or 'can't' as the negative of 'must', rather than 'must not' or 'mustn't', to say that something is not probable or is not certain.

1 When you want to say that something is probably true or that it will probably happen, you use 'should' or 'ought'. 'Should' is followed by the base form of a verb. 'Ought' is followed by a 'to'-infinitive.

We should arrive by dinner time.
She ought to know.

When you want to say that you think something is probably not true or that it will probably not happen, you use 'should not' or 'ought not'.

There shouldn't be any problem.
That ought not to be too difficult.

2 When you want to say that you are fairly sure that something has happened, you use 'should have' or 'ought to have', followed by a past participle.

You should have heard by now that I'm O.K.
They ought to have arrived yesterday.

When you want to say that you do not think that something has happened, you use 'should not have' or 'ought not to have', followed by a past participle.

You shouldn't have had any difficulty in getting there.
This ought not to have been a problem.

3 You also use 'should have' or 'ought to have' to say that you expected something to happen, but that it did not happen.

Yesterday should have been the start of the soccer season.
She ought to have been home by now.

Note that you do not normally use the negative forms with this meaning.

4 When you are fairly sure that something is the case, you use 'must'.

Oh, you must be Sylvia's husband.
He must know something about it.

If you are fairly sure that something is not the case, you use 'cannot' or 'can't'.

This cannot be the whole story.
He can't be very old — he's about 25, isn't he?

WARNING: You do not use 'must not' or 'mustn't' with this meaning.

5 When you want to say that you are almost certain that something has happened, you use 'must have', followed by a past participle.

This article must have been written by a woman.
We must have taken the wrong road.

To say that you do not think that something has happened, you use 'can't have', followed by a past participle.

You can't have forgotten me.
He can't have said that.

6 You use 'will' or '-'ll' to say that something is certain to happen in the future.

People will always say the things you want to hear.
They'll manage.

You use 'will not' or 'won't' to say that something is certain not to happen.

You won't get much sympathy from them.

7 There are several ways of talking about probability and certainty without using modals. For example, you can use:

- 'bound to' followed by the base form of a verb

It was bound to happen.
You're bound to make a mistake.

- an adjective such as 'certain', 'likely', 'sure', or 'unlikely', followed by a 'to'-infinitive clause or a 'that'-clause

They were certain that you were defeated.
I am not likely to forget it.

See Unit 22 for more information on these adjectives.

Unit 63 Can, could, be able to - ability

Main points

- You use 'can' to talk about ability in the present and in the future.
- You use 'could' to talk about ability in the past.
- You use 'be able to' to talk about ability in the present, future, and past.

1 You use 'can' to say that someone has the ability to do something.

You can all read and write.
Anybody can become a qualified teacher.

You use 'cannot' or 'can't' to say that they do not have the ability to do something.

He cannot dance.

2 When you want to talk about someone's ability in the past as a result of a skill they had or did not have, you use 'could', 'could not', or 'couldn't'.

He could run faster than anyone else.
A lot of them couldn't read or write.

3 You also use 'be able to', 'not be able to', and 'be unable to' to talk about someone's ability to do something, but 'can' and 'could' are more common.

She was able to tie her own shoelaces.
They are not able to run very fast.
Many people were unable to read or write.

4 You use 'was able to' and 'were able to' to say that someone managed to do something in a particular situation in the past.

After treatment he was able to return to work.
The farmers were able to pay the new wages.
We were able to find time to discuss it.

WARNING: You do not normally use 'could' to say that someone managed to do something in a particular situation. However, you can use 'could not' or 'couldn't' to say that someone did not manage to do something in a particular situation.

We couldn't stop laughing.
I just couldn't think of anything to say.

5 When you want to say that someone had the ability to do something in the past, but did not do it, you use 'could have' followed by a past participle.

You could have given it all to me.
You know, she could have done French.

You often use this form when you want to express disapproval about something that was not done.

You could have been a little bit tidier.
You could have told me!

6 You use 'could not have' or 'couldn't have' followed by a past participle to say that it is not possible that someone had the ability to do something.

I couldn't have gone with you, because I was in London at the time.
She couldn't have taken the car, because Jim was using it.

7 In most cases, you can choose to use 'can' or 'be able to'. However, you sometimes have to use 'be able to'.

You have to use 'be able to' if you are using another modal, or if you want to use an '-ing' form, a past participle, or a 'to'-infinitive.

Nobody else will be able to read it.
...the satisfaction of being able to do the job.
I don't think I'd have been able to get an answer.
You're foolish to expect to be able to do that.

8 You also use 'can' or 'could' with verbs such as 'see', 'hear', and 'smell' to say that someone is or was aware of something through one of their senses.

I can smell gas.
I can't see her.
I could see a few stars in the sky.
There was such a noise we couldn't hear.

Unit 64 Can, could, may - permission

Main points

- You use 'can' or 'be allowed to' to talk about whether someone has permission to do something or not.
- You usually use 'can' to give someone permission to do something.
- You usually use 'can' or 'could' to ask for permission to do something.

1 You use 'can' to say that someone is allowed to do something. You use 'cannot' or 'can't' to say that they are not allowed to do it.

Students can take a year away from university.
Children cannot bathe except in the presence of two lifesavers.

You use 'could' to say that someone was allowed to do something in the past. You use 'could not' or 'couldn't' to say that they were not allowed to do it.

We could go to any part of the island we wanted.
Both students and staff could use the swimming pool.
We couldn't go into the library after 5 pm.

2 You also use 'be allowed to' when you are talking about permission, but not when you are asking for it or giving it.

When Mr Wilt asks for a solicitor he will be allowed to see one.
It was only after several months that I was allowed to visit her.
You're not allowed to use calculators in exams.

3 In more formal situations, 'may' is used to say that someone is allowed to do something, and 'may not' is used to say that they are not allowed to do it.

They may do exactly as they like.
The retailer may not sell that book below the publisher's price.

4 When you want to give someone permission to do something, you use 'can'.

You can borrow that pen if you want to.
You can go off duty now.
She can go with you.

'May' is also used to give permission, but this is more formal.

You may speak.
You may leave as soon as you have finished.

5 When you want to refuse someone permission to do something, you use 'cannot', 'can't', 'will not', 'won't', 'shall not', or 'shan't'.

'Can I have some sweets?' - 'No, you can't!'
'I'll just go upstairs.' - 'You will not!'
You shan't leave without my permission.

6 When you are asking for permission to do something, you use 'can' or 'could'.
If you ask in a very simple and direct way, you use 'can'.

Can I ask a question?
Can we have something to wipe our hands on please?

'Could' is more polite than 'can'.

Could I just interrupt a minute?
Could we put this fire on?

'May' is also used to ask permission, but this is more formal.

May I have a cigarette?

'Might' is rather old-fashioned and is not often used in modern English in this way.

Might I inquire if you are the owner?

7 You have to use 'be allowed to' instead of a modal if you are using another modal, or if you want to use an '-ing' form, a past participle, or a 'to'-infinitive.

Teachers will be allowed to decide for themselves.
I am strongly in favour of people being allowed to put on plays.
They have not been allowed to come.
We were going to be allowed to travel on the trains.

Unit 65 Can, could, will, would - instructions and requests

Main points

- You use 'Could you' to tell someone politely to do something.
- Imperatives are not very polite.
- You also use 'Could you' to ask someone politely for help.
- You use 'I would like', 'Would you mind', 'Do you think you could', and 'I wonder if you could' to make requests.

1 When you want to tell someone to do something, you can use 'Could you', 'Will you', and 'Would you'. 'Could you' is very polite.

Could you make out her bill, please?
Could you just switch on the light behind you?

'Will you' and 'Would you' are normally used by people in authority. 'Would you' is more polite than 'Will you'.

Would you tell her that Adrian phoned?
Will you please leave the room?

Note that although these sentences look like questions ('Will you', not 'You will'), they are not really questions.

2 If someone in authority wants to tell someone to do something, they sometimes say 'I would like you to do this' or 'I'd like you to do this'.

Penelope, I would like you to get us the files.
I'd like you to finish this work by Thursday.

3 You can use an imperative to tell someone to do something, but this is not very polite.

Stop her.
Go away, all of you.

However, imperatives are commonly used when talking to people you know very well.

Come here, love.
Sit down and let me get you a drink.

You often use imperatives in situations of danger or urgency.

Look out! There's a car coming.
Put it away before Mum sees you.

4 When you want to ask someone to help you, you use 'Could you', 'Would you', 'Can you', or 'Will you'. 'Could you' and 'Would you' are used in formal situations, or when you want to be very polite, for example because you are asking for something that requires a lot of effort. 'Could you' is more polite than 'Would you'.

Could you show me how to do this?
Would you do me a favour?

'Will you' and 'Can you' are used in informal situations, especially when you are not asking for something that requires a lot of effort.

Will you post this for me on your way to work?
Can you make me a copy of that?

5 You also use 'I would like' or 'I'd like', followed by a 'to'-infinitive or a noun group, to make a request.

I would like to ask you one question.
I'd like steak and chips, please.

6 You can also make a request by using:

- 'Would you mind', followed by an '-ing' form

Would you mind doing the washing up?
Would you mind waiting a moment?

- 'Do you think you could', followed by the base form of a verb

Do you think you could help me?

- 'I wonder if you could', followed by the base form of a verb

I wonder if you could look after my cat for me while I'm away?

Unit 66 Could, may, might, shall - suggestions

Main points

- You use 'could', 'couldn't', or 'shall' to make a suggestion.
- You use 'Shall we' to suggest doing something with someone.
- You use 'You might like' or 'You might want' to make polite suggestions.
- You use 'may as well' or 'might as well' to suggest a sensible action.
- You use 'What about', 'Let's', 'Why don't', and 'Why not' to make suggestions.

1 You use 'could' to suggest doing something.

You could phone her.
She could go into research.
We could go on Friday.

You also use 'couldn't' in a question to suggest doing something.

Couldn't you just build some more factories?
Couldn't we do it at the weekend?

2 You use 'Shall we' to suggest doing something with somebody else.

Shall we go and see a film?
Shall we talk about something different now?

You use 'Shall I' to suggest doing something yourself.

Shall I contact the Chairman?

3 You use 'You might', followed by a verb meaning 'like' or 'want', to make a suggestion in a very polite way.

I thought perhaps you might like to come along with me.
You might want to try another shop.

You can also do this using 'It might be', followed by a noun group or an adjective, and a 'to'-infinitive.

I think it might be a good idea to stop recording now.
It might be wise to get a new car.

4 You use 'may as well' or 'might as well' to suggest doing something, but only because it seems the sensible thing to do, or because there is no reason not to do it.

You may as well open them all.
He might as well take the car.

5 You can also make a suggestion by using:

- 'What about' or 'How about' followed by an '-ing' form

What about going to Judy's?
How about using my car?

- 'Let's' followed by the base form of a verb

Let's go outside.

- 'Why don't I', 'Why don't you' or 'Why don't we' followed by the base form of a verb

Why don't I pick you up at seven?
Why don't you write to her yourself?
Why don't we just give them what they want?

- 'Why not' followed by the base form of a verb

Why not bring him along?
Why not try both?

Unit 67 Can, could, shall, will, would - offers and invitations

Main points

- You use 'Would you like' to offer something to someone or to invite them to do something.
- You use 'Can I', 'Could I', and 'Shall I' when you offer to help someone.

1 When you are offering something to someone, or inviting them to do something, you use 'Would you like'.

Would you like a drink?
Would you like to come for a meal?

You can use 'Will you' to offer something to someone you know quite well, or to give an invitation in a fairly informal way.

Will you have another biscuit, Dave?
Will you come to my party on Saturday?

2 You use 'Can I' or 'Could I' when you are offering to do something for someone. 'Could I' is more polite.

Can I help you with the dishes?
Could I help you carry those bags?

You also use 'Shall I' when you are offering to do something, especially if you are fairly sure that your offer will be accepted.

Shall I shut the door?
Shall I spell that for you?

3 You use 'I can' or 'I could' to make an offer when you want to say that you are able to help someone.

I have a car. I can take Daisy to the station.
I could pay some of the rent.

4 You also use 'I'll' to offer to do something.

I'll give them a ring if you like.
I'll show you the hotel.

5 You use 'You must' if you want to invite someone very persuasively to do something.

You must come round for a meal some time.
You must come and visit me.

6 There are other ways of making offers and giving invitations without using modals. For example, you can use 'Let me' when offering to help someone.

Let me take you to your room.
Let me drive you to London.

You can make an offer or give an invitation in a more informal way by using an imperative sentence, when it is clear that you are not giving an order.

Have a cigar.
Come to my place.

You can add emphasis by putting 'do' in front of the verb.

Do have a chocolate biscuit.
Do help yourselves.

You can also give an invitation by using 'Why don't you' or 'How about'.

Why don't you come to lunch tomorrow?
How about coming with us to the party?

How about coming with us to the party?

Unit 68 Would like, would rather, wouldn't mind - wants and wishes

Main points

- You use 'would like' to say what you want.
- You use 'wouldn't like' to say what you do not want.
- You use 'would rather' or 'would sooner' to say what you prefer.
- You also use 'wouldn't mind' to say what you want.

1 You can say what someone wants by using 'would like' followed by a 'to'-infinitive or a noun group.

I would like to know the date of the next meeting.
John would like his book back.

When the subject is a pronoun, you often use the short form '-'d' instead of 'would'.

I'd like more information about the work you do.
We'd like seats in the non-smoking section, please.

In spoken English, you can also use the short form '-'d' instead of 'would' when the subject is a noun.

Sally'd like to go to the circus.

2 You can say what someone does not want by using 'would not like' or 'wouldn't like'.

I would not like to see it.
They wouldn't like that.

3 You use 'would like' followed by 'to have' and a past participle to say that someone wishes now that something had happened in the past, but that it did not happen.

I would like to have felt more relaxed.
She'd like to have heard me first.

You use 'would have liked', followed by a 'to'-infinitive or a noun group, to say that someone wanted something to happen, but it did not happen.

Perhaps he would have liked to be a teacher.
I would have liked more ice cream.

Note the difference. 'Would like to have' refers to present wishes about past events. 'Would have liked' refers to past wishes about past events.

4 You can also use 'would hate', 'would love', or 'would prefer', followed by a 'to'-infinitive or a noun group.

I would hate to move to another house now.
I would prefer a cup of coffee.

Note that 'would enjoy' is followed by a noun group or an '-ing' form, not by a 'to'-infinitive.

I would enjoy a bath before we go.
I would enjoy seeing him again.

5 You can use 'would rather' or 'would sooner' followed by the base form of a verb to say that someone prefers one situation to another.

He'd rather be playing golf.
I'd sooner walk than take the bus.

6 You use 'I wouldn't mind', followed by an '-ing' form or a noun group, to say that you would like to do or have something.

I wouldn't mind being the manager of a store.
I wouldn't mind a cup of tea.

7 You can also express what you want to happen now by using 'I wish' or 'If only' followed by a past simple verb.

I wish he wasn't here.
If only she had a car.

Note that in formal English, you sometimes use 'were' instead of 'was' in sentences like these.

I often wish that I were really wealthy.

When you want to express regret about past events, you use the past perfect.

I wish I hadn't married him.

When you want to say that you wish that someone was able to do something, you use 'could'.

If only they could come with us!

When you want to say that you wish that someone was willing to do something, you use 'would'.

If only they would realise how stupid they've been.

Unit 69 Have to, have got to, must, mustn't - obligation and necessity

Main points

- You use 'have to', 'must', and 'mustn't' to talk about obligation and necessity in the present and future.
- You use 'had to' to talk about obligation and necessity in the past.
- You use the auxiliary 'do' with 'have to' to make questions.
- You use 'have got to' in informal English.

1 When you want to say that someone has an obligation to do something, or that it is necessary for them to do it, you use 'must' or 'have to'.

You must come to the meeting tomorrow.
The plants must have plenty of sunshine.
I enjoy parties, unless I have to make a speech.
He has to travel to find work.

2 There is sometimes a difference between 'must' and 'have to'. When you are stating your own opinion that something is an obligation or a necessity, you normally use 'must'.

I must be very careful not to upset him.
We must eat before we go.
He must stop working so hard.

When you are giving information about what someone else considers to be an obligation or a necessity, you normally use 'have to'.

They have to pay the bill by Thursday.
She has to go now.

Note that you normally use 'have to' for things that happen repeatedly, especially with adverbs of frequency such as 'often', 'always', and 'regularly'.

I always have to do the shopping.
You often have to wait a long time for a bus.

3 You use 'must not' or 'mustn't' to say that it is important that something is not done or does not happen.

You must not talk about politics.
They mustn't find out that I came here.

Note that 'must not' does not mean the same as 'not have to'. If you 'must not' do something, it is important that you do not do it.
If you 'do not have to' do something, it is not necessary for you to do it, but you can do it if you want.

WARNING: You only use 'must' for obligation and necessity in the present and the future. When you want to talk about obligation and necessity in the past, you use 'had to' rather than 'must'.

She had to catch the six o'clock train.
I had to wear a suit.

4 You use 'do', 'does', or 'did' when you want to make a question using 'have to' and 'not have to'.

How often do you have to buy petrol for the car?
Does he have to take so long to get ready?
What did you have to do?
Don't you have to be there at one o'clock?

WARNING: You do not normally form questions like these by putting a form of 'have' before the subject. For example, you do not normally say 'How often have you to buy petrol?'

5 In informal English, you can use 'have got to' instead of 'have to'.

You've just got to make sure you tell him.
She's got to see the doctor.
Have you got to go so soon?

WARNING: You normally use 'had to', not 'had got to', for the past.

He had to know.
I had to lend him some money.

6 You can only use 'have to', not 'must', if you are using another modal, or if you want to use an '-ing' form, a past participle, or a 'to'-infinitive.

They may have to be paid by cheque.
She grumbled a lot about having to stay abroad.
I would have had to go through London.
He doesn't like to have to do the same job every day.

Unit 70 Need to, needn't, not have to - obligation and necessity

Main points

- You use 'need to' to talk about necessity.
- You use 'don't have to', 'don't need to', 'haven't got to', or 'needn't' to say that it is not necessary to do something.
- You use 'needn't' to give someone permission not to do something.
- You use 'need not have', 'needn't have', 'didn't need to', or 'didn't have to' to say that it was not necessary to do something in the past.

1 You can use 'need to' to talk about the necessity of doing something.

You might need to see a doctor.
A number of questions need to be asked.

2 You use 'don't have to' when there is no obligation or necessity to do something.

Many women don't have to work.
You don't have to learn any new typing skills.

You can also use 'don't need to', 'haven't got to', or 'needn't' to say that there is no obligation or necessity to do something.

You don't need to buy anything.
I haven't got to go to work today.
I can pick John up. You needn't bother.

3 You also use 'needn't' when you are giving someone permission not to do something.

You needn't say anything if you don't want to.
You needn't stay any longer tonight.

4 You use 'need not have' or 'needn't have' and a past participle to say that someone did something which was not necessary. You are often implying that the person did not know at the time that their action was not necessary.

I needn't have waited until the game began.
Nell needn't have worked.
They needn't have worried about Reagan.

5 You use 'didn't need to' to say that something was not necessary, and that it was known at the time that the action was not necessary. You do not know if the action was done, unless you are given more information.

They didn't need to talk about it.
I didn't need to worry.

6 You also use 'didn't have to' to say that it was not necessary to do something.

He didn't have to speak.
Bill and I didn't have to pay.

7 You cannot use 'must' to refer to the past, so when you want to say that it was important that something did not happen or was not done, you use other expressions.
You can say 'It was important not to', or use phrases like 'had to make sure' or 'had to make certain' in a negative sentence.

It was necessary that no one was aware of being watched.
You had to make sure that you didn't spend too much.
We had to do our best to make certain that it wasn't out of date.

It was important not to take the game too seriously.

Unit 71 Should, ought, should have, ought to have, had better - mild obligation and advice

Main points

- You use 'should' and 'ought' to talk about mild obligation.
- You use 'should have' and 'ought to have' to say that there was a mild obligation to do something in the past, but it was not done.
- You can also use 'had better' to talk about mild obligation.

1 You can use 'should' and 'ought' to talk about a mild obligation to do something. When you use 'should' and 'ought', you are saying that the feeling of obligation is not as strong as when you use 'must'.

'Should' and 'ought' are very common in spoken English.

'Should' is followed by the base form of a verb, but 'ought' is followed by a 'to'-infinitive.

When you want to say that there is a mild obligation not to do something, you use 'should not', 'shouldn't, 'ought not', or 'oughtn't'.

2 You use 'should' and 'ought' in three main ways:

- when you are talking about what is a good thing to do, or the right thing to do.

We _should_ send her a postcard.
We _shouldn't_ spend all the money.
He _ought_ to come more often.
You _ought not_ to see him again.

- when you are trying to advise someone about what to do or what not to do.

You _should_ claim your pension 3-4 months before you retire.
You _shouldn't_ use a detergent.
You _ought_ to get a new TV.
You _oughtn't_ to marry him.

- when you are giving or asking for an opinion about a situation. You often use 'I think', 'I don't think', or 'Do you think' to start the sentence.

I think that we _should_ be paid more.
I don't think we _ought_ to grumble.
Do you think he _ought not_ to go?
What do you think we _should_ do?

3 You use 'should have' or 'ought to have' and a past participle to say that there was a mild obligation to do something in the past, but that it was not done. For example, if you say 'I should have given him the money yesterday', you mean that you had a mild obligation to give him the money yesterday, but you did not give it to him.

I _should have_ finished my drink and gone home.
You _should have_ realised that he was joking.
We _ought to have_ stayed in tonight.
They _ought to have_ taken a taxi.

You use 'should not have' or 'ought not to have' and a past participle to say that it was important not to do something in the past, but that it was done. For example, if you say 'I should not have left the door open', you mean that it was important that you did not leave the door open, but you did leave it open.

I _should not have_ said that.
You _shouldn't have_ given him the money.
They _ought not to have_ told him.
She _oughtn't to have_ sold the ring.

4 You use 'had better' followed by a base form to indicate mild obligation to do something in a particular situation. You also use 'had better' when giving advice or when giving your opinion about something. The negative is 'had better not'.

I think I _had better_ show this to you now.
You'_d better_ go tomorrow.

WARNING: The correct form is always 'had better' (not 'have better'). You do not use 'had better' to talk about mild obligation in the past, even though it looks like a past form.

I'd better not look at this.

Unit 72 Intransitive and transitive verbs

Main points

- Intransitive verbs do not have an object.
- Transitive verbs have an object.
- Some verbs can be used with or without an object, depending on the situation or their meaning.

1 Many verbs do not normally have an object. They are called 'intransitive' verbs. They often refer to:

> **existence:** appear die disappear exist happen live occur remain vanish
> **the human body:** ache bleed blush faint shiver smile
> **human noises:** cough cry laugh scream sigh snore speak yawn
> **light, smell, vibration:** gleam glow shine sparkle stink throb vibrate
> **position, movement:** arrive come depart fall flow go jump kneel pause run sit sleep stand swim wait walk work

An awful thing has happened.
The girl screamed.
I waited.

Note that intransitive verbs cannot be used in the passive.

2 Many verbs normally have an object. These verbs are called 'transitive' verbs. They are often connected with:

> **physical objects:** build buy carry catch cover cut damage destroy fill hit own remove rent sell use waste wear
> **senses:** feel hear see smell taste touch
> **feelings:** admire dislike enjoy fear frighten hate interest like love need prefer surprise trust want
> **facts, ideas:** accept believe consider correct discuss expect express forget include know mean remember report
> **people:** address blame comfort contact convince defy kill persuade please tease thank warn

He hit the ball really hard.
Did you see the rainbow?
They both enjoyed the film.
She reported the accident to the police.
Don't blame me.

Note that transitive verbs can be used in the passive.

They were blamed for everything.

WARNING 'Have' is a transitive verb, but cannot be used in the passive. You can say 'I have a car' but not 'A car is had by me'.

3 Often, the people you are talking to know what the object is because of the situation, or because it has already been mentioned. In this case you can omit the object, even though the verb is transitive.

accept	draw	iron	phone	study
answer	drive	know	read	type
change	eat	learn	remember	understand
choose	explain	leave	ride	wash
clean	forget	paint	sing	watch
cook	help	park	steal	write

I don't own a car. I can't drive.
You don't smoke, do you?
I asked a question and George answered.
Both dresses are beautiful. It's difficult to choose.

4 Many verbs have more than one meaning, and are transitive in one meaning and intransitive in another meaning. For example, the verb 'run' is intransitive when you use it to mean 'move quickly' but transitive when you use it to mean 'manage or operate'.

call	lose	miss	play	show
fit	manage	move	run	spread

The hare runs at enormous speed.
She runs a hotel.

She moved gracefully.
The whole incident had moved her profoundly.

5 A few verbs are normally intransitive, but can be used with an object that is closely related to the verb.

dance (a dance)	laugh (a laugh)	sigh (a sigh)
die (a death)	live (a life)	smile (a smile)
dream (a dream)		

Steve smiled his thin, cruel smile.
He appears to have lived the life of any other rich gentleman.
I once dreamed a very nice dream.

Note that you normally add more information about the object, for example by using adjectives in front of the noun.

Unit 73 Verbs with two objects

Main points

- Some verbs have two objects, a direct object and an indirect object.
- The indirect object can be used without a preposition, or after 'to' or 'for'.

1 Some verbs have two objects after them, a direct object and an indirect object. For example, in the sentence 'I gave John the book', 'the book' is the direct object. 'John' is the indirect object. Verbs that have two objects are sometimes called 'ditransitive' verbs or 'double-transitive' verbs.

His uncle had <u>given</u> him books on India.
She <u>sends</u> you her love.
I <u>passed</u> him the cup.

2 When the indirect object is a pronoun, or another short noun group such as a noun with 'the', you put the indirect object in front of the direct object.

Dad gave <u>me</u> a car.
You promised <u>the lad</u> a job.
He had lent <u>my cousin</u> the money.
She bought <u>Dave and me</u> an ice cream.

3 You can also use the prepositions 'to' and 'for' to introduce the indirect object. If you do this, you put the preposition and indirect object after the direct object.

He handed his room key <u>to the receptionist</u>.
Bill saved a piece of cake <u>for the children</u>.

When the indirect object consists of several words, you normally use a preposition to introduce it.

She taught physics and chemistry <u>to pupils at the local school</u>.
I made that lamp <u>for a seventy-year-old woman</u>.

You often use a preposition when you want to emphasize the indirect object.

Did you really buy that <u>for me</u>?

4 With some verbs you can only use 'for', not 'to', to introduce the indirect object.

book	cut	make	prepare
buy	find	paint	save
cook	keep	pour	win

They booked a place <u>for me</u>.
He had found some old clothes <u>for the beggar</u>.
They bought a present <u>for the teacher</u>.
She painted a picture <u>for her father</u>.

5 With some verbs you normally use 'to' to introduce the indirect object.

give	pay	read	show
lend	post	sell	teach
offer	promise	send	tell
pass			

I had lent my bicycle <u>to a friend</u>.
Ralph passed a message <u>to Jack</u>.
They say they posted the letter <u>to me</u> last week.
He sold it <u>to me</u>.

Note that you can use 'for' with these verbs, but it has a different meaning. 'For' indicates that one person does something on behalf of another person, so that the other person does not have to do it.

His mother paid the bill <u>for him</u>.
If you're going out, can you post this <u>for me</u>, please?

If you're going out, can you post this for me, please?

Unit 74 Reflexive verbs

For example: I hurt myself

Main points

- Transitive verbs are used with a reflexive pronoun to indicate that the object is the same as the subject.
- Some verbs which do not normally have a person as the object can have reflexive pronouns as the object.

1 You use a reflexive pronoun after a transitive verb to indicate that the object is the same as the subject.

He blamed himself for his friend's death.
I taught myself French.

See Unit 9 for more information on reflexive pronouns.

2 In theory, most transitive verbs can be used with a reflexive pronoun. However, you often use reflexive pronouns with the following verbs.

amuse	help	kill	restrict
blame	hurt	prepare	satisfy
cut	introduce	repeat	teach
dry			

Sam amused himself by throwing branches into the fire.
'Can I borrow a pencil?' - 'Yes, help yourself.'
Prepare yourself for a shock.
He introduced himself to me.

3 Verbs like 'dress', 'shave', and 'wash', which describe actions that people do to themselves, do not usually take reflexive pronouns in English, although they do in some other languages. With these verbs, reflexive pronouns are only used for emphasis.

I usually shave before breakfast.
He prefers to shave himself, even with that broken arm.

She washed very quickly and rushed downstairs.
Children were encouraged to wash themselves.

4 'Behave' does not normally take an object at all, but can take a reflexive pronoun as object.

If they don't behave, send them to bed.
He is old enough to behave himself.

5 Some verbs do not normally have a person as object, because they describe actions that you do not do to other people. However, these verbs can have reflexive pronouns as object, because you can do these actions to yourself.

apply	distance	excel	express
compose	enjoy	exert	strain

I really enjoyed the party.
Just go out there and enjoy yourself.

She expressed surprise at the news.
Professor Dale expressed himself very forcibly.

6 When 'busy' and 'content' are used as verbs, they always take a reflexive pronoun as their direct object. They are therefore true 'reflexive verbs'.

He had busied himself in the laboratory.
I had to content myself with watching the little moving lights.

Unit 75 Reciprocal verbs

For example: We met, I met you, We met each other

Main points

- Some verbs describe two people or two groups of people doing the same thing to each other.
- You use 'each other' or 'one another' for emphasis.
- With some verbs, you use 'each other' or 'one another' after 'with'.

1 Some verbs refer to actions that involve two people or two groups of people doing the same thing to each other. These verbs are sometimes called 'reciprocal' verbs.

We met in Delhi.
Jane and Sarah told me that they met you.
They met each other for the first time last week.

2 The two people or groups of people involved in the action are often mentioned as the plural subject of the verb, and the verb does not have an object. For example, 'John and Mary argued' means that John argued with Mary and Mary argued with John.

argue	combine	kiss	marry
clash	compete	meet	match
coincide	fight	mix	

The pair of you have argued about that for years.
We competed furiously.
Their children are always fighting.
They kissed.

3 When you want to emphasize that both people or groups of people are equally involved, you can use the pronouns 'each other' or 'one another' as the object of the verb. Verbs that refer to actions in which there is physical contact between people are often used with 'each other' or 'one another'.

cuddle	embrace	fight	hug	kiss	touch

We embraced each other.
They fought one another desperately for it.
They kissed each other in greeting.
It was the first time they had touched one another.

4 Some verbs do not take an object, so you use a preposition before 'each other' or 'one another'.

They parted from each other after only two weeks.
We talk to one another as often as possible.

5 With some verbs you have a choice of preposition before 'each other' or 'one another'. For example, you can 'fight with' one another or 'fight against' one another.

with/against:	compete fight
with/from:	part
with/to:	correspond relate talk

Many countries are competing with each other.
Did you compete against each other in yesterday's race?

Stephen and I parted with one another on good terms.
They parted from one another quite suddenly.

6 With some verbs, you can only use 'with' before 'each other' or 'one another'. Note that most of these verbs refer to people talking or working together.

agree	clash	communicate	disagree
argue	collide	co-operate	quarrel

We do agree with each other sometimes.
Have they communicated with each other since then?
The two lorries collided with one another on the motorway.

7 If you want to focus on one of the people involved, you make them the subject of the verb and make the other person the object.

She married a young engineer.
You could meet me at the restaurant.

If the verb cannot take an object, you mention the other person after a preposition.

Youths clashed with police in Belfast.
She was always quarrelling with him.

Unit 76 Ergative verbs

For example: I opened the door, The door opened

Main points

- Ergative verbs are both transitive and intransitive. The object of the transitive use is the subject of the intransitive use.
- A few verbs are only ergative with particular nouns.
- A few of these verbs need an adverbial when they are used without an object.

1 Some verbs can be used as transitive verbs to focus on the person who performs an action, and as intransitive verbs to focus on the thing affected by the action.

When I _opened_ the door, there was Laverne.
Suddenly the door _opened_.

Note that the object of the transitive verb, in this case 'the door', is the subject of the intransitive verb. Verbs like these are called 'ergative' verbs.

2 Ergative verbs often refer to:

- changes

begin	dry	improve	start
break	end	increase	stop
change	finish	slow	tear
crack	grow		

I _broke_ the glass.
The glass _broke_ all over the floor.

The driver _stopped_ the car.
A big car _stopped._

- cooking

bake	cook	fry	roast
boil	defrost	melt	simmer

I've _boiled_ an egg.
The porridge _is boiling._

I'm _cooking_ spaghetti.
The rice _is cooking._

- position or movement

balance	move	rock	stand
close	open	shake	turn
drop	rest		

She _rested_ her head on his shoulder.
Her head _rested_ on the table.

An explosion _shook_ the hotel.
The whole room _shook._

- vehicles

back	drive	reverse	sail
crash	fly	run	

He had _crashed_ the car twice.
Her car _crashed_ into a tree.

She _sailed_ her yacht round the world.
The ship _sailed_ on Monday.

3 Some verbs can be used in these two ways only with a small set of nouns. For example, you can say 'He fired a gun' or 'The gun fired'. You can do the same with other words referring to types of gun, 'cannon', 'pistol', or 'rifle'. However, although you can say 'He fired a bullet', you cannot say 'The bullet fired'.

catch: belt, cloth, clothing, dress, shirt, trousers
fire: cannon, gun, pistol, rifle
play: guitar, music, piano, violin
ring: alarm, bell
show: anger, disappointment, emotions, fear, joy
sound: alarm, bell, horn

I _caught_ my dress on the fence.
My tights _caught_ on a nail.

A car was _sounding_ its horn.
A horn _sounded_ in the night.

4 A few verbs can be used in both ways, but need an adverbial when they are used without an object.

clean	handle	polish	stain
freeze	mark	sell	wash

He _sells_ books.
This book _is selling_ well.

She had _handled_ a machine gun.
This car _handles_ very nicely.

Unit 77 Common verbs with nouns for actions

For example: have a bath, give a shout, make promises, take care

Main points

- Common verbs are often used with nouns to describe actions.
- You use 'have' with nouns referring to eating, drinking, talking, and washing.
- You use 'give' with nouns referring to noises, hitting, and talking.
- You use 'make' with nouns referring to talking, plans, and travelling.

1 When you want to talk about actions, you often use common verbs with nouns as their object. The nouns describe the action. The common verbs have very little meaning.

I had a nice rest.
She made a remark about the weather.

The nouns often have related verbs that do not take an object.

Helen went upstairs to rest.
I remarked that it would surely be better if I came.

2 Different verbs are used with different nouns. You use 'have' with nouns referring to:

meals: breakfast dinner drink lunch meal taste tea   **talking:** chat conversation discussion talk   **washing:** bath shower wash   **relaxation:** break holiday rest   **disagreement:** argument fight quarrel trouble

We usually have lunch at one o'clock.
He was having his first holiday for five years.

3 You use 'give' with nouns referring to:

human noises: cry gasp giggle groan laugh scream shout sigh whistle yell   **facial expressions:** grin smile   **hitting:** kick punch push slap   **talking:** advice answer example information interview lecture news report speech talk warning

Mr Sutton gave a shout of triumph.
She gave a long lecture about Roosevelt.

4 You use 'make' with nouns referring to:

talking and sounds: comment enquiry noise point promise remark sound speech suggestion   **plans:** arrangement choice decision plan   **travelling:** journey tour trip visit

He made the shortest speech I've ever heard.
In 1978 he made his first visit to Australia.

5 You use 'take' with these nouns:

care	decision	photograph	time
chance	interest	responsibility	trouble
charge	offence	risk	turns

He was taking no chances.
She was prepared to take great risks.

6 You use 'go' and 'come' with '-ing' nouns referring to sports and outdoor activities.

She goes climbing in her holidays.
Every morning, he goes jogging with Tommy.

Note that you can also use 'go for' and 'come for' with 'a jog', 'a run', 'a swim', 'a walk'.

They went for a run before breakfast.

7 You use 'do' with '-ing' nouns referring to jobs connected with the home, and nouns referring generally to work.

He wants to do the cooking.
He does all the shopping and I do the washing.

The man who did the job had ten years' training.
He has to get up early and do a hard day's work.

'Do' is often used instead of more specific verbs. For example, you can say 'Have you done your teeth?' instead of 'Have you brushed your teeth?'.

Do I need to do my hair?

Unit 78 Verbs with prepositions

Main points

- Some verbs do not take an object and are normally followed by a preposition.
- Some verbs take an object followed by a particular preposition.
- Some verbs can take either an object or a preposition.

1 Many verbs that are used without an object are normally followed by a prepositional phrase. Some verbs take a particular preposition:

belong to	hope for	listen to	refer to
consist of	insist on	pay for	relate to
hint at	lead to	qualify for	sympathize with

The land belongs to a rich family.
She then referred to the Minister's report.

2 With other verbs that are used without an object, the choice of a different preposition may alter the meaning of the clause.

agree on/with	apologize for/to	result from/in
appeal for/to	conform to/with	suffer from/with

They agreed on a plan of action.
You agreed with me that we should buy a car.

His failure resulted from lack of attention to details.
The match resulted in a draw.

3 With verbs that are used without an object, different prepositions are used to introduce different types of information.

- 'about' indicates the subject matter

care	dream	hear	speak	think
complain	explain	know	talk	write

We will always care about freedom.
Tonight I'm going to talk about engines.

- 'at' indicates direction

glance	grin	look	smile
glare	laugh	shout	stare

I don't know why he was laughing at that joke.
'Hey!' she shouted at him.

- 'for' indicates purpose or reason

apologize	apply	ask	look	wait

He wanted to apologize for being late.
I'm going to wait for the next bus.

- 'into' indicates the object involved in a collision

bump	crash	drive	run

His car crashed into the wall.
She drove into the back of a lorry.

- 'of' indicates facts or information

hear	know	speak	talk	think

I've heard of him but I don't know who he is.
Do you know of the new plans for the sports centre?

- 'on' indicates confidence or certainty

count	depend	plan	rely

You can count on me.
You can rely on him to be polite.

- 'to' indicates the listener or reader

complain	listen	speak	write
explain	say	talk	

They complained to me about the noise.
Mary turned her head to speak to him.

- 'with' indicates someone whose opinion is the same or different

agree	argue	disagree	side

Do you agree with me about this?
The daughters sided with their mothers.

4 Some verbs have an object, but are also followed by a preposition.

The police accused him of murder.
They borrowed some money from the bank.

Some verbs can take either an object or a prepositional phrase with no change in meaning.

He had to fight them, even if it was wrong.
He was fighting against history.

Unit 79 Phrasal verbs

Main points

- A phrasal verb is a combination of a verb and an adverb or preposition.
- The usual meaning of the verb is normally altered.
- Phrasal verbs are used in four main structures.

1 Phrasal verbs are verbs that combine with adverbs or prepositions. The adverbs and prepositions are called particles, for example 'down', 'in', 'off', 'out', and 'up'.

She turned off the radio.
Mr Knight offered to put him up.

2 Phrasal verbs extend the usual meaning of the verb or create a new meaning. For example, if you 'break' something, you damage it, but if you 'break out of' a place, you escape from it.

They broke out of prison on Thursday night.
The pain gradually wore off.

3 Phrasal verbs are normally used in one of four main structures. In the first structure, the verb is followed by a particle, and there is no object.

break out	get by	look in	stop off
catch on	give in	ring off	wait up
check up	go away	start out	watch out
come in	grow up	stay up	wear off

War broke out in September.
You'll have to stay up late tonight.

4 In the second structure, the verb is followed by a particle and an object.

fall for	grow on	part with	set about
feel for	look after	pick on	take after

She looked after her invalid mother.
Peter takes after his father but John is more like me.

5 In the third structure, the verb is followed by an object and a particle.

answer back	call back	count in	order about
ask in	catch out	invite out	tell apart

I answered him back and took my chances.
He loved to order people about.

6 Some phrasal verbs can be used in both the second structure and the third structure: verb followed by a particle and an object, or verb followed by an object and a particle.

add on	hand over	put away	take up
bring up	knock over	put up	tear up
call up	point out	rub out	throw away
fold up	pull down	sort out	try out

It took ages to clean up the mess.
It took ages to clean the mess up.
There was such a mess. It took ages to clean it up.

WARNING: If the object is a pronoun, it must go in front of the particle. You cannot say 'He cleaned up it'.

7 In the fourth structure, the verb is followed by a particle and a preposition with an object.

break out of	keep on at	put up with
catch up with	look forward to	run away with
come down with	make off with	stick up for
get on with	miss out on	talk down to
go down with	play around with	walk out on

You go on ahead. I'll catch up with you later.
Children have to learn to stick up for themselves.

8 A very few verbs are used in the structure: verb followed by an object, a particle, and a preposition with its object.

do out of	put up to	talk out of
put down to	take out on	

Kroop tried to talk her out of it.
I'll take you up on that generous invitation.

Unit 80 Link verbs

Main points

- Link verbs are used to join the subject with a complement.
- Link verbs can have adjectives, noun groups, or 'to'-infinitive clauses as complements.
- You can use 'it' and 'there' as impersonal subjects with link verbs.

1 A small but important group of verbs are followed by a complement rather than an object. The complement tells you more about the subject. Verbs that take complements are called 'link' verbs.

appear	feel	grow	prove	smell	taste
be	get	keep	remain	sound	turn
become	go	look	seem	stay	

I am proud of these people.
She was getting too old to play tennis.
They looked all right to me.

2 Link verbs often have adjectives as complements describing the subject.

We felt very happy.
He was the tallest in the room.

See Units 19 to 22 for more information about adjectives after link verbs.

3 You can use link verbs with noun groups as complements to give your opinion about the subject.

He's not the right man for it.
She seemed an ideal person to look after them.

You also use noun groups as complements after 'be', 'become', and 'remain' to specify the subject.

He became a geologist.
Promises by MPs remained just promises.
This one is yours.

Note that you use object pronouns after 'be'.

It's me again.

4 Some link verbs can have 'to'-infinitive clauses as complements.

appear	get	grow	look	prove	seem

He appears to have taken my keys.
She seemed to like me.

These verbs, and 'remain', can also be followed by 'to be' and a complement.

Mary seemed to be asleep.
His new job proved to be a challenge.

5 You can use 'it' and 'there' as impersonal subjects with link verbs.

It seems silly not to tell him.
There appears to have been a mistake.

See Units 96 and 97 for more information.

You can use 'be' with some abstract nouns as the subject, followed by a 'that'-clause or a 'to'-infinitive clause as the complement.

advice	answer	idea	problem
agreement	decision	plan	solution

The answer is that they are not interested in it.
The idea was to spend more money on training.

Some can only have a 'that'-clause.

conclusion	fact	reason	thought
explanation	feeling	report	understanding

The fact is that I can't go to the party.

Unit 81 Verbs with '-ing' clauses

Main points

- Many verbs are followed by an '-ing' clause.
- Some verbs are followed by an object and an '-ing' clause that describes what the object is doing.

1 Many verbs are followed by an '-ing' clause. The subject of the verb is also the subject of the '-ing' clause. The '-ing' clause begins with an '-ing' form. The most common of these verbs are:

- verbs of saying and thinking

admit	deny	imagine	recall
consider	describe	mention	suggest

He denied taking drugs.
I suggested meeting her for a coffee.

Note that all of these verbs except for 'describe' can also be followed by a 'that'-clause: see Unit 88.

He denied that he was involved.

- verbs of liking and disliking

adore	dislike	enjoy	like	mind
detest	dread	fancy	love	resent

Will they enjoy using it?
I don't mind telling you.

'Like' and 'love' can also be followed by a 'to'-infinitive clause: see Unit 83.

- other common verbs

avoid	finish	miss	resist
commence	involve	postpone	risk
delay	keep	practise	stop

I've just finished reading that book.
Avoid giving any unnecessary information.

- common phrasal verbs

burst out	end up	go round	put off
carry on	give up	keep on	set about

She carried on reading.
They kept on walking for a while.

Note that some common phrases can be followed by an '-ing' clause.

can't help	can't stand	feel like

I can't help worrying.

2 After the verbs and phrases mentioned above, you can also use 'being' followed by a past participle.

They enjoy being praised.
I dislike being interrupted.

After some verbs of saying and thinking, you can use 'having' followed by a past participle.

admit	deny	mention	recall

Michael denied having seen him.

3 'Come' and 'go' are used with '-ing' clauses to describe the way that a person or thing moves.

They both came running out.
It went sliding across the road out of control.

'Go' and 'come' are also used with '-ing' nouns to talk about sports and outdoor activities: see Unit 77.

Did you say they might go camping?

4 Some verbs can be followed by an object and an '-ing' clause. The object of the verb is the subject of the '-ing' clause.

catch	imagine	prevent	watch
find	leave	stop	

It is hard to imagine him existing without it.
He left them making their calculations.

Note that 'prevent' and 'stop' are often used with 'from' in front of the '-ing' clause.

I wanted to prevent him from seeing that.

Most verbs of perception can be followed by an object and an '-ing' clause or a base form: see Unit 84.

I saw him riding a bicycle.
I saw a policeman walk over to one of them.

See also Unit 29 for '-ing' clauses after nouns.

Unit 82 Verbs with 'to'-infinitive clauses

Main points

- Some verbs are followed by a 'to'-infinitive clause. Others are followed by an object and a 'to'-infinitive clause.
- Some verbs are followed by a 'wh'-word and a 'to'-infinitive clause. Others are followed by an object, a 'wh'-word, and a 'to'-infinitive clause.

1 Some verbs are followed by a 'to'-infinitive clause. The subject of the verb is also the subject of the 'to'-infinitive clause. These verbs include:

- verbs of saying and thinking

agree	decide	hope	learn	offer	promise
choose	expect	intend	mean	plan	refuse

She had agreed to let us use her flat.
I decided not to go out for the evening.

- other verbs

fail	manage	pretend	tend	want

England failed to win a place in the finals.

2 Some verbs are followed by an object and a 'to'-infinitive clause. The object of the verb is the subject of the 'to'-infinitive clause.

- verbs of saying and thinking

advise	encourage	invite	persuade	teach
ask	expect	order	remind	tell

I asked her to explain.
They advised us not to wait around too long.

- other verbs

allow	force	get	help	want

I could get someone else to do it.
I didn't want him to go.

Note that 'help' can also be followed by an object and a base form.

I helped him fix it.

WARNING: You do not use 'want' with a 'that'-clause. You do not say 'I want that you do something'.

3 Some verbs are followed by 'for' and an object, then a 'to'-infinitive clause. The object of 'for' is the subject of the 'to'-infinitive clause.

appeal	arrange	ask	long	pay	wait	wish

Could you arrange for a taxi to collect us?
I waited for him to speak.

4 Some link verbs, and 'pretend', are followed by 'to be' and an '-ing' form for continuing actions, and by 'to have' and a past participle for finished actions. See also Unit 80.

We pretended to be looking inside.
I don't appear to have written down his name.

5 Some verbs are normally used in the passive when they are followed by a 'to'-infinitive clause.

believe	feel	know	say	understand
consider	find	report	think	

He is said to have died a natural death.
Is it thought to be a good thing?

6 Some verbs are followed by a 'wh'-word and a 'to'-infinitive clause. These include:

ask	explain	imagine	learn	understand
decide	forget	know	remember	wonder

I didn't know what to call him.
She had forgotten how to ride a bicycle.

Some verbs are followed by an object, then a 'wh'-word and a 'to'-infinitive clause.

ask	remind	show	teach	tell

I asked him what to do.
Who will show him how to use it?

Some verbs only take 'to'-infinitive clauses to express purpose. See Unit 93.

The captain stopped to reload the gun.
He went to get some fresh milk.

See Unit 29 for nouns with 'to'-infinitive clauses.

Unit 83 Verbs with 'to'-infinitive or '-ing' clauses

Main points

- Some verbs take a 'to'-infinitive clause or an '-ing' clause with little difference in meaning. Others take a 'to'-infinitive or '-ing' clause, but the meaning is different.

1 The following verbs can be followed by a 'to'-infinitive clause or an '-ing' clause, with little difference in meaning.

begin	~	try	hate
continue	attempt	~	love
start	bother	fear	prefer

It started raining.
A very cold wind had started to blow.

The captain didn't bother answering.
I didn't bother to answer.

Note that if these verbs are used in a continuous tense, they are followed by a 'to'-infinitive clause.

The company is beginning to export to the West.
We are continuing to make good progress.

After 'begin', 'continue', and 'start', you use a 'to'-infinitive clause with the verbs 'understand', 'know', and 'realize'.

I began to understand her a bit better.

2 You can often use 'like' with a 'to'-infinitive or an '-ing' clause with little difference in meaning.

I like to fish.
I like fishing.

However, there is sometimes a difference. You can use 'like' followed by a 'to'-infinitive clause to say that you think something is a good idea, or the right thing to do. You cannot use an '-ing' clause with this meaning.

They like to interview you first.
I didn't like to ask him.

3 After 'remember', 'forget', and 'regret', you use an '-ing' clause if you are referring to an event after it has happened.

I remember discussing it once before.
I'll never forget going out with my old aunt.
She did not regret accepting his offer.

You use a 'to'-infinitive clause after 'remember' and 'forget' if you are referring to an event before it happens.

I must remember to send a gift for her child.
Don't forget to send in your entries.

After 'regret', in formal English, you use a 'to'-infinitive clause with these verbs to say that you are sorry about what you are saying or doing now:

announce   inform   learn   say   see   tell

I regret to say that it was all burned up.

4 If you 'try to do' something, you make an effort to do it. If you 'try doing' something, you do it as an experiment, for example to see if you like it or if it is effective.

I tried to explain.
Have you tried painting it?

5 If you 'go on doing' something, you continue to do it. If you 'go on to do' something, you do it after you have finished doing something else.

I went on writing.
He later went on to form a computer company.

6 If you 'are used to doing' something, you are accustomed to doing it. If you 'used to do' something, you did it regularly in the past, but you no longer do it now.

We are used to working together.
I used to live in this street.

7 After 'need', you use a 'to'-infinitive clause if the subject of 'need' is also the subject of the 'to'-infinitive clause. You use an '-ing' form if the subject of 'need' is the object of the '-ing' clause.

We need to ask certain questions.
It needs cutting.

Unit 84 Verbs with other types of clauses

Main points

- 'Make' and 'let' can be followed by an object and a base form.
- Some verbs of perception can be followed by an object and an '-ing' clause, or an object and a base form.
- 'Have' and 'get' can be followed by an object and a past participle.
- 'Dare' is followed by a 'to'-infinitive clause or a base form.

1 You can use an object and a base form after 'make' to say that one person causes another person to do something, or after 'let' to say they allow them to do something.

My father made me go for the interview.
Jenny let him talk.

2 Some verbs of perception are used with an object and an '-ing' clause if an action is unfinished or continues over a period of time, and with an object and a base form if the action is finished.

| feel | hear | see | watch |

He heard a distant voice shouting.
Dr Hochstadt heard her gasp.

You normally use an '-ing' clause after 'notice', 'observe', 'smell', and 'understand'.

I could smell Chinese vegetables cooking.
We can understand them wanting to go.

3 You can use an object and a past participle after 'have' or 'get', when you want to say that someone arranges for something to be done. 'Have' is slightly more formal.

We've just had the house decorated.
We must get the car repaired.

You also use 'have' and 'get' with an object and a past participle to say that something happens to someone, especially if it is unpleasant.

She had her purse stolen.
He got his car broken into at the weekend.

4 You use 'have' followed by an object and an '-ing' clause, or an object and a past participle, when you want to say that someone causes something to happen, either intentionally or unintentionally.

Alan had me looking for that book all day.
He had me utterly confused.

5 You use 'want' and 'would like' with an object and a past participle to indicate that you want something to be done.

I want the work finished by January 1st.
How would you like your hair cut, sir?

6 'Dare' can be followed by a 'to'-infinitive clause or a base form in negative or interrogative sentences:

- when there is an auxiliary or modal in front of 'dare'

He did not dare to walk to the village.
What bank would dare offer such terms?

- when you use the form 'dares' or 'dared' (but not 'dares not' or 'dared not')

No one dares disturb him.
No other manager dared to compete.

You must use a base form in:

- negative or interrogative sentences without an auxiliary or modal before 'dare'

I daren't ring Jeremy again.
Nobody dare disturb him.
Dare she go in?

- negative sentences with 'dares not' or 'dared not'

He dares not risk it.
Sonny dared not disobey.

Note that the phrase 'how dare you' is always followed by a base form.

How dare you speak to me like that?

'Dare' is rarely used in affirmative sentences.

Unit 85 The passive voice

Main points

- You use the passive voice to focus on the person or thing affected by an action.
- You form the passive by using a form of 'be' and a past participle.
- Only verbs that have an object can have a passive form. With verbs that can have two objects, either object can be the subject of the passive.

1 When you want to talk about the person or thing that performs an action, you use the active voice.

Mr Smith locks the gate at 6 o'clock every night.
The storm destroyed dozens of trees.

When you want to focus on the person or thing that is affected by an action, rather than the person or thing that performs the action, you use the passive voice.

The gate is locked at 6 o'clock every night.
Dozens of trees were destroyed.

2 The passive is formed with a form of the auxiliary 'be', followed by the past participle of a main verb.

Two new stores were opened this year.
The room had been cleaned.

Continuous passive tenses are formed with a form of the auxiliary 'be' followed by 'being' and the past participle of a main verb.

Jobs are still being lost.
It was being done without his knowledge.

3 After modals you use the base form 'be' followed by the past participle of a main verb.

What can be done?
We won't be beaten.

When you are talking about the past, you use a modal with 'have been' followed by the past participle of a main verb.

He may have been given the car.
He couldn't have been told by Jimmy.

4 You form passive infinitives by using 'to be' or 'to have been' followed by the past participle of a main verb.

He wanted to be forgiven.
The car was reported to have been stolen.

5 In informal English, 'get' is sometimes used instead of 'be' to form the passive.

Our car gets cleaned every weekend.
He got killed in a plane crash.

6 When you use the passive, you often do not mention the person or thing that performs the action at all. This may be because you do not know or do not want to say who it is, or because it does not matter.

Her boyfriend was shot in the chest.
Your application was rejected.
Such items should be carefully packed in tea chests.

7 If you are using the passive and you do want to mention the person or thing that performs the action, you use 'by'.

He had been poisoned by his girlfriend.
He was brought up by an aunt.

You use 'with' to talk about something that is used to perform the action.

A circle was drawn in the dirt with a stick.
He was killed with a knife.

8 Only verbs that usually have an object can have a passive form. You can say 'people spend money' or 'money is spent'.

An enormous amount of money is spent on beer.
The food is sold at local markets.

With verbs which can have two objects, you can form two different passive sentences. For example, you can say 'The secretary was given the key' or 'The key was given to the secretary'.

They were offered a new flat.
The books will be sent to you.

See Unit 73 for more information on verbs that can have two objects.

Unit 86 'It' as impersonal subject

Main points

- You use impersonal 'it' as the subject of a sentence to introduce new information.
- You use 'it' to talk about the time or the date.
- You use 'it' to talk about the weather.
- You use 'it' to express opinions about places, situations, and events.
- 'It' is often used with the passive of reporting verbs to express general beliefs and opinions.

1 'It' is a pronoun. As a personal pronoun it refers back to something that has already been mentioned.

They learn to speak <u>English</u> before they learn to read <u>it</u>.
Maybe he changed <u>his mind</u>, but I doubt <u>it</u>.

You can also use 'it' as the subject of a sentence when it does not refer back to anything that has already been mentioned. This impersonal use of 'it' introduces new information, and is used particularly to talk about times, dates, the weather, and personal opinions.

2 You use impersonal 'it' with a form of 'be' to talk about the time or the date.

<u>It is</u> nearly one o' clock.
<u>It's</u> the sixth of April today.

3 You use impersonal 'it' with verbs which refer to the weather:

| drizzle | pour | sleet | thunder |
| hail | rain | snow | |

It's still <u>raining</u>.
It <u>snowed</u> steadily through the night.
It <u>was pouring</u> with rain.

You can describe the weather by using 'it' followed by 'be' and an adjective with or without a noun.

It's a lovely day.
It was very bright.

You can describe a change in the weather by using 'it' followed by 'get' and an adjective.

It was getting cold.
It's getting dark.

4 You use impersonal 'it', followed by a form of 'be' and an adjective or noun group, to express your opinion about a place, a situation, or an event. The adjective or noun group can be followed by an adverbial or by an '-ing' clause, a 'to'-infinitive clause, or a 'that'-clause.

It was terribly <u>cold in the trucks</u>.
It's fun <u>working</u> for him.
It was a pleasure <u>to be</u> there.
It's strange <u>that</u> it hasn't been noticed before.

5 You use 'it' followed by a verb such as 'interest', 'please', 'surprise', or 'upset' which indicates someone's reaction to a fact, situation, or event. The verb is followed by a noun group, and a 'that'-clause or a 'to'-infinitive clause.

It pleases me <u>that</u> he should want to talk about his work.
It surprised him <u>to realize</u> that he hadn't thought about them until now.

6 You can also use 'it' with the passive of a reporting verb and a 'that'-clause when you want to suggest that an opinion or belief is shared by many people. This use is particularly common in news reports, for example in newspapers, on the radio, or on television.

It was said <u>that</u> he could speak their language.
Nowadays it is believed <u>that</u> the size is unimportant.
It is thought <u>that</u> about a million puppies are born each year.

Note that the passive of reporting verbs can also be used without impersonal 'it' to express general opinions.

The factories were said <u>to be</u> much worse.
They are believed <u>to be</u> dangerous.

See Units 88 and 89 for more information on reporting verbs.

Unit 87 'There' as impersonal subject

Main points

- You use 'there' followed by a form of 'be' and a noun group to introduce new information.
- You use 'there' with a singular or plural verb, depending on whether the following noun is singular or plural.
- You can also use 'there' with modals.

1 'There' is often an adverb of place.

Are you comfortable there?
The book is there on the table.

You can also use 'there' as the impersonal subject of a sentence when it does not refer to a place. In this case you use 'there' to introduce new information and to focus upon it. After 'there' you use a form of 'be' and a noun group.

There is work to be done.
There will be a party tonight.
There was no damage.
There have been two telephone calls.

Note that the impersonal subject 'there' is often pronounced without stress, whereas the adverb is almost always stressed.

2 You use 'there' as the impersonal subject to talk about:
- the existence or presence of someone or something

There are two people who might know what happened.
There are many possibilities.
There is plenty of bread.

- something that happens

There was a general election that year.
There's a meeting every week.
There was a fierce battle.

- a number or amount

There are forty of us, I think.
There is a great deal of anger about his decision.
There were a lot of people camped there.

3 When the noun group after the verb is plural, you use a plural verb.

There are many reasons for this.
There were two men in the room.

You also use a plural verb before phrases such as 'a number (of)', 'a lot (of)', and 'a few (of)'.

There were a lot of people camped there.
There are only a few left.

4 When the noun group after the verb is singular or uncountable, you use a singular verb.

There is one point we must add here.
There isn't enough room in here.

You also use a singular verb when you are mentioning more than one person or thing and the first noun after the verb is singular or uncountable.

There was a man and a woman.
There was a sofa and two chairs.

5 You can also use 'there' with a modal, followed by 'be' or 'have been'.

There could be a problem.
There should be a change in government.
There can't have been anybody outside.
There must have been some mistake.

6 In spoken and informal written English, short forms of 'be' or a modal are normally used after 'there'.

There's no danger.
There'll always be a future for music.
I knew there'd be trouble.
There's been quite a lot of research into it.
I didn't even know there'd been a murder.

7 You can also use 'there' with 'appear' or 'seem', followed by 'to be' or 'to have been'.

There appears to be a vast amount of confusion on this point.
There don't seem to be many people on campus.
There seems to have been some carelessness.

Unit 88 Report structures: 'that'-clauses

Main points

- You usually use your own words to report what someone said, rather than repeating their exact words.
- Report structures contain a reporting clause first, then a reported clause.
- When you are reporting a statement, the reported clause is a 'that'-clause.
- You must mention the hearer with 'tell'. You need not mention the hearer with 'say'.

1 When you are reporting what someone said, you do not usually repeat their exact words, you use your own words in a report structure.

Jim said he wanted to go home.

Jim's actual words might have been 'It's time I went' or 'I must go'.
Report structures contain two clauses. The first clause is the reporting clause, which contains a reporting verb such as 'say', 'tell', or 'ask'.

She said that she'd been to Belgium.
The man in the shop told me how much it would cost.

You often use verbs that refer to people's thoughts and feelings to report what people say. If someone says 'I am wrong', you might report this as 'He felt that he was wrong'. See Unit 89 for more information.

2 The second clause in a report structure is the reported clause, which contains the information that you are reporting. The reported clause can be a 'that'-clause, a 'to'-infinitive clause, an 'if'-clause, or a 'wh'-word clause.

She said that she didn't know.
He told me to do it.
Mary asked if she could stay with us.
She asked where he'd gone.

3 If you want to report a statement, you use a 'that'-clause after a verb such as 'say'.

admit	argue	decide	insist	reply
agree	claim	deny	mention	say
answer	complain	explain	promise	warn

He said that he would go.
I replied that I had not read it yet.

You often omit 'that' from the 'that'-clause, but not after 'answer', 'argue', 'explain', or 'reply'.

They said I had to see a doctor first.
He answered that the price would be three pounds.

You often mention the hearer after the preposition 'to' with the following verbs.

admit	complain	mention	suggest
announce	explain	say	

He complained to me that you were rude.

4 'Tell' and some other reporting verbs are also used with a 'that'-clause, but with these verbs you have to mention the hearer as the object of the verb.

convince	notify		reassure	tell
inform	persuade	remind	

He told me that he was a farmer.
I informed her that I could not come.

The word 'that' is often omitted after 'tell'.

I told them you were at the dentist.

You can also mention the hearer as the object of the verb with 'promise' and 'warn'.

I promised her that I wouldn't be late.

5 Note the differences between 'say' and 'tell'. You cannot use 'say' with the hearer as the object of the verb. You cannot say 'I said them you had gone'. You cannot use 'tell' without the hearer as the object of the verb. You cannot say 'I told that you had gone'. You cannot use 'tell' with 'to' and the hearer. You cannot say 'I told to them you had gone'.

6 The reporting verbs that have the hearer as object, such as 'tell', can be used in the passive.

She was told that there were no tickets left.

Most reporting verbs that do not need the hearer as object, such as 'say', can be used in the passive with impersonal 'it' as subject, but not 'answer', 'complain', 'insist', 'promise', 'reply', or 'warn'.

It was said that the money had been stolen.

See also Units 89 and 47.

Unit 89 Other report structures

Main points

- When reporting an order, a request, or a piece of advice, the reported clause is a 'to'-infinitive clause, used after an object.
- When reporting a question, the reported clause is an 'if'-clause or a 'wh'-word clause.
- Many reporting verbs refer to people's thoughts and feelings.

1 If you want to report an order, a request, or a piece of advice, you use a 'to'-infinitive clause after a reporting verb such as 'tell', 'ask', or 'advise'. You mention the hearer as the object of the verb, before the 'to'-infinitive clause.

advise	command	invite	remind
ask	forbid	order	tell
beg	instruct	persuade	warn

Johnson told her to wake him up.
He ordered me to fetch the books.
He asked her to marry him.
He advised me to buy it.

If the order, request, or advice is negative, you put 'not' before the 'to'-infinitive.

He had ordered his officers not to use weapons.
She asked her staff not to discuss it publicly.
Doctors advised him not to play for three weeks.

If the subject of the 'to'-infinitive clause is the same as the subject of the main verb, you can use 'ask' or 'beg' to report a request without mentioning the hearer.

I asked to see the manager.
Both men begged not to be named.

2 If you want to report a question, you use a verb such as 'ask' followed by an 'if'-clause or a 'wh'-word clause.

I asked if I could stay with them.
They wondered whether the time was right.
He asked me where I was going.
She inquired how Ibrahim was getting on.

Note that in reported questions, the subject of the question comes before the verb, just as it does in affirmative sentences. See Unit 54.

3 Many reporting verbs refer to people's thoughts and feelings but are often used to report what people say. For example, if someone says 'I must go', you might report this as 'She wanted to go' or 'She thought she should go'.
Some of these verbs are followed by:

- a 'that'-clause

accept	fear	imagine	think
believe	feel	know	understand
consider	guess	suppose	worry

We both knew that the town was cut off.
I had always believed that I would see him again.

- a 'to'-infinitive clause

intend	plan	want

He doesn't want to get up.

- a 'that'-clause or a 'to'-infinitive clause

agree	expect	hope	regret	wish
decide	forget	prefer	remember	

She hoped she wasn't going to cry.
They are in love and wish to marry.

'Expect' and 'prefer' can also be followed by an object and a 'to'-infinitive.

I'm sure she doesn't expect you to take the plane.
The headmaster prefers them to act plays they have written themselves.

4 A speaker's exact words are more often used in stories than in ordinary conversation.

'I knew I'd seen you,' I said.
'Only one,' replied the Englishman.
'Let's go and have a look at the swimming pool,' she suggested.

In ordinary conversation, it is normal to use a report structure rather than to repeat someone's exact words.

Unit 90 Time clauses

Main points

- You use time clauses to say when something happens.
- Time clauses can refer to the past, present, or future.
- Time clauses are introduced by words such as 'after', 'when', or 'while'.
- A time clause needs a main clause to make a complete sentence. The time clause can come before or after the main clause.

1 You use time clauses to say when something happens. The verb in the time clause can be in a present or a past tense.

I look after the children while she goes to London.
I haven't given him a thing to eat since he arrived.

WARNING: You never use a future tense in a time clause. You use one of the present tenses instead.

Let me stay here till Jeannie comes to bed.
I'll do it when I've finished writing this letter.

2 When you want to say that two events happen at the same time, you use a time clause with 'as', 'when', or 'while'.

We arrived as they were leaving.

Sometimes the two events happen together for a period of time.

She wept bitterly as she told her story.

Sometimes one event interrupts another event.

He was having his dinner when the telephone rang.
John will arrive while we are watching the film.

Note that you often use a continuous tense for the interrupted action. See Unit 43.

3 When you want to say that one event happens before or after another event, you use a time clause with 'after', 'as soon as', 'before', or 'when'.

As soon as we get tickets, we'll send them to you.
Can I see you before you go, Helen?
When he had finished reading, he looked up.

Note that you use the past perfect to indicate an event that happened before another event in the past.

4 When you want to mention a situation which started in the past and continued until a later time, you use a time clause with 'since' or 'ever since'. You use a past simple or a past perfect in the time clause, and a past perfect in the main clause.

He hadn't cried since he was a boy of ten.
Janine had been busy ever since she had heard the news.
I'd wanted to come ever since I was a child.

If the situation started in the past and still continues now, you use a past simple in the time clause, and a present perfect in the main clause.

I've been in politics since I was at university.
Ever since you arrived you've been causing trouble.

Note that after impersonal 'it' and a time expression, if the main clause is in the present tense, you use 'since' with a past simple.

It is two weeks now since I wrote to you.

If the main clause is in the past tense, you use 'since' with a past perfect.

It was nearly seven years since I 'd seen Toby.

For 'since' as a preposition, see Unit 33.

5 When you want to talk about when a situation ends, you use a time clause with 'till' or 'until' and a present or past tense.

We'll support them till they find work.
I stayed there talking to them until I saw Sam.
She waited until he had gone.

6 When you want to say that something happens before or at a particular time, you use a time clause with 'by the time' or 'by which time'.

By the time I went to bed, I was exhausted.
He came back later, by which time they had gone.

7 In written or formal English, if the subject of the main clause and the time clause are the same, you sometimes omit the subject in the time clause and use a participle as the verb.

I read the book before going to see the film.
The car was stolen while parked in a London street.

Unit 91 Conditional clauses using 'if'

Main points

- You use conditional clauses to talk about a possible situation and its results.
- Conditional clauses can begin with 'if'.
- A conditional clause needs a main clause to make a complete sentence. The conditional clause can come before or after the main clause.

1 You use conditional clauses to talk about a situation that might possibly happen and to say what its results might be.
You use 'if' to mention events and situations that happen often, that may happen in the future, that could have happened in the past but did not happen, or that are unlikely to happen at all.

If the light comes on, the battery is OK.
I'll call you if I need you.
If I had known, I'd have told you.
If she asked me, I'd help her.

2 When you are talking about something that is generally true or happens often, you use a present or present perfect tense in the main clause and the conditional clause.

If they lose weight during an illness, they soon regain it afterwards.
If an advertisement does not tell the truth, the advertiser is committing an offence.
If the baby is crying, it is probably hungry.
If they have lost any money, they report it to me.

WARNING: You do not use the present continuous in both clauses. You do not say 'If they are losing money, they are getting angry.'

3 When you use a conditional clause with a present or present perfect tense, you often use an imperative in the main clause.

Wake me up if you're worried.
If he has finished, ask him to leave quietly.
If you are very early, don't expect them to be ready.

4 When you are talking about something which may possibly happen in the future, you use a present or present perfect tense in the conditional clause, and the simple future in the main clause.

If I marry Celia, we will need the money.
If you are going to America, you will need a visa.
If he has done the windows, he will want his money.

WARNING: You do not normally use 'will' in conditional clauses. You do not say 'If I will see you tomorrow, I will give you the book'.

5 When you are talking about something that you think is unlikely to happen, you use the past simple or past continuous in the conditional clause and 'would' in the main clause.

If I had enough money, I would buy the car.
If he was coming , he would ring.

WARNING: You do not normally use 'would' in conditional clauses. You do not say 'If I would do it, I would do it like this'.

6 'Were' is sometimes used instead of 'was' in the conditional clause, especially after 'I'.

If I were as big as you, I would kill you.
If I weren't so busy, I would do it for you.

You often say 'If I were you' when you are giving someone advice.

If I were you, I would take the money.
I should keep out of Bernadette's way if I were you.

7 When you are talking about something which could have happened in the past but which did not actually happen, you use the past perfect in the conditional clause. In the main clause, you use 'would have' and a past participle.

If he had realized that, he would have run away.
I wouldn't have been so depressed if I had known how common this feeling is.

WARNING: You do not use 'would have' in the conditional clause. You do not say 'If I would have seen him, I would have told him'.

Unit 92 Conditional clauses using modals and 'unless'

Main points

- You can use a modal in a conditional clause.
- You use 'unless' to mention an exception to what you are saying.

1 You sometimes use modals in conditional clauses. In the main clause, you can still use a present tense for events that happen often, 'will' for events that are quite likely in the future, 'would' for an event that is unlikely to happen, and 'would have' for events that were possible but did not happen.

If he can't come, he usually phones me.
If they must have it today, they will have to come back at five o'clock.
If I could only find the time, I'd do it gladly.
If you could have seen him, you would have laughed too.

'Should' is sometimes used in conditional clauses to express greater uncertainty.

If any visitors should come, I'll say you aren't here.

2 You can use other modals besides 'will', 'would' and 'would have' in the main clause with their usual meanings.

She might phone me, if she has time.
You could come, if you wanted to.
If he sees you leaving, he may cry.

Note that you can have modals in both clauses: the main clause and the conditional clause.

If he can't come, he will phone.

See Units 59 to 71 for more information.

3 In formal English, if the first verb in a conditional clause is 'had', 'should', or 'were', you can put the verb at the beginning of the clause and omit 'if'. For example, instead of saying 'If he should come, I will tell him you are sick', it is possible to say 'Should he come, I will tell him you are sick'.

Should ministers decide to hold an inquiry, we would welcome it.
Were it all true, it would still not excuse their actions.
Had I known, I would not have done it.

4 When you want to mention an exception to what you are saying, you use a conditional clause beginning with 'unless'.

You will fail your exams.
You will fail your exams unless you work harder.

Note that you can often use 'if...not' instead of 'unless'.

You will fail your exams if you do not work harder.

When you use 'unless', you use the same tenses that you use with 'if'.

She spends Sundays in the garden unless the weather is awful.
We usually walk, unless we're going shopping.
He will not let you go unless he is forced to do so.
You wouldn't believe it, unless you saw it.

5 'If' and 'unless' are not the only ways of beginning conditional clauses. You can also use 'as long as', 'only if', 'provided', 'provided that', 'providing', 'providing that', or 'so long as'. These expressions are all used to indicate that one thing only happens or is true if another thing happens or is true.

I will come only if nothing is said to the press.
She was prepared to come, provided that she could bring her daughter.
Providing they remained at a safe distance, we would be all right.
Detergent cannot harm a fabric, so long as it has been properly dissolved.

We were all right as long as we kept our heads down.

Unit 93 Purpose and reason clauses

Main points

- Purpose clauses are introduced by conjunctions such as 'so', 'so as to', 'so that', 'in order to' or 'in order that'.
- Reason clauses are introduced by conjunctions such as 'as', 'because', or 'in case'.
- A purpose or reason clause needs a main clause to make a complete sentence.
- A purpose clause usually comes after a main clause. A reason clause can come before or after a main clause.

1 You use a purpose clause when you are saying what someone's intention is when they do something. The most common type of purpose clause is a 'to'-infinitive clause.

The children sleep together <u>to keep</u> warm.
They locked the door <u>to stop</u> us from getting in.

Instead of using an ordinary 'to'-infinitive, you often use 'in order to' or 'so as to' with an infinitive.

He was giving up his job <u>in order to stay</u> at home.
I keep the window open, <u>so as to let</u> fresh air in.

To make a purpose clause negative, you have to use 'in order not to' or 'so as not to' with an infinitive.

I would have to give myself something to do <u>in order not to be</u> bored.
They went on foot, <u>so as not to be</u> heard.

Another way of making purpose clauses negative is by using 'to avoid' with an '-ing' form or a noun group.

I had to turn away <u>to avoid letting</u> him see my smile.
They drove through town <u>to avoid the motorway</u>.

2 Another type of purpose clause begins with 'in order that', 'so', or 'so that'. These clauses usually contain a modal.
When the main clause refers to the present, you usually use 'can', 'may', 'will', or 'shall' in the purpose clause.

Any holes should be fenced <u>so that</u> people <u>can't</u> fall down them.
I have drawn a diagram <u>so that</u> my explanation <u>will</u> be clearer.

When the main clause refers to the past you usually use 'could', 'might', 'should', or 'would' in the purpose clause.

She said she wanted tea ready at six <u>so she could</u> be out by eight.
Someone lifted Philip onto his shoulder <u>so that he might</u> see the procession.

You use 'in order that', 'so' and 'so that', when the subject of the purpose clause is different from the subject of the main clause. For example, you say 'I've underlined it so that it will be easier.' You do not say 'I've underlined it to be easier'.

3 You can also talk about the purpose of an action by using a prepositional phrase introduced by 'for'.

She went out <u>for a run</u>.
They said they did it <u>for fun</u>.
I usually check, just <u>for safety's sake</u>.

4 You use a reason clause when you want to explain why someone does something or why it happens. When you are simply giving the reason for something, you use 'because', 'since', or 'as'.

I couldn't see Helen's expression, <u>because</u> her head was turned.
<u>Since</u> it was Saturday, he stayed in bed.
<u>As</u> he had been up since 4 am, he was very tired.

You can also use 'why' and a reported question to talk about the reason for an action. See Unit 54.

I asked him <u>why</u> he had come.

5 When you are talking about a possible situation which explains the reason why someone does something, you use 'in case' or 'just in case'.

I've got the key <u>in case</u> we want to go inside.
I am here <u>just in case</u> anything unusual happens.

WARNING: You do not use a future tense after 'in case'. You do not say 'I'll stay behind in case she'll arrive later'.

Unit 94 Result clauses

Main points

- You use result clauses to talk about the result of an action or situation.
- Result clauses are introduced by conjunctions such as 'so', 'so...(that)', or 'such...(that)'.
- A result clause needs a main clause to make a complete sentence. The result clause always comes after the main clause.

1 You use 'so' and 'so that' to say what the result of an action or situation is.

He speaks very little English, so I talked to him through an interpreter.
My suitcase had become damaged on the journey home, so that the lid would not stay closed.

2 You also use 'so...that' or 'such...that' to talk about the result of an action or situation.

He dressed so quickly that he put his boots on the wrong feet.
She got such a shock that she dropped the bag.

'That' is often omitted.

They were so surprised they didn't try to stop him.
They got such a fright they ran away again.

3 You only use 'such' before a noun, with or without an adjective.

They obeyed him with such willingness that the strike went on for over a year.
Sometimes they say such stupid things that I don't even bother to listen.

If the noun is a singular count noun, you put 'a' or 'an' in front of it.

I was in such a panic that I didn't know it was him.

Note that you only use 'so' before an adjective or an adverb.

It all sounded so crazy that I laughed out loud.
They worked so quickly that there was no time for talking.

4 When you want to say that a situation does not happen because someone or something has an excessive amount of a quality, you use 'too' with an adjective and a 'to'-infinitive. For example, if you say 'They were too tired to walk', you mean that they did not walk because they were too tired.

He was too proud to apologise.
She was too weak to lift me.

You also use 'too' with an adverb and a 'to'-infinitive.

They had been walking too silently to be heard.
She spoke too quickly for me to understand.

5 When you want to say that a situation happens or is possible because someone or something has a sufficient amount of a quality, you use 'enough' after adjectives and adverbs, followed by a 'to'-infinitive.

He was old enough to understand.
I could see well enough to know we were losing.

You normally put 'enough' in front of a noun, not after it.

I don't think I've got enough information to speak confidently.

6 You also use 'and as a result', 'and so', or 'and therefore' to talk about the result of an action or situation.

He had been ill for six months, and as a result had lost his job.
She was having great difficulty getting her car out, and so I had to move my car to let her out.
We have a growing population and therefore we need more and more food.

You can also put 'therefore' after the subject of the clause. For example, you can say 'We have a growing population and we therefore need more food'.

'As a result' and 'therefore' can also be used at the beginning of a separate sentence.

In a group, they are not so frightened. As a result, patients reveal their problems more easily.
He lacks money to invest in improving his tools. Therefore he is poor.

You can also put 'therefore' after the subject of the separate sentence. For example, you can say 'He left us. He therefore loses his share'.

Unit 95 Contrast clauses

Clauses introduced by: although, in spite of, though

Main points

- You use contrast clauses when you want to make two statements, and one statement makes the other seem surprising.
- Contrast clauses are introduced by conjunctions such as 'although', 'in spite of', or 'though'.
- A contrast clause needs a main clause to make a complete sentence. The contrast clause can come before or after the main clause.

1 When you simply want to contrast two statements, you use 'although', 'though' or 'even though'.

Although he was late, he stopped to buy a sandwich.
Though he has lived for years in London, he writes in German.
I used to love listening to her, even though I could only understand about half of what she said.

Sometimes you use words like 'still', 'nevertheless', or 'just the same' in the main clause to add emphasis to the contrast.

Although I was shocked, I still couldn't blame him.
Although his company is profitable, it nevertheless needs to face up to some serious problems.
Although she hated them, she agreed to help them just the same.

When the subject of the contrast clause and the main clause are the same, you can often omit the subject and the verb 'be' in the contrast clause.

Although poor, we still have our pride. (Although we are poor...)
Though dying of cancer, he painted every day. (Though he was dying of cancer...)

2 Another way of making a contrast is to use 'despite' or 'in spite of', followed by a noun group.

Despite the difference in their ages they were close friends.
In spite of poor health, my father was always cheerful.

WARNING: You say 'in spite of' but 'despite' without 'of'.

3 You can also use an '-ing' form after 'despite' or 'in spite of'.

Despite working hard, I failed my exams.
Conservative MPs are against tax rises, in spite of wanting lower inflation.

4 You can also use 'despite the fact that' or 'in spite of the fact that', followed by a clause.

Despite the fact that it sounds like science fiction, most of it is technically possible at this moment.
They ignored this order, in spite of the fact that they would probably get into trouble.

It is possible to omit 'that', especially in spoken English.

He insisted on playing, in spite of the fact he had a bad cold.

He insisted on playing, in spite of the fact he had a bad cold.

Unit 96 Manner clauses

Main points

- You use manner clauses to talk about how something is done.
- Manner clauses are introduced by conjunctions such as 'as', 'as if', 'as though', or 'like'.
- A manner clause needs a main clause to make a complete sentence. The manner clause always comes after the main clause.

1 When you want to say how someone does something, or how something is done, you use 'as'.

He behaves as he does, because his father was really cruel to him.
The bricks are still made as they were in Roman times.

You often use 'just', 'exactly', or 'precisely' in front of 'as' for emphasis.

It swims on the sea floor just as its ancestors did.
I like the freedom to plan my day exactly as I want.

2 When you want to indicate that the information in the manner clause might not be true, or is definitely not true, you use 'as if' or 'as though'.

She reacted as if she didn't know about the race.
She acts as though she owns the place.

After 'as if' or 'as though', you often use a past tense even when you are talking about the present, to emphasize that the information in the manner clause is not true. In formal English, you use 'were' instead of 'was'.

Presidents can't dispose of companies as if people didn't exist.
She treats him as though he was her own son.
He looked at me as though I were mad.

3 You can also use 'as if' or 'as though' to say how someone or something feels, looks, or sounds.

She felt as if she had a fever.
He looked as if he hadn't slept very much.
Mary sounded as though she had just run all the way.

You can also use 'it looks' and 'it sounds' with 'as if' and 'as though'.

It looks to me as if he wrote down some notes.
It sounds to me as though he's just being awkward.

4 When the subject of the manner clause and the main clause are the same, you can often use a participle in the manner clause and omit the subject and the verb 'be'.

He ran off to the house as if escaping.
He shook his head as though dazzled by his own vision.

You can also use 'as if' or 'as though' with a 'to'-infinitive clause.

As if to remind him, the church clock struck eleven.

5 In informal speech, people often use 'like' instead of 'as if' or 'as' to say how a person feels, looks, or sounds. Some speakers of English think that this use of 'like' is incorrect.

He felt like he'd won the pools.
You look like you've seen a ghost.
You talk just like my father does.

You can also use 'like' in prepositional phrases to say how someone does something.

He was sleeping like a baby.
I behaved like an idiot , and I'm sorry.

6 You also use 'the way (that)', 'in a way (that)', or 'in the way (that)' to talk about how someone does something, or how something is done.

I was never allowed to sing the way I wanted to.
They did it in a way that I had never seen before.
We make it move in the way that we want it to.

7 You can use 'how' in questions and reported questions to talk about the method used to do something, and sometimes to indicate your surprise that it was possible to do it.

'How did he get in?' - 'He broke a window.'
I wondered how he could afford a new car.

Sometimes, you can use 'how' to talk about the manner in which someone does something.

I watched how he did it, then tried to copy him.
Tell me how he reacted when he saw you.

Unit 97 Defining relative clauses

Main points

- You use defining relative clauses to say exactly which person or thing you are talking about.
- Defining relative clauses are usually introduced by a relative pronoun such as 'that', 'which', 'who', 'whom', or 'whose'.
- A defining relative clause comes immediately after a noun, and needs a main clause to make a complete sentence.

1 You use defining relative clauses to give information that helps to identify the person or thing you are talking about.

The man who you met yesterday was my brother.
The car which crashed into me belonged to Paul.

When you are talking about people, you use 'that' or 'who' in the relative clause.

He was the man that bought my house.
You are the only person here who knows me.

When you are talking about things, you use 'that' or 'which' in the relative clause.

There was ice cream that Mum had made herself.
I will tell you the first thing which I can remember.

2 'That', 'who', or 'which' can be:

- the subject of the verb in the relative clause

The thing that really surprised me was his attitude
The woman who lives next door is very friendly.
The car which caused the accident drove off.

- the object of the verb in the relative clause

The thing that I really liked about it was its size.
The woman who you met yesterday lives next door.
The car which I wanted to buy was not for sale.

In formal English, 'whom' is used instead of 'who' as the object of the verb in the relative clause.

She was a woman whom I greatly respected.

3 You can leave out 'that', 'who', or 'which' when they are the object of the verb in the relative clause.

The woman you met yesterday lives next door.
The car I wanted to buy was not for sale.
The thing I really liked about it was its size.

WARNING: You cannot leave out 'that', 'who', or 'which' when they are the subject of the verb in the relative clause. For example, you say 'The woman who lives next door is very friendly'. You do not say 'The woman lives next door is very friendly'.

4 A relative pronoun in a relative clause can be the object of a preposition. Usually the preposition goes at the end of the clause.

I wanted to do the job which I'd been training for.
The house that we lived in was huge.

You can often omit a relative pronoun that is the object of a preposition.

Angela was the only person I could talk to.
She's the girl I sang the song for.

The preposition always goes in front of 'whom', and in front of 'which' in formal English.

These are the people to whom Catherine was referring.
He was asking questions to which there were no answers.

5 You use 'whose' in relative clauses to indicate who something belongs to or relates to. You normally use 'whose' for people, not for things.

A child whose mother had left him was crying loudly.
We have only told the people whose work is relevant to this project.

6 You can use 'when', 'where', and 'why' in defining relative clauses after certain nouns. You use 'when' after 'time' or time words such as 'day' or 'year'. You use 'where' after 'place' or place words such as 'room' or 'street'. You use 'why' after 'reason'.

There had been a time when she hated all men.
This is the year when profits should increase.

He showed me the place where they work.
That was the room where I did my homework.

There are several reasons why we can't do that.

Unit 98 Non-defining relative clauses

Main points

- You use non-defining relative clauses to give extra information about the person or thing you are talking about.
- Non-defining relative clauses must be introduced by a relative pronoun such as 'which', 'who', 'whom', or 'whose'.
- A non-defining relative clause comes immediately after a noun and needs a main clause to make a complete sentence.

1 You use non-defining relative clauses to give extra information about the person or thing you are talking about. The information is not needed to identify that person or thing.

Professor Marvin, who was always early, was there already.

'Who was always early' gives extra information about Professor Marvin. This is a non-defining relative clause, because it is not needed to identify the person you are talking about. We already know that you are talking about Professor Marvin.

Note that in written English, a non-defining relative clause is usually separated from the main clause by a comma, or by two commas.

I went to the cinema with Mary, who I think you met.
British Rail, which has launched an enquiry, said one coach was badly damaged.

2 You always start a non-defining relative clause with a relative pronoun. When you are talking about people, you use 'who'. 'Who' can be the subject or object of a non-defining relative clause.

Heath Robinson, who died in 1944, was a graphic artist and cartoonist.
I was in the same group as Janice, who I like a lot.

In formal English, 'whom' is sometimes used instead of 'who' as the object of a non-defining relative clause.

She was engaged to a sailor, whom she had met at Dartmouth.

3 When you are talking about things, you use 'which' as the subject or object of a non-defining relative clause.

I am teaching at the Selly Oak centre, which is just over the road.
He was a man of considerable inherited wealth, which he ultimately spent on his experiments.

WARNING: You do not normally use 'that' in non-defining relative clauses.

4 You can also use a non-defining relative clause beginning with 'which' to say something about the whole situation described in a main clause.

I never met Brando again, which was a pity.
She was a little tense, which was understandable.
Small computers need only small amounts of power, which means that they will run on small batteries.

5 When you are talking about a group of people or things and then want to say something about only some of them, you can use one of the following expressions:

many of which	none of whom	some of which
many of whom	one of which	some of whom
none of which	one of whom	

They were all friends, many of whom had known each other for years.
He talked about several very interesting people, some of whom he was still in contact with.

6 You can use 'when' and 'where' in non-defining relative clauses after expressions of time or place.

This happened in 1957, when I was still a baby.
She has just come back from a holiday in Crete, where Alex and I went last year.

Unit 99 Changing the focus of a sentence

Main points

- You can sometimes change the focus of a sentence by moving part of the sentence to the front.
- You can also change the focus of a sentence by using an expression such as 'The fact is', 'The thing is', or 'The problem is'.
- You can also use impersonal 'it' to change the focus of a sentence.

1 In most affirmative clauses, the subject of the verb comes first.

They went to Australia in 1956.
I've no idea who it was.

However, when you want to emphasize another part of the sentence, you can put that part first instead.

In 1956 they went to Australia.
Who it was I've no idea.

2 One common way of giving emphasis is by placing an adverbial at the beginning of the sentence.

At eight o'clock I went down for my breakfast.
For years I'd had to hide what I was thinking.

Note that after adverbials of place and negative adverbials, you normally put the subject after the verb.

She rang the bell for Sylvia. In came a girl she had not seen before.
On no account must they be let in.

After adverbials of place, you can also put the subject before the verb. You must do so, if the subject is a pronoun.

The door opened and in she came.
He'd chosen Japan, so off we went to the Japanese Embassy.

3 When you want to say that you do not know something, you can put a reported question at the beginning of the sentence.

What I'm going to do next I don't quite know.
How he managed I can't imagine.

4 Another way of focusing on information is to use a structure which introduces what you want to say by using 'the' and a noun, followed by 'is'. The nouns most commonly used in this way are:

answer	point	rule	trouble
conclusion	problem	solution	truth
fact	question	thing	

The second part of the sentence is usually a 'that'-clause or a 'wh'-clause, although it can also be a 'to'-infinitive clause or a noun group.

The problem is that she can't cook.
The thing is, how are we going to get her out?
The solution is to adopt the policy which will produce the greatest benefits.
The answer is planning, timing, and, above all, practical experience.

It is also common to use a whole sentence to introduce information in following sentences. See Unit 100 for more information.

5 You can also focus on information by using impersonal 'it', followed by 'be', a noun group, and a relative clause.
The noun group can be the subject or object of the relative clause.

It was Ted who broke the news to me.
It is usually the other vehicle that suffers most.

It's money that they want.
It was me Dookie wanted.

There are many other ways of focusing on information:

Ted was the one who broke the news to me.
Money is what we want.
What we want is money.

6 You can also focus on the information given in the other parts of a clause, or a whole clause, using impersonal 'it'. In this case, the second part of the sentence is a 'that'-clause.

It was from Francis that she first heard the news.
It was meeting Peter that really started me off on this new line of work.
Perhaps it's because he's a misfit that I get along with him.

Unit 100 Cohesion: making connections in speech and writing

Main points

- You can use pronouns and determiners to refer back to something that has already been mentioned.
- You use coordinating conjunctions to link clauses.

1 When you speak or write, you usually need to make some connection with other things that you are saying or writing. The most common way of doing this is by referring back to something that has already been mentioned.

2 One way of referring back to something is to use a personal pronoun such as 'she', 'it', or 'them', or a possessive pronoun such as 'mine' or 'hers'.

My father is fat. He weighs over fifteen stone.
Mary came in. She was a good-looking woman.
'Have you been to London?' — 'Yes, it was very crowded.'
'Have you heard of David Lodge?' — 'Yes, I've just read a novel of his.'
'Would you mind moving your car, please?' — 'It's not mine.'

3 You can also use a specific determiner such as 'the' or 'his' in front of a noun to refer back to something.

A man and a woman were walking up the hill. The man wore shorts, a T-shirt, and basketball sneakers. The woman wore a print dress.

'Thanks,' said Brody. He put the telephone down, turned out the light in his office, and walked out to his car.

4 The demonstratives 'this', 'that', 'these' and 'those' are also used to refer back to a thing or fact that has just been mentioned.

In 1973 he went on a caravan holiday. At the beginning of this holiday he began to experience pain in his chest.
There's a lot of material there. You can use some of that.

5 The following general determiners can also be used to refer back to something.

another	each	every	other
both	either	neither	

Five officials were sacked. Another four were arrested.
There are more than two hundred and fifty species of shark, and every one is different.

6 Another common way of making connections in spoken or written English is by using one of the following coordinating conjunctions:

and	but	nor	or	so	then	yet

Anna had to go into town and she wanted to go to Bride Street.
I asked if I could borrow her bicycle but she refused.
He was only a boy then, yet he was not afraid.

You can use a coordinating conjunction to link clauses that have the same subject. When you link clauses which have the same subject, you do not always need to repeat the subject in the second clause.

She was born in Budapest and raised in Manhattan.
He didn't yell or scream.
When she saw Morris she went pale, then blushed.

7 Most subordinating conjunctions can also be used to link sentences together, rather than to link a subordinate clause with a main clause in the same sentence.

'When will you do it?' — 'When I get time.'
'Can I borrow your car?' — 'So long as you drive carefully.'
We send that by airmail. Therefore it's away on Thursday and our client gets it on Monday.

8 When people are speaking or writing, they often use words that refer back to similar words, or words that refer back to a whole sentence or paragraph.

Everything was quiet. Everywhere there was the silence of the winter night.
'What are you going to do?' — 'That's a good question.'

Appendix: Verb forms

Regular verbs have four forms: the base form, the third person singular form of the present simple, the '-ing' form or present participle, and the '-ed' form used for the past simple and for the past participle. The base form is used in the present tense, and for the imperative, and in the 'to'-infinitive. The base form is always given first in dictionaries and is the form used in the lists in this grammar.

Regular verbs

	base form	third person singular of present simple	'-ing' form or present participle	'-ed' form or past participle	EXCEPTIONS
		add '-s'	add '-ing'	add '-ed'	
	join	joins	joining	joined	
		add '-es'			
ending in '-sh'	finish	finishes	finishing	finished	
'-ch'	reach	reaches	reaching	reached	
'-ss'	pass	passes	passing	passed	
'-x'	mix	mixes	mixing	mixed	
'-z'	buzz	buzzes	buzzing	buzzed	
'-o'	echo	echoes	echoing	echoed	
ending in '-e'			omit '-e' before adding '-ing' or '-ed'		age, agree, disagree, dye, free, knee, referee, singe, tiptoe
	dance	dances	dancing	danced	
ending in '-ie'			change '-ie' to '-y' before adding '-ing		
	tie	ties	tying	tied	
ending in consonant + '-y'		change '-y' to '-ies'		change '-y' to '-ied'	
	cry	cries	crying	cried	
one syllable ending in single vowel + consonant			double final consonant before adding '-ing' or '-ed'		not '-w', '-x', '-y': rowing, boxing playing
	dip	dips	dipping	dipped	
two syllables ending in single vowel + '-l'	travel	travels	travelling	travelled	optional in American English: traveling, traveled
the following verbs: equip, handicap, hiccup, kidnap, program, refer, worship	equip	equips	equipping	equipped	optional in American English for: handicap, hiccup, kidnap, program, worship

Regular/irregular verbs

Irregular verbs do not add '-ed' for the past form, and some have different forms for the past simple and past participle. Some verbs have two forms for the past participle.

base form	past simple	past participle
mow	mowed	mowed, mown
prove	proved	proved, proven
swell	swelled	swelled, swollen

Some verbs have two forms for the past simple and two forms for the past participle. If there is a regular form, it is given first, but it may not be the most common one.

base form	past simple	past participle	base form	past simple	past participle
bid	bid, bade	bid, bidden	lean	leaned, leant	leaned, leant
lie	lied, lay	lied, lain	leap	leaped, leapt	leaped, leapt
weave	weaved, wove	weaved, woven	light	lighted, lit	lighted, lit
burn	burned, burnt	burned, burnt	smell	smelled, smelt	smelled, smelt
bust	busted, bust	busted, bust	speed	speeded, sped	speeded, sped
dream	dreamed, dreamt	dreamed, dreamt	spell	spelled, spelt	spelled, spelt
dwell	dwelled, dwelt	dwelled, dwelt	spill	spilled, spilt	spilled, spilt
hang	hanged, hung	hanged, hung	spoil	spoiled, spoilt	spoiled, spoilt
kneel	kneeled, knelt	kneeled, knelt	wet	wetted, wet	wetted, wet

Note that 'gotten' is sometimes used instead of 'got' as the past participle of 'get' in American English. With a few verbs, different forms are used in different meanings. For example, the past form and the past participle of the verb 'hang' is normally 'hung'. However, 'hanged' is used when it means 'executed by hanging'.

Below is a list of irregular verbs which have only one form for the past simple and only one form for the past participle. For some verbs, these forms are the same.

Irregular verbs

base form	past simple	past participle	base form	past simple	past participle	base form	past simple	past participle
arise	arose	arisen	freeze	froze	frozen	shut	shut	shut
awake	awoke	awoken	get	got	got	sing	sang	sung
bear	bore	borne	give	gave	given	sink	sank	sunk
beat	beat	beaten	go	went	gone	sit	sat	sat
become	became	become	grind	ground	ground	slay	slew	slain
begin	began	begun	grow	grew	grown	sleep	slept	slept
bend	bent	bent	hear	heard	heard	slide	slid	slid
bet	bet	bet	hide	hid	hidden	sling	slung	slung
bind	bound	bound	hit	hit	hit	slink	slunk	slunk
bite	bit	bitten	hold	held	held	sow	sowed	sown
bleed	bled	bled	hurt	hurt	hurt	speak	spoke	spoken
blow	blew	blown	keep	kept	kept	spend	spent	spent
break	broke	broken	know	knew	known	spin	spun	spun
breed	bred	bred	lay	laid	laid	spread	spread	spread
bring	brought	brought	lead	led	led	spring	sprang	sprung
build	built	built	leave	left	left	stand	stood	stood
burst	burst	burst	lend	lent	lent	steal	stole	stolen
buy	bought	bought	let	let	let	stick	stuck	stuck
cast	cast	cast	lose	lost	lost	sting	stung	stung
catch	caught	caught	make	made	made	stink	stank	stunk
choose	chose	chosen	mean	meant	meant	strew	strewed	strewn
cling	clung	clung	meet	met	met	stride	strode	stridden
come	came	come	pay	paid	paid	strike	struck	struck
cost	cost	cost	put	put	put	string	strung	strung
creep	crept	crept	quit	quit	quit	strive	strove	striven
cut	cut	cut	read	read	read	swear	swore	sworn
deal	dealt	dealt	rend	rent	rent	sweep	swept	swept
dig	dug	dug	ride	rode	ridden	swim	swam	swum
draw	drew	drawn	ring	rang	rung	swing	swung	swung
drink	drank	drunk	rise	rose	risen	take	took	taken
drive	drove	driven	run	ran	run	teach	taught	taught
eat	ate	eaten	saw	sawed	sawn	tear	tore	torn
fall	fell	fallen	say	said	said	tell	told	told
feed	fed	fed	see	saw	seen	think	thought	thought
feel	felt	felt	seek	sought	sought	throw	threw	thrown
fight	fought	fought	sell	sold	sold	thrust	thrust	thrust
find	found	found	send	sent	sent	tread	trod	trodden
flee	fled	fled	set	set	set	understand	understood	understood
fling	flung	flung	sew	sewed	sewn	wake	woke	woken
fly	flew	flown	shake	shook	shaken	wear	wore	worn
forbear	forbore	forborne	shed	shed	shed	weep	wept	wept
forbid	forbade	forbidden	shine	shone	shone	win	won	won
forget	forgot	forgotten	shoe	shod	shod	wind	wound	wound
forgive	forgave	forgiven	shoot	shot	shot	wring	wrung	wrung
forsake	forsook	forsaken	show	showed	shown	write	wrote	written
forswear	forswore	forsworn	shrink	shrank	shrunk			

Index

Note: numbers refer to Units and paragraphs; entries in **bold** are grammar terms; entries in *italics* are actual words and forms; an arrow ⇨ tells you to look at another entry.